Encyclopædia

of

Religion and Ethics

Encyclopædia of Religion and Ethics

EDITED BY

JAMES HASTINGS

WITH THE ASSISTANCE OF

JOHN A. SELBIE

AND OTHER SCHOLARS

VOLUME V

DRAVIDIANS—FICHTE

T&T CLARK
EDINBURGH

T&T CLARK LTD
59 GEORGE STREET
EDINBURGH EH2 2LQ
SCOTLAND

Edition Completed and Corrected Editions 1926–1976
Reprinted 1994

ISBN 0 567 06505 7

British Library Cataloguing-in-Publication Data
A catalogue record for this book is available from the British Library

Printed and bound in Great Britain by Antony Rowe Ltd, Wiltshire

AUTHORS OF ARTICLES IN THIS VOLUME

ABRAHAMS (ISRAEL), M.A. (Lond. and Camb.).
Reader in Talmudic and Rabbinic Literature in the University of Cambridge; formerly Senior Tutor in the Jews' College, London; editor of the *Jewish Quarterly Review*, 1888–1908.
Family (Jewish).

ADAMS (JOHN), M.A., B.Sc., LL.D.
Professor of Education in the University of London.
Education.

ALEXANDER (HARTLEY BURR), Ph.D.
Professor of Philosophy in the University of Nebraska.
Ethics and Morality (American), **Expediency, Expiation and Atonement** (American).

ANESAKI (MASAHAR).
Professor of Religious Science in the Imperial University of Tokyo.
Ethics and Morality (Buddhist).

ANWYL (Sir EDWARD), M.A. (Oxon.).
Professor of Welsh and Comparative Philology, and Dean of the Faculty of Arts, in the University College of Wales, Aberystwyth; author of *Celtic Religion*, *Grammar of Old Welsh Poetry*, *Welsh Grammar*.
Family (Celtic).

ARMITAGE-SMITH (GEORGE), M.A., D.Lit.
Principal of Birkbeck College, London; formerly Dean of the Faculty of Economics in the University of London; Fellow of Statistical Society; Member of Council of Royal Economic Society; Lecturer on Economics and Mental Science at Birkbeck College.
Employers.

ARNOLD (EDWARD VERNON), Litt.D.
Professor of Latin in the University College of North Wales.
Epictetus.

ASTON (WILLIAM GEORGE), M.A., D.Litt., C.M.G.
Formerly Japanese Secretary of H.M. Legation, Tokyo; author of *History of Japanese Literature*, *Shinto*.
Fetishism (Introductory).

BAILLIE (JAMES BLACK), M.A. (Edin. and Camb.), D.Phil. (Edin.).
Professor of Moral Philosophy in the University of Aberdeen; author of *Hegel's Logic* (1901), *The Idealistic Construction of Experience* (1906), *Hegel's Phenomenology of Mind* (1910).
Ethical Idealism.

BARKER (HENRY), M.A.
Lecturer in Moral Philosophy in the University of Edinburgh.
Duty.

BATESON (JOSEPH HARGER), F.R.G.S.
Secretary, Wesleyan Army and Navy Board.
Festivals and Fasts (Buddhist, Chinese, Nepalese).

BENNETT (WILLIAM HENRY), M.A. (Lond.), D.D. (Aber.), Litt.D. (Camb.).
Sometime Fellow of St. John's College, Cambridge; Professor of Old Testament Exegesis, Hackney College and New College, London; author of *The Religion of the Post-Exilic Prophets*.
Elder (Semitic), **Eve.**

BEVERIDGE (WILLIAM), M.A.
Minister of the United Free Church, New Deer and Maud; author of *A Short History of the Westminster Assembly*, *Makers of the Scottish Church*.
Ebionism.

DE BOER (TJITZE), Philos. Dr.
Professor of Philosophy in the University of Amsterdam.
Ethics and Morality (Muslim).

BOLLING (GEORGE MELVILLE), A.B., Ph.D.
Professor of Greek and Sanskrit Languages and Literatures, and Assoc. Professor of Comparative Philology, in the Catholic University of America.
Dreams and Sleep (Vedic).

BRANDT (Dr. WILHELM).
Formerly Professor of Old and New Testament and the History of Religion in the University of Amsterdam.
Elkesaites.

BROWN (WILLIAM ADAMS), Ph.D., D.D.
Roosevelt Professor of Systematic Theology in Union Theological Seminary, New York; author of *Christian Theology in Outline*.
Expiation and Atonement (Christian).

BULLOCK (THOMAS LOWNDES), M.A.
Professor of Chinese in the University of Oxford.
Ethics and Morality (Chinese).

BURNS (ISLAY FERRIER), M.A.
Tutor and Librarian in Westminster College, Cambridge; formerly Snell Exhibitioner at Balliol College, Oxford.
Faith (Greek, Roman).

CAMPBELL SMITH (MARY), M.A.
Dundee.
Enemy.

CARLETON (JAMES GEORGE), D.D.
Canon of St. Patrick's, Dublin, and Lecturer in Divinity, Trinity College, Dublin; author of *The Part of Rheims in the Making of the English Bible*, *The Prayer-Book Psalter with Marginal Notes*.
Festivals and Fasts (Christian).

CARRA DE VAUX (Baron BERNARD).
Professeur à l'École libre des Hautes Études; Membre du Conseil de la Société asiatique de Paris.
Family (Muslim), **Al-Farabi, Fate** (Muslim).

CARTER (JESSE BENEDICT), Ph.D. (Halle).
Director of the American School of Classical Studies in Rome.
Ethics and Morality (Roman), **Family** (Roman).

CASARTELLI (LOUIS CHARLES), M.A. (Lond.), D.D., and D.Litt. Or. (Louvain), M.R.A.S.
Bishop of Salford; Lecturer on Iranian Languages and Literature in the University of Manchester; formerly Professor of Zend and Pahlavi in the University of Louvain.
Dualism (Iranian).

CHAMBERLAIN (ALEXANDER FRANCIS), M.A. (Toronto), Ph.D. (Clark).
Professor of Anthropology in Clark University, Worcester, Mass.; editor of the *Journal of American Folklore* (1900–1908); author of *The Child and Childhood in Folk-Thought*, *The Child: A Study in the Evolution of Man*.
Education (American).

CLODD (EDWARD).
Corresponding Member of the Société d'Anthropologie de Paris, and Vice-President of the Folklore Society; Fellow of the Royal Anthropological Institute.
Evolution (Ethical), **Execution of Animals.**

COBB (WILLIAM F.), D.D.
Rector of the Church of St. Ethelburga the Virgin, London, E.C.
Faith-healing.

COOK (STANLEY ARTHUR), M.A.
Ex-Fellow and Lecturer in the Comparative Study of Religion, in Gonville and Caius College, Cambridge; author of *The Laws of Moses and the Code of Hammurabi*, *The Religion of Ancient Palestine*.
Edomites.

CRAWLEY (ALFRED ERNEST), M.A. (Camb.).
Fellow of the Royal Anthropological Institute and of the Sociological Society; author of *The Mystic Rose*, *The Tree of Life*, *The Idea of the Soul*.
Dress, Drinks and Drinking, Drums and Cymbals, Eating the God.

CROOKE (WILLIAM), B.A.
Ex-Scholar of Trinity College, Dublin; Fellow of the Royal Anthropological Institute; President of the Anthropological Section of the British Association, 1910; President of the Folklore Society, 1911–12; late of the Bengal Civil Service.
Dravidians (North India), **Dwarka, Education** (Hindu), **Elephanta, Ellora, Fatehpur-Sikri.**

DAVIDS (T. W. RHYS), LL.D., Ph.D., D.Sc.
Professor of Comparative Religion, Manchester; President of the Pāli Text Society; Fellow of the British Academy; author of *Buddhism* (1878), *Questions of King Milinda* (1890–94), *Buddhist India* (1902), *Early Buddhism* (1908).
Elder (Buddhist), **Expiation and Atonement** (Buddhist), **Family** (Buddhist).

DAVIDS (Mrs. RHYS), M.A.
Lecturer on Indian Philosophy in the University of Manchester.
Egoism (Buddhist).

DAVIDSON (WILLIAM LESLIE), M.A., LL.D.
Professor of Logic and Metaphysics in the University of Aberdeen; author of *The Logic of Definition*, *Theism as grounded in Human Nature*, *Christian Ethics*, *The Stoic Creed*.
Dualism (Greek), **Envy and Emulation.**

DENNEY (JAMES), D.D.
Professor of New Testament Language, Literature, and Theology, in the United Free Church College, Glasgow; author of *Studies in Theology*, *The Atonement and the Modern Mind*.
Fall (Biblical).

DHALLA (DASTUR Dr. MANECKJI NUSSERVANJI), M.A., Ph.D.
High Priest of the Parsis of Sind, Panjab, and Baluchistan.
Expiation and Atonement (Parsi).

DORNER (AUGUST), Dr. Theol. und Philos.
Ordentlicher Professor an der Universität zu Königsberg.
Emancipation, Emotions, Fate (Introductory).

DRIVER (SAMUEL ROLLES), D.D., Hon. Litt.D. (Dublin), Hon. D.D. (Glas. and Aber.).
Regius Professor of Hebrew, and Canon of Christ Church, Oxford; Fellow of the British Academy; Corresponding Member of the Royal Prussian Academy of Sciences.
Expiation and Atonement (Hebrew).

DUFF (J. WIGHT), M.A. (Aber. et Oxon.), D.Litt. (Durham), D.Litt. (Oxon.).
Professor of Classics, Armstrong College (in the University of Durham), Newcastle-upon-Tyne; author of *A Literary History of Rome*.
Education (Roman).

DUKES (EDWIN J.).
Minister of St. Paul's Chapel, Kentish Town, London; formerly London Society Missionary in China; author of *Everyday Life in China*.
Feng-shui.

DUNLOP (F. W.), M.A., Ph.D.
Minister at Annandale, Sydney, Australia.
Essence.

EHRHARDT (CHRISTIAN EUGÈNE).
Professeur honoraire de l'Université; Professeur à la Faculté libre de Théologie protestante de Paris; Pasteur à Bourg-la-Reine (Consistoire de Paris).
Equiprobabilism.

ELWORTHY (FREDERICK THOMAS).
Author of *The Evil Eye*.
Evil Eye.

EUCKEN (RUDOLF CHRISTOPH), Dr. theol. u. philos.
Geheimer Rat; ordentlicher Professor der Philosophie an der Universität zu Jena; Verfasser von *Hauptprobleme der Religionsphilosophie der Gegenwart*.
Dualism.

EVANS (JOHN YOUNG), M.A., B.D.
Professor of Church History and Patristic Literature at the Theological College, Aberystwyth.
Erastianism.

FAIRBANKS (ARTHUR), Ph.D. (Freiburg i. B.), Litt.D. (Dartmouth College).
Professor of Greek Literature and Greek Archæology in the State University of Iowa, 1900–1906; in the University of Michigan, 1906–1907; Director of the Museum of Fine Arts, Boston, 1907.
Expiation and Atonement (Greek), **Family** (Greek).

FALLAIZE (EDWIN NICHOLAS COLLINGFORD), B.A. (Oxon.).
Late King Charles Exhibitioner, Exeter College, Oxford; Recorder, Section H (Anthropology) of the British Association for the Advancement of Science.
Family (Primitive).

FORTESCUE (ADRIAN), Ph.D., D.D. (Innsbruck).
Roman Catholic Priest at Letchworth; author of *The Orthodox Eastern Church* (1907), *The Mass: A Study of the Roman Liturgy* (1912).
Febronianism.

FOUCART (GEORGE B.), Docteur ès-Lettres.
Professeur d'Histoire des Religions à l'Université d'Aix-Marseille; Professeur à l'Institut Colonial de Marseille (Religions et coutumes des peuples d'Afrique); Ancien Inspecteur en chef du Service des Antiquités de l'Égypte; auteur de *Histoire des Religions et Méthode Comparative*[2] (1912).
Dreams and Sleep (Egyptian), **Dualism** (Egyptian), **Festivals and Fasts** (Egyptian).

FRAZER (ROBERT W.), LL.B., I.C.S. (Retired).
Lecturer in Tamil and Telugu, University College, London; Principal Librarian, London Institution; author of *A Literary History of India*.
Dravidians (South India).

GARDINER (ALAN HENDERSON), D.Litt. (Oxon.).
Reader in Egyptology at Manchester University; formerly Laycock Student of Egyptology at Worcester College, Oxford, and Sub-editor of the Hieroglyphic Dictionary of the German Academies at Berlin.
Ethics and Morality (Egyptian).

GEDEN (ALFRED S.), M.A. (Oxon.), D.D. (Aber.).
Professor of Old Testament Languages and Literature, and of Comparative Religion, in the Wesleyan College, Richmond, Surrey; author of *Studies in Religions of the East*, *Outlines of Introduction to the Hebrew Bible*; translator of P. Deussen's *Philosophy of the Upanishads*.
Education (Buddhist), **Fate** (Buddhist).

GEFFCKEN (Dr. JOHANNES).
Ordentlicher Professor der Klass. Philologie an der Universität zu Rostock.
Euhemerism, Eumenides.

GERIG (JOHN LAWRENCE), M.A., Ph.D.
Associate Professor of Romance Languages and Celtic in Columbia University, New York.
Ethics and Morality (Celtic).

GERINI (Colonel G. E.), M.R.A.S.
Late Director of Military Education, R. Siamese Army; Honorary Member of the Siam Society.
Festivals and Fasts (Siamese).

GOLDZIHER (IGNAZ), Ph.D., D.Litt., LL.D.
Professor of Semitic Philology in the University of Budapest; Ord. Member and Class-President of the Hungarian Academy of Sciences; Foreign Member of the British Academy, of the Imperial Academy of Sciences, St. Petersburg, of the Royal Academy of Sciences, Berlin, of the Indian Institute, The Hague, of the Jewish Historical Society of England, of the Société Asiatique, Paris.
Education (Muslim).

GRAY (LOUIS HERBERT), Ph.D.
Sometime Member of the Editorial Staff of the *New International Encyclopædia*, *Orientalische Bibliographie*, etc.; Member of the American and German Oriental Societies, etc.; author of *Indo-Iranian Phonology* (1902); translator of *Vāsavadatta, a Sanskrit Romance by Subandhu* (1912).
Duelling, Education (Persian), **Eskimos, Ethics and Morality** (Polynesian), **Eunuch, Expiation and Atonement** (Introductory), **Family** (Persian), **Fate** (Iranian), **Festivals and Fasts** (Iranian).

GRAY (Mrs. FLORENCE LILLIAN [RIDLEY]).
Member of the American Oriental Society.
Easter Island.

HALDANE (ELIZABETH SANDERSON), LL.D.
Author of *Life of James Ferrier* (1899), *Life of Descartes* (1905), and joint-translator of *Hegel's History of Philosophy* (1892), and *The Philosophical Works of Descartes* (1911–12).
Encyclopædists.

HALL (H. R.), M.A., F.S.A.
Assistant in the Department of Egyptian and Assyrian Antiquities in the British Museum.
Expiation and Atonement (Egyptian), **Family** (Egyptian), **Fate** (Egyptian).

HANNAY (JAMES OWEN), M.A.
Rector of Westport, Co. Mayo.
Eustathius.

HARADA (TASUKU), D.D., LL.D.
President of Doshisha University, Kyoto.
Family (Japanese).

HARRISON (JANE ELLEN), LL.D. (Aber.), D.Litt. (Durham).
Staff Lecturer in Classics at Newnham College, Cambridge; Corresponding Member of the German Archæological Society; author of *Prolegomena to the Study of Greek Religion.*
Fan.

HERBIG (Dr. GUSTAV).
Kgl. Bibliothekar an der Hof- und Staatsbibliothek; Privatdozent für indogermanische Sprachwissenschaft und Etruskologie an der Universität zu München.
Etruscan Religion.

HICKS (ROBERT DREW), M.A.
Fellow and formerly Classical Lecturer of Trinity College, Cambridge.
Empedocles, Epicureans.

HILLEBRANDT (A. F. ALFRED), Ph.D. (Munich), LL.D.
Ord. Professor of Sanskrit and Comparative Philology in the University of Breslau; Corresponding Member of the Königliche Gesellschaft der Wissenschaften zu Göttingen, and of the Royal Bavarian Academy of Sciences; Geheimer Regierungsrat.
Dyaus.

HOPKINS (EDWARD WASHBURN), Ph.D., LL.D.
Professor of Sanskrit and Comparative Philology in Yale University; former President of the American Oriental Society; author of *Religions of India.*
Festivals and Fasts (Hindu).

HUGHES (HENRY MALDWYN), B.A., D.D.
Author of *The Ethics of Jewish Apocryphal Literature.*
Experience (Religious).

HULL (ELEANOR).
Hon. Sec. of the Irish Texts Society, London; Member of Council of the Folklore and Irish Literary Societies; author of *The Cuchullin Saga in Irish Literature* (1898), *Pagan Ireland* (1904), *Early Christian Ireland* (1905), *A Text-book of Irish Literature* (1907–8).
Fate (Celtic).

HYSLOP (JAMES HERVEY), Ph.D., LL.D.
Secretary of the American Society for Psychical Research; formerly Professor of Logic and Ethics in Columbia University.
Energy, Equity.

INGE (WILLIAM RALPH), D.D.
Dean of St. Paul's; author of *Faith and Knowledge, Studies of English Mystics, Personal Idealism and Mysticism.*
Ecstasy.

IVERACH (JAMES), M.A., D.D.
Principal, and Professor of New Testament Language and Literature, in the United Free Church College, Aberdeen; author of *Is God Knowable?* (1887), *Evolution and Christianity* (1894), *Theism in the Light of Present Science and Philosophy* (1900), *Descartes and Spinoza* (1904).
Epistemology.

JACOBI (HERMANN), Ph.D.
Professor des Sanskrit an der Universität zu Bonn; Geheimer Regierungsrat.
Durga.

JACOBS (JOSEPH), B.A. (Camb. and Lond.), Litt.D. (Penn.).
Professor of English Literature at the Jewish Theological Seminary of America; formerly President of the Jewish Historical Society of England; formerly editor of *Folklore.*
Fable.

JEREMIAS (ALFRED), Ph.D. (Leipzig), Lic. Theol. hon. c. (Leipzig).
Pfarrer in Leipzig und Dozent an der Universität.
Ethics and Morality (Babylonian).

JOLLY (JULIUS), Ph.D. (Munich), Hon. M.D. (Göttingen), Hon. D.Litt. (Oxford).
Ord. Professor of Sanskrit and Comparative Philology and Director of the Linguistic Seminary in the University of Würzburg; formerly Tagore Professor of Law in the University of Calcutta.
Ethics and Morality (Hindu), **Expiation and Atonement** (Hindu), **Family** (Hindu), **Fate** (Hindu).

JÓNSSON (FINNUR), Dr.Phil.
Professor ordinarius of Northern Philology in the University of Copenhagen.
Eddas.

JOSEPH (MORRIS).
Senior Minister of the West London Synagogue.
Education (Jewish).

JUYNBOLL (TH. W.), Dr. juris et phil.
Adjutor interpretis 'Legati Warneriani,' Leyden.
Eunuch (Muslim).

KEANE (AUGUSTUS HENRY), LL.D., F.R.G.S., F.R.A.I.
Late Vice-President of the Royal Anthropological Institute; late Professor of Hindustani in University College, London; author of *Ethnology, Man Past and Present.*
Ethnology, Europe.

KING (IRVING), Ph.D.
Assistant Professor of Education in the State University of Iowa; Fellow of the American Association for the Advancement of Science.
Ethics and Morality (Australian).

KING (LEONARD WILLIAM), M.A., F.S.A.
Assistant in the Department of Egyptian and Assyrian Antiquities in the British Museum; Lecturer in Assyrian at King's College, London.
Fate (Babylonian).

KNIGHT (G. A. FRANK), M.A., F.R.S.E.
Minister of St. Leonard's United Free Church, Perth.
Feet-washing.

LAKE (KIRSOPP), M.A. (Oxon.), D.D. (St Andrews).
Professor of New Testament Exegesis and the History of Early Christian Literature in the University of Leyden.
Epiphany.

LANG (ANDREW), M.A., D.Litt., D.C.L., LL.D.
Author of *Custom and Myth* (1884), *Myth, Ritual and Religion* (1887), *The Making of Religion* (1898), *Magic and Religion* (1901).
Dreams and Sleep (Introductory).

LANGDON (STEPHEN HERBERT), B.D., Ph.D., Hon. M.A. (Oxon.).
Shillito Reader in Assyriology and Comparative Semitic Philology in the University of Oxford; author of *Neo-Babylonian Royal Inscriptions* (V.A.B. vol. iv.), *Sumerian and Babylonian Psalms, A Sumerian Grammar, Babylonian Liturgies.*
Expiation and Atonement (Babylonian).

LEGER (LOUIS).
Membre de l'Institut de France; Professeur au Collège de France; Professeur honoraire à l'École des langues orientales.
Festivals and Fasts (Slavic).

LEHMANN (EDVARD), D.Theol., D.Phil.
Ordentlicher Professor der Theologie (Religionsgeschichte und Philosophie) an der Universität zu Berlin.
Ethics and Morality (Parsi).

LODGE (RUPERT CLENDON), B.A.
Late John Locke Scholar, Oxford; late Junior Lecturer in Philosophy in the University of Manchester.
Empiricism.

LOEWE (HERBERT MARTIN JAMES), M.A.
Curator of Oriental Literature in the University Library; Director of Oriental Studies, St. Catharine's College, Cambridge.
Expiation and Atonement (Jewish).

MACCULLOCH (JOHN ARNOTT), Hon. D.D. (St. Andrews).
Rector of St. Saviour's, Bridge of Allan; Hon. Canon of the Cathedral of the Holy Spirit, Cumbrae; Examiner in Comparative Religion and Philosophy of Religion, Victoria University, Manchester; Bell Lecturer, Edinburgh Theological College; author of *Comparative Theology; Religion: its Origin and Forms; The Childhood of Fiction; The Religion of the Ancient Celts; Early Christian Visions of the Other-World.*
Druids, Dualism (Celtic), **Earth and Earth-Gods, Eschatology, Euphemism, Fairy, Fall** (Ethnic), **Fasting** (Introductory and non-Christian), **Feasting** (Introductory), **Festivals and Fasts** (Celtic).

MACGREGOR (ANNIE ELIZABETH FRANCES), B.A. (Lond.).
Ethical Discipline.

MCINTYRE (JAMES LEWIS), M.A. (Edin. and Oxon.), D.Sc. (Edin.).
Anderson Lecturer in Comparative Psychology to the University of Aberdeen; Lecturer in Psychology, Logic, and Ethics to the Aberdeen Provincial Committee for the Training of Teachers; formerly Examiner in Philosophy to the University of Edinburgh; author of *Giordano Bruno* (1903).
Fear, Fearlessness.

MACKENZIE (DONALD), M.A.
Minister of the United Free Church at Craigdam; Assistant in Logic in the University of Aberdeen, 1906–1909.
Ethics and Morality (Christian).

MACKENZIE (JOHN STUART), Litt.D., LL.D.
Professor of Philosophy in University College, Cardiff.
Eternity.

MACLAGAN (P. J.), M.A., D.Phil.
Of the English Presbyterian Mission, Swatow.
Education (Chinese), **Family** (Chinese).

MACLEAN (ARTHUR JOHN), D.D. (Camb.), Hon. D.D. (Glas.).
Bishop of Moray, Ross, and Caithness.
Fasting (Christian).

MACLEAN (MAGNUS), M.A., D.Sc., F.R.S.E.
Professor of Electrical Engineering in the Royal Technical College, Glasgow.
Feinn Cycle.

MACLER (FRÉDÉRIC).
Ancien Attaché à la Bibliothèque Nationale; Lauréat de l'Institut; Professeur d'Arménien à l'École des Langues orientales vivantes.
Festivals and Fasts (Armenian).

MACRITCHIE (DAVID), F.S.A. (Scot. and Ireland).
Member of the Royal Anthropological Institute of Great Britain and Ireland; President of the St. Andrew Society, Edinburgh; author of *Ancient and Modern Britons; Fians, Fairies and Picts; Scottish Gypsies under the Stewarts.*
Dwarfs and Pygmies.

MAIR (ALEXANDER), M.A.
Professor of Philosophy in the University of Liverpool.
End.

MARETT (ROBERT RANULPH), M.A., F.R.A.I.
Fellow of Exeter College, and Reader in Social Anthropology in the University of Oxford; author of *The Threshold of Religion.*
Ethics (Rudimentary).

MARGOLIOUTH (DAVID SAMUEL), M.A., D.Litt.
Fellow of New College, and Laudian Professor of Arabic in the University of Oxford; author of *Mohammed and the Rise of Islam, Mohammedanism.*
Expiation and Atonement (Muslim), **Fall** (Muslim).

MARGOLIOUTH (GEORGE), M.A. (Cantab.).
Senior Assistant in the Department of Oriental Printed Books and MSS in the British Museum.
Feasting (Hebrew and Jewish).

MARTIN (ALEXANDER STUART), M.A., B.D.
Formerly Pitt Scholar and Examiner in Theology in the University of Edinburgh, and Minister of the West Parish of St. Nicholas, Aberdeen.
Election.

MARVIN (WALTER TAYLOR), Ph.D.
Professor in Rutgers College, New Jersey.
Equivocation (Logical).

MAVOR (JAMES), Ph.D.
Professor of Political Economy in the University of Toronto; author of *The Scottish Railway Strike.*
Employment.

MOFFATT (JAMES), D.D., D.Litt.
Yates Professor of New Testament Greek and Exegesis, Mansfield College, Oxford; author of *Critical Introduction to New Testament Literature.*
Essenes.

MOGK (EUGEN), Dr.Phil.
Professor der nordischen Philologie an der Universität zu Leipzig.
Expiation and Atonement (Teutonic).

MOORE (WILLIAM), M.A.
Rector of Appleton, Berks; formerly Fellow of Magdalen College, and Lecturer of St. John's College, Oxford; translator of the Philosophical Treatises of Gregory of Nyssa.
Eunomianism.

MORGAN (WILLIAM), D.D.
Professor of Systematic Theology in Queen's College, Kingston, Canada; formerly Minister of the United Free Church at Tarbolton.
Faith (Christian).

MUIRHEAD (JOHN HENRY), LL.D.
Professor of Philosophy in the University of Birmingham; author of *Elements of Ethics, The Service of the State.*
Ethics.

MURISON (WILLIAM), M.A.
Senior English Master in Aberdeen Grammar School; author of 'Education,' in *A Companion to Latin Studies.*
Education (Greek).

MURRAY (GILBERT), LL.D., D.Litt., F.B.A.
Regius Professor of Greek in the University of Oxford.
Euripides.

NEILSON (GEORGE), LL.D.
The Stipendiary Magistrate of Glasgow; author of *Trial by Combat.*
Duelling.

ORR (JAMES), M.A., D.D.
Professor of Systematic Theology and Apologetics in the United Free Church College, Glasgow; author of *The Christian View of God and the World, David Hume* in the 'Epoch Makers' series.
Enhypostasis.

PEARSON (A. C.), M.A.
Late Scholar of Christ's College, Cambridge; editor of *Fragments of Zeno and Cleanthes,* Euripides' *Helena, Heraclidæ,* and *Phœnissæ.*
Ethics and Morality (Greek).

PETRIE (WILLIAM MATTHEW FLINDERS), D.C.L. (Oxon.), LL.D. (Edin. and Aber.), Litt.D. (Camb.), Ph.D. (Strassburg).
Fellow of the Royal Society and of the British Academy; Edwards Professor of Egyptology in the University of London.
Egyptian Religion.

PHILLIPS (DAVID), B.A. (Wales), M.A. (Cantab.).
Professor of the Philosophy and History of Religion in the Theological College, Bala, North Wales.
Ego, Egoism.

PHILLPOTTS (BERTHA SURTEES), M.A. (Dublin).
Fellow of the Royal Society of Northern Antiquaries (Copenhagen); formerly Librarian of Girton College, Cambridge.
Dreams and Sleep (Teutonic), **Ethics and Morality** (Teutonic), **Festivals and Fasts** (Teutonic).

PINCHES (THEOPHILUS GOLDRIDGE), LL.D. (Glas.), M.R.A.S.
Lecturer in Assyrian at University College, London, and at the Institute of Archæology, Liverpool; Hon. Member of the Société Asiatique.
Elamites, Family (Assyro-Babylonian).

PORPHYRIOS II. (LOGOTHETES), Ph.D. (Leipzig), Hon. LL.D. (Cantab.).
Archbishop of Sinai, Paran, and Raitho.
Eastern Church.

POZNAŃSKI (SAMUEL), Ph.D. (Heidelberg).
Rabbiner und Prediger in Warschau (Polen).
Festivals and Fasts (Jewish).

PUNNETT (REGINALD CRUNDALL), M.A.
Professor of Biology in the University of Cambridge; author of *Mendelism.*
Environment (Biological), **Evolution** (Biological).

RADERMACHER (Dr. LUDWIG).
Ordentlicher Professor der klassischen Philologie an der Universität zu Wien.
Enthusiasm.

RADIN (PAUL), Ph.D.
Field Ethnologist, Geological Survey of Canada.
Eskimos.

ROSE (HERBERT JENNINGS), M.A. (Oxon.).
Associate Professor of Classics in McGill University, Montreal; sometime Fellow of Exeter College, Oxford.
Euthanasia, Festivals and Fasts (Greek).

ROSS (JOHN M. E.), M.A.
Minister of St. Ninian's Presbyterian Church, Golders Green, London; author of *The Self-Portraiture of Jesus, The Christian Standpoint.*
Emerson.

ROYCE (JOSIAH), Ph.D., LL.D.
Professor of the History of Philosophy in Harvard University; Gifford Lecturer at the University of Aberdeen, 1898-1900.
Error and Truth.

SALMOND (WILLIAM), D.D.
Professor of Mental and Moral Science in the University of Otago, Dunedin.
Feeling.

SAYCE (ARCHIBALD HENRY), D.Litt. (Oxon.), LL.D. (Dublin), D.D. (Edin. and Aber.).
Fellow of Queen's College and Professor of Assyriology in the University of Oxford; President of the Society of Biblical Archæology.
Dreams and Sleep (Babylonian).

SCHAFF (DAVID SCHLEY), D.D. (Univ. of Geneva, etc.).
Professor of Church History in the Western Theological Seminary, Pittsburgh, Pa.
Evangelical Alliance.

SCHRADER (OTTO), Dr. phil. et jur. h.c.
Ordentlicher Professor für vergleichende Sprachforschung an der Universität zu Breslau; author of *Prehistoric Antiquities of the Aryan Peoples.*
Family (Teutonic and Balto-Slavic).

SCHULHOF (JOHN MAURICE), M.A. (Cantab. et Oxon.).
Clare College; sometime Scholar of Trinity College, Cambridge; late Fellow of St. Augustine College, Canterbury.
Eudæmonism.

SCOTT (CHARLES ANDERSON), M.A. (Camb.), D.D. (Aber.).
Professor of New Testament in Westminster College, Cambridge.
Eudoxianism.

SELL (EDWARD), B.D., D.D., M.R.A.S.
Fellow of the University of Madras; Hon. Canon of St. George's Cathedral, Madras; Secretary of the Church Missionary Society, Madras; author of *The Faith of Islam*, *The Historical Development of the Qur'ān.*
Faith (Muslim).

SHAW (CHARLES GRAY), Ph.D.
Professor of Philosophy in the University of New York; author of *Christianity and Modern Culture*, *The Precinct of Religion*, *The Value and Dignity of Human Life.*
Enlightenment.

SPEIGHT (HAROLD EDWIN BALME), M.A.
Fellow of Manchester College, Oxford; Junior Minister of Essex Church, Kensington; formerly Assistant Professor of Logic and Metaphysics in the University of Aberdeen.
Fichte.

SPENCE (LEWIS).
Edinburgh; author of *Mythologies of Ancient Mexico and Peru*, *The Popol Vuh*, *A Dictionary of Mythology*, *The Civilisation of Ancient Mexico.*
Dualism (American), **Fetishism** (American).

SPILLER (GUSTAV).
General Secretary of the International Union of Ethical Societies; Hon. Secretary of the World Conferences for promoting Interracial Concord; Hon. Organizer of the First International Moral Education Congress.
Education (Moral), **Ethical Movement.**

SRAWLEY (JAMES HERBERT), D.D.
Tutor and Theological Lecturer in Selwyn College, Cambridge; Examining Chaplain to the Bishop of Lichfield.
Eucharist (to end of Middle Ages).

STALKER (JAMES), M.A., D.D.
Professor of Church History in the United Free Church College, Aberdeen.
Evangelicalism.

STARBUCK (EDWIN DILLER), Ph.D.
Professor of Philosophy in the State University of Iowa; author of *The Psychology of Religion.*
Female Principle.

STEVENSON (Mrs. MARGARET SINCLAIR), M.A., Sc.D.
Of the Irish Mission, Rajkot, India; sometime Scholar of Somerville College, Oxford; author of *Notes on Modern Jainism.*
Festivals and Fasts (Jain).

STOCK (ST. GEORGE), M.A.
Lecturer in Greek in the University of Birmingham; author of *English Thought for English Thinkers.*
Fate (Greek and Roman).

STONE (DARWELL), M.A., D.D.
Principal Pusey Librarian, Oxford; author of *A History of the Doctrine of the Holy Eucharist.*
Episcopacy.

STRAHAN (JAMES), M.A.
Edinburgh; author of *Hebrew Ideals.*
Encratites, Euchites, Family (Biblical and Christian).

SUFFRIN (AARON EMMANUEL), M.A. (Oxon.).
Vicar of Waterlooville, Hants.
Dualism (Jewish), **Fate** (Jewish).

SUTHERLAND (J. F.), M.D., F.R.S.E., F.S.S.
Late Deputy Commissioner in Lunacy for Scotland.
Drunkenness.

TACHIBANA (SHUNDO).
Professor in the Soto-Sect College, Tokyo.
Ethics and Morality (Japanese).

TAYLOR (ALFRED EDWARD), M.A. (Oxon.), D.Litt. (St. Andrews).
Professor of Moral Philosophy in the United College of SS. Salvator and Leonard, St. Andrews; late Fellow of Merton College, Oxford; Fellow of the British Academy; author of *The Problem of Conduct* (1901), *Elements of Metaphysics* (1903), *Varia Socratica* (1911).
Dreams and Sleep (Introductory).

TEMPLE (Lt.-Col. Sir RICHARD C., Bart.), C.I.E.
Hon. Fellow of Trinity Hall, Cambridge; late of the Indian Army; Deputy Commissioner, Burma, 1888–94; Chief Commissioner, Andaman and Nicobar Islands, 1894–1903; editor of the *Indian Antiquary* since 1884.
Fetishism (Indian).

THURSTON (HERBERT), B.A., S.J.
Joint-Editor of the Westminster Library for Priests and Students; author of *Life of St. Hugh of Lincoln*, *The Holy Year of Jubilee*, *The Stations of the Cross.*
Extreme Unction.

TURNER (STANLEY HORSFALL), M.A., D.Litt.
Fellow of the Royal Economic Society; Deputy Chief Inspector for Scotland to the National Health Insurance Commission; formerly Lecturer in Political Economy in the University of Aberdeen.
Economics, Fabian Society.

VOLLERS (KARL), Dr.Phil.
Ehemals Professor der Semitischen Sprachen an der Universität, und Direktor des Grossherzogl. Munzkabinets, Jena.
Festivals and Fasts (Muslim).

WADDELL (Lt.-Colonel L. AUSTINE), C.B., C.I.E., LL.D., F.L.S., F.R.A.I., M.R.A.S., I.M.S.
Late Professor of Tibetan in University College, London; author of *The Buddhism of Tibet, Tribes of the Brahmaputra Valley, Lhasa and its Mysteries.*
Festivals and Fasts (Tibetan).

WALSHE (W. GILBERT), M.A.
London Secretary of Christian Literature Society for China; late 'James Long' Lecturer; author of *Confucius and Confucianism*; editor of *China.*
Fate (Chinese).

WARFIELD (BENJAMIN BRECKINRIDGE), D.D., LL.D., Litt.D.
Charles Hodge Professor of Didactic and Polemic Theology in the Theological Seminary of the Presbyterian Church in the U.S.A. at Princeton, New Jersey.
Edwards and the New England Theology.

WATT (HUGH), M.A., B.D.
Minister of the United Free Church at Bearsden, Dumbartonshire; Examiner in Church History to the United Free Church.
Eucharist (Reformation and post-Reformation period).

WHITLEY (WILLIAM THOMAS), M.A., LL.D., F.R.Hist.S., F.T.S.
Secretary of the Baptist Historical Society; formerly Principal of the Baptist College of Victoria, and Secretary of the Victorian Baptist Foreign Mission.
Enthusiasts (Religious).

WISSOWA (GEORG), Dr. jur. et phil.
Ordentlicher Professor an der Universität zu Halle; Geheimer Regierungsrat.
Expiation and Atonement (Roman).

WOODS (FRANCIS HENRY), M.A., B.D.
Rector of Bainton, Yorkshire; late Fellow and Theological Lecturer of St. John's College, Oxford.
Festivals and Fasts (Hebrew).

CROSS-REFERENCES

In addition to the cross-references throughout the volume, the following list of minor references may be useful:

TOPIC.	PROBABLE TITLE OF ARTICLE.
Dutch East Indies	Indonesia.
Dutch Reformed Church	Reformed Church.
Dyaks	Indonesia.
Dyophysitism	Monophysitism.
Dyothelitism	Monothelitism.
Eagle	Animals.
Earth-mother	Earth, Earth-gods.
East	Orientation.
Easter	Calendar (Christian), Festivals and Fasts (Christian).
Ecclesiasticism	Clericalism and Anti-Clericalism.
Eclecticism	Philosophy (Greek).
Eel	Animals.
Effigy	Magic.
Egg	Cosmogony and Cosmology.
Elephant	Animals.
Elves	Demons and Spirits, Fairy.
Emperor-worship	Cæsarism, Deification.
Ephod	Dress.
Epilepsy	Disease and Medicine.
Erigena	Scholasticism.
Eternal Life	Life and Death, Ethics (Christian).
Ethiopian Church	Abyssinia.
Evangelical Association	Sects (Modern Christian).
Evangelical Counsels	Counsels and Precepts.
Evangelical Union	Presbyterianism.
Execration	Cursing and Blessing.
False Witness	Oaths.
Familiar Spirit	Demons and Spirits.
Fanaticism	Enthusiasts (Religious).
Fellowships	Brotherhoods, Communistic Societies, Monasticism.

LISTS OF ABBREVIATIONS

I. General

A.H. = Anno Hijrae (A.D. 622).
Ak. = Akkadian.
Alex. = Alexandrian.
Amer. = American.
Apoc. = Apocalypse, Apocalyptic.
Apocr. = Apocrypha.
Aq. = Aquila.
Arab. = Arabic.
Aram. = Aramaic.
Arm. = Armenian.
Ary. = Aryan.
As. = Asiatic.
Assyr. = Assyrian.
AT = Altes Testament.
AV = Authorized Version.
AVm = Authorized Version margin.
A.Y. = Anno Yazdagird (A.D. 639).
Bab. = Babylonian.
c. = *circa*, about.
Can. = Canaanite.
cf. = compare.
ct. = contrast.
D = Deuteronomist.
E = Elohist.
edd. = editions or editors.
Egyp. = Egyptian.
Eng. = English.
Eth. = Ethiopic.
EV = English Version.
f. = and following verse or page: as Ac $10^{34f.}$
ff. = and following verses or pages: as Mt $11^{28ff.}$
Fr. = French.
Germ. = German.
Gr. = Greek.
H = Law of Holiness.
Heb. = Hebrew.
Hel. = Hellenistic.
Hex. = Hexateuch.
Himy. = Himyaritic.
Ir. = Irish.
Iran. = Iranian.
Isr. = Israelite.
J = Jahwist.
J″ = Jehovah.
Jerus. = Jerusalem.
Jos. = Josephus.
LXX = Septuagint.
Min. = Minæan.
MSS = Manuscripts.
MT = Massoretic Text.
n. = note.
NT = New Testament.
Onk. = Onkelos.
OT = Old Testament.
P = Priestly Narrative.
Pal. = Palestine, Palestinian.
Pent. = Pentateuch.
Pers. = Persian.
Phil. = Philistine.
Phœn. = Phœnician.
Pr. Bk. = Prayer Book.
R = Redactor.
Rom. = Roman.
RV = Revised Version.
RVm = Revised Version margin.
Sab. = Sabæan.
Sam. = Samaritan.
Sem. = Semitic.
Sept. = Septuagint.
Sin. = Sinaitic.
Skr. = Sanskrit.
Symm. = Symmachus.
Syr. = Syriac.
t. (following a number) = times.
Talm. = Talmud.
Targ. = Targum.
Theod. = Theodotion.
TR = Textus Receptus.
tr. = translated or translation.
VSS = Versions.
Vulg. = Vulgate.
WH = Westcott and Hort's text.

II. Books of the Bible

Old Testament.

Gn = Genesis.
Ex = Exodus.
Lv = Leviticus.
Nu = Numbers.
Dt = Deuteronomy.
Jos = Joshua.
Jg = Judges.
Ru = Ruth.
1 S, 2 S = 1 and 2 Samuel.
1 K, 2 K = 1 and 2 Kings.
1 Ch, 2 Ch = 1 and 2 Chronicles.
Ezr = Ezra.
Neh = Nehemiah.
Est = Esther.
Job.
Ps = Psalms.
Pr = Proverbs.
Ec = Ecclesiastes.
Ca = Canticles.
Is = Isaiah.
Jer = Jeremiah.
La = Lamentations.
Ezk = Ezekiel.
Dn = Daniel.
Hos = Hosea.
Jl = Joel.
Am = Amos.
Ob = Obadiah.
Jon = Jonah.
Mic = Micah.
Nah = Nahum.
Hab = Habakkuk.
Zeph = Zephaniah.
Hag = Haggai.
Zec = Zechariah.
Mal = Malachi.

Apocrypha.

1 Es, 2 Es = 1 and 2 Esdras.
To = Tobit.
Jth = Judith.
Ad. Est = Additions to Esther.
Wis = Wisdom.
Sir = Sirach or Ecclesiasticus.
Bar = Baruch.
Three = Song of the Three Children.
Sus = Susanna.
Bel = Bel and the Dragon.
Pr. Man = Prayer of Manasses.
1 Mac, 2 Mac = 1 and 2 Maccabees.

New Testament.

Mt = Matthew.
Mk = Mark.
Lk = Luke.
Jn = John.
Ac = Acts.
Ro = Romans.
1 Co, 2 Co = 1 and 2 Corinthians.
Gal = Galatians.
Eph = Ephesians.
Ph = Philippians.
Col = Colossians.
1 Th, 2 Th = 1 and 2 Thessalonians.
1 Ti, 2 Ti = 1 and 2 Timothy.
Tit = Titus.
Philem = Philemon.
He = Hebrews.
Ja = James.
1 P, 2 P = 1 and 2 Peter.
1 Jn, 2 Jn, 3 Jn = 1, 2, and 3 John.
Jude.
Rev = Revelation.

III. For the Literature

1. The following authors' names, when unaccompanied by the title of a book, stand for the works in the list below.

Baethgen=*Beiträge zur sem. Religionsgesch.*, 1888.
Baldwin=*Dict. of Philosophy and Psychology*, 3 vols. 1901–1905.
Barth=*Nominalbildung in den sem. Sprachen*, 2 vols. 1889, 1891 ([2]1894).
Benzinger=*Heb. Archäologie*, 1894.
Brockelmann=*Gesch. d. arab. Litteratur*, 2 vols. 1897–1902.
Bruns-Sachau=*Syr.-Röm. Rechtsbuch aus dem fünften Jahrhundert*, 1880.
Budge=*Gods of the Egyptians*, 2 vols. 1903.
Daremberg-Saglio=*Dict. des ant. grec. et rom.*, 1886–90.
De la Saussaye=*Lehrbuch der Religionsgesch.*[3], 1905.
Deussen=*Die Philos. d. Upanishads*, 1899 [Eng. tr., 1906].
Doughty=*Arabia Deserta*, 2 vols. 1888.
Grimm=*Deutsche Mythologie*[4], 3 vols. 1875–1878, Eng. tr. *Teutonic Mythology*, 4 vols. 1882–1888.
Hamburger=*Realencyclopädie für Bibel u. Talmud*, i. 1870 ([2]1892), ii. 1883, suppl. 1886, 1891 f., 1897.
Holder=*Altceltischer Sprachschatz*, 1891 ff.
Holtzmann-Zöpffel=*Lexicon f. Theol. u. Kirchenwesen*[2], 1895.
Howitt=*Native Tribes of S. E. Australia*, 1904.
Jubainville=*Cours de Litt. celtique*, i.–xii., 1883 ff.
Lagrange=*Études sur les religions sémitiques*[2], 1904.
Lane=*An Arabic-English Dictionary*, 1863 ff.
Lang=*Myth, Ritual and Religion*[2], 2 vols. 1899.
Lepsius=*Denkmäler aus Ægypten u. Æthiopien*, 1849–1860.
Lichtenberger=*Encyc. des sciences religieuses*, 1876.
Lidzbarski=*Handbuch der nordsem. Epigraphik*, 1898.
McCurdy=*History, Prophecy, and the Monuments*, 2 vols. 1894–1896.
Muir=*Sanskrit Texts*, 1858–1872.
Muss-Arnolt=*A Concise Dict. of the Assyrian Language*, 1894 ff.
Nowack=*Lehrbuch d. heb. Archäologie*, 2 vols. 1894.
Pauly-Wissowa=*Realencyc. der classischen Altertumswissenschaft*, 1893–1895.
Perrot-Chipiez=*Hist. de l'Art dans l'Antiquité*, 1881 ff.
Preller=*Römische Mythologie*, 1858.
Réville=*Religion des peuples non-civilisés*, 1883.
Riehm=*Handwörterbuch d. bibl. Altertums*[2], 1893–1894.
Robinson=*Biblical Researches in Palestine*[2], 1856.
Roscher=*Lex. d. gr. u. röm. Mythologie*, 1884.
Schaff-Herzog=*The New Schaff-Herzog Encyclopedia of Relig. Knowledge*, 1908 ff.
Schenkel=*Bibel-Lexicon*, 5 vols. 1869–1875.
Schürer=*GJV*[3], 3 vols. 1898–1901 [*HJP*, 5 vols. 1890 ff.].
Schwally=*Leben nach dem Tode*, 1892.
Siegfried-Stade=*Heb. Wörterbuch zum AT*, 1893.
Smend=*Lehrbuch der alttest. Religionsgesch.*[2], 1899.
Smith (G. A.)=*Historical Geography of the Holy Land*[4], 1896.
Smith (W. R.)=*Religion of the Semites*[2], 1894.
Spencer (H.)=*Principles of Sociology*[3], 1885–1896.
Spencer-Gillen[a]=*Native Tribes of Central Australia*, 1899.
Spencer-Gillen[b]=*Northern Tribes of Central Australia*, 1904.
Swete=*The OT in Greek*, 3 vols. 1893 ff.
Tylor (E. B.)=*Primitive Culture*[3], 1891 [[4]1903].
Ueberweg=*Hist. of Philosophy*, Eng. tr., 2 vols. 1872–1874.
Weber=*Jüdische Theologie auf Grund des Talmud u. verwandten Schriften*[2], 1897.
Wiedemann=*Die Religion der alten Ægypter*, 1890 [Eng. tr., revised, *Religion of the Anc. Egyptians*, 1897].
Wilkinson=*Manners and Customs of the Ancient Egyptians*, 3 vols. 1878.
Zunz=*Die gottesdienstlichen Vorträge der Juden*[2], 1892.

2. Periodicals, Dictionaries, Encyclopædias, and other standard works frequently cited.

AA=Archiv für Anthropologie.
AAOJ=American Antiquarian and Oriental Journal.
ABAW=Abhandlungen d. Berliner Akad. d. Wissenschaften.
AE=Archiv für Ethnographie.
AEG=Assyr. and Eng. Glossary (Johns Hopkins University).
AGG=Abhandlungen d. Göttinger Gesellschaft der Wissenschaften.
AGPh=Archiv für Geschichte der Philosophie.
AHR=American Historical Review.
AHT=Ancient Hebrew Tradition (Hommel).
AJPh=American Journal of Philosophy.
AJPs=American Journal of Psychology.
AJRPE=American Journal of Religious Psychology and Education.
AJSL=American Journal of Semitic Languages and Literature.
AJTh=American Journal of Theology.
AMG=Annales du Musée Guimet.
APES=American Palestine Exploration Society.
APF=Archiv für Papyrusforschung.
AR=Anthropological Review.
ARW=Archiv für Religionswissenschaft.
AS=Acta Sanctorum (Bollandus).
ASG=Abhandlungen der Sächsischen Gesellschaft der Wissenschaften.
ASoc=L'Année Sociologique.
ASWI=Archæological Survey of W. India.
AZ=Allgemeine Zeitung.
BAG=Beiträge zur alten Geschichte.
BASS=Beiträge zur Assyriologie u. sem. Sprachwissenschaft (edd. Delitzsch and Haupt).
BCH=Bulletin de Correspondance Hellénique.
BE=Bureau of Ethnology.
BG=Bombay Gazetteer.
BJ=Bellum Judaicum (Josephus).
BL=Bampton Lectures.
BLE=Bulletin de Littérature Ecclésiastique.
BOR=Bab. and Oriental Record.
BS=Bibliotheca Sacra.
BSA=Annual of the British School at Athens.
BSAA=Bulletin de la Soc. archéologique à Alexandrie.
BSAL=Bulletin de la Soc. d'Anthropologie de Lyon.
BSAP=Bulletin de la Soc. d'Anthropologie, etc., Paris.
BSG=Bulletin de la Soc. de Géographie.
BTS=Buddhist Text Society.
BW=Biblical World.
BZ=Biblische Zeitschrift.

CAIBL=Comptes rendus de l'Académie des Inscriptions et Belles-Lettres.
CBTS=Calcutta Buddhist Text Society.
CF=Childhood of Fiction (MacCulloch).
CGS=Cults of the Greek States (Farnell).
CI=Census of India.
CIA=Corpus Inscrip. Atticarum.
CIE=Corpus Inscrip. Etruscarum.
CIG=Corpus Inscrip. Græcarum.
CIL=Corpus Inscrip. Latinarum.
CIS=Corpus Inscrip. Semiticarum.
COT=Cuneiform Inscriptions and the OT [Eng. tr. of *KAT*^{2}; see below].
CR=Contemporary Review.
CeR=Celtic Review.
ClR=Classical Review.
CQR=Church Quarterly Review.
CSEL=Corpus Script. Eccles. Latinorum.
DACL=Dict. d'Archéologie chrétienne et de Liturgie (Cabrol).
DB=Dict. of the Bible.
DCA=Dict. of Christian Antiquities (Smith-Cheetham).
DCB=Dict. of Christian Biography (Smith-Wace).
DCG=Dict. of Christ and the Gospels.
DI=Dict. of Islam (Hughes).
DNB=Dict. of National Biography.
DPhP=Dict. of Philosophy and Psychology.
DWAW=Denkschriften der Wiener Akad. der Wissenschaften.
EBi=Encyclopædia Biblica.
EBr=Encyclopædia Britannica.
EEFM=Egyp. Explor. Fund Memoirs.
ERE=The present work.
Exp=Expositor.
ExpT=Expository Times.
FHG=Fragmenta Historicorum Græcorum (coll. C. Müller, Paris, 1885).
FL=Folklore.
FLJ=Folklore Journal.
FLR=Folklore Record.
GA=Gazette Archéologique.
GB^2=Golden Bough^2 (Frazer).
GGA=Göttingische Gelehrte Anzeigen.
GGN=Göttingische Gelehrte Nachrichten (Nachrichten der königl. Gesellschaft der Wissenschaften zu Göttingen).
GIAP=Grundriss d. Indo-Arischen Philologie.
GIrP=Grundriss d. Iranischen Philologie.
GJV=Geschichte des Jüdischen Volkes.
GVI=Geschichte des Volkes Israel.
HDB=Hastings' Dict. of the Bible.
HE=Historia Ecclesiastica.
HGHL=Historical Geography of the Holy Land (G. A. Smith).
HI=History of Israel.
HJ=Hibbert Journal.
HJP=History of the Jewish People.
HN=Historia Naturalis (Pliny).
HWB=Handwörterbuch.
IA=Indian Antiquary.
ICC=International Critical Commentary.
ICO=International Congress of Orientalists.
ICR=Indian Census Report (1901).
IG=Inscrip. Græcæ (publ. under auspices of Berlin Academy, 1873 ff.).
IGA=Inscrip. Græcæ Antiquissimæ.
IGI=Imperial Gazetteer of India^2 (1885); new edition (1908–1909).
IJE=International Journal of Ethics.
ITL=International Theological Library.
JA=Journal Asiatique.
JAFL=Journal of American Folklore.
JAI=Journal of the Anthropological Institute.
JAOS=Journal of the American Oriental Society.
JASB=Journal of the Anthropological Society of Bombay.
JASBe=Journ. of As. Soc. of Bengal.
JBL=Journal of Biblical Literature.
JBTS=Journal of the Buddhist Text Society.
JD=Journal des Débats.
JDTh=Jahrbücher f. deutsche Theologie.
JE=Jewish Encyclopedia.
JGOS=Journal of the German Oriental Society.
JHC=Johns Hopkins University Circulars.
JHS=Journal of Hellenic Studies.
JLZ=Jenäer Litteraturzeitung.
JPh=Journal of Philology.
JPTh=Jahrbücher f. protest. Theologie.
JPTS=Journal of the Pāli Text Society.
JQR=Jewish Quarterly Review.
JRAI=Journal of the Royal Anthropological Institute.
JRAS=Journal of the Royal Asiatic Society.
JRASBo=Journal of the Royal Asiatic Society, Bombay branch.
JRASC=Journal of the Royal Asiatic Society, Ceylon branch.
JRASK=Journal of the Royal Asiatic Society, Korean branch.
JRGS=Journal of the Royal Geographical Society.
JThSt=Journal of Theological Studies.
KAT^2=Die Keilinschriften und das AT (Schrader), 1883.
KAT^3=Zimmern-Winckler's ed. of the preceding [really a totally distinct work], 1903.
KB or *KIB*=Keilinschriftliche Bibliothek (Schrader), 1889 ff.
KGF=Keilinschriften und die Geschichtsforschung, 1878.
LCBl=Literarisches Centralblatt.
LOPh=Literaturblatt für Oriental. Philologie.
LOT=Introduction to Literature of OT (Driver).
LP=Legend of Perseus (Hartland).
LSSt=Leipziger sem. Studien.
M=Mélusine.
MAIBL=Mémoires de l'Acad. des Inscriptions et Belles-Lettres.
MBAW=Monatsbericht d. Berliner Akad. d. Wissenschaften.
MGH=Monumenta Germaniæ Historica (Pertz).
MGJV=Mittheilungen der Gesellschaft für jüdische Volkskunde.
MGWJ=Monatsbericht f. Geschichte u. Wissenschaft des Judentums.
MI=Origin and Development of the Moral Ideas (Westermarck).
MNDPV=Mittheilungen u. Nachrichten des deutschen Palästina-Vereins.
MR=Methodist Review.
MVG=Mittheilungen der vorderasiatischen Gesellschaft.
MWJ=Magazin für die Wissenschaft des Judentums.
NBAC=Nuovo Bulletino di Archeologia Cristiana.
NC=Nineteenth Century.
NHWB=Neuhebräisches Wörterbuch.
NINQ=North Indian Notes and Queries.
NKZ=Neue kirchliche Zeitschrift.
NQ=Notes and Queries.
NR=Native Races of the Pacific States (Bancroft).
NTZG=Neutestamentliche Zeitgeschichte.
OED=Oxford English Dictionary (Murray).
OLZ=Orientalische Litteraturzeitung.
OS=Onomastica Sacra.
OTJC=Old Testament in the Jewish Church (W. R. Smith).
OTP=Oriental Translation Fund Publications.
PAOS=Proceedings of American Oriental Society.
PASB=Proceedings of the Anthropological Soc. of Bombay.
PB=Polychrome Bible (English).
PBE=Publications of the Bureau of Ethnology.
PC=Primitive Culture (Tylor).
PEFM=Palestine Exploration Fund Memoirs.

PEFSt = Palestine Exploration Fund Quarterly Statement.
PG=Patrologia Græca (Migne).
PJB=Preussische Jahrbücher.
PL=Patrologia Latina (Migne).
PNQ=Punjab Notes and Queries.
PR=Popular Religion and Folklore of N. India (Crooke).
PRE[3]=Prot. Realencyclopädie (Herzog-Hauck).
PRR=Presbyterian and Reformed Review.
PRS=Proceedings of the Royal Society.
PRSE=Proceedings Royal Soc. of Edinburgh.
PSBA=Proceedings of the Soc. of Biblical Archæology.
PTS=Pāli Text Society.
RA=Revue Archéologique.
RAnth=Revue d'Anthropologie.
RAS=Royal Asiatic Society.
RAssyr=Revue d'Assyriologie.
RB=Revue Biblique.
RBEW=Reports of the Bureau of Ethnology (Washington).
RC=Revue Critique.
RCel=Revue Celtique.
RCh=Revue Chrétienne.
RDM=Revue des Deux Mondes.
RE=Realencyclopädie.
REG=Revue des Études Grecques.
REg=Revue Égyptologique.
REJ=Revue des Études Juives.
REth=Revue d'Ethnographie.
RHLR=Revue d'Histoire et de Littérature Religieuses.
RHR=Revue de l'Histoire des Religions.
RN=Revue Numismatique.
RP=Records of the Past.
RPh=Revue Philosophique.
RQ=Römische Quartalschrift.
RS = Revue sémitique d'Épigraphie et d'Hist. ancienne.
RSA=Recueil de la Soc. archéologique.
RSI=Reports of the Smithsonian Institution.
RTAP=Recueil de Travaux rélatifs à l'Archéologie et à la Philologie.
RTP=Revue des traditions populaires.
RThPh=Revue de Théologie et de Philosophie.
RTr=Recueil de Travaux.
RWB=Realwörterbuch.
SBAW=Sitzungsberichte der Berliner Akad. d. Wissenschaften.
SBE=Sacred Books of the East.
SBOT=Sacred Books of the OT (Hebrew).
SDB=Single-vol. Dict. of the Bible (Hastings).
SK=Studien u. Kritiken.
SMA=Sitzungsberichte der Münchener Akademie.
SSGW=Sitzungsberichte d. Kgl. Sächs. Gesellsch. d. Wissenschaften.
SWAW=Sitzungsberichte d. Wiener Akad. d. Wissenschaften.
TAPA = Transactions of American Philological Association.
TASJ=Transactions of the Asiatic Soc. of Japan.
TC=Tribes and Castes.
TES=Transactions of Ethnological Society.
ThLZ=Theologische Litteraturzeitung.
ThT=Theol. Tijdschrift.
TRHS=Transactions of Royal Historical Society.
TRSE=Transactions of Royal Soc. of Edinburgh.
TS=Texts and Studies.
TSBA=Transactions of the Soc. of Biblical Archæology.
TU=Texte u. Untersuchungen.
WAI=Western Asiatic Inscriptions.
WZKM=Wiener Zeitschrift f. Kunde des Morgenlandes.
ZA=Zeitschrift für Assyriologie.
ZÄ=Zeitschrift für ägyp. Sprache u. Altertumswissenschaft.
ZATW=Zeitschrift für die alttest. Wissenschaft.
ZCK=Zeitschrift für christliche Kunst.
ZCP=Zeitschrift für celtische Philologie.
ZDA=Zeitschrift für deutsches Altertum.
ZDMG = Zeitschrift der deutschen morgenländischen Gesellschaft.
ZDPV = Zeitschrift des deutschen Palästina-Vereins.
ZE=Zeitschrift für Ethnologie.
ZKF=Zeitschrift für Keilschriftforschung.
ZKG=Zeitschrift für Kirchengeschichte.
ZKT=Zeitschrift für kathol. Theologie.
ZKWL=Zeitschrift für kirchl. Wissenschaft u. kirchl. Leben.
ZM=Zeitschrift für die Mythologie.
ZNTW=Zeitschrift für die neutest. Wissenschaft.
ZPhP=Zeitschrift für Philosophie und Pädagogik.
ZTK=Zeitschrift für Theologie u. Kirche.
ZVK=Zeitschrift für Volkskunde.
ZVRW = Zeitschrift für vergleichende Rechtswissenschaft.
ZWT=Zeitschrift für wissenschaftliche Theologie.

[A small superior number designates the particular edition of the work referred to, as *KAT*[2], *LOT*[6], etc.]

ENCYCLOPÆDIA
OF
RELIGION AND ETHICS

D

DRAVIDIANS (North India).—**1. Meaning of term.**—The term 'Dravidian' (Skr. *Drāviḍa*, the adjectival form of *Draviḍa*) seems to have been primarily an equivalent for 'Tamil,' but was extended by Caldwell (*Dravidian Grammar*², 4 ff.) to denote the family of languages formerly designated Tamulian or Tamulic, practically including all the languages of Southern India,—Tamil, Telugu, Malayālam, Canarese, and Tulu,—which form a group well defined and closely related one to another. Manu (*Institutes*, x. 43, 44) speaks of the Draviḍas as a tribe of Kṣatriyas, or warriors, who had become out-castes; and, as they are the only southern tribe mentioned in his lists, Caldwell supposed that in ancient times the name was loosely applied to the whole of the South Indian peoples. Whether or not this belief was well founded, his invention of the word 'Dravidian' as a generic term for the South Indian group of languages is convenient, and has been generally accepted. By a natural, if not perfectly justifiable, extension the term, primarily philological, has been widely used in an ethnological sense, and we have become accustomed to speak of the Dravidian peoples when we really mean the races speaking the Dravidian languages. Even in this slightly extended sense the term 'Dravidian' is fairly exact and little open to misunderstanding. Risley, however, in his report on the last Census of India (i. 500), has used the term in a much wider sense. He includes in it races 'extending from Ceylon to the valley of the Ganges, and pervading the whole of Madras, Hyderābād, the Central Provinces, most of Central India, and Chotā Nāgpur'; and he regards this as 'probably the original type of the population of India, now modified to a varying extent by the admixture of Aryan, Scythian, and Mongoloid elements.' Nearly all the other existing races of India, except the Indo-Aryans, such as the Rājputs, Jāts, and Khatrīs of the Panjāb, are classed by him as Scytho-Dravidians, Aryo-Dravidians, or Mongolo-Dravidians. In other words, every element in the present population which cannot be classed as Aryan, Scythian, or Mongoloid, is designated 'Dravidian.' This terminology is, as Risley himself is aware, open to much criticism. Like 'Aryan,' 'Dravidian,' originally a purely philological term, is wanting in precision when used in an ethnological sense. But the name, however unsatisfactory it may be, has now passed into popular use, and the writer of the present article is unable to suggest a better alternative. Here it is taken to denote that form of Animism which constitutes the belief of a body of forest tribes occupying the line of hills which forms the backbone of the Peninsula, extending from the Indian Ocean into the lower course of the Ganges. Analogous forms of belief are found among the agricultural, artisan, and menial population of the great northern Plains, and along the lower slopes of the Himālaya. Beliefs and practices of this type form the basis of popular Hinduism as we now observe it. In fact, no clear line of distinction can be drawn between these forms of Animism and much of what is known as orthodox Hinduism. Both have been in contact for an enormous period of time, and each has reacted on the other, Hinduism admitting many of the Animistic beliefs and rites of the darker races, while these in their turn have largely accepted the outward observances of the Hindu faith, worshipping the Hindu gods, who are often only modifications of their own deities, and adopting the rules of caste and the social restrictions concerning food and personal purity which caste enforces.

2. Primitive Dravidian religion.—An attempt has been made by Caldwell in Southern India to investigate on the basis of philology the primitive Dravidian beliefs.

'They were,' he says (*op. cit.* 118), 'without hereditary "priests" and "idols," and appear to have had no idea of "heaven" or "hell," of the "soul" or "sin"; but they acknowledged the existence of God, whom they styled Kō, or king—a realistic title little known to orthodox Hinduism. They erected to his honour a "temple," which they called Kō-il, "God's house"; but I cannot find any trace of the "worship" which they offered to him.'

In another passage (*ib.* 580 ff.) he compares the demonolatry of the Dravidians with the shamanism of High Asia, noting as features of resemblance the absence of a regular priesthood; the acknowledgment of God's existence, combined with neglect of His worship; the non-existence of belief in metempsychosis; the objects of worship being not gods or heroes, but demons, which are supposed to be cruel, revengeful, and capricious, and are worshipped with blood sacrifices and wild dances.

'The officiating magician or priest excites himself to frenzy, and then pretends or supposes himself to be possessed by the demon to which worship is being offered; and whilst in this state he communicates to those who consult him the information he has received. The demonolatry practised in India by the more primitive Dravidian tribes is not only similar to this, but the same. Every word used in the foregoing description of Shamanite worship would apply equally to the Dravidian demonolatry; and in depicting the ceremonies of the one race we depict those of the other also.'

It must, however, be remarked that the belief in metempsychosis, unless Caldwell uses the term in its technical sense, is found among the Northern Dravidians.

3. Shamanism.—Thus, according to Caldwell, the basis of the beliefs of the South Indian Dravidian tribes is shamanism, and many instances of similar customs can be quoted among those of the North; *e.g.* the Kūrs or Muāsīs of Chotā Nāgpur communicate with the evil spirit which they worship through their priest, the *baigā*. He assembles the people, music and dancing commence, and an invocation of the spirit is chanted—

'until one or more of the performers manifest possession by wild rolling of the eyes and involuntary spasmodic action of the muscles. The affection appears contagious, and old women and others who have not been dancing become influenced by it in a manner that is horrible to contemplate. . . . This certainly is the most thorough form of demon worship with which we have met, and one that must appear to its votaries to testify to its own reality each time it was resorted to' (Dalton, 232 f.).

Similar practices employed for the exorcism of diseases are widely spread among the people of the northern Plains. But even among the tribes which occupy the central range of hills this form of shamanistic orgies seems never to have taken the same hold among the people as has been the case in Southern India, where what is known as Devil Dancing may be observed much more frequently than in the north. This has been described among the Shānārs of Tinnevelly by Caldwell (*op. cit.* 585 f.) and by Burnell ('The Devil Worship of the Tulavas,' *IA*, 1894); and in Northern India, at least, shamanism has played a quite unimportant part in the development of the popular beliefs.

4. Animism.—The religion of the Northern Dravidians is mainly a form of Animism, defined by Tylor, who invented the term, as 'the belief in Spiritual Beings' (*Prim. Cult.*[3], 1891, i. 424); or as Jevons (*Introd. to Hist. of Rel.*, 1896, p. 22) defines it: 'All the many movements and changes which are perpetually taking place in the world of things, were explained by primitive man on the theory that every object which had activity enough to affect him in any way was animated by a life and will like his own.' The term has been used by some authors 'to cover the various manifestations of what is commonly but cumbrously styled the "anthropomorphic" tendency of savage thought' (Marett, *Thresh. of Rel.*, 1909, p. 6); and the same author (*ib.* 11) urges that what he calls 'Supernaturalism' is 'not only logically, but also, in some sense, chronologically prior to Animism.' Following the same line of argument, Risley (*Census Report*, 1901, i. 352), while accepting the title 'Animism' for the vague, amorphous conception which he is discussing, endeavours to ascertain the ideas which underlie it:

'What the Animist worships and seeks by all means to influence and conciliate is the shifting and shadowy company of unknown powers or influences making for evil rather than for good, which resides in the primeval forest, in the crumbling hills, in the rushing river, in the spreading tree, which gives its spring to the tiger, its venom to the snake, which generates jungle fever, and walks abroad in the terrible guise of cholera, smallpox, or murrain. Closer than this he does not seek to define the object to which he offers his victim, or whose symbol he daubs with vermilion at the appointed season. Some sort of power is there, and that is enough for him. Whether it is associated with a spirit or an ancestral ghost, whether it proceeds from the mysterious thing itself, whether it is one power or many, he does not stop to inquire.'

And he goes on to suggest that—

'the hypothesis that the earliest beginnings of savage religion are to be sought in the recognition of elemental forces to which, in the first instance, no personal qualities are ascribed, may, perhaps, afford an explanation of a problem which has exercised several inquirers of late—the origin of the *fainéant* unworshipped Supreme beings who figure in savage mythology almost all over the world. . . . When the era of anthropomorphism sets in and personal gods come into fashion, the active and passive powers of the earlier system are clothed in appropriate attributes. The former become departmental spirits or gods, with shrines and temples of their own and incessant offerings from apprehensive votaries. The latter receive sparing and infrequent worship, but are recognized, *en revanche*, as beings of a higher type, fathers and well-wishers of mankind, patrons of primitive ethics, makers of things, who have done their work and earned their repose. The Santāl Marang Buru represents the one; the Bongas or godlings of disease are examples of the other.'

5. Animism in Northern India.—The characteristics of Animism in Northern India have often been described, and do not materially differ from what we observe in other parts of the world. Thus Gait writes of Assam (*Census Report*, 1891, i. 93):

'There is a vague but very general belief in some one omnipotent being, who is well-disposed towards men, and whom therefore there is no necessity of propitiating. Then come a number of evil spirits, who are ill-disposed towards human beings, and to whose malevolent interference are ascribed all the woes which afflict mankind. To them, therefore, sacrifices must be offered. These malevolent spirits are sylvan deities, spirits of the trees, the rocks, and the streams, and sometimes also of the tribal ancestors. There is no regular priesthood, but some persons are supposed to be better endowed with the power of divination than others. When a calamity occurs, one or more of these diviners, shamans, or soothsayers is called on to ascertain the particular demon who is offended, and who requires to be pacified by a sacrifice. This is done either by devil dancing, when the diviner works himself into a paroxysm of drunkenness and excitement, and then holds converse with the unseen spirits around him, or by the examination of omens—eggs, grains of rice, or the entrails of a fowl. There is a profound belief in omens of all sorts; no journey is undertaken unless it is ascertained that the fates are propitious, while persons who have started on a journey will turn back should adverse omens be met with on the way. One peculiarity in connexion with their sacrifices may be mentioned. On all necessary occasions, goats, fowls, and other animals are offered to the gods; but it is always assumed that the latter will be content with the blood and entrails; the flesh is divided among the sacrificer and his friends, the presiding soothsayer usually getting the lion's share.'

From another point of view, dealing with the case of persons gifted with the hereditary powers of healing, Rose (i. 161) shows that—

'as primitive religions have no conception of the distinction between the soul and the life, they reason, logically enough from their standpoint, that, precisely as physical life is transmitted, so too is the soul transmitted from one generation to another, and with the life transmigrate, as it were, all the attributes and powers of the progenitor. On this theory it is quite easy to explain the transmitted hereditary power of curing disease or causing evil by means which we may call supernatural.

Animism, as we observe it in Northern India, develops on various lines, according to the diverse objects which are supposed to be occupied and dominated by spirit agency. It will be convenient to begin with the worship of the celestial bodies, though, as a matter of fact, this type of worship is probably later than the cult of tree-spirits or of the village gods. It is in an advanced stage of religious belief, says Robertson Smith (*Rel. Sem.*[2], 1894, p. 114), that celestial gods predominate.

6. Sun-worship.—Sun-worship prevails widely among the forest tribes of the Central Hills. When they are in trouble, the Kharwārs appeal to the sun; any open space on which he shines serves as an altar. When a sacrifice is needed, the Kisāns offer a white cock to him, according to the laws of mimetic magic. The Bhuiyās and Orāons worship him as Borām or Dharm Devatā. The Korwās reverence him as Bhagwān, 'the wonderful, the divine one'—a term borrowed from the Hindus; his service is done in an open space, where an ant-hill is used as the altar. The Kharriās adore him under the name of Bero.

'Every head of a family should during his lifetime make not less than five sacrifices to this deity—the first of fowls, the second of a pig, the third of a white goat, the fourth of a ram, and the fifth of a buffalo. He is then considered sufficiently propitiated for that generation, and regarded as an ungrateful god if he does not behave handsomely to his votary.'

Worship of a similar kind is done by the Kols and Orāons (*qq.v.*) (Dalton, 130, 132, 133, 141, 157, 159, 186, 223). The Davars, a forest tribe in the Thāna district on the west coast, worship the Sun at the Divālī, or feast of lights, by throwing red lead towards him, and offering fowls, which are not killed, but allowed to fly into the forest (*BG* xiii. pt. i. 157). The Bhīls of the Sātpura Hills have a form of joint worship of the Sun and Moon under the name of Sondal Deo (Luard, i. 72). Among the village population of the Plains this non-Aryan worship of the Sun has been combined with the Aryan cult of Sūrya or Sūraj Nārāyaṇ.

7. Moon-worship.—Moon-worship, though probably earlier in origin than that of the Sun, is much less important. The Binjhiās of Chotā Nāgpur worship Nind-bonga as the Moon, in conjunction with Sing-bonga, or the Sun; and in many other cases the worship of both luminaries is combined, as with the Chandor of the Mundās, known also as Chando Omol or Chanalā, who is worshipped by women, and considered to be the wife of Sing-bonga, the Sun-god, and mother of the stars (Risley, *Tribes and Castes*, i. 136, ii. 103 f.; Dalton, 186). The most curious form is the Chauk Chanda rite in Bihār. On that day the people fast and employ a Brāhman to worship the Moon with an offering of flowers and sweetmeats. It is believed that, if any one looks upon the Moon that day, calamity will befall him. Should any one be unlucky enough to do this, he can repel the dangerous influences by getting himself abused by other people; abuse, like mock fights, being regarded as a means of protection against demons (Frazer, *GB*² iii. 93 f.). He therefore, in order to excite their abuse, flings stones on the roofs of his neighbours' houses (*NINQ* v. 23 f.).

8. Planet-worship.—The worship of the other planets is of much less importance. Their motions are observed chiefly by astrologers, who calculate the horoscopes of children, and examine the figures with a view to determining whether a marriage will or will not be auspicious. Eclipses are supposed to be the work of spirit agency embodied in the demon Rāhu, who can be scared by noise, while the suffering Sun or Moon can be restored to vitality by sacrifice and fasting during the period of the eclipse (see DOSĀDHS).

9. The spirits of water.—According to the theory of Animism, the flow of water in river, stream, or well is considered to be due to spirit action, and floods and whirlpools are the work of a malignant spirit. In the Panjāb, when a village is menaced by floods, the headman makes an offering of a coco-nut (which is probably a form of commutation of an original human sacrifice) and a rupee to the flood-demon. He holds the offering in his hand, and stands in the water until the flood rises high enough to wash it away. Then it is believed that the waters will abate. Some offer an animal victim, a buffalo, horse, or ram, which, after blood has been drawn from its ear as a sign that the offering has been made, is flung into the water (*NINQ* i. 5). At a whirlpool on the Tapti river the Goṇḍs sacrifice a goat before daring to cross the stream (*Berar Gazetteer*, 1870, p. 35). This propitiation of the water-spirit develops in two directions—first, into the worship of rivers held specially sacred, like the Ganges and Narbadā, on whose banks, when the sinner bathes, he enters into communion with the spirit of the stream. As his body is cleansed, so his soul is relieved from pollution. His idea of purification is not spiritual in our sense of the word—that is foreign to primitive habits of thought—but spiritual in the sense of getting rid of evil spirits and their dangerous influence. In the second place, the vague spiritual entity which animates the water is personified into one or other of a host of water-godlings, like Kwāja Khizr or Pīr Bhadr, who are worshipped by fishermen and boatmen whose business is on the great waters. Wells, in the same way, are sacred. Some have underground connexion with a holy river; others are appropriated to the cult of some special god; others are oracular. Hot springs, in particular, indicate the presence of the fire-spirit; of a demon which, if not propitiated, brings disease; of a Rākṣasa or demon slain by a goddess whose blood keeps the water warm (Waddell, *Among the Himalayas*, 203; *BG* xiv. 373).

In the same way the fall of rain is due to spirit agency which, if not conciliated, causes drought. The curious nudity rite, by which women endeavour to repel the evil influence by dragging a plough through the soil—a good instance of mimetic magic—is familiar (Crooke, *PR* i. 69; Frazer, *GB*² i. 98).

10. Wind-spirits.—On the same principle the spirit which causes wind is personified in the Panjāb as Sendū Bīr, the whistling god, whose voice announces the approaching storm. He has now been adopted into Hinduism as an incarnation of Śiva, and is regarded as a malignant deity, causing madness, and burning houses, stealing crops, and otherwise immoral (Rose, i. 130). When a whirlwind comes, the Ghasiyā women in Mirzapur hold the house thatch, and stick an iron or wooden spoon into it as a charm against the demon; if a man were to touch it, the storm would sweep the roof away (*NINQ* i. 68). In the Panjāb, Pherū is the deified saint who rides on the little whirlwinds which blow in the hot weather, and an appeal to him protects the worshipper from harm (Crooke, *PR* i. 81).

11. The hail-demon.—Hail also is the work of a spirit, which, under the rules of sympathetic magic, can be scared by cutting the hailstones with a knife; or the business of repelling it is entrusted to a special magician, like the *śilārī* of eastern Bengal, who, when a storm approaches, rushes almost naked from his hut, with a rattan wand in his right hand, invoking Parameśvara, the Supreme God. He ascends a mound, and, spreading abroad his hands and indicating by a motion of his wand the direction in which he desires the hail to pass away, he recites a series of doggerel incantations (Wise, 368 f.). The Garpagārī of the Central Provinces and the Wolī or Oliyā of Kumaun exercise similar functions (*NINQ* iii. 106; *Central Provinces Gazetteer*, 1870, p. 48).

12. Tree-spirits.—The tree with its waving leaves and branches, apparently dying in the autumn and waking to new life in the spring, providing various medicines and intoxicants, is naturally regarded as inhabited by a spirit. Such spirits, impersonations of the vague terrors of the jungle, the causers of death, accident, and disease to those who intrude within their domains, are generally regarded as malignant. But, when the tribe adopts a settled life, it is provided by the tree-spirit with food and shelter. Tribes like the Mundās take care to preserve a patch of the primitive jungle in which the spirits disestablished by the woodman's axe may repose. Here most of the tribal religious worship is conducted (see ORĀONS). The cult at a later period develops into reverence for one or other of the special varieties of trees, some of which, like those of the fig genus, are regarded as the abode of the collective gods; others are appropriated to the service of individual gods, as the Bel (*Ægle marmelos*) to Śiva, or the Tulasī (*Ocymum sanctum*) to Viṣṇu. Under the shade of the village tree, where the business of the community is conducted, are placed the rude stones which collectively embody the Grāma-devatā, or local gods and godlings (see § 27).

These tree-spirits, in their most primitive conception, form a host of beings without special names, and to whom no special functions are assigned. But in process of time they tend to become concentrated into one or more distinct personalities, like the Silvanus of the Romans. Such is Barām, the forest deity of the Juāngs of Keunjhar, who stands at the head of their system, and is regarded with great veneration (Risley, *Tribes and Castes*, i. 353). We find also, in Bengal, Thānpati, one of the elder gods of the Savarās, 'lord of the sacred grove' (*thān*) (*ib.* ii. 244). In the same category is Sarnā Būṛhī, the 'old lady of the grove' (*sarnā*) of the Orāons, who corresponds to Deswālī, the 'lady of the cleared land' of the Mundās (Bradley-Birt, *Chota Nagpore*, 39). In the United Provinces her place is taken by Bansaptī Mā (Skr. *vanaspati*, 'ruler of the wood'), who is known by the Musahars, a half-civilized jungle tribe, as Bansatī or Bansurī.

'By her command the trees bear fruit, the bulbs grow in the earth, the bees make honey, the tussar worm fattens on the *āsan* leaf, and lizards, wolves, and jackals (useful as food to man) multiply their kind. She is the goddess of child-birth. To her the childless wife makes prayers for the grant of offspring. In her name and by her aid the medicine-man or sorcerer expels devils from the bodies of the possessed. In her name and to her honour the village man kindles a new fire for lighting a brick-kiln. Woe to the man who takes a false oath in the name of Bansatī!' (Nesfield, *Calcutta Rev.* lxxxvi. 264).

So with the Thārūs of the sub-Himālayan Tarāī. They fear the demons lurking in the forest trees, especially the weird cotton tree (*Bombax heptaphylla*).

'Only the terrible cry of fire will bring these poor fear-stricken creatures to open their doors and remove the heavy barriers from their huts at night; and even in the daytime, amid the hum of human life, the songs of the birds, and the lowing of cattle, no Thāru, man, woman, or child, will ever venture along a forest line without casting a leaf, a branch, or a piece of old rag upon the Bansatī formed at the entrance of the deep woods, to save themselves from the many diseases and accidents the goblins and malicious spirits of the forests can bring upon and cause them. The Bansatī, or "good spirit" of the woods, is a square space cut in the ground, six feet by six, and covered with pine branches' (Knowles, 214).

Another form of this cult, already alluded to in the case of the Thārūs, is that of attaching rags to trees. Trees thus decorated are to be found all over Northern India, and are known as Chithariyā or Chithraiyā Bhavānī, 'Our Lady of Tatters,' or in the Panjāb as Lingrī Pīr, or the 'Rag Saint' (Crooke, *PR* i. 161). The question of the motive of these rag-offerings has been fully discussed by Hartland (*LP*, ii. 175 ff.). Discarding the two most usual explanations—either that they are offerings to the god or presiding spirit, or that they contain the disease of which one desires to be rid, and transfer it to any one who touches or handles them—he regards the rite as another application of the same reasoning which underlies various practices of witchcraft and folk-medicine.

'If an article of my clothing in a witch's hand may cause me to suffer, the same article in contact with a beneficent power may relieve my pain, restore me to health, or promote my general prosperity. A pin that has pricked my wart, even if not covered with my blood, has by its contact, by the wound it has inflicted, acquired a peculiar bond with the wart; the rag that has rubbed the wart has by that friction acquired a similar bond; so that, whatever is done to the pin or to the rag, whatever influences the pin or rag may undergo, the same influences are by that very act brought to bear upon the wart. If, instead of using a rag, I rub my wart with raw meat and then bury the meat, the wart will decay and disappear with the decay and dissolution of the meat. In like manner my shirt or stocking, or a rag to represent it, placed upon a sacred bush, or thrust into a sacred well—my name written upon the wall of a temple—a stone or pellet from my hand cast upon a holy image or a sacred cairn—a remnant of my food cast into a sacred waterfall or bound upon a sacred tree, or a nail from my hand driven into the trunk of a tree—is therefore in continual contact with divinity; and the effluence of divinity, reaching and involving it, will reach and involve me. In this way I may become permanently united with the god' (*LP* ii. 214).

The evidence from Northern India corroborates this explanation, which throws much light on the Animistic practices which are discussed in the present article.

One peculiar custom connected with trees is that of marrying the bride and bridegroom to them—of which numerous examples have been collected in Northern India (Crooke, *PR* ii. 115 ff.). The object of this custom is obscure. In some cases the intention may possibly be to communicate to the newly-wedded pair the vigorous reproductive power of the tree. In most cases, however, the intention seems to be to transfer to the tree the malignant spirit influence which menaces them, and, in particular, endangers the fertility of the union (Frazer, *GB*² i. 195 f.).

13. Worship of Mother Earth.—From the worship of the vague spiritual beings with whom the Dravidian peoples the forests amidst which he dwells, and in which he collects the game, roots, and fruits which constitute his only food supply, we pass on to the worship of the Earth-Mother, which marks the adoption of a settled life and his earliest experiments in agriculture. Among many savage races the Earth-deity is spiritualized as female (Tylor, i. 326); and it has been suggested with some degree of probability that the predominance of Mother-worship in India and elsewhere represents a survival from the matriarchate, the prevalence of which has been attested in India by a considerable amount of evidence (J. E. Harrison, *Proleg. to Gr. Religion*, 1903, pp. 261, 499; Risley-Gait, *Census Report*, i. 448). As in the case of the Greek *Thesmophoria*, the gist of which was a mimicking of Nature's processes, in a word, the ritual of sympathetic or mimetic magic—the women fasting seated on the ground because the earth was desolate, then rising and revelling to stir the Megara to imitate the impulse of spring—the North Indian cult of Mother Earth is largely in the hands of women. Again, though we find in the Rigveda the personification of Dyaus and Pṛithivī as respectively gods of heaven and earth, from whom the other deities and even the whole universe were supposed to spring, this cult is quite different from that of the Earth-Mother as we find it among the Dravidians (Monier-Williams, *Brāhmanism and Hinduism*⁴, 1891, p. 182; Oppert, 402).

14. Restoration of the fertility of the Earth-Mother.—The theory of the Dravidians, like that of many primitive races, *e.g.* the Romans (Granger, *Worship of Romans*, 1895, p. 208), is that the Earth after bearing each successive harvest becomes exhausted, and that if she is to continue to discharge her functions she must be periodically refreshed and roused to new activity. In one of the dances of the Kol women of Chotā Nāgpur, they all kneel and pat the ground with their hands in time to the music, as if coaxing the earth to be fertile; and this also doubtless is the intention of the Orāon dance when the performers 'all face inwards and simultaneously jumping up come down on the ground with a resounding stamp that marks the finale of the movement' (Dalton, 198, 255). The same rite was performed at the worship of Demeter Cidaria in Arcadia, and it is found in many other parts of the world (Frazer, *Pausan.*, 1900, iv. 239). Secondly, as among the Celts (Nutt, *Voy. of Bran*, ii. [1897] 150), it was believed that the Earth-spirit needed to be periodically refreshed with human blood. This was one of the ideas underlying the rite of *meriah* sacrifice among the Kandhs (*q.v.*). Thirdly, the fertility of the soil was supposed to depend upon the periodical marriage of Mother Earth with her male consort. The cult of this divine pair meets us throughout the whole range of Dravidian myth, belief, and ritual. Thus in Bengal we find Būṛhā-Būṛhī, 'the old man and the old lady,' whom the Rautiās regard as the ancestors of mankind; they are in Eastern Bengal invoked in times of sickness and trouble; they generally haunt a sacred tree, but in their worship, if a perfect tree be not procurable, a branch of it will answer the purpose (Wise, 132 f.; Risley, *op. cit.* i. 270, 381, ii. 203). The Majhwārs of Mirzapur worship the pair Dih and Deohārin, the impersonated protectors of the village site (*dih*), and they also recognize as crop-guardians the pair Ningo Bāghiyā, the phallic tiger, to whom, when the grain is ripe, the first five handfuls, after being taken home and crushed, are offered; and Hariyārī Mātā, 'the mother of greenery,' to whom a burnt sacrifice is made in the field at sowing and harvest time (Crooke, *Tribes and Castes*, iii. 435, 447). The Pāvrās, a forest tribe in Khāndesh, sacrifice, before harvest, goats and fowls, and make an offering of corn to a pair called Baṛā Kumbā and Rānī Kājhal, who occupy adjoining sacred trees; the pair are invoked at the marriage rites in a song which describes the wedding of these deities of the forest (*BG* xii. 97 f.). The divine pair worshipped by the Kharwārs of the Central Hills are Chandol and Chandā, apparently moon-deities (the moon having a powerful influence over the fertility of the crops), who correspond to the Muṇḍā Desaulī and his wife, Jhareṛā or Maturū (Dalton, 130, 188; Frazer, *GB*[2] ii. 154 ff.). The Kharwārs of Palamāu reverence in the same way a pair known as Darhār and Ḍākin, a boar and country spirits being offered to the male, and a sow and spirits to the female; in Mirzapur, their goddess Devī is associated with the cult of the phallic Gansām (*NINQ* i. 40). In the United Provinces and Bihār we meet a pair of village sprites, Chordeva and his spouse Chordevī, or Jāk and Jakhī, who are known as the thieving deities, because husband and wife live in separate villages, and, when the crops in one village are more productive than those of another, the people think that the Jāk robs the fields of the barren tract to support his wife. This reminds us of the law of the XII Tables, which 'forbade people to spirit away the crops from a neighbour's field by means of spells and incantations' (Crooke, *TC* iii. 447; Frazer, *Pausanias*, v. 57).

In a higher stage of culture among the people of Bengal, Sītalā, a form of the Mother-goddess, who presides over smallpox, has as her husband Ghaṇṭakaraṇa, who is now being adopted into the cult of Śiva; and even the Sun-god is provided with a partner (Gait, *Bengal Census Report*, i. 193). The patron pair in Rājputāna are Eklinga, whose name betrays his phallic origin, now known as Īśvara, the lord Śiva, and Gaurī, the yellow lady, who is identified with Annapūrṇā, 'she that is filled with *or* possessed with food.' At the opening of the year a deputation is sent outside the city to provide earth for Gaurī, thus typifying her as the Earth-goddess. With this image is united one of Īśvara, 'and they are placed together; a small trench is then excavated, in which barley is sown; the ground is irrigated and artificial heat supplied till the grain germinates, when the females join hands and dance round it, invoking the blessings of Gaurī on their husbands. The young corn is then taken up, distributed, and presented by the females to the men, who wear it in their turbans' (Tod, i. 603). This is one of the Gardens of Adonis so fully illustrated by Frazer (*Adonis, Attis, Osiris*[2], 1907, p. 194 ff.). In Southern India even Viṣṇu is associated with the Earth-goddess Bhūmi-devī, as her consort (Oppert, 363); and in a still later development Śiva is represented in his androgynous form as Ardhanārīśa, with a hermaphrodite body, uniting in himself the principles of male and female generation.

15. Marriage of the Earth-goddess.—The rites of symbolic marriage of the Earth-Mother to her partner are periodically performed by many of the Dravidian tribes. Among the Kharwārs of Chotā Nāgpur she is represented by Mūchak Rānī, whose marriage is performed every third year with great pomp and ceremony. The people assemble with drums and horns, and sing wild songs in honour of the bride and bridegroom. The officiant enters a cave, and returns bringing with him the Rānī, who is represented by a small oblong-shaped stone daubed with red lead. This is dressed in wedding garments and carried in a litter to a sacred tree, under which it is placed. The procession then starts for another hill, where the bridegroom, supposed to belong to the Agariyā, or iron-smelter caste, resides. The stone of the goddess is here flung into a chasm; but it is believed that the two hills are connected by an underground passage, by which the bride returns, always in the form of the same stone, every third year to her father's house (*NINQ* iii. 23 f.). Among the Musahars of the United Provinces, Bansaptī, the Forest Mother, is married to Gansām or Bansgopāl, who is represented by a mud pillar in phallic form (Crooke, *TC* iv. 34 f.). In Bihār, Hara or Śiva is combined with his female form in Hargaurī, who is worshipped at marriages (Buchanan, i. 420). In Khāndesh, Rānubāī is a favourite family-goddess. Her marriage and investiture with the sacred thread are performed in a seven days' ceremony, in which the goddess is represented by an image made of wheat flour (*BG* xii. 51). The marriage of Dhartī, or Mother Earth, as performed by the Orāons, is described in the article ORĀONS. In the Panjāb, Darya Sāhib, the god of the river Indus, is married in great state to the goddess, who is embodied in a pot of hemp; and Devī, in the form of Ganggor, represented by an image of clay or cow-dung, is loaded with ornaments, and, after her marriage is performed, is flung into a well (Rose, i. 118, 128). When the tutelary deity of Marwār fell into the hands of the prince of Amber, he married him to his own female deity, and then returned him to his original owner (Tod, ii. 123). As among many savage races, like the Maoris, the legend is told of the severing of the wedded pair, Heaven and Earth, so the Gonds believe that 'formerly the sky lay close down upon the earth. One day an old woman happened to be sweeping, and when she stood up she knocked her head against the sky. Enraged, she put up her broom and pushed the sky away, when it rose up above the earth, and has ever since remained there' (Russell, i. 94; Lang, *Custom and Myth*[2], 1893, p. 45 ff.). It is perhaps possible that we have an echo of the same marriage rite in the tale of the wedding of Ghāzī Miyāṅ, the Muhammadan hero, who has been adopted from Musalmān hagiology into the worship of the Dravidians of the Plains, and whose career ends in untimely death (*NINQ* iv. 70; Crooke, *PR* ii. 324). This is also perhaps the origin of the myth of Dūlhā Deo, 'the bridegroom god,' wedded and slain in the midst of the marriage rites. He reminds us of Attis, god of vegetation, married and periodically put to death in order to promote the fertility of the soil (*NINQ* iii. 39, 93; Crooke, *PR* i. 119 ff.). With this, in the legend of Dūlhā Deo, is combined the world-wide myth of the disappearance of bride or bridegroom in consequence of the infringement of some mystic rule of tabu (Lang, *op. cit.* 64 ff.).

16. Ritual of the worship of Mother Earth.—Among the forest tribes of the Central Hills, Mother Earth is supposed to live with the other village gods in a pile of stones collected round the sacred tree of the hamlet. Worship is done through the *baigā* (*q.v.*), or aboriginal priest, at the chief agricultural seasons—ploughing, sowing, and harvesting—with an offering of flowers and the sacrifice of a goat, the flesh of which is eaten by the men, boys, and unmarried girls, no grown-up girl or married woman sharing in the rite. This is the formal village-worship; but, as we have seen (§§ 9, 14), grown-up women have private services of their own, which are distinct from the tribal celebrations. Other tribes worship her when they begin wood-cutting or collecting thatching-grass, or gleaning the petals of the mahua (*Bassia latifolia*). With some tribes the offering consists of molasses, butter, cakes, a fowl, and some spirits. According to the principles of mimetic magic, the goat should be grey-coloured, and the fowl speckled (*NINQ* i. 77).

17. Her benign and malevolent aspect.—In fact, the character of the offering marks the twofold conception of the goddess. In her benevolent form she is Mother of all things, giver of corn, producer of fertility in man and beast. Accordingly she is presented with offerings of flowers, milk, or the fruits of the earth. In her malevolent and chthonic aspect, which would naturally be recognized by tribes which dispose of their dead by inhumation, she is appeased by blood sacrifices of animals, or even, as in the case of the Kandhs, with human victims. Macpherson, writing of this tribe (*Calcutta Rev.* v. 54), states that in her malevolent form, as the supreme power,

'when a tribe engages in war with enemies of another race, her awful name is invoked, and vows of sacrifice are recorded in the event of success. Her nature is purely malevolent; but she does not seem to interfere with the independent action of other deities in their respective spheres, and she is nowhere peculiarly present.'

On the other hand, in her benign character she

'presides over the operations of nature. . . . Upon her depend the fecundity of the soil and the growth of all rural produce, the preservation of the patriarchal houses, the health and increase of the people, and, in an especial manner, the safety of the flocks and their attendants. She is worshipped by human sacrifices. She has no fixed corporeal shape, form, image, symbol, or temple. But she, together with the other superior gods, may temporarily assume any earthly form at pleasure; as, for instance, that of the tiger as convenient for purposes of wrath.'

In her benign form, among the Kharwārs of Mirzapur she is honoured by sprinkling pulse and rice on the ground, with the prayer: 'Mother Earth! Keep us in prosperity, and protect the ploughman and oxen!' (*NINQ* i. 141); while the orthodox Hindu, at the time of sowing and harvest, prays: 'I salute the Earth, the realizer of all desires, she who is blessed with all kinds of riches and creatures; she who is contented, faithful, and virtuous, the giver of all that one asks for the realization of desires' (*ib.* v. 76). In the eastern Panjāb she takes the form of Shāod Mātā, 'Mother of fertility,' and she is represented by a plough coulter placed between two round balls of cow-dung, probably with a phallic significance. Over these are laid leaves of holy trees, and the peasant, as he measures the corn on the threshing-floor, prays: 'O Mother Shāod! Give us increase, and make our bankers and rulers contented!' (*ib.* i. 173). Her malevolent nature appears in the Kandh prayer: 'We are not satisfied with our wealth; but what we do possess we owe to you, and for the future we hope for the fulfilment of our desires. We intend to go on such a day to such a village, to bring human flesh for you. We trust to attain our desires through this service. Forget not the oblation!' (Macpherson, *Memorials*, 1865, p. 117). Probably the idea of communicating the fertility of the Mother is the object of the curious Maṭmangarā rite at the marriages of the lower castes, when the 'lucky earth' is dug from the village tank, and brought to form the marriage altar and the fireplace at which the wedding feast is cooked (Crooke, *PR* i. 27).

18. The Mother identified with the snake.—In her chthonic aspect the Mother-goddess and her partner are naturally identified with the snake, an animal which lives in holes and moves in the darkness. This was the case at the Greek *Thesmophoria*, where the pigs' flesh thrown into the chasms of the earth seems to have been regarded as in some sort the due of the earth-powers as represented by the guardian snakes; the Erinys, the offended ghost, was considered to be a snake, and this was also the guise of the death hero (J. E. Harrison, *op. cit.* 123, 232, 326 ff.). The Kūrs of Chotā Nāgpur claim descent from Nāga Bhūiya and Nāga Bhūiāin, the male and female earth-serpents (Dalton, 231). The Mother-goddess of South India, Ellammā, has images of snakes in her temple; and Durgammā, another form of the deity, has her temple built over a snake-hole beside a sacred Margosa tree, which, with the snake, if there be one there, is held sacred, and both are symbols of the goddess (Oppert, 469, 497). The Ḍāngīs of the United Provinces worship the Earth-god, Bhūmiyā, as an old snake; and in Bundelkhand snakes are worshipped under the name of Bhiarānī, a form of Devī, a title which is said to mean 'dweller in the earth' (Luard, i. 75). From the same point of view, the snake is the guardian of underground treasure (Crooke, *PR* ii. 134 ff.).

19. The cult of the Earth-Mother developing into a general Mother-cult.—It seems probable that from this primitive conception of the Earth-Mother as either kindly or malevolent has developed the worship of the Mother-goddesses, which forms such an important element in the beliefs of the people of Northern India. As in Greece, the close connexion of the Mother-goddess with the earth is illustrated in sacred art. As in the Greek vases she appears rising out of a mound, so Ellammā's image is a figure hewn in stone, fashioned so that only the head is visible, while the body is concealed in the earth; and the same conception appears in Buddhist bas-reliefs, where we find the Earth-goddess, Mahāpathavī or Pṛithivī, rising out of the ground and supporting the horse of the Master (J. E. Harrison, *op. cit.* 277 ff.; Oppert, 468; Grünwedel, *Buddhist Art in India*, 1901, p. 100 f.).

This conception of the Mother-goddess seems to be the most important element in the Dravidian cultus which has been imported into Hinduism. Like the Earth-Mother, the other Mothers appear in a double manifestation, at once benignant and malevolent. This is shown in the epithets of Devī, who is the most common type of the class—Kanyā, 'the maiden'; Kanyākumārī, 'the youthful virgin'; Sarvamaṅgalā, 'always auspicious'; Śākambharī, 'nourisher of herbs'; and, on the other side, Chāmuṇḍā, 'the demon-slayer'; Kālī, 'the black one'; Ṛajasī, 'the fierce'; Raktadantī, 'bloody-toothed.' It is this contrariety of aspect which renders the cult of the Mother-goddesses so perplexing. In one contrasted and yet identical form they both cause and remove disease. Thus in eastern Bengal the Mother is usually worshipped under the form of Siddhīśvarī, 'perfected queen,' or Vṛddhīśvarī, 'old queen'; but when epidemic diseases break out she is appealed to with an euphemistic epithet as Rākhyā or Bhadrā Kālī, 'Kālī the protector, the auspicious' (Wise, 135). In this benignant form she is one of the favourite objects of worship in Bihār as Kṣemakarnī, 'she who confers blessings' (Buchanan, ii. 49). In the Central Provinces the village-goddess Devī represents the Earth-goddess; she can cause or avert smallpox and cholera, and is incarnate in the body of any one suffering from the former disease; so much so that those who enter the room where the patient lies take off their shoes as a mark of respect to her (Russell, i. 79).

20. Varied manifestations of the Mothers.—Hence the manifestations of the Mothers are infinitely varied. Bahucharājī, who has a shrine at Anjār in Kachchh, is the 'looking-glass goddess,' before whom the votary worships his own image on a sheet of silvered glass; but, to illustrate the elasticity of the cult, in Baroda she is said to have been originally a Chāraṇ woman, who when attacked by robbers committed suicide, and was elevated to the rank of a manifestation of the divinity (*BG* v. 212). Another group of six Mothers in Kāthiāwāṛ are also said to be the daughters of a Chāraṇ who was dismissed from court as unlucky because he was childless. He practised austerities at a shrine of Kālī, and his six daughters, who were born in response to a prayer addressed to the goddess, became Mothers (*ib.* viii. 642 f.). The cult, in fact, is vague in the extreme. The worship of Ekvīrā, the Mother of the Kārli Caves, is mixed up with the original Buddhism, of which this place was a centre, part of the cultus being the circumambulation of a *dagoba*, or Buddhist relic shrine; and the temple of the Turturiā Mother is served by women, who are supposed to be modern representatives of the original Buddhist nuns (*ib.* xi. 383; Cunningham, *Archæological Reports*, xiii. 147). It is in Western India that the Mother-cult most widely prevails. Each Rājput clan in Kāthiāwāṛ has a patron Mother; all Rājputs visit the Mātā with their brides immediately after marriage, and the mint at Navanagar is presided over by the Mother Āśāpurī, 'hope-fulfiller'; but peculation goes on under her very eyes.

21. Ritual of Mother-worship.—The worship at the famous shrine of Becharājī in Baroda may be taken as an example of the ritual of the Mother-cult, which here is almost purely Animistic. Every morning the head officiant, after ablution, enters the adytum and pours a mixture of milk, curds, clarified butter, sugar, and honey—known collectively as *pañchāmṛita*, 'the five divine foods'—over the image, and drops water over it through a perforated metal pot, while a Brāhman chants hymns from the Veda. Coloured powder and flowers are placed upon the image, incense and camphor are burnt, and silver lamps are kept lighted day and night. After the worship, the 'children's food' (*bālabhojya*), consisting of wheat-flour, sugar, and clarified butter, is offered with a coco-nut (a survival of human sacrifice), and the morning service ends with the waving of lamps (*ārti*), burning of camphor, ringing of bells, and beating of gongs. Another meal of sugar and milk is offered to the goddess about 10 a.m., a little being sprinkled over the image, and the rest consumed by the priests. In the evening a passage of the sacred book telling of the exploits of the Devī is read, the figure is washed and worshipped, and more cooked food is presented (*BG* vii. 611 f.).

More usually the Devī or Kālī receives a blood offering, some of which is sprinkled upon the altar (see DEVĪ PĀTAṆ).

Of all the orthodox Hindu cults that of Devī is most akin to Animism, and hence many of the forest tribes of the Central Hills accept as representatives of her many village-goddesses, such as Khermātā, primarily an Earth-goddess; the Desahāī Devī, or goddess of the four quarters of the hamlet; the Chithraiyā Devī, or goddess of rags (§ 12), besides various local incarnations like the Vindhyabāsinī Devī, the goddess of the Vindhyan range (Russell, i. 83). In the Panjāb we find unmarried girls recognized as representatives of Devī, to whom, as to the goddess, offerings are made twice a year. Here, also, girls make images of Śiva and his spouse Pārvatī, Devī in her mountain form, and afterwards throw them into the water. The popular explanation is that this rite commemorates the suicide of a woman married to a boy husband.

'But a different explanation has been suggested. The deities Śiva and Pārvatī are conceived as spirits of vegetation, because their images are placed in branches over a heap of flowers and grass; but this theory leaves many points unexplained, and until we have full details of the rites observed at all the festivals of Devī we cannot hope to discover the ideas underlying these local rites' (Rose, i. 126).

22. The Disease-Mothers.—Mention has been already made (§ 19) of Kālī as the causer and remover of disease. The control of disease is in the hands of a host of these Mothers, to each of whom the power over a certain malady is assigned; Śītalā, for instance, controlling smallpox, Mārī Mātā cholera, and so on (see BENGAL, § 13; Crooke, *PR* i. 123 ff.). These functions are not, however, clearly fixed, and are often attributed to the Mothers of orthodox Hinduism. Thus the Gangotā cultivators in Bihār worship Jagadambā, 'Mother of the world,' twice or three times a month, with offerings of husked rice and incense; while under the title of Bhagavatī, 'the worshipful one,' Devī is propitiated at weddings and in times of sickness, by offerings of kids, butter, basil leaves, and vermilion (Risley, *Tribes and Castes*, i. 269).

Shamanism is an important agency in the cure of disease. The *kaphri*, as Buchanan (ii. 131) calls the exorcist in Bihār, makes an offering to the deity of disease, and becomes violently agitated before he announces the treatment which he recommends. When a person is bitten by a snake he is carried to the shrine of Biṣaharī, 'she who removes venom,' and the practitioner foretells the event by staring into a vessel of water, the troubling of the water indicating the arrival of the deity to take part in the cure. In the eastern Panjāb, the exorcist, who is here called *bhagat*, 'worshipper,' builds a shrine to his familiar, before whom he dances. When he is to be consulted, which should be at night, the inquirer provides tobacco and music. The former is waved over the person of the invalid and given to the *bhagat* to smoke. While the music plays and a butter lamp is lighted, the *bhagat* sometimes lashes himself with a whip, under which treatment he is seized with the afflatus, and, in a paroxysm of dancing and head-wagging, states the name of the malignant influence, the manner in which it may be propitiated, and the time when the disease may be expected to abate. Or he waves corn over the sick man and counts out the grains into heaps, one grain for each spirit which is likely to be at the bottom of the trouble, and that one on whose heap the last grain falls is the one to be attended to (*NINQ* i. 127 f.). In Jalandhar a scape-animal is used; a goat or young buffalo is selected, blood is drawn from its ear, and its face is smeared with vermilion. Then it is taken round and outside the village, bearing the malady with it. It finally becomes the perquisite of the exorcist (*ib.* ii. 191). An important part of the treatment is the muttering of spells and the waving of peacock feathers to scare the spirit (*ib.* iii. 74).

23. Mountain-worship.—'Like the Baal of the Semites, the local Jupiter was commonly worshipped on high places. Wooded heights, round which the rain-clouds gather, were indeed the natural sanctuaries for a god of the sky, the rain, and the oak' (Frazer, *Lect. Kingship*, 1905, p. 208; cf. Farnell, *CGS* i. 4, 51; Fowler, *Roman Festivals*, 1899, pp. 222, 261). The same ideas, combined with the awe and mystery which surround them, doubtless commended the worship of mountains to the Dravidian tribes. Those of the Central Hills imagine each peak to be the haunt of an evil spirit, which they are careful to propitiate before they make an ascent; and it is a common belief that mountains were formed by rival divine or evil powers warring with each other and using the rocks as missiles (*NINQ* i. 47). The cult of mountains has been regarded as purely Dravidian; but this is very doubtful, and at any rate the reverence paid by the Aryans to the mighty Himālayan peaks must have dated from the time when they first came under observation. Many of them became seats of the Hindu gods, and one title of Śiva is Giriśa, while that of his consort is Pārvatī, both meaning 'mountain-dweller.'

In Bengal the Mundās, Santāls, Mahilīs, and other tribes of Chotā Nāgpur revere a mountain-god called Marang Buru or Baṛ Pahāṛ, 'great mountain,' to whom their tribal priest makes sacrifice of buffaloes and other animals. These sacrifices are made at the chief visible habitation of the deity, a bluff near Lodhma (Gait, i. 191). In the Hoshangābād district of the Central Provinces, Sūryabhān, or 'Sun-rays,' is a common name for isolated, round-peaked hills, on which the Sun-god is believed to dwell; and among the Kurkūs, Ḍūngar Deo, 'the mountain-god,' resides on the nearest hill outside the village, where yearly at the Dasahra festival he is worshipped with an offering of two coco-nuts, five dates, and a ball of vermilion paste. They regard him as their tribal god (Elliott, *Settlement Report*, 1867, pp. 121, 254).

24. Animal-worship.—The Northern Dravidians share with other primitive races the belief that animal intelligence is identical with that of man; that animals can, as in the folk-tale world, talk and act precisely as men do; that men and animals may for a time resume the forms which had once been theirs, or, for that matter, take any other. Hence shape-shifting, as it has been called, is widely accepted, and it may even take place by means of death and a new birth, the powers and qualities or even the actual form of a deceased ancestor being reproduced in his descendants. Hence various animals are worshipped within the Dravidian area, of which a few instances will be given here to illustrate the local cults as a supplement to the facts collected in art. ANIMALS.

(*a*) *The horse.*—Some of the Rājput tribes of Gujarāt worship Ghoṛā Deva, 'the horse-god,' in the form of a horse of stone, at their main festivals; and on the sixth day after a birth the Ojhā Kumhār potters of Kachchh form a horse of clay and make the child worship it (Campbell, *Notes*, 292). One of the chief gods of the Goṇḍs is Koḍapen, the horse-god, a stone which is worshipped on the outskirts of the village at the commencement of the rainy season. Only men join in the worship, women being excluded. The *bhūmak* priest besmears the stone with red lead, presents a horse made of pottery, then a heifer, on the head of which he pours spirits and prays: 'Thou art the guardian of the village; we have come and offered to thee according to our ability. If in anything we have failed to please thee, forgive us. Protect our oxen and cows; keep us in safety; let there be no fear in the jungle.' After this the victim is slain and boiled, some of the meat is laid with flour before the god, and the worshippers eat the remainder of the food (Hislop, App. i. p. iii). The Goṇḍs and other Central Indian tribes place earthenware horses on the tombs of ancestors and on the village shrines, which serve as steeds for the sainted dead and for the local gods.

(*b*) *The tiger.*—The tiger is naturally worshipped by the forest tribes. Bāghīśvar, 'the tiger lord,' is a favourite deity along the Vindhyan and Kaimūr ranges. The Santāls and Kisāns worship him as Banrājā, 'forest king,' will not kill him, and believe that he spares them in return for their devotion. Even those who do not actually worship him swear by his name or on his skin, as is the case among the Hos and Juāngs (Dalton, 132, 133, 158, 214). The tribes further west, like the Kurkūs, worship Bāgh or Vāgh Deo, and a female Wāghāī Devī, served by a *bhūmak* priest, who pretends to know spells by which he can protect himself and his parishioners from the beast (*Berar Gazetteer*, 191 f.; Elliott, *op. cit.* 255 f.). The belief in tiger-men, or men who are really metamorphosed tigers, is common, the man-eater being often a person of evil life changed into that form (Gait, *Assam Census*, i. 250 f.; Crooke, *PR* ii. 216 ff.).

(*c*) *The cow.*—Cow-worship, which appears to arise among pastoral tribes which have attained some degree of culture, is naturally not found highly developed among the Dravidians, and the life of the animal is not protected by the effective tabu enforced by orthodox Hindus. The Goṇḍs, for instance, kill a cow at the funeral rites and hang the tail of the victim on the gravestone as a sign that the obsequies have been duly performed; and the Kurkūs sprinkle the blood of a cow on the grave, believing that if this rite be omitted the ghost refuses to rest and returns to earth to plague the survivors (Dalton, 283; *IA* i. 348 f.). See art. COW (Hindu).

It is only among the semi-Hinduized forest tribes that the cult of the cow has made much progress. In Nepāl, where under the present dynasty the rules of Hinduism are rigidly enforced, it is deemed the highest sacrilege to approach the image of the sacred animal, except in a position of adoration, 'insomuch that a malicious person, wishing to suspend the agricultural operations of his neighbour, would be sure to effect his purpose by placing a stone or wooden figure of a cow in the midst of a field' (Kirkpatrick, 100). Further west the cult of the cow is closely connected with that of Kṛṣṇa, and in Central India we have the curious rite of the silent tendance of cattle, in which the performers, drawn from the highest classes of the community, bathe, anoint themselves, put on garlands of flowers, and walk in procession through the grazing grounds, holding bunches of peacock feathers (*NINQ* i. 154 f.).

Special godlings are also worshipped to secure the safety of cattle. Nagar Deo in Gaṛhwāl on the lower Himālaya is supposed to have the cattle in his charge, and he is represented by a trident fixed on a platform to which the first milk given by the animals is dedicated. In Kumāun his place is taken by Chaumū or Baudhān, who recovers stray beasts, receives offerings of milk, and, when a missing animal is found, is honoured by the sacrifice of a goat (*NINQ* i. 56). Among the Kharwārs of the Central Hills, Goraiyā or Gauraiyā, properly a god of boundaries, presides over the herds (Crooke, *Tribes and Castes*, iii. 251).

(*d*) *The dog.*—In common with the Kunbīs of Khāndesh, the Bhīls of that district show extreme reverence to the dog and horse; and the dog is respected by all Marāṭhas, who figure the animal as the companion of their god Bhairoba; and by many Hindus in Western India, who worship the dog of their god Kāla Bhairava (Campbell, *Notes*, 276). At the shrine of Malhārī in Dharwār the Vaggaiyya ministrants dress in blue woollen coats, tie bells and skins round their waists, and meet the pilgrims barking and howling like dogs. They endeavour, in fact, to assimilate their appearance to that of the god whom they serve (Robertson Smith, *Rel. Semites*[2], 437). Each Vaggaiyya has a bowl into which the pilgrims put food; the Vaggaiyyas lay these down, fight with each other like dogs, and then lying on the ground put their mouths, as animals do, into the bowls and eat the contents (*BG* xxii. 212). The cults of Bhairoba or Bhairava, and of Khaṇḍē Rāo, Khaṇḍoba, or

Khaṇḍojī (now promoted to be an incarnation of Śiva), which are widely spread in Western India, have dog-worship as their basis. The Bauris of Bengal will on no account touch a dog, and the water of a tank in which a dog has been drowned cannot be used until an entire rainy season has purified it. Under the influence of the Hindus they have now invented a legend that, as they themselves kill cows and other animals, they deem it right to regard as sacred some beast which is as holy to them as the cow is to Brāhmans; this, as Risley remarks (*Tribes and Castes*, i. 79 f.), being 'a neat reconciliation of the twinges of conscience and cravings of appetite.' But it seems clear that this is an afterthought, and that, the dog being really the sacred animal of the tribe, its 'uncleanness' resulted from its sanctity, as in the case of the pig among the Semites and other races (Frazer, *Pausanias*, iv. 137 f.). 'In general it may be said that all so-called unclean animals were originally sacred; the reason for not eating them was that they were divine' (*GB*² ii. 315).

(*e*) *Birds.*—Many birds are regarded as sacred by the Northern Dravidians; and the sanctity of others, like the crow, the pigeon, and the wagtail, is suggested by the respect paid to omens taken from them. The skin of a species of Buceros or hornbill, known as the 'bird of wealth' (*dhanchiryā*), is hung up in houses by wizards in the Central Provinces, and the thigh bones are attached to the wrists of children as a charm against evil spirits (Hislop, 6). The peacock seems among the Kandhs to impersonate the Earth-Mother, because they placed an effigy of the bird on the top of the *meriah*, or human sacrifice-post (Maltby-Leman, *Manual of Ganjam*, 1882, p. 84).

(*f*) *Fish.*—Fish are regarded in many places as sacred. Some are believed to contain the souls of the dead; all varieties are emblems of fertility, and are therefore used in the marriage rites. At most of the sacred places in Northern India along the sacred rivers, such as Hardwār, Mathurā, and Benares, the fish in that portion of the stream adjoining the bathing places are carefully preserved, and any attempt to catch them is fiercely resented by the Brāhmans. The tabu here enforced is partly due to the sanctity of the holy place which makes things connected with it sacred (Jevons, *Introd.* 63); they are also popularly regarded as impersonations of the divine energy of the stream, and as connected with the dead whose ashes are consigned to its waters. They have now been adopted into the cults of the Hindu gods, and pious people write the name of Rāma on thousands of pieces of bark or paper, which they enclose in little packets and throw to the fish. Once Sītā, wife of Rāma, was bathing in a Deccan stream, when one of the fish bit her leg. If one be now caught and its palate examined, in it will be found a ball of butter (*BG* xviii. pt. i. 93). The crocodile is worshipped as an object of terror. In Baroda the crocodile god, Magar Deo, is worshipped once a year to protect men and animals from the attacks of these monsters, and also as a preventive against illness. The deity is represented by a piece of wood in the form of the animal, supported on two posts (Dalal, i. 157).

25. Totemism.—The respect paid to some of these animals may rest upon a totemistic basis; but it is difficult to say where, in Northern India, the line can be drawn between animal-worship and totemism. In any case the connexion of totemism with the current beliefs of the Dravidians is obscure; and totemism, as we find it at present, generally appears as a mode of defining the exogamous groups, many of which trace their descent from some animal, plant, or other thing which the members of the group regard as sacred and will not eat or injure. The totemistic exogamous groups have been discussed by Risley (*Tribes and Castes*, i., Introd. xlii ff.) and Dalton (254). The latter states that among the Orāons 'the family or tribal names are usually those of animals and plants, and when this is the case the flesh of some part of the animal or fruit of the tree is tabued to the tribe called after it.' This respect for the totem seems now hardly to exist among the totemistic tribes of the Central Provinces, the sacred plants and animals having generally been adopted into the cult of some Hindu deity (Russell, i. 189 f.). The feeling of reverence is still strong in Central India, where the totem tree is never cut or injured; men make obeisance to it, and women veil their faces when they pass it (Luard, i. 198 f.).

26. Local village-godlings.—Writing more particularly of the Semites, Robertson Smith (*Rel. Semites*², 92) remarks that 'the activity, power, and dominion of the gods were conceived as bounded by certain local limits, and, in the second place, they were conceived as having their residences and homes at certain fixed sanctuaries.' In order of time the worship of the village-deities is probably later than that of celestial gods, as they can hardly exist under the conditions of a nomadic life, and their worship probably marks an early stage of tribal settlement. The worship of these gods, as appears from the character of the priesthood (§ 49), has no connexion with Brāhmanical Hinduism. They vary in name, character, and functions all over the country. But all have one distinguishing mark—their influence is confined to a particular area, and it is only when some shrine has, by cures and wonders performed within its precincts, acquired a more than local reputation that it attracts the worship of persons residing beyond its special domain. When this stage is reached, it leads to the establishment of a local cult, which, as it develops and becomes important, is generally annexed by some priest drawn from the orthodox ranks of Brāhmanism, and the local god is gradually promoted to a seat in the regular Hindu pantheon.

27. The village shrine.—The general name for these gods is Grāma- or Grāmya-devatā, 'the godlings of the village,' or in the modern vernacular Gāṅv-devatā or Gāṅv-devī, the last title marking connexion with the Mother-cult. Sometimes, again, they are known as Dih, 'the village,' and the shrine is called Deohār, 'holy place'—a term which is also applied to the whole body of village-gods. In its simplest form the village shrine is a collection of water-worn stones placed under the sacred tree of the settlement. In the Plains, where all stones are scarce, pieces of old carving from a ruined Buddhist or Hindu religious building are often used for this purpose, and occasionally the desecrated image of the Buddha may be seen doing service as the representative of the village Devī or her consort. Sometimes ancient stone axes, looked on with awe by people who now use none but metal implements, have been found in such places. In the more prosperous villages a small square building of brick masonry, with a bulbous head and perhaps an iron spike as a finial, serves as a shrine. Its position is marked by a red flag hung from the adjoining sacred tree; or a bamboo pole is erected close by to serve as a perch for the deity when he deigns to visit the shrine to receive the offerings and attend to the prayers of his votaries. In the hill villages occupied by the purer Dravidian tribes, such as the Kols or Orāons, the shrine is usually a rude mud hut roofed with bamboos and straw, which is often allowed to fall into disrepair until the godling reminds his votaries of his displeasure by bringing sickness or some other calamity upon them. Inside is a small mud platform, on which a jar of water is usually placed and offerings are made.

No clear distinction is made between the various kinds of spirits which occupy such a shrine. First, there are the purely elementary deities, like the Earth-Mother and her consort; secondly, those spirits which are regarded as generally benignant, like the Satī, the spirit of a woman who died on the pyre of her husband, or those which are actively malignant. Thus on the borders of the hill country where Dravidian and Aryan intermix, may be seen what is called a *brahm*, a shrine in honour of some deified Brāhman, where the worshipper makes a libation of milk or curds, lights a lamp, and offers the fire-service (*homa*); and in an adjoining Dravidian village a *baghaut*, a rude shrine or cairn erected on the spot where a man was killed by a tiger, at which a Kol makes an occasional sacrifice (*NINQ* ii. 19). In the eastern Panjāb the fusion of cults is equally obvious. Wilson (*op. cit.* ii. 147) describes at Kāngra a shrine erected by the Chamārs, or menial Hindu leather-dressers, inside which they light a lamp twice a month, and

'when they were ill or in trouble they would come to this shrine and bow down before it, and promise that if their troubles were removed, or their wish gratified, they would present some offering, such as bread, or a coco-nut, or a flag. If the saint fulfilled his part of the bargain, the worshipper fulfilled his vow; if not, the vow was void. Thus I was told that a small flag waving over the shrine had been presented by a Chamār, who had been ill, and who had vowed to offer a flag on his recovery. Often a shrine may be seen outside the village to the village god, or to the smallpox goddess, or some other deity, where at set times the women make offerings of water or grain; and a small lamp may be often seen burning on a Thursday evening at the tomb of a Muhammadan saint. These practices are said to be forbidden in the Korān; but the women especially place some faith in them, and a Rāin is said to have divorced his wife because she persisted in lighting lamps at a Fakīr's tomb, in hope of being blessed with a son.'

This concrete instance admirably illustrates the beliefs of the low-class Musalmān population, who are in the main converts from Dravidian tribes, and whose faith in the tenets of the Prophet is only a thin veneer over their primitive Animistic creed. In the same part of the country we often find the worship of Bhūmiyā, the earth-god, combined with that of one of the great Muhammadan saints; and in one village it appeared that the Hindu Jāts distributed their worship between the saint Shaikh Aḥmad Chishtī of Ajmēr (*q.v.*), Brāhmans, and the Pīpal, or sacred fig-tree.

In many places, again, in the hill country where caves are found, they are utilized as local shrines. They are places of mystery, the fitting abode of the gods, and it is believed that they form an entrance to the nether world. Such cave shrines are numerous in the lower Himālaya, and many of them have been appropriated by the orthodox Hindu gods (*NINQ* iii. 147). They are the prototypes of the great cave-temples of the Buddhists and Hindus, like Ajanta or Elephanta (*qq.v.*).

28. General characteristics of the Grāma-devatā worship.—It is obviously impossible to attempt any precise definition of vague, amorphous beliefs such as these. The creed of the lower classes of the population is, on the one hand, purely Animistic, a cult of the powers of Nature. On the other hand, to it has been added a belief in the necessity of propitiating sundry goblins and evil spirits, many of the latter being the angry ghosts of persons who have perished by a tragical or untimely death. This has, again, absorbed from Hinduism the worship of Brāhmans, and from Muhammadanism the cult of the saints or martyrs of Islām. Further, we occasionally find more than one element united in a single cult. It is, therefore, unnecessary to attempt to compile a list of these village-godlings. A few examples may be given to indicate the general character of this form of worship.

29. Worship of Ganśām Deo.—Ganśām Deo is an important god of the Goṇḍs, Kols, and kindred races. An attempt is now being made to give him a place in Hinduism as a form of Kṛṣṇa; but his Dravidian origin is apparent. In Mirzapur he is protector of the crops, and the *baigā* priest propitiates him, when the rice is ripening, with the sacrifice of a fowl, goat, or sucking-pig, and an oblation of liquor. He generally resides in a tree, and near his shrine is usually placed a rude stone representing Devī. We have here another instance of the cult of the male and female element performed to stimulate the growth of the crops (Crooke, *Tribes and Castes*, iii. 312). But Ganśām has another side, being by some supposed to be a chieftain of the Goṇḍs who was killed by a tiger. His legend tells that after his death he visited his wife, and she conceived by him.

'Descendants of this ghostly embrace are, it is said, living to this day at Amoda, in the Central Provinces. He, about the same time, appeared to many of his old friends, and persuaded them that he could save them from the maws of tigers and other calamities, if his worship were duly inaugurated and regularly performed; and, in consequence of this, two festivals in the year were established in his honour; but he may be worshipped at any time, and in all sickness and misfortune his votaries confidently appeal to him' (Dalton, 232).

30. Worship of Bhairoṅ.—Bhairoṅ, another favourite Dravidian god, is often confounded with Bhūmiyā, who is one form of the consort of the Mother-goddess. He has been partially adopted into Hinduism as Kāla Bhairava, who is often depicted with eighteen arms, ornamented with a garland of skulls, with ear-rings and armlets formed of snakes, a serpent coiled round his head, in his hands a sword and a bowl of blood. He is thus a fitting partner to the blood-stained Mother, Kālī. But it seems clear that in the primitive conception he is one of the divine pair to whose union the fertility of the soil, cattle, and people is due. Even in his Hinduized form as Kāla Bhairava he retains the characters of Animism. As worshipped by the Kunbī cultivators in the Deccan, he is represented as a man standing; in one hand a trident, in the other a drum shaped like an hour-glass, while he is encircled by a serpent, a mark of his chthonic origin. He lives in an unhewn stone smeared with oil and vermilion, and he remains kindly so long as he is supplied with offerings of butter.

'He cures snake-bites, and tells whether an undertaking will do well or will fail. In the chest of the rough figure of Bhairav are two small holes. The person who wishes to consult the oracle places a betel-nut in each of the holes, and explains to Bhairav that if the right betel-nut falls first it will mean that the undertaking will prosper, and that if the left betel-nut falls first it will mean that the undertaking will fail. He asks the god, according as the event is to be, to let the lucky or the unlucky nut fall first. He tells the god that if he will drop the lucky nut, and if his undertaking prospers, he will give the god a cock or a goat. Twice a year, before they begin to sow and before they begin to reap, the villagers come in procession and worship Bhairav' (*BG* xviii. pt. i. 289).

Bhairoṅ or Bhūmiyā is also known as Khetrpāl, or 'field-guardian.' In the Panjāb, when the crop is nearly ripe, Brāhmans are consulted to fix an auspicious time for reaping; and, before the work is begun, five or seven loaves of bread, a pitcher of water, and a small quantity of the crop are set aside in the name of Khetrpāl (Rose, i. 126). Bhūmiyā, again, at times changes sex, and is identified with the Earth-Mother, and provided with a consort in Chandwand or Kherā, the personification of the village site (*NINQ* v. 160). Like his consort, Bhūmiyā has a malignant aspect. He is said to visit with sickness those who show him disrespect, as, for instance, by cleaning their teeth near his shrine.

'Those Bhūmiyās who thus bear the reputation of being revengeful and vicious in temper are respected, and offerings to them are often made; while those who have the character of easy, good-tempered fellows are neglected' (*NINQ* iii. 107).

31. Worship of Hanumān, the monkey-god.—In the same grade is the monkey-god, Hanumān, Hanumat, 'he with the jaws,' also known as Maruti or Mahābīr, 'the great hero,' who has become fully adopted into Hinduism as the helper of the god Rāma in his war against the demon Rāvaṇa, which forms the subject of the epic of the *Rāmāyaṇa*. He is, however, plainly a survival from the old theriolatry. He is represented by a rude image, combining human and monkey characteristics, the animal's tail being specially prominent, and the whole smeared with vermilion. He is an especial favourite with the Marāṭhas; but most villages in Northern India have a shrine dedicated to Hanumān, and the establishment of his image is one of the first formal acts performed at the settlement of a new hamlet. In every fort, built or re-built by Sivajī, the Marāṭha hero, he placed inside the main gate a small shrine with an image of Hanumān (*BG* x. 335). Even now this god has hardly gained full franchise in the Hindu pantheon, and in the greater shrines he acts as warden (*dwārapāla*) to the higher gods. His virile attributes make him a fitting partner of the Mother-goddess, and he is essentially a Dravidian god, bearing in his representation among the Dravidian Suiris of Mirzapur little of the monkey character except his long tail; and he is identified with Borām, or the sun-god, by the wild Bhuiyās of Keunjhar (Buchanan, i. 467; Dalton, 147). Some years ago, when an epidemic broke out among the forest Kāthkaris of Nāsik, they believed that it was a judgment upon them because they used to kill and eat the sacred Hanumān monkeys. They fled the country for a time in order to escape his vengeance (*BG* xvi. 65).

32. Spirit-worship.—Besides local gods of this class, most of whom are associated with the fertility of the land, cattle, and people, the Dravidian is beset by a host of spirits of another kind.

First come the vague terrific forms, the impersonations of awe and terror, spirits of the waste or of the darkness, like the *jinn* of Semitic folk-lore—the Rākṣasa, the Bīr or Vīra, the Dāno, the Daitya. These are now all known by Aryan names, but their representatives were also doubtless found among the Dravidians. Some account of these, and other like vague potentialities, will be found under BENGAL, § 8, ḌOMS, § 2, and DEMONS AND SPIRITS (Indian).

Secondly, there is the host of Bhūts or Bhūtas, the restless spirits of those who have perished by an untimely death, or have failed to reach their longed-for rest, because they have not been honoured with due obsequial rites. They are generally malignant, and if not regularly propitiated bring disease or other suffering on those who neglect their service. Such are Rājā Lākhan, worshipped by the Kols with his sister Belā, and Rājā Chandol, the tutelary god of the Korwās. Most of these seem to be historical personages, Rājā Lākhan apparently having been a leader of the Hindus against the Muhammadan conquerors. They have now been deified and receive constant worship (Crooke, *PR* i. 198 ff.). In the same class are Hardaur Lālā, the cholera godling, and Haridās Bābā, the patron deity of the Ahīrs (*q.v.*). This process of deification of persons, famous or notorious in life, still goes on actively.

'So far as I have been able to trace back the origin of the best-known minor provincial deities, they are usually men of past generations who have earned special promotion and brevet rank among disembodied ghosts by some peculiar acts or accident of their lives or deaths, especially among the rude and rough classes' (Lyall, *Asiatic Studies*[2], 1907, i. 24 ff.).

Thus Hānjū (Dīvān, or Minister, of the Charkari State in Central India) died in A.D. 1768. Though he was not specially famous during his life, a platform was erected at the site of his cremation, and a visit to it is now supposed to cure fever. Hīrā Lāl was killed by robbers some eighty years ago; his decapitated trunk ran three miles to the cremation ground; a cairn was raised on the spot, which is now used as a place of prayer, where boons are granted (Luard, i. 75 f.). Shrines like these are found in all parts of the country.

It is quite impossible to prepare a full catalogue of these Dravidian village-gods. Their names and attributes vary from village to village, and those of any district are unknown even at a short distance from their place of worship. An account of some of the most remarkable deities of this class will be found in Crooke, *PR* i. 83 ff. Some lists of them are given in Elliot, *Supplementary Glossary*, *s.v.* 'Deewar'; Gait, *Census Report Bengal*, 1901, i. 192 ff.; Dalal, i. 156; Campbell, 312 ff.; Ibbetson, 113 ff.; *NINQ* iii. 38 ff., 55, 128, 200, iv. 110, 148, 181.

33. Boundary-worship.—The local character of the worship of the village-gods is shown by the respect paid to boundaries, and in the cult of the deities presiding over them. The Roman worship of Terminus, with the sanctity attached by the Latins to boundary-stones, is one of the most familiar examples of this class of beliefs (Smith, *Dict. Antiq.*[3] i. 90 f.). Among the Goṇḍs the village boundaries are placed in charge of the ancestral ghosts (Sleeman, i. 269 f.). In its most primitive form the cult is found among the Dravidians of the Vindhyan and Kaimūr ranges, who employ their *baigā* priest to perambulate the village annually, and to mark it out with a line of the common liquor, distilled from rice or other grains, in order to prevent the inroad of foreign spirits, who are regarded as necessarily hostile. The boundary, again, is often defined by making a goat walk along the disputed line, and watching it till it gives a shiver, which is regarded as an indication of the wishes of the spirit, whose adjudication is at once accepted (*NINQ* i. 202). The boundary-spirit naturally develops into a deity in whose charge the line is placed. Thus, according to Macpherson, the Kandhs recognized Sundi Pennu as the boundary-god: 'particular points upon the boundaries of districts, fixed by ancient usage, and generally upon highways, are his altars, and these demand each an annual victim, who is either an unsuspecting traveller struck down by the priests, or a sacrifice provided by purchase' (*Memorials*, 90; *Calcutta Rev.* v. 55). Among other tribes, like the Rautiās of Bengal, Goraiyā is regarded as a sort of rural Terminus; the Telī oilmen offer a sucking-pig in the rainy season before the lump of dried mud which symbolizes the presence of the god, the victim after sacrifice being either buried in the ground or given to a Dosādh (*q.v.*), who seems to act as priest of the more primitive deities, and claims the offerings as his legitimate perquisite (Risley, *Tribes and Castes*, ii. 309). Another deity of the same type, Sewanriyā, is the tribal god of the Bhuiyārs and Ghasiyās of the United Provinces, who sacrifice a goat and offer some spirits and a thick cake, the head of the animal and the cake being the perquisite of the *mahto*, or headman, who performs the rite (Crooke, *Tribes and Castes*, ii. 93, 418). Among the Santāls his place is taken by the *sima-bonga*, the collective boundary-gods, who are propitiated twice a year with sacrifices of fowls offered on the boundary of the village where these deities are supposed to dwell (Risley, *Tribes and Castes*, ii. 234). Under the title of *sīmanta-pūjā*, 'boundary-worship,' this has become part of the Hindu marriage-rites, the youth when he comes to fetch his bride being obliged to free himself from the foreign and hostile spirits which have accompanied him, by a rite of worship performed at the boundary of the village of his bride.

34. Implement-worship.—The worship paid to the implements used by the husbandman and the tools of the artisan falls into a different class, which has sometimes been included under the head of Fetishism—a term which possesses no scientific value. In various forms it appears among the rural classes of Northern India. The Bhandārī barbers of Orissa, on the fourth day of the feast to Durgā, lay their razors, scissors, and mirror before the image of Viśvakarma, their patron deity, with offerings of sweetmeats and flowers (Risley, *Tribes and Castes*, i. 93). The Kaibarttā fishermen of Bengal Proper celebrate the feast of Jālpālanī in the early spring, on the last day of which they lay their net, smeared with red lead, on the river bank (*ib.* i. 380). The Kumhār potters arrange their trade implements and specimens of their manufactures on the kiln, ornament them with leaves of the Bel tree (*Ægle marmelos*), and present oblations; while the Pāsī palm-tappers set up their sickles and present offerings of flower and grain (*ib.* i. 525, ii. 167). Perhaps the most remarkable of these so-called fetishes is the *gurdā*, or sacred chain of the *baigā* priest, which is kept in the hut dedicated to the god. With this the *baigā* lashes himself into a state of ecstatic frenzy, and hysterical girls are thrashed with it to drive the devil out of them. This chain, under the name of Sāklā Pen, 'the chain god,' is worshipped by the priests of the Goṇḍs, carried in procession, and solemnly deposited in the shrine (Hislop, App. p. 8; Crooke, *Tribes and Castes*, iii. 441). Among purely agricultural implements, honour is especially paid to the plough, the corn-sieve, basket, and broom used in cleaning and measuring grain, and the rice-pounder, to which a phallic significance naturally attaches (Crooke, *PR* ii. 187 ff.).

35. Stone-worship.—Stones throughout Northern India are recognized as the abode of spirits and deities. One form of this worship, that of the *liṅgam*, or phallus, now appropriated to the cult of Śiva, was formerly believed to have been adopted from the Dravidian tribes of the south by the Aryans (Oppert, 372 f.). This view is now generally rejected (Hopkins, *Rel. of India*, 1896, p. 471). It is said to be alluded to by the writers of the Veda in the *śisna-deva*, 'tail-gods,' but the cult was not openly acknowledged until the rise of Śiva-worship in the Epic period (*ib.* 150, 462). The growth of this form of worship has been attributed to Greek influence, while Fergusson suggests that the *liṅgam* is in origin a miniature Buddhist *dagoba*, or relic-shrine (*Hist. of East. and Ind. Architecture*, 1899, p. 167). The worship of Śiva in this form probably spread throughout India at least as early as the 5th or 6th cent. A.D. (Wilson, *Essays*, 1862–77, i. 224). Śiva, again, is associated with the bull Nandi, and in this form may be compared with the Greek Dionysus in his bull form, as god of fertility, with which his phallic emblem is perhaps associated (J. E. Harrison, *Prolegomena*, 432 ff.). Oppert (378 f.) asserts that the Dravidians were originally adherents of the Śakti-, or Mother-worship, and that 'there exists hardly any evidence to show that these same people worshipped the *liṅga*, or the organ of generation; and even at the present day we cannot point out any aboriginal tribe, which has retained intact its national customs, as revering the Phallus.' This assertion is probably an over-statement of the facts. As we have seen, most of the Dravidian tribes combine with the worship of the Mother-goddess that of her male consort, and the mimic celebration of the union of the divine pair suggests erotic rites. Hislop has collected a long Goṇḍ epic which tells of the creation and adventures of their hero, Lingo. But, as Dalton (282) remarks, this has obviously been compiled under Hindu influence, and cannot be regarded as embodying the real traditional lore of the Goṇḍs. At the same time, it suggests that *liṅgam*-worship was familiar to this tribe, and with them, in the form of the tiger, it was combined with animal-worship in the personification of their deity, Lingo or Ningo Bāghiya (Forsyth, 188). With this may be compared the worship by the Sudhas of Bengal of their goddess Khambeśwarī, who is represented by a peg (Risley, *Tribes and Castes*, ii. 268).

36. Other stone-worship among the Dravidians.—Stone-worship appears in other forms among the Northern Dravidians. Thus we find the worship of cairns. The Bhīls of Rājputana erect on the hill-tops, to the memory of the spirits of deceased relatives, cairns of stone, on which they place rude images of the horse, burn small oil lamps, and sometimes hang pieces of cloth. Goats or male buffaloes are offered here, and the pottery horse-figures are made with holes through which the spirits of the dead are supposed to enter, and then travel up to heaven, when the horse is presented to the deity (Bannerman, i. 53). Conical piles of stone are worshipped in Nepāl as residences of the local gods, and are known as Deorālī, a title also applied to one of the Himālayan peaks (Kirkpatrick, 60). In Mirzapur, in the United Provinces, Anktahā Bīr is the hero impersonated by a pile of rude stones, to which every traveller adds one as he passes by. The hero is now on the way to promotion, as the offerings at his shrine are taken by a family of Brāhman priests (*NINQ* i. 40).

Secondly, we find special worship of particular stones. In all the villages of Central India are stones known by the names of Motī Mātā, 'pearl Mother,' or Lālbāī-Phūlbāī, 'the red flower Mother,' which are worshipped when cholera appears. The Bhīl *barwā*, or medicine-man, officiates; he cuts off the head of a goat, and offers it with some lemons, copper coins, eggs, flowers, etc., in a piece of a broken earthen pot, while a toy cart, apparently used as a vehicle for the goddess, is placed beside the stones. When the head of the goat has been offered, the *barwā* takes up the potsherd and places it on his head. A watchman takes a living goat, an attendant carrying a pot full of country spirits, which drops slowly out of a small hole in the bottom of the jar. Behind this the car of the goddess is dragged by a third officiant. The procession is directed towards the famous shrine of Onkārnātha, until they reach a village, the home of another goddess, Sāt Mātrā, 'Mother of truth.' Here the jar and carriage are left, and by this means the spirit of cholera is supposed to be enticed away beyond the limits of the town, by the aid of her chariot, and attracted by the goat and spirits presented to her (Luard, i. 78). This primitive method of disease-transference illustrates the Animistic character of the cultus. In some cases the stone, which is the home of the deity, is replaced by pillars of wood, blackened by constant offerings of oil and butter. Such are the representatives of Bīrnāth, 'hero lord,' worshipped by the Ahīr cowherds as a protector of their cattle—a worship apparently identical with the cultus of the group of deities known as Bangaramāī, Bangarā Bāī, or, in her Hinduized form, as Devī, who are worshipped in various parts of the Central Provinces (Hislop, 15 f.; Crooke, *Tribes and Castes*, i. 63 f.). This pillar-worship takes various forms. Sometimes we find a stone pillar (*lāṭ*) appropriated to the hero Bhīmsen, who is probably in origin a Dravidian deity, but is now associated with the burly hero of the *Mahābhārata* epic. The Goṇḍs worship him in the form of a shapeless stone covered with vermilion, or of two pieces of wood standing three or four feet above the ground, like those of Bangaramāī. Among the Naikudē, one of the Goṇḍ septs, he is represented by a huge stone rising out of the ground and covered with vermilion.

'In front of this, Naikudē Goṇḍs mingle with Rāj Goṇḍs and Kolāms in acts of adoration. The order of the religious service seems to be as follows. At 5 p.m., having cooked a little rice, the worshippers place it before the god, and add a little sugar. They then besmear the stone with vermilion, and burn resin as incense in its honour; after which all the parties offer their victims, consisting of sheep, hogs, fowls, with the usual libations of arrack. The god is now supposed to inspire the Pūjārī [priest], who rolls about his head, leaps frantically round and round, and finally falls down in a trance, when he declares whether Bhīmsen has accepted the service or not. At night all join in drinking, dancing, and beating tom-toms [drums]' (Hislop, 24 f.).

Passing to the Plains, we find the deity represented by stone pillars, some of those erected by the Buddhist Emperor Aśoka and bearing copies of his edicts being appropriated by the menial Dravidian tribes for this form of worship. In Baroda the forest tribes worship several deities who have their abode in stones. Kavādio Dev, their principal deity, lives in the hollow of a ravine, which, it is believed, will open to receive worshippers of holy life and will reject those who are wicked. Gohāmāya Mādī, the Mother-goddess, is merely a huge boulder which has fallen from the summit of a hill. Before it are placed clay images of men and animals, probably substitutes for the original sacrifice (Dalal, i. 156).

Finally come the pillar stones erected as a home for the spirits of ancestors. Some account of these has been given in connexion with ANCESTOR-WORSHIP (vol. i. p. 431). Such are the *pāliyā*, or guardian stones, of Western India, the heroes inhabiting which are believed to scour the fields and gardens at night, and are consequently much dreaded (*BG* xi. 307 f., xvi. 647). The custom of erecting such stones has probably been borrowed from the Dravidians, because they are erected by the Bhils, and are common among the Muṇḍās and Khāsīs (*Rajputana Gazetteer*, i. 122; Dalton, 55, 203).

37. The development of the pantheon.—The earliest conception of the Dravidian deities whom we have been discussing represents them as gods of all work, to whom no definite functions are assigned. The formation of a pantheon, in which the duties of each god are clearly limited, is a much later development (Robertson Smith, *Rel. Semites*², 39). The current accounts of some of these Dravidian pantheons must be received with some caution, as in the case of Macpherson's account of the Kandh deities. But it seems certain that among some of the wilder tribes this stage of development has been reached, though we may suspect that in some cases it may be traced to Hindu influence. Thus the Malē or Maler Pahāṛias, according to Shaw (Dalton, 268 ff.), are said to have eight gods: Raxie, abiding in a black stone, invoked when a man-eating tiger or an epidemic attacks the village; Chal or Chalnad, with a similar representation and functions; Pow or Pau Gosāin, god of highways; Dwārā Gosāin, protective deity of the village; Kul Gosāin, deity of the sowing season; Autga, god of hunting; Gumū Gosāin, sometimes associated with Kul Gosāin; and Chamdā Gosāin, most important of all, who needs such a great propitiatory offering that only chiefs and men of wealth can provide it. Later inquirers supply a different list, containing Dharmer or Bedo Gosāin, the Sun-god, who rules the world; Bārā Duārī, 'he that has a temple with twelve doors,' the tutelary village-god; Gumū Gosāin, at whose shrine ancestor-worship is performed, and who is represented by the pillars that support the rafters of the shed-like temple; Chalnad, who presides over groups of ten villages; Pau Gosāin (the Pow of Shaw), god of highways; and Chamdā Gosāin, most exacting of all (Bradley-Birt, *Story of an Indian Upland*, 297 ff.). Even here the development of the pantheon is only embryonic, and the duties of the several deities are but imperfectly distributed. The Santāl pantheon is equally vague, having, as some authorities believe, in the background a *fainéant* Supreme Being, known as Ṭhākur, who is occasionally identified with the Sun; deities of Nature, like Marang Buru, the mountain-god, and Jair or Jāhir Erā, goddess of the sacred grove; besides a separate group of family-gods, arranged in two divisions—the Orak-bonga, or regular family-deity, and the Abgē-bonga, or secret god (Risley, *Tribes and Castes*, ii. 232). The other more Hinduized tribes have in the same way developed deities with special functions, like Dārapāt Deo with his wife Angārmatī, the war-gods of the Kharwārs of the Kaimūr range, and Zorbād Deotā, a god of hunting (*NINQ* iv. 36, 77).

38. Theogonies.—Some of the North Dravidian tribes have framed elaborate theogonies with legendary accounts of the creation of man and of the dispersal of the tribes. Thus the Muṇḍās tell how the self-existent primeval deities, Otē Borām and Sing-bonga, created a boy and girl, taught them the art of love, and placed them in a cave to people the world (Dalton, 185). The Kandh legend of the struggle between Būṛhā Pennu, the Supreme Being, god of light, and his consort, Tarī, the Earth-goddess, which ends in the creation of man and all other living things, is more elaborate, and has probably been embellished by the vivid imagination of the natives who supplied Macpherson with his information (*Memorials*, 84 ff.). The Goṇḍ legend of the birth and adventures of Lingo has already been noticed (§ 35). Among the more advanced and Hinduized tribes, legends of this kind seem to have almost entirely disappeared, overlaid by the traditions connected with the Hindu gods, who have gradually displaced or absorbed the tribal deities.

39. Sacrifice.—The theory underlying the practice of sacrifice is, according to the well-known but not universally accepted theory of Robertson Smith, the desire to attain communion with the god by joining with him in the consumption of the flesh of the victim or the fruits of the earth offered at his shrine. In the modern view of the Dravidians, however, it is purely a business transaction, *do ut des*, an arrangement that, if the god fulfils the desires of the worshipper, he will receive a sacrifice in return. Totemism, as we have seen (§ 25), has almost completely ceased to influence the popular beliefs, and it is thus impossible to trace the steps by which, if it was ever the general rule among this people, the slaughter of the totem animal developed into the methods of sacrifice which are in use at present. Here, too, as is the case with all their beliefs and rites, there is no literary evidence of any kind to assist us. There is, however, some scanty evidence to prove that the modern custom may have a totemistic basis. Thus the Parahiyās of the Kaimūr range hold the goat in great respect—a feeling which among the Bengal branch of the tribe applies to sheep and deer. There is a current tradition that, as a means of purification, they in former times used the dung of these animals to smear the floors of their huts; this substance has now been replaced by cow-dung (Dalton, 131). If this be a case of a survival of totemism, not of the ordinary worship of animals, it is noteworthy that in Mirzapur they propitiate the mountain-goddess, whom they now call Devī, with the sacrifice of a goat. Before the animal is slain, it is fed on a few grains of rice, and water is poured upon its head. This they call, not 'sacrifice, but 'goat-worship'; and sometimes, when the Devī is worshipped to avert an epidemic of cholera, the goat is not sacrificed, but released as a scape-animal (Crooke, *Tribes and Castes*, iv. 130). More significant than this is the rule that after sacrifice the flesh of the animal must be consumed by the worshipper and his clansmen, then and there, in the immediate presence of the deity—a rule which is characteristic of totem sacrifices (Jevons, *Introd.* 145 f.). In fact, as was the case in ancient Israel, all slaughter is equivalent to sacrifice (Robertson Smith, *Rel. Semites*^{2}, 241). This, it may be noted, is also the Hindu rule, and many of those who indulge in meat use only that of sacrificed animals, following the rule of Manu (*Institutes*, v. 31) that meat must be eaten only on occasion of sacrifice. The Dravidians are specially careful not to share the sacred meat with strangers, or even with members of their own tribe outside the inner circle of relationship.

40. Methods of sacrifice.—The methods of sacrifice differ among the various tribes. In the more primitive form the ritual is cruel: the Goālās of Bengal turn a pig loose amidst a herd of buffaloes, which are encouraged to gore it to death (Risley, *Tribes and Castes*, i. 290). We occasionally find among the northern tribes the habit of tearing the victim in pieces, as in the Goṇḍ sacrifice to Bāgheśvar, the tiger-god (Dalton, 280). This points to an original habit of eating the flesh of the victim raw, which survived in some of the Greek mysteries and the practices of the Bacchæ, and appears among the southern branches of the tribe, where a lamb is torn to pieces by a man with his teeth (*Bulletin Madras Museum*, iii. 265). At a Devī shrine in Gorakhpur the pigs to be offered are brought to the temple with their hind legs tied; and, the throats of the animals being half cut with a blunt knife, they are allowed to bleed to death before the altar (*NINQ* v. 202). The Tiyars of Bengal, like many of the other menial castes, when they offer a goat to Kālī at the Divālī, or feast of lights, do not decapitate the victim, but stab it in the throat with a sharp piece of wood (Wise, 393). The ordinary method, however, is by decapitation.

In Northern Bengal the usual shrine of Kālī consists of a heap of earth, generally placed under a tree, with a stake to which the head of the victim is fastened, so that the neck may be stretched out for decapitation (Buchanan, ii. 749). The Gorkha custom of sacrificing buffaloes, by one, or at most two blows, is a humane rite; but that of the Newārs, or aborigines of the country, who allow the animal to bleed slowly to death, is very cruel and very disgusting (Oldfield, *Sketches*, ii. 346 ff.). Such was also the custom of the Bhūmij of Chotā Nāgpur at the Binda-parab feast. Two male buffaloes were driven into an enclosure, and on a raised stage adjoining and overlooking it the Rājā and his suite used to take their places. After some ceremonies, the Rājā and his family priest discharged arrows at the victims.

'Others follow their example, and the tormented and enraged beasts fall to and gore each other, while arrow after arrow is discharged. When the animals are past doing very much mischief, the people rush in and hack at them with battle-axes till they are dead. The Santāls and wild Kharriās, it is said, took great delight in this festival; but I have not heard a murmur at its discontinuance, and this shows that it had no great hold on the minds of the people' (Dalton, 176).

It is the general rule that the victim should die from the effects of a single stroke. At the worship of Mārī Mātā, the cholera goddess, at Kāngra, one of the hill districts of the Panjāb, the animal, a ram, he-goat, or cock, must be decapitated with a sharp sword at a single blow. If more than one stroke be needed, it is believed that the goddess has not been duly propitiated and that the ceremony has failed (*PNQ* i. 1). Much importance, therefore, is laid on the act of striking the first blow (Jevons, *Introd.* 291). In Kumāun, in the lower Himālaya, bull buffaloes are offered to Kālī in the event of drought.

'Each buffalo is successively led to the door of the temple for decapitation; the first stroke is inflicted by the principal zemindar [land-owner], and, if not immediately fatal, is followed up by repeated blows from the surrounding crowd, until the animal is despatched, or rather hacked in pieces' (Traill, *Statistical Sketch of Kumaun*, 1828, p. 68).

When a fowl is being sacrificed by the Santāls to the mountain-god, Marang Burū, the sharp national axe is held securely on the ground with the blade pointing upwards, and the priest, taking the bird in both hands, presses its neck heavily upon the upturned edge, severing the head from the body; the blood is then scattered over the stones which form the altar of the god (Bradley-Birt, *Story of an Indian Upland*, 258, with a photograph of a kid sacrifice). In Baroda the ritual of the Animistic worship consists in burning, as incense, some clarified butter before the god, and then sprinkling spirits on small heaps of rice. After this the worshipper kills a cock by cutting its throat, plucks out the feathers, and places bundles of them before the god; he then cooks the fowl, and lays some of the cooked meat on the altar, paints the idol with vermilion, and hangs flags over it. While these rites are going on, the tribal musical instruments are played. When the ceremony is over, the worshippers consume the remainder of the food (Dalal, i. 156).

41. The times of sacrifice.—No special time is appointed for the Dravidian sacrifices. At the more important festivals of the Mother-goddess the victims are slaughtered throughout the day and night. In some Greek shrines it was the custom to slay the victim at night and consume the flesh before the dawn (Pausanias, II. xxvii. 1, X. xxxviii. 4). This was also the rule among the Arabs (Robertson Smith, *Rel. Semites*^{2}, 282). For the Hindu *śūlagava* sacrifice, in which the victim, as the name implies, seems to have been pierced with a spike or lance, the time was fixed after midnight; but some authorities preferred the dawn (Rajendralala Mitra, *Indo-Aryans*, i. 364; Jevons, *Introd.* 146). This rule still prevails among the Prabhūs of western India, who at marriages sacrifice a goat to the family-goddess. In some families the rite is done at midnight on the day before the marriage. The goat is brought into the room and made to stand before the image. One of the married women of the family comes forward, washes the victim's feet, sprinkles red powder on its head, and, after waving a lighted lamp round its face, retires. The eldest man in the household lays a bamboo winnowing-fan with a handful or two of rice in it before the goat, and, taking a sword, stands on one side. While the animal is eating the rice, he cuts off the head with one stroke, holds up the head, lets a few drops of blood trickle over the image of the goddess, and then places the head on a metal plate under the seat of the deity (*BG* xviii. pt. i. 195). At the shrine of Bechrājī in Baroda the victims are slain at dead of night, 'in order not to offend the feelings of Brāhmans and others' (*ib.* vii. 614).

42. The self-surrender of the victim.—The feeding of the victim before sacrifice is probably a means of propitiating it, and suggesting that it is a willing victim. When the Rautiās of Bengal sacrifice an animal to Baṛ Pahāṛ, the mountain-god, the victim is given rice to chew, and is decked with flowers before being slain (Risley, *Tribes and Castes*, ii. 203). At the worship of the Mother-goddess, Bechrājī, when a buffalo is brought for sacrifice, red powder and flowers are sprinkled over the animal, and it is worshipped. A white cloth is thrown over the back of the beast, and a garland of flowers, removed from the image of the goddess, is hung round its neck. A lamp filled from one of those burning in the shrine is brought lighted from the inner room and placed on the stone altar in front of the temple. The buffalo is then let loose, and if it goes and smells the lamp it is considered to be acceptable to the Devī, and is slain at once, if possible by a single stroke of a sword. A blood-stained flower is presented to the deity, and the bystanders apply some of the blood to their foreheads. The blood is believed to bring health and prosperity, and even Brāhmans preserve cloths dipped in the blood, as charms against disease. If the buffalo refuses to smell the lamp placed on the stone altar, it is taken away, after one of its ears has been cut and a drop of the blood offered to the goddess on a flower (*BG* vii. 614).

A more common method is to test the victim by pouring water on it, which was a custom in Greece (J. E. Harrison, *Prolegomena*, 502). When the Ṭhags did sacrifice to Devī, their patron goddess, they used to place on a white sheet the consecrated pickaxe and knives used in their murders, with the spirits provided for the feast. Two goats were selected, black and perfect in all their parts. They were bathed and made to face the west; and, if they shook themselves lustily to throw off the moisture from their bodies, they were considered acceptable to the goddess. If only one shook itself, both were accepted. If neither did so, it was a sign that Devī had rejected both, and the party ate the rice and drank the spirits. But this was regarded in the light of a simple meal, and the sacrifice was postponed to another occasion. When the sacrificial feast took place, the skins, bones, and offal of the victims were thrown into a pit, and they were regarded as so sacred that none but a Ṭhag was allowed to see them (Thornton, *Illustrations of the History and Practices of the Thugs*, 1837, p. 68 f.). The rule that the victim must shake its head in token of acceptance is also found in the Panjāb (Rose, i. 118).

43. Variety, sex, and colour of the victim.—The rules as to the variety, sex, and colour of the victim are not very clearly defined. The animals most commonly sacrificed are buffaloes, goats, pigs, and fowls. The Bhīls of Khāndesh show their complete divorce from Hinduism by sacrificing a bullock to their gods Hātipawā and Vāghāchā Kuṅvar, 'the tiger lord,' while their other deities receive a he-goat or a fowl—a cock for the god, a hen for the goddess (*BG* xii. 93). The Kanjar gypsies of the United Provinces offer a pig to Nathiyā; a lizard to Mānā Gurū; a goat to Devī; a pig to Jakhiyā; a fowl to Madār (Crooke, *Tribes and Castes*, iii. 147). The Muṇḍās offer a male buffalo to Deswālī, their village-god, and fowls to his consort, Jāhir Būṛhī (Risley, *Tribes and Castes*, ii. 103). But this distinction of victims seems to be exceptional.

The colour of the victim offered to the chthonic and malignant powers (like the Greek σφάγιον [J. E. Harrison, *Prolegomena*, 68]) ought to be black. When the forest tribes of the Kaimūr range offer sacrifice to Churel, a malignant female deity, it should consist of a black she-goat and a black fowl; Bansaptī, the forest-goddess, is less actively malignant, and is honoured with a grey or spotted goat (*NINQ* i. 57). Among the Marāṭhas, fowls with ruffled feathers are peculiarly acceptable offerings in cases of disease, and if a cock be sacrificed it should be able to crow (*BG* xi. 34). Following the same laws of symbolic magic, the Kisāns and Bhuiyās of Bengal offer a white cock to Borām, the Sun-god (Dalton, 132, 141).

44. The head of the victim.—The head of the victim is universally regarded as sacrosanct, as was the case with the Semites (Robertson Smith, *Rel. Semites*², 379). Among the Dravidian tribes it is sometimes, when severed, laid upon the altar of the deity in whose honour the sacrifice is being made, but more usually it is the portion of the priest (Dalton, 142; Crooke, *Tribes and Castes*, i. 8). The Bhāṭs of the United Provinces, who pretend to be orthodox Hindus, practise the curious rite of sacrificing a pig to the village-god, Birtiyā, this being done by a low caste Chamār *ojhā*, or medicine-man, who cuts off the head, buries it deep in the ground, and appropriates the remainder of the flesh (Crooke, *TC* ii. 26).

45. Commutation of animal sacrifice.—The animal sacrifice is occasionally commuted in deference to the humanitarian ideas of the Vaiṣṇava and Jain sectaries. In one form of the rite, slaughter of the animal is replaced by merely cutting the ear, letting a few drops of blood fall on the ground or upon the altar, and then allowing the animal to escape (Rose, i. 120). The same custom probably in part explains the rite of letting loose a bull (*vriṣotsarga*), when devotees release an animal in sacred cities like Benares or Gaya, or when a young animal is branded with the trident of Śiva, and released in the course of the *Śrāddha*, or mind-rite (see ANCESTOR-WORSHIP, vol. i. p. 452ᵇ). The more primitive form of the rite was to slay the animal, with the object of providing food for the spirit of the deceased. This rule is still in force among the more secluded tribes, like the Gonds, who kill a cow after the burial, sprinkle its blood upon the grave, and hang up the tail of the victim on the gravestone, as evidence that the funeral rites have been duly performed. In default of this, it is supposed that the spirit is unable to rest, and returns to haunt the survivors (*IA* i. 348 ff.).

46. The scape-animal.—The animal sacrifice, again, is commuted into the scape-animal, with the addition of the belief, common among the Dravidians, that it is 'the vehicle which carries away the collected demons or ills of a whole community' (Frazer, *GB*² iii. 101). This rite is most commonly performed as a means of removing epidemic disease; *e.g.*, in the United Provinces during an epidemic of cholera, a buffalo bull is marked with vermilion and driven beyond the village boundary, thus taking away the disease with him. When the idea is still further worked out by Brāhmans, it develops by painting the beast all over with lampblack and smearing its forehead with vermilion, to represent the 'vehicle' on which Yama, the god of death, rides. To make the charm more effective, the scape-animal is loaded with pieces of iron, as a potent protective against evil spirits (*NINQ* i. 102, v. 116).

47. Human sacrifice.—Human sacrifice was, as is well known, common among the Dravidians, and the best illustration of it is derived from the Kandh (*q.v.*) rite of *meriah* sacrifice. Probably most of the rites of the same kind performed by the allied tribes were done with the same intention (Crooke, *PR* ii. 167 ff.). As was the case in Greece, we find survivals which probably indicate a commutation of the rite (Lang, *Myth, Ritual, and Religion* [ed. 1899], i. 261 ff.). Thus, at Nāsik in the Deccan, when cholera appears, a woman of the Māng, a menial tribe, is solemnly led out of the city as a scape-victim. She remains outside the city limits till the next day, when she bathes and returns. The ceremonial, which closely resembles that of bringing a victim to a shrine, doubtless implies an earlier rite of human sacrifice (*BG* xvi. 521). Another rite resembles that of the self-immolation of pilgrims, who used in former times to fling themselves, in the name of Śiva, over the cliff known as Bhairava Jhāmp, near the famous shrine of Kedārnāth in the lower Himālaya; this rite seems to have prevailed farther west in the hills of the Panjāb (Atkinson, ii. 773; Rose, i. 133). It has now been commuted into paying for the services of a *bādī*, or rope-dancer, who slides on a wooden saddle upon a cable hung from a precipitous cliff, as a means of propitiating Śiva in some Kumāun villages (*NINQ* i. 55, 74 f., 128, iii. 205). In the form of the Bihundā rite the same custom prevails in the Panjāb on the river Sutlej (Rose, i. 133). In Baroda, at the worship of Vāgh Deo, the tiger-god, a man is covered with a blanket, bows to the image, and walks round it seven times. During this performance the worshippers slap him on the back. He then tries to escape to the forest, pursued by the children, who fling balls of clay at him, and finally bring him back, the rite ending with feasting and drinking (Dalal, i. 156).

48. Periodical sacrifices.—The main tribal sacrifices of the Dravidians are not, as a rule, performed annually, and the victims sometimes vary from year to year. The Mundās sacrifice every second year a fowl, every third year a ram, every fourth year a buffalo, to their mountain-god, Marang Burū; and the main object is to induce him to send favourable rain (Dalton, 199). The Tipperās have a legend that their king, Śrī Dharma, enjoined that human sacrifices in honour of Śiva should be offered only triennially (*ib.* 111). This rule of triennial sacrifices is followed by the Kharwārs, Cheros, and Nāgbansīs, while the Kaurs offer a fowl yearly to the tribal Satī, and a black goat every third year (Buchanan, i. 493; Dalton, 129, 135, 138). There are other instances of feasts celebrated at intervals of more than a year, such as the Theban *Daphnephoria* and the Bœotian *Dædala* (Frazer, *Pausanias*, v. 41 f., *GB*² i. 225 f., iii. 328 n.). Those which recur at intervals of eight years seem to be based on an attempt to harmonize lunar and solar time, just as the twelve years' feasts in South India may roughly represent Jupiter's period of revolution round the sun (Frazer, *Kingship*, 294 f.). But it is difficult to suppose that considerations such as these could have influenced people in the state of culture possessed by the Northern Dravidian tribes. It is possible that, in some cases, considerations of economy and the cost of providing the necessary victims may have suggested the rule that the sacrifices should take place at intervals longer than that of a year.

49. The priesthood.—It is said of the Kurkūs of the Central Provinces that 'they have no priesthood, by class or profession, and their ceremonies are performed by the elders of the family' (*Central Pr. Gaz.*, Nagpur, 1870, p. 49). It is true that among many of the North Dravidian tribes the domestic worship, including that of deceased ancestors, is performed by the senior member of the household, or by the house father. But practically all these tribes have reached the stage of possessing priests. The term 'priest,' however, does not usually define with accuracy the functions of this officiant, the duties of medicine-man, sorcerer, exorcist, or witch-finder being generally combined in a single individual or class. Thus, at the Mundā rites in honour of Desaulī, the village patron god, 'the sacrifice and offerings are made by the village priest, if there be one; or, if not, by any elder of the village who possesses the necessary legendary lore' (Dalton, 196). Among the Malēs of Bengal the village headman acts as priest in the worship of Dharmer Gosāin (Risley, *Tribes and Castes*, ii. 57).

The priest, again, among the Kandhs is often identified with the shaman.

'The priesthood may be assumed by any one who chooses to assert a call to the ministry of any god, such call needing to be authenticated only by the claimant's remaining for a period varying from one night to ten or fourteen days in a languid, dreamy, confused state, the consequence of the absence of his third soul in the divine presence. And the ministry which may be thus assumed may, with few exceptions, be laid down at pleasure' (Macpherson, 103).

Their *jannīs*, or priests, he goes on to say, are divided into two classes—

'one which has given up the world, and devotes itself exclusively to religious offices; and one which may still engage in every occupation excepting war. The former class are disposed to hold that they alone are qualified to perform the rites of the greater deities; but the two classes pass insensibly into one another, and many of both are seen to perform every ceremonial,—with two exceptions, namely, the rite of human sacrifice, at which a great and fully instructed priest alone can officiate; and the worship of the god of war, which his own priesthood alone can conduct. And this god, it is to be observed, requires that his priest shall serve him only, while all the other deities accept divided service from their ministers' (*ib.* 104).

The 'great *jannī*,' or ascetic who has given up the world,

'can possess no property of any kind, nor money, nor, according to his rules, even look upon a woman; and he must generally appear and act as unlike other men as possible. He must live in a filthy hut, a wonder of abomination. He must not wash but with spittle; nor leave his door, save when sent for; except, perhaps, when he wanders to draw liquor from some neglected palm-tree, at the foot of which he may be found, if required, lying half drunk. He scarcely ever wears a decent cloth or blanket. He commonly carries in his hand a broken axe or bow, and has an excited, sottish, sleepy look; but his ready wit never fails him in his office. He eats such choice morsels as a piece of the grilled skin and the feet of the sacrificial buffaloes, and the heads of the sacrificed fowls: and, when a deer is cut up, he gets for his share perhaps half the skin of the head with an ear on, and some of the hairy skimmings of the pot.'

The layman priest, on the other hand, has a wife and family, and may accumulate wealth. He eats apart from other laymen, but may drink with them (*ib.* 104 f.). These statements must be accepted with some amount of caution, as Macpherson, relying on information received from his native subordinates, was inclined to attribute a more elaborate system of beliefs and ritual to the Kandhs than the tribe probably ever possessed.

Among the other tribes of the same family this ascetic class of priest does not seem to exist, though, of course, the diviner or witch-finder often adopts the shamanistic tricks which are the common property of his kind. Macpherson also records the singular fact that some Hindus were employed by the Kandhs to assist in the service of the minor deities.

'This alone would indicate that there has been a great change in their religion; but it is probable that the low Hindus alluded to are but the Ojhās or sorcerers whom the witchcraft superstition has called into existence' (Dalton, 296).

50. Priestly titles.—Along the Kaimūr range and in Chotā Nāgpur the tribal priest is known as the *baigā* (*q.v.*). Among the more Hinduized tribes he is known by the titles of *pāhan* (Skr. *pradhāna*, 'leader') or *pūjārī*, 'one who does the service of the gods,' both titles being borrowed from the Hindus of the Plains. No village is without a *baigā*, and such is the superstition of the people, that they would rather leave a village than live without him. Usually he is a member of one of the non-Aryan tribes, and is generally selected from those who live in the more remote tracts, and who, not being contaminated by Hindu beliefs and culture, are supposed to have the most accurate knowledge of the evil spirits, and the modes of placating and repelling them. In the more civilized villages in Palamāu, Forbes found that even Brāhmans and Rājputs were being occasionally appointed to this office—a sign of the progressive process of bringing the tribes under the Hindu yoke. The *baigā* is looked up to with awe by all the residents, is responsible for the appearance of disease in man or beast, and is bound to offer up the sacrifices necessary to repel it.

'He is supposed to be better informed on all that concerns the village than any one else, and to be able to point out each man's tenure. Among the jungle tribes he is invariably the arbitrator in all disputes as regards land or rent, and is the oracle in all discussions affecting the ancient customs and rites of the village, with all of which he is supposed to be intimately acquainted. He is bound at the commencement of each harvest to offer up sacrifices and perform certain ceremonies to propitiate the spirits. For this purpose he levies contributions of money, grain, cloth, fowls, and goats from all villagers. Until these sacrifices have been performed, no one would think of yoking a plough; and the Baiga often takes advantage of the delay to increase his demands' (*NINQ* iv. 5).

The official among the Goṇḍs bears the same name.

'The nuptial, funeral, and similar ceremonies are performed under the lead of aged relations. But generally in every village there is a man who is supposed to have the power of charming tigers and preventing by spells (*mantra*) such calamities as drought, cholera, etc. He is called a Baiga' (*JASB*, 1890, p. 282).

The *pāhan* of the Cheros and Kharwārs, and the *lāyā* or *nāyā* (apparently a corruption of Skr. *nāyaka*, 'leader') of the Korās, exercise similar functions (Dalton, 129; Risley, *Tribes and Castes*, i. 509).

51. Appointment of priests.—In Chotā Nāgpur, according to Forbes (*NINQ* iv. 5), the office of priest is hereditary;

'but in the event of its becoming necessary to appoint a new Baiga, a meeting of the entire community is held, and the successor is appointed by vote; the individual selected is then called on to accept the post, and, in the event of his doing so, a day is fixed for the ceremony of installation. On the appointed day the whole village community meets in solemn conclave: the village headman presides, and the proceedings commence by his calling upon the candidate to state publicly whether he is willing to accept the office, and the duties he will have to perform are explained to him. He is then conducted round the boundaries of the village, the different landmarks of which are explained to him. The whole party then returns to the place of meeting, when the president, taking up the Baiga's instruments of office, which are known as "the knife and dagger," solemnly hands them to the new incumbent, and the installation is complete. These are the sacrificial instruments, and are heirlooms of the village; they are presented in the formal manner above described to each successive Baiga, and are used solely in sacrifice.' In the villages more under Hindu influence these hereditary implements of the Baiga seem to have fallen into disuse.

In other cases a special ceremony is performed to ascertain the will of the local deity regarding the appointment of his priest. In Kunāwar, on the lower slopes of the Himālaya, at one of the greater Hindu festivals, the villagers bathe, and, putting some water in the drinking-cups at the shrine of the local god, invoke him. 'He who is chosen is miraculously rapt or inspired by the god, and, taking up the cup, he is able to distribute grain from it, although it contained nothing but water. The Deotā [godling] may also declare his pleasure in this matter by imbuing one of his votaries with the power of thrusting, unharmed or unmarked, an iron rod through some portion of his flesh. It is the custom in one village to ask the Deotā from time to time after the death of his priest whether he wishes a successor appointed. The image is raised upon the shoulders of the people, and, if the god presses heavily to the left, he wishes the election postponed; if to the right, he wishes it to take place without delay' (*PNQ* i. 12).

Similar ceremonies are performed by the other Dravidian tribes. Among the Muṇḍās the *pāhan* is always selected from among the descendants of the earliest settlers in the village, who alone understand how to propitiate the local gods. He is always selected from one family, but the actual *pāhan* is changed at intervals of from three to five years, by the rite of the sacred winnowing-fan—*mystica vannus Iacchi*. This is taken from house to house by the village boys, and the man at whose house it halts is elected; the same method of selection prevails among the Orāons (Risley, *Tribes and Castes*, ii. 106 f.; Dalton, 247).

52. Priestly tabus.—Among the Malērs the *demāno* is appointed by Divine election. After his call he must spend a certain time in the wilderness, in intimate communication, as his flock believes, with the deity, Bedo Gosāin. From the time that any one devotes himself to the priestly profession, his hair is allowed to grow like that of a Nazirite, because his powers of divination entirely disappear if he cuts it. The cutting of the hair of a holy man is, as Frazer shows (*GB*² i. 368), dangerous for two reasons; first, there is the danger of disturbing the spirit of the head, which may be injured in the process, and may revenge itself upon the person who molests him; secondly, the difficulty of disposing of the shorn locks, which may be accidentally injured, and thus, on the principles of sympathetic magic, may endanger the original owner, or may be used by some evil-minded person to work black magic against him. After admission to full orders the Malēr priest must establish his ability to foretell events, and

'he must prove by the performance of some stupendous work beyond the strength of one man, that he is supernaturally aided by the Supreme Being. The priest may be a married man, but after entering holy orders he must refrain from associating with or touching any woman except his wife. Having undergone all the tests, his nomination is finally confirmed by the Mānjhī [headman] of the village, who ties a red silk thread to which cowries are attached round his neck, and binds a turban on his head. He is then allowed to appear at the periodical sacrifice of buffaloes celebrated by the Mānjhī in the month of January, and must drink some of the blood of the victim' (Dalton, 270).

Another interesting tabu of the Dravidian priests is that enforced at Zindā Kaliānā in the Panjāb, where they are required always to sleep on the ground or on a square bed of grass made on the ground between four posts. This reminds us of the Helloi or Selloi, priests of the Pelasgian Zeus of Dodona, who sleep upon the ground and have their feet unwashed, and of the Prussian priests who sleep in tents near the sacred oak (Hom. *Il.* xvi. 234 f.; Sophocles, *Trach.* 1167; Rose, i. 118 f.; *JAI* xxx. 36).

53. Remuneration of priests.—The methods of remunerating the Dravidian priest vary. Usually he supports himself on the head of the victims and portions of the other offerings which are his perquisite. Among the Muṇḍās he has a glebe of rent-free land, and among the other tribes he receives gifts of grain and other produce at harvest time, and food at the chief tribal feasts.

54. The sister's son as priest.—The fact that inheritance among many of the people in North India is traced through the female has been held to indicate the prevalence of polyandry in ancient times. 'It was probably wide-spread amongst many tribes in other parts of India who at the present day retain no tradition of the practice' (Risley-Gait, *Census Report*, 1901, i. 448). This is specially shown in the case of those tribes among whom the sister's son does sacrifice to appease the spirit of the deceased. Thus among the Hāṛīs of Bengal a pig is sacrificed on the tenth day after a death to appease the spirit of the departed, the flesh being eaten by the relatives, while the nephew (sister's son) of the dead man officiates as priest; and the same is the case among the Ḍoms (*q.v.*), Musahars, Pāsīs, and Tāntīs of the same province (Risley, *Tribes and Castes*, i. 316, ii. 167, 300). Among the Arakhs of the United Provinces, if the services of a Brāhman cannot be secured, the sister's son of the deceased can officiate; the Bhuiyārs hold him in great honour, and make periodical presents to him as the Hindus do to a Brāhman; among the Ḍoms, as in Bengal, he is the funeral priest; among the Kols the marriage rites are performed by the same relative (Crooke, *Tribes and Castes*, i. 83, ii. 95, 325 f., iii. 309; Dalton, 63). This primitive form of priesthood is almost certainly a survival of the matriarchate. A record of the struggle between the matriarchate and the patriarchate has been traced in the Kandh legend, which tells how Tarī, the Earth-goddess, contends with her consort, Būṛhā Pennū. The latter is finally victorious, and as a sign of Tarī's discomfiture imposes, as in the Semitic story, the cares of childbirth upon her sex (Macpherson, 84 ff.).

55. The aboriginal priest adopted into Hinduism.—The process of adoption of these aboriginal priests into Hinduism has been clearly traced in the Central Provinces by Russell (i. 176 f.). Here the class of village priests or astrologers, the *joshī*, *jogī*, *jangam*, and his fellows, occupy for the lower castes the position which Brāhmans hold in the higher strata.

'They are the ministrants of the more primitive form of religion—that of the village gods. In many cases their ritual has probably been derived from a Dravidian source, and they themselves may be the promoted descendants of the tribal priests, medicine-men, or witch-finders. It is true that they are now for the most part employed in the service of the Hindu gods, but this is probably a kind of religious evolution, of a nature akin to the social elevation into Hinduism of the casteless tribes; and, moreover, different authorities have held that many features of the cult of Śiva and Kālī, which represent a great retrogression from the purer nature gods of the Vedas, have been derived from Dravidian sources.'

56. The priestly castes.—Further, we find among some of the Dravidian tribes that certain castes, possibly in imitation of the Brāhman levites of Hinduism, have become specialized for religious purposes, and furnish priests to the lower orders. Thus the Mauliks of Manbhūm and Western Bengal act as priests of the meaner tribes.

'Their offices as priests of the various spiritual powers who haunt the forests, rocks, and fields and bring disease upon man and beast are in great request. A Bhumij or a Kurmi who wishes to propitiate these dimly-conceived but potent influences will send for a Maulik to offer the necessary sacrifices in preference to a Lāyā or priest of his own caste—a fact which speaks strongly for the antiquity of the settlement of the former in the country' (Risley, *Tribes and Castes*, ii. 83).

The *baigā* (*q.v.*) caste in the same way provide priests for the Goṇḍs; and in the United Provinces the Paṭārī branch of the Majhwārs, who perhaps take their name from the *pāṭ*, or sacred plateau, which gives a deity to the Kūrs, Kurkūs, or Muāsīs, act as priests of the whole tribe, and take, like the Hindu *mahābrāhman*, the clothes and other goods of the dead man, by wearing or using which they are supposed to pass them on to the next world for his comfort. Hence they are held in such contempt that their parishioners will neither eat with them nor drink water from their hands (Crooke, *Tribes and Castes*, iv. 153 ff.).

57. The menial priesthood in the Plains.—Among the menial tribes and castes of the Plains the worship of the village-gods is performed by priests drawn from the very lowest ranks, Bhangī, Dosādh, Mālī, or barber; while the semi-Hinduized tribes of the Kaimūr range generally employ a Chero or Bhuiyār. Nor are their services confined to members of the tribes which generally employ them. Women even of high caste use their services in worshipping those local gods, whom the innate conservatism of their sex inclines them to propitiate side by side with the higher Hindu divinities. In time of stress, when famine, disease, or other trouble besets the village, all classes of the community employ them to perform the blood sacrifices and rude ceremonies of propitiation which they themselves do not understand or are unwilling to perform.

58. Promotion of Dravidian gods into Hinduism.—Writing of Greek religion, Campbell (*Religion in Gr. Lit.*, 1898, p. 46) remarks that the reaction of primeval local ceremonies upon the Aryan religious deposit is one of the many causes of the infinite variety in the popular cults of deities reverenced throughout Greece under the same name.

'People at an early stage of culture,' he says, 'are too entirely steeped in the awe and reverence which has descended to them from their forefathers to adopt heartily or entirely a system of worship coming from abroad. The imitative faculty may be active in grafting foreign features on native religion, but the inherent force of that religion will always prevail over such adjuncts, which to begin with are but imperfectly understood.' They remain, as he remarks elsewhere (p. 119), 'as an undergrowth when the tall trees of the forest were felled.'

The survival of these deities among a race of higher knowledge than that which originally worshipped them is further encouraged by the fact that they are to a large extent the impersonations of the awe and mystery of the forest, or the malign manifestations of the primitive Mother-goddess. A new race occupying an unknown land is naturally inclined to insist on the conciliation of those local powers, which, if neglected, are likely to visit them with their displeasure. The Aryan form of Animism was not in its nature different from that of the Dravidians, and hence the acceptance of the local cults presented no difficulty. The spirit of Hinduism has always been catholic, and it has always been ready to give shelter to foreign beliefs, provided it was permitted to assimilate them in its own fashion.

'The homely jungle hero,' says Lyall (*Asiatic Studies*[2], i. 50), 'comes eventually to get brevet rank among regular divinities, whenever his tribe is promoted into Hinduism. The upper class of Brāhmans are prone to deny the existence of this process, and to profess that the proselytizing which goes on should be understood as involuntary on their part, and merely superficial; they would be willing to keep their Olympus classic and above the heads of their low-born intruders. But the local Brāhman has to live, and is not troubled by any such fine scruples, so he initiates the rude Goṇḍ and Mīnā (non-Aryans of the jungle) as fast as they come to him for spiritual advice, sets them up with a few decent caste prejudices, and gives to their rough unfinished superstitions some Brāhmanic shape and varnish. This is vexatious to the refined Vedāntist of the towns, but the same thing goes on everywhere; for a lofty and refined orthodoxy will not attract ignorant outsiders, nor will it keep the mass of a people within a common outline of belief. So the high and mighty deities of Brāhmanism would never draw upward the peasant and the woodlander if he were not invited to bring with him his fetish, his local hero or sage, his werewolf and his vampires, all to be dressed up and interpreted into orthodox emanations. In one part of Rājputāna the Mīnās (an aboriginal tribe) used to worship the pig. When they took a turn towards Islām, they changed their pig into a saint called Father Adam, and worshipped him as such; when the Brāhmans got a turn at them, the pig became identified as the famous Boar Avatār of Vishnu, whose name is Varāha.'

This account admirably explains the process by which these local gods are adopted into Hinduism. A few examples may be given of Dravidian gods promoted in this way. The cases of Bhairoṅ, Ganśām, and Hanumān have been already referred to (§ 29 ff.). Tod (i. 292 n.) describes how the primitive goddess of the Bhīls, who under Hindu guidance was re-named Lakṣmī, goddess of prosperity, gained the title of Sītalā Mātā, the smallpox goddess, whom the women of the tribe invoke in times of danger. Macpherson tells how, when the Hindus occupied the Kandh country, they took over the local goddess, Kandhinī, and, joining in the aboriginal worship at her shrine, 'her worship becomes practically confused with that of Durgā, but it is still discharged with regularity and pomp by this joint ministry' (*Calcutta Rev.* v. 58).

The adoption by the Hindus of these aboriginal gods is often masked by a legend which tells that an image was accidentally found, and the agency by which it is said to have been recovered is often that of a member of one of the non-Aryan tribes. This tale is told of the famous image of Jagannāth, which is said to have been recovered by one of the aboriginal tribe of Savarās. Ball (580) describes how a Kandh found an image said to resemble that of a cat, which is now recognized as that of Narasiṅha, the 'man-lion' incarnation of Viṣṇu. Often the image or *liṅgam* is said to have been discovered as the result of a dream. One of the most famous *liṅgams* in the Central Provinces was recovered in this way, and the same tale is told of an image of Kṛṣṇa in western India, of the great *liṅgam* at Mewār, and quite recently of an image thrown up on the seashore near Bombay (*BG* v. 81; Tod, i. 242; *NINQ* i. 175). The same inference may perhaps be drawn from the fact that the images most valued by modern Hindus are those known as *svayambhu*,

'that is, existing spontaneously and of their own nature pervaded by the essence of deity. They are merely rough stones or rocks supposed to have descended direct from heaven, or to have appeared miraculously on the soil. They are the most sacred of all objects of adoration, and, when discovered, temples are built over them. The most usual idols of this kind are stones supposed to represent the Liṅga of Śiva; and when shrines are built round them, a Yonī (to represent the female organ) is usually added' (Monier-Williams, *Brahmanism and Hinduism*[4], 69).

These Dravidian local gods seem to have supplied much of the coarser elements of modern Hinduism—the lavish blood sacrifices of animals, the occasional immolation of human beings, the use of spirituous liquor in the service of the gods—all of which appear in the Śākta cult, the most degraded form of the current belief. The same was the case in Greece, where 'it must be remembered that the cruder and wilder sacrifices and legends . . . were strictly *local*; that they were attached to these ancient temples, old altars, barbarous *xoana*, or wooden idols, and rough fetish stones in which Pausanias found the most ancient relics of Hellenic theology' (Lang, *Myth, Ritual, and Religion*, i. 252 f.).

59. Dravidian feasts and festivals.—The Dravidian feasts may be roughly divided into two classes: (1) those celebrated at the chief agricultural seasons—ploughing, sowing, harvesting—the object of which is to promote the fertility of the soil and the growth of the crops; (2) those intended as a means of purgation, the periodical expulsion of the malign spiritual powers which menace the community. The line, however, between these two classes of festivals cannot be clearly drawn, and the ceremonies of one occasionally merge in those of the other.

When the hot weather has passed, with the first fall of rain the Santāl performs at seed-time the *Erok Sim* feast, when he craves the blessing of the Mother-goddess who presides over the crops, by making a sacrifice of chickens in her sacred grove. This is followed by the *Hariar Sim*, 'the feast of greenery,' when a sacrifice is again made to secure the favour of the gods (Bradley-Birt, *Indian Upland*, 278 f.). At the transplanting of the rice the Rain-god is again invoked; and at the critical period later on, when the success of the crop depends upon abundant rain, the *Chhaṭ-parab*, or 'umbrella feast,' is held. It is a form of rude mimetic magic.

'A long lithe *sāl* tree shorn of its branches supports the smallest of umbrellas roughly made of gaudy tinsel, and together, amidst the excited shouts of the celebrants, they are raised aloft until, standing perpendicularly, the *sāl* trunk is fixed firmly in the ground. As it slowly settles into place, the people, gathering up handfuls of dust and earth, pelt the umbrella with loud cries and much laughter, dancing round it the while as round a maypole, while the men turn somersaults and perform wonders of athletics and acrobatic skill. Copious drinking of rice beer brings the feast to a close' (*ib.* 280 f.).

Finally, when the rice is in ear and the season of harvest approaches, the *Janthar* feast, or offering of first-fruits, is performed. Tiny sheaves of the half-ripe corn are placed in the sacred grove upon the sacrificial stone, and prayers are made to the gods that they will permit the crop to be safely reaped and garnered. The sacrifice of a pig, the flesh of which is cooked and eaten in the grove, is an essential part of this feast (*ib.* 281). The corn, as Frazer suggests, is eaten sacramentally 'as the body of the corn-spirit' (*GB*[2] ii. 318 ff.). This round of Santāl feasts may be taken as specimens of those performed by the Northern Dravidian tribes, further accounts being reserved for the articles on Muṇḍās, Orāons, and others.

An example of the second class of festivals—the purgation feasts—is to be found in the *Māgh-parab* or *Desaulībonga* of the Muṇḍās. A sacrifice is made to the village-protecting deity, Desaulī.

'At this period an evil spirit is supposed to infest the locality; and, to get rid of it, the men, women, and children go in procession round and through every part of the village, with sticks in their hands as if beating for game, singing a wild chant and vociferating violently till they feel assured that the bad spirit must have fled; and they make noise enough to frighten a legion' (Dalton, 280 f., 196 f.).

We find the same custom amongst the menial castes of the Plains, among whom, after the *Divālī*, or feast of lights, the house-mother takes a sieve and a broom, and beats them in every corner of the house, exclaiming, 'God abide and Poverty depart!' These feasts have been exhaustively discussed by Frazer (*GB*[2] iii. 39 ff.).

The lights used at the *Divālī* feast are probably intended as a means of expelling evil spirits. Among the Pāvrās, an aboriginal tribe of Khāndesh, at this feast four or five stones are brought from a neighbouring river-bed and placed outside the houses but within the village lands. They are painted red, liquor is sprinkled on the ground and freely drunk, and goats and fowls are sacrificed. Dancing begins at nightfall, and two men, holding lighted torches, go from house to house followed by the villagers. Every housewife comes out with a lighted lamp in her hands, waves it before them, marks their foreheads with the lamp oil, and gives beer. In this way every house in the village is purified (*BG* xii. 100). Further south it resolves itself into a means of purifying the cattle. After feasting, a figure of Balindra, god of cattle, is made and hung up in the cowshed, with rice and coco-nuts tied round its neck. The cattle are decorated with splashes of colour and garlands. The fiercest bull and the swiftest heifer in the herd are covered with flowers, and driven through the village, followed by a crowd of shouting youths. The lad who can snatch a garland from the bull or heifer as it rushes along is loudly applauded, and is considered a fit match for the best girl in the neighbourhood (*ib.* xv. pt. i. 207).

60. The Holi.—The most interesting of these Dravidian festivals in North India is that of the *Holī*, known further south as the *Shimgā*. The chief part of the rite is the burning of the *Holī* fire, the primary intention of which is apparently by a sort of sympathetic magic to ensure a due supply of sunshine for the crops (Frazer, *GB*[2] iii. 313 ff.). But there are other incidents which suggest that the rite in its present form is complex, and that more than one train of thought has led to its observance. Returning to that primitive tribe, the Pāvrās of Khāndesh, we find that a pit is dug, and a wooden stake thrust into it, and lighted at night. Every one brings a piece of bread, some rice, and a cock, portions of which are thrown into the fire and the rest consumed on the spot. Drinking and dancing go on till dawn (*BG* xii. 100). In Kumāun each clan erects a tree covered with rags which are begged by the young men from the people of the tribe. Near the tree a fire is kindled and the tree is burned. While it is being burned there is a contest between the clans, each trying to carry off a shred of cloth from the tree of another clan. When the tree is consumed the people leap over the ashes, believing that in this way they get rid of itch and other diseases. The analogy with the custom of hanging rags on trees is here obvious (§ 12). In Gwalior, again, two phallic figures are constructed. One, made of wood, is preserved from year to year; the other, of bricks, after the fire is lighted is broken to pieces with blows of shoes and bludgeons. The wooden figure is placed beside the wedding couch as a fertility charm (*NINQ* iii. 92 f.). A similar rite is the *Khatarhuvā* of Kumāun, when a fire of dry grass and weeds is burned round a pole. Obscene songs are sung, and the purport of one is that the cattle are now safe from demons (*ib.* iii. 135). Among the Dravidian Biyārs, again, a stake of the sacred cotton tree is driven into the ground, and a time is fixed for the Burning of the Old Year. The fire is lit by the village *baigā*, and the people after parching ears of barley at it eat them. They sprinkle the ashes about, and with them mark their foreheads (Crooke, *Tribes and Castes*, ii. 137). An important part of these rites is the leaping over the fire and the driving of the cattle through it, which Frazer (*GB*[2] iii. 312) thinks 'may be intended, on the one hand, to secure for man and beast a share of the vital energy of the sun, and, on the other hand, to purge them of all evil influences; for to the primitive mind fire is the most powerful of all purificatory agents.' Further than this, we find that, in the ceremony as performed in the Mathura district of the United Provinces, the important portion of the rite is that the village priest, apparently as a representative of the community, should walk through the fire not in a perfunctory way, but in a manner which seems to imply that he was expected actually to expose himself to the flames. A similar rite practised by the king of Tyre seems to represent the commutation of an actual fire sacrifice (Frazer, *Adonis, Attis, Osiris*, 38; Crooke, *PR* ii. 317). The *Holī*, then, appears to be a complex rite, the chief intention being to promote fertility and dispel evil influences.

61. The Saturnalia.—It will have been noticed that in connexion with festivals of this kind there is a period of licence, which may be compared to that of the Roman Saturnalia. The *Māgh-parab*, or spring feast of the Muṇḍās, is held in January,

'when the granaries are full of grain, and the people, to use their own expression, full of devilry. They have a strange notion that at this period men and women are so overcharged with vicious propensities that it is absolutely necessary for the safety of the person to let off steam by allowing for a time full vent to the passions. The festival, therefore, becomes a saturnale, during which servants forget their duty to their masters, children their reverence for parents, men their respect for women, and women all notions of modesty, delicacy, and gentleness; they become raging bacchantes' (Dalton, 196).

In the same way the rites of the *Holī* festival are accompanied by indecency of word and gesture, the singing of ribald songs, and the flinging of filth or coloured water on passers-by. Such orgies are commonly associated with the rites of the spring festival or the garnering of the crops (Frazer, *GB*² iii. 118 f., 138). It seems more probable that these acts of indecency are intended as a piece of sympathetic magic to induce fertility, than, as Crawley (*Mystic Rose*, 1902, p. 278 ff.) suggests, a means of purification and breaking with the past by a complete inversion of the normal, decent course of ordinary life.

62. Hunting-festivals.—The last group of the Dravidian festivals which can be considered here is that of the general hunt. In Chotā Nāgpur the Hos, as well as most of the other non-Aryan tribes of the district, have a great national hunting-festival in May. Immense crowds assemble, beat the forests, and kill enormous quantities of game (Bradley-Birt, *Chota Nagpore*, 107 ff.). Among the Rājputs this is represented by the annual spring rite of the *Ahairia*, when the boar, the enemy of the Mother-goddess, Gaurī, is slain (Tod, i. 598 f.). Frazer connects this slaying of the boar with the killing of the corn-spirit (*GB*² ii. 284). This general hunting-festival, again, seems to develop into the Muṇḍā rite, when all the girls of the village arm themselves and make a descent upon a neighbouring village, whence they carry off all the live stock, in the shape of fowls, kids, pigs, and lambs, which they can secure, the village thus raided retaliating by a similar raid upon another; and in the Plains, in Bihār, at the *Jūr Sītal* feast in honour of Śītalā, the smallpox goddess, the people in the forenoon cover themselves with mud, which they shower on every one they meet, and in the afternoon go out with clubs and hunt hares, jackals, and any other animal they can find in the village (*NINQ* iii. 98; Grierson, *Bihār Peasant Life*, 401). The import of these rites is obscure. They may be connected with the totemistic slaughter of sacred animals, as in the case of Hunting the Wren; or they may be purificatory or cathartic (*FL* xi. 250 ff., xvii. 270 ff.).

63. The current religious beliefs of the peasant.—It remains to consider the general views of the so-called Dravidian peasant of the Plains on the subjects of religion and morality. This question was specially considered at the last Census, and much useful information has been collected.

Beginning with the Panjāb, Wilson, a careful observer (*Sirsa Settlement Rep.*, 1883, p. 133), holds that the ordinary Hindu peasant of the Panjāb

'has practically no belief in the transmigration of souls, but has a vague idea that there is a future life, in which those who are good in this world will be happy in a heaven, while those who are bad will be wretched in a hell. His devotional offerings to demons, saints, and godlings are meant rather to avert temporal evils or to secure temporal blessings than to improve his prospects in the world to come. He has an idea that sin will bring evil on himself and his fellows in this life as well as after death. His instincts as to good and evil are much the same as the ordinary European moral distinctions, only they do not take so wide a range; instead of extending to the whole human race, or to the whole nation or sect, they extend only to his own tribe, or village, or family. He thinks it wrong to tell a lie unless perhaps to benefit a relative or friend; he thinks it wicked to injure a man unless he has been injured by him, or to cheat another unless he thinks that that other would cheat him if he got a chance; or to take a bribe without giving the promised consideration for it.' He has a vague idea that it is good for him to meditate on the deity; and, to show that he has not forgotten him, he mutters the name of Rāma, or of some other Hindu god, when he rises in the morning, and, 'if he is piously inclined, at all times also, in season and out of season. Notwithstanding all the numerous saints and deities whom he endeavours to propitiate, he has a vague belief that above all there is one Supreme God whom he calls Nārāyan [Nārāyaṇa] or Parmeshar [Parameśvara], who knows all things and by whom all things were made, and who will reward the good and punish the bad both in this life and in the life to come.'

Fagan, writing of the neighbouring district of Hissar, remarks (*NINQ*, iii. 129) that the peasant is in no sense an orthodox Hindu. He feeds and venerates, though he does not respect, the Brāhman; and he acknowledges the existence and power of the three great Hindu gods, Śiva, Viṣṇu, Kṛṣṇa. Of the more strictly orthodox, but inferior gods, perhaps Sūraj Nārāyan, the Sun-god, is the one most commonly worshipped. His worship consists in bathing at the tank adjoining one of the Hindu temples, obeisance, and pouring water over the *lingam* of Śiva. He worships Sūraj Nārāyan on Sundays; and the more pious fast on that day in his honour, eating only one meal, and abstaining from the use of salt. But these gods are too great for every-day use. 'He lives, as it were, in an atmosphere charged with the spirits of departed saints, heroes, demons, and others who are in a position to, and as a matter of fact do, exercise a benevolent or malevolent influence in the affairs of mankind, and it is from them that he selects those who are to be the recipients of his every-day devotion. It is not so much perhaps the case that he worships them with fixed ceremonies as he does Śiva or Sūraj Nārāyan; but they are always consciously almost present to him as the beings who have the most immediate connexion with his destinies.' In this class Bhūmiyā or Khetrpāl, the Earth-god, and Śītalā, the goddess of smallpox, are most commonly worshipped. Fire he adores by dropping butter into it; he worships the Pīpal, or sacred fig-tree, at dawn, after bathing, by pouring water at its root and making obeisance.

Burn (i. 73 ff.) corroborates the existence in the United Provinces of belief in a Supreme God, called Bhagvān, Parameśvara, Īśvara, or Nārāyaṇa.

'It must not be forgotten, however, that, to the Hindu, religion includes matters which to other people are merely social concerns; and, while he has no idea of congregational worship, such as is usual for instance in Christianity or Islām, ritual enters into his daily life probably to a greater extent than into that of a Christian or Musalmān.'

A cultivator in Bundelkhand thus described his religion to Luard (i. 64): 'All I know about religion is that every day I call Rām morning and night. All my time is taken up in work. I do not do things which would outcaste me, associate with the low, or eat forbidden things. This is all my religion.' In other words, religion amounts to observance of the laws of caste.

LITERATURE.—B. C. Allen, *Census Report Assam*, 1901; Ardasheer Dinshawji Chinoy, *Census Report Berar*, 1901; E. T. Atkinson, *Himalayan Gazetteer*, 1882–4; V. Ball, *Jungle Life in India*, 1880; A. D. Bannerman, *Census Report Rajputana*, 1901; F. B. Bradley-Birt, *The Story of an Indian Upland*, 1905, *Chota Nagpore, a little-known Province of the Empire*, 1903; R. C. Bramley, *Census Report Ajmer-Merwara*, 1901;

F. H. Buchanan, in *Eastern India*, ed. M. Martin, 1838; R. Burn, *Census Report North-western Provinces and Oudh*, 1901; R. Caldwell, *A comparative Dravidian Grammar*[2], 1875; J. A. Campbell, *Personal Narrative of thirteen Years' Service among the Wild Tribes of Kondistan*, 1864; J. M. Campbell, *Notes on the Spirit Basis of Belief and Custom*, 1885; W. Crooke, *Tribes and Castes of the North-western Provinces and Oudh*, 1896, *Popular Religion and Folk-lore of Northern India*[2], 1896; J. A. Dalal, *Census Report Baroda*, 1901; E. T. Dalton, *Descriptive Ethnology of Bengal*, 1872; A. K. Forbes, *Rās Mālā, or Hindoo Annals of the Province of Goozerat in W. India*, 1878; J. Forsyth, *Highlands of Central India*, new ed. 1889; E. A. Gait, *Census Report Assam*, 1891, do. *Bengal*, 1901; *Gazetteers of Bombay, Berar, Central Provinces, Rajputana*; G. A. Grierson, *Bihār Peasant Life*, 1885; F. S. Growse, *Mathura, a district Memoir*[3], 1883; S. Hislop, *Papers relating to the Aboriginal Tribes of the Central Provinces*, 1866; Sir W. W. Hunter, *The Annals of Rural Bengal*, 1868; Sir D. C. J. Ibbetson, *Punjab Ethnography*, 1883; Col. W. Kirkpatrick, *Account of Nepal*, 1811; S. Knowles, *The Gospel in Gonda*, 1889; Capt. E. C. Luard, *Central India Census Report*, 1901; Sir A. C. Lyall, *Asiatic Studies*[2], 1907; Sir J. Malcolm, *Memoir of Central India*, 1824; *NINQ*, 1891–6; H. A. Oldfield, *Sketches from Nepal*, 1880; G. Oppert, *The original Inhabitants of Bharatavarsha or India*, 1893; *PNQ*, 1883–7; H. H. Risley, *Tribes and Castes of Bengal*, 1891; H. H. Risley and E. A. Gait, *Census Report India*, 1901; H. A. Rose, *Census Report Panjab*, 1901, *Glossary of the Tribes and Castes of the Punjab and N.W. Frontier Province*, vol. ii. (1911; all published); R. V. Russell, *Census Report Central Provinces*, 1901; M. A. Sherring, *Hindu Tribes and Castes*, 1872–81; W. H. Sleeman, *Rambles and Recollections of an Indian Official*, ed. V. A. Smith, 1893; J. Tod, *Annals and Antiquities of Rajasthan or the Central and Western Rajpoot States of India*, Calcutta reprint, 1884; L. A. Waddell, *Among the Himalayas*, 1899; W. Ward, *A View of the History, Literature, and Religion of the Hindoos*[2], 1815; Sir M. Monier-Williams, *Brahmanism and Hinduism*[4], 1891; J. Wise, *Notes on the Races, Castes, and Trades of Eastern Bengal*, 1883.

W. CROOKE.

DRAVIDIANS (South India).—**I. Introductory.**—The Southern Dravidians, numbering about 57 millions of people, occupy the portion of India that is bordered on the north by a line which, starting about 100 miles south of Goa, runs along the Western Ghāts to Kolhapur and Hyderābād, then passes south of Berar to the Bay of Bengal on the east. The term 'Dravidian,' irrespective of boundary, is generally used in the sense applied to it by Kumārila Bhaṭṭa in the 8th cent. (about A.D. 725 [Hoernle, *Hist. of India*, 1905, p. 76]) to include those southern peoples who then spoke languages he termed 'Āndhra Drāviḍa,' or 'Telugu Tamil,' among which are now included, as chief languages, Telugu, Tamil, Kanarese, Malayālam, and Tulu. Many attempts have been made to connect this group with other outside families of languages, such as Scythian, Ural-Altaic, and Australian; but, so far as any conclusive evidence is concerned, 'the attempt is now generally regarded as a failure' (*Linguistic Survey of India*, vol. iv. p. 282). The same conclusion seems to have been arrived at with regard to efforts made to connect the Southern Dravidians with other known races of the world, or even with those of North India. Recent head-measurements in South India have led Thurston (*Castes and Tribes of Southern India*, vol. i. p. xli) to the conclusion that

'whatever may have been the influence which has brought about the existing sub-brachycephalic or mesaticephalic type in the northern areas, this influence has not extended southward into the Tamil and Malayālam countries, where Dravidian man remains dolicho- or sub-dolichocephalic.'

It follows that there is no reliable evidence whether the Southern Dravidians are autochthones, or whether in some primitive time they reached their present habitats from some outside country. In South India they were preserved, almost down to historic times, from the outside social and ethnical influences of Aryan, Scythian, or Mongoloid invaders, which in the north submerged the proto-Dravidian races, who spoke some proto-Dravidian language. The barrier of the Vindhya range of mountains warded off for long the pressure of these more vigorous races and of their more advanced civilization. The Southern Dravidians have, therefore, preserved their own indigenous language, diversified in course of time into distinct groups of separate languages. In these languages—Telugu, Kanarese, Malayālam, and especially Tamil—a literature was developed in a peculiar classical form, so archaic and different from the spoken language of to-day that even an educated Southern Indian would now be unable to read or understand this early literature, unless he made it a special study. It enshrines somewhat of the early history of the social organizations and religious conceptions of the pre-Aryan period.

To the east and west of the Vindhyas lay the low coastlands, through which, in due course, Aryan and other newcomers penetrated, settled in the richer river-valleys, and thence advanced through the more accessible passes to the central table-land. These incursions were comparatively late in the lifetime of Dravidian peoples. It is not until the 4th cent. B.C. that mention is made in Aryan literature of the Southern Dravidians. The grammarian Pāṇini in the 5th cent. B.C. merely notes the existence of the Āndhras, who ruled in the Telugu country in the north-east of Dravidian lands, and who, from the account of Megasthenes, held an extensive sway south of the Maurya empire as early as 300 B.C. Kātyāyana, the commentator of Pāṇini, in the 4th cent. B.C., also mentions the ancient Dravidian Pāṇḍya and Chola kingdoms, which had their capitals at Mūdūr and Uraiyūr (*ūr* being Dravidian for 'village' or 'town'). The Edicts of Aśoka in the 3rd cent. B.C. show that the south was then well known, as were the kingdoms mentioned above, and that of the Cheras on the east. Aśoka records in these Edicts that he had conquered the Kaliṅgas as far south as the Kistna River, and killed 100,000 of the inhabitants—which he regretted because 'in such a country dwell Brāhmans and ascetics, men of different sects' (V. A. Smith, *Aśoka*, Oxf. 1901, p. 16). The publication of these Edicts as far south as Mysore 'presupposes a widely diffused knowledge of the art of writing' (V. A. Smith, *Early Hist. of India*[2], do. 1908, p. 154). Inter-communication had so increased by the time of Mahendra, a relative of Aśoka, that he is said to have implanted Buddhism as far south as Ceylon (see CEYLON BUDDHISM).

In the history of religious life—so far as it is of permanent interest—of the Southern Dravidians, it is almost impossible to discriminate exactly between what was the result of the influence of Aryan conceptions and what was of purely indigenous origin. Thought in India loves to work through analogies, and an analogy may be found in the Aryan influence in the south on race and on religion, so far as it affected the higher classes and their literature.

The aboriginal Dravidian was of short stature, of dark skin, with a short broad nose. The Aryan—at least the early Aryan ethnically uninfluenced by the aboriginal races, of whom the pure Brāhman is the best type in India to-day—was of fair complexion and had typical Aryan features. In South India of to-day

'between a Brāhman of high culture, with fair complexion and long narrow nose, on the one hand, and a less highly civilized Brāhman, on the other, there is a vast difference, which can only be reasonably explained on the assumption of racial admixture; and it is no insult to the higher members of the Brāhman community to trace, in their more lowly brethren, the result of crossing with a dark-skinned and broad-nosed race of short stature' (Thurston, *op. cit.* vol. i. p. liv).

This racial mixture of Dravidian and Aryan can be traced all over the south, more marked as one goes northward, where the Aryan influence was more predominant. The same mixture of Aryan and Dravidian can be traced in the literature of the religious life of the people, so far as it is a record of their best thought. There is throughout it an underlying Dravidian substratum, interwoven and covered over with, sometimes almost concealed by, accretions from Aryan culture. Just as Dravidian languages, from their contact with Aryan languages, were enlarged with a new vocabulary and their literature enriched by new modes of expression, so, in a similar manner, Dravidian primitive religious conceptions were refined from dark superstitions and Animism, until they finally reached a living faith[1] in the saving grace of a Supreme Deity. The primitive Dravidian substratum has been described as a form of shamanism (see preced. art. §§ 2, 3). This phase of thought still exists in South India among the wilder tribes and simpler rural folk, who have their own peculiar ecstatic frenzied dances, amid which the votaries, drugged and foaming at the mouth, are held to be in communion with some demon or goddess, and to become soothsayers of the deity thirsting for unholy rites and blood sacrifice. Out of some such phase of thought emerges the pre-historic primitive Dravidian religion, known as some form of Śaivism, or worship of Śiva. The attributes and rites of this deity were gradually brought into conformity, by a process of compromise, with those of some Aryan deity or deities. This was due to the necessity under which an invading race lie of compromising with the people amid whom they make their new homes. There are evidences which tend to show that the Aryans adopted somewhat of the pronunciation of Dravidian languages (*Linguistic Survey*, vol. iv. p. 279). Dravidian languages, on the other hand, north and south, enlarged the vocabulary of the Aryan languages and influenced their inflexions. In a similar manner Dravidian religious conceptions reacted on Aryan modes of thought.

The attributes of the Dravidian deity Siva were found to be most in conformity with those of the Vedic god Rudra, the wielder of the thunderbolt and father of the Storm-gods. The conception thus grew of a half-Dravidian half-Aryan deity—Rudra-Śiva, the Destroyer of the Universe—who became the Supreme Deity, Śiva, of the great mass of the Dravidian people. The term *śiva* is even used in the Vedas as = 'auspicious'—an epithet of the god Rudra. The word *śiva* is, however, the Dravidian word for 'red,' and the word *rudra* in the Rig Veda 'often seems to mean red.' Therefore, at a very early period, 'it seems probable that the conception of the god Rudra had a tinge of Dravidian ideas' (*Linguistic Survey*, iv. 279).

This 'tinge of Dravidian' runs through all Dravidian literature of post-Aryan periods in which the religious ideals of the people were expressed, giving it a distinctive and often perplexing individuality of its own. Aryan influences had, no doubt, a predominating effect alike on the literature, the religious conceptions, and the philosophic modes of reasoning of the Dravidian. Nevertheless, Dravidian genius, roused by contact with an advanced civilization, developed a distinctive religious literature worthy not only to stand side by side with the best of the literature of India, but also to take a place in history as a contribution to the records of the efforts and aspirations of mankind towards the truth.

Evidence for the influence of early Christian beliefs (see *ERE* ii. 548 ff.) on later Dravidian religious conceptions belongs more to the region of feeling than to that of absolute proof. This feeling seems to have impressed itself most strongly on European scholars, who may be said, by their intimate acquaintance with Indian languages and literature, to be almost saturated with the spirit and thought of India (see Grierson, 'Modern Hinduism and its Debt to the Nestorians,' in *JRAS*, April 1907; Pope, Introd. to *Tiru Vāchakam*[2]). The theory of this influence is not further touched on for want of definite evidence or proof: it must suffice to say that, throughout Tamil literature, from the 8th or 9th century, there are to be found ideas and sometimes totally unexpected forms of expression suggestive of some Christian influences on the poetry of the period.

[1] There is no pure Dravidian word for 'faith.' The Skr. word *bhakti* is used (= Tamil *patti*) in Tamil literature as early as the 8th or 9th century.

[2] Sanskrit forms of Tamil words are used throughout, as being more generally known. *Tiru*—the Tamil method of pronouncing the Skr. *śrī*, 'blessed'—is retained, as it is of common occurrence.

2. Early history of Dravidian religion.—Tradition ascribes the earliest Aryan influences on Dravidian religious literature to the Jains, whose writings were usually in Sanskrit, and were translated into the vernaculars for the use of the common people. The *Kural*, a collection of couplets, in the Veṃbā metre, on ethical subjects, is especially claimed by the Jains as their contribution to the earliest efforts to provide the Dravidian cultivators of the soil with moral teachings. This claim seems improbable; the work is more usually ascribed to a weaver named Tiru Valluvar, who lived at St. Thomé, near Madras. It is said to have been accepted by the 3rd *Saṅgha*, or Tamil Academy, at Madura, through miraculous intervention of the god Śiva to establish the revealed character of its stanzas. Divided into three books, on Virtue, Wealth, and Enjoyment, it is still considered by Tamil-speaking people as a masterpiece of literary structure and of profundity of thought, and has received similar praise from many European scholars. It has been ascribed to the 2nd or 3rd cent. (Barnett, *Catalogue*, p. 111), but its style is simple—far more so than works ascribed to a much later period.

The same famed Tamil Academy is also traditionally held to have been responsible for the gathering together, at the court of the king of Madura, of 800 Jain ascetics, who issued a collection of 400 quatrains known as the *Nālaḍiyār*, to serve as a Tamil Veda, or Book of Wisdom, for the daily use of the people. These quatrains are said to have been composed 4000 years ago, but, as a matter of fact, date back, at the furthest period to which they can be assigned, to the 2nd or 3rd cent. A.D. In the outpourings of the soul—tossed from birth to re-birth through the evil of deeds—over the weariness of life and the joy of release from ceaseless transmigrations, there is no evidence of any distinctive school of belief, either Jain, Buddhist, or Śaiva, and no mention of a deity. One quatrain alone (243) gives a faint clue to the existence of a difference between northern and southern faiths, by stating that

'many of the southern people have entered heaven (*svargam*), while many of the northern have lived in vain; the future of every one depends on his own deeds.'

In these early centuries Jainism and Buddhism flourished throughout South India side by side with the rising claims of Śaivism to gather the southern people into one common national faith, founded on the belief in a personal deity able to enter into communion with his votaries. From the beginning of the 1st cent. (A.D. 23) to the beginning of the 3rd (A.D. 218), the Buddhist faith flourished vigorously, especially in the Telugu country. Here, under the rule of the Āndhra-Bhṛtyas, the famed Buddhist tope at Amarāvatī, near the Kistna River, was built. This great Buddhist memorial is now in ruins, and the surrounding country desolate; but in the neighbouring hills are cut out rock-hewn caves, once the abodes of ascetic monks, who must have wandered far and wide, inculcating the faith of their founder and begging alms.

The Jainist negation of the belief in a soul and Buddhist nescience as to the existence of a personal Deity were doomed to failure, removed as these doctrines were in the south from the sources of their birth in far-away Kapilavastu, 200 miles north of Benares. The great revolt of the Dravidian races against both Jainism and Buddhism arose in the 5th and 6th centuries, and continued until the indigenous deity Śiva was left supreme. The land of the Dravidians became henceforth the land of a belief in a First Cause, who by His grace created a cosmos wherein souls might work out the fatality of *karma*, or deeds, and so gain release from the haunting terrors of endless births and re-births, the uncertainties of awards in heavens or terrors in hells.

An account of South India, seemingly authentic, at this period is given by Hiuen Tsiang, a Chinese pilgrim, who travelled all over India to trace the footsteps of Buddha and to learn the condition of the Buddhist faith. It is recorded that this visit took place in A.D. 640, in the reign of the Western Chālukyan monarch, Pulikeśin II. (A.D. 608 to 642), who ruled at Vātāpi, and is said to have conquered the Southern Pallava monarch, Narasiṃha Varma, who ruled (A.D. 625 to 645) at Kāñchī (Conjeeveram). The Chinese pilgrim describes Kāñchī as a city five miles round, containing many Jains, 10,000 Buddhist monks, and 80 Brāhman temples. At Mālākūṭa (country south of the Cauvery) he records that the people did not care for learning, but were given to commercial gain. He says that the country possessed many ruins of old monasteries, but that only the walls were preserved. There were many hundred Deva temples, and a multitude of heretics, mostly Jains. He also describes one Buddhist *stūpa*, or burial-mound, 'in the Chola country, and another in the Drāvida or Pāndya kingdoms, as ascribed to Aśoka' (V. A. Smith, *Aśoka*, p. 47). From this it is clear that the coming struggle was to be between the advancing power of Śaivism as opposed to the Jain belief and the fading influence of Buddhism. There is further internal evidence in the great classical Tamil romances—the *Maṇimēkhalai*, and *Śillapp'adhikāram*—of the 2nd cent. that at that period Buddhists, Jains, and Śaivas lived in harmony, whereas the third great Tamil classic—the *Jīvaga Chintamaṇi* of the 10th cent.—gives evidence of the hostility of both Jains and Śaivas to the Buddhist faith.

3. Sacred hymns of the Śaivas.—The revival of the Dravidian worship of Śiva led to the collection of all the early Śaiva hymns, composed for singing in the temples to Śiva during worship, into what is known as the *Tiru Murai*, or Holy Sayings. The first three books of this collection contain the poems of the most renowned sage and saint of the Tamils, Tiru Jñāna Sambandhar, of the middle of the 7th cent. A.D. (V. Venkayya, *Tamil Antiquary*, No. 3 [1909]), whose image is still worshipped in Śaiva temples of the south. The next three were the poems of Appar, or Tiru Nāvukk'arașu; and the seventh—the last—those of Sundarar, of the 8th and 9th centuries. The poems of this collection, or *Dēvāram*, are held to be Divine revelation, and are daily recited, in Tamil lands in the Śaiva temples, by a special class of priests. To this collection are further added, as the 8th part of the *Tiru Murai*, the poems of Māṇikka Vāchakar, known as the *Tiru Vāchakam*,[1] or Holy Sayings, which date from A.D. 800 to 900 (J. Vinson, *Siddhānta Dīpika*,[2] Aug. 1908; V. Venkayya, *Tamil Antiquary*, No. 3, p. vi). A ninth collection, by nine minor poets, is known as the *Tiru Iṣaipā*, one hymn of which relates to a temple built by Rajendra Chola I. (A.D. 1012) (*IA* xxxvi [1907] 288). The 10th is by a mystic, Tiru Mūlar; and an 11th contains some poems by Nakkīrar Devar of the 5th or 6th cent. A.D. The last ten poems of this 11th collection are by Nambi Āṇḍār Nambi; the last three form the basis of a legendary History of Saints, which is known as the *Periya Purāṇam*, composed by Sēkkirar, under the patronage of Kulottuṅga Chola II. (A.D. 1070–1118) (Sundaram Pillai, *Milestones*, p. 3; see Barnett, *Catalogue*, for a nine-fold collection of the *Tiru Murai*).

[1] Hereafter cited as *T.V.* [2] Hereafter cited as *S.D.*

The collection of early devotional literature, together with the poems of fourteen later Santāna teachers, are sometimes called the 'Sacred Sūtras of the Śaivas.'

The 10th cent. is noted for the sacred Śaiva poems of Paṭṭaṇattu Pillai, while in the 16th or 17th cent. all the floating legends concerning the many manifestations of the energies of Śiva were collected together as 'The Sacred Sports of Śiva,' or *Tiru Vilai āḍal Purāṇam*, by Parañ Jōti. The most popular and sweetest singer of Śaiva mystic raptures was Tāyumānavar, who wrote about A.D. 1650.

This period of revival of the adoration and worship of Śiva exhibits, as an outward expression of the inward devotion of the people to their Deity, the bestowal of an almost incredible amount of labour and skill on the erection in A.D. 985 of the famed temple at Tanjore, the walls of which were covered with inscriptions telling of the great victories of the Chola king, Rāja Rāja Deva (A.D. 985). In the time of the earlier Chola king, Parāntaka I. (A.D. 907), the temple to Śiva at Chidambaram is recorded to have been covered with gold (*S.I. Inscriptions*, vol. i. p. 112).

The most revered of all these early poets was Tiru Jñāna Sambandhar, who is said

'to have looked upon the overthrow of the Jains and Buddhists as the one object of his life—of every one of his numerous hymns the tenth verse is uniformly devoted to their condemnation' (Sundaram Pillai, *Milestones*, p. 70).

He is said to have converted the ruling Pāṇḍya monarch at Madura from Jainism back to the ancient faith in Śiva, to which the monarch's wife and prime minister had adhered. The *Periya Purāṇam* records that not only did he convince the king of the truths of Śaivism, and defeat all the arguments brought forward in support of Jain doctrines, but that he afterwards took care that 8000 Jains should be massacred—a massacre which is still commemorated at Madura. The second greatest of these early poets was Māṇikka Vāchakar, the author of the *T.V.*, who in the 9th cent. A.D. is recorded, in the *Vāthav ūrar Purāṇam*, to have totally defeated the Buddhists, and to have finally established the Śaiva faith in the Chola kingdom. The king of Ceylon is said to have arrived with his surrounding Buddhist missionaries at the court of the Chola monarch, who vowed to exterminate them if Māṇikka Vāchakar could establish the truths of the Śaiva faith in opposition to the arguments of the Buddhists.

It is strange that at this early period one of the keenest philosophical arguments against the whole underlying basis of Buddhism and idealism was raised by the Tamil sage. The Buddhists, in their arguments before the Chola king, stated the cardinal doctrine of their belief that all 'knowledge appears and in an instant of time disappears: all is ceaseless flux.' The answer of Dravidian India came in the retort of Māṇikka Vāchakar, that in all thought, in all perception, there must persist a momentary consciousness, a moment of apprehension, which persistence was in itself evidence of reality. The argument was urged by Māṇikka Vāchakar, who asked how he could reply to a Buddhist who uttered madness, for,

'before thou didst finish uttering forth thy words and meanings, since thine understanding must have passed away, what revelation of truth and virtue can there be?' (Pope, *T.V.* p. lxix).

The Buddhists, after long disputations, had to confess and in despair cry:

'Thou sayest that we possess neither God nor salvation. What, then, is your God and your salvation?'

The best non-doctrinal answer to this question is to be found in the *T.V.* of Māṇikka Vāchakar, now available for English readers in the versified tr. by Pope. These 'Holy Sayings' are, in the words of the translator (p. ix, preface):

'daily recited in all the great Śaiva temples of South India, are on every one's lips, and are as dear to the hearts of vast multitudes of excellent people there as the Psalms of David are to Jews and Christians.'

It is held that in South India the influence of these hymns was such that

'by the close of the 9th century both Buddhism and Jainism had become inert and dead' (*S.D.*, July 1909; Nallaswami Pillai, *Saiva Religion*).

In these hymns, or devotional songs of mystic rapture over the works and grace of Śiva, and telling of the ecstatic joy of release from the bondage of ignorance and deeds, Pope saw everywhere the influence of the Bhagavad-Gītā, the deity Śiva taking the place of Kṛṣṇa, the heroic deity of the Sanskrit poem (dating in its earliest form from 400 B.C. to A.D. 200). The doctrine of *bhakti*, or faith of the Bhagavad-Gītā, finds expression in the Śaiva doctrine of the love and devotion of the soul to the belief and hope that Śiva will, through his grace, grant knowledge of the soul's true nature, by which revelation of knowledge the soul would obtain release (*mukti*) from transmigrations. According to the Śaiva *Āgamānta*, either the position of the soul with regard to the grace of the Deity is helpless, in the position of a kitten towards its mother, until the grace of the Deity seizes it and brings it into salvation—a doctrine known as *mārjārī-bhakti*, or cat-like faith; and this has been described as the lowest (*sā bhakti adhamaḥ*) form of faith. Or, the soul may co-operate in securing salvation, being in the position of a young monkey grasping its mother—a doctrine known as *markaṭātmaja-bhakti*, or monkey-like faith, which is commended (*S.D.*, Oct. 1910, Agamic note, p. 192).

Pope held that this doctrine of *bhakti*, or faith, permeated the whole after-history of Śaivism in a form in which

'the fervent self-negating love and worship of Śiva is represented as including all religion and transcending every kind of religious observance' (*T.V.* p. lxvii).

The flame of revolt against Jainism and Buddhism is said to have been fanned to a fiery persecution in the 8th cent. by Kumārila Bhaṭṭa (a Brāhman from Behār), who preached all over India antagonism to Buddhists and Jains alike, and inculcated a purer Brāhmanism. It was left to Śaṅkarāchārya, towards the end of the 8th or beginning of the 9th cent., to give the death-blow to Buddhism in the south, and to lay the foundations of a wider and more philosophic Śaivism than its earlier forms. Born a Nambūtiri Brāhman, in South India, at Malabar, he died at the early age of 32 in the Himālaya mountains, having crowded into a short life an enormous outpouring of his genius and learning in commentaries on the Upaniṣads, Brahma-sūtras, and Bhagavad-Gītā, while a vast number of revivalist short poems, still recited in the south, are ascribed to him.

In these commentaries India saw its culminating point, in philosophic reasoning, in the doctrine he taught of *advaita*, or non-duality—the Indian form of monistic idealism. The monistic doctrine of Śaṅkara, with its underlying principle of a fictitious *māyā*, conjuring up an unreal cosmos of dream life, with an abstract subject of thought as ultimate entity, was too vague and idealistic to form a basis for a religion sufficient to satisfy the demands of the non-Brāhmanical Dravidians for realism and personal worship and love for a Deity. Śaṅkara, therefore, admitted, as a preliminary to full knowledge of his *advaita* doctrines, the worship of various manifestations of Śiva as forms of the All-God, inculcating a more refined form of the worship, as opposed to the popular worship of the *śaktis*, or female divinities. He founded throughout India four monasteries, and his immediate disciples established ten orders of Śaiva ascetics to carry on the attack against the rival Buddhist monastic orders. The present *guru*, or spiritual head—thirty-third in succession from Śaṅkara—of the monastery he founded at Sriṅgēri, in Mysore, is the acknowledged head of the Tulu-speaking Smārta Brāhmans who adhere to the *advaita* doctrine of Śaṅkara, which is still taught among Smārtā Brāhmans in every considerable village in the south.

The spread of the worship of Śiva was in the 10th cent. further fostered by the conquests by the Chola Śaiva monarch, Rāja Rāja Deva (A.D. 985), of the ancient Chera and Pāṇḍya kingdoms and Ceylon, until finally the whole east coast became a united Chola and Eastern Chālukyan empire by matrimonial alliances between the two kingdoms. In the Deccan a great revival of Śaivism is recorded to have taken place in the time of Bijjala, a Jain who had usurped the throne of the last of the later Chālukyan monarchs, Someśvara IV. An inscription, of about A.D. 1200, gives an account of how the deity Śiva

'specially created a man in order to put a stop to the hostile observances of the Jains and Buddhists' (Thurston, *op. cit.* iv. 239).

There is, further, a tradition that an incarnation of the bull—always associated with Śiva as a form of his energy—was sent to earth in order to restore the worship of Śiva, and that this incarnation appeared as a Kanarese Brāhman, born near Bijapur and called *Basava* (Kanarese for 'bull') (Fleet, *IA* v. [1876] 239). Basava in due course had the usurping Jain, Bijjala, assassinated, after which Chenna Basava, the nephew of Basava, established the Śaiva religion in the Kanarese country. The Śaivas there are known as *Vīra Śaiva*, 'champions of Śiva,' or *Śaiva Bhaktas*, forming the sect of Liṅgāyats, who wear the *liṅgam* and worship Nandi, the bull of Śiva.

4. Vaiṣṇavism and Hindu reformers.—The worship of Viṣṇu, as opposed to that of Śiva, was taught by Rāmānujāchārya, a Brāhman born in the 12th cent. [Barnett, *Bhagavadgītā*, 1905, p. 55, says A.D. 1017], near Madras. Faith in, and worship of, a Supreme Being, Viṣṇu or Vāsudeva, as Cause and Creator of the world as a real objective existing cosmos, were inculcated, with the belief in soul as different from the Universal Soul. The doctrine taught respecting the Deity is that known as *viśiṣṭādvaita*, or qualified non-duality, in opposition to the earlier *advaita* doctrine of Śaṅkara. The Supreme Deity, according to this doctrine, is both the cause of the material world and the substance out of which it was created. Faith in this Deity became the centre of a revived Bhāgavatism. The persecution of Rāmānuja by the Chola monarch, Kulottuṅga or Rājendra Chola II. (A.D. 1070 to 1118), led eventually to the spread of these new Bhāgavat doctrines all over India. This was not finally accomplished until the 14th cent., when a new southern teacher, Rāmānanda, brought up at St. Thomé, near Madras, became a convert to Bhāgavatism in a worship of Rāma Chandra, an incarnation of Viṣṇu, which he preached as a faith for the mass of the people. The contact of Aryan learning and Dravidian religious feeling thus led to a revival of Hinduism all over India, for from Rāmānuja in the 12th century

'were spiritually descended Rāmānanda in the 14th, and Vidyāpati and Chaitanya in the 15th—the three apostles of Vaishnavism in Hindustan, Behar, and Bengal' (Hoernle, *Hist. of India*, 92).

The chief followers of Rāmānuja, known as *Śrī Vaiṣṇavas*, are divided into two schools or sects—those of the North and those of the South, or *Vaḍa galai*, and *Ten galai*. Both schools hold to the Vedas and Vedāntas, the Northern school being more orthodox in holding them as authoritative revelations. The Northern school, further, recognizes a male and a female energy in the Deity, and 'strongly insists on the concomitancy of the human will for securing salvation, whereas the South School maintains the irresistibility of Divine grace in human salvation' (Kennet, *IA* iii. [1874]).

The two schools are thus—like the Śaiva Āgamic schools—divided on the subject of cat-like and monkey-like faith. The Southern school, in place of the Vedas, use their own canonical books of scripture, consisting of 4000 verses in Tamil, known as the *Nālayira Prabandham.* These verses are ascribed to saints called *ālvārs,* held to have been incarnations of the Deity. These *ālvārs* are described as 'those drowned in or maddened with God love' (A. Govindāchārya, *Lives of the Āṛvārs,* Mysore, 1902). The modern Bhāgavata doctrine of faith of the South school of the Śrī Vaiṣṇavas has been raised to sublime heights in the *Artha Pañchaka* of Pillai Lokāchārya (A.D. 1213), until this faith

'in its outward progress becomes more and more intense and rapturous. Instead of compelling it becomes inviting, instead of repelling it becomes bewitching. Effort is merged in craving. Self-assertion gives place to self-abandon. The heart has become poured into the intellect, or rather, the intellect has become fused with the heart' (tr. A. Govindāchārya, *JRAS,* July 1910).

The last great Southern apostle of Vaiṣṇavism was Madhvāchārya, born 1331 as a Śaiva follower of Śaṅkara, who became a fierce opponent of the Śaivas and of the *advaita* philosophy. He preached, in opposition, pure duality, or *dvaita,* holding that the Supreme Being and the soul are different from matter, *māyā,* which he held to be real and eternal. The Supreme Soul of Being was by him held to be Viṣṇu or Nārayaṇa, incarnated as Kṛṣṇa, and salvation was held to be gained by *bhakti,* or love for Vāyu the son of Viṣṇu.

In the South Kanarese country most of the Tulu-speaking Brāhmans are followers of Madhva, and, as might be expected, most of the Dravidian Hindu classes are Śaivas. At present a wide-spread revival of interest in Śaivism is taking place in South India, which demands the close attention of all those interested in the future religious life of India, which seems destined to be influenced by the principle underlying the formulated doctrines of the Śaivas. At a recent Śaiva conference, held in 1909, at Trichinopoly, attended by Śaivas from most of the Southern districts and even from Ceylon and Jaffna, it is reported that the proceedings were opened by the recitation of some verses of the *Dēvāram* and *T.V.*, 'which the Saivites like to call their Psalms.' The report further states that 'the Saiva *Siddhānta* has been from the beginning chiefly the philosophy of the Śūdras.' The spirit of the present revival may be seen from the comments made on the report by the learned editor of the *S.D.*, V. V. Ramaṇan—first, to the effect that there were as many Brāhmans present 'as could possibly be expected in such strictly religious functions'; and, second, that 'the greatest Apostles of God whose teachings constitute the *Śaivādvaita Siddhānta* were for the most part Brāhmans, and they threw open the flood-gates of true spiritual life for all children of God.' A further significant fact in connexion with this revival of interest in the history of the Śaiva religion is the increasing use made by Śaiva writers of Scriptural phrases and analogies. A knowledge of the formulated doctrines of the Śaiva *Siddhānta* will, therefore, become an increasing necessity for all those anxious to understand, or who are brought into contact with, the religious life of South India, which seems to tend towards a change in the direction of greater tolerance for surrounding religious beliefs, and in the direction of purifying Śaivism from the degrading elements contained in the grosser forms of Śakti-worship.

5. Formulated doctrines of the Śaivas.—The scholastic theological doctrines of the Śaivas were in mediæval times set forth in metrical stanzas, with necessary commentaries for their proper interpretation, by a series of poet-philosophers held to have been spiritually descended from the first of these poets who received the earliest form in which they exist in South India, as a revelation from the Deity. This first form is known as the *Śiva Jñāna Bodham,*[1] or 'Enlightenment in Śiva-knowledge.' It was composed—or arranged—by Mey-kaṇḍar Devar, the Divine Seer of the Truth, in or about A.D. 1223. Mey-kaṇḍar was followed by Maṛai Jñāna Sambandhar, who wrote the *Śaiva samayā-neri,* and whose disciple, the famed Kotta-vaṅguḍi Umāpati Śivāchāryar, composed, in or about A.D. 1313, the *Śiva-prakāśam,*[2] or 'Light of Śiva,' the *Tiru Aruṭ Payan,*[3] or 'Fruit of Divine Grace,' and the *Saṅkarpa Nirākaraṇam.* The *S.J.B.* of Mey-kaṇḍar is held to be the most authoritative of all these works, as being a direct revelation from Śiva,

'for the purpose of pointing out the way to proceed from the knowledge of the body full of sorrow to the knowledge of the soul and thence to the knowledge of the Supreme Spirit' (tr. Nallaswami Pillai, Madras, 1895).

It is a free translation into Tamil—in Āśiriyam metre with a commentary in Veṃbā metre—of twelve Sanskrit stanzas said to have formed part of *Raurava Āgama,* of which *Āgamas,* or early works in Sanskrit inculcating the mystic worship of Śiva and Śakti, there are said to be 28, now gradually coming to light, of which two have been translated.[4] The Tamil stanzas of Mey-kaṇḍar are of such

'extreme terseness of diction and brevity of expression that even the ordinary Pundits are not able to understand them without proper commentaries, and very few Pundits can be found in Southern India who are able to expound the text properly even now' (Nallaswami Pillai, *op. cit.* p. viii).

Barnett has recently contended (*JRAS,* July 1910)—and his view has been accepted in Śaiva centres in Madras—that the formulated doctrines of the Śaivas, as they first appear in the *S.J.B.*, reached the Southern Dravidians from the north. His contention is therefore that the

'living faith of the majority of living Tamils is almost in every respect, and certainly in all essentials, the same doctrine that was taught in Kashmir about the beginning of the 11th cent. by Abhinava Gupta.'

Both of the schools he traces to the *Śvetāśvatara Upaniṣad,* and points out that

'the elements of the Tamil Śaiva *Siddhānta,* the Sanskrit *Āgamas,* and the Śaiva theology of Kashmir are all contained in the *Śvetāśvatara Upaniṣad,* which was canonical long before the days of Śaṅkara' (*S.D.*, June 1910).

These ideas of the *Śvetāśvatara Upaniṣad* were in Kashmir formulated into the Spanda and Pratyabhijnā schools, and, according to Barnett,

'meanwhile filtered down through various channels into the lands of the Dravidians, for whose ancient cults it supplied a theological basis.'

Whatever may be the final conclusion on this point, as to whether the formulated doctrines of the Śaivas descended from north to south or ascended from south to north—for the *Śvetāśvatara Upaniṣad* and the various current schools of Indian philosophy, such as the Sāṅkhya, Yoga, and Vedānta, were in the 5th cent. equally well known in the south and in the north, and Sanskrit was used for literary purposes in the south as well as in the north—all the technical terms of the system and its essential features are contained in Śaiva devotional literature of South India from the 7th and 8th centuries. These technical terms and essential features are—as set forth, towards the end of the 8th or beginning of the 9th cent., in Śaṅkara's Commentary on the Brahma Sūtras (ii. 2. 37)—that

[1] Hereafter cited as *S.J.B.*
[2] Hereafter cited as *S.P.*
[3] Hereafter cited as *T.A.P.*
[4] A full account of the *Āgamas* is given by V. V. Ramaṇan in his tr. of Appaya's Commentary on Vedānta-sūtras (Madras; now being printed in parts).

'the Lord (Pati) was the operative cause of the world, and that the bonds (*pāśam*) of the soul (*paśu*, or animal) were broken by the teachings of the Lord.'

The formulated doctrines, as they first appear in the *S.J.B.*, merely give the scholastic explanation of these terms, and teach the means whereby the middle term (in *pati pāśam paśu*), the 'bond,' or *pāśam*, may be sublimated, and how the soul, or *paśu*, free from the fetter, may then unite with its Master, the Lord.

These formulated doctrines, so far as it has been found possible to extract a consistent account from conflicting interpretations, are as follows:—

i. ŚIVA, THE EFFICIENT CAUSE OF CREATION.—A First Cause is postulated from a principle of effect and cause. According to the *S.J.B.*, because the Universe is seen differentiated into forms known as 'he, she, and it,' and undergoes changes of devolution, continuation, and involution, it requires a First Cause; just as, when one sees a pot, a cause—the potter—is required. This First Cause is not, however, reduced to the *advaita*, or non-duality of Śaṅkara—One only without a Second—where the cosmos is a delusion conjured up as a dream by an unreal *māyā*. The Śaiva system is, nevertheless, held to be *advaita*, and to be founded on strict non-duality. Śiva is, accordingly, the Sole Cause, without any other co-operating deity such as Brahmā or Viṣṇu, the Brāhmanic Creator and Preserver, for 'we cannot find out cause for ultimate cause' (*Śiva Jñāna Ratnāvali*[1] [a modern catechism]). Śiva stands supreme; all the deities of later Brāhmanism are merely of the nature of highest souls, dependent on Śiva to carry out his disposition or energy. He alone is the source from which the cosmos is energized throughout its course of creation, preservation, and involution. He is never the object of thought, he remains eternally pure Subject. He is neither spiritual form, nor is he formless (*S.P.* xiv.).

Almost the first—the ever repeated—verse of the *Kural* declares: 'He has neither likes nor dislikes (desires nor non-desires).' To the question, Has God form or no form, or is He both form and formless? we find the answer, 'He has all the above three and none of these' (*S.J.R.*). It is also declared that 'He is form and not form, but to those who know Him he has the form of knowledge' (*T.A.P.* I. iv.). He is also said to be 'incomprehensible by His greatness, by His minuteness, by His great grace, and in the benefits He confers' (*S.J.B.* i. 3). Being neither spirit nor form, but 'being Absolute Being (or *sad*) or pure Subject, he can never be the object of cognition' (Hoisington, *S.P.* xiii.). The full definition of Śiva, considered to be the true and only full One, is: 'That which is perceived by the senses is *a-sat* (not-Being or Changeable). That which is not so perceived does not exist. God is neither the one nor the other, and hence called *Śiva Sat* (pure Being) by the wise, *chit* (pure Intelligence) or *Śiva*, when not understood by the human intelligence, and *Sat* (Being) when perceived by divine intelligence' (*S.J.B.* vi.). He is, as transcendent Being, in inseparable connexion with dispositions or higher energies, the *parā śaktis*, of Being, Intelligence, and Bliss, or *Sat, chit, ānanda*.

Notwithstanding these fundamental doctrines of the *advaita* nature of Śiva as Final Cause and Abstract Subject of Thought, he is, in one form or another, represented in the many Śaiva temples. It is contended, by the modern Śaiva reformer, who sees that 'the worst feature of modern Hinduism is its idolatry' (Nallaswami, *op. cit.*, Preface), that all these forms in temples are merely symbolical of some idea or thought respecting a Deity who eternally remains formless. In popular imagination these temple-forms are viewed as the very abode of a deity, to whom food and offerings are presented for material enjoyment. The two idols to which popular Śaivism pays peculiar adoration are,

'first, the *liṅgam* and *liṅgi*; and, secondly, the image of Śiva accompanied with Umā, whose form is generally combined into one with his. These really represent one idea, Śiva and Śakti, the god and the energy which is inseparable from him, which combine to create, sustain, and destroy the Universe' (Pope, *T.V.* p. xxxv).

[1] Hereafter cited as *S.J.R.*

The worship of the *liṅgam* and *liṅgi* is explained by intellectual Śaivas to be the worship not of phallic emblems, but of the representatives of the pillar or temple of the Deity, and various other ideas told of in the Purāṇas, such as the pillar of fire in which the energy of Śiva appeared before Brahmā and Viṣṇu, to show his supremacy, so that thenceforth

'the worship of the *liṅgam* has been inaugurated in the world. The pedestal (*liṅgi*) is Mahādevi, and the *liṅgam* itself is the visible Maheśvara' (Pope, *T.V.* 152).

(*a*) *The necessity for creation.*—There exists, it is held, an eternal necessity that a cosmos must be created, because souls, which never vary in number and are eternal, require a cosmos wherein to work out the result of *karma*, or deeds, which is also eternal.

The *S.P.*, therefore, says that

'Creation is an act of grace; in the world alone souls are able to eat their *karma* and to rid themselves of impurity and attain *mukti*, union with God' (Goodwill, *S.D.*, March 1903, p. 148).

The underlying principle of this doctrine is that deeds, or *karma*, must be *ripened* before they can be eaten or consumed; and, as a place for this process of ripening is necessary, a cosmos must of necessity be evolved, and this evolution can take place only through the grace, or love, of Śiva. It is not until deeds of the past births, deeds of the present birth, and deeds of the enlightened done between enlightenment and final release are 'balanced' that final union of the soul with Śiva ensues. The *T.A.P.* (vi. 1) clearly states that it is not possible for release to take place until 'the unequal good and evil become balanced.' All deed being an evil, as merely leading to re-births, it becomes necessary that Śiva, through his grace, should evolve a Universe, at the end of each æon, for the benefit of the flock of souls who have not attained the balancing of their deeds and release in previous existences of the phenomenal Universe. At the commencement of each æon

'the unconscious souls shrouded in that primeval darkness are responsible—in some inexplicable fashion—for the old, eternal deeds, the fruit of which must be consumed by each at the time of its maturity' (Pope, *Nālaḍiyār*, p. 67).

The *S.P.*, which of all the texts gives the clearest exposition of this Dravidian method of dealing with the soul's state of 'original sin,' does so by merely saying that it is the soul's natural state; that there is no assignable cause for it; that, while the Deity is pure, the soul is impure in the natural state, just as the coat of rust is natural to copper (Hoisington, p. 149).

(*b*) *Method and source of creation.*—Absolute Being having been accepted by the Dravidians as the highest philosophic truth that could be extracted from surrounding current Yoga, Sāṅkhya, and Vedānta philosophies, it became a necessity to bring this philosophic conception into conformity with the religious wants of the people. The ordinary intelligence of the Dravidian folk—whom it was necessary to enfold in Hinduism—demanded a beneficent Deity, all-powerful and all-gracious, willing and able to save the soul from the haunting terrors of transmigrations in higher and lower forms, the awards of deed, and a real Universe. Realism—the banner of the revolt under which the Dravidian intellect fought against Aryan non-duality—finally conquered, and, as a result, the so-called *advaita*, or non-duality, of the philosophic conception of Śiva had to become graduated down till it became what is virtually a form of *dvaita*, or duality.

The stages of reasoning by which this transition is graduated could hardly ever have appealed to popular imagination, or even to common intelligence. Śaiva philosophy, loth to hold the cosmos as unreal, as the dream product of unreal *māyā*, and still keen to call its system *advaita*, or non-duality, had, nevertheless, to frame a theory to explain Effect from Śiva, Ultimate Cause. To postulate matter (see SĀṄKHYA) would have at once reduced the system to pure duality, inconsistent with the conception of Śiva; accordingly there was postulated merely the existence of an underlying basis of creation, an essence, a form of matter, elemental matter which was called pure (*śuddha*) *māyā*. This pure *māyā*, or elemental abstract matter, is held to co-exist with Śiva eternally, producing differentiated spheres of action for souls. Pure *māyā* has, however, no connexion with souls, which are associated with an impure form of elemental matter (akin to the Sāṅkhya *prakṛti*) known as impure (*aśuddha*) *māyā*. In this impure *māyā* inhere the *malas*, or impurities of souls—those of *karma*, or deed, and *āṇavam*, ignorance, the state or condition of the soul (*aṇu*) (*Tattva Kaṭṭalei*, p. 14).

Śiva, co-existing with pure *māyā* as an efficient cause of creation, is pure thought (*chit*), pure bliss (*ānanda*), as dispositions or energies, as well as having the dispositions or energies of desire or will (*icchā*), action (*kriyā*), and knowledge (*jñāna*). These are the highest of Śiva's energies, his *parā śaktis*, essentially connected with him, but over which he stands aloof and supreme. From the first two of these *parā śaktis*, thought and bliss, are successively developed the *parā śaktis* of desire, action, and wisdom.

All existence, from Absolute Being to earth, is differentiated as possessing essential natures, categories, or properties called *tattvas*. Of these *tattvas* there are 36 primary, which produce a cosmos of 60 subordinate *tattvas*. The 36 primary *tattvas* contain 5 pure *tattvas*, which spring into being by the grace of Śiva's *parā śaktis*. Of the 5 pure *tattvas* the 1st is Nādam, the male energy of Deity, developed from pure *māyā*; the 2nd is Vindu, the female energy of Deity, developed from Nādam; the 3rd, developed from Vindu, is Sadā Śiva, or the state of Śiva before assuming forms for the enlightenment of souls; the 4th is Īśvara, developed from Sadā Śiva, which is the obscuring element; and the 5th, developed from Īśvara, is pure knowledge, the pure element which enlightens souls (Hoisington, 'Tattva Kaṭṭalei,' *JAOS*, 1854). The Sadā Śiva *tattva* is that in which the two energies of action and knowledge are equal, the Īśvara *tattva* is that in which action predominates over knowledge, and the pure knowledge *tattva* is that in which the energy of knowledge predominates over that of action.

It follows from this that Śiva may be taken as the efficient cause of creation, the *parā śaktis* being the instrumental cause, and *māyā* the material cause.

The process is explained, perhaps more clearly than elsewhere, in *S.P.* (xxii.). Here it is stated that the Nādam, or Śivam, or male energy, the first of the Śiva *tattvas*, is developed from *kuḍilei*, or germ, or pure *māyā*, by the operation of Śiva's *parā śakti*, knowledge; and that, by the co-operation of the *parā śakti* of action, Vindu, or separately organized female energy, is developed from Nādam; thence Sadā Śiva, Īśvara, and pure knowledge.

These 5 pure *tattvas* pertain only to the highest order of souls, the *vijñāna kalars*, who have only the single *mala* of *āṇavam*; for souls associated with the impure form of elemental matter—impure *māyā*—there is a five-fold investment, or *pañcha kañchuka*, developed, by the grace of Sadā Śiva, of 5 impure *tattvas*: Kālam (time), Niyati (necessity), Kalā (determination), and—developed from Kalā—Vidyā (finite knowledge), and Rāgam or Icchā (desire). In addition to the above five-fold investment, there is developed—by the grace of pure knowledge—first, *mūla prakṛiti*,[1] the source (material) of all the subsequent developments: (1) *chittam* (the will), (2) *buddhi* (the judgment), (3) *ahaṁkāram* (the individuality or the I-maker), and (4) *manas* (mind or understanding); thence—very much after the manner of all Sāṅkhyan and other Indian metaphysics—the 20 primary elemental natures, *tattvas*, or categories, earth, water, fire, and ether; ears, skin, eyes, tongue, nose; *tanmātras*, or the rudimentary elements of sound, touch, form, smell; and organs of actions, hands, feet, mouth, excretion, and generation. From these primary *tattvas* are developed, in the usual manner of Indian philosophy, the subordinate 60 *tattvas*, or visible physical external organs (Hoisington, *loc. cit.*).

ii. THE SOUL.—The soul is held to be enclosed from eternity in a fine or subtle body, or *sūkṣma śarīra*. This is an inherent covering which persists with the soul through all its transmigrations. It passes with the soul to the various heavens or hells, where rewards or penalties for good and evil deeds are experienced, and it also envelops it during re-birth. The soul is called *aṇu*—a word derived from *aṇu*, 'atom,' because it is exceedingly small; and it is so called because, when associated with ignorance or *āṇavam*, the state of the atom is very small, although it is a Vindu (cosmic germ) in its natural state (Nallaswami, *S.J.B.* p. 4). It is also said that the soul (Skr. *ātmā*) is called *aṇu* ('atom'),

'because the all-pervading nature of the soul (*ātma*) has become limited to an atom by its bondage' (*S.J.R.*).

The soul—from eternity being associated with the impurities, or *malas*, of *āṇavam*, *māyā*, and *karma*—has first to arouse the grace (*arul*) of the Deity to appear as an obscuring energy or *tirodha śakti*, before the soul, freed from its *malas*, can gain knowledge and 'see the truth of its oneness with Śiva' (*S.J.B.* vi.).

The soul is defined in the *S.J.B.* (i.) as '*māyāvi yantra tanuvinul ānmā* (*ātmā*),' or as existing within the body as a *māyā*-made instrument. All souls are divided into (1) *vijñānakalars*, (2) *pralayākalars*, and (3) *sakalars*. The first, or highest, order of souls—the *vijñānakalars*—are freed from *māyā* and *karma* (matter and deeds), and have only one *mala*, or impurity, of *āṇavam*, or nature of the soul. These souls have reached the sphere of the 5 pure *tattvas*, and, being freed from future births and re-births, merely await final union with Śiva. The second class of souls—the *pralayākalars*—are under the influence of the two *malas* of *āṇavam* and *karma*, which condition them to renewed births and re-births. The third class—the *sakalars*—which includes all human beings and the ordinary gods or devas, have the three *malas* of *āṇavam*, *karma*, and *māyā*, and are subject to sense perception, having corporeal existences, wherein *karma* has to be balanced. The soul which has corporeal existences is described as proceeding at death from its physical body, or *sthūla śarīra*, to

'undergo its experiences in heaven or hell, and forgetting such experiences, just as a dreamer forgets his experiences of the waking state, passes as an atom in its Sūkshma Śarīra state into a suitable womb at conception, impelled thereto by the desire created by its previous karma' (Nallaswami Pillai, *S.J.B.* p. 13).

iii. THE BOND AND THE RELEASE OF THE SOUL.—The *pāśam*, the bond, which fetters the soul's intelligence is a rope of three strands made up of *āṇavam*, two-fold deeds, and *māyā*. *Āṇavam*, or state or character of the soul (*aṇu*, 'atom'), is the first strand of the rope which fetters the soul, and it persists beyond the other two strands. This *āṇavam* is an essentially inherent *mala*, or defilement, which darkens the soul's light or

[1] 'The Sāṅkhyas maintain that Prakṛiti is eternal. But that is not correct; for, as it is multifariously varied among all classes of souls, it is not eternal (is perishable) like an earthen vessel. Hence its source or cause is Māyā' (*S.J.B.* xli. [Hoisington]). This is opposed to the Sāṅkhya theory that *mūla prakṛiti*, primordial matter, can self-develop the cosmos.

intelligence, so that it cannot understand its true nature (*S.J.B.* iv.), its oneness with Śiva.

This ignorance or darkness of the soul must receive enlightenment, two-fold deeds must be balanced, and *māyā* sublimated, before the soul gains its final release (*mukti*, Skr.; *mutti* or *vīḍu*, Tamil). The soul was, by the grace of Śiva, sent into sense-perception with a cosmos,

'in order that, the effect of deeds (*a parte ante*) being removed or cancelled, the soul might at length be enlightened by special grace and so become gradually disentangled and purified; the consummation of which is *mutti*, or final emancipation and mystic ineffable eternal union with Śiva' (Pope, *T.V.* p. xlvi).

The Final Cause, Śiva, being pure Subject of thought, could never be an object of knowledge to the soul. Soul being associated with sense-perception cannot 'rise above itself in intelligence.'

The soul can daily become more contemplative; more conscious that there must be some final solution of its unrest; more spiritual (1) by performing all the usual devotional altruistic practices (*charyā*), (2) by practice of religious ritual and worship of the Deity and Divine teachers as symbolized in the temples (*kriyā*), and (3) by practices (*yoga*) of a physical nature to aid in the contemplation of the Deity (see YOGA). All these three—*charyā*, *kriyā*, *yoga*—can only add to *karma* further transmigrations. They, however, so spiritualize the soul that it becomes fit for final leading to enlightenment.

The *S.P.* (sūtra lxxvi.) sums up the final doctrine of release by declaring that the triple bond of *āṇavam*, *karma*, and *māyā* can be destroyed only by the grace of Śiva, which is the same as the *parā śakti* of pure knowledge; this alone will 'cause the soul to unite with the Divine feet of Śiva.' The *S.J.B.* (sūtra viii.) shows how the grace (or *arul*) of Śiva supplies a Divine teacher, or *guru*, to enlighten the soul:

'The Lord, appearing as *guru* to the soul, which has advanced in *charyā*, *kriyā*, and *yoga*, instructs him that he is wasting himself by living among the savage five senses; and the soul, understanding its real nature, leaves its former associates, and, not being different from Him, becomes united to His feet.'

The Śiva system thus ascribes the self-illumination of the soul, as pure subject of thought identical with the supreme subject of thought, to the grace, or highest disposition or energy, of the Deity energizing the soul to this self-illumination by means of a Divine teacher. This knowledge is said to spring up spontaneously to *vijñānakalars*, or highest order of souls; to the *pralayākalars* it comes through a *guru*, or teacher in Divine form; and for the *sakalars* the Deity conceals Himself as a *guru*, or teacher, in human form, and imparts knowledge. The soul, while awaiting final release, must (1) listen with desire to the *guru's* teaching, and must practise (2) meditation, (3) understanding, and (4) abstraction from all objects of sense (*S.P.* xxxiii.). These and the constant inaudible repetition of the five mystic syllables *śi-vā-ya-na-ma* ('salutation to Śiva') will have the result that

'the *tirōdhā*, "energy" (Skr. *tirōdhā*='conceal'), in them will herself remove the *malas* and cause *arul* to appear' (*S.P.* xciii.).

There are ten imperfect forms of emancipation, including that of the gaining of supernatural powers—so commonly professed in India—as the result of acquiring the nature and powers of the Divinity. This power over supernatural powers has been described as the teaching of some Śaivas who profess that

'the soul acquires mystic miraculous powers; that, in fact, the emancipated one is so made partaker of the Divine nature and attributes that he is able to gain possession of and exercise miraculous powers, which are called the eight "*siddhis.*" Persons professing to wield such magical powers are not infrequently found in India, and there is in them a bewildering mixture of enthusiasm and fraud' (Pope, *T.V.* p. xliii).

In the recognized form of emancipation, or union with the Deity, an essential feature of the Śaiva religion is that there is

'no annihilation of the soul, but its individuality or egoism is lost,—its karma having been eaten. Its identity is lost but not itself' (Nallaswami, *S.J.B.* p. 59).

The soul has, as the result of release, this conscious immortality in a separate existence; for, although 'sharing the blessedness and wisdom of the supreme, it is unmingled with His essence' (Pope, *T.V.* p. lxv).

S.P. (lxxxi.) says that the soul, when freed,

'is closely united with the higher knowledge, the *parā śakti*, by whom it is illuminated, and in whom it has a firm footing—and the soul becomes so intimately united with Śiva that they constitute *advaita*, non-duality, and thus it rests in him as the air rests in space, and as salt dissolved in water.'

T.A.P. says (viii. 75) distinctly that, if the soul and Śiva become one, there is nothing; if there is duality, no release, or *mukti*, could arise; therefore, in the mystic union of the soul and Śiva there is neither duality nor non-duality. The union is to be held similar to that seen when the words *tāl*, 'foot' (soul), and *talai*, 'head' (Śiva), are joined; according to the rules of Tamil phonetics, the combined word becomes *tāḍalai*, the *l* and *t* becoming united into *ḍ*; 'so consider the union of soul and Śiva' (viii. 77).

Before the soul passes to its eternal rest in Śiva, it is a *jīvan muttar*, 'freed from life,' but living 'in the body still for a little while, but is one in feeling, soul, and power, and faculty, with the Infinite Eternal. He has put off his rich garments and adornments, is besmeared with white ashes, and wears the peculiar habiliment of the ascetic. From his head depends the braided lock of the Śaiva ascetic; one hand grasps the staff, and the other the mendicant's bowl; he has for ever renounced the world—all the worlds—save Śiva's self' (Pope from *Vāthavūrar Purāṇam* [*T.V.* p. xiii]).

LITERATURE.—L. D. Barnett, *Catalogue of Tamil Books in the Brit. Mus.*, London, 1909, artt. in *JRAS* and *Siddhānta Dīpika*; *Linguistic Survey of India*, vol. iv. 'Muṇḍa and Dravidian Languages'; J. M. Nallāswāmi Pillai, *Śaiva Religion*, Madras, 1909; tr. of *Śiva Jñāna Bodham*, Madras, 1895, *Light of Grace* (*Tiru Aruṭ Payan*), pamphlet, Madras, 1896 (for critical purposes the original must be referred to); G. V. Pope, trr. (London), with valuable notes, of *Kural*, 1886, *Nālaḍiyar*, 1893, *Tiru Vāchakam*, 1900 (original Tamil should always be referred to); V. V. Ramaṇan, Notes and trr. in *Siddhānta Dīpika*, tr. of *Vēdānta-Sūtra-Śaiva-Bhāṣya*, with notes and commentaries, Madras (now being issued in parts); M. Sēshagiri Sāstri, *Essay in Tamil Literature*, Madras, 1897; *Siddhānta Dīpika*, monthly journal, Madras (early parts difficult to obtain: British Museum has copies); Sundaram Pillai, *Some Milestones in Tamil Literature*, Madras, 1895, reprinted with postscript in *Tamil Antiquary*, 1909 (with valuable preface by V. Venkayya); *Tamil Antiquary*; publications of Tamil Archæological Society (established 1903), Madras; E. Thurston, assisted by K. Rangachari, *Castes and Tribes of Southern India*, 7 vols., Madras, 1909; J. Vinson, *Légendes bouddhistes et djainas*, Paris, 1900 (containing summaries of three Tamil classics—*Chintāmaṇi*, *Śillapp'adhikāram*, and *Maṇimekhalai*).

R. W. FRAZER.

DREAMS AND SLEEP.

DREAMS AND SLEEP.—I. General.—From the point of view of psycho-physiology, dreaming is only a part of the more general phenomenon of sleep, and cannot be fully treated except in connexion with the wider topic. The physiology of sleep and dreams is still very little understood, as will be seen by comparing the earliest scientific treatment of the subject, that of Aristotle, with the latest hypotheses of modern physiological psychology.

According to Aristotle (*de Somno*, *de Somniis*, and *de Divinatione per Somnum*), sleep is a periodical phenomenon found in all animals, and in animals only. It is thus an affection of that phase of mental life which is common and peculiar to animals, the faculty of presentation (τὸ φανταστικόν). Its *raison d'être* is the need for periodical recovery of the organs of presentation from the fatigue attendant on long-continued exercise. Since this state of fatigue attacks the whole presentative machinery simultaneously, the conditions characteristic of sleep must be sought principally, not in any of the special sense-organs, but in the κοινὸν αἰσθητήριον, or central seat of presentation, the heart. More precisely the recurrence of sleep is due to changes in the blood consequent on the taking of food. Food, when taken into the blood, evolves heat and evaporation; the evaporation is suddenly cooled on reaching the brain, and a movement of antiperistasis is set up, in which most of the vaporized matter is repelled again downwards. It is to this that the muscular relaxation and sensory inactivity of sleep are due. Aristotle thus anticipates both the views that the immediate cause of sleep is a changed condition of the 'highest centres,' and that the change is due to the temporary presence of toxic substances in the blood. Dreams are affections of the central organ of consciousness (κοινὸν αἰσθητήριον), which must be carefully distinguished from actual sense-percepts. In perception the affection is originated by a real physical stimulus; in sleep such actual perceptions occur sporadically, but they are not the main stuff which dreams are made of. The direct cause of the dream is the persistence in the 'common' or central sensorium of faint relics of the motions formerly aroused by actual stimulation. These residual motions are equally present in waking life, but are not attended to because they are obscured by the more violent motions due to actual present stimulus. In sleep, where actual stimulation is excluded, the more minute affections of the system due to these minimal disturbances become apparent. Hence we are enabled to give a rationalistic explanation of genuine prophetic or 'veridical' dreams, when they are not due, as most of them are, to mere coincidence. Veridical dreams of impending illness, or recovery, or death are 'indications' of the coming event, due to the dreamer's sensibility to minute organic disturbances which are imperceptible in waking life. In other cases a dream may actually be the cause of its own fulfilment, by providing the first suggestion of an action which is afterwards dwelt on and carried out in the waking state. Veridical dreams about the condition of our intimate friends are accounted for on the ground of our special preoccupation with their concerns, which renders the sleeping soul exceptionally sensitive to those minimal disturbances in its surroundings which originate in the friend's organism. It is never permissible to ascribe such dreams to the direct agency of God; if they came from God, they should be specially vouchsafed to the wisest and best men (which is not the case), and their occurrence should exhibit marks of intelligent design instead of being, as it is, sporadic and casual.

The best modern accounts of the subject as a part of general psychology are perhaps those of Volkmann von Volkmar (especially good on the descriptive side) and Wundt (see Lit. below). The following summary is taken from Wundt.

The causes of sleep, as of other periodical functions of the organism, must be looked for in the central nervous system. It is probably a condition due to the temporary exhaustion of the available energies of the nervous system, and has for its purpose the accumulation of fresh 'tensional forces,' which is favoured by muscular inactivity and diminished production of heat. A second condition is the complete or partial abolition of attention. (Animals regularly fall asleep if deprived of their usual sensory stimuli, and so do men of low mental capacity.) It is probable that this nervous exhaustion is merely a general condition favourable to sleep, its direct exciting cause being a specific alteration of condition in the central nervous system which is normally accompanied with the relaxation of attention. It is most likely that narcotics produce their effect by inducing this central change. Hence Purkinje and others have held that the direct cause of sleep is to be found in the partial using up of the oxygen of the nervous system effected by the accumulation of carbonic acid, the final product of respiration. In what region of the brain the assumed 'sleep-centre' lies is not known. The physiological changes induced are in general of the nature of inhibitions, *e.g.* diminution of the activity of heart and respiratory apparatus, probably due to contraction of the smallest cerebral blood-vessels. The period of deepest sleep appears to begin about three-quarters of an hour after its commencement, and to last about half an hour. Then follows a period of lighter slumber of several hours' duration, which forms a preparation for waking. The period of deepest sleep is probably, as a rule, one of complete, or all but complete, unconsciousness. Dreaming, on this view, is an accompaniment of the gradual transition from sleep to waking. Similarly, Volkmann divides the processes into five stages: (1) drowsiness; (2) falling asleep; (3) complete sleep; (4) lighter sleep, attended by dreams; (5) waking. The dream has two chief characteristics: (*a*) the memory images of which it is largely composed are hallucinatory, *i.e.* they are mistaken for real and present physical things; (*b*) the process of apperception is altered, so that the actual percepts which enter into the dream are interpreted in an illusory fashion.

Dream-appearances, which Volkmann classes as hallucinations, are more accurately regarded by Wundt as generally, if not always, based on illusion; *i.e.* they are misinterpretations of actual minimal sense-impressions, such as those due to slight noises, to the position of the sleeper's limbs, to trifling pains, slight difficulties in breathing, palpitations, and the like. A slight intercostal pain is mistaken for the stab of an enemy's dagger, a movement of the foot for a fall from a tower, the rhythm of our own breathing for the rhythmical motions of flying, etc. The visual dream is based on erroneous interpretation of internal retinal stimulations, which appear to the dreamer as flights of birds, butterflies, fishes, etc. (The present writer does not believe that he ever has dreams of this kind, which Wundt regards as remarkably common.) Dreams of water are explained by Wundt as due to *Urindrang* in the sleeper's body. Hence again the exceptional frequency of dreams of fishes. (The present writer, in general a constant and vivid dreamer, never dreams of fishes at all, nor do several persons of whom he has made inquiries.) The common dream in which we hunt for an object that can never be found, or start on a journey and have repeatedly to return for something that has been forgotten, is explained as due to disturbances of the *Gemeingefühl*, the general mass of organic sensations. The successive illusions of the dream are woven into a continuous story by association with memory-images. Wundt attaches special importance to memories from the immediate past, particularly those connected with deep emotional excitement. Thus he accounts for our dreams of the recently dead by the emotion with which we watched their last moments and attended their burial. (This explanation is clearly insufficient. We dream regularly of those for whom we have cared the most, though their death may not have been recent, and may have taken place at the other end of the world. Wundt also omits to take account of the common tendency to dream of events from our early childhood, even when they are of a trivial kind and not likely ever to have been attended with any special degree of emotional excitement.)

In general this account would seem to lay too much stress on the element of illusion and too little on that of hallucination. It is probably true that actual minimal sensations form *points de repère* in all our dreams, but there is no reason to confine the element of genuine hallucination to the one function of establishing links of connexion. Nor is association by itself a sufficient principle to explain the way in which the dreamer interprets his minimal percepts. The individual's habits of diet, no doubt, largely determine the type of his dreams. A man who eats a heavy meal just before going to bed is likely to dream very differently from one whose meals are light and who eats and drinks nothing for several hours before going to sleep. But, in the main, the cue for our interpretation of our dream-sensations is given by our emotional interests: we dream most about the things and persons wherein we are interested. Hence dreams often exhibit a more rigidly logical sequence of events than the facts of waking life. Since the ordinary avenues of intercourse with the extra-subjective world are all but cut off in sleep, the dream can follow its course without interruption, whereas in waking life we have constantly to suspend the working-out of a course of thought or action to attend to wholly irrelevant issues. In much the same way we may explain two of the most familiar peculiarities of dreams—their extraordinary vividness, and the curious foreshortening of time which seems to occur in them. The vividness seems to be due to the absence of the mass of complex and uninteresting detail in which the really interesting experiences of waking life are framed. The interesting presentation stands out alone, or almost alone, and thus engrosses the whole available attention of the sleeper; if we see a sunlit meadow, we see also the shadows that sweep across it, but in a dream we may be aware of the light without the shadow. So with the apparent shortening of time. The dream is wholly made up of the interesting moments, without the uninteresting detail which would form their setting in real life. We may dream, *e.g.*, of eating a dinner, but we do not dream each bite separately, though we should have to perform each separately in real life. Or we dream of an important interview, without dreaming of all the uninteresting and irrelevant 'padding' which would really spin it out. Hence the apparent contraction of events which would really fill hours or days into a dream which occupies a few seconds of real time.

The question whether sleep is always accompanied by dreams or not is one which there seems no means of answering. The general opinion of psychologists appears to be that the deepest sleep is entirely unconscious, and that all our dreams belong to the phase of gradual return to the waking state. This is not, however, proved by the fact that we seem only to remember dreams which immediately precede waking. For it is a common experience to wake, like Nebuchadnezzar (Dn 2), with the firm conviction that we have had a striking dream which we are totally unable to recall. In such cases, it often happens that the lost dream is suddenly remembered towards the evening. The cognate facts of hypnotism also show the fallacy of arguing that an interval from which we can recall nothing must have been one in which we were aware of nothing. Whether 'the mind thinks always,' as Descartes and Leibniz maintain and Locke denies, must, for want of evidence, be left an open question.

One of the most curious features of the dream is the modification of the central personality of the dreamer which not infrequently occurs. We dream that we are committing, with a light heart, misdemeanours or even crimes which would be impossible to us in waking life. Or a man may dream that he is a woman (or *vice versa*), and the assumed rôle may be kept up throughout the dream with remarkable dramatic verisimilitude. Or one may assume, for the purposes of the dream, the personality of some familiar historical character, such as Mary Stuart or Oliver Cromwell. Or, again, if the present writer can trust his analysis of his own dreams, the sense of individual personality may be temporarily completely submerged; the dreamer may drop out of the list of *dramatis personæ* of his dream, which then approximates very closely to Schopenhauer's 'will-less intuition.' The reverse process seems also to occur. One may begin by dreaming that he is reading or hearing a story of adventure, and may then unconsciously become the hero of the incidents dreamed of. Similarly, in the common type of dream in which we are transported back into the time of our childhood, we usually assume a suitable personality. We think and feel as children, not as our adult selves. Presumably these shiftings of personality, which may fairly be called examples of 'alternating personality,' are immediately due to a passing change in the mass of *Gemeingefühl*, or general organic sensation. They may be compared with similar modifications instituted by hypnotic suggestion or by the direct introduction of toxic substances into the nervous system.

2. In Greek literature.—The belief in the Divine and prophetic character of dreams is universal throughout Greek literature. In the classical language the exposition of dreams is regularly subsumed under μαντική, as one special province of the art of the μάντις, or seer. Aeschylus, writing early in the 5th cent., when the rise of 'Sophistic' was giving a special impetus to the glorification of 'culture heroes,' includes the discovery of the rules of oneiromancy among the chief things for which mankind are indebted to Prometheus (*Prom. Vinct.* 485: κἄκρινα πρῶτος ἐξ ὀνειράτων ἃ χρὴ | ὕπαρ γενέσθαι, κτλ.). In Homer the sender of dreams is Zeus; it is, *e.g.*, he who directly dispatches the lying dream to Agamemnon in *Iliad*, ii. 5 ff. [Homer regards dreams as actual beings; there is a 'people of dreams' on the dim path to the land of the dead (*Od.* xxiv. 12). In the case of Agamemnon's false dream, Nestor says: 'Had any other of the Achæans told us this dream, we might deem it a false thing and rather turn away therefrom; but now he hath seen it who of all Achæans avoweth himself the greatest' (*Il.* ii. 80–83). As the over-lord, in Homer, is lord by the will of Zeus, he is apparently supposed (without much positiveness) to receive from Zeus counsel in dreams, while other men's dreams are of no account, unless, indeed, some accepted ὀνειροπόλος, or dealer in dreams, accredits them. The word occurs but once in Homer (*Il.* i. 63: 'some soothsayer or interpreter of dreams, for dream, too, is from Zeus'). In parts of Australia the natives believe that a supernatural being, 'Kutchi of the Dieri, Bunjil of the Wurunjerri, or Daramulun of the Coast Murring,' may visit the medicine-man in dream or vision and reveal to him matters of importance (Howitt, *Native Tribes of S.E. Aus-*

tralia, London, 1904, p. 89). The dream-visitant may also be a ghost; the dreamer then consults the medicine-man, who pronounces on the merits of the vision (*ib.* 434).—A. Lang.]

Elsewhere in Greece we find traces of a cruder and more primitive belief. In Hesiod's *Theogony* (211–213), Night gives birth, without father, to 'Doom and black Weird and Death and Sleep and the family of Dreams'; elsewhere it is Earth who produces prophetic visions of the future (Eurip. *Iphig. in Tauris*, 1261 f.: νύχια χθὼν ἐτεκνώσατο φάσματ' ὀνείρων). This suggests that the original view was that the prophetic character of the dreams got at certain spots, such as Delphi, was due to the inherent virtues of the locality itself; the later and more refined theory was that the dreams are directly inspired by the god to whom the seat of prophecy is consecrated. Thus the oracle of Delphi came into the possession of Apollo, and Apollo, besides revealing the future through the mouth of his 'inspired' prophetess, is the great sender of veridical visions and dreams. It is he who in Aeschylus hounds Orestes on to his revenge by threats conveyed perhaps in horrible dreams, and prepares the way for the enterprise by sending the dream which Clytaemnestra misinterprets as signifying her son's death. Similarly the practice of obtaining prescriptions for ailments by *incubation* (*i.e.* by dreaming on a spot of special and proved prophetic virtue) is, in historical times, peculiarly under the patronage of Asclepius, and his great temple at Epidaurus is the most famous of the sanctuaries at which such dream prescriptions could be received. It was usual for the god in person to 'appear in a dream' to the patient and dictate the remedy, or even leave it behind him. When we remember that there was a widely circulated popular scientific literature of medical works addressed to the lay-public and containing directions for diet and exercise, and prescriptions for common disorders, we can readily understand the considerable repute obtained by sanatoria of this kind. Apart from these great sanctuaries, there were also private professional exponents of the science of interpreting dreams (ὀνειροκρῖται), who were regularly at the service of the credulous. Thus Theophrastus (*Charact.* xvi. 11) notes it as characteristic of the δεισιδαίμων, or *dévot*, that, 'when he sees a dream, he goes to the ὀνειροκρῖται, the μάντεις, or the augurs (ὀρνιθοσκόποι), to ask to what god, male or female, he should offer prayer.' There were also, as with ourselves, handbooks of the science, for private use, one of which, that of Artemidorus, belonging to the 2nd cent. A.D., has come down to us. Even apart from the performance of special ritual purifications (ἀποδιοπομπήσεις) to avert the fulfilment of evil dreams, it was held an effectual method of banishing them, as of baulking the effect of evil forebodings generally, to come out into the open air and 'tell them to the sky,' as Iphigenia does with her sinister dream in Euripides (*Iphig. in Tauris*, 42: ἃ καινὰ δ' ἥκει νὺξ φέρουσα φάσματα | λέξω πρὸς αἰθέρ' εἴ τι δὴ τόδ' ἔστ' ἄκος). The same remedy could be practised against presages of evil of any kind, as is done, *e.g.*, by the nurse of Medea in the prologue to that play (Eurip. *Med.* 57 f.: ἵμερός μ' ὑπῆλθε γῆι τε κοὐρανῶι | λέξαι μολούσηι δεῦρο δεσποίνης τύχας). The complete ritual further involved purification of the bedroom and the dreamer with torches and hot water (cf. the burlesque of the performance in Aristophanes, *Frogs*, 1338: ἀλλά μοι ἀμφίπολοι λύχνον ἅψατε | κάλπισί τ' ἐκ ποταμῶν δρόσον ἄρατε, θέρμετε δ' ὕδωρ, | ὡς ἂν θεῖον ὄνειρον ἀποκλύσω).

The belief in the Divine and prophetic nature of dreams plays an important part in the Orphic religion and its descendant, the Pythagorean philosophy. The familiar Orphic doctrines, that the body is the 'grave' of the soul, and that it is only when free from the body that the soul awakes to its true life, led naturally to the view that in sleep the soul converses with eternal things and receives communications from Heaven to which it is not accessible by day. This doctrine is specially prominent in Pindar and Aeschylus—poets who stood in specially close connexion with Sicily, one of the chief homes of Orphicism and Pythagoreanism. Thus Pindar says in a well-known passage from the Θρῆνοι (fr. 131, ed. Schröder) that the soul 'slumbers while the body is active; but, when the body slumbers, she shows forth in many a vision the approaching issues of woe and weal' (ἐν πολλοῖς ὀνείροις | δείκνυσι τερπνῶν ἐφέρποισαν χαλεπῶν τε κρίσιν); and Aeschylus (*Eumen.* 104) declares that 'in slumber the eye of the soul waxes bright, but by daytime man's doom goes unforeseen' (εὕδουσα γὰρ φρὴν ὄμμασιν λαμπρύνεται, | ἐν ἡμέραι δὲ μοῖρ' ἀπρόσκοπος βροτῶν). So in the speech of Diotima in Plato's *Symposium* (which is demonstrably Orphic in its origin) we are told that it is through the agency of Eros (himself an Orphic figure) that the 'communion and converse of gods with men is effected, for the sleeping as well as the waking' (*Symp.* 203 A). In Aeschylus we further find in several passages a sort of simple naïve psychological theory of the machinery of these prophetic dreams, which is apparently based on the doctrine of the physicist and Orphic prophet Empedocles, that 'the blood surrounding the heart is that with which we think' (αἷμα γὰρ ἀνθρώποις περικάρδιόν ἐστι νόημα). The soul is represented as sitting in the heart, like a μάντις in the prophetic chair, and reading off the visions presented in the blood that drips before it, just as the modern 'scryer' reads off the pictures in his crystal (*Agamem.* 178: στάζει δ' ἔν θ' ὕπνωι πρὸ καρδίας | μνησιπήμων πόνος; 975: τίπτε μοι τόδ' ἐμπέδως | δεῖμα προστατήριον | καρδίας τερασκόπου ποτᾶται, | . . . οὐδ' ἀποπτύσας [*v.l.* ἀποπτύσαι] δίκαν | δυσκρίτων ὀνειράτων, | θάρσος εὐπιθὲς ἵζει φρενὸς φίλον θρόνον [where (?) read ἀποπτύσαν and render: 'Confidence dares not spit it away like a riddling dream and take its wonted seat in my soul']; the θρόνος is not, as in the curiously parallel line of Shakespeare, 'My bosom's lord sits lightly in his throne' [*Romeo and Juliet*, v. i. 3], that of a monarch, but that of a seer or prophet). Presumably the reason why the soul can 'scry' in nightly dreams only, is that by day its attention is diverted from the figures formed in the αἷμα περικάρδιον by the sights of the outer world. The Orphic doctrine of prophetic dreams was apparently, like the rest of Orphicism, refined and spiritualized in Pythagoreanism. Iamblichus refers more than once to the moral discipline exercised by Pythagoras over the sleeping and dream life of the Order. In particular, he tells us that it was the custom of the Society to prepare for sleep by listening to tranquillizing music, with the effect that their unruly passions were stilled, their sleep light, their dreams few and happy and prophetic (*Vita Pythag.* §§ 65, 114). Some writers regarded the famous tabu on beans as intended to banish bad dreams.

A similar theory re-appears in Plato, *Republic*, 571 C ff., where Socrates maintains that the dreams of the good man are pure and prophetic, because even in sleep the lower elements in his soul retain their subjection and leave the noblest element to lead a free and unfettered life of its own. Since the *Timaeus* (71 D ff.) sets a much lower value on dreams, maintaining that in them revelations are made only to the lower and irrational nature, and that the revelation requires subsequent interpretation by reason to be properly understood, the theory of the *Republic* is presumably one held by the actual Socrates but not shared by Plato. Even the account of the *Timaeus* may possibly represent views current among the Pythagoreans of the late 5th cent., to which Plato would not have wholly subscribed. It should be noted that the famous dreams ascribed to Socrates in the *Crito* and the *Phaedo* are clearly of Orphic-Pythagorean *provenance*. The vision which warned Socrates that the trireme had left Delos and would reach Athens on the morrow is manifestly the 'fetch' of the boat itself, which is just leaving the island, and is sent therefore by Apollo of Delos, the great god of Pythagoreanism. The other vision, which bade Socrates 'practise music,' clearly comes from the same source, as he obeyed it by composing a pæan to the Delian Apollo (Diog. Laert. ii. 42). From the Academy the doctrine of Pythagoreanism about prophetic dreams would appear to have passed to the Stoics; hence we find Zeno advising his followers to use their dreams as a test of their advance towards virtue (Plutarch, *de Profect. in Virt.* 12; von Arnim, *Fragmenta Stoicorum*, Leipzig, 1905, i. 56: ἠξίου γὰρ ἀπὸ τῶν ὀνείρων ἕκαστον αὑτοῦ συναισθάνεσθαι προκόπτοντος, κτλ.).

A. E. TAYLOR.

3. Savage and modern dreams.—These Greek beliefs or theories, like most of our theories on such matters, are only more artificial statements of the conclusions of savage reasoners. 'The Narrang-ga think that the human spirit can leave the body in sleep, and communicate with the spirits of others [telepathy] or of the dead' (Howitt, 434). The sleep of the body is the holiday of the spirit, which, in sleep, as after death, can ascend to the spiritual place above the sky, and is free from the bonds of time and space.

Among ourselves, people tell us that they have seen unknown places in dreams, and have later come to and recognized them in scenes which they had never before visited in the body. In the same way Howitt writes (p. 436):

'A Mukjarawaint man told me that his father came to him in a dream, and said that he must look out for himself, else he would be killed. This saved him, because he afterwards came to the place which he had seen in the dream, and turned back to where his friends lived, so that his enemies, who might have been waiting for him, did not catch him' (p. 435). One of the Kurnai tribe, being asked 'whether he really thought that his *Yambo* [spirit] could "go out" when he was asleep . . . said, "It must be so, for when I sleep I go to distant places, I see distant people, I even see and speak with those who are dead."'

These experiences and this philosophy of the experiences are common to most races in the lower culture (see E. B. Tylor, *Prim. Cult.*[4], 1903, vol. i. pp. 397–400). The belief in the interpretation is, of course, reinforced by what Tylor calls 'double narratives,' namely those in which the experience is mutual. A dreams of B, B (awake or asleep) sees A in the circumstances of the dream.

Tylor quotes St. Augustine (*de Civ. Dei*, xviii. 18) for a story told to the saint by a friend. This gentleman, before going to sleep, saw a philosopher of his acquaintance, who came to him and expounded certain Platonic passages which he had previously declined to elucidate. 'I did not do it,' said the philosopher, when questioned, 'but I dreamt I did.' In another case a student in Africa was 'coached' in some Latin difficulties by Augustine, who was in Italy. But Augustine did not dream, or did not remember dreaming, anything about the matter (*de Cura pro Mortuis*, x–xii; *Ep.* clviii.).

There are many modern tales of this 'mutual' experience. One may be mentioned which was written out and signed by the dreamer and his mother, who was in the house at the time of the events:

The Rev. Mr. B. fell asleep in his club, in Princes Street, Edinburgh. He dreamed that he was late for dinner, and that he went home to the house of his father, Sir John B., in Abercromby Place. He could not open the door with his latch-key, but it was opened by his father. He then ran upstairs, and, looking down from the first landing, saw his father below gazing after him. He then awoke, found that he was in his club, and that the hour was ten minutes to midnight. He hurried home, and found the front door bolted. His father opened it and said, 'Where have you been? You came in ten minutes ago and ran upstairs; where have you been since?' Like the Platonic philosopher of St. Augustine's tale, Mr. B. answered, 'I did not do it, but I dreamt I did.' Sir John B. was dead when the written narrative signed by Mr. B. and Lady B. was communicated to the writer. Other cases, equally well attested (by five witnesses on one occasion, and by the dreamer) might be given, but enough has been said to illustrate this mutual type of experience.

It is clear that primitive thinkers could explain their dream experiences only by the belief in an indwelling spirit of each man; and, when the dream proved to be 'clairvoyant' (as of a place not previously seen, but later found), or 'mutual,' the theory would be corroborated. Persons with such experiences must inevitably arrive at the conception of spirits, both incarnate and discarnate, and manifestly this belief has been one of the most potent influences in the evolution of religion. As Tylor says (*op. cit.* p. 445), speculation passed 'from the earlier conviction that a disembodied soul really comes into the presence of the sleeper' (or of persons wide-awake) 'toward the later opinion that such a phantasm is produced in the dreamer's mind' (or in the mind of the wide-awake observer) 'without the perception of any external objective figure.'

There are, practically, the two hypotheses: (1) of an 'astral body,' a real space-filling entity; and (2) of 'telepathic impact.' But rationalistic, if not reasonable, thinkers will dismiss both hypotheses as figments made to account for events which never occurred. These varieties of opinion, however, do not concern us; we merely remark that dreams (with other psychical experiences) account for the animistic or spiritual element in religion.

A man's dream 'comes true'; he finds that what he saw in dream was, though he had no normal means of knowing it, true in reality; he therefore infers: 'something within me can go out of me and wander into places where I have never been.' A modern instance, narrated to the writer by the dreamer, may be given:

At a ball in Stirling, some fifteen years ago, several persons were poisoned by eating ill-conditioned oysters, and some died. The husband of the narrator was among the sufferers. On becoming aware of his condition, he wrote and fastened up two letters to two different firms of stockbrokers in Glasgow, which his wife posted. On the night of his funeral she dreamed, and told the dream to a sister-in-law who slept with her, that she went to two different offices in Glasgow, and in each saw an open ledger, and on a page in each her husband's name at the head of a long list of curious names, of which she mentioned a few. They were the designations of mines in the Transvaal. At the foot of each page figures were written showing the state of the account. In one the loss was smaller, in the other larger; the amount was something over £3000. The lady had no idea that her husband was speculating till she saw the addresses of his letters to the stockbrokers, and, on seeing these, before his death she wrote to them, asking them to wind up affairs. To abbreviate—her dream, unhappily, proved exactly correct.

The interpretation by a professor of psychology in a Scottish University is that the speculator had often told his wife all about his dealings in gold mines, but that she had never listened, and the information, till revived in a dream, slumbered unknown in her sub-consciousness. But a primitive thinker could not possibly hit on this theory, which, in fact, did not commend itself as possible to the dreamer.

When a dream discloses *future* events, it produces a great impression on many minds, and in unscientific ages is explained as a Divine revelation. The Homeric explanation, that true dreams come through the gate of horn, false dreams through the ivory gate, is based merely on a pun in the Greek. We now account for prophetic dreams in the mass by saying that, out of so many shots as our dream-selves make, it would be a miracle if none hit the bull's eye. Moreover, even if a dream, later fulfilled, is recorded contemporaneously, or impels to action taken on the moment, the theory of mere fortuitous coincidence is applied; while every one knows that, in telling a dream, we almost inevitably give rational shaping to what was not rational, and, generally, decorate the anecdote. The number of dreams about winners of any great horse race is so great that some must coincide with the result. In one curious case the explanation is easy.

An Eton friend asked Colonel A. B., 'What is the Latin name for the south-west wind?' 'Favonius,' was the answer. 'I dreamed that a horse with the Latin name of the south-west wind won the Derby, but, when I wakened, I could not remember the Latin name.' The friends found no Favonius in the betting, and none, on the Derby day, was coloured on the card. But it was announced that 'the Zephyr colt' had just been named Favonius. The friends naturally backed Favonius, which won. It is clear that the well-known Zephyr (west wind) colt had, in the dream, suggested the south-west wind by its Latin name, which, when awake, the dreamer could not remember.

Another explanation of a fulfilled dream is that the dream was never dreamt, but was an illusion of memory.

Thus Mr. F. W. Greenwood published and spoke to the writer about a dream of going into a strange house, and finding a human hand on a chimney-piece. He did, next day, visit at a house in which he had never been before; he had forgotten about his dream till he noticed the hand of a mummy on the chimney-piece. When told that, in all probability, he had never dreamed the dream, but only had a sense of the *déjà vu* when he saw the hand, and supposed that 'the previously seen' had been seen in a dream, Mr. Greenwood, a man of sturdy common sense, revolted against the methods of science. This was not unnatural.

It frequently happens that, in the course of the day, some trivial incident reminds us, by association of ideas, of some trivial last night's dream which we had temporarily forgotten. In such cases science does not say that we are under the sense of the *déjà vu*: that explanation is given only in cases where, if it is *not* given, a dream must be recognized as premonitory.

An interesting essay on premonitions in dreams, with examples, by Mrs. Henry Sidgwick, may be read in *Proceedings of the Society for Psychical Research*, vol. v. pp. 311–351. The objections are firmly stated in general terms; especially the objection that memory, if no record be instantly made, improves the case, while the memory of any person to whom the dream was narrated before the coincidence of dream with fact was known is as subject to error as that of the narrator. It will be observed that perhaps the best authenticated premonitory dreams are concerned with quite trivial matters, for example (this case is not given by Mrs. Sidgwick), a series of incidents in a golf match played on links and with an opponent both entirely strange to the dreamer at the time of the dream. (For examples, see Mrs. Sidgwick's essay, pp. 338, 339, 343, 346–351.)

A dream, communicated to the writer at first hand, is picturesque, and may be briefly told. The dreamer one night dreamed that she was in Piccadilly. The street was covered with snow, and a black sleigh was driven quickly past. Looking round, she saw the late Duke of Edinburgh, with whom she was acquainted. He said, 'They are taking the news to Clarence House.' The following day she read in the newspaper the news of the murder of the Duke's father-in-law, Alexander II. of Russia.

This aspect of dreams (if the facts are accepted) may, of course, be viewed from the side of Myers' theory of 'the subliminal self,' as stated in his book, *Human Personality* (1903). By those who accept, more or less, Myers' hypothesis some dreams are taken to be 'supernormal,' and bear witness to unexplained ranges of human faculty. In other cases they merely show that incidents which have left no trace on the ordinary memory are none the less treasured in the subconscious memory, and may be communicated to the upper consciousness through the mechanism of remembered dreams. If no men dreamed, it is probable that religion and philosophy might never have evolved the conception of spirit; while, if only five per cent of mankind dreamed, it is fairly certain that the other ninety-five per cent would regard them as merely mendacious.

LITERATURE.—For a full bibliography, see Baldwin's *DPhP*, vol. iii. pt. 1, *s.vv.* 'Dream' and 'Sleep'; cf. also W. Volkmann von Volkmar, *Lehrbuch der Psychol.*[3], Cöthen, 2 vols. 1884–5; W. Wundt, *Grundzüge der physiol. Psychol.*[5], Leipzig, 3 vols. 1902; Aristotle, *Parva Naturalia*, ed. W. Biehl, Leipzig, 1898; the works of Aristotle, Eng. tr. (general editors, J. A. Smith and W. D. Ross), pt. i. *Parva Naturalia* (tr. of *de Somno, de Somniis, de Divinatione per Somnum*, by J. I. Beare), Oxford, 1908; J. I. Beare, *Gr. Theories of Elementary Cognition from Alcmaeon to Aristotle*, Oxford, 1906; Mary Hamilton, *Incubation, or the Cure of Disease in Pagan Temples and Christian Churches*, London, 1906.

A. LANG.

DREAMS AND SLEEP (Babylonian).—The dream played an important part in the life and religion of the Babylonians. In the dream the deity was believed to reveal himself in a special way to the individual, declaring the will of heaven and predicting the future. The *bârû*, or 'seers,' constituted a particular class of priests, and one of the titles of the Sun-god was *bârû terêti*, 'the seer of the revealed law.' Prophetic dreams, however, might be sent to the ordinary layman as well as to the professional 'seer,' and there were books for interpreting their meaning. It would seem that answers to prayer could be obtained through sleeping in a temple and invoking Makhir, the goddess (or god) of dreams. At all events, in a penitential psalm (*WAI*, iv. 66. 2) we read: 'Reveal thyself to me and let me behold a favourable dream. May the dream that I dream be favourable; may the dream that I dream be true. May Makhir, the god(dess) of dreams, stand at my head. Let me enter E-Saggila, the temple of the gods, the house of life.' The little temple discovered by Mr. Hormuzd Rassam at Balawât (15 miles E. of Mosul) was specially dedicated to Makhir, and may have been frequented by those who thus sought 'favourable' dreams.

In the Epic of Gilgameš dreams play a conspicuous part. In the struggle of the Babylonian hero with Khumbaba three dreams are needed to assure him of success. The loss of his friend Eabani is foretold in a vision of fire and lightning, and in the story of the Deluge the impending destruction of mankind was said to have been revealed to Utu-napištim in a dream. The historical inscriptions are equally full of references to dreams. The will of heaven was made known to Gudea of Lagaš through a dream, and the army of Aššur-bani-pal was encouraged to cross a river by the appearance in a vision of the goddess Ištar, who declared: 'I march before Aššur-bani-pal the king, who is the creation of my hands.' Aššur-bani-pal himself, when overwhelmed with despair at the outbreak of the war with Elam, was similarly reassured with a promise of victory. He prayed to Ištar, and on the self-same night 'a seer (*sabrû*) slept and dreamed a dream,' wherein Ištar of Arbela appeared with a quiver on either shoulder and a bow in her hand, and bade the dreamer announce to the king: 'Eat food, drink wine, enjoy music, exalt my divinity until I have gone to accomplish this deed: I will give thee thy heart's desire; thy face shall not grow pale, thy feet shall not totter, thy strength shall not fail in the battle.' It was in a dream that Aššur commanded Gyges of Lydia to pay homage to the Assyrian king and so obtain help against his Cimmerian enemies, and the prediction that the power of the Manda would be overthrown, as well as the order to rebuild the temple of the Moon-god at Harran, was revealed to Nabonidos in a dream. In the historical framework of the Book of Daniel the dreams of Nebuchadrezzar occupy a leading place, and in one instance the wise men of Babylon were required not only to interpret the dream, but even to recall it to the memory of the king.

Oneiromancy was studied by the Babylonians with that exaggerated devotion to details which otherwise characterized them. The official texts relating to the interpretation of dreams took note of everything, however bizarre or unlikely, which might occur to the imagination of the sleeper. These texts or 'Dream-books,' which were probably collected in a single work, were naturally included by Aššur-bani-pal in his library at Nineveh, and formed the quarry from which Artemidorus drew the materials for his five books of the *Oneirocritica*. The nature of them may be gathered from the following quotations: 'If a date appears on a man's head, it means woe. If a fish appears on his head, that man will be strong. If a mountain appears on his head, it means that he will have no rival. If salt appears on his head, it means that he will apply himself to build his house.' Or, again: 'If a man dreams that he goes to a pleasure-garden, it means that he will gain his freedom. If he goes to a market-garden, his dwelling-place will be uncomfortable. If he goes to kindle a firebrand, he will see woe during (his) days. If he goes to sow a field, he will escape from a ruined place. If he goes to hunt in the country, he will be eminent (?). If he goes to an ox-stall, [he will have] safety. If he goes to the sheepfold, he will rise to the first rank.' Could a pseudo-science end in greater puerilities?

LITERATURE.—A. Boissier, *Choix de textes relatifs à la divination assyro-babylonienne*, ii., Geneva, 1906; F. Lenormant, *La Divination et la science des présages chez les Chaldéens*, Paris, 1875, pp. 127–149; Artemidorus Daldianus, *Oneirocritica*, ed. Reiff, 1805.

A. H. SAYCE.

DREAMS AND SLEEP (Egyptian).—**1. Introduction.**—Although dreams were not considered of such importance in Egypt as in Chaldæa, Phœnicia, or the Hellenic world, the rôle allocated to them was much larger than is generally thought; they occupied a constant place in Egyptian life. The relative scarcity of information is a result of the nature of the monuments at present published. While the epigraphy of the temples furnishes only a very few official examples of dreams, we find (1) that, in spite of this scarcity, dreams are of constant occurrence in the literary papyri; and (2) that the instances of Egyptian dreams mentioned by late authors are proved by a correct exegesis to be of Egyptian origin. These two points give us ground for thinking that the deciphering of the still unpublished papyri and *ostraca* will yield an unknown wealth of information. Further, the study of unpublished *ex voto* stelæ ought, to all appearance, to furnish large additions to the list of cases of miraculous healing obtained by the medium of dreams. If to all this we add the passages in our sources in which dreams are not expressly mentioned, but are implied by the fact that formulæ are employed similar to those used in cases of dreams related expressly as such, we are forced to the conclusion that the current ideas as to the frequency and importance of dreams in Egypt stand in need of considerable modification.

2. Classification of material.—Dreams in which the gods intervene directly may be divided into three groups: (*a*) unsolicited dreams in which they appear in order to demand some act of piety towards themselves; (*b*) dreams in which they give warnings of various kinds spontaneously; and (*c*) dreams in which they grant their worshippers an answer to a question definitely stated. The cases of unofficial magic forcing dreams into its service form a separate class.

This classification has the advantage of arranging the facts in a fixed number of groups, which bring into greater prominence the essentially Egyptian characteristics, and so help to decide whether a certain number of dreams mentioned in the Greek and Roman classics can be regarded as really Egyptian. This is an important question to settle for the general theory of dreams.

3. Unsolicited dreams.—Of this first class the well-known dream of Thothmes IV. is the best specimen contained in our sources. Falling asleep, during the chase, at the foot of the statue of the Great Sphinx, the young prince heard the voice of a god. It promised him the throne of Egypt, and required him to repair the god's temple, which was threatened with ruin. This story leaves no doubt that the dream of Nectanebo, though handed down to us in Greek form (cf. Leemans, *Papyri Græci*, Leyden, 1838, p. 122), is an adaptation of an Egyptian document. As in the case of Thothmes IV., the god (under the form Anhuri) appeared to the king, and complained of the failure to complete certain works at his temple. On waking, the king was greatly perturbed, and gave the necessary orders to have the works completed with all expedition. It is quite certain that this Hellenized legend sprang from the remains of a stela, like that of the Sphinx of Gizeh, on which the priests had had an account engraved of the marvellous incident that caused the repairing of the temple.

The case reported by Plutarch (*de Is. et Osir.* 28) of the dream of Ptolemy Soter belongs to the same category. The king dreams of a colossal statue which orders him to take it back to Alexandria, where it was formerly situated. He makes inquiries on awaking, and finds that Sosebius had once seen an image at Sinope like the one described by the king as seen in his dream. The statue, in short, is found there, and brought back to Alexandria; and Timotheus, as well as Manetho, recognizes it as one of Serapis. Here we see a Hellenized adaptation of Egyptian legends relating to the repair of monuments and the restoration of cults of Divine statues; and this is in complete harmony with the historical fact that the Ptolemys took a great deal of trouble to bring back the national sacred statues which had been carried off from the Nile Valley by Asiatic conquerors.

The question of the absolute authenticity of these documents cannot be discussed here. It was proved long ago that the majority of these stelæ devoted to dreams, miracles, and gifts made after Divine intervention bear inscriptions of a much later date than is attributed to them (*e.g.*, the Stela of Cheops at Gizeh, the Stela 'of the Famine,' Stela of Bakhtan, etc.; the Stela of the Sphinx, in particular, has been shown by Erman to be a new version of an analogous legend attributing an identical dream to another prince). It still remains to be proved, however, that these 'forged' documents are not adaptations of ancient inscriptions or transcriptions on stone of ancient papyri. The only important facts to be kept in view here are: (1) that official Egypt admitted as a regular process this method of Divine warnings by dreams; (2) that numerous restorations of temples and cults were really the outcome of dreams actually experienced, and accepted by the king, on awaking, as certain signs of the will of the gods. An examination of the official texts relating to the restorations of monuments would show, by the parallelism of formulæ, that these cases are much more numerous in Egypt than is usually supposed.

Besides cases like the above, in which the gods may be said to have been working primarily in their own interests, unsolicited dreams were granted also for the benefit of humanity. The revelation by a dream of the hiding-place of some wonderful chapter, for use in funerary or medical magic, seems to have been the traditional origin of a number of formulæ or groups of formulæ inserted later in the great compilations which became the 'Books of the Dead' and the first medical papyri. All that the gods of Egypt did in such circumstances was to show the continuity of their legendary rôle of 'beneficent masters of this whole earth.' Their intervention sometimes took an even more direct form, warnings being given by dreams to the kings, who were the Divine heirs, or to important personages, princes, or even simple mortals loved by the gods. Sometimes they revealed the action to be taken in the man's own interest. It is, *e.g.*, in obedience to a dream that Shabaka (Sabacōs) retires into Ethiopia (Herod. ii. 139). Sometimes they foretell final success, without requiring, as in the case of Thothmes IV., a personal service in exchange.

The famous Ethiopian Stela 'of the Dream' is the typical example of this class. We are told how Tonutamon 'sees in a dream in the night two serpents, one on the left, one on the right,' and how it was explained on his awaking that these two serpents signified the heraldic emblems of the two Egypts (North and South) of which he would soon be master.

In other cases the gods do not scorn to foretell happy events to certain persons in whom or in whose descendants they are particularly interested—perhaps with a view to the good that will result for the whole of Egypt. The story of Satni, father of the great magician Senosiris, is an example:

'Now Satni went to sleep and dreamed a dream. Some one spoke to him, saying: "Thy wife hath conceived, and the child she will bear will be called Senosiris, and many are the miracles that will be done by him in the land of Egypt."'

Sometimes, again, a dream directly reveals the wish of a god. Thus the prince of Bakhtan saw in his sleep a hawk flying away towards Egypt; this was a sign that he had to send back to Thebes the miraculous statue of the god Khonsu, which had formerly exorcized a demon from his daughter. Sometimes, also, the Divine spirit warns the king in a dream to avoid certain projects, either immediate or far ahead, which would turn out harmful to the kingdom. However adapted they may be in non-Egyptian compositions, the dream of Menander and Pharaoh's dream (interpreted by Joseph [Gn 41]) are two good examples, the constituent elements of which are similar to those of Egyptian accounts of such Divine warnings.

The first of these stories has come down to us in fragments of a Coptic romance—the fabulous Life of Alexander: 'Then Menander had the following dream, and saw this vision: he saw a lion loaded with chains and cast into a pit. A man spoke to him: "Menander, why dost thou not descend with this lion, since his purple is fallen? Get thee up now, and seize him by the neck of his purple." Menander's grief at this dream, and his conviction that the lion signified his master, were not mistaken—in the morning a messenger announced the death of Alexander at treacherous hands.' It is highly probable that, if the legend is of late Egyptian date, it borrowed its general form from the ordinary type of historical dreams attributed to the Pharaohs of national legend.

The same remark applies to the Scripture story of the dream of Pharaoh, and the part played by Joseph. In the present state of our knowledge, we cannot assert that this episode belongs to any particular reign in the Egyptian dynasties, nor even that it belongs, for a fact, to some authentic fragment of the national folk-lore relating to the legend of the Pharaohs of the romantic cycle. But Egyptology is in a position to state with assurance that none of the elements of the story is *a priori* in conflict with the Egyptian data relating to dreams. We know from history that the subject itself (the periods of drought and fertility resulting from the annual overflowing of the Nile) was one of the chief interests of the Egyptian monarchy; the famous stela of the island of Sehel (the 'Famine Stela'), *e.g.*, is evidence that facts of this kind were of great importance in monumental religious history, where the gods and the kings both witnessed to the vital importance of this matter—the former by warnings, the latter by acts of piety. The symbolic method of warning, in the figures of fat and lean kine or ears of corn, is analogous to that of the serpents in the Ethiopian 'Dream Stela.' Finally, the calling in of Joseph to interpret the dream, after all the magicians and wise men had been consulted in vain (Gn 41[8]), is likewise in agreement with Egyptian usage: the popular tales relate that, on the failure of the regular interpreters, the king applied at will to private persons noted for their wisdom, as, *e.g.*, in the case of the wise old man consulted by the Pharaoh in the 'Story of Cheops and the Magicians.'

The interpretation of symbolical dreams was the business of special persons—the 'Masters of the Secret Things,' or the 'Scribes of the Double House of Life' (a very poor modern translation; the real meaning of the title is rather 'the Learned Men of the Magic Library'). At no time do these 'official dreamers' seem to have had the prominence they enjoyed in other civilizations. As regards mantic codification of the signification of beings, things, and phenomena seen in dreams, it is hardly likely that Egypt did not possess lists of this kind in the temples; but, as a matter of fact, we do not possess at the present moment a single papyrus of the same kind as the collections of 'omen tablets' of the Chaldæan civilization. It is not a question, of course, of looking for a theoretical work or anything approaching the *Oneirocritica* of Artemidorus; all we could expect would be lists of facts and interpretations conceived on the model, *e.g.*, of the horoscopic calendars.

4. Solicited dreams.—Of more frequent occurrence is Divine intervention by means of dreams sought and obtained, either in exceptional circumstances or in regular arranged form. Good examples of the first class are furnished by the historical cases of kings finding themselves in a difficult situation, and imploring a god to grant them some light on the future or on the course they should follow. The classical inscription of Merenptah (Great temple of Karnak) is a good example:

'Then his majesty saw in a dream as if a statue of Ptah were standing before Pharaoh. He was like the height of. . . . He spake to him, "Take thou (it)," while he extended to him the sword, "and banish thou the fearful heart from thee." Pharaoh spake to him, "Lo . . ."' (Breasted, *Ancient Records of Egypt*, Chicago, 1906, iii. 582).

This passage throws light upon Herodotus' story (ii. 141) of the dream of Sethos, a priest of Hephæstus, during his struggle against Sennacherib:

'The monarch . . . entered into the inner sanctuary, and, before the image of the god, bewailed the fate which impended over him. As he wept, he fell asleep, and dreamed that the god came and stood at his side, bidding him be of good cheer, and go boldly forth to meet the Arabian host, which would do him no hurt, as he himself would send those who should help him.' Cf., on Sennacherib, 2 K 19[35f.].

This is a faithful account—though Hellenized—of what the classical Pharaoh did. He did not 'bewail his fate,' as the Greek author thought, but he stated his case in a prayer, the model of which is given in Maspero, *Contes pop.* (see Lit.); and the appearance of the god in a dream was not an unexpected phenomenon, but a necessary consequence of the prayer. The rest of the story—the entering of the temple, speaking before the statue, incubation, and, lastly, the response of the god—are pure Egyptian characteristics, and are in complete agreement with what we learn on this point from the inscriptions and popular tales.

The various sources of information that have come down to us prove that incubation in the temple in order to obtain a remedy or a mantic response was a current practice, not only among princes, but also among private individuals. It is wonderful to find, once more, and in this connexion, that the Græco-Roman authors were often more accurately informed than is usually believed. Before Egyptological knowledge had supplied the necessary proof, the accuracy of Diodorus (i. 28) was contested (Wilkinson, *Manners and Customs*, Lond. 1878, ii. 356), when he says that 'in Egypt, dreams are regarded with religious reverence, especially as means of indicating remedies in illnesses'; and that 'the prayers of worshippers are often rewarded by the indication of a remedy in a dream.'

The story of Satni tells of Mahituaskhit going to the temple of Imuthes (=Asklepios) in Memphis, praying to the god, then falling asleep in the temple, and receiving from the god in a dream a cure for her sterility: 'When to-morrow morning breaks, go thou to the fountain of Satni, thy husband; there thou shalt find growing a plant of colocasia; pull it up, leaves and all, and with it make a potion which thou shalt give to thy husband; then shalt thou sleep with him, and that very night shalt thou conceive.'

This story is not simply a literary fabrication; for we have the famous Memphite Stela of Psherenptah, of the Augustan period, giving epigraphical evidence of another case of sterility being similarly cured by a remedy revealed in a dream by the same god Imuthes.

By piecing the various texts together, we gradually arrive at a re-construction of the 'processus' of the Egyptian dream by incubation in the temple. The patient entered one of the sanctuaries where the gods were reported to give responses to those who came to sleep within the sacred enclosure.

Our information is fully verified by the texts, at least for the temples of Imuthes in Memphis, and of Thoth in Khimunu. All indications of a scientific nature lead to the same conclusion for the temple of Thoth Teōs at Medinet-Habu, near Thebes (see Disease and Medicine [Egyp.]), and for the celebrated sanctuary of Isis at Philæ (cf. Revillout, in *PSBA* x. [1887] 58). Finally, we are assured by Petrie that there were special places in the temple of Sarbut el-Qadem, in Sinai, for people who desired dreams from the goddess Haithar (Hathor) relating to the locality of turquoise mines (cf. *Egypt and Israel*, London, 1911,

p. 49, and *Personal Religion*, do. 1909, pp. 27, 81). But the same author is probably wrong in thinking that this practice represents a borrowing from ancient Semitic religion.

When inside the temple, the worshipper prayed the deity to reveal himself: 'Turn thy face towards me'; and besought him by his well-known virtues: ''Tis thou who dost accomplish miracles and art benevolent in all thy doings; 'tis thou who givest children to him that hath none,' or ''Tis thou who hast created magic, and established the heavens and the earth and the lower world; 'tis thou who canst grant me the means of saving all.' The god was adjured to '*hear* the prayer' (and this formula is, in the present writer's opinion, decisive proof that the various stelæ on which ears [*sotmu*] are found are, after all the discussion on this point, votive offerings of the worshippers whose supplications the god had heard [*sotmu*] in cases of dreams by incubation). After these invocations, the inquirer waited for the god to come and answer him in sleep.

There is one important point still obscure. We do not know whether, as in so many other savage and semi-savage religions, the coming of the dream was facilitated by the swallowing of some narcotic or intoxicating substance (see Tylor, *PC*[3], London, 1891, ii. 416 f.). Of the two other equally frequent conditions—prayer and fasting—the former has been discussed. As regards fasting, it is almost certain, from a number of evidences and parallelisms, that it was an essential duty of the worshipper desiring a dream. It was originally based, as in uncivilized races, on magical notions which gave a pseudo-scientific interpretation to the hypersensibility to dreams caused by fasting; therefore it developed into the idea of moral purification, as has happened in so many other cases (see Petrie, *Personal Religion*, 'The Ascetics,' p. 70, for the idea of fasting in general in the Egypt of the later period).

The god next appeared in a dream. The usual formula is: 'The god N [or 'some one,' instead of the Divine name *honoris causa*] spake to him, saying. . . .' The deity begins, as a rule, by specifying the identity of the person he is addressing: 'Art thou not *such an one*, son (or father, or wife, etc.) of *so and so*?' (cf. Maspero, *Contes populaires*[3], Paris, 1905, p. 137, for the dream of Mahituas-khit, and p. 147 for the dream of Horus, son of Panishi). When this is settled, the god next tells what should be done 'when morning comes,' and he uses no dark or symbolic language; indeed, it is with most exact details that he tells, *e.g.*, at what place a sealed *naos* will be found, or a certain kind of box, containing a certain book, which must be copied and replaced, to be followed by a certain result, etc. The divinatory dream of an ordinary Egyptian type for incubation is thus a case of oneiromancy, not requiring a metaphysical interpretation, but with the direct instructions of the gods in clear terms. It is by these examples also that the sense of the passage of Hermes Trismegistus is established, referring to 'these prophetic statues which foretell the future by dreams and otherwise.'

5. Dreams evoked by magicians.—Besides these official methods of soliciting dreams from the gods, private magic taught means of obtaining dreams without recourse to the loftier temple procedure. The papyri of later centuries have preserved the pitiable mixture of material details and barbarous jingles of words that form the clearest of those methods.

Papyrus 122 in the British Museum, l. 359 ff., says: 'Take a clean linen bag and write upon it the names given below. Fold it up and make it into a lamp-wick, and set it alight, pouring pure oil over it. The words to be written are: "Armiuth, Lailamchouch, Arsenophrephren, Phtha, Archentechtha." Then in the evening, when you are going to bed, which you must do without touching food, do thus: Approach the lamp and repeat seven times the formula given below, then extinguish it and lie down to sleep.' [The formula is too long to give, but ends thus: 'I require, O lords of the Gods, give me the information that I desire'; cf. Budge, *Egyp. Magic*, London, 1901, p. 216.]

Magic also taught analogous means of getting dreams on unspecified subjects from the popular god of dreams, Bes, whose figure is carved or engraved on numerous pillows on which Egyptian heads reclined. With these formulæ we enter imperceptibly the domain of pure and simple superstition and the current practices of Egyptian society.

The same British Museum papyrus gives, in l. 64 ff., the method of drawing 'on the left hand' a figure of Bes, then writing on a piece of cloth, with ink made of special ingredients, a formula of adjuration; this cloth is then wrapped round the hand, and its end is rolled round the patient's neck. The god of dreams is summoned to come 'this very night.'

It is doubtful whether the more enlightened members of Egyptian society admitted that the gods lent themselves so readily to the commands and threats of men. It is universally admitted, on the other hand, that the dead, who always had power to come and give dreams to the living on their own initiative, were capable, in certain circumstances, of being called into the service of private magic.

Cases of direct intervention by the dead are not of great frequency in the literature at present known to us. The view of Pierret (*Dict. d'arch. égyp.*, Paris, 1875, *s.v.* 'Songe'), that the famous papyrus of 'The Teaching of Amenemhat' has reference to an appearance of the king's father, who came in a dream to instruct his son, is nothing more than hypothesis. The same is true of the interview of Khonsu-m-habi with a dead man (this may have been a waking vision). The most certain cases are those indicated by the formulæ found by Erman in the Berlin magic papyrus, to be employed for driving off the ghosts that torment children in sleep (see art. CHILDREN [Egyptian]). The well-known Leyden papyrus is the type *par excellence* of cases of a dead woman coming to torment her husband in dreams. The way to get rid of this torment was to make a statuette of the dead wife and tie upon its wrist a list of the husband's good deeds during his wedded life, and then a summons to the ghost to stop her persecution, under the threat of proceedings before the god of the dead.

The magicians took full advantage of this readiness of the dead to evoke dreams. They did not employ all ghosts, but only those whose wretched condition had deprived them of their habitations, family-cult, or tomb, and who had consequently to beg assistance of the living and to put themselves at their service in order to exist (see DEMONS AND SPIRITS [Egyp.]); hence the importance attached in necromancy to the spirits of shipwrecked people, suicides, executed criminals, etc. Most of the Egyptian books of magic include private formulæ for sending dreams in this way (cf. the Louvre papyrus 3229, the Gnostic papyrus of Leyden, and the late incantations in Greek). The dreams thus sent belong to two general categories: (*a*) dreams which torment and devour by witchcraft; and (*b*) dreams sent to inspire some one with an ardent love, to encourage a loved one's fidelity, or to bring hostility to a rival or make him physically impotent. In all such cases the sending of the dream is usually complicated by a casting of spells through the medium of a figure of the person to whom the dream is sent (see Maspero, *Histoire*, Paris, 1895, i. 213; and the cases of 'love figures' given by Budge in his *Egyptian Magic*, p. 94 ff.). The whole combines, later on, with Chaldæan, Jewish, and Greek magic to form the involved processes of *tabellæ devotionis*, where dream, incantation, and necromancy are all confused, the dream-sending, however, remaining the chief element (cf., on this difficult question, Maspero, *Études de myth. et d'archéol. égyp.*, Paris, 1893, pp. 297, 311; and the fine studies of Revillout, 'Amatoria,' in *Revue égyptologique*, i. [1881] 69 ff.). A papyrus in the British Museum commends the sending of love-dreams by the method of tracing words with a nail 'taken from a wrecked ship' and then throwing them into the sea; or by making this declaration before a lamp filled with oil of a special composition: 'I desire to appear in the dream of the daughter of N. . . .' By gradual stages the magician adds to these spirits of the dead in his service spirits of demons or of ill-disposed gods, and we see developing the system of black magic which lasted throughout the centuries in the Mediterranean world and in Christian Europe.

This general theory of the dreams sent by magicians fits in exactly with the accounts of pseudo-Callisthenes relating to the legendary birth of Alexander, and proves the Egyptian nature—mistakenly contested—of the dreams that were sent to Olympias and to Philip. The first dream, sent to the queen, is accompanied by a ceremony of spell-casting with a wax figure and unctions of magic herbs analogous to all the practices mentioned above. The dream-visit of Amon to the queen's room is purely Egyptian, and falls in with the theory of Divine conceptions by dreams described at Luxor and Deir el-Bahari for the Thebans of the XVIIIth Dynasty. Finally, the dream in which the hawk is sent from Egypt to announce to Philip the miraculous birth of Alexander is equally in agreement with the mechanism employed by the magicians of the Nile Valley.

6. General.—It will be observed that in none of the cases mentioned as yet do we see an ordinary living person taking any part at all in a dream (giving a warning, coming from a distance, announcing an approaching death, etc.); there is nothing of the nature of the interview of Patroclus and Achilles (*Il.* xxiii. 65 ff.). And, on the other hand, we have no Egyptian examples of the dreamer going to a distant land in his dream, living the past over again, seeing future events, or, in a word, playing any of the parts that are so frequent in dreams of other religions. Besides the dreams already mentioned, in which the dead appear, the only other apparitions seem to have been of gods speaking on definite questions in the clear language of earth, and, sometimes, but more rarely, calling the attention of the sleeper to certain symbolical figures that must be interpreted.

We now come to the final question of what theory was probably held in Egypt as to the mechanism of the dream. No formal explanation has ever been given of this in any Egyptian text known to us, and there is little chance that there ever existed an oneirocritical work analogous to those possessed by the Mediterranean world. The Egyptian dream is not connected rationally either with the mechanism of omens, or with the theory of 'influences,' or with the process of 'intersigns.' It is a tangible reality and is regarded as such, without mysticism and, as a rule, without symbolism. There is not even any allusion, as by Penelope in the *Odyssey* (xix. 500 ff.), to the possibility of a fallacious dream. On the other hand, the absence of dreams in which the soul goes away or in which living persons appear is significant. As it is evident that the Egyptians, like other men, must have had dreams of this type, the fact that they omit to mention them in the texts proves that they did not consider them of importance. Now, if we admit, with Tylor (*Prim. Cult.*³, i. 121, 440, ii. 24, 49, 75, 416), that these types of dreams are included in the list of the fundamental elements of primitive religious phenomena, it must be concluded that Egypt was already far beyond these conceptions, and had travelled far, in this connexion, from the ideas as to the rôle and nature of dreams cherished by the majority of contemporary African peoples. In the last place, the theory of the dream seems to the present writer, after a careful examination of the Egyptian ideas, to be based not upon the separation or the journey of one of the souls of a human being during sleep, but upon the hypersensitiveness of the sleeping man. This fact may be of great interest for the history of comparative religion. There would seem to correspond, in short, to the sleeping state a special sensitiveness enabling the individual to see and hear beings that are always in existence, but cannot be perceived in a waking state because the senses are too gross. This would agree with the belief that on certain occasions or by certain processes man can actually acquire this lucidity, by way of exception, in a waking state (*e.g.* 'to see invisible spirits' by rubbing the eyes with a magic substance; or 'to read sealed writing' through the matter of the case, etc.). The whole hypothesis agrees, however, with the practice that we have established as fact or suspected as preliminary conditions in Egypt of obtaining a dream: prayer (*i.e.* an attenuated form of incantation), fasting, etc. The whole question would thus come under the general theory of the ecstatic process. Far from being, as in other religions, a sort of death, sleep in Egypt was a state of lucid supersensitiveness of the various souls contained in the individual. In support of this view, there is a very important phenomenon to be noted, viz. the ecstatic sleep of the *sam*, so often described or represented in the ritual and in the scenes of the famous ceremony known as the 'Opening of the Mouth' of the dead. It is during this sleep that the *sam* acquires the power of seeing and hearing the soul of the dead 'in all the forms which it takes,' as the dreamer declares on awaking.

LITERATURE.—There is no monograph on the subject. Various facts are briefly given in: A. Erman, *Religion*, Fr. ed., Paris, 1907, pp. 81, 211, 222; V. Ermoni, *Relig. de l'Égypte ancienne*, Paris, 1910, Index; G. Maspero, *Histoire*, i. (Paris, 1895) 213, 266; Ph. Virey, *Relig. de l'anc. Égypte*, Paris, 1910, pp. 129, 226; see, for the examples taken from the classics, J. G. Wilkinson, *Manners and Customs of the Anc. Egyptians*, ed. London, 1878, i. 139, ii. 356, 464, iii. 95. The text of the principal Pharaonic documents is given in J. H. Breasted, *Ancient Records of Egypt*, Chicago, 1904-1907, ii. 815, iii. 582, iv. 922; Maspero, *Contes populaires*³, Paris, 1905, pp. 132 f., 145, 147, 157, 166, 255, 267. The only works in which the subject is approached theoretically are: E. A. W. Budge, *Egyp. Magic*, London, 1901, pp. 94, 206; G. Maspero, 'Imhotep,' in *Journal des Savants*, 1901, and 'Comment Alexandre devint Dieu' (*Annuaire de l'école des hautes études*, 1899), p. 26 f.

GEORGE FOUCART.

DREAMS AND SLEEP (Teutonic).—Dreams played a considerable part in the lives of the Teutons, but their significance was only prophetic. They were thought to foreshadow events in the future of the dreamer or his immediate surroundings, but there is no hint that they played any part in religion. The idea that revelations as to the nature of the gods could be made through the agency of dreams seems to have been foreign to Teutonic conceptions, and the later mystical dreams of the Middle Ages must, therefore, be held to be a Christian growth. In Scandinavia, whence almost all our information for heathen times is obtained, dreams were not only divorced from religion, but also to a great extent from magic. The art of interpreting dreams was in no way connected with magical powers, but was usually found in combination with a philosophical attitude towards life, and a wide knowledge of the world. Thus, in the *Laxdale Saga*, Gudrun appeals to no witch-wife, but to Gest the Wise, a chief universally esteemed for his ripe wisdom, for the interpretation of her dream; and in the *Heimskringla* we find King Halfdan the Black consulting his wisest counsellor about his dream. Every one, however, was acquainted with the rudiments of the art of interpretation, and there seems to have been a general consensus of opinion as to the significance of certain phenomena in dreams: thus Gudrun, in the *Lay of Atli*, says that dreaming of iron portends fire; and Högni, in the same poem, declares that his wife's dream of a polar bear only foretells a storm from the east. The fact that most of the recorded Scandinavian dreams are of ominous import must be ascribed to the selective process exercised by the authors of Saga or poem. The value of dreams, used as a literary device to deepen the atmosphere of doom which surrounds a fated house, was fully appreciated by them. So, before the catastrophic ending of the Atli (Attila) poems, the wives of Högni and Gunnar in vain strive to stay their husbands by the recital of their dark dreams; and the unsuspecting Atli wakes Gudrun to tell her the dream which foreshadows his own death at her avenging hands. In many of the Sagas the suspense before a tragic happening is enhanced by dreams woven into the story, notably in the Saga of Gisli the Outlaw. However, Snorri Sturluson makes good use of a more cheerful type of dream in his histories of the Norwegian kings, shadowing forth the glory of the royal line in the dream of a lofty tree, many-branched, spreading all over Norway and beyond it. Saxo Grammaticus, in his *Gesta Danorum*, tells us of a dream of King Gorm of Denmark which has a similar significance, and one is also recorded from Sweden.

It is worth while to examine a little more closely the various classes of foreboding dreams. The simplest type is merely a dream vision of what is to come; thus a great blaze indicates the burning of a house, and so on. But the dreams most frequently mentioned in the old Scandinavian sources image forth the persons involved under animal form, showing how deeply rooted was the idea of the *fylgja*, the materialization, as it were, in animal form, of a man's spirit, which attended him through life, and could be seen in dreams, or by waking persons before the death of its owner (see SOUL [Teut.]). Thus, in *Njáls Saga*, a dream of a bear followed by two dogs is at once read as showing the presence, in the neighbourhood, of the warlike Gunnar, with two companions. Thorstein Egilsson, in the *Gunnlaugs Saga*, dreams of two eagles fighting over the possession of a swan: the eagles are the *fylgjur* of the two rivals for the love of his daughter, whose *fylgja* is the swan. There is a remarkable similarity between this dream and that in the *Nibelungenlied*, where Kriemhild sees two eagles tear her pet falcon to pieces. Charlemagne's dream of the meeting of a bear and a leopard, recorded in the *Song of Roland*, evidently belongs to this class. In other dreams, again, it is the guardian spirit, or a deceased member of the family, who appears to the living representative to warn him of danger or death—in two stories the warning conveyed is of a landslip, from which the dreamer is thereby enabled to escape. In later Christian times we find St. Olaf or one of the popular Icelandic bishops fulfilling this warning function. In the short Icelandic tale entitled the *Dream of Thorstein*, three female guardian spirits come weeping to Thorstein, imploring him to be wary, for that his thrall Gilli seeks to murder him; but their warning is in vain. Similar is the last dream of Glaumvör, in the *Lay of Atli*, in which she sees dead women, clothed in sad-coloured weeds, come to call her husband Gunnar to the realms of the dead. It is characteristic of the stern Teutonic conception of the workings of Fate that dreams are only seldom warnings to be profited by; oftener they are foreshadowings of an inevitable doom. The gods never appear in dreams until faith in their divinity has been extinguished by Christianity. On the other hand, we must note that evil dreams beset the god Balder before his death (Vegtamskviða, in the Older Edda). Nightmares were not classed as dreams among the Teutonic people, but were (and indeed frequently are) attributed to the actual presence on the bed of a supernatural being, a *mara*, *alp*, or *trude*, or to the witchcraft of an ill-disposed neighbour.

In Scandinavia, where the interpretation of dreams was a secular art, unassociated with either magic or religion, the introduction of Christianity did not lessen the esteem in which it was held. Thus it is evidently no disgrace to the Icelandic bishop St. Thorlák that he took great pleasure in the recital of dreams. In England, however, the study of dreams is denounced by an early archbishop, together with magical practices, soothsaying, and the like. That it held a lower place in England than in Scandinavia seems also clear from the absence of dreams as a literary device in Old English poems. In Germany, as we have seen, the *Nibelungenlied* affords evidence for the same views on dreaming as prevailed in Scandinavia; but, on the other hand, we find Walther von der Vogelweide making fun both of dreams and of the wise women who professed to interpret them. At the present day, however, Germany is full of 'Traumbücher,' giving rules for the interpretation of dreams, and especially as to the methods of detecting, in some detail of a dream, a lucky number in the State lotteries. These books have an immense sale, and it is a significant fact that in some parts of Germany the lottery agents themselves sell 'Traumbücher,' and that in Austria they have been forbidden by law to do so. In Franconia, the interpretation of dreams for lottery purposes is a kind of secret knowledge, very profitable to its professors.

It is a firm belief in most Teutonic countries that to sleep in a new house, or at least in a new bed, is the best method of securing a dream; it was the method known in the Middle Ages, and was recommended to King Gorm of Denmark in heathen times. A curious variant of this practice was adopted by King Halfdan the Black. This Norwegian king slept in a pig-sty in order to cure himself of the habit of dreamless sleep, which was considered a disquieting mental disease. In some parts of Germany it is thought that, if the dreamer refrains from telling a bad dream until after midday, its accomplishment will be prevented. The frequent refusal of persons in the Icelandic Sagas to relate their dreams, or their protests of disbelief in dreams, may possibly be due to a similar idea. Without parallel in Teutonic sources is the death-bringing dream mentioned in the Icelandic *Ljósvetning Saga*, where the dream had such power that the first person who heard it must die.

Certain nights, whose significance dates from heathen times, are considered the most important for dreams almost all over Teutonic Europe, especially the Twelve Nights (the heathen Yule), and Midsummer Night. Both in Sweden and in Germany it is the custom to lay a bunch of nine different varieties of flowers under the pillow on Midsummer Eve, to ensure that the dreams of the night shall come true.

LITERATURE.—W. Henzen, *Über die Träume in der altnordischen Sagalitteratur*, Leipzig, 1890; A. Wuttke, *Der deutsche Volksaberglaube der Gegenwart*³, ed. Berlin, 1900; J. Grimm, *Deutsche Mythologie*⁴, Berlin, 1875–78; O. Schrader, *Reallexikon der indogerm. Altertumskunde*, Strassburg, 1901, *s.v.* 'Traum.'

B. S. PHILLPOTTS.

DREAMS AND SLEEP (Vedic).—The chief passage in Vedic literature for the explanation of the psychology of dreams is *Bṛhadāraṇyaka Upaniṣad*, iv. 3. 9–14. Two theories are advanced: (1) in dreams the soul takes its material from the world and constructs for itself by its own light the objects which it sees; (2) in sleep the soul abandons the body and roams where it will, hence the injunction not to awaken suddenly one who is sleeping, for in that case the soul may not find its way back to the body—an evil which is hard to cure. For the later workings over of this passage in the attempt to harmonize these theories, see Deussen, *Allgem. Gesch. der Philos.*, 1894 ff., I. ii. 271–274. For the present purpose the second hypothesis is the more important. Its difference from the first theory is ascribed by Deussen to the poetic form in which it is presented. More probably the difference is deeper, and we have in these verses a poetic version of an extremely old belief frequently found among peoples at a low stage of civilization, the existence of which among the Vedic peoples must be posited to explain the efforts made, from the Rigveda onwards, to remove the fancied effects of evil dreams.

A number of stanzas both in the Rigveda and in the Atharvaveda speak of an evil dream (*duḥsvapna, duḥṣvapnya*) as a calamity comparable with sin, disease, and witchcraft, or are employed in the ritual for the expiation of evil dreams. From the Rigveda may be cited: i. 89. 8–9, 99. 1, 114. 1, 120. 12, ii. 28. 10, v. 82. 4–5, viii. 47. 14–18, x. 36. 4, 37. 4, 127. 1 (the *Rātrisūkta*, or rather its *khila*), and 164. 1. The thirty-third *Pariśiṣṭa* of the Atharvaveda gives as the *duḥsvapnanāśanagaṇa* (list of hymns that destroy the effects of evil dreams): Atharv. iv. 17. 5, vi. 45. 1, 46. 1, vii. 100. 1, 108. 1–2, ix. 2. 2–3, x. 3. 6, xvi. 5. 1, and, as far as the subject-matter is concerned, might have included also: vi. 121. 1=vii. 83. 4, xvi. 6. 2, 8–9, xix. 56. 1, 57. 1. The last two hymns are employed at a ceremony called *svastyayana*, performed each morning to secure good fortune for the king (cf. Atharv. *Par.* viii. 1. 3). For the most part these stanzas contain little that is distinctive. Typical is Rigveda x. 37. 4: 'O Sūrya, with that light with which thou dost conquer darkness, with that sun with which thou dost rise over all living creatures, with that drive away from us all weakness, impiety, disease, and evil dreams.'

In the hieratic literature the manipulation of these stanzas in the ritual is also quite commonplace. Thus at *Aitareya Araṇyaka*, iii. 2. 4. 18, one who has had an evil dream is ordered to fast, cook a pot of rice in milk, make oblations of it, each accompanied by a verse of the *Rātrisūkta*, feast the Brahmans, and eat the leavings of the oblation. Similar directions are given in *Śāṅkhāyana Gṛhya Sūtra* v. 5. 3–13, with the additional requirement that the milk must be from a cow that is not black and that has a calf of the same colour. Furthermore, Rigveda i. 89. 8–9 must also be recited. In *Āśvalāyana Gṛhya Sūtra* iii. 6. 5–6 the oblation is of rice grains, and is made to the sun with Rigv. v. 82. 4–5, viii. 47. 14–18, or ii. 28. 10. With the first of these verses Sāmaveda i. 141 is identical. Its muttering is prescribed at *Gobhila Gṛhya Sūtra* iii. 3. 32 (cf. *Sāmavidhāna* i. 8. 7) in case of bad dreams. *Hiraṇyakeśin Gṛhya Sūtra* i. 17. 4 orders in a similar case a sacrifice of sesame and *ājya*, accompanied by verses, one of which is equivalent to Atharv. vii. 101. Similar is the practice of *Mānava Gṛhya Sūtra* ii. 15. *Kātyāyana Śrauta Sūtra* xxv. 11. 20 in the same case directs that a *dīkṣita* (one who has taken the bath that consecrates him for the performance of a sacrifice) must mutter a verse practically equivalent to Atharv. vii. 100. 1 (cf. also *Āpastambīya Śrauta Sūtra* x. 13. 11). The *Rigvidhāna* i. 23. 2, 24. 1, 25. 1, 30. 1, ii. 33. 2, iv. 20. 1 also enjoin the muttering of a number of verses to destroy the consequences of evil dreams. Noteworthy also is the fact that *Śāṅkhāyana Gṛhya Sūtra* i. 7. 2 includes most of the verses from the Rigveda in the list of verses to be recited each morning.

In the Atharvan ritual the practices are more striking; of them *Kauśika* xlvi. 9–13 gives a list. While reciting Atharv. vi. 45 and 46, the person who has had a bad dream washes his face. When the dream was very bad, he offers with these hymns a cake of mixed grains, or deposits, while reciting the hymns, such a cake in the land of an enemy. Or after a bad dream one may recite Atharv. vii. 100. 1 and turn on the other side. Whenever any one dreams that he has eaten, he must recite Atharv. vii. 101 and look round about him. Atharv. vi. 46. 2–3 may be substituted for any of the above mantras. Among the *Pariśiṣṭas*, the *Ghṛtāvekṣaṇa* viii. 2. 5 comprises in its effects the destruction of evil dreams, and in Atharv. *Par.* xxxiii. 1. 3 it is stated that Indra formerly suffered from such dreams until the *Ghṛtakambala* afforded him relief.

The ceremonies show that their purpose is not to secure immunity from the actual discomforts of nightmare, and also that the dream is not looked upon merely as a bad omen, but rather as an actual contamination. This view is but the logical result of combining the theory that in dreams the soul leaves the body and actually undergoes the experiences which the waking mind remembers with the Vedic belief that sin is not only a moral delinquency, but much more, a *quasi*-physical contamination. Under these circumstances an excursion into dreamland must have appeared to the Vedic mind as fraught with possible dangers. The methods taken to remove them naturally resemble the attempts to remove actual impurities, physical or spiritual—viz. ablutions and the transferring of the burden to another. The latter means, which is symbolized in the Atharvan ritual by the depositing of the cake in the enemy's land, is expressed in the Rigveda itself, viii. 47. 14 ff., by the prayer to Uṣas (Dawn) to transfer the evil dream to Trita Āptya, the scape-goat of the gods. For this mythological concept the Atharvaveda characteristically shows in its re-modelling of the stanzas a human enemy. In some cases apparently the contamination arises from association with spirits of the dead. Thus at *Śatapatha Brāhmaṇa* xiii. 8. 4. 4, persons returning from a funeral, among other precautions to escape the uncanny influences, wipe themselves with an *apamārga* plant, imploring it to drive away, among other evils, bad dreams. The association with the world of Yama may also be seen in Atharv. vi. 46, xix. 56; and it is most probable that the 'friend' of Rigv. ii. 28. 10 (=*Māitrāyaṇī Saṁhitā* iv. 229. 3) who speaks to one of danger in sleep, and against whom Varuṇa's protection is implored, is a departed spirit.

Auspicious dreams naturally appear much less frequently in the ritual. At *Chhāndogya Upaniṣad* v. 2. 8–9 it is stated that if, during the progress of a sacrifice intended to procure the fulfilment of a wish, the sacrificer sees in his dreams a woman, he may infer the success of his sacrifice.

Divination by means of dreams is attested by *Sāmavidhāna* iii. 4. 1–2, where two ceremonies are described that ensure prophetic dreams.

Dreams as omens.—That the interpretation of dreams must have begun to occupy the attention of the Brahmans at a very early period is implied in the very fact of the recognition of the evil character of some dreams. It is also corroborated by the mention at an early time of certain minute particulars as constituting evil dreams. Thus Rigv. viii. 47. 15 mentions as ominous the making of an ornament, or the weaving of a garland (for explanation of these omens from the later literature, cf. Pischel, *ZDMG* xl. 111). The *Aitareya Āraṇyaka* iii. 2. 4. 16 ff. gives a number of dreams that forebode death: *e.g.*, if a person sees a black man with black teeth and that man kills him, if a boar kills him, if a monkey jumps on him, if he is carried swiftly by the wind, if he swallows gold (emblematic of life) and vomits it, if he eats honey or chews stalks, or wears a single (red) lotus, or drives a chariot harnessed with asses or boars, or, wearing a wreath of red flowers, drives a black cow with a black calf towards the south (cf. Aufrecht, *ZDMG* xxxii. 573 ff.). The explanation of the requirement (see above) that dreaming of eating shall be followed by an expiation is doubtful. Caland regards it as an omen of lack of food, on the principle that dreams go by contraries. But dreaming of eating is in itself a good omen (cf. Pischel, *Album-Kern*, Leyden, 1903, p. 115 ff.). Pischel's explanation, that it is the failure to find in the morning the food dreamed of which constitutes the omen, seems forced. The commentator's remark, that while reciting Atharv. vii. 101 he looks around as if he had eaten food, suggests a different explanation. His soul has incautiously eaten food—an act surrounded by superstitious practices because of the supposed danger of the entrance of a demon (see DISEASE AND MEDICINE Vedic]),—and the dreamer now seeks to take the precautions which his soul omitted in the dream.

LITERATURE.—The minuteness of the omens cited points to a full development of this pseudo-science at an early period. In agreement with them are the systematic expositions of the subject, although the surviving works are of a much later date. First among these is to be mentioned the sixty-eighth *Pariśiṣṭa* of the Atharvaveda, entitled *Svapnādhyāya* (the chapter on dreams). Cf. *The Pariśiṣṭas of the Atharvaveda*, ed. G. M. Bolling and J. v. Negelein, vol. i. Leipzig, 1909–10. Certain phases of the subject are treated in the Purāṇas (cf. *Matsya P.* 242, *Mārkaṇḍeya P.* 43, *Vāyu P.* 19, *Agni P.* 228. 14, *Brahmavaivarta P.* iv. 76) and the astrological works. The Epics also contain tales of prophetic dreams; cf. *Mahābhārata* v. 143. 30 ff.; *Rām.* ii. 69. 15 (Schlegel), v. 27. 14 ff. (Gorresio). The instances of visions mentioned in Indian literature have been collected by L. Scherman, *Materialien zur Gesch. der ind. Visionslitteratur*, Leipzig, 1892; cf. also E. Hultzsch, *Prolegomena zu des Vasantarāja Çākuna*, do. 1879, p. 15 ff. A detailed treatment of the dream superstitions of the Hindus is about to be published by J. v. Negelein.

G. M. BOLLING.

DRESS.—An analysis of the relations of man's clothing with his development in social evolution will naturally be chiefly concerned with psychological categories. When once instituted, for whatever reasons or by whatever process, dress became a source of psychical reactions, often complex, to a greater extent (owing to its more intimate connexion with personality) than any other material product of intelligence. Some outline of the historical development of dress will be suggested, rather than drawn, as a guide to the main inquiry. The practical or, if one may use the term, the biological uses and meaning of dress, are simple enough and agreed upon. These form the first state of the material to be employed by the social consciousness. Its secondary states are a subject in themselves.

1. Origins.—The primary significance of dress becomes a difficult question as soon as we pass from the institution in being to its earliest stages and its origin. For speculation alone is possible when dealing with the genesis of dress. Its conclusions will be probable, in proportion as they satisfactorily bridge the gulf between the natural and the artificial stages of human evolution. The information supplied by those of the latter that are presumably nearest to the natural state, to *Protanthropus*, is not in itself a key to the origin of clothing, but, on the other hand, the mere analogy of animal-life is still less helpful. An animal has a natural covering more efficient for the two uses of protection against the environment and of ornamentation as a sexual stimulus. An animal may become adapted to a change, for instance to an Arctic climate, by growing a thick fur which is white. It may be supposed that, to meet a similar change, man invents the use of artificial coverings. But this old argument is contradicted by all the facts.

It may serve, however, to point by contrast the actual continuity of the natural and the artificial stages, the physical and the psychical stages, of our evolution. If we say that man is the only animal that uses an artificial covering for the body, we are apt to forget that even when clothed he is subject to the same environmental influences as in the ages before dress. Again, there is no hint that the approach of a glacial epoch inaugurated the invention of dress. But it is an established fact that the survivors of immigrants to changed conditions of climate and geological environment become physically adapted by some means of interaction and in certain directions of structure, which are just coming to be recognized. The British settlers in North America have assumed the aboriginal type of the Indian face and head; migrants from lowlands to uplands develop roundheadedness; from the temperate zone to the tropics man develops frizzly hair, and so on. The most obvious of these natural adaptations, physiologically produced, to the environment is pigmentation. The skin of man is graded in colour from the Equator to the Pole. The deeper pigmentation of the tropical skin is a protection against the actinic rays of the sun; the blondness of northern races, like the white colour of Arctic animals, retains the heat of the body.

If we followed the analogy of the animal, we should have to take into account the fact that a mechanical intelligence enables it to obviate certain disadvantages of its natural covering. The animal never exposes itself unnecessarily; its work, in the case of the larger animals, is done at night, not in the glare of the sun. Automatically it acquires an artificial covering in the form of shelter. If man in a natural state followed a similar principle, he would be at no more disadvantage than is the animal. A similar argument applies to the other use mentioned above, namely, sexual decoration. What these considerations suggest is that man was not forced by necessity to invent. The reason is at once deeper and simpler. Again, we get the conclusion that one primary use and meaning of dress is not so much to provide an adaptation to a climate as to enable man to be superior to weather; in other words, to enable him to move and be active in circumstances where animals seek shelter. The principle is implicit in the frequent proverbial comparison of clothing to a house.

Dress, in fact, as a secondary human character, must be treated, as regards its origins, in the same way as human weapons, tools, and machines. Dress increases the static resisting power of the surface of the body, just as tools increase the dynamic capacity of the limbs. It is an extension (and thereby an intension) of the passive area of the person, just as a tool is of the active mechanism of the arm. It is a second skin, as the other is a second hand.

Further, if we take an inclusive view of evolution, admitting no break between the natural and the artificial, but regarding the latter as a sequence to the former, we shall be in a position to accept indications that both stages, and not the former only, are subject to the operation of the same mechanical laws, and show (with the necessary limitations) similar results. These laws belong to the interaction of the organism and the environment, and the results are found in what is called adaptation, an optimum of equilibrium, a balanced interaction, between the two. In this connexion we may take examples from two well-marked stages in the evolution of our subject, the one showing a deficiency, the other a sufficiency, of the artificial covering of the body. A good observer remarks of the Indians of Guiana, not as a result of habituation, but as a first impression of their naked forms, that

> 'it is a most curious but certain fact that these people, even as they wander in the streets of Georgetown, do not appear naked.'[1]

The other case is that of the Chaco Indians:

> 'The Indian is perfectly suited to his environment; even his picturesque costume and the ornamental painting with which he adorns his body is in perfect harmony with his surroundings. The colours blend so beautifully that there is no doubt whatever that the Indian has, in a very great degree, the idea of fitness and harmony.'[2]

If we qualify in the last sentence the word 'idea'

[1] E. F. Im Thurn, *Indians of Guiana*, 1883, p. 194.

[2] W. B. Grubb, *An Unknown People in an Unknown Land: The Indians of the Paraguayan Chaco*, 1911, p. 55.

by the adjective 'automatic' or 'unconscious,' we shall have a sound explanation of a very remarkable phenomenon. The point of the phenomenon is that the evolution of man's artificial covering maintains a balance or harmony with the environment, particularly in respect to light, just as was the case with the naked Indian skins, arrived at just as mechanically, but through the unconscious reaction of the retina. Thus, there is a real continuity between the adaptive colour of the chameleon, and similar cases of so-called protective coloration (which is primarily merely a mechanical attuning to the environment), and the harmony which human dress may show with its surroundings. The selective process has not been conscious, but neither has it been accidental. It is the result of law. Equally unconscious in its first stages was the adaptation of dress to temperature.

This brings us no nearer to the origins of dress, though it clears the ground. Still further to simplify speculation, we may notice some prevalent hypotheses on the subject. Dress being a covering, it assumes, when instituted, all the applicable meanings which the idea of covering involves. But it by no means follows that all of these, or even any, were responsible for its original institution.

There is, first, the hypothesis that clothing originated in *the decorative impulse.* This has the merit of providing a cause which could operate through unconscious intelligence, automatic feeling. Stanley Hall found that of the three functions of clothing whose realization and expression he investigated in a *questionnaire*—protection, ornament, and Lotzean self-feeling—the second is by far the most conspicuous in childhood. The child is unconscious of sex, otherwise this statistical result might be brought into line with the sexual ornamentation of animals. And, though it is unsafe to press any analogy between the civilized child and the savage, the savages known to science are, as a rule, very fond of finery, absolutely, and not always in relation to the other sex.

'The natural man,' says Ratzel,[1] 'will undergo any trouble, any discomfort, in order to beautify himself to the best of his power.'

Dandies, Im Thurn[2] remarks, are about as frequent among the Indians as in civilized communities. At Port Moresby, in New Guinea, young men actually practise tight-lacing, to be smart and fashionable.[3] In these spheres, indeed, it is chiefly the young, if not mere children, who express the impulse to decoration. Of the Dayaks of Borneo a good observer has remarked that a

'love of finery is inherent in the young of both sexes; the elderly are less fond of it and often dress very shabbily, and save up their good clothes for their offspring.'[4]

It is in accordance with the rule among animals that among primitive peoples the male sex chiefly assumes decoration. Ornaments among the Indians of Guiana are more worn by men than by women. The stock ornamentation is paint; scented oils are used as vehicles.

'A man, when he wants to dress well, perhaps entirely coats both his feet up to the ankles with a crust of red; his whole trunk he sometimes stains uniformly with blue-black, more rarely with red, or he covers it with an intricate pattern of lines of either colour; he puts a streak of red along the bridge of his nose; where his eyebrows were till he pulled them out he puts two red lines; at the top of the arch of his forehead he puts a big lump of red paint, and probably he scatters other spots and lines somewhere on his face.' Down is often used with red paint.[5]

But this analogy is not to be pressed, though it is sound as far as it goes. It applies, that is, up to a certain point in social evolution. Beyond that point the balance inclines the other way, and for the last five hundred years of European civilization decorative dress has been confined to women. During a previous period of some centuries—to be regarded as one of unstable equilibrium—not only did the curve of luxury in dress reach its highest point, but there were attempts—spasmodic, it is true—to put down any tendency towards such luxury on the part of women, prostitutes being excepted. The previous stage—one of very considerable length—is still that of Islām; its significance and origin will concern us later. Its chief feature was the principle that female dress should be not ornamental, but protective—of the rights of the husband. Thus we may infer that, in the latest stage, woman as a sex has not only gained freedom, and the right to fascinate, previously possessed by the courtesan alone, but has also shifted the equilibrium of sex to a more permanent and efficient position. The story of woman's unconscious struggle for a monopoly of beauty in dress thus illustrates an important social movement.

In practical investigation it is difficult, as Ratzel[1] observes, to say 'where clothing ends and ornament begins,' or, on the previous hypothesis, where clothing springs out of ornament. Since either may obviously develop into the other when both are instituted, it is idle to examine such cases. Cases where one or the other is absolutely unknown might serve, but there are no examples of this. If an instance, moreover, of the presence of clothing and entire absence of ornament were observed, it would be impossible to argue that clothing cannot be subject to the decorative impulse. In any case, there is the self-feeling, satisfaction in individuality, to be reckoned with, for the impulse to finery is only one phase of it.

The supporters of the ornamentation hypothesis of the origin of dress have an apparently strong argument in the Brazilians and the Central Australians. These recently studied peoples possess no clothing in the ordinary sense of the term. But they wear ornament, and on special occasions a great deal of it. Brazilian men wear a string round the lower abdomen, the women a strip of bark-cloth along the perineum, tied to a similar abdominal thread. This is sometimes varied by a small decorative enlargement. The Central Australian man wears a waist-string, to which is tied a pubic tassel. Corresponding to the last in the case of the women is a very small apron. Leaving the waist-string out of account, we have remaining the question of the erogenous centre. In both the decoration hypothesis and the concealment hypothesis this centre is the focus of speculation. If the Australian tassel of the male sex and the leaf-like enlargement of the Brazilian woman's perineal thread are considered superficially, they may appear to be, if not ornaments, at least attractions. But if this be granted, it does not follow that we have here the first application of the idea of dress.

It would be impossible to make out a case to prove that these appurtenances can ever have satisfied the idea of *concealment*, as on the next hypothesis is assumed. This hypothesis is to the effect that male jealousy instituted clothing for married women. Ratzel[2] observes that, if clothing was originally instituted for purposes of protection only, the feet and ankles would have been protected first. Clothing, he holds, stands in unmistakable relation to the sexual life. 'The first to wear complete clothes is not the man, who has to dash through the forest, but the married woman.' The primary function of her dress is to render her unattractive to others, to conceal her body from other men's eyes. In the lower strata of human evolution he considers that dress as a protection from rain and cold is far less common.

[1] *Hist. of Mankind*, Eng. tr. 1896–8, i. 95.
[2] *Op. cit.* 199.
[3] Haddon, *Head-hunters*, 1901, p. 256.
[4] Brooke Low, in *JAI* xxii. (1892) 41.
[5] Im Thurn, *op. cit.* 195 ff.

[1] *Op. cit.* i. 95.
[2] *Ib.* i. 93 f.

But, if we may argue from the practice of existing savages, this hypothesis cannot hold even of the origin of female clothing. Only by straining can it be applied to that of men. It is certainly a *vera causa*, at a certain stage in barbarism (the stage when wives became 'property'), of the customs of shrouding and veiling women, and of confiscating all a maiden's ornaments and finery when she became a wife. But it does not explain the origin of the small apron worn in very early stages, or of the mere thread in the earliest, and we cannot deny these articles a place in the category of dress.

A frequent corollary of such views is that modesty is a result, not a cause, of clothing (so Sergi). But, as Havelock Ellis observes,

'many races which go absolutely naked possess a highly developed sense of modesty.'[1] Andamanese women 'are so modest that they will not renew their leaf aprons in the presence of one another, but retire to a secluded spot for this purpose; even when parting with one of their *bōd*-appendages [tails of leaves suspended from the back of the girdle] to a female friend the delicacy they manifest for the feelings of the bystanders in their mode of removing it almost amounts to prudishness'; yet they wear no clothing in the ordinary sense.[2] The Guiana Indians, when they want to change their single garment, either retire from sight or put the new over the old, and then withdraw the latter.[3] Modesty is 'in its origins independent of clothing; . . . physiological modesty takes precedence of anatomical modesty; and the primary factors of modesty were probably developed long before the discovery of either ornaments or garments. The rise of clothing probably had its first psychic basis on an emotion of modesty already compositely formed of' these elements.[4]

This last statement, of course, cannot hold of the ultimate genesis of clothing. But, once instituted, it was sure to coincide with emotions of modesty. The general connexion between modesty and dress is a subject of little importance, except in so far as it has involved the creation of false modesty, both individually and socially. Modesty, where there is dress, tends to be concentrated upon it mechanically. When clothing is once established, the growth of the conception of women as property emphasizes its importance, and increases the anatomical modesty of women. Waitz held that male jealousy is the primary origin of clothing, and therefore of modesty. Diderot had held this view. Often married women alone are clothed. It is as if before marriage a woman was free and naked; after marriage, clothed and a slave.

'The garment appears—illogically, though naturally—a moral and physical protection against any attack on his [the husband's] property.'[5]

But the fact of dress serving as concealment involved the possibility of *attraction by mystery*. Even when other emotions than modesty, emphasized by male jealousy, intervene, they may work together for sexual attraction.

'The social fear of arousing disgust combines easily and perfectly with any new development in the invention of ornament or clothing as sexual lures. Even among the most civilized races it has often been noted that the fashion of feminine garments (as also sometimes the use of scents) has the double object of concealing and attracting. It is so with the little apron of the young savage belle. The heightening of the attraction is indeed a logical outcome of the fear of evoking disgust.'[6]

Similarly we find in the most primitive clothing a curious interchange of concealment, protection, decoration, and advertisement. As has been hinted, when an appurtenance has come to be attached to the sexual area, the resulting psychical reactions are significant. In the previous natural stage there is no artificial stimulus; now, there is such an addition to the natural stimulus, first by mere attraction or signification, and later by decoration or veiling. In the mind of the subject also there comes, first, the consciousness of sex, and later the enhancing of self-feeling, which in the case of dress generally, and not merely sexual, is distributed throughout the personality. The subject's material personality is increased by clothing, and his psychical reaction is proportional to this. The result is a rich complex of self-consciousness, modesty, and self-feeling generally, the balance between them varying according to circumstances. But it is highly improbable that such impulses could have led to the invention of dress, much less of mere attachments and appurtenances. Their only means of expression would have been ornament.

[1] *Studies in the Psychology of Sex*, i. (1897) 5.
[2] Man, in *JAI* xii. (1882-83) 94, 331.
[3] Im Thurn, *op. cit.* 194.
[4] H. Ellis, *op. cit.* i. 37.
[5] *Ib.* 41.
[6] *Ib.* 39.

Finally, there is the *protection-hypothesis*. Sudden falls in the temperature, rains and winds and burning sunshine, the danger of injuring the feet and the skin of the body generally when in the forest, and the need of body-armour against the attacks of insects and of dangerous animals seem obvious reasons for the invention of dress. But they do not explain the process of invention, which is the main problem. The cloak, the skirt, the apron, cannot have been invented in answer to a need, directly, without any stages. The invention of cloth was first necessary, and this was suggested by some natural covering. The only line of development which seems possible is from protective ligatures. There are numerous facts which apparently point to such an origin of clothing. One of the most characteristic 'ornaments' of savages all over the world is the armlet. It is quite probable that this has an independent origin in the decorative impulse, like the necklace. But here and there we find bands worn round the ankles, knees, wrists, and elbows, the object of which is clearly to protect the sinews and muscles from strains. The pain of a strained muscle being eased by the grip of the hand, the suggestion of an artificial grip might naturally follow, and a system of ligatures would be the result.

The Nāgas wear black rings of cane round the knee—as some say, to give strength for climbing.[1] The Malays wear bands and ligatures to protect the muscles and prevent strains, as, for instance, round the wrists and below the knee.[2] Ratzel observes that arm-rings may be useful in striking and warding off blows. But the idea of a cestus is unlikely to be the primary motive for ligatures.[3] The Chacos wear anklets of feathers, chiefly to protect their feet against snake-bites.[4]

Wild peoples, in fact, understand quite well the limitations and the capacity of the human organism in respect to the environment. We may credit them with an adequate system of supplying natural deficiencies, and of assisting natural advantages also. For instance, the Malays explain the object of the papoose for infants as being to prevent the child from starting and so straining itself.[5] And it seems probable that there is a connexion between the earlier use of the ligature and the prevalent custom of wearing metal rings or wire as a decoration. Men and women of the Watusi wear round the ankles innumerable coils of iron wire, representing a weight of many pounds. The women wear heavy bracelets of brass.[6] It is possible, also, that in certain cases dress itself might have been developed from the same source. Thus, when we compare the following type of body-dress with the frequent use, in earlier stages, of a pliant bough or cane as a girdle, we can imagine the possibility that the invention of the sheet-form of covering might have been delayed by the extension of the bandage-form.

The garment, termed *lumiet*, of the Sakarang women, is a series of cane hoops covered with innumerable small brass links. The series encasing the waist fits close. It sometimes extends right up to the breasts. The Ulu Ai and Ngkari women wear eight to ten parallel rows of large brass rings round the waist. They are strung on rattans, and fixed to a cane network inside them. Dense coils of thick brass wire are also worn on the legs.[7]

[1] T. C. Hodson, *The Nāga Tribes of Manipur*, 1911, p. 23.
[2] Skeat-Blagden, *Pagan Races of the Malay Peninsula*, 1906, i. 140.
[3] Ratzel, *op. cit.* i. 99.
[4] Grubb, *op. cit.* 262.
[5] Skeat, *Malay Magic*, 1900, p. 335.
[6] L. Decle, in *JAI* xxiii. (1893) 425.
[7] Brooke Low, in *JAI* xxii. (1892) 40 f.

But the ligature as a primary stage of sheet-clothing might have developed merely by adding to its breadth. Given a girdle, we might suppose a natural enlargement of its depth. And among the various bands used by the lowest peoples there is a gradation of the kind. The armlets of the Indians of Guiana are broad cotton bands or string.[1] Yet there is no evidence to show that such a development, from the belt to the kilt, has been the main origin of the skirt-form of dress. A skirt supplying its own belt is generally a late modification.

Examination of the earliest peoples inevitably leads to a rejection of the ligature-hypothesis. Every consideration goes to show that the earliest ligature was not intended to support the muscles. It is inconceivable that the use of string in the Guiana example can be intended for such a purpose. In the next place, it must be borne in mind that the chief area of the organism with which dress proper is concerned is the central part of the body, the trunk. Now, the great majority of the lowest peoples known wear no clothes. Shelter is used instead. But there is very commonly a waist-string, and it is more used by men than by women. We assume that the girdle is the point of departure for the evolution of dress, and the mechanism of that departure will be presently discussed. But for the origin of body-clothing it is necessary to find the origin of the girdle. The civilized idea of a girdle is to bind up a skirt or trousers. This is certainly not its object among the earliest peoples, who have nothing to tie up. It might be supposed that the original purpose of the girdle was that of the abdominal belt, useful both as a muscle-ligature and to alleviate the pangs of hunger. But the earliest girdles are merely strings, and string is useless for such purposes. String, moreover, made of grass or vegetable fibre, or animal sinew or human hair, is an earlier invention than the bandage. Its first form was actually natural, the pliant bough or stem.

It is significant that this waist-string is chiefly a male appendage, and that it is worn neither tight nor very loose. Both facts are explained by the purpose for which the string is worn. It is neither a bandage nor a suspender, but a continuous pocket. The savage finds it indispensable for carrying articles which he constantly needs, and which otherwise would encumber his hands. Once fitted with a waist-string, the body, as a machine, is enormously improved, being able to carry the artificial aids of manual operations ready for use as occasion requires, without hampering the work of that universal lever, the hand.

We can only speculate vaguely as to the series of 'accidents' which led to the idea of the waist-string. It was, no doubt, analogous to the series which ended in the invention of artificial hands in the shape of weapons and tools, but it was certainly much later in time. The varied unconscious ideas of holding, gripping, and encircling, which the muscular experience of the hand imprinted on the brain, might have evolved the principle and practice of a hold-all round the trunk, without the occurrence of any fortunate accidents whatever. The natural position of the hands when at rest would be rejected by unconscious reasoning in favour of a more convenient spot, slightly higher, which would not interfere with the movements of the legs. The downward tapering of the thigh, moreover, renders it impossible to keep a string in position. In this connexion it is worth noting that knee- and ankle-bands are commonly used in various stages of culture for the purpose of holding implements.

The waist-string, therefore, being earlier than clothing proper, and being, as we have suggested, the point of departure for the wearing of coverings, we have next to examine the mechanism of the connexion between them. The use of the string as a holder being given, it would serve not only as a pocket, but as a suspender for leaves or bunches of grass, if for any reason these were required. The point to be emphasized here is that the presence of a suspender would suggest the suspension and therefore the regular use of articles for which there had been no original demand. If, for occasional purposes, a decoration or covering was desired, there was the waist-string ready for use. Central as it was, the decoration or covering would fall below it and be thus applied automatically to the perineal region. Similarly, the hair of the head is a natural holder, though much less efficient, and it is used to support leaf-coverings or flower-decorations.

It is unnecessary to enter upon a description of the various zones of the body which require protection, such as the spine at the neck and in the small of the back, against sun and cold, or the mucous membranes of the perineal region, against insects. The use of clothing of certain textures and colours to maintain a layer of air about the skin at a temperature adapted to that of the body, and to neutralize those rays of light which are deleterious to the nervous system and destructive of protoplasm, is also out of place here. We may note, however, that by unconscious selection the evolution of dress has probably followed a thoroughly hygienic course. But no principles of such hygiene, except the very simplest, can have occurred to primitive man. One of the simplest, however, we may admit for tropical races—the use of a protection against insects. The perineal region is most subject to their attacks when man is naked, owing to the sebaceous character of the surface and its relatively higher temperature. These facts, no doubt, more than anything else, are the explanation of primitive habits of depilation. But depilation is not a complete protection. Something positive is required. The use of bunches of grass or leaves is natural and inevitable, as soon as there is something to hold them, namely, the waist-string. A parallel method is the use of a second string depending from the waist-string in front and behind, and passing between the legs. The Brazilian strip of bast used by women, and the red thread which takes its place in the Trumai tribe, though 'they attract attention like ornaments instead of drawing attention away,' yet, as Von den Steinen[1] also satisfied himself, provide a protection against insects, a serious pest in the forests of Brazil. These inter-crural strings protect the mucous membrane, without, however, concealing the parts, as do leaves and grass. In the present connexion their chief interest is the use made of the waist-string. When cloth was invented, the first form of the loin-cloth was an extension of the inter-crural thread. It may be illustrated from the Indians of British Guiana, though it is practically universal, significantly enough, among tropical and sub-tropical peoples.

The Guiana man wears a narrow strip, called *lap*; it is passed between the legs, and the ends are brought up at back and front and suspended on a rope-like belt. The women wear an apron, called *queyu*, hung from a string round the waist. Very young children before wearing a cloth have a string round the waist. The *lap* is often made of bark, beaten till soft.[2] The *lap* method is employed by the Veddas of Ceylon,[3] and by numerous early races throughout the world.

As the various methods of draping and tying developed with man's familiarity with sheet-dress,

[1] Im Thurn, *op. cit.* 197.

[1] *Unter den Naturvölkern Zentral-Brasiliens*, Berlin, 1894, p. 190 f. For other protective coverings for the organs, against insects, see Wilken-Pleyte, *Handleiding voor de vergelijkende Volkenkunde van Nederlandsch-Indië*, Leyden, 1893, p. 37 f.

[2] Im Thurn, *op. cit.* 194.

[3] C. G. and B. Z. Seligmann, *The Veddas*, 1911, p. 93.

the later form of loin-cloth naturally superseded the earlier. A length of cloth passed round the waist and between the legs, the ends depending, was both more convenient and more comfortable. In the first place it supplied a broader bandage, and, being two articles in one, was more easily kept in position. This is the familiar and widely prevalent 'loin-cloth.' Secondly, it supplied a more efficient method of binding the male organs. There is no doubt that the naked male often finds it desirable, for obvious anatomical reasons which do not trouble the animal (whose organs are practically withdrawn into the perineal surface), to confine these parts. Hence, it may be conjectured, the use of a perineal cloth for men and of a mere apron or skirt for women—a distinction of the earliest date and generally maintained. As showing the practice of such confinement, it is enough to point to a common use of the earlier waist-string. The end of the organ is placed under the string, made tight enough to hold it flat against the abdomen.[1]

The development of the apron and skirt is a simple extension (given the suspensory string and the invention of cloth) of the use of leaves hung from the waist. The frequent use of a rear-apron as a sitting-mat is a later detail, having no influence upon the skirt, which developed independently. A frequent variation is the fringe. A combination of front- and rear-aprons no doubt preceded the complete skirt. When the latter was developed, new methods of suspension were adopted, among them being one similar to that of the loin-cloth, the upper edge serving as a bandage. The use of the waist-string by women, for keeping an inter-crural cloth or tampon in place during the periods, may be referred to; but it did not lead to the development of any article of attire. One example of its use, however, is instructive, as showing how a temporary protection may pass into a regular appendage.

Among the majority of the Nyasa tribes a woman during her periods wears a small piece of calico corresponding to a diaper. The same is worn after childbirth. This is the case generally in Nyasaland. But Angoni women 'always wear them.'[2]

The protection-hypothesis of the origin of dress may thus be adopted, if we qualify it by a scheme of development as suggested above. When once instituted as a custom, the wearing of leaves or bark-cloth upon the abdominal region served to focus various psychical reactions. One of the earliest of these was the impulse to emphasize the primary sexual characters. It is an impulse shown among the great majority of early races in their observances at the attainment of puberty, and it is, as a rule, at that period that sexual dress or ornament is assumed. Among civilized peoples, in the Middle Ages and in modern times, the impulse is well marked by various fashions—the phallocrypt and the tail of the savage having their European analogues. A less direct but even more constant instance of the same recognition is the assigning of the skirt to women as the more sedentary, and trousers to men as the more active sex. The suggestion sometimes met with, that the skirt is an adaptation for sexual protection, need only be mentioned to be dismissed. The Central Australian pubic tassel and similar appendages will here find significance, but it is improbable that such accentuation was their original purpose. Once instituted for protection, the other ideas followed. Another of these, which at once received an artificial focus, was the emotion of modesty. It has been observed among the higher animals that the female by various postures guards the sexual centres from the undesired advances of the male. The assumption of a waist-cloth does not actually serve the same purpose, but it constitutes a permanent psychical suggestion of inviolability. Similarly, the use of any appendage or covering involves the possibility of attraction, either by mere notification, by the addition of decoration, or, later, by the suggestion of mystery.

[1] See Wilken-Pleyte, 38.
[2] H. S. Stannus, *JAI* xl. (1910) 321.

Further than this speculation as to origins need not be carried. The various forms and fashions of dress, and the customs connected with it, will supply examples of the material as well as of the psychological evolution of the subject.

2. Material and form.—It is proposed to describe the types of human dress and the materials of which it has been composed only so far as is necessary to illustrate the religious and social significance of dress as an index to psychological evolution.

If dress be taken to include anything worn on the person other than offensive and defensive armour, there is hardly a single known substance, from iron to air, which has not for one reason or another been employed; while for purposes of decoration or protection against the supernatural, the very utmost use has been made of the natural covering of the organism, in the way of hair-dress, skin-painting, and tatuing, and the wearing of ornaments and amulets on or in the projecting points of the body, particularly various orifices. In the earlier stages two features are prominent—the savage is apt to regard anything he wears as an ornament, though it may be actually a protection. Also, the less body-covering there is, the greater tendency to painting, scarification, and tatuing. 'Having,' as Gautier said, 'no clothes to embroider, they embroider themselves.' As examples of the earliest stages the following are typical:

The Niam-Niam negress wears a single leaf only, suspended by a string from the waist.[1] The Indians of Central Brazil wear a string round the lower abdomen. It is worn after puberty, but it conceals nothing, of course. The women wear a little strip of bast passing between the legs; in some tribes the *uluri*, a triangular decorative piece of bark bast, is worn.[2] 'Except for waist-bands, forehead-bands, necklets, armlets, and a conventional pubic tassel, shell, or, in the case of the women, a small apron, the Central Australian native is naked.' The waist-string is made of human hair. The pubic tassel is a fan-shaped structure of fur-strings, about the size of a five shilling piece. Being covered at corroboree times with gypsum, it serves as a decoration rather than a covering. The Arunta and Luritcha women do not wear even an apron.[3] In the Western islands of Torres Straits the men are naked; the women wear a tuft of grass or split *pandanus* leaves; for dancing, a short petticoat of shred *pandanus* leaves is worn over this.[4] In Samoa the only necessary garment was for men and women an apron of leaves.[5]

The New Ireland men 'go absolutely naked'; the women wear aprons of grass, suspended from cinctures made of beads strung on threads of aloe-leaves. A bonnet of palm leaves is also worn by the women.[6] The Australians of the South show an advance on those of the Centre. The Euahlayi woman's *goomillah* is a waist-string of opossum-sinew, with strands of hair in front. The Central Australian woman has not even a string. The Euahlayi man's *waywah* is a belt, six inches wide, of sinews and hair, with four tufts. Opossum-skin rugs are worn in winter.[7]

Among the Curetu of the Amazons, the men wore a girdle of woollen thread, but the women were entirely naked. The neighbouring Guaycurus reversed the custom, the men being naked and the women wearing a short petticoat.[8] In other tribes of the same region both sexes were quite nude.[9]

'The costume and ornamentation prevalent with the Lower Congo men is principally confined to a grass loin-cloth, and mutilation of the two incisor teeth of the upper jaw; the women wear a small apron in front and behind,' and ear decorations of wood and metal.[10] The Garo petticoat was less than a foot in depth. To allow freedom of movement it was fastened only at the upper corners.[11] The Wankonda men wear nothing

[1] Ratzel, i. 94.
[2] K. von den Steinen, 190 f.
[3] Spencer-Gillen[a], 570, 572.
[4] Haddon, in *JAI* xix. (1890) 368, 431.
[5] Turner, *Samoa*, 1884, p. 121.
[6] A. J. Duffield, in *JAI* xv. (1886) 117.
[7] K. Langloh Parker, *The Euahlayi Tribe*, 1905, p. 120 f.
[8] C. R. Markham, in *JAI* xl. 98, 101.
[9] *Ib.* p. 122.
[10] H. Ward, in *JAI* xxiv. (1894) 293.
[11] E. T. Dalton, *Ethnology of Bengal*, 1872, p. 66.

but a ring of brass wire round the abdomen. The women wear a tiny bead-work apron, exactly resembling that of the Kaffirs.[1] The women at Upoto wear no clothes whatever.[2] In the Shortlands the men are naked; the women wear leaves in a waist-string. In New Britain both sexes are nude.[3] Of Central Africa, Angus gives as his experience: the more naked the people and the more to us obscene and shameless their manners and customs, the more moral and strict they are in the matter of sexual intercourse.[4] The fact should be noted, in leaving the subject of the scantiest form of dress, as being a regular concomitant of nakedness.

Variations of the most opposite character in the same stage of culture are a frequent problem. In some cases they may be accounted for by foreign influence. But any accident may institute a fashion. Thus, the Upoto women are entirely nude;[5] but among the Akikuyu the smallest girl wears an apron.[6]

In tropical countries the use of *leaves* as occasional or permanent garments is regular. Several peoples, such as the East Indian islanders, in Ceram, for example, and the Polynesians, elevated the practice into an art. Noticeable details are the single-leaf head-dress, and leaves fixed in arm-bands.

The Samoans wore girdles of *ti*-leaves (*Cordyline terminalis*), gathered when turning yellow.[7] Adorned with flowers, their figures were a notable example of adaptation to island scenery. The Niam-Niam negress wears a leaf tied to a girdle.[8] Paliyan women are sometimes dressed in a leaf-girdle only. Goṇḍ women wear bunches of twigs round the waist. The Juángs of Chotā Nāgpur are famous for their leaf-dresses. When dry and crackly, they are changed for fresh leaves.[9] The Semangs of the Malay Peninsula wear girdles of leaves. On festive occasions, ligatures of *Licuala* leaf were used to hold flowers on the arms; flowers were also fastened in the girdle and the head-fillet, both made of this leaf. The Sakai wear a waist-cord from which leaves depend in a fringe.[10] This is retained under the cloth *sarong*. At feasts their dress is like that of the Semang, a wreath of leaves or a turban of cloth being indifferently used. The dancing-dress of the Jakun is made of the leaves of the *serdang* palm, and consists of an elaborate fringed head-dress, a bandolier, and belt. Leaf-aprons are still worn by Kōragar women.[11]

Another natural covering is *bark*.

'In tropical regions of both hemispheres, where scanty clothing is needed, certain trees weave their inner bark into an excellent cloth, the climax of which is the celebrated *tapa* of Polynesia.'[12] Taken from the *wauki*, or paper-mulberry (*Morus papyrifera*),[13] the bark was beaten to a soft consistency. In tropical Africa a species of *Brachystegia* (Order *Leguminosæ*) is generally used as a source of bark-cloth. The bark is made into kilts, cloths, band-boxes, canoes, roofing, and various useful articles.[14] The Guiana Indian wears sandals of the leaf stalk of the *aeta* palm (*Mauritia flexuosa*). They are made in a few minutes, and careful measurements are taken. They wear out in a few hours.[15]

The Kayans use bark-cloth, which they dye red and yellow.[16] Throughout Eastern Asia, the Malay Archipelago, and Polynesia, the girdle of bark-cloth is widely diffused. The Sakai hammer the bark of the *ipoh* tree (*Antiaris toxicaria*) and of the wild breadfruit (*Artocarpus*) so as to expel the sap. It is then washed and dried. The loin-cloth made of this by the Semang is the loin-cloth proper, folded round the waist, and tucked through the front after passing between the legs. Both this and the women's fringe of leaves are worn under the Malay *sarong*, where this has been introduced.[17]

The Woolwa Indians make their clothes, the *tounoo* and the sleeping-sheet, from the bark of trees. The women beat this on a smooth log with a mallet shaped like a club and having grooves which give to the bark-cloth the texture and appearance of a mesh. The better sort of garments are made of stout cotton, of many colours and mixed with the down and feathers of birds.[18] Watusi women wear bark-cloth fastened above the breasts and falling below the knees.[19] Formerly the Veddas of Ceylon made bark-cloth from the *riti* (*Antiaris innoxia*).[20]

1 Sir H. H. Johnston, *British Central Africa*, 1897, p. 408 ff.
2 T. H. Parke, *Equatorial Africa*, 1891, p. 61.
3 G. Brown, *Melanesians and Polynesians*, 1910, pp. 202, 310.
4 *ZE* vi. (1898) 479.
5 H. Ward, *l.c.*
6 Routledge, *With a Prehistoric People*, 1910, p. 139.
7 G. Brown, 315.
8 Ratzel, i. 94.
9 W. Crooke, *Things Indian*, 1906, p. 156 f.
10 Skeat-Blagden, i. 53, 142, 364, ii. 118, 124, 136 f.
11 J. M. Campbell, in *IA* xxiv. (1895) 154.
12 O. T. Mason, in *Amer. Anthropologist*, vii. (1894) 144.
13 E. Tregear, *Maori Comparative Dictionary* (Wellington, N.Z., 1891), *s.v.*; *tapa* is the *kapa* of the Hawaiians.
14 *JAI* xxii. (1892) 145, reprint from the *Kew Bulletin*.
15 Im Thurn, 195.
16 Hose, in *JAI* xxiii. (1893) 165.
17 Skeat-Blagden, i. 140 ff., 151.
18 H. A. Wickham, in *JAI* xxiv. (1894) 203 f.
19 L. Decle, in *JAI* xxiii. (1894) 425.
20 C. G. and B. Z. Seligmann, 93.

The 'shirt-tree' of Brazil is a *Lecythis*. Its pliant bark is easily stripped. From a length of the trunk a cylinder of bark is taken, and beaten soft. Two arm-holes are cut, and it is ready for wear.[1] The bark of the 'sacking-tree' is still used for clothes in Western India. The men of the Abors of Assam wear loin-cloths of bark. Bark-cloth was worn by the ancient Hindu ascetics.[2]

Various circumstances, which need not be detailed, make certain peoples adopt *leather* or *fur* garments. Against cold and rain these are still unsurpassed.

The men of the Akamba wore cloaks of ox-hide before the introduction of trade-blankets.[3] The Masai wore dressed skins before cotton cloth was introduced.[4] The only garment of a Chaco Indian woman is a skin petticoat, but in cold weather a mantle of skins is worn.[5] The Ainus use bear-skins for clothing.[6] Arctic and sub-Arctic peoples, like the Eskimo, have made fur-dress into a very perfect covering.

Such ready-made articles of early dress contained both the suggestion and the material of *manufactured cloth.* The animal, insect, and vegetable worlds were gradually exploited for the purpose. Animals like the sheep and the llama, trees like the palm, have both supported man and inspired his invention. Thus from the Mauritia palm the natives of the Orinoco derived wood for building; from its leaf they made clothing, fishing nets, and hammocks. Its sap supplied a fermented drink.[7] Materials which have complex possibilities are more likely to encourage the inventive impulse than is sheer necessity. 'Weaving is the next art, after agriculture and building, to acquire economical importance.'[8] The hair of domesticated animals superseded skins; cotton and linen superseded leaves, grass-matting, and the rougher vegetable fibres, palm, aloe, hemp, and the like. With the introduction of an artificial dress-material the savage stage of the evolution comes to an end. But for various reasons many barbarian peoples draw at times upon the old natural fabrics. In some cases, like that of the Sakai leaf-girdle,[9] it is regularly used in combination with woven material. The earliest stages of the barbarian period are illustrated by the following typical account of home-made fabric, dye, and dress.

The dress of the Fulas is 'universally the cotton cloths made by themselves out of the plants grown in almost every village; it is carded by an instrument, probably imported, which is very much like a wire brush about 8 inches by 9 inches, and woven on an ingenious loom.' The cotton is dyed blue with indigo, cultivated by the natives, and is marked by a white pattern produced by tying portions of the cloth together before dipping it.[10]

It is significant that in these stages the form of the material leads to actualization of its possibilities, and emphasizes simultaneously covering, concealment, and decoration. The third type of the perineal garment becomes regular: namely, for men, the loin and inter-crural cloth combined in one length, and for women the folded petticoat. For example, the ordinary garment of Fula women is a single cloth, either folded round and tucked in under the arms or wound round the waist, leaving the breast exposed.[11] This type has been largely used by both sexes. In an extended form it is the *sarong* of the Malays. The loin-cloth of men is the *maro* of the Polynesians. Both garments have the same method of fastening—a double or treble wrapping round the waist. From it have developed the suspended or belted skirts of women and kilts of men. A combination of this principle with that of the shoulder-wrap leads to the tunic and robes generally. The toga-form of the outer robe is an echo, in its method of wrapping, of the earliest folded garment for the lower body. The loin-

1 Ratzel, i. 96.
2 Crooke, 157.
3 C. W. Hobley, *Ethnology of A-Kamba*, Cambridge, 1910, p. 40.
4 Hollis, *The Masai*, 1905, p. 301.
5 Grubb, 69.
6 Frazer, *GB*², 1900, ii. 375.
7 E. J. Payne, *History of the New World called America*, Oxford, 1892, i. 309.
8 *Ib.* i. 369.
9 See preced. column.
10 G. F. Scott Elliot, in *JAI* xxiii. (1893) 80 f.
11 *Ib.* 81.

cloth proper of the male sex has an extremely wide prevalence.[1]

As an example, the *tounoo* of the Woolwa Indians, or *palpra* of the Mosquitos, is a cloth, 24 inches wide, worn by men round the waist, the ends being passed between the legs, and hanging down in front to below the knee.[2] The *tjawat* of the East Indian Islands is a bark cloth or manufactured cloth twice wound round the waist and then passed between the legs from back to front, the end hanging over centrally. It sometimes survives into early civilization, as among the Hindus.

With improvement in cloth and consequent increase in lightness and folding capacity, a modification was made by many peoples, namely, in the omission of the inter-crural method. Externally there is little difference in appearance except for the greater volume of the newer fashion. The two styles are often confused under the term 'loin-cloth.' The second is the *kain* of the Indonesians, developing into the *sarong* of the Malays.

From the loin-cloth proper were developed drawers and trousers, a type of garment not seldom found among women instead of the petticoat. In all these later extensions of the idea of a loose and modifiable artificial skin, the earliest addition to the natural surface, the primitive waist-string, is still visible. As a girdle and belt it supports various garments; by creating folds it supplies once more its original purpose as a pocket. Mantles, cloaks, and caps in the barbarian stages are confined to their particular purpose, protection against rain, wind, and sun. In the latest civilizations their use becomes regular for outdoor life; the barbarian cloak is duplicated into the coat and the overcoat; the cap into the hat and the umbrella. Of the tribes of Nyasaland it is reported that 'the amount of clothing worn varies very considerably, from nothing to European garments.'[3] Such a case will serve to combine in one short view some of the contrasts of the various stages and some of the principles of dress.

The young children of the Yao and Angoni run naked. Sometimes one has a strip of cloth suspended from the waist-string. A man wears a similar loin-cloth, and a woman an apron, eighteen inches deep. Both are suspended from the waist-string. The more prosperous men wear calico from the waist to the knee, wrapped round the body and held by a belt. Sometimes it is extended to fold across the chest. Women wear a cloth folded across the upper part of the chest. Often men and women have two cloths, one for the waist, the other for the chest. The Angoni wear the latter toga-fashion, a fold being carried on the left arm. A chief wears three such togas—blue, white, and another colour. European calico is now used; formerly bark-cloth and skins. Men now wear a turban, introduced by Arabs. In the house a woman still wears only a bead apron.[4]

In spite of the underlying similarity of principles, universally found, dress more than any external feature distinguishes race from race and tribe from tribe. While distinguishing a social unit it emphasizes its internal solidarity. In this latter sphere there is, again, room for individual distinction. Some types of racial and communal costume may be sketched.

'The ordinary male attire [of the Dayaks of Borneo] consists of a *sirat* or waist-cloth, a *labong* or head-dress, and a *takai buriet* or seat-mat; the full dress consists of the above with the addition of a *klambi* or jacket, and a *dangdong* or shawl.' The female attire is a *bidang* or short petticoat; when out of doors, a *klambi* or jacket is added.[5] The *sirat* (*chawat* of the Malays)[6] is six yards long, but young men wear it as long as twelve or fourteen yards, twisting and coiling it 'with great precision round and round their body until the waist and stomach are fully enveloped in its folds. . . . A practised eye can tell in a moment to what tribe or section of a tribe an individual belongs, not merely by the length of his waist-cloth and the way in which it is wound on, but also by its colour and the fashion in which it is decorated at its extremities.' The *labong* is a cloth a yard or two in length, and worn as a turban, but one end stands up straight from the forehead. Some wear a cap, *selapok*, made of plaited rush or cane. The *takai buriet* is a small mat tied with string round the waist so as to cover the hindquarters and serve as a portable seat. It is made of split cane. The *klambi* (*baju* of Malays) is of home-grown cotton. The sleeves are open under the armpits. There is a great variety of fashions in the cut and colour of the *klambi*. The *dangdong* is slung over one shoulder. The *bidang* is a petticoat reaching from waist to knee, folded over in front and tucked in on one side. The *klambi* is like that of the men, but larger. Marriageable girls wear chaplets of odoriferous berries.[1]

The Kayan petticoat is open on one side to enable the wearer to walk with freedom.[2] This is a general result of the 'natural' petticoat folded round the hips.

The skin garments of North American Indians comprise a skirt of buckskin with a belt, leggings attached to the belt, moccasins, socks of sage-brush, and the skin robe or shawl, generally superseded by the blanket.[3] The only difference between the dress of the two sexes is that the women's skirt reaches below the knee, the men's to the middle of the thigh, and that the coiffure is not the same.

The male Samoyed wears 'a tunic with the hair inside, which is called the *militza*. It is an ample garment reaching below the knee, but in cold weather the Samoyed girds it up round his waist with a leathern girdle of an unusually decorative character, and thus, leaving it baggy round the upper part of his body, secures to himself a layer of warm air.' He wears breeches of deerskin and boots (*pimmies*) of deerskin. This is 'undoubtedly the best form of Arctic boot that we know.' In severe weather he wears over all a *sovik*, a larger tunic, with the hair outside, and a hood.[4]

Among the Malagasy the *salaka* of the men corresponds to the *maro* of Polynesia, the loin-cloth which is inter-crural; the *kitamby* of the women corresponds to the *paru* of Polynesia, the short apron. The upper garment is very distinctive. This is the *lamba*, a toga-like mantle, hung over the left arm by men, over the right by women. The women wear also an upper garment or blouse.[5] The Morocco Berbers wear 'a piece of oblong white blanket or dark blue cotton with a longitudinal slit in the centre for the head—like the Mexican *poncho*.' The women fasten a skirt-cloth over this on the left hip. 'A toga-like arrangement of a light blanket serves as overall.' The *khaneef*, a thick black waterproof cloak of goat-hair, with a hood, is the most characteristic garment. On the back is an assegai-shaped yellow patch denoting the clan. Round the shaven head is worn a band of flannel, cotton, or camel-hair.[6]

The dress of Korean women is a pair of very full white cotton trousers, almost a divided skirt, and over these a very full skirt, tied under the arms. In summer, basket-work frames are worn on the arms, back, and chest, under the robes, to keep the latter clean and also for the sake of coolness.[7] The trousers of Korean, Turkish, and the women of various other peoples is probably, as the term 'divided skirt' suggests, not lineally descended from the trews, but a later application of the principle to the skirt.

The basis of men's dress in India is the *dhoti*. It is a loin-cloth passed round the loins and between the legs in the universal manner. The typical garment for women is the *sārī*. It may be worn round the shoulders and draped over the head.[8] Ten or fifteen yards long, it is wound round the waist first, and then brought gracefully over the shoulder. A bodice is worn underneath the *sārī*, and some women have adopted the Muhammadan fashion of wearing drawers. The men's upper garment, the *uttarīya*, is worn somewhat like a toga. Generally an under-jacket, *aṅgarakṣa* (body-protector), is worn underneath. A scarf for cold weather is carried on the arm. The long coat of calico, usually worn by servants, apparently is a compromise, like the frock coat elsewhere, between the jacket and the toga. The turban was borrowed from the Muhammadans.[9] In fact, throughout parts of India 'all external distinctions have been effaced between Hindūs and Musalmāns,' the only mark often being that 'the former buttons his tunic on the right hand, and the latter on the side of his heart.'[10]

The characteristic male attire in Islām consists of the turban, white cotton drawers or full trousers, the *qamis*, or shirt, the *kaftān*, or coat, the *lungi*, or scarf. The *qamis* corresponds to the Greek χιτών and the Heb. *k^{e}tôneth*; the *kaftān* to the

[1] See Wilken-Pleyte, 39. [2] H. A. Wickham, *JAI* xxiv. 203.
[3] Stannus, in *JAI* xl. (1910) 320. [4] *Ib.* 320 ff.
[5] Brooke Low, *JAI* xxii. 36, 40. The jacket is probably derived from the Muhammadans. It is laid aside for work.
[6] This is the loin-cloth proper, not the *kain*.

[1] Brooke Low, *l.c.* 36, 37, 38, 40.
[2] C. Hose, in *JAI* xxxiii. (1893) 167.
[3] J. Teit, *The Thompson River Indians of British Columbia* Boston, 1898, p. 2.
[4] Montefiore, in *JAI* xxiv. (1895) 402.
[5] W. Ellis, *Hist. of Madagascar*, 1838, i. 278 f.
[6] J. E. B. Meakin, in *JAI* xxiv. (1895) 11, 12.
[7] H. S. Saunderson, in *JAI* xxiv. 303.
[8] Crooke, 158 f.; Monier-Williams, *Brāhmanism and Hindūism*[4], 1891, p. 395 ff.
[9] Dubois-Beauchamp, *Hindu Manners, Customs, and Ceremonies*, Oxford, 1897, p. 326.
[10] Crooke, 163 (Mr. Crooke refers the writer to the following passages, and corrects Dubois' error [*Hindu Manners*, p. 326] in stating that the Musalmān fastens his coat on the right, the Brahman on the left); B. Chunder, *Travels of a Hindoo*, 1869, ii. 374; J. F. Watson, *Textile Manufactures and Costumes of India*, i. (1866) 55.

ἱμάτιον, Heb. *m^e'îl*.[1] The turban, generally of muslin, may be from sixty to seventy yards long. The tarbush and the fez are other forms of head-gear.

Pollux gives a classic account of ancient Greek, and Varro of ancient Italian dress.[2] It is significant, sociologically, that the classic type, characterized by the loose tunic and toga, which with some differences was that chiefly affected by the great Oriental races, and is adapted both to the Oriental ideal of repose and to the classic ideal of aristocratic contemplation, was discarded, as the Empire developed into the States of Europe, in favour of what the Greeks styled barbarian dress, chiefly characterized by trousers—a dress adapted to activity. Trousers, the Sanskrit *chalana*, had been connected in India, as now in the East Indian Archipelago, with the dress of warriors and chiefs.[3]

The early Hebrews, like the Egyptians, wore the loin-cloth, originally, according to monuments of the latter, of the *lap* form. Drawers developing from this were first used as a priestly garment. Together with all Semitic peoples and the barbarians of Europe, they differed from Greek peoples in this one garment, though becoming assimilated in the tunic and mantle. The *sādin* was a shirt. Generally it was of the Greek type, and formed indoor dress. Overlapping by means of the girdle, it provided a pocket; it was slit at each side for ease in walking. The outer garment had two types, the long coat, corresponding to the ἱμάτιον, and the full-dress cloak, the *m^e'îl*, worn by wealthy persons and the priests. Both deserted the toga type in possessing sleeves. It was similar, generally, to the Chinese and Muhammadan long coat.[4]

The early Christians wore the ordinary dress of the country. They always evinced a strong feeling against luxury, display, and immodesty in dress.[5] This is to be attributed not merely to their revolt against Imperial paganism and its luxury and vice, but to their own class-feeling and class-prejudice, an impulse of the pride in lower class conditions of simplicity and poverty. This impulse is paralleled in modern labour and socialist psychology, where the workman's garb becomes a fetish of caste. Early Christian literature contains stories of Christians being tortured for refusing to put on garments indicative of idolatry.[6] All colour was avoided in dress, except the 'natural' colours of the cloth. Under the Frankish Emperors a prohibition was enacted against the wearing of a combination of wool and linen.[7] Such ideas gradually gave way, and the dress of the country, more and more of the 'barbarian' type, even in the South, was still worn by Christian Europeans without any limitations, country and creed being now identical. Among details to be noted are the following:

In Germany and Europe generally, till the 16th and 17th centuries, night garments were not worn; every one slept nude.[8] Sixty years ago in England the use of drawers was almost unknown, and was regarded as immodest and unfeminine.[9] The tight-fitting hose were the men's characteristic garment. The doublet or jacket was replaced among the academic class by the long coat. An extraordinary variety of fashions prevailed from the Middle Ages onwards. Knee-breeches later replaced the long-hose, and the longer jacket the doublet. The peasant's overall, smock, or blouse goes back to early European times. Finally, the modern trousers superseded the knee-breeches.

The evolution of material includes some abnormalities of special interest. Some extreme cases may be selected to illustrate these. Among the Central Australians, human hair is used for various purposes, especially for the manufacture of girdles. The giving and receiving of it constitute an important right and duty. A married man's chief supply is obtained from his mother-in-law.[1] The mediæval use of the hair-shirt as a mode of penance depended on the coarseness of the fabric for the mortification of the flesh. Similar is the use of hempen fabric, sack-cloth, in mourning. In foot-gear an analogy is seen in the use of dried peas to make walking painful.

The famous feather-fabric of the Nahua nations, who lived in a paradise of gorgeously coloured birds, was made by skilled artists, termed *amantecas*. This feather-cloth, with its brilliantly hued and scintillating patterns was used for mantles and dresses by the nobles and the wealthy, as well as for tapestry and similar drapery.[2] The most skilled nation was the Toltec.[3]

The interweaving of precious metal with dress-fabric is a luxurious custom, often merging in superstition. Thus Hindus and Chinese consider it lucky to wear gold, however minute the quantity, in some form on the person.

Colour in dress involves many problems of æsthetic, psychological, and biological importance. Behind fashion in colour there seems generally to be a principle of unconscious adaptation to environment. Æsthetic principles, originally unconscious, were superimposed upon this. The varied symbolism of colour in dress has a psychological foundation. Towards the tropics the tendency to gaudiness becomes marked; subdued tones are preferred by inhabitants of the temperate zone. Conversely, there is adaptation to racial and individual skin-colour.

The Euahlayi Australians think red to be a 'devil's colour.'[4] Such cases show an unconscious appreciation of the powerful stimulus of red. Its erotic connexion no doubt explains its frequent use in marriage ceremonies.[5] A natural association of ideas connects white with the purity of virgins and priests. The following are typical cases of doubtful origin:

Blue was a sacred colour among the Mayas; the priests and the sacred books were clothed in blue. At a certain feast, all instruments used in all occupations, and all children, were painted blue.[6] The Yezidis hate blue. Their strongest curse is 'May you die in blue garments!'[7] In the following example a tabu against mixtures may be involved. According to the Atharvaveda a combination of blue and red savoured of witchcraft.[8] Blue and red, however, were worn in the Hebrew high priest's ephod, which was employed for divination (Ex 28[6] *et al.*).

The special colours of Hindus and Buddhists in Northern India are red and saffron. The Hindu abominates indigo. The Sikh wears blue or white, and abominates saffron. The Musalmān wears indigo, or, if a descendant of the Prophet, green; never red.[9] Tradition, social inertia, and race-feeling perpetuate such preferences when once established.

Superstitious reasons for wearing a particular colour are probably always secondary, as, for instance, in the following cases from India:

For six days before marriage the Indian Musalmān bride wears old tattered yellow clothes, to drive away evil spirits. A wife meeting her husband after a long absence is dressed in yellow. Most Hindus of the West explain the custom of rubbing the body with turmeric in the same way. Among most high-class Hindus the bride's cloth, *vadhūvastra*, is yellow.[10] The Sannyāsī wears yellow clothes.[11] The Lamas of Tibet wear yellow, and yellow is the colour of Buddhist priestly dress universally.

A constant tendency may be observed for the colour, as well as the form, of the dress of the sacred world to be the precise opposite of that of the profane. In later stages, asceticism is also in-

[1] Hughes, *DI*, *s.v.* 'Dress'; see E. W. Lane, *Modern Egyptians*, ed. 1846, i. 36.
[2] Pollux, *Onomasticon*, bks. iv. vii.; Varro, *de Ling. Lat.* bk. v.
[3] Wilken-Pleyte, 42.
[4] G. M. Mackie, art. 'Dress,' in *HDB*; I. Abrahams and S. A. Cook, art. 'Dress,' in *EBi*.
[5] Smith-Cheetham, *DCA*, 1875, *s.v.* 'Dress.'
[6] *Acts of Perpetua and Felicitas*, 18.
[7] Smith-Cheetham, *l.c.*; see *Capitularium*, vi. 46.
[8] W. Rudeck, *Gesch. der öffentlichen Sittlichkeit in Deutschland*, 1897, pp. 57, 399.
[9] E. J. Tilt, *Elements of Health*, 1852, p. 193.

[1] Spencer-Gillen[a], 465.
[2] Bancroft, *Native Races*, 1875–6, ii. 488 ff., who gives the authorities on the 'feather-mosaic' art and its monuments.
[3] Payne, ii. 432. Feather-cloaks and collars were made by the Hawaiians (Frobenius, *Childhood of Man*, 1909, p. 62).
[4] K. L. Parker, 135.
[5] Cf. Gray, *China*, 1878, i. 201.
[6] Bancroft, ii. 697, 700.
[7] Millingen, *Among the Koords*, 1870, p. 277.
[8] Crooke, 165.
[9] *Ib.*
[10] J. M. Campbell, *IA* xxiv. 156 f.
[11] T. Maurice, *Indian Antiquities*, 1806, v. 1008.

volved, and simplicity of form is combined with absence of colour in the ordinary priestly garb.

The purple of the Greek world, as worn by the great, and particularly by royal persons, is an expression of super-personality, as distinguished from the abnormal or the contradictory. Royalty among most races wears special colours as well as special dress. For example, the Malay rajas have a monopoly of saffron, for the Malay royal colour is yellow. White is regarded as 'more exalted and sacred'; it is used to conciliate spirits. It is believed at the same time that the blood of kings is white.[1] As absence of colour, or the 'natural' colour of a fabric, implies negation or contraction of personality, so splendour—as in the various shades of crimson used by the ancient world under the one term of 'purple'—implies expansion of personality, and is suitable for festal occasions, both sacred and profane.

The negation of splendour is often expressed by black or dark blue. Superstition, when using these, relies upon their minimum of attraction rather than upon any optical adaptation. According to the *Rās Mālā*, dark clothes are a protection against the evil eye.[2] The Gujarāt Musalmān believes that black or indigo clothes keep spirits away.[3] In Roman Catholicism, as elsewhere, blue or violet is a colour symbolic of death. Blue is also connected with the external attributes of the Virgin Mary, possibly as mourning her dead Son. Such facts show a sentimental adaptation to circumstances. Red and yellow, being connected with organic growth, are the colours of well-being, and of the affirmation of energy and expanded personality; the blue end of the spectrum represents the negation of these, in proportion to its deleterious influence on the organic world. Where mythological speculation has coloured theology, adaptations in priestly and other garb may occur: blue may represent the sky; yellow the sun; silver the moon; red the sacrificial blood, and so on. In social life, colour no less than dress or uniform becomes a distinguishing mark, either by accident or by design. The gild, the club, the social state (as in the case of the blue blouse and similar status-garb), even the seasons of a Church, are represented by colours.

The following adaptations to sacred circumstances have much the same meaning as the injunction to wear 'decent apparel' on solemn occasions. Among the various tabus affecting tin-miners in Malaysia is one forbidding the wearing of black coats, except for the *pawang*, engineer-in-chief.[4] Local accidents have much to do with the fixing of such rules. In the above it is possible that a sympathetic harmony with the white colour of the sacred metal is alone intended. In the next case, purity alone may be intended. The Druid wore a white robe when cutting the mistletoe. For a similar function the Cambodian priest wears white.[5]

The following is an excellent example of the principle of adaptation. The state to which the person is to be assimilated is, no doubt, the succeeding state of cessation of the blood-flow, white being used by way of contrast with red.

A ceremonial system, termed *beroemboeng*, is followed by some Dayaks in the case of girls at puberty. The girl is washed, and dressed in white. Then she is incarcerated for a year. During this period she eats only white food; the hutch in which she lives is of white wood; at the end she is white herself. A feast is given to celebrate her release; at this she sucks the blood of a young man through a bamboo.[6]

1 Skeat, 51, 18.
2 Balfour, *Cyclopædia of India*³, 1885, v. 29.
3 J. M. Campbell, *IA* xxiv. 153.
4 Skeat, 257.
5 Pliny, *HN* xvi. 249 f.; Aymonier, in *Cochinchine française* xvi. (1883) 136.
6 *Bijdragen tot de Taal-, Land-, en Volkenkunde Nederl.-Indië*, vi. 2, pp. 65–71.

Green has been used to represent sympathy with the growth of green things upon the earth, as in many agriculture rites and spring ceremonies. As a contrast there is the Black Demeter; this is 'plainly a mythical expression for the bare wintry earth stripped of its summer mantle of green.'[1] The use of green is also known to express the non-festal seasons of a religious year. Occasionally green figures as expressive of corruption. The association of green with certain forms of organic decay may explain this.

3. Dress of head and feet.—Foot-gear and head-dress show an evolution as varied, *cæteris paribus*, as dress in general. The constant ideas of dress are seen here, even that of decency. Thus, where special attention is paid to clothing the foot, as among Chinese women, or the face, as among Musalmān women, the resulting modesty is real, but not primary. Decency is a secondary and artificial idea, and there is no biological or psychological difference between its application to the foot or the face and its application to the primary sexual characters. But in the former there is not, while in the latter there is, a primary impulse of modesty, the instinct to protect, though not necessarily to conceal, the sexual centres.

Most natives in India never wear shoes. Even the rich dispense at least with stockings. Leather is avoided for reasons of ceremonial purity.[2] The impulse towards physical cleanliness finds particular expression in foot-gear. It is not so obvious in the case of dress covering the passive areas of the body. The religious rule of removing the shoes before entering a sacred place is identical with that observed in social custom, and the original motive is no doubt merely to avoid carrying dirt or dust into the house either of God or of man.

Head-dress and coiffure involve ideas of ornament and distinction in a more marked degree than any other forms of dress. In so far as these illustrate the principles of dress generally, they are here in point. The Karens wear a head-dress in order to please the *tso*, the soul which resides in the head.[3] The Javanese wear nothing on the head, which is regarded as holy.[4] A Zambesi rain-maker never cuts his hair, for fear the familiar spirits may desert him.[5] Fashions and superstitions are equally innumerable in the matter of coiffure. No part of the external surface of the body has been more variously manipulated than the hair. The coiffure marks differences of race, tribe, clan, sex, age, and social status.

Flowers in the hair are worn by Dayak women; the hair is in a knot at the back of the head. Among Dayak men it is a common practice to grow the back hair long and shave the front hair.[6] The Kayans of Borneo shave all the scalp except a large tuft of long hair which hangs down the back. Hose considers this to be a 'last remnant of the Chinese pigtail.'[7] The latter and the Amerindian tuft are the converse of the priestly tonsure. The hair is either emphasized by concentration or negated by central denudation. Similar principles have been applied in the varying fashions of wearing the beard.

Where the hair is emphasized as a human, or as a masculine or feminine, character, its æsthetic appeal is parallel to that of dress, which also emphasizes by various harmonies of colour and form the æsthetic value of the body. Especially in woman long hair is regarded as beautiful, as her glory (cf. 1 Co 11[15]). From savagery up to modern civilization this attribute has been emphasized by addition, no less than by decoration.

False hair is regularly worn by the Veddas, who never brush, or oil, or wash their heads.[8] The latter fashion, though nearer to the animal, may

1 Frazer, *GB*² ii. 303.
2 Monier-Williams, 396.
3 E. B. Cross, in *JAOS* iv. (1854) 311 f.
4 Frazer, *GB*³ ii. (1911) 261.
5 *Missions catholiques*, xxv. (1893) 266.
6 Brooke Low, in *JAI* xxii. (1892) 41 f.
7 Hose, *JAI* xxxiii. 167.
8 C. G. and B. Z. Seligmann, 98.

be an expression of personal pride in the organism, no less than is scrupulous cleanliness.

The use of the fillet has two purposes—to confine the hair, and to prevent sweat from reaching the eyes. The protection of the eyes and the spine of the neck from the deleterious rays of the sun has been understood in very early stages. The general tendency is towards ornament in female, protection in male, head-gear.

Korean head-gear is remarkable. The men's hats are like inverted flower-pots, with broad, straight brims, similar to the Welsh tall hat. The brims measure two feet across. The hats are made of horsehair, and are varnished. They are stained black, except in half-mourning, when they are string-colour. The court officials wear hats so fantastic that 'it is perfectly impossible to describe them.' The women wear no head-gear, except fur-caps in winter.[1] Such hats as the Korean and the modern European tall hat are the expression of ideas of the dignity of the head, just as was the crown.

4. Ornaments and amulets.—Though dress of the simplest description has an ornamental value, there has always been a precise distinction between dress and ornament. There is little possibility of confusion between them, whether the ornament is directly applied to the body or is actually an addition to the dress, meant to decorate this rather than the wearer. Ornament is often *de rigueur*. No Hindu woman 'would dare to hold up her head' unless well provided with eight kinds of ornaments—nose-rings, ear-rings, necklaces, bracelets, armlets, finger-rings, anklets, and toe-rings.[2]

Lower races are fond of the necklace-method, using shells, seeds, and beads threaded on string. The women of Guiana load themselves with seeds and beads in great ropes.[3] Almost as prevalent is the use of metal cinctures, which subsequently acquire the value of protective armour or amulets. Originally they seem to have been an extension of the ligature-principle.

Amulets are practically innumerable in their variety. They may be worn on the body or on the dress, and are usually abnormal in material. Dress itself may acquire the virtue of an amulet. The Malays write charms on paper or cloth, and wear them next the skin.[4] The Musalmān and Hebrew amulets of sacred texts are familiar examples. The principle employed is that of assimilation of the sacred force by contact. The people of Surinam wear the 'strong metal,' iron, on their bodies, to acquire its strength.[5] In armour dress reaches the climax of its protective functions.

5. Dress as currency.—In the absence of coinage, commercial transactions often take the form of mutual gifts, especially in the case of transactions which are more or less purely financial. At such stages any article representing work and intrinsic value, such as clothing, is an obvious medium for presentation or exchange. In savagery, gifts of clothing are less frequent than gifts of food; in barbarism they are more frequent.

The Trojans placed a robe on the knees of the goddess to induce her to save their city.[6] In the East Indian Islands clothes are a frequent offering to the spirits.[7] Blankets were a common gift among the N. American Indians.[8] To show appreciation of an actor's playing, the Japanese used to throw their clothes on the stage. At the end they were purchased by the donors, and the actor took the money.[9] Blankets form the chief property of the Kwakiutl and Haidas. They are treated as money, and lent at interest.[10] A large proportion of the taxes paid by the Nahuas was in the form of cloths and made-up clothes. The labour involved in providing the tribute was one main aspect of the *Nahua*, 'Rule of Life,' which gave the people their name. Also a considerable amount of dress was annually expended in sacrifices.[11] The remarkable institution of the Indians of British Columbia, known as the *potlatch*, is a distribution of property, such as blankets, undertaken by each member of society in turn, according to his status or opportunity. The system is essentially financial gambling. Similar is the frequent obligation of the king in early culture to redistribute the gifts which his subjects make to him.[1] A *potlatch*, distribution of property, accompanied initiation to the Bear Totem of the Carrier Indians. The candidate gave presents of clothes to all concerned.[2]

[1] Saunderson, in *JAI* xxiv. (1894) 304.
[2] Monier-Williams, 396 f. [3] Im Thurn, 199. [4] Skeat, 567.
[5] Martin, in *Bijd. tot de Taal-, Land-, en Volkenkunde Nederl.-Indië*, xxxv. (1886) 5, pp. 2–4.
[6] Hom. *Il.* vi. 87 ff., 302 ff.
[7] F. Valentijn, *Oud en nieuw Oost-Indiën*, ed. 1862, iii. 13 f.
[8] Dorsey, in *American Naturalist*, Philadelphia, xix. (1885) 678.
[9] Kennedy, in *FL* ix. (1898) 93.
[10] Payne, ii. 376. [11] *Ib.* ii. 465, 476 f.

Ornament and currency are interchangeable, Ratzel points out, in early times. There is no safer place for property than the owner's person. But clothing proper is a parallel form of currency, either as made up into garments, or as prepared material.

Among the Tlingits, seal and other skins are both worn and circulated as money. The fine mat-garments of the Samoans were their most valuable property, and were used as currency. The Wa-ganda use unbleached calico for the purpose, measuring the unit by the length of the forearm.[3] The Garos use cotton cloth as a medium of exchange.[4] Mat-money is used in the Northern New Hebrides. The mats, which are plaited by women, are called by the same term—*malo*—as women's mat-cloths. They are long, narrow pieces, and the value increases with the folds, which are usually counted in tens. In the Banks Islands, crimson-dyed feathers, the favourite decoration, are used as currency.[5] Formerly braid was so used in the Loyalty Islands. In Florida and Saa, disks of shells are used both as ornaments and as money.[6] In Africa, New Britain, Melanesia, among the Californians, Tlingits, and Eskimo, beads, shells, and the like decorations are used for exchange. The Khalkas discontinued the wearing of their valuable silk scarves, and retained them solely as a form of money.

The famous New Britain shell ornaments, termed *dewarra*, were chiefly in the form of extended collars. The wearing of *dewarra* was abandoned as soon as it was found, on the arrival of Europeans, to have commercial value. The shells were tabu. A man's greatest object in life was to collect as large a hoard as possible. 'With *dewarra* they buy their ornaments and their wives; with *dewarra* they buy themselves free from all troubles and complications; with *dewarra* they appease their bitterest enemy, even though they may have killed his nearest relative.' For daily expenses a man carries about with him a yard or a few fathoms of this money. 'The rest is deposited in the *dewarra*-house, a hut specially set apart for keeping the property of all the villagers, the thousands of fathoms belonging to the rich, as well as the smallest savings of the poor. From fifty to a hundred or even two hundred and fifty fathoms are rolled up in a bundle, which is wrapped in bright-coloured leaves. . . . The *dewarra* bank is always guarded by several sentinels.' At the death of a capitalist, his *dewarra* is distributed among the depositors. When a man deposits a large amount, the drum is beaten to summon an audience.[7] Shell arm-ornaments are used as currency by the Southern Massim of New Guinea.[8]

6. Dress symbolism.—Dress acquires ideal valuations from its various uses, materials, and associations. All languages are full of metaphors recording such ideas. According to the *Śatapatha Brāhmaṇa*, 'the priests' fee consists of a hundred garments, for that—to wit, the garment—is man's outward appearance, whence people (on seeing) any well-clad man ask, "Who can this be?"; for he is perfect in his outward appearance; with outward appearance he thus endows him.'[9] This example well illustrates the idea that dress is both an expression and an extension of personality, in its superficial aspect.

The symbolism of the virgin zone, the girdle, the royal robe and crown, needs no illustration. In rare cases, an article of value used in exchange acquires the virtue of such objects as *regalia* and the Australian *churinga*. The *wampum* of the North American Indians

'has, no doubt, grown out of the cords on which were strung shell-beads of divers colours for adorning the neck and arms, and which first served as ornaments, but later circulated in the land as real money. . . . Exchange may have taken place to cement a friendship or a treaty. . . . The *wampum*-belt acquired an extraordinary measure of importance; in it was evolved a certain kind of documentary script.' The speaker at meetings held a *wampum*-belt in his hand. 'Brothers,' he might say, 'with this belt I open your ears that you may hear; I take care and sorrow from your hearts.' At the conclusion of a treaty, tribes exchanged *wampums*, which had a representation of the

[1] Van Gennep, *Rites de passage*, Paris, 1909, p. 43.
[2] A. G. Morice, in *Trans. of Canad. Inst.* iv. (1892–3) 203 f.
[3] H. Spencer, *Principles of Sociology*, 1876–96, iii. 387, quoting authorities.
[4] *Ib.*
[5] R. H. Codrington, *The Melanesians*, Oxford, 1891, p. 323 ff.
[6] Spencer, iii. 388 ff. [7] Frobenius, 57–60.
[8] Seligmann, *The Melanesians of Brit. New Guinea*, 1910, p. 513.
[9] *SBE* xliv. (1900) 353.

event woven into them. The Iroquois supported the office of hereditary *wampum*-keeper, who was more or less a depositary of the history of the people. Every year the whole collection was exhibited and explained to the whole tribe.[1]

The eagle-plumes of American warriors' head-dress signified by their numbers and particular marks the achievements of the wearer. Similar marks of honour were made on their garments.[2] It is, however, misleading to characterize such phenomena as dress-language.

Out of the extensive list of metaphors from dress only one or two types can be included in illustration. A proverbial saying of 16th cent. knighthood contained the phrase, '*Mon harnois ma maison.*'[3] Besides implying the homelessness of the knight-errant, this also involves the application of dress and armour as external shelter no less than as bodily covering. The most prevalent metaphor in all languages, that of dress as a covering, often loses its force as a species of covering, and comes to be a synonym for the genus, owing to its constant use. In proverbs, the wisdom of many and the wit of one employs the simplest and the most complex ideas of dress.

In Masailand the Suahili proverb is used, 'to cut out the tunic before the child is born,' equivalent to the English 'counting your chickens before they are hatched.'[4] A popular Chinese book of moral instruction says: 'Brothers are like hands and feet. A wife is like one's clothes. When clothes are worn out, we can substitute those that are new.'[5]

The metaphorical wealth of Indian literature suggests two points. In the first place, dress is more than covering; it imparts an anthropomorphic value to the object. According to the Vedic texts on 'Soma,' the mixture of *soma* with milk, sour milk, and barley is a 'garment.'[6] Water, say the Upaniṣads, is 'the dress of breath.'[7] In the second place, there is no doubt that a good deal of mythological creation is due to metaphor, not as a disease of language, but as a deliberate use of association of ideas for the purpose of artistic and religious invention. Metaphors, like those of dress, serve, first, to personalize an object, and then to humanize it. There need be no confusion between the two uses; they are simply two methods of viewing one thing. Nor need there be any fetishism behind such cases.

On the other hand, the OT and NT use is purely abstract and literary. But there is no ground for supposing that this is a secondary stage, and that such metaphors were originally material identifications. The lowest savages, for instance, use metaphors merely as such. The pastures 'clothed with flocks'; the heavens 'clothed with blackness'; a woman 'clothed with the sun'; clothed 'with cursing,' 'with vengeance,' 'with drowsiness,' 'with strength and honour'; and flowers clothing 'the grass of the field'[8]—these are examples of Biblical metaphor. Dress-metaphors may be morally applied. Clothed 'with salvation,' 'with righteousness,' or 'with humility'[9] is a pure metaphor. In Zoroastrian texts it is said that the garments of the soul in the life to come are made from acts of almsgiving.[10] A beautiful metaphor like this is not degraded if it becomes concrete; it is merely translated into materiality.

The great bifurcation of dress is sexual. Besides the obvious symbolism and metaphor which this involves (as in phrases like 'petticoat government' and 'wearing the trousers'), there may be mentioned an attempt on the part of asceticism to express the non-sexual idea. The attempt is made both in ideal pictures and in actual priestly garb. The garment selected is the long tunic, which survived here for other reasons, and the colour is white. Thus all indication of primary sexual characters is veiled; the dress not only covers but replaces the body. White is at once pure, free from 'mixture,' as a mixture of all colours, and neutral, between splendour and shame.

It has been suggested[1] that the Egyptian *crux ansata*, the symbol of life, is a picture of the loin-cloth. In the Hervey Islands a frequent name for a god is *tatua manava*, 'loin-belt.'[2] A similar notion is that of the girdle, symbolic of eternity, as the circle is of infinity.

The relation of soul and body is often expressed in terms of dress. The expression may be merely metaphorical; it may also be real. The body is not only a house or a tomb, as in some early Christian literature; more aptly is it an exactly fitting duplicate, covering the soul. Thus, the body, according to Malay psychology, is the *sarong* of the soul. Conversely, the Gnostics spoke of the soul as a 'garment.' In the one case the inner soul, in the other the outer or filmy soul, seems to be intended.[3] In a famous passage St. Paul combines the metaphors of house and dress in reference to the super-terrestrial body: with this man desires to be 'clothed upon,' 'not for that we would be unclothed, but clothed upon, that mortality might be swallowed up of life.' At the same time the body terrestrial is a 'house,' a 'tabernacle.'[4] The Déné Indian when sick regains his soul by the following method. His moccasins are stuffed with down and hung up. If the down is warm next morning the soul has entered the shoes, and it may be reunited with the body if the patient puts them on.[5] Here the presence of personal warmth, associated with actual wearing, represents the presence of the soul in the dress.

The metaphorical and symbolical applications of the idea of dress thus show an oscillation between very distant extremes, which may be summarized as on the one hand a sheltering house, and on the other hand an almost organic skin.

7. The social psychology of dress.—(1) *The dress of mystery.*—The results of the free play of the social mind on the subject of dress in magical, religious, and moral opinion and ritual may be introduced by some such observation as that early folklore regards weaving as a mystical art.[6] In other words, the operation has significance, attracts attention, and may inspire wonder. But the ultimate reason is merely that it is outside the normal plane of ordinary human or, more exactly, animal activity. It is not because there is any reference either to dress or to magic.

The invention of fairy tales illustrates, by extravagant emphasis, various ideas connected with dress, but overlaid with that secondary form of magical belief which is merely æsthetic, literary, or generally fanciful. Stories of magical dresses[7] are numerous. The *motif* illustrates either the connexion of dress with personality or the use of dress as a protection, disguise, or honour. There is, for instance, the shirt of snowy whiteness which turns black when the owner dies.[8] The emphasis on sympathetic connexion is constant. The shirt which never needs mending while the

1 Frobenius, 65–69. 2 *Ib.* 70.
3 De la Noue, *Discours politiques et militaires*, Geneva, 1587, p. 215.
4 Hollis, 245.
5 *Indo-Chinese Gleaner*, Malacca, 1818, i. 164.
6 A. A. Macdonell, *Vedic Mythol.*, Strassburg, 1897, p. 106 f.
7 *SBE* i. 74.
8 Ps 65^{13}, Is 50^{3}, Rev 12^{1}, Ps 109^{18}, Is 59^{17}, Pr 23^{21} 31^{25}, Lk 12^{28}.
9 1 P 5^{5}, Ps $132^{9.16}$.
10 *Shāyast lā-Shāyast*, xii. § 4, in *SBE* v. 341.

1 By Sayce (quoted in March, *l.c.*).
2 H. C. March, in *JAI* xxii. (1892) 314; Gill, *Myths and Songs from the South Pacific*, 1876, p. 35.
3 Crawley, *The Idea of the Soul*, 1909, pp. 125, 216, quoting authorities.
4 2 Co 5^{1-4}.
5 A. G. Morice, 'The Western Dénés,' in *Proc. Canad. Inst.* vii. (Toronto, 1888–9) 158 f.
6 Crooke, in *FL* ix. (1898) 124. 7 *Ib.* 129.
8 M. R. Cox, *Cinderella*, 1892, *passim.*

wearer remains faithful[1] is a contrast to the shirt of Nessus.

In German folklore a shirt spun and stitched by a maiden who has kept silence for seven years can undo spells and render the wearer spell-proof.[2] St. Theresa was presented by the Virgin with an invisible cope which guarded her from sin.[3] The clothes and caps which make invisible were familiar subjects of mediæval lore.

Malay folklore tells of the cloth, *sansistah kallah*, 'which weaves itself, and adds one thread yearly of fine pearls, and when that cloth shall be finished the world will be no more.'[4] An old-time raja 'wore the trousers called *beraduwanggi*, miraculously made without letting in pieces'; also a waistband of flowered cloth, which thrice a day changed colour—'in the morning transparent as dew, at mid-day of the colour of *lembayong* [purple], and in the evening of the hue of oil.' His *sarong* was 'a robe of muslin of the finest kind; . . . it had been woven in a jar in the middle of the ocean by people with gills, relieved by others with beaks; no sooner was it finished than the maker was put to death, so that no one might be able to make one like it. . . . If it were put in the sun it got damper, if it were soaked in water it became drier.'[5]

The idea that dress is a secondary skin, an outer bodily surface, has a connexion with many stories of metamorphosis.

A Javanese magician transforms himself into a tiger by means of a miraculous *sarong*, the Malay garment, half robe and half shirt. This is believed to have such marvellous elasticity that at first it will only cover his great toes, but it stretches till it covers the whole body. It resembles in texture and colour the hide of the Bengal tiger. When it is on, a few muttered charms complete the transformation of the magician into a tiger.[6]

(2) *Dress and personality.*—One of the simplest cases of association is the idea that a person may be represented by his dress. Dress is here analogous to the name, the effigy, and the image.

In China, when a man dies in a foreign land, he is buried in the form of his clothes. The soul is summoned, and then 'the burial of the evoked soul' takes place. In the case, for instance, of an empress in ancient times, her soul was to be evoked 'with the aid of her sacrificial robe; then this robe must be placed on a soul-carriage . . . then the dress must be taken to the sacrificial hall . . . be covered with a corpse-pall, and finally be buried.'[7] If the son of a dead Chinese cannot attend the funeral, he is represented by a suit of sackcloth garments carried on a tray in the procession.[8] At a Celebes festival, a woman's and a man's dress represent deceased ancestors.[9] Among the Eskimo the first child born after a death 'represents' the dead man. These namesakes eat and drink the provisions and wear the clothes offered to the dead at feasts, on their behalf. At the end the shades are sent back wearing the spiritual essence of the clothes, while the gross substance is kept by the namesakes.[10] When the office of high priest in Tonga was vacant, the priestly dress was placed on a chair, and yams were offered to it. It was regarded as an equivalent for the person.[11] If a Zulu lightning-doctor is unable to attend a case, he sends his blanket to be placed in front of the storm as an equivalent for himself.[12]

Bathing in clothes[13] is a form of ceremonial purification which shows the connexion of dress and person. If dress is a part of personality, it follows that it must share in the duties imposed on the natural body. Similarly, if the soul of a dead person is a replica of his ordinary personality in life, the soul after the death of the body is regarded as wearing clothes. This was, for instance, the case with the Egyptian *ka*.

The anointing of garments is a practice found in fashion, ritual, and ordinary life (see art. ANOINTING). As a detail of full dress, the wedding garments of the Masai bride are oiled before being put on.[14] The robes of the Hebrew high priest, no less than his head and person, were anointed with the sacred oil.[15] The hygienic purpose of oiling the skin is also fulfilled by oiling the garments worn.

In many cases the dress is not merely a representative symbol of the person, but a usable substitute for a more or less sacred and therefore unusable reality. A Masai man swears to the truth of a statement 'by my sister's garment,' a woman 'by my father's garment.'[1] The converse of this idea may be seen when regalia or royal robes are more sacred than the person of the monarch. These associations, in connexion with the innate love of finery, are concerned in certain observances during sickness and at death.

In serious illness, a Mongol's best clothes and ornaments are spread round him in order to tempt the absent soul to return.[2] A similar practice is recorded of the Greenlanders and the Todas.[3] In China 'a coat belonging to the sick man, and very recently worn, is suspended on a bamboo.' Incantations are performed to induce the errant soul to enter the coat. When the pole turns round in the hands of the holder, the soul has arrived, and the coat is placed on the sick man's body.[4] For the Chinese ceremony of 'calling back the dead,' the dead man's favourite costume is employed. The idea is to entice the soul into it, for it should be 'inclined to slip into such of its garments as it had been proud to wear during life.' The dress is held out by a mourner, crying 'Ho! come back.' Then, the soul being supposed to have entered, it is placed on the body of the dead man.[5] The Mongols try to persuade the soul of a sick man to return by putting out his best clothes, washed and perfumed.[6] The Maoris enticed the soul of a dead chief by the bait of a piece of its body or its clothes, in order to instal it in the *Wahi Tapu*.[7] Souls are commonly charmed into a cloth or caught in the same receptacle.[8]

The custom of dressing the dead in his best clothes may often be based on similar associations (see below).

The principle of impersonation is easily applied to dress. Particular cases are assimilation to totemic or other animals, and may be regarded as a fusion of personalities, or rather the assumption of a secondary personality.

The natives of the Upper Congo blacken their faces with oil and charcoal in resemblance of a species of monkey; they explain that by so doing they derive 'monkey cunning.'[9] Bechuana warriors wear the hair of a hornless ox in their hair and the skin of a frog on their cloak, that they may be as hard to hold as are these animals.[10] The Bororo of Brazil regard themselves as being identical with red-plumaged birds. They decorate themselves with their feathers.[11] All African tribes, says Schweinfurth (but the statement needs considerable qualification), imitate in their attire some animal, especially those for which they have 'reverence.' 'In this way it frequently happens that their superstition indirectly influences the habits of their daily life, and that their animal-worship finds expression in their dress.'[12] Among the Vaydas of Cutch the bridegroom is dressed as a monkey when he goes to the house of the bride.[13]

The purposes of impersonation are naturally manifold, and require no general illustration. When a sick Eskimo child is made to wear a dog's harness, and is consecrated as a dog to the goddess Sedna,[14] the idea is, no doubt, change of condition as resulting from change of personality.

On a similar principle, the Galelareese, concluding that a barren tree is a male, turn it into a female by placing a woman's petticoat upon it.[15]

Assimilation of dress to person has innumerable gradations, passing ultimately into identity or duplication. The principle is complicated by the belief that inanimate objects have souls. There is an Irish belief that the clothes of a dead man wear out more quickly than those of a living man.[16] The Hindus hold that the dress and ornaments of the gods and deified mortals do not decay.[17] Garments, like other inanimate articles, have souls, as in Fijian and Tongan belief.

(3) *Magical associations.*—All the ideas and

[1] Crooke, *FL* ix. 130.
[2] Grimm, *Teut. Mythol.*, 1880–8, iii. 1098 f.
[3] *Quart. Rev.*, 1883, p. 413.
[4] Skeat, 29.
[5] *Ib.* 29 f.
[6] *Ib.* 161.
[7] De Groot, *Rel. Syst. of China*, 1892 ff., iii. 847, 853.
[8] *Ib.* i. 193.
[9] B. F. Matthes, *Binnenlanden van Celebes*, 1856, p. 5.
[10] E. W. Nelson, in *18 RBEW* (1899), pt. i. pp. 363–379, 424 f.
[11] S. S. Farmer, *Tonga*, 1855, p. 134.
[12] H. Callaway, *Religious System of the Amazulu*, 1868, p. 278.
[13] Manu, xi. 175.
[14] Hollis, 303.
[15] Ex 29[7. 21].

[1] Hollis, 345.
[2] Bastian, *Die Seele*, 1860, p. 36.
[3] Crantz, *Greenland*, 1820, i. 237; Marshall, *A Phrenologist amongst the Todas*, 1873, p. 171.
[4] Doolittle, *Social Life of the Chinese*, New York, 1866, i. 150 f.
[5] De Groot, i. 246 ff.
[6] Bastian, 30.
[7] R. Taylor, *Te ika a Maui*[2], 1870, p. 101.
[8] Crawley, *Idea of the Soul*, 126, 135 f.
[9] H. Ward, in *JAI* xxiv. 293.
[10] E. Casalis, *The Basutos*, Eng. tr., 1861, p. 272
[11] K. von den Steinen, 352, 512.
[12] *Heart of Africa*[2], 1874, i. 406.
[13] Crooke, *PR*[2], ii. 154.
[14] Frazer, *Totemism and Exogamy*, iv. (1910) 208, quoting Boas.
[15] M. J. van Baarda, in *Bijdragen tot de Taal-, Land-, en Volkenkunde van Nederl.-Indië*, xlv. (1895) 489.
[16] *JAFL* viii. (1895) 110.
[17] Monier-Williams, 235.

practices of sympathetic magic are abundantly illustrated by dress. A few typical cases may be cited.

Among the Toradjas of Celebes, when the men are on campaign, those remaining behind may not put off their garments or head-dress, lest the warrior's armour may fall off.[1] The principle of like producing like is frequently applied. A Malay woman explained that her reason for stripping the upper part of her body when reaping rice was in order to make the rice-husks thinner.[2] During the festival of the Mexican 'long-haired mother,' the maize-goddess, women danced with their long hair unbound, that the tassel of the maize might grow in equal profusion.[3] In a Kashmir story, a weaver offers the king some cloth for a shroud. The king held that the man wished his death.[4] A rain-maker in Mabuiag paints himself white and black, with the explanation 'All along same as clouds, black behind, white he go first.' A woman's petticoat also is put on to signify clouds.[5] In ancient India, the Brāhman rain-maker wore black garments and ate black food. He had to touch water thrice a day.[6] Generally it is a rule that to make rain the operator must himself be wet, to make dry weather he must be dry. 'Who drives fat oxen should himself be fat.'

Magical injury is effected upon a person by means of his dress, as having been in contact with or as representing him. The practice of injuring or slaying a man by burning or otherwise destroying fragments of his clothes or food, and the like, is world-wide.[7]

A rejected lover in Burma gets an image of the lady, containing a piece of her clothes or of something she has worn. This is then hanged or drowned.[8] A Wotjobaluk wizard would roast a man's opossum-skin rug before a fire, in order to make him ill or die. The only cure was to soak the rug in water, when the sick felt cooler and recovered.[9] The Tannese wizard practised a similar method with a cloth which contained the sweat.[10] Prussian folklore has it that if you cannot catch a thief you may get hold of a garment he has dropped in his flight. If this is beaten soundly, the thief falls sick.[11] The last case suggests that the dress is regarded as a part of personality, or an exterior and superficial layer of personality. The practices illustrated above are perhaps better explained on this principle than on the hypothesis that things once in contact retain a magical continuity.

The converse method of enforced assimilation produces intimacy and identity by means of dress. To obtain a favour or to conciliate feeling, a Zulu gets some article or fragment from the person he has in mind, and wears it next his skin.[12]

More numerous are cases of actual transmission of properties by means of dress. A South Slavonian woman who desires a child puts a chemise on a fruitful tree. Next morning she places it on her own person.[13] According to Swiss folklore, the dress of a dead child will kill any child who wears it.[14] Such examples need not be multiplied, but their interpretation cannot be found merely in the idea of contagion of physical or magical properties. For early thought it is an obvious inference that a man's nature

'inheres not only in all parts of his body, but in his dress. . . . Probably the interpretation of odour has led to this belief. If the breath is the spirit or other-self, is not this invisible emanation which permeates a man's clothing and by which he may be traced, also a part of his other self?'[15]

But inference from odour does not, any more than the idea of contagion, satisfy all the conditions. There is also, as already suggested, to be taken into account the general ideas derived from the specific idea of dress. A garment is an expression of personality, and, as such, its significance is enforced by its application to other personalities, while this application receives a concrete meaning

1 Frazer, *Early History of the Kingship*, 1905, p. 61.
2 Skeat, 248.
3 Payne, i. 421.
4 Knowles, *Folktales of Kashmir*, 1888, p. 266.
5 A. C. Haddon, in *JAI* xix. (1890) 401.
6 H. Oldenberg, *Rel. des Veda*, Berlin, 1894, p. 420 f.
7 Riedel, *De sluik- en kroesharige rassen*, Hague, 1886, pp. 61, 79, 451; Aymonier, *Cambodge*, Paris, 1900-4, p. 166; Dawson, *Australian Aborigines*, Melbourne, 1881, p. 54.
8 C. J. F. S. Forbes, *British Burma*, 1878, p. 232.
9 A. W. Howitt, in *JAI* xvi. (1886) 28 f.
10 B. T. Somerville, in *JAI* xxiii. (1893) 19.
11 Tettau-Temme, *Volkssagen Ostpreussens*, Berlin, 1837, p. 283 f.
12 Callaway, 142.
13 F. S. Krauss, *Volksglaube und religiöser Brauch der Südslaven*, 1890, p. 35.
14 Ploss, *Das Kind*, Leipzig, 1876, i. 240.
15 H. Spencer, *Principles of Sociology*, i. 336.

and the general idea is concretely realized from the mere fact that the object expressive of personality possesses and may retain the material impress of the person. These ideas enter into many of the superstitious uses of dress. One or two types may be cited:

The Kayans believe that to touch a woman's clothes would enervate them and make them unsuccessful in hunting and war.[1] The Siamese consider it unlucky to pass under women's clothes hung out to dry.[2]

The Queensland natives would take off the skin of a slain enemy and cover a sick man with it, in the hope of curing him.[3] In this and similar cases, as in the practice of blood-drinking, merely the application of organic activity and strength is intended.

It is doubtful if cases like the following imply as much as they seem to do. The desire to have an article clean and new is irreducible, but upon it may be developed habits and beliefs of a mystical nature. The people of Nias, after buying clothes, scrub them carefully in order to rid them of all contagion of the original owners.[4]

The irradiation of ideas of contact has remarkable power and extension, as is shown by beliefs concerning the dress of members of the sacred world. Such garments are impregnated with the *mana* of the wearer, as was Elijah's mantle. But, as pointed out before, metaphors like 'impregnated' cannot always be elevated into reasons. The idea that 'sanctity,' for instance, may inhere in garments as an effluvium or a force is possibly a late explanation, and not the original reason for the practices and beliefs concerned.

The Mikado's clothes, by reason of their 'sanctity,' caused pain and swellings if worn by other persons. Similarly, to avoid injuring others, his eating and drinking vessels were destroyed, immediately after use.[5]

The garments of a Maori chief would kill any man who wore them. In other words, the chief's *tapu*, inherent in them, had the power of destroying.[6] In Fiji there was a special disease, *kana lama*, caused by wearing the clothes of a chief.[7]

The principles of ceremonial purity and defilement have produced some remarkable forms of dress and rules of toilette.

Among the Mekeo of New Guinea, a woman after childbirth must wear gloves made of coco-nut fibre when pouring water.[8] The Tinné or Déné girl during her first period wears a skin bonnet with fringes reaching to the breast, because the sight of her is dangerous to society.[9]

(4) *Personality and state.*—For the psychology of dress a class of facts relating to murderers and menstruous women, and illustrated by the Eskimo theory of tabu, have an important significance.

It is a frequent rule that persons who have shed blood, or emit blood, shall indicate their state in a peculiar way. Thus, the homicide among the Northern Indians of America had to paint his mouth red before eating.[10] The original intention was probably not protective, but merely an unconscious impulse to adapt the person to the particular state. The idea of protection may be superposed upon this. The Omaha murderer was not allowed to let his robe fly open; it was to be pulled close about his body, and kept tied at the neck, even in hot weather.[11] Such cases, if their meaning is protective, are perhaps better explained as reactions to a vague and indeterminate impulse to concealment rather than as direct attempts to evade the ghost of the murderer's victim.

The smearing of the blood-shedder with blood as a means of adaptation to the state of bloodshed is exactly parallel with any investiture with a sacred

1 A. W. Nieuwenhuis, *Quer durch Borneo*, 1904, i. 350.
2 Bastian, *Die Völker des östlichen Asien*, 1866-71, iii. 230.
3 Fison-Howitt, *Kamilaroi and Kurnai*, 1880, p. 223.
4 Nieuwenhuis-Rosenberg, in *Verh. Batav. Genootsch.* xxx. (Batavia, 1863) 26.
5 Frazer, *GB*³, pt. ii. p. 131.
6 R. Taylor, 164.
7 Fison, quoted by Frazer, *GB*³, pt. ii. p. 131.
8 Guis, *Missions catholiques*, xxx. (1898) 119.
9 A. G. Morice, in *Annual Archæological Report*, Toronto, 1905, p. 218.
10 S. Hearne, *Journey to the Northern Ocean*, 1795, p. 204.
11 Dorsey, in *3 RBEW* (1884), p. 369.

dress, as a means of adaptation to a sacred state. The 'dressing' is a frame to the picture.

The Eskimo theory of tabu brings this out. Both personality in general, and particular states of a given personality, form round themselves an expression of their essence. The Eskimo hold that a man who has transgressed tabu appears to animals to be of a dark colour or surrounded by a vapour; for example, the hands of a menstruous woman appear to be red. This colour becomes attached not only to the soul of the agent, but to the souls of the animals with which he has to do; in fact, of everything with which he may establish contact. If a child is sick, the *angekok* removes a black attachment from its soul, caused perhaps by the child having taken oil-drippings from the lamp. A dead man's clothes may not be worn, for a hunter wearing them would appear dark and the seals would avoid him.[1]

Behind all this is the instinct against incongruity, mal-adaptation. A hunter must not wear the dress of a dead man or of a mourner; equally a mourner must not wear the dress of a hunter. The passage from one state to the other, or the transgression of tabu, is not the primary notion. The spiritual garb, resulting from a particular state, is not originally the result of any transgression; it is an automatic effect of the state, a psychological echo of the adaptation, assimilation, or identification of the individual with his particular condition.

Again, it is believed by the Greenlanders that, if a whale-fisher wears a dirty dress, or one contaminated by contact with a dead man, the whales will desert the fishing-grounds.[2]

In such cases it is probable that there is originally no notion of contamination or contagion at all; there is merely the incongruity between the full-dress, and complimentary circumstances of the hunt,—the quarry being approached respectfully and regardfully,—and the undress slovenliness of dirty clothes or the ill-omened and tactless reference to death contained in any connexion with a corpse.

The garment of a particular state must be discarded when that state is past. By this means and by bodily 'cleansing' transition to the new state or to the normal is effected.

The Hebrew high priest after offering the sin-offering had to wash himself and put off the garments he had worn.[3] Similarly the Greek worshipper after an expiation might not enter a city or his house until he had washed himself and his clothes.[4]

Such rules are of world-wide extension. The principle of contamination in its secondary and ordinary meaning cannot cover all the facts. The original meaning of 'mixture,' and conversely the original meaning of 'purity,' as an unmixed state, supply an adequate explanation, in the principle of a psychical (and, as expressed in action, a material) adaptation to state. In customs such as the following the original motive is obscure, but the secondary idea of removal of a dangerous effluvium is suggested.

Among the Berbers of South Morocco, 'persons who have been wrongly accused of a crime sometimes entirely undress themselves in the sainthouse, when going to swear. They believe that, if they do so, the saint will punish the accuser; and I conclude,' observes Westermarck, who reports the custom, 'that at the bottom of this belief there is a vague idea that the absence of all clothes will prevent the oath from clinging to themselves.'[5]

Secondary also is the principle that sacred appurtenances may only be used once; when emptied of their force, they must be destroyed.[6] Nor can we regard as primary the principle that change or removal of dress is a rite of separation from the previous state. The important thing is not the moment of transition (and there is no evidence that any danger is attached to this), but the state itself. Passage from one state to another is marked frequently by change of apparel, but it is unnecessary to labour the point of transition. It is clear that the principle of adaptation to state or circumstance has, as a corollary, the principle of change, which may be more or less emphasized. Thus, the Lapps strip themselves of the garments

1 F. Boas, in *Bull. Amer. Mus. Nat. Hist.* xv. (1901) i. 119-126.
2 Crantz, i. 120. 3 Lv 16[23f.]. 4 Frazer, *GB*² ii. 308.
5 *MI* i. 59. 6 Van Gennep, *Rites de passage*, 85.

in which they have killed a bear,[1] just as after any sacred ceremony the participants put off their ceremonial appurtenances. The particular state is over and done with; therefore its exterior adaptation must likewise be removed. Ideas of removing the sacred and dangerous influence are probably secondary.

These considerations, in connexion with the principle that solemnity in dress must accompany solemnity of circumstance and function, may explain the following types of these customs.

For the harvest festival the two officiating elders of the Nāgas wash carefully and put on new clothes.[2] The Greeks put on clean clothes before worship.[3] Before officiating the Shintō priests of Japan put on clean garments.[4] It is a precept of Islām that the clothes and person of a worshipper shall be clean.[5] A Muhammadan 'would remove any defiled garment before he commences his prayer, or otherwise abstain from praying altogether.'[6] In ancient Christian baptism the novices put off their garments, and clothed themselves in new white robes.[7] At the consecration of a Catholic virgin the novice puts off her ordinary clothes, and puts on the habit and the veil; also the ring on the finger—the ceremony being actually a marriage to Christ.[8] The putting away of the skin dress of the noviciate and the assumption of new clothes were part of the 'ordination' of the ancient Brāhman.[9]

Whether the new state is the extraordinary state of sacredness or the ordinary state of common life, adaptation to it equally involves change of assimilative costume, preceded by removal of that previously worn.

In order to assume the crest of the *Lulem*, the Bear, the Carrier Indian took off all his clothes, and spent some days and nights in the woods. On his return he joined in the Bear Dance, in which he was dressed as a bear. During initiation to secret societies in the Congo States the candidate is naked.[10] In British Central Africa, boys during initiation wear bark-cloth. At the conclusion new clothes are put on. Entrance to the various 'gilds' is marked by a change of costume. Girls after initiation put on new calico.[11] When their initiation ceremonies were over, Kaffir boys were chased to the river, where they washed off the white clay with which their bodies had been painted. Everything about them was burned. They were smeared with the ordinary unguent and were given new karosses.[12]

Frazer has suggested that the practices of depilation, and painting the body white or red, at puberty, are in view of the belief in re-birth.[13] The Kikuyu, for instance, hold that a boy is born again at circumcision, and he pretends so to be.[14] But this idea is *ex post facto*.

When her period is over, a woman puts on new clothes. This is the ordinance of the *Shāyast lā-Shāyast*, of the Mosaic and Hindu law, and of the vast majority of savage and barbarian customary social codes.

Thus, the Kharwar woman after her period bathes and washes her clothes.[15] The Thompson Indian girl has the special dress she wore during her seclusion at puberty burnt on her re-entry into society.[16]

At the end of the *hiri*, the annual trading expedition, which partakes of the nature of a solemn pilgrimage, the Koita of New Guinea bathes, anoints himself, and puts on a new *sihi*, loin-cloth. His wife, who has stayed at home, also bathes and puts on new garments.[17]

A sort of mechanical link between purification by lustration and the assumption of new clothes is made by anointing. After childbirth the Kaffir mother is anointed ceremonially with the ordinary fat and red clay.[18] This is equivalent to the resumption of decent apparel.

New clothes express a new state or condition.

1 Frazer, *GB*³, pt. ii. p. 221. 2 T. C. Hodson, 172.
3 Westermarck, *MI* ii. 352, citing the authorities.
4 W. E. Griffis, *Religions of Japan*, 1895, p. 85.
5 E. Sell, *Faith of Islam*², 1896, p. 257.
6 Westermarck, *MI* ii. 416. 7 Van Gennep, 135.
8 Migne, *Encycl. théol.*, 1844-66, xvii.; Boissonnet, *Dict. des cérémonies et des rites sacrés*, 1846, iii. coll. 539 ff., quoted by Van Gennep, 140 ff.
9 Oldenberg, *Rel. des Veda*, 350.
10 Frobenius, *Die Masken u. Geheimbünde Afrikas*, Halle, 1898, p. 69 f.
11 H. Stannus, in *JAI* xl. (1910) 296, 297.
12 Maclean, *Compendium of Kafir Laws and Customs*, 1858, p. 99.
13 *Totemism and Exogamy*, iv. 230.
14 *Ib.* 228, quoting Hollis. 15 Crooke, in *NINQ* i. 67.
16 Teit, in *Bull. Am. Mus. Nat. Hist.* II. iv. (1900) 317.
17 Seligmann, 110. 18 Maclean, 94.

There is an impulse to rhythmical change in human life, coinciding with later ideas of morality. The Incas, at a purificatory festival which was to banish all evil, shook their clothes, crying 'Let the evils be gone!'[1] In such cases the idea of newness, owing to the contrast between the old state and the new and to the impulsive belief in change as producing good fortune, tends to predominate over the principle of adaptation to the new state. In other words, the important thing is not the succeeding state but the riddance of the old.

At the Creek festival of new fruits, the *busk*, new clothes and new utensils were provided by each person; the old clothes were burned.[2] At the Tongan festival of first-fruits all were clad in new clothes.[3] The Hindus wear new clothes at the festival of the new year, *saṁvatsarādi*.[4] The Chinese ceremony of 'raising the head' is the putting on of special clothes for marriage. A suit of white body-clothes of linen is made for both bride and groom. Brand-new they are, and are worn during the marriage-ceremonies, for on this occasion they themselves 'become brand-new people.' The suits are then put away, only to be worn again in the tomb.[5] In Korea, on the 14th day of the first month, any one entering upon 'a critical year of his life' dresses an effigy of straw in his own clothes and casts it away. Fate is believed to look upon the individual in his new clothes as another man.[6]

Here the secondary principle of disguise intrudes. Ideas of disguise by change of dress have been developed in many cases.

Thus, in the seventh month of pregnancy, a Ceramese woman is rubbed with dough of seven colours. A new ornamental *sarong* is placed on her. This the husband slices in two with a sword and immediately runs away. She is dressed seven times in seven colours.[7] The Bulgarian, to cure scrofula, will creep naked through an arch of boughs, and then hang his clothes on a tree, donning other garments.[8] In Uganda a sick man is made to jump over a stick, and let his bark-cloth fall off. The priest takes the cloth and runs in the opposite direction.[9]

Often it is enough to follow the principle of the fantastic as a strong contrast to the previous state which has suffered misfortune.

Thus, in South Guinea a sick woman is dressed in a fantastic garb, and her body is painted with streaks of red and white. She then stands in front of her hut brandishing a sword.[10] The last detail is a later stratum. The Mosquito Indians believe that the devil (*Wulasha*) tries to seize the corpse. It is hurried to the grave by four men 'who have disguised themselves with paint.'[11] A Siberian shaman will paint his face red when about to accompany a soul to the spirit-land, expressly to disguise himself from devils.[12] The Tongans, when at war, changed their costume before every battle by way of disguising themselves.[13] Similarly, the king of Israel disguised himself at Ramoth-Gilead.[14]

Disguise may take the form of impersonation, and the agent may be a person or a thing.

The people of Minahassa delude the evil spirit by placing on the sick man's bed a dummy dressed in his clothes.[15] Abyssinian kings had a sort of small bodyguard who dressed exactly like their royal master. 'So that the enemy may not distinguish him' was the reason assigned.[16]

The protective value of dress is often expressed merely as that of a covering.

Thus, when the angel appeared to Muhammad, he hastened to his house, crying, 'Cover me with cloth!' Then God spoke to him: 'O thou, enwrapped in thy mantle, arise and warn!' From this point the prophet commenced his composition of the Qur'ān.[17] A Hindu mother passing a haunted place draws her robe over her child. In old Bengal there was a prayer for the protection of children till they were dressed in clothes.[18]

In its sexual and supernatural uses alike the veil protects both the face or head from sight and the eyes from seeing the forbidden or dangerous object. To see and to be seen are often interchangeable, and often combined as media of dangerous influences. In early Arabia handsome men veiled their faces to preserve themselves from

[1] Frazer, *GB*² iii. 75.
[2] W. Bartram, *Travels*, 1792, p. 507.
[3] W. Mariner, *Tonga*², 1818, ii. 197.
[4] J. E. Padfield, *The Hindu at Home*, Madras, 1896, p. 192.
[5] De Groot, i. 47.
[6] Griffis, *Corea, the Hermit Nation*, 1882, p. 298.
[7] *Tijdschrift voor Nederlandsch-Indië*, iii. 2 (1840) 241 f.
[8] A. Strausz, *Die Bulgaren*, Leipzig, 1898, p. 414.
[9] Roscoe, quoted by Frazer, *GB*² iii. 403 f.
[10] J. L. Wilson, *Western Africa*, 1856, p. 28.
[11] Bancroft, i. 744 f.
[12] Radloff, *Aus Sibirien*², Leipzig, 1893, ii. 55.
[13] Wilkes, *U.S. Explor. Exped.* 1852, iii. 10.
[14] 1 K 22³⁰.
[15] N. Graafland, *De Minahassa*, 1867, i. 326.
[16] Krapf, *Trav. in E. Africa*, 1860, p. 454.
[17] E. Sell, 5.
[18] *BG* xviii. 441; Colebrooke, *Essays*, 1858, i. 213.

the evil eye.[1] Here there is no doubt a combination of subjective and objective methods. The veiling of women and the consequent artificial modesty concerning the exposure of the face are a remarkable characteristic of Musalmān social life, and illustrate the secondary habits induced by dress. Ceremonial veiling of a temporary nature is found in the case of puberty, marriage, and widowhood. The novice during initiation to the *Ko'tikili* of the Zuñi wears a veil, and is supposed to see nothing.[2] Similar practices attend initiation to many forms of secret society. The veiling of the bride is more or less universal. A Musalmān woman takes the veil, just as does a nun. Momentary veiling occurs in the presence of death and in approaching a deity. Socrates and Julius Cæsar veiling their faces at the moment of death typified the Greek and Italian national custom. To interpret, as Van Gennep does, these latter cases as rites of passage, with the purpose of separating one's self from the profane world, is fanciful.[3] The habit is more probably a motor reaction to the impulse for concealment before an object of fear. The veil of the bride is a ritual concession to, and a material accentuation of, the sexual character of modesty, rather than a rite of separation from the previous state. To apply the idea of separation from the previous state to the habit of veiling at the moment of death is clearly impossible. In the case of many secret societies veiling is probably intended merely to accentuate the sense of mystery.

In connexion with marriage there are customs of stripping or forcible removal of dress. In some cases these seem to point to a diminution of personality, in others they are preparatory to the assumption of a new dress, often presented by the bridegroom. Among the Roro tribes of New Guinea a nubile girl is tatued, and wears ornaments every day. After marriage, for a few weeks she decorates herself every afternoon. She may not visit her father's village until after a ceremony in which she is stripped of all her finery.[4] The idea, no doubt, is to affirm her subjection to her father's family.

The exchange of presents of dress, a prevalent custom at marriage, may be extended.

Thus, the Koita of New Guinea hold the *heni* ceremony when a first-born child is three weeks old. The infant is decked with various finery, and is carried by the mother, also dressed up, to her mother's house. Her husband follows her with an empty pot, a spear, a petticoat, and a firestick. After smoking and betel-chewing, the wife of the child's maternal uncle strips the ornaments and clothes from the mother and the child. These and the articles carried by the father become the property of the *raimu* and the *wahia*, the grandfather and grandmother on the maternal side. A return present is given.[5]

Customs which prescribe the wearing of best clothes or of rags illustrate the most important psychological result of the invention of dress. This is a secondary human character, the feeling for dress, and is one aspect (consisting in extension of self-consciousness) of the reaction to extension of personality. It is really distinct from the feeling for ornament and the impulse to protection, but is correlated with the more physical impulse to cleanliness, and the dermal and nervous refinement which dress has introduced into the human organism. Connected with the latter development are various reactions in the spheres of art and etiquette. Stanley Hall finds that 'of the three functions of clothes—protection, ornament, and Lotze's self-feeling'—the second is by far the most conspicuous in childhood.[6] But the sense of personal dignity and physical pride is only latent in childhood. Of the psychical resultants of dress this adult character is the most significant. As Lotze

[1] Wellhausen, *Reste arab. Heidentums*², Berlin, 1897, p. 196.
[2] Stevenson, in *23 RBEW* (1904), p. 103.
[3] Van Gennep, 241; also S. Reinach, *Cultes, mythes, et religions*, 1905, i. 299–311.
[4] Seligmann, 266, 270.
[5] *Ib.* 71.
[6] *AJPs*, 1898, p. 366.

put it, clothes extend the limits of self and enable the wearer to feel himself to the extremity of each garment. A precise analogy is found in the psychology of tools. Add the sexual factor, and

'the mere presence or possession of the article [of clothing] gives the required sense of self-respect, of human dignity, of sexual desirability. Thus it is that to unclothe a person is to humiliate him; this was so even in Homeric times, for we may recall the threat of Ulysses to strip Thersites.'[1]

Similarly, to foul a person's garments is a secondarily direct insult. When the sense of well-being is at a maximum, fine dress is an expression of it and an adaptation to it. Also, on momentous occasions a man of any period will dress very carefully, unconsciously intending to affirm and emphasize his personality. Conversely, to express misery, the negation of well-being, or humility, a negative form of dress is employed; value, colour, and style are at a minimum. The diminution of personality is echoed by wearing rags, sackcloth, or colourless or torn or dirty clothes, which act as adaptations to the negative state. Momentary diminutions of personality can only be expressed by partial unclothing or by fouling or tearing the dress. In both cases the dress or its treatment has a reaction on the psychical state of the individual.

On these foundations luxury and superstition have erected a mass of fashions. Two typical cases follow.

Great personages in Siam used to wear clothes of a different colour for each day of the week. As an example, white was worn on Sunday, yellow on Monday, green on Tuesday, red on Wednesday, blue on Thursday, black on Friday, violet on Saturday.[2]

The primary meaning of the dress next cited is not talismanic, but a suggestion of well-being. Its magical content is secondary, and it is therefore considered here particularly. The Chinese *siū i*, 'the garment for a long life,' is a long gown of valuable silk, blue or red-brown, with a lining of bright blue. It is embroidered all over with gold-thread characters, representing the word 'longevity.' 'It purports in the first place to prolong the life of the owner, who therefore frequently wears it, especially on festive occasions, in order to allow the influences of longevity, created by the many characters wherewith it is decorated, to work their full effect upon his person. On the anniversary of his birth he will scarcely ever neglect doing so, it being generally acknowledged among the Chinese that it is extremely useful and necessary then to absorb a good amount of vital energy, in order to remain hale and healthy during the ensuing year. Friends and kinsmen who throng the house to take part in the festivities will then, as a rule, greatly admire the dress and tender their reiterated congratulations to the happy wearer, whose children have been so filial, and so blessed by fate as to have bestowed a present of such delicate and precious description.' The longevity garment is generally the gift of children who are filial enough to wish their parent to live long. There is considerable ceremony about the presentation. The garment should be made if possible in a year which has an intercalary month; such a year naturally has an influence on length. In accordance with Chinese ideas about sympathy between ascendants and descendants, the garment also ensures long life to its wearer's posterity.[3]

In hunting, as in war, the human impulse is to emphasize personality. This is more powerful than the impulse to protection, though the two may be combined.

The Dayaks wear as war-dress a basket-work hat, *katapu*, and a jacket of skin or quilted cotton. The crown of the helmet is adorned with feathers or full plumes. The *gagong*, or war jacket of skin, has the animal's face on the wearer's stomach, and its back hanging over his shoulders. It is little defence, though the head is covered with a plate or shell to protect the pit of the stomach.[4]

The mere fact that in all periods social meetings are the occasion for the wearing of best clothes indicates the social significance of dress. Dress loses half its meaning except in relation to society. The principle of extension of personality refers to the individualistic aspect of dress; the principle of adaptation to state is its social side. The vaguely termed 'festival' of lower cultures is expressive of mutual well-wishing and of common well-being.[5] At festivals the Ainus dress in their best clothes. The statement applies to all peoples. The individualistic form of the social meeting is amphitryonic.

[1] H. Ellis, i. 40; *Il.* ii. 262.
[2] Pallegoix, *Siam*, Paris, 1854, i. 319.
[3] De Groot, i. 61 ff. [4] Brooke Low, in *JAI* xxii. (1892) 53.
[5] Frazer, *GB*[2] ii. 377.

As is the rule with all peoples, the Guiana Indian, 'when expecting guests, grooms himself carefully and puts on his best dress and ornaments, these often, as in this case, consisting only of a narrow waist-cloth by way of dress and of a necklace and armlets of white beads by way of ornament.'[1]

A few types of festal dress may be cited from a variety which exceeds all other forms of human inventiveness—a fact which illustrates both man's physical pride and his tendency to shift its focus to an artificial and variable substitute.

The Manipuri festal head-dress is remarkable. 'A white turban is bound tightly round the head, and over the top and in front is wound round a *shumzil*, a horn-shaped construction of cane bound over with cloth or gold braid, and ending above in a loop and below in three flat loops which are concealed under the turban. The *shumzil* is over a foot high, and curves slightly backwards; from the loop at its end hangs an embroidered streamer. On each side of the head a plume made of peacocks' feathers and the tail feathers of the hornbill are inserted in the turban. . . . The whole structure is bound together by a narrow band of red and white embroidery, wound round and round and tied, under the chin, with ends hanging down nearly to the waist.'[2] On high days Tangkhul men wear a kilt, and the *luhup* head-dress adorned with toucan feathers and tresses of hair.[3] The Woolwa Indians wear on festal occasions coronets made of the curly head-feathers of the curassow, and on the arms, feathers of the macaw, or yellow tail-feathers of the *Ostinops montzuma*.[4] The women wear great masses of beads round the neck, sometimes occupying the whole space from the bosom to the chin. A petticoat of bark-cloth extends below the knee; it is wrapped round the loins, and the end is tucked in over the hip. The exposed parts of the skin are dyed a deep vermilion, the colour being extracted from the pod of the *arnotto* shrub.[5]

The Ackawoi wear for festivals a dress made of the bright, greenish yellow, young leaves of the Aeta palm (*Mauritia flexuosa*). The Macusi wears a head-dress of bright parrot and macaw feathers, a ruff of black curassow and white egret feathers, and a strip of waist-cloth, as a dancing dress.[6] At the feasts of the dead, Quoireng men wear a 'glory.' This consists of bands of yellow and red thread, one and a half inches wide, bound round the head. In them are fixed rays of bamboo with feathers inserted, the structure being eighteen inches in height.[7]

The dance is a social language, a motor expression of individuality in society. As a rule, best clothes are worn. Various circumstances often impose different fashions. For ceremonial dancing the Vedda puts on the *hangala*, a white cloth tied round the waist. Formerly leaf-girdles were used.[8] Probably such costumes are merely for the facilitation of movement. In other cases regard is paid to the dance as such. The female dancing dress of the Fulas is elaborate, made of velvet or ornamental cloth, sometimes decked with bells which sound in time to the music.[9]

Meetings of society in its magical or spiritual character are no less marked by fine clothes. The Qur'ān says: 'Wear your goodly apparel when ye repair to my mosque.'[10] The injunction applies to all religions, with the limitation (due to the difference between well-willing and well-being, and later to the distinction between worshippers and deity) that excess of luxury is forbidden or discouraged. Cleanliness of attire is regularly enjoined, originally, perhaps, for the avoidance not of defilement, material or supernatural, but of mixture of states.

Just as all sacrifice should be precious, so should a dress-wearing victim be well dressed. The human victim sacrificed by the Pawnees was dressed in the richest raiment.[11] The *meriah* of the Khonds was dressed in a new garment before the sacrifice, anointed, and adorned with flowers.[12] For scapegoats the case may be different. When the image of the god is clothed it necessarily wears the richest raiment (see below).

The connexion of fine dress with well-being, and the estimate of clothing as a necessary of existence,[13] are combined in the Hebrew belief that

[1] Im Thurn, in *JAI* xxii. (1893) 190.
[2] J. Shakespear, in *JAI* xl. (1910) 353 f. [3] T. C. Hodson, 22.
[4] H. A. Wickham, in *JAI* xxiv. (1894) 203.
[5] *Ib.* 204. [6] Im Thurn, *JAI* xxii. 195.
[7] T. C. Hodson, 26. [8] C. G. and B. Z. Seligmann, 213.
[9] G. F. Scott Elliott, in *JAI* xxiii. (1893) 81.
[10] *Sūra* vii. 29. [11] Frazer, *GB*[2] ii. 238.
[12] S. C. Macpherson, *Memorials of Service in India*, 1865, p. 118.
[13] See Is 37.

Jahweh was the ultimate donor of food and raiment.[1] The teaching of Christ against 'taking thought' for raiment, illustrated by the natural dress of the lilies of the field,[2] was a wise protest against extravagance in the cult of this secondary body, and a timely rehabilitation of the body itself, no less than of the higher claims of personality.

Diminution of personality is symbolized by various customs of removing part of the dress. In India a low-caste man passing through a high-caste street must take off shoes and turban.[3] That the reason for such uncovering is not the assumption of an unprotected state, by removing a garment of defence, is shown by such a case as the following. All persons when interviewing Montezuma put off their usual costume and 'appeared in plain coarse dresses and barefooted.'[4] The modern European fashion of removing the hat is a salutation of respect of a similar order, and not a removal of defence.

A permanent inferiority of person or status is expressed by inferiority of dress.

'In Flores the sons even of rich families are dressed like slaves at public feasts, so long as the father lives, as also at his funeral. This . . . is apparently the external sign of a strict *patria potestas*, which remains in force till the funeral; until then the son is the father's slave.'[5] It is a very marked custom of the Mpongwe for the young to show deference to the old. 'They must never come into the presence of aged persons or pass by their dwellings without taking off their hats, and assuming a crouching gait.'[6]

An artificial assumption of humility may be employed to emphasize the succeeding magnificence, or to deprecate the ill-luck which may follow pride. For some days before marriage the bride and bridegroom among the Musalmāns of the N.W. Provinces wear dirty clothes.[7] Such practices may soon take on the ideas connected with disguise and protection from the evil eye. Similar, though of more obscure origin, is the custom, found in old English coronation ceremonies, that the king shall appear in poor garments before he is invested with the royal robes. German peasants dress a child in mean clothes to protect it against the evil eye. In Egypt the children who are most beloved are the worst clad. A fine lady may often be seen in a magnificent dress, with a boy or girl, her own child, by her side, with its face smeared with dirt, and wearing clothes which look as if they had not been washed for months. The intention is to avoid attracting the evil eye. The method employed is not disguise, but humiliation, negation of well-being, either deprecatory or to escape notice. The evil eye is stimulated by finery and splendour, and its constant emotion is envy.[8]

Penance and asceticism often coincide in method. Sackcloth is in this connexion the analogue of fasting and humiliation.

For penance, Manu prescribes clothes of cow-hair, with the wearer's own hair in braids.[9] Among the rules of penance in mediæval Christendom was the wearing of dirty clothes.[10] An ancient rule for Buddhist monks was that their dress should be made of rags taken from a dust-heap.[11] Early Christian ascetics disdained clothes, and crawled abroad 'like animals covered only by their matted hair.'[12] Hindu ascetics similarly practised nudity as the least of their mortifications, 'until British law interposed to prevent the continuance of the nuisance.'[13]

A curious question is raised by certain fashions of cleanliness in connexion with dress. Physical cleanliness is a habit which has undergone evolution, and the fact perhaps suffices as an explanation for the following cases.

1 Gn 28[20f.]. 2 Mt 6[25ff.].
3 J. E. Padfield, 73. 4 Payne, ii. 495.
5 Westermarck, *MI* i. 602, quoting von Martens.
6 J. L. Wilson, 392 f. 7 Crooke, in *PNQ* ii. (1886) 960.
8 Ploss, i. 134; Lane, *Modern Egyptians*, 1846, i. 60.
9 *SBE* xxv. (1886) 449.
10 Westermarck, *MI* ii. 356.
11 H. Kern, *Manual of Indian Buddhism*, Strassburg, 1896, p. 75.
12 Westermarck, *MI* ii. 356, quoting Lecky, *Hist. of European Morals*, 1890, ii. 108.
13 Monier-Williams 395.

The ancient Huns and Mongols, and the modern Kalmuks, are reported to avoid the washing of their clothes—in the last case, apparently, for religious reasons.[1] The Sūdras of the Carnatic never leave off a suit of clothes when once it has been put on. It drops off as it rots. The custom is said to have been religiously observed, and persons transgressing it and found changing garments before the old set was thoroughly decayed were excluded from the caste.[2] Jenghiz Khan ordered clothes to be worn till they dropped off in tatters. The wearing of clothes in this way is recorded of several peoples. Cold climates encourage such habits.[3] 'Poverty,' says Westermarck, 'is for obvious reasons a cause of uncleanliness; "a starving vulture neglects to polish his feathers, and a famished dog has a ragged coat."'[4] Cleanliness, again, is frequently 'a class distinction.' Among the Point Barrow Eskimo, as amongst many modern European nations, the poorer people are often careless about their clothes and persons, whereas 'most of the wealthier people appear to take pride in being neatly clad.'[5] Peoples who are much addicted to bathing are not on that account necessarily cleanly in habits of toilet and dress. The Californian Indians are fond of bathing, but are very uncleanly about their lodges and their clothes.[6] The case of the Australian native, who never takes off his girdle of hair, is rather different;[7] the analogy here is the non-removal of such articles as rings. Thus, while her husband is alive, no Masai woman dares to take off her ear-rings, which are part of the symbols of marriage.[8]

Ideas of ceremonial cleanliness have probably had an important collateral influence upon the evolution of habits of cleanliness. Some such idea as the avoidance of mixture of condition and environment may account for the origin of ceremonial purity, whereas during the early stages of the evolution of dress there seems to be no *a priori* reason why clothes, as such, should be periodically cleaned. The case of the Sabæans illustrates the connexion between cleanliness of dress and of person. The candidate for the priestly office is instructed not to dirty himself; and he must change his dress daily.[9] Given the existence of a natural impulse to personal and other cleanliness, its foundation being similar to that of ceremonial purity—an unconscious preference for clearness and distinctness in objects, a preference for the thing itself in its essential, specific, and individual, or unmixed, purity of character—asceticism, when, as is often the case, encouraging uncleanliness, is a biological perversion and a social danger. Early Christianity was largely tainted with this.[10] St. Jerome approves the observation of Paula, that 'the purity of the body and its garments means the impurity of the soul.'[11]

The ritual and emotional removal or tearing of dress is apparently derived from several motives. The Hebrew widow repudiating the levirate takes off her sandal and spits on the ground.[12] In Van Gennep's terminology this is a rite of separation from the husband's family. Among the ancient Arabs, women when mourning not only uncovered the face and bosom, but also tore all their garments. The messenger who brought bad news tore his garments. A mother desiring to bring pressure to bear on her son took off her clothes. 'A man to whom vengeance was forbidden showed his despair and disapproval . . . by raising his garment and covering his head with it, as was done in fulfilling natural necessities.'[13] Among the Chuwashes, Cheremiss, and Wotyaks, the husband effects divorce by tearing his wife's veil.[14] Similar customs, especially the rending of the garments to express indignation or repudiation, were prevalent among the Hebrews. The British

1 K. F. Neumann, *Die Völker des südlichen Russlands*, Leipzig, 1847, p. 27; J. Georgi, *Russia*, London, 1780–3, iv. 37.
2 Dubois-Beauchamp, *Hindu Manners*, p. 20.
3 Westermarck, *MI* ii. 349 ff.
4 *Ib.*, quoting B. St. John, *Village Life in Egypt*, 1852, i. 187
5 Murdoch, in *9 RBEW* (1892), p. 421; Westermarck, ii. 350.
6 S. Powers, *Tribes of California*, Washington, 1877, p. 403.
7 P. W. Bassett Smith, in *JAI* xxiii. (1893) 327.
8 Hollis, 283.
9 N. Siouffi, *Études sur la rel. des Soubbas*, Paris, 1880, p. 68 f.
10 See H. Ellis, iv. ch. 4. 11 *Ep.* cviii. 713.
12 *JE*, *s.v.* 'Ḥaliẓah.' 13 Wellhausen, 195 f.
14 Georgi, i. 42.

Columbian expresses indignation against a wrong by destroying a number of blankets, the native currency. His adversary is expected to destroy an equal number to satisfy honour and heal the quarrel.

The rending of garments is perhaps a development from the reflex impulse to destruction generated by anger, indignation, or despair. When it becomes symbolic it may take on the character of a rite of separation, the rending of the garment indicating the severance of a tie or the isolation of the person from calamity or injury. In the Hebrew custom the latter seems to be the prevailing meaning of the rite—a meaning which might naturally be superposed upon an original unconscious reaction to emotions of resentment or sorrow. Stripping, as an indignity or penance, is applied to any person. Thus, when his guardian-spirit fails to please him, the Eskimo will strip it of its garments.[1]

(5) *Dress of the dead.*—Like other states, death is marked and solemnized by a change of dress. In modern civilization, the corpse, whether embalmed or not, is swathed or loosely wrapped in linen or cotton cloths, and covered with the garment, if any, most typical of the dead person's official position. In particular cases, customs like that of placing the busby on the coffin involve the idea that official dress is more than individual personality, a special covering representing specialized social functions, whereas lay garments represent generalized.

Among earlier peoples it is the general rule to dress the dead person in his best clothes. Typical cases are the American Indians, Burmans, Tongkingese, Maoris, Greeks, and Chinese.[2] Careful washing and scrupulous toilette are no less significant and prevalent parts of the more or less ceremonial investiture of the dead.

Among the Tshi and Ewe peoples the dead body is washed, dressed in the richest clothes, and adorned.[3] The Yorubas dress the corpse in the best raiment. The exposed parts of a woman's body are dyed red. The body is wrapped not in clothes, but in grass mats.[4] Among the Koita of New Guinea the dead man is washed, oiled, and painted; a new loin-cloth and ornaments are put on him.[5] The Greenlanders undress a man when at the point of death, and put his best clothes upon him.[6] This detail recurs in China. The Hindus wash, shave, and dress the corpse in rich garments.[7]

According to Homer, the corpse was covered with a soft cloth, over which a white robe was placed.[8] The Greek dead were shrouded in the handsomest garments the family could afford; there was an idea of keeping them warm on the passage to Hades, and of preventing Cerberus from seeing them naked.[9] The modern Greeks dress the dead in best clothes, but these are rendered useless by being snipped with scissors or drenched with oil.[10]

The grave-clothes of a Chinese are arranged round his dying bed. His boots are by his feet, his hat by his head, and so on. He rejoices, in his last moments of consciousness, 'that he will be fashionably attired in the regions beyond the grave.' It was the old custom to strip the man of his clothes just before expiring, and to put the new clothes on, if possible, before death actually occurred.[11] The Chinese ritual of dressing the dead is most elaborate. The curious point is that the corpse is swathed almost as thickly as an Egyptian mummy, but in suits of clothes, not bands of cloth. A distinction is made between inner and outer garments, the former being specially prepared for wear in the grave, the latter being, as a rule, a person's best or favourite clothes. Five suits of garments are forbidden, because the number five is a synonym of evil.[12] Nine and thirteen are usual numbers. Even numbers symbolize the *Yin* part of Nature, cold, darkness, and evil; they are therefore avoided; and odd numbers typifying the opposite blessings are used.[13] Confucius was buried in eleven suits and one court dress; on

[1] Turner, in *11 RBEW* (1894), p. 194.

[2] Schoolcraft, *Indian Tribes*, 1853-7, ii. 68; Bancroft, i. 86; Lafitau, *Mœurs des sauvages amériquains*, 1724, ii. 389; Shway Yoe [J. G. Scott], *The Burman*, 1896, ii. 338; J. G. Scott, *France and Tongking*, 1885, p. 97; R. Taylor, *Te ika a Maui*, 218; *FLJ* ii. (1884) 168 f.; Frazer, in *JAI* xv. (1886) 75, 86.

[3] A. B. Ellis, *Tshi-speaking Peoples*, 1887, p. 237, also *Ewe-speaking Peoples*, 1890, p. 157.

[4] A. B. Ellis, *Yoruba-speaking Peoples*, 1894, pp. 156, 158.

[5] Seligmann, 159. [6] Crantz, 217. [7] J. A. Dubois, 503.

[8] *Od.* xxiv. 293. [9] Lucian, *de Luctu*, 10.

[10] *FLJ* ii. 168 f. [11] De Groot, i. 6.

[12] *Ib.* 64. [13] *Ib.* 65.

his head was a *chang-fu* cap. But, in accordance with the ancient division of the dressing into three stages, the body-clothes, the 'slighter' dressing, and the 'full' dressing,[1] the eleven suits comprised the first stage only, and over them were the 'slighter' and the 'fuller' dressings.[2] The clothes are exhibited to those present before each suit is put on, and the very elaborate rules of the *Li-ki* about the dressing of the dead are followed.[3] Previously the best or favourite suit is placed round the dying man. Before being placed on the corpse, the clothes are put on the chief mourner. He is stripped, and stands on a tray resting on a chair, 'so as not to pollute the earth'; he wears a large round hat, 'so as not to pollute heaven.' Then each garment is put upon him in its proper order, and afterwards taken off and put on the corpse. In the case of a woman, the eldest son, as chief mourner, still has to put the clothes on.[4] The *Li-ki* explains the custom by the analogy of a dutiful son testing a medicine before his father drinks it.[5] As the dressing proceeds the mourners wail and 'howl.'[6] Wide drawers, lined, for comfort, with silk, are first put on. Stockings and a jacket follow. An ordinary jacket of linen, cotton, or silk, and trousers of the same material come next. A second jacket or even a third—the more there are the more devotion is expressed—may be added. When the body-clothes have been put on, the outer suits follow. The long blue gown of the middle class is a common type. It overlaps to the right, and is buttoned at the side. Over this is a jacket with short sleeves, extending, that is, only to the finger-tips; it is the kind of jacket used in winter as an overcoat. A common skull-cap of silk or horse hair, ordinary shoes and stockings, complete the suit. The costly silk clothes used on festive occasions are preferred by those who possess them. They represent the true sacerdotal attire of the paterfamilias, as high priest of the family.[7] These include an outer and an inner cloak, neither having a collar; the sleeves of the inner cloak project, and are of a horse-hoof shape. The inner is dark blue; for summer wear, white or yellow; the outer is dark blue or brown. A sash is worn round the waist. The boots are of silk. The winter suit alone is used for the dead, even in summer. Women wear their best embroidered clothes, such as the official dress of mandarins' wives, which is the regular bridal costume. It includes a dragon petticoat of green silk, a dragon mantle of red silk, a mantilla of black silk, and boots of red silk. The bride's hood, or phœnix cap, is a quarter-globe of thin twined wire, covered with butterflies, leaves and flowers of thin gilt copper, and symbols of felicity, joy, wealth, and longevity. Great care is taken with the coiffure.[8]

Such is the *tho phao*, attire of the dead. Women, as a rule, wear the 'longevity garment,' but men prefer the true 'sacrificial' robes, the *tho phao*.[9] One prepares them, 'the clothing laid out for old age,' at about the age of 50 or 60. They are preferably cut out and sewn by a very young woman, such a person being likely to live long, and part of her capacity to live 'must surely pass into the clothes, and thus put off for many years the moment when they shall be required for use.'[10]

If these clothes have ever been lent to a friend, not of one's own clan, they may not be used for their chief purpose. Another suit must be prepared. However it may happen, it is a curious fact that the grave-clothes are often cut carelessly, and merely pasted, not sewn.[11] Quite poor people use cheap mats. It is probably Buddhist influence that forbids the use of leather. Metal buttons may not be used, because metal is supposed to injure the body during decomposition.[12]

The Malays shroud the dead body in fine new *sarongs*, sometimes as many as seven.[13]

The bandages of the mummy are a development (for a particular purpose) from the use of the ordinary garments of life. In ancient Egypt the gods were invoked to grant clothing to the dead. The bandaging of the mummy corresponds in its ritualism very much, for example, with the Chinese dressing of the corpse. For instance, a sorrowing husband reproaching his wife for haunting him says: 'I have given clothes and bandages for thy burial. I have given to be made for thee many clothes.' The application of the swathes was 'a divine task.' In funeral rituals there are the chapters 'of putting on the white bandages,' 'of putting on the green,' and 'of the light red and dark red bandages.' The quantity used was a 'measure of the affection of the relatives.'[14]

As a type of simpler customs the following explains itself, and is significant for the whole theory of the subject:

The Samoyeds dress the corpse in the clothes he was wearing at death, and wrap the whole in birch bark or deer skins.[15]

Rare cases occur where derogatory garments are applied. The Avestan horror of death and its defilement sufficiently explains the following rule:

Zoroastrian law ordained 'clothing which is useless; this is that in which they should carry a corpse.' In the case of still useful clothing, which had been touched by a corpse, a very thorough and minute process of cleaning was applied.[16]

[1] De Groot, i. 338 f. [2] *Ib.* 339. [3] *Ib.* 341.

[4] *Ib.* 67 f. [5] *Ib.* 68. [6] *Ib.* 67.

[7] *Ib.* 46 ff., 49. [8] *Ib.* 51-54. [9] *Ib.* 63.

[10] *Ib.* 60. [11] *Ib.* 51. [12] *Ib.* 65 f.

[13] Skeat, 397.

[14] A. Macalister, in *JAI* xxiii. (1893) 107, 103, 111.

[15] Montefiore, in *JAI* xxiv. (1895) 406.

[16] 'Pahlavi Texts' (E. W. West), in *SBE* v. (1880) 269.

When preservatives are not applied to the grave-clothes, some peoples periodically renew them.

The bodies of the Ccapac-Incas were preserved and clothed, new clothes being supplied as required.[1] At stated periods the Malagasy open the tombs of their ancestors, removing the rotten *lambas* and rolling the bones in new ones.[2]

A simpler method is to place changes of raiment in the grave, just as other articles of use are there deposited.

In Vedic times, clothing and ornaments were placed with the dead for their use in the life to come.[3] The Chinese place clothes and silk in the grave, besides the numerous suits in which the dead man is clothed.[4] Clothing, according to Pahlavi texts, was to be put upon the sacred cake of the 'righteous guardian spirit'—both for its use in the other world.[5] The clothing and weapons deposited in the Kayan grave are of the highest value, no broken or damaged article being deemed worthy of a place.[6] On the other hand, many peoples render such articles useless by cutting or breaking them before deposition; and a principle commonly occurs that in this way the souls of the articles are released (as is the soul from the broken body of the dead man), and are thus able to accompany him to the place of the departed.

There is naturally some doubt as to the condition of the soul in its super-terrestrial home.

Thus the soul of the Mexican, at death, entered the new life naked;[7] whereas the soul of the dead Iroquois wears 'a beautiful mantle' when it departs towards the other world in the west.[8] The ghost is believed by Africans to wear the white cloth in which the body was buried.[9] But, as has been seen, the person in the life to come wears similar dress to what he wore on earth. There are refinements; Christian eschatology in its popular aspects is inclined to invest the blessed with fine raiment and crowns of gold.

As for the meaning behind these customs, there seems to be, as usual, a series of moral strata or psychological layers. Various emotions might be supposed to be in competition as soon as attention was directed to the dress of a man just dead. Other things being equal, and before ideas of contagion on the one hand and of a future life on the other had been developed, principles of property and feelings of sorrow would first come into play, together with the principle of dress as an adaptation to state.

Thus the Samoyed type may be one of the earliest. The corpse retains the garments he wore at death. He is prepared for the new state by the protective (both of external and of internal direction) covering of bark or similar substance, which takes the place of the coffin.

Sorrow and affection would make the stripping of the corpse an act impossible for relatives. As the various ideas relating to the state of the dead became clearer, regard would be had to the comfort of the dead. No less than the living they must have the two great necessaries, food and raiment. Naive examples of the idea are numerous.

For instance, the natives of New South Wales wrapped the corpse in a rug, for the purpose, expressed, of keeping the dead man warm.[10] In Voigtland peasants have been known to put an umbrella and goloshes in the coffin, as a protection against the rainy skies of the other world.[11]

Later still there would supervene the idea, of complex origin, that articles in the house of death must be, like the occupant, broken and soulless. One component of this idea is perhaps as early as any, namely, the realization that articles of value, permanently deposited in a place by no means secure, and practically known to be unused, should be rendered useless, to avoid robbery and the attendant distressing results of exhumation.

With the custom of dressing the dead in his richest raiment, and in many suits, the problem becomes less simple. First of all, as soon as the social consciousness realizes that death is a social state, and therefore to be solemnized, a change of garb is necessary. What are significantly termed in various languages 'the last offices' express this principle, as well as the feelings of sorrow and affection, and the desire to do honour to the dead, as for the last time. In such conditions it is inevitable that the best of everything should be accorded to him. But another factor perhaps is included in the complex psychosis, at least in the earlier stages. This is economic. In early culture, clothes are property. Just as a man's property is called in and realized at his death, so a similar process is universal in mankind. The dead man is still a member of society; and the most personal and most distinctive of his property fittingly remains with him—his personal attire. Equally fitting is it that this item should be of the best, as representing him in the last of his social functions. By a pathetic paradox he is arrayed in his best clothes, as if to assert his personality and to express it in its highest terms, for the last time, though actually that personality is no more.

It is not likely that the dressing in fine clothes to tempt the departing or absent soul to return has any reference in this connexion. The custom of using many suits of raiment, carried to logical absurdity by the Chinese, is one of those problems that elude all rationalism. There is the analogy of the mummy-swathings, which suggests that the suits may be intended as a protection; there is also an idea of placing on or with the corpse all his available assets. The custom of dressing the dead in their best clothes, as of placing food with them, has been explained by Frazer as originating 'in the selfish but not unkindly desire to induce the perturbed spirit to rest in the grave and not come plaguing the living for food and raiment.'[1] But the intellectual atmosphere which the explanation assumes is far from primitive or even from early thought. It represents a late, and somewhat abnormal or excessive, development of spiritualistic belief uncontrolled by social custom or dogma, in fact, an anarchic period of individualistic spiritualist licence.

The dress of the dead seems to preserve only in two or three details the principle of adaptation to state. The reason, no doubt, is that affection and other emotions naturally repudiate the physical actuality of that state, and substitute a moral ideal. But the binding of the corpse, or of its limbs, with cords or ropes, and the later swathing with bandages, accentuate the fact that the body is motionless and the limbs quiescent. At a later stage there might intervene the notion that by these means the possibly dangerous activity of the ghost would be checked. But social habits do not originate from such clear-cut rationalistic motives.

Some sporadic customs have probably an original intention that is not dissimilar. The Koreans fasten blinkers over the eyes of the corpse.[2] Various objects, coins and the like, are placed on the eyes of the dead by various peoples. Such habits, no doubt, were in origin intended unconsciously to emphasize, to realize by accentuation, the sightless state of the dead. With this intention is combined the necessity—both from subjective reasons of vague fear of the staring eyes, and from the natural though sympathetic impulse to close them—of mechanically depressing the eyelids after death. Possibly the custom of placing a mask over the face of the dead has a connected origin, as supplying, so to speak, like the swathings of the mummy, a permanent dermal surface over that which is destined to decay.

The ancient Aztecs, the earliest Greek peoples, the Aleuts, Shans, and Siamese, masked the faces of the dead, particularly of kings and chiefs.[3] In some cases, as those of the Greeks and the Shans, the mask is of gold or silver.

1 Payne, ii. 520 f.
2 Matthews, *Thirty Years in Madagascar*, 1904, p. 202.
3 A. A. Macdonell, *Vedic Mythol.* 165.
4 De Groot, ii. 392, 399.
5 'Pahlavi Texts,' in *SBE* v. (1880) 383.
6 Hose, in *JAI* xxiii. (1893) 165.
7 Payne, ii. 407.
8 J. N. B. Hewitt, in *JAFL* viii. (1895) 107.
9 Crawley, *Idea of the Soul*, 175, 179.
10 J. Fraser, *Aborigines of N.S. Wales*, Sydney, 1892, p. 79 f.
11 J. A. E. Köhler, *Volksbrauch in Voigtlande*, Leipzig, 1867, p. 441.

1 *JAI* xv. 75.
2 J. Ross, *History of Corea*, Paisley, 1879, p. 325.
3 Bancroft, i. 93, ii. 606; H. Schliemann, *Mycenæ*, 1878, pp.

(6) *Mourning dress.*—The social significance of dress is well brought out in mourning customs, among which it is the most prominent. The variations are innumerable, but the principles involved are fairly clear. A few types only can be mentioned here.

Among the Masai, as mourning the wife puts off her ornaments, and the sons shave their heads.[1] As mourning, the Andamanese smear themselves with clay; ancient and modern Egyptians throw mud on their heads.[2] In China the near relatives wear a mourning dress of brown coarse sackcloth.[3] As regards other clothes, white is the colour of mourning. The Kiñahs of Borneo 'wear bark cloth round their caps (as we wear crape round our hats) to show they are in mourning.'[4] In New Guinea, women in mourning wear a net over the shoulders and breast. In some parts men wear netted vests; in others, 'when in deep mourning, they envelop themselves with a very tight kind of wicker-work dress, extending from the neck to the knees in such a way that they are not able to walk well.'[5] The Koita widow wears fragments of her dead husband's loin-cloth, locks of his hair, and bits of his tools, as a necklace. She is painted black, and wears a petticoat reaching to the ankles. Over the upper body she has two netted vests, the outer ornamented with seeds and feathers. A network cap is on her head. This costume is worn for six months, after which she is relieved of her mourning by the *robu momomo* ceremony, and the petticoat is burnt. The widower is also painted black all over.[6] Among the Roros, a neighbouring people of New Guinea, bones of the dead are worn by the mourners. A dead man's jaw is often worn as a bracelet.[7]

The principle of adaptation in colour is well exemplified. The most frequent colours used are black, white, dark blue, and the natural colours of, as a rule, cheap and common fabrics.

The mourning colour in Korea is that of raw hemp or string. For a year the mourner wears the well-known mourner's hat. Its shape is that of an enormous toadstool, and the face is completely hidden.[8] Among the Dayaks of Borneo, white, 'as being the plainest and most unpretending, is worn in mourning and during out-door labour; it is cheap and will wash.' Dark blue is the commonest colour for ordinary wear. A white headdress is often worn in mourning.[9] Women wear as mourning a deep indigo blue *bidang* petticoat.[10] Among the Tlingits, mourners blacken their faces, and cover their heads with ragged mats.[11] Calabrian women put on a black veil at the moment when a death occurs. At sunset it is taken off.[12] Roman women put on black *pallæ* after a funeral. Black clothes as mourning are the fashion in ancient Greece and Italy, modern Greece, and modern Europe generally.[13] White mourning is recorded for Korea, Tongking, China, Siam, in Imperial Rome for women, and in various parts of modern Europe.[14] In old England, white scarves, hatbands and gloves were worn at the funerals of infants and the unmarried.[15] At Singapore a white sash is worn, but apart from this there is no mourning costume in Malaysia.

Mourners among the Tshi people wear dark blue clothes, which they assume as soon as the burial is over.[16] Among the Yorubas a dark blue head-cloth is worn.[17] Among the Ewes of Dahomey blue baft is worn, or merely a blue thread is placed round the arm.[18] This fashion is paralleled by the modern European custom of wearing a black band round the sleeve. In parts of Germany blue is worn as mourning by women, and in ancient and modern Egypt a strip of blue is worn round the head by women at funerals. Widows on the Slave Coast wear black or dark blue. Anne Boleyn wore yellow for Catherine of Aragon. Guatemalan widowers dyed themselves yellow.[1] Sophocles wore grey or dark blue clothes in mourning for Euripides. Grey was the mourning colour of the Gambreiotai.[2]

Simultaneous with change of dress are changes of bodily appearance, especially of the coiffure. The practice of cutting the hair short as a sign of mourning is extremely common. On the other hand, some peoples allow the hair to grow long, as the ancient Egyptians, the Hindus, the Chinese, and the Jews.[3]

Mourning as a social state is pre-eminently a suspension of social life; society is avoided, work is discontinued, and the mourner generally is under a ban. The degrees of mourning depend on the degrees of nearness to the dead. The period of mourning is frequently synchronous with the state of death; that is to say, it ends when the corpse is thoroughly decomposed. Throughout early thought there runs the idea that a person is not absolutely dead until every fragment of the viscera has disappeared. At the end of the time the state of ordinary life is re-entered in the usual way.

Thus, the Ewe people burn their mourning clothes and put on new raiment when mourning ends.[4] A widow among the Koossas, at the end of her month of mourning, threw away her clothes, washed her whole body, and scratched it with stones.[5] The last detail is probably merely an extraordinary method of purification. The period of tabu undergone by murderers among the Omahas might be ended by the kindred of the victim. The formula employed was, 'It is enough. Begone, and walk among the crowd. Put on moccasins and wear a good robe.'[6]

The prevalent explanations of mourning dress are based on the fear of the ghost and of the contagion of death. Frazer has suggested that the painting of the body and the wearing of special costumes by mourners are attempts to disguise themselves so as to escape the notice of the ghost.[7] Westermarck is of opinion that 'the latter custom may also have originated in the idea that a mourner is more or less polluted for a certain period, and that therefore a dress worn by him then, being a seat of contagion, could not be used afterwards.'[8] But such customs originate in unconscious motivation. Of course, concealment may be aimed at, unconsciously. But several considerations place the theory of disguise out of court. Savage philosophies seldom hit on correct explanations; being *ex post facto*, they are out of touch with origins. But they do refer to present conscious motives, which again may not be the underlying primary reason. The motive of disguise may often be superposed on some original unconscious motive, but the following case shows that the opposite may exist. In some of the Central Australian tribes it is said that the object of painting the body of a mourner is to 'render him or her more conspicuous, and so to allow the spirit to see that it is being properly mourned for.'[9] Again, the prevalent custom of wearing the clothes or the bones of the dead is an absolute negation of the principle of concealment. On animistic theory these appurtenances should attract the ghost.

Frazer notes that the customs of blackening the face and of cutting the hair after a death are observed not only for friends but for slain foes, and suggests that in the latter case the explanation of their use as being a mark of sorrow cannot apply. They may therefore, he adds, be explained as intended to disguise the slayer from the angry ghost of the slain.[10] The practice of blackening the body

198, 219–223, 311 f.; Benndorf, *Antike Gesichtshelme und Sepulcralmasker*, Vienna, 1878, *passim*; A. R. Colquhoun, *Amongst the Shans*, 1885, p. 279; Pallegoix, *Siam*, i. 247.

[1] Hollis, 306.

[2] E. H. Man, in *JAI* xii. 143; Herodotus, ii. 85; Wilkinson, *Manners and Customs*, 1878, iii. 442.

[3] De Groot, i. 13; J. Doolittle, *Social Life of the Chinese*, i. 134.

[4] Brooke Low, in *JAI* xxii. (1892) 37.

[5] Chalmers-Gill, *Work and Adventure in New Guinea*, 1885, pp. 35, 130, 149.

[6] Seligmann, 162–166.

[7] *Ib.* 719, 721.

[8] Saunderson, in *JAI* xxiv. 304, 306.

[9] Brooke Low, *loc. cit.* 36 f.

[10] *Ib.* 40.

[11] F. Boas, *Fifth Report on the Tribes of N.W. Canada*, 1889, p. 41.

[12] V. Dorsa, *La Tradizione . . . Calabria*, Cosenza, 1884, p. 91.

[13] Homer, *Il.* xxiv. 94; Xenophon, *Hellen.* i. 798; Marquardt, *Privatleben der Römer*[2], Leipzig, 1886, i. 346; Wachsmuth, *Das alte Griechenland im neuen*, Bonn, 1864, p. 109.

[14] Ross, *Hist. of Corea*, p. 318; Scott, *France and Tongking*, 98 (Baron, in Pinkerton, ix. 698, describes it as ash-coloured); Pallegoix, i. 246; Plutarch, *Quæst. Rom.* 26; Köhler, 257.

[15] Brand, *Popular Antiquities*[3], 1870, ii. 283.

[16] A. B. Ellis, *Tshi-speaking Peoples*, 240 f.

[17] *Yoruba-speaking Peoples*, 161.

[18] *Ewe-speaking Peoples*, 160.

[1] Rochholz, *Deutscher Glaube und Brauch*, Berlin, 1867, i. 198; Lane, *Mod. Egypt.* ii. 257; P. Bouche, *La Côte des Esclaves*, Paris, 1885, p. 218; Brand, ii. 283; Bancroft, ii. 802.

[2] Westermann, *Biographi Græci*, Brunswick, 1845, p. 135; *CIG* ii. 3562.

[3] Herod. ii. 36; S. C. Bose, *The Hindoos as they are*, Calcutta, 1881, p. 254; Gray, i. 286; Buxtorf, *Synag. Jud.*, Basel, 1680, p. 706.

[4] A. B. Ellis, *Ewe-speaking Peoples*, 160.

[5] Lichtenstein, *Travels in Southern Africa*, 1803–6, i. 259.

[6] J. O. Dorsey, in *3 RBEW* (1884), p. 369.

[7] J. G. Frazer, in *JAI* xv. 73.

[8] Westermarck, *MI* ii. 545.

[9] Spencer-Gillen[a], 511.

[10] *JAI* xv. 99.

with ashes, soot, and the like is found in America, Africa, New Guinea, Samoa, and very generally throughout the world.[1] The precise reason for the choice of this medium is obscure.

When spiritualism has once become a part of social belief, such views may enter into the complex of current motives without cancelling the deep-seated original motive of the unconscious mind. Mourning dress, for example, may take on the character of a spiritual armour, as a defence against the evil spirits who often act as a syndicate of death, removing and devouring the souls of the living.

At a Chinese funeral the grave-diggers and coffin-bearers tie their shadows to themselves by tying a cloth round their waists.[2] A Northern Indian murderer wraps himself up tightly. The Thompson Indian widow wears breeches of grass to prevent attempts at intercourse on the part of her husband's ghost.[3]

Similarly the principle of contagion may be superposed on the primary meaning of mourning costume.

Maoris who had handled a corpse were tabued, and threw away the special rags they had worn, lest they should contaminate others.[4] It is stated of the Greenlanders that, 'if they have happened to touch a corpse, they immediately cast away the clothes they have then on; and for this reason they always put on their old clothes when they go to a burying. In this they agree with the Jews.'[5] A Navaho who has touched a corpse takes off his clothes and bathes.[6] Such cases fall into line with other extensive groups of ceremonial observances. For example, at an annual festival the Cherokees flung their old clothes into a river, 'supposing then their own impurities to be removed.' A Maori, before entering a sacred place, which would *tapu* him, took off his clothes.[7] But the earliest peoples, like the Australians, actually cover themselves with, and otherwise assimilate, the contagion of death.

On the other hand, de Groot holds that mourning costume in China originated in the custom of sacrificing to the dead the clothes worn by the mourner. In the time of Confucius it was the custom for mourners to throw off their clothes while the corpse was being dressed.[8] But this view cannot be seriously entertained.

There are several considerations to be adduced by way of leading up to a more probable explanation. The complex of emotions produced by the death of a near relative may be supposed to be in the primitive mind composed of awe, sorrow, and, to some extent, indignation. In later culture the chief component is sorrowful affection, and mourning costume is regarded as a respectful symbol of this feeling. In the next place, the dead and the living together form a special society intermediate between the world of existence and the world of nothingness.[9] Again, the principle of adaptation to state has to be taken into account. This particular social state calls for particular solemnization.

'Mourning customs' (and, in particular, costumes), says Frazer, 'are always as far as possible the reverse of those of ordinary life. Thus at a Roman funeral the sons of the deceased walked with their heads covered, the daughters with their heads uncovered, thus exactly reversing the ordinary usage, which was that women wore coverings on their heads while men did not. Plutarch, who notes this, observes that similarly in Greece men and women during a period of mourning exactly inverted their usual habits of wearing the hair—the ordinary practice of men being to cut it short, that of women to wear it long.'[10] The Mpongwes are very fond of dress, but when in mourning a woman wears as few clothes as possible and a man none at all.[11]

This reversal of habit is better explained on the principles we have assumed than on the principle of disguise. Death is a violent break of social life; sympathetic adaptation to it necessitates an equally violent suspension or reversal of ordinary costume. Such adaptation coincides with sorrow and indignation on the one hand, and with diminution or negation of personality on the other. A number of customs, of which the following is a type, confirms this. When a death occurs, Tshi women tear their hair and rend their clothes.[1] From this it is but a step to the assumption of torn or ragged clothes and a shorn coiffure. Sorrow and indignation prompt the mourner to tear and lacerate both his body and his external coverings; sympathy with the state so violently induced prompts him to deny or humiliate his personality; this motive is helped by sorrow. Absence of colour, as in the hue of black, or apparent absence, as in white, and variations of these, as dark blue or self-colour in fabrics, are material reflexes of this motive of self-negation, which also coincide with the symbolism of colour as light and life, and of absence of colour as darkness and death. A particular case is the adoption of an uncleanly habit. Dirty clothes, dirty skin, and unshaven face were the mourning characters of the Romans. The custom of blackening the face with ashes has perhaps the same meaning. In the primitive camp the most obvious medium for dirtying the person is, not the earth, but the ashes of the camp-fire, which with water form, as does coal-dust in coal-countries, a dye as well as a defilement.

A paradox similar to one already noted is the result of this adaptation to state; and sorrow, and with it an equally praiseworthy intention to honour the dead, are the feelings which produce it. The dead man is dressed in his best, arrayed like Solomon in all his glory; for the last time his personality is augmented to superhumanity, while his kin temporarily assimilate themselves to his actual state, socially substitute themselves for him, and practically negate and cancel their living personality and abrogate their social functions.

8. Nudity and dress.—When clothing is firmly established as a permanent social habit, temporary nudity is the most violent negation possible of the clothed state. Ceremonial nudity is a complex problem, but the idea of contrast, of an abnormal as contrasted with a normal state, may go far to explain many of its forms. At ceremonies of fumigation the Malay takes off his *sarong*.[2] Such cases are no doubt to be explained in the obvious way; the purificatory influence has more effect when the body is stripped of all coverings. But other examples of the practice are more obscure.

In time of drought, Transylvanian girls strip naked when performing the ritual for rain.[3] In India the practice is regular.[4] To make rain, Kabui men go on the roof of a house at night, and strip themselves of all clothes. Obscene language is interchanged.[5] To induce rain to fall, Ba-Thonga women strip themselves naked.[6] Baronga women, to make rain, strip themselves of their clothes, and put on instead leaf-girdles or leaf-petticoats and head-dresses of grass.[7] At a festival of Sarasvatī, Bengali students danced naked. A Gujarāt mother whose child is ill goes to the goddess's temple at night, naked, or with only a girdle of *nim* (*Melia*) or *asopato* (*Polyalthea*) leaves.[8]

The principle in the above seems to be that a violent change in the course of Nature may be assisted by a violent change of habit on the part of those concerned. It is adaptation to the desired contrast by instituting a contrast in the officiators. The use of obscene language is, like nudity, a break with the habits of normal life. The use of leaf-girdles is probably no survival of a primitive covering, but merely a method of toning down the

[1] Carver, *Travels through N. America*[3], 1781, p. 407; Bancroft, i. 86, 134, 173, 180, 206, 288, 370, ii. 618; H. H. Johnston, *The River Congo*, 1884, p. 426; Chalmers-Gill, 36 f., 149, 266, 286; Turner, *Samoa*, 308.
[2] De Groot, i. 94, 210 f.
[3] J. Teit, in *Jesup Exped.*, 1900, p. 331 ff.
[4] *Old New Zealand*, by a Pakeha Maori, 1884, pp. 104–114.
[5] H. Egede, *Description of Greenland*, 1745, p. 197.
[6] *1 RBEW* (1881), p. 123.
[7] Frazer, *GB*[2] iii. 74.
[8] De Groot, ii. 475 f.
[9] Van Gennep, 211.
[10] *JAI* xv. 73.
[11] Du Chaillu, *Equatorial Africa*, 1861, p. 9; J. G. Wood, *Nat. Hist. of Man*, 1868–70, i. 586.

[1] A. B. Ellis, *Tshi-speaking Peoples*, 237.
[2] Skeat, 269.
[3] E. Gerard, *The Land beyond the Forest*, Edin. 1888, ii. 40.
[4] *PNQ* iii. 41, 115; *NINQ* i. 210; Frazer, *GB*[2] i. 98 f.
[5] T. C. Hodson, 172.
[6] H. A. Junod, in *REth* i. (1910) 140.
[7] H. A. Junod, *Les Ba-ronga*, Neuchatel, 1898, p. 412 ff.
[8] Ward, *Hindoos*[3], 1817, i. 72, cf. 130; J. M. Campbell, in *IA* xxiv. 265.

violence of the extraordinary state. Similarly, the idea of nakedness is often satisfied by the removal of the upper garment only. Ideas of fertility and outpouring as connected with leaves and with the genital organs are probably later.

The whole subject is illustrated by the following:

The headman of certain New Guinea tribes becomes holy before the fishing season. Every evening he strips himself of all his decorations, a proceeding not otherwise allowed, and bathes near the location of the dugongs.[1] An Eskimo may not eat venison and walrus on the same day, unless he strips naked, or puts on a reindeer skin that has never been worn in hunting the walrus. Otherwise his eating gives pain to the souls of the walrus. Similarly, after eating walrus he must strip himself before eating seal.[2]

The principle of assimilation to special circumstances is here conspicuous. Possibly in the New Guinea example the later extension of the principle to assimilation by contact is involved.

Dress being, as will be more fully illustrated below, not only essentially a social habit, but one of the most distinctly social habits that have been evolved, the public removal of garments and nudity generally come under the regulation of custom and law. Dress, like other habits, is a second nature, and social inertia may fix it more securely; hence such curiosities of legalism as the pronouncement of Zoroastrian law, that it is a sin to walk with only one boot on.[3]

The sexual instincts of modesty and attraction give life to the idea of dress, and a balance is seldom exactly attained between them and legalism. In modern times the missionary movement has practically corrupted many a wild race by imposing upon them, as the most essential feature of Christian profession, the regard for clothing developed in a cold climate among peoples inclined to prudery and ascetic ideals; hence a factitious sentiment of hypocritical decency. In other races, legalism has evolved similar conditions.

In Uganda it is a capital offence to strip naked.[4] In most European countries 'exposure of the person' is a criminal offence. The Roman Catholic Church taught, and still teaches in convent schools, that it is wrong to expose the body even to one's own eyes.[5] 'Moslem modesty was carried to great lengths, insufficient clothing being forbidden. . . . The Sunna prescribes that a man shall not uncover himself even to himself, and shall not wash naked—from fear of God, and of spirits; Job did so, and atoned for it heavily. When in Arab antiquity grown-up persons showed themselves naked, it was only under extraordinary circumstances and to attain unusual ends.'[6] These latter have been illustrated above.

Such excess of the idea of decency renders still more powerful both the magical and the superstitious use of nudity and also its sexual appeal. In the sphere of art it may be the case that peoples accustomed to nakedness, like the Greeks, employ it as a regular subject for artistic treatment, but it does not necessarily follow that it is better understood than among peoples not so accustomed. It lacks the force of contrast. Similarly in the sexual sphere, both natural modesty and natural expansion may be enhanced by the artificial limitations of decency. In this respect dress plays an important part in social biology. By way of showing the contrast, the African and the European conditions may be sketched.

Of the Wa-taveita, Johnston remarks: 'Both sexes have little notion or conception of decency, the men especially seeming to be unconscious of any impropriety in exposing themselves. What clothing they have is worn either as an adornment or for warmth at night and early morning.' Of the Wa-chaga he observes: 'With them indecency does not exist, for they make no effort to be decent, but walk about as Nature made them, except when it is chilly, or if they wish to look unusually smart, in which cases they throw cloth or skins around their shoulders.'[7]

Among Englishmen, a race very observant of the decencies of civilization, Herrick is fairly typical. His attitude to sexual dress is thus described by Havelock Ellis: 'The fascination of clothes in the lover's eyes is, no doubt, a complex phenomenon, but in part it rests on the aptitudes of a woman's garments to express vaguely a dynamic symbolism which must always remain indefinite and elusive, and on that account always possess fascination. No one has so acutely described this symbolism as Herrick, often an admirable psychologist in matters of sexual attractiveness. Especially instructive in this respect are his poems, "Delight in Disorder," "Upon Julia's Clothes," and notably "Julia's Petticoat." "A sweet disorder in the dress," he tells us, "kindles in clothes a wantonness"; it is not on the garment itself, but on the character of its movement that he insists; on the "erring lace," the "winning wave" of the "tempestuous petticoat."'[1] Herrick, of course, is dealing with the dynamic quality of dress, but its static meaning is hardly less explicit in the English and European mind.

[1] R. E. Guise, in *JAI* xxviii. (1899) 218.
[2] F. Boas, *Sixth Report on N.W. Tribes of Canada*, 1888, p. 584.
[3] 'Pahlavi Texts,' i., in *SBE* v. 287.
[4] Ratzel, i. 94.
[5] H. Ellis, iv. 32, quoting authorities.
[6] Wellhausen, *Reste*[2], 173, 195.
[7] *JAI* xv. (1886) 9, 11.

The significance of dress as an expression of the body will be referred to below in the sexual connexion. Meanwhile the general idea thus illustrated may be regarded as the norm in modern civilization. Its opposite or complementary is the increased value given to legitimate nudity. A movement is even proceeding, particularly in Germany, for an extension of this individual privilege into a restricted and occasional social habit—the so-called *Nacktheit* movement.

Such tendencies coincide with the twofold attitude towards the human organism which dress has emphasized—regard for the body in itself and regard for its artificial extension. Periodic social phenomena accentuate one or the other aspect. The Spartan practice of nudity in athletics was based on a reasoned theory of health from exposure and of purity from knowledge. The Papuans have been said to 'glory in their nudeness, and consider clothing fit only for women.'[2] Temporary nudity, when in obedience to natural impulse, should be regarded not as a reversion,[3] still less as a survival of a primitive state, but as a rhythmical movement. The point is well illustrated by the use of nudity as a love-charm.[4]

9. **Dress and social grade.**—Dress is the most distinctive expression in a material form of the various grades of social life. The biological period thus becomes a social period of existence, and the individual is merged in a functional section of the community. The assumption of a grade-dress is, whether explicitly or implicitly, *ipso facto* a social rite—in Van Gennep's term, a rite of aggregation.[5]

(1) *Childhood.*—The swaddling-clothes of infants have their analogue in the earliest cultures, in the form of various modifications of the papoose-system. In this the reasons of protection and cleanliness are obvious. After earliest infancy the children of primitive peoples are quite naked in the warmer climates. Clothing proper is first assumed either at puberty or at the age of six or seven. Probably the former date represents an earlier stratum of fashion. Children, whether first clothed at the earlier age or not, assume adult costume at puberty.

In the New Hebrides, girls and boys are naked till five years of age.[6] Among the Veddas dress is assumed at the age of six or seven.[7] Children of well-to-do Hindus are naked till the third year, those of the poor till about six or seven.[8] Running about uncovered, say the Zoroastrian texts, is no sin, up to the age of 15; and it is no sin to be without the sacred girdle till that age.[9]

In cold climates, where the constant purpose of dress is protection, differences of juvenile and adult costume may be reduced. For example, Samoyed children 'are dressed precisely as their parents, sex for sex.'[10]

There is little to notice in the matter of coiffure in the child-stage. Cases like the following are exceptional:

Young Nāga children have the hair shaved. When a girl is of marriageable age it is allowed to grow long.[11]

[1] H. Ellis, v. 45 f.
[2] Westermarck, *Human Marriage*[2], 1894, p. 118.
[3] As Schurtz argues, *Philos. der Tracht*, Stuttgart, 1891, p. 48.
[4] Ploss, *Das Weib*, Leipzig, 1885, i. 352.
[5] Van Gennep, 77.
[6] B. T. Somerville, in *JAI* xxiii. (1893) 7.
[7] C. G. and B. Z. Seligmann, 90 f.
[8] Monier-Williams, 397
[9] 'Pahlavi Texts,' i., in *SBE* v. 287.
[10] Montefiore, in *JAI* xxiv. 404.
[11] T. C. Hodson, 28.

(2) *Maturity.*—Examples of the ritual assumption of the adult garb may be confined to a few types.

In Florida (Melanesia) the male 'wrapper' is assumed with some ceremony at the age of six or seven. In Santa Cruz the adult male dress is ample. Its assumption is celebrated by a feast and pig-killing. Big boys whose parents are too poor to give a feast may be seen going about naked. The custom in the New Hebrides is the same, and after assumption the boy begins to be reserved towards his mother and sisters.[1] The Koita boy of British New Guinea receives his *sihi*, loin-cloth, from his maternal uncle, *raimu*, to whom in return he owes certain services, such as a share of any fish or animal he kills. The *raimu* makes the cloth, and puts it on the boy in the presence of the relatives on both sides of the family, who then eat together.[2] A similar ceremony of investiture at puberty is practised by the Roro tribes.[3] The last initiation of a New Hebrides boy is the investing of the belt. This is a broad band of nutmeg bark about six inches wide, encircling the waist twice and confined by a small strip of plaited grass. 'An underneath strip of grass cloth or calico supports the very scanty clothing' of the natives. The belt is therefore an ornament, corresponding to the *toga virilis*, but usually not attained (from inability to provide pigs for the feast) until a man is twenty or older.[4] The old Japanese made a ceremony for the 'breeching' of boys and the 'girdling' of girls.[5]

The Hindu *upanayana* is the investiture with the sacred thread, which renders a man 'twice-born,' and before which he is not, in religion, a 'person,' not, as it were, individualized, not even named. The thread is of three slender cotton filaments, white, and tied in a sacred knot, *brahma-granthi*, each of the three consisting of three finer filaments. It is consecrated by *mantras*, and holy water is sprinkled upon it. The wearer never parts with it. As the Catholic priest changes his vestments, so the Brāhman alters the position of the thread. When he worships the gods he puts it over his left and under his right shoulder; when he worships ancestors, the position is reversed; when he worships saints, it is worn like a necklace.[6] The earliest mention of this sacred cord, *yajñōpavīta*, of the Brāhman, is perhaps in the Upaniṣads.[7] Worn over the left shoulder, its position is altered according to the particular act in which the wearer is engaged. This *yajñōpavīta* is of one skein when put on the youth: when he is married it must have three, and may have five skeins. An imitation cord is put on first, then taken off and the real one placed in position. Then the father covers his own head and that of his son under one cloth and whispers the Gāyatrī prayer. A new cord is put on every year at the festival in *Śrāvaṇa*. If one touches a Pariah, the cord must be replaced. The Sannyāsi, having entered the fourth or last stage of the Brāhman's life, does not wear the *yajñōpavīta*.[8] Manu says that the first birth of a Hindu is 'from his natural mother, the second happens on the tying of the girdle of Muñja grass, and the third on the initiation to the performance of a Śrauta sacrifice.'[9] 'Birth' in such contexts as the assumption of the adult state is an almost universal metaphor. In many well-known instances the metaphor itself has been translated into ritual, as being a convenient and impressive mode of affirming the change. But neither the metaphor nor the idea of re-birth is the ultimate reason of initiation ceremonies.

The sacred thread-girdle, the *kōstī*, worn by every member, male and female, of the Zoroastrian faith, after the age of 15, is a badge of the faithful, a girdle uniting him or her to Ormazd and his fellows. Bread and water were to be refused to all who did not wear it. It must be made not of silk, but of goat or camel hair; of 72 interwoven filaments; and it should 'three times circumvent the waist.' The other garment necessary to salvation was the *sudara*, or sacred shirt, a muslin tunic with short sleeves, worn high, not lower than the hips. At its 'opening in front' is a pocket, 'the pocket for good deeds.' When putting it on the faithful looks at the pocket, asking himself whether it is full. Both shirt and girdle are to be kept on during the night, 'for they are more protecting for the body, and good for the soul.' To wear the girdle is to gird one's loins 'with the Religion.'[10]

The distinctive garb of the Athenian *ephebos* was the *chlamys*. It was ceremonially assumed. The Roman boy at sixteen laid aside the *bulla* and the *toga prætexta*, and assumed the white toga of manhood, *toga pura* or *virilis*. The page in mediæval chivalry was made a squire at fourteen. At twenty-one knighthood followed, and new white robes were ceremonially assumed, with a satin vest and a leather collar, over the suit of mail. The Nāga kilt is not assumed till puberty.[11] At puberty the Chaco girl is decorated, and for the first time wears the longer skirt of the women.[12]

There are, of course, exceptions to the rule that the assumption of social dress is a rite. Thus the Mekeo tribes have no ceremony in connexion with the assumption of the male band or the female petticoat.[1] Elsewhere the rite involves such usual complications as the following. Before a boy is circumcised, the Masai father puts on a special dress, and lives secluded in a special hut. On his return he drinks wine and is called 'father of So-and-so.' Then the operation takes place.[2] The designation of the father points to the fact, expressed by the dress, that fatherhood, as elsewhere, is a special social grade.

In many examples there is a distinctive dress worn during the marginal stage of initiation, and discarded at the end for the adult dress proper.

Thus, during the initiation of a Kamilaroi youth he was invested with a kilt of wallaby skin, suspended in front by a girdle. It is described as a 'badge.'[3] The West African boy at initiation is naked and smeared with clay. He may wear a cap of bark, hiding his face. Often he pretends at the conclusion of the sequestration to have forgotten everything and to know nothing.[4] At initiation A-kamba girls wear goat-skins.[5] The Déné girl at puberty wore 'a sort of head-dress combining in itself the purposes of a veil, a bonnet, and a mantlet. It was made of tanned skin, its forepart was shaped like a long fringe, completely hiding from view the face and breasts; then it formed on the head a close-fitting cap or bonnet, and finally fell in a broad band almost to the heels. This head-dress was made and publicly placed on her head by a paternal aunt, who received at once some present from the girl's father. When, three or four years later, the period of sequestration ceased, only this same aunt had the right to take off her niece's ceremonial head-dress. Furthermore, the girl's fingers, wrists, and legs at the ankles and immediately below the knees were encircled with ornamental rings and bracelets of sinew intended as a protection against the malign influences she was supposed to be possessed with.'[6]

Entrance into the grade of social puberty is generally equivalent to nubility.

Among the Tshi-people a girl announces her eligibility for marriage by dressing up and wearing ornaments. She is escorted through the streets, under an umbrella.[7] Infant betrothal complicates this. In the Northern New Hebrides a girl betrothed in childhood wears nothing except on great occasions. When growing up she is clothed, but in the house wears only the *para*, or fringe. In the New Hebrides generally clothing and tatuing are a step towards the marriage of a girl.[8] The Nāga youth, however, is nude until marriage. Only then does he assume the loin-cloth.[9]

Frequently a special dress or modification of the adult dress marks a distinction between maturity and nubility.

Among the Koita of New Guinea tatuing is confined to the women. When a girl is engaged, the region between the navel and the neck, hitherto untouched, is tatued. Just before marriage the V-shaped *gado* is tatued between the breasts.[10]

The passage from childhood to youth, and from youth to nubility, is often marked by a change in the mode of wearing the hair.

As an example, among Nāga women the coiffure is a mark of status.[11] When children, Reharuna girls have their heads shaved, except for the front and a tuft on the crown; at puberty, the hair is allowed to grow, and is worn in chignon-form; when married, they divide the hair into two large plaits hanging down the back; when they become mothers, they wear these plaits over the breast.

(3) *Sexual dress.*—The assumption of dress to initiate the social grade of maturity is the assumption of a social sexual differentiation. The most distinctive social division is the permanent division of sex. Up to puberty this is more or less ignored, and the neutral quality of the previous stage is often indicated by the neutral connotation of the term 'child,' and by a neutral fashion of child-dress. It is natural that the growth and maturity of the primary sexual characters should give these a prominent place in the principles of the distinguishing garb, and that they should, as it were, mould the dress into adaptive forms. The idea of social sexuality is well brought out in the stories of

[1] Codrington, 231 ff. [2] Seligmann, 67 f., 73. [3] *Ib.* 256.
[4] B. T. Somerville, in *JAI* xxiii. (1893) 5.
[5] C. Pfoundes, *ib.* xii. 224. [6] Monier-Williams, 360 f., 379.
[7] 'Upanishads,' in *SBE* i. 285.
[8] Padfield, 76–80. [9] Manu, ii. 169.
[10] 'Zendavesta,' i. 2, in *SBE* iv. 193, 72; 'Pahlavi Texts,' i., in *ib.* v. 287, 289.
[11] T. C. Hodson, 24. [12] Grubb, 177.

[1] Seligmann, 491. [2] Hollis, 294 f.
[3] R. H. Mathews, in *JAI* xxiv. 421.
[4] Dapper, *Description de l'Afrique*, Amsterdam, 1670, p. 288 f.; M. H. Kingsley, *Travels in West Africa*, 1897, p. 531; G. Dale, in *JAI* xxv. (1896) 189.
[5] C. W. Hobley, *Ethnology of A-Kamba*, p. 70.
[6] A. G. Morice, in *Proc. Canad. Inst.* (Toronto, 1888–1889) vii. 162 f.
[7] A. B. Ellis, *Tshi-speaking Peoples*, 235.
[8] Codrington, 241, 233.
[9] Woodthorpe, in *JAI* xi. (1882) 209. [10] Seligmann, 73, 76.
[11] T. C. Hodson, 77; E. Doutté, *Merrâkech*, Paris, 1905, p. 314 f.

children failing to distinguish girls from boys when nude. The adaptation of the distinctive feminine and masculine garments, skirt and trousers, to the activity of the respective sexes has already been referred to. The main idea of dress as a material expression in a social form of the psychical reflexes from personality, and, in this case, sexuality, has here particular prominence. To regard the affirmation, by means of dress, of primary sexual characters as intended to attract the attention of the other sex by adorning them is a superficial view. Such intention is secondary, though, of course, it has an important social bearing. Goethe's remark is in point for the consideration of dress as an affirmation of personality: 'We exclaim, "What a beautiful little foot!" when we have merely seen a pretty shoe; we admire the lovely waist, when nothing has met our eyes but an elegant girdle.'

Special cases of an intensification of sexual characters may be illustrated by the following:

A type of female beauty in the Middle Ages represents forms clothed in broad flowing skirts, and with the characteristic shape of pregnancy. 'It is the maternal function, . . . which marks the whole type.'[1] The type possibly survived in 'that class of garments which involved an immense amount of expansion below the waist, and secured such expansion by the use of whalebone hoops and similar devices. The Elizabethan farthingale was such a garment. This was originally a Spanish invention, as indicated by the name (from *verdugardo*, 'provided with hoops') and reached England through France. We find the fashion at its most extreme point in the fashionable dress of Spain in the seventeenth century, such as it has been immortalized by Velasquez. In England, hoops died out during the reign of George III., but were revived, for a time, half a century later, in the Victorian crinoline.'[2] It is curious, but not exceptional to the view here expressed—it is, in fact, corroborative of it, because of the necessity of emphasizing feminine characters which is characteristic of the class—that this, like most other feminine fashions in dress, was invented by courtesans. The crinoline or farthingale is the culmination of the distinctive feminine garment, the skirt, as a protection and affirmation of the pelvic character.

Augmentation of the mammary character is similar. In mediæval Europe an exception is found in a tendency to the use of compressing garments. The tightening of the waist girth is a remarkable adaptation, which emphasizes at one and the same time the feminine characters of expansion both of the breasts and of the abdominal and gluteal regions. 'Not only does the corset render the breasts more prominent; it has the further effect of displacing the breathing activity of the lungs in an upward direction, the advantage from the point of sexual allurement thus gained being that additional attention is drawn to the bosom from the respiratory movement thus imparted to it.'[3] The development of the corset in modern Europe has been traced from the bands, or *fasciæ*, of Greek and Italian women. The tight bodices of the Middle Ages were replaced in the 17th and 18th centuries by whalebone bodices. The modern corset is a combination of the *fascia* and the girdle.[4]

In the sphere of masculine dress and the affirmation by its means of sexual characters, it is sufficient to note two mediæval fashions:

The long-hose which superseded the barbarian trews and preceded the modern trousers emphasized most effectively the male attribute and social quality of energy and activity as represented by the lower limbs, the organs of locomotion. The *braguette*, or codpiece, of the 15th and 16th centuries is an example of a protective article of dress, originally used in war, which became an article 'of fashionable apparel, often made of silk and adorned with ribbons, even with gold and jewels.'[5] Its history supplies a modern repetition of the savage phallocrypt, and throws light on the evolution of the ideas of dress.

With regard to secondary sexual characters, sexual dress, itself an artificial secondary sexual character, carries on various adaptations. 'The man must be strong, vigorous, energetic, hairy, even rough . . . the woman must be smooth, rounded, and gentle.'[6] These characters are echoed in the greater relative coarseness and strength of fabric of masculine dress, and the softness and flimsiness of feminine. 'A somewhat greater darkness of women is a secondary . . . sexual character;[7] in this connexion a harmony is unconsciously aimed at; the tendency is for men to wear darker, and women lighter clothes. Women tend to 'cultivate pallor of the face, to use powder,' and 'to emphasize the white underlinen.'[1] The attraction of sexual disparity, so important in sexual selection, reaches its culmination in the matter of clothing, and

'it has constantly happened that men have even called in the aid of religion to enforce a distinction which seemed to them so urgent. One of the greatest of sex allurements would be lost and the extreme importance of clothes would disappear at once if the two sexes were to dress alike; such identity of dress has, however, never come about among any people.'[2]

The assumption of sexual dress at maturity raises the question of the original meaning of special coverings for the primary sexual characters. Their probable origin in an impulse towards protection against the natural environment has been suggested. When dress becomes more than a mere appendage and produces the reaction of an affirmation of personality, its meaning inevitably becomes richer. The decorative impulse and sexual allurement take their place in the complex. But the chief, and the distinctively social, factor is always that of affirming by a secondary and artificial integument the particular physiological stage which society transforms into a human grade of communal life. This is well illustrated by such facts as the frequent absence of the skirt, for example, until marriage, and, more significantly, until pregnancy or motherhood. In other cases, as in the frequent confinement of sexual covering to the mammary region, the principle is still logically followed. Thus, among many negro peoples, as the natives of Loango, women cover the breasts especially.[3] Nāga women cover the breasts only. They say it is absurd to cover those parts of the body which every one has been able to see from their birth, but that it is different with the breasts, which appear later.[4]

The evolution of sexual dress involves some side-issues of thought and custom which are not without significance.

The harmony between the ideas of sexual dress and its temporary disuse for natural functions is brought out in many customs and aspects of thought. The following is an instance:

The Mekeo tribes of New Guinea have folk-tales of which the motive is that a man surprising a girl without her petticoat has the right to marry her. After any marriage it is still the custom for the husband to fasten ceremonially the bride's petticoat.[5] The ceremonial loosing of the virgin zone embodies similar ideas.

Savage folklore is full of stories connected with disparity of sexual dress. Difference of custom in different peoples leads to comment when coincidences occur. The Dinka call the Bongo, Mittoo, and Niam-Niam 'women' because the men wear an apron, while the women wear no clothes whatever, getting, however, daily a supple bough for a girdle.[6] Sexual disparity, natural and artificial, has often led to speculation.

Repudiating the sexual element, Clement of Alexandria argued that, the object of dress being merely to cover the body and protect it from cold, there is no reason why men's dress should differ from women's.[7] The Nāgas of Manipur say that originally men and women wore identical clothes. The first human beings were seven men and seven women. 'By way of making a distinction the man made his hair into a knot or horn in front; the woman behind. The woman also lengthened her waist-cloth, while the man shortened his.' As a fact the *dhoti*, loin-cloth, is still the same for both sexes though worn in different ways.[8] The waist-cloth differentiates in evolution very simply into either *dhoti* or skirt, both being fastened in the same way, and differing only in length.[9] It is probably a similar accident of national fashion that makes the 'longevity garment' of the Chinese identical for both sexes.[10]

Spinning, weaving, dress-making, and connected arts have been the work of women until modern

1 Marholm, quoted by H. Ellis, iv. 169.
2 H. Ellis, *l.c.*
3 *Ib.* 172.
4 Léoty, *Le Corset à travers les âges*, Paris, 1893, quoted by H. Ellis, iv. 172 f.
5 H. Ellis, iv. 159; I. Bloch, *Beiträge zur Aetiologie der Psychopathia Sexualis*, Dresden, 1902, i. 159.
6 H. Ellis, iv. 208.
7 *Ib.*

1 H. Ellis, *l.c.*, quoting Kistemaecker.
2 *Ib.* 209. On the phenomenon of interchange of sexual dress, see below.
3 Pechuel-Loesche, in *ZE*, 1878, p. 27.
4 Dalton, in *JASBe* xli. 84.
5 Seligmann, 363.
6 Schweinfurth, i. 152.
7 *Paed.* ii. 11.
8 T. C. Hodson, 15.
9 *Ib.* 27.
10 De Groot, i. 63.

times. Before the rise of organized industry, every family was self-sufficing in the production of clothes for its members. Washing and repairing have been also women's work, equally with cookery. In barbarism, as among the Chaco Indians, all the making of clothes is done by the women. The men's large and cumbersome blankets each take four months to weave.[1]

In the lowest stages each adult prepared and looked after his or her attire. As soon as manufacture began with bark-cloth, the preparation of the material devolved upon women, like other sedentary and domestic arts; but, since the style of the dress depended not upon measurement and cut, but upon folds and draping, women were not actually the makers of dress. In the ancient civilizations the slave-system of industry was applied in two directions. Skilled male artists were employed irregularly by the luxurious; while the regular method of domestic manufacture came to include dress-making and tailoring. Among the ancient Greeks and Italians the making of clothes was carried on in the house by the female slaves under the superintendence of the lady of the house. This system gradually gave way to external production, though female attire still retained its claims upon domestic art up to modern times.

In modern civilization the broad distinction of sexual dress has reasserted itself in the sphere of occupation. The dress of men is prepared by men, that of women by women. Special knowledge rendered this inevitable, as soon as cut and shape superseded draping in both female and male attire. But, as in other arts, the male sex is the more creative, and the luxurious women of modern society are largely catered for by male dressmakers.

In the majority of modern nations the care and repair of the clothes of the family is part of the domestic work of women. The washing of clothes is usually women's work. Yet in Abyssinia it is the man who washes the clothes of both sexes, and 'in this function the women cannot help him.'[2] In the sphere of industry Chinese men provide another exception.

(4) *Wedding garments.*—The sexual dress is at marriage intensified by the principle of affirmation, not of sexuality, but of personality. It is an occasion of expansion, of augmentation; as the social expression of the crisis of love (the culmination of human energy and well-being), it is precisely adapted. Often, for example, the pair assume super-humanity, and are treated as royal persons. A special and distinctive dress for the bride is a widely spread fashion. As a rule, the bride herself is supposed to make the dress. With marriage, housekeeping begins, and, as in Norway, Scotland, India, and elsewhere, the bride supplies the household linen, often including the personal linen of the husband. The variety of wedding dress is endless. Frequently each family supplies the other.

In North India the bride's dress is yellow, or red—colours which 'repel demons.' The Majhwār pair wear white, but after the anointing put on coloured clothes.[3]

English brides wear a white dress. So did Hebrew brides. Old English folklore directed that a bride must wear 'Something old, something new, something borrowed, something blue.'[4] The Hindu bridegroom supplies the cloth for the wedding robes of the bride. The fact is (see below) that there is among the Hindus, not merely a dowry, but an interchange of gifts; furniture and clothes being the principal components. When presented, the clothes are put on; this forms a preliminary marriage-ceremony.[5] The gorgeous flowered embroidery, *phūlkāri*, of the Jāts is prominent in their wedding dress.

[1] Grubb, 69.
[2] Bruce, *Travels to discover the Source of the Nile*, Edinburgh, 1805, iv. 474.
[3] Crooke, *FL* ix. (1898) 125 f.; Smith, *DB* ii. 251; Crooke, *PR*² ii. 28 ff., *TC* iii. 425.
[4] Crooke, *FL* ix. 127 f.
[5] Padfield, 116.

Magnificence, generally, is the characteristic of wedding garments throughout the world; white is frequent, as an expression of virginity. Red is often used, as an unconscious adaptation to the circumstances of expansion.

Special garments or specialized forms of garments are less common than 'best clothes' and ornament.

The Korean bridegroom elect, often betrothed at the age of five, wears a red jacket as a mark of engagement.[1] On the day before marriage the Roman bride put off the *toga prætexta*, which was deposited before the Lares, and put on the *tunica recta* or *regilla*. This was woven in one piece in the old-fashioned way. It was fastened with a woollen girdle tied in the knot of Hercules, *nodus Herculeus*.[2] In European folklore an analogue is to be found in the true lovers' knot, the idea being a magical and later a symbolical knitting together of the wedded pair. The hair of the bride was arranged in six locks, and was ceremonially parted with the *cœlibaris hasta*. She wore a wreath of flowers, gathered by her own hands.[3]

Some cases of investiture follow.

On the wedding night the bride of the Koita people is decorated. Coco-nut oil is put on her thighs. She wears a new petticoat. Red lines are painted on her face, and her armlets are painted. Her hair is combed and anointed with oil, and in her locks are scarlet *hibiscus* flowers. The groom wears a head-dress of cassowary feathers; his face is painted with red and yellow streaks, and his ears are decorated with dried tails of pigs.[4] The Hindu at marriage is invested by the bride's parents with the two additional skeins necessary to make the full complement of the *yajñōpavīta*, the sacred thread, of the married man.[5] The Javanese bridegroom is dressed in the garments of a chief. The idea is 'to represent him as of exalted rank.'[6] The Malays term the bridegroom *rajasahari*, the 'one-day king.'[7] The dressing up of both bride and groom and all parties present, for the bridal procession of the Minangkabauers, is very remarkable.

The bridal veil, originally concealing the face, occurs in China, Korea, Manchuria, Burma, Persia, Russia, Bulgaria, and in various modified forms throughout European and the majority of great civilizations, ancient and modern. In ancient Greece the bride wore a long veil and a garland. The Druse bride wears a long red veil, which her husband removes in the bridal chamber. An Egyptian veil, *boorko*, conceals all the face except the eyes, and reaches to the feet. It is of black silk for married and white for unmarried women.[8] Various considerations suggest that the veil is in origin rather an affirmation of the face, as a human and particularly a sexual glory, than a concealment, though the emphasizing of maidenly modesty comes in as a secondary and still more prominent factor. The veil also serves as an expression of the head and the hair. These are also augmented by various decorations.

The wedding dress often coincides with, or is equivalent to, the grade-dress of the married.

The *stola* as a badge of lawful wedlock was the distinctive garment of ancient Roman wives.[9] It was an ample outer tunic in design, and possibly is to be identified with the bridal *tunica recta*. Among the Hereros, after the wedding meal, the bride's mother puts upon the bride the cap and the dress of married women.[10] The 'big garment,' ear-rings, and the iron necklace distinguish Masai married women from girls.[11]

Further social stages are marked by distinctive dress, such as pregnancy, motherhood, and, more rarely, fatherhood.

As soon as a Wa-taveita bride becomes pregnant, 'she is dressed with much display of beads, and over her eyes a deep fringe of tiny iron chains is hung, which hides her and also prevents her from seeing clearly.' An old woman attends her, 'to screen her from all excitement and danger until the expected event has taken place.'[12] Among Cameroon tribes is found the custom of

[1] Saunderson, in *JAI* xxiv. 305.
[2] Whittuck, in Smith's *Dict. of Gr. and Rom. Ant.*³, 1890, *s.v.* 'Matrimonium.'
[3] *Ib.*
[4] Seligmann, 78.
[5] Padfield, 123.
[6] Veth, *Java*, 1875, i. 632–5.
[7] G. A. Wilken, in *Bijd. tot de Taal-, Land-, en Volkenkunde Nederl.-Indië*, xxxviii. (1889) 424.
[8] Doolittle, i. 79; Griffis, 249; Anderson, *Mandalay to Momien*, 1876, p. 141; *FL* i. 489; Sinclair-Brophy, *Bulgaria*, 1869, p. 73; Ralston, *Songs of the Russian People*, 1872, p. 280; Chasseaud, *The Druses*, 1855, p. 166; Lane, i. 52.
[9] Smith's *Dict. of Gr. and Rom. Ant.*³ *s.v.*
[10] J. Irle, *Die Herero*, Gütersloh, 1906, p. 106 f.
[11] Hollis, 282.
[12] H. H. Johnston, in *JAI* xv. (1886) 8 f.; New, *Eastern Africa*, 1874, p. 360 f.

girls remaining naked until the birth of the first child[1] (see above). The bride in South Slavonia used to wear a veil until the birth of the first child.[2] When the birth of twins takes place, the Herero parents are immediately undressed, previously to being specially attired. The detail shows the importance of immediate assimilation to the new state.

After childbirth the mother passes through a stage of recovery, of isolation, with her babe, often expressed by a costume. At its end she assumes the costume of normal life which has been temporarily suspended, or a special costume of her new grade of maternity.

(5) *Secondary social grades.*—The distinction of dress is carried into all divisions of society that are secondary to the biological. In India the various castes wear clothes differing both in colour and in cut.[3] In ancient times the law was that the Śūdra should use the cast-off garments, shoes, sitting-mats, and umbrellas of the higher castes.[4] All Brāhmans, as all members of each caste, dress alike, except as regards the quality of material.[5] The turban in India, borrowed from the Musalmāns, is folded differently according to caste.[6]

The chief epochs in military uniform are marked by metal-armour, which, when rendered obsolete by fire-arms, gave place to the other component, splendour or gaudiness; and lastly, in recent years, by adaptation, for concealment, to the colour of the country.[7] Amongst the Nahuas the standing of warriors was marked by distinctive costumes. The sole test for promotion was the capture of so many prisoners.[8] A secondary motive of splendour in uniform is illustrated by the grotesque costumes often worn in barbarism, in order to strike terror into the enemy. The Nāgas wear tails of hair, which they wag in defiance of the foe. The hair of the head is long and flowing, and is supposed to be useful in distracting the aim.[9]

The investiture of a knight in the period of chivalry was practically a sacrament, and the arms were delivered to him by the priest.[10] Even in the mimic warfare of the tournament, the armour was placed in a monastery before the jousting began.[11]

The so-called secret societies of the lower cultures have their closest parallel in the masonic institutions. Mediæval gilds and similar corporations, together with the modern club, are, apart from special purposes, examples of the free play of the social impulse. At the initiation to the Duk-Duk secret society of New Britain the novice receives a ceremonial dress; this terminates the process.[12]

Throughout barbarian and civilized history professions and offices of every kind have followed the rule of a distinctive costume. Various factors in social evolution tend to reduce these differences in Western civilization by an increasing use of mufti on official occasions, but the inertia of such professions as the legal resists this. In the East, on the other hand, European dress invades the ancient culture, but the assimilation is still problematic. To the Mandarin, for instance, his dress is a second nature.

(6) *The dress of sanctity.*—One of the longest and most varied chapters in the history of dress is that dealing with the garb of permanent sacred grades, priestly, royal, and the like, and of temporary sacredness, as in the case of worshippers, pilgrims, and victims. Some examples have been incidentally noticed; a brief reference to certain types must suffice here.

In ancient India the ascetic had to wear coarse, worn-out garments, and his hair was clipped. The hermit wore skins or tattered garments—the term may include bark- or grass-cloth—and his hair was braided. The *Snātaka* wore clothes not old or dirty. He wore the sacred string. He was forbidden to use garments, shoes, or string which had been worn by others. The student for his upper dress wore the skin of an antelope or other animal, for his lower garment a cloth of hemp, or flax, or wool. He wore the girdle of a Brāhman, a triple cord of *Muñja* grass. A *Kṣatriya* wore as his cord a bow-string; a *Vaiśya* a cord of hemp.[1] The religious character of this caste-system renders the inclusion of the four last grades convenient.

Temporarily, in worship and on pilgrimage, the ordinary member of an organized faith assumes a quasi-sacerdotal character.

For the *hajj* to Mecca the Musalmān must wear no other garments than the *iḥrām*, consisting of two seamless wrappers, one passed round the loins, the other over the shoulders, the head being uncovered. The ceremony of putting them on at a pilgrims' 'station' is *al-iḥrām*, 'the making unlawful' (of ordinary garments and behaviour and occupations). The ceremony of taking them off is *al-iḥlāl*, 'the making lawful.' The *hajji* shaves his head when the pilgrimage is over.[2] According to some, the *iḥrām* is the shroud prepared in the event of the *hajji*'s death.[3] More likely it is preserved and used as a shroud when he dies.

The most important item in the costume of Japanese pilgrims is the *oizuru*, a jacket which is stamped with the seal of each shrine visited. 'The three breadths of material used in the sewing of this holy garment typify the three great Buddhist deities—Amida, Kwannon, and Seishi. The garment itself is always carefully preserved after the return home, and when the owner dies he is clad in it for burial.'[4]

The dress of worshippers varies between 'decent apparel' and garments of assimilation to the god or the victim or the priest. As in the case of Baal-worship,[5] the garments were often kept in the shrine, and assumed on entrance. In certain rites both Dionysus and his worshippers wore fawn-skins. The Bacchanals wore the skins of goats.[6] The veil of the worshipper has been referred to. In the earliest Christian period a controversy seems to have taken place with regard to female head-dress during worship.[7] In the modern custom the male head-dress is removed, the female is retained. Academies sometimes preserve the rule of a special vestment for worshippers, whether lay or priestly.

It has been noted that the dress of *jogleors*, troubadours, and *trouvères* was an assimilation to the sacerdotal.[8] From the same mediæval period comes the record of 'singing robes.'

(7) *Priestly and royal robes.*—The dress of the sacred world tends to be the reverse of the profane. Apart from the impulse—to be traced in the mentality of medicine-men—to impress one's personality upon the audience by the fantastic and the grotesque, there is here the expression of the fundamental opposition between natural and supernatural social functions.

The garb of Tshi priests and priestesses differs from ordinary dress. Their hair is long and unkempt, while the lay fashion is to wear it short. The layman, if well-to-do, wears bright cloth; the priest may wear only plain cloth, which is dyed red-brown with mangrove-tan. Priests and priestesses, when about to communicate with the god, wear a white linen cap. On holy days they wear white cloth, and on certain occasions, not explained, their bodies are painted with white clay. White and black beads are generally worn round the neck.[9] The Ewe priests wear white caps. The priestesses wear steeple-crowned hats with wide brims. Priests wear white clothes. Priestesses wear 'gay cloths' reaching to the feet, and a kerchief over the breast.[10]

The survival of some antique mode often suffices, through various accidents and modifications, for the priestly garb, other than sacerdotal vestments. Thus, the *ricinium*, a small antique mantle, was

1 Hutter, *Nord-Hinterland von Kamerun*, Brunswick, 1902, p. 421.
2 F. S. Krauss, *Sitte u. Brauch der Südslaven*, Vienna, 1885, p. 450.
3 Dubois, 19. 4 *SBE* ii. (1897) 233.
5 Dubois, 356. 6 Monier-Williams, 396.
7 The principle seems to have been anticipated at various times by the adoption of green uniforms for operations in forest countries.
8 Payne, ii. 481. 9 Woodthorpe, in *JAI* xi. 60, 197.
10 Westermarck, *MI* i. 353, quoting authorities.
11 Sainte-Palaye, *Mémoires sur l'ancienne chevalerie*, Paris, 1781, i. 151.
12 R. Parkinson, *Dreissig Jahre in der Südsee*, Stuttgart, 1907, pp. 582–6.

1 'Laws of Manu,' in *SBE* xxv. ch. vi. 44, 52, 6, 15, iv. 34–36, 66.
2 E. Sell, *Faith of Islam*[2], 1896, pp. 279, 289.
3 Burton, *El-Medinah and Mecca*, ed. 1898, i. 139.
4 B. H. Chamberlain, in *JAI* xxii. (1893) 360.
5 Cf. 2 K 10[22]. 6 Frazer, *GB*[2] ii. 166.
7 Cf. 1 Co 11[5ff.]. 8 H. Spencer, *Prin. of Sociol.* iii. 222.
9 A. B. Ellis, *Tshi-speaking Peoples*, 123 f.
10 Ellis, *Ewe-speaking Peoples*, 143, 146.

worn by the *magister* of the *Fratres Arvales* and by *camilli* generally.

The history of the dress of the Christian priesthood is a striking example of this. Here also we find the principle of opposition to the lay-garb. The democratic and non-professional character of primitive Christianity may be seen in the fact that in A.D. 428 Pope Celestinus censured Gallican bishops who wore dress different from that of the laity. They had been monks, and retained the *pallium* and girdle instead of assuming the tunic and toga of the superior layman.[1] It is curious that the social instinct towards differentiation of dress to mark differentiation of social function was resisted so long. But in the 6th cent. the civil dress of the clergy automatically became different from the dress of the country, since, while the laity departed from the ancient type, the clergy withstood all such evolution. Thus, in the Western Empire the clergy retained the toga and long tunic, while the laity wore the short tunic, trousers, and cloak of the Teutons, the *gens bracata*. Gregory the Great would have no person about him clad in the 'barbarian' dress. He enforced on his *entourage* the garb of old Rome, *trabeata Latinitas*. This cleavage was gradually enforced, and from the 6th cent. onwards the clergy were forbidden by various canons to wear long hair, arms, or purple, and, generally, the secular dress.

The characteristic garb of the Christian clergy, both civil and ecclesiastic, was the long tunic. Originally it appears to have been white. Then its evolution divided; the alb derived from it on the one side, the civil tunic in sober colours on the other. For the civil dress the dignified toga was added to constitute full dress; for use in inclement weather the *casula* or *cappa*, an overcoat (*pluviale*) with a cowl, was adopted. The last-named garment similarly divided into the ecclesiastic *cope*, and the civil over-cloak. The long tunic still survives in three forms—the surplice, the cassock, and the frock coat. Its fashion in the last instance superseded the toga, which again survives in the academic gown.

The evolution of vestments is in harmony with the psychology of dress generally, and in many aspects illustrates it forcibly. With the vestment the priest puts on a 'character' of divinity. By change of vestments he multiplies the Divine force while showing its different aspects. The changing of vestments has a powerful psychical appeal. The dress is a material link between his person and the supernatural; it absorbs, as it were, the rays of Deity, and thus at the same time inspires the human wearer. The dress is accordingly regarded not as an expression of the personality of the wearer, but as imposing upon him a super-personality. This idea is implicit in every form of dress. Dress is a social body-surface, and even in sexual dress, military uniform, professional and official dress the idea that the dress has the properties of the state inherent in it is often quite explicit. Further, the dress gives admission to the grade. In particular cases of solemnity a dress serves to render the person sacrosanct. Thus the Australian messenger is sacred by reason of his red cap.[2]

A temporary sacred garment may even be used sacrificially. At the Zulu festival of the new fruits, the king danced in a mantle of grass or of herbs and corn leaves, which was then torn up and trodden into the fields.[3] In such cases there is perhaps a reverse assimilation of virtue from the sacred person.

Royal dress in civilization tends to combine the principles of military dress and the tradition of the long robes of ancient autocracy. The subject needs a special analysis. The distinctive head-dress, the crown, probably is an accidental survival of a military fillet, confining the long hair which among the Franks was a mark of royalty.[1] But its significance is in line with the general principle, and it is eventually an affirmation of the dignity of the head, the crown of the human organism.

Among the earliest cultures, social authority tends to adopt a specific garb.

The headmen of the Nāgas wear a special dress.[2] The priest-king of the Habbés wears a distinctive costume.[3] The Nyasaland tribes commission the man who buried the dead chief to cover the new chief with a red blanket. 'This he does, at the same time hitting him hard on the head.'[4]

Ideas of purity readily attach themselves to priestly and royal garments. In the following case there seems to be some survival from Zoroastrianism.

Among the Kafirs of the Hindu Kush, men preparing for the office of headman wear a semi-sacred uniform which may on no account be defiled by coming into contact with dogs. These men, *kaneash*, 'were nervously afraid of dogs, which had to be fastened up whenever one of these august personages was seen to approach. The dressing has to be performed with the greatest care in a place which cannot be defiled with dogs.'[5]

Other less prevalent details of royal raiment are such as the girdle and the veil.

In ancient Tahiti the king at his investiture was girded with a sacred girdle of red feathers, which was a symbol of the gods.[6] In Africa veiling the face is a general custom of royalty.[7] The pall of European monarchs, originally bestowed by the Pope, typifies their sacerdotal function.

There is a tendency for each article of a royal panoply to carry a special symbolism, significant of the kingly duties and powers, just as the articles of the sacerdotal dress express Divine functions and attributes.

(8) *The dress of the gods.*—Frazer has shown reason for believing that the costume of the Roman god and of the Roman king was the same. Probably the king was dressed in the garments of Juppiter, borrowed from the Capitoline temple.[8] In the earlier theory of society the gods are a special class or grade in the community. Their dress has not infrequently been an important detail in the social imagination, and has even formed a considerable item in the national budget. In so far as they stand for super-humanity, it goes without saying that their raiment is the costliest and finest that can be obtained.

Amongst the Nahuas, clothes were not the least important material both of sacrifice and of ministration to the gods. 'The finest cotton and woollen stuffs are not only employed in their clothing, but are lavishly burnt in their sacrifices.'[9] The gods of Peru had their own herds of llamas and pacos, whose wool was woven for their robes,[10] and virgin-priestesses spun and wove it and made it up into dress.[11] The Vedic gods wore clothes.[12] The Egyptian and Chaldæan priests dressed their gods and performed their toilet,[13] as Hindu priests do now. The ancient Arabs clothed idols with garments.[14] In Samoa sacred stones were clothed;[15] and the images of the ancient Peruvians wore garments.[16]

The most artistic of races preserved for a long time the non-æsthetic but anthropomorphic custom of clothing statues with real clothes. The image of Apollo at Amyclæ had a new coat woven for him every year by women secluded for the work in a special chamber.[17] Every fourth year a robe woven by a college of sixteen women was placed on the image of Hera at Olympia.

---

1 Cheetham, in Smith-Cheetham's *DCA*, *s.v.* 'Dress.'

2 J. Fraser, 31.

3 J. Shooter, 27; N. Isaacs, ii. 293. Frazer, who cites the custom, suggests that in earlier times the king himself was slain and placed on the fields (*GB*² ii. 328). The suggestion is unnecessary.

1 Frazer, *Early History of the Kingship*, 198.

2 T. C. Hodson, 24.

3 L. Desplagnes, *Le Plateau central nigérien*, Paris, 1907, p. 321 f.

4 Stannus, in *JAI* xl. 316.

5 G. S. Robertson, *The Kafirs of the Hindu Kush*, 1898, p. 466.

6 Ellis, *Polynesian Researches*, 1829, ii. 354 f.

7 Frazer, *GB*³, pt. ii. p. 120.

8 Frazer, *Kingship*, 197.

9 Payne, i. 435.

10 *Ib.* 437.

11 *Ib.* 508, 510, ii. 541.

12 Oldenberg, *Rel. des Veda*, 304, 366 f.

13 G. Maspero, *Dawn of Civilization*², 1896, pp. 110, 679; Ball, in *PSBA*, xiv. (1892) 153 f.

14 Wellhausen, iii. 99; cf. Is 30²².

15 Turner, 268.

16 Acosta, *Hist. of the Indies* (Hakluyt Society, 1880), ii. 378.

17 Pausan. iii. 16. 2, 19. 2.

Before starting work they purified themselves with water and the blood of pigs.[1] The image of Asklepios at Titane wore a mantle and a shirt of white wool.[2] Zeus in an oracle commanded the Athenians to give Dione at Dodona new clothes.[3] The image of Hera at Samos possessed a wardrobe of garments, white, blue, and purple; some the worse for wear.[4] The bronze statue at Elis of a man leaning on his spear, called the Satrap, wore a garment of fine linen.[5] The image of Brauronian Artemis on the Acropolis was covered with many robes, offered by devout women. The same was the case with the image of Ilithyia at Ægium.[6] The magnificent robe, first used as a sail for the sacred ship and then presented to the image of Athene at the Panathenæa, is famous. The image was the old wooden Athene Polias of the Erechtheum. It was clothed in the robe. This was woven every fourth year by two Arrhephoroi.[7]

The dress of the god not seldom becomes a thing in itself, just as the dress of a priest or a king may itself be his substitute.

The Polynesians employed *tapa* in many ritualistic ways. Idols were robed in choice cloths. Every three months they were brought out, exposed to the sun (the term for this being *mehea*), re-anointed with oil, and returned to their wrappings. The god Oro was supposed to be contained in a bundle of cloths.[8] Matting and sinnet were similarly used. Papo, the Savaian god of war, was 'nothing more than a piece of old rotten matting about 3 yards long and 4 inches in width.' Idols were covered with 'curiously netted sinnet,' just as was the ὀμφαλός at Delphi. In Mangaia the gods were 'well wrapped in native cloth'; one god was 'made entirely of sinnet.'[9] The Tahitian word for sinnet is *aha*, and the first enemy killed was called *aha*, because a piece of sinnet was tied to him.[10]

The term 'ephod' in the OT apparently bears three meanings. (1) It is part of the high priest's dress. Worn over the 'robe of the ephod,' it was made of gold, threads of blue and scarlet, and fine linen. Its shape and character are doubtful. Held at the shoulders by two clasps, it was bound round the waist with a 'curious' girdle. (2) The term seems to be used for a garment set apart for priestly use only. (3) There is the ephod which is an image or its equivalent. Passages like Jg 8²⁶ make it difficult to interpret it as a garment. But, apart from questions of verbal interpretation which in some cases are very obscure,[11] it is possible to regard the ephod as a worshipped garment, the practice being found elsewhere, or as a garment enclosing or covering an image.[12]

Various Divine objects, symbols, or emblems may be clothed. In Uganda a jar swathed in bark-cloth, and decorated so as to look like a man, represented the dead king.[13] The Bhagats make an image of wood and put clothes and ornaments upon it. It is then sacrificed.[14] Such cases involve impersonation. Even an emblem like the Cross, when veiled on Good Friday, or sacred centres like the Ka'ba and the ὀμφαλός, when clothed, decorated, or veiled, acquire a certain personal quality. The line is not always easily drawn between covering and clothing.

In the highest stages of theistic imagination the dress of a god tends to be metaphorical. He is clothed with the blue sky,[15] with light, with clouds, or with thunder, with majesty, power, and splendour.

(9) *The dress of victims.*—By dressing an inanimate object, an animal, or a plant, a human quality is placed upon it. It thus becomes a member of society, by which capacity its saving force is enhanced. It does not follow that being so garbed it is a substitute for a previous human sacrifice. Even gifts may be so personalized. The Malays dress and decorate buffaloes which are presented as a gift.[16] But the principle is remarkably dominant in the case of sacrifices and effigies.

1 Pausan. v. 16.
2 Frazer, *Pausanias*, ii. 574 f.
3 Hyperides, iii. 43 f.
4 Curtius, *Inschriften von Samos* (a list is given), pp. 10 f. 17 ff.
5 Pausan. vi. 25. 5.
6 *Ib.* i. 23. 9, vii. 23. 5.
7 Frazer, *Pausanias*, ii. 574 f.
8 Ellis, *Polynes. Researches*, i. 335; Cook, *Voyages*, 1790, p. 1542; Williams, *Missionary Enterprise*, 1838, p. 152.
9 Williams, 375; Ellis, i. 337; Gill, *Myths*, 107, *Jottings from the Pacific*, 1885, p. 206. Sinnet or sennit is plaited palm-leaf strips.
10 Davies, *Dict. of the Tahit. Dialect*, 1857, *s.v.*
11 Jg 17³.
12 S. R. Driver, in *HDB*, *s.v.*; I. Benzinger and L. Ginsberg, in *JE*, *s.v.*; Ex 28⁶ 29⁵ 39², Lv 8⁷; Jos. *Ant.* III. vii. 5.
13 J. Roscoe, quoted by Frazer, *GB*² ii. 58 f.
14 Dalton, *Ethnol. of Bengal*, 258 f.
15 As Christ in Burne-Jones's picture of the Second Advent.
16 Skeat, 39.

There are cases of a reverse impersonation:

After killing a bear, the Koriaks dress a man in its skin, and dance round him, saying that they had not slain the bear.[1] When Nutkas had killed a bear, they put a chief's bonnet on its head and offered it food.[2]

Ordinary impersonation is more frequent.

Russian peasants dress up a birch tree in woman's clothes.[3] At the Little Dædala the Platæans dressed a wooden image made roughly from a tree, and decorated it as a bride.[4] The last sheaf of corn and similar representations of the corn-spirit are dressed in women's clothes at European harvests.[5] The old Peruvians had a similar rite, and dressed a bunch of maize in women's clothes.[6] The effigy called 'Death,' torn in pieces by Silesian villagers, is dressed in their best clothes.[7] The image of 'Death' in Transylvania is dressed in 'the holiday attire of a young peasant woman, with a red hood, silver brooches, and a profusion of ribbons at the arms and breast.'[8] The Iroquois sacrificed two white dogs, decorated with red paint, wampum, feathers, and ribbons.[9] The human scapegoat of Thuringia was dressed in mourning garb.[10] The scapegoat of Massilia was dressed in sacred garments.[11] The human victims of the Mexicans were dressed in the ornaments of the god, in gorgeous attire. In some cases when the body was flayed, a priest dressed himself in the skin to represent the deity.[12] The human victim of Durostolum was clothed in royal attire to represent Saturn. The mock-king in various lands is dressed in royal robes, actual or sham.[13] The reasons for the various dresses just enumerated are sufficiently clear.

Dress, by personalizing a victim, provides a convenient method of substitution. When the oracle ordered the sacrifice of a maiden, a goat was dressed as a girl and slain instead.[14] Such cases may be ætiological myths, but they may well have actually occurred. It does not follow, however, as has already been urged, that all cases of a humanly clothed animal or vegetable victim represent substitution for an originally human sacrifice.

The principle of assimilation to a particular environment, which is the focus of the ceremony, has striking illustrations.

In a folk-drama of Moravia, Winter is represented by an old man muffled in furs, and wearing a bearskin cap. Girls in green danced round a May-tree.[15] A common practice in European and other folk-custom is to dress a person representing the spirit of vegetation in flowers or leaves. 'In time of drought the Servians strip a girl to her skin and clothe her from head to foot in grass, herbs, and flowers, even her face being hidden behind a veil of living green. Thus disguised she is called the Dodola, and goes through the village with a troop of girls.'[16] A remarkable case is seen in Sabæan ritual. When a sacrifice was offered to 'the red planet Mars,' as Longfellow calls it, the priest wore red, the temple was draped with red, and the victim was a red-haired, red-cheeked man.[17] The girl-victim sacrificed by the Mexicans to the spirit of the maize was painted red and yellow, and dressed to resemble the plant. Her blood being supposed to recruit the soil, she was termed *Xalaquia*, 'she who is clothed with the sand.'[18] The similar victim of the Earth-goddess occupied her last days in making clothes of aloe fibre. These were to be the ritual dress of the maize-god. The next victim, a man, wore the female victim's skin, or rather a portion of it, as a lining for the dress she had woven.[19] The victim of Tezcatlipoca was invested for a year with the dress of the god. Sleeping in the daytime, he went forth at night attired in the god's robes, with bells of bronze upon them.[20] At the festival of Toxcatl, Tezcatlipoca's image was dressed in new robes, and all the congregation wore new clothes.[21]

10. Social control of dress.—Dress expresses every social moment, as well as every social grade. It also expresses family, municipal, provincial, regional, tribal, and national character. At the same time it gives full play to the individual. A complete psychology of the subject would analyze all such cases with reference to the principle of adaptation.

The least reducible of all distinctive costumes are the racial and the sexual. For instance, the

1 A. Bastian, *Der Mensch in der Geschichte*, Leipzig, 1860, iii. 26.
2 Frazer, *GB*² ii. 399.
3 Ralston, 234 f.
4 Pausan. ix. 3.
5 Frazer, *GB*² ii. 176 ff.
6 *Ib.* 193 f.
7 *Ib.* 86.
8 *Ib.* 93.
9 *Ib.* 108.
10 *Ib.* iii. 111.
11 *Ib.* 125.
12 Acosta, ii. 323; *GB*² iii. 135 f.
13 Frazer, *GB*² iii. 141, 150 ff.
14 *Ib.* ii. 38, quoting Eustathius on Hom. *Il.* ii. 732, p. 331.
15 Frazer, *GB*² ii. 102.
16 *Ib.* i. 95 ff.
17 Frazer, *GB*² ii. 256, quoting Chwolsohn, *Die Ssabier und der Ssabismus*, St. Petersburg, 1856, ii. 388 f.
18 Payne, i. 422 f.
19 *Ib.* 470.
20 *Ib.* 480; E. B. Tylor, *Anahuac*, 1861, p. 236.
21 Payne, i. 487 f.

Hindu fastens his jacket to the right; the Musalmān to the left.[1] In European dress the male fashion is to fasten buttons on the right, the female on the left. Where a division is central, the former still has the buttons on the right side, the latter on the left, the respective garments thus folding over in opposite directions. The larger differences are obvious, and need not be repeated.

A remarkable tendency is observable at the present day, which is due to increased facilities of travel and inter-communication, towards a cosmopolitan type of dress, European in form.

The sense of solidarity distinguishing social from individual life is sometimes expressed, as culture advances, in laws referring not only to the preservation of social grades as such, but to their economic delimitations. Various particular reasons which do not call for examination here have been the immediate inspiration of sumptuary laws in various races and nations. The sumptuary law proper is often combined with regulations of grade-fashion.

One of the earliest 'laws' of the kind is to be found in the *Lī-kī* of the Chinese.[2] The Koreans have strict 'sumptuary' laws relating to dress. 'The actual design of the dress is the same for all classes; but it is the material of which it is made and its colour that are affected by the law. The lower and middle classes may wear none but garments of cotton or hemp; while silk is the prerogative of the officials, who have the right also of wearing violet, which is a sign of good birth or officialdom.' The dress itself, usually white, consists of an enormous pair of trousers, tied under the armpits, and two or more coats reaching to the ankles. The sleeves of these are large, like those of the Japanese *kimono*. The poor wear sandals, the rich leather-lined shoes. In wet weather work-people wear wooden clogs in shape like the French *sabots*.[3] 'Silk,' according to Zoroastrian law, 'is good for the body, and cotton for the soul.' The former is derived from a 'noxious creature'; the latter acquires from earth and water, which when personified are angels, part of their own sacredness.[4] The Qur'ān forbids men to wear silk or gold ornaments. The Prophet forbade also the wearing of long trousers 'from pride.' His injunction was: 'Wear white clothes . . . and bury your dead in white clothes. . . . They are the cleanest, and the most agreeable.'[5] The military Dorian State passed laws against luxury in female dress. The Solonian legislation apparently followed its example. The *lex Oppia* of the Romans forbade, *inter alia*, the wearing by women of a dress dyed in more than one colour, except at religious ceremonies. The Emperor Tiberius forbade the wearing of silk by the male sex. Philip the Fourth enacted a law against luxury in dress. The law of the Westminster Parliament of 1363 was concerned chiefly with regulating the fashion of dress of the social orders. The law passed in 1463 (3 Edw. IV. c. 5) regulated dress generally, on the lines of the Mercantile Theory of Economics, as had been the case, though less explicitly, in the previous English sumptuary legislation. Luxury in dress (so the theory was applied) merely increased the wealth of other countries. A Scottish law of 1621 was the last of the kind.[6]

It is natural that social resentment should follow breaches of the most characteristic of all social conventions. The mere fact of strangeness as disturbing the normal environment is enough. Thus, in children and uneducated persons, 'anger may be aroused by the sight of a black skin or an oriental dress or the sounds of a strange language.'[7] In accordance with this essentially social instinct, the *Lī-kī* denounces the wearing of 'strange garments' as a sin, adding that it 'raises doubts among the multitudes.' The offence was punishable with death.[8]

Various ideas of personal dignity are apt to be outraged by such breaches. Even in low cultures, carelessness in dress reflects upon both subject and object. Unless a Masai girl is well dressed according to native ideas, and anoints herself with oil, she is not admitted into the warriors' kraals,—a social privilege,—and is regarded as outcast.[9] In view of such social feeling, it is not surprising that in countries like India there is no liberty of the subject as regards dress. Nor is there actually any more liberty in the matter for members of European or American societies. Decency, essentially a social idea, has here its widest meaning: to contravene any unwritten law of dress is an offence against decency—in itself an adaptation to environment and state.

11. Inversion of sexual dress.—The remarks of Frazer may introduce this part of the subject, which is curiously large: 'The religious or superstitious interchange of dress between men and women is an obscure and complex problem, and it is unlikely that any single solution would apply to all the cases.' He suggests that the custom of the bride dressing as a male might be a magical mode of ensuring a male heir,[1] and that the wearing by the wife of her husband's garments might be a magical mode of transferring her pains to the man.[2] The latter mode would thus be the converse of the former. We may also note the importance assigned to the principle of transference or contagion. Such ideas, it may be premised, are perhaps secondary, the conscious reactions to an unconscious impulsive action, whose motivation may be entirely different. The whole subject falls simply into clear divisions, which may be explained as they come. The Zulu 'Black Ox Sacrifice' produces rain. The officiators, chief men, wear the girdles of young girls for the occasion.[3] To produce a change in nature, it is necessary for man to change himself. The idea is unconscious, but its meaning is adaptation. Its reverse aspect is a change of luck by a change of self. The most obvious change is change of sex, the sexual demarcation being the strongest known to society, dividing it into two halves. The following shows this more clearly:

In order to avert disease from their cattle, the Zulus perform the *umkuba*. This is the custom of allowing the girls to herd the oxen for a day. All the young women rise early, dress themselves entirely in their brothers' clothes, and, taking their brothers' knobkerries and sticks, open the cattle-pen and drive the cattle to pasture, returning at sunset. No one of the male sex may go near them or speak to them meanwhile.[4] Here a change of officiators, sexually different, produces a change of luck and of nature. Similarly, among the old Arabs, a man stung by a scorpion would try the cure of wearing a woman's bracelets and ear-rings.[5] In Central Australia a man will cure his headache by wearing his wife's head-dress.

On this principle, as a primary reason, a large group of birth customs may be explained.

When a Guatemalan woman was lying in, her husband placed his clothes upon her, and both confessed their sins.[6] Here and in the next three cases the intention seems to be a change of personality to induce a change of state. A German peasant woman will wear her husband's coat from birth till churching, 'in order to delude the evil spirits.' When delivery is difficult, a Watubella man puts his clothes under his wife's body, and a Central Australian ties his own hair-girdle round her head. In China the father's trousers are hung up in the room, 'so that all evil influences may enter into them instead of into the child.'[7] In the last case the dress itself acts as a warning notice, representative of the father's person.

In the following is to be seen the principle of impersonation, the reverse method of change of personality, combined, no doubt, with an impulsive sympathetic reaction, equivalent to a desire to share the pain.

In Southern India the wandering Erukalavandhu have this custom—'directly the woman feels the birth-pangs, she informs her husband, who immediately takes some of her clothes, puts them on, places on his forehead the mark which the women usually place on theirs, retires into a dark room, . . . covering himself up with a long cloth.'[8] In Thuringia the man's shirt is hung before the window. In South Germany and Hungary the father's smock is worn by the child, to protect it from fairies. In Königsberg a mother puts her clothes over the child, to pre-

1 W. Crooke, *Things Indian*, 163. For the mistake of Dubois (p. 326) on this point, see above, p. 46b, note 10.
2 'Lī-kī' (tr. J. Legge), in *SBE* xxvii. (1885) 238.
3 H. S. Saunderson, in *JAI* xxiv. 302 f.
4 *SBE* xxiv. (1885) 49.
5 *Hidayah*, iv. 92; Hughes, *DI*, 1885, *s.v.* 'Dress.'
6 Guizot, *Civilization*, 1846, ch. 15; J. K. Ingram, art. 'Sumptuary Laws,' in *EBr*9.
7 Westermarck, *MI* ii. 227.
8 *SBE* xxvii. 237.
9 Hollis, *The Masai*, 250.

1 Frazer, *Adonis, Attis, Osiris*2, 1907, p. 432.
2 Frazer, *GB*3, pt. ii. 216, *Totemism and Exogamy*, iv. 248 ff.
3 Callaway, 93.
4 Carbutt, in *S. Afr. FLJ* ii. (1880) 12 f.
5 Rasmussen, *Additamenta ad Historiam Arabum*, 1821, p. 65.
6 De Herrera, *Hist. of America*, 1726, iv. 148.
7 Ploss, i. 123, 254; Riedel, 207; Spencer-Gillena, p. 467; Doolittle, i. 122.
8 J. Cain, in *IA* iii. (1874) 151.

vent the evil *Drud* carrying it off, and to dress a child in its father's smock brings it luck. Among the Basutos, when a child is sick the medicine-man puts a piece of his own *setsiba* garment upon it. In Silesia a sick child is wrapped in its mother's bridal apron. A Bohemian mother puts a piece of her own dress on a sick child. At Bern it is believed that to wrap a boy in his father's shirt will make him strong. Conversely, in some parts of Germany it is unlucky to wrap a boy in his mother's dress.[1]

In the above cases, secondary ideas are clearly present. In particular, the influence of a person's dress, as part of or impregnated with his personality, is to be seen.

A holiday being a suspension of normal life, it tends to be accompanied by every kind of reversal of the usual order. Commonly all laws and customs are broken. An obvious mode of reversal is the adoption of the garments of the other sex.

In the mediæval Feast of Fools the priests dressed as clowns or women. In Carnival festivities men have dressed up as women, and women as men. In the Argive Ὑβριστικά festival men wore women's robes and veils, and women dressed as men. At the Saturnalia, slaves exchanged positions and dress with their masters, and men with women. In Alsace, as elsewhere at vintage festivals and the like, men and women exchange the dress of their sex.[2] In the mediæval feasts of Purim, the Jewish *Bacchanalia*, men dressed as women, and women as men.[3]

The result, and in some degree the motive, of such interchange is purely social, expressive of the desire for good-fellowship and union.

Numerous cases fall under the heading of sympathetic assimilation. Magical results may be combined with an instinctive adaptation, or may follow it.

In Korea, soldiers' wives 'are compelled to wear their husbands' green regimental coats thrown over their heads like shawls. The object of this law was to make sure that the soldiers should have their coats in good order, in case of war suddenly breaking out. The soldiers have long ceased to wear green coats, but the custom is still observed.'[4] The explanation is obviously *ex post facto*. It seems more probable that the fashion corresponds to the European custom of women wearing their husbands' or lovers' colours. Every autumn the Ngente of Assam celebrate a festival in honour of all children born during the year. During this, men disguised as women or as members of a neighbouring tribe visit all the mothers and dance in return for presents.[5] In the Hervey Islands a widow wears the dress of her dead husband. A widower may be seen walking about in his dead wife's gown. 'Instead of her shawl, a mother will wear on her back a pair of trousers belonging to a little son just laid in his grave.'[6] In Timorlaut, widows and widowers wear a piece of the clothing of the dead in the hair.[7]

The custom is very frequent at pubertal ceremonies and at marriage festivities.

At the ceremony of *pollo*, connected with the puberty of their girls, Basuto women 'acted like mad people. . . . They went about performing curious mummeries, wearing men's clothes and carrying weapons, and were very saucy to men they met.'[8] The Masai boy is termed *sipolio* at his circumcision. The candidates 'appear as women,' and wear the *surutya* ear-rings and long garment reaching to the ground, worn by married women. When the wound is healed they don the warrior's skins and ornaments, and when the hair has grown long enough to plait they are styled *il-muran*, or warriors.[9] When an Egyptian boy is circumcised, at the age of 5 or 6, he parades the streets, dressed as a girl in female clothes and ornaments borrowed for the occasion. A friend walks in front, wearing round his neck the boy's own writing-tablet. To avert the evil eye a woman sprinkles salt behind.[10] In the old Greek story the boy Achilles lived in Scyros as a girl, dressed as a girl, to avoid being sent against Troy. He bore a maiden name, Issa or Pyrrha.[11]

In such cases we may see, at the initiation to the sexual life and state, an adaptation to it in the form of an assimilation to the other sex.

The principle of sympathetic assimilation is clearly brought out in the following two examples:

At the ceremonial burying of the placenta, Babar women who officiate wear men's girdles if the child is a boy, but women's *sarongs* if a girl. At the festival celebrating a birth, Fijian men paint on their bodies the tatu-marks of women.[1] In West Africa certain tribes have the custom of the groom wearing his wife's petticoat for some time after marriage.[2] In ancient Cos, the groom wore women's clothes when receiving the bride. Plutarch connects the custom with the story of Heracles serving Omphale and wearing a female dress. The Argive bride wore a beard 'when she slept with her husband,' presumably on the bridal night only. The Spartan bride wore a man's cloak and shoes when she awaited the coming of the bridegroom. In English and Welsh folklore there are cases of dressing the bride in men's clothes.[3]

The custom of inversion of sexual dress is very common at wedding feasts among European peasantry. All these are cases of sympathetic assimilation to the other sex. The principle is brought out by such customs as that mentioned by Spix and Martius, of Brazilian youths at dances with the girls wearing girls' ornaments.[4]

Many cases of the custom at feasts are complicated by various accidents. Sometimes it is meaningless except as a necessity.

Among the Torres Islanders women do not take part in ceremonies. Accordingly, at the annual death-dance deceased women are personated not by women but by men, dressed in women's petticoats.[5]

In other cases the data are insufficient for an explanation.

Thus, at harvest ceremonies in Bavaria, the officiating reaper is dressed in women's clothes; or, if a woman be selected for the office, she is dressed as a man.[6] At the vernal festival of Heracles at Rome men dressed as women. The choir at the Athenian *Oschophoria* was led by two youths dressed as girls.[7]

Cases occur of change of sexual dress by way of disguise; it is more frequent in civilization than in barbarism.

A Bangala man troubled by a bad *mongoli*, evil spirit, left his house secretly. 'He donned a woman's dress and assumed a female voice, and pretended to be other than he was in order to deceive the *mongoli*. This failed to cure him, and in time he returned to his town, but continued to act as a woman.'[8]

The last detail and the psychological analysis of modern cases suggest that a congenital tendency towards some form of inversion is present in such cases. On the face of them, we have to account for the choice of a *sexual* change of dress.

A Koita homicide wears special ornaments and is tatued. The latter practice is otherwise limited to the female sex.[9]

Women's dress may involve the assumption of women's weakness and similar properties.

The king of Burma suggested to the king of Aracan to dress his soldiers as women. They consequently became effeminate and weak.[10]

The Lycians, when in mourning, dressed as women. Plutarch explains this rationalistically, as a way of showing 'that mourning is effeminate, that it is womanly and weak to mourn. For women are more prone to mourning than are men, barbarians than Greeks, and inferior persons than superior.'[11] If the document is genuine, we may apply to the Lycians the principle adopted in regard to mourning costume generally. The state of mourning is an absolute suspension, and it may come to be regarded as an absolute reversal or inversion of the normal state of life.

Death, the negative of life, has taken place and made a violent break with the tenor of existence; hence such an adaptation as an inversion of sexual dress. Occasions might well be conceived when, if change of attire was desired, the only obvious attire presenting itself would be that of the other sex.

One of the most complex cases, at first appearance, is that of the adoption of feminine dress by priests, shamans, and medicine-men. Where for various mythological reasons an androgynous deity

1 Ploss, i. 123, ii. 40; Grützner, in *ZE*, 1877, p. 78; Ploss, i. 62, ii. 217, 221.
2 Dulaure, *Divinités génératrices*, Paris, 1805, xv. 315; Brand, i. 36, 66; Plutarch, *Mul. Virt.* 245 E; Mannhardt, *Der Baumkultus*, Berlin, 1875, p. 314.
3 Frazer, *GB*[2] iii. 156.
4 Saunderson, in *JAI* xxiv. 303.
5 Van Gennep, 69.
6 W. W. Gill, *Life in the Southern Isles*, 1876, p. 78.
7 Riedel, 307.
8 Endemann, in *ZE*, 1874, p. 37 ff.
9 Hollis, *The Masai*, 298.
10 Lane, i. 61 f., ii. 279.
11 Apollodorus, *Bibliotheca*, iii. 13. 8; Ptolemæus, *Nova Historia*, 1.

1 Riedel, 355; Williams, *Fiji*, 1858, i. 175.
2 M. H. Kingsley, *West Afr. Studies*, London, 1901, p. 131.
3 Plutarch, *Quaest. Gr.* 58, *Mul. Virt.* 245, *Lycurg.* 15; T. Moore, *Marriage Customs*, 1814, p. 37.
4 Spix-Martius, *Brazil*, 1824, ii. 114.
5 A. C. Haddon, *Head-hunters*, 1901, p. 139.
6 Frazer, *GB*[2] ii. 227.
7 Lydus, *de Mensibus*, iv. 46 (81); Photius, *Bibliotheca*, 322*a*.
8 J. H. Weeks, in *JAI* xl. (1910) 370 f.
9 Seligmann, 130.
10 Lewin, 137 f.
11 Plutarch, *Consol. ad Apoll.* 22; Valer. Max. xii. §§ 6, 13.

exists, it is natural that the attendant priests should be sympathetically made two-sexed in their garb, and even that the worshippers should invert their dress. Sacrifice was made to the Bearded Venus of Cyprus by men dressed as women, and by women dressed as men.[1]

As a rule, however, the deity is an invention intended, unconsciously enough, to harmonize with a traditional habit of priestly life. This particular habit is of wide extension, and involves a whole genus of psychoses. Some examples may precede analysis:

Chukchi shamans commonly dress as women.[2] The *basir* of the Dayaks make their living by witchcraft, and are dressed as women.[3] The priestesses, *balians*, of the Dayaks dressed as men. Sometimes a Dayak priest marries simultaneously a man and a woman.[4] Among both the Northern Asiatic peoples and the Dayaks it frequently happens that a double inversion takes place, so that of the wedded priestly pair the husband is a woman and the wife a man. It is said by the Koryaks that shamans who had changed their sex were very powerful.[5] The Illinois and Naudowessie Indians regarded such men as had 'changed their sex' as *manitous* or supernaturally gifted persons.[6] But it is unnecessary to assume that the practice is intended to acquire special magical powers attributed to women. This idea may supervene. Possibly the fantastic nature of the change itself, as mere change, has had some influence.

Patagonian sorcerers, chosen from children afflicted with St. Vitus' dance, wore women's clothes. Priests among the Indians of Louisiana dressed as women.[7] In the Pelew Islands a remarkable change of sex was observed. A goddess often chose a man, instead of a woman, to be her mouthpiece. In such cases the man, dressed as a woman, was regarded and treated as a woman. One significance of this is in connexion with the Pelewan social system. Frazer regards this inspiration by a female spirit as explaining other cases when sex is exchanged, as with the priesthoods of the Dayaks, Bugis, Patagonians, Aleuts, and other Indian tribes.[8] It is stated of some North American cases that the man dreamed he was inspired by a female spirit, and that his 'medicine' was to live as a woman.[9] In Uganda Mukasa gave oracles through a woman, who when she prophesied wore clothes knotted in the masculine style.[10] The legends of Sardanapalus (Assur-bani-pal) and Heracles, as well as the cases of the priests of Cybele and the Syrian goddess, would come under the explanation.[11] Heracles' priest at Cos wore a woman's raiment when he sacrificed. The story of Heracles himself may be a reminiscence of such effeminate priests, who were priest-gods. Dionysus Pseudanor is a similar embodiment of the principle.

Eunuchs in India are sometimes dedicated to the goddess *Huligamma*, and wear female dress. Men who believe themselves to be impotent serve this goddess, and dress as women in order to recover their virility.[12] A festival was given among the Sioux Indians to a man dressed and living as a woman, the *berdashe* or *i-coo-coo-a*. 'For extraordinary privileges which he is known to possess, he is driven to the most servile and degrading duties, which he is not allowed to escape; and he, being the only one of the tribe submitting to this disgraceful degradation, is looked upon as "medicine" and sacred, and a feast is given to him annually.'[13]

Among the iron-workers of Manipur, the god Khumlangba is attended by priestesses, *maibi*. But a man is sometimes taken possession of by the god. He is then known as *maiba*, and wears at ceremonies the dress of a *maibi*, viz. white cloth round the body from below the arms, a white jacket, and a sash. A fine muslin veil covers the head. 'The *maibi* is looked on as superior to any man, by reason of her communion with the god; and therefore if a man is honoured in the same way he assumes the dress of the *maibi* as an honour. If a man marries a *maibi*, he sleeps on the right of her, whereas the ordinary place of a woman is the right, as being the inferior side. It appears that women are more liable to be possessed by the god, and the same may be observed among all the hill tribes of these parts.'[14]

The *nganga*, medicine-men, of the Bangala, in certain ceremonies after a death, for the purpose of discovering the slayer dress up as women.[15] Off the coast of Arracan there were 'conjurers' who dressed and lived as women. On the Congo a priest dressed as a woman and was called Grandmother.[1] The Nahanarvals, a tribe of ancient Germany, had a priest dressed as a woman. Men of the Vallabha sect win the favour of Kṛṣṇa by wearing their hair long and generally assimilating themselves to women. The practice is even followed by rajas.[2] Candidates for the *areoi* society of Tahiti were invested with the dress of women.[3]

There is no doubt that these phenomena are cases of sexual inversion, congenital or acquired, partial or complete. Any idea of inspiration by female deities or the reverse is secondary, as also the notions of assimilation of priest to goddess, or of marriage of a priest to a god. The significant fact is that throughout history the priesthood has had a tendency towards effemination. The discussion of this belongs elsewhere.

Sexual inversion has especially obtained among the connected races of North Asia and America. It is marked by inversion of dress.

'In nearly every part of the continent [of America] there seem to have been, since ancient times, men dressing themselves in the clothes and performing the functions of women.'[4] Thus in Kadiak 'it was the custom for parents who had a girl-like son to dress and rear him as a girl, teaching him only domestic duties, keeping him at woman's work, and letting him associate only with women and girls.'[5] A Chukchi boy at the age of sixteen will often relinquish his sex. He adopts a woman's dress, and lets his hair grow. It frequently happens that in such cases the husband is a woman and the wife a man. 'These abnormal changes of sex . . . appear to be strongly encouraged by the shamans, who interpret such cases as an injunction of their individual deity.'[6] A similar practice is found among the Koryaks.[7]

Among the Sacs there were men dressed as women.[8] So among the Lushais and Caucasians.[9] Among the former, women sometimes become men. When asked the reason, a woman so changed said 'her *khuavang* was not good, and so she became a man.'[10] In Tahiti there were men, called *mahoos*, who assumed 'the dress, attitude, and manners of women.'[11] So among the Malagasy (the men called *tsecats*), the Ondonga in South-West (German) Africa, and the Diakité-Sarracolese in the French Sūdan.[12] Of the Aleut *schupans* Langsdorff wrote: 'Boys, if they happen to be very handsome, are often brought up entirely in the manner of girls, and instructed in the arts women use to please men; their beards are carefully plucked out as soon as they begin to appear, and their chins tattooed like those of women; they wear ornaments of glass beads upon their legs and arms, bind and cut their hair in the same manner as the women.'[13] Lisiansky described them also and those of the Koniagas: 'They even assume the manner and dress of the women so nearly that a stranger would naturally take them for what they are not. . . . The residence of one of these in a house was considered as fortunate.' Apparently the effemination is developed chiefly by suggestion beginning in childhood.[14] In Mexico and Brazil there was the same custom. In the latter these men not only dressed as women, but devoted themselves solely to feminine occupations, and were despised. They were called *cudinas*, which means 'circumcised.'[15] Holder has studied the *boté* ('not man, not woman') or *burdash* ('half man, half woman') of the N.W. American tribes. The woman's dress and manners are assumed in childhood. Some of his evidence suggests that the greater number are cases of congenital sexual inversion. 'One little fellow, while in the Agency boarding-school, was found frequently surreptitiously wearing female attire. He was punished, but finally escaped from school and became a *boté*, which vocation he has since followed.'[16] The *i-wa-musp*, man-woman, of the Indians of California formed a regular social grade. Dressed as women, they performed women's tasks. 'When an Indian shows a desire to shirk his manly duties, they make him take his position in a circle of fire; then a bow and a "woman-stick" are offered to him, and he is solemnly enjoined . . . to choose which he will, and ever afterward to abide by his choice.'[17] Something analogous is recorded of the ancient Scythians and the occurrence of a θήλεια νοῦσος among them.[18]

Some of the above cases, difficult to disentangle accurately, are not so much cases of congenital inversion as of general physical weakness. It is a

1 Macrob. *Saturn.* iii. 7. 2; Servius on Verg. *Æn.* ii. 637.
2 W. Jochelson, *Koryak Religion and Myth* (Jesup Expedition, vi. pt. i., Leyden and New York, 1905), p. 52 f.
3 A. Hardeland, *Dajacksch-deutsches Wörterbuch*, Amsterdam, 1859, *s.v.*
4 J. Pijnappel, in *Bijdragen tot de Taal-, Land-, en Volkenkunde van Nederl.-Indië*, iii. (1858) 330; St. John, *Forests of the Far East*, 1863, i. 62.
5 Jochelson, *l.c.*
6 J. Marquette, *Récit des voyages*, Albany, 1855, p. 53 f.
7 Bastian, iii. 309 f.
8 J. Kubary, in Bastian, *Allerlei aus Volks- und Menschenkunde*, Berlin, 1888, i. 35; Frazer, *Adonis, Attis, Osiris*[2], 428.
9 Max. zu Wied, quoted by Frazer, *l.c.*
10 Roscoe, quoted by Frazer, *l.c.* 11 *Ib.* 431 f.
12 Fawcett, in *JASB* xi. (1854) 343.
13 G. Catlin, *N. Amer. Indians*, 1876, ii. 214 f.
14 J. Shakespear, in *JAI* xl. (1910) 354.
15 Weeks, in *JAI* xl. 388.

1 Frazer, *Adonis*[2], 429.
2 Monier-Williams, *Religious Life and Thought in India*, 1883, p. 136.
3 Ellis, *Polyn. Res.* i. 324.
4 Westermarck, *MI* ii. 456, quoting the authorities.
5 *Ib.* 457, quoting Davydow.
6 *Ib.* 458, quoting Bogoraz.
7 Jochelson, 52 f. 8 Keating, *Expedition*, 1825, i. 227 f.
9 Lewin, 255; Reineggs, *Beschreibung des Kaukasus*, Gotha and St. Petersburg, 1796, i. 270.
10 *IA* xxxii. (1903) 413.
11 J. Turnbull, *Voyage round the World*, 1813, p. 382.
12 Westermarck, *MI* ii. 461, quoting authorities.
13 Langsdorff, *Voyages and Travels*, 1814, ii. 47.
14 U. Lisiansky, *Voyage*, etc., 1814, p. 199.
15 Von Martius, *Zur Ethnog. Amerika's*, Leipzig, 1867, i. 74.
16 A. B. Holder, in *N. Y. Med. Journ.*, 7th Dec. 1889.
17 S. Powers, 132 f. 18 Herod. i. 105, iv. 67.

remarkable aspect of certain types of barbarous society that the weak males are forced into the grade of women, and made to assume female dress and duties. Such a practice may, of course, induce some amount of acquired inversion. Payne[1] has suggested that their survival was due to advancement in civilization, and that later they formed a nucleus for the slave-class.

The occurrence of a masculine temperament in women is not uncommon in early culture. In some tribes of Brazil there were women who dressed and lived as men, hunting and going to war.[2] The same practice is found in Zanzibar and among the Eastern Eskimo.[3] Shinga, who became queen of Congo in 1640, kept 50 or 60 male concubines. She always dressed as a man, and compelled them to take the names and dress of women.[4] Classical antiquity has many similar cases of queens wearing men's armour in war, and of women fighting in the ranks, either temporarily, or permanently, as the Amazons. The last case, on the analogy of the West African cases of women's regiments, may be based on fact.[5]

In modern civilization the practice of women dressing as men and following masculine vocations is no less frequent than was in barbarism the custom of effemination of men.[6] Women of masculine temperament are by no means a rare phenomenon to-day, and the balance of sexual reversal has thus changed.

There remain to be considered two classes who form more or less definite social grades, and in some cases are distinguished by dress. These are old men and women.[7] After the menopause, women, as the Zulus say, 'become men,' and the customs of *hlonipa*, or sexual tabu, do not apply to them any longer.[8] Often, instead of the dress of matrons, savage and barbarous women after the menopause dress as men. For instance, in Uripiv (New Hebrides) an old widow of a chief lived independently, and 'at the dances painted her face like a man and danced with the best of them.'[9] Often they engage in war, consult with the old men, as well as having great influence over their own sex.

Various enactments both in semi-civilized custom and in civilized law have been made against inversion of dress. A typical decision is that of the Council of Gangra (A.D. 370): 'If any woman, under pretence of leading an ascetic life, change her apparel, and instead of the accustomed habit of women take that of men, let her be anathema.'[10] The point is noticeable that asceticism here, in the absence of a neutral garb, has recourse to the male dress. Such enactments and the modern laws on the subject are based on the Heb. law of Dt 22^5, and the Christian of 1 Co 11^6, but they embody a scientifically sound principle.

12. Exchange of dress.—This custom is frequent between friends, lovers, betrothed, and as a marriage rite. It is analogous to an exchange of any objects serving as mutual gifts, and its ultimate origin is to be found in this natural and obvious practice. Originally, therefore, it is outside the sphere of the psychology of dress proper; but it at once assumes various ideas of dress, often in an intensified form.

In Homer's story Glaucus and Diomed exchanged armour and became brothers-in-arms.[11] Among the Khamptis an exchange of clothes 'gives birth to or is a sign of amity.'[1] In Amboyna and Wetar and other islands, lovers exchange clothes in order, as it is reported, to have the odour of the beloved person with them.[2] In European folklore it is a very frequent custom that bride and bridegroom exchange head-dress.[3] The Ainu youth and girl after betrothal wear each other's clothes.[4] In South Celebes the bridegroom at a certain stage of the ceremonies puts on the garments which the bride has put off.[5] Among the mediæval Jews of Egypt a custom is recorded of the bride wearing helmet and sword, and the groom a female dress.[6] At a Brāhman marriage in South India the bride is dressed as a boy, and another girl is dressed to represent the bride.[7]

The secondary idea which is prominent in these customs is that of union by means of mutual assimilation. This is shown by such cases as the following:

In Buru a family quarrel is terminated by a feast. The father of the injured woman puts on the shoulders of her husband some of his own family's clothes; the husband puts on him a cloth he has brought for the purpose.[8] Among the Masai murder may be 'arranged' and peace made between the two families by the offices of the elders. 'The family of the murdered man takes the murderer's garment, and the latter [the family of the murderer] takes the garment of one of the dead man's brothers.'[9]

A later stage of development is marked by ideas of contagion of ill-will, or of the conditional curse.

By way of making a guarantee of peace, Tahitian tribes wove a wreath of green boughs furnished by both parties, and a band of cloth manufactured in common, and offered both to the gods, with curses on the violator of the treaty.[10] To establish that contact with a person which serves as a 'conductor' of conditional curses, in the Moorish institution of *l-'ar*, it is enough to touch him with the turban or the dress.[11] The Biblical story is not a case of indignity by mutilation of garments, but a magical act of guarantee. When Hanun, king of Ammon, cut off half the beard and half the clothes of David's ambassadors when he sent them back, he wanted a guarantee of friendly relations. His wise men, Frazer observes, would be muttering spells over these personal guarantees while David was on his way.[12]

Similarly, possession or contact ensures sympathy, whether by mere union or by the threat of injury.

In the Mentawey Islands, 'if a stranger enters a house where children are, the father or some member of the family present takes the ornament with which the children decorate their hair, and hands it to the stranger, who holds it in his hands for a while and then returns it.' The procedure protects the children from the possibly evil eye of the visitor.[13]

Union in marriage and other rites is commonly effected by enveloping the pair in one robe, or by joining their garments together.

In South Celebes the ceremony of *ridjala sampú* consists in enveloping them in one *sarong*, which the priest casts over them like a net.[14] The Tahitians and the Hovas of Madagascar have the same custom.[15] The Dayak *balian* throws one cloth over the pair. Among the Toba-Bataks the mother places a garment over them. A similar ceremony among the Nufoors of Doreh is explained as a symbol of the marriage 'tie.'[16] In north Nias the pair are enveloped in one garment.[17]

Among the Todas, the man who ceremonially sleeps with a girl before puberty covers her and himself with one mantle.[18] The Hindu bride and groom are tied together by their clothes, in the 'Brahma knot.' It is the same knot as is used in the sacred thread. The tying is repeated at various points in the ceremonies. The *maṅgalasūtra*, or *tāli*, is a cord with a gold ornament, worn round the married woman's neck, as a European wears a wedding-ring; and its tying is a binding rite. The bride and groom both don wedding clothes during the ceremonies.[19] The Bhillalas tie the garments of the bride and groom together.[20] Previously to the ceremony of *ridjala sampu* the clothes of the Celebes pair are sewn together—the rite of *ridjai-kamma parukusenna*.[21]

---

1 *Hist.* ii. 16 f.
2 M. de Gandavo, *Historia de Santa Cruz*, ed. 1837, p. 116 f.
3 Baumann, in *Verhandl. Berliner Gesellsch. Anthrop.*, 1899, p. 668 f.; W. H. Dall, *Alaska and its Resources*, 1870, p. 139.
4 W. W. Reade, 364.
5 Pausan. ii. 21; Apoll. Rhod. i. 712; Ptolem. in Photius, 150, v. 33; Mela, i. 19; A. B. Ellis, *Ewe-speaking Peoples*, 183, 290.
6 On sexual inversion in women, see Havelock Ellis, *Sexual Inversion*, 1897, ch. iv., and App. F. (Countess Sarolta).
7 See Van Gennep, 207.
8 Callaway, 440.
9 B. T. Somerville, in *JAI* xxiii. (1893) 7.
10 Cheetham, in *DCA*, *s.v.* 'Dress.'
11 *Il.* vi. 235 f.

---

1 H. B. Rowney, *Wild Tribes of India*, 1882, p. 162.
2 Riedel, 447, 67, 300, 41.
3 Reinsberg-Düringsfeld, *Hochzeitsbuch*, Leipzig, 1871, *passim.*
4 Batchelor, *The Ainu*, 1892, p. 142.
5 Matthes, *Bijdragen tot de Ethnologie van Zuid-Celebes*, The Hague, 1875, p. 35.
6 Frazer, *Adonis*², 434, quoting Sepp, *Altbayerischer Sagenschatz*, Munich, 1876, p. 232.
7 E. Thurston, *Ethnog. Notes in Southern India*, Madras, 1906, p. 3.
8 Riedel, 23.
9 Hollis, *The Masai*, 311.
10 W. Ellis, *Polyn. Res.* i. 318.
11 Westermarck, *MI* i. 586; cf. *ERE* iv. 372.
12 2 S 10^4; Frazer, *GB*³, pt. ii. p. 273.
13 H. von Rosenberg, *Der malayische Archipel*, Leipzig, 1878, p. 198.
14 B. F. Matthes, 31, 33 f.
15 Ellis, *Polyn. Res.* i. 117 f., 270, 272; J. Sibree, *Madagascar and its People*, 1870, p. 193.
16 Grabowsky, in *Ausland*, 1885, p. 785;Ködding, in *Globus*, liii. 91; van Hasselt, *Gedenkboek*, 1889, p. 42.
17 Sundermann, *Die Insel Nias*, Berlin, 1884, p. 443.
18 Rivers, *Todas*, 1906, p. 503.
19 Padfield, 124 ff.
20 Kincaid, in *JAI* ix. 403.
21 Matthes, *l.c.*

In connexion with marriage the custom is hardly intended to unite the woman to the man's family and the man to the woman's.[1] More probably it merely assimilates the two individuals; while, from the social point of view, it unites their respective sexual grades.

It is remarkable that many ceremonies of initiation, particularly those in which a spiritual fatherhood and sonship is established, are analogous in method to a marriage rite. Thus the *guru* of the Deccan Mhārs, when initiating a child, covers the child and himself with one blanket.[2]

Cases where the rite has one side only are natural, but are apt to take on the character of an act of acquisition and possession. In the Sandwich Islands the bridegroom casts a piece of *tapa* over the bride, this constituting marriage.[3] It is analogous to the Hindu 'giving cloth.' In Arabian times to cast a garment over a woman was to claim her. This explains the words of Ruth (Ru 3[9]). In Mal 2[16] 'garment' is equivalent to 'wife.'[4] A similar idea obtains in other circumstances, the dress having the force of a personal representative. The Southern Massim have a custom that a woman may save a man's life when struck down if she throws her *diripa*, grass-petticoat, over him.[5]

LITERATURE.—This is fully given in the footnotes.

A. E. CRAWLEY.

DRINKS, DRINKING.—The sensation of thirst is the psychological correlate of the metabolic functions of water. In direct importance drink comes next to air and before food. Thus in social psychology drink has played a more important part than food, especially since the primitive discoveries of fermentation and distillation made alcohol a constituent of drinkables. After being weaned from his mother's milk—a drink which is also a complete food—man finds a 'natural' drink in water. But, as experimentation in food-material proceeded, the sensation of thirst was supplemented by the sense of taste. The resulting complex 'sense of drink' was satisfied by a series of discoveries which gave to drinkables certain properties both of food and of drugs.

Before they were corrupted by European spirit, the Eskimo drank chiefly iced water, which they kept in wooden tubs outside their houses.[6] But on occasion they drank hot blood, and melted fat. An observer states of the New Hebrideans: 'I have never seen a native drink water (or indeed use it for any purpose). When thirsty, a young coco-nut is split, and then with the head thrown back the whole of the milk is literally poured down the throat without so much as one gulp. . . . The avoidance of the most obvious [drink], fresh running water, which is in great abundance, and generally excellent, is very curious.'[7]

1. Fermented drinks.—(*a*) *Beers.*—It is impossible to trace with precision the order of discovery and invention. Probably one of the earliest steps was the use and storage of fruit-juices. In time the practice of storage would lead to the discovery of fermentation. The use of corn for the preparation of fermented liquor is perhaps almost as early as its use for food. Cereal agriculture itself

'received a powerful stimulus from the discovery that infusions of corn, like drinks made from the juices of fruits and the sap of trees, acquire an intoxicating quality by fermentation. . . . In most parts of the Old and the New World the produce of cereal agriculture was from an early period largely consumed in the manufacture of some species of beer . . . the early cultivators drank it to excess.'[8]

The use of malted grain is probably later than the simpler principle of infusion. The term 'beer' is generally employed to include the products of both. In the majority of early beers, such as the Mexican and Peruvian *chicha*, infusion only is used.

In Eastern Asia an intoxicant made from rice is very general. *Oryza glutinosa* is frequently used for it. The manufacture among the Dayaks is as follows:

The rice is boiled, placed in pots with yeast, *ragi*. This stands for some days exposed to the sun. Then water is added, and the mixture is allowed to ferment for two days. It is then strained through a cloth. This drink is the *tuwak* of the Dayaks, the *tapai* of the Malays, the *badag* of Java. A similar drink is made by the Buginese and Makassars, called *brom*. These drinks are extremely intoxicating.[1] The rice-beer, *zu*, of the Nāgas is said to be soporific rather than intoxicating.[2] This is also largely the case with barley-beers in all their varieties. 'The liquor which plays so important a part in the daily life of the Garo is always brewed and never distilled. It may be prepared from rice, millet, maize, or Job's tears.'[3] Many aboriginal tribes of India drink rice-beer.[4] The term *samshoo*, or *samshee*, in China includes rice-beer. *Saké* or *saki*, the national drink of the Japanese, is made from the best rice-grain by fermentation. It has a slightly acid taste, and is of the colour of pale sherry. Inferior varieties are *shiro-zaké* (white *saké*), and a muddy sort, *nigori-zaké*. There is a sweet variety, *mirin*.

Beer made from varieties of millet (*Andropogon sorghum vulgaris*) is the chief African drink. Its use extends from the Kaffirs to the Egyptians. Under the name of *pombe* it is familiar throughout Central Africa.[5] In Egypt it is known as *durra*-beer. Besides *durra*-beer, the Nubians and Abyssinians make a sour beer from oats.[6]

Where barley is the staple grain for beer manufacture, rye is sometimes used to make a coarser variety. Wheat is occasionally used. In Germany it was once largely employed in what was known as *Weissbier*.

A grain as important regionally as rice and millet for the manufacture of beer is maize (*Zea mais*). Occasionally used in the Old World, as in parts of Africa, it is the staple grain for beer in America, its use extending from the Chaco Indians to the Apaches in the North. The latter made much use of it in their ceremonial life. They called it *tizwin*, and flavoured it with various spices.[7] The Southern and Central America maize-beer is known as *chicha*—a name as familiar as is *pombe* in Africa.

The fermented liquor, *chicha*, is an infusion of cooked maize in water. This is allowed to ferment. Its use was universal throughout ancient Mexico and Peru.[8] *Chicha* boiled down with other ingredients was a particularly strong intoxicant, used only at the *huacas*. To-day the Iquitos of the Amazons brew very excellent *chicha*, flavouring it with the young shoots of a plant which has the effects of an opiate.[9]

In Mediterranean and north European culture, barley has been the staple of beer.

The ancient Egyptians made a beer, *zythum*, from barley. Dioscorides mentions ζύθος, κοῦρμι, and βρῦτον as being used in the Greek world. The Hebrews seem to have included beer in the term *shēkhār* (EV 'strong drink'). Spanish beer (*celia* or *ceria*), Gallic beer (*cerevisia*), and an Illyrian beer were known to the Romans.[10] Germany and England have always been famous for their beers, and in modern times their output is the most important. There was an old distinction between ale (beer without hops) and beer (the hopped liquor). Climate and water, as in the case of wine, have much to do with the production of varieties. English beer is quite a distinct variety from either the light or the dark beer of Germany. The Russian *kvass* is a beer of barley and rye, or of rye alone.

The geographical range of beer, including rice, maize, and millet, as well as barley and rye-beer,

1 As Van Gennep holds (p. 246). On the whole subject of exchange of dress and similar practices, see Crawley, *Mystic Rose*, 1902, *passim*; and for marriage, G. A. Wilken, in *Bijdragen tot de Taal-, Land-, en Volkenkunde van Nederl.-Indië*, xxxviii. (1889) 38–406 ff.

2 *BG* xviii. 441.

3 Ellis, *Polyn. Res.* iv. 435.

4 W. Robertson Smith, *Kinship and Marriage*[2], 1903, p. 105.

5 Seligmann, 547.

6 F. Ratzel, *Hist. of Mankind*, Eng. tr., London, 1896–98, ii. 116.

7 B. T. Somerville, in *JAI* xxiii. (1894) 381 f.

8 Payne, *Hist. of the New World called America*, Oxford, 1892–9, i. 363 f.

1 Wilken-Pleyte, *Handleiding voor de vergelijkende Volkenkunde van Nederlandsch-Indië*, Leyden, 1893, p. 9.

2 T. C. Hodson, *Nāga Tribes of Manipur*, London, 1911, p. 7.

3 Playfair, *The Garos*, London, 1909, p. 52.

4 Sherring, *Mem. As. Soc. Beng.*, 1906, p. 101.

5 Decle, in *JAI* xxiii. 422; Ratzel, ii. 357.

6 Ratzel, iii. 39.

7 Bourke, in *American Anthrop.* vii. (1905) 297; W. B. Grubb, *An Unknown People*, London, 1911, p. 76; Im Thurn, *The Indians of Guiana*, London, 1883, p. 263.

8 Payne, i. 364.

9 C. R. Markham, in *JAI* xl. (1910) 103.

10 S. A. Wyllie, art. 'Brewing,' in *EBr*[9]

under the term, is precisely that of the respective cereals, covering the globe, except the Arctic and Antarctic parallels, and a narrow belt where the vine grows. In this belt, wine has always had precedence over beer and spirits, and it is not a luxury. In northern Europe, beer is more or less a 'national' drink, and everywhere it is a comparatively cheap beverage. Its general characteristic as opposed to wine that it has greater power of refreshment. Improved methods of storage have increased this since the time when beer had to be drunk as soon as it fermented.

(*b*) *Wines.*—There is no reason why the term 'wine' should not be retained to include the many varieties of liquor made by savage and semi-civilized races from the sap of trees. The *latex* of vegetable stems is sufficiently homologous with the juice of fruits, as that of the grape, to be classified with it in a genus distinct from fermented grain. It should be noted, however, that observers sometimes use the terms 'beer' and 'wine' indiscriminately, and do not always distinguish between fermented and distilled liquors.

As soon as vegetable juices, as distinguished from decoctions of grain on the one hand and infusions of leaves and berries on the other, are in question, the difference between the taste of grape-sugar, maltose, and thein is conspicuous. The character of wines may be described as sweet, that of teas as bitter, and that of beers as bitter-sweet. This permanent character is, as will be noted below, generally modified by art.

The discovery of the drink-value of the sap of certain trees was not difficult. Those chiefly used are palms, sugar-canes, and agaves.

In West Africa, palm-wine is the universal drink,[1] and it is commonly used all over the continent. The tree used is the *Raphia vinifera*, a bamboo-palm. The same tree is used for the purpose in Madagascar.[2] Palm-wine is the chief drink in most of the East Indian islands, Celebes, and especially the Moluccas; it is used to some extent in Java, Sumatra, Malaysia, and India. In the Moluccas the chief tree used is the *Arenga saccharifera*. The flower-stalk is tapped and the juice is fermented. Sweetness is sometimes corrected by adding bark. This drink, a typical form of palm-wine, is known as *sagero* in the Moluccas, *tuwak* in Malaysia and among the Bataks and Dayaks, and *legen* in Java.[3] It is the *toddy* of India, which is also made from the coco-palm and date-palm.[4] The *Borassus flabelliformis* is used in Leti, Moa, and Lakor.[5] This palm is the *Palmyra* of India and Africa. In view of the principle that adaptation to climatic conditions is partly effected by diet, it is noteworthy that the people of Tenimber and Timorlaut say that it is impossible to live in these islands without drinking a sufficiency of palm-wine.[6] The Guaraunos of the Orinoco made a fermented drink from the Mauritia palm.[7] The *gwy* of British Guiana is from the *æta* palm.[8] The not distant relative of these palms, the sugar-cane (*Saccharum officinarum*), is an obvious source of drinkables. In Burma, Assam, and Tongking, a fermented drink is made from it together with pineapple juice.[9] The A-kamba make a fermented liquor from the sugar-cane and dried fruits.[10] The A-kikuyu ferment the juice of the sugar-cane.[11]

The ancient Mexicans were very skilful in the preparation of fermented liquors. The chief source of material was the *maguey*, the false or American aloe (*Agave Americana*), the fermented sap of which forms *pulque*. Like palm-wine, *pulque* is obtained by tapping the flowering stalk of the aloe. The sap can be drawn off three times a day for several months, one plant yielding perhaps several hogsheads. To increase its intoxicating qualities, various roots are added. In appearance it resembles milk and water, or soapsuds, and it tastes and smells like rotten eggs. In 1890, 75,000 tons of *pulque* were carried on the main line of the Mexican railway—twice as much as the weight of any other commodity.[12]

The North American Indians made a fermented liquor from maple- and birch-sugar.[13] In England the sap of these trees, as also of the ash and spruce, has been used for the same purpose. Spruce-'beer' is common in northern Europe[1]—a decoction of the young leaves of the spruce-fir. Cider is a fermented liquor made from apples.

The geographical range of the grape-vine makes two narrow belts round the world, extending, roughly, from parallel 30° to 50° N. and S. But various conditions have limited its successful exploitation even here, and its most effective range is confined to southern and central Europe and parts of western Asia. In Italy, Spain, Portugal, Greece, and southern Europe generally the vine grows easily. In northern France and Germany it needs very careful culture. The southern wines, it has been noted, possess a larger proportion of sugar, but often are inferior in bouquet to those of the north. France, the Rhine districts of Germany, Spain, Portugal, Italy, Sicily, parts of Austria-Hungary, and Madeira produce the best wines of the world. Xeres and Oporto have given their names to famous wines of Spain and Portugal. The sack drunk in old England was a sherry. The Johannisberg vintages of Germany and the Tokay vintages of Hungary are particularly famous. The once famous Canary is still produced in the Canary Islands. Greece, Algeria, and Russia make fair wines, and wine is now increasingly grown in Australia, South Africa, and America. In Persia the wines of Shirāz, the produce of an excellent variety of vine, are still famous.[2] In the Græco-Roman world the vines of the Greek Islands, such as Chios, Lesbos, and Cos, produced the most valued wines. The Italian wines never attained their standard of excellence. A good deal of must was used by peasants, and wine turned sour was a favourite drink, and formed part of the rations of troops. The various Græco-Roman drinks were used in Palestine.

2. Distilled drinks.—Distillation, the process of evaporating a fermented liquor, and thus separating alcohol, has been known in the East, especially in China, from the remotest antiquity.[3] It is an invention difficult to trace to its source, but it seems to be attested for a few peoples at the stage of the lower barbarism, and in the higher stages of barbarism it is very generally known. Some of the more primitive American Indians seem to have been acquainted with the process.[4] A primitive form of distillation was found by Cook in the Pacific Islands. It was known to, but little used in, the ancient Mediterranean civilization.

It is recorded that in the 12th cent. the Irish distilled whisky, *uisge-beatha*=*aqua vitæ*, 'the water of life.'[5] In British Central Africa 'spirits used to be made by distilling from beer and banana- and palm-juice by means of a pot and a gun-barrel.'[6] But the process is rare in Africa. In the East it is very common. The Korean native spirits are distilled from rice or millet, and vary in colour, from that of beer to that of pale sherry.[7] The Chinese distil spirits from millet and maize,[8] but chiefly from rice. Rice-spirit and distilled palm-wine are largely drunk in the East. In Sumatra rice-beer is distilled into a spirit.[9] In South India this is also used. *Arrack* proper is a spirit distilled from palm-wine. In the Moluccas it is termed *koli*-water. *Sagero* from the *Arenga saccharifera*, or *Borassus flabelliformis*, is distilled in a primitive fashion.[10] *Arrack*, distilled from *toddy*, or from rice, is largely drunk in India by the lower classes. It is the *surā* of the ancient Hindus. Various peoples, such as the Malagasy, distil spirits from the juice of the sugar-cane,[11] a primitive form of rum.

In modern European civilization the use of spirits has increased, relatively, more than that of beers and wines. The Russian *vodka* is distilled from rye, an inferior sort from potatoes. Scotland and Ireland are famous for their whiskies, France for its brandy of Cognac, Holland for its schnapps, or hollands, a form of gin.

---

1 Ratzel, iii. 110; Torday-Joyce, in *JAI* xxxvi. (1906) 42.
2 W. Ellis, *Hist. of Madagascar*, London, 1838, i. 210.
3 Wilken-Pleyte, 8 f.
4 Rājendralāla Mitra, *Indo-Aryans*, Calcutta, 1881, i. 418.
5 Riedel, *De sluik- en kroesharige rassen*, The Hague, 1886, pp. 15, 382 f., 434.
6 *Ib.* 83.
7 Payne, i. 309.
8 Im Thurn, 268.
9 Ratzel, i. 361.
10 C. W. Hobley, *Ethnology of A-Kamba*, Camb. 1910, p. 31.
11 W. S. Routledge, *With a Pre-Historic People*, London, 1910, p. 62.
12 Payne, i. 374 f.
13 Ratzel, iii. 420.

---

1 The German *Sprossenbier*.
2 Dittmar-Newman, art. 'Wines,' in *EBr* 9.
3 Dittmar-Paton, art. 'Distillation,' in *EBr* 9.
4 Bourke, in *Amer. Anthrop.* vii. 297.
5 Dittmar-Paton, *loc. cit.*
6 Stannus, in *JAI* xl. 322.
7 Ratzel, iii. 470.
8 Saunderson, in *JAI* xxiv. (1894–5) 308.
9 Boers, in *Tijd. Ned.-Indië*, xxiv. 2 (1840), p. 569.
10 Wilken-Pleyte, 9; Riedel, 83, 123, 291, 320, 434.
11 Ellis, *Hist. of Madagascar*, i. 210; Rājendralāla Mitra, i 397.

Portugal and Spain produce a true brandy, known as *aguardiente*. Brandy proper is chiefly made in France. It is distilled from grape-juice alone. Factitious or 'British' brandy is, like gin, made from 'silent,' or unflavoured, whisky. Whisky is made from a fermented infusion of grain, chiefly barley, sometimes rye, malted or unmalted. Rum in its varieties is made from molasses, and can be produced wherever sugar-cane grows. Its chief seat of manufacture is the West Indies. Germany and Russia produce potato brandy from the *fecula* of potatoes.[1]

Mediæval Europe was rich in the lore of making cordials and essences. To the earliest period of the Middle Ages belong the terms *aqua vitæ* and *elixir vitæ*. The search of alchemy for elixirs of life and youth probably gave some impetus to industrial invention.

Civilized taste has declared against the fermented drinks included in the term 'mead.' Fermented liquors made from honey have been largely used from the earliest barbarism. The Bogos and Abyssinians make a variety of mead.[2] What is commonly styled honey-'beer' often is merely a sweet fermented liquor; but true honey-wine is reported for the Hottentots, Feloops, and A-kamba.[3] Certain peoples have made fermented liquors from saccharine substances produced from plant juices by evaporation.

Such are recorded for ancient Syria, made from wine and palm-wine. In Yucatan a fermented liquor was made from *metl*, 'honey,' and in Peru from that obtained by boiling the berries of *Schinus molle*. Honey-mead, *madhu* (=Gr. μέθυ), whatever its nature, is recorded for ancient India. It is said to have been superseded by *soma*.[4]

3. Infusions.—Tea, coffee, and cocoa are stimulants, without the specific effects of alcoholic drinks. Their properties are due respectively to the alkaloids thein, caffein, and theobromin. The use of these infusions and decoctions has increased enormously in modern times. It is significant that China has never been addicted to the use of alcoholic liquor, and that coffee is chiefly grown in Muhammadan countries. Ancient Mexico seems to have had a hard struggle against the national abuse of intoxicants, and its successful crusade was largely due to the presence of cocoa.

The tea-plant (*Thea chinensis*) is a native of China and Assam. Its cultivation in India and Ceylon is only very recent, but has assumed enormous proportions, chiefly in N.E. India and Assam, and S. India, as in Travancore.

Used for centuries in Russia, which derived good tea from China since its connexion with the East, tea is now drunk practically all over the world. Even a people like the savages of the New Hebrides are fond of tea, coffee, and cocoa, provided there is plenty of sugar. But the wilder natives still prefer the milk of the coco-nut.[5] The distinction between black and green tea is due to different methods of drying the leaf. The use of tea among European peoples is relatively recent, while for China it has been traced back to the beginning of the third millennium B.C.

Tradition assigns the discovery of coffee to Abyssinia. It was introduced into Arabia in the 15th cent., and into Turkey in the 16th. In the 17th cent. its use gained a footing in England and France. The coffee of the New World, deriving from one plant sent to Surinam from Amsterdam in 1718, is now the largest production, Brazil supplying the greater part. Arabia, North Africa, and the East Indies are the other great coffee-regions. It is grown also in Southern India.

The best Arabian coffee is grown in Yemen. Besides the infusion of the roasted berry, there is a coffee prepared from the leaves. The green shoots are dried in the sun, and then roasted and powdered. The resulting beverage is the *kishr* of Yemen, the *wedang kopie* of Java, and the *kawah* of Sumatra. The aroma is regarded as being superior to that of ordinary coffee from the berry.[6]

The tree from which cocoa and chocolate are made is indigenous to Central and South America. It was cultivated by the Mexicans, and from them the beverage was introduced to Europe by the Spaniards.

The Mexican cocoa was prepared by mixing the cacao-seed into a paste with maize. Diluted with hot water, and churned into a thick froth, which was the actual beverage, it was drunk when cold only. The Spaniards introduced the practice of drinking it hot. Vanilla was usually added as a flavouring. Chocolate, as thus drunk by the ancient Mexicans, was successful owing both to its aroma and to its fatty constituents. It was known to be a nerve stimulant.[1] In modern times the fat is removed by the screw-press; this and the addition of sugar render it more palatable. Benzoni (1519–1566) describes it as a drink more fit for pigs than for human beings; Linnæus named it *Theobroma* ('food of the gods'), *Theobroma cacao*. It contains the same powerful alkaloid as the kola-nut. As a beverage in Western civilization it is only less important than coffee and tea.

4. Other drinks.—Drinks prepared from roots are not numerous. Some have been incidentally referred to; others are the *kava* of Polynesia, the *paiwari* of Guiana, and the *mishla* of the Mosquitos. The root of the sweet potato (*Batatas edulis*) is occasionally used.[2] *Paiwari* and *mishla* are made from *cassava* (manioc), the root, or bread made therefrom, of the *Manihot utilissima*, which in another form is the tapioca of commerce.

With *mishla* we approach a class of drinks which become pre-eminently social both in preparation and in use. One noteworthy detail reflects the characteristics of communal life, and also illustrates the stage of culture in which the preparation of commodities is *ad hoc*, and storage and artificial production are at a minimum. This is the fact that the communal drink is prepared only for special feasts, which are, however, frequent, and is all consumed.

The *mishla* of the Mosquito region includes all kinds of strong drink, but particularly that prepared from cassava or manioc.[3] The famous *kava* of Polynesia and Melanesia is in many regions becoming obsolete, owing to the introduction of European drinks. The *soma* of the ancient Indians, and the identical *haoma* of the ancient Parsis, are the most conspicuous examples of the communal drink becoming religious, and being apotheosized.[4] *Amṛta*, the nectar conferring immortality, was produced, along with thirteen other valuable entities, from the churning of the milky ocean. It was, however, an unguent rather than a drink (see ANOINTING [Hindu]).[5] The Homeric *ambrosia* was the food of immortality; the *nectar* was the drink of the gods. Sappho and Anaxandrides speak of ambrosia as a drink; it is also employed as an unguent like the Vedic *amṛta*. Alcman speaks of nectar as a food. Later, it was a synonym for wine, and acquired the special connotation of fragrance. The Homeric nectar conferred immortality; hence it was forbidden to men. It was described as ἐρυθρόν, and, like Greek wine, was mixed with water. Apparently by etymology (νή and root of κτείνω) its meaning is the same as that of ambrosia.[6]

5. Tendencies of evolution.—The evolution of taste is perhaps not altogether a sociological, but partly an ontogenic process. It is correlated with the evolution of manufacture. One or two tendencies may be observed. For example, man's drinks tend to the condition of water. Thus, many beverages of primitive peoples are prepared in a thick soup-like form. Chocolate, for example, was drunk very thick.[7] In Tibet and many Mongol districts tea is prepared with butter. Turkish coffee is characterized by the inclusion of grounds. English beer has passed from a muddy consistency to a sparkling clearness. The thick sweet character of *pulque* resembles the inspissated must of Græco-Roman wine production. The ancient wine itself in its ordinary form was very thick, almost of the consistency of treacle, and probably for that reason it was generally drunk diluted with water. The sparkling nature of the best water has during the last century been suggested both in wines and in water by the method of effervescence. First applied to the wines of Champagne, it was adopted for certain of the Rhine

1 Dittmar-Paton, *loc. cit.*
2 Ratzel, iii. 211.
3 Mungo Park, *Travels*, London, 1860, i. 7; T. Hahn, *Tsuni-Goam*, London, 1881, p. 38; Hobley, 31.
4 Payne, i. 377 f., quoting authorities; A. A. Macdonell, *Vedic Mythology* (*GIAP*, Strassburg, 1897), 114.
5 Somerville, in *JAI* xxiii. 382.
6 Wilken-Pleyte, 8; Ratzel, i. 433, iii. 211, 334.

1 Payne, i. 380.
2 Im Thurn, 263, 268.
3 See H. A. Wickham, in *JAI* xxiv. 203 f., 206 f.
4 J. Eggeling, in *SBE* xxvi. (1885), introd.; Macdonell, 104, 110 f.
5 Monier-Williams, *Brāhmanism and Hindūism*[4], London, 1891, p. 108.
6 Liddell-Scott, *Greek-English Lexicon*[8], 1901, *s.vv.*
7 Cf. Wickham, in *JAI* xxiv. 207.

vintages. The production of artificial mineral waters, in which an access of carbonic acid gas causes sparkling, is characteristic of the last half-century. One result of fermentation is thus obtained, without, in the case of mineral waters, any fermentation at all.

Another tendency is towards the reduction of sweetness. Old wines in which no sugar is left have been preferred in recent centuries. Such, however, have a corresponding excess of alcohol. Dryness in modern wines is increasingly sought after. Thick, sweet drinks, like mead and malmsey, are typical in barbarism, and in ancient and mediæval culture. Malmsey, the French *malvoisie*, was originally a Greek wine, and carried on the tradition of the thick wines of ancient Greece. The Greeks themselves corrected sweetness by various methods, among them being the use of salt water. Savagery and barbarism had no lack of experiments in the production of varied flavours, if not of the correction of sweetness.

The rice-beer of the Nāgas is flavoured with jungle herbs, such as *Datura*,[1] while the neighbouring Garos dilute theirs with water.[2] The natives of the Moluccas correct the sweetness of their *sageru* by adding barks of a bitter flavour. The addition of hops to barley-beer gives it a tonic and more refreshing character. In old English life spices were largely used in both ale and wine. Mulled drinks were taken hot.

A similar tendency, found very early in culture, is to be noted in the preference for sour milk.

6. Animal drinks.—Drinks, other than milk and blood, produced from animal substance, are in the lower cultures not merely soups or broths, but actual beverages. The credit of the invention and use of the only animal spirit known to the world belongs to the Tatar tribes of Asia. Their *koumiss*, distilled from the milk of their mares, has been known since Greek times.

Human milk is the natural food of the human infant. Though differing in some important respects, the milk yielded by various animals is a satisfactory diet for children, and, especially in its products, a valuable food for adults. The use of milch-animals was a great step towards civilization.[3]

When Dayaks kill a pig or an ox, which is done to music and singing, they scramble for the blood. Men, women, and children drink of it; they smear themselves all over with it, and behave like maddened animals, burying their faces in the bleeding carcasses.[4] Blood, in fact, is to the savage 'a perfectly natural food; scarcely less so, perhaps, than milk, which is nothing but blood filtered through a gland.'[5]

7. Drinking customs and ideas.—The natural care bestowed upon the preparation of drinkables is guided and developed by growing intelligence, and inspired at certain stages of culture by religious emotion.

'The Hindu is very particular as to the water he drinks. It must be ceremonially pure, though not necessarily chemically pure.' It has to be very carefully fetched. If the carrier touches or comes near an out-caste or anything impure, the water is thrown away, and the vessel broken, or scoured with sand and water.[6] The kings of ancient Persia had their drinking-water brought from particular rivers, especially the Zab.[7]

Water, in Zoroastrianism, is sacred. It is a 'dress for breath,' physiologically and physically. It is a sin to drink water in the dark, or to pour it away.[8] Water is the 'dark spirit'; for sacrifice it is more valuable than spirituous liquors.[9]

A good deal of myth has gathered about the palm-wine tree (*Arenga saccharifera*) in the East Indies.

Many stories are told of how the juice of the nut has brought the dead to life again.[10] The Dayaks of South-East Borneo figure palm-wine as milk, flowing from the tree as if from a woman.[1] The Niasers hold that a palm-tree planted by a woman yields more sap than one planted by a man. A folk-tale runs that a woman after delivery, feeling she was about to die and not wishing her babe to starve, cut off one of her breasts. Out of this grew the palm-wine tree.[2] In Angkola a woman prayed to be turned into a tree. When she died, the *Arenga* tree came from her navel, the opium plant from her forehead, the *pisang* from her feet, milk from her breasts.[3]

Besides the stimulating and expansive properties of wine and spirits, the process of fermentation has naturally engaged the popular mind. A good deal of superstition is, no doubt, to be referred to speculation upon this mysterious change.

Among the Masai, 'when honey-wine is to be brewed, a man and a woman are selected for the purpose, neither of whom has had sexual intercourse for two days. A tent is set apart for them to live in until the honey-wine is ready for drinking (six days), during which time they may not sleep together. As soon as the honey-wine is nearly ready they receive payment, and go to their respective homes. Were they to have sexual intercourse during the six days that the honey-wine is brewing, it is believed that the wine would be undrinkable, and the bees that made the honey would fly away.'[4]

The ultimate reason for such a rule is probably merely an unconscious impulse towards concentration of purpose and avoidance of anything that might divert attention. The prohibition is particularly enforced in delicate operations. From the original impulse would develop ideas about the danger of mixing interests, no less than material; and, later on, ideas of sympathetic influence, among which may be some comparison of the sexual function with the process of fermentation.

In old Mexico the men who prepared *pulque* might not touch women for four days previously; otherwise the 'wine' would go sour and putrid.[5] The brewing of beer (*sheroo*) is regarded by the Kachins 'as a serious, almost sacred, task; the women while engaged in it having to live in almost vestal seclusion.'[6]

In the Mexican example may be seen a possible explanation of the way in which a comparison of the processes of fermentation and of sex was applied. Mixing of personality has attached to itself various terms and ideas of 'impurity.' Similarly the ingestion of leaven has been regarded as resulting in an impure condition of the material acted upon. Leaven itself is a symbol of corruption. Thus, an impure state in the persons engaged may induce a similar impurity in the object of their labours. Conversely, in other circumstances, it may expedite a desired change, as from barrenness to fertility.

A similar objection to mixture may be seen in an Australian custom. If we compare with it the rule of the Timorese priest[7] which forbids him in war-time to drink cold water, and orders him to drink hot water only, so as not to cool the ardour of the warriors, we may see how a rule arising naturally from an aversion to anything exciting or disturbing, when important operations are in progress, may be sophisticated subsequently. The Australian case shows an earlier stratum of psychosis.

The Euahlayi people believe that, if a medicine-man have many spirits in him, he must not drink hot or heating drinks. These would drive them away. Also, spirits would never enter a person defiled by the white man's 'grog.'[8] The Zambesi rain-maker, in order to keep his spirits with him, never touches alcohol.[9]

When the savage has reached the idea of a spirit informing his own organism, he has usually also reached the idea that heating or spiritous liquor is itself possessed of a spirit. Thus, if he wishes to concentrate the attention of his own spirit, he must, in sober earnest, refrain from mixing it with others.

The care bestowed on the preparation of liquors

1 Hodson, 60 f. 2 Playfair, 52. 3 Payne, i. 290.
4 *Tijdschrift voor Nederlandsch-Indië*, I. i. (1838) 44.
5 Payne, i. 393. See, for further instances, New, *East. Africa*, London, 1874, p. 397; Hollis, *Masai*, Oxford, 1905, pp. 257, 317 f.; De Goguet, *Origin of Laws*, Edinburgh, 1761, ii., art. 3; New, 189; *Journ. Ethn. Soc.* i. (1869) 313; H. Ward, in *JAI*, xxiv. 292.
6 Padfield, *The Hindu at Home*², Madras and London, 1908, p. 41 f.; Dubois-Beauchamp, *Hindu Manners*³, Oxford, 1906, p. 187.
7 Ratzel, iii. 401. 8 *SBE* iv. (1895) lxii., i. (1900) 74.
9 *SBE* xxiv. (1885) 292, xxvii. [1885] 435.
10 A. C. Kruijt, *Het animisme in den ind. Archipel*, The Hague, 1906, p. 150.

1 Kruijt, 153. 2 Sundermann, p. 412.
3 Kruijt, *loc. cit.* 4 A. C. Hollis, in *JAI* xl. 481.
5 Sahagun, *Hist. générale* (Jourdanet-Siméon), Paris, 1891, p. 45.
6 J. Anderson, *From Mandalay to Momien*, London, 1876, p. 138.
7 H. O. Forbes, in *JAI* xiii. (1884) 414.
8 K. L. Parker, *The Euahlayi Tribe*, London, 1905, p. 46.
9 *Missions catholiques*, xxvi. (1893) 266.

is also evidenced in the ceremonial handselling of the new wine.

Thus, among the Mexicans, the priest of the god Ixtlilton, a healer of children, invested with the god's robes, opened the new wine annually in the houses of the people, and ceremonially tasted it.[1] New liquor is made by the Nāgas at the feast of *Reengnai* in January. This is a *genna*, or occasion of tabu, and men carry their own water for the rice-beer, and during the manufacture men and women eat separately.[2]

From this 'tasting' develops the sacrifice of the first-fruits of the vine. The Romans sacrificed the first of the new wine to Liber; until this was done, the new wine might not be generally drunk.[3]

The mechanism of drinking as practised by Europeans is more or less identical with that of eating. The liquid does not fall down the pharynx and œsophagus, but each gulp is grasped by the tongue and passed down. Thus a man is able to drink while standing on his head. Many peoples, however, either have not reached this method or have modified it.[4]

The wild men of Malaysia drink by throwing the water from the hand into the mouth. The Orang Laut do this with unerring aim, at a distance of more than a foot, without splashing. Even children are expert. A mother gives her infant water by dripping it from her hand. A New Hebrides native throws his head back, and literally pours the liquid down his throat without gulping. The ordinary drink in Oceania is the juice of the half-ripe coco-nut. The nut is held up and the juice allowed to fall into the mouth. It is unmannerly to touch the shell with the lips. The Lake Victoria tribes drink their beer through a tube.[5] In the Hindu ritual of meals, food is eaten with the right hand, but water is drunk with the left; the vessel is taken up with the left hand. The vessel must not touch the lips. It is held a little way above the upturned mouth, and the water is poured from it into the mouth. To allow the vessel to touch the lips would be indecent. The Fijians never put a vessel to the lips when drinking. They regard it also as objectionable for several persons to drink out of the same vessel. A Maori chief would not touch a calabash with his hands when drinking; he held his hands close to his mouth, and another man, a slave, poured the water into them. It was a grave crime to let any one use a cup rendered sacred by having touched his lips.[6]

Muhammad forbade drinking water in a standing posture. Three breaths are to be taken before a draught, for the reason that thus the stomach is cooled, thirst is quenched, and health and vigour are imparted. Drinking from the mouth of a leather bag was forbidden. 'He who drinks out of a silver cup drinks of hell-fire.' The faithful may not drink out of green vessels, large gourds, or vessels covered with pitch, the last being used for wine. During the fast of Ramaḍān it is held that even to swallow saliva between sunrise and sunset is a sin.[7]

The natural tendency against mixing re-appears in the custom of not eating and drinking at the same time. This is only partially identical with physiological law, since certain foods require a liquid vehicle, and certain drinks stimulate digestion.

When eating rice the Malagasy drink water. But otherwise they rarely drink at meals.[8] The Hindu does not drink until the meal is finished.[9] The natives of Borneo usually drink only after they have finished eating. 'They contend that by abstaining from taking liquid with their food they prevent indigestion.'[10] In British Central Africa the native drinks between meals, but chiefly water.[11] The A-kikuyu never drink at meals, but drink at any time when thirsty.[12] The Abyssinians drink nothing at meals.[13]

Eating, especially in the somewhat rapid method used by early peoples, is hardly compatible with conversation; hence many rules against eating and talking at the same time. Drinking does not labour under this disability. When drink is alcoholic, there is still less restraint of the tongue. In 15th cent. England 'people did not hold conversation while eating, but the talk and mirth began with the liquor.'[1]

[1] Bancroft, *NR*, San Francisco, 1882, iii. 410. [2] Hodson, 171.
[3] Festus, *s.v.* 'Sacrima'; Pliny, *HN* xviii. 8.
[4] The 'lapping' method of Gideon's three hundred (Jg 7[5f.]) was not 'as a dog lappeth,' but consisted merely in using the hand as a cup.
[5] Skeat-Blagden, *Pagan Races*, London, 1906, i. 110 f.; Somerville, in *JAI* xxiii. 382; Ratzel, i. 259; Hobley, 31.
[6] Padfield[2], 41; Dubois-Beauchamp, 183; Wilkes, *U.S. Exped.*, 1845–58, iii. 115; Shortland, *Southern Districts of New Zealand*, London, 1851, p. 293; Colenso, in *Trans. New Zealand Institute*, 1868, p. 43.
[7] T. P. Hughes, *DI*, *s.v.* 'Drinkables'; A. Leared, *Morocco and the Moors*, London, 1876, p. 204.
[8] W. Ellis, *Madagascar*, i. 190–210.
[9] Dubois-Beauchamp, 183.
[10] Hose, in *JAI* xxiii. 160. [11] Stannus, *JAI* xl. 322.
[12] W. S. Routledge, *With a Pre-Historic People*, 61.
[13] Ratzel, iii. 228.

When existence, as in the middle stages of social evolution, is threaded with superstition, methods of drinking and habits associated with drinking are either emphasized or inverted on special occasions which call for peculiar regard. As already suggested, it is probable that the ultimate psychological reason for these tabus is merely the instinct for concentration and the exclusion of foreign and disturbing interests. Ideas of supernatural danger are developed later, in order to give an explanation of the instinctive rule. Possibly the arbitrary prohibitions of 'individual' tabus are due to the same instinct; at any rate, the observance of such prohibitions helps to form the sense of responsibility.

On the Gold Coast, among individual tabus is the prohibition against drinking palm-wine on certain days of the week.[2] During a *genna* in January the Kabuis forbid young men to drink anything outside the house. On the occasion of the erection of a village monument the villagers may not use drinking-cups, but have to drink from leaves.[3] Among individual tabus of the Bangala are, 'You must not drink native wine except through a reed, and never straight out of a vessel of any kind.'[4] The cook of the party on the *hiri*, or trading expedition of the Massim, may not drink water, but only coco-nut milk.[5] A Massim sorceress drinks no water, but coco-nut milk only for eight days, by which time she is sacred and able to heal the sick.[6] In Celebes the priest who is responsible for the growth of the rice may not drink with any one or out of any person's cup.[7] In S.E. Australia a visitor to another tribe was under certain restrictions for a time. He was allowed to drink muddy water, three mouthfuls on each occasion. He had to drink these very slowly, or his throat would swell up.[8] The Thompson Indian girl, during the first four days of her seclusion at puberty, drank water, while otherwise fasting, from a birch-bark cup painted red. She sucked up the liquid through a tube made of the leg of a crane or swan; her lips were not allowed to touch the surface of the water. Subsequently she was permitted to drink from streams and springs, but even here she had still to use her tube, otherwise the spring or stream would dry up.[9] The Tlingit girl in the same condition had to drink through the bone of a white-headed eagle.[10]

On his first campaign the North American brave was very sacred. Especially was it essential that no one should touch his eating and drinking vessels. When on the outward journey warriors drank from one side only of the bowl; on the return, from the other. When within a day's march of home they hung their vessels on trees or threw them away.[11] In another account a functionary named *elissu* is mentioned. His duty was to hand to the warriors everything that they ate or drank; they were not allowed to touch these themselves.[12]

Among the Tring Dayaks mourners may not drink ordinary water, but only water collected in the leaves of creepers. This is called 'soul-water.'[13] Before setting out on a trapping expedition, the Carrier Indian abstains from drinking out of the same vessel as his wife.[14] In Chotā Nāgpur and the Central Provinces of India men abstain from alcohol and women when rearing silkworms.[15]

The last case may be compared with the Masai tabu during the making of wine. There chastity is observed in order that the wine may not be spoiled. If the reason be that by magical 'sympathy' a sexual process may taint the wine, that reason and any idea of the sympathetic action of

[1] T. Wright, *Domestic Manners in England*, London, 1862, p. 396.
[2] C. H. Harper, in *JAI* xxxvi. 184 f.
[3] Hodson, 173, 182. [4] J. H. Weeks, in *JAI* xl. 366.
[5] Seligmann, *The Melanesians*, etc., London, 1910, p. 102.
[6] Romilly, *From my Verandah in New Guinea*, London, 1889, p. 94 f.
[7] *Med. Nederl. Zendeling-Genootschap*, xi. (1867) 126.
[8] Howitt, 403.
[9] Teit, in *Mem. Am. Mus. Nat. Hist.* ii. pt. iv. (1900) 311–317.
[10] Langsdorff, *Reise um die Welt*, Frankfort, 1813, ii. 114; cf., for similar instances from other peoples, Morice, in *Proc. Can. Inst.* vii. (1889) 162 ff.; Frazer, *GB*[2] iii. 215, quoting Schomburgk and von Martius; G. Hamilton and J. Rae, in *JAI* vii. (1878) 206 f.; G. Dawson, 'The Haida Indians,' in *Geolog. Survey of Canada*, App. A, p. 131; Guis, in *Missions catholiques*, xxx. (1898) 119.
[11] *Narrative of John Tanner*, N.Y. 1830, p. 122 f.
[12] J. Adair, *Hist. of the American Indians*, London, 1775, p. 380; cf., for further instances, Frazer, *GB*[2] i. 331, quoting Bourke, and i. 342, quoting Boas; D. Kidd, *The Essential Kafir*, London, 1904, p. 309 f.; S. Hearne, *Journey . . . to the Northern Ocean*, London, 1795, p. 204; F. Russell, in *26 RBEW* (1908), p. 204 f.
[13] Kruijt, 282.
[14] A. G. Morice, in *Trans. Canad. Inst.* iv. (1892) 107.
[15] *Indian Museum Notes*, Calcutta, 1890, i. 3, p. 160.

alcohol on the larvæ can hardly apply to the Chotā Nāgpur tabu. Some explanation more in accordance with the evolution of mind seems to be required.

In the following, ideas of sympathetic adaptation appear:

During the preliminary ceremonies for making rain among the Arunta no water may be drunk, else the magic would fail[1]—no doubt because of the premature use of liquid. So in Java, when proceedings are taken to prevent the fall of rain, the person interested may not drink anything while the ceremonies are in progress,[2] otherwise the rain would at once commence. Conversely, medicine-men sometimes drink, and generally cultivate wetness, when making rain.

Permanent caution in the act of drinking is often found in the case of important persons, and sometimes it is a social habit. Africa is remarkable for such observances.

In the Congo State 'there is hardly a native who would dare to swallow a liquid without first conjuring the spirits. One of them rings a bell all the time he is drinking; another crouches down and places his left hand on the earth; another veils his head; another puts a stalk of grass or a leaf in his hair, or marks his forehead with a line of clay. This fetish custom assumes very varied forms. To explain them, the black is satisfied to say that they are an energetic mode of conjuring spirits.' When a chief drinks he rings a bell at each draught: and at the same moment a boy brandishes a spear in front of him, 'to keep at bay the spirits which might try to sneak into the old chief's body by the same road as the *massanga* (beer).'[3]

When the king of Loango 'has a mind to drink, he has a cup of wine brought; he that brings it has a bell in his hand, and, as soon as he has delivered the cup to the king, he turns his face from him and rings the bell, on which all present fall down with their faces to the ground, and continue so till the king has drunk.' The king would die if he were seen in the act of drinking.[4] When Winwood Reade offered the king of Canna a glass of rum, the monarch hid his face and the glass under a towel.[5] When the king of Dahomey drinks in public, a curtain is held up to conceal him. Bowdich describes the scene when the king of Ashanti drank wine; music played, and the soldiers, brandishing their swords with the right hand, covered their noses with the left, singing meanwhile the monarch's victories and titles, as he drank behind an extemporized curtain. A man of consequence never drinks before his inferiors without hiding his face. It is said in Ashanti that an enemy can most easily impose a spell on the faculties of his victim when drinking. A son of the king of Congo was put to death for having accidentally seen his father drink. A Pongo chief never drinks in the presence of others except behind a screen.[6] When the king of Unyoro in Central Africa went to the royal dairy to drink milk, the men dispersed and the women covered their heads. No one might see him drink. A wife handed him the milk-bowl, but turned her face away.[7] The Thompson Indians believe that enemies can injure a man by magic when he drinks.[8] A Warua when drinking holds a cloth before his face. The habit is particularly strong in the presence of a woman. 'I had,' says Cameron, 'to pay a man to let me see him drink; I could not make a man let a woman see him drink.'[9]

In these cases the development takes the form of a real, though secondary, sense of modesty. Von den Steinen found in Central Brazilian tribes a sense of modesty, attended by shyness and blushing, exhibited when alimentary functions were in progress, a sense as keen as that shown by the majority of the human race in the matter of sexual functions.[10] In similar rules cited below there may be seen not merely habits of etiquette, but a sense of modesty and a law of decency, involving the fear of exciting disgust. The idea that such practices hinder the entrance of evil influences, or prevent the soul from escaping,[11] is a later sophistication, and cannot explain their origin.

[1] F. J. Gillen, in *Horn Sci. Exped. to Central Australia*, iv. (1899) 177 ff.; Spencer-Gillen[a], 189 ff.
[2] G. G. Batten, *Glimpses of the Eastern Archipelago*, Singapore, 1894, p. 68 f.
[3] *Collections ethnographiques du Musée du Congo*, Brussels, 1902–6, p. 164, quoted by Frazer, *GB*[3], pt. ii. (1911) p. 120.
[4] Frazer, *GB*[3], pt. ii. p. 117 f., quoting authorities.
[5] W. Reade, *Savage Africa*, London, 1863, pp. 184, 543.
[6] J. L. Wilson, *Western Africa*, London and N.Y. 1856, pp. 202, 308, 310; R. Burton, *Mission to Dahome*, London, 1864, i. 244; Reade, 53; Bowdich, *Mission to Ashantee*, London, 1873, pp. 438, 382.
[7] Frazer, *GB*[3], pt. ii. p. 119, quoting Roscoe.
[8] Teit, in *Amer. Mus. Nat. Hist.* i. (1900) 360.
[9] Cameron, in *JAI* vi. (1876) 173.
[10] K. v. den Steinen, *Unter den Naturvölkern Zentral-Brasiliens*, Berlin, 1894.
[11] Frazer, *GB*[3], pt. ii. p. 120.

When the Indian of Cape Flattery falls ill, he often ascribes it to a demon which entered his body when he was drinking at a stream.[1] Bulgarians before drinking make the sign of the Cross, to prevent the devil entering the body with the drink.[2] Devout Russians used to blow on the glass to drive Satan from the liquor.[3] Conversely, the soul may be tempted to remain, though the mouth is dangerously open, by offering it a share in the beverage. When the hair of the Siamese boy is cut, there is a danger lest the *kwun*, the guardian spirit of the head, may depart. It is enticed and captured; then coco-nut milk is presented to it. This is drunk by the boy, and thus by absorbing the drink of the *kwun* he retains the *kwun* itself.[4]

Rules of drinking, more or less impregnated with superstition, occur all over the world.

In Wetar it is a serious offence to use a chief's drinking-cup.[5] A Maori who drank from the cup of a man who wished him ill became bewitched.[6] The Niam-niam, who are said to be 'particular at their meals,' that is, to observe alimentary decency, wipe the rim of a cup before passing it on.[7] Great care was taken by the Fijians that no one should touch the king's cupbearer. They regarded it as objectionable for several persons to drink out of the same vessel, and held that pollution was carried by saliva.[8] The civilized man has the same instinct of isolation and of excluding foreign elements from his drinks.

Contact with particular persons is avoided.

According to the rules of Kaffir *hlonipa*, relatives of a husband will not drink milk at any kraal connected with the wife, nor will the wife's relatives at a kraal connected with the husband. For some time after marriage the wife will not use milk. The principle is that she was paid for with cattle, and would be *insila* ('defiled') if she consumed her own purchase. After a visit to her father, from whom she brings a goat or an ox, the tabu is removed. The animal is slain, and the 'defilement' passes from the milk into the animal. She has 'cleaned her spoon.'[9]

In the above case we have probably little more than a phase of etiquette. In others there is a distinct fear of contamination resulting in various conceptions of real or imaginary injury.

In Tonga, inferior persons might not drink in the presence of superiors,[10] and the various 'ranks' could not drink together.[11] In India, water cannot be accepted by high-caste from low-caste persons.[12] Even Pahariahs will not drink with Keriahs.[13] Among the Nāgas, with whom village feuds are frequent, one village may often be found refusing to drink from a running stream which supplies another.[14] New Guinea natives refused to drink water offered to them by Europeans.[15]

In cases like the last there is perhaps no definite conception, merely a vague uneasiness about the unfamiliar. A similar sensitiveness occurs in the case of unfamiliar or untested drinks.

When the Eskimo find a new spring, an *angekok*, or the oldest man present, drinks of it first to rid the water of any *torngarsuk*, or malignant quality which might make them ill.[16] Similar ideas are connected with the hospitable practice of 'tasting,' though it is not clear that they are the primary reason of the custom.[17] At palm-wine drinkings the Kruman hostess takes the first and last drink herself, in order to 'take off the fetish.'[18] The same notion may be involved in the ceremonial tasting by an official of the new wine and the new fruits.[19] In Eastern Central Africa, at beer-drinkings given by the chief, the priest or 'captain' of the chief tastes the liquor, to show the guests that it is not poisoned.[20] New Guinea natives taste the water they offer to a stranger, to prove that it is free from poison.[21] Among the Zulus it is not etiquette to offer beer to any one without first tasting it.[22]

Drinking with a woman is avoided by many peoples in various stages of evolution. The Beni-Harith would not take drink from the hands of a

[1] J. G. Swan, in *Smithsonian Contributions*, Washington, xvi. (1870) 77.
[2] Sinclair-Brophy, *A Residence in Bulgaria*, London, 1877, p. 14.
[3] G. A. Erman, *Siberia*, London, 1848, i. 416.
[4] E. Young, *The Kingdom of the Yellow Robe*, Westminster, 1898, p. 64 f.
[5] Riedel, 455.
[6] J. S. Polack, *New Zealand*, London, 1838, i. 263, 280.
[7] G. Schweinfurth, *The Heart of Africa*[2], 1874, ii. 19.
[8] Wilkes, iii. 115, 349.
[9] D. Leslie, *Among the Zulus and Amatongas*[2], Edinburgh, 1875, pp. 173, 196.
[10] D'Urville, *Voyage pittoresque autour du monde*, Paris, 1834–5, ii. 77.
[11] W. Mariner, *The Tonga Islands*[3], Edinburgh, 1827, ii. 234.
[12] Monier-Williams, 453.
[13] V. Ball, *Jungle Life in India*, London, 1880, p. 89.
[14] Hodson, 8.
[15] H. von Rosenberg, *Der malayische Archipel*, Leipzig, 1878, p. 478.
[16] H. Egede, *Descript. of Greenland*[2], London, 1818, p. 185; D. Crantz, *Hist. of Greenland*, London, 1820, i. 193.
[17] See below. [18] J. L. Wilson, 124. [19] See above.
[20] D. Macdonald, *Africana*, London, 1882, i. 191.
[21] Von Rosenberg, 470. [22] D. Leslie, 205.

woman on any consideration.[1] An artificial horror is generated in such cases. The Muskhogeans held it equivalent to adultery that a man should take a pitcher of water from the head of a married woman. It was permissible for him to drink if the woman removed the pitcher herself, and retired after setting it on the ground.[2] Following another line of thought, the Arunta hold that a draught of woman's blood will kill the strongest man.[3]

Among the Kaffirs and the Bahima a menstruating woman may not drink milk; if she does, the cows will be injured. She is restricted to beer.[4] At his daughter's first period, however, a Kaffir father sets apart an old cow for her exclusive use, and its milk constitutes her only food.[5] After being delivered, the Greenland mother observes tabus. She has a water-pail for her own use; if any one else drinks from this, the rest must be thrown away.[6] Pliny mentions the belief that, if a menstruous woman touches wine, it turns to vinegar.[7] 'In various parts of Europe it is still believed that if a woman in her courses enters a brewery the beer will turn sour; if she touches beer, wine, vinegar, or milk, it will go bad.' In Calymnos a menstruous woman 'may not go to the well to draw water, nor cross a running stream, nor enter the sea. Her presence in a boat is said to raise storms.'[8]

On the face of these customs and ideas there is a regard both for the woman's own safety and for that of others. She is rendered harmless by being insulated, and at the same time is removed from danger.[9] It has been further suggested, for the explanation of similar cases, that any taint of sexual functions may injure the milk of cows, and that the sympathetic link between the milk and the cow may be snapped by any process which converts the milk into another substance, such as curds. Members of the 'sacred world' may therefore use these substances without injuring their source.[10] On this principle the Wanyamwesi practice of mixing vaccine or human urine with milk has for its object the safeguarding of the source.[11]

The Jbāla of Northern Morocco believe that a murderer is permanently unclean. 'Poison oozes out from underneath his nails; hence anybody who drinks the water in which he has washed his hands will fall dangerously ill.'[12] Among the Zulus a wounded man may not touch milk till a ceremony has been performed.[13]

The sources of contamination dangerous to drinkables are almost universally the same. There are some variations, as perhaps the law of Muhammad that a vessel from which a dog has drunk is to be washed seven times before it is used by human beings.[14]

A universal source of contamination is death.

After a death the Zulus drink no milk for a day; the mourners not for some time. Widows and widowers apparently are permanently forbidden its use.[15] A Nandi who has handled a corpse may not drink milk until he has been purified.[16] The Déné who has touched a corpse has to drink out of a special gourd.[17] In the same circumstances the Thompson Indian has to spit out the first four mouthfuls whenever he drinks.[18]

For the classification of the various magical properties of drinks the Zulu theory is instructive. But neither here nor elsewhere can a line be drawn between inherent and acquired characteristics. The Zulus logically distinguish between two complementary species of magical drinks. These are 'black' and 'white,' negative and positive. The former removes, for instance, everything that causes a man to be disliked; the latter gives him 'brightness,' and produces liking and admiration in others. The former is emetic in its operation. The ejected matter is placed in the fire; thus the 'badness' is consumed. The white drink, when used, for instance, to command the affections of a girl, or to conciliate a great man, should contain some object that the person referred to has worn next the skin.[1]

Drinks of the first class have the properties of liquids when used for washing; those of the second have the positive qualities, stimulant or nutritive, which drinks share with food and drugs. A distinction is clearly to be drawn between the latter class and drinks which have been contaminated by alien or dangerous substances.

Just as mythology developed the generic idea of drink into a water of life or of immortality, so it has developed the idea of cleansing into a water of oblivion. The 'Drink of Forgetfulness' is found in Greek, Hindu, Norse, and other mythologies.[2]

In Fijian mythology the spirit of the dead man on his way to the other world drinks of a spring. As soon as he tastes the water, he ceases weeping, and his friends at home cease weeping, forgetting their sorrows. This savage Water of Lethe is called the *Wai-ni-dula*, the 'Water of Solace.'[3] The Fijian idea is significant when compared with certain ceremonial drinking which terminates mourning. Among the Kacharis of Assam an elder distributes to the mourners 'the water of peace,' *santi jal*; the drinking of this terminates the mourning.[4] The Kathkars effect 'purification' after birth or death by means of water touched by a Brāhman.[5] In South India holy water is drunk to terminate mourning. In Roman Catholic ritual a sick man drinks water in which the priest has washed his hands.[6] At the end of mourning the Kaffir widow rinses her mouth with fresh milk.[7] Chaco Indians 'purify' themselves after a funeral by drinking hot water and washing themselves,[8] cleansing thus both the outer and the inner man. In Central Africa the possessing spirit is driven out of a man by drinking an intoxicant. The Goṇḍs believe they purify themselves by drinking spirits.[9] Among the Orāons a man is re-admitted to caste after he has drunk the blood of a goat to wash away his sin.[10] When the Bijāpur Bedars re-admit an adulteress, they touch her lips with a red-hot twig of *Asclepias gigantea*, and give her liquor to drink.[11] In Mexico during the 'bad days,' which recurred every four years, children were made to drink spirits.[12]

In these and similar cases there is a preference for 'strong' water, whether it be hot or spirituous, or blood, or containing some added virtue. It is difficult, therefore, always to distinguish 'purification' from the ingestion of virtue or *mana*. Many magical drinks certainly have both negative and positive properties. This is the case, whether literally by acquisition or metaphorically by imagination, with water itself.

The Musalmān Nawab of Savanur drank Ganges water only, not from piety, but because of its medicinal properties. The water of which a Brāhman sips thrice before a meal is 'Vishnu's feet-water.' The Kenaras drink water in which the priest has washed his feet.[13] In early England a cure for demoniac possession was water drunk out of a church-bell.[14]

From this aspect drinks are suitable for purposes of consecration and institution. Their virtue gives a vigorous set-off in the new state.

In old Scandinavia the new king drank a horn of liquor before taking his seat on the throne.[15] European monarchs after coronation take the Sacrament. So in Catholicism do married couples. Interesting variants are the following. In Avestan times the first food given to the new-born child was the *haoma*-juice.[16] Among the Tshi peoples the father gives his son a name by squirting rum from his mouth upon him. Rum is poured out on the ground for the ancestors on the same occasion.[17]

1 W. R. Smith, *Kinship and Marriage in Early Arabia*, London, 1885, p. 312.
2 Adair, 143.
3 F. J. Gillen, *loc. cit.* iv. 182.
4 J. Macdonald, in *JAI* xx. (1891) 138.
5 Roscoe, in *JAI* xxxvii. (1907) 107.
6 H. Egede, 196.
7 *HN* vii. 64 f., xxviii. 77 ff.
8 Frazer, *GB*² iii. 232 f., quoting authorities.
9 *Ib.*
10 Frazer, in *Anthrop. Essays presented to E. B. Tylor*, Oxford, 1907, p. 163 f.
11 *Ib.*
12 Westermarck, *MI* i. 378.
13 N. Isaacs, quoted by Frazer, in *Anthrop. Essays*, 158.
14 Hughes, *DI*, *s.v.* 'Drinkables.'
15 Frazer, in *Anthrop. Essays*, 160 f.
16 A. C. Hollis, *The Nandi*, Oxford, 1909, p. 70.
17 C. Hill-Tout, *The Far West*, London, 1907, p. 193 f.
18 Teit, *Amer. Mus. Nat. Hist.*, 1900, p. 331 ff.

1 H. Callaway, *Rel. System of the Amazulu*, Natal, 1868, p. 142 f.
2 W. Crooke, *FL* ix. (1898) 121; Dasent, *Tales from the Fjeld*, London, 1874, p. 71; M. Frere, *Old Deccan Days*, London, 1868, p. 143.
3 B. H. Thomson, in *JAI* xxiv. 352.
4 Frazer, *Totemism and Exogamy*, 1910, iv. 298. See below.
5 J. M. Campbell, in *IA* xxiv. (1895) 30.
6 *Ib.* p. 58; *Golden Manual*, p. 721.
7 H. Lichtenstein, *Travels in Southern Africa*, Eng. tr., London, 1812–15, p. 259.
8 Grubb, 168.
9 Campbell, in *IA* xxiv. 30.
10 *Mem. As. Soc. Beng.* i. (1905) 157.
11 *BG* xxiii. 94.
12 Bancroft, iii. 376.
13 Campbell, *loc. cit.* 29 f.
14 Tylor, *PC*³, 1891, ii. 140.
15 P. H. Mallet, *Northern Antiquities*, London, 1770, p. 196.
16 *SBE* v. (1880) 322.
17 Ellis, *Tshi-speaking Peoples*, London, 1887, p. 233.

When a child is received into the Kok-ko of the Zuñi, his 'godfather' drinks 'holy water' and gives it to the child to drink. This godfather acts as a sponsor, and takes the vows in place of the child.[1] These customs explain themselves.

As part of his initiation the Southern Massim boy drinks salt water mixed with unripe mango-flesh. He bathes in the sea, and drinks some sea-water. Then he drinks some coco-nut milk. Whatever the meaning of these drinks, they play a considerable part in the process of man-making.[2] In savage pubertal ceremonies milk is sometimes drunk in connexion with a pretended new birth. Ancient religion had this fiction. After the new birth of the *taurobolium* (*q.v.*) the initiate was fed on milk, like a new-born babe.[3]

Ideas of invigoration are one of the most obvious reactions to the effect of strong drinks. 'Dutch courage' has been an important factor in history. At a ceremony previous to war the Tobelorese give their headmen palm-wine outside the temple. After drinking the wine the generals run seven times round the temple.[4] This custom is possibly a naive way of inspiring the leaders of the people. Ancient classical authors give several accounts of races whose practice it was to go into battle drunk.

'It is extremely probable that the funeral sacrifice of men and animals in many cases involves an intention to vivify the spirits of the deceased with the warm, red sap of life.'[5] The shades in Hades renew their life by drinking blood.[6] The offering of a drink is a frequent method of animating a fetish, and is thus analogous to the use of drink as an institutional rite. The Tshi negro squeezes rum upon his new-made *suhman*, saying 'Eat this and speak.'[7]

In metaphor and mythology drink plays a more considerable part than food. From similes like 'as cold water to a thirsty soul'[8] to the metaphorical description of Spinoza as 'a God-intoxicated man,' all the psychical reactions of drinks are expressed in language.

In religion the story of wine constitutes a distinctly ideal element, and it is here that the function of drink receives not only a sort of apotheosis, but perhaps a sound physiological explanation.

The Vedic gods were originally mortal; immortality was acquired by, among other methods, the drinking of *soma*.[9] Similarly the Homeric gods attained immortality by drinking nectar and eating ambrosia.[10] In the mythology of ancient Babylonia, Hasisadra brought into the ark a supply both of beer and of wine.[11] According to the Mexicans, the first human beings created by the gods fed on *pulque*.[12]

The sociological significance of orgiasticism has not yet been studied.

'Wine or spirituous liquor inspires mysterious fear. The abnormal mental state which it produces suggests the idea that there is something supernatural in it, that it contains a spirit, or is perhaps itself a spirit.'[13] The Siamese, intoxicated by the spirit arrack, says he is possessed by the 'spirit,' in the Animistic sense, of the liquor.[14] Thus the juice of the grape is the blood of the vine, its soul or life. 'The drinking of wine in the rites of a vine-god like Dionysus is not an act of revelry, it is a solemn sacrament.'[15]

Some typical cases of the religious and social uses of strong drink remain to be mentioned. No attempt is made to define stages of evolution. The earliest Brāhmanism used spirituous liquors in acts of worship. Arrack was offered to the gods. The *Sautrāmaṇī* and *Vājapeya* rites were typical for the drinking of *surā*, and the *soma* rite was in celebration of the *soma* itself. The later Vedas prohibited the worshipper from drinking the ceremonial liquor for a sensual purpose. The Śāktas to-day have actually the same principle, and purify the liquors before worship.[16] The followers of Zarathushtra have clung to the old way more consistently than the Hindus. Liquor-drinking forms part of almost all Parsi ceremonies to-day. Liquor is specially consecrated on New Year's Day.[1]

The Eucharist in its early form has the mark of a periodic wine-drinking, breaking up the 'fast' of work-a-day life. It was necessary for organizers like St. Paul to prohibit excess[2]—a fact which shows that wine was freely taken. The wine represented the blood of Christ and conferred immortality. In the course of history the use of wine has been denied to others than the celebrant, and in Churches which allow all worshippers to partake of the chalice the wine is not drunk but tasted. The Hebrew Cup of Blessing is an analogue of the Christian wine of the Eucharist. The early Christians made a free communal use of the sacred drink; it was given to the dead; vials of it were placed in the grave, with cups inscribed with toasts, such as 'Drink and long life!'[3]

For very special offerings to a god the Bhīls make *kuvari*, 'virgin liquor.' The distillers in this case must bathe and wear newly washed clothes before commencing operations.[4]

For special purposes, other than inspiration, a priest may become intoxicated. On certain days the high priest of the Zapotecs was obliged to be drunk. On one of these he cohabited with a Virgin of the Sun.[5]

Gods reflect in an intensified form the ideals and habits of their worshippers. If a god is housed, clothed, and fed, he is also supplied with drinks.

A difficult problem is presented by various customs of eating the dead. Their discussion belongs elsewhere; but they show variation even in the case of drinking.

The Cocomas of the Amazons ground the bones of their dead to powder and drank this in their beer. They said 'it was better to be inside a friend than to be swallowed up by the cold earth.'[6] The Ximanas mingled the ashes of the dead with their drink.[7] Here there can be no survival of cannibalism. The Angoni make the ashes of the dead into a broth. This must be lapped up with the hand, and not drunk in the ordinary way.[8] The native practice, generally confined to the women, of drinking some of the fluids drawn from the decaying body of a dead relative is a commonplace of Australian anthropology.

As a preliminary to the problem may be mentioned the frequent occurrence of morbid perversions of appetite in cases of strong emotion. If such perversion be applied to a psychosis of affection or respect, the Australian and similar practices are more easy to understand.

The Irish wake is a familiar example of the practice of drinking to celebrate death. In West Africa the Tshi people drink heavily during the fast which follows a death, and the mourners are generally intoxicated.[9] The same is the case among the Yorubas.[10] But it is chiefly after the funeral that drinking is the rule of the feast.

At funerals among the Woolwa Indians there is much drinking of *mishla*. A long line of cotton is stretched, like a telegraph wire, from the house of the dead, where the drinking takes place, to the burial-ground where the body has been deposited. 'I have seen the white thread following the course of the river for many miles, crossing and re-crossing the stream several times.'[11] As soon as a Bangala man dies, the family gets in large supplies of sugar-cane wine. Dancing and drinking are carried on for three or four days and nights, or until the wine is finished.[12] The Guiana Indians drink and dance at the funeral feast.[13]

Among the Tshinyaï of the Zambesi the native beer, *pombe*, plays a considerable part in post-funeral rites. For the ceremony of *Bona*, a large quantity is prepared. Holes are bored above the grave and *pombe* is poured in. In one hole, in front of the house where the grave is, the mourners wash their hands with *pombe*. As the procession retires, a widow of the deceased (she is called *musimo*, the spirit), her head covered with calico, constantly calls out for *pombe*, which she drinks beneath the

1 Stevenson, in *5 RBEW* (1887), p. 553.
2 Seligmann, 495.
3 *Fragmenta Phil. Græc.* (ed. Mullach, Paris, 1860–81) iii. 33.
4 Kruijt, 409.
5 Westermarck, *MI* i. 475.
6 Homer, *Od.* xi. 153.
7 Ellis, *Tshi-speaking Peoples*, 100 f.
8 Pr 25[25].
9 Macdonell, 17.
10 *Il.* v. 339 ff., *Od.* v. 199.
11 G. Smith, *Hist. of Babylonia* (ed. Sayce, London, 1895), p. 41.
12 Bancroft, iii. 347.
13 Westermarck, *MI* ii. 344.
14 Tylor, *PC*[3], ii. 181.
15 Frazer, *GB*[2] i. 358 f., ii. 366, *GB*[3], pt. ii. p. 248.
16 Rājendralāla Mitra, i. 397, 407 f., 417 ff.

1 J. M. Campbell, in *IA* xxiv. 319.
2 1 Co 11[20ff.].
3 Smith, *DB* ii. 142; Smith-Cheetham, *DCA* i. 40, 253, 308, 535, 732, ii. 1434.
4 Campbell, *loc. cit.* 320.
5 Bancroft, ii. 142.
6 C. R. Markham, in *JAI* xl. 95.
7 *Ib.* 132.
8 J. Macdonald, in *JAI* xxii. (1893) 111.
9 A. B. Ellis, *Tshi-speaking People*, 239.
10 Ellis, *Yoruba-speaking Peoples*, London, 1894, p. 156.
11 Wickham, in *JAI* xxiv. 207.
12 J. H. Weeks, *JAI* xl. 380.
13 Im Thurn, 225.

covering. At the house of the head widow a large hole is dug and well cemented. This is filled with *pombe*, and every one lies down and drinks it without help of spoon or vessel. A feast follows, consisting of *pombe* and meat.[1]

Various considerations, some of which are supplied in the above-cited cases, suggest that drinking at funerals and their anniversaries is motivated by a double impulse, or rather by two complementary impulses, namely, the desire to stifle sorrow, and the desire to give the dead a share in the good things of the world to which they still belong, though absent in the body. These two expressions of feeling, coupled with the 'sympathy' shown by the community, render funeral drinking a typical case of social instinct. Secondary ideas necessarily supervene.

The universal employment of a drink of fellowship to institute and also to terminate a social process is found in the case of pubertal ceremonies, though rarely. The reason is that, in this case, the process does not include a pair of persons. In the case of marriage and covenants this essential condition of a social act is patent. It may be said that the reciprocal process in the former class is between the novice and the members of the social state to which he is admitted. And in many analogous cases this is recognized, though the mind in its more primitive stages is slow to recognize by concrete expression such abstract ideas as that of community. But in these stages the other member of the couple may be found in the 'godfather' or sponsor, on the one hand, and individual members either of the same or of the other sex, the latter being the indirect objective of the initiation. Thus among many early peoples the boys after initiation drink with the girls. Similar ceremonies are performed in connexion with the sponsor. After initiation the A-kamba youth makes honey-beer, and gives it to the elder who looked after him during the ceremonies.[2] At the end of the *ntonjane*, the Kaffir ceremony performed to celebrate a girl's arrival at puberty, the girl's nearest female relative drinks milk, and then hands the bowl to the girl to drink.[3] From such practices there may easily develop ideas of tabu, which is to be ended by drinking or other rite of passage. Thus, in Central Australia the man whose blood has been taken to supply another with health or strength is tabu to him until he releases him from the 'ban of silence' by 'singing over his mouth.'[4]

Marriage is universally the occasion of a social feast, and the rite in which the bridal pair drink together is one of the most prevalent methods of tying the knot. There is thus both individual and social drinking at weddings. Sometimes the latter is not shared by the marrying parties; sometimes the individual drinking rite is extended to relatives; and sometimes it is carried out by them as sponsors for the bride and bridegroom. Naturally there is considerable variation in the ritual of the act of union.

At Tipperah weddings the bride receives a glass of liquor from her mother. She takes this to the bridegroom, sits on his knee, and, after drinking some of the liquor, gives the rest to him.[5] Among the Kaffirs, milk from the bridegroom's cows is presented to the bride. Her drinking of this milk renders the marriage complete, and the tie indissoluble. The guests exclaim, 'She drinks the milk! She has drunk the milk!'[6] Among the Nakrī Kunbīs of Thana, liquor is given to the pair when the wedding ceremony is completed.[7] The girl relatives of the Khyoungtha bride bar the entrance to the village against the bridegroom with a bamboo. Across this he has to drink with them a 'loving-cup of fraternity' before he is allowed to enter.[1] At weddings in Morocco the priest hands to the pair a cup of wine which he has blessed. When both have drunk of it, the glass is dashed to the ground by the bridegroom, with a 'covert meaning that he wishes they may never be parted until the glass again becomes perfect.'[2] In the Manuahiki Islands the priest gives the man a coco-nut containing its milk. The man drinks, and the woman after him.[3] Among the Larkas, a cup of beer is given to each of the two parties; they mix the beer, and then drink it. This completes the marriage.[4] In the Moluccas, Japan, Bengal, Brazil, Russia, Scandinavia, and many districts of Europe, the bridal pair drink, as the marriage ceremony or part of it, wine or beer from one vessel.[5] At Beni-Israil weddings the bridegroom pours wine into the bride's mouth.[6] In Korea and China the pair drink wine from two cups, which are tied together by a red thread.[7] In Christian countries the rite is separated from the marriage ceremonial proper, but is carried out indirectly when the pair receive together the wine of the Communion, which is to be partaken of immediately or soon after the marriage itself. Among the Goṇḍs, the respective fathers of the bridal pair drink together.[8]

Drinking together at marriage is a rite which applies to two parties the principles of social drinking. Sharing in an act is a sort of reciprocity, and together with interchange of gifts constitutes the fundamental principle of society. The more abstract ideas of similarity, union, and identity follow, and the simple ritual of sharing has a corresponding development. From the beginning there are also involved in the process, but unconsciously, the reactions to the physiological feelings of refreshment, and in particular to the effects of alcohol, which increase both self-feeling and altruism.

Pure altruism is the primary motive of many a custom which involves a simple sharing of drink. Here is the virtue of the man who gives a cup of cold water to a little one (Mt 10[42]). The natives of India have the custom of erecting sheds for the giving of water or butter-milk to poor wayfarers.[9]

Secondary motives, such as a general desire to conciliate or a wish to avoid the injury of a curse or an evil eye, come to obscure the primary. In the procession preceding the circumcision of an Egyptian boy is a servant carrying a skin of water and brass cups. Now and then he fills a cup and offers it to a passer-by. Another servant carries a tray with materials for coffee. It is his business, when they pass a well-dressed person, to fill and present him with a cup; the person gives him something, perhaps a half-piastre.[10] The analogy of other Egyptian customs suggests here the avoidance of the evil eye.

Even towards slain animals and the human objects of social resentment pure altruism is shown. Indians of the Orinoco, after killing an animal, pour into its mouth some liquor, 'in order that the soul of the dead beast may inform its fellows of the welcome it has met with, and that they, too, cheered by the prospect of the same kind reception, may come with alacrity to be killed.'[11] One may take leave to assign a worthier motive as the origin of this custom. Similarly, though primitive peoples share their drink with the dead, some have learnt to explain the custom of placing such things in the grave as a method of inducing the dead to be quiet, and not to come and pester the living for anything they want.

The co-operative totems of Australia are perhaps the earliest instance known of the principle of co-

1 L. Decle, in *JAI* xxiii. 421. For further instances, see Stannus, in *JAI* xl. 315; de Groot, *Rel. System of China*, Leyden, 1892 ff., i. 79, 141; W. Munzinger, *Ostafr. Studien*, Schaffhausen, 1864, p. 473; J. Perham, in *JRAS*, Straits branch, 1884, p. 296 ff.; H. Ling Roth, *Natives of Sarawak*, London, 1896, i. 208 ff.; Sheane, in *JAI* xxxvi. 153.
2 Hobley, 76.
3 G. McC. Theal, *Kaffir Folk-lore*, London, 1882, p. 210.
4 Spencer-Gillen a, 462.
5 T. H. Lewin, *Wild Races of South-Eastern India*, London, 1870, p. 202.
6 Lichtenstein, i. 262.
7 *BG* xiii. 129.

1 Lewin, 127.
2 A. Leared, 37.
3 G. Turner, *Samoa*, London, 1884, p. 276.
4 H. B. Rowney, *Wild Tribes of India*, London, 1882, p. 67.
5 Riedel, 460; Westermarck, *Human Marriage* 2, London, 1894, p. 419; E. T. Dalton, *Ethnol. of Bengal*, Calcutta, 1872, p. 193; Ploss-Bartels, *Das Weib* 3, Leipzig, 1891, ii. 442 ff.
6 *BG* xviii. 520.
7 W. E. Griffis, *Corea*, London, 1882, p. 249; J. Doolittle, *Social Life of the Chinese*, London, 1866, i. 86.
8 S. Hislop, *Tribes of the Central Provinces*, Nagpur, 1866, App. i. p. iv. On the subject generally, see A. E. Crawley, *Mystic Rose*, London, 1902, p. 383 ff.
9 Padfield 2, 190.
10 E. W. Lane, *Modern Egyptians* (ed. London, 1836), ii. 279.
11 Frazer, *GB* 2 ii. 402, quoting Caulin.

operative industry elevated into a system. Among the totems of the Central Australians is a water-totem. A member of this may drink water when alone; but, if he is in company, it is necessary for him to receive it, or the permission to take it, from an individual who belongs not to that totem, but to a moiety of the tribe of which the water-man is not a member—a complementary moiety. The principle, according to Spencer–Gillen, is that of mutual obligation between complementary food-totems, regulating the supply of food and drink.[1]

But the principle of reciprocal service is at the root of all social phenomena. Some of its forms are curious; others seem totally unlike the original type. Secondary ideas, once more, are responsible for these fluctuations. An African wife drank the medicine intended for her husband, in the belief that he would be cured.[2] A similar notion is seen in the belief that what a man drinks may affect the child whose birth is expected. A further development is reached in such customs as that of the Kwakiutl Indian, who, after biting a piece of flesh from the arm of a foe, drinks hot water in order to inflame the wound.[3] At this stage of sophistication there is often a choice of absurdities. The Indian might be supposed anxious for his own digestion rather than for the increase of suffering on the part of his foe.

Another case of the intrusion of a secondary idea is to be seen in the Australian custom of drinking human blood before starting on an *atninga* (avenging expedition).

'Every man of the party drinks some blood, and also has some spurted over his body, so as to make him what is called *uchuilima*, that is, lithe and active. The elder men indicate from whom the blood is to be drawn; and the men so selected must not decline, though the amount drawn from a single individual is often very great; indeed, we have known of a case in which blood was taken from a young and strong man until he dropped from sheer exhaustion.'[4]

The beginning of a venture or expedition is universally celebrated by drinking, on the principle of invigoration, as in the old English 'stirrup-cup.' But in the Australian example a further notion has come in. If on such an occasion a man joined who had some connexion with the tribe to be visited, he was forced to drink blood with the party, and, 'having partaken of it, would be bound not to aid his friends by giving them warning of their danger.'[5]

The Indians of the Cordilleras drink of the water of a river, and pray the god to let them pass over. So did the old Peruvians.[6] Dingan's army at the banks of the Ubulinganto strewed charcoal on the water, and then drank of it, 'the object perhaps being to deprecate some evil power possessed by the river.'[7] More probably the aim is to adapt one's self to the object by contact, to produce fellow-feeling and sympathy by communion.

Ideas of union similar to those concerned in marriage ceremonies of drinking, but involving from the outset, or at least producing, *ipso facto*, the secondary ideas of mutual responsibility by means of inoculation, or ingestion of the other's substance, or a conditional curse, have built up what may be described as the legal forms of social drinking. 'The drinking of human blood, or of wine mixed with such blood, has been a form of covenant among various ancient and mediæval peoples, as well as among certain savages.'[8] 'He who has drunk a clansman's blood is no longer a stranger but a brother, and included in the mystic circle of those who have a share in the life-blood that is common to all the clan.'[9] Robertson Smith's induction is actually a tertiary stage of thought on the subject, but present and powerful in the social consciousness of Arabs and other peoples. Among other details in point is the fact that blood-brotherhood itself is often produced by drinking any substance other than blood. See BROTHERHOOD (artificial).

[1] Spencer-Gillen[b], 160.
[2] R. Moffat, *Mission. Labours*, London, 1842, p. 591.
[3] F. Boas, in *Rep. U.S. Nat. Mus.*, 1895, p. 440.
[4] Spencer-Gillen[a], 461. [5] *Ib.* [6] Tylor, *PC*[3] ii. 210.
[7] Callaway, *Nursery Tales of the Zulus*, London, 1868, i. 90.
[8] Westermarck, *MI* ii. 567. [9] W. R. Smith, *Rel. Sem.*[2] 315.

The ordeal, often termed 'drinking the oath,' is a legal application of a secondary idea.

To extract the truth from a man, the Negro dips a *bohsum* in rum. This rum is then offered to the man, and, if he lies, makes his belly swell. A man claiming a debt due to a deceased person drinks the water in which he has washed the corpse. In legal actions before the chief, the *odum* drink is drunk as an oath and ordeal. It is a poisonous emetic.[1] A Masai accused of a crime drinks blood, and repeats these words: 'If I have done this deed, may God kill me.'[2]

Hospitality, a virtue of universal occurrence, is often complicated by superstitious accretions due to fear of the stranger within the gates.

As soon as a stranger enters the house of a Jivaro or Canelo Indian, each of the women offers him a calabash of *chicha*. A guest is welcomed by the Herero with a cup of milk.[3] These are simple acts of fellow-feeling. It is particularly among Arab races that the custom attains complexity.

Among the nomadic Arabs of Morocco, 'as soon as a stranger appears in the village, some water, or, if he be a person of distinction, some milk, is presented to him. Should he refuse to partake of it, he is not allowed to go freely about, but has to stay in the village mosque. On asking for an explanation of this custom, I was told that it was a precaution against the stranger; should he steal or otherwise misbehave himself, the drink would cause his knees to swell so that he could not escape. In other words, he has drunk a conditional curse.'[4] Zaid-al-Khail refused to slay a thief who had surreptitiously drunk from his father's milk-bowl.[5]

Health-drinking, the *propinatio* of the Latins, has some variations. One form is the sharing of a drink; the person doing honour drinks first, and hands the cup (in Greek life this became the property of the person honoured) to the other. Another is drinking alone, with a look or a sentiment of goodwill towards the person honoured. The projection outwards of the drinker's will is typified in many languages, as in most of the customs, by emphasizing the fact that he drinks first.

Among the Ba-Yaka and Ba-Huana, the host drinks first, and the guest after him.[6] At Abyssinian mead-drinkings the host drinks first, by way of showing that the liquor is not poisoned. He notifies a servant which guests need their cups replenished. On receiving the drink, the guest rises and bows.[7] Among the Kaffirs, it is not etiquette to give beer to a guest without first tasting it. This, according to the account given, is intended to safeguard the guest against poison.[8]

Terms like 'pledge' connote the idea of guaranteeing goodwill. The poison-test is obviously not the origin of the custom of the host or pledger drinking first. When that custom took on secondary ideas, one of these would be the affirmation that what the host offers is his own, and that it is of his best.

In barbarism the drinking-bout so called is often the form of political discussion. The chief of the A-kikuyu gives his people the news at beer-drinkings, to which he invites them.[9]

With agricultural drinking-feasts we return to man's immediate relations to intoxicating or refreshing drink. Drinking is a social rite in connexion with the ceremonial eating of the new crops.

Lithuanian peasants observe a festival called *Sabarios*, 'the mixing or throwing together,' when the sowing of the new corn has taken place. The Cheremiss celebrate the baking of the first bread from the new corn by a ceremonial drinking of beer. 'The whole ceremony looks almost like a caricature of the Eucharist.' At the cutting of the rice the Coorgs of South India drink a liquor of milk, honey, and sugar.[10]

[1] A. B. Ellis, *Tshi-speaking Peoples*, 197 f.
[2] Hollis, *The Masai*, Oxford, 1905, p. 345.
[3] Simson, in *JAI* ix. (1880) 391; Ratzel, ii. 480.
[4] Westermarck, *MI* i. 590.
[5] W. R. Smith, *Kinship*, London, 1885, p. 149 f.
[6] Torday-Joyce, in *JAI* xxxvi. 42, 279.
[7] Ratzel, iii. 228, 329. [8] D. Leslie, 205. [9] Routledge, 63.
[10] Frazer, *GB*[2] ii. 319-323, quoting Prætorius, *Deliciæ Prussicæ*, Berlin, 1871, pp. 60-64, and Georgi, *Beschreibung aller Nationen des russischen Reichs*, St. Petersburg, 1776, p. 37.

In such rites there is the social consecration, implicit or explicit, of wine itself and its sources.

It is perhaps merely an abnormality that fasting among many peoples does not exclude drinking strong liquor. This is notably the case in West Africa. Spirits are largely drunk during the fast after a death, and mourners are generally intoxicated. During the fast-days of the yam harvest the people drink hard, and the king and chief distribute brandy and rum.[1]

For various obscure reasons, great personages of the sacred world are often restricted to pure water.

The ancient kings of Egypt were restricted to a prescribed quantity of wine *per diem*. Plutarch says they never drank it at all, because it is the blood of beings who fought against the gods.[2] The chief of the Karennis of Burma 'attains his position not by hereditary right, but on account of his habit of abstaining from rice and liquor. The mother, too, of a candidate for the chieftainship must have eschewed these things . . . so long as she was with child. During that time she might not . . . drink water from a common well.'[3] The Bodia, or Bodio, the pontiff of the Grebo people of West Africa, may not drink water on the highway.[4] Here there is clearly a reference to 'purity.' Priests in Abyssinia drink neither wine nor mead.[5] Wine might not be taken into the temple at Heliopolis, and no one might enter the temple at Delos unless his system were free from wine.[6]

Asceticism naturally would interdict stimulating drinks, as it interdicts all tendency to expansion.

'Water was the pure and innocent beverage of the primitive monks; and the founder of the Benedictines regrets the daily portion of half a pint of wine, which had been extorted from him by the intemperance of the age.'[7]

Many peoples low in the scale of culture emphasize by law the natural aversion of childhood, not to speak of womanhood, to intoxicants. The A-kikuyu, for instance, allow no one to drink beer until he has reached the status of 'elder.'[8] The Chaco Indians forbid women and children, even youths, the use of intoxicants.[9]

LITERATURE.—This is fully given in the footnotes.

A. E. CRAWLEY.

DRUIDS.—The elaborate system of theology and philosophy ascribed to the Druids by the older school of writers, and the esoteric doctrines supposed to have been handed down from pagan times in the bardic schools of Wales, have no foundation in fact, though they still have a hold upon the popular fancy, which loves to think of the Druids as a mysterious Celtic priesthood, guardians of pure doctrines—the relics of a primitive revelation. Much of this is due to the classical writers themselves, who had strange notions about the Druids. A strictly scientific examination of the evidence proves that there was little that was mysterious or esoteric about them; nor, though we may regret the paucity of the evidence, is it likely that, had it been fuller, it would have given any support to those unscientific opinions. Our knowledge of the Druids rests mainly upon what Cæsar, in a passage of some length (*de Bell. Gall.* vi. 13 f.), and Pliny and other writers in shorter notices, have handed down, and upon occasional references in the Irish texts. The monumental and epigraphic evidence is practically *nil*, although Dom Martin (*Rel. des Gaulois*, Paris, 1727) and others insisted that the figures on various bas-reliefs in Gaul were Druids engaged in ritual acts.

1. Origin of the Druids.—Opinion is still divided regarding the origin of the Druids, whether they arose in Gaul or in Britain, and whether they formed a pre-Celtic or simply a Celtic priesthood. Nothing was known definitely by the classical observers. While Pliny (*HN* xxx. 1) seems to think that Druidism passed from Gaul to Britain, Cæsar (vi. 13) says: 'The system is thought to have been devised in Britain and brought thence into Gaul; and at the present time they who desire to know it more accurately generally go thither for the purpose of studying it.' Possibly, however, Cæsar is relating what was a current opinion rather than an actual fact, since he says 'is thought' (*existimatur*). This opinion may have been based on the fact that the system was held to be purer in Britain than in Gaul, where, in the south at least, it had perhaps come in contact with other influences, *e.g.* Greek philosophy, through the colonies at Marseilles. Taking Cæsar's words as a statement of fact, D'Arbois de Jubainville (*Les Druides*, Paris, 1906, p. 23 f.) and others (Desjardins, *Géog. de la Gaule rom.*, Paris, 1876–85, ii. 518; Deloche, *RDM* xxxiv. 446) hold that Druidism originated in Britain. The former maintains that the Druids were the priests of the Goidels, who, when conquered by the Celts from Gaul, in turn imposed their priesthood upon their conquerors. The Druidic system then passed over into Gaul about 200 B.C., where it was equally triumphant. All this is based upon no other evidence than Cæsar's statement. Valroger (*Les Celtes*, Paris, 1879, p. 158) further derives British Druidism from the Phœnicians, for reasons which are purely fantastic; and equally fantastic is its derivation from Buddhistic sources (Wise, *Hist. of Paganism in Caledonia*, London, 1884).

A growing school of writers has on various grounds adopted the theory that Druidism was pre-Celtic in origin, and imposed itself upon the Celtic conquerors in Gaul and Britain. The Druids are not found in the Danube area, in Cisalpine regions, or in Transalpine Gaul outside the region occupied by the 'Celtæ,' *i.e.* the short, brachycephalic race of the anthropologists (Holmes, *Cæsar's Conquest of Gaul*, London, 1899, p. 15). But the references to the Druids are so casual, especially as no classical writer professed to write a complete account of this priesthood, that this negative evidence cannot be taken as conclusive. Moreover, it cuts both ways, since there is no reference to Druids in Aquitania—a non-Celtic region (Desjardins, ii. 519). On the other hand, the earliest reference to the Druids in two Greek writers *c.* 200 B.C., cited by Diogenes Laertius (i. 1), seems to testify to their existence outside Gaul; while Celtic priests, though not formally called Druids, were known in Cisalpine Gaul (Livy, xxiii. 24). Professor Rhŷs postulates Druidism as 'the common religion of the aboriginal inhabitants from the Baltic to Gibraltar,' from whom the incoming Celts adopted it (*Celt. Brit.*², London, 1884, p. 72); and in this he is followed by Gomme, who finds many of the Druidic beliefs and practices—the redemption of one life by another, magical spells, shape-shifting, the customs of the Druids in settling property succession, boundaries, and controversies, and in adjudging crimes—opposed to Aryan sentiment (*Ethnology in Folk-lore*, London, 1892, p. 58, *Village Community*, London, 1890, p. 104). This begs the whole question of what was Aryan and what was non-Aryan; and, indeed, there is every reason to believe that Aryan sentiment was as backward, if not more so, in such matters as that of the pre-Aryan folk. Nor is it easy to understand why the Aryan Celts were conquered by the Druidic priesthood, if their 'sentiment' was so opposed to the beliefs and practices of the Druids. On the other hand, the arguments used by Reinach (*RCel* xiii. 189, 'L'Art plastique en Gaule et le druidisme') in support of the pre-Celtic origin of the Druids suggest a higher religious outlook on the part of the pre-Celtic people. The Celts, he says, had no images, and this argues that images were forbidden, and only a powerful

[1] A. B. Ellis, *Tshi-speaking Peoples*, 229, 239, *Ewe-speaking Peoples*, London, 1890, p. 152.
[2] Diod. Sic. i. 70; Plutarch, *de Is. et Osir.* 6.
[3] *IA* xxi. 317.
[4] H. H. Johnston, *Liberia*, London, 1906, ii. 1077.
[5] Ratzel, ii. 329.
[6] Plutarch, *de Is. et Osir.* 6; Dittenberger, *Syll. Inscr. Græc.*², Leipzig, 1898–1901, no. 564.
[7] Gibbon, *Decline and Fall*, ch. xxxvii.
[8] Routledge, 62.
[9] Grubb, 184.

priesthood could have forbidden them. But the pre-Celtic peoples in Gaul had equally no images, while, on the other hand, they had vast megalithic structures. Therefore, again, only a powerful priesthood could have forbidden the one and forced the people to erect the other. The same priesthood, the Druids, continued to exercise that power over the Celts which they had exercised over the aboriginal race. The Celts adopted the Druidic religion *en bloc*; but, when the Celts appear in history, Druidism is in its decline, the military caste rebelling against the foreign priesthood and taking its place. In answer to these arguments it may be pointed out that the Celts do not appear to have had a religious prejudice against images (see CELTS, § XIV.); again, the adoption of the aboriginal religion *en bloc* would be credible only if the Celts had no religion and no priests of their own, while it leaves unexplained the fact that they did not adopt the custom of erecting megalithic structures; finally, the opposition of the military to the priestly caste is no argument for the foreign origin of the latter, since such an opposition has been found wherever these two castes, existing side by side, have each desired supremacy.

2. The 'gutuatri.'—Besides the Druids, the Celts had certain priests, called *gutuatri*, attached to certain cults like the Roman *flamens*. D'Arbois (p. 2 ff.) argues that the *gutuatri* were the only native Celtic priesthood, and that, when the Druids, whose functions were more general, were adopted by the Celts, the *gutuatri* assumed a lower place. It is much more likely that they were a special branch of the Druidic priesthood, attached to the cult of some particular god. Ausonius calls Phœbitius *Beleni æditιuus* (perhaps the Latin equivalent of *gutuatros*), while he was of a Druidic stock like another servant of Belenus mentioned elsewhere (*Prof.* v. 7, xi. 24); and this suggests a connexion between the two. Livy distinguishes the *sacerdotes* from the *antistites* of the temple of the Boii (xxiii. 24), and this may refer to Druids and *gutuatri*. Classical evidence tends to show that the Druids were a great inclusive priesthood, with priestly, prophetic, magical, medical, legal, and poetical functions. Most of these functions are ascribed to the Druids by Cæsar. Elsewhere we hear of different classes—Druids (philosophers and theologians), diviners, and bards (Diod. Sic. v. 31; Strabo, IV. iv. 4 [p. 197]; Amm. Marc. xv. 9). Strabo gives in Greek form the native name of the diviners as οὐάτεις, which was probably in Celtic *vâtis* (Irish *fáith*). The bards in all three writers are a class by themselves, who sing the deeds of renowned warriors; but since *vâtis* means both 'prophet' and 'poet,' the diviners may not have been quite distinct from the bards. The connexion between Druids and diviners is still closer. No sacrifice was complete without a philosopher or Druid, according to Diodorus and Strabo, yet both speak of the sacrificial functions of the diviners; while, though the Druids were of a higher intellectual grade and studied moral philosophy as well as Nature (Timagenes), according to the same writer and Strabo, the diviners also studied Nature. Augury was a specialty of the diviners, yet the Druids also made use of this art (Cic. *de Divin.* i. 41, 90; Tac. *Hist.* iv. 54), while Pliny refers to 'Druids and this race of prophets and physicians' (*vatum medicorumque*, xxx. 1). Thus the diviners seem to have been a Druidic class, drawing auguries from the sacrifices performed by Druids, while standing in relation to the bards, whom we may regard as another Druidic class. In Ireland we trace the same three classes. There are the Druids who appear in the texts mainly as magicians, though their former priestly functions can here and there be traced. There were the *filid* (from *velo*, 'I see' [Stokes, *Urkelt. Sprachschatz*, Göttingen, 1894, p. 277]), learned poets who occupied a higher rank than the third class, the bards. The *filid* were also diviners and prophets, while some of their methods of divination implied a sacrifice. The Druids, who likewise were certainly sacrificial priests, were also diviners and prophets in Ireland. Hence the two classes stood in close relation, like the Druid and *vâtis* of Gaul. With the overthrow of the Druids as a priestly class, the *filid* remained as the learned class. D'Arbois (p. 108) assumes that there had been a rivalry between the two classes, and that the *filid*, making common cause with the Christian missionaries, gained their support. But this is unlikely. The *filid*, less markedly associated with pagan priestly functions, were less obnoxious, and may willingly have renounced purely pagan practices. At an earlier time they may have been known as *fáthi* (=*vates*), or prophets—a name applied later to the OT prophets and sages (Windisch, *Táin bó Cúalnge*, Leipzig, 1905, Introd. p. xliv); but, as they now applied themselves mainly to poetic science, thus apparently reducing the bards to a lower position, the name *filid* designated them more aptly.

The connexion of the *filid* with the Druids is further witnessed to by the fact that the former had an *Ard-file*, or chief-poet, and that, when the office was vacant, election was made to it, and rival candidates strove for it (Stokes, *Trip. Life*, London, 1887, i. 52, ii. 402; Windisch and Stokes, *Ir. Texte*, Leipzig, 1880 ff., i. 373; 'Colloquy of the Two Sages,' *Book of Leinster*, 187). This resembles what Cæsar tells of election to the office of chief-Druid (vi. 13), while there was probably a chief-Druid in Ireland (§ 8). The *filid* acted as judges, as did also the Druids, while both had a long novitiate to serve, lasting over several years, before they were admitted to either class.

The *gutuatri* are known mainly from inscriptions, but Hirtius (*de Bell. Gall.* viii. 38) speaks of one put to death by Cæsar. An inscription at Mâcon speaks of a *gutuater Martis*, i.e. of some Celtic god identified with Mars (*Rev. Epig.*, 1900, p. 230); two *gutuatri* of the god Anualos occur in inscriptions from Autun, and another in one from Puy-en-Valay (see Holder, *Altcelt. Sprachschatz*, Leipzig, 1891 ff., i. 2046). The *antistites templi* mentioned by Livy, xxiii. 24, as found among the Boii, may have been *gutuatri*, like Ausonius' *æditιuus*. *Gutuatri* may mean 'the speakers,' *i.e.* they who invoked the gods (D'Arbois, p. 3), and it is derived from *gutu*, 'voice' (Zeuss, followed by Holder, i. 2046; for another explanation, see Loth, *RCel* xxviii. 120), the Gaulish *gutuatros* being Latinized as *gutuater*.

3. The Druids a native Celtic priesthood.—There is, therefore, little ground for the theory that the Druids were a pre-Celtic priesthood imposed upon or adopted by the Celtic conquerors. With it is connected the theory that the Druids had a definite theological system and worshipped only a few gods, while they merely gave their sanction to the Celtic cults of many gods or of various natural objects—wells, trees, etc. (Bertrand, *Rel. des Gaul.*, Paris, 1897, pp. 192 f., 268 f.; Holmes, *op. cit.* p. 17). All this is purely hypothetical, and we conclude that the Druids were a native priesthood common to both branches of the Celtic people, and that they had grown up side by side with the growth of the native religion. On the other hand, it is far from unlikely that many of the pre-Celtic cults were adopted by the Celts because they resembled their own native cults, and that the aboriginal priesthood may, in time, have been incorporated with the Druidic priesthood, just as the pre-Celtic people themselves were Celticized. A detailed examination of the functions of the Druids leaves little doubt that they took part in the cult of natural objects, and that they were much addicted to magical practices. Possibly in the south of Gaul, where they felt the influence of Greek civilization, and employed Greek characters in writing (Cæsar, vi. 14), some of these cults and practices may have been abandoned, and the Druids may have become more definitely a learned class. But as a class the Druids were not a philosophic priesthood, possessed of secret knowledge, while the people were given over to superstition and magic. Some of the cults of Celtic religion and much of its magic may have been unofficial, in the sense that any one could perform them, just as a Christian can pray without the intervention of priestly help. But the Druids themselves probably practised those cults and used that magic, and doubtless the people themselves knew that greater success was likely to be obtained if a Druid were called in to help on these unofficial occasions. The Druids never lost the magical character which is found in all primitive priesthoods. Hence it is a mistake to regard 'Druidism' as an entity outside of Celtic religion in general, and, on the whole, opposed to it. The Celtic religion, in effect, was Druidism.

The native Celtic name for Druid was probably *drúis*, gen. *drúidos*. In Irish it is *drúi*, *drái*, or *draoi* (cf. Gaelic *draoi*, 'sorcerer'). The etymology is obscure. Pliny, connecting it with the Celtic oak-cults, derived it from Gr. δρῦς, 'oak,' an impossible derivation. Thurneysen (*Keltoromanisches*, Halle, 1884, *s.v.*) analyzes 'Druid' into *dru-uids*, regarding the first part of the word, *dru-*, as an intensive, and connecting *uids* with *uid*, 'to see *or* know.' The resulting meaning would be 'greatly *or* highly knowing,' a meaning consonant with the position of the medicine-man or priest everywhere as one who knows more than his fellows (see also Osthoff, *Etymol. Parerga*, Leipzig, 1901, i. 133 ff., 153). Stokes (*Urkelt. Sprachschatz*, p. 157) regards the etymology as uncertain, but compares θρέομαι, 'to cry aloud,' ἀθρέειν, 'to look,' although the etymology of the latter Gr. word is still very uncertain (cf. Boisacq, *Dict. étymol. de la langue grecque*, Heidelberg, 1907 ff., p. 18 f.). For ogham inscriptions in which the name Druid occurs, see Holder, *s.v.* 'Druida,' i. 1330.

4. Were the Druids a philosophic priesthood?—The earliest reference to the Druids by name is found in a passage of Diogenes Laertius (i. 1), who, when referring to the philosophic character of barbaric priesthoods, cites Sotion and pseudo-Aristotle (*c.* 2nd cent. B.C.) as saying, 'There are among the Celtæ and Galatæ those who are called Druids and Semnotheoi.' Cæsar, Strabo, Diodorus Siculus, Timagenes, Lucan, Pomponius Mela, and many other later writers speak of the philosophic science of the Druids, their schools of learning, and their political power; but, on the other hand, most of these writers refer to the cruel human sacrifices of the Druids, Mela characterizing these as savagery (iii. 18), while Suetonius also describes their religion as cruel and savage (*Claud.* 25). Pliny does not regard them as philosophers, but his description of the mistletoe rite suggests their priestly functions, though here and in other passages he associates them with magico-medical rites (*HN* xxiv. 63, xxix. 12, xxx. 1). The difference in these opinions shows that a closer practical acquaintance with the Druids revealed their true nature to the Roman Government, which found them more cruel and bloodthirsty and superstitious than philosophical. For these reasons, and on account of their hostility to Rome, the latter broke their power systematically (see below, § 12). Thus, it is unlikely that the Druids were reduced to a kind of medicine-men to gain a livelihood (D'Arbois, 77). Pliny's phrase, *Druidas . . . et hoc genus vatum medicorumque*, appears to refer rather to their position before the Roman edicts and to the fact that there were different grades among them—some priests, some diviners, and some practising a primitive medical science. Pliny's acquaintance with the Druids seems to have been superficial, but he evidently realized that their magical practices belonged to them from the first, and were not the result of Roman suppression. On the other hand, it is probable that the Druids were not all at the same level over the whole Celtic area. But the opinion that they were lofty philosophers seems to have been repeated by a series of writers, without any inquiry whether there was any real ground in fact for their opinion.

The facts upon which what may be called 'the Druidic legend,' as it appealed to the classical world, was based were these: the Druids were teachers, unlike the Greek and Roman priests (*e.g.* they taught the doctrine of immortality), they were highly organized, they were skilled magicians, and their knowledge was supposed to be Divinely conveyed (they 'speak the language of the gods,' Diod. Sic. V. xxxi. 4). On the other hand, we must beware of exaggerating the descriptions, themselves probably exaggerated, in classical writers. Cæsar (vi. 14) and Mela (iii. 19) say, 'They profess to know the motions of the heavens and the stars'—a knowledge which need not imply more than the primitive astronomy of barbaric races everywhere. Thus Cicero's Druid, Divitiacus (*de Div.* i. 41, 90), though professing a knowledge of Nature, used it to divine the future. Strabo (IV. iv. 4 [p. 197]) and Mela (iii. 19) tell of their knowledge of 'the magnitude and form of the earth and the world,' of their belief in successive transformations of an eternal matter, and in the alternate triumph of two elements, fire and water. This need have been no more than a series of cosmogonic myths, the crude science of speculative minds wherever found. Similarly, the Druidic doctrine of metempsychosis had certainly no ethical bearing, and, from what may be gathered of it from Irish texts, did not differ from similar beliefs found, *e.g.*, among American Indians and Negroes. The philosophy of the Druids, if it existed, was elusive: no classical writer ever discovered it fully; it exerted no influence upon classical thought. For the same reason the theory of a connexion between Druidism and the Pythagorean system must be rejected, though again we must not overlook the fact that Greek philosophic teachings may have penetrated to some of the Druids *via* the Massilian colonies. Probably the origin of this fabled connexion is to be found in the fact that the Druids taught a future existence in the body, and that they had myths, such as are found in the Irish texts (see CELTS, § XVI.), regarding transmigration. It was at once assumed that there must be a link between these Celtic beliefs and the Pythagorean doctrine of metempsychosis. There are, however, very real differences. The Druidic doctrine of immortality was not necessarily one of metempsychosis properly so called, for the myths of transmigration mainly concerned gods and not men; and in neither case was there any ethical content such as the Pythagorean doctrine insists on. But, the belief in this connexion once started, other apparent resemblances were exaggerated and made much of. Hence such statements as those of Timagenes, that the Druids 'conformed to the doctrines and rules of the discipline instituted by Pythagoras' (*ap.* Amm. Marc. xv. 9; cf. Diod. Sic. v. 28); or of Ammianus, that they lived in communities, their minds always directed to the search after lofty things; or of Hippolytus, long after Druidism had disappeared in Gaul, that Zamolxis, a disciple of Pythagoras, had taught his doctrines to the Celts soon after his death (*Philos.* ii. 17). There is no evidence that the Druids lived in communities; they certainly did not do so in Ireland, and probably the fact that they were a more or less organized priesthood with different grades and functions (see above, § 2) gave rise to this opinion. We have seen how far their philosophic researches probably extended, and Hippolytus' statement is obviously fabulous, especially as it stands alone and refers to a period eight centuries before his time. On the other hand, there is no reason to doubt that the Druids sought after knowledge, but it was of an entirely empiric kind, and must have been closely connected with their practice of divination and magic, their human sacrifices, and their belief in the power of ritual.

5. The Druids as teachers.—To the Druids, says Cæsar (vi. 13), 'a great number of the young men flock for the sake of instruction'; but the next paragraph (14) suggests that it was the privilege of exemption from military service and from tribute that encouraged many to go to them of their own accord for instruction, or to be sent to them by parents and relatives. Whatever the reason, the fact that the Druids were teachers cannot be doubted; but, since their course of instruction lasted 20 years, some of their pupils were probably under training for the priestly life rather than for general instruction. The Irish texts show that the insular Druids were also teachers, imparting 'the science of Druidism' (*druidecht*) to as many as 100 pupils at one time, while they also taught the daughters of kings, as well as the fabulous heroes of the past like Cúchulainn (*Leabhar na hUidhre*, 61; *Trip. Life*, 99). Cæsar writes that the subjects of knowledge were the doctrine of immortality, 'many things regarding the stars and their motions, the extent of the universe and the earth, the nature of things, and the power and might of the immortal gods' (vi. 14); and verses, never committed to writing, were also learned. Strabo (*loc. cit.*) also speaks of their teachings in 'moral science.' The teaching of immortality had a practical end, for it was intended to rouse men to valour and make them fearless of death. Their scientific teaching was probably connected with magic and divination, and doubtless included many cosmogonic myths and speculations; their theology was no doubt mythological—stories about the gods such as are found in the Irish texts; their moral teaching was such as is found in most barbaric communities. An example of it is handed down by Diogenes Laertius (*proem.* 5): 'The Druids philosophize sententiously and obscurely—to worship the gods, to do no evil, to exercise courage.' Ritual formulæ, incantations, and runes would also be imparted. These last may be the verses to which Cæsar refers, but they probably also included many myths in poetic form. They were taught orally, in order to keep them from the common people (a curious reason, as the common people could not read), and in order to exercise the memory. The oral transmission of the Vedas is a parallel with this. Writing, however, was known, and the Greek characters were used; but this can hardly apply to a wide region. Perhaps there was also a native script, and the ogham system may have been known in Gaul as well as in Ireland, if we may judge by the existence of the god called Ogmios (see CELTS, § V.). The Irish Druids appear to have had written books, to judge from an incident in the life of St. Patrick (*Trip. Life*, 284). Beyond what Cæsar says of the verses kept secret from the common people, and consisting of incantations and myths, there is no evidence that the Druids taught some lofty esoteric knowledge, some noble philosophy, or some monotheistic or pantheistic doctrine. The secret formulæ were kept secret save to the initiated, lest they should lose their magical power by becoming too common, as in the parallel cases of savage and barbaric mysteries elsewhere.

6. Religious functions of the Druids. — The Druids 'take part in sacred matters, attend to public and private sacrifices, and expound the principles of religion' (Cæsar, vi. 13). Their priestly power being so great, the Druids would let no important part of the cult pass out of their hands. All details of ritual—the chanting of runes, the formulæ of prayers, and the offering of sacrifices—were in their hands; in a word, they were mediators between the gods and men. Every known kind of divination was observed by them, and before all matters of importance their help in scanning the future was sought (see CELTS, § XIII.). As to sacrifices, none was complete 'without the intervention of a Druid' (Diod. Sic. V. xxxi. 4; cf. Cæsar, vi. 16). This was probably also the case in Ireland, though little is said of sacrifices in the texts; we do, however, find Druids taking part in the sacrifices at Tara (D'Arbois, *Cours de litt. celt.*, Paris, 1883, i. 155) and at the Beltane festival (Cormac, *Gloss.*, ed. Stokes, in *Three Irish Glossaries*, London, 1862, *s.v.*). The cruel sacrifices of the Druids horrified the Romans, and this largely discounts the statements about their philosophic doctrines. An instance of their power is seen in the fact that those who refused to obey their decrees were interdicted from all sacrifices—a severe punishment in the case of so religious a people as the Gauls (Cæsar, vi. 13 and 16). The Druids played an important part in the native baptismal and name-giving rites (see BAPTISM [Ethnic], § 7), and also in all funeral ceremonies. At burial, runes were chanted, and sacrifices were offered by the Druid, who also arranged all the rites and pronounced a discourse over the dead. The Druids would also regulate all myths regarding the gods. Many of these would be composed or arranged by them, but, save on Irish ground, all trace of them is lost. They also composed and arranged the various magic formulæ, incantations, and prayers. Besides this, they who knew the language of the gods (Diod. Sic. V. xxxi. 4) probably claimed to be incarnations of these gods, in this occupying the place of those earlier priest-kings upon whom the order of the universe depended. With the differentiation of king and priest some of the Druids may have been invested with such divinity, although in Ireland it was still apparently attributed to kings (see CELTS, § VIII.); but this may not have debarred the Druids from claiming similar powers. Such divine pretensions would accord with the claim of the Druids to have created heaven, earth, sea, and sun (*Antient Laws of Ireland*, Dublin, 1865–1901, i. 22), while it would also explain the superiority of their rank over that of kings as alleged by Dio Chrysostom and discovered in Irish instances (see § 9).

7. Medical and magical practices. — Pliny's words, *Druidas et hoc genus vatum medicorumque*, may suggest that the Druids practised the healing art, or that a special class attached to them did so. In Ireland, Druids had also medical skill, and some who are not called Druids, but may have been associated with them, practised this profession (O'Curry, *MS Mat.*, Dublin, 1861, pp. 221, 641; Windisch, *Ir. Texte*, i. 215). And, as there were gods of healing in Gaul, so in Ireland the god Díancecht was supreme in this art. But, in so far as the Druids were doctors, it was probably the magical aspect of medicine with which they dealt. Thus the plants which Pliny mentions as in use by the Druids, or the use of which they recommended (*HN* xxiv. 11, xxv. 9), may have had healing properties, but it was apparently the magical ritual with which they were gathered, quite as much as their own powers, that counted, while the use of them was in some cases magical. The gatherer must be clothed in white, he must have his feet naked, must make a sacrifice, and must cull the plant in a particular way and at a certain time. The mistletoe was also used for healing, but it is evident that the plucking of it had a much wider importance (for the ritual, see CELTS, § X.). The classical observers were so dominated by their preconceptions of the Gaulish Druids that we hear little from them regarding their magical practices. The Irish Druids, however, were quite evidently magicians, and their practices included shape-shifting and invisibility, control of the elements and the weather, the producing of fertility, the use of all kinds of spells, and the causing of sleep, illness, or death by magical means (see CELTS, § XV.). Though it is possible that the Druids of Gaul may have been more advanced than those of the islands, it is most unlikely that they did not also pose as magicians, and it is more than likely that it is this side of their functions to which Suetonius refers when he speaks of the 'savage' nature of the Druidic religion; or Pliny, when he calls the Druids *magi* (xvi. 44, xxiv. 11) or *genus vatum medicorumque* (xxx. 1); or Posidonius, when he says (in Diod. Sic. v. xxxi. 5) that 'they tamed the people as wild beasts are tamed.' How far is this from the attributing of a lofty philosophy to the Druids! Moreover, the wide-spread use of human sacrifices among the Druids of Gaul makes it extremely probable *a priori* that they were also wielders of magic, while, as we have seen, they certainly used the art of divination.

8. Druidic organization.—The enormous power wielded by the Druids both in religion and in politics, as well as the privileges which they claimed, makes it evident that they were a more or less closely organized priestly corporation; and this conclusion receives support from the fact that they had fixed annual meetings in Gaul (see below, § 9), and that, as Cæsar says (vi. 13), there was one chief-Druid wielding authority over all the others. On the death of the chief-Druid, he who had pre-eminent dignity among the others succeeded to the office; but, if there were several of equal rank, the selection was made by vote, while sometimes they even contended in arms for the presidency. Though there were Druidic families, the priesthood was not necessarily hereditary, since, as has been seen, entrance to it was permitted after a long novitiate. There is no direct evidence that the insular Druids were similarly organized; but, in spite of the denials of some recent writers, the fact that there were chief-Druids in Ireland is seen from the texts, and such a chief-Druid, *primus magus*, summoned the others together when necessary, *e.g.* against St. Patrick (*Trip. Life*, ii. 325). A passage of Timagenes, cited by Ammianus Marcellinus (xv. ix. 8), and connecting the Druidic organization with the authority of Pythagoras, speaks of the Druids as *sodaliciis adstricti consortiis.* This points to them as a religious corporation (*sodalicium*), and perhaps as dwelling in cœnobitic communities, if *consortium* is to be taken in that sense, which is not certain. Cæsar, on the other hand, who gives the fullest account of them, says nothing of communities of Druids, and the passage of Timagenes may simply be an exaggeration due to the fact that they had some kind of organization or that there were Druidic families, and to a supposed following of the Pythagorean associations by them. The theory has, however, been revived by Bertrand (*Rel. des Gaul.*, p. 280), who maintains that the Druids lived in communities like the Tibetan or Christian monks, devoted to abstruse studies, and that the Irish monastic system was simply a Christian transformation of this Druidic community life. The Irish texts give no support to this view; on the contrary, there are numerous references to the wife and children of the Druid; nor is it likely that the Druids, in all cases hostile to the Christian faith, would be transformed into Christian monks. The Irish monastic system was formed on Continental models, and owed nothing to paganism.

9. Political and judicial functions of the Druids.—The political power of the Druids would certainly be augmented by their position as teachers; and, though in individual cases it may have owed much to a commanding personality, the evidence leaves little doubt that it was exercised officially. Rulers and chiefs were apparently elected by their choice, and Cæsar (vii. 33) speaks of the magistrate Convictolitanis who, on a vacancy occurring in the office, had been elected by the priests 'according to the custom of the State.' It was evidently a customary power which was thus exercised. In Ireland the Druids also intervened in the choice of a king. They sang runes over a sleeping man who had been fed with the flesh of a white bull slain perhaps as a sacrifice, the runes being 'to render his witness truthful.' The man then dreamt of the person who was to be king, and saw where he was and what he was doing at the time. When the man awoke, the subject of his vision was elected king (Windisch, *Ir. Texte*, i. 213). Perhaps the Druids hypnotized the man and suggested to him the person whom they desired to be elected. We have no evidence as to the method of election in Gaul. Dio Chrysostom (*Orat.* xlix.) says of the Druids that kings were their ministers and servants of their thought, and could do nothing apart from them; and, although his witness is late and may be exaggerated, it receives corroboration from the Irish texts, in which the king is always accompanied by his Druid, and is influenced by him. Moreover, a singular passage in the *Táin bó Cúalnge* (Windisch's ed. p. 672 f.) shows King Conchobar giving no response to the bringer of important tidings until the Druid Cathbad had spoken to him. 'For such was the rule in Ulster. The men of Ulster must not speak before the king, and the king must not speak before his Druids' (*Antient Laws of Ireland*, i. 22). The political power of the Druids, though great, is exactly paralleled by that of other priesthoods, and may have served to keep in check the position of the warrior class. They frequently intervened in combats, and by their exhortations made peace (Diod. Sic. v. 31. 5), even when two armies were about to join battle. This probably refers to inter-tribal warfare. As to their judicial functions, Cæsar writes (vi. 13): 'They are held in great honour, for they decide generally regarding all disputes, public and private; and, if any crime has been perpetrated, or a murder committed, or if there be a dispute about property or about a boundary, they decide it. If any one, whether a public or private individual, has not submitted to their decrees, they interdict him from the sacrifices.' Such interdicted persons were regarded as criminals, and all shunned contact with them; in effect they were tabu. Cæsar also adds that they met together yearly in a consecrated spot in the territory of the Carnutes, the central district of all Gaul, and thither came all who had disputes and submitted to their judgments. Cæsar may be referring to a bygone past rather than to existing practice, since he himself mentions disputes not settled by Druids, while nothing is said regarding any obligation to refer to Druidic judicature. That judicature was, however, far-reaching, and its judgments were upheld on magico-religious grounds. It is possible that the immolation of criminals taken in theft and other crimes was a punishment ordered by the Druids (Cæsar, vi. 16), who would thus obtain a supply of sacrificial victims. If, as is here contended, the Druids were a purely Celtic priesthood, the existence among the Galatian Celts of a council of 300 men who met in a place called *drunemeton*, and judged crimes of murder, may mean that this was a council of Druids (Strabo, XII. v. i. [p. 567]). *Nemeton* means 'a sacred place' like that in which the Gaulish Druids sat as judges, whether *dru* is connected with the first term of *dru-uidos* or not. It should here be observed that Diogenes Laertius quotes a fragment of Aristotle in which the existence of Druids among the Galatians is asserted; and there is also a later reference to this by Clement of Alexandria, who may, however, be simply echoing this passage. The Irish texts assign judicial functions to the *filid*, not to the Druids; and, unless this is due to Christian influence desirous of slighting the importance of the Druids, they may not have acted there as judges. If this be so, it is not easy to understand why, if Druidism came to Gaul from Britain, the Druids were able to assume judicial functions there. D'Arbois (p. 103) thinks, however, that the exercise of such functions by early Christian clergy in Ireland may be due to the fact that the pagan priests had a judicial position, and, if the *filid* were a Druidic class, they would then be carrying on the judicial functions of the Irish Druids.

10. Supposed differences between Irish and Gaulish Druids.—The often-quoted differences between the Druids of Gaul and those of Ireland are perhaps more apparent than real. We know the former only from pagan observers; the latter only from Christian observers, or from documents which have passed through Christian hands, and it is probable that Christian influences may have endeavoured to reduce the Druids to the lowest possible level.

Stress is sometimes laid upon the supposed lack of judicial functions and of organization among the Irish Druids, but it has been seen that it is possible to account for this discrepancy. More vital still is the assertion that the Irish Druids were only magicians and not priests (Hyde, *Lit. Hist. of Ireland*, London, 1899, p. 88; Joyce, *Soc. Hist. of Anc. Ireland*, London, 1903, i. 239). It is true that in the Irish texts they have the appearance of mere wizards, but they are also teachers and possess political influence like the Druids of Gaul. The probability is, therefore, that they were also priests, as the Druids of Britain certainly were (Tac. *Ann.* xiv. 30, where the sacred grove, the human sacrifices, the altars, and the rites of divination of the Druids of Mona are mentioned). Why, then, are they not more frequently represented in that aspect? Probably for the same reason that there are such scanty references to ritual and religion in the texts, and where these do exist they have evidently been tampered with. That reason appears to be that there was a deliberate suppression of all that related to religion or to the exercise of priestly functions. Thus, where in connexion with some rite there is recorded the slaughter of animals, it is most probable that the slaughter implies a sacrifice, though nothing is said of it. In such cases (*e.g.* that of the election of a king, above, § 9) the Druids take a considerable part; hence, if there was a sacrifice, we can hardly doubt that they were the sacrificers, and were, therefore, priests. In other notices of ritual which may have escaped being tampered with, the Druids at least take part in sacrifice and in other ritual acts. Finally, if the Druids were not priests, what other body of men exercised that function (for it is incredible that the Irish Celts were priestless)? The opposition of the Christian missionaries to the Druids shows that they were opposing not mere magicians, but men who were the determined upholders of the old religion, viz. its priests.

Possibly the insistence on the magical powers of the Druids may account for the somewhat loose way in which the word 'Druid' is used in the texts. It is applied to kings and heroes, not merely to the strictly Druidic class, because they had learned and practised Druidic magic, while it is also applied to the priests or medicine-men of the successive colonists of Ireland. It is also said that the Tuatha Dé Danann, the euhemerized gods, were masters of Druidism; in other words, those gods possessed in a full degree one of the functions of the priests who served them, viz. magic. Priests and gods were confounded together. Another difference between the Druids of Gaul and those of Ireland is that the former absented themselves from war (Cæsar, vi. 14), while the latter certainly took part in it; yet we find the Gaulish Druids on the battle-field exercising priestly or magical functions, while Cæsar refers to the warlike prowess of the Druid Divitiacus.

11. Druidesses.—Towards the beginning of the 4th cent. A.D., Lampridius (*Alex. Sev.* 60) and Vopiscus (*Aur.* 44, *Numer.* 14) speak of certain women called *Druis*, usually translated 'Druidess,' who, as prophetesses or wise women, foretold events in the lives of the emperors or were consulted by them. As this is the first occurrence of the name, it is likely that such wise women assumed the Druidic name when the Druids as a class had died out. There is no evidence in earlier classical texts of the existence of a class of women called Druidesses with functions corresponding to those of the Druids, and such women as are here referred to were apparently divineresses, those Celtic women whom Hannibal desired to arbitrate in certain matters being probably an earlier example of this class (Plutarch, *Mul. Virt.* 246). In Ireland divineresses seem to have been associated with the *fáthi* or *filid*, and were called *ban-filid* or *ban-fáthi*, while they were consulted on important occasions (Windisch, *Táin*, 31; Meyer, *Contributions to Irish Lexicog.*, Halle, 1906, p. 176). They are probably the 'pythonesses' against whom the Patrician canons utter a warning (Joyce, *Soc. Hist. of Anc. Ireland*, i. 238), and whose spells the saint prays against in his hymn (Windisch, *Ir. Texte*, i. 56). Solinus (xxxv.) says women as well as men in Ireland had a knowledge of futurity; and the women whose fury, along with the prayers of Druids, was directed against the Romans in Mona may have been of the same class. Others, called *ban-tuathaig* in the tale of the battle of Magtured, had magical powers of transformation (*RCel* xii. 93). Possibly all such women may later have been called 'Druidesses,' since this name is occasionally met with in the texts, usually where the woman (in one case the goddess Brigit) is also called *ban-fili*, or 'poetess,' unless they were wives of Druids (Windisch, *Táin*, p. 331; *Book of Leinster*, 75*b*; *RCel* xv. 326, xvi. 34, 277). But in Ireland women also seem to have had certain priestly functions, since the nuns who guarded the sacred fire at Kildare had evidently succeeded to virgin guardians of a sacred fire, the priestesses of a cult which was tabu to men (Gir. Camb. *Top. Hib.* ii. 34 ff.; Stokes, *Three Irish Glossaries*, p. 33), while other guardians of sacred fires existed elsewhere in Ireland (G. Keating, *Hist. of Ireland*, ed. Ir. Texts Soc., 1908, p. 331). In Britain, Boudicca performed priestly functions, invoking the gods and divining (Dio Cass. lxii. 6). Inscriptions in Gaul show the existence of priestesses called *antistes* or *antistita* and *flaminica sacerdos* (at Arles and Le Prugnon [Jullian, *Recherches sur la rel. gaul.*, Bordeaux, 1903, p. 100; Holder, *s.v.* 'Thucolis']), who, like the priestess of Artemis among the Galatian Celts, whose priesthood was hereditary (Plutarch, *Mul. Virt.* 20), were attendants on a goddess. On the other hand, the Metz inscription referring to a *Druis antistita* is spurious (Orelli, 2200; Robert, *Epig. de la Moselle*, Paris, 1883, i. 89). The nine virgin priestesses of a Gaulish god on the Isle of Sena foretold the future, raised storms, and healed diseases, while they were said to transform themselves into animals (Mela, iii. 48). Other women, who practised an orgiastic cult on an island in the Loire, probably had priestesses among their number who directed the cult, as perhaps did also the virgins of Sena (Strabo, IV. iv. 6 [p. 198]). Though perhaps pre-Celtic in origin, these cults were acceptable to Celtic women, who must have had similar rites of their own. Reinach regards the references to these island cults as based on the myth of Circe's isle (*RCel* xviii. 1 ff.); but there is no reason to believe that they had not been actually observed, even though the accounts are somewhat vague. If, as is likely, Celtic divinities were at first female, and agricultural rites were first in the hands of women, even when a strong priesthood had arisen, conservatism would here and there leave the ritual and its priestesses intact, while goddesses with a more or less strong personality may still have been served at local shrines by women. In the magical powers of witches we may further see the survival both of Druidic magic and of the priestly, prophetic, and magical powers of such priestesses.

The fact that Cæsar speaks of priestesses among the Germans but not among the Celts is sometimes regarded as proving that there were no Celtic priestesses. But we cannot suppose that Cæsar gave a full account of Celtic religion, while the notices above referred to and the improbability that women had no religious functions among the Celts must be set against his silence. Though the Druids may have been an organization of priests, and, though there were no 'Druidesses,' there may yet have been priestesses for some particular purposes, just as there certainly were divineresses.

12. Disappearance of the Druids.—The extinction of the Druids was due to two causes: (1) in Gaul and S. Britain, to Roman opposition and the Romanizing of the native religion, and perhaps in some degree to Christian influences; (2) in Britain beyond the Roman pale and in Ireland, entirely to the introduction of Christianity and the opposition of the Christian priesthood. Rome did not attack the Druids on religious grounds, strictly speaking, but (*a*) on political grounds, because the Druids had such power in politics and in the administration of justice, and opposed the majesty of Rome; (*b*) on grounds of humanity, because the Druids offered human sacrifices; and, finally, (*c*) because of their magical superstitions. But this opposition implied little more at first than the application of existing laws against these things. Augustus prohibited Roman citizens from taking part in the *religio Druidarum* (Suet. *Claud.* 25); and Pliny (xxx. 1) asserts that Tiberius interdicted 'the Druids and that race of prophets and doctors,' though it is probable that this was no more than putting into force the existing law against human sacrifices. If it meant a suppression of the Druids as such, it entirely failed of its object; for they were still active in the reign of Claudius, who completely abolished the cruel religion of the Druids ('Druidarum religionem apud Gallos dirae immanitatis, et tantum civibus sub Augusto interdictam, penitus abolevit,' Suet. *Claud.* 25). Here it is doubtful whether more than an abolition of human sacrifices and magical practices was intended, for Claudius put to death a Roman citizen of Gaul for appearing in court with a Druidic amulet, the so-called serpent's egg (Pliny, xxix. 3), and Aurelius Victor says that Claudius merely abolished the 'notorious superstitions' of the Druids (*de Cæsar.* 4). The Druids were still in existence at a later time, the native religion still went on, and Mela (iii. 18) expressly says that human sacrifice was commuted to a little harmless blood-letting. The actual disappearance of the Druids was undoubtedly due less to such laws than to the Romanizing of Gaulish religion begun under Augustus, and to the institution of the State religion, with its own priesthood. Whether the Druids were still allowed to assemble yearly at the consecrated place in the territory of the Carnutes (Cæs. vi. 13) is doubtful, but they would certainly not be allowed to act as judges; and the annual assembly of deputies from the towns of the three Gauls at Lugdunum (Lyons) round the altar of Augustus, with its obviously religious character, was probably intended to take the place of that assembly. A *flamen* of the province was elected by the deputies, and there were *flamens* for each town. If the Druids wished to be recognized as priests, they would have to become priests of the new Gallo-Roman religion.

Their position as teachers was also attacked by the establishment of schools, as at Autun, where sons of noble Gauls are found receiving instruction as early as A.D. 21 (Tac. *Ann.* iii. 43). Thus, by an adroit ignoring of the Druids, as well as by the direct attack upon certain of their functions, the Roman power gradually took away from them their occupation as native priests. D'Arbois (p. 73), however, maintains that there was a steady persecution of the Druids, and, citing passages of Lucan and Mela, says that this caused them to retreat to caverns and forests, where they hid themselves, and still continued to teach the sons of noble Gaulish patriots. Lucan (*Phar.* i. 453), however, makes no reference to such a flight, and refers merely to the resumption by the Druids of their rites and teaching in forest glades where they dwelt, not where they hid themselves, after Cæsar's war, and he makes no reference to what took place after the laws against the Druids had been passed. Mela (iii. 19), though writing in Claudius' reign, does not appear to refer to secret teaching as a result of the laws, but, either amplifying Cæsar's words or citing Posidonius, says that the Druids taught the sons of noble Gauls during a period of twenty years secretly in caverns or forest depths. He has obviously confused the twenty years' novitiate of those who intended to become Druids with the teaching given to others. The secret forest recesses were simply the consecrated groves where Druidic rites were carried on. There the Druids may have continued to teach, but probably the sons of noble Gauls took advantage of the Roman schools. This teaching would be permitted by Rome, so long as the Druids did not interfere in politics or practise human sacrifices. Moreover, Mela does not appear to hint that the commutation of human sacrifice was a secret rite; it was rather part of the still permissible Druidic religion. Those who practised the forbidden rites would certainly be liable to punishment, but probably the bulk of the Druids succumbed to the new order of things. But Druids were still active after Nero's death, and took a prominent part in the revolt against Rome, while some prophesied a world dominion for the Celts at the time of the burning of the Capitol at Rome in A.D. 70 (Tac. *Hist.* iv. 54). The mistletoe and herb rites of the Druids described by Pliny may have still existed in his day; but he may be referring, like Lucan, to a former state of things. After this date the Druids seem gradually to have disappeared in Gaul and S. Britain, and were remembered only as philosophers. But even in the 4th cent., as the verses of Ausonius show (*Prof.* v. 12, xi. 17), men counted it an honour to have a Druid for an ancestor.

In independent Britain, Druidism remained as it had been (cf. Pliny, xxx. 1), and after the evacuation of Britain by the Romans the Druids seem to have re-appeared south of the Roman wall. Nennius (*Hist. Brit.* 40) describes how Vortigern, after being excommunicated for incest, called together his 'wise men' (*magi*, tr. 'Druids' in the Irish Nennius), who advised him to offer a human sacrifice at the building of a fortress. But neither in Christian nor in pagan Britain could the Druids withstand the growing powers of the Christian clergy. The lives of Celtic saints show how the Druidic magic arts were equalled and surpassed by the miracles of the saints, and how they were inevitably overcome, as is vividly seen in the encounters of Columba with the Druids in the north of Scotland, described by Adamnan. Similarly in Ireland, Christianity also destroyed the Druids; and the Lives of St. Patrick, who combated 'the hard-hearted Druids' (Windisch, *Ir. Texte*, i. 23), and other Lives of saints, are full of the magical or miraculous deeds by which the heathen priests were discomfited. The victory of Christianity over the Druids was, in popular belief, accomplished by a more powerful magic; but, at the same time, though the Druids passed away, many of their beliefs remained among the people as superstitions to which, perhaps, they attached as great importance as to Christianity (cf. Reeves' ed. of Adamnan, *Vita S. Columbæ*, Dublin, 1857; Stokes, *Three Middle-Irish Homilies*, Calcutta, 1877, p. 24 f.; *Antient Laws of Ireland*, i. 15).

LITERATURE.—The older writers, J. Toland, *Hist. of the Druids*, London, 1726; J. Martin, *Rel. des Gaulois*, Paris, 1727; E. Davies, *Myth. and Rites of the British Druids*, London, 1809; G. Higgins, *The Celtic Druids*, London, 1829, must be used with caution. More useful are D'Arbois de Jubainville, *Cours de litt. celtique*, i., Paris, 1883, *Les Druides*, Paris, 1906; T. Mommsen, *Röm. Gesch.*[8], Leipzig, 1889, iii. 237, v. 94 ff.; A.

Bertrand, *Nos Origines*, iv. 'La Religion des Gaulois,' Paris, 1897; E. Lavisse and M. G. Bloch, *Hist. de France*, I. ii. 'Les Origines,' Paris, 1900; A. Lefèvre, *Les Gaulois*, Paris, 1900; G. Dottin, *Manuel pour servir à l'étude de l'antiquité celt.*, Paris, 1906; C. Renel, *Les Religions de la Gaule avant le christianisme*, Paris, 1906; C. Jullian, *Recherches sur la relig. gaul.*, Bordeaux, 1903; P. W. Joyce, *Soc. Hist. of Anc. Ireland*, London, 1903; J. Rhŷs, *Celtic Heathendom*, London, 1888, *Celtic Britain*[2], London, 1884; Duruy, 'Comment périt l'institution druidique,' *RA* xv. 347; De Coulanges, 'Comment le druidisme a disparu,' *RCel* iv. 44; J. A. MacCulloch, *Religion of the Ancient Celts*, Edinburgh, 1911.

J. A. MACCULLOCH.

DRUMS AND CYMBALS.—The drum is 'a musical instrument of the percussive class, consisting of a hollow cylindrical or hemispherical frame of wood or metal, with a "head" of tightly stretched membrane at one or both ends, by the striking of which and the resonance of the cavity the sound is produced.'[1] This definition hardly includes two types of drum which have played a more important part in social and religious evolution than any other—the incision-drum and the tambourine. The ordinary membrane-drum is composite in principle, combining in one structure the chief characteristics of both the tambourine and the homogeneous incision-drum. The actual genesis of the membrane-drum cannot be traced, though some speculations have been made on the suggestions supplied by various temporary drums and drum-substitutes. Clearly, like its two components, it has been independently invented by a fair proportion of the races of mankind.

Methods directly or indirectly suggestive of drumming are either obvious or recondite to civilized experience.

The Veddas have no musical instruments of any kind. In their dances they mark the rhythm by beating with the hands their chests, flanks, or bellies.[2] The Andamanese women beat time for the dancers by slapping the hollow between the thighs, as they sit squatting on the heels, with the palm of the right hand, which is held at the wrist by the left.[3] The same method is employed among the Australian aborigines, whose women invariably form the orchestra.[4] This method is analogous to that of cymbals, as the Vedda method of beating the belly or chest is to that of the membrane-drum. Another method is common to several races. Thus, for an extemporized drum, the Chaco Indians, who also employ a far more highly developed drum, sometimes use a bundle of skins tied into a package. This they beat with a stick.[5] In Australia the instrument, being the native rug or cloak of opossum-skin stretched across the hollow of the thighs, is analogous to the membrane of a drum. The women are said to keep faultless time.[6] At Australian corroborees 'the women of the tribe, who take the part of musicians, are seated in a semicircle, a short distance from the large fire lit on these occasions, holding on their knees opossum rugs tightly rolled and stretched out. These are struck by the right hand, in time with the action of the master of the ceremonies, usually one of the old men. He carries in each hand a corroboree stick, and these are struck together. . . . This use of the opossum cloak and clanking of the sticks appears to be the most primitive form of musical instrument, if it can be so termed, amongst our aborigines.'[7] Mitchell speaks of the rolled opossum-skin rug as 'the tympanum in its rudest form.'[8] In Western Victoria the rolled rug contained shells, producing a jingling sound.[9]

The Samoans at their dances used stretched mats, which were beaten with sticks, as well as the drum.[10] This method may or may not involve the ideas of a resounding cavity or vibrating membrane. For there may be no cavity, or the mat may be spread on a hard surface. But either cavity or membrane may be supplied by the accident of imitating the making of cloth. For beating bark into cloth the Polynesians used a beam of wood with a groove on the lower side. This rested on the ground, and a wooden mallet was used to strike the bark. Owing to the groove, made for the purpose of steadiness, 'every stroke produces a loud sound. . . . Heard at a distance, the sound of cloth-beating is not disagreeable.'[11] In Mangaia, of the Hervey Islands, the cloth-beating mallet was used for drums, and mimic cloth-boards were beaten as drums at certain feasts.[1] The Bechuanas, who are the finest leather-makers in Africa, use at initiation feasts the method of the free membrane An ox-hide is held and tightly stretched by several men. This is beaten with sticks.[2] The process is a repetition of one used in skin-preparation, here employed to produce ceremonial music. In old days the Chippewa made their war-drums by stretching a hide over stakes driven in the ground, and binding it in place by means of strong hoops.[3] Covering a pot or clay cylinder with a head of skin is a common method of making both permanent and temporary drums.[4]

Among historical peoples the drum is of very great antiquity. Its invention belongs to their pre-history; its forms are the membrane-drum, tambourine, and kettle-drum. It was known in Vedic India, and a hymn in the *Atharvaveda* celebrates its praises.[5] The earliest records of China are familiar with the drum.[6] The tambourine and double-headed drum were used by the Assyrians and Egyptians. The latter was supported against the drummer's body and played with both hands. Such an instrument is represented in a relief of Ashurbanipal (668–626 B.C.), in which women and children are clapping their hands.[7]

Certain peoples representing the lowest stages of culture known have failed to invent the drum, but in savagery generally, in all the stages of barbarism, and in civilizations like that of India, its use corresponds with its importance as the chief, and sometimes the only, instrument of music.[8] The structural variations presented by the instrument are endless, but the types are clearly marked. These are eight in number.

(1) The *incision-drum* is a hollow cylinder, varying in length from a few inches to twelve or more feet, and in diameter proportionally. Made from a bamboo internode or hollow tree, the ends are closed by the nodes or by the trunk sections. A narrow longitudinal slit, of varying length, but generally nearly as long as the cavity, is made on one side of the drum. Its width in the larger instruments is about three inches. The tapering of the lips is important, for the drumstick is applied to them, and the tones vary according to the thickness of the substance struck. This drum may be placed either in a vertical or in a horizontal position. The best results are produced from the latter.

(2) The *stamping-drum* is a long hollow cylinder, one end of which is closed and the other left open. The 'heading' of the closed end is either natural, as the node of a bamboo, or artificial, as a 'membrane' of skin. This instrument usually has a handle, by which the closed end is struck on the hard ground.

(3) The *single-headed membrane-drum* is a wooden cylinder, whose length is not much more than its diameter. The tightly stretched membrane of hide is beaten with the fingers, the hand, or a stick. The stick, usually knobbed, sometimes of a hammer-shape, becomes a heavy-headed club for the larger drums. The other end of the drum is closed.

(4) The *double-headed membrane-drum* is the single-headed with the closed end removed and converted into a 'head.' This drum is placed in a horizontal position and both heads are used.

(5) The *friction-drum* is (3) or (4) with a thong or cord stretched across the diameter of the head (one head in the case of the double-headed drum), or along its radius, being fixed in the centre. A

1 Murray, *OED*, s.v. 'Drum.'
2 C. G. and B. Z. Seligmann, *The Veddas*, Cambridge, 1911, pp. 214, 217.
3 E. H. Man, in *JAI* xii. (1883) 131.
4 A. W. Howitt, in *JAI* xiv. (1885) 304.
5 J. W. Fewkes, in *15 RBEW* (1897), p. 276.
6 K. L. Parker, *The Euahlayi Tribe*, 1905, p. 122.
7 R. Etheridge, in *JAI* xxiii. (1894) 320 f.
8 F. L. Mitchell, *Eastern Australia*, 1838, ii. 5.
9 J. Dawson, *Australian Aborigines*, Melbourne, 1881, p. 80.
10 G. Pratt, *Dict. of the Samoan Language*, 1878, s.v. 'Tata.'
11 W. Ellis, *Polyn. Researches*, 1829, i. 179, 184.

1 W. W. Gill, *Myths and Songs from the South Pacific*, 1876, pp. 262, 259.
2 F. Ratzel, *Hist. of Mankind*, 1896–98, ii. 329.
3 F. Densmore, 'Chippewa Music,' *Bull. 45 BE*, 1910, p. 11.
4 See *20 RBEW* (1903), p. 34 f.; L. Frobenius, *Childhood of Man*, 1909, pp. 95–98; W. B. Grubb, *An Unknown People in an Unknown Land*, 1911, p. 178; Ratzel, ii. 329.
5 A. A. Macdonell, *Vedic Mythology* (*GIAP* iii. [Strassburg, 1897] 155, quoting *Atharv.* 20).
6 *SBE* xxviii. (1885) 90.
7 J. D. Prince, in *EBi*, s.v. 'Music.'
8 See Crantz, *Greenland*, 1820, i. 162; T. C. Hodson, *The Nāga Tribes of Manipur*, 1911, p. 64; A. Simson, in *JAI* xii. (1883) 24; Ratzel, ii. 329.

small piece or splinter of wood may be inserted beneath the thong.

(6) The *pot-drum* is an earthenware vessel headed with a membrane.

(7) The *kettle-drum* is a metal vessel headed with a membrane. Both (6) and (7) are single-headed closed drums. Type (6) tends towards the hemispherical shape of body; (7) in its developed form is quite hemispherical.

(8) The *tambourine* is a head of membrane attached to a cylindrical rim. On this are generally hung pieces of metal, according to the *sistrum* principle. The membrane is struck by a stick, more usually with the hand.

'The drum,' says Codrington, 'in many forms, may be said to be the characteristic instrument of Melanesia.' It is, however, absent from Florida and Santa Cruz. The incision-type is employed. A joint or internode of bamboo, or a tree-trunk of suitable size, for the largest, is selected, and a longitudinal slit of varying degrees of narrowness is made along one side. The lips of this slit are very carefully tapered; apparently the tone of the drum depends largely upon this detail. Small drums are held in the hands by dancers, but the large bamboo drums are held by an assistant. Most of these big drums have a special hut in which they are stored. They are valued very highly and certainly are in a sense sacred. They are described as 'very resonant and well toned, and can be heard at a great distance.'[1]

Big drums were made from hollowed trees throughout Polynesia. The lips being thick, and the whole instrument more or less a mere 'dug-out,' a heavy club was used by the drummer.[2]

The *canoe-drum* is a remarkable type, used in the Fiji Islands, Java, and Assam. A hollowed tree-trunk, often twenty-five or thirty feet in length, with closed ends tapering upwards, and an orifice along its upper length just wide enough to admit the body, is obviously both a canoe and an incision-drum of a large type. With two wooden mallets the operator beat on the lips of the incision, which were curved inwards. In Fiji these drum-canoes are the *lali*, and are kept in sacred houses.[3] The signal drums of New Pomerania and South Congo are identical. They are small, being not more than two feet in length.[4] The Malay peoples use a bamboo-stem with several internodes, each of which has the incision. As the diameter of the internodes increases, the scale, as with organ-pipes, descends.[5]

The Maori war-drum was of the incision type, but flat. It was hung from a cross-bar on a high scaffold, with the slit side underneath, and played from a platform half-way up the scaffold.[6] This *pahu*, hung in a sort of watch-tower, approximates in a fashion to the bell. In the Philippines the Jesuits have not only used old signal-drums of incised bamboo as church-bells, but have reproduced them in wood for the same purpose.[7] In the Tongan drums, from two to four feet in length, the chink ran nearly the whole length and was about three inches in breadth. The drum being made from a solid tree-trunk, all the hollowing-out was done through the incision—a long and difficult operation. In playing this drum, the drummer with his stick, a foot long and as thick as his wrist, varied the force and rate of his beats, and changed the tones by beating 'towards the end or middle of the instrument.' This drum was the *naffa*, the *kaara* of the Hervey Islands.

In Tahiti the drum used was the upright one-headed closed drum. A tree-trunk section was hollowed out, leaving a closed base. Shark's skin was stretched over the open top. This was the *pahu*; its sacred form was the *pahu ra*. One in Tahiti was eight feet high, and was beaten with two sticks. 'The thrilling sound of the large drum at midnight, indicating a human sacrifice, was most terrific. Every individual trembled with apprehension of being seized.'[8] The *kendang* or *gendang* of Indonesia, as used by Dayaks, Bataks, Macassars, Buginese, and Javanese, in Borneo, and throughout the countries east of India, is of the Hindu type, a single-headed closed wooden drum, played with the fingers.[9] The American drum was either the pot-drum or the wooden single-headed membrane-drum.[10]

There is more variety of drums in Africa than elsewhere. Practically every form is found, and variations occur which are in some cases unique or extremely rare.[11]

[1] R. H. Codrington, *The Melanesians*, Oxford, 1891, pp. 336 f., 175, 332, 340.

[2] G. Brown, *Melanesians and Polynesians*, 1910, p. 419.

[3] S. E. Peal, in *JAI* xxii. 252; Frobenius, 83, 91; Brown, 419.

[4] Frobenius, 84.

[5] Skeat-Blagden, *Pagan Races of Malay Penin.*, 1906, ii. 140.

[6] Frobenius, 92 f.

[7] *Ib.* 90 f.

[8] Cook, *Voyages*, 1790, p. 1419; W. Ellis, i. 193, 195.

[9] See Ratzel, i. 194; Playfair, *The Garos*, 1909, p. 42; Wilken-Pleyte, *Handleiding voor de vergelijkende Volkenkunde van Nederlandsch-Indië*, Leyden, 1893, p. 111.

[10] See E. F. Im Thurn, *Among the Indians of Guiana*, 1883, p. 309; A. C. Fletcher, in *22 RBEW* (1904), pt. ii. p. 257; F. Densmore, 12.

[11] For various African drums, see Hobley, *Ethnology of A-Kamba*, Cambridge, 1910, p. 32 f.; A. Werner, *British Central Africa*, 1906, p. 225; A. B. Ellis, *Tshi-speaking Peoples*, 1887, p. 326, *Yoruba-speaking Peoples*, 1894, p. 115.

The Baganda drum was made from a section of tree-trunk, conical in form; the base of the cone alone was open. This was headed with a cow-hide, and this was the end kept uppermost. Some were ten inches high, others five feet, and four in greatest diameter. Some were beautifully decorated with cowries and beads. Except in the case of the very large drums, they were hung on posts, so as to get the full benefit of the sound. The skins were kept soft and elastic by being rubbed with butter.[1]

The essential character of the snare-drum and friction-drum is the presence of a string or thong of leather across the membrane or drum-head. A simple form is from British Guiana. A fine double thread, with a slip-knot in the centre, is stretched across the membrane. Before it is drawn tight, an exceedingly slender splinter of wood is secured in the slip-knot, so as to rest on the membrane at right angles to the line of the thread. The other head of the drum being unaltered, the instrument gives two different sounds. The friction-head produces, by the vibration of the splinter against the skin, a 'metallic sound.'[2] In another form the string extends along a radius only of the membrane.[3] Such drums, besides producing different tones from the two heads, can be muffled by placing a wad beneath the string.

Small hand-drums are commonly used by various peoples.[4]

The old English tabor is a type of these. The kettle-drum is not frequent. In the East the gong is preferred.[5]

The Greek and Roman drum (τύμπανον, *tympanum*) comprised two varieties of the tambourine type. The one was the flat tambourine; the circumference was hung with bells. The other resembled the Lapp form, the under side being closed by a convex hemispherical bottom. This variety was also played with the hand like a tambourine.[6]

The Heb. *tōph* (Gr. τύμπανον, EV 'tabret,' 'timbrel') was a simple tambourine, probably without bells or rattles.[7] The same Heb. word represents both the English, and probably there was only one form.

The tambourine, 'which was once among the chief instruments of the Lapland wizards, is now a great curiosity.' Two types were in use. One was a wooden hoop strengthened with two cross-pieces and covered on one side with reindeer-skin; the other was an oval box with a convex under side, hewn out of a tree-trunk, and with a reindeer-skin head. In some there was a slit serving as a handle. Each tambourine had an 'indicator' (*arpa*) consisting of a large iron ring, on which smaller rings were linked, for the purpose of divination by means of pointing to the symbols on the membrane. The hammer was made of reindeer-horn. The Lopars treated their tambourines with great respect, and kept them, with the indicator and hammer, wrapped up in fur. No woman dared to touch them.[8]

The cymbal varies in form, from a disk of metal to a shallow hemispherical or half-oval cup, with or without a flange. Cymbals were known in early India, and are still used by the Hindus in ordinary and temple orchestras.[9] The Garos use two sorts of cymbals: the *kakwa*, like the Euro-

[1] J. Roscoe, *The Baganda*, 1911, pp. 26, 407 f.

[2] Im Thurn, 308.

[3] See H. Balfour, 'The Friction-Drum,' in *JAI* xxxvii. (1907) 67.

[4] See G. Brown, 329; J. O. Dorsey, in *13 RBEW* (1896), p. 282; Skeat-Blagden, ii. 140; J. J. M. de Groot, *Rel. Syst. of China*, Leyden, 1892 ff., i. 157; Ratzel, iii. 388.

[5] See Ratzel, iii. 231; Wilken-Pleyte, 111.

[6] Pliny, *HN* ix. 109.

[7] Prince, *l.c.*

[8] G. Klemm, *Kulturgesch.*, Leipzig, 1843–52, iii. 90–99; J. Scheffer, *Lapponia*, Frankfurt, 1673, pp. 109 f., 130 f.; V. M. Mikhailovskii, 'Shamanstvo,' in *JAI* xxiv. (1894–95) 62, 126; W. Radloff, *Aus Sibirien*[2], Leipzig, 1893, ii. 18 ff.

[9] A. A. Macdonell, 134; J. E. Padfield, *The Hindu at Home*, Madras, 1896, p. 182.

pean, and the *nengilsi*, a smaller kind resembling in shape two small cups of brass.[1] The European type is derived from the Græco-Roman. These were quarter- or half-globes of metal with a flange. An older form is possibly indicated by the 'bronze vessels' used in the ceremonial dismissal of family *manes* by the Roman *paterfamilias*.[2] The Roman cymbals were either without handles or provided with a knob or ring or metal handle; others had a hole for the insertion of a cord. The unflanged, early Semitic type was also known.[3] The Khasias use cymbals in combination with drums.[4] The Chinese drummer usually employs one pair of cymbals.[5] The Abyssinians have tambourines, cymbals, and various drums.[6]

In modern European orchestras they hold a not unimportant place.

Only in the case of one people, the Hebrews, have cymbals attained independent importance. They were employed in dances and singing with the *tōph*, but in the Temple were used alone.

The cymbals of the Hebrews (*m^eṣiltayîm, ṣelṣ^elîm*, κύμβαλα) were used in the temple-worship to mark time for chants. They were bronze 'disks,' held, one in each hand, and clashed together. *Ṣelṣ^elîm* is used only in 2 S 6^{5} and Ps 150^{5}. In the latter passage the epithets 'loud' and 'high-sounding' are applied. It has been supposed, therefore, that the *ṣelṣ^elîm* were the conical flangeless cymbals, as used by the Assyrians, giving a highly-pitched note. In 1 S 18^{6} *shālîshîm*, κύμβαλα, cannot refer to cymbals. According to the Mishna and Josephus, one pair only was used in the Temple. It is not likely that κρέμβαλα, *sistra*, castanets, are ever connoted by the terms *m^eṣiltayîm* and *ṣelṣ^elîm*. It is possible that in the case of the Temple cymbals one disk was fixed, and was beaten by the other like a clapper. In later Mishnaic the noun used is in the singular number. The cymbalists were Levites. In the Second Temple a special officer had the charge of the cymbals, which are stated to have been of great antiquity. Their sound is described as high, loud, and far-carrying. It has been suggested that the 'tinkling cymbal' of St. Paul's simile implies the metallic spheres worn on bridles and by courtesans on their belts. This agrees better with the epithet ἀλάλαζον.[7]

The use of the drum as an instrument of society, and probably the art itself of drum-playing, have their highest development in Africa. The only national instrument that can approach the drum of the African is the pipes of the Scot. But the skill with the drum is more widely diffused among the Africans. Uganda in the old days supplies a typical example of a drum-conducted community.

The chief drums of the Baganda were the royal, called *mujaguzo*, ninety-three in number. Fifty-one of these were small. They were guarded by a chief, *kawuka*, and his assistant *wakimwomera*. Drummers took their turn of a month's residence each year in the royal court for beating the drums. A particular drum belonged to each chieftainship. The numerous totem-clans had each special drums; the leading members defrayed the expense. Every chief, besides his drum of office, had his private drum. This was beaten from time to time to ensure his permanent holding of office. Each clan had a special rhythm which was recognized.[8]

Drum-playing calls for considerable executive skill, particularly on account of the rebound of the membrane. It is in the utilization of this rebound that the essence of the drummer's art consists. Even with the heaviest drums no great force is required. The weight of the blow varies as the thickness of the membrane. In the case of large incision-drums, where the body serves as a membrane, the lips are finely tapered, and very resonant notes are produced by the use of a light stick. Various forms of drum-stick have been mentioned incidentally.

The Baganda drummer used two short but heavy sticks, club-shaped. 'The vibration from the large drums was so great that a man who did not understand how to beat them might have his shoulder dislocated by the rebound of the leather when struck. Music could be got from these drums, so much so that any one a mile away would scarcely believe that a drum, and not some other instrument, was being played.'[1] In the New Hebrides big wooden billets are used for beating the largest incision-drums. High notes, in concerted music, are supplied by small horizontal incision-drums. These are beaten 'in brisk syncopated time, to the loud boomings of the bigger drums.'[2]

For the psychological study of music by which the social and religious importance of the artistry of sound is destined to be explained, the music of drums and cymbals supplies unique data, and the drum-music of such races as the Central African, the American Indian, and his congener the Northern Asiatic (the Melanesians are, artistically, in a lower class) forms one of the most indispensable documents.[3]

The fact is that the music of the drum is more closely connected with the foundations of aurally generated emotion than that of any other instrument. It is complete enough in itself to cover the whole range of human feeling, which is not the case with its subordinate, the cymbals, while it is near enough to the origins of musical invention to appeal most strongly to the primitive side of man's nature. The investigator will need a long experience and adaptation to the atmosphere in which the vibrations of drum and tambourine produce their emotional waves. To compare, as an early explorer did, the orchestral drum-music of negroes to 'the raging of the elements let loose,'[4] is no longer an explanation of primitive music. To put it briefly—the emotional appeal of music is to a very large extent muscular. Rhythm is practically a neuro-muscular quality, and it is the fundamental form of musical sound. Most of our emotions tend to produce movement.[5] Harmonious rhythm in movement and action is the soul of society, as it is the soul of the dance.

'In all primitive music, rhythm is strongly developed. The pulsations of the drum and the sharp crash of the rattles are thrown against each other and against the voice, so that it would seem that the pleasure derived by the performers lay not so much in the tonality of the song as in the measured sounds arranged in contesting rhythm, and which by their clash start the nerves and spur the body to action, for the voice which alone carries the tone is often subordinated and treated as an additional instrument.'[6] Helmholtz observed: 'All melodies are motions. Graceful rapidity, grave procession, quiet advance, wild leaping, all these different characters of motion and a thousand others can be represented by successions of tones. And, as music expresses these motions, it gives an expression also to those mental conditions which naturally evoke similar motions, whether of the body and the voice, or of the thinking and feeling principle itself.'[7]

To increase muscular power the strongest stimulus is muscular movement; to produce emotional intoxication the combination of muscular movement that is rhythmical with rhythmical sound (or motion translated into music) is the most efficient. One great sphere of drum-music has been the social emotions. Not only military, religious, and sexual excitement, but every possible form of social orgiasticism has been fostered and developed by its influence. It is a significant coincidence that the boom of the modern cannon and the boom of a primitive drum mean war. In contrast to this large, impressive sound, which is so essentially organic in its nature and its production, may be placed the exclusively religious use of cymbals by the Hebrews, and the prominence of cymbal-music in the perverted sexualism

[1] Playfair, 44 f.
[2] Frazer, *GB*[2] iii. 89.
[3] Smith, *Gr.-Roman Ant.*[3], *s.v.* 'Cymbalum.'
[4] *Trans. Ethn. Soc.* vii. (1869) 309.
[5] De Groot, i. 157.
[6] Ratzel, iii. 231.
[7] Prince, in *EBi*, *s.v.* 'Music'; Ezr 3^{10}; Jos. *Ant.* VII. xii. 3; E. G. Hirsch, in *JE*, *s.v.* 'Cymbals'; Mishn. *'Ar.* 13 *a*; 1 Ch 16^{42}, Ps 150^{5}, 1 Co 13^{1}. Cf. 1 Ch 15$^{16. 19. 28}$ 16^{5} 25^{6}, 2 Ch 5^{13} 29^{25}, Neh 12^{27}.
[8] J. Roscoe, 25–30.

[1] *Ib.* 26 f.
[2] B. T. Somerville, in *JAI* xxiii. 11 f., 384.
[3] See F. Densmore, 6, 137.
[4] G. Schweinfurth; see Ratzel, ii. 329.
[5] See J. B. Miner, 'Motor, Visual, and Applied Rhythms' (*Psychological Review*, Monograph Supplements, v. 4 [1903]); S. Wilks, in *Medical Magazine*, Jan. 1894; Wundt, *Völkerpsychologie*, Leipzig, 1904 f., i. 265; R. Wallaschek, *Primitive Music*, 1893, *passim*.
[6] A. C. Fletcher, 'Love Songs among the Omaha Indians,' in *Proc. Internat. Congr. of Anthropology*, Chicago, 1893.
[7] Helmholtz, *On the Sensations of Tone*, tr. A. J. Ellis[2], 1885, p. 250.

of the cult of Attis.[1] These two last cases are isolated phenomena. The music of the drum is more completely human.

Lastly, the muscular appeal of the drum is made powerful by the very limitations of the instrument. The player is practically confined to rhythm, and the influential manipulation of this depends on his personality. He is one with his drum. It is this translation of human meaning and will into sound that explains the so-called 'drum-language.' Further, the player's muscular skill and muscular life are at their highest efficiency; he is for his hearers an inspirer, a leader, and a prophet, the individual representative of the social body in movement and in emotion. It is on this principle that the drum in so many races gives the summons for all social functions. The blow of the drum-stick translates itself not merely into sound, but into a spiritual reverberation, an impulsive stroke upon the social consciousness.

The meaning of drum-sounds is thus of a universal, undifferentiated character; they appeal primarily to the muscular sense, and secondarily to all that is built up on that foundation. An instance of the simplest possible application may be contrasted with others more or less elaborate:

Explaining the route to Spirit-land to the soul of a dead chief, the Chippewa punctuates his words with sharp drum-taps.[2] 'To a European,' says Ellis, 'the rhythm of a drum expresses nothing beyond a repetition of the same note at different intervals of time; but to a native it expresses much more. To him the drum can and does speak, the sounds produced from it forming words, and the whole measure or rhythm a sense. In this way, when company drums are being played at an *ehsudu*, they are made to express and convey to the bystanders a variety of meanings. In one measure they abuse the men of another company, stigmatising them as fools and cowards; then the rhythm changes, and the gallant deeds of their own company are extolled. All this, and much more, is conveyed by the beating of drums, and the native ear and mind, trained to detect and interpret each beat, is never at fault. The language of the drum is as well understood as that which they use in their daily life. Each chief has his own call or motto sounded by a particular beat of his drums.'[3]

Klark declares that 'the sound of the tambourine, the convulsive antics of the shaman, his fierce screams, his wild stare in the dim light, all strike terror into the hearts of semi-savage people, and powerfully affect their nerves.'[4] The character of this tambourine-music has been thus described: After some preliminary sounds such as that of a falcon or a sea-mew, which concentrate attention, 'the tambourine begins to make a slight rolling noise, like the buzzing of mosquitoes: the shaman has begun his music. At first it is tender, soft, vague, then nervous and irregular like the noise of an approaching storm: it becomes louder and more decided. Now and then it is broken by wild cries; ravens croak, grebes laugh, sea-mews wail, snipes whistle, falcons and eagles scream. The music becomes louder, the strokes on the tambourine become confused in one continuous rumble; the bells, rattles, and small tabors sound ceaselessly. It is a deluge of sounds capable of driving away the wits of the audience. Suddenly everything stops; one or two powerful blows on the tambourine, and then it falls on the shaman's lap.'[5]

To peoples like the Central Africans, the drum, apart from its directly emotional use in social gatherings, as an instrument of social intoxication, plays the part of the church-bell, the clock, the town-crier, and the daily newspaper, besides being used for religious music and the exhortation of the sick.

In Africa (Lake Nyasa) the drum is used at dances, at feasts religious and secular, at wakes, by doctors at the sick-bed, by boatmen to time the paddles, and to send messages over the country.[6] Among the Woolwa Indians the drum is played when drink is offered to the guests at *mishla*-drinkings.[7] Of the Baganda drums, Roscoe writes: 'The drum was indeed put to a multitude of uses, quite apart from music: it was the instrument which announced both joy and sorrow; it was used to let people know of the happy event of the birth of children, and it announced the mourning for the dead. It gave the alarm for war, and announced the return of the triumphant warriors who had conquered in war. It had its place in the most solemn and in the most joyous ceremonies of the nation.' The royal drums were beaten to announce the coronation of a king, and his entry into a new house, and also at the new moon. Drums were carried on journeys and beaten to encourage the walkers. A young man would beat the drum with his hands and sing meanwhile. 'The people when carrying loads, or when on a march, loved to be accompanied by the drum, and, if they had no drum, they sang songs, and set the time for marching by the song.'[1]

Its co-operative and socializing importance is here well suggested. Its most spectacular use is that of a postal, telegraphic, and telephonic service.

The carrying power of these fine instruments renders communication very rapid. The big drum of the Anyanja can be heard at a distance of six miles.[2] The Chippewa drum, which is not two feet high, can be heard at a distance of ten miles.[3] As the drum-telephone is used to-day in Central Africa, it depends on an elaborate code, which to one reared in the atmosphere is perhaps more dependent on social understanding and mutual recognition of 'tone-variations' than on a colourless translation of sounds into letters. At any rate, throughout a very large tract of Central Africa, daily by means of the drum two or more villages exchange their news. Travellers, even Europeans, have obtained food and lodgings by its means. The notes used can be imitated by tapping the cheek when the mouth is open.[4] An apt method is here implied for native practice, since it is the aperture- or incision-drum that is used for the sound-messages. Dennett's account of actual messages sent by drum is all the more valuable because it is free from any attempt to heighten the effect.[5] He notes that this system gives the key to a perennial puzzle, revived during the Boer War, How does news travel among the natives in the speedy way it does? The drum-message system is found in New Guinea, and among the Jivaros of South America, the old Mexicans, and some Indians of the North-West. It is particularly developed in Oceania, the countries north-west and north-east of New Guinea, especially New Pomerania. Signalling by means of the incision-drum, but without any highly developed code, was used in Borneo, Java, the Philippines, New Zealand, the New Hebrides, Fiji, and the Hervey Islands.[6]

Throughout Melanesia, drums are part of a rich man's establishment. The top of these drums is fashioned into a grinning face. When the drum is an image of a venerated ancestor, the taps are made on the stomach.[7] In Melanesia, ancestor-worship is linked to the civil and military authority by these instruments, half-drum and half-image. It is natural also for rulers and important persons to collect round them as many sources of *mana* as possible, though they may leave the more recondite applications of supernatural power to the shamans. In the Upper Nile regions the 'sacred' official drums hang in front of the chief's house, or under the sacred tree of the village. They are regarded with awe.[8] The regalia of a chief are, as it were, his *sacra*. These may come to be identified with the mysterious power of his office. In other cases, the drum may be regarded as the mouthpiece of a god or spirit, as containing the voice of the god or the god himself. This voice, in the lower cultures, derives impressiveness not from stillness or smallness, but from loudness and resonant power.

Some miscellaneous examples are appended of

---

[1] The general use of cymbals in the worship of Dionysus and in the Eleusinian Mysteries belongs rather to the category of the impressiveness of noise, as such.
[2] Densmore, 54.
[3] *Tshi-speaking Peoples*, 326 f.
[4] Mikhailovskii, in *JAI* xxiv. 65.
[5] Anonymous writer in the *Sibirskii Sbornik*, quoted by Mikhailovskii, 94.
[6] H. S. Stannus, in *JAI* xl. 297, 333 f.; J. H. Weeks, *ib.* 380, 402, 404.
[7] H. A. Wickham, in *JAI* xxiv. 204.

[1] J. Roscoe, *The Baganda*, 25, 27, 29.
[2] A. Werner, p. 225.
[3] Densmore, 12.
[4] Frobenius, 84 f.
[5] R. E. Dennett, *At the Back of the Black Man's Mind*, 1906, p. 77 ff.
[6] Ratzel, i. 37, ii. 22; Frobenius, 86–93.
[7] Codrington, in *JAI* x. (1881) 295.
[8] Ratzel, iii. 39.

the beliefs and ritual connected with the sacredness of drums.

The regalia of Malay States includes the court and official drums, which are sacred. The royal drums of Jelebu are said to be 'headed' with the skins of lice, and to emit a chord of twelve different sounds; the royal trumpet and the royal gong also emit the chord of twelve notes. The Sultan of Minangkabau wakes daily to the sound of the royal drum (*gandang nobat*). These drums are regarded as having come into existence by their own will. 'Rain could not rot them nor sun blister them'; any person who even 'brushed past them' would be felled to the ground by their magic power. In the State drum of Selangor resided the *jin karaja'an*, or 'State demon'; and powerful *jinn* dwelt in the other royal drums.[1]

Each temple and house of a chief in West Africa has a tall drum (*gbedu*) covered with carvings. This drum had a protecting spirit, that, namely, of the slave who was sacrificed on it when it was made. It is beaten only at religious ceremonies. Before being struck, it receives an offering of blood and palm-wine, which is poured on the carvings.[2]

Tane, the Polynesian god, was more or less represented by his sacred drum. These drums were often surmounted by carved heads; and possibly the evolution here is from drum to idol. While the drum retained its membrane, a connexion would be traced between its sound and the voice of the god.[3] When the special royal drum, *kaula*, of the Baganda received a new skin, the blood of the cow whose skin was used was run into the drum. Also a man was beheaded, and his blood was run into it. The idea was that, when the drum was beaten, the life of the man added fresh life and vigour to the king. When any drum was fitted with a new skin, the ox killed for the purpose also supplied the blood for pouring into the drum.

Every drum contained its fetish. Renewing the fetish was as necessary as renewing the skin, and the two operations were simultaneous. These fetishes were concrete objects of the familiar African type. It was not every man who knew how to make a drum-fetish. A characteristic drum-fetish was that of the drum of Dungu, god of hunting. It was composed of portions of every kind of animal and bird hunted; all kinds of medicines used in making charms for hunting; miniature weapons, and pieces of cord used in making traps. This fetish was fixed upright in the drum.[4]

The clan Gomba of the Baganda had a drum, *nakanguzi*. A runaway slave, if he reached its shrine, became the servant of the drum, and could not be removed. Any animal straying thither became the property of the drum, a sacred animal, free to roam.[5] A criminal among the Marotse of Africa escapes punishment if he can reach and touch the drums of the king.[6]

In Vedic India the drum was not only beaten, but invoked, to drive away danger, demons, and enemies. It was used in sacrifices, and in battle; the warrior offered it worship. Before being played, a *mantra*, or charm, was spoken into it.[7] The analogy between thunder and the boom of the drum is obvious. Russian peasants used the drum to imitate thunder, by way of a charm for the production of rain.[8] The natives of Guiana prefer the skin of the baboon or 'howling monkey' for the heads of their drums, believing that a drum so fitted possesses 'the power of emitting the rolling, roaring sounds for which this monkey is celebrated.'[9] The Timorese regard cymbals as the home of spirits.[10] Such beliefs are found with all musical instruments.

The essential instrument of Christian temple-worship has been, from a very early period, the organ. No doubt an impulse of antagonism to pagan ritual prevented the early Christians from adopting pagan instruments. Only perhaps in Abyssinia, and in the modern Salvation Army, has the drum found a place. Drums do not appear to have been used by the Hebrews in temple-worship. The usual drum, *tōph*, of the tambourine type, was used in processions, at weddings, and feasts, and to accompany religious music of a joyous and popular character.[11] But in the great Oriental religions, particularly in Hinduism and Buddhism, the drum has an important place in

1 W. W. Skeat, *Malay Magic*, 1900, pp. 25–28, 40 f.
2 A. B. Ellis, *Yoruba-speaking Peoples*, 100.
3 H. C. March, in *JAI* xxii. (1893) 328.
4 J. Roscoe, 27 f., 312.
5 *Ib.* 167.
6 A. St. H. Gibbons, *Exploration and Hunting in Central Africa, 1895–96*, 1898, p. 129.
7 Macdonell, 155; *SBE* xli. 23, 26, xlii. 77, 117, 130; Oldenberg, 39.
8 W. Mannhardt, *Antike Wald- und Feldkulte*, Berlin, 1877, p. 342.
9 E. F. Im Thurn, 308 f.
10 Riedel, in *Deutsche Geographische Blätter*, x. 278 f.
11 Prince, *l.c.*; 1 Mac 9^39, Ex 15^20, Ps 81^2, 2 S 6^5, 2 Ch 5^12f.

the temple-worship; nor is it unknown in the worship of Islām. In lower cults the drum serves as a church-bell, an organ, and a direct vehicle of supernatural power.[1]

The Baganda temple-drums were next in importance after the royal drums. Each had its particular rhythm and particular fetish. They were beaten at feasts and at the time of the new moon, warning the people of the monthly rest from work.[2] In New Guinea, drums are beaten to drive away the ghosts of men slain in battle; in New Britain, to stop earthquakes.[3] Demons are expelled by South African drummers.[4] In the Moluccas the drum is employed against evil spirits causing difficult child-birth.[5] In Central Africa demons are driven away with guns and drums at funerals and before death.[6] Dayak women and shamans alike use the drum to cure the sick.[7] In China, scapegoats are driven away to the music of drums.[8] Greek historians record the 'disinfecting' of ambassadors by Turkish shamans by means of the drum;[9] and the use of it to drown the cries of children offered to Molech.[10] The *ska-ga*, or shaman, of the Haidas undertakes to drive away the evil spirit which possesses the sick. His chief implements are the drum and the rattle.[11] The exorcism of an evil spirit causing disease is carried out by the Wanika medicine-man in the centre of a band, playing drums and shouting.[12] The Patagonian doctor beats a drum by the sick man's bed to drive out the spirit.[13] The Asiatic shamans use the drum to cause spirits both to appear and to disappear.[14]

There is always something very human about the use of drum-music, even when applied to spiritualities. At an Eskimo feast the drums are beaten softly when the traders' goods are brought in; loudly when the guns are brought, so that the shades of animals present may not be alarmed.[15] For induction of spirits, the principle may be that of a summons or of an invitation.[16]

An old Motu-motu man observed to Chalmers: 'No drums are beaten uselessly; there are no dances that are merely useless.' The young men, for instance, are bidden to beat the drum and dance that there may be a large harvest.[17] The Papuan's remark applies universally. Tshi priests work themselves into an inspired state by dancing to the music of the drums. Each god has a special hymn accompanied by a special beat of the drum.[18] In ancient Israel the priests prophesied to the music of harps, psalteries, and cymbals.[19] Among the Chaco Indians the boys during initiation are called 'drums,' from the fact that during this period the village drums are beaten incessantly day and night by relays of men.[20] Among the Port Moresby natives (New Guinea) the boys at initiation have only one serious duty, which is for each to make his drum. They are tabu, and live in the forest until the drums are completed; this may be a week or a month. Several boys go together. 'A straight branch is selected and cut to the requisite size; this is next scraped with shells till the orthodox shape is arrived at; finally, the cavity is carefully and laboriously burnt out.' During the whole period they observe minute rules: if they were seen by a woman 'the drum would have to be destroyed, otherwise it would be certain to split, and would sound like an old cracked pot.' If they eat fish the skin of the drum will burst; red bananas cause a dull tone. They may not touch fresh water, but only that found in the stems of bananas, or coco-nut milk. Should they touch water inadvertently before the drum is hollowed out, they break it, crying: 'I have touched water, my firebrand is extinguished, and I can never hollow out my drum.' The sorcerers instruct them that water extinguishes the 'fire' of the music; a fish-

1 Cf. J. Mooney, in *14 RBEW* (1896), p. 725; J. G. Kohl, *Kitchi-Gami* (Eng. tr. 1860), i. 59 ff.
2 J. Roscoe, 28, 297, 312.
3 Haddon, *Head-hunters*, 1901, p. 308; van der Roest, in *Tijd. voor Ind. Taal-, Land-, en Volkenkunde*, xl. (1898) 157 f.
4 J. Macdonald, *Religion and Myth*, 1893, p. 100 ff.
5 Riedel, *De sluik- en kroesharige rassen tusschen Selebes en Papua*, Hague, 1886, pp. 265, 449, 175.
6 J. Macdonald, in *JAI* xxii. 114 f.
7 G. A. Wilken, in *Bijd. tot de Taal-, Land-, en Volkenk. van Ned.-Indië*, v. 2 (1887), p. 610.
8 J. H. Gray, *China*, 1878, ii. 306.
9 *FHG* (ed. C. Müller) iv. 227.
10 Plut. *de Superstitione*, 13.
11 G. M. Dawson, 'The Haida Indians of the Queen Charlotte Islands,' in *Geol. Surv. Can.*, 1878–79, p. 122.
12 J. L. Krapf, *Eastern Africa*, Eng. tr. 1860, p. 189.
13 M. Dobrizhoffer, *Account of the Abipones*, Eng. tr. 1822, ii. 262.
14 J. Georgi, *Les Nations samoyèdes et mandshoures*, St. Petersburg, 1777, p. 140.
15 *18 RBEW* (1899), p. 383.
16 Cf. Stannus, in *JAI* xl. 313: A. B. Ellis, *Tshi-speaking Peoples*, 125; Im Thurn, 339; Skeat, 512; Kruijt, *Het Animisme in d. ind. Archipel*, Hague, 1906, p. 445; J. H. Meerwaldt, in *Med. N.Z.G.* i. (1907) 98; G. A. Wilken, *l.c.*; Frazer, *GB*[2] ii. 196; Sheane, in *JAI* xxxvi. (1906) 152; Weeks, in *JAI* xl. 372, 404.
17 J. Chalmers, *Pioneering in New Guinea*, 1887, p. 181.
18 A. B. Ellis, *Tshi-speaking Peoples*, 120 ff.
19 1 Ch 25^1-3, 2 S 6^5.
20 Grubb, 178.

bone tears the tympanum; and the sight of a woman destroys the tone.[1]

The basket-drum of some American tribes recalls not only primitive substitutes for the drum, but certain features of agricultural rituals.

In their sacred rites the Navahos use an inverted basket in lieu of a drum. It is finely made by the women from twigs of sumach, wound in helix form, and when inverted the basket is nearly hemispherical. During ceremonies it is beaten with the sacred drum-stick. This is made according to elaborate rules from the leaves of *Yucca baccata*. The Navahos say, 'We turn down the basket,' when they refer to the commencement of a song; 'We turn up the basket,' when a song is finished. As it is raised, hands are waved in the same direction, to drive out the evil influence which the sacred songs have collected and imprisoned under the basket.[2]

It is no sacrilege to serve food in this sacred drum. To do so is common enough, but without ceremonial meaning. In Græco-Roman cults, such as the mysteries of Attis, eating sacred food from the sacred drum and cymbal was probably a reversion to primitive times, when platter, drum, basket, and winnowing-fan were interchangeable.

The use of the tambourine by the shamans of Northern Europe and Asia is remarkable. This instrument and its shamanistic manipulation are found in a belt which almost completely surrounds the world in northern parallels, through Asiatic Russia, Greenland, Northern America, and Lapland, and among Amerindians, Mongols, Tatars, and Lapps.[3] The structure of this hand-drum has already been described. Those used by Americans, Tatars, and Mongols have pictorial designs on the drum-head. The designs are supposed to produce or modify the sounds, and each, being thus a sort of word or sentence accompanied by pure sound, has its particular influence on the spirits who are invoked by the music.[4] The Lapp shaman's drum has small brass rings fastened loosely on the head. These move and dance over the designs inscribed when the head is beaten with the hammer; and, according to their movements in relation to the magic signs of sun, moon, and planets, the shaman predicts the future.[5] The origin of this method, which, it is to be noted, is always secondary to the musical or 'suggestive' use of the instrument, may be from the following practice: the Yakut shaman places a ring or coin on the palm of the inquirer's hand, moving it about in various directions, and then foretells the future.[6] The Votyak *tuno* moved beans on a table for the same purpose.[7]

It is suggestive of hypnotism rather than of music to find that the drum is tuned up by holding it in front of the fire. A drumstick or the hand is used in playing. The tambourine plays the main part in the *kamlanie*, the invocation of spirits and subsequent prophesying. The Chukchi shaman in his *kamlanie* taps the tambourine with a piece of thin whalebone. The *kam* uses the tambourine in various ways, and produces the most varied sounds. The spectators recognize the various rhythms, such as the tramping of horses' feet, during which the *kam* is supposed to be riding with his guards. As he taps, he collects spirits in the tambourine. Sometimes during the collection of spirits the tambourine becomes so heavy that the *kam* bows under the weight.[8]

LITERATURE.—This is fully given in the footnotes.

A. E. CRAWLEY.

DRUNKENNESS.[9]—**1. Definition.**—Drunkenness has never been satisfactorily defined in a legal or ethical sense. In any attempt to define it legally, difficulties at once present themselves, and the judge has to reach his conclusions from the evidence. Drunkenness might in general, if not in scientific, terms be defined as that condition of mind and body produced by a sufficient quantity of alcohol (varying according to the susceptibility of the individual to the toxic agent) to bring about distinct changes in the intellect, the emotions, the will (volition), the motor mechanism, and the functions of the cerebellum, or small brain, indispensable to the accurate execution of any movement. On the various stages and symptoms of intoxication, and forms of alcoholism, see art. ALCOHOL (vol. i. p. 300). The definition of 'habitual drunkard' first appeared in the Habitual Drunkards Act of 1879. It runs as follows:

'a person who, not being amenable to any jurisdiction in lunacy, is, notwithstanding, by reason of habitual intemperate drinking of intoxicating liquors, at times dangerous to himself or herself, or to others, or is incapable of managing himself or herself, and his or her affairs.'

2. Racial degeneration: heredity.—Of as great moment as individual and family wreckage wrought by drunkenness is the degeneracy of the innocent offspring. About this degeneracy, until quite recently, there has never existed a doubt. The all but universal testimony of competent observers and of the medical profession all over the world, based upon extensive experiments, and the general impressions of the profession on the question remain to this hour unshaken. And it may be said at once that these impressions as to bodily, nervous, and mental degeneration are not to be lightly set aside by any conclusion or opinion based upon the very restricted investigation by one or two authorities, however eminent. In 1910 the Galton Eugenics Laboratory issued two papers by Professor Karl Pearson on the influence of parental alcoholism on the physical health and mentality of the offspring. These papers were supposed to set forth lax and subversive views on the subject of temperance—views which, if capable of proof and acceptance, would indisputably have given a decided set-back to the believed and accepted doctrines of clinicians, and of scientific men and of social reformers in every land, as to the undoubted racial degeneration of the alcoholic individual and his or her offspring. If the first dictum of these observers, to the effect that on the whole in regard to degeneration the balance turns as often in favour of the alcoholic as of the non-alcoholic parentage, could be upheld, the outlook for the nation could not be otherwise than ominous. These opinions, apart from their calamitous effect on the race, shocked orthodox believers in the classical view hitherto held, and Sir Victor Horsley and others entered the lists in its support. If Professor Pearson and his collaborateurs could have established their proposition to anything like the extent to which their opponents have established theirs, it would have to be seriously entertained, no matter what might be the consequences to society and the race. But they have not done so, and it is not much to the point for them to impugn the investigations of their opponents on the ground that no trouble was taken to ascertain whether the alcoholism or the parentage came first. Indeed, the same charge of laxity of methods of investigation must be brought against Professor Pearson's own inquiry, for the 'Preliminary Study of Extreme Alcoholism in Adults' is based on reports made in connexion with a very restricted investigation. In any study, whether for or against, some fixed and definite standards are needed by which all cases can be tested. Such would have averted the con-

[1] Haddon, 257.
[2] Washington Matthews, in *Amer. Anthrop.* vii. 202–208.
[3] Mikhailovskii, 91, 93 f.
[4] G. Mallery, in *10 RBEW* (1893), p. 514, referring to Potanin.
[5] H. M. Aynsley, in *IA* xv. (1886) 67.
[6] Mikhailovskii, 95 (quoting Gmelin). [7] *Ib.* 154.
[8] Mikhailovskii, 68 (quoting Krasheninnikov and Erman), 72, 75 f.
[9] This art. deals almost exclusively with the ethical aspect of drunkenness. Full information as to its geographical distribution, the intoxicants used by different races, etc., will be found in the art. DRINKS, DRINKING. Cf. also the art. ALCOHOL.

flicting meanings attached to the terms 'drinking' and 'sober' applied to masses of the population. Many excessive drinkers are never 'drunk,' and many have a reputation for sobriety who consume in one debauch as much as the man called a 'drinker' would in months without apparent injury to themselves and others. Hence the need for rigid definitions and limitations applied to investigations which, to be of value, would require to be of a comprehensive character, and extended over a series of years. The effect of the 'Study,' however, is to demonstrate the close connexion between alcoholism and mental defectiveness, but the question is left unsolved whether this large proportion of mental and physical defectives, which is much greater than is found in the general population, is attributable to alcohol, or to the pre-existing mental defect.

In the second paper, the theory of the first—that there is no close relation between mental defect in the children and alcoholism in the parents—has been abandoned, and a close relationship is admitted, while segregation is called for on the ground of its hereditary character. Nothing specific, it will be observed, is said with reference to the undoubted physical stigmata of such degenerates.

Professor Pearson contends that mental defect is antecedent to alcoholism. But what, it may be asked, antecedes the mental defect? Unless this can be answered satisfactorily, one must come full circle to the original standpoint, and be confronted by the old problem. The Pearsonites have abandoned the position that 'the balance turns as often in favour of the alcoholic as of the non-alcoholic parentage,' and practically admit that alcoholism and mental defectiveness are associated; but whether the one precedes the other, and which precedes the other, they do not know. As far as the controversy has gone, there can be no doubt that the authorities who believe that alcoholism, not gross alcoholism—about that no doubt exists—but that fairly general kind of free indulgence which takes place daily, with frequent 'week-end' bouts, does lead to the physical and mental impairment of the offspring, are in the right, and can produce unquestioned evidence in support of their view. Than this no controversy of greater moment in regard to alcoholism has been started. To make the investigation referred to of the least value, a statistical and clinical research into the comparative physique and capacity of the descendants of alcoholic and non-alcoholic parents respectively in several carefully chosen districts would be required, and it is not too much to anticipate what the conclusion would be. It would finally determine whether there is any marked correlation between parental alcoholism and inferiority of offspring manifesting itself not only in childhood but in adolescence; and it would dissipate views calculated to do infinite harm to the race and to the commonwealth.

The degeneracy of alcoholic offspring is attested by such authorities as Magnan, Morel, Lancereaux, Crichton-Browne, Legrand du Saulle, John Macpherson, etc., and it comes about in many ways. The male parent who is a 'soaker'—we need not consider the physical state of the progenitor suffering from the effects of an occasional bout at the time of conception—undoubtedly begets a weak offspring, made surer if his habits worry and impoverish the sober mother during pregnancy and lactation. When both parents are 'swillers,' the bad effects are still more marked. It has been alleged, although little evidence has been adduced in support of it, that when fathers are addicted to drunkenness the female offspring are more likely to be the subjects of hereditary alcoholism, and when the mother is the offender the males perpetuate the parental failing (*hérédité croisée*). It is thought, and there are strong grounds for the presumption, that the female progenitor is the surer and more general transmitter of the hereditary alcoholic taint and of the neuroses which eventuate in insanity, imbecility, and nervous diseases. The prepotency of the alcoholic mother, in handing on to her offspring a constitution not only physically defective but mentally unstable, cannot be gainsaid. This view accords with common sense, even if exact statistical records are wanting, for not only is her condition at conception of moment, but so also is the fact that during utero-gestation and lactation the blood is charged with the toxic agent, specially so during pregnancy. The heredity may be 'immediate' from one or both parents, or 'mediate' from grandparents, the 'immediates' having been free from the taint. And the heredity may be homogeneous or heterogeneous: in the one group inebriety begets neurotic children; in the other the inebriety of members of a family springs from neurotic parentage, which may not, and frequently does not, owe its existence to alcoholic excess.

Four of the foremost advocates of the non-transmission of personally acquired characters are Galton, Weissman, J. A. Thomson, and Archdall Reid—recognized authorities on the principles and laws of heredity. In their view environmental influences play a secondary part; heredity is everything. One may ask the question in this connexion, Are the bad mental effects of vicious habits and alcoholic excess passed on to descendants, thus setting up racial degeneration? Dr. Ford Robertson, following Darwin, Maudsley, and Hartwig, traverses Dr. A. Reid's proposition that 'inborn characters are known to be transmissible from parent to offspring,' and postulates for himself the remarkable doctrine and dogma that 'offspring, as far as can at present be determined, inherit no character whatever from their parents. . . . The distinction between inborn and acquired characters has really no justification in modern scientific fact. . . .' Although there is no inheritance of parental characters, there is of environmental influences, to which all that is of any importance in human ontogenetic evolution (*i.e.* the development of the individual) is directly due. There is here evidence of acute dialectic diversity, as well as of uncertainty.

3. Statistics.—The following statistics, which have a profound significance, are submitted in order to give some idea of (1) the annual mortality, sickness, and unemployment consequent upon excessive indulgence; and (2) the prevalence and cost of pauperism, pauper lunacy, criminality, and delinquency due to the same cause.

(*a*) *Mortality.*—It was calculated twenty years ago (Dr. Norman Kerr) that 40,000 persons die annually in the United Kingdom from drunkenness and habitual drunkenness; and Dr. Wakley, Editor of the *Lancet* and Coroner for Middlesex, not only confirmed this estimate, but put it higher. Of 1500 inquests he attributed 900 at least to hard drinking, and he believed that from 10,000 to 15,000 persons died annually in the Metropolis from drink, upon whom no inquest was held. For the United Kingdom this calculation would easily justify a total of 50,000. Deaths from suicide, drowning, and exposure totalled 7372 in one year in Great Britain and Ireland, and of these one may safely reckon that alcohol was responsible for 50 per cent. Of deaths from accidents and negligence (13,386), 15 per cent may be attributed to the same cause.

Infant mortality.—For the declining birth-rate in this and other lands, to which of late attention is constantly drawn, many causes are assigned, but in the present connexion we are concerned only with the great wastage occurring in the depleted birth-rates through overlaying by drunken parents, especially mothers, parental neglect arising from over-indulgence and improper feeding, no cognizance being here taken of premature births attributable to drunkenness, and to accidents arising therefrom. In regard to the suckling of infants, the milk of the alcoholic mother is both deficient in quantity and inferior in quality, in spite of the popular belief to the contrary in favour of stout and wines; and, further, there is defective ovulation and sterility.

Comparative mortality for various trades and occupations, including the Licensed Trade itself.—According to Dr. Newsholme, if the comparative mortality figure for all men equals 1000, an equal number of gardeners would yield only 568 deaths, teachers 571, grocers 664, doctors 957 (midway), while at the other end of the scale are brewers 1407, innkeepers and men-servants 1665, and file-makers 1682. Comparing employees in inns, etc., with all other occupied males, it is found that, out of a given number in each group, 8 times as many die from alcoholism, 5 times as many from gout, $1\frac{3}{10}$ times as many from nervous diseases, $1\frac{1}{5}$ times as many from suicide, and $2\frac{1}{2}$ times as many from consumption. Regarding the liability of drunkards to consumption, Prof. Brouardel (Paris) observes: 'Alcoholism is, in fact, the most powerful factor in the propagation of tuberculosis,' and Dr. R. W. Philip (Edinburgh) agrees: 'The most vigorous man who becomes alcoholic is without resistance before it.'

Actuarial calculations made with great care and exactitude by insurance offices are significant. The best offices increase the premium as much as 50 per cent, and a few absolutely decline proposals of persons in the drink trade. And, as regards abstainers and non-abstainers, the chances of life are no less than 2 to 1 in favour of the former. The ratio is much the same in regard to sickness, recovery being speedier among the former. The moral clearly is that he who desires to live long, wisely, and well should either be a total abstainer or exceedingly temperate. For many persons total abstinence is a necessity of their being if they are not to make early shipwreck of their lives.

(*b*) *Crimes and petty offences.*—In the United Kingdom there were 636,340 apprehensions in the year 1903. These figures do not represent so many individuals as is often concluded, the same individual figuring more than once in returns. A total of 318,000 persons who have been in the hands of the police for homicide, assaults, petty thefts, prostitution, drunkenness, disorderly conduct, etc., would be nearer the mark. The total admits of a further reduction to 273,000 as the number in which alcohol plays a chief part; but, as many persons commit petty offences without being officially listed, it would be safe to put the number requiring, although not receiving, the attention of the police at 80,000—in all 353,000, or 1 to 128 of the population. In Scotland it is reckoned that there are 4700 recidivists, both of the criminal and of the petty offender classes, waging (especially the former) an aggressive war against society, of whom 2500 are feeble-minded, debauched, parasitic, petty offenders, or 5 per 1000 of population—a ratio somewhat similar to that estimated by Mr. C. S. Loch, C.B., for England.

The sex-ratio of these parasitic offenders is remarkable as the frequency of convictions advances. Thus from 11 to 20 convictions, males are to females 100 : 70; 21 to 50 convictions, 100 : 90; 51 to 100 convictions, 100 : 180; 101 and upwards, 100 : 330.

In Scotland, 2500 have been convicted and sent to prison 20 times, and 1330 more than 50 times. Referring to the 1330, Dr. John Macpherson, Commissioner in Lunacy, makes the following trite observations as to the mental irresponsibility of such cases:

'It is only the shortness of human life which limits the number.' Chronic drunkenness, habitual or periodic, he says, is 'a neurosis closely allied in its symptomatology and heredity to the other neuroses and to insanity'; and the true cause is 'a defective heredity which (1) induces the subject to crave for a particular mental state—not for alcohol, but for the state which alcohol most conveniently produces; (2) which provides the subject with a constitution which is particularly susceptible to the influence of such poisons as alcohol; and (3) which is in many cases the cause of a mental unsoundness independent of alcohol.'

(*c*) *Cost of prisons.*—In the year 1909 the cost of prisons was: in England, £720,340; Scotland, £95,790; Ireland, £114,660 — being a total of £930,790. It is safe to assume that, but for alcohol, not one-third of the whole cost, or £310,000, would be required for this purpose. The daily prison population amounts to 26,000, of whom 17,000 are interned for crimes and offences directly connected with casual and habitual drunkenness.

(*d*) *Pauperism.*—The number of paupers in England, Scotland, and Ireland, and the cost to the country locally and imperially, may be roughly expressed as follows: paupers, 1,083,470; cost, £7,389,000. It is no exaggeration to say that 50 per cent of pauperism and its cost may be ascribed to drunkenness and habitual drunkenness—in other words, 541,700 paupers and dependents are maintained at a cost of £3,695,000.

(*e*) *Police.*—Maintenance of the police force in England, Wales, Scotland, and Ireland, numbering 62,400 picked men (England and Wales 46,000, Scotland 5670, Ireland 10,740), falls little short of £6,000,000 per annum. Of this enormous sum, drunkenness, and offences and crimes connected directly with drunkenness, may be credited at least with one-third, £2,000,000, met from local taxation and imperial subventions. But this is not all. From the Civil Service Estimates (Class iii., 'Law and Justice,' pp. 229–353), consideration must be given to another set of heavy imperial charges under this head, amounting in all to £1,600,000 for County Courts, Supreme Court of Judicature, Reformatories and Industrial Schools, Criminal Asylums, etc. If to this enormous imperial total under the head of 'Law and Justice' be added the burdens falling upon local authorities under the same head, the total would not fall short of £2,600,000, of which drunkenness and allied offences may be debited with 33 per cent, or £860,000.

(*f*) *Pauper lunatics.*—In the year 1910 these were: England 130,550, Scotland 18,340, Ireland 24,140—a total of 173,030. The annual (approximate) cost of maintenance, inclusive of interest on buildings and land, was £6,000,000. Assuming that alcohol directly and indirectly is responsible for 20 per cent of the insane poor, it follows that £1,200,000 per annum from rates and Government grants are required to meet the burden of providing for a daily population of 34,000 lunatics.

(*g*) *Excise and Customs Revenue for one year.*—On the other side of the ledger must be placed the revenue raised by the duties on spirits, beer, wines, brandy, rum, etc., which may be put down at £35,000,000. When over against this revenue is put the cost and loss to the nation of £27,200,000 (see Summary) in consequence of intemperance, the benefit of the enormous revenue sinks into insignificance. £170,000,000 is spent annually on drink by the nation. In the light of the facts and statistics submitted it is hardly possible to contemplate a graver ethical problem than this one of drunkenness, affecting as it does so prejudicially the individual, the family, the community, and the commonwealth.

SUMMARY OF THE FOREGOING STATISTICS.

	Numbers.	Cost and Loss.
1. Annual Mortality . . .	‡ 50,000	£10,000,000
2. Sickness and Unemployment .	..	£3,000,000
3. Law and Justice . . .	..	£860,000
4. Police	⊙ 273,000 † 62,400	£2,000,000
5. Pauperism	* 541,700	£7,389,000
6. Pauper Lunacy . . .	= 34,000	£1,200,000
7. Prisons	‖ 17,000	£620,790
8. Cost of collecting Excise and Customs Duties . . .	..	£2,130,800
		£27,200,590

‡ Value of each life £200. ⊙ Apprehensions. † Police Force. * Paupers. = Pauper Lunatics in daily population. ‖ Daily population.

4. Responsibility in drunkenness: anomalies of the Civil and Criminal Law.—There would be no responsibility if intoxication following one bout were recognized as temporary insanity, or, after many bouts, with resultant organic disease of the brain, nervous system, and the bodily viscera (liver, lungs, kidneys, etc.), as something more than temporary insanity. The civil law is inclined to throw its shield over the drunkard; the criminal law, while not now in practice considering drunkenness an aggravation, does not consider it an excuse, in spite of the fact that the sale of drink is unfettered; it will step in to save the drunkard only when grave crimes are committed, and then (until quite recently) only to punish him with the view of reforming him and deterring others—the latter a vain delusion, as people do not drink to commit crimes. Crime is an accident of the intoxicated state. A crime of violence is not in the drunkard's thoughts at the start, and, after inhibition has gone and intoxication is established, the idea of deterrence for him is as absurd as the notion that he had any true conception of his conduct. In 1843 the Bench of Judges laid down the law for England in regard to all forms of insanity, to the effect that to establish a defence it must be proved that, at the time of committing the act, the accused was labouring under such a defect of reason of the mind as not to know the nature and quality of his act, or, in other words, as not to know that he was doing wrong. Accepting in relation to responsibility the test thus laid down, it must be apparent to the most ordinary observer that the intoxicated authors of crime (especially homicide, serious assaults, cruelty to children, etc.), and therefore of 80 per cent of all crimes (minor and petty offences due to drink are excluded in this connexion) implying violence and recklessness, would not be held responsible, and would either be dealt with as persons insane at the time of committal, or in the public interest would be detained in prison for long periods because of the drunkenness which led to the injury. In either case society would be protected against such potentially dangerous elements detected in its midst, and justice would be fully satisfied. But what of the drunkards *in posse*? Do they take warning from those *in esse*? Not at all. Later, in 1886, Justice Day said: 'Whatever the cause of the unconsciousness, a person not knowing the nature and quality of his act is irresponsible for it.' The existing law recognizes that, if the drunkenness has not been voluntarily induced, responsibility has not been incurred. But who is to decide when drunkenness is voluntary? A ruling which has been viewed with much satisfaction was that given by Lord Low at Glasgow in 1891. He expressed his willingness to give the accused the benefit of the belief that there was no malice and no deliberation, but that he committed the crime while maddened by strong drink. While that was sufficient to take the case out of the category of murder, it still left the charge of culpable homicide. There have been several recent rulings of quite another kind in the United Kingdom; and the 'wilful' nature of the crime, as well as the 'voluntarily' induced state of mind, has been much dwelt upon. The United States legal view is well put by an eminent New York jurist, Clark Bell, when he states that

'the better rule of law undoubtedly now is that if the person at the time of the commission of the act was unconscious and incapable of reflection or memory by intoxication, he could not be convicted. There must be motive and intention.'

Before leaving the 'wilful' nature of the crime and the 'voluntarily' induced state of mind, it may with reason be asked, Do such cases admit of other interpretations? Might it not be argued, both on its own merits and in the light of more enlightened judicial rulings, (1) whether a man drunk can legally do a wilful act; (2) whether at any stage of a habitual or periodic drunkard's bout the drinking was 'voluntary,' for that would imply the certainty of the absence of latent or patent physical and mental degeneration; and (3) whether, admitting, as in the case of the occasional drunkard, that the imbibing of a moderate quantity was 'voluntary,' the moment inhibition is sufficiently impaired—sooner in some than in others, by reason of temperament and habit, by a partial paralysis of the higher nerve centres by the toxic agents—further drinking, leading up to the paroxysmal and frenzied states revealed *ad nauseam* in our criminal courts, becomes 'involuntary.' And these seem cases where a plea of 'insane at the time' would be a good and valid one, or the resultant crime would be reduced from murder of the first degree.

The anomalies which emerge when the civil and criminal laws are examined in regard to drunkenness are remarkable. As the capacity to perform intelligently an important act is liable to be seriously impaired, the plea of intoxication is admissible to vitiate civil acts. Witnesses in civil as well as in criminal trials, when visibly under the influence of drink, have been asked by judges to stand down; or, if they are permitted to give evidence, it is properly discounted. In Scotland an intoxicated prisoner's declaration is considered invalid. In England, the Lord Chancellor acting in Lunacy may, if an inquiry in lunacy has established that any one has been unable to manage his affairs through confirmed intoxication, take the person and property into his custody. Wills are voidable if made when the testator is drunk, whether the bout indulged in be by a casual or a habitual drunkard. Property sold or disposed of under such conditions may be followed by restitution when sobriety is attained. Contracts are now also voidable when the law discovers that the drunkenness was connived at by the other party for purposes of fraud. They become valid if ratified when sober. Intoxication implies incapacity to consent, and a contract involves the mutual agreement of two minds, so that, if one party has no mind to agree, he cannot make a valid contract. It is not a question of two sober persons differing in bargaining astuteness. This will always be; but it is different when one of the two is drunk. In the United States it is held that, if the bargaining is fair and free from fraud and not over-reaching, it will stand, even although one of the parties was intoxicated. The Judicial Committee of the Privy Council, in a Canadian case, held that the present view taken of drunkenness rendered habitual drunkenness a sufficient ground for setting aside paternal rights. In British law it has been ruled that, if either party to a marriage had been so far under the influence of drink as not to understand the nature and consequences of the act, proof of this would render the act invalid. It is presumed in such a case that there was no consummation. Thus, to all intents and purposes, the civil law shields the drunkard from the consequences of civil acts, testamentary dispositions, and contracts made in a state of intoxication—thus practically admitting the condition as one of *non compos mentis* for the time being.

5. **Legislation affecting drunkenness.**—(1) *Great Britain.*—In Great Britain, the Legislature, stimulated by Reports of Royal and Departmental Commissions on Licensing, Poor Law, the Feeble-minded, and Habitual Offenders and Inebriates, has in recent years done a good deal with the object of removing temptation in congested slum areas. For the casual drunkard, the laws provide slight penal treatment involving a few days in prison or a small fine, for the payment of which time may be allowed by the Stipendiary, Justice, or Magistrate before imprisonment takes effect; or the offender may be liberated after imprisonment by part payment of the fine equivalent to the time still to be served in prison, the partial fine being provided by friends or by his own labour. For the reformation and protection of habitual drunkards, many of whom are feeble-minded, mentally unstable, and degenerate, the punishment meted out to 'casuals' is, in the vast majority of cases, applied to them, and only in a very few cases after conviction are the habituals sent to Certified or State Reformatories. The latter, maintained solely by the State, receive the worst, although not necessarily less reformable (the refractory and intractable), cases; the former, with its semi-penal atmosphere, the quieter and more hopeful cases, who for misconduct and insubordination may be transferred to the latter. The inmates, on cause shown, may be transferred from one to the other by order of the Secretary of State. The State Reformatories are supported by Government grants, the Certified by local rates and Treasury subventions; but, down to the time of writing, neither has been the success anticipated, or anything like it, owing to the working of the Acts. Stipendiaries and Magistrates have taken little advantage of the Act of 1898 as to Certified Reformatories, and, when they have taken advantage of it, they have hitherto selected wholly unpromising material in many cases. As regards cases suitable for the State Reformatories, Sheriffs and County Court Judges have not availed themselves of the power conferred upon them. There is also a reluctance, on rating grounds, on the part of local authorities, singly or in combination, to build Certified Reformatories, or to contribute to the support of those in existence. To the Legislature the public must look for amendments of the Acts of 1879, 1888, and 1898, the serious defects of which experience has shown to exist. A change is clamantly urged, so that the law may become effective, and not, what it is, practically a dead letter. Further compulsion is also required in regard to well-to-do habitual and periodic drunkards (dipsomaniacs), under the Acts of 1879 and 1888, who do not come under the notice of the police, in order that they may enter licensed Retreats. The effect of compulsion would certainly be that many such habituals now fully qualified for segregation and treatment would enter these Retreats voluntarily in terms of the law as it is at present, and would thus be saved from themselves, while their families and substance would be protected against folly and prodigality of the worst kind, which a century ago could be promptly met by interdiction. The Act of 1898 makes voluntary entrance easier, in so far as the signature of the applicant need only be attested by one Justice instead of two, as formerly. The *institut* of the family council, known to French, Canadian, and Jersey laws, would be, for Great Britain, a step in the right direction.

(2) *America.*—The United States passed the first Inebriate Act in 1854, under which patients could enter a Retreat either voluntarily or by order of the Committee of the Habitual Drunkard. In 1867, King's County, N.Y., established a Home. Entrance was voluntary or by order of the Trustees of the Home, who were empowered to visit the County jail and select fit subjects. Further, on the report of a Commission of Inquiry to the effect that any person was a habitual drunkard, and incapable of managing his or her affairs, a Justice could commit to the Home such person for one year. The Home received 12 per cent of licence monies. In 1892 a Home for alcoholic and drug females was set up in Manhattan Island. The victims of either habit were admitted voluntarily or under compulsion. When compulsion was resorted to, two medical certificates were necessary and the order of a Judge, who could call for affidavits or take proof. In 1867 the Washington Home, Chicago, was erected. This Home received, till expiry of original sentence, any person convicted of drunkenness or any misdemeanour occasioned thereby. In the same year the Pennsylvania Sanitorium opened its doors. When there was no Committee of the Habitual Drunkard, the institution could receive him on presentation, by his guardian or friend, of the certificates of two doctors attested by a judicial officer. In Connecticut, in 1874, the Court of Probate, on the application of a majority of the Select men of the town, could order an inquiry as to the allegation of habitual drunkenness arising from drink or drugs. This is the first reference to the need for investigating judicially the pernicious drug habit—unfortunately a growing one in every civilized country. If habitual drunkenness was proved, the patient was conveyed to an inebriate asylum for a period of from 4 to 12 months; if dipsomania, for 3 years. The dipsomaniac was thus viewed in a worse light than the other. Superior courts had the right to interfere and discharge at any time. In New Jersey the application of a 'voluntary' requires to be attested by one Justice, or the applicant may present himself at the Home, and fill up a form, which is as binding as when attested by a Justice. A person drunk when received may, on becoming sober, sign a valid and binding application. The Massachusetts Home has accommodation for 200 patients. If one is unable to pay for maintenance, the Municipality may be called upon to meet the cost. Fort Hamilton Home, Brooklyn, is the principal institution receiving pauper inebriates. Although there is, on the whole, fairly good legislation in the United States in the interests of inebriates who are either well or comfortably off in the matter of resources, there is, as in Great Britain, practically no provision made for the impecunious, except for those falling into the hands of the police, and for them the provision is miserably inadequate.

(3) *British Colonies.*—(*a*) *Canada.*—Nearly all the Provincial Legislatures have enacted effective measures for habitual inebriety. Ontario in 1873 passed an Act to set up a Home for voluntary and involuntary inmates—the term of stay not to exceed 12 months. A petition is presented to the Judge by relatives or, in default, by friends, to the effect that the patient cannot control himself or his affairs; the Judge grants a hearing; a copy of the petition is served on the habitual drunkard; the Judge summons witnesses; he can interrogate the drunkard, who has the right to call as well as to examine witnesses; the Judge forwards his decision and a copy of the evidence to the Provincial Secretary, who directs removal to a Home. In Quebec, in 1870, an Act was passed to provide for the interdiction and cure of habitual drunkards. Any Judge of the Superior Court of Lower Canada can pronounce interdiction, and can appoint

a curator to manage the drunkard's affairs, and control his person as in interdiction for insanity. A family council is called by the Judge to investigate the truth of allegations, and a petition is served on the alleged 'habitual,' who may be relieved of interdiction after one year's sobriety and regain civil rights. Wilful and knowing sale of drink to the interdicted is finable and punishable. The curator, sometimes termed the guardian, may place his charge or ward in any licensed Home, and may remove him at any time. The Quebec Province law of interdiction closely resembles what obtained in Scotland 100 years ago, but fell into desuetude, although there are competent authorities who say it could, without statutory enactment, be revived again. In Manitoba the petition is presented by a public officer. There is much to be said for the creation of such an official, as relatives are often placed in an invidious position, and will not move. Relatives and neighbours are summoned and put on oath. The interdicted may be confined in any place the Judge may think proper, and be visited once a month by a County Sheriff. While interdiction lasts, bargains, sales, and contracts made are null and void. The interdicted may be discharged and re-vested after proof of 12 months' abstinence.

(*b*) *Australia.*—In 1874 the Legislature of South Australia set up a Home at Adelaide, and voted £3000. Voluntary admission could be obtained for 12 months on application of the 'habitual' to any Justice. For involuntary admission, application was made by relatives or friends. The inebriate could be summoned before a Judge or special Magistrate or two Justices, and requested to show cause why he should not be committed to a Retreat for 12 months. Whether present at, or absent from, the trial to which he has been invited, if it is proved that he is an inebriate, he can be sent to the Retreat. Two medical certificates are necessary. In Victoria, the legal machinery, like the provision made, is much the same, except that for voluntary entrants only one Justice is required. In New South Wales there are two kinds of Homes—one for those who can pay, the other a mixed penitentiary and inebriate asylum for quasi-criminal offenders.

(*c*) *New Zealand.*—Admission is either voluntary or involuntary. Residence is in a ward or division of a lunatic asylum, quite apart from the insane. Great difficulties, as might be looked for, have been experienced in complying with this part of statutory requirement, and special accommodation has long been considered urgent.

6. Prophylaxis and therapeutics.—One of the few hopeful features of the drink problem is the gradual diminution in the use of alcohol in society and in the treatment of disease in hospitals and in private practice, until now it is at the vanishing point as a drug, stimulant, or tissue-builder. In 7 of the principal London Hospitals from 1872 to 1902, although the daily resident population has varied little, the expenditure on alcohol has fallen *62 per cent.* No less striking and satisfactory are the figures for the Wandsworth Union, in which the number of inmates, inclusive of the sick, has increased 288 per cent, while the spirit bill has fallen from £371 to £2, 7s. Equally interesting are the figures for the Hospitals of the Metropolitan Asylum Board for 1894 to 1905. The total under treatment for 'fevers' rose from 19,900 to 27,160, or 36 per cent, while the cost of stimulants fell *63 per cent*, from £1388 to £515. The same tale could be told of every hospital in the land; and it is especially significant, since the fall is the outcome of the best clinical experience and scientific research. In surgical wards of hospitals and in maternities, patients operated upon rarely get alcohol, except for 'shock' and severe hæmorrhage, especially *post-partum* (Dr. W. L. Reid, Glasgow), and in these directions alcohol is being superseded by other and better substitutes.

During a drinking bout numerous untoward or fatal accidents may occur, viz. gastritis (inflammation of stomach, which is perhaps the least to be feared, as the poison may be rejected), retention of urine, suffocation resulting from the position of the body (head resting on the chest), coma (when death takes place from deep toxic narcosis), exposure, drowning, or bodily injuries. Apoplexy is frequently mistaken for drunken coma, the person with the apoplectic seizure, it may be, smelling of alcohol.

In regard to treatment, something requires to be said of what one might term orthodox medical treatment, and of the many puffed 'secret cures,' freely advertised, regardless of expense, of which only the rich can avail themselves. Before admittance into any of the Homes in which the 'secret' cure is practised, a bargain is struck, and a big sum of money is paid down. Benevolence or philanthropy does not enter into the matter. The nature of the remedy, so far as the vendor is concerned, is kept 'secret.' But there is no secret about it, as nearly all such remedies have been analyzed by competent chemists, and their contents are known. As a rule, the composition of the best of them in no way differs from the composition of those prescribed by physicians who act for the good of the drunkard, and have no interest in the profits from the sale of the remedies.

Strychnine, atropine, nux-vomica, hyoscine, bromides, quinine, digitalis, capsicum, and apomorphia for sleeplessness, in very minute doses, are the chief ingredients of the physician's prescription, as they are of many of the 'secret' remedies; and they are said to create a distaste for alcohol by restoring and bracing up the tissues to a healthy state. If by any of the remedies that are really 'quack' a cure is said to have been effected, the 'cure' is by 'suggestion,' which sometimes is of good effect when aided by long abstinence, by the tonics alluded to, and by healthy regimen, employment, and recreation.

LITERATURE. — Allbutt-Rolleston, *System of Medicine*, London, 1910; A. Baer, *Der Alcoholismus*, Berlin, 1878, *Ueber Trunksucht*, Berlin, 1880; Thomas Barlow, in *Brit. Med. Journ.* 1905; James Barr, 'Alcohol as a Therapeutic Agent,' *ib.*; Charles Booth, *Pauperism and the Endowment of Old Age*, London, 1892; T. Lauder Brunton, *The Action of Medicines*, London, 1897; John Burns, *Labour and Drink*, London, 1904; T. S. Clouston, *Unsoundness of Mind*, London, 1911; T. D. Crothers, *Diseases of Inebriety*, New York, 1893; W. T. Gairdner, *Morison Lectures*, Edin. 1890; A. Hill, *Primer of Physiology*, London, 1902; Victor Horsley and M. D. Sturge, *Alcohol and the Human Body*, London, 1907; R. Jones, *Evidence before Dep. Com. on Physical Deterioration*, London, 1904; T. N. Kelynack, *The Alcohol Problem in its Biological Aspect*, London, 1906; N. Kerr, *Inebriety, its Etiology*, etc.[3], London, 1894; M. Legrain, *Dégénérescence sociale et alcoolisme*, Paris, 1895; W. Bevan Lewis, *Textbook of Mental Diseases*[2], London, 1899; J. Macpherson, *Morison Lectures*, Edin. 1905; T. A. M'Nicholl, 'A Study of the Effect of Alcohol on School Children,' in *Med. Temp. Rev.*, 1905; V. Magnan, *Alcoolisme*, Paris, 1874, and *Recherches sur les centres nerveux*, Paris, 1876 and 1893; H. Maudsley, *Heredity, Variation and Genius*, London, 1908; F. W. Mott, *Alcohol and Insanity*, 1906, and 'Heredity and Disease,' in *Brit. Med. Journ.* 1905; A. Newsholme, *Elements of Vital Statistics*[3], London, 1899; C. F. Palmer, *Inebriety*, London, 1896; Archdall Reid, *Principles of Heredity*, London, 1906, and *Alcoholism; Study in Heredity*, do. 1901; Rowntree-Sherwell, *Temperance Problem*[9], do. 1901, App. p. 465; G. H. Savage, *Increase of Insanity*, London, 1907; E. A. Schäfer, *Textbook of Physiology*, Edin. 1898–1900; P. Smith, Address to British Med. Assoc., 1900; E. H. Starling, *Elements of Human Physiology*[4], London, 1900; J. Steeg, *Les Dangers de l'alcoolisme*[3], Paris, 1901; J. F. Sutherland, artt. 'Recidivism,' in *Journ. of Ment. Science*, 1908–9, 'Jurisprudence of Intoxication,' in *Edinburgh Juridical Rev.*, 1898, 'The Insanities of Inebriety' (legislative and medico-legal standpoints), read to Brit. Med. Assoc., 1898, *Urgency of Legislation for Well-to-do Inebriates*, 1899, and 'Crime from the Economic, Sociological, Statistical, and Psychological Standpoints,' *Trans. Brit. Assoc.*, 1892; A. Taillefer, *L'Alcoolisme et ses dangers*, Paris, 1904; J. E. Usher, *Alcoholism and its Treatment*,

London, 1892; G. S. Woodhead, *Recent Researches in Action of Alcohol in Health and Sickness*, London, 1904; see also Registrar-General's Returns; Judicial Statistics; Reports of Inebriate Retreats and Reformatories, of Prisons, of Local Government Boards (Pauperism), of Lunacy Commissions; Report of Sel. Com. on Habitual Drunkards, 1872; Report of Eng. Dep. Com. on Treatment of Inebriates, 1893; Report of Scot. Dep. Com. on Habitual Offenders, Inebriates, etc., 1895; Report of Dep. Com. (Eng.) on Inebriates and their Detention in Reformatories, 1908; Report of Dep. Com. (Scot.) 1909; Report of Roy. Com. on Licensing, 1899; Report of Brit. Med. Assoc. Whisky Com. 1903; Report of Roy. Com. on Care and Control of Feeble-minded, 1908; Report of Com. on Physical Deterioration, 1904.

J. F. SUTHERLAND.

DRUSES.—See SECTS (Christian).

DRYADS.—See HAMADRYADS.

DUALISM.

DUALISM.—The term 'dualism' appears for the first time in Thomas Hyde's *Hist. religionis veterum Persarum* (*e.g.* cap. 9, p. 164), published in 1700, and is there applied to a system of thought according to which there exists an Evil Being co-ordinate and co-eternal with the primal Good. The word was employed in the same sense by Bayle (cf. art. 'Zoroastre,' in his *Dict.*, ed. Paris, 1820) and Leibniz (in his *Théodicée*; cf. Erdmann's ed., Berlin, 1839–40, pp. 547*b*, 565*a*). It was then transferred from the sphere of ethics and religion to that of metaphysics by Christian Wolff (1679–1754). Wolff applies the term 'dualists' to those who regard body and soul as mutually independent substances,[1] and contrasts such thinkers with the monists, who would derive the totality of the real either from matter alone or from spirit alone. The Wolffian usage of the term is now by far the most generally recognized, although we still sometimes find the word applied to certain theories in ethics, epistemology, and the philosophy of religion.

In its application to the relation between soul and body, spirit and Nature, the term 'dualism' recalls a problem which goes back to a very early period, and which has received various solutions in the evolution of human thought. Among the ancient Greeks the tendency was to bring the physical and the psychical into very close relations with each other. Thus their philosophy begins with a naive monism—hylozoism; and, in particular, their artistic achievement reveals a marvellous harmony of the spiritual and the sensuous. But dualistic tendencies likewise began to manifest themselves at an early stage, as, *e.g.*, in the teaching of the Orphics and Pythagoreans regarding the transmigration of souls—a doctrine which implies that the soul is independent of the body. In philosophy, however, it was Anaxagoras (*q.v.*) who first explicitly disengaged spirit or mind (*νοῦς*) from matter, setting the former, as the simple, the pure, the unmixed, in opposition to the latter;[2] and we may, therefore, speak of Anaxagoras as the first philosophical dualist. But the dualistic mode of thought finds its most magnificent expression in the philosophy of Plato, with its rigid separation of the world of Ideas from the manifold of sense. Aristotle, on the other hand, inclines rather towards monism, as appears from his definition of the soul as the entelechy of the body.[3] But his conception of the spirit (*νοῦς*) as something added to the process of Nature from without, and separable from the body, bears an unmistakably dualistic character.[1] It is certainly true that in the later period of the ancient world the Stoics advocated a monistic hypothesis, bringing force and matter (*δραστικὸν καὶ ὑλικόν*) into close connexion with each other, and affirming the material nature of all reality; but when, in the further evolution of ancient social life, the old ideals began to lose their fervour, and the dark and painful aspects of experience more and more engaged the minds of men, and when, above all, dire moral perplexities began to be felt, matter gradually came to be regarded as something obstructive and evil—something from which the individual must try his best to deliver himself. Thus arose the ascetic ideal of life, and, hand in hand with it, a rigid dualism. Accordingly we find that the last great system of ancient thought, that of Plotinus, is pervaded by a vehement disparagement of sensuous matter, while the intelligible world and the world of sense are set in rigorous opposition to each other. See, further, the 'Greek' section of this article.

Christianity, in its essential principles, has no affinity with a dualism of this kind. Looking upon all that exists as the handiwork of God, it cannot regard matter as something unworthy. Its firm contention is that the source of evil lies, not in matter, but in voluntary action, in the apostasy of spiritual beings from God. Another element which militates against the dualistic tendency is the fact that in Christianity the body ranks as an essential constituent of human nature, as is shown, in particular, by the doctrine of a bodily resurrection. Notwithstanding these facts, however, Greek and Oriental dualism forced their way into the early Church on a wide scale, and, as appears from the prevalence of asceticism (see ASCETICISM [Christian]), gained a vast influence over the Christian mind. As we might expect, its grasp was still further strengthened by the Platonism which prevailed in the first half of the mediæval period. On the other hand, the ascendancy of the Aristotelian philosophy in the culminating stages of mediæval thought was, in the domain of natural science, rather favourable to monism, since it did not permit of any hard and fast antagonism between body and soul. But the Aristotelian view at length underwent a certain modification, in so far as the champions of mediæval Aristotelianism, Albertus Magnus and Thomas Aquinas, held that the vegetative and animal faculties of the soul, which Aristotle himself assigned wholly to the body, are conditioned by the bodily organs only in their *temporal* functions, and therefore also share in the immortality of the spirit. This view was officially recognized as the doctrine of the

[1] *Psychologia Rationalis*, Frankfort, 1732, § 39: 'Dualistae sunt, qui et substantiarum materialium et immaterialium existentiam admittunt.'

[2] Cf. *e.g.* Aristotle, *Metaph.* i. 8 (Bekker, p. 989*b*, 14): φησὶ δ' εἶναι μεμιγμένα πάντα πλὴν τοῦ νοῦ, τοῦτον δὲ ἀμιγῆ μόνον καὶ καθαρόν; *Phys.* viii. 5 (256*b*, 24): διὸ καὶ Ἀναξαγόρας ὀρθῶς λέγει, τὸν νοῦν ἀπαθῆ, φάσκων καὶ ἀμιγῆ εἶναι, ἐπειδήπερ κινήσεως ἀρχὴν αὐτὸν ποιεῖ εἶναι· οὕτω γὰρ ἂν μόνως κινοίη ἀκίνητος ὢν καὶ κρατοίη ἀμιγὴς ὤν; *de Anima*, i. 2 (405*a*, 13): Ἀναξαγόρας δ' ἔοικε μὲν ἕτερον λέγειν ψυχήν τε καὶ νοῦν, χρῆται δ' ἀμφοῖν ὡς μιᾷ φύσει, πλὴν ἀρχήν γε τὸν νοῦν τίθεται μάλιστα πάντων μόνον νοῦν φησὶν αὐτὸν τῶν ὄντων ἁπλοῦν εἶναι καὶ ἀμιγῆ τε καὶ καθαρόν.

[3] *De Anima*, ii. 1 (412*b*, 4): εἰ δή τι κοινὸν ἐπὶ πάσης ψυχῆς δεῖ λέγειν, εἴη ἂν ἐντελέχεια ἡ πρώτη σώματος φυσικοῦ ὀργανικοῦ.

[1] Cf. *de Animal. Gen.* ii. 3 (736*b*, 27): λείπεται δὲ τὸν νοῦν μόνον θύραθεν ἐπεισιέναι καὶ θεῖον εἶναι μόνον· οὐδὲν γὰρ αὐτοῦ τῇ ἐνεργείᾳ κοινωνεῖ σωματικὴ ἐνέργεια; *de Anima*, ii. 2 (413*b*, 25): ἔοικε (*scil.* ὁ νοῦς) ψυχῆς γένος ἕτερον εἶναι, καὶ τοῦτο μόνον ἐνδέχεται χωρίζεσθαι καθάπερ τὸ ἀΐδιον τοῦ φθαρτοῦ.

Catholic Church by the Council of Vienne (A.D. 1311).

Modern philosophy, as inaugurated by Descartes (*q.v.*), opened with an unqualified dualism. The conceptions of matter and mind were now for the first time precisely defined, and clearly distinguished from each other. Descartes' definition of body and soul respectively as *substantia extensa* and *substantia cogitans* obviously made it impossible to bring the two under a single concept, since the 'thinking substance' is stated to be absolutely indivisible, while the spatially extended substance is capable of infinite division. Body and soul have thus no internal principle of unity, but are simply joined together by the will of God. A distinction so absolute could not, of course, remain permanently unchallenged, but it sufficed at least to put an end to the hitherto prevailing confusion between the physical and the psychological interpretation of phenomena, and made it henceforth necessary to explain Nature by Nature, and the psychical by the psychical. The natural sciences, in particular, had suffered serious detriment from a theory which explained physical and physiological processes—more especially the formation, growth, and nutriment of organic bodies—as immediately due to the workings of the soul; for, of course, the practice of tracing natural phenomena to psychical causes stood in the way of all advance in exact science, and it was the dualism of Descartes, with its precise delimitation of concepts, that first brought such advance within the range of possibility.

This dualism maintained its ground as the dominant hypothesis of the period of Illumination, and Wolff himself claimed unequivocally to be a dualist. But Descartes' accentuation of the antithesis between mind and matter evoked an endeavour to bridge the gulf in some way, and to find some explanation of the connexion that actually obtains. Descartes himself manifests this striving in his doctrine that the physical and the psychical have their point of contact in the pineal gland; and further instances are found in occasionalism, with its belief that material and spiritual processes are maintained in mutual harmony by Divine agency; in the system of Spinoza, who regarded the two great divisions of phenomena as the attributes of a single substance; and in Leibniz's doctrine of monads, which derives all reality from spirit, and explains the body as simply a congeries of souls.

A defection from the prevailing belief in dualism, however, ensued only with the break-up of the Illumination and the emergence of new currents of thought. Various factors combined to make a stand against it. First of all, the movement towards an artistic interpretation of life and a more natural conception of reality—as found alike in the neo-humanism represented by Goethe and in romanticism—intensified the need of an inherent connexion between Nature and spirit, the sensuous and the non-sensuous. Then came the speculative philosophy of Germany, with its interpretation of all reality as but the evolution of spiritual life.[1] But the most potent factor of all was modern science, which demonstrated in countless ways the dependence of psychical life upon the body and bodily conditions, alike in the experience of the individual and throughout the entire range of organic being. This forms the starting-point of the theory which with special emphasis now claims the name of monism, and rejects everything in the nature of a self-sustained psychical life. Nevertheless, as has been well said by so eminent a contemporary thinker as Wundt, this monism is in essence simply a reversion to the hylozoism of the Ionic philosophers: and it is certainly open to doubt whether the question is quite as simple as monists make out, and whether the entire intellectual movement of centuries has, in so fundamental a problem, been barren of all result, as monists must perforce maintain. This point will be further dealt with, however, in the article MONISM; and it need only be said meanwhile that it is one thing to think of the world as in the last resort sundered into absolutely diverse provinces, and quite another to regard human experience as embracing different starting-points and different movements, which can be brought into closer relations only by degrees and in virtue of progressive intellectual effort. It is impossible that dualism should constitute the final phase of human thought; but, in view of such consummation, it has an important function to perform, viz. to put obstacles in the way of a premature synthesis, and to insist upon a full recognition of the antitheses actually present in human experience. Dualism, in virtue of its precise definition of concepts, acts as a corrective to that confusion into which monism so easily lapses; and, to realize the value of such a rôle, we need but recall the aphorism of Bacon: 'veritas potius emergit ex errore quam ex confusione.'

[1] Cf., *e.g.*, Fichte, *Werke*, iv. 373: 'One who in any wise admits the existence of a material world, though only along with and beside the spiritual—dualism as they call it—is no philosopher.'

LITERATURE.—R. Eisler, *Wörterbuch der philos. Begriffe*[3], Berlin, 1900, *s.v.* 'Dualismus'; L. Stein, *Dualismus oder Monismus? Eine Untersuchung über die doppelte Wahrheit*, Berlin, 1909; R. Eucken, *Geistige Strömungen der Gegenwart*[4], Leipzig, 1909, p. 170ff. (an English translation will appear shortly).

R. EUCKEN.

DUALISM (American).—The view which has obtained in several quarters, that an ethical dualism exists in the religions of many of the American Indian tribes, is a wholly mistaken one. No ethical contrast existed in the native mind between those deities who assisted man and those who were actively hostile to him; and it has been made abundantly clear that such dualistic ideas as have been found connected with other religious conceptions of American Indian peoples owe their origin to contact with the whites. The view that dualism did exist arose from the misconceptions of early missionaries, assisted in many instances by the mistranslation of native words.

'The idea that the Creeks know anything of a devil is an invention of the missionaries' (Gatschet, *op. cit. infra*, i. 216). 'The Hidatsa believe neither in a hell nor a devil' (Matthews, *op. cit. infra*, p. xxii).

In some cases the same word which the missionaries have employed to translate 'devil' they have been compelled to use to render 'spirit.' The early missionaries regarded the gods of the Indians as devils, and taught their converts to look upon them as such, but in some cases the natives disagreed with their teachers, attempting to explain to them that their deities were the bringers of all good things, and by no means evil. This, of course, implied not that their gods were 'good' in the ethical sense, that they loved righteousness and hated iniquity, but that they conferred on man the merely material blessings necessary to savage existence. Winslow, in his *Good News from New England* (1622), says that the Indians worship a good power called Kiehtan, and another 'who, as farre as wee can conceive, is the Devill,' named Hobbamock, or Hobbamoqui. The former of those names is merely the word 'great' in the Algonquin language, and is probably an abbreviation of *Kittanitowit*, the 'Great Manitou'—a vague term mentioned by Williams and other early writers, and in all probability manufactured by them (see Duponceau, *Langues de l'Amérique du Nord*). On the other hand, the god whom Winslow likens to the power of evil was, in fact, a deity whose special function was the cure of diseases;

he was also a protector in dreams, and is explained by Jarvis as 'the *Oke*, or tutelary deity, which each Indian worships.'

In the religious conceptions of some tribes the same god is both 'good' and 'evil,' in the sense that he distributes equally joy and sorrow. Thus Jurupari, worshipped by the Uapes of Brazil, is the name for the supernatural in general, from which all things come, good and evil. In the majority of American religions, however, the supreme deity is 'good' in a purely material sense. Thus Aka-Kanet, sometimes mentioned as the father of evil in the mythology of the Araucans of Chile, is, in reality, a benign power throned in the Pleiades, who sends fruits and flowers to the earth. In the same way the Supay of the Peruvians and the Mictla of the Nahuatlacans were not embodiments of the evil principle, but simply gods of the dead, corresponding to the classical Pluto. The Jesuit missionaries rarely distinguish between good and evil deities, when speaking of the religions of the northern tribes; and the Moravian Brethren, writing of the Algonquins and Iroquois, state that 'the idea of a devil, a prince of darkness, they first received in later times through the Europeans.'

'I have never been able to discover from the Dakotas themselves,' writes the Rev. G. H. Pond, a missionary to them for eighteen years, 'the least degree of evidence that they divide the gods into classes of good and evil, and am persuaded that those persons who represent them as doing so do it inconsiderately, and because it is so natural to subscribe to a long-cherished popular opinion' (*ap.* Schoolcraft, *Indian Tribes*, p. 642).

Myths have arisen in several Indian mythologies since the tribes in whose religions they occur have come into contact with Europeans. In these myths the concepts of good and evil, as known to civilized nations, are introduced; and several myths have been altered to bring the older conceptions into line with the newly-introduced idea of dualism. The comparatively late introduction of such views finds remarkable confirmation in the myths of the Kiche (Quiché) of Guatemala, which are recorded in the *Popol Vuh*, a compilation of native myths made by a Christianized Kiche scribe of the 17th century. Dimly conscious, perhaps, that his version of these myths was coloured by the opinions of a lately-adopted Christianity, he says of the Lords of Xibalba, the rulers of the Kiche Hades: 'In the old times they did not have much power. They were but annoyers and opposers of men, and, in truth, they were not regarded as gods.' Speaking of the Mayas, Cogolludo says: 'The devil is called by them Xibilba,' the derivation of which name is from a root meaning 'to fear'; it relates to the fear inseparable from the idea of death, and has no connexion in any way with the idea of evil in the abstract. The gods of the American Indians, like those of other savages, are too anthropomorphic in their nature, too entirely savage themselves, to partake of higher ethical qualities. Personal spite or tribal feuds may render some more inimical than others, but always purely from self-interest, and not through a love of evil for evil's sake. Some, again, favour man, but always from similar motives, and not from any purely ethical sense of virtue.

LITERATURE.—D. G. Brinton, *Myths of the New World* (3rd ed. revised), Philadelphia, 1905; A. S. Gatschet, *Migration Legend of the Creek Indians*, Philadelphia, 1884; P. S. Duponceau, *Langues de l'Amérique du Nord*, Paris, 1838; Jarvis, 'Discourse on the Religion of the Ind. Tribes of N. America' (in the *Trans. of N.Y. Hist. Soc.*, 1819); G. H. Loskiel, *Gesch. der Miss. der evang. Brüder*, Barby, 1789; Schoolcraft, *Indian Tribes*, Philadelphia, 1851–59; L. Spence, *Popol Vuh*, London, 1908; W. Matthews, *Grammar of the Hidatsa*, New York, 1873.

LEWIS SPENCE.

DUALISM (Celtic).—Little or nothing is known to us of the religion of the ancient Celts as an ethical religion. The references to it in classical writers, the evidence of inscriptions, the Welsh and Irish texts, and the witness of folk-survivals reveal it almost wholly as a Nature-religion. To some extent the dualism which is more or less present in all Nature-religions characterized Celtic mythology, but how far it was also an ethical dualism is quite obscure. As the religion of a people who were largely engaged in agriculture, there was a cult of divinities and spirits of growth and fertility whose power and influence might be aided by magical ritual. Opposed to growth and fertility were blight, disease, and death, the evidence of which was seen in pestilence, in bad seasons, and in the desolation of winter. As growth and fertility were the work of beneficent deities, so those evils were probably regarded as brought about by personal agencies of a supernatural and evil character. The drama of Nature showed that the sun was sometimes vanquished by cloud and storm, though it soon renewed its vigour; that summer with all its exuberant life died at the coming of winter, but that it returned again full of vitality; that vegetation perished, but that it revived annually in ample plenitude. But what was true of Nature was true also, in mythology, of the personal and supernatural forces behind it. Beneficent and evil powers were in conflict. Year by year the struggle went on, year by year the gods of growth suffered deadly harm, but appeared again as triumphant conquerors to renew the struggle once more. Myth came to speak of this perennial conflict as having happened once for all, as if some gods had perished in spite of their immortality. But the struggle, nevertheless, went on year by year. The gods might perish, but only for a time. They were immortal; they only seemed to be wounded and to die.

Such a dualistic mythology as this seems to be represented by the euhemerized account of the battles between Fomorians and Tuatha Dé Danann in the Irish texts. Whatever the Fomorians were in origin, whether the gods of aboriginal tribes in Ireland, or of a group of Celtic tribes at war with another group, it is evident that they had come to be regarded as evil and malicious, and could thus be equated with the baneful personages already known to Celtic mythology as hostile to the gods of growth and fertility. It is evident that the Irish Celts possessed a somewhat elaborate mythical rendering of the dualism of Nature, and this seems to survive in the account of the battle or battles of Magtured. But, after the Christianizing of Ireland, the old gods had gradually come to be regarded as kings and warriors, and this euhemerizing process was completed by the annalists. Hence in the account of the battles, while it is evident that in some aspects the hostile forces are more than human, the gods are described as kings and great warriors or as craftsmen. The Fomorians appear as the baneful race, more or less demoniac, inhabiting Ireland before the arrival of the Tuatha Dé Danann. But we also hear of the Firbolgs and other peoples, who are clearly the aboriginal races of Ireland, and whose gods the Fomorians are sometimes said to be. The Tuatha Dé Danann are certainly the gods of the Irish Celts or of some large group of them.

Early Irish literature knew only one battle of Magtured, in which Firbolgs and Fomorians were overthrown together. But in later accounts the battle is duplicated, and the first fight takes place at Magtured in Mayo, and the second at Magtured in Sligo, twenty-seven years after the first. In the first battle the leader of the Tuatha Dé Danann, Nuada, loses his hand, and for this reason the kingdom is temporarily taken from him and given to Bres, the son of a Fomorian by a woman of the Tuatha Dé Danann. There is the usual inconsistency of myth here and elsewhere in these notices. The Tuatha Dé Danann have just landed in Ireland, but already some of them have united with the Fomorians in marriage. This inconsistency escaped the euhemerizing chroniclers, but it clearly points to the fact that Fomorians and Tuatha Dé Danann were supernatural and Divine, not human races successively arriving in

Ireland, and, though in conflict, yet, like conflicting barbarous tribes, occasionally uniting in marriage. The second battle took place on Samhain (Nov. 1st), the festival which began the Celtic winter (see FESTIVALS [Celtic]). Meanwhile the Tuatha Dé Danann had been forced to pay tribute to the Fomorians and to perform menial duties for them, in spite of their having been conquerors. This shows that the euhemerists probably misunderstood the old myths, which may have been known to them only in a garbled form. Myths must have told of the temporary defeat and subjection of the beneficent Nature-gods, followed by their final triumph, not of a subjection after a victory. Following the annalistic account, we find that the exactions demanded by Bres led to discontent. For his niggardliness he was satirized by a poet, and 'nought but decay was on him from that hour.' Meanwhile Nuada had recovered his hand, and Bres was forced to abandon the throne. In grief and anger he went to collect an army from his father, who sent him to Balor and to Indech. These assembled their forces and prepared to attack the Tuatha Dé Danann. In the course of the battle which followed, Indech wounded Ogma (probably a culture-god), and Balor (a personification of the evil eye) slew Nuada, but himself received a mortal wound from Lug (perhaps a sun-god). This put an end to the battle; the Fomorians were routed, and fled to their own part of the country.

Another inconsistency in the euhemerized account is that, while the first battle is fought on Beltane, the beginning of summer, the second is fought on Samhain. One would naturally expect that powers of blight would be represented as vanquished not on a winter but on a summer festival. Perhaps the old myths told of the defeat and subjection of the gods on Samhain, and of their victory over the powers of blight on Beltane.

It is clear that the Fomorians, in their opposition to the Tuatha Dé Danann, and from the sinister character assigned to them in folk-tradition, had come to be regarded in mythology as identical with beings who, to the Celts of Ireland, represented the powers of Nature which were hostile to man and to his gods. Blight, disease, fog, winter, the raging sea, and all influences of evil are personified in the Fomorians. Before them men trembled, yet they were not wholly cast down, for they knew that the bright immortal gods, who gave light and caused growth, were on their side and fought against their enemies.[1]

A similar euhemerized version of old dualistic myths, though presented in a more romantic form, is perhaps to be found in the Welsh story of *Llûdd and Llevelys.*

Llûdd is an old divinity (perhaps the equivalent of the Irish Nuada) who, in this story, figures as a king of Britain. His country is subjected to three plagues: that of the race of the Coranians, who hear every whisper wherever it is spoken; that of a shriek heard all over the island on May Eve, which scares every one, and leaves animals, trees, earth, and water barren; and that of the mysterious disappearance of a year's supply of food. From these three plagues Llevelys by his advice releases Llûdd and his people. He gives him insects which he must bruise in water. Then, having called together his people and the Coranians, he is to throw the water over them. It will poison the Coranians, but do no harm to the men of his own race. The second plague is caused by the attack made on the dragon of the land by a foreign dragon, and Llevelys instructs Llûdd how to capture both. This is done, and Llûdd buries them in a *kistvaen* at Dinas Emreis in Snowdon. The third plague is caused by a mighty magician who, while every one is lulled to sleep by his magic, carries off the store of provisions. Llûdd must, therefore, watch, and, whenever he feels a desire to sleep, must plunge into a cauldron of cold water. Following this advice, he captures and overpowers the magician, who becomes his vassal (Loth, *Mabinogion*, Paris, 1889, i. 173). The Coranians are described in the *Triads* as a hostile race of invaders, and, contrary to this story, they are said never to have left the island (Loth, ii. 256, 274). But the method of getting rid of them, as well as the incidents of the dragons and the magician, shows that we are not dealing with actual tribes. As Rhŷs has shown, they may be a race of dwarfs, their name probably being derived from *córr*, 'dwarf.' They also survive in Welsh folk-belief as a kind of mischievous fairies (*Celtic Heathendom*, London, 1888, p. 606; cf. the Breton dwarf fairies, the *Corr* and *Corrigan*).

The question arises whether there is not here something analogous to the strife of Fomorians and Tuatha Dé Danann. In all three incidents we have a whole realm suffering from plagues; in the last two, fertility and plenty are destroyed, women lose their hope of offspring, animals and vegetation are blighted, and food is stolen away. The dragon plague occurs on May-day (Beltane), and in a *Triad* the plague of the Coranians has its place taken by that of March Malaen from beyond the sea, and is called 'the oppression of the 1st of May.' Rhŷs has pointed out the similarity of *March* to *Morc*, a Fomorian king who levied a tax of two-thirds of their children, corn, and milk on the Nemedians every Samhain eve, and has also shown that *Malaen* is perhaps connected with words denoting something demoniac (*op. cit.* 609).

The incidents of the Welsh story may be based on earlier myths or on ritual customs embodying the belief in powers hostile to growth and fertility and to their gods. Llûdd, like Nuada, is probably a god of growth, and this may be referred to in the tale, not only in the fact that he overcomes beings who cause dearth and barrenness, but in the fact that his generosity and liberality in giving meat and drink to all who sought them are particularly mentioned. It is not clear, however, why the hostility should have been most active on May-day, but this may be a misunderstanding, as in the Irish story, and it is said that the dragons are overcome on May-eve.

It is not unlikely that these dualistic myths were connected with ritual acts. Another romantic Welsh story, based upon an earlier myth, is strongly suggestive of this.

Llûdd had a daughter Creidylad, who was to wed Gwythur, but before the wedding Gwyn abducted her. A fight ensued, in which Gwyn was victorious, forcing one of his antagonists to eat his dead father's heart. On this, King Arthur interfered, and commanded that Creidylad should stay at her father's house, while Gwyn and Gwythur were to fight for her every year on the 1st of May until the Day of Judgment. Then the victor should gain her hand (Loth, i. 269 f.).

The myth on which this story is based may have arisen as explanatory of actual ritual combats in which the beneficent and hurtful powers were represented dramatically. Traces of these ritual combats survived in folk-custom.

Thus, in the Isle of Man on May-day a young girl was made Queen of the May, and was attended by a 'captain' and several other persons. There was also a Queen of Winter and her company. Both parties were symbolically arrayed, and met in mimic combat on the May festival. If the Queen of the May was captured, she was ransomed by her men for a sum of money, which was then spent on a feast in which all joined (Train, *Isle of Man*, Douglas, 1845, ii. 118).

Such mimic fights between human representatives of Summer and Winter are common in European folk-custom, and are survivals from primitive ritual, which was intended magically to assist the beneficent powers of growth in their combat with those of blight and death, while at the same time auguries of the probable fertility of the season were no doubt drawn from the course of the fight (for examples, see Grimm, *Teut. Myth.*, Eng. tr., London, 1880–8, ii. 764 f.; Frazer, *GB*², 1900, ii. 99 f.). The ritual was connected with the dualistic idea of

'a quarrel or war between the two powers of the year. . . . Summer and Winter are at war with one another, exactly like Day and Night; Day and Summer gladden, as Night and Winter vex the world.' In the ritual 'Summer comes off victorious, and Winter is defeated; the people supply, as it were, the chorus of spectators, and break out into praises of the conqueror' (Grimm, 762, 764).

But, as the true meaning and purpose of the ritual were gradually forgotten, the mythical ideas which they dramatized would be expressed differently—in some cases, perhaps, more elaborately. Both myth and ritual of a dualistic kind probably gave rise to the story of Creidylad, the daughter of a god of growth. Nor, indeed, is it impossible that the stories of the battle of Magtured may have owed something to the suggestiveness of those ritual combats. These took place at the beginning of summer, when the vigour of the powers of growth had increased, and that of the powers of blight had as clearly decreased. This, which was regarded as the result of a long combat, was so represented in the ritual and described in myth.

In general the ritual of the Celtic festivals was largely directed to aiding the sun and other powers by which fertility was increased. The bonfire which had so prominent a place on these occasions was a kind of sun-charm (see FESTIVALS [Celtic]). It is probable also that the human victims slain at an earlier time at these festivals, as representatives of the spirit or god of vegetation, were later regarded as sacrifices offered to propitiate the evil powers which arrayed themselves against man and his beneficent deities, unless they were simply regarded as propitiating the latter.

[1] For the account of the battles, see Harl. MS 5280, text and tr. in *RCel* xii. [1891] 59 ff. Cf. d'Arbois de Jubainville, *Cours de litt. celt.*, vol. ii. [Paris, 1884] *passim*; and for the probable original character of the Fomorians, see art. CELTS in vol. iii. p. 282ᵃ.

The activity of hostile powers of blight was naturally greater in winter, and this appears to be referred to both in tales in Irish texts which are the débris of old myths, and in popular traditional beliefs. In these, demoniac beings of all kinds are regarded as peculiarly active and malevolent at Samhain (the beginning of winter). 'Malignant bird-flocks' issue from the hell-gate of Ireland every Samhain-eve, to blight the crops and to kill animals. 'Demon women' always appear on that night, and they resemble the *Samhanach*, a November demon believed in the Highlands to steal children and work other mischief. The activity of witches and other evil beings, of fairies who abduct human beings, and of the dead at that time is also suggestive in this connexion (see Joyce, *Social Hist. of Anc. Ireland*, 1903, ii. 556; *RCel* x. [1889] 214, 225, xxiv. [1903] 172; *Celtic Magazine*, ix. [1883] 209). Nor is it unlikely that some of the demoniac beings of later Celtic superstition were not simply older beneficent gods or spirits to whom an evil character had been assigned as the result of the adoption of a new religion; it is probable that already in pagan times they represented the powers of Nature in its more hostile aspects.

Thus, though the evidence for Celtic dualism is not extensive, and is largely inferential, there is no reason to doubt that a certain belief in opposing powers, such as is a necessary part of all Nature-religions, did exist. How far that ever became a more ethical dualism is quite unknown.

LITERATURE.—This is sufficiently given in the article. See also MacCulloch, *Religion of the Ancient Celts*, Edin., 1911.

J. A. MACCULLOCH.

DUALISM (Egyptian).—**1. General.**—Egyptian religion exhibits, 'fossilized' in the different stratifications of its various religious periods, the whole series of dualistic notions that we find to-day in all the other religions. Thus, in a good many of the chapters of the different 'Books of the Dead,' we find traces of a pre-historic period when dualism, in the humblest sense of the term, may be seen in process of formation, and in a form analogous in many respects to what exists at present among numerous black tribes of the African continent. Every good or bad incident experienced or observed by the individual is the work of 'spirits,' visible or invisible (see DEMONS AND SPIRITS [Egyp.]); every occurrence of which man feels the counter-blow is the result of these encounters. In this Egyptian realm of primitive religion, as in every other part of creation, no single spirit is specifically good or bad (generally speaking, however, the tendency is towards the pessimistic side, as is the case with the majority of savage notions); all spirits are irritable, and hungry, and simply try to gratify their instincts, which are the same as those of all other beings of the visible world. But the personal experiences gathered from generations of Egyptians, and collected by sorcerer-priests, led to the notion that these spirits were under the command of stronger spirits, who were their masters. It is not even said that these masters are good; they are simply the controllers of beings whose attacks are feared by man.

Men's business is to try to steal from the most powerful spirits the knowledge of the means employed by them, to seize their arms, and, above all, to disguise themselves as these very spirits themselves. Men, therefore, always pretend to 'be' such and such spirits or gods, in order to have more power; but such substitution does not involve any conclusion as to a permanent character of good-will or even of protection so far as the spirit is concerned in whose name they act or claim to act. Fugitive traits of dualism appear. Alliance or identification with the most powerful spirits necessitates an attempt at classification and the attributing to a certain number of them of the permanent characteristics of beings useful, or even to a certain extent favourable, to man. They are not yet called beneficent. A tacit alliance is formed between certain spirits and certain men, with a tendency to mutual obligations, based on experimental utility. At the same time, the classification of 'spirits' (and of the good and bad forces controlled by them) ceases to be an individual appreciation. The knowledge acquired, by traditional teaching, of the means (formulæ, talismans, mimetic disguises, etc.) of working upon these spirits brings into existence, for the advantage of the initiated, a list of the powers that are generally hostile or sympathetic. The use of this seems to have been reserved at first to a social class or tribal group.

In certain chapters of the Book of the Dead, which are evidently of less remote composition, we see the properly so-called dualistic notion of a *permanent* conflict between the different kinds of important spirits very nearly taking definite separate shape, with an idea of an *earthly* opposition (giving, of course, the word 'earth,' or 'universe,' the very narrow sense of that patch of ground inhabited by the group in question). The observation of the actions of animate beings, and of natural incidents and phenomena, and the efforts to connect cause and effect, lead to a more or less laboured adjustment of this elementary co-ordination. Light and darkness, health and sickness, calm and storm, abundance and want, range themselves in two armies, into whose ranks step the various visible beings (fauna and flora), then the terrestrial invisible beings, then the beings of the 'regions,' and of the winds and the stars (these last three classes having a tendency to assume the characteristics of ordinary beings well- or ill-disposed to men; the Cat of the Ashdu-tree in Heliopolis, the Ibis, and the cow-goddesses, *e.g.*, opposing the reptiles and lizards, who are the constant enemies of man). Gods analogous to the *Mo-acha* and *Shi-acha* of the Ainu (gods of calm and of the tempest, and mutual enemies; see AINUS, § 16, vol. i. p. 242), or to the South-West Wind of Chaldæa, appear in the Nile Valley.

This dualism, crude as it is, may reach a rough grouping of opposed deities, with a relative hierarchy of spirits or secondary beings enrolled in the ranks of the two armies. The first attempts at cosmogonical explanations lead to the appearance in the texts of the same quasi-necessary grouping, on the side of the good army, of the beings who preside over the creation and the preservation of light, of the fertilizing waters, and the supply of nourishment and necessary things. The notion—still obscure, but in existence—presents itself of a state of things, an 'order,' over which these beings preside, which is their work; and, as life and the continuation of species depend upon this order, an alliance necessarily springs up between the Divine beings controlling it and the man of Egypt.[1]

Of course this dualism is exclusively naturalistic, and there can be no question of a moral element. All that we have as yet is certain permanent 'beneficent' functions associated with certain gods, and continuous hostile energies associated with certain others. The hierarchies are confused and badly organized, because of the widely dissimilar sources from which the different combatants come: a number of Divine beings were neutral, or only intermittently active; and, as a

[1] This curious process—necessarily a long one—may be seen fairly well in the efforts of the successive commentators on ch. 17 of the Book of the Dead, or in certain ancient parts of the Pyramid texts.

more general rule still, their character of good or bad arose from what they had accomplished by their energy (killing, stinging, devouring, tearing, etc.) in the service of a good or bad god—not by their free choice, but by the fact that they were slaves, or forcibly detained spirits, in the service of such and such a master. This is the condition of most of the 'spirits' bequeathed by pre-historic times to the Theban descriptions (paintings or writings) of the Other-world; and likewise of nearly all the genii and demons of animal aspect.

Poor as a dualistic classification based on such processes may appear to us, nevertheless, once this point is reached, the system already contains the fundamental element—the antagonism of the forces upon which the world's progress depends. Though it seems at first a difficult thing to admit, still it may be affirmed that the mastery of the idea of a *moral* dualism is much less difficult to attain from this point than was the original comprehension of the idea of the antagonism of purely material order and disorder.

2. Conditions peculiar to Egypt.—A system of cosmogonic dualism like the above, generally achieved through the creation of myths, has been formed nearly everywhere by different religions. But it has stopped, as a rule, among savage peoples, at the limits of ascertained knowledge, and has usually tended to end in pessimistic inaction. The future of a dualism which has reached this point in development lies in the idea of the possible, then necessary, co-operation of man—and that without assuming any idea of a moral element; it is the much simpler case of the conviction that man can help the superior beings to maintain order in the material world, and even, in a more humble way, that he can render material aid to the useful beings in their struggle against their enemies. This idea, though instinctive, cannot be crystallized without important preliminary indications supplied by Nature. These enable even elementary religions to abstract from the tumult and chaos of the innumerable phenomena of Nature a relatively clear vision of the great struggles of the elements, climatic and geographical. In this respect Egypt has been truly a privileged country (see § 3, and CALENDAR [Egyptian]).

3. Principal elements.—If we now turn to investigate the separate elements that united to form a dualistic system in Egypt, we find (leaving out of account the innumerable secondary formative elements) three chief groups: (1) the Nile and its valley as opposed to the desert; (2) the supposed strife of the stars in the vault of heaven or in the invisible sky of the 'lower world'; and (3) the struggle between the sun and the powers of darkness, taking the place of the struggle of the stars. The whole becomes gradually more closely bound together.

It is difficult to decide whether the first group is the most ancient. A negative evidence seems to follow from the positive fact that the antagonism of the desert and the verdant soil of the valley is not mentioned in the ritual texts, legends, or iconography down to a very late date. Even the assimilation, affirmed throughout Egyptology, of Osiris with the valley, and of his enemy Set with the lonely destructive desert, is found, on thorough examination, to be an assertion of very late date, due to naturalistic symbolism; and Plutarch is still the best authority to refer to in this matter.

Whatever its actual date, this 'naturalistic' division of dualism never came into the complete body of doctrine except in the form of a complementary explanation. A goodly proportion of the pre-historic texts preserved in the Pyramid versions is, on the other hand, devoted to the motions and supposed struggles in the firmament, and their direct influence upon the rest of the world can be clearly deduced from an examination of Egyptian beliefs. The positions of the planets and constellations, the sudden appearance of such bodies as meteors, shooting stars, and comets, are regarded as manifestations of opposing shocks, of struggles to maintain or to destroy the order of the universe. It is worth observing that, at this stage of development, the sun has very little importance in itself; its beneficent influence is hardly mentioned in the oldest beliefs, and there is, of course, no question of its filling any creative rôle whatever. This fact can be explained, partly at least, by the small importance, in a country like Egypt, of the gradual disappearance of the heating force, or of the period of its stay, light being as yet the sun's chief beneficent activity. The Egyptian had not yet connected its visible course with the succession of the various seasons of the year—these were the work of the stars, of Sothis, the Great Bear, etc. The moon seems early to have attained a more definite character; its name of *Ahi* ('the Combatant') is a relic of a time when this planet held an important place in the Egyptian's studies.

On a close examination of the dualistic organization based upon the orbits and influences of the heavenly bodies, two periods can be distinguished in these times at once so remote and yet so far in advance of the starting-point. In one of these periods, the principal rôle is still in the hands of groups of demons and spirits who control a certain part of the celestial world—a region, a constellation, etc. (see DEMONS [Egyp.])—and ensure the safe journey of the sun, moon, and planets, constantly guarding them from the various monsters lying in wait throughout the whole firmament. (About a fifth of the Pyramid texts relate to this subject.) Groups of secondary spirits or vassals, with no individual personality, are ranged around the combatants in each encounter, or are localized in a certain spot (bands of jackal spirits, monkey spirits, etc.); others, such as the *hunmamit*, form a bodyguard for the sun; and their importance decreases proportionately as the sun assumes a personality and importance for itself. These spirits gradually become groups of angels with no definite function, and in the end are practically confounded with the rays, or vital forces, of the sun.

In the second period, the antagonism of the world becomes accentuated, and the sun's beneficent protective rôle is defined over against a certain number of stars. These play a more active part, while the spirits of the regions fall into the background. These stars are early deified and regarded as figures or images of the gods rather than as the dwellings of groups of spirits. They are described in the texts as accompanying the sun, preparing the way for it, defending it, battling unceasingly. Several deities of the Nile Valley, who were not stellar deities originally, show a tendency to become confused with these gods of the sky, and take a position on board the sun's barque. They all employ their time guiding the barque, reciting incantations, and pointing out dangers. The paintings of the Theban period, though of very much later date, contain an exact picture of that period, and on the whole agree in essentials with the Pyramid texts. A steady succession of dangers (in which the pikes, harpoons, arrows, and lances of the gods play as important a part as the magic formulæ) is painfully surmounted by virtue of untiring efforts. The sun is guided, protected, and sustained, but never directs anything itself. It is not a chief; it simply submits passively to attacks and defences. The cosmogonic order and well-being always win the day, but never decisively. For, although the army of the good gods is steadily getting into better order, so also is that of the bad gods. The conception is not yet formed that the κόσμος is the *personal* work of the sun, but the fundamental idea is already there—that the κόσμος (*maāit*) depends upon the maintenance of the sun's action. On the other hand, Apōpi, the single giant adversary of the sun, to begin with, gathers round him as his helpers all the isolated spirits who had been warring on their own account in the primitive struggle. These were the serpent gods of every kind, the boa (*e.g.*, Book of the Dead, ch. 40) or serpent *naja*, and all those serpents so vividly portrayed in the group of curious texts of the Pyramid of Unas against serpents; also a whole section of the crocodile gods of the marshes of the sky; and, finally, the earliest adversaries of the good stars: the ass who tried to destroy the sun in the heavenly deserts, the sow who tried to devour the moon, the giant tortoise, the fantastic monsters of the Theban frescoes, the gazelles with serpents' heads, etc. Thus narrowed down into a duel between light and darkness, the struggle between good and evil is imagined and described as taking place during the hours of the night, when the sun was invisible to the eyes of the Egyptians. The lower world is peopled with 'friends' and 'enemies,' under the form of thousands of spirits helping or attacking the groups of gods who protect the sun in its course. The upper and lower heavens are thus peopled, like the earth, by representatives of the two great opposing forces.

The evolution of this originally stellar dualism ends, after several thousands of years, in solar dualism. The sun Rā gradually ceases to be a protected god, and becomes a protector. The κόσμος is no longer merely the result of his existence; it is his work. He becomes the type of every beneficent energy; he becomes the creator; he is, therefore, the natural chief of everything that contributes to confirm his work. The magnificence of the hymns of the Theban period, when describing Rā (the classic sun) or Aten (the sun of Amarna religion), gives a good idea of the conception then formed of the rôle of the sun, the supreme god. The fresco of Siphtah and the paintings of Seti I. in the royal hypogees of Thebes, show very well, though with too much mysticism at times, the very strenuous struggle which the sun carries on without a break against the disturbers of his work; and in the world of darkness, where the 'enemies of Rā' are undergoing all sorts of punishments, the notion already appears that 'hostility to Rā' could consist not only in a struggle against material light and order, but also in the combat with everything that is in any way whatever a consequence or necessary complement of this light and order. This step, which was of the highest importance for the broadening of the nature of dualism, was due to the combination of solar dualism with the idea that the demiurgical work of the sun went on after the creation, through the descendants placed by the sun on this earth. If the Egyptian Rā, Lord of Order, was developed by means similar to those producing the earthly rôle of the Chaldæan Shamash, and if the disturbers of the Egyptian κόσμος are the same essentially as those of the Delta of the Euphrates, this new and final element would appear to be peculiar to the Nile Valley. It rests upon the fundamental legend of Osiris, son of Rā, a god with human shape, and the first king of the Egypt which Rā organized and civilized. Osiris, continued in Horus, left the carrying on of his task to the Divine continuations placed 'upon the throne of Horus'—the Pharaohs, 'sons of the sun.' See EGYPTIAN RELIGION.

Osiris, organizer of the Nile Valley, originator of the first institutions of civilization, inventor of the chief things that are good and useful for man (agriculture, trades, etc.), becomes the archetype of the good being (*uōnnofir*), round whom gradually gather all the elements and creatures who do any good and salutary work in the world. The necessity of a counterpart gives rise to the romance of his struggle against Set. The slaying of Osiris, his resurrection, and his departure to the Otherworld at once connect this myth with that of the sun's journey into the lower world, and also make it possible to continue the rôle and reign of Osiris beyond the terrestrial life. At the same time, the legend of Horus succeeding his father Osiris on this earth, after avenging him, shows that the work once begun does not come to an end. In short, the fact that Set is not destroyed, but only conquered, is the solution of what is perhaps our most difficult problem—the present existence of evil in the world. A dualism which is confined to the origin of the world, with a struggle completed at the world's inception, cannot explain the persistence of evil. This becomes clear only when we admit that the struggle goes on indefinitely; and the conception of the battle of Osiris's successors against Set and his followers fits in with the parallel continuity of the ancient solar struggle in the celestial regions.

This parallelism gradually leads to a fusion of the characters of Osiris and Rā, which, we might almost say, was fated from the beginning. Osiris becomes one of the aspects of the struggling sun, apparently dying and coming to life again every day; and his work on the earth gets confused with the creative function of the sun. On the side of the evil forces there is even greater confusion between Set and Apōpi, chief of the powers of darkness. Rā-Osiris, chief of all good forces, becomes more and more clearly opposed, as the centuries pass, to Set-Typhon-Apōpi, chief of evil. The picture is completed in the last period by the assimilation of Osiris to the beneficent Nile and of Set to the hostile desert.

4. Final aspect of Egyptian dualism.—From this stage it is a comparatively easy step to the relative realization of a dualism with moral elements. The king of Egypt, grandson of Osiris and successor of Horus, in whom there lives, in virtue of his coronation, a portion of the soul of Rā, is strictly required to continue everything his ancestors have done on the earth and are still doing in the sky. The enemies of Rā and Osiris are his enemies, and, inversely, the enemies of the king are the enemies of Rā and Osiris. The gods and men of Egypt owe each other strict allegiance at every moment against the opposing forces. By force of circumstances the purely human enemies of the king of Egypt, one of whose titles is 'the Good God' (*Notir Nofir*), are assimilated to the evil and destructive gods and spirits, as adversaries, of the very same kind, of one and the same κόσμος—cosmogonic as much as political or administrative. The foreign enemy of the Egyptian becomes 'cursed,' a 'plague,' a 'son of rebellion,' a 'child of darkness,' whom gods and men must reduce to impotence along with the enemies of Rā and Osiris; and the pictures of the lower world show the former confounded with the latter. Two mighty armies of good and evil appear before Egyptian thought, which, however, never arrived at a clear determination of the separate characters of this vast picture. On one side we have Rā-Osiris, Horus, the king, and along with them—the product of all periods and of all the stages of formation—the ancient stellar spirits, the heavenly gods befriending light, the earthly gods proceeding from beings friendly to man, the followers of Horus, the initiated worshippers of the Osirian teaching, the faithful accompanying or representing the living king, all upright and trusty functionaries, and—down to the lowest peasant—every man who carries on the task assigned to him in the maintenance of a country organized (like the world) according to normal order (*maāit*). On the other side are Apōpi and his followers, monsters and demons, Set with his Divine and human partisans, the spirits of evil, of disease, and of darkness, the troublesome dead, and the millions of hostile spirits of the other world, and, lastly, amalgamated with these (or sometimes even confused with them), there are the tribes of the desert and frontiers which prehistoric Egypt had to drive back at the beginning of her political organization. The Egyptian's enemies have naturally become the enemies of good, the natural allies of Set-Apōpi; and, in the Other-world, Rā continues to destroy them, delivering over their shades to heat, the sword, and the fire, commanding his spirits to 'proceed to their destruction.'

A less savage conception of the place of foreign races in the world appears later. In the famous sarcophagus of Seti I., *e.g.*, the sun discourses with a noble benignity to the four races of the world (Egyptians, Libyans, Asiatics, and Blacks), and the only condition necessary in order to have a claim upon his protection seems to be to acknowledge the uncontestable supremacy of Egypt. The classification of 'foreigners' in the army of evil forces seems now to become confined to the traditions of legendary wars, in which there is no longer any clear distinction between the human and demoniac character of the ancient 'enemies of Egypt' of legendary times.

The inclusion of the nation's human adversaries among the forces of evil has, as a symmetrically necessary counterpart, the notion that the internal enemies of Egyptian order are equally adherents of the evil forces. Just as the sun Rā cannot maintain the order he created without discipline, the hierarchy, and the submission and co-operation of all ranks of his collaborators, in the same way the king requires identical conditions before he can carry on in Egypt the work of Osiris, 'the Good Being,' and that of Horus; the duties expected of the Egyptian of every degree, proportioned according to his circumstances, are thus based upon the idea of this ever-present and necessary task. The imperative and more and more minute duties of the good chief or the good administrator presuppose a firm authority, prudence, and equity, then a love of justice and truth, pity for the weak, charity, and an ever-increasing number of social virtues. These obligations, confined at first to those in power, are soon extended to the more humble citizens. Any violation of these duties means a blemish upon the order (*maāit*), which is already partially an administrative order, then becomes a social, and finally a moral, order. In mimetic processions and dramas we undoubtedly see magic battles going on just as among primitive peoples; but symbolism attaches a more and more esoteric significance to these representations—the significance of a victory of good over evil which could not be attained by magic pure and simple; or the significance of a commemoration of the initial work accomplished by the gods in days gone by which it is man's duty to carry on (individually or in groups) by the struggle against everything evil. Figures as early as those of the 'Stelæ of Horus,' in which the god crushes, tramples upon, or destroys crocodiles, serpents, and monsters, are significant, to the thinker, of the beneficent rule of a god who abhors evil, and whom every man ought both to assist and to imitate. When Ptolemy Soter, at his coronation in a papyrus barque, captures the water-fowl in the marshes, he means by this to symbolize that, under his sway, he guarantees the destruction of all evil things, in the highest meaning of the words.

LITERATURE.—There is no monograph on the subject. The opposition of Osiris and Set, or of Rā and Apōpi, is, of course, mentioned in all works dealing with Egypt and Egyptian religion. A number of useful observations may be found in E. A. W. Budge, *Osiris and the Resurrection*, London, 1911. The question is briefly treated in G. Foucart, *Méthode comparative*[2], Paris, 1912, p. 310 ff.

GEORGE FOUCART.

DUALISM (Greek).—**I. The pre-Socratic pluralists.**—The view of the universe taken by the pre-Socratic philosophers was for the most part monistic, and materialistically monistic. This applies to the Ionian hylozoists (Milesian and Ephesian alike)—to Heraclitus as much as to Thales, Anaximander, and the others; for, though Heraclitus laid stress on *logos* as well as on primitive 'fire,' since the explanatory term *logos* was to him merely an aspect of fire, it was only one side of the primary stuff or material out of which the world was formed. It applies also, although with a difference, to the Eleatic School; for, although Parmenides and his followers emphasized Unity and denied Change, making the one Being and the other Non-being, the teaching is still materialistic and monistic (for the unity of Parmenides is 'corporeal'), but the monism rests on the intellectual apprehension of Unity, not on the manipulation of a primary substance. It is the result of the philosophical intellect exercised on the world of our experience, as distinguished both from the scientific intellect and from the poetic imagination, as well as from mere sense-perception. In 'the Many' the intellect perceives only the illusory and 'a path that none can learn of at all'; 'the One' alone is true, and it alone exists. Dualism emerges first with the early pluralists—Empedocles, Anaxagoras, and Democritus; and it indicates the fact that a more scientific view of the world was now being reached, and that the conception was clearly growing of the distinction between man as a thinking subject and the world as the object of thought. It has, therefore, both a cosmological and a psychological significance.

(1) *Empedocles.*—The first great principle on which Empedocles based his philosophy was that bodies in the universe, and the universe itself, consist of the four elements (he called them 'roots of things')—fire, air, water, earth; and that these are held together or kept in separation, as the case may be, by the two contrary forces Love and Hate. Regarded as a completed Sphere, this world is conceived as broken up by degrees, through the interference of Hate or Discord, till the moment comes when Discord is supreme and chaos reigns, out of which order is again produced by the gradual influence and alternate dominance of Love, to be again succeeded by the disintegrating agency of Strife; and this alternate process goes on time without end. Here explicit expression is given to the dualistic conception of existence; for, as the world is composed of elements, these need to be moved; but they have no power of movement in themselves; consequently, they must be moved from without—that is, Love and Hate are needed as movent forces. See, further, art. EMPEDOCLES.

(2) *Anaxagoras.*—The reputation of Anaxagoras in the history of philosophy rests mainly on two things: (1) his physical doctrine of *homoiomeria*; and (2) his enunciation of the seemingly spiritualistic position that νοῦς, or intellect, is the interpreting factor in the universe. In place of four elements, out of which everything was formed, as Empedocles had taught, Anaxagoras posits an infinite number of primitive substances, each composed of homogeneous particles, 'which neither come into being nor perish, but persist eternally.' These Aristotle designated ὁμοιομερῆ; whence the substantive ὁμοιομέρεια was formed (though not by him) to designate existence by ὁμοιομερῆ and the doctrine thereof as set forth by Anaxagoras. Each homœomery is unique and unlike every other; yet none can exist apart from the others—each is mixed with each. Consequently, if everything is mixed with everything (πᾶν ἐν παντί), a body is what it is simply because of the elements that are *predominant* in its structure.

But the world is not explained by these conceptions alone. We require also to take account of νοῦς, or intelligence. 'At the beginning,' Anaxagoras says, 'all things were together; then came mind (νοῦς ἐλθών) and set them in order (αὐτὰ διεκόσμησε).' It is evident that, if we interpret νοῦς spiritualistically, we have here the assertion of a non-materialistic principle in the universe ruling and guiding all, operative both in the whole and in the individual—a presentation of a teleological view of the world that anticipated Plato and Aristotle. It is the first clear statement in Greek thought that there is a plan and purpose in existence, that Nature has a meaning and is interpretable, and that physics is subordinate to metaphysics.

How far Anaxagoras himself realized the true import of his own doctrine is disputable. On the one hand, notwithstanding the fact that he himself designates νοῦς as absolutely pure and unmixed, and ascribes to it the function of imparting motion originally to things and of acting though itself incapable of being acted upon, it is doubtful whether νοῦς to him is really a spiritual substance. Many interpreters, supported by implications in his own phraseology, read it materialistically, though they allow that the noëtic matter is not gross, but subtle and refined: they say that, though it may be taken after the analogy of what we find in human consciousness, it was only, after all, a natural force—simply on the line of the spiritual conception, but not yet itself spiritual. On the other hand, there can be little question that Anaxagoras did not use his conception to the full, either in his cosmological or in his psychological teaching. It is the complaint both of Plato and of Aristotle that, in his philosophy, it simply occupies the place of a *deus ex machina*; or, otherwise, that he uses it as a kind of impressive badge or motto, and accords it a position of *otium cum dignitate*. At all events, the principle of mind (νοῦς) is present in the Anaxagorean philosophy as something distinct from matter, thereby bringing into view a dualistic interpretation of the universe that was to influence Western thought for all time.

Dualism is further apparent in Anaxagoras's doctrine of sense-perception. Accepting the principle that 'everything is mixed with everything,' he proceeds to explain perception by the additional principle that 'unlike is recognized by unlike' (the exact opposite of what Empedocles had laid down): *contraries* are the indispensable condition of sensuous cognition. Take sight, for example. This is effected, according to Anaxagoras, 'by reflexion of an image in the pupil of the eye, but this image is not reflected in a part of the pupil of like colour with the object, but in one of a different colour. . . . The colour which predominates in the object seen is, when reflected, made to fall on the part of the eye which is of the opposite colour' (Theophrastus, *de Sensu*, § 27). Cf. also art. ANAXAGORAS.

(3) *Democritus.*—The grandest attempt in early Greek thought to give a thoroughgoing account of the universe on the basis of purely materialistic and mechanical principles was the Atomic Theory, associated chiefly with the name of Democritus. It was essentially scientific, but it is also philosophical. It so far reproduced the teaching of Parmenides that it allowed that there can be no motion or becoming without Non-being; but, in order to conserve motion and becoming, it further maintained that Non-being (the Void) is equally real with Being (the Plenum). On the other hand, it owed much to Empedocles, whose doctrine of effluvia it adopted, though not without important modifications. For a full exposition of Democritus's theory, see art. DEMOCRITUS.

2. The Pythagoreans.—The kinds of dualism that we have been dealing with are distinctly philosophical and scientific. A different type confronts us when we turn to the Pythagoreans. We have now a dualism of an ethical and religious stamp, based on the contrast of soul and body, and of the principles of good and evil. The body was regarded by the Pythagoreans, not as the auxiliary and instrument of the soul, but as its sepulchre and prison-house, even as the seat and source of sin. 'Mortify the body then' became the great injunction; and a religious order was instituted, and a system of abstinence devised for the purification of the soul and the development of its higher life. This was conjoined with the doctrine of metempsychosis, which taught that life here in the body is a penance for sin committed in a previous state of existence, and that only by successive incarnations can the soul be restored to purity and bliss. This view of the body as essentially 'vile,' and a hindrance, not a help, to the soul, had great influence in Greek philosophy: it was in large measure accepted by Plato, and it was the basis of the teaching of the mystical Greek Schools of later times—especially the neo-Platonists. See, further, art. PYTHAGOREANS.

3. Plato.—The dualism of Plato centres in his Theory of Ideas, but assumes various aspects according to the context or the point of view from which that theory is regarded. Besides its distinctively epistemological significance, it has a well-marked psychological bearing, depending on Plato's sharp-cut distinction between the soul and the body, conjoined with his doctrine of the soul as pre-existent as well as immortal, and of the necessity of its gradual purification and ultimate return to its original home through re-incarnations or metempsychoses. It has also a cosmological reference, both in connexion with the creation of the world, where Necessity or Fate plays a part as well as design or purpose, and in connexion with the creation of the Soul of the World and the creation of Man, whose composite nature presents special difficulties.

(1) If, as Aristotle tells us, and as may very well be seen from a perusal of the Platonic *Dialogues* themselves, the three great influences that told on Plato in the formation of his philosophy were the Heraclitean doctrine of the perpetual flux of sensible things, the Parmenidean insistence on Unity as the key to truth, and the Socratic unyielding demand for definitions and clear concepts pursued on a dialectic method that almost inevitably gave permanence to the concepts attained, the Platonic Ideology naturally takes the following shape:

There are two worlds—the world of sense and the world of intelligence. The first is the sphere of change, of the fleeting and the fallacious; the second is the sphere of the permanent and the true. It is to the second of these worlds that Ideas belong; and they are not mere subjective representations, but transcendent self-subsistent entities, immutable and eternal—real independent objective existences, though the existence is timeless and spaceless, and so noumenal. Being the universal, they are not derived from experience, but are presupposed in it: they are the only true and knowable realities, all else being but show and appearance—objects of 'opinion,' but not of 'knowledge.'

Yet sense *is*, and the Ideas must have a relation to it. What is the relation? Speaking generally, the answer is that Ideas are the causes of what reality sense-objects possess; or, in other words, sense-objects 'participate' in Ideas. This is Plato's famous doctrine of 'participation' (μέθεξις or τὸ μετέχειν), which is intended to express the immanence of Ideas—known also as 'communion' (κοινωνία) and 'presence' (παρουσία). If, further, it be asked how sense-objects participate in the self-existent and eternal Ideas, the answer is given in the *Philebus*, that 'the One' is manifested in 'the Many' in a graded system of knowledge. This does not explain the *fact* of participation, but it throws light upon the *mode*. More suggestive still is the figure of 'the Line,' as representative of the cognitive process, in the sixth book of the *Republic*. Knowledge proper is thus shown to be absolutely distinct from opinion, which is the highest that sense in any of its forms can achieve. The Idea of the Good is all-pervasive; while transcendent, it is also immanent; although itself above intellect and above sense, it is the cause of both (like the sun in the heavens) and permeates both. But *how* this should be is not shown.

(2) The Platonic dualism is further seen when we raise the question with regard to Ideas, How do we come to know them? The answer to this is given in the *Phædo* and the *Phædrus*, and, again, in the *Meno*, viz. by reminiscence (ἀνάμνησις). In a previous state of existence, the mind viewed the eternal Ideas; and, after its descent to earth and its union with the body, it is able to revive them in part. Only thus, it appeared to Plato, could we explain the facts that truth is attainable by

man at all, that learning is possible, and that virtue can be taught. There is metempsychosis (so, too, Pythagoras had said); and the explanation of knowledge is here. But our birth into this world, the union of the soul with the body, is a descent; and the full ascent is made only when the union is dissolved. Although the body is not regarded by Plato, except in the *Timæus*, as essentially vile (sin, to Plato, was simply a disease, arising either from ignorance or from madness), yet it is the prison-house of the soul—a clog and hindrance to its complete development and highest perfection. It is mortal and, therefore, a restraint to the immortal, obstructing its clear vision and retarding its perfect acquisition of virtue. On the side of intellectual knowledge, it drags down the soul to the fleeting and transitory, for the body operates through the senses, and these deal with the fleeting and the changeful only. On the side of ethical achievement, it is apt to lower morality and to replace virtue by pleasure, and so to render the perception of ethical ideas faint.

That there is truth in this conception of the body is obvious, but it is clearly not the whole truth. There is another side to it, namely, that which Browning has so finely expressed in *Rabbi Ben Ezra*, where it is maintained that

> 'All good things
> Are ours, nor soul helps flesh more, now, than flesh helps soul!'

Nor does the doctrine of metempsychosis meet the real difficulty. It does not explain how the mind that has had pre-natal sight of the eternal Ideas should come to be joined to a body at all—how the clear vision of the pre-existent state should come to be lost. As to how the soul of man came to fall from its pristine condition, Plato simply says, metaphorically, that some pre-existent souls are unable to keep up with the gods in the pursuit of reality, 'and through some ill-hap sink beneath the double load of forgetfulness and vice, and their wings fall from them, and they drop to the ground' (see the Myth of the Charioteer in the *Phædrus*). But what *rational* necessity there is in this, making a fundamental difference among pre-existent souls, is not obvious. Once metempsychosis gets a start, then the fact of a partially impure life here may explain the necessity of a return, for purposes of purification and of spiritual progress, to earthly life; but how metempsychosis should ever begin, or, in other words, how the state of matters necessitating metempsychosis originates, is not shown. Yet this should be shown, if Plato's theory is to be rational throughout.

(3) Into the details of the Platonic cosmology as elaborated in the *Timæus*, it is impossible here to enter. The problem is—Given the Platonic Forms or Ideas as eternal immutable existences, and given also the eternal existence of Matter (matter orderless, chaotic, ruled by necessity), how were the order and the beauty of the former to be imparted to the latter? The answer is that the Divine Reason, the Demiurge or Creator, produced the marvellous effect that we know as the world by working upon matter according to an eternal archetype or pattern existing in the Divine mind. According to this intelligible archetype the visible universe was formed, and it owes its existence simply to the goodness of the Creator. The result is that the Universe is an animated rational existence, a God; having a Body (σῶμα), a Soul (ψυχή), and a Mind (νοῦς). Yet, the cosmos is not perfect. This arose from the fact that the Demiurge, in working upon matter, met with the pre-cosmical and extra-cosmical resistance of Necessity (Ἀνάγκη). Necessity ruled Matter (the πρῶτον σῶμα): how could it be vanquished? Not, according to Plato, by coercion, but by persuasion. In so far, then, as the Creator could gain Necessity by persuasion, to that extent could he freely execute his design on matter; but, at the point where Necessity resisted and refused to be persuaded, the Demiurge was powerless; hence the imperfection of the cosmos. However metaphorical this is, it is the acknowledgment of a radical dualism in Plato's thinking.

Similarly, the dualistic conception comes out in Plato's account of the creation of man. The mortal part of him is the workmanship of 'the gods,' but the rational and immortal part is supplied by the Demiurge himself. This division of functions was necessary because nothing mortal could be created by the Demiurge, and, had man been wholly his creation, it might have been possible to cast the blame of man's sin and folly upon the Creator. As formed by the gods, man is a miniature of the cosmos—a microcosmos; but, as his constructors had only mortal elements to work with, their handiwork had flaws and imperfections in it peculiar to the situation. It was theirs simply to create the body and the two mortal souls, the spirited and the appetitive (τὸ θυμοειδές and τὸ ἐπιθυμητικόν), and to effect the junction of these with the immortal soul, or νοῦς. As the mortal and immortal souls were antagonistic to each other, the best that the formative gods could do was to place them in such positions within the body (the skull, the breast, the belly) that the action of each upon the others should be as conducive as possible to good. This is pictorially attractive, but it does not remove the difficulty. The curious relation of the Demiurge to matter and to man, as represented in the *Timæus*, is practically an acknowledgment of inability to solve the riddle of the universe.

4. Aristotle. The greatest critic of the Platonic Theory of Ideas in ancient times was Aristotle. His criticisms are many and various, but they all centre in the objection that the two worlds—the world of sense and the world of intellect—are left by Plato apart, and that no real explanation is given of change in the world of phenomena. Either the Ideas are an unnecessary duplicate of the facts of experience, or they are useless, inoperative. Nevertheless, Aristotle had been the pupil of Plato, and the doctrine of Ideas left its permanent mark upon him. Hence, a metaphysical dualism, no less real than, though not quite so obvious as, that of Plato, permeates the Aristotelian philosophy; it is the dualism of Form and Matter, of Actuality and Potentiality. To Plato and Aristotle alike, knowledge lay in the Universal; but, while the Universal was to Plato outside of and prior to experience, it was to Aristotle immanent in experience: universal there is, yet it is not transcendentally existent, but is realized in individuals, in the concrete particulars of sense—it is the Form (essence), which Matter (the sense element) embodies.

This dualism assumes various aspects as the different parts of Aristotle's philosophy are passed in review. It is specially prominent in his Psychology, in that part of it which deals with the metaphysics of the soul (for psychology was by no means all empirical to Aristotle), and in his Theology or First Philosophy—his treatment of the relation of God to the Universe.

(1) The psychological dualism appears in the very definition that Aristotle gives of the soul itself, and in the distinction that he makes between soul and body. Soul he defines as 'the first entelechy [the earlier or implicit realization] of a natural body possessing life potentially': ἐντελέχεια ἡ πρώτη σώματος φυσικοῦ δυνάμει ζωὴν ἔχοντος (*de An.* 412*a*, 27). The body here is regarded as matter, to which soul stands in the relation of

form: as Spenser puts it (*Hymn in Honour of Beauty*, line 132),

> 'For of the soul the body form doth take,
> For soul is form, and doth the body make.'

'Life' is the power of the body to nourish itself, to grow of itself, and to decay of itself; so that, if for 'matter' and 'form' we substitute 'potentiality' and 'actuality,' and distinguish the first stage of actuality from the second, as we distinguish *knowledge* from the *exercise* of knowledge, or the *visual power* of the eye from *actual seeing*—i.e. if we distinguish between *power* or *faculty* and *actual use*, of which the second must be preceded by the first—then we get the foregoing definition. As applied to the soul of man, the conception that underlies the definition is that the human body is the specific organ whereby the human soul or mind realizes itself. This clearly distinguishes Aristotle's view from Plato's. Plato opposed soul to body, regarding the latter as the prison-house of the former, and allowed only that the body could be trained by gymnastic and music to obey the soul. To Aristotle, on the other hand, the body is the natural instrument of the soul, and so is pre-adapted to it. The two are necessary to form the concrete particular which we know as the individual human being. Yet, Aristotle adds:

> 'It is, however, perfectly conceivable that there may be some parts of it [the soul] which are separable [from the body], and this because they are not the expression or realization of any particular body. And, indeed, it is further matter of doubt whether soul as the perfect realization of the body may not stand to it in the same separable relation as a sailor to his boat' (*de An.* 413*a*, 6).

Dualism comes out sharply when Aristotle reaches the handling of the highest function of the soul, viz. intellect or νοῦς, where he discriminates between the active and the passive νοῦς, and between νοῦς generally and the other psychic functions. His scheme of functions, beginning with the lowest, is: nutritive or vegetative soul (τὸ θρεπτικόν); sentient soul (τὸ αἰσθητικόν), including the conative soul (τὸ ὀρεκτικόν), which he sometimes makes a separate function; and intellectual or noëtic soul (νοῦς or τὸ νοητικόν), divided, as above, into passive νοῦς (νοῦς παθητικός) and active νοῦς (νοῦς ποιητικός). Each higher function presupposes the lower, though the lower does not presuppose the higher. Thus, the sentient soul presupposes the vegetative soul, and both sentient and vegetative souls are presupposed by the noëtic soul; but the vegetative does not presuppose the sentient soul, nor does the sentient presuppose the noëtic. It is characteristic of νοῦς that it is eternal and immortal—at any rate, this applies to the active or poietic νοῦς: it is introduced into the individual human being *ab extra*, and the difficulty is to find what connexion it has, on the one hand, with the passive νοῦς and with the other functions of the soul generally, and, on the other hand, with the body. As has been said above, it is distinctive of Aristotle that he recognizes the intimate and indissoluble relation of soul to body, and the necessity of taking account of the physiological as well as of the psychical aspect of mental facts and processes. His great objection to the Pythagorean doctrine of the transmigration of souls was that it assumes that any body is suitable to any soul, whereas the human body is specially fitted for the soul. To maintain the opposite, he says, is like maintaining that the carpenter's art 'clothes itself in flutes; the truth being that, just as art makes use of its appropriate instruments, so the soul must make use of its fitting body' (*de An.* 407*b*, 25). But, when he comes to treat of the active νοῦς, this intimate relationship is ignored; and the conclusion is reached that this higher soul can exist altogether apart from the body—it is 'a different kind of soul' (γένος ἕτερον) from the others, and 'it alone admits of separation, as the eternal from the perishable' (καθάπερ τὸ ἀΐδιον τοῦ φθαρτοῦ).

Still further, the dualism of form and matter enters into Aristotle's theory of sense-perception.

(2) The theological aspect of the Aristotelian dualism has been brought out in the art. DESIRE (Greek), and need only be referred to here. On the one side is God, who is the prime unmoved movent, to whom the universe evermore looks desiringly; and on the other side is the universe, which, though dependent on the Deity and derived from Him, is, nevertheless, regarded as not created at one particular time but as eternally existent. This might be interpreted as simply Aristotle's way of indicating his belief in impersonal reason as permeating the universe, and yet he at times has glimpses of a personal God, apart from the universe and ruling it, as a general does his army.

> 'We must consider also,' he says, 'in which of two ways the nature of the universe contains the good or the highest good, whether as something separate and by itself, or as the order of the parts. Probably in both ways, as an army does. For the good is found both in the order and in the leader, and more in the latter; for he does not depend on the order, but it depends on him' (*Met.* xii. 10. 1075*a*, 10).

Moreover, God is in Himself conceived by Aristotle as Thought, and God's Thought is defined as 'the thinking upon thought' (καὶ ἔστιν ἡ νόησις νοήσεως νόησις [*Met.* xii. 9. 1074*b*, 30]). Personality is involved in this.

5. In later Greek systems.—Besides the dualisms that have been now considered, it is to be observed that there is frequently a dualistic note in Greek monism, which need not, however, be more than adverted to here. This applies particularly to the post-Aristotelian schools. For example, the Stoics found a difficulty in adjusting their doctrine of the primitive material substance 'fire' to the requirements of man's rationality; and, in especial, the neo-Platonists disclosed a distinct dualism in their system of the Absolute when they came to evolve their famous Triad of Absolute Unity, Absolute Intelligence, and Absolute Soul, and therefrom matter and all that is finite (see the neo-Platonic section in art. DESIRE [Greek]). The problem of how to derive Matter from Mind on a mystical basis is a difficulty that is inherent in every doctrine of Emanation and seems to be insurmountable.

SUMMARY.—The foregoing are the leading types of dualism in Greek philosophy. The term 'dualism' is one, but it has diverse significations. (1) It has a cosmological application, as is seen in the attempts of the pre-Socratic Pluralists to explain existence dualistically. (2) It is applied (*a*) in connexion with empirical psychology in explanations of the relation of subject and object in sense-perception, such as we find in Empedocles on the one hand, and in Aristotle on the other; and (*b*) in connexion with rational psychology in such a doctrine as that of the νοῦς in Aristotle. (3) It has (*a*) a metaphysical application, as expressive of the doctrine which maintains the absolute disparity between Mind and Matter and the impossibility of reducing the one to the other, and designates the opposite of monism; and (*b*) an epistemological application, as in Plato's grand attempt to explain the possibility of knowledge in his Theory of Ideas and in Aristotle's doctrine of Form and Matter. (4) There is an application of the term that is ethical and religious, which has reference to the sharp-cut distinction between soul and body, and to the view that the body is a clog or hindrance to the development of the soul and may be the seat of sin and degradation. (5) Lastly, there is a theological application, when (as by Plato in the *Timæus*) the world is set forth as the product of opposing principles—God and necessity—and an explanation is offered of the seeming defects in creation which shall minimize the difficulty of a purely teleological rendering of the universe. These various meanings, though not mutually exclusive, are distinct, and they should be kept distinct, if the positions of the Greek thinkers are to be understood.

LITERATURE.—Practically all the books specified under 'Literature' in the art. DESIRE (Greek), to the end of the list on Aristotle. In addition: Henry Jackson, *Texts to illustrate a Course of Elementary Lectures on the Hist. of Gr. Philos.*, London, 1901; W. E. Leonard, *The Fragments of Empedocles*, London, 1908; R. D. Archer-Hind, *The Timæus of Plato*, London, 1888; Walter Pater, *Plato and Platonism*[2], London, 1896; R. L. Nettleship, *Philosophical Lectures and Remains*, London, 1897; G. Croom Robertson, *Elements of General Philosophy*, London, 1896; Lewis Campbell, *Plato's Republic*, London, 1902; John I. Beare, *Greek Theories of Elementary Cognition from Alcmæon to Aristotle*, Oxford, 1906; Marie V. Williams, *Six Essays on the Platonic Theory of Knowledge*, Cambridge, 1908; E. Vernon Arnold, *Roman Stoicism*, Cambridge, 1911; James Adam, *The Vitality of Platonism*, Cambridge, 1911.

WILLIAM L. DAVIDSON.

DUALISM (Iranian).—A tendency towards dualistic conceptions, or, perhaps we may say, towards bilateral symmetry, seems to be an essential characteristic of the Iranian mind. This is to be seen in the constantly recurring distinction of the 'two worlds,' the world of Spirit and the world of Matter—a common concept in the Gāthās (*e.g.* *Yasna* xxix. 5); or, again, in the two lives, the present and the future (cf. 'uvaēibya . . . ahubya,' *ib.* lvii. 25; 'ubōyō aṅhvō,' *ib.* xli. 2). This symmetrical dualism, or 'polarity,' as S. Laing would probably style it, finds quaint expression in a curious diagram, attributed to the celebrated minister of Yazdagird I., Atrōpat, preserved in the *Dīnkarṭ* (iv. 137, ed. Peshotan, Bombay, 1883), which is represented thus:

material	wealth	sovereignty	honour	prosperity	body	BEING	soul	merit	beneficence	religion	knowledge	spiritual
stihīk	hūdahīshnīh	pātōkhshāyīh	ajarm	khvāstīk	tanū	YEHEVUN	rūbāno	kerfak	frārūn tvakhshīha	dīno	danākīh	mnōīk

It will be seen that this curious table divides the whole notion of Being into two correlative worlds of Spirit and Matter, with terms relatively corresponding to one another on opposite sides of the central notion. But it is particularly the *religious* dualism which is ordinarily considered to be the chief characteristic of the Zoroastrian religion. Yet there is no point in connexion with that faith which has given rise to so much controversy among both native and Western scholars. The modern Parsis stoutly deny that their faith is, or ever was, dualistic; and a similar view is held by more than one distinguished European authority. E. W. West attempted to defend Mazdæism from the accusation of dualism, 'made in good faith by Muhammadan writers, and echoed more incautiously by Christians,' though he blames the Parsis themselves for having admitted it, at least during the Middle Ages (see 'Pahlavi Texts,' pt. i. in *SBE*, vol. v. p. lxviii f., also pt. ii. *ib.* vol. xviii. p. xxiv). Quite recently J. H. Moulton, in a lecture on Mazdæism, asserted that,

'if we judged Parsiism by Zoroaster, there was nothing that could be called dualism. There were two powers, it was true. We were told that in the beginning one of them chose good and the other chose evil. They began a long, continuous struggle, which was to go on to the end of time, but the end was to be the final victory of the power of good and the final destruction of the power of evil. That was not dualism. If it was, Christianity would be about equally open to the charge.'

It appears to the present writer that the whole question is one of terms. It cannot, of course, be denied that the Supreme God of the Avesta is Ahura Mazda, conceived as essentially good, and the author and creator of all that is good, who is also repeatedly spoken of as Spenta Mainyu (the Holy Spirit), and that in opposition to him is Aṅra Mainyu (the Destroying Spirit). These two opposing principles are, of course, the Ormazd and Ahriman (*qq.v.*) respectively of later Persian literature. As is well known, the whole religious system of Mazdæism may be said to consist in the perennial warfare between these two powers. Certainly the mere fact of antagonism between a good and an evil spirit and their respective followers would not of itself constitute a real dualism in the Avestan, any more than in the Christian, system. But the real point of the matter is that, according to the Avestan system, (1) there exists a Being, evil by his own nature, and the author of evil, who does not owe his origin to the creator of good, but who exists independently of him; and (2) this Being is an actual creator, who calls into being creatures opposed to those of the Good Spirit and contrary to his will.

Here is seen the fundamental difference between the Avestan and the Christian (or Muhammadan) theology. In the latter the evil spirit, so far from having an origin independent of the God of good, is actually His creature, though fallen and rebellious, and certainly is never conceived as creating any beings whatsoever. The distinction seems to be decisive. So far is the idea of the creative power of the evil spirit carried in the Avesta, that not only is Aṅra Mainyu represented as creator of a vast host of demons (*daēva*), but even this physical world and its inhabitants are divided into creatures of the good and the evil spirits respectively—to the latter being attributed cold, sickness, and even noxious animals, such as wolves, poisonous snakes, etc. The very beginning of the *Vendīdād* is an enumeration of the various plagues created by Aṅra Mainyu in opposition to the various good lands and countries created by Ahura Mazda, a special verb (*fra-keret*, translated by Darmesteter as 'counter-create') being employed in opposition to the verb *dā*, attributed to the good spirit. This conception of a double creation was continued, and even enhanced, during the post-Avestan, or Patristic period, as it has been termed. Even among the heavenly bodies, the planets are considered as creatures of the evil spirit and opponents of the constellations and the stars created by the good spirit. Similarly in some of the Pahlavi treatises, such as the *Būndahish*, lists are given of the animals, arranged in two hostile armies, among those of the good creation being the falcon, magpie, crow, kite, mountain-ox and goat, wild ass, dog, fox, etc., whilst the serpent, locust, wolf, and intestinal worms are of the evil creation. There can, we think, be no doubt that all through the Zoroastrian system, from the Avesta down to the Pahlavi theologians, the evil spirit is considered as a real creator, and for this reason, even apart from the question of his origin, the system may justly be termed dualistic. It is quite true that, according to the general teaching, Aṅra Mainyu and his hosts are to be entirely and utterly destroyed at the last day; but it can scarcely be denied that, at least in the original system, his origin is quite distinct from that of Ahura Mazda, and that the two spirits are coexistent from eternity. We have thus a monotheism limited and modified by dualism, as well as a dualism modified by an ultimate monotheism. These theories may seem to us inconsistent. No doubt the origin of evil has been in all ages the principal difficulty which all religions have had to face, and the form given to this solution characterizes the divergences which distinguish them from one another. The Mazdæism of every age has sought this solution in the doctrine of two independent hostile and diametrically opposite principles—the principle or spirit of Good, and the principle or spirit of Evil. The inconsistency which we readily see in such a solution did not fail to present itself to the Iranian mind, and from early times we find that theories were devised as a means of escaping from the difficulties of this dualistic solution. These may be grouped generally under two hypotheses: (1) that the two spirits have sprung from a single, indifferent, pre-existing source; (2) that the Evil Spirit proceeds from the Good Spirit, by generation or creation. The former is the doctrine of the Zervanists, the latter that of the Gayomarthians. The Zervanists, according to the descriptions preserved by the Armenian historians, went back to a primeval being, Zervan Akarana, lit. 'Unlimited Time,' sometimes apparently identified with Destiny; and this primordial being was supposed to have generated both Ormazd and Ahriman. The second school, the Gayomarthians, seem to have held that the Evil Spirit was produced by an evil thought in the mind of the Good Spirit. This is practically the solution of the modern Parsis, who make a sharp distinction between the names Ahura Mazda and Spenta Mainyu. They point out that, especially in the Gāthās, Aṅra Mainyu is constantly opposed, not to Ahura Mazda, but to Spenta Mainyu. Ahura Mazda, they hold, is the one supreme and primordial spirit and sole creator. He is, however, possessed of two 'faculties'—Spenta Mainyu, or the faculty whose function is beneficent, and Aṅra Mainyu, whose function is destructive. One cannot but suspect that this modern Parsi solution has been unconsciously suggested by the Hindu doctrine of the functions of Viṣṇu and Śiva in the Hindu triad. A quite recent Parsi theologian has advanced a new theory, holding that Spenta Mainyu and Aṅra Mainyu denote the good and evil spirits respectively of *man*, and not of the Divinity (Rastamji Edulji, *Zarathushtra and Zarathushtrianism in the Avesta*, Leipzig, 1906, pp. 140–159); but we are not aware that this is anything more than a peculiar view of the author. It is an approximation to the Christian doctrine of the origin of evil in the *free will* of the creature.

LITERATURE.—E. W. West, 'Pahlavi Texts,' pts. i. ii. in *SBE*, vols. v. [1880], xviii. [1882]; C. de Harlez, *Avesta*², Paris, 1881, Introd. pp. lxxxiv–lxxxvii; A. V. Williams Jackson, 'Die Iran. Religion,' in *GIrP* ii. [1900] 627–631 (Dualism is a characteristic trait of Zoroaster's faith, and in its widest sense—whatever its ultimate source—was doubtless the product of his own genius. This dualism is monotheistic and optimistic, in that it postulates the final triumph of Ormazd and the destruction of all evil); L. C. Casartelli, *Phil. of the Mazdayasnian Rel. under the Sassanids*, Eng. tr., Bombay, 1889, pp. 50–54; 'The Zoroastrian Theology of the Present Day,' in *Babylonian and Oriental Record*, viii. (1900) 222-229, embodying a 'nineteenth century *rivāyat*' by a modern Parsi theologian; and all the writers on the Avesta and Zoroastrianism. Cf. Literature at end of art. AVESTA.

L. C. CASARTELLI.

DUALISM (Jewish).—Traces of a belief in two conflicting supernatural beings striving for the mastery are nowhere found in the pre-exilic writings of the OT. In the oldest religious belief of the Israelites, Jahweh's jurisdiction extended over Palestine, and He was not at war with any neighbouring god or demon. There was no evil spiritual being endeavouring to subvert His moral government. While dualism ascribes evil to a diabolic agent, the ancient pre-exilic writers found no difficulty in making it emanate from Jahweh Himself (cf. Am 3⁶). No doubt the Israelite was subject to the same psychological laws which raise a horror of the dark and of unfrequented and desert places, and he peopled them with more hurtful beings than are recorded in the OT; but his mythology was of his own creation and associated with his surroundings. Observing a multiplicity of wild life on the edge of the desert, such as monstrous serpents, jerboas, and wild goats, his imagination endowed them with superhuman intelligence, and assigned them a habitation in the interior of the desert. There arose the *śeʻîrîm*, the *ʻalûḳā*, the *lilîth*. It is doubtful, however, how far he considered them possessed, or only, like the serpent of Gn 3¹, 'subtil.' They were physically injurious to man when he entered their domain, but did not come into his religious and cosmic views. The monotheism of the OT writers kept the popular belief in demonology entirely in the background. The solitary mention of ʻ*Azazel* (*q.v.*), to whom a goat was sent out on the Day of Atonement, is too obscure to justify any conclusions as to the origin of that rite or the person of ʻAzazel. In Lv 16 the act is viewed as symbolic of a transference of the nation's sins to another land. The nature and habitation of ʻAzazel are left undefined, as if unknown or of no consequence. Nor is the OT Satan an independent Divinity. The root שׂטן signifies 'to oppose' (by standing in the way), not necessarily in a bad cause. In Nu 22²²· ³² the angel of Jahweh was a *saṭan* to Balaam. A personal Satan occurs first in passages of post-exilic date, but even in these he is not yet an independent being. See DEMONS AND SPIRITS (Heb.), in vol. iv. p. 597 f. The 'host of the high ones' of Is 24²¹ are not spiritual beings, but astral bodies to the worship of which the Israelites were addicted.

How far Babylonism affected Jewish belief before the Exile is difficult to decide. Although the history of Israel and Judah was closely connected with Assyria and Babylon, it had not contaminated the strong monotheism of the pre-exilic Prophets and Psalms. It is not likely that the theomachy of Marduk-Tiamat was so widely known as to penetrate into the popular faith of the Israelite peasantry, who were 'a people who dwelt alone,' and who as late as the reign of Hezekiah were ignorant of Aramaic (2 K 18²⁶).

The ubiquitous arch-Satan of later Jewish theology, with his diabolic subordinates standing in hostile array against God and good, and planning man's temporal and eternal destruction, is a post-exilic development, evolved primarily from foreign, chiefly Persian, sources, and grafted on Jahwism. Thus early Judaism became tinged with a tendency to dualism. The Jewish conception of the nature and work of Satan, and the hope and manner of his overthrow, leave no doubt that Ahriman was the original model. The place of contact between Judaism and Parsiism was Babylon, whither Mazdæism had already penetrated, and where probably it received accretions from Babylonism (see Cheyne, *Jewish Relig. Life*, N.Y. and London, 1898, p. 259). This would account for the Bab. element in Jewish Satanology and eschatology. Since, however, Judaism absorbed only so much of foreign religions as it could assimilate and invest with a Jewish colouring, ancient allusions to defiant evil in the OT were resuscitated and applied to the newly developed ideas of a Satan. He was crystallized in Jewish literature under various appellations. He is connected with the 'evil imagination' of Gn 8²¹. As Tiamat he had his prototype in Gn 3 and in the obscure passage Is 27¹, and plays an important part in the Qabbāla as נָחָשׁ הַקַּדְמוֹנִי. For the Bab. *Bel Dababi*, the accusing God, the Enemy (Aram. בְּעֵל דְּבָבָא), a voucher and a name were found in Pr 28²¹. The Egyptian Typhon suggested his designation of צְפוֹנִי in Jl 2²⁰, although in *Suk.* 52*a* derived from צפן, 'hidden.'

In analogy with Jahweh's angels he was supplied with subordinates to execute his will, the connecting link with the OT being the *nᵉphîlîm* of Gn 6⁴.

Already in Tobit (3^8)—an early pre-Maccabæan romance—an evil spirit, no longer, according to Hebrew idiom, 'from Jahweh' (1 S 16^{14}), but of foreign origin, slew seven innocent men. Asmodæus was banished by fumigation into the wilderness of Egypt, but survived in Jewish tradition as king of the *shēdîm*.

It must, however, be remembered that, whereas the growing belief in the transcendence of God created the demand for a solution of the problem of the origin of evil, the new conception of a Satan after the model of Ahriman entered Judaism, not by means of literature (for there are no traces of Jewish acquaintance with the Avesta), but through popular belief; and much of it remained folk-lore and private opinion, and was not shared by the sober practical legalist. This renders it impossible to systematize Jewish Satanology. Nevertheless, dualistic views existed in popular belief, and came strongly to the surface in the Apocalyptic literature. In the *Book of Enoch* the introduction of evil into the world is ascribed to the *nᵉphîlîm* under their leaders, Shem'aza and 'Azael (see DEMONS AND SPIRITS [Heb.], vol. iv. p. 600^b). In the *Book of Jubilees*, Mastema is the head of the fallen angels. At the request of Noah, nine-tenths are imprisoned, and the remainder are the Satans at large, the authors of idolatry, of every kind of evil, of destruction and bloodshed ($11^{4f.}$). In none of the Apocalyptic writings is Persian influence so prominent as in the *Testaments of the Twelve Patriarchs*. There the source of all evil is Beliar and his seven spirits (see DEMONS AND SPIRITS [Heb.], vol. iv. pp. 599^a, 601^a).

The political commotions of the age, the scanty resources of the nation, the repeated disappointments on numerous occasions when the realization of cherished hope seemed near, the success and prosperity of surrounding nations, and the power of evil intensified the spirit of pessimism which had already commenced in the Exile. The pious looked forward to a compensation in another æon, and assigned this world to the author of evil, which the pious must hate (Enoch 48^7). God and Satan, good and evil angels, the upper and the lower world (*ib.* 25 ff.), heaven and hell (Abr. 21 ff.), children of light and children of darkness (En. $108^{7.\,11}$), are contrasted. In human nature itself there are antitheses—spirit and flesh, soul and body (Wis 9^{15}, En. 108^7). Satan and his angels have sown the seed of evil in the world and in man. There lies in man the propensity to sin, the יֵצֶר הָרָע of Rabbinism. Even in the Ezra Apocalypse, where Satan is not mentioned, the flesh is made to be the source and seat of sin (Volz, *Jüd. Eschatol.* 7, 60, 77, 82).

Prayers for protection from Satan occur in Jewish liturgy in collects of ancient date, and are quoted in Ber. 60*b* as well known: 'May it be thy will . . . to deliver me this day, and every day, from a bad man . . . from Satan the destroyer!'

The popular tendency to dualism met with opposition from early times. According to La 3^{38}, good and evil alike proceed from God. The repeated assertion of the unity of God in Is 45 sounds like a polemic against Zoroastrianism. The 7th verse, 'I form light and create darkness; I make peace and create all,'[1] is the *Yozer Or* in the Jewish liturgy and the creed of normal Judaism. The practice of uttering a blessing on every occasion is an institution referred to Ezra (Maim. *Ker. Sh.* i. 7), or to the men of the Great Synagogue (*Ber.* 33), but is in reality a pious imitation of Zoroastrians. Yet no prayer is valid without a שֵׁם and מַלְכוּת, *i.e.*, it must be said in the name of Jahweh, and His Sovereignty must be acknowledged (*Ber.* 40). Suriel, the Prince of the Countenance, who taught R. Ishmael three charms against the power of evil spirits (*Ber.* 51), has been conjectured to be the Sraosha of the Avesta, who contends with the Devs night and day (*Yasna* lvii. 10–23; cf. *Rel.-gesch. Lesebuch*, ed. Bertholet, Tübingen, 1908, p. 339). But it is not he who causes the cock to herald the approaching light, but 'Blessed art Thou, O Lord our God, King of the Universe, who hast given to the cock intelligence to distinguish between day and night' (Daily Morn. Pr.).

The contest in favour of monotheism was carried on by the Rabbis in their combats with Magianism, Gnosticism, and the Minim who believed in שְׁתֵּי רְשׁוּיוֹת, 'two powers,' a duality in the Godhead (Friedländer, *Die relig. Bewegungen*, Berlin, 1905, pp. 169–234; Bergmann, *Jüd. Apologetik*, Berlin, 1908). The Mishna enacts that God should be blessed for evil no less than for good (*Ber.* ix. 5). A reader in the synagogue should be silenced if he says, 'Thy name be remembered concerning good,' or 'We praise Thee, We praise Thee' (*ib.* v. 3). 'Whosoever associates the name of heaven with another object is rooted out of the world' (*Suk.* 45*b*). In the Passover service the redemption from Egypt and the slaying of the first-born are emphatically stated as accomplished by God in person: 'I and not an angel, I and not a saraph, I and not a messenger.'

The strong assertions of the Divine unity and the all-importance of legalism left no room in the Halakha for Satanology. Hence the Mishna is free from it. Where Satan does occur in the Haggada of the Talmud and Midrash, the description is coarse, puerile, and inconsistent. At one time he is a fallen angel. When God threw him from heaven, 'he caught hold of Michael's wing, but the Holy One, blessed be He, rescued Michael' (*Yalḳ. Shim.* 68; see Kohut, *Angelologie*, 1866, p. 63). Then he is the 'Great Prince in Heaven' (*Pirḳe d. R. Eliezer*, 13). He is קַטֵּגוֹר, Michael being סַנֵּגוֹר. He is סַמָּאֵל, 'the poison of God,' because of his identity with the angel of death.

The Qabbāla and the mediæval Mystics restored Satan to his Ahrimanic dignity. The piut מי יתנה חוקף, still said by some Jewish communities on the Day of Atonement, reads like a chapter from the Avesta.

If the person of Satan is undefined in Jewish theology, the existence of the *yēṣer ha-rā'* (in *Baba bathra*, 16*a*, identical with Satan and the angel of death) is a Jewish dogma. This theologoumenon is based on the *yēṣer* of Gn 6^5 8^{21}, rendered in the AV 'imagination,' and connoting that faculty of the soul which is the cause of rebellion against God. The *yēṣer* became very early hypostatized in Jewish theology (cf. the antithesis in אוֹי לִי מִיּוֹצְרִי, וְאוֹי לִי מִיִּצְרִי, 'Woe to me because of my Creator, woe to me because of my tempter' [*Ber.* 61*a*]). He is the 'strange god' of Ps 81^9, dwelling in man (*Shabb.* 105*b*). As the source of sin, he was already known to Sirach as ἐννόημα (21^{11}), ἐνθύμημα (37^3), διαβούλιον (15^{14}). In these passages, as well as in others in the Apocrypha, where human dichotomy is asserted, such as Wis 9^{15}, an approach was made towards metaphysical dualism; yet the spirit of legalism checked its further development. Whereas the very virtues of the wicked (= Gentiles) are vices in the eyes of the righteous (*Yeb.* 103*a*), a Jew can keep the Law and be sinless. 'Blessed are Israelites. When they are occupied with the study of the Law and the performance of good works, the *yēṣer* is delivered into their hands, and not they into the hands of the *yēṣer*' ('*Abōda zara*, 5*b*; *Ḳid.* 30*a*; cf. Sir 21^{11}). He is not a human faculty and therefore not ante-natal, but an adjunct

[1] The substitution of 'all' for 'evil' is 'for the sake of euphony' (*Ber.* 11*b*), probably also from an aversion to terminate anything with a word of evil omen.

at birth (*Sanh.* 91*b*). He is situated at the left,[1] the other *deus ex machina*, the *yēṣer ṭôb*, being at the right (*Ta'an.* 11*a*). According to *Ber.* 61*b*, he resembles a fly,[2] and is placed between the valves of the heart. He was Divinely created for a benevolent purpose. Unless he existed, 'no man would build a house, or marry or beget children, or transact any business' (*Gen. R.* 89^{7}). At the end of the world God will slay him in the presence of the righteous and wicked (*Suk.* 52*b*).

LITERATURE.—Artt. 'Apocalyptic Literature,' 'Asmodæus,' 'Demon,' 'Demonology,' 'Devil,' 'Dualism,' 'Satan,' 'Zoroastrianism,' in *HDB*, *EBi*, *JE*, and their equivalents in *PRE*^{3} and Hamburger's *RE*; P. Volz, *Jüd. Eschatol.*, Tübingen, 1903; W. Bousset, *Rel. des Judentums*^{2}, Berlin, 1906; E. Stave, *Ueber den Einfluss des Parsismus auf d. Judentum*, Haarlem, 1898; M. Jastrow, *Rel. of Bab. and Assyria*, Boston, 1898; H. Gunkel, *Schöpfung und Chaos*, Göttingen, 1895, and his Com. on *Genesis*^{2}, Göttingen, 1902; I. H. Weiss, *Zur Gesch. d. jüd. Tradition*, vol. ii., Vienna, 1876; H. Duhm, *Die bösen Geister im AT*, Tübingen, 1904; N. Krochmal, *More Nebuche ha-Zeman*, Warsaw, 1898; F. Weber, *Jüd. Theol.*^{2}, Leipzig, 1897.

A. E. SUFFRIN.

DUELLING. — I. Under civilization. — Although early Schoolmen declared that the judicial duel was Divinely instituted when David fought Goliath (1 S 17), the point never ceased to trouble the conscience of Christendom. Invested with sanctions of the highest antiquity, the origins of the duel elude definite ascertainment as completely as do the various ordeals among the oldest peoples, of both East and West. Found in various forms, from Japan to Ireland, and from the Mediterranean to the northern latitudes, it was yet no universal practice, but mainly European 'where the hazel grew,' and its traces are scattered. The solemnities preceding the single combat of Menelaus and Paris (*Il.* iii. 38 ff.) are marked indications of ancient custom and ceremonial in Homeric times. Historic Greek examples fail, but the usage existed among the ancient Umbrians and among the Slavs (Nicolaus Damascenus [Didot, *Frag. Hist. Græcorum*, iii. 457]; Kelly, *Hist. of Russia*, London, 1878, pp. 33, 53; Lea, *Superstition and Force*^{4}, Philadelphia, 1892, pp. 108, 110). While the legendary battle of the Horatii and Curiatii (Livy, I. xxiv. f.) may point to an archaic practice among the Romans, the system of trial by battle has neither any tradition in the fragments of early Roman law nor any countenance from the jurists or the code. Roman civilization knew the duel as a Barbarian institution. Scipio Africanus (206 B.C.) met it in Spain (Livy, XXVIII. xxi.); it flourished among the Celtic and Germanic tribes (Velleius Paterculus, ii. 117 f.; Tacitus, *Germ.* 10); and a particular tradition, unusually circumstantial, associates it with the Burgundians, and ascribes its revival to king Gundobald (A.D. 501) as an antidote to forsworn oaths induced by Christian compurgation (*Leges Burgundionum*, tit. xlv.). Wide diversity of application and form existed; but, with the overthrow of the Empire, the duel as part of the Barbarian codes became a sort of common law of Europe, fostered by the martial traditions which were developing into feudalism and were to culminate in chivalry.

Norse sagas have many records of *hólmgang* (as the duel was called in Iceland—from the islet [*hólmr*], its customary arena) or *hazle-field* (as it is called in Norway—from the posts demarking the ground); there were champions who made it a profession; the saga of Kormak, at once poet and champion, contains regulations of battle in which there are traces of sacrificial rites or incantations. *Orrostuhólmr*, Kormak's name for the place of combat, may be compared with *eornst* or *orreste*, the term for the duel in Anglo-Saxon and early Welsh laws. Ireland knew the institution as *comrac* or *comrac fri óenfer* ('battle against one man'; cf. Joyce, *Soc. Hist. of Anc. Ireland*, London, 1903, i. 152–54). Singularly enough, the evidence for the duel in England prior to the Norman conquest has failed to satisfy the historians. Thus, while elsewhere, through the influence of Christianity, the duel was being abolished early (*e.g.* in Iceland in A.D. 1006, and in Norway in 1012), in England there is the anomaly of its not becoming an undoubtedly national mode of trial till half a century later. The Conquest certainly established it; that it was unpopular with the English is a current inference without a very solid foundation. The laws of William the Conqueror gave an accused person, whether Norman or Englishman, the option between ordeal and duel, reserving a third choice—compurgation (*q.v.*)—to the Norman. The earliest English instance recorded is dated 1077; Norman examples occur forty years earlier. In that epoch it had a very wide application, both in civil matters and in charges of crime. In character it was, by its essential feature of self-help, not really an ordeal. How elaborate was the tradition for the forms of the duel as well as for the substantial law administered by its agency, can be seen from the *Assises of Jerusalem*, drawn up by Godfrey of Bouillon in 1099 for the Latin kingdom established by the First Crusade. This ordinance is equally full and precise regarding the modes of battle, the causes and conditions, the oaths against magic, and the distinctions of rank, whereby only knights fought in mail on horseback with helm and lance, while common folk fought in jackets (*bliant*), on foot, and with batons.

Before the close of the 12th cent. the jurisdiction of the duel was considerably restricted in England by Glanvil's 'great assise,' a sort of magnified jury. The tendency expanded; gradually the duel was superseded in civil causes except land-rights; burghal charters from Henry I. to Henry III. gave numerous exemptions; and by the time of Edward I. the practice was largely confined to trials on the writ of right to land and to 'appeals' for manslaughter and serious crime. Although trial by jury grew fast, the duel was long to remain. The importance of land litigations explains the origin of the professional 'pugil,' or champion, kept sometimes at a regular retaining fee by a religious house. 'From the quhilk consuetude,' said Sir John Skene (*Exposition of Difficill Wordes*, 1597, *s.v.* 'Campiones'), 'cummis the common saying,

"Do thou richt, do thou wrang,
Cheis thou a champion strang."'

In criminal causes a kindred but more corrupt product was the 'approver,' an informer, frequently infamous, who in making his charge underwent the risk of a challenge to battle. The loser in appeals of battle, being convicted of perjury by the fact of defeat, was hanged; and there is extant a contemporary picture of an approver who thus came to the bad end he had earned (Maitland, *Select Pleas of Crown*, Selden Soc., London, 1888).

From the 9th cent. the Church was continuously denouncing the duel, and as continuously giving it countenance. The latter process took many forms, one being the acquisition of jurisdiction by ecclesiastical dignitaries over trials by combat. Perquisites of court deflected even clerical minds from the true path. Sometimes clerics themselves fought duels in person, and it was as hard to stop the practice as to keep churchmen from bearing arms in war. A Glasgow pontifical in 1180 includes the liturgical common form for blessing the shield and baton for a duel, and some saints were esteemed especially efficacious to be invoked for success in such combats. In the First Crusade,

[1] Hence his name in the *Zohar*, סִטְרָא אַחֲרָא, 'the other side,' 'sinister.'

[2] Like Ahriman in the Avesta.

Peter the Hermit himself bore a challenge for a duel of ten, six, or three crusaders against an equal number of Saracens (*Tancredi*, cap. 81). As usual, practice belied precept, and anathema was useless. Indeed, an old French authority on the duel in the 15th cent. (Olivier de La Marche, in *Traité du duel judiciaire*, ed. Prost, Paris, 1872, p. 44) declares that ecclesiastics, like other people, were bound to fight if the case was treason or involved a point of the faith. The sanctions of the duel occasioned much deep discussion. Nicolas de Lyra wrote a treatise on the classic precedent of David and Goliath ; Cain and Abel admittedly furnished a less satisfactory example.

Until the end of the 13th cent. the duel was a duel of law, but in the 14th it blossomed anew as a duel of chivalry, once more emphasizing its aristocratic and military impulses. The duel, rapidly decaying in other matters, became the fashion for appeals of treason, and this newer chivalric duel took on fresh splendour, especially in the courts of England and France. An important ordinance of King Philip the Fair in 1306 was a characteristic code, containing regulations most of which passed into general use in chivalric courts. Notable editions of such duel codes were the ordinance drawn up by the Constable of England under Richard II., and the reproduction of it in the Order of Combats preserved by the Constable of Scotland from a MS belonging to James I. The formalities were evidently known to Chaucer, who reproduced them in the *Knight's Tale*.

Mere tilting matches, different as they were in principle from duels, are easily confounded with them, especially when they were 'jousts of war,' in which the combat was *à outrance*. Some of these are historic, such as the 'Combat des Trente' in 1351 between thirty Bretons and thirty Englishmen. It is the subject of a French *chanson de geste*, and its interest is the greater from its having supplied a model for the clan duel (in 1396) of thirty Highlanders of Clan Chattan against thirty of Clan Kay. Not a few fruitless challenges of 100 knights against 100 are extant, and there were many actual duels of numbers, such as of 13 Frenchmen against 13 Italians, and of 7 Frenchmen against 7 English. The duel, strictly construed as a combat of two, adjudged by and fought before a court invariably noble and usually royal, had long a distinct place, chiefly for trials on charges of treason where legal proofs were inadequate. It suited the times. Fourteenth century England devised a Court of Chivalry in which the historical importance of the duel culminates in the wager of battle between the Dukes of Hereford and Norfolk in 1398. This duel was stopped at the outset by Richard II., who arbitrarily and illegally exiled both combatants. Hereford returned from his exile next year to depose Richard and take the throne as Henry IV., and it was he who at his coronation jocularly assured his champion that he would himself see to the defence of his right to the crown. The 'champion of England' was one of the institutional inventions of English chivalry in the 14th century.

Meanwhile, alongside of chivalry the old duel of law was taking an unconscionable time to die. Law in the 13th and 14th cent. had no shudder for its brutality, and Bracton could calmly record (*de Legibus Angliæ*, ed. 1640, fol. 145) that the loss of a front tooth maimed a man and gave him an excuse from the duel, 'for such teeth help much to victory.' Pitiful records in the 15th cent. show this, gruesomely enough, to have been literal fact, for graces attendant on chivalry encountering before kings were absent when humble combatants in inferior courts mauled each other with baton or 'biscorne,' and tore each other with their teeth. One does not marvel that Pope Nicholas, in 867, had denied the Divine institution of the duel, but one does marvel that nearly seven centuries afterwards, John Major's protest, that 'God did not settle questions in that bad way,' was a mere voice in the wilderness. Yet humane opinion was ripening, and in 1549 the Council of Trent (Sess. XXV. cap. 19) denounced the duel, and decreed excommunication against all participators, even including seconds, spectators, and the lords temporal who assigned a place for a duel. The property of duellists and seconds was to be sequestrated, and they were to be delivered to the secular arm as murderers, while the funeral rites of the Church were to be denied to those who fell.[1] This denunciation had had innumerable predecessors, and was to be as little regarded, for the 'detestable use' had then entered on a new phase and was raging in Europe, as if to show that the Reformation of creed wrought little to reform humanity.

There had arisen in that new epoch the private duel, as distinguished from the duel under form of law or chivalry. Its vogue is usually ascribed to the consequences of the personal quarrel in 1528 between Francis I. of France and Charles V. of Spain. The constitutional interest of the new type was that it dispensed with the intervention of a judge or a court, and the great prevalence of this private duel for about two centuries in Europe was doubtless in part a consequence of the fashion of carrying light side-arms. Just as the two-handed sword of mediæval warfare was succeeded by the rapier, so the formal wager of battle with all its ceremonial procedure gave place to the lighter, easier form more apt for the 'sudden and quick in quarrel.' So there was bred the gauntlet-gatherer, the duellist, who inherited and developed all the pretensions of class privilege and other bad points of chivalry. Thus by additions was constructed a new code of the 'point of honour,' largely of Italian manufacture, which was a constant menace to domestic peace in Europe. The 'bons docteurs duellistes,' as Brantôme called them (*Mémoires*, p. 183), devised the pestiferous doctrine of the 'satisfaction of a gentleman,' which for three hundred years exacted a heavy toll of human life. If it fostered courage, it also fostered the bully. 'Men may account a duello,' said Bacon (*Letters and Life*, ed. Spedding, London, 1872, vi. 108), 'an honourable kind of satisfaction, yet it is but a scarlet or a grained kind of murdering.'

One stage of the duel, half-way between the old judicial combat and the new private duel, was the duel by licence, permitted in France and practised in Scotland under James VI. Later, as James I., he issued his edict against the duel in 1613, seconded by Bacon, who insisted that by the law of England the killing of a man in a duel was murder, however fair the duel might have been. Bacon saw the root of the matter in the point that the law gave no sufficient reparation for insult and libel—a consideration which weighs heavily still in estimating the place of the duel in modern Europe.

Wager of battle, dramatically resurrected in an appeal of murder in England in 1818, was repealed by statute in the following year. In all its forms, both judicial and unjudicial, the duel is now extinct in Great Britain and in the United States; in the latter for a time it was one of the most curious importations and survivals of European feudalism. Arising under military conditions, it naturally persists the longer where militarism

[1] Cf. also the unqualified condemnation of duelling by Benedict XIV. (Const. *Detestabilem*, 10 Nov. 1752), the punishment of surgeons and confessors intentionally administering to duellists (excommunication, by response of the Holy Office, 31 May 1884), and the renewed disapproval of the whole system, including even student duels, by Leo XIII. (Brief *Pastoralis officii*, 22 Sept. 1891).

is a determinant of public life. Among German students it has sunk to a rather savage athletic sport; and in Europe generally it has run, and is running, a course parallel to that of private wars —possibly prophetic of that of national wars. Its endurance is determined, not by enactment of law, but by the spirit of society. It is bound up with ideas of private revenge and family blood-feud, not with the conceptions of a State with justice as its primary function. It is instructive, therefore, to compare briefly the law in Britain and in Europe, and to diagnose certain causes of contrast. In Great Britain the duel has in general, since King James's edict, and more particularly during the last century and a half, been treated with far greater severity than was shown to it elsewhere. In this country practically alone is it now the law that to kill in duel is murder, involving the capital penalty. In almost all the rest of Europe this stringency holds only when traditional rules have been infringed, or when there has been some unfairness in the combat. Challenges, preliminary steps, and wounding in duel are, in like manner, much less heavily punished on the Continent than in Britain. On the other hand, exponents of the honour-code of Europe themselves declare that British courts make far more effective provision than Continental courts for the primary pecuniary protection for wrongs to personal honour, this scale being, for instance, contrasted with the slight reparation made in France. Bentham (*Works*, London, 1843, i. 379, 543), soberly balancing the merits and demerits of penal policies in general and 'honorary satisfaction' in special, points out the partiality, uncertainty, and inconvenience of the duel considered as a punishment, although he thought it might be proper to be indulgent to it if the alternative was revenge by poison or the bravo. Duels, he pointed out, were less common in Italy than in France and England, but poisoning and assassinations were much commoner. Like the historian Robertson, Bentham as a moralist thought that duelling tended to preserve 'politeness and peace,' and seems to have had little foresight of its swift decline. In recent times, the conditions, *e.g.* in France, often appeared to ensure immunity from injury but not from ridicule. The facts seem to justify the inference that for once British laws have doubly—by repression of the duel and by adequate civil reparation for injured honour—tended to suppress the duel and to make it unnecessary. *Frapper fort sur la bourse, c'est frapper juste* is the dictum of a modern 'docteur duelliste' (Croabbon, *op. cit. infra*, 399). In Britain the spirit of trial by jury has proved a better guardian even of honour than the sword. Perhaps it is not among the things they manage better in Germany and France that men continue, in however restricted a degree, to countenance the duel, which ranks as probably the oldest barbaric inheritance among the institutions of Europe. Probably Bentham himself did not sufficiently reflect that what had so long been abandoned by Europe as an utterly capricious and irrational mode of justice, where substantial interests were concerned, stood thereby already grotesquely out of court for the finer task, in modern civilization, of healing the sores of honour.

Significant indications of current tendencies, illustrating some of the foregoing views, have appeared in Germany, the centre of modern militarism, especially since 1897, when Kaiser Wilhelm II. issued a Cabinet order declaring his will that duels among officers should be more effectively prevented by remitting private quarrels to Councils of Honour with appeal to Courts of Honour, commanding officers, and the Kaiser himself. These Councils of Honour for a regiment consist of three officers, while the Courts of Honour comprise all the officers. This order by its terms did not prohibit duelling, but it enlarged the province of Courts of Honour. Reconciliation by intervention of such Councils and Courts, however, was, and still is, declared permissible only when not forbidden by the honour of the class to which the officer belongs or by good morals. At first hailed as an abolition of the duel, the order was soon found not to warrant any such hopes. Critics in 1897, and since, have pointed out that the Kaiser had never departed from recognition of the duel as the *ultima ratio* in affairs of honour; they bluntly stated that the so-called scandal of duelling would not be ended, that the order would entirely depend for its efficiency on the spirit of its enforcement, and that it was puerile to anticipate the eradication of so deep-rooted a practice at one stroke. Yet on the whole the order was recognized as a very considerable attempt at restriction in the army. It was subsequently made applicable also to naval officers.

The critical forecast was justified by events. Scandals continued to arise periodically over duels under painful circumstances and with fatal consequences. In 1901 sharp controversy sprang from the discovery that, in violation of an Imperial order, candidates for choice as officers in the reserve had been subjected to questions regarding their opinions on duelling, and had suffered prejudice for answers opposed to the practice. The Minister of War declared in the Reichstag that, while duels were justifiable for such cases as charges of cowardice, insult by violence, or imputation upon an officer's moral integrity or family honour, everything was done to prevent the duelling abuse. These explanations did not satisfy friends of reform, who protested that every officer punished for taking part in a duel should be dismissed from the army. Afterwards, in the same year, a manifesto was influentially signed demanding the prohibition of all duels and the institution of Courts of Honour in their stead. It was expressly urged that the best means of prevention was to afford more effective legal protection against attacks on the honour of individuals. Direct legislative action does not seem to have followed, but the agitation has served a useful purpose in elevating public opinion in Europe.

LITERATURE.—*Traité du duel judiciaire* [by Olivier de La Marche and others], ed. B. Prost, Paris, 1872; *Arbre des Batailles*, in Scots tr. *Buke of Bataillis* of Gilbert of the Haye (ed. Stevenson, Scottish Text Soc., 1901); Paris de Puteo, *Duello*, Venice, 1525; P. de B. de Brantôme, *Mémoires . . . touchant les duels* (ed. princeps, 1665), London, 1739; J. Selden, *The Duello*, London, 1610; E. A. Kendall, *Argument . . . on Trial by Battle*, London, 1818; H. C. Lea, *Superstition and Force*[4], Philadelphia, 1892; Pollock-Maitland, *Hist. of Eng. Law*, Cambridge, 1895; Alfred Hutton, *The Sword and the Centuries*, London, 1901; G. Neilson, *Trial by Combat*, Glasgow, 1890. Leading authorities on the duel in Europe include Comte de Chateauvillard, *Essai sur le duel*, Paris, 1836; F. Patetta, *Le Ordalie*, Turin, 1890; and, as regards the state of modern laws and regulations affecting the duel, A. Croabbon, *La Science du point d'honneur*, Paris, 1894. General reference may also be made to Carl A. Thimm, *Bibliography of Fencing and Duelling*, London, 1896; Fougeroux de Champigneulles, *Hist. des duels anciens et modernes*[2], 2 vols., Paris, 1838; E. Cauchy, *Du Duel, considéré dans ses origines et dans l'état actuel des mœurs*, 2 vols., Paris, 1846; G. von Below, *Das Duell in Deutschland, Gesch. u. Gegenwart*[2], Kassel, 1896; H. Fehr, *Der Zweikampf*, Berlin, 1908; M. Liepmann, *Duell u. Ehre*, Berlin, 1904; E. Kohlrausch, *Zweikampf*, Berlin, 1906; M. Rade, art. 'Zweikampf' (with copious Literature) in *PRE*[3].

GEORGE NEILSON.

2. Among primitive peoples.—However much the duel has degenerated from its once high estate, as has just been shown, it must yet be adjudged to have been once one of the numerous forms of ordeal (*q.v.*), although still another factor plainly contributed to its rise and tenacity—the frequent failure of primitive jurisprudence to secure in any other way the ends at which it aimed. The purely religious side of the duel, which, from this point of view, is more commonly termed 'the wager of battle,' may be reserved for art. ORDEAL, but certain primitive forms of legal duels, as summarized by Post (*Grundriss der ethnolog. Jurisprudenz*, Oldenburg, 1894–5, ii. 236, 351 f., 504–506), may be briefly mentioned here.

In the simplest type, as among the S. American Charruas and Botocudos, the duellists pommel each other with fists or sticks, with scant danger to life or limb, this being the case even in old Bohemian and Polish law. A more interesting form is that in which, as among the Australians, the parties strike each other alternately; and the highest is that in which deadly weapons are employed with intent to kill, as among the Californian Korusi, the Dayaks, the Bataks, the Australians, the Tunguses, the Grusinians, and in Europe generally. An interesting instance of the duel as a proof of guilt is to be found in Nias.

When a girl is found to be pregnant and the man whom she accuses denies his share in her guilt, each of the pair is given a knife, the one first wounded in the ensuing duel being adjudged in the wrong. In this case it is, moreover, interesting to see that the girl may be represented, quite as was the case in Europe, by a champion, this being in Nias one of her kinsmen. Elsewhere, where women are allowed to participate in duels (a privilege normally reserved for the male sex), their opponents may be compelled to have some handicap, as when, in old Bohemian law, they were obliged to stand in a pit dug in the ground. Elsewhere, however, as among the Slavs and Bohemians, the services of a champion were expressly forbidden, on the ground that a man really innocent might be killed.

The cycle of development of the duel would seem to be somewhat as follows: in its ultimate origin it is simply a fight, more or less serious, between two men concerning some real or fancied injury. From this point of view it is precisely like any modern fight between two men for the settlement of some difficulty between them, or even for mere revenge. But at an early time these fights become hedged about, for the welfare of society, with various restrictions; *e.g.* formal witnesses (the later 'seconds') may be required to see fair play, or certain cases alone may be settled by the duel, or certain formalities are required by the authorities before a duel may be fought. There is also doubtless present, even in the most primitive form of duel—or mere fight—the conviction, on the part of at least one of the combatants, that he has been wronged, and he feels that the victory will decide which of the two has been right. Though the methods employed are far different, the underlying principle is the same as in the most highly polished modern controversy of any sort whatever. From this feeling that 'truth is mighty, and will prevail,' comes the concept that the duel has a religious sanction, that Divine powers aid the party in the right, and that it is, indeed, an ordeal, in the technical sense of the term. On the other hand, the increasing scope of law imposes ever narrowing bounds upon the duel, and, as other modes of redress are evolved, the duel becomes more and more needless, especially as it is felt that it involves a useless waste of valuable lives, besides interfering with the majesty of the law. Thus the duel finally decays as an institution, and comes to be treated as a crime, even a challenge, except in time of war, being punished with death among the Aztecs. Yet the duel dies hard, for there lingers a persistent belief among many of fine fibre that there are wrongs for which no court of law can give redress, and it must be confessed that pecuniary damages or even imprisonment of an opponent is thin salve for wounded honour. Church and State have alike condemned the duel, and justly; yet perhaps the duellist's side of the argument should not, in fairness, be utterly ignored.

The peculiar nature of the duel from the point of view of early jurisprudence is well illustrated by its relation to the blood-feud (*q.v.*), to which a man killing another in a duel is rarely liable, this being probably due to the fact that both parties were held to be fighting in self-defence, while, where the duel was a recognized form of procedure, there would be no room for blood-feud.

The extreme degeneration of the duel is almost ludicrously illustrated by the 'nith-songs' of the Greenland Eskimo.

'When a Greenlander considers himself injured in any way by another person, he composes about him a satirical song, which he rehearses with the help of his intimates. He then challenges the offending one to a duel of song. One after another the two disputants sing at each other their wisdom, wit, and satire, supported by their partisans, until at last one is at his wits' end, when the audience, who are the jury, make known their decision. The matter is now settled for good, and the contestants must be friends again and not recall the matter which was in dispute' (Chamberlain, in *Handbook of Amer. Indians*, ii. 77 [*Bull. 30 BE*, Washington, 1910]).

Lastly, it may be noted that any attempt to trace the duel to a single people is hopeless. It had its origin in the fighting spirit of the human race, and that spirit is as universal as mankind.

Louis H. Gray.

DUNKARDS.—See Sects (Christian).

DUNS SCOTUS.—See Scholasticism.

DURGĀ.—Durgā is one of the commonest names of Śiva's consort. Other names are Devī, Umā, Gaurī, Pārvatī, Chaṇḍī, Chāmuṇḍā, Kālī, Kapālinī, Bhavānī, Vijayā, etc. (for a very full list, see Dowson, *Classical Dict. of Hindu Mythol.*[4], London, 1903, *s.v.* 'Devī'). The name Durga originally designated that goddess in her terrific character. As has been shown in art. Brāhmanism (vol. ii. p. 813), she is, like her husband Śiva, a combination of several deities and local varieties of similar mythological conceptions. It is, therefore, natural that she should present very different aspects.

The worship of such goddesses as ultimately were combined in, and made up, as it were, the great goddess Durgā, seems to have become more popular about the end of the Vedic period, for some of their names occur already in Vedic literature, especially in the latest works belonging to it. Ambikā is called Rudra's sister in the *Vājasaneyī Saṁhitā*, but in *Taittirīya Āraṇyaka*, x. 18, she has already become the spouse of Rudra, just as in later times. In the same work, x. 1 (p. 788 of the *Bibl. Indica* ed., Calcutta, 1864–72), we find an invocation of Durgā devī, who is there styled *Vairochanī*, daughter of the Sun or Fire; and in x. 1, 7, among verses addressed to Agni, we meet with two more names of Durgā (here called Durgī), viz. Kātyāyanī (the text has the masculine form, Kātyāyana) and Kanyakumārī.[1] Umā, daughter of Himavat, is mentioned in the *Kena Upaniṣad*, iii. 25, as a heavenly woman conversant with Brahman, on which account the commentator regards her as a personification of Brahmavidyā; but in *Taitt. Ār.* x. 18 (according to the Draviḍa text) Rudra is invoked as Umāpati, 'husband of Umā.' Kālī and Karālī, two names of Durgā, occur in the *Muṇḍaka Upaniṣad*, i. 2, 4, among the names of the seven tongues of Agni. Finally, it may be mentioned that, in Weber's opinion, there is some connexion between Durgā and Sarasvatī, since the epithets Varadā, Mahādevī, and Sandhyāvidyā, given to Sarasvatī in *Taitt. Ār.* x. 26, 30, belong, at a later period, exclusively to the consort of Śiva (cf. Muir, *Orig. Skr. Texts*, 1858–72, iv. 428 f.).

From the testimonies adduced, it seems certain that about the end of the Vedic period several goddesses had come to be acknowledged who then or later were promoted to the rank of wives of Rudra-Śiva; and that some of them may, with more or less probability, be connected with mountains and with the element of fire. They have all been blended in the one consort of Śiva, whose character obviously betrays the diversity of her origin. In her terrible aspect she seems to represent fire as the devouring and, at the same time, expiating element; and in her more benign character we seem to catch sight of a goddess of the mountains. But there were probably other goddesses or female demons, belonging to different parts of India and worshipped by different classes of people, who in the course of time were combined into one great goddess, the spouse of Śiva. Yet this coalescence of various elements in the one great goddess does not seem ever to have been complete, since a kind of consciousness of their disparity appears to have lingered in the mind of her worshippers as late as the composition of the *Devīmāhātmya* (assigned by Pargiter to the 6th or perhaps 5th cent. A.D.). In the story of her victory over Śumbha and Niśumbha, related below, Chaṇḍikā (here identified with Ambikā and Chāmuṇḍā) as well as Kālī is said to be an emanation from Durgā; through them, and not in her own

[1] From Kumārī, Cape Comorin, the southernmost point of India, is supposed to have got its name, which we find already in the *Periplus Maris Erythræi* (Κωμάρ, cap. 58).

person, she performed those deeds for which she is chiefly celebrated.

This syncretistic process, begun in the Vedic period, is all but complete in the Epics, which, however, do not contain explicit accounts of Durgā's deeds. The divinity of Śiva's spouse was then generally acknowledged, and the ideas concerning her were very much the same as, though less extravagant than, in later times. What they were will best be seen from a hymn of Arjuna to Durgā in *Mahābhārata*, vi. 23, which is here transscribed (tr. Muir, iv. 432):

'Reverence to thee, Siddhasenānī [generaless of the Siddhas],[1] the noble, the dweller on Mandara, Kumārī, Kālī, Kāpālī, Kapilā, Kṛṣṇapiṅgalā. Reverence to Bhadrakālī; reverence to thee, Mahākālī; reverence to thee, Chaṇḍī, Chaṇḍā; reverence to thee, O Tāriṇī [deliveress], O Varavarṇinī [beautiful-coloured], O fortunate Kātyāyanī, O Karālī, O Vijayā, O Jayā [victory], who bearest a peacock's tail for thy banner, adorned with various jewels, armed with many spears, wielding sword and shield, younger sister of the chief of cowherds [Kṛṣṇa], eldest born in the family of the cowherd Nanda, delighting always in Mahiṣa's blood, Kauśikī, wearing yellow garments, loud-laughing, wolf-mouthed; reverence to thee, thou delighter in battle, O Umā, Śākambharī, thou white one [or Śvetā], thou black one [or Kṛṣṇā], O destroyer of Kaiṭabha. Reverence to thee, O Hiraṇyākṣī, Virūpākṣī, Dhūmrākṣī [golden-, distorted-, dark-eyed], O Vedaśruti [tradition of the Veda] most pure, devout, Jātavedasī [female Agni], who dwellest continually near to Jambū, mountain-precipices, and sepulchres. Of sciences, thou art the science of Brahman [or of the Veda], the great sleep of embodied beings, O mother of Skanda, divine Durgā, dweller in wildernesses. Thou art called Svāhā, Svadhā, Kalā, Kāṣṭhā [minute divisions of time], Sarasvatī, Sāvitrī, mother of the Vedas, and the Vedānta [or end of the Vedas]. Thou, great goddess [Mahādevī], art praised with a pure heart. By thy favour let me be ever victorious in battle. In deserts, fears, and difficulties, and in the preservation of thy devout servants, and in Pātāla, thou constantly abidest, and conquerest the Dānavas in battle. Thou art Jambhanī [destroyer], Mohinī, Māyā, Hrī, Śrī, Sandhyā, the luminous, Sāvitrī, the mother, Tuṣṭi [contentment], Puṣṭi [fatness], Dhṛti [constancy], Dīpti [light], increaser of the sun and moon, the power of the powerful in battle,—[all this] thou art seen by the *Siddhas* and *Chāraṇas* [to be].' The translator adds that in *Mahābhārata*, iv. 6, there is another hymn addressed by Yudhiṣṭhira to Durgā, very similar to the preceding. Among other things, she is there said to 'have her perpetual abode on the Vindhya mountains, and to delight in spirituous liquor, flesh, and sacrificial victims.' In the sequel, Muir quotes a remarkable line from the *Harivaṁśa* (v. 3274), according to which Durgā was worshipped by the savage tribes of Śabaras, Barbaras, and Pulindas.

We now proceed to relate the chief mythological data and the deeds of Durgā which are found in Sanskrit literature. Usually she is stated to be the daughter of Himavat (Umā Haimavatī already in the *Kena Upaniṣad*) by Menā. The latter is, according to *Rāmāyaṇa*, I. xxxv. 14, the daughter of Meru, and, according to the *Purāṇas*,[2] the mental daughter of the Manes. According to *Rāmāyaṇa*, I. xxxv. 15, Umā was the younger sister of Gaṅgā, but, according to *Harivaṁśa*, 943 ff. (where she is called Aparṇā), she was the eldest daughter of Himavat, and had two sisters, Ekaparṇā and Ekapāṭalā, wives of Jaigīṣavya and Asita Devala respectively. Sometimes, however, Durgā is addressed as sister of Viṣṇu[3] and of Indra,[4] whence she is said to be called Kauśikī. Her epithet *Vairochanī*, in *Taitt. Ār.* x. 1. 7, seems to make her a daughter of the Sun or perhaps of Fire, while the epithet Gautamī would connect her with one of the seven Ṛṣis. Some of these statements were perhaps prompted by a desire on the part of the worshippers of Śiva to provide their supreme and primeval god with a consort of more equal rank than belonged to a daughter of the Himālaya. Such a tendency almost certainly gave rise to the Paurāṇic story that Śiva's wife originally was Satī, daughter of Dakṣa, the creator, and that in her wrath she abandoned her bodily existence through *yoga*, when Dakṣa slighted her husband by not inviting him to his sacrifice.[1] For this accident is not yet alluded to in the earliest account of Dakṣa's sacrifice in *Mahābhārata*, xii. 284, where Śiva's wife is called Devī and Umā.

The story of Umā's marriage with Śiva forms the subject of Kālidāsa's famous poem, *Kumārasambhava*.[2] The gods, defeated by the Asura Tāraka, consulted Brahmā; he predicted that Śiva's son by Umā, who was not yet betrothed to him, would vanquish their enemy. In order to cause Śiva, who was practising austerities on the Himālaya, to fall in love with Umā, Indra dispatched Manmatha, the god of love, to the spot, where just then the beautiful daughter of the Himālaya, Śiva's host, was offering flowers to the divine ascetic. Manmatha drew his bow at him, and detached his mind from contemplation. Śiva waxed wroth, and reduced the god of love to ashes; but afterwards he was moved by Umā's constancy as she submitted to the severest austerities in order to win him, and wooed her. The product of their love was Kumāra, who on his birthday killed the Asura.[3] It may be added that the Paurāṇic etymology of Umā is based on this story: when she engaged in austerities, her mother dissuaded her from this course, saying, *u mā*, 'no, no.'

Another son of Durgā is Gaṇeśa, the god with the elephantine head. His miraculous birth has been related in art. BRĀHMANISM.[4]

The most famous deeds of Durgā are her victories over several Asuras; they form the subject of the *Devīmāhātmya*, an episode of the *Mārkaṇḍeya Purāṇa*,[5] which has become the text-book of her worshippers. In this work Durgā is said to have been formed, under the name Chaṇḍikā, by the combined energies of the gods, which they put forth in their wrath when the Asura Mahiṣa had vanquished the gods, and had set himself up as the Indra of the heavenly dominions. The goddess did battle with the host of Asuras, and killed them wholesale. Then ensued a single combat between Chaṇḍikā and Mahiṣāsura, who assumed many forms, especially his buffalo shape, from which he derived his name. At last Chaṇḍikā stood on the demon, and cut off his head; but out of the trunk grew the Asura in his natural shape, and then he was killed by the goddess. It is in this act of dealing the last blow to the Asura who comes out of the beheaded buffalo that Durgā is usually represented in Indian art, not only in numberless pictures and sculptures, but also in poetry; for the great poet Bāṇa, who lived in the 7th cent. A.D., describes this scene in nearly every verse of his *Chaṇḍīśataka*, a hymn to that goddess (ed. Durgāprasāda and Parab[2], Bombay, 1899; a new ed. and tr. forthcoming by G. Payn Quackenbos, in the Columbia University Indo-Iranian Series).

Besides the killing of Mahiṣāsura, the *Devīmāhātmya* celebrates the victory of Chaṇḍikā over the Asuras Śumbha and Niśumbha. These two demons had routed the gods, and had usurped the government of the three worlds. The gods implored the aid of Pārvatī, who had come to bathe in the water of the Gaṅgā; from her body issued another goddess who is called Ambikā or Chaṇḍikā. Now, it happened that Chaṇḍa and Muṇḍa, two servants of Śumbha and Niśumbha, had seen this goddess, and had been struck by her beauty. They, therefore, advised Śumbha to take her as his wife,

[1] The form in the original is *siddhasenāni*, not *siddhasenānīḥ*, 'generaless of the Siddhas,' the interpretation given by Muir, following Nīlakaṇṭha. The name might be explained as 'wife of Siddhasena'; Siddhasena, however, is a name of Kumāra, not of Śiva.

[2] *Kumārasambhava*, i. 18, com.

[3] *Harivaṁśa*, 10235.

[4] *Ib.* and 3260.

[1] *Viṣṇu Purāṇa*, tr. Wilson, i. 117, 127, n. 1; cf. *Kumārasambhava*, i. 21.

[2] The same story is also told in the *Śiva Purāṇa* and the Śivarahasya of the *Skanda Purāṇa*. For references, see *ZDMG* xxvii. (1873) 178 ff.

[3] See *ERE* ii. 807.

[4] It may be added here that Gaṇeśa is first mentioned in *Taitt. Ār.* x. 1, 5, where a *mantra* is addressed to him under the name Danti. Cf. also art. GANAPATYAS.

[5] Eng. tr. by Eden Pargiter, *Bibl. Ind.*, 1904.

upon which the latter sent a messenger to invite her to marry him. She consented, on condition that he should vanquish her. Thereupon Śumbha sent Dhūmralochana with a host of Asuras to seize her; but she destroyed them all. Then Chaṇḍa and Muṇḍa were dispatched with another army. When Ambikā saw them, she waxed exceedingly wroth, so that from her forehead issued a terrible goddess Kālī, of emaciated body, clad in a tiger's skin, with a garland of skulls hanging from her neck, and her tongue lolling out from her wide mouth. After a frightful battle, she killed both Chaṇḍa and Muṇḍa, from which feat she received the name Chāmuṇḍā.[1] Now Śumbha himself, at the head of an enormous army of Asuras, went to meet Ambikā, on whose side fought the energies of all gods, which had taken bodily form. Among the Asuras was Raktabīja; when a drop of his blood fell on the ground, it was at once changed into an Asura of his form. Thus innumerable Asuras soon came into existence, and increased the army of the enemies of the gods. Chaṇḍikā then ordered Chāmuṇḍā to drink up the blood of Raktabīja before it fell to the ground, and at last killed the exhausted and bloodless Asura. Now Niśumbha attacked the goddess, while her lion caused great havoc in the army of the demons. The battle was terrible, but at last Niśumbha fell, and Śumbha also was killed by Chaṇḍikā.

There is yet another form of Durgā as Yoganidrā or Nidrā Kālarūpiṇī, which connects her worship with that of Viṣṇu-Kṛṣṇa, and is apparently intended to bring it under the protection and patronage of Viṣṇu.[2]

In the *Harivaṁśa*, 3236 ff., it is related by Vaiśampāyana that, with the view of defeating the designs of Kaṁsa in regard to the destruction of Devakī's offspring, Viṣṇu descended into Pātāla, where he sought the aid of Nidrā Kālarūpiṇī [Sleep in the form of Time]; and promised her in return that through his favour she should be a goddess adored in all the world. He desired her to be born as the ninth child of Yaśodā on the same night on which he was to be born as the eighth child of Devakī, when he would be carried to Yaśodā, and she to Devakī. He told her that she would be taken by the foot, and cast upon a rock, but would then obtain an eternal place in the sky, becoming assimilated to himself in glory; would be installed by Indra among the gods, received by him as his sister under the name of Kauśikī, and would obtain from him (Indra) a perpetual abode on the Vindhya mountains where, thinking upon him (Viṣṇu), she would kill the two demons, Śumbha and Niśumbha, and would be worshipped with animal sacrifices.[3]

The same story is told in several *Purāṇas*, e.g. in the *Viṣṇu Purāṇa*, v. 1 (tr. Wilson, iv. 260 ff.).

In another myth the goddess is made to share the glory of Viṣṇu.[4] When this god, at the end of the *kalpa*, 'wooed the sleep of contemplation' on the universal ocean, the two demons, Madhu and Kaiṭabha, approached him, with the intention of killing Brahmā, who stood on the lotus that grew out of the navel of Viṣṇu; but the latter cut them asunder with his discus. The part played by Yoganidrā in this transaction was this: that she left Viṣṇu's eyes on being invoked by Brahmā; thus the god was awakened, and could slay the demons. In the hymn quoted above from the *Mahābhārata* she is styled 'destroyer of Kaiṭabha,' which seems to attribute the victory entirely to her.

From the quotations given above, it is evident that in the period of the Epics, probably towards the end, the worship of Durgā was already firmly established; and that it was further developed in the time of the *Harivaṁśa* and the *Purāṇas*. But it is in another branch of later Sanskrit literature, the *Tantras*, that her worship is at its height. The *Tantras*, says Wilson,[5]

'always assume the form of a dialogue between Śiva and his bride, in one of her many forms, but mostly as Umā and Pārvatī, in which the goddess questions the god as to the mode of performing various ceremonies, and the prayers and incantations to be used in them.'

They furnish the rites and formulæ in a new form of worship, which has largely superseded the older one based on the Veda.

There was yet another cause at work to give the worship of Durgā its present form, viz. the theory of *śakti*. *Śakti* is the energy of a god, especially of Viṣṇu and Śiva; it is personified as his female partner, and is identified with the *prakṛti* of Sāṅkhya philosophy, whereby a mystical and speculative foundation is given to the *śakti*-theory, which is already taught in several *Purāṇas*. By far the most popular *śakti* is that of Śiva as Pārvatī, Bhavānī, or Durgā; and the majority of the Śāktas, or followers of these doctrines, worship this goddess.

We have seen above that already, in the *Mahābhārata*, Durgā is said to delight in spirituous liquor, flesh, and sacrificial victims. These have always been characteristic of the worship of Durgā.

'In Bengal,' says Colebrooke,[1] 'and the contiguous provinces, thousands of kids and buffalo calves are sacrificed before the idol, at every celebrated temple; and opulent persons make a similar destruction of animals at their private chapels. The sect which has adopted this system is prevalent in Bengal,[2] and in many other provinces of India. . . . But the practice is not approved by other sects of Hindus.'

Even human sacrifices were offered to the goddess in some places. Bāṇa (7th cent.), in a lengthy description of a temple of Chaṇḍikā,[3] alludes to human sacrifices; Bhavabhūti (8th cent.) introduces, in the 5th act of his play, *Mālatī and Mādhavā*, a temple of Chāmuṇḍā and her votaries, who try to sacrifice a human victim; in the *Samarāichcha Kahā*, by Haribhadra (9th cent.), a temple of Chaṇḍikā and the offering of a human sacrifice by Śabaras are described (p. 435 ff., *Bibl. Ind.* ed.); in the *Kālikā Purāṇa*, 'minute directions are given for the offering of a human victim to Kālī, whom it is said his blood satisfies for a thousand years.[4]

Finally, mention must be made of the most degraded worship of Durgā and other *śaktis* by the Vāmīs, or 'left hand' worshippers; in it debauchery and gross immorality are admitted, so that the worship is perverted into a most scandalous orgy.[5]

LITERATURE.—This has been sufficiently indicated in the article.

HERMANN JACOBI.

DUTY.—If taken in a wide sense, the notion of duty is essentially implied in every system of morality and every ethical theory. For all morality and all ethics turn upon the contrast between the inclinations of the individual and some objective and authoritative standard to which these inclinations must be subordinated; and it is just this objective control that is emphasized in the notion of duty. Duty comes to us with a claim; it is a thing laid upon us to do whether we like it or not. But, although the element of objective authority is necessarily implied in every moral standard, the notion of duty is far less prominent and exclusive in some systems of morality than in others; and, of course, is also far less distinctly abstracted and analyzed, and occupies a far less fundamental place, in some types of ethical theory than in others.

1. In **Greek ethics**, for instance, the moral life is, for the most part, presented as a good to be realized or a type of virtue or excellence to be attained. Man's good or true happiness, the health of the soul, is shown to lie in the life of virtue, the performance of the work or function which his own nature and the part he has to play in the general life of the community mark out for him. To see

[1] This name occurs first here and in the *Mālatīmādhava*, and a *rākṣasā* named Chauṇḍa appears in *Pauma*, v. 263.

[2] Muir, iv. 434.

[3] *Ib.* 433 f.

[4] *Mārkaṇḍeya Purāṇa*, tr. Pargiter, p. 469 f.

[5] *Select Works* (1861), i. 248.

[1] *Miscellaneous Essays*, 1873, i. 101, n. 1.

[2] A full description of the festival of Durgā as celebrated in Bengal is given by Pratapchandra Ghosha, *Durgā Pūjā*, 1871.

[3] *Kadāmbarī*, ed. Peterson[2], Bombay Sanskrit Series, 1889, p. 223 ff.

[4] Wilson, *Select Works*, ii. 268.

[5] *Ib.* i. 254.

in this life of virtue his real happiness or good is man's true wisdom, whereas the scepticism which sees in it only a burden and a restraint imposed for the advantage of others is short-sighted folly. The restraints of the virtuous life are only the restraints which any man must exercise who would be master of himself and would live a truly human life among his fellows. So long as this mode of presenting the moral life prevailed, the element of duty was completely absorbed into, and subordinated to, the thought of good or achievement. A man must be courageous, temperate, and just, because in no other way can he achieve his good or true happiness.

It was only when, in *Stoicism*, this good was conceived to be determined by, and to be realized in obeying, a cosmical law of universal reason that the notion of duty emerged into a new distinctness and prominence. Not that the Stoics could not, or did not, use the same general formulæ as the older schools had done. The change, apart from details, is rather one in the whole philosophical atmosphere. The same formulæ might be used, but they were used with a different meaning. Everything was coloured by the pantheistic necessity of the Stoic system. The life which it behoved the good or wise man to lead was one determined for him by the law or reason of the universe, which prescribed to man his place in the system of things and the duties pertaining to that place. It was for man to recognize the place and duties assigned to him, and thus consciously to live in accordance with nature, or the immanent reason of the universe. Hence the notion of duty entered into the Stoic system in a double sense, expressed by the two terms *καθῆκον* and *κατόρθωμα*. The former term was applied to right actions regarded simply as fitting or prescribed by nature, the latter to the same actions when consciously done for this reason by the good or wise man;[1] hence only an action which deserved the latter epithet was completely good or virtuous.

2. Thus it was when morality came to be regarded mainly in the light of conformity to a law that the notion of duty became prominent. The Stoic law of nature, however, was also a law of reason, which the same reason in man enabled him to recognize. And this conception of the law of nature, as the law which reason affirms, continued even after the law of nature had come to be, in a manner, identified with positive law in the shape of the *jus gentium*, or equity of Roman jurisprudence. Now, **Christianity**, like Stoicism, represented morality in the light of obedience to a law, but the Christian law was the revealed commandments of God—not a law which man's reason had to discover, but one which was given to man by Divine revelation, and had simply to be obeyed. Hence the strictly authoritative aspect of duty stands out much more prominently in Christian than in Stoic morality. Of course, it did not follow that, because the Moral Law was thus authoritative, it was in any sense arbitrary; this mistaken inference was a product of later reflexion. The natural assumption was that, being God's law, it could not but be a wise and good law. But the law was to be obeyed by man because it was laid upon him by God, not because man himself saw his good or true happiness to consist in obedience to such a law. Man's eternal welfare—his entrance into the Kingdom of God, as the primitive Christians would have said—was bound up with his obedience to God's law, but so bound by God's own ordinance, not by any sort of connexion which man's own reason discovered to him.

[1] These terms were also used, however, to express a distinction between absolute and conditional duty (see Zeller, *Stoics*, Eng. tr., pp. 287-290, and notes).

Now, this kind of separation between duty and good, this reference of the connexion between them to a hidden Divine source, remains characteristic of the Christian morality and ethics throughout, whereas it was quite absent from Stoicism. The Stoic, in fact, simply identified the good or happiness with the virtuous life. Christianity makes the former depend upon and involve the latter, but does not identify them; it rather represents man's eternal good or happiness as the Divine seal or reward of obedience to God's commandments. In this sense, then, the performance of duty remains, on the Christian view, always a matter of obedience rather than of insight; the *good* of obedience is not our concern. On the other hand, as regards the actual contents of the law which is to be obeyed and the mere rightness of obeying it, the tendency of the more philosophical expositions of Christian ethics has usually been to assert that man's own reason or conscience not merely assents to, but itself also affirms, the fundamental precepts of revealed morality. That is to say, God has not only revealed the Moral Law by express commandment, but has also implanted it in man's conscience, or made him capable of discovering it by the due use of his natural reason. Revelation only reinforces or amplifies the dictates of conscience or the natural reason.[1] On this view, therefore, the authority of duty is by no means a matter of merely external command; it is no less a matter of internal perception and recognition. We see the rules of duty to be in themselves right, or such as we ought to obey (Intuitionism) without needing to know wherein the good of obedience consists; conscience has an intrinsic authority which makes itself immediately felt. The coarser expositions of Christian ethics, on the other hand, have tended to represent the rules of duty, even when it was acknowledged that they may be *known* by the light of nature, as depending for their *authority* on rewards and punishments (*e.g.* Paley). The same tendency in secular ethics leads to the representation of morality as good policy, and seeks to back up the claims of duty by an appeal to the enlightened self-interest, or at best to the finer sensibilities, of the individual. The prevalence of this type of ethics in the 18th cent. partly accounts, by way of reaction, for the severity of the classical exposition of the conception of duty which we owe to Kant.

3. Kant.—The rigid distinction, with which Kant's exposition opens, between action done from duty and action done from inclination is one which, no doubt, lends itself to such caricatures as that drawn in Schiller's well-known lines, but it was really necessary for Kant's purpose. This was—to make absolutely clear the objectivity of duty. What is right is right whether we like it or not, and, were it not that the right thus stands out as something objective and authoritative over against our private inclinations, the notion of duty would have no meaning. Morality does not begin to exist until this contrast is felt and takes effect. As Kant puts it, an action has no moral worth unless it is done from duty, *i.e.* in the consciousness of its rightness. Paradoxical as this proposition has often been found—for good actions surely are often done without any thought of duty—it is, from the point of view of Kant's analysis, a truism. An action that expresses nothing but the present inclination of the agent tells us nothing about his character. What he does from inclination to-day, he may likewise from inclination refuse to do to-morrow. The commands of duty do not wait upon

[1] So, *e.g.*, Butler, *Analogy*, pt. ii. ch. i. The conception of a law written in the heart and conscience is already present in St. Paul (Ro 2[15]), who may owe it indirectly to the diffused influence of Stoical ideas.

our inclinations, or strike a bargain with us; the imperative of duty, in Kant's terminology, is a Categorical Imperative.

Some other features of Kant's ethical doctrine which are closely connected with his analysis of the notion of duty may be noted. (1) He regards the Moral Law, or Categorical Imperative of duty, as a formal law, that is to say, as a law which prescribes the spirit in which actions are to be done rather than the objects at which they are to aim, or, at any rate, prescribes the latter no further than is involved in prescribing the former. (2) He regards the conception of the Moral Law as the first and fundamental conception of ethical theory, and that of the good as subsequent to and dependent upon it; in fact, the good is for him, one might say, a religious rather than a strictly ethical conception. From all this it is evident that Kant was not far wrong in supposing himself entitled to look upon his ethical theory as a philosophical version of the Christian morality. (3) He lays great stress upon what he calls the 'autonomy of the will,' *i.e.* the necessity that we should be able to see in the command of morality, not a foreign compulsion, but that self-constraint of our own spiritual nature which is our true freedom. And this conception, again, if less directly related to the ethics of the Gospels, is closely parallel to St. Paul's conception of Christian freedom.

4. The one kind of ethical problem which interested Kant was to find an abstract formula or expression for the moral consciousness, and to determine what were the ultimate conditions involved in this formula. The genetic inquiries, psychological and sociological, which have become so prominent in our time were beyond his horizon. It is not surprising, then, that one of the facts about duty which are most obvious to the present-day moralist, viz. its social origin and basis, does not figure with quite the same kind of prominence in Kant's abstract analysis of the conception. What Kant is concerned to show is that the consciousness of duty is the consciousness of an objective law of conduct, which is, of course, a social law, because it is equally binding upon all men, and pays no regard to the private inclinations or selfish interests of individuals. It does not enter into the scope of his inquiries, however, to ask how this consciousness of a law of conduct grew up, what forces maintain such a law in its actual power over men's minds and actions, and how the individual is brought to a consciousness of his duty to observe it. And it is from the point of view of these questions that an appeal to 'the social factor' becomes so obvious and indispensable. Whatever capacities we may suppose the child needs to be endowed with, in order that he may develop a moral consciousness, it is at all events clear that this consciousness is actually developed by means of the constant commands and instructions of his elders, backed up by punishments and other milder forms of suasion. The sense of duty is, to this extent, at any rate, and so far as the individual is concerned, a product of the social factor. Nor is it less clear that the rules of duty depend, to a very considerable extent, for their actual efficacy over men's minds and actions, on the pressure of law and social opinion. The good man, of course, will need this pressure less than others, but every man is made to feel that society expects from him the performance of certain duties, and resents any conspicuous failure to perform them. It is, further, clear enough that the particular requirements of duty, so far as they have varied from age to age and from people to people, have depended on the historical conditions of social progress, while, so far as in other and more fundamental respects they have remained constant, they have depended on the essential conditions of all social life; so that the requirements of duty have an unquestionable relation to some kind of social utility, if we use this term in a sufficiently wide sense. And, finally, an attempt has been made to show that the very existence and origin of a moral consciousness or sense of duty in the race can be traced, along similar lines, to the operation of the social factor.

One of the best known of these attempts is that of Herbert Spencer, which traces the origin of the sense of duty in large measure to primitive man's experiences of fear of the vengeance of his fellow-savages, his chief, and his gods. This, however, is to invoke the social factor in a rather inadequate form, for we are not really shown how such a fear of the vengeance either of particular individuals or even of unseen powers can generate any sense of duty properly so called. To recognize that we are likely to suffer for doing an action is not just the same as, however closely connected it may be with, recognizing that the action itself is wrong. Referring the sense of duty in this too easy way to the experience of external coercion, Spencer was led to his 'very startling' conclusion, that 'with complete adaptation to the social state'—that is to say, in the future golden age when man will spontaneously do actions that benefit himself without injuring his neighbour, or, still better, actions that benefit both, and will never feel inclined to do any actions that would injure others and so call forth coercion—'the sense of duty . . . will diminish as fast as moralization increases,' and will eventually disappear altogether (*Data of Ethics*, § 46). This paradise of evolution, it need hardly be said, has as little relation to scientific ethics as the paradises of mythology have to scientific history. But the imperfections of Spencer's social psychology and the extravagances of his prophetic ardour do not affect the genuineness of the problem of origins which he endeavoured to solve, or the right of scientific thought to look for a solution of it in some such direction as he took.

5. It makes a great difference whether we take, on the one hand, the objective, social, and historical point of view appropriate to the inquiries just outlined, or, on the other, the point of view of Kant's abstract analysis of the moral consciousness of the individual. Statements which are significant and even obvious from the one point of view become paradoxical or untenable from the other. When we regard duty from the point of view of social expectation, it is evident that there is a more or less definite sum of duties to be performed by any person, a certain minimum requirement the performance of which is sufficient for social respectability. And in this sense it is perfectly possible, not merely to do one's duty, but to go beyond it. We call Grace Darling a heroine because she did more than we could possibly have said it was her duty to do. There are, in fact, 'counsels of perfection' which the average person is not obliged to follow. From the Kantian point of view, on the other hand, this naturally appears to be a pernicious doctrine, and Kant is never tired of inveighing against the 'moral fanaticism and exaggerated self-conceit that is infused into the mind by exhortation to actions as noble, sublime, and magnanimous,' as if the actions could be done 'as pure merit, and not from duty' (*Critique of Practical Reason*, bk. i. ch. iii., Abbott's tr. p. 178). If Grace Darling's conscience laid it upon her to undertake her perilous task, then for her it *was* duty, from which it would have been cowardly and wrong to shrink. Yet we may safely assume that the moral judgment of 'common sense' would not have accused her of wrongdoing if she had shrunk from the attempt, and would even have regarded remorse for such a shrinking as fantastic and overstrained.

6. When the various duties are regarded in an objective way, it is natural to seek for some kind of classification of them in order to make a systematic survey of the field. But it is difficult or impossible to find any quite satisfactory *scheme of division.* Perhaps the most common and obvious division is that between self-regarding and social duties. But, unless we understand very clearly what we are about in using it, it may easily involve us in somewhat gross confusion and error. Both terms used in the division are treacherous. The term 'self-regarding duties' is apt to be taken in the sense of duties to oneself, and this was, in fact, one of the heads under which duties were ranged in the threefold scheme favoured by the older moralists, viz. duties to oneself, to one's neighbours, and to God. But it is evident that, in any sense in which we can owe it to ourselves to perform some of our duties, we owe it to ourselves to perform them all; while, in the more literal sense, in which a debt or obligation is owed from A to B and involves *two* parties, we cannot properly be said to owe any one of our duties to *ourselves.* The term 'social duties,' again, is apt to suggest that there are other duties which are non-social or concern only the individual, and we may even be led to infer, with J. S. Mill, that 'the only part of the conduct of any one for which he is amenable to society is that which concerns others,' while 'in the part which merely concerns himself, his independence is, of right, absolute' (*Liberty*, People's ed. 1865, p. 6[a]). But such a view is really contrary to the actual tenor of our moral judgments, which condemn, and assert a right to condemn, extravagance, and drunkenness, and idleness in themselves, without waiting to see their directly or indirectly harmful consequences for other persons than the agent. Moreover, it assumes a discrimination between injury to self and injury to others, which, in the case of habits so important as the moral habits, cannot really be made. The spendthrift, drunkard, and idler are inefficient members of society, and as such cannot but do social harm which is much more than 'contingent' or 'constructive.' And, finally, any supposed right to an *absolute independence*, however limited, on the part of the individual is contradicted by the very meaning of a right, which, of course, implies social recognition and social value. But, in spite of the misunderstandings to which the division into self-regarding and other-regarding duties is exposed, it does point to a palpable enough distinction between the objects or spheres of the respective duties. We can practise the duty of temperance by ourselves; the duty of truth-speaking can be practised only in relation to others. This distinction—between what we might call immanent and transeunt duties—is clearly valid enough; but it is not a distinction in the source or basis of the obligation. The performance of both duties alike is owed (metaphorically) to ourselves and (literally) to the moral community of which we are members. The duties which are practised in relation to others may be subdivided into those which are of a more general kind, such as veracity or promise-keeping or honesty, and those which depend upon some more specific relationship or institution, such as parental or filial duty, which depends on relationship within the family. (The distinction between duties of strict or perfect, and duties of imperfect, obligation can hardly be regarded as a distinction of principle, except in so far as it is identified with the distinction of legal obligation and moral duty.)

7. When they are thus classified from the objective point of view, we can hardly deny the possibility of a real **conflict between duties.** The individual, of course, can do only one thing at a time, and, in face of warring claims, has for his one duty to make the best he can of the situation before him. What this best will be must clearly depend on the particular nature of the situation in question, and, therefore, no general solution of the problem of the conflict of duties is possible. But not merely is no *general* solution possible. When we look at the conflict of duties from the objective point of view, we have no right to assume that every such problem is capable even of a *particular* solution, at all events of one which will be final and complete. From the fact that the individual has to satisfy the claims upon him as best he can, *i.e.* has to find out what is the solution of the problem *for him*, it does not by any means follow that he can reconcile the rival claims completely, or can find a solution of the problem *which will satisfy them.* The problems of conduct are practical problems, and we have no right to assume *a priori* that any practical problem can be solved without remainder.

LITERATURE.—W. Wallace's *Natural Theology and Ethics*, Oxford, 1898, contains a characteristic general essay on 'Duty.' As specimens of the treatment of Duty in the textbooks the following may suffice: Dewey-Tufts, *Ethics* (London, 1908), ch. xvii.; F. Paulsen, *System of Ethics* (Eng. tr., London, 1899), bk. ii. ch. v. For the Stoic conception, see E. Zeller's *Stoics, Epicureans, and Sceptics* (Eng. tr., London, 1892), pt. ii. chs. x. and xi. For a comparison of Stoic and Christian ideas, see E. Hatch's *Hibbert Lectures* of 1888 on *The Influence of Greek Ideas and Usages upon the Christian Church* (5th ed., London, 1895), Lect. vi. Kant's analysis of the conception of Duty is contained in the First Section of his *Grundlegung zur Metaphysik der Sitten*, along with which work must be used *Kritik der praktischen Vernunft* (both translated in T. K. Abbott's *Kant's Theory of Ethics*[3], London, 1879). With Kant's own exposition may be compared pt. i. of the *Ethik*[2] (in *Grundriss d. theol. Wissenschaften* series, Tübingen, 1901) by W. Herrmann. For a representative account of the sense of Duty as a product of social influences see Bain's *Emotion and Will* (London, 1859), ch. x. § 7 ff. H. Spencer's account is given in *Data of Ethics*, London, 1879, §§ 44–46. T. H. Green's *Prolegomena to Ethics*, Oxford, 1883 ([3]1890), bk. iv. ch. ii., deals with the question of conflict of duties.

HENRY BARKER.

DWARFS AND PYGMIES.—These terms are nowadays interchangeable in the diction of ethnology,[1] and are indifferently applied to those undersized races which exist, or have existed, in various parts of the world. In addition to tribes or nations of dwarfs, there are also small-statured individuals, occurring sporadically among the taller races, who may fitly be styled dwarfs. Their low stature is often attributable, however, to morbid physical conditions; although it might be regarded, in the case of healthy persons, as an inheritance from a line of ancestors of dwarfish type. The present inquiry is limited to those who are indubitably dwarfs by race.

In the Teutonic languages, the word 'dwarf' can be traced back for at least twelve centuries, appearing under such forms as O.N. *dvergr*, Anglo-Sax. *dweorh*, O.H.G. *twerg*, Germ. *Zwerg*. It occurs also in Gaelic as *droich* and *troich*, but these are probably borrowed from Teutonic sources. The other Gaelic synonyms, *e.g.* O.Ir. *abacc*, have quite a different etymology, as have also the Cymric terms, *e.g.* Welsh *pegor*. The word 'pygmy' is recognized at much earlier dates, being derived from the Gr. *pygmē*, a measure of length from the elbow to the knuckle or fist (πυγμή)—13½ inches. Similar in connotation is the O.Pruss. *parstuck*, etymologically connected with Lith. *pìrsztas*, 'finger'; and a like idea may be present in Lat. *pumilio* (cf. Walde, *Etymolog. Wörterb. der lat. Sprache*[2], Heidelberg, 1910, p. 625), while Lat. *pusilio* is a formation from *pusus*, 'boy.' In Gr. *νάννος*, Lat. *nanus* (whence Fr. *nain*, etc.), a 'Lallname' is present (cf. Gr. *νάννη*, 'auntie'). The Balto-Slavic group, represented by Russ. *karla*, Lith. *karlà*, is doubtless borrowed from O.H.G. *karal*, 'man' (cf. Eng. *churl*). Cf., further, Schrader, *Reallex. der indogerm. Altertumskunde*, Strassburg, 1901, pp. 1000–1002.

The fact that the term 'pygmy' was originally held to denote a people of the preposterously small stature of 13½ inches renders that term not so acceptable as 'dwarf' in any serious discussion.

[1] The present art. deals with the subject mainly from the anthropological side. A fuller treatment of dwarfs in folk-belief will be found in the 'Teutonic' and 'Slavic' sections of art. DEMONS AND SPIRITS, and in the art. FAIRY.

It is to be noted, however, that 'pygmy' has now lost its first meaning, and merely denotes the members of a race visibly below the stature of the ordinary races of man. Windle, who has made a careful study of the facts relating to these people, allows a somewhat high level as the upward limit, laying down the definition that 'any race in which the average male stature does not exceed 4 feet 9 inches may fairly be described as pygmy' (Introd. to Tyson's *Pygmies*, reprint of 1894, London). This is the height of the West African Obongos of the Gaboon region, described fifty years ago by Paul du Chaillu, and quite recently by Poutrin (*L'Anthropologie*, 1910, pp. 435–504), who places the average stature of the men at 4 ft. 8 in. (1·43 m.), and of the women at 4 ft. 6 in. (1·37 m.). This indicates a much taller race than the Akkas encountered by Sir H. M. Stanley, who estimated their adult height at from 3 ft. to 4 ft. 6 in. (*In Darkest Africa*, London, 1890, ii. 92). A. B. Lloyd (*In Dwarf Land*, London, 1899, pp. 310, 323) gives a similar report of those whom he met. Even lower is the stature of a race, presumably Eskimo, inhabiting the north-western shores of Hudson's Bay in the 17th cent., for Captain Foxe records (1631) the finding of a native cemetery in that region in which the longest corpse did not exceed 4 feet.[1] Windle (*op. cit.* p. xxxiii) cites the case of a Bushman woman, the mother of several children, who was only 3 ft. 8 in., while another woman of her race measured 3 ft. 3 inches.

The distribution of dwarf races seems to have been at one time world-wide; but at the present day they are found chiefly in the equatorial regions of Africa and Malaysia. Classic writers, such as Pliny, Pomponius Mela, Aristotle, Ctesias, Herodotus, and Homer, make several references to African pygmies, and they also figure prominently in the records of Ancient Egypt. The most important of the tombs at Assuan explored by E. A. W. Budge is that of a provincial governor, Her-Kheef, who lived in the reign of Pepi, in the VIth dynasty (*c.* 3300 B.C.), and who was sent on an expedition to the Sudan to bring back a dwarf for the king. Brugsch (*Hungersnoth*, Leipzig, 1891, p. 141) cites an inscription at Karnak, belonging to the Ptolemaic epoch,—the three centuries before Christ,—which states that 'the dwarfs of the southern countries come to him [the reigning Ptolemy], bringing their tributes to his treasury.' Ed. Naville, in his account of the festival-hall of Osorkon II. in the great temple of Bubastis (*10 EEFM*, 1892, p. 30), refers to a picture which seems to show that racial dwarfs were specially selected as the vergers of the temple. A very interesting and suggestive comparison between the pygmies of the classic writers and existing dwarf races has been made by Paul Monceaux in his treatise on 'La Légende des pygmées et les nains de l'Afrique équatoriale' (*Revue Historique*, xlvii. [1891] 1–64), the inference drawn being that the pygmies of the Greek and Roman writers, sculptors, and painters are memories of actual dwarfs seen by their forefathers in Africa and India. He further points to the resemblance between the modern Akkas of Africa and the dwarfs portrayed at Pompeii, Rhodes, and Cyprus, and to the 'Patakas' placed as figureheads on Phœnician ships. The supposition that the Jews as well as the Egyptians were acquainted with dwarf races underlies more than one tr. of the term *Gammādîm* which occurs in Ezk 27[11]. In the Vulgate this term is rendered by *Pygmæi*, in Aquila by πυγμαῖοι, and the 'Bishops' Bible' of 1572 and 1575 translates it as 'Pygmenians.' The reason for this identification of 'Gammadim' with dwarfs appears to be so far unexplained, though it may well be due to folk-etymology with *gōmed*, 'cubit' (Jg 3[16]). (For other interpretations, see *HDB* and *EBi*, art. 'Gammadim.') According to the later Jewish *Gen. Rabba* (xxxvii. 5), the Caphtorim of Gn 10[14] were dwarfs, and in Rabbinical literature Nebuchadnezzar is often called 'the dwarf of Babel,' or 'the little one-ell dwarf' (with reference to Dn 4[17]; for further data, see Kohler, in *JE* v. 22 f.).

One of the earliest modern descriptions of African pygmies is that given in 1625 (see *Purchas his Pilgrimes*) by Andrew Battel, an English sailor who had spent nearly eighteen years in the Congo region; and they have been subsequently described by many travellers. Those living on the eastern border of the Congo State are distinguished by their long, shaggy beards and hirsute skins. E. S. Grogan, who encountered many of these pygmies in 1898, in the volcanic region of Mushari, near Lake Kivu, thus pictures one of them:

'He was a typical pygmy as found on the volcanoes—squat, gnarled, proud, and easy of carriage. His beard hung down over his chest, and his thighs and chest were covered with wiry hair. He carried the usual pygmy bow made of two pieces of cane spliced together with grass, and with a string made of a single strand of a rush that grows in the forests' (*From the Cape to Cairo*, London, 1900, p. 194).

The same writer speaks of their amazing swiftness of foot, and of their 'combination of immense strength necessary for the precarious hunting life they lead, and of compactness, indispensable to rapid movements in dense forest' (*op. cit.* p. 178). According to Sir H. Johnston (*The Uganda Protectorate*, London, 1902, pp. 473, 513, 530), the Congo pygmies are often very ape-like in appearance, this effect being, no doubt, partly produced by their hairy skins, their long arms, the strength of their thick-set frames, their furtive ways, and the rapidity with which they move among the branches of the forest trees.

A. B. Lloyd actually mistook his first pygmy for a monkey, and was about to shoot him as such when his native guide arrested his arm. The dwarf was perched high up in a lofty tree in the equatorial forest; and, when he saw he was observed, he swung himself from branch to branch with the ease and swiftness of an ape. This arboreal pygmy was equipped with bow and arrow, and had been himself hunting at the time.

In spite of some outward simian traits, however, the African pygmies seem to be intellectually not inferior to their taller neighbours. This is the testimony of Poutrin with regard to the Obongo dwarfs and the neighbouring Bantus; and another French writer, Breschin, employs even more favourable terms in referring to the Congo pygmies:

'Far from being degenerates, they are, on the contrary, superior to the neighbouring negroes in acuteness of sense, agility, courage, sociability, and family affection' (*La Géographie*, Paris, 1902, p. 443).

Sir Edwin Ray Lankester, speaking of the whole pygmy race collectively, observes (*Daily Telegraph*, Aug. 1910):

'They have all short, round skulls of full average brain capacity. To a great extent their corporeal features suggest an infantile or child-like stage of development, and the same is true of their intellectual condition and of their productions.'

It must be understood, of course, that this is a general statement, not necessarily applicable to every division of the race.

In his *Histoire naturelle* (Paris, 1778, v. 505) Buffon reports the existence of a hill-tribe in Madagascar, known as Kimos, whom he describes as '*nains blancs*,' although this term is subsequently modified by the statement that their complexion is lighter than that of the neighbouring blacks; probably a light brown colour is indicated. Their arms are said to have been so long as to reach below the knee when they stood erect. They are characterized as vivacious in mind and body, and as very brave, using assegais and darts or arrows

[1] Lafitau (*Mœurs des sauvages amér.*, 12mo ed., Paris, 1724, i. 55) records that an Eskimo girl, captured on the Labrador coast in 1717, declared that in her country were entire tribes of men three feet high, the slaves of those of taller stature. On American Indians of low stature (160–165 cm.), see Hrdlička, in *Bull. 30 BE*, i. 55; and on popular fallacies concerning Indian pygmies, Holmes, *ib.* ii. 285.

('*traits*'). They reared cattle and sheep, and lived also upon vegetables and fruits. A woman of this tribe, seen at Fort Dauphin, measured about 3 ft. 8 inches. Windle, in referring to these accounts (*l.c.* p. xxxvi), adds: 'It is stated that people of diminutive size still exist on the banks of a certain river to the south-west.'

The existence of a pygmy race in New Guinea has been known for a considerable time. The Italian traveller Beccari encountered them in 1876, and they have been seen by d'Albertis, Lawes, Cayley Webster, and other travellers. But much interest was aroused in the summer of 1910 by the information sent home by a British exploring expedition with regard to a tribe of dwarfs whom they found inhabiting the Charles Louis Mountains in New Guinea, at an elevation of about 2000 feet above sea-level. Four of the men were temporarily captured by Captain Rawling's party, and on being measured they proved to be respectively 4 ft. 6 in., 4 ft. 4 in., 4 ft. 3 in., and 4 ft. 2 in. in height. They were naked, except for a grass helmet, a bag, and a tiny strip round the waist. They are described as good-looking and well-proportioned, and of a lighter complexion than the natives of the lowlands. The general average stature of these Tapiro pygmies is 4 ft. 8¾ in., while that of their lowland neighbours is 5 ft. 6⅔ inches.

In several other parts of Eastern Asia there are, or have been, dwarf races. In ancient Chinese records there is mention of black or brown dwarfs in the province of Shan-tung in the 23rd cent. B.C. At the present day, the Pulas, a people whose stature varies from 4 ft. to 4 ft. 9 in., are found living beside the tall Lolo race, in Western China. The northern parts of Japan were at one time inhabited by a pygmy race, from whom the existing Ainus (*q.v.*) of Yezo may be in part descended. The accounts from India, Ceylon, and Persia all point to former dwarf peoples, represented to-day, in a modified form, by races of low stature, although taller than actual dwarfs. It is reasonable to infer that the tall races have frequently intermarried with those of dwarfish type, producing a hybrid race combining the qualities of both lines of ancestry.

[An interesting instance here in point is the description of the 'Pygmies' of Central India, as given by Ctesias, i. 11 (in Photius, *Bibl.* lxxii. 144 ff.). Swarthy in colour, and speaking the same language as the other Indians, 'they are very diminutive, the tallest of them being but two cubits in height, while the majority are only one and a half. They let their hair grow very long—down to their knees, and even lower. They have the largest beards anywhere to be seen, and, when these have grown sufficiently long and copious, they no longer wear clothing, but, instead, let the hair of the head fall down their backs far below the knee, while in front are their beards trailing down to their very feet. When their hair has thus thickly enveloped their whole body, they bind it round them with a zone, and so make it serve for a garment. Their privates are thick, and so large that they depend even to their ankles. They are, moreover, snub-nosed, and otherwise ill-favoured. . . . They are eminently just, and have the same laws as the Indians. They hunt hares and foxes, not with dogs, but with ravens and kites and crows and vultures' (tr. McCrindle, *Ancient India as Described by Ktêsias the Knidian*, Calcutta, 1882, p. 15 f.). To this Megasthenes (in Strabo, p. 711, and Pliny, *HN* vii. 2) adds that they are the 'men of three spans' against whom the war of the cranes, mentioned in *Il.* iii. 3–6, was waged. These accounts have been carefully analyzed by Lassen (*Ind. Alterthumskunde*, ii.², Leipzig, 1874, pp. 661–664), who comes to the conclusion that these 'pygmies' represent the Kirātas, a race of dwarfs as compared with the Aryan invaders, long-haired (though beardless), flat-nosed (though light in colour), brave hunters, and exposed to the constant enmity of the mythical bird Garuḍa. Moreover, in Sanskrit *Kirāla*, their national name, is one of the terms for 'dwarf.'—L. H. GRAY.]

The accounts from America are not so definite as those furnished by the Old World, but dwarf types are reported from Argentina, Peru, the Amazon basin, and Central America. In North America, the Arapaho Indians of Oklahoma and of Wyoming have many traditions of a fierce race of cannibal dwarfs with whom their forefathers fought. They are described as a little under 3 ft. in height, dark-skinned, pot-bellied, and powerfully built, with large arms and legs—this last statement being scarcely consistent with dwarfish stature. They were expert trackers, very nimble and fleet of foot, and of a low order of intelligence. The Crow Indians of Montana have similar traditions.

'A long time ago,' they say, 'there lived a very dwarfish people who lived in cliffs and had no fire. Their bows were made of deer antlers, and their arrow-heads of flint. Their aim was true and unerring. They were so powerful that they could carry buffalo on their backs.'[1]

These, it is true, are only traditions, and the last statement cannot be accepted literally, although it testifies to the quality of great bodily strength so often attributed to dwarf races. But, in view of the wide-spread distribution of the dwarf type, the traditions may rest upon a sound basis. It is certain that Arctic America can show many undoubted evidences of a race whose stature was well below the maximum limit of dwarfism. Buffon, indeed, ascribes to the most of the Arctic races a stature not exceeding 4 ft. 6 in.; but this is too sweeping a statement, although much of his information is derived from good authorities. He includes the Lapps in this category, whereas their average stature is from 5 ft. to 5 ft. 2 inches. They may, however, be held to represent a crossing with an earlier and truly pygmy race.

Of pygmy races in Europe, the skeletons discovered at Schaffhausen, in Switzerland, and described by Virchow and Kollmann, the numerous specimens found in cemeteries in Silesia and France, described by Thilenius and others, and the Mentone skeletons described by Verneau and de Villeneuve all afford tangible evidence. An early 'Mediterranean race' of pygmy stature has also been deduced from a study of existing types by the Italian anthropologists Sergi, Mantia, and Pullé. All these results are obtained from anatomical research during the past quarter of a century, and the effect has been to create new views of European anthropology. In this study, Kollmann has played a leading part. His earlier monograph, 'Pygmäen in Europa' (in *ZE* xxvi. [1894] 189 ff., 230 ff.), was followed by several others on the same subject, one of which, 'Die Pygmäen und ihre systemat. Stellung innerhalb des Menschengeschlechts' (in *Verhandl. d. naturforsch. Gesellsch. in Basel*, xvi. [1902]), sums up his conclusions. These are as follows, in the words of W. L. H. Duckworth (*Man*, 1903, no. 62):

'(1) Pygmy races can be recognized in all continents. Their stature varies from 120 to 150 cm., and their cranial capacity is between 900 and 1200 c.c. (2) The material collected in Peru by Princess Theresa of Bavaria yielded evidence of pygmies in the New World. (3) The number of localities in Europe whence evidence of the existence of pygmy races in prehistoric times is available, is still increasing. France and Germany must now be added to the list of countries whence such evidence has been obtained. (4) The view which regards the pygmy races as originating through the degeneration of races of normal size is combated. (5) The author regards the pygmy races as representative of the primitive stock whence all the human races have been evolved. (6) The occurrence of the remains of pygmy peoples in interments of the epoch of the first dynasty in Egypt adds a new interest to the historic references made by the ancients to the existence of pygmy races in Africa.'

The rapid development of thought, since 1903, in relation to the pygmy races, is well illustrated by several of the sentences just quoted—perhaps even by all. That these races can be recognized in all continents is no longer a matter for discussion, any more than the statement that there are, or were, pygmies in the New World. That France and Germany furnish evidence of pygmy peoples within their borders is a fact that no one would now dispute. And 'combated' is a verb that would

[1] For these various American Indian traditions, see accounts by S. Culin, in the *Science and Art Bulletin*, Philadelphia, Jan. 1901, vol. iii. no. 1; and by G. A. Dorsey, A. L. Kroeber, and S. C. Simms, in Publications 81 and 85 of the *Field Columbian Museum*, Chicago, 1903.

not now be employed to express a protest against a theory that healthy living dwarf races have originated through the degeneration of races of normal size. The very adjective 'normal' would be ruled out of court in this connexion. On the other hand, Kollmann's conclusion, that the pygmy races represent the primitive 'normal' stock of mankind, is an idea which is received with increasing favour.

It is, of course, too soon for such ideas to have obtained complete recognition, especially among those whose mental bias is innately conservative. In a recent number (April 1911) of *Petermanns Mitteilungen*, R. Andree refers to certain expressions of dissent aroused by Schmidt's new work, *Die Stellung der Pygmäenvölker in der Entwicklungsgesch. des Menschen* (Stuttgart, 1910), which follows the lines laid down by Kollmann. Among the opponents of the new ideas, Schwalbe, Keith, and Czekanowski are specially named by Andree. The leading arguments in Schmidt's book are thus referred to by a reviewer in the *Times*, Literary Supplement, 16th June 1910:

'Dr. Schmidt's long and careful study of the physique, the language, and the culture of the dwarf races of mankind . . . is certainly one of the most interesting works of anthropological investigation that have appeared in recent years. Its conclusions are nothing less than revolutionary: they are arrived at over the graves of many current theories, and, if confirmed, they place the question of the physical and spiritual origin of man in a new light. Dr. Schmidt's minute investigation of all the pygmy races known when his book was being written, has led him to support, with some modifications, the view maintained by the well-known anatomist of Basle, J. Kollmann, who holds the pygmies to be the oldest of peoples on the earth—the child-race of mankind. The child-race, not a half-bestial race. The distinction is shown very clearly when one regards as a whole the characteristics of the pygmy races. They are entirely men, but undeveloped men. Their mind is a human, a thinking mind; they possess human feeling, and a distinct ethical will. Morally, although, like children, they are a prey to many fleeting impulses and wanting in perseverance, they stand often much higher than many of the tall races, and they have a religion which stands in close relation to their ethics. They are anything but vicious or malignant. Their intellectual attainments are very low, but they are capable of responding to demands made upon them, and the mental powers they have evolved are adequate for their way of life. . . . In physical indications, there are, of course, many marks of a non-human ancestry, but the upright or projecting forehead and the frequently large and expressive eyes mark a distinction which cannot be overlooked. . . . Spiritually, the pygmies "stand in no way nearer to the beast than any other race of man"; they "do not give us the smallest encouragement to suppose that in and by them a bridge can be thrown across the gulf between the human and the beast soul." . . . We may close by expressing our hearty concurrence with Dr. Schmidt in one sentence at least of his interesting work: "It is my firm conviction that the investigation of the pygmy races is, at the present moment, one of the weightiest and most urgent, if not the most weighty and most urgent, of the tasks of ethnological and anthropological science."'

The conclusion arrived at by Kollmann, Schmidt, and others has been steadily gaining ground during recent years. It is interesting to note, although the circumstance will have no value in the domain of science, that the same belief was held by the early Scandinavians, who asserted that the dwarfs were created before men. The late Charles Godfrey Leland, by an intuitive process, had arrived at the same conclusion. 'I believe mankind was originally a dwarf,' he observed many years ago, in a letter to the present writer. But the assertions of tradition, and the intuition of a man of genius, are negligible quantities in scientific controversy.

The opposite contention is that the taller races represent normal man, of whom the pygmy type is merely a stunted *Kümmerform*, degraded in body and mind by certain accidents of environment. Those who take this view will find strong support in the statements made by E. Torday in his paper on 'The Land and Peoples of the Kasai Basin' (Belgian Congo), which appeared in the *Geographical Journal* (London) for July 1910. Torday and his party visited a village of pygmies near Misumba, in the country of the Bu Shongo. These pygmies, instead of leading the wandering, forest life of their ancestors, are settled agriculturists, and have been so for the last two or three generations. Now, it seems that a result of this alteration in environment and habits is that the sedentary pygmies are considerably taller than their kindred who still lead the nomadic life of the forest. It has been suggested that their superior stature, and their readiness to take to agriculture, are both due to a possible admixture of blood in a previous generation, and that the settled pygmies are not typical pygmies. This may be so, and the facts of the case must be strictly ascertained before any satisfactory deduction can be made. There is one conclusion, however, that seems inevitable: if these pygmies are of pure, undiluted stock, and have grown in stature by abandoning the forest, then the converse would hold, and the tall Bu Shongo among whom they live would, if driven into the forest by a stronger race, begin to approximate in stature and physique to the forest pygmies, should they be forced to live their life for a similar period of time. The question of environment cannot be overlooked, but it may be doubted whether its potency is so great as to produce such results.

One or two other facts connected with the Bu Shongo and the nomadic pygmies of their region must be noticed here. Each Bu Shongo kinglet has a group of pygmies under his suzerainty, who supply him with game in exchange for vegetable food. But, although the Bu Shongo utilize the pygmies in this way, they regard them as beings of a different nature from themselves. They are held in awe as 'half-ghosts'—spirits born from trees. This attitude is by no means confined to the Bu Shongo; there is a wide-spread dread of the pygmies among other African tribes. When a pygmy arrow is found in a bunch of growing bananas, no man, even the owner, would be bold enough to take away either the arrow or the bananas.

These facts lead naturally to the subject of the reverence paid to dwarfs in many lands. In passing, it may be observed that this reverence tends to support the idea that mankind generally regarded the dwarf races as in some sense beings of a special order. Mention has already been made of the Kimos of Madagascar, a race of long-armed dwarfs. They are known also as Vazimbas, and under this name E. B. Tylor refers to them (*Prim. Cult.*[3], 1891, ii. 114 f.) in the following connexion:

'In Madagascar, the worship of the spirits of the dead is remarkably associated with the Vazimbas, the aborigines of the island, who are said still to survive as a distinct race in the interior, and whose peculiar graves testify to their former occupancy of other districts. These graves, small in size and distinguished by a cairn and an upright stone slab or altar, are places which the Malagasy regard with equal fear and veneration. . . . To take a stone or pluck a twig from one of these graves, to stumble against one in the dark, would be resented by the angry Vazimba inflicting disease, or coming in the night to carry off the offender to the region of ghosts.'[1]

In Southern India a similar attitude is observed towards the dwarfish Kurumbas of the Nilgirī hills. Popular tradition asserts that the megalithic cromlechs of the district were reared by the ancestors of the Kurumbas.

'Though they are regarded with fear and hatred as sorcerers by the agricultural Badagas of the table-land, one of them must,

[1] [A similar belief existed among the pagan Lithuanians regarding the *kaukai* (Lith. *kaũkas*, 'dwarf,' 'elf'), concerning whom Lasicius (*de Diis Samagitarum*, Basel, 1615, p. 51 [new ed. Mannhardt, Riga, 1868]; cf. also Solmsen, in Usener, *Götternamen*, Bonn, 1896, p. 92) writes: 'Sunt lemures quos Russi Uboze ['mannikins, goblins'] appellant; barbatuli, altitudine unius palmi extensi, iis qui illos esse credunt conspicui, aliis minime; his cibi omnis edulii apponuntur, quod nisi fiat, ea sunt opinione ut ideo suas fortunas, id quod accidit, amittant' (quoted by Schrader, *l.c.*). For further allusions to Balto-Slavic beliefs on dwarfs, reference may be made to Hanusch, *Wissenschaft des slaw. Mythus*, Lemberg, 1842, pp. 229, 327–330, although the work must be used with extreme caution.—L. H. Gray.]

nevertheless, at sowing-time be called to guide the first plough for two or three yards, and go through a mystic pantomime of propitiation to the earth deity, without which the crop would certainly fail. When so summoned, the Kurumba must pass the night by the dolmens alone' (Windle, p. xxvi).

Here we have the recognition of dwarfs as a kind of Levite caste, possessed of a peculiar supernatural power. Possibly the idea of employing dwarfs as temple-vergers in Ancient Egypt may be due to a similar belief. In view of the association between dwarfs and megalithic structures in Southern India, it is of interest to record Captain Meadows Taylor's statement (*Cairns, etc., in the Dekkan*, Dublin, 1865, p. 1) that the cromlechs of the Deccan

'were called by the people, in the Canarese language, *Mori-Munni*, or Mories' Houses; and these Mories were believed to have been a dwarf race of great strength, who inhabited the country in very remote ages.'

A very full account of the Kurumbas, with copious references, will be found in Gustav Oppert's *Original Inhabitants of India*, Madras, 1893, ch. xii.

Mention has already been made of the resemblance, pointed out by Paul Monceaux, between the modern Akkas and the dwarfs portrayed at Pompeii, Rhodes, and Cyprus, as well as the 'Patakas' of the Phœnicians.

'In most of the negrillo races,' he further says (*loc. cit.*), 'are strongly accented the characteristic traits of the classic pygmies, as of the dwarf gods of Egypt or of Phœnicia, the huge head, the thick hanging lips, the prominent belly, the excessively long arms, the excessively short legs, twisted and bowed.'

No doubt there is exaggeration in all this; but the significance of the comparison lies in the indication that the dwarf gods of Egypt and Phœnicia had their origin in a veneration paid to living dwarfs of a similar nature to that accorded in Madagascar and Southern India.

The question of dwarf races is manifestly more circumscribed in Europe than it is in countries where there are living specimens to be studied. Osseous remains there are, certainly, as well as many references in tradition; but the field of conjecture is confessedly wide. Many observers of the African pygmy races have been reminded of European traditions which seem to point to a similar race in Europe.

'Other dwarf races of humanity belonging to the white or the Mongolian species may have inhabited Northern Europe in ancient times, or it is just possible that this type of Pygmy Negro, which survives to-day in the recesses of Inner Africa, may even have overspread Europe in remote times. If it did, then the conclusion is irresistible, that it gave rise to most of the myths and beliefs connected with gnomes, kobolds, and fairies. The demeanour and actions of the little Congo dwarfs at the present day remind one, over and over again, of the traits attributed to the brownies and goblins of our fairy stories. Their remarkable power of becoming invisible by adroit hiding in herbage and behind rocks, their probable habits, in sterile or open countries, of making their homes in holes and caverns, their mischievousness and their prankish good-nature, all seem to suggest that it was some race like this which inspired most of the stories of Teuton and Celt regarding a dwarfish people of quasi-supernatural attributes' (Sir H. Johnston, in *Pall Mall Mag.*, Feb. 1902, p. 178).

Of the dwarf skeletons found in Europe, scientific accounts are furnished in the works of Kollmann and Schmidt, already cited. Special mention may also be made of an article on 'Prähistor. Pygmäen in Schlesien,' by G. Thilenius, which appeared in the Brunswick journal *Globus* in 1902 (Bd. lxxxi. no. 17). A recent addition to the list of European dwarf skeletons is that of a young woman, 4 ft. 6 in. in height, which was found in Scotland in 1907, at the bottom of a pit in the Roman fort at Newstead, Roxburghshire. The skeleton is thus referred to by James Curle, who conducted the excavations of the fort during the period 1905–1910:

'The most curious of all these human relics was the nearly complete skeleton of a dwarf, found in one of the pits. Professor Bryce estimates the age at from twenty-two to twenty-three years, and yet the height cannot have exceeded four feet six inches. Though the creature must have been a dwarf, the bones show no signs of rickets or other bone disease, being well formed, but slight and slender to a remarkable degree. How it came to lie in the pit beneath the bones of nine horses is a problem of which no solution can be hoped for' (*A Roman Frontier Post and its People*, Glasgow, 1911, p. 111).

LITERATURE.—In addition to the works mentioned in the text, the following may be cited: **A. de Quatrefages**, *Les Pygmées*, Paris, 1887 (Eng. tr. by F. Starr [London, 1895], who supplements its copious bibliography); **W. H. Flower**, 'The Pygmy Races of Men' (*Proc. Soc. Roy. Inst. Gt. Brit.* xii. [1888] 266–283); **H. Schlichter**, 'The Pygmy Tribes of Africa' (*Scot. Geogr. Mag.*, June–July 1892); **Paul du Chaillu**, *Great Forest of Equatorial Africa, and Country of Dwarfs*, London, 1890; **G. Schweinfurth**, *The Heart of Africa* (Eng. tr., do. 1874); **Stuhlmann, Barrow, and Junker**, *Travels* (Eng. tr., do. 1890); **A. Werner**, 'The African Pygmies' (*Pop. Science Monthly*, xxxvii. [1890] 658–671); **Broca**, 'Akkas' (*RAnth*, 1874); **Cornalia**, 'Akkas' (*Archivio por l'antrop.*, 1874); **Max le Clerc**, 'Les Pygmées à Madagascar' (*REth* vi. [1887] 323–335); 'Chimpanzees and Dwarfs in Central Africa,' by **J. F.** (*Nature*, xlii. [1890] 296); **R. G. Haliburton**, *The Dwarfs of Mount Atlas*, London, 1891. All of these relate primarily to Africa. Asia is treated by Flower, Fichte, Man, Fruer, Hamy, Semper, and by **R. Lydekker** in his 'Pygmies of Asia' (*Knowledge*, Sept. 1900). For America, see **Kollmann**, 'Pygmäen in Europa und Amerika' (*Globus*, Brunswick, 1902, no. 21); **Clements Markham**, in *JAI* xxiv. (Feb. 1895); **R. G. Haliburton**, in *Proc. Amer. Assoc. for Advancement of Science*, xliii. (1894). Other works, in which the subject is largely treated from the standpoint of popular tradition, are: **D. MacRitchie**, *Testimony of Tradition*, London, 1890, *Fians, Fairies, and Picts*, do. 1893, and 'Zwerge in Geschichte und Überlieferung' (1902 [*Globus*, lxxxii. no. 7]); **Gath Whitley**, 'Present Dwarf Races and Prehistoric Pigmies' (*London Quart. Rev.* xii. [1904] 139); **Mackenzie**, 'The Picts and Pets' (*The Antiquary*, London, May 1906); **Elizabeth Andrews**, 'Ulster Fairies, Danes, and Pechts' (*ib.* Aug. 1906), and 'Traditions of Dwarfs in Ireland and in Switzerland' (*ib.* Oct. 1909); **A. S. Herbert**, 'The Fairy Mythology of Europe in its Relation to Early History' (*NC*, Feb. 1908); **W. Y. E. Wentz**, *The Fairy Faith*, Rennes, 1909, 2nd ed. London, 1911. The Tapiro pygmies of New Guinea are described by **C. G. Rawling** in *The Geographical Journal*, xxxviii. 3 (London, Sept. 1911), 245–247. An account of pygmy remains found in a cave in Southern Spain is contributed by **Willoughby Verner** to the *Saturday Review*, London, Sept. 30 and Oct. 21, 1911.

DAVID MACRITCHIE.

DWĀRKĀ (Skr. *Dvārakā*, *Dvāravatī*, 'the city of many gates').—The famous city and place of pilgrimage associated with the life of Kṛṣṇa, situated in lat. 22° 14′ 20″ N., long. 87° 21′ E., in the native State of Okhāmaṇḍal in the peninsula of Kāthiāwār in Western India. In the usual form of the legend, Kṛṣṇa is said to have been assailed by the hosts of Rājā Jarāsandha, whom he repulsed seventeen times. Jarāsandha, finding it vain to continue the struggle alone, called in the aid of Rājā Kālayavaṇa, who with his hordes from the far west bore down upon the doomed city of Mathurā (*q.v.*). On that very night Kṛṣṇa bade arise on the remote shore of the Bay of Kachh (Cutch) the stately city of Dwārkā, and thither in a moment of time transferred the whole of his faithful people. The first intimation that reached them of their changed abode was the sound of the surf beating on the shore when they awoke the next morning. The legend probably represents some attack by forces from the west on the people of the Jumnā valley, and their retreat before their enemies southwards in the direction of the sea. Kṛṣṇa, it is said, reigned in splendour in his new city, and there, by his wife, Jāmbavatī, daughter of the king of the bears, had a son named Sāmba. The latter, by an indecent prank, insulted the Ṛṣis, or saints, who cursed him and his family. To remove the curse they went on a pilgrimage to Somnāth (*q.v.*), and there Kṛṣṇa was accidentally slain by the arrow of a Bhīl hunter. Hearing of his death, the Gopī milkmaids, the companions of his revels, buried themselves alive at a place called the Gopī Talāv, or 'milkmaids' tank.' Their ashes, it is believed, turned into the white clay still found at the place, which is called *gopīchandan*, 'the sandal wood of the milkmaids,' and used by members of the Vaiṣṇava sect to make their forehead marks. J. Kennedy (*JRAS*, October 1907, p. 951 ff.) distinguishes the more ancient Kṛṣṇa of Dwārkā from the Mathurā deity.

Two places are specially venerated in connexion with the life of Kṛṣṇa—the first, Mūl Dwārkā, the 'original Dwārkā,' a little mound on the seashore between the mouths of the rivers Somat and

Singāvrā, surmounted by the ruins of a temple, which popular belief declares to be the original Dwārkā where Kṛṣṇa reigned, and whence he transferred himself to the new Dwārkā in Okhāmanḍal. Here are many sacred spots which have their counterparts at modern Dwārkā. The temple at the latter place is situated on the north bank of the Gomatī creek, and its erection is ascribed by some to Vajranābha, grandson of Kṛṣṇa; while others assert that it was built in a single night by supernatural agency. It is on the plan of all ancient Hindu temples, containing a shrine, a spacious audience-hall, the roof of which is supported by sixty columns of granite and sandstone, and a conical spire 150 feet in height. The body of the temple and the spire are elaborately carved from base to pinnacle, but internally they are characterized by excessive plainness and simplicity of style. The figure of Gaṇapati, or Ganeśa, carved over the entrance door, indicates a dedication to Śiva, which makes it difficult to assign the original building to the Vaiṣṇava cult of Kṛṣṇa.

LITERATURE.—F. S. Growse, *Mathura, a District Memoir*³, Allahabad, 1883, p. 65 f.; *Bombay Gazetteer*, viii. 267 ff., 552; *Vishṇu Purāṇa*, bk. v. ch. 20 ff., tr. H. H. Wilson, 1840, v. 53 ff.

W. CROOKE.

DYAUS.—Dyaus plays no rôle of importance in Vedic mythology. The more intensively felt activity of gods like Agni and Indra probably threw into shade the personification of the heavenly vault. All that the Rigveda says of him has been collected by Macdonell in his *Ved. Myth.* § 11. Though he is often mentioned and styled 'father,' the father of Agni, Parjanya, Sūrya, and especially of the goddess of Dawn, there is no single hymn addressed to him. He is generally invoked along with Pṛthivī as *Dyāvāpṛthivī* or *Dyāvākṣāmā*, etc. In the *Nivid*, or solemn formula inserted in the Dyāvāpṛthivīya hymns, which form part of the *Vaiśvadevaśāstra* of the *soma* sacrifices, they are called father and mother, bull and cow—he, the *dyaus*, being rich in seed, she in milk (*Śāṅkh. Śrauta S.* viii. 19). The small importance attached to him in the hymns is reflected by the ritual, which rarely mentions offerings bestowed on him apart from his female partner. Together with her he receives his share in the animal and *soma* and other sacrifices (cf. *Ś. Śr. S.* iii. 12. 3, vi. 11. 7, viii. 3. 11, xiv. 6. 3, etc.).

It is well known that *Dyaus* as name and as deity goes back to the Aryan period, and is related to the Ζεύς of the Greeks, the Latin *Juppiter*, and also to the German *Zio-Tŷr*, if the latter word is not better combined with *deva*, as some scholars assert. Though, for want of proofs, he cannot be said to have been a very important or characteristic god of the Aryan pantheon, the mere fact that there was such a god in those times of remotest antiquity is a striking argument against the exaggerations of the one-sided ancestor theory. It was formerly generally supposed that Varuṇa was a synonym of Dyaus, or developed from an epithet of Dyaus into an independent deity of Heaven. This opinion, though still upheld by scholars of distinction, has fallen under suspicion, as it does not answer all objections brought forward against it: and in its place Oldenberg (*Religion des Veda*, Berlin, 1894, pp. 48–50, 193, 287) and the present writer (*Ved. Mythologie*, Breslau, 1891–1902, iii. 45–52; so also Hardy, *Vedisch-brahmanische Periode*, Münster, 1893, pp. 47 ff.) have put forward the moon theory for Varuṇa.

LITERATURE.—A. A. Macdonell, *Vedic Mythology*, Strassburg, 1897, § 11 (where the reader will find all the earlier literature); L. v. Schröder, *WZKM* xix. [1905] 1 ff.

A. HILLEBRANDT.

E

EARTH, EARTH-GODS.—Man's ideas concerning the earth may be divided into three classes—cosmological, mythical, and religious. In some cases these mingle strangely; and, while man thinks of the earth as a created or artificially formed thing, he also regards it as more or less alive.

1. Form of the earth.—The cosmological ideas entertained by various peoples were a mythico-scientific deduction from man's observation of what he saw around him. In no case had he any conception of the extent of the earth. To him it was merely the district in which he lived. He saw the sea, and believed that it encircled the earth like a vast river. Earth was usually thought of as a flat disk or oblong box floating on the ocean, while the heavens were regarded as a kind of dome, stretching above the earth and resting upon it or upon the waters, or propped up by poles or pillars. Such beliefs are found among lower races—Australians, Eskimo, the wild tribes of the Malay Peninsula, the Ewe of W. Africa, and others.[1] In some cases the surface of the earth covers an under world, accessible from various points.[2] Frequently, too, the earth is supposed to rest on pillars, or on a tree, or on the body of a giant or hero, or a god or gods, or on a huge animal.[3] Such primitive ideas as these survive in higher mythologies—Semitic, Egyptian, Greek, Hindu—though parallel with these more philosophic views prevailed.[1]

2. Origin of the earth.—Man's speculations did not limit themselves to the form of the earth; he busied himself also with the problem of its origin, and the various solutions of that problem are found with wonderful similarity amongst widely separated peoples. In some cases direct creation by a divinity seems to be asserted.

Thus in the sacred myths of the Quichés, preserved in the *Popol Vuh*, it is said that in the beginning there existed Divine beings called 'they that give life.' They spoke the word 'Earth,' and earth came into existence. An old hymn of the Dinka of the Upper Nile tells how, 'at the beginning,' Dengdit (on whom see *ERE* iv. 707 f.), a god dwelling in heaven, made all things.[2] Similarly a native hymn from the Leeward Islands tells of Toivi who 'abode in the void. No earth, no sky, no men. He became the universe.'[3] So, too, a hymn of the Zuñis describes Awonawilona, the Creator, forming everything by thinking 'outward in space.'[4]

But, generally speaking, where the making of the earth by a god is referred to, it is rather the framing of existing matter than creation that is meant. Thus some Australian tribes speak of Bunjil going over the earth, cutting it with his knife in many places, and thus forming creeks, rivers, valleys, and hills.[5] As man himself shaped

1 Howitt, 426 f.; Rink, *Tales and Traditions of the Eskimo*, London, 1875, p. 37; Skeat-Blagden, *Pagan Races of the Malay Peninsula*, London, 1906, ii. 239, 293, 355; Ellis, *Ewe-speaking Peoples of the Slave Coast*, London, 1890, p. 30.

2 Rink, 37; Man, *JAI* xii. [1882] 101 (Andaman Islanders).

3 Keane, *Man Past and Present*, Cambridge, 1899, p. 421; Tylor, *PC*⁴, 1903, i. 364 f.; cf. *ERE* i. 491ᵇ.

1 See artt. on COSMOGONY AND COSMOLOGY; Warren, *The Earliest Cosmologies*, New York, 1909; Jensen, *Kosmologie der Babylonier*, Strassburg, 1890.

2 Lejean, *RDM*, 1862, p. 760.

3 Lang, *Making of Religion*, London, 1898, p. 275.

4 Cushing, *13 RBEW*, 1896, p. 379.

5 Brough Smyth, *Aborigines of Victoria*, Melbourne, 1878, i. 423.

things out of clay or wood, so he imagined the Creator to have acted, and hence the native word for 'Creator' often means 'cutter-out,' 'moulder,' 'builder,' or 'forger.'[1] In a whole series of myths from different parts of the world, but very common among American Indian tribes, the earth is formed out of a little mud or clay fished up out of the waters by a Divine being, often in animal form. This mud or clay is formed or grows into the earth. Of this myth there are Vogul, American Indian, and Hindu versions.[2] In many cases the waters are those which have overwhelmed a previously existing world, and sometimes it is the earth itself which is fished up or rises out of the deep.

This is found in an Athapascan myth in which the raven flies down to the sea and bids earth rise out of the waters.[3] In a Polynesian myth the god Tangaroa fished up the world, but his line broke and it was again submerged, save a few portions now forming the South Sea Islands.[4] Cf. the Japanese myth of Izanagi and Izanami thrusting a spear from heaven into the ocean, the brine dropping from which coagulated and formed an island on which they now dwelt.[5]

In another series of myths the earth is formed out of part of the body of a gigantic being, who is sometimes hostile to the gods and is slain by them, as in the Bab. myth of Tiamât, out of whose body, cut in two, Marduk made heaven and (apparently) earth.

Cf. the account preserved by Berosus of the gigantic woman Omoroka whom Belos cut in two, making heaven of one part and earth of the other;[6] and the Scandinavian myth of the giant Ymir, from whose flesh Odin, Vili, and Ve made the earth.[7] In the Hindu parallel to these myths the gods offered in sacrifice the gigantic first man Puruṣa, and out of him made earth, as well as sky, sun, moon, etc.[8]

3. Heaven and Earth as a Divine pair.—The expanse of heaven and the broad earth were early regarded as personal beings, and also as husband and wife; Earth, from which so many living things sprang, being thought of as female. Their union was the source of all things in Nature, and, when the gods of departments of Nature were evolved, these were regarded as their children. Generally also they are parents of gods and men. In most cosmogonies Earth is the fruitful mother impregnated by Heaven, though in some cases the Sun or the 'Great Spirit' is her husband, and they are universal parents. Mythology also solved the problem of their separation by saying that it had been forcible, and (in many instances) brought about by their children.

Myths of Earth and Heaven as a Divine pair are found among African tribes, and, as among the Yorubas, they are represented by the male and female organs of generation, the symbolism pointing to the mythic origin of all things from them.[9] Similar myths are found among the American Indians, though with them the Great Spirit sometimes takes the place of Heaven. In one myth the hero god Mateito causes the removal of Heaven from Earth by magic.[10] Similar ideas are wide-spread among the Polynesians, and in the Maori myth of Rangi and Papa it is their children, especially the father of forest-trees, who cause their separation. In other islands, gods, a sea-serpent, plants, or the first human beings, bring this about.[11] Occasionally the Sun is Earth's husband, and, as in Timor, his union with her is the source of fertility.[1]

In Egypt, Seb (Earth) was male, and Nut (Heaven) was his wife, united with him in the primordial waters before creation. Shu separated them, but the hands and feet of Nut still rest on Seb, and her legs and arms thus correspond to the sky-supporting pillars of another myth. In some myths they were re-united at night, and conceived the sun, which was born of Nut every morning and swallowed by her at night.[2] In Vedic mythology Dyaus and Pṛthivī are parents of gods and men, but are separated by Indra, their child.[3] Hesiod has preserved the well-known myth of Uranus and Gaia, of Gaia visited by Uranus from a distance, and of the mutilation of Uranus by his son Kronos. Gods and men are their children, and this is recalled in the Orphic conception of man as the child of Earth and starry sky.[4] Zeus and Gaia may have been regarded as a Divine pair, and they were invoked in a liturgy at Dodona. But usually Hera, in some aspects an Earth-goddess, or Demeter, goddess of the fruitful earth, takes her place. A Chinese myth tells of Puang-ku separating T'ien and Ti, the universal parents.[5] Cf. Aston, 84, for a Japanese myth.

4. Earthquakes.—The movements of the animal who supports or exists within the earth are supposed to cause earthquakes (cf. ANIMALS, § 10). Where a god or giant is the supporter, they are similarly produced,[6] or a god or giant within the earth or an earthquake deity causes them.[7] In other cases the dead are supposed to cause them, *e.g.* by shaking the palm on which the earth rests,[8] or by struggling to reach the earth's surface.[9] According to Pythagoras, the dead fought and shook the earth.[10] In the naive belief of the Caribs, an earthquake was held to be Mother Earth dancing and signifying to her children that they also should dance.[11]

5. Disturbing the Earth.—The idea that it is dangerous to disturb the Earth or to intrude into her domain, and that, when this is done, Earth must be appeased by sacrifice, is seen in the common custom of foundation sacrifices (see FOUNDATION), in which a human or animal victim is placed below the foundation when the earth is dug out. Frequently this is done to provide a spirit-guardian for the building; but there is no doubt that the propitiatory aspect came first. The analogous custom of sacrificing to rivers when crossing them makes this certain (cf. also art. BRIDGE), and reference may be made to the Japanese *ji-chin-sai*, or 'earth-calming-festival,' for propitiating the site of a new building.[12] Similarly the sacrificial ritual before ploughing, though it has the intention of assisting fertility, doubtless was connected with this idea, and is expressly implied in such rites as those of the Chams, in which ploughing is begun secretly, and is then carefully atoned for with sacrificial and lustral rites, after which it may be proceeded with.[13] The thought is expressed in Sophocles' *Antigone* (339 f.), 'Earth . . . man wears away.' In India, ploughing does not take place on certain days when Mother Earth is asleep.[14] We find the same idea in Celtic myths of lakes which burst forth when a grave was dug;[15] and in India, Earth is worshipped

1 See Brinton, *Relig. of Primitive Peoples*, N.Y., 1897, p. 123.
2 de Charencey, *Une Légende cosmogonique*, Havre, 1884; Lang, *Myth, Ritual, and Religion*2, London, 1899, i. 176 f.; Muir, *Orig. Skr. Texts*, i. [London, 1858] 52; for a modern Bulgarian folk-version, see Chodzko, *Contes des paysans slaves*, Paris, 1864, p. 374.
3 Brinton, *Myths of the New World*3, Philadelphia, 1896, p. 229.
4 Réville, *Rel. des peuples non civilisés*, Paris, 1883, ii. 46; for other versions in which an island is fished up, see Grey, *Polynesian Myth.*, ed. London, 1909, p. 29 f.; Taylor, *Te Ika a Maui*, London, 1855, p. 115 f.
5 Aston, *Shinto*, London, 1905, p. 87.
6 Lenormant, *Origines de l'histoire*, Paris, 1880–4, i. 42, and appendix.
7 *Edda*, chs. 2, 3.
8 *Rigveda*, x. 90; cf. the remarks of Bousset, *Hauptprobleme der Gnosis*, Göttingen, 1907, p. 211 f.
9 Ellis, *Yoruba-speaking Peoples*, London, 1894, p. 41; see also Taylor, *African Aphorisms*, London, 1891, p. 140; *ARW* xi. [1908] 403 f.
10 2 *RBEW*, 1881, p. 25; Cushing, 379; Gregg, *Commerce of the Prairies*, New York, 1894, ii. 237.
11 Grey, 1 f.; Turner, *Samoa*, London, 1884, p. 285 f.; Gill, *Myths and Songs from the S. Pacific*, London, 1876, p. 59; Thomson, *Savage Island*, London, 1902, p. 85.

1 Frazer, *GB*2, 1900, ii. 206; see § 7, below.
2 Maspero, *Études de myth. et arch. ég.*, Paris, 1893, i. 160, 330, 340, ii. 216, 227; Budge, *Papyrus of Ani*, London, 1891, p. ciii.
3 Muir, v. [1872] 11 f.
4 Hesiod. *Theog.* 44 f.; Pindar, *Nem.* vi. 1 f.
5 Tylor, *PC*4 i. 325–6, ii. 270.
6 Muyscas (Keane, 421); Tongans (Mariner, *Tonga Is.*, London, 1817, ii. 112); Tlascalans (Bourbourg, *Hist. des nations civilisées du Mexique*, Paris, 1857–59, iii. 482); Karens (Mason, *JASBe* xxxvii. [1868], pt. 2, p. 182).
7 Meitheis (Hodson, *The Meitheis*, London, 1908, p. 111); Tshis (Ellis, *Tshi-speaking Peoples*, London, 1887, p. 35); Scandinavia (Grimm, *Teut. Myth.*, Eng. tr., London, 1880–88, p. 816); Japan (Aston, 147); cf. Ovid, *Met.* v. 356, xii. 521; Hesiod, *Theog.* 931; Paus. I. xxix. 7.
8 Man, *Andaman Islands*, London, 1883, p. 86.
9 Bastian, *Indonesien*, Berlin, 1884–94, ii. 3.
10 Aelian, *Var. Hist.* iv. 17.
11 J. G. Müller, *Amer. Urrel.*, Basel, 1855, p. 221.
12 Aston, 143.
13 Aymonier, *RHR* xxiv. [1891] 272 f.
14 Crooke, *PR*2, 1896, ii. 293.
15 *RCel* xv. [1894] 421, xvi. [1895] 277.

before a well is dug.[1] Propitiatory sacrifices were frequently offered before gathering various plants.

6. Earth as Divinity.—Earth is generally known as 'Mother Earth,' depicted by the Aztecs as a many-breasted woman,[2] like the Ephesian Artemis, who was in origin an Earth-goddess. Hesiod spoke of 'broad-bosomed' Gaia,[3] and the Zuñis of Earth with her 'four-fold womb.'[4] In primitive agricultural communities Mother Earth was propitiated with sacrifices, or worshipped with orgiastic rites, or her processes were assisted by magic. Among many tribes of W. Africa she is the object of an extensive cult.[5] Such titles as 'Mother,' 'the good Mother from whom all things come,' as well as a cult of the Earth, were wide-spread among American Indian tribes, who also had many myths of man's origin from the Earth. Offerings—from those of food to human victims—were usually buried in the ground, and, as among the Algonquins, roots, medicines, and animals were supposed to be in the care of Mother Earth.[6] Among the aborigines of India, Mother Earth is worshipped mainly in connexion with agricultural seasons. Sacrifices are offered, and she is begged to be propitious, while she has often a special festival, or, as among the Oraons, a spring festival celebrates her marriage with Heaven.[7]

A typical instance of Earth-worship is found among the Khonds, with their cult of Tari Pennu, the spouse of the Sun-god. Her cult is orgiastic and is intended to promote fertility. For this purpose, and in order to recruit her energies, a victim representing her was slain at a great festival and hacked in pieces, and portions of the flesh were buried or placed on the fields.[8]

Among the Teutons, Nerthus (=Terra Mater) was specially worshipped by certain tribes in spring, her waggon being drawn about the land by cows, and attended by her priest, probably in order to make the land fertile.[9] Other goddesses worshipped elsewhere—Frija, Tamfana, and Nehalennia—were probably in origin Earth-goddesses, while the giantess Jordh, mother of Thor, is simply the Earth. Freyr, in some aspects a god of fruitfulness,[10] had also a procession in spring, attended by his priestess, regarded as his wife. After this procession a fruitful year was looked for. Freyr was the son of Niordhr, perhaps a male double of Nerthus, who would thus be his mother. Both Niordhr and Freyr may be regarded as later male forms of an earlier Earth-goddess.[11]

Traces of the cult of an Earth-mother among the Celts are probably to be found in such goddesses as the consort of the Celtic Dispater, Stanna, Divona, Domnu, Berecynthia, and others; while the *Matres* with their symbols—fruit, flowers, and a child—are threefold extensions of the primitive Earth-mother. But, in accordance with a tendency for gods to take the place of goddesses which is not confined to Celtic religion, certain gods, primarily Earth-gods—those equated with Dispater, and Dagda in Ireland—are prominent. They are

[1] Crooke, i. 49. [2] Brinton, 257.
[3] *Theog.* 117. [4] Cushing, 379.
[5] Struck, *ARW* xi. [1908] 403; Waitz, *Anthrop.*, Leipzig, 1860, ii. 170; Leonard, *Lower Niger and Its Tribes*, London, 1906, p. 349 f.
[6] Müller, 56, 110, 221; Brinton, 258 f.; de Smet, *Oregon Missions*, New York, 1847, pp. 341, 359; Dorsey, *11 RBEW* (1894), pp. 438, 534.
[7] Crooke, i. 30 f.; Hopkins, *Rel. of India*, Boston, 1895, p. 532.
[8] Campbell, *Thirteen Years' Service amongst Wild Tribes of Khondistan*, London, 1864, p. 52 f.; MacPherson, *Memor. of Service in India*, London, 1865, ch. 6.
[9] Tac. *Germ.* 40.
[10] Adam of Bremen, iv. 26.
[11] Krohn, 'Finn. Beitr. zur germ. Myth.' [*Sonderabdruck aus den finnisch.-ugr. Forschungen*, 1904 and 1905], Helsingfors, 1906, p. 244 f.; Mogk, *Germanische Mythologie*², Strassburg, 1907, iii. 366 f.; Jaekel, 'Die Hauptgattin des Istvaeen,' *Ztschr. f. deutsch. Phil.* xxiv. [1891] 289 f.; de la Saussaye, *Rel. of the Teutons*, Boston, 1902, pp. 248 f., 269 f.

also under-earth gods. The older goddess now generally appears as the consort of one of these.[1]

The Vedic Earth-mother Pṛthivī was usually worshipped along with Dyaus, and their epithets show their greatness and productivity, as well as their moral and spiritual character. But she is sometimes referred to alone, and one hymn is devoted to her.[2] The cult of Dyaus and Pṛthivī is recalled in the present Indian marriage ritual, and Earth is still revered in the morning ritual, before sowing, ploughing, at milking, etc., while she is worshipped by some tribes as a household goddess. Bhūmi, the soil, has a place in village cults, and to this divinity—now male, now female—cakes, sweetmeats, and fruits are offered.[3]

In Babylon, En-lil was god of the earth, but it is probable that an Earth-goddess had been first worshipped. Such a goddess may be seen in his consort Nin-lil, or in Damkina, 'lady of the earth,' consort of Ea. Probably the great mother-goddesses of the Semitic area—Ashtart (*q.v.*) in Canaan, Atargatis (*q.v.*) in Syria, Ishtar (*q.v.*) in Babylonia, etc.—had been Earth-goddesses. They are connected with fertility, maternity, and the giving of children (hence they are often represented holding a child), and are called 'mother of men.'

Ishtar, at whose descent to Hades fertility ceases, in part symbolizes the death of earth in winter. But, since Earth and under-Earth are closely connected, Allatu, goddess of Hades, may also have been an Earth-goddess, one name of Hades being Irṣitu, 'the earth.' From earth sprang man, according to an old Semitic belief, and thither he returned. Ishtar, mother of men, and Allatu, receiver of men, are thus different aspects of one being.[4] Earth is called *E-sharra*, 'house of fertility.'[5] In popular view the gods had sprung from the Earth, and Ishtar is also the mother of the gods.

The cult of Earth was primitive in Greece. Ge or Gaia was the Mother who sent up fruits.[6] She had local cults and temples, and the fruits of the earth, as well as animal and perhaps human victims, were offered to Γῆ καρποφόρος. The title κουροτρόφος, applied to an otherwise unnamed goddess,[7] is connected with Γῆ,[8] and recalls the belief that children or the first men come from the earth. Other goddesses were derived from or associated with the old Earth-goddess—Aphrodite, Semele, Artemis, Pandora, Aglauros, etc.—and in some instances an epithet of Γῆ (κουροτρόφος, θέμις) was separated from her and became a new goddess. Demeter, 'Earth-mother' (Δη=Γῆ), or 'Grain-mother' (δηαί, 'barley'),[9] is certainly also a form of the Earth-goddess, but now rather of the cultivated earth. She is specifically a corn-goddess, but also, more generally, καρποφόρος, as well as 'she who sends up gifts' ('Ανησιδώρα),[10] while her functions concern vegetation and the fruits of the earth as well as flocks and herds. She is also equated with Rhea-Cybele, herself a primitive Earth-mother.

The ritual of the *Thesmophoria* points to Demeter, with Kore, as Earth-goddess. Live pigs, along with dough images of serpents and of the φαλλός, were thrown into underground sanctuaries, and the rite was intended to promote the growth of fruits and of human offspring.[11] The flesh of the pigs was afterwards mixed with the seed-corn, to promote an abundant harvest. All these offerings symbolized fertility, and the throwing of them into underground places resembles the custom of burying offerings to the Earth-goddess.

Kore has also characteristics of an Earth-goddess, and was once probably one with Demeter. She, too, is καρποφόρος, and in the representations of her return from Hades, the return of an Earth-goddess,

[1] MacCulloch, *Rel. of the Ancient Celts*, Edinburgh, 1911, pp. 31, 37, 40 f., 57, 58; cf. *ERE* iii. 80b, 280, 283b, 287a.
[2] *Rigveda*, v. 84.
[3] Crooke, i. 29, 105; Colebrooke, *Essays*, London, 1873, i. 220.
[4] See Jastrow, *Rel. of Bab. and Assyr.*, Boston, 1898, p. 587.
[5] Jensen, *Kosmol. der Bab.* p. 199.
[6] Paus. x. xii. 10. [7] Aristoph. *Thesm.* 295.
[8] Paus. I. xii. 3.
[9] Mannhardt, *Myth. Forsch.*, Strassburg, 1884, p. 292; cf., further, on the meaning and the various forms of the name, Gruppe, *Gr. Mythol. u. Religionsgesch.*, Munich, 1906, p. 1164 f.
[10] Paus. I. xxxi. 4.
[11] Schol. on Lucian; see Rohde, *Rhein. Mus.* xxv. [1870] 549.

the awakening of the Earth in Spring, evoked by ritual actions, *e.g.* striking the earth with hammers, may be seen.[1] While Demeter is said to have visited the earth with dearth, in anger at Pluto's rape of Kore, an older myth may have explained this as the result of her own disappearance, as in the case of Ishtar. The Phigaleian myth of her retirement to a cave because of Poseidon's violence, and the consequent death of vegetation, points also in this direction.[2]

The great goddess of the old Cretan religion was probably an Earth-mother, the prototype of the Great Mother of the gods, the goddess identified with the Cretan Rhea and the Phrygian Cybele, and who is primarily the fruitful earth, mother of gods and men. The Great Mother is often identified with Demeter and Gaia.

Among the Romans the primitive Earth-spirit, who was personified as Terra Mater, or Tellus, may also be seen behind such female divinities as Ops, Ceres (the equivalent of Demeter), Bona Dea, and Dea Dia. At the *Fordicidia* pregnant cows were sacrificed to Tellus, the unborn calves being torn from them and burnt, while the ashes were used at the *Parilia* along with the blood of the 'October horse.'[3] This savage piece of ritual, in which the Vestals were concerned, is clearly of ancient date and intended to assist Earth's fertility, or 'to procure the fertility of the corn now growing in the womb of Mother Earth.'[4] Tellus was also invoked with Ceres at the *Sementivæ* to protect the seed, and offerings of cakes and a pregnant sow were made.[5] Tellus was associated with the under world and the *manes*, as Demeter was with the dead, and she was invoked in the marriage ritual.[6] Earth was thus to the early Romans, as to the Greeks, the giver of fruits, as well as of children, while to her, as to a kind mother, men returned at death (see the grave-inscriptions). The cult of Tellus and other divinities connected with the Earth was carried far and wide by the Romans, who assimilated them to local earth-divinities of other lands.[7]

The ancient Mexicans knew Earth as 'Mother of all,' and invoked her at oath-taking, eating some earth sacramentally. Centeotl, goddess of the maize, must be regarded as an Earth-goddess. She was 'nourisher of men,' as well as 'our revered mother,' and was sometimes represented as a frog, the symbol of the moist earth, with many mouths and breasts. She was also the bringer of children, and was represented bearing a child. Her festivals fell in spring and summer, and at the latter a woman representing her was slain.[8] In Peru, where, as in Mexico, myth told how the first men came out of the earth, Pachamama, Mother Earth, was worshipped, *e.g.* at harvest, when corn and *chicha* were offered to her. A cult of Earth was also carried on in grottos and caves, and oracles were sought there.[9]

Sacrifices to earth-deities are laid on the ground, buried, or thrown into a hole.[10] Human victims were often slain in agricultural ritual; the earth or seed was watered with their blood, or their flesh was buried, to promote fertility, whether the victim was a propitiatory offering or, as Frazer[11] maintains, a representative of the deity of vegetation. Examples from N. America, Mexico, Africa, Indo-China, and India are cited

[1] See Harrison, *Prol. to the Study of Greek Rel.*^{2}, Cambridge, 1909, p. 276 f.; *Hellenic Journ.*, 1900, p. 106 f.
[2] Paus. VIII. xxv. 42; see below, § 8.
[3] Ovid, *Fasti*, iv. 631 f., 733 f.
[4] Fowler, *Roman Fest.*, London, 1899, p. 71.
[5] Ovid, *Fasti*, i. 658 f.
[6] Servius on *Aen.* iv. 166.
[7] Toutain, *Les Cultes païens dans l'empire romain*, Paris, 1907, i. 338 f.
[8] Müller, 491; Réville, *Rel. of Mex. and Peru*, London, 1884, pp. 73, 95.
[9] Müller, 312, 369; Réville, 197.
[10] Besides the examples referred to, see also Ling Roth, *Nat. of Sarawak*, London, 1896, i. 190; de Smet, 351; Lang, *Myth, Ritual and Rel.*^{2} ii. 281: Tylor, ii. 273 (Germany, Gipsies).
[11] *GB*^{2} ii. 245.

by him,[1] and he is also of opinion that the myth of Osiris' members scattered over Egypt may point to a similar custom there,[2] as suggested by the scattering of the ashes of red-haired victims over the fields.[3]

7. Earth as Mother.—The belief in the earth as the mother of men may be seen in the myth which told how the first men came out of the earth, of which there are many N. and S. American, Zulu, Eskimo, aboriginal Indian, Mexican, and Peruvian instances.[4] Greece also had myths of earth-born tribes (*αὐτόχθονες*), as well as of Erichthonius, the son of Earth. In other myths, men emerge from stones, trees, plants, etc., or, again, the creator moulds them from earth or clay. These are divergent forms of the same myth.

Cf. the Bab. myth of Ea-bani created from clay, and the suggestion of similar myths in Gn 2^7 3^{19}. In Ps 139^{15} and Job 1^{21} there appear to be traces of the myth of man's emergence from earth.[5]

The belief is further seen in the idea that children buried in the Earth may be re-born,[6] and a connexion between the two ideas is found in the custom of barren women resorting to the place whence men first emerged from earth.[7] Dieterich has shown[8] that the Roman and Hindu custom of cremating children arose from the belief that Earth could give to the child's soul a new birth, and that the common folk-answer to the question, 'Where do the children come from?'—viz. 'Out of stones, holes,' etc.—may be a relic of the myth of Earth as mother of men. But Earth is not only the womb but the tomb of all, and men return to her womb, from which they may be re-born. Hence the belief in the restlessness of the shade whose body is left unburied may be connected with the idea that burial in the womb of Earth is necessary to re-birth. Hence also it is often sufficient to throw a little earth on the corpse to ensure rest to the spirit. Men were often buried in the position in which the child rests in the womb; or, again, the dying were laid on the earth, or a little earth was placed on them to facilitate the passage of the soul to its true home. Analogous is the custom of laying the newly-born child on the ground—probably as a consecration to Mother Earth, or to obtain her protection and strength.[9]

All these beliefs and customs, and the myth of Heaven and Earth as a Divine pair, are the result of the analogy which man saw between the processes of conception and birth, and those by which the earth brings forth. Hence in many languages the words for begetting, sowing, and ploughing, for *semen* and the seed sown in the earth, for woman or the female organ of generation and the field or furrow, for the male organ and the ploughshare, are the same, or are used metaphorically one for the other (*ἀρόω*, *σπείρω*, Heb. *zeraʿ*, Bab. *zêru*, etc.).[10] Hence Earth was regarded as fertilized by Heaven, or by the rain (cf. the Eleusinian formula *ὕε*, 'Rain,' addressed to Heaven, and *κύε*, 'Be fruitful,' to Earth); hence, too, the myth of Earth sown with stones which spring up as men, or of plants growing from human *semen* spilt on the ground. Earth, as a fruitful mother impregnated like a female, was easily regarded as mother of men and *κουροτρόφος*. For this reason the process or symbols of begetting are believed to react magically on Earth's productive powers, and conversely the rites for Earth's fruitfulness on that of man. The

[1] *GB*^{2} ii. 238 f.
[2] *Ib.* ii. 142.
[3] Plut. *de Is. et Osir.* 73; Diod. Sic. i. 88.
[4] Brinton, 261 f.; Lang, *Myth, Rit. and Rel.*^{2} i. 174; *FL* xx. [1909] 377, 391, 392 f.; Preuss, *ARW* vii. [1904] 234; Balboa, *Hist. du Pérou*, 4 (in vol. vii. of Ternaux-Compans, *Voyages*, Paris, 1837–41).
[5] See *ARW* viii. (1905) 161 f., 550 f.
[6] See *ERE* iv. 331, and Spencer-Gillen^a, 336.
[7] Brinton, 268.
[8] *Mutter Erde*, Leipzig, 1905, p. 21 f.
[9] Dieterich, 6 f.; *ARW* x. (1907) 158, xi. (1908) 402 (African); *ERE* ii. 640^a, 662^a (Teutons), 649^b (Romans).
[10] Cf. *ARW* x. 158 f.; Lucret. iv. 1266–7; Vergil, *Georg.* iii. 136; Shakespeare, *Antony and Cleopatra*. II. ii. 233; *Qur'ān*, ii. 223; Dieterich, 47, 109.

rites of the 'Ἀρρητοφορία helped the fruitfulness of Earth and man, and during them φαλλοί of dough were flung into the earth. Symbolic sexual acts, as well as sexual union, often performed on the fields, are held to assist fertility, and the myth of the union of Iasion and Demeter on a thrice-ploughed field probably arose out of such ritual acts.[1] The marriage of Heaven and Earth is sometimes celebrated ritually, as in the Leti Islands, where the sun is supposed to come down and fertilize Earth at the rainy season, this being made the occasion of a festival in which the sexes unite.[2] Women, because of the analogy of their fruitfulness with that of Earth, or because they first practised agriculture, have usually a prominent place in agricultural ritual. And, again, because of Earth's influence on human productiveness, or because children were supposed to come from earth, Earth is sometimes invoked in marriage rites.

8. Earth and under-Earth.—Earth as the tomb of all became the abode of the dead; and hence many Earth-divinities are associated with the latter, since there is little difference between Earth and under-Earth, things growing on it springing from below the surface. Traces of this are found in Celtic religion; and in Greece, Gaia was associated with festivals of the dead, and was also called Γῆ χθονία—an epithet also shared by Demeter, whose cult at Phigaleia proves her connexion with the under world; while the dead were called Δημήτριοι. More obvious still is the connexion of Kore with Pluto, lord of Hades and giver of all blessings which come from the earth, just as Trophonios, an under-world deity, was the 'nourishing' god. Most Greek Earth-divinities have this twofold character.[3] The Roman Tellus was also associated with the under world. Allatu, the Bab. lady of Hades, may have been an Earth goddess (§ 6), and, contrariwise, Ishtar may have been a goddess of the under world. Her images have been found in Phœnician graves; and Aphrodite, her counterpart in Greece, was occasionally associated with the under world.[4] The death of Earth in winter would also help to suggest a connexion of the Earth-goddess with the region of the dead. Mythology, however, tended to separate Earth from under-Earth, and the death of vegetation was explained by saying that the Earth-goddess was detained in the under world by its ruler—Ishtar by Allatu, Kore by Pluto.

The connexion is further seen in the similar methods of evoking the return of the Earth-goddess in spring and the spirits of the dead, *i.e.* by striking the ground.[5]

LITERATURE.—This is indicated in the article.

J. A. MACCULLOCH.

EARTHQUAKES.—See PRODIGIES AND PORTENTS.

EASTER ISLAND.—1. Name, geography, and ethnology.—Easter Island is the most easterly inhabited island of the Polynesian group, situated in the Pacific Ocean about 1100 miles south-east of Pitcairn Island, and forming an irregular triangle with an area of about 34 sq. miles. Its name is derived from the current belief that it was discovered by Roggeveen on Easter Day (6th April), 1722. The natives call it 'Te Pito te Henua,' or 'the navel and uterus,' from a seeming resemblance of the volcanoes Rana Roraka to the navel (*pito*) and Rana Kao to the uterus (*henua*). In 1770 the Spaniards named the island San Carlos, and throughout southern Polynesia it is known as Rapa Nui, though this name dates back only to the seventh decade of the nineteenth century. It has also been called Teapy and Waihu by the natives. Many explorers have visited the island, but none stayed long enough to make a thorough investigation, previous to the expedition of the United States Steamship *Mohican*, which remained there from 18th to 31st Dec. 1886. The natives of Easter Island are of comparatively small stature, the largest skeleton measured on the *Mohican* expedition being somewhat less than six feet in length. The women are smaller-boned, shorter, and fairer than the men. The children have somewhat the complexion of Europeans, but grow darker with age from constant exposure to sun and trade-winds, although the covered portions of the body retain their light colour. The coarse black hair is straight, or wavy, but never kinky, the nose straight, eyes dark-brown with thin dark brows and lashes, cheek-bones prominent, lips thin, and beard scanty. The general facial appearance thus corresponds (making due allowance for sculptural exaggerations) with the physiognomy of the statues. The breasts of the women are round, rather large, well up on the chest, and with small nipples but large areolas, though neither so great nor so dark as in many other Polynesian islands. In the oldest adult males the pilage on the body is often very thick.

2. Tatuing, which was introduced by immigrants from the Marquesas Islands some two centuries ago, is not practised at the present time, but the older natives are thus decorated, chiefly on the face, neck, waist, and legs, although no special design is adhered to, and its object is solely ornamental. The women are more elaborately and extensively tatued than the men. The bodies were also painted in early times, while the clothing consisted of scant garments, chiefly of *tappa* cloth, over the shoulders and about the loins. Feather hats were worn on various occasions, but without apparent religious significance, except possibly in cases of marriage-feasts, and when the chiefs used them as insignia of office.

3. The early **population** of Easter Island is unknown, but it is practically certain that it was never very great. It is known, however, that their numbers have suffered serious depletion in consequence of the brutal deportation of the islanders by Peru in 1863. In 1868 there were 900, but 500 were removed to Tahiti in 1875, and three years later 300 more emigrated to the Gambier Archipelago. At the time of the *Mohican's* visit in 1886 the natives still on the island numbered 155.

4. The general **ethical status** of the Rapa Nuis, at least in modern times, is relatively high. The women are modest and of a higher moral standard than almost any of the other Polynesians. In disposition the natives are cheerful, contented, and hospitable. Intoxicating drinks, even *kava*, are wholly unknown. Thieving was common, but was not regarded as immoral. The thief was under the protection of a special divinity, and was believed to be detected only when the theft did not meet with the deity's approval. A system of retaliation existed, by which the person wronged might regain the property plundered, the thief in no wise forfeiting social respect or position. A darker side of their ethics, however, is presented by the cruelty which was meted out to their conquered foes after the conclusion of their wars. Pre-nuptial unchastity was common, and after marriage the husband was at liberty to lend or sell his wife to another for as long a time as he wished, receiving her back without detriment to the self-respect of any concerned. Adultery, on the other hand, was punished with death. Divorce depended on the will of the married pair. Suicide was extremely common, infanticide was rare, and

[1] See Dieterich, 94; Mannhardt, *Wald- und Feldkulte*, Berlin, 1877, i. 469 f., 480 f.; Frazer, *GB*² ii. 205.
[2] *GB*² ii. 205.
[3] Rohde, *Psyche*⁴, Tübingen, 1907, i. 205.
[4] Perrot-Chipiez, iii. 202; Farnell, *CGS*, 1896 ff., ii. 627.
[5] Cf. Harrison, *Hellenic Journal*, 1900, p. 106 f.; Paus. VIII. v. 1; *CF*, 207; *TS* ii. 3. 89.

puberty rites were unknown. The aged found little respect or consideration. Despite Christian influences, there are obvious traces of an earlier custom of marriage by purchase, the price, which generally consisted of sugar-cane and other edibles, being consumed in honour of the betrothal.

5. **Amusements** to-day, except at a marriage-feast or on the arrival of a vessel, are very rare; but the ancient dances are still retained. These are essentially pantomimic, and in them the arms are employed more than the legs. A small dancing-paddle, or wand, is a prominent feature of the posturing. There are also *hula-hula* dances of an erotic type, but the sexes seldom dance together. The *hula-hula* seems to have been danced chiefly at the annual election of a military chief, the celebration in honour of it lasting a month.

6. In ancient times the **government** of Easter Island was an arbitrary monarchy. The supreme authority, which was *quasi*-priestly, was vested in a king, and was hereditary in his family. He ruled over the entire island, which was divided into districts, each named and presided over by a chief. There was no special code of laws, custom defining the rights of the natives. Each tribe was entirely independent of any other, and in the continual conflicts which took place the king and his family were held sacred and were not troubled by either victory or defeat. Since the kidnapping of the principal chiefs and of Maurata, the last of a long line of kings, by the Peruvians in 1863, and their subsequent death in slavery, there has been no acknowledged authority among the Rapa Nuis.

7. In **war** the only weapons known to the natives were obsidian-pointed spears, short clubs, and stones, all of which were used with great skill. Shields were unknown, and there was no class of trained warriors.

8. The ancient islanders **buried their dead** lying at full length, usually with the head towards the sea. The bodies were wrapped in dried grass bound together by a sedge mat; but later *tappa*, or native cloth, was used instead of the mat. There seems to have been no special place of burial, although the platforms and the caves were favourite depositories for the dead. The bodies are now frequently exposed to animals and the elements, and are later thrust into their final places of interment without ceremony. The skulls of chiefs seem to have been marked with special clan-tokens, and numbers of such crania have been found.

9. **Cannibalism** was practised until a recent date, and an old legend states that children were sometimes devoured by their parents to satisfy the craving for human flesh. There is no evidence, however, that cannibalism was a ritual ceremony.

10. The general style of **architecture** seems to have been of two kinds. The more temporary form was that of the rectangular house built of bark or reeds and supported by posts set in the interstices of the stone foundation. These structures were from 10 ft. to 15 ft. in length and 6 ft. to 8 ft. in width. They had a thatched gable roof and nearly straight sides, one of which contained the door. In constructing the stone hut, which formed the second type, a convenient hill or rock was generally taken for the back wall. From this were laid side walls varying in thickness from 3 ft. to 7 ft., the shape being determined in great part by topographical conditions, and no definite plan was adopted. The front wall was constructed in the same way as the side, with the exception of the door, which was formed of two stone posts over which was laid a slab of stone, the entrance averaging a height of 20 inches and a width of 19 inches. In some houses two doors are found. The material used was basaltic rock. The average proportions of these dwellings are as follows: height from floor to ceiling, 4 ft. 6 in.; thickness of walls, 4 ft. 10 in.; width and length of rooms, 4 ft. 6 in. and 12 ft. 9 in. respectively. The ceiling was made of slabs reaching from wall to wall. This was topped by a mound of earth, which was covered with sod, making the hut effectually rainproof. In a few instances there are dwellings having one or more rooms opening from the main one. A small place was hollowed out of the wall of every dwelling, to hold the household gods and any valuables which the inhabitants might possess. This *quasi*-closet is remarkable in that it is frequently roofed by a true arch of lava with a keystone. Near Anahoirangaro Point there is a round tower 12 ft. in diameter and 20 ft. in height, supposed to have been used as a look-out to observe the movements of turtles. Another such tower, whose shaft measures 24½ ft., may be seen near Ahuakapu. It stands in the centre of a narrow platform 67 ft. long.

In Easter Island, as elsewhere in the Polynesian Islands, an important form of architecture was the construction of long, narrow platforms which correspond to the Polynesian *marais*. The platforms are usually near the beach on high ground, and are built with parallel walls of squared stones laid together, but uncemented. Inside these walls, at irregular intervals, were built small tombs. Between these, and extending to the top of the retaining walls, were thrown small stones until the horizontal plane of the platform was completed. Into this rubble were set the rectangular stones upon which the images stand. Finally, wings were built sloping from the horizontal plane to the ground. There are 113 platforms in all on Easter Island, each with a name. The largest, Tongariki, is 150 ft. long, 9 ft. wide, and 8 ft. high, excluding the wings, but with these it measures 540 ft., and the platforms vary in character and condition from this to mere shapeless masses of stone. Tongariki was adorned with fifteen statues, all but one of which have fallen face downward on the inshore side and are mostly broken. Another platform, named Vinapu, has six wings. Behind this is a round area 225 ft. in diameter. There is evidence to suggest that this was the ancient place of assembly for feasts and native ceremonies, and other platforms show similar spaces, the platform of Anaoraka having behind it a large triangle paved with cobbles.

Altars, which are said to have been erected for sacrifice, are found in the rear of some of the platforms. They are built of a single shaft, generally of vesicular lava, or sometimes of the material from which the images and crowns were made, and vary in height from 5 ft. to 10 ft., squared from 3½ ft. to 4 ft. on each face. They stand in the centre of a smoothly-paved terrace, and the sides and plinth are covered with figures sculptured in low relief, which, unfortunately, are too worn to be determined. There are traces of fire on the top of these stones, but no charred human bones have been found, so that the idea that they were used for human sacrifice may be discarded, especially as they are unlike the altars used in the other Polynesian islands for this purpose.

11. The **art** seems to have been of a crude and simple type. Slabs painted white, red, and black have been discovered. Some of the figures upon them resemble birds, while others are remarkable reproductions of European ships. Sculptured rocks, some of which seem to be prior to all remains except a ruined village west of Kotateke Mountain, have also been found. These are covered with fishes, turtles, and a bird-like figure which probably represents Meke Meke. On the wooden clubs and wide-bladed paddles designs of heads

may be plainly seen. Carved necklaces, which were worn during the dances, also exist.

All the stone for the monoliths of Easter Island was quarried either in the southern part of the crater of Rana Roraka or else on the western slope of the mountain. The workshops of the image-builders were situated in both of these places. The workman first chose an appropriate rock, then made a rough drawing of his subject in a recumbent position, and finally carved and completed the statue with the exception of cutting it loose from the rock. This was done last of all, and with caution, to avoid breakage. There are about 248 statues in, or very near, the crater of Rana Roraka, in various states of preservation. Their weight varies from ten to forty tons. An unfinished image, the largest on the island, measures 70 ft. in length and 14½ ft. across the body. The head itself is 28½ ft. long. The faces of these images, which alone are finished with any degree of care, have receding foreheads, high cheek-bones, straight noses, firm lips, long orthognathous chins, and ears of an exaggerated oval shape, possibly representing an early custom of elongating the lobes by means of pendants. The backs of the heads are square, on account of the way in which the statues were freed from the living rock. Little care, if any, was given to finishing the body, which in no case extended below the hips. The heads were invariably flat on the top, to allow for the adjustment of the red tufa crowns with which all the images were originally adorned. Of these crowns the largest is 12½ ft. in diameter. In three or four instances female statues occur. In feature the images correspond closely with the household gods already mentioned, except that the latter are made of wood, with eyes of bone and obsidian; and, unlike the images, they have the body entirely finished. They range from 2 ft. to 8 ft. in length, and are more modern than the stone household gods. The usual view is that they were images of noted persons; but from the analogy of Polynesian religion in general they seem originally to have been closely connected with the cult of deceased chiefs, or, in other words, were the outgrowth of ancestor-worship.

12. The **language** of Te Pito te Henua is unmistakably Polynesian, being most closely akin to the Maori of New Zealand, and this is the only island of the group which has an alphabet. There are numerous wooden tablets in the possession of the natives, each of which is believed to contain a different tradition. The characters on them are pictorial symbols, and were incised with obsidian points in straight lines on a sunken channel. Some of these tablets seem to have been made of drift-wood, very possibly parts of a canoe. They vary in size from 5½ in. by 4 in. to 5½ ft. by 7 inches. The art of reading them was hereditary in the families of the kings and chiefs, although in isolated cases a priest or teacher might decipher them. Ure Vaeiko, an old inhabitant of Easter Island, related the traditions contained in the tablets, and his version was afterwards corroborated by another man, Kaitae by name, who claimed to be directly descended from the last king, Maurata. At least approximate translations of these are given by Thompson and Geiseler (*opp. citt. infra*).

13. The early **religion** of Rapa Nui was distinctly Polynesian in type. The chief god was Meke Meke, who was the creator of all, and who is represented in the sculptures of Orongo, and in the paintings, as a bird-like figure. In his honour a feast was held annually in July, at Orongo, when eggs of sea-birds were brought from the rocky islets of Mutu Rau Kau and Mutu Nui, a few hundred yards from Rapa Nui itself—he who first brought an egg unbroken having certain rights to food and other privileges, as being especially honoured of Meke Meke. This god is evidently the Polynesian Tangaloa, the sky-god, who is represented in many Polynesian cosmogonic myths as a bird, originally imprisoned in a gigantic egg (see COSMOGONY [Polynesian]). There were numerous other gods and goddesses, to whose conjugal union was ascribed the origin of all existing things, as told by one of the tablets. Unfortunately the account is too brief for any re-construction of the mythology, since it is merely a list of such statements as 'God Agekai and goddess Hepeue produced obsidian.' It is known, however, that there was a god of fish named Mea Ika. There was also a god of birds called Era Nuku, whose wife was Manana, and who had the shape of a fish. Another bird-god was Mea Moa, while the *bonito* fish had a distinct deity, Mea Kahi. The god of theft has already been mentioned. Legend traces the coming of the Rapa Nuis, under their king Hotu-Matua, in two *proas* from the west, and likewise tells of a conflict between the Vinapu and Tongariki clans which resulted in the destruction of platforms and the overthrow of statues, so that the fallen images are still called 'dead,' while those yet standing are 'alive,' and are believed to have slain their prostrate foes. This tradition may well represent an actual internecine war, which would not be unprecedented in Easter Island, although some explorers prefer to explain the desolation of Te Pito te Henua by the hypothesis of a seismic disturbance. The date of this destruction, whatever its cause, seems to have been about the middle of the 17th century.

The exact import of the statues is a matter of doubt. They are acknowledged to represent chiefs and men of prominence; yet, on the other hand, it is said that they, like the household gods, received no worship. *A priori*, however, this is extremely doubtful, especially as the platforms where they are placed are favourite places of burial. It is more probable that the statues and, at least to some extent, the household gods, through whom communication was held with the spirits, represent the ancestor-cult of the early Rapa Nuis, and that they thus find their analogue in the Melanesian images erected as memorials of *tindalos*, although having in themselves no *mana*, or supernatural power (cf. Codrington, *The Melanesians*, Oxford, 1891, pp. 173–174). The statues are still objects of veneration to the natives of Easter Island, and are even believed to possess *mana*. They are protected by tabu (called *rahui* in this island), which is indicated in Rapa Nui by a white stone set on three common stones. The household gods seem to have received some sort of homage at the principal feasts, especially at the time of the ripening of the fruits, the fishing season, and the gathering of eggs. Temples were unknown, and worship was performed in the open air. The problem of altars has already been discussed.

Fetishism was also part of the religious belief of the island. The *timoika*, or fetish-board, was a whalebone paddle, 30 in. long by 14 in. wide, which was waved to the accompaniment of incantations to injure an enemy, while the *rapa*, or potato-fetish, a double-bladed paddle some 2 ft. long, was employed in similar fashion to protect the potato crops against drought or insects. Still more interesting are the *atua mangaro*, or fetish stones, small pebbles, either rough or fashioned, which were buried beneath the houses to ensure good fortune.

In early times the Easter Islanders had many superstitions, and had recourse to prayers, charms, incantations, and amulets to ward off evil and to bring good luck. They believed in a future life, to which, after death, the soul departed, there to be rewarded or punished as it deserved. For this reason a small hole was left near the top of the burial-place, so that the spirit of the dead might pass forth. Deified spirits were supposed to be constantly roaming about the earth and to influence human affairs. They appeared to, and communicated with, sleeping persons in visions or dreams. Gnomes, goblins, and ghouls were said to live in inaccessible caves and to prowl around after dark. The islanders of to-day are extremely superstitious, and live in constant dread of the baneful power of demons and supernatural beings. Circumcision is unknown to the Rapa Nuis, and there is no word equivalent to it in their language.

14. The **antiquities** of Rapa Nui are not without their parallels in other Polynesian islands, although the monuments decrease in importance as one advances eastward. Thus the island of Rapa, some 2000 miles west of Easter Island, contains terraces of massive turretted stone forts, while the tombs of the Tui-Tongas in Tongatabu, the chief island of the Tonga group, form nineteen truncated pyramids, each about 100 ft. square at the base and 25 ft. high, many of the coral concrete blocks measuring 18 ft. in length by 5½ ft. in height, and 3 ft. in width, and weighing over twenty tons. A megalithic dolmen, each of whose sides weighs fifteen tons, and with a top, brought, according to tradition, by boat from Wallis Island, more than 600 miles distant, is also found in the same island. In Tinian, one of the Ladrones, are two rows of columns resembling the uprights of the dolmen in Tongatabu, each capped with a hemisphere, flat side up, and weighing four tons. Ponape, in the Caroline group, contains marvellous cyclopæan ruins of basaltic prisms brought from a quarry ten miles distant, and ruins are also found in various other islands of the same group (see Guillenard, *Australasia*, ii., London, 1894, pp. 452, 500, 515, 519, 522, 527, 549, 554).

LITERATURE.—Philippi, *Isla de Pascua y sus habitantes*, Santiago de Chile, 1873; Stolpe, *Pask-ön*, Stockholm, 1883; Geiseler, *Die Oster-Insel*, Berlin, 1883; Thompson, 'Te Pito te Henua, or Easter Island,' in *Report of the United States National Museum* (for 1889), pp. 447-552, Washington, 1891; Cooke, 'Te Pito te Henua,' *ib.* (for 1897) i. 689-723, Washington, 1899; Gana, Viaud, and Ballesteros, *La Isla de Pascua*, Santiago de Chile, 1903 [reprint of work published between 1870 and 1875; bibliography, pp. 149-161]; Lehmann, 'Monographie bibliographique sur l'île de Pâques,' in *Anthropos*, ii. (1907) 141-151, 257-268; Roussel, 'Vocabulaire de la langue de l'île de Pâques ou Rapanui,' in *Muséon*, new ser. ix. (1908) 159-254.

FLORENCE L. GRAY.

EASTERN CHURCH.[1]—The Church which believes herself to be the canonical heir of the ancient undivided Church, remaining in the Faith and Orders of the first ages of Christianity, is called 'Orthodox' or 'Eastern.' Both these names distinguish her from, and contrast her with, her sister, the Western Church, which has excommunicated her, as well as from all the Protestant communities which have seceded from the latter. The name 'Orthodox Church,' on the one hand, expresses the idea that she is the Church of Christ which maintains the correct belief; the appellation 'Eastern Church,' on the other hand, in connexion with the division of the ancient Roman Empire, points primarily to the Eastern half in contrast with the Western, of which the centre is the Church of Rome. Yet, inasmuch as the Western Church, under the Pope, by introducing innovations regarding the foundations of government and regarding faith, at length separated herself from the Eastern Church, the name 'Eastern' acquired a moral significance, pointing to the Church as the possessor and champion of the ancient traditional faith, in contrast with the deviating *Western* Church. Thus also, though she has long ago extended greatly towards the North and includes the Russians, she continues none the less to give herself the title of 'Eastern,' and thus to recall, on the one hand, the former eminence of the Orthodox Church of the East, and to bind herself, on the other hand, to the ancient Church of which she claims to be the canonical and genuine heir.

[1] Besides this general article, there will be separate articles under the titles GREEK CHURCH and RUSSIAN CHURCH, to which this article is intended to be an introduction.

Besides the Christians of those ancient lands in which the Orthodox Church prematurely extended her bounds, she numbers now about a hundred million believers, including, since the 9th cent., the Russians. She consists of fourteen self-governing Churches, that is, Churches completely independent and autocephalous in regard to internal administration. These are as follows:

1. The Ecumenical Patriarchate of Constantinople.
2. The Patriarchate of Alexandria.
3. The Patriarchate of Antioch.
4. The Patriarchate of Jerusalem.
5. The Archiepiscopate of Cyprus.
6. The Church of Russia.
7. The Church of Greece.
8. The Metropolis of Carlovics.
9. The Church of Roumania.
10. The Church of Servia.
11. The Archiepiscopate of Montenegro.
12. The Metropolis of Hermannstadt.
13. The Metropolis of Bukowina and Dalmatia.
14. The Holy Monastery of Sinai, of which the Archbishop, whilst independent as Abbot, is as Archbishop attached for spiritual matters to the Patriarchate of Jerusalem.

All these Churches, though separate and independent, yet constitute one body, inasmuch as they possess (1) the same Faith, (2) the same principles of government, and (3) the same bases of worship.

1. The common Faith.—The common Faith of the Orthodox Churches is drawn from the two sources of revelation, according as the infallible Church has understood and interpreted them through her hierarchy, either assembled in Synods, or by themselves teaching each the same doctrine. The founts and the rule of dogmatic instruction are the dogmatic decisions of the Ecumenical Councils, or those of local Synods confirmed by an Ecumenical Council. As secondary sources, Expositions of the Faith are used, such as have been ecclesiastically accepted, inasmuch as they agree with ecclesiastical doctrine. Such are the so-called Symbolical Books of the Eastern Church, especially the Orthodox Confession of Mogilas and that of Dositheos. The chief points of Orthodox doctrine are as follows:—Man, having transgressed the commandment of God, fell from his original righteousness, on the one hand throwing off the true knowledge of God, on the other hand leaning generally towards evil. But the Son of God, having become incarnate, and having been sacrificed on Golgotha, reconciles sinful mankind with God, and establishes His Church for the continual supply of the benefits of the Cross. Thus the Church is the storehouse of truth and of sanctifying grace; through her the believer is taught the genuine contents of the Faith, and by means of her seven Sacraments (Baptism, Anointing, the Eucharist, Repentance, Ordination, Marriage, Extreme Unction) he is both justified and edified, through faith working by love, in the work of sanctification and in advancement towards all that is good. The Saints are honoured as models of faith and virtue (by feasts, pictures, and relics), and their intercession with God is requested (cf. the Symbolical Books of the Eastern Church, published by Kimmel in two vols., Jena, 1843). The reader may further consult the numerous Orthodox Catechisms, of which the principal is that of the Russian Plato; and the dogmatical works of the Russians Antonios, Makarios, and Sylvester, and in Greek those of Rossi's *System of Dogmatics of the Orthodox Eastern Catholic Church* (vol. i., Athens, 1903), and Androutso's *Symbolics* *from an Orthodox Point of View* (Athens, 1901), and *Dogmatic of the Orthodox Eastern Church* (Athens, 1907).

2. Church government.—The second chain binding the autocephalous Churches into one whole is the common principles of government. These principles are supported by the holy Canons, by the Fathers, and by the administrative laws of the Emperors, referring to the Church and completing the Canons. Among these canonical collections, entitled *Nomocanon*, the most important is the Code given to Photius, which was sanctioned in 920 by a great Council in Constantinople, and proclaimed as having authority over all the Eastern Church, constituting the fundamental collection of her laws. More modern collections are, on the one hand, the so-called *Rudder of the Intelligent Ship of the one Holy Catholic and Apostolic Church of the Orthodox*, published first at Leipzig in 1800; and, on the other hand, the *Constitution of the Divine and Holy Canons*, published by Ralli and Potli at Athens, in six volumes, in 1852 (Greek).

According to the principles of Orthodox government, the head of the Church is Jesus Christ; but believers are distinguished into *clergy*, consisting of three grades (archpriests, priests, and deacons), and *laity*. Monastic life, without any division into grades, is a single organism resting upon the monastic arrangements of Basil the Great, reduced to order by means of legal commands of ecclesiastical and political legislation.

The monks (whose first and second orders wear cassocks) are spiritually subject to their local bishops, excepting the monks of the *stauropegia*[1] and of the Imperial monasteries. The monasteries are distinguished, according to their regimen, into *cenobitic* and *idiorythmic.*[2]

The centre of each Church is the bishop, but the basis of administration of the autocephalous Churches is the Synodical system, all questions of ecclesiastical administration and discipline being solved in regular or periodically convoked Synods. Not only spiritual questions affecting ecclesiastical life and hierarchical organization are regulated by Church law, but partly also many relations of social life, which are bound up closely with that of the Church, such as questions of marriage, divorce, etc. In spite of all the differences which, owing to their relations towards the civil government, Canon Law presents from this point of view in the various autocephalous Churches, the common spirit of administration appears everywhere. Many Canon Laws have been published among the Orthodox, the best of them being *Ecclesiastical Law*, composed by Milasch at Zara in 1902, of which a second edition has appeared.

3. Worship.—The third mark of the unity of the Orthodox Churches is the common basis of worship. No one liturgical language holds the place in the Orthodox Church that Latin does amongst the Roman Catholics; every race performs its service in its own tongue. The Table of Feasts of the Orthodox Church rests on the Julian Calendar, which has thus an ecclesiastical significance; hence a reform of it, bound up as it is with ecclesiastical life among the Orthodox, cannot take place by means of a political enactment.

The churches are nearly all built on the same plan; the holy place is separated from the rest of the temple by the shrine for pictures.

The feasts are distinguished either as 'great,' because they relate to the Lord Jesus or to the Mother of God, or as Saints' days; but the central one is the Paschal feast (Easter). Easter, Christmas, the Assumption of the Virgin, and the anniversaries of the death of the Holy Apostles are preceded by fasts of many days; other fast-days being also Wednesdays and Fridays, the 14th of September, the 29th of August, and the Eve of the Epiphany.

The stronghold and centre of the whole worship is the Liturgy, of which two types are used—that of Basil the Great, recited on fixed days, and that of Chrysostom, which is usual throughout the year. The Liturgy of the Pre-sanctified, called, after the nomenclature of Gregory, the *Dialogos*, is recited only in Lent. Preaching of the Divine word, for the explanation and imparting of Christian truth, which was anciently an inseparable part of public worship, has now disappeared, and only in Russia does it show some signs of life. Common to all the Churches are certain books for the offices of the Feasts and the Sacraments. (1) Τυπικόν. The *Typicon* is a book which fixes the canonical psalms and hymns to be used, as well as the mode of conducting the services of the Church on the different festivals. (2) Εὐχολόγιον. The *Euchologion* contains the order of prayers for the seven Sacraments, and other prayers for different occasions. (3) Ὡρολόγιον. The *Horologion* contains the seven kinds of petition for the seven hours of prayer, that is, the first, the third, the sixth, the ninth, Vespers, Midnight, and Dawn. (4) Τριώδιον. The *Triodion* contains the hymns to be sung during the whole of the forty days which precede Easter. (5) Πεντεκοστάριον. The *Pentecostarion* contains the hymns to be sung from Easter to Whitsuntide. (6) Παρακλητική. The *Paracletice* contains the hymns of John of Damascus and others, which are sung from Whitsuntide onwards. (7) Μηναῖα. The *Menæa* contains hymns for all the Saints' days and festivals of the year which are not contained in the *Triodion* and the *Pentecostarion*. (8) The Psalter, the Gospel, and the 'Apostle.' The music is vocal and idiorythmic, and is pleasing when it is well performed. Instrumental music and graven images are forbidden (cf., for the Table of Feasts, the Calendar of Nilles, and for the music the Literature of Krumbacher, in *Byzantinische Litteratur*[2], Munich, 1897, p. 599 ff.).

4. Character of the Orthodox Church.—The essential features of the Orthodox Church are two: (*a*) *theoretical*, that she preserves and keeps unchanged doctrine handed down by her (Traditionalism); and (*b*) *practical*, that she avoids excess or bias in external ceremonies (Ritualism). The first of these marks is generally in agreement with the marvellous beginning of Christianity, because this, according to the Orthodox, is not something empty and invisible, but a revelation having a firm and definite content in regard to faith and the bases of worship and administration; and the Orthodox Church, tolerating no innovation, claims to preserve and exhibit as much as possible the supernatural essence of Christianity. From her point of view, the Western Church came to a rupture with ancient tradition, and Protestantism is a subversion of traditional foundations, whereas she herself claims to teach essentially what was taught by the Church of the first ages. Certainly, that keeping of the traditional Faith does not exclude theological development and the many-sided investigation of Divine truth. And if, from the 8th cent. onwards, treatises about Christian truth are lacking in life and independent thought, this must be attributed not to the principles of Orthodoxy being insusceptible of development, for in the first period of the Church they were shown to be the inexhaustible source of rich theological research, but to external causes, to well-known political circumstances.

All who visit the Churches of the East are

[1] Σταυροπήγιον is a monastery in foreign lands depending on the Ecumenical Patriarchate of Constantinople.

[2] Monks of the former class have common meals and a common purse; in the latter each dwells apart from his fellows, but is under the spiritual direction of his Abbot.

forcibly struck by the attention to external forms. Whereas the main aspect of the Western Church is that of an administrative institution, having a well-formed system of obedience to the authority of the Church, and whilst among Protestants Christianity is principally a matter of teaching and preaching, the Orthodox Church, having on the one hand a loose administrative system, and on the other hand a lifeless preaching, appears now to be chiefly a society for worship. Thus dogma is put aside or hidden in the external forms of adoration; the whole religious being of the Orthodox appears generally in reverence and submission to her numerous rites. But surely religious ceremonies are the necessary expression of the internal spirit; and is it not reasonable that the Orthodox Church, having been distinguished of old by her rich religious life, should afterwards have turned to create appropriate rites to express the living Faith? And if, since the 8th cent. sacred ceremonies multiplied and then came to be incomprehensible to the common understanding, so that their performance by the lips and the simple listening to them are now assumed to be the fulfilment of religious duties, such a zeal for ritual is not a product of the Orthodox spirit, but shows the unfavourable circumstances of which the Orthodox Church was formerly the victim, and under whose power she still remains. The lack of missionary work among the Orthodox must also be attributed to the same unfavourable circumstances, and not to 'the self-complacency of the Orthodox Church or the satisfaction of a glutted possessor,' or the sense of her own weakness, as some modern theologians declare without examination (*e.g.* Loofs, *Symbolik*, Tübingen, 1902, i. 167, and Boulgaris, Θεολογικοί, Vienna, 1872, p. 25.

LITERATURE.—See lists appended to artt. GREEK CHURCH and RUSSIAN CHURCH.

PORPHYRIOS, *Archbishop*.

EATING THE GOD.—The idea that the properties of an organism are acquired by eating its substance is widely spread among semi-civilized peoples.[1] It forms a prevalent explanation of ceremonial cannibalism (*q.v.*), and is probably the chief among the reasons given for the correlated rite of theophagy. This rite is not frequent, though the history of religion and magic teems with examples which just fall short of the definition. The vague and indeterminate conception of deity in the lower religions helps to explain both of these facts.

Communion in the flesh or blood of a god is necessarily indirect. Even when the man, animal, or plant, sacrificed for the purpose, is divine, only the individual is used; the species remains. The nearest approach to actual theophagy is in the employment of a man-god.

'The sacrificial form of cannibalism obviously springs from the idea that a victim offered to a supernatural being participates in his sanctity, and from the wish of the worshipper to transfer to himself something of its benign virtue.'[2]

Sacrificial cannibalism has been a regular institution among the peoples of Central America, in parts of Peru, in Nigeria and various tracts of Equatorial Africa, and in certain islands of Polynesia and Melanesia.[3]

The most remarkable development was in Mexico. At every sacrifice the victim bore the name and filled the rôle of the god. Acosta observes:

'Afore they did sacrifice him, they gave him the name of the idol to whom he should be sacrificed, and apparelled him with the same ornaments like their idol, saying that he did represent the same idol.'[4]

The annual representative of Tezcatlipoca, after a year's luxurious living, was sacrificed at the great festival. His heart was offered to the sun. His legs and arms were served up at the tables of the lords. The 'blessed food' was chopped up small.[1] At the feast of Xipe, prisoners of war were eaten. They were termed *tototecti*, 'dying in honour of *Totec*.' A thigh was sent to the king's table. The dish was called *tlacatlaolli*. The giver of each feast did not eat of his own captive, but of those of others.[2] In Cholula a slave of fine physique was sacrificed as the representative of Quetzalcoatl, and eaten.[3] The Mayas ate the flesh of human victims sacrificed to the gods, as 'a holy thing.'[4] In Caranque, a province of Peru, it was the custom to eat the flesh of persons sacrificed to the gods.[5] In Nigeria, human victims offered to gods are eaten by both priests and people; the flesh is distributed throughout the country.[6] Traces of the rite are found in Vedic India.[7]

Where the god is a deity of the corn, he may be eaten in his anthropomorphic substance or in the form of grain or bread. The Mexican theophagy of Huitzilopochtli is an important example of the rite, though the cult is apparently composite.

A colossal statue of the god Huitzilopochtli in dough was broken up and distributed among the worshippers. The ceremony was described as 'killing the god Huitzilopochtli so that his body might be eaten,' and was termed *teoqualo*, 'god is eaten.' Women were not allowed to partake.[8] The dough was made of all kinds of seeds and the blood of children. After being exhibited in the temple, the image was 'slain' by the priest, who pierced it with a dart. The heart was eaten by the king. The rest of the 'flesh' was broken up small, and all males received a portion.[9] Smaller images of dough were eaten at other feasts. Reasons assigned were to secure good health, and, in the case of warriors, to increase their strength.[10]

Analogous cases of the offering of images of divine beings made of bread are adduced by Frazer.[11] Holy cakes are often in the form of wafers on which the divine image is stamped in relief. This method may clearly arise without reference to the principle of substitution, as may be seen in the case of the Christian Eucharist, where it is unnecessary to assume that the stamped wafer is a substitute for an actual lamb.

In so far as the fruits of the earth are conceived as the embodiments of divine beings, the sacramental eating of the new fruits is a form of the rite of eating the god.[12] In some cases this solemn act of assimilation is preceded by a purgation, both physical and moral. The intention in the former aspect is 'to prevent the sacred food from being polluted by contact with common food in the stomach of the eater. For the same reason Catholics partake of the Eucharist fasting.'[13] It is unlawful to partake of it after a meal. Lent was originally regarded as the fast preparatory to the Easter communion. Continence, often associated with fasting, was also prescribed before communion.[14] A transition from sacrament to sacrifice in this connexion has been suggested.

'At a later age, when the fruits of the earth are conceived as created rather than as animated by a divinity, the new fruits are no longer partaken of sacramentally as the body and blood

1 Frazer, *GB*², London, 1900, ii. 353-361.
2 Westermarck, *MI*, London, 1906-8, ii. 563. 3 *Ib.* ii. 562 f.
4 Bancroft, *Native Races of the Pacific States*, New York, 1875-6, ii. 307, iii. 267, 278, 342, 353, 355; Acosta, *History of the Indies* (Hakluyt Soç. 1880), ii. 323.

1 Sahagun, *Hist. gén. des choses de la Nouvelle Espagne*, Paris, 1880, pp. 61 f., 96-9, 103; Bancroft, ii. 319 f.; Brasseur de Bourbourg, *Hist. des nations civilisées du Mexique*, etc., Paris, 1857-59, iii. 531 ff.
2 Sahagun, 584 f.; Bancroft, ii. 309. 3 Bancroft, ii. 397.
4 *Ib.* ii. 689; for other examples, see Sahagun, 75, 116, 123, 158, 164, 585.
5 J. Ranking, *Hist. Researches on Conquest of Peru, Mexico*, etc., London, 1827, p. 89.
6 C. Partridge, *Cross River Natives*, London, 1905, p. 59; A. F. Mockler-Ferryman, *British Nigeria*, London, 1902, p. 261.
7 A. Weber, *Indische Streifen*, Berlin and Leipzig, 1868-79, i. 72 f.
8 Bancroft, iii. 297 ff., 440, quoting Torquemada.
9 Sahagun, 203 f. See also art. DEICIDE.
10 Clavigero, *Hist. of Mexico* (Eng. tr., London, 1807), i. 311; Sahagun, 33, 74, 156 f.; Bancroft, iii. 316; Br. de Bourbourg, iii. 539.
11 *GB*² ii. 344. 12 See examples in *GB*² ii. 318-335.
13 *Ib.* ii. 335 f.
14 *Cat. of Council of Trent*, ii. 4, 6; Jerome, *in Jonam*, § 3, also *Epp.* xlviii. § 15, quoted by Westermarck, ii. 295.

of a god; but a portion of them is presented as a thank-offering to the divine beings who are believed to have produced them. Sometimes the first-fruits are presented to the king, probably in his character of a god. Till the first-fruits have been offered to the deity or the king, people are not at liberty to eat of the new crops.'[1]

In Wermland (Sweden), the peasants eat loaves made from the grain of the last sheaf. The loaf is in the shape of a girl, and 'represents,' according to Frazer, 'the corn-spirit conceived as a maiden.' Similarly in France, at La Palisse, a man of dough is broken in pieces and eaten, at the end of harvest.[2] The Lithuanian festival of Sabarios included the eating of loaves ceremonially made from all kinds of seeds. One little loaf was given to each member of the household.

'In one part of Yorkshire it is still customary for the clergyman to cut the first corn; and my informant believes that the corn so cut is used to make the communion bread. If the latter part of the custom is correctly reported (and analogy is all in its favour), it shows how the Christian communion has absorbed within itself a sacrament which is doubtless far older than Christianity.'[3]

In Buro, at the end of rice-harvest, each clan holds a sacramental meal to which each member contributes some of the new rice. It is termed 'eating the soul of the rice.'[4] Similar rites are observed in Celebes, among the Hindus, Burghers, and Coorgs of South India, in the Hindu Kush, and among the Chams of China.[5] In Scotland, grain from the Old Wife, the last sheaf cut at harvest, is given to the horses, in order to secure a good harvest next year.[6]

Such worship as the Ainus of Japan paid to the bear 'appears to be paid only to the dead animal.'[7] Though, whether alive or dead, it is described as *kamui*—a term similar to the *ngai* of the Masai, the *orenda* and *wakan* of the North Americans, and the *mana* of the Melanesians—it is slain whenever possible; its flesh is a staple food, and its skin furnishes clothing. But at the annual bear-festival a bear was 'worshipped' and then ceremonially slain. Its blood was drunk by the male members of the family. The liver was eaten raw by women and children as well as by men. The brain was eaten with salt. The heart also was eaten. The rest of the flesh was kept for a day, and then divided among all who had been present at the feast.[8] Similarly the Gilyaks of Siberia pay a certain measure of 'worship' to a bear, prior to its solemn sacrifice.

After being shot to death with arrows, it is prepared for food. The flesh 'is roasted and eaten in special vessels of wood finely carved. They do not eat the flesh raw or drink the blood, as the Ainos do. The brain and entrails are eaten last; and the skull ... is placed on a tree near the house. Then the people sing, and both sexes dance in ranks, as bears.'[9]

A more detailed account supplies a valuable type of such theophagous ceremonies:

'The broth obtained by boiling the meat had already been partaken of. The wooden bowls, platters, and spoons out of which the Gilyaks eat the broth and flesh of the bears on these occasions are always made specially for the purpose at the festival, and only then; they are elaborately ornamented with carved figures of bears and other devices that refer to the animal or the festival, and the people have a strong superstitious scruple against parting with them. While the festival lasts, no salt may be used in cooking the bear's flesh, or indeed any other food; and no flesh of any kind may be roasted, for the bear would hear the hissing and sputtering of the roasting flesh, and would be very angry. After the bones had been picked clean they were put back in the kettle in which the flesh had been boiled. And when the festal meal was over, an old man took his stand at the door of the house with a branch of fir in his hand, with which, as the people passed out, he gave a light blow to every one who had eaten of the bear's flesh or fat, perhaps as a punishment for their treatment of the worshipful animal.'[10]

[1] *GB*[2] ii. 459. [2] *Ib.* 318 f. [3] *Ib.* 320 f.
[4] G. A. Wilken, quoted by Frazer, *GB*[2] ii. 321.
[5] *GB*[2] ii. 322 ff.
[6] Maclagan, in *FL* vi. (1895) 151. See Jamieson, *Dict. Scottish Lang.*, *s.v.* 'Maiden.'
[7] *GB*[2] ii. 375 f., quoting authorities.
[8] *Ib.* 376–80, and *ERE* i. 249. [9] *Ib.* 380 ff.
[10] L. von Schrenck, *Reisen und Forschungen im Amur-Lande*, iii. (St. Petersburg, 1867) 696–731, quoted by Frazer, ii. 385.

In ancient Greece the worship of Dionysus seems to have included theophagy. Bulls, calves, goats, and fawns were torn to pieces and devoured raw by the worshippers. They believed, Frazer infers, 'that they were killing the god, eating his flesh, and drinking his blood.'[1]

At the Athenian *Bouphonia* the flesh of the slain ox was eaten by the participants in the ceremony.[2] The oxen slain at Great Bassam in Guinea annually to secure a good harvest are eaten by the chiefs.[3] Similarly, at a spring festival in China, the flesh of a sacrificed buffalo is eaten by the mandarins.[4] It is possible that at the *Thesmophoria*, Athenian priestesses ate the flesh of sacrificed swine as a communion of the body of the god.[5] Near Grenoble the harvest supper is made from the flesh of a goat killed ceremonially. Similarly, in the case of a slain ox near Dijon.[6] The ancient Egyptians partook of the flesh of a pig sacrificed to Osiris. Instead of the pig, poor persons offered a cake of dough.[7]

The Kalmuks consecrate a ram as 'the ram of heaven' or 'the ram of the spirit.' The animal is tended carefully and never shorn. When it is old, and the owner bethinks him of consecrating a young ram, the ram of heaven is slain, and its flesh eaten.[8] The Todas, by whom the buffalo 'is to a certain degree held sacred,' and is treated 'with a degree of adoration,' never eat its flesh, except at a sacred meal celebrated once a year. A calf is killed in a secret place of the jungle, and its flesh roasted on a sacred fire. Women are not allowed to be present.[9]

Frazer distinguishes two types of 'sacramental killing' of the 'animal god'—the Ainu and the Egyptian types. In the former the animal is one which is habitually killed, and the special sacrifice is a 'special annual atonement' for the habitual slaughter, the individual 'god' of the species 'deity' being 'slain with extraordinary marks of respect and devotion.'[10] The Toda ceremony is an example of the Egyptian type.

The prohibition against the use of salt or of leaven, or other modifying constituents, is noteworthy in the case of the ceremonial consumption of 'strong,' or 'sacred,' foods. The bread of the Passover and the Catholic host are unleavened. Sacred foods generally may not be mixed, and the prohibition of salt and leaven is no doubt a result of the same principle. 'Strong' foods, again, are as a rule forbidden to women, various reasons being assigned. Male selfishness, ideas of male superiority, connected with the androcentric structure of society, are sufficient reasons for the prohibition, taken together with woman's natural aversion to such foods, and, in particular, to strong drink. In the 6th cent. the Council of Auxerre forbade women to receive the Eucharist with the naked hands.[11] Here a complication is introduced by the then prevailing notion of the natural impurity of woman.

As sacred bread is to the flesh of the god, so is sacred wine to his blood. As the 'worshipper' in the hunting stage of social evolution acquired strength and 'inspiration' by drinking the fresh blood of slain animals, so in the agricultural stage the process is repeated by drinking wine.

[1] Arnobius, *adv. Nationes*, v. 19; F. Maternus, *de Errore*, § 6; Euripides, *Bacchæ*, 735 ff.; Schol. on Aristoph. *Frogs*, 357; see *GB*[2] ii. 165 ff.
[2] *GB*[2] ii. 294, with authorities.
[3] *Ib.* 296. [4] *Ib.* 297.
[5] Schol. on Aristoph. *Frogs*, 338; see *GB*[2] ii. 301 f.
[6] Mannhardt, *Ant. Wald- und Feldkulte*, Berlin, 1877, p. 166, *Mythol. Forschungen*, Strassburg, 1884, p. 60.
[7] Herod. ii. 47 f.; Ælian, *de An. Nat.* x. 16; Plutarch, *de Is. et Osir.* 8.
[8] Bastian, *Völker d. östl. Asien*, Leipzig, 1866–71, vi. 632.
[9] W. E. Marshall, *A Phrenologist amongst the Todas*, London, 1873, pp. 80 f., 129 f.
[10] *GB*[2] ii. 437; see *MI* ii. 605. [11] *MI* i. 666.

'Whoever drinks the blood of an animal is inspired with the soul of the animal or of the god, who . . . is often supposed to enter into the animal before it is slain; and whoever drinks wine drinks the blood, and so receives into himself the soul or spirit of the god of the vine.'[1]

In ancient Brāhmanism and Zoroastrianism the worshipper drinking the *soma* or *haoma* was in communion with deity. In the former case, as in the case of the Greek Dionysus, the wine itself had come to be anthropomorphized into a god.

Among totemic peoples it is a general rule that the totem may not be slain or ill-treated in any way. But there are a few exceptions. The Narrinyeri of South Australia were in the habit of killing and eating their totemic animals.[2] In the Euahlayi tribe it is lawful to kill and eat the hereditary totem, which is derived from the mother; but it is forbidden to treat the individual totem, *yunbeai*, in this way.[3] Among the Arunta and other tribes of Central Australia the totem animals are eaten by the members of the totem group at the *Intichiuma* ceremonies, but at no other time, except sparingly. This ceremonial eating is connected with the purpose of multiplying the numbers of the totem animal which forms a staple food for other totem groups.[4] There seems to be no *a priori* reason why a totem animal regularly killed should not on occasion serve as a mystic food. At the *Intichiuma* of the kangaroo totem the members eat a small portion of the flesh of a kangaroo, and anoint their bodies with the fat.

'Doubtless the intention alike of the eating and of the anointing is to impart to the man the qualities of his totem animal, and thus to enable him to perform the ceremonies for the multiplication of the breed.'[5]

But these Australian sacraments, so called, are not only in the magical stage, but, to all appearance, devoid of any sentiment of loyalty to the totem or of solidarity in the clan. They seem to show the mechanical and business-like aspect of magic rather than its emotional aspect.

There is no evidence of any rite of sacramental communion with the totem by eating its flesh, in cases where the totem may be regarded as a divinity. The 'mystic meal' of the Australian *Intichiuma* is not a mode of religious communion, but merely an application of sympathetic magic, both in the mechanism and in the results of the ceremony. All that can be said is that it may be a case of theophagy in the making.

'The totemic animal or plant is not regarded exactly as a close relative, whom it would be wrong to kill.'[6] The Wolf clan of the Tlingits hunts wolves, but, when in danger from them, prays to them as 'relatives.'[7]

The principles on which theophagy rests are apparently simple, when we consider the early views as to the transmissibility of supernatural power and the meaning of the assimilation of nutriment.

'The divine qualities of a man-god are supposed to be assimilated by the person who eats his flesh or drinks his blood. This was the idea of the early Christians concerning the Eucharist. In the holy food they assumed a real bestowal of heavenly gifts, a bodily self-communication of Christ, a miraculous implanting of divine life. The partaking of the consecrated elements had no special relation to the forgiveness of sins; but it strengthened faith and knowledge, and, especially, it was the guarantee of eternal life, because the body of Christ was eternal. The holy food was described as the "medicine of immortality."'[8]

But, even in the early stages of human thought, the distinction between substance and accidents is clearly held. The soul of man is nourished (hence the strength and life of his body) by the soul of the food.[9] The accidents on both sides are either ignored or explained away. As materialism and spiritualism or animism become separated, the necessity is felt of bridging the gulf between substance and accidents; hence theories of transubstantiation. Along other lines of thought come the ideas of symbolism and commemoration. The rite is symbolic of spiritual assimilation; or it is done in memory of a divine being.

In spite of meagre data, not likely to be augmented, the rite is a very logical corollary of several series of ideas. It is a case of convergence; the patent results of the assimilation of food are the basis of the homology. The animism and vitalism so deeply ingrained in religious thought and emotion seem to have a permanent warrant in the facts of nutrition. It is quite natural that the primitive mind should attach magical and animistic ideas to food, as such, and in particular to flesh. Raw flesh is 'living flesh';[1] warm blood is instinct with life and soul. From the point of view of the magical assimilation of properties, human flesh and blood are the most valuable nutriment possible. But, in spite of occasional lapses into cannibalism, man has generally shown an instinctive repulsion to the habit or the perversion. And, if there is some mystery about flesh and blood generally, there is still more about the flesh and blood of men. Hence sacrificial cannibalism is an act fraught with supernatural crisis. Probably all such acts are a form of orgiasticism. So much is suggested by the psychology of cannibalism dictated by revenge, or even by love. Popular expressions such as 'I could eat you' show that a normal tendency of this kind may exist.

Besides the fascination derived from mystery and even from repulsion, there is no doubt that human flesh is preferred by cannibals to any other. Moreover, man being the lord of creation, his flesh is regarded as correspondingly 'strong,' and hence more nutritious and strengthening than any other. The Euahlayi Australians hold that what strengthens them more than anything, both physically and mentally, is the flesh of men.[2]

'It is easy to understand why a savage should desire to partake of the flesh of an animal or man whom he regards as divine. By eating the body of the god he shares in the god's attributes and powers. And when the god is a corn-god, the corn is his proper body; when he is a vine-god, the juice of the grape is his blood; and so by eating the bread and drinking the wine the worshipper partakes of the real body and blood of his god. Thus the drinking of wine in the rites of a vine-god like Dionysus is not an act of revelry, it is a solemn sacrament. Yet a time comes when reasonable men find it hard to understand how any one in his senses can suppose that by eating bread or drinking wine he consumes the body or blood of a deity. "When we call corn Ceres and wine Bacchus," says Cicero, "we use a common figure of speech; but do you imagine that anybody is so insane as to believe that the thing he feeds upon is a god?"'[3]

It has been suggested that the killing of divine men and animals may itself be due expressly to a desire for assimilating, by eating, the divine properties. In order to assimilate these properties the surest method is that of physiological absorption, and slaughter is a necessary preliminary.[4] On this view certain difficulties, such as that noted by Cicero, are apparently lessened.

'It is not the spirit of the corn and vine, as such, but the life-giving virtue of bread and wine that is the essence of the sacrament.'[5]

Among early agricultural peoples, strong meat, such as flesh, is eaten but rarely. Often it is eaten only, as strong drink is drunk only, at feasts. Similarly, the ancient Hindus allowed pregnant women the use of beef by way of strengthening the child.[6] But not all theophagy is of the flesh of

1 *GB*[2] i. 360.
2 Taplin, in Woods, *Native Tribes of S. Australia*, Adelaide, 1879, p. 63.
3 K. L. Parker, *The Euahlayi Tribe*, London, 1905, p. 20.
4 Spencer-Gillen[a], ch. vi.,[b] ch. ix. f.
5 *GB*[2] ii. 365; Spencer-Gillen[a], 204 f.
6 Spencer-Gillen[a], 207.
7 F. Boas, *Fifth Report N.W. Tribes of Canada* (1889), 23.
8 *MI* ii. 563 f., quoting Harnack, *Hist. of Dogma* (Eng. tr., London, 1894-99), i. 211, ii. 144 ff., iv. 286, 291, 294, 296 ff.
9 See A. C. Kruijt, *Het Animisme in den ind. Archipel*, The Hague, 1906, pp. 50-60.

1 W. R. Smith, *Rel. Sem.*[2], London, 1894, p. 339.
2 K. L. Parker, 38.
3 *GB*[2] ii. 365 f.; Cic. *de Nat. Deor.* iii. 16 (41).
4 A. E. Crawley, *The Tree of Life*, London, 1905, p. 105; *MI* ii. 605.
5 Crawley, 223.
6 Rājendralāla Mitra, *Indo-Aryans*, Calcutta, 1881, i. 360.

animals or men. It was in the case of bread and wine that Cicero noted a difficulty.

While, therefore, by stretching the idea of godhead to include victims to the god, many animal and human sacrifices may be regarded as theophagous rites, in which there may be a belief that 'god is eaten,' it requires an effort of imagination to hold such belief in the case of eating bread. But a comparison of the facts, both of spirit-belief and of the psychology of eating, shows that the custom is a development rather of the latter than of the former set of ideas and practices. All the ideas of eating, but few of theism, are found in theophagy. For instance, as Westermarck shows,[1] it includes the conception of the conditional curse. A significant case is the ordeal of the Eucharist, in which the swearer, after communicating in the body of Christ, prayed that in case of perjury the bread might choke and slay him.[2] By the nature of the case, on the other hand, there must be either substitution, transubstantiation, symbolism, or analogy, in order to identify the food with the god. In the greater number of instances it would seem that this identification is rather with the divinity of the god than with the god himself.

The two most important instances, the Christian Eucharist and the Mexican sacrifices, are in strong contrast. The latter is evidently a development from human sacrifice to ceremonial cannibalism, unless it was that a habit of cannibalism developed along with a habit of slaughter. It can hardly be regarded as a 'survival' of cannibalism. Much less can the Eucharist be so regarded, in spite of such analogies as may be hinted at in West Asian religions. On the face of it, and in view of parallel sacraments with bread and wine, it began in the form of analogy. The words, 'This is my body,' 'This is my blood,' are no survival of earlier and cruder rubrics, but an imaginative direction to identify the sources of physical with those of spiritual nutriment.

LITERATURE.—In addition to the authorities cited in the footnotes, see W. R. Smith, art. 'Sacrifice,' in *EBr*[9]; F. Liebrecht, *Zur Volkskunde*, Heilbronn, 1879, pp. 436-439.

A. E. CRAWLEY.

EBIONISM.—I. *NATURE AND ORIGIN.*—'Ebionism,' taken generally, is the name given to certain tendencies of thought, which crystallized into sects, within Judæo-Christian circles, in the early centuries of Christianity. The sects could have arisen only on Jewish soil, and apart from Judaism it is impossible to understand them. When we remember that Judaism was a national religion, holding within itself a special revelation and a Law enshrined in the sacred treasure of its past; when, further, we recall with what tenacity Judaism had clung to its Law, and what sacrifices it had made to preserve its historic identity and nationality—it will be understood what a ferment the new ideas of Christianity set up, and what a reaction of strenuous opposition they were calculated to raise. Ebionism, looked at historically, takes its place as one of the resultants of the fierce antagonism of Judaism to the simplicity and universality of the religion of Jesus Christ. The Ebionites had moved out of strict Judaism, but they had not moved into the Catholic faith. In a sense they were Jewish Christians; but their Christianity was nominal, and held by such a feeble thread that the slightest tension might snap it. So nominal was their hold of Christianity in its essence that the tendency of Ebionism was away from the Catholic faith. As the years went on, it became more and more heretical, until by the 5th cent. it had become practically extinct.

1. Name and general interest of the sect.—As we shall see, the name 'Ebionism' was given to more than one tendency of thought within Judæo-Christian circles. Some Ebionites were hardly distinguishable from the first Jewish Christians, from men like St. Peter and St. James, who endeavoured to combine the faith of Christ with the obligations of the Law and their national hopes. Others became strenuously antagonistic to the Catholic faith, and, while retaining the name 'Christian,' became really hostile to the spirit of Christ. Finally, there were others who held a faith of a mixed or syncretistic character. While they accepted Christ, they accepted Him only as a revived Moses; and they combined in their creed elements of a heterogeneous character, in which Essenism and Gnosticism are plainly recognizable. But, amid all the elements which we describe as Ebionitic, and notwithstanding the heterogeneous teachings which gather round the name, there were two points common to all Ebionites. The first had regard to the Law, the second to Christ. Ebionites were at one in exalting the Law and in depreciating Christ. The first point of agreement betrays the Judaism in which they had been reared; the second explains how they drifted outside the current of the Catholic faith and were at last stranded.

Why the name 'Ebionites' was given to those Judæo-Christian sects is not very clear. The tendency of the Church Fathers was to trace back such sects as the Ebionites to a *personal founder*. Tertullian (*de Præscr. Hær.*) in the 3rd cent. appears to have been the first to give currency to this view, which was held also by Epiphanius (*Hær.* xxx. 1. 17), who, without much critical judgment, regards Ebion ('callidus ille serpens animoque mendicus') as the author of the heresy. This explanation, which is without foundation, has been abandoned in modern times, though Hilgenfeld advocated it (*Ketzergesch.* 422 f.). There can be little doubt that the name is derived from the Heb. אֶבְיוֹן, 'poor.' But, while this is clear, it is not equally clear on what ground the Ebionites were so designated. The name gave scope for 'Patristic scorn,' and its bearers were denounced for poverty of intellect, poverty of faith, or poverty of Christology (Origen, *c. Celsum*, ii. 1; cf. *de Princip.* iv. 22, and *in Matth.* I. xvi. 12, τῷ Ἐβιωναίῳ καὶ πτωχεύοντι περὶ τὴν εἰς Ἰησοῦν πίστιν). Though the designation gave a convenient handle for Patristic sarcasms, it is improbable that its origin was so subtle. It is much more likely that it was originally a nickname given by the Jews to describe those who attached themselves to the religion of Jesus Christ, and who actually were among the poorer classes. The epithet, given originally in contempt, came to be used by Jewish Christians themselves, and gloried in, as describing sufficiently a characteristic of their order. By and by it lost its original signifiance, as names do; and in course of time it came to describe the sections of Jewish Christians who either failed to advance towards Catholicity or receded into more or less of antagonism to it.

2. Origin of sect.—When we endeavour to account historically for the pseudo-Jewish-Christians known as Ebionites, we are brought face to face with well-known facts in the nature and history of Judaism. Judaism, with its inheritance from the past, and its altogether unique appreciation of the Mosaic Law, was essentially a national religion. It might become the soil in which there should grow a Catholic faith, but in itself the religion of the Jews was intensely particularistic and national. From the records of the NT we see how there arose a form of faith, known as Jewish Christianity. In substance this was an endeavour to combine what was characteristic in Judaism with a faith in Jesus as the Messiah, the Son of

[1] *MI* ii. 622 ff.

[2] F. Dahn, *Bausteine*, Berlin, 1879, ii. 16, quoted by Westermarck, ii. 690.

God, and the Saviour of the world. To begin with, this Jewish Christianity must have held, as one of its presuppositions, that the observance of the Mosaic Law was necessary to Christianity (cf. Harnack, *Hist. of Dogma*, Eng. tr., i. 289); and, so far as we can trace its history, this remained one of its characteristics, though, as we shall see, some Jewish Christians were much more tolerant than others. How, then, did this Jewish Christianity develop in contact with the facts of history?

If we read aright the history of the Apostolic age, we see in it the gradual process whereby Christianity freed itself from the swaddling bands of Judaism—a process which was not achieved without struggle. To the first leaders of the Jerusalem Church the truth was not always clear that the Christian religion was independent of Mosaism. The first concession wrung from Jewish Christians was that, while the Law was binding on themselves as Jews born, it was not essential for Gentile Christianity to observe its enactments. That concession was the emancipating act of the Jerusalem conference, and it was due in large measure to the labours and propaganda of St. Paul. While the work and the teaching of the latter were intelligible to the spiritually-minded men at the head of the Jerusalem Church, and, however revolutionary, were accepted by them, it by no means followed that they were intelligible or acceptable to the mass of the Jews who had become converts to the Messiahship of Jesus. This is clear from the hostility which dogged St. Paul's footsteps from city to city; and it becomes clearer in after-history, when that hostility developed into Ebionism, which is simply the residuum of the struggles and heart-burnings of the age when the religion of Jesus Christ shook off the trammels of Judaism.

At this point we are able to estimate the influence of the national upheaval which ended in the fall of Jerusalem in A.D. 70. It was an age of passion, perplexity, and agitation; an age when extreme men clamoured for extreme views; an age which naturally gave birth to sectarianism. After the fall of Jerusalem, the Christian Church was re-constituted at Pella; but it was a changed Church. The Jewish element in it had ceased to be predominant. The passing away of the Temple, the rude triumph of the Gentile, and the cruel hands that had been laid on the sacred memorials of the past combined to cause a shock under which Mosaic ritual staggered. Further, at Pella the Church was recruited from the Essenes, and an Essene element began to penetrate it. By and by the Church came back to Jerusalem; and then came a final crash. Under Hadrian the Jews rebelled; Bar Cochba led a forlorn hope (A.D. 132); the Jews were expelled from Jerusalem; sacrifices were prohibited; Ælia Capitolina was founded (A.D. 138); and in place of the old Judaism, which in turn had yielded to Judæo-Christianity, there was a Church presided over by a Gentile bishop—a Church in which Jews and Gentiles had become one. Jewish Christianity had passed; and those who still clung to their national forms, and tried to combine them with a belief in the Messiahship of Jesus, were driven into heresy. When the Church discards a belief which it has outgrown, the tendency of those who retain that belief is to become heretical. The Church having outgrown Jewish Christianity, Judæo-Christians tended to return to Judaism. The time came when Judaism simply masqueraded in the guise of Christianity. 'Orthodoxy, when left behind by the culture of the age, and deserted by public opinion, becomes heresy' (Hase; see Hagenbach, *Hist. of Doctrines*, i. 68).

II. *Forms of Ebionism.*—When we begin to inquire narrowly into the divisions of the sect, we encounter considerable difficulties. These arise from the fact that the Fathers on whom we rely for our information are not agreed as to who were or were not Ebionites, and as to what precisely constituted the heresy of Ebionism. Probably at one period the nicknames 'Ebionites' and 'Nazarenes' were given indiscriminately to Judæo-Christians. When the names lost their original significance, and when Jewish Christianity in the Apostolic sense passed away, it was not always easy to say what or where were the heretics to whom the designation 'Ebionites' had come to be applied. Moreover, when it is remembered that these obscure sects were found in places as far apart as Syria and Rome, and that writers had few facilities for exact verification, it can be understood that divergences in description were liable to creep in. At the same time, it will be seen that, as a whole, the testimony is singularly consistent.

We may begin with a passage from Justin Martyr in the middle of the 2nd cent., who, in his *Dialogue with Trypho*, tells us that in his day there were two distinct classes of Jewish Christians. The one observed the Mosaic Law themselves, but associated with believing Gentiles, and did not insist on the observance of the Law by them. The other class refused to have fellowship with Gentile Christians until they had complied with the requirements of the Mosaic Law (*Dial. c. Tryph.* ch. xlvii.). Thus, we find the antagonism, already apparent in the NT, perpetuated and intensified in the middle of the 2nd century. One section of Judæo-Christianity had a tendency towards a Catholic faith, the other had a tendency back to Judaism; and in following this tendency the second class fell out of the Catholic movement and became heretical. Probably Justin had in view the developed tendency of the second class when, in ch. xlviii. of the *Dialogue*, he refers to some of the Jewish race who 'admit that He [our Lord] is Christ, while holding Him to be man of men.' Subsequent writers describe these Jewish Christians of Justin as 'Ebionites,' and give to the tolerant section the name 'Nazarenes.' The distinction was clear in the 4th cent. to Epiphanius (*Hær.* xxix.), and to Jerome. The latter found the Nazarenes dwelling in Peræa beyond Jordan, and classed them with the Ebionites, although they held to the Virgin Birth and the Divine Sonship: 'dum volunt et Judaei esse et Christiani, nec Judaei sunt, nec Christiani' (*Ep. 112 ad August.* c. 13).

It is remarkable that in the writers who follow Justin, towards the end of the 2nd cent. and the first half of the 3rd,—Irenæus, Hippolytus, and Tertullian,—there is only one section of Ebionites known, viz. those who deny the Divinity of our Lord. Irenæus, in the end of the 2nd cent., is the first to use the name *Ebionæi* (I. xxvi. 2, III. xi. 7, III. xv. 1, xxi. 1, IV. xxxiii. 4, V. i. 3). He is closely followed by Hippolytus (*Hær.* vii. 34; cf. Tert. *de Præscr. Hær.* 33), while Origen in the middle of the 3rd cent. has several references to the Ebionites. In one he says: 'Those Jews who have received Jesus as Christ are called by the name of Ebionites' (*c. Cels.* ii. 1). In another he makes reference to the Ebionites as 'deriving their name from the poverty of their intellect' (*de Princip.* iv. 22). In a third reference, he writes of 'the twofold sect of Ebionites [οἱ διττοὶ Ἐβιωναῖοι], who either acknowledge with us that Jesus was born of a virgin, or deny this, and maintain that He was begotten like other human beings' (*c. Cels.* v. 61). This is so far clear, and Origen's distinction is entirely in agreement with that of Jerome, to which we have already referred. But in a subsequent passage (*c. Cels.* v. 65) Origen says that 'both classes of Ebionites' (Ἐβιωναῖοι ἀμφότεροι) reject the Epistles of St. Paul. It is probable that he is somewhat confused here, because it is clear from other sources that the Nazarenes, who held the Virgin Birth, did not reject the Pauline Epistles. A simple explanation would be that Origen had not the same opportunity as Jerome of ascertaining the distinctive tenets of the Nazarenes (cf. Ritschl, *Entstehung der altkath. Kirche*, 1857, p. 156 f.). Lightfoot (*Com. on Galatians*, p. 318) approves of the further suggestion that, if originally the names 'Nazarenes' and 'Ebionites' were applied to Jewish Christians, it was inevitable that some confusion should enter into the Patristic narratives (cf. Ritschl, *op. cit.* p. 158).

If, then, we are to accept Origen's distinction (in which he is followed by Eusebius, *HE* iii. 27), we find that the Ebionites fall into two classes, the first acknowledging the Virgin Birth, the other holding that Jesus was simply the son of Joseph and Mary. To the first alone is the name 'Nazarenes' given; the second class are never known except by the name 'Ebionites.' There is another form of Ebionism described to us by Epiphanius (*Hær.* xxx.). It is sometimes known as *Essene* or *Gnostic* Ebionism, sometimes as syncretistic Judæo-Christianity. Apart from Gnostic influences, therefore, pseudo-Jewish Christianity appears in various shades and forms, tolerant or otherwise—forms known as 'Nazarenism' and 'Ebionism.' In Nazarenism, Jewish Christianity became 'stationary' (Uhlhorn, *PRE*[3], art. 'Ebioniten'); in Ebionism, as distinct from Nazarenism, it became highly heretical, and this aspect of Ebionism may be described as *Pharisaic*. Under Gnostic and Essene influences,

Jewish Christianity became highly syncretistic, as well as heretical. We may group the characteristics of all the Ebionites under the three divisions 'Nazarenes,' 'Pharisaic Ebionites,' and 'Gnostic Ebionites.' The relations between the different parties may be outlined in a table, such as the following:

A. Gentiles	(1) Non-Christian = Heathenism.			
	(2) Christian			Merged in *Christian Church* after A.D. 138.
B. Jews	(1) Christian	Non-heretical = Judæo-Christianity		
		Heretical	(*a*) Those who accepted supernatural birth of Jesus, with undeveloped Christology	= *Nazarenes.*
			(*b*) Those who accepted Messiahship of Jesus, denied Virgin Birth, and hated St. Paul	= *Pharisaic Ebionites.*
			(*c*) Those who became gnosticized	= *Essene* or *Gnostic Ebionites.*
	(2) Non-Christian = Judaism.			

1. Nazarenes.—The authorities for our knowledge of the Nazarenes are mainly Epiphanius (*Hær.* xxix.) and Jerome (*de Vir. Illus.* § 3, and various passages in his commentaries). Epiphanius includes the Nazarenes in his list of heretics, but his account is confused; and in regard to their Christology in particular he confesses that he does not know much (*Hær.* xxix. 7). He is aware, however, that the Nazarenes were execrated by the Jews, and that they used the Gospel of Matthew complete (εὐαγγέλιον πληρέστατον) in Hebrew (*ib.* 9). According to Epiphanius and Jerome, these Nazarenes were to be found in the 4th cent. mainly about Pella beyond Jordan. Jerome had unusual facilities for knowing about them, and, when we piece together the various passages in which we have any account of them (cf. Schliemann, *Clement*, p. 445 ff.), we learn that they entertained the following beliefs. They accepted the Divinity of Christ, holding that He was born of the Virgin Mary. They admitted the Apostleship of St. Paul (cf. Jerome, *in Is.* III. ix. 1, 'qui novissimus Apostolorum omnium fuit'). Although they wished to remain Jews themselves and to retain the obligation of the Mosaic Law, they did not desire to bind these obligations on Gentile Christians, nor did they refuse to have fellowship with them. They mourned over the unbelief of the Jewish nation, and eagerly looked for the time when the Jews who loved them not should believe in Christ. It is difficult to describe their Christology, except that, as compared with the Catholic doctrine of Christ, it was primitive and undeveloped. They held to the supernatural birth of Christ. They described Him as 'the first-born of the Holy Spirit.' The Holy Spirit was the μήτηρ Ἰησοῦ from the hour of His birth. At His baptism the 'omnis fons Spiritus Sancti' descended on Jesus (Jerome, *Com. in Is.* IV. xi. 1). It is difficult to describe such an indefinite Christology, but probably Dorner is right when he says: 'They did not hold a pre-existing hypostasis of the Divine in Christ, but only His pre-existence in God generally and His Spirit' (*Person of Christ*, I. i. 193). Anyhow, it is clear that, while their view of Christ had risen far above Judaism and had not degenerated into Pharisaic Ebionism, it had not developed into the Catholic doctrine. It was an arrested belief. It may be added that there is a strong probability that the work called *The Testaments of the Twelve Patriarchs*, written not long after the fall of Jerusalem, and while the memory of that event was fresh, belongs to the circle of the Nazarenes. This is the view of Ritschl (*Entsteh. d. altkath. Kirche*, p. 172) and of Lightfoot (*Gal.* p. 319 ff.); Ritschl, indeed, holds that the author was a Nazarene (*op. cit.* p. 173).

2. Pharisaic (non-Gnostic) Ebionism.—(1) Our authorities for this form of Ebionism are chiefly the following: Irenæus (*adv. Hær.* I. xxvi., III. xv., V. iii.); Hippolytus (*Hær.* vii. 22, x. 18); Epiphanius (*Hær.* xxx.); Eusebius (*HE* iii. 27); Tertullian (*de Præscr.* xlviii.); and Theodoret (*Hær. Fab.* ii. 2). Our first authority is Irenæus, according to whom the views of the Ebionites corresponded closely with the teachings of Cerinthus, whose personality and influence, as we shall afterwards see, were of great significance in the history of heresy. In a sense Cerinthus (*q.v.*) may be described as the father of heresy. The views of Cerinthus are thus stated by Irenæus:

'He represented Jesus as having not been born of a virgin, but as being the son of Joseph and Mary according to the ordinary course of human generation, while he nevertheless was more righteous, prudent, and wise than other men. Moreover, after his baptism, Christ descended upon him in the form of a dove from the Supreme Ruler, and then he proclaimed the unknown Father, and performed miracles. But at last Christ departed from Jesus, and then Jesus suffered and rose again, while Christ remained impassible, inasmuch as he was a spiritual being' (Iren. I. xxvi.; Hipp. vii. 21).

With these views of Cerinthus the Pharisaic Ebionites agreed. In their Christology they further taught that 'Jesus was justified by fulfilling the Law. And therefore it was that he was named Christ of God, and Jesus, since not one of the rest [of mankind] had observed completely the Law. For, if any other had fulfilled the commandments in the Law, he would have been that Christ' (Hipp. vii. 22). Further, according to Hippolytus, they alleged 'that they themselves also, when in like manner they fulfil [the Law], are able to become Christs; for they assert that our Lord Himself was a man in a like sense with all' (Hipp. vii. 22). Apart from their Christology, we learn that the Pharisaic Ebionites rigorously adhered to the Mosaic Law; that they used the Gospel according to St. Matthew only; that they repudiated the Apostle Paul; and, indeed, that they were so Judaic in their style of life that they even adored Jerusalem as if it were the house of God (Iren. I. xxvi.).

(2) From what is thus told us by Irenæus and Hippolytus we can gather an accurate conception of the general character of Pharisaic Ebionism. It was a mutilated Christianity, false to the spirit of the Christ in whom it professed to believe. Its adherents were true to the monotheism of the OT, but, when they refused to harmonize the Person of Christ with historical monotheism, they became false both to the spirit of Christianity and to the true spirit of the OT. They betrayed the soil in which their teaching was bred by their clinging to the Law, their exclusion of the Gentiles, their ostracism of St. Paul, and their reverence for Jerusalem. They showed also their Pharisaism in their denial of the supernatural birth of Christ, in place of which they put His baptism. Their Christology contains certain speculative elements which show influences outside Judaism. Indeed, this form of Ebionism, as a whole, shows a certain vitality and power of progress, though the progress was in the wrong direction—away from the Catholic faith, not towards it.

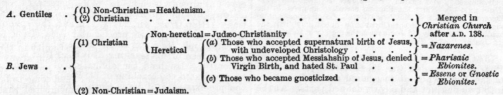

Not much need be added from subsequent writers to complete the picture as it is given us by Irenæus and Hippolytus. Epiphanius, however, gives a few details which may be referred to. We learn from him that Pharisaic Ebionites were much more widely scattered than the Nazarenes, who were found mainly in the neighbourhood of Pella. Pharisaic Ebionism had travelled as far as Rome (*Hær.* xxx. 18). We learn, also, from Epiphanius something of the silly scurrilities in which the Ebionites indulged about the Apostle Paul. They circulated the story that he was really a Gentile by birth, who, after coming to Jerusalem, endeavoured to marry the high priest's daughter, but failed, even though he had become a proselyte. His wounded vanity, according to the Ebionites, drove him into bitter hostility to the Jews (*Hær.* xxx. 18, 25). We have seen that these Pharisaic Ebionites used a Gospel of Matthew, and Epiphanius gives us an interesting glimpse of the Baptism narrative in the recension of the Gospel used by them. The most striking point is the account of the voices heard from heaven at the baptism of Jesus: 'Thou art my beloved son; in thee I am well pleased'; and again: 'I have this day begotten thee' (*Hær.* xxx. 13). Thus, the Baptism narrative, as given in the Ebionitic recension of Matthew's Gospel, was clearly meant to show that the day of the Christ-birth dated only from the baptism. Then only did Jesus reach the dignity of Messiahship (cf. Justin, *Dial. c. Tryph.* ch. xlix.).

(3) Certainly the most characteristic feature of Pharisaic Ebionism was its *Christology*. The life of the Jesus whom it recognized as the Christ fell into two distinct and clearly defined parts. At the point of cleavage stood the baptism. Up to the moment of His baptism Jesus was a man, on the level of common humanity, and inheriting the tendency of human nature to sin. His sonship up to the point of His baptism was purely ethical, and along the line of that ethical sonship it was possible, so the Ebionites said, for any man to be a Christ. Jesus was pre-eminent, in that first part of His life, for virtue. He was, like other men, justified through the Law, but so pre-eminent was He 'in justice, prudence, and wisdom' that He became worthy to be the Messiah, and at His baptism that seal of worthiness was placed on Him. It was His birthday as Messiah. Then did He become worthy to be the Messiah, and then only did He Himself become conscious that He was the Messiah; for, at that moment when the voice from heaven said, 'This day have I begotten thee,' there descended on Jesus, and entered into Him, a new power, viz. the Christ. This power was not God, and could not be God, for God was infinitely supreme and could not stoop to union with a man. Ebionism at this point returns to the monotheism, in all its rigidity, which it conceived to be the master-thought of Judaism. What then was this power? It was not God, but, though created, it had 'a proper pre-existing hypostasis.' This power was the Christ, who entered into union with Jesus, not to redeem the world, but to be the prophet of a new order, and to make known the Father. Then only, after the Christ had united with, and entered into, the man Jesus, was He able to perform miracles. It ought, therefore, to be kept clear, in connexion with Pharisaic Ebionism, that the office of the Christ, so united with Jesus, was not redemptive, but prophetic. The union of the Christ, who was no mere impersonal power, with the man Jesus was not an indissoluble union, for the Christ before the death of Jesus departed from Him. Only Jesus suffered and rose again; the Christ had re-ascended and returned to 'His own Pleroma' (Iren. III. xi. 1; and cf. Lightfoot, *Colossians*, p. 264 f.).

It is clear that Gnosticism had already begun its work in connexion with the doctrine of the Church. If, according to Gnostic speculation, matter was essentially evil, it was impossible that a spiritual Being, such as God, could come into union with it; and therefore the way must be found by the in-dwelling for a time in Jesus of One who was above the angels and a created power. Thus Gnosticism passed over into Jewish Christianity in the form of Ebionism, the link being Cerinthus.

3. Gnostic or Essene Ebionism.—This form of Ebionism may be described (as by Harnack) as *syncretistic Jewish Christianity*. It is differentiated from Pharisaic Ebionism by the fact that it has incorporated in it elements which were not indigenous to Jewish soil. But the problem is not altogether simple—to trace, either as to their origin or as to their character, the speculative elements which are found in this type of Ebionism. The chief authority for a knowledge of these Gnostic Ebionites is Epiphanius (*Hær.* xix., xxx.). Characteristics of their teaching are found also in Hippolytus (*Hær.* ix. 8–12, Clark's tr.), Origen (Euseb. *HE* vi. 38), and the pseudo-Clementines.

(1) We may best approach Gnostic Ebionism through the teaching of Cerinthus, to whom reference has already been made. This heresiarch was a Jew, 'disciplined in the teaching of the Egyptians' (Hipp. *Hær.* vii. 21, x. 17), and the sphere of his activity was in proconsular Asia (Iren. I. xxvi.; Epiph. *Hær.* xxviii. 1). From what we have already seen of his teaching, it is clear that it was Ebionitic. He held the obligation of the Law; he repudiated the teaching of St. Paul; he rejected the pre-existence of Jesus Christ; and he taught the millennial reign of the Messiah in Jerusalem.

The one point in which his teaching departed from typical Pharisaic Ebionism was in regard to his doctrine of creation. Cerinthus taught that 'the world was not made by the primary God, but by a certain power far separated . . . from that Principality who is supreme over the universe, and ignorant of him who is above all' (Iren. I. xxvi.). According to Cerinthus, an immense gulf yawned between God and this world. He bridged it by the conception of a power, inferior to God and ignorant of Him, the world-maker or *demiurge* (cf. Lightfoot, *Col.* p. 107 ff.; Neander, *Ch. Hist.* ii. 42 ff., Bohn's ed. 1850–58). The affinity of this conception of a demiurge with Gnostic speculations on the evil inherent in the physical world is apparent. In Cerinthus we have the first historical representative of Gnostic speculation linked with Judæo-Christianity. He sets forth a teaching which is certainly heretical Jewish Christianity or Pharisaic Ebionism; but on that teaching he has grafted a speculation which is certainly not Jewish. When the tendency thus shown in Cerinthus—the tendency, namely, to incorporate with Jewish Christianity speculative elements not indigenous to Jewish soil—is further developed, we have *Gnostic Ebionism.*

(2) The character of Gnostic Ebionism may be ascertained from Epiphanius, though his account is somewhat confused. We learn, however, that these Ebionites agreed with those of the Pharisaic type in holding the validity of the Law, especially of circumcision and the Sabbath, in repudiating St. Paul, and in denying the Virgin Birth of Jesus Christ (Epiph. *Hær.* xxx. 2, 4, 16). Their Christology was not uniform, and is somewhat indefinite. Some of them affirmed that Adam and Christ were one. Others regarded Christ as a spiritual Being, created before all things, and higher than the angels. This spiritual Being descended in Adam, was made visible in the patriarchs, and at last, clothed with Adam's body, came to earth, suffered on the cross, rose again, and ascended back to heaven (*Hær.* xxx. 3, 16). We learn, further, that they spoke of Christ as 'the successor of Moses'—the only prophet whom they recognized. Christ was 'the Prophet of Truth.' Jesus himself was a mere man, who, because of super-excellent virtue, deserved to be described as Son of God (*Hær.* xxx. 18; cf. Ritschl, *op. cit.* p. 211; Harnack, *Hist. of Dogma*, i. 309). Christianity, therefore, with these Ebionites was simply true Mosaism, and Christ was the successor of the prophet of Sinai. The only part of the OT which they accepted was the Pentateuch, and even it only in part. Perhaps the most remarkable feature of their treatment of the OT was their rejection of the whole sacrificial system. In their recension of Matthew's Gospel (which Gospel alone they accepted) they made Christ give, as one of the objects of His coming, the abrogation of the sacrificial system (*Hær.* xxx. 16: *ἦλθον καταλῦσαι τὰς θυσίας, καὶ ἐὰν μὴ παύσησθε τοῦ θύειν, οὐ παύσεται ἀφ' ὑμῶν ἡ ὀργή*). Further, they were vegetarians and ascetics. They refused to partake of flesh or wine, taking as their pattern St. Peter, whose food, they said, was bread and olives (*Hær.* xxx. 15; cf. *Clem. Homilies*, xii. 6). They also followed St. Peter in his custom of daily lustrations (*Hær.* xxx. 15, 21). The Lord's Supper they partook of with bread and water (*ib.* 16). Their asceticism on the point of marriage was originally strict, but it had been modified so much in course of time that the majority of them esteemed marriage highly (*ib.* 2; cf. *Clem. Hom.* iii. 68).

If, then, we take the picture of these Ebionites, as given us by Epiphanius, we note at once that they have departed from the Pharisaic type in three pronounced directions: (*a*) their Christology, while fundamentally alike, is mixed with elements of Gnostic speculation; (*b*) their asceticism is rigid, except on the point of marriage; (*c*) for their abandonment of the sacrificial system the annals of Pharisaism contain neither precedent nor preparation.

(3) How, then, are we to account for these divergences from Pharisaic Ebionism? The problem is intricate, but the solution seems clear. There can be little doubt that the influences incorporated in the form of Ebionism we are considering come through *Essenism*. In this article it is not necessary to enter into a detailed description of the characteristics, origin, or history of the Essenes (see art. ESSENES), nor need we concern ourselves with the perplexing questions arising round this sect, so well described as 'the great enigma of Hebrew history' (Lightfoot, *Colossians*, p. 82). It will be sufficient to point out a few of the characteristics of the Essenes, as these are indicated by our primary authorities (mainly Philo, *Quod omnis probus liber*, § 12 f.; Josephus, *BJ* II. viii. 2–13, *Ant.* XVIII. i. 5; and Pliny, *HN* v. 17). These characteristics may be given in the words of Josephus, which are followed closely by Hippolytus (*Hær.* ix. 13–22):

'These Essenes reject pleasures as an evil, but esteem continence and the conquest over our passions to be virtue. They neglect wedlock, but choose out other persons' children while they are pliable and fit for learning' (*BJ* II. viii. § 2). 'These persons are despisers of riches. . . . There is, as it were, one patrimony among all the brethren' (§ 3). 'As for their piety toward God, it is very extraordinary; for before sun-rising they speak not a word about profane matters, but put up certain prayers, which they have received from their forefathers, as if they made a supplication for its rising' (§ 5). After describing their daily bath in cold water, and their measured eating and drinking, Josephus says: 'They dispense their anger after a just manner, and restrain their passion' (§ 6). 'They inquire after such roots and medicinal stones as may cure their distempers' (§ 6). He further says that novices are tried for three years. 'If he [the novice] appear to be worthy, they then admit him into their society. And before he is allowed to touch their common food, he is obliged to take tremendous oaths . . . and that he will neither conceal anything from those of his own sect, nor discover any of their doctrines to others, no not though any one should compel him so to do at the hazard of his life . . . and will equally preserve the books belonging to their sect, and the names of the angels' (§ 7). 'What they most of all honour, after God Himself, is the name of their legislator [Moses], whom if any one blaspheme he is punished capitally' (§ 9). 'They are stricter than any other of the Jews in resting from their labours on the seventh day' (§ 9). 'They contemn the miseries of life, and are above pain by the generosity of their mind' (§ 10). Their doctrine of anthropology, according to Josephus, is 'that bodies are corruptible, and that the matter they are made of is not permanent, but that the souls are immortal, and continue for ever' (§ 11). Josephus, further, tells us that 'there is another order of Essenes who agree with the rest as to their way of living, and customs, and laws, but differ from them in the point of marriage' (§ 13). In another passage he makes this remark: 'The doctrine of the Essenes is this, that all things are best ascribed to God. They teach the immortality of souls, and esteem that the rewards of righteousness are to be earnestly striven for, and when they send what they have dedicated to God into the temple, they do not offer sacrifices, because they have more pure lustrations of their own' (*Ant.* XVIII. i. 5).

Much of what Josephus records is confirmed by Philo, and a single remark may be quoted from Pliny: 'There flock to them from afar many who, wearied of battling with the rough sea of life, drift into their system' (*HN* v. 17). We are able, without further detail, to understand the leading characteristics of the Essenes. They were brethren of a common order—an order characterized by a rigid asceticism, more especially in regard to food and marriage. They cultivated medicinal and magical knowledge. They preserved their books with absolute secrecy. Their devotion to Mosaism was fervent. They practised a rudimentary sun-worship. They rejected animal sacrifices. They believed in the immortality of the soul only. On one side, they were true to their Jewish faith, for, in their regard for Moses and the Law and the Sabbath, they were simply 'Pharisees in a superlative degree' (Schürer, *HJP* II. ii. 210). But, on the other side, in the secrecy of their monastic life, in their scorn of marriage, in their incipient sun-worship, in their magical arts, in their rejection of animal sacrifice, and in their anthropology and doctrine of immortality they show remarkable and emphatic divergences from the Pharisaic type of Judaism, and such an influence from extraneous tendencies of thought that Essenism may deservedly be called *Gnostic Judaism*; and one has difficulty in believing that it could be wholly a growth from Jewish soil (as Frankel), although it may be that it was the carrying out of the idea of a universal Jewish priesthood (as Ritschl). It is not material for us to inquire here as to the sources of these foreign customs and tendencies of thought—whether from Pythagorean sources (as Zeller), or from Parsi influences (as Lightfoot), or from both (as Schürer). One point, however, must be kept in view: that the Essenes, in their withdrawal from worldly pursuits, and in their doctrine of the immortality of the soul, show the influence of the speculative idea that matter is essentially evil —an idea which reached a full development in Gnosticism.

We may conclude, then, that Gnostic Ebionism, in the form we have described, and as given in Epiphanius, has assimilated elements from Essenism. Its asceticism in meat and in drink, its persistent rejection of sacrifice, and its speculative elements have come through Essenism. In the matter of marriage the Ebionites of Epiphanius go back to Pharisaism, or to that milder party of Essenes to which Josephus refers. If it be asked when the combination could have taken place, the answer is clear. Before the fall of Jerusalem a filtering down of Christian thought must have taken place. After the fall of Jerusalem the Essenes disappear as a separate party, and it is reasonable to believe that many of them attached themselves to the Judæo-Christian Church at Pella, observing, as they must have done, the fulfilment before their eyes of prophecies uttered by Christ in regard to the doom of Jerusalem (cf. Ritschl, *op. cit.* p. 223). When they took this step, it would be hard to imagine that they left their Essenism behind them; and it would be incredible that an order and a system of thought so definite and so masterful as Essenism should have been without influence in the development of Jewish Christianity.

(4) The form of Ebionism which we have described may be illustrated further from the *Book of Elkesai* and the *pseudo-Clementine literature*. In the one we see not merely the essential features of Essene Ebionism, but the indications of an effort to propagate the system westwards; in the other we see Essene Ebionism assuming a literary dress. In regard to both, while we have the features of Essene or Gnostic Ebionism, as we have already described them, we seem to be standing at an advanced stage of non-Christian and syncretistic Judaism, in which an effort is made to eliminate from Mosaism its more national and limited elements, and to commend it to the world as a universal religion. While the book of *Elkesai* and the pseudo-Clementine literature have their distinctive peculiarities, yet in both we discern, with some modifications, the features of the Essene Ebionism presented to us by Epiphanius. It will not be necessary here to do more than to indicate generally the system of thought in the book of *Elkesai* and in the pseudo-Clementines, with their differences and agreements one with the other, and with Essene Ebionism as a whole. See, further, art. ELKESAITES.

The chief authority for our knowledge of the book of *Elkesai* is Hippolytus (*Hær.* ix. 8–12, x. 25), whose account is in the main confirmed by Epiphanius (*Hær.* xix., xxx., liii.) and Origen (Eus. *HE* vi. 38). Hippolytus came into personal contact with the Elkesaites, met them point by point in argument, and felt no little satisfaction with himself over the issue. He tells us that in the time of Callistus (that is, about the year 222) there came to Rome from Syria 'one called Alcibiades, a cunning man, and full of desperation' (*Hær.* ix. 8), who brought with him a book, *Elkesai*, the contents of which had been the subject of direct revelation by an angel. Alcibiades asserted that the angel was 'Son of God,' and with the angel went a female called 'Holy Spirit.' He also declared that 'there was preached unto men a new remission of sins, in the third year of Trajan's reign' (*i.e.* A.D. 100). Hippolytus characterizes this as the 'operation of a spurious spirit, and the invention of a heart inflated with pride.' The book, according to Hippolytus, insisted on circumcision and the Law. Its doctrine of Christ was partly Judaistic and partly Gnostic. It taught that Christ was born as other men, 'but that both previously and that frequently again He had been born and would be born' (ix. 9). '[Christ] would thus appear and exist, undergoing alternations of birth, and having His soul transferred from body to body.' Hippolytus further tells us that the Elkesaites 'devote themselves to [the] tenets of mathematicians, and astrologers, and magicians, as if they were true' (ix. 9). The chief point in the system of *Elkesai* was its doctrine of the forgiveness of sins. Hippolytus gives us a clear account of its teaching on that point. The book taught forgiveness of sins on renewed baptism 'in [the] name of the Great and Most High God, and in [the] name of His Son, the Mighty King,' provided, further, that the person being baptized 'adjure for himself those seven witnesses that have been described in this book—the heaven, and the water, and the holy spirits, and the angels of prayer, and the oil, and the salt, and the earth' (ix. 10). Such a renewed baptism, along with the magical incantations of *Elkesai*, was effectual, not for sins only, but for sickness, such as consumption, or for accidents, such as a dog-bite. The book, finally, enjoined that its mysteries should be kept secret: 'Do not recite this account to all men, and guard carefully these precepts, because all men are not faithful, nor are all women straightforward' (ix. 12).

From the account of the Elkesaites thus given by Hippolytus—an account confirmed by Epiphanius and Origen—it is clear that there were the strongest affinities between their tenets and those of the Essene Ebionites. Indeed, it may be said that the Elkesaites were a step in the development of Essene Ebionism (cf. Ritschl, *op. cit.* p. 222). The Christology, which is the surest test of affinity, is in most respects alike. In both, Adam and Christ are identified, and there is the same belief in successive incarnations. The Elkesaites also agreed with the Essene Ebionites in holding the obligation of the Law, in rejection of sacrifices (with a consequent free handling of the OT), hatred of St. Paul, abstinence from flesh and wine, frequent lustrations, approval of marriage, and secrecy in regard to their books, customs, invocations, and magical rites. The peculiar element in the book and in the beliefs of the Elkesaites is the doctrine of forgiveness through renewed baptisms and magical invocations. Undoubtedly, there is present here a heathen influence, foreign to Jewish soil. Uhlhorn has correctly described it as 'a strong heathen naturalistic element' (art. 'Elkesaiten,' in *PRE*[3]). Probably this doctrine of forgiveness through renewed baptism was meant to take the place of the OT sacrifices (cf. *Clem. Recog.* i. 39).

On the whole, then, we may conclude that the differences between the Essene Ebionites and the Elkesaites were small, practically the only point of divergence being the new doctrine of forgiveness. The roots of Elkesaism, as of Essene Ebionism, go back to that period after the fall of Jerusalem which, according to Hegesippus, was the birthday of sectarianism (Eus. *HE* iii. 32). In *Elkesai*, Essene Ebionism in the beginning of the 3rd cent., and under strong heathen influences, took a step in a direction away both from Judaism and from Catholic Christianity, the impelling influence probably being a desire to commend its tenets to the world by the fiction of a new revelation. In the pseudo-Clementine literature, as we shall see, Essene Ebionism developed in other directions, equally removed from Judaism, but less out of touch with the spirit of Catholic Christianity.

(5) *The pseudo-Clementine literature* consists of three works—one containing twenty *Homilies*; another generally known as the *Recognitions*, and preserved in a translation by Rufinus; and, thirdly, an *Epitome* of the Homilies—a work of little significance. The literature, which is spurious but of great importance, goes under the name of the well-known Clement of Rome. The problems connected with this literature are varied and intricate, while the uncertainties associated with it are among the most numerous in Church history and doctrine. Indeed, the only statements which may be made with certainty are that the literature is not from the hand of Clement of Rome, and that it is the literary dress of a Gnostic Ebionism. It may, further, be said that the Ebionism is not so stringent as in Elkesaism, and that much greater stress is laid on Christian elements. The pseudo-Clementine literature cannot be ignored by any historian of the early Church, though we may rightly refuse to agree with the extravagant claims of Baur, and may doubt if it gives such 'brilliant disclosures' (Hilgenfeld) as some critics imagine.

The problems connected with the pseudo-Clementine literature may be briefly stated, though a discussion of them cannot find a place here. There is, for one, the problem as to whether the pseudo-Clementines or the book of *Elkesai* has the priority in time. The conclusion accepted generally (though not by Ritschl) is that the pseudo-Clementines presuppose the book and doctrine of the Elkesaites. Connected with this is the problem of date, which it is impossible to solve until the further problem is settled as to the priority of the parts. How difficult and intricate the latter problem is becomes at once clear when it is seen how divided opinion is among 'the most eminent critics.' Baur, Schliemann, Uhlhorn (at first), and Lightfoot give the priority to the *Homilies*; Ritschl, Lechler, Hilgenfeld, and Salmon, to the *Recognitions*. If the *Recognitions* is first in point of time, its date may be as early as A.D. 140; if second in point of time, the date may be towards the middle of the 3rd century. On the whole the position may be assumed here that the literature, at least in the present form, belongs to the earlier part of the 3rd century. The trend of opinion is in favour of the view that both the *Hom.* and the *Recog.* are based on a common source such as the *Kerygma of Peter*, the historical contents of which may be best seen in the *Recog.*, the doctrinal in the *Homilies*. There is a further problem as to the aim of the writer or writers. It is conceded that the literature is coloured throughout by Ebionism, but it is not clear if it was meant solely as an Ebionitic propaganda. On this point very diverse views are held, as Harnack's, that in the *Homilies* we have a Catholic revision of a heterodox original, or Bigg's, that we have an Ebionitic revision of an older Catholic original. There is, finally, the problem of the place of writing—whether Rome or Syria, or both.

In this welter of opinions and tangle of problems, one hesitates to express any opinion; but it seems to the present writer, on the whole, most probable that the *Recognitions* is prior in time, as it is certainly nearer to Catholic sentiment, and less anti-Pauline, than the *Homilies*. Further, it is probable that the literature, as a whole, hails from Syria, that it belongs to the earlier part of the 3rd cent., and that it bears a close relation to Essene Ebionism, whether the Ebionism was in the original or engrafted on it. Probably, also, the pseudo-Clementines have some connexion, but by way of repulsion, with the Marcionites, with their developed dualism, and their extravagant ultra-Pauline tendencies. To the authors of the pseudo-Clementine literature Christianity was not the sudden and unhistorical thing Marcion supposed it to be; Christianity was purified Mosaism, and Adam and Christ were one.

When we consider the teaching of the pseudo-Clementines, apart from questions of origin and apart from the literary form in which the teaching is dressed ('Tendenz-roman'), we cannot fail to observe the Ebionism in which the literature is steeped. Certainly its parts are not all equally Ebionitic, for it is plain that in the *Recognitions* the stamp of Ebionism is much less marked than in the *Homilies*. The writer of the *Recognitions* is, on the one hand, much less Judaistic, as in his practical ignoring of circumcision; and, on the other, much nearer the Catholic standpoint, as in his rejection of the anti-Pauline passages which he probably found in the original of his work. But, as a whole, the literature presents us with the features already familiar to us in Essene Ebionism. Compared, for instance, with the book of *Elkesai*, the pseudo-Clementines hold substantially the same Christology. They view Jewish law and custom from the same standpoint. In their rejection of sacrifice, in their refusal to accept St. Paul's teaching, in their encouragement of marriage, in their abstinence from animal food, and in the concealment and secrecy enjoined on their adherents, they attach themselves to the same syncretistic and Judæo-Christian type of thought which we have seen to be characteristic of the Elkesaites and of Essene Ebionism generally. As a whole, the system departs from the book of *Elkesai* mainly on two points: (*a*) in the toning down of the rigid demand for circumcision, and (*b*) in its silence with regard to the peculiar doctrine of *Elkesai* on forgiveness.

In the Christology of the pseudo-Clementines, the most striking feature is the doctrine of the *True Prophet*. If the aim of life is to obtain the highest good, knowledge is essential. God has, indeed, revealed Himself at the beginning, but sin has intervened. The True Prophet, therefore, becomes necessary. He has come again and again. He has come in the seven pillars of the world—Adam, Enoch, Noah, Abraham, Isaac, Jacob, and Moses; and finally, he has come in Christ. Christ, Moses, and Adam are incarnations of the True Prophet (*Hom.* ii. 6, iii. 11, 20, 49; *Recog.* i. 16, 40, 41; cf. *Recog.* i. 45, 'a man over men, who is Christ Jesus'). Thus to follow Moses or to believe Christ leads equally to salvation, for, 'there being one teaching by both, God accepts him who has believed either of these' (*Hom.* viii. 6). According to the pseudo-Clementines, therefore, 'Christianity is simply reformed Judaism' (Baur, *Dogmengesch.* vol. i.), or, as Niedner puts it, 'Christianity is only a restoration of the primitive religion in time, and an enlargement of it in space' (*Kirchengesch.*², Berlin, 1866, p. 246). Clearly, however, in the Christology thus presented there is no room for the Deity of Christ. He is simply a created being. On the point of Christ's Deity, the pseudo-Clementines leave no doubt, for Peter is made to say: 'Our Lord neither asserted that there were gods except the Creator of all, nor did He proclaim Himself to be God, but He with reason pronounced blessed him who called Him the Son of that God who has arranged the universe' (*Hom.* xvi. 15).

Reference has already been made in this article to 'the brilliant disclosures' which Baur and the Tübingen school have found in the pseudo-Clementine literature. With Baur it holds a pre-eminent place. The theory of the development of Catholicity, so earnestly advocated by Baur and so candidly abandoned by Ritschl, gives a central place to this literature. Baur's theory was that the early Church was profoundly Ebionitic. Between Jewish Christianity and Ebionism there was 'a very close identity,' and 'Jewish Christianity in general was a kind of Ebionitism' (*Kirchengesch.* i. 182 [Eng. tr.]). Baur postulated a conflict in the early Church between Ebionism, *i.e.* Jewish Christianity, and Paulinism. Catholicity at the close of the 2nd cent. was intelligible only as the result of a conflict between two opposing forces—Ebionism on the one hand, and Paulinism on the other; and through this conflict the particularism of Judaism ('the aristocratic claims of Jewish particularism' [*op. cit.* p. 113]) developed into the universalism of Christianity. To Baur the conflict was clearly discernible in the pseudo-Clementines, and in the controversy between Simon Peter and Simon Magus. The one was a representative of Jewish Christianity (*i.e.* Ebionism); the other was the representative of Paulinism (*i.e.* Gentile Christianity). Simon Magus was unmistakably a pseudonym for St. Paul (*op. cit.* p. 86). Simon Magus was nothing but a caricature of the Apostle Paul. Such was Baur's theory, which it is needless to criticize at length. It will be sufficient here to say that such a theory destroys the historical personality of Simon Magus, who is regarded in the pseudo-Clementines as the historic embodiment of all heresy. It is not denied here that this literature, as a whole, rejects St. Paul, and one passage in the *Homilies* (xvii. 19) has an unmistakable reference to the Apostle of the Gentiles. Nothing else could have been expected from the Ebionism in which the pseudo-Clementines are soaked. Further, it is absolutely clear that Ebionism was something more than Jewish Christianity, and the Ebionites, instead of being co-extensive with Jewish Christians, were really confined to a small area, and had little influence west of Syria.

III. *CONCLUSION.*—Our inquiry is almost over. The Ebionites as a sect continued into the 5th cent., and gradually disappeared (Theodoret, *Hær. Fab.* ii. 11). Nothing else could have been looked for. They had taken a false direction, which led them more and more away from the channel in which the Church's life flowed full and free. Catholic Christianity swept past them. They moved further and further away until all progress was barred against them. While the Church's life and doctrine developed into Catholicity, strong and clear, Ebionism more and more degenerated, until its elements were absorbed either in bitter Judaism or in truculent heathenism. Catholic Christianity gained nothing from Ebionism, unless in that reflex way which heresy often has of causing the Church to make sure of its ground and to mature its Christology.

LITERATURE.—The ancient authorities are referred to in the course of the article. In modern literature the following are important in a study of Ebionism: Gieseler, 'Ueber die Nazaräer und Ebioniten' in Städlin-Tzschirner's *Archiv*, iv. 2 (1819); Baur, *de Ebionitarum Origine* (1831), also *Kirchengesch.* (1853, Eng. tr. 1878), and *Vorles. über die christl. Dogmengesch.* (1865–68); Schliemann, *Die Clementinen, nebst den verwandten Schriften und dem Ebionitismus* (1844); Schwegler, *Das nachapost. Zeitalter* (1846); Hilgenfeld, *Die Clement. Recognitionen und Homilien* (1848), also *Ketzergesch. des Urchristenthums* (1884); Uhlhorn, *Die Homilien und Recognitionen* (1854); Ritschl, *Die Entstehung der altkathol. Kirche* ² (1857); Dorner, *Hist. of the Development of the Doctrine of the Person of Christ* (Eng. tr. 1861–3); Hagenbach, *Hist. of Doctrines* (Eng. tr. 1880–1); Lightfoot, *Galatians* (1881), *Colossians* (1882); Lechler, *Apostolic and Post-Apostolic Times* (Eng. tr. 1886); Schürer, *GJV* ³ (*HJP*, 1885–90); Zahn, *Gesch. d. NT Kanons* (1888); Harnack, *Dogmengesch.*³ (1893, Eng. tr. 1894–9); Fisher, *Hist. of Christian Doctrine* (1896); Rainy, *The Ancient Catholic Church* (1902); artt. in *PRE* ³ ('Ebioniten,' 'Elkesaiten,' 'Clementinen'), *DCB* (1877–80), *DCG* (1906); also *Church Histories* of Gieseler, Neander, Hase, Robertson, Schaff, Moeller, Kurtz.

W. BEVERIDGE.

ECLIPSE.—See PRODIGIES AND PORTENTS.

ECONOMICS.—1. Connotation of the term.—Economics originally meant the administration of household resources, being the English form of οἰκονομική (*sc.* τέχνη). Aristotle, in the first book of the *Politics*, thus defines it as household management, including the treatment of slaves. The word 'economy' is, however, now used in a much wider sense, being applicable to the prudent management of all kinds of resources and possessions—the utilization of material goods, of time, of thought, or of labour, in such a manner as to avoid waste. It is not confined to a special department of human activity, but denotes a feature that may appear in any branch. To Aristotle 'Political Economy,' which is now synonymous with Economics, would have appeared to be a contradiction in terms; and even in the present usage of the word 'economy,' the prefixing of 'political' is apt to suggest the science or art of managing the resources, and especially the finances, of a State. This would lead to quite an inadequate conception of the subject, for, though Economics includes the management of State resources in such directions as taxation, and is intimately concerned with State regulation of industrial and commercial activities by factory legislation, tariff policies, land laws, and the like, it considers also the ways in which individuals, groups, and organizations within the State establish relations with one another for the purpose of increasing their means and administering their resources. As the resources of the community are managed far more by the spontaneous activities of individuals and groups than by the direct intervention of Governments, Economics is concerned chiefly with the former. It inquires how man obtains the goods which satisfy his wants, explains the causes upon which the material well-being of mankind depends, and treats of all activities by which goods are produced, exchanged, and distributed among the individuals and classes of which society is composed. Economics has frequently been described as the science of wealth, but this, like most brief definitions, is apt to mislead; and indeed, economists themselves have sometimes carelessly written as if mankind existed for the purpose of increasing the quantity of material wealth. This over-emphasis on one phase of the study was responsible for its being dubbed by Carlyle 'the dismal science,' and for the view still sometimes expressed that it is 'sordid.' But the economist, of all men, should most clearly understand that wealth is subservient to a further purpose, and is not in itself the final goal of man's activity. Thus, while in one aspect it is true to say that Economics is the science of wealth, in another, and more important, aspect it is a part of the study of man. Wealth is for his consumption, is a necessary basis of his activities; but it is only in so far as it becomes subservient to man's interests that it is of importance in economic study.

2. The social and political aspects.—The change of standpoint which accounts for the preference for the broader term 'Economics' is due to the increasing emphasis upon social rather than upon political activities. At first economic literature was distinctively political, its aim being the attainment of a sound system of public finance, and even the increase of the wealth of the citizens was considered a matter for State regulation as a means to the replenishment of the public exchequer and the provision of the sinews of war. Gradually, however, the promoting of the material welfare of the people began to be considered less from the point of view of politics and public finance, a great impetus being given to this movement by the French Physiocrats in the latter half of the 18th cent., who insisted that the network of State regulations for the enrichment of the people defeated its own end, and that it was not the business of the statesman to make laws for the increase of wealth, but to discover the laws of Nature which themselves operate for the highest welfare of the people, and to guard these laws from violation and encroachment. Hence to Quesnay (*Droit naturel*, in E. Daire, *Physiocrates*, Paris, 1846) and his followers, Economics became the theory of how natural laws worked in an orderly sequence for the establishment of the greatest well-being of the people; and the chief object of the science was the understanding of the conditions imposed by Nature upon human action in the promoting of material welfare. Under this mode of thought, freedom of industry and trade became the dominant doctrine as against the detailed regulation of every branch of economic activity by the State; and in its most extreme form it led to the maxim of *laissez-faire* (*q.v.*).

The influence of these Physiocratic preconceptions upon Adam Smith was very considerable, for, although it is a great exaggeration to say that he was completely under the dominance of the French speculations, he also formulated much of his teaching in terms of the 'system of natural liberty,' and urged that if Nature were only left alone it would enrich the people much more effectually than did the method of governmental interference. However defective this view may subsequently have proved (cf. COMPETITION), the immediate result was that Economics became a study of the processes of production, distribution, and exchange of wealth as accomplished by the spontaneous co-operation of men rather than by the action of Governments. Indeed, the revolt from State regulation tended to pass towards the opposite extreme of non-interference in matters of industry and commerce, save for the provision of the necessary revenue to the public exchequer and the prevention of fraud. Economics became a social science, and, despite important changes during the last century, it is still more concerned with social than with political or private activities. This by no means implies that economic writings had less effect upon politics; they had more. Pitt, Huskisson, Peel, and Cobden took Adam Smith as their authority in the abolition of restrictions on foreign commerce, on domestic trade, and on freedom of combination. Ricardo exercised a profound influence upon banking legislation and the abolition of the corn laws; Malthus upon the reform of the poor laws. Nevertheless, in the early stages of the development of Economics as a social science there was a certain narrowness that arose partly from the simplified presupposition of the beneficence of natural forces, and partly from the fact that the economists were so few in number and so closely agreed that adequate criticism was lacking. The industrial conditions of England in the early years of the 19th cent. were also somewhat exceptional, peculiar both to the time and to the country, so that doctrines derived from the study of them were found to be defective when applied to other times and places.

During the latter half of the 19th cent., criticism and opposition arose both within and without the ranks of professed economists, and the development of fuller analysis has led to changes in both the mental and the moral attitude. There has been an abandonment of inelastic dogmas, so that it is no longer possible to formulate brief economic creeds and catechisms; the modifications due to changes of conditions have shown that the application of principles is relative to time and place. Modern economists could no longer be appealed to against all forms of State interference, as politicians appealed to economic writings in the early 19th cent. as a weapon against factory legislation. Economics, too, had come to be traditionally regarded as concerned with the increase of riches, and there was some warrant for the complaints of Carlyle and Ruskin that, while abundant attention was devoted to the production of wealth, too little thought was given to its distribution in such ways as to improve the condition of the poorer classes. To-day there is a perceptible shifting of emphasis from the acquisition of wealth to the abolition of poverty, from production to distribution; and the most recent text-books treat the subject-matter throughout with constant reference to the material and moral welfare of humanity. Though his primary business is the scientific study and interpretation of facts, the economist never loses sight of this practical aim of affording guidance for social life and reform.

3. Relation of Economics to Ethics.—As a social science, Economics is concerned with the intricate and complex actions and motives of man, and therefore it is closely related to Ethics. It is true that it is no part of the function of a positive science to pronounce ethical judgments, but even the positive science cannot neglect the fact that moral considerations often affect man's conduct in business life, and must be given a place in the same manner as the facts of physical Nature which also condition economic activity. But the relation is much closer in passing to applied Economics, and the increased attention devoted to the problem of distribution of wealth has brought questions of justice into greater prominence, as in the demand for a 'fair wage.' Some have denied that Economics is at all concerned with this ethical aspect of problems, and would confine it rigidly to the positive science. Others, indeed, have carried abstraction still further by excluding even those moral factors which admittedly influence man's conduct in business life, thus creating a purely fictitious person, 'the economic man,' who pursues wealth along the line of least resistance, and is not deflected from this course by any other motive than aversion to labour and the desire for enjoyment. No such man exists, and no social science worthy of the name can confine itself to the study of such an abstraction. Yet even those who readily admit that man must be dealt with as he is sometimes deny that questions of justice can be treated by the economist, so that the result for a long time was that many of the most vital problems of social welfare were treated neither by Ethics nor by Economics. There was even a prevalent idea that the two were in conflict, and that an elastic conscience was an economic virtue. Clearly, however, such a sharp division cannot be maintained. It cannot be a matter of indifference to the economist whether capitalistic combinations and trusts adopt immoral practices, or whether the adoption of a protective policy leads to corruption. Still less can he ignore the question whether a more equal diffusion of wealth is conducive to the highest welfare, even though it should involve a slight check to wealth production.

This intermixture of ethical and economic considerations need not lead the economist into the deeper controversies that lie entirely beyond the scope of his science. For his practical purposes the precise meaning of 'the good' is less important than the fact that among moralists of different schools there is a general consensus of opinion regarding the desirability of such and such a change in social life. A problem relating to monetary media or banking practice may present little or no ethical aspect, but labour problems which are claiming an increasing share of public attention cannot be regarded as adequately treated without due consideration of ethical factors, and those who speak with authority in the name of Economics now fully recognize the necessity for this wider outlook.

Whether, indeed, ethical and economic considerations may come into conflict in particular cases is doubtful. Honesty is not necessarily the best policy for a particular individual from the standpoint of the acquisition of wealth; illustrations to the contrary are too numerous to admit of doubt. But for society as a whole, honesty is an economic as well as a moral virtue. No doubt, too, a community may sometimes gain immediately in material wealth by actions that the moralist would condemn, and it is surely true that an act which marks a moral gain to society may result in immediate material loss. But in the long run it is doubtful whether the conflict can subsist; and, as a rule, if not universally, that which is from the standpoint of society economically injurious is likely to be ethically wrong, while that which is ethically good is likely to be economically advantageous. This consideration suggests that it is quite as important for the moralist to give due weight to the economic forces as it is for the economist to recognize the ethical aspects of social problems. The former is probably suffering from greater neglect than the latter.

4. Economic method. — Disputes regarding method at one time threatened to divide economists into different schools, but they have now almost ceased. There is no peculiarly economic method of study, and, though the relative importance of analysis and the search for facts varies with the problem under discussion, each is as ineffective alone as is a single blade of a pair of scissors. The controversies about the inductive and deductive, historical and analytical, concrete and abstract methods have yielded place to a general agreement that every method is correct in proportion to its fruitfulness in solving the particular problem, and that in most cases a combination of methods proves most valuable. Thus, while generalization from historical or statistical data is predominantly employed in most of the problems of production, deduction is relatively more important in dealing with the complexities of distribution or such related matters as the incidence of taxation, where the plurality of causes and intermixture of effects baffle purely inductive treatment. There was unquestionably a tendency among the economists of the first half of the 19th cent. to employ the abstract method too exclusively, and to apply the resulting generalizations too hastily, and the protests of the historical school, combined with the advance of statistical science, have led to the fuller application of quantitative and comparative tests. Much progress has still to be made in such quantitative analysis before a thorough estimate can be made of the relative strength of various economic forces, but the economist is frequently handicapped on this side by the inadequacy of existing statistical data. Nevertheless, there has been a marked advance in this direction, which might well be illustrated by a comparison of the English Poor Law Report of 1834, proceeding almost exclusively on *a priori* methods of reasoning, with the Report of the Royal Commission on the same subject in 1909, in which quantitative analysis plays a much larger part. The same feature is evident in comparing the Free Trade controversy of to-day with that of Cobden's time.

In other directions economic method has been influenced by psychological analysis. Jevons in England, Walras in Switzerland, and Menger in Austria simultaneously worked out a theory of value from the side of demand, on the basis of the psychology of choice, which proved complementary to the older theory that started from the side of cost of production. It supplied the fundamental principles of a theory of consumption. Hitherto the economist has generally been compelled to establish his own psychological principles, since they were not sufficiently prepared for his use by the psychologist; but it seems probable that the future development of Experimental Psychology will have an important bearing upon deductive Economics.

Even more fruitful has been the application of biological conceptions to social and economic life, though their uncritical use has sometimes been mischievous by pushing analogies so far that they become untrue. Formerly economists had attempted to explain man's actions by the categories of Physics, and society was treated as if it were a machine. The interactions of men's wills and motives in economic life were explained in terms of stress and strain, attraction and repulsion. The principle of the composition of forces was thought by J. S. Mill (*Autobiography*, London, 1873, p. 159 f.) to afford a key to economic method by adding 'the separate effect of one force to the separate effect of the other.' But, while this method is frequently useful as a first approximation, it generally makes the invalid assumption that economic problems are concerned with external forces operating upon objects which themselves remain unchanged. This was felt to be much too external a conception for a social science. Thus, the effects of an increase of wages in a trade might be studied on the mechanical method by showing how relative wages and profits act as forces attracting or driving away labour and capital; but this would not yield a complete analysis, because the increased wage would tend to affect the efficiency of the worker and possibly of the business organization, so that there is an obvious analogy to functional adaptation in Biology. The step from physical to biological analogies has thus marked a great advance, emphasizing the mutual dependence of the welfare of the whole and the parts, of differentiation and integration, and humanizing economic study. But it has also led to much inaccurate thought, the difference between biological and economic phenomena having frequently been ignored in the first enthusiasm of the discovery of analogies. The 'struggle for existence' in economic life has been treated in a narrowly individualistic way, and the 'survival of the fittest' has been said to necessitate unrestricted competition, while it was forgotten that morally inferior men sometimes display greater ability in obtaining for themselves advantages from the environment, and that many competitors are favoured, while others are irrationally handicapped, before they enter upon the economic 'struggle.' These crude uses of biological categories, however, are confined to the minor writers, and intelligently construed biological methods have contributed greatly to economic advance, for the two sciences have a subject-matter which is similar, in respect that the internal structure and nature change as well as the external conditions and outward form.

5. Economic laws.—Two circumstances have combined to create much popular misunderstanding regarding the nature of economic laws. On the one hand, the close relation of Economic Science to Ethics and Politics has frequently given rise to the erroneous impression that economic laws prescribe or forbid certain courses of conduct. On the other hand, the old association of the science with the 18th cent. beliefs regarding the natural and with the policy of *laissez-faire* led to the idea that, if only economic forces were left alone, they would work for the highest social welfare. Once it was understood, however, that the beneficence which was claimed for the natural and unfettered action of economic forces presumed that most of the institutions of the time, like rights of property, inheritance, and a criminal law, were 'natural,' while only certain ill-defined kinds of regulations were violations of Nature, this conception was abandoned. For the economist is no longer under the impression that, with the exception of a few details which he does not like, the institutions of the present day are natural, so that economic forces may safely remain unchecked within the limits of the existing social system. On the contrary, the social problem is very largely one of regulating and directing the economic forces so that they may work more surely towards social well-being, and this may involve considerable changes in the institutions which were formerly regarded as natural and taken for granted. Economic laws are, like the laws of Physics, merely statements of the relations between phenomena expressed in the indicative mood, as contrasted with laws in the moral and juristic senses of the word. When, therefore, a proposal is condemned as violating economic laws, the speaker is almost certainly confusing the different meanings of the word 'law.' It is true that no Government can change or destroy an economic law, though it may change the economic conditions that give significance to it. All that it asserts is that given causes will, *ceteris paribus*, lead to certain results; and in that sense the law is inviolable. Yet the statesman may get rid of the causes or introduce other forces which counteract the effect. But, whether it is desired to strengthen or to check the action of economic laws, it is obviously important first to understand their working, since it is usually far easier to accomplish a desired result by harnessing and directing them into proper channels than by struggling against them.

6. Development of economic thought.—In the foregoing remarks upon its meaning, scope, and method, reference has been made to some of the more prominent changes in economic thought. Although used by Aristotle, it remains true that in the present sense of the term 'Economics' is essentially a modern science. It is, indeed, usual to refer to Adam Smith as its founder, but this does not mean that he was the first to write upon economic subjects. On nearly every part of Economics there had been previous writers, and some topics, such as foreign trade, money, and taxation, had quite a considerable literature of their own. But he so entirely recast the subject, combining the English and French doctrines and weaving them into a connected scientific whole, that the *Wealth of Nations* (1776) marks as great a departure in Economics as the system of Copernicus did in Astronomy.

The industrial life of Greece and Rome was based upon slavery, domestic manufacture, and petty commerce. Discussions on the principle of private property are found, division of labour had been utilized to a moderate degree, but the chief feature of modern industry was lacking, for industrial capital played no large part in production. Public finance and the nature of money certainly occupied the attention of writers of antiquity; but, apart from an occasional anticipation of modern theories, there is little in Greek and Roman literature that has any direct significance for modern economic life. The industrial conditions were not such as to direct attention to the problems which present themselves most acutely at the present day. In mediæval times the slave was disappearing before the free labourer, but industry was still on a petty scale and there was little industrial capital. Economic speculation was intermingled with theological and moral questions—the determination of a just price, usury doctrines, and luxury exemplifying the topics discussed. On the whole it became little more than a casuistical system of rules for business conduct. After the Reformation, the introduction of printing, the discovery of trade routes to the East, and the influx of precious metals from the New World, there were hundreds of books and pamphlets on economic subjects before the middle of the 18th cent., usually relating to particular controversies connected with monetary matters and foreign trade. As local industrial regulation gave place to national, the Mercantile Theory (cf. COMMERCE) became dominant, with its demand for freedom of exportation and its doctrine of the balance of trade. There was a great advance in the analysis of problems of production and exchange, but the separation of a wage-earning class and the rise of capital were only beginning to turn attention to problems of profit, wages, and labour.

It was when the old industrial order was thus passing away and capitalism was in its infancy that Adam Smith's *Inquiry into the Nature and Causes of the Wealth of Nations* appeared. Much of it is polemical, being aimed against the innumerable rules and regulations for the conduct of trade which had lost any justification they may formerly have had in the conditions of the time. The Physiocratic writers in France had already laid stress upon the natural law of freedom before the publication of the *Wealth of Nations*, but it has now been made clear, by the publication of the notes of his lectures taken by a student, that Adam Smith was teaching very similar ideas in the University of Glasgow as early as 1763 (*Lectures on Justice, Police, Revenue, and Arms, delivered in the University of Glasgow, reported by a Student in 1763*, and edited by Edwin Cannan, Oxford, 1896). Despite an occasional confusion of economic laws with ethical precepts, which arose from the preconceptions regarding the natural, his exposition of the principles of freedom of trade was so forcible and so opportune that it profoundly affected legislation.

But the *Wealth of Nations* also contained a scientific treatise on value and the distribution of wealth, and here the French economists had anticipated him and exercised a strong influence upon him. Turgot, in his *Réflexions sur la formation et la distribution des richesses* (1770; Eng. tr. edited by W. J. Ashley, New York, 1898), gave a theory of wages, profits, interest, and rent which was largely coloured by the Physiocratic doctrine that agriculture alone yielded a net product over the expenses of production, while manufacture merely changed the shape of materials already produced, adding a value corresponding strictly with the useful materials consumed by the artisans during the period of labour; and commerce merely changed the place of materials without increasing the wealth of the country. The theory of distribution received fuller development at the hands of Adam Smith, and, though he did not accept the view that agriculture alone was productive, but extended the conception to manufacture and commerce, he still thought that the first was productive in a special sense.

'In agriculture nature labours along with man; and, though her labour costs no expense, its produce has its value, as well as that of the most expensive workmen'; while 'no equal quantity of productive labour employed in manufactures can ever occasion so great a reproduction. In them nature does nothing; man does all' (*Wealth of Nations*, bk. ii. ch. v.).

The basis of this assertion appears to be that land yields a surplus in the shape of rent in addition to wages and profits; yet this fact is not due to the greater bounty of Nature in work on the soil than in other industrial pursuits, but rather to the limitations and variations of that bounty. Now, when natural forces have been exploited on a large scale for manufacturing and mercantile purposes, it is futile to ask whether Nature contributes more to production on the land than to other forms of production. The main doctrines of Smith regarding the distribution of wealth did not differ essentially from those of Turgot, though he departed further from the Physiocratic theory and gave more emphasis to the industrial, as distinguished from the agricultural, system. Francis Hutcheson, Hume, Steuart, and other English writers had also made important contributions to economic theory before 1776, but, as Marshall (*Principles of Economics*[5], London, 1907, i. 757) says,

'Adam Smith's breadth was sufficient to include all that was best in all his contemporaries, French and English; and, though he undoubtedly borrowed much from others, yet, the more one compares him with those who went before and those who came after him, the finer does his genius appear, the broader his knowledge, and the more well-balanced his judgment. . . . Wherever he differs from his predecessors, he is more nearly right than they; while there is scarcely an economic truth now known of which he did not get some glimpse. And, since he was the first to write a treatise on wealth in all its chief social aspects, he might on this ground alone have a claim to be regarded as the founder of modern economics.' His highest claim to have made an epoch in thought, according to the same authority, is that 'he was the first to make a careful and scientific inquiry into the manner in which value measures human motive'—a theory which gave a common centre and unity to the science.

The Industrial Revolution, which was only beginning in Adam Smith's time, soon proceeded apace, for Watt discovered the steam-engine in the same year that the *Wealth of Nations* was published. New problems arose as the factory system superseded the domestic system of production, and, as England was industrially far in advance of any other nation, the discussion of them took place chiefly in that country. In the hands of Ricardo and Malthus, therefore, the development and extension of Adam Smith's principles had the directly practical aim of contributing towards the solution of the special problems of the early years of the 19th cent., and this work they did very effectively. Freedom of trade was now more necessary than ever; questions of distribution became more acute with the growth of the business unit and the increased number of wage-earners, so that the relation of wages to profit was a prominent feature of discussion; the condition of the poor and the influence of the poor-laws were seen in the contributions of Malthus; the effects of the restrictions upon importation of corn led to an elucidation of the theory and nature of rent; while the financial difficulties of the period of the French war and the suspension of specie payment by the Bank of England caused a development in monetary theory. The Malthusian theory seemed to warrant the view that the poor condition of the labouring classes was due to the fact that when wages rose above the level of subsistence there was a tendency for population to increase and force them down again. Ricardo strengthened this view in one way by his theory of rent, which showed the tendency to diminishing returns from increased applications of labour to land, and also that the surplus produce above the margin of cultivation went to the owners of the soil. By a careless expression to the effect that wages could not rise above the level of necessaries he also provided the basis for the Socialistic doctrine which represented the margin of cultivation as the margin of necessary wages, generalized it to the whole of industrial life, and held that capitalists and land-owners swept off all surplus produce.

7. Recent development.—Later economic doctrine has been mainly an amplification and modification of that which flourished in England under Ricardo, Malthus, MacCulloch, and Mill. But, since the middle of the 19th cent., other countries have been overtaking England in industrialism, and have begun to contribute also to the development of economic thought. Prior to that time France and England were almost the only countries which had contributed anything of importance, but during the last half-century American, German, Austrian, and other writers have applied themselves to the science with such skill and success that they have rid it of much of its former insularity and widened its outlook. The increased concentration of capital and the immense growth of commerce, following upon improvements in railways and steamships, have brought about newer conditions, so that problems of transport, international trade, monopoly, and speculation have assumed a larger place in economic treatises. The doctrine of non-interference has been greatly modified, and the latest phase of this movement of thought, which promises to be the most important for some time to come, is the use of the machinery of the State for social amelioration, partly by means of restrictive legislation regarding the conditions of employment, partly by the utilization of the system of taxation for improving the condition of the labourers, and partly by extending the collective ownership and operation of industrial enterprises.

The subject of distribution of wealth is claiming fuller investigation, and the desire for raising the economic condition of the less fortunate members of the community is tending to overshadow all minor controversies. The economists of the first half of the 19th cent. treated distribution from the standpoint rather of abstract classes like capitalists and labourers than of individuals, and did admirable work in explaining the nature and variations of each category of income—rent, profits, and wages. But to-day the emphasis of popular discussion is upon the great inequalities of incomes which arise largely from inequalities of inherited property and inequalities of opportunity, and economic inquiry has tended to follow the same direction. Consequently, greater stress has been laid upon the fact that the increase of aggregate wealth is not the same thing as the increase of material well-being; and, through the work of Jevons and the Austrian school, the theory of value has been re-stated from the side of consumption and utility in such a way that no modern economist can fall into the common error of earlier authorities of confounding the two conceptions. It is now of fundamental importance, not only in general economic theory but also in its application to the principles of taxation and socialistic proposals, to recognize the simple psychological fact that the relative urgency of wants depends largely upon the extent to which they have already been satisfied, so that it cannot be a matter of indifference in estimating the amount of well-being whether a particular quantity of material goods accrues to the rich or to the poor. No doubt recent economists in elaborating this profoundly significant principle have sometimes attempted to give it an air of mathematical precision which it cannot sustain, and such calculations of pleasure or utility are apt to raise the suspicions of the philosopher. But, while it is impossible to give absolute proof that a particular poor man suffers more from the loss of a shilling than does a particular rich man, and it may even be quite untrue in special cases, yet in dealing with large numbers any scruple regarding the matter vanishes, for no one would find much comfort in the fact that the aggregate of material wealth was the same whether a million sterling went to the working-classes or to the payers of super-tax. The earlier economists, partly under a false impression regarding the relation of capital to wages as expressed in the doctrine of the 'wages-fund,' partly from lack of an adequate theory of demand and consumption, usually thought that if a policy increased or diminished what is now called the 'national dividend,'—the quantity of goods produced in a year,—it was *ipso facto* good or bad, economical or wasteful. But the principle that the utility of a good depends upon the quantity possessed makes it clear that even a policy which injures the national dividend may yet promote material welfare if it modifies the distribution of wealth to the advantage of the poorer sections of the community; and a policy that increases the dividend may likewise fail to promote material welfare if it alters the distribution of wealth to the disadvantage of the poorer classes. Hence among economists, as well as by socialists, a more even distribution of wealth is considered to be desirable, and modern controversy turns rather upon the advisability of particular methods of achieving it, and upon the magnitude of their effects on productive efficiency and the like, than upon the desirability of the end.

This conception of utility or psychic significance has affected not only the standpoint from which the distribution of wealth is regarded, but also many of the aspects of the production of wealth. The fuller recognition of the distinction between material wealth and material welfare has made it necessary to take account of the disutility involved in excessive and uninteresting toil as a deduction from the material gain. Consequently, it is no longer considered a sufficient answer to claims for the reduction of hours of labour in particular employments merely to assert that the national dividend will be injured thereby. Often, of course, such an injury does not result from curtailing the hours of labour; but, even though it should be so, the economic aim is the maximizing not of material goods, but of material welfare, and it is possible that the latter may be achieved by means which slightly injure the former. On the other hand, everything that increases the interest in, and satisfaction directly derived from, an occupation is a gain of material welfare, even though it may not similarly increase the output of goods.

Apart from this elaboration of the principles of utility and demand, which has exercised a larger influence upon recent Economics than is commonly realized, there have been a number of other changes of a more limited nature in general economic theory. The distinction between capital and land was too sharply drawn by the older writers, not merely because capital becomes incorporated with the soil,—for that they knew,—but because the incomes yielded by the two are not so strictly distinguishable as they thought. Marshall has shown that the rent of land is not a thing by itself, but a leading species of a larger genus, and to the other species he gives the name of 'quasi-rent.' The distinction between rent and quasi-rent depends chiefly upon the possibility of increasing or diminishing the supply of the article, but economically they are otherwise similar. The doctrine of the pressure of population upon the available means of subsistence from land has also been modified since the time of J. S. Mill, partly by a clearer understanding of the influence of a rising standard of life upon the birth-rate and upon the efficiency of labour, partly by a more complete analysis of the factors which may counteract the tendency to diminishing returns from land, and partly also by the opening up of new countries and the consequent increase of the area of food supply. The wages-fund theory—that some rather ill-defined fund of capital constituted the source of wages, and that if one workman obtained more of it another must get less—flourished with slight modifications down to 1870, and was frequently set up as a barrier against any pretence on the part of a Trade Union that it could increase wages without equally injuring those employed in other trades. It was, however, directly attacked by Longe (*A Refutation of the Wage Fund Theory of Modern Political Economy*, London, 1866) and by Thornton (*On Labour*, London, 1869), so that Mill himself abandoned it. The increasing differentiation between the capitalist and the entrepreneur in business life has been coincident with a clearer distinction of their respective functions and gains. In Germany and America careful work of a similar nature has been done by a number of brilliant scholars who have produced thorough analyses of particular branches, added greatly to the available historical and statistical material, and widened the boundaries of the science. The names and works of the more important of these recent writers will be found in the 'Literature' at the end of this article. Suffice it to say here that modern economic theory has not only been brought more closely into touch with the facts of industrial life, and thrown aside the insular narrowness which characterized the first half of the 19th cent., but has become, partly through the influence of socialistic criticism, though chiefly by development from within, more closely associated with social reform.

8. Problems of Economics.—A summary of all the various subjects that are treated in a text-book on Economics would yield but a dry table of contents. What is here proposed is rather to explain, without unnecessary technicalities, the essential features of the science at its present stage of development, dealing first with the more general principles upon which the material welfare depends, and secondly with their application to particular policies for the furtherance of material welfare through the action of the State.

(*a*) The primary requisites of material welfare are *labour* and *natural agents*; without the co-operation of these no production of any kind is possible. In a secondary place come *capital* and *organization*—meaning by 'secondary' not that they are less important in the process of production as now carried on, but that production of some sort is possible without them and they become important at a later stage of industrial development. Labour cannot create material things; but, by operating upon the materials which Nature gives, changing their form, place, or qualities, it adapts them to man's needs. In Nature there is remarkably little suitable for human provision until it has thus been re-made according to man's own plan. Down to the second half of the 18th cent. this adaptation, which is called the production process, had to be performed almost wholly by man's muscular force aided by that of domesticated animals. There were tools, but, the motive-power being muscular, their range of operation was definitely limited by the physical and nervous energy of man. In a very few directions, which now seem by comparison almost negligible, the earlier period had attempted to progress beyond the merely muscular, as in utilizing the wind for ocean traffic and for small mills; but since the advent of the age of inventions we have looked more and more to the intelligence of man curbing and directing the forces of Nature in such forms as steam and electricity to perform most of the heavier work.

This perfecting of the agencies of production, which is still proceeding rapidly, removes the former limit of physical endurance, and the only bounds to the increase of material goods are the far-distant one when all natural forces shall have been economically exploited, and the improbable one that man's inventive capacity will come to a halt. This rapid adaptation of the world to man's requirements, by which natural forces are made to work for us, should, if rightly directed, result in a much higher general level of living. A community is not, however, well-off merely because of the increase of the aggregate output of goods; these are only instruments that may contribute much or little to welfare and to the raising of the standard of living according to the manner in which they are divided and utilized, and to the number of people embraced in the community. As man's wants are never fully satisfied, or likely to be, the first principle of production is that a people should strive to obtain the goods it requires with the minimum expenditure of effort. This is sometimes questioned by those who are painfully conscious of the fact that people are often to be found who have no work to do, and projects for 'making work' are sometimes advocated. Yet there can be no such thing as a general scarcity of work until mankind is supplied with everything it desires. Defective organization of industry shows itself in maladjustments of the labour force between different trades; in the inability to predict with certainty the future supply of raw produce or food, and the character of future demand for goods; in the spasms and reactions of credit, as well as in the temporary displacements that accompany all progress and change. Such causes as these lead to unemployment; but there is no lack of work to be done, and it is wasteful to spend more effort upon making any class of goods than is absolutely necessary.

The effectiveness of labour in production is greatly increased by the advance of science, which teaches men how to make the most of the natural environment by applications of chemical and physical discoveries, and by the general raising of the level of skill and intelligence. It is also increased by the fact that the stock of appliances for production is growing faster than the population, so that every generation bequeaths to its successor a much larger quantity of the products of past effort, in the shape of machinery and other forms of capital, than it received from the preceding generation. And the effectiveness of labour depends, too, upon the manner in which individuals co-operate for the supply of their wants through the separation of employments and division of labour, allowing each to perform the work for which he is most suited by nature or training; through the combination of labour, which can perform what would be quite impossible to any single individual; through the localization of industries in the places best suited to the particular branch of production. If one man can weave more cloth in a day than can another, while the second can produce more or better boots than the first, the productivity of their labour will be increased when they specialize their work and exchange their products. Similarly if, for climatic or other reasons, one district can produce cotton goods more easily than another, while the second can produce coal or granite more easily than the first, it is economical that the districts should specialize their production and exchange their products. Indeed, even if a man possessed such excellent abilities that he could do a dozen things better than most other people, it would still be most beneficial to production that he should devote himself to the occupation in which his superiority was most marked, for it is not economical for a successful lawyer to do his own typewriting, even though, with practice, he might be able to do it expertly.

These commonplaces are seldom directly denied, but it is often forgotten that they are not changed by political boundaries and lines of latitude, and that the advantages of territorial division of labour are not essentially different in comparing two nations from what they are in comparing two towns or counties. If, by hindrances to exchange, a community is compelled to make for itself the goods in which it has little or no superiority, it must make fewer of the goods in which its relative superiority is great; and such hindrances, by impeding the territorial division of labour, lower the productivity of industry. No doubt there are some incidental disadvantages in all forms of localization of industry, as there certainly are when labour becomes so specialized that it is difficult to readjust the amount of it in different lines of production as the demand changes; but on the whole the productivity of industry increases when the localization of industry is unimpeded, for much the same reasons as when each man is performing the work for which he has the highest aptitude.

It follows from this conception of localization also that the effectiveness of labour depends upon the condition of the land or other natural agent with which it operates. Different areas are very unequally fitted for assisting labour, because of their variations of fertility, climate, geological formation, or geographical position; and, though some of these natural circumstances may be altered by man's action through the incorporation of capital with the soil, others admit of no great modification. In any case, the labour required for producing a given quantity of goods in a favourable locality is less than in an unfavourable one, so that labour is more productive when applied under the former circumstances than under the latter. This gives rise to variations of rent, for those who control the superior sources will naturally reap higher gains than those who control the inferior. Besides variations in natural endowments affecting the productivity of labour applied to land, it is also affected by the response that land makes to intensive cultivation, so that there was at one time a fear that the number of people would increase to such a point that the supply of food and other products of the land would not keep pace with the growth of population. In other words, the effectiveness of labour depends on the amount of land available, for after a certain point, as cultivation becomes more intensive, there is a lower and lower return of produce to the successive increments of labour, unless changes have meantime occurred in the arts of agriculture. If it were not so, there would be no limit to the intensity of the cultivation that could be profitably carried on. The earlier economists may have given too little weight to the possible improvements in agricultural methods, facilities of transport from abroad, and the like; but it remains true that, if population increases in an old country while no change occurs in these respects, greater difficulty must be experienced in producing the food required for the additional numbers, and therefore it is quite possible that there may be too many people in comparison with the area of land available, though the limit may be pushed back by various kinds of improvements. There may also be the opposite phenomenon of under-population, where the addition of every immigrant tends to increase the productivity per head of the community.

(*b*) Specialization and localization are obviously dependent upon the facilities for *exchange of products*, and the problem arises why a quantity of one commodity exchanges for another quantity of a different commodity. If each person worked with his own land and instruments, producing only those goods which he directly consumed, there would be no exchange, and the income of each would be merely the goods he made. The complexities of exchange and of the distribution of wealth arise because a man's income depends not only upon what he personally produces, but also on the ratio of exchange of his produce with that of other people, and on the payments that must be made for the use of factors of production like land and capital lent to him by others. To facilitate exchange a monetary system is required, both as a standard of value and as a means of transfer from one person to another, and, though a host of commodities, such as furs, feathers, cattle, grain, shells, and tobacco, have in different communities performed the functions of money, these have all tended to give way to the precious metals, especially to gold, which is peculiarly suited to the purpose because of its portability, homogeneity, divisibility, and similar qualities. But such a medium as gold can only serve as a means of comparing the values of different commodities at one particular time, and not at different times, because the value of gold itself changes from period to period for the same reasons as ordinary goods change in value, viz. from circumstances affecting the supply or the demand for it. One of these circumstances in the case of gold is the extent to which exchange takes place without the intervention of actual metal. The most important forms of credit documents are connected with banking, which assists production further by facilitating the transfer of capital from those who can make little or no use of it, to those who can employ it to great advantage, and by affording credit on the security of future repayment.

The problem of value is not, however, settled by the adoption of a monetary medium; for, when the question is asked why six different commodities all sell for a shilling, it is futile to answer that money balances them, since money is merely one of the seven things balanced. Some socialists have asserted that goods are of equal value because they embody equal amounts of labour; but that is not only untrue of goods the supply of which is definitely fixed, as its upholders often admit; it does not apply even to those goods which are being constantly produced for meeting the demands of the market. To explain value by means of labour it is necessary to resolve all kinds and qualities of labour to some common unit, and, when any attempt is thus made to weigh different forms of labour against one another, the only way of doing it is by the price paid for their results, and this involves a *petitio principii*. The true answer is that the value of goods depends, from the side of demand, upon the relative estimate of their utility or significance in the satisfaction of human desires; and, from the side of supply, upon their relative abundance, which again depends upon the cost of production. As regards the demand side, the fundamental factor is that, the greater the quantity of a good we possess, the lower is the significance to us of any further addition to the stock of it, until, when superfluity is reached, no satisfaction is dependent upon any one item of the good, and therefore its value is zero, as in the case of air. There can be no value in the absence of utility, and the value of any good depends upon the marginal utility—that is, upon the utility of the final increment of the commodity which we are just induced to purchase. Cf. art. CONSUMPTION. Thus, the nearer the quantity of the commodity approaches to the amount required for complete satiety of the wants dependent upon it, the smaller will be the marginal utility and the lower the value of any single increment of it. Hence it may be briefly stated that, other things being equal, the demand price of a commodity decreases with every increase of supply, because the marginal utility falls. It is by analysis of the conditions affecting the supply of the goods that the complementary truth is explained, viz. that the price reacts upon the amount produced and determines the extent to which labour and capital will be devoted to the production of the particular article. Goods will not permanently be produced unless they 'pay,' and so account must be taken of the cost of production as well as of utility. Cost of production, in the sense of an irrevocable fact that capital and labour have been devoted to producing an article, has no real influence on the value; nevertheless, there is a constant tendency for value to conform to cost of production, because capital and labour will turn to the production of those goods which offer the best remuneration. Instead of making more of a good when the price of it is below the cost, industrial resources will be shifted to other lines of production where the price is above the cost, thus lowering the supply and raising the marginal utility of the former, while increasing the supply and lowering the marginal utility of the latter until they balance. The fact that under competitive conditions the value of a good is normally very near its cost of production has led many to assert that it is the cost of production that causes value. But this is a confusion of mind. Value depends upon utility and scarcity, while cost of production is important inasmuch as it affects the degree of scarcity, but in no other manner. Values change when either of these factors changes, unless, perchance, both change in such directions as to neutralize one another. An increase in the supply, while the demand remains the same, will lower the value of each unit of the commodity; a diminution of the supply will raise the value. An increase in the demand, while the supply is unchanged, will raise the value of each unit; a fall in the demand will lower it.

(*c*) The problem of the *distribution of income* in the form of wages, rent, interest, and profits is an application of these principles of value. The relative incomes of different people depend upon the value of the produce of their labour and the value of the use of their property, so that a full explanation of the fact of wide differences of income would involve a statement of all the reasons why some own more property than others, why some properties yield a higher return than others, and why different forms of exertion, from unskilled labour to the organization of a huge industry, are so variously valued. This can only be here indicated in the broadest outline. In existing conditions there is no pretence to reward moral worth or even intellectual merit as such: what is rewarded is simply an economic service. Many are paid not for any work that they personally perform, but for the service of factors of production which they own. The variations in the magnitude of incomes from the possession of such property depend upon the amount and the efficiency of the property possessed, and these again depend upon individual providence, judicious choice of investments, luck, and the quantity inherited, as well as upon the magnitude of the individual's earnings, which largely determine the possibility of saving. Within any one class of property incomes there are variations: one landed estate yields a higher income than another of equal size, because of its superior situation, natural endowments, and the improvements made upon it by expenditure of capital and labour in the past; one use of capital yields a higher income than another because the different uses to which capital is put vary in their productiveness, in their security, and in their marketability; and people are willing to accept a lower return on an investment which has a high security and is easily marketed. Similarly, the wages of labour depend upon the value which the public attaches to the goods or services produced by it, and consequently upon the number of workers ready to perform the tasks. In each trade the wages will be fixed by the value of the product of the marginal worker—the worker, that is, whose presence or absence makes little appreciable difference to the employer. If the number of labourers increases while other things remain the same, the remuneration of each will be lowered, because the value of the marginal product will fall as more of it is placed upon the market, unless the industry happens to be one in which the addition of workers makes production so much more efficient that the increased output per head is more than sufficient to counterbalance the fall in the price of each unit of produce. In this way it emerges that the importance of an occupation to society is no test of the wages that will be paid in it, any more than the relative value of corn, air, and diamonds is explained by their importance to human well-being. Precisely as goods rise in value if there are few in the market when many are wanted, so the value of a particular kind of labour rises when there are few labourers in comparison with the demand for their work. Hence the reason why wages in one trade are higher than in another depends upon the number of people and the demand for their produce in each case. If all workers were equal and all trades equally desirable, there could be no such differences of wages. But not only do occupations vary in the advantages, other than money wages, which they afford; the workers are also differentiated into classes who can rarely do each other's work, and the main reasons for the relative over-supply of labour in some occupations as compared with others are therefore to be sought in the circumstances that render labour immobile, and that prevent workers from entering the more highly paid trades. For some temporary reason, such as a change in the nature of demand, too many people may have become specialized to a particular trade and too few to another, but the error cannot be quickly rectified, because of the time required to train new workers. In the course of time it may be expected that the higher wages will attract to the one occupation, and the lower wages will repel workmen from the other; but in the meantime the maladjustment of the labour force between the trades will cause a corresponding variation of wages.

Of more permanent and serious import is the fact that the choice of a trade is not free. The people become distributed between different occupations in a rather unsatisfactory manner, and it would promote welfare if more people followed some, and fewer other, occupations than at present. Since many employments call for lengthy and expensive training, it depends upon the number of parents who are both willing and able to undertake this preliminary expenditure for their children, whether the supply of labour of that kind will be great or small. The chief reason why those kinds of work that any ordinary person can perform are at present paid for on a very low or miserable scale is that there is a very large number of parents who either have not the power or have not the will to bear the expense involved in training their children. Customs of various kinds also limit the freedom of choice in some cases, and this is particularly important in fixing women's wages, for women are by custom excluded from many employments, and so relatively overcrowd others. The difficulty of gauging in advance the comparative advantages of employments when conditions are rapidly changing, the differences of physique and mental strength, also give rise to differences of wages from trade to trade, while the last-mentioned factor also causes variations of earnings within the same trade.

Besides competition of workers and the relative supply of them in different trades, there is still another factor tending to fix the limits of wages, viz. the principle of substitution. Men compete with machinery, and different combinations of labour and capital with other combinations. It is the employer's function and interest to keep down the expenses of production by choosing those factors and groupings which are most economical. Thus land, labour, and capital are all needed in farming, and no one of them can be wholly substituted for the others; but they can be substituted for one another at their margins. The farmer may conceivably produce the same crop from a given area with more labour but less machinery or manure, with less labour and more machinery or manure; or he may produce the same crop from a smaller area of land by still further increasing the labour and machinery. Land, labour, and capital are here being balanced against one another as factors of production, and, if the price of one rises considerably, the others may be chosen to take its place in some measure. So it is in every industry. Each factor and subfactor, however necessary to production, may find a substitute at the margin in some other factor or subfactor; and in this fact there is found some justification for the hard and misleading saying that 'most men earn just about what they are worth,' that being calculated as their economic factor-worth. The wages in a trade tend to equal the marginal worth of the labour in that trade, and that marginal worth is fixed both by the number of workers in the occupation relatively to the demand for their produce and by the competition of other factors capable of performing similar work. Unfortunately, however, the saying just quoted is often used to support the very different idea that a man's income measures his personal efficiency. That is by no means justified by economic analysis. Through the method of substitution the portion of the aggregate produce of the community which goes to remunerate any particular agent or factor of production tends to be adjusted to the efficiency of that factor in supplying the wants of mankind, so that distribution depends upon factor-worth. But, besides labour and organizing ability, capital and land are factors of production; and, though these earn in proportion to their efficiency in the supply of wants, they cannot be said to acquire incomes; their owners receive the reward whether personally efficient or the reverse. Moreover, the theory of distribution takes the wants of mankind as they are, not as they ought to be; so that, if the popular demand requires successive editions of a sensational novel, while a book embodying the profound researches of the scholar will not sell, the author of the former is the more efficient in supplying the wants of mankind, and accordingly obtains a greater share of income. In a deeper sense, no doubt, a man may be so very efficient that the people are unable to appreciate his wares; but that is only to reiterate that intellectual merit and moral worth do not, as such, constitute a claim upon the national dividend under existing conditions.

9. State action for the promotion of material welfare.—After this survey of the general principles, it remains to exemplify their application to particular proposals for State action in furtherance of material welfare. This section cannot pretend to systematic completeness, and selection can only be made of two samples from the multiplicity of projects and activities. The subjects chosen as sufficiently representative and widely debated are the raising of the economic condition of the worst-paid labour, and the imposition of import duties for the protection of home industries

(*a*) *The problem of very low earnings.*—The subject of low earnings connects itself with the general principles of wages already enunciated. The tendency of economic forces, in so far as they are not impeded, is to pay to workers their marginal worth in the particular trade. Clearly they cannot permanently get more than this, because, if the marginal worth of a class of men were 20s. a week while the wages were 21s., it would be to the advantage of an employer to dismiss men up to the point at which the gain resulting from a further dismissal would be equalled by the loss. On the other hand, competition for labour among employers should normally prevent wages from falling below the marginal worth of the labour.

Hence, when a large class of work-people is found to obtain very low earnings, two questions arise to the mind of the economist: Are the low wages to be accounted for by the low marginal worth in that occupation, or are they due to special circumstances which prevent the general economic forces from operating properly in the trade in question?—more briefly, Are the workers not obtaining as much as their marginal worth? In some cases both questions may admit of an affirmative answer. Thus, in the case of sweated home-work among women, the supply of labour relatively to the demand for it is very high, so that its marginal worth is low. Much of the work is of a kind that can be performed with the aid of machinery in factories, and the cost of production in the factory fixes a limit to the wages that can be paid in the home. Many of the articles may be made by the consumers themselves, and, if their price rises, this method of production will be stimulated. There is thus an excessive supply and a limited demand, and these facts alone warrant the conclusion that the marginal worth of the labour must be low. At the same time there are also reasons for believing that the wages, in some cases at least, fall below the marginal worth, because the bargaining power of the home-workers is very weak; they know little of one another, and cannot take combined action in resistance to a fall of wages. So far the conditions of a true market are absent, and in practice different piece-rates are sometimes paid for precisely the same work by different employers. It is chiefly in this latter fact that the institution of minimum wages by law for such industries may be expected to have a good effect; for, if the home-workers were already in all cases obtaining their marginal worth, any raising of the wage must inevitably displace some of them, unless, indeed, their worth immediately rose in proportion to their higher wages. But in the case of unskilled men there is little reason to believe that the payment of wages below their marginal worth is very common or important. The main cause of their low earnings is that their marginal worth is low on account of the magnitude of the supply of such labour relatively to the demand for it. The idea that the prescription of a minimum wage by law will in such circumstances suffice to remove the evil cannot be sustained, for it is impossible to force employers to give more for labour than it is worth, and a man is not worth more simply because the Government declares that he must not be employed for less than a given sum. The result of a minimum wage in these circumstances must be to throw a large number of men out of work altogether. Conceivably this may be desirable as an incident in a larger scheme of reform where the gain is more than sufficient to counterbalance this loss, but the legislative prescription of a minimum wage alone is no remedy. Far more hope lies in an attempt to make the men worth more by raising some of the members of the overcrowded class to a higher level of efficiency, or by checking the degradation of members of the higher grades. The economic reason for the deplorable state of things is that there is a maladjustment of supply to demand, and the best course to pursue is to rectify this, for economic forces will then work with us in raising the wages of the poorer classes. This means that some of the sources of the over-supply of such labour must be stopped up, and in particular that at the adolescent age boys must be trained to fill some positive function in industrial life, instead of being allowed to drift into any uneducative job that offers good wages at the moment but leads to nothing in the future.

A serious objection is frequently raised to this course by the skilled workman, who asserts that the drafting of boys from unskilled and casual to skilled and regular trades can do no real good, because the skilled trades are already over-stocked; and a number of anti-social policies by Trade Unions and others have been dictated by this view. It arises largely from the practice of thinking about values and wages only in terms of money; as soon as one goes behind the money expressions, it is seen to be fallacious. The bootmaker's objection to the training of more boys for his trade, instead of allowing them to drift into casual and unskilled labour, is that the want he exists to satisfy will be more fully met while the other wants that he himself feels will not be more fully met, so that society gives him less of general commodities for a week's work than before. The objection would be partially valid if all the boys were diverted into this one skilled trade, though it might still be said that, when a set of men who would otherwise be doing little work, or casual work of very low worth, are making boots that are much needed instead, society as a whole will be enriched by the change, despite the fact that the price of boots and the wages of boot operatives would fall. But it is not proposed to draft all the boys into any single skilled industry; they would be distributed over industries of all kinds, so that all wants would be somewhat more fully met in due proportion. Then, despite the fact that boots are rather less urgently required than before when the supply increases, the bootmaker will not suffer because the same is true of the things he wants in exchange for boots. The only qualification to this is that by withdrawing labour to a large extent from casual occupations the price of such unskilled labour would rise, and, unless it increased in efficiency fully in proportion, or unless there were progress and invention in the work performed by the unskilled, their produce would rise in price and they would be relatively favoured by obtaining a greater command of general commodities for each unit of their labour. But in any case the economist will not quarrel with this result; it makes real wages more equal as between skilled and unskilled trades by raising the earnings of the latter, and welfare is thereby promoted. The function of State action in this matter is, therefore, to carry its educational policy further into the more adequate training of youths, the suppression and regulation of undesirable forms of boy labour, and the more thorough direction of the labour force into the most desirable channels by the diffusion of information regarding occupations and the like. In such ways it can raise the marginal worth of the workers in unskilled trades, by reducing the supply and by raising the efficiency, so that economic forces themselves will then raise the wages. The State may also bring pressure to bear upon employers in order to regulate work as far as possible, instead of offering it in a casual fashion, and this will likewise tend to diminish the supply, as people will see that the chances of picking up a living by odd jobs are reduced, and they will have a stronger inducement to prepare themselves and their children for regular occupations. The surest means that the State can employ for improving the position of the poorest classes are those which directly or indirectly increase the efficiency of the workers, and distribute them more evenly among different trades in comparison with the demand, so that their marginal worth is at least sufficiently high to give them command over the necessaries for decent living.

(*b*) *Free Trade and Protection.*—The object of foreign trade is to render it possible for the people of a country to obtain goods more easily than they could otherwise do. That exchange is a gain to both parties, and that it realizes the economies of division of labour and localization of industries, is always admitted in regard to domestic trade; consequently no one questions the advantages of a policy of free exchange within the limits of a single country. The doctrine of freedom in international trade rests upon the same elementary facts. If each nation devotes its resources to those forms of production for which it has a relative superiority, and exchanges such goods for those which it cannot produce with equal facility, the income of its people will be higher than if they were compelled to produce for themselves all the goods consumed within the country. The idea that one country gains at the expense of another is absurd, and a country that will not buy cannot sell. Hence impediments to trade diminish the productivity of labour and capital within the protected area by nullifying the advantages of territorial division of labour. There is a *prima facie* presumption that it pays Britain better to produce the goods she is producing and exporting rather than to divert some of her productive forces from these to making the goods she is now importing. The burden of proof, therefore, lies upon the protectionist to demonstrate the falsity of this simple general principle, or its inapplicability to some particular circumstances. Broadly, protectionist arguments may be divided into two classes: those which urge that impediments to trade will increase the wealth, employment, or productivity of the country imposing them; and those which appeal to wider considerations such as national defence or imperial sentiment.

The oldest and the crudest of the arguments arises from the conception that foreign trade benefits a nation only when the value of the exports exceeds that of the imports, because it is then supposed that the difference must come in gold and so enrich the country. The refutation of the argument is manifold. The excess of imports or of exports is usually fully explicable without the passing of gold, by taking account of such items as shipping services and interest on investments abroad. It is impossible to obtain a surplus of exports by the imposition of import duties; and, even if the balance did come in gold, it does not follow that the country is richer. No economist to-day advances the balance of trade argument.

One of the strongest economic arguments is that temporary protection may encourage the development of infant industries. Under free importation an industry for which a new country is naturally adapted might not be able to obtain a footing, but once sufficiently protected it would grow up, obtain the economies of production on a large scale, and after an 'apprenticeship' period be able to stand without tariff support. The validity of this argument has been allowed by many free traders. Its best exponents grant that the immediate effect of the restrictions will be to lower the income of the community, but they look to a greater gain in the future from the more rapid development of the industries. The limitations to its validity, however, are that the industries to be fostered must be such as are likely to become self-supporting after a limited period, otherwise the loss is permanent; and that the protective support must be withdrawn after the 'apprenticeship.' In practice these two conditions are seldom fulfilled. The new country gives protection indiscriminately instead of to a few well-chosen industries; and, as the industries become important, they come to have a vested interest in the maintenance of the tariff, using the political machinery rather to increase than to lower the duties. Hence, while it is quite possible that temporary protection of this sort, if wisely administered, might yield a net advantage in the long run to a new country, it is doubtful whether it has in practice ever achieved as much good as harm. What strength it possesses lies in its being strictly limited both in scope and in duration.

The argument upon which the greatest stress is generally placed is the benefit of protection to the working classes by increasing the quantity of employment or of wages. For this various reasons are assigned. The first consists in pointing to specific instances in which a trade could be made to employ more people if the competing foreign goods were excluded. But the free trader has never denied that the amount of employment in a particular industry may be contracted by allowing imports to compete with it, and charges the protectionist with the fallacy of *ignoratio elenchi*. The position of the free trader is that those industries that would gain by a tariff would do so at the expense of a greater aggregate loss to other trades by diverting productive forces from more to less remunerative channels. In political campaigns, however, this argument for protection is one of the most effective. It appeals to the economic truth that it is to my interest that the goods I make should be scarce while everything else is plentiful, and if a tariff will bring about that state of things I shall gain. But, as soon as the promise of making goods scarce by a tariff ceases to be confined to a particular trade and is generalized to all trades, it becomes flagrantly absurd.

Another form of the same method of argument is to point to the effects of a tariff in leading to the investment of capital—sometimes foreign capital—in the protected industry. Even granting that the cases cited were always attributable to the tariff, it does not follow that protection has attracted more capital to the industries of the country as a whole. On the contrary, it causes a diversion of capital to an equal or greater extent from other trades which are directly and indirectly injured by the tariff.

A different kind of argument in support of the protectionist view is that workmen in particular may be benefited by such a tariff as would exclude manufactured goods while permitting importation of raw materials, because the factor of labour is more important in the former than in the latter. Quite apart from the difficulty of distinguishing raw materials from manufactures in a state of industry where the product of one trade becomes the raw material of another, the argument appears to rest on a confusion of thought. More labour has, of course, gone to the production of a ton of steel than to the production of a ton of coal; but, then, nobody exchanges a ton of the one for a ton of the other. The question is whether labour has played a greater part in producing £100 worth of steel than in producing £100 worth of coal, and in point of fact a higher proportion of the value of coal goes to remunerate labour than in the case of steel. The comparison of values alone is relevant here; and, value for value, it is not the case that manufactured goods embody more labour than raw materials.

The most recent plea under this head is that protection might steady employment by lessening the fluctuations of industry. Statistical comparison of countries in regard to unemployment is very difficult to make at present, and, even if it were not so, it would fail to be convincing, because at most the fiscal policy can be but one among many factors influencing the intensity or recurrence of depressions of trade. The protectionist, however, asserts that the 'dumping' of surplus goods by foreign countries into a free trade country at very low prices is a cause of instability. Cf. art. COMMERCE. The extent of such operations by foreign trusts and kartels has been greatly exaggerated, but they do occur; and on the one side is the gain to the industries that use the cheap imports, which are almost always half-finished goods, while on the other side is the injury to the industries with which the dumped goods compete. The free trader tends to emphasize the former, the protectionist the latter, but the net gain or loss to the importing country depends on the circumstances of the particular time at which the dumping takes place. It is possible that on the whole the loss may predominate, inasmuch as dumping is intermittent: if it were steady and calculable, the gain would be greater. But the burden lies upon the protectionist to show that a tariff would cure the evil by preventing any unsteadiness of employment that it may occasion, and he is apt rather to take this for granted than to prove it. It is quite untrue to say that a free trade country alone is subject to dumping, for similar complaints have been frequently made in protected areas. Moreover, if the price of the goods in a protected country is higher by about the amount of the tariff than in a free trade country, there is no more inducement to dump into the latter than into the former. Indeed, if a country A habitually sends goods of a certain class to B, a free trade country, and to C, a country with a ten per cent tariff, and A now finds itself with a temporary surplus to get rid of without lowering prices at home, dumping will be slightly easier into C than into B, because in C the tax per ton falls as the price falls, and so stimulates sales the more. Further, low protection of about ten per cent, which is all that the Tariff Reform Commission in Britain has suggested, would not check dumping, because, on the authority of that unofficial Commission itself, the dumping prices are already dropped by a much larger percentage. Very high protection that stopped imports of that class altogether would, of course, prevent dumping; but, so far from securing stability of employment, it would increase instability by raising new causes of fluctuations which free trade prevents. It is a steadying influence that, when the price of iron in a free trade country falls, importation is checked, and when the price rises more is sent. If this influence is removed, every industry dependent upon iron will be subject to greater disorganization and fluctuation of employment, so that a tariff sufficiently high to prevent dumping would create much worse conditions for the workers, quite apart from the other injuries of high protection.

The wages argument, especially in the United States, takes the form of ascribing high wages to the tariff, and appeals for the exclusion or taxation of the products of low-waged European labour. That some fallacy is here involved is suggested by the facts that the countries with low wages are among those which adopt protection, and indeed sometimes urge the necessity for tariff aid against their highly paid competitors, and that no country in the world has ever differentiated in its tariff by favouring imports from countries where wages are high as against those from countries where wages are low. The argument does not allow for the difference between money wages and real wages, and generally in a protected country the cost of living is relatively high. Also, low wages do not mean low cost of production, for commonly, where high wages are found, the output per worker is at least as high in proportion. The true economic relation has thus been inverted. High real wages are due to the high productivity of labour, and that in turn depends chiefly on the superior natural resources of a country, the efficiency of its workers, and its business organization. It also depends upon foreign trade to the extent that productivity is increased by the exchange of goods between countries, but this point would favour free exchange. In fine, wages are dependent upon the effectiveness of labour; and, since the artificial inducement of industries in which labour is not sufficiently effective to render them profitable without a tariff results in lowering the general effectiveness of the labour force of the country, the average level of real wages will be thereby reduced.

It is occasionally proposed that a nation should adopt free trade only towards the countries granting to it the same privilege. In so far as this arises from the belief that trade must be free on both sides if it is to be at all advantageous to both, it is fallacious; but, in so far as it is based on the view that a tariff may be used for purposes of bargaining, and thus may lower or remove foreign restrictions, it was admitted by Adam Smith as a possible exception to the general free trade doctrine. It involves immediate loss in the hope of future compensation through freer trade. Its validity depends upon the probability of success, as it can be justified only when it removes the hindrances to trade; and in estimating this probability the nature and conditions of the export and import trade of the particular country must be considered. Experience has generally shown that retaliation creates animosities which lead to still higher protection, so that a balance of injury commonly results to the country using the weapon as well as to those retaliated upon.

It may be urged that, even though the wealth of the nation is diminished by protection, this loss may be off-set by political considerations, increased national security, or the like. Such arguments were at one time urged in favour of the Corn Laws and Navigation Acts in Britain, and each particular case can be treated only on its own merits. On general grounds it may be said, however, that, while a loss to the aggregate wealth does not alone suffice to condemn a policy, wealth is now a very important factor in national security.

LITERATURE.—The chief works of the so-called Classical School of economists and their immediate followers are: **Adam Smith**, *Wealth of Nations*, London, 1776 (last ed. by E. Cannan, 2 vols., London, 1904); **T. R. Malthus**, *On Population*, London, 1798, and later editions; **D. Ricardo**, *Principles of Polit. Econ. and Taxation*, London, 1817 (ed. E. C. K. Gonner, London, 1891); **J. R. MacCulloch**, *Principles of Polit. Econ.*, Edinburgh, 1825; **J. S. Mill**, *Principles of Polit. Econ.*, London, 1848 (ed. W. J. Ashley, London, 1910); **J. B. Say**, *Traité d'écon. polit.*, Paris, 1803. As representing the reaction of the Historical School, the following may be mentioned: **Cliffe Leslie**, *Essays in Political and Moral Philosophy*, Dublin, 1879; **A. Toynbee**, *The Industrial Revolution*, London, 1884; **G. Schmoller**, *Grundriss der allg. Volkswirtschaftslehre*, 2 vols., Leipzig, 1900–4.

The best works of the Austrian School are: **E. von Böhm-Bawerk**, *Capital and Interest* (tr. by W. Smart), London, 1890, and *Positive Theory of Capital* (tr. Smart), do. 1891; **F. von Wieser**, *Natural Value* (tr. C. A. Malloch), London, 1893. English writers who have emphasized the same doctrines are: **W. S. Jevons**, *Theory of Polit. Econ.*, London, 1871; **W. Smart**, *Introd. to the Theory of Value*, London, 1891; **P. H. Wicksteed**, *The Commonsense of Polit. Econ.*, London, 1910.

On the subject of logical method the best work is **J. N. Keynes**, *The Scope and Method of Polit. Econ.*, London, 1891.

On the history of economic theory the chief works are: **E. Cannan**, *Hist. of Theories of Production and Distribution*[2], London, 1903; **J. Bonar**, *Philosophy and Polit. Econ. in their Historical Relations*, London, 1893; **L. Cossa**, *Introd. to the Study of Polit. Econ.*, London, 1893; **J. K. Ingram**, *Hist. of Polit. Econ.*, London, 1907. The following are among the best recent treatises: **A. Marshall**, *Principles of Economics*, vol. i. (last ed. Lond. 1910); **H. Sidgwick**, *Principles of Polit. Econ.*, London, 1883; **A. W. Flux**, *Economic Principles*, London, 1904; **J. S. Nicholson**, *Principles of Polit. Econ.*, 3 vols., London, 1893–1901; **M. Pantaleoni**, *Pure Economics*, London, 1898; **H. R. Seager**, *Introd. to Economics*, New York, 1909; **E. R. A. Seligman**, *Principles of Economics*, New York, 1905; **J. B. Clark**, *Distribution of Wealth*, New York, 1899; **A. Wagner**, *Grundlegung der polit. Ökon.*, 3 vols., Leipzig, 1892–4; **G. Cohn**, *System der Nationalökonomie*, 3 vols., Stuttgart, 1885–98; **P. Leroy-Beaulieu**, *Traité théorique et pratique d'écon. politique*, 4 vols., Paris, 1896; **V. Pareto**, *Cours d'écon. polit.*, 2 vols., Lausanne, 1896–7.

The subjects of Free Trade and Protection are treated in most of the foregoing general works; the following deal specifically with the problem from various standpoints: **C. F. Bastable**, *Theory of International Trade*[3], London, 1900; **W. Smart**, *Return to Protection*, London, 1904; **P. Ashley**, *Modern Tariff History*, London, 1904; **W. J. Ashley**, *The Tariff Problem*, London, 1903; **F. W. Taussig**, *Tariff History of the United States*, New York, 1888; **J. A. Hobson**, *International Trade*, London, 1904.

On Poverty in its economic aspects, the *Reports of the English Poor Law Commission*, 1909, with their voluminous appendixes, are the amplest source of information. The special phases touched upon in this article are treated more fully in: **W. H. Beveridge**, *Unemployment*, London, 1909; **R. A. Bray**, *The Town Child*, London, 1907; **E. Cadbury**, *Women's Work and Wages* [in Birmingham], London, 1906; and the *Report on Home Work* (no. 246 of 1908), issued by a Committee of the House of Commons.

It is impossible to indicate here the vast literature on other parts of the field of Economics, such as Taxation, Monetary Problems, Trusts, Socialism, Trade Unions, Industrial History, etc. A good bibliography, entitled *What to Read on Social and Economic Subjects*, compiled by the Fabian Society and published by King, London, 1910, may be recommended for those desirous of guidance on particular topics. The two best Cyclopedias are: **R. H. I. Palgrave's** *Dict. of Polit. Econ.*, 3 vols., London, 1894–99, Appendix 1908; and **Conrad's** *Handwörterbuch der Staatswissenschaften*[2], 6 vols., Jena, 1898–1901.

Among the leading periodicals devoted exclusively to Economics, and in which much of the contemporary literature appears, may be mentioned *The Economic Journal*, London, quarterly from 1891; *The Quarterly Journal of Economics*, Boston, from 1886; *The Journal of Polit. Econ.*, Chicago, quarterly from 1892; *Journal des Économistes*, Paris, monthly since 1843; *Jahrbücher für Nationalökonomie*, Jena, monthly since 1863; *Revue Économique Internationale*, Brussels, monthly since 1904.

STANLEY H. TURNER.

ECSTASY.—1. Definition and forms.—'Ecstasy' (ἔκστασις) may be defined as an abnormal state of consciousness, in which the reaction of the mind to external stimuli is either inhibited or altered in character. In its more restricted sense, as used in mystical theology, it is almost equivalent to 'trance.' During ecstasy, the visionary is impervious to messages from without, and can even feel no pain. In the wider sense, all self-induced excitement may be called a kind of ecstasy.

Among human beings in every stage of culture there is a natural tendency to seek some means of exalting the consciousness above the ordinary level of daily experience. The satisfaction which is sought from this heightening of the consciousness may be of a sensuous, or of an intellectual, or of an æsthetic kind. It is generally, but not always, associated with religion, since the experience is most easily explained by supposing that the soul has been brought into communication with higher powers. The means used to induce this mental rapture are very various, and have all been discovered empirically. The *kava*-drinking of the Polynesians, the inhalation of tobacco-smoke by the North American Indians, the use of *hashish* (Indian hemp) by some two hundred millions of Asiatics and Africans, and the use or abuse of alcohol—the favourite medium of intoxication among the white races—and of opium by the Chinese, are all expedients for artificially altering the state of consciousness in such a way as to produce pleasurable sensations; and most of them are used to induce quasi-religious ecstasy. Very different methods of liberating the mind from the trammels of ordinary sensation are protracted fasts, flagellation, orgiastic dancing, whirling, or jumping, and self-hypnotization by the mechanical repetition of words, such as 'Om' by the Buddhists, 'Ḥasan Ḥusain' by Muhammadan Shīʿites, and the Paternoster or Ave Maria by Roman Catholics, or by gazing steadily at some bright object (see CRYSTAL-GAZING), or at some part of one's own body (the tip of the nose, by some Indian contemplatives; the navel, by the monks of Mount Athos). It is difficult to describe the generic type of ecstasy, especially in what may be called its lower forms, since its manifestations are determined partly by the nature of the means employed and partly by the mental state and character of the experimenter. The phenomena of drunkenness differ from those of opium intoxication; the dancing dervish works himself into a different state from the howling dervish; the dreams of the Persian mystic, inspired partly by wine and strongly tinged with sensuality, are very unlike the raptures and torments of the Roman Catholic *ecstatica*; and these again differ widely from the vision of the all-embracing and all-transcending unity which gave to the neo-Platonic philosopher the assurance that his quest of the Absolute had not been in vain. The *yogi* in ecstasy feels the blissful void of Nirvāna; the celibate ascetic experiences the indescribable mysteries of *les noces spirituelles*; Swedenborg saw heaven and hell opened to his view; the Roman Catholic fanatic sees heretics torn with hot pincers; the Platonist sees the forms of earthly beauty transfigured into their eternal and more lovely archetypes. In every case the dominant interest and aspirations of the inner life are heightened and intensified, and in every case the enhanced force of auto-suggestion seems to project itself outside the personality, and to acquire the mysterious strength and authority of an inspiration from without.

2. History.—The historical manifestations of ecstasy fill so large a place in the records of religious experience that only a few typical examples can be given. The ancient Greeks were no strangers to what Plato calls θεία μανία; but orgiastic religion was scarcely indigenous in Hellas, and was especially associated in the minds of the Greeks with the barbarous land of Thrace. The *Bacchæ* of Euripides is a magnificent study of the sinister aspects of religious ecstasy. Under the Roman Empire, Oriental cults of an ecstatic type were widely diffused; but by this time the population even of the European provinces was largely of Asiatic or African origin. Descriptions of religious frenzy are to be found in Lucretius, Catullus (the *Attis*), and Apuleius. The mystery-cults of the Empire were designed to induce both higher and lower forms of ecstatic feeling. Meanwhile a sober and deeply religious use of the mystical state was encouraged by the later Platonism. Ecstasy was for Plotinus the culminating point of religious experience, whereby the union with God and perfect knowledge of Divine truth, which are the conclusion and achievement of the dialectical process and the ultimate goal of the moral will, are realized also in direct, though ineffable, experience. Plotinus enjoyed this supreme initiation four times during the period when Porphyry was with him; Porphyry himself only once, he tells us, when he was in his 68th year. It was a vision of the Absolute, 'the One,' which, being above even intuitive thought, can only be apprehended passively by a sort of Divine illapse into the expectant soul. It is not properly a vision, for the seer no longer distinguishes himself from that which he sees; indeed, it is impossible to speak of them as two, for the spirit, during the ecstasy, has been completely one with the One. This 'flight of the alone to the Alone' is a rare and transient privilege, even for the greatest saint. He who enjoys it 'can only say that he has all his desire, and that he would not exchange his bliss for all the heaven of heavens' (*Enn.* vi. 7. 34, vi. 9 *passim*). From neo-Platonism this philosophic rapture passed into Christianity, though we seldom again find it in such a pure and elevated form. We trace the succession of metaphysical mystics from pseudo-Dionysius to Erigena, Eckhart, Boehme, and Swedenborg. Some modern poets have described an experience similar to that of Plotinus. Wordsworth, for instance, speaks of being led on

> 'Until, the breath of this corporeal frame
> And even the motion of our human blood
> Almost suspended, we are laid asleep
> In body, and become a living soul:
> While with an eye made quiet by the power
> Of harmony, and the deep power of joy,
> We see into the life of things'
> (*Lines composed above Tintern Abbey*).

Tennyson records:

> 'A kind of waking trance I have frequently had, quite up from boyhood, when I have been all alone. This has generally come upon me thro' repeating my own name two or three times to myself silently, till all at once, as it were out of the intensity of the consciousness of individuality, the individuality itself seemed to dissolve and fade away into boundless being, and this not a confused state, but the clearest of the clearest, the surest of the surest, the weirdest of the weirdest, utterly beyond words, where death was an almost laughable impossibility, the loss of personality (if so it were) seeming no extinction, but the only true life' (H. Tennyson, *Tennyson: A Memoir*, 1897, i. 320).

This experience is utilized by the poet in his 'Ancient Sage.' In his case, though not in Wordsworth's, acknowledged methods of self-hypnotism are recorded as inducing the trance. Boehme, too, prepared for his visions by gazing intently at some bright object. The mystics of the cloister often spent hours before a crucifix (so St. Francis of Assisi and Julian of Norwich) or an image of the Virgin, till they were half-hypnotized. When these artificial methods are resorted to, ecstasy is a much more frequent phenomenon than Plotinus would lead us to expect. So far from being the crown and goal of the contemplative journey, an experience hardly to be looked for in this life, it came to be regarded, by the directors of Roman Catholic piety, as an act of grace accorded by God as an encouragement to beginners. Aspirants after holiness are bidden not to be disquieted by the cessation of such favours, since this is the normal course of education in the inward life. It should be added that the best directors deprecate any great importance being attached to ecstasy as a sign of progress in holiness, and discountenance recourse to mechanical methods of inducing it.

There are two periods in the history of Christianity in which the mystical experience was unusually frequent and intense. These are the 14th and 17th centuries. In both cases the great ecstatics came soon after a great spiritual and intellectual awakening—in the earlier period the culmination of the scholastic theology and the revival of mental activity which accompanied it, and in the later the Renaissance and the Reformation. Unless at exceptional epochs like these, ecstasy seems to be more common in the lower levels of culture. We find it at present very common in Russia; while in Western Europe and America it appears from time to time as a phenomenon of 'revivals,' which spread chiefly among the semi-illiterate peasantry. Individual ecstatics are often men and women of high cultivation, though with unusual and partly abnormal psychical endowments. But, as a social phenomenon, ecstasy breaks out like an epidemic among normal people, chiefly belonging to the lower classes. The study of psychical epidemics is still in its infancy, and is a subject of great interest and importance. From this point of view, the individual is rather the patient than the creator of psychical storms, which sweep over whole populations. Ecstasy is communicated by direct contagion, just as panic invades whole crowds. Salient examples are the waves of religious excitement which produced the Crusades, in which millions of ignorant folk met with their death; the outbreaks of the dancing mania (St. Vitus' Dance), which in Central Europe followed the devastating pestilence called the Black Death; the *tarantula* epidemics in Italy in the 14th and 15th centuries, which were attributed to the bite of a spider, but were certainly due to psychical contagion; the 'convulsionists' in France at the beginning of the 18th century; the 'Jumpers' among the English Methodists; and the trances which were not uncommon during the recent Welsh revival.

In extreme cases, ecstasy produces complete insensibility. 'Schwester Katrei,' who is spoken of as a pupil of Eckhart, is said to have been carried out for burial when in a cataleptic trance. Anæsthesia of the skin is very common; the ecstatic feels nothing when pins are driven into his flesh. A poor girl in Germany persuaded her friends to crucify her, and expressed only pleasure when the nails were driven through her hands. Here there was no loss of consciousness, but only extreme spiritual exaltation, inhibiting the sensation of pain. It is almost certain that many of the martyrs endured their terrible tortures with but little suffering; and even so base a criminal as the assassin of William the Silent bore his cruel punishment with the same unnatural fortitude. In the account of the martyrdom of St. Perpetua we read that a catechumen named Rusticus, who suffered with her, asked when they were going to be gored by the wild cow of which they had heard, and could hardly be convinced, by the sight of his own wounds, that he had just undergone this ordeal.

The duration of ecstasy is extremely various. Half an hour is frequently mentioned by the Roman Catholic mystics; but St. Teresa on several occasions 'remained for the space of above six hours as if dead'; and of one of the 'Friends of God,' Ellina von Crevelsheim, we read that, after remaining dumb for seven years, absorbed in the thought of the Divine love, she fell into an ecstasy which lasted five days, during which she had a revelation of 'pure truth,' and was exalted to an immediate experience of the Absolute. She 'saw the interior of the Father's heart,' was 'bound with chains of love, enveloped in light, and filled with peace and joy' (Underhill, *Mysticism*, p. 441).

Although there is a natural tendency to ascribe these abnormal states to Divine influence, the experts in this strange science were constrained to admit the frequency of 'diabolical counterfeits,' and to caution the aspirant against the wiles of our ghostly enemy. It was observed that unwholesome ecstasy was generally the result of too impatient craving for supernatural favours, though it might assail even the truest saint, especially after too rigorous self-discipline. It was also a matter of common observation that self-induced trances were frequently followed by intense mental depression, and by that sense of abandonment by God which was called 'the dark night of the soul.' These reactions were, indeed, expected by all mystics, and were explained as the last death-pangs of the lower nature, before the final illumination. They were frequently merely the result of nervous exhaustion, caused by too intense concentration of the mind, ecstasy being (from the psychological point of view) an extreme variety of mono-ideism.

In conclusion, we must ask a question which to the religious mind is of the greatest importance. What is the value of ecstasy as a revelation of objective truth? Has it any of the transcendent value which has so long been claimed for it? Two opinions may be hazarded. First, the notion that the *emptiness* of the trance is a sign that the subject is in contact with absolute truth may probably be dismissed as an error, though it has the sanction of many great mystics. The doctrine implied may be stated in the words of Aquinas:

'The higher our mind is raised to the contemplation of spiritual things, the more it is abstracted from sensible things. But the final term at which contemplation can possibly arrive is the Divine substance. Therefore the mind that sees the Divine substance must be wholly divorced from the bodily senses, either by death or by some rapture' (*Summa contra Gentiles*, iii. 47).

The argument is that, since we can see only what we are, we cannot apprehend the Absolute without first being divested of all that belongs to particular individual existence. We must sink into the abyss of nothingness in order to behold that which is deeper than all determinations. The warning of Plotinus, 'to seek to rise above intelligence is to fall outside it,' is very pertinent here. And, secondly, the apparent *externality* of a revelation is no guarantee of its truth. The subliminal consciousness has no peculiar sacredness; it may be evil as well as good, and probably, as a rule, echoes racial memories of mixed value. Malaval, the author of *La Pratique de la vraye théologie mystique* (Paris, 1709, i. 89, quoted by Underhill, *op. cit.* p. 431), distinguishes true from false ecstasy as follows:

'The great doctors of the mystical life teach that there are two sorts of rapture which must be carefully distinguished. The first is produced in persons but little advanced in the way, who are still full of selfhood; either by the force of a heated imagination which vividly apprehends a sensible object, or by the artifice of the devil. . . . The other sort of rapture is, on the contrary, the effect of pure intellectual vision in those who have a great and generous love for God. To generous souls who have utterly renounced themselves God never fails in these raptures to communicate high things.'

A very typical statement of the mystical doctrine of ecstasy is the following from Ruysbroek, a writer who lived in the richest flowering-time of mysticism, the 14th cent., and who is perhaps the most characteristic of all the Roman Catholic mystics:

'When love has carried us above all things, above the light into the Divine darkness, we are transformed by the eternal Word who is the image of the Father; and, as the air is penetrated by the sun, we receive in peace the light incomprehensible, embracing and penetrating us. What is this light, if it be not a contemplation of the infinite and an intuition of eternity? We behold that which we are, and we are that which we behold, because our being, without losing anything of its own personality, is united with the Divine truth which includes all diversity' (*de Contemplatione*).

It is unnecessary to be sceptical about such testimony. Ecstasy can never be reproduced in description, because it could be described only by one who was at the same time inside and outside the mystical state; and this is impossible. But the fact of intuition into Divine truth, during states of spiritual exaltation, seems to the present writer incontrovertible, and the admission can cause no difficulty to a theist. We can, however, maintain that the saner forms of ecstasy, which are not propagated by contagion, and which contain a strong moral and intellectual as well as emotional element, are at once the rarest and the most trustworthy. The νοῦς ἐρῶν (Plotinus) sees healthier visions than the excited and half-morbid imagination of the cloistered devotee. Cf. also artt. ENTHUSIASTS (Religious), MYSTICISM, ṢŪFĪISM.

LITERATURE.—T. Achelis, *Die Ekstase*, Berlin, 1902; E. D. Starbuck, *Psychology of Religion*, London, 1899; F. Granger, *The Soul of a Christian*, London, 1900; T. Ribot, *Les Maladies de la mémoire*, Paris, 1881, and other works; E. Underhill, *Mysticism*, London, 1911; W. R. Inge, *Christian Mysticism* (*BL*, 1899); E. Récéjac, *Essai sur les fondements de la connaissance mystique*, Paris, 1897.

W. R. INGE.

EDDAS.—**1. The name.**—The meaning of 'Edda' is the subject of much dispute. According to the older view, the name is identical with *edda*, 'great-grandmother,' and was bestowed on account of the supposed high antiquity of the Eddic songs. But, this being considered somewhat far-fetched, modern scholars have proposed other explanations. Konrád Gíslason tried to show that the name is derived from *óðr*, 'song,' 'poem,' so that the proper meaning of 'Edda' would be 'Manual of Poetics,' assuming, as we shall see, very justly, that the name really was the title of the work of Snorri Sturluson. Eiríkr Magnússon has sought to connect the word with *Oddi*, the old seat of learning in Iceland, and the place where Snorri himself was educated. Both these explanations are, indeed, exposed to philological objections, but the former is the better and more natural. Originally Edda was only the title of the didactic work of Snorri, in one of the chief manuscripts of which we read: 'This book is called Edda; it was composed by Snorri Sturluson, and in this arrangement' (Cod. Upsaliensis). This manuscript was discovered by the famous bishop of Skálholt, Brynjólfr Sveinsson († 1675), who was also the possessor of the chief manuscript of the Eddic poems. The discovery of these manuscripts led to the theory, based upon the intimate relation of their contents, that the two books were closely connected, and the manuscript of poems was also called 'Edda,' without any sufficient reason. The manuscripts came to be spoken of as 'the Elder' and 'the Younger' Edda, the former of those appellations being given to the manuscript containing the ancient poems; this manuscript was also called *Sæmundar Edda*, as the songs were erroneously supposed to have been collected by the famous priest Sæmundr fróði († 1133). This last name has come into general use, but in our own times the poems are mostly called 'the Eddic poems'; and, as these are the chief source of Snorri's work, the appellation is not altogether incorrect.

2. The Edda of Snorri Sturluson.—This work was composed by the famous Icelandic historian and chieftain Snorri Sturluson (1178–1241), one of the most cultured and highly gifted men of his time. Besides his chief historical work, the *Heimskringla*, he left another, the *Edda*, a manual for young beginners in the art of poetry. In the poetry of all the old Teutonic peoples there had been developed a special poetic language, consisting of simple or composite words, which either had become obsolete in prose or never had belonged to the spoken language (cf. in A.S. such words as *béaggyfa*, 'a munificent prince,' *hringedstefna*, 'a ship,' etc.). In Norway and Iceland this peculiar poetic language, especially in the matter of the intricacies of the metrical art, attained its highest development, and was elaborated systematically at an early period. The composite appellations called *kenningar* were derived from many different sources, partly from everyday life, and partly from Nature; and a great many of them were founded on the old mythology and its legends. Thus gold was called 'Sif's hair' because the goddess Sif, according to a myth, had her hair made of gold. Another appellation of gold was 'the bed of Fáfnir' (the serpent), on account of the legend of the serpent Fáfnir and his bed of gold. In order to form and use these *kenningar*, a certain amount of knowledge was indispensable; we also meet with certain cases indicating that the younger scalds learned from their older colleagues the mysteries of their art. Snorri, himself a poet, felt called on to write a manual of the art of poetry, his *Edda*. That work consists of three parts.[1] The middle part is called *Skáldskaparmál* ('the Language of Poetry'), and gives general rules for poetic denominations of living beings and dead things. First there are the composite denominations of Odin and poetry, gods and goddesses; and the appellations of heaven, earth, sea, sun, wind, fire, winter, summer, man, gold, battle, weapons, ships, God (of the Christians), kings. Then follows a list of the simple and uncomposite names in a similar order, all accompanied by scaldic verses, serving as examples. Lastly, there is a third list of appellations (synonyms from everyday language). Two manuscripts add some lists of names (in verse), but they are interpolations and did not originally belong to Snorri's work. The author sometimes inserts longer stories to explain the origin of some of these names; but, as already mentioned, the old myths were the basis of the whole, and so Snorri found it convenient to write as an introduction to the work a complete survey of the old mythology, based on the best sources—the ancient poems relating to the gods (the 'Eddic poems'), and various living traditions. In those times this was a bold thing to do, but he succeeded in giving such a view of the whole subject that his work could hardly have been done better, considering the circumstances. He proceeds systematically, beginning with the cosmogony, and its accessaries; then follows a description of the oldest times of the gods, the golden age, and the Ash of Yggdrasil (the world-tree). This is followed by an account of the gods and goddesses, their place of abode, Valhalla, and everything connected with it; he then relates more fully two myths of Thor's exploits, and proceeds with the story of the death of Balder, the imprisonment of Loki, the wonderful things foreboding the approach of Ragnarök; and, finally, he gives a wonderful description of that last fight of the gods and the regeneration of the world. All these things are presented in a dialogue between a Swedish king, Gylfi, and the trinity of Odin. The name *Gylfaginning* ('the Delusion of Gylfi') alludes to this, as Gylfi does not know with whom he is speaking.

Snorri's sources were principally the three important Eddic poems, *Völuspá*, *Vafþrúðnismál*, and *Grímnismál*, and a few of the other poems; he chiefly used the *Völuspá*, from which he probably got the idea of the arrangement of the whole. He often quotes verses from these poems, but not so frequently as he might have done. Snorri treats the myths critically, sometimes in a somewhat arbitrary fashion, and he has not escaped the influence of Christian ideas, especially at the beginning. His greatest fault is that the punishments, which in the *Völuspá* come before Ragnarök, are placed by him after that event—a total misconception. Another source was the oral tradition, so strong and vigorous in Iceland. The style is magnificent, everywhere adapted to the varying contents—earnest and solemn, or playful and jocose, always full of life. The author reveals himself as the great master of Icelandic prose.

Between the first and the second part—as an introduction to the latter—there is a very interesting chapter on the origin of the 'drink of the poets,' and how Odin became the owner of it. Thus Odin, alone of all gods and men, was the owner and giver of the poetic faculty, and *he* was said to give 'the drink of the poets' to his favourites.

The third chief part of the Edda is Snorri's own poem, the *Háttatal*, consisting of 102 strophes in praise of Hákon the Old, king of Norway († 1263), and Earl Skúli. The peculiarity of this poem is that it is written in various kinds of metre, arranged systematically; Snorri has, however, missed the true historical development of Icelandic metrics; he begins with the 'most perfect' kind of metre (*dróttkvæðr háttr*), which in reality is the youngest, and places at the end the oldest kinds of metre, those used in the Eddic poems, and some other metres closely related to them. Of course, Snorri everywhere uses the scaldic phraseology. The reason why he placed his own poem at the end of his work was that he desired to show how his theories looked when carried out in practice. The poem exhibits the technical finish of Snorri, and his complete mastery of the language and the difficult metres.

This poem gives us a hint regarding the time of the composition of the work, but only a *terminus ad quem*. It cannot have been composed earlier than the winter of 1222–23, and certainly not very much later. Snorri had lived between 1218 and 1220 at the courts of the princes he praised. The poem is a thanksgiving for the honours bestowed on him. It is most probable that the two earlier parts of the work were written, partly at least, before 1218, although the whole may have been written in the years 1221–23.

The *Edda* of Snorri is one of the principal works of Icelandic literature, admirable both in form and in contents, and quite unique in the latter regard. Of course, it does not give us a perfectly accurate picture of the old heathendom which had then been practically extinct for 200 years; but, on the other hand, it is certain that it always must remain one of our principal sources of information regarding that faith, as the old traditions were preserved in Iceland with a singular tenacity and faithfulness, owing to the remoteness of that country and its very limited intercourse with the outside world.

In one MS (A. M. 242) there are added four grammatical treatises, of which the second is found also in the Upsala MS, and the third also in two fragments. Their contents are linguistic, rhetorical, and didactic, but they have nothing to do with Snorri or his *Edda*. The first of these treatises is on the phonetical system of the Icelandic language in the 12th cent., and is of extreme value. The third treatise is written by Snorri's nephew, Óláfr þórðarson.

[1] The form varies in the chief MSS—Codex Regius 2367, 4° in the Old Royal Collection in the Royal Library, Copenhagen; Codex Arnamagnæanus 242, fol., in the University Library, Copenhagen; and Codex Upsaliensis, Delagardie 11, in the University Library, Upsala—and partly in some other MSS.

LITERATURE.—(1) *EDITIONS*: The great Arnamagnæan ed., 3 vols., Copenhagen, 1848–87, with Latin tr.; special ed. of Cod. Upsaliensis and other fragments (in vol. ii.), and an ed. of the so-called *Skáldatal* with the biographies of the poets and a survey of their poems; critical ed. of the text by Finnur

Jónsson, Copenhagen, 1900, and Reykjavik, 1907.—(2) *TRANSLATIONS*: Danish: *Gylfaginning*, by F. Jónsson, Copenhagen, 1902; German, by H. Gering, Leipzig and Vienna, 1892; English, by G. W. Dasent, Stockholm, 1842.—(3) *CRITICAL TREATISES*: E. Mogk, 'Untersuchungen über die Gylfaginning, i.–ii.,' in Paul-Braune, *Beiträge*, vi.–vii. [Halle, 1879–80]; see also K. Müllenhoff, *Deutsche Altertumskunde*, v. [Berlin, 1883]; E. Wilken, *Untersuchungen zur Snorra Edda*, Paderborn, 1878; F. Jónsson, 'Edda Snorra Sturlusonar,' in *Aarböger for nordisk Oldkyndighed og Historie*, Copenhagen, 1898: K. Gíslason, in *Aarböger*, 1884; Eiríkr Magnússon, 'Edda,' in *Sagabook of the Viking Club*, London, 1896.

3. The Eddic poems (the 'Elder Edda,' 'Sæmundar Edda').—These famous poems are for the most part found in a single MS, 2365, 4°, in the Old Royal Collection in the Royal Library in Copenhagen (Codex Regius). The MS consists of 45 leaves, but a whole sheet (8 leaves) is wanting, thereby causing a deplorable lacuna. The MS dates from about 1270, and it was discovered shortly before the middle of the 17th century. It is a very fine one; a phototype edition, with the text printed on opposite pages, was published by L. Wimmer and F. Jónsson in 1891. The first known owner of the MS, Bishop Brynjólfr Sveinsson, presented it to the king of Denmark. We have now only six leaves of another MS, A. M. 748, 4° (Univ. Libr. Copenh.), containing some of the same poems as Codex Regius, with one addition, but partly defective.

The contents of Cod. Regius may be divided into two groups: (1) mythical and (2) heroic poems, arranged in a certain, but imperfect, chronological order, which could more easily be applied to the last group of the legendary poems, as the persons described there are all genealogically connected. In the mythical group this was generally impossible, except in one case. Here the interest of the poems centres in the two principal gods, Odin and Thor. One heroic poem, the *Volundarkviða*, has been incorrectly inserted in this group. In each group there may be observed a tendency to subdivisions, beginning with certain important poems of a more general character. The collector has in many places, especially in the last group of poems, given explanatory and connecting prose pieces. The MS is a copy, not the original collection, which must have been compiled in the end of the 12th century. The MS A. M. 748 is another copy of the original collection, with some additions. A third collection (or copy) was in the possession of Snorri.

The collection begins with the *Völuspá*, a grand poem, a kind of world drama having for its subject the mythical life of gods and men from the beginning of the world to Ragnarök; the death of Balder is the central event. The dominating thought of the author is that all evil deeds breed fighting and death. The poem is written throughout in a tone of stern morality. It was composed about the middle of the 10th century. The next in order is the *Hávamál* ('The Song of the High One'), a collection of several fragments of poems, all of a more or less ethical and moral character. The first poem is the principal one; in it Odin gives counsels to the human race, as to what is best for man, and how to behave in the different conditions of life, ending with pointing out that after death a good name is the best. Another poem contains the magical songs of Odin; and a third has counsels to a young man, of a similar character to the first. Then follow some poems, which are pre-eminently Odin lays: *Vafþrúðnismál* ('Lay of Vafthrúdhnir'), describing a trial of intellectual strength between Odin and a giant; the giant is defeated, and loses his life; in *Grímnismál* ('Lay of Grímnir'), Odin reveals his terrible character to a blind and hard-hearted mortal king, his own foster son; in *Hárbarðsljóð* ('Lay of Hárbardh'), Thor quarrels with the disguised Odin, whom he does not know—a struggle between wisdom and mere strength, where wisdom prevails. Thor is the special hero of *Þrymskviða* ('Song of Thrym'), which tells of how he lost his hammer and recovered it. *Hymiskviða* ('Song of Hymir') tells how Thor got a brewing cauldron large enough for the gods, and records other instances of his trials of strength; *Alvísmál* ('Lay of All-wise') is the story of a word-duel between Thor and a dwarf. The beautiful poem *Skírnismál* ('Song of Skírnir') describes Freyr's vehement love for the giant maiden Gerðr; while in the *Lokasenna* ('Scolding of Loki'), Loki, the enemy of the gods, scolds all the gods and goddesses, but is obliged to fly before Thor and his hammer. In *Baldrs draumar* ('Dreams of Balder' [found only in A. M. 748]), the dreams of Balder are related, and the ride of Odin to the under world to consult a dead sibyl.

To these lays of the gods there are generally added some poems found in other MSS: *Hyndluljóð* ('Song of Hyndla') (from the Flatey Codex), relating how Freyja procures information from a giantess regarding the family of her favourite, Óttar. Here is found inserted a fragment of a mythical poem, *Völuspá in skamma* ('The Short *Völuspá*'). *Rígsþula* ('Song of Rígr' [found in A. M. 242]) is a philosophical poem on the origin of the different social orders of men, and the supposed development of social life. The poem, which ends by mentioning kingship, was possibly composed in honour of Harald Fairhair. *Grógaldr* ('Magical Song of Gróa') and *Fjölsvinnsmál* ('Song of Fjölsvinnr') go together and treat of a young man, Svipdagr (probably a mythical person), who gets good advice from his dead mother Gróa, and then starts on a dangerous journey in pursuit of his ladylove Menglöð.

To the second group of Eddic poems, the heroic lays, belongs first of all the important poem, mentioned above, *Völundarkviða* ('Lay of Wayland'), describing the smith Völund, his imprisonment by king Níðuð, and his revenge on the king and his family. Then there follows a group of *Helgakviður* ('Helgi Lays'), two poems about Helgi Hundingsbani, and one treating of Helgi Hjörvarðsson, two different heroes, chiefly describing their revenging their fathers, their martial deeds, and specially their love affairs with the Valkyries (Sváfa, Sigrún). Next comes the long cycle of poems about the Völsung family, especially Sigurðr Fáfnisbani—a kind of verified historical narrative; *Grípisspá* ('Prophecy of Grípir'), a comparatively young poem, giving a view of Sigurd's life in the form of a prophecy; *Reginsmál* ('Lay of Regin'), fragments of two poems—on the first great deed of Sigurd; *Fáfnismál* ('Lay of Fáfnir'), on the slaying of the serpent Fáfnir; *Sigrdrífumál* ('Lay of Sigrdrífa'), on Sigurd's meeting with the Valkyrie Sigrdríf, and the good counsels which she gives him. Here comes the lacuna mentioned above; there must be at least two long poems wanting (cf. the *Völsungasaga*). The text begins again with a poem relating the murder of Sigurd; he had been married to Guðrún, daughter of king Gjúki, and had been brought (by magical means) to forget the Valkyrie Sigrdríf (Brynhildr), a sister of Atli Buðlason (Attila), who had been treacherously married to Gunnar Gjúkason. In a following poem the characters of these two ladies, the principal female actors of the story, are contrasted psychologically. *Sigurðarkviða in skamma* ('Short Lay of Sigurd') relates briefly the death of Sigurd; then follows a long monologue by Brynhild, who kills herself; and in *Helreið* ('Brynhild's Ride to Hel') she goes to Hel and defends her deeds against the censure of a giantess. In the *second and third Guðrúnarkviða* ('Songs of Guðrún') Guðrún surveys her own tragical fate; she is now married to king Atli; and the poem closes with dark dreams of their future relations; in the last poem Guðrún, by a kind of ordeal, proves her conjugal fidelity to Atli. There follows a poem with an entirely new heroine, *Oddrúnargrátr* ('Lament of Oddrún'). Oddrún, Atli's sister, has loved Gunnar, but a union between them has never been brought about;

she gives a survey of her tragical story. The next two parallel poems, *Atlakviða* and *Atlamál* ('Songs of Atli' [the latter called the Greenlandic, because composed in the Icelandic colony in Greenland]), describe, each in a slightly different way from the other, the relations between Atli and Guðrún and her brothers: the brothers are killed at Atli's command, and Guðrún in revenge causes his death. Now, one would think the tragedy would be at an end, but the last act remains. Guðrún contracts a third marriage with Jónakr, and bears to him three sons, Sörli, Hamðir, and Erpr. Her daughter by Sigurd, Svanhildr, has been given in marriage to King Jörmunrekr, who has accused her of infidelity, and at his command she is trampled to death by horses; she is revenged by her brothers, who also are killed. Such are the contents of the two last poems in Cod. Reg., *Guðrúnarhvöt* ('The Urgings of Guðrún') and *Hamðismál* ('Lay of Hamðir'). *Gróttasöngr* ('Song of the Grótti') must also be reckoned with the heroic lays; it is found in a MS of Snorri's *Edda*, and treats of the giant maidens grinding gold, peace, and, at last, death to Fróði, king of Denmark.

The legends of the heroic poems were originally, for the most part, German importations into Scandinavia, where they have been transformed and imbued with the true Northern spirit, and combined with each other without regard to original times or places. They are of primary importance for German and Teutonic legendary history. The persons are idealized; they are typical heroes and heroines, a quintessence of the people of the Viking age. Some of the minor characters are, however, drawn from common life. The descriptions of persons and events are exceedingly clear and racy and strictly logical, and the language is correspondingly so. The sentences are short and pithy, everything superfluous is banished; still, the poems differ in this, that some are more wordy than others; difference in age may be inferred from this.

The *age* of the poems is, on the whole, the period from A.D. 900 to 1050. This may now be regarded as beyond all doubt. But within the limits of this period there may be discerned older and younger groups of poems, when we consider the more or less elaborate descriptions, stories, the persons mentioned, etc. Thus *Þrymskviða*, *Völundarkviða*, and *Rigsþula* are among the oldest; *Sigurðarkviða in skamma*, *Atlamál*, and *Oddrúnargrátr* among the youngest. Only a few are very young, from the 12th cent. (*Grípisspá*, *Völuspá in skamma*), and belong to a late renaissance of Icelandic poetry.

The *home* of the poems has been the subject of much dispute. Some maintain that they are all Icelandic, others think they are all Norwegian, or composed in the Norwegian colonies in the British Islands. One poem can definitely be proved to be Greenlandic (*Atlamál*). The truth is that everything of value for deciding the question of the home of the poems points decidedly to Norway, Norwegian life, Norwegian culture, and Norwegian nature. The poems must, therefore, be Norwegian for the most part. We have no certain way of deciding what is Norwegian and what possibly may be Icelandic. It is not right to consider poems as Icelandic merely because they lack outward signs pointing to a Norwegian origin; all these poems are on the same level; there is, on the whole, the same way of considering life, and the same manner of thinking; one might say they are all of the same school in spite of their different age.

The metres of the poems are chiefly the three oldest: *fornyrðislag*, verses of four syllables, in the epic poems; *ljóðaháttr*, strophes of six verses of different length, in the moral and didactic poems; *málaháttr*, verses of five syllables, in epic poems. One poem, *Hárbarðsljóð*, is very irregular in its metre. All the poems are strophical, each strophe as a rule consisting of eight verses—six in *ljóðaháttr*; when strophes of more or less than eight verses are found, this is probably due to corruptions of the text. The tradition was only oral for perhaps more than 200 years, and, of course, as might be expected, rather bad. Strophes or verses are often lacking, or words are so corrupted that it is very difficult, sometimes impossible, to emend them critically, metrically, or linguistically. Some verses are in the tradition given in duplicate form, and the collectors have written down both without choosing between them.

The poems are all anonymous, probably because the authors considered themselves only as re-narrators of known subjects. It may, however, be considered as certain that they gave the poems certain individual colours, and moulded the characters with their psychological peculiarities. How far they invented new persons or events has not been decided conclusively. On the other hand, it is certain that they were very independent in their combinations of the old legends.

LITERATURE.—(1) *EDITIONS*: S. Bugge, *Norræn fornkvæði*, Christiania, 1867 (of fundamental value); phototype ed. of the Cod. Reg., with the abbreviation in italics, by L. Wimmer and F. Jónsson (Copenhagen, 1891), of A. M. 748 by F. Jónsson (Copenhagen, 1896); ed. of the text by K. Hildebrand (Paderborn, 1873 and 1904), with a dictionary by H. Gering (3rd ed., Halle, 1907); editions with commentary by H. Lüning (Stuttgart, 1859), R. Heinzel and F. Detter (Leipzig, 1903), and, above all, B. Sijmons (Halle, 1888–1906, vol. i., text with variants; vol. iii., a complete dictionary by Gering; vol. ii., commentaries, has not yet been edited; vol. i. contains a long and excellently written introduction, treating critically the MSS, the age and home of the poems, etc.). (2) *TRANSLATIONS*: Danish, by O. Hansen (Copenhagen, 1911); Dano-Norwegian, by G. Gjessing (Christiania, 1899); Swedish, by P. A. Gödecke (Stockholm, 1881); German, by H. Gering (Leipzig, 1892); English, by B. Thorpe (London, 1865); an ed. with an Eng. tr. is also found in G. Vigfusson's *Corpus poeticum boreale*, Oxford, 1883 (tr. in prose, bad text). Besides the dictionary by Gering, already mentioned, Sveinbjörn Egilsson's *Lexicon antiquæ linguæ septentrionalis* (Copenhagen, 1860) deserves to be noted. (3) Of other works useful to the student may be mentioned: E. Jessen, 'Über die Eddalieder, Heimat, Alter, Character,' in *Ztschr. f. deutsche Philologie*, iii. (Halle, 1871, of fundamental value); K. Müllenhoff, *Deutsche Altertumskunde*, v. (with an analysis of several of the mythical poems and a critical survey of the heroic lays); F. Jónsson, *Den norske og islandske litteraturs historie*, i. (Copenhagen, 1897), and polemics between him and B. M. Olsen, in *Tímarit hins íslenzka Bókmentafjelags*, xv.–xvi. (Reykjavík, 1894–95); E. Mogk, 'Norwegisch-isländische Litteratur,' in Paul's *Grundriss*, ii.[2] (1902); E. H. Meyer, *German. Mythol.* (Berlin, 1891), pp. 36–45, 51–53; Chantepie de la Saussaye, *Religion of the Teutons* (Boston, 1902), p. 194 ff.; A. Heusler, *Die Lieder der Lücke in Cod. reg.* (Strassburg, 1902), also 'Heimat und Alter der eddischen Gedichte' (*Archiv f. neuer. Sprachen*, xvi. [Brunswick, 1905]); S. Bugge, *Home of the Eddic Poems* (London, 1899): G. Neckel, *Beiträge zur Eddaforschung* (Dortmund, 1908). On syntax: Wisén, *Ordfogningen i den äldre Eddan* (Lund, 1865); M. Nygaard, *Eddasprogets syntax*, i.–ii. (Bergen, 1865–67). On metrics: E. Sievers, 'Beiträge zur Skaldenmetrik,' ii. (in *Beiträge*, vi. [Halle, 1879]), and *Altgermanische Metrik* (Halle, 1893). Regarding the great number of treatises on special subjects the reader may be referred to Sijmons' edition.

F. JÓNSSON.

EDOMITES.—1. Introductory.—'Edom' is the name of a people frequently mentioned in the OT, and generally located to the south of the Dead Sea. They are regarded as a 'brother' of Israel, and this relationship is vividly expressed in the popular stories in Gn 25, 27, 32 f., which represent Esau—*i.e.* Edom—as the elder twin-brother of Jacob, who is otherwise known as 'Israel.' Apart from the direct and indirect evidence for Edomite culture and religion, there is good reason to believe that the Edomites and allied peoples of the area lying outside Israelite territory, and especially in N.W. Arabia, played a somewhat prominent part in Israelite religion and history. This has often been emphasized since the earlier observations of Wellhausen, Kuenen, Stade, and Robertson Smith; and in recent years has come more to the front in Biblical research. In discussions of the origin of the Israelite Jahweh, the tribes of Israel, the rise of the kingdom of Judah, the locale of the patriarchal stories, the extension of the term 'Egypt' (Heb. *Miṣrayim*, Assyr. *Muṣri*) outside the limits of Egypt—in these and other questions the Edomite area, its population and history, and its relations with Israel invariably enter into the field of inquiry; and it is therefore necessary to premise that a treatment of the *religion* of the Edomites unavoidably raises certain problems of the OT which cannot be discussed in these pages.

The Edomites are otherwise known as 'Esau,' or 'sons of Esau,' after their reputed 'father'; and as 'sons of Seir,' after the district of Mt. Seir. Their land may be described as the district between the Dead Sea and the Gulf of ʻAḳabah, bordered by Moab, Judah, S. Palestine, the Sinaitic peninsula, N. Arabia, and the Syrian desert; the more precise boundaries varied from time to time according to the larger political circumstances affecting the surrounding States or confederations. Thus, for purely geographical reasons, it was entirely exposed to the political, social, and religious movements in Western Asia; and its vicissitudes cannot be understood apart from the history and thought of the old Oriental world. An important fact is the very close relationship which, as the Horite and Edomite genealogies in Gn 36 represent, was felt to subsist between the Edomites and their neighbours; Edom, Midian, and Ishmael are intimately connected, and names of Edomite origin or affinity can even be traced in the Israelite tribes of Judah, Dan, and Benjamin. It has long been recognized that the tribe of Judah as constituted in 1 Ch 2 and 4 was 'half Arab,' and of its two main divisions—Caleb and Jerahmeel—the former is explicitly connected with the Edomite Kenaz (Gn 36^{11}, Jg 1^{13}, 1 Ch 4^{13}), while Edomite or 'Horite' elements are somewhat strong in the latter (see Meyer and Luther, *Die Israeliten u. ihre Nachbarstämme*, Halle, 1906, p. 406). The whole body of evidence, when carefully studied, is such as to suggest that a closely inter-related group (which may be called Horite, Seirite, or Edomite-Ishmaelite) extended westwards into S. Palestine, and that some portion separated and was ultimately incorporated in Judah, thus becoming truly Israelite (see *ib.* p. 446). This relationship, to which the genealogies testify, is to be supplemented by numerous features of 'Edomitic' influence in the OT, the full significance of which can as yet be only imperfectly understood.

2. The gods.—Although there is little direct evidence for Edomite culture and religion, there is much that is indirectly valuable, and, even though it is often of a somewhat hypothetical character, it cannot properly be ignored.

(*a*) *Edom* itself may be the name of a deity. This is suggested partly by the name of the Gittite *Obed-Edom* in the OT (2 S $6^{10ff.}$, 1 Ch $15^{18.\,24}$, 2 Ch 25^{24}, *et al.*), who becomes prominent as a Levitical singer and doorkeeper. The interpretation 'servant of [the god] Edom' is not to be rejected, although it is open to dispute whether the deity in question is necessarily identical with the familiar Edom. Further, Egyptian evidence for a place-name *Shemesh-Edom* in the Lebanon district (time of Thothmes III. and Amen-hotep II.) seems to equate Edom with the sun-god; and the deity reappears in an obscure Egyp. passage, together with Resheph, the warrior-god of fire and lightning (W. M. Müller, *Asien u. Europa nach altägypt. Denkmälern*, Leipzig, 1893, p. 315 f.). This would suggest a deity of the Hadad-type, fairly well distributed, who became the god of a group or people which called itself by his name.[1]

(*b*) *Esau.*—This obscure name, perhaps found in an old Arabian inscription (Hommel, *Südarab. Chrestomathie*, Munich, 1893, p. 39 f.), has been plausibly connected with that of the goddess ʻA-si-ti, represented on Egyp. monuments as a wild, warlike rider of the desert (Müller, 316 f.). The Biblical story of Esau, the wild hunter, is commonly associated with the Phœnician myth of Usōos and his brother Samēmrum or Ὑψουράνιος ('high heaven').[1] The strife between the more civilized brother and the hunter Usōos naturally recalls the account of the twin-brothers Jacob and Esau, and the various points of resemblance between the late euhemeristic Greek record and the older, simpler, and more primitive story in Gen. are sufficiently close to suggest some common Canaanite cycle of tradition. In its present form, the story of Esau and Jacob clearly shows the influence of other elements, and Gressmann has drawn attention to features in Esau which are suggestive of some satyr-like figure (*ZATW*, 1900, p. 22, n. 3); a considerable modification of the original tradition must in any case be recognized. There is other evidence for some survival of old Canaanite myth in the Cainite genealogy (see J. Skinner, *Gen.*, 1910, p. 123 f.); and consequently, both here and again in the stories which the Danites told of their hero Samson, the present forms are the outcome of a very intricate development. Hence, although the above evidence may be used to prove that primarily Esau was not a distinctively Edomite figure, it is clear, nevertheless, that the Biblical story in its present form belongs to a time when Esau stood for some section (at least) of Edom, and that this fact alone explains its preservation in the Biblical history.

(*c*) The Edomite king *Ai*(AN-AA)-*rammu* ('Ai is high'), mentioned by Sennacherib, has a name compounded with a deity who may possibly be identified with Jahweh (cf. in this case the Biblical name *Jehoram*). But the equation is very uncertain (Zimmern, *KAT*^{3}, 1903, p. 467), although on other grounds the appearance of Jahweh in Edom might be expected.

(*d*) More specifically Edomite is the god *Ḳaush*, in the names of two Edomite kings: *Ḳ.-malaka* ('Ḳ. is king *or* reigns'), in the time of Tiglath-Pileser IV. (after the middle of the 8th cent. B.C.), and *Ḳ.-gabri* ('Ḳ. is mighty *or* a hero' [cf. the name *Gabriel*]), in the 7th century. Nothing is known of the god. The name may be identified with the common Arab. *ḳais*, 'lord, 'husband' (cf. the appellative *baʻal*).[2] It is conjecturally connected with the Biblical *Ḳīsh* (Benjamite and Levitical), with the place-names *Ḳishion* and *Ḳishon*,[3] and with *El-ḳōsh*, the home of Nahum (according to one old tradition, in Judah). More interesting are the Levitical *Ḳishi* or *Ḳushaiah*, if the latter may be interpreted 'Jah[weh] is K.' on the analogy of *Bealiah*, 'Jah[weh] is Baal'; but this interpretation is not certain. In the form קיש (with vocalic endings) it occurs in Nabatæan names, and also as a deity (together with other gods) at el-Ḥejra (in N. Arabia, south of Tēma). It is doubtless the *Kus* in Assyr. contract-tablets of the reigns of Darius I. and Artaxerxes I., where we meet with *K.-yadaʻ* ('K. knows'), *K.-yaḥabi* ('K. gives'), and *bar-K.* ('son of [an Aram. form] K.'). With the last it is natural to compare *Barḳōs*, one of the temple Nethīnīm (Ezr 2^{53}, Neh 7^{55}), whose names often betray a foreign origin.[4] These forms can scarcely be severed from *Kos*, met with in Greek sources, especially among a family of Sidonian origin settled in the Idumæan Marissa or Mareshah (close of 3rd cent. B.C.); and in a rather later inscription from Memphis, remarkable for the variety of foreign names and the prominence of Kos.[5] The names comprise Κοσμάλαχος, Κοστόβαρος (Jos. *Ant.* XV. vii. 9, XX. ix. 4, probably for Κοσγόβαρος); cf. the two Edomite compounds of Ḳaush (above); Κοσάδαρος ('K. helps,' an Aram. form) and Κοσνάτανος ('K. gives,' explicitly *not* Aram.), both also in Nabatæan and Sinaitic inscriptions (spelt קס and קוס); Κόσβανος ('K. builds'), Κασβάρακος ('K. blesses' [*CIG* 5149]), Κόσραμος ('K. is high'), Κόσγηρος (? 'K. a sojourner'), and perhaps Κόσαδος (doubtful [Peters and Thiersch, *op. cit.* p. 46 f.]).

---

1 See Meyer, *Gesch. d. Altertums*^{2}, Stuttgart, 1909, i. § 343. Edom appears elsewhere as a place-name, and as a personal name is found in Phœnician and the Ṣafa inscriptions (cf. perhaps also Lidzbarski, *Ephemeris f. semit. Epigraphik*, Giessen, 1901, i. 41 f.).

1 Philo Byb., in Euseb. *Præp. Ev.* i. 10; see esp. Lagrange, *Études sur les relig. sém.*^{2}, Paris, 1905, p. 415 f.

2 W. R. Smith, *Rel. Sem.*^{2}, London, 1894, p. 170, n. 4, and J. Wellhausen, *Reste arab. Heid.*^{2}, Berlin, 1897, p. 67.

3 See R. J. H. Gottheil, *JBL* xvii. [1898] 199–202.

4 See Zimmern, *op. cit.* 473.

5 For the former, see J. P. Peters and H. Thiersch, *Painted Tombs in the Necropolis of Marissa*, 1905; and for the latter, E. Miller, *Rev. archéol.*, 1870, pp. 109–125, 170–183; and cf. Lidzbarski, *Ephem.* ii. [1903] 339.

(*e*) Quite distinct, on the other hand, is the Idumæan *Kozeh*, to whose hereditary priesthood the ancestors of the patriot Costobaros (see above) belonged (Jos. *Ant.* xv. vii. 9, Κοζέ; ed. Niese, Κωζαί). The god is identified with the Arab *Ḳozaḥ*, who was venerated in the vicinity of Mecca; and, since the rainbow is called the 'bow of K.' (cf. Jahweh's words 'my bow,' Gn 9^{13}), he was apparently the head-deity of the district. It is tempting to suppose that *Kozeh* was the Idumæan Apollo of Jos. *c. Ap.* ii. 10 (see W. R. Smith, *Kinship* 2, 1903, p. 302).

(*f*) Some indirect evidence is furnished by the Edomite proper names in the OT, where the common Ḳaush or Ḳos is conspicuously absent. On the other hand, *Hadad* occurs thrice as the name of a king; and this at least points to a knowledge of the well-known god of storm, rain, etc.

(*g*) *Bĕdad*, the father of Hadad I. (Gn 36^{35}), may represent *Bir-dadda* (also the father of the Arab. Uaite, 7th cent.), in which case Hadad is again involved (see Zimmern, *op. cit.* 443 f.).

(*h*) Acquaintance with *Baal* appears in the king *Baal-ḥanan* ('B. is gracious' [Gn 36^{38}]), as also in the inscription from Memphis (φασάβαλος, 'B. has opened *or* saved'?) and in a Nabatæan inscription from Petra. This throws no light upon the particular deity intended by the appellative 'lord,' although there is some evidence that the Baal of Western Asia was a god of battle of the Hadad-type.[1]

(*i*) Equally vague is *El*, 'god,' in the names *Eliphaz* and *Reuel*, and later at Memphis (where, however, others than Idumæans may be meant).

(*j*) *Uz* (עוּץ), connected with Edom (Gn 36^{28}, La 4^{21}), may be conjecturally identified with the Arab. god *'Auḍ* (see W. R. Smith, *Kinship*2, 61, and his defence, against the criticisms of Nöldeke, in *Rel. Sem.*2, 43 n.).

(*k*) *Jeush* (יְעוּשׁ), identified by W. R. Smith with the Arab. lion-god *Yaghūth* ('he protects'), is found also in Nabatæan and Tamud inscriptions, and is doubtless represented by ἰέγουθος at Memphis.[2] Purely conjectural is the identification with Iauta', a king of Kedar in the 7th century. See, further, W. R. Smith, *Kinship* 2, 224 f.; Wellhausen, *Reste arab. Heid.*2 17–19; Nöldeke, *ZDMG* xviii. 869.[3]

3. Miscellaneous evidence for Edomite religion.—Evidence of another sort is furnished by those Edomite (and allied) names which may be interpreted, with more or less probability, as animal-names.[4] Here are to be included *'Achbōr* ('mouse), *Ărān* (perhaps 'wild-goat'), *Ayyah* ('falcon'), *Cālēb* ('dog'), *Dishān*, *Dishōn*, and *Ja'lām* ('mountain-goat'), *Shōbāl* ('young lion,' though phonetically difficult), *Zibeōn* ('hyæna'), and others. The animal-names found in the OT are connected especially with people (or clans) and places with Judæan, S. Palestinian, and Edomitic connexions (note, *e.g.*, the Midianite *'Ōrēb* and *Zĕēb*, 'raven' and 'wolf'). It is disputed whether they point to the former existence of totemism (so W. R. Smith), or whether they may be explained merely as 'natural poetry' (Nöldeke; see Gray's discussion, pp. 98 ff., 113 ff.). On the whole, it may be said that a more definite explanation is needed than the latter, but that the former is not proved by the evidence alone. The question turns upon the meaning and development of totemism (*q.v.*), and in the meanwhile it is enough to notice that *a priori* objections based alike upon low ideas of totemism and upon elevated conceptions of Oriental religious thought and practice are untenable. As bearing on the sociological aspect of the inquiry, it may be remarked that J. G. Frazer, observing that the eight kings of Edom are not hereditary, infers that 'in Edom, as elsewhere, the blood royal was traced in the female line, and that the kings were men of other families, or even foreigners, who succeeded to the throne by marrying the hereditary princesses.'[5] It is probable, also, that the Edomites practised circumcision. It is true that, according to Jos. (*Ant.* XIII. ix. 1), the Idumæans were circumcised by John Hyrcanus, but the custom could hardly have been introduced then for the first time (see Jer $9^{25f.}$, cf. Ezk 32^{29}, and the circumcision of Ishmael in Gn 17^{23-27}). It is more likely, therefore, that, as Nöldeke suggests (*EBi* ii. 1188), 'the Jewish rite of circumcision shortly after birth was substituted for the rite in use among the kindred peoples, namely, circumcision shortly before puberty, the former alone being recognised as real circumcision by the Jews.'

On *a priori* grounds it is reasonable to assume that Edomite religion was not isolated from that of the surrounding peoples. The traces of Egypto-Semitic cult found by Petrie in the south of the Sinaitic peninsula date before the age of the Israelite monarchy, but point to the antiquity of definite religious ideas in the desert region outside Palestine.[1] It is interesting to notice that about the 6th cent. B.C., in an Aramaic inscription from Tēma (Ishmaelite, Gn 25^{15}, named with Dedan, Is $21^{13f.}$, Jer 25^{23}), contact with Egypt is shown by the name *Pet-Osiris*, the father of a priest who ministers to Ṣalm of M-ḥ-r-m (evidently a local form of a more prominent deity), Shingala (שנגלא, perhaps a form of Astarte), and Ashira (apparently the well-known Ashirat, Ashirta). But the inscription also shows linguistic and art indications of Bab.-Assyr. influence. Moreover, Edomite contact with Arabia, the presence of a Minæan colony in N. Arabia at el-Ōla, and the fact that the name *Ḳēnān* (Gn 5^{9}, son of Enosh, and corresponding to Cain) is that of an old S. Arabian deity afford ground for further speculation. Although there is no trace in Edom of the deity Sin, the name is familiar both in ancient Arabia and in the Edomite area (the wilderness of Sin, Mt. Sinai). So also there is no trace of the cult of Ishtar-Astarte; but the male 'Athtar or 'Attar is found in Arabia, and is joined with Chemosh in Moab; and Atar-Samain ('Ishtar of the heavens') was venerated by the Kedar tribes in the 7th century. The corresponding 'lord of the heavens,' found in Palestine and later among the Nabatæans, and with an equivalent in ancient Arabia, may also have been familiar in Edom, though perhaps under one of the more definite names (*e.g.* Hadad, Ḳaush) already noticed. Finally, some indirect evidence is afforded by the points of contact between Israelite and old Arabian religion, a noteworthy example of which is the Minæan title לוא, fem. לואה. These terms apparently mean 'priest,' 'priestess,' and, with Hommel and others, may explain the words 'Levi,' 'Levite' (לוי). If so, the word probably entered into Israel through the 'Edomitic' connexions which the genealogies represent, and it is significant that the Levitical traditions and personal names agree in manifesting a peculiar relationship with S. Palestine, Ḳadesh, and that area which is connected more closely with the Edomites generally than with Israel.[2]

4. Edom and Israel.—Suggestive hints for the older religion of the Edomite area may be gleaned from the Nabatæan evidence, notably in the cults at Petra, which obviously were not entirely novel growths (see, further, NABATÆANS; on the later evidence for Idumæan cultus at Adora, see Büchler, *ZATW*, 1909, p. 224 f.). A more intricate inquiry is involved in Hebron and Mamre, the persistent heathenism of which is proved by the statements of Sozomen (*HE* ii. 4). The practices were presumably Idumæan; but such is the vitality and

[1] S. A. Cook, *Rel. of Ancient Palestine*, 1908, pp. 84, 89–91.

[2] The LXX ἰεούς for *Jeush* does not prove that the translators were acquainted with a Semitic pronunciation of the name which distinguished it from the form which the Greeks at Memphis transliterated with γ.

[3] Smith's suggestion that *Jă'ăḳān* (1 Ch 1^{42}; cf. Gn 36^{27}) may be identified with the Arab god *Ya'uḳ* (*Kinship*2, 242, 254) is too doubtful to be included in the above list.

[4] See, in the first instance, W. R. Smith, *JPh* ix. [1879] 75–100, with the qualification in *Kinship* 2, 253 f. For criticisms, see Nöldeke, *ZDMG*, 1886, pp. 148–187; J. Jacobs, *Studies in Bibl. Archæol.*, 1894, p. 64 ff.; Zapletal, *Totemismus*, Freiburg, 1901, p. 29 ff.; Kautzsch, in *HDB*, vol. v. p. 613 n.; and the clear and convenient analysis by G. B. Gray, *Heb. Proper Names*, 1896, p. 86 ff.

[5] *Adonis, Attis, Osiris*2, 1907, p. 12, n. 6.

[1] See W. M. F. Petrie, *Researches in Sinai*, 1906, ch. xiii.

[2] See, for the old Arabian data, F. Hommel, *AHT* (Eng. tr., 1897), and his study in Hilprecht's *Explorations in Bible Lands*, Edinburgh, 1903, pp. 735 f., 746 ff.; also art. ARABS (Ancient); for the Levitical relationships, see S. A. Cook, *Critical Notes on OT History*, 1907, p. 84 ff.

persistence of religious observance that some of them may have gone back to Israelite times (cf. Nöldeke, *EBi* ii. 1188). Moreover, Hebron had not always belonged to Israel; it had been taken by Caleb (Jos $15^{13ff.}$), who, though subsequently reckoned to Judah-Israel, was originally a Kenizzite, and therefore of Edomite affinity. It is also evident from the Biblical narrative that the Edomites could reckon the ancestors of Esau as their ancestors: Abraham and Sarah at Hebron and Mamre, or Isaac at Beersheba. Have any of their legends persisted? Meyer has suggested that some features in the stories of Abraham point to a heroic figure who was Calebite before his adoption into the common Judæan-Israelite tradition (*Die Israeliten*, p. 262 f.), and both Isaac and Ishmael are more naturally located outside Israel and Judah, in the ordinary sense of the terms. Hence, while elements of myth and legend of wide distribution appear in Genesis in a localized form, attached to definite figures and places, it is very noteworthy that much of the material is S. Palestinian. As Meyer and Luther have emphasized, the true popular Israelite tradition is scanty, whereas many traditions concern S. Palestine or could only have arisen there (pp. 227, 259, 279, 305, 478); to call them Judæan is too restrictive (pp. 386, 443); the interests are those of the Seirite and Edomite connexions (as illustrated by the genealogies) rather than of the Israelites.[1]

This tendency to discover in the OT data which primarily were 'Edomitic' rather than Israelite involves the recognition that their presence is not fortuitous; they have stamped themselves upon Biblical (*i.e.* Israelite) tradition as surely as certain 'Edomitic' groups became—as is seen in 1 Ch 2 and 4—Israelite. The process may be illustrated by Gn $4^{17ff.}$, the account of the aboriginal patriarchs and the beginning of civilization. This is evidently a piece of distinctively Cainite (*i.e.* Kenite) lore, and the natural inference is that it was brought into the common stock of Israelite tradition by the Kenites when they entered Judah; so, A. R. Gordon (*Early Trad. of Genesis*, Edinburgh, 1907, pp. 74 f., 168, 188), who ascribes to them also the account of the origin of the world (Gn $2^{5ff.}$). These fragments testify to some larger and more organic body of tradition, which, in its present modified form, has points of contact with old Canaanite or Phœnician culture-myths (see Skinner, *Gen.* p. 123 f.); and, since the invocation of Jahweh is dated from Adam's grandson Ĕnōsh ('man' [Gn 4^{26}]), its view of Jahwism ran upon lines quite different from the prevailing Biblical view. But, as comparative research has shown, divers peoples or tribes have their own beliefs of origins, and consequently the Kenite lore not only illustrates material brought into the Israelite stock from a S. Palestinian ('Edomitic') area, but also shows, by its very presence, that through certain vicissitudes the Kenites were able to impress *their* tradition upon the literature.[2]

Edom and the desert peoples enjoy a reputation for wisdom (Ob ^{8}, Jer 49^{7}, Bar 3^{23}), and the superlative wisdom of Solomon is emphasized by placing him above certain sages whose names have Edomite connexions (1 K 4^{31}—Ethan the Ezrahite, Heman, Mahol). The names recur in 1 Ch 2^{6} as sons of Zerah (an Edomite clan affiliated to Judah [Meyer, 350]); and thus, quite apart from the question of value, the *claim* of a Judæan relationship is unmistakable. This, however, is not more striking than the presence of other 'Edomitic' Judæans in 1 Ch 2 and 4. The un-Israelite names in Pr 30^{1} 31^{1} are too doubtful for the conjecture that these chapters contain specimens of Edomite wisdom. On the other hand, the background of the grand book of Job lies outside Israel and Judah, possibly in the Edomite area,[1] and there is no *a priori* reason why the thought of the book should be regarded as exclusively Israelite. Further, Israelite tradition itself explicitly ascribes to the Midianite Jethro the inauguration of the judicial system (Ex 18), and the father-in-law of Moses subsequently appears in Israel (Jg 1^{16}, cf. 4^{11}). The Levites also have connexions with S. Palestine, and it is noteworthy that such names as *Obed-edom*, *Korah*, *Ethan*, *Heman*, etc., link the temple of Jerusalem, its officers and its singers, with features which take us away from Judah and Israel.

5. Edom and Jahweh.—That Israel and Edom were very closely connected at certain periods is clear from the history of Palestine. In later times the Idumæans bear such names as *Jacob* (the rival of their ancestor!), *Phinehas*, *Simon*, and *Saul*—names familiar in Israelite tradition. On the other hand, the repeated occurrence of names in *Ḳaush* and *Kos* from the 8th cent. onwards points to tradition more distinctively Edomite; and it is noteworthy that, while the district and clan-division of Edom would favour local and minor cults, the names of the kings include such more prominent and widely distributed deities as Hadad (thrice), Ḳaush (twice), and Baal (once, in *B.-ḥanan*, son of 'the Mouse'). It is a striking fact that, although the Edomites, like the other peoples, had their gods, they are placed by Israel apart from other heathen neighbours. The third generation after inter-marriage had full Israelite privileges, whereas Ammon and Moab were banned for ever (Dt $23^{3.\,7f.}$); these two lands are regarded as stumbling-blocks, but there is no warning against Edomite idolatry except in relatively late passages. Nor is allusion made to any Edomite national deity corresponding to Milcom, Chemosh, and Jahweh, in Ammon, Moab, and Israel. Although the gods Hadad, Baal, and possibly Ḳaush were or had been known in Israel, Jahweh could be worshipped by the Edomite Doeg (1 S 21^{7}), and was, no doubt, known in Edom, as He also was—to judge from personal names—in N. Syria. Indeed, according to one very favourite view, Jahweh was the god of the Kenites;[2] and, since Gn 4^{26} refers to His immemorial worship, it would seem that their clan claimed to possess the cult from the earliest times. But the evidence does not confine Jahweh to the Kenites. His rise is connected with Sinai, Mt. Paran, Seir, Teman, and probably Ḳadesh (Dt 33^{2}, Jg $5^{4f.}$, Hab 3^{3}); and the persistence of this belief is shown partly by the tradition that Elijah was impelled to visit Horeb, the mount of God, in search of the true Jahweh (1 K $19^{8ff.}$), and partly by the lateness of the reference in Habakkuk. It is clear that the Edomite area was, in some very special sense, regarded as the home of Jahweh. In addition to this, with the Kenites are associated the Rechabites (1 Ch 2^{55}; Calebite in 4^{12} [reading 'Rechab' for 'Rechah,' with LXX]), and these certainly held that desert conditions were proper to the religion of Jahweh (Jer 35). Their uncompromising zeal, as suggested in the account of Jehu's revolt (2 K $10^{15ff.}$), illustrates a reforming spirit, which finds a parallel when the Levites take their stand for Jahweh and put their brethren to the sword (Ex 32^{26}). Thus, with S. Palestine are connected, directly or indirectly, traditions of the

[1] See, further, Meyer, pp. 83, 305; Luther, p. 107 ff., and esp. 129 ff., 158 f.; cf. also H. Gressmann, *ZATW*, 1910, pp. 15, 26, 29. N. Schmidt (*HJ*, 1908, p. 339) does not hesitate to regard Aaron as originally 'an Edomitish divinity, having his shrines on Mosera and Hor,' the traditional scenes of his death.

[2] 1 Ch 2^{55} refers to families of scribes connected with the Kenites. With the tracing of mankind to Ādām, 'man,' compare the suggestion that the name Ĕdōm is a dialectical form of *ădām* (Nöldeke, *EBi* ii. 1181).

[1] Uz is named with Edom in La 4^{21}; and, for Eliphaz of Teman, cf. the names in Gn 36^{11}.

[2] Tiele, Stade, Budde, Guthe, Moore, H. P. Smith, and others; see Paton, *BW*, Aug. 1906, p. 116 ff.

origin of Jahweh and certain impetuous reforms which are bound up with Rechabites and Levites, both of whom have S. Palestinian relationship. It is very difficult to find an adequate explanation of all the data. The Jahweh of the south, from the Edomite area, became *the* Jahweh of the Israelites; and, since the deities Hadad (or Addu) and Shemesh (the sun-god) are most conspicuous in Palestine in the age of the Amarna Letters (*c.* 1400 B.C.),[1] it may be inferred that only some sweeping change in the history of the land can account for the subsequent appearance of Jahweh as the sole recognized god of Israel. But there is no good evidence for any early wide-spread movement from the south, such as is represented in the Israelite conquest, nor is there any reference to apostasy to Hadad or Shemesh. The evidence suggests rather that the south was responsible for a new era in Jahwism, for the inauguration of a new stage in the development of conceptions of Jahweh's nature. It is intelligible that, just as a new stage may be inaugurated by a new name (*Abraham* for Abram, *Hebron* for Kirjath-arba, etc.), the adherents of a purer worship of Jahweh might regard Him as a new god; and, in point of fact, the reformers of Israel view the heathenish worship of Jahweh as Baal-worship. It is another question whether Jahweh had actually been a recognized god in Edom. If, for example, the cult of Jahweh in Palestine had been enforced over S. Palestine, it might have existed in a purer form among the wild but simpler desert tribes. It is also possible that allowance must be made for reflexion, and that southern groups, afterwards incorporated in Israel, held the belief that their purer worship of Jahweh had been brought with them from their earlier seats. Finally, the traditions may imply that certain Edomite groups separated themselves from their brethren, and ranged themselves under the banner of Jahweh; and, if Jahweh was not originally Edomite, the relations between Him and these new adherents would be without naturalistic traits—they would be rather a matter of free choice. The relationship in such a case would be more of an ethical character.

In conclusion, there is a very close relationship between Esau (Edom) and his twin-brother Jacob (Israel); this is enhanced by the genealogical data in Gn 36, and by the evidence linking Israel with an area which is Edomite rather than Israelite. Certain clans in Israel appear to have come direct from Ḳadesh, on the Edomite frontier, and with such a movement as this may be associated the presence of specifically S. Palestinian traditions, which are now Israelite in the ordinary sense. There is no reference to a national Edomite god, no condemnation of the cults or of the people in the earlier literature; the Edomite area appears to have influenced Israelite legal and ecclesiastical institutions; and Jahweh Himself, or perhaps rather the purer form of Jahwism, is closely connected with this district. The bearing of this Edomite evidence upon the wider questions of OT criticism has yet to be worked out.[1]

LITERATURE.—In addition to the authorities cited in the article, see artt. on 'Edom,' by A. H. Sayce, in *HDB*, Nöldeke, in *EBi*, and S. A. Cook, in *EBr*[11]; F. Buhl, *Gesch. d. Edomiter*, Leipzig, 1893 (an excellent pioneering work); geographical and archæological information by Gray Hill and Sir Charles Wilson, in *PEFSt*, 1896–98; Brünnow-Domaszewski, *Provincia Arabia*, Strassburg, 1904–6; Libbey-Hoskins, *The Jordan Valley and Petra*, London, 1905; A. Musil, *Arabia Petræa*, Vienna, 1908. See, further, P. Thomsen, *Palästina-Literatur*, Leipzig, 1905–9, ii. 170, and Index, *s.vv.* 'Edom,' 'Petra'; and the opening articles by G. A. Smith, in *Expositor*, Oct.-Dec. 1908.

S. A. COOK.

¹ See S. A. Cook, *Rel. of Anc. Pal.*, p. 88 ff.

¹ On some of the questions involved, the writer may be permitted to refer to the articles 'Genesis,' 'Jews,' 'Levites,' and 'Palestine,' in *EBr*[11], and the Introduction to 1 Esdras, in R. H. Charles' edition of the Apocrypha (1912).

EDUCATION.

EDUCATION (Introductory).—**I.** The meaning attached to the word 'Education' varies greatly. According to some writers it includes all the forces that influence human development. According to others it is limited to something so narrow as to be equivalent to nothing more than *teaching*. The widest meaning is well expressed in the words of John Stuart Mill, who tells us that education

'includes whatever we do for ourselves, and whatever is done for us by others for the express purpose of bringing us nearer to the perfection of our nature; in its largest acceptation it comprehends even the indirect effects produced on character, and on the human faculties, by things of which the direct purposes are different; by laws, by forms of government, by the industrial arts, by modes of social life; nay, even by physical facts not dependent on human will; by climate, soil, and local position' (Rectorial Address, St. Andrews, 1867).

He himself seems to feel that this is rather too wide a view to be of practical application, so he restricts it in the same address to

'the culture which each generation purposely gives to those who are to be its successors, in order to qualify them for at least keeping up, and, if possible, for raising, the level of the improvement which has been attained.'

In both definitions it will be observed that the idea of Purpose is involved in the process of education. 'To have loved her' may have been 'a liberal education,' but the epigram owes its point to the very omission of this idea of purpose, which is always felt to be essential in education.

If we examine a large number of the definitions supplied by eminent writers, we shall find that there is one term present in almost all of them. This term is 'Development.' The word itself is seldom absent, and the idea implied by it is always present. Thus Pestalozzi states his views in the familiar plant metaphor:

'Sound Education stands before me symbolized by a tree planted near fertilizing water. A little seed, which contains the design of the tree, its form and proportion, is placed in the soil. See how it germinates and expands into trunk, branches, leaves, flowers, and fruit! The whole tree is an uninterrupted chain of organic parts, the plan of which existed in its seed and root. Man is similar to the tree. In the newborn child are hidden those faculties which are to unfold during life' (see Address on Birthday, 1818).

Froebel as a loyal disciple naturally follows:

'So the man must be viewed not as already become perfect, not as fixed and stationary, but as constant yet always progressively developing, . . . always advancing from one stage of development to another' (*Menschenerziehung*, Vienna, 1883, § 16).

Besides the ideas of development and deliberate purpose, there are always present in some form or other two additional ideas, those of System and of Knowledge or Culture. In a certain sense a child is educated by the process of living, even when there is no purpose of educating him, and no system in the process; but, in so far as Education is treated as an art or as a science, it must be carried on with the deliberate purpose of modifying development by means of knowledge systematically imparted.

Of the four ideas that we have found to be essential to the connotation of the term 'Education,' that of Development applies to the pupil, and must be accepted as a datum in the problem; the other three are more or less under the control of the educator.

The idea of Development involves the correlative idea of organism, and organism implies the existence of an inherent law that is brought to light in the development of the organism. The idea of life, literally or figuratively, is always implied when we speak of an organism. This, indeed, would compel us to hunt for the meaning of this mysterious thing called Life, but we must here assume a knowledge of the general meaning of the vital principle. Whatever it is, it pervades the whole of the structure in which it is found. Of it may be said, as is said of the soul, 'it is all in the whole, and all in every part.' This distinction, indeed, is of great value in marking off an organism from a machine. Only an organism can develop. As we discriminate between an organism and a machine, so we must discriminate between development and growth. Growth may take two forms—accretion and multiplication—but neither increase in bulk nor increase in number of parts of itself implies development. Increase in complexity of structure must be added to adaptation to function, before we have genuine development. Development, then, is a process of differentiation correlated with adaptation to function.

This brings us to the third essential element in the connotation of the term 'Development.' It always implies self-determination on the part of the developing organism. This, indeed, is implied in the idea of an organism. It begins, flourishes, and decays, all according to laws that are inherent in its own nature. The laws of its development are indeed part of itself. Its life is simply the exemplification of these laws. The question may be asked, in fact, Which is the butterfly; is it the egg, the larva, the chrysalis, or the imago? The answer clearly is that it is all four. The idea of the butterfly is incomplete unless it includes all the stages through which the creature passes in the process of its development. We cannot define a developing being unless we take into account what it has been and what it is going to be. A frog both is and is not a tadpole. The acorn, the seedling, the sapling, and the full-grown tree are all essential to the true idea of the full-grown oak. The oak is implicit in the acorn; the acorn is explicit in the oak. The acorn realizes itself only by becoming an oak.

2. Theories and problems of education.—The true fundamental aim of every individual is self-realization in the widest and truest sense of the term; but here at the very threshold a serious difficulty arises. The mere phrase 'self-realization' suggests an objection of the first importance in Education. If true development is self-development —development from within in accordance with the laws of our nature,—is there room in the process for an educator? Does it not seem almost self-evident that an educator, so far from aiding in true development, must of necessity hinder it by imposing on the developing self an influence other than that of the developing ego? This difficulty is at the bottom of the popular saying that all true education is self-education. But even Jacotot, an ingenious French teacher who, in his writings, took great pains to depreciate the work of teachers, does not go to the root of the matter. It is a strange demonstration of the uselessness of teachers that results in perhaps the most absurd of all methodologies, as Jacotot's system turns out to be. The same difficulty is felt in Rousseau's scheme, but is evaded by the inept plan of overt inaction. Why write a volume on Education, as Rousseau does, to prove that the teacher figures as a practically negligible element?

The radical difficulty shows itself to be what it is in Pestalozzi, and still more clearly in Froebel. The cause of this recognition of the difficulty and the attempt to meet it is to be found in the fact that these writers based their theory of education upon more or less clearly conceived Idealistic principles.

It is true that Rousseau usually gets the credit of being the philosopher who won Pestalozzi for Education. But Pestalozzi lived a long life, and the force that impelled him to Education was not the only one that modified his thought. Kant was just finishing his University studies when Pestalozzi was born, and by the time the educator had found his vocation, and was actually engaged in it, the Kantian thought was beginning to make itself felt. The germs of Idealism were in the air; Pestalozzi could not hope to escape the infection. The plant metaphor, which has since been so overworked, appears to have had considerable influence in modifying his principles; but the metaphor was, after all, only a concrete statement of the Idealist position.

As Kant was followed by Hegel, so Pestalozzi was followed by Froebel,' and in both cases an advance in Idealism has been made. For our present purpose, principles, not persons, interest us. We are not specially concerned with either the Pestalozzian or the Froebelian development. The important thing is that the development of the whole school has given a clear demonstration of the educational effect of the theory of self-realization.

There exists at this moment a large and important school of educationists who ground their opinions on a more or less intelligent interpretation of the life and works of Pestalozzi and Froebel. They have outlived the philosophical difficulties that troubled their later master. They have a system which experience has proved to be valuable, and they are inclined to rest content without going into uncomfortable details. It was otherwise with Froebel. He felt keenly the initial difficulty of his system, and throughout the whole of his *Education of Man* he struggles with more or less success to justify the educator in interfering in the work of education at all. The ordinary Kindergarteners dabble in the mechanism of Idealism without in the least understanding the nature and necessity of the primary assumption that gives it life and meaning. Naturally, as soon as they set themselves to think at all, they come to a deadlock. The child is like a plant, it can grow and develop: it is growing, but only in a determinate way. True education, therefore, must aim at permitting and encouraging the child to develop in the greatest possible freedom. Froebel sees this very clearly:

'Therefore Education, instruction, and teaching should in the first characteristic necessarily be passive, watchfully and protectively following, not dictatorial, not invariable, not visibly interfering.' Further, in the following section we are told: 'The still young being, even though as yet unconsciously, like a product of nature, precisely and surely wills that which is best for himself, and, moreover, in a form which is quite suitable to him, and which he feels within himself the disposition, power, and means to represent' (*op. cit.* § 7 f.).

If, then, the child thus makes for what is for his good as certainly as a duckling makes for water, it is obvious that the occupation of the teacher is in a parlous state. Why employ a man to make a child do what the child cannot help doing? The usual reply is botanical. A given seed can produce nothing but a particular plant, and yet there may be work for a gardener. The very elaborate scheme of gifts and occupations that characterizes the Kindergarten system shows that Froebel regarded education as at least possible, and, by inference, desirable. We are therefore entitled to a better argument than a mere analogy. The problem is how to find a place for a teacher between a developing nature, with a determination towards good, and a world that is by hypothesis good, inasmuch as 'all has proceeded from God, and is limited by God alone.'

Froebel's answer rises above Botany. The educator, he tells us, is himself a part of the world in question: he has, therefore, a place. That this place is consistent with the rest of the theory is manifest, because the teacher who is found imposing laws and restrictions on the child 'himself is strictly and inevitably subjected to a perpetually governing law; to an unavoidable perpetual necessity; thus all arbitrariness is banished.' The educator must at every moment act under two different influences, which yet lead him to the same line of conduct. He must guide and be guided. His consistency as governed and governor is guaranteed by the continual reference of himself and his pupil to an invisible and invariable third. The teacher, while seeking to enable the pupil to attain to self-realization, must seek at the same time to realize himself. Only by rightly guiding the pupil can the master himself be right. If the boy's nature and the master's are each developing freely, then their actions must of necessity fit into each other, and produce a harmony which *is* the invisible and invariable third, in other words, the inherent rationality of the universe.

In Education, as in some other directions, the Idealist position has been accepted timidly and incompletely. Instead of boldly accepting the whole of the doctrine thus enunciated in the *Education of Man*, later Froebelians have selected for special emphasis the principle, '*Find what Nature intends for the children, and follow that.*' 'A passivity, a following,' has become their watchword; and so true are they, in theory at least, to this view-point that it is hardly to be wondered at that a sort of general paralysis is the result. So passive must the Froebelians become, if they are true to their theory, that they must cease to have any influence over their pupils at all.

When we consider the bewildering paraphernalia of gifts and occupations in the Kindergarten, we are inclined to think that the Froebelians have hardly been loyal to their principle of non-interference. The justification usually offered is that the various exercises have been discovered by experiment to be exactly the sort of thing that Nature demands, and that the teacher in applying his methods is, after all, only 'passive, following.'

It would be unfair to the system, and not to our present purpose, to argue from the fact that anything more unnatural than many of the practical applications of the principle, it would be impossible to find. The principle can hardly be held responsible for the rigid, and, therefore, irrational application made by unsympathetic teachers. Yet it is surely not unreasonable to maintain that a benevolent superintendence is too modest a name for the complicated system the Froebelians have now elaborated. The value of the Kindergarten is not the point at issue. The question is—Can the 'passive, following' theory be held to be consistent with the system as now developed?

By observation it is found that children are fond of making things, of expressing thus their own ideas, of 'making the inner outer.' When the teacher gives them the opportunity of exercising this power or gift, he feels that he is 'passive, following.' He is but the jackal that provides the meat. The eating is the part of the child. If the teacher is content with this function, nothing more need be said. Education is recognized as a mystery. Given a child and certain materials, it is found that a certain result is produced. This may be interesting as a fact in Natural History; it cannot be held to explain anything. The educator does not educate; the child is his own educator.

There is obviously a sense in which it is true that all education is self-education. No man can learn for another; no man can be moral for another. Jacotot's definition of teaching, 'causing another to learn,' has been discredited. Can the definition of Education, 'causing another to develop himself according to the laws of his own nature,' be defended? By the conditions of the case, the subject must develop somehow: the only point left for consideration, therefore, is, Can we modify this development so as to produce the best result possible in the given case? This again involves two distinct problems: First, we have to discover what the highest form of development possible in the given case really is. Secondly, we have to discover some means of attaining this form.

The first problem, as it is stated above, is insoluble. No doubt, were all the conditions of the case known, the highest form of development possible for the given subject would be at once evident. But such knowledge is absolutely beyond our finite minds. Viewed *sub specie æternitatis*, the problem ceases to be a problem, and becomes a mere statement of fact. Unfortunately, this point of view is not attainable.

The case is not yet altogether hopeless. The second problem, which seems to depend upon the first for its very conditions, may itself supply the solution of the first. In working out its own development, the ego may indicate its own ideal, indeed must indicate that ideal. The important question that now arises is, Does it indicate that ideal soon enough for the educator to profit by the indication? Even if this question be satisfactorily answered, there remains the final problem, Can an external mind have any share in determining the development of a self-determining organism? To face the question fairly, we must give up all metaphors, however convenient. Above all, we must give up that wearisome acorn with its resulting tree. It has to be admitted that the tree is implicit in the acorn, and that certain laws can be discovered which aid us in furthering the development of the oak; but a child is not an acorn: a man is not a tree. We may endow an acorn with life—organic life; we may, if we will, endow it with a sort of generalized consciousness; but in the case of the child there is something quite new, and much higher than the highest we can possibly attribute to the tree. The oak is, no doubt, as absolutely self-determined as is the child, but it is not consciously self-determined. The developing human being is not only self-determined, he is self-conscious.

How does this new element affect the case? Can external influences modify self-development characterized by self-consciousness in the same way as they modify self-development not so characterized? Manifestly they can, in a negative sense at least. The environment, conscious or unconscious, can and does interfere with the full and free process of self-realization. A force that can hinder may reasonably be assumed to be able to help, if only in a negative way. By merely withholding its action, the environment may be said to produce a positive effect; nature is clearly dependent on nurture. It must not be forgotten that in the process of development there are two forces—an outer and an inner—the nature of the developing ego, and the nurture supplied; and any influence must differ according as it is allied to the inner nature or to the outer nurture.

We have the antagonism between two forces—the self-developing ego on the one hand, and the environment against which it strives on the other. It is in and through this strife that the ego realizes itself, so far as it rises above the antagonism, and attains an ever higher and higher unity. If the educator is to exercise any influence at all, he must throw in his force either with the ego or with the environment.

The natural thing is to throw in his influence with the struggling ego; but what is the result? Suppose that by his help a higher unity is obtained: how does the self-realizing ego fare? The unity thus attained may be real for the educator: it is empty for the struggling ego. This mistake in moral training is exactly parallel with the popular blunder in intellectual education. The blunder in question is the supplying of cut and dry definitions and rules, which certainly introduce order among the confused mass of presented ideas, but an order that is meaningless. The child, for example, is struggling to understand the meaning of the concept 'Abstract Noun.' There is a manifold of presented ideas. The teacher may give his cut and dry definition which produces an appearance of order. This definition, which imposes a mechanical unity on the hitherto rebellious manifold, may be perfectly accurate, and may represent a real unity to the teacher. To the child it is a hindrance. No general principle can be of use to a child till he has worked for it, that is, till he has made it his own by rising above the antagonism of the particulars it combines.

To seek to aid the ego, then, by directly helping it, is to weaken it. Even if we understand the ideal the ego seeks to attain, we cannot directly aid it in its efforts, for in so doing we reduce the development below the level of conscious self-realization.

The place of the educator is, therefore, limited to the environment. He is but one element of the manifold against which the ego reacts. We must influence the ego by means of its limitations. If we can so modify the environment that the ego must react upon it in a determinate way, we seem to be able to influence the ego directly, and to restrict its power of self-development. Yet the very power thus exercised is possible only because of the laws according to which the organism develops itself. If the developing organism responded capriciously to given forces, it could not be said to be self-determined. A perfectly unlimited self ceases to be a self at all, and loses all meaning. If, then, the child answers the educator's stimulus exactly as the educator expects, it is because the nature of the child demands that this reaction and no other shall follow this stimulus.

It may be here objected that, if this be so, man-making is really possible. The child is clay in the hands of the potter. All the educator has to do is to discover the laws according to which the child develops, and apply this knowledge. To this a cheerful assent may be given. So far as the educator knows the laws according to which a child develops, so far is that child clay in his hands, to make of him what he will. Nor does this admission in the least endanger the independence of the child as a self-determining organism. The educator can make of the child what he will only by obeying the laws of the child's development. The very freedom that marks the self-development of the child is the necessity which impels him to act as the educator leads him to act. The child realizes himself fully and freely in the environment that has been modified by the educator. No less freely and fully does the educator realize himself in the environment which he has modified.

Viewed from too close a standpoint, there seems here to be a distinct contradiction. How can a child be at the same time self-determined and determined by another? Viewed from a higher level, the contradiction disappears, and the two forces—the child ego and the educator ego—are seen to form parts of a wider organism in which each finds its only possible freedom in attaining a harmony with its surroundings—in acting thus and thus and not otherwise. If this be so, it may be asked, Why do educators as a matter of fact so often fail to obtain that determining power over their pupils? It is generally admitted that within certain narrow limits the educator does mould the character of the pupil as a potter does the clay; and, when the matter is looked into with any degree of care, those limits are found to be constituted by the bounds of the educator's knowledge of the laws according to which the pupil's ego is self-determined.

The objection of the loss of freedom of the child, whose nature is guided by the skilful teacher, may be met by the correlative objection of the loss of freedom on the part of the teacher. If the child must react in a fixed way to certain stimuli, he seems to lose his freedom; but what of the freedom of the educator? In order to modify in a given direction the development of a given organism, the educator must modify his own energies in a definite direction—must, in short, to some extent give up the freedom of his own development. There is here no fatalism. Educator and educated develop alike according to the laws of their being. The fact that a complete knowledge of the nature of the educated would enable the educator to modify the development in no way interferes with the free self-development of the educated. Such complete knowledge is admittedly unattainable. But, supposing it to be attained by the educator, he would by that very knowledge have ceased to be an educator. He would have risen to a point of view from which he could look with full comprehension upon both parties in the work of education. He would see that master and pupil in their action and reaction upon each other are gradually working out their differences, and are attaining ever higher and higher levels at which certain antagonisms of the process disappear. What causes it to appear that the ego of the educator is dominating the ego of the educated is that the former always works from a slightly higher level. He cannot, indeed, rise to such a height as to be able to envisage at one sweep all the antagonisms and reconciliations that make up the entire sphere of education, but he is always working from a level high enough to resolve the immediate antagonism that makes up the now of education at any given moment.

Underlying all this is the great assumption of Idealism which we must be content to receive and to acknowledge as an assumption. We cannot transcend thought; we cannot prove the organic unity of the universe; but, if the universe be not an organism, if there be no reason underlying the manifold of experience, then philosophy has no meaning for us. All the same, it must be admitted that these wide generalities, while showing that explanation is possible, that a system of education is within the grasp of complete knowledge, give little help in the practical work of education. Within this rounded whole that makes up the Idealist's universe, we must begin our work somewhere. We must have a system that fits into the limited area within which we live. Our practical method does not require to supply a complete explanation of its principles. The essential thing is that it shall not contradict any of the findings of the more general theory set forth above.

To come down from the clouds—let us see how the thing works out. Given a newly-born child, how can the educator bring his influence to bear upon it? The faculty psychologist is at once busy with talk about exercising the faculty of discrimination by changes of light and temperature. This exercise demands, he tells us, a rudimentary form of memory and judgment. And thus the building up of the ego proceeds. The whole process may be summed up in the one word 'training.' In modern educational works this word has acquired a sort of sacred meaninglessness. Few words labour under such a weight of assumptions. Naturally its use is marked by a great deal of vagueness; but, as often as it occurs, it appears to connote a process that is peculiarly philosophical yet practical. Despite its ordinary vagueness it is not left without a fairly well defined special meaning. R. H. Quick, for example, would divide all educators into the three great classes: Realists, Humanists, and Trainers; and the school of educators who follow David Stow claim to form what they call '*the* training school.' If we have regard to the results of the process of education, this classification obviously implies a cross-division; for each of the schools claims to train its pupils, though they differ regarding the means to be used to accomplish the training. Without pressing the distinction too closely, it may be said that teaching lays stress on the knowledge to be conveyed, training rather on the process of conveying it, and particularly on the effect of this process upon the mind of the pupil.

Sometimes, indeed, a lower view of training is held. It is regarded as more or less physical. In his *Introduction to the Pedagogy of Herbart* (London, 1895), p. ix, we find Ufer saying:

'Animals cannot in any true sense be educated: they can only be trained. Education is an influence upon man. When a person is spoken of as well-educated, we do not think of bodily qualities. The educating influence has reference to the soul, and concerns itself with the body only in so far as the care of the latter is immediately serviceable to the former.'

The very existence of the training school of educators proves that this comparatively low view of training is not universal; yet there is clearly an element of truth in it. At college there are *trainers* for the river, and *tutors* for the schools. As usual, whatever difficulty there is arises from a metaphor. The process represented by the word is carried over from the body to the mind. Fortunately there is more than the usual attenuated connexion between the two terms of the metaphor. In the last resort physical training consists in teaching an animal to perform certain acts easily by making it do them frequently. Here it is the first step that costs. After the act has been performed once, there is little difficulty in having it repeated, till it can be done perfectly. *Faber fabricando* is the trainer's motto. In physical training this first step causes no real difficulty. A dog is taught to pretend to smoke a pipe by having the pipe placed in his mouth; the rest of the training resolves itself into biscuits and blows. In the region of morals the same thing may be applied to a limited extent. We may make a child act in certain ways by sheer physical force, and then by rewards and punishments transform isolated acts into habits. This is probably all that is implied in the aphorism adopted by the training school: 'Train up a child in the way he should go: and when he is old, he will not depart from it.'

But this is not enough. If it were, we should not have got beyond the idea of virtue as a bundle of good habits. Many writers, among them Locke, are content to accept this view of moral training, at any rate in the earlier years. At this stage the young mind is regarded as incapable of reasoning: there can be no real thought about morals; the practice of virtue must precede the principles. It need not, of course, be denied that there is in life room for automatic virtue, not merely in bodily habits, but in those intangible influences that make up so great a part of moral and intellectual life. But such a virtue is a *terminus ad quem.* It explains nothing, and indeed increases the need for explanation. No system of moral training can recognize mere habit as the ultimate moral aim. If the soul becomes a mere self-acting machine, morality is impossible. We attach no blame to the dynamiter's clockwork.

Are we then driven back upon the Socratic 'Virtue is *knowledge*'? Can we not be moral without being consciously moral? The answer is Yes or No according to the time element involved. An act that is purely a reflex act is in itself unmoral, neither moral nor immoral; but the process by which a deliberate act has been changed into a reflex one is a moral process. Without making too much of the distinction, it may be maintained that all acts that are originated in the cerebrum are moral; those that can trace their origin no further back than the cerebellum are in themselves unmoral. Botanists tell us that at the tip of each budding twig there is a point at which all the cells that are generated come into being undifferentiated. In all the other parts of the plant the cells begin their existence with a definite bias: they are bast cells, or sap cells, or fibre cells, or cambium cells; they are that and can be nothing else. Only the undifferentiated cells at the growing point are fitted to become any sort of cell that the plant stands most in need of at the time. The part of our being that deals with new cases is our moral growing point. Most of our nature soon gets a set which is moral only from what it implies in the past; the real living morality must be looked for in the application of principles to new cases. In ordinary life, every time a drunkard gives way to his craving we believe that he is guilty of an immoral act, and hold him responsible for it; yet our condemnation should in fairness fall not upon the individual act, but upon the series of acts that rendered this individual act inevitable. It is true that the drinking habit hardly reaches the purely reflex stage, but in some cases it comes extremely close to it, and the closer it comes to this point the less the responsibility of the subject for each individual act.

Underlying all the theories of training is the fundamental assumption of capacity. We can train only within the limits of this assumed capacity. The relative importance of capacity and training, however, varies considerably in the theories of different writers. On the one side we have the Idealists, with their theory of development which places capacity in the very forefront; on the other we have the Atomistic school, which all but eliminates faculty in favour of training. According to Herbart, 'The soul has no capacity or faculty whatever, either to receive or to produce anything' (*Lehrbuch zur Psychologie*, Leipzig, 1851, § 152). This startling statement does not block the way of the educator so completely as at first sight appears: for what Herbart takes from the soul he gives to the ideas; and whatever may be the metaphysical and psychological rights of the matter, the educational process does not suffer. It is sometimes objected to Herbart that his educational theories cannot be deduced from his psychology; but as a matter of fact his educational theories were elaborated before his psychological, and there can be little doubt that the needs of education had a great deal to do with the peculiar form his psychology took. Carried out to its logical issue, the Herbartian system of education implies the possibility of man-making not only on the intellectual but also on the moral side. As Locke demolished the theory of innate ideas, so Herbart demolished the theory of innate faculties. His educational system may not unfairly be said to be a process by which faculties can be supplied. His evolution of the will from the conflict of ideas really amounts to the creation of the will by circumstances if no educator deliberately interferes, or by the educator if there be one who cares to modify the interaction of the conflicting ideas. If, as Herbart maintains, 'Action generates the will out of desire,' there is evidently room in education for a more effective application of the maieutic art than even Socrates ever imagined.

The positions of the Herbartian metaphysic and psychology are untenable, but the educational applications are in themselves very useful, and are really not involved in the condemnation that their supposed foundation deserves. Herbart distinguished between mere instruction and 'educative instruction,' the distinction depending upon the nature of the connexions involved in the subjects taught. Those subjects that touch human life at the greatest number of points form the best kind of *Gesinnungsstoff*, as he names the material for educative instruction. In estimating the value of the Herbartian system, the mistake is commonly made of attaching too much importance to the purely intellectual aspect, sometimes even to the exclusion of the moral, though, as a matter of fact, the moral side bulked very largely in Herbart's mind. No doubt Herbart does attach very great importance to Knowledge as an educational organon, but no competent critic can read his educational work without at once seeing the moral implications of the system. The whole value of instruction, indeed, from Herbart's point of view, consists in its moral bearings. So far does he go in this direction that he has given rise to a great deal of indignation by his well-known saying, 'The stupid man cannot be virtuous.' A view of the Herbartian system as a whole makes it clear that he did not mean the word *stumpfsinnig* to be understood as referring to capacity, but rather to the use made of capacity, though it has to be admitted that the word is not the best he could have chosen to convey this meaning. He is continually emphasizing the need of supplying the mind with healthy ideas in order that a full life may be possible. We are too apt to set up a purely negative ideal of virtue. Our favourite moral axioms consist of prohibitions. Herbart is more inclined to demand positive goodness. His advice is not so much 'Avoid evil' as 'Do good.' The dull untutored man cannot be virtuous because he has not made the most of himself. He is not what he might have been. *Ignoti nulla cupido,* quotes Herbart, and the remark applies to good as well as to evil. All temptation in the last resort comes from within. We have here the psychological explanation of the saying, 'To the pure all things are pure.' The 'circle of thought,' by which Herbart means the organized content of the mind, determines the character of a man. If all Herbartianism could be gathered up into one sentence, that sentence would be: 'The will has its root in the circle of thought.'

At the present moment the great need of the Science of Education is a synthesis of the Herbartian and Froebelian systems, and signs are not lacking that such a synthesis is well within sight. Each supplies the defects of the other, each corrects the other's errors.

3. **History of education.**—From a certain point of view, the history of Education is the history of the development of civilization. All moral and intellectual progress results from educational processes that need not, however, be conscious processes. At the earliest stages of civilization, Education is confined to the ordinary influences of intercourse. The child is educated by the mere process of living. He learns by the reactions on his environment, and particularly by imitation, both in its positive and in its negative form. It is true that parents and other adults do at this stage give a certain amount of instruction to the growing child; but all this instruction is given with an immediate and definite aim, and has no intentional relation to the development of the character of the child. True education begins when the community attains to a sort of collective self-consciousness, and, as it were, turns itself back upon itself and takes itself in hand, with the deliberate intention of guiding development. The mere existence of schools is no proof that there is any attempt at education. These may exist only as a means of imparting a certain dexterity that will increase the value of the children to the community, or to some section of the community.

Since religion was the first of the social forces that led to a special organization, it is very natural that it should be the first to see the need of education. To secure the proper observance of religious rites, it was essential that there should be a body of skilled priests, and this body could be maintained only by a system of carefully selecting and training young men to take the place of those who succumbed to age or disease. Experience would show that the earlier the training began, the more effective it proved, so what began as a professional college gradually developed a sort of preparatory department. Two influences would at once begin to act in such a way as to keep the school and the college distinct. First, the priests would come to regard the school as an excellent means of sifting out all the characters that gave promise of proving good subjects for the religious life. It was obviously desirable, therefore, to mark off the school from the college by means of certain rites that came to be essential to full admission into the religious community. In the second place, it would soon be found that pupils who had gone through the school had benefited by the training, even though they had not been deemed worthy to enter the college. A desire would accordingly arise among the more ambitious parents that their children should share in the advantages of the school, even though there was no desire that they should take up the religious life. This tendency would be strongest where the Church was most powerful, and where the lay nobility was weakest. The connexion between the Church and Education is maintained throughout the ages, though the nature of the connexion varies according to the spiritual state of the Church. When the Church was predominantly a political organization, the schools became little better than technical colleges, preparatory to the clerical profession. When the Church reached a high spiritual level, the schools gave their attention to human beings in general, and became places to fashion the raw material of humanity into its noblest forms, literally *officinæ hominum.*

Of the history of Education among the primitive races we know very little with certainty. The only point that is quite clear is that Education has taken a form in each case determined by the prevailing ideals of the race. Caste in India,

Tradition and Ancestor-Worship in China, Dualism in Persia, Practical Common Sense in Egypt, all leave their mark on the kind of education adopted, and the lines along which it was developed. The Theocracy among the Jews, with its consequent enhancement of the value of the individual, resulted in a wide-spread popular education, which was fundamentally moral and religious, but did not neglect the purely literary side. From the Old Testament record we gather that among the Hebrews as a nation a knowledge of reading and writing was wide-spread, and in this respect they stand out in a most favourable light compared with their contemporaries. See EDUCATION (Jewish).

With the Greek States, we enter upon a new phase of the history of Education. Not only do we have written records of the actual state of education at the time, but we have more or less detailed discussions of the theory of education and of educational ideals. Among the Greeks generally, the individual was entirely subordinated to the State, the man was lost in the citizen. The subjects taught were classed under the two heads, Music and Gymnastics, corresponding generally to literary and physical training. For it must be remembered that Music among the Greeks included not only what we understand by that term, but also poetry, which in due course involved a knowledge of reading and writing and the literary arts generally, though, of course, those arts were cultivated in very different degrees in the different Greek States. Among the Thebans, for example, Gymnastics meant mainly the training necessary for war, and Music was limited to the attainments that gave a charm to the orgies they loved. The Spartans had higher ideals; but even among them the aim of Gymnastics was to give skill and endurance in warfare. The literary training was confined to the three R's, and some warlike Music. It is difficult to say under which head the peculiar educational subject of larceny is to be placed. Probably this form of training in dexterity and cunning is most fitly classed as Gymnastic. The training of citizens fell naturally into four periods: *childhood* at the mother's knee up to 7 years of age; *boyhood* up to 18, during which period the boys were at public training schools, but each had to have some grown man as his special friend and trainer; *youth* up to 30, during which time the young men were trained in the practice of war; *manhood*, during which they practised what they had been trained to do. It is to the credit of the Spartans that female education was fairly well organized in their State. Among the Athenians, the literary side received more attention, though Gymnastic retained its prominence, the recognized physical exercises being now grouped together in the *pentathlon*: running, leaping, quoit-throwing, wrestling, and boxing. The wider life of Athens, and the influence of the foreign element there, favoured the development of individualism. In his great educational work, *The Republic*, Plato sets himself to combat this individualism, and constructs an ideal scheme of Education in which the best elements of the actual Spartan and Athenian education are worked up into a system in which the individual is again overshadowed by the State. The Sophists, against whom Socrates was never tired of girding, were teachers rather than educators. They professed to communicate a certain amount of valuable knowledge rather than to form character. See EDUCATION (Greek).

This class of teacher became popular in Rome, which owed most of its culture to Greece. Among the Roman teachers were some notable men who deserve to rank as genuine educators. Chief of these is Quintilian, who, though his book professes to limit itself to the training of an orator, gives us a treatise on Education which Professor Laurie is inclined to regard as the best ever written. The Public Schools of Rome were secular and political, rather than religious; but with the introduction of Christianity a new system of education was established among the early believers, the main object of which was to enable converts to understand the new religion, and, if occasion favoured, to promulgate it. Hence arose the Catechetical Schools of the early Christians. By and by, the establishment of permanent places of worship led to the appearance of Monastery and Cathedral Schools, which were able to carry on the work of education after the fall of the Roman Empire. In the time of Charlemagne we find the value of Education recognized in the existence of a famous institution known as the Palace School. This was an itinerant institution which accompanied the Court in its wanderings, for the purpose of providing a suitable education for the sons of the nobility. Though probably not founded by him, it certainly attained its fame mainly through the intelligent patronage of Charlemagne. To him is also due the honour of issuing the famous Capitulary of 787, probably drawn up by Alcuin, then Master of the Palace School. This is a sort of general order sent to all the abbots of the monasteries under the great king, giving them his views on education, and his instructions regarding it. It has been described by Mullinger as 'perhaps the most important document of the Middle Ages,' and by Ampère as 'the charter of modern thought.'

The subjects taught in the mediæval schools formed the seven 'liberal arts.' They were divided into two groups, named respectively the *Trivium* and the *Quadrivium*. The 'trivial' arts were Grammar, Rhetoric, and Dialectics (the last corresponding to what we usually call Logic). The 'quadrivial' arts were Geometry, Arithmetic, Astronomy, and Music. These seven arts were held to include all that was worth knowing in the mediæval world. The first reference to the seven liberal arts, as matter of study or discipline, has been traced to Varro, but the credit of dividing them into the two groups is claimed for each of two writers—Augustine, and a certain Carthaginian named Martianus Capella. The truth probably is that Augustine made the distinction, while Capella, by his more picturesque style, called attention to and perpetuated it.

Universities as institutions were not founded; they really founded themselves; they grew out of the nature of things. The tendency of learned men to gather together for mutual help led to a process of segregation in suitable districts. No doubt in many cases favourable centres were found at certain schools connected with Cathedrals or Abbeys. In most cases the Cathedral School proved more attractive to learned men in search of intellectual freedom than did the Abbey School. A University was originally known as a *studium publicum vel generale*, but this phrase does not occur frequently till about the end of the 12th century. The *studia generalia* differed from schools inasmuch as they were meant for men. They were further distinguished by claiming and exercising the right of free teaching and free self-government. The teaching was not limited to students from one district or one country, hence the charter of a University had to come from one who had an authority recognized in different kingdoms. The only two such authorities in Europe were the Pope and the Emperor. To these, therefore, it became customary to apply for a charter to establish a new University, though some of the oldest and most famous Universities never had any charter, but claimed and exercised the privilege of granting to their graduates the *jus ubique docendi* by right of old custom. The *studia generalia* were very early identified with specialized instruction. Indeed, the idea of a *studium generale* very soon included the possession of at least one of the higher faculties in addition to the Arts faculty, which in those early times corresponded really to a preparatory course for one of the three higher—Theology, Law, and Medicine.

Parallel with the education of the Monastery, the School, and the University, was that of the Castle, where, instead of the seven 'liberal' arts, were taught the seven 'free' arts—those of Riding, Shooting, Hawking, Swimming, Boxing, Chess-playing, and Verse-making. The contrast between the free and the liberal arts emphasizes the weakness of the *Trivium* and the *Quadrivium*—their unwholesome aloofness from the affairs of everyday life. The mediæval scholars, as scholars, held themselves jealously apart from the common things of life; they lived in a world of their own, in a world of abstractions. When we consider that for nearly five centuries the finest intellects of Europe were applied to the discussion of the question of the relation of the general to the particular, we can understand the peculiar intellectual atmosphere in which mediæval scholars lived. On its educational side the Renaissance manifested itself in a revolt against this arid scholasticism. The charge of bookishness is sometimes made against the Renaissance education, and it must be confessed that in some of its developments it afterwards yielded to the tendency towards abstraction which is inherent in most forms of teaching. But on its first appearance the Renaissance education valued books mainly for their contents and their general style. It was a later generation that fell into the slough of 'scholarship' and grammatical pedantry.

By the time of the Renaissance the writers and thinkers on educational questions had developed their subject so much that different schools of thought have to be recognized among them. A triple classification is frequently made, the divisions being into Humanists, Realists, and Naturalists. The distinction is based largely upon the nature of the material upon which the mind is exercised as a means of training. The Humanists are those who prefer language and other specially human functions on which to nurture their pupils. They did not, as a matter of fact, at first confine themselves to language, but rather treated language as one means among many of expressing human aspirations. Painting, Music, Sculpture, Literature, and all that had a direct bearing on human life and action formed the materials with which the Humanists dealt. It is only when the Humanistic view is carried to excess that it leads to the pedantry associated with the mere language drill condemned by Carlyle under the name of *gerund-grinding*.

(1) Among the most distinguished *Humanistic* educators was **Vittorino da Feltre** (1378–1446), a schoolmaster at Mantua, who exercised a very considerable influence on education in Italy. **John Sturm** (1507–1589) was the master for many years of a famous grammar school at Strassburg, where he elaborated a procrustean system of instruction, in which the amount of work for each year was absolutely regulated, so that to exceed the amount prescribed was as great an offence as to fall short of it. By his pedantry Sturm did a great deal to obscure the real merits of Humanism. The English Humanists, **Roger Ascham** (1515–1568) and **Richard Mulcaster** (1531–1611), exemplify a better form of Humanism, and it has been remarked that it would have greatly benefited the education of Europe if the example of Mulcaster had been followed instead of that of Sturm. When the **Jesuits** saw the political importance of education, and deliberately set themselves to become the teachers of the governing classes of Europe, they founded their teaching on a Humanistic basis. Their work has been variously estimated. Religious prejudice no doubt plays a considerable part in the criticism to which the Order has been subjected, but the general view appears to be that their teachers more or less deliberately sacrificed matter in favour of form. This did a good deal to bring Humanism into disrepute, since it was regarded as an elegant but useless basis of education. The 'little schools' of the **Port-Royalists** in France adopted a more satisfactory form of Humanism. Their main contribution to Education was an excellent series of text-books, some of which have only recently become obsolete. It is well known that the education supplied at the present day in our great Public Schools in England is mainly Humanistic.

(2) The *Realists* prefer things to words. They maintain that the Humanists spend their time in a mere vapouring with signs, while neglecting the things signified. Underlying the Realistic reaction was the educational principle, now universally recognized, that in learning we pass from the concrete to the abstract, and that we must learn by direct contact with the material of our study. The saying of the old schoolmen, *Nihil in intellectu quod non prius fuerit in sensu*, is nowhere better exemplified than in the work of a Moravian bishop, **John Amos Comenius** (1592–1671), who gave his long life almost entirely to the cause of education, though his basal interest lay in a scheme of pansophy which he never found time to develop. Some of his ideas were anticipated by a peculiar personage called **Wolfgang Ratke** (1571–1635), who in those early days believed he had made discoveries in Education that had a great commercial value, and who tried to make money by selling his educational secrets. Probably the best work of Comenius consisted in his introduction of the vernacular as a means of teaching, and his recognition of the national importance of Education. He proclaimed the importance of all kinds of schools, from the village school up to the University, and maintained that no educational system could be complete which provided merely for one class of the community. Comenius wrote and published many class-books. Although these exemplify many breaches of educational principle, they were much ahead of anything then available; and one book in particular, the *Orbis Pictus*—a small picture-book in which the exercises in speech are founded upon the pictures supplied—had a phenomenal success, being indeed the first illustrated book for children. In direct succession from Comenius comes the Swiss educational enthusiast, **Pestalozzi** (1746–1827), whose self-denying labours have done wonders for educational theory and practice. He succeeded more by his intense human sympathy than by either his knowledge or his intellectual capacity. His great principle was, as he maintained, to psychologize education; but his writings and his practice have done little towards this end. His follower, **Froebel** (1782–1852), extended and elaborated the Pestalozzian principles. He carried the plant metaphor of his master to its legitimate conclusion by establishing the Kindergarten system, in which the school is treated as a garden, and the children as the plants. Among quite modern writers the most prominent realist was **Herbert Spencer** (sometimes, however, classed as a Naturalist), whose little book on *Education*, though decidedly weak in certain directions (clearly indicated by Professor Laurie in a criticism to be found in his *Educational Opinion from the Renaissance*, 1903), has probably had more effect in

modifying public opinion on Education than any other publication of the Victorian period.

(3) The *Naturalists* lay less stress on the mere subjects to be taught, and more upon the training supplied by life itself. Their aim is not so much to teach this, that, or the other subject as to bring the pupil into direct contact with life at the proper points, and thus enable him to work out his own education. Instruction is not lacking in the Naturalistic system, but it is not the only thing, nor even the most essential thing. The first Naturalist may be said to be **Rabelais** (1483–1553), who, as soon as he had escaped from his monastery, set himself in his more serious moments to the study of the possibilities of education in producing the kind of man that the world requires. His attitude is largely destructive, though in his *Eudœmon* (a well-endowed and well-trained youth used as a contrast to Gargantua) we find the ideal at which we ought to aim; and in certain passages we get fairly clear hints towards the method of attaining that ideal. The second Naturalist is **Montaigne** (1533–1592), who in the learned leisure of an easy life set himself to develop his theories of what education should be. **Locke** (1632–1704), on the other hand, went out of his way to publish a somewhat unmethodical and easy-going essay under the title of *Thoughts concerning Education.* In this we have the fruits of the observation of the medical man, the private tutor, and the philosopher. What the book lacks in system is more than made up for by its practical common sense and by its suggestiveness. **J. J. Rousseau** (1712–1778), in his pedagogical story of *Emile*, presents probably the most influential work on Education that has been written in modern times. He believes that man is by nature good and has been corrupted by civilization. The cry of the book is therefore 'back to Nature.' The educator must learn to lose time wisely, and to keep himself in the background, letting the educand develop in his own way. All initiative is to come from the pupil. **Fichte** (1762–1814), so far as he can be classified at all, must be ranked with the Naturalists. His claim to special notice is his famous *Reden an die deutsche Nation*, in which he deliberately set forth the claims of education as a regenerator of nations. **Goethe** (1749–1832) treated of Education as he treated of almost everything else. His contribution is to be found in the section on the educational province in *Wilhelm Meister*. This marks him out as Naturalistic. It was formerly customary for every German professor of Philosophy to deliver a course on Education, so most of the best known German writers on Philosophy have written something on the subject, Kant among others. At the present moment there is a prolific literature on educational subjects. While each country contributes to the general problem, each has acquired a specific character by emphasizing some aspect. Thus in the United States, Child Study and the relation of education to social life have received their fullest development. France has done exceptionally good work in tracing out the relations of temperament to education. In France, too, the educational applications of 'Suggestion' are best developed. Germany is specially strong in dealing with the philosophical bases of education, but has also given a great deal of attention to the methodology of the subject, particularly in connexion with the relation between the Froebelian and the Herbartian Systems. In Great Britain there is less interest in the philosophical bases, and the subject is usually treated in a more or less empirical way.

LITERATURE.—G. Stanley Hall and John M. Mansfield, *Hints towards a select and descriptive Bibliography of Education* (Boston, 1886); W. S. Monroe, *Bibliography of Education* (New York, 1897). These have naturally a strong American reference. E. P. Cubberley's *Syllabus of Lectures on the History of Education* (N.Y., 1902) is useful. In *National Education* (London, 1901), Laurie Magnus gives a very useful 'Bibliographical Note.' Reference may also be made to the catalogues of the various Educational Libraries, such as the Board of Education Library at the Whitehall Office, the Library of the College of Preceptors, the Teachers' Guild Library. There are some more or less commercial publications, such as the *Führer durch die pädagogische Literatur* (Vienna, 1879), that are not of much general utility. Of Educational Encyclopædias the following are the most important: Kiddle and Schem, *Cyclopædia of Education* (New York, 1877); Sonnenschein, *Cyclopædia of Education* (London, 1892); F. Buisson, *Dictionnaire de pédagogie* (Paris, 1882); Wilhelm Rein, *Encyklopädisches Handbuch der Pädagogik* (Langensalza, 1902). [This great work in seven large volumes is excellent.] Paul Monroe's five-volume *Cyclopedia of Education* published its first volume in 1911. On the development of Education, Letourneau writes well in his *L'Évolution de l'éducation* (Paris, 1898). The two most comprehensive Histories of Education are the *Geschichte der Pädagogik* of K. v. Raumer (Gütersloh, 1902), and the *Geschichte der Pädagogik* of K. Schmidt (Köthen, 1876). Of a more popular character is the *Histoire de la pédagogie* of Gabriel Compayré (Paris, 1883). Both Raumer and Compayré appear in English translations. Friedrich Paulsen's *Geschichte des gelehrten Unterrichts* (Leipzig, 1896) is now a standard work. The Herbartian controversy is admirably treated by F. H. Hayward in his *The Critics of Herbartianism* (London, 1903). The chief writers on the Herbartian side are: F. W. Dörpfeld, *Denken und Gedächtnis* (Gütersloh, 1904); T. Ziller, *Grundlegung zur Lehre vom erziehenden Unterricht* (Leipzig, 1884); W. Rein, *Outlines of Pedagogics* (Eng. tr., new ed., London, 1899). The 'critics' of Herbartianism are represented by H. Wesendonck, *Die Schule Herbart-Ziller und ihre Jünger* (Vienna, 1885); E. v. Sallwürk, *Gesinnungsunterricht und Kulturgeschichte* (Langensalza, 1887); O. Hubatsch, *Gespräche über die Herbart-Ziller'sche Pädagogik* (Wiesbaden, 1888); August Vogel, *Herbart oder Pestalozzi* (Hanover, 1893); P. Natorp, *Herbart, Pestalozzi, und die heutigen Aufgaben der Erziehungslehre* (Stuttgart, 1899). A good general book is P. Monroe's *Text-book in the History of Education* (London, 1905). French writers deal less specifically with Education; the following are typical works: M. J. Guyau, *Education et hérédité* (Eng. tr., London, 1901); P. F. Thomas, *L'Education des sentiments* (Paris, 1898), and *La Suggestion* (Paris, 1898); Frédéric Queyrat, *L'Imagination* (Paris, 1896), and *L'Abstraction* (Paris, 1894); J. Payot, *L'Education de la volonté* (Paris, 1894); C. A. Laisant, *L'Education fondée sur la science* (Paris, 1904). Three French writers who have most profoundly affected the Science of Education, without directly writing upon it, are: Alfred Fouillée, *Tempérament et caractère* (Paris, 1895); Fr. Paulhan, *L'Activité mentale* (Paris, 1889), and *Les Caractères* (Paris, 1902); G. Tarde, *Les Lois de l'imitation* (Paris, 1895). In English there is a large and rapidly increasing literature on the subject. Herbert Spencer's *Education* (1861); A. F. Leach's *English Schools at the Reformation* (London, 1896); W. T. Harris's *Psychologic Foundations of Education* (New York, 1898); S. S. Laurie's *Institutes of Education* (Edin. 1900), and H. G. Wells's *Mankind in the Making* (London, 1903), are probably the works that have produced most effect on educational opinion. Educational theory is now becoming consolidated, and the results appear in such works as E. N. Henderson's *Text-book in the Principles of Education* (1910), and F. E. Bolton's *Principles of Education* (1911). The *Great Educator Series* (Heinemann) and the *International Education Series* (Appleton) contain some excellent contributions.

J. ADAMS.

EDUCATION (American). — **1. Primitive teachers.**—As elsewhere throughout the world, the teachers of children among the American Indians include the *father*, who early instructs his sons in the arts and activities which more especially concern the male half of the tribe; and the *mother*, who in like manner teaches her daughter the domestic activities and industrial arts belonging to women. The *grandfather* and the *grandmother* are also teachers, particularly of the mythic lore, tribal legends, wealth of story and proverb; and often certain other aged men and women devote themselves more or less completely to giving such instruction, so that they are practically professional teachers, such as we have among ourselves to-day. The *medicine-man*, or shaman, appears likewise as teacher, often in connexion with secret societies, for admission into which children are prepared at an early age. Other interesting phases of teaching in aboriginal America are the following, where in some cases a high appreciation of the value of the 'profession' is involved in the actions indicated.

(*a*) *The captive.*—It is a great mistake to suppose, as some writers have done, that in their wars savage and barbarous peoples refrain from killing prisoners only to enslave or to debauch them. Even as

> 'The great Emathian conqueror bid spare
> The house of Pindarus, when temple and tower
> Went to the ground' (Milton, Sonnet viii.),

so many an uncivilized tribe spared the teacher amid the wild turbulence of strife. Woman's rôle as the mother and disseminator of so many forms of primitive culture, from ceramic art to the mysteries of religion, caused her, even in very remote ages of human history, to be thus spared; sometimes, too, when she was the apostle of the darker side of knowledge, she was feared rather than loved for her skill and cunning. J. W. Fewkes tells us that, when, in 1700, the Indians of the Pueblo of Oraibi, in New Mexico, took and destroyed the Pueblo of Awatobi (both settlements of the Tusayan people), the conquerors 'spared all the women who had song-prayers and were willing to teach them.' Among those saved was the *Ma-zrau-moñ-wi*, or chief of the Ma-zrau society, who declared her readiness to 'initiate the women of Walpi in the rites of the Ma-zrau'; and it was in this way that the observance of the ceremonial known as the *Ma-zrau* came to Walpi. We learn further that 'some of the other Awatobi women knew how to bring rain, and such of them as were willing to teach their songs were spared and went to different villages.'[1] The learning of men, too, made them safe amid the horrors of war, though not always so conspicuously as was the case with women. At the same conquest of Awatobi,

> 'the Oraibi chief saved a man who knew how to cause the peach to grow, and that is why Oraibi has such an abundance of peaches now. The Mi-çoñ-iñ-o-vi chief saved a prisoner who knew how to make the sweet *so-wi-wa* (small-eared corn) grow, and this is why it is more abundant here than elsewhere.'[2]

Captive women who married their captors have often been not merely teachers of individuals, but of families, clans, and even tribes. They have in not a few cases influenced the social customs and the religion of the peoples among whom their new lot was cast.

(*b*) *The pedlar*.—The pedlar, who survives now only in the more backward of our modern civilizations or on the fringes of the more advanced cultures of to-day, still retains traces of his former importance as an educator. He has often been quite as noted for his dissemination of intellectual wares as for the distribution of creature comforts or other material things. As O. T. Mason well says,

> 'itinerants and peddlers and tramps have marched about the world over, and men and women have been enslaved and wrecked. These have transported things and ideas and words. They have set up a kind of internationalism from place to place.'

These itinerant primitive 'tradesmen' are to be found among the American aborigines, where they served as dispensers of knowlege, distributors of tales and legends—in fact, as 'teachers' of a great variety of human lore.

(*c*) *The stranger and the foreigner*.—Among primitive peoples the stranger is often welcome, not because he brings with him good luck, fine weather, and the like, although such things also cause him to be happily greeted, but because he is a bringer of news. This characteristic is noted also among civilized races, particularly where they inhabit regions more or less cut off from the culture-centres of the world. Here the stranger really takes rank as an educator, being an important channel for the dissemination of knowledge of all sorts. Westermarck says: 'During my wanderings in the remote forests of Northern Finland I was constantly welcomed with the phrase, "What news?"'[3]

It is by no means true, as is often believed, that all primitive or uncivilized peoples are utterly averse to receiving knowledge from outside their own tribal bounds, and look with disfavour on any practical recruiting of their own intellectual resources from foreigners or strangers within their gates. In all probability, however, races, like individuals, have differed widely in their sense of receptivity, and in their attitude towards the exotic in all fields of human activity—mental, moral, social, and religious. What is true to-day of civilized races in this respect is true of the uncivilized peoples now existing, and we are justified in believing the same of their ancestors of the earliest human times. *Heterophilia* and *heterophobia* find their representatives at all stages of man's progress, from pre-historic 'savagery' to the culture of the twentieth century. Nor has the most progressive of modern nations exceeded some primitive peoples in eagerness to receive and absorb the new, the strange, and the foreign. Indeed, the same people, race, or even tribe may contain within itself these two diverse types, the neophobes and the neophiles—those who hate and those who love the new. Uncivilized peoples, likewise, are well acquainted with the condition of mind indicated by the famous couplet of Pope—

> 'Be not the first by whom the new are tried,
> Nor yet the last to lay the old aside'
> (*Essay on Criticism*, pt. 2, line 133 f.).

Among the American Indians, for example, all varieties of attitude towards the new and the reception of exotic objects and exotic knowledge can be found. Some of the Athapascan tribes of north-western Canada are extremely neophile. Some ethnologists (*e.g.* F. Boas) attribute this receptive attitude to lack of intensity of culture rather than to race.

2. Social institutions in relation to education.—Some Indian tribes, like the Kutenai, *e.g.*, have few, if any, secret societies and kindred social institutions; but with many other aboriginal peoples of America these abound, and children are carefully prepared for membership in them. These societies are of various sorts—social, political, religious, etc. In many of the tribal ceremonies and dramatic performances of the Indians, children have their regular rôles, for which they receive due training at the hands of their elders. As in some other parts of the globe, the advent of manhood and womanhood (see art. PUBERTY) is prepared for by much instruction of the young in special ways, among various American Indian peoples. Marriage, likewise, among many tribes has certain educational pre-requisites. Concerning the Omaha, one of the principal tribes of the Siouan stock, Miss Fletcher informs us (*27 RBEW* [1911], p. 330):

> 'In olden times no girl was considered marriageable until she knew how to dress skins, fashion and sew garments, embroider, and cook. Nor was a young man a desirable husband until he had proved his skill as a hunter and shown himself alert and courageous.'

3. Educational processes, institutions, etc.—The scope and general character of education among the American aborigines are thus described by Mason (*Handb. Amer. Ind.* i. [1907] 414):

> 'The aborigines of North America had their own systems of education, through which the young were instructed in their coming labours and obligations, embracing not only the whole round of economic pursuits—hunting, fishing, handicraft, agriculture, and household work—but speech, fine art, customs, etiquette, social obligations, and tribal lore. By unconscious absorption and by constant inculcation the boy and girl became the accomplished man and woman. Motives of pride or shame, the stimulus of flattery or disparagement, wrought constantly upon the child, male or female, who was the charge, not of the parents and grandparents alone, but of the whole tribe. Loskiel (*Mission of United Brethren*, Lond. 1794, p. 139) says the Iroquois are particularly attentive to the education of the young people for the future government of the state, and for this purpose admit a boy, generally the nephew of the principal chief, to the council and solemn feast following it.
>
> The Eskimo were most careful in teaching their girls and boys, setting them difficult problems in canoeing, sledding, and hunting, showing them how to solve them, and asking boys how they would meet a given emergency. Everywhere there was the

[1] *Amer. Anthrop.* vi. (1893) 366. [2] *Ib.*
[3] *MI* i. 581.

closest association, for education, of parents with children, who learned the names and uses of things in nature. At a tender age they played at serious business, girls attending to household duties, boys following men's pursuits. Children were furnished with appropriate toys; they became little basket makers, weavers, potters, water carriers, cooks, archers, stone workers, watchers of crops and flocks, the range of instruction being limited only by tribal custom. Personal responsibilities were laid on them, and they were stimulated by the tribal law of personal property, which was inviolable. Among the Pueblos, cult images and paraphernalia were their playthings, and they early joined the fraternities, looking forward to social duties and initiation. The Apache boy had for pedagogues his father and grandfather, who began early to teach him counting, to run on level ground, then up and down hill, to break branches from trees, to jump into cold water, and to race, the whole training tending to make him skilful, strong, and fearless. The girl was trained in part by her mother, but chiefly by the grandmother, the discipline beginning as soon as the child could control her movements, but never becoming regular or severe. It consisted in rising early, carrying water, helping about the home, cooking, and minding children. At six the little girl took her first lesson in basketry with yucca leaves. Later on decorated baskets, saddle-bags, bead work, and dress were her care.'

Miss Fletcher informs us that among the Omahas of olden times no 'baby talk' was in vogue; and special attention was given to the grammatical use of language. The Twana Indian children 'are taught continually, from youth until grown, to mimic the occupations of their elders' (Eells, *Bull. U.S. Geol. and Geogr. Survey*, iii. [Washington, 1877] 90). Among the Seminoles of Florida, 'no small amount of the labor in a . . . household is done by children, even as young as four years of age' (MacCauley, 'Seminole Indians of Florida,' in *5 RBEW* [1887], p. 498). With some of the Indian tribes of Guiana, 'while the women are shaping the clay, their children, imitating them, make small pots and goglets' (Im Thurn, *Among the Indians of Guiana*, 1883, p. 278). Among the Kato Pomo Indians of California, 'the chiefs, especially, devote no little care to the training of their sons as polyglot diplomatists,' and sometimes send them away from home to learn foreign dialects (Powers, *Indian Tribes of California*, 1877); the Mattole of California were reputed to give their children careful lessons in topography and geography of a primitive sort, resembling the excursion lessons now in vogue since the currency of 'Nature-study' in the schools of to-day in civilized lands. Among the Algonquians and other peoples of N. and S. America, professional story-tellers existed, whose business it was to instruct both adults and children in the mythic lore of the race. Forms of education corresponding somewhat to those in use among European peoples of the Middle Ages, including schools for special professions, existed among the more or less civilized peoples of Ancient Mexico, especially in connexion with the training of priests and nuns and attachés of the temples and similar institutions. Here we can speak of 'schools'—Mason (*Woman's Share in Prim. Cult.*, p. 208) even states that 'annexed to the temples were large buildings used as seminaries for girls, a sort of aboriginal Wellesley or Vassar.' There were seminaries for boys also. Barnes (*op. cit. infra*, p. 79) says:

'In ancient Mexico, the instructors were the priests, parents, and elders; the schools, the temples of the gods; the curriculum, careful courses in manners and morals.' Moreover, 'the method of instruction was didactic precept, and its aim the formation of an obedient, kind, submissive character.'

For several Indian tribes we have now interesting sketches of child-life (often of an autobiographical nature), which give many details as to the early education of the young of both sexes.

In Jenks' *Childhood of Jishib* is to be found a sympathetic account of the progress of an Ojibwa boy from birth to manhood, treating especially of his association with the animal world. For Indians of the Siouan stock (here the child's growth in primitive religious relationship with the *wakanda* or *manitous* is more or less emphasized) we have various writings of C. A. Eastman, himself of Indian descent, including his *Indian Boyhood* and *The Soul of the Indian*; also F. La Flesche's *The Middle Five*, and the writings of Miss A. C. Fletcher. The educational literature concerning the Pueblo Indians (with these peoples the effects of conservative sacerdotalism are much in evidence) is represented by Mrs. Stevenson's 'Religious Life of the Zuñi Child' (1887), and Spencer's 'Education of the Pueblo Child' (1889). The ceremonial education of the ancient Mexicans and the ritual of infancy, as recorded in some of the hieroglyphic manuscripts, have been treated by Hagar in his 'Four Seasons of the Mexican Ritual of Infancy' (1911), and Dr. and Mrs. Barnes in their brief article on 'Education as seen in Aztec Records,' based on Clavigero, Sahagun, etc.

4. Proverbs and sayings of pedagogical import.—Comparatively few American Indian proverbs are upon record (see Mrs. O. Morison, *op. cit. infra*, and Cushing's *Zuñi Folk-Tales*, N.Y., 1901).

Instruction by 'wise proverbs' was practised by many Indian tribes, as, *e.g.*, the Omaha, amongst whom the old men of the tribe had long talks with boys and girls, emphasizing the need of good manners, consideration for others, industry, etc. These talks were illustrated with proverbs condensing and strengthening their significance.

5. Song and story as pedagogical material.—Amongst American Indians there are numerous instances of the more or less direct employment of song and story as pedagogical material for the young of both sexes. The great ritual songs and ceremonies of primitive peoples often contain sections that are directly pedagogical. Such, *e.g.*, are the 'parables' of the Pawnee Indians, concerning which Miss Fletcher, who has penetrated some of the deepest secrets of these American aborigines, says (*Indian Story and Song*, p. 30):

'Scattered through an elaborate ritual and religious ceremony of the Pawnee tribe are little parables, in which some natural scene or occurrence serves as a teaching to guide man in his daily life. . . . The words of the song are purposely few, so as to guard the full meaning from the careless, and to enable the priest to hold the interpretation as a part of his sacred treasure. They are sufficient, however, to attract the attention of the thoughtful; and such a one who desired to know the teaching of the sacred song could first perform certain initiatory rites, and then learn its full meaning from the priest.' In the *Hako*, which is 'a prayer for children, in order that the tribe may increase and be strong, and also that the people may have long life, enjoy plenty, and be happy and at peace,' a Pawnee ceremony celebrated 'in the spring when the birds are mating, or in the summer when the birds are nesting and caring for their young, or in the fall when the birds are flocking, but not in the winter when all things are asleep' (A. C. Fletcher, in *22 RBEW*, pt. 2, pp. 26, 23 f.), there are a number of these 'parables.'

In these 'parables,' or brief-worded songs, as interpreted by the *kurahu*, the genius of the Pawnee Indians, as we may term the high-minded and thoroughly human 'priest' of this tribe, who revealed to Miss Fletcher the true religion professed by his fathers, we get a glimpse into the mind of the aboriginal American in one of its most didactic moments.

Among the things condemned in Indian stories (as recorded by G. A. Dorsey, *Pawnee Mythology*) are: making fun of poor children by rich ones, making fun of or maltreating animals, betraying friendship, meddling with ceremonial objects, quarrelling of children (especially brothers and sisters), wandering away from home, too great pride, needless sacrifices to the gods, false reports of 'buffalo in sight,' etc. Things approved and recommended are: respect for poor boys on the part of rich girls, belief in success through continued effort, hope of greatness and power being attained, obedience to and reverence for the gods, taking care of one's clothing, attention to things while travelling, friendship among young men, high aims in life, marriage of the maiden of one's choice, kindness to birds, listening courteously to everything but not believing all one hears, recognition of the fact that a chief is not, by the mere fact of being such, a great man, and that a prophet is without honour in his own country.

It was upon such devices rather than upon corporal punishment (see CHILDREN [American]) that the American aborigines relied for the ethical results of manhood and womanhood.

LITERATURE.—Besides the material on the American Indian child-life and education to be found in the monographs on various tribes published in the Annual Reports, Bulletins, etc., of the Bureau of Ethnology at Washington, the Memoirs of the American Museum of Natural History (New York), and in the numerous ethnological publications of the Field Museum of

Chicago, the University of Pennsylvania, Harvard University, the University of California, etc., the following may be cited: E. and M. S. Barnes, 'Education as seen in Aztec Records,' in *Studies in Education*, 1896–7, pp. 73–80; F. Boas, *The Mind of Primitive Man*, N.Y. 1911, *Ind. Sagen von der nord-pacif. Küste Amerikas*, Berlin, 1895; D. G. Brinton, *Rel. of Prim. Peoples*, N.Y. 1897, *Amer. Hero-Myths*, Philad. 1882; D. I. Bushnell, Jr., 'The Choctaw of Bayou Lacomb' (*Bull. 48 BE*, 1909); A. F. Chamberlain, *The Child and Childhood in Folk-Thought*, N.Y. 1896, 'Indians, North American,' in *EBr*[11]; G. A. Dorsey, *Pawnee Mythology*, pt. i., Washington, 1906 (Carneg. Inst. Publ., no. 59); C. A. Eastman, *Indian Boyhood*, N.Y. 1902, *The Soul of the Indian*, Boston, 1910; A. C. Fletcher, *Indian Story and Song from North America*, Boston, 1900, 'The Hako: a Pawnee ceremony' (*22 RBEW*, 1904, pt. 2); S. Hagar, 'The Four Seasons of the Mexican Ritual of Infancy,' *Amer. Anthrop.*, N.S. xiii. [1911] 229–234; G. W. James, *Indian Basketry*, Pasadena, Cal., 1902; A. E. Jenks, *Childhood of Jishib, the Ojibwa*, Madison, Wis., 1900; F. La Flesche, *The Middle Five*, Cambridge, 1901; O. T. Mason, *Woman's Share in Primitive Culture*, N.Y. 1894, *Origins of Invention*, Lond. and N.Y. 1895, 'Primitive Travel and Transportation' (*Rep. U.S. Nat. Mus.*, Washington, 1894, 1896), also art. 'Education,' in *Handb. of Amer. Indians*, pt. i. [1907] pp. 414–418; O. Morison, 'Tsimshian Proverbs' (*JAFL* ii. [1890] 285–286); F. C. Spencer, 'Education of the Pueblo Child' (*Contrib. to Philos., Psychol. and Educ.*, Columb. Univ., N.Y., vol. vii., no. 1, 1899); S. R. Steinmetz, *Ethnol. Studien zur ersten Entwickl. der Strafe*, 2 vols., Leyden, 1894; T. E. Stevenson, 'The Religious Life of the Zuñi Child' (*5 RBEW*, 1887); E. Westermarck, *MI*, Lond. 1906 ff.

ALEXANDER F. CHAMBERLAIN.

EDUCATION (Buddhist).—To present a consecutive history of educational theory or practice among Buddhist peoples is hardly possible in the absence of historical records or material. It is probable that the practice, if not the theory, has varied much in different countries and at different periods of time. There is, moreover, no evidence at how early a date, or under what circumstances, the monasteries of Buddhism became in general centres of instruction and training, not only in the precepts and observances of religion confined to those who had entered upon the religious life, but in more secular branches of education and study. And, if the training offered has been within all recent years of the most elementary description, there is reason to believe that limitations of this nature have not always ruled—certainly in India and Ceylon, and also in the lands of the Further East. The eagerness with which the Chinese pilgrims and students during many centuries sought access to the great Indian schools of learning, and, for the sake of the advantages which they offered, were prepared to face the dangers and endure the privations of long and distant journeyings, is proof not only of the reputation, but of the real worth of these schools. They were in all probability carrying on an educational practice which they had inherited from Hindu ancestry and precedent. They worthily maintained, however, the legacy of regard for learning and zeal in its pursuit; and they seem to have extended its scope—if a safe inference may be made from the practice of later centuries—beyond the confines of the purely religious or philosophical to subjects of a more general and popular interest.

Buddhist literature, however, is silent with regard to all such practices and developments. Wholly dominated by the religious interest, and occupied with matters of doctrine and philosophical speculation, it is even less informing than is the Hindu with regard to matters of historical detail, of the constitution and condition of the lay community, and of the opportunities open to all to obtain the training in knowledge or the arts which would suffice for the needs of daily life. Independently of the monasteries, such educational opportunities did not exist. Nor indeed, so far as is known, have they ever existed in Buddhist countries until recent times, unless in isolated and exceptional instances. Secular as well as religious education was in the hands of the monks, who alone possessed, and had the leisure to impart, knowledge. It was the duty of the senior monks to teach; the subject-matter of their teaching was for the most part religious faith and doctrine; and in cases in which it went beyond these subjects it is not probable that the curriculum embraced at any time much more than the rudiments of general knowledge. There are traces also of the beginning of an industrial training on a small scale. Manual toil was honourable to the layman, and was an obvious necessity if he was to minister to the support of the numerous inmates of the monasteries.

I. *EARLY RECORDS.*—The writings of the Chinese Buddhist monks and pilgrims who visited India afford abundant proof of the active pursuit of learning there carried on, and the many opportunities for study. The purpose of their travels was to secure copies of Buddhist sacred books, which on their return to China were translated into Chinese; and for several centuries a close and active intercourse appears to have been maintained between the two countries with this object. The earliest of these students whose narrative has been preserved, Fā-Hian, was absent from home in the early part of the 5th cent. for a period of fifteen years, visiting the sacred sites of Buddhism. He remained for two or three years at a time at monasteries in Pāṭaliputra (Patna) and Tāmralipti (Tamlūk), and spent two years also in Ceylon. In all these places he occupied himself in study, and secured copies of Sanskrit and other sacred texts. Many of the monasteries were large, containing 600 or 700 monks; and he describes how students resorted to these centres of piety and learning in search of truth. In Northern India, by which is meant the Panjāb and adjacent districts, Fā-Hian found that all the instruction was oral, and the rules of the various Buddhist schools were transmitted only by word of mouth. Further to the east, however, the monasteries preserved written copies of the Vinaya, the Sūtras of the schools, and also the Abhidharma. The utmost freedom appears to have been permitted to him in every place, every facility being afforded for study and the copying of the manuscripts. Some of the Buddhist books he is said to have himself translated into Chinese after his return to China. There is also in his narrative a single passing reference to Nāla or Nālanda, the site near Gayā of the Buddhist monastery or university which in later years was so widely renowned. In Fā-Hian's time the place had apparently not yet attained the greatness or importance which subsequently belonged to it. He refers to it as a village a *yojana* east of Rājagṛiha, and the birth-place of Sāriputta, where also he died and was buried; but he makes no mention of the presence of monks or a monastery.[1]

About two centuries after Fā-Hian a second and more famous Buddhist monk from China, Hiuen Tsiang, visited India, and during a period of sixteen years (*c.* A.D. 629–645) travelled widely in Central Asia and the northern parts of India, returning home, at the close of his wanderings, by land across the continent without seeing the monasteries of Ceylon or the south, of which he gives a merely hearsay account. During the interval of two centuries there had been frequent intercourse and exchange of visits between India and China, but no record of the experiences of the travellers appears to have been preserved. The most striking feature of Indian religious life, as Hiuen Tsiang found it, was the revival of Brāhmanism, and the growth and extension of the

[1] *Record of Buddhistic Kingdoms*, ch. xxviii. Beal identifies Nāla or Na-lo not with Nālanda, but with Kālapināka, on the ground that the latter is stated by Hiuen Tsiang to have been the name of the place where Sāriputta was born (see *Buddhist Records of the Western World*, i. p. lviii, ii. 177).

Mahāyāna school of Buddhism accompanied with a decline in numbers and influence of the Hīnayāna. Numerous monasteries of both sects, however, existed, some with as many as a thousand resident monks, engaged in the study of the law and the discussion of questions of religion and philosophy. For example, at the 'Golden Hill' (*Hiraṅyaparvata*), a city on the Ganges, there were ten *saṅghārāmas*, with about 4000 priests, belonging for the most part to the Sammatīya school of the Hīnayāna. At Tāmralipti, also, there were about ten monasteries with 1000 monks; and similarly in many towns of which he makes mention. Hiuen Tsiang further records, as Fā-Hian had done, the continual movement of students from all parts of India to these centres of learning and interest.

The most important and flourishing school of Buddhist learning, however, was at Nālanda, identified by Cunningham with the modern village of Barāgāon near Gayā,[1] about nine miles from Rājgir. Here there existed an ancient *saṅghārāma*, or monastery, built in memory of the Buddha, who had made the place his capital in a former existence; and numerous monasteries and temples, maintained out of the royal revenues, in which were several thousands of monks, of great distinction and fame, belonging to the eighteen principal Buddhist sects, engaged from morning to night in the study of the sacred books and the discussion of religious questions. Learned men from different cities resorted in large numbers to the schools of Nālanda for study and the resolution of their doubts and questionings. And the name itself was held in honour far and wide.

It is a proof of the intensive character of this love of learning, as well as of the power and influence of Buddhism, that Hiuen Tsiang reports the existence of a great monastery only about twenty miles west of Nālanda, with a thousand priests studying the Mahāyāna, the resort of scholars and learned men from distant countries.

In Central Asia also, Buddhism was possessed of a wide-spread influence. The devotion to learning and to the copying and study of the sacred books seems to have maintained itself for a considerable period. In his recent travels in the districts bordering upon China on the west, M. Aurel Stein found that the name and memory of the Chinese monk were still known and revered as of a scholar and saint.

In the latter part of the 7th cent. a testimony to the extension of Buddhist learning to Malaysia is given by a third Chinese traveller and monk, **I-Tsing**, who spent more than six years in Srībhoja, or Sumatra, engaged in the study of the law and the collection and translation of manuscripts, Sanskrit and Pāli. I-Tsing made his way to Sumatra and India by sea, sailing from a southern Chinese port in or about the year A.D. 671. His absence from home extended over a quarter of a century, during which time he is said to have travelled in more than thirty different countries, and to have brought or sent home to China four hundred Buddhist texts, of which after his return he himself, with the help of native Indian scholars who accompanied him to China, published translations of more than two hundred. I-Tsing gives a more detailed account of the manner of life in the monasteries and the doctrines of the different schools than either of his predecessors. And his narrative conveys the same impression of great activity of discussion and thought, and a wide-spread interest in knowledge, both religious and secular.

Within the boundaries of India itself the travels of I-Tsing were not so extensive as those of either Fā-Hian or Hiuen Tsiang. He spent, however, ten years at the university of Nālanda, which he describes as possessed of considerable wealth, receiving the revenues of land with more than two hundred villages—an endowment for which the monasteries were indebted to the generosity of the rulers of many generations. The monastic regulations at Nālanda were more strict than in other monasteries that I-Tsing visited, and the time and habits of the monks were all subject to rule. The hours of worship and work were determined by a clepsydra. Within the monastery itself there were more than 3000 resident priests, and the building contained eight halls and three hundred apartments. Besides the ordinary religious services of the monastery, the time of the monks was occupied in reading and study, and in the composition of religious poems and of expositions and commentaries on the sacred texts.

The course of instruction for boys began at the age of ten with the study of grammar, to which three years were devoted. This was followed by the reading of commentaries and works of a more advanced character on grammatical science, logic, and philosophy, which were all committed to memory. Thus far the course of study was alike for priests and laymen; and no one could claim to be well educated who had not made progress to at least this extent. The priests further studied works on the Vinaya, with the Sūtras and Śāstras. More than once I-Tsing compares the stages or attainments of the student with the several degrees of the Confucian scholar, and enforces the duty of unremitting study by the example of Confucius himself. The treatises of the Abhidharma were also made subjects of study; and public discussions were held, at which heretical opinions were considered and refuted.

It is evident that I-Tsing was imbued with a great respect for the learning, ability, and devotion of his teachers. Of one to whom he was indebted in his early years he writes that he was equally learned in both Confucianism and Buddhism, and was well versed in astronomy, geography, mathematics, and other sciences; and that he took the greatest pains in giving instruction, whether his pupil were a child or a full-grown and capable man. A second teacher was never wearied of teaching from morning to night. The personal attention and counsel which I-Tsing himself received from these and other men elicited his warmest gratitude.

With the cessation of intercourse between India and China, or in the absence at least of written records of such intercourse, direct evidence of the prosecution of Buddhist learning and of the study of the sacred books in the monasteries and at the courts of Northern India fails. There is no reason to believe, however, that the monasteries in any sense ceased to be centres of education and discipline, where facilities were to be found for literary study, and where the mind and habit were trained in the discussion of the theological and philosophical questions of the time. With the gradual decay and disappearance of Buddhism from India, its influence on literary culture and the thought and life of the people also passed away. To some extent, however, and in some centres, at least, it is probable that there were maintained to the end the tradition and practice of learning, and the devotion to study, which made the monasteries influential in forming

[1] *Ancient Geography*, 1870, p. 468; see *IGI*, *s.v.* 'Barāgāon.' The site has been marked for excavation by order of the Government of India. It is perhaps hardly probable that remains exist dating from as early a time as the visit of Hiuen Tsiang. In a note on the name and site (*JRAS*, 1909, p. 440 ff.), Bloch describes a statue of the Buddha still standing, with attendant Bodhisattvas, and writes that the modern name of the place would be more correctly spelt, as pronounced, *Baṛgāv*. The origin and meaning of the name Nālanda are uncertain.

the character and giving direction to the thought of successive generations of students. It is true that of the long lists of Buddhist authors and teachers which are recorded many of the names cannot be identified, and the date or even the existence of the writers is problematical; but the lists are nevertheless proof of the respect in which learning was held, and of the prevalence of a manner of life which gave opportunity for the cultivation of knowledge and rewarded its possessors.

There is sufficient evidence also that in Ceylon and Burma, no less than in India and China, and probably in other Buddhist countries, the literary tradition was well maintained. In Ceylon, in particular, the life and labours of Buddhaghoṣa (5th cent.) would have been impossible except on the basis of a well-established and long-continued practice and tradition of learning, which held literary pursuits in esteem, tested literary worth, and gathered together and carefully preserved the materials for literary study. How far during these early centuries of intense and fruitful monastic life the education and culture of the monasteries were in touch with, or influenced, the common people, it is impossible to determine. Perhaps not to any very great extent. The usage of later times, however, would indicate that, in some Buddhist countries at least, education was not confined to those whose lives were spent, or intended to be spent, in the comparative seclusion and leisure of the monasteries; that these last were in a real sense schools of general learning; and that in some instances, and possibly universally, where Buddhist control was sufficiently strong to enforce the rule, the entire population received a measure of education at the hands of the monks, all the boys being required by law or custom to pass a certain length of time within the walls of a monastery, and to submit to the discipline of a training in the elementary principles of knowledge. That the consequences of Buddhist zeal for knowledge, freedom of thought, and speculation were very great and beneficial, it is impossible to doubt. Alone of the great religions of the East, Buddhism stood for liberty of individual thought and action. To a high appreciation of knowledge for its own sake and to principles of generous tolerance the Buddhist faith owed in large part the influential position which it held so long among the nations of the East, and the attraction which it has never ceased to exercise upon minds of a more reserved and contemplative character.

II. *IN MODERN TIMES.*—In some Buddhist countries, notably in Japan and Burma, the tradition of scholastic learning and educational practice has been maintained in connexion with the monasteries down to the present time; and it is reasonable to suppose, although detailed proof cannot in the nature of the case be forthcoming, that the tradition has never been broken. Until the revival of interest in recent years, however, the education given had become increasingly perfunctory, greatly degenerate both in form and substance from what has been shown to be the zeal and habit of early days. The revival of interest in the sacred books and in Buddhist literature and teaching generally, which the closing years of the 19th and the beginning of the 20th cent. have witnessed in Ceylon and other countries, can hardly be counted altogether to the credit of Buddhism itself. In many, perhaps most, instances, it has been stimulated by external influence and example, and has often been inspired by a polemical aim, to counteract the growth and progress of Christianity as an alien religion. A real literary and historical interest has by no means always been wanting. The initial impulse, however, has been supplied by the West, widely as it may have been fostered and extended by native industry and research. These movements, at their present stage at least, hardly enter into consideration as contributions to the history or practice of Buddhist education. Where, as in Ceylon, they are under Buddhist and priestly control, they are imitative of Christian procedure in missionary and other schools, and have as their primary and avowed aim the counteracting of Christian propaganda, which they seek to meet with its own weapons. Elsewhere, as in Japan, the education is national in the fullest sense of the term, and Buddhism shares in it only as it has become and remains part of the national life. The following brief survey, therefore, of modern practice and achievement in regard to education in Buddhist countries takes account as far as is possible of what has been or is being done by native effort alone, independently of suggestion or pressure from the outside.[1] It should be added that there is nowhere any trace in Buddhism of a secular system of education, that is, of one independent of the monasteries or conducted by laymen. The monks have apparently always been the sole teachers, as they have been without exception the sole custodians of sacred learning.

1. **Ceylon.**—In Ceylon systematic instruction is given in the monasteries to both monks and laymen. There are, further, two native Buddhist societies, the Theosophical and the Mahābodhi, which possess schools at which children receive instruction; and others have been established under local or private management. The stimulus to this extra-monastic educational work, which is all of recent date, has undoubtedly been given by European incentive and example. To the same cause, and to the desire to retain in their own hands the religious control of their children, are due the numerous Buddhist Sunday schools in the island, at which the subjects of instruction are, of course, purely religious. In the monastery schools the senior monks undertake the office of teacher, not necessarily but of choice. They receive no stipend, but in many instances gain a wide reputation and influence. In the other schools salaried lay teachers are employed. Both monks and laymen teach in the Sunday schools, but the latter are always understood to be men of proved knowledge of the Buddhist scriptures. The ordinary schools come under Government control, and receive a grant-in-aid. In the latest year for which statistics are available, about 30,000 children were thus being trained in Buddhist aided schools. In these the subjects of instruction are necessarily those of the Government Code; but in addition a catechism of Buddhist doctrine is taught, and the life-history of Gautama Buddha himself is studied. In the monastery schools the education is, as a rule, entirely religious, but includes a knowledge of the sacred languages, Pāli and Sanskrit, and also classical Siṅhalese (Elu); in some instances astrology is included in the curriculum, and the elements of a science of medicine. Attendance at the Sunday schools is entirely voluntary; and, in addition to Buddhist doctrine, ethical teaching of a more general character is given. Apart from Government aid the Buddhist schools are supported by the gifts and liberality of the Buddhists themselves.

The Government of Ceylon has recently adopted a system of compulsory elementary education, but as yet (1911) it has hardly had time to become completely effective. Probably it is correct to state that about 60 per cent of the children of school-going age are in actual attendance at school. It

[1] Grateful acknowledgment is here made of information and help received from many correspondents in the different lands where Buddhism prevails. Without such aid, freely and generously afforded, the following account could not have been written.

has proved less difficult in general to carry out the ordinance in the country districts than in the towns; and greater progress in this direction has been made in the Southern Province than in the Northern. The system tends, and will increasingly tend, to eliminate private schools, whether belonging to the Buddhist or to any other community.

The general estimate of the moral influence of the education given does not seem to be high, especially of that in the monasteries. The deficiency is ascribed to the character of the teachers employed, in many of whom a lack of moral fibre and strength communicates itself with injurious effect to their scholars. With the monastic schools under present circumstances it would be impossible to interfere; but elsewhere it would seem that it ought not to be difficult to apply a remedy. The pride and power of Buddhism have been in her ethical system. And a practical failure in this direction would be a confession of failure in the whole.

The education of the girls, as in Eastern countries generally, is greatly deficient as compared with that of the boys. In the monasteries, of course, only boys and young men are received and taught. To the other schools and to the Sunday schools both boys and girls are admitted, but the latter form a small minority. Nor do any nunneries exist, as in other Buddhist lands, with the exception of a recent establishment near the centre of the island, in which an education and training might be given to Buddhist girls, parallel with that which is offered freely to all the male population in the monasteries.

2. Burma.—Buddhist educational practice in Burma has been more systematic and complete than in Ceylon, although perhaps hardly more advanced. Instruction is given in connexion with all the monasteries by the senior monk *hpongyī*, a title frequently given by courtesy to all monks in Burma, but properly restricted to the senior monks of more than ten years' standing; from among these the abbot or head of the monastery is selected, and is known as *sayadaw*, 'royal teacher'; and he is assisted usually by one or more probationers, *upasins*, unordained monks who are still in their novitiate. Before the country came under British control, with the consequent establishment of a system of independent vernacular schools under lay teachers, the whole male population of Burma passed through the monasteries, and for a longer or shorter period of time received instruction at the hands of the monks. Every Burmese boy entered the *kyaung*, or monastic school, at an early age, and remained for some years resident in the monastery. If it was intended that he should return to the life of a layman, he left school at the age of twelve or earlier, having, in addition to religious instruction, been taught reading and writing and the elementary rules of arithmetic. The boys who were designed for a monastic life remained permanently in the monasteries, and received further instruction in the Vinaya and Abhidharma, and later also in the Suttas. In the ordinary curriculum the religious teaching was confined to the life and sayings of Gautama and the stories of his previous existences (*Zats*, 'Jātakas'); the latter were committed to memory, and also a few simple prayers and hymns of praise in Pāli.

The establishment of Government and mission schools has had the effect of withdrawing the boys to a great extent from the monastery schools; and of those who have never been resident in the *kyaungs*, but have received their entire education in other institutions, it is generally true that through life their knowledge of, and attachment to, Buddhist rule and doctrine are of a much less marked character than is the case with most of their fellow-countrymen. In some instances also the *kyaung* serves the purpose of a preparatory discipline, and after three or four years at the monastery the boys pass on to complete their education at a school under Government or mission control. It is still true, however, that the great majority of the people owe their training and knowledge to the monasteries. The last Census Report states that 95 per cent of the whole male population of the country is literate, and this result must be ascribed almost entirely to the monastic teaching. Within recent years attempts have been made from without to raise the standard of the monastic schools, and those that have been willing to submit themselves to Government inspection and accept the Government conditions and code have been placed on the list for a grant-in-aid. These overtures, however, have been received with a measure of reluctance and suspicion; and no great progress has been made. As in Ceylon, and under the influence of similar motives, a few independent Buddhist schools have been founded on native initiative, where instruction in Buddhist doctrine and practice takes the place of the Christian teaching in the schools established by missionary agencies.

That the general effect upon the Burmese nation of the monastic instruction in the past has been beneficial there can be little doubt. The results of the system were twofold. Although the teaching was very elementary, and, as regards the lay portion of the population, ceased at an early age, it nevertheless imparted a character and tone of literacy, and placed the whole people on a higher level of interest and knowledge. No Burman need be, or as a rule was, entirely ignorant. He was at least able to read and write. And thereby, both by the mental discipline and by the stimulus to sympathy and thought, his outlook was widened and opportunities were afforded of further development of mind and character. The cumulative effect of a universal training in the elements of knowledge, perpetuated and enforced by custom and religious sanction through many generations, although it might not carry the individual very far, could not but exercise a broadening and elevating influence upon the nation as a whole. The Burman stands, and has stood, on a high level as compared with most of the surrounding peoples who are probably of the same origin and kin. And it is reasonable to place a part at least of his progress and superiority to the credit of his schools.

The second result has been on the side of ethics and religion. The teaching of the monastic schools has tended powerfully to the support of the national Buddhist faith. Every Burmese boy was instructed in the history and doctrines of Buddhism, and left school with a more or less intelligent knowledge of the principles of his religion, and a reverence for its ideals. The 'three jewels'—the Buddha, the Law, and the Community (Buddha, Dharma, Saṅgha)—represented a reality to him; and his sympathies and interest were enlisted at the most impressionable age in favour of the interpretation of life and duty which Buddhism offered. The hold of the Buddhist religion upon the heart and thought of the people has been very greatly strengthened thereby, and the faith itself preserved in comparative purity. Morally the teaching has not perhaps exercised the restraining influence that might have been expected. At the present day the evil example and the low standard of living of many of the monks counteract the good effects which might have been anticipated from the lofty theory and precepts of ethics which Buddhism inculcates. It is probable that in early times the moral power of the religious teaching of the schools was greater, less embarrassed and thwarted by the inconsistent lives of the monks themselves. It has, moreover, been preservative of much that is good in the national life, and through all has declared a standard of correct living, and has promoted and maintained a national consciousness of right and wrong.

Until the establishment of British rule no systematic instruction was provided for Burmese girls, as for the boys in the monastic schools. Nunneries, however, existed, and an order of nuns, *methilah*, but they were comparatively few in number and of little knowledge or influence. Part of their duty was to visit the women in their homes and give religious teaching. In a few instances also schools on a small scale were established in connexion with the nunneries, where an elementary education was offered on similar lines to that of the monasteries. There was no regular system, however, and it appears to have depended on the inclination or caprice of the nuns themselves whether any teaching work was undertaken. Little is done in this direction at the present time. Since the introduction of British Government, lay schools for girls as well as for boys have been established in considerable numbers under native Buddhist auspices, and these are found frequently in competition with the Government or mission schools. The work done in them is of a similar character, and the curriculum is the same as in the schools for boys. The standard also of effectiveness is being raised under the stimulus of competition and the influence of example, and in larger numbers the teachers employed are of certificated rank.

3. In **Annam** and **Cochin China** native schools are found widely distributed in some instances, but apparently they have had no direct relation to Buddhism. In **Sikkim** also and the Buddhist States on the north and north-east border of India the monks occasionally undertake the duty of giving instruction, or gather around them a few pupils as opportunity offers. There exists, however, no system or rule, and the occasional practice can hardly be regarded as having exercised any appreciable influence on the character or capacity of the people.

4. **China.**—The Buddhist zeal for learning, which was dominant in China in the early centuries, appears to have been entirely lost at the present time. The monks themselves are almost without exception uneducated and ignorant men, who are not held in any respect by the people, and are incapable of giving instruction in any real sense of the term, even if they possessed the will. There are, therefore, no native Buddhist schools in which a directed and definite attempt might be made to inculcate the principles of religion or to spread knowledge. The education of the country is entirely Confucian and based upon Confucian ideals (see EDUCATION [Chinese]), with which the Buddhist monks have no concern; and the children trained in the national schools learn to regard the monks with indifference and even contempt. Within recent years large numbers of the monasteries have been reclaimed by the Chinese Government, to be used as secular schools on modern lines, and the monks have been ejected.

Within the monasteries also the training given to the novices has been of the scantiest description, and confined to almost elementary necessities. For the most part the pupils who entered the monasteries with a view to the monastic life were drawn from the lowest classes of the population. They were, therefore, as a rule possessed of little aptitude or desire for learning. The usual vows are imposed, and the pupils are then taught by the abbot or senior monk sufficient to enable them to take their part in the general services and ritual of the monastery and in the recitation of masses. Beyond this the training seems never to go. The result has been, and is, that among a nation by whom learning is held in high honour the Buddhist monks as a class are despised, and they exercise no influence for good. Buddhist nunneries also exist; but the nuns no more command the respect of the people in general than do the monks. Novices are received in the temples and undergo the usual ceremonies of initiation, with shaving of the head; but no schools for girls are found in connexion with them, nor are any of the nuns definitely engaged in teaching.

The revival of interest in Chinese Buddhist literature on the part of some native scholars is due almost entirely, as in Ceylon, to example and incentive from the West. The literature is very extensive, and consists of translations of sacred books made from the Sanskrit or Pāli, of many of which the originals are no longer extant. It is, therefore, of the greatest value from the point of view of Buddhist doctrine; but it has been almost entirely neglected by the Chinese people themselves in favour of the Confucian Classics, and has exercised no educative influence upon the nation at large, or been a source of moral or religious progress of any kind. Buddhism in China, in contrast to its attitude and standing in some other countries, seems to have been overcome by mental and spiritual inertness and lethargy, and to have long ceased to be an element of account in the intellectual life and history of the nation.

It is not without interest, also, to note that the defective condition of Buddhism in China has aroused the sympathy of some of the more active and spiritually minded Buddhist churches of Japan. Proposals have been made to send Buddhist missionaries from Japan to open Buddhist mission schools in China, where a free training should be given to the children of the poor, with the object not only of extending a true knowledge of Buddhist principles and teaching, but of promoting civilization and education in general. It is very probable that thus, and in other ways, the newly awakened readiness in China to admit Western learning and instruction from without will show itself in a revived interest in and appreciation of a faith to which the people and land have owed much in the past, and the present atrophy and neglect be followed by a period of awakening and activity.

5. **Japan.**—In the larger sense of the term, Japan owes more educationally to Buddhist influence and instruction than perhaps any other nation, with the possible exception of the Burmese; and the Japanese have shown greater power of assimilation of teaching and example, both intellectual and moral. B. H. Chamberlain, whose knowledge of 'Things Japanese' was unrivalled, writes:

> 'All education was for centuries in Buddhist hands; Buddhism introduced art, introduced medicine, moulded the folklore of the country, created its dramatic poetry, deeply influenced politics and every sphere of social and intellectual activity. In a word, Buddhism was the teacher under whose instruction the nation grew up.' [1]

The same writer adds that Japanese scholars are usually forgetful of the fact of the paramount influence of Buddhism during the early and formative centuries of the national life. That influence has been deep and strong and lasting. And, although Buddhism as a religion was disestablished and disendowed in Japan forty years ago in favour of Shintoism, its moral teaching and ideals, which are those of the Mahāyāna school, remain effective, and are probably increasing their

[1] *Things Japanese* [3], London, 1898, p. 71 f.

hold upon a large proportion of the more thoughtful minds of the nation. As a formal religion, Buddhism is now to a considerable extent ignored in Japan, and is not likely to re-assert an extended sway. During the twelve or thirteen centuries, however, of her more or less continuous ascendancy, the Buddhist missionaries were the instructors of the nation in every department of learning, and the leaders in all progress; and they have left a deep and permanent mark upon almost every department of the national life. In no country, not even in Ceylon or Burma, has Buddhism had a greater opportunity, or made a more effective and, on the whole, beneficent use of the opportunity put into her hands.

The details of the educational history it is impossible to trace in the absence of direct evidence or of documentary records. Buddhism was introduced into Japan from Korea in the middle of the 6th cent.; and it is probable, therefore, that Korean monks took a large part in the preaching and dissemination of Buddhist principles. Korean civilization was itself, however, of Chinese origin, and was wholly, or almost wholly, exotic. Although it entered Japan by way of Korea, it was essentially Chinese in method and character, and Chinese teachers took the lead in conveying to the people both the Buddhist religion and a knowledge of the arts and sciences which it had made its own in the land from which it was derived. What might have been the effect of the introduction of Chinese civilization apart from the refining and gentle influence of Buddhist teaching it is impossible to determine. The two were intimately conjoined. And the latter was the agent or medium through which the former reached the hearts of the people, and moulded their habits and lives.

Before the opening of Japan there existed schools taught by the monks, known as *terakoya*, 'temple-huts.' They were not universal, or in connexion with every monastery; but that they were to be found in effective working in most parts of the country is proved by the fact that nearly all the male population were able to read. Attendance at these schools was entirely voluntary, and it is probable that the education given did not, in the country districts at least, go much beyond the elements of reading and writing. There were also schools open for girls, which were, it may be assumed, always under the direction of nuns. As a result of these schools a large proportion of the women under the old régime in Japan were literate in the sense of being able to read. In more recent times the system of national education, with compulsory attendance in the primary grade schools from the age of six to the age of twelve years, has for the most part superseded these schools, which find it difficult to maintain themselves in competition with the Government institutions. A few remain, chiefly for the benefit of the poorer classes; and some Buddhist schools of a higher grade have been established, supported by private interest and contributions. In these lay teachers are employed as well as monks. The total number, however, is small, and their influence upon the general education of the country is very restricted; for the Government system is so complete in its provision for education, from the lowest grade to the highest University and post-graduate requirements, that there is little room or opportunity for private enterprise. The curriculum of the schools in secular subjects conforms to that of the Government regulations. In addition, Buddhist doctrine is taught—probably in no instance to any great extent—and the principles of Buddhist morality are inculcated. There are also a few girls' schools of this class, but they have little or nothing to do with the nunneries, and the nuns do not teach in them.

In all the monasteries, provision is made for the training of the younger monks in Buddhist doctrine and practice. The sacred books are studied and expounded, and the principles of the faith explained and enforced. Many of the monks are men of considerable learning as well as of piety. An increasing interest also is taken in the history and tenets of the various sects; and in no direction has the tendency to a religious revival shown itself more clearly than in the emphasis laid upon the devotional and spiritual element in the teaching of the Buddhist books. In the country districts there has been little movement or awakening of interest. In the larger towns, however, partly no doubt with the polemical aim of counterworking Christian teaching and the influence of Christian missionary schools, a considerable increase of zeal and activity has been manifest, which endeavours by direct instruction, as well as by the Press, to confirm the principles of the faith in the minds of the people. And the monasteries have become, at least in some instances, centres of religious thought and of a real literary culture, which cannot fail to be of influence on the nation.

Buddhist *Kindergarten* schools also exist, but in no great numbers. The suggestion of these has been adopted from the Christian missionary institutions, and both in form and methods the model of the latter has been followed. Within the limits of age and training there is naturally hardly any opportunity for distinctively Buddhist teaching, although the schools are under Buddhist control. In some instances Christian instructors have been employed, in view of their superior technical capacity and knowledge.

6. Korea, etc.—In countries where Buddhism has been a secondary influence, at least in recent times, as in Tibet, Korea, Manchuria, and Mongolia, it is not easy to determine how much of educational practice and the teaching of the young, where this has been carried out at all, has been due to Buddhist example and effort. Training in doctrine and ritual is always given in the monasteries to the younger monks and novices, and usually includes a knowledge of at least the elements of reading and writing. It is hardly probable that in any of these lands the education was carried beyond the most elementary stage. During the most flourishing period of Buddhism in Korea, from the beginning of the 10th to the end of the 14th cent. of our era, all learning was concentrated in the hands of the monks, and politically, as well as ecclesiastically, their influence was dominant. They cultivated the sciences and shared in the government of the country, using the power and prestige of knowledge to secure temporal advancement. There was no attempt, however, to extend the advantages of learning to the laity, or any evidence that the schools of the monasteries were open to others than the resident monks and novices. In **Siam** also learning was cultivated, and in recent years has revived under royal patronage. It was confined, however, to a minority; and its influence upon the nation as a whole was small, although it undoubtedly tended, as in Burma, to the preservation of Buddhism as the national religion and a permanent force in the national life. Astrology and magic also in some instances, especially in Tibet, have entered into the curriculum. But the introduction of these has been due not to Buddhism but to the primitive Nature or other worship upon which Buddhist forms and doctrine were imposed.

Under ordinary circumstances there did not exist in any of these countries a system of education for the Buddhist laity. Individual monks might, and probably did, gather around them a few pupils, to whom of their own free will they imparted elementary instruction, teaching them out of the limited store of their own knowledge. The practice, however, was infrequent, and seems to have entirely died out. The almost universal condition of comparative ignorance and neglect is, indeed, in striking and not pleasant contrast to the habit and life of the early centuries, when, in Central Asia at least, the Chinese travellers make reference to a stirring intellectual life in the large cities, and monastic establishments on a considerable scale with eager students of the Buddhist writings. It is evident that the influence of Buddhism was at that time much greater than at the present day, and was exerted in the direction of literary culture and pursuits. Recent discoveries by M. Aurel Stein and others have tended to corroborate the Chinese accounts of the flourishing condition of the Buddhist faith.

The conclusion to be drawn from a survey of the whole is that, with the exception perhaps of Burma, the early efforts of Buddhism for the promotion of educational training and advancement have not been maintained. Japan ranks next to Burma in regard to the degree in which Buddhist discipline and intellectual training have continued to exercise a real influence upon the general population; and it is far in advance of Burma in the richness and variety of its intellectual interest. Ceylon is overshadowed by the antagonistic influence of the religions of India; but partly for that reason, partly in opposition to the religion of the West, Buddhism is there making a great effort to free itself from foreign admixture, to re-establish the purity of its own teaching, and to keep and strengthen its hold upon the thought and training of the young. It is, indeed, too early as yet to determine, or even to forecast, what the effect will be of the religious revival within Buddhism. It is not a little remarkable that after a long period of stagnation and decay there is an almost universal awakening on the part of Buddhists themselves to an interest in their own history and doctrines, and a zeal for the maintenance of the faith, and even for its extension amongst foreign peoples. Nor is the movement by any means confined in the East to Buddhism alone. The efforts of the latter, however, are more markedly on the lines of a literary culture and the education of the mind and thought. Such an appeal, made on behalf of an ancient faith with a widely renowned and honourable past, cannot fail to command sympathy and respect, even among those who believe that the practice and discipline of the faith are inconsistent with the best interests of mankind, and its teaching out of harmony with the highest truth.

LITERATURE.—There is not much literature that can be cited upon the subject of education in Buddhism, and there is no work that attempts to give a connected view of the whole. The narratives of the Chinese monks have all been translated into English as follows: Fā-Hien, *Record of Buddhistic Kingdoms*, tr. J. Legge, Oxford, 1886; Hiuen Tsiang, *Si-yu-ki, Buddhist Records of the Western World*, tr. S. Beal, 2 vols., London, 1906, also *Yuan Chwang's Travels in India*, tr. T. Watters, 2 vols., London, 1904–1905; I-Tsing, *A Record of the Buddhist Religion*, tr. J. Takakusu, Oxford, 1896. Works on Buddhism in the various countries usually contain more or less detailed reference to the training of the monks, *e.g.*, R. S. Copleston, *Buddhism in Magadha and Ceylon*[2], London, 1908, pts. v. and vi.; H. Kern, *Manual of Indian Buddhism*, Strassburg, 1896, pp. 73–85; Shway Yoe, *The Burman, his Life and Notions*[3], London, 1910, chs. iv., xii., xiii.; H. Hackmann, *Buddhism as a Religion*, London, 1910, *passim*; W. E. Griffis, *Corea, the Hermit Nation*[7], London, 1905; J. H. Langford, *Story of Korea*, London, 1911; M. Aurel Stein, *Ancient Khotan*, Oxford, 1907, and *Ruins of Desert Cathay*, London, 1912. The recent policy and practice of education in Japan are most fully expounded by Baron Kikuchi, *Japanese Education*, London, 1909, where will be found also references to earlier practice, p. 33, chs. x., xiii., etc. The Governments of Ceylon, Burma, and Japan issue annual reports on education, which are the authoritative statements in the several countries. See also the artt. on BURMA AND ASSAM (Buddhism in), CEYLON BUDDHISM, CHINA (Buddhism in), etc.

A. S. GEDEN.

EDUCATION (Chinese).—As no nation can vie with China in the alleged antiquity of her literary origins, so perhaps no nation surpasses her in the importance attached throughout her history to education.

'If he [a ruler] wish to transform the people and to perfect their manners and customs, must he not start from the lessons of the school? The jade uncut will not form a vessel for use; and, if men do not learn, they do not know the way (in which they should go). On this account the ancient kings, when establishing states and governing the people, made instruction and schools a primary object' (*Li Chi*, xvi. 1 f. [*SBE* xxviii. 82]). 'Without education the nature deteriorates.' 'If in youth one does not learn, how will he do when he is old?' (*Three Character Classic*).

From these quotations it is already evident that, as is right, education is taken to mean more than the imparting of knowledge. Its aim is the formation of character so as to fit a man to play his part in society, and more particularly in State employment. Previous to the T'ang dynasty (A.D. 618), 'letters were valued solely as an aid to politics, and scholarship as a proof of qualification for civil employment'; and, if in later times 'letters began to assume the position of a final cause,' still civil employment was the incentive proposed. Of the four classes into which Chinese society is divided —scholars, agriculturists, artisans, and traders— scholars take precedence. But for the word translated 'scholar' the dictionaries give the meanings 'officer, soldier, minister, learned man, scholar, gentleman'; and 'gentleman' perhaps best covers all that a Chinese scholar should be. The ideal scholar is thus described:

'Early and late he [the scholar] studies with energy, waiting to be questioned. . . . The scholar's garments and cap are all fitting and becoming; he is careful in his undertakings and doings; . . . he seems to have a difficulty in advancing, but retires with ease and readiness; and he has a shrinking appearance, as if wanting in power.' He guards against death, that he may be in waiting for whatever he may be called to; he attends well to his person, that he may be ready for action. 'With the scholar friendly relations may be cultivated, but no attempt must be made to constrain him; . . . he may be killed, but he cannot be disgraced; . . . he may be gently admonished of his errors and failings, but he should not have them enumerated to him to his face. The scholar considers leal-heartedness and good faith to be his coat-of-mail and helmet; propriety and righteousness to be his shield and buckler; he walks along, bearing aloft over his head benevolence; he dwells, holding righteousness in his arms before him; the government may be violently oppressive, but he does not change his course—such is the way in which he maintains himself. . . . If the ruler respond to him, he does not dare to have any hesitation (in accepting office); if he do not respond, he does not have recourse to flattery. . . . The scholar lives and has his associations with men of the present day, but the men of antiquity are the subjects of his study. . . . The scholar learns extensively, but never allows his researches to come to an end; he does what he does with all his might, but he is never weary. . . . The scholar, when he hears what is good, tells it to (his friends); and, when he sees what is good, shows it to them. . . .' Gentleness and goodness, respect and attention, generosity and large-mindedness, humility and courtesy, the rules of ceremony, singing, and music, these are the qualifications and manifestations of humanity. 'The scholar possesses all these qualities in union, and has them, and still he will not venture to claim a perfect humanity on account of them—such is the honour (he feels for its ideal), and the humility (with which) he declines it (for himself). The scholar is not cast down, or cut from his root, by poverty and mean condition; he is not elated or exhausted by riches and noble condition. . . . Hence he is styled a scholar' (*Li Chi*, xxxviii. 3–19 [*SBE* xxviii. 403–409]).

Such a sketch shows us the *ethos* of Chinese education, and is the more interesting as purporting to come from Confucius himself.

In very ancient times there was an official whose title has been translated 'Minister of Instruction.' His functions, as summarized by J. Legge, were to teach the multitudes 'all moral and social duties, how to discharge their obligations to men living and dead, and to spiritual beings' (*SBE* xxvii. 231 n.). It is not easy, however, to discover through what machinery he discharged these functions. The most vivid glimpse we get of ancient education is in the *Analects*, which records the intercourse between Confucius and his disciples. In his 22nd year Confucius came forward as a public teacher. He taught all who, attracted by his reputation, were willing and able to receive his instructions, however small the fee they could afford. His school was peripatetic, and the teaching conversational. Its note is struck in the opening sentences of the *Analects*: 'The Master said, Is it not pleasant to learn with a constant perseverance and application? Is it not delightful to have friends (fellow-students) coming from distant quarters?' His themes were the Book of Poetry, the Book of History, and the maintenance of the Rules of Propriety. He taught ethics, devotion of soul, and truthfulness. He attached great importance to the ancient poetry as an instrument for stimulating the mind and assisting in self-contemplation, and to music, which, in his opinion, as in that of Plato, could, according to its kind, either deprave or correct the mind (cf. *Shun Tien*, ch. v.).

Such instruction as that given by Confucius to his disciples may be compared with tutorial instruction of University students, and implies some preliminary opportunities of learning. We find surviving from ancient times the names of schools of various grades, but little definite can be learned of their organization and scope. Perhaps they were only for the children of men of rank, though they may have been imitated by the non-official classes. Probably in those early times education was left largely to private enterprise, as it has been in later periods. The Sacred Edict expressly commends the founding of a family school. A wealthy man may invite a teacher and start a school for the children of himself and his friends, perhaps even for all the children of his clan or village; or a whole village may unite and open a school, the expenses of which are met by fees or by a contribution from the public funds of the village. In the larger towns colleges may be started pretty much in the same way. Such schools, not otherwise graded than by the ability of their teachers, have been the nursery of all China's scholars. Home education, in the narrower sense of the imparting of book-lore by parents to their children, has never counted for much in China. The mothers of China are for the most part too ignorant to give instruction, and, even where the same reason does not hold good for the fathers, still, opinion is rather against a parent acting also as teacher (Mencius, bk. iv. pt. i. ch. 18). Home influence, however, does count, and to tell a child that he has had 'no home training' is reckoned a severe rebuke by reason of its oblique reflexion on his parents. One of the Odes contains the lament of a father over his indocile son; in another it is said, 'Our mother is wise and good; but among us there is none good.'

A well-known anecdote of Mencius' mother both exhibits her solicitude to exert a right influence on her son's character, and dates the beginning of that influence in his pre-natal days. One day Mencius asked his mother what the butcher was killing pigs for, and was told that it was to feed him. Her conscience immediately reproved her for the answer. She said to herself, 'While I was carrying this boy in my womb, I would not sit down if the mat was not placed square, and I ate no meat which was not cut properly—so I taught him when he was yet unborn. And now, when his intelligence is opening, I am deceiving him—this is to teach him untruthfulness.' Accordingly she went to the butcher's and bought a piece of pork for Mencius.

The education of a Chinese youth was thus left to the home, and to what schools, of this unofficial sort, might be accessible to him. But, though there have been no Government schools, it would ill become one who writes from the Chao-Chow Prefecture, which still remembers the great debt it owes to Han Wên-kung (A.D. 768–824), to forget how powerfully education in any district may be fostered by an intelligent and energetic official. Moreover, it must not be supposed that the influence of the Chinese Government has not ever been effectively in favour of education. That influence has been brought to bear on the nation through the great system of competitive examinations. The germ of the system may be found in the post-official examinations already in existence in the time of Shun (2255 B.C.), who every three years examined into the merits of those holding office under him, degrading the undeserving and promoting the deserving (*Shun Tien*, ch. v.). But in its development this post-official examination system has been overshadowed by the pre-official. The system may be said to have reached its full development in the Ming period, and was until recently continued under the Manchu rule. The whole Empire was knit together in a great network of examinations for an ascending scale of degrees, *hsiu-tsai*, *chu-jen*, *chin-shih*, held periodically in each county, prefecture, and province, and culminating in an examination for admission to the Imperial Academy (Hanlin), held in the capital under the immediate supervision of the Emperor. To the lower examinations all subjects of respectable birth were admissible, and to the higher examinations all who had passed the lower. Indeed, once a student had, by passing his examination, got his name on the register of scholars, he was bound to present himself periodically at the examinations for the degrees he held, even though he did not aspire to a higher.[1]

The primary object of this system of examinations was to obtain able men for State service. While securing this, it gave a great stimulus to education, but at the same time reduced it, latterly at least, to a narrow uniformity. In more ancient times, candidates were examined in the rules of propriety, music, archery, horsemanship, writing, and arithmetic, to which were afterwards added such subjects as law and military science. But latterly, however the ancient names have been retained, what has been sought is neither varied accomplishment nor a mass of acquired knowledge, but rather an intimate acquaintance with the classical books and an exquisite facility in Wen-li (the literary language) both in prose and verse, together with skill in penmanship.

A boy who begins to attend school—usually at the age of 7 or 8—enters on a new epoch of his life, marked by the bestowal on him of a new name chosen by his teacher. He starts at once, with loud-voiced repetition, to memorize the books which are the scholar's equipment, beginning with the *Thousand Character Primer* or the *Three Character Classic*, and passing on to the more strictly classical books. Not till the memory has been well drilled is a beginning made in explaining the meaning of the books memorized, the explanation being a midrash founded, in the case of the classical books, on the commentaries of Chu Hsi (A.D. 1130–1200). The necessity of such explanation is obvious if it is borne in mind that Wen-li, in which the books studied are composed, never has been a vernacular medium anywhere in China at any time of her history. *Pari passu* with his reading, the pupil is taught penmanship and composition in all the approved rhetorical forms, specially with a view to excelling in the famous 'Eight-legged Essay.' The result of years of such training is the production of a ripe Chinese scholar, 'in knowledge a child, in intellectual force a giant, his memory prodigious, his apprehension quick, and his taste in literary matters exquisite' (Martin, *Hanlin Papers*, 1st ser., p. 38). The fact already mentioned, that Wen-li is not the mother-tongue

[1] A somewhat parallel system of examinations for degrees in military subjects needs only to be mentioned.

of any Chinaman, helps to explain why, in spite of all the importance attached to education, the percentage of illiteracy in China is so high. Martin estimated that the proportion of those who can read understandingly is not more than 1 in 20 for the male sex, and 1 in 10,000 for the female. Not even in China are all boys sent to school; still, in deference to the maxim that it is culpable for a father to bring up a son without education, even very poor parents will make shift to send their sons to school for a year or two. Unfortunately, what is acquired in that time is, for the most part, merely the ability to recognize and pronounce, but not to understand, a number of characters; and to repeat verbatim, but equally without understanding, some portion of the books studied. If poverty then compels the withdrawal of the boy from school, the knowledge acquired is apt to be evanescent, and is in any case useless. As might be expected, however, among a people so painstaking as the Chinese, and attaching so much importance to education, there are not wanting examples of learning successfully pursued under the severest stress of poverty.

In considering Chinese pædagogics we must never forget the underlying psychology. According to the orthodox view, human nature is radically good, and is corrupted, not by the breaking out of an internal taint, but by external infection. This failure to reach the deep root of evil explains the exaggerated view which meets us everywhere of the power of example and of instruction. Reference may also be made to Mencius' interesting discussion of the passion nature (bk. ii. pt. i. ch. 2), and to the account given by Confucius of his own intellectual and moral development (*Anal.* ii. 4).

In educational method what is most noticeable is the prominence given to memory discipline, the effects of which are seen not only in the frequent apt quotation of classical phrases, but in a perfect plague of recondite allusions. Some suggestive hints as to method are found in *Li Chi*, xvi. 13 (*SBE* xxviii. 87): 'He [the skilful teacher] leads and does not drag, so producing harmony; he strengthens and does not discourage, so making attainment easy; he opens the way but does not conduct to the end, so making (the learner) thoughtful.' The catechetical method is reversed, the pupil questioning the teacher, who, as he skilfully waits to be questioned, is compared to a bell which gives a sound, great or small, corresponding to the hammer with which it is struck. If the pupils are not able to put questions, the master should put subjects before them; and, if then they do not show any knowledge of the subject, he may let them alone. So we find Confucius saying, 'When I have presented one corner of a subject to any one, and he cannot from it learn the other three, I do not repeat my lesson' (*Anal.* vii. 8).

A teacher's position is regarded with respect, and gives him great authority over his pupils; and the latter are supposed to cherish a life-long deferential regard for their teachers. A well-known line in the *Three Character Classic* gives the Chinese 'dominie' sufficient warrant for severity, and 'the cane and the thorns' are noted as part of the awe-inspiring apparatus of ancient schools.

What has been said has reference almost exclusively to boys. A girl has always been at a discount (*Odes*, II. iv. 5), and is not supposed to require book-lore. According to the *Li Chi*, it was sufficient if she learned pleasing speech and manners, to be docile and obedient, and to deal with hemp and silk and viands. The Chinese have ever been imitators of the ancients, and female literary education has therefore been neglected, though, of course, literary ladies are by no means unknown.

Of more informal educational influences may be mentioned the constant issue of old and new tracts, hortatory and dehortatory, some of which, such as the 'Family Instructions' of Chu Tzŭ, are accepted as standard works. One would like to include that solitary example of Chinese preaching, the official expositions of the Sacred Edict on the 1st and 15th of each month; but the exposition is a formality, and its influence nil. Of the Sacred Edict itself it is said (Martin, *Hanlin Papers*, 2nd ser., p. 325) that 'nothing, since the discourses of Mencius, gives us a better view of the kind of morals inculcated by the head of the nation.' Of incalculable, but doubtless great, effect in moulding character are the numerous proverbs, with their pithy statements of morality and prudence.

The present condition of education in China is very different from that outlined above. Under the new régime, which may be conveniently dated from 1902 (establishment of Ministry of Education; note also decree of Oct. 1905 abolishing the old system of examination for degrees), the Government has issued an educational programme, with schools of all grades up to a University. The published code is interesting as showing what is aimed at, but has less in it that is peculiarly Chinese, being based on Western systems. One notes with satisfaction the wider range of studies, the place given to ethics and to physical drill, and the recognition of female education. The approved lesson-books also indicate an advance in educational methods. The working of the scheme varies according to the interest of the officials in each locality. There is an inevitable shortage in the supply of competent teachers, so that we find schools well equipped with apparatus which no one can use; and further obstacles easily arise from the fact that each locality has to bear the financial burden of its own schools. But, if there are difficulties at present, still, with all drawbacks, the situation is full of promise; and one may hope that, when things have settled down under the republican regime, more rapid advance will be made in organizing a system of national education. In view of the importance in education of the religious element, which is ill provided for by the teaching of ethics supplemented by a perfunctory worship of Confucius, much may depend on the attitude that the educational authorities take up towards Christian pupils and teachers, and towards schools under Mission auspices which have shown the way and are still in the front rank. Existing Mission schools of all grades (if they are educationally efficient) and the projected Christian University may be most useful, directly and indirectly, even though they fail to secure recognition as part of the Government educational system. And, indeed, in complaining of the non-recognition of educational institutions under foreign control, and teaching a religion the foreign associations of which are still prominent, it is easy to become unreasonably forgetful of the point of view naturally taken by the rulers of an ancient and proud people inspired by a lately awakened patriotism.

LITERATURE.—*The Chinese Classics* (tr. by Legge, *SBE* iii., xvi., xxvii., xxviii., Oxford, 1861–85); Morrison, *Dict.*, ed. 1815, i. 746, *s.v.* 'Heŏ'; *Variétés sinologiques*, no. 5: 'Pratique des examens littéraires,' Imprimerie de la Mission Catholique, Shanghai, 1894; Martin, *Hanlin Papers*, 1st ser., London, 1880, 2nd ser., Shanghai, 1894; Graybill, *The Educational Reform in China*, Hongkong, 1911.

P. J. MACLAGAN.

EDUCATION (Greek).—*Introductory.*—What form education took in the first period of Greek history, we have no means of knowing; and, even when we come to later times, our information is often without precise dates. But, making allowance for that, we have a considerable body of ascertained facts to rely on for the latter part of the 6th cent. B.C., for the whole of the 5th, and for the 4th till about 322, the year of Aristotle's death. With him ancient Greek thought and ideals ended; though the spirit of the Athenian system of education did not die, but was destined to spread and to exercise a powerful influence in Rome and in other cities of the Mediterranean region.

1. Homeric times.—Attempts have been made to picture Greek education during the period when the Homeric poems arose (850–750 B.C.). The evidence in Homer, however, is meagre, and any inferences must be very uncertain. The speeches of Achilles, Nestor, Odysseus, and other heroes, with their perspicuous argument, their repartee, irony, and pathos, imply that, while the *Iliad* was taking shape, orators existed who could speak, and audiences existed who could appreciate the spoken word. Phœnix claims (*Il.* ix. 443) to have taught Achilles to be a speaker of words and a doer of deeds: μύθων τε ῥητῆρ' ἔμεναι πρηκτῆρά τε ἔργων. In those days, however, mental culture came mostly from singing and lyre-playing. Bodily training consisted of dancing, wrestling, swimming, running, and such like; and these would be acquired chiefly through practice with comrades. By precept and example, the father would instil religion and morality into his boys; while the girls would learn household duties and the rules of an upright life from their mother.

2. Dorian.—(*a*) *Crete.*—'In the normal Greek conception,' says Jebb (*Attic Orators*, 1893, ii. 14), 'Society and the State were one. The man had no existence apart from the citizen.' And, as an indigenous type of education inevitably harmonizes with the national ideal, Greek education is closely related to the Greek idea of citizenship. Hence, to take one aspect, we find education restricted to the free population possessing full civic rights. Among the Dorians, whether in Crete or in Lacedæmon, all whose birth entitled them to citizenship were bound to undergo the complete course of training. In Crete the males of a certain number of families shared the common meals (ἀνδρεῖα = συσσιτία) in a common dining-hall (Aristotle, *Pol.* ii. 10. 3). There the boys of those families lived, and received an education from observing the conduct and listening to the conversation of their elders, one of whom was the παιδονόμος, or superintendent of the boys of that house (Athenæus, 143 E). Scantily clad both summer and winter, they passed through a hard training to teach them skill and endurance. They were exercised in gymnastics, in handling the bow and other weapons, and in fighting—sometimes single combats, sometimes house with house. They learned also to read; to sing hymns in honour of the gods, and songs to the fame of the brave; and to chant the laws, which were set to music (Strabo, x. 480, 482, 483; Ælian, *Var. Hist.* ii. 39). At the age of seventeen, having sworn to serve the State loyally and to hate its enemies, they were freed from the supervision of their elders and gathered in ἀγέλαι, or droves. They remained members of these till marriage. Each drove was under a captain (ἀγελάτης), who had full powers to punish. He led them to the gymnasium for practice, and to the open country on hunting expeditions. One drove fought mimic battles with another. The sole aim of the Cretan training was military.

(*b*) *Sparta.*—The military ideal was still more prominent in Sparta, where the Dorians tenaciously clung to a traditional system which had arisen when they were a comparatively small band of invaders in the Peloponnese, keeping men of alien race in subjection by main force. In Sparta, the Dorians possessed of full citizenship were outnumbered by the περίοικοι, who were personally free but politically unenfranchised, and by the helots, who were serfs attached to the land; and it was, therefore, necessary that the citizens should be made, as far as training could make them, men of courage and endurance.

As soon as a child was born, it was inspected by the elders of the tribe. If weakly, it was exposed (cf. art. CHILDREN [Greek], in vol. iii. p. 540); if strong, it was handed to the mother to remain in her care till the age of seven. Spartan discipline began early. The child was taught to fast, to keep from screaming, and to overcome the fear of being alone in the dark. The boys were taken to the public dinners (φιδίτια), where they learned to be Spartans like their fathers.

When they reached the age of seven, the State intervened and carried them off to be educated in public boarding-houses. They were arranged in βοῦαι, droves, and ἶλαι, troops, under the strict charge of a State official, the παιδονόμος. Sleeping on beds of straw or reeds, with no blankets, going about barefooted, clad in a single garment, and stinted in regard to food, they became inured to hardship. Food they were encouraged to steal; but, if caught in the act, they were punished, to make them cunning foragers in war. The boys in each house were under a βουάγορ, who was one of the εἴρενες, or men over twenty years of age. It was his duty to superintend their mimic battles, to stimulate them to smartness in foraging, and to train them in concise answering of problems on behaviour and conduct. Severe punishment was all-pervading. Floggers (μαστιγοφόροι) attended the παιδονόμος; any citizen might inflict a beating; the βουάγορ punished disobedience. Flogging-competitions were held to decide who could stand the greatest number of strokes (Xenoph. *Resp. Laced.* ii.). The chief means of education was gymnastics, which aimed solely at developing warlike qualities, such as bodily activity and powers of endurance. The boys learned to run, leap, play ball, swim, throw the javelin and the discus, ride, and hunt. They also practised dancing. Some of the dances were religious; but most were war-dances, *i.e.* rhythmical marchings and evolutions (Lucian, *de Saltatione*, 10–12; Athenæus, 630 E, 631 A). The gymnastic training hardened, but it brutalized (Aristotle, *Pol.* v. [viii.] 4; Xenoph. *op. cit.* v. 9). Yet the Spartans were not without humanizing influences, though these had not free play. Their music was meant to form character; and the Dorian mode was regarded as inspiring the hearer with firm and deliberate resolution which kept the mean between pusillanimity and fool-hardiness (cf. Milton, *Par. Lost*, i. 550 ff.). They sang hymns in praise of the gods, and chanted the laws of Lycurgus. Their other poetry, designed mainly to stir up bravery and patriotism, consisted of songs eulogizing their heroic ancestors and jeering at cowards. Reading, writing, and arithmetic were not in great repute, and seem to have been introduced comparatively late. Even in the 4th cent. B.C. many Spartan citizens were declared to be unable to read or write (Isocr. *Panathen.* 276 D, 285 C). But, apart from reading, the Spartans possessed literary equipment, acquired by memory; nor were they without a turn for pithy and terse speech—what Plato calls βραχυλογία τις Λακωνική (*Protag.* 342 E, 343 B). In addition to their national songs and hymns, they knew and valued Homer (Plato, *Laws*, 680 C).

In their eighteenth year, the youths left the boys' houses, and, for the next two years, were styled μελλείρενες, *i.e.* those who were to be εἴρενες. They were still under strict discipline. They were trained in arms and in military evolutions; in organized battles, team against team; in hunting; in musical drill and choral dancing. They were also dispatched on secret service (κρυπτεία), when they prowled about the country, scouting, and, if necessary, slaughtering helots. On this service they learned to rough it, and had opportunity to display courage and resource (Plato, *Laws*, 633 B, C).

In Sparta the girls had a training similar to that of the boys (Xenoph. *op. cit.* i. 4). They practised physical exercises—dancing, running, wrestling, leaping, throwing the javelin and the discus—to make them worthy mothers of a sturdy race. They were instructed in music. Youths and maidens joined in choral songs and dances. The other Greeks remarked that, in spite of this training, Spartan girls were not less modest or well behaved. In the capacity of sisters, wives, and mothers, their opinion was respected, their censure dreaded, their commendation sought.

This system of education, with the stern discipline that pervaded Spartan life as a whole, created a nation of soldiers—brave, self-sacrificing, reverencing old age, devoted to the State, ready with a jest and a smile to die for their country. But their morality was *of* the State, not *in* the individual. When the Spartan was free from public constraint, *e.g.* when he went abroad, he was apt to degenerate. The system failed to develop the intellect and the imagination, and personal power of initiative (see, for various points, Plutarch, *Lycurgus*, xiv–xxviii).

3. Athenian.—(1) *Aim and scope.*—Athenian education can be treated in detail, for the sources of information are fuller. This is fortunate, for two reasons. First, the Athenian type was, with modifications, the general Hellenic type, except among the Dorians. Then, it is of greater intrinsic worth: it gave more play to the individual nature, and sought to effect a full and harmonious development of the man. Its aim, especially at first, was distinctly ethical. The different branches of education were designed not to produce scholars or musicians or athletes, but to develop and build up moral qualities. It is true that this goal was not always reached. Sometimes balance was upset by too much devotion to one or other of the branches, sometimes the end was lost sight of in the means. No better statement in brief of the Athenian aim can be found than a passage from Plato's *Protagoras* (325 C–326 E). When the problem 'Can virtue be taught?' is started, Protagoras declares the teaching of virtue to be the main intention in education, and man's life, from the cradle to the grave, to be one round of instruction and admonition. Then follows the description of the Athenian training of the young:

'As soon as a boy understands what is said to him, his nurse, his mother, his *pædagogus*, and even his father, spare no pains for the sole purpose of making him as good as possible. At the very moment when he does any act or speaks any word, they point out to him that one thing is just, another is unjust; this is beautiful, that is ugly; this is holy, that is unholy; and they say "Do this," "Do not do that." If he obeys willingly, well and good: if not, they correct him with threats and with blows, like one straightening a piece of wood that is bent and warped. Then, when it is time for boys to go to school, their parents enjoin upon the masters to pay far more attention to training in proper behaviour (εὐκοσμία) than to teaching letters and lyre-playing. The masters attend to this; and, when the boys have learned their letters and are sure to understand what is written, just as formerly they understood what was said, the master places beside them on the benches the works of good poets for them to read—poems abounding in moral admonitions and in narratives, eulogies and panegyrics of the brave men of old. These the boys are forced to learn by heart, that they may zealously imitate those heroes and desire to be like them. The music-master, in turn, does exactly the same. He gives heed to inculcating self-control (σωφροσύνη), and sees to it that the boys do no evil. In addition, when they have learned to play the lyre, he teaches them the works of other poets—lyric poets this time—and sets the verses to music. He causes the rhythms and harmonies to dwell as familiar friends in the souls of the boys, that they may be more refined, and, becoming more permeated with good rhythms and good harmonies, may be more effective for speech and for action. Further, the boys are sent to the palæstra that their bodies may be strengthened to do yeoman service to their efficient intellect, and that a bad condition of body may not force them to play the coward either in war or in any other of life's activites. This is what is done by the parents who can best afford it, that is to say, by the wealthy, whose sons are the earliest to go to school and the latest to leave.'

With this cf. Aristophanes, *Clouds*, 961 ff., where the old system is eulogized as the nurse of the men of Marathon; and Lucian, *Anacharsis sive de Gymnasiis*, 20 ff.

It should be noted that in Athens, as in Greece generally, the priest as priest had nothing to do with education, and that there was no direct religious teaching. What religious training there was came through learning hymns to the gods, through the ritual of worship at home and in the temples, and through the public festivals. In Athenian education it was the poet, not the priest, that exercised a paramount influence. This enables us to understand Plato's attack upon poets and dramatists for the pernicious effect of their works on young and growing minds (*Republic*, 377–397).

In Athens, as in Sparta, education was not for all; but, since Athenian citizenship had come to be on another and a wider basis than Spartan, a larger proportion of the male inhabitants were educated.

(2) *Mothers, nurses, pædagogi.*—It was the father, and not the tribal elders, that in Athens decided whether or not the child should be reared. Till the age of seven, children were cared for by mothers and nurses, who imparted the rudiments of learning in the form of lullabies and nursery rhymes, myths about the gods, and tales of heroes, beast fables, as well as stories of ghosts and goblins—μορμώ, ἔμπουσα, ἐφιάλτης, λάμια (Xenoph. *Hellen.* iv. 4. 17; Lucian, *Philops.* 31. 2; Theocr. xv. 40; Strabo, i. 19). Theorists like Plato (*Rep.* 377 A) had much to say about the ethical danger lurking in the myths and stories. To interest the child at this stage as well as later, there were the usual toys, amusements, and games—rattles,[1] dolls, dolls' houses, boats, tops, hoops, swings, hobby-horses, balls, leap-frog, ducks and drakes, blindman's buff (μυίνδα, χαλκῆ μυῖα), beetle-flying (μηλολόνθη), balancing on an inflated wineskin well greased (ἀσκωλιασμός), knucklebones, hide-and-seek (Pollux, ix. 99 ff.). About the age of seven, the boy had assigned to him an elderly slave as his moral supervisor—παιδαγωγός. It was the attendant's duty to accompany the boy to school, to the gymnasium, or elsewhere; to look after his manners; and to beat him if necessary. At times, the slaves selected were those who from age or physical disablement were unfit for other tasks; or they were boorish and spoke with a bad accent. Such disqualifications made them incompetent to manage the older lads. The supervision lasted till the boys reached the age of sixteen or even eighteen (Plato, *Lysis*, 208 C, *Laws*, 808 C; Plutarch, *de Educ. Puer.* vii.).

(3) *Schools, schoolmasters, State supervision.*—The rise of schools followed the employment of writing for literary purposes. We hear of school buildings in the beginning of the 5th cent. (Herod. vi. 27; Plutarch, *Themis.* x.); and they existed a hundred years earlier, if we may trust the statements of Æschines (*c. Timarch.* 9 ff.) and Diodorus (xii. 12). In Athens, schools were private ventures and varied in kind, being sometimes very inferior (Demosth. *de Coron.* 257 ff. = 312 ff.). Teaching might be conducted in the open air—in some convenient nook of street or temple. Even the best schoolrooms were not grand structures or elaborately furnished. The head master sat in a high-backed chair, the other masters and the boys on stools and benches. The walls were hung with

[1] The renowned Archytas invented a rattle, πλαταγή (Aristotle, *Pol.* v. [viii.] 6 *ad init.*).

writing-tablets, rulers, cases for manuscripts, and lyres (see, for example, the vase-paintings). The room might at times be adorned with statues of gods, muses, and heroes, and with pictures illustrating scenes from Homer. The *Tabula Iliaca*, now in the Capitoline Museum at Rome, is regarded as part of a series of these illustrations. The school day began soon after sunrise,—not such a variable hour in Athens as in our northern latitudes,—and, with a break at midday, continued till just before sunset. How the day was portioned out among the various subjects is unknown. Nor can the number of holidays be precisely stated. Schools would not open on public festivals and other general holidays. We find fugitive records of prizes given after public competition, chiefly for athletics, but also for music and letters.

The teacher of letters (γραμματιστής) was not highly honoured, and consequently the best type of man was not always obtainable. 'He is dead, or he is teaching letters,' was a byword of any one who had unaccountably vanished. The presence in schools of pet leopards and dogs belonging to pupils (see vase-paintings) indicates laxity of discipline or general contempt for teachers. Lucian (*Necyom.* xvii.), speaking of what poverty drives kings and satraps to, classes elementary teaching (τὰ πρῶτα διδάσκοντας γράμματα) along with the hawking of smoked fish.

According to Plato (*Crito*, 50 D), parents were ordered by law to educate their sons in music and gymnastics; but the method of enforcing this is not on record. The Areopagus would exercise a general oversight—a function which the officials called σωφρονισταί seem to have performed in later times. Custom, however, if not law, made a certain tincture of literary education general in Athens. How much that was would vary with the standing and the desire of the parent. Though the Spartan severity of flogging did not exist in Athens, punishment was common and severe in all departments of education. In the home, too, the rod was not spared. The general opinion agreed with Menander's saying, 'A man unwhipped is a man untrained' (Xenoph. *Anab.* ii. 6. 12; Herondas, *Mimes*, iii.).

(4) *Early education: letters.*—For many generations the complete Athenian course consisted of letters, music, and gymnastics. At different periods and according to the boy's social position, these branches occupied a varying number of years of his life. Whether the three began simultaneously or not, we cannot tell. In later times, for those who were able and willing, a more or less definite curriculum of higher education[1] filled the years immediately preceding manhood at eighteen.

The Athenian boy learned, first of all, to read intelligently—a considerable mental discipline, since in Greek writing the words were continuous as well as without punctuation. Next, he was taught to read with proper articulation and accent, and to bring out the melody and rhythm of the sentence. He also learned to write. The scarcity of books in early times necessitated much oral work. It was not till the age of Pericles (469-429) that books became common. Slave labour made them tolerably cheap, and they speedily came into school use. In spite of Plato's outcry (*Protag.* 329 A, *Phædrus*, 275 ff.) against the written word as lifeless compared with the spoken word, books played an important part in later Greek education. A good memory, then, was very important, particularly in the earlier period; and a great amount of poetry was learned by heart. Besides strengthening the memory, this roused the imagination, cultivated literary taste, stored the mind with moral maxims and homely wisdom, and stirred the boy to emulate the brave deeds of heroes. In poetry, Homer stood supreme, reverenced as the educator of Greece, the matchless guide in all affairs of life (Xenoph. *Sympos.* iii. 5, iv. 6; Plato, *Rep.* 606 E). Other poets were Hesiod, Theognis, Phocylides, Solon, Mimnermus, and Tyrtæus. Æsop's prose fables were also popular.

At first arithmetic was not taught as a mental discipline, but was learned as of practical utility. The Greek symbols for counting were clumsy to manipulate, and calculation was performed on the fingers, or with pebbles, or by means of the *abacus*. Later, when the educational value of mathematics was better appreciated, geometry as well as arithmetic was taught. Drawing did not become a school subject till the 4th century. Aristotle approved of it, because it trained the eye to appreciate beauty and enabled one to judge the money value of statuary, and thus escape cheating (Aristotle, *Pol.* v. [viii.] 3; Plato, *Laws*, 818).

(5) *Music.*—Originally μουσική had a wide meaning, and was often used to include literature (Plato, *Rep.* 376 E) as well as music, the narrower sense to which the word came later to be restricted. In Greek schools, music was both vocal and instrumental. Though the music-master was called κιθαριστής, it was not on the κιθάρα—a professional instrument—but on the λύρα that boys learned to play. After the Persian War the αὐλός, or pipe, was in vogue, but later it fell into disfavour. It distorted the player's face (Plutarch, *Alcibiad.* ii.); he could not sing while playing; and its music was held to be exciting. The last reason is the strongest, and harmonizes with the Greek conception that music should be studied, not merely as an accomplishment to occupy leisure moments or entertain a social circle, but mainly as the chief developer of character. For music did more than stir the feelings, it created ethical qualities. The different modes of music produced each a particular type of character. The Dorian, for example, was manly, strong, and dignified; the Lydian, soft and effeminate; the Phrygian, passionate and exciting. The Greeks, however, did not love instrumental music by itself. Sounds without words never appealed to them as the highest art. The boys diligently learned by heart the verses of the lyric poets for the purpose of singing. They were carefully instructed in rhythm and metre, and in enunciation. It is this belief in the ethical importance of music that explains Plato's and Aristotle's demand for the State to regulate music in the schools, since only thus would proper rhythm and harmony be produced in the soul (Aristotle, *Pol.* v. [viii.] 3 and 5-7; Plato, *Rep.* 398-401, *Laws*, 654, 812; Polybius, iv. 20. 4).

(6) *Gymnastics.*—The Greeks attached particular importance to physical education. It began at an early age: exactly when, we do not know. From about the age of fifteen on to eighteen, a very large amount of time was devoted to gymnastic exercises; and all through life a citizen was expected to keep himself in training. It was his duty to be fit for war (Xenoph. *Memor.* iii. 12; Plato, *Phædrus*, 239 C); and it was an object of ambition, especially for the leisured, to possess a fine physical frame. Perfect bodily condition, also, was necessary for good health, and as a basis for a sound and vigorous mind (Lucian, *Anacharsis*, 15).

While using the term γυμναστική, we must distinguish the παλαίστρα from the γυμνάσιον. The former means, regularly, a private school for train-

[1] To distinguish the higher subjects from the others, the terms 'secondary' and 'primary' have sometimes been employed. We should, however, remember that, if used, the terms cannot bear their present-day precision of meaning.

ing boys; the latter was a public resort for practice by the *ephebi* and older men, as well as a training-place for competitors in the games and for professionals. In later days we find the words used indifferently: γυμνάσιον being also applied to the boys' training-school, and παλαίστρα to part of the γυμνάσιον. The latter name indicates that those exercising were γυμνοί, naked or lightly clad. The palæstra, in charge of a παιδοτρίβης, was an enclosure with a floor of sand, open to the sky—to inure the boys to the sun—and, if possible, near a running stream. A plunge in the stream or a cold bath concluded the exercises, after the sweat and dust had been scraped off by the στλεγγίς—especially needful for wrestlers, whose bodies were always oiled.

We do not know the exercises for different ages, but they would be graduated from easy to difficult. Wherever possible, the movements were performed to the sound of music. Among the earliest exercises were ball-playing, swimming, and deportment. Boys, for example, were carefully trained to sit properly and to walk gracefully (Pollux, ix. 103 ff.; Lucian, *Lexiph.* 5). The course included also χειρονομία, or rhythmic movement of the arms, leap-frog, rope-climbing, running, jumping, throwing the discus and the javelin, wrestling and boxing (Athenæus, 629 B; vase-paintings). To the Greeks, dancing meant the measured motion of the whole body, often mimetic of some action or scene. In Athens, dancing fell into disfavour in the education of boys, except for those who took part in the chorus at some public festival (Xenoph. *Sympos.* ii. 15 ff.).

The last years of the boy's training were very hard in regard to diet as well as exercises. And it became clear to the wisest thinkers that this severe physical strain militated against intellectual work. The idolizing, also, of the athlete led to professionalism. Pure athleticism, instead of creating brave and strong warriors, merely brutalized; and the result was a body useless to the State, because disproportionately developed (Aristotle, *Pol.* v. [viii.] 4; Eurip. fr. *Autolycus*; Xenophanes, *Elegies*, ii.).

While the Athenians sought to foster the exercises that would develop pluck and intelligence, we miss among them what is considered an invaluable part of our school games—the forming of clubs, the members of which discipline themselves in self-government.

(7) *Higher education: the Sophists.*—In early days, as we have seen, instruction in γράμματα and μουσική generally ceased when the boy was about the age of fourteen. The sons of the wealthy might then do as they pleased; others must think of fitting themselves to earn a living. We should remember, however, that Athenians of all ages and ranks, though not at school, were always under the intellectual and æsthetic influences of their common life—influences emanating from rhapsodists and orators, from statues and architecture, from dramas and festivals. But about 450 B.C. the feeling arose that ability to read and write, to sing and play the lyre, to recite poetry, was not a complete education. The demand for a wider and more advanced course called forth a supply of instructors in all kinds of subjects—mathematics (comprising the science of number, geometry, astronomy, theory of music); rhetoric, political and forensic; the art of disputation; literary criticism; grammar; etymology; correct diction; discrimination of synonyms; geography; natural history; rhythm and metre; dialectic; ethics. For a century the lecturers on these subjects—collectively designated the Sophists—dominated the general or liberal education of Greece. Some of the best known Sophists were Protagoras, Prodicus, Gorgias, Polus, Thrasymachus, Evenus, Hippias, and Isocrates. The hearers who flocked to them were of all ages, and many of the lectures must have been beyond the comprehension of younger minds. But much was suitable for boys, and came to be part of the ordinary school curriculum. The Sophists sometimes claimed not only to supply knowledge, but also to prepare a man for civic life, besides imparting accomplishments and general culture (Plato, *Rep.* 518 C, 600 C; *Protag.* 314, 318, 349; *Apol.* 20 B). Plato and Aristotle vigorously assailed the Sophists on the score of superficiality and for believing education to be identical with the absorbing of intellectual results. But what the Sophists taught—especially grammar, style, interpretation of poetry, and oratory—had positive merits.[1] Their method, however, was often marred by their preference of style to matter and of dazzling effect to accurate statement or reasoning (Plato, *Protagoras*, *Gorgias*, *Sophist*; Aristotle, *Soph. Elench.* i., xi., xxxiv.; Aristoph. *Clouds*; cf. H. Jackson, art. 'Sophists,' in *EBr*[11]).

In the 4th cent. the philosophers ousted the Sophists from their domination over the higher learning. Plato lectured in the Academy at Athens, where he was succeeded first by Speusippus and then by Xenocrates. In the Lyceum, Aristotle was head of a seminary of universal knowledge.

The deep interest in education at that period, as well as the searchings of heart amid the conflicting subjects and methods, may be gathered from the theories of education then set forth—Plato's in the *Republic* and the *Laws*; Xenophon's in the *Cyropædia*; Aristotle's in the *Politics* and the *Nicom. Ethics*. Though it belongs to much later times (*c.* A.D. 100), we may here mention Plutarch's sketch, *de Educatione Puerorum*.

(8) *The ephebi.*—On reaching the age of eighteen, the Athenian boy, though he did not yet receive full rights of citizenship, was no longer a minor. The State took complete charge of his training for two years. He had first to pass the scrutiny (δοκιμασία) of his township (δῆμος), to see if he was of flawless descent and of mature age (Aristotle, *Athen. Constit.* xlii.). If he passed, he was registered in the roll (ληξιαρχικὸν γραμματεῖον), and was now ἔφηβος.

Though this custom must be ancient, its origin is buried in obscurity The word ἔφηβος does not seem to occur in literature before Xenophon (*c.* 370 B.C.); and the earliest of the inscriptions—the chief sources of information about the *ephebi*—belongs to 334-3 (*CIA* IV. ii. 574 D).

In the temple of Aglaurus the youth swore never to disgrace his arms or desert a comrade; to fight for home and temple; to leave his country better than he found it; to obey the magistrates and the laws; to oppose any violation of the constitution; and to honour the national temples and religion (Pollux, viii. 105 f.; Plutarch, *Alcibiad.* xv.; Demosth. *Fal. Leg.* 346 = 303). The *ephebi* of each tribe were under a superintendent (σωφρονιστής), who looked after their discipline and morality. Over all the *ephebi* was the κοσμητής, or president. The σωφρονισταί were paid by the State, which also provided money for the maintenance of the youths in training. As uniform, these wore a cloak, or χλαμύς, and a broad-brimmed hat, or πέτασος (Pollux, x. 163 f.). They were sent to do garrison duty at Munychia and Piræus. They had now much harder gymnastic exercises, and began regular military training under military officers. Their heavy duties, however, were lightened by the festivals and games, in which they took a prominent part, and by visits to the theatre, where special seats were allotted to them. At the end of the first year of training, the *ephebi* displayed their proficiency at the Great Dionysia, when each was presented

[1] Notably the work of Isocrates (see Jebb, *Attic Orators*, ii. 36 ff.).

with a shield and a spear. Any one whose father had died on the field of battle received a complete suit of armour. They now acted as patrols (περίπολοι), patrolling the frontiers (Xenoph. *de Vect.* iv. 52), and occupying the guard-houses (περιπόλια). The *ephebi* of each tribe were in succession stationed at the various points, and thus became familiar with the different localities. At the end of the two years, they were available for military duty at home and abroad.

Toward the close of the 4th cent. this service seems to have become voluntary, and, as a consequence, restricted to the wealthy. The number of *ephebi* decreased. Foreigners were admitted, and there was no age-limit. As time went on, intellectual studies were added,—literature, rhetoric, philosophy,—which by and by displaced the military training. We find a staff of professors, numerous students and students' clubs, a library—in fact, what has been termed the University of Athens, drawing its members from all quarters of the civilized world (see W. W. Capes, *University Life in Ancient Athens*, 1877).

(9) *Girls.*—Unlike the Spartans, the Athenians permitted no kind of public education for girls. This was in keeping with the seclusion, almost Oriental in character, in which Athenian women of the upper classes were kept—a seclusion more or less common throughout Greece except among the Dorians. A girl-wife, fifteen years of age, is described by Xenophon (*Oeconom.* vii. 5) as having been very carefully brought up to see and to hear as little as possible, and to ask as few questions as possible. In Athens, then, what girls learned they learned at home. Though some could read and write, very few received any intellectual training. They were taught to sing, to play the lyre, and to dance; bands of girls danced at the festivals. But it was chiefly in household duties that the Athenian girl was drilled. She must be able to spin and weave, to knit and sew, to cook, to superintend the female slaves, to nurse the sick, and generally to manage the household (Xenoph. *op. cit.* vii. 6 ff.). Wise mothers were also examples to their daughters in purity of life and propriety of behaviour. Neither in private nor in public had Athenian women the status or the influence of their Spartan sisters. Plato's proposal (*Rep.* 451 ff.), that women should be educated along with men, was extremely audacious. No less audacious was his admission of women to his lectures in the Academy (Diog. Laert. iii. 31). What provision was made in later centuries for female education, we cannot tell. An inscription from Teos, of late but uncertain date, records the selection of three masters to teach girls as well as boys. That the higher learning was unusual for Greek girls *c.* A.D. 100 may be inferred from Plutarch's emphatic recommendation (*Conjug. Præcept.* xlviii.) that they should study geometry and philosophy, to preserve their minds from frivolity and superstition.

(10) *Athens and Sparta.*—Contrasted with Sparta and its narrow but definite aim of creating a nation of sturdy warriors, Athens, while ever keeping in view the needs of the State and rounding off the boy's education with a military training, sought to develop the whole man. The Spartans learned reading and writing because of their practical utility; the Athenians held that to hunt everywhere after the useful is, as Aristotle remarks (*Pol.* v. [viii.] 3 *ad fin.*), by no means befitting the high-souled and the free. In Sparta nothing was relied on but continual espionage: Spartan boys, writes Xenophon (*Resp. Laced.* ii. 11), could never evade a ruler's eye. The Athenians allowed the utmost liberty, and trusted to the restraining influence of their common civic life (Pericles' speech [Thucyd. ii. 37 ff.]).

LITERATURE.—L. Grasberger, *Erziehung und Unterricht im klassischen Alterthum*, Würzburg, 1864–1881; A. S. Wilkins, *National Education in Greece*, London, 1873; art. 'Education,' in *A Companion to Greek Studies*, Cambridge, 1905; Becker-Göll, *Charikles*, Berlin, 1877; J. P. Mahaffy, *Old Greek Education*[2], London, 1883; P. Girard, *L'Education athén. au ve et au ive siècle avant Jésus-Christ*, Paris, 1889; S. H. Butcher, *Some Aspects of the Greek Genius*, London, 1891; R. L. Nettleship, 'Theory of Education in Plato's Republic,' in *Hellenica*[2], London, 1898; S. S. Laurie, *Historical Survey of Pre-Christian Education*[2], London, 1900; T. Davidson, *A History of Education*, Westminster, 1900; P. Monroe, *Source Book of the History of Education for the Greek and Roman Period*, London, 1902; K. J. Freeman, *Schools of Hellas*, London, 1907.

W. MURISON.

EDUCATION (Hindu).—**1. Hindu education associated with religion.**—From the earliest period of their history the Hindus have been accustomed to associate education, like all the other departments of their social life, with religion. As we shall see (§ 6), the youth of the 'twice-born' classes were prepared for admission into the Hindu ranks by a solemn rite of initiation, which was immediately followed by a course of instruction in the sacred literature, dogmas, and ritual of the national religion; and they were thus trained to share with their brethren the privileges and obligations of the caste to which they belonged. This practice, sanctified by that devotion to usage and custom which is one of the predominating influences that guide the course of the Hindu's life, has persisted down to the present day; and, though the people have now readily accepted the system of national education which the British Government, pledged to an attitude of neutrality towards the multitudinous beliefs and usages of the native population, has organized, the duty of the parent to carry out the religious rites of education and moral training remains unaffected. The difficulty of reconciling the wide-spread desire of the people for the religious and moral training of the child with the danger of State interference with the divergent religious beliefs of its subjects, is one which the Government of India shares with those of many other peoples in the West.

2. Education during the Vedic and Brāhmaṇa periods.—The Vedic literature, composed or compiled by various poets, naturally involved a course of training in the due recitation of the hymns; and, as these formulæ came to be adopted in religious and magical rites, where every word was momentous, each gesture and movement of the reciter fraught with mystery, the need of training to fit the priest or medicine-man for the due performance of his office became increasingly apparent. We thus find in the Veda records of the meetings of priests to discuss religious topics, and of the issue of diplomas to students qualifying them for admission to the sacrificial rites, while those who failed to attain the necessary standard of knowledge were degraded to the rank of ploughmen (*Rigv.* x. 71, vii. 103. 5; M. M. Kunte, *Vicissitudes of Aryan Civilization*, 1880, p. 129 f.). This form of instruction, as the contents of the Veda underwent the criticism of interpreters, developed into the establishment of various schools of commentators (A. Weber, *Hist. of Ind. Lit.*, 1882, p. 88; H. T. Colebrooke, *Essays on the Rel. and Philos. of the Hindus*, 1858, p. 189; *Vishṇu Purāṇa*, cap. iii. iv., tr. H. H. Wilson, 1840, p. 272 ff.). This tendency increased, with the advancing development of ritual in the Brāhmaṇa period, when the education of the Brāhman student (*brahmachārī*) became fully organized.

'Instruction is no longer merely concerned with domestic traditions. The student travels to a distance, and attaches himself to now one, now another teacher of renown; and the itinerant habits thus produced must have contributed not a little to imbue the Brāhmans with the feeling that they formed a class by themselves, in the midst of the small tribes of people into which Aryan India was at the time divided. This apprenticeship, which was at the time a noviciate in morals, was a very protracted one, for "science," they used to say, "is infinite"'

(A. Barth, *Religions of India*, 1882, p. 45; for the *Wanderjahre* of Brāhman students, see C. H. Tawney, *Kathā-sarit-sāgara*, 1880, i. 196, quoting G. Bühler, Introd. to the *Vikrimānkade-vacharita*). Among these schools, those at Taxila or Takshaśila, the modern Shāhdherī, Kurukshetra in the E. Panjāb, and the famous schools of logic in the East were the most important (V. A. Smith, *Early Hist. of India*², 1908, p. 57, n. 1; J. W. M'Crindle, *Anc. India as described in Classical Lit.*, 1901, p. 33, n. 4; T. W. Rhys Davids, *Buddhist India*, 1903, pp. 8, 203; R. W. Frazer, *Lit. Hist. of India*, 1898, pp. 4, 67).

3. Education in Buddhist times.—When Buddhism became fully organized in N. India, the establishment of the monastic communities gave a powerful influence to education. One of the most important of these seats of learning was the monastery (*saṅghārāma*) at Nālanda, near Rājagriha, the modern Rājgir in the Patna District, the headquarters of Indian Buddhism, founded by Aśoka (V. A. Smith, *Asoka*, ed. 1909, p. 110; *IGI* xxi. [1908] 72), the system of training at which is described by the Chinese pilgrim, Hiuen Tsiang (S. Beal, *Buddhist Records of the Western World*, 1884, ii. 170 ff.). Cf. the account of the monastery at Benares (*ib.* ii. 45 f.). Hindu and Buddhist learning attracted the attention of Megasthenes during his mission (302 B.C.) to the court of Chandragupta (Strabo, xv. 58–60, in J. W. M'Crindle, *Anc. India as described by Megasthenes and Arrian*, 1877, p. 97 ff.).

This system of Buddhist education survives to the present day in the monasteries of Ceylon, Tibet, and other parts of Eastern Asia. See, further, art. EDUCATION (Buddhist).

4. Hindu monastic education.—The modern Hindu monasteries (*maṭh*), such as those of the Jains and the ascetic orders like the Yogīs, Sannyāsīs, or Udāsīs, are so carefully guarded from intrusion by European observers that little is known of the monastic organization or of the system under which the novices are trained. For a general sketch, see H. H. Wilson, *Essays and Lectures on the Religions of the Hindus*, 1861, i. 48 ff.; *BG* xv. pt. i. 147 ff. The training, such as it is, is supervised by the prior (*mahant*). High priests, called Tambirans, of monasteries (*mattam*) in the Tamil country lecture to students (*Comm. Rep. Educ. Madras*, 1884, p. 67).

5. Education under neo-Brāhmanism.—When Brāhmanism revived in a new and more vigorous form after the decay of Buddhism, the education of the youth was regulated by the code of social legislation which has come down to us in the *Institutes of Manu* and the other law literature, the former being originally a local code which assumed its present shape not later than A.D. 200, and is now generally accepted as the rule of religious and social life among all the higher classes of Hindus (A. Macdonell, *Skr. Lit.*, 1900, p. 428). The restoration of Brāhmanism to popular favour, and the associated revival of Sanskrit learning during the Gupta period, first became noticeable in the 2nd cent. A.D., were fostered by the Western satraps in the 3rd, and made successful by the Gupta emperors in the 4th cent. (V. A. Smith, *Early Hist. of India*², 287).

'The systematic cultivation of the sacred sciences of the Brāhmans began and for a long time had its centre in the ancient Sūtrakaraṇas, the schools which first collected the fragmentary doctrines, scattered in the older Vedic works, and arranged them for the convenience of oral instruction in Sūtras or strings of aphorisms. To the subjects which these schools chiefly cultivated belongs, besides the ritual, grammar, phonetics, and the other so-called Aṅgas of the Veda, the sacred law also. The latter includes not only the precepts for the moral duties of all Āryas, but also the special rules regarding the conduct of kings and the administration of justice' (G. Bühler, 'The Laws of Manu,' *SBE* xxv., Introd. xviii.; cf. the same author's Introd. 'Sacred Books of the Āryas,' *SBE* ii. and xiv.).

6. Education according to the Laws of Manu.—It must be remembered that this legislation applies only to the Aryan or 'twice-born' man, the Sūdra being forbidden to fulfil the sacred law, except certain portions of it (x. 126, 127); to hear, learn, recite, or teach the Veda (iii. 156, iv. 99, x. 127); to receive spiritual advice from a Brāhman; but in times of distress a student may learn the Veda from one who is not a Brāhman.

The student who devotes himself to sacred learning should first undergo initiation (*upanāyana*), *i.e.* investiture with the sacred thread (*yajñopavita*), in the fifth year after conception (ii. 37); he should wear the skin of a black antelope, spotted deer, or he-goat as an upper garment, while his under dress should be of hemp, flax, or wool (ii. 41); he should procure his food by begging under strict regulations, and eat it with special precautions (ii. 49 ff.); after the rite of initiation, the teacher (*āchārya*, *guru*, his assistant being called *upādhyāya*) should instruct his pupil in the rules of personal purification, conduct, fire-worship, and twilight devotions; but, before the student begins the study of the Veda, he must sip water in accordance with the sacred law, join his hands (*brahmāñjali*), clasp the feet of his teacher, and touch his right and left foot with his hands (ii. 71 f.); he must begin and end the lesson when ordered to do so, and he must at the beginning and end recite the mystic syllable *Oṁ*, because, unless this precedes and follows, his learning will slip or fade away (ii. 73 f.). The rules of behaviour of the pupil towards his teacher are carefully prescribed. He must, during the period of instruction, *i.e.* until he is allowed to return home (*samāvartana*) after completing his course of instruction, do what is beneficial to his teacher; never offend him; fetch water, firewood, flowers, cowdung, earth, and the sacred *kuśa*-grass for his use; controlling his body, speech, organs, and mind, he must stand before him with joined hands; he must eat less than usual in his presence, wear less fine garments and ornaments, rise earlier, and go to bed later; he must not converse with his teacher while reclining, sitting, eating, or with averted face; he must observe strict rules of meeting and addressing him (ii. 108, 144, 182, 192 ff.); whenever persons justly censure or falsely defame his teacher, he must cover his ears, or leave the place, and he who defames a teacher shall be amerced in a heavy fine (ii. 200 f., viii. 275). He is subject to various tabus, all things savouring of a luxurious life being specially prohibited (ii. 175 ff.). 'A Brāhmaṇa who serves his teacher till the dissolution of his body, reaches forthwith the eternal mansion of Brahman' (ii. 244). During the course of instruction he must study the whole Veda with the Rahasyas, or secret explanations of the Veda, that is to say, the Upaniṣads, and perform at the same time various prescribed austerities and vows (ii. 165). He must give no fee to his teacher while under instruction, but provide a suitable reward for the venerable man when his course is complete (ii. 245). The vow of studying the Veda under a teacher must be kept for thirty-six years, or for a half or a quarter of that period, or until the student is proficient (iii. 1). Elsewhere it is ordained that the pupil shall live with his teacher for the fourth part of his life, and the second quarter at home as a married householder (iv. 1). Casting off a teacher is one of the most deadly sins (xi. 60); and the penalties for violation of the bed of the teacher by his pupil are of the most stringent kind (ix. 235, 237, xi. 49, 55, 104 f.). Such an offender is liable to numerous transmigrations into grasses, trees, creepers, or noxious animals; but a form of penance secures purification (xii. 58, xi. 252). Brāhman students on the completion of their course are to be honoured, for money given to Brāhmaṇas is 'an imperishable treasure for kings' (vii. 82). The king shall protect the property of a pupil while he is under instruction; the pupil is incapable of being a witness in a court of justice, and he is relieved from the payment of ferry tolls (viii. 27, 65, 407). Education was thus regarded as the first of the four stages (*āśrama*) into which the life of the Hindu was divided (M. Monier-Williams, *Brahmanism and Hinduism*⁴, 1891, p. 362 f.). An interesting survival of this rule is found in the custom at a modern Hindu marriage, when the bridegroom makes a formal attempt to start for Benares to undergo a period of study (*kāśiyātra*), from which he is with difficulty dissuaded by his relations. (See a more detailed analysis of these regulations in *Calcutta Review*, iii. [1845] 216 ff.)

7. Hindu education in later times.—(*a*) *Under Muhammadan rule.*—The effect of the Muhammadan conquest was disastrous to the Brāhman caste; the springs of princely liberality were dried up, many of the sacred texts were destroyed, and the great periodical festivals were in a great measure discontinued (A. Barth, 89 ff.). Their sacred places, temples, monasteries, and colleges were in many places destroyed. As an example, when Bakhtiyār Khiljī captured Bihār about A.D. 1297,

'most of the inhabitants of the place were Brāhmans with shaven heads. They were put to death. Large numbers of books were found there, and, when the Muhammadans saw them, they called for some persons to explain their contents, but all the men had been killed. It was discovered that the whole fort and city was a place of study' (Sir H. M. Elliot, *Hist. of India*, 1867–77, ii. 306).

The enlightened emperor Akbar, however, was a patron of learning, and directed that translations of several of the sacred books of the Hindus should be prepared (G. B. Malleson, *Akbar*, 1890, p. 166 f.;

H. Blochmann, *Aīn-i-Akbarī*, 1873, i. Introd. vii. f., 103 ff.).

(*b*) *Under British rule.*—When the British, by virtue of a grant from the emperor Shāh 'Ālam, in A.D. 1765, obtained the civil authority (*dīvānī*) of Bengal, Bihār, and Orissa, they found classical education in a depressed condition, the result of the long period of anarchy which prevailed during the decay of the Mughal Empire. A number of scattered institutions (*ṭol*) were devoted to Sanskrit instruction according to the ancient system. Colleges of this type still survive in the Ṭols of Nadiyā or Nabadwīp, which are finishing-schools for Brāhman students of logic, as Rārhī or Bardwān is for grammar, and Krishṇagaṛh for law, receiving many students of middle age who come from places as far distant as Assam (*Calcutta Review*, vi. [1846] 421 ff.; Report of Prof. E. B. Cowell, Calcutta, 1867; *IGI* xviii. [1908] 281). The Governor-General, Lord Minto, in his Minute of 6th March 1811, proposed that Sanskrit Colleges should be opened at Nadiyā and Tirhūt, a project to which sanction was refused (*Calc. Rev.* iii. [1845] 257). An instructive account of the state of classical learning in W. Bengal, which proved that the instruction was feeble and unscientific, will be found in the survey of that portion of the province carried out by F. Buchanan Hamilton between A.D. 1807 and 1814 (M. Martin, *Eastern India*, 1838, i. 134 f., 485 ff.; ii. 101 ff., 428 ff., 705 ff.; iii. 128 ff.). The controversy between classical and Western education was finally closed by the celebrated Minute by Macaulay in 1835, in which he wrote:

'The question before us is simply whether, when it is in our power to teach this language, we shall teach languages in which, by universal confession, there are no books on any subject which deserve to be compared to our own; whether, when we can teach European science, we shall teach systems which, by universal confession, wherever they differ from those of Europe, differ for the worse; and whether, when we can patronize sound philosophy and true history, we shall countenance, at the public expense, medical doctrines which would disgrace an English farrier, astronomy which would move laughter in girls at an English boarding-school, history abounding in kings thirty feet high and reigns thirty thousand years long, and geography made of seas of treacle and seas of butter.'

During the last century these Vedic schools have steadily lost ground.

For instance, in Bombay 'the main object of the Veda schools of the Hindus is to teach young Brāhmans to recite *mantras* [mystical verses, spells] and portions of the Vedas, and thus to fit them in after-life to assist at the various rites and ceremonies of the Hindu household. The instruction given in these schools is limited to the correct recitation of the Sanskrit text. The pupil reads each passage aloud to the *guru* [teacher], who carefully corrects his mistakes, and when the youth has accurately apprehended the words, he commits them to memory. No detailed explanation is given of the subject-matter; and much of what is learnt is not understood by the pupil. . . . The Vedic schools, which were almost purely religious institutions, have lost ground from causes which are only remotely due to the operations of the Educational Department. An increasing carelessness in the performance of the complex rites and ceremonies of the Hindu religion is generally admitted on all sides; and by Hindus themselves it is believed to point to a time not very remote, when the services of a priest, well acquainted with the sacred mysteries, will no longer be in any great demand. Already the employments to which pupils in these schools used to aspire are much fewer and less lucrative than they once were' (*Rep. Educ. Comm.* 59; *ib.* Bombay Appendix, i. 1884, 71, 75; *ib.* Panjāb, 35). The course at Sanskrit schools in Benares at the present day consists of grammar, philosophy, and logic (*nyāya*), the Vedānta, law, rhetoric, literature, the beliefs of the Mīmāṃsā, Sāṅkhya, and Yoga philosophies, medicine, astronomy, and astrology (*ib.* North-West Provinces, 86; cf. *ib.* Bombay, i. 72).

The study of Sanskrit received an impetus in Bengal by the recognition by the State during the Permanent Settlement of 1793 of rent-free grants made by the older Government for their support (*ib.* Bengal, 3). With a view to improving the indigenous system of classical education, various institutions were founded by the British Government.

The Benares College was founded by Jonathan Duncan in 1791, and under the direction of a succession of scholars, such as J. Muir, J. R. Ballantyne, and G. Thibaut, has secured a large measure of success in the study of Sanskrit according to Western methods (*ib.* North-West Provinces, i. ff.). The same may be said of the Poona, now the Deccan, College, founded in 1821 (*ib.* Bombay, i. 5, ii. 22), and of similar institutions in other parts of the country. But, on the whole, the study of Sanskrit, though in some provinces, Bengal for instance, it has been to a certain extent stimulated by the establishment of examinations in the indigenous schools and by the conferment of titles of honour upon the most proficient pupils, remains in an unsatisfactory condition. The five Universities—those of Calcutta, Madras, and Bombay founded in 1857, that of the Panjāb in 1882, of Allahabad in 1887—provide courses for the classical languages, and encourage the study of them by scientific methods. But the attractions of Western learning surpass those of the classical type. At the more important centres of Hindu religious life, Benares, Mathura, Nāsik, Madura, learned Brāhmans still pursue the study of the Veda on Oriental lines. But the average town or village Brāhman Paṇḍit knows little more Sanskrit than a few verses, which without understanding them he recites at the domestic ceremonies of his clients. The use of English is at once more fashionable and lucrative, and the ambitious student devotes himself to it in preference to Sanskrit.

'With the Hindus the decline of their higher institutions is due in a great measure to the natural quickness and practical instincts of the Brāhmans, who have realized the altered circumstances which surround them, and have voluntarily abandoned a classical education for one more suited to produce conditions of success' (*Rep. Educ. Comm.* 60).

It is, of course, possible that the growth of a spirit of nationality among the Hindus may tend to arrest the decay of the classical teaching. Already increased attention is being given to the study of the Vedānta, and some enthusiastic believers in it have endeavoured to popularize it in Europe and America as a substitute for the out-worn faiths of the Western world. A few younger scholars are investigating with enthusiasm the history, antiquities, and ancient languages of the country. Projects have recently been announced for the establishment of a Hindu University in connexion with, and in extension of, the Hindu College at Benares, of which the leading spirit is Mrs. A. Besant. The Association known as the Bharata Dharma Mahāmaṇḍala proposes to found a University on more strictly orthodox lines, with Colleges and schools at Benares, Nadiyā, Mathura, Poona, and Conjeevaram, in which no fixed text-books are to be used, all courses of study are to be optional, and diplomas will be granted by boards of local Paṇḍits. The ultimate result of these projects must for the present remain uncertain (*The Pioneer Mail*, 25th Aug. 1911).

8. Indigenous primary education.—When the British occupied the country, primary education was represented by the schools known in N. India as *pāṭhśālā* (from Skr. *paṭh*, 'instruction,' *śālā*, 'hall'), in the Panjāb as *śāl* or *śālā*, in Southern India as *pial*, the last term being taken from the raised platform used for sitting in front of a house on which the school is held; the word is ultimately derived from Port. *poyo*, *poyal*, 'a seat *or* bench' (Yule-Burnell, *Hobson-Jobson*, 1903, p. 703).

In Bombay 'the ordinary daily routine of a Hindu indigenous school is nearly the same in all parts of the Presidency. Each morning at about 6 o'clock the Pantoji, who is in some cases a Brāhman and the priest of many of the families whose children attend the school, goes round the village and collects his pupils. This process usually occupies some time. At one house the pupil has to be persuaded to come to school; at another, the parents have some special instructions to give the master regarding the refractoriness of their son; at a third, he is asked to administer chastisement on the spot. As soon as he has collected a sufficient number of the pupils, he takes them to the school. For the first half-hour a Bhupālī or invocation to the Sun, Saraswatī, Gaṇpati, or some other deity, is chanted by the whole school. After this the boys who can write trace the letters of their *kittas* with a dry pen, the object of this exercise being to give free play to the fingers and wrist, and to accustom them to the sweep of the letters. When the tracing lesson is over, the boys begin to write copies; and the youngest children, who have been hitherto merely looking on, are taken in hand either by the master's son or by one of the elder pupils. The master himself generally confines his attention to one or two of the oldest pupils, and to those whose instruction he has stipulated to finish within a given time. All the pupils are seated in one small room or verandah, and the confusion of sounds which arises from three or four sets of boys reading and shouting out their tables all at the same moment, almost baffles description. One of the Educational Inspectors writes: "Each pupil recites at the top of his voice, and the encouragement to noise is found in the fact that the parents often compute the energy of the master from the volume of sound proceeding from the school. This is no exaggeration. I have myself heard villagers complain that our Government schools lack the swing and energy of the indigenous schools." The school breaks up about 9 or 10 o'clock, and re-assembles at 2 in the afternoon. The concluding lesson is given at 4 P.M. For this the boys are ranged in two rows facing each other, while two of the older pupils are stationed at one end between the two rows, and dictate the multiplication tables, step by step, for the rest of the boys to shout after them in chorus. When this is over, the school is dismissed, and the master personally conducts the younger children to their homes. The school nominally meets every day of the week, Sundays included. But the frequent holidays on account of the Hindu feasts and fasts, and the closure of the school twice a month on Amāvāsyā or new-moon day and Paurnimā or full-moon day fairly take the place of the weekly and other holidays in English schools. In harvest-time, also, many of the rural indigenous schools are entirely closed. It is still the practice in some indigenous schools, though the custom is rapidly dying out, for the pupils on the eve of Amāvāsyā and Paurnimā to perform the ceremony of Pāṭīpūjā or slate-worship. A quarter of an anna [one farthing], a betel-nut, half a seer [the regulation *sīr*=2·057 lbs. avoirdupois] of grain, a little saffron and turmeric, and a few flowers are laid upon the slate of each pupil as offerings to Saraswatī, the goddess of learning. Before these each boy reverently bows down, and then places the slate for a few minutes on his head. The master afterwards appropriates the offerings. Crowded, noisy, and ill-regulated as the schoolroom is, the majority of these schools fairly accomplish their main object, which is to teach reading, writing, and the native multiplication tables. Our return shows that nearly one-third of the pupils are able to read and write, and that about one-sixth know their tables. These statistics, however, are not based on any actual examination of the pupils, but on the opinions of the Pantojīs themselves. It appears to be generally agreed that the punishments inflicted upon the pupils of indigenous schools are less barbarous and severe than they were twenty years ago. There is still, however, room for improvement in this respect' (*Rep. Educ. Comm.*, Bombay, i. 73 f.). For similar accounts of the methods of instruction, see *ib.* North-West Provinces, 278; *Calc. Rev.* xiv. (1850) 193. An early account of a Pial school in S. India will be found in the Travels of P. della Valle in 1623 (ed. Hakluyt Society, 1892, ii. 227 f.); for modern accounts, E. C. Glover, *IA* ii. (1873) 52; *Rep. Educ. Comm.*, Madras, 68; S. Mateer, *The Land of Charity*, 1871, p. 154.

9. Origin and development of indigenous primary education.—The question of the origin of this indigenous system of education has been much debated. Though, as we have seen (§ 6), the Sūdras were excluded from the education provided for the 'twice-born' classes, it is possible that some kind of elementary education was organized by the village communities; and some authorities, arguing from the character of the instruction provided and the methods by which the teacher is appointed, controlled, and remunerated, accept this view, which, however, is disputed by Mr. J. C. Nesfield as regards the United Provinces (*Rep. Educ. Comm.*, Bengal, 363; *ib.* Panjāb, 497; *ib.* North-West Provinces, 85 f., 256). In Bengal the origin of the village school is connected with the worship of the village tutelary idol, in charge of a Brāhman, who added to his priestly duties that of education. The early history of the schools in Bengal is fully detailed in the report by W. Adam (1838; summarized in *Calc. Rev.* ii. [1844] 301 ff.). In this province the policy has been to win the confidence of the indigenous schools, to aim at amalgamating them into the State system, and cautiously and gradually to introduce necessary improvements (*Rep. Educ. Comm.* 103 f.). In the United Provinces and other parts of N. India they have been generally replaced by the circle (*ḥalqabandī*) school, which provides for the wants of a group of villages (*ib.* 106).

10. Problems of Indian education.—The question of the extension of Western knowledge among the Hindu population is beyond the scope of this article. It is exhaustively discussed in the *Report of the Education Commission*. It may be well to indicate some of the more pressing problems of education in India which still in a great measure await solution.

(*a*) *General illiteracy.*—The most pressing difficulty is that, in spite of the efforts made to promote education during the last century, there is still a large amount of illiteracy among the Hindus. Of the total population only 53 persons per 1000 are literate in the limited sense in which this term was used at the Census of 1901; in the case of Hindus the average is 50 per 1000 (94 males, 5 females) (*CI*, 1901, pp. 158, 177). The causes which have contributed to this failure are exhaustively discussed by Sir H. Risley and Sir W. Hunter (*ib.* 162 ff.; *Rep. Educ. Comm.* 112 ff.). This specially applies to female education (*CI* 163 f.; *Rep. Educ. Comm.* 521 ff.). In 1911 a bill was introduced in the Legislative Council of India by Mr. Gokale for the gradual introduction of free and compulsory education. This proposal was sympathetically received by the Secretary of State (*The Times*, 25th July 1911); but the state of the finances and the economic situation, which renders the employment of child labour necessary among the agricultural and pastoral tribes, prevent it from becoming, for the present at least, a practicable policy.

(*b*) *Jealousy between Hindus and Muhammadans.*—The progress of education is at present much hampered by the jealousy between Hindus and Muhammadans, as shown by the controversy whether Urdū, a language which largely combines Perso-Arabic words with those derived from Sanskrit, is to be adopted in N. India as the medium of instruction in place of Hindī or other languages of Sanskrit origin (*Rep. Educ. Comm.* 69; *ib.* Bengal, 47 f., 276 f., 398 ff.; *ib.* Panjāb, 549).

(*c*) *Special education of chiefs and nobles.*—The special education of native chiefs and nobles is an ancient problem, Manu (vii. 43) directing that the king should learn the threefold sacred science from those versed in the three Vedas—the primeval science of government, dialectics, and the knowledge of the Supreme Soul—while from the people he should acquire the theory of the various trades and professions. Teaching such as this was imparted by the sage Droṇa to the Pāṇḍava princes in the epic of the Mahābhārata. Under the British Government, Chiefs' Colleges, of which the most important are those at Ajmer, Rājkot, and Lahore, have been established, 'where some of the features of the English public school system have been reproduced, with the object of fitting young chiefs and nobles, physically, morally, and intellectually, for the responsibilities that lie before them' (*IGI* iv. [1907] 435; *Rep. Educ. Comm.* 480 ff.).

(*d*) *Education of forest tribes and menial classes of Hindus.*—The education of the non-Aryan forest tribes and the depressed classes of the Hindu population presents special difficulties. The migratory, semi-savage habits of the former render the establishment of special schools difficult; but some progress has been made in this direction (*Rep. Educ. Comm.* 507 ff.; *ib.* Central Provinces, 3, 191 f.; *ib.* Bengal, 53 ff.). In the case of the depressed classes and menial castes special arrangements are needed, on account of the refusal of the higher classes to associate with them in a common school (*Rep. Educ. Comm.* 513 ff.). For instance, only a few years ago the Chānda school was closed because nearly all the masters resigned on account of the admission of a few Dheṛ boys (*ib.* Central Provinces, 2).

(*e*) *Missionary and secular education.*—Since the time of the Portuguese government, and more especially during the British occupation, the various missionary bodies have taken an active and honourable share in the work of education. Mr. W. Carey at Serampore, Dr. Duff at Calcutta, and Dr. Wilson at Bombay are among the many names of those who were conspicuously engaged in translating the Scriptures and other valuable literature into the Indian dialects, and in the general control of schools and colleges (*IGI* iv. [1907] 409 f.). The older missionaries were strongly opposed to the native systems of education (Abbé J. A. Dubois, *Hindu Manners, Customs, and Ceremonies*³, 1906, p. 376 ff.; W. Ward, *A View of the History, Literature, and Religion of the Hindoos*², i. [1818] 583 ff.). The attitude of the modern missionary is more tolerant, because he finds that a knowledge of native modes of thought is essential to the success of his work. The question of the withdrawal of the State from the control of the higher education was raised before the Commission presided over by Sir W. Hunter; and a tendency was shown by the orthodox Hindu party to advocate the dissociation of the State from the higher missionary schools, on the ground that the support of them by Government was inconsistent with the policy of neutrality which is the basis of the Indian educational system (*Rep. Educ. Comm.*, Madras, Summary of Evidence, 176). The missionary view is defined in a series of memorials addressed to the Commission (*ib.* 303 ff.). The Commission observed (*ib.* 454):

'Missionary institutions may serve the great purpose of showing what private effort can accomplish, and thus of inducing other agencies to come forward. They should be allowed to follow their own independent course under the general supervision of the State; and so long as there are room and need for every variety of agency in the field of education, they should receive all the encouragement and aid that private effort can legitimately claim. But it must not be forgotten that the private effort which it is mainly intended to evoke is that of the people themselves. Natives of India must constitute the most important of all agencies if educational means are ever to be co-extensive with educational wants.'

LITERATURE.—The history of Hindu education still remains to be written. The leading authorities have been fully quoted in the course of this article. For the present aspects of the subject much material will be found in the *Report of the Education Commission*, with Sir W. Hunter as president, which was issued at Calcutta in 1883, with appendixes dealing with provincial details published in the following year. Each of the Provincial Governments issues an annual Educational Report, and these are periodically reviewed by the Government of India. The Reports of the Census of 1901 give full statistical details of the progress of literacy. The *Calcutta Review* (1844 ff.) contains numerous important articles on the subject, those in the earlier volumes generally reflecting the views of the Serampore missionaries. The official view of the subject is given in the article on 'Education,' *IGI* iv. (1907) 407 ff., with a bibliography.

W. CROOKE.

EDUCATION (Jewish).—**I. In OT and Apocrypha.** —(1) The child is a conspicuous figure in the Old Testament. No systematic provision for his education and general training is mentioned; but the importance of his personality, and the need of safeguarding his higher welfare and, with it, that of the community, by wisely planned discipline, is fully recognized. Of secular teaching there is scarcely a trace; all the ordinances relating to education deal with it in its larger aspects as a preparation for the moral and religious life, as a means of developing character. Similarly, while both teacher and scholar are mentioned in connexion with the musical training of the Levites (see 1 Ch 25⁸), the professional teacher, as an instructor of the young generally, has no place in the Hebrew Scriptures, unless we are to see a reference to him in such passages as Ps 119⁹⁹ and Pr 5¹³: the teacher is the father. In the exceptional case of a child being dedicated from birth to the Divine service, he was made over, at an early age, to the care of the chief priest, and lived with him in or close by the sanctuary (1 S 3¹ᶠᶠ·). Princes of the royal house likewise had their guardians, who possibly were their tutors (2 K 10¹ᶠᶠ·). There is allusion, moreover, to 'schools of the prophets,' in which youths were trained for the prophetical office, probably by religious teaching and by instruction in music (1 S 10⁵). The moral and religious training of his children became one of the most weighty of the father's obligations; and, though no system is prescribed for the discharge of this duty, thoroughness in its performance is attained by the injunction to make religious teaching an integral constituent of the daily life. The father is exhorted to teach the Divine commands 'diligently' to his children, and to speak of them 'at all times'—when he sits in his house, when he walks by the way, when he lies down, and when he rises up (Dt 6⁷ 11¹⁹). Great events, moreover, in the national life and their anniversaries are to be used as opportunities for impressing the great verities of religion upon the child's mind (4⁹). The Passover is indicated as such an opportunity (Ex 13⁸ᶠᶠ·, Dt 6²⁰ᶠᶠ·). But the entire history of Israel seems to have been utilized as a basis for religious teaching. The father would recount the 'wondrous works' of God, that 'the generations to come might know them, even the children which should be born, who should arise and tell them to their children, that they might set their hope in God and keep His commandments' (Ps 78⁴ᶠᶠ·, cf. Dt 32⁷). Josephus especially instances this study of history as an element in the education of the child in his time (*c. Apion.* ii. 25). If, as H. Gunkel holds (see the Introd. to his Com. on *Gen.*², 1902), the stories in Genesis are saga which were originally told to delight and move the primitive Hebrews, we must imagine the wondering children as among the listeners, sharing the pride of race and the consciousness of the Divine providence aroused by the recitals.

On the other hand, the maxims of the Wisdom Literature are examples of more formal teaching, not a few of which are addressed directly to the young. Wisdom is declared to be 'the principal thing'; 'therefore,' exhorts the Sage, 'get wisdom' (Pr 4⁷). And for him wisdom is moral science, the knowledge of right methods of living. But in his view, too, the moral life is stable only when it is rooted in religion: 'the beginning of wisdom is the fear of the Lord' (Pr 9¹⁰, cf. Job 28²⁸, Sir 19²⁰). It is this higher wisdom which is commended to the young, for their own sake and for the sake of their parents. Wisdom is life (Pr 9¹¹), and its possessors win it to their own profit (v.¹²), and to the joy of their parents (10¹). And parents include the mother. 'My son,' says a Sage, 'hear the instruction of thy father, and forsake not the doctrine of thy mother' (Pr 1⁸ 6²⁰); and the last chapter of Proverbs contains a string of moral precepts of King Lemuel 'which his mother taught him.' The parental doctrine, moreover, must have the child's true well-being for its aim; it must not be subordinated to other considerations, even to the child's immediate comfort. If necessary, discipline must be severe. Even corporal punishment is legitimate; to eschew it is cruelty. 'He that spareth his rod hateth his son' (13²⁴). The Biblical maxims on this matter reflect the tone and temper of contemporary thought. None the less, the superiority of moral suasion as a disciplinary influence was fully recognized (see 17¹⁰).

(2) The educational ideas of the Bible receive some development in the Apocrypha. Wisdom is again lauded as the *summum bonum*, though with greater exuberance of phrase; but it connotes intellectual, as well as ethical, excellence. 'The fruits of wisdom's labour are virtues, for she teacheth soberness and understanding, righteousness and courage'; but 'she understandeth' also 'subtilties of speeches and interpretations of dark sayings; she foreseeth signs and wonders, and the issues of seasons and times' (Wis 8⁷ᶠᶠ·). Astronomy, meteorology, natural history, botany, and medicine are all parts of wisdom (7¹⁷ᶠᶠ·). Education, then, must have included those branches of learning in the early post-Biblical period, among the Greek Jews at any rate. Again, since Ben Sira has some maxims about behaviour at 'a concert of music' (Sir 32⁴), it is probable that music during that period was a subject of study among

the well-to-do classes. It was certainly taught systematically to the choristers of the Temple, and a certain Chenaniah is named as one of their instructors (1 Ch 15[22]).

2. In the Talmud.—Education looms large in the Talmudic literature. The solemnity and sanctity of training children for the duties of life receive the amplest recognition. The Rabbinic ideas on the subject echo the Biblical teachings. The formation of character is still the supreme aim of training; the fear of God, or, as it is usually expressed, 'the study of the Torah,' directed towards the fashioning of the good life, is still the foundation of wisdom. The child's nature is receptive, like wax in the hands of the teacher; he may make of it what he will. The child, when learning, 'writes, as it were, on clean paper.' Hence the responsibility of the teacher's office and the necessity for beginning instruction early, when receptivity is at its best. Indeed, a passage in the Talmud (*Niddah*, 30*b*) would seem to imply that the Rabbis were not unfamiliar with the conception of education as a process of drawing out the child's latent capacities, rather than the mechanical implanting of knowledge *ab extra*. Before a child is born, they say, he is taught the whole body of religious lore; but at the moment of birth an angel touches his lips, and he forgets everything. The child should begin to learn as soon as he is capable of being taught. 'Our principal care of all,' Josephus remarks, 'is to educate our children well' (*c. Apion.* i. 12), and he adds that 'the teaching is to begin in infancy' (*Ant.* IV. viii. 12). Philo, too, boasts that Jewish children are taught religion in 'their very swaddling clothes' (*ad Gaium*, 16, cf. 31). The child's incipient powers of speech were consecrated by his being taught to utter simple verses from Scripture. Two such verses are mentioned in the Talmud: 'Hear, O Israel, the Lord is one' (Dt 6[4]), and 'Moses commanded us a law, an inheritance for the congregation of Jacob' (33[4]). The age prescribed for beginning systematic instruction is the fifth or sixth year; at ten the Mishna was studied, at fifteen the Gemara (Talmud) (see *Aboth*, v. 24; *Kethuboth*, 50*a*).

The value attached to education by the Talmudic Rabbis is exemplified by many utterances. 'The world is upheld by the breath of the children in the school-house'; their instruction must not be interrupted even for the re-building of the Temple (*Shab.* 119*b*). The monition, 'Touch not mine anointed ones' (1 Ch 16[22]), is allegorically interpreted as signifying the school-children; the exhortation, 'Do my prophets no harm' (*ib.*), as an allusion to the teachers. 'Dearer to Me,' God is pictured as saying, 'is the breath of the school-children than the savour of sacrifices' (*Ḳoh. Rab.*). 'So long as there are children in the schools Israel's enemies cannot prevail against them' (*Ber. Rab.* 65). Of a great Rabbi it is told that he would never break his fast until he had taken his child to school in the morning (*Ḳid.* 30*a*). The teacher's office is regarded with the utmost veneration. Rabbi Judah, 'the Prince,' when on a pastoral visit, asks for the watchmen of the city; they bring him the beadles and the town-guard. He rebukes them; 'Not these,' he says, 'but the school-teachers are the city's watchmen' (*Jer. Ḥag.* i. 7). Teachers must be married, males, and of unblemished character. They must not hesitate in speech, and must be painstaking. One teacher is named who would go over the lesson hundreds of times until the pupil had mastered it (*Erubin*, 54*b*). A teacher who knows a little thoroughly is to be preferred to one who knows much superficially (*Bab. bath.* 21*a*). The teacher is warned against favouritism, especially against making a distinction in favour of the children of rich parents, and also against bad temper (*Taanith*, 24*a*). 'An irritable man cannot teach' (*Aboth*, ii. 5). The teacher, moreover, is to beware of compromising his dignity before his pupils; he should not jest, nor should he eat or drink in their presence (*Yorĕ Deah*, cxlv. 11).

Systematic provision for the education of the young seems to have existed in Palestine at the beginning of the Christian era. Simeon ben Sheṭaḥ, the president of the Sanhedrin, is said to have decreed that children should be taught at school instead of being instructed at home by their parents as hitherto. The inadequacy of the father's instruction, and regard for the educational needs of orphans, necessitated the ordinance. A century or two later this school system had extended from Jerusalem to all parts of the country. The credit for the extension is given to one Joshua ben Gamla, a high priest (*Bab. bath.* 21*a*). The Greek terms σχολή and παιδαγωγός often meet us in the Rabbinic literature. Whether the school in the Talmudic age was anything more than a religious school is very doubtful. The 'three R's' and, it would seem, foreign languages, geography, history, mathematics, astronomy, and gymnastics were also learnt by children; but all, or most of them, at home. Among foreign languages the Talmud (*Meg.* 18*a*) gives the preference to Greek; it is 'the beauty of Japhet' (the Aryan races—a reference to Gn 9[27]), 'the language of song.' The parent was further enjoined to teach his boys swimming and also a cleanly trade (*Ḳid.* 9*b*, 29*a*). 'He who does not teach his son a trade virtually teaches him to steal' (*ib.*). In the schools, however, the Bible and its Rabbinical interpretations were the chief, if not the exclusive, subjects of instruction. Mention is made of tablets on which the letters of the alphabet were written for beginners. These tablets were of two sizes, corresponding to the modern slate and blackboard. The elder children learnt from scrolls. Home tasks appear to have been set (*Ḳid.* 30*a*). The school was held either in the synagogue itself or in some adjoining building. It was kept open all day and long after nightfall; even on the Sabbath it was closed for only a small part of the day. The scholars were taught in unsystematic relays—an unpractical arrangement which necessarily led to confusion and to needless labour on the part of the teacher. A Rabbi of the 4th cent. directed attention to the evil, and the hours of instruction were limited to five daily, and were fixed for the early morning and the evening (*Erubin*, 54*b*). An average class consisted of twenty-five children; if the number reached forty, an assistant teacher was appointed. The pupils sat on benches arranged in a semicircle, so that each child might see and hear the teacher. The teacher was sometimes the reader (*ḥazzan*) of the synagogue, sometimes a Rabbi, who might be very eminent indeed. Discipline was to be maintained, but punishments should be mild. For physical chastisement a light strap only was to be used. Persistent insubordination was not to be visited with expulsion; the offender was rather to be subjected to the salutary influence of his more tractable school-fellows. Lenity was preferred to rough measures. 'Repulse the child with the left hand; draw him to thee with the right' (*Ṣoṭah*, 47*a*). The stimulus of rewards was also recognized. One Rabbi is said to have distributed sweetmeats as an incentive to the smaller children. In the earlier Talmudic period teachers received no fixed payment for their work; its performance was regarded as a pious duty. By the 2nd or 3rd cent. payment was made for instruction in reading, but it was still deemed improper to accept a salary for religious instruction. Later on this self-denying rule had to be relaxed. The teacher, when unpaid, was exempt from public service and from taxation. Systematic provision for higher religious study also existed in the Talmudic period, notably in Babylonia. The academies of Sura and Pumbeditha were famous.

3. In the post-Talmudic period Jewish educational ideals and methods varied with the fortunes of the Jews themselves. Tolerant treatment and a civilized environment yielded fruit after their kind in Jewish culture, of which a liberal education was the necessary condition. In North Africa and in Spain, under Muslim rule, the Jews evinced a marked enthusiasm for secular learning, without, however, losing their traditional love for Hebraic and religious studies. It was otherwise in Christian countries. In France, which, so far as the Jews are concerned, included England during the centuries immediately previous to the expulsion under Edward I., and in Germany, Jewish education was, generally speaking, at a low ebb. The Jews, proscribed or ostracized by their neighbours, were thrown back upon themselves, and forced to seek their intellectual sustenance exclusively in their religious literature. Nor would the example of the general population, even if they had been accessible to its influence, have enlarged their educational outlook. When even elementary learning was confined to the clergy of the Church, it is not surprising that, with some rare exceptions, the Jews of Northern Europe should have shown no ardour for profane knowledge. On the other hand, their zeal for the one possible study was intensified; the stream was all the deeper because it was shut up in a narrow channel. Nor was this limitation of intellectual ideals unmixed loss. Immersion in the study of the Talmud, with its keen dialectic, sharpened the Jewish mind and fitted it to take full advantage of social and intellectual enfranchisement when its hour struck. Every congregation had its communal school supported by the contributions of the members. Instruction was also given by private teachers either in their own homes or at the houses of the pupils.

The act of bringing the child to school for the first time was elevated into a solemn rite. It took place when the child was five or six years old, and preferably on Pentecost, the Feast commemorative of the giving of the Law at Sinai, the prototype of the child's induction into the knowledge of the Torah. Attired in holy vestments, he was brought into the synagogue, where the Decalogue was recited as the lesson for the day. Thence he was taken to the teacher, who thereupon began to teach him the Hebrew alphabet from a tablet smeared with honey which the child ate as he pronounced the letters, so that the sacred lore might be sweet in his mouth. The solemnity of the ceremony foreshadowed the character of the entire course of instruction, which was made a very momentous business, rarely interrupted by holidays or games. 'For there was no greater disgrace than that of being called an *'am ha-areṣ* (an ignoramus)'! Having mastered the Hebrew alphabet, the child was taught to spell and to read. Thus three months passed, at the end of which he was taught passages from the Bible and the Prayer Book, which took up a second three months. The first Scripture lessons were supplied by the three introductory chapters of Leviticus, which treat of the sacrifices, whose purity matched that of the child. But a merely superficial familiarity with the sacred text did not suffice; for six months the pupil was exercised in the translation both of the Pentateuch and of the Prayer Book into the vernacular. A knowledge of writing the vernacular would also seem to have been imparted, but this was probably acquired privately. It was called the 'Christian script.' Hebrew grammar was usually neglected. The pupil, when reciting his lesson, swayed his body to and fro as old-fashioned Jews still do at prayer, and used a peculiar sing-song or cantillation. At the end of the first year he was taken from the Pentateuch to the Prophets and the Hagiographa, in the fourth year to the Mishna, and thence to the Talmud. Lessons began at an early hour of the day—in the winter while it was still dark—and continued till the time of morning prayer, when the children would either go to the synagogue or attend service in the teacher's house. After breakfast at home they returned to school, and lessons went on again until eleven o'clock. Then came the midday meal, and at noon the instruction was resumed once more, to last, with a short interval in the afternoon, till the time of evening prayer, which closed the school day. At the age of sixteen, if the pupil decided to make religious study his vocation, his *Wanderjahre* began, during which he visited various towns in turn, in order to sit at the feet of famous teachers. This extended course of study was not undertaken only by those who intended to become Rabbis; love for the Torah would fire many a youth who could hope to gain nothing from his study save the knowledge itself. Even the Rabbis would scorn all pecuniary remuneration for the exercise of their office, deeming it shameful to use the Torah, in Talmudic phrase, 'as a spade to dig withal.' They relied for a meagre livelihood upon some secular occupation, often the humble calling of the artisan.

Güdemann (*op. cit. infra*, vol. i. p. 92 ff.) reproduces from an Oxford MS an interesting scheme, dating from the 13th cent., for founding a systematic course of Jewish instruction in the north of France. The scheme contemplates the establishment of an upper and a lower school, suggested respectively, perhaps, by the cathedral seminaries and the parochial schools which existed in France at that period. The document mentions an order of students which it styles the 'separatists' or the 'dedicated,' because they have made religious study the chief or sole occupation of their lives. For these the upper or 'greater' school is to be instituted. 'That,' echoing the Talmud, the scheme premises, 'is the true learning for which a man slays himself'; so the student must give himself wholly to study, taking up his abode in the seminary so as not to lose time in coming and going, and remaining there seven years. It is the duty of every Jew, the document continues, to dedicate one of his sons to this holy vocation, just as he would set apart a portion of his property to the service of Heaven. The lower school was intended for day-scholars. The institution is to be supported by the community, each member of which is to subscribe twelve deniers half-yearly. These contributions are to be supplemented by the fees of the pupils. The staff is to consist of a rector and tutors, of whom the former is to lecture to the students, and the latter to 'coach' them. Each tutor is to be limited to ten pupils, in contradistinction to the twenty-five prescribed by the Talmud, 'which was intended only for Palestine, where the climate favours mental development, and for times when Jews were free'; for, the author of the scheme adds pathetically, 'the free are strong and clear of brain, and absorb knowledge more readily than do the downtrodden, whose higher energies are sapped by service of cruel masters.' The pupils are to be taught from a book, not *viva voce*, and they are to be encouraged to hear each other's lessons every evening as a means of sharpening their intelligence. Systematic repetition is recommended. In winter only a fourth of the night is to be devoted to the instruction, for lights are dear. The student, however, is at liberty, when he so desires, to spend the entire night in private study. Only promising pupils are to be retained in the school. If a boy proves to be dull, the rector should send for the father and discreetly say: 'God aid thy son to do good deeds; for study he has no aptitude.' The teachers are not to follow any other occupation; they are to live in the upper school all the week, returning home for the Sabbath only. They must have a special suit of clothes for school hours, so that they may teach in unsoiled garments, as befits the sanctity of their task.

As in the Talmud, so in the mediæval literature generally, much stress is laid upon moral and religious training as the final aim of education. The 'Book of the Pious' (*Sepher Ḥasîdîm* [13th cent.]) is full of maxims illustrative of this fact.

'Children copy their parents; if the latter are dishonest, they will be dishonest too, and all study of the Torah is useless. . . . It is not good to give children much money. . . . A wealthy father, whose children do not heed his moral and religious precepts, should see that they work for a living;

perhaps they will be brought back thereby to the right path. . . . Even if a child can only read, he should be made to understand what he reads. When he reads the Bible, the teacher should strive to arouse his piety. He should tell him that it is God who gives him food; later on, he should be told of everlasting rewards and punishments. . . . In choosing an occupation for his son, the father should have regard to the boy's character. If he is disposed to take the study of religion seriously, let him be dedicated to it; but if he would study from sordid motives, let him rather be taught some secular occupation.' Then some rules about education generally meet us: 'A teacher must not encourage a sneak, or gossip either in school or in the street. He must not say, "As I have to teach all day, I will rise early and study for myself"; for he may be drowsy whilst teaching and so neglect his duty. What one teacher forbids another should not allow. The child should be taught the subjects for which he has most aptitude; if he makes good progress in Bible, do not force him to the Talmud. If a child stammers, he should be told to bring his questions to the teacher after the other pupils have gone away, or to bring them in writing, so that he may not be mocked at by his school-fellows.'

Maxims of similar import are to be found in all the mediæval moralists, and they are given a prominent place in the 'ethical wills' which pious Jews were accustomed to leave—not seldom it was all they had to leave—for the edification of their children. Most teachers, moved doubtless by the doctrine of Proverbs and the Talmud, put in a plea for corporal punishment; but they are careful to add that it must be used with discrimination. On the other hand, a famous Rabbi of comparatively modern times (Elijah Wilna [18th cent.]) left word in his ethical will that those of his children who were addicted to scandal-mongering or untruthfulness should be unsparingly chastised. Another ethical will, to which we may here refer, though its origin was Spain, is that of Judah ibn Tibbon (12th cent.).

Judah reminds his son that he travelled to the 'ends of the earth' to find teachers for him in science and other profane studies. He exhorts him to read every Sabbath the weekly lesson from the Pentateuch in Arabic in order to perfect himself in that language. He is to take great care of his books, so that they may not be lost or damaged. 'Make thy books,' he says, 'thy companions, and thy library thy garden. Pluck the fruit that grows therein; gather the roses, the spices, and the myrrh. If thy soul be satiate and weary, roam from one bed to another, and desire will renew itself.'

Knowledge, however understood, was a precious thing for every Jew. A father would deny himself the common necessaries of life in order to secure for his son a good education. This self-denying zeal still characterizes the Jewish poor to-day.

On the other hand, the standard of education for *girls* was decidedly lower than it was in the case of boys. In this respect the mediæval Jews fell below the level of their Christian neighbours. The Talmud (*Ṣôṭah*, 21*b*) deprecates the study of the Torah by women, and the mediæval Rabbis fully shared this attitude. It was the custom to marry girls at a very early age, and there was, therefore, little time, as well as small inclination, to give them more than a mere smattering of religious knowledge. Attention was concentrated upon their domestic training and upon instructing them in those precepts of the ritual law which would especially concern them as wives and mothers. The average Jewish girl in the Middle Ages knew little or nothing of Hebrew; and, even if she was able to read the Prayer Book, she did not understand it. Thus we find Jewish women generally, in common with illiterate males, recommended by the authorities to pray in the vernacular. Later on (about the 15th cent.) the vernacular took the form of a jargon, in which devotional and religious books were written for their especial benefit. While intellectually Jewish women suffered from these narrow educational ideals, their *morale* remained unharmed. Female excellence was maintained at a high level. The Jewish woman vied with her husband in an admiration for a religious culture which she was not permitted to share; her greatest pride was to have sons learned in the Torah. She was, above everything, modest and chaste, and she could immolate herself as a martyr when the need arose. Occasionally, too, she could break her traditional bonds, and give herself to study. Jewish history tells of learned women, later Huldahs, to whose knowledge and opinions distinguished Rabbis did not disdain on occasion to appeal, and even of women who taught boys and preached in the synagogues. In the ethical wills already mentioned the testators' daughters receive the same attention as their sons in the matter of moral training.

Among the Jews in Muhammadan Spain, education, as has already been said, received a wider interpretation than it enjoyed among their brethren of Northern Europe. Joseph ibn Aknin of Barcelona (12th cent.) recommends the following subjects of instruction to be studied in the order named: reading, writing, Torah, Mishna, Hebrew grammar, poetry, Talmud, religious philosophy, logic, mathematics, astronomy, music, mechanics, medicine, and metaphysics. Jewish literature of the Spanish period witnesses to the liberal culture of its authors, and therefore to a high educational standard. Whether Rabbi or man of business, the Spanish Jew was often a poet or a philosopher, sometimes a physician also. In Italian Jewry, which was largely influenced by Spanish ideas and practice, a strong desire for secular learning manifested itself. It was discernible before the Renaissance, and when, in the 16th cent., intellectual darkness had descended upon the Jews of Germany and Russia, a sketch of a curriculum was framed by David Provenzale in Mantua which, besides the usual Hebrew and theological subjects, includes Latin and Italian philosophy, medicine and mathematics.

As time went on, the general standard of education among the Jews in Northern Europe deteriorated rather than improved. By the 15th cent. it reached its lowest point. Young children were handed over more frequently than before to the private teacher, who was often only a little less ignorant than his pupils, and who taught his class, without method or discipline, in an overcrowded and stuffy room (*ḥeder*)—an arrangement which still obtains in Russia, and is favoured by the Jewish immigrant from that country into England. A boy remained in the *ḥeder* until he reached the age of thirteen, the age of religious responsibility (*bar-mitzvah*), the advent of which was marked by his publicly reading a passage from the Pentateuch in the synagogue, and by his delivery of an address upon some Talmudic subject to an assembly of his friends at home. With the age of Moses Mendelssohn (18th cent.), however, a new intellectual era dawned for the Jews of Germany and of Europe generally. Mendelssohn's great aim and work was the rescue of the Jewish mind from mediævalism, and among the first fruits of his influence was the foundation in 1778 of the Jewish Free School in Berlin, where the instruction embraced Hebrew, German, French, and the usual commercial subjects. About the same time a movement aiming at the improvement of Jewish education, favoured by the tolerant policy of the Emperor Joseph II., was initiated in Austria. The efforts of the reformers in all countries had a twofold direction; secular teaching was to go hand in hand with Jewish instruction, but the scope of the latter itself was also to be enlarged. The tuition, more or less mechanical, in Bible and Talmud, to which it had hitherto, as a rule, been restricted, was to be supplemented by systematic instruction in Jewish history and theology. Text-books on these subjects, previously almost unknown, now appeared in rapid succession. Greater regard was likewise paid to grammar in the teaching of Hebrew. Technical schools, moreover, began to spring up. Since that time Jewish educational ideas have gradually widened in all countries where civilization co-exists with religious liberty. In Russia and Roumania and Turkey, those ideas, except where they are leavened by salutary influences from without—by those, for example, of the Anglo-Jewish Association in England and the Alliance Israélite in France—are still antiquated; but elsewhere there is nothing to differentiate Jewish educational aims and methods from those of other religious bodies. Even Palestine, hitherto the home of reactionary tendencies, gives evidence of an educational awakening. Enlightened conceptions of teaching and a liberal curriculum are becoming the order of the day; secondary schools are springing up, and, in Jerusalem, there are to be found an arts and crafts school and a normal school for teachers. In Europe the latest tendency is to entrust the secular teaching of Jewish children to the State or to the municipality, and to restrict voluntary education to instruction in Hebrew and religion and cognate subjects. The Jews, taxed as citizens for the maintenance of general elementary and secondary teaching, deem themselves discharged from the duty of making special provision for the secular instruction of the children of their poor. They are concentrating their efforts in an increased degree upon the provision of religious training. This tendency is especially marked in England, where the first Jewish school was founded in London about the middle of the 17th cent., though nearly a hundred years had to elapse before any attempt was made to add some rudimentary secular teaching to the ordinary elements of Jewish instruction. At the present time there are eight Jewish denominational schools, including the great 'Free School' in Bell Lane, Spitalfields, with its 3000 scholars, in the metropolis. State-aided, they provide secular as well as religious instruction; but, while they are supported with hardly relaxed generosity by the Jewish community, no disposition is manifested to increase their number. The religious education of the many thousands of Jewish children who now attend the public elementary schools is undertaken by the Synagogue, with its religious classes connected with the various places of worship, and, in London, in addition, by the Jewish Religious Education Board, which maintains an organized system of religious teaching at certain County Council schools, mainly in the East End, where Jewish children form the great majority of the scholars.

LITERATURE.—I. Abrahams, *Jewish Life in the Middle Ages*, London, 1896; M. Güdemann, *Gesch. des Erziehungswesens der abendländ. Juden*, 4 vols., Vienna, 1873–88; Hamburger, artt. 'Erziehung,' 'Lehrer,' 'Lehrhaus,' 'Unterricht,' 'Schule,' 'Schüler'; *JE*, artt. 'Education,' 'Ḥeder,' 'Pedagogics'; *JQR* ix. [1896–97] 631 ff.; S. Maybaum, *Methodik des jüd. Religionsunterrichts*, Breslau, 1896; J. Picciotto, *Anglo-Jewish History*, London, 1875; S. Schechter, *Studies in Judaism*, London, 1896; B. Strassburger, *Gesch. der Erziehung bei den Israeliten*, Stuttgart, 1885.

MORRIS JOSEPH.

EDUCATION (Muslim).—**I. Education in the early history of Islām.**—The value set upon education in Islām is indicated by certain *ḥadīth* sayings which, though they may have no claim to rank as authentic, yet undoubtedly reflect the educational ideals of Islām in its early days, and may be taken as representing the prevailing views of the first generations. Thus it is handed down as a saying of the Prophet himself, that 'A father can confer upon his child no more valuable gift than a good education'; and, again, 'It is better that a man should secure an education for his child than that he bestow a *ṣā'* in charity.'[1] The boon thus commended extends also to slaves. It is regarded as a work of specially meritorious character 'to educate a slave-girl well, then set her free, and give her to a husband.'[1]

1 Tirmidhī, *Ṣaḥīḥ*, Cairo, A.H. 1292, i. 354.

It may be safely said that Islām raised the Arabs to a higher level of civilization, and at the same time introduced amongst them the elements of education, in which they had hitherto been rather deficient.[2] That Muhammad himself—partly, it may be, on utilitarian grounds—attached considerable importance to the acquisition of the most indispensable elements of knowledge, may be inferred from the conditions on which he released prisoners of war after his victory at Badr. He employed several Quraish captives to teach the boys of Medīna to write, and this service counted as their ransom. Twelve boys were assigned to each of the Meccan prisoners who were capable of giving the required instruction, and, as soon as the pupils had attained the stipulated degree of progress, their teachers were set at liberty.[3] The Quraish, as a people largely engaged in commerce, had naturally more occasion to practise writing than the date-planters and husbandmen of Medīna,[4] and it was, therefore, easier to find penmen among them than in Yathrib—a consideration which may perhaps also dispose us to accept the view held by certain Muslim theologians,[5] though condemned as heresy by the orthodox school, viz. that Muhammad was not the 'illiterate' that Muslim orthodoxy, with its mistaken interpretation of the epithet *ummī*, tries to make out.[6] Mention is even made of a list of contemporary Meccan women who were familiar with the art of writing; but this group did not include the youthful 'Ā'isha, who, though she had the advantage over her companions in being able to read, yet had never learned writing.[7] We may, therefore, infer that among the men of Mecca the ability to write was nothing out of the common.[8] Mu'āwiya distinguished himself as the Prophet's secretary. Penmanship was not quite so common among the Arabs of Medīna. To the Khazrayite Ubaiy b. Ka'b, who made a name for himself by recording the revelations of the Prophet, is ascribed the exceptional distinction of having been skilled in penmanship before the rise of Muhammad.[9] In Medīna, those who, in addition to certain other accomplishments, possessed also the art of writing—acquired perhaps from the Jews resident there[10]—were deemed worthy of the title of *kāmil* ('perfect').[11]

It would also appear that, once the young Muslim community had been constituted, a primitive system of education, embracing at least the bare elements of knowledge, was set on foot. In no long time we begin to meet with references to the *kuttāb* ('elementary school'). We would cer-

1 Bukhārī, *Kitāb al-'atq*, no. 16; Jāḥiẓ, *Kitāb al-ḥayawān*, Cairo, A.H. 1323, i. 28, mentions a slave-girl who was conversant with Euclid.

2 Cf. the present writer's *Muh. Studien*, i. (Halle, 1889) 112.

3 Sprenger, *Mohammad*, Berlin, 1861–9, iii. 131; D. S. Margoliouth, *Mohammed and the Rise of Islam*, London, 1905, p. 270, at foot.

4 Cf. Caetani, *Annali dell' Islam*, Milan, 1907, ii. 702 ff.

5 *e.g.* the Andalusian Abu-l-Walīd al-Bāji († A.H. 474=A.D. 1081), who incurred great hostility in consequence; cf. the present writer's *Ẓāhiriten*, Leipzig, 1884, p. 171, note 1; Dhahabī, *Mīzān al-i'tidāl*, Lucknow, A.H. 1301, ii. 41, *s.v.* ''Abdallāh b. Sahl of Murcia' († A.H. 480=A.D. 1087); 'Between him and Abu-l-Walīd al-Bājī there were great disputes over the writing question.'

6 On this question, see Nöldeke-Schwally, *Gesch. d. Qôrans*², i. (Leipzig, 1909) 12.

7 Balādhorī, ed. de Goeje, Leyden, 1870, p. 472.

8 Cf. Lammens, 'La République marchande de la Mècque,' p. 24 (*Bull. de l'inst. égyp.*, 1910, p. 46, note 7).

9 Ibn Sa'd, III. ii. 59; Caetani, *op. cit.* iv. 201.

10 Balādhorī, 473.

11 Cf. the passages quoted by Lammens, *Études sur le règne du Calife Mo'āwiya*, Beirūt, 1906, p. 630; also *Aghānī*, ii. 169, at foot; Ṭabarī, *Annales* (ed. Leyden, 1879 ff.), i. 1207, where the reference is not to Arabs in general, but to natives of Medīna. For the full connotation of *kāmil*, see Ibn Sa'd, v. 309, line 7 ff.

tainly not lay much stress upon the mention of a 'companion' called Mirdās,[1] and surnamed *al-mu'allim* ('the teacher'),[2] as there is but little evidence to show that such a person ever existed.[3] Even in the early period, however, we find better attested notices of the *kuttābs* and the *mu'allims* who taught in them. Umm Salīm, mother of Anas b. Mālik, the Prophet's attendant (or, according to other accounts, Umm Salama, one of the Prophet's wives), asks a *mu'allim kuttāb* to send her some schoolboys—preferably of the slave class—to assist her in wool-carding.[4] 'Amr b. Maimūn al-'Audi († c. A.H. 74–77 = A.D. 693–6) gives the text of an apotropæic formula which the 'companion' Sa'd b. abī Waqqāṣ taught his children, 'as the teacher instructs his scholars in writing.'[5] Another reference tells how Abū Huraira, Ibn 'Omar, and Abū Usaid (who fought at Badr) on one occasion passed by a *kuttāb*, and attracted the attention of the boys.[6] There is also evidence to show that the *lauḥ* (tablet for practice in reading and writing) was in use at a very early period; the female 'companion' Umm al-Dardā writes on such a tablet some wise sentences as reading lessons for a boy ('Abd Rabbihi b. Sulaimān b. 'Omar).[7]

Elementary education seems to have been thoroughly established in Islām by the early Umayyad period.[8] It is true that we cannot decide whether sound evidence on this point can be drawn from an anecdote telling how the facetious grammarian Sa'd b. Shaddād jocularly sold the pupils of his elementary school as slaves to 'Ubaidallāh b. Ziyād, governor of 'Irāq.[9] We are on surer ground when we read that the poet Kumait and the formidable vicegerent and commander Ḥajjāj b. Jūsuf were schoolmasters—the last named, of course, in the years before his remarkable political career. Just before the time of Ḥajjāj, again, Jubair b. Ḥayya taught in a school at Ṭā'if, and likewise rose afterwards—in 'Irāq—to high rank, being promoted by Ziyād from the position of a clerk to that of administrator of Iṣfahān.[10] Ḍaḥḥāq b. Muzāḥim († A.H. 105 = A.D. 723) kept a *kuttāb* in Kūfa, making no charge for instruction.[11] In the 2nd cent. A.H.—the date cannot be fixed more precisely—we even hear of a Bedawi of the tribe of Riyāḥ who settled as a *mu'allim* in Baṣra, and conducted a school for payment (*bil-ujra*).[12] There is, of course, nothing surprising in the fact that in the lands conquered by Islām, such as 'Irāq, a Muslim system of education should take root and develop in the centres of an older civilization; but the foregoing references to schools in Arabia proper are more pertinent to the subject in hand.

Even in the early Umayyad period the education of the young princes at court had reached a high standard of excellence, but it is not necessary here to describe it in detail. A spirited account of it, dealing with all its phases, and furnished with copious references to sources, has been given by H. Lammens, and we need only call the reader's attention to his work.[1] The *mu'addib* ('instructor') was a standing figure at the Umayyad court, and was admirably supported in his work by the fathers of the princes.

'Omar II. took his children severely to task when they violated the rules of grammar.[2] He had, in his own youth, a most lugubrious *mu'addib*, and the ascetic character of the future khalif might perhaps have been anticipated from the fact that this tutor is described as a person negligent of externals; he wore a coat that reached to his heels, and his moustache hung down over his lips[3]—a trait at variance with Arabic ideas of elegance, which, in accordance with a primitive *sunna*, enjoined the trimming of the moustache (*qaṣṣ al-shārib*).[4]

The development of scientific knowledge under the Abbāsids in the 2nd cent. A.H. naturally carried with it a corresponding advance in preparatory education. There is also evidence of the fact that the younger generation were encouraged, by the prospect of public recognition, to give themselves heart and soul to the task of acquiring the elements of learning. It is recorded that in the early years of this period deserving pupils of the elementary schools in Baghdad were rewarded by being carried through the streets on camels and having almonds thrown to them. It was on an occasion of this kind that the poet 'Akawwak lost his sight, his eyes having been seriously injured by the almonds meant for the clever scholars. In this period, moreover, we find mention of institutions for higher education (*majālis al-adab*).[5] About the same time the Fāṭimid administration, now established in Egypt, took steps towards founding academies (*dār al-ḥikma* or *al-'ilm*) in Cairo, where the theological tenets of the Shī'ite school, as also—in eclectic fashion—the rich stores of learning inherited from the Greeks and the Persians, were studied. When the Fāṭimid dynasty was overthrown, the Ayyūbids superseded their academies by high schools conducted on Sunnite principles, and the wide spaces of the mosques were utilized for teaching purposes. This use of the mosque as a *madrasa* had a notable influence upon the architecture of the mosque itself.[6] The sultanates under the sway of the Abbāsids continued to vie with one another in the promotion of higher education—largely confined, it is true, to theology and its subsidiary sciences[7]—as also in the erection of suitable *madrasas*,[8] which find mention from the 4th cent. onwards. An epoch-making advance in the development of the higher school was made by the enlightened Seljūḳ vizier Niẓām al-mulk (middle of 5th cent. A.H. = 11th cent. A.D.), whose institutions—the *Niẓāmiyya*-academies—in various parts of the empire were devoted chiefly to the higher theological studies.[9] In the same period, however, we note a growing tendency to free the studies of the *madrasas* from their theological onesidedness. Separate institutions were founded, and became famous, for the study of the exact sciences. The observatories which sprang up everywhere became centres for the teaching of astronomy, while the numerous

1 Ibn Ḥajar, *Iṣāba*, no. 2008, iii. 818 (Calcutta ed.).

2 This title might also, as in Ibn Sa'd, III. ii. 103, lines 7–9, signify one who instructed the people in the citation of the Qur'ān.

3 The doubtful traditions referring to him are given by Suyūṭī, *Al-La'ālī al-maṣnū'a fi-l-aḥādīth al-mauḍū'a*, Cairo, A.H. 1317, i. 107.

4 Bukhārī, *Diyāt*, no. 27.

5 *Ib.* no. 24.

6 Ibn Sa'd, IV. i. 133, line 4; cf. the present writer's *Vorlesungen über d. Islam*, Heidelberg, 1910, p. 148, at top.

7 Nawāwī, *Tahdhīb*, ed. Wüstenfeld, Göttingen, 1842–47, p. 860, line 6 from foot.

8 Kremer, *Culturgesch. d. Orients unter d. Chalifen*, Vienna, 1875–7, ii. 132.

9 In Suyūṭī, *Bughjat al-wu'āt*, Cairo, A.H. 1326, p. 253.

10 Ibn Ḥajar, *Iṣāba*, i. 460.

11 Ibn Sa'd, vi. 210, line 12.

12 Yāqūt, *Dict. of Learned Men*, ed. Margoliouth, 1909 ff. (*Gibb Memorial Series*, vi.), ii. 239.

1 *Études sur le règne du Calife Mo'āwiya*, p. 331 ff.

2 Yāqūt, ed. Margoliouth, i. 25, at the foot.

3 Ibn Qutaiba, *'Uyūn al-akhbār*, ed. Brockelmann, Berlin, 1900 ff. (in the series *Semitische Studien*, ed. C. Bezold), p. 351, line 15.

4 Bukhārī, *Libās*, no. 63.

5 *Aghānī*, xviii. 101.

6 See Max v. Berchem, art. 'Architecture,' in *Spécimen d'une encyclopédie musulmane*, Leyden, 1899, col. 16; also artt. ARCHITECTURE (Muhammadan in Syria and Egypt), above, vol. i. p. 757 f., and ART (Muhammadan), p. 878 f.

7 For Muslim higher education in the periods referred to, cf. Haneberg, *Über d. Schul- u. Lehrwesen d. Muhammedaner im Mittelalter*, Munich, 1856; Kremer, ii. 479 ff.; Winand Fell, *Über d. Ursprung u. d. Entwickelung d. höhern Unterrichtswesens bei d. Muhammedanern* (*Program d. Marzellen-Gymnasiums in Köln*, for the year 1882–83).

8 Important data regarding the older types of *madrasa* which preceded the *Niẓāmiyya*-schools are found in Subkī, *Ṭabaqāt al-Shāfi'iyya*, Cairo, A.H. 1324, iii. 137.

9 Julian Ribera, 'Origen del Colegio Nidami de Bagdad,' in *Homenaje a Francisco Codera*, Saragossa, 1904.

hospitals now being instituted—served as they were by the most renowned physicians of the day—attracted students of medical science, as is shown by numerous references in Ibn abī Uṣaibi'a's *Biographies of the Physicians.* In the present article, however, we propose to confine our discussion largely to elementary education.

2. The subjects of primary education; forbidden books.—In a series of sayings showing no trace of theological influence, advice is given regarding the subjects which should have a place in the education of children. Khalīf 'Omar I., for instance, is said to have counselled parents in these words: 'Teach your children to swim and to throw darts; charge them that they must be able to mount a horse securely, and make them recite appropriate verses.'[1] 'Omar was himself a renowned horseman, and is said, in picturesque phrase, to have sat in the saddle 'as if he had been created on the horse's back.'[2] Amongst these attainments the art of swimming was specially prized. Khalīf 'Abdalmalik gave his sons' tutor the following injunction: 'Teach them to swim, and accustom them to sleep little.'[3] Ḥajjāj (who, according to another report, laid most emphasis upon the religious training of his children, and therefore refused to engage a Christian teacher)[4] gave a similar charge to the preceptor whom he had selected for his sons: 'Instruct them in swimming before you teach them writing, for they can at any time easily find one who will write for them, but not one who will swim for them.' Jāḥiẓ, to whom we owe this item of information about Ḥajjāj, supplies further details indicative of the importance attached to the art of swimming in the educational practice of the higher ranks. A saying of Ibn al-Tau'am commends writing, arithmetic, and swimming as the accomplishments which, above all others, a prudent father should seek to procure for his children. As between writing and arithmetic, the latter should have precedence, since it is not only of more value in business, but is actually more easily learned, while its eventual advantages are also greater.[5] The traditional view, with a slight variation, finds expression in a modern Arabic proverb current in 'Irāq: 'Learn to write, to make the calamus, and to swim in the river.'[6]

It would, of course, be absurd to suppose that the educational maxims which assign so prominent a place to swimming had their origin in Arabia, as that country could provide but few opportunities for practising the art.[7] The present writer is of opinion that—as is suggested by the grouping together of riding, dart-throwing, and swimming—such educational ideals were largely influenced by foreign, and especially Persian and Greek, views; and, indeed, the pedagogic maxims in question are but the echoes of such views.[8] In especial, the importance ascribed to swimming is doubtless to be traced to Greek ideas: to be able 'neither to swim nor to read' (μήτε νεῖν μήτε γράμματα [Plato, *Leg.* iii. 689 D]) was a Greek equivalent for the absolute lack of culture. It was likewise under the same influence that swimming found a place in the educational maxims of the Talmud.[9]

The subjects recommended in the sayings just quoted form no part of the distinctively Muslim theory of education, which was governed by principles of an entirely different character. The general course of training for young males is set forth in the *ḥadīth* as follows:

'On the seventh day after the child's birth, the *'aqīqa* ("hair-cutting," together with the sacrifice of an animal) is performed, and he receives his name and is made secure against all harm; when he is six years old, his education begins; at the age of nine, he is given a separate sleeping-place; at thirteen years of age, he receives corporal punishment when he omits his prayers; at sixteen, his father gives him in marriage, then grasps him by the hand and says: "My son, I have trained you and had you taught, and I have given you in marriage: now I beseech God for help against your temptations in this world, and against your being punished in the Last Judgment."'[1]

As regards the elementary curriculum in particular, the relevant sources furnish us with the following details. When the child begins to speak, he should be taught to repeat the Muslim article of belief, *Lā ilāha ill' Allāh*; he must then learn the words of Qur'ān, xxiii. 117*b*: 'Exalted is Allah, the king in truth; there is no god but Him, the Lord of the stately throne of Heaven'; then the 'throne-verse' (*āyat al-kursī*, ii. 256), and the last two verses of sūra lix. (*sūrat al-ḥashr*): 'He is Allah; there is no deity but Him, the Holy King,' etc. Those who teach their children so will not be brought to judgment by God.[2] At the age of seven, when the child becomes responsible for the *ṣalāt*, he is to be sent to school, and the teacher must begin to instruct him systematically in the Qur'ān itself. Children should not be sent to school before the age of seven, as is the practice of some parents, who wish merely to spare themselves the trouble of looking after their offspring.[3] The teaching of the Qur'ān should be combined with instruction in the more important religious precepts and usages: the proper response to the *ādhān*, the different kinds of washings, the prayers in the mosque to which children should be taken whenever possible; they must without fail be familiarized with the practice of joint-prayer (*ṣalāt al-jamā'a*), even in the school, where one of the older boys acts for the time as leader in prayer (*imām*). Instruction in reading and writing, of course, must also be proceeded with. The children practised writing on tablets (*lauḥ*, pl. *alwāḥ*); the words employed were usually taken from passages in the Qur'ān.

Ibn Jubair († A.H. 614 = A.D. 1217), in his sketch of the state of education in Damascus, says that in the elementary schools of that city—where writing (*taktīb*) and recitation (*talqīn*) of the Qur'ān were taught by different masters—the passages for exercise in reading and writing were taken, not from the Qur'ān, but from poetical texts of secular character, as the act of wiping inspired words from the tablets seemed to cast dishonour upon the sacred book.[4] The cleansing (*maḥw*) of the tablets marked the close of the first period of morning school: the allotted hour for this was eight o'clock a.m., and the teacher must then grant a short pause (*tasrīḥ*, 'leave').[5] For the act of wiping the *alwāḥ*, when they contained verses of the Qur'ān, various precautions are recommended by the more strait-laced theologians. It must be performed in a clean and well-guarded place, not open to be trodden upon, so that the water used in wiping out the sacred words shall not subsequently suffer any desecration. The best way to dispose of the water is to pour it into a river or a pit, or to collect it in a vessel for those who wish to use it medicinally,[6] as it is believed to possess magical virtues. A pious resident of Cairo, Muhammad Tāj al-dīn († A.H. 707 = A.D. 1307), who founded a school in the Qarāfa, inserted in the deed of foundation a clause to the effect that the water used in that institution for cleansing the *alwāḥ* was to be poured upon his grave.[7] Even the pieces of rag with which the tablets were wiped must be wrung out with the greatest care, lest the water that dripped from them should be profaned.[8]

Concurrently with exercises in reading and writing from the Qur'ān, the pupils were taught the rudiments of arithmetic. To these were added

[1] Mubarrad, *Kāmil*, ed. Wright, Leipzig, 1874, p. 150.
[2] Jāḥiẓ, *Bayān*, ii. 54, line 8 from foot.
[3] Mubarrad, p. 77, line 6.
[4] *Aghānī*, xviii. 37, line 20 ff.
[5] Jāḥiẓ, *Bayān*, i. 213.
[6] Weissbach, 'Irāḳ-arab. Sprichwörter,' no. 121, in *Leipziger Semitistische Studien*, iv. (Leipzig, 1908).
[7] Lammens, *Études*, p. 330.
[8] The like holds good of the *kāmil* ideal current in Medina (see above, p. 198[b]).
[9] Bab. *Qiddûsh*. fol. 29*a*.

[1] In Ghazālī, *Iḥyā 'ulūm al-dīn*, Būlāq, A.H. 1289, ii. 198.
[2] MS in the Ducal library of Gotha (Arab.), no. 1001, fol. 34*a*.
[3] 'Abdarī, *Madkhal al-shar' al-sharīf*, Alexandria, A.H. 1293, ii. 164, line 7.
[4] Ibn Jubair, *Travels*, ed. Wright and de Goeje, *Gibb Memorial Series*, v. [1907] 272, line 17.
[5] *Revue africaine*, xli. [1897] 283, at the foot.
[6] *Madkhal*, ii. 165.
[7] Ibn Ḥajar al-'Asqalānī, *al-Durar al-kāmina* (MS in Vienna Hofbibliothek, Mixt. 245), iii. fol. 350*b*.
[8] *Madkhal, loc. cit.*

also legends of the prophets (*aḥādīth al-anbiyā*) and anecdotes from the lives of godly men (*ḥikāyāt al-ṣalīḥīn*).[1] In early times the parts of the *ḥadīth* most in favour for educational purposes were the legends about the *Dajjāl* (Antichrist),[2] by which are probably meant the traditions regarding the Mahdī period and the Last Things. Finally, the children had to learn selections from the poets; and with these the elementary curriculum seems to have reached its term. In an ordinance regarding the education of the young, 'Omar I. enjoined that popular proverbs (*al-amthāl al-sā'ira*) and beautiful poems should form subjects of instruction.[3] As regards the kind of poetry to be selected for children, the writers who discuss the course of elementary education are all most emphatic in demanding that moral pieces alone should be allowed, and that verse of an erotic character should be strictly excluded. It is interesting to read what the philosophers—to leave the theologians out of account—have to say on this subject.

Ibn Sīnā (Avicenna) recommends the following course of instruction: 'When the boy's limbs have become firm and he has attained to some readiness of speech, when he is able to assimilate the coherent materials of language and his ear has become perceptive, he should begin to receive instruction in the Qur'ān, the letters of the alphabet should be drawn for him to copy, and he should be taught the precepts of religion. As regards poetry, it is desirable that the boy should acquire the *rajaz* poems to begin with, and only afterwards the *qaṣīdas*, for the recitation of the *rajaz* is easier and its retention in the memory more certain, as its verses are shorter and its metre simpler. The teaching of poetry should commence with pieces which find themes in the advantage of good morals, the praise of science, the reproof of ignorance, and the rebuke of stupidity, and which enforce the honouring of one's parents, the practice of good deeds, and other noble qualities.[4]

Ibn Miskawaih reproaches parents for teaching their children to recite licentious poetry, to repeat the lies found in such poems, and to take pleasure in what they tell of vicious things and the pursuit of lewdness, as, *e.g.*, the poems of Imru-ul-Qais, al-Nābigha, and others like them: 'one so taught will go to live with princes, who summon him to their presence in order that he may recite such poems, and even compose in a similar strain.'[5] And in the directions drawn up for the *muḥtasib* ('chief of police'), as recorded by Ibn Bassām (13th cent. A.D.), that official is charged to see that schoolboys do not learn the poems of Ibn Ḥajjāj or the *Dīwān* of Ṣarī' al-dilā, while boys who read such poems by stealth must be deterred by corporal punishment.[6]

The strictness with which the young were guarded from the influence of erotic poetry will not surprise us when we remember the attitude of the Sunnite theologians towards narrative literature of a secular stamp. In the extant *fatwā* of a fanatically orthodox theologian of the 11th cent. A.D., people are warned against the possession not only of metaphysico-theological and philosophical works, but also of poetic and entertaining writings, and especially of certain frivolous books of the day. Contracts relating to such literary products are null and void. Writings of this character should rather be destroyed by fire and water.[7] Muhammad al-'Abdarī goes so far as to maintain that a paper merchant should not sell his wares to one who, to the best of his belief, will use the paper for reproducing the stories of 'Antar or Sīdī Baṭṭāl, and similar tales, as the diffusion of such writings falls under the category of *makrūhāt* ('reprehensible things').[8]

There were, however, other grounds upon which certain kinds of poetry were withheld from the young. Thus 'Abdallāh b. Ja'far b. Abī Ṭālib forbade his children's tutor to read with them the *qaṣīdas* of 'Urwa b. al-Ward, as they might thereby be incited to leave their native soil and seek their fortunes elsewhere.[1] There is also a *ḥadīth* saying which assigns the 'books of the Christians' likewise to the class of writings that must not be taught to the young.[2]

3. Status of the elementary teacher.—The importance attached to the work of the elementary teacher—the person from whom the young received their earliest knowledge of Allāh—is by no means reflected in his social status. The prevailing attitude of Muslim society towards the teacher of children (usually called *fiqī*; in the Maghrib also *dārrār*, 'little child,' from *dhurriyya*, pl. *dharārī*) is represented in Arabic literature as one of extreme disrespect. His position is on a level with that of weavers, blood-letters, and other despised trades.[3] Teachers were universally spoken of as a stupid and brainless class. 'Seek no advice from teachers, shepherds, or those who sit much among women'[4] an adage which, as applied to teachers and weavers, and with the addition of the explanatory clause, 'for God has deprived them of reason and withheld His blessing from their trade,' is quoted as a saying of the Prophet.[5] The phrase *'aḥmaq min mu'allim kuttāb* ('stupider than a schoolmaster')—with variations in the wording—has passed into a proverb.[6]

There is also a group of anecdotes, forming a permanent element in the Adab literature, which turn on the same point—the teacher as dunce.[7] 'How should we look for sagacity in one who is beside his wife in the evening, and in the early morning goes back to the society of little children?'[8] This contemptuous attitude found expression in the epigram:

Kafā-l-mar'a naqṣan an juqāla bi'annahu
Mu'allimu ṣibyān^{in} wa'in kāna fāḍilā,[9]

i.e. 'It is a sufficient indication of a man's inferiority—be he never so eminent—to say that he is a teacher of children.' The teacher's occupation, in fact, works almost like a specific for generating stupidity. Ibn al-Jauzī († A.H. 597 = A.D. 1200), who wrote two books, treating respectively of 'the shrewd' and 'the stupid,' sets forth in the second of these the relative stupidity of various classes of people according to the following table: 'The rationality of women [who are universally regarded as *nāqiṣāt al-'aql wal-dīn*,[10] i.e. 'deficient in rationality and religion'] equals that of seventy weavers; that of a weaver equals that of seventy schoolmasters.'[11] When 'Abdallāh b. al Muqaffa' was asked to give a weekly lesson to the son of Ismā'īl b. 'Alī, a dignitary of State, he refused the engagement, with the remark, 'Do you really wish me to have a place on the register (*dīwān*) of numskulls?'[12] It is not surprising, therefore, that the satirical poems directed against Ḥajjāj b. Jūsuf take full advantage of the fact that he, as well as his brother, was once a schoolmaster at Ṭā'if, and remind him of the time when he was still 'a humble slave, who early and late kept company with the village boys';[13] a person whose loaves were always of different shapes—'one without any visible rounding, another round as the full moon'—because he received them as payment from the parents of the children whom he primed with the *sūrat al-kauthar*.[14]

This literary mockery of the elementary teacher, however, was not so damaging as the scorn which found its way into the *ḥadīth* in the form of sayings ascribed to the Prophet; for here the criticism was no longer confined to humorous sallies against the

1 Ibn al-'Arabi, in 'Abdarī, iii. 311, line 15.
2 Nawāwī, *Tahdhīb*, ed. Wüstenfeld, p. 239, line 6 from foot.
3 Jāḥiẓ, *Bayān*, i. 213, 3 from foot.
4 *Risālat al-siyāsa*, MS in Leyden University Library, no. 1020, fol. 67*a* = *Mashrīq*, ix. 1074.
5 *Tahdhīb al-akhlāq*, p. 44, foot.
6 *Nihāyat al-rutba fī ṭalab al-ḥisba*, in *Mashrīq*, x. 1085.
7 Cf. *ZDMG* lviii. (1904) 584.
8 *Madkhal*, iii. 127, 131, line 1.

1 *Aghānī*, ii. 191, 9. The reference is probably to such verses as are found in the *Dīwān*, ed. Nöldeke, Göttingen, 1863, iii. verse 5 ff., v. 1 ff., vi. 7 ff., xxxii. 4.
2 *Lisān al-'arab*, *s.v.* 'Bkr,' v. 145, line 3: *lā tu 'allimū abkāra aulādikum kutuba-l-naṣārā.*
3 Cf. the present writer's art. 'Die Handwerke bei d. Arabern, in *Globus*, lxvii. (1894), no. 13.
4 Jāḥiẓ, *Bayān*, i. 180, line 1.
5 Dhahabī, *Mīzān al-i'tidāl*, i. 66.
6 Burton, *Unexplored Syria*, London, 1872, i. 285, no. 132.
7 Ibn Qutaiba, *'Uyūn al-akhbār*, p. 442; Ibn al-'Adīm, in *Thalāth rasā'il*, ed. Stambul, p. 33; the same anecdote, as told of *mollāhs* in Turkestan, appears in F. Duckmeyer, 'Unbefangene Beobachtungen aus Russisch-Turkestan,' in the *Beilage zur Münchener Allgem. Zeitung*, 1901, no. 250.
8 Jāḥiẓ, *loc. cit.*
9 *Muḥāḍarāt al-udabā*, Cairo, 1287, i. 29.
10 *Musnad Aḥmed*, ii. 67, at top; *Ṣaḥīḥ Muslim*, i. 159; cf. Goldziher, *Muh. Studien*, ii. 296; the idea is elaborated in a poem ascribed to 'Alī, and found in Bahā al-dīn al-'Āmilī, *Mikhlāt*, Cairo, A.H. 1317, p. 72.
11 *Thamarāt al-aurāq* (ed. in margin of *Muḥāḍarāt al-udabā*), i. 194 (with many anecdotes about teachers).
12 *Muḥād. udabā*, i. 29.
13 Mālik b. al-Raib, in Ibn Qutaiba, *Poesis*, ed. de Goeje, Leyden, 1904, p. 206, line 14; cf. Lammens, p. 360, note 2.
14 Jurjānī, *al-Muntakhab min kināyāt al-udabā*, Cairo, 1908, p. 118.

intellectual poverty of teachers, but fastened with special keenness on their moral shortcomings.

'The teachers of our children are the vilest among you; the most deficient in pity for the orphan, the most churlish towards the poor.' 'What thinkest thou of teachers?' asked Abū Huraira of the Prophet, whose answer was: 'Their *dirham* is forbidden property, their livelihood is unjust gain, their speech hypocrisy.'[1]

The odium thus expressed made itself felt also in the treatment meted out to teachers. Yaḥyā b. Aktham († A.H. 243 = A.D. 857), judge under Khalīf Ma'mūn, even refused to accept teachers as satisfactory witnesses in a court of law.[2] This disqualification has been explained on the ground that the profession taught the Qur'ān for hire. But the teacher could, of course, make the retort that the judge himself takes a reward for dispensing Divine justice.[3] The hapless pedagogue gave further offence by drawing attention to the better treatment accorded to his calling among other peoples. Such comparisons evoked severe strictures from the religious standpoint, and were actually declared by the Meccan theologian, Ibn Ḥajar al-Haitamī († A.H. 973 = A.D. 1565)—on the authority of earlier writers—to be one of the recognized criteria of unbelief:[4]

'When a teacher of children says, "The Jews are a great deal better than we Muslims, for they fulfil the obligations due to the teachers of their children,"—any one who so speaks is to be regarded as a *kāfir*.'[5]

It is possible, of course, that this depreciation of the indispensable profession of teacher may be due simply to the haughtiness inherent in the Arabic race.[6] In passing judgment upon it, however, we must not forget that analogous features appear in the educational annals of Greece and Rome.[7] Moreover, it may be said in favour of Muslim society as a whole that this far from creditable attitude towards the elementary teacher was by no means universal. We know of Muhammadans of unbiased mind who made a stand against the hackneyed judgments of the populace, and attained to a more appreciative estimate of an undeservedly maligned vocation. As the representative of this point of view, we may single out Jāḥiẓ († A.H. 255 = A.D. 869), who in this, as in other matters, criticized the prejudices of the masses in an independent spirit.

Jāḥiẓ maintains that the traditional estimate of the schoolmaster held good only of those in the lowest ranks of the profession—the ignorant *fellāḥ* teachers; and he points to the men of high intellectual distinction who had taught in schools, and had in some cases exercised great influence as the instructors of princes.[8] He also cites an imposing list of illustrious scholars, poets, and theologians (Kisā'ī, Quṭrub, Kumait, etc.) who had adorned the profession, and he sets beside them a number of contemporary teachers. 'Here in Baṣra we have never had men of greater learning in various branches of science, or of more lucidity in the expression of thought, than the two teachers, Abu-l-Wazīr and Abu-l-'Adnān.' Hence it was sheer folly and crying injustice to reproach the profession as a whole with stupidity.[9]

1 In Zurqānī, on *Muwaṭṭa*, Cairo, A.H. 1279–80, iii. 7.

2 *Thamarāt al-aurāq, loc. cit.*

3 *'Uyun al-akhbār*, p. 91, line 9; cf. Bukhārī, *Aḥkām*, no. 17 (Qasṭallānī, x. 268).

4 *Al-I'lām bi-qawāṭi' al-islām* (ed. in margin of this writer's *Zawājir*, Cairo, A.H. 1312, ii. 74).

5 As illustrating the reverse side of the matter, we may quote what Wilhelm Burchard, a native of Saxony, who was held captive by the Turks in the 17th cent., says with regard to the position of teachers in Turkey: 'Man hält die Schulmeister in Türckey sehr wehrt und thun kein Überlast, lassen auch nicht geschehen, dass ihnen ein eintzig Leid wiederfahre, worinnen sie uns Teutschen hefftig beschämen, als da viele gar Fuszschemel aus ihren Schuldinern machen und alles Hertzeleid den armen Leuten zufügen' (W. B., *Eines in die 19 Jahr von Türcken gefangen gewesenen Sachsen auffs neu eröffnete Türckey*, Magdeburg, 1688, ²1691, cap. ix.).

6 Cf. Goldziher, *Muh. Studien*, i. 110.

7 Ussing, *Darstellung d. Erziehungs- u. Unterrichtswesens bei d. Griechen u. Römern*, Altona, 1870, p. 102.

8 The tutor sometimes took his *nisba* from a family of repute in which he had served: thus the philologist, Abū 'Amr al-Shaibānī, who taught the son of Yazīd b. Manṣūr, adopted the surname Yazīdī (Suyūṭī, *Bughjat al-wu'āt*, p. 192).

9 Jāḥiẓ, *Bayān*, i. 100 ff. = *Khams rasā'il*, Stambul, A.H. 1301, p 187.

In order to gain the prestige of authority for this more favourable view of the teacher's calling, attempts were made to trace it likewise to utterances of the Prophet himself. Al-Qurṭubī († A.H. 671 = A.D. 1272), the great commentator on the Qur'ān, gives his imprimatur to one such deliverance, viz.

'The best of men, and the best of all who walk the earth, are the teachers. When religion falls into decay, it is the teachers who restore it. Give unto them, therefore, their just recompense; yet use them not as hirelings, lest you wound their spirit. For, as often as the teacher bids the boy say, "In the name of Allāh, the merciful, the compassionate," and the boy repeats the words after him, God writes for the teacher, and for the boy and his parents, a record which shall surely save them from the Fire.'[1]

It is true that the scholar who thus lent his sanction to a *ḥadīth*[2] usually branded as apocryphal was an Andalusian. In Andalusian Islām, no doubt, a higher value was placed upon the function of the teacher than was the case in the East—a result due in great measure to the flourishing system of elementary education that had grown up in the Western khalifate.[3] Here, therefore, the alleged utterances of the Prophet in honour of teachers would tend to be more favourably received. The same thing holds good of Islām in Sicily.

Speaking of Palermo, the Arab traveller Ibn Ḥauqal († A.H. 367 = A.D. 977) puts on record that he found over three hundred elementary schools in that city, and that the inhabitants regarded their teachers 'as their most excellent and distinguished citizens,' speaking of them as 'the people of Allāh, their witnesses [before God], and their trusty friends.' It is true that Ibn Ḥauqal, in explanation of the scornful attitude towards the intellectual capacities of teachers prevalent elsewhere, adds that 'they choose this profession in order to evade enrolment in the army.'[4]

4. Payment of teachers.—As has been indicated in the foregoing, the gravamen of the strictures urged against the teaching profession from the religious side was the fact that teachers asked and took payment for giving instruction in the Qur'ān. The moral propriety of taking wages for religious teaching was a question frequently debated among Muslim jurists. It is to be presumed that in Islām, as in other religions,[5] the devout were in favour of gratuitous religious instruction. In spreading the knowledge of Divine things the teacher should have no other design (*niyya*) than that of doing a work well-pleasing to God, and thereby attaining nearness to Him. No financial consideration should attach to such 'near-bringing works' (*qurāb*), any more than—on similar grounds—to the *ādhān*,[6] the *ṣalāt*, the diffusion of the *ḥadīth*, etc. All such acts must be done only *iḥtisāban* ('for God's sake'), not *iktisāban* ('for gain'). In support of this view, and in evidence of its being the only legitimate one, there were numerous traditions to hand;[7] nor were typical examples lacking to commend its acceptance.

One such example was found in 'Abd al-Raḥmān al-Sullami, a man of devout spirit, who had actually heard *ḥadīths* from the lips of 'Othmān and 'Alī, and who, at the time of his death (during the khalifate of 'Abdalmalik), was *imām* of a mosque in

1 Quoted by 'Abdarī, *Madkhal*, ii. 158.

2 Ibn al-Jauzī pronounces the following verdict on this *ḥadīth*: 'It is not permissible to use this saying as an argument [in the question as to payment of teachers], for it is a concoction of Aḥmed b. 'Abdallāh al-Harawī al-Jūyībārī, who was a liar, and fabricated *ḥadīths*—a matter in which all critics of tradition agree' (MS in Leyden Univ. Library, no. 1772, fol. 132*a*). In Suyūṭī's work on spurious traditional sayings likewise, this and other similar utterances regarding *mu'allim* are marked with a warning rubric (*Al-La'ālī al-maṣnū'a fi-l-aḥadīth al-mauḍū'a*, p. 103 ff.).

3 Cf. Schack, *Poesie u. Kunst der Araber in Spanien u. Sicilien*, Berlin, 1865, i. 52; Dozy, *Gesch. d. Mauren in Spanien*, Leipzig, 1874, ii. 68.

4 *Bibl. Geogr. Arab.*, ed. de Goeje, Leyden, 1870 ff., ii. 87, top.

5 Cf. Manu, xi. 63, where the act of teaching the Veda for hire, or learning it under a paid teacher, is declared to be a sin of the second degree.

6 Goldziher, *Muh. Studien*, ii. 390.

7 These traditional testimonies were collected by the Ḥanbalite Ibn al-Jauzī (MS in Leyden Univ. Library, no. 1772, fol. 131*b*).

Kūfa, and in that capacity had devoted himself to teaching the Qur'ān. It is recorded that once, on coming home, he found a number of cattle which a grateful father had sent him as a honorarium for instructing his son in the sacred volume. He at once returned the gift, with the message: 'We take no payment for the Book of God.'[1] Other teachers of the Qur'ān gave similar practical expression to this point of view;[2] and, in support of the theory that religious instruction should be given *majjānan* ('gratuitously'), appeal was made also to an admonition 'from the ancient books' which, in point of fact, may be identified as a Talmudic maxim.[3]

But, while the demand for free religious teaching might be good enough as an ideal, and while some even tried to carry it into effect, it was naturally left behind in the march of practical life. It was, after all, necessary that the wretched beings who, without much moral support from their fellows, engaged in the work of teaching should at least make a bare subsistence out of it. In this, as in many other things, the religious injunction, with its ascetic ideal, could not be put in practice so ruthlessly as to maintain a universal interdict against the merest pittance of payment.[4] As a matter of fact, besides the more austere *ḥadīths*, there are others of a more humane character, and more favourable to the practice of taking wages for religious instruction; and the teacher who was not in a position to prosecute his calling for a purely spiritual reward could always derive comfort from these.[5]

Even Bukhārī himself finds a place in his *Corpus Traditionum* for a saying ascribed to Ibn 'Abbās: 'Nothing has a better right to be rewarded than [instruction in] the Book of God.' It is true that he appends to this the condition laid down by Sha'bī, viz. that the teacher may on no account negotiate for his wages, but may accept what is voluntarily given him. Bukhārī finally cites the testimony of Ḥakam b. 'Uyaina: 'I have never heard it said of any of the *fugahā* that he disapproved of the teacher's remuneration. Even Ḥasan Baṣrī paid a teacher ten dirhams.'[6] From Mālik b. Anas comes the still more decisive statement that in the holy city of Medina none has ever taken umbrage at the teacher's receiving a reward even in this world —and that not merely as a voluntary honorarium from the parents, but as a fixed monthly fee (*mushāhara*).[7]

Accordingly the payment of teachers became the rule actually recognized in practice by Muslim law,[8] and was vindicated, with the support of the sources quoted above, by authorities of the highest repute.[9]

The adherents of the more rigid view, in giving their consent to the practice of paying teachers—this payment, however, they preferred to call '*iwaḍ* ('recompense')—sought to solace their feelings by qualifying the teacher's right by certain *pia desideria*, which, it is true, made very little difference. They appealed to the moral sense of the teacher. He must look upon his wages, not as professional emoluments, but as a gift (*fatḥ*)[10] Divinely bestowed upon him in order that he may pursue a calling well-pleasing to God.[11] The all-important thing is the inward purpose (*niyya*); he must devote himself to the work from purely spiritual motives, and without any worldly considerations whatever. To this 'Abdarī adds the naive admonition that the teacher should make no public profession of his motives, as it is quite like 'the people of our time' to take him at his word, and deprive him of his material recompense.[1] Further, he must not let his continuance at work depend rigidly upon his being paid regularly. Should his allowance cease in any particular case, he must attend all the more zealously to the children of parents who, owing to their poverty, have fallen behind in their payments.[2] From the children themselves he must not receive presents without the knowledge of their parents or guardians.[3] In general, he must be satisfied that the money tendered him is above suspicion as to its source, and that it has not been gained dishonestly, or by methods obnoxious to religious precept; he should, for instance, have nothing to do with the money of a tax-gatherer. With respect to this counsel—it was, of course, simply a wish—it is interesting to note the qualifying clause annexed to it, viz. that in such cases the teacher need not refuse money from the hands of the mother or grandmother of his pupil, so long as he can assure himself that the immediate source has the warrant of religious law.[4] But he must avoid all intercourse with fathers whose occupation is at variance with the strict demands of religion; and, as long as they make their living in that way, he must not greet them, or hold himself accountable to them.[5]

Stories of the exorbitant charges made by eminent teachers come down from every period, though it must be admitted that this applies only to those branches of learning which were not in the strict sense religious.

The grammarian Muhammad b. 'Alī al-Mabramān († A.H. 345 = A.D. 956), pupil of Mubarrad, had a name for excessive avarice. He would not give instruction in the *kitāb* of Sībūyah under a fee of one hundred dīnārs.[6] Muhammad Shams al-dīn al-Suyūṭī († A.H. 808 = A.D. 1405) charged a dirham for every line of the grammatical poem *Alfiyya*,[7] which comprises about a thousand lines.

5. School administration.—Muslim literature treats in great detail of the teacher's demeanour towards his scholars,[8] and the conditions applying to the conducting of schools. As regards the relation of teacher to pupil, the fundamental principle is the just and equal treatment of all scholars. Laith b. Mujāhid affirms that at the Day of Judgment God will subject the schoolmaster to a special interrogation as to whether he maintained strict impartiality between pupil and pupil, and that, if he is found guilty in this respect, he will be set beside the workers of iniquity.[9] A whole series of apparently trivial points relating to the child's presence in school are brought by 'Abdarī under the principle that no distinction shall be made between children of the rich and children of the poor.[10] Nor must the scholars be employed in the private service of the teacher's household, without the express sanction of their parents;[11] and from this it was argued that the teacher must not make use of orphan children for such work *under any circumstances*.[12]

It is the law in Islām that all teachers should be married;[13] a similar requirement is found in the Talmud.[14] A typical indication of the ethical standpoint of Eastern peoples is seen in the regulations designed to obviate the very suspicion of evil communications. The rule that the work of elementary teaching must be done, not at the teacher's own

[1] Ibn Sa'd, vi. 120, line 3 ff.
[2] *Ib.* p. 210, line 12; 213, line 14.
[3] Goldziher, *Muh. Studien*, ii. 181 f.; also quoted as from 'ancient writings,' in Māwardī, *Adab al-dunyā wal-dīn*, Stambul, A.H. 1304, p. 71.
[4] Cf. Lammens, *Études*, 360.
[5] The *ḥadīths pro* and *con* are brought together in the Ahlwardt MSS, Berlin Royal Library, no. 145.
[6] Bukhārī, *Ijāra*, no. 16. That giving instruction in the Qur'ān might have a pecuniary equivalent is shown by a story which relates how a man who was too poor to give his bride money or money's worth as a wedding-present (*mahr*) was allowed by the Prophet to teach her several sūras of the Qur'ān in lieu thereof (Bukhārī, *Nikāḥ*, no. 40; cf. Zurqānī on *Muwaṭṭa*, iii. 7).
[7] The present writer has not succeeded in tracing this regulation, as cited by Mālik, in the *Muwaṭṭa*.
[8] *Revue africaine*, xli. 281.
[9] Kamāl Pashāhzādah wrote a special *risāla fī jawāz al-istījār 'alā ta'līm al-Qur'ān* (Ahlwardt, Berlin MSS, no. 439).
[10] For this term, see *WZKM* xiii. (1899) 49.
[11] 'Abdarī, *Madkhal*, ii. 158, line 13.

[1] *Madkhal*, ii. 159.
[2] *Ib.* i. 345, line 14 ff.
[3] *Ib.* ii. 161, line 17.
[4] *min wajhin mastūrin bil-'ilmi* (*Madkhal*, ii. 159, at the foot).
[5] *Ib.* 160, line 2.
[6] Suyūṭī, *Bughyat al-wu'āt*, p. 74.
[7] *Ib.* 37.
[8] Ghazālī has a short paragraph on the *ādāb mu'allim al-ṣibyān* ('manners of the teacher of children') in his *Al-ādāb fi-l-dīn* (*Majmū'at*, ed. Ṣabrī al-Kurdī, Cairo, A.H. 1328, p. 67).
[9] Ibn Qutaiba, '*Uyūn al-akhbār*, p. 98, line 6.
[10] *Madkhal*, ii. 158, 162, 167.
[11] Ibn Bassām, in *Mashriq*, x. 1084; *Rev. africaine*, xli. 283.
[12] *Madkhal*, ii. 166, line 19.
[13] *Ib.* 167.
[14] Mishn. *Qiddūsh*. iv. 13.

residence, but in a specially appointed public place (*ḥānūt*, pl. *ḥawānīt*) within sight of the people was intended to prevent every suggestion of scandal.[1] Nor could the halls of the mosques be used for this purpose, as little children might unwittingly defile the walls and flooring of the sacred edifice. This prohibition was supported by a saying of the Prophet: 'Keep your boys and your lunatics away from your mosques'; but the precept was not strictly observed in practice. It has been a favourite custom from olden times to conjoin the elementary school and the public fountain (*sabīl*); the institution of the latter is often combined with that of a school in the upper storey (*maktab sabīl*). It is interesting to note 'Abdarī's criticism of certain practices common among teachers in his day. He holds it unworthy of the profession that a teacher, at the inauguration of his school—or afterwards, if he finds his undertaking insufficiently supported—should try to draw the attention and invite the patronage of the public by setting up placards before the school-gate. It is likewise unbecoming that a teacher, in requesting the parents to attend the school-festivals (*afrāḥ*), should in his letters of invitation (*aurāq isti'dhānāt*) flatter them with high-flown epithets and titles, or compose the invitations in verse.[2]

The pupils must also have their off-days. The school must be closed for two days of every week, viz. Thursday and Friday, and also for a period of from one to three days before and after the *'īd* festival.[3] The Thursday holiday gave occasion to the proverbial phrase, 'to be as happy as a teacher on Thursdays' (*kamā fariḥa al-mu'addib bil-khamīs*).[4] The scholars are also granted a whole or partial holiday whenever any one of them has finally mastered a section of the Qur'ān.[5] The parents of a boy who has succeeded in doing this celebrate the event by a festivity (*iṣrāfa*),[6] and bestow upon the teacher a special gift, the acceptance of which is not frowned upon even by the precisians. When a youth completes his study of the Qur'ān, the occasion is celebrated in a feast called (in Mecca) *iqlāba*, or (in the Maghrib) *takhrīja*.[7] 'Abdarī's minute account of the more extravagant—and to him obnoxious—forms sometimes assumed by these functions reveals an interesting phase of contemporary life.

The question of corporal punishment was also discussed among those with whose educational methods we are now dealing. The 'rod' is regarded as a valuable auxiliary of the teacher's art. The 'strap'—quite characteristically—becomes an object of comparison: 'In the Prophet's hand was a whip, like that used in school' (*ka-dirrat al-kuttāb*)—a simile often employed.[8] The teacher is sometimes held up to derision by being described as 'one who brandishes the whip' (*ḥāmil dirra*) and takes reward for the book of God.[9] Even the philosopher Ibn Sīnā, in his treatise on the education of children, speaks of the 'assistance of the hand' (*al-isti'āna bil-yad*) as a useful adjunct of instruction.[10] The tutors of the young sons of khalīfs did not spare the rod,[11] nor did the fathers disapprove.

Al-Mubarrad describes a scene in which the Khalīf 'Abdalmalik leads by the hand Prince Marwān, 'crying because of the whipping his teacher had given him.'[12] Abū Maryam, preceptor of the Abbāsid princes Amīn and Ma'mūn, was apparently given to a too drastic use of the ferule. On one occasion he chastised Prince Amīn so severely as to make his arm black and blue. The prince complained to his father, and showed him the maimed arm. The Khalīf invited the stern pedagogue to dinner; and when the latter, in no little apprehension, specified the offence for which the prince had been so sharply dealt with, the father reassured him with the words: 'You are at liberty even to kill him: it were better that he die than remain a fool.'[1]

A further form of punishment was 'keeping in'; but, in the one instance of this known to us, it is the father, not the teacher, who administers the correction.[2]

It was to be expected that, in order to protect the children against the undue severity of irascible masters, Muslim jurisprudence would endeavour to regulate the penalties applied, both as to their form and as to their degree. It sanctioned corporal punishment, especially for religious offences,[3] but only in the case of children over ten years of age; while, as to the amount of punishment, the extreme limit was variously laid down as between three[4] and ten 'light strokes.' Nor must the teacher resort to any instrument used by the judge in administering legal penalties (*ḥadd*). The *Madkhal* speaks severely of contemporary teachers who chastise with 'dry almond rods, bushy palm-branches, Nubian switches, and even the instrument called the *falaqa*'[5] ('stocks'), and used for the bastinado. The supervision of the teacher in this, as in other matters, was assigned to the chief of police. In the directions drawn up for this officer he is instructed to be observant of the way in which children are treated at school, and to protect them from maltreatment by hot-tempered teachers.[6]

6. Education of girls.—It must be borne in mind that the maxims relating to the training and instruction of the young apply only to boys (*ṣabī*). The education of girls did not fall under these rules except in one single particular, viz. that, as set forth in the police directions recorded by Ibn Bassām, the female teachers of girls (*mu'allimāt al-banāt*) are to be more strictly looked after in regard to the poetical pieces which they set before their pupils.[7] While it was deemed necessary to instruct girls in moral and religious things, there was no desire to lead them through the portals of intellectual development. Woman's proper sphere centres in the spindle,[8] and this requires no training in letters. Even the philosophic thinker and poet Abū-l-'Alā al-Ma'arrī († A.H. 449 = A.D. 1057) endorses this maxim,[9] which became a veritable household word in the ancient Muslim world. The following utterance of the Prophet regarding females—said to rest on the authority of 'Ā'isha—is frequently quoted: 'Do not let them frequent the roofs; do not teach them the art of writing; teach them spinning and the *sūrat al-nūr*.'[10] But it were surely preposterous to regard this sūra

1 Ibn Bassām, in *Mashriq*, x. 1084; *Madkhal*, ii. 163; *Rev. africaine*, xli. 281.
2 *Madkhal*, ii. 169 f.
3 *Ib.* 168.
4 Balawī, *Kitāb Alif-bā*, Cairo, A.H. 1287, i. 208.
5 *Rev. africaine*, xli. 284, at top.
6 We find also the term *ḥudhāqa* (*Madkhal*, ii. 179, line 16).
7 Snouck Hurgronje, *Mekka*, Hague, 1889, ii. 146; Marçais, *Le Dialecte arabe parlé à Tlemcen*, Paris, 1902, p. 246.
8 *Usd al-ghāba*, iii. 50, line 6; iv. 234, line 9; v. 553, line 1.
9 Yāqūt, ed. Margoliouth, i. 60, line 7 from foot.
10 *Mashriq*, ix. 1074.
11 Yāqūt, i. 223.
12 *Kāmil*, p. 573, line 11.

1 *Muḥāḍarāt al-udabā*, i. 30.
2 *Aghānī*, ix. 111, line 6 from foot.
3 In the instructions regarding the training of children it is usually stated that 'they shall receive corporal punishment for neglecting prayer from the age of thirteen' (*e.g.* Ghazālī, as above); in other versions (e.g. *Mīzān al-i'tidāl*, ii. 364) the *terminus a quo* is given as ten years.
4 The maximum of three was deduced from the *ḥadīth* by certain Mālikite theologians; see Qasṭallānī, x. 40, line 12 (on Bukhārī, *Muḥārabūn*, no. 29).
5 *Madkhal*, ii. 165. Regarding the instruments of punishment employed in Oriental schools, cf. the interesting notes, with illustrations (including the *falaqa*), in the *Rev. du monde musulman*, xiii. [1910] 420-423, and xiv. [1911] 67, from which we learn that in one Muslim country or another the various penalties mentioned by 'Abdarī were all in actual use.
6 Ibn Khaldūn, in *Mashriq*, x. 963; cf. *ib.* 966; Ibn Bassām, *ib.* 1084.
7 *Mashriq*, x. 1085.
8 Mubarrad, *Kāmil*, 150. An almost verbally identical saying of the Rabbis occurs in the Bab. Talmud, *Yōmā*, fol. 66*b*, on which cf. S. Krauss, *Talmud. Archäol.* i. (Leipzig, 1910) 558, note 260.
9 Kremer, *Culturgeschichte*, ii. 133.
10 *Mīzān al-i'tidāl*, ii. 335. This *ḥadīth* is reproduced in the *Mustadrak* of Ḥākim as an authentic saying of the Prophet.

(xxiv.) as suitable for the training of young girls, containing as it does the revelations which refer to women of known or suspected immoral life. The most emphatic warnings of all are uttered against teaching women to write. Ibn Miskawaih († A.H. 421 = A.D. 1030), in spite of all his schooling in philosophy, finds nothing strange in this prohibition. In his *Jāwidān Khirad* he adopts a pronouncement of 'Omar I. which, in counselling the stringent control of women, lays an interdict upon their being taught to write.[1]

It is told of Luqmān the sage that, when on one occasion he passed a school, and noticed that a girl was being taught, he asked, 'For whom is this sword being polished?' implying, of course, that the girl would be her future husband's ruin.[2] It is not surprising to find this view reflected in the police instructions handed down by Ibn Bassām: 'He [the teacher] must not instruct any woman or female slave in the art of writing, for thereby would accrue to them only an increase of depravity.' It is a current saying that 'a woman who is taught to write is like a serpent which is given poison to drink.'[3]

Girls must be kept from the study of poetical literature; here there is no concession whatever, such as is made in the literary education of boys.[4]

These views, however, belong rather to the sphere of ethnology than to that of religion, and it would be absurd to regard them as expressing principles inseparable from the fundamental teachings of Islām. The history of Muslim civilization, even in periods which show no deviation from the line of strict orthodoxy, would supply many a refutation of such a theory. When we bear in mind how many women had a share in the transmission of *ḥadīth* works,[5] we see the untenability of the view that in religious circles the art of writing was withheld from women on principle. The daughter of Mālik b. Anas was able to correct the errors of those who recited and transmitted her father's *Muwaṭṭa*.[6] That the rule against teaching women to write was of universal validity is disproved by the very name of a learned lady of Damascus, viz. *Sitt al-kataba* ('mistress of the writers') *bint abi-l-Ṭarḥ*, who supplied Jūsūf b. 'Abdal-mu'mīn of Nābulūs with traditions.[7] The learned woman is found even among remote tribes in the heart of the Southern Sahara, where women are apparently not prohibited from cultivating Muslim learning.[8]

'The nomads of this region of the Sahara possess books, precisely as do the settlers; nor do they abandon them even in their wanderings; their migratory habits do not prevent their devoting themselves to intellectual activities, or allowing their children, *even girls*, to share in such studies.'[9]

Above all, however, it is the position of women in the learned life of Andalusian Islām, as portrayed by such writers as al-Marrākushī,[10] and verified by the facts of literary history, that shows to what a small extent the prohibitory maxims were applied in actual religious practice. Besides the women who attained eminence in various branches of science and literature, and especially in poetry, we find several who were active in civic service, as, *e.g.*, 'Muzna (secretary to the Emīr al-Nāṣir li-dīn-Allāh [† A.H. 358 = A.D. 969]), the learned, gifted with a beautiful handwriting.'[1] Such examples show at least that the prohibitive sayings referred to were a dead letter in practical life; and they also prove that the education of women actually attained a very high standard, and went far beyond the prescribed limit of the *sūrat al-nūr*. Hence the endeavours made within recent times in various parts of the Muslim world to raise female education to the level of Western civilization may be justified by an appeal to the past history of orthodox Islām.

7. Education in ethical and political writings.—The problem of elementary education has not been ignored in the literature of ethics and politics. The somewhat mechanical precepts of the older theological writings have been furnished with a deeper foundation in ethics and philosophy, and enriched with the ideas of a more worthy conception of life. As in ethics and philosophy generally, so also in education, we must recognize the powerful effects of that Hellenistic influence which we have already noted in some matters of detail. Reference was made above to an educational excursus which Avicenna († A.H. 428 = A.D. 1037) incorporated in his tractate on government (*risālat al-siyāsa*).[2] But Avicenna dealt with little more than the formal elements of the question, and it was really al-Ghazālī († A.H. 505 = A.D. 1111) who first brought the problem of education into organic relation with a profound ethical system. Starting from the Hellenistic idea of the infant mind as a *tabula rasa* susceptive of objective impressions,[3] he urges upon parents and teachers their solemn responsibility for the principles which they may stamp permanently upon the young soul. The child is given them as a trust, and it is their part to guard it well and faithfully. They must not only fill the young mind with knowledge, but—and Ghazālī lays special emphasis upon this—must seek to stimulate the child's moral consciousness, and train him to the proprieties of social life.[4]

It is somewhat remarkable that in the discussion of problems in the theory and practice of education the literature of Western Islām (the Maghrib) takes the lead. In the East, it is true, Ghazālī's vigorous dissertation makes up for the more abundant products of the West, and has, moreover, had a great influence upon the latter. As early as the 4th cent. A.H., however, we find a reference to a work called *Kitāb al-tafḍīla fī ta'dīb al-muta'allimīn* ('On the Education of Pupils'), by 'Alī b. Muhammad b. Khalaf al-Qābisī († A.H. 403 = A.D. 1012), of Gabes in Southern Tunis,[5] who enjoyed a high repute as one of the Mālikite traditional school.[6] The present writer has, however, sought in vain for any further mention of this presumably pedagogical work of al-Qābisī. In regard to the legal provisions bearing upon education, again, the great authority

1 MS in Leyden Univ. Library, no. 640, p. 202.
2 Ibn Mas'ūd, in Ibn Ḥajar al-Haitamī, *Fatāwī ḥadīthiyya*, Cairo, 1307, p. 63, among other warnings against educating girls.
3 *Mashriq*, x. 1085. Cf. Muhammad ben Cheneb, *Proverbes arabes de l'Algérie et du Maghreb*, ii. (Paris, 1906) 246 f., no. 1685.
4 Jāḥiẓ, *Bayān*, i. 214, line 1; Ibn Bassām, *loc. cit.*
5 The instances given in the present writer's *Muh. Studien*, ii. 405–407, might be largely added to. We take occasion to refer only to the many women mentioned by Tāj al-dīn al-Subkī († A.H. 771 = A.D. 1370) among the sources of his knowledge of tradition; see, *e.g.*, *Ṭabaqāt al-Shāfi'iyya*, i. 49, lines 16, 17; 51. 16; 69. 7; 72. 16; 74. 12; 76. 6; 80. 3 from foot; 82. 3; 107. 7 from foot, etc. The number of women referred to as sources of tradition by al-Suyūṭī († A.H. 911 = A.D. 1505) in the list of his *Isnāds* (in appendix to his *Bughyat al-wu'āt*, pp. 440–461) is surprisingly large.
6 *Madkhal*, i. 179.
7 Ibn Rajab, *Ṭabaqāt al-Ḥanābila* (MS in Leipzig Univ. Library, Vollers, no. 708), fol. 149*a*.
8 For a notable example from the 17th cent. see *Rev. du monde musulman*, xiv. [1911] 7.
9 Ismā'īl Hamet, 'La Civilisation arabe en Afrique Centrale' (*ib.* 11). The author contrasts the ignorance prevalent among women in the Northern Sahara with the culture which is widely diffused among those of the Southern tribes (*ib.* 22).
10 *Hist. of the Almohades*², ed. Dozy, Leyden, 1881, p. 270.

1 *Al-Dabbī*, ed. Codera, no. 1590 (*Bibl. Arab. Hisp.* vol. iii.).
2 Published in the Arab magazine *Mashriq*, ix.
3 Cf. the Arabic proverb *Al-ta'allum fi-l-ṣighar kal-naqsh fi-l-ḥajar* ('Learning in youth is like engraving upon stone'), Jāḥiẓ, *Bayān*, i. 102, line 10 from foot.
4 This most important treatise by Ghazālī has been translated into English and appreciatively criticized by D. B. Macdonald, 'The Moral Education of the Young among the Muslims,' in *IJE* xv. [1905] 286–304; cf. also al-Ghazālī, *Lettre sur l'éducation des enfants*, tr. by Muhammad ben Cheneb, in *Rev. africaine*, xlv. [1901] 241 f.
5 Balawī (likewise a native of the Maghrib), *Kitāb Alif-bā*, i. 76, line 6.
6 Ibn Khallikān, ed. Wüstenfeld, Göttingen, 1835–40, no. 457 (tr. de Slane, London, 1843–71, ii. 263); Abū Bakr ibn Khair (*Bibl. Arab. Hisp.* ix. x.), p. 296.

is Abu-l-Walīd ibn Rushd the elder († A.H. 520 = A.D. 1126), qāḍī of Cordova, and grandfather of the famous philosopher of the same name (*i.e.* Averroës). Abū Bakr ibn al-'Arabī († A.H. 543 = A.D. 1148), qāḍī of Seville, who expounded his educational ideas in a work entitled *Marāqī al-zulfā* ('Stages of approach,' *i.e.* to God), is also frequently indebted—even in his language—to Ghazālī's treatise. The *Marāqī* is apparently lost, but numerous excerpts are quoted in a work by another Maghrib writer, the *Madkhal al-shar' al-sharīf* ('Introduction to the Sublime Law' of Muhammad ibn al-Ḥājj al-'Abdarī († A.H. 737 = A.D. 1336–7). This work, which has in view the reform of Muslim life on the basis of the ancient Sunna, devotes a number of sections to the subject of education and training, and has on this account been used as one of the sources of the present article. It is worthy of remark that in the scheme of education set forth in 'Abdarī's quotations from the *Marāqī* of Ibn al-'Arabī, the latter lays great stress upon hardening the body: the young should sleep in hard beds, and be trained in physical exercise; they should be urged to bodily activity, and inured to pain by corporal punishment. He also pleads strongly for games and hours of recreation.

'If a child is kept from play, and forced to work at his tasks without intermission, his spirit will be depressed; his power of thought and his freshness of mind will be destroyed; he will become sick of study, and his life will be overclouded, so that he will try all possible shifts to evade his lessons.'[1]

Ghazālī likewise had spoken emphatically on the evils of overpressure. Next in order after 'Abdarī comes another Maghrib authority, Ibn Khaldūn († A.H. 808 = A.D. 1405), renowned as a writer on the philosophy of history, who devoted great attention to educational problems, and especially to the spirit of primary education, its gradation, the methodics of teaching the Qur'ān and philological subjects, and even the question of school-books (*mutūn*);[2] a lucid account of his educational ideas will be found in D. B. Macdonald's *Aspects of Islam.*[3] A work treating of married life (*muqni' al-muḥtāj fī ādāb al-ziwāj*) by the Maghrib writer Abu-l-'Abbās b. Ardūn al-Zajlī († A.H. 992 = A.D. 1584) contains a long chapter on the education of children; this was published recently by Paul Paquignon.[4] Reference may also be made to a compendium of the maxims relating to education, the work of a Maghrib author whose name is not given; it is based largely on the treatise of 'Abdarī, and has been published in the original, together with a French translation, by the Algerian professor, Muhammad ben Cheneb.[5]

A word may be added, for fullness' sake, regarding the educational 'guide' of Burhān al-dīn al-Zarnūjī (*c.* A.H. 600 = A.D. 1203), introduced into Europe under the title of *Enchiridion Studiosi.*[6] This work, the author of which was a native of the East, deals, not with primary education, but with the study of theology, and gives pious counsels for the successful prosecution thereof. From the educational standpoint the sixth chapter is worthy of attention, as it contains suggestions regarding the first steps in study, the amounts to be mastered in the early stages, the repetition of what has been learned, etc. The author, conformably to time-honoured maxims, advises students to begin a study so far as possible on a Wednesday, as it was on that day that God created light.[7]

8. Modern movements towards reform.—So long as the social life of Islām remained impervious to Western influence, and even to-day in circles that are still unaffected by it, the instruction of the young proceeded mainly on the lines laid down in the older theological writings (see above, § 2). The best descriptions of this traditional stage are found in the works of E. Lane[1] and Snouck Hurgronje[2] (for Arabic countries), and H. Vámbéry[3] (for Turkey proper).[4] But, while this primitive and patriarchal form of instruction still holds its place—even amid the influences of foreign culture with which it will have nothing to do—there has meanwhile arisen in various Muslim countries a system of education which comes more and more into harmony with modern requirements. The new movement was initiated by the Egyptian pasha Muhammad 'Alī, the founder of modern Egypt, whose educational reforms, begun in 1811, were at first, it is true, of a somewhat circumscribed character. A further advance was made in 1824 by the erection of training schools in various departments, and the movement was partially organized and consolidated in 1836.[5] On this basis all branches of education have made rapid progress in Egypt. In Turkey, the reform of primary education was inaugurated in 1845, under Sultan 'Abdulmajīd, by the institution of the so-called *Rushdiyya* schools, while in 1868 his successor, 'Abdul 'Azīz, established a lyceum in Galata-Serai.[6] But, in spite of ceaseless efforts to raise the standard and widen the scope of education throughout Turkey, the results still fall far short of a general diffusion of knowledge, and in many parts of the Ottoman Empire there has been no advance whatever upon the crude institutions of primitive times. It should be added, however, that in Turkey and elsewhere the more liberal-minded Muhammadans, in default of adequate institutions of their own, send their children of either sex to non-Muslim schools established by European and American agencies.

It will be readily understood that, in countries under European rule having a Muslim population, the various Governments have greatly promoted the cause of education by the establishment of distinctively Muslim schools, as, *e.g.*, in India,[7] and, since the English occupation, also in Egypt. In the Muslim colonies of France and Holland likewise,[8] the respective administrations have devoted great efforts to the task of bringing the native educational methods nearer to the standards of modern culture. It is a remarkable fact that the Muhammadan subjects of the Russian empire (Tatars) are spontaneously and independently making strenuous and successful efforts to develop a modern system of education,[9] and, under the leadership of enlightened co-religionists, are able, in all social and intellectual concerns, to combine an unswerving loyalty to their faith with an earnest striving after progress on modern lines. The advance thus being made in various branches of education embraces also the instruction of girls, which is coming to be recognized more and more

1 In *Madkhal*, iii. 312 ff.

2 *Prolégomènes*, ed. Quatremère, Paris, 1858, iii. 248; tr. de Slane, Paris, 1862–68, iii. 271 f.

3 New York, 1911, pp. 309–316.

4 *Revue du monde musulman*, xv. [1911] 118–123.

5 'Notions de pédagogie musulmane,' *Rev. africaine*, xli. [1897] 269–285.

6 ed. Caspari, Leipzig, 1838.

7 *Ta'līm al-muta'allim ṭarīq al-ta'allum*, with a commentary by Shaikh ibn Ismā'īl 'Alī (dedicated to Sultan Murād III. [1574–1595]), Maimaniyya Printing Office, Cairo, A.H. 1311, p. 31.

1 *Manners and Customs of the Modern Egyptians*[5], i. (London, 1871) ch. ii. ('Early Education'), p. 73 ff.

2 *Mekka*, ii. 143 ff. For East India, cf. the same writer's *De Atjéhers*, Leyden, 1894, ii. 1 ff.

3 *Sittenbilder aus dem Morgenlande*, Berlin, 1876, p. 120 ff.

4 Cf. also *Voyages du Chevalier Chardin en Perse*, ed. Langlès, Paris, 1811, iv. 224 ff.

5 Cf. Dor, *L'Instruction publique en Égypte*, Paris, 1872; Yakoub Artin Pasha, *L'Instruction publique en Égypte*, Paris, 1890. The latest statistical information regarding Muslim and Coptic education in Egypt is given in a little work entitled *Al-ta'līm fī Miṣr*, Cairo, A.H. 1329, by Shaikh 'Alī Jūsuf.

6 The main particulars are given by Carra de Vaux, *La Doctrine de l'Islam*, Paris, 1909, p. 210 ff.

7 On the present state of Muslim education in India, see *Revue du monde musulman*, xv. [1911] 118–123.

8 J. G. Hockman, 'L'Enseignement aux Indes Orientales Néerlandaises,' in *Bibliothèque Coloniale Internationale* (Institut Colon. Intern., Brussels), 9th ser., vol. i.

9 See Molla Aminoff, 'Les Progrès de l'instruction publique chez les Musulmans russes,' in *Rev. du monde musulman*, ix. 247–263, 295; Sophie Bobrovnikoff, 'Moslems in Russia,' in *The Moslem World*, ed. Zwemer, i. (1911) 15 ff.

as a matter of vital moment for the Muhammadan world. The more important phases and incidents of the whole movement are chronicled in the *Revue du monde musulman* (Paris, since 1906), which deals with all Muslim countries, and has now completed its sixteenth volume.

Among specifically Muhammadan tendencies making for educational reform, we may mention the Bābī movement, which arose in Persia in 1844 (see art. BĀB, BĀBĪS, vol. ii. p. 299 ff.), and which, as Bahā'ism, has since then been constantly extending its influence. From the outset the principles of this sect have embraced an endeavour to raise primary education to a higher level and to relieve it of its long legacy of prejudice—aims which have been most strenuously pursued by the Bahā'ī. Their more exalted conception of woman and of her function in family life, and their abolition of the restraints placed upon the female sex by ancient convention, are naturally coupled with efforts to improve the education of girls.

With the progress of primary education the development of the higher grades of instruction goes hand in hand. In many parts of the Muslim world, indeed, the latter has outstripped the former. A considerable number of colleges for the study of special subjects—military, medical, legal, and technical—and designed primarily to meet economic and political requirements, have been established, and in some centres these are combined to form a kind of university (*dār al-funūn*).[1] A large institution, designed to perform the function of a university, was quite recently erected in Cairo[2] (President-Rector, Prince Aḥmed Fu'ād Pasha, great grandson of Muhammad 'Alī). In Aligarh, India, the endeavour to form the academy founded there in 1875 into a university is within sight of success—a movement which, with Agha Khān at its head, finds generous support among adherents of Islām throughout India.[3] Ṭeherān likewise has a college which does its work under the style of a *dār al-funūn*. By way of providing stepping-stones towards such higher institutions, effective progress is being made in Turkey and Egypt with the system of preparatory or *i'dādī* schools.

These institutions are all conducted according to detailed instructions of the respective Governments, and the instructions are printed and made public. Various reforms, especially in regard to the system of examination and granting diplomas, have been recently effected by the Government in the great *madrasa* of the Azhar mosque in Cairo, in which the study of the various branches of theology is pursued on traditional lines; as also in the schools associated with that *madrasa* at Ṭanṭa (the Aḥmediyya mosque), Damietta, and Alexandria.[4] The need for reform in higher theological education has asserted itself also in more sequestered localities.[5] Among other agencies aiming at the diffusion of culture among Muhammadans, mention may be made of the Khaldūniyya institution at Tunis,[6] which takes its name from the Ibn Khaldūn referred to above. All these manifold activities are but so many endeavours to arouse, strengthen, and apply in practice, among the Muhammadan peoples, the conviction that their religion does not prohibit them from rising to the demands of a progressive civilization, or pursuing the intellectual life.

LITERATURE.—This has been given fully in the footnotes.

I. GOLDZIHER.

EDUCATION (Persian).—The Persians, like all other Orientals, attached high value to education, so that Hōrmazd (afterwards Hormisdas IV.) could reply to his teacher, the sage Buzurjmihr, that 'wisdom is the best thing, for the sage is the greatest among the great' (*Shāh-nāmah*, tr. Mohl, Paris, 1876–78, vi. 425), and the Pahlavi *Pandnāmak-ī Vajōrg-Mitrō* (ed. and tr. Peshotan Behramji Sanjana [under the title *Ganjesháyagán*], Bombay, 1885, p. 11) makes the same sage say: 'Education makes man noble, . . . education is a corrector of man'; while the 9th cent. *Dīnkarṭ* (ed. and tr. Sanjana, Bombay, 1874 ff., p. 585) declares that 'men ought to raise themselves to illustrious positions by worldly knowledge and by education, (which enables them) to read and write.' So vital was this matter, especially as regards religion, that even an adult was advised by Buzurjmihr (*Pandnāmak*, p. 21) to spend a third of every day and night 'in getting religious training and in asking sensible questions of pious men,' the second third being devoted to agriculture, and the remainder to eating, sleeping, and recreation. The legal code of the Avesta, in like manner, enjoins that the 'holy word' (*māθra spenta*) be pronounced to those who come 'seeking (religious) instruction' (*xratu-činah* [*Vend.* iv. 44]), and it is especially mentioned as a desirable characteristic of children that they be 'of good understanding' (*hvīra* [*Yasna*, lxii. 5; *Yašt*, xiii. 134]).

Thus far there is the unity of all generalities; but, when we turn to the data concerning the actual training of children, much confusion confronts us. The reason doubtless is that, just as in modern times, education was not absolutely uniform; and, in addition, the passages on which we must rely are largely concerned (especially in the classical authors) with the early training of royal children; while some accounts, notably those of Xenophon's *Cyropædia*, are not free from the suspicion of exaggeration in the interests of political romance.

The *Vendīdād* states (xv. 45) that the care (*θrāθra*) of the child should last seven years. Until the age of four (Bahrām Gūr, *Shāh-nāmah*, v. 400), five (Herod. i. 136), or seven (Valer. Max. ii. 6), the infant passed his time in the women's apartments, and his first training was received from women and eunuchs (Plato, *Legg.* 695 A; cf. the pseudo-Platonic *Alcibiades Primus*, 121 D). From five until seven the child should be under its father's tuition (*Shāyast lā-Shāyast*, v. 1 [West, *SBE* v. 290]), although, as in the case of Bahrām Gūr, who was sent to Arabia in infancy (*Shāh-nāmah, loc. cit.*), this rule was not always observed. Real instruction began about the age of seven (Bahrām Gūr), or even as early as five (Herod. i. 136; Strabo, p. 733), and lasted until the age of twelve (Bahrām Gūr, who, however, seems to have been exceptionally brilliant), fifteen (Artaxshīr Pāpakān, the founder of the Sasanian empire [*Kārnāmak-ī Artaxshīr-ī Pāpakān*, ed. and tr. Darab Peshotan Sanjana, Bombay, 1896, p. 5]), sixteen or seventeen (Xenophon, *Cyropæd.* I. ii. 8), twenty (Herod. i. 136), or even twenty-four (Strabo, p. 733); but all essential instruction should be given by parents to their children by the age of fifteen (*Pandnāmak*, p. 25). It was a man's duty to instruct his child, for thus it might rise to some superior station in life (*Dīnk.* ed. Sanjana, p. 263); and he should teach not only his child, but his wife, his countrymen, and himself

1 As regards Turkey, cf. M. Hartmann, *Unpolitische Briefe aus der Türkei*, Leipzig, 1910, p. 127 ff.

2 *Rev. du monde musulman*, xiii. [1911] 1–29. The courses given in Cairo University by native and European scholars (Guidi, Littmann, Nallino, etc.) in Arabic have now been published.

3 *Ib.* xiii. 570–573; as to the objects of the university, cf. *ib.* xiv. [1911] 100 ff.

4 P. Arminjon, *L'Enseignement, la doctrine, et la vie dans les universités musulmanes d'Égypte*, Paris, 1907.

5 As, *e.g.*, in Bukhāra; cf. *Rev. du monde musulman*, xiv. [1911] 143.

6 The official organ of this establishment is *Al-madrasa*, edited by 'Abdalrazzāq al-Niṭāsī; it contains reports of the courses in the various subjects taught in the Institution.

(this probably refers especially, as Sanjana remarks, to religious rather than secular knowledge; see *Āndarj-ī Āṭūrpāṭ*, ed. and tr. Peshotan Behramji Sanjana, Bombay, 1885, p. 2); while it is enjoined upon him: 'If you have a son, send him to school from his early years, for education is the light-giving eye of man' (*ib.* p. 5). The *Pandnāmak* (p. 25) adds a further inducement for a parent to teach his child to practise virtue and to shun vice: 'Those parents that give a certain amount of education of this kind to their children obtain their recompense from whatever good deeds their children do; but those that do not give it draw upon their own heads whatever iniquities their children, devoid of the strength it affords, commit.' It is also especially recommended to marry one's daughter 'to an intelligent and learned man; for her union with such a person is like the seed sown in a fertile soil and producing grain of a superior quality (*Āndarj*, p. 7).

In its original extent the Avesta contained accounts of the subjects and methods of education, but these records have now vanished, and the sole information regarding them is contained in the *Dīnkarṭ* (VIII. xxii. 2; xxxvii. 4 [tr. West, *SBE* xxxvii. 77, 114]).

The former of these *Dīnkarṭ* passages—on the second section of the *Ganabā-sar-nijaṭ Nask*—contained information 'about arrival at the period for the teaching of children by a guardian or father, and the mode of his teaching; . . . the sin due to not teaching a child who is to be taught, and whatever is on the same subject.' The other passage—on one of the concluding sections of the *Hūspāram Nask*—touches on matters pertaining to 'the association of priestly instructor and pupil, and their meritoriousness together; the fame of the priestly instructor for priestly instruction, and that of the disciple for every kind of learning derived from the priestly instructor, and every kind that the priestly instructor imparts to the pupil; and the happy effects of the priestly instructor, of every kind, in similar matters.'

According to a famous passage of Herodotus (i. 136; cf. Strabo, p. 733), Persian boys were taught 'three things only—to ride, to shoot, and to speak the truth'; and it is clear from Strabo's account that their training was physical rather than mental. The Iranian sources imply (as was doubtless the case) that intellectual instruction was carried to a far higher degree. Thus Artaxshīr Pāpakān 'became so proficient in literary knowledge, riding, and other arts, that he was renowned throughout Pārs' (*Kārnāmak*, p. 5); and for Bahrām Gūr were chosen three teachers: one for the prince's instruction in letters; the second to teach him falconry, battledore, archery, swordsmanship, vaulting, and 'to hold his head high among the brave'; and the third to acquaint him with all royal and administrative duties (*Shāh-nāmah*, v. 401 f.). Some idea of the mental attainments which the *beau ideal* of a Persian prince was supposed to possess may be gleaned from the examination of Hōrmazd, on the completion of his education, by Buzurjmihr (*ib.* vi. 425–430).

Strabo states (*loc. cit.*) that the Persian boys were trained in companies of fifty each; and Xenophon (*Cyropæd.* I. ii. 2 ff.) ascribes to the Persians an elaborate system of education, which however, is probably far from being historic.

According to him, the Persians were the only nation who taught their future citizens from the very first to abstain from evil and to do good. They had a 'free market,' from which all trading was excluded as causing a confusion inimical to good training; and of its four parts one was occupied by children, and another by youths. Both classes were divided into twelve parts, aged men directing the children, and men of mature years the youths. The children studied justice as the Greek schoolboys studied their letters, and the most of their time was passed in holding mock courts. Besides this, the children learned self-control (σωφροσύνη), and to all this training they were subject until the age of sixteen or seventeen, when they were graduated into the number of the youths, their duties now being of a more practical nature, such as mounting guard, hunting, warlike exercises, and tests of endurance, this period of their lives lasting twenty-five years. The whole account seems to be a thinly-veiled picture of what Xenophon would gladly have seen carried into actual effect in Greece.

Persian children of noble and princely families were often educated at court (Xenoph. *Anab.* I. ix. 3, *Cyropæd.* VIII. vi. 10), although it was by no means unusual for high-born children to be sent for their training to other families of rank, as was the case with Zames (Jām), the second son of Qubād (Procopius, *de Bell. Pers.* i. 23), and with Bahrām Gūr, the latter being educated in Arabia (*Shāh-nāmah*, v. 400). Tutors for the latter prince were sought from all civilized countries, including Greece, India, China, and Arabia, the choice being finally awarded to two sages from the country last-named (*ib.* p. 398 f.). Besides this, we are told by Clemens Alex. (*Pæd.* i. 7) that the Persians had 'royal pedagogues' (βασίλειοι παιδαγωγοί), who, four in number, were chosen from all the Persians by the king and placed in charge of the instruction of his children. The pseudo-Platonic *Alcibiades Primus* (*loc. cit.*) adds that these men were appointed when the princes had reached the age of fourteen, and details their duties as follows:

The first, who was 'the most wise,' taught the 'magic' (μαγεία) of Zoroaster, 'which is the service of the gods,' and royal duties; the second, who was 'the most just,' taught the child to practise truthfulness throughout life; the third, who was 'the most prudent,' taught control of all passions and contempt of bodily pleasure; and the fourth, who was 'the most manly,' taught the prince to be fearless and brave (cf. the three teachers of Bahrām Gūr, though their branches of instruction, as noted above, were quite different from those detailed in the Greek source).

Of the personal relations between teacher and pupil there is little record in the extant Iranian texts, although, from the respectful and affectionate attitude maintained towards the instructor in the *Shāh-nāmah*, it is to be inferred that the feeling between the two was one of tenderness and devotion. It has already been observed that a section of the lost Avesta *Hūspāram Nask* devoted attention to 'the association of priestly instructor and pupil, and their meritoriousness together' (*Dīnk.* VIII. xxxvii. 4); and the Avesta, as now preserved, itself has a significant indication of the closeness of this relation (*Yašt*, x. 116 f.):

'Twentyfold is Miθra [here the godling of alliance and fidelity] between two friends from the same district; thirtyfold between two from the same community; fortyfold between two from the same house; fiftyfold between two from the same room; sixtyfold between two from the same priestly gild; *seventyfold between priestly pupil and priestly teacher* (*aēθrya aēθra-paiti*); eightyfold between son-in-law and father-in-law; ninetyfold between two brothers; hundredfold between parents and child; thousandfold between two countries; ten thousandfold is Miθra to him who is of the Māzdayasnian religion.'

LITERATURE.—Brisson, *de Regio Persarum Principatu*, ed. Lederlein, Strassburg, 1710, pp. 165 ff., 429 ff., 510; Rapp, in *ZDMG* xx. (1866) 103–107; Modi, *Education among the Ancient Irānians*, Bombay, 1905: Karaka, *Hist. of the Parsis*, London, 1884, vol. i. ch. vi.; Jackson, *Persia Past and Present*, New York, 1906, pp. 379 f., 427.

LOUIS H. GRAY.

EDUCATION (Roman).—The history of Roman education is that of an evolution from a simple to a complex and comparatively encyclopædic kind of instruction; from what we should call 'primary' education through a stage when 'secondary' education was gradually combined with higher learning of a 'University' stamp; from the ancient discipline of the home to an Imperial system of officials appointed under the cognizance of the Emperor; from an unpaid instruction by parent or slave to an organization where, at least in the higher grades, large salaries were paid; and from a narrowly Roman training to a cosmopolitan culture. To illustrate the development in biological terms, there was an original Roman strain, there was subsequent crossing with Greek influences, accompanied by vigorous adaptation to environment, and followed gradually by a fixing of the type, which became more and more effete. So practical a people as that of Rome was certain to have its own way of fitting each new generation for the struggle and duties of life, and the equipment which was sufficient for the burgher of a city-State needed wide expansion before it could suit the citizen or civil servant of a world-Empire. The altering aims and methods of Roman education are easily discernible in a chronological survey of the subject, which may be conveniently examined in three stages:

(1) Earlier period—Republican times, to the age of the Punic Wars, *c.* 240 B.C.
(2) Middle period—*c.* 240 B.C. to the reign of Hadrian, A.D. 120.
(3) Final period—from A.D. 120 to the end of the Empire.

One may at once point out that, amidst the ferment of the fresh ideas of Hellenic culture, Roman education was most progressive in the middle period, while in the later period the rhetorical training, on the contrary, became stereotyped; that is to say, education in the end ceased to secure so well the practical aims which it previously had in view, and the acceptance of traditional culture and methods as absolute rendered the system impervious to health-giving conceptions of change and advance.

1. Earlier period—to the Punic Wars.—For the earlier centuries of the city, evidence regarding education is scanty and untrustworthy.

Not much value can be attached to statements of a later age about the school attendance of Romulus and Remus at Gabii (Plut. *Romul.* vi.), about Numa's Sabine training, or about the education, partly in Greek, given to Servius Tullius (Cic. *de Rep.* II. xxi.). The advanced culture of Etruria, we know, influenced Roman religion and customs; but the probability of its having influenced Roman education (Cic. *de Div.* I. xli. 92; Jullien, *Les Professeurs de litt.* etc., pp. 29–33), and, in fact, the state of general education in regal times, are matters beyond our ken. It is true that Mommsen considers reading and writing to have been widely spread in Rome at an early period (*Röm. Gesch.* i. 211 f. [Eng. tr., 1875, i. 224]); but even so one cannot positively assert the existence in the 5th cent. B.C. of schools at Rome regularly attended by girls of mature years, although that would be the literal inference from Livy's account of Virginia going to school among the shops of the forum (Liv. III. xliv.; Dion. Hal. *Ant. Rom.* XI. xxviii.); nor can one on similar evidence positively assert the existence of schools at Falerii and Tusculum in the times of Camillus (Liv. V. xxvii., VI. xxv.).

The character of education, however, during many generations of the older Republic can be readily grasped. The clearest conception of it is to be obtained from what Plutarch tells us (*Cat. Maj.* xx.) of the way in which Cato brought up his son. Although this applies to the period of the Punic Wars, yet Cato's rigid attachment to traditional usage impels one to take it as representative of the education after the ancestral fashion which preceded the Punic Wars. Cato kept a slave to teach the elements to the young people in his establishment; but he disliked the notion of having his own son scolded or reprimanded by an inferior; so he himself undertook the training of his boy in literature, law, and gymnastics (αὐτὸς μὲν ἦν γραμματιστής, αὐτὸς δὲ νομοδιδάκτης, αὐτὸς δὲ γυμναστής). The physical education was in riding and the use of weapons, boxing, and exercises likely to test endurance. With his own hand and in large letters he wrote out historical narratives for the boy's use, and showed such scrupulous regard for decency of behaviour and language in the interests of the youth's moral welfare that Plutarch expressly alludes to the noble work of moulding a young life to virtue.

This practical, physical, and moral training was long in vogue. The younger Pliny regretfully recalls those happy ages when instruction was more a matter of the eye than of the ear, and his concise formula expresses a central feature of the primitive training—'suus cuique parens pro magistro' (*Ep.* VIII. xiv. 6), as does Seneca's allusion to the 'domestic magistrates' (*de Ben.* iii. 11) as agents of education. Close companionship of parent and son characterized the manners of times which encouraged youths to listen to a father's discussion of legal questions raised by his *clientes* in the *atrium*, to take part in his religious observances as *camilli*, to attend him to the senate (as was the usage at one period), to hear momentous speeches delivered, and even to accompany seniors to dinner-parties, where they might sometimes chant the praises of bygone heroes (Cic. *Brut.* xix. 75, *Tusc. Disp.* IV. ii. 3; Val. Max. II. i. 10; Varro *ap.* Non. 77, *s.v.* 'Assa voce'), and where their very presence might prove a salutary check upon licence (Plut. *Q. Rom.* xxxiii.), on the principle worthily formulated by Juvenal—'maxima debetur puero reverentia' (xiv. 47).

In the Latin sense *educatio* was applied to the process of training a child how to live—how to confront the problems of material existence (Varr. *ap.* Non. 447, 33, *s.v.* 'Educere': 'educit obstetrix, educat nutrix, instituit paedagogus, docet magister'). In this sense, education began with the father's recognition of the newly-born infant's right to live, which was conceded if he formally raised it in his arms; and most of this early care for the young fell to the mother or to near kinswomen, or, in an increasing degree as society developed, to nurses. In the time of the Empire, Tacitus could still use the phrase 'in sinu matris educari'; and it should be remembered that a Roman matron was well equipped to impart sound physical, moral, and often intellectual training to sons and daughters. Her position was one of greater dignity than that of the Athenian wife, and some have ventured to think that 'the whole social fabric was moulded by the forceful character of house-mothers in the serene atmosphere of the home' (C. W. L. Launspach, *State and Family in Early Rome*, 1908, p. 199). This is but a modern version of that 'regiment of women' (γυναικοκρατία) which so alarmed Cato (Plut. *Cat. Maj.* viii.).

Although primitive usage preferred that mothers should suckle their own babes, there is good evidence for the early employment of both foster-mothers and dry nurses. At a later period the number of nurses employed can be gauged from the records of inscriptions (see 'Monumenta columbariorum,' in *CIL* vi. 4352, 4457, 6323, 6324, 8941–43; cf. occurrences of *nutrix* and similar words in Indexes of the *CIL* ix. and x., under 'Parentelae et necessitudines'). Their importance was not restricted to questions of the proper feeding of infants, although this was not overlooked by the Romans (Varro, *Cato* [for older readings *Catus* or *Capys*], *aut de liberis educandis*, cited Aul. Gell. IV. xix.; Nonius, 201, *s.v.* 'Cepe'). It was recognized that they had much power in shaping the character for better or worse, and in securing the avoidance of many bad habits, foolish beliefs, and objectionable pronunciations. This is the reason for the stress laid upon the choice of a nurse in Quintilian and in the *de Educatione Puerorum* ascribed to Plutarch.

About the age of seven a Roman boy in the earlier period came more definitely under his father's tuition, to be taught on the lines which we have seen were followed by the elder Cato—namely, the elements of reading, writing, and reckoning, and such bodily exercises as would best fit him for military service. Boys belonging to the simpler and more agricultural times of Rome also took part in farm-work and in the rural religious ceremonials; while girls learned, under their mother, spinning and other domestic accomplishments, except the menial tasks of corn-grinding and cookery. The two main careers were war and politics; and the object was to train a man of action, with no claims to rival the intellectual and æsthetic accomplishments of an Athenian, but well-developed in body, reverential towards the gods, mindful of ancestral custom (*mos maiorum*), regardful of the laws which he learned as a boy by rote from the Twelve Tables (Cic. *de Leg.* II. xxiii. 59), inclined, therefore, by the force of precept and example to follow virtues like obedience, temperance, bravery, and industry, which may always be inculcated independently of an organized system of education, if parents can be relied upon to perform their duty. There was nothing more distinctive of the native Roman education than its training of character, and the store set by morality —*e.g.* modesty (*τὰ δ' αἰσχρὰ τῶν ῥημάτων οὐχ ἧττον εὐλαβεῖσθαι τοῦ παιδὸς παρόντος ἢ τῶν ἱερῶν παρθένων ἃς Ἑστιάδας καλοῦσι* [Plut. *Cat. Maj.* xx.]; cf. Cicero's terms of praise 'adulescenti pudentissimo et in primis honesto' [*pro Cluent.* lx. 165]); or obedience (Dion. Hal. *Ant. Rom.* ii. 26). In fact, the outstanding qualities in a model young Roman may be taken, as summarized in Cicero's words, as 'self-control combined with dutiful affection to parents and kindliness towards kindred' ('modestia cum pietate in parentes, in suos beneuolentia' [*de Off.* II. xiii. 46]). Such were the moral results attained by an education entrusted without reserve to the *familia*, in consonance with a characteristically Roman regard for the *patria potestas*. By the time that a youth reached the age of 20, a training deemed adequate for all likely calls upon him had been given through the home, through exercise, through the companionship and experience of seniors, and through observation of the ways of men in the forum. The formal training of the mind, at first often undertaken by a father himself, tended, as claims on time became more insistent, to be delegated to a cultured slave, acting under the parental supervision.

While robust frames, disciplined minds, stolid gravity, and unyielding courage bore testimony to the strength of the ancient upbringing, it had its defects. It provided little to induce refinement, artistic tastes, or kindlier emotions. It produced a Cato, ready to recommend the prompt sale of a slave worn out by faithful service, or a Mummius, who sacked Corinth without compunction, and saw nothing extraordinary in laying down a stringent condition that his contractors for transporting unrivalled masterpieces of Greek art to Rome should replace any lost or damaged *en route*! Yet, despite limitations, it was an admirable method of training patriotic warriors; and it yielded the constancy and energy requisite for the victors in the Punic Wars. Leaving such liberty to the family, and eschewing State infringement upon private instruction, the older Rome succeeded in drawing the bonds of citizenship closer than Greece had done through theories of systematized education.

2. Middle period—240 B.C.-A.D. 120.—The most momentous alien factor in the development of Roman education was the influence of Greece. The whole action of Hellenic culture upon Rome was of high significance; but its details cannot be considered here (see 'The Invasion of Hellenism,' in J. W. Duff's *Lit. Hist. of Rome*², pp. 92-117). Some salient facts, however, must be given. Relations between Rome and Magna Graecia led to contact with Greek civilization at an early but not exactly determinable date. The borrowing of the alphabet is a well-known instance; and commerce and diplomacy obviously ensured acquaintance with Greek, at any rate in its spoken form. Thus Postumius in 282 B.C., as Roman envoy at Tarentum, could make a speech in the language, even if it was a ludicrously bad one; and Cineas, the representative of Pyrrhus, seems to have addressed the Roman Senate in Greek without an interpreter. But this does not necessarily imply acquaintance with Greek literature, or presuppose a highly developed literary education; and it is fully a century later when we find the father of the Gracchi (consul in 177 and 163 B.C.) addressing the Rhodians in good Greek. Certainly, the literary education had long been in operation before the days of Licinius Crassus, who, as proconsul of Asia in 131, proved his command of no fewer than five Greek dialects. A date of lasting import for education, as it was for literature, was the year 240 B.C., when Livius Andronicus realized and supplied the need of a literary text for Roman schools by translating the *Odyssey* into Latin saturnians. It remained in use till the days of Horace. The period of Livius was evidently one of educational activity; for he and Ennius, Suetonius says, were poets and 'half-Greeks,' but at the same time teachers who gave instruction in both languages (*de Gram.* i.). Another sign of the times was the opening, about 231 B.C., by Sp. Carvilius, of the first school where regular fees were charged. Apparently as early as 173 B.C. the teaching of Epicurean philosophy had excited so much attention that the Government, alarmed at its seductive plausibility, banished two of its professors. Soon after, Aemilius Paulus brought the royal library from Macedon to Rome (Plut. *Aem. Paul.* xxviii.; Isid. *Orig.* VI. v. 1), and the access of the 'Scipionic Circle' to its volumes must have influenced education, as it did literature. The residence of the thousand Achæan hostages in Italy for sixteen years after 167 B.C. is memorable, not only for the intellectual stimulus so given, but also for the recorded advice tendered by the most famous of the hostages, Polybius, to the younger Scipio—that he should take advantage of the educational facilities obtainable owing to the number of Greek teachers in Rome (Polyb. XXXII. x.). Nearly at the same date Crates, the renowned librarian of Pergamum, came on an errand of state from King Attalus, and, being detained in Rome owing to a broken leg, spent some time in lecturing. A man of broad scholarship, he so improved the method of teaching by his lectures on Greek literature that Suetonius declares him to have been the introducer of 'grammar' (*de Gram.* ii.). Meanwhile Greek philosophy and rhetoric were making great headway — too much headway in the eyes of many patriotic Romans; for in 161 the *philosophi* and *rhetores* were banished, probably for reasons similar to those which in 92 B.C. prompted the censors Ahenobarbus and Crassus to interdict the *rhetores Latini*, namely that, in handling rhetoric, they did not lecture in Greek and according to genuine Greek methods, but transferred their attention to Latin, and reared students in a cheap 'school of impudence.' A similar distrust animated Cato's hostility to letting the dangerously brilliant philosopher Carneades prolong his diplomatic visit and continue his discourses in 155 B.C. In fine, what we discover before the middle of the 2nd cent. B.C. at Rome is an acquaintance with the principles of Greek rhetoric on the part of the upper classes, and the emergence of three grades of education—in the hands of the *litterator*, the *grammaticus*, and the *rhetor* respectively. Roughly, they correspond to our elementary, secondary, and University standards (Apul. *Flor.* xx. 'prima craterra litteratoris ruditatem eximit, secunda grammatici doctrina instruit, tertia rhetoris eloquentia armat'). The consideration of these must now occupy us.

(1) *Elementary education.*—The ***litterator*** was in charge of the education in reading, writing, and ciphering. He was the teacher of the rudiments (*γραμματιστής*), and must not be confused with the more advanced *grammaticus*, who was sometimes, in virtue of his fuller learning, called *litteratus* (Orbilius, quoted by Suet. *de Gram.* iv.). St. Augustine draws a clear distinction between these elementary 'letters' and the *belles lettres* which once attracted him so powerfully—'adamaueram latinas (litteras), non quas primi magistri, sed quas docent qui grammatici uocantur' (*Conf.* I. xiii. 1). In private houses, failing the parent, a trained slave, or in some cases the child's own attendant (*paedagogus*), taught the rudiments; but elementary schools kept by a *ludi magister* (who was usually

a freedman) were, despite the unconcern of the Government, on the increase. The percentage of illiteracy was less than might be supposed; for primary education must have been pretty widely diffused, to admit of the circulation of military orders in writing by the time of Polybius. The scribblings on the walls of Pompeii, too, argue a wide-spread faculty of reading and writing in the 1st cent. A.D. The methods of elementary teaching are discussed in Quintilian's work, the fullest educational treatise which has come down from antiquity. The lack of literary texts had vanished long before his day, and he counsels early lessons on good authors (he prefers Greek [I. i. 12]), even before pupils can grasp the entire meaning. Simple fables and extracts from authors made convenient reading-books. The initial recognition of the shapes of letters can be, he points out, aided by ivory models given to children to play with (I. i. 26; for instruction in reading, see Grasberger, *Erziehung*, etc., ii. 256–300). Writing was started by guiding the pupil's hand, as he followed with the *stilus* characters traced on wax-covered tablets, or by a sort of stencil process in which the letters were cut on wood (Quint. I. i. 27; Vopisc. *Tac.* vi.). Later came the copying of specimen letters, and more advanced pupils would use a *calamus* with *atramentum* to write upon vellum from Pergamum, or *charta* manufactured from the papyrus plant of the Nile (for instruction in writing, see Grasberger, *op. cit.* ii. 300 ff.). The *dictata magistri*, selections for dictation, gave practice in writing, and could be used afterwards to train the memory. In arithmetic many references show that the fingers were freely used for calculations. As at all times, tables had to be got up by rote, and St. Augustine recalls with an evident shudder of dislike the refrain of 'one and one make two,' etc. (*Conf.* I. xiii. 'unum et unum duo, duo et duo quatuor, odiosa cantio mihi erat'). Harder sums were done with the help of the *abacus* and its *calculi*, the board being marked out into columns for units, fives, tens, fifties, hundreds, etc. The difficulties due to the awkwardness of the Roman figures were considerable (Marquardt, *Das Privatleben der Römer*², 97–104, or Fr. tr. *La Vie privée des Romains*, 1892, i. 115–123); but this fact did not prevent the attainment of high arithmetical skill by the capitalists, tax-farmers, money-lenders, and traders of a shrewd, hardheaded, and frequently covetous race, which had largely diverted its attention from farming to money-getting.

(2) '*Grammar School' education.*—Training under the *grammaticus* succeeded to elementary instruction commonly when the pupil was 12 or 13; and lasted until he passed at about 16 into the hands of the *rhetor*. It should be noted that age-limits for the different grades of study cannot be regarded as constant; for undoubtedly there was overlapping between the grades; then, as now, pupils of the same age exhibited marked disparity in mental capacity; and the abandonment of the *bulla* of boyhood and the assumption of the *toga uirilis* varied, with individuals and at different times, from 14 to 17, when military service usually began. At the 'Grammar School' the aim was to teach intelligent and effective reading of standard authors in both Latin and Greek. Of the series of *grammatici* mentioned by Suetonius, most were of Hellenic origin, and many were freedmen (*de Gram.* xv., xvi., xix., xx.); but there were Romans who applied the methods of Crates' lectures on Greek literature to their own poets, so that Naevius, Ennius, and Lucilius soon became school authors (*op. cit.* ii.). On the whole, the profession received scant honour and scant pay. The magistrates' officer (as in the case of Horace's master Orbilius), the pantomime actor, and the boxer might all turn teacher (Suet. *op. cit.* ix., xviii., xxii.); and yet there were instances of Roman knights taking up the work; and the educational demands must have been considerable when the city had over twenty flourishing Grammar Schools (*op. cit.* iii.). Under the Empire, good schools had a *grammaticus Latinus* and a *grammaticus Graecus*—a special teacher for each language, one lecturing in *toga*, the other in *pallium*. Though their subject-matter was different, the method was the same for both (Quint. I. iv. 1).

This specialization and style of description are abundantly clear from inscriptions found in Italy and the provinces (*e.g.* the *Graecus* in *CIL* ii. 2236 [Corduba], vi. 9453, 9454, x. 3961 [Capua]; the *Latinus*, ii. 2892 [Tricio in Spain], iii. 406 [Thyatira in Asia Minor, ΡΩΜΑΙΚΩ], 3433 [Verona], 5278 [Como], vi. 9455 [Rome], ix. 5545).

Greek *grammatici*, who taught in Rome towards the end of the Republic, understood and wrote Latin also. The freedman Ateius Philologus, a native of Athens, was described by Asinius Pollio as 'nobilis grammaticus Latinus' (Suet. *de Gram.* x.), and Gnipho, Cicero's teacher, was 'non minus Graece quam Latine doctus' (*op. cit.* vii.). Professors who took the simple title of *grammatici* were usually *grammatici Latini* (*e.g. CIL* ii. 5079 [cf. 3872, 'magistro artis grammaticae'], vi. 9444–9452, ix. 1654).

'Grammar' (*grammatica*) covered a wider field than in our acceptation. Its two functions were 'recti loquendi scientia' and 'poetarum enarratio,' in other words, the knowledge of the correct employment of language and the appreciation of literature (Quint. I. iv.–ix.). The first division involved study of the parts of speech, accidence, metric, and discussed faults in use of words, in idiom, pronunciation, spelling. The second division, which aimed at elucidation of the poets, involved far more than literary study. Besides the geographical, historical, or mythological implications of the matter, subsidiary subjects, like music, geometry with astronomy, and philosophy, were necessary for successful teaching or study (Quint. I. iv. 4, I. x.). Prose was much less lectured upon than verse; so that Cicero with reason complains of the comparative neglect of history (*de Leg.* I. ii.). For linguistic study, pupils used the Latin grammar of Remmius Palaemon, or the Greek handbook by Dionysius of Thrace, a work which held its ground at Constantinople till the 13th cent. A.D. Inquiry into the phenomena of language appealed to generations of eminent Romans, to *savants* like Varro, to statesmen like Cæsar, and to some of the Emperors; while the *Corpus* of the grammarians (ed. Keil), taken along with such representative commentators upon Virgil as Macrobius and Servius, will suffice to indicate the range and methods of Roman grammar.

The tasks set included the re-telling of Æsop's fables as an oral and a written exercise, paraphrasing, training in *sententiae* (moral maxims), *chriae* (anecdotes with moral bearing), *ethologiae* (personal character-descriptions), *narratiunculae* (short stories on poetic themes, to teach matter rather than style [Quint. I. ix. 6]). The study of literature—the coping-stone of ancient grammar—involved *lectio* (expressive reading without sing-song or provincial accent [Quint. I. viii. 2, VIII. i. 3, XI. iii. 30]); *enarratio* (erudite explanation of the subject-matter); *emendatio* (textual criticism); *iudicium* (literary criticism).

The authors prescribed by the *grammaticus* were largely identical with those prescribed by the *rhetor* at a later stage, as handled by Quintilian in his tenth book; only, the standpoint of study ultimately altered to oratorical effectiveness. In Greek the rule was to begin with Homer, as in Latin with Virgil. Homer was approved as an indispensable text for the study of language, history, myth, religion, manners, geography; and wide knowledge—with sometimes the most meticulous recollection of details—was demanded from a lecturer. Other Greek authors popular in schools were Hesiod, for his practical maxims; the lyric poets in selections, excluding or minimizing the erotic; the great tragedians; and the comic poets, especially Menander. Among Latin texts which had a prolonged vogue were Andronicus' verse translation of the *Odyssey*, the older epic poets Naevius and Ennius, and the dramatists Plautus, Caecilius, Terence, Pacuvius, Accius, Afranius. Virgil was introduced into the school course by Caecilius Epirota, a freedman of Atticus, not long after the poet's death, and took among Roman authors a place parallel with Homer's among the Greeks. Horace, too, was soon found in the schools; and a desire to escape from archaic models accounts for the lectures which were given on the poems of Lucan, Statius, and Nero himself, during the lifetime of the authors. The literary reaction of the 2nd cent. A.D. led to a revival of interest in ante-Augustan poets. This predominance of poetic study, which is so marked a feature of the course in grammar, had great effects upon Latin style. But prose authors received more attention from the *rhetor*. Cicero became a model in his own day, and Quintilian holds him up as 'iucundus incipientibus quoque et apertus.' Among historians he recommends Livy in preference to Sallust, who, he maintains, needs a more advanced intelligence; but here Quintilian is thinking more especially of the training for declamation.

(3) *The highest education.*—In the final stage of formal education, namely, under the *rhetor*, the training was designed to fit directly for the duties of public life—for deliberative and forensic oratory; and, its faults notwithstanding, rhetoric turned out, in the time of the Empire, men of affairs, magistrates, civil servants, and advocates, equipped with an admirable power of effective speech. The Roman turn for oratory ensured an early and favourable attention to the practice and theory of Greek rhetoric, which inherited old traditions from Sicily, Athens, and Asia Minor. The Greek rhetor was, therefore, heard gladly, and his lessons were acceptable to an extent not always conceded to *rhetores Latini*, who had been viewed with suspicion by the authorities in 92 B.C., and who did not in Quintilian's time do their work so well as their Greek colleagues (I. ix. 6). Referring to the relation between grammar and rhetoric, Quintilian touches on the constantly recurrent phenomenon of overlapping in education (II. i.). In this case it was nothing new, for Suetonius tells us that in ancient times the same teacher often taught both departments (*de Gram.* iv. 'ueteres grammatici et rhetoricam docebant'); and Quintilian says that boys were often kept too long by the grammarian before being sent on to the rhetorician. With his usual good sense he recognizes that the time for passing into the rhetor's hands should depend on capacity rather than on years (II. i. 7). The secondary teachers, however, were tempted to trench on the superior province, and to give boys practice in what were really rhetorical exercises, so that pupils might go on to the professor of rhetoric creditably equipped (Suet. *de Gram.* iv. 'ne scilicet sicci omnino atque aridi pueri rhetoribus traderentur').

By the middle of the 2nd cent. B.C., as has been seen, the principles of Greek rhetoric were familiar to the upper classes at Rome; but a new departure was the introduction of 'declamations' on imaginary themes—perhaps by Molon of Rhodes about 84 B.C., as Bornecque thinks (*Les Déclamations et les déclamateurs*, p. 42). This hypothesis is not at variance with the probable date of the earliest systematic treatise in Latin upon rhetoric, *ad Herennium* (86 to 82 B.C.), or with the fact that it touched on declamation, and furnished subjects for debate of the *suasoria* type. It was only, however, towards the end of Cicero's life that *declamatio* came to be transferred from its old sense of vehement delivery of a speech to the sense of an oratorical exercise upon an invented subject. Declamation subsequently became the crowning exercise in rhetoric, and spread from Rome through Italy to the schools of Gaul and Spain.

To lead up to declamation the rhetorician prescribed a definite series of preliminary exercises, and for effective educational results Quintilian insists that the professor must be of excellent character, as well as of the highest possible intellectual ability, and tact in dealing with a class (II. ii.–iii.). The preliminary exercises (II. iv.) include composing narratives of a less poetic stamp than in the 'Grammar School,' discussion of matters of historic doubt, panegyric and invective, comparison of characters, *communes loci* (traits of character useful for attacking vices), *theses* (questions of a general type for deliberation, *e.g.* 'Is town or country life preferable?' 'Is the glory of law or of warfare the greater?'), *coniecturales causae*, which Quintilian remembered as a pleasant exercise of his own student days (*e.g.* 'Why is Cupid winged and armed with arrows and torch?'), and criticism of laws. Prose models in oratory and history are to be lectured on, and here Cicero and Livy can be used with most profit. For repetition, select passages from great authors should be got up by heart, rather than the student's own show-pieces, which the proud parent, to the detriment of true oratory, was only too anxious to have declaimed over and over again (Quint. II. vii. 1).

The two culminating exercises were the *suasoria* and the still more difficult *controuersia*, the former deliberative, the latter forensic in its bearing.

Their character is best illustrated by the seven *suasoriae* and five complete books of *controuersiae* which survive from the collection of Seneca the elder; there exist also excerpts from these five and from the five lost books, along with the declamations of the pseudo-Quintilian and excerpts from Calpurnius Flaccus. The *suasoria* was a fictitious soliloquy by some historic personage at a crisis in his life—'Alexander debates whether he should cross the Ocean,' 'The three hundred at Thermopylæ consider whether they should retreat,' 'Cicero deliberates whether he should beg his life from Antony.' The most familiar instance of all is Juvenal's recollection of the cane in the rhetorical academy where he declaimed his exercise purporting to advise the dictator Sulla to abdicate (*Sat.* i. 16–17).

For complete success such exercises demanded historical knowledge of circumstances and character, with considerable gifts of imagination and style. An interesting fact is recorded about Ovid, that as a student he enjoyed the *suasoria* but disliked the *controuersia*. The latter was an exercise in arguing for or against—sometimes, to attain versatility, for and then against—the claims put forward in an invented case. The cases, the laws, and the types of person introduced came very often from a sphere of imagination which certainly provoked ingenuity in treatment, but called forth the strictures of Quintilian for their remoteness from practical life.

Suetonius (*de Rhet.* i.) quotes two examples of the less extravagant *controuersiae*—the one concerning the disputed ownership of gold found in a fishing-net after the particular cast which certain youths have purchased from the fishermen in advance; the other concerning the disputed freedom of a valuable slave who had been disguised and declared as a free man by his importers to cheat the Customs officers at Brindisi (similar to cccxl. in the Quintilianean *Declamationes*, ed. Ritter, 1884). But many were much more unreal, and involved incredible situations in which a great part was played by tyrants, pirates, unnatural fathers, and so on. Take a case—'A kidnapped youth writes asking his father to ransom him; when the father declines, the daughter of the pirate-chief offers to free the prisoner, if he will swear to marry her. He consents, is set free, goes back to his father, and marries the girl. The father afterwards sees an heiress who would make a desirable match for his son, and orders him to divorce the pirate-chief's daughter. The son refuses, and is disinherited' (Sen. *Contr.* I. vi.).

This kind of exercise sharpened the wits by a sort of mental gymnastic; it produced marvellous subtlety of argument, and great readiness and finish of speech. But it had serious drawbacks. Its range was narrow and artificial; its subjects were hackneyed—so that the dreary round of declamation on the same subject by youth after youth rising in turn from the bench was, as Juvenal remarks, enough to kill teachers with boredom ('Occidit miseros crambe repetita magistros' [vii. 154]). Old material had to be dressed in apparently fresh form; and this caused an excessive concentration upon style and expression, to the inevitable detriment of subject-matter and sound sense. The system was calculated to produce an indifference to truth, to the rights or wrongs of a case, and so was morally deleterious; it fostered, too, that glibness of speech which seemed so detestable to the sensible author of the *de Educatione Puerorum*; and—most notorious and most wide-reaching of all in effect—it accounted for a large amount of the tinsel, staginess, and artificiality of the Roman literature of the Silver Age.

It was a complaint with good judges, like Quintilian and Tacitus, that the licence and ignorance of declaimers had corrupted true eloquence. Like Cicero before him, Quintilian contemplated an ideal oratory on a basis morally and intellectually sound (Quint. XII. i. 1), and he cites Cicero's requirement of wide knowledge as an indispensable equipment ('omnium rerum magnarum atque artium scientiam' [II. xxi. 14]). Quintilian's requirements are stated more modestly when he says that the orator must at least study the subject on which he is to speak 'sed mihi satis est eius esse oratorem rei de qua dicet non inscium.' But he does desiderate acquaintance with many subjects outside the professional training—*e.g.* ethics, physics, and dialectic (I. *prooem.* 16; XII. ii. 10), law (XII. iii.), and history (XII. iv.). It was, indeed, largely in philosophy that Roman students of ability followed their 'post-graduate' course, either in the capital itself, where Epicurean, Academic, and Stoic thought had long been represented, or in Athens as the traditional headquarters of the schools. The education of great authors must not be taken as absolutely typical; yet it proves the educational facilities available for leisured people of some means. Thus Virgil added to literature the study of philosophy, rhetoric, medicine, mathematics, and law. Cicero had able Epicurean and Academic teaching in Rome; but at the age of 27, partly for health, partly for culture, he went abroad and studied under eminent Greeks in Athens, Asia Minor, and Rhodes. Cæsar was 25 when he visited Rhodes, mainly for advanced rhetoric. The age for study at a foreign 'University,' however, was usually earlier. The younger Cicero and Ovid were 20 when they went to Athens; Horace was studying philosophy there at 18.

Encyclopædic learning became obviously less attainable as knowledge advanced, and distinct progress in education between the 2nd cent. B.C. and the close of the Republic is evident on a comparison of Cato's list of subjects of general culture and Varro's list in his *Disciplinarum libri ix.* In the Roman gentleman's education, Cato included oratory, agriculture, law, war, and medicine; while Varro's nine were grammar, dialectic, rhetoric, geometry, arithmetic, astronomy, music, medicine, and architecture. The significant point is that war, law, and agriculture had become professional studies. It will be observed that the first three in Varro's list correspond with the *trivium*, or elementary course of the Middle Ages, and the four succeeding subjects with the *quadrivium*, or advanced course pursued from the time of Martianus Capella.

The practical outlook of the Roman developed an education different in conception from that harmonious training of the faculties of mind and body contemplated by the Greek μουσική and γυμναστική. Literature came slowly to the Roman, and, even when it had entered the schools, it was subservient to rhetoric, which, in turn, was taught at first as an instrument of success in life. Cicero makes a suggestive remark, in noting certain contrasts between Greek and Roman education, when he adds that the Greeks held geometry in the highest honour, while his own countrymen studied it only as far as it was useful (*Tusc. Disp.* I. ii. 4). The gymnastics, music, and dancing of the Greeks became known to Rome only in their decadence, and so missed their chance of full influence. Physical exercise the Romans preferred to limit by practical aims; to them the idleness of the *palaestra* was a thing suspect, and nudity immodest. As for music and dancing, they remained, to the mass of the Romans, accomplishments which clever performers might be paid to learn, but which formed no essential part of a free man's education. A count against a Catilinarian lady-conspirator was that she danced too well for a woman of good reputation (Sall. *Cat.* xxv.); and the associations of the term *saltator* are plain in the light of Cicero's declaration: 'nemo fere saltat sobrius nisi forte insanit' (*pro Mur.* vi. 13; cf. Hor. *Od.* III. vi. 21).

(4) *Education of women.*—Women of good family were often highly educated. The mother of the Gracchi was well able to superintend her boys' education (Cic. *Brut.* lviii. 211); and Pompey's wife was expert in literature, geometry, philosophy, and lyre-playing (Plut. *Pomp.* lv.). There were ladies in the time of Lucretius, as in the time of Juvenal, who liked interlarding their Latin with Greek expressions (Lucr. iv. 1160–1170; Juv. vi. 195). Ovid's gay set contained women with pretensions, if not claims, to literary tastes (*de Arte Am.* ii. 282). Seneca considered feminine capacity for mental training equal to masculine (*ad Helv.* xvii., *ad Marc.* xvi.); and Quintilian favours the intellectual development of women for the sake of their children (I. i. 6; for ancient frescoes from Herculaneum and elsewhere illustrating girls at study, see references in art. 'Educatio,' in Daremberg-Saglio). The mark made by women in authorship testifies to emancipation from, or expansion of, the ancient ideal of the Roman matron who was *lanifica* and *domiseda*. Agrippina's memoirs, Sulpicia's poems, and the literary tastes of Pliny's wife are among the proofs and fruits of this higher education among women. But it is disputed whether girls and boys were educated in mixed classes in ancient Rome.

According to some authorities, both sexes got the same training from the grammarian, and studied their Homer and Ennius together (Friedländer, *Darstellungen*, I. v. 'Die Frauen,' p. 246; Boissier, *Rel. rom.* ii. 215). Marquardt cites several passages in support of this view (*Das Privatleben*², i. 110, n. 8; Hor. *Sat.* I. x. 91; Mart. VIII. iii. 15–16, IX. lxviii. 2). But it is combated by Jullien (*op. cit.* pp. 147–150; cf. Hulsebos, *De educ. et instit.* p. 98), who holds that the passages relied upon do not refer to training under the *grammaticus*. It is, however, significant that Livy sees nothing uncommon in representing Virginia, a girl of mature years, as attending school. Many girls were, of course, taught at home, like the daughter of Atticus (Suet. *de Gram.* xvi.; Cic. *ad Att.* XII. xxxiii. 2), by a private tutor, or in some cases by a governess (*CIL* v. 3897, vi. 6331; cf. Ovid, *Tr.* ii. 369–370; Juv. vi. 185 ff.).

(5) *Schools and equipment.*—The more concrete side of education, such as schools, equipment, pay of teachers, can receive only brief treatment here. A school (*ludus*) was often simply in a room on the ground-floor of a building, separated from the

street by a curtain, or in a room above, open on one side like a veranda or Italian loggia (*pergula*). Thus, if there was no inspection, there was publicity; and the noise of school lessons, which began at an early hour, was a subject of complaint in Rome (Ovid, *Amores*, I. xiii. 13–14; Mart. IX. lxviii. 1–4). There is evidence for the educational use of models, maps, and busts. The *tabula Iliaca*, now in the Capitoline Museum at Rome, was a sort of concrete aid to study for a class working upon Homer; it may have been used by Augustus when a boy. We hear surprisingly little of the buildings used in higher work: halls, porticoes, theatres, baths, and wrestling-schools could be used for largely attended declamations. We read, too, of 'roomy *exedrae* furnished with seats, whereon philosophers, rhetoricians, and the rest of the study-loving world may sit and debate' (Vitruv. V. xi. 'exedrae spatiosae in quibus philosophi rhetoresque reliquique qui studiis delectantur sedentes disputare possint'). Hadrian's Athenæum was a noble edifice, in the amphitheatres of which Greek and Latin rhetors could lecture to crowded audiences (Aurel. Victor, *de Caesaribus*, xiv.; Lamprid. *Alex. Sev.* xxxv.; Capitol. *Pert.* xi., *Gord. Tres*, iii.). As to fees, the eight asses per month of the country school mentioned by Horace (*Sat.* I. vi. 75) show that elementary education was not handsomely paid. Masters seem in early days to have depended chiefly on freewill offerings from pupils or their parents at times of festivals like the Quinquatrus in March (when the *Minerval* was presented to the teacher), or the Saturnalia in December. Carvilius, towards the end of the 3rd cent. B.C., seems to have introduced the innovation of regularly charging school fees; but probably many adhered to the old custom of trusting to the gratitude and generosity of patrons. Thus Gnipho, Cicero's master, never stipulated for a fee (Suet. *de Gram.* vii.). Suetonius records the extreme poverty of some famous grammarians; *e.g.* Orbilius, Valerius Cato, and Hyginus the freedman of Augustus and librarian of the Palatine (Suet. *de Gram.* ix., xi., xx.). On the other hand, some were fortunate enough to secure favour in high places; thus, Verrius Flaccus was nominated by Augustus preceptor to his grandsons, had his school housed in the Palatium under the condition that he would accept no new pupils, and received a salary of 100,000 sesterces a year (*op. cit.* xvii.). Remmius Palaemon made 400,000 sesterces annually from his school (*op. cit.* xxiii.). In Imperial times, especially in the later period still to be considered, with the emergence of municipal schools there appears the feature of local endowment of education; and, where the municipality did not act, it was possible for a few private individuals to guarantee the salary of a master, as the younger Pliny suggested when he found that boys had to be sent from Como to Milan for their education. The first Emperor to appoint State-paid professors of rhetoric was Vespasian (Suet. *Vesp.* xviii.); and thenceforward, in the higher teaching of rhetoric or philosophy, especially if directly encouraged by Imperial favour, men like Quintilian could count on making a good income.

(6) *Punishments and holidays.*—The Roman schoolmaster was a severe disciplinarian, and unsatisfactory pupils were punished with the rod (*ferula* [Juv. i. 15]) or with the severer *scutica*. A famous fresco from Herculaneum represents a pupil 'horsed' by another, while a third holds his feet and the master flogs him. Quintilian expresses his objection to corporal punishment (I. iii. 14). As to holidays, climatic conditions must have necessitated a considerable break in the hottest time of the year; and during harvest and vintage there can have been little or no attendance at country schools.

The old notion of a four months' summer holiday, based on a false reading in Horace (*Sat.* I. vi. 75), is an error, but one which apparently dies hard (*e.g.* A. Meissner, *Altröm. Kulturleben*, Leipzig, 1908, in section on education, p. 77 ff.: 'Das Schulgeld wurde, da während der Monate Juli bis Oktober Ferien gegeben wurden, nur für acht Monate berechnet').

The *nundinae* and the greater public festivals brought a cessation of school-work. Apart from minor feasts and extraordinary occasions for rejoicing and shows, the more important festivals alone accounted for over sixty holidays every year.

3. From Hadrian to the end of the Roman Empire.—The State, which had concerned itself with morality by repeatedly enacted sumptuary laws and by encouraging marriage, was much slower to take education under its direct cognizance. Yet it is the Imperial concern for education which makes the distinctive feature of this closing period; for neither in East nor in West did the substance or method of education alter much. Thus, in the Greek portions of the Roman world the 'Second Sophistic' was represented by travelling rhetoricians, who found critical audiences—indicative of a wide diffusion of the old intellectual culture (Dill, *Rom. Soc. from Nero to Marcus Aurelius*, 1905, p. 372; Mommsen, *Provinces of Rom. Emp.*, Eng. tr., 1886, i. 362–367; cf. Philostr. *Apoll. Tyan.* i. 7, *Vit. Soph.* i. 220). Again, in the West, Africa (especially at Carthage), Spain, and the Gallic seats of learning maintained the ancient training in grammar and rhetoric. Marseilles, Autun, Lyons, Bordeaux, and, later, Toulouse, Narbonne, and Trèves were representative centres. It was the continuance of an old movement. Agricola had in early life realized the benefits of a good education at Marseilles, and about A.D. 80 established schools in Britain for chieftains' sons. In the 2nd cent. Juvenal glances at the craze for culture signified by the influence of Gallic eloquence on British lawyers, and by the talk in the 'Farthest North' about appointing a professor of rhetoric (*Sat.* xv. 111–112). Marcus Aurelius went through the normal three stages with certain additions: lessons from his *litterator* were amplified by others from an actor and a tutor who was both musician and geometer; at the next stage he had one Greek and three Latin *grammatici*; at the third stage he had three Greek masters of eloquence (including Herodes Atticus), and one Latin master, Fronto. He studied under many philosophers, and worked hard at law. He also attended public declamations (Capitol. *M. Ant. Phil.* ii.–iii.). A broadly similar course, though less full, was followed early in the 3rd cent. by Alexander Severus, first in the East, and afterwards at Rome (Lamprid. *Alex. Sev.* iii.).

The persistence of the ancient pagan learning meets us in an interesting way when we note the course of training followed by Christian Fathers and well represented in the *Confessions* of St. Augustine, which, as the utterances of one who had been a student in Africa and a professor at Milan, place vividly before us at once the æsthetic attractions and the moral defects of classical literature.

The characteristics of Roman education in Gaul during the 4th and 5th cents. are best known to us through the works of Ausonius and Apollinaris Sidonius (Dill, *Rom. Soc. in last Cent. of W. Empire*², pp. 385–451). The rhetorical training had suffered inevitable degeneration, thanks to its extravagant display of conventional cleverness in handling unrealities; but one pleasant feature in the literary education is its tendency to form a ground of common interest between Christian and non-Christian friends. Another and a less pleasant feature, suggestive of the coming disruption of the Empire, and anticipative of the training of the Middle Ages, is the gradual decline of the study of Greek in the West. This is quite noticeable both in Gaul and in Africa, where, in the time of Apuleius and Tertullian, educated men had known Greek as proficiently as Latin. St. Augustine, for example, had little hold upon or affection for Greek, and studied Plato chiefly in Latin translations (*Conf.* I. xiii.-xiv., VII. ix., VIII. ii.).

The attitude of the central authorities towards education, which is the salient feature of this period, had been foreshadowed from the very beginning of the Empire. Julius Cæsar granted the franchise to medical men and teachers of the liberal arts (Suet. *Div. Iul.* xlii.)—a great testimony to the dignity of learning as a passport for foreigners to Roman citizenship. A similar spirit prompted Augustus' exemption of teachers from a decree banishing foreigners (Suet. *Div. Aug.* xlii.); and his establishment of Verrius Flaccus in the Palatium has been mentioned. Tiberius and Claudius were interested in schools and in grammatical learning; but the next practical step in the direction of Imperial patronage was Vespasian's fixing of an annual stipend of 100,000 sesterces for Greek and Latin rhetors (Suet. *Vesp.* xviii.). This stipend of about £800 a year probably would not hold good outside the capital itself, and it may not have been till the reign of Domitian that Vespasian's arrangements came into actual force; for one of Jerome's entries under Domitian's reign (*Euseb. Chron.* ad ann. 2104) is: 'Quintilianus Calagurritanus ex Hispania primus Romae publicam scholam et salarium e fisco accepit et claruit.' Trajan's decision to confer education upon 5000 poor boys was a recognition of the gain to the community from having its future citizens trained (Plin. *Paneg.* xxvi.-xxviii.). Then, under Hadrian, came that expansion of educational policy from Rome to the Empire at large which marks his reign as the opening of a new era. Himself a widely read student, accomplished in painting and music, with a taste for declaiming, and fond of having learned men in his *entourage*, he showed liberality to all professors, and he superannuated teachers who were beyond their work (Spart. *Hadr.* xvi.). Besides giving rhetoric a home at his Athenæum in the capital, he established schools in the provinces, granted them subventions, and appointed teachers.

Hadrian's policy was continued and extended by Antoninus Pius (Capitol. *Ant. Pius*, xi.: 'rhetoribus et philosophis per omnes prouincias et honores et salaria detulit'), who also exempted rhetors, philosophers, grammarians, and doctors from certain State imposts, laying down the number of professors to be thus favoured in each town—*e.g.* in the smallest within the scope of the decree, 5 doctors, 3 sophists, 3 grammarians (*Digest.* xxvii. 1, 6). This measure proves the relationship of municipal and central authorities with the *personnel* of the teaching body. In reality, the expense of such schools fell on the municipalities, and the Emperors by special benefits simply encouraged and supported the towns in their educational policy. As Pottier remarks: 'C'est vraiment une organisation municipale de l'enseignement' (art. 'Educatio,' in Daremberg-Saglio; cf. Boissier, 'L'Instruction publique,' *loc. cit. infra*, pp. 331–335).

In A.D. 176, Marcus Aurelius made payments to establish professorships at Athens (Dio Cass. lxxi. 31. 3, ed. Bekker; Lucian, *Eun.* iii.). In the 3rd cent. with Alexander Severus appeared a bursary system; for, while increasing the schools and fixing salaries for rhetors, grammarians, and others, he arranged that their lectures should be attended by poor students aided by exhibitions (Lamprid. *Alex. Sev.* xliv.: 'discipulos cum annonis, pauperum filios, modo ingenuos, dari iussit'). The recurrence of enactments in the 4th cent. proves the tendency of municipalities to be mean or dilatory in paying salaries to teachers, education always appearing to offer a tempting field for economy. In 301, monthly payments were fixed by edict of Diocletian; *e.g.* 50 denarii per pupil for a *magister institutor*, 75 for a *calculator*, 200 for a *grammaticus Graecus siue Latinus* and for a *geometres*. Constantine ordained the regular payment of salaries, and by edicts of A.D. 321, 326, and 333 he granted indulgences to teachers 'quo facilius liberalibus studiis multos instituant.' When Constantius Chlorus appointed Eumenius to be principal of the resuscitated school at Autun about A.D. 297, the town had accepted the Emperor's right to choose as quite natural; and in 362, Julian claimed the nomination of professors throughout the Empire as a prerogative of the Emperor, but delegated the sifting of candidates to the local bodies (*Cod. Theod.* xiii. 3. 5). His forbidding of Christians to teach in schools was the first definite restriction imposed by the Emperor upon the freedom of local choice. Different rescripts of Gratian and of Theodosius regulated the stipends and the number of chairs (*Cod.* xiii. 3. 11, xiv. 9. 3). Gratian's policy possesses a special interest, because it was probably guided by his adviser and former tutor, Ausonius; his edict left the appointments of teachers to the municipalities, but fixed the emoluments; *e.g.* a rhetor was to have twice the amount due to a grammarian. Now, this was equivalent to ear-marking money in the municipal budgets for professorial salaries.

The last notable advance in the Imperial organization of public instruction is the foundation by Theodosius II. at Constantinople in 425 (little over a century before its dissolution by Justinian) of a University staffed by 31 professors, viz. 3 Latin rhetors, 10 Latin grammarians, 5 Greek rhetors, 10 Greek grammarians, 1 philosopher, 2 jurisconsults. The professors were treated as State-functionaries, and a monopoly in public teaching was secured to the University. The staffing is significant for its omissions. Neither science nor medicine figures in the list, and philosophy is poorly represented; yet Constantinople had a wider curriculum than most other institutions, which in the main concentrated their work, as Bordeaux did, upon grammar and rhetoric. Thus philosophy, never truly a passion with the Romans, and certainly losing ground in the Gallic schools of the 4th cent., came to be fully represented only at Athens, which in this respect outshone Massilia, Naples, Alexandria, Antioch, Seleucia, Smyrna, Ephesus, Rhodes, Tarsus, and Rome itself; while law, though not forgotten in centres like Cæsarea, Antioch, Alexandria, Carthage, Arles, and Narbonne, was most effectively taught at Berytus, outside the two capitals of the Empire; and medicine—a separate branch of study which had only by degrees risen out of the hands of slaves and freedmen, and could be best learned by assisting a practising doctor of repute—was specially professed in the schools of Rome, Alexandria, and Athens.

A law of Valentinian I. (A.D. 370) illustrates the concern of the Government for another aspect of education. It lays down rules for the supervision of students at Rome. On arrival, they were required to deliver to the *magister census* a passport from the governor of their own province, stating their antecedents; they must declare their intended course of study; misconduct might render them liable to public chastisement and expulsion; and permission to reside in Rome up to the age of 20 was made conditional on good behaviour and diligent study. Such regulations were necessary; for idlers and rowdies, like the *euersores* of St. Augustine's *Confessions*, could and did make themselves terrors to professors and to fellow-pupils in the schools of Europe, Africa, and Asia Minor. The amenities and the troubles of student life in the 4th cent., both in West and in East, are brought home to us in the pages of Ausonius, Augustine, Eunapius, and Libanius. We read of a cultured society looking back with pleasure and gratitude to 'college' lectures and companionships; students flocking to the lectures of a famous professor, especially, as Eunapius shows, if he came from their own part of the world; professorial schemes to attract students, or timidity in rebuking them, or jealousy over a rival's reputation; corporations of students formed, as Libanius discovered, to further the interests of a favourite professor, to waylay new-comers, and by rough ordeals initiate them into membership, under oath that they would take no lessons except from sophists recognized by their worshipful association (see A. Müller, *loc. cit. infra*).

If we take Gaul as typical of the survival of the old Roman education, we find in the 5th cent. that studies have ceased to make any advance, and that the classical tradition is on the eve of disappearance before irruptions of barbarism and the distrustful attitude of the Christian monastic schools.

LITERATURE.—**W. A. Becker**, *Gallus oder römische Scenen*, Leipzig, 1838, [3]1863, ed. Göll, 1881, Eng. tr.[10], London, 1891, by F. Metcalfe (esp. Sc. I. Excurs. ii.); **G. Bernhardy**, *Grundriss d. röm. Litteratur*[5], Brunswick, 1872 (Einleitung, Kap. iii.: 'Erziehung, Unterricht u. Kultur der Römer'); **H. Blümner**, *Die röm. Privataltertümer*, in Iwan v. Müller's *Handb. d. klass. Altertumswissenschaft*[3], IV. ii. 2, 1911 ('Erziehung u. Unterricht d. Knaben,' pp. 312–340); **G. Boissier**, art. 'Declamatio,' in Daremberg-Saglio, also 'Les Écoles de déclamation à Rome,' in *RDM*, 1st Oct. 1902, pp. 481–508 ('The Schools of Declamation at Rome,' in *Tacitus and other Roman Studies*, tr. by W. G. Hutchison, London, 1906, pp. 163–194), 'L'Instruction publique dans l'empire romain,' in *RDM*, 1884, pp. 316–349, and *La Religion romaine d'Auguste aux Antonins*[16], 2 vols., Paris, 1906 (education of women, ii. 212 ff.); **H. Bornecque**, *Les Déclamations et les déclamateurs d'après Sénèque le père*, Lille, 1902; **G. Clarke**, *Educ. of Children at Rome*, London, 1896; **F. Cramer**, *Gesch. d. Erziehung u. d. Unterrichts im Altertume*, 2 vols., Elberfeld, 1832–1838; **S. Dill**, *Roman Society in the last Cent. of the Western Empire*[2], London, 1899 (ch. v. 'Characteristics of Rom. Educ. and Culture in the Fifth Cent.' pp. 385–451); **J. Wight Duff**, *A Literary History of Rome*[2], London and Leipzig, 1910 (see references in Index under 'Roman Education,' 'Grammar,' 'Rhetoric'); **E. Egger**, *Étude sur l'éducation et particulièrement sur l'éduc. littéraire chez les Romains*, Paris, 1833; **W. Warde Fowler**, *Social Life at Rome in the Age of Cicero*, London, 1908 (ch. vi. pp. 168–203, 'The Educ. of the Upper Classes'); **L. Friedländer**, *Darstellungen aus der Sittengesch. Roms in der Zeit von August bis zum Ausgang der Antonine*[6], 3 vols., Leipzig, 1888, [7]2 vols., 1901 (teachers and schools, I. iii. 156–164; women's educ. I. v. 245–248, 269–274; educational courses, II. iv. 373–389; philosophy, II. vi. 551–603); **L. Grasberger**, *Erziehung u. Unterricht im klass. Altertum*, 3 vols., Würzburg, 1864–81; **G. A. Hulsebos**, *De educatione et institutione apud Romanos*, Utrecht, 1875; **E. Jullien**, *Les Professeurs de littérature dans l'ancienne Rome et leur enseignement*, Paris, 1885; **J. H. Krause**, *Gesch. d. Erziehung, d. Unterrichts u. d. Bildung bei d. Griechen, Etruskern, und Römern*, Halle, 1851; **S. S. Laurie**, *Historical Survey of Pre-Christian Educ.*, London, 1895; **W. Liebenam**, *Städteverwaltung im röm. Kaiserreiche*, Leipzig, 1900, pp. 73–82, 349–353; **J. Marquardt**, *Das Privatleben der Römer*[2], Leipzig, 1886, pp. 80–126 (French tr., *La Vie privée des Romains*, Paris, 1892, pp. 96–157, in tome xiv. of *Manuel des antiquités romaines*, by Mommsen and Marquardt); **P. Monroe**, *Source Book of the Hist. of Educ. for the Greek and Roman Period*, London, 1902; **A. Müller**, 'Studentenleben im 4 Jahrhundert n. Chr.,' in *Philologus*, lxix. (Leipzig, 1910) 292–317; **R. Pichon**, 'L'Éduc. rom. au premier siècle,' in *Revue Universitaire*, 15th Feb. 1895; **E. Pottier**, art. 'Educatio,' in Daremberg-Saglio; **J. P. Rossignol**, *De l'Éducation et de l'instruction des hommes et des femmes chez les anciens*, Paris, 1888; **J. E. Sandys**, *A Hist. of Classical Scholarship*, vol. i., Edinburgh, 1903, 2nd ed., Cambridge, 1906 (esp. chs. x., xi., xii. for Roman age of Latin scholarship, grammarians, etc.); **J. L. Ussing**, *Darstellung des Erziehungs- u. Unterrichtswesens bei d. Griechen u. Römern* (Germ. tr. from Danish by P. Friedrichsen), Altona, 1870, new and corrected ed. as *Erziehung u. Jugendunterricht bei d. Griechen u. Römern*, Berlin, 1885; **A. S. Wilkins**, *Roman Education*, Cambridge, 1905.

J. WIGHT DUFF.

EDUCATION, MORAL.—I. Definition and scope.—The concept 'moral education' requires to be clearly defined; otherwise much confusion is bound to arise in discussion. We shall consider first what the definition should exclude, then what it should include.

(*a*) *Religious and denominational duties.*—The differences between the members of the human race are altogether insignificant compared with the differences between a man and his Deity. We may, therefore, profitably distinguish, at least for practical purposes, between moral and religious duties; and, since a man's duties to his Church are corollaries to his duties to his Deity, it would be well also to include denominational under the head of religious duties. Moreover, neither a man's relation to his Deity nor that to his fellows is a purely ethical one; therefore, just as we do not look upon every human question as an ethical one, so we must bear in mind that every religious problem is not necessarily a moral one. We are thus justified in distinguishing between theological and moral duties, and in confining, for all intents and purposes, theological duties to the religious lesson, and moral duties to the moral lesson.[1] Both religious and moral education would be gainers by such a separation, since the duties towards our fellows and those towards the Deity, which differ in several respects, could be more exhaustively and more fruitfully treated. This would be all the more important because opinions on theology vary so widely in the 20th century.

The objection that morality is connected with, and dependent on, theology is beside the point, for a similar connexion exists between theology and most other subjects in the curriculum—history, science, and literature, for instance. Accordingly there is no compelling reason why morality, any more than history or science, should form part of the religious lesson. To the particular extent that the objection is justifiable, it may be met by occasional references in the religious lesson to ethics, history, and science, as the case may be, and, in denominational schools, by occasional references to theology when treating of the same subjects. For example, one chapter in the official Portuguese Moral Instruction Manual for Primary Schools is devote to theological duties, including duties to the Church, while, conversely, the Portuguese Catechism treats to some extent of moral duties. Each, morality and theology, comes in this way to its own. For the common school, however, it would be sufficient for the teacher to make it plain that the religious lesson will deal with religious and denominational duties. If it is argued that the principal motives to right conduct are theological, the reply must be that the trend of modern times is to appeal to human motives in conduct, and that an ethics which is primarily other-worldly is on that account out of place in education. Our literature, our press, our social and political life, and the whole spiritual structure of our schools imply the sufficiency of human motives for right action. The argument is further weakened by the fact that non-theological moral lessons of one kind or another are becoming frequent all over the world.

Finally, it is held by some that the Bible alone (or the Catechism) is the proper text-book of moral instruction, and that true morality is one with Bible morality. The remarks in the last paragraph partly dispose of this objection. In addition, it may be stated that the books comprising the Bible reflect a certain civilization which is widely removed from ours: *e.g.* our political and social life vastly differs from that of Judæa, and men live now—not as in that period of history—on an international plane. Our scheme of virtues and our moral teaching must, therefore, be based on the conditions of modern existence. Let any one compare, for this purpose, the Portuguese Catechism with the Portuguese Ethical Manual, or the syllabuses of the English Moral Instruction League with an ordinary religious instruction syllabus, or the Ten Commandments, as they stand in the Bible, with the explanations of them given in most Protestant and Roman Catholic catechisms, and the difference between Bible morality and modern morality will be obvious. This is not a question as to whether the Bible is abstractly correct in its morals (though even this is disputed by recognized theologians).[2] Different civilizations

[1] 'Religion itself I take to mean a body of truths or beliefs respecting God and our relation to Him; and flowing from these a collection of duties which have God as their primary object. These are, in the main, functions of the will in the form of exercises of internal and external worship. Out of these beliefs and volitions there emerge feelings and emotions which we call religious sentiments. They include love, gratitude, sorrow, fear, joy, hope, awe, veneration, and allied forms of consciousness' (Father Michael Maher, S.J., in *Papers on Moral Education communicated to the First International Moral Education Congress*, 1908, p. 178).

[2] 'If the Jehovah who instructed Jacob to cheat Laban, bade Joshua to massacre the women and children of Canaan, sent bears to kill the children who mocked Elisha, or accepted such

must be interpreted in different moral terms, and a person brought up strictly on Bible morality would be fitted only for Bible times and not at all adapted for our age. The Bible, therefore, may be used by the teacher of morals as one only out of many sources of moral insight and inspiration.

We conclude, therefore, that for all practical purposes moral must be separated from religious education.

(*b*) *Intellectual, physical, æsthetic, and professional education.*—The closer study of educational problems demonstrates more and more that the concept 'education' has various aspects which can be separated with comparative ease. Moral education has consequently come to be regarded as a distinct branch of education. To this the objection is still sometimes offered, that since, as is alleged, intellectual education tends to make children truth-loving and true, or physical education makes them courageous and upright, therefore separate moral education is superfluous. A careful examination, for which we have no space here, would show that there is little truth in these contentions, and that, on the whole, each branch of education has to look to perfecting itself, if it is to achieve solid results, although it may justly rely on some support being given to it by each of the other branches.

It might further be argued that ethics should not be treated as a special subject, but should permeate the whole of education. To this the reply is that these two means are non-exclusive. Just as the teacher in every class promotes the physical education of the children by insisting on proper postures and movements, and by touching on aspects in his subject connected with physical culture, even though there be a separate gymnastic class, so discipline and indirect moral instruction do not exclude systematic moral teaching. They are complementary and interdependent. As to the fact that the formation of character is generally judged to be the chief aim in education, this can make no difference to the need of separate teaching for the purpose of conveying clear and connected impressions on the way of life.

We have seen that moral education is to be distinguished from religious, intellectual, physical, æsthetic, and professional education. We must inquire now what this form of education aims to compass.

(*c*) *Support of the present regime.*—If moral education demanded obedience solely, its purport would be readily divined, for children would simply be taught to do what they are commanded by parents, teachers, masters, and magistrates, and to be satisfied with the economic and social position in which they may happen to find themselves. This code of morals is not by any means a rarity to-day, and its inculcation, in part at least, is favoured in many quarters. For instance, the large majority of French text-books on moral instruction were, until recently, emphatic on the point that the Great Revolution had achieved everything of moment for the good of France, and that dissatisfaction with present conditions argued, therefore, an unethical state of mind. There is no future in the schools for such a non-progressive morality.

(*d*) *Abstract moral conceptions.*—It is also easy to define moral education in abstract moral terms. Obedience to the commands of duty, hearkening to the voice of conscience, belief that our will is free, the heinousness of sin, the hauntings of remorse, and the necessity for repentance are such abstract moral conceptions. Even general references to truthfulness, kindness, or courage do not alter materially the effect of the teaching, for in all these cases the moral lessons do not tell the young what to do and what to leave undone. The bigot, the oppressor, the pleasure-hunter, the idler, and the ignorant are in no way morally enlightened by the recollection of such teachings, but rather tend to be confirmed in their respective courses of conduct by an accommodating conscience. The moral education of the present has no sympathy with such an abstract theory.

homage as is offered in the 69th Psalm, were to be regarded not as a conception relative to a barbarous age, but as an authoritative picture of the one true God, then it would inevitably follow that the ruler of the world was not, in the modern sense, a moral being' (Canon Glazebrook, in *Papers on Moral Education communicated to the First International Moral Education Congress*, p. 155 f.).

(*e*) *The aim of moral education.*—Moral education, as conceived to-day, aims in the main at communicating a deep sense of personal, social, civic, and international responsibility. The duties implied in this responsibility may be comprehended in twelve categories of social relationship: (1) home and family (including relatives, guests, near neighbours, household helps, and domestic animals); (2) companionship (including sociability, acquaintances, friends, and courtship); (3) the school (including love of knowledge and science); (4) social life; (5) animal life; (6) self-respect (including regard for moral, intellectual, and physical health); (7) the ethics of work; (8) leisure and pleasure; (9) love of nature; (10) love of art; (11) citizenship and internationalism; (12) respect for the past, the present, and the future. Courage, prudence, temperance, and justice would be regarded as the general virtues which guide and inspire personal and social endeavour, and the teacher would sum up, with the Stoics, all the duties and virtues in the one duty and virtue of manliness, that is, of being a man or woman guided by careful reflexion and wide sympathies. The features peculiar to such instruction are: it should be positive rather than negative in its injunctions, and draw its material from reality rather than from fiction; it should concern itself with motives as well as with acts; it should keep in view both the desirability and the danger of cultivating habits of thought and action; it should not restrict itself to inculcating duties suitable to the child stage; it should not consist of mere analysis or strict logical treatment; it should cultivate the active side, and enforce the importance of example; it should lay stress on complete faithfulness to the ideal, and the rejection of even the faintest compromise with sin; and its prime test should be its effect on the character and the conduct of the taught.

2. The place of moral education.—It is almost universally agreed that the supreme object of education is the formation of character, and this agreement is due to the common conviction that morality is the unifying bond of society, without which social harmony and happiness are impossible. Moral education is, consequently, held to be of supreme importance.

3. Departments of moral education. — Moral education may be divided into home education, school education, and self-education.

(*a*) *Moral education in the home.*—The problem of moral education in the home is more complicated than that of moral education in the school. In the home there are, besides assistant teachers, two teachers—the parents (who often do not agree in their views on education); there are usually several children of different ages; the children have no set tasks to perform as at school; the home schooling extends practically over the twenty-four hours at first; the parents have not usually been prepared for their duties, and they have other than educational duties to fulfil; and there are no authoritative manuals to inform them how to educate their children morally. Under these circumstances it is only the general pressure and influence of the environment which guide and correct the education given.

One striking exception alone exists up to the present—that referring to the education of infants. Here a multitude of definite rules are followed which simplify the problem and almost solve it. Perfect cleanliness, proper food, plenty of fresh air, prescribed regularity and proportion in everything, and never-failing gentleness remove nearly all educational obstacles, to the great relief and benefit of both parents and infant. Accordingly it is wisely suggested that every young woman (and perhaps every young man) should visit for a few weeks a crêche (or other scientifically conducted nursery) for the purpose of learning the 'trade' of parent. A second significant step is being already taken. Young women, trained in kindergartens, learn how to amuse and employ young children, and how to depend completely, in the exercise of their profession, on intelligent anticipation, cheerfulness, serenity, loving care, courtesy, and respect for the child's love of liberty. No corporal punishment, no pushing or pulling, no scolding, shouting, or argumentation, no harshness, teasing, or bribing, no alternation between forbidding and granting everything, no appeals to low motives, no false promises or excuses are resorted to, and yet the educational results are far more satisfactory than they used to be. The evident conclusion is that prospective parents should train themselves or be trained as are kindergarten nurses and teachers; and, considering the simplicity of the training and the thoroughly unwise education which is only too common, opinion should not be divided on the matter. The only drawback—which is, however, a serious one—is that this education, as now given, does not prepare for any high calling. A positive scheme of ethics, such as we have sketched, must supplement the mere training in cheerfulness and correct behaviour; for the building up of a strong character bent on playing a worthy part in life must be the objective.

The above method of dealing with infants and young children indicates the general lines of a sound system of moral education. The children, at all stages of development, must have something to do both in the way of amusement and employment, and the parents must know how to treat them. The children should be trained in self-help, in helping in the home, and in helpfulness generally. Devotion to the right, love of justice and tolerance, courage, perseverance, courtesy, modesty, exactitude in observation and in giving accounts or making statements, independent thought, carefulness in generalizing, love of truth and of learning, of nature and of art, strenuousness and love of work, temperance in the classic sense, and simplicity of living should be, among other virtues, inculcated in the home according to the stage of development of the young. Children should learn, too, to do what is right and reasonable unhesitatingly, intelligently, perseveringly, cheerily, and rapidly. In the adolescent period the parent should be the trusted friend of the youth or maiden; and purity, sobriety, industry, desirable companions, love of nature, art, and learning, and devotion to good causes should be particularly encouraged.

We may divide moral education into four periods: (i.) from birth to the age of two-and-a-half; (ii.) from two-and-a-half to seven; (iii.) from seven to about twenty-one; and (iv.) from twenty-one onwards. In the first period, when the child cannot as yet be easily reasoned with, we consider more especially the formation of good *habits*; in the second, when the child possesses just about sufficient understanding to comprehend commands, his character is to be moulded chiefly by *obedience*; in the third, when the mental powers and self-possession are more developed, *commendation* should be the principal means of moral training; and, naturally, *self-direction* is the main motive fitting the last period. Yet the formation of good habits must be continued throughout the second, third, and fourth stages; the appeal to obedience throughout the third and fourth stages; the method of commendation throughout the fourth stage; and, indeed, the four methods are applicable, in varying degrees, to all the four stages.

The following aspects are discernible in a well-considered system of moral education:—

(1) The nature of the morality taught and the principal methods employed have to be fixed, as we have done above.

(2) Since the child has two teachers in his parents, and since harmony and efficiency in the teachers are essential, two conditions at least require to be satisfied. In thinking of marriage, the suitability of the contemplated partner should be weighed from this point of view. Secondly, husband and wife must seek to eliminate any points of differences in educational conceptions which may exist between them. The parents must also do their utmost to prepare themselves for the task of educating their offspring. Perhaps in time a voluntary and afterwards a compulsory service for about a year or more, probably divided into separate periods, will take the place of the present military service, and prepare men and women for the duties of adult life.

(3) The general organization of the home requires attention. The treatment of the children will be consistent, and show neither rigidity nor weakness. The children should be supplied with everything necessary for their moral, intellectual, and physical welfare. They will have convenient rooms and places to be in and to play in. Things will be so arranged in the home that the children are not tempted into mischief. The songs, the toys, the games, the picture-books, the stories told, the readings, the amusements, the employments, and the domestic animals should, as is becoming increasingly the case, largely promote the moral aim of home education. In short, an ethical spirit should determine the whole organization.

(4) Example is of far-reaching importance with the young. Dependent on their environment, they adopt the ideas of those surrounding them; they imitate their actions, their bodily attitudes, their tone of voice, and, what is sometimes not recognized, their feelings. Overflowing with energy and living in the present, the young child possesses, it is true, little self-control; but intelligent anticipation and organization, and unvarying serenity, consistency, and cheerfulness on the parents' part prevent passionateness and vacillation from becoming permanent in the child, and thus pave the way for the acquisition of whatever virtues his guardians possess.

(5) Incidental moral teaching was almost continuous under the old conditions. The child is eager to act, and also soon gets tired of any particular course of action; therefore, when his amusements are not scientifically regulated, he appears to be thinking of nothing but mischief, and remonstrances become incessant. Still, even under the most favourable conditions, many an occasion presents itself for pointing a moral. We can thus, by noting the moral successes and failures in conduct, impress the need for doing what is right and reasonable unhesitatingly, intelligently, and so forth.

(6) Indirect moral teaching should not be left entirely to chance. Various personal and social problems should be discussed (with due regard to the age of the child) from an ethical point of view, and provision should be made in order that such opportunities should not be lacking. Occurrences in the home, public events, the reading of a story, and the learning of a lesson may all be made occasions for indirect moral teaching.

(7) Direct moral teaching should also be given. The young are interested in issues concerned with conduct, and, if we approach them intelligently and sympathetically—sentimentality and sermonizing being excluded—we can talk over with them their own conduct, the conduct of others, and moral ideas and ideals generally. In this way, a lively sense of their duties and of their strong points and failings may be generated in them, and their character to a large extent determined. This would make superfluous many rebukes, and prevent the child from forgetting what he is to do and what he is to leave undone. How to do better than well rather than how not to do ill should be the burden of incidental, indirect, and direct moral teaching.

(8) Systematic moral teaching would be implied in the above so far as special instruction in morals is concerned, but systematic teaching proper involves teaching where the various ideas are, so far as possible, co-ordinated and comprehended in a system. Systematic teaching in the home, taking for granted rising stages of development, would mean that one important problem after another would be approached, and its bearing on present

and future life and conduct investigated. The aim of such set talks is the attaining of clear and comprehensive moral ideas, and the communication of a general enthusiasm for the right. Given a reasonable family life and a simple ideal, this should not prove unattainable. Systematic teaching being the rule in every subject, there can be no objection to systematic moral teaching.

(9) Environmental factors have important bearings. In (1) and (8) we have tacitly assumed a certain economic affluence in the family, and a certain social environment favourable to right conduct. These assumptions fall wide of the mark if the average family is considered, where the income is generally so meagre that scarcely anything beyond the barest necessities can be procured, while bad economic conditions and low moral standards lead to much misery and unrighteous dealings. Owing to these and other causes—not least the absence of efficient moral education—impurity, intemperance, idleness, ignorance, lack of sympathy and economic exploitation are widespread. Consequently, the average family is almost bound to fail to a considerable extent in the task of moral education, whilst the unpropitious social conditions create further obstacles. The moral educator is thus commonly also a social reformer.

(*b*) *Moral education in schools.*—The problems of school and home are largely the same, and we have, therefore, implicitly dealt to some extent with the school in speaking of the home and of moral education in general. Let us summarize the points. (1) There must be a system of morals which the teacher can utilize; (2) the teacher must be efficiently trained; (3) he should have a strong personality; (4) the school should be effectively organized for ethical purposes; there should be (5) incidental, (6) indirect, (7) direct, and (8) systematic ethical teaching; (9) the environment must not be decidedly unfavourable to right conduct; and (10) school and home must be properly correlated. We shall deal with these points separately.

(1) The nature of the ethics to be taught at school will naturally be the same as that inculcated in the home, only that the school life lends itself better to the practice of the social virtues. The principles governing the discipline will also be precisely the same, except that greater care will be requisite to do justice to the sensibilities and individuality of children who come from various homes, and that special care is necessary since the children are usually massed together for nearly an hour at a time. To ensure adequate attention to the pupils' needs, the teachers should preferably be class-teachers, and should remain some three years with the same set of children.

(2) The moral training of the young must be undertaken by efficient teachers. Moral education demands, therefore, that the teaching profession should be sufficiently respected and remunerated to attract men and women of character and ability, and that prospective teachers should be thoroughly prepared in training colleges and otherwise. This preparation should include special training and teaching in morals, in order that teachers should be familiar with the meaning and the task of moral education.

(3) The personality of the teacher, and particularly that of the headmaster, is of importance, especially where the school, as used to be the case, makes no organized provision for moral training. In the latter case almost everything depends on the influence of the headmaster, and to this is due the altogether exaggerated estimate of the teacher's personality which still largely survives. The personality of the teaching staff, however, has no small significance even to-day, considering that the teachers are to the child the living embodiment of the purpose for which the school exists.

(4) We need not enumerate here the various factors which go to the making of a well-organized school. These are well known. We lay stress on only a few points, assuming that the moral training of the pupils is the school's chief aim. The average number of children in a class should not exceed twenty-five; no more in the way of teaching results is to be expected than is consistent with thoroughness in training and teaching; the teacher should have sufficient leisure to continue his education; the teaching staff should be actively interested in the welfare of the pupils, and should also organize games and amusements; self-reliance and co-operation among the pupils should be encouraged; and a decided ethical tone should be traceable in the school decorations. Following the practice of the American School Republics, many tasks should devolve upon the pupils, and a strong and healthy corporate spirit should be cultivated among them. The school should be in close touch with the home, and it should introduce the pupils to the larger world by visits and excursions of various kinds. The ethical atmosphere of the class-room needs, however, special mention. Just as every teacher is at all times expected to watch over the pronunciation of his pupils, and to make sure that they express themselves clearly, intelligently, fluently, and concisely, so the ethical purpose of the school demands that at least the following moral qualities be kept constantly and consciously in view by the teacher: courtesy, love of truth, broad-mindedness, strenuousness, courage, orderliness, kindliness, uprightness, and simplicity of living.

(5) Incidents are uncommon to-day in a good school, and consequently little room is found for incidental moral teaching. Even where an 'incident' occurs, the good teacher usually finds it far more effective to confer privately with the culprit than to play to the gallery. It is inconceivable that in a well-conducted school the moral teaching should be confined to incidental moral instruction, though it can be easily understood why in former days, when the teaching methods were ill-devised and the disciplinary measures harsh, incidental moral teaching had a large scope.

(6) Indirect moral instruction is moral instruction arising out of the treatment of one subject or another of the curriculum. The history and the literature lessons are peculiarly suited to this. In addition, the physiology lessons are sometimes made the channel for inculcating general rules of health, the natural history lessons for kindness to animals, and the domestic science lessons for the household virtues.

Until recently such indirect moral instruction was rare, and there were many warnings uttered against it: *e.g.* educationists urged that one must not introduce an irrelevant subject; that it is not practical to attempt to kill two birds with one stone; that one must beware of falsifying facts to suit ethical ends; and that the class is not the place for moralizing and sermonizing. There used to be legitimate grounds for this objection, the chief one being that the school was at that time intellectualistic and opportunistic in aim, and that the recognized way of treating a subject and the matter itself almost precluded indirect ethical teaching. This is rapidly changing. The Belgian history-syllabuses, the attitude towards history of the English and Scottish Boards of Education, and that of many historians and educationists imply that history must be conceived as a record of the growth of civilization, and not merely as an account of military exploits. Illustrative of this fundamental change is also the fact that the New York City Education Authority conceives of geographical teaching as tending primarily to show the solidarity of the human race and its interdependence. Similarly, German and French School Readers now supply plentiful material of an ethical character, while frequently one of the main tests of a piece of literature to-day is whether or not an ethical spirit pervades it. Even arithmetic will soon be looked upon as a training in exact and cautious thinking rather than as a meaningless juggling with figures; and in high educational quarters the permeation of æsthetic culture—music, singing, drawing, painting, modelling—with an ethical spirit is coming to be taken for granted. In a word, the whole curriculum is about to be ethicized, and in a generation or two we may expect every subject to be primarily ethical in character, with signal advantage to the particular subject (since ethics is life, and life is interesting) and to the race (since conduct, as Matthew Arnold said, covers three-fourths of life). It was because the school was narrowly patriotic, because it was too much concerned about turning out factory heads and hands, because its text-books were often written by near-sighted specialists who did not perceive the social meaning and bearing of the several school subjects, and because there was no strenuous attempt to make it serve its chief aim—character-building—that indirect moral instruction was rare, and frequently out of place. With educational advance, genuine opportunities for indirect moral instruction are multiplying; and such indirect instruction will appear more and more important, until every subject will ultimately prepare the pupil for promoting the cause of progress and well-being—individual, social, and racial. Ethics will be taught as the leading fact in history and life, and largely take the place of the facts favoured by militarism, commercialism, specialism, and intellectualism. The recent Education Codes of most countries illustrate this trend.

(7) Direct moral instruction in special subjects is now not infrequently given. Hygiene, with special reference to the drink question and to non-smoking, is a popular subject; temperance is a separate subject widely favoured; patriotism, citizenship, purity, good manners, and kindness to animals are also subjects to be met with in curricula. Such courses are of recent origin, and are rapidly multiplying in the school systems of the civilized world. It is, however, already felt that these separate courses require co-ordination and correlation, and that individually they do not supply the requisite ethical momentum to make the lessons effective for character-forming.

(8) Systematic moral instruction means direct or separate teaching, where the whole subject is treated in a comprehensive manner. This, however, does not exclude systematic treatment of selected subjects; it rather presupposes it, just as it assumes indirect moral instruction and the proper organization of the school for ethical ends. Such systematic instruction—common to all school subjects from the beginning of school life—alone provides clear and comprehensive ethical ideas, and covers the whole field of right doing. The other kinds of instruction — incidental, indirect, and direct—favour particular virtues instead of virtue, and cannot do justice to many aspects of conduct which may require detailed treatment. The ethics of home, of work, of the proper use of leisure, of friendship, and of much else could only in this systematic way be adequately and usefully dealt with. Sole reliance on the other methods—which is never the case with any other school subject—argues an unpedagogical procedure because the children do not correlate what they hear on the various occasions, and consequently soon forget it. Accordingly, systematic moral teaching, for the whole of the school period and in agreement with the ordinary pedagogic principles, is bound to come.

Already France, Italy, Portugal, and Japan possess such teaching; the English Board of Education strongly recommends it in its Code; many British colonies and over fifty English Local Education Authorities provide it; and individual schools and systems of schools in the United States and elsewhere also supply such teaching. The Ethical Societies have done much to popularize the idea of courses in general morals for the young, and the English Moral Instruction League is almost wholly responsible for the rapid advance made in this direction in England.[1] See MORAL EDUCATION LEAGUE.

The content of this instruction we have already outlined in speaking of the aim of education and of home education. Its tendency, as indicated in those passages, will be to produce men and women whose wills are good, strong, firm, and enlightened, men and women inspired by the widest sympathies.

(9) The school must prepare for social life; but what is to be done if the social life of the present in many ways discourages right conduct? The answer that every man must rise above circumstance has led to much preaching and little doing, and is, therefore, to be ruled out of court. On the contrary, we are bound to recognize that for one person whom nothing daunts, nineteen are, for good or evil, sensibly affected by their environment. Accordingly, we must admit that home and school to-day are not all-powerful, and cannot send out into the world ideal men and women, or ensure that their charges will not morally suffer when plunged into the whirling stream of social life. There is need, therefore, for the social reformer, and the school must create him. Much, indeed, in the school itself depends on the spirit which pervades society: *e.g.* scholars are herded together—50, 60, or 70 in a class—and leave school several years before they should, and teachers are poorly trained and ill paid. Probably, until the national expenditure on education is at least doubled, the school will not be able to grapple effectively with the problems it has to face, nor until then will it yield a 'high rate of interest.'

(10) *School and home.*—A child well brought up at home is, as educationists testify,[1] an excellent scholar, for such a child eagerly and easily learns. If the home does its duty, the task of the teacher is, therefore, incalculably simplified. In fact, if home education approached perfection, school education would either be superfluous or follow lines different from the present ones. Well-bred children would possess the intellectual virtues (so far as the stage of development they had reached permitted) which the school is now inculcating with infinite pains and with relatively small success: *e.g.* careful observing, judging, and generalizing, a good memory, and vigorous independent thinking; and conciseness, readiness, polish, and clearness in speech and writing. They would also possess in a high degree the school virtues of punctuality, regularity, orderliness, neatness, attentiveness, industry, and courtesy; and, accordingly, the educational methods might demand much more of the child—working without supervision, co-operating with other children—making the influence of the school co-terminous with waking existence. Under these circumstances the school would not feel obliged to cram the children with 'necessary' knowledge; it would chiefly teach them how to learn, and the school's work it would mostly leave to the consultation of dictionaries, encyclopædias, maps, and books of statistics at home and at school; to observation, experiments, private reflexion, art galleries, museums, travel; and, not least, to the reading and the study of the great literary, scientific, and philosophical classics. This being the relation between school and home, it is essential that the two should come into close contact, and even be co-ordinated.

At present, in spite of various efforts, the school has succeeded only to an insignificant degree in keeping in touch with the home. Parents may call on the teacher; they are occasionally invited to attend lessons, examinations, and festive functions; they receive periodical accounts of the children's progress and conduct; they are asked to assist the children with their 'home' work, and to interest themselves in the children's school life; occasional parents' evenings are organized; in a few instances teachers visit the parents and the children, and also organize the children's amusements outside school; and in rare cases the parents of the scholars are asked to be represented on the school's committee of management. The subject of the relation between school and home is of sufficient importance to warrant a special investigation being undertaken with a view to making far-reaching proposals, since scarcely anything could be of such advantage to the school as that the pupils should have

[1] For full details regarding Moral Instruction (theological and non-theological) in eighteen countries, with complete syllabuses in use and an exhaustive bibliography, see Gustav Spiller, *Report on Moral Instruction and on Moral Training*, 1909. See also *Moral Instruction in Elementary Schools in England and Wales, A Return compiled from Official Documents* by H. Johnson, Secretary of the Moral Instruction League, 1908.

[1] 'Little difficulty is felt in securing good work from boys who have had the invaluable advantage of a good home training' (Collar and Crook, *School Management and Methods of Instruction*, 1900, p. 53).

a first-rate home education. Among the objects more particularly to be realized is the professional encouragement of home education by the preparation of manuals, by the holding of classes and courses of lectures, and by full readiness to give counsel and assistance to parents. Ultimately the Education Authorities will concern themselves probably with home as well as with school education.

(*c*) *Moral education of adults.*—Adult life offers a number of special moral problems—the question of gaining a livelihood, the relation of superior to subordinate, of partner in marriage, and of parent, of civic responsibility, of influencing others by our ideas and activities, and so forth. The home and the school may develop a good character in those they have charge of, but this character is likely to deteriorate markedly when, adult life being reached, there is no inclination to continue the education received. The test of the moral man as well as of the business man is success in his particular sphere, and therefore the good man must ask himself: 'Does every one who knows me, near and far, think that I am all that I should be? Is my influence on all those I come in contact with, near and far, a beneficial one? Do I succeed as partner in marriage, as parent, as employer or employed, in friendship, in social intercourse, and in civic life? And to what extent do I succeed?' Experience proves that these searching questions are more easily put than satisfactorily answered.

Certain reasons for this relative non-success in life are not difficult to discover. We do not fully understand and appreciate others; passing impressions and feelings dominate us instead of the broadest considerations; we are unaware of the priceless value of simple living and cheerfulness, of uprightness and devotion to the common good; and we make innumerable distinctions between men, when one undeviating rule—to assist all according to their need—should be followed. Yet the mere being conscious and convinced of these reasons will avail little. They must be expanded in a series of works which show the way to act in the various relationships of life. We shall not, for instance, understand others by earnestly wishing to understand them, or live the simple life without knowing in what it consists. Unfortunately, writers on ethics have not generally appreciated the moral difficulties which are due to painful ignorance of details. No man will think of telling a man, 'Be forthwith a musician or poet'; but the writings of ethical thinkers only too often imply the command, 'Be forthwith a good man.' The truth is that the good life is a fine art which requires unceasing study and practice. The Church, Ethical Societies, and similar organizations have sought, with comparatively little success, to act as ethical schools for adults, and the reading of the great moralists, essayists, and devotional writers (of whom we cite some below) has been recommended for the same reason, and wisely; but what would render the most signal service would be scientific manuals on right conduct, dealing fully with the various relationships of life, especially if these manuals were used in connexion with classes, where views could be exchanged and definite advice might be received. The 20th century needs Doctors of Morals as well as Doctors of Medicine. Cf. ETHICAL DISCIPLINE.

LITERATURE.—(1) *SCHOOL EDUCATION*: Felix Adler, *Moral Instruction of Children*, New York, 1895; Sophie Bryant, *The Teaching of Morality in the Family and the School*, London, 1897; F. W. Foerster, *Jugendlehre*, Berlin, 1904–6; F. J. Gould, *Life and Manners*, London, 1906; Edward Howard Griggs, *Moral Education* (with bibliography), New York, 1904; J. N. Larned, *A Primer of Right and Wrong*, New York, 1902; Jules Payot, *Cours de morale*, Paris, 1906; Rudolph Penzig, *Ernste Antworten auf Kinderfragen*, Berlin, 1904; M. E. Sadler (editor), *Moral Instruction and Training in Schools* (with bibliography), London, 1908; Gustav Spiller, *Report on Moral Instruction and Moral Training in Eighteen Countries* (with full bibliography), London, 1909, also *Papers on Moral Education communicated to the First International Moral Education Congress*, London, 1908; A. J. Waldegrave, *A Teacher's Handbook of Moral Lessons*, London, 1904.

(2) *SELF-EDUCATION*: Xenophon's *Memorabilia*; Plato's *Republic*; Aristotle's *Nicomachean Ethics*; the Greek dramatists; the *Analects* of Confucius; the Buddhist *Suttas*; Cicero's *de Officiis*; St. Paul, Seneca, Epictetus, Marcus Aurelius; Augustine's *Confessions*; Boethius' *Consolations of Philosophy*; à Kempis' *The Imitation of Christ*; Luther's *Table Talk* and *Large Catechism*; Essays of Montaigne, Bacon, Emerson, Carlyle, Ruskin; Taylor's *Holy Living*; Seeley's *Ecce Homo*; Gizycki's *Moral-philosophie*, etc. GUSTAV SPILLER.

EDWARDS AND THE NEW ENGLAND THEOLOGY.—Jonathan Edwards, saint and metaphysician, revivalist and theologian, stands out as the one figure of real greatness in the intellectual life of colonial America. Born, bred, passing his whole life on the verge of civilization, he has made his voice heard wherever men have busied themselves with those two greatest topics which can engage human thought—God and the soul. A French philosopher of scant sympathy with Edwards' chief concernment writes:[1]

'There are few names of the eighteenth century which have obtained such celebrity as that of Jonathan Edwards. Critics and historians down to our own day have praised in dithyrambic terms the logical vigour and the constructive powers of a writer whom they hold (as is done by Mackintosh, Dugald Stewart, Robert Hall, even Fichte) to be the greatest metaphysician America has yet produced. Who knows, they have asked themselves, to what heights this original genius might have risen, if, instead of being born in a half-savage country, far from the traditions of philosophy and science, he had appeared rather in our old world, and there received the direct impulse of the modern mind. Perhaps he would have taken a place between Leibniz and Kant among the founders of immortal systems, instead of the work he has left reducing itself to a sublime and barbarous theology, which astonishes our reason and outrages our heart, the object of at once our horror and admiration.'

Edwards' greatness is not, however, thus merely conjectural. He was no 'mute, inglorious Milton,' but the most articulate of men. Nor is it as a metaphysician that he makes his largest claim upon our admiration, subtle metaphysician as he showed himself to be. His ontological speculations, on which his title to recognition as a metaphysician mainly rests, belong to his extreme youth, and had been definitely put behind him at an age when most men first begin to probe such problems. It was, as Lyon indeed suggests, to theology that he gave his mature years and his most prolonged and searching thought, especially to the problems of sin and salvation. And these problems were approached by him not as purely theoretical, but as intensely practical ones. Therefore he was a man of action as truly as a man of thought, and powerfully wrought on his age, setting at work energies which have not yet spent their force. He is much more accurately characterized, therefore, by a philosopher of our own, who is as little in sympathy, however, with his main interests as Lyon himself. F. J. E. Woodbridge says:[2]

'He was distinctly a great man. He did not merely express the thought of his time or meet it simply in the spirit of his tradition. He stemmed it and moulded it. New England thought was already making towards that colorless theology which marked it later. That he checked. It was decidedly Arminian. He made it Calvinistic. . . . His time does not explain him.'

Edwards had a remarkable philosophical bent; but he had an even more remarkable sense and taste for Divine things; and, therefore (so Woodbridge concludes, with at least relative justice), 'we remember him not as the greatest of American philosophers, but as the greatest of American Calvinists.'

1. The period of Edwards' preparation.—It was a very decadent New England into which Edwards was born, on 5th Oct. 1703. The religious fervour which the Puritan immigrants had brought with them into the New World had not been able to

[1] Georges Lyon, *L'Idéalisme en Angleterre au xviiie siècle*, Paris, 1888, p. 406 f.

[2] *The Philosophical Review*, xiii. [1904] 405.

propagate itself unimpaired to the third and fourth generation. Already in 1678, Increase Mather had bewailed that 'the body of the rising generation is a poor, perishing, unconverted, and (except the Lord pour down His Spirit) an undone generation.'[1] There were general influences operative throughout Christendom at this epoch, depressing to the life of the spirit, which were not unfelt in New England; and these were reinforced there by the hardness of the conditions of existence in a raw land. Everywhere thinking and living alike were moving on a lowered plane; not merely spirituality but plain morality was suffering some eclipse. The churches felt compelled to recede from the high ideals which had been their heritage, and were introducing into their membership and admitting to their mysteries men who, though decent in life, made no profession of a change of heart. If only they had been themselves baptized, they were encouraged to offer their children for baptism (under the so-called 'Half-Way Covenant'), and to come themselves to the Table of the Lord (conceived as a 'converting ordinance'). The household into which Edwards was born, however, not only protected him from much of the evil which was pervading the community, but powerfully stimulated his spiritual and intellectual life. He began the study of Latin at the age of six, and by thirteen had acquired a respectable knowledge of 'the three learned languages' which at the time formed part of the curricula of the colleges—Latin, Greek, and Hebrew. Before he had completed his thirteenth year [Sept. 1716), he entered the 'Collegiate School of Connecticut' (afterwards Yale College). During his second year at college he fell in with Locke's *Essay concerning Human Understanding*, and 'had more satisfaction and pleasure in studying it,' he tells us himself,[2] 'than the most greedy miser in gathering up handfuls of silver and gold from some new-discovered treasure.' He graduated at the head of his class in 1720, when he was just short of seventeen years of age, but remained at college (as the custom of the time was) two years longer (to the summer of 1722) for the study of Divinity. In the summer of 1722 he was 'approbated' to preach, and from Aug. 1722 until April 1723 he supplied the pulpit of a little knot of Presbyterians in New York City.[3] Returning home, he was appointed tutor at Yale in June 1724, and filled this post with distinguished ability, during a most trying period in the life of the college, for the next two years (until Sept. 1726). His resignation of his tutorship was occasioned by an invitation to become the colleague and successor of his grandfather, Solomon Stoddard, in the pastorate of the church at Northampton, Mass., where, accordingly, he was ordained and installed on 15th Feb. 1727.

By his installation at Northampton, Edwards' period of preparation was brought to a close. His preparation had been remarkable, both intensively and extensively. Born with a drop of ink in his veins, Edwards had almost from infancy held a pen in his hand. From his earliest youth he had been accustomed to trace out on paper to its last consequence every fertile thought which came to him. A number of the early products of his observation and reflexion have been preserved, revealing a precocity which is almost beyond belief.

On this ground, indeed, Lyon, for example, refuses to believe in their genuineness. It is futile to adduce the parallel of a Pascal, he declares; such a comparison is much too modest; the young Edwards united in himself many Pascals, and, by a double miracle, combined with them gifts by virtue of which he far surpassed a Galileo and a Newton; what we are asked to believe is not merely that as a boy in his teens he worked out independently a system of metaphysics closely similar to that of Berkeley, but that he anticipated most of the scientific discoveries which constitute the glory of the succeeding century.

It is well to recognize that Lyon has permitted himself some slight exaggeration in stating his case, for the renewed examination of the MSS which he, and, following him, A. V. G. Allen asked for, has fully vindicated the youthful origin of these discussions.[1] There is, for instance, a bantering letter on the immateriality of the soul, full of marks of immaturity, no doubt, but equally full of the signs of promise, which was written in 1714-1715, when Edwards was ten years old. There are some very acute observations on the behaviour of spiders in spinning their webs which anticipate the results of modern investigation,[2] and which cannot have been written later than his thirteenth year. There are, above all, metaphysical discussions of 'Being,' 'Atoms,' and 'Prejudices of Imagination,' written at least as early as his junior year at college, that is to say, his sixteenth year, in which the fundamental principles of his Idealistic philosophy are fully set out. And, besides numerous other discussions following out these views, there is a long series of notes on natural science, filled with acute suggestions, which must belong to his Yale period. It is all, no doubt, very remarkable. But this only shows that Edwards was a very remarkable youth.

It is in these youthful writings that Edwards propounds his spiritualistic metaphysics, and it is chiefly on the strength of them that he holds a place in our histories of philosophy. His whole system is already present in substance in the essay 'Of Being,' which was written before he was sixteen years of age. And, though there is no reason to believe that he ever renounced the opinions set forth in these youthful discussions—there are, on the contrary, occasional suggestions, even in his latest writings, that they still lurked at the back of his brain—he never formally reverts to them subsequently to his Yale period (up to 1727).[3] His engagement with such topics belongs, therefore, distinctively to his formative period, before he became engrossed with the duties of the active ministry and the lines of thought more immediately called into exercise by them. In these early years, certainly independently of Berkeley,[4] and apparently with no suggestion from outside beyond what might be derived from Newton's explanations of light and colour, and Locke's treatment of sensation as the source of ideas, he worked out for himself a complete system of Idealism, which trembled indeed on the brink of mere phenomenalism, and might have betrayed him into Pantheism save for the intensity of his perception of the living God. 'Speaking most strictly,' he declares, 'there is no proper substance but God Himself.' The universe exists 'nowhere but in the Divine mind.' Whether this is true 'with respect to bodies only,' or of finite spirits as well, he seems at first to have wavered; ultimately he came to the more inclusive opinion.

He could write of the rise of a new thought: 'If we mean that there is some substance besides that thought, that brings that thought forth; if it be God, I acknowledge it, but if there be meant some thing else that has no properties, it seems to me absurd.'[5] Of 'all dependent existence whatever' he comes at last to affirm that it is 'in a constant flux,' 'renewed every moment, as the colours of bodies are every moment by the light that shines upon them; and all is constantly proceeding from God, as light from the sun.'[6] He did not mean by this, however, to sublimate the universe into 'shadows.' He was only attempting to declare that it has no other substrate but God: that its reality and persistence are grounded, not in

[1] H. M. Dexter, *Congregationalism in its Literature*, New York, 1880, p. 476, n. 36.

[2] Dwight's *Memoir*, prefixed to his ed. of Edwards' *Works*, i. 30.

[3] See E. H. Gillett, *Hist. of the Presbyterian Church*², Philadelphia, 1864, p. 38.

[1] See esp. Egbert G. Smyth, *Proc. Amer. Antiq. Soc.*, 23rd Oct. 1905, 'Some Early Writings of Jonathan Edwards, 1714-1726'; also *AJTh* i. [1897] 951; cf. H. N. Gardiner, *Jonathan Edwards: a Retrospect*, 1901.

[2] On these observations, see Egbert G. Smyth, *The Andover Review*, Jan. 1890; and Henry C. McCook, *PRR*, July 1890.

[3] Cf. President T. D. Woolsey, *Edwards Memorial*, Boston, 1870, pp. 32-33; and E. G. Smyth, *Proc. Amer. Antiq. Soc.*, 23rd Oct. 1905, p. 23; H. N. Gardiner, p. 117.

[4] So E. G. Smyth and H. N. Gardiner, *locc. citt.*; it is now known that he had not read Berkeley before 1730 (Dexter, *Some MSS of Jonathan Edwards*, as below).

[5] Dwight's *Memoir*, i. 713, 48; *AJTh* i. 957.

[6] *Original Sin* (*Works*, 4 vol. ed., New York, 1886, ii. 490).

some mysterious created 'substance' underlying the properties, but in the 'infinitely exact and precise Divine idea, together with an answerable, perfectly exact, precise, and stable will, with respect to corresponding communications to created minds and effects on their minds.'[1] He is engaged, in other words, in a purely ontological investigation, and his contention is merely that God is the *continuum* of all finite existence. He is as far as possible from denying the reality or persistence of these finite existences; they are to him real 'creations,' because they represent a fixed purpose and an established constitution of God.[2]

Edwards was not so absorbed in such speculations as to neglect the needs of his spirit. Throughout all these formative years he remained first of all a man of religion. He had been the subject of deep religious impressions from his earliest boyhood, and he gave himself, during this period of preparation, to the most assiduous and intense cultivation of his religious nature. 'I made seeking my salvation,' he himself tells us, 'the main business of my life.'[3] But about the time of his graduation (1720) a change came over him, which relieved the strain of his inward distress. From his childhood, his mind had revolted against the sovereignty of God: 'it used to appear like a horrible doctrine to me.' Now all this passed unobservedly away; and gradually, by a process he could not trace, this very doctrine came to be not merely a matter of course to him but a matter of rejoicing: 'The doctrine has often appeared exceedingly pleasant, bright, and sweet; absolute sovereignty is what I love to ascribe to God.' One day he was reading 1 Ti 1^{17} 'Now unto the King, eternal, immortal, invisible, the only wise God, be honour and glory, for ever and ever, Amen,' and, as he read, 'a sense of the glory of the Divine Being' took possession of him, 'a new sense, quite different from anything he ever experienced before.' He longed to be 'rapt up to Him in heaven, and be, as it were, swallowed up in Him for ever.'[4] From that moment his understanding of Divine things increased, and his enjoyment of God grew. There were, no doubt, intervals of depression. But, on the whole, his progress was steadily upwards and his consecration more and more complete. It was this devout young man, with the joy of the Lord in his heart, who turned his back in the early months of 1727 on his brilliant academic life and laid aside for ever his philosophical speculations, to take up the work of a pastor at Northampton.

2. Edwards the pastor.—Edwards was ordained co-pastor with his grandfather on 15th Feb. 1727, and on the latter's death, two years later, succeeded to the sole charge of the parish. Northampton was relatively a very important place. It was the county town, and nearly half of the area of the province lay within the county. It was, therefore, a sort of little local capital, and its people prided themselves on their culture, energy, and independence of mind. There was but the one church in the town, and it was probably the largest and most influential in the province, outside of Boston. It was not united in sentiment, being often torn with factional disputes. But, under the strong preaching of Solomon Stoddard, it had been repeatedly visited with revivals. These periods of awakening continued at intervals during Edwards' pastorate; the church became famous for them, and its membership was filled up by them. At one time the membership numbered 620, and included nearly the entire adult population of the town. Stoddard had been the protagonist for the laxer views of admission to Church-ordinances, and early in the century had introduced into the Northampton church the practice of opening the Lord's Supper to those who made no profession of conversion. In this practice Edwards at first acquiesced; but, becoming convinced that it was wrong, sought after a while to correct it, with disastrous consequences to himself. Meanwhile it had given to the membership of the church something of the character of a mixed multitude, which the circumstance that large numbers of them had been introduced in the religious excitement of revivals had tended to increase.

To the pastoral care of this important congregation, Edwards gave himself with single-hearted devotion. Assiduous house-to-house visitation did not, it is true, form part of his plan of work; but this did not argue carelessness or neglect; it was in accordance with his deliberate judgment of his special gifts and fitnesses. And, if he did not go to his people in their homes, save at the call of illness or special need, he encouraged them to come freely to him, and grudged neither time nor labour in meeting their individual requirements. He remained, of course, also a student, spending ordinarily from thirteen to fourteen hours daily in his study. This work did not separate itself from, but was kept strictly subsidiary to, his pastoral service. Not only had he turned his back definitely on the purely academic speculations which had engaged him so deeply at Yale, but he produced no purely theological works during the whole of his twenty-three years' pastorate at Northampton. His publications during this period, besides sermons, consisted only of treatises in practical Divinity. They deal principally with problems raised by the great religious awakenings in which his preaching was fruitful.

Such, for instance, are the *Narrative of Surprising Conversions*, published in 1736, the *Thoughts on the Revival of Religion in New England in 1740*, published in 1742, and that very searching study of the movements of the human soul under the excitement of religious motives called *A Treatise concerning Religious Affections*, published in 1746. Then there is the *Humble Attempt to Promote Explicit Agreement and Visible Union of God's People in Extraordinary Prayer for the Revival of Religion*, etc., published in 1749, which belongs to the same class, and the brief *Account of the Life of the Rev. David Brainerd*, published in the same year. There remains only the *Humble Inquiry into the Rules of the Word of God, concerning the Qualifications requisite to a Complete Standing in Full Communion in the Visible Church of God*, published in 1749, along with which should be mentioned the defence of its positions against Solomon Williams, entitled *Misrepresentations Corrected and Truth Vindicated*, although this was not published until somewhat later (1752). No doubt there was much more than this written during these score or more of years, for Edwards was continually adding to the mass of his manuscript treasures; and some of these voluminous 'observations' have since been put into print, although the greater part of them remain yet in the note-books where he wrote them.

It was in his sermons that Edwards' studies bore their richest fruit. He did not spare himself in his public instruction. He not only faithfully filled the regular appointments of the church, but freely undertook special discourses and lectures, and during times of 'attention to religion' went frequently to the aid of the neighbouring churches. From the first he was recognized as a remarkable preacher, as arresting and awakening as he was instructive. Filled himself with the profoundest sense of the heinousness of sin, as an offence against the majesty of God and an outrage of His love, he set himself to arouse his hearers to some realization of the horror of their condition as objects of the Divine displeasure, and of the incredible goodness of God in intervening for their salvation. Side by side with the most moving portrayal of God's love in Christ, and of the blessedness of communion with Him, he therefore set, with the most startling effect, equally vivid

[1] Dwight, i. 674.

[2] On Edwards' early Idealism, see esp. Egbert C. Smyth, *AJTh* i. 959–960; G. P. Fisher, *Discussions in Hist. and Theol.* 229–30; H. N. Gardiner, 115–160; J. H. MacCracken, 'The Sources of Jonathan Edwards' Idealism,' in the *Philosophical Review*, xi. [1902] 26 ff.; also G. Lyon, *loc. cit.*; and I. W. Riley, *American Philosophy: The early Schools*, New York, 1907.

[3] Dwight, i. 59.

[4] *Ib.* 60.

pictures of the dangers of unforgiven sin and the terrors of the lost estate. The effect of such preaching, delivered with the force of the sincerest conviction, was overwhelming. A great awakening began in the church at the end of 1735, in which more than 300 converts were gathered in,[1] and which extended throughout the churches of the Connecticut valley. In connexion with a visit from Whitefield in 1740 another wave of religious fervour was started, which did not spend its force until it covered the whole land. No one could recognize more fully than Edwards the evil that mixes with the good in such seasons of religious excitement. He diligently sought to curb excesses, and earnestly endeavoured to separate the chaff from the wheat. But no one could protest more strongly against casting out the wheat with the chaff. He subjected all the phenomena of the revivals in which he participated to the most searching analytical study; and, while sadly acknowledging that much self-deception was possible, and that the rein could only too readily be given to false 'enthusiasm,' he earnestly contended that a genuine work of grace might find expression in mental and even physical excitement. It was one of the incidental fruits of these revivals that, as we have seen, he gave to the world in a series of studies perhaps the most thorough examination of the phenomena of religious excitement it has yet received, and certainly, in his great treatise on the *Religious Affections*, one of the most complete systems of what has been strikingly called 'spiritual diagnostics' it possesses.

For twenty-three years Edwards pursued his fruitful ministry at Northampton; under his guidance the church became a city set on a hill to which all eyes were turned. But in the reaction from the revival of 1740–1742 conditions arose which caused him great searchings of heart, and led ultimately to his separation from his congregation. In this revival, practically the whole adult population of the town was brought into the church; they were admitted under the excitement of the time and under a ruling introduced as long before as 1704 by Stoddard, which looked upon all the ordinances of the church, including the Lord's Supper, as 'converting ordinances,' not presupposing, but adapted to bring about, a change of heart. As time passed, it became evident enough that a considerable body of the existing membership of the church had not experienced that change of heart by which alone they could be constituted Christians, and indeed they made no claim to have done so. On giving serious study to the question for himself, Edwards became convinced that participation in the Lord's Supper could properly be allowed only to those professing real 'conversion.' It was his duty as pastor and guide of his people to guard the Lord's Table from profanation, and he was not a man to leave unperformed a duty clearly perceived. Two obvious measures presented themselves to him—unworthy members of the church must be exscinded by discipline, and greater care must be exercised in receiving new applicants for membership. No doubt discipline was among the functions which the Church claimed to exercise; but the practice of it had fallen much into decay as a sequence to the lowered conception which had come to be entertained of the requirements for church membership. The door of admission to the Lord's Supper, on the other hand, had been formally set wide open; and this loose policy had been persisted in for half a century, and had become traditional. What Edwards felt himself compelled to undertake, it will be seen, was a return in theory and practice to the original platform of the Congregational churches, which conceived the Church to be, in the strictest sense of the words, 'a company of saints by calling,' among whom there should be permitted to enter nothing that was not clean.[1] This, which should have been his strength, and which ultimately gave the victory to the movement which he inaugurated throughout the churches of New England,[2] was in his own personal case his weakness. It gave a radical appearance to the reforms which he advocated, which he himself was far from giving to them. It is not necessary to go into the details of the controversy regarding a case of discipline, which emerged in 1744, or the subsequent difficulties (1748–9) regarding the conditions of admission to the Lord's Supper. The result was that, after a sharp contest running through two years, Edwards was dismissed from his pastorate on 22nd June 1750.

3. Edwards the theologian.—By his dismissal from his church at Northampton, in his forty-seventh year, the second period of Edwards' life—the period of strenuous pastoral labour—was brought to an abrupt close. After a few months he removed to the little frontier hamlet (there were only twelve white families resident there) of Stockbridge, as missionary of the 'Society in London for Propagating the Gospel in New England and the Parts Adjacent' to the Housatonic Indians gathered there, and as pastor of the little church of white settlers. In this exile he hoped to find leisure to write, in defence of the Calvinistic system against the rampant 'Arminianism' of the day, the works which he had long had in contemplation, and for which he had made large preparation. Peace and quiet he did not find; he was embroiled from the first in a trying struggle against the greed and corruption of the administrators of the funds designed for the benefit of the Indians. But he made, if he could not find, the requisite leisure. It was at Stockbridge that he wrote the treatises on which his fame as a theologian chiefly rests: the great works on the Will (written in 1753, published in 1754), and Original Sin (in the press when he died, 1758), the striking essays on *The End for which God created the World*, and the *Nature of True Virtue* (published 1768, after his death), and the unfinished *History of Redemption* (publ. 1772). No doubt he utilized for these works material previously collected. He lived practically with his pen in his hand, and accumulated an immense amount of written matter—his 'best thoughts,' as it has been felicitously called. The work on the Will, indeed, had itself been long on the stocks. We find him making diligent studies for it already at the opening of 1747;[3] and, though his work on it was repeatedly interrupted for long intervals,[4] he tells us that before he left Northampton he 'had made considerable preparation and was deeply engaged in the prosecution of this design.'[5] The rapid completion of the book in the course of a few months in 1753 was not, therefore, so wonderful a feat as it might otherwise appear. Nevertheless, it is the seven years at Stockbridge which deserve to be called the fruitful years of Edwards' theological

[1] More than 550 members were added to the church at Northampton during Edwards' pastorate (see Solomon Clark, *Histor. Catalogue of Northampton First Church*, 1891, pp. 40-47).

[1] According to the organic law of the Congregational churches (the Cambridge Platform), 'saints by calling' are 'such as have not only attained the knowledge of the principles of religion, and are free from gross and open scandals, but also do, together with the profession of their faith and repentance, walk in blameless obedience to the word.'

[2] Cf. H. N. Gardiner, *Selected Sermons*, p. xii.

[3] Letter to Joseph Bellamy, 15th Jan. 1747, printed by F. B. Dexter, *The MSS of Jonathan Edwards* (reprinted from the *Proc. of Mass. Hist. Soc.*, Mar. 1901), p. 13; Letter to John Erskine, 22nd Jan. 1747, reconstructed by Dwight, i. 249-250, but since come to light (*Exercises Commemorating the Two-Hundredth Anniversary of Jonathan Edwards, held at Andover Theological Seminary*, p. 63 of the Appendix).

[4] Dwight, i. 251, 270, 411.

[5] *Ib.* 506, 532, 537.

work. They were interrupted in the autumn of 1757 by an invitation to him to become the President of the College of New Jersey, at Princeton, in succession to his son-in-law, Aaron Burr. It was with great reluctance that he accepted this call; it seemed to him to threaten the prevention of what he had thought to make his life-work—the preparation, to wit, of a series of volumes on all the several parts of the Arminian controversy.[1] But the college at Princeton, which had been founded and thus far carried on by men whose sympathies were with the warm-hearted, revivalistic piety to which his own life had been dedicated, had claims upon him which he could not disown. On the advice of a council of his friends,[2] therefore, he accepted the call and removed to Princeton to take up his new duties, in January 1758. There he was inoculated for smallpox on 13th Feb., and died of this disease on 27th March in the fifty-fifth year of his age.

The peculiarity of Edwards' theological work is due to the union in it of the richest religious sentiment with the highest intellectual powers. He was first of all a man of faith, and it is this that gives its character to his whole life and all its products; but his strong religious feeling had at its disposal a mental force and logical acuteness of the first order; he was at once deeply emotional, and, as Ezra Stiles called him, a 'strong reasoner.' His analytical subtlety has probably never been surpassed; but with it was combined a broad grasp of religious truth which enabled him to see it as a whole, and to deal with its several parts without exaggeration and with a sense of their relations in the system. The system to which he gave his sincere adhesion, and to the defence of which, against the tendencies which were in his day threatening to undermine it, he consecrated all his powers, was simply Calvinism. From this system as it had been expounded by its chief representatives he did not consciously depart in any of its constitutive elements. The breadth and particularity of his acquaintance with it in its classical expounders, and the completeness of his adoption of it in his own thought, are frequently underestimated. There is a true sense in which he was a man of thought rather than of learning. There were no great libraries accessible in Western Massachusetts in the middle of the 18th century. His native disposition to reason out for himself the subjects which were presented to his thought was reinforced by his habits of study; it was his custom to develop on paper, to its furthest logical consequences, every topic of importance to which his attention was directed. He lived in the 'age of reason,' and was in this respect a true child of his time.[3] In the task which he undertook, furthermore, an appeal to authority would have been useless; it was uniquely to the court of reason that he could hale the adversaries of the Calvinistic system. Accordingly it is only in his more didactic—as distinguished from controversial—treatise on *Religious Affections*, that Edwards cites with any frequency earlier writers in support of his positions. The reader must guard himself, however, from the illusion that Edwards was not himself conscious of the support of earlier writers beneath him.[4] His acquaintance with the masters of the system of thought he was defending, for example, was wide and minute. Amesius and Wollebius had been his text-books at college. The well-selected library at Yale, we may be sure, had been thoroughly explored by him; at the close of his divinity studies, he speaks of the reading of 'doctrinal books or books of controversy' as if it were part of his daily business.[1] As would have been expected, he fed himself on the great Puritan divines, and formed not merely his thought but his life upon them. We find him in his youth, for instance, diligently using Manton's *Sermons on the 119th Psalm* as a spiritual guide; and in his rare allusions to authorities in his works, he betrays familiarity with such writers as William Perkins, John Preston, Thomas Blake, Anthony Burgess, Stephen Charnock, John Flavel, Theophilus Gale, Thomas Goodwin, John Owen, Samuel Rutherford, Thomas Shephard, Richard Sibbes, John Smith the Platonist, and Samuel Clark the Arian. Even his contemporaries he knew and estimated at their true values: Isaac Watts and Philip Doddridge as a matter of course; and also Thomas Boston, the scheme of thought of whose *View of the Covenant of Grace* he confessed he did not understand, but whose *Fourfold State of Man* he 'liked exceedingly well.'[2] His Calvin he certainly knew thoroughly, though he would not swear in his words;[3] and also his Turretin, whom he speaks of as 'the great Turretine';[4] while van Mastricht he declares 'much better' than even Turretin, 'or,' he adds with some fervour, 'than any other book in the world excepting the Bible, in my opinion.'[5] The close agreement of his teaching with that of the best esteemed Calvinistic divines is, therefore, both conscious and deliberate; his omission to appeal to them does not argue either ignorance or contempt; it is incident to his habitual manner and to the special task he was prosecuting. In point of fact, what he teaches is just the 'standard' Calvinism in its completeness.

As an independent thinker, he is, of course, not without his individualisms, and that in conception no less than in expression. His explanation of the identity of the human race with its Head, founded as it is on a doctrine of personal identity which reduces it to an 'arbitrary constitution' of God, binding its successive moments together, is peculiar to himself.[6] In answering objections to the doctrine of Original Sin, he appeals at one point to Stapfer, and speaks, after him, in the language of that form of doctrine known as 'mediate imputation.'[7] But this is only in order to illustrate his own view that all mankind are one as truly as and by the same kind of Divine constitution that an individual life is one in its consecutive moments. Even in this immediate context he does not teach the doctrine of 'mediate imputation,' insisting rather that, Adam and his posterity being in the strictest sense one, in them no less than in him 'the guilt arising from the first existing of a depraved disposition' cannot at all be distinguished from 'the guilt of Adam's first sin'; and elsewhere throughout the treatise he speaks in the terms of the common Calvinistic doctrine. His most marked individualism, however, lay in the region of philosophy rather than of theology. In an essay on *The Nature of True Virtue*, he develops, in opposition to the view that all virtue may be reduced ultimately to self-love, an eccentric theory of virtue

1 Dwight, i. 251.
2 Dwight (i. 576) was not able to ascertain all the facts concerning this council; Ezra Stiles, *Diary*, New York, 1901, iii. 4, supplies interesting details.
3 Cf. the discussion of Edwards' 'rationalism,' by Jan Ridderbos, *De Theologie van Jonathan Edwards*, 310–313.
4 Hopkins tells us that 'he had an enormous thirst for knowledge, in the pursuit of which he spared no cost or pains. He read all the books, especially books treating of theology, that he could procure, from which he could hope to derive any assistance in the discovery of truth.' From his youth up, however, he disliked a display of learning. In his earliest maxims, by the side of 'Let much modesty be seen in the style,' he sets this other: 'Let it not look as if I was much read, or was conversant with books, or with the learned world' (Dwight, i. 41 f.).

1 Dwight, i. 93. 2 *Ib.* 242.
3 Preface to the treatise on the Will, Dwight, ii. 13.
4 *Works*, New York ed. 1856, iii. 123.
5 Letter to Joseph Bellamy, 15th Jan. 1747, printed by F. B. Dexter, 13.
6 *Works*, 4 vol. ed., ii. 486 ff.; Dwight, ii. 555 f.
7 *Works*, 4 vol. ed., ii. 483 f.; Dwight, ii. 544.

as consisting in love to being in general. But of this again we hear nothing elsewhere in his works, though it became germinal for the New England theology of the next age. Such individualisms in any case are in no way characteristic of his teaching. He strove after no show of originality. An independent thinker he certainly claimed to be, and 'utterly disclaimed a dependence,' say, 'on Calvin,' in the sense of 'believing the doctrines he held because Calvin believed and taught them.'[1] This very disclaimer is, however, a proclamation of agreement with Calvin, though not as if he 'believed everything just as Calvin taught'; he is only solicitous that he should be understood to be not a blind follower of Calvin, but a convinced defender of Calvinism. His one concern was, accordingly, not to improve on the Calvinism of the great expounders of the system, but to place the main elements of the Calvinistic system, as commonly understood, beyond cavil. His marvellous invention was employed, therefore, only in the discovery and development of the fullest and most convincing possible array of arguments in their favour. This is true even of his great treatise on the Will. This is, in the common judgment, the greatest of all his treatises, and the common judgment here is right.[2] But the doctrine of this treatise is precisely the doctrine of the Calvinistic schoolmen. 'The novelty of the treatise,' we have been well told long ago,[3] 'lies not in the position it takes and defends, but in the multitude of proofs, the fecundity and urgency of the arguments by which he maintains it.' Edwards' originality thus consists less in the content of his thought than in his manner of thinking. He enters into the great tradition which had come down to him, and 'infuses it with his personality and makes it live,' and the vitality of his thought gives to its product the value of a unique creation.[4] The effect of Edwards' labours was quite in the line of his purpose, and not disproportionate to his greatness. The movement against Calvinism which was overspreading the land was in a great measure checked, and the elimination of Calvinism as a determining factor in the thought of New England, which seemed to be imminent as he wrote, was postponed for more than a hundred years.[5]

4. The New England theology.—It was Edwards' misfortune that he gave his name to a party; and to a party which, never in perfect agreement with him in its doctrinal ideas, finished by becoming the earnest advocate of (as it has been sharply expressed[6]) 'a set of opinions which he gained his chief celebrity by demolishing.' The affiliation of this party with Edwards was very direct. 'Bellamy and Hopkins,' says G. P. Fisher,[7] tracing the descent, 'were pupils of Edwards; from Hopkins West derived his theology; Smalley studied with Bellamy, and Emmons with Smalley.' But the inheritance of the party from Edwards showed itself much more strongly on the practical than on the doctrinal side. Its members were the heirs of his revivalist zeal and of his awakening preaching; they also imitated his attempt to purify the Church by discipline and strict guarding of the Lord's Table—in a word, to restore the Church to its Puritan ideal of a congregation of saints.[8]

[1] Dwight, ii. 13.
[2] Cf. F. J. E. Woodbridge, in *The Philosophical Review*, xiii. [1904] 396; and G. Lyon, *op. cit.* 412.
[3] Lyman H. Atwater, *Biblical Repertory and Princeton Review*, xxx. [1858] 597.
[4] H. N. Gardiner, *Selected Sermons*, p. xvii.
[5] Cf. Williston Walker, *Ten New England Leaders*, 232.
[6] Lyman H. Atwater, 589; cf. J. Ridderbos, 320 f.
[7] *A Discourse Commemorative of the History of the Church of Christ in Yale College during the First Century of its Existence*, 1858, p. 36.
[8] On the 'rigidity' of the New Divinity men in 'Church administration' and 'discipline,' see the interesting details in Ezra Stiles' *Diary*, iii. 273 f., 343 f., 358 f.

Pressing to extremes in both matters, as followers will, the 'Edwardeans' or 'New Divinity' men became a ferment in the churches of New England, and, creating discussion and disturbances everywhere, gradually won their way to dominance. Meanwhile their doctrinal teaching was continually suffering change. As Fisher (p. 7) puts it, 'in the process of defending the established faith, they were led to re-cast it in new forms and to change its aspect.' Only, it was not merely the form and aspect of their inherited faith, but its substance, that they were steadily transforming. Accordingly, Fisher proceeds to explain that what on this side constituted their common character was not so much a common doctrine as a common method: 'the fact that their views were the result of independent reflection and were maintained on philosophical grounds.' Here, too, they were followers of Edwards; but in their exaggeration of his rational method, without his solid grounding in the history of thought, they lost continuity with the past and became the creators of a 'New England theology' which it is only right frankly to describe as provincial.[1]

The men who worked out this theological transmutation were men of high character, great intellectual gifts, immense energy of thought, and what may almost be called fatal logical facility. Any people might be proud to have produced in the course of a century such a series of 'strong reasoners' on religious themes as Joseph Bellamy (1719–1790), Samuel Hopkins (1720–1803), Stephen West (1759–1818), John Smalley (1739–1820), Jonathan Edwards, Jr. (1745–1801), Nathaniel Emmons (1745–1840), Timothy Dwight (1752–1817), Eleazar T. Fitch (1791–1871), and Nathaniel W. Taylor (1786–1858)—all, with the single exception of the younger Edwards, graduates of Yale College; not to speak of yet others of equal powers, lying more off the line of direct development, like Leonard Woods (1774–1854), Bennet Tyler (1783–1858), Edward D. Griffin (1770–1837), Moses Stuart (1780–1852), Lyman Beecher (1775–1863), Charles G. Finney (1792–1875), Leonard Bacon (1802–1881), Horace Bushnell (1802–1876), and Edwards A. Park (1808–1900).

It is a far cry from Jonathan Edwards the Calvinist, defending with all the force of his unsurpassed reasoning powers the doctrine of a determined will, and commending a theory of virtue which identified it with general benevolence, to Nathaniel W. Taylor the Pelagianizer, building his system upon the doctrine of the power to the contrary as its foundation stone, and reducing all virtue ultimately to self-love. Taylor's teaching, in point of fact, was in many respects the exact antipodes of Edwards', and very fairly reproduced the congeries of tendencies which the latter considered it his life-work to withstand. Yet Taylor looked upon himself as an 'Edwardean,' though in him the outcome of the long development received its first appropriate designation—the 'New Haven Divinity.' Its several successive phases were bound together by the no doubt external circumstance that they were taught in general by men who had received their training at New Haven.

The growth of the New Divinity to that dominance in the theological thought of New England from which it derives its claim to be called 'the New England Theology' was gradual, though somewhat rapid. Samuel Hopkins tells us that at the beginning—in 1756—there were not more than four or five 'who espoused the sentiments which since have been called "Edwardean" and "New Divinity"; and since, after some improvement was made upon them, "Hopkintonian" or "Hopkinsian" sentiments.'[2] The younger Edwards still spoke of them in 1777 as a small party.[3] In 1787, Ezra Stiles, chafing under their growing influence and marking the increasing divergence of views among themselves, fancied he saw their end approaching.

[1] Cf. Woodbridge, 394.
[2] Park, *Life of Hopkins*, Boston, 1854, p. 23; Fisher, *Discussions*, etc., 80.
[3] Ezra Stiles, ii. 227; Fisher, *loc. cit.*

'It has been the Ton,' he writes,[1] 'to direct Students of divinity these thirty years past or a generation to read the Bible, President Edwards', Dr. Bellamy's, and Mr. Hopkins' writings—and that was a good sufficiency of reading.' But now, 'the New Divinity gentlemen are getting into confusion and running into different statements.' 'The younger Class, but yet in full vigor, suppose they see further than those Oracles, and are disposed to become Oracles themselves, and wish to write Theology and have their own books come into vogue.' He thought these 'confusions' the beginning of the end.

In this he was mistaken: the New Divinity, in the person of Timothy Dwight, succeeded him as President of Yale College, and through a long series of years was infused into generation after generation of students.[2] The 'confusions' Stiles observed were, however, real; or, rather, the progressive giving way of the so-called Edwardeans to those tendencies of thought to which they were originally set in opposition.

We note Hopkins already conscious of divergence from Edwards' teaching—a divergence which he calls an 'improvement.' Ezra Stiles tells us that in 1787 the New Divinity men were beginning to 'deny a real vicarious Suffering in Christ's Atonement,' and were 'generally giving up the Doctrine of *Imputation* both in *Original Sin* and in *Justification*'; and some of them, 'receding from disinterested Benevolence, are giving in to the idea that all holy Motive operates as terminating in personal happiness,'[3]—a very fair statement of the actual drift.

The younger Edwards drew up a careful account of what he deemed the (ten) 'Improvements in Theology made by President Edwards and those who have followed his course of thought.'[4] Three of the most cardinal of these he does not pretend were introduced by Edwards, attributing them simply to those whom he calls Edwards' 'followers.' These are the substitution of the Governmental (Grotian) for the Satisfaction doctrine of the Atonement, in the accomplishment of which he himself, with partial forerunners in Bellamy and West, was the chief agent; the discarding of the doctrine of the imputation of sin in favour of the view that men are condemned for their own personal sin only—a contention which was made in an extreme form by Nathaniel Emmons, who confined all moral quality to acts of volition, and afterwards became a leading element in Nathaniel W. Taylor's system; and the perversion of Edwards' distinction between 'natural' and 'moral' inability so as to ground on the 'natural' ability of the unregenerate, after the fashion introduced by Samuel Hopkins[5]—a theory of the capacities and duties of men without the Spirit, which afterwards, in the hands of Nathaniel W. Taylor, became the core of a new Pelagianizing system.

The external victory of the New Divinity in New England was marked doubtless by the election of Timothy Dwight to the Presidency of Yale College (1797); and certainly it could have found no one better fitted to commend it to moderate men; probably no written system of theology has ever enjoyed wider acceptance than Dwight's *Sermons*.[6] But after Dwight came Taylor, and in the teaching of the latter the downward movement of the New Divinity ran out into a system which turned, as on its hinge, upon the Pelagianizing doctrines of the native sinlessness of the race, the plenary ability of the sinner to renovate his own soul, and self-love or the desire for happiness as the spring of all voluntary action. From this extreme some reaction was inevitable, and the history of the so-called 'New England Theology' closes with the moderate reaction of the teaching of Edwards A. Park. Park was of that line of theological descent which came through Hopkins, Emmons, and Woods; but he sought to incorporate into his system all that seemed to him to be the results of New England thinking for the century which preceded him, not excepting the extreme positions of Taylor himself. Reverting so far from Taylor as to return to perhaps a somewhat more deterministic doctrine of the will, he was able to rise above Taylor in his doctrines of election and regeneration, and to give to the general type of thought which he represented a lease of life for another generation. But, with the death of Park in 1900, the history of 'New England Theology' seems to come to an end.[1]

1 Ezra Stiles, iii. 273–5.

2 Young Theodore D. Woolsey in 1822 can speak of 'Hopkinsianism' as 'a sort of net which catches all but the Presbyterian eels, who slip through.' It had become, he says, 'a general term which comprehends all who are not Arminians and disagree with Turretin on the Atonement' (*Yale Review*, Jan. 1912 [i. 2], p. 246).

3 iii. 273 f.

4 Published in Dwight, i. 613 ff.

5 Cf. G. N. Boardman, *Hist. of New England Theology*, 50.

6 Cf. G. P. Fisher, *A Sermon*, etc., 57: 'No work in systematic divinity has had such currency and authority in Great Britain, at least outside the Established Church of England, as the Sermons of Dr. Dwight. In that country they have passed through not less than forty editions.'

LITERATURE.—(*A*) A list of Edwards' works is given by Dwight, i. 765 ff.; S. Miller, 254 ff., and Ridderbos, 327 ff. (*opp. citt. infra*). A brief bibliography will be found in Allen, *op. cit. infra*, 391 ff. The first edition of Edwards' Works was in 8 vols., ed. S. Austin, Worcester, Mass. 1808–1809. This edition has been frequently reproduced in 4 vols.: New York, 1844, 1852, 1856, 1863, 1881. A new and enlarged edition in 10 vols., ed. S. E. Dwight, vol. i. being a Memoir, appeared at New York, 1829. An edition was published at London in 8 vols., 1837, to which 2 supplementary vols. were added, Edinburgh, 1847. Later British editions are: London, 1840, with Dwight's Memoir and an Essay by H. Rogers; London, 1865 (Bohn), in 2 vols. Additional writings of Edwards have been published: *Charity and Its Fruits*, ed. Tryon Edwards, London, 1852 (subsequently re-issued under the title *Christian Love in the Heart and Life*[6], Philadelphia, 1875); *Selections from the Unpublished Writings of Jonathan Edwards*, edited with an introduction by A. B. Grosart, Edinburgh, 1865; *Observations concerning the Scripture Economy of the Trinity*, edited with an introduction by Egbert C. Smyth, New York, 1880; *An Unpublished Essay of Edwards on the Trinity*, edited with an introduction by George P. Fisher, New York, 1904; *Selected Sermons of Jonathan Edwards*, edited with an introduction and notes by H. N. Gardiner, New York and London, 1904 (contains one new sermon).

(*B*) For life, etc., see S. Hopkins, *Life and Character of the late Rev. Mr. Jonathan Edwards*, Boston, 1765, Northampton, 1804; S. E. Dwight, *Memoir*, being vol. i. of his edition of the Works (see above), New York, 1829; S. Miller, *Life of Jonathan Edwards*, Boston, 1837 and 1848 (vol. viii. of first series of Jared Sparks' *The Library of American Biography*); A. V. G. Allen, *Jonathan Edwards*, Boston, 1889; Williston Walker, *Ten New England Leaders*, Boston and New York, 1901, pp. 215–263, also *Hist. of the Congregational Churches in the U.S.*, New York, 1894, chs. vii. viii. ix.; [Joseph Tracey] *The Great Awakening*, etc., Boston, 1842.

(*C*) The most comprehensive survey of Edwards' theological teaching is given by Jan Ridderbos, *De Theologie van Jonathan Edwards*, The Hague, 1907; see also G. P. Fisher, *Discussions in History and Theology*, New York, 1880, pp. 227–252; Noah Porter, 'Edwards' Peculiarity as a Theologian,' in *The New Englander*, xviii. 737 f.; H. N. Gardiner, *Jonathan Edwards: a Retrospect*, etc., Boston and New York, 1901; *Exercises Commemorating the Two-Hundredth Anniversary of the Birth of Jonathan Edwards, held at Andover Theological Seminary*, Andover, 1904.

(*D*) The New England Theology should be studied in the works of its chief exponents. Lives of many of them are also accessible. See also F. H. Foster, *Genetic Hist. of New England Theol.*, Chicago, 1907; G. N. Boardman, *Hist. of New Eng. Theol.*, New York, 1899; C. Hodge, *Princeton Essays*, first series, 1846, pp. 285–307, second series, 1847, pp. 206–235, *Essays and Reviews*, 1856, pp. 539–633; Lyman H. Atwater, *Biblical Repertory and Princeton Review*, xxvi. (1854) 217–246, xxx. (1858) 585–620, xxxi. (1859) 489–538, xl. (1868) 368–398; Edwards A. Park, *The Atonement*, etc., Boston, 1859; G. P. Fisher, *Discussions*, etc., 285–354; H. B. Smith, *Faith and Philosophy*, New York, 1877, pp. 215–264.

BENJAMIN B. WARFIELD.

EGO (a term [Lat. 1st personal pronoun = 'I'] for 'self,' used in various languages).—The conception of the Ego is very perplexing. It is difficult to describe its content, and to discover a fundamental principle which will serve to distinguish it satisfactorily from the non-Ego. If, starting from its etymology, we say an Ego is a self-conscious being, one who knows himself and is able to say 'I,' and proceed to ask what the Ego so defined is, we get different answers. Descartes called it a

1 Cf. F. H. Foster, *Genetic History*, etc., Chicago, 1907, 'Conclusion,' pp. 543–553, where the fact is fully recognized, though the reasons assigned for it are questionable.

'thinking thing,' including, under the term 'thinking,' understanding, affirming, denying, willing, refusing, imagining, perceiving (*Meditation II.*). Thinking is a quality; qualities inhere in substances; for it cannot be that a quality is a quality of nothing. By substance is meant a 'thing existing in such a way as to stand in need of nothing else in order to its existence' (*Principles*, § 51). There is only one absolutely independent being, namely, God. A finite mind, however, is dependent on nothing but the 'concurrence of God.' It is not dependent on body; for, Descartes contends, it can be thought to exist when the existence of body is doubted; and it does not need a place in order that it may exist. Its existence is involved in thinking—'as long as I think, I am' (*Med. II.*). Yet Descartes has to recognize that bodily and mental substances are so intimately related in man that some of the experiences of the Ego—pain, hunger, thirst, etc., which he calls confused modes of thinking—arise from this union. He tends to deny mind to animals.

An examination of the content of self-consciousness, however, shows that the line drawn between the self and the not-self is not always drawn by Egos themselves in the way Descartes draws it. At times some of our inner states are excluded from our conception of ourselves. We identify ourselves, *e.g.*, with what we want to be, with the ideals we have taken as our own. When we forget these and act on other motives, we say that we have forgotten *ourselves*. At other times the body and even objects outside the body are included in the conception of self.

'Between what a man calls *me* and what he simply calls mine the line is difficult to draw. We feel and act about certain things that are ours very much as we feel and act about ourselves. Our fame, our children, the work of our hands, may be as dear to us as our bodies are, and arouse the same feelings and the same acts of reprisal if attacked. And our bodies themselves, are they simply ours, or are they *us*? Certainly men have been known to disown their very bodies, and to regard them as mere vestures, or even as prisons of clay from which they should some day be glad to escape.

We see, then, that we are dealing with a fluctuating material, the same object being sometimes treated as a part of me, at other times as simply mine, and then again as if I had nothing to do with it at all. *In its widest possible sense, however, a man's* ME *is the sum-total of all that he* CAN *call his*, not only his body and his psychic powers, but his clothes, and his house, his wife and children, his ancestors and friends, his reputation and works, his lands and horses, and yacht and bank account. All these things give him the same emotions. If they wax and prosper, he feels triumphant; if they dwindle and die away, he feels cast down—not necessarily in the same degree for each thing, but in much the same way for all' (W. James, *Text-book of Psychology*, 1892, ch. xii. p. 176 f.).

Philosophical reflexion seems to confirm the conclusion drawn from a psychological analysis of the content of self-consciousness. The self cannot be separated from what it knows, feels, and reacts upon, without being destroyed. If it knew nothing of the world, it would apparently be empty of content. It lives and grows by the dual process of appropriating all things related to it, and at once distinguishing itself from them. Its nature, as MacTaggart observes, is very paradoxical.

'What does it include?' he asks. 'Everything of which it is conscious. What does it exclude? Equally—everything of which it is conscious. What can it say is not inside it? Nothing. What can it say is not outside it? A single abstraction. And any attempt to remove the paradox destroys the self. For the two sides are inevitably connected. If we try to make it a distinct individual by separating it from all other things, it loses all content of which it can be conscious, and so loses the very individuality which we started by trying to preserve. If, on the other hand, we try to save its content by emphasising the inclusion at the expense of the exclusion, then the consciousness vanishes, and, since the self has no contents but the objects of which it is conscious, the contents vanish also' (*Studies in Hegelian Cosmology*, 1901, § 27).

Descartes' assertion that the Ego, as we know it now, is a thinking substance independent of its own and other bodies cannot therefore be justified by an appeal to immediate consciousness, psychological analysis, or philosophical reflexion. That after death other objects take the place of bodies may, of course, be quite possible. But dependent relation to objects seems an inexpugnable element of our conception of it. Whether bodies have themselves substantial existence is a question which will concern us again. At present we have to consider the question whether the Ego can be intelligibly called a substance. Substance is represented by Descartes as that in which qualities inhere. It is, in Locke's words, their 'unknown support.' We do not know, Locke says, what a substance is. It cannot be perceived by the outer or inner sense. There is no idea of it in the mind, and so we can give no intelligible account of its relation to the qualities which it is supposed to support. Hence, to say that qualities inhere in substances is, according to Locke, to say nothing more than that they exist together.[1] Why, then, assume the existence of substances? Berkeley, following after Locke, asked this question regarding material substance, and denied its existence. Hume asked it of mental substance, and denied the existence of the Ego.

'I have no immediate intuition [of matter],' said Berkeley; 'neither can I immediately from my sensations, ideas, notions, actions, or passions infer an unthinking, unperceiving, inactive Substance—either by probable deduction, or necessary consequence.' The physical world is nothing but a floating system of ideas (*Third Dialogue between Hylas and Philonous*).

'For my part,' said Hume, 'when I enter most intimately into what I call *myself*, I always stumble on some particular perception or other, of heat or cold, light or shade, love or hatred, pain or pleasure. I never can catch *myself* at any time without a perception, and never can observe anything but the perception.' A mind is 'nothing but a bundle or collection of different perceptions, which succeed each other with an inconceivable rapidity, and are in a perpetual flux and movement' (*Human Nature*, bk. i. pt. iv. sec. 6).

'The final result of Hume's reasoning,' says Huxley, 'comes to this: As we use the name of body for the sum of the phenomena which make up our corporeal existence, so we employ the name of soul for the sum of the phenomena which constitute our mental existence; and we have no more reason, in the latter case, than in the former, to suppose that there is anything beyond the phenomena which answers to the name. In the case of the soul, as in that of the body, the idea of substance is a mere fiction of the imagination. This conclusion is nothing but a rigorous application of Berkeley's reasoning concerning matter and mind, and it is fully adopted by Kant' (*Hume*, 1879, p. 171 f.).

The last quotation represents Huxley's own opinion also. The individual mind is held to be a series of mental phenomena parallel with the series of material phenomena which compose the corresponding individual body. The series do not interact. In place of Descartes' dualism of substances we have a dualism of material and mental phenomena. (For an adverse criticism of this theory, see J. Ward, *Naturalism and Agnosticism*², 1903, vol. ii. pt. iii.; and McDougall, *Body and Mind*, 1911, ch. xii.)

Reflexion on Descartes' conception of substance led Spinoza also to deny the substantial existence of the Ego. His method was different from that of the English Empiricists. Emphasizing the idea that substance is conceived through itself and exists in itself, he concluded that there is only one Substance—God. Minds and bodies are but modes of its two attributes—thought and extension—respectively (*Ethics*, ii. prop. 10).

The substantial nature of the Ego has been maintained by other thinkers holding more adequate notions of substance than that held by Descartes. The universe, according to Leibniz, consists entirely of indivisible, mutually exclusive substances, or 'monads,' as he calls them. The content of these monads consists of their perception of the universe. They differ according to their point of view and the clearness of their perception. The rank of a monad in the scale of being depends on the clearness of its perception, on the degree of adequacy with which it mirrors or reflects the universe. What appears to us as inert matter is an

[1] *Essay concerning Human Understanding*, bk. ii. ch. xxiii. § 102.

aggregate of monads whose perceptions are faint and obscure. The bodies of men and animals are orderly aggregates of monads belonging to various grades of being, dominated by one monad—the self or soul. Extended bodies have no existence as such. Their extension is but an appearance to conscious beings. These do not, therefore, interact with matter; neither do they interact with one another. They develop from within. The order of the world is due to the pre-established harmony in which they were created by the supreme monad, God (Leibniz, *Monadology*). In G. H. Howison (cf. his *Limits of Evolution*, N.Y., 1905) we have a modern disciple of Leibniz. For Lotze also the universe consists of Egos. They are not mutually exclusive, as with Leibniz. They are related to one another through inclusion in the one absolute Person, God. God is the only absolute Substance, but finite Egos have relative independence. They are not mere modes of the being of another, or of others, as material things are. The latter do not exist in themselves, because they do not exist *for* themselves. Only beings that exist *for* themselves have self-existence. What is essential for self-existence is feeling. Thought is not essential, although it is necessary in order to develop the full meaning of selfhood, to enable an Ego to know itself and to say 'I.' But whatever has a feeling of self, the worm, *e.g.*, writhing in pain, has the fundamental characteristic on which substantial or self existence depends. For it 'undoubtedly distinguishes its own suffering from the rest of the world, though it can understand neither its own Ego nor the nature of the external world' (*Microcosmus*, Eng. tr., 1885, vol. i. bk. ii. ch. v. § 3). J. Ward develops a theory along lines suggested by Leibniz and Lotze (cf. his *Realm of Ends*, Cambridge, 1911, *passim*).

We have so far discussed the term 'Ego' as applied to the complete conscious individual, or to what psychologists call the 'total self.' But it has another application which is important. Since Kant wrote, many have recognized within the Ego so conceived a duality, variously described as a duality of subject and object, of subject-consciousness and object-consciousness, of the 'I' and the 'Me,' of the pure Ego and the empirical Ego—not a dualism of essentially different substances, be it understood, but a duality of such a nature as to form together one individual conscious being.

Hume's 'bundle of perceptions,' Huxley's 'sum of phenomena,' are capable of being analyzed, described, and related to one another. They are constituents of the Ego as object-consciousness, the Me, the empirical Ego; not, however, the only constituents of the object Ego. As already noted, a line cannot be drawn between what is included in the Ego and what is not. The body is often included by a man in his consciousness of himself, and even objects outside the body. A mystic may feel at one with the universe, or consciously identify himself with God.[1]

But distinct from the self as known and possessed is the self or subject which knows and possesses it. Knowing implies two terms in relation. An idea or perception which is perceived by no one is a contradiction. The centrality and organization of experience is unintelligible apart from the synthetic act of an interested subject (Ward).[2] Simple ideas

[1] Cf. Deussen, *The Philosophy of the Upanishads*, Eng. tr., Edin. 1906, p. 39: Brahman, the 'eternal infinite divine power is identical with the *ātman*, with that which, after stripping off everything external, we discover in ourselves as our real most essential being, our individual self, the soul. This identity of the Brahman and the *ātman* . . . is the fundamental thought of the entire doctrine of the Upanishads. It is briefly expressed by the "great saying": "thou art thou" and "I am Brahman."' To know self as Brahman is to achieve salvation.

[2] Art. 'Psychology,' in *EBr*[11] xxii. 550, *Naturalism and Agnosticism*, vol. ii. bk. iv. lect. xiv. f. *passim*.

are not combined into complex ideas by mere association; a combining is necessary (James).[1] A 'bundle of perceptions' or a 'sum of phenomena' cannot know itself as a bundle or sum respectively. How is that which is, *ex hypothesi*, a series to know itself as a series? (J. S. Mill).[2] Experience is not a mere series of perceptions. It is a unity. 'That the different kinds of empirical consciousness must be connected in one self-consciousness is the very first and synthetical foundation of all our thinking,' whether of ourselves as individuals or of the world as systematically connected according to law.[3] And the unity of self-consciousness depends on the synthetic activity of the Ego, the 'I think' which accompanies each of its synthetic acts.[4]

In Kant's philosophy three Egos may be distinguished—the pure Ego (the subject of knowledge), the empirical Ego (the succession of our conscious states, Hume's flux of perception), and the noumenal Ego (the subject of moral action). The first is needed to account for the objective unity and necessity of knowledge; the second is a verifiable fact; the third is postulated to make morality possible. The pure Ego is a logical principle, and the source of all theoretical principles; the empirical Ego is a part of the order of Nature, and all its states are determined according to the scientific law of causation which, with other theoretical principles, has its source in the pure Ego. The noumenal Ego does not belong to the world of sense, and is not subject to the order of Nature; it is free, and must be so if morality is to be possible. For morality implies the categorical imperative 'Thou oughtest,' and 'ought' implies 'can.' The categorical imperative is a command of the Practical Reason, or of reason in its practical application. Hence the freedom of the Ego is a postulate of the Practical Reason. And, since freedom is impossible in a world determined throughout according to the law of causation, as the world of sense-experience is thought by Kant to be, the ethical Ego belongs to the noumenal or intelligible world—a world which transcends the phenomenal.[5] The ethical Ego is the same as the logical Ego, but its transcendent existence can be asserted only by the Practical Reason. For the theoretical reason the Ego is an utterly empty idea. Nothing more can be said about it than that it is self-consciousness in general, the bare form of consciousness—the 'I think' which accompanies all knowledge of objects, and is the possibility of the knowledge of objects, but which has itself no content to distinguish it, and is not separable from the consciousness of objects.[6]

One obvious objection to Kant's conception of the Ego in its logical and ethical form is that it is too abstract to account for the concrete unity and organization of experience. Sentiency is excluded from it. Perceptions and sense-impulses must be assumed as somehow given. Kant made this assumption at first. He saw later that synthesis was implied in simple apprehension. But the conception of the Ego was not modified by him. He did much to overcome the opposition between sensibility and reason which had been developed by previous thinkers. One of his main purposes was to show that both were necessary for knowledge. But the dualism persists in his philosophy as two elements of opposite nature that had to be brought together. Later thinkers have carried out more thoroughly what Kant attempted. J. Ward maintains that the subject of sense-ex-

[1] *Text-book of Psychology*, p. 198.

[2] *Examination of Sir W. Hamilton's Philosophy*, 1872, p. 248.

[3] Kant's *Critique of Pure Reason*, Max Müller's tr.[2], 1896, p. 96 n.

[4] *Ib.* 745–751.

[5] *Critique of the Practical Reason*, Abbot's tr., 1879, p. 131 ff.

[6] *Critique of Pure Reason*, 278 ff.

perience is one and continuous with the subject of knowledge. So also the subject of simple impulsive actions is one and continuous with that of purposive actions.

Because experience at all levels depends on active as well as on passive factors, and because the conception of an object without a subject is a contradiction, Ward believes that the duality of subject and object in unity is a fundamental and underivative characteristic of experience, present alike in cognition, conation, and feeling. It is true even of the experience of God—the Supreme Person.[1] Other thinkers who recognize that experience shows this duality deny its fundamental character. Bradley, *e.g.*, says that the distinction is derivative. There is no ground for asserting that it is true of experience at all levels—the highest and the lowest. The consciousness of activity is not primary. 'The perception of activity comes from the expansion of the self against the not-self.' There is no consciousness of activity as distinguished from mere change apart from the idea of change. Moreover, subject and object have contents and are actual psychical groups. The contents of subject and object are interchangeable. Ideally, every conation and the most inner feelings may be made objects; we can, *e.g.*, think of changing them (*Appearance and Reality*[2], 1897, chs. ix. and x.; cf. also A. E. Taylor, *Elements of Metaphysics*, 1903, bk. iv. ch. iii.).

Ward replies that Bradley confounds reality with the perception of it, experience with a reflective knowledge of it. The relation subject-object must exist before it can be perceived. To show how the idea of activity arose is not to show that the consciousness of activity itself is derivative. The so-called 'expansion of the self' is the activity of the subject, and is presupposed in the perception of it. The relation subject-object cannot be reduced to relation between presentations.

The strongest objection to Ward's theory is that based on the ability of the mind to reflect on its own conations and feelings, thus apparently transferring them to the object Ego. But a subject, it may be urged, is implied even in reflexion. True. Is it, however, the same object? May there not be several Egos? W. James maintains that this is the case.

'Consciousness,' he says, 'may be represented as a stream; things which are known together are known in single pulses of that stream. The pulse of the present moment is the real subject. It is not an enduring being; each subject lasts but for a moment; its place is immediately taken by another which exercises its function, that is, to act as the medium of unity. The subject for the time being knows and adopts its predecessor, and by so doing appropriates what its predecessor adopted.' 'It is this trick which the nascent thought has of immediately taking up the expiring thought and adopting it which leads to the appropriation of most of the remoter constituents of the self. Who owns the last self owns the self before the last, for what possesses the possessor possesses the possessed' (*Text-book of Psychology*, 205). 'If there were no passing states of consciousness, then indeed we might suppose an abiding principle absolutely one with itself to be the ceaseless thinker in each one of us. But, if states of consciousness be accorded as realities, no such "substantial" identity of the thinker need be supposed. Yesterday's and to-day's states of consciousness have no substantial identity. For when one is here the other is irrevocably dead and gone. But they have a functional identity, for both know the same objects, and so far as the by-gone me is one of those objects they react upon it in an identical way, greeting it and calling it *mine*, and opposing it to all the other things they know. This functional identity seems really the only sort of identity in the thinker which the facts require us to suppose. Successive thinkers numerically distinct, but all aware of the same past in the same way, form an adequate vehicle for all the experience of personal unity and sameness which we actually have. And just such a stream of successive thinkers is the stream of mental states . . .' (*ib.* 202 f.).

This theory is not open to the objection made to that of Ward. But another difficulty presents itself when we consider the relation between the Egos. Assuming that the present pulse of the stream is able to exercise all the functions attributed to the Ego at any moment, the question arises, How are we to account for its special characteristics, and for the selection made out of the total complex presented at any moment, and thus account for the concrete unity or unities then manifested? The present Ego, according to the account given, is not derived from its predecessors; it does not 'inherit' the past, but possesses it by an act of appropriation. An Ego is not continued in its successor, for it has no substantial identity with it. Each Ego is described as an isolated individual, which appears for a moment as a medium of unity, and then vanishes, leaving its complex object and conative and reactive accompaniments—why have these not vanished?—to be appropriated by another, and this in turn gives place to still another which appropriates it.

Does this theory enable us to understand the relative permanence and unity of experience? Perhaps we should not take James's words too literally when he says that there is no substantial identity between yesterday's and to-day's states of consciousness. The words 'substantial' and 'identical' are ambiguous. James is here refuting the theory that the Ego is a substance which exists independently of what it knows, and remains one and the same over against the flux of experience. But his statements do not simply deny such a subject. They affirm also that the successive subjects are different beings, and that there is no continuity of existence between them; when one is here the other is irrevocably dead and gone. That the past conditions the present he would not deny. Yet how can this be if there is no identity between past and present states? And how can a past state which is irrevocably dead and gone be known and welcomed by the subject as its own?

James seems to make too much of his metaphor. A stream is not adequate to represent conscious life. It emphasizes its continuity, and over-emphasizes its transitoriness. Our experience contains relatively permanent elements. The past endures in the present. A state of consciousness is not a momentary existence merely. As a passing phase, of course, it endures only for a moment. But its whole being is not summed up in the term 'passing phase.' Experience is process; so is all else. 'All things flow.' No state of the existence of a tree or stone ever, as such, recurs. But the stone or the tree does not cease to exist, and every mode it has assumed shows itself in a more or less permanent modification of being. A subject which knows a tree as an enduring thing must itself be a relatively permanent being.

But we are not obliged to attribute absolute unchanging permanence to the subject, and define it as a simple indivisible principle or entity. It must have at least as much concreteness and variety of character and as much complexity of structure, so to speak, as its objects. Moreover, the character of the Ego is a changing one. The fabric or material of experience is undergoing frequent transformation, and we cannot but suppose that the Ego is similarly transformed. Indeed, it is obvious that our capacity for knowing, feeling, and doing is being continually modified. What appeals to us and compels attention, what we choose and reject, our conception of the world and our estimate of the things in it, change from day to day. The unity and identity of the subject cannot, therefore, exclude change. Why should a simple and indivisible element be asserted to exist in us? One motive is the desire to give to the Ego characteristics quite opposite to those

[1] *Naturalism and Agnosticism*, Lect. xv., *The Realm of Ends*, 191 ff.

possessed by body. MacTaggart argues, on metaphysical grounds, that such an element gives to finite experience its peculiar centrality or unity of centre.[1] But, if this simple element exists, it cannot be the subject which knows, feels, and does.

Once we recognize that the subject is not simple and indivisible and that it can change, it is no insuperable objection to Ward's theory to say that the subject may reflect on its activities and may desire to change them, thus transferring them for the time to the object consciousness. For subject and object are not two substances—entities different in kind. They enter into the unity of one experience and are inseparable.

'What a subject without objects, or what objects without a subject, would be, is indeed, as we are often told, unknowable; for in truth the knowledge of either apart is a contradiction' (Ward, *Naturalism and Agnosticism*, ii. 112). 'Let what may be outside experience, if there can be anything, and the supposition is not nonsense, at least there cannot be bare subjects lying in wait for objects, nor objects that by definition never are positively objects' (*ib.* 128 f.).

See also artt. CONSCIOUSNESS, PERSONALITY, SELF-EXISTENCE.

LITERATURE.—In addition to the works already cited, reference may be made to monographs and commentaries on the works of the authors mentioned, and also to the Histories of Philosophy under their names. For a psychological account of the processes by which the consciousness of self originates and develops, see W. K. Clifford, *Seeing and Thinking*[2], London, 1880; J. Royce, *Studies of Good and Evil*, New York, 1898; G. F. Stout, *Manual of Psychology*, London, 1898-99; J. M. Baldwin, *Social and Ethical Interpretation*[4], New York, 1907; W. McDougall, *An Introduction to the Study of Social Psychology*, London, 1909.

DAVID PHILLIPS.

EGOISM.—A distinction may be drawn between theoretical and practical egoism. (*a*) Theoretical egoism, usually called Subjective Idealism or Solipsism (*q.v.*), is the theory which maintains that his own individual Ego is the only being that a man can logically assert to exist. For he can know only what is in his own mind; and, since his knowledge does not extend beyond the states of his own being, he has no valid ground for asserting the existence of other beings. Of course, it is absurd for any one to think that he is the only being in existence; and, in order to escape the absurdity and to make it intelligible how we know beings other than ourselves, we must assume, it is maintained, that our experience is not of our own states merely.

'The escape is simple once we recognize that experience from the outset involves both subject and object, both self and other; and that the differentiation of both factors proceeds *pari passu*' (J. Ward, *The Realm of Ends*, 1911, p. 129; cf. also F. H. Bradley, *Appearance and Reality*[2], 1897, ch. xxi.).

(*b*) Practical Egoism, according to Kant (*Anthropologie*, § 2), has three forms—logical, æsthetic, and moral respectively. The *logical* egoist considers it unnecessary to bring his own judgment to the test of another's understanding. Protagoras, for example, is said to have taught that 'man is the measure of all things, of the existence of things that are, and of the non-existence of things that are not'; that 'things are to you such as they appear to you, and are to me such as they appear to me, for you and I are men' (Plato, *Theætetus*, 152 A, Jowett's tr.). The *æsthetic* egoist is fully satisfied with his own taste (cf. the saying, 'De gustibus non est disputandum'). The *moral* egoist makes himself the end of all his activities. Nothing is valuable unless it benefits him. Its moral application is what we have usually in mind when we speak of egoism. In ethical works it is contrasted with altruism (*q.v.*), concern for the good of others.

Egoism, as an ethical theory, maintains that the standard of conduct for the individual is his own good on the whole. It should be distinguished from the directly egoistic or egotistic attitude of mind to life = mere selfishness. A man is usually called egoistic or egotistic in so far as his inclinations and purposes are immediately and exclusively directed towards himself (cf. Meredith's *Egoist*). Such egoism may be independent of any theory as to what is right or reasonable. It may be exemplified by a child or by a thoughtless man; and may take the form of choosing what is most agreeable or least painful at the time of action, without any thought of life as a whole. On the other hand, it may be the result of cool deliberation and concentrated purpose. Thoroughgoing egoism of this kind is seldom or never met with. 'Selfishness' is not, indeed, a logical consequence of ethical egoism. It is not inconsistent with the latter to cultivate a 'disinterested' regard for others and for their welfare. For too great and direct regard for self-interest may lead to a narrowing of the scope of life which is incompatible with the greatest individual well-being. The hedonistic egoist who seeks his own happiness too keenly is in danger of defeating his own end.[1] A man concerned to save his soul may attain his end most effectively by trying to save others, and by forgetting that he has a soul to save: losing interest in himself, he finds himself. By dying he lives. Hence Ethical Egoism, or Egoism as a theory of the good or of what is right and reasonable, does not necessarily imply 'selfishness.'

Ethical egoists are generally dogmatic; *i.e.* they do not seek to justify the individual's right to make his own good the standard of life, or, in other words, to show that such a view is a reasonable one for him to take. Such justification is not, perhaps, thought to be necessary. The reasonableness of seeking our own good is taken for granted. A reason is supposed to be needed for considering the good of others when inclination does not induce, or necessity compel, a man to do so. Even Butler says

'that our ideas of happiness and misery are of all our ideas the nearest and most important to us . . . that, though virtue or moral rectitude does indeed consist in affection to and pursuit of what is right and good, as such; yet, when we sit down in a cool hour, we can neither justify to ourselves this or any other pursuit, till we are convinced that it will be for our happiness, or at least not contrary to it' (Sermon xi.).

That the egoist should seek his own good as one of his ends requires no justification. Every justification is secondary and derivative; whereas the appeal for his own good is to each one immediate, and it is intuitively evident that he should seek it. The appeal of the good of others is not so direct; nor is it so immediately evident that one should promote it except when others are bound to him by such intimate ties as make their welfare interesting to him in the same way as his own is. Consequently, when, from any cause, natural and social claims are weak or repudiated, egoistic theories of life tend to win recognition. The Cynics, *e.g.*, lived during the decline of the Greek city-State, and Hobbes (1588-1679) during the social disorganization attending the Revolution in England. Spinoza was ostracized for his theological views; Schopenhauer and Nietzsche were constitutionally Ishmaelites.

Egoism is based, explicitly or implicitly, on an 'atomistic' conception of society; every social whole is composed of individuals, the nature of each one of whom is to preserve his own life, to seek his own good, to satisfy his own desires; and good and evil are relative to the individual. There is nothing good or evil absolutely. Both presuppositions are explicit in Hobbes:

'The object of the voluntary acts of every man is "some good to himself"' (*Leviathan*, ch. xiv.). 'Whatsoever is the object of any man's appetite or desire, that is it which he for his part calleth "good"; and the object of his hate and aversion "evil"; and of his contempt "vile" and "inconsiderable." For these

[1] *Studies in Hegelian Cosmology*, § 85 ff.

[1] Cf. Sidgwick, *Methods of Ethics*, 1893, p. 49.

words of good, evil, and contemptible are ever used with relation to the person that useth them; there being nothing simply and absolutely so; nor any common rule of good and evil, to be taken from the nature of the objects themselves; but from the person of the man . . .' (*ib.* ch. vi.). 'The "right of nature," which writers commonly call *jus naturale*, is the liberty each man hath, to use his own power, as he will himself, for the preservation of his own nature; that is to say, of his own life; and consequently, of doing anything which in his own judgment and reason he shall conceive to be the aptest means thereunto.' 'Whensoever a man transferreth his right, or renounceth it, it is either in consideration of some right reciprocally transferred to himself or for some other good he hopeth for thereby' (*ib.* ch. xiv.).

Social life was impossible while men exercised this liberty. Consequently they divested themselves of the right of doing what they liked in consideration of the fact that others did the same. This 'social contract' is the basis of community life. Through it men passed from the natural state, in which every man was at war with every other man, to a state of peace. The obligation to obey laws rests on this contract and on the authority and power which the Government possesses in virtue of it to enforce them. Obedience to Divine ordinances (whether learned from Nature or Revelation) likewise depends on a recognition of the Divine authority and power to enforce them by pains and penalties.

The relativity of good and evil to desire and aversion respectively is taught by Bentham and his followers. They maintain, moreover, that each one desires pleasure only and freedom from pain.[1] Thus J. S. Mill writes:

'I believe that these sources of evidence [practised self-consciousness and self-observation, assisted by observation of others], impartially consulted, will declare that desiring a thing and finding it pleasant, aversion to it and thinking of it as painful, are phenomena entirely inseparable, or rather two parts of the same phenomenon; in strictness of language, two different modes of naming the same psychological fact: that to think of an object as desirable (unless for the sake of its consequences), and to think of it as pleasant, are one and the same thing; and that to desire anything, except in proportion as the idea of it is pleasant, is a physical and metaphysical impossibility' (*Utilitarianism*, ed. 1901, ch. iv. p. 58).

Nietzsche's account of the good aimed at by the individual differs from the accounts both of Hobbes and of the Hedonists:

'Psychologists should bethink themselves before putting down the instinct of self-preservation as the cardinal instinct of an organic being. A living thing seeks above all to *discharge* its strength—life itself is the *Will to Power*; self-preservation is only one of the indirect and most frequent *results* thereof' (*Beyond Good and Evil*, Eng. tr., Edinburgh, 1907, § 13).

On comparing the representative opinions given above, it becomes evident that Egoism is not necessarily associated with any particular theory of the nature of the good; and that, moreover, in any of its forms it cannot be established by a psychological analysis of the nature of desire, or by an examination of the ends that men actually seek. Modern psychological investigations have, indeed, made it increasingly evident that the human consciousness is not under the control of any one principle except at a highly reflective stage of intellectual life. Men have various impulses directed to different objects, and they are not reduced to the unity of a system, or subordinated as means to one end. And, even when such unity exists, the governing principle is regulative only in a general way. It does not enter as a constituent element into all purposive actions and directly subordinate them as means to itself. Unity of aim is an ideal rather than an actual principle—a fact to which the conception 'ought' bears witness. It would be a more correct account of what actually happens to say that psychological egoism, whenever it exists, is a consequence of a more or less conscious ethical egoism, than to say that ethical egoism is based on psychological egoism. For men aim consistently at their own good, to the extent that they have definite conceptions of themselves and of the nature of the good which will satisfy them. Ethics is the systematic study of this good; and its teaching will acquire scientific exactness only when the nature of the individual man in relation to his fellows and the rest of the universe is clearly understood.

If the egoist's attitude is dogmatic, his ethics is fundamentally merely a statement of his own convictions, and he cannot be reasoned with. But, when he tries to justify his conviction, he may be reasoned with, and, possibly, convinced of error. The egoist is trying to give a reasonable basis to his theory when he rests it on a psychological analysis of the nature of desire. His attempt is, as we have seen, not successful. He might yet maintain that he has an immediate and ultimate intuition that he should seek his own good whether he actually does so or not. It may be safely said, in reply to this, that other men would not recognize the validity of the egoist's intuition, especially if his good is to be obtained at their expense. Further, he ought consistently to admit that every other individual's good is an ultimate end for himself, and that it should be recognized as such by all. And, if this be admitted, does it not follow that the good of all should be respected by each, and that, therefore, a limit is set to individual self-seeking? The egoist's contention would then be qualified into the statement that he should seek his own good, but in such a way as not to interfere with similar self-seeking on the part of others.

Further, it may be urged that the atomistic conception of human life is false. Human societies are not mere aggregates. A man is not self-contained; no sharp line of division can be drawn between his life and interests and those of others (cf. art. EGO). He is a member of an organic whole. The complete good is the good of the whole of which he is a member. The full realization of his interests is at the same time the full realization of the interests of others. Hence his good is no purely private and personal matter. It is true that sometimes there is an appearance of conflict. Whether the conflict is necessary is a large question which cannot be discussed here. In an ideal state, as H. Spencer (*Data of Ethics*[2], 1879, ch. xi.) points out, there would be no conflict. And even now men exist who seem to find that they more nearly realize their true good by denying what appear to be their private interests and acting for the sake of others. They so identify themselves with their State or Church that they are content to die in order that the institution may live and flourish. The surrender of life is not felt to be self-sacrifice but self-realization, and it is often made with no thought of recompense in a future life.

LITERATURE.—Most modern writers on Ethics discuss Egoism. In addition to the works already cited the reader may consult: **F. H. Bradley**, *Ethical Studies*, London, 1876; **Felix le Dantec**, *L'Egoïsme base de toute société*, Paris, 1912; **G. E. Moore**, *Principia Ethica*, Cambridge, 1903; **F. Paulsen**, *A System of Ethics*, London, 1899; **H. Rashdall**, *The Theory of Good and Evil*, Oxford, 1907; **Max Stirner**, *Der Einzige und sein Eigenthum*, Leipzig, 1892; **A. E. Taylor**, *The Problem of Conduct*, London, 1901; artt. CYNICS, NIETZSCHE, SCHOPENHAUER.

DAVID PHILLIPS.

EGOISM (Buddhist).—The inquiry whether the motives, sources, or springs of action are or are not exclusively egoistic, or self-interested, whether or not 'altruism' may rank as a twin in such springs, or whether there are yet other sources, is so characteristic of modern ethics that it is not strange if no corresponding discussion be found in early Buddhism, any more than in other early philosophical and religious traditions. Such discussions are the corollaries of a synthesis which belongs

[1] Hobbes also says that desire is always accompanied by some pleasure more or less; pleasure is the 'appearance or sense of good,' and 'displeasure' the 'appearance or sense of evil' (*Leviathan*, ch. vi.). Spinoza's view is similar. But both writers lay stress on self-preservation as the fundamental impulse.

more essentially to the past two centuries than to any others we can name—that of individuals and of peoples as *solidaires* one of another. They have sprung from a time, when, in George Eliot's words,

'ideas were making fresh armies of themselves, and the universal kinship was declaring itself fiercely; . . . when the soul of man was waking to pulses which had for centuries been beating in him unheard, until their full sun made a new life of terror or of joy' (*Daniel Deronda*).

Herein may possibly lie a sounder basis of historical division in ethical theory than, with Martineau, to find in a psychological basis the true dichotomizing principle of the ethical systems of pre-Christian and post-Christian thought. His generalization is sound only as long as we turn our back on not only one part of pre-Christian ethical thought, but on by far the most considerable part. In his strange statement, 'It is curious that psychological ethics are *altogether peculiar to Christendom*' (italics his), the whole world of Oriental thought is ignored.[1] To take India only: in Vedāntist ethics, the ethical ideal, growing up with the evolution of thought, is emphatically subjective. The creative and presiding power of the universe became identified with the psychical principle in man; salvation lay in the personal recognition of this identity—'the finding self to be Ātman' (Deussen); and the ethical value of actions was reckoned less according to an objective scale of utility than according to a subjective calculus of their significance, in cost and result, to the doer.[2]

Buddhist ethic is no less strongly and consciously psychological (see DESIRE [Buddhist]). Its views on the self were different from those of Vedāntism. It denied any immanence, in the wholly and constantly changing living organism, physical and mental, of an eternal, unchanging, impassive (*i.e.* super-passive) principle. The 'I' (*ego, aham*) of agency was a convenient abstraction of thought, a convention of popular speech, as when we say '*it* rains.' As a metaphysical, rather than an ethical, subject, but one of cardinal importance in Buddhist doctrine, the Ego is dealt with under SELF, SOUL. Under the present title we are concerned with the attitude of its ethical doctrine towards that which, in theory or practice, is called 'egoism.' All the materials, in fact, for our modern ethical *discussion* of egoism and altruism are present in Buddhism; and, since the sources of those materials are still so imperfectly accessible, and so inadequately exploited, it is by no means impossible that we may yet discover, or come upon, such discussion. We may nevertheless affirm this much: that it forms no such predominant feature as is the case in modern ethical works. It is as if the pulses of that full social consciousness to which we have referred above were beating latent and unheard. The struggle of early culture was for the individual to 'find himself,' even as it is to-day. The intervening struggle has been to find one's brother. In a brief provisional inquiry like the present, the best course suggesting itself is to indicate: (1) the presence in Buddhist scriptures of the materials aforesaid, or, let us say, of channels in ethical thought on the lines of the modern cleavage; (2) any modification in that thought due to the a-psychic or anti-animistic standpoint; (3) any evolution in Buddhism with respect to egoistic and altruistic theory.

1. We find in the Pāli Piṭakas a definite theory with respect to the 'springs of action.' These are termed *hetu* ('condition,' 'cause'), or *mūla* ('root'), or *nidāna* ('source'). They are six in number, three being 'roots' of good, three of bad action.[3]

[1] Martineau, *Types of Ethical Theory*, Oxford, 1885, i. 14.

[2] P. Deussen, *Allgem. Gesch. d. Philosophie*, i.² (Leipzig, 1907), p. 327 ff.

[3] *Aṅguttara Nikāya*, i. 134 f.; C. A. F. Rhys Davids, *Buddhist Psychological Ethics*, London, 1900, p. 274 ff.; S. Z. Aung, *Compend. of Philosophy*, London, 1910, p. 279 ff.

And, though bad and good actions are so termed in virtue of the painful or pleasurable results they entail respectively on the agent, yet they are shown actually to consist in immoral and moral actions respectively—that is to say, in actions considered as affecting others.

The three bad 'roots' are greed, hate, and want of intelligence; the other three are their opposites—detachment, love, and intelligence. In Pāli they read *lobha, dosa, moha*; *alobha, adosa, amoha*. A frequent synonym for the first is *rāga* ('lust,' 'passion,' understood very generally); for the third, *avijjā* ('ignorance'); for the fifth, *mettā* ('love,' 'charity,' 'amity'); for the sixth, *paññā* ('insight,' 'wisdom'). So radical and inclusive, as sources of all human faults and follies and consequent suffering, are the first three held to be, that the extinction of them, that is to say, letting action proceed solely from their three opposites, is one of the few positive definitions given of *nibbāna* (*nirvāṇa* [*q.v.*]).

No reduction is attempted of either triplet to any more ultimate ground of action. But the first named of the six approximates closely to that manifestation of organic life, so significant in Buddhist ethics, called *taṇhā*, unregenerate desire, want, appetite, craving (see DESIRE [Buddhist]). *Taṇhā* is—by the great scholastic, Buddhaghosa (*q.v.*)—termed *mūla* also, but it is of the whole round of re-birth that it is called the root (*vaṭṭa-mūlabhūtā taṇhā*). It is itself rooted in, or the effect of, sensuous contact—'because of contact, sensation, because of sensation, craving.' The result of craving is grasping (*upādāna*)—a term which, in its double sense of the *act* just named, and the *fact* of requisite stuff or fuel, becomes a mental hieroglyphic or word-picture, to indicate how the *taṇhā*-prompted will and action serve to re-kindle once more, in a new 'becoming' or coming-to-be (*bhava*), the fires of life. This *taṇhā* is fairly approximate to egoism, considered as the instinct and impulse of self-preservation. But in that one form of it as *vibhavataṇhā*, described by the commentators as the lust of self-annihilation, its connotation is wider than that of the lust of life, and it is perhaps better to consider its meaning as wanting, lusting, or craving in general; the lust of life and the pleasures of life, earthly or celestial, being its predominant manifestation.

Now, if the hundred equivalent terms and metaphors describing *lobha* in the *Dhamma-saṅgaṇi*[1] be consulted, it will be seen that *lobha* and *taṇhā* are practically coincident in meaning. Still, the latter term is not used in describing the three roots or conditions of bad *kamma* or action, as is *lobha* or *rāga*. In parables drawn from plant-life, *taṇhā* functions not as root, but as the moisture which is, together with suitable soil, an essential *condition* of growth.[2] As related to the other two roots, *lobha* or *taṇhā* is itself a root or condition of inimical actions.

'Thus it is, Ānanda,' the Buddha is described as saying, 'that craving comes into being because of sensation, pursuit because of craving, gain because of pursuit, decision because of gain, desire and passion (*chhandarāga*) because of decision, tenacity because of desire and passion, possession because of tenacity, avarice because of possession, watch and ward because of avarice, and many a bad and wicked state of things arising from keeping watch and ward over possessions—blows and wounds, strife, contradiction and retort, quarrelling, slander and lies' (Rhys Davids, *Dialogues*, Oxford, 1899, ii. 55)—a passage that was a few centuries later paralleled by St. James's account of the relation between *taṇhā* and strife (Ja 4[1f.]).

But the root-principle of *dosa*, here shown as co-operating with that of *lobha*, is deeper seated than such hostile acts, and is the temperamental state or disposition of natural aversion, misanthropy, anti-social feeling, expressed in Buddhist psychology by *paṭigha*, resistance, opposition, aversion.[3]

[1] Tr. in C. A. F. Rhys Davids, *Bud. Psychol. Ethics*.

[2] *Saṃyutta Nikāya*, iii. 54; *Aṅg. Nik.* i. 223.

[3] S. Z. Aung, *op. cit.* 83.

As related to *moha*, *lobha*, or lusting after false goods and ends, is aided by the errant groping and dim vision, denoted by the former term. Thus the verses ascribed to Mahāpajāpatī (aunt and foster-mother of the Buddha) run:

'Oh! but 'tis long I've wandered down all time,
Not knowing how and what things really were,
And never finding what I needed sore.
But now mine eyes have seen th' Exalted One,
Now have I understood how ill doth come.
Craving, the cause, in me is driéd up. . . .'
(*Therigāthā*, 157 f.)[1]

2. Taking next the three causes of good or moral action, it is not possible to reduce them to simpler terms. They are at least as ultimate as conation, feeling, and cognition. *Alobha*, or detachment, is not so negative as it sounds. Essentially a state of mind and heart which does not grasp at, or cling to, it is the condition of all generous and disinterested action.[2] Such a state is likened to the free mobility of a dewdrop on the glaucous surface of a lotus-leaf. *Adosa* is sympathy, altruistic tenderness, care, and forbearance, the ἀγάπη of St. Paul. *Amoha* is the clarity of mind affirmed in the foregoing verses. Any one of these three, according to the *Paṭṭhāna*, may condition, involve, and lead to the other two—'Because of *alobha*, [arises] *adosa*, *amoha*,' etc. (*Duka-paṭṭhāna*, 1); but this is all.

We may trace self-interested and other-interested motives in acts conditioned by one or more of these six, but the six are not reducible to the one principle or the other. The good of self and that of others, as the end and result of action, are frequently met with in the Pitakas, but not as basic principles. For instance, the two form part of a fourfold cleavage in classifying human beings:

'There are four classes of persons in the world: those, namely, who live neither for their own good, nor for that of others; those who live for the good of others, not for their own good; those who live for their own good only; those who live for the good both of themselves and of others.'

Of these four, the first are compared to a charred and rotten log, good for nothing. Of the rest, the scale of value is noteworthy. The second, or altruist, is better than the first; the third, or egoist, is better than the altruist. The fourth, whom H. Sidgwick would have called a universalistic hedonist, is the best of all. When, however, we read further, the explanation of living for, or being concerned with, one's own and others' good shows that we are not dealing with egoists as we should understand them. The class who study their own good only are those persons who, while seeking to extirpate *rāga*, *dosa*, *moha* in themselves, do not habitually exhort others to do the same. Those who study others' good only are such as exhort others to extirpate the conditions of bad acts, while not themselves trying to do so. A similar distinction is drawn with respect to other moods of ethical endeavour, showing that the Dhamma contained no encouragement for unenlightened, worldly, or sensual self-interest.[3]

Another classification in self- and other-regard, occurring several times, is that of persons who inflict pain or hardship on self and their fellowmen. The same fourfold division is followed, but only the doubly negative class is commended. To these belong the self-conquerors, the saints, those who have won *nibbāna*.[4] Especially is the dual regard for self and others put forward as conduct conditioned by the sixth 'root,' *amoha* (or *paññā*). One who is mastered by greed, etc., devises what is injurious to himself, to others, to both. One who has not cleared away the 'five hindrances'—sensual desire, ill will, ignorance, etc.—has too

[1] Tr. in C. A. F. Rhys Davids, *Psalms of the Early Buddhists*, London, 1909, i. 89.
[2] S. Z. Aung, *op. cit.* 279 f.
[3] *Aṅg. Nik.* ii. 95 ff.
[4] For instance, *ib.* 205 ff.

weak insight to know his own good, others' good, or both; he who has cleared them away 'knows what is the good of both even as it really is.'[1] Generally speaking, the balance of ends is stated in such words as the verse, 'He seeketh both his own and others' good';[2] and in the Buddha's words: 'Contemplating either one's own good, or that of others, or both, is sufficient motive for setting about it strenuously.'[3] But, while the early Buddhist held that morality was the basis of all spiritual growth, and that benevolence was essential to the increase of one's own happiness, he did not, as Sidgwick says of Comte, 'seriously trouble himself to argue with egoism, or to weigh carefully the amount of happiness that might be generally attained by the satisfaction of egoistic propensities duly regulated' (*History of Ethics*, London, 1887, p. 257). Thus the Buddha is represented as giving ethical advice to questioners perplexed by rival doctrines, as follows:

'Let your verdict not be guided by tradition, precedent, custom, or dialectic. Test the doctrines, each for himself, whether they will conduce to happiness or the reverse. For you know well that the conduct conducive to happiness is the conduct that is conditioned by detachment, by love, by intelligence; and that the conduct conducive to sorrow is conditioned by greed, hate, and illusion. These impel men to take life, steal, live unchastely, tell lies, and stir others up to do the like. Those impel men to avoid doing these things.'[4]

In more detailed expositions of ethical disposition and conduct, the term nearest to our 'selfishness' is perhaps *macchariya*. The derivation is from a stem signifying madness or infatuation, but the dominant feature in the disposition so called seems to be meanness, the opposite of magnanimity, a grudging spirit. The content of the term is, however, expounded in part by other terms indicative of a selfish nature, of one that, spreading itself over all its own gettings, says 'Mine be it, not another's,' and of one that would hinder generosity in others. Another such ancillary term signifies a styptic or contracted state with regard to others' needs.[5]

Other aspects of egoism—self-interest, self-conceit, self-seeking, self-reference—are all represented in Buddhist doctrine. The term *sadattha*, one's own good, advantage, or interest, is used invariably, we believe, in the approved sense of 'enlightened' self-interest, including 'personal' salvation. Thus, in one of the usual descriptions of the elect or perfected, it is said:

'They who are arahants, who have destroyed the intoxicants (*āsavas*), who have lived the life, have done that which was to be done, have laid aside the burden, have won their own salvation (*anuppatta-sadattha*),' etc.[6]

Self-conceit, or *māna*, is thus described:

'Conceit at the thought "I am the better man,"—"I am as good [as they],"—"I am lowly"—all such fancies, overweening vanity, arrogance, pride, flag-flaunting, assumption, desire of the heart for self-advertisement:—this is called *māna*.'[7]

Now, *māna* was quite incompatible with *sadattha*. Self-conceit did not arise in the bosom of him who had won his highest gain. As with some phases of evangelical Christianity, so with Buddhism, it was customary for one attaining to the consciousness of salvation to testify to the same. Two disciples thus attaining are related to have waited on the Buddha, and repeated the formula quoted above:

'Lord, he who is arahant, who has . . . won salvation, who has utterly destroyed the fetters of becoming (re-birth), who is by perfect knowledge emancipated, to him it does not occur—"There is that is better than I, equal to me, inferior to me." And, they saluting and passing out of the congregation, the Buddha speaks: "Even so do men of true breed declare *aññā* (gnosis): they tell of their salvation (*attha*), but they do not bring in the ego (*attā*)."'[8]

Two other disciples, more notable than these,

[1] *Aṅg. Nik.* i. 158, 216, etc.
[2] *Saṁy. Nik.* i. 222.
[3] *Ib.* ii. 29; *Aṅg. Nik.* iv. 134.
[4] *Aṅg. Nik.* i. 188 ff.
[5] C. A. F. Rhys Davids, *Bud. Psychol. Ethics*, 299 f.
[6] *Saṁy. Nik.* v. 145.
[7] C. A. F. Rhys Davids, *Bud. Psychol. Ethics*, 299.
[8] *Aṅg. Nik.* iii. 359.

testify in their talk to this contrast between saintship and self-reference. Ānanda comments on Sāriputta's beautiful expression and demeanour, and asks:

'What have you been occupied with to-day?' 'I have been dwelling apart, practising *jhāna*, brother, and there arose in me never the thought, "It is *I* who attain or *I* who emerge."' 'That is because all egoistic tendencies in the venerable Sāriputta have long been rooted out,' responds Ānanda.[1]

Not only do we find this unobtrusion of the ego commended, but we also read of the Buddha, when the self had been obtruded, diverting the point of the episode to altruistic regard. The story is told in the *Udāna*, a little manual of short episodes framing a metrical *logion*, how the king of Kosala and his wife discuss the possibly current Vedāntist text, that the self, the immanent deity, is dearer than all else.[2] It is possible that the metaphysic implied is more in line with that of the Christian text, 'What shall a man give in exchange for his soul?' (Mt 16[26]). Anyhow, the king mentions the conversation to the Buddha, who thereupon replies:

'The whole wide world we traverse with our thought,
Nor come on aught more dear to each than Self.
Since aye so dear the Self to other men,
Let the Self-lover harm no other man.'[3]

Etymologically speaking, ego-ism is more than paralleled in Indian linguistic. The oblique cases of the personal pronoun yield derivatives as well as the nominative. Thus we have *ahaṁ-kāra*, 'I-maker,' and also *mamaṅkāra*, 'mine-maker,' *mamattaṃ*, 'mine-ness,' *a-mama*, 'having nought of "mine",' *i.e.* calling nothing, or wishing nothing to be, mine, etc. It is in connexion with these last terms that we find egoism as self-seeking dealt with, that is to say, with that larger self which has annexed and identified with itself the things a man possesses (W. James, *Princ. Psychology*[2], London, 1905, i. 292 ff.).

'Unlike, these two, and far apart they dwell:
The goodman keeping wife, and he who naught
Doth call his own (*amamo*), the saint. Unchecked
The layman hurteth other lives, the sage
In self-restraint protecteth all that lives.

He who doth never think "'Tis mine!";
Nor "Others have gotten something!"; thinketh thus:
There's naught for me! no "mineness" (*mamattam*) being found
In him, he hath no cause to suffer grief.'[4]

3. The first-named term of these derivatives, *ahaṁ-kāra*, undergoes an interesting evolution in Indian thought, but the ethical part it plays is slight. In the (older) Chhāndogya Upaniṣad, it is equivalent to the *Ātman*, or soul conceived as the immanent Divinity. Put into our metaphysical idiom, the one passage referring to it runs thus: 'Under the aspect of a *plenum*, the sum total of our perceptions is Self, is I-making.'[5] In several later Upaniṣads the term recurs, but in the psychological sense attached to it in the Sāṅkhyā philosophy. That is to say, it is a mental organ, or function, evolved from matter, and mediating between the material and the spiritual, or presenting external experience as so many 'intelligibles' to the soul or self.[6] Its occurrence in the Buddhist scriptures is confined practically to one phrase repeated in a few *suttas* of two Nikāyas. The meaning of the phrase is invariably that of the older Upaniṣad. It has two slightly varying forms: 'mind involved in I-making-mine-making conceit (*māna*),' and 'the bias of I-making-mine-making conceit.' The context is concerned with the problem of practical philosophy and religion: how, given the recipient organism and the world of external impressions, to attain spiritual freedom, and not to suffer the conceit of self-reference to arise. All assumption of a self, soul, or ego (*attā*, *aham*), as any part of the organism or its impressions, is to be extruded.[1]

It is possible that the function assigned to *ahaṁ-kāra* in animistic psychology was contemporary with the foregoing. But there is no allusion to it, as a psychological fallacy or otherwise, in Buddhist psychology.

But anti-egoistical teaching nowhere resolves itself into a positive doctrine of altruism. The solvents applied, in Buddhism, to the animistic creed of immortal, unchanging Divine soul within one body after another have been described as the destruction of individuality. The object, however, was not expressly the breaking down of spiritual barriers between one individuality and those of its fellow-men. We may, again, apply to the Buddha Sidgwick's description of Comte's views (*op. cit.* p. 257):

'A supreme unquestioning self-devotion, in which all personal calculations are suppressed, is an essential feature of his moral ideal.'

The self-devotion, however, is not altruistic, but to the highest good, for self and others, as he conceived it: the good that lay in the perfecting and the perfection (and thereby the completion) of life. And this was ultimately a task to be carried out by each man for himself.

'I only may achieve the task; herein
None other may accomplish aught for me.'[2]

On the other hand, the accomplishing lay essentially in a life based on other-regarding virtues, and, in all cases where temperament or infirmities did not forbid, in ministering to the spiritual and temporal needs of others. Combined, moreover, with moral conduct and service was the altruistic side of the contemplative disciplines, on which considerable emphasis is laid. This consisted in a systematic irradiation or mental suffusion (*pharaṇa*) of other beings, starting from one person or group and expanding the range, with *love*, then *pity* (or sympathy with sorrow and pain), then *sympathy* with the happy, finally *equanimity*, each emotion to be realized as practically elastic to an infinite degree. Lastly, the rejection by the Buddha of all validity in rank, caste, or birth, as standards of personal value, was conducive to fraternity in general. A discourse on the altruistic duties of the layman has this peroration:

'Liberality, courtesy, benevolence, unselfishness, under all circumstances and towards all—these qualities are to the world what the linchpin is to the rolling chariot.'[3]

And the fraternal affection among members of the Order is frequently mentioned.

'Behold the company who learn of him—
In happy concord of fraternity . . .
The noblest homage this to Buddhas paid.'[4]

One of the most elevated and best known of Piṭakan expressions of universal benevolence is that inculcating mother-love to all beings—perhaps the finest outburst of altruism in all ancient literature:

'E'en as a mother watcheth o'er her child,
Her only child, as long as life doth last,
So let us, for all creatures, great or small,
Develop such a boundless heart and mind.
Ay, let us practise love for all the world,
Upward, and downward, yonder, hence,
Uncramped, free from ill will and enmity.'[5]

Those among modern Buddhists who call themselves Mahāyānists claim that, in developing and progressing beyond original Buddhism, the sentiment of altruism as opposed to egoism takes a more prominent position in their teaching, notably in what is termed the Bodhisattva (*q.v.*) theory. In this the goal of *nirvāna* becomes one not of personal salvation but of transferred

[1] *Saṁy. Nik.* iii. 235 f.
[2] *Bṛhadāraṇyaka*, I. 4, 8.
[3] *Udāna*, 47.
[4] *Sutta-Nipāta*, verse 951.
[5] *Chh. Up.* 7. 25.
[6] R. Garbe, *Die Sāṃkhya-Philosophie*, Leipzig, 1894, p. 7 ff.

[1] *Saṁy. Nik.* ii. 253, etc.; iii. 80, etc.
[2] C. A. F. Rhys Davids, *Psalms of the Early Buddhists*, ii. verse 542.
[3] *Digha Nik.* iii. 192.
[4] C. A. F. Rhys Davids, *Psalms of the Early Buddhists*, i. 89; *Majjhima Nik.* ii. 103, iii. 156.
[5] *Sutta Nip.*, verses 148-150; *Khuddakapāṭha.*

merit, saintly aspiration being for the salvation of all beings. Negatively, writes Daisetz Suzuki, *nirvāṇa* 'is the annihilation of [the belief in] the notion of ego-substance, and of all the desires that arise from this erroneous conception. . . . Its positive side consists in universal love or sympathy for all beings.'[1]

LITERATURE.—This is given in the footnotes.

C. A. F. RHYS DAVIDS.

EGOTISM.—See VANITY.

EGYPTIAN RELIGION.—I. *CONDITIONS.*—

1. Length of time.—The very long history of Egypt is traceable through more than 7000 years in writing, and it has a pre-history of which details can be recovered from 1000 or 2000 years before writing; hence the changes of religious thought can be followed over a wider range than in classical lands. In place of a very full account, covering a few centuries, as in Greece and Italy, we have a scattered and fragmentary account of as many thousand years. The scope and the treatment, therefore, must be very different from that applied to other religions.

2. Character of the land.—The peculiar nature of the country reacted on the religion, as upon all other interests of man. The continuous contrast of desert and of cultivation impressed the whole Egyptian character. It produced those contrasts which seem so contradictory—a people who had the reputation of gloomy stubbornness, and who yet covered their tombs with scenes of banquets, dancing, and gaiety: a people to whom the grandeur of the tomb was one of the great objects during life. The constant presence of the dead in the cliffs and desert overlooking the scenes of their lives, or, in later times, more familiarly kept surrounding the family life in the atrium of the house, preserved a sense of the continuity with the Other-world which made a far more contrasted life than we see elsewhere. As opposed to the luxuriance and fatness of the rich plain, there was always visible on either hand the desert, little known, dreaded, the region of malevolent gods, of strange monsters, of blinding, suffocating storms, of parching thirst and heat.

3. Form of the land.—The form of the country also acted on the religion by favouring isolated communities, which preserved distinct beliefs. Not only was the long, narrow valley readily cut up into distinct principalities, which warred on one another and promoted separate forms of worship, but there was also a strong antipathy between the two sections of the population, east and west of the river. To this day a man of one side will dislike those just opposite to him more than those ten times as far away on his own side. The Nile valley not only holds a streak of population a hundred times as long as it is wide, but even two incompatible streaks side by side all the length of it. Thus there was every facility for the isolation of local worships. Before a strong continuous monarchy existed, or whenever it was eclipsed, there appeared a long row of antagonistic tribes and cults, each of which defended its local worship as the bond of its union. To kill and eat their neighbour's sacred animal was the regular assertion of independence and vigour. Whatever antagonisms we now see remaining beneath the unification of Islām are mere shadows of the intense antipathies between the partisans of rival cults in ancient times.

4. Political rivalry and fusion.—Religion was thus essentially a part of politics. Fanatical fervour is the product of the political necessity of union. Small bodies, which are liable to be broken up, need a test of true membership, and a moral consciousness that they are in the right and their enemies are in the wrong, foul, miserable, and despicable. All this is given by a religious antipathy. The god is the rallying cry; the triumph of his followers is his triumph. Hence the mythic victories of the gods, one over another, are the records of the victories of their worshippers; and even the marriages of the gods are in many cases the expression of the marriages of the tribes who upheld them.

Besides the violent conquest of one god or tribe over another, there was the peaceful fusion of tribes, who became blended both in blood and in religion. This led to the fusion of gods who were alike, and who henceforward bore compound names, as Ptah-Sokar-Osiris, or Osiris-Khentamenti. This fusion also led to the acceptance of several gods and the uniting of them in groups, triads, or enneads. Thus Horus was originally an independent god, known later as the 'elder Horus' or 'greater Horus,' son of Hathor and not of Isis (Lanzone, *Diz. di mitol.* 603); from whom Hat-hor, 'the dwelling of Horus,' took her name. Isis 'was an independent deity . . . she had neither husband nor lover' (Maspero, *Dawn*, 131). Thus the best known triad of Egypt was compounded of the gods of three independent tribes, Osiris, Isis, and Horus, who were linked as a family when the tribes became fused together.

5. Resulting mixture.—Not only was the theology thus compounded by multiple names for a god, and forming groups of connected gods, but the fusion also led to the acceptance of incompatible beliefs, particularly about the future life. The interaction and combination of these formed a chaotic mass of contradictions, which were continually in flux, and accepted differently by each age, each district, and even each person. There is no such thing as 'the Egyptian Religion'; during thousands of years there were ever-varying mixtures of theologies and eschatologies in the land.

Such may exist even under the far more exclusive dominance of Christianity. The old Pictish *Bucca Gwidden*, or 'bright spirit,' is still named among us as 'Puck,' while the *Bucca Dhu*, or 'dark spirit,' has become the familiar 'Bogey Bo.' If we even retain these in London at present, much more were they realities in the West country during past centuries. They are as totally incompatible with Christianity as one theology in Egypt was irreconcilable with another; yet here they have co-existed for eighteen centuries.

II. *SOURCES.*—**6. Classifications and publications.**—The sources of our knowlege of the religion are but fragmentary; the ten books on worship, and ten on the laws and the gods, have disappeared since the days of Clement. Taken in the order of age, the materials may be classed, with the chief modern publications, thus:

1. *FIGURES OF SACRED ANIMALS OF PRE-HISTORIC AGE*: **J. Capart**, *Primitive Art in Egypt*, Eng. tr., London, 1905, figs. 125–139; **W. M. F. Petrie**, *Naqada*, do. 1896, *Diospolis Parva*, do. 1901.

2. *AMULETS, ANIMATE AND INANIMATE*: **Petrie**, *Deshasheh*, London, 1897, *Dendereh*, do. 1900, xxvi., *Abydos I.*, 1902, xxxviii.; **G. A. Reisner**, *Cairo Catalogue*, xxxv. [1907] 'Amulets.'

3. *TITLES OF PRIESTLY OFFICES*: **M. A. Murray**, *Names and Titles of Old Kingdom*, London, 1908; **H. Brugsch**, *Dict. géogr.*, Leipzig, 1877–80; **G. Legrain**, *Répertoire*, Cairo, 1908; **J. D. C. Lieblein**, *Dict. de noms*, Leipzig, 1871, i.–iv.; Petrie, *Royal Tombs*, London, 1900, i. and ii.

4. *NAMES OF PERSONS, SHOWING THE USUAL GODS AND IDEAS*: same sources as for 'Titles.'

5. *DEATH-SPELLS TO ENSURE SAFETY FOR THE BODY AND SOUL*: **P. le Page Renouf**, *Book of the Dead*, London, 1907; **G. Maspero**, *Inscr. des pyr. de Saqqarah*, Paris, 1894; **E. A. W. Budge**, 'Book of Gates,' and 'Book of Am-Duat' (Under World), in *The Egyp. Heaven and Hell*, London, 1906; **G. Jéquier**, *Livre de ce qu'il y a dans l'Hadès*, Paris, 1894; **H. Schack-Schackenburg**, *Das Buch von den zwei Wegen*, Leipzig, 1903; **R. V. Lanzone**, *Le Domicile des esprits*, Paris, 1879; **Brugsch**, 'Sai an Sinsin' (*RP* iv. [1905] 121); **Ed. Naville**, *Tomb of Sety I.*, Paris, 1886; **F. Guilmant**, *Le Tombeau de Ramsès IX.*, Paris, 1908; **E. Lefébure**, *Hypogées royaux*, Paris, 1886–9.

6. *TEMPLE SCENES OF RELIGIOUS SERVICE, AND TEMPLE*

[1] *Outlines of Mahāyāna Buddhism*, London, 1907, p. 51.

WRITINGS: A. Moret, *Du Caractère religieux de la royauté pharaonique*, Paris, 1903; C. R. Lepsius, *Denkmäler*, Berlin, 1897 ff.; A. Mariette, *Abydos*, Paris, 1869–80, *Dendérah*, do. 1880; A. Gayet, *Le Temple de Louxor* (*Mém. Mission Archéol. au Caire*, xv.).

7. *HYMNS*: Petrie, *History*, i. (1894) 182, ii. (1896) 215–8; *RP* ii. [1903] 129, iv. [1905] 99, 107, vi. [1907] 97, viii. [1909] 129; Naville, 'Litany of Ra' (*RP* viii. 105).

8. *POPULAR FIGURES OF GODS, MAINLY OF ROMAN AGE*: A. Erman, *Egyp. Religion*, Eng. tr., London, 1907, pp. 218–227; Petrie, *Roman Ehnasya*, London, 1904; V. Schmidt, *De graesk-aegyptiske Terrakotter i ny Carlsberg glyptothek*, 1911.

9. *GENERAL WORKS*: Lanzone, *Diz. di mitol. egiz.*, Turin, 1881–6; A. Wiedemann, *Rel. of the Anc. Egyptians*, London, 1897; Maspero, *Dawn of Civilization*², London, 1896, *Études de mythol.*, Paris, 1893 ff.; Budge, *Gods of the Egyptians*, London, 1904; Erman, *op. cit.*

III. *POPULAR RELIGION*. — **7. Pre-historic figures.**—The popular religion is the earliest form that we can trace in the remains of the pre-historic ages. In the graves and town-ruins are found various animal figures which seem to show the adoration of different species. The human figures of the same age seem to be distinctly servitors to satisfy the wants of the dead, and not to represent higher beings. The lion is the most usual of such animals, and the figures are distinguished from those of later ages by the tail turning up the back, with a small hook at the end. The bull's head was often carved, but rather of a small size, as an amulet. The hawk is the next commonest sacred animal. The hippopotamus is rarely found. The frog is usual, of various sizes. Serpents were specially honoured; the more usual form is coiled round, with the head in the centre, and was made of limestone or glaze nearly a foot across, to hang up in the house, and of a small size to wear on the person. Two intertwined serpents—as on a *caduceus*—are also represented, and a serpent coiled closely to fit on a stick. The scorpion occurs as a large separate figure, and also the locust. Among animals represented, but perhaps not regarded as religious, are the elephant, stag, bull, and hare. The baboon may not be pre-historic, but is one of the commonest figures in the Ist dynasty. The dog is not represented in carving, but was frequently buried in tombs. It is notable that some of the most usual sacred animals of later times never appear in the pre-historic period, such as the cat, jackal, vulture, and crocodile. That there were definite religious beliefs, fixed in common acceptance, is indicated by the constant posture of burial, and the regularity of the offerings buried, as we shall notice further on.

8. Magic.—Magic apparently began in the pre-historic age. A small box was found containing three little flat carvings in slate tied together, and two carved ivory tusks, none of which had any use for work. Such ivory tusks were carved with a human head at the pointed end, and kept in pairs, one solid, one hollow. They are probably connected with the present African belief in charming a man's soul into a tusk. Many small amulets were in use—not only the figures of sacred animals, but also such as a fly, a claw, a lance-head, or a vase.

In the early historic age magic appears as the basis of the popular tales: the forming of a crocodile of wax and then throwing it into the water to pursue a victim; the bringing together the head and body of a decapitated goose and restoring it to life; the turning back of the waters and descending to the river-bed to find a lost jewel—such are the pivots of the earliest tales. There appears to have always been a strong belief in the virtue of words and names. Creation was attributed to the word or speech of the Creator, as among the Hebrews. Even animals and objects had names given to them, to render them effective; without a name there could hardly be existence. In the close of Egyptian literature there is a protest against its translation into Greek: 'out of the solemn, strong, energetic speech of names . . . we do not use words, but we use sounds full filled with deeds.' In the later magic writings and inscriptions, names—generally corrupted and mistaken—are the moving power of the spells. In the later Ramesside times a conspiracy turned upon making wax figures, and sending them into the harim, to compass the death of the king. The latest tales, of the Ptolemaic age, turn entirely upon the use of magic. It seems not too much to say that an Egyptian was dominated throughout his life by the belief in the magical control exercised upon the gods, upon spirits in life and in death, and upon material objects. Cf. MAGIC (Egyp.).

9. Domestic worship.—The customs of domestic worship can only be gleaned from some occasional remains. In the pre-historic age the larger disks, carved with a coiled serpent, are pierced with a hole for suspension, showing that they were probably hung up in the houses; and in the Ist dynasty the usual border to the hearth was a pottery fender in the form of a serpent, doubtless copied from the serpent which they would find at dawn coiled round the ashes for the sake of warmth. In the XVIIIth dynasty there was usually a recess in the hall of the house, coloured red; and in one case, where it is preserved to the top, it had a scene of adoration of the tree-goddess above it. This was, doubtless, the focus of the domestic worship, probably having different deities painted over it according to the devotion of the master. On reaching Roman times, we have many interesting details preserved by the terra-cotta figures which were then so widely developed. The domestic shrine is represented as a wooden cupboard containing the figure of the household god, with a lamp burning before it. For poorer families, figures were made to hang up by a hole in the back to fit on a nail in the wall. The figure often had at its feet a small lamp, made all in one piece. Such figures are found by the thousand in towns of the Roman age, showing that they were probably in use in every house, or every room, like figures of saints at present among Roman Catholic populations. Of the prayers to the gods there is evidence in the epithets of Amon, 'who cometh quickly to him who calls on him'; and of Ptah, 'who hears petitions,' and whose tablets have ears carved on them.

10. Birth, marriage, and death.—The ceremonies at birth have not been recorded; but, as the names are often compounded from those of gods, it is probable that some religious ceremony attended the naming of the child, as in Egypt at present (see BIRTH and CIRCUMCISION [Egyp.]). Of marriages we know scarcely any more. The settlements of the XIIth dynasty are purely business documents. The demotic marriage-contracts are without any religious reference. The terms in the XXVIth dynasty agreed on for divorce by the man are confirmation to the wife of her marriage portion, and control of her children's share of paternal property, also a third of all property acquired by the pair during marriage; but in one case the divorce terms were five times the marriage gift. For divorce by the woman, she must return one-half of the marriage portion given to her. Divorce simply consisted in renouncing claims, and authorizing the woman to live with another man. In Ptolemaic times the terms were very similar. The only trace of religious terms is in one case, beginning the divorce clause by swearing by Amon and Pharaoh (Griffith, *Demotic Papyri, Rylands*, London, 1909, p. 115). In Coptic times it is said: 'Since God willeth that we should unite one with the other'; but either party could divorce freely on paying seven times the marriage gift, and no provision was stipulated for the children. The religious sanction of marriage seems, therefore, unknown in the pagan and scarcely named in the Christian contracts, which accords with the temporary view of the deed, and the constant provision for divorce.

The great religious event to an Egyptian was his death. There is no trace of spiritual preparation or *viaticum*. The body was simply handed to the embalmers, and they prepared it without the slightest reverence or sentiment. After the seventy days came the greatest ceremony of private life—the funeral; the procession, the wailers, the recitation, the incense, the ceremony of opening the mouth of the mummy; and, after the burial, the ritual service of funeral offerings, for which endowments were left, like those for masses in Europe. See, further, art. DEATH (Egyptian).

11. Dancing.—Another development of popular religion was dancing. In the earliest royal monuments the dance of men in the festival of Osirification of the king is represented; this took place, apparently, in an enclosure formed by cloth hangings placed on poles, and the conventional figure of this was represented behind the prince, down to the latest times. Dances of the servants are often represented in the tombs of the Pyramid age; but such were probably only festive, and not religious. In the XIIth dynasty the princesses are described as dancing with their ornaments before the king, and singing his praises. The sculptures and paintings of the XVIIIth–XXth dynasties show many scenes of funeral dances; usually one woman held a tambourine aloft and beat out a rhythm on it, while others danced round. Exactly this dance may be seen now when parties of women go up to the cemetery a fortnight or a month after a funeral; an old negress is often the drummer, and the party stop every few hundred yards along the road for a dance. The dances are mentioned by Herodotus (ii. 60) among the parties going to the great festival at Bubastis. Dancing was a considerable part of the public worship of the ascetic Therapeutæ in the Roman age. At their great gatherings, held every seven weeks, they 'keep the holy all-night festival . . . one band beating time to the answering chant of the other, dancing to its music . . . turning and returning in the dance' (Philo, *de Vita Contemplativa*; see G. R. S. Mead, *Fragments of a Faith Forgotten*, London, 1900, p. 80 f.). This must have been much like an orgiastic modern *zikr*, only performed by men and women in opposite companies. That so scrupulous and ascetic a community, generally devoted to solitude, should make religious dancing so important and so mixed points to a much freer use of dancing by the unrestrained public.

12. Wayside shrines.—The individual worship took place not only in the house, but also in the wayside shrines. The open-air shrines common now in Italy are represented in Egypt by covered shrines, where shelter from the heat may be enjoyed by the devotee. These shrines, or *welys*, at present abound in Egypt, being small cubical chambers of brick covered with a domed roof, and usually containing a cenotaph of some local holy man. The native passing them will utter a short ejaculation, or will stop for a recitation, or, further, will walk round the cenotaph either inside or outside of the building. Similar shrines are frequently reproduced in the Roman terra-cotta figures, and were evidently as familiar in ancient times as now. The simplest was a low dwarf wall with a little entrance on one side, enclosing a square; a column placed at each corner supported an arched roof over it. A similar form, entirely of wood, was mounted on wheels for the purpose of carrying an image. The more solid shrines were built up in brickwork on all sides, with latticed windows, and covered by a double-sloping roof, with gable in front. When a village or town extended round an earlier shrine, and enveloped it, the little sanctuary became richer, and needed a dwelling for the priest and a storeroom. But the site could not be enlarged around; so the building was carried upward, as shown by another model. Here the open shrine was raised by two or three steps, and lamps burned on either side of the door; above it were two rooms, one over the other, and at the top was inserted a large panel bearing the figure of the god. Thus the little hovel had grown into a four-storey building, on a level with the houses around it. Sometimes the priests used to carry a portable shrine through the streets, to collect the alms of the devout; this was a small cupboard shrine about two feet high, carried between two priests side by side, probably on a yoke resting on the shoulders. From Lucian's account of the wandering devotees of the Syrian goddess, and the prevalence of wandering dervishes in Egypt at present, doubtless the alms-collecting was carried on from village to village. A figure of Horus sitting in a low-wheeled basket-chair—perhaps personified by a living boy with the attributes—shows what was taken to perambulate the country.

13. Festivals of fertility and harvest.—The popular worship on a collective scale was seen in the great festivals. How large and important they might be, we know from the size of the gathering at the festivals of the present day. The great feast at Tanta is estimated to attract 200,000 people. That it is an occasion for general licence to the loose-living part of the population doubtless descends from the customs of the ancient festivals, as shown by the accounts of Herodotus. The two great festivals kept everywhere were the fertility feast and the harvest feast. At the first the 'gardens of Osiris,' like the 'gardens of Adonis' in Syria, ornamented the house. These are sometimes found preserved, as bowls full of Nile mud, and pierced with the holes left by innumerable sprouts of corn. Another method was to make clay figures of Osiris, stuffed with corn, as sometimes found; on wetting these, the corn would sprout from the body of the god. Still larger figures are represented, doubtless from the official feast, where the statue of Osiris is lying on a bier surrounded by a large bed of sprouting corn. As the planting in Upper Egypt is stated in the calendar to begin on the 14th Oct., millet on the 18th, and barley on the 19th, this feast of the growing corn was probably that named on the 21st Oct. (Choiak 11) in the Sallier calendar as the 'day of the panegyry of Osiris at Abydos'; the following day was 'the day when he transformed himself into a *bennu* bird,' probably a bird liberated from the green couch of Osiris to represent his resurrection.

The second general festival—that of harvest—fell during April, as the harvest is reckoned to begin with this month in the south, and end with it in the north. This was celebrated by offerings to Rannut, the serpent-goddess of harvest. After the threshing the grain was piled up, as it may now be seen in immense heaps lying in the open air at the large stores; the winnowing shovels were stuck upright with the handles buried in the heap, the tossing boards or scoops were held on high before it, the corn-measure crowned the heap, and Rannut was adored (stele in Bologna Museum).

14. Great temple feasts.—The details of provision for the great Theban festivals to Amon have been preserved to us in the Harris papyrus (see Petrie, *Hist. Studies*, London, 1911). From that we gather the details of a festival of 20 days in March, and another of 27 days in August. In the March feast 10,000 persons were present on the great day, and 4000 on other days; in the August feast 4800 on the great day, and 1000 on others. The great hall, or temple-court, was decorated with tamarisk branches, reed-grass, and hundreds of bouquets and chains of flowers. Tables of provisions of meat and cakes were set out for the priesthood and the nobles. Large quantities of food were provided for the people, mainly various breads, cakes, and fruit. Flowers for each person, to be offered by each, were supplied. Such was the general character of the great temple-festivals in honour of the local gods.

The festival of the New Year has a remarkable feature in the appointing of a mock king and his being sacrificed. This is not referred to in the ancient calendars, as it was a popular rather than a religious anniversary; but, happily, an account of the survival of it has been preserved. Klunzinger records (*Upper Egypt*, Eng. tr., 1878, p. 184):

'For those days it is all up with the rule of the Turks; every little town chooses for itself . . . a ruler who has a towering fool's-cap set upon his head, and a long spectral beard of flax fastened to his chin, and is clothed in a peculiar garment. With a long sceptre in his hand . . . he promenades. . . . Every one bends before him, the guards at the door make way, the governor of the province . . . lets himself be ousted, while the new dignitary seats himself on his throne. . . . At length he, that is, his new dress, is condemned to death by burning, and from the ashes creeps out the slavish Fellah.'

The modern copy of the crown of Upper Egypt, the false beard worn by kings, and the sceptre point to the descent of this custom.

15. 'Sed' festival.—In connexion with this should be noticed the great Sed festival. It appears to have been normally celebrated every 30 years, and to have been on the occasion of the king being deified as Osiris, and the Crown Prince being appointed and married to the heiress of the kingdom. Such a usage appears to be the amelioration of a custom of killing the king after a fixed interval, in order that his royal maintenance of the public life and prosperity should not deteriorate. Such a custom of king-killing was usual in Ethiopia, until abolished in the 3rd cent. B.C. It is still practised by the Shilluks in the Sudan; also in Unyoro, in Kibanga, in Sofala, and formerly among the Zulus. Thus it is strongly an African custom. Nor is it peculiar to Africa, as it occurred in Prussia, and at fixed intervals of 12 years in Southern India. There is thus abundant parallel for such a feast in pre-historic Egypt; but, before the use of records, this custom gave place to the deification of the king, who lived on with his successor. The king became Osiris, was clad as the god, held the Divine emblems, and was enthroned in a shrine at the top of a flight of steps. Before him danced the Crown Prince, and at a different point in the ceremony the assembled men danced in the same enclosure of hangings upon poles. Sacred standards were carried in procession. In some connexion with the festival there is the record of 400,000 oxen, 1,422,000 goats, and 120,000 captives. These numbers show the national character of the ceremony, whether they were dedicated or sacrificed. In the late times of the XIXth dynasty this festival of Osirification was performed much oftener, and after his 30th year Ramses II. repeated it every third year (Petrie, *Stud. Hist.* iii. 69). See, further, art. FESTIVALS AND FASTS (Egyptian).

16. Religious calendar.—The religious calendar of Egypt has never been studied, or even collected together. The materials are: (1) early lists of feasts, which were seasonal, and which usually do not exceed half a dozen occasions for funeral offerings; (2) the Ramesside papyrus Sallier iv., of which two-thirds of the year remains, stating the luck and the mythical or legendary events of each day (F. Chabas, *Le Calendrier*, Paris, 1870); (3) the Ptolemaic temple-calendars of Edfu, Esneh, Dendereh, etc., translated by Brugsch (*Drei Fest-Kalender*, Leipzig, 1877); (4) a few feasts noted by Plutarch (*de Is. et Osir.*); and (5) the modern Coptic calendar (published by R. N. L. Michell and E. Tissot). Cf. art. CALENDAR (Egyptian).

The ancient calendars are strongly local, those of the temples referring mainly to the festivals held in the temples on which they were recorded. On comparing the lists of Edfu and Esneh, which were of the same age and region, we find but six feasts identical, out of about a hundred entries. When we try to connect calendars of different periods, the shifting of the month-names through all the seasons presents the first difficulty. Owing to not observing leap-year, the nominal calendar rotated through the year in about 1460 years. Hence the question arises, which of the religious anniversaries were attached to the nominal month and day, and which to a day in the fixed year, both classes being named in inscriptions. The seasonal anniversaries must necessarily belong to the fixed year. On comparing the Sallier papyrus (of the age of Ramses II. or a little earlier) with the Ptolemaic lists, we find not a single festival or event attached to the same day in these earlier and later calendars.

That the festivals were attached to the fixed year is shown by six entries in the earlier and later calendars. We here denote the months by Roman numerals, I. to XII. for Thōth to Mesore, so as to read the intervals more readily:

	Sallier.	Ptolemaic.	Interval.
Going forth of Isis . .	13 III.	10 I.	302
Feast of Shu . . .	21 III.	19 I.	303
Isis and Nebhat weeping .	14 V.		308
Osiris slain (Plutarch) .		17 III.	
Feast of Sokar . . .	27 VI.	26 IV.	304
Smiting the wicked . .	22 VIII.		304
Feast of the Strong . .		21 VI.	
Feast of Horus . . .	1 IX.	1 VII.	305

Excepting in Plutarch, who wrote later than the Ptolemaic calendars, the interval between the early and late lists is 304 days; and this shift of the calendar on the seasons would occupy about 1255 years. The date on which the Esneh calendar was compiled is fixed by the New Year feast, of the fixed year by Sothis, falling on 26 X., which occurred in 138 B.C. The date of the Sallier calendar is, therefore, 1255 years earlier, or 1393 B.C.; and this agrees well with its having the name of Ramses II. scribbled on the back of it, as he began to reign 1300 B.C. Hence for any connected view of the calendars it is needful to translate the dates of the shifting months into fixed days of the year, corresponding with the epoch of the calendar. To compile a detailed religious calendar would be beyond the scope of this article, but the principle of fixed dates is here stated, as it has not yet been published.

We will now state the nature of the religious events which were notified in the calendars. The principal classes are

	Sallier.	Ptolemaic.
Festivals and myths of great gods .	98	72
Events of the war of Set . . .	37	4
Minor gods and myths . . .	37	30
Local worships	8	69
	180	175

17. Lucky and unlucky days.—Personal directions are given only in the Sallier papyrus. Originally every day was noted as favourable, cautionary, or evil, with some days of mixed character. Of these 223 remain, and there are also applied to these days 96 general directions as to going out or beholding things, 54 specific directions as to acts, and 15 prognostications of the course of life or manner of death, from birth on a given day. As Chabas shows, these directions are similar to the directions for action on different days of the month given by Hesiod, the list of unlucky 'Egyptian days' observed in Rome in the time of Constantine—25 in all—and the list of unlucky Jewish days stated by Salmasius—24 in all. It might be expected that the bad 'Egyptian days' of the Romans would be the same as among the Egyptians. On a comparison of the lists, the only adjustment of calendars which yields continuous connexion is from 18 Makhir to 25 Pharmuthi, coinciding with the unlucky days 25th Feb. to 3rd May. This also is exactly the connexion between the calendars when the vague year was finally fixed, as stated by Chabas. Hence these 7 of the unlucky days retained their character from the time of Ramses to that of Constantine.

The break between Paganism and Christianity has swept away nearly all traces of connexion between the calendars. The Coptic calendar is mainly seasonal, and very seldom mentions the luck of a day. There are, however, a few days when marriage is prohibited, in both the Ramesside and the Coptic calendars; and the intervals between these appear to be connected.

Sallier.	Coptic.	Interval.
5 II.	26 IX.	231
7 V.	24 XII.	227
17 V.	2 I.	230
19 V.	2 I.	228

As these days in the Sallier calendar are connected with other evil events, they must have belonged to the fixed year, like the rest; hence it is difficult to see how a shifting calendar could have transported them 229 days. If it be so, then these fixed seasons must have become attached to the shifting calendar in 434 B.C. and have been carried on with it till its arrest in 30 B.C.; since that date it has shifted only by the difference between old and new style. The dates mentioned in the myth of Horus of Edfu do not in any way agree with the Edfu or other calendars.

18. General feasts.—The seasonal dates of the feasts which are found in any two calendars, and which were, therefore, general, may be taken as within a day of the following:

Feast of Sokar	Jan. 15
Setting up the Dad	„ 19
Feast of the Strong	Mar. 11
Feast of Ptah	„ 21
Feast of Horus	„ 21
Feast of Horus	Apr. 21
Birth of Horus	May 21
Going forth of Isis	Oct. 1
Feast of Shu	„ 11
Feast of Isis	„ 27
Isis and Nebhat weeping	Dec. 3.

IV. *FUNERARY RELIGION.*—**19. Cause of its prominence.**—The funerary branch of the religion has become better known than any other, owing to the prominence of the tombs among the other remains. This is merely a casual prominence due to the Nile deposits. The laying down of ten to twenty feet of mud over the river-valley since the flourishing ages of history has buried the remains of daily life almost entirely; only a few small towns on the desert, or the later parts of the cities which were built high up on their mounds, have remained exposed. By far the greater part of the dwellings and buildings have passed under the Nile soil and the advancing water-level, while the cemeteries, being on the desert edge, have mostly remained as accessible as at first. Hence the disproportion in which we view the Egyptians, as being more concerned with death than with life. Probably the Egyptian saw and thought much less about his forefathers' graves, miles away in the desert, than an English rustic does who walks through the graveyard every Sunday.

20. Its importance.—The tomb was essentially the house of the dead, where the soul would live; and the intrinsic fact which has made the Egyptian tombs so important to us is the custom of representing the ordinary course of life in sculpture and painting on the walls of the funerary chapel, in order to gratify the deceased with the pleasures of life. No other people except the Etruscans and the early Chinese have thus recorded their civilization. The magnificence of some of this work must not, however, be put down as entirely for the dead. The great halls cut in the rock which astonish us at Syut or Beni Hasan were the quarries whence stone was taken to build the palaces of the living down in the Nile plain. It needed but little more labour and device to cut the quarry so as to serve for the tomb, and the painting of its walls was a trifling work compared with the excavation.

21. Reason of offerings.—An essential question is whether the provision for the dead depended on fear or on love; was it to prevent the ghost's returning or to gratify it in its new life? Can we view Egyptian customs as akin to those of the Troglodytes, who bound the body round from neck to legs, and then threw stones on it with laughter and rejoicing (Strabo, xvi. 4. 17)? On the contrary, we see, from the earliest times onward, that weapons were placed by the dead, which would arm them if they attacked the living; we find in the pre-historic times the skull frequently removed and subsequently placed with honour in the grave, as if it had been kept with affection, as it is among some races at present; the successors frequently visited the tomb and held feasts there; in Roman times the mummies were kept around the hall of the house; and to this day a widow may be seen going to her husband's tomb, removing a tile, and talking down a hole into the chamber. The treatment of the body, and the provision for it, all show no trace of repugnance or fear, but rather a continued respect and affection. We are bound, therefore, to look at the other offerings, of food and drink, of model houses and furniture, of concubines and slaves, as equally dictated by a wish for the future happiness of the deceased.

22. Pre-historic ritual.—In the pre-historic age there was a fixed ritual of burial, which implies an equally wide-spread group of beliefs as to the use and efficacy of the funerary provision. The body was placed in a contracted position on the left side, the hips and knees bent, with the hands together before the face. The direction was with the head to the south and the face to the west. The main classes of provision had each their regular place. The weapons were usually behind the back; the bag of malachite, and the slate and pebble for grinding it to paint the face, were before the face; the wavy-handled jar of ointment was at the head end; a small pointed jar stood at the feet; at either end of the grave beyond the body, or in a row along the side, stood the group of great jars full of ashes of the burning of offerings made at the funeral.

There was also an entirely different treatment of the body, often referred to in the oldest religious formulas of the Pyramid texts. The head was removed, the flesh taken off, the bones separated and cleaned, and then re-composed in right order, and the whole body put together again. This was supposed to purify the dead so that he should be fit to associate with the gods (see *Gerzeh, the Labyrinth, and Mazghuneh*, 1912). The traces of these customs, which probably belonged to the Osirian worshippers at very remote times, are found in a small proportion of bodies down to historic times. The latest clear group, in the Vth dynasty, had one-third of the bodies partly dismembered, with the hands and feet cut off and laid on the stomach beneath the swathing of the body, or with every bone cleaned and wrapped separately (Petrie, *Deshasheh*, 1897, p. 20, pls. xxxv., xxxvii.).

In almost all ages, from the pre-historic to the present, the Egyptians were equally averse to throwing earth on the dead. The earliest graves were pits roofed over with poles and brushwood, so as to leave a chamber. Later a recess was made in the side of the pit to hold the body, and fenced across the front by a row of jars. In the early dynasties a rock chamber was usual, later a brick shaft with a chamber at one side of it. Only in Christian times does the chamber seem to have been abandoned, and the open grave preferred. Under Islām, the chamber, with room for the corpse to sit up in it, is considered essential. Cf. artt. ANCESTOR-WORSHIP (Egyptian) and DEATH AND DISPOSAL OF THE DEAD (Egyptian).

23. The 'ka.'—Before we can follow the different views of the future life, we must look at the beliefs on the nature of man. The earliest tombstones, those of the Ist dynasty, show the *khu* bird between the *ka* arms; thus there was then recognized the *khu*, the 'glorious' or 'shining' intelligence, as dwelling in the *ka*, the activities of sense and perception; both of these were the immaterial entities in the *khat*, or material body. The idea of the *ka* is difficult to define, as we have no equivalent. It was closely associated with the material body, as it had parts and feelings like the body. All funeral offerings were made to the *ka*. If opportunities of satisfaction in life were missed or neglected, it was said to be grievous to the *ka*; also the *ka* must not be needlessly annoyed. Here it seems to stand for the bodily perceptions and powers of enjoyment. The *ka* could not resist the least physical force after death, although it retained consciousness and could visit other *kas* and converse with them. The *ka* could also enjoy the offerings and objects of life in representation; hence the great variety of funeral offerings, and the detail of the sculptures and paintings representing all the actions of daily life, the hunting in the desert, fishing on the river, beholding all the farm-yard, and the service of retainers, dancers, and musicians. A recent discovery adds to the complexity. Not only is the *ka* of the king represented as born as an infant at the same time, being nursed and growing up, and following the king holding a standard of 'the king's *ka*,' but we even see the *ka* holding the feather fan and fanning the king on his throne. This suggests that the king's *ka* may have had a separate physical body; and, as the Egyptian believed in horoscopes, so a child born at the same hour as the king would have the same fate, partake of the same soul, and was perhaps selected to accompany the king as his double and serve him for life. One being might have many *kas*; Rā had 14 *kas*, Tahutmes I. was the first king to have more than one *ka*, and Ramses II. had 30. The *ka* being so far separate could be taken by the Semitic mind as the equivalent of the Semitic guardian angel—an idea entirely foreign to the Egyptian: and thus it comes that we find the Semitic king Khyan with the title 'beloved by his *ka*.' Later this deification of the *ka* proceeded, and on the sarcophagus of Panahemisis we read, 'Thy *ka* is thy god, he parted not from thee, and so thy soul lived eternally' (Bissing, *Versuch . . . des Ka'i*, 1911). Here the *ka* has become a Divine principle, indwelling, and saving the soul. This comes fully into touch with the doctrine of the Logos in its developments. 'They possess Logos only and not Mind' (*Pers. Rel. in Eg.*, London, 1909, p. 92) is the stage of the purely human soul as the *ka*. Next, 'Thou art being purified for the articulation of the Logos' shows the Logos as a saving Divine principle, like the last view of the *ka* (*ib.* 93). The later growth was 'The Logos is God's likeness,' and 'The Logos that appeared from Mind is Son of God.'

24. The 'ba.'—An entirely different pneumatology is that of the *ba*, which is the disembodied soul figured as a human-headed bird. This is associated with the tree-goddess of the cemetery; out of her great sycamore tree she pours drink and gives cakes to the *ba*, who receives the food on the ground before the tree. Thus the *ba* is the entity that wanders about the cemetery requiring food, whereas the *ka* was thought to be satisfied with the model foods placed in the tomb. The *ba* is associated with the *sahu*, or mummy, as the *ka* is connected with the *khat*, or body. Some beautiful figures of the XIXth dynasty represent the mummy on its bier, with the *ba* resting on its side and seeking to re-enter its former habitation. Other figures in papyri show the *ba* flying down the tomb-shaft to reach the mummy lying in the chamber below. The actual source of the idea of the bird-like soul was doubtless in the great white owls which haunt the tomb-pits, and fly noiselessly out, their large round faces looking with a human expression. As to the different sources of these ideas, the *ba* belongs to the tree-goddess and the cemetery—apparently the earliest and most primitive kind of belief; the *ka* is always said to go to Osiris, or to the boat of the sun, or to the company of the gods, and belongs, therefore, to the more theologic views.

25. The 'ab.'—Other concepts were also associated with man, though seldom with any further religious views. The most important of these was the *ab*, the will and intentions symbolized by the heart. It was used much as we use the term 'heart' in 'good-hearted,' 'hearty,' or 'heartfelt'; so the Egyptians said that a man was 'in the heart of his lord,' or spoke of 'wideness of heart' for satisfaction, or 'washing of the heart' as expressing plain speaking or relieving the feelings by saying what was thought. The idea of the heart was prominent in later times, as it enters into all the throne names of the Saite period. Besides the metaphorical term of the heart for the will, the physical heart was also named as *hati*, the chief organ of the body, mentioned most frequently on the heart scarabs which were put in the place of the heart in the mummy, and inscribed with ch. xxx. of the Book of the Dead, called the 'Chapter of the Heart.'

The ruling power of man, decision and determination, was separated by the theorists, who multiplied these divisions, and was called *sekhem*, the sign for which was a baton or sceptre. The shadow was also named a *khaybet*, for which the sign was a large fan used to shade the head.

26. The 'ran.'—The essence of a name (*ran*) was very important, being the essential for true existence, both for animate and inanimate bodies. To possess the true name of a person gave power over its owner; without the name no magic or spell could affect him. A great myth, found in New Zealand as well as Egypt, is the gaining of the true name of the sun-god by stratagem, and so compelling him. Isis thus gained the two eyes of Rā—the sun and moon—for her son Horus. This importance of the name led in Egypt, as elsewhere, to the real name being avoided and kept secret, while some trivial name was currently used. On monuments it is usual, especially in the IVth and XXVIth dynasties, to find the 'great name' given, and also the common or 'little name': the great name is often formed from that of a god or a king, so as to place the person under divine protection in his future life.

27. The under world.—The under world (Erman, *Egyp. Rel.*, London, 1907, pp. 109–114), through which the dead had to pass, was divided into the twelve hours of night, so entirely was it associated with the sun's course. These twelve spaces are variously called 'fields' or 'caverns,' the latter idea obviously because of the sun going under the solid earth. Each space has a large population of gods, of spirits, and of the dead. The special goddess of each hour acted as guide, through that hour, to Rā and his company of gods. The first hour is said to be 800 miles long, till Rā reaches the gods of the under world. The second hour is 2600 miles long. The third is as long, and here Osiris and his followers dwell. In the fourth and fifth hours dwells the ancient god of the dead, Sokar, and his darkness cannot be broken by Rā, the later god. 'Rā does not see who is therein.' Rā has his boat changed into a serpent, to crawl through the earth. In the sixth hour is the body of Osiris. In the seventh is the great serpent Apap—a tradition of the boa-constrictor. The flesh of Osiris is here enthroned, and his enemies lie beheaded or bound before him. Here also are the burial mounds of the gods—Atmu, Rā, Khepera, Shu, Tefnut, and others. In the ninth hour the rowers of the sun-boat land and rest. In the tenth a beetle alights by Rā. In the eleventh hour the ship's rope becomes a serpent, and the ship is dragged through a serpent nearly half a mile long, and, as it emerges, Rā becomes the beetle, the god of the morning—Khepera. It is notable that the Egyptian had even an exaggerated idea of the size of the earth, as that is only 1000 miles to each hour on the equator, while the hours of the under world are reckoned as 2600 miles each.

Another version of these ideas imposed great gates between the hours, each guarded by watchers and fiery serpents. Another form was that of the fields of Aalu, which had 15 or 21 gates, each guarded by evil genii, with long knives in their hands (Petrie, *Gizeh and Rifeh*, 1907, pls. xxxvi. D, E, F). Yet an earlier idea was that of a great variety of roads, which had to be known to the soul, and for which an account of sixteen roads was placed upon the sarcophagus. Another chapter concerns eight nets or snares which have to be avoided. There was also a chapter for ensuring that the head should be restored to the body after it had been cut off in the early dismemberment usage. The earliest form of these texts is in the VIIth dynasty (see Petrie, *Dendereh*, 57 f.).

28. The 'ba' in the cemetery.—The Egyptian beliefs regarding the future life were very incongruous, and various elements were mingled, regardless of their consistency or relative possibility, much as present beliefs in England mix together the Old and New Testament, Milton, and folklore, the paganism of our ancestors. To have any intelligible view of the subject we need to disentangle the complex, and regard each system of belief apart.

The most simple view was that of the continued existence of the soul in the tomb and about the cemetery. This belief still survives in Egypt, in spite of Christianity and Islām. In Middle Egypt there is still a custom of placing jars of water and plates of food in the tomb, though it is considered so unorthodox that only by casual inquiry can this be learned. In one case a mattress was put beneath the dead; but it was said that on no account was any metal put in the tomb. This survival of the primitive belief and custom shows us how easily it continued to be held throughout, along with the later dogmas of the kingdom of Osiris and company of Rā.

The soul then was thought of as a human-headed bird, the *ba*, flying in and out of the tomb. It required access to the food provided for it, which was stored in, or around, the chamber. In the pre-historic age the offerings were placed close round the body. When the larger tombs of the earliest kings were developed, the body was enclosed in a wooden chamber of beams, and the offerings were placed round it. The space was afterwards subdivided into a line of store chambers, which were later built of brick. Jars of water, wine, corn, grapes, and other food were provided by the hundred; haunches and heads of oxen, trussed geese, cakes, dates, pomegranates, all abounded; chambers full of knives and weapons, for hunting and for fighting, succeeded to the flint-knife and mace-head of the earlier years; while finely wrought stone dishes and bowls of the most beautiful materials, including also the rare copper, were stored for the table service. The servitors were all quickly buried to go with their king to the under world; there was not even time for their dozens of tomb-chambers to dry before they were sacrificed and placed in rows around the great tomb.

The soul required a way of access to its provision and to the outer air. In some large tombs of the IInd dynasty a model gallery was made on the ground surface covered over by the *mastaba*; in this was placed a row of model granaries of mud, extending for ten or fifteen feet, and a little passage a few inches square led from the tomb-pit to this gallery of provisions. In tombs of the Vth dynasty a similar little opening is provided from the tomb-shaft out to the funeral chapel. In later times other provision was portrayed, though the idea was probably older than that described. The great shady sycamore trees which stood over the cemetery were looked on as the house of a kindly goddess, who was later identified as a Hathor. She provided food and drink for the wandering souls, and is shown looking out of her tree, pouring from her vase and dropping cakes from her tray to feed the *ba* before her.

29. The 'ka' and its imagery.—A different and less material view of the soul arose, and in place of a human-headed bird it was thought of as the *ka*, or will and consciousness of the person, coinciding with the sensations of the body, and therefore filling exactly the same form, but incorporeal. As the body had a *ka*, so all animals had *kas*, as they also felt; then everything that existed was by a feeling of Animism endowed likewise with a *ka*. Proceeding from this, the *ka* world was held to be self-contained, and in the full sense a duplicate of the corporeal world in which it resided. Hence the *ka* could enjoy the models of food which contained the *ka* of the food; it could enjoy the figures of men and animals, as it had enjoyed the corporeal forms when in the body. A whole world of imagery could thus be provided for the life of the *ka*; and that it was intended for this conception is shown by every part of it being stated to be for the *ka* of so-and-so. The life-like statues were for the *ka* to dwell in, that it might not wander disembodied; the more closely like life, and the more the clear eye glittered and the mouth seemed ready to speak, the happier the *ka* would be residing in it. The doctrine of the *ka* was, therefore, the great inspiration of Egyptian art.

Both of those views of the future life are so entirely free from any theological touch, or connexion with any god, that it seems difficult to suppose that they arose along with belief in any great Divinity. They seem to belong entirely to an animistic world, and to be, therefore, probably older than any of the theologies which entered Egypt. The idea of the immortality of the soul seems older than any belief in a Superior Being (see, further, 'Egyptian' sections on BODY, NAME, SOUL, etc.).

30. The kingdom of Osiris.—The oldest theology of the future life is that of the kingdom of Osiris. The dead were thought of as going down to the cool and misty north, to the realm of Osiris, in the Delta. After that region became familiar the scene was moved to Byblos, in Syria; and lastly, it became the heavenly kingdom in the north-east of the sky, and the Milky Way was looked on as the heavenly Nile which watered it. In every respect it was thought of as a double of the life in the Nile valley. Agriculture was the main occupation: the souls ploughed the land with a yoke of oxen as here; they sowed the grain broad-cast, reaped the harvest of corn or gigantic maize, and threshed it out by the oxen treading the threshing-floor. All this labour was done by the dependents of the great man, who meanwhile sat at ease in the shade, and played draughts with his wife, or rowed in a skiff on the meandering canals.

31. The Judgment.—Before the dead could be admitted to this kingdom, some examination was needful; it was not supposed to render the evil good, but the wicked required to be set aside, and only the good might enter. This examination was the Judgment of Osiris, which is a familiar scene in the funeral papyri. The dead were brought in by the jackal-headed Anubis before the presence of Osiris enthroned, with Isis and Nebhat standing behind him. The protestation of innocence was then made by the dead, each one denying that he had committed any one of 42 crimes. This list is commonly but strangely called 'the Negative Confession' (see, for details, artt. CONFESSION [Egyp.] and ETHICS [Egyp.]). Then came the 'weighing of the heart' in a great balance which the ibis-headed Thōth read and recorded. The heart was placed in one pan, and the feather of Maat—Truth—in the other. As the ostrich feather was the emblem of lightness (being also an emblem of Shu, god of space, or the atmosphere), it is evident that the heart needed to be light, and not weighed down by sins. The ideal of innocence was being 'light-hearted,' as we say. Those who could not bear the test were condemned. Their fate was to be devoured by a female hippopotamus, which stood waiting at the feet of Thōth in these scenes. Another fate of the wicked in the Rā theology was to be beheaded and burnt in a lake of fire; but that does not seem to belong to the Osiris system.

32. The 'ushabti' servants.—Whether the serfs and servants of an estate were supposed to be so often bad that the supply of labour would be short, or whether each justified person was necessarily a master in the future, it was thought needful to supply images of servants to do the agricultural work. Whether these originated in the figures of servants engaged in domestic work, found in tombs of the Vth and VIth dynasties, is not clear. In the XIIth dynasty single figures of a mummy form are rarely found, engraved with the name of the dead. These do not seem to descend from the servant figures; but by their forms they appear to originate the serfs for the Osiris kingdom of the XVIIIth–XXXth dynasties. It would appear, then, that in the XIIth dynasty the mummiform figure was for the *ka* of the person himself, and was supposed to act in the future. Then, to save him labour, a group of figures of serfs was substituted. These serfs have a chapter of the Book of the Dead as a spell to vivify them into action. They were furnished with bronze models of baskets and hoes at first, which soon after were carved or painted, held in the hands of the figures or resting on their shoulders. The water-pot was added rather later. The spell on the figures commanded them to carry the sand and the water when ordered, and to do the cultivation. To accompany women there are sometimes pottery figures of girls without tools, not mummy forms like those of men, but nude. These have an older woman robed to oversee them, as the male figures have often an overseer dressed in a waist-cloth or robe. The number of the figures varies, but in the most complete tombs of the Saite age 400 was the regular supply; sometimes there is one overseer to each ten workers. The name *ushabti* is usually understood as an 'answerer' who responds to the demand for service; it has also to be explained, in the shorter form *shabti*, as referring to the figures being made of sycamore wood. The history of the changes of form and material hardly belongs to the religion.

In Greek times, after these figures ceased to be made, it was usual to write that a deceased man had 'gone to Osiris' in such a year of his age.

33. The fellowship of Rā.—Another complete theology of the future was connected with the sun-worship of Rā and the gods associated with him. This was bound up with the soul's going to the west; and probably Khentamenti, 'he who is in the west,' was a god of the dead in this system. Certainly he was the god of Abydos for ages before Osiris was worshipped there, and Abydos was the place specially where the desert valley in the west led to the abode of the dead. In the dark world of the dead there were innumerable perils to be avoided; and the necessary protection could be obtained by joining the boat of the sun, and so being safely led through the successive gates of the hours guarded by their evil spirits. The dead is figured sometimes as just entering the boat and approaching the company of the gods who sail with Rā through the hours of day and night. In order to enable the dead to reach the boat of the sun, it was needful that he should have a boat to go forth and intercept it in its daily round. Hence a model boat with a crew upon it was provided in the tomb, especially in the Vth–XIIth dynasties. It had all the fittings—a sail for going up the Nile, and oars for rowing down—or sometimes two boats were differently rigged according to their direction; a peg for tying up at the shore, a mallet to drive the peg, and a landing plank were also provided.

34. The mummy and amulets.—In none of these views—of the *ba*, the *ka*, the Osirian or the Rā company—has the material body any part. These views were probably all formed before historic times, and after the earliest dynasties we find arising, about the end of the IIIrd dynasty, a system of mummifying. Before that the body was often perfectly dried in the soil, but not artificially preserved. This embalming, therefore, was apart from all the views which we have described. It developed another system—that of protective amulets. In the Vth dynasty we find strings of amulets of carnelian or ivory placed around the wrists and the neck. The most usual forms are the jackal head, lion-head, frog, bee, clenched hand, open hand, leg, *uza* eye, and scarab. After this age the amulets diminish, and in the XVIIIth–XXIIIrd dynasties only one or two glazed figures of gods were used. With the XXVIth dynasty there burst out an enormous development of the system. Figures of the gods in glazed pottery or lazuli, *uza* eyes, and scarabs in all stones and materials, rarely gold *ba* birds with inlaid wings, and gold seal rings, were arranged in rows upon the body, often fifty or more figures in all. By Ptolemaic times the amulets were larger and coarsely made in blue pottery, and they seem to disappear entirely before Roman times (cf. art. CHARMS AND AMULETS [Egyptian]).

This elaborate armoury of amulets was designed to preserve the body from being attacked or broken up, and to ensure that it should remain complete for the habitation of the *ka*. This preservation of the body led to an entire reversal of the older ideas. In all the dynastic ages the construction of a costly tomb for the dead was quite as needful as the preparation of the corpse; in the Roman age, however, the corpse was embalmed and very elaborately wrapped, often with a portrait over the face, and then kept for many years in the house, after which it was roughly buried, without any care, in the cemetery.

V. *THEOLOGY*.—**35. Animal-worship.**—In considering the worship of the gods, we shall endeavour to separate the successive stages which have ruled in Egypt. Maspero has pointed out how the jackal-worship predominated at Thinis before the rise of the jackal-headed Khentamenti, or the still later Osiris-worship, at Abydos. He notes also how the Osirian conception of the fields of Aalu is earlier than the solar view in the *Book of Knowing Duat*, or the under world. From such traces of the growth of the theology, and the proofs of independence of the sources of the gods, shown by their compounded names, we arrive at the historical view of the successive strata of the theology. We have: (1) the pure animal-worship; (2) the animal-headed gods with human bodies; (3) the human gods of the Osiris cycle; (4) the cosmic gods of the Rā cycle; (5) the abstract gods of principles; (6) the gods brought in from foreign sources, and not originally belonging to a part of the Egyptian population.

The animal-worship is based on two main ideas: (1) the sacredness of one species of animal to one tribe; (2) the sacramental eating of an example of the sacred animal at stated intervals. That the whole of a species was sacred among a tribe is shown by the penalties for killing any animal of the species, by the wholesale burial and even the mummifying of every example, and by the plural form of the names of the gods who were later connected with the animals, such as *Heru*, 'hawks'; *Khnumu*, 'rams'; *Bau*, 'birds.'

The sacramental slaying or eating is known in the case of the bull at Memphis (Mariette, *Le Sérapéum de Memphis*, Paris, 1882, pp. 11, 14, 16) and the ram at Thebes (Herodotus, ii. 42). From that appears to have sprung the keeping of an example of the sacred animal. It is well known that, in countries where human sacrifices were offered, it was usual as a compensatory measure to keep the victim for a long time—as much as a year—in the greatest indulgence and luxury, and to deny him no pleasures. This principle naturally resulted in keeping the sacred animal which was destined to be sacramentally eaten, and feeding and honouring it in every way. The keeping of a sacred animal will not account for its being consumed, rather the contrary; but the intended sacrament on the animal will be ample reason for keeping it with all honour. Hence we seem bound to accept the sacrament as the primary idea: the tribe needed at intervals to unify itself with its sacred species by absorbing the substance of one example, like the Norse burial of portions of a king in the fields to ensure their prosperity and fertility.

36. Sacred animals.—The sacred animals whose local worships are known have obvious qualities for which they might have been venerated; but whether those qualities were the sole cause of their celebrity or whether the tribe had a totemistic belief in its connexion with the animals is difficult to determine. That only one species was honoured by one tribe does not prove a belief in a connexion, because the earliest stage of theologic belief has similarly only one god for one tribe. So far as this evidence goes, the animal species was just in the position of the later god to the tribe. Nor does the use of the figure of an animal as a standard prove a totemistic connexion, as many of the nomes had standards which were reverenced—such as the crook and flail at Heliopolis, or the mace at Memphis—but which could hardly be regarded as totems of the people. The principle of reverence sufficiently accounts for the standards without supposing any closer connexion in some cases.

The *baboon* was adored as the emblem of wisdom, and of Tahuti, the god of wisdom. The appearance and ways of the baboon naturally originated this belief. Four baboons were kept as sacred in the temple at Hermopolis; they are often represented as adoring the sun, from their habit of chattering at sunrise. Figures of the baboon abound in the Ist dynasty at Abydos.

The *lion* and *lioness* are found in the pre-historic figures, and in later amulets, but are not shown on monuments or with names. The goddesses with the head of a lioness are named as Sekhmet of Memphis and Nubia; Bast of Bubastis, Leontopolis, Tell el-Yehudiyeh, and Letopolis; Mabes of Nubia; and Tefnut of Dendereh, el-Kab, Elephantinē, and Nubia. The spirit of the peak of Thebes—or Mert-seker—is also said to 'strike as a fascinating lion.' The destructive power of Rā, the sun, was personified as the lioness Sekhmet, who destroyed mankind from Herakleopolis to Heliopolis, at the bidding of Rā.

The lesser *felidæ* were also reverenced. In Sinai the *cheetah* and *serval* are figured as being sacred to Hathor. The *cat* was sacred to Bast, especially at Bubastis and Speos Artemidos, where Bast was equated with Artemis the hunter. The cat was also sacred to Mut, probably reverenced as a maternal emblem, at Thebes. The intensity of the popular worship of animals, even in the latest times, is shown by the well-known story of the fanatical mob tearing a Roman soldier to pieces for killing a cat.

The *bull* was worshipped mainly in the Delta, where four nomes used it as a standard. The four bull-gods most recorded are: (1) *Hapi*, or *Apis*, of Memphis, whose temple lay south of that of Ptah; (2) *Ur-mer*, or *Mnevis*, of Heliopolis, which was a more massive breed; (3) *Ka-nub*, or *Kanobos*, from whom the city was named; and (4) *Bakh*, or *Bakis*, of Hermonthis. These bulls were later connected with the gods who were worshipped at those cities. Hapi was the incarnation of Ptah, and also of Osiris as Osir-hapi; Rā was incarnate in Mnevis, and Mentu in Bakis; but these are evidently syncretic adaptations of rival worships.

The *cow* was apparently not worshipped (unlike India) except as an emblem of Hathor, probably from her source as the cow-goddess, the horned Ashtaroth, the Ishtar of Sumerian origin.

The *ram* was also worshipped as a procreative god; at Mendes in the Delta he was later identified with Osiris; both there and at Herakleopolis he became Hershefi—the strong chief; at Thebes he became Amon, and was specially the emblem of Amon to the Ethiopians; at the cataract he was Khnumu the creator. This diversity of connexions of the ram proves how his earlier worship was independent of the later gods. The burial-places and sarcophagi of the sacred rams have been found at Mendes and at Elephantinē.

The *hippopotamus* was called 'the great one,' Taurt, and always remained an entirely animal-god, never partly humanized. She was the patroness of pregnancy. Rarely the hippopotamus also appears in connexion with Set, probably from its devastation of crops, and thus it was theologized as Taurt, wife of Set. No local worship or temple of Taurt is known.

The *jackal* was the god of the dead, owing to his haunting the cemeteries and the Western desert where the soul was supposed to pass. At

Memphis he was described as 'on his hill' of the desert, and received later the name of Anpu, and a place in the Osirian family. At Asyut he was regarded as the maker of tracks in the desert, for the jackal-paths are the best guides, avoiding the valleys and precipices; thus he could guide the soul to the blessed West, and was called the 'opener of ways,' *Up-uat*, and also entitled 'he who is in the Oasis.' At Abydos he was called 'he who is in the West,' *Khentamenti*; and is later shown as a jackal-headed human figure seated on the judgment-seat of the future world. The *dog* was honoured in the pre-historic age, buried with the dead, and sometimes in special tombs of dogs; but we cannot say how far this was a part of the general canine worship, which was later confined to the wild species.

The *ichneumon*, or mongoose, was sacred at Herakleopolis; and was in antagonism to the neighbouring worship of the Fayyum crocodile, as it fed on the beast's eggs.

The *shrew-mouse* was sacred at Buto and Athribis, and also embalmed at Thebes.

Of birds, the *hawk* was that mainly adored, almost entirely in Upper Egypt. The hawk *Behudet* was worshipped at Edfu; another hawk at Hierakonpolis near el-Kab; two hawks were the standard of Koptos, and the nome of Hierakonpolis just south of Tehneh and opposite Asyut shows other centres. These hawks were later identified with Horus and with Rā, who are shown in that form. The hawk was also a god of the dead in a mummified form, as the god Sokar of Memphis. It is shown in a boat which is rowed by small hawks; these may perhaps be the deceased kings, as the king's soul was believed to fly up as a hawk to heaven (*Sanehat*). The mummy hawk was also venerated in the region of Suez, being the emblem of *Sopdu*, god of the East, found in Goshen and in Sinai.

The *vulture* was the emblem of maternity, worshipped mainly at Thebes, where the idea was later embodied as a mother-goddess, *Mut*. The vulture head-dress was worn by the queen-mother; and the vulture is represented spread out for protection over the king, and across the passages of the tombs to protect the soul. The vulture *Nekhebt* was also the goddess of the southern kingdom centred at Hierakonpolis, and was used to the latest times as the emblem of the southern dominion, as the serpent of Uazet was of the northern.

The *goose* and the *wagtail* continued to be adored at Thebes down to the XVIIIth dynasty, as is shown on tablets; the goose was then connected with Amon.

The *ibis* was identified with *Tahuti*, the god of wisdom, at Hermopolis, probably from its habit of searching and examining the ground for food. It was also mummified at Memphis, Abydos, and Thebes.

The *crocodile* flourished especially in the marshy levels of the great lake of the Fayyum, and was worshipped as the god of the province. In later times it was here united with Osiris and with Rā. It was also worshipped at Onuphis in the Delta, and at Nubti, or Ombos, where it was united with Set. The men of the neighbouring city of Tentyra carried on a tribal warfare against this god of the next nome, as described by Juvenal (*Sat.* xv. 35 ff.).

The *frog* was an emblem of multitudes or reproduction, and of *Heqt*, the goddess who assisted at birth; but there is no trace of its being worshipped, though it was a frequent amulet in the prehistoric age and the XVIIIth–XXIInd dynasties.

The *cobra* serpent was much reverenced in prehistoric times, when it appears coiled up as a house amulet to hang up, or as a necklace amulet, or coiled round a stick, or in pairs twisted together, or curled round the hearth as a pottery fender. The great pythons are shown in the mythological serpent *Apap*, and combined in the serpent-necked monsters upon the slate carvings. The *uraeus*, or cobra with expanded hood, became the emblem of judgment and death, and appears on the cornice of the judgment-hall and on the royal head-dress. An immense serpent was carved as the guardian of the temple of Athribis in the XVIIIth dynasty. Serpents were commonly mummified, and even a bone or two were encased in bronze, with a serpent figure on the top, in the XXVIth–XXXth dynasties. The serpent was looked on as the 'Agathodaimon' of the house in Ptolemaic and Gnostic beliefs. Serapis and Isis were identified with serpents, and bracelets or finger-rings ending in two *uraei* were the commonest ornament. Serapis also is figured as a human-headed *uraeus* on the popular terra-cottas for domestic use. Three goddesses were in the form of the *uraeus*: *Uazet*, worshipped at Buto in the Delta, and the symbol of the northern kingdom; *Mert-seker*, 'the lover of silence,' the goddess of the dead at Thebes, supposed to reside on the peak of Thebes; and *Rannut*, the harvest-goddess, doubtless originating from the serpents left in the last patch of corn in the harvest-field.

Several *fish* were sacred: the *Oxyrhynkhos* at the city named after it, now Behnesa; the eel, or *Phagrus*, at Phagroriopolis and Syene; the *Latus* at Latopolis; the *Maeotes* at Elephantinē; the *Lepidotus* at various places.

37. **Animal-headed gods.**—The animal-headed gods form a distinct class, as—with the exception of Horus—they are found only in this form and never with human heads. They appear to belong to the earliest theologic stage, when gods with human qualities were introduced, and blended with the earlier animal-worship. The habit of combination of forms was already usual in the close of the pre-historic age, before any figures of gods that we know. On the slate palettes are compound animal figures and human-animal figures, with habitual symbolism of standards of tribes acting as the tribes, in fighting or holding captives. The animal-headed gods are less violent in symbolism than the figures which were already usual. The earliest figure of such a god is on the seals of the IInd dynasty.

Khnumu, the creator, bears the head of the ram; and the long twisted horns of the ram are often attached to the head-dresses of Osiris, and of the kings who became Osiris, as showing their creative functions. Khnumu was especially the god of the cataract; he is represented seated as a potter and framing man on the potter's wheel. Besides his local importance he was greatly thought of in later times, when the amulets of his standing figure are often found on mummies.

Hershefi, another ram-headed god, was purely local, and is not found outside of the region of Herakleopolis, except at Mendes.

Sekhmet, the lioness-goddess, represented the fierceness of the sun's heat; she is the agent of the wrath of Rā in the myth of the destruction of mankind. Her statues are common, especially at Thebes, where hundreds of them adorned the temples. She was worshipped at Memphis, where she became the consort of Ptah.

Bastet had the head of a cat; but it is difficult, without names, to distinguish her figures from Sekhmet. She represented the ardour not of heat, but of animal passion, and her festivals at her city of Bubastis were very popular and licentious. Her name is found in priesthoods of the early Pyramid age, but her great period was during the political ascendancy of her city under the Shishaks. As a cat-goddess, she was also the patroness of hunting, and so became identified by the Greeks with Artemis.

Anpu, or *Anubis*, was the jackal-guardian of the cemetery, and the guide of the dead. His figures when acting are always human, with a jackal head, and he is most often shown as leading the dead into the judgment of Osiris, or bending over the bier attending to the mummy. His statuettes were often placed on mummies. On the other hand, no temples or local worships of Anubis are known; but he passed into the Roman adaptations from Egypt, and is figured on the Gnostic gems.

Set, or *Setesh*, was the god of the pre-historic inhabitants, and probably one with the Asiatic god who appears as *Sutekh* of the Hittites—an illustration of the Asiatic origin of the second pre-historic culture in Egypt. He is shown in the IInd dynasty and at various later times in an entirely animal form, but, when associated with other gods, in a human figure with animal head. What animal is intended is uncertain; the body form is most like a greyhound, but the peculiar upright tail with a tuft at the end is like that of the wart-hog when excited; other comparisons with the okapi, etc., have also been made. Probably the original form was lost to the Egyptians, and conventional changes hide it. At first the god of the Egyptians, his worshippers were conquered, after a long struggle, by the followers of Horus. Set yet retained some adoration in the Book of the Dead and in calendar feasts. The two worships were put on an equal footing by the last king of the IInd dynasty. After suppression, Set appears again favoured in the early XVIIIth dynasty; and in the XIXth the kings Seti I. and II. were even named after him. In later times the great popularity of Horus led to Set being entirely suppressed, and looked on solely as the evil spirit.

Sebek, or *Sobk*, or *Soukhis*, rarely appears, being only a local god. Statues of the human figure with a crocodile head were in the Labyrinth of the Fayyum in the XIIth dynasty. Rarely the converse is shown, and a crocodile with a human head, as Sebek-Osiris, appears as the Fayyum god of the dead.

Tahuti, or *Thōth*, appears with the head of the ibis, never that of the baboon; but both animals were equally used as his emblems in all periods. He is seldom figured alone, but is usual in groups of gods as the recorder of the judgment, and as performing rites over the king. As the god of learning, he was specially the patron of scribes, but was not worshipped in temples, except at his cities of Hermopolis in Upper Egypt and in the Delta.

Mentu was the hawk-god of the region from Kus to Gebalayn, but was later restricted to Hermonthis when Amon became the god of Thebes.

Hor, or *Horus*, was the hawk-god of Upper Egypt, especially of Edfu and Hierakonpolis. This form, with a human body and hawk head, was that of the conqueror of Set; the entirely hawk form is not found associated with other gods, and the purely human form appears only as the son of Isis. The hawk-headed form was popular till very late times, as Horus is so represented as a Roman warrior on horseback slaying a dragon—the prototype of St. George. The figure of Horus apart from the Osiris cycle is that of Hor-ur, Horus the elder, as a tribal god before being merged in the Osiris family.

38. Human gods: Osiris cycle: Theban triad.—The entirely human gods belong to two great groups—the Osiris family and the Amon family, besides the goddess Neit. These are marked off by not adopting animal forms, or being cosmic or Nature gods, or representing single abstract ideas. (*a*) *Asar*, or *Osiris*, though so familiar to us, is mainly known from late sources, which were modified by other ideas. In the Book of the Dead, the Osirian portions are earlier than the solar portions, yet both are so early that they are mingled in the Pyramid texts. We cannot doubt that the Osiris worship arose in the pre-historic age; the oldest list of Osiris centres does not include Memphis. In the early Pyramid age, Anubis only is named in the funeral-formula, but in the Vth dynasty Osiris takes his place. In the earlier dynasties only kings are entitled 'Osiris,' having undergone apotheosis in the Sed festival; but in the XVIIIth dynasty, and later, every deceased person was entitled the 'Osiris,' as having been united to the god. Neither at Abydos nor at Philæ is Osiris named on the earlier monuments, although in later times he was specially the god of both places. It seems that the extent of Osiris-worship was growing throughout the historic period; this may be due to Osiris gradually regaining an earlier position, from which he had been ousted by the new gods of invaders.

The myth of Osiris is preserved in its late form by Plutarch; the main outlines, which may be primitive, are as follows. Osiris was a civilizing king of Egypt, who was murdered by his brother Set and seventy-two conspirators. Isis, his wife, found the coffin of Osiris at Byblos in Syria, and brought it to Egypt. Set then tore up the body of Osiris and scattered it. Isis sought the fragments, and built a shrine over each of them. Isis and Horus then attacked Set and drove him from Egypt, and finally down the Red Sea.

Another view of Osiris is that of a god of fertility (see Frazer, *Adonis, Attis, Osiris*[2], 1907, p. 268). He is represented as lying surrounded with green plants and sprouting corn, and his figures were made full of corn. This was probably a view resulting from his being the ever-living god of the dead, who might be regarded as the source of returning life. The division of his body into fourteen or more parts, each buried in a different nome, appears to belong to the idea of dividing a body of a king or great man, and burying portions in various places to ensure the fertility of the land. For lists of the Osiris relics and places, see Petrie, *Historical Studies*, pl. vii.

Aset, or *Isis*, was originally an independent goddess, but by political changes she became united with the Osiris myth, as the sister and wife of Osiris. Her worship was far more popular than that of Osiris. Persons were more often named after her, and she appears more usually in affairs. Her devotion to Osiris appealed to the feelings, and her combination with Horus, as her son, led to a great devotion to her as the mother-goddess. She is seldom shown as the nursing mother till the XXVIth dynasty; but from that time the worship of the mother and child became increasingly general, and spread to Italy and over the whole Roman Empire. The temples of Isis, like those of Osiris, are of late date; the principal one was the great red granite Isaeum, now known as *Behbit el-hagar*, in the east of the Delta. Generally Isis was more a divinity of the home and person than of the temple and priest, until in Roman times her worship spread immensely through the world, and temples and priests of Isis are found in most lands of the West.

Nebhat, or *Nephthys*, is placed as the sister of Osiris and Isis, but is figured as only a complementary second to Isis. Yet she was worshipped at Letopolis, Edfu, Diospolis Parva, Dendereh, and the Isaeum. This worship and her name—*Neb-hat*, 'mistress of the palace'—seem to show that she was originally a more important consort of Osiris, who was pushed aside by the amalgamation of the Isis-worship in the group. She usually appears opposite to Isis, in the same attitude, mourning over Osiris.

Horu, or *Heru*, *Horus*, is a most complex divinity, in the various worships that were mixed together, and in the different aspects under which he became popular. The different alliances of tribes at various times led to three human forms: (1) the greater Horus, *Hor-ur*, brother of Osiris, and older than the rest of the group; (2) Horus, son of Osiris, avenger of his father; (3) Horus, the child, *Har-pe-khroti*, Harpocrates, son of Isis.

(1) Hor-ur was the son of Hathor, whose name, 'the dwelling of Horus,' shows that she derives her position largely from her son. He was specially the god of Letopolis, north of Memphis, also worshipped at an upper centre of Hathor-cult, the cities of Dendereh, Qus, and Nubti, and in the Fayyum. (2) Horus, son of Osiris, is the 'avenger of his father,' usually hawk-headed, spearing the evil crocodile, trampling on Set, driving his party out of Egypt, establishing smithies of his band of *shemsu*, or followers, and, lastly, attendant on Osiris in the judgment. He was also *Hor-sam-taui*, 'Horus, uniter of both lands,' as conquering Egypt from the Set party. (3) The most popular form of Horus was that of the child of Isis. Figures of Isis and Horus are known from the VIth dynasty, but the great spread of this form was in the later times of the XXVIth dynasty, and on to Christian changes. A cognate form was the boy Horus, trampling on crocodiles, and grasping serpents, scorpions, and noxious animals. This was a type commonly carved in relief on tablets to be placed as amulets in the house, and covered with long magical texts. The infant Horus also appears seated on a lotus-flower; but it is doubtful if this arose in Egypt before the type of Buddha, jewel in the lotus, might have been imported. Figures of Horus the child, seated in Indian attitudes, point to a connexion. Horus, as an infant carried by Isis, or being suckled by her, is the most general late type, continued till the 4th or 5th century. The absorption of this type, as an entirely new *motif*, into Christian art and thought took place under the influence of Cyril of Alexandria, by whom Mary was proclaimed as Mother of God in A.D. 431. Henceforward these figures are not of Isis and Horus, but of the Madonna and Child.

(*b*) The Theban triad were also entirely human, without any animal connexion until later times.

Amon was the local god of Karnak. He was probably closely connected with Min, the god of the neighbouring desert of Koptos; and a late legend points to Min being the earlier and Amon being a variant, as Isis is said to have divided the legs of Amon, who could not walk before, but had his legs growing together (Plutarch, *Is. et Os.* lxii.). Min is always shown with the legs joined, Amon with the legs parted. Moreover, Amon is often shown in the ithyphallic form of Min. Had the princes of Thebes not risen to general dominion, probably Amon would have been as little known as many other local gods; but the rise of the XIth and XIIth dynasties brought Amon forward as a national god; and the XVIIth dynasty from Nubia, holding Thebes as its capital, entailed that Amon became the great god of the most important age of Egypt—the XVIIIth–XXth dynasties. He thus became united with Rā of Heliopolis, the greatest god of the Delta; and Amon-Rā became the figure-head of Egyptian religion, king of the gods, and 'lord of the thrones of the earth.' Important as Amon was, he was never intruded upon the worships of older cities, and his temples are rare. Of all the territorial titles which he has, only those of Memphis as the capital, Asfun, and Habenan touch other worships. The rest are in the new cities of the Delta marshes, in the desert, or in Nubia. A special feature of his worship was the devotion of the queens of the XVIIIth dynasty and onward to the XXVIth. The queen was his high priestess; and, as such, Amon (personated by the king) was her husband, and father of her children, who were consecrated from birth by this divine paternity. The temple of Deir el-Bahri portrays the divine birth of Hatshepsut, that of Luqsor the divine birth of Amenhotep III. The family of high priests next married the royal heiress, and became the priest-kings of the XXIst dynasty. In the XXVIth dynasty the line of high priestesses of the Ethiopian family was kept in possession of Thebes, but the Memphis kings never married them, but required them to adopt a daughter of the king. Thus the high priesthood was carried on in a fictitious line. In Ethiopia, where Amon was the national god, the high priestess was always the daughter of one king, and wife of the next in unbroken female succession; during the Ethiopian rule of Egypt, a second high priestess also ruled at Thebes. The ram, which was the sacred animal of Thebes, was worshipped in combination with Amon by the Ethiopians, and Amon appears with a ram's head at Napata and Naga. The ram was specially adored by the Ethiopian dynasty (XXVth), and ram-headed scarabs are usual at that time.

Mut was the goddess of Thebes, probably even before Amon was localized from his desert form of Min. Her greatest temple was that in the quarter of Thebes called Asheru, and she is always named 'lady of Asheru.' She was also worshipped in the desert of Hammamat, and at Mendes and Sebennytos, but not imposed on the general adoration. She is shown as leading and protecting the kings, and queens often appear in her character, and with the vulture head-dress of the goddess.

Khonsu is closely parallel with Tahuti in his character as a god of time, a moon-god, and 'the executor of plans,' or god of knowledge. He is identified with Tahuti, as *Khonsu-Tahuti*, at Edfu, and so obtains the head of the hawk of Edfu. Otherwise Khonsu is always a human child, while Tahuti is a man with the ibis head. His place at Thebes is as the son of Amon and Mut, and a large temple was built to him by Ramses III. at Karnak, to which Euergetes added the immense gateway so well known.

(*c*) *Neit*.—This goddess was always represented in entirely human form, holding bow and arrows, and bearing on the head crossed arrows or shuttle. There is, however, no trace of her being connected with weaving, and it has been supposed that the shuttle was only a mistake of the Egyptians in later times, the primitive form being a long package crossed by two arrows (see Petrie, *Royal Tombs*, 1900, i. front.). The package might well be the skin of an animal rolled up, as in the sign *shed*, and so the whole might belong to a goddess of hunting. In later times the shuttle with thread upon it is clearly used for the name of the goddess. Neit was the most popular divinity in the Ist dynasty, queens being named *Neit-hotep* and *Mer-neit*, and many private persons also used the name. She was probably a goddess of the primitive Libyan population, and was the special divinity of the later Libyan invaders of the XXVIth dynasty at their capital Sais. During the Pyramid period the priesthood of Neit was the most usual; and in the XIXth dynasty her emblem is shown as the tatu mark on the Libyan figures. She was worshipped only in the Delta, at Sais Athribis and Zar (Sebennytos), except in the Ptolemaic temple of Esneh.

39. **Cosmic gods.**—The cosmic gods were apparently a later stratum of theology than those already described. They belong mainly to the Eastern Delta, and probably are due to an Asiatic immigration.

Rā, the sun-god, was specially worshipped at Heliopolis, and, when that older centre rose again above the invasion of the earlier dynasties and gave the Vth dynasty to rule Egypt, each king took a name on accession which embodied a quality of Rā, in much the same Semitic style as the 99 names of Allah. Every king of Egypt afterwards had a Rā-name, such as *Rā-men-kau*, 'Rā establishes the *kas*'; *Rā-sehotep-ab*, 'Rā satisfies the heart'; *Rā-neb-maat*, 'Rā is the lord of truth.' Rā was thus more constantly recognized than any other god, yet he has no temples in the great centres; beyond his own city of Heliopolis he is named only in connexion with Babylon in the same nome, at Xois in the Delta, and at Edfu, owing to his union with the hawk-god. He was, however, united with Amon, as the compound god *Amon-Rā*, in universal honour; and thus shared in the great worship of Amon. The need of uniting these two names shows that these gods originally belonged to different races.

Rā was not the primitive god, even of Heliopolis, as the worship of another sun-god, Atmu, underlay that of Rā. The collateral facts point to Rā having come in as the god of Asiatics; the title of the ruler there was *heq*, the Eastern title known later through the Semitic invaders; the *heq* sceptre was the sacred treasure of the temple; the 'spirits of Heliopolis' are more akin to Babylon than to Egypt; and the city was always a centre of literary learning. The obelisk of the sun seems connected with the Syrian worship of conical stones and stone pillars; and the 'city of the sun,' Baalbek, shows a similar worship.

Rā is shown as a purely human figure—as in his union with Amon; or as a hawk-headed figure owing to his union with the hawk-god of Edfu; or simply as the disk of the sun, especially when in his boat for floating on the celestial ocean. The disk has various emblems usually associated with it: the cobra in front, as king of the gods; two cobras, one on each side, which may refer to the double kingdom of day and night, or both banks of the Nile; two ram's horns as the creation-god; two vulture wings as the protecting god, or sometimes only one. The disk is often placed on the head of the hawk-god or the hawk-headed human figure.

Atmu, or *Tum*, was the god of the Eastern Delta, from Heliopolis round to the gulf of Suez. Whether he was a sun-god originally, or only became so by union with Rā, is not known. He is always shown in a purely human form. He was regarded as the setting sun, in some connexion with the Semitic origin of his name, 'the completed, *or* finished, *or* closed.' His special place was Pa-tum (Pithom, the city of Ramses).

Khepera is the rising sun, 'he who becomes *or* arrives'; only secondarily, from this name written with the scarab, was the sun represented as a scarab. He is shown mainly about the XIXth dynasty, and was otherwise scarcely known.

Aten was the radiant disk of the sun, entirely separate from the theology of Rā. It is never represented by any human or animal figure, and the worship of Rā was proscribed by the devotee of Aten. The object of worship was not so much the disk of the sun as its rays, or radiant energies; these are shown each ending in hands, which give life and dominion and accept offerings. This worship was restricted within half a century or less, traces of it appearing under Amenhotep III., the full development under his son Akhenaten, and the end of it under Tut-ankh-amon. As it appears when Syrian influence was at its height, the connexion of the name with *Adon* (Sem. 'Lord') seems clear, especially as Adonis was worshipped in Syria. From the hymns to the Aten, the worship appears to be that of the solar energy, and to have been a scientific idea apart from the usual type of Egyptian religion. Aten was regarded as a jealous god, who would not tolerate any other worship or figure of a divinity. Aten is the source of all life and action; all lands and peoples are subject to it, and owe to it their existence and allegiance.

Anher, 'he who leads heaven,' was the god of Thinis in Upper Egypt and Sebennytos in the Delta. He is always in human form, and carries a sceptre. His name shows that he was a sun-god, and he was later identified with Shu, son of Rā. He does not appear to have been regarded at all beyond his own centres of worship.

Sopdu was identified with the cone of light of the zodiacal glow, which is very clearly seen in Egypt. He represented the light before the rising sun, and was specially worshipped in the eastern desert, at Goshen, and Serabit in Sinai.

Nut was the embodiment of heaven, represented as a female figure, dotted over with stars. She was said to dwell at Diospolis Parva and near Heliopolis, but there are no temples to her, and she is usually not worshipped but grouped in a cosmic scene. She bends over, resting on her hands and feet, usually supported by Shu, the god of space, on his uplifted hands; below lies the earth, Seb, as a man. This seems to show the lifting of heaven from the embrace of the earth by the power of space.

Seb, or *Geb*, was the embodiment of the earth. He is called 'the prince of the gods,' as going before all the later gods. He thus is analogous to Saturn; and, like him, doubtless Seb and Nut belong to a primitive cosmic theology earlier than any other in Egypt. Seb is called the 'great cackler,' and the goose is placed upon his head. There seems in this the idea of the egg (named in Book of the Dead, liv.) of the sun being produced from the horizon by the earth. He is called 'lord of food,' as being provided by the earth. He was honoured at Memphis and Heliopolis, but no temples of his are known. It seems that Seb, Nut, Shu, and Tefnut remained as the cosmogony of Egypt, but had long ceased to be worshipped or to have any offerings or temples in their honour.

Shu, the god of space, was symbolized by an ostrich feather, the lightest object for its bulk that was known. His function was the lifting of the heaven from the earth; and as a separate figure he is usually shown kneeling on one knee with uplifted arms. He was honoured in the south of Egypt, at Pselcis, Bigeh, Esneh, and Dendereh, and also at Memphis; but no temples were built to him. Shu is often grouped with his sister Tefnut, and sometimes both appear together as lions.

Tefnut was also honoured in the South, in Nubia, Elephantinē, el-Kab, Erment, and Dendereh, as well as at Memphis. She appears in human form, like Shu, but is often lion-headed.

After the sun-, sky-, and earth-gods must be added the Nile-god, *Hapi*. He is always shown in human form, a man, but with female breasts, and often barred all over with wavy blue water-lines. Owing to the division of Upper and Lower Egypt, the Nile was similarly divided into two entities. Figures of the Upper and Lower Nile, distinguished by papyrus and lotus plants, are commonly shown as holding those plants entwined around *Sma*, the hieroglyph of union, as an emblem of the union of the whole country. Hapi was worshipped at Nilopolis and at the 106 little river-side shrines which marked the towing stages on the Nile. The dates of inscriptions in honour of the Nile at Silsileh do not refer to the festivals, except that of Merenptah on 5 Paophi, =19 July, in 1230 B.C., which might be at the rising of the Nile. A long hymn to the Nile does not throw light on the worship, but praises the productiveness of the river (*RP* iv. 107).

40. Abstract gods: Ptah, Min, etc.—The abstract gods stand quite apart in character from those whom we have noticed. They have no history or legends like Osiris and Rā; and, as abstractions, they stand at a higher level than the Nature-gods of the simpler ages. There are no great festivals connected with them, or any customary celebrations. Some were probably tribal gods, but on a different plane from those already noticed, and seem to be of a late and advanced character.

Ptah was the great god of Memphis, and became the head of the Memphite triad, and later of the ennead. He has two apparently contradictory characters—that of the creator acting by moulding everything from primeval mud, and that of the mummiform god. Whether these are not two separate beliefs fused together we cannot yet discern. The mummy form strongly implies a deified human being, and one of the dynastic race, as all the earlier peoples buried in a contracted position. There is also the duplicate belief of Ptah creating by the spoken word. A further complication arises from his fusion with the old primitive animal-worship of the bull Apis at Memphis. He was also united to the primitive Memphite god of the dead, Sokar, in the form of a mummified hawk; and was likewise associated with the later human god of the dead, Osiris, appearing as Ptah-Sokar-Osiris. As a further complication, the late figures of this fused god as a bandy-legged dwarf are entirely different from the mummiform Ptah and from the figures of the other two gods. If we were to analyze these incongruities so far as our present information goes, they might be arranged thus:

Sokar, hawk-god of dead—primitive.
+ Osiris, god of dead—pre-historic.
+ Ptah, therefore a mummy—dynastic.
later + *pataikoi* of Phœnicia—dwarf.

Apis, the bull creator—primitive.
+ Ptah, creator by the word—dynastic.

Khnumu, the ram-creator—primitive.
+ Ptah, creator by moulding, as Khnumu at Dendereh and Philæ.

Hence Ptah the artificer was simply a creator-god of the dynastic race, who became assimilated to the earlier gods of various kinds. It is impossible to dissociate from Ptah the *pataikoi*, dwarf figures which were worshipped by the Phœnician sailors (Herod. iii. 37), identified with Ptah, and given the same name. These, again, have some relation to the bandy-legged or lame god of artificers, Hephaistos. Ptah was worshipped mainly at Memphis, and also at the next nome, Letopolis, as well as at Bubastis and Mendes.

Min, or *Amsu*, as the name is sometimes transliterated, was the abstract father-god. He appears, as we have shown, to be the earlier form of Amon. Like Ptah, he is enveloped in bandages; and, as Ptah has his hands projecting and holding a sceptre, so Min has his right arm raised holding a flail, and his left hand holding the phallus. The origin of this god is indicated in a late text, where the form of a sanctuary in the land of Punt is exactly that associated with the god (*Athribis*, 8, xviii, xx). This shrine is a conical hut, like those of Punt, and the god has a black face (*Deir el-Bahari*, lxix–lxxi). These details point to Min having been introduced by immigrants from there. The oldest figures of Min are three colossi of limestone found in the bottom level of the temple of Koptos, with designs upon them, including Red Sea shells and sword-fish, agreeing with the source stated above. He was particularly the god of the desert, worshipped at Hammamat, at the end of the desert road at Koptos; at Ekhmin, which was probably the end of the other desert road from Myos Hormos; at Dendereh opposite Koptos; and at Edfu, Thebes, and Saqqareh. His figures are common in the XIIth and XIIIth dynasties; in the XIXth he was united with Amon-Rā, but in Ptolemaic times he again became important.

Hat-hor was the abstract mother-god, probably introduced as a correlative deity with Min. Her head is seen on the column in front of the shrine of Min (*Athribis*, xxiii). Her peculiar position, as being worshipped over the whole country and identified with other goddesses, points to her belonging to the latest immigrants. The myth of Horus striking off the head of his mother Isis, and replacing it by a cow's head, points to the Horus clan accepting Hathor of the dynastic people and uniting her with Isis. Hathor's head appears as the favourite emblem of the dynastic people (palette of Narmer, top, and kilt of king [*Hierakonpolis*, xxix]), and the priesthood of Hathor and the love of Hathor are often named in the early dynasties. The Hathor head appears as a capital to columns at Deir el-Bahri, and in Nubia in the XVIIIth dynasty. It formed the base of the sistrum used in her worship, and the whole sistrum and head were used as the model for capitals of columns in the XXVIth dynasty down to Ptolemaic times (see esp. Dendereh). Hathor was fused with other deities, particularly Isis as the mother, and she appears in most sites of Egypt. The fates presiding over birth and destiny were called the seven Hathors.

Maat was the goddess of truth. She had no temples, and received no offerings. On the contrary, the image of Maat is often shown as being offered to the other gods by the king. There is also a double form, the two Maats presiding over justice and truth (Maspero, *Dawn*, 187). These were shown usually one at each end of the shrines of the gods; and they appear to be the source of the cherubic figures, one at each end of the mercy-seat, known apparently as 'Mercy' and 'Truth' (Ps 25^{10} 61^{7} 85^{10} 86^{15}, Pr 3^{3} 14^{22} 16^{6} 20^{28}). Maat appears in the judgment scenes of weighing the heart, as a pledge of truth, and she is linked with Rā and Thōth, and especially with Ptah, who is 'the lord of truth.' So little personality was attached to this abstraction of 'truth' that, when Akhenaten proscribed the names of all the gods in favour of the Aten, he still kept the name of Maat 'associated with his own' in placing his motto after his name, *ankh em maat*, 'living in truth.'

Nefertum is a youthful god in human form, with a lotus flower on his head. He appears to be a god of vegetation and growth, and was associated as son of Ptah and Sekhmet at Memphis. He appears only from the XXIInd dynasty and onwards, when bronze statuettes of him and relief figures on *situlæ* are common. No temple of his is known, or any offerings to him.

Safekht was the goddess of writing. She is named as early as the Pyramid times, and often appears in the XIXth dynasty recording the festivals of the king, and holding a scribe's outfit. Her emblem was a seven-pointed star on the head, with a pair of horns inverted above it. This has some connexion with *safekh*, 'seven,' and the seven-pointed star which appears as one of the earliest emblems of divinity (*Hierakonpolis*, xxvi B, C, xxix). The group may well read *upt safekh*, 'she who has the seven upon her head'; if so, she was an early goddess marked by the early sign of divinity, and hence 'crowned with the seven' came to be her title. Her true name thus appears to be lost.

Cosmogonic pairs of elemental gods were venerated at Hermopolis, each pair male (with frog heads) and female (with serpent heads); the male names were *Heh*, 'eternity'; *Kaku*, 'darkness'; *Nu*, 'the heavenly ocean'; *Nenu*, 'the inundation.' The female names were merely the feminine of these. Maspero regards them as the equivalents of Seb and Nut, Osiris and Isis, Shu and Tefnut, Set and Nebhat, respectively (*Dawn*, 149). There are various views of the meaning of the eight; but their names seem to harmonize with the 'majesty of light,' the succession of ages, the water used in modelling creation, named in the *Kore Kosmou*, the earliest of the Hermetic books, which retains most of Egyptian thought. These elements were called 'the eight,' *khmunu*; and Tahuti made the ninth, the god who dominated the elements. They gave the name to the city Khmunu, now modified to Eshmuneyn.

Other abstractions are occasionally named, the more usual of which are *Hu*, the god of taste, and *Sa*, the god of perception. The rarer abstractions remind us of the Roman personifications of *Pavor*, *Pallor*, etc.

41. Foreign gods.—The foreign gods are those which were brought into Egypt apart from an immigration of their worshippers, and which always remained exotic.

Bēs, or *Bēsa*, was originally a dancing figure of Sudanese type, dressed in the skin of the *bēs* animal, the *Cynœlurus guttatus*. He is often shown beating a tambourine. How such a figure came to be associated with the protection of infants and with birth is not known; but this connexion is seen in the XVIIIth dynasty (*Deir el-Bahari*, li) and on to the Ptolemaic age (Birth-house, Dendereh). The earliest example of the figure is female, in the XIIth dynasty (Petrie, *Kahun*, viii. 14, 27); it is male in later times, but in the Roman age a female Bēs appears as a consort. Bēs had no temples or offerings, but in Roman times there was an oracle of Bēsa at Abydos. A curious intimation of this worship by the Phœnicians is the figure of Bēsa on the coins of Ai-besa, 'the island of Besa,' the modern Iviça.

Dedun was another African god, worshipped in Nubia. He was apparently a creation-god, since he was fused with Ptah, the combination Ptah-Dedun being often worshipped in the XIXth dynasty. He is always in human form.

Sati seems to have been the goddess of a tribe at the cataract. She is similar to Hathor, with cows' horns, and was called the queen of the gods.

Anqet was the local goddess of Seheyl, the island in the cataract, and is shown wearing a high crown of feathers.

Turning now to the Asiatic gods, the principal one was *Sutekh*, who may originally have been one with the Set or Setesh of the Egyptians, but the separation was pre-historic. When we meet with Sutekh in the XIXth dynasty, he is the national god of the Kheta, and has many cities devoted to him on the Upper Euphrates in Armenia (Petrie, *Student's History*, iii. 66). The Egyptians represented him with a tall pointed cap bearing two horns projecting in front and a long streamer from the peak descending to his heels (Petrie, *Sinai*, fig. 134). Similar figures of Sutekh, standing on the back of a lion, are found on some scarabs.

Baal was also sometimes identified with Set, or combined with Mentu as a war-god. Names compounded with Baal are sometimes found, as *Baal-mahar* ('Hasten, Baal'), the Punic *Maharbal* (*Pap. jud.* ii. 2, v. 3–6).

Reshpu, or *Reseph*, appears on some steles, wearing a pointed cap with a gazelle head bound on in front. He was a god of war, armed with spear and shield in the left hand, brandishing a halbert, and with a full quiver on his back (Wilkinson, *Manners and Customs*, 1878, iii. 235).

Anta, or *Anaitis*, was a goddess of the Kheta (the Aryan *Anahita*, imported like Mitra and Varuna), represented as seated on a throne or on horseback, holding a spear and shield, and brandishing a halbert. Her name appears in that of a favourite daughter of Ramses II., Bant-antha, 'daughter of Anaitis.'

Astharth, or *Ashtaroth* (Ishtar), was worshipped at Memphis, where is a tomb of a priestess of hers. She is represented at Edfu as lion-headed and driving a chariot. Ramses called a son Merastrot, 'loved of Ashtaroth.'

Qedesh appears as a nude goddess standing on a lion, her hair like the wig of Hathor, and lotus-flowers and serpents in her hands. She is placed with Min, and therefore seems to be a form of the Mother-god or Hathor; she has no weapons like Anaitis and Ishtar.

42. Tribal history in the myths.—Owing to the early age at which sculpture and writing began in Egypt, it is possible to trace the tribal history passing into religious myth. The war of the worshippers of Horus expelling those of Set was recorded as history, and places retained the name *samhud* as 'united to the Hud' or Behudet, hawk-god of Edfu, allies of the Horus tribe. Yet the whole of this also appears as mythology—Horus warring on Set and driving him out of Egypt. As we see, on the earliest slate carvings, the standards of the tribes represented acting as the emblem of the tribe, breaking down fortresses, holding the bonds of captives, or driving the prisoners, so, by the same habit of symbolism, the god of a tribe was said to conquer another god when his tribe overcame another tribe. The contest of Poseidon with Athene for Attica and Troezene, with Helios for Corinth, with Hera for Argolis, with Zeus for Aegina, with Dionysos for Naxos, and with Apollo for Delphi, seems equally to mark the yielding of the worshippers of Poseidon to the followers of the other gods. This is an important principle for the understanding of religious myths, but it belongs to history rather than to the present subject.

43. Nature of the gods.—The nature of divinity was perhaps even more limited in the Egyptian mind than it was to the Greek. The gods were not immortal: Rā grew old and decrepit; Osiris was slain. In the Pyramid texts, Orion is stated to hunt and slay the gods and to feed upon them. The gods can suffer, for Rā was in torment from the bite of a magic serpent. The gods are not omniscient; they walk on earth to see what is done; it takes time for them to learn what has happened; Thōth has to inform Rā about what he has heard, and cannot punish men without Rā's permission. Nor can a god act directly on earth; he sends 'a power from heaven' to do his bidding. The gods, therefore, have no divine superiority over man in conditions or limitations; they can be described only as pre-existent, as acting intelligences, with scarcely greater powers than man might hope to gain by magic and witchcraft of his own (cf. art. GOD [Egyptian]).

See also art. WORSHIP (Egyptian).

LITERATURE.—The literature is given throughout the article, especially in § 6.

W. M. FLINDERS PETRIE.

ELAMITES.—*Introductory.*—Elam, in Gn 10[22], is said to have been the eldest son of Shem. The tract occupied by the nation descended from him is a portion of the mountainous country separating the Mesopotamian plain from the highland district of Iran, including the fertile country at the foot of the hills. It is the Susis or Susiana of classical geographers (Strabo, xv. 3, § 12; Ptol. vi. 3, etc.), and was so called from its capital, Susa (Assyr.-Bab. *Šušu* or *Šušan*, Heb. *Shūshan*). The country itself was called in Assyr.-Bab. *Êlamtu* or (without the case-ending) *Êlammat* (Heb. *'Elām*). The native name is given by the Assyr. inscriptions as *Anšan* or *Anzan*, also *Aššan* (*Anzhan*, *Azhzhan*), and in the native Elamite texts the kings call themselves 'of *Anzan-Šušun*' (Anzan and Susa, or Susian Anzan). Another name for the country was *Ḫapirti*. In early times two languages were current in the country—Semitic Babylonian, and Elamite, the affinities of which have still to be determined, though, from the vocabulary, Aryan roots may be suspected. As far as we can at present judge, Semitic Bab. ceased to be used officially at a comparatively early date.

Though numerous Elamite and Bab.-Elamite inscriptions have been found, it cannot as yet be said that we know much of Elamite religion. There is hardly any doubt, however, that it resembled closely that of Babylonia, influenced as it was not only by the Semitic-speaking inhabitants of Elam, but also by their Assyro-Bab. neighbours. The connexion of Elam with Babylonia probably goes back to pre-historic times, as witness the conflict of the Erechite Gilgameš with the Elamite Ḫumbaba, guardian of the stolen statue of Ištar (see *ERE* ii. 315[b]). From time to time, also, not only did Bab. kings rule in Elam, but Elamite rulers extended their sway over Babylonia and all its dependencies, as is stated in the Biblical account of Chedorlaomer (Gn 14).

1. From what has been stated, a true history of the Elamite religion is practically impossible. In all probability, like that of Babylonia, it was animistic in its origin, and gradually developed into a polytheistic creed. As in Babylonia, each city had its special protective deity, who, however, was honoured all over the land, and in many cases had been received into the pantheon of the neighbouring countries of Babylonia and Assyria. Thus, the patron-deity of Susa was *In-Šušinak*, identified by the Babylonians with their Ninip (*ERE* ii. 312[b]); *Aa-ḫupšan* was the deity of Ḫupšan; *Tišpak* (also identified with Ninip) was the deity of Dungi-Nannar; *Bêl* was lord of the neighbouring State of Ešnunnak; *Armannu* was worshipped in Rapiqa, *Lagamal* (Lagamar, La'omer) in Maur; and *Aamiltu* was 'queen of Parṣi' or Marza. Gods worshipped at other Elamite cities will be referred to farther on.

2. (*a*) The chief figures of the Sem.-Elamite pantheon were naturally those of the Babylonians —Anu and Anatu, Enlil (Ellil, Illil), and Ninlil, Êa and Damkina, Sin, Šamaš and Aa, Ištar, Merodach and Zērpanîtu, Nebo and Tašmêtu, Ninip, Nergal, Nusku, Girru, Addu or Adad (Rammānu) and Sala, Tammuz (Ištar's spouse), the *Igigi* and the *Anunnaki*, etc. (*ERE* ii. 310–313). To these may probably be added such minor Bab. deities as the son of Šamaš, *Kittu* ('righteousness'), and his minister *Mîšaru* ('justice'); *Zagaga*, one of the gods of war; *Išum*, 'the glorious sacrificer'; *Lugal-girra* and *Meślamta-êa*, aspects of Nergal; *Ma'metu*, the goddess of fate; *Gu-silim*, 'the pronouncer of well-being'; *Uraš*, Ninip as god of planting; *Sugamuna*, explained by the Babylonians as 'Merodach of water-channels'; and many others. Though little real information concerning the Elamite gods is available, it is practically certain that many of them had their equivalents in the Babylonian pantheon, to which we owe valuable details concerning them.[1]

(*b*) The principal deity of the non-Semitic Elamites was *In-Šuš(i)nak*, called by the Babylonians *En-Šušinak*, possibly = 'the Susian Lord' *par excellence*. To all appearance he was originally the local deity of Susa. The Assyro-Babylonians identified him with Ninip, regarded as the son of Enlil, and one of the most important deities of their pantheon—indeed, he was worshipped as far west as Beth-Ninip, apparently near Jerusalem. Silḫak-In-Šušinak (*c.* 1060 B.C.) calls him 'the great lord, ruler (?) of the divinities,' 'lord of heaven and earth,' 'creator of the entire universe.' Other Elamite names of this deity quoted by the Babylonians are Laḫuratil, Šimeš, Adaene, Šušinak, and Dagbak.

Another of the great gods of the Elamites is he whose name is written with the Sumerian character *GAL*. Scheil suggests that this deity is the Bêl of the Babylonians, and associated with *Bêlti-ya*, 'my lady,' in which case this divine pair would represent Merodach[1] and Zēr-panîtu, worshipped at Babylon. From the great inscription of Šilḫak-In-Šušinak, it appears that her Elamite name was *Kiririša*, described as the lady who dominates the goddesses. This, in the Bab. pantheon, is a title of Ištar, who, however, was identified with Zēr-panîtu (*ERE* ii. 643[b]). The etymology of Kiririša is interesting, being apparently from the Elam. *kirir*, 'Ištar' or goddess in general, combined with Usa(n), seemingly standing for Ištar in particular (*Cun. Texts*, xxv. 18, rev. 17, 18). Zēr-panîtu, called by the Babylonians 'the lady of the gods,' has, with the name of *Nin-siš*, the explanation 'the lady of the gods, the lady of Susa.' The principal passages for the identification of the Sumerian Gala with Merodach are *Cun. Texts*, xxiv. pl. 50, 47406, obv. 12, where he is explained as 'Merodach of *kirzizi*'; but, as the document is only the 'monotheistic list' (*ExpT* xxii. [1911] 166), this identification has apparently but little value. On pl. 36 of *Cun. Texts*, xxiv. he appears as one of the *utukku*, or spirits of Bau the goddess of healing, so that there, at least, Gala was one of the minor deities.

Important as being, apparently, one of the components of the name Chedorlaomer (Gn 14[1]) is the name *Lagamar*, *Laqamar*, or *Lagamal*. Except in Aššurbanipal's account of his 3rd Elamite campaign, this name always appears in Assyro-Bab. texts under the form of *Lagamal*, and his principal place of worship was Dailem near Babylon. If line 15 of *WAI* ii. 60 be rightly arranged, he was 'king of Maur,' a district probably on the Elamite border. He is described as the son (not the daughter) of Êa, and this agrees with the form, which, accepting Scheil's suggestion that it is of Sem.-Bab. origin, and means 'the unsparing,' is masculine. The *ḫiel* of Lagamal at Susa was restored by the Elamite king Kutir-Naḫḫunte (Scheil, *Textes élam.-anzan.* [=vol. iii. of *Mémoires de la délégation en Perse*, Paris, 1901], p. 49), who calls upon In-Šušinak to protect it.

Naḫḫunte or *Na'ḫunte* was identified with the Assyro-Bab. Šamaš, the sun-god, and was probably regarded, like the Bab. Šamaš, as the god of judgment, righteousness, and justice, as well as the god of the light of day. The Assyro-Bab. scribes mention him under the name *Naḫḫundi* or *Nanḫundi*, implying a nasal sound before the second syllable. In the list of the seven Elamite gods in *Cun. Texts*, xxv. pl. 24, *Naḫundi* appears last but one; and after the summation comes that of *Narundi*, their (the 7 gods') sister, and *Zammaḫundi* was *alam dua-nene*, possibly = 'their announcing image.' If Scheil's suggestion that *Naḫḫunte-utu* means 'Naḫḫunte brings forth' (from the Sumerian *utu*, 'to beget') is right, Naḫḫunte may have been an Elamite god of generation. Probably, however, the name simply identified him with the Sumer. *Utu* = *Šamaš*.

[1] The boundary-stones found at Susa, which mention many Babylonian gods, were probably carried off from Babylonia by Šutruk-Naḫḫunte at the end of the 12th cent. B.C.

[1] See below, § 3.

Hadad (Assyr. *Adad*, Bab. *Addu*, also called *Rammānu* or Rimmon) seems to have been known to the Elamites chiefly by his Mitannian (Hittite) name of *Tešup*, but the Assyr. list (*Cun. Texts*, xxv. pl. 16, l. 20) gives the Elamite equivalent as *Kunzibami*, compared by Scheil with the Bab. *Kuzzubu* or *Kunzubu*, 'abundant,' or the like. With the Assyro-Babylonians he was not only the god of wind, thunder, and lightning, but also of fertilizing rain. Another Elamite name given by the same text is *Š(?)iḫḫaš* (*ib.* pl. 17, obv. 40).

Ḫumban, Ḫuman, Umman. As this is a very common deity in the composition of men's names, he must have been one of the most popular of the Elamite pantheon. According to Scheil, this name is, like others, of Sem.-Bab. origin, being composed of the name Ḫum, and *ban* (from *banû*, 'to form *or* create')—'Ḫum is a creator.'[1] Ḫanni of Aiapir speaks of 'Ḫuban the great, god of the gods' (Scheil, iii. 103), and the same inscription has the divine name Ḫuban-šunkik, 'Ḫuban the king.'

The Elamite *Šimut* is identified by Scheil with *Sumudu*, who appears first on the list given by Aššurbanipal of Assyria, and is immediately followed by *Lagamaru*. As Nin-uru precedes Lagamal (Lagamaru) in *Cun. Texts*, xxiv. 49, l. 4, and xxv. 1, l. 14, Scheil suggests that Simut or Sumudu and Nin-uru are the same. If this be the case, Simut was a goddess, spouse of *Guanna-si-ila* or *Uraš*, the god of planting (*ExpT*, 1911, p. 165), among the Sumero-Babylonians.

Ḫišmedik and *Ruḫurater.* These are apparently two male deities, not a male and a female (Scheil, iii. 19). The variant *Išmetik* leads Scheil to suggest that the former may be a corruption of the Sem. *Ištemik*, '(the god who) hears thee.' Similar names occur in Babylonia, and another in Sem.-Elamite is *Išni-* (for *Išmi-*) *qarab*, 'he has heard the prayer.' Scheil points out that *Ruḫurater* is probably the *Laḫuratil* of *WAI* ii. 57, 43 *cd*, where it appears as one of the names of Ninip in Elam, as stated above.[2]

Noteworthy among the goddesses is *Belala*, who, as Scheil points out, is the *Bilala* of Aššurbanipal, vi. 41. She is possibly the *Bulala* of *WAI* ii. pl. 60, l. 27, where the city which stands opposite her name is Ubasu. The nearest name in Sumer.-Bab. is *Belili* or *Belili-alam*, spouse of *Alala* or *Alala-alam*, two of the numerous male and female personifications of the heavens (Anu and Anatu). *Belili* appears as the sister of the sun-god Tammuz, who was probably as well known to the Elamites as to the Babylonians.

The common Elamite name for 'god' was *nap*, which was borrowed, to all appearance, by the Assyro-Babylonians. Whether there is any significance in the fact that *nap* is the character for 'god' doubled, is uncertain, but, if admitted, its fundamental principle would seem to be dualistic—probably male and female. In *Cun. Texts*, xxiv. pl. 39, l. 10, *Nap*, as the name of a deity, is explained as *Enlil šamê*, 'Enlil of the heavens,' the name of Enlil being written with the character for 'old'—as though 'the ancient.'

Whether this root has anything to do with the *Napratip*, a group of deities (Scheil) to whom a temple, restored by Untaš-*GAL*, was dedicated, is uncertain. Scheil regards *Napratip* as being the *Napirtu* of Aššurbanipal, vi. 43, and prefers a Sem. etymology, namely, *napiru*, 'covering,' 'protecting,' or the like. The occurrence of *Napiram*, in the same text with *Šadî*, 'my (protecting) mountain'—names which he quotes—seems to bear upon the Median mountain of *Nipur*, where the ark was regarded as having rested, and suggests a reason for the temple named *Ê-kura*, 'the house *of the mountain*' at the Bab. *Nippur*. In the Assyrian list of native and foreign deities (*WAI* iii. pl. 66, rev. 10*d*) the apparently Elamite *Napriš* occurs, and is immediately followed by 'Nergal of *Ḫupšal*,' which is, as Scheil states, the Elamite *Ḫupšan*.

3. Noteworthy among the figures of deities derived from Elam are the reliefs on the Babylonian boundary-stones of the Kassite period, by means of which the emblems on those monuments have been identified. It is now known that the emblem of Merodach was a spear—perhaps that with which he slew the dragon of Chaos; that Nusku was represented by a lighted lamp, similar to the Roman; that a stock terminating in an eagle's head was the god Zagaga (Zamama); that a seated female figure represented Gula; and that a thunderbolt stood for Addu or Hadad. A variant showing Merodach's spear-head surmounting a kind of house set on a dragon is described as Merodach combined, apparently, with the name of the god *GAL*, confirming what has been said (p. 251[b]) as to the identification of these two deities. The above, with other emblems, were probably used by the Elamites as well as by the Babylonians.

4. Concerning the Elamite gods, Aššurbanipal, the Assyrian king, in his cylinder-inscription above quoted (Rm. 1, col. vi. lines 27 ff.), gives some interesting details. The *ziqqurat*, or temple-tower, of Susa was built of enamelled brick imitating lapis-lazuli, the sacred stone of the Assyro-Babylonians, and evidently also of the Elamites. This his soldiers destroyed, as well as the pinnacles of bright bronze apparently attached to it. Šušinak, the god of their oracle, dwelt (he states) in a secret place, and no one ever saw the work (workmanship, form) of his divinity. Six deities, Sumudu, Lagamaru, Partikira, Amman-kasipar, Uduran, and Sapak, were worshipped only by the Elamite kings, and (the statues of) these, together with 12 others—Ragiba, Sungam-sarâ, Karsa, Kirsamas, Šudānu, Aapaksina, Bilala, Panin-timri, Sila-garâ, Napsâ, Napirtu, and Kindakarpu—with their priests and property, were carried off to Assyria. After this come references to the winged bulls and genii of the temples, and the guardian wild bulls (*rêmē*) protecting the gates of the shrines. There were also sacred groves—secret places—into which no stranger penetrated, and the burial-places of the kings. That the Elamite kings should have had their own deities presupposes a dynasty in early times which did not belong to the same district as the people over whom they ruled, resulting in the establishment of two pantheons, afterwards more or less united.

LITERATURE.—See especially **P. V. Scheil**, *Textes élamites-sémitiques (anzanites)*, 1900 ff. (vols. ii.–vi., ix., etc., of de Morgan, *Mémoires de la délégation en Perse*); and cf. also **A. H. Sayce** in *ExpT* xii. (1900–01) 155 f. and xiii. (1901–02) 65; and art. 'Elam,' in *HDB* and *EBi*.

T. G. PINCHES.

ELDER (Buddhist).—Certain members of the Buddhist Order took rank as elders, and, as such, had considerable weight in the management of its business, and in the preservation of the doctrine. It was not, by any means, all the seniors in the Order who were technically so called, though the word 'elder' (*therā*) is occasionally used in its ordinary sense of such members of the Order as were of longest standing in it (*Aṅguttara*, i. 78, 247). Four qualities are mentioned as making a man an elder, in the technical sense. These are: (1) virtue; (2) memory and intelligence; (3) the practice of ecstasy; (4) the possession of that emancipation of heart and mind which results from the rooting out of the mental intoxication arising from cravings, love of future life, wrong views, and

[1] The Assyro-Bab. lists contain a god *Ḫumba* or *Ḫumma*, who, with *Ḫadaniš* (possibly Elamite), is described as one of the spirits (*utukku*) of the Nippurite temple *Ê-kura*.

[2] In the proper name *Šamši-Ruḫurater*, 'my sun is Ruḫurater,' there is probably no identification of this deity with Šamaš, the Bab. sun-god.

ignorance (*Aṅg.* ii. 22; no. 4 in this list, it should be noticed, is the stock description of an *arahat*).[1]

The number of those who were thus entitled to be called elders is not given as very large.[2] There is a frequently repeated short list of the most distinguished amongst them, 'the elders who are disciples' (*therā sāvakā*). The full number is twelve, and their names usually follow one another in the same order. They are (1) Sāriputta, (2) Moggallāna, (3) Kassapa, (4) Kachchāna, (5) Koṭṭhita, (6) Kappina, (7) Chunda, (8) Anuruddha, (9) Revata, (10) Upāli, (11) Ānanda, (12) Rāhula. But the lists are not consistent. Sometimes one, sometimes another name, especially of those at the bottom of the list, is omitted; and there are slight variations in the order. It is quite clear that neither the number nor the names were fixed at the time of the earliest tradition (*Vinaya*, i. 354–55, ii. 15, iv. 66; *Aṅg.* iii. 299; cf. *Majjhima*, i. 212, 462).

In one passage (*Aṅg.* i. 23–25) we have a much longer and very interesting list of those members of the Order who were disciples (*bhikkhū sāvakā*), specifying after each name the good quality or mental expertness in which the Buddha had declared him pre-eminent. Forty-seven men and thirteen women are mentioned, and Buddhaghoṣa (*q.v.*), in his commentary on the passage, calls them all 'elders.' All the twelve disciples except no. 7 recur in this list, and are said to be pre-eminent respectively in the following ways—that is, according to the order of the names given above: (1) in great wisdom; (2) in the powers of *iddhi* (*q.v.*); (3) in discussions as to extra (optional) duties; (4) in power of expanding that which has been stated concisely; (5) in the fourfold knowledge of the texts—the knowledge of their philological meaning, of the doctrine they contain, of the derivation of words and ideas, and, finally, in the power of extemporary exposition of them; (6) in ability in exhorting the brethren; (7) not mentioned; (8) in inward vision; (9) pre-eminent among those who dwell in the forest; (10) the best of those who knew the canon law; (11) the most distinguished among those who learned the texts, who were self-possessed, whose conduct was right, who had moral courage, and who were of service to others; (12) the best among those of the brethren who were willing to learn.

There is a touch of historical probability in the fact that no better distinction could be found for no. 12, who was the Buddha's only son, than that he was willing to learn. And, when we notice that only one or two of the whole sixty in this list were among the first disciples to be admitted to the Order, so that there were many others senior to them, we must conclude that the title 'elder' was more dependent on other qualities—such qualities as are given in the list, and in the passage quoted above—than on the mere fact of seniority in the community. Even in the *Vinaya* (the Rules of the Order), in which, as a general rule, so much weight is laid on precedence by seniority, we find the word 'elder' (*therā*) used in this technical sense (*Vinaya Texts*, i. 228, ii. 17, 61, 237 [*SBE* xiii., xvii.]).

It is sufficiently clear how this happened. In the ordinary meetings of the local chapters administering the affairs of the Order, the senior *bhikkhu* present (reckoning not by age, but by the date of ordination) presided, and the members present were seated in order of such seniority. But, when it came to talking over questions of ethics and philosophy, or discussing details in the system of self-training based on psychology and ethics, something more than seniority was required.[1] A certain number of the brethren became acknowledged as leaders and masters in these subjects. Their brethren called them 'elders' as a courtesy title. There was no formal appointment by the Order itself, or by any external authority; nor is there any evidence that a *bhikkhu* became a *therā* merely by age, or by seniority in the Order.

So far had this secondary and special meaning of 'elder' driven out the etymological meaning that it is the only one dealt with in Dhammapāla's exposition of the word at the beginning of his commentary on the *Therā-gāthā*; and the unknown commentator on the *Dhammapada*, in his explanation of the word at verse 261 (see above, note 1), actually derives *therā*, by a fanciful and exegetical, not philological, argument, from *dhīra* in the sense of 'having moral courage.' The canonical Buddhism contained in the Pāli texts was called, in the tradition, the *Therā-vāda*, that is, 'the opinion of the *therās*,' where the word is again used in the secondary sense, and refers especially to the *therās* who held the First Council (see Childers, *Pali Dict.*, 1875, *s.v.* 'Vāda').

In one passage we find the phrase *Saṅgha-therā*, that is, 'the elder of the Order.' The present writer has translated this (*Vinaya Texts*, iii. 404) by 'the eldest Therā (then alive) in the world.' This is probably right, as the number of years of his standing in the Order is immediately added. But it may also mean 'the most distinguished and venerable of the then living Therās.'

The Buddhist elders had no more authority in the Order than such as followed from the natural deference paid them for their character and accomplishments; and they had no other authority over laymen. Such slight discipline as was customary was carried out, not by the *therās*, but by the local chapters (see DISCIPLINE [Buddhist]). The *therās*, as such, had no special duties or privileges in connexion with the temporalities of the Order.

In mediæval and modern times, the kings of Ceylon, Burma, and Siam have from time to time recognized some distinguished *bhikkhu* as Saṅgha-therā; and quite recently the English Government in Burma has followed their precedent, though it left the choice of the *bhikkhu* to be so distinguished to the local Order in chapter assembled. The title *therā* is still used, in these three countries, of any *bhikkhu* of distinction. There is still, as in olden times, no formal grant of the title. In other Buddhist countries it has fallen out of use, and even in these three it is used mainly, though not exclusively, when writing or speaking in Pāli. The modern native languages have other terms, such as *nāyaka*, 'leader,' which tend to take its place.

LITERATURE.—The references to the texts are given in the article. The question has not been hitherto discussed by European scholars.

T. W. RHYS DAVIDS.

ELDER (Semitic).—**1. Connotation of the term.**—The importance of the 'old men' or 'elders' was a natural development of the authority of the head of the family, and of the reverence felt for parents and for the aged in primitive times. Note the position assigned to Abraham, Isaac, and Jacob in all the documents of the Hexateuch. The reverence due to parents and to the aged is a favourite theme of both the OT and the NT; *e.g.*, Eliphaz the Temanite is confident, because 'with us are both the grayheaded and very aged men' (Job 15^{10}); and in Sir 3^{3} 'He that honoureth his father maketh atonement for sins' (cf. Pr 30^{17}, Mk $7^{10ff.}$ etc.).

[1] So at *Dhammapada*, verse 261, an elder is defined as a man in whom there is truth and religion, kindness, self-command, and training.

[2] There is an anthology of verses ascribed to elders, both men and women, included in the canon under the title, *Therā-therī-gāthā*. It contains poems of 263 male and 74 female poets. *Therās* are also often mentioned in the various episodes in the other books, but most of them occur among the above 337.

[1] The same difficulty was felt when the *bhikkhu* presiding at a chapter had to recite the Pātimokkha. If he could not do so, a junior *bhikkhu*, who could, took his place (*Vinaya Texts*, i. 267).

Similarly in the Code of Ḥammurabi (*e.g.* § 195) severe penalties are prescribed for those who fail in respect and duty towards parents.

Here, therefore, we have one of the many cases where a word in common use acquires a technical meaning while its ordinary meaning still persists, so that a difficulty may arise as to whether it simply means an old man or an 'elder' in the technical sense. Very early there must have been many old men who were not 'elders,' although all 'elders' would be old. Later on, an 'elder' came to mean simply a chief, usually mature or elderly, not necessarily old. There might be shaikhs, just as there are aldermen, in the prime of life; Presbyterian elders are not always old.

Amongst the nomad Arabs there is one supreme shaikh for a tribe, but there is also a *Diwān*, or council of shaikhs. In the OT, the 'elders' almost always, if not invariably, appear as a group or council; and the Heb. term *zākēn* in the technical sense is used in the plural.[1] Is 3^{2} 9^{15} are not real exceptions even if *zākēn* means 'elder' in these passages, for the word in each case is collective. Gn 24^{2} (cf. below) seems a real exception; but possibly *zākēn* here means 'senior' and not 'elder.' Gn 43^{27}, taken alone, might be 'your father, the shaikh,' but this is unlikely in view of the stress laid in 44^{20} etc. on the advanced age of Jacob.

In primitive society the head of a family or clan, like the captain of a ship, would discharge many functions which are assigned to separate individuals in a more advanced civilization. He would be leader in war and peace, priest, judge, often the repository of, and chief authority on, tribal tradition, and possibly doctor. It is natural, therefore, that, as society developed, the title 'elder' or 'shaikh' was sometimes borne by various people in authority and by the members of different professions. Thus in the OT we read not only of elders of cities, tribes, etc., but also of Eliezer as the 'elder' of Abraham's household (Gn 24^{2}), of the elders of Pharaoh's household (Gn 50^{7}), of the elders of David's household (2 S 12^{17}),[2] of the elders of the priests (2 K 19^{2}, Is 37^{2}, Jer 19^{1}).

In later Judaism, *zākēn* is a scholar or teacher of Rabbinical law, and the synonym *ṣîbh* is used in the same sense.[3] Amongst the modern Arabs 'shaikh,' or 'elder,' is used with a wide variety of meaning.[4] It has, of course, the familiar meaning of leader of a tribe; the name is also applied to the heads of the great Muslim sects, to the magistrates set over districts of a city, and to the chiefs of various trades and industries, and even of thieves. A professional devotee, or 'saint,' is also called a shaikh, and the title is also borne by priests[5] and schoolmasters, the title 'shaykah' being given to a female teacher.

Thus the 'elders' or 'shaikhs' would be of very different degrees of importance. In the OT, where we nearly always find them acting in groups, and not as individuals, we have the elders of a district or city (1 K 21^{8}), of a tribe (Gilead, Jg 11^{5}; Judah, 2 S 19^{11}, 2 K 23^{1}), and of Israel (1 S 4^{3} etc.). If we may regard Succoth as typical, the elders of a country town were fairly numerous, and probably included the heads of all families of any standing, for we read that in Succoth there were 77 princes and elders (Jg 8^{14}).

Both the name and the institution of 'elder' or 'shaikh' were wide-spread; we find them not only in Israel, but in Egypt (Gn 50^{7}); amongst the Canaanites (Jos 9^{11}); Moabites and Midianites (Nu 22^{7}); and at the Phœnician town of Gebal (Ezk 27^{9}). According to Winckler, one of the Amarna letters[1] is from Irkata, a Phœnician city, 'and its elders.'

The available evidence suggests that the quasi-patriarchal authority or influence associated with the term 'elder' usually existed at an early stage of social development. Robertson Smith, for instance, speaks of 'the senates of elders found in the ancient states of Semitic and Aryan antiquity alike.'[2] Probably in some cases persons corresponding to elders or shaikhs bore titles not derived from a root meaning 'old,' more especially later, when 'elder' had become a technical term equivalent to 'chief' or 'counsellor.' Thus it is often suggested[3] that the Canaanite noble, met with in Egyptian inscriptions, and referred to as *marna*, 'our lord,' corresponded to the Israelite elder.

Nevertheless, the title 'elder' for a person of authority, learning, or other distinction continues to this day. The Gr. γερουσία and the Rom. *senatus* are still represented by the 'senates' of modern States and Universities. The elders can be traced through the whole history of Israel and Judaism; the title and the office were taken over by Christianity, and are still found in priests, presbyters, and elders; and modern Semites still have their shaikhs.

On the other hand, it seems probable that various other titles are synonyms of 'elder'; we have already referred to the Syr. *marna*, and may note also the N. Sem. *malk* (see below). In Hebrew there are many titles more or less synonymous with *zāqēn*. The interchange of terms in the narratives of Gideon and of the relief of Jabesh-Gilead by Saul suggests that *'îsh* in the sense of 'householder' or 'head of a family' may be such a synonym.[4] Then there are *rā'shê hā'ābhôth*, 'chief fathers,' heads of the clans (Nu 36^{1}); the 'prince' or 'captain,' *nāsî'*, the head of the tribe (Nu 2^{3}); the chiefs or, lit., 'corner-stones' of the people, *pinnôth hā'ām* (Jg 20^{2}, 1 S 14^{38}); and, in Ex 24^{11} only, the *'ăṣîlîm*, 'nobles,' of the Israelites.[5] Other terms for chiefs, rulers, officials, such as *sārîm*, *ḥōrîm*, *sᵉgānîm*, seem sometimes equivalent to 'elders.' *Zᵉkēnîm* is also coupled with *rā'shîm*, 'heads,' *shōphᵉṭîm*, 'judges,' *shōṭᵉrîm*, 'officers,' to make up a description of the leaders (Dt 29^{10} 31^{28}, Jos 8^{33}). Probably these terms are partly synonymous. But 'father' in such phrases as 'father of Tekoa' (1 Ch 2^{24}) means 'founder' rather than 'chief.'[6]

2. History of the institution.—In early times, *e.g.*, in Israel in the nomadic and pre-monarchical periods, the position of the elder corresponded with that of the shaikh amongst the modern Bedawīn. He was the head, or one of the heads, of his family, clan, village, or district; the leader in war; the chief counsellor in war and peace; the arbitrator in disputes; but his power was moral, and depended on the force of his personality; he could advise but not command, persuade but not coerce.[7] As Doughty says, 'The sheykh of a nomad tribe is no tyrant'; 'the dignity of a sheykh in free Arabia is commonly more than his authority.'[8]

According to Doughty, the office of supreme shaikh descends by inheritance. McCurdy,[9] however, quotes authorities to show that the office was rather elective, seldom remaining in the same

[1] Benzinger, art. 'Aelteste,' in *PRE*³.
[2] Seesemann (*op. cit. infra*) holds that *zākēn* = 'senior' in these three passages.
[3] Marcus Jastrow, *Dict. of the Targumim*, etc., London and N.Y. 1886–1903, *s. vv.*
[4] Lane, *Manners and Customs of the Modern Egyptians*, London, 1846, pp. 74, 132, 139, 146, 238.
[5] Curtiss, *Ursem. Rel.*, Leipzig, 1903, p. 165

[1] *Tell-el-Amarna Letters*, 1896, p. 122.
[2] *Rel. Sem.*², London, 1894, p. 33.
[3] For instance, by Nowack, *Lehrb. der heb. Arch.* i. 304.
[4] Seesemann, 25 ff., 32 ff.
[5] *'Āṣîl* may also mean 'corner,' 'side,' 'support.'
[6] Cf. Ewald, p. 245.
[7] McCurdy, i. 36; Benzinger, *Heb. Arch.* 296.
[8] Doughty, *Travels in Arabia Deserta*, Cambridge, 1887–88, i. 251, ii. 662.
[9] ii. 187.

family for four generations. No doubt customs differed; the application of the hereditary principle would depend on the qualifications of the heir, and it would sometimes be modified by election within a given circle. Thus, amongst primitive nomads, the elders or shaikhs represented three different kinds of influence or authority: that of the father or head of the family—patriarchal; that of 'age or reputed wisdom'—personal; that of a legitimate government—official. These three were not necessarily associated in the same persons in the more advanced and complex social order of agricultural and city life; the title 'elder' attached itself often to the office apart from age or hereditary right. At the same time, the status and character of the elders were not always or altogether changed by the abandonment of nomad life. McCurdy states[1] that the habits and relations of the old patriarchal life were not discarded in the permanent institutions of the fixed settlements. The influence of the patriarchal system can be traced in the establishment and regulation of the Semitic cities; and we may find there a reproduction in type, if not in name or in detail, of the essential elements of the old tribal government. Throughout the N. Sem. realm the simple constitution of the city or State included a head, *malk*—a name corresponding with the Heb. *melek*, 'king'; a circle of nobles or 'great men'; and the general body of the common people. The *malk* and the 'great men' were usually hereditary. As the word *malk* in Aramaic is lit. 'counsellor,' McCurdy suggests that the *malk* was originally the chief elder of the clan which founded the settlement.

We have already pointed out that the title 'elder' persisted through the whole course of Jewish history; and it is a familiar fact that, within certain limits, the paternal authority was equally persistent.

Nevertheless, the changed conditions gradually modified the social life. The family remained the unit, but the group of families, the kindred, the clan more or less gave place to the community of the district, village, or town.[2] The fixed home, the regular cycle of agriculture, involved a more stereotyped social life, a greater authority on the part of the local chiefs. In Israel, for instance, as we have said, the elders appear in groups, each group forming the ruling council of a district, city, tribe, or even of the nation. Apparently, local government always remained largely in the hands of the elders,[3] though, with the development of society, there was a differentiation of offices; and other notables—priests, judges, military leaders—shared the authority of the elders. In Arabia there is sometimes the *ḳāḍī*, or judge, side by side with the shaikh.

The rise and increase of the royal power further limited the authority of the elders, by the interference of the financial, military, and judicial activity of the king, his ministers and representatives. We may summarize what can be gathered from the earlier documents as to the elders in Israel under the 'judges' and the monarchy.

In the history of the Exodus in JE,[4] we frequently meet with the 'elders of Israel' or 'of the people,' as associated with Moses in the leadership of the people, or as intermediaries between him and the people (Ex $3^{16.18}$ 4^{29} 12^{21} $17^{5.6}$ 19^{7} etc.). In Ex 18^{12-27} [E], Moses, Aaron, and all the elders of Israel entertain Jethro; and Moses by his advice appoints 'heads over the people, rulers of thousands, rulers of hundreds, rulers of fifties, and rulers of tens.' It is not clear how far we have here an organization and supplementing of the elders, or how far this is meant to be an independent, parallel set of officials. In Nu 11^{24b-30} [from an early source not certainly identified], seventy elders are associated with Moses in his prophetic inspiration. There is no mention of elders in E's code, the Book of the Covenant (Ex 20–23), but there are 'judges' (21^{22}). We meet with the 'elders of Israel' or 'of Judah' at intervals throughout the history (Jos 7^{6}, 1 S 4^{3}, 1 K 8^{1}; in D, Dt 27^{1};[1] Ezk 14^{1} [during the Exile], Ezr 6^{7-14}, 1 Mac 12^{6} *γερουσία*, 14^{20} *τοῖς πρεσβυτέροις*), associated with the high priest (cf. Mt 21^{23}). The members of the Sanhedrin were called 'elders,' *zᵉkēnîm*.[2]

This body of 'elders of Israel' exercised great influence in the early monarchy; they command the army (1 S 4^{3}), demand a king from Samuel (8^{4}), and confer the kingdom (2 S 5^{3}). They are less prominent in the later monarchy, power falling more and more into the hands of the royal ministers and officials (1 K 4), but become important again in and after the Exile; and, finally, the Sanhedrin claimed to represent the 'elders of Israel,' more especially the 'seventy elders' associated with Moses. In the 3rd cent. A.D., R. Joḥanan says that the members of the later Jewish council, the *Bêth-dîn*, must be 'tall, of imposing appearance, and of advanced age; and they must be learned, and must understand foreign languages as well as some of the arts of the necromancer.'[3]

We have seen that, over against the 'elders of Israel' we have the local elders of a city or district, who are the local authorities of whom we hear most. For instance, the elders act on behalf of Succoth (Jg 8^{14}) and Gilead (11^{5}). In the legislation of D the elders are prominent as the local authorities; they deliver up the murderer for punishment (Dt 19^{12}); they represent their city in the ritual for the expiation of murder by an unknown hand ($21^{2ff.}$); the disobedient son, the wife charged with infidelity, and the man who refuses to marry his deceased brother's widow are brought before them ($21^{19ff.}$ $22^{15ff.}$ $25^{7ff.}$, cf. Ru $4^{2ff.}$). After the Exile we have the 'elders of every city,' in Ezr 10^{14}.

On many points we have no express information as to the elders. We are told nothing as to their qualifications, and very little as to their rights, privileges, authority, or duties. Probably throughout the history the local elders were the heads of the leading families; but it is not clear who the 'elders of Israel' were. They may have been in theory a gathering of all the local elders, and in practice a gathering of such as were able or inclined to be present on a given occasion. If so, the elders of a district would usually be represented in proportion to their proximity to the place of meeting. If we read anywhere of *the* elder or shaikh of a town or district, we might think of the 'elders of Israel' as being made up of such district elders, but the latter do not appear in our documents. It is, nevertheless, possible that the 'elders of Israel' formed a national council with a comparatively small number of members, each with a definite official status, acquired by inheritance, or some principle of selection or election.

As to number, the Sanhedrin (*q.v.*) comprised about seventy, perhaps because seventy elders are mentioned in the account of the Exodus; but these are seventy *out of* the elders (מִזִּקְנֵי יִשְׂרָאֵל), implying that the total was much greater (Ex 24^{1}, Nu 11^{16}). Seventy-seven 'princes' and 'elders' are mentioned at Succoth.

Probably the authority of the body of elders, whether local or national, was largely of the same undefined character as that of the shaikh of an

1 i. 35 f.
2 Cf. the present writer's essay in *Christ and Civilization*, London, 1910, p. 49 ff.
3 McCurdy, ii. 124.
4 According to Benzinger, *PRE*³ (*loc. cit.*), only in J; but this is doubtful.

1 Perhaps a later stratum of D.
2 *HDB*, art. 'Sanhedrin,' iv. 399.
3 *JE*, art. 'Sanhedrin,' xi. 43ᵇ.

Arab tribe (see above). It was liable to be set aside by that of the king or any leader of an armed force, and it depended largely on the personality of the elders and the extent to which they represented public feeling.

A combination of our various pieces of evidence, Babylonian, Israelite, Arab, etc., suggests lines of development which are probably typical for the Semitic peoples generally. We have first the shaikh or shaikhs of a nomad tribe, then the elders of a town or district in a settled community. These furnish in some way a council of elders for an entire State. In a more advanced stage of social development the influence of the elder is subordinated to that of royal and other officials, but the elders long persist as a local institution, and recover much of their importance in such crises as the Captivity of Israel. On the other hand, the term 'elder' or 'shaikh' sometimes lost its original meaning, and came to be used for a chief of any kind.

LITERATURE.—Artt. 'Elder,' in *HDB*; 'Law and Justice,' 'Government,' in *EBi*; 'Elder,' 'Elder, Rebellious,' 'Family,' 'Judge,' 'Sanhedrin,' in *JE*; 'Aelteste,' in *PRE*^{3}; 'Shaikh,' in Hughes' *DI*; I. Benzinger, *Heb. Arch.*, Freiburg, 1894, pp. 296–320; G. H. A. v. Ewald, *Antiquities of Israel*, Eng. tr., London, 1876, p. 245 ff.; J. F. McCurdy, *Hist., Proph., and the Monuments*, London, 1894–1901, §§ 36, 443, 486, 560, 1092, 1310 f.; W. Nowack, *Lehrb. d. heb. Arch.*, Freiburg, 1894, i. 151, 301–324; O. Seesemann, *Die Aeltesten im AT*, Leipzig, 1895.

W. H. BENNETT.

ELEATICS.—See PHILOSOPHY (Greek).

ELECTION.—**1. Definition.**—Election is a purely religious idea, originating in an interior necessity of the spiritual life, as the natural explanation of the source of its saving impulses. The movement in the soul against sin is directly traced to a cause supernatural to the sinner. Righteousness is never an ordinary thing, or a common privilege that may be ranked beside others. It is laid to the responsibility of God, whose peculiar work it is. And, as it is of His inception, its continuance and successful fruition likewise are by His agency. It began with Him, and He will perfect it, by that faithfulness which, if it be too strong to describe it as 'irresistible grace'[1]—the compulsion of sovereign might—is indeed the pertinacity of unwearied love, of strong, wise, unerring Fatherhood over erring, weak, and foolish childhood. This is the very nerve of the doctrine in all the stages of its growth. The free return of man to God springs from the passionate communication of God to man. Election is the antecedent to revelation.

Election is to be distinguished from predestination (*q.v.*), with which it is at times confounded. The terms are not synonymous (for election, Heb. בָּחַר, Gr. *ἐκλογή*; for predestination, יָעַץ, יָצַר, Gr. *προορίζω*), nor is their connotation identical. The idea of predestination runs through Scripture, if that idea be understood in the sense of the all-creating, all-controlling activity of God over and in and through all things, but it is in no respect so central and essential to the revelation of His redemptive purpose as the idea of election. They are, however, closely related. Predestination has reference to the all-embracing, comprehensive design of the Divine will in all its work—creation, providence, salvation; election refers to the special application in redemption. Again, while predestination and election embrace speculative and religious contents, they retain them in different proportions; predestination being the more speculative, election the more religious. The problems of the former arise first in the reflecting stages of religious development, when an answer is required to the question, 'How is the individual related to the universe?' Election is not due to the philosophical instinct; it is an affirmation of the religious consciousness, expressing its certitude of the Divine, and therefore objectively valid, foundation of its religious experience. It meets the interior anxieties of the soul for saving grace. The discussion of predestination belongs to theodicy, of election to dogmatics. Further, the doctrine of election is Biblical and theistic. It occupies a foremost place in the Scriptures of both the OT and the NT. It derives its meaning and force solely from the system of revelation they record. It is grounded in the insistent conviction of the saved soul that salvation is derived from God. It is inconsistent with any view of the Divine Being which denies His personality and the beneficent character of His relation to men. It implies the reality of man's alienation from God, his sinfulness, his inability to work out his own salvation, and looks to the mercy of God to manifest a way of escape from sin and of return to Himself in reconciliation. It is thus also the presupposition of His gracious operation in the hearts of those who believe, prescribing its method and determining its result. Its definition can be gathered only inductively from the Scriptural data and believing experience, where alone we have the actual facts as they are presented in the history of His elect servants. Few doctrines have suffered so much from neglect of this consideration. Its treatment has been constantly vitiated by the intrusion of associations extraneous to its vital character and the Biblical premisses, and prejudicial to its truthful exposition. What these last are must be discovered in accordance with the canons and principles applicable in all doctrinal formulation, viz. the gradual evolution of the idea, the close connexion with the history of events, the emergence into ever-increasing purity and universality, and the fulfilment with self-consistent and complete form in Christ, 'the Elect One'[1] (Lk 9^{35}).

2. Systematic statement.—(*a*) The systematic presentation of election may begin with *its source in the Divine love.* God is Love. Love is His nature. It is to be viewed not so much as one of His attributes—it is the one quality concerning which it is predicated of God that He *is* (1 Jn 4^8)—but rather as the Divine constitution in which all the attributes are combined. It is the substance of His character, regulating the relationships within the Godhead. It is also regulative of His relation towards His creatures, including mankind. It is possible to trace God's righteousness, faithfulness, mercy, and justice to love as their foundation and essence. But, even where this conception of the Divine nature appears untenable and love is viewed as an attribute, all other attributes must be regarded as reconcilable with love. Whether essence or attribute, the love of God is the fountain of His electing grace. On the former hypothesis, it is more manifestly so; on the latter, God's love is liable to be subordinated to His glory identified with His righteousness or holiness, and a moral severity, inspired by ideas of earthly sovereignty and justice, is infused into His gracious acts, so absolute as to rob them of tenderness, compassion, and beneficent efficacy. Where this procedure is followed, election is, as a rule, described as an act of the Divine sovereignty—the Calvinist tendency.[2]

Although, under stress of criticism, every suggestion of caprice or arbitrariness is properly excluded from the idea of sovereignty, and its exercise is asserted to be conditioned by the Divine Attributes, it is, nevertheless, the case that love is conceived by Calvinism as a constituent of holiness, possessing but slight constraining force, and powerless to furnish those motives of the most persuasive sort that are requisite to enable sinful men to succeed in the work of salvation, *i.e.*, in exercise, sover-

[1] Calvin's phrase, as it was Augustine's.

[1] This is usually regarded as the genuine reading.

[2] Cf. Shedd, *Dogmat. Theol.*, 1889–94, i. 424; Cunningham, *Hist. Theol.*, 1863, ii. ch. 25 (where also the sphere of Divine sovereignty is argued for as the sphere of Divine mercy); Candlish, *Fatherhood of God*^{5}, 1870.

eignty is more judicial and retributive than gracious and salutary. Nor, on this view, has philosophic Calvinism yet offered an adequate rationale of the origin of election. It seeks refuge in mystery. It is forced to look for God's ultimate reasons for His acts in a sphere inaccessible to human understanding—'He has sufficient reasons secret to us.' Doubtless; but that is reasoning on abstract principles, and not from His actual procedure, His manifested nature and character. The Scriptures give no hint of such secret resort. There the goodness of God is exhibited as revealed in its highest exemplification in redemption, wherein He seeks to win sinners from their depravity to His own life of holiness and happiness, and Himself supplies the means whereby they attain those blessed ends. In that work mere justice has no concern. God is just; and, while the punishment of the sinner who clings to his sin is in accordance with justice, the notion of distributing to every transgressor exactly what he deserves is a different matter; the notion that the justice of God, or the claims of His law, must needs be satisfied by the sinner's endurance of punishment, is an un-Scriptural notion. God is not a Shylock. The punishment for sin administered by His righteous love has quite other motives. It is a means to an end. His holiness is a constituent of His love—not love a constituent of His holiness. His righteous love desires for the sinner his highest good, the Divine life itself, a holy displeasure against sin, a sincere penitence for participation in sin, a separation from its unholy influences, and liberation from the penalties incurred by yielding to them. This desire is the permanent condition of the heart of God towards sinful man. His attitude towards men and His activity on their behalf are directed by this desire. It prompts Him to His methods for its satisfaction. It precedes and creates the evil-doer's repentance. It provides the means enabling God to surrender His resentment. It leads to His self-sacrificing effort to regain men, and restore them to a better state of mind and heart. The desire issues from love. That love is conditioned by nothing in God that can act as a restraint on its exercise or hinder its operation. Holiness is its centre. But holiness enters in to hold it to the right thought of what is to be imparted, and to the right means of imparting it. The Divine mercy and righteousness are not antitheses, and need no reconciliation; they spring from the same root in the Divine love. Calvinism has high merit in having vindicated God's nature, as the source of election, against the claims of man's works or faith; for grace is the free and undeserved gift of God's love. But Calvinism fails in its analysis of the Divine nature. Modern theology here abandons its guidance; sees in the dispensation of grace something higher than a dispensation of justice; and, in the glory of God for which it works, the good of His creatures; and ascribes to the Divine Personality, as its most essential and fundamental content, a holy compassion, whose most imperative necessity is to seek the salvation of all men[1] (Jn 3[16], Ro 3[22], 1 Ti 2[4] etc.).

(*b*) The idea of election is *progressively unfolded in the history of redemption.* It pervades both the history and the prophecy of the OT. The story of the Hebrews is the story of Divine grace striving against human sin. It begins with the promise of restoration made to primitive man after his fall (Gn 3[15]), the appreciation of Abel's sacrifice over Cain's (4[4]), and the rescue of Noah from the Flood (ch. 6). It takes more definite shape in the calling of the patriarchs, Abraham (12[1-3] 13[14-17] 18[18]), Isaac (26[2-5]), Jacob (28[13-15] 46[3]), Judah (49[10]), and Joseph (45[7] etc.)—a calling which detached them from their heathen surroundings, and impressed upon them, and, through them, on the race that was to spring from their loins, the ineffaceable stamp of their separateness. In the promises made to them, and in the so-called Blessing of Jacob (Gn 49), we possess the earliest testimony to the nature of the hopes inspired by the Divine choice. It was an election to *blessing* and *influence*: 'I will bless thee, and in thee shall all the families of the earth be blessed' (Gn 12[2. 3]).

The patriarchs were made to understand that God was with them, directing their destiny, and through their instrumentality fulfilling His purpose of goodwill to the peoples. The blessing they were to receive and bestow was of material good. The warrant for their conviction rested in the Divine covenant, whose corroboration was recognized at once in outward event and inner assurance. To the minds of the patriarchs the facts of their lives pointed plainly to this one unmistakable inference. A Divine order is discerned in their troubled lives, wherein even the evil was made subservient to the Divine plan. Their narratives close with the intensest faith in God's goodness to their race. All their experience was solely of God's favour and in pursuance of His own counsel. His counsel, however, is not inscrutable; it is a counsel of blessing (32[26] 43[14] 48[4]) and help (48[15] 49[25] 50[20]), first to the chosen people and, through them, to all peoples.

[1] Cf. Fairbairn, *Christ in Mod. Theol.*[6], 1894, p. 406: 'the essential graciousness of His Being and the necessary grace of all His acts.'

A fresh stage was introduced by Moses. He laid the foundations of a civic and religious polity creative of a sense of *corporate* or *national individuality*, based on the election of Israel by Jahweh to be His chosen people. A new covenant was established, with the object of nurturing a new spirit, under a new and more exalted conception of God's name. The ritual and moral ordinances were designed to educate this consciousness. They imparted a unity of feeling and sense of benefit and of responsibility—but not in themselves, for they were merely the institutions of the neighbouring peoples; the new enrichments were to be traced to the new name of Jahweh (Ex 3[14]). Israel's God was never a reflexion of the national spirit; the national spirit received its impress from His image. Jahweh was the framer of Israel, and the mould in which He cast it was that of His own nature. Its institutions had little in them that was peculiar; what gave them meaning, transfiguring them and rendering them serviceable media for conveying Israel's formative influence, was anterior to them—the revealed name of their God. Corresponding to Jahweh must be His people; that was the substance of Mosaism. To produce that correspondence, and to realize its specific obligations, was the task of Mosaism. Henceforth the idea of election comprises both concepts. With the Divine goodness rests the credit. The signal proof of it was the deliverance from Egypt. Jahweh sends His servant Moses. He is compassionate. He spares the people and averts His judgments. His chastisements witness to the same; they are the inflictions of solicitous care and guidance. Individual election to specific service is not lost sight of, as, *e.g.*, in the consecration of one tribe to discharge priestly duties, and in the nomination of persons extraordinarily gifted to exercise their gifts in the common interest. It is, however, national and political election for which Mosaism stands.

Throughout the monarchical period significant modifications appear. They are associated, first, with the foundation of the theocratic kingdom, and, next, with the progress of prophecy. The conception of the king as the 'Lord's anointed' (1 S 16[13]) powerfully influenced expectation in the direction of a more *personal*, *spiritual*, and *universalist* interpretation. The anointing set forth the visible embodiment of the true relation between the chosen and God. The true king was God Himself; but He appointed another to rule for Him. He stood to His substitute in the most intimate connexion. Nothing less was involved in the solemn transference of the title 'son' from Israel to Israel's king than the assumption that henceforth the holder of the promised sovereignty was to be an individual of the reigning house.

It is not easy to fill up the outline of the 'son' with its just content. But, under the teaching of the prophets, it may be held to include similarity of nature, closeness of fellowship, identity of aim, unity of honour, and heirship. 'Thou art my Son'—likeness; 'Ask of me, and I will give thee the heathen for thine inheritance'—universal sway (Ps 2[7f.]). Both ideas are embodied in material form, to begin with, in the king; and become the starting-point of what is sometimes termed 'figurative prophecy,' in which they are presented as existing in him, not as he then was, but *ideally*—a process consummated in the picture of the perfect Servant of Jahweh (Is 53-66), in whom election is to the graces of the Spirit (61[1-3]), by a new covenant (59[21]), embracing all hearts and lives filled by the Spirit (ch. 60, Jer 11, etc.) who fulfil the one condition of repentance and whose names are written in the book of life (Ezk 13[9], Dn 12[1], Mal 3[16])—a process not substantially altered, if in detail enriched, until the baptism of John.

Thus from Adam to Christ—first in a man, then in a family, then in a nation, then in a kingly dynasty within the nation, then in prophets, and finally in Christ—the Divine choice runs. There is an evolution of stages that set forward a continuous progress, each prognostic of the next, and all in organic line, from ideas material and political to an idea more ethical and spiritual, whereby the hope of earthly prosperity is transformed into yearning for the blessings of the inner life of love and suffering—an evolution palpitating throughout with the truth of human experience and feeling as well as with the impulse of supernatural movement. Everywhere these two factors converge in election—the Divine will and the nation's conformity to it. The election is never absolute or unconditioned. Jahweh is a moral ruler, and deals with the elect as with all, on moral principles, the eternal principles of His own nature.[1] Nor is it conceived in theoretical interests; it is not a mere satisfaction to intellect; it is a revelation to piety, the simple setting of practical facts in their proper relation to God.

(*c*) Election comes to *its perfect expression in Christ.* Historical in Israel, it becomes personal in Christ. The NT teaching derives its specific features from His, and His teaching founds itself on the OT development. We may summarize it as follows. The Jewish nation had been the recipients of special privilege, and were truly the elect people of God (Jn 4^{22}; cf. Mt 15^{26}, Lk 7^{30}, Ro 9$^{4.16}$, Gal 3$^{4-9}$, Ac 7), exhibiting a stage in the realization of the Divine purpose. Their election was purely of His grace (Jn 1^{12} 17$^{2-6}$, Ro 9^{11}, Ac 13^{17}), and was forfeitable through unfaithfulness to its conditions. By them its blessings were to be extended to all peoples. The official religious leaders had been unfaithful, and had failed to retain the nation in its privileged position. Election now centres in Christ and in all who, through Him, are the true 'seed of Abraham,' not by physical descent simply, but by doing His works and following after the righteousness that is of faith. The association of the benefits of salvation with Christ entails new positions of great interest, prompting new affirmations of faith and hinting at new problems of speculation. With Him the type yields to the reality. He establishes a new covenant founded on a new relation—the Kingdom of God, which for the elects' sake has been prepared before. He, the Elect One, also has been prepared before from the foundation of the world (1 P 1^{20}, He 7).[2] The nature of election is in conformity with the nature of the Kingdom, viz. election into a common life under one rule. It is a universal Kingdom; the choice is made by God's love of humanity, not by favour to any particular nation. It is boundless in extent and everlasting, being for man as man. There is therefore a universal call, the manifestation of God in Christ coming into contact with the minds of men. It is also a spiritual Kingdom. The call to enter it can be complied with only by fulfilling its spiritual conditions—repentance and faith. Christ is the pattern and exemplar of it. He is the Elect One (Lk 9^{35} 23^{35}), with whom, the Servant of the Lord, He explicitly identifies Himself (Lk 4$^{16-24}$), and who is upheld in His election by the Father. The call is addressed to all men (Ro 1^{6}, 2 Th 2^{13} etc.), but all do not continue in it (Mt 20^{16} etc.). Those who do are the true elect (κλητοί, ἐκλεκτοί), for whom the Kingdom was prepared from before the foundation of the world (25^{34} etc.); for whose sake God shortens the sufferings of the last times; whose prayers He hears, whom He knows, and who are to rejoice because their names are written in heaven. To give the Kingdom to them is the Father's good pleasure. They prove themselves the elect of God in that they are obedient to the call of Christ. The origin of their faith is carried back to the eternal counsel of God. This faith itself originates not so much in their own receptivity as in the work of Christ and power of God. The process of their election is their continuous discipleship, referred, like its inception, to the will of God. Not only in purpose, but in fact, are these in election.

In all the foregoing no attempt is made to solve the implicit difficulties; the knots are there, not for solution, but for combination. In St. John we find that the result of Christ's work is due to Divine cause: those come whom the Father gives, those who do not come to Christ are the children of the devil. Again, those who come are those who love the truth and light, those who come not love darkness. All, *i.e.*, that happens here happens in human freedom, yet under Divine causality. According to St. Peter, election fulfils itself in sanctification of spirit (1 P 1$^{1.2}$ [in 1 P 2^{8} reprobation seems indicated; the ethical condition of 'disobedience' is not to be excluded]). St. James sees Christians to be what they are by God's election, begetting by the word of truth, and working in them faith (Ja 1^{18}–2^{5}). St. Paul's doctrine comprises so many elements that very divergent views of it have been taken. On close examination it will be found to add nothing radically new. The Thessalonians (1 Th 1^{4}) know themselves elected of God, because they have accepted the message of salvation (with 2 Th 2^{13} etc., cf. 1 P 1$^{2.5.23}$ etc.). The kernel of the Apostle's teaching is to be found in Ro 8$^{28-30}$ (rather than in 9–11),[1] where election is the strongest assertion of assurance. Amid the anxieties of the age, the believer is not to be dismayed, since to those whom God loves, and who are His elect, all things work together for good—a certainty which opens out a broad prospect into the deepest thoughts of God, who foreknows and foreordains; and whom He foreknows and foreordains He calls, justifies, and glorifies. It is a pure triumph-song of faith, declaring its own eternal salvation for its own comfort and strengthening. In the other *locus classicus*, Eph 1$^{4-6}$, the ground of election is God's good pleasure and free grace; its aim the holiness of the elect and their standing in the adoption of children. According to Eph 4^{4}, election accomplishes itself by incorporation into the one body, the believing community, which is effected by the acceptance of the Gospel. In the Pastorals the Apostolate is ordained to work faith in the elect. In other Epistles the assurance of election is confirmed in the conceptions of it as a πρόθεσις τῶν αἰώνων, and as being bound up with the world-plan. The ideas throughout are moral, not theoretical, expository rather than explanatory: the statement of present experience and undeniable personal conviction that the action of God, the protection of God, and the purpose of God are upon the believer, within him, and around him, going before him and preparing him unto the eternal issue. It is a thought in entire harmony with the general doctrine of the NT. Humanity is fallen, is incapable of saving itself by its own forces, and can be redeemed only by an act of pure grace. Election has followed a course of evolution, the realization of God's plan, since the call of Abraham, in the history of his nation, culminating in Christ. St. Paul clearly formulates the intention of the Jews' election, that 'all may be saved.' There is no mention of the exclusion of any by Divine decree. He, indeed, never suggests that men may not resist God's will; nor does he ever allow us to suppose that they may not defeat God's purpose. But salvation is offered to all. Its determining cause is the free decision of the individual. Its condition is faith in the gospel. God confers on man the power to believe through the presentation of the gospel. Unbelief arises from neglect of the use of the means of grace. There is, at this point, a moment of determinism in the Pauline doctrine.

[1] In the well-known chapter of Jeremiah (18), Israel is not mere clay, nor is God a mere potter; the heart of the parable is the Divine desire to secure the Divine impress on the clay.

[2] These are points in which the NT teaching is in direct affinity with later Jewish apocalyptic; cf. *Book of Enoch*.

[1] See p. 259^{b}, small print.

Man is so fast in the bondage of sin, so turned towards evil, that God's Spirit must accompany the word to produce saving faith. The Apostle thus asserts both election and man's liberty. He makes no attempt to reconcile them. Was the necessity urgent? St. Paul was a mystic in the higher reaches of his thought. The religious life to him was, in its last analysis, a rhythm of life within life, in which desire determined the flow of gifts from the including greater to the included less. So God meets man in the many phases of his shadowed mind, and gives Himself or what is His as man will receive; and, as He gives, the inner springs of man's self are touched, yielding the secrets of freedom and faith. The God-possessed life is the self-possessing life. Of the mechanism of the soul that sets itself against God, St. Paul had no experience: he could not describe it. Still less could he posit a decree of reprobation to explain it. In the case of the sole rejection he knew—that of the Jews—the casting away was temporary, and to be wrought against. Even so it might fare with evil, when its meaning should be taken up into the master-meaning of good, and its whole history, while playing a real part, should be known as but an episode in the history of good.

From the foregoing we deduce these three assured positions: (1) the ideal Son, who is the Mediator of the Divine life, the bestower of the Divine Spirit, the express image of the Divine Person; (2) the ideal community, the elect race, the chosen body, which is to exhibit the virtues and graces of the Son; (3) Jesus, pre-ordained in the eternal counsel to be the agent of its election, its Head, Lord, and Christ, through whom God calls, begets, and sanctifies the elect. In the Person, Work, and Church of Christ the many-sided foreshadowings and hopes of the OT find fulfilment. The correspondence of the fulfilment with the prophecy is not forced. We see the great lines of thought of the history and prophecy proceeding to an unknown, unimaginable end, and in the NT meeting in Christ in a wholly new combination, the spring of fresh forces and larger hopes for mankind. It is the consummation in Life of what was prepared in life.

If the Divine purpose is to be read in the light of its evolution, *can we justly speak of non-elect*? The term has no warrant in Scripture. Has the idea? In answer, the following considerations may be deemed relevant: (1) Election is always of *some* with the benefit of *all* in view, the special *few* for the universal *many*. (2) Election is neither in the OT nor in the NT rigorously restricted to the elect body: other nations besides Israel do work for Jahweh in the execution of His redemptive purpose—as, *e.g.*, Egypt, Cyrus, etc.; similarly in the NT 'in every nation he that feareth God' (Ac 10^{35}) and 'all nations of men on all the face of the earth,' concerning whom God 'hath determined the times before appointed, that they should seek the Lord, if haply they might feel after him and find him' ($17^{26.\,27}$; cf. Eph 3^{6}). (3) The Christian hope is universal, 'not for us only, but also for the whole World' (1 Jn 2^{2}; cf. 1 Ti 2^{4} 4^{10}, Tit 2^{11}). (4) The prophecy of 'a dispensation of the fulness of the times' (Eph 1^{10}; cf. Ph $2^{10.\,11}$, Col $1^{19.\,20}$), when whatever shall ultimately exist shall be reconciled to God, is an idea including the redemption of physical nature, with the destruction of suffering and death; the redemption of human nature, with the destruction of sin; and the redemption of the world of angels, with the destruction of the spiritual forces opposing themselves now to the Kingdom. (5) Although there is a limit to absolute universality of salvation, the cause of limitation is not in God or His counsel. Intimations of impossibilities occur, but these are not referred back to God's ordainment; they arise from the condition of the spirit of men themselves. To the wicked God shows mercy—giving time and place for repentance. All shall be made alive who *can be*. If it should be that God's judgments pass from a disciplinary stage to a penal, it is through the impenitence of those who are the subjects of them. A decree of non-election is unthought of (in Ro 8, Eph 1, the reference is to believers only). Election is to life. And the life of the elect is the leaven of all. Yes, but all are not receptive; what then? The problem is not solved. God wills all men to be saved. But all are not saved. Is the Divine will then frustrated? An intractable residuum in human nature is contemplated. Before it does God's resourcefulness fail? There will be a restitution of all things. Can it tolerate on its borders a quenchless Gehenna? The antinomy is left—a position acceptable perhaps to the practical religious mind, but perplexing to the reason. The final relation between the elect and the reprobate, and between the reprobate and God, is unknown. There is no experiential material on which to construct; and God's procedure is hid. Conscience, not intellect, adjusts the problem.

The well-known chapters 9–11 of Romans are best understood as a parenthesis, treating of a very special objection. Its theme was a burning problem to the Apostle, hence the length at which he treats it. Its argument is wholly apart from his central experience, and in line with the current Judaic scholastic teaching. It reminds us that St. Paul was a Jew, 'learned in the traditions'—as well as a Christian. Its principal elements are these: (1) The recognition of the absolute sovereignty of God; the Jews who rejected Christ and those who accepted Him both made their respective choices in subjection to the Divine appointment. (2) This Divine election was for a certain definite purpose; the unbelieving Jews were blinded in order that the Gentiles might obtain the salvation that was through Christ. (3) The blinding thus inflicted upon a portion of the Jews was temporary, and, when the purpose was accomplished for which this Divine appointment had been made, the ban would be removed; through the ministry of the Gentile Christians the unbelieving Jews would be converted to the true faith and all Israel would be saved. The absolute result was sure: if any failed it was because they did not make their calling sure. That this line of thought on election had its exponents in the Jewish schools may be felt in the Book of Wisdom (cf. the interesting essay by Eduard Grafe in *Theol. Abhandlungen Carl von Weizsäcker gewidmet*, Freiburg, 1892). 'Double predestination' is affirmed, but whether in the Augustinian or in the Calvinistic sense is another question. The Apostle's object is to set forth a wider election-doctrine than that of the Pharisees (cf. Gore, *Romans*, 1899, ii.; Sanday-Headlam, 'Romans,' in *ICC*, 1895, *ad loc.*), and to reduce every motive for Judaic pride. He has not in view either the relation of God's causality and man's freedom or the 'double predestination.'

3. Subsequent theological reflexion.—Until the time of St. Augustine this is neither profound nor precise. Patristic thought is unspeculative. It is pervaded by a strong practical sense which shrinks from theoretical problems suggested, but not solved, by the Apostolic teaching. The mental attitude of the Fathers is determined by a close adherence to the received sacred pronouncements, and by the endeavour to repel whatever in contemporary cults appeared plainly contrary to them. In their view the unit of election tends to be not the individual destiny, but the redeemed race. Again, their point of departure is not the decree of God, but the believing experience of the saved. Moreover, personal election being a moment of personal faith—faith's assurance of its own eternal worth—it cannot conjoin with itself any assertion of reprobation, since that can be no element of faith. That Jesus is 'the Elect' of God, that His election has no other object than the election of His Church, that the Church lives to bring the world to God—these are the primary contentions. Both the Greek and Latin doctors maintain the Divine sovereignty, man's liberty and responsibility, and the reconciliation of both in God's foreknowledge.[1] Differences first appear in the meanings attached to those doctrines; and the

[1] Not necessarily foreknowledge of man's merit. The question was not seriously discussed.

meanings emerge in their particular cast from alien prepossessions, *e.g.* in the East from philosophy, in the West from law. The Greek divines, influenced by the universalist strain in St. Paul's teaching, formulate a more genial concept of man's freedom; the Latins, appealing to his determinist strain, dominate man's will by God's sovereignty.

Tertullian [1] is an exception. He unites with the Alexandrians in a view of the will which erects it into an independent faculty, having 'freedom in both directions,' knowing both good and evil, and able to choose between them. This is not St. Paul's doctrine: he asserts of the will simply freedom from conflicting motives. East and West alike inculcate a doctrine of synergism, according to which the renewal of the soul is the result of two factors—Divine grace and man's freedom. But what is the part taken by each factor? Does the mercy of God take the initiative, or the will of man? Does the exertion of man's will precede the Divine aid? In what sense is the will free? Increasingly the West exalts the Divine goodness; the East enlarges the range of human freedom, and accords saving merit to man's effort. In harmony with such positions, election is a pre-ordination of blessings and rewards for such as are foreseen to be worthy of them. There is no predestination to sin, although there is foreknowledge of it. Justin Martyr is strenuous in repudiating Stoic fatalism. Men, he affirms, have it in their power to cast off sin by exerting their will. With Irenæus sin in men and angels is a free act. Why some fall and others do not is a mystery. There is no interference with human freedom. The blindness in those who reject the Gospel is the result of their own character. It is the same with the Greeks; Methodius expresses this common conviction when he writes that 'sin is an act of personal freedom.' Of special interest is Victorinus the Rhetor, who pushes the logic of the West to its extreme limit, short of Augustine's, of whom he is the direct precursor. Much varying comment is made on isolated statements [2] in St. Paul's Epistles, which often assume a greater importance than in the original context, and are usually discussed less in relation to the Apostle's system of doctrine than under personal predilections.

With Augustine the whole subject assumed new and front-rank prominence. His doctrine has little historical background. It was mostly a new creation from a new standpoint, drawn not from earlier Christian sources, but from the ideas which he had imbibed from his philosophical studies operating on the convictions of an intensely awakened conscience. The secret of Augustine lies in his inner growth. To appreciate aright his contribution to Christian philosophy, two considerations must be kept in view—his peculiar spiritual discipline, and the subordination of his reason to his faith. His philosophy, if he has one, is ancillary to his religion, which is real, positive, and profound. It was gradually, as polemical occasion incited, worked out; it cannot be presented as a systematized whole, bristles with unreconciled antitheses, offers unceasing suggestion, and is to be interpreted in its spirit and method rather than in its immediate conclusions. Amidst the enervation and confusion which resulted from his doubt and despondency, and from the secular catastrophes of his age, there were two truths that continued to cast an absorbing image on his mind—a conviction that the human mind was a thing apart in the universe, and that a Divine mind embraced the whole in an all-seeing vision. How reconcile this incarnate perversity of a world with the being of God? The two foci of his 'system' are a monistic doctrine of unity and the theory of original or racial sin. The world is but the expression of God; God's own immediate will is the sole cause of all things. In the view of God's eternal knowledge the natural man is evil, wholly depraved, morally insufficient, and helpless, from the identity of the race and Adam (so tremendous an effect is attributed to the Fall): 'the will has power indeed for evil but not for good, except as helped by the Infinite Good.' Original sin is the basis of predestinating election. The whole human mass was so justly condemned in the apostate root that, were none rescued from that damnation, none could blame God's justice. Those who are rescued are rescued gratuitously; those who are not only show what the whole lump, even the rescued themselves, deserved, had not undeserved mercy succoured them (*Enchiridion*, 99; cf. *Ep.* cxciv. 6, 8). If the will of man turns to good, that is due to gracious Divine efficiency. Man's regeneration is entirely the work of grace. Grace is efficacious and irresistible; its action on the soul is the result of direct Divine agency. Only those predestinated to eternal life are regenerated; they are also endowed with the gift of perseverance. Grace is indefectible. They are the elect. The elect are few in comparison with the non-elect (a doctrine attributed to Scripture, and confirmed by observation); yet the latter are somehow created for the benefit of the former. Election is not grounded on foreknowledge of human faith or conduct; no account is given as to why some are elected and others not; there must be two classes to manifest the Divine mercy and justice. 'Over the mass of corruption there passed two acts of the will of God—an act of favour and grace, choosing part to be partakers of everlasting glory; and an act of justice, forsaking the rest and adjudging them to endless perdition; these, vessels of wrath, those, of mercy.' There was no positive and efficient decree of any to eternal death; the decree of God was simply to leave the wicked in the state of perdition to which they had come. Augustine teaches preterition.

The Augustinian doctrine depressed several positions hitherto unquestioned, and initiated a controversy which proved of unequalled influence throughout the mediæval period, and which at the Reformation still interested the intellectual world. God as Will, not Mind; man's free will as dependent on Divine causation and not inalienable in its own constitution; grace as controlling, not assisting, human effort; and all the logical consequences of the conceptions of absolutism in God and determinism in man—these ideas fill the horizon of the Middle Ages, partly by way of attraction, partly of repulsion. The strict Augustinian argument is well sustained by such theologians as Gottschalk, Aquinas, Bradwardine, and others, who exalt the Divine grace, and at times teach the twofold predestination. The doctrine of merit is represented in such commanding minds as Rabanus Maurus, John Scotus Erigena, Duns Scotus, etc. The dominant point of view, however, is seen in Aquinas, who looked upon merit in the strict sense of the term as the effect of grace, and grace as the effect of predestination. He argues with Augustine that the reason why grace is rejected is man's own fault—not on the ground of the existence of man's free will, but on account of his disinclination to grace by reason of original sin. He places the rejection in the faulty will of the race and not in the choice of the individual.

Throughout the period the controversy shifts its base from the sound facts of experience; and its net results are of less value for the idea of election than for that of predestination. Logical considerations are the determining factors. Little of practical import accrues. The modern world tacitly settled down to a modified Augustinianism. In the Roman communion strict Augustinianism, while not formally repudiated, has, under the influence of Jesuit ascendancy, not been favoured. The Council of Trent made no further definitions. Various hypotheses as to the connexion between electing grace and man's free will have been ad-

[1] The phrase 'liberum arbitrium' is due to Tertullian.

[2] As, *e.g.*, 'Whom he did foreknow he also did predestinate' (Ro 8^{29}); 'Whom he will he hardeneth' (9^{18}); 'Jacob have I loved, Esau have I hated' (9^{13}).

vanced by Roman divines, and only those of the Jansenists have been condemned. The general current of opinion has been against unconditional election, in favour of synergism. In the Reformation teaching the general spirit of Augustinianism has been maintained; at first more faithfully with Luther and the Lutheran Church in its subjective value; with Zwingli and Calvin in its objective worth; more recently with both Lutheran and Reformed unconditional election has been abandoned. Yet synergism has not won fresh credit. Pelagianism, it is universally felt, has been finally refuted. God is sovereign, and man is free; both truths are to be retained, as Augustine blunderingly argued. The path to their reconciliation, according to modern thought, is to be found in a less juristic and more moral conception of Divine sovereignty, and in a less indifferent and more determinate theory of the human will. Present-day mental science, even with the help of the doctrines of heredity and environment, has not succeeded in rendering any form of materialistic determinism cogent to the modern mind. In so far it helps to confirm the belief of the bulk of the Christian Church in all ages that man's destiny is in his own hands. It prevents us equally from any assertion of predestination in its extreme personal sense. Election in the sense of our circumstances and surroundings being made for us and not by us—this is simple and obvious enough. But that we are not the necessary result of our circumstances and surroundings is the plain testimony of our conscious life. That conscious life which speaks saying, 'Thou oughtest,' wakes a no less certain echo within, which says, 'Because I ought, I can.' That 'can' abides for ever, however enfeebled it may become.[1] The social pressure may as a matter of fact be made subservient to its increase: since social coercion, if it be reasonable, is a condition of moral robustness. Similarly man's independence is secured in dependence on God. The essence of freedom is self-surrender to the Divine will.[2]

LITERATURE.—There is a very large literature on the subject, in the major part of which 'election' and 'predestination' are used interchangeably. A copious bibliography will be found at the end of W. A. Copinger, *Treatise on Predestination, Election, and Grace*, London, 1889. Every modern writer on NT theology and every commentator on 'Romans' and 'Ephesians' deals with the subject—largely by way of simple exposition. The two most notable writings of the modern period are Thomas Erskine of Linlathen, *The Doctrine of Election*, London, 1837, and Schleiermacher, *Lehre von der Erwählung*, Berlin, 1836.

A. S. MARTIN.

ELEMENT.—See ATOMIC THEORY.

ELEPHANTA.—Elephanta is an island on the W. coast of India; lat. 18° 58′ N.; long. 73° E.; about 6 miles from the city of Bombay, and 4 from the mainland. The native name of the island is *Ghārāpurī*, which has been interpreted to mean 'city of purification,' or, in the form *Gārāpurī*, 'city of excavations,' of which *Purī* was probably the earlier form. The Portuguese gave it the name of *Elephanta*, from a life-sized figure of an elephant, hewn from an isolated mass of trap-rock, which formerly stood in the lower part of the island, not far from the usual landing-place. This figure fell down many years ago, and was supposed to have disappeared; but it was discovered in 1864–5, and was removed to the Victoria Gardens, Bombay, where all that remains of it now stands. The elephant had originally a small figure on its back, called by some a young elephant, by others a tiger (Yule-Burnell, *Anglo-Indian Gloss.*, *s.v.* 'Elephanta'). Another image, that of a horse, which once stood S.E. of the Great Cave, has disappeared. The island is famous for a splendid series of rock-cave temples, which, according to local tradition, were excavated by the Pāṇḍava heroes of the *Mahābhārata* epic, while a still wilder legend attributes them to Alexander the Great, to whom popular tradition ascribes many great and ancient structures, even in parts of the country which he never reached in the course of his invasion. Fergusson, comparing them with other works of the same type, assigns their construction to the 10th cent. A.D.; Burgess dates them earlier—in the latter part of the 8th or the beginning of the 9th century. There is said to have been an inscription over the entrance of the Great Cave, which, if discovered, would probably decide the date and the name of the king under whom they were excavated. This slab, according to Diogo do Couto, the Portuguese annalist, was removed by his countrymen; but, if it ever existed, it has now disappeared.

The temple in the Great Cave is, like all Brāhmanical rock-temples in W. India, dedicated to Śiva; and, according to Stevenson, it belongs to the Smārtta school of that sect. Burgess, however, is inclined to believe that it may be older than the present sectarial divisions, and that it was excavated when all the Śaivas held nearly the same doctrines.

In all there are six caves, of which four are fully or nearly complete; the fifth is almost entirely filled up, and the sixth is supposed to have been intended merely to provide cells for anchorites. The most important of all is the Great Cave, which, excluding the porticoes and back aisle, forms an irregular square of about 91 ft. in both directions. This contains that striking piece of sculpture, a colossal bust, known as the *Trimūrti*, or 'triad' ('trinity' being an inappropriate expression for this Hindu combination of gods), which stands at the back of the cave, facing the entrance. It undoubtedly represents Siva as the supreme deity; but there has been much difference of opinion as to the designation of the three faces. That in the centre is probably Śiva, the creator of the universe; or, as some say, Brahmā, who, according to the legend, sprang from the left side of Śiva to create the world. That on the left of the spectator is believed to be the Vedic Rudra, in later times identified with Śiva, the Destroyer. The third face of the triad, that on the right of the spectator, has a gentle, placid, almost feminine look; and, though generally, and perhaps rightly, regarded as that of Śiva in the character of Viṣṇu, has by some been identified with Pārvatī, the *śakti*, or consort, of Śiva. Like many of the Elephanta sculptures, this group has been sadly mutilated, even in recent times, by thoughtless or mischievous visitors. It has now been placed under the protection of a guard. Enough, however, remains to show the wonderful beauty and dignity of the sculpture. On each side of the recess in which the *Trimūrti* stands are figures of the giant warders, minor gods on their promotion, who act as protectors (*dvārapāla*) of the god. The shrine (*garbha*) of the temple contains in the centre a base, or altar, in the middle of which is the *liṅgam*, or phallic emblem, of Śiva, cut from a stone of harder and closer grain than that out of which the temple has been excavated.

'This plain stone, the mysterious symbol representative of Śiva as the male energy or production, or source of the generative power in nature—as the *yoni*, or circle in which it stands, is of the passive or female power—is *the idol* of the temple, the central object of worship, to which everything else is only accessory or subsidiary' (Burgess, p. 9).

In the compartment east of the *Trimūrti* is a

[1] Cf. Henley, 'I am the master of my fate;
I am the captain of my soul.'
For a splendid assertion of the same from the side of mysticism, see Maeterlinck's *Wisdom and Destiny*, Lond. 1902.

[2] Cf. Tennyson, 'Our wills are ours, we know not how;
Our wills are ours, to make them thine.'

group of many figures surrounding a representation of the androgynous Śiva, an image half male and half female, known as Arddhanārīśvara, accompanied by Viṣṇu riding on the bird Garuḍa (whom Fergusson would connect with Assyrian beliefs), Indra, and Brahmā, who are here represented as in attendance upon Śiva. The similar compartment on the west side is occupied by Śiva and Pārvatī, the mountain-goddess, his consort. The figures are not really nude (which is a Jaina rather than a Brāhmanical habit), the drapery being carved in the conventional style, which represents only the thicker folds and hems.

Passing to the west porch, we come to the famous group of the marriage of Śiva and Pārvatī, who here represent the primordial pair from whose union the fertility of the soil and the increase of the human race, cattle, and crops are assured. The scene, unfortunately now much damaged, seems to depict the meeting of the bridal pair, accompanied by Brahmā, Viṣṇu, or Sūrya, the sun-god, the mother of the bride, and Sarasvatī, the goddess of eloquence, who blesses the union. Following this scene come representations of Śiva and Pārvatī in Kailāsa, the paradise of the god; and under it the ten-faced Rāvaṇa, king of Laṅkā or Ceylon, whose exploits are recorded in the *Rāmāyaṇa*.

Opposite the marriage of Śiva is one of the most remarkable sculptures in the cave—the face of the principal figure indicative of rage, the lips set, with tusks projecting from the corners of the mouth. This has usually been considered to represent Vīrabhadra, one of the Śaiva incarnations (*avatāra*). It is more probably Bhairava, an incarnation of Rudra, who seems to be derived from the non-Aryan demonolatry—one of the most common objects of worship among the Marāthā people, by whom he is also known as Kapālabhṛt, 'skull-wearer,' or Mahākāla, Time personified as the Great Destroyer. In this aspect Śiva was worshipped by the Kapālika sect, naked mendicants who wore skulls round their necks, and drank from a cup formed out of a human skull (see AGHORĪ). Farther on, Śiva is depicted performing the Tāṇḍava dance, which he does in the character of Bhūteśvara, 'lord of ghosts and goblins,' haunting cemeteries and places of cremation, attended by troops of imps, trampling on rebellious demons, heated by drink, and followed in the dance by his spouse Devī—another example of the absorption, in the cult of the god, of much of the non-Aryan devil-worship. Here he also appears as Mahāyogī, the 'great ascetic,' his image closely resembling that of Buddha, with whom this side of his cultus was doubtless closely associated. Burgess (p. 41) explains this resemblance as

'due in part to the circumstance that the Brahmans excavated their cave temples in imitation and rivalry of the Bauddhas. The Bhikshus or Bauddha ascetics wore yellow robes, and in imitation of them probably the Shaiva Yogis and mendicants adopted tawny-coloured clothes. Buddha was regarded by his followers as the Great Ascetic, and this may have tempted the early Shaivas to give prominence to a similar characteristic in the representation of their favourite object of worship.'

The second rock-temple has been injured, and little of the sculpture remains capable of description or identification. The third temple is still more dilapidated. In the fourth there were, according to Diogo do Couto, two images of Vetāla, lord of demons, and of Chaṇḍī, or Durgā in her malevolent aspect; but these have long since disappeared. The Great Cave is still used at Śaiva festivals, and a fair is held at the feast of the *Śivarātri*, or 'Śiva's night,' on the 14th of the dark half of Māgha (about the middle or end of February), when a fast is observed by day and a vigil by night, and there is special worship of the *lingam*.

LITERATURE.—The literature connected with Elephanta is voluminous. The best account of the place, on which this article is largely based, is that of J. Burgess, *The Rock-Temples of Elephanta or Ghārāpurī*, with excellent photographs by D. H. Sykes (Bombay, 1871; reprinted, without illustrations, in 1875). This is supplemented by Pandit Bhagvānlāl Indrajī, in *BG* xiv. 59 ff. The earliest traveller's account is that of Van Linschoten (1598), ed. A. C. Burnell, Hakluyt Society, i. 291. This was followed by Diogo do Couto (1616), *Do muito notavel e espantoso Pagode do Elefante*, quoted by Yule-Burnell, *Anglo-Indian Gloss.*, p. 341. Among accounts by other travellers may be noted: Fryer, *New Account of E. India and Persia* (1698), p. 75; Ovington, *Voyage to Suratt* (1696), p. 155 f.; Grose, *Voyage to E. Indies* (1757), i. 59 ff.; Ives, *Voyage from England to India* (1773), p. 45; Niebuhr, *Voyage en Arabie et en d'autres pays circonvoisons* (1774), ii. 25 ff.; Macneil, *Archaeologia* (1783), viii. 270 ff.; Goldingham, *Asiatick Researches* (1795), iv. 409 ff.; Lord Valentia, *Voyages and Travels* (1809), ii. 159 ff.; Forbes, *Oriental Memoirs* (1813), i. 423, 452 ff., 441 ff. (2nd ed. 1834, i. 265 ff.); Erskine, *Trans. Literary Society* (1813), i. 189 ff.; Maria Graham, *Journal of a Residence in India* (1812, 2nd ed. 1813), p. 45 ff.; Fergusson, *Rock Temples of India* (1845), p. 54 f.; Fergusson-Burgess, *Cave Temples of India* (1880), p. 465 ff.; V. A. Smith, *A Hist. of Fine Art in India and Ceylon* (1911), p. 215 f.

W. CROOKE.

ELKESAITES.—The adherents of a form of religion having baptism as its leading feature, which arose *c.* A.D. 100, probably in trans-Jordanic Palestine. It was intended to mark a renewal in Judaism, and was originally a Jewish sect.

1. The literary tradition.—(1) *Sources.*—The sources of our information regarding the Elkesaites and their founder are far from abundant.

Eusebius (*HE* vi. 38) speaks of the 'perversion of the Elkesaites' as something quite ephemeral in character, and quotes from a homily of Origen on Ps 82 a passage which refers to the proceedings of Elkesaite missionaries, to their sacred book, and to their offer of remission of sins. For any more definite knowledge regarding the sect, as well as for light upon its not wholly insignificant history, we are entirely dependent upon the heresiologists Hippolytus and Epiphanius. The former narrates the doings of the Elkesaite Alcibiades in Rome, while the latter recounts the results of the Elkesaite propaganda in Syria; but to both writers we are even more indebted for their extracts from the Elkesaite book of revelation. This document was known to them only in its Greek form; in a passage containing references to dimensions which is quoted by both, the reduction of the Oriental measures to Roman miles is given by each in identical terms. The copy of the book which Hippolytus used was that which Alcibiades had taken to Rome. It contained some lines referring to Elkesai as a righteous man, who had received the book (see below, § 3) and delivered it to others. These lines, and other two or three passages of which we shall speak below, were wanting in the copy used by Epiphanius, and were, in fact, written by Alcibiades himself in Rome. The style of the Gr. translation, or else the condition of the MS, was such that both Hippolytus and Epiphanius were now and again compelled simply to guess at the construction, with the result that mistakes have crept into their accounts. But their references and quotations are in the main of such a character as to give us the impression that the book was not a large one, and that hardly anything of real importance in its contents has been wholly overlooked. As yet, however, the task of using the fragments as materials for a connected history of Elkesai and his work has never been taken in hand, and it is the aim of the present article to make good this defect.

In connexion with the various points dealt with in what follows, cf. Hippolytus, *Philosophoumena* (*Refutatio omnium hæresium*), ix. 13–17, x. 29 (Miller, pp. 292–297, 330); Epiphanius, *Hær.* xix. xxx. 17, liii. (pp. 40–44, 141, 397, 461 f.), *Epitome*, xix. xxx. (ed. Dindorf, i. 352, 359). The account given by Theodoret (*Hær. Fab.* ii. 7) is wholly dependent upon these older authorities, and contributes nothing to the emendation of their texts. The Arabic records of the Mughtasila (see below) are given in the original, with a German tr., by D. Chwolsohn, *Die Ssabier u. der Ssabismus*, ii. 543 f., and by G. Flügel, *Mani, seine Lehre u. seine Schriften*, Leipzig, 1862, pp. 48, 83 f., 133 f.

(2) *The name.*—The Elkesaites are so named from an Aram. formation which the Gr. tradition represents as ηλχασαι (Hipp.) or ηλξαι (Epiph.). The second element of this word may quite likely be a transliteration of Aram. כסי, 'hidden.' The first syllable, according to Epiphanius, corresponds to חיל, 'power.' The name as a whole would thus mean 'hidden power,' and one may quite reasonably believe that the founder of the sect—if, let us say, he was, like the Apostle Paul (2 Co 10^{10}), a man of insignificant presence—was so designated by his followers; the epithet applied to Simon Magus (Ac 8^{10}) would furnish an analogy. But the Arab. form of the name borne by the founder

of the Mughtasila (baptists of the Euphrates), viz. الحسيح, as read in the manuscripts of *Kitāb al-Fihrist*, precludes the aspiration of the first letter, and therefore also the derivation of ηλ from חיל, 'power.' The Arab. spelling, in fact, seems rather to suggest that the original expression was אל כסי, 'hidden God.' Still, as the Arab. name bears no vowel-signs, and also lacks the diacritical points without which the last three consonants cannot be exactly determined, it may be pronounced in various ways, and its real meaning may have been something quite different. The conventional form 'Elkesai' makes its appearance for the first time in Theodoret, who derived it from Origen's Ελκεσαιται; this, again, is a variation of Ελκεσαιοι, and the form Ελκεσαιος gained currency only through a confusion between the name of the sect and the surname of the prophet Nahum, האלקשי, of which it is the regular Gr. transliteration in the LXX.

A view that has received considerable support is that the name 'Elkesai' applies to the sacred book itself, and not to its author at all. But there are no good grounds for accepting this theory, which, moreover, involves a quite useless distinction. As we shall see presently, there was a real personality behind the book.

(3) *The Book of Elkesai.*—Tradition affirms that Elkesai was in possession of the volume—as a book of revelation—from the very outset of his career, but it gives widely varying accounts of the means by which he obtained it. The Elkesaite missionaries with whom Origen was acquainted are said to have held that it fell down from heaven. Another account—or perhaps two—was inserted by the above-mentioned Alcibiades in his own copy of the work, immediately before the text, which began with the chapter describing a vision vouchsafed to Elkesai. Hippolytus deciphered as much of this inserted note as he was able, and reproduces it thus:

'The righteous man Elchasai received the book from Sera [or Serai (? a city or 'the Seres,' *i.e.* the Chinese)] in Parthia, and entrusted it to one named Sobiai, as having been revealed by an angel who was twenty-four σχοῖνοι in height, six in breadth,' etc.

On this we would remark that the original writer of the note obviously did not know how the book had come into existence, and that his fictitious statement was really designed to stimulate interest in the work, on the principle that curiosity plays most assiduously around things of remote origin; while, again, the phrase 'revealed by an angel,' so far as regards the words ὑπὸ ἀγγέλου, merely represents an idea in the mind of Hippolytus himself, who thus sought—unwarrantably and wrongly—to connect the statement of Alcibiades with the vision recorded in the text of the book: probably a few words at the end of the note were illegible.

Apart from these prefatory lines, and a few passages subsequently interpolated or recast, the book undoubtedly owes its existence to the founder of the sect. But it would, of course, be altogether wrong to suppose that the founder delivered no fresh oracles (commandments, directions about ritual, predictions, etc.) while engaged in disseminating his teachings and governing his adherents. The deep veneration accorded to his descendants at a later day goes to show that in his lifetime he had acquitted himself among his intimate disciples as a man of God, while many features of his book point so clearly to the speaker's conviction regarding his Divine call as a prophet that it is impossible to believe otherwise. Now, if we examine the extant passages of his work in the light of this idea, and take into account not only their diction but also the diversified character of their matter, we come inevitably to the conclusion that the Book of Elkesai came into existence by some such process as subsequently took place in the case of the Qur'ān, *i.e.* by piecing together the separate sheets on which the prophet's utterances had from time to time been transcribed. After Elkesai's death his followers could fall back upon the written record, and could promise salvation to all sinners 'as soon as ye hearken unto this book'; but, while he still lived, he must assuredly have insisted—as did, of course, also his disciples—upon submission to himself as Divinely inspired. The theory that the prophet, as occasion arose, uttered his oracles, commandments, decisions, etc., which were then written down upon separate sheets and circulated among his followers, is that which best accords with the contents of the extant texts.

2. Personality and work of Elkesai.—As regards the life and personality of Elkesai, all that the literary tradition tells us is that he was a product of Judaism, was regarded as a righteous man, and announced the new means of obtaining remission of sins in the third year of the Emperor Trajan. We learn, further, that the Essenes and Ebionites accepted him, *i.e.* either the man himself as a prophet, or, at a later period, his distinctive teaching. But the surviving extracts and other citations from the sacred book give us so definite an impression not only of his doctrines, but also of his personality and his labours, that we are able in many cases to reconstruct the attendant circumstances without great risk of error.

(1) *Doctrine and ritual.*—Elkesai required his adherents to practise circumcision, to observe the Sabbath, and, in general, to live according to the Jewish Law. He also sanctioned marriage. It is probable that the prohibition of flesh-eating ascribed to him, perhaps erroneously, by Epiphanius extended only to participation in the sacrificial meals of the heathen. He insisted strongly on the practice of turning towards Jerusalem in prayer, and forbade that of praying towards the East—an injunction meant, no doubt, for the heathen, and perhaps also the Essenes, among his followers. He believed in the One God of Judaism and in the Last Judgment. He also shared the Jewish belief in various classes of angels, and he identified the evil angels with the stars in the northern region of the sky.

Elkesai was not a learned man. The extant fragments of his book show not the slightest evidence of his having studied the Jewish Scriptures. He imagined that he was proficient in astrology, and he had heard of the elements of which the world is composed; but in these things likewise his knowledge was of the scantiest. In an astrological passage of his book the days 'when the moon travels past, or in the same path with them [the stars of the north],' are designated 'days of the dominion of the evil stars,' on which accordingly no task should be begun. One of these days was the Sabbath. But the third day was also evil: 'when another three years of the Emperor Trajan have elapsed . . .' war would break out among the ungodly angels of the north, and a convulsion of all ungodly kingdoms would ensue. The prophet had, of course, the Roman Empire in his mind, and, as the catastrophe did not take place, this unfulfilled prediction is a positive corroboration of the tradition that Elkesai lived and taught before the end of the reign of Trajan.

The principal feature of the Elkesaite form of religion was its practice of baptism. Elkesai proclaimed that total immersion of the body—the garments being retained—in the waters of a river or a spring was the means whereby the Divine remission of all sin was to be appropriated. That which other forms of religion sought to secure by sacrifice on altars was effected here by the waters of baptism. The rite must be performed 'in the name of the great and most high God,' or [? conjectural reading] with adoration of Him; and the candidate had to declare, immediately before his immersion, that he would henceforth abstain from all sin and all improbity in life and conduct.

Precisely the same ceremonial was to be observed when immersion was resorted to for the cure of disease and similar troubles, as, *e.g.*, the bite of a mad dog or of a venomous animal. Those who suffered from phthisis and those who were possessed with demons were ordered to immerse themselves in cold water, *i.e.* in a river or a well, forty times in the course of seven days; and, if they were unable to do this for themselves, the immersion had to be performed, and the requisite vows uttered, on their behalf, by others. This sacramental bath, as we interpret it, was designed to expel the demons and disease-spirits who seek to destroy the body. In all religions, no doubt, certain sacramental ceremonies, such as baptism, laying on of hands, anointing, communion, are believed to work similar effects on the bodily condition, but among the Elkesaites the belief was an officially formulated doctrine. One of their formularies for immersion survives in full. But, as it contains a reference to 'this book,' *i.e.* the Book of Elkesai, and also gives the series of the Elkesaite 'witnesses to the oath' (see below) in a later transcript dating from a time when the Greek translation was about to appear, the rubric in question has not come down to us in its original form.

We do not venture to affirm that the use of the sacrament set forth in this fragment was not appointed by Elkesai himself and first arose in the community at a later date (see 2 K 5^{14}).

Elkesai must have instituted still another sacramental ceremony—of which, however, we hear only indirectly (see below)—viz. a communion with bread and salt. A ceremony of this kind, designed to ratify a covenant, was known among the Jews (cf. Lv 2^{13}, Nu 18^{19}, 2 Ch 13^{5}); it betokened fellowship at the same table, and thus expressed a solidarity of life or interest amongst the parties. In the Elkesaite celebrations, however, the bread and salt must have been credited with magical virtues—beneficent in their nature, of course, yet capable of producing the opposite effects in the case of faithless or otherwise unworthy participants, just as is said with regard to the Christian Eucharist (1 Co $11^{29f.}$). The precise nature of the beneficent effects in the case before us remains unknown; the *Contestatio Iacobi* (in the [pseudo-] *Clementine Homilies*), cap. 4, reads like a reminiscence of the Elkesaite practice.

(2) *The 'witnesses to the oath.'*—The Elkesaite practice of invoking the elements as witnesses of the baptismal vow presupposes the belief that the saving effects of sacramental rites might be changed into the opposite effects; it was supposed that they would prove fatal to those who took the oath falsely. Elkesai enjoined that such an invocation should be made at the ceremonial bathings, the elements being called to witness the vow of a holy and upright life that had to be uttered, before immersion, by all desirous of securing the promised boon.

With the ceremonial elements (bread and salt) he here associated those of the cosmos, to which mankind must likewise look as the source not only of blessing but also of the worst of evils. Elkesai knew of the pentad of elements—earth, water, fire, air, and æther, as enumerated in the teaching of the Greek schools from Aristotle's day. In his ignorance, however, he substituted for 'air' its most palpable manifestation, viz. wind, or the winds. 'Earth,' again, he interpreted as 'the earth,' and maintained accordingly that the heaven likewise should have a place among the elements; while, to balance this addition, he rejected fire, which, from its association with sacrifice, he was unwilling to admit into his scheme. The ceremonial and cosmic elements, as thus elucidated, formed the series of the 'seven witnesses' to which the Elkesaites made appeal when they performed the rite of immersion. The underlying idea, as we may surmise, was that those who did not keep their vow became liable to all the evils which these elements might produce. Hence, if an Elkesaite fell again into sin, it was a matter of the utmost moment that he should repeat the ceremony without delay.

(3) *Personality of Elkesai.*—The baptism of Elkesai alike in its object—the remission of sins—and its preliminary condition—the pledge of a changed life—reminds us of the mission of John the Baptist. But there was little in common between the two men. It is true that, in the earlier period of his career, Elkesai, like John, believed in an impending convulsion which would dissolve the existing world-order. But tradition furnishes no ground for believing that he expressly set before himself the task of preaching repentance to his own people and arousing their conscience. The general tone of his admonitions (as, *e.g.*, when he gives a reason why fire should not be trusted, and why water is better) scarcely suggests the impassioned propagandist. With perfect composure of spirit he enjoins that proselytes—his converts from heathendom had first of all to embrace Judaism—shall not be baptized on the Sabbath. He looked for success not to some sudden thrill of emotion which predictions of woe would excite among the people, but to the approval which those who believed in a Divine retribution would accord to his teaching. He thus counted upon the convincing power with which his declarations and arguments, instinct as they were with the note of assurance, would impress all who were prepared to listen to them with a serious mind. As one who received revelations, he must have been an 'ecstatic,' but he was no less a man of practical judgment, with a clear eye for ways and means.

On the other hand, Elkesai did not lack that inner experience which forms the dynamic of all outstanding personalities in the religious sphere. We have an evidence of this in his secret watchword, which, it is true, he communicated to his disciples for use in their prayers, though in the wholly unintelligible form obtained by reversing the sounds of each several word. The proper form of the saying was אנא מסהד עליכון ביום דינא רבא, *i.e.* 'I am a witness over you in the day of the Great Judgment.' He thus cherished the expectation that at the Last Day his personal testimony would be accepted as decisive before the great tribunal—an idea which reveals the intensity of his religious conviction.

(4) *His converts and followers.*—The prophet found disciples not only among the Jews, but also among the heathen whom the Jews called 'God-fearing' (φοβούμενοι τὸν θεόν). He laid upon his heathen converts the obligations of circumcision, Sabbath-keeping, turning towards Jerusalem in prayer, and abstinence from the flesh of pagan sacrifices. When, after having given him their allegiance, they were tempted by their relatives to return again to the sacrificial feasts, he cautioned them kindly with the words, 'Children, go not unto the gleam of fire, but follow rather the voice of water.'

(*a*) *The baptized.*—There is reason to believe that Elkesai at first directed his attention mainly to the 'God-fearing,' or, at least, that he drew the majority of his followers from their ranks. This seems to be implied by the concluding words of the lines prefixed to the copy of his book used by Hippolytus: words to the effect that the author had entrusted the work, as a revelation, to a certain 'Sobiai.' Now, this name (Σοβιαί) is—apart from the terminal vowel, which is wanting—an exact transliteration of the Aram. *ṣᵉbīʿaiyā*, which is the passive participle of a verb signifying 'to stain,' 'to wash,' and also 'to bathe'; and, as a definite plural, it would in this case mean 'the bathed,' 'the baptized.' This term, then, as found in the prefatory note regarding the book, *i.e.* regarding its actual contents, the utterances of Elkesai himself, may be taken as indicating that his earliest adherents were not of Jewish race, but heathens who had submitted to the proselyte baptism of Judaism only in order to secure the salvation proclaimed by him. His injunction against baptizing proselytes on the Sabbath proves beyond question, indeed, that he not seldom gained accessions from the ranks of heathenism.

(*b*) *The Essenes.*—Among the Jews the sect of the Essenes (*q.v.*) accepted the teaching of Elkesai. From the time of the Jewish war this group of zealous baptists had settled in the district to the east of the Jordan, where they had opportunity to follow their practice of ritual bathing in streams and wells. Elkesai's teaching was in many points akin to their own. Burnt-offerings had already been discarded by their fathers, even while the altars of the true God were still burning at Jerusalem. It is likely enough, too, that a belief in astral deities would prevail in a community which worshipped the sun at his rising. Whether the Essenes abandoned that worship in compliance with Elkesai's general injunction against turning to the East in prayer, we do not know. That in their other prayers they observed the *qibla* towards Jerusalem may be inferred from the fact that they had been in the habit of sending dedicated offerings to the Temple.[1] Nevertheless, they must have in some degree maintained their distinctive character and their separate existence as a community, else Epiphanius could not have spoken of the remnant of their adherents in his day as a definite group among the Elkesaites.

(*c*) *The Jewish Christians.*—The teaching of Elkesai found an open door also among the Jewish-Christian communities whose language was Aramaic. Amongst these—the existing representatives of the earliest churches founded by the Apostles of Jesus and their associates—the recollection of the baptism preached by the forerunner of Jesus would still be of some influence; and, moreover, their long-protracted waiting for the Saviour's return from heaven, as well as their disappointment that one 'sign of the time' after another had proved abortive, must inevitably have tended to predispose them to welcome a new revelation. With a view to winning their whole-hearted allegiance, Elkesai circulated among them a document in which he related how there had appeared to him two figures of monstrous size, a male and a female, facing each other like a pair of statues; the male was the Son of God, the female was the Holy Spirit.[2] In order to gain credence for this story, he averred that the figures—of equal magnitude—stood between two mountains, and that he was thus enabled to ascertain their dimensions: they were twenty-four σχοῖνοι high (ninety-six Roman miles), etc. He also took care to represent the vision as a token of God's approval of himself and his work, stating that these beings are invisible to man, and had manifested themselves to him only by way of exception. The story was quite in keeping with the religious notions of these Jewish Christians. The 'Gospel' of the Nazaræans in Berœa, according to Origen and Jerome, contained a reputed saying of Jesus in these words: 'My mother, the Holy Spirit, took me by one of my hairs, and conveyed me to the top of the lofty mount Tabor.' In any case the imposture—we can call it nothing else—was successful. Epiphanius asserts that the Ebionites and the 'Nāṣōræans,' like the Essenes and the 'Nazaræans,' were imposed upon by the heresy of Elkesai, and, while this statement does not apply to all Nazarenes or Jewish Christians, we can quite well believe that a large proportion of the pre-Catholic Christians of Syria, and especially those occupying the district to the east of the Jordan—probably it was the latter only who as yet called themselves *'Ebyōnîm*, 'the poor'—yielded their allegiance to Elkesai. In a later age the Catholic Christianity of the East surrendered in similar fashion to Islām, and with less excuse. Cf. art. EBIONISM.

(5) *The presumptive close of Elkesai's career.*—Elkesai had thus become the hierarch of a confraternity which, if it did not count its members by tens of thousands, had nevertheless a considerable influence, and enjoyed a fairly wide expansion. Presently he had, of course, to deal with the cares and troubles incident to a position like his. The members of his communities came to him with their grievances. As Jews, they were subject to the tyranny and chicanery of special taxation; as monotheists, who would not bow to the gods of the State or the statues of the Emperor, they were exposed to persecution of all sorts. Elkesai, willing to save them from the worst possibilities of these oppressions, issued a further document to his faithful followers, permitting them in the last resort to deny their faith with the lips, while still loyal to it in their hearts. So long as they withheld their inward assent, it was no sin, in times of persecution, to worship idols, to take part in the sacrificial meals associated with such worship, and, in short, to renounce their religion in words. Elkesai vindicated this policy by adducing the example of a Jewish priest called Phinehas, who, during the Babylonian captivity—under King Darius in Susa—was saved from death by an act of homage to Artemis.

When we bear in mind that this was a case where a religious leader of strongly self-reliant character granted to others an indulgence which promised no personal advantage to himself, we cannot but see in the action a certain humane consideration and a high degree of tolerant kindliness. But leniency in religious things is not what we look to find in the founder of a sect—not, at least, until the closing stages of his career, when the fires of enthusiasm are quenched and the mind has attained to peace. We may thus venture to surmise that this dispensation was Elkesai's last proclamation—the message of a man no longer young, whose sole remaining wish was to prove an attentive shepherd to his flocks, and leave among them a legacy of gracious memory. Are his people persecuted? Be it so; let them hoodwink the ungodly, and the devil. In the great Day of Judgment it is their leader's testimony that will count. He, Elkesai, will then bear witness, on behalf of his faithful ones, that their denial was but make-believe, not the expression of their inmost thought. It must have been in some such frame of mind and with some such conviction that he issued his permission to deny their faith.

It is probable that this dispensation in its original form included an instruction which Hippolytus wrongly interprets as referring to the whole book. The instruction is in these words:

[1] Jos. *Ant.* XVIII. i. 5.

[2] We must remember that the Semitic mind quite naturally represented the Holy Spirit as female, the Semitic equivalents of 'spirit' being feminine.

'Read not this discourse before all persons, and guard these precepts carefully; for not all men are trustworthy, nor are all women upright.' The phrase 'all persons,' as we think, was meant to be restricted to the Elkesaite fellowship; since, if it be taken unconditionally, the reminder that 'not all are trustworthy or upright' would be a pointless truism. The message which thus sanctioned, under special pressure, a feigned denial of the faith was intended only for those members of the sect whose loyalty and uprightness were beyond question. To have delivered it to all the members without discrimination would have been to risk such a misapplication as might in no long time have brought Elkesai's whole life-work to nought.

The silence of tradition as to the close of Elkesai's life may be taken as an evidence that he died a natural death. We cannot so much as guess when he died, nor would it be of any great moment even if we knew the exact date. Suffice it to know that he ended his days with his faith unperplexed, and at peace with his followers, as may be inferred from the fact that the veneration accorded to him as a religious leader was still maintained towards his descendants. The form of religion associated with his name continued to flourish for centuries after his death.

3. Elkesaism after the death of its founder.—(1) *The translation of the sacred book.*—We have already seen how the separate sheets issued by Elkesai, so far as they could be recovered, were gathered together to form a book. Now, at that period many people in the larger towns of Syria understood and spoke Greek as well as Aramaic, and in this way the teaching of Elkesai must have become known also to Syrians who spoke Greek only. Among these, *i.e.* in the more cultured circles of the cities, it found friends and adherents, who at length began to express a desire for a Greek rendering of the highly-revered document.

The Greek version of the Book of Elkesai, as Epiphanius records, enumerated the seven witnesses to the oath in two diverse forms. The series given in the surviving directions for immersion we recognize as the later. In this list, owing to the twofold meaning of the Semitic word רוּחַ, we find 'spirits,' and even 'holy spirits,' instead of 'the winds'; for 'the æther' we have the inhabitants thereof, angels, 'the angels of prayer,' who receive the prayers of men and convey them to the throne of God—a Jewish as well as a Christian belief. Instead of 'bread,' again, we have 'the oil,' which may have been meant to suggest a sacrament of unction, but probably denotes here—together with the salt—simply the material used in the preparation of nearly all foods, for it is evident that the Elkesaites amongst whom these changes had been effected were not aware that the series of witnesses ought to include only cosmical and ceremonial elements, and did not know what the practice of invoking them had originally signified. 'Holy spirits' and 'angels of prayer' are not elements, nor are they the sort of beings who would wreak injury on perjured souls. Hence the fact that Epiphanius, in the other passage which dealt specially with the seven witnesses, and which has not survived, still found the original designations—the winds, the æther, the bread—need not surprise us: it can mean only that the translator felt what was there said about these things to be quite inapplicable to holy spirits, angels, and oil.

(2) *Progress among Greek-speaking Jewish Christians.*—The Elkesaite faith, thus equipped with the Greek version of its sacred book, exercised an influence also in certain circles which did not accept it fully, and this influence was by no means slight. A considerable number of the Greek-speaking Jewish Christians of Syria felt attracted by the strange work, and appropriated many things—ideas as well as practices—they found in it. Now, Epiphanius possessed a volume which, as he supposed, contained the teachings of a certain 'Ebion'—it was, of course, simply an Ebionite work—and from which he quoted a commandment requiring that after cohabitation a man shall bathe 'often, and in his clothes,' as also a prescription for sick people and those who had been bitten by a venomous animal, directing them to bathe in water and invoke four pairs of names, these being compiled from the two lists of the seven Elkesaite 'witnesses' (*Hær.* xxx. 2. 17, pp. 126 A, B, 141 B).

(3) *The Elkesaite mission to the West.*—About the year 220 of our era a group of Elkesaites in the Syrian littoral who possessed the Greek version of their sacred book were of a spirit so vigorous and enterprising that they sought scope for it in an attempt to propagate their doctrines in other parts of the Roman Empire. They proposed to send missionaries to the West, and that these should appeal to the Catholic Churches and show their book to the members, asking them to hearken to its message and assent to it, and should then, on condition of their doing this, invite them to undergo immersion for the remission of sins. Upon one chapter of the book in particular they placed no small reliance, as it seemed to be precisely of such a character as would dispose the Christians to look favourably on the book as a whole. This was the Christological section, which probably does not go further back than the Greek version, and which contained the doctrine that 'Christ' had appeared often in the course of the world's history.

Epiphanius confesses that he did not fully understand the passage in question, and that, in particular, he could not make out whether the Christ spoken of was the Lord Jesus or another. Finally, or rather by way of supplement, in *Hær.* liii. he adds a short note connecting—on quite fallacious grounds—the figment of the two gigantic forms with a certain doctrine of Jewish-Christian gnosis, according to which Christ was the Adam created in Paradise, and in his several advents simply assumed for the time the body of Adam. Hippolytus, on the other hand, says explicitly that the Elkesaite Christology proceeds upon the Pythagorean idea of transmigration, and actually quotes in this connexion a word (μεταγγίζεσθαι) associated with that doctrine. But, when he tells us that in the Christological teaching of the Elkesaites Christ was said to have been 'born of the Virgin this time,' we feel that he is supplementing from his own creed; for, had this been expressly stated in the document, Epiphanius could scarcely have had any dubiety in the matter, but would have known that by 'Christ' the Elkesaites meant the Lord Jesus.

From the remaining data of the two heresiologists, so far as they agree, we infer that the later Elkesaite Christology was somewhat as follows: Christ is a higher being; was fashioned in Paradise as Adam, and since then has been born—not merely once, as now, but repeatedly in the course of previous ages—in various personalities as a man like other men, or has appeared as a phantom. It is hardly open to doubt that in the fragment under consideration it was implied that not only Jesus, but also Elkesai, was an incarnation of the Christ, and, indeed, that the latest and most notable manifestation of the great being was none other than Elkesai, not Jesus of Nazareth. Now Elkesai himself cannot have believed this, as he had made it known that the Son of God had appeared to him in a form of enormous proportions; and it is much more likely that this fact was overlooked by the later generation of his adherents. The Christological section, as the present writer thinks, first saw the light at the time when the Elkesaites—in Apameia or elsewhere—were preparing copies of their book for their Western mission. The period and the locality both tended to favour the delusion that the Catholic communities would be satisfied with such a Christology. It seems to have been at this time also that an addition was made to the directions for the sin-purging rite of immersion, the formula 'in the name of the great and most high God' being supplemented by the words 'and in the name of his son, the Great King.' The smaller interpolation was meant, of course, to serve the same purpose as the larger.

The apostles of the Elkesaite faith, thus furnished with a revised edition of their book, then set forth to the conquest of Catholic Christendom. Origen, in a discourse directed against them, says that they ventured to approach 'the Churches.' But they were quite unable to win a firm footing anywhere. Nor is this to be wondered at, as the enterprise rested upon a wholly defective apprehension of the doctrines, the rites, and the general conditions of the Catholic world.

Our further knowledge of the undertaking is restricted to the efforts of Alcibiades, a citizen of the important town of Apameia on the Orontes, who directed the Elkesaite mission in Rome. He found the Roman Church in a condition that seemed altogether favourable to his designs, and he determined to take full advantage of the fact. Bishop Callistus (A.D. 217–222) had shown himself unwilling to exclude sinners from the fellowship of the Church, even for sins of the flesh, the usual penalty of which had been excommunication. It was asserted by his opponents that this leniency had caused the prevalence of precisely that kind of sins; but Callistus maintained that Christ forgave all whose intentions were good, and so would *he* forgive all. The learned Hippolytus, who is our informant here, and who was chosen bishop by the dissatisfied party, deplores that the sinners were now arrogating to themselves the name 'Catholic Church'; he also states that the attempt to introduce a second baptism was first made in the time of Callistus (*Philosophoumena*, ix. 8, p. 290 f.).

The circumstances thus noted by Hippolytus find a striking echo in two of his quotations from the Greek book of Elkesai—the only passages with which we have not yet dealt. They are as follows:

'My children! if one has lain with any kind of beast, or with a male, or with his sister, or his daughter, or has committed adultery or fornication, and desireth forgiveness of his sins, so let him, as soon as he has hearkened to this book, be baptized the second time in the name of the great and most high God, and in the name of his Son the great king, and purify and cleanse himself, and take to witness the seven witnesses recorded in this book: the heaven and the water and the holy spirits and the angels of prayer and the oil and the salt and the earth.'

'Again I say, O adulterers and adulteresses and false prophets [*i.e.* heretical teachers], if ye will be converted, that thereby your sins may be forgiven, so ye likewise shall have peace and a portion with the just, as soon as ye have hearkened to this book and are baptized the second time, in your clothes' (*Philos.* ix. 10, p. 294 f.).

Here we recognize at a glance the hand of the reviser: the reference to 'this book,' the name of the Son of God added to that of the most high God, the list of witnesses in its later form. But we also note, as something altogether new, the passive use of 'baptize'; the sinner is to 'let himself be baptized,' or 'be baptized,' and, moreover, 'for the second time.' We cannot well imagine that the latter changes in the two texts had been made in Syria in anticipation of the projected mission to the Christians of the West. For one thing, it is quite incredible that any missionary religion would from the outset entertain the thought of finding its converts in a class of persons that could only cover it with odium. For another, it is certain that the text used by Epiphanius either did not contain these particular directions for the sin-cancelling ablution at all, or, at least, did not contain them in the form which Hippolytus found in the copy originally belonging to Alcibiades—the form, that is to say, providing expressly for sinners usually regarded as of the grossest type, and containing the summons to the second baptism. Neither of these features could have escaped Epiphanius, nor would he have failed to denounce them. In point of fact, the two passages—or, so far as regards the first, its extant version—must have been composed by Alcibiades himself, after he had made approaches to the dominant party, the Callistians. He addresses the Christians in exactly the same manner as their own teachers, viz. as 'children' (a form which, it is true, had been used also by Elkesai), seeking thus to coax them to his side, and keep them there; for he had but one end in view—the formation among them of a community that should hold the Book of Elkesai in reverence. The idea of the second baptism must have struck him as full of promise for his purposes; and so, with a view to its adoption, he composed the two verses quoted above, containing respectively the ritual for gross sinners and the invitation or summons to the second baptism. For the former he found a pattern in Elkesai's prescription for the bite of a mad dog, and the style of the original is cleverly imitated in the successive 'or . . . or . . .' of the interpolation.

But it was all a beating of the air: these accommodations to Roman Christianity were of no avail. Under Bishop Callistus, sinners were sure of lenience and remission without exorbitant penances, and this, moreover, within the pale of their ancestral Church; what further end could be served by their becoming Elkesaites?

The sole remaining expedient of the Syrian missionaries was to make a prodigy of the Book of Elkesai, which, as a matter of fact, they themselves no longer fully understood. It is possible that some inexperienced or uneducated or unintelligent Christians were drawn to them by a liking for the occult and the fantastic, and here and there formed a little Elkesaite group. But any such community must have been short-lived, for there was no practical interest to bind the members together. In short, the result of the Elkesaite propaganda in Catholic Christianity was such that Eusebius could speak of the movement as having arisen, and then presently died away.

(4) *Later fortunes of the sect in the East.*—In those parts of Syria where Catholic Christianity supplanted Jewish Christianity Elkesaism gradually dwindled away, and in the Hellenized section of the inhabitants it became completely extinct. But in that district of the country which lay at a distance from the main highways, and in which it won its earliest victories—among a population speaking Aramaic exclusively—it stood its ground, and even made a further advance.

(*a*) *The Sampsæans.*—Before Epiphanius left Palestine (A.D. 367), he heard of a sect living in the country eastwards from the Jordan and the Dead Sea, viz. the Sampsæans (Sampsenes, Sampsites), who believed in one God, and worshipped Him by ablutions. They held that life arose from water. They vaunted Elkesai as their teacher, and in their midst lived two women, sisters, who were descended from him. The members were accustomed to bend the knee to these women, and even to follow behind them for the purpose of securing their spittle and the dust from their feet, preserving these in capsules, which they carried as amulets. In most matters of creed and ritual they were at one with Judaism; nevertheless they were not Jews. Their distinguishing peculiarity was their reverence for the Book of Elkesai, and they did not own the authority of either the Old or the New Testament. Incorporated with them were the Ebionites, the Nāṣōræans, the Nazaræans, and the Ossæans. With reference to this point, Epiphanius states that the last-named sect, *i.e.* the Essenes, had 'now' renounced Judaism, and no longer lived in the manner of the Jews.

The only conclusion we can draw from these data is that the Elkesaites had given up that particular feature of Judaism which formed at once a bond of union and a principle of isolation for the Jewish people, *i.e.* their observance of legal purity in food and drink, and their consequent refusal to eat with the heathen. Now the coincidence of this defection with the occurrence of a new name of a decidedly heathen cast forms a sufficient ground for thinking it probable that a group of Syrians of non-Jewish race had united with the Elkesaite baptists, and accepted their sacred book, but did not observe the Jewish regulations about food. The name 'Sampsæans,' if we may trust the accuracy of its traditional form, means 'the sunny ones,' or 'the sunlike,' not 'sun-worshippers' or the like. It prompts the conjecture that the 'Sampsæans' were really a family, and indeed one of high standing. They would seem likewise to have been well-to-do, perhaps also on a good footing with the civil authorities, and on these grounds to have rapidly risen to great influence in the Elkesaite fellowship. The two great-granddaughters of the prophet willingly accepted their obeisance, while the Elkesaites by birth did not refrain from sitting with their new associates at meals; and it was for the sake of the latter that the former discarded the Jewish laws regarding food, and thus broke away from the community to which they—as a somewhat unacceptable party, it is true—had hitherto belonged. Socially, therefore, the older group may be said to have united with the newer, rather than the newer with the older, and this circumstance took effect also upon the nomenclature. The Sampsæans did not surrender their high-sounding name. They were the most eminent section of the order; they became its leading group, and, when outsiders occasionally spoke of the whole community as the 'sun-like ones,' the older Elkesaites actually felt flattered, and, indeed, soon began to apply the new name to themselves.

The Elkesaite baptists may have maintained for centuries their tranquil existence in the little-visited district watered by the Eastern tributaries of the Jordan, but the voice of tradition is henceforth silent with regard to them.

(*b*) *The Mughtasila.*—The name of Elkesai—but only the name—crops out once more in an ethnographic note in the *Kitāb al-Fihrist* by Ibn Abī Ja'qūb al-Nadīm (ed. Flügel, Leipzig, 1871–72, p. 340). The note refers to a religious community whose adherents inhabited the wide-spreading swampy region traversed by the Euphrates in its lower course, and were locally known to the Arabs as *al-Mughtasila*, i.e. 'those who wash themselves.' We are informed that 'these people are numerous in the marsh-lands, and they are, in fact, the Sabæans of the marshes.' They must accordingly be regarded as identical with the Sabians (also meaning 'baptists') mentioned in three passages of the Qur'ān (ii. 59, v. 73, xxii. 17) as a people who, together with Jews and Christians, are to have liberty in the exercise of their religion. This privilege was accorded to them in virtue of their monotheism and their possession of sacred writings. The note continues: 'They maintain that people should wash [often], and they also wash all they eat. Their leader is called الحسيح; he is the person who founded their faith.' Chwolsohn reads the name as *al-Ḥasaiḥ*, Flügel as *al-Ḥasīḥ*; but, as we have already seen, this transliteration can rest upon conjecture only. The note also ascribes a dualistic cosmology to the sect, stating that they believed in a male and a female order of beings, and asserts that at an earlier time, as regards the two original principles, they agreed with the Manichæans. On this point al-Nadim makes another interesting statement (Chwolsohn, i. 125 f.), viz. that the father of Mani (who founded Manichæism in the 3rd cent. A.D.) joined the Mughtasila, and educated his son in their faith, and that the latter began to proclaim his own doctrine at the age of twenty-four. The baptists of the Euphrates can thus be traced back to the end of the 2nd century. They were known to Muhammad as monotheists and possessors of sacred writings; and some time afterwards an inquirer learned from them that their founder and lord was called Elkesai—or some such name. Now, not every religion has a lord and founder. Islām, however, tolerated only such forms of religious belief as were like itself in this respect. Thus the Mughtasila, in meeting inquiries regarding their origin, had the most cogent of reasons for putting forward some name that might stand as co-ordinate with names like Moses, Jesus, and Muhammad, and accordingly the reference in the *Kitāb al-Fihrist* cannot rank as historical evidence. All that the note proves is that the priestly or learned class among the Mughtasila had heard of the name of Elkesai as that of a religious leader, or teacher, while this again may signify nothing more than that a copy of the Book of Elkesai, inscribed with his name, had fallen into their hands. If, moreover, the volume was for a considerable period their sole possession of the kind, they would come to honour it as their oldest document; and in this way might arise the tradition that the book contained doctrines which its author had delivered to their ancestors at the birth of their religion. A religious document of that kind, even when its possessors do not follow it in practice—and almost, indeed, in proportion to their inability to understand it—tends to become a holy thing, whose very name inspires reverence. Thus we need not assume that the Mughtasila ever really lived as Jews, observing circumcision, the Sabbath, or the *qibla* towards Jerusalem.

The monotheism of the Mughtasila was, with some of them, only a pretext; 'to this day,' says the Arabic writer, 'they have among them some who worship the stars'; besides, it was combined with dualistic tenets, and accordingly, like that of Mani, must have been derived, not from Judaism, but—either by means of actual contact, or through the studies of the priests—from Parsiism. That the Mughtasila performed their ablutions by bathing may be presumed from the fact that they lived in a marshy district; but on the same grounds it seems unlikely that they deemed it essential to use river or spring water. We cannot say whether or not they practised immersion. That Elkesai himself had proclaimed his doctrine among them is *a priori* improbable, even if it should be thought possible that in his day they were Jews, or had provisionally become Jews. Success among them would have induced him to remain in their midst, just as his success in the district to the east of the Jordan kept him there; and, moreover, it was in the latter locality that his descendants lived.

4. Origin of Elkesaism and its place in the history of religion.—With reference to the historical connexion of Elkesaism with other religions of similar character, the main question turns upon its practice of baptism. Let us state at once that what we have to deal with is not the mere fact of religious washing or bathing, but the requirement of total immersion in a river or spring, with the garments on, as a necessary condition of remission of sins or bodily healing.

Judaism never at any time made such a demand, although the Essenes, it is true, bathed in loin-sheets, and must in cis-Jordanic Palestine have had to content themselves with the water of ponds. We meet with the practice in Southern Babylonia, among the Mandæans, and also in the far East, among the Hindus. As regards the latter, we find Manu enjoining that those guilty of certain sexual sins must expiate them by bathing in their clothes (*Laws*, xi. 175 [*SBE* xxv. 466]); and the Hindus, from similar motives, practise immersion in rivers. The Mandæans likewise bathe in the river Euphrates for remission of sins, being clothed in white for the occasion, just as they formerly wore white garments in their daily life (see W. Brandt, *Mandäische Religion*, Leipzig, 1889, pp. 91, 92, 224).

That this religious rite was brought to Palestine by way of the Euphrates from India we cannot believe, if for no other reason than that it is not again alluded to in the code of Manu, which probably attained its present form *c.* A.D. 1000, so that the practice can hardly have been at that date a long-established or popular one in India. The probability is rather, indeed, that it migrated from the Euphrates towards the East, just as the Mandæans themselves spread eastwards from that river into the interior of Persia.

The resemblance between the practice of the Mandæans and that of Elkesai is striking. But in the former we do not find anything to correspond with the vow which Elkesai demanded from his adherents at their immersion, or with the invocation of the seven witnesses. Nor did the sacramental elements of the Mandæans consist of bread and salt. Their oldest sacred writings were composed in the period of the Sasanians, or even earlier, but they contain no mention of Elkesai. The Mandæans believed that their deity dwelt in the North, beyond the mountains whence the great rivers come, and it was towards that point that they turned in prayer. These facts forbid the assumption that they owed their religious ritual to Elkesai.

Nor are we able to affirm that, contrariwise, the Elkesaite ritual was derived from Babylonia. We may, indeed, regard it as possible, and even probable, that the Mandæan cult was the older, but this does not admit of proof. For his doctrines Elkesai did not need to go so far. Babylonia was the cradle of astrology, but this 'science' had already spread over a great part of the world. In conformity with the belief that water is the source of life and health, the Parsi theologians fancied that the two trees 'All-seed' and 'All-heal' germinated from the sea, or from the waters of a wholesome spring. A similar idea, however, had long found a footing on Jewish soil, where it can be traced back to the passage in Ezk 47 describing the future glory of the land.

Do we find any light from Bab. antiquity upon the Elkesaite immersion? In the ancient Babylonian texts hitherto published, though we there find mention—in a religious connexion—of such acts as drinking clear water, suffusing, laving, washing, cleansing, and sprinkling with the waters of wells or springs, of the Euphrates, the Tigris, or the sea, we have as yet discovered no definitely attested instance of immersion. The earliest known reference to the practice in the Semitic world is still the case of Naaman the Syrian, who dipped himself seven times in the Jordan in order to be healed of his leprosy (2 K 5[14]).

In the civilized belt of country around the Mediterranean Sea, which extended on the East beyond the Jordan, we find the religious rite of immersion associated with that conception of the new birth which enters largely into the mysteries. With that idea, therefore, it is no doubt genetically connected, and, like the mysteries generally, is to be traced to the esoteric doctrines of priests. The association of immersion with the vow and the seven witnesses, as found among the Elkesaites, seems to imply that their founder had become acquainted with the ceremonial of one or other of the mystery-cults practised by a priesthood or a religious association. His own ritual is modelled after some such solemnity, and he may well have taken the practice of immersion—the central feature of the ceremony—from the same source.

So far as we can judge, it did not fall to the lot of the Elkesaites to have an active share in the rise or development of any religion that survived their own. It has been asserted that their doctrines had an influence upon the system of ideas embodied in Islām, but this has never been proved.

LITERATURE.—D. Chwolsohn, *Die Ssabier u. der Ssabismus*, St. Petersburg, 1856, i. 100–138; A. Hilgenfeld, *Nov. Test. extra canonem receptum*, fasc. iii. ('*Hermae Pastor*'), Leipzig, 1867, pp. 153–167 [[2]1881, pp. 227–40]; E. Renan, *Histoire des origines du christianisme*, v. (Paris, 1877) 454–461; W. Bousset, *Hauptprobleme der Gnosis*, Göttingen, 1907, *passim*; W. Brandt, 'Die jüd. Baptismen' (*Beihefte zur ZATW* xviii. [1910] 99 ff.), *Elchasai; ein Religionsstifter und sein Werk*, Leipzig, 1912 (contains also a survey of former studies of Elkesaism).

W. BRANDT.

ELLORA.—Ellora is a town in the dominions of the Nizām of Haidarābād; lat. 20° 21′ N.; long. 75° 13′ E.; famous for its rock-caves and temples. There is some doubt as to the true form and derivation of the name. The form accepted by Burgess is *Verulā* or *Elurā*, which has been identified with a place called *Vellūra* in the *Bṛhat Saṁhitā* of Varāhamihira (xiv. 14; *IA* xxii. 193); or with *Elāpura*, which may mean 'cardamom town'; while others connect it with Tamil *Elu-ūru*, 'rule village' (see Fleet, *BG* i. pt. ii. 391). Fleet writes the name *Ellōrā*. The place is still considered sacred, and is the site of a shrine of Gṛṣneśvara, one of the twelve sacred *liṅgam*-temples of India. This was probably connected originally with the caves, but, when these were desecrated by Aurangzīb (*q.v.*), it was transferred to the neighbouring village. The caves, according to Burgess (p. 4), are about half a mile E. of the village, and lie nearly N. and S. along the W. face of the hill, on the summit of which the modern village of Rozah stands. They extend a little over a mile in a straight line. The caves at the S. end are Buddhist; those at the N. end Jaina; while those between these groups are Brāhmanical.

1. The Buddhist caves. The Buddhist group at the S. end consists of twelve excavations, which were constructed in the period between A.D. 450 and 650 or 700. Of this group three caves are especially important. That numbered X in the list of Burgess is the great *chaitya*, or rock-temple, the only one of the kind at Ellora, and locally attributed to Viśvakarma, the architect of the gods.

'It is a splendid temple, with a fine façade and large open court in front, surrounded by a corridor, and worthily concludes the series of Buddhist Chaitya caves, which, taken together, are perhaps the most interesting group of buildings or caves in India. We can now trace the sequence of these, from the early wood-fronted examples at Pitalkhorā, Kondāṇē, and Bhājā, through the stone-fronted caves of Beḍsā and Kārlē (*q.v.*) to the elaborately decorated façades of the two latest at Ajantā (*q.v.*), till at last it loses nearly all its characteristic external features in this one at Ellora' (Burgess, p. 9).

It contains a great *dāgoba*, or relic-shrine, and on the front of it an immense mass of rock is carved into a large image of Buddha, attended by the Bodhisattvas, Avalokiteśvara and Mañjuśrī.

The second is the *Doṅ Ṭhāl* cave, so called because it was long supposed to consist of only two storeys. In 1876, however, the lower storey was cleared of the earth which had completely buried it. This cave seems to have been left partially incomplete, and was intended to serve both as a temple and as a monastery.

The third great Buddhist cave, known as the *Tīn Ṭhāl*, or three-storeyed cave-temple, was suited rather for worship than for use as a monastery.

'This is of its class,' writes Burgess (p. 16), 'one of the most important and interesting caves at Elurā. In no other series do we find a three-storeyed Vihāra carried out with the same consistency of design and the like magnificence as in this example, and from these circumstances there is a grandeur and propriety in its appearance that it would be difficult to surpass in cave architecture. The greatest interest, however, lies in its being a transitional example between the styles of the two great religions which divide between them the architectural magnificence of the place. On comparing it with the Das Avatāra cave, that all but immediately succeeds, it seems almost as if the builders of this cave had been persuaded to change their faith, and by gentle means to adopt the new religion, and not that they had been converted by persecution, as has been very generally supposed. So gently, indeed, does the change seem to take place, that we can hardly detect it in the architecture, though the sculptures announce it with sufficient distinctness. But the mode in which sculpture is substituted in the upper story of the cave for the arrangement of cells in the older and genuine Vihāras shows that a change was creeping over the form of the religion long before it pronounced itself by the acceptance and adoration of the new gods.'

2. The Brāhmanical caves.—The *Das Avatāra* cave, as its name, 'the Ten Incarnations,' implies, is purely Brāhmanical. It contains sculptured images of all the greater gods. An inscription indicates that it was finished, or was at least in an advanced condition, in the middle of the 8th cent. A.D. The other chief Brāhmanical caves are the *Rāmeśvara* and the *Dumar Lenā*, the latter one of the finest of its kind, and interesting as being almost a duplicate of that of Elephanta (*q.v.*).

But of all the Brāhmanical monuments none is more remarkable than the *Kailāsa*, named after the paradise of Śiva, also known as *Rang Mahal*, 'painted hall,' which was constructed in the reign of Krishna (Kṛṣṇa) I., the Rāṣṭrakūṭa king of Mālkhed (*c.* A.D. 760–783; see ARCHITECTURE [Hindu], vol. i. p. 742ª). The Kailāsa is an undoubted copy of the old structural temple of Virūpākṣa at Paṭṭadakal in the Bījāpur District, and this again, a temple in the Dravidian style of S. India, is strikingly like the old temple of Kailāsanātha at Conjeeveram (J. H. Marshall, *Arch. Survey Report*, 1905–6, p. 112; Smith, *Early Hist.*[2] p. 386 f.). 'It is,' says Burgess (*op. cit.* p. 26), 'by far the most extensive and elaborate rock-cut temple in India, and the most interesting as well as most magnificent of all the architectural objects which that country possesses.' Fergusson (*Indian and Eastern Arch.* [1899], p. 334, ed. 1910, i. 342 ff.), says:

> In it 'we have a perfect Dravidian temple, as complete in all its parts as at any future period, and so advanced that we might have some difficulty in tracing the parts back to their originals without the fortunate possession of the examples on the Madras shore. Independently, however, of its historical or ethnographical value, the Kylas is in itself one of the most singular and interesting monuments of architectural art in India. Its beauty and singularity always excited the astonishment of travellers, and in consequence it is better known than almost any other structure in that country, from the numerous views and sketches of it that have been published.'

And he goes on to show that it reverses the methods of the Buddhist caves which adjoin it, being not a mere chamber cut in the rock, but a model of a complete temple, such as might have been erected on the plain. In other words, the rock has been cut away both externally and internally, leaving the structure completely isolated from the cliff, of which it once formed a part. The disadvantage of this mode of construction naturally is that the building stands in a pit. But it remains an example, probably unique, of unsparing labour devoted to the construction of a religious edifice. Among the important groups of sculpture which it contains are that of the destruction of Mahiṣāsura, or the buffalo-headed demon (which gives its name to Mysore), slain by Chaṇḍī or Durgā; those of Śiva in his various manifestations; and the shrines of the river-goddesses—Gaṅgā, Sarasvatī, and Yamī or Yamunā.

3. The Jaina caves.—Lastly come the Jaina caves. Of these the two principal are

> 'very extensive works, superior both in extent and elaboration to any of the Brāhmanical caves, excepting, of course, the Kailāsa, and the Viśvakarma among the Buddhist ones. Though two storeys in height and extremely rich in decoration, the Indra and Jagannāth Sabhās are entirely deficient in that purpose-like architectural expression which characterized the works of the two earlier religions. They have no cells, like the Vihāras, and are nothing like the Chaitya halls of the Buddhists, nor do they suggest the Chāvaḍis, like the Dumar Lenā of the Hindus. Rich and elaborate though they certainly are, the plan is compressed, and all their arrangements seem to result more from accident than from any well-conceived design, so that they lose half the effect that might have been produced with far less elaboration of detail' (Burgess, p. 44).

They are much later in date than either the Buddhist or the Brāhmanical caves. It seems that the Jainas occupied the place after the decadence of the Rathoḍ dynasty in the 9th or 10th cent. A.D., and their only desire was to mark the superiority of their religion, then becoming important, by rivalling the works of their predecessors.

LITERATURE.—This article is based on the excellent monograph, 'Report on the Elura Cave Temples and the Brāhmanical and Jaina Caves in Western India,' by J. Burgess, forming vol. v. of the *ASWI*, 1883, which is fully illustrated with photographs, drawings, and plans. This is in continuation of Fergusson-Burgess, *Cave Temples of India* (1880), in which see pp. 367–384 for the Buddhist caves; 431–463 for the Brāhmanical; 495–502 for the Jaina. Also see J. Fergusson, *Hist. of Indian and Eastern Architecture* (1899), pp. 127, 334–337, 445, ed. 1910, i. 120 ff., 127 f., 159, 201 ff., 342 ff., ii. 19 f.; V. A. Smith, *A Hist. of Fine Art in India and Ceylon* (1911), p. 210 ff. The place is fully described by Syed Hossain Bilgrami and C. Willmott, *Historical and Descriptive Sketch of H.H. the Nizam's Dominions* (1883), ii. 440 ff. For illustrations also see W. H. Workman, *Through Town and Jungle* (1904), p. 158 ff. The earlier account by J. B. Seely, *The Wonders of Elora* (1st ed. 1824), has been superseded by later investigation.

W. CROOKE.

ELYSIUM.—See BLEST (ABODE OF THE), STATE OF THE DEAD.

EMANCIPATION.—*Definition.*—Emancipation in its more general sense signifies the liberation of the individual from the yoke of the community and its institutions, or from that of tradition and custom; or, again, the liberation of a smaller and weaker community from the coercion of a larger and more powerful. As the restrictions in question may vary greatly in kind, and may relate to various aspects of life, emancipation, too, may assume different forms. Before we discuss the moral character of the movement towards freedom, we shall make a general survey of the whole field. We may distinguish between the emancipation of thought and emancipation in the sphere of action, though for the most part the two have proceeded hand in hand.

1. Emancipation of thought.—Thought becomes emancipated when it casts aside the traditional views and prejudices which have impeded its free movement in the past. We do not, of course, apply the term 'emancipation' to every case where erroneous traditions are abandoned, but only to cases where the general consciousness of a community is concerned, and where the restrictions upon thought had the sanction of some coercive authority. Thus, in particular, the moral consciousness may become emancipated from ethical conceptions hitherto hallowed by tradition and established by public opinion; religious thought may similarly pass from under the bondage of sacred traditions and ecclesiastical authority; there may also be an emancipation of science, as when it frees itself from the fossilized prejudices that have erewhile hampered its progress; or of art, as when it is delivered from some hoary religious tradition, or from the incubus of an antiquated school or style. Emancipation of this sort is always allied with the spirit of criticism, as in Greece, for instance, where the Sophists impugned the morality of tradition and of popular religion, and the philosophers sought to undermine current beliefs regarding the gods, and where hieratic art was at length overthrown by the great artists. Similarly Buddhism brought about an emancipation from the ascendancy and authority of the Brāhmans by proclaiming a *universal* redemption from suffering; while Christianity broke the yoke of the OT legalism by imbuing the mind with the life-giving spirit, in place of the dead letter. Thus, too, the sciences freed themselves from the despotism of mediæval theology—by the device, first of all, of a twofold truth, and then by the growing conviction that they must pursue truth by their own methods, and must treat this pursuit as an end in itself. Finally, the human mind attained to the conception of complete liberty of thought in all its phases, and in course of time this was claimed as a right. The prerogative of freedom in religious belief, in scientific inquiry, in the utterance of one's convictions, came to be regarded as inalienable, and the State was called upon to preserve it inviolate. True, a certain liberty of thought had been conceded in the Greek world; nevertheless, charges of impiety (ἀσέβεια) were not unknown, as in the case of Protagoras, Diagoras, Anaxagoras, Stilpo—to say nothing of Socrates; and at length the Athenian schools were closed by Justinian. Complete emancipation of thought was first claimed as a legal right by the modern champions of Natural Law, and has been won only after the severest conflicts. Only in modern times, too, has æsthetic thought sought to deliver itself from ecclesiastical and national influences, by insisting upon a free secular art.

2. Emancipation in practical life.—The process of emancipation, however, bears not only upon thought but upon practical life, and its progress in this sphere seems to accelerate as we approach the present day. To begin with, the individual has become more and more independent.

(*a*) In ancient times *slavery* was defended even by Aristotle; it was viewed with disfavour by the Stoics, while in the Roman Empire it was greatly mitigated by law; it was still recognized, as, *e.g.*, by Aquinas, in the Middle Ages, and was maintained even in the 19th cent. by the Southern States of N. America; now, however, it is entirely abolished in Christian lands, and, outside Christendom, prevails only amongst the Muhammadans. But the caste system of India is for the lower classes almost worse than slavery, and in the United States, where slavery no longer exists, there still remains the negro question, as also the problem of conferring civil rights upon the liberated race under conditions which will ensure a proper exercise of the privilege. In fact, the general policy of the higher races in regard to the lower is one of the most formidable questions of the day, as it can hardly be denied that the developed civilization of the former, allied as it is with superior physical resources, has often been employed in oppressing the latter. In these respects the process of emancipation still lags far behind.

(*b*) The emancipation movement embraces also the question of *women's rights*. Among ancient peoples the position of woman was a very limited one. In *China* her subordination to man is in line with the principles underlying the entire social order. Women, according to Confucius, are not easily dealt with.[1]

'If you are intimate with them, they will not obey; if you keep at too great a distance, they are angry with you. Woman is always dependent—as a daughter, upon her father or elder brother; as a widow, upon her son. She is under tuition and discipline to her husband.' She ought to keep within the house; her duty lies there. 'On the higher side, she must give due homage to her father-in-law; on the lower, she must serve her husband, and nurture her child.'

Nevertheless, Confucius holds that marriage is the be-all and the end-all of mankind; that woman is the paramount person in the sphere of love, and that reverence is her due. Certainly divorce is easily procured by the husband: infectious disease, antipathy, excessive loquacity, form sufficient grounds. But the man may not disown his wife if her parents be dead, or if, though now rich, she was originally poor and of mean extraction. Confucius also enjoins the care of widows.

Nor did *Buddhism*, in spite of its universalism, place women on a level with men; its highest morality demands entire abstinence from sexual intercourse. Nuns, by the rules of their order, rank lower than monks. 'Inscrutable as the way of a fish in water is the nature of women, those thieves of many devices, with whom truth is hard to find' (*Chullavagga*; cf. Oldenberg, *Buddha*[5], 1906, pp. 169 f., 385 f.).

In *Brāhmanism*, again, marriage is made much more of: every one ought to marry. Still, according to the *Laws of Manu*, the husband is the head of the wife; she must do nothing to displease him, even if he give himself to other loves; and, should he die, she must never utter the name of another man. If she marry again, she is excluded from the heaven where her first husband dwells. Unfaithfulness on the wife's part is punished with the utmost rigour. 'A woman is never independent.' She cannot inherit, and after her husband's death she is subject to their eldest son. The husband may even chastise her with the bamboo-rod. It is Brāhmanism, nevertheless, which gives us the saying: 'If the wife be made unhappy, the sacred fire soon dies out; if she execrates her home, its end is at hand' (*Laws of Manu*).

Among the *Persians* the recognized necessity of preserving the germ of life is in full harmony with their views of life in general. Marriage is, therefore, reckoned a duty; and every marriageable young woman must ask her parents to give her a husband. Chastity is well guarded, but, as in the *Laws of Manu*, the woman is subject to the man. Every morning the wife must nine times ask her husband what he wishes her to do; she must honour him as the pure honours the pure. In the later Gāthā period, however, women are more on an equality with men; they are not to be excluded from communion with Ahura Mazda, but are to rank along with men in every respect.

In *Muhammadanism*, women are secluded in the harim. They are denied all freedom of action, and all participation in matters intellectual. Certainly the Prophet raised the status of women above that assigned to them in ancient Arabia; in particular, the woman was no longer a mere heritable chattel of her deceased husband's estate, but was herself capable of inheriting; while, again, a free woman could not now be forced into marriage, and, in cases of divorce, the husband was required to let the wife retain what he gave her at marriage. Moreover, women of the upper classes might occupy themselves with poetry and science, and even act as teachers, while those of lower rank not seldom shared the joys and sorrows of their husbands, as mistresses of their households. The mother likewise must be treated with respect. Nevertheless, the seclusion of the harim tends to keep women in a subordinate position; their intercourse with one another is limited, and their education is neglected, though in the higher orders of society their existence is not devoid of comfort. The compulsory practice of veiling shows how little they are trusted.

Among the ancient *Jews* polygamy still persisted, and divorce, more especially in the later period, was easily procured. The wife was placed in subjection to her husband; still, marriage was reckoned honourable, and a virtuous wife was deemed of more value than rubies (Pr $31^{10ff.}$). The mother was highly esteemed, and the widow was regarded as a worthy object of benevolence.

While polygamy was the rule among Oriental peoples, the case was otherwise in Greece and Rome. Among the *Greeks* women were certainly confined to their own apartments, and they did not share in the education given to men; the only exception to this is found in the *hetæræ* of a later time. Yet Greece was not without cultured women, such as Sappho, while Penelope's constancy and Antigone's sisterly affection were proverbial. The *Ecclesiazusæ* of Aristophanes depicts women as so

[1] Cf. *SBE* iii. 26, 27, 28; Plath, in *Abhand. bayr. Akad. d. Wissensch.*, hist.-phil. Kl., esp. xiii. (1875).

far emancipated that they became a ruling power in the State. In the *Republic* Plato would have the State assume the task of distributing the women amongst the men, but at the same time he puts them in a position of perfect equality, insisting only upon their physical inferiority. Notwithstanding all this, however, it remains true that in Greece genuine intellectual intercourse was sought not in married life, but in friendship amongst men.

In *Rome*, according to the law of the XII Tables, the wife was under the absolute control of the husband—like a daughter, in fact. At a subsequent period, however, the matron was accorded a higher homage; witness, *e.g.*, the definition of marriage: *Matrimonium est maris et feminae coniunctio, omnis vitae consortium, iuris humani et divini communicatio* ('Marriage is the union of man and woman, complete community of life, joint-participation in Divine and human law'). The growing independence of women is also indicated in the laws regarding inheritance. According to the XII Tables, women could not inherit at all; by the Prætorian law they inherited in the third class; Justinian placed them on an equal footing with men in cases of intestacy. Further, the right to dispose of property by will, at first denied to women, was at length granted, in the event of their having detached themselves from their own family in due legal form. But the institution of marriage was much impaired by the egoistic tendencies of Roman law. Celibacy became common. Women were allowed no choice in the matter of marriage, and they had no effective safeguards against being repudiated. Even Cicero put away his first wife, in order to pay his debts with the inherited property of a second. But it was always possible for women to evade their legal disabilities by underhand means, and even to intermeddle with political affairs—a state of things attended with the direst moral results.

Christianity, emphasizing from the outset the value of personality in the sight of God, proclaimed the equality of the sexes. This is shown by the injunction regarding divorce, which, recognizing no justification for that proceeding save *porneia* (Mt 5^{32} 19^{9}), left nothing to the man's caprice. The fact that the principle of equality was not pushed forthwith to its full consequences is due to the ascetic temper of the Early Church. While marriage was regarded as a symbol of the relation between Christ and the Church (Eph $5^{22ff. 31f.}$), St. Paul also views it as a safeguard against immorality (1 Co $7^{2.9}$). Widows took a prominent part in the life of the Early Church, and an order of deaconesses was instituted, but the idea of man and woman as complementary to each other was not urged so strongly as their equality. It was but natural, therefore, when the moral factor was at length overridden by that of religion in the narrower sense, that monks and nuns should be placed on a level, and that, in particular, as marriage was counted inferior to the celibacy of the *religiosi*, the distinctive character of women should be ignored. When, further, the less estimable estate of marriage was made a sacrament, and declared to be indissoluble, the effect was, on the one hand, to subordinate the individual to the institution, and, on the other, to extrude the ethical element altogether. As it was the special prerogative of the mediæval monks to make methodical pronouncements upon moral questions, this theory of marriage continued to hold its own; though Aquinas laid stress upon the element of friendship between man and wife, and upon the woman's freedom to marry or to remain single, even against the will of her parents; and though Duns Scotus declared that matrimony was a more exacting state than monachism. While woman's place in the marriage relation was thus one which ill consorted with her distinctive nature, a kind of counterpoise was provided by the romantic and enthusiastic love which inspired the chivalry of the Middle Ages, though its object was not the wedded wife. Chivalry, however, was in part an expression of the ancient Teutonic idea that women have a mysterious power of prescience denied to men. Virginity and maternity were combined in the homage paid to Mary, who represents the love and grace of God. Such conceptions of the female nature, however, were not carried into the sphere of moral practice; they existed only in the imagination of knights-errant and monks—or of poets, such as Dante, whose Beatrice becomes his guide to heaven (cf. also the *Vita nuova*), and Petrarch, whose Laura forms the theme of his muse. This pseudo-spiritual severance of the visionary ideal from moral reality has a merely æsthetic value, and fails to bring the true dignity of women into definite and practical recognition. The two disparate views regarding women are just what might be expected from the dualistic spirit of the Middle Ages—a period in which religion and morality were not as yet in harmony, and solicitude regarding the other world led to disparagement of the present.

A change in the position of women was ushered in at the Reformation. Married life now came to be looked upon as the sphere in which their true vocation was to be realized, and its proper realization, moreover, was regarded as a mode of serving God. Further, divorce was sanctioned in cases of adultery, and the innocent party was permitted to marry again. But, while it was fully recognized that woman, as a moral personality, had a right to a sphere of active service, yet her distinctive value was no better appreciated than the value of individuality in general. Her real independence, as resting upon her peculiar nature, was explicitly enunciated for the first time by J. G. Fichte, who gave prominence to the idea that, in virtue of her emotional temperament, her function is to give herself freely for others, and that to love and to be loved are necessities of her nature. Schiller likewise extols the dignity of women, holding that their peculiar gift lies in their ability to combine the moral and the gracious—in a natural harmony of spirit denied to men. Schleiermacher, too, attaches special importance to the female character, regarding it as designed both to enrich and be enriched by the male, so that a true marriage is the only means of making good the defects of each, and of developing an all-round human being. It was Schleiermacher in particular, who, after the example of Goethe, pointed to the refining influence of women—*die Virtuosin der Geselligkeit*—upon social life and morals. It is beyond question that the vindication of women's rightful status, and of their proper vocation in the home and in society, was due to these writers. No doubt, the distinctive character of woman was urged by the Romanticists in such a one-sided way as to imply that for any given individual there is one, and *only* one, definite partner, and the institution of marriage was sapped by romantic subjectivity—the theme of Goethe's *Wahlverwandtschaften*—though Goethe does not pander to inconstancy. Others followed with philippics against compulsory marriage, which, as was alleged, frequently results in the moral and physical ruin of the woman; while, on the other side, Schopenhauer contended that women should be put under restriction, on the ground that in their very nature they require a guardian, and are made for obedience.

In the process of the emancipation of women, however, the problem of the wife eventually gave place to that of the unmarried, and in recent times this question has been taken in hand by women themselves. In Germany married life was until lately regarded as the normal vocation of women, but this view was obviously irrelevant in regard to those who remained single simply because there are more women than men. In England the modern movement began with Mary Wollstonecraft's *Vindication of the Rights of Woman*[2] (1792)—a work which drew its inspiration largely from France; but it is rather to the whole-hearted advocacy of J. S. Mill, half a century later, that we must trace recent advances in the cause of female emancipation, as also perhaps the present agitation for full political rights. More particularly in the United States the stage has been reached where women no longer look upon marriage as their specific calling, but seek complete equality with men as a matter of principle. Endeavours are accordingly being made to give them access to all the various professions, in order that they may gain an independent footing in society; and even to grant them the franchise, as a step to public life in State and Church—in a word, to remove every disability of sex. When this state of things is appealed against by pointing to the physical difference between the sexes—a difference which reveals itself also on the mental side—the theory of evolution is brought into court for the purpose of showing that by habit, heredity, etc., women may in time develop those particular qualities of which their circumscribed position has till now impeded the cultivation. But in truth the differentiating tendencies of Nature herself may well be regarded as depreciating such factitious development. We dare not disregard the inherent heterogeneity of the sexes. After all, marriage is grounded in the natural order, and any other career for women is but an expedient which, as adapted to her individual capacity, will, in default of marriage, secure for her a position of economic and moral independence such as a moral personality requires. The 'free love' which some propose to substitute for marriage would differ from prostitution only in degree. 'Marriage reform' still lacks clear definition. The true method of emancipation is that which assigns to each sex the task adapted to its peculiar character and gifts, thereby investing it with its own moral dignity and honour; and which, in particular, places women in a position to understand the distinctive life of men, and to share their interests, while men on their part undergo the correlative discipline. Marriage must continue to rest upon the intimate friendship which gains moral stability in fulfilling the common task of maintaining the home and rearing children.

We learn from the above outline that there has been a gradual advance in the emancipation of women, an advance which is based upon a proper estimate of their personality, but which also tends to assume debased and unnatural forms when the distinctive qualities of the sex are ignored. The probable result of disregarding these qualities would be a recrudescence of the ancient view of women, viz. that they are essentially equal to men, though of weaker mould and, accordingly, of lower status—a view which was discarded only by allowing for the specific characteristics of womanhood, and by conceding to women a position of equality in keeping with their special gifts.

(*c*) We see a corresponding development of freedom in the relation of the individual to the *family*. In Rome, the law of the XII Tables invested the father with authority to sell his children, and even with the power of life and death; and in the era of the Republic a son of full age was still under paternal jurisdiction in domestic matters, though otherwise a free citizen. So strongly was the unity of the family insisted upon, that a son could neither possess nor acquire independent property during his father's lifetime. The procedure in connexion with a son's emancipation (here we have the original usage of the word) was, according to the XII Tables, that the father sold his son three times to the so-called *pater fiduciarius*, who had promised not to take the contract in earnest. But the power of the *paterfamilias* was circumscribed by use and wont. In the event of a capital sentence, the father invoked a family assize; and eventually, in the Imperial period, even this right was annulled, and the father was compelled to carry the case to the authorities. The legal authority of the father over his descendants, and the amenability of the individual to family jurisdiction were still further modified by Christianity, which paid higher regard to the individual, making him more and more independent of the family; while it based the family on a moral and emotional, rather than on a purely legal, foundation, the legal aspect being now attended to by the State. The Christian principle that spiritual qualities are of more value than corporeal, and that even children, as souls in the making, are of infinite worth, was a condemnation of the savage custom of exposing weak infants—a practice defended even by the most enlightened Greek philosophers. The Christian view necessarily led to a restriction of the right to punish children, and to the civil protection of their life and health, even against their parents. With this we may compare the modern law, which prevents careless parents from standing in the way of their children's education.

The ideal of education upheld by the great thinkers of Greece was that the family should transfer its responsibilities to the State—a position natural enough in view of the defective condition of family life in Greece. Among Christian peoples the place of the State was in a measure assumed by the Church, which took in hand the work of education—an arrangement which still to some extent prevails in Roman Catholic countries. The family thus became subordinate to the Church and the *religiosi*, and education was handed over to the monastery and the convent. The countries of the Reformation, however, where the family had maintained its independence in a markedly higher degree, recognized the educative value of home life, as specially adapted to train the heart and the disposition. Provision was made, however, both for attaining knowledge and for developing talent and intelligence by the institution of public schools, the maintenance of which fell upon the State; though in England private education was still recommended by Locke. The augmented demands for intellectual culture, and for its dissemination (within limits) amongst the people at large—as even Luther had desiderated—practically made it incumbent upon the State to undertake the development of natural talent, and more particularly of the mental faculties. In some countries school-attendance was made compulsory, the children's right to be educated being thus enforced even against the parents, while reformatories and industrial schools were provided by the State in the interests of children whose moral training was criminally neglected at home.

In all this we discern a progressive liberation of the individual from the ascendancy of the family, though the latter by no means ceases to operate as a genuine educative factor. Similar progress has been made in regard to the *aim* of education. The conviction that a man's education should be directed towards making him an independent personality has become more and more explicit.

Recent educational science pays special attention to the transition stage between youth and full manhood, and regards it as the definitive task of education that the pupil, once he has outgrown the discipline of home and school, should be trained with a view to the attainment of his ethical majority.

In this connexion Schleiermacher draws a distinction between aristocratic and democratic families, pointing out that the family relationship is much more effectively maintained in the former than in the latter. But he specially urges that parental authority on its moral side should gradually pass into friendship, while the filial respect he insists upon is not meant to exclude freedom of decision on the part of those who have reached maturity; the parents, in short, shall then be no more than counsellors.

Thus the family, once a legal institution, has become the moral community of the home, enjoying, nevertheless, the protection of the law; the rights of the individual members, especially of those under age, are protected by the State, even against the family itself; while, in a moral and legal respect, increasing regard is paid to those who have attained maturity and independence, more particularly with a view to their becoming founders of new families.

(*d*) The emancipation of the individual has also a *social* reference. In *India* a man is bound to his caste, and cannot rise above it. In *China*, where the system of caste does not prevail, the individual's position in the social organism is defined by religion and by a most elaborate ceremonialism, which tend to impede the spontaneity of social life. In regard to property, however, the conditions are more favourable, and land can be tilled or sold as the proprietor pleases. In ancient *Greece* social life had not as yet freed itself from national life; the individual, as Aristotle expresses it, was primarily a ζῶον πολιτικόν, while the theory and practice of the State set forth in the Dorian system of Plato's *Republic* hardly left room for personal independence in social and economic relations. Nevertheless, in regard to social life, Greece shows a certain advance upon Brāhmanic India, since it no longer made birth the criterion for participation in public life—a reform explicitly decreed in the laws of Solon, which, however, still countenanced slavery. In the period after Alexander the Great interest in the State began to wane before social life and friendship, which had been extolled by Aristotle, and especially by Epicurus, in whose opinion the State was simply a contract for the attainment of mutual security. This social fellowship, however, did not embrace family life: it was friendship amongst men, or occasionally, with *hetæræ*. Nevertheless, the interests of the individual came gradually to the front.

In *Muhammadanism* the Qur'ān is the great authority in matters not only of religion, but of morality, law, and social order as well. The Prophet, or his vice-gerent, the Khalīf, is invested with power to regulate the tenure of property; the system, more particularly as regards the land, may be called socio-theocratic. Social life is at a low level, resting as it does on the separation of the sexes; and, wherever a better state of things prevails, it is not due to Islām.

The theocratic standpoint likewise dominated social life among the *Jews*. But, while the land was regarded as belonging to God, yet the social and religious legislation, though not always carried out in practice, served to strengthen the family on its economic side, as is shown, for instance, by the regulations regarding the jubilee, the Sabbatical year, gleaning, etc., which were designed to avert utter impoverishment. With some exceptions the various crafts, such as tillage and cattle-rearing, were held in high respect. The consciousness of being the chosen people of God bound the Israelites more closely together, while the simultaneous festivals, the observance of the Passover, and the Sabbath, with its mandate of rest for man and beast, tended to promote the social side of family life. The moral import of the social and economic independence of the family and its head is set forth in the Law, and it was in view of this ethical end that statutory barriers were raised against impoverishment.

In *Rome*, again, we see a certain progress in the realization of social independence. The long-continued conflict between plebeians and patricians, the outcome of which was to equalize the two parties, bore rather upon political than upon social life; yet it was not without significance for the latter, as it made clear that social privileges were no longer to be the appanage of birth, but the reward of meritorious public service. The later period of Roman history, however, was marked by the formation of numerous associations, which, on the whole, were an expression of the desire for freedom in social matters; in fact, Julius Cæsar recognized not only the ancient gilds and the autonomous societies, but also the independence of municipalities. By making life secure, and by giving the *paterfamilias* the right to dispose of his property, Roman law maintained a formal freedom; it also guarded the right of association for social and religious ends. But, as those liberties were without ethical character, the relative enactments simply led to an increase of selfishness, enabling the privileged few to reduce the rest to penury.

In *Christianity*, which so strongly emphasized the ethical value of personality, even property was viewed in a moral light, and men became aware that they were responsible to God in the management thereof. The conception of Christian equality in social and economic relations found expression first of all in a magnificent benevolence, and the great end of riches was believed to be relief of the poor. But the idea of equality in the sight of God had also a vast influence upon the social life of Christian communities. Certainly distinctions of class were not done away with; nevertheless, all were equal in the eyes of religion—a thought which had found expression in Stoicism, though without any practical issue. Christianity also effected a deliverance in the sphere of custom, Christians either breaking away from heathen practices, or else, as was often the case, transforming them, and feeling themselves individually responsible for the reform—a line of action urged especially by Tertullian in the one-sided, but all the more powerful, appeals of his shorter ethical works, and also by Clement of Alexandria, who, however, treated ancient usages with a more tender hand. Doubtless men were then so profoundly concerned with the world to come that they retained but little interest in earthly goods, and social life was largely confined to religious intercourse. Even in the primitive Church we find warnings against wealth and its perils, and in no long time it came to be believed that property was grounded in selfishness (Ambrose), and that voluntary poverty was a mark of superior sanctity; while, similarly, those who abandoned the world and the family for the desert or the cloister were held in high repute. Be it remarked, however, that the endeavour to escape from the world and to be inwardly free from its enticements was itself the outgrowth of a genuine emancipative movement.

Even in the mediæval feudal system with its class divisions, and in the system of trade gilds which prevailed in the cities, there grew up a renewed interest in social life, the general trend of which was likewise favourable to individual security. Notwithstanding a man's class disabilities and his dependence upon his gild, and in spite of frequent conflicts between the various ranks of society, his economic freedom was promoted by the expansion of agriculture, commerce, and the industrial arts. The peasantry, too, had access to tribunals established on their behalf; and, while the gilds frequently imposed restrictions upon freedom of action, they also afforded protection and security.

As against the Church's authority over the individual, the Reformation asserted the 'freedom of a Christian man' as the watchword of personal liberty, thereby universalizing, on religious ground, the advantages which, on social and political ground, the powerful had arrogated to themselves in the previous century. Moreover, the Reformation, affirming on principle the moral dignity of labour and of the secular calling, laid the foundation of a new organization of society, which was wrought out in subsequent centuries. Luther's contention that wages should be proportionate to work has a wonderfully modern ring. Then the Mercantile System, laying stress upon manufactures, commerce, and the use of money (in place of barter), helped to facilitate the transport of goods, the process being furthered also by the Physiocrats, who, notwithstanding the importance they assigned to agriculture, yet contended for complete freedom of trade, made war upon gilds, Government concessions, and the burdens of the peasantry, and thereby helped to forward the liberty of the subject. Finally, Adam Smith and his school, repudiating the compulsory element in the gilds, and advocating open competition, set the seal upon individual freedom, and their investigations were doubly important from the fact that, as regards both the acquisition of property and the liberty of the subject—matters in which they had the support of the philosophy of Natural Law from the time of Locke—they bore upon the natural foundations of society, and served to assign to the individual his rightful place in the larger system of national and international life. In the French Revolution, the principles of freedom and equality advocated by Natural Law brought about the abrogation of innumerable privileges, and the emancipation of the 'third estate.' But the weak point in the movement was the people's lack of moral preparation, and the failure to recognize natural differences among men. The general rights of man, which from the religious point of view are based upon the equality of all before God, but which were traced by the Revolutionists to men's equality in the eyes of moral and civil law, were urged so ruthlessly, that the actual disparity of men in their moral, mental, and physical qualities was ignored.

While the principle of open competition freed the individual from the limitations of his class and his trade, yet the new system of production, with the requirement of capital, introduced fresh difficulties, the solution of which has been undertaken by Socialism. Socialism (*q.v.*) begins by recognizing the actual inequalities of men, tracing these not to diversities of natural gift—this being assumed rather to be equal in all—but to disparities in the possession of productive capital. Though an open door has been set before the individual, and the obstacles to the development of his faculties cleared away; though equal political rights have been conceded to all, and the class distinctions which stood in the way of social advancement removed; of what avail is it all, asks the Socialist, if men have no choice but to enter the lists of competition with unequal resources? The individual's dependence upon capital must, therefore, be brought to an end if his emancipation is ever to be complete; and this object is to be attained by making productive capital a national asset. In order to give practical effect to the idea, it is proposed to turn the State into a great industrial company, which would guarantee to every man the due remuneration of his labour. In point of fact, however, such an emancipation would result in the loss of personal freedom; and, as the worker would then possess no capital, but gain at most sufficient wages—in the form of work-certificates—to procure him the means of enjoyment, the system would but pander to the selfish desire for happiness, and check the impulse to produce, which thrives only where it is free. We must, nevertheless, recognize that both the policy of open competition, which emanated from England, and the Socialistic movement, which first arose in France, were prompted by the spirit of emancipation; only, these movements are concerned with the material rather than with the moral side of man's nature, and with what is common to all rather than with the peculiar qualities of the individual. A higher respect is, therefore, due to those who emphasize the ethical aspect of the social problem and the ethical significance of property, and who desiderate a true personal independence, guaranteed by such a system of ownership as would enable each to discharge his proper function in the social organism, and, so far as possible, remove that financial servitude which keeps him from fulfilling his vocation as a man and as an individual. A similar object is aimed at by the renascent tendency to form corporate societies standing midway between the individual and the State—societies in which a man may act as a voluntary member, and from which he derives a certain support and security. A practical attempt to deliver the working man from the power of capital is made by the Trade Unions, which secure a proper representation of his interests, and treat with capitalists and their combinations upon equal terms. Again, provision is made in Germany for old age and sickness by compulsory insurance, while in Great Britain old age pensions are now paid by the State, and there and in America the same purpose is served in part by funds accumulated independently of the State. The emancipation of factory-workers, miners, and rural labourers is sought in ameliorative legislation.

The emancipation movement makes itself felt in the sphere of social intercourse precisely as in that of economics. Social intercourse is regulated by custom; and here also a beginning has been made with that levelling process which looks to the worth of personality as such. While formerly distinctions of rank were rigorously observed, in modern times the sense of equality has been intensified by international intercourse, by the recognition of human rights and of the ethical value of labour in general; and this manifests itself in the respect and courtesy shown even to social inferiors. It is, of course, true that this tendency towards the democratization of society is counteracted by a tendency towards differentiation, which is constantly splitting society into new and mutually exclusive groups. But, as the various ranks are arranged no longer according to birth, but according to occupation or profession, there may grow up in the professions themselves an ethic and etiquette which do away with the distinction of birth, while, again, the equal respect paid to the several professions—the moral value set upon work in general—practically opens to every man the door of any calling for which he may be qualified, and so breaks down the rigidity of professional caste. Both of these modifications may have an effect upon custom, and in this respect, too, modern society exhibits a movement towards the emancipation of the lower classes from the thraldom of their position—a movement which has made most headway in the United States. Recent ethics has made it increasingly clear, however, that custom is not a thing fixed and stable, but is ever being moulded afresh by the action of individuals, and that every man shares in the responsibility for its right development.

Coming now to the larger communities, the State and the Church, we find the process of emancipation at work in various forms. It may manifest itself in the relation between the individual and either of these communities, or, again, in the relation of these communities to each other.

(*e*) First of all, as regards the tie between the individual and *the Church*, we must distinguish between countries like Judæa and Persia, where there was a national religion established by law, and where every citizen was bound to conform to its authority, alike in belief and in practice, and countries like Greece and Rome, where religion was, indeed, a matter of the State, but where no pressure was put upon a man so long as he did not overtly violate the sacred institutions. In Rome, the devotees of the *religiones licitæ* were allowed absolute liberty, on condition that they observed the worship of the Emperor; while in Greece it was possible for a free philosophical religion to develop from the popular cults. Christianity was at first a voluntary association of believers, in which every man could act a part congenial to his gifts; but in process of time it was transformed into an infallible school of doctrine, a sanctuary through which salvation flowed, a seminary which prepared men for heaven. The Roman Church, in particular, insisted upon the spiritual incapacity of the people, and held all its members in thrall to its dogma and its discipline alike. The emancipation of the individual really began with the Reformation, which made the *personal* assurance of salvation, the *testimonium Spiritus Sancti internum*, a matter of superlative moment, and regarded the Church as *principaliter* the community of believers. But the Churches of the Reformation had their own fixed Confessions and Liturgies, and presently came to take their stand upon the infallibility of Scripture. In no long time, therefore, personal liberty fell again into abeyance, and all the more completely that the task of maintaining doctrinal purity was practically handed over to the State. At length, however, under the influence of modern philosophy, and of natural and historical science, the religious spirit wrenched itself free from ecclesiastical authority; the Church itself became the subject of critical inquiry, and the system of National Churches was partly superseded by the policy of public tolerance for all religious communities. It is, again, the United States which has made most progress in the latter direction, for there the individual may choose at will among the various denominations, and move as he pleases from one to another; though, on the other hand, diverse tendencies within the various communities themselves are less willingly tolerated. In Europe the system of privileged Established Churches is still very general—Churches which more or less strenuously maintain their traditional worship, doctrine, and usage, and hold their members in a position of dependence. Yet within these Churches we find various types of thought existing side by side, more especially in the Protestant communities of Germany and Switzerland, and in the Church of England; and religious freedom broadens out more and more, though not altogether without opposition. It is worthy of special note that the right of the individual to take part according to his abilities in reforming the Church from within is more and more recognized.

(*f*) Again, the sphere of individual participation in *the national life* has been gradually enlarged. The great monarchies of the East—Babylon and Egypt—gave the mass of the people no voice in the control of public affairs. True, the Greek States and the Roman Republic obliged their citizens to take part in the government, but the enfranchised classes were small in number, and their privileges were subject to the condition that the State should superintend their moral training. As a matter of fact, it was the feudal State of the Middle Ages that made a beginning with personal enfranchisement with respect to the law, and with the people's right to vote supplies—witness the English Magna Charta of 1215; to the same period we must also trace a weakening of the central authority by the growing independence of territorial and local rulers—a state of matters exemplified by the *condottieri* of Italy. To these signs of progress we must add the nascent theories of Natural Law, according to which the State derived its authority from the people, as was held by Occam and others. The severance between social and national life which is gradually being effected in the modern world is an index of the increasing prestige of the individual and the class in relation to the State. Finally, comparing the views of Natural Law held by a man like Locke with ancient theories of the State, we see how great an advance has been made in the matter of personal interests; for, according to Locke, the function of the State is merely a legal one, viz. to protect the individual and the family in life and property.

Reference must also be made to the view that the State is based upon a contract of its citizens, and that, accordingly, its part is to act in their interests. The French Revolution was an attempt to carry out the principles of liberty, equality, and fraternity, and to abolish the privileges of the favoured classes; and since then most European countries have adopted constitutions which not merely compel the citizen to obey and to pay taxes, but also enable him to take a greater or smaller share in the national life by the exercise of his vote. Schleiermacher in his *Politik* puts the matter thus: government on the one hand and subordination on the other should be shared by all, every man being in one aspect a ruler, and in another a subject; while W. von Humboldt, in his work entitled *Ueber die Grenzen der Wirksamkeit eines Staates*, makes it incumbent upon the State to furnish the strongest possible guarantee of the citizen's right to free self-development. When we consider the expansion of the leading States of to-day, and the share in their government which is nevertheless guaranteed in varying measure to their inhabitants, we see what an advance has been made upon ancient conditions; for, after all, the democracies of old correspond rather with the oligarchies of modern times. Once more, it is the United States which has gone furthest in applying the principle of personal liberty, inasmuch as, on the one hand, the Government has its functions circumscribed, no longer holding the citizen in tutelage, while, on the other, every citizen is free to take a part in public life. At the same time, the experience of that country shows that civil emancipation requires a certain standard of education in the citizens, and that its necessary complement is compulsory school attendance. In Europe, on the other hand, more especially in countries where the monarchy still bears a despotic and autocratic character, we find a growing tendency to Anarchy (*q.v.*), manifesting itself either in a nihilistic onslaught upon the existing organization of society, or in the subversive theories of thinkers like Tolstoi, who would abrogate all State authority in favour of the freely rendered love of one's fellow-man. Certainly the warrant for personal participation in the government of one's country, to which at the same time obedience must be rendered, is to be found alone in the right of moral self-determination: in fact, the growth of the sense of moral responsibility amongst the people, and of their respect for the constitution and the law, forms an accurate index of their capacity for a responsible share in the national administration. Accordingly, in reference to the French Revolution, Schiller and other German writers maintained that the nation which would take its destiny into its own hands must possess an inwrought moral character, lest liberty of action should degenerate into pure caprice and unreason. Similarly, it was Kant's conviction of the ethical value of personality—the idea of moral autonomy —which led him to urge that free moral action was based upon law, and that a legally constituted State was essential to the realization of moral freedom. Since in the modern State the first principle of legal administration is the equality of all before the law; since punishment has lost much of its former barbarity, and is designed mainly to preserve law and order; since the State makes it its task to protect the common rights of man, and since this protection covers not only life and property, but also liberty of conscience, of thought, of inquiry, and the freedom of the press; we may regard it as certain that the law-abiding citizen may claim public protection for his most sacred interests, whether material or spiritual, and may look upon the law as the sponsor of his absolute right to cultivate his mental and physical faculties to the best of his ability. Perhaps the South American Republics afford the most striking illustration of how little is gained by a purely formal freedom, *i.e.* a freedom unsupported by that moral responsibility which manifests itself in unconditional reverence for the law—not that the law need be regarded as incapable of improvement or as unalterably and finally fixed, but it ought to be obeyed so long as it stands. This aspect of the matter was admirably set forth by Schleiermacher when he said that the most perfect form of national life is that in which freedom as such is never sought after.

(*g*) *The emancipation of the State from the Church* comes into consideration only in cases where the former has been dominated by the latter. In antiquity the two communities, the political and the religious, were as a rule too closely identified for any attempt on the part of the former to free itself from the latter. In Egypt the State passed under the ascendancy of the priesthood in the period of the Theban domination. Amenhotep IV. transferred his court from Thebes to Tell el-Amarna, and sought to throw off the priestly power and even to introduce, on his own initiative, a solar monotheism, letting himself be worshipped as the reflexion of the sun. This drastic proceeding, however, proved ineffective, and gave place to an absolute theocracy, the priesthood again gaining the upper hand in the Ethiopian dynasty. A similar movement manifests itself in the Jewish theocracy, as when Saul set himself in opposition to Samuel, while David came to the throne as the true theocratic king. In Greece the State was in no way subject to the hierarchy, save at Delphi, where for a time the constitution was theocratic, while in Rome the religious interest was really subordinate to the political. Once the Christian Church in the Western Empire had become a power co-ordinate with the State, Augustine laid the foundations of a theory which actually exalted the theocratic community above the civil, and the Middle Ages witnessed an attempt to carry the theory into practice.

The Church, it was declared, fulfils a higher function than the State: the latter has to do with the *terrena felicitas*, the former with eternal salvation. The secular purpose of the State can, therefore, be consecrated only when the civil power places itself at the disposal of the religious. Views of this tenor, aiming at the ascendancy of the Church, come more and more into vogue until the rise of Jesuitism. Indications of the movement had begun to show themselves in the pseudo-Isidorian *Decretals*, at the Synod of Paris (A.D. 829), the *de Institutione Regia* of John of Orleans, and the *Constitutio* of Odo of Canterbury. While Aquinas, in his *de Regimine Principum*, apparently assigns an independent position to the State, he nevertheless holds that, as the Church has the superior function, the civil power must give way whenever the Church so enjoins, and also that the Church itself must in all cases decide when its own higher interests justify such a demand. In fact, the prevailing idea of the Middle Ages was that the Church and the State were as sun and moon, the latter deriving its light from the former. In the reign of Ludwig of Bavaria this view was maintained in the *Summa de Potestate Ecclesiæ* of Augustinus Triumphus, as also in the *Summa de Planctu Ecclesiæ* of Alvarus Pelagius, the Spanish Franciscan. The Jesuits contended that all authority belongs primordially to the Church, which receives the same directly from God, whereas the power of the State is wholly derived from the people. Endeavours to carry out these theories in face of the Imperial authority were made by Gregory VII., who was filled with the ideals of the Clugniac order, and also by Innocent III., while Boniface VIII. even claimed the right to parcel out territory by a stroke of the pen. The State was gravely imperilled in its own domain by the spiritual jurisdiction and the sway of the priests as exercised in the confessional. Above all, the Church's claim to release the subject from an oath given to an unbeliever—some refractory ruler, let us say—and even to depose princes, was a standing menace to the sovereignty of the State.

Such views, however, did not even then pass unchallenged. For one thing, the Saxon and Salic emperors, down to Henry IV., deemed themselves the guardians of the Church, while the Hohenstaufens, especially Frederick I. and Frederick II.—the latter in his Sicilian Laws—tried to emancipate the State from the Church; for another, writer after writer took up the controversy in defence of the State's rights. Early in the 9th cent., for instance, Abbot Smaragdus of Verdun, in his *de Via Regia*, spoke of the king as the earthly counterpart of God; Henry IV. found a champion in the Italian jurist Petrus Crassus; while Frederick II. in his own *Letters* upheld the national prerogative, and had the support of Peter of Vineis and Thaddæus of Suessa. Dante's *de Monarchia* had a similar end in view. In the time of Ludwig of Bavaria the independence of the State was still more strenuously advocated by the Franciscan William of Occam, by Marsilius of Padua in his *Defensor Pacis*, by Leopold of Babenburg in his *Tractatus de Iuribus Regni et Imperii*; and in France, in the time of Philip IV., the cause was maintained by Dubois in his *de Recuperatione Terræ Sanctæ*. As against the assumptions of the Church, Machiavelli asserted the absolute independence of the State; as against the idea of the universal empire, he advocated the unity of the Italian nation, though all he claimed for the State was its supremacy in regard to its finance and its external power and prosperity.

The emancipation of the State from the Church in countries dominated by Roman Catholicism can come about only through conflict with the Church itself. Even to the present day the Roman Catholic Church claims to be absolutely supreme in all questions which it regards as bearing upon its interests—a contention which finds frank expression in the Syllabus of Pius IX. The result is that, whenever a Roman Catholic State unfetters itself from ecclesiastical bondage, it assumes an openly irreligious character: the views of Machiavelli afford a typical illustration. But, as it is impossible that a people can live permanently without religion, Roman Catholic nations tend to pursue a policy of vacillation between the two extremes: on the one hand, an irreligious and secular standpoint, where there is no concern for anything but material prosperity, and, on the other, a position of subjection to the Church; Spain and France furnish instances (cf. CONCORDAT). The liberation of the political from the ecclesiastical interest can in fact attain a permanent footing only when the State aims at something higher than material prosperity and enjoyment, and when at the same time the Church confines itself to spiritual affairs, and is concerned solely with the fostering of the religious life. The numerous tentative statements of this conception made in the Middle Ages, as, *e.g.*, by Frederick I. of Hohenstaufen, Dante, William of Occam and his allies, could win no real acceptance while the Church remained unreformed, as was shown in the case of France, which had to renounce the ancient Gallican liberties of Louis IX. in favour of modern Ultramontanism, and is now endeavouring to free itself from the latter. Cf. art. ERASTIANISM.

In the process of emancipation of State from Church, a crucial and epoch-making stage was reached at the Reformation. The Church's function was now in principle limited to the religious nurture of the soul; the Church itself was viewed as the community of faith. It was, therefore, impossible for the Church to obstruct the State, as the latter too had a Divine commission—to foster justice, to maintain order, to ensure liberty of moral action on the basis of law. In point of fact, as the individual depended no longer upon the Church's mediation, but could win the assurance of salvation for himself, and as he recognized that he had been elected to realize himself as a free moral agent, and thus to become something more than a passive unit in the national life, his new-born conviction was really an augury not only of his own personal liberty as a citizen, but also of the emancipation of the State itself. Calvinism, which interpreted the consciousness of election to life as an incitement to moral practice, was marvellously adapted to endow the nations with a freedom based upon personal responsibility, and thereby to procure the liberation of the State from the Church, as is well shown in the history of Calvinistic lands.

(*h*) Finally, we must consider *the emancipation of the Church from the State*. In ancient Greece and Rome the civil power was paramount in religious things; religion was, in fact, an affair of the State. This is still the case in China, where the machinery of government is regarded as a Divine manifestation, and where the moral and religious training of the people is in the hands of public officials. Within Christendom, too, the Eastern Church was subject to the State; doctrine was a State concern, and was frequently enforced by Government authority. The Donatist controversy turned not only upon the idea of the Church, but upon the Church's liberation from State control (see DONATISTS). While the mediæval Roman Church claimed the right to dominate the State, it was rather the Byzantian principle which re-emerged in Lutheran countries at the Reformation: it was held that the State, as a Christian entity, ought to concern itself even with the defence of the faith; and the territorial principle *cujus regio ejus religio* held its own for a time. Once more, however, it was Calvinism that upheld religious liberty against the usurpations of the State: witness the history of Holland, Scotland, and the United States. These countries actually carried out the idea that religion, being a matter of the inmost heart, should in no way be constrained by the civil power—a principle which, it is true, had been strongly advocated in Reformation times by dissenters like Denk and Sebastian Frank. Even the system of Established Churches was set aside, notably in the United States. It was held that the Churches should be quite independent of the State, requiring nothing from it save legal protection: only on these conditions could the freedom of the Church as a *societas fidei* be realized. Certainly, were the Churches to attempt to suppress freedom, and to dragoon the people to accept their formulæ, the civil power would be called upon to safeguard the liberty of the subject, since it is of the very essence of a free Church that the members should belong to it voluntarily, and should not be coerced in any way. The outcome of such a freedom is that the religious spirit unfolds itself in the most varied forms. State Churches, in fact, can compete in this respect with voluntary Churches only by admitting a wide variety in their doctrine and practice. Cf. art. ERASTIANISM.

(*i*) Bare mention may also be made of the fact that emancipation is understood by some in an absolute sense, *i.e.* as *personal liberty without any qualification whatever*. Such freedom is conceded to the man of genius, as, *e.g.*, by Romantic writers like Schlegel—in his theory of Irony; or to the man of power, as in Nietzsche's *Herrenmoral*. But all this really amounts to an emancipation from morality—a condition 'beyond good and evil.' Such an emancipation, like the Solipsism of Max Stirner's *Der Einzige und sein Eigentum* (Leipzig, 1893), is sheer delusion.

3. Moral and religious bearings of emancipation.—From the foregoing survey we see how emancipation has broadened out more and more, manifesting itself now as the liberation of thought, now as the deliverance of the individual from the bondage of society and of organized communities, and again as the liberation of one community from another, each exhibiting a growing sense of its peculiar function, and striving to fulfil the same in its own way. It is admitted by the various schools of thought—whether as a subject for blame or for praise—that the process of emancipation is in the last resort the supersession of authority by autonomy. In this striving after freedom many read hostility to religion, a tendency to break away from the Divine government, the atomizing and levelling of society, the growth of the notion that justice is to be determined solely by the individual (who appropriates what rights he can), the imminent dissolution of discipline and order—all ending at length in moral chaos. To others, however, as to J. G. Fichte for instance, the real tenor of the process seems to consist in the transmutation of authority into liberty, of natural gifts into qualities personally acquired and developed, of tradition into freedom of thought and act; in the ceaseless renovation of communities—not as dead institutions but as living organisms—by the unobstructed effort of their members; and in the growing capacity of each separate community to undertake and execute its specific work, without alien interference, but with its own resources, and according to the principles of its constitution—no community having authority over any other, but each being supreme within its own domain, and each in reality best serving the interests of the rest by attending to its own affairs.

It is a fact beyond question that the human personality must possess the moral right to express itself in action, and is, therefore, entitled to a measure of emancipation adequate thereto. Moral personality has two sides. There is first of all the universal side, in virtue of which every man ought to have an equal right to practical self-expression, and upon this postulate rest the general rights of man asserted by the advocates of Natural Law—including not merely protection of life and property, but freedom of conscience and thought as well. Then there is the individual side, which postulates that each person, as such, should possess the right to develop his special talents in his own way; nor is he to be levelled to the general average of society, as is demanded by certain schools of Socialism. It is clear, nevertheless, that an emancipation of the individual issuing in a ruthless self-assertion at the cost of others would subvert the real rights of the latter, while, as a matter of fact, men are meant to work as complementary to one another. It is, therefore, of capital importance that an adjustment be made between the general rights of moral personality and the right of the individual to act for himself. Every human being must be free to act in his proper vocation, and must at the same time pay due regard to the corresponding right of others.

The relation subsisting between the individual and the various groups—the family, the corporate body, the class, civic society, the State, the Church, custom—is conditioned by the postulate that as a moral personality he shall have the right to act spontaneously, and according to his abilities, in these several relationships, and hence also to assist in the continuous renovation of the communities themselves; emancipation is, therefore, necessary as a means to that end. Again, however, the various communities must preserve a certain continuity, must demand that recognition be given by the individual to the constitution and order without which they could not exist. Hence there emerges once more the need of an adjustment, the condition of which is that, while the existent economy of these communities is treated with respect, it shall leave room for development and reform, and consequently for efforts directed thereto, such progress shaping its course according to the distinctive character of the several communities.

Finally, as regards the interrelations of the various communities, it is required that each of these shall possess such a measure of freedom as will enable it to develop according to its own principles, and to do justice to its specific aim and object. But, since none of these communities is absolutely independent, since, in fact, they circumscribe one another, they must enter into mutual relations. So far as their external activities are concerned, the province of each must be delimited in such a way as to obviate the possibility of collision with any other. This end is secured by the law, the guardian of which is the State, while it is the State likewise which must guarantee the complete liberty required by each community in the working out of its peculiar task.

In a word, emancipation is a necessary moment in that liberation of the moral personality and the moral community without which they cannot adequately realize their appropriate moral end. But this fact also indicates the limit of the process, viz. that the individual and the community alike must regard themselves as each having a place in the whole moral organism, and as working towards the Highest Good, or—in terms of religion—the Kingdom of God. Emancipation taken as an end-in-itself, and as the repudiation of moral responsibility, is worse than useless, and results in moral chaos; but, if we regard it as a means of setting the moral powers free for action, so that they may most efficiently contribute their special quota to the realization of the whole ethical process, then emancipation is seen to be a demand of the moral law itself.

LITERATURE.—H. Münsterberg, *Die Amerikaner*, 1904, i. 459 f., ii.; Helene Lange and Gertrud Bäumer, *Handbuch der Frauenbewegung*, i. (1901), ii. (1902), iii. (1906); A. Bebel, *Die Frau u. d. Sozialismus*[28], 1897; J. J. Baumann, *Sechs Vorträge aus d. Gebiete der prakt. Philos.*, 1874, Vortrag 2; Ellen Key, *Ueber Liebe und Ehe*[12], 1906; J. S. Mill, *The Subjection of Women*, 1851, new ed. 1883, *On Liberty*, 1859 (for the general question); T. Stanton, *The Woman Question in Europe*, 1884; A. Kuyper, *Reformation wider Revolution*, 1904, chs. iii. iv. v.; W. E. Lecky, *Hist. of Rationalism*, 1865, II. iii. v. vi.; E. v. Hartmann, *Phänomenol. des sittl. Bewusstseins*, 1879, p. 624 f.; Luther, *Werke* (Erlangen ed., 1826–57), i. 22, xiii. xv. xix. xx.; Adam Smith, *Wealth of Nations* (publ. 1776); W. Roscher, *Gesch. der Nationalökonomik in Deutschland*, 1874; L. Stein, *Socialismus u. Communismus d. heut. Frankreichs*, 1848; L. Brentano, *Die Arbeitergilden der Gegenwart*, 1871; Schleiermacher, *Entwurf ein. Syst. d. Sittenlehre*, ed. Schweizer, 1835, pp. 275–327, *Die christl. Sitte*, 1843, pp. 178–217, 237 f., 264 f.; A. Vinet, *Manifestation des convictions religieuses et sur la séparation de l'église et de l'état*, 1842; J. P. Thompson, *Church and State in the U.S.*, 1873; M. Minghetti, *Stato e chiesa*, 1881; R. Mariano, *Cristianisimo, cattolicismo, e civiltà*, 1879; E. Zeller, *Staat u. Kirche*, 1873; J. J. Baumann, *Die Staatslehre des Th. v. Aquino*, 1873; H. Höffding, *Ethics*, Eng. tr. 1888, pp. 257 f., 280 f., 310 f., 338 f., 374 f., 439 f., 478 f., 578 f.; H. Spencer, *Principles of Sociology*, 1876–96, 'The Man *v.* the State'; A. Dorner, *Das menschl. Handeln*, 1895, pp. 421 f., 645 f., also *Individ. u. soz. Ethik*, 1906; K. C. F. Krause, *Lebenlehre od. Philos. d. Geschichte*[2], 1904, pp. 366 f., 376 f., 388 f.

A. DORNER.

EMERSON.—I. Life and writings.—Ralph Waldo Emerson, essayist, poet, and the most famous representative of the Transcendentalist school of thought in New England, was born, the third of seven children, in Boston, Mass., on 25th May 1803. His father, William Emerson, was minister of the First Church (Unitarian) in Boston; his mother, Ruth Haskins, was a woman of strong and gracious character. Emerson took a genuine pride in his descent from a long line of Christian ministers. It gave him 'a certain normal piety, a levitical education'; he counted himself happy in having a star which rained on him influences of ancestral religion. His aunt, Mary Moody Emerson, did much to shape his character and thought —'the kind aunt whose cares instructed my youth, and whom may God reward!'

He was educated at the Boston Grammar School and Latin School, and then at Harvard, where he graduated without any great distinction in 1821, two of his brothers proving much more brilliant than he. The family circumstances being straitened by his father's early death, he had to teach in a school in order to help himself through college, and again after graduation; but it was a task in which he was not happy, feeling himself shy and awkward, 'toiling through this miserable employment without even the poor satisfaction of discharging it well.' His thoughts turned towards the Christian ministry. A month before he came of age he wrote: 'I deliberately dedicate my time, my talents, and my hopes to the Church.' He studied theology at the Harvard Divinity School, was approved as a preacher in 1826, and in 1829 was settled as colleague-minister of the Second Church in Boston. This chapter in his history was not to be a long one. He gradually conquered the chest weakness which at first made public speaking difficult. But in 1832 he resigned his charge, feeling that he could no longer conscientiously administer the Lord's Supper in the accustomed form. His grounds were partly those of criticism and interpretation—he did not think that Christ designed a perpetual commemoration with the help of symbols; and partly those of personal taste and experience:

> 'This mode of commemorating Christ is not suitable to me. That is reason enough why I should abandon it. . . . I will love him as a glorified friend, after the free way of friendship, and not pay him a stiff sign of respect, as men do those whom they fear.'

In other ways he felt that in the pulpit, and amid the accepted traditions of worship, his wings were bound. This year he wrote in his Journal:

> 'I have sometimes thought that, in order to be a good minister, it was necessary to leave the ministry. The profession is antiquated. In an altered age we worship in the dead forms of our forefathers.'

The same year there occurred the death, from consumption, of his young wife, Ellen Louisa Tucker, whom he had married in 1829. Thus set free from all ties, he paid his first visit to Europe (described in the beginning of *English Traits*), and returned to America to write and lecture, sometimes also preaching as occasion offered. In 1834 he settled at Concord, occupying first for some years the 'Old Manse,' made famous by Hawthorne, and in 1835 married Lidian Jackson (*d.* 1892). For a time he preached on Sundays to the Church in East Lexington, but more and more he felt that the lecture-platform was his real pulpit, and in 1838 he gave up preaching. None of his sermons has been published except that on the Lord's Supper, preached at the time of his resignation from his Boston charge; but we may judge of the tone and quality of his preaching from many passages in his essays and lectures, in which the preacher reappears scarcely disguised. There are many testimonies to the sweetness of his voice, the dignity and sincerity of his manner, and the beauty of his language in preaching and in prayer. But probably his preaching, like his poetry, appealed to a select circle.

The clearest light on these earlier years, and indeed one of the most valuable means we possess for the knowledge of the essential Emerson, has recently been given in the long-delayed publication of his private Journal, edited by his son and grandson. Four volumes have, so far, been issued, covering the years 1820–38. Early in life he began a notebook system, one chief purpose of which was, apparently, to enrich his conversation and deliver him from 'cheap, extemporaneous, draggle-tail dialogue.' He included quotations which had impressed him; his own comments on these and other matters; extracts from letters written by him and to him, especially from his correspondence with his aunt Mary; and all the spontaneous overflow of his mind according to the outlook and feeling of the moment. It was, in part, a deliberate literary exercise as well as a storehouse of memories and seed-thoughts, as when he took a fancy to imitate for a time the *Rambler* or *Spectator*. This Journal was the foundation of his published writings, and contains the rough-hewn outlines of some of his most famous utterances. The whole is of the most intense interest as a revelation of the man. The lover of Nature is here continually—and the indomitable optimist, except at a certain youthful period of ill-health and depression. Here are the gravity and dignity that gave to so many of his later utterances an oracular and prophetic tone: 'Why has my motley diary no jokes? Because it is a soliloquy, and every man is grave alone.' Here are hints of the remoteness and reserve which were characteristic to the end: 'Aristocracy is a good sign . . . no man would consent to live in society if he was obliged to admit everybody to his house that chose to come.' Here is his own confession of the wayward and disconnected thinking which some of his critics have regarded as his chief defect: 'My wayward Imagination. . . . I have come to the close of the sheets which I dedicated to the Genius of America, and notice that I have devoted nothing in my book to any peculiar topics which concern my country.' Here may be traced the beginning of the Swedenborg influence, which left so deep a mark upon him, especially in its feeling for the unity of Nature and its foreshadowing of the idea of Evolution; it reached him first through a 44-page pamphlet, entitled *The Growth of Mind* (Boston, 1826), by Sampson Reed, a young apothecary. The pamphlet does not contain much that would now arrest attention, but to Emerson it had the 'aspect of a revelation.' But the most interesting ingredient in the Journal is the youthful anticipation of doctrines of which, in later years, he was to be the prophet. The Essay on Compensation is here in germ. When he was 22 he wrote:

'I say that sin is ignorance, that the thief steals from himself, that he who practises fraud is himself the dupe of the fraud he practises: that whoso borrows runs in his own debt, and whoso gives to another benefits himself to the same amount.'[1]

The doctrine of self-reliance is equally prominent; cf. this (*æt.* 20): 'I see no reason why I should bow my head to man, or cringe in my demeanour.' This, again, in a letter to his aunt, anticipates his frequent championship of the individual soul, its rights and dignities:

'I hold fast to my old faith, that to each soul is a solitary law, a several universe. The colours to our eyes may be different,—your red may be my green. My innocence to one of more opportunity shall be guilt.'

So we watch in these volumes the gradual unfolding of the thinker and the man. At 17 he dreams of standing 'in the fair assembly of the chosen, the brave and the beautiful'; at 20 he writes: 'I burn after the *aliquid immensum infinitumque* which Cicero desired.' And, as we turn these pages, we feel that he is already far upon the way.

From the time of his settling in Concord his life ran a comparatively easy and peaceful course, not without its financial struggles and its private sorrows, such as the death of his eldest boy in 1842 (commemorated in *Threnody*). His second visit to Europe was in 1847, when the lectures on *Representative Men* were delivered, and his third in 1872. The rest is summed up in his lecturing tours; his correspondence, notably with Carlyle; his reception of innumerable visitors; his happy communion with his family and with Nature; and the publication of his various works. The first of these—*Nature*, published in 1836—deserves special notice because of its relation to the movement of which Emerson became the principal seer. Though the little book was greatly admired by a few, twelve years passed before 500 copies were sold.[1] Its value lies not only in its intrinsic beauty and suggestiveness—it contains some of the most poetic prose that Emerson ever wrote—but also in that we look back upon it now as a kind of preface to all that is covered by the word 'Transcendentalism.' It is difficult to frame this movement in any exact definition; it was more a spirit that could be felt than a set of doctrines which might be tabulated. It had links of connexion with Kantian idealism; it owed much to the influence of Coleridge, Carlyle, Goethe; also to Edward Everett, who popularized in Boston the newer stirrings of European thought. But there was at least as much in it of New England as of Europe: it was a reaction against the intellectual conventionality that reigned in Unitarian as in Calvinistic circles; it was a cry for new life, or partly a cry and partly a breath that came in answer to the cry. The movement gathered to itself supporters, some that were notable, such as Margaret Fuller, some eccentrics and extremists, many that were obscure in name but lofty and eager in spirit.

To get the essence of the Transcendentalist spirit, one might take this sentence from *The Dial*:

'They [the Editors] have obeyed, though with great joy, the strong current of thought and feeling which, for a few years past, has led many sincere persons in New England to make new demands on literature, and to reprobate that rigor of our conventions of religion and education which is turning us to stone, which renounces hope, which looks only backward, which asks only such a future as the past, which suspects improvement, and holds nothing so much in horror as new views and the dreams of youth. With these terrors the conductors of the present journal have nothing to do.'

The same spirit is more briefly and positively expressed in the first paragraph of *Nature*:

'The foregoing generations beheld God and Nature face to face; we, through their eyes. Why should not we also enjoy an original relation to the Universe?'

It is obvious that this relates itself closely to Emerson's favourite gospel of self-reliance: the Transcendentalist is one who trusts the deepest voices of his own being, and holds himself gladly free to follow the new light that new days bring to him. Yet he, of all men, is most truly loyal to the past; he is but doing what great souls of all ages have done before him.

'This way of thinking, falling on Roman times, made Stoic philosophers . . . falling on superstitious times, made prophets and apostles . . . and, falling on Unitarian and commercial times, makes the peculiar shades of Idealism which we know.'

This sentence from the lecture on *The Transcendentalist* hints at the way in which Emerson reconciled to his own mind his reverence for the past with his still greater reverence for the intuitions and revelations of the living present.

Nature was followed by two public utterances, which were also significant and prophetic. The oration on *The American Scholar* was delivered at Cambridge in 1837—an event, Lowell says, 'without parallel in our literary annals.' It has been described as an intellectual declaration of independence for America;[2] it was a call to the sluggard

[1] There is a passage to the same effect written when he was 19. Cf. the opening of the Essay itself: 'Ever since I was a boy . . .'

[1] Cf. a sentence in the Journal, when he was 18: 'Greatness is a property for which no man gets credit too soon; it must be possessed long before it is acknowledged.'

[2] Cf. Emerson, in *The Dial*, April 1843: 'The American Academy, the Historical Society, and Harvard University

intellect of the American continent to look from under its iron lids:

'We have listened too long to the courtly muses of Europe; . . . we will walk on our own feet; we will work with our own hands; we will speak our own minds.'

The influence of this address in calling forth an American literary consciousness can scarcely be over-estimated; the mind of a nation challenged itself through the voice of a man; the younger thinkers of the time heard it as a call to courage and self-respect—the 'Stand upright' of the angel in Daniel (10^{11}) repeated for modern ears. This was followed the next year by the *Address* to the Divinity Class in Cambridge—an utterance which caused much controversy, in which Emerson took no part. Its significance for us lies in its revelation of his religious position. It was the doctrine of self-reliance applied to the loftiest things—a re-assertion of the great Stoical doctrine, 'Obey thyself'; a prescription, 'first soul, and second soul, and evermore soul,' for the deadness of conventional thoughts and forms; a call to rise to Christ's conception of the greatness of a man. The address shocked the orthodox by seeming to belittle the historic basis of Christianity and the accumulated witness of the past; it alarmed some who did not count themselves specially orthodox, by its sheer courage of reliance upon instinct and intuition. Many things here are characteristic, and the reader who knows this utterance well knows much that came after. There is the deep and passionate moral sense, which to Emerson was the very nerve of religion; when a man attains to say, 'Virtue, I am thine, save me, use me . . . then is the end of creation answered and God is well pleased.' There is a glimpse of his critical and independent relation to historical Christianity,—his feeling that he has hold of something larger than the Churches were giving,—his conviction that the best method of honouring Jesus was to show the same courage as He showed and to live as He did, by intuition and conscience, and faith in the grandeur of the soul. There is also a note which may almost be called Messianic: 'I look for the new Teacher, that shall follow so far those shining laws, that he shall see them come full circle.'[1]

But Emerson's religious position as a whole is best summarized in a phrase from one of his letters to his aunt Mary: 'I belong to the good sect of the Seekers'; and his relation to all the dogmas is in one sentence in his Journal (1830): '*Alii disputent, ego mirabor*, said Augustine: it shall be my speech to the Calvinist and the Unitarian.' Perhaps he read a little of himself into the 'bright boys and girls in New England,' when in 1842 he wrote to Carlyle: 'They are all religious, but they hate the Churches.' It is evident from the *Address* and from other utterances that the historical element in Christianity never appealed much to him: 'We shall look back, peradventure, to Christianity as to a rosary on which, in the morn of existence, we learned to count our prayers.' It was this which enabled him to delight in Swedenborgian interpretations of Scripture, which were utterly inaccurate and unhistorical; it was enough for him that the sentiment was true and eternal. Apparently, however, even he was sometimes afraid lest the temper of negation and criticism might carry men too far.

'It is not good to say with too much precision and emphasis that we are encroached upon by the claims of Jesus in the current theology: it brings us into a cold, denying, unreligious state of mind.'

That state of mind was never Emerson's own. His positive assertions were always so essentially religious and believing that they have lent wings to many who have small sympathy with the more negative side of his position.

Emerson's writings appeared in the following sequence: in 1841, *Essays* (including 'History,' 'Self-Reliance,' 'Compensation,' 'Spiritual Laws,' 'Friendship,' 'The Oversoul,' etc.); in 1844, *Essays*, 2nd Series (including 'The Poet,' 'Experience,' 'Character,' 'Manners,' 'Nominalist and Realist,' 'New England Reformers,' etc.); in 1849, *Miscellanies* (including 'Nature,' 'The American Scholar,' the 'Address to the Divinity Class,' 'Man the Reformer,' 'The Times,' 'The Conservative,' 'The Transcendentalist,' etc.), and in the same year *Representative Men*. In 1851 he united with W. H. Channing and J. F. Clarke in the *Memoirs of Margaret Fuller Ossoli*. In 1856, *English Traits* appeared; in 1860, *Conduct of Life*; in 1870, *Society and Solitude*; in 1875, *Letters and Social Aims*; in 1878, *Fortune of the Republic*. His first volume of *Poems* was published in 1846; *May-day and other Pieces* appeared in 1867; *Selected Poems* in 1876. After his death the following appeared: in 1884, *Poems* (new and revised edition), another volume of *Miscellanies*, and one of *Lectures and Biographical Sketches*; in 1893, *The Natural History of Intellect*, and other papers. In 1903, the re-issue of the *Complete Works* began in the Centenary edition; and in 1909–10 the first four vols. of the *Journal* were published.

Emerson died at Concord, where his peaceful home had been for nearly half a century, on 27th April 1882.

2. Characteristics.—Emerson's works are a collection of miscellaneous counsels and oracles, and not the logical working out of any system of thought. But a few things stand out visibly through the whole.

(*a*) One is his immense and inexhaustible value as *an ethical teacher*. Even those whose religious position is different from his owe him in the ethical realm a vast debt of gratitude—not least for his gospel of self-reliance, his insistence on the duty of self-respect and the obligation to listen to the imperial voice of one's own soul. Linked with this there is his deep sense of the worth of the individual.

'God enters by a private door into every individual. . . . Everybody knows as much as the *savant*. The walls of rude minds are scrawled over with facts, with thoughts. They shall one day bring a lantern and read the inscription' (*Intellect*).

If this emphasis on self-trust has its dangers, Emerson guards against them by instilling a sense of responsibility and of the greatness of life; he shows us in prose and poetry the scorn that is in the eyes of the passing days if we do not make good use of their gifts:

'Truly it demands something godlike in him who has cast off the common motives of humanity and has ventured to trust himself for a taskmaster' (*Self-Reliance*).

Two qualities make him an ethical teacher most bracing and helpful to the young. One is his note of good cheer—his sense of the ethical value of hope. Here comes in the doctrine of compensation; his sense of the utility of scepticisms; his vision of the glory of living in the present age.

'I rejoice that I live when the world is so old. There is the same difference between living with Adam and living with me as in going into a new house, unfinished, damp, and empty, and going into a long-occupied house where the time and taste of its inhabitants has accumulated a thousand useful contrivances, has furnished the chambers, stocked the cellars, and filled the library. . . . O ye lovers of the past, judge between my houses! I would not be elsewhere than I am' (*Journal*, ii. 71).[1]

The other is his general manliness and closeness to life, his insistence on concentration, on thoroughness, on discipline; this is even clearer in the later writings, where there is perhaps less mysticism and more guidance for the highway—his head is

would do well to make the Cunard steamers the subject of examination in regard to their literary and ethical influence. . . . We go to school to Europe. We imbibe a European taste. Our education, so-called—our drilling at college and our reading since—has been European, and we write on the English culture and to an English public, in America and in Europe.'

[1] On this, see art. by W. Robertson Nicoll, mentioned under Literature. Cf. the passage at the end of 'Worship' (*Conduct of Life*) on the new church to be founded on moral science, 'at first cold and naked, a babe in a manger again.'

[1] Cf. *The Problem*, the poem in which, after his praise of 'the Shakespeare of Divines,' he concludes:

'And yet, for all his faith could see,
I would not the good bishop be.'

less in the clouds and his feet are more upon the earth. He can be very searching, this sage of the highway:

'A day is a more magnificent cloth than any muslin; the mechanism that makes it is infinitely cunninger; and you shall not conceal the sleezy, fraudulent, rotten hours you have slipped into the piece, nor fear that any honest thread, or straighter steel, or more inflexible shaft, will not testify in the web' (*Power*).

(*b*) Along with this ethic there goes a something that is not quite a theology: let us call it an *almost theology*—a firmament that is not fashioned according to the ancient star-maps, but is real enough to provide a sky for the earth and a dew for the tender grass. The typical piece here is the *Oversoul*. Why should I so boldly trust my intuitions? Because intuition is reception: one chief part of our business in this world is to receive. Emerson had been a critic of the accepted theologies from his youth up:

'It seemed to me when very young that on this subject (*Compensation*) life was ahead of theology, and the people knew more than the preachers taught.'

The critic in his turn has often been criticized for his theological indifferentism and for his leanings towards Pantheism. Yet, if he leaves God vague and undefined, readers of different standpoints can read their own beliefs into his large conceptions and get great help from his essentially religious spirit. 'Shall I not call God the Beautiful, who daily showeth Himself so to me in His gifts?' That is almost enough theological definition for him. If a Christian preacher were turning Emerson's pages in search of illustrations for Scripture texts, there are two texts that would draw to themselves a special number of thoughts and phrases. One is St. Paul's counsel, 'Let each man be fully assured in his own mind' (Ro 14^{5}); the other is the Psalmist's prayer, 'Let the beauty of the Lord our God be upon us' (Ps 90^{17}). Here at least is much to live by—a glory in the heavens and a firm path upon the earth. In regard to the doctrine of immortality, he was also lacking in definition, though he was optimistic throughout. Sometimes he spoke vaguely and impersonally, sometimes more warmly and in terms of a personal hope.

'All the comfort I have found teaches me to confide that I shall not have less in times and places that I do not yet know.'

In his later years he is said to have spoken sometimes of reunion with those who had gone on before.

(*c*) Through all the writings there appears most vividly *the man*. The very limitations and defects of the teaching, which are plain enough, are the limitations of the man. He had not the gift of ordered and consecutive thinking: he wrote once to a friend:

'I do not know what arguments are in reference to any expression of a thought. I delight in telling what I think; but if you ask me how I dare say so, or why it is so, I am the most helpless of mortal men.'

A good deal of criticism is disarmed by this frank confession. Beside his avoidance of life's more tragic and terrible themes in his teaching, there may be placed the fact that in common life he hated to hear people speak of their ailments. Some may regard this as a virtue and others as a defect; but most people who speak of their distempers weaken themselves by so doing, and he may have deliberately chosen in his writings to leave the shadows to others and to point the sunlit path where men could have the maximum of courage and strength. There are indications in the earlier pages of the Journal that he was by no means without a sense of personal sin, especially at the time when his life was first enriched by love, and humbled by his call to the ministry. Did he outgrow these feelings as if they were 'the soul's mumps and measles and whooping-coughs'? One thing is sure, that, even if he left behind the shadow of sin, he did not leave behind the shadow of sorrow; and his journals give hints of a life not all complacency, with veiled depths of brooding and pain. But through it all there breathes the spirit of a singularly lofty character—the man who is more than all his words. His later years were surrounded by a reverence such as is given to few men while they are still alive. Lowell wrote in 1868:

'For us the whole life of the man is distilled in the clear drop of every sentence, and behind each word we divine the force of a noble character, the weight of a large capital of thinking and being.'

Even to those who are much further removed, that force and weight still make themselves felt; to few writers are they bound by so strong a tie of personal admiration.

3. Poetical genius.—Widely different estimates have been made of Emerson's worth as a poet. Some tell us that here is the Emerson who counts, and that all else is nothing by comparison: others again are offended by his comparative lack of form and music, and deal with his poetry in the somewhat condescending and ungracious fashion adopted by Matthew Arnold. Appreciation will always vary according to the value placed by the critic upon melody or upon thought: some will despise the ship because she labours in making progress; others will prize her because of the wealthy freight she bears. Emerson's description of one of the Persian poets who influenced him so greatly might be applied to himself—'a river which makes its own shores': when the river is doing that, it may break through the ordinary channels of expression, and cut across the conventional and ordered beauties of the lyric landscape; but he who has eyes for force and fullness will find something here to study and to admire. Yet even the critic who seeks form and melody might find something to haunt his heart in the slow undulations of the poem beginning—

'I heard or seemed to hear the chiding Sea
Say, Pilgrim, why so late and slow to come?'

or in the severe dignity of *Days* and *Terminus*, or in the tenderness of *Threnody*, or in the lyric simplicity of *Thine eyes still shined*, and *If my darling should depart*. Lord Morley's estimate is just: 'Taken as a whole, Emerson's poetry is of that kind which springs, not from excitement of passion or feeling, but from an intellectual demand for intense and sublimated expression.' It will, therefore, have its appeal to a limited number. The Muse is here who

'ransacks mines and ledges
And quarries every rock,
To hew the famous adamant
For each eternal block';

and, though there is at least a little of the kindred Muse who

'lays her beams in Music,
In music every one,
To the cadence of the whirling world
Which dances round the sun,'

the impression left on the whole is one of grave severity which will always find a fit audience, though never a large one.

4. Influence.—Few writers of the 19th, or indeed of any century, have exerted a wider influence than Emerson. 'A strain as new and moving and unforgettable as the strain of Newman or Carlyle or Goethe'—so M. Arnold describes the impression made in England when Emerson's message first began to sound across the sea. That influence has grown steadily, and has left its mark on many notable lives of varying type; it would be easy to gather testimonies from many biographies (*e.g.* those of Tyndall, R. W. Dale, Henry Drummond) where this indebtedness is confessed. And, though there are some who feel that he did not do complete justice to certain great happenings of long ago which are still 'towering o'er the wrecks of time,' they will join with others in their gratitude for an influence so high, so pure, and so helpful. And they will put Emerson among the most accessible of the books which are able to lead them away from the shallows and the common-places, 'into the heart of sacred cities, into palaces and temples.'

LITERATURE.—The *Journal* alluded to above, 4 vols. 1909–10; the authorized Life by J. E. Cabot, Boston, 1887; the monograph by O. W. Holmes (*American Men of Letters* series, Boston, 1885); *Correspondence of Carlyle and Emerson*, 1834–1872, ed. C. E. Norton, Boston, 1883. There is an excellent bibliography of Emerson by G. W. Cooke (Boston, 1908). The following are also useful: O. B. Frothingham, *Transcendentalism in New England*, Boston, 1876; Moncure D. Conway, *Emerson at Home and Abroad*, Boston, 1883; A. Bronson Alcott, *R. W. Emerson, Philosopher and Seer*, Boston, 1882. Of articles, lectures, etc., the following may be mentioned: Lecture by A. Birrell, 1903; art. by W. Robertson Nicoll in *N. Amer. Review*, clxxvi. (May 1903); J. M. Robertson in *Modern Humanists*, London, 1895; Morley's preface to *Collected Works*, London, 1883; M. Arnold in *Discourses in America*, London, 1885; Lowell in *My Study Windows*, Boston, 1871, and subsequent editions. The works have been published in the Riverside ed. (12 vols., Boston, 1883–94); and the Centenary ed., Boston and New York, 1903, etc.; also in England, 6 vols. ed. Morley (1883).

J. M. E. ROSS.

EMOTIONS.—The present article will deal with the emotions in their ethical bearings, *i.e.* considered as springs of moral action. For the more strictly psychological aspect, see art. MIND. Emotion may be regarded as a compound of feeling and impulse. It belongs to the natural constitution of man, and is distinguished from both intelligence and moral volition. The significance we assign to the emotions in Ethics will vary according to our view of the foundations of morality.

I. *HISTORICAL SKETCH.*—**1. The emotions in Greek ethics.**—Greek ethics from the time of Socrates was essentially based upon knowledge; and as this intellectual conception more and more prevailed, the place of the emotions tended of necessity to become correspondingly less.

(1) *Plato* enumerates three faculties of the soul, viz. the appetitive (ἐπιθυμητικόν), the impulsive or spirited (θυμοειδές), and the rational (λογιστικόν), each having its appropriate virtue; and these three re-appear in the State (which is but a magnified personality) as the several ranks of artisans, warriors, and philosophers. This view gives due recognition to the emotions, since each faculty has its own virtue, and the harmony of all is justice, defined as τὰ αὑτοῦ πράττειν ('each doing its part'). In accordance with his theory of 'goods,' which does not exclude pleasure, Plato aims at the harmony of all the faculties, declining to suppress either desire or courage. Thus the virtue of the appetitive faculty is its obedience to and service of the rational; the same holds good of the spirited part, whose independence, however, is to some extent recognized in Plato's demand that it shall side with reason. Just as in the individual the supremacy must belong to reason—the charioteer of the two steeds—so is it in the human macrocosm, the State, which ought to embody the Idea of the Good. Here, then, neither pleasure, nor desire, nor courage is discarded; they are but subordinated to the harmonizing rule of the rational faculty. Again, however, since Plato really regards the latter alone as authoritative, and since in the State the classes corresponding to the ἐπιθυμητικόν and the θυμοειδές, more especially the former, exist only to obey,—the philosophers having within themselves a sufficiency of light, and being, in fact, the only true men,—desire and emotion now appear as something supplementary, having no concern with the pure Idea or with virtue as such. Thus Plato's estimate of the emotions varies according as the ideal he contemplates is absolute, or one accommodated to the actual world. In relation to the former, the emotions have no value; in relation to the latter, they fill a necessary place in a harmonious earthly life, so long as they discharge their function under the control of reason, and thereby contribute to the harmonious activity of the good man and of the State. Plato's sincere concern for the realization of such a harmony is seen in his theory of education, which prescribes Gymnastic, that valour may be braced for the task of keeping desire in leash; and Music, that it may be preserved from truculence. Yet he is equally emphatic in holding that Music must not enervate, as the strains of the Phrygian mode are wont to do, and that, in particular, the drama must not inflame the emotions, which ought rather to be restrained by reason.

(2) A still greater influence is assigned to the emotions by *Aristotle*. For him, as for Plato, the highest virtue consists in knowledge, which in its perfection is Divine; but he differentiates the ethical from the dianoetic virtues, and associates morality with the natural life. Just as he finds true happiness in a virtuous activity, and yet recognizes other sources of happiness,—the organic appetites, or, at all events, wealth, honour, friendship, absence from pain,—so he attaches the ethical virtues to the natural impulses and the πάθη. The πάθη belong to the good side of human nature, but require training. The emotions are, therefore, not to be suppressed, but to be kept within proper bounds. In this way he distinguishes between θηριότης (sub-human grossness) and virtue. The intermediate stage is self-denial, in which the desires, not yet overcome and still active, are being fought against; while true virtue is first attained in the 'mean,' in which the desires are reduced to due proportions, and thereby brought under the sway of reason. Thus, according to Aristotle, none of the πάθη, *i.e.* the affective states of the soul, which give rise to pleasure or pain—covetousness, anger, fear, love, hate, desire, sympathy, envy—are in themselves bad: they are simply natural; but, in order to become ethical, they must be duly restrained. He thus recognizes certain psychical states which are capable of virtue, but not fully virtuous, *e.g.* modesty, which stands midway between shamelessness and bashfulness. They are all, in fact, natural emotions, which provide the requisite raw material for morality, but are not themselves moral. As contrasted with the dianoetic virtues, the ethical consist in the restraining of desire and emotion within the limits of the mean through rational intelligence and discipline—an end partly subserved by Art, whose function it is to purify from passion. Aristotle simply proceeds upon the theory that, as human beings, we require the goods of the body as the means of happiness, and that human virtue can rest only upon the measured control of our natural endowments and impulses. From human nature itself there issues a sort of non-purposive, instinctive action, but this is marked by instability. Virtue, on the other hand, is a stable and permanent condition, a proficiency based upon conscious volition (ἕξις προαιρετικὴ ἐν μεσότητι οὖσα τῇ πρὸς ἡμᾶς, ὡρισμένη λόγῳ); as ethical virtue, therefore, in contrast to dianoetic, it is the facility with which the πάθη and desires are brought within rational measure by habit. The particular virtues are then set in relation to such goods as pleasure, wealth, honour, society. Thus, valour has to do with pain, temperance with pleasure; in social intercourse, liberality stands midway between avarice and prodigality; meekness stands in the mean with respect to anger, as does the love of honour with respect to glory. Nevertheless, even Aristotle ranks the dianoetic virtues higher than the ethical, and follows Plato in regarding knowledge as the supreme good.

(3) This characteristic attitude to knowledge is adopted also in the later Greek systems, viz. Stoicism and Epicureanism. (*a*) The *Epicureans*, indeed, base their ethics on pleasure, but with them the supreme end is not, as with Aristippus, the mere momentary enjoyment, but *ataraxia*, which is not so very remote from the *apathia* of the Stoics. It is remarkable that, while, after the age of Phidias, Art tends to become more emotional, philosophy seeks salvation in freeing itself from the πάθη. Though Epicurus rejects sensual pleasure, he is still concerned with pleasure of a kind, namely, that which lasts beyond the momentary thrill. Since, however, the goods which yield pleasure are liable to change, he lays great emphasis upon the feeling of security, which is partly supplied, and indeed guaranteed, by the State; and also upon the *ataraxia* which can be maintained in the face of death itself. Epicurus desires to eliminate the transient factor in the emotions, to guard against both pain and fear, to oust the passions as being the source of suffering. In the condition of *ataraxia* the emotions are really restrained by knowledge, though pleasure is not excluded when unattended by pain. Rational intelligence must teach us how to live content with little, and without such pleasures as are not indispensable. This assumes a certain antagonism between the world and the pleasure-seeking man; and thus the latter must pass from all momentary excitement to the mood of *ataraxia*, which lasts, and is to be won by means of intelligence. Here we have a restriction of emotion which contrasts with the views not only of the Cyrenaics, but also of Aristotle; the idea of an actual mastery of the passions, or of using them as a means of self-realization, is alien to Epicurus; but, as his criterion of judgment is simply pleasure or pain, and since pleasure is not to be had, the sole aim of virtue is the utmost possible avoidance of pain, *i.e.* the independence of outward circumstances guaranteed by *ataraxia*. It is specially noteworthy that emancipation from fear is here regarded as the aim of the wise. The more timid the Epicureans are, and the more inclined they are, as eudæmonists, to shrink from the perturbations of pleasure and pain, the more eagerly do they shun every occasion of fear and press towards *ataraxia*.

(*b*) In this negative aim the Epicureans are at one with the *Stoics*. The moral problem of the Stoics is how to attain to *apathia*. They set the emotions at the very heart of individual morality; in fact, as their cosmopolitanism is no more than an ideal, their morality is simply the morality of the individual. The Stoic wise man is one who is free from all sorrow, engaged in purely rational action, and perfectly blessed therein. Moreover, a man must either be entirely wise, or else a fool. The passions constitute for the latter a false form of judgment, which springs from suffering, from dependence upon earthly things, for, under passion, everything is judged from a transient and limited point of view. The wise man, on the contrary, places himself in the articulate system of nature, and lives in harmony with nature's order. Thus, according to the Stoics, the passions are pleasure and pain, and, in regard to the future, fear and desire. Their grand aim is the attainment of *apathia*, *i.e.* complete freedom from the emotions. But the perfect happiness which the Stoics find in the perfect knowledge of the wise man is a stable condition of mind, which does not depend upon suffering, but is rather the agreeable sensation that accompanies freedom and energy, while even the pleasure yielded by the external world is unwarranted, being a kind of suffering. It is true that the Stoics did not carry their view of the exclusive value of virtue, any more than their theory of *apathia*, to its logical issues. After all, there do exist certain minor objects of human desire, such as health, riches, friendship, etc.; and, though happiness does not depend upon these, yet there is a certain gratification in possessing them—hence the doctrine of *apathia* cannot be fully carried out. Nevertheless, the Stoics hold that the wise man will not become the slave of such things. In reality, virtue is sufficient for happiness, and, though the wise man cannot evade the feelings of pleasure and pain, he can rise above them. Like the Epicureans, the Stoics stand at the culmination of Greek thought; they withdraw from the external world to the internal, and find the 'life according to nature' in that life alone which is in harmony at once with the law of nature and with that of reason. They set a high value upon self-preservation—an end which, being in full accord with perfect freedom, manifests itself in indifference to painful experiences, and permits the wise man to evince his oneness with the supreme, all-pervading Deity.

The main trend of Greek ethics is towards the supremacy of reason, and, while in Plato and Aristotle reason appears as the harmonizing principle that controls emotion, it is for the Stoics and Epicureans the sole principle, since all natural enjoyment of the world and its goods has ceased, and a mood of pessimism dominates everything. There had been, as the Stoics believed, but few wise men in the past, and a multitude of fools. Their ideal is to be wholly free from all painful experiences whatsoever—in a word, from the πάθη. Thus, wherever knowledge is regarded as the formative ethical force, and the will is associated with the process of judgment, the emotions can have no proper place in Ethics at all, and, in fact, must be assigned finally, as in the Stoa, to defective understanding.

2. In Jewish and Early Christian ethics.—The emotions perform a very different function in a sphere where morality is an affair of the will, as, *e.g.*, in Judaism. In Jewish ethics the will is determined by the emotions of fear and hope—fear of punishment and hope of reward. The commandments are given by God's absolute will, and, as it is the same authoritative Will, and no mere natural nexus, which determines alike the penalty of transgression and the recompense of obedience, it is clear that the moral dynamic of volition cannot be knowledge of the Good as something in itself valuable, but only fear and hope. It is true that trust in God and love to God had also a place in Judaism; but it was a subordinate one, and they were much obscured by the other two.

The emotions had a recognized place also in the primitive Christian ethic, and have retained this in sundry forms till the present day. Despite the ascetic, pessimistic strain intermittently heard in the NT ethic, the emotions fill an important rôle. For one thing, love is looked upon as the supreme ethical motive: love, as an amalgamation of feeling with a definite and permanent direction of the will, is the emotion which in Christianity is exalted to the grand creative affection of the soul. Love to God is the standing motive of the moral and religious life. The natural impulses and feelings are, indeed, reckoned sinful—not, however, because they are intrinsically corrupt, but because they have assumed the command and taken the wrong way. Self-seeking and love of the world have supplanted the love of God. Emotion, accordingly, is not to be eradicated, but simply turned to its proper use, and this is achieved when it becomes the support and inspiration of good volition. But such volition is directed towards God, and love to God embraces love to man, since all men are called to become the children of God, while, on His part, God is the Father of all. Thus, according to the Fourth Gospel, the Christian is filled with an enduring joy, a happiness that cannot be taken away. His besetting emotion is a permanent and blessed spirit of love, which predisposes him to good works. Fear of punishment and hope of reward may still remain—vestiges of Jewish ethics,—but perfect love driveth out fear. Nevertheless, the pre-eminence of love in primitive Christianity does not involve the suppression of other emotions; they, too, are to be made auxiliaries of the spiritual life. St. Paul is a man of singularly fervid emotion—one in whom even anger is made to subserve his great task. And although, *inter alia*, the expectation of the Parousia was a specially potent factor in causing men to set less store than they now do by such earthly boons as marriage, social position, property, art, etc., and so to repress the natural feelings that cluster around these things, yet, as a compensation, the peculiar heritage of the individual was placed upon a new basis, inasmuch as every man had a vocation of infinite value, and every condition of life could be consecrated by the operation of a right spirit within. Here, then, provision was made for a deepening of spirit and a refinement of feeling such as are possible only where so high an estimate is placed upon personality.

In its further development, Christian morality presently shows a tendency to coalesce with Greek ideas, at least on the native soil of the latter. In *Clement of Alexandria* the Stoic *apathia* coalesces with the Christian principle of love. Along with the distinction between *gnosis* and *pistis*, between the esoteric, intellectual religion and the popular, there emerges the demand that the Christian Gnostic must be εἰς ἀπάθειαν θεούμενος ('deified unto *apathia*'), *i.e.* delivered from all passion—from the πάθη which originate in the distractions of sense. He must rise to the sphere of calm, clear knowledge; and, while not spurning the goods of the natural life, he must be independent of them. Nevertheless, he does not show himself apathetic towards his fellow-man; he, too, has a heart. Thus the possessor of *gnosis* does not repudiate his relations with the natural, and his *apathia* is toned down to something not unlike the Platonic 'temperance.'

In the West, the challenge of Christianity to the older civilization is much more emphatic. True, we find *Tertullian* speaking of the *anima naturaliter Christiana*; nevertheless, his ethical teaching—particularly in his Montanistic period—is hostile to all culture, and is directed towards the complete excision of desire, so that he might almost be called a Christian Cynic. Personally, however, he is highly emotional and passionate, and, especially as a Montanist, prone to let himself be carried away—even to the point of ecstasy—by feelings commonly thought to be symptomatic of inspiration. As a protest against the moral degeneracy of his age, he demands that Christians shall withdraw themselves from the public life of heathendom, which fosters the passions the Christian must eschew. Theatrical performances and second marriages are special perils. Tertullian advocates a stringent penitential discipline, and revives the opposition to all æsthetic culture of one's natural powers. He aims, not at the regulation, but at the complete exclusion, of all that culture bestows, even the culture of the emotions. Hence, too, the impassioned character of his renunciation of the heathen world. His fervour concentrates itself upon moral reform of a Christian, *i.e.* first of all, an anti-pagan type. In the white heat of his enthusiasm, 'conformity to nature,' which he regards as also in line with Christianity, appears to him to consist in perfect simplicity of life, in the repression of *cupiditas* and *concupiscentia*. Pagan civilization has fanned the flames of passion and desire, and has taken man away from his natural and simple condition.

As this antagonism to heathen culture develops, however, it eventually becomes an antagonism to all that is natural, which is declared to be corrupt. *Ambrose* desiderates a complete independence of earthly joy and sorrow: 'non in passione esse sed victorem passionis esse beatum est.' Property is grounded in selfishness: 'pecuniae contentus est iustitiae forma.' Our possessions are to be placed at the disposal of love by works of beneficence. *Augustine* knows only of a human nature that is entirely corrupt with original sin—a *massa perditionis*. With him, emotion has no standing save in religion, in man's ardent love of God, which at its highest he combines with the eudæmonistic anticipation of future reward and the fear of future punishment.

3. In monastic and mediæval ethics.—Monasticism rejects all earthly goods—as a condition of entire consecration to the love of God. Since the natural is here regarded as wholly alien to the Divine, or at least as of no concern in religion, all natural propensities and feelings die away in love to God. Morality being in itself inadequate, all the more decisively is emotion transferred to the sphere of religion; and the monastic mysticism of the West allows a much greater scope to the emotional element in that sphere than does that of the East, just because the West lays the main emphasis upon a will wholly surrendered to God, and the East upon knowledge. Even the ecstatic love of God spoken of by Dionysius the Areopagite is much less emotional than the Divine *furor* of many a mediæval mystic, and the subjective factor comes out still more forcibly when the enjoyment of God, the exuberant bliss of Divine intercourse, is emphasized. According to Plato, it was a blessed thing to gaze upon the Idea; but Augustine and the mystics of the Middle Ages lay yet more stress upon the will which is zealous for God and brings beatitude to man. But while religious emotion thus threatens to absorb every other concern of life—just as the fervent zeal of the Church counted earthly interests as nothing in comparison with religious interests, and so sent the heretic to the stake—yet mediæval morality is not without a mundane aspect, as appears in the ethics of Abelard and Aquinas.

(*a*) *Abelard*, indeed, lays all emphasis upon the disposition, but he sees in Christianity the assertion of that law of nature which was recognized and obeyed by the philosophers of old. The good is to be willed for its own sake; hence penitence must be something more than external works, and must have, not fear of punishment, but love to God, for its motive. Abelard accepts the ancient cardinal virtues; in short, he does not propose to set up an antithesis between natural and Christian morality, and so he traces all the virtues to their one source in character—to love—while he also regards sin as issuing from the heart, and holds that even penitence must spring from love. But this deriving of morality from love does not involve a contradiction between love and human nature, for he gives no recognition to original sin.

(*b*) We find a different estimate of natural morality and the emotions in *Aquinas*: with him, indeed, *gratia infusa* and love are supernatural gifts of the Spirit; still, he accepts the cardinal, as well as the theological, virtues; and, since in his doctrine of goods he is ready to do justice to the State (though ultimately subordinating it to the Church), he discerns various stages in the cardinal virtues themselves. Nevertheless, even the highest of these stages only serves to accentuate his antagonism to the natural. The cardinal virtues are *exemplariter* in God; the lowest grade is political virtue; and, as it is the duty of man to turn to God, so far as in him lies, there are, between the *exemplares* and the *politicæ*, intermediate forms, viz. the *purgatoriæ* and those of the *purgatus animus*. Whereas the political stage is bound up with earthly things, and chastens the natural emotions, the *purgatoriæ* work negatively towards making man like God, so that, e.g., *temperantia* relinquishes earthly things, so far as nature permits; while, again, *temperantia* at the level of the *purgatus animus* has done with earthly cares altogether. Aquinas's doctrine of the several grades of virtue amounts, then, to this: the political virtues are genuine virtues; the higher species curb desire and feeling as far as possible, while the highest of all do away with them entirely. Nevertheless, he still thinks in terms of dualism, for, according to him, true perfection consists in withdrawing from the world: 'Nutrimentum caritatis imminutio cupiditatis.' Thus, on the one hand, the ancient virtues, even in the political sphere, are recognized, and the natural affections not proscribed; yet, on the other, both are in the end construed ascetically, under the idea of grace, so that there remains at last only love to God in contradistinction to all that is of the world, and the cardinal virtues are merged in the grace that is poured from above.

Not only, however, was it impossible in mediæval ethics to suppress the affections, or deny their claims on a lower stage of virtue; they were actually made subservient to religion and the Church. A supernatural love to God, annulling every earth-born affection, was, of course, the ideal; but, when this ideal failed the Church in her capacity of teacher, she appealed to fear, menacing the transgressor with penalty—in hell or purgatory or the present world—and so engendering a spirit not so much of hostility to evil as of mere abject terror. Such emotions as love, fear, hope, and repentance in the ecclesiastical sense, operated with tremendous power in the Middle Ages, while the actual moral practice of life was but little regarded.

4. In modern ethics.—In the modern period down-trodden human nature comes to its own, so that morality is now based entirely upon it. Philosophical ethics has at length cast off the trammels of theology, and we may distinguish three tendencies in its development, viz. the *Rationalistic*, which in sundry forms bases morality upon human reason, and is thus akin to the classical view; the *Naturalistic*, which would find a foundation in impulse and feeling; the *Synthetic*, which aims at combining the other two. Alongside of these has existed since the Reformation a *Theological* ethics, in both a Protestant and a Roman Catholic form. We commence with this.

(*a*) In *Roman Catholic ethics* the bilateral view of a fully-developed monastic morality and a virtue that is political and earthly has been not only maintained but strengthened. On the one hand, in the monastic system all the natural affections are repressed; the *Jesuits*, in fact, demand the obedience of a corpse, and so train the whole man that, deprived of all personal volition, he hears his conscience in the command of his superior, in face of which every desire and emotion must be still. On the other hand, just because such a vocation is not possible for all, and because a morality of that type is uncontrolled by any unifying principle, the widest possible scope is given to casuistry; and this likewise has been carried to its furthest limits by the Jesuits.

(*b*) *Protestant ethics*, it is true, started from the assumption of the radical corruption of human nature, not, however, as seeing in religion something alien to man, but actually conceding a certain intrinsic value to the goods of this life. Thus, *Melanchthon*, in the first edition of his *Loci*, holds that selfishness, as contrary to the love of God, is the cardinal propensity of man in his state of original sin, and that the unchastened affections are but the various aspects of this selfishness, constantly repressing or modifying one another according to their several degrees of intensity, yet never attaining to any moral worth; still, we cannot fairly infer from his words that the emotions are incapable of being utilized in the service of love. Above all, the Christian has assurance of his salvation; he has the internal testimony of the Holy Spirit, with the attendant feeling of security and blessedness from which he acts—just as, according to *Calvin*, the motive of moral conduct is found in the consciousness of election, since the indwelling Spirit manifests Himself in a man's will and feeling, and he acts from courage, as one assured of final triumph. A Christian's activity, however, is not confined to the Church, or wholly directed to religious ends, for every calling is sacred, and love to one's neighbour, as *Luther* maintained, can be practised in every sphere of life.

Now, all this might have led to an ethic which would touch the character to its noblest issues, which would do justice to the earthly life, and which, accordingly, far from crushing the natural promptings of feeling and desire, would enlist them in the service of love—a consummation exemplified, for instance, in the Protestant estimate of conjugal love. But as man's inherent corruption came to be increasingly emphasized, and as his relation to God gradually came to dwarf every other relation, it became more and more difficult to vindicate the natural, emotional, impulsive life, or to see anything but sin in its spontaneous manifestations. This tendency is exemplified in *Pietism* (*q.v.*), which, in its timid scrupulosity, looked upon the natural life as full of temptations and obstacles to religion. All that is bright and genial in life was frowned upon; courage and joy were crushed by fear and repentance—though these, it is true, had to do with sin rather than with punishment. Protestantism, in fact, with its emphatic assertion of man's native corruption and its all-absorbing interest in the Divine, on the one hand, and with its lofty estimate of the earthly calling and of the culture of the Christian's natural disposition, his feelings, affections, and desires, on the other, had not even yet emancipated itself from an inner conflict—the antinomy which strikingly re-appears in the most recent expositions of Protestant ethics (cf. Luthardt, Franck, H. Weiss, and others).

(*c*) *Naturalistic ethics*, having freed itself from theology, finds its starting-point in the instinctive feelings themselves. This school has found its main expansion in England and France.

Agrippa of Nettesheim had called attention to the function of hate and love in the realm of nature generally, as also to their effects upon human nature, and the influence of passion upon conduct. *Thomas More*, in his *Utopia*, had promised the highest possible degree of unruffled gratification for one and all. The sensualistic *Telesius* had drawn attention to the impulse of self-preservation, to which he traced the emotions, thus recognizing their function in the interests of life itself, and finding virtue in the rational perception of what is useful or injurious. The Aristotelian *Cremonini*, too, had asserted that the dynamic of life was not the intelligence *simpliciter*, but rather the soul which knows and *loves*, and that, the emotions being rooted in the bodily frame, morality must needs rest upon a natural science of the soul; conduct, in fact, is connected with matter, and is dependent upon the natural warmth of the temperament, and the feelings arising from it. *Montaigne* also would connect morality with nature, and insists that it is tied to the *complexions et inclinations naturelles*.

It was *Bacon* who first tried, by the scientific method of historical and psychological induction, to derive morality from experience, who combined it with the natural impulses, with the *lex suitatis* and the *lex communionis*, and maintained that the emotions must be taken into consideration as being the stimuli of the will, which is the grand factor in morality. According to Bacon, the proper function of ethics is so to regulate the emotions as to secure their obedience to reason, that is, to the laws won from experience, which enable us to harmonize the interests of self-preservation with the interests of social life. He thus discriminates the two fundamental impulses, the self-regarding and the 'other-regarding,' which have continued to play their part in Naturalistic ethics till the present day.

Hobbes, with his 'homo homini lupus,' emphasized the impulse of self-preservation in its most extreme form, making it the rationale of the State, whose function it is to keep the self-directed impulse within bounds. The social motive, he holds, is not primordial, but springs from fear, which, begotten by the individual's desire to protect himself, and by his sense of weakness, compels him to compromise with society. The State exists for the sake of peace and security, which enable the individual to live according to nature within the limits prescribed by the law; in other words, the individual, in virtue of that security, should have all the enjoyment the State can allow. Hobbes's politics and ethics are thus based upon the desire of self-preservation and fear—the necessary results of the war of each against all others.

The doctrines of Hobbes form a standing element in *English Utilitarianism*, though the latter lays a stronger emphasis upon the idea of political liberty. Utilitarianism received its classical expression from the hands of *Bentham*: its cardinal principle is the greatest possible good for each and all. It bases morality upon the pursuit of happiness, and its sole aim is the greatest happiness of the greatest number.

In support of his thesis, Bentham appeals to psychology; he tests pleasure and pain by reference to differences among individuals, as a means of discovering rules by which pleasure may be most effectively secured and pain avoided, and thereby the highest possible amount of happiness obtained. These rules attain to universal validity by means of the various sanctions—the natural, that of public opinion, the political, and the religious—the authority of which, again, is derived from the pleasures or pains associated respectively with obedience or disobedience to the rules themselves. Thus pleasure and pain, hope and fear, are made the motives for the observance of the very rules of conduct which are designed to secure the greatest pleasure. Here morality becomes a doctrine of prudence—the art of calculating the greatest happiness.

A simpler and less artificial form of the theory that the ethical motive is formed by the pleasures and pains connected with the instinct of self-preservation is found in the doctrine that unrestricted competition always gives the victory to the fittest, and that, accordingly, moral progress is the result of natural selection. For, after all, it is the instinct of self-preservation which produces that struggle for existence in which the strongest survive. The dynamic of social progress is thus found in the desire for power.

Another form of naturalistic ethics would found morality upon a combination of self-love with the *social instinct*—a favourite resource with the *Scottish School*, who, after the example of *Cumberland* and others, put natural benevolence on a level with selfishness. According to the Scottish School, moral goodness springs from benevolence—the sympathetic impulse—which produces the immediate reflex-feeling of approbation.

This principle holds a special place in the theories of *Hutcheson*, *Hume*, and *Adam Smith*. Morality rests upon sympathy—sympathy first of all with one's own motives; it is really the retributive impulse—whether in the form of gratitude or of revenge—that we commend. Similarly, the sympathetic emotion has to do with those who come into active relations with us. The immediate emotional judgment assumes in particular cases an ethical character, and is formulated in general rules. Of decisive importance for morality are those sympathetic emotions which are designed to temper the others, particularly hope and fear. *Hume* traces national character, love of fame, and the imitative faculty to sympathy, and he likewise regards custom and tradition as expressions of the sympathy that subsists between successive generations. The State, too, owes its existence to sympathy—to the sense of a common weal; and to custom, in the form of loyalty to the laws and the authorities.

But, just as Hobbes was unable to ignore the social factor in morality, so those who ground their ethics upon sympathy cannot leave the purely individual interest out of account; and thus, while sympathy with what produces the good or evil of others is the determinative factor, stress is also laid upon the satisfaction experienced by the individual who yields himself to that sympathy.

Herbert Spencer, too, places altruism, which rests upon the social impulse, above egoism, though from a somewhat different point of view, asserting that man, after long experience and by means of the discipline which connects pleasure and pain with the growth of the social and sympathetic propensities, finally comes to see that, by aiming at the good of others and the common good, he really serves his own ends better than by indulging his egoistic impulses. *J. S. Mill* also makes happiness the leading principle of his ethics, and lays the chief emphasis upon the adjustment of the individual interest to the social. *Helvetius*, one of the French representatives of the ethics of emotion, called attention to the fact that in the last resort it is self-love which prompts us to act for the common good—though in such manner that we combine private with public ends. Man, indolent by nature, is roused to a sense of personal interest only by passion, and it is, therefore, of importance that the higher passions be regulated by habit, and that, in particular, the State, by its appeal to pleasure and pain, shall mould them, and by its discipline counteract the work of chance. *Holbach* (*Système de la nature*, 1821) believes that reason is nothing but the capacity for selecting the passions which conduce to happiness. At a later period *Comte*, *Taine*, and *Littré* based ethics upon the principle that the sympathetic impulse of altruism ought to prevail over egoism, thus emphasizing, in contrast to the English view, the ascendancy of the social over the individual factor. *Feuerbach* likewise held that morality reposes upon the desire of happiness, upon a reconciliation of the claims of the *I* and the *Thou* ('Tuism'). The pessimistically tinged theory of *Schopenhauer*—practically that of Buddhism also—which regards pity as the source of morality, may be classed as a variety of the 'sympathetic' hypothesis.

(*d*) In sharp antithesis to the foregoing views stands *Rationalistic ethics*, which would reduce the emotions to their lowest level. But if the ethics of emotion cannot entirely dispense with the intellect, neither can the Rationalistic school disregard feeling; for it is a fact of everyday observation that emotion is controlled only by emotion, and that the will is never moved by pure reason alone.

Spinoza and Kant may be taken as representatives of this Rationalistic view. *Spinoza* sets out from self-conservation. The absolute Substance, with its attributes of thought and extension, is something active, and the various modes share, and maintain their existence, in this activity; in so far, however, as these modes are finite, they are wrought upon by others, and suffer. To this suffering correspond confused ideas, imaginations; and from these proceed the perverted emotions that rest upon the errors of an understanding subject to suffering. The primary affections are pleasure, pain, and, in relation to the future, desire. Pain we associate with some external arrest of power; pleasure, with an increment. But we judge things wrongly, in so far as we regard them from our own restricted point of view. Spinoza gives a magnificent exposition of the way in which the various affections are derived from the primary forms—by their relations either to time, to their respective objects, or to each other. The characteristic idea of this deduction is that, when man is under the inexorable control of the affections which may co-exist in a state of strife, he is in a condition of servitude. Accordingly, these affections are without value for moral ends, and must be cast aside. This is accomplished when we regard all things *sub specie æternitatis*, by means of the *amor Dei intellectualis*, the adequate ideas which dissolve the imaginations, and the activity of our rational essence, as directed upon the passions. The true good does not war against happiness; it shares in the active self-conservation of God, and reveals itself as creative intelligence. In this activity man is satisfied and blessed; he has the *acquiescentia in seipso*, and its concomitant *hilaritas*. Spinoza thus excludes the affections in so far as they rest on suffering, and will recognize only the happy consciousness that is bound up with the soul's own pure activity. So long as man is subject to the domination of the affections, it is well for him, in the interests of society, to let the more harmful be kept in check by the less harmful; as, for instance, when the State resorts to the fear of punishment, or concedes a partial indulgence to the less noxious affections, in order to counteract a greater danger by a less. The ethical view, however, goes deeper; it has regard only to the pure activity of the soul, with its attendant blessedness. According to Spinoza, therefore, the essential constituent of morality is the subjection of the affections to the authority of reason, which frees itself from the imaginations and keeps watch upon their inner movements. It is unnecessary to point out how closely he is allied to the Stoics.

The ethics of *Kant*, based upon the autonomy of the *a priori* practical reason, sets aside every motive which springs from inclination and passion. The only true ethical motive is reverence for the moral law. Kant's aversion to desire is such as lays him open to the charge of dualism, and gives an ascetic character to his ethical teaching. On analysis of this reverence for the law, however, we find that the element of feeling is by no means ignored. For, according to Kant, the moral law ought to kindle our hearts to a nobler pleasure, imbuing us with a true pride in the majesty of our practical reason, while also humbling us for our shortcomings. It is, in fact, this inner discord which gives rise to the sense of reverence for the law. Further, in the *Critique of Judgment*, Kant assigns an even more important function to emotion, basing the æsthetic judgment upon a spontaneous feeling, which he holds to be purely intellectual in character. This æsthetic judgment of emotion, again, with its claim to universality, he regards as preparatory to morality, as it habituates us to the love of the beautiful apart from any sensuous interest, and even to admire the sublime in opposition to any such interest.

A corresponding intellectual interpretation of morality was upheld in England by *Cudworth* and *Clarke*, who take their stand upon the intrinsic necessity of the moral relationships. According to Clarke, there exist eternal, unchangeable, and rationally instituted laws of righteousness, equity, goodness, and truth, which, like Kant, he combines with the idea of future retribution.

(*e*) *Synthetic or Mediating ethics*.—In *England*, however, the representatives of an *a priori* Rational ethics are eclipsed by those who would *combine* reason and emotion, of whom the most outstanding is *Shaftesbury*. Shaftesbury goes back to a 'moral sense'—a feeling of self-approval which attaches to the equipoise between selfishness and benevolence. When this equipoise, this inner adjustment, with its accompanying sense of satisfaction, becomes the object of thought, a judgment of approval is the result. In the harmony of our being, therefore, we discover an ideal of perfection, which, as appropriate to our nature, also involves a state of happiness. Religion, too, is estimated according to its capacity of strengthening or weakening our moral feelings. The Deity, being immanent in Nature, is the source of that cosmic harmony which finds an echo in our moral constitution. In fact, philosophy itself, according to Shaftesbury, is a passion for all that is good and beautiful. We are always seeking for unity and articulation amidst the manifold, and it is likewise these that we aspire to in the moral field—especially in the sphere of our emotions. We ought never to be moved to action save by inclinations that are worthy of the good disposition, and are at the same time in harmony with the system of which we form a part. Hence the propensities which make for the good of the whole should restrain those that are self-centred, since our individual good is involved in the general good. It is love, it is enthusiasm for the good, that elevates man; the enjoyment of love and friendship is really a participation in the harmony of the universe. Shaftesbury was wholly optimistic, believing, as he did, in a world-soul that works towards universal harmony and animates mankind. As against the sensualistic tendencies of his time, he speaks in the name of the rational, insisting upon harmony and unity, and yet not repudiating the affections, without which a moral life is, as he thinks, impossible.

While Shaftesbury holds strongly to the conviction that virtue is the manifestation of what is good in us, *Price* would rather emphasize the idea of duty. The latter derives morality from the primordial consciousness of obligation, and thus makes it its own support; it is not to be traced to states of feeling, since these are always controlled by reason. But though the ethical rests upon the rational, yet its operation is so far conditioned by emotion—by a lively spontaneous feeling that gives intensity to the process of rational intuition.

The *intuitive Scottish School* likewise founds morality upon immediate rational perception. Thus *Dugald Stewart* defines the ethical as a tendency—now become a principle—to act under the authority of conscience. The moral can be apprehended only by a direct intuition in conscience. Pity and sympathy lend support to this intuition, and beget an inclination to follow the lead of conscience. A similar attempt to conjoin rational intuition with emotion was made by *James Mackintosh*, who held that feelings of pleasure and displeasure in matters of character, so far as these feelings become springs of action, are given in conscience, which contains the norm for our conduct, and which is perfected by a process of reflexion that clarifies these immediate judgments of feeling; while, again, the natural altruistic tendencies urge us to obey the behests of the inner monitor.

In *Germany* the endeavour to bring the emotions within the scope of ethical rationalism has been made in various ways by Leibniz, Schiller, J. G. Fichte, Herbart, Schleiermacher, and others.

Like Shaftesbury, *Leibniz* is an optimist, and has a very mild view of evil. He believes in the pre-established harmony of the monads, the highest of which, since they can increase the intelligence which constitutes their nature, are capable of development. Each intelligent monad aims at perfection, at becoming an increasingly clear and rich reflexion of the world. Moreover, each will have regard to the others; each will rejoice in its own self-preservation only as it yields itself to the social impulse—the craving for the universal, for the all, for the harmony of love. This longing exists in every rational being, and is rooted in the nature of the universe. In this way Leibniz combines the natural and rational desire for perfection with the desire for happiness. The two are not at variance, for the intelligent monads cannot attain happiness save in harmony with all. Reason is thus in full accord with the natural impulses, and both work into each other's hands in the ethical sphere. Even the endeavour after perfection, belonging, as it does, to the very nature of spiritual beings, is bound up with pleasure. The feeling of perfection, or rather of advance towards perfection—for we never get beyond the process—is the highest pleasure; it is the joy of enhancing our own being; but along with this personal progress must always go a development of our interest in the good of others, since that is the only way in which we can become clear and truthful mirrors of the world. Self-love and love to others are quite compatible, and each is rooted in our rational constitution. Clearness of knowledge gives us insight into our own nature, and teaches us how to set our various emotions in right and natural relations by cultivating a stable disposition of heart appropriate to our nature, and by subordinating the momentary promptings of feeling to that permanent quality of soul which lays hold upon the highest. The possibility of this is given in our nature, which ever presses towards a universal harmony; and it is the part of religion, as faith in the pre-established harmony of the world, to reduce the discordant elements to unity.

Schiller also, following the lead of the ancients, intones the inner harmony of reason and sense. Obedience to reason must be amalgamated with joy. Sensuous desire must retain its function in the moral field; sense adds to the intensity of the ethical factor. Here, in fact, emotion is utilized as a means of deepening the moral law; reason exercises her authority so infallibly that she can safely admit the feelings to a subsidiary place in the ethical life. This condition is realized in the refined soul, while the truly noble spirit can adjust the claims of the sensuous and the moral in such a way as to make manifest the absolute superiority of reason to sense.

Of *Fichte* also it may be said that, though his ethics is of an entirely rationalistic cast, he does not take up so rigid an attitude towards desire as did Kant. He insists upon the free activity of reason, and the transformation of authority into liberty, into the spontaneity of intelligence. By treating our nature, however, as the material of duty, he is able not only to set forth a profusion of goods as the fruit of human activity, but also, by bringing into prominence the creative aspect of the moral character—its power of original production—to find a place for emotion in the moral realm. He recognizes a feeling of freedom and love, which, with the impulse of reason, furnishes a motive for conduct. Although we cannot on any account let pleasure have the last word, yet the complex of impulse and feeling in our nature forms the 'material of duty.' In point of fact, Nature herself has made provision for the ethical life; thus, the distinction of sex is the necessary antecedent of the family, and the hereditary resemblance between child and parent is the postulate of all fruitful education. Fichte does justice to individuality and its aspirations by his demand that every one should take up his peculiar ethical call with the insight of genius, and choose his profession freely; as also by tracing conjugal love, especially on the woman's side, to an act of willing surrender.

Herbart, too, unites emotion and reason. To begin with, he deduces five ethical ideas[1] from our judgments of pleasure or displeasure regarding relations of will. These five are inner freedom, perfection, benevolence, justice, and equity. He does not regard these relations of will as being even qualitatively free from emotion. But in the same way the ideas which are connected with the relations of individual wills have as their correlatives the various 'systems' of society; for example, the administrative system corresponds to benevolence, the system of culture to perfection—the highest possible development of every capacity; and spiritualized society—as presenting a great harmonious whole in which the individual as well as the various systems are articulated in perfect unity—to inner freedom. Here Herbart formulates, in contrast with Kant, an ideal doctrine of goods which has in view the highest good of each and all in its harmonious embodiment. If he thus gives prominence to the æsthetic view, he also explains that other pleasurable feelings may be enjoyed in the spiritualized society. He is not so far from the Scottish School. Moreover, he is at pains to show how the psychological mechanism may be enlisted in the service of these ideas, namely, by so utilizing all educational resources in their favour as to enable them to expel the antagonistic states of mind—feelings or motives—and permanently to maintain the upper hand.

[1] Herbart's five ideas are connected with Whewell's 'five axioms.'

We come, finally, to *Schleiermacher*, who still more pointedly combines the rational theory of ethics, as a speculative science, with the natural life as a whole and with the emotions. We see this in his general definition of ethics as the science whose task it is to exhibit the action of reason upon man's nature; in his derivation of all the natural endowments, all the psychical faculties of man, from that action; in the emphasis he lays upon natural individuality; and in his doctrine of goods, which makes human nature the symbol or organ of reason. In particular, we see it in the position which he concedes to feeling and the emotions; witness the fact that, in the main, he traces religion itself to feeling. Nevertheless, he too lays it down that the emotions must not of themselves stimulate to action; the feelings must be controlled by reason, and should act merely as indicators (*Anzeiger*) for our knowledge of particular moral tasks. After all, however, he is as little disposed to repress the emotions as to repress human nature itself. Emotion itself must become the organ of the ethical. Schleiermacher expressly opposes the Stoic *apathia*, and holds with Schiller that virtue shows itself in the facility with which the emotions are put into requisition. Thus he refuses to identify chastity with *apathia*, and maintains that, while sensual gratification should never be a motive *per se*, it is not to be discarded; it comes to its natural right when permeated by the spiritual. Patience, too, is something more than *apathia* towards unpleasant experiences. Such experiences cannot be allowed to stimulate the senses to independent action, but ought rather to prompt men to manifest their moral refinement. In a word, Schleiermacher desiderates the moral beauty which appears when the emotions are brought into harmony with the moral character, and work congenially in the service of the moral reason. Again, while he will not allow the attainment of pleasure and the avoidance of pain to rank as an independent moral end, yet—more particularly in his *Christian Ethics*—he regards serenity of soul, the bliss that attaches to the Christian consciousness of God, as yielding a motive for conduct. This quite accords, moreover, with the standpoint of his *Philosophical Ethics*, in which he even describes reason as a creative energy which is combined with pleasure with a view to action. In his *Monologues* he had already spoken with enthusiasm of the ethical genius of the individual who spends himself and all he has in the service of the community.

Summary.—The antithesis between rational and emotional ethics is of outstanding importance for the *development* of ethical theories. Those who find the basis of morality in reason alone insist most strenuously upon the immutability of ethical principles. Such is the case with Greek intellectualist ethics throughout, as well as with the modern rationalistic schools of Spinoza, Clarke, and Kant. The same holds good of those who find the ethical foundation in the Deity, and who place the emotions of hope and fear in the service of His established laws. But the case is completely altered when morality is founded upon the emotions. Here, in place of immutable norms fixed in reason, we find the psychological investigation of the origin of morality. To speak of an unchangeable moral law now becomes a mere irrelevancy, since moral law has no unconditional validity, but merely shows how the desire for happiness may best be satisfied, and how private or public good may be most effectively furthered. The emotions depend upon the external ever-changing world, finding their satisfaction in it alone, or, at least, not apart from it. An ethical doctrine which is founded upon emotion has, therefore, never more than a relative validity, and such injunctions as it gives apply only to particular circumstances. The naturalistic theory must, accordingly, have regard to the various forms of the moral consciousness, and must investigate that consciousness psychologically and historically both in its origin and in its variations, yet without ever reaching an absolutely valid moral law. For happiness can never get beyond the relative, as is shown by English and French Eudæmonism, and, most clearly of all, by Bentham's Utilitarianism.

It is a different matter when rational ethics gives recognition also to the emotional side of human nature. Here, on the one hand, the unconditional character of morality is upheld; while, on the other, the way in which the moral law is actually and concretely realized is not always the same. This suggests the idea of a historical progress, and thus arises the problem of how to harmonize, *by a process of moral development*, the whole natural endowment of impulse and feeling with reason. Accordingly, we find Schleiermacher maintaining that ethics must lay down the base-lines of the philosophy of history; but it was pre-eminently Hegel who gave currency to the idea of development, viewing the whole process of history as the evolution of reason. Though he gave, it is true, an intellectual interpretation of Nature, regarding it merely as a stadium of the Idea (a view which, of course, does not concern us here), he nevertheless distinguishes between Nature and Spirit *in concreto*, and sees the consummation of ethics neither in a natural Eudæmonism nor in the Kantian Rationalism, but in *Sittlichkeit*, 'established observance,' in which the antithesis between Nature and Spirit is reconciled, *i.e.* raised to a higher unity. If, according to Hegel, reason realizes itself in the State, yet he does not regard civic life as incompatible with the community of feeling, *i.e.* marriage; or with the community of interests and its complex of needs; or with the community of citizenship, or, in fact, with any particular relationship of the individual life that is partly conditioned by emotion; on the contrary, he finds a place for all of these, just as he finds the characteristic feature of the Christian period in the fact that it gives due recognition to the interests of the individual and his desire for happiness. The course of history shows us that the tendency to combine the rational and the emotional aspects of morality is constantly gaining ground.

II. *ANALYSIS AND EXPOSITION.*—It remains to consider the nature of the emotions and their varieties, as a step towards inquiring how we are to estimate them ethically and to utilize them in practice.

1. Nature and structure of the emotions.—What are the emotions? It is safe to say, for one thing, that they belong not to the theoretical but to the practical, side of our psychical life; not to thought or imagination,[1] but to feeling and volition. In what respects, then, do they differ from feelings and volitions, seeing that they are not identical with either, but rather form a connecting link between them? The emotions often arise as immediate reactions upon particular feelings. But such immediate and instantaneous reactions may, by dint of repetition, superinduce a permanent condition. Anger, for instance, is a transitory state, but there is also an irascible disposition, *i.e.* a propensity to react in an angry way. Accordingly, the manner in which the subject reacts upon his feelings will be determined by his peculiar nature, his temperament, or his peculiar blend of temperaments, by character, sex, etc.—in a word, by his individuality, which, again, is modified by his family, national, or racial type. Moreover, this individual disposition is by no means limited to one's natural constitution; it may be acquired—a fact that underlies the plasticity of the emotions. But, while the emotions are thus reactions upon feeling, we must not forget that there are also moods of feeling, involving a permanent tendency towards certain forms of action; and these moods must likewise be reckoned amongst the emotions.

The emotions have often been called passions, and traced back to 'suffering' (*passio*); here, again, we must bear in mind that such suffering is not always momentary, and that the influence of an object may last beyond the period of direct stimulus. Here the influence is really that of the *representation* of the object; and in this case the imagination works towards the expansion and intensification of the emotion; and, indeed, may become so habituated to represent certain objects as to produce fixed ideas, which, again, by becoming fused together with the feelings that evoke them and the volitions that issue from them, may act as a permanent stimulus to the emotions.

The emotions have also been frequently identified with the impulses; but impulse is really a mode of the will, and may either spring from the nature common to man or be the resultant of a long series of volitions, which, gathering strength by hereditary transmission, at length become established in the later generation. Thus, for instance, the desire of fame and of power, in their nobler forms at least, seems to presuppose a social life of some permanence, and a certain degree of culture. Impulse as such, however, is not emotion; rather it becomes emotion only when the object to which it is directed affects the feeling, and prompts the will to act. This is what takes place in particular instances; but, as has been said, the object may be so persistently present to the mind as to give a sustained tone to the feelings, which, again, gives a definite bias to the will. The emotions, then, are distinguished from spontaneous impulses by the fact that they are traceable to some impression, or feeling, and emerge as a tendency to react upon this stimulus. We may say, therefore, that the emotions are combinations of feeling with movements or acts of will, and that they may have either a transitory or a lasting character, according as they are immediate reactions upon a definite object, or upon habitual states of the soul which rest upon a more or less persistent combination of feeling and volition; these, in turn, depending upon the object affecting the soul. Moreover, it goes without saying that these habitual states may find vent in momentary outbursts.

Then we must also distinguish between the momentary strength of an emotion and its durableness. An emotion may be strong for the moment, but have no persistence, as, *e.g.*, when it is evoked by a merely passing stimulus from the object; and, conversely, an emotion may never manifest anything like intensity, and may yet work all the more pertinaciously; compare, for instance, an angry outbreak with cool, calculated hate.

2. Varieties of emotion.—The emotions exhibit a multitude of variations, quite apart from the distinction between transience and permanence. Thus, the feeling and its accompanying tendency to react may, as called forth by the object, be one either of pleasure or of pain. If pleasurable, the motive will be one of sympathy with the object; if painful, one of antipathy. Then the emotions may be classified with reference to time—according as they are related to the past, the present, or the future. In connexion with the past, pain produces repentance, while pleasure brings satisfaction, with a wish for renewal of the conditions; and either of these, again, may be transitory or enduring. Pleasure in regard to the present calls forth desire; while pain arouses aversion, or, in a more intense form, anger. Pleasure in regard to the future becomes hope, with the inclination to make the thing hoped for a reality; pain in relation to the future becomes fear, with the inclination to obviate or ward off the thing feared. Obviously these emotions may also vary in intensity, *i.e.* they are susceptible of quantitative differentiation. But these quantitative differences must not be confounded with differences which depend upon whether a man is by the bent of his mind stronger in feeling than in will-power, or *vice versa*. Should feeling predominate, then, *e.g.*, repentance will be

[1] Imagination, of course, may influence our emotional life *indirectly*.

not so much a motive prompting a change of will for the better as a sentimental regret, which, as it inhibits the will, has an enfeebling effect; similarly, contentment will degenerate into luxurious remembrance, instead of inciting the will to hold fast in the present by what the past has given. If volition, however, be the stronger, the reverse will be the case. Moreover, pleasure and pain may, so far as their influence on the will is concerned, become quite neutral, and less dependent upon time-differences; desire will then become love, and aversion hate. Again, all these modifications of emotion may be further differentiated by reference to the kind of object that excites them. Thus, feeling in passing over to volition will always be initially a feeling of self, a feeling of excitation; but this feeling of self may be of very different kinds. In the first place, one may be affected either in body or in soul. But the bodily frame itself has different aspects: there is the need, for instance, of self-preservation, or of preserving one's peculiar type. Should it be affected by a corresponding body, a fresh group of emotions displays itself, associated with food or sex. When reflexion has been sufficiently developed to raise a man above mere momentary sensations, he will desire permanently satisfying objects; the sexual impulse will become love, and hunger will be transformed into the desire for possessions sufficient to satisfy permanently his bodily needs. The latter emotion may likewise vary as one wishes to use, to preserve, or to augment one's property. Prodigality, niggardliness, and avarice have their source here; but also liberality, thrift, and diligence. It is personal differences alone which prompt one man to liberality or prodigality, another to thrift or niggardliness, and a third to avarice or diligence.

Again, the affective state of the mind has to do with its relations to other minds. The fundamental fact is that the mind is influenced by others in such a way as to experience pleasure or pain, and thus arises sympathy or antipathy. Sympathy and antipathy also involve the feeling of self, springing respectively from the sense of being attracted or repelled by others, according as the impressions which are received work upon the will in a pleasurable or a painful manner. Here, also, of course, individuality counts for much. Further, we must take into consideration whether sympathy or antipathy in regard to another is aroused by his personality as a whole or only by certain aspects thereof—some being attractive, others repellent; in the latter case we have an unstable emotion, one vacillating between sympathy and antipathy. Once more, from the sympathetic emotion, so far, at least, as it rests upon the consciousness of others' equality with ourselves, springs the desire to recompense. Should another afford us pleasure, we incline to return the favour: this is gratitude. But should he pain us by doing us a disadvantage, the result is the feeling of revenge. A further principle of division might be found in the question whether our sympathy and antipathy relate to individuals or to communities.

Finally, a man's sympathy or antipathy may either be such that his thoughts dwell most upon his own pleasure or pain; or such that the feeling for others predominates in his mind. In the former instance, he will be sympathetically moved towards another only in so far as the experience is absolutely free of pain, and, in fact, when the sympathy itself affords pleasure. In the second case, he is so much at one with the other as to enter into his feelings. The former kind of sympathy goes no further than a man's own advantage, changing even to antipathy when that disappears. He really seeks his own advancement in his recognition of the other; his authority over the other will enhance his sense of his own power. The desire for glory or power rests upon a sympathy of this sort, which vanishes whenever the other ceases duly to respond. Such sympathy may in an extreme case manifest itself as compassion, for this is, of course, directed upon suffering, which, however, should properly arouse antipathy. Compassion is, in fact, a sympathetic antipathy. But the sympathy will at once become something else if the other's feeling causes me discomfort. Indeed, if I am pained in any way while another is pleased, there may emerge antipathy towards him in the form of ill-will and envy; and, if I am in any degree inferior to him, my antipathy may show itself in a desire to disparage; while, again, if I am conscious of my merits in comparison with him, the result will be pride.

It is otherwise if I can enter into the feelings of another. I then recognize his superior merits (should these exist), and in the frank admission of them I have a feeling of admiration—something higher, that is to say, than a recognition whose aim is merely to have oneself recognized, to use another as a means to one's own glory. Similarly, I can now regard another's defects or misfortunes with pity, which disposes me to help in amending his defects or alleviating his misfortunes. These two kinds of sympathy may also manifest themselves when two individuals fix upon a single object, which one alone can have. If the feeling of self prevails, jealousy will arise; if sympathy predominates, the one individual will be ready to renounce for the other's sake. Again, however, one may have a very weak or a very strong feeling of self-reliance. If the former, there will emerge a tendency to belittle one's own merits in comparison with another's—the sympathetic emotion of self-abasement, which often appears as sensitiveness. Very different is the emotion which arises when sympathy is associated with self-confidence. In this association the self-confidence may be by no means insignificant in itself, as, *e.g.*, in benevolence, which in no way implies uncertainty as to one's own merits, or any inclination to self-disparagement. Similarly, a self-esteem in reference to others may not lead to conceit and ambition, when a man desires to convince others of his own merits without seeking to underrate theirs.

There may thus be an extraordinary variety amongst the emotions. For the sake of completeness, we may also note that one emotion may restrain another, either for a time or permanently. Desire of power or of fame, for example, may keep the appetites in abeyance. Similarly, certain emotions may coalesce and thereby strengthen each other; thus, revenge may join hands with envy, domineering with pride, or greed with ill-will.

3. Moral value of the emotions.—What ethical value shall we set upon the emotions? Are they simply evil, or partly good and partly evil, or, again, are they in themselves morally colourless, but, like other faculties of the mind, capable of being made subservient to the moral life? These questions find various answers. Naturalistic ethics must necessarily regard the emotions as morally indifferent: they exist *before* morality. On this view, it is the psychological mechanism which gradually secures an adjustment among the conflicting emotions. We learn by experience, it is said, even in our own interests, to prefer the other-regarding impulses to the self-regarding, the permanent to the transient, the spiritual to the corporeal. By formulating rules in virtue of our faculty of abstraction, it is said, we set up a standard by which the emotions are consciously valued, and a choice amongst them consciously made; all this, however, has meanwhile been done, unconsciously, by our psychological mechanism. The result is called the *moral* standard; though, in point of fact, what we so designate is only a fingerpost pointing to the greatest possible advantage. But this theory, according to which the choice amongst our emotions is really made for us in experience—the understanding merely deducing the laws from the facts—is founded upon error. For, if the psychological mechanism establishes a certain hierarchy among the emotions by natural selection, we have not really transcended egoism at all. For, even if the egoistic emotion is overpowered by the altruistic, it is simply because, as a matter of experience, the former fares all the better thereby. In reality, therefore, it is not so overpowered; on the contrary, the psychological mechanism is actually guided by it. Along this line, therefore, no genuine adjustment can ever be arrived at. The truth is, moral life begins only when the understanding forms universal laws, when the difference between the ideal, the 'ought,' the law, on the one hand, and, on the other, the actual condition of things is first realized. Then there appears something *new*, viz. the craving of our nature for unity, which the adjustment made by our psychological mechanism cannot satisfy. Such adjustment, in fact, will always be precarious, as the egoistic emotions will ever and anon break out in spite of all our altruism. The desire for unity, however, spontaneously presses towards harmony and activity; while, on the contrary, the emotions are unstable, and, being stimulated by external objects, have no true spontaneity, and always end in mere enjoyment, mere passivity.

Hence we need not wonder that the naturalistic theory has been challenged again and again by a rigid and one-sided rationalism, which will countenance no rule in the moral realm except that of reason alone, and spurns the emotions as something irrational. But this standpoint is shown by history to be untenable. The Stoics were compelled to abandon the rigorism of their *apathia*, and to concede that in some degree even the wise man feels pain—though he does not allow himself to be mastered by it—and that he too may have εὐπάθεια, such as good-will and joy. Further, the Stoics doubted whether the life of the wise man were meanwhile possible, and spoke of an approximation merely, in which a man should be immune from diseases of the spirit, but not free from emotion. Spinoza also, while discarding the emotions, was unable to regard them as other than a necessary product of the *natura naturata*; and Kant came at length to the conclusion that the propensities are not evil in themselves, just as in the sphere of the beautiful and the sublime he recognizes a certain mutual relationship between the sensuous and the spiritual.

If the moral reason, then, cannot be merely the inductive reading of our psychological mechanism on its emotional side, and if it does not necessarily involve a rigid exclusion of the emotions, or, in other words, if we can neither identify it with the formulated results of our psychological mechanism nor concede a dualism between it and emotion, the only course open to us is to grant an independent, co-ordinate position to both reason and emotion—with the proviso, however, that reason be always credited with the power of harmonizing and unifying the emotions for its own ends. As we have seen, this view is held by a large number of modern thinkers. They regard the emotions as the data and material which reason has to elaborate. If the emotion arises from a movement of the will combined with feeling and prompted by an object, it is the function of reason to examine and regulate the process.

The question as to the moral character of the emotions is, therefore, to be answered generally by asserting that in themselves they are neither good nor evil, but become so only as they respectively submit to or repudiate the supervision and guidance of reason. This holds good of all kinds of emotion. Reason must assign the limit of their momentary intensity, and likewise regulate their duration and persistence, for it tolerates the continuance of such kinds only as coincide with its own fundamental aims. Emotions of pleasure are no more proscribed as such than those of pain. What is alone of moment is, on the one hand, to determine their measure, and, on the other, to take account of their object. Anger, for example, as excited volition, is not to be summarily condemned; only it must be made subservient to reason, and be directed against that which is truly reprehensible. Again, neither the impulse of self-preservation nor that of sympathy is *per se* blameworthy; they require only to have their respective scope and their mutual relationship defined by reason. Under such conditions the emotions will not become demoralized. Love of power rests upon an exaggerated, but in itself perfectly innocent, desire for influence; envy, upon the complete subjection of the altruistic impulse to the in itself quite legitimate impulse of self-preservation—all sympathy being crushed by the selfish wish to possess what is another's. Similarly, the organic emotions have their rightful place, requiring only that adjustment which reason must make in view of organic needs; they must be brought into proper relations with one another and with the spiritual emotions. The emotion attaching to property, as regards both its preservation and its use, must be reduced—in conformity with the function which reason assigns to property in the moral sphere—to its due proportions in the desire to earn.

In short, the emotions as such are not evil when subject to the guidance of reason, but, just as human nature must be brought into harmony with reason, so must they be made to minister to the ends of reason. If left to themselves, they tend to degenerate, since they cannot then be kept within due measure, or be fully harmonized with one another.

4. Rational control of the emotions.—Finally, if it be asked how reason acquires dominion over the emotions, we look first of all to its power of framing ideals. Its task, alike as regards the guidance of the several emotions—with due allowance for their individual modifications—and as regards their mutual relations, must be clearly defined in the light of actual, concrete ethical ideals. It is obvious that a proper comprehension of the meaning and value of emotion for moral life is the necessary condition of right conduct. Such comprehension, however, does not guarantee its being realized in practice. It is often asserted that emotion is modified only by emotion, that reason without emotion remains a dead letter; and this is certainly the case. The dictates of reason, therefore, must be combined with love, which we may call the positive norm of emotion; then will reason become effective. The ideal must become the object of love; then will this supreme affection—enthusiasm for the ideal—work its effect upon the other forms. Such enthusiasm cannot, of course, be manufactured. It is something free—the unforced persistent glow of love for perfection, the practical interest in the ideal of reason.

To generate this archetypal affection is the business of education, which, however, would be all in vain unless human nature provided something for it to work upon. But reason and its ideal are not alien to man. It is man's *own* reason which exhorts him to follow its behests. So long as he refuses to identify himself with this consummate affection —with his own ideal—he feels an inner discord. Education may prompt towards this enthusiasm, but it cannot furnish, still less force it. If we appeal to such motives as fear of punishment or hope of reward, we may succeed in curbing certain emotions, and even in partially establishing a habit of restraint in others, and thus prepare the way for real moral conduct by removing obstacles to the attainment of the good will; but enthusiasm for the ideal is not to be acquired in this way; for, if we confine ourselves to such motives, we have not passed beyond selfishness after all. The ideal must be loved for its own sake. This supreme affection is engendered only through the individual's own act, for which education provides but the stimulus. Like devotion to the beautiful, or ardent love to the Divine, enthusiasm for the good is absolutely free. Ought we, then, to call it an emotion at all, since emotion always springs from some impression on the mind, which feeling transmutes into a motive? We must remember, however, that such an impression has a place even in the affection we speak of. For one thing, the educator may hold up the example of those who, possessed by this enthusiasm, are capable of moving our hearts. For another, while we recognize the ideal as our own, yet it always towers above our actual attainment, as if to impress us with love for our better part. Finally, the ideal comes to us in the impressions wrought by God within the soul. The mental impression in question, therefore, results, not from any external object, but from our being apprehended by our reason's own ideal or by the Divine spirit within us. The same thing lies at the root of what is called moral passion, though this is likewise a free motive to action.

Without moral passion the moral ideal cannot be realized. But it is far from adequate in itself. When the emotions, excited by the various experiences of life, are asserting themselves in their full strength, to attempt to oppose them by moral passion alone is futile. But enthusiasm for the moral ideal has undoubtedly a restraining effect upon the urgency of emotion; and, this being so, such restraint makes it possible for reflexion to intervene before the response to stimulus takes place. Thus reason, which both determines the end to be attained and apprehends the actual conditions, can assign the measure and the course of the emotion, and, taking advantage of the congenial enthusiasm for the ideal, can carry its purposes into effect. But even something more than this is required in the task of controlling the emotions, namely, a certain psycho-physical habituation. With these resources, then, it is possible for reason to subject impulse to its own all-embracing ideal, to attain, by habit, ever nearer to a complete harmony of the emotions amongst themselves and to the right proportion of each, and so to utilize them in practical life as to give them the place which, in the light of the moral ideal, is rightly theirs.

We note, in closing, the recent spread of a romanticism which would base morality upon the instincts, and declares war upon all intellectual interpretations; which yields the ascendancy to spontaneous feeling, and would exclude all *ratio* in favour of the Unconscious that is revealed in emotion—a new form of ethical and æsthetic naturalism. Such a theory, however, cannot possibly discover the proper measure of the emotions, as it really keeps the moral reason out of its rights.

See also FEELING, MIND.

LITERATURE.—Spinoza, *Ethics*, iii.; Leslie Stephen, *The Science of Ethics*, 1882; A. Bain, *The Emotions and the Will*, 1859, *Mental and Moral Science*, 1868 [esp. bk. iii. pt. ii., in which he gives a historical survey, chiefly of English Ethics]; F. Jodl, *Gesch. der Ethik in der neueren Philosophie*, 1882; Schleiermacher, *Entwurf eines Systems der Sittenlehre*, ed. Schweizer, 1835 [esp. the 'Tugendlehre'], and *Christliche Sitte*, 1843 [esp. pt. ii., 'Der Gottesdienst im weiteren Sinne,' pp. 599–620]; Fr. Schiller, vols. xi. and xii. [in particular 'Anmuth und Würde,' xi. 323 f., and 'Die æsthetische Erziehung des Menschen,' xii. 1 f.]; A. Dorner, *Das menschliche Handeln*, 1895, pp. 73 f., 356 f., 573–598; A. Fouillée, *Critique des systèmes de morale contemporains*, 1883, i. and ii.; M. J. Guyau, *La Morale anglaise*, 1879; H. Münsterberg, *Der Ursprung der Sittlichkeit*, 1889; J. Bentham, *Introduction to the Principles of Morals and Legislation*, 1789; J. Sully, *The Human Mind*, 1892, vol. ii.; J. McCosh, *The Emotions*, 1880.

A. DORNER.

EMPEDOCLES.—Empedocles was a Sicilian philosopher who was famous also as a statesman, poet, orator, physician, and wonder-worker.

1. Life and writings.—Empedocles belonged to a wealthy and distinguished family of Agrigentum (the Greek *Akragas*). His grandfather, also called Empedocles, won a victory with a racehorse at Olympia in 496 B.C. The philosopher himself took an active part in the troublous politics of his native city, after the expulsion of its tyrants (Diog. Laert. viii. 63–67; cf. Plut. *adv. Col.* 32. 4, p. 1126 B). He was a resolute democrat, and is said to have refused an offer of royal power; yet we read that in later years his enemies caused this champion of the people to be banished. There is much that is marvellous, much that is vague and contradictory, in the accounts of his life which have come down to us, principally in Diog. Laert. viii. ch. 2. The Sicilian historian Timæus, who lived in the 3rd cent. B.C., and preserved many such notices, did not know for certain the place or the manner of his death. Even his date is not exactly determined. Aristotle (*Met.* i. 3. 984*a*, 11) speaks of him as a younger contemporary of Anaxagoras (*q.v.*); Gorgias is said to have been his pupil (Diog. Laert. viii. 58; Quint. iii. 1). Apollodorus fixed his birth in 484; and his death, at the age of 60, in 424. But Zeller (*Pre-Socratic Phil.* ii. 117 ff.) has adduced grounds for placing his birth from eight to ten years earlier, *i.e.* in 492 or 494.

The chief works of Empedocles were two poems with the titles περὶ Φύσεως τῶν ὄντων and Καθαρμοί. The former, dealing with physical science, was in two books, if, with Diels, we prefer the reading βίβλια β′ in Suidas *s.v.*, although Tzetzes (*Chil.* vii. 522) erroneously makes them three. Of these poems we have fragments extending to 440 lines. Aristotle, who in a lost dialogue gave Empedocles full credit for Homeric inspiration and forcible diction (Diog. Laert. viii. 57), nevertheless took him for his illustration when maintaining, in the *Poetics* (i. 1447*b*, 17), that metrical form does not convert prose into poetry. Empedocles was the last to use verse as the vehicle of philosophic exposition; and Anaxagoras reverted to prose, with which the Milesians had started.

2. The four 'roots.'—In his physical theories Empedocles was an eclectic. Like Leucippus, he had studied the Eleatic philosophers; but he rejected their chief doctrine, that of the One, and reverted to pluralism. He assumed four primary matters—Fire, Air, Earth, and Water; or, mythologically expressed, Zeus, Hera, Aidoneus, and Nestis. These primary matters, which are as indestructible and unchangeable as the Sphere of Parmenides, he called the 'roots' (ῥιζώματα) of all that exists. The term 'element' (στοιχεῖον) did not come into use until later, but it is clear that Empedocles had grasped the conception of an element, in the sense of modern chemistry, as opposed to a compound body; for by the mingling and separation of these four roots the world of particular things is produced. Thus he made bone, flesh, and blood—which last is the seat of intelligence

—consist severally of air, earth, fire, and water united in determinate proportions.

Besides the four roots there were two other constituents of the universe, called Love or Friendship (φιλία, φιλότης, Ἀφροδίτη) and Strife (νεῖκος, κότος). These were moving causes answering to attraction and repulsion respectively; but also, it would seem, corporeal substances which rush into and out of the 'Sphere' (Diels, 21 B, 35 [i.[2] 185], Ar. *Met.* xii. 10, 1075*b*, 3). Alternately predominating, they govern the rhythmical evolution of the world, which passes from a state of complete aggregation of the elements to the opposite state of their utter disintegration, and back again in an unending cycle. When Love has succeeded in expelling Strife, the four roots are entirely aggregated in a chaotic medley, termed, from its shape, the Sphere; but at this epoch all particular existence is extinct. Again, particular existence is just as impossible when Love is expelled by Strife, and the four roots so completely severed that there is no mingling. But in the intervals between these epochs Love and Strife work together, and a world of particular things results from their joint action.

3. Cosmogony.—The formation of our world, it would seem from Aristotle (*de Cœlo*, ii. 301*a*, 15), began when Strife forced its way into the Sphere, and brought about its disruption by creating a vortex motion which successively separated off (1) air, (2) fire, and (3) earth saturated with moisture. Thus first of all 'bright ether' (air) flew off to the extremity, and became a crystal vault or encircling shell, to which the fixed stars are attached. Within this again was formed a sphere consisting of two hemispheres, the one filled with fire, the other, which is dark, with a mixture of fire and air. The revolution of these two hemispheres round the earth produces at each point on its surface the succession of day and night, and also keeps the earth in its place in the centre, in the same way as a cup with water in it may be swung round and round at the end of a string without the water being spilled. The analogy is at fault, for it is centrifugal force which keeps the water in the revolving cup, whereas the earth is presumably at rest.

According to Empedocles, there are two suns, or, rather, he held the apparent sun to be a sort of burning-glass, equal in size to the earth, wherein are collected those fiery rays which come from the true source of light, the fiery hemisphere. These rays first strike the earth, and are thence reflected on the hemisphere opposite, if the text of Aetius (ii. 20. 13; Diels, 21 A, 56 [i.[2] 162]) be sound. Empedocles thus wrongly extended to the sun the recent discovery that the moon shines by borrowed light. The moon itself he held to be mainly composed of 'air' condensed or congealed, obviously assuming that its phases correspond with actual changes in its shape. One great achievement of modern astronomy he certainly anticipated; for he held that light travels, and takes time to travel, from one point to another (Ar. *de An.* ii. 7. 418*b*, 20; *de Sensu*, 6. 446*a*, 26). He thought that the axis of the universe, originally perpendicular so that the north pole was in the zenith, had been displaced by the pressure of the air.

4. Organic life.—Empedocles also had his views on the origin of life. Plants and animals alike spring out of the earth, and grow because the terrestrial heat tends upwards. Existing species, however, in no way resemble the crude and shapeless structures first evolved, such as men with oxen's faces, which were incapable of maintaining or reproducing themselves. This wild fancy differs from the modern doctrine of evolution in overlooking modification by inheritance, and in assuming separate organs to have been evolved before the wholes they combined to form. Its single point of agreement is the truism that no species has survived which was not adapted in some degree to its environment. Empedocles' scientific imagination may also be seen in his mechanical theory of respiration, on the analogy of the water-clock (Diels, 21 B, 100 [i.[2] 200]), and of the spinal vertebræ (Ar. *de Part. An.* i. 1. 640*a*, 19); but more particularly in a theory of sense-perception based upon the entrance, through symmetrical passages or pores (πόροι), of films (ἀπόρροαι) emanating from external objects. This account of the mechanism of sensation best suits taste and smell; it may have been, as Diels thinks, derived from Leucippus; the application to vision (though adopted in great part by Plato) is beset with difficulties. The unique fact of perception proper Empedocles sought to explain by means of another principle, that like moves towards, and is recognized by, like. The sentient subject knows earth, water, air, and fire because these elemental substances are found in his own composition. This principle must be carefully distinguished from the attraction of like to unlike personified in φιλία, or Love. Thought, again, is a corporeal process (Ar. *de An.* iii. 3. 427*a*, 26); there is no such gulf as Parmenides presumed between sense and reason. The value of the senses as sources of knowledge is implied throughout the poems, and the passage (Diels, 21 B, 4 [i.[2] 174]) which, as interpreted by Karsten and Zeller, would concede superior claims to reason has been set right by Stein's punctuation.

5. Religion and Ethics.—In the cosmos as here set forth there would seem to be no place for religion; yet Empedocles speaks of gods. (1) There are the 'long-lived gods, greatest in honour,' who are products of the mingling of his four elements, and, as such, are set down side by side with 'trees and men and women, beasts and birds, and fishes bred in the waters' (Diels, 21 B, 21 [i.[2] 180]). These, be it remarked, are not deathless, but merely long-lived; it is not impossible that they are what he elsewhere calls the daemons. (2) As already noted, he also deifies the four elements and the two efficient causes. (3) Further, we find the Sphere spoken of as a 'blessed god,' but this again may be merely a poetic description. It need not imply monotheism, any more than the parallel expressions of the pantheist Xenophanes.

In his other poem, the *Purifications* (Καθαρμοί), Empedocles poses as a moral teacher and religious reformer. He is the favourite of heaven, and the inspired votary of Apollo; he lays claim to a Divine origin and superhuman powers. He recounts his successive transmigrations. The tone of the whole poem is mystic, as opposed to the scientific spirit of the περὶ Φύσεως, and bears many resemblances to Orphic and Pythagorean doctrines. There is one passage where a god is described in terms perhaps borrowed from Xenophanes: 'He is not provided with a human head upon his limbs; two branches do not spring from his shoulders; he has no feet, no swift knees, no hairy members; he is only a sacred and unutterable mind shooting with swift thoughts through all the world' (Diels, 21 B, 134 [i.[2] 212]). This god has been by some identified with the Sphere; but how could the Sphere be said to shoot with swift thoughts through all the world? It would seem, therefore, more reasonable to follow Zeller and Diels, who think that Apollo is meant; for from an early date, as J. Adam remarks (*Religious Teachers of Greece*, Edinburgh, 1908, p. 249), 'Greek religious thought naturally tended to spiritualise Apollo.' Empedocles also tells us of demons, who, 'having polluted their hands with blood,' are condemned to wander for thrice ten thousand seasons in all manner of mortal forms through the universe until their sin is expiated; 'and one of these,' he says, 'I now am, an exile and a wanderer from the gods' (Diels, 21 B, 115 [i.[2] 207]). Here is the doctrine of retribution for guilt, and here, too, that of metempsychosis.

The moral teaching of the Καθαρμοί consists mainly of tabus based upon the belief in transmigration, and its corollary, the kinship of all animate and inanimate things. Empedocles describes a period when men lived at peace with each other and all the world, and bids his followers abstain from all animal food, and from beans and laurel-leaves.

It is an interesting, though perhaps insoluble, problem to determine how the *Purifications* is related to the poem upon *Nature*. Are we to suppose, with Diels, that in the one Empedocles taught science to a circle of students, and afterwards in the other addressed a popular audience with religious fervour? Or is Bidez right in assuming that the Καθαρμοί was the work of his youth, and the περὶ Φύσεως the fruit of riper study in mature life? That the same thinker should at the same time have endorsed the apparently contradictory doctrines of both poems is advocated by Burnet (*Early Greek Philosophy*[2], p. 269 ff.). Such a view is possible only to those who recognize in Empedocles not so much a philosophic mind as an enthusiastic poet and seer, careless of logical consistency.

LITERATURE.—**H. Diels**, *Poet. philos. fragm.*, Berlin, 1902, also *Fragm. der Vorsokratiker*, Berlin, 1906-10 [i.[2] 149–219]; **F. G. Sturz**, *de Emped. Agrig. vita et philosophia expos., carminum reliq. coll.*, Leipzig, 1805; **S. Karsten**, *Emped. Agrig. carminum reliq.* (vol. ii. 'Reliq. phil. vet. Græc.'), Amsterdam, 1838; **H. Stein**, *Emped. Agrig. fragmenta*, Bonn, 1852; **H. Diels**, 'Studia Empedoclea,' in *Herm.* xv. (Berlin, 1880), 'Gorgias und Empedocles,' in *SBAW*, 1884, 'Ueber die Gedichte des Emped.' *ib.* 1898; **P. Tannery**, *Pour l'Histoire de la science hellène*, Paris, 1887, pp. 304–339; **E. Zeller**, *Philos. der Griechen*, i.[5], Leipzig, 1892 (Eng. tr. [of 4th ed.] by S. F. Alleyne under title *Zeller's Pre-Socratic Philosophy*, London, 1881); **J. Bidez**, *La Biographie d'Empéd.*, Ghent, 1894, 'Obs. sur quelques fragm. d'Empéd. et de Parm.' in *AGPh* ix. (1896) 190-207; **T. Gomperz**, *Gr. Denker*[2], i., Leipzig, 1903 (Eng. tr. by L. Magnus, *Gr. Thinkers*, London, 1901); **von Arnim**, in *Festschr. f. Gomperz*, Vienna, 1902, p. 16; **E. Rohde**, *Psyche*[3], Tübingen and Leipzig, 1903; **J. I. Beare**, *Gr. Theories of Elementary Cognition*, Oxford, 1906; **J. Burnet**, *Early Gr. Philosophy*[2], London, 1908, ch. 5, pp. 227–289 (includes a tr. of the fragments); **W. E. Leonard**, *The Frags. of Empedocles tr. into Eng. Verse*, Chicago, 1908.

R. D. HICKS.

EMPIRICISM.—Empiricism denotes primarily the scientific investigation of the world which we experience through our senses. In the world so experienced we are continually apprehending uniformities of different kinds; scientific empiricism brings together groups of sense-phenomena apprehended as exhibiting the same uniformities, and endeavours, by further observation and experiment, to apprehend more clearly the special nature of the uniformities within each group, and the precise conditions on which their presence depends.

Thus, to study the nature of two-dimensional space, we bring together figures in two dimensions, and by a further process of minute sub-grouping obtain figures in which we apprehend more distinctly the nature of the triangle, the circle, etc., and from the mutual relations of their parts in definite figures apprehend as necessary certain further conclusions with regard to the nature of those figures. In all cases it is through the construction that we come to apprehend the nature of the figure; we apprehend, *e.g.*, the universal truth 'Things which are equal to the same thing are equal to one another' only by considering a particular instance. But in some cases the construction is more elaborate; *e.g.*, in Euclid i. 47 the figure is extremely complex, and presupposes the construction of triangles, etc. Empiricism, therefore, aims at re-grouping the phenomena studied, according to their uniformities, in continuous series, beginning with the relatively simple and passing to the progressively complex. Progress in Mathematics and the other empirical sciences depends on finding the right 'construction,' in discovering a method which will enable us to apprehend more definitely the way in which the elementary parts are connected in any given case. What is aimed at is precise formulation, such as, *e.g.*, the exact reciprocal relation between the sides and angles of the equilateral triangle; but in the present state of all the sciences this exact formulation is rare, and it is only by the examination of fresh groups of problems that we are enabled gradually to reform our present inexact formulations.

By proceeding, then, in these two ways: (1) by continually attacking fresh problems, and (2) by perpetually revising the stock of acquired formulations, Empiricism hopes to obtain an ever wider and deeper knowledge of the world which we come to experience through our senses; it admits that the uniformities hitherto studied have very rarely received adequate formulation, and that its 'laws' are only relatively true; but it hopes to advance, within this sphere of relative truth, to laws which ever more adequately express the nature of the reality which it studies.

In one direction this ideal of ever-improving, but ever-relative, knowledge is definitely limited. There is one main presupposition of Empiricism which, as such, it cannot question or even examine, but must simply accept. This presupposition is expressed, on the objective side, as the 'Law of the Uniformity of Nature'; this means that the apprehensible world, as such, has a definite nature of its own, and works according to laws which remain universally valid, though only partially apprehended by us, through unstable sense-organs and at particular moments of time; the stars continue to revolve in definite orbits through all the advances of science, from Aristotle to Copernicus, from Copernicus to the present day; the stream pours forth its waters into the sea, the sea still dashes upon its rocky strand, though every living eye is closed in slumber.

From the side of the subject, this presupposition is expressed by saying that the mind is a *tabula rasa*, a waxen tablet upon which the external world imprints its forms. Its *esse* is *percipere*; more than that we cannot say. There can be no scientific 'theory of knowledge'; for Empiricism maintains that our apprehensions appear to contain uniformities only because they are apprehensions of objective uniformities; that the so-called 'Necessities of Apprehension'—causation, substance, etc.—are so only because they are apprehensions of necessities in the Object; that the 'Laws of Thought' are laws for thought only because they are laws of the things which thought apprehends. In short, the uniformities and necessities belong wholly to the apprehended Object; on the side of the Subject we have simply apprehension—apprehension of just those objective uniformities and necessities.

The main principle of Empiricism being, then, that through sense-experience we come to apprehend the universal laws which express the nature of the apprehensible world, it follows that error, or false thinking, is impossible. We may fail to apprehend; we cannot misapprehend. Where we have not yet found the right construction, the right method for observing the nature of a certain uniformity, we fail so far to apprehend its full nature. But, when we say, *e.g.*, '2+2=5,' the possibility of self-correction shows that we did not really *think* so, that we were simply not attending, and so failed to apprehend. When we attend and have the features of the problem clearly before us, we cannot fail to apprehend the correct conclusion. In fact, error is always due to some sort of inattention, *i.e.* to psychological causes, against which scientific Empiricism has its special safeguards.

A proposition is 'proved' when we have discovered the right construction, the method which enables us to apprehend clearly the connexion of the elements within the given problem; the statement of the conclusion so apprehended is said to be 'true.' In the present state of the sciences, many propositions are held to be 'provisionally true' if a few advanced scientists confirm each other's observations; but the aim of science is always to present its results in such a form that the observations can be verified by any intelligent student. This aim is most clearly attained in the text-books of Mathematics and Physics. A statement, then, is true when we find the right construction and observe its truth directly. It follows that the claims of the 'Law of Contradiction' or of the 'Principle of the Inconceivability of the Opposite' to present us with a 'formal criterion of truth' are inadmissible. These so-called 'criteria' are, in fact, virtual re-statements of the general principle of Empiricism, viz. that the apprehensible world has certain definite characteristics; but truth consists just in particular truths, in apprehension of just these particular definite characteristics. Consequently, in order to apply to particular cases, the 'criteria' have to become particularized, in which case there is no longer one criterion, but as many criteria as there are problems to which they are to be applied. Moreover, Empiricism insists that a particular statement is not true because its opposite is inconceivable, but that its opposite is inconceivable because the statement is true. There can thus be no formal criterion of truth, and progress in knowledge depends always on our possessing insight into the particular nature of particular scientific problems.

Owing to a number of historical causes, these main outlines of Empiricism have been seriously misunderstood by Empiricists themselves, as well as by their opponents. Hume's separation of the particular sense-experience from the universality and necessity apprehended through that experience makes these appear mere fictions of our imagination; a too mechanical adherence to the *tabula rasa* metaphor has misled many into supposing that they can apply physical laws to the explanation of apprehension itself; and J. S. Mill attempted to prove empirically the presupposition of Empiricism itself—the Uniformity of Nature. But these and similar vagaries in the writings of the Empirical School are to be regarded as aberrations from the simple tenets of scientific Empiricism.

See, further, such artt. as EPISTEMOLOGY, HUME, LOCKE, MILL, IDEALISM, PHILOSOPHY, and the Literature cited under them. R. C. LODGE.

EMPLOYERS.—The term 'employers' is a relative term; it connotes employees and a relation of contract between the two parties; corresponding terms in common use are 'masters' and 'men,' 'capitalists' and 'labourers,' though the latter are not now exact equivalents. The fundamental facts from which the relation springs are that one set provides work and pays for it, the other performs the work and receives payment. The classification is a result of an economic division of labour according to function in the operations of wealth-production or conduct of business; and it gives rise to a parallel distribution or division of the proceeds of production as profits and wages. To be more precise, the function of the employer is to find out the work to be done, to plan, to organize, and direct it; he takes the risk contingent upon its performance, and on this account is often called the *entrepreneur*, or undertaker; he becomes a kind of middleman or go-between in the equalization of demand and supply—the demand being that of the consumer for goods, and the supply that of the various kinds of labour necessary to satisfy that demand. The employer is thus an essential factor in the refined and intricate system of modern industry.

In earlier times, and under simpler conditions of life, when the market was quite local and small, the employer provided the capital for the undertaking; under modern conditions, with wide markets and large production, he very frequently conducts the enterprise with the aid of borrowed capital. The facilities afforded by a widely diffused system of banking and a highly organized money market, together with the method of combining many different capitals on the joint-stock principle of enterprise, have enabled large amounts of capital to be placed under the direction of men who have special ability for controlling it for purposes of business. Under such circumstances the employer becomes mainly the manager of capital or the agent of its owners; he is entrusted with its command because he possesses in a peculiar degree the special faculty of business management, together with technical knowledge of the industry of business in which the capital is embarked. The separation of the functions of capitalist and employer is the outcome of an economic evolution which has introduced greater complexity and subdivision into the methods of production and exchange. It has proved a highly efficient form of differentiation, firstly in securing the direction of affairs by specialists, and secondly by utilizing much capital which might otherwise only be hoarded and would therefore be idle, or which indeed might not have been saved at all, did not such openings for its employment arise.

The function of the employer has become so important in modern industry that he is often regarded as a fourth factor in production; land, labour, and capital being the three factors formerly recognized as the requisites of wealth-production. The huge scale on which manufactures, commerce, and transport are now organized has created a demand for great financial and technical skill, and as a consequence single individuals of exceptional talent now control a vast number of financial interests and determine the employment of multitudes of labourers. On their good management depend the success of the venture, the return to the savings invested in it, and the earnings of a host of employees. These 'captains of industry' receive very high remuneration, and many of them, from their superior ability, derive a surplus profit of a kind which has some of the chief economic characteristics of rent.

Many important problems arise out of the relations of employer and employed. In the Middle Ages the apprentice to a craft duly became a journeyman, and in course of time generally evolved into a master on a small scale; that is, he became an independent producer and an employer of other apprentices and journeymen. Under modern conditions only a small percentage of workmen can ever become employers, and, indeed, the employer class tends to be confined to specially trained men drawn from those ranks which enjoy unique opportunities for acquiring the wide and varied knowledge and experience which are requisite for successful organization. The employees constitute a large and distinctive class, whose common interests as wage-receivers lead them to combine in special organizations. Trade Unions have been devised in order to secure for the employees greater power by bargaining collectively for their share of the product; other functions are to provide mutual help in times of sickness or want of employment, and a machinery for regulating the conditions which affect their safety, comfort, and health, and determine the hours of labour in their several industries. Trade Unions obtained legal recognition only in 1825; they have advanced gradually in power and influence, and are now a very potent instrument in determining the economic conditions of industry. Their evolution has been attended with many struggles and disastrous strikes, which have at times paralyzed the activities of industry and entailed much suffering and economic loss. They are, however, now a recognized and important institution in the negotiations between employers and employees.

The perfect co-operation of capital and labour in production is a matter of universal interest, since on it depends the supply of wealth. It is to the advantage of both capital and labour that each should be highly efficient; divergence of interests arises in the division of the proceeds, and it is in the determination of the shares that the conflicts of capital and labour arise. At the period of the Industrial Revolution, and for a long time after the introduction of machinery and power into industry, the exploitation of labour by capital worked very unjustly for the employee. Trade Unionism introduced a new principle in collective bargaining, and strengthened labour in its attempts to secure its fair proportion. Meanwhile many economic reforms have taken place, and a century of factory legislation, the spread of education, and the increase of skill have all contributed to advance the position of labour, and have enabled the employees in organized industries to compete on equal terms with the employer. At the bottom of the scale of workers there is still a class whose wages are abnormally low and whose industry is often described as 'sweated.' Their condition is due to the low efficiency of their labour, the extreme ignorance and weakness of the employees themselves, and their inability to organize and combine. Social investigation has been active in exposing the circumstances of these labourers, and legislative action has been adopted for amending their position. This is, however, a problem which cannot be considered here.

Various schemes have been devised to diminish the friction between employers and employed, and to provide means for fair distribution of the product. The system of co-operation (*q.v.*) originated in an attempt to free labour from the control of capital, and to combine the interests of employer and employed in the same set of individuals, the labourers themselves providing the capital for their own employment. The weak point, however, resides in the difficulty of management. Experience has shown that no large industry can be successfully conducted without the guidance and direction of highly qualified managers. The kind of ability which they possess is relatively scarce and always commands a high price. Thus, though co-operation does in some respects curtail the functions of the employer, it does not dispense with his services; a price has to be paid for efficient management, and to the manager must be entrusted authority and discretion. Thus the employer as organizer becomes inevitable in co-operation of any kind, but most of all in productive industry where the commodity has to compete in the open market with the produce of rival firms.

The profit-sharing system is another method for reconciling the conflicting interests of intelligent workers and employers. It makes for higher efficiency by a combination of good feeling with an assurance of fuller reward, yet it is dependent upon the excellence of management and the skill and ability of the employer. No better instance of the economic working of this more fraternal system of production can be adduced than the case of the South Metropolitan Gas Company, so admirably conducted for many years by Sir George Livesey.

Socialism, again, seeks to replace private enterprise by State-production and to substitute for competition the principle of public control of capital and the means of production; it also encounters the same economic necessity for skilled management. The employer may be theoretically the State, but actually business of every kind is dependent for its success upon the organizing skill of individuals, and the problem of efficient management will become very serious if the position, direction, and control of State employees becomes dependent upon political influence or a bureaucracy. The equivalent of the employer must be found, and in the absence of the test of competition other avenues to the appointment of the directing staff would endanger the economic success of the proceedings. All organization involves grading, and officers are as essential to an industrial army as to a military force. Work must be organized; some persons must have authority to direct and command; their class becomes virtually an employing class as regards discipline and management; and, if it does not determine absolutely the rate of wages, neither can it guarantee that degree of efficiency which must ultimately determine the wages in amount.

From this brief review of the chief modes of conducting industrial enterprises, it will be obvious that the employer plays a vital part in the system of large industry, and that its success depends in a great degree upon his specialized skill. Competition for the rank of employer in business concerns which are conducted on a huge scale is exceedingly acute. The successful employer is a case of the survival of the fittest in a contest where no quarter is given. A large proportion of those who start as employers in smaller businesses fail in the struggle and disappear, their places being taken by others more able, or, in some instances, less scrupulous. The magnitude of modern industrial concerns offers to men of extraordinary business faculty great opportunities; it has also led to a grading of employers. Much of the work of direction is relegated by the chief to subordinates and heads of departments. The highest controllers of industry resemble a great general or chief engineer. In some cases this faculty amounts to genius; success depends upon the combination of many attributes —judgment, foresight, grasp of circumstances, promptitude, decision, firmness, and resourcefulness. The reward of success is proportionally high, and consists of wages plus a high rent of ability. The share of profits which recoups capital and risk will go as gross interest to the shareholders who provide the capital; the share which passes to the chief organizer is determined by his talent. This analysis reduces the employer in large production to a wage and rent receiver; he is really a worker of exceptional capacity receiving a high monopoly rate of pay for his services, like an eminent physician or a distinguished barrister. Thus the conflict in sharing is not merely between labour and capital, but also between groups of labourers of different degrees of ability; capital, as such, getting a return which covers interest and risks, the remainder being distributed between ordinary labours and the special labour of organization and control—all under the play of competition.

It is evident that many of the problems of modern industry cluster round the functions of the employer and the relations they involve; their fuller analysis and discussion, however, would go much beyond the proper limits of the present article, which is mainly descriptive and suggestive of the field of inquiry. See, further, artt.

ECONOMICS, EMPLOYMENT, SOCIALISM, TRADE UNIONS.

LITERATURE.—The subject is discussed under the divisions of Production and Distribution in all systematic treatises on Political Economy. The Works of J. S. Mill, Walker, Marshall, Sidgwick, and Nicholson should be consulted. W. Bagehot, *Economic Studies* 2 (1888), A. Toynbee, *Industrial Revolution* 5 (1890), W. S. Jevons, *The State in relation to Labour* 3 (1882), and S. Webb, *Industrial Democracy* (new ed. 1902), throw valuable light on the relations of capital and labour.

G. ARMITAGE-SMITH.

EMPLOYMENT.—1. Connotation of the term.—'Employment' may be held to mean the exercise of a function of any kind. The function in question may be exercised by a person on his own initiative and to his own advantage, or it may be exercised voluntarily or obligatorily by one person for the advantage of others or for mutual advantage. For the purposes of the present article 'employment' may be considered as the rendering of service through the exercise of a function in accordance with mutual obligations implied, imposed, or voluntarily assumed.

2. Relation of employer and employed.—In primitive slavery there is an implied obligation of protection and of opportunity to acquire maintenance on the part of the slave-owner, in correspondence with an obligation of service imposed upon the slave. In modern serfdom there is at least a similarly implied obligation on the part of the serf-owner, and in some cases an obligation of maintenance of the serf is imposed upon him by the State, when the opportunity in question has not been productive. (Thus for a long period in Russia the serf-owner was obliged by law to provide his serfs with grain when harvests were deficient.) In voluntary employment of free labourers by employers, there is an implied obligation of civil treatment and facility for the rendering of the service agreed upon; there are the obligations imposed upon both master and servant by customary and by statute law; and there are the explicit obligations in respect to hours of labour, remuneration, and notice of quittance, which form the subject of a written or verbal contract.

The incidents of the transition from voluntary or quasi-voluntary employment to personal bondage, and from that condition, through land bondage or otherwise, to hereditary serfdom and back to the system of voluntary employment, have no doubt varied in different countries and according to the different periods over which the process extended.

The economic history of Russia affords by far the most luminous details of the course of development, chiefly because the main incidents of it occurred during a comparatively recent period, and because they have been indicated in a large number of formal documents. From that history it may be gathered that the debt dependence of the free hired labourer arising from advances for the building of his dwelling, or for expenses during sickness or other incidents involving absence of earnings, led to a contract by which he obliged himself to work for his creditor, the wages otherwise due for his work being placed against the interest only, or against the principal of the debt and the interest together; or, alternatively, wages and loan alike being cancelled and the debtor entering formally into serfdom. The immobility of the propertyless debtor was secured by police measures, and the peasant was thus tied to the soil, while the piling upon him of obligations and taxes completed his ruin. This process was in effect fully worked out in the 18th cent., and the decay of the system followed. The introduction of mechanical industry on the large scale rendered the employment of skilled labourers necessary, and although, in the early stages of Russian industrial enterprise, forced labour was largely employed by *ascription* of peasants to factories, there was, from the beginning of the 18th cent., some employment of free hired labourers in industrial establishments. The presence, in the same factory or mill, of free and of obligatory labourers was anomalous, and from this and other causes the decay of serfdom began. The system of factory employment was subjected, in the end of the 18th and the beginning of the 19th cent., to the competition of the isolated industry of the cottage (*kustarni ězba*), under which the cottage craftsman manufactured for sale to the merchant, who offered an immediate market for his product. The profitable character of the business, together with the absence of large accumulated capitals, prevented the merchants from becoming also employers. The exploitation of the independent and isolated craftsman was simpler and less exposed to risk than the exploitation of grouped workmen in a factory. The advent of steam power threw the economical advantage on the other side, and gradually the factory gained at the expense of the cottage. In the factories to which peasants were ascribed, wages were credited to them against their taxes, and against their obligations where these were defined; where the latter were not defined, nothing was usually paid. The practice of defining obligations having increased, and in some cases the practice of paying taxes directly to the State having been introduced, a class of free hired labourers seeking employment gradually emerged. The emancipation of the serfs in 1861 did not at once throw the whole of the peasant masses into this class, but it greatly reinforced it. When this event occurred, large numbers of the peasants who had been ascribed to factories immediately abandoned their employment and returned to their villages, creating a temporary scarcity of artisan labour and an advance of industrial wages.

The system of serfdom, with its attendant industrial ascription, was undoubtedly subversive of human dignity; but it involved employment for every one. Where there were few or no free labourers, and where every one was either master or servant, there could be no unemployment.

This at all events was the theory. Flights of peasants, however, occurred from estates (in Russia) when, owing to deficient harvests or mismanagement, the peasants were unable to subsist on their own earnings and their proprietors were unable or unwilling to support them; and these fleeing peasants were of course landless and unemployed.

The phenomenon of unemployment may be regarded as coincident with the development of free hiring. Unemployment—occasional, periodical, or permanent—may be considered as the price which the working masses have paid for the abolition of obligatory labour. The conditions of employment have historically been subjected to determination —by the State, by the municipality, by justices of the peace, by the gilds, by unions of the employers, and by trade unions—as regards hygienic conditions and protection from machinery in factories, as regards safety of mines and ships, and as regards the amount of wages either by way of fixing a minimum or a maximum wage, or, in respect to the periods and methods of payment, to the attachment of wages for debt, or to the security for their payment in case of the bankruptcy of the employer.

3. The State and employment.—The policy of the modern State with reference to factory legislation was in general opposed by the advocates of *laissez-faire* in the first half of the 19th century. The expediency of sanitary legislation for factories, etc., can no longer be regarded as matter of controversy, so far as the general principle is concerned, although every extension of it is necessarily subjected to criticism. The expediency of the control of the State over the terms of the contract which is made between the employer and his workpeople is by no means so universally acknowledged, although the State does, as a rule, prevent by law the payment of wages in the form of goods (under the Truck Act) or in public-houses. It does not now prescribe the rate of wages.[1] An argument for a national minimum has, however, been advanced by Mr. Sidney Webb (*Industrial Democracy*, London, 1897, ii. 766 ff.). He considers such a measure as the only means of putting an end to 'industrial parasitism,' and as a natural complement to the national hygienic minimum which he thinks has already been carried into effect in factory legislation (see, however, Zwiedineck-Südenhorst, 384–385). The *principle* of a minimum wage for the mining industry obtained legislative sanction from the British Parliament on the occasion of the great coal strike of March 1912.

The policy of an authoritative fixation of a minimum wage is open to the criticism that such a measure would tend to the non-employment of those whose labour might be insufficient to justify the minimum payment, unless the minimum were fixed at a very low point; yet such persons might be able to earn a part at least of their sub-

[1] Justices of the Peace are, *e.g.*, forbidden to fix wages by 5 Geo. IV. c. 96.

sistence by being permitted to work for inferior wages. Mr. Webb might answer that such cases of 'industrial parasitism' should be otherwise provided for, because their presence in the labour market tends to depress the wages of the group to which they belong.[1] The reactions of a minimum wage would, however, be extremely difficult to forecast even if much more numerous data than now exist were available (cf. Zwiedineck-Südenhorst, *l.c.*). The policy of fixing a minimum wage by a trade union is open to the objection that the minimum is also a maximum, and that the highly efficient workman is obliged to work at the same rate as the less efficient. Even when the wages are paid by piecework, the workman who works harder than his fellows and makes more money finds it difficult to continue to do so because of the opposition of his comrades, who conceive that his proceeding may tend to bring down the piecework rate (see, however, on the whole subject, 'The Device of the Common Rule,' in Webb, *op. cit.* ii. 715 ff.). The policy of fixing a maximum wage by the public authority is open to the objection that, unless the maximum is placed at or above the rates current in other districts to which workmen may migrate, there will be a tendency for workmen to go where there is no legal maximum.

In the 14th cent. the municipal governments of some of the Italian towns fixed, in the assumed interests of the employers, a maximum rate of wages. Venice did not do so, with the result that labourers flocked there, and wages in that city became lower than elsewhere.

4. The ethical aspect.—On its ethical side, the relation between employers and employed appears at present to be passing through important phases, although the direction of the movement is not always obvious. The principle known in Scotland as *ca' canny*, involving the performance by the workman of as little work as possible, may not be widely or frequently, but is certainly in some industries occasionally, applied both in Europe and in America. On the other hand, remorseless exploitation of the workers probably still exists in both industrial continents and in Japan, especially with regard to unskilled or inferior skilled labour. Apart from the possibility of improvement, from an ethical point of view, on both sides, of the relation, there is to be considered the certainty of economic deterioration which must follow in the event of these tendencies going far, with consequent reaction towards a relation sounder alike from an economic and from an ethical point of view. The 'class conscious' working mass, which, according to the Marxist doctrine, must eventually completely overcome its antagonist, the 'class conscious' employing class, may carry the process to the bitter end, or the conflict of classes may be arrested by a sense of *la solidarité humaine* arising in both classes. Particular schemes like those of Godin and Leclaire, the movement for co-operative production, and the like, must be regarded as of less importance than the mass movement. Whether or not this movement is making for increased social, as opposed to class, consciousness, is at present extremely hard to determine. There appears, however, to be a certain general tendency in that direction—the ethical relations of the classes being probably somewhat improved by the gross increase in production, and by the consequent mitigation of the struggle for existence. A check to this increase, considered in relation to the growth of the population, would undoubtedly involve a check to the ethical advance.

5. Concentration of capital and industry.—The rôle of the employer in modern industry becomes more important, and his corresponding responsibilities become greater, with the accumulation and concentration of industrial capital. The employer also becomes more impersonal. Although very large enterprises are frequently associated with the name of one individual (especially in the United States), the actual share of that individual in the management of the enterprise is usually confined to the determination of some matter of wide policy, and even in this his course is generally influenced by his partners. The ultimate control of all large enterprises must rest with the body of its stock-holders at a particular moment. In many large industrial concerns the number of stockholders is at least as numerous as the number of employees. Both are highly fluctuating bodies,—one body changes its *personnel* daily in the bourses, and the other changes daily in the workshops. The concentration of industry, which has gone far in the United States, has been accompanied by grave difficulties of management, the bold financier being rarely patient enough in respect to detail to secure the economies which have been anticipated from the concentration. The mere fact of concentration does not, however, appear to have been adverse to the interests of employees; the chief antagonism to it has arisen from the small trader, whose profits have been reduced by the competition of the large joint-stock company or group of companies combined in a merger or trust. From a theoretical point of view, the function of the employer, as such, is to administer his business in such a way as to secure its continuity by the creation of a sufficient reserve against the accidents of trade, and to secure the goodwill of his employees in such a way as to retain an efficient working *personnel*. The increasingly impersonal character of employment may not improbably mitigate the class struggle, because of the diffusion of the capitalistic interest, and even its transfusion into the working class itself.

In the United States and Canada, for example, the relatively high wages in some industries enable certain groups of workmen to accumulate considerable sums of money. These sums are invested by them not merely in houses or in land, but also sometimes in industrial securities, probably rarely in the industries to which they themselves belong, generally rather in others.

Four important recent incidents in the evolution of employment demand mention in this place; these are: (*a*) the appointment of Arbitration and Conciliation Boards, either by the Government or voluntarily by agreement between the parties; (*b*) collective bargaining between groups of employers and groups of workmen; (*c*) the establishment of Labour Exchanges; and (*d*) the project of insurance against unemployment.

(*a*) *Arbitration Boards* in England probably owed their existence to the *conseils des prud-hommes* of France and Belgium, which were organized early in the 19th century (cf. H. Crompton, p. 19 ff.). The first Board of this kind in England appears to have been formed in 1849, for the purpose of dealing with a dispute in the silk trade at Macclesfield (*ib.* 124); another followed in 1853 in the printing trade (*ib.* 131); but the most important early Arbitration Board was that formed in 1860 for the purpose of dealing with disputes in the hosiery trade at Nottingham (*ib.* 19). The practice has been widely adopted in Great Britain, in New Zealand, and in Canada—with qualified success. In none of these countries has it altogether prevented strikes; but it has in some measure diminished their number. The various inquiries which have followed the appointment of arbitrators or the action of a permanent Conciliation Board have shown conclusively the impossibility of arriving at a just wage. The decision of the Board must, therefore, invariably involve either a compromise, in which both sides give way somewhat, or a victory for one party or the other. In

[1] The employment of pensioners, of persons of independent means, and of women and children who do not require to earn the whole of their subsistence, undoubtedly depresses the wages of their groups.

the first case, neither party is wholly satisfied; and in the second case, if one is satisfied, the other is not. This is true of all litigation; but in industrial disputes arbitration is expected to conduce to peaceful settlement in a sphere in which positive law and even precedent afford no guide, which in litigation they do. The decision of the arbitrators has not, and cannot have, the force of law, because, under present industrial conditions, a large body of men cannot be forced against their will to work for a particular employer for wages determined by a third party (see, however, *Labour Laws of New Zealand* [as cited in Lit.] and *New Zealand Year-Book*). The history of the great strikes in England in 1911 and 1912 is significant in this connexion.

(*b*) *Collective bargaining* grew out of the practice of arbitration. It has been strenuously objected to by employers, but in most of the staple trades it has come to be recognized. It is frequently accompanied either by periodical fixation of rates of wages, or by an automatic sliding scale (as in the coal and iron trades).

(*c*) *Labour Exchanges, Labour Registries, or Labour Bureaux* of a private character are of long standing, and so is their regulation by law. Of late years there has been an increasing hostility to such agencies, especially those which concern themselves chiefly with the employment of sailors. In order to replace private agencies and to extend the functions of Labour Exchanges, public institutions have been established in Germany, France, Belgium, and Great Britain. In all these countries the operations of such institutions have now become very extensive. (Cf. Board of Trade Reports, cited in the Lit.)

(*d*) *Insurance against unemployment* has existed, in fact, for many years in the unemployed benefit funds of the Trade Unions. Local Unemployment Insurance Offices were established in Berne in 1893, in Cologne in 1896, in Leipzig in 1903, and elsewhere. (Cf. Board of Trade Reports, as above.) Insurance against unemployment was included in the National Insurance Bill (cd. 5989, London, 1911). In certain trades, insurance against unemployment is, under the Insurance Act, compulsory. The total Unemployed Insurance Fund is provided partly from contributions by the workmen, partly from contributions by employers, and partly from moneys voted by Parliament. The effects of the new Act will not be observable earlier than the end of the year 1912.

6. Causes of unemployment.—The emergence of a class of free hired labourers, or of persons voluntarily seeking employment, usually makes itself manifest by the migration of numbers of such labourers to periodical or permanent centres of employment.

Instances of such periodical migrations are to be found in the movement of hop-pickers to Kent; in that of Irish harvesters from Ireland to the Lowlands of Scotland; in that of Italian *contadini* from Lombardy and Piedmont to the south of France; in the immense migration (annually about one million) of harvest labourers from various parts of northern and central Russia to the Black Soil Region; in the 'harvesters' excursions' from Ontario and Quebec to the Prairie provinces of Canada; and in the annual migration, which now assumes considerable proportions, of workmen from Scotland and from Italy to America in the spring, and to Scotland and Italy in the autumn. The colonization of America and of Australia, the partial colonization of Africa by Europeans, and the colonization of the Straits Settlements by Chinese, afford instances of permanent settlement of migrants.

Migration from the rural districts to the towns is a phenomenon common to all regions where no insurmountable obstacles exist against the mobility of labour. The relatively higher scale of nominal wages in the towns, as compared with the scale of wages in the country, and the relatively greater attraction of social centres, in general, conduce to this movement. This process customarily denudes the small towns, diminishing in them the demand for labour, and then denudes the villages. The stream of labourers seeking employment in the industrial centres under conditions of free mobility is uncontrolled, and is sometimes in excess of the demand for them. An excess of labourers seeking employment may of itself produce, through a series of reactions, the phenomenon of unemployment. This result is reached in two ways: the reduction of population in the country towns and villages diminishes the demand for commodities there; and the surplus of labourers in the industrial towns tends to reduce wages, and thus to reduce effective demand in them. Migration of labourers, in the absence of means of organizing their labour or the labour of others whom they displace, may, therefore, if conducted on a considerable scale, result in depression of trade, in so far as that is due to diminished capacity for consumption caused by diminished employment.

Diminution of employment may also result from the rise of the rate of interest upon capital devoted to industrial enterprises. Such a rise in the rate of interest may be caused by an increase in the demand for industrial capital over the supply of such capital in the market; or by increase of demand for funds in the market for commercial capital, or in the market for public funds; or the rise may be due to restriction of credit from any one or all of very numerous causes, such as over-speculation in land, in buildings, in industry, commerce, or otherwise, over-production of certain important commodities; or to disproportionate investment in enterprises which do not immediately yield a return adequate to meet the normal rate of interest upon the invested funds.

Examples of unemployment resulting from reactions of this kind are to be found in the depression in Great Britain in 1878 and subsequent years, which arose in part from the over-investment of capital in railways in the United States and in New Zealand.

Unemployment may also occur, upon an extended scale, through the cutting off of the supply of raw material which is necessary for the production of an important commodity.

Such a phenomenon may be caused by a war, as in the case of the Cotton Famine; or by a strike, as in industrial suspension due to a strike of coal miners.

Unemployment may also result from the falling off of demand for commodities, due to deficient harvests; resulting in advance in the price of necessaries of life, and in consequent diminishing general purchasing power as applied to commodities other than necessaries, so far as concerns the industrial centres; and, if the advance in price of agricultural produce does not offset the deficiency, in diminished purchasing power in the rural districts. Unemployment may also be caused by changes in tariffs, in technical processes (as in the displacement of hand labour by machinery, and the substitution of one machine for another), or in transportation routes, or by the opening up of new ports.

Instances of the latter are to be found in the creation of a new port of entry at Montreal in 1832, which immediately diminished by about one-half the port trade of Quebec; and the extension of the docks at Antwerp, Hamburg, and Havre, which more recently diminished the *entrepôt* trade of the port of London.

Periodical unemployment is also produced by seasonal trades, and by the interference of weather conditions with the normal course of outdoor labour.

The causes which have been enumerated are of a general character; and they affect, directly or indirectly, large numbers of men who, but for their operation, would be in constant employment. There are, however, two series of causes of unemployment in addition to these general causes: one series relates to the efficiency of the directive power of the employing class, and the other to the efficiency of the labouring power of the working class.

Competent management may, through the creation and intelligent use of reserves, distribute labour force in such a way as to secure continuity of employment under any but long-continued abnormal conditions; whereas incompetent management may result in the idleness of large groups of men, even in a period of brisk trade. Similarly, the efficient worker is, in general, likely to secure employment, while the inefficient, dissolute, or ill-tempered workman may find it difficult to procure employment at any time.

7. Recent attempts to solve the problem of unemployment.—The steps which have been taken during recent years to deal with the problem of unemployment have, in general, been characterized by the policy of separating those who are unemployed owing to causes over which they have no control from those whose unemployment is caused by personal deficiency. Temporary relief, accompanied by employment upon public or private work not otherwise demanded at the time, has been devised for the relief of workmen temporarily out of employment (as in Distress Committees and like organizations). A more difficult problem is presented by the casual labourer who has lost the faculty of continuous labour, and whose employment by private employers is for that reason discontinuous. Very frequently, physical and mental deficiencies combine to make the labour of such unemployed unproductive. The very measures which have been taken for the employment of the employable unemployed have probably rendered it more difficult for the unemployable unemployed to obtain the charity which is, after all, what they need, since work in any serious sense is not possible for them.

The Labour Colonies of Germany, Holland, and Belgium have been devised for such cases; and similar institutions have more recently been established in Scotland (in Ayrshire), and in England (at Hollesley Bay). The Labour Colony is an expensive, and not wholly satisfactory, form of poor relief; but it does, undoubtedly, present a means of preventing begging, and of avoiding the waste of indiscriminate charity (see, however, references in the Lit.).

Contemporaneously with the efforts which have been made by the public authorities (in England by the Local Government Board and by the municipalities) to grapple with the question of relief of the unemployed, certain steps of a positive character have also been taken.

In Germany, the enrolment of every workman in a society of his trade is practically compulsory. He is also under obligation to make periodical payments. Should he be sick or unemployed, he is entitled to certain benefits. In Great Britain, a scheme of insurance against unemployment is now before the country.

8. The right to work.—Such positive steps may or may not involve the recognition by the public authority of the right of the labourer to the opportunity for labour. Where such a right is recognized, and where machinery is provided for rendering it effective, it is difficult to see how the corollary of obligatory labour can be evaded.

An interesting experiment in this connexion is at present in progress. An Employment Committee has been appointed in Glasgow, under the auspices of the Board of Trade. The functions of this Committee involve the examination of every young person who is brought before it, and the provision of employment, after the manner of Plato's guardians. Should this plan be widely adopted, it is difficult to avoid the conclusion that there is a risk of fixing, by such means, hereditary occupations to an even greater extent than is now the case.

It is important to notice that, under existing police administration in Great Britain, it is usually possible in practice to compel young persons to work, whether they desire to do so or not. The extension of these powers to the obligatory employment of adults, excepting where they are sentenced by law to penal servitude, does not appear to have been carried out in practice.

The Unemployed Workmen Bill of 1907, promoted by the Independent Labour Party, contained an obligatory clause by which unemployed men might be sentenced to work under the control of the local authority for six months (cl. 7, sec. 3).

9. Socialism and employment.—It remains to be noticed that from the socialist point of view (promulgated especially by Saint Simon) all private employment is exploitative; and that from the anarchist point of view State and private employment are alike exploitative. The growth of the former idea has led to a propaganda of collectivism in which the principal point is that a democratic State should be sole employer; and the growth of the latter has led to the idea that the exploitative element in State and private employment alike should be checked by *l'action directe*, expressing itself in general strikes repeated as often as may be considered necessary.

It should be observed, however, that the general strike is a weapon with a double edge, and that the edge which is turned away from the striker is likely to be blunted before the other. The so-called third general strike in Russia proved this to the satisfaction of the leaders of it.

From the socialist point of view also it should be observed that the labourer has a right to the whole of the produce of his labour. A method of division which should be devised with a view to secure this condition, under modern circumstances of division of labour, and the eventual evaluation of the product—frequently at a long distant time and in widely distant places—presents cardinal difficulties. Such a plan appears to be applicable only to a limited and self-contained society. It might be held that the strenuous competition of modern commerce and industry tends to the elimination of unearned increments of value, although it is open to doubt whether any system would eliminate the possibility of adventitious gains due either to chance or to shrewd anticipation of economic reactions. A careful analysis of the phenomena of employment and of unemployment must show that mere alteration in the system or in the amount of the taxation of land, as is proposed in the Single Tax propaganda, or even the nationalization of the land, would not necessarily solve, or even seriously influence, so complex a problem as that of unemployment. Even in an agricultural country, not merely is access to land requisite, but a sufficient endowment of agricultural capital and skill are necessary to enable the landless unemployed to avail themselves of the land which might even be freely placed at their disposal. The phenomenon of near proximity of unemployed men and of land which may be cultivated rent-free is not unknown. It must be allowed, however, that, where scarcity of land really exists, peasants who might prefer to remain cultivators are driven into the towns because they have insufficient or no land. (This condition exists undoubtedly in some parts of Russia.) Whether even confiscatory taxation or immediate nationalization of the land would in any country necessarily result in increased cultivation, either extensively or intensively, is at least doubtful.

See also artt. ECONOMICS, SOCIALISM.

LITERATURE.—The subject of Employment is treated in all systematic treatises on Political Economy. The emergence of a class of free labourers seeking employment may be studied, for Western Europe, in the following: **M. Kowalewsky**, *Die ökonom. Entwickelung Europas bis zum Beginn der kapitalist. Wirtschaftsform* (tr. from the Russian), Berlin, 6 vols., 1901 ff., and, for Russia, **V. O. Kluchevsky**, *Hist. of Russia* (tr. C. J. Hogarth), London, 1911, vol. i., *Course of Russian History*, vols. i.[2]–iv. (Russian), Moscow, 1908–10.

For the economics of employment, see **J. A. Hobson**, *Evolution of Modern Capitalism: A Study of Machine Production*, London, 1894; **L. Brentano**, *The Relation of Labor to the Law of To-day* (Eng. tr.), New York and London, 1891; **E. v. Böhm-Bawerk**, *Capital and Interest: A Critical Hist. of Economical Theory* (Eng. tr.), London, 1890; **E. v. Philippovich**, *Grundriss der polit. Ökonomie*, 2 vols., Freiburg i. B., 1893 and 1899; **J. Conrad**, *Handwörterb. d. Staatswissenschaften*, Jena, 1901, art. 'Unternehmer und Unternehmergewinn,' etc., vol. vii.[2] pp. 338–361.

For wages, see **A. Marshall**, *Elements of Economics of Industry*, London, 1892, p. 267 ff., and *Principles of Economics*, do. 1907, vol. i.[5] p. 505 ff.; **O. v. Zwiedineck-Südenhorst**, *Lohnpolitik und Lohntheorie mit besonderer Berücksichtigung des Minimallohnes*, Leipzig, 1900.

For unemployment, see Board of Trade—Labour Department: Report on Agencies and Methods for Dealing with the Unemployed (Parl. Paper C.—7182), London, 1893 (contains Bibliography of Labour Colonies); continuation of above [cd. 2304], London, 1904; *La Disoccupazione, Relazioni e discussioni del 1o Congresso Internazionale per la lotta contro la disoccupazione 2–3 Ottobre 1906*, Milan, 1906; A. Agnelli, *Il Problema economico della disoccupazione operaia*, Milan, 1909; Unemployed Workmen Act, 1905 (5 Edw. VII. ch. 18); Circulars, etc., connected therewith, London, 1905, Orders, nos. 48,677–79; London Unemployed Fund, 1904–5; Report of Central Executive Committee, London, 1905; Report upon the Work of the Central (Unemployed) Body for London (Unemployed Workmen Act, 1905), do. 1906; Report of the Queen's Unemployed Fund, 1905–6, do. 1906; J. Burns, speech in House of Commons on vote for Local Gov. Board, 19th July 1906.

For arbitration and conciliation, see H. Crompton, *Industrial Conciliation*, London, 1876; L. L. F. R. Price, *Industrial Peace: its Advantages, Methods, and Difficulties*, London, 1887; Reports by Board of Trade of Proceedings under the Conciliation (Trade Disputes) Act, 1896 (59 & 60 Vict. c. 30), 7th Report, London, 1910; and Report on Collective Agreements between Employers and Workpeople (*ib.*), do. 1910.

For Labour Exchanges: Report on Agencies and Methods for Dealing with the Unemployed (*ib.*), London, 1904; Abstract of Labour Statistics (*ib.* annually); *The Labour Laws of New Zealand*[2], compiled by direction of the Hon. the Minister of Labour, Wellington, N.Z., 1896; New Zealand Official Year-Book; and Dominion of Canada, *The Labour Gazette* (issued monthly).

For the socialist point of view, see esp. W. Thompson, *An Inquiry into the Principles of the Distribution of Wealth*, London, 1824, and *Labour Rewarded: the Claims of Labour and Capital Conciliated; or, How to secure to Labour the whole Products of its Exertions*, do. 1827; K. Marx, *Das Kapital: Kritik der polit. Ökonomie*[6], Hamburg, 1909, vol. i. *passim*, vol. iii., 1st and 2nd pt., 1904[2], *passim*, also *Theorien über den Mehrwert*, vol. ii. 1st pt., Stuttgart, 1910[2], pp. 1–159, and vol. ii. 2nd pt., do., 1905, pp. 233–319; A. Menger, *The Right to the Whole Produce of Labour*, London, 1899; K. Vorländer, *Die Neukantische Bewegung im Sozialismus*, Berlin, 1902.

J. MAVOR.

EMULATION.—See ENVY.

ENCRATITES (Ἐγκρατεῖς [Iren.]. Ἐγκρατηταί [Clem. Alex.], Ἐγκρατί(ῖ)ται [Hippol., Epiph.]).—Christians of the early Church who made abstinence from flesh, wine, marriage, and possessions their rule of life. From the middle of the 2nd cent. they 'stood midway between the larger Christendom and the Marcionite Church as well as the Gnostic schools' (Harnack, *Hist. of Dogma*, Eng. tr., London, 1894–99, ii. 43). Without holding one form of creed, or being organized as a body, they practised everywhere the same kind of asceticism. Their spirit was widely diffused. Epiphanius, in his chapter, κατὰ Ἐγκρατιτῶν (*Hær.* 47), names seven countries, mostly of Asia Minor, in which they abounded (πληθύνουσι). Irenæus (i. 28) says that some of the earliest of them were followers of Saturninus and Marcion. Eusebius (*HE* iv. 28) appears to be mistaken in calling Tatian, the eminent Apologist, their founder (ἧς παρεκτροπῆς ἀρχηγόν), and Epiphanius (*loc. cit.*), in placing the Encratites after the Tatianites. What Tatian did was to join the sect, and to give it a more complete canon, including the Epistles of St. Paul, whose teaching other leaders, especially Severus, rejected. There must have been a considerable Encratite literature. Several writers, both for and against the principles of the sect, are now little more than names.

In the time of Marcus Aurelius, 'Musanus . . . is said to have written a very elegant work (ἐπιστρεπτικώτατος λόγος), addressed to certain brethren who had swerved from the truth to the heresy of the Encratites, which had even then made its appearance, and which introduced a singular and pernicious error into the world' (Euseb. *HE* iv. 28). Theodoret (*Hær. Fab.* i. 21) mentions Apollinaris, another writer of the same period, who wrote against the Severian Encratites. Macarius Magnes (iii. 43) states that an Encratite leader, Dositheus, a Cilician, wrote a defence in eight books, contending that 'by sexual intercourse the world had had its beginning, and by continence would receive its end.' Clement, in whose *Stromata* (bk. iii.) Encratism can best be studied, states that Julius Cassianus, whom he calls the founder of the Docetic heresy, wrote Περὶ ἐγκρατείας ἢ περὶ εὐνουχίας, and quotes three Encratite passages from this work (iii. 13, 91, 92).

The influence of the Encratites may be ascribed to three causes. (1) Their renunciation of the world was strikingly complete. They had the great merit of being logical. Having grasped a principle, they applied it with the utmost rigour and vigour. They rejected the prevalent distinction between a higher and a lower, though sufficient, morality. The Church, which applauded their counsel of perfection in the few, resolutely declared war against their principle when they sought to make it an inflexible law for all. Therefore they refused to follow the Church, scorning the weak compromise she offered. They insisted that, if ἐγκράτεια was right at all, it was right universally. To be a Christian was to be an Encratite.

(2) The Encratites pointed to the example of our Lord. They made the 'evangelic' life their standard, urging that the Christian system of morals must be founded on the actions of Christ, and take its laws from Him. The life of celibacy and the renunciation of all worldly goods, after His pattern, was the essential mark of Christian perfection. Tatian wrote a book, Περὶ τοῦ κατὰ τὸν Σωτῆρα καταρτισμοῦ (Clem. Alex. *Strom.* iii. 12), in which he showed that the Christian ideal can be attained only by the imitation of Christ, and rallied the Church to the duty of walking in His steps. The writer forgot, as Clement wisely observes, that Christ was 'not a common man' (οὐδὲ ἄνθρωπος ἦν κοινός).

'He was deficient in a right understanding of the life of Christ in its completeness, and in its relation to His mission as the redeemer of mankind, and the author of a new creation of Divine life, which, in the further course of its development from Him, was designed to embrace and pervade all human relations' (Neander, *Church Hist.*, ed. London, 1884, ii. 127).

Tatian wrongly regarded Paul as teaching (1 Co 7[5]) that marriage and unchastity are one and the same thing—both equally the service of Satan. 'With Marcion and Saturninus he asserted that wedlock was only corruption and fornication' (φθορὰν καὶ πορνείαν [Eus. *HE* iv. 29]). In forming his opinions, it is probable that he made use not only of the canonical Gospels, but of apocryphal histories, in which the delineation of the Person of Christ had been modified under the influence of theosophical and ascetic principles. Epiphanius states that the Encratites used the *Acts* of Andrew, John, and Thomas; and the fragments of Cassianus found in Clement seem to reflect the *Gospel according to the Egyptians*.

(3) Encratism generally based itself on the same prevalent doctrine of God and the world as Gnosticism. Some Encratites, indeed, professed to be orthodox. Those whom Hippolytus describes (*Phil.* viii. 20) are admitted by him to have been sound in their teaching regarding God and Christ, differing from the Church only in their manner of life. But most Encratites were philosophical dualists. Taking the gloomy view that matter is essentially evil, and the body the cause as well as the occasion of sin, they denied the identity of the supreme God with the Creator of the world. Tatian learned a kind of dualism from his master, Justin Martyr, and afterwards developed it into the ordinary full-blown Gnostic doctrine of Æons (Euseb. *loc. cit.*). He then felt logically bound to connect himself with the Encratites, seeing no way of redemption except the subjugation of all the natural impulses and appetites. Tertullian would have become an Encratite, if this mode of life had not been associated with heresy (Harnack, *Hist.* ii. 103). A form of this morbid error is already combated in 1 Ti 4[3-5]. When men were 'forbidding to marry, and commanding to abstain from meats,' the healthy-minded writer of the Epistle refuted them by denying the first principle of Gnosticism and Encratism. God is the Creator of the world, and none of His work is to be despised. 'Every creature of God is good, and nothing is to be rejected, if it be received with thanksgiving: for it is sanctified through the word of God and prayer' (4[4. 5]). Christianity is

not the eradication but the consecration of nature. In the right sense of the word, every Christian must, of course, be ἐγκρατής (used only once in NT, viz. Tit 1[8]). Paul reasoned of ἐγκράτεια till the Roman governor trembled (Ac 24[25]); he names it as part of the fruit of the Spirit (Gal 5[23]); and another writer mentions it as one of the graces which are to be added to faith (2 P 1[6]). But true self-control (ἐγκράτεια ἑαυτοῦ [Plato, *Rep.* 390 B], ἐγκράτεια ἡδονῶν καὶ ἐπιθυμιῶν [*ib.* 430 E]) is not to be attained by an otherworldliness which shirks life's duties, and shuns its pleasures as temptations of the devil. This 'fugitive and cloistered virtue' is far from according with the mind of Christ, who wished His followers to be the leaven of society, the salt of the earth, the light of the world (Mt 5[13ff.]).

Sozomen (v. 11) mentions the Encratites as a sect existing in Galatia in the time of Julian, when Busiris, one of their number, suffered. One of the laws of the Theodosian Code (A.D. 381) was directed against the Manichæans, who sheltered themselves under the name of Encratites. But 'the Encratite controversy was, on the one hand, swallowed up by the Gnostic, and, on the other hand, replaced by the Montanistic' (Harnack, *Hist.* i. 238).

LITERATURE.—In addition to books already named, see A. Hilgenfeld, *Ketzergesch. des Urchristentums*, Leipzig, 1884, esp. p. 543 ff.; cf. also art. 'Encratites,' in Smith-Wace, *DCB*; and Krüger, 'Enkratiten,' in *PRE*³.

JAMES STRAHAN.

ENCYCLOPÆDIA OF THEOLOGY.—See THEOLOGY.

ENCYCLOPÆDISTS.—1. Rise of the Encyclopædic movement.—It may truthfully be said that the appearance of Hume's *Treatise of Human Nature* (1739–40) was the starting-point of a new school of thought. Locke had devoted himself to the explanation of the origin of our ideas; he told us that we owe our conception of substance to the long-continued habit of seeing certain modes in association one with the other; or—to put it in a word—Locke denied the existence of innate ideas, and declared that all our knowledge springs from experience. But Hume asked the question, How do we know that two things stand to one another in the relation of causality? Because we usually see one thing follow another thing, we simply come to the conclusion that it must so follow. Self is merely a complex of swiftly succeeding ideas, under which we imagine an illusory soul or self to exist. Soul, this complex of ideas, must hence cease when the ideas cease, and when bodily movement comes to an end. Thus it was that Hume's scepticism naturally followed Locke's empiricism in the order of thought, and all our knowledge was reduced to perception of sense, leaving us with sensation alone to take the place of the old determination of universality and necessity. The point of view arrived at had a close affinity with the philosophy of the 18th cent. in France. Of the school of thought known as the Illumination, or the Philosophy of the Enlightenment (see ENLIGHTENMENT), the Encyclopædists form a noteworthy part, inasmuch as they represent its spirit in its most characteristic form. In France this attitude of mind was unaccompanied by the pietistic tendency, wherein inward spiritual experiences were given a value as distinguished from the literal teaching of authority. This tendency was a feature in the movement towards intellectual liberation in the *Aufklärung* in Germany, even while it seemed to be in opposition to its conclusions. The Enlightenment of the Understanding there concluded its period of clear intellectual conceptions, by means of reason alone, by giving place to a period of sentimentality. In France, as we shall see, this concentration on the value of feeling, as advocated by Rousseau, ended in momentous results on the practical side of politics; while in Germany, where the call for action was not in the same way demanded, it found vent in intellectual and æsthetic interests, in the period of *Sturm und Drang*, and in Romanticism in literature.

It was in France, however, that the empirical or Lockian school of thought was carried to its ultimate and logical consequence of sensualism and materialism. Empiricism developed in France as it never did in England, despite its being derived so largely from the writings of Englishmen. The French relentlessly faced the practical consequences of the speculative position which they adopted with the clearness and logic characteristic of their race; and this resulted in a thoroughly materialistic conception of the system of the world, and in an egoistic morality.

But the growth of the speculative and sceptical attitude of mind that took the place of the idealism which had proceeded from Cartesianism gives us but one aspect from which the rise of the new school of the 'Illumination' can be explained. Along with the speculative side, there were two other influences at work which had as great an effect on contemporary thought as that which was purely intellectual, and which was complementary to it. The first was the rise of the scientific spirit, which, though it may have begun in France with Descartes, was developed in a remarkable way by Isaac Newton. Newton made men realize that the 'physical laws which hold good on the surface of the earth are valid throughout the Universe.' The mechanical conception of Nature formulated by Kepler, Galileo, and Descartes became, through Newton, intelligible to all. Men were shown how the machine works, while it was also demonstrated to them how it is held together by means of the law of gravitation. Newton's philosophy, on its speculative side, did not have much influence on contemporary thought, but practically his teaching and method had an effect which can hardly be overestimated. He popularized the so-called scientific view of Nature and made it intelligible, and this scientific outlook had the effect of making the world around of immense interest and importance in every one of its aspects, and presented infinite possibilities for those who were prepared to open their eyes, and have unveiled to them the things that had hitherto seemed hidden or mysterious. It also held up before them the hope of attaining the happiness sought by all, through knowledge of a kind that was free to every seeker after truth. It was Voltaire, in his *Lettres sur les Anglais*, who introduced his countrymen at large to this new way of looking at the world; it was he who contrasted the old learning and the old religion with the new; it was he who popularized the views which he had adopted, applying scientific methods to supernatural and superstitious beliefs. The light of day was to shine out unobscured by the accretions of the ages. Voltaire expounded Newton's theory of Physics, and wrote a *Dictionnaire philosophique portatif* (1764), which set forth his views on these and similar subjects from the standpoint (though officially contradicted on occasion) of a sceptic in religion and a materialist in philosophy. The visits of Voltaire and Montesquieu to England had great results, for they brought home with them new ideas in religion, philosophy, and the relations of man to man.

But there was still another cause in operation which made for the new empirical point of view. It is to be found in the general social and political condition of France at the time. A dissolute court and a despotic government, on the one hand, and a Church both hypocritical and tyrannical, on the other, had, each in its respective sphere, alienated not only the poor and suffering, but all thinking men, such as were the *philosophes* of the 18th century. The impulse on their part was to resist the tyranny and corruption that everywhere abounded. When they applied their clear reasoning powers to the corrupt order of things that obtained at the time, there was little doubt of the result. The unjustifiable condition of matters then existing was to them the order of things established by authority, and, if they were to vindicate for rational mankind the possession of its reason, the first thing to be done was to show forth the irrationality of a state of affairs whose existence was a disgrace to a nation, and revolting to every intellectual principle and moral feeling. The *philosophes* did their part effectually, and possibly prepared the way for the nation to do the rest in a manner as yet undreamed of.

2. The Encyclopædic spirit.—Thus had the way been paved, and men had now reached a frame of mind in which they were ready to accept the scientific and sceptical doctrines as expounded by the new philosophers. It had at last come home to them what was the significance of the point of view from which it is recognized that law governs everything, and consequently that a knowledge of this law is what is most desirable for the welfare of mankind; and they apprehended the notion in the somewhat abstract fashion in which it was presented, for it was undoubtedly presented in a way which fell far short of being completely true. The 'law' which was well-nigh exalted to the place of the Deity of former days, arbitrary enough though that Deity might have seemed, was regarded too much as a power working outside of us, and independently of any ideal or developing force which might guide its operations and bring with it a unifying influence. The way was perhaps made too plain and clear to be accepted as the way of Truth, so evasive to those who search after it as an end. The mysteries remained mysteries even after the artificial wrappings were removed, and the very superstitions were found to conceal certain aspects of truth, in addition to the falsehood that could not be overlooked. Nevertheless, the wrappings had to be removed, and it was rightly thought that an organized systematization of all known knowledge in the arts and sciences would help in bringing about this end in the most effectual and practical way possible. Goethe says in his *Dichtung und Wahrheit*: 'If we heard the encyclopædists mentioned, or opened a volume of their monstrous work, we felt as if we were going between the innumerable moving spools or looms in a great factory.' But, though the knowledge of the process by which his coat was made at length disgusted Goethe with the coat itself, that knowledge had to be acquired along with the rest of the scientific and systematic knowledge of the day.

3. The Encyclopædia.—What, then, was this work which gave a name to a whole group of thinkers in the middle of the 18th century—that time of which d'Alembert remarked that 'the middle of the century was apparently destined to form an epoch in the history of the human mind by the revolution in ideas which appeared to prepare for this event'? The first volume of the Encyclopædia appeared in 1751, and at this time the *philosophes* who took part in it were considerable in number. They were also, as a matter of fact, not all of one mind: there were among them atheists and deists, and the personal jealousies and antipathies that existed among them were not small. But a splendid optimism carried them along in their great work—an optimism which meant belief in the best elements of humanity, in natural goodness instead of natural depravity, and in the possibility of human perfection under suitable conditions. Helvetius expressed their point of view when he said: 'The good law-giver makes the good citizen.'

The task of producing a complete exposition of all the scientific knowledge of the day was, indeed, a difficult one; it was one that occupied twenty years, and it comprehended, in the first edition of the work, seventeen volumes of text, eleven volumes of plates, four volumes of supplement, and two volumes of index, while a further supplement of five volumes appeared in 1776. There had, of course, been many encyclopædias of various sorts before this time; the most ancient extant is usually stated to be Pliny's *Natural History*, in thirty-seven books. In 1727, Ephraim Chambers, a Quaker born in Kendal, published his *Cyclopædia: or an Universal Dictionary of Arts and Sciences*, in two volumes; and this, which resembled a Dictionary more than what we understand by a Cyclopædia, ran through many editions. The famous French *Encyclopédie* really originated in a French translation of Chambers's *Cyclopædia*, begun in 1743 and completed in 1745 by John Mills, an Englishman settled in France, assisted by Gottfried Sellius, a native of Dantzig. This work was termed the *Encyclopédie ou dictionnaire universel des arts et des sciences*—a work in four volumes of text and one of plates. Owing to the unscrupulous action of his publisher, Mills was despoiled of the work he had carried out, and he returned to England. Jean Paul de Gua de Malves, an abbé, was then engaged as editor, and, in order to revise the work in a thorough fashion, he called in certain learned men as assistants, amongst whom were Condillac, Diderot, and d'Alembert. Disputes followed with the publishers, and de Gua resigned the editorship. Consequently, in 1745, the editorship was offered to Diderot, who had edited the *Dictionnaire universel de médecine*, and, curiously enough, had also issued a translation of an English work. Diderot (1713–1784) had much larger views of what the compass of the work should be than that first contemplated by the publishers, le Breton and his associates, for he aimed at making it a complete compendium of the whole of human knowledge, while at the same time it was to be the manifesto of a great philosophic party. D'Alembert (1717–1783) was associated with Diderot in this undertaking, and to him the portion relative to Mathematics was more especially assigned.

Of other writers there were twenty-one, each of whom received the original article on his subject in Mills' translation to serve as a guide for his work. But these articles were found to be useless for the purpose, and the work was done in most cases independently. D'Alembert wrote the *Discours préliminaire* to the book, explaining therein the origin and succession of the different branches of human knowledge, and classifying, after the Baconian method, the various arts and sciences according as they depended on memory, reason, or imagination—the three principal human faculties. This Preface was much admired at the time as a great effort after system, and it was delivered before the Academy on the author's reception, which was itself regarded as a triumph. Diderot undertook most of the articles on the Arts and Trades, to which he gave a large place in the Encyclopædia, revising what he did not absolutely write; indeed, this portion of the work was perhaps the most original of the whole. He was assisted by the Chevalier de Jaucourt, a modest writer, who rejoiced in the drudgery entailed in such an undertaking, and himself wrote nearly half the Encyclopædia; many specialists were also brought in, such as Daubenton for Natural History, Barthèz and Tronchin for Medicine, du Marsais and Beauzée for Grammar, Marmontel for Literature, and Rousseau for Music. But all the contemporary *grands esprits* of the time were called upon to assist in some way or other—Voltaire, Euler, Morellet, Montesquieu, d'Anville, d'Holbach, Quesnai, and Turgot, the leader of the new school of economists whose teaching was first proclaimed in the Encyclopædia. In the supplementary volumes, Haller, the great physiologist, took part, and Condorcet, whose fate was to be so tragic in the days of the Terror. History and Biography were excluded except when they came in incidentally, and, the object of the book being frankly utilitarian, knowledge was held to be worthy of the name only if it led to some useful invention or discovery.

The prospectus describing the work as one which would form 8 volumes, with at least 600 plates, appeared in November 1750, but before that time Diderot had had much trouble with his pledged contributors, who were mostly in arrears with their articles. To make his difficulties greater, he himself was imprisoned at Vincennes on 29th July 1749 for 28 days, and then kept for three months and ten days a prisoner on parole at the castle, on account of his book entitled *Lettre sur les aveugles*. This, however, did not stop the printing, though, of course, it caused delay.

The clerical party was not long in realizing the dangers that threatened it through a work which preached the negation of the doctrine of innate ideas, and gave a new outlook on the world. It saw that a powerful influence was coming into being with the view of attacking its preserves, and the Jesuits especially were jealous of the fact that they had not been consulted regarding the articles on Theology or Religion. They were not appeased by the fact that Diderot and d'Alembert themselves signed articles most orthodox in character. The more cautious amongst the Encyclopædists likewise became alarmed as time went on. Montesquieu declined the articles 'Democracy' and 'Despotism'; Buffon, though he wrote on 'Nature' in 1765, did not love the Encyclopædists; Voltaire, Duclos, Rousseau, and Turgot gradually separated themselves from the atheistical party, though they had been identified with the new movement at the beginning. The first volume of the Encyclopædia appeared in 1751, and the second in January 1752. Jansenists vied with Jesuits in attacking it. The Abbé de Prades, one of the collaborators, was the first to suffer. He had sustained a thesis in which he was supposed to criticize miracles, comparing certain of them with the cures of Æsculapius. Diderot was suspected of being its true author. It was found to be materialistic and atheistic by the authorities, and the Abbé was condemned by the Sorbonne, without a hearing, by 82 votes against 54. He was degraded, and fled to Germany to escape further punishment. Diderot wrote an 'Apology' in his favour—a moderate and well-argued document—but the two volumes of the Encyclopædia that had so far appeared were ordered to be destroyed, by a decree of the King's Council on 7th Feb. 1752.

As a matter of fact, the real effect was to advertise the work. Indeed, the freethinkers were evidently gaining ground. Jansenist and Jesuit were alike reproached for the intestine rivalries which made the Church and its ceremonies fall into contempt. The Government did not long maintain its rigorous attitude, and tried to support first one side, then the other. But the incompetence of the Church favoured the growth of the liberal spirit. Malesherbes, Director-General of the Librairie, almost openly favoured the philosophers, and it was reluctantly that he was forced to issue the decree of 1752. This decree, however, contained no prohibition of the continued publication of the Encyclopædia, or of carrying on an active propaganda by means of brochures warmly accepted by the public, who delighted in finding the Episcopal mandates denounced. The publication of the Encyclopædia itself was regularly continued from 1753 (when vol. iii. appeared) until vol. vii. was reached in 1757. In the meantime Diderot had a remarkable triumph. Just after the decree he was compelled to hand over his papers to the Jesuit cabal, who thought they could themselves have carried on the work. In this they soon found themselves mistaken, and the Government was forced to make application in May 1752 to Diderot to continue the work which his genius was alone able to accomplish.

With the publication of the seventh volume the ferment was renewed, and storms arose which brought the whole agitation to a crisis. The popularity of the book was extending. The subscribers had increased from barely two thousand for the first volume to double that number for the seventh, and the indignation of the clerical party grew in proportion. Diderot, d'Alembert, Voltaire, Rousseau, and Buffon were all supposed to be united in the desire to form a conspiracy to overthrow the existing society. D'Alembert, after being the guest of Voltaire at Ferney and visiting Geneva, wrote an article in which he praised the Genevan ministers for the purity of their lives and supposed heterodoxy of their opinions, in a way which was held to reflect on the Jesuits and Jansenists. Thus a flood of passion was let loose, which was, if possible, increased by the publication by Helvetius of his book *De l'Esprit* in 1758. Helvetius, a generous protector of the *philosophes*, set forth, in four dissertations, opinions often stated in his hearing, and his book was published under royal privilege. The Sorbonne condemned it; it was regarded as an abridgment of the Encyclopædia, and was said to be scandalous and licentious. Helvetius finally retracted his statements and left the country, and the *philosophes* themselves felt that harm had been done to their cause by the book. The Council of State suppressed the privilege conceded to the Encyclopædia in 1746, prohibited the sale of the seven volumes already printed, and on 8th March 1759 disallowed the publication of any further volumes. This was after a commission of theologians and lawyers had been appointed by the court to examine the work, but before they had reported. Yet, curiously enough, the Government did not wish actually to destroy the movement, but merely to adopt such a policy of encouragement or repression as was most convenient to the politics of the time, or possibly such as the caprices of a royal mistress might dictate. An enormous amount of money was involved in the concern, which was an additional complication. The 4000 subscribers had paid in advance their subscriptions of 114 livres apiece. Diderot had prepared 3000 plates, for which, by an absurd anomaly, a privilege was given, as though they could be of value without the text. The printing, however, went on as before, 50 compositors being constantly engaged upon the work.

It was in 1758 that Rousseau severed his connexion with the Encyclopædists by his celebrated letter to d'Alembert on 'Stage Plays,' in reply to the latter's article on 'Geneva,' wherein he had assailed the doctrine that the theatre is an invention of the devil. But this was, of course, only the reason assigned for what implied a real break between the emotional school and that of pure reason. The beginning had been reached of that reign of sentimentalism which, while maintaining the cult of the primitive man as against the product of civilization and reason, introduced the theory of government by means of the sovereign 'general will,' which was soon to be carried to its extreme consequences with such momentous results.

Rousseau's secession was, indeed, a severe blow to Diderot, who had struggled so bravely against continual difficulties and adversity. But a harder blow still was to follow. D'Alembert, his fellow-worker, exhausted by continuous persecution, at last declared his intention of resigning his task, and advised Diderot to do the same. 'I am worn out,' he says, 'with the affronts and vexations of every kind that this work draws down upon us.' Even Voltaire was persuaded that d'Alembert was right, but it was in vain that he pressed his views on Diderot. The latter felt that to abandon a work so begun would be to play into the hands of his opponents and to show a pusillanimous and feeble spirit. Weary as he was of insults from the enemies of reason, he resolved to 'go back to the Encyclopædia.'

It was seven years more before the enormous task was brought to a close, and this consummation was made possible only by the protection of Mme de Pompadour, de Choiseul, and Malesherbes. And it was to Diderot himself that the labour of carrying it to a conclusion fell. Not only had he to write articles on every sort of subject, to edit the articles, and to make explanations of the engravings as well as supervise their production, but he had to do all this in constant fear of interruption by the police. And in the end the production of this immense enterprise, which enriched three or four publishers, left him who had done so much for it a poor man. He himself asks if it is not strange that this is so, but characteristically adds that, after all, he is 'too happy to have lived.' And undoubtedly his reputation spread throughout civilized Europe, along with that of his stupendous work. It was towards the close of it that one of the hardest trials of the many that he had suffered had to be endured. After the delay of 1759, le Breton was entrusted with the printing of the ten remaining volumes in a single issue. Instead of carrying out his orders, he altered the articles in such a way as to delete every reference or statement that might be provocative to the Government, and consequently he mutilated the whole so that it was deprived of all that was most valuable in it. To make matters worse, the original manuscripts were put into the fire. Diderot's wrath and indignation knew no bounds, and for weeks he could neither eat nor sleep. Yet, though his first impulse was to give up his task, he resolutely persevered in it, and in 1765 the last ten volumes of letterpress were issued, though the eleven volumes of plates were not completed till 1772. The general assembly of the clergy on 20th June 1765 condemned the book. This sentence was quashed by the Parliament from hatred to the clergy, but all who owned the Encyclopædia were called on to deliver it to the police, by whom, however, it was eventually returned after some small alterations had been made.

4. The contributors to the Encyclopædia.—As regards those who took part in this great work, we must always place **Diderot** at the head. He was the man amongst the rest who thought out not only his plan of operation, but the scientific method of which the book was the exponent. He was, indeed, the great Encyclopædist, he of whom Goethe says that 'whoever holds him or his doings cheaply is a Philistine,' for it would be to show a truly limited understanding not to appreciate at its just value the great idea which Diderot tried to expound—that we must rise not only above the artificialities of the stately classic school of literature associated with the great French dramatists of the previous century, but also above the artificialities of an arbitrary standard of orthodoxy in religion and an untenable theory of government. 'Enlightenment of the understanding' meant, above all, the clear vision that penetrated through these mists and condemned all that could not be distinctly comprehended as unworthy of further notice. It was Diderot, with his very manifest faults of life and modes of expression, who brought unity into a plan in which many men of very different outlook took part. His articles fill 4132 pages, and number 1139; the greater number of them appear in the last ten volumes of the Encyclopædia. His special department in the work was supposed to be Philosophy and the Arts and Trades, but he undertook articles on a miscellaneous number of subjects besides. The minutest care was expended by him in the reproduction of the plates, and it is said that in the chief departments of industry these would serve for practical specifications and working drawings. Diderot himself visited the workshops, examined the machines, had them taken to pieces and put together again, and even learned to work them. In the Encyclopædia attention was, of course, specially concentrated on the physical sciences and the practical arts. Things which can be seen and handled, ideas which do not indicate mere verbal distinctions, as with the schoolmen, or whose essence is found in form rather than in matter, as in some of the great writers of the age just preceding, are the subjects which most attracted the famous Encyclopædist.

D'Alembert (Jean le Rond), 1717–1783, Diderot's fellow-editor, wrote mainly on scientific subjects; and his works on Mechanics and on Natural Science placed him in the front rank amongst the *savants* of his time. Moreover, though to us he may seem heavy and dry in his style, he was said to have the gift of making interesting all that he wrote or said. In any case he obtained great popularity in the salons of the day, more especially in that of Mlle de Lespinasse. But intolerance was his bane, and the anti-religious bent of his mind became a real passion within him. His loss, however, when he retired, disgusted with the difficulties of his work, was a very serious one.

Of the other writers besides Diderot and d'Alembert, **Voltaire** comes first to our mind; he was incessant in his industry and ready to accept any article submitted to him, of whatever kind, and he grumbled at no editorial modification, while he was honest and helpful in telling his friends where he thought they had erred either in taste or in fact. He had the good sense to maintain his objections to the unfortunate policy which the editors sometimes adopted, of allowing statements which they could not justify to appear because of the exigencies of the time. 'Time will enable people to distinguish what we have thought from what we have said,' d'Alembert had to confess. But, before condemning this attitude of trimming the sails to suit the wind, we must recollect the courage that had been already required to say what had been said in face even of physical danger, in days when, as in the time of Louis XV., the Government claimed the right to direct not only the conduct but also the opinions of the subject. The existence of this right, still maintained by him, was one of the causes of the breach which took place with another of the original contributors, **Jean Jacques Rousseau.** He upheld the right of suppressing, by means of the secular arm, opinions that were anti-social. But what really distinguished Rousseau from the Encyclopædists was the fact that his ideas were determined by feeling, while the philosophy of the Enlightenment declared that they ought to be determined by reason only. The artistic renaissance called Romanticism was to come as a reaction from, and at the same time as a comprehensible development of, the rationalistic doctrines of the French philosophers. Rousseau had the power of sympathizing with the unenlightened, the outside people whom Voltaire designated as 'la canaille,' because he rested his philosophy on those elemental sentiments which were common to all; and the intellectualists consequently failed to comprehend him, as he certainly did not understand them.

Among the other notable Encyclopædists, **Helvetius** must be mentioned. Of his book *De l'Esprit* we have spoken; it roused keener resentment than perhaps any other book of the time, as tending, in the minds of the orthodox, to engender hatred against Christianity. Even the friends who, like Diderot, admired his work most declined to support the principles on which he rested his judgment. Helvetius' diatribes against the existing Government and the Roman Catholic religion made for revolution rather than for reform, and self-interest and pleasure were frankly advocated as the basis of justice and morality. His philosophy, if philosophy it may be called, was founded on sensationalism in its extremest form. But it is interesting to know that, if his arguments are not profound or convincing, without being the author of a thought-out doctrine of Utilitarianism he helped to inspire Bentham, its great advocate.

Holbach, the author of the *Système de la nature* (1770), which was often ascribed to his intimate friend Diderot, and part of which the latter probably composed, or at least inspired, was the prosperous and hospitable friend of the poorer Encyclopædists, while he also entertained friends from every part of Europe, including Hume, Priestley, and other Englishmen. He gave vent in no stinted terms to his indignation at the existing form of government. Indeed, institutions that had grown up through centuries were alike condemned by him without any effort on his part to determine their real meaning or value; and, unlike some of the other Encyclopædists, he did not restrict his attacks to superstitions or mere sentiments, but boldly advocated war between the governors and the governed. Intellectual deliverance was to him but the first step to converting thoughts into deeds. In reading Holbach now we come to understand how, when these doctrines were drunk in with avidity, the revolutionary maxims so soon became converted into facts.

But Helvetius and Holbach were but one type of Encyclopædists. We have, on the other hand, **Turgot**, who wrote anonymously some of the most valuable and weighty articles in the book, which he regarded, until he came to distrust its sectarian spirit, as a great instrument for the enlightenment of mankind. Then there was **Montesquieu**, who died in 1755 and left behind him an unprinted article on 'Taste'; and there were others who, until division arose, contributed to give dignity to the undertaking.

5. Value of the Encyclopædia.—The Encyclopædia itself was unequal, as might be expected from the difficulties under which it was composed and from the scarcity of money with which to pay contributors; some articles were inferior, and, as Voltaire pointed out, they constantly suffered from verbosity and dogmatic modes of expression. D'Alembert himself confessed that this was the case, and Diderot was dissatisfied with the work. The attitude adopted to religion is not by any means consistent any more than the rest. It would be untrue to say that dogmatic atheism was preached, though on the whole the attitude of the book is, of course, critical of orthodox beliefs. The main attack is, however, against Sacerdotalism, against a Church that was corrupt, and against priests who were enemies to society. The object was to teach the value of Science and the reign of Law, and, thereby, to take away interest from the miraculous. The Encyclopædists found such continual occupation in the world as it revealed itself to them that they were content to leave alone what was beyond. The goodness of human nature was taken for granted, and, as was developed in a way more thorough by Rousseau and his followers later on, bad education was held to be responsible for social failure, as bad laws and bad government were blamed for a corrupt State. The earth in which we live is of more interest than a heaven of which we can know nothing surely. Francis Bacon's idea of the systematic classification of knowledge made it seem possible that such classification should be made, and Bacon may be said to have inspired the idea of the Encyclopædia. Diderot himself said that he had 'taught his fellow-citizens to read Bacon.' Newton and Bacon were in the ascendant in the century which produced what Carlyle calls the 'Polemic of a Mechanical Era.'

It is interesting to reflect that from the Encyclopædists proceeds much of the social spirit of modern days. When Diderot teaches us to prevent misery rather than supply refuges for the miserable, he is preaching the latest doctrines in social economics. This, indeed, implies more than at first appears, because it means a break from the churchly doctrine of merely helping the weak and poor because it is a Christian duty, and setting to work instead to see where the 'machine' is working badly and producing these sad and suffering mortals. The one attitude is perhaps as abstract as the other, because, just as we think the machine is being brought into perfect working order, we are pulled up sharply by finding that the individual rebels at having himself regarded as only a part of a beautiful mechanical contrivance, and insists on asserting his individuality. Still, on the whole, the new science is the more hopeful and inspiring of the two, especially to those whose minds require some logical reason for their actions, and who do not want to be controlled simply by sentiment or by the ascetic spirit of religion.

All who played their part in this 'Encyclopædic workshop,' as Comte named it, were bound together in a common fellowship by their work on a common book, in a way probably never known before. But their failing was doubtless that of being abstract in their views of life and the world. The Liberalism of the Enlightenment had the faults as well as the virtues of certain forms of Liberalism in a later age. It freed itself from shackles that were impeding progress in the search for truth. It failed, however, to see that there were in the old rejected forms certain elements of truth that had been overlooked. The Encyclopædists did not consider that, even if knowledge of the useful arts and sciences were brought to perfection and the abuses that menaced society swept away, there would still be the eternal desire for some further explanation of the how and why, some fresh effort to comprehend the mind that understands and gives a unity to the conglomeration of facts presented to it.

LITERATURE.—*Encyclopédie: Discours préliminaire*, vol. i., Paris, 1751; John Morley, *Diderot and the Encyclopædists*, 2 vols., London, 1878; K. Rosenkranz, *Diderot's Leben und Werke*, 2 vols., Leipzig, 1866; L. Ducros, *Diderot*, Paris, 1894, also *Les Encyclopédistes*, Paris, 1900; J. L. F. Bertrand, *D'Alembert*, Paris, 1889; E. Lavisse, *Hist. de France*, vol. viii., Paris, 1909; D. Diderot, *Œuvres complètes*, Paris, 1875–1877; T. Carlyle, Essay on 'Diderot'; F. M. Grimm, *Correspondance littéraire*, Paris, 1829; E. J. F. Barbier, *Journal*, Paris, 1849–56; F. Brunetière, *Études sur le xviiie siècle*, Paris, 1911; J. F. Marmontel, *Mémoires*, ed. Tourneux, Paris, 1891; C. A. Sainte-Beuve, *Causeries*, Paris, 1857–62; C. P. Duclos, *Mémoires secrets sur le règne de Louis XV.*, Paris, 1846; M. Roustan, *Les Philosophes et la société française au xviiie siècle*, Paris, 1906; the works of Rousseau, Voltaire, d'Alembert, Helvetius, Holbach, etc.

E. S. HALDANE.

END (Germ. *Zweck, Ziel, Ende* [primarily spatial]; Fr. *fin, but*).—The point towards which a process or act is directed; the object of a desire or purpose; the completion or culmination of a process or act. The concept of end is one which enters specially, though not exclusively, into the interpretation of human action. Thus, the scientific worker is said to be aiming at the accurate determination of some aspect of reality, the artist to be striving after a satisfactory form of expression, the moral agent to be attempting to adjust his conduct to certain standards of right living—in each case, that is to say, there is an end in view which is a determinant of action, just as the artificer's operations are determined by the kind of mechanical construction which it is in his mind to produce. The efforts made to express the content of these ends and to relate those in each move to one another in a systematic manner are referred to as constituting a normative or a regulative science. Thus, Logic, which deals with the ends or ideals of scientific activity, Æsthetics, which deals with those of artistic production, and Ethics, which deals with those relating to moral action or conduct, are spoken of as essentially normative sciences. Aristotle made the conception of end familiar to philosophy through his well-known doctrine of the four causes (ἀρχαί), in which he distinguishes the '*final cause*'—to give it its scholastic name[1]—'the purpose or goal,' from the formal cause, the material cause, and the efficient cause. 'The final cause,' he says, 'operates like a loved object' (*Metaph.* 1072*b*, 3). He applies this conception not merely to the interpretation of organic process and moral behaviour, but to the interpretation of the whole of reality, including the physical universe.

'Material causes are only intermediate—merely the means and indispensable conditions of phenomena. Above them stand final causes; above material necessity, the design of the universe; above the physical explanations of nature, the teleological' (Zeller's *Aristotle*, Eng. tr., 1897, i. 458 f.).

We thus have the arduous debate between Mechanism and Teleology explicitly opened—a debate which continues to our own time, and to which the most recent interesting contributions are those of the Neo-Vitalists and H. Bergson (see TELEOLOGY).

A distinction may be made between an end which can be consciously presented or envisaged as the object of voluntary process and an end which is not so presented, but is inferred from the facts of experience. The 'final purpose' of Nature, the 'goal' of progress, the *Summum Bonum*, would be instances of this type. Sidgwick has this distinction in view when he contrasts the Good attainable by human effort and the notion of an Ultimate Good (*Methods of Ethics*[3], p. 3). These two types of end are distinguished by Baldwin respectively as 'subjective end' and 'objective end'—a distinction which is not to be confused with Kant's distinction of subjective and objective finality in the *Critique of the Judgment*. This terminology is liable to misinterpretation under the ordinary acceptation of 'subjective' and 'objective.' 'Subjective' generally implies an element of contingency and arbitrariness, and these characteristics are not necessarily attached to ends of the first type; these ends may satisfy all the tests of objectivity. It would seem to be closer to the facts to distinguish them as 'explicit' and 'implicit' ends.

It is the explicit end of which we have direct experience. This is a cognizable element in the conscious process. In purposeful activity we are aware, on introspection, of an idea or image of some situation or object which is controlling the process. We are conscious of an orientation of the conscious stream in that direction, of a desire for it, of a striving towards it. This conative tendency, as it is called, is maintained and furthered by the presence, in consciousness, of the end; and the striving will continue, through hindrances and difficulties, until the idea is 'realized,' *i.e.* until it becomes literally (or, more precisely, temporally) the end-state or terminus. 'The end after which consciousness strives is, when attained, the termination of the striving' (Stout, *Manual of Psychology*, p. 66). It has to be borne in mind that, while we may say that the striving ceases when the end is reached, it would be injudicious to say that the end is reached *because* the striving ceases. The striving may cease because the end is reached; it may also cease before the end is reached. The end, the attractive idea, may lose its attractiveness and be abandoned, and *ipso facto* we cease to aim at it. On the other hand, there are ends so extensive and complex that we never completely attain them. The striving may not terminate while life continues, but we do not refuse the name of 'end' to the idea which keeps this tendency alive, though in current speech the term generally employed in this case is 'ideal.'

Ethical theory is always theory of ends. It has to do with ends of both the types referred to above. Motived actions, *i.e.* actions into which reference to an explicit end enters, are its data. Its conclusions have reference to implicit ends. A man need not be a moral philosopher in order to be moral. Even the moral philosopher in his daily details of conduct may safely be said to make no explicit reference to the *Summum Bonum*. The ends which regulate the specific acts, however, may appear as the constituents of that system of ends which we call the moral ideal. The acts are valued according to the nature of the explicit end, which is valued in turn by reference to the total system. The reality of this Moral Ideal is not affected by the fact that it is implicit and is not and cannot be an element of immediate experience. See, further, artt. on ETHICS AND MORALITY.

LITERATURE.—Aristotle, *Physics*, ii. 3. 194*b*, 23, *Metaphysics*, i. 3; P. Janet, *Final Causes*, Eng. tr., Edinburgh, 1878; J. M. Baldwin, *Handbook of Psychology*, 'Feeling and Will,' New York, 1891, ch. ix. § 7; G. F. Stout, *Manual of Psychology*, London, 1898–99, bk. i. ch. i. § 4, ch. ii. § 3; H. Sidgwick, *Methods of Ethics*[3], London, 1884 [[6] 1905], ch. i. § 2. See also Literature appended to art. TELEOLOGY.

A. MAIR.

ENEMY.—The significance of the term 'enemy' has altered with the course of centuries. From being ill-defined, it has become highly technical; from being wide of application, it has been confined to the designation of States at war.[1] A sentence in Cicero tells us what was the history of the word in the period within his knowledge: 'Hostis enim apud majores nostros is dicebatur quem nunc *peregrinum* dicimus' (*de Off.* i. 12). The word *hostis*, that is to say, originally meant a stranger, whence it may be inferred that strangers and enemies were at one time practically classed together.

In the earliest times, when there was no such thing as political society, strictly so-called, primitive man gave the name 'enemy' to every one who was not connected with him by ties of blood. Every such alien to the family or tribe he pursued with tireless hatred; he regarded him as lawful prey to be plundered or slain. The tribe was thus a union, on the basis of consanguinity, for purposes of defence and attack. The instinct of co-operation, of which it was partly the expression, gave place only very slowly to a spirit of union of a wider kind. Men became conscious of interests binding together those who worked on a common soil and made it their own by their labour. A

[1] Aristotle himself does not use the term. He speaks of 'the end' (τὸ τέλος), or 'that on account of which' (τὸ οὗ ἕνεκα).

[1] For 'enemy' in the private sense, see HATRED, LOVE, etc.

state of society emerged in which they stood to one another not as kinsmen, but as fellow-citizens. The tribe became the nation, and the ties of kinship lost much of their compelling and restraining power. But the old feeling against aliens persisted under the new determining principle of the spirit of nationality. Among the ancient States, especially in the East, all foreign nations were regarded practically as enemies. In the case of some peoples, as, for instance, the Jews in post-exilic times, this animosity towards strangers was partly due to religious reasons, the monolatry of Judaism stamping all outsiders as heathen and idolaters, enemies of Jahweh, the one God. But the feeling was not very different both in the Greek city-States and at Rome, where a stranger, unless specially commended to protection, was regarded as having no rights at all. In Greece he was everywhere distrusted, and from Sparta excluded altogether. In Rome he could obtain justice only by the friendly offices of a citizen.

In considering the writings of Plato and Aristotle, so far as they bear upon this question, we have to keep in mind that the precept 'Love your enemies' has no place in Greek ethics. In the *Philebus* (49), we find Socrates remarking that it is not wrong to feel joy in the woes of enemies, while it would be very unjust to rejoice in the misfortunes of friends. He also describes barbarians, that is, foreigners, as natural enemies of the Greeks, and condemns war (and the common methods of warfare) only when waged between the Hellenic tribes, which were bound together by the ties of race and religion (*Republic*, v. 470). In the *Laws* (v. 729; ix. 879; xii. 949 f., 952 f.), Plato goes on to discuss the treatment of strangers in Greece, and makes several suggestions of reform. But the high-water mark of Greek thinking on this subject is perhaps attained by Aristotle in his criticism of the guardian class in Plato's ideal State (*Repub.* ii. 375 f.). He complains that the guardians are to be savage to strangers, although affectionate towards their friends, and he uses these words: 'It is not right to be fierce towards any one, nor are magnanimous natures ever savage, except towards persons who injure them' (*Pol.* iv. 7). Aristotle presumably is thinking of direct personal injury, or of the feeling of enmity which Socrates regards as justifiable between the inhabitants of the ideal Republic and the *individuals* in a foreign State who are responsible for initiating war against them (Plato, *Repub.* v. 471).

In these and earlier times the utmost cruelty was permissible towards enemies. Ferocity and lawless savagery characterized all phases of primitive society. Revolting customs were sanctioned by highly civilized States. Hence, even in Aristotle, whose views on war were far in advance of his time, inasmuch as he disapproved of it as an end in itself, we find no criticism of methods of warfare and conquest which we should describe as barbarous. He saw the land of the conquered pillaged and devastated, and non-combatants subjected to slaughter and outrage or sold with their children to slavery; but he seems to have found a sufficiently satisfactory explanation in the consideration that these atrocities were committed against 'barbarians,' people who were 'by nature' slaves. Plato, too, found such practices revolting only between Hellenic tribes, and he makes Socrates express the wish that in the ideal Republic the Hellenes should reserve for war with barbarians the treatment which Greeks now mete out to each other (*Repub.* v. 471).

The responsibility of beginning and conducting war has not long been the prerogative of States. Under the feudal system of the Middle Ages it was especially common for war to be declared by powerful lords, by cities, or provinces. Gentilis, the predecessor of Grotius, was the first publicist who defined war, much as we should define it now, as the just or unjust conflict between States. In Roman law the term 'enemy' was applied to States or individuals between whom had passed a formal declaration of war. But the Roman jurists, except for certain rules regarding the person of ambassadors, hostages, the keeping of treaties, and the like, laid down few regulations as to the treatment of a foe. Ideas of justice to an enemy and humanity to the conquered appear for the first time in Cicero (*de Off.* i. 11). But not until the 16th cent., when Grotius laid the foundation of the modern law of nations in his work *de Jure Belli ac Pacis*, did more humane principles influence the practice of States. At the present day, a traveller or resident in foreign territory is protected by, and answerable to, the law of the land. If, when he is abroad, war arises between his own nation and the country whose hospitality he is enjoying, he is generally allowed to remain where he is, so long as he conducts himself peaceably and loyally. An individual, indeed, is not usually accounted the *enemy* of the State with which the government to which he owes allegiance is at war. War is understood by the law of nations to be between States, not between individuals as such, although an individual may during war acquire what is termed enemy character, either as the owner of property or because of acts done by him as a private person. On the other hand, in so far as business relations are concerned, the subjects of belligerent States are enemies. All ordinary intercourse must cease until the war is at an end.

Hostilities are now carried on subject to a code of general rules which combatants cannot violate without exciting the reprobation and risking the interference of the civilized world. Prisoners and non-combatants alike are free from the severities of warfare, and in defeat their persons can be subjected neither to slaughter nor to outrage. Only such methods are legitimate as are absolutely necessary to weaken the forces of the enemy and compel him to seek peace; and all such as inflict useless suffering are rigidly excluded. Rules relating to the practices of assassination and devastation, and to the use of poison and of arms and projectiles which inflict needless torture, were laid down by the Brussels Conference of 1874. The Brussels code has not yet been made law, but nations which have since that date engaged in war have adhered to the principles embodied in it. See, further, art. WAR.

LITERATURE.—Text-books on International Law; Aristotle's *Politics*; Plato's *Republic* and *Laws*. A very interesting account of what in early times constituted a relation of hostility is found in Sir Henry Maine, *Early History of Institutions*, London, 1875; and reference may also be made to O. Schrader, *Reallex. der indogerm. Altertumskunde*, Strassburg, 1901, p. 256, and A. H. Post, *Grundriss der ethnolog. Jurisprudenz*, Oldenburg, 1894–95, i. 448 f. M. CAMPBELL SMITH.

ENERGY.—A term borrowed from the Greek to express the mechanical idea of the 'power to do work.' Its etymological import is *something in action* or a name for *action itself*. It is thus the equivalent of 'matter in motion.' Sometimes it is a synonym for 'force' (*q.v.*), which has the same definition, and so means to denote the fact that effects do not take place without causal action, and this causal action for Mechanics is substance or matter in action or motion. But energy also, as denoting 'power,' implies capacity to do work without representing the 'force' or matter as actually in motion. Hence it was divided into 'potential' and 'kinetic' energy. Potential energy is force or matter in a static condition, one which represents the mere capacity of producing work, but not the actual fact of producing it. Kinetic energy is 'force' in action or actually producing work. Thus snow lying on the mountain side may be conceived as potential energy. But when melted into water and flowing down the stream it is kinetic energy. A spring resting without strain is potential energy; the same spring bent or pressed down and exerting strain is kinetic energy. Hence any matter or force in a passive or static condition is potential energy; the same substance in motion or exerting pressure, strain or pulling power, is kinetic or dynamic energy.

In the practical problems of Mechanics it becomes important to measure energy, and some standard for the purpose had to be obtained. The first step in the direction of obtaining such a standard was to assume some constant form of energy and measure it in some way. It was known that it took a certain amount of energy, not measured, to raise 1 lb. a foot high, and twice this amount of energy to raise 2 lb. the same distance, or 1 lb. two feet high. This relation served as a means of determining some criterion to measure the amount of energy doing work, and this criterion could be found in the amount of work done. This unit of work done is called the 'foot-pound.' Gravity is the constant by which we may determine this; hence we may take the energy employed in moving an object a given distance vertically as the equivalent of gravity, and so obtain a standard for its measurement.

In fixing this standard 'we must choose our unit of work,' says Balfour Stewart, 'but in order to do so we must first of all choose our units of weight and of length, and for these we will take the *kilogramme* and the *metre*, these being the units of the metrical system. The kilogramme corresponds to about 15,432·35 English grains, being rather more than two pounds avoirdupois, and the metre to about 39·371 English inches. Now, if we raise a kilogramme weight one metre in vertical height, we are conscious of putting forth an effort to do so, and of being resisted in the act by the force of gravity. In other words, we spend energy and do work in the process of raising this weight. Let us agree to consider the energy spent, or the work done in this operation, as one unit of work, and let us call it the *kilogrammetre*. In the next place, it is obvious that if we raise the kilogramme two metres in height, we do two units of work, if three metres, three units, and so on. And again, it is equally obvious that if we raise a weight of two kilogrammes one metre high we likewise do two units of work, while if we raise it two metres high we do four units of work. From these examples we are entitled to derive the following rule:—*Multiply the weight raised (in kilogrammes) by the vertical height (in metres) through which it is raised, and the result will be the work done (in kilogrammetres).*'

By a process based upon the velocity which gravity gives falling bodies it is possible to calculate this energy, and so to determine a formula for practical use in mechanical operations. This calculation shows that *energy is proportional to the square of the velocity of objects.* Taking M to stand for the mass and V for the velocity, this formula is MV^2. Now gravity accelerates the velocity of falling bodies at a certain constant rate. One half of this divided into this formula gives the actual amount of energy expended in the operation. Hence $\frac{1}{2} MV^2$ represents the formula for measuring the amount of energy in any special case.

The total amount of energy in the world is supposed to remain the same at all times. This conception has given rise to the doctrine of the Conservation of Energy. The sense in which Mechanics or Physics asserts this doctrine is that the sum of potential and kinetic energies remains the same in all operations, and not that there may be no increase or decrease of either of them. If a ball is propelled upwards at a certain velocity its energy will be measured by the formula above given, and it will come to rest when gravity has overcome the energy of propulsion. Its initial velocity represents energy of the kinetic sort. When completely arrested its energy will be potential. At any point between the initial motion and its stoppage the sum of the potential and kinetic energies will be equal to the kinetic energy at the outset, the potential energy being nil at that point. This is what is meant by a conservative system of forces, and the expression Conservation of Energy expresses the fact.

Another import has been given to this doctrine in the idea that the kinetic energy of a system remains the same in all transformations, and it gives rise to some difficulties in accounting for the phenomena of change, especially of change from kinetic to potential, from dynamic to static conditions. The best conception of this situation is *Correlation* rather than Conservation of Force or Energy. The former suggests a conception of identity which seems not to be a fact in the transformations. Hence, in consequence of this equivocation in the doctrine of the Conservation of Energy, a controversy arises between philosophy and mechanical science. But, with the correction of the phrase suitable to the different problems involved, there is no occasion to do more than insist upon the equivocation, and so question the relevance of the physicist's inference from his mechanical use of conservation to the denial of the philosopher's doctrine of change, especially of facts that involve qualitative change.

Recently a doctrine of 'energy' has arisen which regards it as a 'substance.' The mechanic treated it as a property or quality of matter for doing work. But certain metaphysical propensities, on the one hand, and the implications lying at the basis of the distinction between kinetic and potential energy, on the other hand, created the need of a term for something which the scientific metaphysician—for that is what he was—wanted to distinguish from matter, on the one hand, and its properties, on the other. 'Energy' was thus made distinct from 'force' and 'matter.' It might lie at the basis of both, but it was distinct from them. Ostwald is perhaps the leading representative of this school. It does not express anything different, however, from that of those physicists who conceive the ultimate basis of material phenomena in terms of matter or ether, and only serves to eliminate the idea of inertia where 'matter' seems to imply it. We see, therefore, no reason for attaching any special importance to the doctrine.

LITERATURE.—Balfour Stewart, *The Conservation of Energy*[2], Lond. 1874; A. Daniell, *Principles of Physics*, do. 1884; Lord Kelvin, *Elements of Natural Philosophy*[2], Camb. 1879; *EBr*[11], art. 'Energy.'

JAMES H. HYSLOP.

ENHYPOSTASIS.—The term is one of a series—'hypostatical union' 'anhypostasis,' 'enhypostasis'—used to cast light on the constitution of the Person of Christ. The Christology of the Council of Chalcedon (A.D. 451) postulates in Christ the unity of two distinct natures—the Divine and the human—in a single person. This is called in theology the 'hypostatical union.' Since, however, the personality is assumed to belong exclusively to the side of the Divine—*i.e.* it is the eternal, pre-existent Son who has entered humanity—it would seem to follow that the humanity of Christ must be conceived of as impersonal. Church doctrine, therefore, has very generally affirmed the impersonality (*anhypostasia*) of the humanity of Christ. But the difficulty is obvious—How can an impersonal humanity be conceived of as a real or entire humanity? Does not the very peculiarity of man as rational lie in his possession of self-consciousness and will? And is a being possessing these attributes not already personal? To avoid this difficulty, the idea was hit upon of describing the humanity of Christ not as 'im-personal,' but as 'en-personal.'

The doctrine of *enhypostasis* is already met with in Leontius of Byzantium (A.D. 483–543), but is specially developed by John of Damascus (*c.* A.D. 750). It agrees with the other view in holding, in opposition to Nestorianism, that the human nature of Christ never subsisted in a personality of its own; that it was assumed by, and subsisted only in, the person of the Divine Logos or Son. But it avoids the unfortunate suggestion (which is not in the least intended) in the word *anhypostasia* of a possible independent impersonal existence of Christ's human nature, and lays emphasis on the idea that the humanity from the beginning subsisted 'in' the person of the Logos. Plainly, however, this does not remove the essential difficulty that it is a Divine, not a human, personality that we have in Christ. Many modern theologians would solve this by rejecting altogether the doctrine of the two natures, and boldly affirm that the personality lies wholly in the humanity; but it is very difficult to keep this view from passing into pure humanitarianism. If a solution is to be found, it is probably in the line of recognizing the essential kindredness of humanity to the Logos in which it is grounded, and which, in the Incarnation, appropriates humanity to itself as the organ of its own personal manifestation. The Logos is the personal centre, but under conditions truly and perfectly human—'The Word *became* flesh, and dwelt among us.'

LITERATURE.—A. Harnack, *Hist. of Dogma* (Eng. tr.[3], Lond. 1894–99), iv. 232, 264; I. A. Dorner, *Person of Christ* (Eng. tr., Edinb. 1861–63), div. ii. vol. i. p. 210 ff.; J. Orr, *Progress of Dogma*, Lond. 1901, p. 205 f.

JAMES ORR.

ENLIGHTENMENT, THE.—In its most general sense the term 'Enlightenment' (Germ. *Aufklärung*) indicates the first of the two periods through which modern thought has passed; or the development of philosophy from Bacon's *Novum Organum* (1620) to Kant's *Kritik der reinen Vernunft* (1781). But a more critical view of the period, with its characteristic ideals, reveals the fact that the beginning of the period must be dated from Hobbes (1588–1679) rather than from Bacon, whose freer and more cultural philosophy belongs to the Renaissance. As a further limitation, it must be observed that the Enlightenment hardly included the greater philosophic works which appeared contemporaneously with it. Though Locke (1632–1704) was connected with the movement, it was not by means of the *Essay concerning Human Understanding* (1690), but through his minor works on rights and religion, that the relation was sustained. Spinoza (1632–1677) in his *Ethica* (1677), with its Cartesian foundation, was innocent of the movement; but in his theologico-political writings, inspired as they were by Hobbes, he takes up some of its peculiar problems. In his *Treatise on Human Nature* (1738), Hume was as studious as Locke to avoid the rationalism of the Enlightenment, whose principles he criticized in his *Dialogues concerning Natural Religion* (1777). Kant's relation to the movement is discoverable, not in the *Kritik*, but in his lesser works on natural rights. Thus appearing in the minor writings of the great thinkers, the philosophy of the Enlightenment was elaborated by a host of semi-philosophical thinkers, who ignored the fundamental problems of logic and ethics, for the sake of settling practical questions of Church and State. Nevertheless, the Enlightenment possessed the spirit of the larger philosophy, even where it was unable or unwilling to pursue its method. This spirit was a regressive one, according to which the age endeavoured to return to fundamentals. With Descartes (1596–1650) the tendency manifested itself in the desire to premise a first principle of all thinking, the *cogito, ergo sum* (*Meditation II.*); Locke was equally anxious to elucidate the native principle of cognition when he styled the mind a *tabula rasa* (*Essay*, bk. i.). The same radical spirit was shown in practical philosophy, as when Herbert of Cherbury sought the true faith in the original *religio naturalis* (*de Veritate*, 1624), and Grotius attempted to find the true principle of law in the *jus naturale* (*de Jure Belli ac Pacis*, 1625). In a manner less definite and logical, the Enlightenment insisted upon 'nature' and 'reason,' without precisely stipulating what these ideas should denote. The method of the movement, guided as it was by the regressive spirit of the 17th cent., consisted in establishing contrasts between things established by authority and tradition and those erected through freedom and reason. This conflict between reason-rights and tradition-authority thus recalled the ancient Sophist contrast between φύσις and νόμος, the exact reiteration of which may be found in Cudworth's *Treatise concerning Eternal and Immutable Morality*, 1678 (bk. i. ch. i.). The practical result of this method of thought was to create an opposition to history, the source of tradition and authority, and to instil a belief in the eternity of 18th cent. ideals; coupled with this dogmatism was an attack upon positive religion and an antipathy to the idea of progress. Emancipating itself from the past, and feeling no need of a future, the Enlightenment was possessed of an optimism which believed that human reason was able to solve all problems and cure all ills. The leading questions of the Enlightenment had to do with (1) Natural Rights, (2) Free-thought and Toleration, (3) Rational Christianity, and (4) Natural Religion.

1. Natural rights.—It is with the name of Hugo Grotius (1583–1645) that the history of Natural Rights begins. Anticipated by Bodin's *Six Livres de la République* (1575), with its insistence upon the historical theory of rights, as also by Gentilis' *de Jure Belli* (1588), with its direct deduction of rights from Nature, Grotius' great work, *de Jure Belli ac Pacis*, was able to make use of the empirical in the one and of the rational in the other. The psychological basis upon which Grotius rears his juristic system was found in man's natural tendency towards the formation of society; this is attributed to the social instinct within him, as also to the particular gift of language, with its social possibilities (*op. cit.*, Prolegomena, §§ 7–8). From the logical standpoint Grotius argues, from both *a priori* and *a posteriori* principles, that natural rights are in harmony with human nature. *A priori* it was urged that *jus naturale* was so native to man that he could not be conceived of as existing without it, while the common consent of mankind argues, as from effect to cause, that, since the principle of rights is universal, it is also necessary to the human race (*ib.* I. cap. i. xii. § 1). In his enthusiasm over the rational principle of rights, Grotius was led to assume a radical position in theology, in accordance with which he asserted that the principle of rights would hold though we should assume that there is no God (*ib.* Proleg. § 1). Natural law is thus conceived of as following from the nature of things, while the law of God is dependent upon His will. The blunt way in which Grotius expressed this Thomism seems to produce the impression of atheism, and it was to the dual extremes of *ni dieu, ni maître* that this philosophy was destined to evolve. The Divine law was conceived as coming to man by means of tradition as something authoritative; having thus expressed himself, Grotius creates the dualism of *jus* and *lex*, *ratio* and *traditio*. It was in this way that the Enlightenment learned to despise the historical and to repose in the purely rationalistic.

In England, the philosophy of rights was continued by Hobbes, who developed a theory alien in character to that of Grotius. The failure of Bacon to participate in the discussion is one of the striking features of 17th century thought. Lerminier says:

'Chose remarquable! Bacon n'emploie pas une seule fois le mot *jus* comme représentant le droit même dans sa nature et dans sa substance. Le droit, *jus*, n'est pour lui que la collection des lois positives: il n'a donc pas traité de la justice universelle' (*Hist. du Droit*, 1829, p. 113).

In the hands of Hobbes the Grotian principle of rights underwent a double transformation; where Grotius was optimistic in measuring man, Hobbes was pessimistic; and where the one had been inclined to the social, the other turned abruptly to the egoistic. According to Hobbes, man is so constituted as to seek his own private benefit, being urged on by inexorable forces, and being further incapacitated to appreciate the condition of another's mind. The pessimistic conclusion drawn from these egoistic premisses appears when Hobbes, adding to Grotius' idea of *jus naturale* that of *status naturalis*, concludes that the native condition of man was one of 'war of all against all' (*Leviathan*, 1651, ch. xiii.). Such were the principles upon which Hobbes sought to erect a philosophy of the State, the essence of which consisted in the idea that the passage from the natural condition of *jus*, or *libertas*, to the civil condition of *lex*, or *obligatio*, is by means of contract, in accordance with which each individual surrenders his rights in consideration of a similar act on the part of others (*de Cive*, 1642, i. § 2). In connexion with this mechanical theory of the origin of the State, Hobbes introduced an ethical philosophy in which good and bad, instead of being conceived of as intrinsic, were looked upon as relative to the well-being of mankind—a view which was opposed by the absolutism of Cudworth and Clarke. For the development of the philosophy of rights the Enlightenment was indebted to Pufendorf (1632–1694), who sought to combine the social in Grotius with the selfish of Hobbes.

In the preparation for the schemes of free-thought and toleration, rational Christianity and natural religion, the juristic theories of Spinoza and Locke were of much moment, however secondary they may have been in the theory of natural rights as such. In his theory of rights, Spinoza stands closely related to Hobbes, although his own conception of Being as an all-inclusive substance in which all particular things participate (*Ethica*, pt. i.) was influential in the deduction of a principle of absolute rights as lodged in the Deity, to be derived from Him by the rational creatures which participate in His being (*Tractatus Politicus*, 1677, ii. § 18). Spinoza is quite frank in his assertion that right is equivalent to power, as this reposes in the Deity and is further found in man. In man appear the functions of desire and reason; in the former are found hope and also the instinct of self-preservation; in the latter, the wisdom that enables man to form the State and thus free himself (*ib.* ii. § 18). As Spinoza had carried out the harsh ideas of Hobbes, Locke advanced a theory of rights suggestive of Grotius' mildness. In particular, he put forward a more temperate view of the natural state of mankind, as well as a more rational conception of the origin of society. With Locke, the state of nature no longer signified the 'bellum omnium contra omnes,' but indicated a condition of things marked by the absence of external authority. Accordingly he says:

'Men living together according to reason and without authority to judge between them is properly the state of nature. But force, or the declared design of force upon the person of another . . . is the state of war' (*Two Treatises of Government*, 1690 [*Works* 11, 1812, v. 348–349]).

Like Grotius and unlike Hobbes, Locke believed that man has a natural appetite for society, so that his natural condition is not the impossible *status naturalis*. In this connexion, Locke attempted to show that the state of nature had existed in human history, and thus, in his work *On the Roman Commonwealth* (1660), he says:

'Romulus at the head of a numerous colony from Alba was the first founder of the Roman State; this colony was in the original state of nature, free and independent of any dominion whatsoever' (*Life of John Locke*, by Fox Bourne, N.Y. 1876, i. 148).

This conception of man's original condition made it possible for Locke to give a more plausible explanation of the origin of the State in a contrast between man and man rather than between man and the magistrate.

The juristic element in the thought of the Enlightenment, fated as it was to become an important factor in the development of Deism (*q.v.*), was not overlooked by the Deists themselves, however little they had to contribute to the philosophy of rights as such. Indeed, the common ground upon which the greater modern thinkers, like Locke and Spinoza, and the uncultured Deists, like Tindal and Chubb, were to meet was the juristic one. Free-thought was thus a great leveller; hence Warburton, quoting Swift, said:

'No subject but religion could have advanced Toland into the class of reputable authors . . . no subject but religion could have sunk his lordship [Bolingbroke] so far below it' (*Divine Legation of Moses* 5, 1746, v. 440).

Among the Deists, Tindal was the first to identify himself with the natural-rights movement, in connexion with which he shows himself to be a follower, first of Hobbes, then of Spinoza, and finally of Locke. In his *Essay concerning the Laws of Nations and the Rights of Sovereigns* (1694), he urges 'egoism' as the 'source of all man's actions and the foundation of his duty to God and man' (*op. cit.* 121). The *Essay on the Rights of Mankind* (1697) discusses the *status naturalis*, while the author's more complete philosophy of rights appears in *The Rights of the Christian Church* (1706), a work which connects the political philosophy of the Enlightenment with Deism. In this work, Tindal contends against established religion, on the ground that men are in a religious state of nature, 'subject only to God and their own consciences' (*op. cit.* 2). Without analyzing the inner nature of the principle of rights, Toland (1670–1722) advanced principles of practical rights and freedom. These appear in his *Life of Milton* (1699), as also in *Amyntor* (1699), the defence of it. A more definite relation to the philosophy of rights was sustained by Toland in his *Paradoxes of State* (1707), and *The Art of Governing by Parties* (1707); while more philosophical views are expressed in his *Anglia Libera* (1707), wherein he discusses questions of political contract and the ideals of a commonwealth (*op. cit.* 92). Chubb had a very meagre relation to the movement, as appears from his *Enquiry concerning Property* (1717), and *Some Short Reflections on the Ground and Extent of Authority and Liberty* (1728). Insignificant as were these Deistic attempts at elaborating a philosophy of rights, they are of great value in showing how closely connected were the principles of theology and politics—a connexion which will appear more convincing in relation to the question of free-thought and toleration. The purely political philosophy of the Enlightenment, dependent as it was upon Hobbes and Locke, underwent a development which in France was practical, in Germany speculative. Rousseau carried out Locke's idea of government by contract, the theory of which he projected in *Le Contrat social* (1762). In Germany, Kant attempted a theoretical deduction of *jus naturale* in his *Metaphysische Anfangsgründe der Rechtslehre* (1797), in which he reasons from the *status naturalis*, not as though it had been a real condition of mankind, but as a hypothetical condition upon the grounds of which human rights might be deduced. The process is continued in Fichte's *Grundlage des Naturrechts nach den Prinzipien der Wissenschaftslehre* (1796), in which the relation of ego to non-ego is transformed into the relation of the individual to society. A similar application of the Enlightenment's philosophy of rights was made by Schopenhauer, who interpreted the Hobbist 'state of nature' in the light of the 'will to live' (*Welt als Wille und Vorstellung*, 1819, § 62).

2. Free-thought and toleration.—Free-thought was the minor premiss in an argument wherein natural rights was the major premiss and natural religion the conclusion. Inherent in Protestantism, the principle of freedom had further been employed by Grotius when he elaborated his principle of rights, especially at the point where he asserted the validity of 'jus naturale non esse Deum.' Hobbes had defined *jus* as *libertas*, and had contended against the 'captivity of the understanding' (*Leviathan*, ch. xxxii. p. 360). Spinoza, however, was the first to perfect an argument for freedom as something native to the human mind. According to the Spinozistic theory of natural rights, right is equivalent to power, so that one may do whatever he is able. Now thought, by its very nature an inner and individual process, is something over which no one but the individual himself can possibly exercise power (*Tractatus Theologico-politicus*, 1670, cap. xvii.). As with thought, so likewise with worship; its inner nature is such that it can be conceived of as undergoing no interference from an external power, although the magistrate may with power and right enjoin duties of justice and charity (*ib.* cap. xviii.). In making this distinction of the inner and outer, Spinoza sought to free science from religion, and to separate philosophy from faith, such a separation constituting the essential aim of his work (*ib.*). To arrive at this end, he defines one in terms of speculation, the other in those of practice: 'Ratio regnum veritatis et sapientiae; theologia autem pietatis et obedientiae' (*ib.* cap. xv.). Not only as a matter of natural rights in the individual, but likewise as the most rational law for the State, is the principle of toleration to be upheld. Such was the motto of Spinoza's work. His relation to Deism was an indirect one, for he made little appeal to the average free-thinker, hence the omission of his name from the list of free-thinkers from Socrates to Locke which Collins gave in his *Discourse of Free Thinking* (1713). Nevertheless, Deism was not unaware of Spinoza, while his logic of free-thought sometimes appears in its literature. Evidence of Spinoza's direct connexion with natural religion as a system is found in Kortholt's *de Tribus Impostoribus* (Herbert, Hobbes, Spinoza), 1680. Connected as was his name with these two greater thinkers, Spinoza was supposed to have influenced Toland and Tindal. Warburton called Toland the 'mimic of Spinoza' (*Divine Legation of Moses*[5], iv. 273), and both the pantheism and free-thought of this Deist may serve to indicate the nature of the imitation. With regard to Tindal, the controversy over natural religion brought forth the following rhyme:

> 'Spinoza smiles and cries, the work is done.
> Tindal shall finish (Satan's darling son)—
> Tindal shall finish what Spinoza first begun.'

Without any theoretical preliminary, Hobbes had anticipated Spinoza in proposing principles of toleration, the result of whose application was destined to become momentous in the history of Deism. The principles upon which Hobbes sought to base toleration consisted of two articles of Christian faith: the Deity of God and the Messiahship of Jesus. Belief in the existence of God as an existence, with attributes of a negative, superlative, or indefinite nature, involves the end of all true worship. That Jesus was the Christ was regarded by Hobbes as the other article of free faith, and this simple creed was in his mind the burden of the Gospels and the testimony of the Apostles as recorded in the Acts (*de Cive*, cap. xviii.). Rational Christianity and natural religion, with their maxims of the mere Deity of God and the mere Messiahship of Jesus, were thus practical political principles used in a controversy over Church and State, rather than speculative ones deduced in a disinterested fashion. This practical tendency reappears in Locke, whose sensationalism would have been as ineffective as Hobbes' materialism if their authors had been called upon to employ speculative instead of practical methods in the controversy. Like Spinoza, Locke insists upon the inwardness of religious belief, and thus argues that,

> 'although his (the magistrate's) opinion in religion be sound and the way that he appoints truly evangelical, if I be not thoroughly persuaded in my own mind, then there will be no safety for me in following it' (*A Letter for Toleration*, 1689 [*Works*[11], vi. 17-26]).

In insisting that speculative articles and opinions should not be imposed by law, Locke was not prepared to consent that the right of toleration should extend to the atheist, for the reason that with him the oaths and bonds of civil society could be of no avail. 'The taking away of God dissolves all,' declared Locke, who was still anxious to reduce the idea of Deity to a minimum (*ib.* 47). Having thus indicated the lower limit of religious belief, Locke furthered the formation of the Deistic code when he contended that the minimum of Christian belief which the State might enjoin consisted in the death and resurrection of Christ (*A Third Letter for Toleration*, 173–177). On the negative side, he insisted that it was not necessary for the subject to believe in the Athanasian Creed (*ib.* 410), so that his Deism was a mean between the extremes of atheism and orthodoxy. The magistrate cannot enforce a religion as true, 'unless the Law of Nature deliver into his hands the xxxix. articles of the one and only true religion' (*ib.* 428).

Among the Deists, who were beginning to make an impression as free-thinkers, the work of toleration was taken up when Tindal wrote his *Essay concerning Obedience to the Supreme Powers* (1694), in which he declares himself a follower of Locke, when he says:

> 'The author of the *Letters for Toleration* is the first who has ventured to assert the justice and necessity of toleration in its due and full extent' (*op. cit.* 130).

Tindal's more independent argument for freedom appeared in his tract, *A Discourse on the Liberty of the Press* (1698), wherein he pleads for freedom on the ground that, since reason is the only light that God has given man, he will be held responsible for the proper use of his faculties; whence the necessity of a free press, in order that men may perfect their faith by the free interchange of opinion (*op. cit.* 294). In his *Essay concerning the Power of the Magistrate* (1697), Tindal attempts a practical definition as the 'belief of a God, and the sense and practice of those duties which result from the knowledge we have of Him and ourselves' (*op. cit.* 130). But the most characteristic work on free-thinking that Deism was to produce appeared in 1713, when Anthony Collins (1676–1727) produced his *Discourse of Free-Thinking*, in which toleration, instead of being derived *a priori*, was based upon practical grounds. According to Collins, free-thinking in theology is as necessary as in other sciences, for the reason that theology involves these in its treatment of Nature and history (*op. cit.* 12). As with science, so with religion; since uniformity of opinion among men is impossible, it is best for each to judge independently, so that the 'surest and best means of arriving at truth lies in free-thinking' (*ib.* 33). Collins even goes so far as to assert that the manifest design of the gospel was to set all men free-thinking, as the Apostles urged them to abandon an established religion for a faith wholly new to them. With regard to his own day, Collins contends that, in view of various alleged revelations, as the Zend-avesta and the Bible, and owing to the different views of God and the Scriptures within the Church itself, it has become necessary to adopt free-thinking as the only possible means of setting one's self right in religion (*op. cit.* 48–90). In the hands of Collins the principles of free-thought were separated from the juristic philosophy of the Enlightenment and transformed into the special pleading peculiar to Deism.

3. Rational Christianity.—From its beginning in Hobbes, the theory of toleration had proceeded upon the assmption that the principles of Christianity may be stated in a manner so simple that it will satisfy the State in its demand for law and at the same time content the free-thinker in his claims for the rights of toleration. It was in this mediatorial spirit that Hobbes and Locke had sought to base rational Christianity upon the idea of God as mere existence, and Christ in His mere Messiahship. Now was to follow an independent treatment of the problem. Before Locke had written *The Reasonableness of Christianity* (1695), Arthur Bury published *The Naked Gospel* (1690), the aim of which was to advance the interests of natural religion, whose primary principle was faith (*op. cit.* 10). In the particular case of Christianity this general religious function operates as a belief in Christ as the Messiah (*ib.* 39). Such was also the view of Locke, who outlined his theology against the background of his philosophy of toleration. By appealing to primitive Christianity, Locke argued that the original article of belief and the sole test of discipleship among the Apostles consisted in the creed that Jesus was the Christ, so that to believe in Christ meant to credit His claims to Messiahship. The first principle of Christian ethics was that of repentance.

'These two,' says Locke, 'faith and repentance, *i.e.* believing Jesus to be the Messiah, and a good life, are the indispensable conditions of the new covenant, to be performed by all who would obtain eternal life' (*The Reasonableness of Christianity* [*Works*[11], vii. 105]).

This simple gospel was in Locke's mind the burden of St. Paul's preaching, and all that he advanced as necessary to salvation. With regard to the Pauline theology, as developed in the Epistles, Locke can only plead that these writings were intended for those who were already Christians; hence they 'could not be designed to teach the fundamental articles and points necessary to salvation' (*A Vindication of the Reasonableness*, etc., 1695, p. 167). As an empiricist, Locke would have had no right to use the term 'reasonableness,' but his employment of the term was political rather than philosophical, his contention practical rather than speculative. A century later, on the decline of Deism, Kant followed a similar course, except that, instead of passing from rights to religion, he reversed the process; and, having written a rationalistic treatise on Christianity, *Die Religion innerhalb der Grenzen der blossen Vernunft* (1793), he followed it up with a juristic defence of freedom, the principles of which are found in his *Rechtslehre* (1797). Thus, from Hobbes to Kant the principles of theology were closely connected with those of natural rights.

As the practical phase of Locke's philosophy had been of great moment in the formulation of the Deistic creed, so the speculative part of his system received Deistic recognition when Toland produced his *Christianity not Mysterious* (1696), a work suggestive of Bury's *Naked Gospel*. Toland's contention was that there was nothing in the gospel contrary to or above reason, so that no Christian doctrine could be called a mystery (*op. cit.* 6). [For a full account of Toland's views, see art. DEISM, in vol. iv. p. 534 f.] The next step in Deism was to attack the accounts of the miraculous as given in the Gospels. Accordingly, Collins, who had completed his theory of free-thought, inaugurated the attack upon mystery when he sought to invalidate the testimony of the prophets. Where William Whiston, in the Boyle Lectures of 1707, had contended for a single, Messianic sense in the interpretation of prophecy, Collins contended that the prophecies usually cited have in them a sense which is not Messianic at all, and that the application to the life of Christ, as in the case of the citations made in Mt 1 and 2, is to be understood in a purely allegorical or mystical manner (*The Grounds and Reasons of the Christian Religion*, 1724, p. 106). The reply to this Deistic work which was made by Edward Chandler, in *A Defence of Christianity from the Prophecies* (1725), so involved the question of miracles that it formed the starting-point for William Woolston's *Discourses on Miracles* (1727–1729), inaugurated as they were by his work, *The Moderator between an Infidel and an Apostate* (1725). With some of the miracles recorded in the New Testament, Woolston resorts to the allegorical method of interpretation (see *Discourses* i., ii., iii., iv.); others, which deal with the raising of the dead and the resurrection of Christ, are regarded as incredible. This negative attitude towards miracles formed the basis of Peter Annet's attack upon the credibility of the resurrection, the Gospel account of which he deemed a forgery (*The Resurrection of Jesus Considered*, 1744, p. 22).

This destructive treatment of Christianity was accompanied by an attempt to construct a rational Christianity, based upon the teaching rather than the person of Christ. The way for this had been prepared by Hobbes and Locke, in their plea for toleration upon the basis of the mere Messiahship of Jesus, while it was also an expression of the Socinian element in Deism. Locke's *Reasonableness of Christianity* had come in for some criticism as a Socinian work when John Edwards wrote his *Socinianism Unmasked* (1696), while in Warburton's mind Deism was a 'modern fashionable notion, not borrowed from, but the same with the Socinian' (*The Divine Legation of Moses*[5], i. 56). The most characteristic defender of this milder form of Deism was Thomas Chubb (1679–1747), who had made his entrance into the field of controversy by means of his Socinian work, *The Supremacy of the Father* (1715). Chubb's chief contribution to Deism was *The True Gospel of Jesus Christ* (1738), in which materials suggestive of Hobbes' hedonism are expressed in a form peculiar to Herbert's natural religion. The essence of Christianity and the person of Christ are treated in a purely utilitarian manner; accordingly, Chubb asserts that what fits a man for future felicity tends to make him happy here, so that, when the gospel is found to subserve man's present and future well-being, it may be called 'true' (*op. cit.* 4), just as the author of it may be called the 'greatest benefactor of our species' (*ib.* 16). Chubb's more precise formulation of his rationalistic Christianity involved three articles, as follows: (1) conformity of life to the rule of action founded upon the nature of things; (2) repentance and reform where one has violated this rule; (3) a future judgment where requital or condemnation will be meted out according to conformity or non-conformity to the rule of right action (*ib.* 17). In adopting these principles of natural religion, Chubb abandoned the hedonism of Hobbes for the rationalism of Cudworth and Clarke. In the same spirit Thomas Morgan († 1743) attempted to connect the gospel with the religion of Nature, by regarding Christ as the Teacher who brought to light the 'true and genuine principles of nature and reason' (*The Moral Philosopher*², 1738, p. 144). Bolingbroke (1698–1751) attempted a distinction between the natural religion of Christ and the spurious religion of St. Paul and his followers; and, just as Lessing distinguished between the religion of Christ and the Christian religion, so Bolingbroke declared that 'the Gospel of Christ is one thing, the Gospel of St. Paul and all those who have grafted after him on the same stock, another' (*Philosophical Works*, 1754, p. 313). Christianity was to Bolingbroke 'a complete but plain system of natural religion' (*ib.* 316). Thus shorn of its mysteries of prophecy and miracle, the Christianity of Deism had become identified with the system of natural religion.

4. **Natural religion.**—As the doctrine of natural rights, with its corollaries of free-thought and toleration, had led to the formulation of rational Christianity, so natural religion employed a different logic to arrive at the same conclusion. The first movement, inaugurated by Grotius, was practical; the second, which sprang from Herbert, was speculative. Herbert's work *de Veritate*, appearing one year before that of Grotius, investigated natural instinct in its logical form as Grotius examined its ethical nature. Both thinkers attempted an *a priori* deduction of a natural principle, whose existence in human nature was then corroborated by an *a posteriori* investigation of human history; in both alike we find the appeal to the *instinctus naturalis* and the *consensus universalis*. [The contentions of the *de Veritate* will be found in art. DEISM, vol. iv. p. 533.] Herbert's view of religion, naively conceived, and wanting in the inexorable rationalism and secularism of the Enlightenment, was destined to be prophetic rather than constructive in the career of natural religion, whose fundamental principle was that of the 'reason of things.' Hence, after the appearance of Herbert's work, the interest of the Enlightenment pursued the juristic of Grotius rather than the rationalistic of Herbert, the two tendencies uniting in the first quarter of the 18th century. This unity of natural religion and natural rights appeared in Charles Blount († 1693), who considered Herbert's five articles of universal belief to be the best ground for toleration (*Religio Laici*, 1683). In Blount's *The Oracles of Reason* (1693), the term 'Deist' is found, this being one of the earliest instances of its occurrence.

Without any dependence upon Herbert, Samuel Clarke exercised the same speculative freedom manifested in the former's *de Veritate*, while he enriched Deism with something like a theistic philosophy. Written in opposition to Spinoza, as also to Hobbes, Clarke's *Demonstration of the Being and Attributes of God* (1704–1705) was so devoted to the 'nature of things' as a first principle that it never freed itself from a kind of Spinozistic pantheism—a fact which did not escape the notice of William Carroll in his *Remarks upon Mr. Clarke's Sermons* (1705), while in recent years its importance has been re-considered by R. Zimmerman (*Samuel Clarke's Leben und Lehre*, Vienna, 1870). With Clarke the idea of God is thus closely connected with that of the reason of things, so that his theism or Deism tends to uphold a noetic system, Thomistic and Cudworthian in the extreme. With his implicit faith in the mathematical analogy, Clarke asserts that God must be thought of as eternal and necessary, just as twice two must be thought of as equal to four; as a necessary Being, God is thus the ground of His own existence (*Works*, 1732–1742, iii. 5). Identified with the nature of things, the Deity is called upon to will in accordance with the necessities which these things impose. In this connexion Clarke introduces the ethical as a determinant of the real; thus he says, 'To will things to be what they are not is as absurd as to believe that twice two is not equal to four' (*ib.* ii. 586). In thus arguing, Clarke was contending for a complete and self-sufficient natural religion, but the emphasis laid upon the ethical seems to involve as its consequence the abrupt change to revealed religion, for the reason that the will cannot perform what the intellect recognizes as fit and necessary. Accordingly, Clarke's metaphysical dogmatism is pursued by a moral scepticism, which declares that, perfect as the reason of things may be, the fallacy of acting contrary to such a standard is not sufficient to deter man from vice, because its pursuit is often accompanied by pleasure and profit, while pain and calamity may follow upon virtue.

'This alters the case, and destroys the practice of that which appears so reasonable in speculation, and introduces the necessity of rewards and punishments' (*ib.* 630).

This apparent lapse into hedonism was really an appeal to the idea of future rather than present happiness, as will become evident from the following plea:

'It is neither possible nor reasonable that by adhering to virtue men should part with their lives, if thereby they deprive themselves of all possibility of receiving advantage from that adherence' (*ib.* 679).

The doctrine of future rewards was thus the connecting link between natural and revealed religion, for, on the side of the Deity, this idea was fundamental, since

'God by express declaration of His will in Holy Scripture has established and confirmed the original difference of things' (*ib.* 697),

while from the human standpoint the principle of reward and punishment is necessary as a motive to impel the will towards that which the understanding recognizes as right in itself.

Early in the field of natural religion, Shaftesbury (1670–1713) elaborated an optimistic and æsthetical view of the world, which had something of that tendency towards pantheism which Deism ever betrayed. Shaftesbury uses the term 'Deist,' which he considers the 'highest of all names' (*The Moralists*, 1709, pt. 2, sect. 3). He has a word of praise also for the free-thinker, whom he characterizes as the 'noblest of characters' (*Characteristics*, 1711, iii. 311), but the more strenuous methods of rights and reason were foreign to his thought. The leading motive with Shaftesbury seems to be that of harmony within and without; to perceive this harmony constitutes religion, to promote it is the chief concern of morality. On the ethical side, he pursues the idea of harmony in connexion with his analysis of human nature, which is supposed to evince three tendencies: natural affections which tend to public good; self-affections which lead to private benefit; and unnatural ones which are harmful both to self and to society. To these, conscience or the moral-sense is added (*ib.* ii. 98, 119). The nature of virtue is such as to relate man to the world as a whole; hence, as Shaftesbury says, 'If any creature be wholly and really ill, it must be with respect to the universal system' (*ib.* 20). Furthermore, he speaks of virtue as 'proportionable affection' (*ib.* 40), while he asserts that the

'affection of a creature towards the good of the species or common nature, is as proper or natural to him as it is to any organ, part, or member of an animal body or mere vegetable to work in its known course and regular way of growth' (*ib.* 78).

At the same time, the mind is called upon to perceive the harmony in the world without, for virtue is impossible in a 'distracted universe' (*ib.* 70). Here is the point where the systems of Shaftesbury and Clarke are in conflict; for, where Clarke sought to advance to the realm of revelation through the cracks in the natural order, Shaftesbury postulates a perfect world-order whose inner and outer harmony is in striking contrast to the distracted universe of the other system, and claims that without this the practice of virtue is in vain.

The influence of Clarke is to be observed in the most important of Deistic works, *Christianity as Old as the Creation; or the Gospel a Republication of the Law of Nature* (1730), written by Matthew Tindal (1656-1733). [See art. DEISM, vol. iv. p. 535 f.]

The famous reply to Tindal and to Deism in general which Butler (1692-1752) framed in *The Analogy of Religion, Natural and Revealed* (1736), was not so much opposed to or free from the elements of Deism as has usually been supposed; Butler, indeed, like Clarke, contributed to a system which he affected to attack. In his ethical philosophy, Butler defends egoism when he declares that self-love stands in need of furtherance, while its dignity is such as to place it upon a level with conscience (*Sermon* ii.); both principles are based upon the Stoical principle of harmony with Nature (*ib.*). After assuming that no revelation would have been given had the light of Nature been sufficient, Butler reiterates Tindal's favourite motto: 'Christianity is a republication of natural religion' (*Analogy*, ii. ch. i. § 1). Here, natural religion is the standard; for, if in revealed religion there are ideas whose meaning is contrary to natural religion, such meaning cannot be the real one (*ib.* § 2). In the same manner reason stands supreme, and Butler in his determined rationalism declares:

'I express myself with caution, lest I should be mistaken to vilify reason; which is indeed the only faculty we have wherewith to judge concerning anything, even revelation itself' (*ib.* ch. iii. § 1).

Butler's position, however, differs from that of the Deist, in that he is pessimistic where the exponent of perfect natural religion is ever optimistic; he thus contends that the imperfection attending revealed religion is one which natural religion is called upon to share, so that all that may be said against the one is valid as a criticism of the other. Indeed, Butler's ethical pessimism and his armed resistance to it are the permanent results of his traditional system. In his ethical sermons, he utters an ever-memorable lament over conscience, when he says:

'Had it strength, as it has right; had it power, as it has manifest authority, it would absolutely govern the world' (*Serm.* ii.);

and, when in the world he discovers 'infinite disorders,' he is still able to postulate a theory of the moral government of God, the actual operation of which in the present militant condition of things is manifest as a 'tendency' (*Analogy*, I. ch. iii. §§ 4-5). [Cf. art. BUTLER.]

The decline of Deism is to be noted in Thomas Morgan and Bolingbroke. Morgan is of historical value in connecting Clarke with the controversy, for it was from Clarke that he derived his Deism. In speaking of the famous expression, 'the reason of things,' Morgan says:

'I mean the same thing by it that Dr. Clarke does, while he grounds the whole of natural religion upon this principle' (*The Moral Philosopher*[2], 1738, iii. 314).

Morgan further reveals the influence of natural rights, for he criticized the Mosaic law in the light of the Grotian *jus naturale*, and expressed Jezebel's attitude towards Elijah after he had slain the prophets of Baal by saying: 'She thought this method contrary to the law of nature and nations' (*ib.* ii. 314). Bolingbroke began to cast suspicion upon the authenticity of natural religion by searching for evidences of it in history. The Hobbist *status naturalis* he regarded as a condition of the world in which man was, not irrational, but 'artless'; when he searches this native condition of mankind for traces of the religion of Nature, he can only say:

'It cannot be proved without the help of the Old Testament, nor very well with it, that the unity of God was the primitive Belief of Mankind; but I think it sufficiently evident . . . that the first and great principle of natural theology could not fail to be discovered as soon as men began to contemplate themselves and all objects that surrounded them' (*Works*, 1754, iv. 203). A glance at the ancient Egyptian religion, the worship of the Chinese, and the faith of King Melchizedek seems to suggest the possibility of this.

With the application of history to the scheme of natural religion the end of Deism begins; at the same time, the rationalistic force of the Deistic argument began to lessen, as was shown by the appearance of Dodwell's *Christianity not Founded upon Argument* (1742). With no theory of knowledge to guide him, Dodwell assumed the standpoint of intuition, or religious consciousness, whence he was able to offset all rationalism in religion by saying, 'There is no medium between believing and not believing' (*op. cit.* 6). With the actual content of religion as the basis of his argument, Dodwell turns away from a 'boasted rational faith,' and asserts that this is 'without the least foundation to support it in either nature or revelation' (*ib.* 7). Fitted for actual life in the world, the human soul is not adapted to the unfruitful work of speculation, while a rational faith could never produce the effects attendant upon real religion (*ib.* 24). As with the content of religion, so with revelation; here the command is, 'Believe'; the appeal is direct and compromising (*ib.* 37). Dodwell's work, which constantly touches the fringe of a genuine philosophy of religion, was of great importance as a human document, while it amounted to little as a controversial production, for the reason that it took a stand against both Deism and orthodoxy; Dodwell himself seems to have possessed something of the humanism of both Lessing and Rousseau, while his particular mood was one of mysticism.

The complete downfall of Deism was due to the scepticism of Hume (1711-1776), who applied to the rationalism of his fellow-countrymen the results of national empiricism. He thus undid the work of Herbert of Cherbury. [See art. DEISM, vol. iv. p. 537 f.] Another attack upon reason in religion was made by Rousseau, while the historical content of human worship was emphasized by Voltaire in his *Essai sur les mœurs des nations* (1756). [See, further, art. ENCYCLOPÆDISTS.] Deism in Germany was organized by H. S. Reimarus (1694-1768) in his *Wahrheiten der natürlichen Religion* (1754). Lessing (1729-1781) was involved in the religious controversy, and in so far assumed the rôle of a Deist; but his humanism and sense of historical values saved him from being submerged in the troubled waters of natural religion. His attempt at a philosophy of revelation was made in his booklet, *Die Erziehung des Menschengeschlechts* (1780). In addition to the opposition to the static philosophy of the Enlightenment, the late 18th cent. began to emphasize the thought of 'progress'—an idea wholly alien to the speculations and political ideals of the period. Bodin (1530-1597) had attempted this problem in his philosophy of rights; Vico (1668-1744) introduced it into his *Scienza nuova* (1725); Turgot expressed it more definitely in his *Les Progrès successifs de l'esprit humain* (1750). The rationalistic method of the Enlightenment, which had accompanied this static conception of things, was set at naught by Kant's *Kritik der reinen Vernunft*. In spite of its blind faith in what is called 'Nature,' the Enlightenment had the advantage and performed the service of emancipating the human spirit from authority and tradition; moreover, it laid the foundation for philosophy in things necessary in themselves and universal in their application, as appears most convincingly in its systems of rights and religion. The thought of the present age is at the very antipode of the Enlightenment, which glorified the static and rationalistic where the present upholds the dynamic and realistic.

See also artt. HUMANISTS, GOETHE, SCHILLER, RENAISSANCE, ROMANTICISM.

LITERATURE.—In addition to the sources and authorities cited in the article, the following general works may be consulted: J. E. Erdmann, *A History of Philosophy*, tr. W. S. Hough, London, 1897, §§ 285, 293; R. Eucken, *Die Lebensanschauungen der grossen Denker*[2], Leipzig, 1897, pp. 342–403; A. S. Farrar, *Critical History of Free Thought (BL)*, London, 1862; J. G. Hibben, *The Philosophy of the Enlightenment*, London, 1910; J. Hunt, *Religious Thought in England*, London, 1870–73; G. V. Lechler, *Geschichte des englischen Deismus*, Leipzig, 1841; F. C. Schlosser, *Geschichte des achtzehnten Jahrhunderts*[4], Heidelberg, 1861; L. Stephen, *English Thought in the Eighteenth Century*[2], London, 1881; W. Windelband, *Geschichte der neueren Philosophie*, Leipzig, 1876, §§ 28–56.

CHARLES GRAY SHAW.

ENTHUSIASM.—The word ἐνθουσιασμός[1] is of relatively late origin. The only term in the earlier Greek vocabulary that could be used to denote a condition of vehement psychical excitement or inordinate exaltation was μανία, a word of very general connotation. It is characteristic of the Greeks that they spoke even of the 'madness' of poets, corresponding to the *furor poeticus* of the Romans. Subsequently the word μέθη was sometimes used in the same sense, and the term 'intoxication,' therefore, is not to be too literally interpreted. Intoxication emanates from Dionysus, the god who re-incorporates himself in wine; and, accordingly, the μέθη αἰώνιος, the guerdon of Orphic mystics in the other world (cf. A. Dieterich, *Nekyia*, Leipzig, 1893, p. 80, note), really signifies their final union with the deity, and is thus, as we shall see, identical with an eternal enthusiasm. We find mention likewise of an intoxication in which the poet creates his work—an idea which is connected in a special way with Æschylus, the most impassioned of the Greek tragedians; legend even tells us that, while he was still young, Dionysus appeared to him and kindled in him the fire of poetic creation (Athenæus, 22*a*). Æschylus is the first writer known to us who uses the verb ἐνθουσιᾶν in intimate connexion with βακχεύειν (frag. *Edonoi*, 58 [Nauck]); then comes Euripides (*Troades*, 1284), with whom ἐνθουσιᾶν virtually means 'to rave.' The earliest use of the substantive ἐνθουσιασμός, with its doublet ἐνθουσίασις, occurs in Plato; and the correlative idea operates largely in his writings. But even the root from which these various forms are derived, viz. ἔνθεος, with its corresponding verb ἐνθεάζειν, 'to be enraptured,' is not found, so far as we know, before the 5th cent. B.C., the earliest instances of their usage being respectively Æschylus, *Septem con. Theb.* 497 (ἔνθεος Ἄρει), and Herodotus, i. 63.

It can hardly be doubted that these terms came into use with the rise of the Mysteries and the spread of prophecy, for here the idea of a union with deity that exalts the favoured ones above all earthly concerns plays a prominent part: when the deity enters into a man, the resultant state is enthusiasm. The word ἔνθους, which occurs in Proclus, *in Timæum*, i. 64, 14. 23, and other writers, is equivalent to ἔνθεος, 'having God in oneself' (Boisacq, *Dict. étymol. de la langue grecque*, Heidelberg, 1907 ff., p. 254). The term may have reached Plato by way of the Orphics, and the reason why Proclus (*in Tim.* i. 7, 27 [Diehl]) applies the adjective ἔνθεος to the Pythagoreans as well is simply that the line of demarcation between Orphic and Pythagorean views was for him indistinguishable (Rohde, *Psyche*[3], Tübingen, 1903, ii. 108, 2). At all events ἐνθουσιασμός was from the first mainly a theological conception, while ἔκστασις, on the other hand, comes from the domain of medical terminology, and, so far as known, was not applied till long after Plato's day to the rapturous state of a soul delivered from earthly conditions. Ecstasy (*q.v.*) involves the separation of the soul from the body, since in it the soul presses towards God, and strives to become one with Him; it is something fundamentally different from enthusiasm, though the two ideas go hand in hand, and are often confused with each other (A. Dieterich, *Eine Mithrasliturgie*, Leipzig, 1903, p. 98). Enthusiasm, as we saw above, denotes the state of a man in whom a god dwells; but here we must, of course, make the further reservation that, when the indwelling power is a noxious or evil spirit, the result is 'possession' (θειασμός, δαιμονισμός), which may likewise be spoken of as μανία, 'madness,' but never as ἐνθουσιασμός. The connotation of the latter term is thus clear and distinct. The mystic is ἐνθουσιαστικός; so is the seer, in the frenzy of prophecy (cf. *e.g.* Plutarch, *de Defect. Orac.* 432 D, *Solon*, 12, Firmicus, *Math.* viii. 21), and also the poet, in whom dwell Apollo and the Muses (cf. Democritus; see Zeller, *Phil. d. Griechen*, i. [Leipzig, 1869], 645; Plato, *Phædr.* 245 A; Tambornino, *de Antiquorum Daemonismo*, Giessen, 1909, p. 6); seer and poet are also styled νυμφόληπτοι (cf. Bloch, in Roscher, iii. 513 ff.).

The mode of generating that union with the deity which produces the enthusiastic state was represented at first in a very crude way—as eating the god or having sexual intercourse with him (A. Dieterich, *Eine Mithraslit.* 97 ff.). Enthusiasm was brought about also by drinking wine, since Dionysus materializes himself therein (*ib.* 173). Seer and poet drink inspiration with the water of the Castalian fountain, for here the nymph dwells in bodily form. The erotic union of the Delphic priestess with Apollo has been vividly portrayed by ancient witnesses (Bethe, *Rhein. Mus.* lxii. [1907] 467; cf. schol. on Aristoph. *Plut.* 39, and the passages in A. Dieterich, *Eine Mithrasliturgie*, 2nd ed. enlarged, Leipzig, 1910, p. 14). Another act of amatory union was the dance of the Bacchantes with Dionysus (cf. *e.g.* Aristoph. *Frogs*, 324 ff.), which likewise assumed enthusiastic forms; in explanation of this, reference may be made to an Esthonian custom recorded by Weinhold ('Zur Geschichte des heidnischen Ritus,' in *ABAW*, Berlin, 1896, p. 30; cf. Fehrle, *Kultische Keuschheit*, Naumburg, 1908, p. 11, 1). Further, the phenomena of the dream were also brought into connexion with enthusiasm, as the soul of the dreamer develops higher powers of vision and anticipates the future. According to Aristotle (frag. 10), the first impression of the idea of God is imparted by the ἐνθουσιασμοί and μαντεῖα of the soul in sleep, and we know that the Stoics found warrant for oracles and dream-reading in the Divine origin of the soul as manifested in ἐνθουσιασμός (Zeller, *op. cit.* iv. 320).

A peculiar function is assigned to enthusiasm in the philosophy of Plato, who distinguishes several phases of a frenzy (μανία) that imparts gifts of the highest order. There is the frenzy of the seer, who unveils the future; that of the consecrated mystic, who absolves men from sin; and that of the poet, who is possessed by the Muses—these three forms have already been noted, while a fourth is found in the frenzy of the philosopher (*Phædr.* 244 ff.). Every human soul has in a former life beheld the

[1] The present article is intended merely to trace the origin and ethical usage of the (Greek) term; cf., further, ECSTASY and ENTHUSIASTS (Religious) for the part that 'enthusiasm' has played in religion.

true reality, but only a few are able to summon up the remembrance thereof. Those to whom this privilege is vouchsafed, however, hold themselves aloof from the ordinary pursuits of life, and, uniting themselves with God, are reviled by the multitude as mad, while, as a matter of fact, they dwell apart in the enthusiastic state. In Plato's judgment, accordingly, enthusiasm is the medium of a direct intuition of the Divine—a vision which is granted to the philosopher alone (*Phædr.* 249 C).

Platonic and Stoic views, combined with popular ideas, reappear in Plutarch (Zeller, *op. cit.* v. 173 ff., with relevant quotations). According to Plutarch's exposition, when the soul is in a state of enthusiasm, it receives immediate intimations from God; upon enthusiasm, indeed, rests all higher revelation. The more effectively the soul represses its own activities, preserves its tranquillity, and frees itself from the sensuous, the more delicate becomes its receptive faculty; and consequently the best medium of Divine revelation is sleep or an abstemious life. The intimations of the gods are conveyed to the soul by dæmons, while material agencies, such as the vapours of the Pythian grotto, may also avail, with the consent of the gods and the aid of dæmons, to induce the enthusiastic state. Enthusiasm always comes spontaneously, and the suddenness of the illumination it brings is the guarantee of the truth thereof.

Plutarch defines enthusiasm as an affective state (πάθος) of the soul, but Aristotle had characterized it more precisely as a *pathos* peculiar to the psychical *ethos* (*Pol.* viii. 55). The special power of inducing the enthusiastic condition is ascribed by Aristotle to the music of Olympus (*loc. cit.*)—a view that suggests other related phenomena. In ancient Hellas an important factor in orgiastic celebrations was boisterous music (cf. *e.g.* Eurip. *Bacch.* 126 ff.), which was regarded, no doubt, as a means of exciting emotion, just as it forms an accompaniment to ecstatic actions among the less civilized races of to-day. The Greeks could not but feel, however, that the music of the orgies was of a barbaric kind. Their own music was always marked by the quality of dignified repose, and did not naturally lend itself to the expression of joy, or pain, or enthusiasm (Gevaërt, *Hist. et théorie de la musique de l'antiquité*, Ghent, 1875–81, i. 37 ff.). The power of producing enthusiasm was associated with the Phrygian and Lydian modes and with the music of flutes (Arist. *Pol.* viii. 6. 5), and here we have the explanation of the above reference to the music of Olympus. It would seem, moreover, that the Aristotelian school were specially interested in investigating the influence of music upon the emotions; for, apart from Aristotle's own disquisitions in *Pol.* viii., we hear of a work by Theophrastus, 'On Enthusiasm,' in which, according to frag. 87 (Wimmer), the effects of music were discussed. The subject was, of course, one of special importance, as music was a leading element in ancient education (Arist. *loc. cit.*).

At the close of the classical period of philosophy stands the imposing figure of Plotinus, in whose writings, as in those of his pupils, the terms ἔνθεος and ἐνθουσιασμός play a great part (cf. Diehl in the Index to Proclus, *in Timæum*, iii. 425; Proclus, *in Rem Publicam*, ed. Kroll, Leipzig, 1901, ii. 440). But it is quite evident that for Plotinus the union of the human soul with the deity properly means its separation from the body, and thus implies the condition of ecstasy, not of enthusiasm at all.

LITERATURE.—This is indicated in the article.

L. RADERMACHER.

ENTHUSIASTS (Religious).—This article deals with certain teachers of religion, who have believed themselves to be directly inspired by God to impart new truth. They may be classified according to their attitude to previous revelation. Some have attached themselves closely to previous literature, frequently concentrating on apocalyptic, or interpreting on special lines—as the Catholic Apostolic Church. Others, in supplementing existing revelations, tend to supersede them—as Muslims and Mormons. Others believe themselves in such close touch with God that they do not value previous prophecy; of such are the Bābīs. Thus not all the new theologies are immutable; Muggleton, Swedenborg, and Ann Lee have had no successors, but the Doukhobors believe inspiration to be generally diffused. All these classes of theological Enthusiasts are treated separately; and the Hebrew Prophets, noblest of the type, will be dealt with in art. PROPHECY (Hebrew).

1. Our study may begin with **Christian prophecy**, a phenomenon of great importance for some two centuries. From the first it was avowed that the prophet would not be a permanent feature in Christian life (1 Co 13[8]), but meantime prophecy was a gift of Christ (Eph 4[11]) to men and women (Ac 21[9]), for the benefit of the Church and occasionally of outsiders (1 Co 11[22-25]). Like their Jewish prototypes, the Christian prophets could use symbols (Ac 21[11]); but, unlike the Greeks possessed with spirits of divination (Ac 16[16]), they had their spirits under control (1 Co 14[32]). In Greek circles there was clearly a risk of confusion, causing hesitation in some quarters (1 Th 5[20]), and authoritative repudiation of some false prophets (1 Jn 4[1]). A typical product of such Enthusiastic ministry is seen in the Apocalypse, with visions and predictions which yet, in their literary form, show manifest signs of elaborate study (cf. 1 P 1[10. 11]). This book is the only one in the NT which puts forth explicit claims to inspiration (Rev 1[11] 22[18]); but these were pitched very high, and, being accompanied with orders for public reading (1[3]), they at once ensured acceptance, even outside Asia and its seven Churches.

Another specimen of an Enthusiast's work is the *Shepherd*, with its visions to Hermas, leading up to the coming of an angel, who imparted much information which the seer was told to commit to writing and circulate. Some of the more striking doctrines are the importance attached to guardian angels (*Mand.* 6[2]) and the elaboration of the terms of salvation; baptism is the means of forgiveness (*Sim.* 9[16]), and sins after baptism can be forgiven only once more (*Mand.* 4[3]); those who died before Christ have their opportunity by the preaching of the apostles and teachers when they themselves died; but, even then, baptism in Hades is necessary (*Sim.* 9[16]). Sins are carefully classified (9[19-28]), and works of supererogation are admitted (5[2]). Great stress is laid on the doctrine of the Church, and the risk arising from false prophets is frankly recognized (*Mand.* 11). This tendency became more pronounced with Ignatius, who hoped that God might reveal something to him (*Eph.* 20); but he pointed emphatically to a new path when he claimed that the preaching of the Spirit prompted the message (*Phil.* 7): 'Do nothing without the bishop.'

2. The conflict foreshadowed in 3 John came to a head on the uplands of Asia Minor, when the **Montanists** objected to the new officialism. They claimed that for generations they had not lacked inspired prophets; and the revelations that came from their leaders were akin to Biblical prophecy and apocalyptic, in that they demanded a most strict morality, and foretold the speedy ushering in of a new age. But it would appear that their prophets wrought themselves up to receive these revelations, and combined the old methods of asceticism and physical exertion with the Indian method of intense introspection. In a discussion

about A.D. 178, some bishops hardly appeared to advantage; the Montanists thereupon rallied all the conservatives throughout the Empire, with the combined appeal for separation from the world to high morality, and reliance on the sure word of prophecy. For a generation they held their place within the general federation of churches, but at Rome and at Carthage the prophets were obliged to step out, leaving the officials to perfect the machinery of the Great Church. After the days of Zephyrinus and Tertullian, Montanism shrank to the dimensions of a mere local sect, almost negligible; even in Phrygia the succession of the prophets ceased. [Cf. art. MONTANISM.] Henceforward, in the West, all claims to direct inspiration were steadily discountenanced by the orderly instinct of Rome, and until the disruption of the 16th cent. all effervescence was speedily checked.

3. A few cases may be noted. Towards the end of the 12th cent. arose **Joachim of Fiore,** in Calabria, who won the ear of four successive Popes, until a new religious order was sanctioned, and his writings were widely read. He taught that the age of the Spirit would begin with A.D. 1260, and he sketched in detail the events of the sixty years preceding. Starting from the Apocalypse, he and his many disciples added new revelations. The Franciscan order was permeated with his views, and, when it divided, the Spirituals clung to them; with their suppression, and the obvious failure of Joachim's predictions, the school died a natural death. A Lombard enthusiast, **Wilhelmina 'of Bohemia,'** claimed to be an incarnation of the Spirit to save the Jews, Saracens, and false Christians; her sect was exterminated soon after her death in A.D. 1281. In Thuringia, *c.* A.D. 1360, from the midst of the Flagellants (*q.v.*) came **Conrad Schmid,** an incarnation of Enoch, who founded the Brethren of the Cross; the Inquisition prevented the unfolding of a constructive programme. Among the **Taborites,** prophets appeared who foretold the speedy end of the age, and incited to war in order to clear the way for the reign of Christ. This intensified the resolve of the authorities to nip all such movements in the bud, and they burned Hans Böhm, who in A.D. 1476 claimed a commission from the Virgin Mary. **Savonarola's** claims to angelic visions won him great popularity, till he flinched from the demand to submit his claims to the ordeal of fire. The **Alumbrados** of Spain, professedly holding intercourse with the Lord and with the Virgin, were equally put down; even **Teresa of Castile** was viewed askance, and her writings were severely censured, though they deal with practical religion more than with theology, and side with the Counter-Reformation.

4. The Hussite leaven showed striking results in A.D. 1521. At Zwickau, midway between Prague and Eisleben, dwelt a Silesian weaver **Nicholas Storch,** who had apparently lived among the Taborites. When he was backed by **Thomas Münzer,** an educated Saxon sent by Luther, he soon blossomed into a prophet. Luther having disappeared after the Diet of Worms, Storch went to Wittenberg, and convinced the leaders of the reality of his mission. Luther hastily returned, and adopted the old device, demanding a miracle to substantiate Storch's claims. The latter withdrew to Silesia and Southern Germany, dying at Munich in 1525, accepted on all hands as inspired, though his enemies adopted Luther's addendum that it was Satan who inspired him. Meanwhile Münzer went to Prague, and announced the dawn of the new dispensation, with the redress of all social grievances. Returning to Saxony, he initiated a communistic system, which he declared to be Divinely ordered. Banished by Luther's influence, he spread his views in Nüremberg and Switzerland, and then returned to Mühlhausen, through districts where the Peasants' War was raging. Here he convinced them of his mission, so that their social programme was backed by the conviction that God was directing them through this prophet. With the massacre of Frankenhausen in 1525, Münzer died, and the first phase of this prophetic movement ended, Hans Hut confining himself to mere exposition of the Apocalypse in his book on the *Seven Seals.*

5. A leather-dresser from Swabia, **Melchior Hoffmann,** was teaching east of the Baltic; then in 1526, at Stockholm, he published a short *Exhortation to his Livonian Converts,* containing an application of Dn 12; and he proceeded to calculate the end of the age, which he fixed for 1533. From Sweden he worked through Denmark and Friesland to Strassburg, where he arrived in 1529. Here he devoted himself further to exposition of the Apocalypse, expanding the idea that the few years left were the period of the Two Witnesses. Presently he recognized inspired prophets in Leonard and Ursula Jost, he himself becoming Elijah, the inspired interpreter. Driven out from the city, he toured through the Netherlands and Westphalia, quite transforming the northern Anabaptist movement till it was thoroughly impregnated with Millennial views. He announced that Strassburg was the New Jerusalem, whence the armies of the Lord would destroy His enemies; and he returned thither to get ready. In a few weeks he was imprisoned, and lingered for ten years, revising his calculations; and, though he heard of the outbreak of civil war resulting from his teachings, he never recognized any fundamental error.

6. Hoffmann being silenced, the second witness appeared promptly in a Haarlem baker, **Jan Matthys;** Hoffmann was Elijah, Matthys was Enoch. Strassburg being clearly impossible, missionaries to Münster, in Westphalia, announced that the Millennial Kingdom was at hand; in eight days 1400 people pledged themselves to the new state of things. Matthys sent two more missionaries to take the lead, and the quieter citizens speedily left the place. Matthys announced the revelation that Münster, and not Strassburg, was the New Jerusalem, and he sent out messengers to direct a general concentration of his followers thither. Amsterdam, Lübeck, Bremen, and other cities responded promptly; and then, although it does not appear that Matthys contemplated any military propaganda, any more than do Second Advent bodies of to-day, the authorities took alarm, inaugurated a reign of terror, intercepted immigrants, and murdered many. The Münster citizens who remained were mostly won to the prophetic side, and the February elections threw all authority in the city into the hands of the Chiliastic Anabaptists. Matthys soon came to take personal charge, and then arose other prophets and prophetesses. When an episcopal army appeared to besiege the city, communism was adopted, as in many other cities under similar conditions; it does not appear that this was ordered by revelation. Visions came to many; and, when Matthys went forth as Samson against the Philistines, and fell in the sortie, his chief apostle, **Jan of Leyden,** was soon recognized as prophet. He gave forth a revelation, whereby the Council was superseded by the Twelve Elders. A few months later, another prophet, **Johann Dusentschuer,** proposed that Jan be made king; and this was done. In October, Dusentschuer gave forth a revelation that 27 apostles were to be sent out, preaching the doctrine of the Kingdom; and all started, mostly to martyrdom. They were preachers making no pretensions to prophecy; but they breathed the same atmosphere, and nearly

the last propaganda work from Münster was Rothmann's book, *A wholly consolatory Witness of the Vengeance and Judgment of the Babylonian Abominations*, etc. Early in the New Year, King Jan issued a code of law, closing with the claim, 'The voice of the living God has instructed me that this is a command of the All Highest.' To the end, he was believed in and obeyed; but the city was captured, and all the inhabitants were massacred. So closed the most remarkable of all the mediæval Enthusiastic movements.

7. The doctrines did not die out at once, for ten years later Calvin published a tract *Against the fanatical and furious Sect of the Libertines who call themselves Spiritual*. His version was that they deemed themselves appointed to usher in the last dispensation, that of Elijah or the Spirit, when every Christian should have direct revelation, and the dead letter of Scripture would be discerned to have a double meaning. Calvin also accused them of teaching that there was no outward law and no principle of evil, for every believer was identified with God.

8. More lasting was the movement inaugurated by **Heinrich Niclaes** of Münster, in 1540. He had hitherto been a Roman Catholic; at Amsterdam he had met Anabaptists and declined to associate with them; but he now received a revelation to establish himself at Emden as a prophet, and publish three Divine communications: 'For this purpose have I borne thee on My heart from thy youth, for a house for Me to dwell in.' For twenty years he carried on a quiet propaganda with three companions supernaturally pointed out to him, Daniel, Elidad, and Tobias; then he was driven out, and worked in England and up to Cologne. A fourth revelation came in 1565, largely concerned with the organization of his followers; but it led to their doubting his inspiration. Apart from a most elaborate framework for the Family of Love, and a decided opposition to Lutheranism, the chief peculiar theological tenet was that 'there are some now living which do fulfil the law in all points.' Niclaes died in 1570, leaving no prophetic successor, but in 1606 the English adherents appealed to King James for toleration, repudiating all sympathies with the Puritans, insisting that they valued the Scriptures and believed in salvation through Christ Jesus the only Saviour, on repentance and newness of life. Two years later, Henry Ainsworth at Amsterdam felt it wise to refute the *Epistle to Two Daughters* of Warwick. Yet they held on, only disappearing after 1645, when an outburst of new revelations attracted Englishmen susceptible to such influences, and left the Family of Love to wither away. There seems to be no more recent study than F. Lippold's, in *Zeitschr. f. d. hist. Theol.*, Gotha, 1862.

9. Britain was slower than the Continent to evolve prophets, but about 1633 **Arise Evans** began his career with warnings to King Charles that he and the kingdom were doomed. For a second message, two years later, he was imprisoned. When the Civil War broke out, he received a revelation to uphold the Established Church, and therefore attacked the General Baptists; they challenged his inspiration, and he offered a prediction to be fulfilled in a week. Its success confirmed him, and he continued to admonish the ruling powers, but met no acceptance.

10. Another isolated prophetess was **Anna Trapnel**, who entered on her career about 1643, and joined the Allhallows Fifth-Monarchy church in 1650. After the dissolution of the Nominated Parliament, three books of her prophecies were speedily published, and for a year before the death of Cromwell she was again active. She went into trances, and spoke in rude rhyme so fast that she could hardly be reported, calling herself the poor Instrument, or the Voice. The burden of the new teaching was the imminent return of Christ, as soon as the 3½ times were fulfilled. No organization resulted from her work. The most recent study of her is in the *English Historical Review* for July 1911. More successful were the Ranters, the Muggletonians, and, a century later, the Southcottians; for these see the separate articles.

11. Meantime fresh prophets arose on the Continent. **J. W. Petersen**, a Lutheran dignitary, devoted himself to apocalyptic interpretation, and then, with his wife and another lady, announced new revelations, which seem to have contained nothing fresh except the modification of a dogma of Hoffmann, that Christ had a double human nature—one eternal, the other originating with the Virgin. Though Petersen spent half a long life publishing, his death in 1727 showed that no effect had been produced; and equally unimportant were other prophets, from the German artisan class. Two Bernese who professed to be the Two Witnesses, and in their teachings revived the Gnostic idea that, while the soul was regenerate, the doings of the body did not matter, were cut short by the law in 1754. For all these, consult Hagenbach, *Hist. of the Church in the 18th Century* (Eng. tr., N.Y. 1869).

12. In Russia an old inheritance from the Paulicians of Armenia was touched with new life. One sect is the **Khlysti** ('Flagellants'), followers of a man who in 1645 proclaimed: 'I am the God announced by the prophets, come down on earth the second time for the salvation of the human race, and there is no God but Me.' They hold, however, that a succession of Christs has been maintained ever since, elevation to this rank being by perfect surrender to the influence of the Spirit, who subdues the flesh. Their ecstatic methods of worship produce much prophesying, and, as they are expressly forbidden to write, lest inspiration be trammelled, they have made no permanent addition to dogma. As a reaction from them, about 1770, arose the **Skoptsi** ('Castrators'), founded by one who declared himself God incarnate: they are strongly chiliastic, and look for the return of Christ when their number reaches 144,000; the sealing into this number consists of castration. For these and similar sects, see Leroy-Beaulieu, *Empire of the Tsars* (Eng. tr., N.Y. 1893–6, vol. iii.). The most important of the movements in east and north Europe are the Doukhobors and Swedenborgians, both of whom have spread beyond the country of origin (see separate articles).

13. The Convulsionist outgrowth of the Jansenists at Paris left no mark in theology; nor is it otherwise with the Cevennes Prophets (see CAMISARDS). But the latter are responsible for the Manchester movement of the Wardleys, and Ann Lee, 'Bride of the Lamb,' who migrated to America and founded the Shakers (*q.v.*). These are not to be confounded with an English body founded in 1864 by **Mary Anne Girling**, who gave herself out as the final revelation of God. Her teachings dealt chiefly with conduct, inculcating celibacy and communism. The most singular dogma was her own immortality, and her death in 1886 ruined these second Shakers, who had styled themselves 'Children of God.' About the same time the 'New and Latter House of Israel' was organized in Kent by **James White**, whose revelations are published in the *Flying Roll*. The most remarkable point is that Christ redeemed souls only to a limited extent; bodies must be redeemed by acceptance of the Mosaic Law, and at Christ's appearing, 144,000 of these will greet Him and reign with Him. An enormous unfinished building near Gillingham is the chief relic of these Jezreelites. More lasting has been the Catholic Apostolic Church (see

IRVINGISM), springing out of a movement at Port Glasgow in 1829; while the proceedings of Prince and Smyth-Pigott have not yet destroyed the Somerset Agapemone (*q.v.*). Far more influential results have followed the enthusiasm of two remarkable Americans, Joseph Smith and Mary Baker Glover Eddy, for which see articles MORMONISM and CHRISTIAN SCIENCE, though the latter does not emphasize the point that the system came by revelation; as to which see *Science and Health*, p. 34, line 7; p. 109, line 20; p. 123, line 19.

[America has also been the home of other enthusiasts besides those just mentioned. The Amana Society (*q.v.*) is of German provenance, but the very small sect of Angel Dancers (*q.v.*) is purely American in origin, and, despite its evanescent character, it is not without interest psychologically as illustrating the rise of a sect based entirely upon enthusiasm. **Ballou's** curious 'American Bible' *Oahspe* (*q.v.*) will be considered in a separate article. Like the work of Ballou, the activity of **Andrew Jackson Davis**, the 'Poughkeepsie Sage,' whose *Principles of Nature, Her Divine Revelation, and a Voice to Mankind*, published in 1845, marks the foundation of Spiritualism (*q.v.*) as a separate cult, must be considered as outside the realm of Christianity, though Jackson was not, like Ballou, directly hostile to it. He claimed to have received his inspiration, during a trance of sixteen hours, from inhabitants of the other world, and alleged communications from the departed spirits form a leading feature in all spiritualistic *séances*. Within the sphere of Christianity mention should first be made of **Mrs. Ellen G. White**, the wife of James White already mentioned. She was born in Portland, Maine, in 1827. Before her marriage, in 1846, she began to have 'visions,' at least some of the phenomena manifested by her clearly being attributable to hysteria. To her was due in great part the rise of the sect of Seventh-Day Adventists, who in the earlier days believed her to possess the gift of prophecy, and who have always maintained that she received 'messages of instruction for the Church from time to time by the direct inspiration of the Holy Spirit.' The extent to which this sect holds this belief is shown by the fact that in 1865 a sub-sect, the Church of God (Adventist), was formed on the single new tenet of rejection of acknowledgment of Mrs. White's alleged inspiration. A still more remarkable phenomenon is afforded by the creation of the Christian Catholic Church in Zion by **John Alexander Dowie** (1847–1907), a Scotsman by birth. He was for some years a Congregational minister in Australia; but at Melbourne, where he had established an 'independent' church, he became a believer in Divine healing through prayer. For several years he inculcated these tenets in the United States and Canada, and finally, in 1896, he organized his new sect, assuming the title of 'general overseer.' In the latter part of 1899 he claimed to be the 'Messenger of the Covenant,' in 1901 he was 'Elijah the Restorer,' and from 1904 until a revolt against him in 1906 he was 'First Apostle' of his sect.

To the number of American enthusiasts must be reckoned **Frank W. Sanford** (b. at Bowdoin, Maine, 1862), who was for several years a Free Baptist minister in New England. At a convention of his denomination in 1893 he announced that he had received Divine revelations commanding him to preach to the whole world before the 'coming of the end.' He accordingly founded at Shiloh, Maine, the Holy Ghost and Us Society, which holds most pronounced chiliastic views, while Sanford himself claims to be Elijah. After having conducted a disastrous voyage to Africa, during which a number of his followers died from insufficient food and care, Sanford was convicted, 9 Dec. 1911, of causing the death of six of these persons, and was confined in a Government prison. A single sentence from his statement before the court is of psychological interest in this connexion:

'I said: "Father, what next? What next, now that we have this company on board?" I received this answer—and I make this statement advisedly, knowing what I am doing—I received this answer: "Continue."'

In the latter part of 1896 yet another enthusiastic sect sprang into existence, the Church of God and Saints of Christ (popularly known as 'Black Jews'). The founder was **William S. Crowdy**, a negro who had been a railway cook until he received a revelation as 'a prophet of God sent to the whole world.' The new sect for a time made a profound impression on the negroes who attended its services, where even the local preachers were termed 'prophets.' The 'bishop,' or 'prophet' (at present Crowdy himself),

'is not elected, but holds his position by virtue of a Divine call. He is believed by his followers to be in direct communication with the Deity, to utter prophecies by the will of God, and to perform miracles. On his death the prophetic office lapses until a new vision appears' (Special Census Report [1906] on *Religious Bodies*, ii. 202, Washington, 1910).—LOUIS H. GRAY.]

14. All the Enthusiasts yet mentioned arose in a Christian atmosphere; it remains to glance at some in the near East. The Jews have been peculiarly liable to ebullitions of this kind, owing to their Messianic expectations; Bar Cochba and David Alroy have attracted some Christian attention, but the career of **Shabbethai Ṣebi** in the 17th cent. is the most recent. He was a Spanish Jew, born at Smyrna of a family in close commercial touch with England. Since Qabbalists had calculated A.D. 1648 as the year of salvation, he then privately announced himself as the Messiah, but met no local acceptance. At Gaza he was acknowledged by a famous rabbi, who took up the part of Elijah, herald of the Messiah; and for thirteen years he quietly strengthened his position at Jerusalem. A visit to Cairo brought him into contact with a rich young Jewess of good family, who expected to be the bride of the Messiah, and they married. Elijah now announced the speedy restoration of Israel after a bloodless victory, and the Messiahship was openly proclaimed. This necessitated his fleeing the land, and he returned to Smyrna. Here the English Fifth-Monarchy movement had induced the belief that A.D. 1666 was to usher in the Millennium. The whole Jewish world was disturbed, and embassies came from all quarters, hailing him as King of the Jews. Though miracles were reported on all hands, he remained entirely passive. The Sultan naturally desired to test his claims, and he preferred to become a Muslim, afterwards stating to his followers that thus Messiah 'was numbered among the transgressors'! His apostasy wrecked their faith in him, and a vigorous persecution by Shah Abbas in the same eventful year ended the movement in Persia, though for a century the European Jews remained on the alert for a national restoration to their Holy Land.

15. Far more important to the whole world has been the appearance of **Muhammad** as the Prophet of God. He began only as a teacher, but, when his authority was challenged, he was reassured by the angel Gabriel, who bade him 'recite in the name of the Lord who created.' From that time till his death he had frequent revelations, received usually in artificial darkness; these were generally written down by hearers. More than once these communications referred with respect to the Law and the Gospel, to Noah, Abraham, Moses, and Jesus as true prophets; but the implication was increasingly that former books were superseded. His revelations were put into an authorized edition within three years of his death, and a revised Qur'ān sixteen years later has proved final for the Sunnite sect, now the most influential. The transplantation of Islām to Persia, where high views of hereditary right were common, produced a schism soon after the Prophet's death, and the Shī'ites are legitimists not only in politics but in theology, holding that the hereditary successors of Muhammad are inspired. Three times this has had important results, with the Ṣūfīs, the Assassins, and the Bābīs (*qq.v.*).

LITERATURE.—Besides books mentioned in the text, see **E. C. Selwyn**, *The Christian Prophets and the Prophetic Apocalypse*, London, 1900; **G. N. Bonwetsch**, *Gesch. des Montanismus*, Erlangen, 1881; **H. Weinel**, *Die Wirkungen des Geistes und der Geister im nachapost. Zeitalter*, Freiburg, 1899; **J. F. K. Hecker**, *Epidemics of the Middle Ages*, tr. Babington, London, 1844; **C. A. Cornelius**, *Gesch. des münster. Aufruhrs*, Leipzig, 1855–60; **R. Heath**, *Anabaptism*, London, 1895; **R. Barclay**, *Inner Life of the Religious Societies of the Commonwealth*, London, 1877; **Rufus M. Jones**, *Studies in Mystical Religion*, London, 1909. Much additional material, including biographical, may be gleaned from the artt. in *PRE*[3] on 'Joachim von Flore' (by Deutsch, ix. 227–232), 'Geisselung, kirchliche, v.' (by Haupt, vi. 440 f.), 'Böhm, Hans' (by Haupt, iii. 271 f.), 'Alombrados' (by Zöckler, i. 388–390), 'Hut, Hans' (by Hegler, viii. 489–491), 'Hoffmann, Melchior' (by Hegler, viii. 222–227), 'Münster, Wiedertäufer' (by Köhler, xiii. 542 ff., on Rothmann), 'Familisten' (by Loofs, v. 750–755), 'Petersen, Johann Wilhelm' (by Bertheau, xv. 169–175), and also from the pertinent biographies in the *DNB* and the relative artt. in *Cath. Encyc.*; see also art. 'Verzückung' (by Thieme), in *PRE*[3] xx. 586–593, and cf. art. ANABAPTISM, above, vol. i. pp. 406–412. On Mrs. White, see *Life Sketches of Elder James White and his Wife, Mrs. Ellen G. White*, Battle Creek, Michigan, 1880; on Dowie, R. Harlan, *John Alexander Dowie and the Christian Catholic Apostolic Church in Zion*, Evansville, Wisconsin, 1906; and on Shabbethai Ṣebi, *JE* xi. 218–225 (by Malter).

W. T. WHITLEY.

ENVIRONMENT (Biological).[1]—For the biologist the problems raised by the term 'environment' are largely concerned with the part this factor or collection of factors may play in the process of evolutionary change. To what extent can the characters of living things be changed by changes in the conditions under which they live; and, if such changes occur, how far can they become permanent? That a definite change in the nature of the environment—temperature, moisture, food supply, or some other factor—will frequently bring about a change in the organism is beyond dispute. But whether the impress left on the organism can be transmitted to the next generation—whether so-called 'acquired' characters can be inherited—has been, and still is, a subject of keen controversy.

In his theory of evolution, put forward in 1809, Lamarck laid it down as one of his laws that the functional changes produced by a change in the environment during the life of the organisms are transmitted to the offspring; and during the next half century, in so far as the doctrine of evolution was accepted, it was accepted on this basis. By the publication of his *Origin of Species* in 1859, Darwin introduced another factor to account for evolutionary change, and the acceptance of 'natural selection' released the evolutionist from the burden of ascribing all specific difference to the direct action of the environment on the living thing. Darwin, however, remained to some extent a follower of Lamarck. Without variations upon which to work, natural selection cannot be effective in producing evolutionary change. As to the origin of such variations he did not venture upon any general statement, holding that in some cases they might be brought about by the direct action of a changed environment, while in others they must be attributed to some innate tendency on the part of the organism to vary, due to causes of which we are quite ignorant. Nevertheless, he did not hesitate in many instances to state his opinion, that a change in the conditions of life led to modification through the increased use or disuse of certain parts or organs, and that these modifications were accentuated and gradually rendered permanent through a continuous process of selection.

As an example may be taken the relatively smaller size of the wing structures, with their lessened powers of flight, in domesticated fowls, ducks, and pigeons—a peculiarity which Darwin considered to have been directly initiated through the effects of disuse consequent upon a change of environment, and ultimately exaggerated and fixed by long-continued selection.

As compared with Lamarck on the one hand, and most modern biologists on the other, Darwin may be said to have held an intermediate position. For Lamarck the increased use or disuse of organs consequent upon a changed environment was the only source of variation, and therefore the sole factor in the transformation of species. For Darwin there were two classes of heritable variation—variations arising through increased use or disuse, and variations arising spontaneously in the organism through causes not understood, though in either case the co-operation of natural selection was necessary to bring about a permanent change in form. Cf. art. EVOLUTION (Biological).

More recently the tendency among biologists has been to deny the transmissibility of modification acquired by the individual through a change of environment during its lifetime. This was largely brought about through the teaching of Weismann, who introduced a new conception of the relation of the reproductive tissues to the rest of the body. Hitherto this relation had been regarded as an alternating one. The germ-cells gave rise to the individual, and the individual in turn produced the germ-cells. Weismann introduced the idea of the continuity of the germ plasm through successive generations, and regarded the body, or *soma*, as an offshoot specialized for carrying and protecting the all-important germ plasm. By its formation the body is, as it were, sidetracked off the main course of evolution. Its chief function is that of a trustee for the germ plasm which it contains. Moreover, the germ plasm carried by a given body belongs to the same generation as the body itself, and is of equal age, both being the direct offspring of the germ plasms carried in the bodies of the common parents. It is obvious that this conception of the relation between an individual and its contained reproductive tissue renders it difficult to conceive how a modification brought about by an environmental change in the former can induce such a change in the latter that, when it comes to throw off a somatic offshoot, it will convey to it the impress of a modification just produced in a group of cells in which it lived but from which it was not derived. Weismann, therefore, challenged the evidence for the supposed transmission of 'acquired' characters, and showed that when critically examined it broke down. He also brought forward direct experimental evidence against the transmissibility of a definite group of acquired characters, and showed, from a long series of experiments on mice, that mutilations are not in the least degree inherited.

Nevertheless, heritable variations are continually arising in animals and plants, and it is in the seat of such variations that Weismann's views differed from those earlier current. For Weismann, the seat of heritable variation was in the germ plasm, and not in the *soma* by which the germ plasm was carried. Any new variation first arises through some abnormal occurrence in the germ plasm. Having once arisen, its tendency is to become permanent, and it is expressed in each of the sequence of somatic offshoots to which that germ plasm gives rise. Fresh variations can, on Weismann's view, be directly due to an environmental

[1] For the ethical aspects, see EDUCATION (Moral), p. 216, and ETHICS (Rudimentary), p. 426.

change, but they owe their origin to the effect of the changed conditions on the germ plasm and not on the body which carries the germ plasm (cf. art. HEREDITY). The action of a changed environment on a living thing may induce a change either in the *soma*, or in the germ plasm, or in both; but, even if both are affected, it does not necessarily follow that the changes are corresponding ones. The change in the germ plasm can, of course, be appreciated only on its forming a somatic offshoot, and this may present modifications differing from those shown by the antecedent *soma*, though the modifications in each case may have been brought about by the same environmental change. In the one case the change acts directly upon the somatoplasm, in the other it acts upon the germ plasm which transmits the effects of the stimulus to the *soma* that subsequently arises from it.

Discussions on the transmission of environmental changes frequently arise out of cases in which the developing young, as in mammals and plants, are parasitic for a time upon the maternal parent. Decreased vigour in the parent, resulting from unfavourable conditions of nutrition, often leads to an abnormal lack of vigour in the offspring, and this has sometimes been held to show that the direct effect of altered conditions on the parent is transmitted to the next generation. For example, two similar plants may be taken, of which one is grown under favourable, and the other under unfavourable, conditions. The seeds of both are collected and grown under similar conditions, and it is found that those derived from the latter plant give rise to less vigorous offspring than those derived from the former. In such cases it is apt to be overlooked that the relation of the parent to the offspring is twofold. Not only does the parent carry the germ plasm from which the offspring arise, but at the same time it acts as the environment of the developing young. It is in the latter capacity that a modification in the parent following upon changed conditions brings about a modification in the offspring. The question is not one of the transmissibility of increased or decreased vigour from parent to offspring; it is simply a question of the direct effect of altered environment on the developing young.

Weismann's views may be said to have met with general acceptance among biologists, though here and there were to be found a few supporters of a somewhat modified form of Lamarckianism. Little further advance was made until the 20th cent. brought with it a fresh stimulus to experimental work on living things, and within the last few years the question of the inheritance of 'acquired' characters has been re-opened, largely through the researches of Przibram, Kammerer, and others. The experiments of the last-named were for the most part made with amphibia and reptiles, and are concerned principally with colour modifications or with modifications of the normal instincts resulting from a changed environment. In several such cases it is claimed that the modifications produced re-appear in the offspring even when they are reared under normal conditions. The possibility is not precluded that the germ plasm was altered simultaneously with, but independently of, the somatoplasm in the individuals used for experiment; and the results cannot be regarded as conclusive evidence for the transmission of acquired characters, until it can be shown that they are reversible at will through the alteration of the environmental conditions. Though this has not yet been done, the experiments are full of suggestion, and there is reasonable hope that the work of the next decade will go far towards providing the answer to the old and much debated question of the inheritance of modification brought about by an alteration in the environment.

LITERATURE.—In addition to the writings of Lamarck and Charles Darwin, the following will be found of interest to English students: S. Butler, *Life and Habit*, London, 1877, also *Evolution, Old and New*, do. 1879; E. D. Cope, *The Primary Factors of Organic Evolution*, Chicago, 1896; T. H. Morgan, *Experimental Zoology*, London, 1907; A. Weismann, *The Germ Plasm* (Eng. tr., do. 1902), also *The Evolution Theory*, do. 1904. A succinct and illustrated account of the most recent experimental work is given in H. Przibram's *Experimental-Zoologie*, iii. 'Phylogenese,' Vienna, 1910. The most recent discussion from the Lamarckian standpoint will be found in R. Semon's *Die Mneme*, Leipzig, 1908, and in his art. in the *Fortschritte der naturwissenschaftl. Forschung*, vol. ii., Vienna, 1911.

R. C. PUNNETT.

ENVY AND EMULATION.—1. Envy.—Envy is an emotion that is essentially both selfish and malevolent. It is aimed at persons, and implies dislike of one who possesses what the envious man himself covets or desires, and a wish to harm him. Graspingness for self and ill-will lie at the basis of it. There is in it also a consciousness of inferiority to the person envied, and a chafing under this consciousness. He who has got what I envy is felt by me to have the advantage of me, and I resent it. Consequently, I rejoice if he finds that his envied possession does not give him entire satisfaction—much more, if it actually entails on him dissatisfaction and pain: that simply reduces his superiority in my eyes, and ministers to my feeling of self-importance. As signifying in the envious man a want that is ungratified, and as pointing to a sense of impotence inasmuch as he lacks the sense of power which possession of the desired object would give him, envy is in itself a painful emotion, although it is associated with pleasure when misfortune is seen to befall the object of it. As Dryden puts it,

> 'Envy, that does with misery reside,
> The joy and the revenge of ruin'd pride.'

It is obvious that envy and *jealousy* are closely allied. They have much in common, though they are perfectly distinct emotions. They are both selfish and malevolent, they are both concerned with persons, and both imply hatred of their object and a desire to harm him. But there is a deeper malevolence in jealousy than in envy, and the former is the stronger and more imperious passion. For this there are various reasons. In the first place, it is owing to the fact that jealousy is grounded on some estimate of what is due to self: it is not a mere consciousness of inferiority, as in envy. In the next place, there is a *twofold* source of irritation and displeasure to the jealous man, arising from the circumstance that *three* persons are involved in the situation, so that he is dealing, not with one rival, but with two (individuals or groups of individuals). When I am jealous of a person, it is because he has gained possession of the regard of another whose attachment I claim. This means that I hate the usurping person, but also that I am annoyed with the other who has allowed him thus to intrude. And so, also, when I say that I am jealous of a man's popularity with a party or a section of the community, my meaning is that I hate him for taking away a popularity that I myself claim or aspire to, and that I resent the pliability of the section or party who have allowed themselves to come under his influence.

It is characteristic of jealousy that it distorts the nature of him who harbours it, depriving him of the power to see things as they really are, rendering him unjust in his judgments and over-suspicious, leading him to catch at straws and make much of trifles, and driving him on to acts of cruelty.

> 'Jealousy is cruel as the grave:
> The flashes thereof are flashes of fire,
> A very flame of the Lord' (Ca 8[6]).

Great poets, like Shakespeare, know well how to represent this emotion in its nature, play, and offensiveness (see, *e.g.*, *Othello* and *Winter Night's Tale*), and they mark its outward expression also, and elucidate it by similes. Says Chaucer, in 'The Knight's Tale':

'Therewith the fyr of jealousie up-sterte
Withinne his brest, and hente him by the herte
So woodly, that he lyk was to biholde
The boxtree, or the asshen, dede and colde'
(lines 1299–1302 in vol. i. of A. W. Pollard's ed. of the *Canterbury Tales*).

Jealousy seems to be present to some degree in the lower animals, as well as in men.

'A favourite dog will be emotionally moved by the sight of his master fondling a kitten or another dog; he will sometimes slink away and hide himself and sulk, or he will keep pushing himself forward to be caressed, with sidelong glances at the kitten. Some very young children behave in a similar way, when their mother nurses another child. And in both cases the jealous creature is apt to exhibit anger towards the intruder' (W. McDougall, *Introd. to Social Psychology*, p. 138).

2. Emulation.—Very different from envy, though often taken as synonymous with it, is emulation. The latter is not, properly speaking, either selfish or malevolent, and it is not of the essence of it to be associated with hatred. It is characterized more by contrasts with envy than by similarities. It is an exhilarating emotion, drawing forth and strengthening our activity, and is the condition of progress and healthy development in the individual, as it is the result of aspiration or the pursuit of an ideal. It is a species of rivalry or competition, and, therefore, presupposes antagonists or opponents. But an opponent need not be viewed as an enemy to be hated: rather, he is our friend, if he braces our nerves and calls forth our energies and helps us to develop ourselves. Egoistic, indeed, emulation is, and has to be classed under the natural desire of superiority or power, but it is not selfish: it is compatible with generosity of character and good-will, which neither envy nor jealousy is. It stimulates us like play or the chase, and invigorates our nature; and, by the fact that there is in it an element of uncertainty (if not of hazard), it adds to the zest of life, as pursuit and enterprise in general do.

The emotion seems not to be confined to man, but is shared in by the lower animals, as we see in the competition in racing between horses and the like; and it is intense in children, entering into many of their games.

Emulation must not be confused with *ambition* (*q.v.*). Ambition, too, reposes on the love of power, and, when nobly directed, is a valuable and laudable impulse, achieving great things: it is simply an eager desire (with effort to actualize it) to rise in place or to increase in influence; and so far it is good. 'To take a Soldier without *Ambition*,' says Bacon, 'is to pull off his spurres' (*Essays*, 'Of Ambition'). But if, as Plato represents it in the *Republic*, it be the dominance of the will over the reason, then it is *inordinate* desire, and is ready to make a wrong use of rivals or those that stand in the way, ignoring the fact that every man is an end in himself, and must not be treated simply as a tool. The ambitious man, we often say, has no conscience: at any rate, his conscience is subservient to his own purposes, and not necessarily to rectitude. It is not well with us when our principle becomes, '*I* must rise, whoever falls, and whatever be the means.' The evil consequences of ambition on character have been the theme of preachers and poets alike all down the ages: 'by that sinne fell the Angels' (*King Henry VIII.*, III. ii. 440).

3. Emulation degenerating.—Distinct though emulation and envy are, the one may readily lapse into the other. It is manly and proper to wish to excel in a race, and to strain every nerve to accomplish that end; but, when the runner, finding himself likely to be outstripped by his opponent, tries to jostle him or to trip him up, that is emulation degraded to envy: honourable rivalry has been replaced by conduct that is dishonourable and mean.

'Emulation,' says Butler (Serm. i. note 20), 'is merely the desire and hope of equality with, or superiority over others, with whom we compare ourselves. . . . To desire the attainment of this equality or superiority by the particular means of others being brought down to our own level, or below it, is, I think, the distinct notion of envy. From whence it is easy to see, that the real end, which the natural passion emulation, and which the unlawful one envy, aim at is exactly the same; namely, that equality or superiority: and consequently, that to do mischief is not the end of envy, but merely the means it makes use of to attain its end.'

The lapse into envy brings its own nemesis. The envy of the envious man reacts upon himself: it is apt to bring him more pain than pleasure—as the common phrase has it, it 'gnaws' his soul.

4. Implication of society.—It only remains to add that the emotions here considered—envy and jealousy, emulation and ambition—presuppose society; *i.e.* they could not exist except in a social environment or setting. They are essentially egoistic, inasmuch as they centre in the self or Ego, being concerned primarily with the individual's interest; but they are conditioned for their existence by the fact that there is an 'other' over against the individual, competing with him and possessing different and, it may be, antagonistic interests. They all imply relations to other human beings, and the conception of a pure 'individual'—of an isolated conscious unit, absolutely divorced from every other conscious unit—is an absurdity: egoism (*q.v.*), in that sense, there can be none.

LITERATURE.—Aristotle, *Rhetoric*, II. x. and xi. (tr. Jebb, Cambridge, 1909); Francis Bacon, *Essays*, IX., XXXVI.; Descartes, *The Passions of the Soul* (tr. E. S. Haldane and G. R. T. Ross, in *The Philosophical Works of Descartes*, vol. i., Cambridge, 1911); Spinoza, *Ethica*, pars iii. (tr. W. H. White and Amelia Hutchison Stirling, 3rd ed., London, 1899); Leibniz, *New Essays concerning Human Understanding*, bk. ii. ch. 20 (Eng. tr. by Alfred G. Langley, New York and London, 1896); Joseph Butler, *Sermons*, ed. J. H. Bernard, London, 1900, i.; David Hume, *A Treatise of Human Nature*, bk. ii. pt. ii. sec. viii.; Thomas Reid, *Works*, ed. Hamilton, Edinburgh, 1854, p. 566 ff.; James Beattie, *Elements of Moral Science*, Edinburgh, 1817, i. 215–218; Dugald Stewart, *The Philosophy of the Active and Moral Powers of Man*, Edinburgh, 1828, i. 66–72; Thomas Brown, *Lectures on the Philosophy of the Human Mind*, Edinburgh, 1820, Lect. lxxii.; A. Bain, *The Emotions and the Will*[3], London, 1875; Th. Ribot, *The Psychology of the Emotions*, London, 1897, p. 268; James Martineau, *Types of Ethical Theory*, Oxford, 1885, ii. 170; W. James, *The Principles of Psychology*, London, 1891, ii. 409; David Irons, *A Study in the Psychology of Ethics*, Edin. and London, 1903, p. 90; G. F. Stout, *The Groundwork of Psychology*[2], Cambridge, 1903, p. 189; W. McDougall, *Introd. to Social Psychology*, London, 1908, pp. 136, 138.

WILLIAM L. DAVIDSON.

EPICTETUS.—Epictetus of Hierapolis (*c.* A.D. 50–130) was a distinguished pupil of the Roman philosopher Musonius. Though not possessed of the originality or daring of his teacher, he has attained much greater fame through the fact that the substance of a great number of his discourses was preserved and published by his pupil Arrian. From the date of their first publication down to the present day these 'discourses of Epictetus' have enjoyed an extraordinary popularity; they have been many times translated into various European languages; and they constitute an authority of the first importance, both as to the teaching of the Stoic philosophy which Epictetus professed, and as to the social atmosphere of Rome in the 1st cent. A.D.

Epictetus was brought up as a slave in the house of Epaphroditus, a freedman of Nero, and presumably the same who became his secretary, remained faithful to him upon his fall, assisted him in his last hours, and was afterwards put to death by Domitian. Epaphroditus recognized the talent of the young slave, gave him the liberal education which was at that time the privilege of the humblest members of the great Roman households, and sent him as a young man to study under Musonius. He then gave him his freedom, and Epictetus took up with success the profession of popular philosopher. Young men from all parts of the Empire listened to his teaching, and men of rank and position sought his advice. In the year A.D. 89 he fell a victim to the edict of Domitian against the philosophers, and was exiled from Rome and Italy; he withdrew to Nicopolis, and lectured there till his death in a ripe old age. The Emperor Trajan held him in special honour, and the records of his teaching exercised a great influence on the youth of Marcus Aurelius.

Epictetus was well schooled in the orthodox teaching of the Stoic philosophy, and it has been shown that both in his principles and in his use of technical language he is loyal to it. It is, however, only with difficulty and by a careful rearrangement of the material that a philosophical system can be deduced from his recorded utterances. Each of these is complete in itself, and has as its direct aim the enforcement of some moral principle by an appeal to the conscience of his hearers. Thus the practical application of ethics outweighs all other parts of the philosophy; and, whilst there is constant repetition within this field, the rest of the system is only hinted at by casual allusions. The ethical principles of Epictetus are strongly coloured by the circumstances of the time. He urges that, although political and personal freedom may be wanting, no man can be deprived of true freedom, which consists in pursuing virtue, the only good. Fortune has no power over the philosopher, because the things that she can give and take away are indifferent. The exercise of virtue consists in attention to the homely duties which result from human relationships, such as those of master and slave, parent and child, magistrate and citizen. In all his troubles the good man is comforted by the nearness of God, whose will he gladly obeys, and to whose decrees he is resigned. Epictetus holds up to our admiration the picture of the ideal Cynic, who, disdaining home or comfort for himself, becomes the servant of all, and enters every family to reconcile or to console; but he avoids the paradoxes in which the early Stoics and Cynics alike delighted, is gentle and reasonable in his teaching, and seldom engages in sharp controversy. He asserts his personal convictions most definitely in an uncompromising denial of the doctrine (towards which his hearers were strongly inclined) of the continuance of personality after death.

The discourses of Epictetus are so often considered typical of Stoicism that it is necessary to observe that he was Stoic with a difference. In temperament he had little in common with Zeno and Cleanthes, who were enthusiasts and revolutionaries; and hardly more with Panætius and the 'middle Stoics,' who were gentlemen and statesmen. Epictetus, even when his position was highest, was at heart a slave; his talents lay at the disposition of others. He accepted Stoicism at command; and in the same spirit he accepted the religion, the politics, and the social circumstances of his time. No man could be more precise in insisting upon the regular and contented performance of all actions approved by the general opinion; around these he threw the glow of a religious submissiveness which certainly forbade him to do wrong at the bidding of any earthly master, but at the same time predisposed him to consider as right any burden that others might lay upon him. Domitian was unduly anxious if ever he imagined that political danger could arise from such a philosopher.

The study of the discourses of Epictetus is an indispensable starting-point for a true understanding of the teaching of St. Paul. Better than any work of antiquity they reveal to us the inner thoughts of the social circles to which the Apostle chiefly addressed himself. See, further, art. STOICISM.

LITERATURE.—*Epict. dissertationes*, ed. H. Schenkl, Leipzig, 1898 (here the ancient references to the life of Epictetus are also collected); tr. of the *Dissertationes*, with notes, a Life of Epictetus, and a view of his philosophy, by G. Long, London, 1848; H. von Arnim, art. in Pauly-Wissowa, 11th half-volume, 1907; R. Asmus, *Quæstiones Epicteteæ*, Freiburg, 1888; A. Bonhöffer, *Epictet und die Stoa*, Stuttgart, 1890, also *Die Ethik des Stoikers Epictet*, do. 1894; Ivo Bruns, *de Schola Epicteti*, Kiel, 1897; H. Schenkl, *Die epiktet. Fragmente*, Vienna, 1888; J. Stuhrmann, *de vocabulis notionum philosophicarum ab Epicteto adhibitis*, Jena, 1885: T. Zahn, *Der Stoiker Epiktet und sein Verhältnis zum Christentum*², Leipzig, 1895; W. L. Davidson, *The Stoic Creed*, Edinburgh, 1907, *passim*.

E. V. ARNOLD.

EPICUREANS.—The Epicureans are properly the adherents of the Greek philosopher Epicurus. But the term is popularly and less correctly used with reference to thinkers of later times who did not belong to his school, and were not directly influenced by his teaching.[1] Thus hedonistic ethics, the rejection of purpose in Nature, and the denial of a moral government of the world, were vaguely called 'Epicurean,' from whatever quarter such views were put forward. The school is interesting as the heir to the doctrines of the Ionian philosophers, and as the exponent of ancient materialism in its final form.

1. Life and writings of Epicurus.—Epicurus (341–270 B.C.) belongs to an age when the first speculative impulse of the Greek intellect had already subsided. The chief facts of his life are collected by Diog. Laert. (x. 1–28).

He was born at Samos (where his father Neocles had received a grant of land when the Athenians occupied the island) on the 7th day of Gamelion, 341. Though he traced his descent to the famous clan of the Philaidæ, his family was poor, and he is said to have assisted his father, who was a schoolmaster as well as a farmer, and his mother, who performed certain religious rites of purification. When he was twelve years old he began to study philosophy, probably at Teos, under Nausiphanes, a Democritean. He also heard Pamphilus, a Platonist, at Samos. After the death of Alexander the Great, at the time when Epicurus was completing the military service required of every Athenian citizen as an ἔφηβος in Attica, his father, with the other Athenian settlers, was expelled from Samos by Perdiccas, and went to Colophon. The following years seem to have been spent in private study, until, at the age of 32, he began to teach, first at Mytilene, then at Lampsacus; next, from 306 onwards, at Athens. From Mytilene he drew Hermarchus, afterwards his successor. The adherents won at Lampsacus formed the kernel of his school. Such were Idomeneus, and Leonteus with his wife Themista, among the richest and most influential of the citizens; such, too, were Metrodorus, Polyænus, and Colotes, who became his ablest pupils. At Athens he gathered a community about him in the famous garden, where the members met as friends and pupils of a common master. Shut off from the world around, and closely united to each other by their fervent belief in his teaching, they resembled a religious sect rather than a philosophic school; and their affection for Epicurus bordered on adoration. He accepted such respect and veneration as a matter of course, assumed the responsibility of a spiritual director, and by his whole behaviour consciously imposed on them an absolute devotion to his person. He drew up for them catechisms of his doctrines, which they were bidden to learn by heart. By example and precept he condemned excess and recommended a simple mode of life, discouraged ambition, and counselled retirement from the world. His whole day was taken up with study, authorship, and correspondence. His health had always been delicate; only an invalid racked with pain could have rated painlessness so high. Having outlived Metrodorus and Polyænus, his favourite disciples, he succumbed to a painful malady in his 72nd year (270 B.C.). A scrap of his letters shows that he bore the agony of the last fortnight with cheerful confidence.

Of the 300 rolls which this industrious recluse lived to complete, no fewer than 37 belonged to his *magnum opus*, περὶ φύσεως, of which fragments of books ii., xi., xiv., xv., and xxviii. have been recovered, though in a very imperfect state, from Herculaneum. The work proceeded slowly; in 300–299 it had reached book xv., and, four years later, book xxviii. Of his other works only scanty fragments are preserved, sufficient, however, to

[1] It is interesting to note that, in Rabbinical Judaism, 'Epicurean' (אפיקורוס) is a stock synonym for 'infidel,' 'materialist' (Deutsch, in *JE* i. 665 f.).

show their great variety. Many were scientific treatises, some physical (περὶ ἀτόμων καὶ κενοῦ, περὶ τῆς ἐν τῇ ἀτόμῳ γωνίας, περὶ ἁφῆς, περὶ τοῦ ὁρᾶν), others ethical (περὶ αἱρέσεων καὶ φυγῶν, περὶ βίων, περὶ δικαιοσύνης καὶ τῶν ἄλλων ἀρετῶν, περὶ ἡδονῆς, περὶ ὁσιότητος, περὶ τέλους), and one, the famous Κανών, dealt with the standards of truth in scientific inquiry. Others treated of lighter topics, *e.g.* the dialogue Συμπόσιον, in which both Epicurus and Metrodorus were interlocutors. Of those which took their titles from the names of men and women, some were most likely eulogies of friends or, it may be, tributes to their memory, *e.g.* Ἀριστόβουλος, Νεοκλῆς, Χαιρέδημος (named after the three brothers of Epicurus), Εὐρύλοχος, Ἡγησιάναξ, Θεμίστα, Μητρόδωρος. Others were certainly controversial: Ἀντίδωρος, Τιμοκράτης, Ἐπιτομὴ τῶν πρὸς τοὺς φυσικούς, περὶ παθῶν δόξαι, πρὸς Τιμοκράτην, πρὸς Δημόκριτον, πρὸς Θεόφραστον, πρὸς τοὺς Μεγαρικούς. His correspondence was from an early time passed round from hand to hand, and highly valued for its didactic tone; but there are personal traits in the letter to his mother discovered at Œnoanda, and in another to a little girl, possibly the daughter of Metrodorus. This mass of writing is represented now by the three epistles: (i.) to Herodotus, an epitome of physics (Diog. Laert. x. 35–83); (ii.) to Pythocles, περὶ μετεώρων, a similar epitome treating of atmospheric and celestial occurrences, including earthquakes (*ib.* 84–121); (iii.) to Menœceus, on religion and ethics (*ib.* 122–135); to which may be added (iv.) Κύριαι δόξαι, an arbitrary selection or anthology of striking sentences from the larger works, put together on no obvious principle, and as remarkable for repetitions as for omissions (*ib.* 139–154). This, though the most famous, was not the only anthology of the kind: another, Γνωμολόγειον, containing eighty-one sentences or maxims by Epicurus, many of them new, was recently found, and published by C. Wotke in *Wiener Studien*, x. 175 ff.

The epistles to Herodotus and Menœceus are unquestionably genuine. Usener doubted whether Epicurus himself compiled the epistle to Pythocles, though he admitted that it was drawn from his works, citing in support of his contention Philodemus in *Voll. Herc. coll. alt.* i. 152. H. von Arnim (Pauly-Wissowa, vi. 137 ff.) defends the authenticity of this compendium also.

Modern readers find the style of Epicurus difficult; but this was not the judgment of antiquity. He was so lucid a writer, says Diogenes Laertius, that in his work on Rhetoric he makes clearness the sole requisite. This one merit is granted him by Cicero, who criticizes severely his neglect of those graces of style which give to the works of Plato, Aristotle, and Theophrastus a perennial charm. But the truth is that, like other philosophers, notably Aristotle, Epicurus had two styles. So voluminous an author was almost bound to vary his mode of expression, according as he addressed an esoteric circle of disciples or a wider public. For the former, clearness and precision sufficed; but the epistle to Menœceus, in its avoidance of hiatus and its fervid, if restrained, eloquence, remains to show that upon occasion Epicurus could write for effect.

2. The School.—Our authorities are unanimous that there never was a more united school. The doctrine of the founder was passed on unaltered, and it is difficult to detect any material divergence from orthodoxy in the expositions of succeeding ages. Of the immediate disciples, three, Metrodorus (330–277 B.C.), Polyænus, and Hermarchus, were in later times joined with the master as the four pillars or standards of orthodoxy.

Polyænus had been an eminent mathematician; and Metrodorus, who after his first introduction never left Epicurus except once to spend six months at his old home, was the favourite and the most gifted. We have a list of fourteen works by him, and they were cited in later times as of all but equal authority with the master's own. Several of them appear from the titles to have been controversial works; for even Metrodorus found his scientific activity limited by the very completeness and finality of the system which he embraced. Loyalty to the master was incompatible with free inquiry, and in all succeeding generations Epicureans who wrote on philosophy at all were bound either to expound and expand his original statements, or to expose and refute those who did not accept them. Metrodorus had a brother Timocrates, who first embraced and then abandoned the faith—almost the only instance of a renegade in the annals of the school. It was in a polemic against this heretic that he somewhat coarsely avowed that a sound digestion is the standard of all that pertains to man's wellbeing—an avowal of which the enemies of the school were not slow to take advantage.

From Hermarchus, who succeeded Epicurus, the headship of the school passed to Polystratus, of whose work περὶ ἀλόγου καταφρονήσεως we have fragments, deciphered by Gomperz (*Herm.* ii. 398 f.); from him it passed to Dionysius (200 B.C.), and next to Basilides; and then in unbroken succession for several centuries, though our information is so scanty that many of the scholarchs are not known to us even by name. About 100 B.C. Zeno of Sidon, who is mentioned by Cicero, succeeded Apollodorus (ὁ κηποτύραννος), who was the author of some 400 treatises. Zeno was followed by Phædrus, whose successor, Patron, was head from 78 until after 51 B.C. But the most conspicuous Epicurean in the Roman society of that day was Philodemus of Gadara, tutor and guest of Piso, the consul of 57 B.C. His poetical skill is admitted by Cicero (*in Pis.* 28 f.), and over thirty of his epigrams are included in the *Anthologia Palatina*. He was also a prolific prose writer; the library of an Epicurean at Herculaneum contained works by him—περὶ εὐσεβείας, περὶ μουσικῆς, περὶ ῥητορικῆς, περὶ ποιημάτων, περὶ σημείων καὶ σημειώσεων, περὶ κακιῶν, περὶ ὀργῆς, περὶ θανάτου—fragments of which have been in part, but very imperfectly, deciphered. He also wrote on the Philosophic Schools, in at least ten books (Diog. Laert. x. 3). In the 1st cent. B.C. also lived at Rome Asclepiades of Bithynia, a celebrated medical practitioner, who put forward a new theory of the origin and classification of diseases, which he based upon an adaptation of the Epicurean doctrine of atoms and void. The Roman poet Lucretius (*q.v.*) hailed Epicurus as the deliverer of mankind from superstition and the fear of death. The same passionate enthusiasm marks the outpourings of a certain Diogenes, who had spent his life in propagating Epicurean doctrine in Œnoanda, an obscure Pisidian town, where, in 1884, two French scholars, Holleaux and Paris, discovered inscriptions on the walls of the market-place. From them we learn that the aged teacher, knowing his end to be near, left a sermon in stone where it was bound to catch the eye of every resident and every casual visitor. The inscription includes tracts by Diogenes himself (i.) *On the Nature of Things* (34 columns); (ii.) *On the Infinity of Worlds*, addressed to Antipater (12 columns); (iii.) an ethical discourse (36 columns); and (iv.) a fragment *On Old Age*, addressed to the young. To these are appended maxims of Epicurus, and what is apparently a citation from a letter to his mother.

3. Philosophy and its divisions.—As a child of his age, Epicurus emphasized the importance of conduct, defining philosophy as 'a daily business of speech and thought to ensure a happy life.' The loss of national independence and the decay of civic life are often alleged as causes why the later Greek philosophy became more and more practical, and the needs of the individual its chief preoccupation; but this change of direction had set in long before, with the Sophists and the Socratics. The older physicists sought knowledge for its own sake; Epicurus and his school sought it as a means to happiness.

'If we had never been molested by alarms at celestial and atmospheric phenomena,' he says, 'or by the misgiving that death somehow affects us, or by neglect of the proper limits of pains and desires, we should have had no need to study natural science' (Diog. Laert. x. 142). And again, 'Vain is the discourse of that philosopher by whom no human suffering is healed' (Porphyrius, *ad Marcellam*, xxxi. p. 209, 23 [Nauck], fr. 221 [Usener]).

By these and similar utterances he attests the predominance of the practical aim, and by implication prescribes limitations to the necessary task of physical inquiry. We must study Nature because we ourselves are part of it, and, until we have gained some acquaintance with the whole, we shall not understand our relations to it, or learn on what conditions our happiness depends. So far from encouraging the extension of research, Epicurus was impatient of such studies as poetry, rhetoric, and mathematics, which had their place in the ordinary education of the day, because they did not contribute to happiness. 'Hoist all sail,' he writes to a young friend, 'and give a wide berth to culture (παιδεία).' In his system there is no great originality; he borrowed his physics from

Democritus (*q.v.*), to whom he stands in much the same relation as do the Stoics to Heraclitus. To him the value of the discoveries of the Atomists lies in their utility; they free us from the errors of popular belief and false philosophy. Thus they are directly subservient to a happy life. Philosophy had been divided into Logic, Physics, and Ethics; but the great mass of logical doctrine was rejected by Epicurus as superfluous. Like men of science in more recent times, he wished to concern himself not with words but with things. However, besides Physics and Ethics, he recognized what he called Canonic, a study of the standard, or canon, of truth. The aim of this study was to convince us that our knowledge of Nature is trustworthy. It was not so much an independent division of the system as—what it is sometimes called—an appendix or special part of Physics (*accessio naturalis partis* [Sen. *Ep.* 89. 11]).

4. Physics.—(*a*) *General principles.*—The two epitomes mentioned above, the epistle to Herodotus and that to Pythocles, are the most trustworthy sources for Epicurean physics. Like all his Ionian predecessors, Epicurus starts with the axiom that matter is indestructible. Nothing can arise out of that which is not; nothing which actually exists can be altogether annihilated. Moreover, the sum-total of things was always such as it is now, and such it will ever remain. For there is nothing into which it can change, since outside the sum of things there is nothing that could enter into it and bring about the change. The whole of being, then, consists of bodies and space. Experience through sense attests the existence of bodies, and without space (τόπος)—which we also call an intangible existence (ἀναφὴς φύσις), vacuum (κενόν), or room (χώρα)—the motion of bodies, which is also a datum of experience, is inconceivable. Beyond bodies and space there is nothing—no *tertium quid*—which can be conceived to exist, so long, that is, as we fix our attention upon wholes or separate things, in contradistinction to the qualities, whether essential or accidental, which belong to things. But a distinction must be drawn between those bodies which are composite and those which are simple. The former are unions of particles—unions which can be again dissolved; the latter, the particles of matter themselves, must be unchangeable and indivisible (hence their name, ἄτομοι, ἄτομα). All apparent becoming and perishing of things depends upon the alternate uniting and separating of such ultimate indestructible particles. The All, or sum of things, is by its very notion infinite. For, if finite, it must be bounded by a something outside it, which is inconsistent with the notion of the All. It is infinite, not only spatially, but in respect of the number of indivisible particles or atoms contained in it; for, if space were infinite and bodies finite, they would not have stayed anywhere, but have been dispersed and lost in the void; whereas, if space were finite, it could not find room for infinite matter. The atoms resist disintegration because they are all matter; they contain no void within them. In Lucretian language, they are strong in solid singleness. They vary in shape; the atoms of each shape are absolutely infinite, but the variety of shapes, though indefinitely great, is not absolutely infinite. The atoms are eternally in motion, rebounding after collision, or again oscillating when imprisoned in a mass with other atoms which temporarily form a composite thing. This is because every atom is in void space, which offers no resistance; and there was no beginning to all these motions, because both matter and space are infinite. Hence, too, there must be an infinity of worlds—some like this of ours, others unlike it. A world is defined (§ 88), after Leucippus, as a sort of envelope of sky enclosing an earth and stars and all visible things, which is cut off from the infinite, and terminates in a boundary which may revolve or be at rest, which may be round or triangular, or of any shape whatsoever.

After thus laying down the principles of matter and motion, Epicurus proceeds to deal with the films (εἴδωλα) which emanate from bodies, by which he, like Democritus, explained perceptions of external objects, and mental activity in general. Such husks of films are incessantly streaming from the surface of all perceptible bodies, the waste being as constantly repaired by the accession of fresh atoms from the infinite store of matter. Their velocity through space is enormous, if they encounter no resistance; and, so long as this is the case, they preserve the relative shape, with projections and depressions, of that object from which they were parted. This degree of resemblance entitles them to be called images, in spite of their lack of depth. Our sensations of seeing, hearing, and smelling depend upon the entrance of these films into the appropriate organs of sense. Our belief in the permanence of visible external objects is due to the constant succession of images of the same shape and colour which reach us from them. And, as with the eyes, so with the mind. The mental perception of shape, whether in dreams or in intuitive thought, is due to the impact of the εἴδωλα upon the finer substance of the mind. But not all the films which strike upon the senses or the mind reach us unimpaired. In the course of their passage the outlines may have been blurred, distorted, or mutilated. Further, in the air atomic structures may arise which never formed the superficial layer of any actual body, *e.g.* a Centaur, and these, coming in contact with the senses or the mind, give rise to erroneous judgments.

(*b*) *Canonic.*—At this point the purely physical exposition naturally passes over into Canonic. In his treatment of the problem of truth and error, Epicurus inflexibly adheres to one main position: that perceptions of sense and mental intuitions are always true, and that error creeps in with judgment or opinion (δόξα). Judgment undertakes to interpret sensation. If we want to test the truth of a judgment about an external object, we compare the sensations which we receive in succession from it. If, then, the earlier interpretation is confirmed (ἐὰν ἐπιμαρτυρηθῇ) by a subsequent observation, the judgment was true; if, however, it be not so confirmed (ἐὰν μὴ ἐπιμαρτυρηθῇ), the judgment was false, as when the tower which seemed round at a distance is discovered on a nearer approach to be square. This is a case where subsequent examination is possible (τὸ προσμένον); but many judgments deal with the unknown (ἄδηλον), about which we draw inferences from the known. Here the ἄδηλον, which cannot be directly perceived, must be made the subject of an inference by connecting it with another object which can be perceived. There are also cases, within the region of known and knowable fact, where, owing to circumstances, the test of sensation cannot be directly applied a second time. Where for any of these reasons further confirmation (ἐπιμαρτύρησις) is inapplicable, Epicurus falls back upon a feebler test—the absence of contradictory experience: cf. οὐκ ἀντιμαρτύρησις δέ ἐστιν ἀκολουθία τοῦ ὑποσταθέντος καὶ δοξασθέντος ἀδήλου τῷ φαινομένῳ (Sext. *adv. Math.* vii. 213, fr. 247 [Usener]). The judgment upon its trial is acquitted of error because no fact (ἐναργές) can be adduced to witness against it. Thus applied, the Canon allows the strangest hypotheses concerning atoms, images (εἴδωλα), and gods to pass unchallenged. It should be noted also that the procedure by way of induction and analogy presupposes something answering to a law of uniformity—'as are the instances under our observation, so too are the instances inaccessible to observation.' Sometimes, it is true, Epicurus does reason in this way: the imperceptible atoms and their movements are construed as if, under the microscope or some more potent aid, they could be directly observed. At other times the Canon is differently applied. Somewhere in infinity all possibilities are realized, for nothing in our experience contradicts either this general proposition, or particular cases affected, such as the shapes of the worlds, or the alternative explanations of celestial phenomena. A mutilated tract by Philodemus of Gadara on signs and inferences (περὶ σημείων καὶ σημειώσεων) is a proof that, two centuries after the death of its founder, the school was still interested in analogical and inductive reasoning. Again, Epicurus laid down a criterion for the practical as well as for the theoretical sphere. This consisted in the peculiar sensations of pleasure and pain, in which he recognized the same clear evidence (ἐνάργεια) which belongs to perceptions of external objects (Diog. Laert. x. 34; Aristocles *ap.* Euseb. *Præp. evang.* xiv. 21, p. 768*d* ff.; Cic. *de Fin.* i. 23, fr. 243 [Usener]). This is of the highest importance when he comes to Ethics.

Besides immediate perception, and the feelings of pleasure and pain, a further standard of true judgments is to be found in preconception (πρόληψις). This term denotes primarily a notion based upon and derived from perception, and therefore, like it, valid, which has found expression in some common term in daily use (*e.g.* 'man'). The utterance of the term calls up in those who understand the language a clear and distinct mental image (πρόληψις) already formed from previous clear and distinct perceptions. Sometimes, however, true judgments so universally recognized as not to require further testing by experience are also called preconceptions (προλήψεις). In any case, both their validity as tests of truth, and the mark of clearness and distinctness which they present, must be of a secondary and derivative kind, as compared with sensation.

(*c*) *The atoms.*—Returning now (§ 54) to the unchangeableness of the atoms, Epicurus thence deduces the distinction between primary and secondary qualities long before announced by Democritus (*q.v.*). All qualities (ποιότητες) are changeable; but the atoms must be thought of as unchangeable, for all changes must have something permanent underlying them. Hence the atoms possess only weight, shape, and magnitude, to which may be added impenetrability (ἀντιτυπία: Sext. *adv. Math.* x. 240, fr. 275 [Usener]). They have not colour, smell, taste, heat, cold, dampness, or dryness. These changeable qualities arise, not in the atoms but in the composite wholes (συγκρίσεις), through the varying union and arrangement of atoms (ἐν τῇ ποιᾷ συνθέσει τῶν ἀτόμων ταῦτα: Simp. *Categ.* 14, fr. 288 [Usener]). But, while Democritus made the secondary qualities relative (νόμῳ χροιή, νόμῳ γλυκύ), Epicurus by his unshakable belief in the reality of present sensation is bound to attribute them to the composite objects or perceptible things. The leaf is yellow, though its atoms have no colour, for my sensation of yellowness upon seeing it is real and objective, due to an image, of the same colour as the leaf (ὁμοχρόων: Diog. Laert. x. 49, p. 11 [Usener]), which enters my eye. The whole variety of changing qualities present in experience can, Epicurus maintains, be derived from shape and magnitude, the qualities which are left to the atoms, if due account be taken of variety in atomic arrangement and motion. Another point of difference from Democritus is that, whereas he made his atoms of all sizes, Epicurus objects to the assumption as unnecessary for the explanation of differences of quality, and as involving the absurdity of visible atoms. Nor, again, can any atom be infinitely small, for no body of finite size can contain an infinity of constituents, nor can subdivision go on indefinitely, for then some part of matter would be annihilated. Though the atom is the least body separately existing, it has itself minimal parts, which must be conceived on the analogy of the corresponding minimal parts of bodies of finite size. Space and time, as well as matter, are conceived as made up of minimal parts not further subdivisible. In infinite space all bodies move with uniform velocity (ἰσοταχεῖς [Diog. Laert. x. 61]), so long as they encounter no resistance, which is made to account for all variation in velocity (βράδους γὰρ καὶ τάχους ἀντικοπὴ καὶ οὐκ ἀντικοπὴ ὁμοίωμα λαμβάνει: *ib.* x. 46, p. 10 [Usener]). The free atoms move with the swiftness of thought over the very greatest distances, and this uniform velocity is maintained, whether the atom falls from above downwards under the influence of weight, or recoils from collision with another atom, or oscillates in the entangled mass of atoms which make up a sensible thing. The downward motion due to weight presumes that up and down are somehow empirically determined. Now, in infinite space there can be no up or down in the sense of a highest or lowest point or surface beyond which a body cannot move. At the same time, the opposite directions up and down, which we distinguish in any line of finite length, remain equally opposed when the line is prolonged to infinity.

5. The soul.—The materialism of Epicurus is prominent in his treatment of the soul. It is a corporeal substance, a compound of atoms of four different species, distributed throughout the frame, but more densely massed in the breast. It most resembles warm breath, *i.e.* wind mixed with heat. Elsewhere it is said to contain air as distinct from wind, and a fourth nameless substance which is the seat of sensation, memory, love, hate, and intellect in general (τὸ γὰρ ᾧ κρίνει καὶ μνημονεύει, καὶ φιλεῖ καὶ μισεῖ, καὶ ὅλως τὸ φρόνιμον καὶ λογιστικὸν ἔκ τινός φησιν ἀκατονομάστου ποιότητος ἐπιγίνεσθαι: Plut. *adv. Col.* 20, p. 1118*d*, fr. 314 [Usener]). Portions of this subtle substance may leave the body, as in sleep, or through the effect of a deadly blow, and yet the patient may recover, and receive new accessions of soul-substance from outside. Its mobility is shown in thought, feeling, and the bodily motions which it originates. The connexion and mutual dependence of the two corporeal substances, soul and body, are conceived as follows. We derive sensation, sentience, feeling, mainly from soul, partly from body; for our soul would not be sentient unless it were confined in our body. Being so confined, it confers this quality on the body, which it renders sentient; but the body does not share in the other functions of the soul, such as memory and thought. The peculiar motions of the soul's substance, on which these higher functions depend, are also conditioned by the body which encloses and holds it together. At death the lifeless corpse ceases to feel; but the soul, too, can no longer retain sensation when separate from the body, but is dispersed in air.

Essential attributes and accidents.—That the soul is not an incorporeal substance is proved by the fact that it acts and is acted upon. There is nothing incorporeal to Epicurus except empty space. Whatever else we call incorporeal is found, upon examination, to be, not an independent thing, but an attribute or quality. And here a distinction must be drawn between essential attributes (συμβεβηκότα), which are inseparable from (ἀεὶ παρακολουθοῦντα) the conception either of a body in general or of a visible body, and the fortuitous transitory states, or accidents (συμπτώματα), with which this is not the case. The former, Epicurus holds, are not independent substances, or incorporeal entities, or simply non-existent; in their entirety they constitute the permanent nature of the whole body, though not in the sense that they are parts of it spatially divisible (ὡς τὸ ὅλον σῶμα—ἐκ τούτων ἁπάντων τὴν ἑαυτοῦ φύσιν ἔχον ἀΐδιον: Diog. Laert. x. 69, p. 23 [Usener]), and are never perceived apart from it. As shape and size are qualities of body as such, which we cannot think away, so it is with single bodies: each has its inseparable essential attributes, which we cannot think away from it without annihilating its nature. Of accidents (συμπτώματα) the most important are motion and rest; and, as motion and rest are related to corporeal things, so time in its turn is related to them. Hence time is properly defined as an accident of accidents (σύμπτωμα συμπτωμάτων).

6. Human progress.—The infinity of worlds already mentioned implies that incessantly some come into being, and others perish. The Epicurean cosmogony, which in the main follows the lines laid down by Democritus, is most exactly given by Lucretius (*q.v.*). Neither the creation nor the destruction of worlds is the work of Divine agency, but both are merely a product of the eternal motion of atoms, of natural laws working independently of any plan or purpose. As with our world at large, so with human civilization. That, too, is a product of undesigned natural development. Activities originally exercised instinctively came, in course of time, to be matured and perfected by intellect, and thus all the arts of life were successively evolved. Intellect itself is a product of Nature, and, in long ages, has acquired, under the pressure of need, its whole store of knowledge and aptitudes. The origin of language had given rise to fierce discussion. Some sought it in Nature, others in convention. Epicurus does not wholly accept either view. He traced language back to those instinctive cries, expressive of emotion, which are as purely reflex as a sneeze or the bark of a dog; but he recognized that these cries would not be everywhere the same, but would vary in different tribes according to varying conditions. Out of these primitive words language gradually developed—and mainly by conscious effort, in order that the meaning of each term used in a local dialect should be quite unmistakable, and intelligible throughout the whole tribe. The last terms to be invented would, of course, be the names of things which are not visible and corporeal. In other words, language is another case where the natural instinctive product was shaped under stress of necessity, and adapted to its purpose by human intellect.

7. μετέωρα.—The epistle to Herodotus ends with a brief summary of the principles regulating the attitude of Epicurus in regard to those natural phenomena which in all ages have excited curiosity and terror, such as eclipses, comets, tempests, and the like. The general name for such phenomena is *μετέωρα*, because, with the exception of earthquakes, they occur overhead in the sky. We are bound to believe, he says, that such events do not occur by the command of any being who enjoys bliss and immortality, *i.e.*, they are not the work of the gods. Whether such Divine interference be conceived as perpetual, and the cause of regularity, or as spasmodic, and producing abnormal and irregular events, the care and anxiety implied by it is incompatible with our notion of perfect bliss, and the mere belief in such an inconsistency is enough to poison our peace of mind. Our happiness does, indeed, depend upon accurate knowledge of the most important principles, and from that sphere of physics plurality of causes or contingency must be absolutely excluded. But exact knowledge of details does not contribute to happiness. Thus in astronomy we must learn what the heavenly bodies really are. On this point no uncertainty is permissible; we must be quite clear, *e.g.*, that the Stoics are wrong in holding them to be orbs of fire, endowed with life, reason, and purpose; but, when we come to their risings and settings, their solstices and eclipses and the like, exact knowledge on these points is unnecessary to happiness, and, as a fact, does not relieve from terror and misgivings the experts who claim to possess it. Their curiosity can never be quite satisfied. Some things still remain unknown, and therefore excite no less alarm in the experts than in the ignorant multitude. If our researches into celestial phenomena lead us to assume, not a single definite cause, but a plurality of possible causes, each sufficient to account for the phenomenon in question, such a result is accurate enough for our purpose, which is to ensure our own peace of mind. In such investigation we must take account of the various ways in which analogous phenomena occur within our terrestrial experience. When we know that a given effect can be produced in several ways by several distinct causes, while we are uncertain to which of these causes it is to be referred in any particular case, then, if we are sure that the question whether it should be referred to cause A or to cause B does not affect our tranquillity, we need not carry the investigation any further. How this method worked is shown in detail in the epistle to Pythocles. For each phenomenon several alternative explanations are set down side by side, and no preference is given to any of these over the others. Many of them are known to have been put forward in all seriousness by one or other of the early Ionians—Anaximander, Anaximenes, Xenophanes, Anaxagoras, Metrodorus of Chios, and, of course, Democritus. Thus the document, properly used, has its value as a contribution to the history of Greek science. The industry with which all previous explanations are collected is creditable, and may be set off against the writer's indifference as to which of them is true, so long as they dispense with the subsidiary assumption of Divine interference. Once, indeed, the record drops its habitual tone of impartial neutrality and takes sides with all the ardour of personal conviction. Heraclitus had declared the size of the sun to be the breadth of a man's foot (Diels, 12 B 3 [i². 62]). Epicurus, ignoring the wide divergence of opinion upon this interesting problem, lays down a similar view (Diog. Laert. x. 91) respecting sun, moon, and stars, which are all alike stated to be, in relation to us, just as large as they appear, though we are still left with three alternatives as to the actual size, which may be a little larger, a little smaller, or precisely as large as it appears. The grounds of this dogmatic statement, as given in περὶ φύσεως xi. (fr. 81 [Usener]), are that, if the apparent size, the size in relation to us, had diminished owing to the distance, the colour or brightness would have diminished still more: and this from the supposed analogy of fires seen at a great distance upon earth. In this summary (for the two epistles to Herodotus and Pythocles may be treated as a single whole) Epicurus did not think it worth while to include his famous hypothesis of atomic declination, or his account of the origin of life, while there is only a passing reference to such important topics as the history of our world, and of mankind upon it.

8. Theology.—From the foregoing it is abundantly clear that to Epicurus the gods are not supernatural beings controlling Nature from outside. His denial of Divine providence and Divine interference with the world is unqualified. That he should have believed in gods at all is probably due in part to the influence of Democritus (*q.v.*), who postulated gigantic long-lived phantoms (δαίμονες), powerful for good or ill. The Epicurean gods differ from such δαίμονες in three particulars. (i.) They do not dwell in this or any world, but in the *intermundia* (μετακόσμια), or interspaces between world and world, where multitudes of gods and goddesses in human form hold converse. (ii.) They are not divided into beneficent and maleficent beings, but are all alike utterly indifferent to human interests. No benefits are to be expected from their favour, no punishments to be dreaded from their anger. Free from all tasks and occupations, they live solely for their own enjoyment. (iii.) They are not merely long-lived, but indestructible and eternal. The proof of their existence is the universal belief in them, which is declared to be no false opinion, but a genuine preconception (πρόληψις), which cannot have arisen except through many previous impressions of gods, all of them corresponding to an outward reality. Thus we are bound to think of them as blessed and eternal. To such superhuman excellence our reverence is due; but neither prayers, nor vows, nor prophecies have any part in true piety. These theological dogmas are declared to be just as certain, just as important in their bearing upon human happiness, as the fundamental principles of physics. But they involve a difficulty which baffles explanation. The bodies of the gods, like all συγκρίσεις, ought to be dissoluble by the separation of those atoms which united to form them. This difficulty is treated by the Epicurean speaker in Cic. *de Nat. Deor.* (I. xviii. 49, fr. 352 [Usener]), but the passage is the despair of commentators. According to Lachelier, Scott, and Giussani, the Divine bodies are eternal because continually renovated by fresh matter, waste and repair being equal and co-instantaneous (cf. ὁμοιότητες, Aet. I. vii. 34 [*Doxogr. Gr.* p. 306]).

9. **Ethics.**—(*a*) *Psychological prolegomena.*—Before proceeding to Ethics, it is convenient to sum up the conclusions already reached which most affect our happiness. Correct theology rids us of fear of the gods, by teaching that they do not interfere with the order of Nature; correct psychology rids us of the fear of death, by teaching us the true nature of the soul, which is seen to be incompatible with immortality. Further, the study of Nature can alone teach us what are the true limits of pleasure and pain. As we saw, for action and conduct, feelings (πάθη) are the test and touchstone, as sense-perception is for knowledge and opinion. There are definite limits to the increase of pleasure and pain alike. For pleasure they consist in the removal of every painful want. When this has been attained, pleasure cannot be heightened, it can only be varied (ποικίλλειν). Pain also has its limits fixed by Nature; the intensity of pain is in inverse ratio to its duration. The worst pains bring themselves to a violent end by killing the sufferer outright. Further, in pleasure it is necessary to distinguish the goal from the path which leads to it. The former is a permanent state of tranquillity or rest (καταστηματικὴ ἡδονή); the latter consists in movement (ἐν κινήσει), or progress, or excitement. Such movements are fugitive states, as contrasted with the permanent peace and serenity at which they aim, their object being either to get rid of painful want or to vary the pleasure which ensues upon its removal. Similarly, there are two sorts of desires, the first natural and necessary (φυσικαὶ καὶ ἀναγκαῖαι), aiming at the removal of all pain, the second natural but not necessary (φυσικαὶ καὶ οὐκ ἀναγκαῖαι); and these latter may be prompted by the false opinion that pleasure can be heightened, not merely varied, when all pain has been removed. This would explain preference for luxurious over simple fare, which Epicurus holds to be a mistake. Lastly, the pursuit of that which affords no pleasure at all—the miser's love of gold, the conqueror's love of glory—is a third class of desires, neither natural nor necessary, and entirely based upon false opinion. This psychological view, that there are two species of pleasure, is in sharp contrast with the doctrine of the Cyrenaics (*q.v.*), who held that pleasure is always a state of motion, and hence denied that the painless state of rest is pleasure at all. Another point on which Epicurus is at issue with the Cyrenaics is the comparison of mental with bodily pleasures. As to origin, the Cyrenaics pointed to certain mental pleasures and pains as not derived from the body (Diog. Laert. ii. 89, fr. 451 [Usener]). Epicurus held that all mental pleasure is derived from and related to the bodily pleasures of sense, affirming, in a much cited passage, that apart from these latter he had no idea whatsoever of the meaning of good (*ib.* x. 6, fr. 67 [Usener]). As to relative intensity, the Cyrenaics pronounced unhesitatingly for the pleasures and pains of the body. Epicurus contended that mental pleasure extends to past and future objects, while bodily pleasure is confined to the present. Past pleasures stored in the memory continue to be enjoyed; and, reinforced by them, even feeble present pleasure can outweigh greater present pain. Again, an assured hope and confident anticipation of the future is a similar makeweight on the side of pleasure. On these grounds he reverses the decision of the Cyrenaics, and pronounces that mental pleasures, although they merely mirror in the faculty of thought the bodily pleasures of sense, nevertheless exceed them in intensity as well as in range.

(*b*) *The end of action.*—In his theory of life and conduct (περὶ βίων) Epicurus starts (as did Bentham long after him) from the principle that pleasure and pain are the sole, the only possible, motives for our actions. This follows from our physical constitution. That pain must be avoided and pleasure pursued is a dictum as plainly evident as that fire is hot and ice cold. Internal sense guarantees the one, external perception the other, and each in its own sphere is a valid criterion. All experience confirms this: every animal as yet uncorrupted by false opinion naturally and instinctively pursues pleasure, and seeks to ward off pain. If all our striving, willing, and acting thus relate to pleasure and pain, we may call pleasure the highest good, and pain the worst evil, where by good we mean simply the end sought for its own sake, which is never a means to something else. Or, as J. S. Mill puts it, what better proof can be adduced that a thing is desirable than the fact that it is desired? Epicurean ethics is thus seen to be a system of egoistic hedonism, in which the maximum pleasure of the agent, after due subtraction of pains, is the supreme standard. Thus peace of mind and body, or the health of the entire man, is the only true and permanent satisfaction in which all minor and subordinate aims are embraced. Reason enables us to foresee and take into account the consequences, pleasurable or painful, which follow from our actions, so that we sometimes choose present pain in preference to pleasure, because by so doing we ensure a greater pleasure later on. For, though, considered in itself, every pleasure is a good, and agreeable (οἰκεῖον) to human nature, yet not all are to be chosen indiscriminately. Nor are all pains to be avoided, although pain is always an evil, and alien (ἀλλότριον) to our constitution, for their after-effects may be salutary. It is necessary, before acting, to measure or weigh the consequences, pleasurable and painful, one against the other. Reason will choose and avoid, upon a sober calculation of the maximum pleasure attainable, after subtracting whatever pain is involved in and consequent upon its attainment.

(*c*) *The virtues.*—To the end thus defined, the virtues are related as indispensable means. No one can live pleasantly who does not live prudently, honourably, and justly; and, conversely, no one who lives prudently, honourably, and justly can fail to live pleasantly. At the same time, apart from this relation to the end, the virtues are worthless; and Epicurus was not slow to ridicule the absolute and unconditional value which the Stoics claimed for morality (*καλόν*, *honestum*) as an end in itself. If this morality has nothing to do with pleasure, what, he asks, can it stand for, unless it be the object of popular applause (*populari fama gloriosum*: Cic. *de Fin.* ii. 15, 48, fr. 69 [Usener])? It was easy for him to show the utility of three of the cardinal virtues. Prudence (*φρόνησις*), the root of all the other virtues, teaches what is to be sought and what to be avoided; Temperance (*ἐγκράτεια*), that we must not be seduced from a prudent choice by the bait of a pleasure known to entail painful consequences. The function of Courage is to keep us firm against those fears of the gods, of death, and of pain which *φρόνησις* has proved to be groundless. But the case is different with the social virtue of Justice, and the duties which by it a man owes to his neighbours. How are we to prove that honesty is the best policy? How can disinterested conduct be justified in a system which makes self-love the mother of all virtues? For, if it is a psychological truth that all men by instinct and reason pursue their own pleasure and avoid their own pain, all duties must be self-regarding. The egoistic effort of every individual competes with that of every other. Again, what makes actions just, and why does Epicurus enjoin obedience to the rules of justice? He holds that injustice is not in itself an evil, and that, in the state of nature, man was predatory. But he is no longer in the state of nature; Epicurus, like Hobbes and Hume, assumed a social compact, which, once made, is ever afterwards binding. But why should the wise man observe this compact if he find secret injustice pleasant and profitable? Because he can never be sure that he will not be found out. If he escapes detection by his fellow-men, there remains the fear of Divine vengeance, which, even if groundless, does more to disturb man's peace of mind than the fruits of injustice to promote it. That such motives do not weigh with criminals is irrelevant; we are dealing now with the wise and prudent man. In his judgment, compliance with the demands of justice, honour, and equity is a small price to pay for a pleasant life, or rather a moderate premium to ensure it. As things are, through justice and equity we gain the goodwill, love, and support of our fellow-men, which contribute so much to make us happy. Thus Epicurus first stated the utilitarian defence of justice. Its rules are wisely framed to procure for each the maximum of pleasure, to adjust conflicting interests with the minimum of friction; but, if all men were shrewd enough to see this and profit by it, laws would no longer be needed. Their present function is rather to protect the wise from suffering injustice than to deter them from committing it.

(*d*) *Friendship.*—Whereas the Stoics saw in justice and philanthropy the bonds which hold society together, Epicurus augured the happiest results from the voluntary association of friends. We must make friends, as we must obey the laws, because without them we cannot live safely and fearlessly, and therefore cannot live pleasantly. We promote our own happiness by conferring benefits on our friends; it is sweeter to give than to receive (*τὸ εὖ ποιεῖν ἥδιόν ἐστι τοῦ εὖ πάσχειν*; Plut. 'non posse suaviter vivi secundum E.': 15, p. 1097*a*, fr. 544 [Usener]). When an admission apparently so compromising to egoism is once made, it is easily pushed further; it is, therefore, not surprising to be told that we should make sacrifices for friends, and even undergo the greatest hardships on their behalf. In all ages the school was famous for the devoted friendships of which it could boast.

10. Fate and free will.—The epistle to Menœceus closes with the lofty claim that the man who follows its precepts will live the life of a god upon earth. At every moment the pleasures he enjoys far outweigh his pains; his future is secure; even on the rack he will be happy; give him bread and water, and he will not fall short of Zeus in enjoyment. The Stoics made promises no less extravagant, and Epicurus could not afford to be outdone by his rivals. But he differed from them fundamentally in his view of the future. The Stoics retained the doctrine of natural necessity as laid down by Democritus, that all events are equally determined, and linked together in one unending series of causes and effects; that the future is thus inevitably fixed, and could conceivably be foretold with complete accuracy at any point in the series. Epicurus rebelled against this doctrine. The past, he admitted, was determined, but not the future. So tenacious was he of this distinction, that he would not allow the validity of a disjunctive proposition relating to the future, such as: 'Hermarchus will either be alive or not alive to-morrow.' He was afraid (Cic. *de Fato*, x. 21, fr. 376 [Usener]) that in granting this he would be granting by implication that all events are necessarily determined. His own view is that some things happen by chance, and some are due to human agency (*ἃ δὲ ἀπὸ τύχης, ἃ δὲ παρ' ἡμᾶς*: Diog. Laert. x. 133, p. 65 [Usener]), where the context shows that *ἀπὸ τύχης* and *παρ' ἡμᾶς* must imply some sort of spontaneity and free will. This is a direct denial of Leucippus' maxim, *οὐδὲν χρῆμα μάτην γίνεται.* With pointed allusion to Leucippus and Democritus, Epicurus exclaims that it would be better to believe the tales about the gods than to become the slaves of the inexorable Fate of the physicists (*ἐπεὶ κρεῖττον ἦν τῷ περὶ θεῶν μύθῳ κατακολουθεῖν ἢ τῇ τῶν φυσικῶν εἱμαρμένῃ δουλεύειν*: *ib.* 134, p. 65 [Usener]). To what limitations this doctrine of contingency was subject is not known; but it is very improbable that it was carried as far as Guyau (*La Morale d'Épic.* ch. ii.) supposed. See also LUCRETIUS.

LITERATURE.—*Voll. Herc.*, 1st series, 1793–1855, 2nd series, 1862–1876, Naples, also Oxford, 1824–25; **H. Usener**, *Epicurea*, Leipzig, 1887, 'Epik. Schriften auf Stein,' in *Rh. Mus.* xlvii. [1892] 414–456; **Th. Gomperz**, 'Die herc. Rollen,' in *Zeitschr. f. d. österr. Gymn.* xvii. [1866] 691–708, 'Neue Bruchstücke Epicurs,' *ib.* xviii. [1867] 669–672, *Neue Bruchstücke Epic., insbesondere über d. Willensfrage*, Vienna, 1876; **M. Guyau**, *La Morale d'Épic.*, Paris, 1878; **W. Wallace**, *Epicureanism*, London, 1880; **W. Scott**, 'The Physical Constitution of the Epic. Gods,' in *JPh*, 1883, pp. 212–247; **A. Brieger**, 'de Atomorum Epic. motu principali,' in *Philol. Abhandl. für M. Hertz*, 1888, 'Epik. Lehre von der Seele,' *Progr. Halle*, 1893; **C. Wotke**, in *Wiener Studien*, x. [1888] 175–210; *Metrodori Epicurei fragmenta collegit, scriptoris incerti Epicurei commentarium moralem subjecit* Alfredus Koerte, in Supplementband, xvii. [1890] 529–597, of *Neue Jahrbücher für Philologie*; **F. Picavet**, 'Epic. fondateur d'une religion nouvelle,' in *RHR* xxvii. [1893] 315–344; **A. Goedeckemeyer**, *Epik. Verhältnis zu Dem. in der Naturphilosophie*, Strassburg, 1897; *Diog. Oenoand. Frag.*, ord. et expl. Io. William, Leipzig, 1907; **H. von Arnim**, *Epikur's Lehre von Minimum*, Vienna, 1907, and in Pauly-Wissowa, 1909; **R. D. Hicks**, *Stoic and Epicurean*, New York, 1910, pp. 151–311.

R. D. HICKS.

EPIPHANY.—This is the name usually given to the Christian feast held on January 6th. The early history of the feast is obscure, but it certainly was generally observed by A.D. 325, and was probably not yet universal in 311. This is shown by the evidence of the Arians and the Donatists. The Arians appear to have celebrated the feast, for Greg. Naz. says that in 372 the Arian Emperor Valens visited the church at Cæsarea in Cappadocia, and shared in the Epiphany feast.[1] Considering the intensity of feeling between Arians and Orthodox, it is extremely improbable that either party would have accepted a feast which had been introduced by the other (cf. also Usener, 'Weihnachtsfest,' p. 192 f.). Thus it is probable that the Epiphany feast belonged to the services of the undivided Church, and, therefore, must have been introduced before 325. On the other hand, it can scarcely have been universal before 311, when the Donatists broke away from the Church; for Augustine in preaching about the Epiphany complained that the Donatists did not celebrate it.[2] It is not probable that the Donatists abandoned any established Christian custom, and it seems, therefore, to be almost certain that the Epiphany was introduced after their schism; but, of course, the proof is stringent for Africa only; and, although it justifies the view that the feast was not generally observed before 311, it does not exclude the possibility that it was celebrated in some churches at an earlier period. This possibility is, indeed, turned to certainty by a reference to the Epiphany in the *Martyrium* of Philip of Heraclea († 304), and by the statement in Ammianus that, when Julian was in Vienne in Gaul, he visited the church at the Epiphany.[3]

Some writers have quoted the homily of Hippolytus, *εἰς τὰ ἅγια θεοφάνια*, as a proof that the Epiphany existed in Rome in the middle of the 3rd cent.; but this evidence must probably be abandoned. It is very doubtful whether this tract belongs either to Hippolytus, to the West, or to the 3rd century. Internal evidence shows that it was more probably a sermon delivered at the baptism of some distinguished person in the Eastern Church, and probably in the 4th century. It may have been at the feast of the Epiphany; this is probable not only on internal evidence but also because the Epiphany was a favourite day for baptism.[4]

Still earlier is the evidence of Clem. Alex., who states that the Basilidians observed the feast of the Baptism on Jan. 6,[5] but his words seem distinctly to imply that the feast was not observed in Catholic circles. The evidence for the celebration of the feast among Gnostics is, therefore, about a century earlier than that for its existence among Catholics.

As was shown in art. CHRISTMAS, it is certain that in the East Jan. 6 was the feast of the Nativity as well as that of the Baptism, and it is probable, though not quite so certain, that the same is true of the West. But in the 4th and 5th centuries Dec. 25 was gradually adopted as the feast of the Nativity, and ultimately became universal, except in Armenia.

The history of the feast on Jan. 6 after the acceptance of Dec. 25 for the Nativity is not quite the same in the East as in the West. In the East it remained the feast of the Baptism, as may be seen, apart from the liturgical arrangements for the day, from the sermons of the Eastern Church Fathers, and from the hymns. But in the West it came to be chiefly associated with the visit of the Magi to Bethlehem, though the connexion with the Baptism was never entirely forgotten; in addition to this, the miracle of Cana was associated with the feast, and later there was a tendency to regard it as a celebration of all manifestations of the Divine nature of Christ.

So far there is no doubt. The problems which arise are: (1) Was Jan. 6 originally a feast of two distinct events, the Nativity and the Baptism, or of one only; and if the latter, what was the course of its development? (2) Why was Jan. 6 chosen as a special feast, apart from the question as to which event was celebrated on it?

I. The original character of the feast of Jan. 6 and its modification.—There is no sufficient evidence to justify a confident answer to this question. What is clear is that in the 4th cent., in Constantinople, Antioch, Alexandria, and probably elsewhere, before Dec. 25 was accepted as the date of the Nativity, Jan. 6 was observed as the feast both of the Nativity and of the Baptism. Jerusalem offers a possible exception. Here it is quite plain, from the evidence of Silvia, that Jan. 6 was a feast of the Nativity; it is less certain whether it was also a feast of the Baptism. The researches of F. C. Conybeare (at present unpublished) tend to show that the Armenian rites, which combine the Baptism and the Nativity, represent a combination of a Jerusalem rite celebrating the Nativity, and a Greek (Alexandrian, or Antiochene?) rite celebrating the Baptism.

Now, it is tolerably plain that in connexion with the doctrinal controversies of the 4th and 5th centuries there was a tendency to emphasize the Nativity and distinguish it from the Baptism, and that this was one of the reasons which led to the establishment and exaltation of a separate feast on Dec. 25. To go farther is difficult. The points which stand out are that in the West the feast came to be connected with the Magi, and that Jerusalem, which, if we are to trust Macarius, had originally celebrated the Baptism on Jan. 6, partially or completely changed the character of the feast and connected it with the Nativity. So far did this go that Epiphanius not only maintains that Jan. 6 is the date of the Nativity, but says that a different date, Nov. 8, was that of the Baptism.[1] Obviously these changes were made because the Church was contending with some disputed doctrine concerning the Baptism of Christ, and desired to exclude it, or the danger of it, from the celebration of the Epiphany. The exact proof is difficult to obtain, in the absence of any direct statement; but there are enough indirect allusions to show that the danger was the doctrine that Jesus became Divine at the Baptism rather than at the Nativity, or that He obtained regeneration through baptism in the same manner as Christians. The evidence for this view is too scattered to be given in full. The following must serve as an indication of its character.

Among the correspondence of Leo (440–461) there is a letter to the Sicilian bishops (no. 18), and it is clear from his protests that there was in Sicily a tendency to regard the baptism of Jesus as having conveyed the same grace to Him, and having borne the same import for Him, as the baptism of believers

[1] *εἰς γὰρ τὸ ἱερὸν εἰσελθὼν μετὰ πάσης τῆς περὶ αὐτὸν δορυφορίας, ἦν γὰρ ἡμέρα τῶν Ἐπιφανίων καὶ ἀθροίσιμος, καὶ τοῦ λαοῦ μέρος γενόμενος οὕτως ἀφοσιοῦται τὴν ἕνωσιν κ.τ.λ.* (Greg. Naz. *Or.* xliii. 52 [i. 808d, ed. Bened.]).

[2] 'Merito istum diem nunquam nobiscum haeretici Donatistae celebrare voluerunt, quia nec unitatem amant, nec orientali ecclesiae, qua apparuit illa stella, communicant; nos autem manifestationem domini et salvatoris nostri Iesu Christi, qua primitias gentium delibavit, in unitate gentium celebremus' (Aug. *Serm.* 202, 2 [v. 915c]).

[3] 'Feriarum die quam celebrantes mense ianuario Christiani Epiphania dictitant' (Ammianus, xxi. 2. 5).

[4] See H. Achelis, *TU* xvi. 4, p. 210 ff.; P. Batiffol, *RB*, 1898, p. 119 ff.; N. Bonwetsch, in *PRE*³ viii. 130; Harnack, *Chronol.* ii. 217 f.

[5] *οἱ δὲ ἀπὸ Βασιλείδου καὶ τοῦ βαπτίσματος αὐτοῦ τὴν ἡμέραν ἑορτάζουσι, προδιανυκτερεύοντες ἀναγνώσει . . . τὴν πεντεκαιδεκάτην τοῦ Τυβὶ μηνός, τινὲς δ' αὖ τὴν ἑνδεκάτην τοῦ αὐτοῦ μηνός* [*i.e.* Jan. 6 or Jan. 10] (*Strom.* i. 21).

[1] *καὶ ἐβαπτίσθη ἐν τῷ Ἰορδάνῃ ποταμῷ, τῷ τριακοστῷ ἔτει τῆς αὐτοῦ ἐνσάρκου γεννήσεως, τουτέστι κατὰ Αἰγυπτίους Ἀθὺρ δωδεκάτῃ, πρὸ ἓξ εἰδῶν Νοεμβρίων* (*Panarion* 51, ed. Dindorf, ii. 482 ff.).

conveys to and bears for them. The vigour with which Leo protests shows that this doctrine existed in Sicily. It is also not improbable that a similar feeling underlies Pope Siricius's letter to Himerius of Tarracon in 385, in which he protests against the custom of baptism at the Epiphany. More definite traces of this type of heresy may be found in various homilies on the Epiphany, among the *Spuria* of Augustine, Ambrose, and Maximus. In pseudo-Augustine 136, for instance, the writer says: 'Let us celebrate Christ's baptism, keeping watch over our purity; because this is the regeneration of Christ and a strengthening of our faith.' It is difficult to define its exact limits, but there is no doubt that the view, ultimately derived from early Adoptianist sources, lingered on for a long time, that Jesus was in some sense regenerate, or even that He became Christ, in the Baptism, and that this heresy necessitated the efforts of the Church so to handle the feast that its heretical explanation should be excluded. Hence, especially in the genuine homilies of Augustine, the Epiphany is treated as primarily the celebration of the coming of the Magi, and not of the Baptism.

2. The original choice of Jan. 6.—The solution of this problem is unattainable at present. The fact which stands out is that the earliest evidence for the feast is that of the Basilidians. We have every reason for believing that these Gnostics were syncretistic in their methods, and this draws attention to a story in Epiphanius (*Panarion* 51) as to the feast which used to be held in Alexandria in the Koreion, or Temple of Kore, on Jan. 6. He says that on the eve of that day it was the custom to spend the night in singing and attending to the images of the gods. At dawn a descent was made to a crypt, and a wooden image was brought up, which had the sign of a cross, and a star of gold, marked on hands, knees, and head. This was carried round in procession, and then taken back to the crypt; and it was said that this was done because 'the Maiden' had given birth to 'the Aeon.' With this may be compared the statement of Macrobius (i. 18. 9.):

'Sol ut parvulus videtur hiemali solstitio, qualem Aegyptii proferunt ex adyto die certa quod tunc brevissimo die veluti parvus et infans videatur,'

and the statement in Cosmas Indicopleustes (*PG* xxxviii. 464):

ταύτην ἦγον ἔκπαλαι δὲ τὴν ἡμέραν ἑορτὴν Ἕλληνες καθ' ἣν ἐτελοῦντο κατὰ τὸ μεσονύκτιον ἐν ἀδύτοις τισὶν ὑπεισερχόμενοι ὅθεν ἐξιόντες ἔκραζον· ἡ παρθένος ἔτεκεν, αὔξει φῶς.

It is possible that Cosmas himself believes this to be Dec. 25, but, as he refers to Epiphanius, it is not improbable that it was really Jan. 6. In this connexion the usual name for the Epiphany in Greek, ἡ ἡμέρα τῶν φώτων, obtains a new importance (see further F. Cumont, 'Le Natalis Invicti,' in *CAIBL*, 1911). The existence of a heathen feast of this kind would afford ample explanation of the growth of a similar Christian feast, either by way of syncretism or of rivalry; and a more or less Docetic or Adoptianist form of Christianity would naturally regard the Baptism as the spiritual birth of Christ.

Another line of possibility is contained in the constant connexion of Epiphany with the rite of 'Blessing the Waters.' In the earliest Syriac, Coptic, Armenian, and Greek Epiphany rites there is a ceremony of consecrating water, usually that of the local river, for baptism. There is reason to think that this represents an originally pagan custom. According to Epiphanius (*Panarion* 51), there was in Alexandria a festival called ὑδρεῦσις (see F. Chabas, *Le Calendrier des jours fastes et néfastes de l'année égyptienne*, Paris, 1870, p. 69). This festival was on Tybi 11 (Jan. 6), and it was the custom to draw water and store it because of the especial merit which it then acquired. Aristides Rhetor in the 2nd cent. also mentions this custom, though he does not specify the date. He also states that the water used to be exported for use abroad, and that—unlike all other water—it was supposed to improve with age, like wine (*Orat.* ed. Oxford, 1730, ii. 573 [p. 341] and 612 [p. 361]). Epiphanius goes still further, and says (*loc. cit.*) that the water actually became wine; and he connects this fact with the celebration of the miracle of Cana at the Epiphany. It is also probable that this custom was not confined to Egypt or the Nile; Epiphanius goes on to state that at that season many fountains turned to wine. There was at Cibyra in Caria a fountain of this sort, and another at Gerasa in Arabia. Epiphanius had actually drunk of the fountain at Cibyra. In Rome libations were made by the priest of Isis with Nile water; and Plutarch tells us that the water which used to be carried before the priests in procession was in some sense an effluence of the god himself (*de Is. et Osir.* 36; cf. also Clem. Alex. *Strom.* ed. Sylburg, p. 634).

Behind all these customs there is probably (though it is scarcely susceptible of proof) an ancient belief to the effect that at the turn of the year water was especially dangerous, owing to evil spirits; and that it became propitious once more when the sun had begun clearly to lengthen his day. Even to the present day the Coptic calendar (published in 1878 at the Feluch Printing Office in Alexandria by A. Mourès) issues a warning not to drink water from the river on Tybi 5 (and it is better not to do so a whole month previously), but on Tybi 9 the blessing of Heaven descends on the river.[1]

Probably nothing will in the end throw so much light on the origin of the Epiphany feast, and also on that of Baptism, as a general study of the primitive belief of the connexion between water, the spirit world, and the cycle of the sun.

LITERATURE.—H. Usener, *Religionsgeschichtl. Untersuchungen*, i. 'Das Weihnachtsfest,' Bonn, 1889, ²1910; P. de Lagarde, *Mittheilungen*, Göttingen, 1884–91, iv. 241 ff. There is a valuable article in *PRE*³ v. 414–417 by Caspari; but much more may be expected if, or when, Conybeare's collection of material is published.

KIRSOPP LAKE.

EPISCOPACY.—The term 'episcopacy' is used in the present article to denote that system of the Church in which bishops (in the ordinary modern sense of the word 'bishop') fill the offices on which the continued life of the Church depends.

1. New Testament.—In the NT the word 'bishop' (ἐπίσκοπος) is used to denote the same officer as the word 'presbyter' (πρεσβύτερος). See Tit 1^{5-7}, where Paul, in directing Titus to appoint presbyters in every city, and describing those who are fit to be presbyters, says: 'For one who is a bishop must be blameless, as God's steward,' thus using the word 'bishop' to apply to the person who has been called 'presbyter' immediately before; Ph 1^{1}, 1 Ti 3^{1-13}, where bishops and deacons are mentioned side by side without any reference to presbyters, and where the passages would plainly demand some mention of the presbyters if they were different from the bishops; Ac $20^{17.28}$, where those described in the narrative as the presbyters of the church are addressed by Paul as bishops (cf. also 1 P $5^{1.2}$ in TR and RV text, where 'exercising the office of bishop'—ἐπισκοποῦντες—is used for those who are addressed as presbyters; but RVm and WH omit). A comparison of these passages affords adequate evidence that in the NT the terms 'bishop' and 'presbyter' are used interchangeably.[2] The use of the word 'bishop' in

[1] Owing to the change of calendar, the equivalence of the months is now different; and Tybi 9=Jan. 16, but this is, as it were, only a modern accident.

[2] Against this, see von Weizsäcker (ii. 326-331, Eng. tr.), who distinguishes the terms; and Hort (pp. 190–194), who regards

the NT then does not itself denote the existence of episcopacy in NT times.

It remains to inquire whether there are other indications to show that episcopacy existed. Of such indications there are the following: (1) the position and work of the Apostles; (2) the suggestions about the position of James, the Lord's 'brother,' at Jerusalem: see Ac 12^{17}, where Peter directs that his release from prison be announced to 'James and to the brethren'; $15^{13.19}$, where James appears to be represented as having presided at the Council of Jerusalem;[1] 21^{18}, where the statement about Paul, that he 'went in' 'unto James; and all the presbyters were then present,' shows that James was then presiding in the church at Jerusalem; Gal 2^{9}, where Paul, referring to Jerusalem, mentions James before Peter as well as before John, contrary to the usual order in the NT; (3) the rule of the Apostolic delegates Timothy and Titus at Ephesus and Crete: see the Pastoral Epistles, *passim*; (4) the use of the laying on of hands as a link in the ministry by the original Apostles and Paul and the Apostolic delegate Timothy: see Ac 6^{6}, where the seven men of good report were ordained by the Apostles laying their hands on them with prayer; 1 Ti 4^{14}, 2 Ti $1^{6.7}$, where Paul refers to Timothy having been ordained *with the accompaniment of* the laying on of the hands of the presbytery (*μετὰ ἐπιθέσεως τῶν χειρῶν τοῦ πρεσβυτερίου*), but *by means of* the laying on of his hands (*διὰ τῆς ἐπιθέσεως τῶν χειρῶν μου*);[2] 1 Ti 5^{22}, where Paul urges Timothy not to lay hands hastily on any one;[3] (5) the appointment of presbyters by Paul and Barnabas in the churches of Asia Minor, whether, as analogy makes more probable, by the laying on of hands or by some other method: see Ac 14^{23}. These indications point to the rule and the exercise of ordaining power on the part of officers of a higher order than the presbyters and corresponding to the bishops of later times.[4]

2. Early Church.—There is very clear evidence that in Asia Minor the government of the Church was episcopal, and episcopacy was regarded as necessary from, at any rate, the beginning of the 2nd century. Ignatius of Antioch, writing about the year 110, expresses himself in terms which imply that he did not know of recognized Christian bodies anywhere without bishops, and that he regarded the latter as necessary to the existence of the Church. He says that, apart from bishops, presbyters, and deacons, 'there is not even the name of a Church' (*χωρὶς τούτων ἐκκλησία οὐ καλεῖται*). He refers to the necessity of bishops, (1) that there may be a centre of unity for discipline and prayer, (2) that the bishop may be the representative of Christ and of God, and (3) that the Eucharist may be securely, and Baptism and other rites lawfully, administered.

'Be careful, therefore, to observe one Eucharist . . . there is one altar, as there is one bishop together with the presbytery and the deacons my fellow-servants'; 'Let that be held to be a valid (*βεβαία*) Eucharist which is under the bishop or one to whom he shall have committed it'; 'It is not lawful apart from the bishop (*οὐκ ἐξόν ἐστιν χωρὶς τοῦ ἐπισκόπου*) either to baptize or to hold a love-feast': see *Eph.* 2, 3, 4, 5, 6, 20; *Magn.* 2, 3, 6, 7, 13; *Trall.* 2, 3; *Philad.* 3, 4; *Smyrn.* 8.[1]

Towards the end of the 2nd cent., about the year 185, the need of episcopal succession from the Apostles is emphasized by Irenæus in Gaul as a guarantee for the preservation of the truth: see *adv. Hær.* III. iii. 1. There is like evidence from Africa in a passage from Tertullian, writing about the year 199 and referring to episcopal descent from the Apostles as affording the proof of the life of the Church: see *de Præscr. Hæret.* 32. The ordinary belief of the 3rd cent. is expressed by St. Cyprian when he says: 'Any one who is not with the bishop is not in the Church' (*Ep.* lxvi. 8). The rites which lie behind the *Canons of Hippolytus* (Roman or African, 2nd or 3rd cent.), the *Liturgical Prayers* of Serapion (African, 4th cent.), and the *Apostolic Constitutions* (Syrian, 4th cent.) contained a clear distinction between the offices of bishop, presbyter, and deacon. (For what may be a different element in the *Canons of Hippolytus*, see below.) As to Rome, the lists of the bishops of Rome afford weighty testimony to episcopal government, and to the episcopal government being that of a single bishop. The value of these lists has often been questioned; but Bishop Lightfoot in his essay on the early Roman succession showed with great conclusiveness that there was really one (and not, as many had thought, more than one) tradition as to the early bishops of Rome, and that this tradition went back to the middle of the 2nd century (see his *Apostolic Fathers*, I. i. [1890] 201–345). A reference to 'Clement,' to whom is entrusted the charge of sending to the foreign cities (*πέμψεις ἐν Κλήμεντι καὶ ἐν Γραπτῇ· πέμψει οὖν Κλήμης εἰς τὰς ἔξω πόλεις, ἐκείνῳ γὰρ ἐπιτέτραπται*), in the *Shepherd* of Hermas, a Roman document of the end of the 1st cent. or of the middle of the 2nd, may allude to a bishop as chief ruler at Rome (*Vis.* ii. 4 (3)). The lists of bishops of Jerusalem, Antioch, and Alexandria given by Eusebius may also be mentioned. They have much less authority than the list of the bishops of Rome, but have some importance; and the evidence of the Antiochene list is corroborated by the testimony in the *Epistles* of St. Ignatius (see the lists collected from the *Ecclesiastical History* and *Chronicle* of Eusebius by McGiffert in his tr. of Eusebius in *Nicene and Post-Nicene Fathers*, p. 402).

If the evidence which has so far been mentioned stood alone, it would hardly be possible for any scholars to hold an opinion other than that episcopacy was the form of Church government in Rome and throughout the West as well as in Asia Minor from the earliest times. A different opinion, however, has been based on other evidence and linked with the references to the 'prophets' in the NT already alluded to. In the *Teaching of the Twelve Apostles*, a Syrian or Alexandrian document of the 1st or 2nd cent., probably composed for Christian use on the basis of a Jewish manual, the prophets fill an important place. A true prophet is said to 'speak in the Spirit,' and to 'have the ways of the Lord.' The prophets are called 'your chief priests' in connexion with the reception of first-fruits—a phrase which suggests a comparison between the position occupied by the prophets among Christians and that occupied by the priests among the Jews. The local ministers are described as 'bishops' (*i.e.* presbyters, as in the NT) and deacons; an indication of their dignity is that 'they perform the service (*λειτουργοῦσι . . . τὴν λειτουργίαν*) of the prophets and teachers,' and that they are 'your honourable men along with the

the word 'bishop' not as denoting an office, but as simply meaning generally one who is in a position of oversight.

[1] Against this, see Hort, pp. 79–81.

[2] F. H. Chase, *Confirmation in the Apostolic Age*, London, 1909, pp. 35–41, with less probability interprets 2 Ti $1^{6.7}$ as referring to Confirmation, not Ordination.

[3] With less probability this is interpreted as alluding to Absolution, not Ordination, by C. J. Ellicott, *in loco*; Hort, pp. 214, 215; Chase, *op. cit.* p. 65.

[4] Against this it has been maintained that the existence and work of the prophets, or prophets and teachers, and especially the statements about them in 1 Cor. and the notice in Acts of their laying hands on Paul and Barnabas at Antioch and sending them away on their missionary journey, show a ministry independent of anything corresponding to episcopal rule and ordination both in its origin and in its work: for the prophets, see Ac 11^{27} 13^{1} 15^{32} 19^{6} $21^{9.10}$, Ro 12^{6}, 1 Co $11^{4.5}$ $12^{4-11.28.29}$ $13^{2.8.9}$ $14^{1-6.22-39}$, Eph 2^{20} 3^{5} 4^{11}, 1 Th 5^{20}, 1 Ti 1^{18} 4^{14}.

[1] Ignatius does not, it may be well to notice, specify the method by means of which the bishop receives his office. He says nothing about succession, and he does not mention the laying on of hands.

prophets and teachers.' Instruction is given that the prophets are to be allowed to 'offer thanksgiving as much as they desire' (εὐχαριστεῖν ὅσα θέλουσιν)—a phrase which probably means to celebrate the Eucharist at such length and with such forms as they wish (cf. Justin Martyr, *Apol.* i. 67; *Const. Ap.* viii. 12). There is no indication that the local ministry of 'bishops' and deacons was ordained by a higher order as well as chosen by the people; and there is nothing to show whether the prophets were or were not ordained. Some writers hold that this silence is a proof that there was no ordination in either case, but in connexion with such matters the incomplete and fragmentary character of the book must be borne in mind (*Teaching of the Twelve Apostles*, x. 7, xi. 3–12, xiii., xv. 1, 2, xvi. 3). The *Shepherd* of Hermas contains instruction how to distinguish a true from a false prophet by the observation of character; but does not show whether the prophet was in any way appointed to his office (*Mand.* xi.). Prophets held a prominent place in the Montanist movement which began from Phrygia in the second half of the 2nd cent.; and the Montanists maintained that the prophets and spiritual persons possessed the powers which were wrongly claimed by the officials of the Church. For instance, Tertullian in his Montanist days writes: 'The Church will indeed forgive sins; but it will be the Church the Spirit by means of a spiritual man, not the Church the number of the bishops' (*de Pud.* 21). It is a theory of some writers that in this respect the Montanists preserved the original tradition of the Church.

With the references to the prophets in the NT and the later evidence from the *Teaching of the Twelve Apostles*, Hermas, and the Montanists, the privileges ascribed to the 'confessors' in some quarters have been associated by writers who hold that the original constitution of the Church was not episcopal. A study of the Church Orders brings out the existence and alteration of a provision that a confessor might be accounted a presbyter without receiving ordination. The *Canons of Hippolytus* enact that one who has been tortured for the faith is to be regarded as a presbyter without ordination by the bishop if he is a freeman, and that if he is a slave he must be ordained, but the bishop is to omit the part of the prayer which relates to the Holy Ghost. A confessor who has not suffered torture must be ordained if he is to become a presbyter; and no one can become a bishop without ordination even if he had been tortured for the faith (canons 43–45 in Achelis, *Canones Hippolyti*, 1891). The later *Egyptian Church Order* contains confused and inconsistent statements, which show traces of a similar provision to that in the *Canons of Hippolytus* as well as of its reversal (canons 24, 25, 54, 55 of the Ethiopic text; and canons 34, 67 of the Saidic text in Horner, *The Statutes of the Apostles*, 1904). The *Apostolic Constitutions* prohibit a confessor from acting as a bishop or presbyter or deacon unless he has been ordained (viii. 23). A similar line of thought to that indicated by the allowance of this privilege to the confessors may have underlain the claim made at Carthage in the 3rd cent. that those who had suffered persecution and torture and danger of death for the sake of the faith might re-admit to communion Christians who had apostatized (see, *e.g.*, Cyprian, *Ep.* xv. xvi.).

With this group of evidence may be taken an obscure sentence in the *Canons of Hippolytus* which occurs in the description of the rite of consecrating a bishop, a canon of the Council of Ancyra of 314, some alleged instances of ordination by presbyters, and statements about the Church of Alexandria. The sentence in the *Canons of Hippolytus*, 'Then, from among the bishops and presbyters let one be chosen who is to lay his hand on his head and pray, saying,' has been thought to form part of the older strata incorporated in the present text of the *Canons*, and to embody a primitive custom, according to which ordination was not restricted to bishops prior to the clear distinction between bishops and presbyters already mentioned, and to the regulation by which the power of ordaining is explicitly said not to be committed to presbyters (*Canons of Hippolytus*, 30–32). The thirteenth canon of Ancyra, according to the text adopted by J. B. Lightfoot and as translated by him (*Philippians*, pp. 232, 233), enacts that 'it be not allowed to country-bishops (χωρεπισκόποις) to ordain presbyters or deacons, or even to city-presbyters (μηδὲ πρεσβυτέροις πόλεως), except permission be given in each parish (ἐν ἑκάστῃ παροικίᾳ) by the bishop in writing'—an enactment which has been understood to mean that episcopal ordination can in some cases be dispensed with, if there is episcopal sanction, which on such an interpretation would testify to episcopal government as a fact, but would imply that no necessity for episcopal ordination exists as a matter of principle. To the present writer the true text and translation of the canon appear to be: 'Country bishops may not ordain presbyters or deacons, no, nor town presbyters either (μηδὲ πρεσβυτέρους πόλεως), without the written consent of the bishop, in another diocese (ἐν ἑτέρᾳ παροικίᾳ).'[1] The alleged instances of ordination by presbyters of Felicissimus in the West in the middle of the 3rd cent. by the presbyter Novatus (Cyprian, *Ep.* lii. 2), of Daniel in the East in the 4th cent. by the abbot Paphnutius (Cassian, *Conl.* iv. 1), and of St. Aidan in the 7th cent. by the abbot and monks of Iona (Bede, *HE* iii. 5) are probably all cases in which the phrases 'appointed' (*constituit*), 'made' (*fecerat*) a deacon, 'was preferred (*est prælectus*) to the office of deacon,' 'he promoted (*provexit*) him to the honour of the presbyterate,' 'ordaining (*ordinantes*) him,' refer not to the act of ordination but to the making of arrangements for that act. As regards Alexandria there is a series of statements which need careful consideration. Jerome, after speaking of the identity, according to his theory, of bishops and presbyters, proceeds:

> 'When afterwards one was chosen to preside over the rest, this was done as a remedy for schism, and to prevent one individual from rending the Church of Christ by drawing it to himself. For even at Alexandria, from the time of Mark the Evangelist to the episcopates of Heraclas and Dionysius, the presbyters used always to appoint as bishop one chosen out of their number, and placed on a higher grade, as if an army should make a commander, or as if deacons should choose one of themselves whom they know to be diligent, and call him archdeacon. For, with the exception of ordaining, what does a bishop do which a presbyter does not?' (*Ep.* cxlvi. 1).

In a letter written by Severus, the Monophysite Patriarch of Alexandria between 518 and 538, it is said that formerly at Alexandria the bishop was appointed by the presbyters, and that it is by a later custom that his 'solemn institution has come to be performed by the hand of bishops' (see E. W. Brooks, in *JThSt* ii. [1901] 612, 613). In the collection *Apophthegms of the Fathers*, parts of which are probably as old as the second half of the 4th cent., 'certain heretics' are said to have abused the Archbishop of Alexandria 'as having received his ordination from presbyters' (*Apophthegm. Patrum*, 78, in *PG* lxv. 341). The 10th cent. writer Sa'īd Ibn al-Baṭrīq, the Melkite or Uniate Patriarch of Alexandria, who took the name of Eutychius, gives a circumstantial account that

> 'the Evangelist Mark appointed, together with Ananias the Patriarch, twelve presbyters to be with the patriarch, so that, when the patriarchate was vacant, they should choose one of the twelve presbyters, and that the other eleven should lay

[1] See R. B. Rackham, in *Studia Biblica et Eccles.* iii. (1891) 149, 187–193; cf. Routh, *Rel. Sac.*², 1846–8, iv. 121, 144–157.

their hands on his head and bless him and make him patriarch, and afterwards should choose some eminent man and make him presbyter with themselves in the place of him who had been made patriarch, so that they might always thus be twelve,' and adds that this custom was changed for the later custom in the time of the Patriarch Alexander in the first half of the 4th cent. (*Annals* in *PG* cxi. 982 [Lat. tr.]; Arab. text of the treatise in Pocock's ed., Oxf. 1658; and of this passage in Selden, *Eutychii Ægyptii Orig.*, Lond. 1642).

None of this evidence appears to the present writer to counterbalance the testimony which indicates that episcopacy was part of the ordinary system in the Church from the first. It is easy to exaggerate the importance of the *Teaching of the Twelve Apostles*; and it is very questionable what inferences can rightly be drawn from its silence. Apart from a comparison with the *Teaching*, no conclusions contrary to episcopacy could be derived from the references to the prophets in the *Shepherd* of Hermas. The general history of the Church in the 2nd and 3rd centuries does not support the opinion that the Montanists retained a survival of the original tradition. The privileges allowed to the confessors seem to have been merely an outcome of the exaggerated value which was sometimes attached to sufferings on behalf of the faith. If the text and translation of the canon of Ancyra are as already suggested, the canon does not allow of ordination by any except bishops, but is simply a disciplinary measure designed to prevent the bishops appointed to supervise the Christians in country districts from encroaching on the rights of the diocesan bishops. The alleged instances of ordination by others than bishops do not, in the light of the consideration which has been already urged, bear examination. The case of the Church at Alexandria is much more important than the others. But here there is great doubt about the facts. In the midst of his statement on the equality of bishops and presbyters, Jerome, by introducing the sentence, 'With the exception of ordaining, what does a bishop do which a presbyter does not?' appears to restrict ordination to bishops; for it is hardly an adequate interpretation of his words to suppose that they merely indicate the practice which had come to be in his time, and are not in any way an assertion of a principle. Eutychius, apart from corroboration of his statements, is not regarded by any one as a trustworthy authority. It is not unlikely that the whole story arose out of Arian slanders against Athanasius, who is known to have been episcopally ordained; and it may be observed that Origen, who had plenty of opportunity for knowing the facts about Alexandria, does not show that he was acquainted with any such method of appointing the patriarch as Eutychius mentions.[1]

The state of things at Rome and Corinth at the end of the 1st cent. and in the first half of the 2nd cent. needs separate consideration. The epistle of Clement of Rome to the Corinthians, written about the year 95, lays strong stress on succession from the Apostles as a part of the ordered system of the Church. The ministry, says Clement, is from the Apostles, and so, through the Apostles, from Christ, and, through Christ, from God. His epistle does not afford any clear evidence whether he regarded this Apostolical succession as necessarily preserved by means of bishops. The word 'bishop' is used in it, as in the NT, to denote the same persons as the presbyters. The presbyters are spoken of as filling posts of authority at Corinth. It is not clear whether these were the posts of chief authority. In two passages (3, 6) there is a doubt as to the meaning of the words 'rulers' (ἡγούμενοι, προηγούμενοι) and πρεσβύτεροι, and in another passage (3–5) there is a doubt about the meaning of the phrase 'men of account' (ἐλλόγιμοι ἄνδρες). Of these passages taken by themselves there are three possible interpretations. (1) The phrases 'rulers' and 'men of account' are used in a specific sense to denote the holders of a specific office; the word πρεσβύτεροι in chs. 3, 6 denotes the presbyters and not simply older men; it follows that the 'rulers' held an office superior to the presbyters, corresponding to that of diocesan bishops. (2) The phrases 'rulers' and 'men of account' are not used in a specific sense, but are simply synonyms for the presbyters; the word πρεσβύτεροι in chs. 3, 6 denotes older men, not the presbyters; it follows that the presbyters held the highest rank in the ministry at Corinth and ruled the Church there, but there is no reason to suppose that they had not been ordained in such a way as to receive the episcopal powers which in Asia Minor and at a later time in the West were limited to the diocesan bishops. (3) The presbyters held the highest rank and exercised the chief rule, and there is no reason to suppose that they were ordained in any different method from the presbyters of later times. A like question arises about Rome in connexion with the *Shepherd* of Hermas. Alluding to a past generation, Hermas speaks of apostles, bishops, teachers, deacons. In referring to the ministry of the present, Hermas mentions deacons, presbyters, bishops (about whom nothing shows whether they are to be identified with the presbyters, as in the NT and St. Clement of Rome, or to be distinguished from them), prophets apparently itinerant, 'rulers of the Church' (οἱ προηγούμενοι τῆς ἐκκλησίας), and Clement (*Vis.* ii. 2 (6), 4 (2), (3), iii. 5 (1), 9 (7), *Mand.* xi. 7, *Sim.* ix. 25, 26 (2), 27 (1), (2)). Apart from the reference to Clement, which has already been mentioned, there is the same doubt as in the epistle of Clement of Rome whether the 'rulers of the Church' are to be identified with the presbyters or to be distinguished from them. The presbyters are said to preside over the Church (τῶν πρεσβυτέρων τῶν προϊσταμένων τῆς ἐκκλησίας); and the 'occupants of the chief seats' (τοῖς πρωτοκαθεδρίταις) are either identified with or closely associated with the 'rulers of the Church.' Here again there are three possible interpretations: (1) there are three groups of officers, Clement the bishop, the 'rulers' as a special class under him, the presbyters; (2) there are two groups, Clement the bishop, and the presbyters also called 'rulers'; (3) there is one group only, described as presbyters or as 'rulers,' of whom Clement was in the chief place as the presiding presbyter, but was not the holder of any different office from the rest. It is probable that decisions in regard to the interpretations to be placed on the epistle of Clement and the *Shepherd* of Hermas concerning this matter will be largely influenced by views of the evidence as a whole; and that in forming this general view the determining factor will be the importance attached to the list of the bishops of Rome as indicating a succession of single bishops at Rome from the first on the one hand, or to the position of the prophets regarded as a ministry independent of official rule on the other hand.

3. Later times.—It is clear that from the middle of the 2nd cent. onwards the settled system of the Church was episcopal, and the episcopacy that of a single bishop, everywhere (on the theory of an exception at Alexandria, see above), and that this was the case at Rome and in the West as well as in Asia Minor and the East. Episcopacy and the rule of a single bishop then remained as the constant and universal tradition until the 16th cent., when the need of it was challenged in some quarters, and considerable bodies of Christians

[1] See a note by Bishop Gore in *JThSt* iii. [1902] 278–282; cf. C. H. Turner, in *Cambridge Medieval History*, vol. i. [1911] p. 160 f.

who were without episcopal government gradually grew in numbers and in importance. The existing state of affairs is the outcome of influences derived from the pre-Reformation tradition and of new influences which arose in the course of the Reformation. In the churches of the East, episcopacy is regarded as of Divine origin, and as the Divinely appointed means for the preservation and rule of the Church and the transmission of sacramental grace, and as essential in those who ordain. In the Church of Rome, bishops are held to be of Divine institution and appointment, and are the only ministers of ordination. Their position as rulers has been greatly modified by the claims and practice of the Popes. It has been much disputed whether the episcopate is a distinct order from the priesthood or only an extension of it. Most of the great schoolmen, including Aquinas (*Sent.* IV. xxiv. 3; *Sum. Theol. Suppl.* xi. 5), but not Duns Scotus (*Sent.* IV. xxv. 1, 2 ad 3), held that it is not a distinct order. The Council of Trent, while asserting that the hierarchy is Divinely instituted and consists of bishops, presbyters, and deacons, and that bishops are superior to presbyters and have the power of confirming and ordaining, and that the power of bishops is not common to them with the presbyters, was careful not to make any decision on this disputed point (Sess. xxiii. can. 6, 7). Of late years the prevailing opinion has been that the episcopate is a distinct order. In the Church of England great care has been taken to prevent the ministrations of any ministers who are not episcopally ordained, and it is declared that 'from the Apostles' time there have been these orders of ministers in Christ's Church, bishops, priests, and deacons' (preface to the ordinal); but the phraseology used in the twenty-third Article of Religion, by not defining 'men who have public authority given unto them in the congregation to call and send ministers into the Lord's vineyard,' stops short of requiring an opinion that in the abstract episcopacy is necessary to the maintenance of the ministry. Anglican divines have agreed that episcopacy is right; they have differed in the degree of emphasis with which they have asserted this; and they have not been agreed on the question whether episcopacy is actually necessary to a valid ministry as well as the proper means of conferring it. The German and Swiss Old Catholics and the Old Episcopal (popularly known as 'Jansenist') Church of Holland have retained episcopacy. The German Lutherans have abandoned it. The Danish and Norwegian Lutherans, though retaining the title 'bishop,' are clearly without an episcopal succession, and 'bishop' is merely a name for a chief officer or superintendent. The case of the Swedish Lutherans stands on a different footing from that of the Danes and Norwegians, and there has been much discussion whether they have really preserved the episcopal succession which they believe that they possess. The Moravians claim an episcopal succession; but in their case also there is considerable doubt about the facts. Their bishops are simply an ordaining body; the rule is in the hands of boards; they recognize the validity of presbyterian ordination, and do not regard bishops as necessary for the administration of confirmation. The various Nonconformist bodies in Great Britain and Ireland and the allied communities in America do not possess episcopacy.[1]

4. General considerations.—It is necessary to set aside some confusions of thought which are often made, and to notice arguments of a general character which, in one direction or the other, have influence with many minds. (1) The principle of episcopacy is not necessarily bound up with the rule of a single bishop, which is often called monepiscopacy or monarchical episcopacy. It might equally be preserved by a college of bishops and by a single bishop, by a collegiate or collective episcopate and by monepiscopacy. For instance, the principle is unaffected in regard to the Church of Rome in the 1st and early 2nd cent., whether the present writer is correct in holding that during this period one bishop bore rule, as in later years, or whether J. Langen held rightly that the chief government was in the hands of a college of bishops. Episcopal succession from the Apostles might exist apart from that particular form of episcopacy which has been termed monepiscopacy. (2) Further, as episcopacy does not necessarily involve one particular form, so succession does not in the abstract necessarily involve one particular method. As a matter of fact, the laying on of hands is found wherever there is evidence one way or the other. But, supposing it were the case that what is termed tactual succession did not exist in a particular period, this would not necessarily invalidate that succession whereby a bishop succeeds his predecessor in the see which he occupies. To take an instance, even if the precarious argument that, since the laying on of hands is not mentioned between the NT and the *Canons of Hippolytus*, therefore it was not practised between the end of the 1st cent. and the end of the 2nd, were sound, this would not necessarily prove that episcopal succession from the Apostles did not exist. Indeed, the natural inference from the passages in Irenæus and Tertullian, in which they emphasize the succession of the bishops (see above), is that the succession on which they lay stress is that of the succession in the sees. (3) Nor, again, must the principle that the continuity of the Church is maintained by means of the episcopal succession be confused with the quite different question of episcopal rule. To the present writer the evidence for both is cogent; but, whatever the evidence for either may be, the preservation of the Church's life through bishops is one thing and the government of the Church by bishops is distinct and different. (4) The antithesis between spirit and form, which has often been used for the purpose of minimizing the importance of any kind of outward ministry, is not of weight in view of human conditions in the present stage of existence, and of man's bodily nature. (5) It is obvious that there is much in the history of the 1st and early 2nd cent. in regard to the ministry which is obscure. There are difficulties of interpretation, difficulties of correlating one part of the evidence with another, difficulties in deciding which section of evidence is of more value than another. On some historical matters it may be too much to hope that agreement will ever be reached. To the present writer the consideration of the historical questions suggests the conclusion that episcopacy was continuous in its essential features from the time of the Apostles, and that the ordinary method, at least, was that of a single bishop. But he is conscious that the really decisive argument to his mind for episcopacy as a practical system is derived from its continuous and universal acceptance in the Church, from at any rate the middle of the 2nd century to the 16th century. Whether we speak of the witness of the Spirit in the mystical body of Christ, or of the

[1] The 'Protestant Episcopal Church in the United States of America' (in communion with the Church of England) owes its orders to Bishop Seabury, who was consecrated by three Scottish bishops in 1784, and to Bishops White, Provoost, and Madison, who were consecrated by English archbishops and bishops in 1787 and 1790. The first 'bishop' of the so-called 'Methodist Episcopal Church' in America was Thomas Coke, who was set apart as a 'superintendent' by John Wesley in 1784, and received the title 'bishop' from the American Methodist Conference in 1787.

sense of the Christian consciousness, or of the voice of the Catholic Church, this universal acceptance throughout so many centuries makes a strong claim. It may well be said that for the practical Christian the operations of the Spirit in the Church must decide how the life of the Church is maintained; and a question on this subject receives a very emphatic answer in the long-continued unanimity with which it has been believed that without the bishop there is not the Church. (6) Yet an argument of a different kind may be drawn from the signs of spiritual life which have been observed in non-episcopal bodies of Christians since the 16th century. There are those who say that this fact weighs with them more heavily than the unanimity of many past centuries, even when this unanimity of the past is coupled with the impressive spectacle of the theory and practice of the churches of the East, of the Church of Rome, and of the Church of England at the present time. Those who so think do not consider that their contention is adequately met by any considerations derived from the unquestioned truth that 'the power of God is not tied down to visible sacraments' (Aquinas, *Sum. Theol.* III. lxviii. 2; cf. Hooker, *Laws of Ecclesiastical Polity*, V. lvii. 4), and that His grace may overflow the channels of the covenant. (7) It is probable that the decision between the two conflicting lines of thought, the one of which attaches most importance to the vast agreement through the Christian centuries among episcopal Christians, and the other to the life which has been manifested in non-episcopalians, really rests on pre-suppositions which run very deep in fundamental thought, and are connected with doctrines outside the scope of the present article, and in particular those concerning the whole question of Church authority. See CHURCH, vol. iii. p. 624.

LITERATURE.—Lightfoot, 'The Christian Ministry,' in his *St. Paul's Ep. to the Philippians*, 1868 (reprinted in his *Dissertations on the Apostolic Age*, 1892); Hatch, *Organization of the Early Chr. Churches*, 1881; Gore, *The Church and the Ministry*, 1889 (4th ed. revised, 1900), also *Orders and Unity*, 1909; Hort, *The Chr. Ecclesia*, 1897; Moberly, *Ministerial Priesthood*, 1897; Wordsworth, *The Ministry of Grace*, 1901; Lindsay, *The Church and the Ministry in the Early Centuries*, 1902; Bigg, *The Origins of Christianity*, 1909; Durell, *The Historic Church*, 1906; Stone, *The Chr. Church*, 1905, also *Episcopacy and Valid Orders in the Prim. Church*, 1910; Gwatkin, art. 'Bishop,' in *HDB*, also *Early Church Hist. to A.D. 313*, 1909; Robinson, art. 'Bishop,' in *EBi*; Simpson, art. APOSTOLIC SUCCESSION, in the present work; Schaff, art. 'Episcopacy,' in *New Schaff-Herzog Encyclopædia*; Döllinger, *Christentum und Kirche in der Zeit der Grundlegung*², 1868; Langen, *Gesch. der röm. Kirche bis zum Pontifikate Leo's I.*, 1881; Duchesne, *Hist. anc. de l'Église*, 1906 ff.; Scheeben-Atzberger, *Handbuch der kathol. Dogmatik*, 1873–1901; Wilhelm-Scannell, *Manual of Cathol. Theology*, 1890–1898; Borkowski, *Die neueren Forschungen über die Anfänge des Episcopats*, 1900, also art. 'Hierarchy,' in the *Cathol. Encycl.*; Mertens, *De hierarchie in de eerste eeuw des Christendoms*, 1908; Sobkowski, *Episkopat und Presbyteriat in den ersten christl. Jahrhunderten*, 1893; Weizsäcker, *Das apostol. Zeitalter*, 1886, 3rd ed. 1902 (Eng. tr. 1893–1895); Harnack, *Mission und Ausbreit. des Christentums in den ersten drei Jahrhunderten*, 1902, 1906 (Eng. tr. 1908), also *Entsteh. und Entwickel. der Kirchenverfassung und des Kirchenrechts in den zwei ersten Jahrhunderten*, 1910 (Eng. tr. 1910); Sohm, *Kirchenrecht*, 1892; Lowrie, *The Church and its Organization in Primitive and Catholic Times: an Interpretation of Rudolph Sohm's 'Kirchenrecht,'* 1904; Réville, *Les Origines de l'épiscopat*, 1894; Schwarze, art. 'The Moravian Church and the Proposals of the Lambeth Conference,' in *CQR*, Oct. 1909; Lambeth Conference Reports, 1888, 1897, 1908.

DARWELL STONE.

EPISTEMOLOGY.—I. Introductory.—Epistemological problems are at present the most interesting subjects of philosophical inquiry. Many books have recently been written on the problem of knowledge, many have been devoted to the history of attempts to solve it. These attempts have been made from various points of view, and there is a wide difference between the solutions offered. With some, Epistemology is merely a branch of a particular problem of logical inquiry, for it is thought that the bounds of knowledge, its method, and its validity are given when Logic has found its proper place and is duly acknowledged. But in their case Logic has, like Aaron's rod, swallowed up all the other sciences, and logical processes are the whole both of knowledge and of reality. With others, knowledge is only a branch of psychological inquiry; and, when Psychology has completed its work—in its description of the origin, the growth, the nature, and the result of knowledge—Epistemology is also held to find its place and its justification. In all these cases, and in others which we do not mention, Epistemology is denied to be a separate discipline, and its problems are submerged in other inquiries. But it is not possible for these problems to be merged in Logic, in Psychology, or in Metaphysics, as the history of modern philosophy abundantly shows.

It may, however, be granted that the epistemological problem is not the first for the individual mind or for the race. Historically we find that philosophy begins with Metaphysics. What is the form of the universe? What is its origin? What is reality? What is the nature of the soul? What is the body? And what is the relation of the soul to the body? These were the first questions that men asked, and they gave such answers as were possible. It was the difficulty of answering them or of resting satisfied with the answers given that led to the further inquiry as to the nature of knowledge and its possibility. For the answers were not only many but contradictory, and they gave rise to the further question, Is the human intellect able to solve such problems? From the historical point of view, Epistemology is a critical reflexion on Metaphysics. It is an endeavour to ascertain why and how the contradictory answers which have arisen in metaphysical inquiry have emerged, and whether these are not due to a disregard of the limits of the human mind, and an unwarranted application of cognitive processes to matters beyond its ken.

While it is true that the epistemological problem arises out of the failure of metaphysical inquiry, it is also true that it emerges elsewhere and otherwise as soon as men begin to reflect on knowledge itself. At the outset knowledge is not a problem. Its nature and validity are taken for granted. Men assume naively that they are in contact with reality, that the objects which they know they know surely and immediately, and all that is needed is that the knowledge be verified in practice. They regard this first and immediate knowledge as certain, and objectively true; or rather, since the question of objectivity and subjectivity has not yet arisen, and their thinking and its outcome have never been questioned, they abide in the conviction that the knowledge they possess is adequate and true. At first, both in the individual and in the race, knowledge is not concerned with itself, or with its processes; it is simple, immediate, and direct. It is only when difficulties arise in the practical application of knowledge that the mind begins to reflect on knowledge itself, its origin, its nature, and its limits. The external attitude is first: men look outwards; they do not question the reality of common experience, or conceive of themselves as thinking beings at all. They are lost in the object, in the endeavour to master the means whereby they may subserve their ends. The question of the self, of themselves as experiencing subjects, and of the bearing of the nature of themselves as the subjects which make knowledge does not arise until reflexion has well begun. Apart from the distinctions which have emerged between Logic, Psychology, Metaphysics, and the Theory of Knowledge, there is no doubt that at the basis of all knowledge there is first the experience which is more or less indefinite. For experience does not begin with a recognition of the distinctions which subsequent reflexion finds within it. At first it is vague and indefinite. The elements within it are not distinguished. These distinctions are the work of reflexion: we find within experience elements which we call feeling, thought, and volition. These we discover to be ultimate, that is, we cannot identify thought with feeling or with volition, though all three are present in every experience. Similarly, we find in the sphere of knowledge that there are many elements which can be distinguished, and processes which can be considered in abstraction from the others—sensation, perception, imagination, conception, general laws, and so on; so that we may regard sensations becoming associated together, and by the apperceptive activity of the mind worked into perceptions; and perceptions by the same activity becoming images; images becoming conceptions; and conceptions being worked up till they become ideas (*Begriffe*). Ideas in their turn give rise to newer and wider judgments, till the whole contents of consciousness are organized and placed in sure and definite relation with reality. Such is the kind of picture sometimes painted of the process and outcome of knowledge on its subjective side; and on the objective side objects keep pace with the subjective evolution, being bound together in order, so that the subjective and objective are only opposite sides of reality.

But many questions arise, such as the relation of sensation to perception, of perception to conception, of conception to judgment and to idea, and these questions are not yet answered. One fundamental question is, Can we consider any of these mental activities without involving all the others? Does not the simplest intellectual experience involve the whole activity of the mind, and is not the whole experience of the rational being implicitly present in the first rudimentary experience? When we concentrate attention on, say, perception, is not the rational activity of the perceiving subject involved in every perception?

2. Solidarity of mental movements.—Leaving these questions unanswered for the present, let us look for a little at the first abstraction which we make when we separate the cognitive activities from the volitions and from the feeling experience of man. Can we have a real Epistemology when we take the cognitive activities by themselves, and separate them from the other experiences inseparably bound up with them?

'In knowledge, the knower appears to himself as an active and sensitive intellect. The knower feels sure of the existence of himself and of his object, the thing known; he is certain of his painful or pleasurable feelings, and of those feelings we call sensations, which are in him, but which he nevertheless attributes to the objects as their *external* cause. The knower is, above all, an intelligent will. He knows his object; the thing known, as he acts upon it, moves it, moulds it, makes or destroys or modifies it; and is himself moved, moulded, or otherwise affected by it. Without intellect there is no knowledge; without feeling there is no knowledge; without doing and experiencing the effects upon ourselves and our object, of this doing, there is no knowledge. And yet these elements, or factors, are all given together in the unity of the act or process of cognition' (Ladd, *Knowledge, Life, and Reality*, p. 61).

It would seem, then, that Epistemology must be careful lest, in dealing with its own problems, it may treat them in so abstract a fashion as to make the solutions untrue or inadequate. It must not proceed on the supposition that a purely cognitive experience is possible. It must accept from Psychology the facts which it establishes regarding the complexity of every act of cognition, and the further fact that not cognition but conation is the fundamental element in experience. It cannot investigate of itself, or inquire into the origin of experience, or go back to the first beginning of cognition. No science can go back to its own origin. Nor is there any science of origin. We cannot recall the beginning of our experience, nor can we say what experience is the simplest possible. But we can say that all experience is process. What we can discern as we look back on our experience is just this continuous process of change—change felt and experienced—and also processes in which there is continuous interchange. There seem to be interchanges between external happenings and subjective feelings, interchanges between our acts and external changes in the objects we act on. And all along the process there is the constant play of feeling, cognizing, acting, none of which takes place without the others. We note also that, at the outset, feeling, acting, and thinking take up the whole field; the subject is so occupied with these interests and processes, its whole range of consciousness is so focused on the object in view, that it is not aware of itself or its changes, or of the interest which led it to make selections or to form a world for itself to which it would direct its attention. Likes and dislikes are there, desire and aversion are present, and the objects which are primarily attended to are those which one longs for, or desires to avoid. In the activity aroused by objects which excite feeling, objects grow so as to be defined as desirable or undesirable, and this activity is directed towards the attaining of the one set or the destroying of the other; and, in order to do this, the various objects are classified, recognized, known, so as to be brought, as far as possible, within the moulding influence of our action. All these processes may go on, and, in fact, have gone on, ever since men began to be or act; and yet a man may not have reflected on himself as the subject which feels, thinks, and acts. The subject is wholly occupied at the outset, and for long after, with the objects of its knowledge, desire, or action; it is so busy with their recognition, classification, and arrangement, so as to master them for its own use, that it scarcely ever regards its own nature, its own activity, or its own aims at all. Least of all has it discriminated among its own states, or distributed its own activity into its several kinds. Feeling, thinking, willing, are there, but only in the form of undistinguished activity. Nor ought reflective analysis ever to forget that, while it may distinguish the several elements in thought, they are inseparable in reality.

It may well be, then, that knowledge, will, and feeling are indispensable aspects of consciousness. Knowledge always involves an act of attention (see art. ATTENTION, vol. ii. p. 212), and attention as mainly aroused by interest, or stimulated by feeling. While attention thus expresses an attitude of the mind, it is equally certain that it also expresses an act of will. For will invariably involves some awareness—a means to be used in order to reach an end. An act of will looks at a present situation in order to modify it, with the view of reaching a goal. This is emphatically true when one pursues a reasoned course in order to reach a desired end, but it is also true of the most impulsive act of will. Even in an impulse there is some apprehension of a situation, and some desire to change it in order that it may better fit our purpose. It may further be said that every actual process of consciousness involves awareness, and this awareness is of a purposive kind. It is not possible to enter into a full analysis of this purposive element in every act of consciousness, but reference may be made to such writers as Stout, Royce, and Ward for a full account of this interesting analysis. Knowledge is itself teleological, it is selective of its own content, and its selection is determined by interest, and by a desire to control the world for its own purpose. Knowledge and action are thus correlative to each other, and each must have its place in a systematic exposition of the activity of consciousness. On the other hand, both knowledge and will must be considered in relation to a basis of immediate feeling which arouses attention and prompts to endeavour, with a view to an increase of pleasurable feeling, or an avoidance of an experience which is painful. Feeling is thus an inspiration to endeavour, whether in the region of thought or of action. It is the signal to awareness, it arouses the attention, it inspires the action, it prompts towards the realization of a fuller experience. According as we lay stress on knowledge, will, or feeling, we shall have in the first place a world of truth or fact, in the second place a world of ideals more or less realized, and in the third place a world of appreciations, in which values and worths are the main feature. These three worlds ought to be one, and the present endeavour of philosophy is to make them one; and thus the worlds set forth in their exclusiveness by idealists, empiricists, and pragmatists must finally appear as aspects of that real world to construct which is the ultimate aim of philosophy.

While we thus caution ourselves that an abstract Epistemology must in its very nature be one-sided, and must ever be held in control by the other aspects of consciousness, it is yet a legitimate aim to consider knowledge in itself, apart from those implications which are inseparably bound up with it as a matter of fact. It is legitimate to consider the operations of Logic apart from Psychology, and also to deal with problems of Metaphysics by themselves. But each of these involves the others, and each is constantly applying to the others for help and guidance. So, abstract Epistemology, or the discussion of the nature of knowledge, its limits, and its validity, may so far be considered in separation from the other philosophical sciences; yet the conclusions to be drawn from the discussion are themselves abstract, and are not forthwith to be regarded as true and adequate for the description of concrete reality.

3. Cognition as 'awareness.'—Let us try then to get back to the simplest possible cognitive position. Even this will have elements in it which we shall be obliged to neglect, if we are to have only a cognitive position to attend to. When we seek the simplest possible cognitive position, we are not seeking the origin of knowledge. We have already said—and it is a commonplace—that inquiry into origins is beyond the business of science. But we may ask, What is the fact about knowledge which involves the latter in its most elementary form? We obtain knowledge in its simplest form when we go back to the most elementary description of consciousness which we possess. It is simply that of *awareness*, or of simple apprehension. We may neglect for the moment the fact that awareness has in it a voluntary and a feeling element, and concentrate our attention on the fact that it has a cognitive element. Both Locke and Kant agree that all knowledge begins with experience, and from this there is no dissent on the part of any philosopher. What then is the simplest form of experience, or the ultimate datum from which knowledge starts? Have we any state of mind which may, for this purpose, be regarded as ultimate, which, itself unexplained, may afford the explanation of everything else? The ultimate fact seems to be, not a stimulus of any kind, or a dependence of a state of consciousness on any sense organ, but an immediate presence to consciousness. What I feel, what I taste, what I see, need no further evidence of their existence than the fact that I feel, taste, or see them. I am aware of them, and this awareness is a primary act of knowledge. It depends on nothing but itself. Here, if anywhere, we have an act of knowledge seemingly concerned with present reality, and with that alone. It is to be remarked again, by way of caution, that we isolate, for the purpose of study, the act of knowledge from the other elements in the complex state of consciousness which we call awareness. When we speak of knowing, of willing, or of doing, we abstract these from the normal state of consciousness which usually involves all three. Pure thought, pure feeling, pure will, are abstractions, not names of any concrete reality. Awareness is a state of consciousness which possesses all the elements of experience. Here we concentrate attention on the cognitive aspect of awareness. We may from this point of view name it *apprehension*, which is the simplest and the most ultimate of all cognitive acts. At the same time, it is contended that even the simplest state of consciousness has a cognitive aspect. The consciousness of the present is itself an act of knowledge. If at this stage we may use language more applicable to a subsequent stage of the argument, a state of consciousness is the state of any conscious subject, and it has an object. But, it may be said, is every conscious state one which may be described as knowledge? Would not this be a contradiction of the statement that knowledge, feeling, and volition are not to be derived from one another, that they are primary and underivable? It may be granted that each of these aspects of intelligence has peculiarities inseparable from its very existence, which must be described from attributes peculiar to itself. On the other hand, it may be justly contended that every state of feeling has its cognitive aspect, that every state of knowledge has its feeling tone, and that every volition has its emotional and cognitive aspect. Still we may concentrate attention on the cognitive aspect which is present in every mental state. Awareness is mainly cognitive, even if it be also volitional and emotional. This awareness at its simplest implies the consciousness of a content present to us, and an assurance that we are so far in possession of a knowledge of it. It seems to be the simplest of all the acts of knowledge, and cannot be derived from anything more simple.

We are aware that the last statement is deeply contentious, and one which is attacked fiercely and from different standpoints. Idealism contends that the simplest act of knowledge is constituted by thought-relation, and we cannot have an act of knowledge which does not involve relations constituted by thought. Empiricists, on the other hand, tend to isolate sensations, and to make these the sole foundation of possible knowledge. We have not space fully to argue the question, but it may be said, in answer to the former, that even Idealism must have some data from which to start. Something must be given if thought is ever to make a start. And the common starting-point of all the subsequent explanations of experience is just this position of awareness. Awareness may be so interpreted as to involve the whole outcome of completed experience. It may, indeed, be truly said of it that it is the awareness of a subject, and this is sufficient to justify all the claims of idealism. On the other hand, empiricism may contend that the first thing is the sensation, and that the awareness is second, and the effect of the sensation. But it seems more consistent with the fact of experience, and with the whole analysis of the case, to take awareness as the first thing we meet with; it seems to be the ultimate fact beyond which we cannot go, itself unexplained, yet the explanation of everything else. From this primary and underived fact we may explain all the phenomena, whether these take the form of the ordered world of knowledge known as science, on the one hand, or all the facts which are formed into the ordered knowledge which we call by the name of Logic, Psychology, or Metaphysics, on the other. Awareness is the pre-condition of all the systems, and it is well to take it as the starting-point of any theory of knowledge which can in any way be adequate to the fact.

4. Contents of knowledge.—Taking, then, this attitude of awareness as the starting-point for the discussion of knowledge, what do we find? The consciousness of a here and now, with a content more or less defined. This is the irreducible minimum, the ultimate datum of all experience. Apart from all subtlety of argument and all attempts at explanation, this is sure. There is a present experience, and from immediate experience every theory of knowledge must start. The simplest form of immediate experience is just this awareness. No doubt the latter is a property of every form of life. It seems to lie at the bottom of adaptation, and may be considered as a characteristic of life in general, or a property of organic life, which helps an organism to adapt itself to its environment. As life becomes more organized, awareness is there in increasing measure. Organic habits and interests grow up, and in higher organizations they are the means by which the organism adapts itself to its environment. It is a matter of observation that every organism has a working knowledge of Nature, and is so far aware of the hindrances and helps towards its self-preservation. This is a characteristic of all life, and without it life would be impossible. How far adaptation to environment may be regarded as something which flows out of intelligence on the part of life is a question which does not admit of any definite answer; but the fact of adaptation is undoubted. Yet in a self-conscious being adaptation to environment must in the long run become a conscious process, and intelligent foresight will take the place of instinctive adaptation. At the same time it must be conceded that adaptation to environment, even in a being implicitly self-conscious, consists in adjustments common to men and the lower organisms. Men are practising science even before they recognize it. Even the tracks made by sheep up a hill-side are wonderfully engineered, taking the line of least resistance. The people of a village who have never heard of Euclid, in making their paths through the fields, act on the principle that the two sides of a triangle are longer than the third side.

We must recognize, then, that organic habits and instincts have a significance for knowledge, and that knowledge of a kind has made some progress before reflexion begins, or at least while reflexion is in a rudimentary condition. Instincts, beliefs, habits, are part of that original endowment of man in virtue of which he is able to make himself at home in the world in which he has to live. Those habits and beliefs develop in man in interaction with the environment, and, before reflexion begins, he is prepared for the recurrence of day and night, for the succession of the seasons, and can anticipate the procession of natural events in the emergencies of his daily life. Organic habits and beliefs, increased by the experience of many generations handed down from father to son and recorded in language, may grow to so great an extent that, in virtue of them, men may learn to obtain control over the world so far as immediate necessity requires. This must be taken into account when we seek to understand the mystery of knowledge. Analyzing this complex body of knowledge with which an individual starts, we see that so much is due to the primary endowment of the individual, which enables him to make himself at home in the world in which he is to dwell. We may not exactly measure the extent and limits of this primary disposition, or inquire how much of it is due to traditional lore and how much to instruction on the part of parents and friends. It is not possible for one to tell how much is due to nature and how much to nurture. But, at all events, for every individual born into this world a portion is assigned; he obtains an inheritance of nature and culture which enables him to start, by no means ill-furnished, on the work of living. No doubt much of this knowledge is uncritical, unsifted, and much of it must be cast aside as untrustworthy, but it is there, and this unsifted knowledge is what an individual must start with.

Coming back, then, to awareness as the simplest datum of a possible knowledge, let us ask what is implied by it. Of course the two elements which are combined in every act of knowledge are present here in their most rudimentary form. There is the attitude of the mind which is aware, and the object of which it is aware. What the nature of the object may be it is premature to inquire. It may be its own feeling of pleasure or of pain; it may be the change from one state to another; it may be an impression from without; but in every case there is an awareness of an object. And then there is the awareness itself, considered simply as an attitude of the subject. This awareness, thus simply considered, gives us the starting-point of knowledge. It passes through the various grades of experience, until, as the outcome of growing experience and of reflexion on itself, it becomes the full-orbed distinction which we call the distinction between subject and object, which is implied in all human knowledge. The subject has its own nature, characteristics, modes of action, its rules, its principles, and its laws which condition all knowledge. Objects have also their own characteristics, their own natures, and their own correspondences. So all knowledge is conditioned by the knowing subject and by the objects which are known. The two are in relation to each other, and the whole question is as to what is the relation, or what are the relations, of subject and object within the world of knowledge. Are we to think of subject and object as a distinction which is ontological? Are we to think of this distinction as the same which we name 'self' and 'not-self'? Are we to place the two under the law of causality, and name the one 'cause' and the other 'effect'? Are we to look at the object as the governing element in the formation of knowledge? Or, are we to look at the subject as the maker of Nature, and to state our theory of knowledge in consistency therewith? All these questions confront us as we begin to wrestle with the epistemological problem, and the history of philosophy may be called the history of the attempt to answer them. Other questions also arise. There is the question of the possibility of knowledge, and of the various attitudes assumed thereto on the part of the human spirit. These attitudes are, or have been, mainly three. There is the attitude called *scepticism*, which denies the possibility of knowledge, and which has appeared in various relations in the history of human thought. There is the attitude, also common, which we call *dogmatism*; and, finally, there is *criticism*, or an examination of the principles which are implied in the possibility of knowledge both on the side of the subject and on that of the object. All these attitudes must obtain recognition in a discussion of knowledge, its possibility, and its existence as fact. Further, there are questions as to the relation of knowledge to the object that is known. Is the object of knowledge independent of the fact that it is known? Is knowableness an essential quality of things? And, if the object is knowable, what is the machinery by which it is knowable? Is knowledge in immediate relation to its object, or is it representative?

It is clearly out of the question in this article to give anything like an adequate account of the various attitudes of the mind towards the epistemological problem, or to institute an inquiry into the characteristic features of scepticism, dogmatism, or criticism. It is equally impossible within any reasonable limits to set forth the various theories which have appeared in history regarding the relation of thought towards its object, or to give a full account of naturalism, empiricism, idealism, or the theories of knowledge contained under these or similar names. To deal with empiricism fully would be to give a complete account of English philosophy from Hobbes down to J. S. Mill, with a glance at the philosophy of Shadworth Hodgson. One main characteristic of this philosophy is that it regards the object as the determining element in knowledge, and looks at the relation of object to subject as one of causality. Nor can we give a full account of idealistic constructions of experience, whether subjective or objective, for that would be to attempt to write the history of philosophy since Kant, not to speak of the contribution made to thought by the splendid achievements of Greece.

We must travel by a shorter route, which will not leave the above questions without an answer. We shall look at them first from the point of view of mind, or of the subject, and second from that of the content of knowledge, or of knowledge as affected by the nature of the object. On the one side, all knowledge is the product of the active subject; and, no less, knowledge, if it is valid, must correspond with reality. Under the first head all questions regarding the successive steps by which the subject articulates its knowledge into an ordered whole might well be discussed, and under the second all questions as to the validity of knowledge or its relation to its objects might find a place. All questions regarding the activity of the subject in organizing its knowledge —whether these are materialistic, realistic, or idealistic—would find a place in the inquiry into the nature of intelligence and its mode of working; while those relating to validity, and the attitude of the mind towards knowledge, whether this is sceptical, dogmatic, or critical, would find their fitting place under the latter heading.

5. Epistemology and sense-experience.—Starting afresh from the concrete fact of our experience, which must be considered the primary fact of our mental life—the awareness of a content—we must seek to show how this really involves, or contains implicitly, what is evolved into the structures of Metaphysics, Psychology, Logic, and Epistemology. All the mental sciences spring out of this fact of awareness—a fact of which the simplest analysis gives position, discrimination, and comparison. These are not independent acts or processes, nor can they be regarded as constituting the fact of awareness. They are simply aspects of this fact, and are not before it in point of time. They are in themselves abstractions, and are to be viewed as strictly subordinate to the reality out of which they spring, and apart from which they have no meaning. On the other hand, the simplest facts of mind, even sense-impressions and ideas, cannot be facts of mind at all unless they have in them, implicitly at least, the rudimentary forms of those features of distinction and relation which have become articulate in the elaborated forms which we find in our highest thought. To make explicit what is involved in the simplest form of experience is the function of philosophy.

Here we are at the parting of the ways; and, according as we take the one path or the other, we are committed to a system or a mode of interpretation of experience which is far-reaching. What is the fact of which we are aware, and what does it mean? In modern language, is it a simple 'that' or is it a 'what'? Is the whole duty of man, as a thinker, simply to write shorthand descriptions of his own sensations, their order, their organization, and their outcome? This is the view held in some quarters: the objective relations of these sensations are regarded as something unknowable. To inquire into this view would necessitate an investigation into the nature of sensation and its meaning, into the relation of a sensation to the mind which has it, and into the nature of the relation to the occasion of its being felt. On this head we refer to the masterly discussion by Ward in his article 'Psychology' (*EBr*[11] xxii. 547) and to his Gifford lecture, *Naturalism and Agnosticism* (ii. 116 f.):

'Sensations *have* form; in other words, they have inalienable characteristics, quality, intensity, extensity; as people say again nowadays, they have a "what" as well as a "that." Again, they are not isolated; but, as I have already urged, they are changes in what—for want of a better word—I have been fain to call a presentational continuum. The so-called "pure sensation" of certain psychologists is a pure abstraction; as much so as the mass-point of the physicist, but without perhaps the same warrant on the score of utility. The whole doctrine of the gradual elaboration of perception out of purely subjective material is fast being relegated to the region of psychological myth. . . . It is physiology rather than psychology that has kept the notion of sensations as subjective affections in vogue. Primary or perceptual presentation is all we mean, and such a term has the advantage of making the objective character explicit, and of ignoring physiological implications with which we have nothing to do.'

Taking this, then, as the view which Psychology presents to us, we may neglect the controversy as to simple sensations, and take for granted that every sensation has an objective as well as a subjective reference. What shall we say as to the relation of thought to sensation, perception, conception, and to all the categories in which thought seems to sum up the contents of knowledge, and the nature of experience in general? Will the analysis of thought give to us the interpretation of experience, and will obedience to the categories of thought ensure the validity of our thinking? Is thought responsible for matters of fact? What is the function of thought in relation to experience? In particular, what (to use the language of Ward) has thought to do with perceptual presentation? Instead, therefore, of following up in detail the description of the elaboration of the forms of our knowledge from perceptual presentation through perception, image-making, and conception, to the highest forms of Logic and Metaphysics, let us look at the part which thinking may be said to play in the making of knowledge.

Before considering this question, we must have some conception of what sense-experience means and implies. For, on any view, there is such a thing as sense-experience or a consciousness of objects in a world of sense.

'It is because in our experience there is given a broad distinction between two features of the contents [of consciousness] —on the one hand that of extension, on the other hand the negative thereof (the absence of extendedness) with, probably, as its positive associate, the element of feeling—that we are first enabled to make a distinction between subjective and objective' (Adamson, *Development of Modern Philosophy*, i. 291).

Here Adamson found the simplest form of experience, the most rudimentary form of objectivity on the one hand and of subjectivity on the other. At this stage of experience both the objective and the subjective are undefined, but from it the development of both subject and object proceeds, until we come to full self-consciousness on the one hand, and full consciousness of a defined object on the other; and these are the complementary aspects of complete knowledge. The first aspect of sense-experiences which forces itself on the mind is their opposition. On the one side there is extension, and on the other there is feeling or a state of consciousness; and how are these to be reconciled? The objects which affect us seem to be out there, beyond us; are they really what they seem to be? We need not recall the story so picturesquely written in the history of human thought, of how the relation of the mind to its objects, as this is set forth in sense-experience, has culminated in Scepticism on the one hand and Solipsism on the other. Doubt as to the very existence of an external world, followed by doubt as to the existence of an internal world, has arisen from the attempt to make sense-experience the whole experience of man. Yet sense-experience is a fact, and has to be taken into account on any theory of knowledge. The characteristic quality of it is the simple immediate existence of a conscious content. 'I see,' 'I hear,' 'I feel,' 'I taste,' and so on, simply give, so far as sense is concerned, the present experience and nothing more. 'This,' 'that,' 'here,' 'now,' are indications of the presence to consciousness of a sense quality. No doubt, there is a difference between these indications—'here' is one thing, 'now' is another—but they are only variations of the same kind of conscious life. Take any object of perception, and abstract from it all that has been evolved by conscious activity in elaboration of it in former experience, and what is left for pure perception is only an experience of a 'here' and 'now.' What is perceived is not an articulated object, say a horse, with all the characteristic marks of a horse as it is to a scientific mind, or even to a practical mind, with all the implications of a gathered knowledge; it is only a difference of colour which is presented to sense. This is commonplace ever since Berkeley's classic analysis of the nature of vision—an analysis which is true of all our interpretations of sense-experience. When we strip sense-experience bare of all that is added to it by interpretation, we have only a present content of consciousness—in practical experience it is not possible to make so drastic an abstraction.

On the other hand, it is vain to say that the nature of things is to be perceived. The statement *Esse est percipi* is without meaning unless we add to bare perception those perceptual judgments by which a mere presentation of difference of colour and shape becomes a judgment of distance, of character, and so on. But, when we do so, we have come to a perception which is charged with the meanings introduced into it by a long experience, functioned by interpretations gathered by a mind in contact with reality, and which has formed judgments in accordance with its own nature and the nature of things. It has been customary to refer to perception as the standard and norm of knowledge. But, when this is done, we have passed from perception as simple sense-experience, and have introduced into it all the series of interpretations which have been gathered from the action of the mind in interaction with the objects of its experience. Perceptual presentation (to use the phrase of Ward) implies more than can be justified from sense-experience. It is possible, indeed, on the basis of the latter to arrive at something like a universal. That universal is precisely what Ward calls a 'presentational continuum'; or, as the same thing is expressed by Baillie,

'The universal is just the *continuity of the process which makes up the life-history of immediate sense-experience.* This may, by selective interest or otherwise, appear in distinct phases or parts. But each as readily becomes its opposite, and this fluent interchangeableness constitutes the identity between them. The incessant change of sense-life is due to its being a mere variation of the same simple form of existence, is due, in fact, to the interchangeableness of its content: a "this" can equally well become a "that," a "now" a "then," and so on. This incessant change of similar elements is all that sense-life consists in. Hence its variability, its endless fleeting character, its instability, its inadequacy to satisfy the desire for a stable ideal, or constant organizing universal. Hence, so far from being the ultimate touch-stone of reality, as some have held, it is just what is perpetually slipping from our grasp. Its being is change, its life the death of its moments. As for constituting a support, which some have tried to make it, against sceptical attack, it is bound to prove the best weapon scepticism can use. The incessant change, which constitutes its life as a universal, makes it impossible for a "this" or "that" to maintain a substantial permanent reality external to the subject. A "this" or "that" has no reality of its own at all: its nature falls into the universal process of change' (*Idealistic Construction of Experience*, p. 152 f.).

Even in sense-experience, then, there is something at work which transcends it. In the formation of percepts, in the process of perception, there is already an activity of the subject at work. Nor is it possible to isolate the process of perception, or to consider it in abstraction from the more elaborate processes through which mind works. The sharp distinction so often drawn between perception and conception cannot be maintained. For, as men now are, with their inherited culture, with their social life in family and school, perceptions are charged through and through with trans-subjective meanings; and it is not possible for us to get face to face with a pure perception. The very fact that we have to name the various perceptions, and that names are words charged with meanings, makes it impossible for us to regard perception as the norm of knowledge. Here thought has been at work, and the very giving of names proves that we can no longer interview consciousness in its naked simplicity. We may seek to isolate the process of perception, and may, indeed, note its characteristics; but at the best we only succeed in proving that it is a stage in the development of the subject on its way to complete self-consciousness, and a stage of the objects on the way towards complete organization in a world of knowledge. It is almost axiomatic that the evolution of the subject towards its ideal is also the evolution of the world of knowledge into an organized form. The subject is growing, and, as it evolves, so does the world of knowledge, for these are aspects of the same reality.

6. Thought and sense-perception.—If, then, even in sense-experience we have traces of interpretation—and interpretation is the work of thought—we may formally ask, What is the function of thinking in the growth of knowledge? It is necessary to note here that, in the case of sense-presentations coming to us from the objective world, they come and go without any control over them on the part of the subject. Whatever passes within our sphere of vision makes its own impression on the eye, and the visual image is there, whether we attend to it or not. Sounds are heard, and the hearing of them is beyond the control of the ear. So with all sense-presentations. Even the flow of ideas in the mind itself seems sometimes to be unregulated, informed by no principle, and uncontrolled by any reference either to the objective world or to the interests of the self. Both in the case of sense-presentations, and of ideas associated in a mere flow without inner connexion, and uncontrolled by reference to purpose, we have illustrations of conscious movements which seem to have no rational connexion. This is obvious both in sense-presentations and in the case of ideas, as may be shown by a reference to the laws of association. What has once come together somehow in experience tends to come together again. The most unlike things which have come together tend to recur together. Illustrations of this abound. Take the relation of thought to words, or of words to the music of the song, and we find that thought and word are inseparably united, and the words of a song are wedded to the music. This is one order of the contents of consciousness. But there is another order, in which we seek to establish not contingency but necessity, not accidental conjunction but inner connexion. Over against the uncontrolled flow of sense-presentations, and the unregulated flow of ideas accidentally associated, we place the exercise of a mental activity of our own. We seek to place together the things which, we think, belong together. We may recognize that they belong together, not because they have happened to come together in some passing phase of our experience, but because they are fixed in changeless relations. The properties of a circle belong together, and cannot be separated without destroying the notion of a circle. Thus, science is the attempt to ascertain the things and qualities which belong together, and to replace a contingent and accidental order by one that is fixed and connected. Nor is the activity of thought limited merely to the recognition of the things which belong together in the objective order of the world—whether that order is fixed by the peculiar constitution of the actual world to be ascertained by experiment and observation, or fixed by ideal combinations (as in pure mathematics) constructed solely by the mind. For mind is creative. In the normative sciences there is not merely recognition of things which belong together; there is the power of saying that some things *shall* belong together. In the one case, the self is the discoverer and the interpreter of an order which it has not instituted; in the other case, it is a law-maker, determining both the end which it has in view and the means by which it is to be accomplished. Here it is possible to 'give to airy nothing a local habitation and a name.' In this sphere we certainly find the activity of the subject, the expression of itself and of its own purpose, where the train of thought is dominated by a purpose, and the means are arranged by which a new meaning is given to the material so arranged as to fulfil a purpose. As Adamson has remarked: 'Taken in the mass, our thinking appears (1) as a subjective activity; (2) as the expression of some purpose, and therefore as self-conscious; (3) as relating together the materials supplied by presentations and representations' (*op. cit.* ii. 258).

Leaving the discussion of the first two characteristics of thinking for the moment, we shall dwell on the third, namely, that of relating together materials supplied by presentations and representations. We have already seen that the aim of thinking is to bring together what belongs together. Now, it is clear that the presentational continuum does not bring together what belongs together; it presents experiences as they happen to come. It, therefore, gives no principle of rational connexion. Nor do the happenings which are merely associated together supply the linkage which we are in search of. What are the criteria of things which belong together? How are they to be related? In the first place, we connect them according to the rational principles of the mind which links them together, and, in the second place, according to the native connexions of the things themselves. But in every product of knowledge these are together. True, in dealing with the two factors of knowledge, we may neglect one or other for the sake of convenience; but we must always try to restore the wholeness of what we have thus disrupted for the time.

7. The conceptual and perceptual order.—In his latest book, unhappily unfinished, W. James says, with all the emphasis of italics: 'The intellectual life of man consists almost wholly in his substitution of a conceptual order for the perceptual order in which his experience originally comes' (*Some Problems of Philosophy*, p. 51). And on the previous page he says: 'If my reader can succeed in abstracting from all conceptual interpretation and lapse back into his immediate sensible life, . . . he will find it to be what some one has called a big blooming buzzing confusion, as free from contradiction in its "much-at-onceness" as it is all alive and evidently there.' The phrase has all the picturesqueness which we expect from its author. But is it true or adequate? The sensible life is, so far, an ordered life. Impressions which come to us through the senses are filtered as they come. Eye, ear, and all the other senses select out of 'the big blooming buzzing confusion' those waves of sight and sound which can be transformed into sensations; and, even at the very beginning, the eye does not see sound, or the ear appreciate light. But the eye does have a picture of a coloured something, which is not confused, or blooming, or buzzing. At the outset, therefore, there is not confusion, but something which is already full of order; sense-impressions are definite and ordered, and the work of science is to ascertain, define, and describe the order.

But can it be fairly said that the order in which our experience originally comes is the perceptual order? Or, if it is, can we separate thus abruptly the perceptual from the conceptual order? Can we have percepts by themselves? James evidently thought that we could, for in all his books he refers constantly to the perceptual order as the norm and criterion of valid knowledge. To us, on the other hand, a percept is as much the work of thought as a concept. Even sensation itself, in so far as it has a meaning, is a work of thought.

8. Thought and reality.—It may be well to guard ourselves at this stage against a possible misunderstanding, which might arise from speaking in separate terms of thought and reality, and the relation between them. We do not mean by Epistemology, or the theory of cognition, an examination of the nature of knowledge as something apart from the reality which is then taken as an external standard. Rather we regard the treatment of thought, and the analysis of reality itself, as the attempt to reach a world of reality considered as a system of ideas, which may actually become the world of reality. It is our interpretation of reality, and is part of the reality which is constructed by intelligence in response to the whole universe of experience. The environment of thought is neither an external world nor a supposed world of action; it is the whole world of experience, which is to be articulated into system, and made such as to answer to our intelligence. Not, indeed, that we may ever hope to transfer all reality into our system of thought, which for the thinker is the reality he can command and use. Yet our system of thought falls far short of reality. For, while the world which each mind constructs for itself out of its own experience is the world of which it is the centre, there must be a world common to all intelligences, or, in other words, a higher experience than ours, which in its organized state is the supreme world of reality. All the worlds which seem separate and unconnected, as constructed by each for himself, have common ground and purpose in that experience which is higher and deeper than ours. In this view, reality is independent of our judgment, and is something which far transcends our experience. Yet our judgment and its outcome must be held to be an element in that higher experience, and the world we construct is part of the world that is what it is for the higher experience.

As, on the one hand, reality must be held to transcend the final worlds which knowledge builds out of our experience, so, on the other hand, there is a something given before thought can begin its constructive work. Our immediate feeling has a content of its own, something which is there in a sort of unity and simplicity which we have not made, but only experience. It is a mode of contact with a world not yet realized or resolved into its elements. We do not confer on that immediate experience either its immediacy or its individuality; we experience it in its unity. The first step of the action of thought on that immediate feeling is to break up its formal unity, to distinguish elements within it, and to pass beyond it into another kind of unity, namely, that which is conferred by thought. But to restore the lost unity is very difficult, and the whole task of philosophy is to restore that unity which is first given in feeling, disrupted by thought, and made diverse by the analysis which thought has performed upon it. Thus, in the end, we strive to attain, by the exercise of discursive thought, to something like intuition of unity, the unity of a whole, what life started with in that intuition of unity which is the characteristic of our feeling life. For the mind, in its constructive attempt to think the world, finds that it passes its strength either to attain to intuition which envisages the world as a whole—that is only for a higher experience than ours—or to rest content in the simple immediacy of feeling which gives us a sense of wholeness in our simplest experience.

It is the province of Logic (*q.v.*) to set forth the categories of mind, or the machinery by which it does its work, as it is the province of Psychology to set forth cognition considered as a merely mental process. It is the part of Epistemology to accept from the sister sciences the description of the process of knowledge considered as an internal fact, and to accept from Logic the deduction of the categories, their inter-relations, and their worth as instruments for the organization of knowledge. We need not, therefore, dwell here on the significance of space and time as the forms within which all our intuitions take place. Nor need we inquire into the subjectivity or objectivity of space and time. Sufficient for our purpose is the fact that all our mental life is conditioned by these forms; at least all our sense-presentations are of such a kind as never to transcend the boundaries of space and time. Into the origin and nature of our conceptions of these we are not called to enter. It is sufficient to say that they are forms into which mind gathers its experiences, and that it is constrained to regard all things as things in one space, and all events as happening in one time. In these forms it finds the first possibility of a unity of experience.

9. Thought and self.—The notion of space, then, dominates all our thinking with regard to things, and time does the same with regard to the inner life. It is another matter, however, when we ask ourselves how the notion of time governs all the phenomena of the inner life. Can we in this relation do without the supposition that the very possibility of time depends on the fact that there is a continuity of the thinking subject to which the events that happen to it, or in it, are referred? Is not the permanence of the thinking subject the condition of the possibility of the notion of time? We are aware that this is a keenly contested question.

'It is a fact recognized explicitly or implicitly by every one, that the manifold and constantly changing experiences that enter into the life history of an individual mind are in some sense owned by a self or ego which remains one and the same throughout their vicissitudes. But, when we begin to inquire into the precise nature of the unity and identity ascribed to the self, and the precise sense in which its experiences belong to it, we are confronted with a fundamental divergence of views. On the one hand, it is maintained that, just as the unity of a triangle, or of a melody, or of an organism consists merely in the special mode in which its parts are connected and correlated so as to form a specific kind of complex, so the unity of what we call an individual mind consists merely in the peculiar way in which what we call its experiences are united with each other. On this view, when we say that a desire is some one's desire, we merely mean that it enters as one constituent among others into a connected totality of experiences having a certain sort of unity and continuity which can belong to experiences only, and not to material things. In opposition to this doctrine, it is strenuously maintained by others that the identical subject is not merely the unified complex of experiences, but a distinct principle from which they derive their unity, a something which persists through them and links them together. According to these writers, it is an inversion of the truth to say that the manifold experiences through their union with each other form a single self. On the contrary, it is only through their relation to the single self as a common centre that they are united with each other. Of these two conflicting theories, I feel bound to accept the first and to reject the second. The unity of the self seems to me indistinguishable from the unity of the total complex of its experiences' (Stout, 'Some Fundamental Points in the Theory of Knowledge,' p. 6 [one of the Essays published by the University of St. Andrews in connexion with the Five Hundredth Anniversary of its Foundation, 1911]).

With his usual felicity of diction and lucidity of argument, Stout states the grounds of his rejection of the second view and his acceptance of the first. Yet even his subtlety and power cannot prevent his argument from appearing paradoxical.

'The rôle which they ascribe to the subject of consciousness ought rather to be ascribed to its object. The general principle is that the changing complex of individual experience has the unity and identity uniquely distinctive of what we call a single self or ego, only in so far as objects are apprehended as one and the same in different acts or in different stages and phases of one and the same act. In other words, the unity of the self is essentially a unity of *intentional* experience, and essentially conditioned by unity of the object as meant or intended' (*ib.* p. 7).

We humbly suggest that in this quotation, and in the subsequent reasoning, Stout has virtually taken up the position of the theory which he has formally rejected. How can the unity of the self be a unity of intentional experience if there is no subject to form the intention? If objects are apprehended as one and the same, surely there must be a subject which apprehends them. The present writer feels bound, therefore, to accept the second of the above views and to reject the first. Without arguing the question further, he would simply say that 'I am not the thoughts I think,' in other words, 'I am not thought, but I think, and I who now think am the same who thought yesterday.' The conclusion—to lay stress on the epistemological interest—is that thought exists only in relation to a conscious and abiding subject. But the latter is not merely an abstract identity; it lives, and moves, and grows, and realizes itself just in proportion as it masters its objects, and is able to fit them into the unity of a world of truth. Still we may express our indebtedness to Stout for the emphatic way in which he brings out the close connexion between the unity of the subject and that of the object. For it is a characteristic of thinking, or of thought, that, in addition to its being a mental event, it claims to represent a truth which is independent of the latter. It is no doubt true that every thought as a mental event is particular; in fact, all the contents of consciousness as mental events are particular; but the mystery of knowledge lies just here, that a particular mental event, or a series of such, claims to be valid for an order of fact or of reason which our thought does not make but discovers—an order which is common to all and not special to one.

10. Judgment the category of thought.—This order, which I do not make but discover, is one which I am able to discover because it is in itself in relation to my intelligence, and can be construed by me in accordance with those principles on which I act as an intelligent being. These rational principles are implicit in every act of judgment, and the rational principles of my judgment are found to be at work in the order which I discover. What these principles are it is the business of Logic to set forth. For our purpose it is necessary to refer to only one of these categories, namely, that of Judgment, which is the form which thought uses in the apprehension of truth. Logic is coming more and more to recognize judgment as the one category which involves all other categories in its operation, and in its discussion of logical principles the doctrine of the judgment holds the foremost place. We refer to Sigwart's *Logic* in illustration. The various forms of the judgment may be found in treatises on Logic, and need not be detailed here. But the fundamental conditions of the judgment are fundamental conditions of thought itself. Judgment in every form of it involves a relation to the thinking self or to the unity of the mental subject. This holds good even on the hypothesis of Stout, as quoted above. It is the self that judges, and it judges in consistency with the totality of its rational experience, or at least it ought to do so. In the second place its judgments must be consistent with each other; in other words, all judgments must have regard to the law of identity and contradiction. If we are to have a constant and consistent meaning, we must think according to that law. Again, our judgment must have regard to the fact of connexion among the objects of thought. The irresistible belief that things are connected, and that the connexion may be discovered, lies at the basis of every judgment. What the connexion is the mind may not know, and sometimes finds it hard to discover, but that such a connexion exists is a conviction without which there can be no judgment.

In dealing with the judgment in its various forms and applications, we ought to remember that there is one element common to all, which no judgment can explicitly set forth. In all judgments, reference is explicitly or implicitly to the subject which judges. It is the subject which supposes, affirms, judges. The subject may itself be the object of reflexion. Thought itself may be the object of thought, and it may be reflected on till all its implications become explicit, and its modes of acting may be articulately set forth. But that does not exhaust the meaning of the subject. Is thought capable of exhausting in its own way all the meanings which are implied in the function of 'self,' 'subject-self,' 'knower,' as over against the objects of thought, object-self, and so on? We may think about the subject, may make it an object of thought; but, the more we do so, the more is the reference to a subject a persisting relation. Exhaust the meaning of self by making it an object of thought as much as we please, yet at the end the self persists as the final condition under which knowledge of the self as object is possible. The meaning of self or subject as capable of statement as object of thought does not exhaust its subjective meaning.

'The great attempts of philosophers have been, on the one hand, to show that the self as "subject" is nothing but the self as "object"; and, on the other hand, to show that the self as "object" is only a sort of re-statement of the self as subject; or, yet again, to show that the self as object arises as a sort of cognitive screen or blind before the self as subject, so that the latter is hopelessly obscured or hidden—the subject disappearing in the realm of the "unknowable," or the "thing-in-itself"' (Baldwin, *Thought and Things, or Genetic Logic*, ii. 407).

In this relation we may quote from the essay of Stout (*l.c.* p. 8):

'The self is the same self, inasmuch as throughout the process of pursuit it is aware of the desired object as the same, and inasmuch as it is aware of the object attained as identical with the object pursued. The best example, however, is supplied by continuity of attention. Attention is continuous when it is throughout directed to the same total object from varying points of view, so as to distinguish successively its different partial features, aspects, and relations. For instance, in observing a flower with a view to its classification as a botanical specimen, the stamens, root, and leaf arrangement may be successively distinguished. The total object is a flower as a specimen to be classified, together with the whole body of botanical science so far as this may be relevant to the classification. The partial features of this total object are successively discriminated, and in their turn cease to be discriminated. But there is continuity of attention, inasmuch as the partial features successively discriminated are throughout implicitly apprehended as being partial features of the same complex unity.'

As a description of the work done by the mind in the classification of a flower, this leaves nothing to be desired. But to speak of attention as continuous because it is throughout directed to the same object seems a rather inadequate account of attention considered as a mental process. Nor does it describe the attitude of attention as continuous; for, as a matter of fact, the process of attention by which the flower is classified may not be continuous: it may be distributed over many times, and is so when we work on any subject and resume it after an interval. But the main point is that the process of attention as described by Stout is attended by a consciousness of the strain of attention. I may be absorbed in the attempt to classify the flower, but on reflexion I am conscious that I was attending all the time. In fact, all the objective meanings—even those in which the subject or thought itself has been thought of—are over against a subject-self. The self is not to be merged in its own products, and the unity of the object seems to be inadequate to produce that unity of the subject which is the presupposition of knowledge. For, push the matter back as far as possible, even after all is done there will remain the fact of a subject over against all the objects of thought or objective meanings, as the very ground of the possibility of knowledge. In the last resort it is the self that makes knowledge, it is the self that judges, and the series of judgments organized according to the nature of the subject and according to objective conditions form the kingdom of truth, which it is the aim of thought to work out. The first condition of the possibility of knowledge is just this reference to a subject, which becomes, in the process of working out the kingdom of truth, a self-conscious subject, to which all the objects of knowledge finally assume the form of a coherent world of truth. In this ideal goal, truth and fact become one; and the content of mind, articulated into system, becomes the content of reality as well. But such a goal is never attained by the finite mind; it remains an ideal, but one that influences and shapes all our lesser and more partial systems of actual knowledge. So, the real question becomes not how to attain to the notion of the unity of the subject from the object, as Stout really does, or to attain the unity of the object world from the subject, but how to construe both subject and object as related unities in a wider unity which transcends and yet contains both. Are not subject and object subsumed in the wider world of experience? Are they not really given in the earliest experience possible to a subject which finally becomes a thinking subject? Are not both factors really present in the first cognitive experience, which we have already found to be present even in the sense-life? No doubt in our reflective analysis we place the subject over against the object and the object over against the subject, and make their relation to each other one of utter opposition; yet the relation of opposition is a relation after all, and even in opposition the two are really held together in the unity of one experience.

11. Intelligibility of the objects of knowledge.—In any case, there is a conformity between cognition and its objects. What is the meaning of that conformity? Are we to say that cognition must conform to objects, or are we to say that objects must conform to cognition? This is the experiment of Kant, who, finding that the assumption that cognition must conform to objects had led to scepticism, asked what would be the outcome of the supposition that objects should conform to cognition. His question and the answer to it were epoch-making in the history of thought, and every theory of knowledge must take them into account.

In answering his question, Kant endeavoured to discover the nature of reality from the conditions of its intelligibility, and in doing so he constructed the world of objects, step by step, on the plan of the world of knowledge. If there is such a world intelligible to us, the conditions of its intelligibility, Kant says, are such and such. Whether the actual world was of the kind which answered to these conditions was, and is, a question which Kant could not answer. For his solution had regard only to the conditions of intelligibility, and not to the actual world of human experience. So his intelligible world remained a phenomenal world, purely hypothetical; and the question of the relation of this phenomenal world to reality remained unanswered, or, rather, the answer was farther removed than ever. Instead of the old dilemmas, we find ourselves in the presence of a new one, and one more radical than ever; for we have removed the older difficulties, only to be confronted with a new contrast between reality and appearance, between phenomena and things-in-themselves, between the world of the knowable and its relation to the world of the unknown and the unknowable. How did the new hypothesis of the conformity of objects to cognition, and the consequent setting forth of the conditions of knowledge, lead to this contrariety of the world of reality as beyond the phenomenal world? If conformity to our cognition, as in the new question asked by Kant, and its answer, removes reality from our knowledge, and restricts our knowledge to phenomena, there is time to ask another question as to the relation of thought and things. When and where in experience does intelligibility begin? Are we to regard intelligibility as something impressed on things by the action of the mind? Does mind constitute objects? Of course, if objects are to be intelligible, they must conform to the nature of the intelligence which apprehends them. But is the intelligibility conferred on the object, or is it to be supposed intelligible in itself? Are objects really what Hume—and in this Kant seems to be at one with him—calls independent facts, and are events really disconnected which are outwardly and contingently gathered together in our minds by purely mental relations? Kant did in his philosophy show that the Nature known by us as knowable is systematic, and finally came to the conclusion that this systematic character is analogous to the unity of self-consciousness. But consistent thinking leads us back to the conception that this systematic character of Nature is not conferred on it by us, that, in fact, it is implicit in the earliest experience of rational beings; and the business of our thinking is to make explicit what is implicit there, and to articulate in detail what is inchoately present at the beginning.

And yet, while we regard as true the relation of thought to an intelligible world, it must not be supposed that the world of thought and the systematic world discovered by it are identical. Nor can we suppose that the two are so connected that the analysis of thought and its action will give us the real world. While thinking is a real factor in the making of the world, as we know it, it does not follow that the real world is one thing when real thinking begins, and another when it ends. For us, as thinkers and actors, it is so, and the reality for us expands with its explanation, and, through the operations of thought in the processes of conceiving, judging, inferring, the indefinite becomes definite, and the vague contents of first impressions are articulated into a systematic whole, and differences are held together in a unity which contains and explains them, and so for us the world is made. Yet the law of gravitation was at work before Newton formulated the law of inverse squares, and the conservation of energy was a law of things before Joule made his experiments and expounded its meaning.

It is not possible, then, to identify the movements of the world, or the succession of events, with the dialectical movements of our thoughts. Yet the latter may render explicit what lies before us in the world of mere concrete experience. It is necessary for the philosophy of the present time to go further back in its analysis than where Kant began, and to show that the world of ideas into which thought has gathered its experience had relations with fact long before reflexion began, and that the difference between sense and understanding, between fact and truth—in whatever way we put this ever-recurring contrariety—is less absolute than empiricism has supposed. The correspondence between the perceptual and the conceptual worlds is closer than has been supposed. As we have already said, percepts are a product of the activity of thought, and concepts are in touch with perceptual reality. The processes which we may describe in our text-books as if they were separate and in isolation are, after all, continuous, and are put into operation as the mind in interaction with its objects comes to self-realization.

We must, then, set aside the assumption that knowledge begins with a series of subjective states, and from these strives to reach a world beyond itself. Subjective states as such are never present without some objective reference, whatever that reference may be. Even feeling, which has been described as subjectively subjective, has in it a content which cannot be explained without a reference which leads beyond that state considered in itself. Pleasure and pain, though subjective states, have an objective reference. More clearly is this true of the states of consciousness which we describe as conation and cognition. These have objects, desires, aims, purposes; and they reach forth towards their objects. Thus we are justified, from the psychological point of view, in saying that there are objective and subjective elements in the simplest cognition. All the changing states of consciousness have objective references, which may be described as both subjective and objective; and the process of thinking is just the articulation of these correlated elements into the fabric of our thought, whether that thought is occupied with the analysis of itself, or with the body of knowledge which is the full possession of mankind. Thus we seek to advance from thought to things, not from things to thought; these are together at the outset of cognition, and full cognition ideally realizes them as one. Instead of holding that thought determines reality, it would be better to say that reality determines our thought, and that, when reflexion uses the apparatus of notion, judgment, and reasoning, it is guided by principles which are true of reality as well as characteristic of thought.

More especially it may be affirmed that the aim of the mind in its judgments is always objective. It seeks universality and necessity, and strives to connect together what belongs together. But there is a distinction in its procedure, which marks also a distinction in the form of judgment. There are judgments which involve the constraint of belief, or active endorsement and acknowledgment. There are judgments which are attended by active belief, and with the conviction that it is impossible not to believe. This attitude of genuine belief, of acceptance, of control over the mind, is characteristic of certain judgments. Here the mind is in an attitude of certainty; it knows, and can act on the assurance that this judgment is true. But there are judgments which seem only probable. Here the mind is in a state of suspense; it questions, assumes, and comes to a conclusion from which it withholds that position of certainty which in other situations it asserts. It is not possible here to enter fully into the positions of those who have been called lately the Austrian school, or to dwell on the suggestive work of Meinong and others. (As to the meaning of assumption, see Meinong, *Über Annahmen* [1910], and Baldwin, *Genetic Logic.*) It is sufficient to say that judgment, when it coerces belief, is always, or is always regarded as, of objective reality and validity. It regards itself as true, and as valid in the sphere of fact.

12. Connectedness of objects of thought: significance of mathematics for Epistemology.—We come now to what we stated to be the third mark of true knowledge—the assumption of connectedness among the objects of our thought. That there is such a connectedness, which we do not make but discover, we regard almost as axiomatic. What the connectedness really is has to be discovered in every case. The postulate of the mind is that there is a connectedness; this is its formal attitude in relation to all the objects of its knowledge. With regard to things, it postulates the relation of cause and effect, and other universal axioms which it regards as necessary. No doubt there has always been a tendency to press universality and necessity in their abstract form to extremes, and to bind all experience into these unities of abstract thinking. As an illustration of this, we may instance the tendency to make that necessity, of which mathematics may be cited as the symbol, the type and norm of all experience. We see this tendency at work in the attempt to reduce all the sciences to a mathematical form, and in particular to reduce biological problems to physical and chemical terms.

Yet, after all, the study of the history of mathematics, especially in some of its more recent developments, is not without interest to the student of the theory of knowledge. In his *Prolegomena to all Future Metaphysic*, Kant asks the questions, 'How is pure mathematics possible? How is pure science possible? and How is pure metaphysic possible?' He thought he had established the validity of the mathematical sciences by showing that they are confined to phenomena, and do not apply to things-in-themselves. In mathematical science the mind is in contact with things which may be regarded as constructed by the mind itself, and the knowledge of such things does not apply to things-in-themselves. Whether this really involves the doctrine of the relativity of knowledge and of the unknowable we do not stay to inquire. Our present aim is to look at mathematics and physical science generally, in the interest of Epistemology. For in mathematics we may distinguish between the thinker and his thought, as we do in other branches of science. We may look at science from the point of view of a record of the mind that thinks, relates, elaborates, and as a record of the inter-relations of the facts of Nature as these are understood and interpreted. It has been held that in mathematics the mind is creative, that it has made the facts with which it deals, and that in this sphere there is no difference between mathematical science and mathematical thought. We make our definitions, we state our axioms, we claim our postulates, we have our intuitions; and, reasoning from these, we have framed our geometry, elaborated our algebra, and constructed our calculuses. In this sphere, at all events, it is claimed that the mind has constructed its objects, and has not only constructed them, but has also called them into being. But it has to be borne in mind —and here the pragmatist has something to say which is relevant—that geometry, algebra, and all the other branches of mathematical science have arisen in response to the demand of practical need. Geometry arose to meet the demands of land-measurement, and algebra arose simply as an extension of arithmetic. These sciences arose out of practice, and even in its highest forms mathematics may be viewed as a measuring and calculating instrument invented by the mind in its desire to make Nature subservient to its own purpose. There are those who regard this as the main interest of mathematics, and there are others who regard mathematics as the type of true knowledge. The latter look at the applications of mathematics as of interest only in so far as they suggest problems in pure mathematics. They are inclined to think that all the sciences remain imperfect and crude until they have come under the mathematical yoke and submitted themselves to its rule and method. But the ultimate question in Epistemology is, Does thought determine reality, or does reality determine thought, or what is the relation between thought and reality? Granted that mathematics is so far a mental product, in fact much more a mental product than the more concrete sciences are, still we may ask, What is the relation of the constructive mind to the science which it has constructed?

If we go back to the first beginnings of mathematical science, we find that it grew out of practical need. It was an instrument made for the overcoming of Nature. Man had to master his environment, and in the struggle he came to those constructions which we find used as a means for measuring and counting. But, when man drew his first circle or saw the mystery of parallel lines, a new view burst upon him. The figures became something in themselves and to be studied for their own sake; so we find various demonstrations discovered by many thinkers, various problems solved, until at length Euclid gathered the geometrical science of his time into that book which still remains the foundation of geometrical science. We find men also studying the various properties of the sections of the cone, and setting them forth, largely for practical use, but also with a desire to know all the possible meanings of the construction which they themselves have made. Numbers were useful for counting, but their characteristic features were themselves the object of abiding interest. So it has been through all the history of mathematical science and mathematical thought. Mathematical formulæ may be regarded as concepts, and they play the part in mathematical thinking which concepts play in other thinking. But the meaning and scope of concepts or of mathematical formulæ, and their worth and validity, are things not given when they are formed. In both cases the intent and meaning are the objects of endless research. Thus we find, throughout the ages, those thinkers to whom mathematical thoughts owe their advance towards systematic coherence occupied with examining and strengthening the foundations of mathematical reasoning, purifying its methods, submitting them to proofs ever increasing in rigour, and putting to stringent tests the scope and range of current conceptions. Geometry by itself made progress, algebra by itself became more and more comprehensive and thorough; and, by their union in the hand of Descartes and their cross-fertilization, a new era in mathematical science began. Analytical geometry arose, and out of it sprang the calculus. Here, too, men were occupied with the meaning of the new formulæ which they had invented. For a new formula, though the work of mind, obtains an objective value as soon as it is formulated. Mathematicians had to study their own formulæ, to follow out their implications, and they were often surprised at the new and strange worlds which opened out to their investigation. For the new formulæ not only solved old questions, but opened up new problems to solve. Analytical geometry advanced; and, were we writing on mathematics, we should see how geometry also responded on its part, and learned a method of a breadth and generality similar to those at the command of the analytic method. A new geometry arose, beautiful in itself, and useful as the test and illustration of the more abstract method of analysis. The significance of this growth is that here we see how the product of thought becomes in turn the object of thought, and also how concepts may become enlarged and purified, and be made more universal and more particular by the exercise of that thinking power which first constructed them. This is one feature of the epistemological value of mathematics.

But there is another aspect equally significant. Mathematical formulæ, as we saw, arose out of practical need, and were invented in order to obtain control over Nature. Equally every new departure and every extension of mathematical formulæ were dictated by practical need, and their validity was tested by ability to solve the problems which were presented to men by the practical difficulties they encountered in the course of their widening experience. On the one hand, men strove to make their formulæ more consistent, more logical, more flexible, and more comprehensive; and, on the other hand, they applied them to the solution of practical problems. We may note here the great advance which Newton made by the conception of fluxions—a new conception, by the use of which he passed beyond the static world of concepts, in which every concept was regarded as eternally one and the same, to a world of motion, of change, of continuity. Even change had been regarded before him as discrete, discontinuous, made up of steps, each step being regarded as equal to another. By the use of the concept of fluxions Newton enabled mathematics to accommodate itself to the notion of continuous change.

'All applications of mathematics consist in extending the empirical knowledge which we possess of a limited number or region of accessible phenomena into the region of the unknown and inaccessible: and much of the progress of pure analysis consists in inventing definite conceptions, marked by symbols of complicated operations; in ascertaining their properties as independent objects of research; and in extending their meaning beyond the limits they were originally invented for,—thus opening out new and larger regions of thought. A brilliant and most suggestive example of this kind of reasoning was afforded by a novel mode of treating a large class of physical problems by means of the introduction of a special mathematical function, termed by George Green, and later by Gauss, the "Potential" or "Potential Function." All the problems of Newtonian attraction were concentrated in the study of this formula: and when the experiments of Coulomb and Ampère showed the analogy that existed between electric and magnetic forces on the one side, and Newtonian forces on the other; still more when Fourier, Lamé, and Thomson (Lord Kelvin) pointed to the further analogy which existed between the distribution of temperature in the stationary flow of heat and that of statical electricity on a conductor, and extended the analogy to hydrostatics and hydrodynamics,—it became evident that Nature herself pointed here to a mathematical dependence of the highest interest and value' (Merz, *History of European Thought in the Nineteenth Century*, ii. 698 f.).

We might give many instances of the advance of mathematical thought, and note how, as knowledge widened, new problems arose, and, as they arose, new inventions or modifications of old methods were made in order to grapple with them. Our present interest is not, however, in the development of mathematical thought, but in the light which that development casts on Epistemology. That interest may be illustrated by the concluding phrase of the foregoing quotation: 'Nature herself pointed here to a mathematical dependence of the highest interest and value.' Mathematical formulæ have an interest in themselves as products of thought—a world in themselves, self-contained—and they can be exhibited as logical illustrations of consistent thinking. But they have a deeper interest in the fact that they represent the actual, and are interpretative of a real world beyond themselves. The mind is interested in its own work, and seeks to understand it; but it is more deeply interested in the world, and ever desires to direct its attention to those hints which Nature herself points out. With this view Science is ever ready to modify her conceptions, to discard her notions which have proved inadequate, to revise and subject to criticism every concept which is found unfit to follow the intimations of Nature. All mathematical formulæ may be regarded as concepts, and the way in which mathematics is ever revising her concepts gives a useful lesson to thinkers on other spheres of knowledge, no longer to regard their concepts as fixed, unchangeable, eternally the same, but fluid, ever ready to adapt themselves to fresh problems. Abundant illustrations might be given of the way in which mathematics is ever modifying, changing, enlarging her concepts, but these may be taken for granted here. Still more striking illustrations might be derived from the history of physics and chemistry in recent years. If a student of these sciences fifty years ago, familiar with the language of text-books at that period, were to open a text-book written at the present day, he would find that he had to learn a new language and furnish himself with a new set of concepts. The latter we need not enumerate, for the fact is obvious to every student. What is insisted on here, in the light of recent physics and chemistry, is the lesson they teach us with regard to the epistemological problem. Here at least concepts are not regarded as of fixed, unchangeable content. We may note also how mathematics strives to recognize the ever-changing flexibility of Nature and the subtle flow of reality; and the progress of this science has been from the static and the fixed to the variety and the flexibility which in its way seeks to correspond with the manifoldness of Nature. So also in chemistry, and in physical chemistry—a new science made by the cross-fertilization of physics and chemistry.

The lesson is that concepts are not fixed, unchangeable, and static, but that they are, or ought to be, as definite, yet as fluid, as the world they deal with. But, if the identical meaning and fixed content which have been characteristic of a concept persist and cannot be changed, then we let it remain to characterize a certain meaning interesting in the history of thought; and for the new meaning a new term is found, fit to express it. What we learn from the story of science and its practice is that our concepts ought ever to be in active commerce with the widening experience of man, and must always be held in subjection to that experience. We are not to pour Nature into the mould of our concepts, and regard them as the measure of the possible and the limit of what is actual; rather are we to regard our concepts as tentative, as attempts to gather into a convenient form what we have already learnt from the indications of Nature as to its own meaning. We learn from mathematics that it is possible to construct a world of logical consistency and logical meaning worthy of the highest admiration for its symmetry and beauty, but we learn also that this mathematical world by no means gives us that particular world in which we dwell, and which we must learn to know. The mathematical world is consistent with many kinds of worlds, whereas ours is a particular world, and has its own character and meaning. No doubt it is consistent with the mathematical world, which is a comfort. Yet the very triumph of mathematical science points out its limitations. Is there a knowledge which is not mathematical? In other words, are there realities which cannot be counted, measured, weighed? If there are, and if these are such as can somehow be known, clearly we are in a sphere in which mathematical reasoning is inept. Even in the spheres in which mathematical reasoning has been so triumphant, it is found, as in physics, that the changes in Nature depend not so much on the quantity of mass and energy as on their distribution and arrangement. While there are thus truths of reason which are valid for all objects, whatsoever they may be, and while there are what we call laws of Nature, valid for the physical world in which we live, there are actual facts of collocation and facts of distribution and arrangement which cannot be deduced from the necessities of reason, or from the laws of Nature; these have to be ascertained. Any fact is consistent with the laws of Nature and with the ideas of reason, but what the fact is must be otherwise discerned than by deductive compulsion. Concepts, as we say, are and must be subject to constant revision; but, revise them as we may, there are many things and experiences which escape their grasp.

13. Limits of mathematical thought.—Mathematical science has, therefore, its limits; experience is not to be measured by them, however great and far-reaching they may be. Dissatisfaction with mathematics, physics, and chemistry, as the norm and measure of experience, has been variously expressed. For instance, Baldwin gives energetic expression to his dissatisfaction in the following note:

'The essential requirement, I take it, if one would accustom oneself to thinking in genetic terms, is that one free himself from the compulsion of the mechanical and a-genetic concept of causation. We have all been hypnotized by the thought of cause of the type of impact, transfer of energy fixed in quantity, with a formulation of effect in terms of an equation with composition of forces issuing in a resultant—as in the "parallelogram of forces." We are told that nothing can be in the effect that is not already in the cause. All this is a partial and forced interpretation of nature. If science deals only with such causation series, then the great body of what we may in the large sense call "conditioning," or "sequence," remains uninterpreted. The Adaptations, Growths, Novelties, in nature are as much in evidence to the scientific observer as are the Identities, Conservations, and Effects. Why may not the subsequent term of a sequence have something in it not already present in the antecedent term? It usually does. The causal interpretation commonly gives an abstract meaning reached by excluding certain phases or characters of the event called the effect. The genetic progression recognizes *all the characters* of the event, allows the causal interpretation as an abstraction, but attempts to reconstitute nature in the fullness of her processes of change from the mode that conditions to the richer mode—be it what it may—that succeeds' (*op. cit.* i. 25, note).

The protest is emphatic enough, but it might have been accompanied by a recognition of what has been accomplished by the assumptions it criticizes. By the use of mathematical formulæ, by the study of physics and chemistry, by the evolution of mathematical thought, science has penetrated far into the arcana of Nature. Assuming, as it did, that there were an order and arrangement to be found out in Nature, science, by inventing mathematical formulæ ever more comprehensive and more subtle, was able not only to set forth the more conspicuous elements of the natural order, but to set it forth in its continuity, and in so doing advanced towards the conception of unity. These mathematical formulæ also raised fresh problems, which, in being solved, led to interpretations of natural phenomena the existence of which lay far beyond the unaided vision of man. So the content of knowledge, the control of Nature by knowledge, and the validity of knowledge as illustrated by its practical verification have been abundantly justified by the sciences. Yet mathematical science has its limitations as well as its temptations. Its very success as an instrument for the enlargement of knowledge within its own sphere led to that abuse against which Baldwin has protested so emphatically. It is limited, we again say, to what can be numbered, weighed, and measured. But there is valid knowledge of what cannot be dealt with in these ways. Still further, those things which lend themselves to mathematical treatment can be set forth as externally related to each other. They act and react on each other, and influence each other in ways that can be measured. They attract or they resist each other, and then behave as if all that is characteristic of them could be summed up in a statement of their external relations. From the point of view of physics the world is made up of matter, of energy, and so on. Individuality does not appear in the world of physics. Rudiments of it begin to appear in the fact that one chemical element will combine with others only on its own terms, and from the facts of crystallization. But mathematical science becomes helpless when anything like true individuality begins. Given a thing with an inner nature of its own, with predilections, or with anything which would make it something for itself, and then we need concepts for its description which pass beyond mathematical formulæ. Science abundantly recognizes this; but, when it does, it ceases to be quantitative and becomes qualitative. It is no longer a science of magnitudes, it deals with qualities, which are quite beyond the scales of magnitude. For not only can science deal with the great generalizations like the laws of gravitation, conservation of energy, and the like, it can also recognize the uniqueness of the unique, the particularity of the particular. There is a process of scientific thought which passes from the general to that which appears only once, and to events which occur only once and never again.

14. The determinant and the teleological judgment.—But these particular events and singular occurrences require to be described, description needs language, and language is conceptual. True, but there are conceptions and conceptions, and the mind is flexible enough to coin new concepts to express its new experiences. So it is when we pass from the inorganic world to a world which presents us with objects which cannot be fully described from an external point of view, to those which have a meaning within themselves and cannot be explained as mere points in a system of forces. We may deal competently with physical masses when we regard the mass as concentrated at the centre of gravity; we can deal with chemistry as a system of combining weight, and from other abstract points of view; but when we deal with living matter we are in a world of peculiar actions and reactions, which cannot be stated in terms of attraction and resistance. So we have here to ask a different question. Kant asked, How is science possible?, and he gave his characteristic answer, which had regard both to mathematics and to physical science. We have to ask, How is biology possible? Here, too, the formal answer of Kant as to the function of the mind may be carried over without differentiation. For the attitude of mind is the same towards all its knowledge. The difference between the physical and the biological sciences is determined not by the character of the subject but by the character of the object. So in biological sciences we have to use not the determinant judgment but the teleological. In this sphere we have quite a different series of reactions, and we have to change our method and our nomenclature accordingly. For now we have something which can be called selections, choices, adaptations to environment, growths, changes along definite lines; and we must construct suitable concepts for their expression. Yet men are unwilling to take the trouble, or to yield up the control which the use of quantitative concepts apparently gave them over the world to which they were applied. Hence we have had the extension of mathematical and physical formulæ to cover the field of life. Biological phenomena were attenuated till they were brought under the formulæ of mathematics, physics, and chemistry. No doubt this attempt was so far a just one, because living forms, so far as they are quantitative, are subject to measurement, and are, therefore, fit subjects for mathematical analysis. What cannot be mathematically analyzed are simply the internal states even of the protozoa. If a thing has an inside, and its relation to other things in space is not determined merely by its outside, then that relation must, if it is to be adequately described, take into account the inside as well as the outside. But that means a new calculus, a new set of concepts, and one does not see why science should not set itself, without prejudice, to make concepts fitted to express the new relations. It is interesting to quote in this connexion the following distinction drawn by Paulsen:

'It is worthy of note that a peculiar relation exists between our external or phenomenal knowledge and our understanding of phenomena which rests on interpretation. We may express it in the form of a paradox: *The better we conceive things the less we understand them*, and conversely. We conceive the inorganic processes best, that is, we can define them so accurately as to make them calculable. The vital processes are not so easily reduced to conceptual mathematical formulæ and calculation. Biology works with empirical laws altogether, the complete reduction of which to ultimate elementary laws of Nature has so far proved to be impossible. Man is the most incalculable being in existence. Hence it is that his acts are still regarded as absolutely indeterminate, or as the effects of an indeterminate agent, the so-called free will, which is simply equivalent to denying the possibility of conceiving or defining him. The reverse is true when it comes to understanding. Human life is the only thing that we understand perfectly. We reach the maximum of understanding in history: it is less complete in zoology and botany, and vanishes altogether in physics and astronomy, where we have the most perfect mathematical conception of things' (*Introd. to Philosophy*, Eng. tr., 373 f.).

15. 'Begreifen' and 'Verstehen.'—Paulsen's distinction between *Begreifen* and *Verstehen*, as thus set forth, is an interesting one, and may be regarded as both useful and convenient, from a popular point of view. But it is difficult to make the distinction good from a logical, a psychological, or an epistemological point of view. For, in the first place, what he regards as 'understanding' and as 'conceiving' are both mental processes, and are both the work of mind; and the distinction between them is one not of kind but of degree. In the second place, mathematics and physics, and especially chemistry, are not sciences which depend on calculation alone. Both physics and chemistry are experimental sciences, and, so far as they are experimental, they belong to what Paulsen calls 'understanding.' No physicist would limit his knowledge of any substance merely to what he can calculate about it. He feels he knows radium in its particularity, and is face to face with it as a real thing. He conceives it, and he understands it in its nature and in its behaviour. So here the distinction is inept. In the third place, when he says that man is the most incalculable being in existence, and refers to free will, one would like to know what is his view of free will. To be fair, he does not say that he holds that view of free will which he describes in the passage. But he so far identifies himself with that indeterminate view as to use it as an element in the position that man cannot possibly be conceived or defined. Is man intelligible? Can a doctrine of freedom be intelligibly set forth, and used as a principle of explanation in a description of man? We submit that all that can be inferred from the distinction between *Begreifen* and *Verstehen* is that mathematical, physical, and chemical concepts have their limits, and have to give place to other concepts when we pass from the physical sphere to the sphere where quantity ceases to obtain, and quality takes its place.

So, then, when we strive to obtain controlling knowledge of beings which are something for themselves and cannot be set forth merely in relation to other things in a world in space and time, we have to change our mode of conceiving them in order to suit the altered circumstances. The determinant judgment must give place to the teleological. We have to conceive a kingdom of means and ends, of things inter-related with a view towards a purpose. A new form of causation or linkage must be found. And the new concepts are forthcoming if only they have fair play. Final causes may be sneered at as vestal virgins, and may be discredited from many points of view, yet in modern times teleology has come to its own. The theory of evolution, and all that it implies, has reinstated purpose as the ruling idea of modern thought; and in all spheres of inquiry we have learned to value history as the key to the explanation of the world of external things. Evolution makes room for novelties, for something in the effect which was not in the cause, and we have to alter our conceptions to make them fit the facts. The processes of the world are not repetitions of former happenings; they are growths, developments, evolutions; and the growths are intelligible and may be stated in terms which may be understood.

16. Objects as linked together by the teleological judgment.—Our Logic, Psychology, Epistemology, must be made flexible enough to meet the new situation. Not that the situation is new in reality, for the processes of evolution have gone on from the beginning; only men had changed the flowing, growing, evolving world into a static world which could be calculated in numbers, weights, and measures. Now that we have come to a better understanding of the world, let us alter our formulæ to correspond. In seeking to do so, we may not cast all the blame of former failures on our conceptual modes of thought. For we have no other means of thinking than by concepts, and our vigilance ought to be directed towards the endeavour to make them adequate to their task. This can be done by the recognition of the differences between the objects which we think about, and by the recognition of the fact that notions fitting and adequate in one sphere are not applicable to others with different qualities and characteristics. For example, a little ago, we spoke of order, continuity, and unity as notions which have a meaning within physical science. In physics, however, order may mean nothing more than arrangement, but in the biological sciences, and especially in the sciences which deal with man, order means something more: *e.g.* when we speak of the social order, where the conception is bound up with the highest social, ethical, and religious interests. Continuity has also to take on a larger meaning, as the subject with which it deals becomes more complex. For here it is not the continuity of cause and effect, nor is it the linkage of mere sequence; we have to think of continuity as constituted by a purpose which seems to gather the contingent into something which gives it a reasonable meaning. So also with unity and with individuality. In truth it is only when we come to the action of life, only when we study things that have an inside, that we can attach a definite meaning to individuality. There is a certain indefinite nuance of individuality attached to an atom of matter, but then its individuality is limited by the fact of its inertia: it moves only as it is moved. It has its attractions and its repulsions, but it moves in response to them without any hesitation or choice. In living matter the response seems to be of a different kind; the organism responds according to its own nature. As we ascend the scale of organization, individuality receives wider and more precise meanings until it becomes personality, of which we cannot speak now. In living creatures we do not speak of inertia, but of self-preservation—a very different conception. We can speak also of reproduction, and of heredity, and of those sentiments which seem to lie at the basis, or to accompany the fact, of self-preservation—of love, and hunger, which assume deeper and deeper meanings as the human race moves onward to higher progress.

This does not mean, therefore, that, when we pass from the sciences which are mainly occupied with inorganic matter, we are to do without concepts; it means only that we must form our concepts fitly to represent the new facts. It is essential to hold that new concepts may be formed, or old concepts may be modified, and that new ideas may be evolved to meet the new needs. But with regard to these concepts, the laws of reason and the principles of Logic still hold good; only we may regard them as outside the scope of quantitative measurement. That is simply to say that sentiments are not to be calculated in foot-pounds, and that we do not measure love by the yard. It may be measured in intensity, if not in extensity. There is needed a treatise to deal with the teleological judgment, which will place it on the same level as the determinant judgment. It is not enough to regard the determinant judgment as the type of judgment in general, and to place it on a platform of its own, as the only form of universal and necessary implication, and to regard the teleological judgment as merely empirical. This was the way of Kant. But it may be doubted whether the distinction between empiricism and idealism is as absolute as it has been assumed to be. If there is an order of the world, if that order can be understood, and if there are principles of arrangement in the world, then it may be postulated that the empirical order is also rational; and the judgments which have been regarded as purely empirical may also have a meaning in relation to the ideas of reason. That is too large a question to be discussed here. But, if the assumption of idealism that the real is the rational has any truth in it, then the distinction between empiricism and rationalism tends to disappear. What is empirically true may not be rationally false. Mathematics has shown us that facts and relations experimentally discovered may, with proper assumptions, be expressed with the utmost generality and necessity. Faraday's electric discoveries were mathematically explained by Clerk-Maxwell, and his mathematical formulæ were physically verified by Hertz, and applied to practical uses by Marconi.

17. Relation of the determinant to the teleological judgment.—This may be variously illustrated. Indeed, so copious are the sources of illustration that we are at a loss which to select. They are not opposed to each other. Rather the relation is that the teleological judgment steps in to afford an explanation where the determinant judgment ceases to be intelligible. The teleological presupposes the determinant judgment. In the case of the latter we are occupied with the understanding of things as they are—their nature, their modes of action, their inter-relations, and so on; but when these are so far understood, we are prepared for a new kind of action. Just in proportion to our knowledge of things as they are, are we able to impress new meanings on them, and make them subservient to our purposes. We investigate Nature, and transform it into our sciences of astronomy, dynamics, physics, and chemistry; or we measure and calculate heat, light, electricity; and, having so far mastered these, we proceed to new constructions, the explanation of which is not found in the abstract sciences, but in their applications. It is here that teleology begins, and it has a place in the theory of knowledge, not merely on empirical but also on other grounds. The whole system of efficient causes is implied in every machine, in every work of art, and in every construction which man has impressed on Nature. So we mould, alter, control Nature, and make her do our will; and she lends herself to the expression of new meanings which have been impressed on her former system of working. We make our harbours, build our ships, construct our roads and railroads, invent all the instruments of peace and war, sow and reap and gather into barns, build our houses, and plan cities; beyond these, we have our arts and sciences, our poetries and philosophies, and we seek to set forth our relations to the unseen powers on which we depend; and in all these efforts of man the distinguishing and guiding principle is the teleological judgment. The assumption is that Nature makes room for us and for our efforts, does not resent our attempts to mould her to new meanings, or refuse to carry out our purpose, when we ask her intelligently to do so. A machine is a new meaning impressed on Nature, in order that man may do his work. It is possible to explain a steam-engine as a system of mechanical forces; or we may write a history of its invention, and trace the course of its evolution from the kettle of Watt to the engines which drive Atlantic liners across the sea. In this history no mention need be made of the minds which successively made those changes which increased the complexity, efficiency, and usefulness of the steam-engine. But every step of the process, looked at from another point of view, illustrates the action of the teleological judgment. Applied science is always teleological. Machines are constructions with a meaning which goes beyond the machine regarded only as a mechanical construction. The meaning is impressed on a system of efficient causes, in order to make it work out a purpose. Thus in the case of any machine we pass beyond the sequence of cause and effect, and beyond the linkage of mechanical explanation; we are in the presence of things of another kind—things which require new concepts for their description and interpretation.

18. Validity of teleological knowledge.—Here, too, we may instance something which is of significance for knowledge. We may recognize that there is a valid knowledge of the individual. Individuality is a valid concept, though in our logical and psychological systems there is apparently no room left for it. Psychology tells us formally that it has no place for biography; and Logic tends, on almost every scheme, to pass away from what it calls the mere individual. But, on any theory of knowledge, room must be left for the idiosyncrasies of the individual. Surely a biography may be written, and may contain true and adequate knowledge, and there may be a description of the uniqueness of the unique. Hamlet and Macbeth have been described, and attempts have been made to understand Julius Cæsar and Napoleon; nor have Plato, Aristotle, Kant, and Hegel been set aside as unintelligible, though all of them have risen above the commonplace; and we still seek to comprehend the great poets, not by subsuming them under general categories, but by diligently studying them in the circumstances of their life. We place such men under the subsumptions of the teleological judgment, with its categories of purpose and freedom; we find room for the study of individuality and personality as something which really appears in the world of phenomena.

But it is in the biological sciences that the teleological judgment is conspicuously present. Here the categories of unity, individuality, purpose, come into view. An organism cannot be defined without implicating all these at least. We cannot describe an organism without the recognition of it as a whole. Nor can we describe any organ in it without the implication that the organ has a meaning only in relation to the whole organism. We may, for descriptive purposes, reduce the phenomena of an organism to a number of systems, such as the circulatory, the muscular, etc.; but, after this description, we have to go back to the recognition of the organism as a living system, all the parts of which are in relation to the whole, and the whole is realized through the inter-relations of the parts. Still further, there is the fact that for the understanding of the organism the principle of unity and of action is within it. It has an inside. It is an old observation, 'Plant the skill of the shipbuilder within the timber, and you will see how Nature works.' The skill of the shipbuilder is within the timber in the case of every organism. This conclusion has been forced on us more and more ever since the epoch-making work of Darwin. It is not necessary to point out how, even contrary to the tendency of Darwin himself, teleology has been enthroned in the highest place in the sciences which deal with life, and Epistemology recognizes the significance of the concept, and has to make room for it. In every organism considered in its individuality, in every species considered as a concept descriptive of a certain kind, in the slow process of the evolution of living forms, we have been taught to see, in the growth of living things, a tendency towards a goal, a means towards an end; and this tendency has all the system of efficient causes at its service. It is not necessary to dwell further on the story of evolution as it is told to us at present; the great epistemological interest of it lies in the fact that a new set of concepts is at the service of the theory of knowledge—concepts which have the merit of recognizing a sphere of knowledge and of action, which had been inadequately recognized in our logical and psychological inquiries. A study of the theory of evolution and its procedure will yield fruitful results for Epistemology.

19. Criticism of the teleological judgment.—A critical inquiry into the teleological judgment would necessitate, in the first place, an investigation into the psychological conditions of its exercise, and, in the second place, an inquiry into the objective products which are the outcome of that exercise. Psychologically, we should need to investigate the whole field of purpose, the phenomena of means and ends, the fact of aim and desire, the power of forming ideals, and the means at our disposal in order to carry them out. For it is indisputable, it is, indeed, a fact of common experience, that living creatures have some power of using Nature for their own ends. It is a fact that rational creatures have a certain power of self-guidance, and of modifying Nature, and of making Nature subserve their ends. They sow and reap, they can use the changing of the seasons in order to store up food for future need, they can adapt themselves to their environment, not merely by organic modifications as lower animals do, but by adapting the environment to their needs. They clothe themselves in heavier raiment when the seasons change, they build houses, they seek their food, and everywhere in human life we see men moulding Nature in order to make life more easy, more comfortable, and more successful. We need not dwell on the fact of the teleological process; it is manifest. It is one element in adaptation, and it is thus a proof of the validity of the scheme of means and ends which is characteristic of life in general.

In the second place, a critical analysis of the teleological judgment would lead us into the objective investigation of all the works of man. These, again, are of the most important kind for the purpose of Epistemology. We might look at these works of humanity from various points of view. We might look at them as bodies of truth, and seek to test their scientific value. We might regard them from the point of view of description, and set them forth in that descriptive process which is another name for explanation. Or we might seek to appreciate them, to estimate their worth, and their æsthetic, logical, psychological, and metaphysical values. But, from our present point of view, our aim is to regard them as a set of human ideals concretely realized in the art, the science, the poetry, the philosophy, and the religion of mankind. Teleology would thus become a history of the ideals of mankind, as these are embodied in the history of literature, to use a comprehensive word which includes all the works of man enumerated above. Teleology studied in this comprehensive sense would give us most valuable material for a complete view of human knowledge, and would set us free from the tyranny of mere science, with its exclusiveness and its incompleteness. It would enable us to set its proper value on history as the supreme record of human endeavour, and to realize from a new point of view that distinction which Paulsen sought to establish in the quotation already made. The study of ideals, as these have been objectively realized in the life of a people, as realized in art, in sculpture, and in painting, as realized in the great poets of the world, as also in the philosophies of all nations, would open out to us the objective realizations of the teleological processes of the human mind and their several worths.

20. Teleology and ideals.—The power to frame ideals, and to appreciate them when they are set before us, is one of the characteristics of man. If this be so, then there must be some way of setting forth the procedure of the mind in the formation of ideals, and some way by which their validity and influence may be tested. This involves an investigation into the whole subject—an investigation which can hardly be said to have begun. For it would mean an investigation into the whole of human creations, as these are embodied in institutions, constitutions, political activities, national characteristics, and international influences. All these may be regarded as embodiments of characteristic ideals, and their sources and influences would have to be considered. Again, art, science, poetry, literature—in fact, all the achievements of man in the world he has made—would have a place in the great analysis of ideals, their nature and influence. Out of this investigation there would issue a new set of concepts, to describe the experience of mankind in this relation, to supplement and correct, or at least to modify, conclusions drawn from the system derived from man's primary intercourse with the world around him. Here, then, there may be great gain for the theory and nature of knowledge, if one could only find a way to utilize it. It is the glory of ideals to be great and broad and comprehensive, too rich and full to be the same to all, too wide to be realized in any single form or mode. Take the ideal in any sphere of human aspiration—architecture, for example—and we find it to be made up of certain qualities, none of which can be neglected in any building worthy of the name—qualities such as strength, beauty, dignity, fitness, durability. Each of these may be realized in different ways: there may be many varieties of architecture. But each style has its ideal; architects have their visions, and they have examples in which former ideals have been realized; and so, out of the grandeur of their vision, and out of the fullness of their knowledge, they build, and the building remains an illustration of the working out of an ideal. So in art we may make a study of the vision which the artist saw, examine the way in which he realized his vision in the concrete form of painting or of statue, and note the limitations and restrictions laid on him by the material in which he has worked. So also in poetry, and in literature generally, we may trace the sources of the ideal; we may note how it grew, what it fed on, and how it was realized; and we may be persuaded that in these investigations we have a real illustration of the growth and law of human knowledge. Here we are delivered so far from the bondage of the actual. We are in a sphere where the human mind, master of its own experience, or so far master of it, sets itself to embody its own meaning and its own vision in a real objective form, so that it is no longer a private meaning, but one that can be the common possession of all men. This translation of a private, individual vision into forms which become a common possession is one of the characteristic ways of human achievement, and one of the ways of raising men to a higher level. We may study the work of the great masters in painting, sculpture, architecture, poetry, science, metaphysic, and in the study of them learn a lesson in the characteristics of what knowledge is and means, which we could never learn from the abstract discussions by which men have sought to delimit knowledge, and to assign to it bounds beyond which it cannot pass. Here, too, we may study in concrete form that great subject of individuality and personality which eludes the analysis of discursive thought. We may allow Psychology to occupy the place of the abstract spectator, and to say that Psychology is not biography; we may allow Logic to lay down the conditions of thought, and to elaborate the categories under which all fruitful thinking is to be conducted; and we may allow Metaphysics to deal with the ultimate problems of reality, and need not refuse generous recognition of their validity and worth, and yet claim that in the work of men there are revealed principles of thought and action and fields of knowledge of which they take but little cognizance. For there is real knowledge in this sphere, which all must recognize as real.

In this sphere we are not independent of Psychology, Logic, Metaphysics, or Ethics. For these supply the principles upon which our study of the achievements of men must proceed. In all our actions we must be logical, psychological, metaphysical, and even mathematical; but the sciences mentioned do no more than prescribe the conditions under which we work; they do not fix the vision which the seer sees or the ideal which he seeks to realize. In order to understand the vision, we must postulate the man who sees, and the mind which has been in the presence of the ideal. But the vision has been seen, the ideal has been set forth, and these are as much facts as are the facts of physical or chemical science, and as such they may be known and set forth in practice. Here, too, we may study the activity of man in its creative aspects, and note the conditions under which such activity is possible, for it works under conditions. In art the conditions are primarily those set by the material in which the artist works. The sculptor must have regard to the marble or other material in which his creative faculty labours. He has also to work under the mathematical, physical, and chemical conditions to which all human creations are subject. Mental conditions are also present, but need not again be enumerated. Yet, when the artist respects all these conditions—and if he neglects any of them, his work must fail—within them, indeed by means of them, he embodies his vision and realizes his ideal. The conditions do not fix the vision, nor do they contain the ideal; they only say that, if the artist is to work, these conditions must be fulfilled. If we are to understand the new product, the only cause to be assumed is the artist. And to understand him, if we can, we must pass from the general conditions under which he has worked, and study him as something which cannot be subsumed under general rules. For the proof of this we must refer to the critical studies of artists and poets, which, happily, are not non-existent, though they too often lose sight of their particular subject, and get lost under the general rules which are applicable to all men, and therefore are not illustrative of the singular genius they seek to describe in his habit as he lived. There must be some way of studying and understanding great men, for great men have appeared on the earth, and have been active in making history; and such a study is not without significance for the theory of knowledge.

21. **Teleology and history.**—The mention of history leads us to the recognition of what it is, what it means, and how it is to be understood. Paulsen, as quoted above, says that this is what we all understand but cannot conceive. This presupposes that conceiving is only of the general, the abstract, the universal, and necessary. But concepts may be changed, and their range enlarged, and they may be made such as to represent the reality with which we have to deal. We see how, in physics and chemistry, we have a new set of names to represent the new understanding of Nature to which men of science have come. Why should it not be so in the sphere of history? Are we to say that our failure to conceive belongs essentially to the very nature of conceptual knowledge? Even in that case, the limitation and the imperfection of knowledge are not determined by the knower or by the known, but by the imperfection of the instrument by which the knower seeks to express himself. If this is so, then there is hope for knowledge. It must revise its instruments, and make them more elastic and more fit for their purpose. The naked eye must be aided by the microscope, and the language must become more precise and more fluid at the same time. We must find a way of expressing the particular as well as the general, nor ought we to preach agnosticism until we have exhausted the possibilities of expressing the knowledge which we plainly possess, though it has escaped the meshes of our previous formulæ.

The study of the productions in which the human spirit has objectively expressed itself ought to give rise to the science of ideals. There is true and real knowledge to be found in this line of investigation, however great may be the difficulty of bringing it under rules and categories. Above all, in the sphere of religion and ethics we are face to face with sets of facts which have not yet been formulated. Here, too, we are in the sphere of creative personalities, though there are other spheres in which these have reigned. It is curious to observe that in the history of mathematical thought we are ever in the presence of creative personalities. From Pythagoras to Lord Kelvin every advance in mathematics is connected with a personality; and, when we get an account from the Town Council for electric light, we are charged for so many units called by personal names illustrious in the history of electric discovery. But in the sphere of religion and ethics personalities dominate. Ideals are created by them, are appreciated by other men, and become the living influence by which history is determined and character is formed.

'Real, deep devoutness, such as controls the whole life, is certainly a power that is only to be found in a few. But it is on the basis of those few that the nature of an age's piety must be determined, just as we must determine the art of a period on the basis of the real artists. For in those devout men, as in those artists, lives the eternal, ever-moving spirit of religion and of art, and they compel the rest, even though slowly and gradually, to follow after them, and at least to acknowledge as form and authority that which they cannot receive as spirit. But many out of the throng do receive a ray of the spirit, and warm their cold life with it. Any one, therefore, who desires to depict the piety of the West in the fifth century must describe the piety of Augustine; whosoever wishes to understand the piety of the twelfth and thirteenth centuries must study the piety of Bernard of Clairvaux and Francis; he who seeks to grasp the piety of the sixteenth century must make acquaintance with the piety of Luther, Calvin, and Knox; and so throughout.

But these names show what a power piety has been in the history of the world and of civilization; these names show that the fear of the Lord was the beginning not only of wisdom but also of might. Ought I to add the name of Cromwell or of Muhamed? The greatest events and changes in the history of the world have had their origin in religion—not in the public religion, but in the purely personal, in that secret religion which remains hidden in the individual, until it suddenly jets forth as if from a newly breaking spring' (Harnack, *HJ* x. [Oct. 1911] 70 f.).

We quote this interesting and profound passage as an illustration of our thesis that the knowledge of individuals and of personalities is real and valid knowledge, even though it cannot be predicted, and cannot be calculated. Harnack has shown that piety, purely personal, has been the source of the greatest events and changes in the history of the world; and this is true not only of piety, but of every characteristic of creative personalities who have been centres of influence for their age and generation. Rightly to understand the influence of man on man, and the receptiveness of the average man towards the personal influence which streams forth from the exceptional man, would be to see the inner connectedness of history, and to differentiate history from the mechanical action which is the rule of the lower world.

'As there exist graded series of special and more general laws for the things, there are also numberless steps between the influence of the average man, whose will is included only in the will of his neighbours, and the will of the religious leader, or the artistic genius, or the hero whose will tunes the will of millions, and enters in pure identity into the minds of whole nations. As nothing is entirely disconnected, nothing is absolutely unimportant there; but only by this emphasizing of the important and decisive does the system of identities become an organized whole, in which the fate of peoples, in their leading spirits and in their quiet masses, can be understood' (Münsterberg, *The Eternal Values*, 152).

Leaving now the study of the products of mankind in the light which they cast on the problems of knowledge, let us look for a little at history, and endeavour to find why the methods and assumptions of natural science are inapplicable to history. We assume, indeed, a connectedness in history, but we soon find that the connectedness is not that of cause and effect, or mere temporal perseverance, as the causal judgment finally amounts to. In the historical world, or in the world in which men live and work, objective things assume a new form. They become not only a system of causes and effects, but one of means and ends. They are objects of desire or aversion, objects to be attained, or somehow moulded to subserve human purposes. The ultimate aim of natural study, in order to know the external connectedness of things, is to use that knowledge in order to institute a new connectedness, the explanation of which is to fulfil the aim of the worker. The transformation of the actual into the ideal always follows the track of human effort. When the actual becomes an object of desire, it is invested at once with new properties, and is transformed into an object which has a new meaning—a meaning arising out of the relation placed on it by the fact that it has become an object of desire. In history all objects are considered as objects of will, and their natural qualities are transformed accordingly.

In history, therefore, what is dealt with is no longer objects as seen in their scientific connectedness, but objects seen in their new transformation as interesting in their relation to the fulfilment of human need. Thus a new science arises, with new methods and aims, also with new categories to set forth all that newness, which yet has a connectedness that can be understood. It will become a science which deals with subjects, with wills in action and interaction with the world in order to transform that world into a world of values and worths. The new science will take into account the fact of individual wills and personalities, and endeavour to show how these wills become the general will, or how individualities, while maintaining their distinctness and their peculiarity, become a conscious part of an organic whole, which will have its own reality. We shall have to widen our conception of organism to express this new form of it. Just as politically we have to find a new conception for the British Empire, which is a system of relatively independent nationalities, bound in a unity such as the world has never seen before, so it is with regard to the new conception of organism.

Real objects or objects out in the world of space become ideal when they enter into the world of desire. It is just the fact of this transformation which marks out the science of history from other sciences, and it is in this sphere that we are to look for the connectedness which obtains and must obtain in history as in other sciences. The connectedness does not lie in the thought of the tendency of things to persist in their present state, but in the capacity of being transformed to meet human desire. It is not in connexion with the past that in history we seek explanations; it is in the unity impressed on natural objects when seen in the light of the possibility of their transformation to meet and to fulfil the purposes of man. That there is here an actual connectedness admits of no doubt, and to set forth this connectedness is an important task for knowledge. In history, then, there exists a real world which has arisen through human effort; and, if it is to be understood, it must be regarded in the light of the characteristic activities of man. How human wills agree to act in common, how ideals can be impressed on the average man, how men act together, have a common purpose—are questions of great interest. How meanings arise, how they are communicable, and how ideals may become the common possession of a people—are questions which we may put but which we cannot answer here. Looking back over the past, we find that all ideals have been traced by the peoples to their great men. All religions trace themselves ultimately to a personal founder; all laws have been ascribed to a personal legislator. And, in general, every advance in civilization has been ascribed to individual discoverers, inventors, or thinkers. In the transformation which takes place in objects when they become objects of desire, a great function is discharged by those who are great enough to indicate to the common mind what objects they ought to submit to this transformation. What ought men to desire? What ought they to avoid? Here come in all the ethics and all the religions of the world, and the transformations which they have effected on the common world.

We may instance also the ideals which in the history of the world have become national—Hebrew, Assyrian, Babylonian, Indian, Greek, Roman, Teutonic, English, Scottish. Ideals are there, with all their greatness, and also with all their limitations; and the influence of a national ideal on the members of the nation can be described. That ideal every individual within the nation makes his own, shapes his conduct according to it, and thus makes the national will his own will. Again, one may arise within the nation who transcends the national ideal, yet is within it; and so he may modify it, and, without breaking with the past, open out new paths in which the feet of the ordinary man can safely tread. The main thing insisted on here is that history has to be understood from the point of view of ideals, that these are descriptive of the varied desires of man, and that the outcome of historical endeavour is determined by the efforts of men to realize their ideals. For these they suffer, strive, work; in the accomplishment of them they find themselves and their lasting joy. In a word, the sphere of history is the sphere of the teleological, and history is the story of the strivings of men to reach the ideal which somehow they possess.

22. The teleological judgment as a system of values.—Here, again, we see how mind changes its methods and its language as it comes into new fields of study. It does so in consistency with the laws which regulate its own procedure, and also in consistency with the nature of the objects it seeks to understand. In the fields of ethics, religion, and history it has to construct a system of values, for these are of essential importance in a world of ideals. But as a discussion of them will be found in art. VALUE, we need not deal with the subject here. Nor do we find it possible to discuss the problem of ignorance or of error. The problem of error lies alongside the problem of truth, and accompanies it all the way (see art. ERROR AND TRUTH). The subject need be discussed here only in so far as it bears on the task and nature of knowledge. Of course, all along the line of the effort to complete the task of knowledge there lies the possibility of mistake. The epistemologist may make a mistake in Psychology when he considers knowledge as a mental process. He may make a mistake in his description of the process through which the subject elaborates its objects, classifies them, transforms them. He may make universals which are not really such and land himself in the perplexity of those who work with inadequate instruments. In the sphere of Logic many mistakes may also be made, which may be found treated in detail in any treatise on Logic, under the name of 'fallacies.' Mistakes also occur in the metaphysical field which may render unfruitful the whole discussion of the epistemological problem. In our attitude towards the problem of knowledge we may be dogmatic, or we may be sceptical. We may have an attitude of belief towards that which is essentially incredible, or we may refuse belief to truth which can be shown to be valid and trustworthy. All these things are possible, and many of them have been present as matters of fact in every age. What then? Are we to despair of knowledge, or of the possibility of coming to a right apprehension of knowledge, its worth, its validity? What are we to say of those systems which mark out a certain boundary and declare that beyond it there is the unknowable? Is it possible to say what are the bounds of knowledge, and if so, how far is it possible? Can this be done from the point of view of the nature of the knower, or from the nature of the known? We have not found this to be the case. We have not found it possible to delimit the sphere of knowledge, or to set it aside as a process inapplicable to anything which can fall within experience. We have found its methods to be often inadequate; we have seen that it is apt to make conceptions which have proved powerful and adequate within one range applicable, without further inquiry, to another set of things, and to make one aspect of experience dominant over all experience, just because this has been more manageable and useful in its endeavour to control its objects.

23. Teleology and criticism.—Along all these lines knowledge has to be vigilant if it is to fulfil its purpose. Here, too, eternal vigilance is the price of safety; if knowledge is to hold itself and its products in secure possession, it must subject all its assumptions, its categories, its processes, to a criticism which must grow ever more stringent as knowledge increases. Criticism of beliefs must ever be undertaken anew as the experience of man widens, and his power of separating the true from the false increases. Criticism of the mind and of the axioms which it has held as absolutely true must be looked at afresh in the light of increasing knowledge, and of a fuller consciousness of the mind itself. Logical procedure will need revision constantly; and, if criticism is ever called for with regard to knowledge regarded as the work of the knower, it is always in order also with regard to knowledge as it is determined by the nature of the object. For not all that passes under the name of knowledge, but only that which has been tested, sifted, and weighed in the balance of criticism, is worthy of the name.

Add to this that criticism is not a fixed, unchangeable process of appreciation or of evaluation. It is an evolution which goes on from more to more. We are to learn what it means. It has grown to considerable proportions in other spheres; and literary, historical, and scientific criticism has already performed a great work in the way of purging our knowledge and of purifying our conceptions of what has happened in the past. Philosophical criticism, or the criticism of philosophical systems, has helped to make clear the problem of philosophy, and to define what it can wisely attempt. The great work which Kant began is not yet completed, and there must be a criticism of the critical philosophy itself. It has been criticized, but mainly from partial points of view, and in the interests of a philosophy constructed on a different basis. But the thing which is most needed is *a criticism of the process of criticism itself*. This also is, or may be, a constructive work of the highest philosophical importance. For it would give us an instrument of the utmost value for the determining of philosophical tendencies, and provide us with a test of their worth, truth, and validity. But the critical view of criticism itself is also subject to growth, and evolves; and, as it evolves, it helps us in the process of distinguishing the true from the false, and helps us to sift out of our judgments the inadequate, the unreal, and the untrue.

Meanwhile knowledge grows, and the power of the mind to grasp its objects grows. Nor can we assign any limits to this growth, for mind grows by the exercise of its functions, and with this growth there goes the evolution of knowledge, and with the growth of both there goes the growth of criticism, or the examination of all that is concerned with knowledge. The story of later philosophy is instructive in this respect. Idealism is learning to appreciate worths, and to hold a high respect for matters of fact. Empiricism is learning to have respect to rational principles, and is ceasing to look at mental processes as mere effects wrought on the mind by an objective world. Other signs of a more hopeful tendency to look at philosophy as able to recognize all the elements of experience are not wanting. Most hopeful of all is the growth of criticism itself, or the earnest scrutiny bestowed on all its processes by philosophy itself, and the resultant purification of our methods. May we not take it that the long processes of building up our knowledge step by step may be hastened as man becomes master of his methods? Eminent mathematicians have been able to see the outcome of lengthened demonstrations in a brilliant flash of intuition; their mathematical formulæ have been again turned into pictures, and they read them as the ordinary man reads the pages of a book. May not intuitions be the goal of all our discursive reasoning?

Meanwhile, from the subject or from the object there is no hindrance to the hope of the indefinite increase of our knowledge. Intensively it will increase as we learn more of ourselves, of the world, and of the Maker of the world; extensively it may increase until it stands over against the world, and recognizes that through and through it is an intelligible world, a world that may be understood. With the increase of knowledge the knower grows, and the mastery of the world grows also.

'I am a part of all that I have met;
Yet all experience is an arch wherethro'
Gleams that untravell'd world, whose margin fades
For ever and for ever when I move'
(Tennyson's *Ulysses*).

LITERATURE.—This is so vast that only a selection from the more recent can be given here. The great systems from Plato and Aristotle downwards have a close bearing on the subject of Epistemology, but only a general reference to these is necessary. The same remark applies to the Histories of Philosophy; nor do we enumerate all the recent works on the problem of knowledge. The following selection is offered, mainly because of the indebtedness of the present writer to the works named:—R. Adamson, *The Development of Modern Philosophy*, 2 vols., London, 1903; J. B. Baillie, *Idealistic Construction of Experience*, Edinburgh, 1906; J. M. Baldwin, *Thought and Things, or Genetic Logic*, London, vol. i. (1906), vol. ii. (1908); H. Bergson, *Time and Free Will*, Eng. tr., London, 1910, also *Matter and Memory*, do. 1911, and *Creative Evolution*, do. 1911; B. P. Bowne, *Theory of Thought and Knowledge*, New York, 1897; E. Cassirer, *Das Erkenntnisproblem*, Berlin, vol. i. (1906), vol. ii. (1907); T. M. Forsyth, *English Philosophy*, London, 1910; T. H. Green, *Collected Works*, 3 vols., do. 1885; W. James, *Some Problems of Philosophy*, do. 1911; W. Jerusalem, *Introd. to Philosophy*, Eng. tr., New York, 1910; H. Jones, *The Philosophy of Lotze*, Glasgow, 1895; G. T. Ladd, *Knowledge, Life, and Reality*, London, 1909; A. D. Lindsay, *The Philosophy of Bergson*, London, 1911; J. T. Merz, *Hist. of European Thought in the Nineteenth Century*, Edinburgh, vol. i. (1896), vol. ii. (1903); H. Münsterberg, *The Eternal Values*, London, 1909; F. Paulsen, *Introd. to Philosophy*, Eng. tr., New York, 1907; R. B. Perry, *The Approach to Philosophy*, London, 1905; R. Reininger, *Philosophie des Erkennens*, Leipzig, 1911; J. Royce, *The World and the Individual*, New York, vol. i. (1900), vol. ii. (1901); C. Sigwart, *Logic*, Eng. tr., London, 1895; J. Ward, *Naturalism and Agnosticism*, do. 1899.

JAMES IVERACH.

EQUIPROBABILISM.—1. Definition.—Equiprobabilism is a form of probabilism (*q.v.*) which stands midway between simple probabilism and probabiliorism. The equiprobabilistic principle may be stated thus: the *opinio minus tuta, i.e.* the opinion *quæ libertati favet*, may be followed, on condition that it is as probable as the *opinio tuta*, *i.e.* the *opinio quæ legi favet*; we may not, on the contrary, follow the *opinio minus tuta* if it is considerably less probable than the *opinio tuta*. Probabiliorism does not admit of following the *opinio minus tuta* unless it is more probable than the *opinio tuta*. Simple probabilism demands only a strong probability in favour of the *opinio minus tuta*.

2. Founder.—Alfonso Maria di Liguori (*q.v.*) is generally regarded as the founder of the equiprobabilistic system. This theologian was originally a rigorist, as he tells us in his *Morale Systema*. He afterwards went over to simple probabilism, and then to equiprobabilism. There are signs of the latter evolution in several of his writings prior to the year 1762, but it was openly completed at that date, for it was in 1762 that the founder of the order of Redemptorists published his *Breve dissertatione dell' un moderato dell' opinione probabile*. It is difficult to say whether this change of opinion was suggested to him by the thought of the abuses to which simple probabilism gave rise, or by the desire to avoid seeing his doctrine suffer the discredit into which the ethics of the Jesuits had fallen at that time. St. Alfonso, in his equiprobabilistic system, rests on the authority of Eusebius Amort, who published a *Theologia scholastica et moralis* in 1753. Junius († 1679), Antony Mayer the Jesuit, author of a *Theologia scholastica* which appeared in 1729, and Rasslar, author of a *Norma Recti*, published in 1713, are also regarded as forerunners of equiprobabilism, but equiprobabilism as a theory distinct from simple probabilism makes a definite start only with Alfonso di Liguori. In ch. iii. ('de Conscientia') of his *Homo apostolicus ad audiendam confessionem instructus* (see the 1837 ed., Paris and Besançon), Alfonso formulates his opinion as follows:

'Tertia igitur, quae nostra est sententia, dicit quod quum opinio quae libertati favet est aeque probabilis atque opinio illa quae legi favet, sine dubio et licite sequi potest.' Nevertheless he calls attention to the fact that, in a matter of faith, one must always follow the *opinio tutior*.

3. Controversies.—Towards the end of the 18th and the beginning of the 19th cent. probabiliorism and even tutiorism became predominant, and remained so until the time when the Jesuits and other scholars revived the doctrine of St. Alfonso. Among his modern disciples special mention is due to Father Gury, the author of a very well-known *Manuel de théologie morale*, and to Gousset, who insists strongly upon the equiprobabilism of his master. In 1864, Antonio Ballerini, the Jesuit, published a *Dissertatio de morali systemate S. Alphonsi* for the purpose of showing that Alfonso di Liguori had never taught equiprobabilism, and of claiming him absolutely for the side of the simple probabilists. This dissertation called forth an answer from the Liguorians, and in 1872 the *Vindiciæ Alphonsianæ* appeared. This great work is a special plea in favour of St. Alfonso and equiprobabilism. It seeks to prove that this theologian was the inventor of the equiprobabilistic system, and that this system was always his. The authors relied chiefly on the dissertation of Liguori, written in 1749, entitled *De usu moderato opinionis probabilis in concursu probabilioris*. No one before Liguori, they said, had ever spoken of a moderate use of probable opinion. In their eyes equiprobabilism was the most correct, most sensible, and easiest rule of moral conduct. They summed up their master's doctrine as follows. (1) In a case of doubt as to the existence of a law, the *opinio quæ libertati favet* must be as probable as the *opinio quæ legi favet*. (2) In doubt with regard to the extinction of a law which has certainly existed, the *opinio quæ libertati favet* must be sufficient ground for moral certitude. (3) In doubt concerning a fact which involves a non-moral danger, the surest opinion must always be followed; in other words, one has no right, under pretext of probability, to endanger, in any given case, the interests of a third person.

The *Vindiciæ Alphonsianæ* led to a lengthy controversy. In 1873 a pamphlet was published in Belgium, entitled *Vindiciæ Ballerinianæ*, in support of the argument of Ballerini (his dissertation is reprinted in the pamphlet) that Liguori was always a defender of simple probabilism. In the same year a discussion took place in the newspaper *L'Univers* (see the issues of 8 May, 25 June, 29 July, 28 Oct. 1873), in which Ballerini himself participated. He took his stand upon Liguori's early writings, and recalled the fact that even Liguori's own partisans had claimed that he never changed. Besides, if he did change, says Ballerini, it would be better to follow his original opinion. The same author recurs to the subject in the 1893 edition of Gury's *Manuel*, to claim the authority of St. Alfonso in favour of the argument: one may follow an opinion which is truly and wholly probable, rather than a sure opinion which is equally or even more probable, in the purely moral sphere, when no question of fact comes into consideration.

Numerous books and articles were devoted to this controversy. It is both historical and theoretical. The points at issue were: (1) What exactly did Alfonso di Liguori teach? and (2) What value is to be put on equiprobabilism as a directing principle of conscience?

As far as the first point is concerned, it may be remarked that this historical question is interesting mainly to biographers of Alfonso di Liguori. The Jesuits and their partisans maintain that St. Alfonso never taught anything but moderate probabilism, and that he repudiated laxity only; the majority of Liguorians assert, contrary to the evidence of facts, that the founder of their order was always an equiprobabilist. Some Liguorians, however, admit that the equiprobabilism of their master dated only from 1762. On account of the want of precision that characterizes St. Alfonso's terminology, it is quite easy to find arguments in his writings in support of all these different opinions.

As regards the second point, equiprobabilism has certainly had more opponents than supporters. Among the former we may mention—besides Ballerini—Lehmkuhl, Huppert, Le Bachelet; and among the partisans of equiprobabilism may be named Aertnys, Ter Haer, and Jansen.

Some of the opponents of the equiprobabilistic system claim that it is only an attenuated form of simple probabilism; others acknowledge the original character of equiprobabilism, but only to demonstrate that this principle is illogical and inapplicable. They hold strictly by the three fundamental rules of probabilism: (1) liberty is prior to law, and cannot be dispossessed of its rights except by an absolutely certain law; (2) a doubtful law is not obligatory; and (3) if a *vere et solide probabilis* reason exists against law and on the other side of liberty, the law becomes doubtful. The substance of their reasoning is as follows: it is impossible to measure exactly the degrees of probability of different opinions, and therefore a comparison between the reasons which militate for and against liberty is of little value; besides, even if there is a more probable opinion in favour of law, the latter remains none the less doubtful. One may act even with a certain *formido malitiæ*, for only moral certainty, in favour either of the law or of liberty, excludes this *formido*, because it excludes every hesitation of judgment. Between a simply probable opinion and a morally certain opinion there are no intermediate degrees. In most cases only the so-called reflex principles, and in particular the principle *lex dubia non obligat*, have practical certitude, which, of course, must not be confounded with theoretical certitude.

To these arguments the equiprobabilists reply that only a comparison between different opinions can decide if one of them is *vere et solide probabilis*. Practical certitude is of a subjective kind, and to obtain it we must consult our personal feeling. If the law is more probable than the opinion favourable to liberty, there is no real doubt. Now, nothing but real doubt removes the obligatory character of law. It is perfectly possible to determine, in a given case, that such and such an opinion is more or less probable than another. It should be noted that equiprobabilists as a rule admit the general principles of probabilism formulated above. Jansen, however, calls attention to the fact that it is incorrect to claim that liberty, being prior to law, has a presumption in its favour (*libertas possidet*), and that it is always the existence of law that has to be demonstrated. According to him, liberty exists only by virtue of law, the source of our rights as of our duties. He does not, as the Roman Catholic moralists usually do, place liberty in opposition to law, but he affirms that law is in itself more probable than liberty, and that, consequently, it must prevail if there is another reason in its favour.

Considering the general principle of probabilism, simple probabilism is unquestionably more logical than equiprobabilism. The latter is a timid protest against a purely legal morality, in favour of the subjective conscience, an attempt to stay the abuses inherent in simple probabilism which degenerates almost certainly into laxity. What makes the controversy which we have just summed up interesting is that at the present time, in the sphere of Roman Catholic morality, equiprobabilism is the last intrenchment behind which a small number of defenders are fighting against the principles and morals of the Jesuits. Probabiliorism and tutiorism have now no supporters.

LITERATURE.—Döllinger-Reusch, *Gesch. der Moralstreitigkeiten in der röm.-kathol. Kirche seit dem sechszehnten Jahrhundert*, Munich, 1889; the works of Liguori, esp. his *Theologia moralis* and *Homo apostolicus ad audiendam confessionem instructus*, and his letters: *Lettere di S.A.M. di Liguori . . . pubblicate nel primo centenario della sua beata morte*, 3 vols. Rome, 1887; Gousset, *Théol. morale*, Paris, 1844; *Vindiciæ Alphonsianæ seu Doctoris Ecclesiæ S. Alphonsi de Ligorio, episcopi, et fundatoris Congregationis St. Redemptoris doctrina moralis vindicata a plurimis oppugnationibus C.P. Antonii Ballerini, Soc. Jesu in Collegio Romano professoris, cura et studio quorumdam Theologorum e Congregatione St. Redemptoris*, ed. altera, Paris, Tournai, Brussels, 1874; *Vindiciæ Ballerinianæ seu gustus recognitionis Vindiciarum Alphonsianarum*, Bruges, 1873 (see review by H. Dumas, in *Études . . . publiées par quelques Pères de la Compagnie de Jésus*, Jan. 1873); Gury, *Compend. theol. moralis, ab auctore recognitum et ab Antonio Ballerino adnotationibus locupletatum*[11], Rome, 1893; Le Bachelet, *La Question liguorienne*, Paris, 1899; Ter Haer, *De systemate morali antiquorum Probabilistarum dissertatio historico-critica*, Paderborn, 1894; Matignon, artt. in *Études* (cited above), 1866, the *Mont*, Feb. 1874, the *Civiltà Cattolica* (on the 'Vindiciæ Alphonsianæ' and the 'Vindiciæ Ballerinianæ'), and the *Revue Thomiste*, July and Sept. 1898; Jansen, 'L'Equiprobabilisme,' in *Revue des sciences ecclésiastiques*, 1873; various artt. by Grandclaude and Didiot, *ib.* 1874, tom. 1; Desjardins, 'De l'Equiprobabilisme de saint Alphonse de Liguori,' and two articles signed A.O. entitled 'St. Alphonse de Liguori et le probabilisme,' *ib.* 1878; Leboucher, 'Le Probabilisme de saint Alphonse de Liguori d'après le Rév. Père Cath.' in *Der Katholik*, 1893, ii.; Huppert, 'Der Probabilismus,' *ib.* 1874, ii.; two series of these signed R., *ib.*; Aertnys, 'Zur Rechtfertigung des Aequiprobabilismus,' in *ZKT*, 1895; Huppert, 'Probabilismus u. Aequiprobabilismus,' in *Jahrb. f. Philosophie u. speculat. Theol.* 1896, p. 37 ff.; Jansen, 'Der Aequiprobabilismus u. seine philos. Begründung,' *Pastor Bonus*, 1895; Lehmkuhl, 'Probabilismus u. Zweifel,' p. 161 ff.; Jansen, 'Probabilismus u. Kritik,' p. 316 ff.; and various other articles by the same authors continuing this controversy. The *Theol. Quartalschrift*, 1897, contains an art. by Koch, entitled 'Die Entwickelung des Moralsystems des hl. Alfons v. Liguori, auf Grund seiner Briefe dargestellt'; see also artt. 'Liguori' and 'Probabilismus,' in *PRE*[3].

E. EHRHARDT.

EQUITY.—In common usage, 'equity' denotes what is right as distinct from what is according to law. The law represents what is enacted by Parliament or the legislature, and, though it may intend to embody the right, it does not always do so, and men then judge the case according to 'equity.' 'Equity' thus comes to mean some 'law of nature,' as it did in Roman Law, or the consensus of opinions of what is right in the circumstances. The distinction is an old one familiar to Greek philosophers and Roman jurists.

Aristotle (*Nic. Eth.* v. 10) remarks that the equitable and the just are sometimes identified and sometimes distinguished. This is because 'justice' and 'equity' are in common parlance regarded as synonymous with the right, but in legal parlance the 'just' is merely according to positive law or legislative enactment, and the 'equitable' is something in accordance with some other supposed 'law' or principle. This supposed 'law' is the mind's sense of right, or some standard assumed to represent it. In speaking of the obscurity and equivocation of the terms, Aristotle says: 'What obscures the matter is that, though what is equitable is just, it is not identical with, but a correction of, that which is just according to law. The reason of this is that every law is laid down in general terms, while there are matters about which it is impossible to speak correctly in general terms.' Hence, when a positive law does not strictly apply to the special case in hand, an appeal has to be made to 'equity,' which means some principle of 'justice' or right on which the legal enactment is supposedly based or which it is intended to serve. For instance, the law may be that a person convicted of murder shall be hanged, but the conviction may be wrong, and, when there is reason to believe this, 'equity' may come in, when process of law will not deal with the matter and remit the punishment.

Sir Henry Maine (*Anc. Law*, p. 60 ff.) suggests that the distinction between 'justice' and 'equity' grew out of the contradictions in the positive law which recognized class distinctions, and the growth of a sense of equality in the application of the right.

'It is remarkable,' he says, 'that the "equality" of laws on which the Greek democracies prided themselves . . . had little in common with the "equity" of the Romans. The first was an equal administration of civil laws among the citizens, however limited the class of citizens might be; the last implied the applicability of a law, which was not civil law, to a class which did not necessarily consist of citizens. The first excluded a despot; the last included foreigners, and for some purposes slaves. On the whole, I should be disposed to look in another direction for the germ of the Roman "Equity." The Latin word "aequus" carries with it more distinctly than the Greek ἴσος the sense of *levelling*. Now its levelling tendency was exactly the characteristic of the Jus Gentium, which would be most striking to a primitive Roman. The pure Quiritarian law recognized a multitude of arbitrary distinctions between classes of men and kinds of property: the Jus Gentium, generalized from a comparison of various customs, neglected the Quiritarian divisions. The old Roman law established, for example, a fundamental difference between "Agnatic" and "Cognatic" relationship, that is, between the Family considered as based upon common subjection to patriarchal authority and the Family considered (in conformity with modern ideas) as united through the mere fact of a common descent. This distinction disappears in the "law common to all nations," as also does the difference between the archaic forms of property, Things "Mancipi" and Things "nec Mancipi." The neglect of demarcations and boundaries seems to me, therefore, the feature of the Jus Gentium which was depicted in Æquitas. I imagine that the word was at first a mere description of that constant *levelling* or removal of irregularities which went on wherever the prætorian system was applied to the cases of foreign litigants. Probably no colour of ethical meaning belonged at first to the expression; nor is there any reason to believe that the process which it indicated was otherwise than extremely distasteful to the primitive Roman mind.'

The ethical colouring which the conception obtained was probably due to the influence of Christianity, with its sense of the value of individual men and their equality before God and so before the law. It thus came to represent the basis upon which positive law at least pretended to stand. It was at first the mere correction of anomalies in the application of the law, but the rise of the idea that all laws had a basis higher than mere legislative enactment, and did not rest on the arbitrary will of the lawgiver or a capricious contract, gave it an ethical meaning superior to all others in authority, and made it the ground on which common law had to rest for its justification.

LITERATURE.—Aristotle, *Nicomachean Ethics*, bk. v.; H. Maine, *Ancient Law*[10], Lond. 1907, ch. iii.; T. E. Holland, *Jurisprudence*, Oxf. 1880. See also art. 'Equity,' in *EBr*[11].

JAMES. H. HYSLOP.

EQUIVOCATION (Logical).[1]—Equivocation is one of the verbal fallacies, that is, one of those in which a conclusion is not validly inferred, because of the improper or ambiguous use of words in the course of the argument. In particular, equivocation is that verbal fallacy which is due to the employment of the same word in two senses. For example, 'The holder of some shares in the lottery is sure to gain the prize; and, as I am the holder of some shares in the lottery, I am sure to gain the prize'; or, again, the old illustration, 'Who is most hungry eats most, who eats least is most hungry, therefore who eats least eats most.' As there are three terms in the syllogism, and as each of these terms appears twice, there are three possible places where equivocation may be located: on the one hand, in the middle term, or wholly in the premisses; on the other hand, in either the major or the minor term; and so, in part, in the conclusion. But it is usually to be found in the middle term. Since in equivocation we use the words denoting one of these terms in two senses, we really have not one term but two, and so altogether four in our syllogism. Thus equivocation, as is true of so many other fallacies, is but a species of the fallacy of four terms.

Jevons gives three causes which especially lead to equivocation: (1) the accidental confusion of different words, *e.g.* mean (the average) and mean (the despicable); (2) the giving of the name of one object to another object with which that object is associated, *e.g.* church, house, court; (3) the giving of the name of one object to a second object in some respect similar to the first, *e.g.* sweetness (of music), light (of knowledge). But behind the equivocal use of words there is always of necessity some ignorance regarding the things for which the words stand; and in some cases it is difficult to decide whether to call the fallacy equivocation or one of the material fallacies, especially accident (*q.v.*). Hence it happens that the complete exposure of an equivocation is often far more than merely a matter regarding the meaning of a word, being rather an analysis and discrimination of the objects themselves denoted by the word. For example, to make clear the meaning of such words and phrases as 'identity,' 'I,' 'laws of Nature,' 'the freedom of the will,' in philosophy—not to mention ambiguous words and phrases which have played an important part in the history of theology, ethics, economics, and other sciences—has proved not only a difficult task for the student, but also an important step forward in the development of his science. See, further, art. LOGIC.

LITERATURE.—J. S. Mill, *Logic*, ed. London, 1884, pt. v. ch. vii.; A. Sidgwick, *Fallacies*, London, 1883, N.Y. 1884; W. S. Jevons, *Lessons in Logic*[2], London, 1890, Lessons iv. and xx.; and other text-books in Logic.

W. T. MARVIN.

[1] For equivocation in the ethical sense, see CASUISTRY, LYING.

ERASMUS.—See HUMANISTS.

ERASTIANISM.—I. Definition, derivation, and delimitation of the term.—The opening of Figgis's brilliant essay, 'Erastus and Erastianism' (in *JThSt* ii. [1900] 66 ff.), 'Was Erastus an Erastian?' suggests, on the one hand, the distance between the views actually propounded by Erastus and the principles of modern Erastianism; and, on the other hand, the difficulty of fixing the meaning of an elusive term in political nomenclature; while the title of Bonnard's invaluable monograph, *Thomas Éraste et la discipline ecclésiastique* (Lausanne, 1894), fixes the attention upon the limited area of the controversy with which Erastus was concerned. Robert Lee, in his historical Preface to *The Theses of Erastus touching Excommunication*[1] (Edinburgh, 1844), labours to exhibit the ignorant abuse of the terms 'Erastian' and 'Erastianism' by those who, in the heat of the Disruption, applied them to the Established

[1] The translation published by Lee is a revision of the first Eng. tr. of the *Theses*, entitled, *The Nullity of Church Censures* (London, 1659), and containing an account of Erastus taken from Adam Melchior's *de Vitis Germanorum Medicorum*. Another tr., *A Treatise of Excommunication*, appeared in 1682 (London, printed for L. Curtis).

Church of Scotland. With this defence of the Church of Scotland we may compare the words of R. I. Wilberforce, *Sketch of the Hist. of Erastianism* (London, 1851):

'It will be found that Presbyterianism, to whatever other evils it has been open, is at least a deadly enemy of Erastianism. Beza was the first to write against Erastus, and no ecclesiastical body is more hostile at present to the encroachment of the civil power than the Scottish Kirk' (ch. i.).

We may quote also the following passage from Figgis:

'The real object of Erastus was to give clear expression to the denial of any right to coercive authority in the religious society apart from the State.[1] He decided, in fact, to prevent the Evangelical churches becoming what one of them claimed to be in Scotland and actually became in Geneva, a *societas perfecta*, with all its means of jurisdiction complete and independent' (*Camb. Mod. Hist.* ii. [1902] 743; cf. also Lee, Pref. p. xxix, and W. Cunningham, *Discussions on Church Principles, Popish, Erastian, and Presbyterian*, Edinburgh, 1863, pp. 164, 207).

Figgis's reference to 'the simpler definition of Erastianism as the theory that religion is the creature of the State' (*JThSt* ii. 83) is hardly the account of the matter which modern religious Erastians like Fremantle and Gwatkin would admit, though it expresses the tendency of mere political Erastianism which Hobbes propounded in the great forty-second chapter of the *Leviathan*, 'Of Power Ecclesiastical.'[2] As Machiavellianism[3] subordinates morality to political exigencies, so Erastianism, pushed to extremes, subordinates religion.

An attempt at even the most cursory review of the operation of Erastianism is rendered difficult, not only by the persistence and variety of political intervention in ecclesiastical affairs since Christianity was 'licensed' by Constantine, but still more by the notorious fluidity of the term, and by the contradictory judgments of historians and political philosophers as to the determining factors of the ecclesiastical policies of the princes and statesmen —even of churchmen—whose acts are called in question. In the criticism of theorists, too, as we have seen in the case of Erastus, the application and justification of the epithet are often matters of debate. How far a monarch, for instance, was actuated by a genuine desire to propagate Christianity and to extirpate heresy in his dominion; how far he merely subordinated the organization, the influence, and the sanctions of the Church to the aggrandizement of his personal power or the prosperity of the State—these are problems which not only must frequently remain insoluble puzzles of regal psychology and casuistry, but will always be differently treated according to different conceptions of the mutual relations of Church and State.

The divergent verdicts recorded on the careers of Constantine the Great, Clovis, and Charles the Great furnish conspicuous instances of the difficulty of estimating the quantity or the quality of the Erastianism that has actuated the great makers of Church history. It is necessary, too, to distinguish between the home and the foreign policy of monarchs like William I., Henry II., and Henry VIII. of England; for statesmanship that was Erastian in its treatment of the Church of England was not necessarily Erastian in its attitude towards the claims of Rome. The anti-Papal Statutes of Edward I. and Edward III. were but patriotic and enlightened efforts to check the disintegration of the body politic that was increasingly threatened by the alienation of jurisdictions and temporalities, by the extension of judicial and fiscal immunities, and by the still further weakening of the sovereignty of the State through the legative system and the intrusion of foreigners into even the metropolitan sees. The problem of the Erastianism of bishops need not detain us. As regards some of the most famous of these, the question of the master they elected to serve has received different answers. Thomas Becket changed sides on his translation from a civil to an ecclesiastic office; whereas Lanfranc, in his support of the Conqueror, furnishes an example, not so much of Erastianism, as of the defence of the autonomy of a national see. The famous epigram of James I., 'No bishop, no king,' not only enunciates the principle that in the first half of the 17th cent. the permanence of episcopacy was the condition of the stability of the monarchy, but furnishes the diagnosis to the embitterment of the struggle between the religious parties of the following reign. *Prima facie*, the subserviency of Laud to Charles I. appears as treason to the Church, when contrasted with the independence exhibited by Peckham towards Edward I. But, so far as Episcopalians accept the implication of Erastianism for Laud's contemporaries or successors, the charge is admitted only through a certain inversion of the term (cf. Patterson, *Hist. of the Church of England*, London, 1909, p. 334 f.).

We should be inclined to say that, so far as clerical Erastianism co-exists with the maintenance of the spiritual and even the political claims of the Church, such Erastianism can only regard the State as being itself ultimately the minister, not the master, of the Church; the tributary, not the patron. State oversight and support of the Church are, according to this view, not only advantageous to the prestige, the welfare, and the morality of the State; they conduce to the efficiency and prosperity of the Church, which would be imperilled by disestablishment or any form of self-supporting autonomy. Nor has the operation of Erastianism proved invariably injurious, however problematic we may regard the advantage of the State's tutelage of the Church. Often has the secular power limited hierarchical tyranny, to the advantage of true religion as well as in its own interests. Even the decadent Byzantine Empire furnishes, in the persons of Leo the Isaurian and his hyper-iconoclastic son, Constantine V., instances of monarchs whose efforts to extirpate superstitions—especially the worship of images—which the Church successfully maintained against all Imperial measures range them among the champions of progress and enlightenment. Bury has shown that Constantine V. was animated by true statesmanship in his aversion to the depopulating practice of monachism, and much of the ecclesiastical policy of the later Byzantine Emperors was, like that of Constantine I. at Nicæa, dictated by an honest desire to heal the schisms made in the State itself by the virulence of Christological controversy. Finally, we have to observe that, once the Edict of Milan (313) had reversed the injunction, 'Non licet esse vos,' Constantine the Great had no option but to become *episcopus episcoporum* (though he claimed to act as such only in the externals of religion), for the care of the State religion was as much a duty as a prerogative of the Emperor. On the other hand, while Constantine was politic enough to see the advantage of availing himself of such an auxiliary to government as Christianity presented—an aid which heathenism in its totality was unable to render—he could no longer allow

1 '"Erastianism," as a by-word, is used to denote the doctrine of the supremacy of the state in ecclesiastical causes; but the problem of the relations between church and state is one on which Erastus nowhere enters. What is known as "Erastianism" would be better connected with the name of Grotius' (art. 'Erastus,' in *EBr*[11]).

2 'Many of us—most of us, in fact—are Erastians with certain limitations; Hobbes was an Erastian without limitations' (W. G. Pogson Smith, in Essay prefixed to *Hobbes's Leviathan reprinted from the Edition of 1651*, Oxford, 1909, p. xxx).

3 How Machiavelli was 'caught up in the growing controversy between Church and State, and identified with the party who maintained that the political authority must outweigh the religious,' is discussed by Burd, *Il Principe*, Oxford, 1891, p. 57 f.

the greatest of all *sodalicia* to operate throughout the Empire independently of his superintendence.

2. Life and work of Erastus.—

Thomas Lüber was born at Baden, in Switzerland, on 7th September 1524. On his matriculation at the University of Basel in 1542 he adopted, in accordance with the fashion of the time, the Greek equivalent (*Erastus*) of his family name. In 1544 he quitted Basel and proceeded to Italy, where the generosity of a rich patron enabled him to spend nine years—three at Bologna and six at Padua. First he studied philosophy, and afterwards medicine, graduating as doctor in the latter. In 1557, while he held the appointment of physician to the court of the Count of Henneberg, in South Germany, he received almost simultaneous invitations from two German princes. Declining the offer of the Duke of Saxony, he accepted the professorship of medicine which Otto Henry, the Elector Palatine, offered to him at the University of Heidelberg. He was attached to the new faculty of medicine, in the capacity of professor of therapeutics, on 3rd May 1558. At the end of the same year he was unanimously elected to the Rectorship for the following year, having already, as Bonnard suggests, received at Heidelberg the degree of doctor of philosophy. He immediately exhibited great ability and energy in the development, not only of the study of medicine, but of culture and science generally, while his election to the Church Council of the Palatinate drew him forthwith into the vortex of those Confessional conflicts in which Heidelberg, 'a refuge for theological eccentrics of all nations' (Figgis, p. 69), enjoyed an unenviable pre-eminence.

Erastus, who remained throughout his life attached to the Zwinglian party, of which he was the leading layman at Heidelberg, incurred the hatred of the Lutherans at the beginning of the year 1559 by his opposition to the intolerant action of Hesshusius, the Lutheran dean of the faculty of divinity, in attempting to refuse the doctorate to Stephen Sylvius. On 12th February the Elector Otto Henry was succeeded by Frederick III. The former had been a tolerant Lutheran, whereas Frederick was strongly anti-Lutheran. In the Colloquies of 1560 between the Reformed theologians of the Palatinate and the Saxon representatives of the Lutheran confession, Erastus, at the request of the Elector, defended the Reformed doctrine of the Supper, gaining the approbation of the Calvinist Olevianus (1536–1587), who had been appointed director of the College of Wisdom at Heidelberg. In August the Reformed faith was introduced, both Lutheranism and the residual Roman Catholicism of the Palatinate being proscribed by edict. Two years later Erastus supported in a synod the introduction of the Reformed Catechism of Heidelberg, which Olevianus and Ursinus had composed, and in the same year (1562) was printed, by the Elector's command, the *Büchlein vom Brotbrechen* ('Pamphlet on the Breaking of Bread'), of which Erastus was undoubtedly the author. John Marbach of Strassburg issued the Lutheran rejoinder, which evoked, in 1565, the second contribution of Erastus to the sacramental quarrel.

An account of the part taken by Erastus in the theological disputes at Heidelberg before the controversy that gave his name a dubious renown is not only indispensable for the right appreciation of his standpoint on the question of excommunication and discipline, but also advantageous for the study of what may be called the normal 'Erastian' character of the Protestant States of Germany. In April 1564, Erastus, as one of the Elector's theological lieutenants, was prominent at the Colloquy with the Württemberg doctors at Maulbronn, and two years later he accompanied Frederick on his mission to Amberg. The 10th of June 1568 was the red-letter day in the discipline-controversy at Heidelberg, when George Withers of Bury St. Edmunds, afterwards Archdeacon of Colchester, but at present a refugee in consequence of the Vestiarian controversy in England, maintained before the University his theses in defence of the authority of the ministers, along with the Presbytery, to perform all that related to church discipline (including excommunication) upon all offenders, not excepting princes. The Heidelberg Catechism (Articles 81–85) had already enunciated the principle of the excommunication of impenitents and hypocrites, and had been followed by two successive ordinances, of which the first was drawn up by Olevianus, who, however, was opposed to the second, because it reserved to the prince the right of pronouncing excommunication in the strict sense, namely, that of exclusion from the Lord's Supper. It was the debate begun by Withers that fanned the long-smouldering flame. Erastus opposed Withers on the second day, a friend having taken his place in his absence on the first. In the dispute thus inaugurated, Olevianus, on the side of Withers, was supported by his fellow-Calvinists, Ursinus, Zanchius, Tremellius, and Dathenus. Chief among the allies of Erastus were Neuser, Sylvanus, and Willing, with Simon Grynæus, the brother of J. J. Grynæus, who had married the sister of the wife of Erastus. The first two were subsequently accused of heresy and even of infidelity. Sylvanus was executed; and, though no complicity with their errors can be proved against Erastus, the odium in which these associates involved him accelerated the defeat of the anti-disciplinarian party, the discipline being established by an edict dated 13th July 1570, and the pleas of Erastus rendered nugatory.

Before the end of August 1568, Erastus had all but completed a *commentarium*—as he called it in his letter to the Zürich theologian Bullinger—against the proposed discipline. His arguments were thrown into the form of one hundred Theses on excommunication. Copies of the work, which he had no intention of publishing, were circulated in manuscript. Soon afterwards the Theses were reduced to seventy-five. From Zürich he was supported, from Geneva assailed. In the course of the first half of the following year appeared, also in manuscript, Beza's reply, which, as printed in 1590, bore the title, *Tractatus pius et moderatus de vera excommunicatione et christiano presbytero*. On Christmas Eve 1569, Erastus completed his longer work in six books—five in reply to Beza, and the sixth in reply to Ursinus, Zanchius, and (probably) Boquin, dean of the faculty of theology at Heidelberg. This manuscript bore the title, *Thesium (quæ de excommunicatione positæ fuerant) Confirmatio*.

Erastus, though again elected Rector for 1572, was two years later put under the ban of the Heidelberg consistory, and in 1575, the year before his excommunication was revoked, he was accused, but unsuccessfully, of anti-Trinitarian tenets. On 26th October 1576, Frederick III. was succeeded by Ludwig VI. A violent Lutheran reaction ensued; Luther's Catechism supplanted that of Heidelberg, and the Reformed theologians were dislodged from Court and Church. On 31st July 1579, the Elector, having subscribed the Formula of Concord, commanded the University professors to adopt the new confession or to resign. Erastus, like the majority of his colleagues, chose the latter alternative, thus proving that he was no 'Erastian in the ordinary sense.' In 1580 he removed to Basel, where his brother-in-law Grynæus had been professor of theology since 1575. At the beginning of 1581 he was admitted into the *collegium medicorum* of Basel, and in the summer began to teach ethics, of which he was appointed professor in the following January. He died on the last day of the year 1583, two days after the first anniversary of his election on the governing council of the University. Though inferior in spiritual insight and moral enthusiasm to many of the second generation of the Reformation, his career justifies the epitaph in St. Martin's Church at Basel, 'Acutus Philosophus, Elegans Medicus, Sincerus Theologus, Heidelbergensis Academiae Columen, Basiliensis Lumen.'

More than five years after the death of Erastus appeared a volume containing: (1) the seventy-five *Theses*, with a preface, (2) the *Confirmatio*, and (3) thirteen letters relating to discipline and the controversy at Heidelberg, addressed to Erastus by Bullinger, Gwalther, and others. The work bore the title: '*Explicatio gravissimae quaestionis, utrum excommunicatio, quatenus religionem intelligentes et amplexantes, a sacramentorum usu, propter admissum facinus arcet, mandato nitatur divino, an excogitata sit ab hominibus.* Autore clariss. viro Thoma Erasto D. medico. Opus nunc recens ex ipsius autoris autographo erutum et in lucem, prout moriens iusserat, editum . . . Pesclavii. Apud Baiocum Sultaceterum, Anno Salutis MDLXXXIX.' 'Pesclavii' (Poschiavo) was merely a pseudonym for London, and the following name the anagram for Jacobus Castelvetrus, who had married the widow of Erastus.

The two main questions in dispute between Erastus and Beza were those of Excommunication and the Organization of Discipline. Erastus, while recognizing the existence of exceptional cases where excommunication may be lawfully exercised, denies any right of withholding the Sacrament from professors of the Christian faith who, notwithstanding a moral lapse, are nevertheless desirous of participating, such desire being, in his opinion, sufficient proof of their repentance, and the Sacrament being, like the Word, a means of grace intended to benefit all, whereas it is an abuse of it to make it an occasion or instrument of punishment by withholding it. Nowhere, he holds, in the Law of Moses[1] or in Jewish history is excommunication the penalty for moral offences as distinct from ceremonial disqualification. Further, by a minute exegesis (according to the hermeneutics of the time) of NT passages, Erastus eliminates from the latter also all authority for excluding believers from the Lord's Supper, concerning the significance and efficacy of which sacrament his views are consistently Zwinglian.

Erastus emphatically disclaims any desire to weaken Church discipline. 'Nihil desidero magis quam ut severissima in Ecclesia morum disciplina servetur' (*Thes.* xvii.). But the question at issue is, Who, in a Christian State, is the depositary of disciplinary authority? It is here that we reach the problem of Erastianism and of Erastus' relation thereto. As men are subject to two governments—the invisible, whereof God is the Head, and the visible, whereof the magistrate is the head (and he, *ex hypothesi*, a Christian)—a State containing two or more distinct visible authorities is an anomaly, as much a monstrosity as a two-headed body:[2]

'God having entrusted to the Christian magistrate the sum-total of the visible government, the Church has by no means the right to exercise (in a Christian country) a power of repression distinct and independent of that of the State' (Bonnard, 134).

Erastus holds that such is the teaching of the OT and the NT. To claim visible power for the Church is tantamount to robbing Cæsar of what belongs to Cæsar, and the height of usurpation is to summon princes to the Church's tribunal and to excommunicate them. The Christian magistrate, though he may be admonished according to the word of God, and may profitably choose pious laymen to assist the ministers in superintending public morals on his behalf, is not to be set in antithesis to the Church as the profane power by the side of the sacred. The Church may warn and censure offenders, but punitive action belongs to the magistrate alone.

Without inquiring how far the objection of Erastus to the exercise of disciplinary jurisdiction by the Church was conditioned by his dislike of the Genevan tribunal of 'godly elders' at Heidelberg, we must endeavour to trace the connexion between his views on the specific question of the right of the Church to exercise discipline, especially that of exclusion from the Sacrament, and the wider question of the supremacy of the temporal power in matters spiritual—a question touched but incidentally by Erastus, who is more interested in Scriptural disquisitions than in the discussion of principles in politics and history. Both the extent and the boundaries of his contention may be defined as follows. In a State where all profess the true religion, all coercive authority (from which excommunication, however, is excluded[3]) resides in the magistrate alone, the functions of the Church being restricted to teaching, exhortation, and the due performance of worship. (Only where the magistrate is not a Christian or is unorthodox may the Church set up her own tribunals; but from these, also, the power of excommunication is withdrawn.)

[1] The fallacy involved in the analogy assumed between the Jewish and Christian dispensations is noted in the art. 'Erastus,' in the *Catholic Encyclopædia* (London, 1883).

[2] Contrast Keble's observations on 'Supposed Erastianism in some Parts of Hooker: real Amount of his Concessions in that Way,' in his ed. of Hooker's *Works*[7], Oxford, 1888, vol. i. p. lxxx; also p. lxxxvii: 'All Erastian reasoning implies that *co-ordinate authorities are incompatible.*'

[3] The views of Erastus on the right of a citizen to communicate are diametrically opposite to those expressed by Locke, while in some measure like them as regards the efficacy of the Sacrament: 'The whole force of excommunication consists only in this . . . the participation of some certain things, which the society communicates to its members, and unto which no man has any civil right, comes also to cease. There is no civil injury done unto the excommunicated person by the Church ministers refusing him that bread and wine, in the celebration of the Lord's Supper, which was not bought with his, but other men's money' (Locke, *Letter concerning Toleration*, London, 1714, ii. 237).

Our sketch of the life and teaching of Erastus presents him as a Zwinglian whose opposition to the Lutheran doctrine of the Supper underlay his antagonism to excommunication, and whose antipathy to the Calvinistic discipline was the exciting cause of his denial, in favour of the magistrate, of the Church's right to any coercive action. Yet his true relation to Erastianism must be sought, not so much in the propositions which the *Explicatio* and the *Confirmatio* actually formulate, as in the common orientation, of Lutherans and Zwinglians especially, towards the rival claims of Church and State, a theocracy being rather the Calvinistic ideal. It was not so much the opportune publication of the writings ('alowed' by Whitgift's *imprimatur* in 1589) as the appeals to the authority of Erastus by the Arminians against the Calvinists in Holland that gave Erastianism the varying connotation which, since the politico-ecclesiastical debates of the Stuart period, it has possessed in Great Britain. The opponents of Arminius and his friends reproached them for appealing 'to the superior magistrate against the ecclesiastical authority' (Figgis, p. 78, note). Both Grotius (who published in 1614 his Erastian treatise *de Imperio Summarum Potestatum circa Sacra*) and Althusius (whose view of the holiness of the State places him, with Luther, the Anglicans, Zwingli, and Erastus, against the Jesuits and the Presbyterians with their theory of the Church as *societas perfecta*) regard a Christian commonwealth as a State wherein the clergy form but one class of officers. Though it was Grotius who elaborated what we call Erastianism, he himself does not mention Erastus, and holds other views on excommunication. Nevertheless, the fact that Erastus was the first to assert in a Protestant country the principle of the subordination of the Church to the State entitles him to what ambiguous fame attaches to his memory in the name 'Erastianism.'

3. Erastianism in history.—(I.) *FROM CONSTANTINE TO THE REFORMATION.*—(*a*) *The period of the Ecumenical Councils.*—Concern with the affairs of the Church was for Constantine and his successors a political necessity. Yet it is easy to exaggerate the actual amount of Imperial interference exercised, and to forget the extent to which the motives of the State were in the interests of peace.

Though it was the great African sectary, Donatus, who asked the famous question, 'Quid Imperatori cum Ecclesia?' the Donatists set the precedent of an appeal to the State by one section of the Christian Church against another, thus necessitating the reference of the controversy to the Council of Arles (314 or 315). The Donatist schism was destined, despite Imperial generosity and coercion, commissions and conferences, to rend Africa until it was conquered by the Vandals after the death of Augustine. The Nicene Council, convened by Constantine for the purpose of allaying the strife that already threatened the peace of Egypt, proved to be rather the beginning of a world-wide controversy that continued to harass Church and State until Theodosius gave Arianism its death-blow. 'Arianism was put down as it had been put up, by the civil power' (Gwatkin, 'Arianism,' in *Camb. Med. Hist.* i. [1911] 141). The so-called Second Ecumenical Council held at Constantinople in 381—to which only Eastern bishops had been summoned—was convened primarily for the purpose of coping with religious disorders in the capital itself. Not the least justification for the use of the term 'Byzantinism' (the usual synonym for 'Erastianism' on the Continent[1]) is found in the fact that,

[1] For the equivalence of the terms 'Erastianism' and 'Byzantinism' (the latter being regarded as preferable), see Figgis, p. 101, and Hobhouse, *The Church and the World in Idea and in History*, London, 1910, p. 392 ff. 'This doctrine [of the superiority of the civil power to the ecclesiastical] is often called by Continental writers Byzantinism, a name suggested by the

ever since Constantine transferred his capital from Nicomedeia across the Bosporus to Byzantium, which henceforth bore his name, Constantinople became not only the storm-centre of the strife of creeds, but also, for the most part, the *venue* of the Emperor's negotiations with the Church in the Eastern Empire.

In the entourage of the Arian prelate Eusebius of Nicomedeia, with their allies (including Eusebius the historian, bishop of Cæsarea), we have the first instance of what may be called an Erastian party, their aim being to support the form of Christian faith guaranteed to give them most influence at Court, and, on the other hand, to strengthen the Imperial supremacy over the Church. Foakes-Jackson has suggested that the support of Arianism by Constantius, to whom the problem of Church and State presented great difficulties, was an endeavour to secure peace by the Emperor's endorsement of what appeared to be the creed of the majority. Nor must we forget that Athanasius, as Patriarch of Alexandria, was regarded as wielding an authority that might be detrimental to the unity of the Empire. Perhaps even the pagan reaction under Julian (361–3) was to some extent motived by a desire to substitute for Christianity, which Julian had forsworn, a non-contentious system of belief founded upon a popularized Neo-Platonism. The orthodox Valentinian (364–375), unlike his brother the Arian Valens (364–378), endeavoured to maintain as much neutrality as possible, neither protecting the persecuted orthodox of the East nor permitting Hilary to remain in Milan to challenge the orthodoxy of the Arian bishop, Auxentius. Like Hosius of Corduba, whose influence with Constantine at Nicæa was probably the principal factor in securing the Emperor's insistence upon the homoousian Creed, Theodosius the Great (379–395) was an orthodox Spaniard, the sincerity of whose religious zeal is proved less by his anti-pagan and anti-heretical legislation than by his acceptance, as penance for his responsibility for the massacre at Thessalonica (391), of a temporary excommunication at the hands of Ambrose. 'His proclamation *de Fide Catholica* is one of the most important legal documents in the annals of the Christian Church. It declares the Imperial will that all nations and peoples in the Empire shall follow the religion which the Apostle Peter introduced into Rome, and "which the Pontiff Damasus and the Bishop of Alexandria now profess."'[1] Gratian (374–383) had already broken the last official link of the Empire with paganism by abdicating the title of Pontifex Maximus, and Theodosius had supported his youthful colleague (an apt disciple of Ambrose) in refusing to replace the altar of Victory in the Senate. Honorius (395–423) and Arcadius (395–408), the sons of Theodosius, who succeeded to the rule of the West and the East respectively, differed, like the brothers Valentinian and Valens, in the extent of their intervention with the Church—the Western Emperor, according to the rule that prevailed, henceforth being the less pragmatical. Nevertheless Honorius, besides convening the conferences with the Donatists (411), whose recalcitrancy he vainly sought to repress, by an edict of 418 banished Pelagius and his principal followers, notwithstanding their recent acquittal by Zosimus, the vacillating Pope who forthwith marked his recantation by calling upon the Italian bishops to subscribe his anti-Pelagian *Epistola Tractoria* (417). But more importance, for our inquiry, attaches to the reprimand addressed by Honorius to Arcadius after the condemnation of Chrysostom, Patriarch of Constantinople, at the Synod of the Oak, near Chalcedon (404). Chrysostom's deposition and tragic exile were the result, not so much of the displeasure of Arcadius, fomented though it was by the patriarch of the jealous see of Alexandria, as of the offence which his fearless denunciation of frivolities and delinquencies had given to the 'monstrous regiment of women' (as John Knox called the government of Mary Stuart), now for the first time, in the person of the Empress Eudoxia, becoming a force in the Eastern Empire. The importance of the letter of Honorius lies, as Bury has pointed out, in the fact that it contains a declaration by an Emperor of the principle which Hosius and Hilary, in their opposition to Constantius, had first asserted, namely, that the interpretation of Divine things was the concern of churchmen, while it was the due observance (*obsequium*) of religion that concerned the Emperors.[1] Here is anticipated the later distinction between *ius in sacris* and *ius circa sacra*.

unwarrantable control exercised by the Emperors of the East over the Patriarchs of Constantinople and the Greek Church during the Middle Ages, while in this country it is generally known by the name of Erastianism' (Cunningham, p. 164; see also p. 207).

[1] Hobhouse, 103.

Not without reason did Nestorius, the Patriarch of Constantinople, who, soon after his transference from Antioch to the capital, inaugurated the bitter controversies of the succeeding centuries, give to his autobiography the title 'Tragedy.' The vehement wrangles about the Two Natures in Christ occasioned in the first place the Council of Ephesus (431), at which Nestorius was condemned. Seventeen years later Eutyches propounded the opposite heresy, asserting but One Nature of Christ after the Incarnation; and this first form of Monophysitism triumphed in the tumult of the 'Robber Synod,' as Pope Leo (*Ep.* xcv. 2) designated the Council summoned by Theodosius II. to Ephesus in 449. The change of attitude in Theodosius, who was at first inclined to favour the Dyoprosopic teaching of Nestorius, was probably due to the influence which, before the Council of 431, Cyril had succeeded in exercising upon the Imperial ladies. But the death of Theodosius in 450 brought about a speedy reversal of his policy. The Empress Pulcheria and her consort Marcian, supporters of the doctrine of Two Natures, decided to summon another Ecumenical Council, and that, too, against the wishes of Leo, who preferred that the question at issue should be determined by the authority of his *Tome*, rather than by the decision of a Council dominated by the Emperor and Empress. Thus Monophysitism, in its Eutychian form countenanced by Theodosius II., was repudiated by Pulcheria and Marcian, the *Definition* of Chalcedon inclining more to the teaching of Nestorius than to that of his successful persecutor, Cyril. Yet the pressure which Marcian at Chalcedon (like Constantine at Nicæa) put upon the majority of the Eastern bishops only embittered the reaction, for the Nearer East remained Monophysite. In 482, the Emperor Zeno issued the *Henoticon*, which, though probably composed by the Patriarch Acacius, was resented by a number of bishops for the very reason that it was issued on the authority of the Emperor alone. 'Zeno tried the autocratic short cut out of controversy by the prohibition of technical terms.'[2] Nestorius and Eutyches were both anathematized and the anathemas of Cyril against Nestorius approved, the doctrine of Chalcedon being implicitly condemned and the symbols confirmed at Ephesus (431) asserted to be adequate. Needless to say, the *Henoticon* proved but an abortive Eirenicon, and the next Pope, Simplicius, excommunicated the Emperor. Seventy years after the issue of Zeno's *Henoticon* to the bishops of Egypt, the Fifth

[1] Bury, *Hist. of the later Roman Empire*, London, 1889, i. 105.

[2] Alice Gardner, 'Religious Disunion in the Fifth Century,' in *Camb. Med. History*, i. [1911] 516.

Ecumenical Council (Constantinople, 553) was held at the bidding of Justinian, and in connexion with the form which the Monophysite controversy had now taken through the Emperor's action in condemning, in the edict known as the 'Three Articles' or 'Three Chapters' (*Tria Capitula*), to wit, the works of the three leading theologians of the Antiochene School, Nestorius, Theodore of Mopsuestia, and Ibas of Edessa. Pope Vigilius, who had for some time been practically a prisoner in the East and had refused to sign the 'Three Articles,' recanted after his condemnation at the Council, thus finally subordinating to the Imperial will the theological opinion of the West. The basis—the agenda—of the Fifth General Council

'was an edict drawn up by the Emperor; it adopted theological tenets formulated by the Emperor. This is the most characteristic manifestation of Justinian's Cæsaro-papism' (Bury, ii. 5).

So far did Justinian push his ecclesiastical absolutism that just before his death he deposed the Patriarch of the capital for rejecting the edict in which the Emperor, who had lapsed into the heresy that Christ's earthly body was incorruptible, commanded the assent of all patriarchs and bishops to the Aphthartodocetic doctrine.

For the disaffected Monophysites of the East, Justinian had not gone far enough in the assertion of One Nature, and Sergius sought to win them over by the admission that the Two Natures operated by means of one theandric energy. Exactly a hundred years from the time when Pope Vigilius was the prisoner of Justinian, Pope Martin was brought to Constantinople, whence he was banished to the Crimea by the Emperor Constans II., who, in accordance with his conservatively Roman attitude towards the doctrine of the Church, had prohibited, in his *Ecthesis* (638) and his *Typos* (648), the employment of such technical theological terms as engendered strife. Martin paid with his life the penalty of condemning both Monothelitism and the Emperor's two edicts. Constantine IV., on the other hand, displayed a genuine impartiality in leaving to the bishops at the Council of 680 untrammelled power to decide the issue. However great was the doctrinal importance of their condemnation of Monothelitism, greater historical interest attaches to their anathema of Pope Honorius, who was adjudged to have supported the Monothelite heresy in 635.

It is unnecessary to follow the Erastian policy of the Eastern Emperors (whose Cæsaro-papism became the inheritance of the Czars of Russia) after the Seventh Ecumenical Synod, held at Nicæa in 787. Leo the Isaurian (718–741), who attempted to suppress the superstition of image-worship, was confronted both by a revolt under Cosmas, and with the ban of Pope Gregory II. But his most illustrious opponent was John of Damascus, who, himself the subject of the Khalif, maintained in three apologies that Emperors had no prerogative to manage the affairs of the Church.[1] Constantine Copronymus, the son of Leo, continued his father's policy with an iron hand. He was, as we have already mentioned, a hater of monks as well as of images, and anticipated the policy of those later Emperors in the West who sought to overthrow the power of the Pope. Constantine strove, not to enforce doctrines, but to abolish those customs or institutions of the Church which he regarded as detrimental to the State. Twelve years after his death the Second Ecumenical Council—supported by the astute and cruel Irene, the widow of his successor—established the worship of images; and in 842, Theodora—the disloyal widow of another iconoclastic Emperor, Michael Balbus—celebrated the Feast of Orthodoxy on the restoration of the worship which her husband had temporarily checked.

[1] Harnack, *Dogmengesch.*, Eng. tr. iv. [1898] 323, 328.

For the orthodox Eastern Church, because of her cultus, her Monophysitism, and her dependence upon the Emperor, 'it was easy to be,' as Oman says, 'as no other Church has ever been, the State Church, and at the same time non-political' (*The Church and the Divine Order*, London, 1911, p. 134)—words that recall the statement of Freeman (*Historical Essays*, Third Series, London, 1892, p. 265):

'To the Eastern Roman the orthodoxy of the Eastern Church made up for the lack of nationality in the Eastern Empire. The sway of Christ and Cæsar went together. In the true Byzantine mind the two ideas could hardly be conceived asunder.'

(*b*) *The struggle of the Empire and the European kingdoms with the Papacy.*—The iconoclastic controversy forms a significant transition, from the history of the developing Byzantinism that dominated the religious life of the later Roman Empire in the East, to the history of the titanic conflict of the Romano-German Empire with the Papacy. As King of the Franks, Charles the Great had already vindicated his headship over the Frankish Church, nor had he hesitated to reject the decisions of the Ecumenical Council of 787. He presided at all the Frankish ecclesiastical councils, and even in the Papal domain exercised all the rights of the lord of the land. The fact that there was at the moment no Emperor in the East may, apart from the necessity of securing Charles's personal support, have been a factor in determining the action of Pope Leo III. (795–816) in crowning him Emperor on Christmas Day, 800. On the death of Charles (814), we pass from the rarely challenged supremacy of the Emperor over the Church to the Church's assertion of her right to temporal supremacy as well as to absolute spiritual authority over Emperors and princes. The interests of the monarchs of the separate countries, too, both within and without the Empire, were all alike imperilled by the growing claims of the Papacy, from Nicholas I. (858–867) to Innocent III. (1198–1216); but the question of Erastianism itself, in any given circumstance of domestic policy, is complicated by the phenomena of feudalism and the rise of national Churches. Notwithstanding the strong hand with which monarchs like William the Conqueror dealt with ecclesiastical affairs, a very real limitation of regality was involved in a recognition, however grudging, of the Papal supremacy.[1] An obvious effect of the success of the Papal pretensions was the curtailment of Erastian statecraft throughout the West. The brunt of the struggle fell upon the German Emperors, because of the unique relation which they bore to the Popes, who were regarded, by princes outside the Empire, as foreign potentates exercising in the separate realms a jurisdiction more or less resented. To the Emperors the Popes were colleagues, for neither the rivals themselves nor the theorists who severally supported them envisaged the struggle as a contest waged by two different societies. But, though it would be a misreading of history to speak of the conflict as between Church and State—having regard to the prevalent theocratic conception of the Holy Roman Empire as one society with two functions, *sacerdotium* and *imperium*, discharged by different officers—the crux of the struggle was, nevertheless, the recurrent question of the supremacy of the spiritual or of the temporal power in the State. The representative anti-Papal theories,[2]

[1] Freeman holds that, had it not been for the Romanizing influence of Edward the Confessor and William, the Church of England would have become as subordinate to the State as was the Eastern Church (*The Norman Conquest*, v. [Oxford, 1876] 494 f.).

[2] The magnitude of the mediæval literature relating to the controversy may be inferred from the fact that Gierke enumerates no less than 160 Publicists, Legists, and Canonists from the 11th to the 16th cent. (Gierke-Maitland, *Political Theories of the Middle Age*, Cambridge, 1900, pp. lxiii–lxxvi).

which we shall briefly summarize, demonstrate the strength of the dialectical defence of the right of princes, and the force of public opinion allied with them. Time after time did the temporal power at bay display its *de facto* if not its *de jure* superiority, as is instanced by the death in exile of Gregory VII. (Hildebrand, 1073–1085), who abased Henry IV. at Canossa (1077), and of Alexander III. (1159–1181), who humbled Frederick I. (Barbarossa) at Venice (1177). So, too, the French kings avenged, by the Babylonian captivity of the Popes at Avignon, the blow to regal prestige that was involved in the fall of Frederick II., the last of the Hohenstaufens (1212–1250). From the earlier doctrine of the Church herself, that the State was co-ordinate with her, and from the original idea of a pre-existent harmony between the two powers, both policy and speculation drifted to the more and more emphatic assertion of their distinctness and even opposition. It will suffice for our present purpose to review the anti-Papal theories of two great Italians and two great Englishmen—Dante (1265–1321) and Marsilius of Padua (died after 1342); William of Occam (died in 1347) and John Wyclif (1324–1387).

(*a*) The *de Monarchia* of Dante is not only 'the most purely ideal of political works ever written' (Edmund G. Gardner, *Dante*, London, 1900, p. 66), but is at once the epilogue or epitaph of the Empire as the earthly Kingdom of God, and 'a prophecy of the modern State, and of that doctrine of the Divine Right of kings, which formed for long its theoretical justification against clerical pretensions' (Figgis, *From Gerson to Grotius*, Cambridge, 1907, p. 28). The first book shows that the temporal monarchy—whereof the Empire is the unique embodiment—is necessary for the well-being of the world; the second, that the Roman people, under the jurisdiction of whose Emperors Christ deigned to be born and to suffer, succeeded by Divine Will to the empire of the world; the third, that the authority of the Roman Monarch or Emperor depends immediately (*sine ullo medio*) upon God. The Supreme Pontiff and the Emperor are man's two necessary guides of life, corresponding to the two ends of life—eternal life and temporal felicity. It was the conflict between John XXII. (1316–1334) and Ludwig of Bavaria (1314–1347), who attempted to depose each other, that made the *de Monarchia*, hitherto almost unknown, an armoury of Imperialist arguments, the supporters of Ludwig including William of Occam, whom Pope Clement regarded as having inspired Marsilius of Padua.

(*b*) Marsilius of Padua (whose *Defensor Pacis* was, by the command of Henry VIII., published in an English translation, *The Defence of Peace*, by William Marshall, in 1535) anticipates, in his views on excommunication, the radical attitude of Erastus. He maintains not only that coercive power belongs exclusively to the State, but even that no compulsion may be exercised in the matter of religious belief. Sovereignty rests with the whole body of citizens, acting as the faithful lawgiver, and the prince appointed by them. The civil ruler has full regulative and judicial power over the Church. Papal decrees have no temporal effect, and all bishops are equal.

(*c*) William of Occam espoused the cause of Ludwig of Bavaria against John XXII., by whom Occam and Michael of Cesena, the General of the Franciscan Order, were banished from Avignon during the Minorite quarrel on the subject of clerical poverty, this being the cause of Occam's opposition to the Papal claim to unlimited *plenitudo potestatis*, both temporal and spiritual. He contends that the whole hierarchy, from the Pope downwards, is a human order, and not immediately Divine. Were the Pope's power unlimited, he could depose princes, and reduce Christianity to an unprecedented slavery. Occam would even advocate a college of Popes in preference to a monarchical Papacy. The ordinary judge of the Pope is the Emperor, but the Church at large has jurisdiction over him. In case of heresy he could be deposed by a General Council representing the whole Church. Inasmuch as every society can make laws for itself, the Church, assembled as a General Council on the basis of parishes, could appoint a successor. Occam maintains that Christ alone is Head of the Church, and his principles are not only subversive of Papal domination but also assertory of the fact that the true faith resides among the pious. He anticipates both Wyclif's conception of grace as the ground of dominion and Calvin's conception of the true Church as consisting of the spiritual community.

(*d*) Wyclif has been accounted more Erastian than Erastus. In his *de Officio Regis* and other tractates he asserts the king's Divine right to disendow the Church. Even the laity have the right to withhold revenues from unworthy ecclesiastical superiors. Wyclif's advance upon contemporary anti-Papal theories consists in his extension of the State's *dominium*. Not content with maintaining the State's autonomy in civil affairs, he asserts both its right and its duty to intervene in the administration of the Church when she neglects her duty. The spiritual office is a *ministerium*, not a *dominium*, but this *ministerium* the secular lords may take away from irreligious clerics. The link between Wyclif and Luther is supplied by John Hus (1373–1415), whose treatises, *de Ecclesia*, *de Potestate Papæ*, and *Determinatio de ablatione temporalium a clericis*, show how completely he had absorbed Wyclif's anti-Papal teaching.

(ii.) *THE REFORMATION.*—(*a*) *Germany.*—It was inevitable that the Reformation should be established in the various German States, as in other countries, only by the help of the secular power. If the German princes and nobles had not responded in sufficient numbers to Luther's appeals in 1520, and if Charles V. had not honoured Luther's safe-conduct to Worms, the attempts of Luther at reform would have proved as fatally futile as did the premature efforts of Arnold of Brescia and Savonarola. Luther's *Address to the Christian Nobles of the German Nation* (1520) bore immediate fruit in the list of grievances against the Roman see which the States drew up two years later at the Diet of Nuremberg. On the ground of the priesthood of all believers, Luther appealed to the German princes to undertake the reformation of the Church—the duty which the bishops refused to perform.[1] At the Diet of Speier (1526) the principle was adopted which forms a land-mark in the history of the Reformation—that, in the matter of putting in force the Edict of Worms, whereby Luther was placed under the ban, each component part of the Empire should act as it pleased. The principle afterwards formally ratified at Augsburg (1555), *cujus est regio, ejus est religio*,[2] secured the religious autonomy of each Catholic and Lutheran State independently of the Emperor, whilst investing the prince with absolute authority to impose upon his subjects the religion professed by himself. The German Reformation, in its political aspect, heralded the modern State, and resulted in a new conception of the authority of the territorial prince in ecclesiastical affairs.

Luther's opinions on the relation of the Church to the State form one of the most debated themes connected with the history of the Reformation. Zwingli and he were in practical agreement as to the functions of the secular power in matters ecclesiastical, and on this subject in general—apart from the specific question of excommunication—the views of the Zwinglian Erastus, as we have seen, present no material divergence from those of Luther. Difficulty has been experienced in reconciling apparently discrepant judgments of Luther at different epochs, but these may be harmonized by taking cognizance of the change which his earlier opinions underwent after the Peasants' War and the outbreak of the Anabaptists. 'To Luther it always remained clear that the work of the magistrate in the Church could never be more than a help to the task of ruling purely by the word of God. But Luther has no successor in this protest' (Oman, 227 f.).

(*b*) *England.*—So closely is Erastianism interwoven with the history of the Church of England, that the record of its operation here is to a great extent conterminous with the ecclesiastical history of the kingdom, the English kings having always claimed a visitatorial authority over the Church. Before Henry VIII. the greatest assertors of the independence of the Crown against Papal jurisdiction from without and clerical immunities within were William the Conqueror, Henry II., and Edward III.[3] The first two were concerned with the problems of civil and ecclesiastical tribunals, William being also occupied with the matter of

[1] A fundamental theory of the German Reformation was that of the transference of episcopal jurisdiction from the bishops to the Protestant princes, or, rather, that of the recovery by the princes of the power which, though naturally theirs, had been usurped by the bishops. The 'Episcopal System,' ratified by the Compact of Passau (1552), professed merely to restore to the prince his inherent ecclesiastical rights. See Wilberforce, *op. cit.*, with reff. to Carpzovius, Gerhard, and Stryk.

[2] '*Cujus regio ejus religio* is a maxim as fatal to true religion as it is to freedom of conscience; it is the creed of Erastian despotism, the formula in which the German territorial Princes expressed the fact that they had mastered the Church as well as the State' (Pollard, 'Religious War in Germany,' in *Camb. Mod. Hist.* ii. [Cambridge, 1903] 278). On the important diplomatic consequences of the Peace of Augsburg to England, see Lindsay, *Hist. Reformation*, Edin. 1906, i. 398, note 2.

[3] Longman, *Life and Times of Edward III.*, Lond. 1869, ii. 92–96.

investitures. Hildebrand recognized the right of lay investiture as a privilege enjoyed by English kings, while William rejected Hildebrand's claim to suzerainty over England. The conflict of Church and State waged between Becket and Henry II. centred in the question of the validity of the Canon Law, together with the numerous claims to privileges or immunities made by the Church on the basis thereof, especially as regards the civil impunity of criminous clerks.[1]

The sixth session of Henry VIII.'s Reformation Parliament (1534–1535) witnessed the culmination of the breach with Rome, the *Act of Supremacy* giving the King the title of 'Supreme Head on earth of the Church of England,' while the *Treason Act*, under which Fisher and Moore were condemned, included, under the category of treason, maliciously depriving the sovereign of any of his royal titles or calling him a schismatic. With Henry's ecclesiastical legislation, Erastianism in England enters upon a new phase. Even before the rupture with Rome had been consummated by Clement VII.'s refusal of the divorce with Katherine, Convocation had recognized the King as 'Supreme Head,' and reluctantly acquiesced in the 'Submission of the Clergy' (1532). In Elizabeth's *Act of Supremacy* (1558) her father's claim to the headship of the Church was modified. She was declared to be 'Supreme Governor of this realm as well in all spiritual or ecclesiastical things or causes as temporal'; but section 20 of the Statute recognized the limitation of the royal prerogative in matters of doctrine, reserving the right of the clergy in Convocation to assent.[2] While the professed purpose of the Statute was to restore 'to the Crown the ancient jurisdiction over the State ecclesiastical and spiritual, and abolishing all foreign power repugnant to the same,' it was the monarch's personal authority, rather than that of Parliament, that was herein enhanced, and the *Acts of Supremacy*, both of Henry VIII. and of Elizabeth, were important factors in Tudor absolutism. On the other hand, the developments of Protestantism in Puritanism, Independency, Quakerism, and other movements towards religious and political liberty and equality, effected the ultimate overthrow of the Stuart dynasty. Now were laid the foundations both of modern Erastianism and of the manifold opposition to it. Even when Hooker published his *Laws of Ecclesiastical Polity* (1593–94), the fundamental assumption of his Erastianism (not unlike the basis of Arnold's idea of a Broad Church co-extensive with the nation) was already falsified by the fact that the State, even viewed as Protestant, was no longer of one religion. From the beginning of Elizabeth's reign the interminable controversy of Church and State assumes a new significance. It no longer hinges upon the rival claims of Pope and Emperor or King. The vindication of the spiritual autonomy of presbyters, of congregations, and even of individuals against the authority of Sovereign, Parliament, or Magistrate compelled inquiry into the true nature of the Church of Christ. Yet it must not be forgotten that, as Hutton[3] says, 'the English Revolution was thoroughly Erastian in its treatment of the Church question,—a complete contrast to the Scots.' The Erastianism of the Independents was in great measure due to their anti-Presbyterianism. The House of Commons, despite its suspicion of king and bishop, refused to abdicate its supremacy *circa sacra*.

(*c*) *Scotland*.—In no Protestant country has greater opposition been shown to the very suggestion of Erastianism than in Scotland. Not only the Secession of 1733 and the Disruption of 1843 (the latter especially being, in the first instance, a protest against lay patronage and intrusion), but also the growing effort on the part of the Established Church to free itself from State control, shows how deeply engrained in the Scottish religious consciousness is that idea of the essential autonomy of the Kirk which John Knox acquired during his exile in Geneva. The revolt against Erastianism in Scotland may be said to have begun when the Scottish Estates, on 25th Aug. 1560, abolished the Papal jurisdiction and the Mass.[1] But it was especially in connexion with the repeated attempts of the Stuart kings of England to establish prelacy that the term 'Erastianism' acquired in Scotland its evil connotation.[2] Resistance to successive Acts which were understood to be aimed against the Presbyterian Church of Scotland after the Restoration inspired the heroism of a series of movements—those of the Covenanters, the Protesters, the Conventiclers, the Hamiltonians, and the Cameronians.

Nor have the principles that underlie the discussion of the relation between Church and State been in any country more learnedly, eloquently, and judiciously handled than in Scotland. Probably no Church in Christendom is in this respect more ecclesiastically-minded, in the true sense of the term, than the Presbyterian Church of Scotland, whether Established or Free. The current opinion of many modern English ecclesiologists, that the Established Church of Scotland enjoys almost complete autonomy, is a mistake. On the question of State aid it has been tersely expressed that the Established Church of Scotland was non-voluntary, the Free Church was voluntary on conditions, and the United Presbyterian Church was voluntary without conditions.[3] Apart from the Disruption of 1843, when resentment at the decision of a legal tribunal was of the essence of the movement, in more recent times similar resentment was shown on the part of the United Free Church against the claim of a majority of the lay tribunal of the House of Lords (1st Aug. 1904) to control and determine the development of doctrine in the Free Presbyterian Churches of Scotland. Thus the religious history of Scotland exhibits opposition to Erastianism, whether the State control be exercised legislatively or administratively.

LITERATURE.—A. V. G. Allen, *Christian Institutions*, Edin. 1898, esp. bk. i. chs. 10–12; J. Bannerman, *The Church of Christ*, do. 1868; W. Binnie, *The Church*, do. 1882, esp. pp. 33–35; A. Bonnard, *Thomas Éraste et la discipline ecclésiastique*, Lausanne, 1894; J. H. Blunt, *The Book of Ch. Law*[7], Lond. 1894; J. Bryce, *Holy Roman Empire*[8], do. 1889; J. B. Bury, *Hist. of the Eastern Roman Empire*, do. 1912 (important for the history of ecclesiastical policy); S. Coit, *National Idealism and a State Church*, do. 1907; M. Creighton, *The Church and the Nation*, do. 1901; W. Cunningham, *Discussions on Ch. Principles*, Edin. 1863, also *Histor. Theol.*, do. 1862, esp. vol. i. ch. xiii. § 3, and vol. ii. ch. xxvii.; R. W. Dale, *Hist. of Eng. Congregationalism*, Lond. 1907; J. N. Figgis, 'Erastus and Erastianism,' *JThSt* ii. [1900] 66–101, also *Divine Right of Kings*, Camb. 1896; G. P. Fisher, *The Reformation*, new ed., Lond. 1906, esp. ch. xiv., 'Relation of the Prot. Churches to the Civil Authority' (with valuable bibliography on p. 410); W. H. Fremantle, *The World as the Subject of Redemption*, Lond. 1885; F. H. Geffcken, *Church and State*, Eng. tr., Lond. 1877; H. M. Gwatkin (and others), *The Church, Past and Present*,

[1] Maitland, *Roman Canon Law in the Church of England*, London, 1898, esp. Essay ii., 'Church, State and Decretals,' and Essay iv., 'Henry II. and the Criminous Clerks.'

[2] Prothero, *Select Statutes and other Constitutional Documents illustrative of the Reigns of Elizabeth and James I.*[3], Oxford, 1906, p. xxx ff., 'Church and State.'

[3] W. H. Hutton, *History of the English Church from the Accession of Charles I. to the Death of Anne*, London, 1903, p. 128 ff.

[1] Hume Brown, *Hist. of Scotland*, Cambridge, ii. (1905) 71 f.

[2] 'To many a Scot prelacy will always suggest another word of evil sound: to wit, Erastianism. The link is Anglican. The name of the professor of medicine at Heidelberg . . . won a fame or infamy in Britain that has been denied to it elsewhere' (Maitland, 'The Anglican Settlement and the Scottish Reformation,' in *Camb. Mod. Hist.* ii. [1903] 595).

[3] J. A. Paterson, 'The Ecclesiastical Situation in Scotland,' *HJ* x. (1912) 2.

do. 1900; H. H. Henson, *The National Church*, Lond. 1908, also *Church Problems* (ed.), do. 1900, and *English Rel. in the Seventeenth Cent.*, do. 1903; W. M. Hetherington, *Hist. of the Ch. of Scotland*, Edin. 1847; W. Hobhouse, *The Church and the World in Idea and in History*, do. 1910 (perhaps the most comprehensive work on the whole subject, both theoretical and historical; contains copious reff. to Patristic, mediæval, and modern literature); Hooker, *Works*, ed. Keble, Oxford, 1888, with valuable comments; W. H. Hutton, *William Laud*, Lond. 1895; A. Taylor Innes, *Church and State*, Edin. 1890; A. Lang, *Hist. of Scotland*, Edin. and Lond. 1900–07, vols. ii.–iv.; Lechler-Stähelin, art. 'Erastus,' in *PRE*[3]; R. Lee, *The Theses of Erastus touching Excommunication*, Edin. 1844: T. McCrie, *Story of the Scottish Church*, Lond. 1875; P. MacFarlan, *Vindication of the Ch. of Scotland*, do. 1850; J. H. B. Masterman, *Rights and Responsibilities of Nat. Churches*, do. 1908; H. W. Moncrieff, *The Free Ch. Principle*, Edin. 1883; J. B. Mozley, *Essays*, Lond. 1878, those on Strafford, Laud, Cromwell, Luther, Arnold; J. Oman, *The Church and the Divine Order*, do. 1911; R. L. Ottley, *Christian Ideas and Ideals*, do. 1909, ch. xvii., 'The Church and the State'; H. W. Parkinson, *Modern Pleas for State Churches examined*, do. 1874; M. W. Patterson, *Hist. of the Church of England*, do. 1909; A. P. Stanley, *Essays on Ch. and State*, do. 1870; J. Stoughton, *Ch. and State Two Hundred Years Ago*, do. 1862, also *Eccles. Hist. of England*, do. 1874; K. Sudhoff, 'C. Olevianus u. Z. Ursinus,' in pt. viii. of *Leben u. ausgewählte Schriften der Väter*, etc. (Elberfeld, 1857), bk. iii. ch. iii., 'Die Kämpfe wegen der Kirchenzucht,' p. 339 f.; C. F. Vierordt, *Gesch. d. Reformation im Grossherzogtum Baden*, Carlsruhe, 1847, p. 456 ff.; W. Warburton, *Alliance of Ch. and State*, summarized in Watson's *Life of Bp. Warburton* (Lond. 1863); R. I. Wilberforce, *Sketch of the Hist. of Erastianism*, Lond. 1851, also *Relations of Ch. and State*, do. 1848; W. Wilson, *Free Ch. Principles*, Edin. 1887. See also *The Free Ch. of Scotland Appeals 1903–4*, Authorized Report, Edin. and Lond. 1904.

JOHN YOUNG EVANS.

ERINYES.—See EUMENIDES.

ERROR AND TRUTH.—Both in its philosophical and in its popular acceptation the word 'error' is applied to false opinions. But popular usage also gives to the term a still wider meaning, whereby it includes not only false opinions, but numerous forms of practical failure, and of defective conduct, whose relations to conscious beliefs are by no means constant or easily discoverable. The derivation of the word illustrates the naturalness of associating the conception of a false opinion with the idea of some such act as wandering, or straying, or missing the way. It seems, therefore, as if a first approach to a sharper definition of 'error' would be aided by clearly distinguishing between the practical and the theoretical applications, and then confining the philosophical use of the term, so far as possible, to theoretical errors. But we shall find it impossible to define even theoretical error without reference to some genuinely practical considerations. However much we try to avoid popular confusions, we shall be led in the end to a concept of error which can be stated only in teleological terms, and which involves the idea of action for an end, and of a certain defect in the carrying out of such action.

The present article, after distinguishing, as far as possible, the concept of theoretical errors, or of false opinions, from the popular concept of practical errors, and after stating some of the best known views regarding what a false opinion is, will seek to indicate the nature of a solution of the problem in terms of a doctrine about the relation of the cognitive to the volitional processes.

1. Practical errors and false opinions.—When one emphasizes the practical aspect of an error, one sometimes makes use of the more drastic word 'blunder.' A blunder is something which involves serious maladjustment, defect in conduct. Errors in the sense of blunders may be due to false opinions, or may even very largely consist of such. On the other hand, they need not involve false opinions, and *must* involve actions which do not attain their goal. These actions may be only partly voluntary; but the relation of their defective aspects to the accompanying voluntary processes is what makes us call them errors. Thus, we speak of the error or blunder of the marksman who misses his mark; of the player who fails to score, or who permits his opponent to score when the game calls for some device for hindering the opponent from scoring. We speak of the musician's error when he sings or plays a false note. Such errors may, but often do not, result from, or accompany, false opinions or misjudgments. Thus one may fail as marksman, as player, or as musician, either through misjudgments or through defects of physical training, of temporary condition, of mood, or of attention—defects which may involve no false opinions whatsoever.

In the moral realm, the relations between such practical errors on the one hand and false opinions on the other are especially momentous and intricate. Here, in fact, the theory of moral error involves all the main problems about the relations between knowledge and action. A sin is very generally called an error. 'We have erred and strayed from thy ways like lost sheep.' The error is, first of all, practical. It has also some relation to knowledge. Yet, since sin appears to depend upon some degree of knowledge of the right, the 'error' in question does not merely result from a false opinion about what one's duty is. On the other hand, that sin involves 'unwisdom,' and so does in some respect depend upon false opinions, is very generally asserted. Any careful discussion of those practical errors which have a moral significance will, therefore, show that it is no merely accidental confusion which has led to our use of a word derived from our experience of wanderings from the right path as a term which is also to be applied to false opinions. Opinions certainly express themselves in actions; and voluntary actions are guided by opinions. The resulting relations of cognition and volition, especially in the moral world, are amongst the most complex and intimate which are known to us anywhere. They are relations which we can neither ignore nor wholly disentangle. Hence the clear separation of theoretical error and practical error, at least in the moral world, is impossible. For sin involves both theoretical and practical defects.

We can, however, make some approach to such a separation of the theoretical and practical aspects of error if we turn for aid to a very different realm, namely, formal logic. The distinction between true and false propositions involves certain well-known general relations, such as formal logic considers and analyzes. We may use these relations for what they are worth in attempting to define what a false opinion is. Having thus laid a basis for further analysis, we may attempt to clear the way through some of the more complex regions of the problem of error.

The distinction between true opinion and false opinion obviously depends upon, but also is obviously not identical with, the formal logical distinction between true and false propositions. This close relation and important difference between these two distinctions appear upon a brief study of the considerations which formal logic employs in dealing with the concepts of truth and falsity. True and false are, for the formal logician, predicates belonging to propositions, quite apart from any question as to whether anybody believes or asserts those propositions. With regard to the predicates 'true' and 'false,' formal logic uses, upon occasion, the following well-known principles, which we may here provisionally accept as a basis for further inquiry: (1) every proposition (supposing its meaning to be precise) is either true or false, and cannot be both true and false; (2) to every proposition there corresponds a determinate proposition which is the contradictory of the first proposition; (3) the relation of contradictories is reciprocal or 'symmetrical'; (4) of two contradictory propositions, one is true and the other is false. These may be here regarded, if one chooses, merely as defining principles, explaining what one means by propositions, and how one proposes to use the logical predicates 'true' and 'false.'

Granting these purely formal principles, of which all exact reasoning processes make constant use, it is obvious that propositions taken collectively as a system constitute an ideal realm wherein to every truth there uniquely corresponds its contradictory falsity, and to every false proposition its contradictory true proposition. The realms of truth and falsity are thus formally inseparable. To know that a given proposition is false is to know that the corresponding contradictory is true, and *vice versa*. Omniscience regarding the realm of truth would, therefore, equally involve knowing true propositions as true and false propositions as false; nor could the one sort of knowledge be defined or real without the other.

But no such formal logical necessity appears to connect true opinion and error. No one can know that $2+2=4$ is true without thereby knowing that $2+2\neq4$ (that is, the contradictory of the former assertion) is false. But we can conceive of a computer who should never make any errors in computation; and such a computer might even be supposed so perfect, in the possession of some superhuman infallibility of computation, as not even to know what it would be to err in his additions. We ourselves, when we use the assertion $2+2=4$ as an example of a peculiarly obvious proposition of computation, find this bit of summation one about which it is rare or difficult for a man 'in his sober senses' to err. Yet for us the knowledge of the truth of the proposition $2+2=4$ is logically inseparable from the knowledge of the falsity of the contradictory of this proposition.

In sum, then, true and false propositions are logically inseparable. To possess a knowledge of truth is, therefore, inseparable from the possession of a knowledge of what falsity is, and of what false propositions mean. But a being can be supposed to know truth and falsity, and their distinctions and relations, without having any tendency to fall a prey to error. At all events, no purely formal logical reasons, such as for the moment concern us, can be given for supposing that a being who is capable of knowing truth should be capable of falling into error. The more concrete distinction between true opinion and error must, therefore, be different from the formal logical difference between truth and falsity. The latter may be viewed as a logically necessary distinction between inseparable objects. The former must be due to motives or causes, and must imply mental tendencies and situations of which formal logic, taken in its deliberate abstraction from the fullness of life, gives no account.

The concept of a false opinion is thus obviously distinct from that of a false proposition, and not every true opinion requires that the corresponding false opinion should be held by somebody. It is the purpose of advancing science, of education, of the propagation of truth, to diminish and, so far as may be, 'to banish error' from the minds of men. If this purpose were somehow miraculously attained, there would be as many false propositions in the formal logician's ideal realm of truth and falsity as there ever were; but human errors would have ceased.

2. The leading definitions of error.—To define false opinion, hereupon, as the acceptance or the mistaking of false propositions for true ones, or of true for false ones, is a familiar device of philosophers, but it throws no light upon the real nature of error. For, to mistake a falsity for a truth, to accept a false opinion as true—what is this but simply to make a mistake, or to hold a false opinion? This supposed definition is but a tautology. Not thus is the nature of error to be clarified. Further light upon the subject can be obtained only through (1) defining more exactly the distinction between true and false propositions; and (2) showing upon what further distinctions the conception of error depends. Some of the best known efforts to accomplish this result must next be summarily stated and criticized.

(i.) *The 'correspondence theory of truth and falsity'* and the definitions of error based upon it deserve to be stated, because they are familiar, and because they have formed the starting-point for supplementary doctrines and definitions and for corrections. According to the view now in question, a proposition is true if it reports, or describes, or portrays 'facts as they are.' The emphasis is laid upon the 'as.' A true idea 'corresponds' in its structure to the thing, or reality, or fact of which it is a true idea; a true proposition is one which asserts that an idea does thus correspond to the facts, when it actually so corresponds. Or, again, if the account given by a proposition conforms to the structure of the facts of which it attempts to furnish an ideal portrayal, the proposition is true. Thus, a proposition may relate to the number in a real flock of sheep. In this case an idea, gained by counting the sheep, is first formed, and then the assertion is made that this numerical idea represents the real number of sheep present in the flock. The correspondence of the idea with the facts constitutes that to which the assertion is committed. If the correspondence exists, the assertion is true.

Such being (according to the 'correspondence' theory) the nature of truth, error takes place when, because of inadequate observation of the sheep, or because of some other psychological defect on the part of the one who counts, a numerical idea which does not correspond to the real number of the sheep arises in the mind that is subject to the error; while, because of these or of still other psychological motives, the false proposition, 'Such is the number of the sheep,' comes to be asserted. That the correspondence does not exist makes the proposition false. That this non-existent correspondence is asserted and believed to exist constitutes the essence of the error.

In order to understand what error is, and how it arises, one therefore needs, according to this view, to analyze the nature of belief, and the motives which lead the erring mind to make assertions. From this point onwards, the definition and the theory of error have always required the consideration of various associative, affective, or volitional factors of the process of making and believing assertions—factors of which pure logic, considered in its usual abstraction, can give no account. In brief, the nature of truth and falsity once having been thus defined, the nature of error depends upon some disposition to accept or to assert an untrue proposition—a disposition which cannot be due to the merely logical nature of the untruth itself, but must be referred to the prejudices, the feelings, the ignorance, the wilfulness, or the other psychological fortunes of the erring subject.

What further accounts, upon this basis, have been attempted as explanations of the essence of error, there is here no space to set forth at length. A few points must be noted. One may assert: (1) that error in such a case as the foregoing, or in the more complex cases of superstitions, supposed theological heresies, false philosophies, errors in scientific opinion, false political doctrines, etc., may be mainly due to a negative cause—the mere ignorance of the erring subject, his lack of 'adequate ideas,' the absence of correct and sufficient portrayals of fact. What a man lacks he cannot use. If he has no ideas that correspond with the facts in question, how can he make true assertions? Error is then, at least in the main (according to the view now in question), due to privation. For instance, I may not even attempt to count the sheep in the flock. I may merely guess at random. In such a case, error seems to be due merely, or mainly, to my lack of ideas. Such a negative theory of error was worked out by Spinoza, and applied by him, as far as possible, to decidedly complex cases. Naturally, according to Spinoza, 'the order and connexion of ideas' corresponds to 'the order and connexion of things.' This, for Spinoza, is the case with even the most worthless of our human imaginations. But, for psycho-physical reasons, which Spinoza discusses at length, most ideas of the ordinary man, relating to his world, are extremely 'inadequate'; that is, such deas correspond only to very fragmentary aspects of the real world. The majority of men live 'ignorant of God and of themselves, and of things.' This ignorance prevents them from possessing the stock of ideas which could furnish the basis for true opinions. Men fill the void with errors. Yet none even of their errors is without basis in fact. They simply judge, without restraint, concerning that of which they know not, just because they know so little. This doctrine of error as ignorance, if accepted, would give us the most purely and completely theoretical definition of error which has ever been offered.

Plainly, however, ignorance is not of itself error. I cannot err concerning facts of which I know so little as to have no idea whatever about them; just as I cannot, in a speech, make grammatical blunders of whose existence I have never heard. Some other factor than ignorance determines the actual acceptance and utterance of false propositions. This even Spinoza himself has in the end to recognize. In his study of the errors of human passion, he makes the mechanical associative process, and the resulting passions themselves, factors in the genesis of error. Thus we are inevitably led to further theories.

One may assert: (2) that error is due to whatever moves the will of the erring subject to make assertions even in the absence of ideas that correspond to real objects. This volitional theory of error played a considerable part in Scholastic doctrine; was obviously useful in giving reasons for the moral condemnation of the errors of heretics, infidels, and schismatics; and has, in fact, an obvious and important basis in the psychology of opinion. Descartes recognized it in connexion with his own form of the doctrine of the freedom of the will. Spinoza, who rejected the theory of free will, and defined both intellect and will in terms of his psycho-physical theory of the associative process, still on occasion was obliged, as just pointed out, to use his own version of the doctrine of 'human bondage' as an explanation of the fatal errors into which the play of our inadequate ideas and of our passions leads us. In other forms this theory of error is widely accepted. From this point of view an error is a wilful assertion of a false proposition —an assertion made possible, indeed, by the erring subject's ignorance of the ideas that do correspond with reality, but positively determined by his willingness to assert. False beliefs are thus due to a combination of ignorance with the will to believe.

One may insist: (3) that the affective processes which condition the mood called 'belief' are the principal factors in making a false proposition, when it chances to be suggested, seem plausible. Where error is propagated by social contagion, or is accepted through reverence for authority, not so much the will as the emotional life of the erring subject seems to be the factor which makes error possible. Here, according to the previous view, ignorance of ideas that do correspond with reality is a condition of error, but constitutes neither its essence nor its sufficient cause. An error, according to the present view, is a false opinion which, because of its appeal to the sentiments, the feelings, the prejudices, of the erring subject, because it is harmonious with his social interests or with his private concerns, wins the subject over to the state of mind called belief.

One may further maintain: (4) that the principal cause of error is whatever associative, perceptual, or imaginative process gives such liveliness, strength, and persistence to ideas which as a fact do not correspond with reality, that the erring subject is forced, in the absence of sufficient corrective ideas, or (to use Taine's expression) for lack of 'reductors,' to regard these ideas as representatives of reality. Theories of error founded upon this view have played no small part in the psychiatrical literature which deals with the genesis of pathological forms of error, and have been prominent in the teachings of the Associationist school generally. From this point of view, an error is a false proposition whose assertion is forced upon the erring subject through the mechanism of association, and mainly because no other ideas than those which this assertion declares to correspond with the facts can win a place in the subject's mind when he thinks of the topic in question.

The foregoing accounts of the nature and source of error have all been stated with explicit reference to the 'correspondence' theory of truth. This theory supposes that the test of truth is the actual conformity of a representative idea with the object which it is required to portray. Idea and object are viewed as distinct and separable facts, just as a man and his portrait or photograph are possessed of a separate existence. The representative idea is external to the object. Truth depends upon a certain agreement between such mutually external facts. And, just as the idea to whose truthfulness as a representation a proposition is committed is external to its object, so, as we have now seen, the motives which lead to error appear, in the accounts thus far given, to be external to the meaning, and to the truth or falsity, of ideas and propositions. The falsity of a proposition, so far as we have yet seen, gives no reason why the error involved in believing that proposition should be committed. The truth of a proposition, also, in no wise explains why the true proposition comes to be believed—unless, indeed, with Spinoza, one comes to accept, for metaphysical reasons, a theory that ideas are by nature in agreement with objects. In case, however, one does accept the latter theory without any limitation, then error can be defined only in negative terms as due to mere absence of ideas. Such an account of error, as we have also seen, is incapable of telling us what it is, and is inadequate to explain the most familiar facts about its occurrence.

If, then, the truth or the falsity of a proposition does not of itself explain why we come to get a true or a false belief, the existence of error, for one who accepts the correspondence theory of truth, has to be explained by psychological motives which are as external to the logical meaning of true and false propositions as the ideas of the correspondence theory of truth are external to their objects. Some propositions are true. Their contradictories are false. So far, we have a system of facts and relations that seems, according to this account, to be wholly independent of the psychological processes of anybody. But of these true and false propositions, some are believed by men. If the propositions believed are true, we have not explicitly considered in the foregoing the psychology of the process by which they come to be believed. But, if the beliefs are beliefs in false propositions, some accounts of how the errors arise have been suggested. These accounts all appeal to motives which do not result from the falsity of the propositions, but from the feelings, the will, or the associative processes of the erring subject—all of them influences which are due not to the logical distinctions between true and false, but to the mental fortunes of the believer.

Unfortunately, however, since the true beliefs of the subject must also have their psychology, quite as much as the false beliefs, and since the will, the feelings, the associative processes, the conditions which determine 'lively ideas,' and the like, must be equally effective when true propositions are believed as when false beliefs triumph—all the foregoing accounts leave us dissatisfied should we be led to ask: What are the processes which prevent error and give us true beliefs? For, apart from Spinoza's assumption of the universal agreement between 'the order and connexion of ideas and the order and connexion of things'—an assumption which makes error in any but a purely negative sense impossible—the truth of a proposition is a fact which in no wise explains why we mortals should come to believe that proposition to be true. And, if we explain the true belief as due to the will, the feelings, the associative or other psychological processes of the subject, these factors, as the theories of error so far stated have insisted, work as well to produce error as to beget true opinion. The one thing of which we have so far given no account is the way in which the difference between true opinion and error arises—the factor which is decisive in determining whether a given state of opinion, in a given subject, shall be one which accepts true propositions or, on the contrary, embraces errors.

Of course, the need of such an account has frequently been felt by the partisans of the 'correspondence' theory of truth. Innumerable portrayals exist of the ways in which conformity of idea and object can be furthered or attained by psychological processes. Ideas can be made 'clear and distinct,' observations of the object can be rendered careful, prejudice can be kept in abeyance, feeling can be controlled, judgment can be suspended until the evidence is incontestable, and so on. By such means error can be more or less completely avoided, and agreement with the object can be progressively obtained. There is no doubt of the practical importance of such advice. There is also no doubt that the processes of control and of clarification which are in question are psychological processes, which the inquiring subject can find or produce within himself. It becomes plain, however, as one reflects, that to insist upon such matters is more or less to modify, and in the end to abandon, the representative theory of truth as consisting merely in the conformity of ideas to objects that are external to these ideas.

For how does one know, or why does one judge, that clear ideas, careful observations, the avoidance of prejudice, the suspension of judgment, and the other psychological devices of the truth-seeker, actually tend to make the subject escape from error, and win true opinion? Is it because, from some point of view external both to the object and to the ideas of the subject, one observes how the subject gradually wins a closer conformity with his object through using the better devices, and through avoiding the mental sources of error? If so, then whoever has this point of view, external both to the object and to the cognitive process, is already somehow acquainted with the constitution of the object, and is aware what propositions are true about the object quite apart from the psychological fortunes of the poor subject, whose escape from error is to be aided by such wise counsels. As a fact, philosophers who give such counsels very often behave for the moment as if they, at least, had not to wait for a slowly acquired conformity with the nature of reality, but were already assured of their own grasp of the object, and were therefore able to give such good advice to the erring psychological subject. No purely psychological theory of the way in which a conformity to an external object can be gradually acquired through clear ideas, freedom from prejudices, and so on, can serve to explain how the critic of human truth and error has himself acquired his assumed power to see things as they are, and thus to guide the psychological subject in the right path. That sort of attainment of truth which this theory attributes to the philosopher who teaches it is just what it does not explain.

In fact, a little reflexion shows that, when we hold, as we very rightly do, that a certain wise conduct of our ideas, feelings, will, observations, processes of recording observations, and other such mental enterprises helps us towards truth, and aids us to avoid error, we are comparing, not ideas with merely external objects, so much as less coherent with more coherent, unified, clear, and far-reaching forms of experience, of cognition—in general, of insight. If we once see this fact, we have to alter our definition of truth, and herewith our definitions both of true opinion and of error.

Truth cannot mean mere conformity of idea to external object: first, because nobody can judge an idea merely by asking whether it agrees with this or with that indifferent fact, but only by asking whether it agrees with that with which the knowing subject meant or intended it to agree; secondly, because nobody can look down, as from without, upon a world of wholly external objects on the one hand, and of his ideas upon the other, and estimate, as an indifferent spectator, their agreement; and thirdly, because the cognitive process, as itself a part of life, is essentially an effort to give to life unity, self-possession, insight into its own affairs, control of its own enterprises—in a word, wholeness. Cognition does not intend merely to represent its object, but to attain, to possess, and to come into a living unity with it.

Accordingly, the theories of error which have been founded upon the 'correspondence' theory of truth must be, not simply abandoned, but modified, in the light of a richer theory of truth. A true proposition does, indeed, express a correspondence between idea and object, but it expresses much more than this.

(ii.) Another definition of truth, which has its foundation far back in the history of thought, but which has been of late revised and popularized under the names of Pragmatism, Humanism, and Instrumentalism, may next be mentioned.

According to this view, an idea is essentially something that tends to guide or to plan a mode of action. A proposition expresses the acceptance of such a mode of action, as suited to some more or less sharply defined end. Now, a mode of action inevitably leads to consequences, which arise in the experience of the active subject. These consequences may be called the 'workings' of that idea which tended to guide or to plan this mode of action. These workings may agree or disagree with the intent of the idea. If the idea agrees with its expected workings, that idea is true, and with it the proposition which accepts that idea as suited to its own ends is true; otherwise the idea and the proposition are erroneous. Such is the definition of truth which is characteristic of Pragmatism.

The case of the right or wrong counting of the flock of sheep will serve to illustrate the present theory of true opinion and of error quite as readily as to exemplify the representative theory of the same matters. A flock of sheep is not merely an external object to be portrayed. It is, to the one who counts it, an interesting object of human experience. He counts it in order to be ready to estimate his possessions, to sell or to buy the flock, to know whether he needs to hunt for lost sheep, or because of some other concrete purpose. His counting gives him an idea, perhaps of what he ought to ask of a purchaser, or of a plan for the shearing or for the market, perhaps of whether he ought to search for missing sheep. When he accepts and asserts that some determinate number represents the actual number of the flock, he, no doubt, takes interest in the correspondence between the idea and the object; yet his real object is not the indifferent external fact, but the flock of sheep as related to his own plans of action and to the practical results of these plans. The only test of the truth of his count, and, in fact, the only test that, when he counts, he proposes to accept, is that furnished by the workings of his count. Does his idea of the number of sheep, when accepted, lead to the expected results? One of these results, in many cases, is the agreement of his own count with that made by somebody else, with whom he wishes to agree concerning a sale or some other enterprise. Or, again, he expects the enumeration which he makes at one time to agree with the result obtained at some other time when he counts the flock anew. Furthermore, a habit of inaccurate counting betrays itself, in the long run of business, in the form of failure to get expected profits, or in the form of a loss of sheep whose straying is at one time not noticed because of the inaccurate counting; while later experience shows, in the form of the experience which traces the loss, the non-correspondence of expectations and results. Such expectations, tests, and agreements define the sort of truth that is sought.

What so simple and commonplace an instance illustrates, the whole work of the natural sciences, according to the pragmatist, everywhere exemplifies. The Newtonian theory of gravitation is accepted as true because its ideas lead, through computations, to workings which agree with observation. The older corpuscular theory of light was rejected because certain of its consequences did not agree with experience. The same process of testing hypotheses by a comparison of expectations with outcome can be traced throughout the entire range of empirical investigation.

As to the cause and essence of error, upon the basis of this theory of truth, there can be, according to the pragmatist, no very subtle difficulties to solve. The whole matter is, upon one side, empirical; upon the other side, practical. Experience runs its course, however it does. We, the truth-seekers, are endeavouring to adjust our actions to empirical happenings by adapting our expectations, through the definition of our ideas, and through the forming and testing of our hypotheses, to the observed facts as they come. As we are always in our practical life looking to the future, and are seeking the guidance which we need for our undertakings, our propositions are hypotheses to the effect that certain ideas will, if tested, agree with certain expected workings. If the test shows that we succeed, then, just when and in so far as we succeed, our propositions prove to be then and there true. If we fail, they prove to be errors. Truth and falsity, and, consequently, true opinion and error, are not 'static' properties or fixed classifications of our ideas or of our hypotheses. Both the ideas and the propositions 'come true' or 'fail to come true' through the fluent and dynamic process of the empirical test. Thus every truth is true, and every falsity false, relatively to the time when, and the purpose for which, the individual idea or hypothesis is tested.

Absolute truth or permanent truth, and equally absolute falsity or permanent falsity, are, from this point of view, purely abstract and ideal predicates, useful sometimes for formal purposes, when we choose to define our purposes in terms of logical or of mathematical definitions. 'Concrete' truth and error are of the nature of events, or series of events, or of 'the long run' of experience. That many of our ideas should not 'work,' or that many of our hypotheses should result in disappointed expectations, is, for the pragmatist, merely an empirical fact, requiring a special explanation no more than do the marksman's misses or the player's failure to score. We are not perfectly skilful beings; experience is often too fluent or too novel for our expectations. The wonder is rather that this is not more frequently the case. That man is as skilful a player as he is of the game of ideal expectations and anticipated consequences is a matter for congratulation. But failure is as natural an event as is success.

The traditional accounts of the psychology of error mentioned above are readily accepted by Pragmatism, precisely in so far as they are indeed accounts which experience justifies. No doubt, ignorance is a source of error. We are, in fact, ignorant of all except what experience, in one way or another, permits us upon occasion to prove by actual trial. This ignorance permits errors, in the form of false expectations, to arise. Prejudice, emotion, wilfulness, and the associative process unite to engender expectations which may prove to be false. Nor is there any known cause that uniformly ensures the attainment of truth. The difference between success and failure in our adjustment to our situation is simply an empirical difference. We have to accept it as such. No deeper account can be given than experience warrants.

The result of the pragmatist's definition of error obviously forbids any sharp distinction between theoretical and practical errors. The presence or absence of conscious ideas, of definite expectations, of articulate hypotheses, remains (in case of our always more or less practically significant maladjustments of our acts to our situation) as the sole criterion for distinguishing between erroneous opinions, on the one hand, and blunders that are made, on the other hand—merely as the fumbling player may fail to get the ball, or as the nervous musician may strike the false note—blindly, and without knowing why one fails, or what false idea, if any, guided one to the failure. This reduction of all errors to the type of practical maladjustments is a characteristic feature of Pragmatism.

If the 'correspondence' theory of truth makes the distinction between true and false opinions something that is quite external to the logical distinction between true and false propositions, the pragmatist's theory of truth and error in propositions seems, on the contrary, to go as far as is possible to annul altogether the difference between these two sorts of distinctions. For the pragmatist it is merely a formal device of the logician to regard truth and error as in any sense permanent properties, or predicates of the supposed entities called propositions. What actually occurs, what empirically happens, is a series of concrete agreements and disagreements between expectations and results. These happenings, or 'the long run' of such happenings, constitute all that is concretely meant by truth and error. Whether one says, 'This proposition is true or false,' or, 'This opinion is true or false,' the concrete fact to which one refers is the sequence of testings to which ideas are submitted when their expected workings are compared with the expectations. Since logicians like to abstract certain 'forms' from the matter of life, they may, if they choose, define the entities called true and false propositions, and then leave to the students of the concrete the study of the fortunes of mere opinions. As a fact, however, according to Pragmatism, propositions live only as opinions in process of being tested. The distinctions with which we began this discussion have their own provisional usefulness, but only as abstractions that help to prepare the way for understanding life. A proposition becomes true in the concrete when the opinion that it is true leads to expected workings, and becomes false when the belief in it leads to workings which do not agree with expectations.

Such, in sum, is the pragmatist's solution of our initial problem. It emphasizes very notable facts regarding the relations between logic and life, and between thought and volition. Yet it fails to satisfy. For it can only be stated by constantly presupposing certain assertions about experience, about the order, the inter-relations, the significance, and the unity of empirical facts to be true, although their truth is never tested, in the pragmatist's sense of an empirical test, at any moment of our experience.

Thus, it has been necessary to assume, even in stating the view of Pragmatism about truth, that ideas can be formed at one time, and submitted to the test of experience at another time, and perhaps by another person, just as Newton's hypotheses were formed by him, but were tested, not only by himself, through a long course of years, but by later generations of observers. It has been necessary to assume that one can form expectations to-day, and compare them with facts to-morrow, or next year, or after whatever length of time the conditions make possible. But this assumption requires the truth of the proposition that the meaning, the object, the purpose, the definition of the ideas and expectations of one moment, or period of time, or person, not only can be but are identical with the meaning, object, purpose, definition of the ideas and expectations of another moment, temporal region, or person. Now such an assertion, in any one case, may be regarded with scepticism, since it is, for human beings, unverifiable. Nobody experiences, in his own person, or at any one time, the identity of the ideas, meanings, expectations, of yesterday and to-day, of himself and of another person, of Newton and of the later students of Nature who have tested what they believe to be Newton's ideas. One may, in each special case, doubt, therefore, whether the idea formed yesterday is the same in meaning as the idea tested to-day, whether two men mean the same by the hypotheses which they are trying to verify together, and so on. But this much seems clear: however doubtful, in the single case, any such proposition may appear, unless some such propositions are true, there is no such process as the repeated testing of the same ideas through successive processes of experience, occurring at separate moments of time, or in the experiences of various human observers. But in that case it is not true that the proposition, 'Such a testing of ideas by the course of experience as Pragmatism presupposes actually takes place,' expresses the facts. If, however, this proposition is not true, the whole pragmatist account of truth becomes simply meaningless. On the other hand, if the proposition is true, then there is a kind of truth whose nature is inexpressible in terms of the pragmatist's definition of truth. For there are propositions which no human being at any moment of his own experience can ever test, and which are nevertheless true.

Much the same may be said of the pragmatist's assertion regarding the 'workings' that an idea is said to 'possess,' or to which it is said to 'lead.' These 'workings,' by hypothesis, may extend over long periods of time, may find a place in diverse minds, and may involve extremely complex reasoning processes (*e.g.* computations, as in the case of the Newtonian theory of gravitation) which are very hard to follow, and which no human mind can survey, in their wholeness, at any moment, or submit to the test of any direct synthetic observation. The proposition, however, 'These are the actual, and, for the purposes of a given test, the logically relevant workings of the idea that is to be tested,' must itself be true, if the empirical comparison of any one of these workings with the facts of experience is to be of any worth as a test. The truth of the proposition just put in quotation marks is a truth of a type that no one man, at any instant, ever personally and empirically tests. In every special case it may be, and in general must be, regarded as doubtful. Yet, unless some such propositions are true, Pragmatism becomes a meaningless doctrine; while, if any such propositions are true, there is a sort of truth of which Pragmatism gives no account.

What holds of truth holds here, in general, of the conditions which make falsity possible. And the whole theory of true and false opinion, and consequently the definition of error, must be modified accordingly. In brief, Pragmatism presupposes a certain unity in the meaning and coherence of experience taken as a whole—a unity which can never at any one moment be tested by any human being. Unless the propositions which assert the existence and describe the nature of this presupposed unity are themselves true, Pragmatism has no meaning. But, if they are true, Pragmatism presupposes a sort of truth whereof it gives no adequate account. To say this is not to say that Pragmatism gives a wholly false view of the nature of truth, but is only to insist upon its inadequacy. It needs to be supplemented.

(iii.) Over against the theory of truth as the correspondence between a wholly external object and an ideal portrayal, and also in contrast with Pragmatism, there exists a theory of truth which defines that concept wholly in terms of a harmony between the partial expression of a meaning which a proposition signifies and the whole of life, of experience, or of meaning, which, according to this theory, ideas and propositions intend to embody so far as they can. A proposition is true in so far as it conforms to the meaning of the whole of experience. Such conformity can never be attained through the mere correspondence of a portrayal with an external object. It can exist only in the form of the harmonious adaptation of part to whole—an adaptation that can best be figured in the form of the adaptation of an organ to the whole of an organism.

If one reverts to the comparatively trivial instance of the sheep and the counting, the present view would insist, as Pragmatism does, upon the fact that, in counting sheep, one is attempting to adjust present ideas to the unity of an extended realm of experience, in which the observed sheep appear, now as grazing in the field, now as having their place in the herdsman's enterprises, now as passing from one ownership to another, and so on. The one who counts wants to get such a present idea of the sheep as will stand in harmonious unity with all else that can be or that is known with regard to them. The truth involved in the process of counting is itself of a relatively abstract and lower sort; and hence is ill adapted to show what truth really is. For, in fact, to treat sheep merely as numerable objects is to treat them as what, on the whole, they are not; hence to say, 'They are so many,' is to utter what is in some respects false. For they are sheep, and to say this is to say that each is a living organism, a unique individual, a product of ages of evolution, and a being possessing values beyond those which commerce recognizes. Hence a numerical account of them has only 'partial truth,' and therefore is false as well as true. The only wholly true account of the sheep would express (not merely portray) their character as facts in the universe of experience and of reality. One can say, at best, of the proposition about their number that it is true in so far as it expresses a view about them which harmonizes, to the greatest extent possible for a numerical statement, with what experience, viewed as a whole, determines the place and the meaning of one's present experience of the flock of sheep to be.

Truth, from this point of view, is an attribute which belongs to propositions in a greater or less degree. For single propositions, taken by themselves, give us abstract accounts of facts, or rather of the whole in which every fact has its place, and from which it derives its characters. A proposition is an interpretation of the whole universe, in terms of such a partial experience of the nature of the whole as a limited group of ideas can suggest. This interpretation is always one-sided, precisely in so far as the group of ideas in question is limited. In so far as the partial view harmonizes with the whole, the proposition is true. Since the partial view, being one-sided, can never wholly harmonize with the whole, each separate proposition, if taken in its abstraction, is partially false, and needs to be amended by adding other propositions.

This general theory of truth and falsity, while its sources run back into ancient thought, is especially characteristic of modern Idealism. That the truth of propositions about experience is a character determined by their relation to the ideal and virtual whole of experience, to the 'unity of apperception,' is a thesis which forms part of Kant's 'Deduction of the Categories.' The later developments of the 'Dialectical Method,' by Fichte and Hegel, and the analogous features of Schelling's thought, led to more explicit theories of the relations between truth and falsity, and to the doctrine that every proposition, considered in its abstraction, is partially false, and needs amendment. Hegel, in the preface to his *Phänomenologie*, asserted that 'Das Wahre ist das Ganze,' and interpreted this as meaning that only what a survey of the total process of experience signifies enables us to know truth, while 'partial views,' such as we get on the way towards *absolutes Wissen*, are at once true and false—true, as necessary stages on the way to insight, and therefore as in harmony with the purposes of the whole; false, as needing supplement, and as showing this need through the contradictions which give rise to the dialectical process. In Hegel's *Logic* this view of truth is technically developed. With a different course of argument, with many original features, and with a more empirical method of investigation, a view of truth and error which belongs to the same general type has in recent times been developed by Bradley.

If one accepts such a theory of the 'degrees of truth and falsity,' and of truth as the harmony or organic unity between a partial view and the ideal whole of experience or of reality, the essence of error—that is, of false opinion—must receive a new interpretation. In the history of the development of Absolute Idealism, the theory of error has taken, on the whole, two distinct forms.

(1) According to the first of these forms, usually emphasized by Hegel, error exists merely because it is of the essence of a partial view to regard itself as the total and final view, precisely in so far as the partial view inevitably passes through the stage of 'abstraction,' in which it defines itself to the exclusion of all other points of view than its own. Did it not pass through this stage, it would not be a live or concrete view of things at all. It simply would not exist. But (according to Hegel) the whole, in order to be an organism at all, requires the parts to exist. And, if the parts are—as in the case of opinions—partial views of the whole, and if the whole requires them to exist, each in its place in the system of spiritual life, it is the whole itself, it is the Absolute which requires the partial view to make, as it were, the experiment of regarding itself as true—that is, as an absolutely whole view. If a man is merely counting, he takes his objects simply as numerical; and then real things seem to him, as to the Pythagoreans, to be merely 'numbers.' Such a view, as an abstraction, is false; but as a stage on the way to insight it is inevitable; and as a concrete phase of opinion it is an error, that is, a positive belief in a falsity, or, again, a taking of a partial view for the whole. To be sure, this 'dwelling on the abstraction,' this *beharren* or *verweilen* in the midst of falsity, is a phase; and since, for Hegel (just as much as for the Pragmatists), the apprehension of truth is a living process, not a static contemplation, this phase must pass. An experience of the 'contradictions of finitude' must in its due time arise, and must lead to the recognition that the partial phase is false. This is what happens in the course of the history of thought, when the successive systems of philosophy—each a partial truth, required by the necessity of the thought-process and by the life of the *Weltgeist* to regard itself as absolutely true—succeed one another with a dialectical necessity that tends to larger and truer insight. The same sequence of necessary errors, which are all of them partial truths taking themselves to be whole and final, appears in the history of religion.

(2) To Bradley, and to others among the more recent representatives of Idealism, to whom the dialectical method of Hegel appears in various ways unsatisfactory, this account of the way in which error arises, and, as a phase of experience and of life, is necessary, does not appeal. For such thinkers, error is, indeed, defined as a partial and (in so far) false view, which is not merely partially false and partially true, but takes itself to be wholly true. The existence of such a disharmony between part and whole, in a realm of experience where the metaphysical presuppositions which these writers accept seem to require organic wholeness and harmony to prevail, and to be of the essence of reality, is an inexplicable event, which must be viewed as in some unknown way a necessary 'appearance,' not a reality.

As a statement of the ideal of truth which is alone consistent with rational demands, the Idealism thus summarized seems to be, in great measure, successful. But its success is greatest with respect to the conception of truth as the teleological harmony or adjustment of a partial to a total view of experience and of its meaning. Precisely with regard to the problem of the possibility of error, that is, of disharmony between the demands of any partial interpretation of experience and that which is revealed and fulfilled by the whole of experience, the idealistic theory of truth and of error has proved to be, thus far, most incomplete.

3. Conditions of a solution of the problem of error.—The foregoing survey shows that a satisfactory theory of error must meet the following requirements:

(1) It must be just to whatever interest in a decisive and unquestionably 'absolute' distinction between true propositions and their contradictory false propositions is justly urged by formal logic. That is, no account of truth and error in terms of 'partial views' and 'the total view' of experience must be used to render the contrast of true and false anything but a decisive contrast, as sharp as that between any proposition and its contradictory.

(2) The theory of error must take account of the actual unity of the cognitive and the volitional processes. It has been the office of recent Pragmatism to insist, in its own way, upon this unity. But Hegel, in his *Phänomenologie*, also insisted, although in another fashion, upon the fact that every insight or opinion is both theoretical and practical, is an effort at adjustment to the purposes of life, an effort to be tested by its genuine rational success or failure.

(3) The theory of error must recognize that truth is a character which belongs to propositions so far as they express the meanings which our ideas get in their relations to experience, and not in their relations to wholly external objects.

(4) That the rational test or the success of ideas, hypotheses, and opinions lies in their relations not to momentary experiences, but to the whole of life, so far as that whole is accessible, must also be maintained.

(5) The existence of error, as disharmony between the partial view which actively and, so to speak, wilfully asserts itself as the expression of the whole, must be explained as due to the same conditions as those which make possible finite life, evil, individuality, and conflict in general.

(6) Theoretical error cannot be separated from practical error.

(7) A revision of Hegel's dialectical method, a synthesis of this method with the empirical tendencies of recent Pragmatism, a combination of both with the methods of modern Logic seem, in their combination, to be required for a complete treatment of the problem of error. An error is the expression, through voluntary action, of a belief. In case of an error, a being, whose ideas have a limited scope, so interprets those ideas as to bring himself into conflict with a larger life to which he himself belongs. This life is one of experience and of action. Its whole nature determines what the erring subject, at his stage of experience, and with his ideas, ought to think and to do. He errs when he so feels, believes, acts, interprets, as to be in positive and decisive conflict with this *ought*. The conflict is at once theoretical and practical.

LITERATURE.—Aristotle, *Metaph.* vi. 4, 1027*b*, ix. 10, 1051*b*. On the Scholastic concept: Thomas Aquinas, *Summa c. Gent.* i. 59, *Summa Theol.* i. 17. 1. In modern philosophy: Descartes, *Princ. Phil.* i. 48, *Med.* v. 42; Spinoza, *Ethica*, i. prop. xxx., ii. prop. xxxiv., and *de Emend. Intell.*; Locke, *Essay on the Human Understanding*, iv. chs. 5, 20; Kant, *Kritik der reinen Vernunft*, Riga, 1781, p. 81. On recent discussions: W. James, *Pragmatism*, London, 1907, *The Meaning of Truth*, do. 1909; F. C. S. Schiller, *Humanism*, do. 1903, *Studies in Humanism*, do. 1907, art. 'Pragmatism' in *EBr*[11]; H. H. Joachim, *The Nature of Truth*, do. 1906; F. H. Bradley, *Logic*, do. 1883, *Appearance and Reality*[2], do. 1897; art. 'Truth' in *DPhP* (contains an important statement of the views of C. S. Peirce).

J. ROYCE.

ESCHATOLOGY.—The principal subjects treated of in this article are the 'last things' strictly so called—the idea of judgment and retribution, or of a Day of Judgment, Millennial ideas, the catastrophic end of the world and its renewal, and how the dead are related to that end of all things. The different views regarding the state of the dead are discussed in the article STATE OF THE DEAD (see also BLEST [ABODE OF THE], MESSIAH, RESURRECTION).

1. Savage races.—(*a*) *Retributive notions.*—The question of the existence of the idea of future retributive justice among savages is not easily settled, as certainly, in some cases where it is believed in, it may be traced to outside influences—Hindu, Buddhist, Muhammadan, or Christian. Still, even here the idea must have been latent or already expressed in some form, else it would not so easily have been adopted. While a mere continuance of present earthly conditions is frequently believed in, distinctions according to rank, wealth, or power are commonly found. The future of the soul is also dependent upon the nature of the funeral offerings, or upon burial or non-burial, or upon the person having been tatued, circumcised, mutilated in some particular way, or provided with certain amulets. An approach to a retributive doctrine is found in the wide-spread view—extending upwards to the ancient Teutons and Mexicans—that cowardice debars from Paradise or incurs actual punishment; courage being here a savage virtue which is rewarded. Again, since gods and spirits frequently punish in this life sins (not necessarily strictly moral shortcomings) against themselves—tabu-breaking and the like—it was easy to extend this to the future life. Hence, neglect or contempt of worship, ritual, tabu, etc., is frequently punished in the Other-world, or keeps souls out of the more blissful state.

This is a common belief in Melanesia and Africa (see *ERE* ii. 683 f.; Brown, *Melanesians and Polynesians*, 1910, p. 195), in Polynesia (Ellis, *Pol. Researches*[2], 1832, i. 396 f.), and in S. America (Naupós [Coudreau, *La France équinoxiale*, Paris, 1887, ii. 195 f.]).

In certain cases crimes which are detested by the tribe, and therefore by the tribal gods, and which are severely punished on this earth by torture or death, are also believed to be punished beyond the grave—a natural deduction. These crimes are mainly murder or theft committed against fellow-tribesmen, sorcery, adultery, incest, as well as lying, and even niggardliness.

For examples, see Brown, *op. cit.* 195; Codrington, *Melanesians*, Oxford, 1891, p. 274; *ERE* ii. 685[a]; Post, *Grundriss der ethn. Jurisprudenz*, Oldenburg and Leipzig, 1894–5, i. 41 (Amer. Ind.); Rink, *Tales and Trad. of the Eskimo*, 1875, p. 41; see also *ERE* iv. 255[b], 256. Actual retribution (apart from outside influences) is also alleged among the Andaman Islanders (Man, *JAI* xii. [1883] 158, 162), Australians (Parker, *More Aust. Legendary Tales*, 1898, p. 96), Haidas, Salish, and other Amer. Indian tribes (Harrison, *JAI* xxi. [1891–2] 17; Wilson, *TES* iii. 303), Mintiras of Malacca (Steinmetz, *AA* xxiv. 582), Ainus (*ERE* i. 252[a]), Masai (Merker, *ZE* xxxv. [1903] 735). In most of these instances the nature of the punishments points to native ideas. In some cases the 'wicked' are simply annihilated (Grinnell, *Pawnee Hero Stories*, 1893, p. 355).

A judgment is necessarily implied where a division on various grounds, or actual punishment by the gods, or exclusion from Paradise is believed to take place in the Other-world; but it is only sporadically that it is expressly stated to occur (Khonds [Hopkins, *Rel. of India*, Boston, 1895, p. 530], Chippewas [Dunn, *Oregon*, 1844, p. 104], Guinea Negroes [Pinkerton, *Voyages*, xvi. 401], Ainus [*ERE* i. 252]). Some of the West African secret societies probably teach a future judgment. Out of such primitive views the idea of judgment in the higher religions was evolved.

The judgment may simply be an examination by some being or animal, to discover whether the person has the necessary distinctive mark which admits to Paradise, or has done certain things according to custom in this world (Codrington, *op. cit.* 256, 257, 265, 280; Pinkerton, iii. 303 [Massachusetts Indians]). In other cases some ordeal, appointed occasionally by a divinity or spirit, has to be undergone, which tests the man's fitness for the blissful region (Schomburgk, *Reisen in B. Guiana*, Leipzig, 1848, iii. 318; Thomson, *The Fijians*, 1908, pp. 121, 125, 128). Or it may consist in sending the good by one road leading to Paradise, and the bad by another leading to a place of pain (Mooney, 'Siouan Tribes,' *Bull. 24 BE*, 1894, p. 48; Bancroft, *NR* iii. 524 [Karok]; Coudreau, *op. cit.* ii. 195 f.). Or, again, the bridge which the dead must cross becomes an ordeal, the bad being unable to cross it, or they are repelled by its guardian (Landau, *Hölle und Fegfeuer*, Heidelberg, 1909, p. 60; *ERE* i. 493[a], ii. 854). 'Bad' does not always here mean the morally bad; but the beings who examine and test the soul are primitive judges of the dead. Sometimes the spirits of the dead debar murderers and other undesirable persons from the blissful region, and force them to remain apart or in an undesirable place, or to wander restlessly on earth, and in some cases it is the spirits of persons injured in life by the new arrival who inflict such punishments—a natural extension of the idea of blood-revenge, surviving also in higher religions (Codrington, 269, 274 f., 279, 288; Brown, 444 [New Guinea]; Couard, *RHR* xlii. [1900] 268 [Algonquins]; cf. Landau, 186 f.).

(*b*) *The Final Catastrophe.*—The Andaman Islanders believe that spirits, apart from souls, go to a gloomy jungle below the earth, which is flat. But a time will come when a great earthquake will cause the world to turn over. The living will perish and change places with the dead. Spirits will be re-united with souls, and live on the renewed earth, in which sickness and death will be unknown (Man, *JAI* xii. 161 f.). Many American tribes (north and south) expected a catastrophic end of all things—frequently by fire, as the world had before been destroyed by water. But in such cases it was believed that, as certain persons escaped the flood to re-people the earth, so some would be hid from the fire and re-people the new world (Schoolcraft, *Indian Tribes*, 1853–56, i. 319, iv. 240, 420; Brinton, *Myths of New World*[3], Philad. 1896, p. 253 f.). In a Choctaw legend the dead were to resume their bodies and live on the renewed earth. A similar re-peopling of the purified and renewed world after its final destruction by water was believed in by the Eskimos (Brinton, 302; Egede, *Nachrichten von Grönland*, 1790, p. 156; Boas, 'Central Eskimo,' *6 RBEW* [1888] 588 f.). Probably Christian teaching has here influenced existing native beliefs. The Mexican belief in a series of world-ages or 'suns'—each terminated by a catastrophe, from which only a few were saved for the new age—is akin to these. The Mexicans did not know when the existing age would terminate, but only that it would be at the end of a cycle of 52 years; nor does it appear how the dead would fare at this consummation. This conception of the end of the world-age seems to have been unrelated to the myth of the return of Quetzalcoatl and the renewal of the Golden Age (J. G. Müller, *Amer. Urrel.*, Basel, 1855, p. 511 f.; see AGES OF THE WORLD [Prim. and Amer.]). The Peruvians also believed in a former destruction of the world by water, and in its future destruction, signalized by an eclipse of sun or moon, in which the sun would vanish, the moon fall on the earth, and a conflagration or drought would follow, in which all would perish (Müller, 396; Brinton, 254). It is obvious that such myths are extensions of the observation of actual catastrophes and unexplained natural phenomena, and of the terrors inspired by them.

2. Egyptian.—Of any Egyptian doctrine of a final catastrophe there is no record. The idea of judgment of the soul after death appertained to the Osirian faith from the time of the XVIIIth dynasty, though it is found in connexion with the Rā doctrine in the *Book of the Gates*. In this the judgment takes place in the Hall of Osiris—the sixth domain through which the sun passes on his nightly journey; but in the *Book of the Dead* the judgment was preparatory to entering the true paradise of Osiris—the Fields of Aalu.

The soul was brought into the presence of Osiris the judge, by Anubis. Before him stood the balance in which Thōth the scribe would weigh the heart of the deceased against the feather which symbolized righteousness, or the image of Maat. Thōth was also the scribe who registered the result with tablet and style. Around were seated the 42 Divine assessors to whom the famous 'negative confession' was made. If the soul passed through the ordeal of the balance, which may have been a test of the truth of the confession, it was rewarded by Osiris; but if not, it is possible that it was eaten by the monster Am-mit, 'Eater of the Dead,' or shared the fate of annihilation with the enemies of Osiris, who were hacked to pieces or thrown into pits or a lake of fire. How far such a retribution could be overcome by 'words of power' is uncertain. These punishments are referred to in the *Book of the Gates*; but, so far as they concerned souls, they could not be eternal, for the soul was annihilated. How judgment on the followers of Rā was pronounced is uncertain, but again in the *Book of the Gates* and the *Book of That which is in Duat* we hear of the horrible punishments by which the annihilation of Rā's enemies was brought about, and these enemies almost certainly included the wicked. This annihilation, according to Budge (*Gods of the Egyptians*, 1903, p. 265), was the misinterpretation of a Nature-myth of the sun attacking with his rays and fiery glance. See also the whole scene of the judgment described in a story of a visit to Amenti, where annihilation, as well as fearful punishments of the wicked, is found (Griffith, *Stories of the High Priests of Memphis*, Oxford, 1900, p. 45 f.). Cf., further, artt. EGYPTIAN RELIGION, p. 243[a], and ETHICS AND MORALITY (Egyp.), p. 475.

3. Teutonic.—Though the general view of the division of souls at death among the Teutons is non-moral, glimpses of a more ethical division and of a daily judgment after death by the gods are obtained. Crimes, such as offences against kinsmen and gods, murders, adultery, and perjury, were punished (see BLEST, ABODE OF [Teutonic], vol. ii. p. 708). Much more detailed is the picture of the final world-catastrophe as found in *Völuspá* and *Gylfaginning*; and, since it involves gods, but is not produced by them, it is automatic—a proof of its originality; while the whole picture of the catastrophe includes various elements in the mythology.

All the regions and beings hostile to the Æsir, or gods, prepare for the final conflict, and those enemies whom the former had bound break forth to take part in it—the Midgard serpent, the Fenris wolf, Hel, and Loki. The world has become wholly evil, and this evil is especially marked by the loosening of the ties of kindred. Signs in Nature—storms, floods, and the three-fold Fimbul winter—precede the end. Those beings now unbound, along with Surtr and his train from Muspelheim, attack the gods; and Odin, Freyr, and Thor fall before their onslaught. The sun is darkened, the stars vanish, earth sinks into the sea, and fire bursts forth. After this a new earth springs from the waves, with green meadows. Its fields bring forth without labour, evil and sorrow are unknown, and the gods renew their youth on Idavöllr. Perhaps this new earth is the hidden paradise of Mimir's grove, in which Líf and Lífthrasir are hidden and survive the great winter, according to one myth, or this catastrophe, so that a new and blessed race may spring from them and re-people the earth (*Vafthrudnismál* [Vigfusson-Powell, *Corpus Poet. Boreale*, Oxford, 1883, i. 67]; *Gylfag.* § 53). But there is also added the conception of a final judgment by 'a mighty one from above.' The righteous now dwell in Gimlé, the wicked are condemned to Ná-strand.

How far all this has been moulded by Christian influences is still uncertain. Most probably floating eschatological myths have been fixed in an orderly narrative by the poet of *Völuspá* under such influences. There is a certain resemblance to Persian eschatology, while a world-catastrophe is hinted at in tales which have no connexion with *Völuspá* (Grimm, *Teut. Myth.*, Eng. tr., 1880–88, pp. 429, 815).

4. For **Celtic** eschatology, see art. CELTS, in vol. iii. p. 302 f.

5. Greek and Roman.—In the earlier Greek poets, Homer and Hesiod, nothing is said of judgment. But such enemies of the gods as the Titans are shut up in Tartarus (Hes. *Theog.* 713 ff.; Homer, *Il.* xiv. 279, cf. viii. 13), while Tityus, Tantalus, and Sisyphus suffer torments (*Od.* xi. 576 f.). Minos in the under world gives laws to the dead (θεμιστεύοντα νέκυσσιν), but he does not appear to act as judge (*Od.* xi. 567 f.). But, under the influence of the Mysteries and of the Orphic and Pythagorean cults, the ideas of judgment and retribution became prevalent, and are found in later writers. Pythagoras taught a judgment of souls (Iambl. *Vita Pyth.* 29 f.), and the Orphic judgment is depicted on the vase on which Æacus, Triptolemus, and Rhadamanthus appear as judges (J. E. Harrison, *Prol. to Study of Greek Rel.*[2], Cambridge, 1908, p. 599). In the Mysteries it was also taught that the uninitiated, the profane, and the unjust were punished in the Other-world.

Generally the judges, who exist independently in Pluto's kingdom, are three in number—Minos, Rhadamanthus, and Æacus—and they were appointed to this office because they had acted justly on earth (cf. Plato, *Gorgias*, 523). But the Mysteries added a fourth, Triptolemus, and Plato refers to all four as true judges in Hades (*Apol.* 41). They give judgment in a meadow at the parting of the ways, one of which leads to the abode of the blessed, the other to Tartarus.[1] Their sentences or symbols (σημεῖα) of their deeds are bound upon souls (Plato, *Gorg.* 523, *Rep.* x. 614 f.). Their shadows were the accusers of souls, according to the satire of Lucian (*Menippus*, 10)—probably a popular idea.

The ideas of the Orphics and Pythagoreans are reproduced by Pindar (see *Ol.* ii. 55 f.; *Thren.* frag.) and Plato, but the conception of judgment and retribution is connected with that of metempsychosis. Ten thousand, or, in the case of pure souls, three thousand, years elapsed before the soul returned to its primal home. Judgment took place at the end of life, when the soul was rewarded, or punished in places of correction (εἰς τὰ ὑπὸ γῆς δικαιωτήρια). At the end of a thousand years the soul chose a new body, human or animal, and was born on earth, to undergo further probation there, and to be rewarded or punished once more at death. Some souls, however, were too wicked ever to return, and remained for ever in Tartarus (Plato, *Phædrus*, 248 f.; *Rep.* x. 614 f.; cf. *Gorg.* 523; and, for a reference to similar teaching in the Mysteries, *Laws*, ix. 870).

In the *Phædo* (107, 113) the soul is led by its dæmon to the place of judgment, and is then sent to bliss, or to purgatorial punishments followed by rewards for good deeds. Incurable sinners never leave Tartarus.

Such beliefs as these were probably widely diffused among the Greeks, as we may gather even from the numerous passages referring to judgment and the fate of souls in Lucian's satires and from the caricature of Aristophanes. The dramatists seldom speak of a judgment of the dead (cf. Æsch. *Suppl.* 218 f., *Eum.* 263 f.), but it is referred to sporadically in other authors and on grave inscriptions. The Stoics held that evil souls were punished after death. Punishment was, however, purgatorial, though bad souls might become extinct. Seneca speaks of death as a day of judgment when sentence will be pronounced on all (*Ep.* xxvi., *Herc. fur.* 727 f.; see Zeller, *Stoics*, 1870, p. 205 f.). The Epicureans rejected all such views, and taught that the soul died with the body (Lucr. iii. 417 f.; cf. Hippol. *Refut. Hær.* i. 19). While among the Roman people their native religion taught nothing of judgment and future penalties, the poets accepted the Greek ideas and the names of the judges of the dead, and frequently referred to them. Thus in Vergil's picture of the under world, Minos judges certain crimes, and Rhadamanthus judges in Tartarus (*Æn.* vi. 426 ff., 540 ff.; see other passages collected in Ruhl, *De mortuorum judicio*, Giessen, 1903, p. 76 ff.).

The conception of the end of all things was philosophical rather than popular and mythical, but the Stoic doctrine of the ἐκπύρωσις became popular. How was the conception of the future life related to the cyclic change?

In Plato's theory of the two ages ever recurring, those who died in the period of disorder, when the universe was left to itself, were in the new age—the Golden Age—born from the earth as old men, and grew ever younger. The end of each period, when the earth began to move in an opposite direction, was marked by great convulsions of Nature. In the Stoic doctrine of the cyclic conflagration, all souls (or those which have not become extinct) are then resolved into the World-Soul or Primal Fire. This world-catastrophe over, the formation of a new universe begins (Cicero's *renovatio*), and all things repeat themselves as in the previous cycles, and every person again plays his part in it. Did this include personal identity? Some answered that the persons were distinct without a difference, others regarded them as different (see Zeller, 155 ff.). Seneca, who gives a vivid picture of this world-conflagration (*Consol. ad Marciam*), seems to have looked forward to living again in the next cycle (*Ep.* xxxvi. 10). See AGES OF THE WORLD (Greek and Roman).

6. Hindu.—Although in the *Rigveda* no clear statement of judgment is found, and Yama appears mainly as king of the region of bliss, yet he is to some extent an object of terror, and a dark underground hell is spoken of as the fate of evil-doers (iv. 5. 5, vii. 104. 3, ix. 73. 8). In the *Atharvaveda* the torments of this place are also referred to (v. 19). The later views differ widely from this, through the gradual introduction of the belief in transmigration, while Yama is now the judge of the dead. The popular view is represented by various passages in the *Śatapatha Brāhmaṇa*. The dead pass two fires, which burn the wicked, but let the good go by: they are weighed in a balance, and their fate is thus decided. The good pass to bliss; the wicked suffer in hell, or are re-born as a punishment. In the *Upaniṣads* re-birth in various conditions, in heaven, hell, or on earth, appears as the result of ignorance of the true end of existence, viz. release from the chain of cosmic existence and absorption in the world-soul. Hinduism in all its forms endorses this view. All go to Yama over a dreadful road, on which the pious fare better than the wicked. Yama or Dharma judges and allots the fate. Through endless existences and re-births—in human, animal, or plant forms—alternated with lives in the heavens or hells, the soul must pass. The Hindu doctrine of the Four Ages is connected with eschatology. The Four Ages—*kṛta*, *tretā*, *dvāpara*, and *kali*, each with its dawn and twilight periods—form a *mahāyuga* of 12,000 years, each of which is equivalent to 360 human years, thus resulting in a period of 4,320,000 years. A hundred such periods form a *kalpa*. At the close of the *Kali* age, or more usually now at the close of the final *kali* of a *kalpa*, there is an apparent destruction of the world by fire and flood. The gods are absorbed by Brahma, along with their heaven and all good persons in it. Then follows the age-long sleep of Brahma (equal to the length of a *kalpa*), after which he re-creates the world. The process of transmigration begins anew, and all are re-born in higher or lower forms, to renew their cosmic existence, save those who desire final and absolute absorption in the Supreme (see *SBE* vii. 77 f.; xxv. pp. lxxxiv, lxxxvii; xxxiv. 212; Hopkins, *op. cit.* 419 f.; Barth, *Rel. of India*, 1882, p. 93; AGES OF THE WORLD [Indian]).

7. Buddhist.—In Buddhism the idea of *karma* afforded an automatic principle of judgment, whereby the person after death entered upon an existence, higher or lower, according to his actions. At death, the force resulting from actions combined with clinging to existence causes creation of the five *skandhas*, or constituent elements of being. This is so swift that there is hardly any break in the continuity of personality, which is thus re-created in one of the six states—gods, men, *asuras*, animals, plants, *pretas*, or inhabitants of one of the hells. The shortest term of punishment in a hell is 500 years, but one may rise from that to life in a higher state, while a life in heaven may be succeeded by a life on earth or in one of the hells. But already in early Buddhism we find the idea—taken over from Brāhmanism—that the warders of hell drag the wicked before Yama, who condemns them to one of the hells (Monier-Williams, *Buddhism*, 1889, p. 114 f.). But it is in Northern Buddhism that this idea is more particularly developed. Here there is the conception of a judgment of the soul after death in the courts of the ten judges of the dead, one of whom is Yenlo (Yama). He judges with strict impartiality, and also fixes the hour of dissolution.

After the deceased is clad in the black garment of sins, or in the shining garment of good deeds, the latter are weighed against evil in a balance. If the sins exceed, punishment follows; if good deeds, reward. Scenes of the judgment and of punishments are painted on the walls of temples, depicted in books, or formed with clay figures. The judgment-halls are arranged like earthly tribunals. There is also a belief in a bridge over which souls pass; the good cross it easily, but the wicked fall from it to torments. Souls are subject to re-birth after existence in heaven or hell, this also being fixed by the judges. This conception of judgment is also found among the

[1] Plato says that Rhadamanthus judges souls from Asia, Æacus those from Europe, while Minos, as the oldest, decides difficult cases (*Gorg.* 524).

Taoists (Edkins, *Chinese Buddhism*, 1880, *passim*; *As. Journ.* xxxi. [1840] 209 f.; Legge, *Rel. of China*, 1880, p. 119 f.; de Groot, *Actes du 6me Cong. Intern. des Orient.*, sect. iv. [1885] 97 f.).

The Buddhist conception of *kalpas* has already been discussed (AGES OF THE WORLD [Buddhist]). Each great *kalpa* ends with the destruction of the present universe—by water, fire, or wind. Creatures do not perish with the universe. Most of them are re-born in higher spheres, which cannot be destroyed. Others still in hell are re-born in the hell of some universe, the time for the destruction of which has not yet come.

8. Parsi.—Some of the various elements of the eschatology of the *Bundahiš* and other later documents are already found in the *Avesta*, but it is quite uncertain how far all are primitive, and it is more than likely that the earlier belief was one in mere continuance of the soul. After death the soul hovered near the body for three days and nights—if righteous, assisted by Srôsh against demons; but if evil, tormented by evil angels. Then, according to its condition, it started for the Other-world with an escort of good or evil beings. Now the Chînvat bridge was reached. Here the righteous met a beautiful virgin—the sum of his good deeds—who conducted him to Paradise, where he was introduced to Ahura, welcomed by Vohumano, and given heavenly raiment and a golden throne (*SBE* iv. 373 f.); and (according to later belief) the wicked met an ugly hag—embodying his evil deeds—who led him to hell, 'the obscure world' (*SBE* iv. 219, xviii. [*Dâṭistân-î Dînîk*, xxv. 5]). A weighing of the deeds of men at the bridge in the balance of Rashnû Razista, or a decision by three judges—Mithra, Rashnô, and Srush—is spoken of in later documents. Those whose good deeds balanced their evil deeds were kept in Hamêstakân, a kind of intermediate state (*SBE* xxiv. 18; *Book of Ardā Vīrāf* [ed. Haug and West, Bombay, 1872], v., vi. 9 f.).[1] The bridge extended over hell and led to Paradise. For the souls of the righteous it widened, but for the wicked it narrowed to the breadth of a thread or a razor-edge, and they fell off or were cast into hell (*SBE* iv. 219).

Here we may glance at the Iranian theory of the world-ages, each of four periods of 3000 years. Towards the beginning of the final 3000 Zarathushtra is born. Towards the beginning of the second millennium of this period, evils increase, there are signs in heaven and earth, and now Hûshêṭar is born. Religion is restored, and he brings back the creatures to their proper state. Towards the beginning of the final millennium Hûshêṭar-mâh is born. In his time creatures become more progressive and men do not die. But now evils again increase. The serpent Azhi-Dahâk, confined in Mt. Demavend by Freṭun, breaks forth, but is destroyed by Sâm; and at the close of the period Sôshyans, the Persian Messiah, 'who makes the evil spirit impotent and causes the resurrection and future existence,' is born (*Bahman Yašt*, iii. 1 ff.; *Bundahiš*, xi. 6 f.; *Dînkarṭ*, vii. 9 f.; for the chronology, see West, *SBE*, v. Introd. lv f.). Now begins the new order of things. All mankind, beginning with Gâyômarṭ, followed by Mâshya and Mâshyôî, are raised from the dead (cf. 1 Co 15[23], and *Vita Adae et Evae*, 42; *Apoc. Mosis*, 13[41] [Adam is first raised, then his descendants]). Then follows the great assembly, in which each sees his good and evil deeds. The righteous are set apart from the wicked; the former are taken to heaven, and the latter cast back to hell for 'the punishment of the three nights'—their final punishment. Fire now melts the earth and remains like a river. All must pass through it, but to the righteous it is like warm milk, to the wicked like molten metal. Ahriman and his hosts are defeated by Ahura and his angels, and perish in the conflagration (cf. *SBE* xxiii. 306 f.). Now all come together; relations recognize each other; men have the age of 40 years and children of 15 years. All are now immortal and clad in spiritual bodies, and awards are apportioned according to merit. Hell becomes pure, and is brought back for the enlargement of the world. The earth is renewed and made immortal and extends to heaven (*Bund.* xxx.; *Dînk.* ix.; *Dâṭistân-î Dînîk*, xxxii. 14). The anticipated joys both of heaven and of the renewed world are of a highly spiritual character (Söderblom, *La Vie future d'après le mazdéisme*, Paris, 1901, pp. 128, 269; for the Yima legend, see *ERE* i. 208).

9. Muhammadan.—Muhammadan is based upon Jewish and Christian (and possibly Parsi) eschatology, though there are some important differences. After death all persons are visited in the grave by two angels, who examine them as to their faith. If the answer is satisfactory, the dead sleep on in peace; otherwise, they are struck with a hammer and the earth pressed down upon them.

There is a general belief that before the judgment the faithful dead are in a state of repose. They are said to enter *al-Barzakh*. They dwell in or near the grave, but the wicked are tormented there or in a foul dungeon (*SBE* vi. p. lxix; Sale, *Koran*, Prel. Discuss. § iv.; Hughes, *DI*, 1895, *s.v.* 'Barzakh').

Many wonderful signs precede the Last Day or the Day of Judgment (*yaum ad-dīn*; cf. *as-Sā'a*, 'the Hour'), the time of which is known only to God. The Mahdi will establish a reign of righteousness; ad-Dajjâl, or Antichrist, will appear and be slain by Jesus, who will become a Muhammadan; Gog and Magog will be released. . . . Then the angel Isrâfîl will sound the trumpet, which will be followed by frightful convulsions in Nature. At the second blast all creatures will die. At the third the resurrection will take place, and all will rise to give an account of themselves out of the book of their deeds. God is set on His throne with His angels. The recording angels who follow men all through life witness against them, and the works of men are weighed in a balance. The judgment lasts 1000 or 50,000 years. All must now cross the bridge as-Ṣirāṭ, which passes over hell to Paradise, and is finer than a hair and sharper than the edge of a sword. The righteous cross it easily, but the wicked fall or are thrown from it to hell. Earth and heaven are changed.

The righteous pass to the seven regions of Paradise, the sensual joys of which, as described in passages of the Qur'ān (dating, curiously enough, from Muhammad's monogamous period), are such as would appeal to people living in a desert region, and are often direct transcripts of old pagan verses (Jacob, *Altarab. Beduinenleben*[2], 1897, p. 107 f.). They are often spiritualized by Muhammadans, while in the Qur'ān itself more spiritual joys are set forth (xiii. 20–24). Many also regarded the torments of the seven regions of hell as purgatorial, at least for sinful believers and perhaps for all (Macdonald, *Development of Muslim Theol.*, 1903, p. 130; Bukhārī, *Ṣaḥīḥ*, viii. 170). Some hold that heaven and hell did not come into existence until the Judgment, and Jahm ibn Safwan taught that both would finally pass away and God would remain alone (Macdonald, 138). Many deny that men are judged by their works, and the corporeal resurrection is also often set aside.

10. Hebrew and later Jewish.—(*a*) Not till a comparatively late period of Hebrew history is there any idea of a retributive judgment at any period after death.[1] The soul passes to Sheol, but 'death is itself a final judgment; for it removes man from the sphere where Jehovah's grace and judgment are known' (W. R. Smith, *Prophets of Israel*, 1897, p. 64). Retribution is limited to this life, and eschatology is almost invariably connected with the development of history; its subject is the

[1] This state appears to have two parts, one for the not *quite* righteous, and one for the not wholly sinful (*Dâṭ. Dînîk*, xxiv. 6, xxxiii. 2). But souls of some sinners are often said to remain in hell 'till the resurrection'—perhaps implying that others are released from it. Or a specified time in hell is mentioned (*SBE* iv. 37 f., 81, 82, 135).

[1] While the general Bab. view of the after-life seems to have regarded it as unconnected with morality, it has been thought that some traces of a retribution-doctrine and of a judgment of the dead may be found, *e.g.* in the poem of the Descent of Ištar (see Jeremias, *Bab. Conception of Heaven and Hell*, 1902, p. 49).

nation. Many of the elements of later Jewish eschatology are already found in the prophetic books, even in the earliest, although some of the passages in Amos, Hosea, Micah, etc., relating to the Messianic Kingdom are later interpolations. Jahweh appears in judgment upon Israel and also the nations, though this judgment is less a process of investigation than actual vengeance. The time of judgment, preluded by or including various woes, is summed up comprehensively as 'the Day of Jahweh' (see below), the day of Jahweh's vindication against the sinful nation. He punishes it or the wicked in it with the scourge of the Gentiles and with captivity; but, as in Zephaniah and later prophets, there is a wider retribution. The Gentiles, sometimes conceived as His instruments in punishing Israel (Hab 1^{12}), are themselves punished because of their mad pride and idolatry (cf. Is 14). Famine and pestilence and the sword lay the people waste. The wicked, whether of Israel or of the nations, are objects of Jahweh's fury; they flee before Him and are destroyed (Am 3^{2}, Is 8^{22} 11^{4} 13^{11} 17^{9} $24^{21f.}$ $37^{22f.}$, Zeph $1^{17f.}$, Nah 1^{8}). Nature itself is convulsed at His presence—sun, moon, and stars are darkened; the heavens are shaken or rolled together; mountains and hills are scattered; the earth is burned or destroyed by water, or shaken, removed, or dissolved (Am 9^{5}, Zeph $1^{2f.\ 14f.}$, Nah $1^{3f.}$, Hag $2^{6.\ 21f.}$, Hab $3^{6f.}$, Is $2^{12f.}$ $13^{10f.}$ 24. $34^{4f.}$, Ezk 38^{19}).

This conception of Nature convulsed at Jahweh's appearing is connected with the idea that, behind the great phenomena of Nature—earthquake, fire, flood, storm, lightning—are His power and presence. These are manifestations of Him (Ps $18^{7f.}$, Hab 3, Jg $5^{4f.}$). This idea is rooted in the old Nature religion, which had its storm-, thunder-, and earthquake-gods, or personified these phenomena themselves.

An additional historical feature in the midst of eschatological ideas is that of the Captivity as a punishment or part of the judgment. Jahweh's controversy with His people is that because of their neglect of Him they must be punished, while through punishment, even that of captivity, lies the way to restoration and the establishment of His will in the hearts of a regenerate nation. Punishment is the means of reformation for Israel, as well as for the nations (Hos 6. 10^{12} 14, Jer 24^{7} $31^{33f.}$). Or, more generally, through all those woes which are the expression of His judgment He is preserving a faithful remnant who survive because of their faithfulness (Mic 7^{8}, Am 3^{12} 5^{15} $9^{8f.}$, Is $4^{2f.}$ 6^{13} $10^{20f.}$ $11^{11f.}$ 27^{13} $28^{5f.}$ 44^{22}, Zeph 2^{3} $3^{13f.}$, Hab 2^{4}), or who are the nucleus round which gathers the reformed and repentant nation (cf. the repentance of the *nation* in Hos 2^{14} $6^{1f.}$ $11^{10f.}$ 13^{14}). They are restored to the land, or they remain in it because the destruction of the kingdom would not agree with the accomplishment of the Divine purpose (Isaiah). Now begins the reign of peace and safety on earth. Throughout, Jahweh is regarded as the Deliverer, and it is He or the manifestation of His glory (Is 4^{5}) that continues to dwell under the new conditions among His people as Ruler and Judge, and to be their 'everlasting light' (Is $2^{2f.}$ $4^{2f.}$ 40^{3} 60^{19}, Zeph $3^{17f.}$, Zec 2^{11}); He reigns in Jerusalem (Is 24^{23} $65^{17f.}$). But in some prophecies Jahweh sets over the restored people an ideal warrior—or priest-king, semi-Divine (cf. *El Gibbôr*, 'Mighty God,' Is 9^{6}), or endowed with the Divine spirit (Is 11^{2}), or of David's line, to sit on the throne of David and to execute justice. Under him (or perhaps under a line of such kings) the righteous nation will dwell in peace, and his whole delight will be in the fear of the Lord (Is $9^{1.\ 5.\ 6}$ $11^{1f.}$ 32^{1}, Jer $23^{5f.}$ 33^{15}, Mic 5^{2}, Zec $6^{9f.}$ $9^{9f.}$; cf. Ps 110). This king is the 'Messiah' or 'anointed one' of later Judaism.

In Is 42 to 53 *passim*, we find the servant who suffers, not for his own sins but for the sins of others, who dies and is then highly exalted. He is the deliverer of Israel, as well as the light and teacher of the nations. By him an ideal Israel, or the righteous remnant, or even an individual (as in 52^{13}–53), may be intended. But, though the passages have a close bearing on Christ's Messianic work, they were not certainly regarded by the Jews as Messianic before the time of our Lord. In the Talmud the Suffering Servant is sometimes regarded as equivalent to Messiah suffering with His people; and Justin (*Dial. with Trypho*, 68, 69) makes his Jewish interlocutor accept the doctrine of the Suffering Messiah. But this does not point to a general Jewish belief, nor is there any trace of the latter in the Gospels.

Zion will now be re-built and become the spiritual metropolis of the earth, an immovable city and a quiet habitation, established on the top of the mountains; and to it shall all nations flow (Is 2^{2} 4^{5} 33^{20} 40. 65^{18}, Mic $4^{1f.}$, Jer 30^{18}, Zec 2, Ezk $40^{1f.}$). Nature will be changed; there will be new heavens and new earth (perhaps a later conception); the moon will shine as the sun, and the sun's light will be increased sevenfold. There will be abundance of waters and of provender for flocks and herds. These, as well as men, will multiply exceedingly, and there will be marvellous fertility and increase in corn and wine. The desolate land will become like the garden of Eden (Am $9^{13f.}$, Is $30^{23f.}$ $35^{1.\ 2.\ 7}$ 65^{17} 66^{22}, Hos 1^{10} $2^{18f.}$, Zec 8^{12}, Ezk $34^{14.\ 27}$ $36^{8f.\ 30.\ 35}$). According to Ezk $47^{1f.}$, a river will flow from the temple. It will be full of fish, and on its banks will stand trees with unfading leaves and continuous fruit—the leaves used for medicine, the fruit for food (cf. Ps 46^{4}, Rev $22^{1.\ 2}$). Further, the wildest animals will live at peace with each other, and 'a little child shall lead them'; or there will be no more any evil beasts (Hos 2^{18}, Is $11^{6f.}$ 35^{9} 65^{25}, Ezk 34^{25}). All human ills will be done away; the lame will walk, the deaf hear, the dumb speak, the blind see; and there will be no more weeping, sorrow, or sighing (Is 30^{19} $35^{3f.}$, Ezk 34^{16}). The ransomed will obtain joy and gladness; the members of the restored nation will be given a new heart and spirit, they will no more do iniquity, the law will be written in their hearts, and all will know the Lord (Is 35^{10}, Ezk 36^{26}, Zeph 3^{13}, Jer $31^{31f.}$ 'the new covenant').

While the picture of the happy future on earth is now more sensuous, now more spiritual, there is no doubt that it is largely described in terms of the mythical Eden and the past Golden Age, according to a principle which emerges more clearly in later Apocalyptic—that of renewal, or of restoring the present state to its former condition (cf. § 15, and *Ep. Barn.* 6^{3} ἰδού, ποιῶ τὰ ἔσχατα ὡς τὰ πρῶτα). (1) Peace among animals, no ravenous beast, the child (=Adam) leading them; cf. Is $11^{6f.}$ 35^{7}, Ezk 34^{25} with Gn $2^{19.\ 20}$. (2) Desert and waste become beautiful and fertile; cf. Is $35^{1f.}$, Am 9^{13} with Gn 2^{9}, Ezk $31^{8.\ 9}$. (3) Abundance without labour; cf. Gn $3^{17\text{-}19}$. (4) The waters and the trees; cf. Ezk $47^{1f.}$, Ps $46^{4f.}$ with Gn $2^{9f.}$. (5) The new state is on a mountain, in accordance with the idea that Paradise was on a mountain; cf. Is 2^{2} 11^{9} with Ezk 28^{14}, Gn 2^{10} (where the presence of a river suggests a height), Is $14^{13.\ 14}$ (the north and heaven are the same, cf. Ezk 1^{4}). This mountain is now to be Mt. Zion (Is 35^{10}, Ps 48^{2}).[1] (6) There is to be no bodily defect or sorrow (Is $35^{5f.}$) or war (Is $2^{2f.}$ 11^{9}, Mic $4^{1f.}$, Zec $9^{9.\ 10}$, Jer $23^{5.\ 6}$), but everywhere happiness and contentment (Is 25^{6} $55^{1\text{-}3}$), while Jahweh will be present among men—all features of the past Golden Age. (See Gunkel, *Schöpfung und Chaos*, Göttingen, 1895; Oesterley, *Evol. of Mess. Idea*, London, 1908, pp. 135 f., 252 f.; Volz, *Jüd. Eschat.*, Tübingen, 1903, p. 296 f.) These ideas of future earthly bliss correspond also with the picture of Otherworld bliss as conceived in later Judaism and in Christianity. They suggest, in effect, heaven on earth; hence they could be directly transferred to the picture of the heavenly Paradise seen in Jewish and Christian visions.

Throughout these prophecies the blessings of the future are on this earth and for the righteous remnant of Israel—the living in whom the nation finds its true immortality, a future rather than the present generation. But it is obvious that, since the state of the dead in Sheol was a dreary one, the question must have pressed for solution—Are the righteous dead to have no share in the future joy? Hence the gradual emergence of the belief that they would rise to share in this earthly felicity. This satisfied, to some extent, the growing and passionate desire for communion with God after death. What had been already used as a

[1] Cf. Bab. myth of the mountain of the gods in the north (Hommel, *Die Insel der Seligen in Mythus u. Sage der Vorzeit*, Munich, 1901, p. 35 f.).

daring metaphor to describe the restoration of Israel (Hos 6^{2}, Ezk 37) now, possibly under Persian influences (though it is not absolutely necessary to assert those), became a vital doctrine, stated for the first time in Is 26^{19}. Thus, after the judgment was accomplished, the righteous remnant, or the purified nation along with the righteous dead, would form the Kingdom of God in the renewed earth, of which a renewed Jerusalem would be the spiritual centre.

When the restoration was completed, and when these blessings seemed as far off as ever, the prophets still spoke of a time of judgment as imminent, in which the nations and the wicked would be destroyed. According to Haggai, it would be a day of destruction for the heathen, followed by the establishment of the Messianic king ($2^{6f. 22f.}$). In Joel there is the first appearance of an actual scene of judgment, preceded by signs in the heavens. The nations are assembled in the Valley of Jehoshaphat, judged, and destroyed; but Israel, already purified and restored, now enjoys peace and blessing. In Malachi ($3^{1f.}$), Jahweh will come, preceded by Elijah (an idea perhaps suggested by the story in 2 K 2)[1] or His messenger, to judge and destroy the wicked, to recognize those who had trusted in Him, and to dwell in Jerusalem. Out of this conception of a judgment still in the future arises the later eschatology, which, however, made use of all the elements of the earlier, as detailed above.

Thus in Daniel, following the vision of the four beasts (=the world-powers of Babylon, Media, Persia, and Greece), there is a judgment scene. The Ancient of Days sits with His hosts, and the books are opened. Dominion is taken from the beasts, and the fourth beast is slain. Now begins an eternal kingdom on earth possessed by the saints (regenerate Israel), typified by 'a Son of Man' or a human being, to whom all nations are subject ($7^{9ff.}$). But, according to another picture, there is a period of great trouble, in which Michael delivers Israel, or every one whose name is written in the book. There is also a resurrection, of some of the righteous to everlasting life, and of some of the wicked to everlasting shame and contempt (probably in Gehenna)—the latter an entirely new conception (12^{2}).

Occasional references to the blessed future on earth occur in the Apocryphal books. God will arise to judge and destroy the heathen and unrighteous (Sir 35^{18} $36^{8f.}$). Israel is delivered and the gathering of the dispersed follows (36^{11} 50, cf. Bar 2^{34} $4^{36. 37}$ 5^{5-9}, 2 Mac 1^{27} 2^{18} 7^{37}, cf. 1 Mac 2^{57}), and the kingdom endures for ever. In Tobit $13^{1f.}$ the people are scourged and then brought out of all lands. Jerusalem is restored in beauty, and the nations bring gifts and serve God ($13^{11f.}$ $14^{5f.}$). The resurrection of the just only is taught in 2 Mac, in a somewhat material fashion ($7^{9. 11. 14. 22. 23}$ 12^{44} 14^{46}). But it is uncertain whether they are raised up to the future kingdom on earth, though 7^{24} as well as the date of the book seems to support this view.

(*b*) A doctrine of future retribution emerged gradually in Hebrew thought. It is adumbrated in Ps $49^{14. 15}$ $73^{17f.}$, and more clearly in Is $24^{21. 22}$ (4th cent.?), 50^{11} 66^{24} (5th cent.?), and in Dn 12^{2}. Besides retribution in this life, the wicked are punished in the other world according to 2 Mac 6^{26} $7^{34f.}$ In Wisdom the wicked are punished after death ($4^{19f.}$) and judged by the righteous dead. These ideas appear more definitely in Apocalyptic literature.

(*c*) *The Day of Jahweh.*—In its earliest conception the Day of Jahweh must have meant a mythical manifestation of Jahweh in the majesty of terrible natural phenomena conquering hostile evil powers. The whole conception is based on mythical ideas, and to the end the Day was regarded as accompanied with dreadful convulsions

[1] Cf. Sir 48^{10}, *Sib. Or.* ii. 187 f., Mk 6^{15} 9^{11} etc.; see also § 8, where it is shown that two prophets precede the Persian Sôshyans.

in Nature out of which a new order was evolved.[1] This primitive view gave place to another popular idea. The Day would be one in which Jahweh would judge and destroy Israel's enemies, who now (and also in the Prophets) take the place of the hostile evil powers. It would be a day of battle like the 'day of Midian' (Is 9^{4}; for the corresponding Arab idiom, see W. R. Smith, *Prophets*, 398). There was no ethical element here; Israel was to be avenged because of her devotion to outward ritual. Jahweh would manifest Himself in light (Am 5^{18}); there would be abundance in the land and festival gladness ($5^{16f. 18}$). There would be a renewal of the conditions of the Golden Age. To this conception Amos, followed by other prophets, gives a direct denial. Israel must also be judged and suffer in the Day of Jahweh, a day of darkness, sorrow, and fear, because she has neglected the ethical side of His religion ($5^{18f.}$). The unrighteous nations hostile to Israel, and regarded often as the instruments of Israel's punishment, would also suffer, but mainly Israel (3^{2}). Thus Jahweh's character as a righteous God would be vindicated. If the passages in Amos and Hosea referring to a restoration following upon these judgments be later interpolations, then they, like Micah, regard the Day as one issuing in nothing but doom. But this idea soon gave place to another. The nation purified, or a righteous remnant, and in some cases the heathen nations also, would find the Day ultimately issue in blessing. Here the prophets in part take over the popular view of the Golden Age issuing out of the manifestation of Jahweh in the convulsions of Nature, but at the same time they spiritualize it, and limit this bliss to those who survive because of their righteousness. The restoration is to be not on a natural but on a righteous foundation.

This is more particularly seen in Nahum and Habakkuk, in whom a conception of the Day is found which somewhat resembles the popular one in form, but differs from it in essence. Judah is now regarded as already righteous (Nah 1^{15}, Hab 1^{4}), and the Day of Jahweh is His terrible vengeance against her wicked foes. Thus His righteousness and that of Judah are vindicated.

In Jeremiah and Ezekiel the relation of the individual to Jahweh is emphasized (Jer 9^{24} $31^{29. 30}$, Ezk $14^{12f.}$ $18^{4. 20f.}$). Hence with them the Day of Jahweh was less a manifestation of His judgment on the nation than on the individuals composing it, and it issued in the restoration of righteous individuals (Jer $3^{13f.}$ 24^{7} $31^{33. 34}$, Ezk $6^{8f.}$ 7^{16} 11^{19} $14^{13f.}$ 33^{18} $39^{28f.}$). The nations as such also share in the judgment (Jer $25^{15f.}$ 46 ff.). The relation of the nations who survive the judgment to the blissful Kingdom is differently viewed in these Prophets, and their differing views were reproduced in later works.

According to Jeremiah, the nations participate in the Kingdom (3^{17} $4^{1. 2}$ 12^{16} 16^{19})—a view which is followed by other prophets (Mic $4^{1f.}$, Zec 2^{11}), for some of whom the idea of a Day of Jahweh hardly exists, its place being taken by that of Israel as the means of the world's restoration (cf. Is 45^{14} $49^{22f.}$ 2^{2-4} [post-exilic] $19^{21f.}$, cf. Ps $22^{27f.}$ 65^{2} 87). In Malachi, where the same hope is found, there is a Day of Jahweh. According to Ezekiel, while the righteous remnant will be restored, the nations will be utterly destroyed in the Day of Jahweh's vengeance ($21^{25f.}$ 25 ff. 35; cf. 38. 39). This view has already been found in Nahum and Habakkuk. It is found also in other prophets, who look forward after the Return to a destruction of the nations (Is 34, Hag 1^{2} $2^{6f. 20f.}$, Zec $1^{18f.}$) previous to the establishment of the new era. Or the nations or such of them as survive the Day will become servants of Israel (Zec 2^{11} $8^{20f.}$, Dn 7^{14}, and see above). In Ezk 38. 39 hosts coming from the north, Gog from the land of Magog, against *restored* Israel, are utterly destroyed (cf. Zec $14^{1f.}$)—an idea destined to play an important part in later eschatology, Jewish and Christian (see Bousset, *Rel. des Judentums*, Berlin, 1903, p. 206 f., *Antichrist*, 1896, p. 128 f.).

The idea of the Day as an actual judgment-scene or assize is found in Jl $3^{2f.}$, when the heathen are assembled in the Valley of Jehoshaphat, where

[1] See Gunkel, *Zum religionsgesch. Verständnis des Neuen Test.*[2], Göttingen, 1910, p. 22; Gressmann, *Der Ursprung der israelitisch-jüd. Eschat.*, Göttingen, 1905.

Jahweh sits to judge them, after the restoration of His people to whom they have been hostile and who are now penitent. The nations are destroyed. A world-judgment is already suggested in Zeph $1^{2.3.18}$ 3^{8}, Is 34, Jer $25^{15ff.}$, Hag 2^{22}, and it reappears in Daniel.

Various names for the Day of Jahweh in the OT are 'the Day' (Ezk 7^{10}), 'that Day' (Is 30^{23}), 'the time' or 'that time' (Ezk 7^{12}, Jer 31^{1}), 'the Great Day' (Jl 2^{11}, Zeph 1^{14}), 'the Day of wrath' (Zeph 1^{15}, cf. Ro 2^{5}); cf. 'the Great Day of His wrath' (Rev 6^{17}). In Apocryphal and Apocalyptic literature the phrase which refers to the time of judgment, either before or after the Messianic Kingdom, varies, but it covers ideas similar to those already found in the Prophets—'the Day of Judgment' (*Enoch*, *Secr. of En.* 39^{1}, 4 Ezr 7^{39}, *Apoc. Bar.* 60^{8}, *Test. xii. Patr.* [Levi 3^{2}], Jth 16^{17}, *Jub.* 10^{17} 22^{21}), 'the Day of the Great Judgment' (*Jub.* 23^{11}, *Secr. of En.* 50^{4}). Other titles are 'the Day of the Great Consummation,' 'the Day of tribulation, darkness, or slaughter,' 'that Great Day' (see Charles, note to *En.* 45^{2}, p. 125 f.); 'the Day of the Great Condemnation' (*Jub.* 5^{10}), 'the Day of the Lord's judgment' (*Ps. Sol.* 15^{13}), 'the Day of the Wrath of Judgment' (*Jub.* 24^{30}), 'the Day of turbulence and execration and indignation and anger' (*Jub.* 36^{10}), 'the Day of the Mighty One' (*Apoc. Bar.* 55^{6}), 'the Consummation of the times' or 'of the ages and the beginning of the Day of Judgment' (*Apoc. Bar.* 13^{3} 60^{8}, cf. 29^{8}, also 23^{7} 'My redemption [=Day of Judgment] has drawn nigh,' cf. Lk 21^{28}, 1 P 4^{7}), 'the Visitation' (*Ass. Mos.* 1^{18}), 'the Day of the Ordinances,' or 'the Day of the Ordinance of the Lord in the righteous judgment of God' (*Test. xii. Patr.* [Levi 3^{3}]). Sometimes God, occasionally Messiah (*En.* 62^{2} 69^{27}), acts as judge. In the NT the phrase passes over to our Lord's Parousia with which is joined the Judgment, and it appears in the forms 'the Day of the Lord Jesus' (1 Co 5^{5}, 2 Co 1^{14}), 'the Day of Jesus Christ,' 'the Day of Christ' or 'of our Lord Jesus Christ' (Ph 1^{6} 2^{16}, 2 Th 2^{2}, 1 Co 1^{8}), 'the Day of the Lord' (1 Th 5^{2}, 2 P 3^{10}), 'the Day' or 'that Day' (1 Co 3^{13}, 2 Ti $1^{12.18}$ 4^{8}, 2 Th 1^{10}), 'the Day of Judgment' (Mt 10^{15} 11^{22}, 2 P 3^{7}, 1 Jn 4^{17}), 'the Great Day of God' or 'of his Wrath' (Rev 16^{14} 6^{17}); cf. Lk 17^{24} 'so shall the Son of Man be in his Day,' and St. Paul's pregnant phrase, 'the Day of Wrath, and revelation of the righteous judgment of God' (Ro 2^{5}).

(*d*) *Apocalyptic eschatology*.—In approaching the period of Apocalyptic literature, it must be borne in mind that, while its roots are fixed in and nourished by OT prophecy (where also Apocalyptic ideas are not unknown, *e.g.* Ezk 37 ff., Zec 1 ff.; cf. also Dn.), its anticipations are of a much more detailed character, and announce coming events in a formal manner. It also occupied a different standpoint from that of the orthodox Pharisaic schools. This literature was of a popular character, and did much to quicken that belief in the Messiah and the coming of the Kingdom, as well as the individual hope of the future, which were so characteristic of the people's thoughts in Christ's time. Moreover, it can hardly be doubted that He and those who wrote of Him were familiar, if not with that literature, at least with the popular views to which it had given birth. This raises a strong presumption that the eschatology which He taught or which was attributed to Him followed the lines of current ideas, but, as will be seen, with important differences.

(i.) In Apocalyptic writings the coming of Messiah, or the advent of the new order, often inaugurated by God Himself, or the final judgment, is preceded by terrors and sorrows (the 'Messianic woes') and by frightful convulsions in Nature. God or Messiah destroys the enemies of Israel, and spiritual foes—Beliar, demons, evil angels—are also destroyed. Meanwhile, through all these horrors, the true Israel is concealed (cf. Is 26^{20}, *Enoch* 96^{2}, *Ass. Mos.* 10). Then follows the eternal or temporal Kingdom on earth, the somewhat sensuous description of which—great fruitfulness, eating and drinking, begetting numerous children—together with more spiritual ideas—the absence of sin, the nearness of God to His people—reproduces the thought of the Prophets. While in some writings Messiah has no place (certain sections of *Enoch* and *Apoc. Bar.*, *Ass. Mos.*, *Secrets of Enoch*), in others he is introduced mechanically, but in others again he has a most important place (*Test. xii. Patr.*, *En.* 37 ff., *Ps. Sol.*, 4 Ezra, sections of *Apoc. Bar.*), and, as in *En.* 37 ff., he acts as Judge. The destruction of Israel's enemies easily passes over into the thought of a Last Judgment of Israel and the actions already adumbrated in the Prophets; and this, in necessary association with ideas of Resurrection, is a dominating conception of Jewish eschatology. Prominent, too, in some writings is the thought of future and final bliss or torment in the Other-world.

The Apocalyptic writings show three well-defined notions of the future: (1) continuing the prophetic conception, there is judgment followed by the establishment of a blissful Kingdom on earth or on a renewed earth (*En.* 1-36. 37-70 [new heaven and earth], 83-90; *Sib. Or.* iii. 194 f.; *Test. xii. Patr.*); (2) the Kingdom is temporary, and at its close Judgment begins, followed by the dawn of the eternal world (*En.* 91 f., *Apoc. Bar.* [various sections], *Secrets of Enoch*, 4 Ezr., and possibly *Ps. Sol.*, *Jub.*, *Ass. Mos.*); (3) no Kingdom on earth, but an imminent future Kingdom in the Other-world.

(1) *The eternal earthly Kingdom*.—In *Enoch* 1-36 (*c.* 170 B.C. [so Charles, ed. *Book of Enoch*, 1893, p. 26]) there is a preliminary judgment. Azazel and the angels who lusted after women are set in the place of darkness ($10^{4f.}$) until the judgment. Disobedient stars are confined in a waste place over an abyss of fire. Sinners have a place apart in Sheol till the judgment. The consummation and judgment are accompanied by shaking of the mountains and rending of the earth. God appears with ten thousands of His holy ones, and executes judgment on Mt. Sinai (ch. 1). Azazel and the angels are cast into an abyss of fire, along with all others who are condemned, including the wicked in Sheol (10^{6} 13. $21^{1f.}$ 27^{2}). The righteous dead are raised and, with the righteous who are alive, dwell in peace on earth, which will be full of desirable trees and vines, yielding seed and wine in abundance. The righteous will live till they beget a thousand children, and will know neither sorrow, pain, nor trouble. Labour will be a blessing. Righteousness and peace will be established, and the earth will be cleansed. The righteous eat of the Tree of Life, which gives them long life. They enjoy the presence of God, who will sit on a throne in a high mountain, and they never sin again. The remaining Gentiles become righteous and worship God.

A not dissimilar picture is found in *En.* 83-90, but here a human Messiah, symbolized by a white bull (90^{37}), is described vaguely as dwelling in the Kingdom, though not introducing it. Still more important, the idea of a new Jerusalem—not a purified earthly Jerusalem, but an entirely new city set up by God—is found (90^{29}; see § 14). The Judgment is depicted under the figure of God sitting on a throne. Sealed books are opened and set before Him. The stars and angels are judged and condemned to an abyss of fire, along with apostate Jews ($90^{20ff.}$). The risen righteous are transformed into the likeness of Messiah and live eternally.

In the *Testament of the Twelve Patriarchs* (109–105 B.C.) the dispersed of Israel, or Israel after repentance, are restored. God appears (Sim. 6, Asher 7^{3}) on the earth and destroys the spirits of deceit. But in other parts a sinless Messiah—king, prophet, and priest—appears and wars with the enemies of Israel or with Beliar, from whom he takes the captivity (Dan $5^{10.11}$), binds him (Levi 18), or casts him into the fire (Jud. 25^{4}). Sin now comes to an end (Levi 18). The resurrection of Enoch, Noah, Shem, Abraham, Isaac, Jacob, the twelve patriarchs, and all men (Benj. $10^{6f.}$), some to glory, some to shame, follows. All are judged, and the judgment is accompanied by convulsions of Nature (Levi $4^{1f.}$). There are snow, ice, and fire, and spirits of retribution preserved in the heavens, as well as armies for vengeance on the spirits of deceit and Beliar (Levi 3). The Gentiles share in the Messianic Kingdom which is on this earth. The saints are said to rest in Eden and the New Jerusalem (Dan $5^{10.11}$), or in Paradise which Messiah opens (Levi $4^{1f.}$).

In *En.* 37–70 (1st cent. B.C. [so Charles, p. 29]) there is a preliminary judgment on the dead ($41^{1f.}$). The righteous are oppressed and cry for help. The supernatural and pre-existent Son of Man appears with the Head of Days. He sits on the throne of his glory, set there by the Lord of Spirits, that he may judge (45^{3} $48^{2f.}$ 49^{4} 61^{8}–62). The dead (Israelites?) are raised. Angels, good and evil, are judged before him, as well as the kings of the earth and all who dwell in it (51. 54. $61^{5.8}$; cf. 49^{4}). The wicked are consigned to Gehenna or driven off the face of the earth (38^{3} 41^{2} 45^{6} 53. 54). God transforms heaven and earth as a place for the righteous to dwell in (the first time heaven is categorically mentioned as an abode for the righteous). The Kingdom is here not conceived sensuously, though the righteous 'eat with that Son of Man' (62^{14}). The Elect One dwells with the righteous, who are clothed with garments of His glory (62^{15}), and live for ever. They find righteousness with the Lord of Spirits ($58^{1f.}$).

In the third book of the *Sibylline Oracles* God sends a king who brings all war to an end. Now the kings of the earth assemble about Jerusalem, but are destroyed. Israel dwells safely under God's protection. Earth yields boundless wheat, wine, and oil. There is abundance of trees, cattle, and sheep. There is no more drought or famine. Is 11^{6-9} is here paraphrased. The eternal Kingdom, with Jerusalem as its centre, extends over the whole world, for the heathen now worship God and live at peace (vv.$^{65^2 ff.}$). The eternal Messianic Kingdom is referred to in Jn 12^{34}.

(2) *The temporary earthly Kingdom.*—(*a*) Meanwhile a temporal Messianic Kingdom had been brought into prominence. The eternal earthly Kingdom had its incongruous elements—sensuous and earthly, spiritual and heavenly; and the separation of these was perhaps aided by the influence of Hellenistic Judaism and its eschatology—the immediate entrance of souls into their state of bliss or torment at death. The idea of a temporal Messianic Kingdom, which ultimately issued in that of a Millennium, was 'a compromise between the old hope of the prophets, which they expected to be realized in the present world, and the transcendental hope of later Judaism' (Gunkel, in Kautzsch, *Die Apokr. und Pseudepigr. des AT*, Tüb. 1900, ii. 370). The first appearance of this idea is in one of the sections of *Enoch* (91–104, c. 134–94 B.C. [so Charles, p. 28]). Here, under the influence of the 70 years of Jer 25^{12}, the doctrine of 10 world-weeks is found. The first 7 of these are increasingly wicked; at the end of the 7th the 'elect of righteousness' receive revelations concerning the whole creation ($93^{3f.}$). Now begins the Kingdom, and in the 8th week sinners are delivered into the hands of the righteous for destruction; the latter acquire houses, and the temple is built in glory. The righteous judgment is revealed to the whole world in the 9th week. Sin vanishes from the earth, which is, however, written down for destruction. At the end of the 10th week the great Judgment occurs. The earth is destroyed; the first heaven departs, and the new heaven appears ($91^{12f.}$). The righteous dead rise to it from their intermediate abode (91^{10} 92^{3} 103^{4} [? resurrection of the spirit]); they live in goodness and righteousness, and walk in eternal light in Heaven (104^{2}). In this book the wicked at death are cast into Sheol (98^{3}), and here they are confined for ever ($103^{7.8}$). Sheol has thus become hell.

In some other works of this period it is not clear whether the Kingdom is temporal or not. Thus in the *Book of Jubilees* (c. 135–96 B.C.), after the usual 'Messianic woes,' there is a return to righteousness and a Messianic Kingdom, with God dwelling in Zion in a new sanctuary ($1^{26.29}$ $23^{13f.}$). Heaven and earth are gradually renewed as a conditional result of man's being transformed spiritually (4^{26}). There will be no Satan or any evil destroyer, and men will attain to 1000 years ($23^{27.29}$). The verse which says that God will 'descend and dwell with them throughout eternity' (1^{26}) seems to point to the eternity of this Kingdom; but, on the other hand, it seems to terminate with the great Judgment (see *Bk. of Jub.*, ed. Charles, 1895, p. 150, note on 23^{30}), in which the fallen angels and their children, Mastema or Satan, and all sinners are to be judged ($4^{19.24}$ 5^{10} 10^{8} 23^{11}). The resurrection is not definitely mentioned.

The same uncertainty characterizes the *Psalms of Solomon* (c. 70–40 B.C.), with their vivid presentation of the Messianic hope, and of a personal Messiah, Χριστός, who will appear and drive out from Israel the heathen and sinners, but with spiritual weapons, and gather together the holy people, and rule them in holiness. The earth will be divided among them. The heathen will serve him as vassals, and Jerusalem, purified and made holy, will be the centre of his holy and wise rule (*Pss* 17. 18). There is to be a final day of judgment ($15^{13.14}$); but, as this is never said to precede the Messianic Kingdom, and as the duration of the latter is probably 'conterminous with that of its ruler' (Charles, *Crit. Hist. of Doct. of Fut. Life*, 1899, p. 223), we may assume that it occurs at its close. It is a day of mercy for the righteous,[1] who rise to life eternal (3^{16} 13^{9}) and inherit life in gladness (14^{7}), but of recompense for the wicked, who receive Hades (the abode of sinners, 16^{2}), darkness, and destruction for ever (3^{13} 14^{6}).

The temporal Kingdom is probably also to be found in the *Assumption of Moses*, dating from the beginning of the Christian era. After a time of repentance (1^{18}), God arises in wrath, and, amid convulsions of Nature, interferes on behalf of Israel. Satan will be no more. 'Then thou, O Israel, wilt be happy' (10^{8}). Finally, Israel is exalted to the firmament, and thence looks down upon its enemies in Gehenna (or on earth?) ($10^{3ff.}$). There is no Messiah in this book.

A clearer view of the temporal Kingdom is to be found in some of the constituents of the *Apocalypse of Baruch* (A.D. 50–70). It will be preceded by tribulations and convulsions of Nature which do not affect Palestine (27–29^{2}). Messiah is then revealed (29^{3} 39^{7}). In two of the sections he slays (1) the leader of the hostile fourth empire, Rome (39^{5}–40^{3}; the 'leader' is a kind of Antichrist [see *ERE*, vol. i. p. 578^{b}]); or (2) the hostile nations which have trodden down the seed of Jacob. The others he spares ($72^{2f.}$). The Kingdom is temporal (εἰς τὸν αἰῶνα), and lasts until 'the world of corruption' is at an end (40^{3} 73^{1}). It is also sensuous. Behemoth and Leviathan serve as food for the righteous remnant—the 'Messianic banquet' (cf. 4 Ezr $6^{49f.}$).[2] The earth yields fruits 10,000-fold; each vine has 1000 branches, each branch 1000 clusters, each cluster 1000 grapes, each grape produces a cor of wine. Winds bring aromatic perfumes, clouds distil the dew of health, and the treasury of manna again descends ($29^{4f.}$; cf. Is 25^{6-8}). There is joy, no weariness, disease, anxiety, or sin. No one dies untimely; women have no pain in childbirth. Wild beasts minister to men. There is no toil in labour (73. 74). At the close of this period, 'the Consummation of the times' (30^{3}), Messiah returns to heaven (? see 30^{1}), and the righteous rise. Now begins the Day of Judgment (59^{8}), and the time of increased perdition and torment for the wicked ($54^{15.21}$).

(β) But with this period there arose attempts at giving the exact duration of this temporal Kingdom, connected with the growing view of the world-ages.[1] Jeremiah's prophecy of the coming of the Kingdom after 70 years (25^{12}) had not been fulfilled. At a much later time (c. 168 B.C.) the writer of Daniel returns to the number 70, but re-interprets it as 70 weeks of years (see Cornill, *Die siebzig Jahrwochen Daniels*, 1889), looking for the establishment of the Kingdom after 3½ years (9^{24}). The writer of *Enoch* 83–90 also re-interprets it, and speaks of 70 shepherds, to whose care the nation is given from the beginning of the heathen attack until the establishment of the Kingdom ($89^{59f.}$), the period of their rule being subdivided into 12, 23, 23, 12 (=70) times (89^{72} 90^{5}). A more exact method of dating is found in *En.* 91–104 (early in 1st cent. B.C.). Here the world's history is divided into 10 week-periods ($93^{3f.}$). At the close of the 7th begins the Messianic Kingdom, in the 9th the revealing of Judgment, and in the 10th the Judgment and the end, opening up a period of limitless weeks ($91^{2f.}$). The writer is living towards the close of the 7th period (93^{10}). In the *Secrets of Enoch* (c. A.D. 1–50), the author, perhaps basing upon the Persian conception of the duration of the human race during 6 millenniums,[2] uses an argument which was to become popular in later times (§ 15). The world having been created in 6 days, these days, each of 1000 years (Ps 90^{4}), represent the course of the world's history, followed by the Sabbath rest of 1000 years. This 'rest' is the duration of the temporal Messianic Kingdom (without a Messiah) now first regarded as a millennium. It is followed by the Day of Judgment, which the righteous escape, receiving a final award in Paradise (9); but the wicked are cast into hell in the third heaven (10). There is no resurrection.

In 4 Ezra, after many signs, wonders, and evils, Enoch and Elijah are revealed, and evil is blotted out ($6^{18ff.}$). Then Messiah, God's Son, is revealed 'with those that be with him,' and his Kingdom lasts for 400 years (this period was arrived at by comparing Gn 15^{13} with Ps 90^{15}; see Gfrörer, ii. 253). Those who have escaped the woes and evils rejoice in it, as well as 'those revealed with him'—possibly the righteous dead now raised (Charles, 286; cf. 13^{52}, where Messiah is revealed with certain OT saints). Messiah now dies, along with all men. There is a 7 days' silence, followed by the resurrection of ***all mankind***, and the last Judgment, a day in which none of the phenomena of Nature is existent, only the splendour of the Most High. It endures a week of years. The righteous enter Paradise and the wicked Gehenna (5. 6. 7). Messiah is here conceived of as a semi-Divine and a mortal being, and he has no part in the Judgment. If the idea of a first resurrection is really to be found here, it is obviously carried over from those earlier views, in which all the righteous rose to share in the eternal Messianic Kingdom. It is also found in the Talmud (Weber ^{2}, 364 f.).

(3) *The Other-world Kingdom.*—Although the persistence of the hope of the Kingdom is one of the most remarkable features of Judaism, and one shared by no other ethnic religion, yet an extremely pessimistic view of the world led in some quarters to a complete abandonment of any hope of a Messianic Kingdom. This is found in two of the sections of *Apoc. Bar.*, written after the fall of Jerusalem (see Charles's ed., 1896, p. lv). The Final Judgment is soon to take place (20^{2} 23^{7} 25). Souls will be brought forth, of the righteous from their 'treasuries,' of the wicked from their place of temporary punishment (30^{2-5}). The earth gives back their bodies in the form in which it received them in order that they may recognize each other. Then follows the Judgment, at which books are opened in which sins are written (24^{1} 49. 50; cf. 21. 23. 24^{1}). Afterwards the bodies of the righteous are transformed to glory, and they receive 'the world which does not die,' and dwell in the heights of that world (51). The wicked suffer torment (30^{5} 51^{6} 52^{3}). The transitory creation is renewed; there appears 'a world which does not die' (32^{6} 48^{50} 51^{3}). For a similar but less detailed picture of the future, see ch. 85, also the so-called 'Apoc. of Salathiel' in 4 Ezr $4^{34f.}$, and 4 Maccabees.

(ii.) In later prophetic books the *Resurrection* includes the righteous and also wicked Israelites. In Apocalyptic books it generally excludes the wicked (*Test. xii. Patr.*; 2 Mac., *En.* 83 ff. 87 f. 90^{33} 91 f. [resurrection of the spirit], *Ps. Sol.* 3^{16} [bodily or spiritual]). But it sometimes includes the wicked Israelites or some of them, though their resurrection may not be a bodily one (*En.* 22^{11} $51^{1.2}$; but cf. 61^{5} [righteous in a spiritual body] 51^{4} $62^{15.16}$). Again, in others, perhaps as a result of Christian influences, there is taught a resurrection of all, both Jews and Gentiles, righteous and wicked (*Apoc. Bar.* 30^{2-5} 50. 51, 4 Ezr $7^{32f.}$,

---

[1] The Judgment is a 'day of mercy' for the righteous, but so also is the day when Messiah appears (18^{6}). Does this mean that the Judgment takes place on that 'day'?

[2] Cf. Ps $74^{13f.}$, Ezk 29^{5} $32^{4f.}$. In *Enoch* 60^{72} Leviathan and Behemoth are said to be 'parted.' In the Talmud (*Baba bathra*, 74*a*) the saints are to feast on Leviathan in the time of Messiah. In the Targum of pseudo-Jonathan on Nu $11^{26f.}$ Israel will feast on the ox prepared for them from the beginning (see Gfrörer, *Gesch. des Urchristent.*, Stuttgart, 1888; Weber, *Lehre des Talmud*, 1880, pp. 156, 195, 370, 384). In Persian eschatology the marrow of the ox Hadhayôsh serves as food of immortality to the righteous (*Bund.* xix. 13, xxx. 25; cf. also *JE* viii. 38 f.).

[1] In *Apoc. Bar.* 23^{4} f., when Adam sinned, the multitude to be born was numbered; and, until it is fulfilled, the resurrection cannot take place. Cf. 4 Ezr 4^{36}, Rev 6^{11}.

[2] Six millenniums preceded these (see § 8).

Test. xii. Patr. [Benj. 10]; cf. *Sib. Or.* iv. 181 f.). The Talmud looks forward to a resurrection of the righteous only, though occasionally a resurrection of the righteous Gentiles, or even of all Gentiles, is taught (Gfrörer, ii. 276 f.; Volz, 247; Eisenmenger, *Entdecktes Judenthum*, Königsberg, 1700, p. 908 f.). In *Jub.* 23$^{30.\,31}$ the *spirits* of the righteous are glorified; cf. *Ass. Mos.*, and the Alexandrian Jewish school—Sirach, Philo, also the Essenes and Sadducees. In *Secrets of Enoch* 22$^{8f.}$ righteous souls are clad in 'the raiment of God's glory' (cf. the Pharisaic belief in Jos. *BJ* II. viii. 13 [good souls receive 'other bodies']; see Schwally, *Leben nach dem Tode*, Giessen, 1892, p. 171 f.).

Dn 12 is the first place in the OT where the Final Judgment includes the dead. A not dissimilar idea of a final judgment for certain of the dead, already subjected to a preliminary judgment, appears in Is 24$^{21.\,22}$. In these Apocalyptic books, where punishments are allotted to evil angels or the dead before the Final Judgment, a preliminary judgment is also implied or stated. Such a judgment is often inflicted on the living by Messiah, or the saints, at the beginning of the temporal Kingdom. In either case it is followed by the Final Judgment, which allots the last and worst condition of the wicked. Where the Messianic Kingdom is eternal, the Final Judgment usually precedes it. But, where it is temporal, it occurs at its close.[1]

(iii.) The *condition of the dead* between death and the Resurrection or Final Judgment may be summarized as follows. Sheol is an intermediate state in which the righteous are separated from the wicked. From it the righteous rise to the eternal Messianic Kingdom (*En.* 1–36; cf. 2 Mac). Occasionally it becomes also the final state of punishment for the wicked or for some of them, though Gehenna is the more usual term for this state (*En.* 22^{13} 99^{11}, *Ps. Sol.* 14^{6} 16^{2}, *Ass. Mos.* 10^{10}, *Jub.* 7^{29} 22^{22}, Talmud; cf. also the fiery abyss in *En.* 18$^{11f.}$ 21$^{8f.}$ for wicked angels). A similar conception of Sheol as an intermediate abode is found in *En.* 91 f., 4 Ezr 4^{41}, *Apoc. Bar.* 11^{6} 23^{5} 52^{2}, Josephus; but here the righteous rise to a Kingdom in heaven, or to a Messianic Kingdom in a new heaven and earth (*En.* 37 f.), although, as in 4 Ezra, there is a first resurrection to a temporal Kingdom. Where Sheol is regarded as a place of torment for the wicked at death, the righteous go to a separate division of it as an intermediate abode, or else to an intermediate Paradise (*Jub.* 7^{29}, *En.* 61^{12}, *Secrets of En.* 32^{1}). The older conception of Sheol as a general place of the dead is still found sporadically, unassimilated with the newer ideas (see Volz, *Jüd. Esch.* 289). The final reward of the righteous is generally 'everlasting life' (Dn 12^{2}, *En.* 40^{9}, *Secr. of En.* 65^{9}; cf. Mk 10^{17} etc.)—usually in heaven, or in the new heaven and earth. That of the wicked is 'everlasting destruction' (*Ps. Sol.* 15$^{12f.}$). They remain in Sheol or suffer torments in Gehenna or the 'abyss of fire.' Annihilation by fire which goes forth from God is referred to in *Asc. Is.* 4^{18}. Torments, fire, and darkness are frequently mentioned; and fire, ice, and snow, as well as spirits of retribution reserved for the Day of Judgment, occur in *Test. xii. Patr.* (Levi 3^{2}). In later Judaism, Gehenna is the purgatory of faithless Jews, but Gentiles are eternally punished in it.

(iv.) The place of the *Gentiles* in the earthly Messianic Kingdom varies in Apocalyptic books. The righteous heathen worship God (*Sib. Or.* iii. 710 ff.). Those who have not been enemies of Israel are spared, and are subject to Messiah or Israel (*En.* 10^{21} 90^{30}, *Apoc. Bar.* 72$^{2f.}$, *Ps. Sol.* 17^{32}; cf. Rev 21$^{24f.}$ 22^{2}), or those who repent and accept the light of Messiah are gathered in with Israel and enlightened (*En.* 48$^{4.\,5}$ 50$^{2-5}$, *Test. xii. Patr.* [Levi 18^{9}, Naph. 8$^{3f.}$]). But in other cases (mainly 1st cent. B.C.) the Gentiles are doomed to destruction and punishment (*En.* 37 f., *Ass. Mos.* 10, 4 Ezr 13$^{37f.}$, and also in later Judaism). In *Jub.* 23^{30} (cf. 50^{5}) they are driven out of Palestine (cf. *Sib. Or.* v. 264, Jl 4^{17}).

(v.) *The two ages.*—The present state of things (temporal, evil, and corruptible) is often contrasted with the future state (blissful, eternal, and incorruptible). Hence arose the doctrine of the two ages—this and that æon, ὁ αἰὼν οὗτος (cf. Ro 12^{2}, 1 Co 1^{20} 2$^{6.\,8}$), הָעוֹלָם הַזֶּה; and ὁ αἰὼν ὁ μέλλων or ὁ ἐρχόμενος (Mk 10^{30}, Eph 1^{21}, cf. 2^{7}), הָעוֹלָם הַבָּא (cf. 'the great æon,' *Secr. of En.* 58^{5} 61^{2}). This age corresponds, on the whole, with the transient world-ages (see above). The new age begins either with the Messianic reign—eternal or temporal—or (a later view) at the end of the Messianic Kingdom which introduced a still higher order, or the heavenly state (4 Ezr 7$^{30.\,31}$, *Apoc. Bar.* 44$^{9ff.}$). In *Apoc. Bar.* 74$^{2f.}$ the temporary Kingdom is mediant between the two ages. The end, completion, or consummation of the age, or the times, or of all things, is often referred to and is confidently awaited; and these phrases are very common in the NT (Dn 7^{26} 12^{13}, *Apoc. Bar.* 27^{15}, Mt 13^{39} 24^{3} 28^{20} ἡ συντέλεια τοῦ αἰῶνος; cf. He 9^{26} συντέλεια τῶν αἰώνων, 1 Co 10^{11} τὰ τέλη τῶν αἰώνων, 1 P 4^{7} πάντων τὸ τέλος).

A common Jewish expression, from the 1st cent. onwards, was 'to take possession of the future æon.' For a similar idea, cf. *En.* 48^{7}: the Son of Man 'shall preserve the portion of the righteous,' and Col 1^{12}. See Gfrörer, ii. 212 ff.; Schoettgen, *Horae Hebr.*, Dresden, 1733, i. 1153 ff.; Schürer, *HJP* II. ii. [1885] 133, 177.

(vi.) *Parsi influences on Jewish eschatology.*—Darmesteter (*SBE* iv. [1880], Introd. lvii ff.) and others saw a strong Jewish influence on the Avesta. Other scholars have maintained that there was a considerable borrowing from Parsiism in the formation of Jewish eschatology, just as in other beliefs. The question is complicated by the fact that we do not know whether the later Parsi beliefs also existed in earlier times. There are certainly profound differences between the two eschatologies. Moreover, though superficially there appear to be strong resemblances between them,—*e.g.* the idea of world-periods, the binding and conquest of evil powers, preliminary judgments and awards after death, the belief in a Messiah, the destruction of the world in connexion with resurrection and judgment, the resurrection, the renewal of the worlds,—a detailed comparison of these general likenesses reveals many discrepancies. Many elements of Jewish eschatology have their roots in Semitic mythology, and it is probable that the Parsi influence was not generally fundamental, but merely formative in the case of beliefs which were already in existence or in process of being born, with occasional transmission of details.

On this subject, see Böklen, *Die Verwandtschaftsverhältnisse der jüd.-christl. mit der pars. Eschatologie*, Göttingen, 1902; Stave, *Ueber den Einfluss des Parsismus auf das Judentum*, Haarlem, 1898; Cheyne, *Origin of the Psalter*, 1891, p. 381 ff.; Mills, *Avesta Eschatology*, Chicago, 1908; Söderblom, *op. cit.* 301 ff.; Bousset, *Rel. des Judentums*, 473 ff.

II. **Eschatology in the Gospels.**—(*a*) The interpretations given to our Lord's eschatology have been many. It has been taken with absolute literalness; it has been spiritualized; it has been regarded as subject to interpolation, greater or less; or its originality is admitted, but its ex-

[1] In the Jewish-Christian *Test. of Abraham* (2nd cent.) there are 3 judgments—the 1st at death, by Abel; the 2nd by the 12 tribes of Israel, at the Advent; the 3rd by the Lord Himself (§§ 13, 14; see *TS* ii. 2. 29 ff.).

pected fulfilment is regarded as a mistake and an illusion which, however, does not disannul Christ's real greatness. In reviewing our Lord's teaching, we must keep before us certain important probabilities: (1) that He used the current Apocalyptic language as the vehicle of a greater truth; (2) that Apocalyptic language which He did not use has been attributed to Him; and (3) that His sayings were misunderstood and a wrong colouring given to them. M. Arnold's maxim is here of importance: 'Jesus above the heads of His reporters.'

Christ's teaching points to two separate ways of regarding the Kingdom of God. It is a present spiritual reality (Mt 11[12] 12[28] 13[16. 17], Lk 17[20f.] ἐντὸς ὑμῶν). But it has also a future consummation—the 'glory of His Kingdom,' the παλιγγενεσία. The one condition is a preliminary to the other. The present Kingdom revealed in righteousness is to spread until it is universal.[1] St. Paul's conception of the Kingdom is similar. It is a present and purely spiritual state (Ro 14[17], Col 1[12f.]), but our full inheritance of it is in the future (1 Co 6[9] 15[50], Gal 5[21], Eph 5[5]). But in some sayings of Christ the future Kingdom is introduced suddenly and is catastrophic. How are these different aspects—development and catastrophe—to be reconciled? The eschatological theory that Christ thought that the Kingdom would be inaugurated immediately after a short period of 'Messianic woes,' He Himself being revealed as Son of Man, or Messiah, after a supernatural removal and transformation, but that, having seen this to be impossible, He began to speak of a future Kingdom and brought on His death in order that the catastrophic coming of the Kingdom might at once follow, cannot be proved.[2] Moreover, there was no Jewish precedent for such a conception of Messiah. Nor can it be certain that Christ looked forward to an immediate coming of the (future) Kingdom.

In Mt 10[23] a coming of the Son of Man before the disciples go over all the cities of Israel is foretold. This completes a section (vv.[17-23]) which has no parallel in the Mk. (6[7f.]) and Lk. (9[1f.]) accounts of the mission of the Twelve, these ending with the command to shake off the dust from their feet (cf. the parallel mission of the Seventy, Lk 10[1f.]). This discourse in Mk. and Lk. (=Mt 10[1-16]) is thus complete in itself. This is seen in the fact that the additional section in Mt. (v.[17ff.]) has parallels in the Eschatological discourse in Mt 24=Mk 13=Lk 21. Verse [23] has thus nothing to do with the mission of the Twelve, and is perhaps a mistaken form of the formula found in Mt 24[14], Mk 13[10], unless it refer to Pentecost or the destruction of Jerusalem. Hence it cannot have the meaning given to it by Schweitzer (*Quest*, p. 357), that the Parousia will take place before the return of the Twelve from their hasty journey. Further, the sufferings prophesied (v.[17ff.]) are thus not those which will befall the Twelve on their mission, but refer to a state of things after Christ's death and before the unknown future Parousia (cf. Jn 16[2]). They are the 'Messianic woes' of current eschatology.

The two methods of regarding the Kingdom, present and future, correspond to the Jewish conception of a temporary, followed by an eternal Kingdom (§ 10 (*d*)), but with important differences. Christ has come and established a Kingdom of God on earth—not, however, a sensuous Kingdom, but a reign of righteousness; and not a reign of righteousness mechanically produced, but the result of the gradual yielding of human wills (cf. 2 Co 5[17]). But the consummation of the Kingdom was not on earth but in heaven. To this our Lord looked forward, but He probably accepted and taught that the consummation would have its catastrophic beginning, here following Apocalyptic eschatology. But we do not know how far this adoption of current thought is original, or how far it is merely attributed to Christ. Eschatology has an important place in Christ's teaching *as we have it*, yet there are other elements, and it is too often forgotten that we have not a complete record of all He taught.

The present Kingdom is not sensuous or introduced by catastrophic or other signs (save the coming of Elias=John Baptist), but spiritual and 'not of this world' (Jn 18[36]). The future Kingdom is heavenly, and thus, as far as men are concerned, the two aspects, present and future, are one and the same. Cf. Mk 10[5], where men's method of receiving the Kingdom is the condition of their enjoying its future consummation. The future Kingdom corresponds to the heavenly Kingdom of later Apocalyptic, but is far more spiritually conceived (see Oesterley, *Doctrine of the Last Things*, 1908, p. 190 ff.).

A prophecy of the Parousia and Judgment is already found in Mk 8[38]—the Son of Man is to come in the glory of His Father with His holy angels. But we shall consider first the eschatological discourse Mk 13=Mt 24[1ff.]=Lk 21[5ff.]. It opens with a prophecy of the destruction of the Temple, followed by the question as to the time and sign of 'these things,' viz. the Temple's destruction. The discourse answers the question, but it goes much further.

In Mk 13[4] and Lk 21[7] the question refers only to the destruction of the Temple. Therefore the eschatological form of the question in Mt 24[3]—'the sign of thy coming and of the end of the age'—may be regarded as an interpolation. The reply must simply have been one referring to the destruction of Jerusalem—a subject often spoken of by Christ—as well as the doom of unbelieving Jews. It is specifically referred to in Lk 19[41f.], and less clearly in 23[28f.], where it is near at hand. Cf. also Mt 12[43f.], 23[37f.], Mk 12[1], Lk 11[51] 13[1f. 34f.].

In Mk 13, with the prophecy of signs preceding and accompanying the fall of Jerusalem is mingled a prophecy of an event of much wider significance, preceded by signs of more world-wide importance.

The most striking difference in these two prophecies is that, while the one peril is imminent (vv.[9. 11. 29. 30]), the other is at an unknown date (v.[32]), this passage following on the other and offering a strange contradiction to it if both refer to the same event (cf. Lk 12[40]). Hence probably v.[10] belongs to the second prophecy—before the end, not before the fall of Jerusalem, must the gospel be preached among all nations. Again, v.[24] 'after that tribulation . . .' must refer to the wars and convulsions of vv.[7. 8], not to the destruction of Jerusalem, if we follow the line of traditional Apocalyptic. Thus the mingling of two prophecies—one referring to Jerusalem, the other to the Parousia—by some one who believed in the imminent coming of the Son of Man, confirmed or gave rise to the current view that it would take place soon after the destruction of Jerusalem.

The composite character of this passage is also seen in the fact that in the parallel passage in Mt 24 are inserted vv.[26-28. 37-41]. These are not found in the parallel passage in Lk., but occur with him in a different connexion, viz. after the saying that the Kingdom cometh not with observation, etc. (17[20-22]). In Mt. they break the continuity of the passage and occur separately, while in Lk 17 they are brought together (vv.[23. 24. 37. 26. 27. 34. 35]) with some additions (vv.[28. 29. 32. 33]), which have parallels elsewhere in Mt 10[39] 16[25] (cf. Mk 8[35]). Again, Lk 17[31] occurs in a different context in Mt 24[17. 18]=Mk 13[15. 16]. (In Lk. the sections describing an outward coming of the Kingdom are surely out of place in a description of the Kingdom as 'within you.') Mk 13[9-13] occurs in Mt 10[17-23] in connexion with the mission of the Twelve, where it is clearly out of place, and it is much shortened in Mt 24[9. 13. 14]. The passage regarding the coming of the Son of Man and the sending forth of His angels (Mk 13[26. 27]) may combine words spoken separately, viz. Mk 8[38], Mt 13[40f.], in which the final day is differently described as a coming of the Son of Man on clouds with angels, and a sending forth of angels (though for a different purpose—'to gather out all that offend,' as against 'to gather in the elect').

The composite character of the discourse may thus be assumed. By many critics vv.[7. 8. 14-20 (21-23?) 24-27. 30. 31] are regarded as a Christian adaptation of a Jewish Apocalypse, written just before the fall of Jerusalem, or a Christian Apocalypse using Jewish materials, and containing many direct parallels with Jewish Apocalypses (see Charles, p. 326 f., ed. *Ass. Mos.* pp. 80, 87), as well as with prophetic eschatology. The reference to the coming of the Son of Man shows that it is at an unknown (cf. Lk 12[35. 39. 43], Mt 25[1f.]) and possibly distant time (cf. 'at even,' etc.). Hence it is unnecessary to include vv.[14-20] in this Apocalypse, for they form a natural sequel to the verses dealing with the signs of the fulfilment of 'these things,' *i.e.* the destruc-

[1] Cf. Harnack, *Sayings of Jesus*, 1908, p. 232: 'If any one finds it impossible to accept the antinomy "the Kingdom is future and yet present," argument with him is useless.' See also Sanday, *HJ* x. [1911] 102.

[2] For these views, see Weiss, *Die Predigt Jesu vom Reiche Gottes*, Göttingen, 1910; Schweitzer, *Von Reimarus zu Wrede*, Tübingen, 1906 (Eng. tr. *The Quest of the Historical Jesus*, 1910); Tyrrell, *Christianity at the Cross Roads*, 1909. Cf. also F. C. Burkitt, 'The Parable of the Wicked Husbandmen' in *Trans. 3rd Intern. Cong. Hist. Rel.*, Oxford, 1908, ii. 321 ff.

tion of the Temple, which is near at hand. Whether they are original to the answer is a different question, and the probability is that they are not (cf. v.^{14} 'readeth,' not 'heareth,' and the completely different form in Lk 21^{20} 'compassed with armies').

Thus the prophecy relating to Jerusalem contains—

vv.$^{5.6}$ Appearance of false Christs.
vv.$^{9.11.13}$ Persecution of disciples.
v.^{12} Family quarrels.
vv.$^{14-20}$ Warnings and woes.
vv.$^{21-23}$ Appearance of false Christs and prophets.
vv.$^{28-31}$ Near approach of these events.

Probably this discourse has been coloured by the eschatological thoughts of its reporter, for it is unlikely that our Lord would give details of the event. Lk $19^{43f.}$ $21^{20f.}$ would then also be so coloured or interpolated.

This leaves the purely eschatological passage—

vv.$^{7-8}$ Wars, earthquakes, famines; the *beginning* of sorrows, but the end is *not yet* (ἀλλ' οὔπω τὸ τέλος; Lk 21^{9} οὐκ εὐθέως).
v.^{24} After *that* tribulation, further phenomena in Nature (cf. Lk $21^{25.26}$), which are not so much a sign as an accompaniment of
vv.$^{26-27}$ The coming of the Son of Man.
vv.$^{32-37}$ The unknown time of the coming. Warnings to watch.

The inconsistency of an unknown coming being heralded by signs is inevitable in Apocalyptic, and occurs in 1 and 2 Thess.

Thus the eschatological passage, vv.$^{7.8.24-27.32f.}$, gives a clear picture in prophetic and apocalyptic style of the Parousia at an unknown and probably distant time.[1] That it was spoken as it stands need not be asserted, but it is unnecessary to suppose that it has been taken bodily from an existing Apocalypse. Christ's references elsewhere to the Parousia are less detailed, but their language corresponds.

The sudden but unknown Parousia of the Son of Man is often mentioned—Mt 24^{44}=Lk 12^{40}; Lk 17^{24}; cf. Mt $24^{27.37f.}$ The Son of Man is to come in the glory of His Father and in His own glory with His holy angels, or in the clouds of heaven, to reward every man according to his works, or to be ashamed of those ashamed of Him (Mk 8^{38}=Mt 16^{27}=Lk 9^{26}; cf. Mt 25^{31}, Mk 14^{62}). The Son of Man is to send His angels to gather out of the Kingdom all that offend, but the righteous will shine as the sun (Mt 13^{41-43}). The judgment is further described in the discourse of the Sheep and the Goats (Mt 25^{31-46}). For other references to the Day of Judgment, see Mt $12^{41.42}$=Lk $11^{31.32}$; Mt 11^{22}=Lk 10^{14}; Mt 11^{24}.

To these passages there are parallels in Dn 7^{13} 'came with the clouds of heaven,' and in *Enoch*, where the Son of Man is described as sitting on the throne of His glory to judge (45^{3} 61^{8} 62^{5} 69^{27}). Angels of punishment take the wicked and execute judgment upon them (62^{11}). Thus these, as well as the passage in Mk 13, echo the language of Apocalyptic.

The passage, 'When in the regeneration,' etc. (Mt 19^{28}), does not occur in the parallel passage Mk $10^{28f.}$=Lk $18^{28f.}$. But it occurs in a different connexion in Lk $22^{29.30}$, where it is obviously out of place with what precedes. It may be an eschatological addition suggested by such an incident as Mt $20^{20f.}$; cf. Mt 25^{21}. It is the natural result of speaking of inheriting the Kingdom of Heaven (Mt $25^{33.34}$), but it is found in older Apocalypses; cf. *En.* 108^{12} 'I will seat each on the throne of his honour'; *Test. xii. Patr.* [Jud. 25^{1}], at the resurrection Judah and his brethren will be chief of the twelve tribes; cf. Benj. 10^{7}; cf. also Rev 3^{21}. The idea of judgment by the righteous is already found in Dn 2^{44}, *En.* 91^{12} 95^{7} 96^{1} 98^{12}; Wis 3^{8}, cf. 1 Co $6^{2.3}$.

Christ spoke so often of the judgment on Jerusalem that we can hardly doubt that in His mind it was a Divine judgment, and, as such, a coming of the Son of Man to the city which had rejected Him.[2] Much of the detail is obviously interpolated, and it was not the Final Judgment (as Wendt [*Teaching of Jesus*, 1892, ii. 364 f.] insists), though the horror excited by the fall of Jerusalem caused an inevitable mingling of the two events in Synoptic tradition. Possibly, therefore, Mt 10^{23} may have been spoken with reference to this event as a 'coming.' (One may here compare the punishments on the unfaithful churches in Rev $2^{15.16}$ 3^{3}, which are regarded as a 'coming' of Christ.) After this 'coming,' Christianity would shake itself free of Judaism and enter on that long period

[1] The time unknown to the Son is recalled in Rev 14^{15}, where the angel carries the message to the Son of Man announcing that now the time has come.

[2] See Durell, *Self-Revelation of our Lord*, 1910. For the different suggestions in Christ's teaching about the Kingdom—present, near future, more distant future—see Sanday, *HDB* ii. 620.

of growth which is pointed to in Mt $13^{24f.36f.47f.}$ 25^{19}, Mk $2^{19.20}$ $4^{26f.}$. Thus, in a sense, the present Kingdom on earth has its catastrophic coming or point of development, analogous to the catastrophic coming of the future heavenly Kingdom.[1]

The emphasis laid on the unknown time of the coming, as well as the mingling of two events in Mk 13, helps to elucidate those passages which look forward to it within 'this generation.' In Mk 8^{38} 9^{1} (=Mt $16^{27.28}$, Lk $9^{26.27}$) 'some shall not taste of death till they have seen the kingdom of God come with power' (Lk. 'see the kingdom of God'; Mt. 'see the Son of Man coming in his kingdom') immediately follows on a reference to the Parousia and Judgment. The latter, said elsewhere to occur at an unknown time, is here combined with an event said to be near at hand. Two different things are spoken of, or were spoken of, at different times and combined by one who believed in the imminent catastrophic coming and establishment of the Kingdom. It is impossible to suppose (as Dobschütz does, *Eschat. of the Gospels*, 1910, p. 116) that there is here no real contradiction because, in putting the date at the end of His generation, Christ gives no real date. It should be noted, however, that Mt. is more eschatological than Mk., who again is more so than Luke. This is an example of the way in which to a non-catastrophic saying regarding the Kingdom there may be given such a colouring. The Kingdom coming, or coming in power, was not necessarily catastrophic, like the 'coming' of the previous verse. Already it had come as an unseen power; the future coming with power within 'this generation' might quite well refer to a spiritual outpouring, such as Joel foretold and such as occurred on the Day of Pentecost (cf. Jn 14^{26} $15^{26.27}$ $16^{7f.}$). This was seen by the disciples. It was also a judgment, marking out the Christian community, the faithful, who were rewarded with a deeper spiritual life, from those who put Christ to shame by not accepting His message.

That this is the case may be seen from the fact that the Parousia is invariably spoken of as a coming of the Son of Man with His angels, followed by a judgment (Mk 8^{38}, Mt 13^{49} 16^{27} 25^{31}, Lk 9^{26}). This differentiates it from the simple seeing the Kingdom, or coming of the Kingdom with power (Mk 9^{1}, Mt 16^{28}, Lk 9^{27}), and suggests that these phrases do not refer to the Parousia properly so called. Similarly, the Kingdom is already come in the presence of Christ in the world (Lk $17^{20f.}$), and His invisible presence might also be felt in all future spiritual, moral, or national crises.

That the future unknown coming may also be a distant coming is seen from the form of the saying, Mk 13^{35} 'at even, or at midnight, or at cock-crowing, or in the morning.' Similarly in Lk $19^{11f.}$, to those who thought the coming of the Kingdom of God imminent Christ spoke the parable of the Talents, with the phrase 'Occupy till I come.' Cf. the parallel passage Mt 25^{19} 'after a long time the lord of those servants cometh.'[2] Again, the words to the high priest, ἀπ' ἄρτι ὄψεσθε (Mt 26^{64}), or simply ὄψεσθε (Mk 14^{62}), do not necessarily denote that he would see the coming of the Son of Man in his lifetime, but may mean after death, at the resurrection, when the unjust as well as the just would rise, according to a well-known opinion of Jewish Apocalyptic. Cf. *En.* 51^{1}, where at the coming of the Son of Man all Israel rises. It should be noted also that the parallel Lk 22^{69} says nothing of a coming of the Son of Man (cf. Ac 7^{56}). Thus the exhortation to watch for the unknown coming did not imply that it would be in the hearers' day, since Christ Himself did not know when it would be. It might be then, therefore they should be watchful. But the words are spoken also to future generations of disciples.

[1] In one of the sections of the *Apoc. Bar.* the fall of Jerusalem is antecedent to and preparatory for the Judgment (20^{2}).

[2] Cf. Mt $24^{48.50}$ 'tarrieth,' 25^{5} 'tarried.'

In its present form the Kingdom fulfils the anticipations of the past, but these are generally spiritualized by Christ (cf. Dobschütz, 138 f.). Why, then, does He use the current ideas and language regarding the future catastrophic Parousia, without also clearly spiritualizing it? If He is correctly reported, His purpose may have been to show that the Son of Man would be the principal figure in the Kingdom, and to point to His own future justification as well as to the necessity of an ethical division before the establishment of the heavenly Kingdom—a division begun and ended by Himself. Although His disciples anticipated a literal fulfilment of these sayings in their own time, they also caught the spiritual sense, and their eschatological hopes did not interfere with their Christian life and conduct. In their discourses in Acts, though judgment is spoken of, the main stress is not eschatological. Indeed, though Christ used the language of His time as well as of past time, He did not necessarily mean that He would actually come on clouds, or that a great visible assize would take place. His hearers had no 'celestial language,' and perhaps to Him there was open only the inadequate language of His time—metaphor and pictorial imagery. It was the vehicle of His thought, and it expresses more than appears. Moreover, even the thoughts which lay in the depths of His personality, and which came into being through His deep consciousness of His relation to the Father, could perhaps only shape themselves as they rose to the surface from time to time, through the medium of His surface thoughts, while yet they always indicated their presence, or from time to time forced aside the refracting medium. Perhaps for this reason His eschatological conceptions bear the appearance of an imminent as well as of a catastrophic coming. Intense convictions loom large on the mental horizon and assume a nearness of fulfilment which is illusory. In times of intense thought we 'can crowd eternity into an hour.' This was true of many prophetic utterances,[1] and it was much more true of Apocalyptic convictions, which frequently speak of the nearness of the last things, as if they could not be otherwise conceived of (cf. *En.* 51^{2}, *Apoc. Bar.* 20^{4} 23^{7} 82^{2}). Yet combined with this is an uncertainty as to the time (*Apoc. Bar.* 24^{4} 4 Ezr 6^{59}, *Sib. Or.* iii. 55). Still, what is emphatic is less the thought of nearness than the absolute certainty of the reality of the things of the end.[2] For these reasons Christ's deeper knowledge and conviction of His position as Judge of men's thoughts and deeds took shape in His surface thoughts, mainly, though not always (see below), in intense eschatological convictions, which (if the nearness of the Parousia in His teaching is insisted on) then assumed the form of an imminent and catastrophic Parousia. We must, therefore, search for the rich meaning of which Christ's eschatology is full, and which its association with the past already connotes.

(1) Thus it is not necessary to assume that Christ taught absolutely an imminent Parousia. This overcomes the theory that such a prophecy was falsified, as well as the necessity of resorting to sophistical methods of explaining away the falsification.

(2) The literal acceptance of the Parousia teaching robs it of much of its meaning. Is there not rather here an impulse to moral conduct, because Christ comes as Judge not finally but always? So the sentence, 'Enter . . . joy . . . depart . . .,' suggests what is true in the course of human life. Those whose life is approved have a present joy, while the unrighteous already feel the self-imposed curse of separation from God. Present and future merge into one, and these conditions may be permanent if men choose to make them so. We may well see in Christ's eschatological language a picture of truth, not a reference to actual future events—a picture of His present and continuous judgment on mankind. Before Him, not at a 'Last Day,' but always, are gathered all nations; and in this, as in another sense, the saying is true, 'Lo, I am with you always.' The imagery of coming on the clouds of heaven is not too much for the splendour of this thought of a perennial and present judgment. OT prophecy was not fulfilled literally, but fulfilled far more effectively in the vindication of the eternal rule of righteousness, and its triumph over human pride and sin. This was pictured in concrete images, in elements drawn from the field of political, social, and cosmic life, forming one single and vast dramatic situation. Thus it gained in force. Isaiah recasts his details from time to time as new circumstances in history arise, but his main contention remains unchanged. So the dramatic action in Christ's picture of the last things is a representation of the continuous course of the Divine judgment. Hence, whether the language is His own or due to the additions of His reporters, such a line of interpretation is unaffected. It is also confirmed by the Gospel of St. John (see below), as well as by passages in the Synoptics (cf. Mk 2^{5}, Mt $10^{34f.}$ $11^{21f.\,27}$ $23^{37f.}$).

[1] Cf. A. B. Davidson, *Old Test. Prophecy*, 1903, p. 353.

[2] Cf. Baldensperger, *Das Selbstbewusstsein Jesu*, Strassburg, 1888, p. 148.

In this connexion it should be noted that, while Christ is careful to preserve the prophetic and Apocalyptic ideas of the Kingdom, at the same time He spiritualizes them.

Thus the coming of the Kingdom is preceded by Elijah (John Baptist, Mt 11^{14} 17^{10-13}). Satan's (=Beliar's) power is destroyed (Mt $12^{27f.}$, Lk 10^{18}). Human ills are done away with—the blind, lame, deaf, healed; sinners brought to repentance. The conception of the Messianic banquet is not lost sight of: Mt 8^{11} (=Lk 13^{28} [Q)]), Mk 14^{25}, Lk $22^{16.\,30}$ (cf. Mt 22^{1-14} 26^{29}). But it is obvious that the latter passages are not to be taken literally; they are symbols of spiritual ecstasy and union (cf., for this, Rev 3^{20} 'will sup with him'), since elsewhere the sensuous conception of the Kingdom is excluded, the relations of sex are abolished, and men are as the angels (ἰσάγγελοι) (Mk $12^{24.\,25}$).[1] We may compare the parables where the festival is used as a type of the Kingdom (Lk $14^{16f.}$), and also Christ's action in sitting down with publicans and sinners (Mk 2^{15}); cf. also Lk 14^{15}, description of the Kingdom as a marriage supper, though here it is the present Kingdom which is thus typified (v.[17]). The Kingdom is finally consummated in an entirely new order, the παλιγγενεσία (Mt 19^{28}). They who attain that æon are τῆς ἀναστάσεως υἱοί (Lk $20^{35.\,36}$).

But it can hardly be doubted, as a comparison of parallel passages in the Synoptics abundantly suggests (cf. Dobschütz, 91 f.), that a great deal of eschatological colouring has been given to Christ's words by His reporters. In this connexion it is significant that Q contains less eschatological matter, and that coloured less highly (cf. Mk 8^{38} with Mt 10^{33}, Lk 12^{9}) than the others,[2] though still sufficient to show that Christ did speak in Apocalyptic language: Lk 22^{28-30} = Mt 19^{28}, a passage which bears evidence of a common original, somewhat freely treated by the two writers ('continued with me,' 'followed me'; 'eat and drink' [Lk.]; 'in the regeneration . . .' [Mt.]). Mk. contains more, Mt. most of all. There is less in Lk., and least in Jn. (see B. H. Streeter, in *Oxford Studies in the Synoptic Problem*, 1911). Perhaps the destruction of Jerusalem deepened the colouring given to Christ's words in Mk. and Mt., if these Gospels date *c.* A.D. 70 (see Harnack, *Date of the Acts and the Synoptic Gospels*, 1911). Christ's reporters also more or less combined the idea of a coming of the Kingdom at a near date (destruction of Jerusalem, Pentecost) with the coming of the Son of Man at an unknown and remote date. This gave rise to the idea of a near Advent and Judgment, as we see it in the Epistles and in early Christian literature.[3] But this idea did not hinder the first followers from regarding the development of the Church as an historic process (cf. Inge, *Guardian*, 13 May 1910, p. 680, col. 3).

As has been seen, the conception of an immediate coming did not act upon the mind of Jesus. 'If we eliminate His eschatological ideas, His ethics remain unchanged' (Dobschütz, 13). There is no real evidence that the ethic of Jesus is an *Interimsethik*, as Schweitzer insists, but it is for all time, as is also the

[1] These ideas occur also in *En.* 62^{14} 'With that Son of man will they eat'; 51^{4} 'They will become angels in heaven'; cf. $104^{4.\,6}$.

[2] Cf. Harnack, *Sayings of Jesus*, 1908, p. 250 f., 'The tendency to exaggerate the apocalyptic and eschatological elements in our Lord's message, and to subordinate to this the merely religious and ethical elements, will ever find its refutation in Q.'

[3] It is obvious that men who thought, after the Resurrection, that Christ would now restore the Kingdom to Israel (Ac 1^{6}) might err regarding the time of the Parousia.

ethic of St. Paul. The ethic of Jesus is an ethic of the Kingdom considered as a present reality, and its essence and influence still remain in the future heavenly Kingdom. The hopefulness of the early Christians, their belief that they were living in a new order, which would not be changed, but consummated, by the Parousia, gave them confidence to live on the ethical plane of this new state, with glad alacrity. (See F. G. Peabody, 'NT Eschatology and NT Ethics,' *Trans. 3rd Inter. Cong. Hist. Rel.*, Oxford, 1908, ii. 305 ff.)

That the actual sayings of Christ regarding both the destruction of Jerusalem and the Future Coming have been highly coloured by the Apocalyptic ideas of His reporters is seen (1) in the fact that in Jn. little allusion is anywhere made to the 'impending judicial calamities of the Judæo-Roman war, and the destruction of Jerusalem and of the temple' (Wendt, ii. 273); and (2) in the Johannine conception of judgment.

Christ knew what was in men (Jn 2^{25}); hence there is a present judgment, regarded as automatic and self-induced, which has results for the future (3^{36} 5^{24}). Unbelievers are judged already (3^{18}). But believers are not judged (3^{18} 5^{24}); the fact of their acceptance of the Light has freed them from judgment. Though the judgment is self-induced, and Christ in this sense does not judge (cf. 8^{15} $12^{47f.}$), yet, because He is the Light, He 'reproves' the dark deeds of men (3^{20}), while those who do the truth in presence of the Light have the Divine working in their deeds made manifest (3^{21}). Thus He, as the Light, does judge (cf. $5^{22.\ 24.\ 30}$ 9^{39} 12^{31}). But, throughout, judgment is a *present* process—no doubt with future results, but still working in the present. The judgment is not conceived as a future, catastrophic coming. That future judgment is simply a confirming of the continuous judgment of the present.

The passage, Jn $5^{28.\ 29}$, is so obviously interpolated that it has no bearing on this subject. The formula, 'at the last day,' which occurs in various connexions—resurrection ($6^{39f.\ 44.\ 54}$), judgment (12^{48})—is perhaps also an interpolation, as its omission rather adds to than takes from the force of the passages. (Note 12^{48} 'the word that I have spoken, the same shall judge him,' as parallel with the ideas of $3^{18\text{-}21}$ 5^{24}, when 'at the last day' is omitted.) Thus St. John gives us a closer approximation than the Synoptists, not only to the meaning but also to certain aspects of the form of Christ's Apocalyptic teaching. No doubt he looked forward to the near end of the age, preceded by antichrists (false teachers, 1 Jn $2^{18.\ 19.\ 22.\ 26}$ 4^{3}), and to the Parousia; but he usually describes it differently from the Synoptists (cf. 14^{3} 'I will come again, and receive you unto myself,' although the Parousia is also connected with judgment [1 Jn 2^{28} 4^{17}]).

The saying to St. John (21^{22}) does not necessarily show that Christ taught a near coming such as would be involved within the period of a human life. The words are purely conditional rather than affirmative, and are intended to check curiosity (cf. v.^{23}).

The authenticity of the Johannine conception of judgment and its roots in Christ's actual teaching are seen in this, that, while the Synoptics set forth the Final Parousia and Judgment—a conception which dominated the early Church—John gives such a different and more spiritual conception. This did not originate with him, unless we are to regard him as greater than Christ. On the other hand, just as God's judgment is shown in the Synoptics to be present and continuous (Mt $6^{4.\ 6.\ 14.\ 15.\ 18}$ 10^{40}) as well as future (Mt 10^{28} 18^{35}), they also show that this is true of Christ (Mt 9^{2} $10^{34f.}$ $11^{20.\ 27}$), thus proving that dramatic eschatology was not the only aspect of Christ's teaching. The passage, Jn 5^{22} 'He hath committed all judgment unto the Son' (cf. *En.* 69^{27} 'The sum of judgment was committed unto him, the Son of Man'), shows how a simple statement of the connexion of the Son with judgment might be expressed either by Christ or His reporters in the form of an eschatological picture.

(*b*) *Christ as Judge.*—In the OT, Jahweh is Judge, as also in Apocalyptic books, save *En.* 37–70, where the Son of Man judges. But in the Gospels, while the Father is spoken of as Judge (Mt 10^{28} 18^{35}), Christ's influence at the Judgment is also spoken of (Mk 8^{38}), and more generally He Himself is Judge, and exercises this function on all men.

(*c*) *The Son of Man.*—It is noticeable how, in nearly all directly eschatological passages, this is the title used by Christ.[1]

See Mk 13^{26}=Mt 24^{30}=Lk 21^{27}; Mt 24^{27}=Lk 17^{24}; Mt $24^{37.\ 39}$=Lk 17^{26}, cf. ^{30}; Mt 24^{44}=Lk 12^{40}; Mt $25^{13.\ 31}$; Lk 21^{36}, cf. 12^{40}; Mk 14^{62}=Mt 26^{64}=Lk 22^{69}; Mt 10^{23}; Mk 8^{38}=Mt $16^{27.\ 28}$=Lk 9^{26}; Lk $12^{8.\ 9}$; Mt 19^{28}; Lk 18^{8}.

As has been seen, the phrase, 'one like unto a son of man,' occurs in Dn 7^{13}, and there sums up comprehensively the 'people of the saints of the Most High,' who are exalted in glory, and to whom judgment is given. There may also be a reference to one who represents the saints, and a Messianic meaning was given to the phrase by the Jews. We can hardly avoid the conclusion that Christ, in using 'the Son of Man,' refers back to Dn., and regards Himself as typifying the saints of the Most High (the people of His Kingdom), who are in Dn. first humiliated, then exalted. In two passages there is a strong suggestion of the origin of the title in Dn. (cf. Mt 24^{30} 26^{64} with Dn $7^{13f.}$). But, again, in *En.* 37–70 the title 'Son of Man' occurs with imagery similar to that which our Lord uses. This document may represent a larger literature in which the title also occurred, and it was probably understood by many of His hearers.[1] We can hardly avoid the conclusion that Christ deliberately transferred this title to Himself, giving it a richer and fuller meaning (cf. passages in which it suggests not glory, but humiliation, and see Charles, *Bk. of Enoch*, p. 315, for the reference of the latter to the Isaianic conception of the Servant of Jahweh).

The argument in favour of Christ's using a title from *Enoch* rests on the pre-Christian date of this section. (See Charles, pp. 107, 113; and, against, Hilgenfeld, *ZWT*, 1892, p. 445 f.; Drummond, *JThSt* ii. 545.) The title may have been a popular, not a Pharisaic, one, and its use in Christian circles would explain the fact that it is sparsely, if at all, found in Rabbinic writings. (See Dalman, *Die Worte Jesu*, 1898, i. 201 ff.; Sanday, *Exp.* 4th ser. iii. [1891] 27 f.) In Ps $8^{4.\ 5}$ the 'son of man' is crowned with glory and honour. This passage is thought by some to have also suggested Christ's use of the phrase (Bartlet, *Exp.* 4th ser. vi. [1892] 434 f.; Dalman, i. 218).

The use of the phrase, 'the Son of Man,' where the first person might be expected, is 'an exceedingly strange mode of speech,' and has given rise to the question whether Christ here meant Himself in all cases, especially in the reference to a future coming (Drummond, 566, 568). But in Mt 16^{13}, even if $\mu\epsilon$ is omitted, the disciples' answer shows that they had identified Christ with the Son of Man. Again, the fact that in some parallel passages 'I' takes the place of the corresponding 'Son of Man' shows that the two were regarded as identical, and that Christ used the phrase alternatively with 'I.' It is obvious that in Mt 26^{64} the high priest at once believed that Christ was speaking of Himself, while in Mt $25^{31f.}$ who could be referred to but Christ? (See v.$^{35ff.}$) See, further, JESUS CHRIST.

The future coming of the Son of Man, as contrasted with the passages where it is said He has come, though it is never spoken of as a *second* coming, need present no difficulty, in spite of the fact that it has been asked, 'Can Jesus mean Himself in these passages?' (Drummond, 567). The usage is parallel with that which speaks of the Kingdom both as present and as future.

(*d*) *State of the dead.*—The parable of Dives and Lazarus points to the current popular Jewish view of different states in Sheol after death, better or worse. Paradise, as used in Lk 23^{43}, probably means the better part of Hades, for it is evidently not Heaven (cf. Jn 20^{17}, Ac 2^{31}).[2] Hades, or Sheol, is a temporary abode, for it is cast into the lake of fire after giving up the dead (Rev $20^{13.\ 14}$; cf. 1^{18}). Meanwhile, the righteous dead enjoy communion with God. After the Judgment, the righteous with their risen bodies go into life eternal in the Kingdom of the Father, and are as the angels, and shine forth like the sun. They will never die (Mt 13^{43} 22^{30} 25^{46}, Lk 20^{36}). Their felicity is spiritual, though this is set forth occasionally in more or less sensuous images (Mt 8^{11} 19^{28} $22^{2f.}$ 25^{10}). In Jn., eternal life as well as resurrection is a present possession of believers (5^{24} $6^{40.\ 47.\ 54}$ 11^{25} 17^{3}, 1 Jn 5^{11}); but the contradiction with the Synoptics is more apparent than real. The promised 'life' is bound up with the Kingdom of God, and, in so far as that is present, 'life' is also a present posses-

[1] For the arguments for and against the theory that Christ never used the title of Himself, see Drummond, *JThSt* ii. [1901] 545 f.

[1] The form of the question in Jn 12^{34} does not suggest ignorance of the title, but curiosity regarding a Son of Man who will be 'lifted up.'

[2] In 2 Co 12^{4} Paradise is in one of the heavens. Cf. *Secrets of Enoch* 8^{1}: Paradise in the third heaven is the final abode of the righteous.

sion. Whether Christ teaches a resurrection of the wicked has been questioned, but their fate is clearly set forth (Mt $5^{22. 29. 30}$ 8^{12} $13^{42. 50}$). Punishment will be proportionate (Mt $11^{21f.}$, Lk $12^{47f.}$). This and other passages (Mt 5^{26} 12^{32}), as well as the general drift of Christ's teaching regarding the love of the Father, raise the question whether these punishments are eternal in the sense of unending, or only in the sense of lasting till their work of purification is accomplished. It is not impossible that here, as elsewhere, our Lord was simply using the language and beliefs of His own time, to enforce moral truth; and probably His reporters have further coloured His sayings with their own beliefs. The parables of the Supper—'compel them to come in'—and of the Draw-net are suggestive, and we are also forced to view these problems in the light which Christianity as an ethical faith and a religion of progress supplies. We cannot limit our views of the future by the crude and material images of older beliefs from which Christianity has too often borrowed.

12. Eschatology of St. Paul.—St. Paul was imbued with ideas regarding the Apocalyptic coming derived from his Jewish training and from Christian tradition—especially the traditional form of Christ's eschatological discourses,[1] and he is concerned with three main events, (1) the Parousia, (2) the resurrection of the dead and transformation of the living, and (3) the Judgment. The emphasis on the first two varies in different epistles, and his teaching on each is called forth by varying circumstances.

(1) In 1 Th., St. Paul has to do with Christians who were anxious, regarding those who had died, with respect to Christ's Parousia, which they, with St. Paul, deemed to be close at hand. He answers that the Day of the Lord will come as a thief in the night, and that Christ will come suddenly from heaven with the voice of the archangel and with the trumpet. The dead in Christ shall rise; the faithful living shall be caught up to meet the Lord in the air ($4^{13ff.}$ $5^{1ff.}$). The whole passage is of a primitive character. In 2 Th. there is to be a revelation (*ἀποκάλυψις*) of Christ from heaven with His mighty angels. But the Day is not so near as the exaggerated anticipations of the Thessalonians expected. There will be first a great falling away (cf. Dn 8^{23-25} LXX, *πληρουμένων τῶν ἁμαρτιῶν αὐτῶν*), and the revelation (*ἀποκαλυφθῇ*) of the man of sin, who as God sits in the temple of God (cf. Dn 7^{8} 11^{36}, Mk 13^{14}, 2 Co 6^{15}), and who is at present hindered. But he will be destroyed by Christ at His Parousia ($2^{3ff.}$). St. Paul thus still expected the Parousia in his lifetime.

The Pauline Antichrist resembles in many points that of the Apocalypse, and goes back to the opposing power in Dn $7^{7f.}$ $11^{28f.}$, and Mk 13 (cf. *Apoc. Bar.* 41). But, while Antichrist in the Apocalypse is Rome, or Rome represented in its Emperor, the Pauline Antichrist has a much more ideal symbolism, and is non-political and probably Jewish (a pseudo-Messiah), though it recalls Caligula, who tried to set his statue in the temple. The restraining power (*τὸ κατέχον*), or the restrainer (*ὁ κατέχων*), is probably the Empire and its rule. This in itself sets the Parousia at some distance off.

In 1 Cor. there is little difference from the above account, save that there is no reference to Antichrist. The time is short; men are living at the ends of the ages (7^{29} 10^{11}). After short tribulations ($7^{26. 29}$), Christ will come with the sound of a trumpet. Meanwhile, during this short period before His Parousia, Christ reigns and strives with His enemies, the last of which, Death, shall be destroyed at His coming, through the resurrection of believers (cf. 2 Th $1^{8. 9}$ 2^{8}). His temporal, mediatorial Kingdom will then come to an end, and God will be all in all ($15^{24ff.}$).

While this temporal and short rule of Christ is not equivalent to a millennial reign of Christ on earth, following on the Parousia (coming between the *ἔπειτα* of v.^{23} and the *εἶτα* of v.^{24}), as some have maintained, probably the thought is here coloured by the Jewish idea of the temporal Messianic Kingdom, though the latter is enriched and spiritualized (cf. also 15^{25} with Mk 12^{36}). In later epistles, Christ is 'all in all,' and His Kingdom is one with that of God (Eph 1^{23} 5^{5}).

In Rom. and 2 Cor. the Parousia is still regarded as near (Ro 13^{11}), but the idea of a general apostasy preceding it gives place to that of the inclusion of the Gentiles in the Kingdom ($11^{25. 26}$). This anticipates a speedy conversion of the world. But St. Paul is no longer confident of living to see the Parousia (Ro 14^{8}, 2 Co $4^{14. 16}$ $5^{6f.}$, but see Ro $13^{11f.}$). At first he expected to be alive at the Parousia. But, as time went on, the stress of his teaching lay elsewhere, and now he only *hoped* to be alive. Finally, he regarded it as far better to die, though it was needful that he should live, not to see the Parousia, but to benefit his people (Ph $1^{23. 24}$, cf. 3^{11}). Yet he could still look for the coming from heaven (Ph 3^{20}). Its nearness was to him guaranteed by the extension of the Christian faith and the great spiritual awakening consequent upon that. For he follows the prophetic belief in spiritual outpouring as immediately preceding the Day of the Lord. Contrariwise, with the Prophets and later Apocalyptists he saw in the opposing increase of evil another herald of the nearness of the Day.

(2) At the Parousia the dead in Christ rise, and the living are caught up to meet the Lord in the air, or transformed (*ἀλλαγησόμεθα*, 1 Co 15^{51}). The dead rise with a *σῶμα πνευματικόν* bearing *τὴν εἰκόνα τοῦ ἐπουρανίου* ($15^{45ff.}$; cf. Ph 3^{21}: the body is to be changed into the likeness of *τὸ σῶμα τῆς δόξης αὐτοῦ*). Some have thought that St. Paul now came to regard the resurrection from another point of view, or that the latter was already latent in his mind in 1 Co 15. This view, based mainly on 2 Co $5^{1ff.}$, presupposes that he now taught that the soul *at death* receives in heaven a new body or organism (*ἔχομεν*; cf. Bousset, *ARW* iv. 144; so also Pfleiderer, Holtzmann, Reuss, Charles, etc.). In accordance with this view, not a resurrection but a manifestation of the already glorified righteous dead took place at the Parousia (Ro 8^{19}, Col 3^{4}).

This theory does not seem to be supported by 2 Co 4^{14}, where a future resurrection is in question. Nor need *ἔχομεν* imply immediate entrance into possession of the *οἰκίαν ἀχειροποίητον*. It is for the believer a sure inheritance, but it is not necessarily received at death. St. Paul almost certainly believed in an intermediate state (cf. Eph $4^{9. 10}$); but, since the Parousia was so near at hand, the experience of that state (being found naked [*γυμνοί*], disembodied spirits) could be but a short one. It would be better to survive to the Parousia and then not undergo the process of 'unclothing' (*ἐκδύσασθαι*), but that of being 'clothed upon' (*ἐπενδύσασθαι*), so that mortality might be swallowed up of life—the transforming of 1 Co 15.

(3) The Judgment, with Christ as Judge, is associated with the Parousia. In 1 Th. it is not directly mentioned (but see 1^{10} *ἐκ τῆς ὀργῆς τῆς ἐρχομένης*, 4^{6} 5^{3}), as it is not involved in the argument. In 2 Th., at the Parousia, Christ takes vengeance in flaming fire on the wicked, who are punished with *ὄλεθρον αἰώνιον*, and destroys Antichrist ($1^{8. 9}$ 2^{8}). In 1 Cor. there is a judgment on men's works and a revelation of the counsels of the hearts ($3^{13f.}$ 4^{4}). The saints shall judge the world, also angels ($6^{2f.}$). The universality of the Judgment and its reference to deeds are emphasized in Ro $2^{5f.}$ 14^{10}, 2 Co 5^{10}. There is, however, no condemnation (*κατάκριμα*) of those in Christ (Ro 8^{1}). This does not contradict the former view, and a mediant position is found in 1 Co $3^{12ff.}$, where a judgment according to spiritual capacity and results is taught.

13. Eschatology of other epistles.—Although the epistles of St. Peter, St. James, St. Jude, and St. John, and that to the Hebrews, differ in details, yet, as far as the broad outlines of eschatology are concerned, they may be grouped together. In

[1] Cf. 1 Co 6^{2} and Mt 19^{28}, 2 Co 5^{10} and Mt $25^{31. 32}$. See also Kennedy, *St. Paul's Conceptions of the Last Things*, 1904, pp. 167, 180.

general the old Jewish views prevail, but there is no doctrine of a temporal Kingdom.

Judgment and punishment have already befallen (1) angels (Jude ^{6}, 2 P 2^{4}), (2) the unrighteous (2 P 2^{9}), though 1 P 3^{19} suggests an intermediate state in which progress is possible. The end of all things and the Parousia are near at hand (1 P 4$^{5.7}$, Ja 5^{8}, He 10^{25}). It will be preceded by wickedness (Jude ^{18}), or by a fiery trial (1 P 4^{12}), or by the appearance of antichrists (unbelievers and false teachers, 1 Jn 2$^{18f.}$ 4^{3}). On the other hand, the day may be distant, since one day is with the Lord as a thousand years (2 P 3$^{8f.}$), but in any case it will be sudden and unexpected (3^{10}). At the Parousia the Judgment will take place either (1) by God (He 10^{31} 13^{4}), or (2) by Christ (1 P 4^{5}), who will come with thousands of His saints[1] (Jude ^{14}), to judge the living and the dead, but especially the ungodly, and also the angels who sinned (1 P 4^{5}, 2 P 2$^{4.9}$, Jude $^{6.14.15}$; cf., for the angels, 1 Co 6^{3}, Mt 8^{29}). The righteous will be rewarded in their risen bodies (He 11^{35}, cf. 1 Jn 3^{2}) with eternal life in the promised kingdom (Ja 2^{5}, Jude ^{21}), and with a crown of glory or of life (1 P 5^{4}, Ja 1^{12}). This Kingdom is in heaven (He 6$^{19.20}$ 11^{16}, 1 P 1^{4}). The wicked will be destroyed in a consuming fire (2 P 3^{7}, He 10$^{27.39}$). Heaven and earth will be shaken and removed, that those things which cannot be shaken may remain (He 12$^{26.27.28}$ cf. 1^{10}). The world will pass away (1 Jn 2^{17}), or it will be destroyed by fire (2 P 3$^{7.10.12}$, the only reference to this in the NT). There will be a new heaven and earth wherein dwelleth righteousness (2 P 3^{13}).

14. Eschatology of the Apocalypse.—The earlier chapters of this book describe in a series of visions, which are concurrent rather than successive, the woes which fall upon men, catastrophes on earth and convulsions of Nature, judgments upon Jews and Gentiles, and the preservation of the elect. The Parousia is said to be near at hand (3^{11} 16^{15}, cf. 22$^{7.12.20}$); the Messiah or one like the Son of Man will come with the clouds (1^{7} 14^{14}; cf. Dn 7^{13}, Mk 13^{26}); and the Judgment is described under different figures—(1) convulsions of Nature and terror of mankind at the approach of 'the great day of his wrath' (6$^{12-17}$); (2) reaping wheat by Christ—probably the gathering of the righteous (14$^{14-16}$); (3) gathering the clusters of grapes by an angel and treading them in the winepress of God's wrath (14$^{17-20}$, the judgment of the wicked by Christ; cf. 19^{15}). Judgment of the dead is mentioned (11^{18}).

In these the Lamb or one like the Son of Man is a prominent figure. But after each there are several interludes, followed by a vivid description of the judgment upon Rome (chs. 17. 18).

There now follows a connected but compressed account of the last things. The marriage of the Lamb and the Church, and the Banquet, are announced (19$^{6f.}$). Messiah comes from heaven as a judge and as a warrior with armies. He is withstood by Antichrist and his armies, who are defeated and destroyed. Antichrist and the False Prophet are cast into the lake of fire,[2] and Satan is bound in the abyss for a thousand years (19^{11}–20^{3}). During these thousand years the martyrs and such as had resisted Antichrist live and reign with Christ. This is the first resurrection, and the rest of the dead do not live until the end of the thousand years (20$^{4-6}$). Satan is now loosed and stirs up the nations, Gog and Magog (cf. Ezk 38^{3}), and these compass Jerusalem, the camp of the saints, but are destroyed by fire from heaven. The devil is cast into the lake of fire (20$^{7-10}$).

The idea of overcoming Antichrist and the binding of Satan goes back to mythic conceptions of the strife of Divine powers with evil chaotic powers. Traces of this are found in Is 24$^{21f.}$ 27$^{1f.}$, Dn 7^{11}, *Ps. Sol.* 2$^{29.30}$. In *En.* 10$^{4ff.}$ evil angels are fettered, and finally punished at the Day of Judgment (cf. *Jub.* 5^{10}, *Secrets of Enoch* 7^{1} 18). Death, or the angel of Death, and Hades are brought to an end at the end of the days (Is 25^{8}, cf. 4 Ezr 8^{53}, *Apoc. Bar.* 21^{23}, *Test. xii. Patr.* [Levi 18], Rev 20^{14}, 1 Co 15$^{25f.\ 55}$.[3] Death and the devil are brought into connexion (cf. 1 Co 5^{5}); the devil is the lord of death, just as the Greeks made the Persian Ahriman = Hades. We may also compare the idea of later Parsiism, that the dragon Azhi Dahak was overcome and bound by Thraētaona and then loosed by Angra Mainyu to war against Ormazd. The Jews regarded the world-powers as under the rule of Beliar, and he, like Antichrist and the devil, is conquered at the end of the age (cf. *Test. xii. Patr.* [Levi 18^{12}, Dan 5$^{10.11}$, Sim. 6^{6}, Jud. 25^{4}]), evil spirits are overcome, and Beliar is bound and cast into the fire by Messiah (*Ass. Mos.* 10^{1}, the devil's rule comes to an end; *Jub.* 10^{8}, Mastema [Satan], overcome at Day of Judgment; *Sib. Or.* ii. 168, Beliar comes before the end; iii. 65 ff., he will be burned with a fiery blast from heaven). This conception of the strife with and destruction of supernatural powers of evil, as signifying the approach of the Kingdom, is also found in Mt 12^{28} = Lk 11^{20}, cf. 4^{13}; Jn 12^{31} 14^{30} 16^{11}. (For Antichrist, see *ERE* i. 578 f.; Bousset, *Antichrist*, also *Rel. des Jud.* 242 f.; Charles, *Ascension of Isaiah*, 1900, p. 51 f.)

In this account the new feature is the 1000 years' reign of the martyrs with Christ, perhaps already adumbrated in Rev 7^{9} 14$^{1f.}$ 15$^{2f.}$ This reign is not said to be on earth, nor is the first resurrection said to be a bodily one (cf. 20^{4} *souls*), and no *second* resurrection is mentioned, a *general* resurrection being inferred (20^{13}). If the martyrs restored to life are the saints dwelling in Jerusalem who are attacked by Gog and Magog, it is curious that Christ (with whom they reign) does not attack those enemies. Their destruction comes from heaven (20^{9}). Those saints are the righteous now freed from Satan's power, and the nations are subject to them. This, rather than the martyrs' reign of 1000 years, is the equivalent of the temporal Messianic Kingdom of Jewish Apocalyptic (e.g. *En.* 91 ff.). Possibly, by the conception of the martyrs living and reigning with Christ for 1000 years, while the rest of the dead do not 'live' until the general resurrection at the close of this period, the writer anticipates the view of Tertullian (*de An.* 55, *de Res. Carn.* 43) and Irenæus (i. 31. 2) that martyrs at death went to Paradise, all others to Hades. But, whether this or 'the duration of the triumph of Christianity' (Swete, *Apoc.* 1906, p. 263) is intended, the conception lent itself as a *point d'appui* to the Chiliastic ideas brought over from Judaism into Christianity—the idea of a temporal Kingdom on earth to which some of the dead rise (4 Ezra), and which lasts 1000 years (*Secrets of Enoch*).[1]

Now follow the resurrection, and the Judgment of each and all by God, who sits on a great white throne (20$^{11f.}$, cf. 4$^{2.9}$ etc.). The judgment is according to works and the record of these in the books. The wicked, whose names are not in the Book of Life, are cast into the lake of fire and endure the second death (20^{14} 21^{8}). Hades and Death are also cast into it. The first heaven and earth as well as the sea (cf. *Ass. Mos.* 10^{6}, *Sib. Or.* v. 158 f., 447) having passed away, there is a new heaven and earth, which, with the New Jerusalem which descends from heaven, becomes the abode of the blessed (21. 22, cf. 3^{12}). The city is characterized by holiness (τὴν ἁγίαν 21^{2}).

An ideal or a re-built Jerusalem is a characteristic of OT prophecy and of some Apocalypses (Is 54. 60, Ezk 40. 48, Hag 2$^{7-9}$; *Sib. Or.* iii. 290). This gave place to the Apocalyptic idea of a New Jerusalem[2] to be set up by God (*En.* 90^{29}; cf. *Jub.* 1^{29}), or a heavenly Jerusalem revealed by Him (*Apoc. Bar.* 4$^{3f.}$ 32^{2}, 4 Ezr 7^{26} 10$^{27f.}$ 13^{36}) or built by the Messiah (*Sib. Or.* v. 420 ff.). These ideas recur in He 11^{10} 12^{22} 13^{14}, Gal 4^{26}, and are the familiar theme of Rabbinic theology (Gfrörer, ii. 245 f.; Weber, 373, 404).

15. Eschatology of the Church; the Millennium.—The prevalent beliefs of the early centuries may be summarized as follows. At death the soul was carried by angels into the presence of God, who, by a temporary judgment, assigned it a place in an intermediate state according to its condition.[3] In several writers these intermediate states were different parts of Hades (Tertullian, Irenæus). But another view prevailed—in part the result of the release of souls by Christ's Descent to Hades—to the effect that now righteous souls passed to Heaven or a heavenly region called Paradise (this is sometimes on earth, the Paradise of Adam).[4] This is already found in Ignatius and in the *Ascension of Isaiah* (ix. 7 f.), and Cyprian appears to have shared it (cf. *adv. Demetr.*; *de Mortal. passim*), while it had many adherents, for it is vigorously combated by Justin (*Dial.* 80, 93), Irenæus, and Tertullian. Tertullian maintained

[1] This is a citation from *En.* 1^{9} 'He comes with ten thousands of His holy ones [=angels] to execute judgment upon them'; cf. Dn 7^{10}.

[2] Cf. *En.* 90$^{24.25}$ (stars and shepherd angels cast into a fiery abyss).

[3] Death, also personified, is a species of lord in Hades; cf. Ps 49^{14}.

[1] Possibly a temporary Messianic Kingdom is taught in Ac 3$^{19f.}$

[2] The 'New Jerusalem' is first mentioned by name in *Test. xii. Patr.* [Dan 5].

[3] This was already a Jewish notion (Weber[2], 339; *Test. Abraham*, § 20), but it is met with mainly in popular Christian writings (see Conybeare, *Monuments of Early Christianity*, 1894, p. 311 f.; Coptic documents in *TS* iv. 2; *Visio Pauli*, § 12 f.; cf. Justin, *Dial.* 105; Hippolytus, *Discourse against the Greeks*; *Hom. of S. Macarius*, in Gallandius, *Bib. Vet. Patr.*, Venice, 1765–81, iii. 237; *Passio Perpetuæ*, § 11; cf. *TS* ii. 2. 127).

[4] This would then be revealed at the millennial coming of Christ and the dissolution of the earth (*Apoc. Pauli*, § 21).

that none but martyrs passed at once to Paradise (*de An.* 55; *de Res. Carn.* 43)—a belief perhaps shared by Irenæus (iv. 38. 9) and Justin (cf. *Mar. of the Holy Martyrs*, 4). Besides the conception of a fire through which all pass either after death or at the Judgment (see § 17), the idea of repentance and of purification after death, aided by prayer or sacrament, is found sporadically.[1] But anything approaching the later doctrine of Purgatory is not found, apart from Augustine's conjecture that some of the faithful might have to be purified, as by fire, from sinful affections (*de Civ. Dei*, xxi. 26; *Enchir.* 69), until Pope Gregory's time (see his *Dial.* iv. 30, and *passim*—a purgatorial fire for lighter faults).[2]

In the Early Church there was a general belief in the approaching end of the world and the Parousia. This would be preceded by great troubles and by the revelation of Antichrist (*Didache*, xvi. 4; *Ep. Barn.* 15; Iren. v. 25 f.; Hipp. *de Christo et Antichristo*; Lactant. vii. 17 f.). But at Christ's advent Antichrist and the wicked would be destroyed. The chronology adopted by most of the writers of this, and indeed of later periods, was that of the six periods of a thousand years (= six days of creation [*Ep. Barn.* 15, followed by Irenæus, Hippolytus, Lactantius, etc.]). Christ had come in the last thousand-year period, and His second coming would be at its close; hence calculations were made to discover its exact time. According to Hippolytus, the world had still 250 years to run; according to Lactantius, 200. Another common idea, based on the expected duration of the Roman Empire (Ῥώμη = 948), was that the end would come in A.D. 195 (*Sib. Or.* viii. 148). The end of the 6000 years and the second coming would inaugurate the seventh period of 1000, the Millennium, to enjoy which the righteous dead would be raised (the first Resurrection). In spite of the fact that, save in the Apocalypse, the NT did not speak of the Millennium, and that Christ does not connect the Parousia with the establishment of an earthly Kingdom, this belief had an extraordinary hold on the minds of Christians. Doubtless a misunderstanding of the Apocalypse gave the belief a certain authority, but it is rather from its Jewish antecedents that its popularity and the elaboration of its details are to be explained.[3]

The general picture of the millennial Kingdom on earth, 'the day of the supper of 1000 years' ('Bohairic Death of Joseph' [*TS* iv. 2. 142]), includes such features as that the earth would be renewed and Jerusalem re-built and glorified. Men would be perfectly righteous and happy, and would have numerous offspring. There would be no sorrow and no labour. The earth would produce abundantly, and a table would always be spread with food. A passage of Papias, cited by Irenæus (*adv. Hær.* v. 33), derives a picture of this fruitfulness from Christ Himself, though it is now known to have been copied from a document (perhaps a midrash on Gn 27^{28} [Harris, *Exp.*, 1895, p. 448; *AJTh*, 1900, p. 499]), used also in *Apoc. Bar.* $29^{5f.}$, and in *En.* 10^{19} (see Charles, *Ap. of Baruch*, 54). The moon would have the brilliance of the sun, and the sun would be seven times brighter than the moon. Some of the wicked would be left on earth, subjected to perpetual slavery.

This sensuous aspect of the Kingdom is directly taken over from Judaism. Tertullian tried to spiritualize it, but he still used many sensuous metaphors in describing it; and it is probable that with most of those who taught it the more sensuous view prevailed, since it was held that the saints reigned in the flesh. The doctrine is found clearly stated in *Ep. Barn.* (4, 15), Hermas, *Didache* (10, 16), Justin (*Dial.* 80, 81), Irenæus (v. 32 f.), Tertullian (*adv. Marcion.* iii. 24), Hippolytus (Overbeck, *Quæst. Hipp.* 70), Lactantius (vii. 20 ff.), Methodius (*Conviv.* ix. 1. 5), Commodian (*Carm. Apol.* v. 979 ff.).

It was, of course, contrary to the Gnostic scheme of eschatology, and as such was upheld against them, *e.g.* by Irenæus (v. 33); but Cerinthus, who admitted the real humanity of Christ and the resurrection, is alleged to have taught that, after the latter, Christ's Kingdom would be an earthly one of an extremely sensuous and carnal kind (Caius, *ap.* Eus. *HE* iii. 28).

The Ebionites (Jerome, *Com. on Is.* 66^{20}) and Montanists also cherished millennial views of an unspiritual kind. With the latter, Christ was speedily to come and found an earthly Kingdom of the saints in the New Jerusalem, which would descend visibly out of heaven and be established at Pepuza in Phrygia. This would be the sign of Christ's coming. Montanus wished to separate believers from all worldly affairs, and so prepare them for the Kingdom, by gathering them together in the region where Christ would have His seat (see Eus. *HE* v. 16; Tert. *adv. Marc.* iii. 24; Epiph. xlix. 1; *Oracle of Prisca*).

Yet there was a strong opposition to this belief from comparatively early times: Justin (*Dial.* 80) says that many, otherwise orthodox, were opposed to it; and this statement seems to be supported by Irenæus (v. 31. 1). The doctrine is not mentioned in Clement, Ignatius, or Polycarp, or in many of the Apologists; but we can hardly argue from their silence that they disbelieved it, while, in the case of the Apologists, policy may have dictated silence. The Alogi also attacked the doctrine, while denying the Johannine authorship of the Apocalypse and attributing it to Cerinthus (Epiph. xxxii., xxxiii., li.). The excesses of Montanism helped to discredit the doctrine in the East, and to stamp it as Jewish rather than Christian.

Caius at Rome opposed the Montanist Proclus, and maintained that Cerinthus had invented the Millennium (Eus. *HE* ii. 25). For his views on Cerinthus and the Apocalypse, see Eus. vii. 25; Gwynn, *Hermathena*, vi. 397 f.

But it was largely the influence of Alexandrian philosophical ideas, and especially those of Clement (*Strom.* vii. 12. 74) and Origen (*de Princ.* ii. 11 f.; *c. Cels.* viii. 30), which gave the death-blow to chiliastic views in the East. This teaching was followed up by Dionysius of Alexandria, who has left us an interesting picture of his success in combating the chiliastic views of Egyptian Christians, probably of the rural districts, who had been much influenced by a writing of Nepos of Arsinoë (Ἔλεγχος τῶν ἀλληγοριστῶν), teaching a Millennium of bodily enjoyment. A schism was threatened in the Egyptian Church, but Dionysius, by wise arguments and instruction, averted this, and his opponents, headed by Coracion, gave up their views (A.D. 225; Eus. *HE* vii. 24). Chiliasm was still defended by Methodius of Tyre (*Conviv.* IX. i. 5) and by Apollinaris (Basil, *Ep.* cclxiii. 4, cclxv. 2; Greg. Naz. *Ep.* cii. 4), and accepted by Egyptian monks (Harnack, *Hist. of Dogma*, ii. 300, note).

In the West, chiliastic views prevailed until the time of Augustine, who had himself once cherished them in a spiritual rather than a sensuous form, but who now attacked them and formulated an interpretation of Rev $20^{4f.}$ which was accepted by the Church for many centuries. Millenarianism now became a heresy.

Augustine holds that the 1000 years = the duration of the Church on earth; the reign of the Saints = the reign of the Kingdom of Heaven; the First Resurrection = the spiritual share which the baptized have in Christ's Resurrection (*de Civ. Dei*, xx. 6 f.). His theory regarding the duration of the Church, literally interpreted, gave rise to the view that the end would come in A.D. 1000.

[1] *Shepherd of Hermas*, Sim. ix. 16; *Acta Pauli et Theclæ*, § 28; *Pass. Perp.* § 7; *Test. Abrah.* § 14; Tertullian, *de An.* 35, 58, *de Monog.* 10, *de Cor. Mil.* 3.

[2] For the doctrine of the sleep of the soul (ψυχοπαννυχία), see Tatian, who held that it died with the body (*ad Græc.* 13) and (Arabians) Eusebius (*HE* vi. 37).

[3] A preliminary judgment at the First Resurrection of those who had known God is taught by Lactantius (vii. 20). Those whose evil deeds outweighed their good deeds would be condemned. A judgment by fire would burn those whose sins exceeded in number and weight, but would not be felt by the righteous. The former would then have their place with the wicked who do not arise to this judgment (Ps 1^5). Tertullian appears to teach that the pure would rise at once, but those who had contracted some guilt would rise later, or perhaps not till the Second Resurrection, when the wicked rise (see *de An.* 35, 55, 58; *adv. Marc.* iii. 24).

The comparative ease with which millenarianism disappeared shows that, generally speaking, it had never interfered with the ethical and spiritual life of Christianity, or with the life of the Christian as a citizen. Men were content to wait, and thus the notion passed insensibly from their minds, as its baselessness and the extravagance of some who held it became apparent.[1] Expectations of the Millennium were revived in the Middle Ages by mystical sects; and after the Reformation, mainly among Anabaptists. Millennial views, varying in their expectations of a more sensuous or more spiritual Kingdom, have been revived from time to time since then, and owe their great modern development to Bengel. Many distinguished theologians have held millenarian views, but it is mainly in America that the doctrine has given rise to separate sects (Seventh Day Adventists, Second Adventists, etc.). These, as well as the millenarians of the Early Church, believe that, at the close of the 1000 years, Satan will be unbound, and that he will make war against the Saints, only to be destroyed.

The close of the world-drama was described in similar terms by both Chiliasts and non-Chiliasts, and the description probably is cherished in a literal sense by many Christians still—Roman Catholic, Anglican, and Protestant. The main features are the second coming of Christ in majesty as Judge of all mankind, the resurrection of all (or of the wicked, the Second Resurrection of the Chiliasts), the Judgment (to take place, as some thought, in the Valley of Jehoshaphat), the doom pronounced—eternal punishment in hell for the wicked, and eternal bliss for the righteous in heaven or in the new heaven and earth.[2] Connected with these views was that of the passing away of heaven and earth, their destruction or their transformation, and the appearance of a new universe of which the Heavenly Jerusalem would be the centre.

Clement of Alexandria taught a probation which ceased at the Last Judgment (*Strom.* vii. 2. 12). With Origen the Judgment—of which he says nothing as to its immanence (the Gospel prophecy is not to be taken in its literal sense [*in Matt. Com.* sec. 49])—is hardly a final act; rather is it a 'moment' in an age-long process, in which the wicked, including demons, will be restored by a remedial process of punishment, though there will be various degrees of blessedness, and the sinner's soul can never again be what it was. This is the doctrine of the ἀποκατάστασις, in which he is followed by many Greek Fathers, especially by Gregory of Nyssa, Theodore of Mopsuestia, and—less emphatically—Gregory Nazianzen. The monasteries of Egypt and Palestine also supported this doctrine for long after, and it is more or less followed by many modern theologians.

The doctrine of Conditional Immortality (*q.v.*) and the annihilation (*q.v.*) of the wicked after the Judgment, already found in Arnobius, was stated by Hobbes and Locke, and, since the teaching of White (*Life in Christ*, 1846), has obtained a large following.

In the Gnostic systems the conception of the final consummation does not include the idea of Divine Judgment. The judgment is automatic, according to the inherent nature of souls—a species of conditional immortality. Those who were neither πνευματικοί nor ψυχικοί simply perished, and, as the æon Christ had passed to the Pleroma, there could be no second coming. The consummation results from the complete restoration of all the sparks of light to that high region whence they came. The created universe, deprived of them, must wax old and decay, and will be destroyed by fire (§ 16).

A Last Judgment and hell-pains are taught in *Pistis Sophia*—an unusual aspect of Gnosticism. In Marcion's system the good God does not judge or punish, except in so far as He keeps the evil at a distance from Him. The wicked are punished in the fire of the Demiurge. There are only two issues—the heaven of the good God, and the hell of the Demiurge. 'Either Marcion assumed with Paul that no one can keep the law, or he was silent about the end of the "righteous" because he had no interest in it' (Harnack, i. 273, note 2).

[1] There were some in Syria and Pontus who, like Montanus, thought they should cut themselves off from all ties and go forth to meet the Lord, or sell all their goods and cease from work because He was near at hand (see Bratke, *Das neu entdeckte vierte Buch des Daniel-Comm. von Hippolytus*, Bonn, 1891, p. 15; Conybeare, *op. cit.* 21 f.).

[2] One of the earliest descriptions is found in the *Apoc. of Peter* (see the citation from Macarius Magnes in James and Robinson's ed., 1892, p. 71).

16. The new heaven and earth.—A belief in the catastrophic end and renewal of the world and the universe has already been found among some savages, the Mexicans, Norsemen, Hindus, Buddhists, Parsis, Stoics, and Muhammadans. We shall now trace this belief as it is developed among the Jews and in Christian eschatology. In the Prophetic books the way is prepared for such a doctrine by the account (1) of convulsions in Nature accompanying the judgments of the Day of the Lord, while the earth even returns to its former condition of chaos (Jer 4^{23}); and (2) of the exuberant fertility and beauty of the heaven and earth afterwards (Hab 3^{5}, Am 9^{5}, Mic 1^{4}, Is 51^{6} 34^{4}). At the same time, the stability of the earth was sometimes referred to (Ps 93^{1} 104^{5}). The doctrine of the new heaven and earth—the final corresponding to the former state—appears for the first time in Is $65^{17f.}$ 66^{22}, cf. 51^{16}; but whether it is there an intrusion on the context or not is difficult to decide (cf. 66^{22b} with 65^{20}).[1] A similar idea is found in Ps $102^{25f.}$, which perhaps dates from Maccabæan times. Passing outside the limits of the OT, we next find this doctrine in *En.* $45^{4f.}$, where a transformation of heaven and earth is taught. The new earth becomes the scene of the Messianic Kingdom, and sinners have no place in it. In $91^{14f.}$, after the end of the earthly Kingdom the world is 'written down for destruction,' and the heaven gives place to a new heaven after the Judgment. Into this the righteous pass (104^{2}), but nothing is said of a new earth. Cf. 72^{1} 'till the new creation is accomplished, which endureth till eternity.' In *Jub.* (4^{26}) the heavens and earth are to be renewed, and a sanctuary will be made in Jerusalem. The earth and all in it will be sanctified, and men will live 1000 years. Such a renewal had already occurred twice—at the Deluge (5^{12}), and with Jacob and his seed (19^{25}). In *Apoc. Bar.* the world returns to its nature of aforetime (3^{7}), is renewed at the Final Judgment, and becomes everlasting, incorruptible, and invisible (32^{6} 44^{12} 48^{50} 51^{8} 57^{2}). In 4 Ezr $7^{30f.}$ the world is turned to the 'old silence' for seven days, and is then 'raised up.'

Similar teaching is found in the Rabbinic and Talmudic writings. The new heaven and earth are the abode of the righteous, and from them all pain, sorrow, sin, and evil beings are banished (Gfrörer, ii. 273 f.; Wünsche, *Der bab. Talmud*, 1889, ii. 3. 194).

In the NT a similar conception is found. There will be a παλιγγενεσία (Mt 19^{28}), or an ἀποκατάστασις πάντων (Ac 3^{21}).[2] Heaven and earth will be shaken or removed, but what is permanent will remain (He $12^{26f.}$, cf. 1^{10}). In 2 P $3^{5f.}$ the destruction of the world by water in the past is referred to, and a future destruction of heaven and earth by fire is foretold—the only reference to such a destruction in the NT (cf. Jos. *Ant.* I. ii. 3 [water, fire]). This doctrine is already found in Bab. belief (see AGES OF THE WORLD [Bab.], vol. i. p. 183^{b}). Then a new heaven and earth, in which dwelleth righteousness, will appear.

This resembles the Stoic doctrine of the ἐκπύρωσις (§ 5), and there may have been a borrowing from it. But already in the OT the idea of fire destroying the earth is found (Dt 32^{22}), and that in connexion with God's judgment—a fire which burns up the wicked (Ps 97^{3}, Zec 13^{9}, Jer 15^{14}, Zeph 1^{18}, Mal 4^{1}; cf. Ps 50^{3}, Hab 3^{5}). In Dn 7^{10} a fiery stream issues below the throne; so

[1] Charles (p. 123) regarded these verses as an interpolation, because they do not agree with the context; but, in his edition of *Jubilees*, p. 9, he thinks them original, because they point not to a catastrophic, but to a gradual, change, conditioned by man's ethical conduct, as in *Jub.* 1^{29} 4^{26} $23^{26f.}$

[2] Cf. 2 Co 5^{17}, Gal 6^{15} καινὴ κτίσις.

En. 14^{19} 71^{2}. In 4 Ezr $13^{2f.}$ a fiery stream issues from the mouth of the 'man from the sea,' and burns his enemies. Cf. *Jub.* 36^{10}, *Asc. Is.* 4^{18}. The idea of judgment by fire is continued in the NT (Mt 3^{12}, He 10^{27} 12^{29}, 1 Co 3^{13}, 2 Th 1^{8}).

Again, in the Apocalypse, at the Last Judgment earth and heaven flee away (cf. Mk 13^{31}), or they pass away along with the sea, and give place to a new heaven and earth, the seat of the blessed (Rev 20^{11} 21^{1b}; cf. 6^{14} and § 14). In Ro $8^{19f.}$ a new creation is suggested; cf. 1 Co 7^{31} παράγει γὰρ τὸ σχῆμα τοῦ κόσμου τούτου.

From these sources the idea passed over into Patristic theology. The present universe will be annihilated, or its external order will be changed, and give place to a more glorious structure.[1] Following 2 P $3^{5f.}$, Justin (*Apol.* ii. 7), Tatian (ch. 25), and Minucius Felix (ch. 34) teach the destruction of the world by fire. Hippolytus describes the river of fire which will consume the earth, while heaven is rolled together like a scroll. After this there is a new heaven and earth (*Discourse*, § 37; cf. Tert. *de An.* 55, *de Spect.* 30). Origen also refers to this (*c. Cels.* v. 15), but elsewhere he speaks of a transformation and renewal of the material world (*de Princ.* i. 6. 4; cf. ii. 1. 3). He also speaks of the blessed passing beyond the planetary spheres to the true heaven and earth (ii. 3. 7, iii. 6. 8). Methodius also speaks of a renewal of the world by fire, and Lactantius speaks of fire burning up the world and the wicked. Meanwhile the righteous are hid in caves, and then come forth. The heavens will be folded together, and the earth changed (vii. 26). These ideas occupy a prominent place in the *Sibylline Oracles*. At the Judgment, a stream or cataract of fire flows from heaven and consumes earth, sea, and sky; but all things come out purified, or God takes out that which tends to purity. This (or another) stream issues from a pillar by God's throne, and all pass through it after the Resurrection (ii. 196 ff.; cf. iii. 79 ff., iv. 161 ff., v. 158 ff., vii. 28 f., viii. 217 ff.). The whole conception in the Sibyllines, whether Jewish or Christian, is strongly reminiscent of Parsi eschatology (see Bousset, *Der Antichrist*, 163 f.).

Irenæus (v. 36. 1), in opposition to Valentinus, does not believe in the annihilation of the world by fire, but in its transformation. Augustine taught that what is perishable in the world will be destroyed by fire; then will appear a new world, the fit dwelling of a renewed humanity (*de Civ. Dei*, xx. 16).

According to the Valentinian doctrine, fire lies hidden in the world, and at the end will blaze forth and destroy all matter, being extinguished itself along with it (Iren. i. 7. 1). This was probably borrowed from the Stoics. The Simonians taught the dissolution of the world (Iren. i. 23. 3; cf. the Basilidean system [Hipp. x. 10]), and it is also hinted at in the Peratic system—'the formal world' is to perish (Hipp. v. 7). Here, of course, there was no renewal. In *Pistis Sophia* occurs also the doctrine of a Last Judgment and a world-conflagration (Schmidt, *Kopt. Gnost. Schr.*, 1905, p. 48). In the Manichæan system, fire which endures for 1468 years burns up the world—a doctrine, doubtless, borrowed from Parsiism. The Gnostic doctrine, on the other hand, has rather Heraclitean and Stoic affinities.

17. The final fire.—In Patristic writings, before the doctrine of Purgatory was fully established, various ideas regarding fire are found. Setting aside the conception of this fire—material or symbolic, according to the writer's point of view—as purifying certain persons between death and judgment (see Origen, *de Princ.* ii. 10. 6; Cyprian, *Ep.* 60; Greg. Nyssa, *Orat. Catech.* 26, 35, πῦρ καθάρσιον; Aug. *Enchir.* 69, *de Civ. Dei*, xxi. 26),[1] there are two other prevalent conceptions of it.

(1) At death, souls pass through a river or sea of fire. It does not harm, but only purifies, the righteous and penitent. All others suffer in it (Coptic documents, *TS* iv. 2; cf. *Hist. of Joseph*, *Acts of John*). In *Test. of Abraham* (§ 12), at the preliminary judgment after death, souls are tried by fire by the angel Puriel. If their works are consumed, they are carried to the place of sinners; but, if the fire approve their works, they pass to the place of the just.[2] (2) The same conception of a river of fire is brought into connexion with the Final Judgment, as in the Parsi doctrine (§ 8). This is found in the Sibyllines (see above). Origen occasionally regards the purifying fire as that which will consume the whole world. To it all must come, but it causes no pain to the pure. Lactantius (vii. 20) teaches that at the pre-millennial coming of Christ there will be a judgment by fire, which will burn those whose sins exceed in number or weight, but it will not be felt by the righteous. Ambrose (*Serm.* iii. 14, xx. 12; *in Ps.* xxxvi. 26) taught that fire would prove souls at the Last Judgment, purifying and refreshing the righteous, but eternally torturing the wicked. A purifying fire for sinners after the Judgment is found in the teaching of Ambrosiaster (*in Ep. i. ad Cor.* xv. 53; *in Ep. ad Rom.* v. 14).

The idea of the fire through which all pass is connected by most of these writers with the fire of 1 Co 3^{13}, but there are many passages in OT and NT where the fire at Judgment is spoken of (see above). Probably the classical conception of Pyriphlegethon, the Egyptian idea of a fiery lake in Amenti (Budge, *Book of the Dead*, 288 f.), and the Parsi myth of the world-fire, which is to the righteous as warm milk, to sinners as molten metal (§ 8)—have all helped to shape this Patristic notion.[3]

18. Psychostasia.—In connexion with the idea of Judgment, that of the *psychostasia*, or weighing of souls or of their deeds, is found in many eschatologies. We have already met with it in Egyptian, Indian (cf. *Śat. Brāh.* xi. 7; Weber, *Ind. Streifen*, Berlin, 1868, i. 21. 2), Persian, and Muhammadan eschatologies. It is also found among the Mandæans, as a loan from Parsiism (Brandt, *Die mand. Rel.*, Leipzig, 1889, pp. 76, 195). Among the Hebrews, the idea of weighing in a balance by God is at first confined to this life (Job 31^{6}, Pr 16^{2} 21^{2} 24^{12}, Ps 62^{9}, Dn 5^{27}, 4 Ezr 3^{34}, *Ps. Sol.* 5^{4}), and is generally spiritualized (cf. *Il.* viii. 69 f., xxii. 204 f.). In Apocalyptic literature the conception is transferred to the future Judgment, when the actions of men will be weighed in a balance by the Elect One (*En.* 41^{1} 45^{3} 61^{8}; cf. *Apoc. Bar.* 41^{6})—a conception found in a very materialized form in the Talmud (Weber, 269 f.). The first reference to this idea in Christian literature is found in *Test. Abr.* (§ 12), where, at the preliminary Judgment after death, the angel Dokiel weighs souls. Their fate is in accordance with this and other tests, but a soul with equal sin and righteousness is set apart,[4] to await the Final Judgment. This idea of the weighing of souls by Michael, whose function has been suggested by that of Hermes, weigher of the fates of men, became a popular one in early and later mediæval Visions of the Other-world; and, in iconography, frequently Satan or a demon tries to depress the scale, and so to win the soul (see

[1] Cf., e.g., *Ep. Barn.* 15; Hipp. *de Christo et Antichr.*; Iren. v. 35 f.; Aug. *Enchir.* 85 f., *de Civ. Dei*, xxii.; Ambrose, *Sermo* iii. 14 f., xx. 12 f.

[1] This conception is found in Rabbinic theology (cf. Gfrörer, ii. 78 f.).

[2] Cf. *Test. of Isaac* [*TS* ii. 2. 146 f.]: the fiery river has intelligence not to hurt the righteous, only sinners. Cf. the πῦρ φρόνιμον of Clement, *Pæd.* iii. 8; Origen, *Strom.* vii. 6; Min. Felix, 35, 'sapiens ignis.' This idea is found in Heraclitus and the Stoics.

[3] The natives of Santa Cruz believe that ghosts go to a certain volcano, and are there burned and renewed (Codrington, *Melanesians*, Oxford, 1891, p. 264).

[4] This idea is probably of Egyptian provenance. It is found in an Egyptian story of a visit to Amenti (Griffith, *Stories of the High Priests of Memphis*, 1900, p. 45 f.).

Maury, *RA*, 1844, i., ii.; Wiegand, *Der Erzengel Michael*, Stuttgart, 1886, p. 38 ff.; Landau, *Hölle und Fegfeuer*, p. 114 f.).

A sign or mark set on a person distinguishes him as doomed to, or saved from, a dread judgment (Ezk 9^{4}; *Ps. Sol.* $15^{8.}$ 10^{8} 'the mark of the Lord is on the righteous, to their salvation,' 'the mark of destruction is upon their forehead'; Gal 6^{17}, Rev 7^{3} 9^{4} 14^{1}; this may be suggested by Ex 12^{13}, Gn 4^{15}). In Rabbinic literature, circumcision is the mark which saves from Gehenna (*JE* iv. 93). These ideas are reproduced in the Gnostic conception of the ascent of the soul through the spheres, and its free passage because it bears certain marks, or is baptized or sealed, or knows magic formulæ. Similar conceptions have already been met with in savage eschatology (§ 1). Cf. also the idea of Baptism as a test or mark. Sins make marks on the sinner, and by these he is recognized in the Other-world (Plato, *Gorgias*, 523; Lucian, *Katapl.* 23; cf. Origen, hom. *in Jer.* 16).

19. Books of Fate and Judgment.—In Bab. belief, Marduk had a scribe who wrote down, at his dictation, the fate of the living, and the decrees of the ruler of Hades were also written down by a scribe (Jastrow, *Rel. of Bab.*, Boston, 1898, p. 587). In the OT a Book of Life or of Remembrance contains the names of those who belong to Jahweh's people, and from it their names may be blotted out (Ex 32^{32}, Ps 69^{28}, Is 4^{3}, Ezk 13^{9}, Mal 3^{16}; cf. Ps 139^{16}, Jer 22^{30}, Is 48^{19}). This, then, becomes the book of those who are admitted to the future blessedness (Dn 12^{1})—an idea found fully in the NT (Lk 10^{20}, Ph 4^{3}, He 12^{23}, Rev 3^{5} 13^{8} 17^{8} $20^{12.15}$ 21^{27}). Books in which good and evil deeds are recorded are also referred to (Mal 3^{16}, Is 65^{6}), and they are opened at the Judgment (Dn 7^{10}, Rev 20^{12}). These ideas recur in Apocalyptic literature. Books of the living exist (*Jub.* 36^{10} 30^{22}), and are opened at the Judgment (*En.* 47^{3}; cf. 104^{1}). There are also books wherein the deeds of men are recorded, and these also are used in the Judgment (*En.* 81^{4} 90^{20} $98^{7.8}$ 104^{7}, *Jub.* $30^{20f.}$ 36^{10}, 4 Ezr 6^{20}, *Apoc. Bar.* 24^{1}). Enoch is said to be the scribe who records the deeds (*Jub.* 4^{23} 10^{17}; cf. *Secrets of Enoch*, 40^{13} 53^{2} 64^{5}); elsewhere it is an archangel (*En.* 89^{61}; Michael, *Asc. Is.* 9^{21}). In *Test. Abr.* (§ 12) two angels or Enoch record the deeds and the judgment passed on souls. Similar ideas are found in early Christian literature (Book of Life or of Righteous [*Apoc. Petri*; Hermas, *Vis.* i. 3, *Mand.* viii. 6, *Sim.* ii. 9; cf. *PG* xxviii. 589]), and in Visions of the Other-world, early and later (*Apoc. Petri; Apoc. Pauli*; Bede, *Eccl. Hist.* v. 13), and are a matter of popular belief. The recorders are very frequently angels—a conception already found in the Greek belief regarding demons (Hes. *Op.* 251 f.) or shadows (Lucian, *Menip.* 13). Similar ideas regarding books or registers which decide the future fates of men are found in some of the higher ethnic religions—Hindu, Buddhist, and Muhammadan (§§ 6, 7, 9; cf. § 2, for the scribe Thōth). See Scherman, *Materialien zur Gesch. der indisch. Visionslitt.*, Leipzig, 1892, p. 89; Landau, *Hölle und Fegfeuer*, 114 ff.; cf. also artt. BOOK OF LIFE, and FATE.

CONCLUSION.—The ideas regarding the end of the world which are found in most eschatologies may be regarded as mythical speculations prompted by knowledge of actual catastrophes in Nature and of its phenomena. The world, as science teaches, and as the speculations of men suggested, must have an end; but they pictured that end in lurid colours, while generally anticipating after it a new order. But only in a few eschatologies is the conception of a great Final Judgment found (Parsi, Jewish, Christian, Muhammadan); and this is joined to the doctrine of the world-end, the final catastrophe being the prelude to, or even a part of, the action of judgment. Moral and natural events were thus connected, because it seemed fitting to men that the time when their final fates were being decided should synchronize with the close of the world-order. Christianity, and, if we accept Christ's eschatological teaching literally (though, as has been seen, it is not necessary to do so), Christ Himself, taught this view; but the tendency is now more and more to seek the more spiritual conception of judgment, and for men to concern themselves less and less with the close of the world-order as an event to which has been attached, more or less mechanically, the idea of a Last Judgment. The manifestation of God's judgment in the soul of man is regarded as of more importance than the lurid phenomena which have so long been believed to accompany a Final Judgment, and which can have no relation to the soul or the organism with which it is clothed in a future state.

LITERATURE.—1. SAVAGE.—E. L. Moon Conard, 'Idées des Ind. Algonq. relatives à la vie d'outre-tombe,' *RHR* xlii. [1900] 244 ff.; T. Koch, 'Zum Animismus der südamer. Ind.,' *Intern. Arch. f. Ethnog.*, Leyden, xiii. [1900] Suppl.; L. Marillier, *La Survivance de l'âme et l'idée de justice chez les peuples non-civilisés*, Paris, 1893; R. Steinmetz, 'Continuität, oder Lohn und Strafe im Jenseits der Wilden,' *AA* xxiv. [1897] 577 ff.; E. B. Tylor, *PC*⁴, London, 1903.

2. ETHNIC.—(*a*) Egyptian: E. A. Wallis Budge, *Papyrus of Ani*, 1895, *Book of the Dead*, 1898, *Egyp. Heaven and Hell*, 1906; G. Maspero, *Études de myth. et d'archéol. égyp.*, Paris, 1893; A. Wiedemann, *Anc. Egyp. Doct. of Immortality*, 1895.—(*b*) Teutonic: Vigfusson-Powell, *Corpus Poet. Boreale*, Oxford, 1883; G. W. Dasent, *The Prose or Younger Edda*, Stockholm, 1842; De la Saussaye, *Rel. of the Teutons*, Boston, 1902: F. Jónsson, *Den oldnorske og oldislandske Litteraturs Historie*, Copenhagen, 1901.—(*c*) Greek and Roman: E. Rohde, *Psyche*⁴, Tübingen, 1907; A. Dieterich, *Nekyia*, Leipzig, 1893; L. Ruhl, *De Mortuorum Judicio*, Giessen, 1903; G. Wissowa, *Rel. und Kult. der Römer*, Munich, 1901.—(*d*) Hindu and Buddhist: *SBE*, *passim*; J. Muir, *Orig. Skr. Texts*, 1858–72; E. W. Hopkins, *Rel. of India*, Boston, 1896; A. Barth, *Rel. of India*, 1882: C. F. Köppen, *Rel. des Buddha*, Berlin, 1857–59; R. S. Hardy, *Manual of Budhism*², 1880; M. Monier-Williams, *Buddhism*, 1889; J. Edkins, *Chinese Buddhism*, 1880; J. Legge, *Rel. of China*, 1880; J. J. M. de Groot, *Rel. System of China*, Leyden, 1892 ff.—(*e*) Parsi: *SBE*, *passim*; N. Söderblom, *La Vie future, d'après le mazdéisme* (*AMG* ix.), Paris, 1901.—(*f*) Muhammadan: *SBE*, vols. vi., ix.; A. A. Bevan, *JThSt* vi. [1904] 20 f.; D. B. Macdonald, *Development of Muslim Theol.*, London, 1903; J. B. Rüling, *Beitr. zur Eschat. des Islam*, Leipzig, 1895.

3. HEBREW AND LATER JEWISH.—A. Jeremias, *Bab.-Assyr. Vorstell. vom Leben nach dem Tode*, Leipzig, 1887; F. Schwally, *Das Leben nach dem Tode*, Giessen, 1892; W. R. Smith, *Prophets of Israel*², 1897; W. Bousset, *Rel. des Judentums*², Berlin, 1906, 'Beitr. z. Gesch. d. Eschatol.,' *Ztschr. für Kirchengesch.* xx. (1889) 2; R. H. Charles, *Crit. Hist. of the Doct. of a Future Life*, 1899, ed. *Apoc. Bar.*, 1896, *Asc. of Isaiah*, 1900, *Assump. of Moses*, 1897, *Book of Enoch*, Oxford, 1893, *Book of Jubilees*, 1902, *Test. xii. Patriarchs*, 1908; Charles and W. R. Morfill, *Book of the Secrets of Enoch*, Oxford, 1896; Beasley and M. R. James, *Fourth Book of Ezra* (*TS* iii. [1895] pt. 2); H. E. Ryle and M. R. James, *Psalms of Solomon*, Cambridge, 1891; C. Alexandre, *Orac. Sibyll.*, Paris, 1841–56; E. Kautzsch, *Apoc. und Pseudepig. d. AT*, Tübingen, 1900; H. Gressmann, *Ursprung der isr.-jüd. Eschat.*, Göttingen, 1905; E. Schürer, *GJV*³, iii. 1898 (*HJP*, Eng. tr. of 2nd ed., 1886, II. iii.); A. Gfrörer, *Das Jahrhundert des Heils*, Stuttgart, 1838; F. Weber, *Jüd. Theol.*², Leipzig, 1897; W. O. E. Oesterley, *Doctrine of the Last Things*, London, 1908.

4. CHRISTIAN.—The works of Beyschlag, Holtzmann, and Weiss on NT Theology; E. A. Abbott, *The Son of Man*, Camb. 1910; L. Atzberger, *Gesch. d. christl. Eschat.*, Freiburg, 1896; R. H. Charles, *Crit. Hist. of the Doct. of a Future Life*; C. W. Emmet, *Eschatol. Question in the Gospels*, 1911; G. Dalman, *Die Worte Jesu*, Leipzig, 1898; L. Guy, *Le Millénarisme dans ses origines et son développement*, Paris, 1904; H. Gunkel, *Schöpfung und Chaos*, Göttingen, 1895; A. Harnack, *Hist. of Dogma*, Eng. tr. 1894–99; E. Haupt, *Eschatol. Aussagen Jesu*, Berlin, 1895; R. Kabisch, *Eschatol. des Paulus*, Göttingen, 1893; H. A. A. Kennedy, *St. Paul's Conceptions of the Last Things*, 1904: M. Landau, *Hölle und Fegfeuer*, Heidelberg, 1909; J. A. MacCulloch, *Early Chr. Visions of the Other-World*, Edinburgh, 1912; S. D. F. Salmond, *Chr. Doct. of Immortality*², 1896; W. Sanday, 'Apocalyptic Element in the Gospels,' *HJ* x. [1911] 83–109; A. Schweitzer, *Von Reimarus zu Wrede*, Tübingen, 1906; E. F. Scott, *The Fourth Gospel*², Edinburgh, 1908; H. B. Sharman, *Teaching of Jesus about the Future*, Chicago and London, 1909; L. J. Tixeront, *Hist. des dogmes*, Paris, 1909; E. von Dobschütz, *Eschatol. of the Gospels*, 1910; J. Weiss, *Die Predigt Jesu vom Reiche Gottes*², Göttingen, 1900; H. H. Wendt, *Die Lehre Jesu*², Göttingen, 1901, Eng. tr. *Teaching of Jesus*, Edinburgh, 1892.

J. A. MACCULLOCH.

ESKIMOS.—**1. Ethnology.**—The Eskimos form, with the Aleuts (*q.v.*), a distinct linguistic stock of N. Amer. aborigines, and, as far as all evidence goes, have inhabited their present territory at least from the time when they were first visited by the whites. This habitat extends along the coasts and islands of Arctic America, from eastern Greenland and the north end of Newfoundland to the westernmost Aleutian islands; and a small section, the Yuit, have even crossed, apparently at no very distant time, to the Asiatic coast, where they are settled about Indian Point, Cape Chukotsky, Cape Ulakhpen, and on St. Lawrence Island. Of their migrations little is known, but 'it is supposed that their original home was the district around Hudson's Bay (Boas) or the southern part of Alaska (Rink), and that from these regions they migrated eastward and westward, arriving in Greenland a thousand years ago, and in Asia barely three centuries ago' (Deniker, *Races of Man*, London, 1900, p. 520).

The evidence for the early presence of Eskimos in Greenland is afforded by the discovery there, by Eric the Red (*c.* 980), of ruins of buildings, remains of boats, and stone implements, which the Norsemen ascribed to *skrœllingar* ('little folk,' 'weaklings'), who are probably to be identified with the Eskimos. It is even possible that in 1004 they were found by Thorvald about Kjalarnes, which has been held to be the same as Cape Cod (Keane, *Man Past and Present*, Cambridge, 1900, p. 370).

It is clear, from remains found in Smith Sound, that Eskimo bands formerly wintered as far north as lat. 79°, and that they had summer camps up to 82°. They have, however, receded from their extreme northern range, and have also abandoned, in the south, the northern shores of the Gulf of St. Lawrence, the northern end of Newfoundland, James Bay, and the southern shores of Hudson's Bay, while in Alaska one tribe, the Ugalakmiut, has become practically Tlingit through intermarriage.

The Eskimos may be divided into nine fairly well-marked ethnological groups, as follows (Boas, *ap.* Henshaw and Swanton, art. 'Eskimo' in *Handbook of Amer. Ind.* i. 435 f.):

'i. The Greenland Eskimo, subdivided into the East Greenlanders, West Greenlanders, and Ita Eskimo—the last transitional between the Greenland Eskimo proper and the next group.

ii. The Eskimo of South Baffin Land and Labrador, embracing the following divisions: Akudnirmiut, Akuliarmiut, Itivimiut, Kaumauangmiut, Kigiktagmiut, Nugumiut, Okomiut, Padlimiut, Sikosuilarmiut, Suhinimiut, Tahagmiut.

iii. The Eskimo of Melville Peninsula, North Devon, North Baffin Land, and the north-west shore of Hudson's Bay, embracing the Agomiut, Aivilirmiut, Amitormiut, Iglulirmiut, Inuissuitmiut, Kinipetu, Koungmiut, Pilingmiut, Sauniktumiut.

iv. The Sagdlirmiut of Southampton Island, now extinct.

v. The Eskimo of Boothia Felix, King William Land, and the neighbouring mainland. These include the Netchilirmiut, Sinimiut, Ugjulirmiut, Ukusiksalirmiut.

vi. The Eskimo of Victoria Land and Coronation Gulf, including the Kangormiut and Kidnelik, which may, perhaps, be one tribe.

vii. The Eskimo between Cape Bathurst and Herschel Island, including the mouth of Mackenzie River. Provisionally they may be divided into the Kitegareut at Cape Bathurst and on Anderson River, the Nageuktormiut at the mouth of Coppermine River, and the Kopagmiut of Mackenzie River. This group approximates the next very closely.

viii. The Alaskan Eskimo, embracing all those within the American territory. This group includes the Aglemiut, Chingigmiut, Chnagmiut, Chugachigmiut, Ikogmiut, Imaklimiut, Inguklimiut, Kaialigmiut, Kangmaligmiut, Kaniagmiut, Kaviagmiut, Kevalingamiut, Kiatagmiut, Kinugumiut, Kowagmiut, Kukpaurungmiut, Kunmiut, Kuskwogmiut, Magemiut, Malemiut, Nunatogmiut, Nunivagmiut, Nuwukmiut, Nushagagmiut, Selawigmiut, Sidarumiut, Tikeramiut, Togiagmiut, Ugalakmiut, Unaligmiut, Utukamiut, and Utkiavimiut.

ix. The Yuit of Siberia.' (These have four linguistic groups: Noökalit of East Cape; Aiwanat of Indian Point; Wuteëlit of Cape Ulakhpen; and Eiwhuelit of St. Lawrence Island [*Handbook*, ii. 1007 f.].)

2. Designation. —Like so many primitive peoples, the Eskimos name themselves *Innuit*, 'people,' 'men.' Their usual appellation, *Eskimo*, seems first to have been given them by the Jesuit Father Biard in 1611, under the form *Excomminquois*, which appears to be taken from their Abenaki designation, *Eskimantzik* (or the Chippewa equivalent, *Ashkimeq*), 'eaters of raw flesh.' Two other interesting names applied to them are the Kutchin *Ta-Kutchi*, 'ocean people,' and the Seneca *Tciěck-rúněn*, 'seal people,' while the Hudson's Bay jargon, *Husky*, is simply a corruption of their familiar designation. (For a complete list of appellations applied to the Eskimos, see *Handbook*, i. 436 f.) The entire Eskimo population is estimated at some 27,700, of whom about 10,900 are in Greenland, 15,600 in North America, and 1200 in Asia.

3. Physical characteristics.—Of the physical characteristics of the Eskimos, Deniker writes as follows (p. 520 f.):

'Physically, the pure Eskimo—that is to say, those of the northern coast of America, and perhaps of the eastern coast of Greenland—may form a special race, allied with the American races, but exhibiting some characteristics of the Ugrian race (short stature, dolichocephaly, shape of the eyes, etc.). They are above average stature (1 m. 62), whilst the Eskimo of Labrador and Greenland are shorter, and those of southern Alaska a little taller (1 m. 66), in consequence perhaps of interminglings, which would also explain their cranial configuration (ceph. ind. on the living subject, 79 in Alaska, against 76·8 in Greenland), which is less elongated than among the northern tribes (average cephalic index of the skull, 70 and 72). Their complexion is yellow, their eyes straight, and black (except among certain Greenland half-breeds); their cheek-bones are projecting, the nose is somewhat prominent, the face round, and the mouth rather thick-lipped.' To this may be added, from Henshaw and Swanton (p. 434), that the Eskimos 'possess uncommon strength and endurance; their skin is light brownish yellow with a ruddy tint on the exposed parts; their hands and feet are small and well formed. . . . They are characterized by very broad faces and narrow, high noses; their heads are also exceptionally high.' Their hair is straight and black; the beard is at best scanty, and often is entirely lacking. They are not long-lived, seldom living much beyond sixty. The most common cause of death is inflammatory rheumatism. In this connexion it should be stated, in addition to the theories of their origin already noted, that Chamberlain (*Internat. Encyc.* vi. [New York, 1903] 858), following Dall, Olivier, Nordquist, Krause, and others, is inclined to think that 'the Eskimo were derived directly from peoples of the Asiatic polar regions, some of whom came to America across the narrow Bering Strait. The Koriak and Chukchi, who inhabit the extreme eastern portion of the peninsula of Siberia, are regarded as an Asiatic branch of the Eskimo race.' The latter statement is, however, extremely doubtful (see Keane, 299).

4. Language.—The Eskimo language belongs to the general type of American languages usually, but not very accurately, termed polysynthetic or incorporating. Naturally, in its long history, this language has split up into a number of dialects, rather, it would appear, through phonetic and semasiological changes than through the influence of other tongues.

'The dialectic differences are important, although not so extensive as to obscure the identity of the Eskimo languages of Alaska and of Greenland. We even find dialectic deviations from fiord to fiord. Nowadays an East Greenlander does not understand a West Greenlander until both have become accustomed to each other's speech; and the Greenlander has to learn the peculiarities of the dialect of the Baffin-land Eskimo to carry on conversation with him. The dialects of western Alaska differ fundamentally from the Greenland dialects, about as much as English and German or English and French differ from each other' (Thalbitzer, *Handbook of Amer. Ind. Languages*, i. 971).

5. Material culture, occupations, organization.—The Eskimos have always occupied a special place in the study of American aboriginal tribes. As the most northerly tribe in the world, their habitat itself has attracted to them more than usual attention; yet it is not to this accidental fact that the interest manifested in them is due, but rather to the fact that ethnologists and sociologists saw in them what appeared to be a classical example of the adaptation of a people to a special, unfavourable environment. They have found, corresponding to the vast, uniform, and monotonous Nature around them, a remarkable uniformity in the customs, culture, and language of all the tribes scattered over the enormous area of the Arctic archipelago and the mainland; they have discovered in the ingenious devices for catching their prey, in the specialized *kayak*, in the snow houses, and in the sledge with the dogs trained for drawing it, convincing proof that here was a perfect adaptation of man to his environment. There can, indeed, be no doubt that in the domain of material culture the adaptation of man to his environment is remarkable, especially if we regard it from a broad point of view. But even here, as soon as we look at details, the adaptation does not appear so perfect, and the play of individual variation and the conservative force of customs, in no way connected with the adaptation of man to any special environment, are apparent at every point. What relation is there between adaptation to environment and the religious custom which compels a man to destroy all that he owns, objects whose loss, in winter, for instance, might mean starvation and death, if his father dies in the house where they are deposited? What is unquestionably true is that the special climatic conditions of the Eskimo habitat demanded, perhaps, more than a 'working adaptation' to environment; but when this was once secured—and it was secured long ago—it permitted the play of forces that in themselves had no relation to the problem of adaptation, but were the direct result of the individual and social cultural potentialities of the Eskimos, no matter what part the physical environment may have played in shaping and upbuilding them.

The material culture of the Eskimos has been described many times, so that it will here be sufficient to quote the admirable summary of Rink, in his introduction to his *Tales and Traditions of the Eskimo* (London, 1875):

The Eskimo are entirely dependent upon seals and cetaceous animals for food, and the peculiar hunting contrivances used in securing them are the following: (1) *kayaks*, boats which consist of a framework of wood joined together principally by strings, and provided with a cover of skins impenetrable to the water. (2) The adjustment of the *kayak* itself and the *kayak*-coverings, with a view to provide an entire shelter for the *kayaker* or seal-hunter, with exception only of the face, to protect him against the water. Only a small number of Eskimos have *kayaks* fitted for more than a single man; and still more exceptionally, in the farthest north, some are found who have no *kayak* at all, because the sea is almost continually frozen. (3) Adaptation of a bladder filled with air to the harpoons or javelins, in order, by retarding the animals, to prevent them from escaping after being struck, and to prevent the harpoon from sinking should the hunter miss his aim (cf. Mason, *Rep. U.S. Nat. Mus.*, 1900 [Washington, 1902], p. 236 ff.). (4) The ingenious way in which the points of the weapons and of the spears with which the animals are finally killed are fitted into the shaft, so that, having penetrated the skin of the animal, the point is bent out of the shaft, which is either entirely loosened while only the point with the line and the bladder remains attached to the animal, or keeps hanging to the point. Without this precaution, the animal in its struggle would break the shaft or make the barb slip out of its body again. (5) The sledge with the dogs trained for drawing it (cf. Mason, *ib.* 1894 [Washington, 1896], p. 552 ff.).

It should also be noted that, besides bows made of drift-wood and strengthened with sinew (see Murdoch, *RSI*, 1883–84, ii. 307 ff.), the Eskimos are acquainted with a number of forms of the trap, including cage-, door-, and pit-traps, and dead falls for foxes, etc., whalebone nooses for waterfowl, and nets of sinew, rawhide, or baleen for fish (Mason, *RSI*, 1901, p. 467 ff.). Nor would any account of the material culture of the Eskimos be complete without some allusion to their lamps, made chiefly of soapstone (or some other sort of stone), less usually of earthenware, clay, bone, or wood. The Eskimos were the only Americans who possessed the lamp, and with them it assumes the duties not merely of illumination, but also of the cooking stove, besides heating the *igloos*, melting water, drying clothing, bending wood, and the like. Each house-wife possesses her own lamp, and 'a woman without a lamp' is an Eskimo synonym for the most wretched and destitute of beings. It has even been suggested that the architecture of the Eskimo *igloo* has been influenced by the use of the lamp (see on the whole subject, Hough, 'The Lamp of the Eskimo,' *Rep. U.S. Nat. Mus.*, 1896 [Washington, 1898], pp. 1025–1056).

There are two general types of habitation, the summer and the winter type, of which the latter contains a number of subdivisions that serve as rooms. In summer, when travelling, the Eskimos occupy tents of deer- or seal-skins stretched across poles. The winter houses are varied in structure. They are generally built of stones and turf, the roof-spars and the pillars which support the middle of the roof being of wood. Only the Eskimos of the middle regions have vaults of snow for their habitations, whilst the western Eskimos build their houses chiefly of planks covered on the outside with green turf. Some of the far northern divisions are obliged to use bones or stone instead of wood (cf. also *ERE* i. 684[b]).

The normal occupations of the men are hunting and fishing and the care and manufacture of their hunting gear, especially the *kayak*; the women are busied with the usual household tasks; the duty of skin-dressing devolves among some tribes on the men, and among others on the women. The clothing is of skins, with little variation for the two sexes. Personal adornment is rare, although in most tribes the women tatu their faces, and some of the Alaskan tribes wear small labrets under the corners of their mouths.

The social organization is extremely loose, the village being the largest unit. There is no real chief, although there is in each settlement some advisory head, who has, however, no power to enforce his opinion.

The standard of sexual morality is low, except where Christianity prevails; but, on the other hand, the Eskimos are peaceable, honest, truthful, and faithful; they are, moreover, generous and hospitable, kind to the stranger, the infirm, and the aged, cheerful and light-hearted. They are fond of singing and of music, although, except where they have come into contact with the whites, their sole musical instrument is a sort of little tambourine made of membrane stretched over an oval frame. They are also exceedingly fond of games.

The Eskimo games are described and discussed by Culin (*24 RBEW* [1907]). They are: ball juggling (p. 712), buzz (751 f.), cat's cradle (767 f.), dice (102 ff.), football (699 ff.), hoop-and-pole (472 ff.), ring-and-pin (544 ff.), tops (736 ff.)—these common to all. The Labrador Eskimos alone have the hand game, the object of which is to guess, like our 'hot and cold,' what object is concealed in the hand (283); peculiar to the Central Eskimos are ball-tossing (709), running after hoops on the ice (783), playing sealing (783), and a sort of roulette (783); and to the Western Eskimos arrow-tossing (386 ff.), hand-and-foot ball (706 f.), jackstraws (729 f.), quoits (723 f.), running races (805), and shinny (629).

The Eskimos, as is well known, are masters of realistic design on bone, one specimen, for instance, given by Deniker (*Races of Man*, p. 138) from Alaska being a series of 12 figures on an ivory whip, recording the fact that the owner paddled to an island with a single hut, where he slept one night, then went to another inhabited island and there spent two nights, and, after sealing and hunting with a bow, paddled back with a comrade to his own hut.

6. Religion.—Until the publication of Knud Rasmussen's *People of the Polar North* (Lond. 1908), Eskimo mythology occupied a peculiar place in the religious systems of the American aborigines, in that it was supposed to deal exclusively with human heroes and human activities. Indeed, it might be said that the 'myth' had been almost entirely displaced by the 'tale,' the latter connoting any plot that, from the Eskimo point of view, falls within the domain of earthly happenings, while 'myth' stands for a plot that does not. It was believed, previous to Rasmussen's work, that the animal played no part whatever in Eskimo mythology, and it assuredly does not do so in the areas not described by him; yet there can be no doubt that for the northern areas, with which the first part of his book deals, animal myths are found; and this fact lifts Eskimo mythology out of the position which it had long occupied in relation to the mythologies of other American tribes.

It is extremely difficult to describe even the essentials of Eskimo religious belief in the present state of our knowledge; for, with the exception of Rink, Boas, and Rasmussen, no observers have spent enough time among any given band really to get at the bottom of their religious system—or lack of it. Rink was under the disadvantage of having to rely on interpreters all the time and of not getting his material from texts; and this, combined with his tendency towards over-systematization, renders his accounts of Eskimo religious beliefs unsatisfactory in many respects. Rasmussen, on the other hand, although he obtained everything from texts and approached his subject with the utmost sympathy, suffers at times from the tendency to look at his subject too exclusively from the literary point of view, and from his failure to differentiate clearly between the esoteric point of view, as embodied by the shamans, and the exoteric, as represented by the laymen.

Briefly put, the Eskimos believe in spirits inhabiting both animals and what we should term inanimate objects. Their chief 'deity' is called *Tornassuk*, and he rules over all the helping and guardian spirits, or *tornat*, of all of whom he disposes at will. His figure and power are not, however, definitely marked. The chief deity in connexion with the food supply is an old woman who resides in the ocean, and is called *Sedna* among the Central Eskimos, and *Arnaknagsak* among the other divisions. She causes storms or withholds seals or other marine animals, if any of her tabus are infringed, her power over these animals arising from the fact that they are sections of her fingers cut off by her father at the time when she first took up her abode in the sea. It is the chief duty of the shaman, or *angakok*, to discover who has infringed the tabus and thus brought down the wrath of the supernatural beings; and it is likewise his duty to compel the offender to make atonement by public confession to him. Among the Central Eskimos it is believed that two spirits reside in a man's body, one of whom stays with it when it dies and may temporarily enter the body of some child, who is then named after the departed; while the other goes to one of the several lands of the souls, some of which lie above, and some below, the surface of the earth.

According to the statements of Rink, the whole visible world is ruled by supernatural powers, each of whom holds sway within certain limits, and is called *inua* ('man,' 'owner').

'Strictly speaking, scarcely any object existing either in a physical or spiritual point of view may not be conceived to have its *inua*. Generally speaking, however, the notion of an *inua* is limited to a locality, or to the human qualities and passions, *e.g.* the *inua* of certain mountains or lakes, of strength, of eating,' etc.

Perhaps the best idea of Eskimo religious beliefs can be obtained from Rasmussen's work mentioned above.

'We do not all understand the hidden things,' one old man told him, 'but we believe the people who say they do. We believe our *angakok*, and we believe them because we . . . do not want to expose ourselves to the danger of famine and starvation. We believe, in order to make our lives and our food secure. If we did not believe the magicians, the animals we hunt would make themselves invisible to us; if we did not follow their advice, we should fall ill and die. . . . We observe our old customs, in order to hold the world up, for the powers must not be offended. . . . We are afraid of the great Evil. Men are so helpless in the face of illness. The people here do penance, because the dead are strong in their vital sap, and boundless in their might' (p. 123 f.).

Here is a magician's description of how he obtained his power: 'I wanted to become a magician, and went up to the hills and slept up there. There I saw two hill-spirits as tall as a tent. They sang drum-songs. I kept silent. I was ashamed. The day after I went home and I was a little of a magician; but to the many I said nothing of it, for I was still very little of a magician. Another time I started for the hill and lay down to sleep, and, as I lay, I heard again the song of the hill-spirits. One now began to speak to me, and asked me for a ladle of wood. When I returned to men, I still did not speak about it, but carved a ladle of wood for the spirit. The third time I saw the hill-spirits it was in my own house, and a great dog was running after them; it, too, became my helping spirit. It was only when many people fell sick that I revealed myself as a magician. . . . My helping spirits know my thoughts and my will, and they help me when I give commands. Once I was very ill, and then I lost a great deal of my magic power. My helping spirits began to despise me. Now I am again a great magician. Even my wife can hear the spirits when they come to me, and I know when people are going to fall ill, and I know when they can recover' (cf. Rasmussen, p. 147 f.).

Rasmussen himself thus sums up their religion:

'Their religious opinions do not lead them to any sort of worship of the supernatural, but consist—if they are to be formulated in a creed—of a list of commandments and rules of conduct controlling their relations with unknown forces hostile to man' (p. 125). 'Their religion does not centre round any divinity who is worshipped, but vents itself in a belief in evil, in a dim perception of certain mystical powers who are easily offended and whose anger is dangerous. Man would be overwhelmed by the consideration he has to pay to the forces of Nature and by the rules governing his relations with these forces, were it not that he has the power, by forethought, to be the stronger, and, despite all, to control dangers. And this he does by himself taking the dreaded forces into his service. For the magicians, who are the leaders of the people, can, by their arts and skill, make the powers who are masters of life and death subject to them, not by prayer but by command. . . . Every man is at his birth endowed with a certain supply of vital force which is to be used up on earth. When this supply is exhausted, the person grows old and, by death, passes over into another existence. In such a case no magician endeavours to retain life in the invalid, for he is "worn out," and it is better that he should die' (p. 126 f.).

From these beliefs those of the Eskimos of Ammassalik Fiord, East Greenland, differ in some noteworthy regards, as is detailed by Thalbitzer ('The Heathen Priests of East Greenland,' in *XVI. Internat. Amerikanisten-Kongress*, Vienna, 1910, ii. 447–464):

'The Eskimo religion knows two supreme divinities: the moon, Aningáhk, which is regarded as a man, a hunter, who catches sea-animals, who has his house, his hunting grounds, and his implements of the chase in the sky; and the old nameless woman of the sea [the Sedna or Arnaknagsak of the other Eskimos], whose house lies far away at the bottom of the ocean, and who rules over the marine seals, whales, and polar bears. Finally, the people of Ammassalik speak of a third power in the sky, an old woman of the name of *Asiak*, who procures rain by shaking a skin drenched in urine down upon the earth, so that a shower of drops is sprinkled upon it.' Besides the *angakoks*, the Greenland Eskimos have an inferior and less esteemed class of shamans, the *qilalik*, the most of whom are women. The mystic language in which the *angakok* holds converse with the spirits is 'not sheer abracadabra, but obsolete or metaphorically used Eskimo words, a kind of inherited art language, which contributes in a high degree to the solemn and mystical character of the spiritual gathering. The religious forms or expressions themselves are made no secret of: only the way in which the disciple receives his training is wrapped in mystery.' During his questioning of the spirits, the soul of the *angakok* is believed to sink below the earth (or sometimes to go to the moon), his body being meanwhile occupied by his *taartaat* (apparently 'successor'). He is aided by his spirit monsters, or the manlike animals belonging to the sacred ritual, which enter the hut while the *angakok's* soul is still in his body, these being *Timerseet*, living in the interior of the country; *Eajuätsaat*, dwelling under the ground close to men's huts; and *Innertiwin*, living on the beach under the rocks of the coast. Besides these there comes from the sea the 'consulted one,' *Apergit*, who serves as the intermediary between the *angakok* and *Toornartik*, a sea-monster which guides him to the woman of the sea, and informs the *Apergit* (who then tells the *angakok*) as to what souls have abandoned the sick man on whose behalf the consultation is made, and where they may be found; whereupon the attendant spirits are to search for and bring back the deserting souls. 'For, according to Eskimo notions, all disease is nothing but loss of a soul; in every part of the human body (particularly in every joint, as, for instance, in each finger-joint) there resides a little soul, and, if a part of the man's body is sick, it is because the little soul has abandoned that part. In most cases the loss of the soul is regarded as due to one of the following causes: either that evilly disposed persons have driven it out by means of magic, or that higher powers, the moon, for instance, have removed it as a punishment for men's sins (some sacrilege, breach of tabu, or other).'

There can be no doubt that the native religion of the Eskimos is gradually becoming extinct, and in Western Greenland (as also in East Greenland) the Danish missionaries have practically extinguished it. The same thing is true of Labrador, where Moravian missionaries have long been active; and in Alaska the Russians have laboured for more than a century, with good success, for the Christianization of the Eskimos, their work being assisted by missionaries of other communions. Among the central groups, on the other hand, the native religion has remained practically untouched by missionary endeavour.

Taken all in all, Eskimo culture, despite a remarkable specialization in certain aspects of material civilization, shows sufficient fundamental similarities in all other aspects to warrant its inclusion in the cultural areas of North America.

LITERATURE.—The older records are summarized in Waitz, *Anthropol. der Naturvölker*, Leipzig, 1862, iii. 300 ff. Besides the works mentioned in the text, reference should be made to Boas, 'Central Eskimo' (*6 RBEW* [1888]), and 'Eskimo of Baffin Land and Hudson Bay' (*Bull. Amer. Mus. Nat. Hist.* xv. pt. i. [1901]); Dall, 'Tribes of the Extreme Northwest' (*Contrib. to N. Amer. Ethnol.* i. [1877]); Nelson, 'Eskimo about Bering Strait' (*18 RBEW*, pt. i. [1899]); Murdoch, 'Ethnolog. Results of the Point Barrow Expedition' (*9 RBEW* [1892]); Kroeber, 'Eskimo of Smith Sound' (*Bull. Amer. Mus. Nat. Hist.* xii. [1899]); Turner, 'Ethnol. of the Ungava District' (*11 RBEW* [1894]); Holm, 'Ethnologisk Skizzen af Angamagsalikerne' (*Meddelelser om Grönland*, x. [1887]); Rink, 'Eskimo Tribes' (*ib.* xi. [1887]); Nansen, *Eskimo Life*[2], London, 1894; Bolles, 'Cat. of Eskimo Collection' (*Rep. U.S. Nat. Mus.*, 1887); Pilling, 'Bibliog. of the Eskimo Language' (*1 Bull. BE* [1887], to be supplemented by the list of Thalbitzer, 'Eskimo,' in *Handbook of Amer. Ind. Lang.* (*40 Bull. BE* [1911]) i. 969 ff.; D. MacRitchie, 'Eskimos of Davis Straits in 1656' (*Scottish Geographical Magazine*, xxviii. [1912] 281–294.

PAUL RADIN and LOUIS H. GRAY.

ESSENCE.—All human striving seeks the essential. Cognitive energy, from its first instinctive stirrings to its most highly developed and clearly conscious forms, is a process of selection impelled by deep-lying vital necessities. The senses are organs of selection, reacting characteristically upon the multitudinous stimuli of the physical world. On the selected material they present, the mind carries out a further process of sifting and combination, in accordance with its immanent norms and ends. The whole discriminative and elaborative activity is vital self-expression of the mind. In biological terms, cognition may be described as a mode of the mind's vital adjustment to environment—an adjustment which utters the nature and at the same time subserves the realization and conservation of the self. In other words, cognition so far satisfies the primal need of personal life, namely, to assert and maintain itself (cf. art. EPISTEMOLOGY). Thus, thinking and human activity in general are purposive through and through. Behind it all is the will to live, to be a self. In illustration, it may be pointed out that the very ideas of truth and reality are possible only in relation to an interest or purpose. Apart from an informing aim to attain the true or to grasp the real, thinking or intellection could have no intelligible relation to truth or reality.

As Stout puts it (in *Personal Idealism*, ed. Sturt, 1902, p. 10), 'a person cannot be right or wrong without reference to some interest or purpose.' Similarly, Royce asserts that an idea appears in consciousness as having the significance of an act of will, and that the inner purpose is the primary and essential feature of an idea (*The World and the Individual*, 1st ser., New York, 1900, Introd., *passim*).

Thus, the objective world furnishes the occasion and material for the progressive self-fulfilment of the Ego; or, to put it otherwise, it is the correlate of man's self-activity; and the essential is what is specially relevant to a particular interest or purpose of the mind at work on the organization of experience.

'The essence of a thing is that one of its properties which is so important for my interests that in comparison with it I may neglect the rest' (W. James, *Text-Book of Psychology*, 1892, p. 357). Or, 'it is merely such aspects of the whole behaviour of the thing as are selected from among the rest, by reason either of their relative permanence or of their importance for our purposes' (F. C. S. Schiller, *Humanism*, 1903, p. 225).

This fairly represents our ordinary work-a-day attitude towards things. It does not follow, however, that the things of sense-experience are absolutely plastic material. On the contrary, they exercise a certain control. They may be variously conceived, but misconception is checked by its discovered unworkableness. In our practical intercourse with things we have to reckon with certain invariable modes of action and reaction; and these constitute for us their essential characteristics or nature (cf. G. Jacobi, *Pragmatismus*, 1909, p. 33). Science represents a systematized and critical form of the common-sense view of the world. Armed with its weapons of precision, it stands for enhanced mastery over Nature, for enlarged human efficiency. It is this quality of exactitude, expressed in measurement, that distinguishes scientific procedure most sharply from the rough and ready methods of common sense. The constant endeavour to attain the maximum of accuracy, order, connexion, consistency, and completeness in the different provinces of knowledge makes science necessarily critical of the looseness and incoherence of ordinary thinking, and is apt to beget the impression that the scientific attitude is antithetic to that of the practical man (see, *e.g.*, J. Arthur Thomson, *Introd. to Science*, London, 1911, p. 38 f.). Nevertheless, in spite of the undeniable contrast, science may best be described as a critical development of common sense. The further organization of experience is due to the working of the same organic impulse of self-realization, with its inherent selective interests, which makes the synthesis of knowledge possible at all. It is very generally recognized that at all events the physical and natural sciences aim at 'the description of events by the aid of the fewest and simplest general formulæ' (*ib.* p. 47); they limit themselves to descriptive formulation in contradistinction to explanatory interpretation.

This phenomenalism of method is self-imposed in the interests of the special disciplines and of science as a whole. In order to deal with the facts of experience in their immeasurable complexity, certain aspects must be mentally isolated and fixated, and the whole body of relative data envisaged from this point of view. Thus, the particular sciences carry through methodically the abstraction which is the other side of all intellectual concentration. They are methods of intellectually attacking and mastering an otherwise unmanageable mass of experiential material. The same group of facts may be worked over by many sciences from their own distinctive view-points, yielding to each its special concepts, classification, and laws. Merz, in his monumental *History of European Thought in the Nineteenth Century* (1896–1903), regards the various lines of scientific advance as characteristic modes of viewing Nature, and classifies them accordingly as the astronomical, the atomic, the mechanical or kinetic, the physical, the morphological, the genetic, the vitalistic, the psycho-physical, and the statistical views of Nature.

Clearly, then, it is not the business of the sciences to determine the real essence of their subject-matter. The very notion lies outside their purview. For that reason it is grossly fallacious to construe this methodological ignorance as metaphysical negation. It is impossible to negate what is not considered; it is impossible to answer a question which is never raised. Empirical science is no more anti-metaphysical because it ignores the metaphysical than geometry is anti-biological because it does not concern itself with the phenomena of life. On the other hand, the empirical sciences contribute valuable and indispensable material for the solution of the strictly philosophical problems.

Science does not, in point of fact, satisfy the

irrepressible demand for real explanation. A pure scientist has never lived. Philosophy recognizes that the questions regarding ultimate explanations and meanings, final causes, and eternal values must be faced. It recognizes, further, the inherent limitations and instrumental character of scientific method, and perceives that it is but a partial expression and satisfaction of the cognitive impulse, and but one phase in the total life of the human spirit. Philosophy represents a resolute endeavour after completeness in thought. It seeks to take cognizance of all the facts and factors that enter into human experience, and hence does not limit itself to facts amenable to ordinary scientific treatment, or assume as ultimate and finally valid the working principles and underlying assumptions of the sciences. The particular sciences and science as a whole form part of its total datum, which embraces the whole range of human culture, both as result and as process. This huge aggregate —as it at first sight appears—must somehow be conceived as a whole, and to this end the facts must be graded according to their causative efficiency and explanatory value. The result is an ultimate synthesis, on the basis of a thoroughgoing resolution, of the phenomenal complex into its constituent factors and ends. Not, of course, that the philosopher is bound to consider his view of the world as an adequate intellectual formulation of ultimate reality; the fact that the life which energizes in the thinker is in continuous movement and development should be enough to hold him back from the presumption of absolutist gnosticism. Yet this admission does not carry with it adhesion to relativism. The philosopher cannot help believing that, though he has not grasped and cannot grasp the whole truth, he has, nevertheless, reached essential truth, that permanent validity attaches to the substance at least of his central affirmations, and that his efforts will make for a fuller apprehension of the truth by future generations. To claim less than this would mean an intellectual self-renunciation tantamount to suicide. In its metaphysical insistence philosophy expresses the outreaching in one direction of the spiritual life—a reality wider and deeper than mere thought—towards self-fulfilment. The essential is an ideal to be realized; it is also a substantial reality, impelling and attractive; or it would not be sought. Only that which is in some sort our own moves us. Essence in its large signification is the all-comprehensive problem of humanity, alike theoretical and practical. Its solution will not be furnished by the subtlest reflexions of the theoretical reason, but by the forward movement of life as a whole, by the active realization and explication of a truth of humanity which is vastly more than any theory (see R. Eucken, *Geistige Strömungen d. Gegenwart*,^{4} 1909, p. 36 f.). The problems are internal and vital, and are progressively resolved by the self-unfolding of the vital process, which they have challenged and stimulated.

See also artt. ACCIDENT, BEING, EPISTEMOLOGY, ONTOLOGY, PHILOSOPHY, SUBSTANCE.

LITERATURE.—On the part the term and concept have played in the history of philosophy, see Eisler, *Wörterbuch der philos. Begriffe*^{2}, 1904, art. 'Wesen.' For Greek philosophy, see the Histories of Philosophy by Zeller, Erdmann, and Uberweg-Heinze. Good accounts of Scholastic usage are given in T. Harper, *The Metaphysics of the School*, 1879–84, vol. i. bk. ii., and the *English Manuals of Catholic Philosophy*, Stonyhurst series, esp. those on Logic (Clarke), First Principles (John Rickaby), General Metaphysics (do.). For modern times, besides the works already referred to, the following may be consulted: Locke, *Essay on Human Understanding*, bk. iii.; J. McCosh, *Intuitions of the Mind*, 1860; A. Bain, *Mental and Moral Science*^{3}, 1884; J. F. Ferrier, *Institutes of Metaphysic*, 1854, p. 249 f.; Hegel, *Encyklopädie*, 1845, 'Lehre vom Wesen' (cf. W. Wallace, *Logic of Hegel*^{2}, 1894, p. 177 f.); Lotze, *Metaphysics*, Eng. tr. 1884, *passim*, and *Microcosmus*, Eng. tr. 1885, vol. ii. bk. ix.; B. P. Bowne, *Metaphysics*, 1882, ch. ii.; G. T. Ladd, *Theory of Reality*, 1899; W. Windelband, *Hist. of Philos.*, 1893. A novel and strikingly suggestive development of the idea of essence is given by R. Eucken, in his philosophy of the Spiritual Life set forth in many vols., e.g. *Grundlinien einer neuen Lebensanschauung*, 1907, pp. 174 f. and 259 f. (cf. J. Goldstein, *Wandlungen in der Philosophie der Gegenwart*, 1911). A lucid discussion of real kinds or 'essence' is given by Mellone, *Introd. Text-Book of Logic*^{2}, 1905.

F. W. DUNLOP.

ESSENES.

ESSENES.—The *Epulones* of Artemis at Ephesus were called 'Essenes' (Paus. viii. 13. 1: *τοὺς τῇ Ἀρτέμιδι ἱστιάτορας τῇ Ἐφεσίᾳ γινομένους, καλουμένους δὲ ὑπὸ τῶν πολιτῶν Ἐσσῆνας*), or 'king bees'; but the name is specially applied to a remarkable pre-Christian order of Jewish monks, whom Josephus calls *Ἐσσηνοί* or *Ἐσσαῖοι*. Philo adheres to the latter name, which, as more Semitic, was probably the original formation of their title.

1. Sources of information.—Neither the Bible nor the Rabbinical literature mentions the Essenes, but their mode of life is described by (*a*) Jewish, (*b*) Christian, and (*c*) pagan writers.

(*a*) Philo and Josephus devote unusual attention to their customs; and as the former was a contemporary, while the latter spent three years in their neighbourhood and had other opportunities of gaining acquaintance with individual Essenes, the narratives of both writers, although liable to qualifying criticism on the score of tendency, furnish indispensable materials for an estimate of the order.

(i.) Two Philonic statements are extant. The first and longer occurs in the treatise, *Quod omnis probus liber* (§§ 12–13), a youthful work, perhaps written when Philo was studying in Alexandria. He has just been proving that the world is not wholly destitute of virtuous people; after pointing to the Persian Magi and the Indian gymnosophists, he proceeds to quote a salient example from his own countrymen:

§ 12. 'Nor are Palestine and[1] Syria barren of moral excellence (*καλοκἀγαθία*)—countries inhabited by a large portion of that most populous race, the Jews. There are among them people called Essenes, numbering over 4000, and in my judgment so called from their piety (*ὁσιότητος*)—though the derivation is not strictly Greek—since they are pre-eminently worshipping servants of God (*θεραπευταὶ θεοῦ*); they do not sacrifice animals, but study to keep their minds in a saintly frame (*ἱεροπρεπεῖς*). In the first place, they reside in villages, shunning town-life on account of the lawless manners of townsfolk, since they are well aware that such associations are as able to infect their souls with incurable disorder as tainted air is to infect their bodies with deadly disease. Some of them till the ground. Others practise such arts and crafts as are consonant (*συνεργάτιδες*) with peace, and thereby benefit themselves and their neighbours. They do not treasure up silver and gold, nor do they acquire large tracts of land in an eager desire for income, but only make provision for the absolute necessities of life. They are almost the only people who remain destitute of money and possessions, by use and wont rather than by any lack of prosperity; yet they are esteemed wealthy, for they consider that to be frugal and contented is, as indeed it is, ample abundance. You would not discover among them any maker of arrows, spears, swords, helmets, corselets, or shields, any maker of arms or war-engines, any one busied in the slightest with military avocations or even with those which, during peace, slip easily over into mischief; they are totally ignorant of trade and commerce and sea-faring, abhorring, as they do, all inducements to covetous gain.[2] There is not a single slave among them; all are free and exchange kind offices with each other. They condemn the position of master, not only as unjust, being a breach of equality, but as impious, since it violates the order of Mother Nature, which gives birth to all alike and rears them as genuine brothers, not as nominal, whereas crafty covetousness disorganizes this natural kinship by its desire to outshine others, it engenders hostility instead of affection, and enmity instead of friendship.

Logic is a department of philosophy which they leave to word-catchers, as unnecessary for the acquiring of virtue; physical science they regard as too lofty for human nature, and so they

[1] Schürer, omitting *καί*, confines the Essenes to Palestinian Syria. They were, at any rate, local, as the Therapeutæ were not. No trace of Essenic propaganda is to be found in Asia Minor or Italy.

[2] Hippolytus (*Hær.* ix. 21) adds that some carried their religious objection to idolatry so far that they refused to use coins, and even to enter cities in case they passed below statues at the gate (cf. *ERE* iv. 849).

leave that to high-flying theorists,[1] except as it includes the study of God's existence and the formation of the universe. It is Ethics to which they devote all their strength, under the guidance of their ancestral laws, which no human soul could have devised apart from Divine inspiration. In these laws they are instructed, particularly on the seventh day, as well as at other times. For the seventh day is held sacred; on it they cease all work,[2] and repair to sacred places called synagogues,[3] where they sit arranged according to age—the young below the older persons—and listen with due order and attention. One reads aloud the sacred books, whereupon another of their most experienced members comes forward to explain whatever is not clear; for the greater part of their lore is conveyed figuratively[4] (διὰ συμβόλων) after their time-honoured fashion. They are taught piety, holiness, justice, the management of affairs (οἰκονομίαν), citizenship, the knowledge of what is truly good or bad or indifferent, how to choose the right and how to shun the contrary; and in all this they employ three rules and standards, namely, the love of God, the love of virtue, and the love of man. Thus they furnish thousands of examples of the meaning of love to God, by a close and continuous purity maintained throughout life, by abstinence from oaths and falsehood, and by regarding the Deity as the cause of all good but of no evil. As for the love of virtue, they point us to freedom from the love of money (ἀφιλοχρήματον),[5] fame, and pleasure, to self-control, to endurance, and also to contentment (ὀλιγόδειαν), simplicity, good humour, modesty, regard for the laws, firmness of character, and such-like qualities. As for the love of man, they give proofs of goodwill, impartiality, and an indescribable bond of fellowship. About this last it will not be amiss to say a few words. First of all, no one has a house of his own, which does not belong to all; in addition to residing together in companies, they keep open house for associates who arrive from other quarters. Then, they have a common treasury, and share all expenses; they also share their clothes, and their meals are common, as they mess together. Among no other people would you find that community of residence, life, and food is more of a reality. This is perhaps only natural, for they put their daily wage into a common fund, instead of keeping it for themselves, and thus provide for any who want help. Their sick members are not neglected because they can contribute nothing, for their ample funds enable them to make lavish provision for all such. Their seniors are treated with respect and honour and attention, as parents are by their own children; their old age is cherished bountifully by the toil and endless thought of the younger members.

§ 13. Such are the masters of virtue (ἀθλητὰς ἀρετῆς) turned out by a philosophic system which has nothing to do with research into Greek terms, but which essays to train them by means of laudable actions as the basis of a freedom which is not to be subdued. Here is a proof of this. From time to time their country has been seized by many rulers, men of varied characters and aims; some of them have tried unceasingly to outdo wild beasts in their ferocity, exhausting every form of savagery, massacring hordes of their subjects, and even cutting them up limb from limb when they were alive, like very butchers, until at last they suffered the same doom at the hands of the justice which supervises human life. Others put their frenzy into a fresh form of malice; unspeakably venomous was their device. Their words were smooth, but the gentle tones they adopted only revealed their bitterness of mind; they would fawn upon men like treacherous dogs, and yet prove the authors of fatal evils. They have left monuments of their impiety and hatred of men in the ever-memorable disasters suffered by their victims in the cities. Yet none of these bloodthirsty creatures, none of these treacherous and cunning tyrants, was able to lay any charge against the company of the Essenes, or "holy men" (ἢ ὁσίων). Their moral excellence triumphed, and everybody treated them as independent and free by nature, praising their common meals and their indescribable good-fellowship—the clearest proof of a life which is perfect and exceedingly happy.'

The second Philonic passage is from the author's lost *Apology for the Jews* (ὑπὲρ Ἰουδαίων ἀπολογία), excerpted in Eus. *Præp. Ev.* viii. 11 (ed. E. H. Gifford, 1903):

'Our Lawgiver has trained to community of living many thousands of disciples, who are called Essenes, because of their holiness, I believe. They dwell in many cities of Judæa and many villages, and in large and populous societies. Their sect is formed not on family descent, for descent is not reckoned among matters of choice, but on zeal for virtue and philanthropy. Accordingly, there is among the Essenes no mere child, or even a scarce-bearded lad, or young man; since of such as these the moral dispositions are unstable and apt to change in accordance with their imperfect age; they are all full-grown men, already verging upon old age, as being no longer swept away by the flood of bodily impulses, or led by their passions, but in the enjoyment of the genuine and only real liberty.

And their mode of life is an evidence of this liberty; none ventures to acquire any private property at all, no house, or slave,[1] or farm, or cattle, or any of the other things which procure or minister to wealth; but they deposit them all in public together, and enjoy the benefit of all in common. And they dwell together in one place, forming clubs and messes in companies (κατὰ θίασους, ἑταιρίας καὶ συσσίτια), and they pass their whole time in managing every kind of business for the common good. But different members have different occupations, to which they strenuously devote themselves, and toil on with unwearied patience, making no excuses of cold or heat or any change of weather; before the sun is up they turn to their usual employments, and hardly give up at its setting, delighting in work no less than those who are being trained in gymnastic contests. For, whatever occupation they follow, they imagine that these exercises are more beneficial to life, and more pleasant to soul and body, and more permanent than athletics, because they do not become unseasonable as the vigour of the body declines. Some of them labour in the fields, being skilled in matters relating to sowing and tillage, and others are herdsmen, being masters of all kinds of cattle; and some attend to swarms of bees. Others, again, are craftsmen in various arts, who, in order to avoid any of the sufferings which the want of the necessaries of life imposes, reject none of the innocent ways of gaining a livelihood.

Of the men, then, who thus differ in occupation, every one on receiving his wages gives them to one person who is the appointed steward; and he, on receiving them, immediately purchases the necessary provisions, and supplies abundance of food, and all other things of which man's life is in need. And they who live together and share the same table are content with the same things every day, being lovers of frugality, and abhorring prodigality as a disease of soul and body. Not only have they a common table, but also common raiment; for there are set out in winter thick cloaks, and in summer cheap tunics, so that any one who will may easily take whichever he likes, since what belongs to one is considered to belong to all, and the property of all to be, on the other hand, the property of each one.

Moreover, if any of them should fall sick, he is medically treated out of the common resources, and attended by the care and concern of all. And so the old men, even if they happen to be childless, are wont to end their life in a very happy and bright old age, inasmuch as they are blest with sons both many and good, being held worthy of attention and honour by so many, who from free good will rather than from any bond of natural birth feel it right to cherish them.

Further, then, as they saw with keen discernment the thing which alone, or most of all, was likely to dissolve their community, they repudiated marriage and also practised continence in an eminent degree. For no Essene takes to himself a wife, because woman is immoderately selfish and jealous, and terribly clever in decoying a man's moral inclinations, and bringing them into subjection by continual cajoleries.[2] For when, by practising flattering speeches and the other arts, as of an actress on the stage, she has deluded eyes and ears, then, as having thoroughly deceived the servants, she proceeds to cajole the master mind. And, should she have children, she is filled with pride and boldness of speech, and what she formerly used to hint under the disguise of irony, all this she now speaks out with greater audacity, and shamelessly compels him to practices, every one of which is hostile to community of life. For the man who is either ensnared by the charms of a wife,[3] or induced by natural affection to make his children his first care, is no longer the same towards others, but has unconsciously become changed from a free man to a slave.

So enviable, then, is the life of these Essenes that not only private persons, but also great kings, are filled with admiration and amazement at the men, and make their venerable character still more venerable by marks of approbation and honour.'

(ii.) The principal passage in Josephus occurs in *BJ* II. viii. 2 ff. He opens by noting the reputation of the Essenes for moral earnestness (ὃ δὴ καὶ δοκεῖ σεμνότητα ἀσκεῖν) and brotherliness (φιλάλληλοι), in both of which qualities[4] they compare favourably with the Pharisees and the Sadducees.

§ 2. 'They eschew pleasures[5] as vicious, and regard continence (ἐγκράτειαν) and mastery over the passions as virtue. Marriage they despise; they select other people's children, when their characters are still fresh enough to be indoctrinated, adopt them,[6] and mould them after their own tenets, since,

[1] The term (μετεωρολέσχαις) is used in a depreciatory sense by Plato (*Rep.* 489 C) and Lucian (*Icar.* 5).

[2] Hippolytus (*Hær.* ix. 20) adds that some stayed in bed all the Sabbath, to avoid the temptation of work.

[3] Diettrich (*Die Oden Salomos*, 1911, p. 9) detects a reference to these places of worship in the fourth Ode of Solomon (vv. 1–4: 'No one, O my God, changeth thy holy place . . . for thy sanctuary thou hast established before thou didst make other places; the older shall not be put below the younger').

[4] *I.e.* allegorically. This feature attracted Philo.

[5] Cf. He 13^{5} and *ERE* iv. 87.

[1] The context seems to imply that the Essenes had slaves in common, whereas elsewhere (see above) Philo asserts that they had no slaves at all; but the phraseology is loose, and the discrepancy is too slight to serve as a ground for suspecting the authenticity of either passage.

[2] D. Plooij (*De Bronnen voor onze kennis van de Essenen*, 1902, p. 96 f.) regards this misogynism as Eusebian rather than Philonic.

[3] Cf. 1 Co 7^{33}, Rev 14^{4}.

[4] This comparison is upset if καὶ τῶν ἄλλων πλέον is taken with what follows (so Lat., Holwerda), instead of with what precedes.

[5] Cf. *ERE* iii. 272^{a}, 486 f.

[6] A non-Jewish trait (see *ERE* i. 115). No information is given as to how these children were procured.

although they do not repudiate marriage with its function of carrying on the race, they shun the licentiousness of women, and are convinced that no woman keeps faith with a man.

§ 3. They despise wealth,[1] and their socialism is remarkable; you cannot find any of them who has more than his fellows. The rule is that all who enter the sect must divide their property among the common body, so that there is not a trace among them of abject poverty or of excessive wealth; the distribution of every one's possessions creates, as it were, a common stock for all the brotherhood. Oil they regard as defiling, and, if any one is involuntarily smeared, he wipes his body clean; to be unanointed (αὐχμεῖν),[2] and always to wear white, are highly esteemed by them. They also elect managers of their common property, whose sole business it is to look after the wants of all and sundry.

§ 4. They have no single city, but large numbers of them inhabit every city; they freely put whatever they have at the disposal of any fellow-members who may arrive, and the latter enter the houses of people they have never seen before, just as if they were on the closest terms of intimacy. Consequently, although they travel armed in case of robbers, they never carry anything with them on a journey. In every city a special relieving officer is told off for strangers, to provide them with clothing and supplies. As regards their dress and person, they act like boys in terror of their tutors (τοῖς μετὰ φόβου παιδαγωγουμένοις παισίν). They never change their clothes or shoes till they are quite torn to pieces or worn out. They never buy or sell amongst themselves; each gives what he has to any one who is in need (τῷ χρῄζοντι διδούς),[3] getting from him in return what he himself requires; they are free to take what they want from any one they choose, apart from any question of paying back (χωρὶς τῆς ἀντιδόσεως).

§ 5. Yet they are peculiarly scrupulous in matters of piety. Before sunrise they never speak a word about profane affairs, but offer some ancestral prayers, as if[4] they besought the sun to rise. After this they are dismissed by the managers to the tasks in which they are respectively proficient, working assiduously till the fifth hour, when they once more gather in one spot, and, clothing themselves in linen veils, take a cold bath;[5] after this act of purification they assemble in an apartment of their own, from which all outsiders are excluded; they enter the dining-room pure (καθαροί) as they would enter a sacred precinct, and take their seats quietly. Then the baker puts loaves before them in order (ἐν τάξει), while the cook sets before each a plate containing one kind of food.[6] But no one is allowed to taste it until the priest offers a prayer, and after they have breakfasted [reading with Porphyry ἀριστοποιησαμένοις] he prays again. At the beginning and at the end of the meal they do honour to God as the supplier of life (ὡς χορηγὸν τῆς ζωῆς, *v.l.* τροφῆς).[7] After this they lay aside their garments as sacred, and resume their tasks till evening, when they return home to sup in similar fashion, sitting down with any strangers who may be present. No brawling or uproar ever defiles their house; they let every one speak in turn (ἐν τάξει, as above). To outsiders, indeed, the silence of the inmates seems full of awe and mystery, but it is due to their unbroken sobriety, and to the fact that food and drink are measured out for them to satisfy their needs, and no more.[8]

§ 6. While in all else they act only at the bidding of the managers, two things are left to their own initiative, namely, succour and charity. They are free to help any deserving cases and to give food to the starving, but they are not allowed to share anything with one another except by the permission of their superintendents. Just in the exercise of anger, they keep a check upon all passion; they are champions of trustworthiness (πίστεως) and promoters of peace. A word of theirs is stronger than an oath; they shun swearing, which they consider worse than perjury, since, they argue, what needs a Divine oath to accredit it is condemned already (ἤδη κατεγνῶσθαι).[9] They also take exceptional pains to select from the writings of the ancients (τὰ τῶν παλαιῶν συντάγματα) what is good for soul and body, which leads them to discover medicinal roots and stones which have the property of curing ailments (cf. *ERE* iv. 757).

§ 7. If any one is eager to join their sect, he is not admitted at once. He is given a spud, a girdle [omitting, with Porphyry, τὸ προειρημένον], and a white robe, and ordered to practise their mode of life for a whole year, remaining still an outsider. After thus giving proof of his continence, he gets closer to their way of living, and shares their baths of purification,[1] though still excluded from their common fellowship. This evidence of endurance[2] is followed by a further period of probation, lasting two years, after which, if he seems worthy, he is enrolled in their band. But, before touching their common food, he takes fearful oaths: first of all to be pious to the Deity; then to practise justice towards men; never to injure any one either of his own accord or under compulsion; always to hate the wicked and to side with the just; at all times to show fidelity to all men, and particularly to those in authority, since no one acquires power apart from God; never, if he is in power himself, to vaunt his authority or to outshine his subordinates in dress or finery; always to love the truth and denounce liars; to keep his hands clean from theft and his soul from unhallowed gain; never to keep any secret from his fellow-members or to betray any of their secrets to other people—no, not even under threats of death. He swears, moreover, to communicate their principles precisely as he himself has received them, to abstain from brigandage, and to preserve with like care the sacred books of the society and the names of the angels. Such are the oaths by which they make sure of their adherents.

§ 8. They expel any members found guilty of heinous sins, and the expelled person often perishes miserably; for by the bond of his oaths and habits he is prevented from receiving food at the hands of other people, so that, reduced to eating herbs, he languishes under starvation and perishes. Hence, out of compassion, they take many a man back when he is at his last gasp, considering that he has been sufficiently punished for his sins by being thus brought to the verge of death.

§ 9. They are extremely strict and just in the matter of inflicting penalties; no sentence is passed by a court numbering less than a hundred; but such a decision is irrevocable. Next to God the name of their legislator is highly reverenced, and the punishment for any blasphemy of him is death. They obey their elders (τοῖς πρεσβυτέροις) and a majority of their society [reading, with Destinon, κοινῷ for καλῷ]; thus, when ten are in session, no one would speak if the other nine objected. They eschew spitting[3] in front of them or on the right side, and avoid work on the seventh day more strictly than any other Jews. Not only do they prepare their food on the previous day, to avoid lighting fires on the seventh day, but they do not even venture to move a vessel or to evacuate. On other days[4] they dig holes a foot deep with the spud—a sort of spade given to all who enter the society,—cover themselves with a cloak, to avoid offending the rays of God, and ease themselves into the hole, after which they put back the earth they had dug out. Even for this they choose out-of-the-way spots; and although the voiding of excrements is a natural process, they make a practice of washing afterwards, as if it defiled them.

§ 10. They are divided into four classes, according to the length of their service, and the juniors are so inferior to the seniors that, should the latter be touched by the former, they wash themselves as if they had been sullied by contact with a foreigner.[5] They are long-lived, many of them reaching the age of a hundred—thanks, I suppose, to their simple diet and regular habits; but they despise the ills of life. Their spirit enables them to rise superior to pain; and death, encountered with glory, is preferred to length of days (ἀθανασίας ἀμείνονα). The Roman war[6] showed what great souls they all had; for, though racked and twisted, burnt and mutilated, and subjected to every instrument of torture, to make them blaspheme their legislator or eat forbidden food, they stoutly refused to do either; not for a moment would they cringe to their tormentors or shed a tear, but, smiling through their anguish, they scornfully laughed at the torturers and cheerfully gave up their souls, to receive them once again.

§ 11. For it is their firm opinion that, while the body is corruptible, and its substance transient, the soul is permanent and immortal; that the soul comes from the thinnest air by a sort of natural spell to be imprisoned, as it were, within the body; and that, on being released from the fetters of the flesh,[7] it joyfully soars away into freedom from the long bondage (μακρᾶς δουλείας). They believe, like the sons of the Greeks,

---

1 Possibly this was an anticipation of the Gnostic repugnance to money as part and parcel of the evil material principle.

2 In spite of Bousset, this aversion to oil is most naturally taken as an ascetic trait, rather than as a note of the Essenes' antipathy to the Jewish priesthood or to an oil-sacrament.

3 Cf. Lk 6^{30}; ct. the Pharisaic *Pirqe Aboth* v. 16.

4 The phrase (ὥσπερ ἱκετεύοντες) does not mean sun-worship (see on this, E. A. Abbott, *Notes on NT Criticism*, 1907, pp. 188–192); at most it is *invocatio*, not *adoratio*.

5 Cf. *ERE* iii. 489b.

6 Cf. Lk 10^{42}.

7 It is not quite clear that these meals were sacramental in the strict sense of the term, or equivalent to the θυσίαι, which the Essenes regarded as superior to the temple-sacrifices.

8 Jerome (*adv. Jovin.* ii. 14) misquotes Josephus, as if he declared that the Essenes abstained from flesh and wine. Josephus merely says they ate and drank in moderation; his point is that their glory lay in their temperance, not in total abstinence.

9 Like some of the Pharisees, they enjoyed exemption from the oath of loyalty, as a special mark of Herod's favour (*Ant.* xv. x. 4).

1 That is, from the defilement of sin, more searching (καθαρωτέρων) than the cold baths of § 5. Cf. Bousset, *Hauptprobleme der Gnosis*, Göttingen, 1907, p. 283.

2 Cf. *ERE* ii. 228 f.

3 'Every hidden thing' in Ec 12^{14} was interpreted by R. Samuel (3rd cent. A.D.) as referring to a man spitting in the presence of his neighbour so as to disgust him (*Hagig.* 5a).

4 Cf. Conybeare's ed. of the *de Vita Contemplativa*, Oxford, 1895, p. 198 f.

5 This is one of the practices which suggest the influence of the Indian caste-system. 'So an Indian Brahman is polluted by the touch and even the sight of a low-caste native' (F. C. Conybeare, *HDB* i. 769).

6 In this some Essenes, like John (*BJ* II. xx. 4), took an active part, although their peaceful principles forbade warfare. For an analogous instance of patriotism overbearing such principles, Holtzmann (*Neutest. Theologie*, Freiburg, 1896–97, i. 109) quotes the action of the Mennonites and some Quakers in the American War.

7 For the conception of immortality apart from the resurrection of the body in Hellenistic Judaism, see Wis $3^{1\text{-}4}$ $4^{8\text{-}10}$, 4 Mac $9^{8\text{ff.}}$ etc. Hippolytus (*Hær.* ix. 22) erroneously attributes to the Essenes the Pharisaic doctrine of the body's resurrection.

that good souls dwell beyond the Ocean, in a land unvexed by rain or snow or oppressive heat (καύμασι), but refreshed by the gentle breath of the West wind blowing steadily from the Ocean; to bad souls they allot a gloomy, stormy den, full of punishments unending. The Greeks, in my judgment, hold the same view, when they assign the Isles of the Blest [1] to their braves, whom they call heroes and demi-gods, and consign the souls of the wicked to the abode of the impious in Hades, where people like Sisyphus, Tantalus, Ixion, and Tityus are being punished, according to their mythology; the idea is, in the first place, that souls are eternal,[2] and, in the second place, that people may be dissuaded from vice and prompted to virtue. For the good are supposed to behave better if they can hope for reward even after death, while the impulses of the vicious are checked by the dread anticipation of suffering everlasting punishment after their decease, even if they escape notice in the present life. Such is the Essenes' theology of the soul, and it exercises an irresistible fascination over those who have once tasted their philosophy (τοῖς ἅπαξ γευσαμένοις τῆς σοφίας αὐτῶν) of life.

§ 12. Some of them also undertake to predict the future, by perusing sacred books, by performing various acts of purification (ἁγνείαις), and by digesting prophetic oracles. Rarely, if ever, are their forecasts wrong (cf. *ERE* iv. 806 f.).[3]

§ 13. There is also another order of Essenes, who share the life, habits, and customs of the others, but take a different view of marriage. They argue that celibates excise the main function of life,[4] which is to perpetuate the race, and that, if everybody declined to marry, the race would soon cease to exist [reading, with Destinon, μέλλειν for μᾶλλον]. They take wives: only, they put them on probation [5] for three years, and marry them when, by menstruating three times, they have attested their power to conceive. These Essenes have no intercourse with their wives during pregnancy, showing that they marry for the sake of offspring and not for pleasure. In the bath the women wear gowns, and the men drawers. Such are the customs of this order.'

In *Ant.* XVIII. i. 5 also Josephus gives a brief outline of the doctrine of the Essenes, which has only three distinctive items: (1) the remark that, in sending their ἀναθήματα to the temple at Jerusalem, they do not offer the usual sacrifices, since, in their opinion, they have superior lustrations (διαφορότητι ἁγνειῶν), and that this refusal excludes them from the common court (τοῦ κοινοῦ τεμενίσματος) of the Temple, as ceremonially defiled persons;[6] (2) the description of their relieving officers as 'good priests';[7] and (3) the comparison of them to 'the Dacæ who are called Polistæ' (Πολίσται, cf. Strabo, vii. 33).

(*b*) The Christian references are all later, and, for the most part, of little independent value. Epiphanius (*Hær.* xix. 1–2, xx. 3, xxx. 3, etc.), who appears to name them 'Ossenes,' describes what he calls a surviving remnant of them in the Sampsæans, or sun-worshippers, a sect among the infusoria of Eastern Christianity, who occupied the shores of the Dead Sea and honoured the book of Elkesai. Hippolytus preserves one or two more credible items of information (*Hær.* ix. 14–23), particularly the fact (which is, on other grounds, probable) that some Essenes identified themselves with the active methods of the Zealots and the Sicarii. But both Hippolytus and Porphyry (*de Abstin.* iv. 11–13) go back, in the main, to the former account of Josephus.

(*c*) A solitary notice occurs in Latin literature, which is interesting rather than important. Pliny (*HN* v. 17), after describing the Dead Sea, continues:

'On the West side the Essenes avoid the baleful shoreline. They are a race by themselves, more remarkable than any other in the wide world; they have no women, they abjure sexual love, they have no money, and they live among palm-trees. Still their membership (*turba convenarum*) is steadily recruited from the large number of people who resort to their mode of existence because they are wearied of life's struggle with the waves of adversity. In this way the race has lasted (strange to say) for thousands of ages, though no one is born within it; so fruitful for them is the dissatisfaction with life (*vitæ pœnitentia*) [1] which others feel. Below them lay the town of Engedi, once second only to Jerusalem in fertility and palm-groves, now simply a second sepulchre. Then comes the rock-fort of Masada, which also is not far from the Dead Sea.'

2. Characteristics.—The above sources, upon the whole, confirm and supplement one another. Repeated attempts have been made to discredit one or both of the Philonic passages (*e.g.* by Ausfeld, Ohle, and Hilgenfeld), but their authenticity may be considered to be established (cf. Treplin's special essay in *SK*, 1900, pp. 28–91, and the argument of Plooij, in *Theol. Studiën*, 1905, p. 205 f.).[2] When De Quincey first read the narrative of Josephus, he leant back in his chair and denounced the tale as 'a lie, a fraudulent lie, a malicious lie' (*Works*, vi. 275). Others before him and after him, with better reason, have suspected the Essenic paragraphs of the Jewish historian (notably Ohle, in *JPTh*, 1888, pp. 221 f., 336 f.), but their suspicions have failed to make any serious impression. The sources may be accepted as coming from Philo and Josephus. It is another question, however, whether they are trustworthy in every detail. Eusebius may colour his quotation from Philo, but Philo's predilections probably have led him to arrange the figure of the Essenes for his picture in the *Quod omnis probus liber*, just as Josephus is likely to have read into the beliefs and customs of the order slightly more than was actually present. Thus it is noticeable that Philo, for example, omits any reference to the presence of Essenes in the cities of Palestine; his aim is to bring out their semi-monastic existence. The ordinary impression of the Essenes is, indeed, that they were a community of celibate recluses; Newman's lines,

'Now truant in untimely rest,
The mood of an Essene' (*Lyra Apostolica*, clxix.),

indicate the popular estimate of these Jewish monks. But, while the sources corroborate this general verdict, they also attest, as we have already seen, the existence and activity of certain Essenes outside the pale of the strict settlements. Josephus, who assigns their rise to the 2nd cent. B.C. (*Ant.* XIII. v. 8–9),[3] tells an anecdote which proves incidentally that in the beginning of the next century there were Essenes who did not eschew city-life and did not reside permanently in retired, monastic communities. It is a twice-told tale (*BJ* I. iii. 5=*Ant.* XIII. xi. 2) of how the murder of Antigonus was foretold by Judas the Essene,

'who had never made a mistake or been deceived hitherto in his predictions. He saw Antigonus passing through the temple (διὰ τοῦ ἱεροῦ) and called out to his friends, a number of whom were sitting beside him to receive instruction (μανθανόντων): "Ah! I had better die now, since truth has died before me, and a prediction of mine has proved false. Here is Antigonus alive when he should have been dead to-day; he was fated to be killed at Straton's tower, six hundred furlongs from this. It is now the fourth hour of the day, so the time has played havoc with my prophecy." These were the words of the old man; his spirits were down-cast and remained so. Shortly afterwards, however, word came that Antigonus had perished in a subterranean place, which, like Cæsarea on the coast, was called Straton's tower. It was this identity of names which disconcerted the seer.'

In Jerusalem,[4] therefore, as well as in the other townships of Palestine, Essenes were to be found, no doubt preserving their close brotherhood, but still not wholly detached from the interests of the larger world. Another Essene, called Menahem, exercised his prophetic gifts in a more auspicious fashion, by saluting a schoolboy as king of the

[1] Cf. *ERE* ii. 696 f.

[2] The pre-existence of souls is taught in Wis $8^{19f.}$, Slav. En. $23^{4f.}$ etc.; but cf. F. C. Porter in *AJTh* xii. 53–115.

[3] Josephus himself records several cases; *e.g.* Simon's Joseph-like interpretation of the dream of Archelaus (*BJ* II. vii. 3), Menahem's prediction to Herod (*Ant.* XV. x. 5), and the forecast of Judas (see next col.).

[4] The school of Shammai quoted Is 45^{18} to prove that 'the world was created only that men might be fruitful and multiply' (*Ḥagig.* 2*b*).

[5] Experimental cohabitation (cf. *ERE* iii. 32, 815^{a}).

[6] At an earlier period (cf. *BJ* I. iii. 5) the regulation was not quite so strict.

[7] When a comma is put after ἀγαθούς, however, the following ἱερεῖς τε may refer to the function of preparing their meals (διὰ ποίησιν σίτου τε καὶ βρωμάτων)—another reminiscence of the caste-system.

[1] Cf. *ERE* iii. 778^{a}.

[2] With Wendland's special essay on the authenticity of the *Quod omnis probus liber*, in *AGPh* i. [1888] 509 f., *ib.* [1892] 225 f.

[3] Pliny's 'per millia saeculorum' is, of course, an exaggeration.

[4] There was a Gate of the Essenes (*BJ* v. iv. 2).

Jews, and predicting his royal career. When the schoolboy succeeded to the throne as Herod the Great, he remembered Menahem, and for his sake honoured the order of the Essenes (*Ant.* XV. x. 5). Later on, some Essenes helped to make history as well as to foretell its course. The Jewish war saw at least one Essene heading the rebels, and others in the ardent ranks of the Sicarii and the Zealots. Still, the independent action of individuals must have been restrained by the *disciplina arcani* and the close socialistic union which bound an Essene for life to his fellows. Banus, the anchorite with whom Josephus spent three years, lived in the vicinity of the Essenes, but the Essenes were not lonely anchorites. Even in the cities they hung together. A closely knit system of mutual support prevented them from becoming exposed to the temptations of trade, on the one hand, and of a solitary recluse existence, on the other.

The probability is, therefore, that the Essenes were a set of small, communistic, religious groups on the shores of the Dead Sea. While their nucleus was decidedly monastic in character, both beyond and even within their membership there were grades—not simply novices and initiates, priests and lay brothers, but even some who practised marriage in a fashion, and others who dwelt abroad, in cities where the agricultural life was impossible. It is evident that some Essenes were in the habit of travelling within certain limits, and we can only conjecture the object of their journeys; as it could hardly be trade, it probably was connected with the business of the order—possibly with the promulgation of their tenets and propaganda in a mild way, in order to recruit their ranks. It is chronologically impossible and psychologically unnecessary to assume that Essenism passed from a looser to a closer bond, or *vice versa*. Both phases existed simultaneously, and their relative importance depended upon the special conditions of the age. We cannot speak either of a gradual withdrawal from society or of a gradual expansion of interest, on the part of some Essenes, in the world beyond their farms and settlements.

A perusal of the sources will give a more vivid idea of the general characteristics of the Essenes than any summary. Through the windows of Philo and Josephus and Pliny—for they are not too much coloured to be fairly transparent—we can look down upon this little Jewish order of over 4000 souls, a league of virtue, with their agricultural settlements, their quaint, semi-ascetic practices, their strict novitiate, their silent meals, their white robes, their baths, their prayers, their simple but stringent socialism, their sacerdotal puritanism, their soothsaying, their passion for the mystical world of angels, their indifference to Messianic and nationalistic hopes, their esoteric beliefs, and their approximation to sacramental religion. If the modern student only knew their genesis and exodus as well as he does their numbers, he would be satisfied; but they appear and disappear in a mist, leaving barely a clue to their existence. None of their sacred books has survived[1]—that is, if these included, as they probably did, more than the books of Moses. We do not even know whether they were written in Greek or Aramaic. By the time that the Rabbinic and the Christian literature arose, the literature, and almost the very name,[2] of the Essenes had vanished from the Eastern world. It is thus impossible to approach them with any clearness through the Christian tradition. De Quincey, indeed, once wrote an essay to prove that the Essenes were Christians organized in a secret society for the purpose of self-preservation; but his essay belongs to English literature, not to historical criticism. At one time ingenious attempts were made to trace the affinities of the Essenes with the early Christians, and to discover the influence of the former in the ascetic tendencies, the incipient communism, the eschewing of oaths, and the common meals of the primitive Churches. But the day for such labours of criticism is over; it is no longer necessary to prove that Jesus was not an Essene, and that early Christianity was not Essenic. Even in the errors combated in the Epistle to the Colossians it is hardly possible (cf. Hort, *Judaistic Christianity*, 1894, p. 128) to detect any specifically Essenic features. It is only through later and inferior traditions that we can surmise the existence of Essenic survivors among the medley of the sects who swarmed within the pale of Eastern Christianity after the fall of Jerusalem.[1] They become less obscure as they are approached not from the Rabbinical literature so much as from their sources in contemporary Judaism.

1 Unless apocalyptic collections like Enoch and the Sibylline Oracles contain fragments of them.

2 Hegesippus mentioned them (Eus. *HE* iv. 22. 7) along with Galilæans, Hemerobaptists, etc., among the pre-Christian γνῶμαι διάφοροι of Judaism. The so-called 'Essenic' traits in his description of James, the Lord's brother, are not specifically Essenic.

The Essenes have been called 'the great enigma of Hebrew history,' and the enigma begins with their very name. It is not derived from the founder, or from the locality, of the order. The choice lies open between 'the holy ones' (ὅσιοι [so Philo fancifully]), 'the silent ones' (חשאים), 'the pious ones' (Syr. *ḥasyā*), and 'the healers' (אסיא = 'physician'). The second, advocated by Lightfoot, C. Taylor (*Sayings of the Jewish Fathers*[2], 1897, p. 79), and E. Mittwoch (in *ZA* xvii. [1903] 75 f.), is more probable than the first, just as the third (favoured, *e.g.*, by Lucius, Ermoni, and Schürer) is more likely than the fourth (Baur, Derenbourg, Keim, etc.), which would single out an isolated trait as distinctive of the order. In any case they were a τάγμα of Judaism. Even their loose relation to the Temple-cultus does not invalidate this primary fact. But, if they are an enigma of Hebrew history, they are an insoluble enigma, unless we look beyond the confines of Judaism. The Jewish traits of the Essenes, especially their rigorous care for purity, their reverence for the Mosaic law, and their strict sabbatarianism, certainly ally them with the Pharisees rather than with the Sadducees. Their passion for an ascetic, simple life, in contrast to the dangerous comforts of Greek civilization in the cities, might seem to stamp them as descendants or revivers of a movement like that of the Rechabites (cf. *ERE* ii. 63[b], 66[a]); but against this we must set their avoidance of marriage, their tolerance of wine and agriculture, and their unnomadic attitude to fixed dwellings. Essenism was not hereditary. It was a γένος, in the sense of a gild or corporation, not in the sense of the older Rechabite clan. Its ranks were recruited from without, like a monastic brotherhood, and its ascetic practices were different from those of the Rechabites. Although parallels with many separate details of Essenic belief and praxis can be found in Rabbinic literature,[2] the synthesis of these on Jewish soil is a phenomenon by itself, and—in spite of the efforts made by Jewish and Christian (*e.g.* Ritschl and Lucius) scholars—it contains elements which point to a Palestinian syncretism enriched from some foreign and possibly Oriental sources.

The Essenes, as Josephus admits, were ἑτερόδοξοι within Judaism; they took their own way of life and worship. They were more than ultra-Phari-

1 Cf. Hilgenfeld, *Ketzergesch. des Urchristenthums*, Leipzig, 1884, p. 87 f.; and Lightfoot, *Galatians*[6], 1880, p. 322 f.

2 Cf. Lehmann, 'Les Sectes juives mentionnées dans la Mischna' (*REJ*, 1895, pp. 187–203), and M. Simon in *Jewish Rev.*, 1912, p. 527 f.

saic, or Hasidæan (Kohler, Weinstein, etc.), for the latter were not organized in separate communities (*ERE* ii. 98[a]). Their election of their own priests, their avoidance of marriage, their turning to the sun, their practice of adopting children, and the distrust of matter which appears in their dualistic anthropology ('To be set free from matter was the grand problem of Essenism' [Keim]), are among the plainest indications that we have to do with influences which were originally non-Jewish. It was only natural that the remark of Josephus (*Ant.* XV. x. 4) about the Essenes practising the same customs of life as the Pythagoreans should be developed by those who, like Zeller especially (cf. *ZWT*, 1899, p. 195 f., 'Zur Vorgeschichte des Christenthums: Essener und Orphiker'), fix attention upon their invocation of the sun, their prohibition of oaths, their doctrine of the soul, their communism, their aversion to animal sacrifices, and similar features, which recall Pythagorean and Orphic traits. But some of these were not distinctively Pythagorean, and the Essenes lacked other features (*e.g.* vegetarianism, and a belief in the journey of the soul after death) which were characteristic of the Pythagorean and Orphic faith. The origin of Essenism cannot be wholly derived from the infiltration of the Pythagorean and Orphic spirit, much less from Zoroastrianism (Lightfoot, Cheyne; cf. *ERE* ii. 110 f.), for asceticism at any rate does not belong to the *Vendīdād*, and none of the alleged parallels is particularly striking by itself (cf. Moulton, in *HDB* iv. 992). Hellenistic influence may be sought in other directions (cf. Herzfeld, Friedländer, Pfleiderer, Hoennicke, Conybeare); for, although Philo and Josephus presented practical and speculative Essenism in semi-Hellenistic colours, they were probably doing no more than deepen features of an Egyptian Hellenism which was already present in the order. At the same time, it is not improbable that some weight should be assigned also to the conjecture (which Hilgenfeld eventually abandoned, but which is being revived at the present day in several quarters) that Buddhistic tendencies helped to shape some of the Essenic characteristics as well as some of those in 2nd cent. Gnosticism. The discussion of this hypothesis, however, must be reserved for art. THERAPEUTÆ.

LITERATURE.—In addition to what has been cited already in the course of this article, the following may be noted as including most of the more recent or important studies: Z. Frankel, 'Die Essäer nach talmud. Quellen,' in *MGWJ* ii. 1853] 30 ff., 61 ff.; A. Ritschl, *Entstehung der altkathol. Kirche*², Bonn, 1857, p. 179 f.; L. Herzfeld, *GVI*, Nordhausen, 1847–57, ii. 368 ff., 388 ff., 509 ff.; H. Grätz, *Gesch. der Juden*⁴, iii. (Leipzig, 1888) 91 f., 697 f.; G. H. A. v. Ewald, *Hist. of Israel*, Eng. tr., London, 1878–86, v. 370 f.; F. C. Baur, *Church Hist. of the First Three Centuries*³, Eng. tr., London, 1878–79, i. 20 f.; T. Keim, *Gesch. Jesu*³, Zürich, 1873, i. 282 f. (Eng. tr.², London, 1876, i. 358 f.); J. Derenbourg, *Hist. de la Palestine*, Paris, 1867, pp. 166 ff., 460 f.; R. Tideman, *Het Essenisme*, Leyden, 1868; A. Hausrath, *Neutest. Zeitgesch.*², Munich, 1873–77, i. 132 ff. (Eng. tr., London, 1878–80, i. 164 f.); Lauer, *Die Essäer u. ihre Verhältnisse zur Synagoge und Kirche*, Vienna, 1869; C. Clemens, *ZWT* xii. [1869] 328 ff. [on sources], xiv. [1871] 418 f.; J. B. Lightfoot, *Colossians*², London, 1876, p. 347 ff.; P. E. Lucius, *Der Essenismus in seinem Verhältniss zum Judenthum*, Strassburg, 1881; A. Hilgenfeld, *Judenthum und Judenchristenthum*, Leipzig, 1886, p. 20 f.; R. Ausfeld, Essay on *Quod omnis probus liber*, in *Dissert. philos.*, Göttingen, 1887; R. Ohle, in *JPTh* xiii. [1887] 298 f., 376 f., and xiv. [1888] 221 f., 366 f.; P. Wendland, *JPTh* xiv. 100 f.; N. I. Weinstein, *Beiträge zur Geschichte der Essäer*, Vienna, 1892; M. Friedländer, *Zur Entstehungsgeschichte des Christenthums*, Vienna, 1894, p. 98 ff.; A. Réville, *Jésus de Nazareth*, Paris, 1897, i. 135 f.; J. Wellhausen, *Isr. u. jüd. Geschichte*⁵, Berlin, 1901, p. 309 f.; E. L. Stapfer, *RThPh*, 1902, p. 385 f.; P. Chapuis, 'L'Influence de l'essénisme sur les origines chrétiennes,' *RThPh*, 1903, pp. 193–228; D. Plooij, 'De Essenen,' in *Theol. Studiën*, 1905, pp. 205 f., 313 f., and 1907, p. 1 f.; M. Friedländer, *Die relig. Bewegungen innerhalb des Judenthums im Zeitalter Jesu*, Berlin, 1905, pp. 114–168; D. W. Bousset, *Rel. des Judentums*², Berlin, 1906, p. 524 f.; V. Ermoni, 'L'Essénisme,' *Revue des questions historiques*, 1906, pp. 5–27; E. Schürer, *GJV*⁴ ii. (1907) 651; O. Pfleiderer, *Primitive Christianity*, Eng. tr. 1906 ff., vol. iii. pp. 1–22; G. Hoennicke, *Das Judenchristentum*, Berlin, 1908, pp. 40 f., 78 f. The chief dictionary articles are by Dähne, in Ersch-Gruber's *Allgem. Enzykl.* xxxviii. [1843] 173 f.; Ginsburg, in *DCB* ii. [1880] 198 f.; Westcott, in Smith's *DB* i. 996 f.; Lipsius, in Schenkel, ii. 181–192; Uhlhorn, in *PRE*³ v. [1898] 524 f.; Conybeare, in *HDB* i. [1898] 767 f.; Jülicher, in *EBi* ii. [1901] 1396 f.; K. Kohler, in *JE* v. 224–232; E. P. Graham, in *Cath. Encycl.* v. 546–547; and P. Fiebig, in *Rel. in Gesch. u. Gegenwart*, ii. 646 f.

JAMES MOFFATT.

ETERNITY.—I. Meaning of the conception.—There are three main senses in which 'eternity' may be understood: (1) as an unending extent of time; (2) as that which is entirely timeless; (3) as that which includes time, but somehow also transcends it.

The first of these is the popular meaning of the term. In ordinary discourse, when people speak of passing from time to eternity, they appear, in general, to imply nothing more than the transition from a state in which special objects of interest (such as human personalities) have only a limited duration to a state in which they may be supposed to persist for ever. This sense of the term is also to be found sometimes in philosophical writings. The eternal process, for instance, which Kant conceives to be necessary for the realization of the moral ideal is primarily to be thought of as a process that is to be carried on without end.

It is generally recognized in philosophy that such a conception has no positive significance. Kant, for instance, acknowledges that his way of thinking of the realization of the moral ideal contains no real solution of the difficulties involved in the conception of that realization; and he accordingly supplements it by the idea of a Divine point of view, from which the unending process appears as a timeless attainment of the end to which it points. But he does not show how this idea is to be reconciled with the conception of an endless process. On the whole, however, it may be fairly stated that the conception of eternity which has prevailed throughout the history of philosophy is not that of an unending process, but that of a state of existence which is completely independent of temporal conditions. Such a conception is that to which the mind is most naturally driven as soon as the difficulties involved in the idea of an unending process have been fully brought home to it; and it is a conception that is strongly supported by the apparent timelessness of those 'laws' and other general statements with which science and philosophy are largely concerned. The fact (or apparent fact) that there is such a thing as timeless truth leads very naturally to the view that there may also be such a thing as timeless existence. It soon appears, however, that all the existences known to us in our ordinary experience are subject to temporal conditions; and a little reflexion is enough to convince most people that no timeless existence is even conceivable under the ordinary conditions of our conscious experience. Hence the conception of timeless existence leads inevitably to some such distinction as that of Kant between phenomena and noumena, appearance and reality, the sensible and the intelligible world, or however else the antithesis may be expressed. But the history of philosophy shows quite conclusively that, if any such antithesis is pressed, it becomes impossible to understand any connexion between the two modes of being that are thus opposed; so that, in the end, the opposition comes to be one not simply between the intelligible and the sensible, but between the intelligible and the unintelligible, or rather between two terms which are in truth both alike unintelligible.

If we are to avoid such a result as this, it seems necessary to interpret 'eternity' in the third of the three senses to which we have referred, *i.e.* to regard it not as the mere negation of time conditions, but as containing those conditions within itself, though in a form in which their limitations are transcended. It will be our object in this article to indicate briefly how such a conception of eternity is possible. But we must first give a glance at some of the chief difficulties that have been brought out, in connexion with this problem, in the course of the development of philosophy.

2. Difficulties connected with the conception, and attempts to solve them.—Kant is undoubtedly the writer who did more than any other to make the difficulties in connexion with the ideas of time and eternity prominent and clear; and it is accordingly to his views that we intend chiefly to refer. But the significance of his work cannot be properly understood without reference to at least a few of his precursors, among whom Parmenides, Plato, and Spinoza seem specially important in connexion with this particular problem. Valuable contributions have been made to the subject by some of the recent followers of Hegel, among whom T. H. Green, F. H. Bradley, Josiah Royce, and J. M. E. McTaggart are perhaps especially deserving of attention. From a different point of view, the work of Henri Bergson contains valuable suggestions. After noticing what has been done by these writers, it will be possible to sum up the conclusions to which the discussion of the subject seems to point.

Of **Parmenides** it is not necessary to say much. He is important only as showing how the difficulties of the problem present themselves at the beginnings of speculative inquiry. Unfortunately, there is still the possibility of considerable difference of view with regard to the exact meaning of his most important utterances; but there cannot be much disagreement as to the general nature of his influence on the development of philosophic thought. It seems clear, at least, that he affirmed the eternal and unchangeable reality of being, as it is conceived by pure thought (or reached by the 'Way of Truth'), as against the uncertain and fluctuating appearance of that which is the subject-matter of opinion. **Zeno** appears to have further emphasized this aspect of the teaching of Parmenides, by urging the self-contradictions into which we fall when we try to think definitely of change as a motion from point to point in space, taking place from moment to moment in time. **Melissus**, the other chief follower of Parmenides, would seem to have brought out still more explicitly the eternity of that which really exists, turning the poetry of Parmenides into plain prose, but perhaps, in so doing, approaching somewhat more nearly to the conception of eternity as an endless duration, rather than as that which is in its essence timeless. There is no evidence, however, that any of these members of the Eleatic school made any real attempt to explain the apparent changes in the world of our ordinary experience, on the supposition that ultimate reality is unalterable and free from time conditions. Like most of the early Greek thinkers, they were content to set the real in opposition to the apparent, the object of clear thought in opposition to the deceptiveness of the senses, without reflecting that even what only appears to us must have some kind of reality, or at least without adequately recognizing that it was any part of their problem to explain the precise relation between the absolutely real and this specious appearance.

It was **Plato**, as we believe, who first definitely recognized that some account has to be given of appearance as well as of the ultimately real. His conception of the ultimately real, like that of Parmenides (by whom he was undoubtedly very greatly influenced), is the conception of that which exists eternally. More definitely than in the case of Parmenides, this conception is based primarily upon the eternity of universal truths, such as those of geometry or ethics. But what is specially noticeable here is the attempt that is made by Plato to give a place in his system to the changing as well as the eternal. He does this by the recognition of a certain reality in becoming as well as being—in short, by the recognition of the relative truth of the view of the universe set forth by Heraclitus, as well as that set forth by Parmenides. It can hardly be maintained, however, that Plato is really successful in making clear the relation between these two sides of his philosophy. There is too much force in the complaint of Aristotle that it is only by a sort of poetic metaphor—the metaphor of the world-architect and his imperfect material—that Plato is able to give any kind of plausibility to the view that he wishes to convey. It would seem that he thought that the world of appearance had too little reality to be really grasped and explained by thought. 'Alles Vergängliche ist nur ein Gleichnis'; it is, after all, only a shadow of the eternal reality; and it is in accordance with this conception that Plato characterizes time itself as 'the moving image of eternity.' Why there should be such an image at all, and why it should move, seems in the end to be quite unexplained. If, in accordance with the magnificent imagery of Shelley,

> 'Life, like a dome of many-coloured glass,
> Stains the white radiance of Eternity' (*Adonais*, stanza 52),

it is hard to see why the brightness of eternity should submit to such defilement.

In the philosophy that followed Plato, and especially in the Neo-Platonic school, there are perhaps some hints of a possible solution. But we pass over these, as being hardly sufficiently definite for our present purpose. Nor does there appear to be in the writings of **Aristotle** and his commentators anything sufficiently illuminating on this subject to deserve special attention. Among more modern writers, it is chiefly with **Spinoza** that the conception of eternity gains once more a position of preeminent importance. Spinoza's point of view, indeed, bears a very obvious resemblance to that of Parmenides, at least as modified by Plato, of whose general theory of knowledge that of Spinoza is a fairly direct adaptation. Nor can it well be maintained that Spinoza is much more successful than Parmenides and Plato in escaping from the difficulties that are involved in this position. He thinks of eternity as meaning the essential and permanent nature of reality, as distinguished from its varying modes. All real existences, to be truly known, must be viewed *sub specie quadam æternitatis*. It is the deceptiveness of the imagination, as contrasted with the clear light of thought, that tends to separate off the special modes from their intrinsic place within the infinite whole. But it is in this apparent separation that the chief difficulty in Spinoza's system lies. The deceptiveness of imagination in the theory of Spinoza seems to require explanation quite as much as the vagaries of opinion in that of Parmenides. We may, no doubt, find hints in Spinoza's writings of some possible explanation of this—some suggestion of the view that the eternal reality has to express its completeness through changing modes; and that a certain deceptiveness must, from the nature of the case, appear in these changing modes. But there is certainly nothing more than a hint of this; and it is fairly clear that the development of any such suggestion would transform the whole nature of the Spinozistic system.

To a certain extent it may be said that **Kant** is to Spinoza what Zeno was to Parmenides. The positive idea of eternal reality underlying the system of Kant—so far as it can be held that there is any such positive idea at all—is in its essence Spinozistic. It is the idea of a reality undetermined by any of the limitations of our ordinary experience, and hence, in particular, undetermined by any conditions of time. But the strength of Kant, like that of Zeno, lies not in the unfolding of any positive conception of such reality,—which, indeed, he believes to be quite impossible,—but in the thoroughness with which he brings out the difficulties involved in the thought of any kind of reality that is subject to change in time. In order to realize the significance of his work, it is necessary to notice exactly the essential points in his contention, though they must be stated here with the utmost possible brevity. In stating these points, the present writer will express them in his own language, though endeavouring to include nothing that is not really contained in Kant's argument.

The first point that seems essential in Kant's argument is the contention that Time is simply the form of change, not anything that can be regarded as in itself substantial. Kant has a somewhat peculiar way of expressing this, which it is not necessary for us to consider here. He calls Time the form of the inner sense, and urges that it is of the nature of perception rather than of conception. All this is extremely questionable, and does not seem to affect the central part of his argument. The essential thing is that Time is to be regarded as a certain order—an order which may be most simply characterized as being of such a kind that its antecedent parts pass out of being as the succeeding parts come into being.

The next important point is that such an order as this cannot be regarded as ultimately real. Here, again, Kant's argument is somewhat complicated by modes of statement that are open to question. What is essential seems to be the contention that the order involved in time presupposes either a first member in the series of events or an unending extent in the antecedent members of that series. Neither of these suppositions, it is urged, is really conceivable. A first member in the series of events would have nothing before it to determine its place, and consequently would not really have a place in the time-order at all. It could only be thought of as being preceded by empty time, which is nothing at all. On the other hand, a series of events that never began would simply be a series that never existed at all. It may be possible to think of a series as going on without end, but not as having gone on without beginning, since this implies that an endless series has been completed.

The only escape from these difficulties, Kant contends, is to be found in the recognition that the time-series is unreal. It is only a mode of our imperfect experience, and must not be ascribed as a condition to the ultimate reality that underlies our phenomenal world. Hence, as we have already noted, if immortality is found to be a postulate of the moral consciousness, this can only be interpreted as pointing to some kind of eternity of existence which is independent of time conditions. Such an existence is, however, for us completely incomprehensible.

It is with this ultimate incomprehensibility that the Kantian view of eternity ends. Now, in the opinion of the present writer, the **Hegelian philosophy** contains the suggestion of a possible solution of the difficulties that are here raised. The general nature of that solution is to be found in the conception of a real process in ultimate reality—a conception which is entirely subversive of the Parmenidean or Spinozistic theory of an Absolute at rest. If, however, the Absolute contains process, it would seem that this process must be thought of as eternal. There may be a real order in that which is ultimately real, but it can hardly be supposed to be an order of transient occurrences. The view, therefore, as we understand it, to which Hegel's theory points is that the order of time is real, but that its apparent transience is unreal. But Hegel himself did not definitely work out this conception. His own statements seem rather to favour the view that the eternal is to be conceived as timeless; and most of his followers have adopted this interpretation. It may be profitable to notice briefly the views of some of the most recent exponents of this position.

T. H. Green, who connects more immediately with Kant than with Hegel, endeavours to overcome the difficulties involved in a real temporal existence by the conception of an Eternal Being who reproduces Himself in the form of a world in time. Like Plato, he is led to this conception largely by the consideration of the timelessness of universal truths, such as those of geometry. But the idea of a reproduction in time is almost as obviously metaphorical as Plato's image of a world-architect; and, when we try to translate it from poetic imagery into exact science, it is very hard to see what its precise significance would be. How can anything be *re*produced when it has never been produced at all, and when the whole idea of production or reproduction is in contradiction with its timeless nature? Green himself quite frankly admits that the existence of a finite world is inexplicable on his theory; but it appears to be not only inexplicable, but even self-contradictory. Moreover, as the reproduction of the Eternal seems to be thought of by Green as a real process in time, and as connecting with a real time development towards the goal of human perfection, the Kantian difficulty about the possibility of any real beginning of a time-series would appear still to stand in need of solution. It may be doubted whether, with regard to this particular problem, Green has really advanced much further than Parmenides, Plato, and Spinoza.

F. H. Bradley has, on the other hand, certainly advanced the subject a little by the emphasis which he has laid on degrees of truth and reality. This conception is by no means a new one in philosophy. It is perhaps implicit in the Parmenidean distinction between truth and opinion; it is already explicit in Plato's antithesis between being and becoming; it was a good deal emphasized by some of the Schoolmen, and is used both by Descartes and by Hegel. But Bradley has certainly done much to revive it, and has given it a special prominence as the means whereby an Absolute which is essentially timeless may yet be conceived as more or less adequately expressed in a process that appears in time. The value of this conception, however, as thus applied, would depend on the extent to which the elements of reality and unreality in a time-series could be discriminated; and Bradley—who is generally more successful in stating difficulties than in removing them—does not appear to have contributed much to the solution of this particular problem.

One of the most interesting attempts to carry the matter a step further is that which has recently been made by **J. M. E. McTaggart.** Few writers have been more emphatic than he in maintaining that absolute reality must be conceived as timeless. Yet he is also one of those who have been most insistent on the recognition of a certain independence in individual personalities, which have to be thought of as, in some sense, differentiations of the Absolute, and as persisting, in different phases of their development, throughout the whole extent of time. This apparent combination of absolute reality and absolute unreality in the time-process has long been a stumbling-block to the readers of McTaggart's extremely attractive writings; but an explanation has recently been offered by him in two papers in *Mind*—'The Unreality of Time' (Oct. 1908) and 'The Relation of Time and Eternity' (July 1909). The essential points in his contention can be very briefly stated. The process of development in time, he urges, is to be regarded as leading up to an end that is timeless; in such fashion that each subsequent stage in the development is nearer to the nature of eternity than the antecedent stage; and so that, in fact, it is this progressive realization of the timeless reality that determines the position of each point in the time-series. Thus, the intelligence which is developing through a process in time does eventually become completely timeless in its nature; so that, in a sense, the eternal has a place at the end of the time-series.

In some respects we believe that the elements of a true solution are contained in the theory of McTaggart. Its chief defect lies in the fact that a process in time is still thought of as leading up to a result which—so far at least as this particular aspect of its being is concerned—is simply the negation of time altogether. There seems to be a contradiction in ascribing so much importance to a time-process, and yet excluding this process from the nature of ultimate reality. This defect could, however, be readily removed by recognizing frankly that the time-process is to be taken as an essential aspect of the eternal reality, which is not negated in the being of the eternal, though, in a sense, it is transcended. In short, while McTaggart maintains that eternity is in a certain sense in time, the present writer would seek to hold rather that time is in a certain sense in eternity. What we mean by this will, we hope, become more apparent in the sequel.

There are some other attempts to deal with this problem that have very considerable importance, especially the brilliant investigation of the general meaning of 'Infinity' contained in **Josiah Royce's** work on *The World and the Individual*, and since reproduced to some extent, though in a somewhat popular way, in the work of R. B. Haldane, and, with considerable modifications, in that of A. E. Taylor. Royce's main contention is that the world in time, regarded as a whole, is eternal; though, from the point of view of its parts, it is a series that can never be completed. This view is extremely helpful; but the antithesis between the whole and its parts presents difficulties that do not appear to be satisfactorily removed. It would be impossible, however, to discuss these difficulties without an examination of Royce's doctrine of infinity, of which his doctrine of eternity is a special application.[1] Hence it seems best to reserve what has to be said about this conception for the art. INFINITY.

The philosophy of **Henri Bergson** does not at first appear to throw any fresh light on the conception of eternity. It is a philosophy of change, and is apt to seem like a reaffirmation of the Heraclitean flux, against the eternal Being of Parmenides. But the conception of 'real duration' that is emphasized by Bergson involves the view that there is no actual transience in the time-process. The present, according to him, contains the past and anticipates the future. This certainly comes very near to the doctrine that time is eternal; but, if this implication were brought out, his philosophy would cease to be a philosophy of change. It would then have to be recognized that the whole within which change takes place does not itself change. A view of this kind, however, does not seem to be directly maintained by Bergson; and the consideration of his general theory of time is beyond the scope of this article.

3. A possible solution of the problem.—It may be well to state at the outset that the present writer fully accepts the presentation of the difficulties set forth by Kant, at least in the form in which they have already been summarized above. But he would urge at once that one of the difficulties is by no means so great as Kant makes it appear. A real beginning of a time-series is not strictly inconceivable. Such a beginning, no doubt, would not itself be in time: it would, in truth, be the beginning *of* time. But this is no real objection to it. As soon as we clearly recognize that time is simply the form of succession in a developing process, it becomes apparent that, if that process has a real beginning and a real end, time itself must have a real beginning and a real end. There is no time outside of the process. Hence the process as a whole might be said to be eternal, though every particular part in it has a place in time. The eternal, thus conceived, would not be the timeless, but rather that which includes the whole of time. Time would not be, as with Plato, 'the moving image of eternity,' but eternity itself.

Another way of putting this is to say that the order of time is real, but not its apparent transience. Order that does not involve transience is, of course, sufficiently familiar. The colours of the spectrum are arranged in a certain order, but the appearance of one does not involve the disappearance of the others. A locomotive engine usually goes before or after the carriages to which it is attached; but they all exist simultaneously and in the same sense. But there is one kind of order that appears inevitably to involve transience, viz. that in which what goes before is identical with what comes after. Two different states of the same identical object cannot exist simultaneously. The father and the child may exist together; but the child who is father of the man does not exist at the same time as the man of whom he is the father. Now, the world of our experience may be said to maintain its identity throughout the whole of time; but it is continually changing its states. Hence its successive stages are not merely in a certain order, but the order is such that the successive stages do not exist together. This would seem to be the general significance of the time-process as we commonly know it. But now we might raise the question, whether this mutual exclusiveness of successive stages in the time-series is a uniform and necessary characteristic of that series. A little reflexion might raise doubts on this point; and perhaps the following illustration may help us to give a more correct answer to the question thus suggested.

Taking the case of the relation between child and man, we may note that, while these different stages in the life of a single personality are mutually exclusive, they are not reciprocally exclusive in a quite equal degree. The child contains the anticipation of the life of the man, but contains it only implicitly: it is for the man that the anticipation is contained, rather than for the child itself. The man, on the other hand, contains in himself the unfolding of the child's potentialities, and is capable of an explicit recognition and appreciation of these potentialities. The child-life has passed away, yet it is still in a real sense present, and is capable of being made present to an almost indefinite extent. The man includes the child in a sense in which the child does not include the man. Now, if it is right to think of the whole universe of our experience as a developing

[1] For some criticisms on Royce's view, reference may be made to J. Ward, *The Realm of Ends*, 1911, and B. Bosanquet, *The Principle of Individuality and Value*, 1912.

system, proceeding from a definite beginning to a definite end, the illustration of child and man may be regarded as furnishing us with more than a mere analogy. Here, also, the beginning and the end are really distinct, and, in a sense, mutually exclusive; though, in another sense, each of them contains or implies the other. But the end contains the beginning in a sense in which the beginning does not contain the end. The present includes the past in a sense in which it does not include the future. The end might be said, as it were, to return upon the beginning like a 'serpent of eternity'; while yet the beginning and the end would, as thus conceived, retain a real distinction. The process from beginning to end would be a process in time, in which each stage (with the exception of the last) excludes the others. But this mutual exclusiveness of the successive parts would become progressively less as the process advances towards its end. And as the beginning and the end would both be real, and yet both, on their outer side, free from time determinations, the whole process would be an eternal one. There would be no time at which the process is not going on. The process, as a whole, when we thus conceive it, is not in time; rather time is in the process. Time is simply the aspect of successiveness which the eternal process contains.

This conception of an eternal process has not hitherto played much part in purely philosophical speculation, but it has long been familiar enough in theology. In the Christian doctrine of the Trinity, the Son is conceived as eternally begotten of the Father, and in the Fourth Gospel we find the declaration: 'Before Abraham was, I am' (Jn 8[58]). And, if philosophy is to escape from those difficulties and self-contradictions which have been brought out in the course of its history, it must, we think, return to something more or less akin to this doctrine of the Trinity. There remain difficulties enough, it must be confessed, in the attempt to realize such a conception of the universe; but we believe, at least, that those fundamental difficulties which are summed up in the antinomies of Kant are completely removed by it. It enables us to think of the world as having a real beginning and end, and yet as being truly infinite; as a progress and a struggle towards a 'far-off Divine event,' and yet as the eternal realization of that for which it strives. But to pursue this further would carry us beyond the limits of our present subject, to the consideration of the being of God and His relation to the world.[1]

LITERATURE.—Almost every systematic treatise on Metaphysics contains, more or less explicitly, some theory of eternity. The following may be mentioned as some of the most important references: J. Burnet, *Early Greek Philosophy*², 1908, chs. iv. and viii.; Plato, *Timæus*, chs. x. and xi.; E. Caird, *Evolution of Theology in the Greek Philosophers*, 1904, esp. Lect. ix.; Augustine, *de Civ. Dei*, xi. 5; Aquinas, *Summa Theol.* i. 10; Spinoza, *Ethics*, esp. pt. i., def. 8, and pt. v.; H. H. Joachim, *A Study of the Ethics of Spinoza*, 1901, esp. bk. i. ch. i., bk. ii. Append., and bk. iii. ch. iv.; Kant, *Critique of Pure Reason*, esp. the statement of the antinomies in the 'Transcendental Dialectic,' also *Crit. of Prac. Reason*, 'Dialectic,' ch. ii. sect. 4; E. Caird, *Critical Philosophy of Kant*, 1889, vol. ii. bk. ii. ch. v.; Hegel, *Encycl.*, esp. 'Natur-Phil.,' I. i. B; Lotze, *Metaph.* 1884, bk. ii. ch. iii.; T. H. Green, *Prolegomena to Ethics*³, 1890, esp. bk. i.; F. H. Bradley, *Appearance and Reality*², 1897, chs. iv. and xviii.; J. Royce, *The World and the Individual*, 2nd series, 1901, esp. Lect. iii.; J. M. E. McTaggart, *Studies in Hegelian Dialectic*, 1896, ch. v., *Studies in Hegelian Cosmology*, 1901, ch. ii., and the articles referred to above; R. B. Haldane, *The Pathway to Reality*, 1903, vol. ii., Lects. ii. and iii.; A. E. Taylor, *Elements of Metaphysics*, 1903, bk. iii. ch. iv.; H. Bergson, *Time and Free Will*, Eng. tr. Lond. 1910, and *Creative Evolution*, do. 1911; H. Münsterberg, *The Eternal Values*, do. 1909.

J. S. MACKENZIE.

[1] The view of eternity set forth in the above article seems to its author to be in its essence Hegelian; but the particular way in which it is conceived is one for which he is alone responsible. The general lines of its treatment have been previously indicated in a paper in *Mind* (July 1904) on 'The Infinite and the Perfect,' and somewhat more fully developed in a subsequent paper on 'The Problem of Time' (July 1912) and in the closing chapter of *Lectures on Humanism*, London, 1907.

ETHICAL DISCIPLINE.

1. History of the term.—'Discipline' is the English form of the Lat. *disciplina*—the abstract noun formed from *discere*, 'to learn,' whence also comes *discipulus*, 'a disciple.' Thus 'discipline' is properly instruction,—that which belongs to the *discipulus* or scholar,—and is antithetical to 'doctrine,'—that which pertains to the doctor or teacher. Hence, in the history of the words, 'doctrine' is more concerned with abstract theory, and 'discipline' with practice or exercise. In this sense Wyclif (1382) renders Pr 3[4] 'Thou shalt find grace and good discipline (1388 'teching'; AV 'understanding') befor God and men'; and Chaucer has, 'Thanne shaltow understonde, that bodily peyne stant in disciplyne or techinge, by word or by wrytinge, or in ensample' (*The Persones Tale*, Skeat's Student's edition, p. 716). But under the influence of the Vulgate and the Church, 'discipline' came also to be used for 'chastisement,' and the term in this more restricted sense is early found in English, and sometimes in the same authors, in parallel use with the term in its classical signification. Thus Wyclif renders Pr 3[11] 'The discipline (AV 'chastening') of the Lord, my sone, ne caste thou away'; and in Chaucer we find 'As it fareth by children in schoole, that for learning arne beaten when their lesson they foryeten, commonly after a good disciplining with a yerde, they kepe right well doctrine of their schoole' (*The Testament of Love*, fol. 306).

2. Theory of the idea.—(1) *Ethical inquiry recognizes the need of discipline in the formation of character, and points to self-discipline as the ideal form.*—The Socratic formula 'Virtue is knowledge' is found to be an inadequate explanation of the moral life of man. Knowledge of what is right is not coincident with doing it, for man, while knowing the right course, is found deliberately choosing the wrong one. Desire tends to run counter to the dictates of the reason; and the will, *i.e.* the whole personality, *qua* selective and active, perplexed by the difficulty of reconciling two such opposite demands, tends to choose the easier course and to follow the inclination rather than to endure the pain of refusing desire in obedience to the voice of reason. Hence mere intellectual instruction is not sufficient to ensure right doing. There arises the further need for 'chastisement,' or the straightening of the crooked will, in order to ensure its co-operation with reason in assenting to what she affirms to be right, and its refusal to give preference to desire or the irrational element in man's nature, when such desire runs counter to the rational principle.

This doctrine is clearly developed by Aristotle in his division of the faculties into rational and irrational:

> 'In the case of the continent and of the incontinent man alike,' he says, 'we praise the reason or the rational part, for it exhorts them rightly, and urges them to do what is best; but there is plainly present in them another principle besides the rational one, which fights and struggles against the reason. For, just as a paralyzed limb, when you will to move it to the right, moves on the contrary to the left, so is it with the soul; the incontinent man's impulses run counter to his reason' (*Nicom. Ethics*, Peters' tr., bk. i. 13 [15. 16]). Again, he speaks of 'the faculty of appetite or of desire in general, which partakes of reason in a manner—that is, in so far as it listens to reason and submits to its sway. . . . Further, all advice and all rebuke and exhortation testifies that the irrational part is in some way amenable to reason' (*ib.* bk. i. 13 [18]).

Moral virtue, for Aristotle, is a habit of choice or purpose, purpose being desire following upon deliberation. A right purpose then involves both true reasoning and right desire. Hence the final end of moral discipline is the reform, and not the suppression, of desire.

'Discipline' we may provisionally define as the systematic training of our faculties, through instruction and through exercise, in accordance with some settled principle of authority. It is with the discipline which is guided by intellectual and moral ideals that we are here more particularly concerned. In the early years of life the principle which guides the moral training takes the form of an external authority which the child obeys, at first altogether blindly, having no understanding of a principle *qua* principle, but seeing only the authority which represents it in the person of parent or teacher, who demands in its name and interest an unquestioning obedience.

'The imposition of commands, by exercising the child in self-restraint and by inducing a habit of obedience, is the great means by which the early training of the will is effected, and the foundation of moral habit and good character established' (see *Cyclopædia of Education*, *s.v.* 'Discipline').

Such discipline may meet with a voluntary submission, the parent or teacher receiving the spontaneous co-operation of the child, or it may, on the contrary, be necessary to enforce an obedience to the parent's commands when such commands meet with resistance. In either case the distinguishing mark which characterizes this external discipline or outward conformity to rule is the absence of all reasoned grasp, on the part of the child or other subject undergoing it, of the principle which inspires its application. That the ideal towards which the discipline is directed should not even be conceived by the child is an obvious limitation, and it is only when regarded as a prelude to a higher type of moral training that such discipline can justify its existence. The educator, who, through fear of the dangers besetting the yet untrodden path of personal liberty, unduly prolongs this early stage, pays the penalty of a dwarfed and enfeebled character in the child he desires to train.

We find a similar tendency in the history of the race illustrated by the systems of Communism and Casuistry (*qq.v.*)—notable attempts to systematize, and thus to render permanent, this stage of external authority. *Communism*, with a view to curtailing the liberty of the individual, relieves him as far as possible of any personal responsibility; and, the responsibility for his maintenance being vested in the State, all functions are performed through him and on his behalf, but none on his own initiative. In *Casuistry* we find 'an attempt to work out a body of authoritative moral precepts in detail, so as to show that every case of conduct, actual or possible, may consistently find its place under one or other of such precepts' (MacCunn, *Making of Character*, 1900, p. 153). The Casuists, as the moral advisers of the people, have been called the jurists of morality, to whom they need never turn in vain for the solution of a moral problem, however complex, since the casuistical teacher with his body of moral rules is always ready to work out their application in detail, and to show how the particular case in question falls under his scheme of life. It is unnecessary for our present purpose to pursue further these two systems of morality. Suffice it to say that they are both open to the objection of attempting to extend the first stage of morality far beyond its natural limits, and, by thus depriving the individual of personal responsibility, they directly thwart the development of the individual judgment.

The necessity for advancing from this early stage of moral training to the higher stage of *self*-discipline is based on nothing less than a fundamental demand of our nature as self-conscious beings.

'In proportion as self-consciousness develops,' says Sigwart, 'it strives for unity of the will, for subordination of all particular aims under one which is higher than all and embraces all, for the determination of every practical question by one supreme law' (*Logic*, Eng. tr., 1895, vol. ii. p. 13).

It is evident that such an ideal can never be realized as long as the moral training of the individual is enforced merely by an external authority to which he renders a more or less voluntary submission. It may be that in course of time he will come to see the reasonableness of certain duties thus imposed upon him, *e.g.* respect for private property; yet, as long as these duties remain isolated and detached from one another, and lack a unifying principle which may find expression in them all, so long will the higher needs of the moral nature remain unsatisfied, and the character stunted and undeveloped. Then the individual must bring these duties under an ideal which he has made his own, and be self-governed by the idea of the law which he thus adopts. It is further to be noted that moral habits are not formed by merely outward actions, and that no habit which can truly be considered moral will grow apart from voluntary effort, desire, and intelligent appreciation of its character, although the action on its physical side be repeated again and again. According to MacCunn,

'even faultless outward conformity to the noblest of social ideals would be a miserable substitute for the freely given admiration, and the spontaneous loyalty, which are at once root and fruit of the moral independence of the individual' (*op. cit.* p. 141).

It is, then, only in the voluntary discipline of the self that we find that true morality which is inspired by an indwelling principle expressing itself in all the details of conduct. Such discipline alone can lead to true self-control, which we may regard as its final end.

'Self-control,' says Stout, 'is control proceeding from the Self as a whole and determining the Self as a whole. The degree in which it exists depends upon the degree in which this or that special tendency can be brought into relation with the concept of the Self and the system of conative tendencies which it includes' (*Manual of Psychology*[2], 1901, p. 626). 'Self-control is greatest in the man whose life is dominated by ideals and general principles of conduct; but this involves a development of conceptual consciousness which is absent in children and savages' (*ib.* p. 628). And we have seen that it also involves a degree of moral discipline which is likewise absent in the earlier life of man and of the race.

(2) *Psychology demands that such discipline shall embrace the whole nature of man, in its threefold aspect of knowing, desiring, and willing.*—Bearing in mind this ideal of moral unity, we return once again to the Aristotelian conception of virtue, which we found to be 'a habit of choice or purpose, purpose being desire following upon deliberation.' This conception of virtue, as an expression of the whole self in its threefold aspect of knowing, desiring, and choosing, implicitly contains the idea of the unity of man's moral life—an idea rendered explicit by modern writers in their insistence that an adequate treatment of the moral life can be attained only by basing ethical theory on a concrete psychology, which shall take into account the whole nature of man.

This idea of moral unity, though implied in the teaching both of Plato and of Aristotle, was not rendered so explicit as to influence the schools of moral philosophy which immediately succeeded these fathers in ethical teaching. On the contrary, we find, in Aristotle as in Plato, the latent conception of moral unity so overshadowed by their insistence on a dualism of the moral life, answering to the rift in human nature between the rational and irrational elements, that their immediate successors can find no better way of unifying the life than by sacrificing the one element to the other. The Cynics, and the Stoics after them, make the Reason supreme, and entirely subordinate the life of feeling. The Cyrenaics and Epicureans, on the contrary, while exalting the sensibility, practically ignore the life of Reason. In both schools we find an unsatisfactory conception of the moral life of man, owing to the abstract, and consequently inadequate, psychology which underlies it. 'Man is not a merely sentient being,' says James Seth, 'nor is he pure reason energising. He is will; and his life is that activity of will in which both reason and sensibility are, as elements, contained, and by whose most subtle action they are inextricably interfused' (*Ethical Principles*[10], 1908, p. 40).

Such a conception of the moral life, based on a

concrete psychology, can alone give rise to a true conception of self-control, which we have found to be the final end of moral discipline. Hence the discipline which has this for its goal must be the discipline of the whole nature of man; and, while each element requires its specific training, the training must in no case be such as to detach the interests of one faculty from those of another.

Ethics, then, recognizes the need for a discipline of man's nature, which shall bring unity where there is schism, and so harmonize the opposing elements of his soul. Such discipline must be a discipline of the self proceeding from the self, for thus alone can it meet the demand of self-consciousness for its own inward unity. Moreover, a concrete psychology, as we have seen, shows the organic complexity of the nature, the ethical demands of which are to be met by moral discipline.

Without losing sight of the fact that knowing, feeling, and willing are inseparably blended in consciousness, we may now proceed briefly to examine the lines on which man must discipline himself in order to acquire the self-control which will enable him to know the Truth, to desire the Good, and to will the Right, and thus to realize Reality in its threefold aspect.

(*a*) *Discipline of the intellect.*—We find, in the case of the intellect, that the datum is already given in the sensational basis of knowledge. Out of this vague presentational *continuum* man must, by his own intellectual activity, construct a world for himself. The complete determination of this originally chaotic sphere, when reduced by the mind to the cosmos of intelligence, would be the Truth; and herein lies the intellectual ideal which all mental discipline must keep in view. According to Bosanquet,

'we must learn to regard our separate worlds of knowledge as something constructed by definite processes, and corresponding to each other in consequence of the common nature of these processes' (*The Essentials of Logic*, 1895, p. 17).

Now it is in the interest of this process of thought, by which the mind gradually constructs for itself a world of knowledge, that a definite training is required; since it is in the treatment of the fresh data constantly presented to consciousness that the difference between the disciplined and the undisciplined mind reveals itself. To the former only belongs that control which makes possible the reduction of these data to a world of unity and system, or, to use a technical expression, it is the trained mind alone which can be trusted to fulfil its normal function of 'apperception' (*q.v.*). This process Stout defines as that 'by which a mental system appropriates a new element, or otherwise receives a fresh determination' (*Analytic Psychology*, 1896, vol. ii. p. 112). The apperceptive process is essentially one of selection, and the man who by mental discipline has acquired control over his thought-activity will give evidence of the fact by the way in which, through processes of inhibition and attention (*q.v.*), he selects his data. By mental inhibition we mean the suspension of judgment with regard to any fresh fact, so as to allow time for the mind to grasp the true nature of the fact, to perceive its relation to an apperceptive system already at work, and, finally, to appropriate the new element, by allowing such a system to be modified by this fresh determination. Such a pause for deliberation, though a suspension of judgment, is by no means a suspension of mental activity. On the contrary, it is often a time of the sharpest conflict, arising from the apparently rival claims of the old mental group and the new element which confronts it—a conflict which is continued until their true relation is discovered. By attention or concentration we mean the power to develop any particular topic.

'What is called sustained voluntary attention,' says James, 'is a repetition of successive efforts which bring back the topic to the mind. . . . It is not an identical *object* in the psychological sense, but a succession of mutually related objects forming an identical *topic* only, upon which the attention is fixed' (*Principles of Psychology*, vol. i. [1907] p. 420 f.).

In striking contrast to this process of mental apperception stands the readiness of the undisciplined mind to pass hasty judgment upon the facts presented, before their import is fully understood, being either so blinded by prejudice that further evidence with regard to a particular topic appeals to it in vain, or so lacking in strength and vigour that it shirks the strenuous conflict which must often be faced before the new element can find its place within the system of knowledge already acquired. Against this mental prejudice we find scientific, ethical, and religious teachers of all ages directing their keenest shafts, regarding it as a deeply rooted evil which saps all mental life, and makes impossible an honest search for truth. Thus Bacon says:

'The human understanding, when any proposition has been laid down (either from general admission or belief, or from the pleasure it affords), forces everything else to add fresh support and confirmation; and although most cogent and abundant instances may exist to the contrary, yet either does not observe, or despises them, or gets rid of and rejects them by some destruction with violent and injurious prejudice, rather than sacrifice the authority of its first conclusions' (*Nov. Org.* Aph. 46).

Again, in the words of Locke: 'He must not be in love with any opinion, or wish it to be true, till he knows it to be so, and then he will not need to wish it; for nothing that is false can deserve our good wishes, nor a desire that it should have the place and force of truth; and yet nothing is more frequent than this' (*Conduct of the Understanding*, p. 32).

Finally, to quote from a theologian of our own day: 'We must all train ourselves in the very rare quality of submission to good evidence, when it runs contrary to our prejudices at any point' (Gore, *The Permanent Creed and the Christian Idea of Sin*, 1905, p. 17).

And yet again the mind reveals its lack of discipline in its proneness to mind-wandering or lack of concentrating power. We may state this in psychological terms by saying that, while the disciplined mind is governed by noetic synthesis—the essential characteristic of the apperceptive process—the undisciplined mind is governed by the mere association of ideas. In reference to the development of a train of thought, Stout remarks:

'In so far as it is determined by the special idea which has last emerged, the principle of association is operative; in so far as it is determined by the central idea of the whole topic, noetic synthesis is operative. . . . It is mere association, for instance, which would lead a man in a conversation about peace and war to begin to talk about Peace the murderer' (*Analytic Psychology*, vol. ii. p. 3).

(*b*) *Discipline of the will.*—Turning now to the sphere of the will, we find, as in the case of the intellect, that the datum of volition is already given in the impulsive tendencies or propensities to act. It is then the work of will, not to create fresh data, but so to direct and control these natural impulses as to bring unity and system into this originally chaotic motor *continuum* of vague desire, of which the complete determination and definition would constitute the Right. Now we find that the will, in thus organizing impulse, fulfils a function analogous to the intellectual activity of 'apperception.'

'We must "apperceive,"' says James Seth, 'the contemplated act, place it in the context of our life's purposes, and, directly or indirectly, with more or with less explicit consciousness, correlate it with the master-purpose of our life' (*Ethical Principles*[10], p. 48).

It is not the natural and unformed but the disciplined will which habitually performs this activity of moral apperception. Here again, as in the sphere of the intellect, moral training reveals itself in the power to select from among various possible lines of conduct, by means of the inhibition of impulsive tendencies, or the pause during which alternative activities are suspended, and by attention to the probable result of such activities in the light of the moral end. When a man has thus learned to control his actions, he is no longer at the mercy of the dominant idea of the moment; he ceases to be the slave, and has become the master, of his impulses. Such mastery, however, is not the result of one day's effort. He who would have the self-control which will enable him to resist the wrong action to which he is most strongly impelled can acquire this power only by a daily self-discipline, in learning to refuse the demands of impulses, even though these be good in themselves. It is the need for such discipline which Westcott has in mind when he says:

'We yield to circumstances without the ennobling consciousness of self-sacrifice, or the invigorating exercise of will. We fail to test our powers betimes by voluntary coercion or effort, that so we may be supreme masters of ourselves when the hour of struggle comes' ('Disciplined Life,' in *Words of Faith and Hope*, 1902, p. 4).

Attention, too, plays a no less important part in our volitional than in our intellectual life. It is as we consider alternative ends of conduct in the context of our life's purposes that, on account of the appeal which it makes to the whole self, the one which has at first the least attractive force often becomes the stronger; while others, which had at first much compelling power, retreat into the background when considered in the light of our moral ideal. See ATTENTION.

(*c*) *Discipline of the emotions.*—On the emotional side of man's nature we find no less necessity for training, and no less demand for an acquirement of such control as will give the individual power over the passion which otherwise will master him, thus enabling him to make a choice, in the light of his moral ideal, from among the innumerable channels into which his emotional life may flow. To emphasize this point, we cannot do better than quote the words of Ruskin:

'As the true knowledge is disciplined and tested knowledge,—not the first thought that comes,—so the true passion is disciplined and tested passion,—not the first passion that comes. The first that come are the vain, the false, the treacherous; if you yield to them, they will lead you wildly and far, in vain pursuit, in hollow enthusiasm, till you have no true purpose and no true passion left. Not that any feeling possible to humanity is in itself wrong, but only wrong when undisciplined. Its nobility is in its force and justice; it is wrong when it is weak, and felt for paltry cause' (*Sesame and Lilies*, ed. 1882, p. 55).

It is hardly necessary to add that such dissipation, and also such redemption, of passion are possible, both through the world of fiction and in the world of fact.

'For the noble grief we should have borne with our fellows,' says Ruskin, 'and the pure tears we should have wept with them, we gloat over the pathos of the police court, and gather the night-dew of the grave' (*ib.* p. 89).

And with confidence we may say that they who have been truly moved by the sorrows of Antigone and the grief of Andromache are not likely to be affected by the tragedy of a second-rate novel, or to grieve much over the petty vexations of life.

We conclude, therefore, that, whether we regard man's nature in its emotional, its volitional, or its intellectual aspect, true moral discipline reveals itself, not in the annihilation of the natural forces, but in their subjugation to a unifying principle which controls the life. The duty of self-discipline has always a positive as well as a negative side. While, negatively, it is the refusal to permit any single tendency of our nature to act in isolation and to dominate the life, on the positive side we find not merely the conquest of natural impulsive energy, but its pressure into the service of the total purpose of the life. Then, the stronger the natural impulses, the stronger will be the purpose which they serve, when engaged in the pursuit of an end which can utilize them all. The search for Truth demands the force and passion of Socrates and Newton, while nothing less than the energy of Luther's nature can accomplish the task of Reformation.

LITERATURE.—J. Sully, *The Human Mind*, 2 vols., London, 1892; W. James, *The Principles of Psychology*, 2 vols., London, 1890–1891, and *Talks to Teachers on Psychology; and to Students on some of Life's Ideals*, do. 1899–1900; G. F. Stout, *A Manual of Psychology*[2], London, 1901, and *Analytic Psychology*, 2 vols., do. 1890–1896; C. Lloyd Morgan, *An Introduction to Comparative Psychology*, London, 1894; J. F. Herbart, *The Application of Psychology to the Science of Education*, Eng. tr., London, 1898; J. S. Mackenzie, *A Manual of Ethics*[4], London, 1900; W. R. Boyce Gibson, *A Philosophical Introduction to Ethics*, London, 1904: H. Sidgwick, *The Methods of Ethics*[7], London, 1907; A. E. Taylor, *The Problem of Conduct*, London, 1901; Sophie Bryant, *Short Studies in Character*, London, 1894; J. Welton and F. G. Blandford, *Principles and Methods of Moral Training*, London, 1909.

ANNIE E. F. MACGREGOR.

ETHICAL IDEALISM.—1. Definition of the term.—The term 'ethical idealism' has two distinct meanings. It may signify a theory of reality as a whole, the fundamental principle of which is drawn from the nature of the moral life. Here morality supplies the clue to the meaning of reality. In this sense 'ethical idealism' designates a metaphysical theory based on a prior analysis of the moral life. On the other hand, 'ethical idealism' also signifies the theory of the moral life derived from an 'idealistic' conception of reality. In such a case an idealistic metaphysic is presupposed, and the metaphysical principle must be more general than, or at any rate of a different kind from, that obtained by an analysis of the moral life alone. Morality is a deduction from such a principle.

These two meanings are, therefore, logically quite distinct. In the first, metaphysics rests on morality; in the second, morality rests on metaphysics. Kant's metaphysical theory may be regarded as an illustration of the first; Aristotle's theory of ethics may be considered as typical of the second. No doubt the two meanings may approximate, as, for example, in Plato's *Republic*, where the moral good leads the way to the apprehension and interpretation of the metaphysical 'idea of the good,' which is shown to transcend the moral good and to include it as a particular manifestation of the supreme principle. But in general it is important to keep separate the two meanings of the term 'ethical idealism'; and for purposes of discussion it is essential to do so. In the present article we are concerned with 'ethical idealism' primarily in the second of these senses, *i.e.* with the moral life as interpreted in terms of idealism, 'idealism' being a specific metaphysical view of reality.

2. Meaning of Idealism.—To begin with, we have to consider the meaning of idealism. Idealism has taken different forms in the history of speculation; but there are certain features common to all. (*a*) *Negative.*—In the first place, idealism is negatively described by contrast with 'naturalism.' Naturalism is sometimes indistinguishable from materialism, and in that case designates a theory or point of view which seeks to explain all known events and facts, human experience included, in terms of the elements of physical Nature. It lays stress on the ultimate material origin of the world, and, again, on the mechanical necessity which holds sway throughout the processes of the world, however complex these processes are. Apparent differences in kind amongst phenomena, *e.g.*, inorganic and organic, chemical and conscious, are held to be resolvable into differences of complexity of manifestation of the same identical elements, matter and motion. Sometimes, however, naturalism is applied specifically to the reduction of all mental processes, more particularly the higher mental life of man, to organic elements and conditions, nothing being affirmed about a further reduction of the organic to inorganic material elements. In this case, it may even be said that such a further reduction is impossible, that organic Nature and purely physical Nature are in reality heterogeneous. When naturalism is used in this sense, we have again explanation in terms of origin; but here the 'original elements' of the mental life are restricted to organic elements and processes; laws of the more complicated mental life are reducible to the fundamental laws of organic life in general, but these organic laws and elements are not reducible either to material elements and laws or to a substratum common to the two.

In both forms of naturalism we have the same general characteristics—explanation by the reduction of the complex to ultimate elements and their laws; the connexion of all events by the principle of the causal continuity of the temporal antecedent with the temporal consequent; and the absence of the use of any conception of end as a final principle of interpretation. The only 'ends' admitted are results, not pre-conditions; they are effects, not grounds. Idealism affirms the opposite of all this. It seeks to interpret the simple and primordial by reference to the more complex and later in time; it does not explain in terms of origin but in terms of completion; and it does not connect by causal sequence in time, but by controlling ends.

No doubt there is a sense in which the 'nature' of anything may be identified with the end rather than with the pre-conditions; in this case there can be no contrast between idealism and 'naturalism.'

(*b*) *Positive.*—Idealism on its positive side may in general terms be described as the theory which regards the ultimate principle of reality as one which operates by conscious reference to an end or system of ends. An unconscious end could not be the principle of idealism, even though it were admitted that the unconscious end might be quite distinct from a mechanical principle. For the conception of 'ideal' is essential to the meaning of idealism, and an 'ideal' is a *conscious* end of some sort. The conception of an ideal is subordinate to that of end, which is more general; and the differentia is found by reference to a consciousness. An end, more particularly a supreme end, when it as such becomes consciously sought and consciously operative, becomes an ideal. The various applications of the term 'ideal' will be found to bear out this interpretation, whether these applications are figurative, *e.g.*, an 'ideal rose,' or literal.

3. Types of Idealism.—It is clear from the above description that a metaphysical idealism may take different forms, according to the way in which the content of the end is present in consciousness, and according to the kind of consciousness to which the end is present. If the universe is interpreted idealistically, its principle of unity must be a supreme consciousness aware of a supreme final end, and aware of this as its own end. Since this principle cannot be subordinate to some further principle, in some sense this supreme end must be one with the supreme consciousness, not external to it. This is sometimes expressed by saying that the ultimate principle is a supreme self-consciousness, making itself its own end. In relation to the finite world, this end may be either transcendent of finitude, or immanent in finitude; and it has also been maintained that this end can be both transcendent and immanent. In any and every case, however, this supreme end covers all reality, finite and infinite alike.

Again, the supreme principle may be regarded as realized wholly and solely in every part and domain of reality. In this case the supreme self-consciousness is realized in a differentiated plurality of individual self-consciousnesses, and hence there would be as many self-consciousnesses as there are individuals. This is the view of idealistic 'pluralism.' On the other hand, the supreme principle may be regarded as single and unique, combining in itself all finite individuals not necessarily themselves self-conscious, and making all individuals contributory to the complete realization of its own end known only to and realized only by its own self. This is the view of idealistic 'singularism,' to use the term applied to this doctrine in a recent volume.[1]

4. General nature of Ethical Idealism.—Whatever be the form of idealism adopted, the conception of the moral life derived therefrom has the same general features and follows much the same lines in each case. The fundamental nature of the moral life on this view of reality is that it is the expression, in the case of man, of the supreme principle of the whole, and an integral indispensable moment in the realization of that principle. This may be put in various ways, but the same idea is involved. Whether the idea is presented in the vague and indefinite form that human purposes are 'rooted in the nature of things,' that the 'soul of the world is just'; or in the characteristically religious expressions 'the righteous shall be had in everlasting remembrance' (Ps 112^6), man is 'God's fellow-worker' (1 Co 3^9); or, again, in the systematic attempt to show that the moral order is an adumbration of the orderly unity of the world, and a specific realization of the ultimate 'reason' in the 'matter' of man's sense-life,—in all these ways and in various ethical theories the same thought is contained. Whenever we find the moral life regarded as working and leading in man's life towards the spiritual principle unifying all reality, or wherever the source and ground of the moral life are derived from such a principle, there we have an ethical idealism. The moral end, on this view, is one expression of the supreme end, not a *means* to that supreme end but a literal manifestation of it, one way in which the supreme spiritual principle is conscious of itself, or conscious of its *own* end. In so far as man's moral end is taken to be a fundamental constitutive element of man's being, man's conscious realization of his end is at once a consciousness of the supreme principle in himself and a condition of making his individuality an integral part of the supreme principle; and, in so far as man becomes conscious of the supreme principle in himself, his life becomes determined by the moral end, and set to moral issues. The two statements reciprocally involve each other: hence we have the constant oscillation, in this type of ethical theory, between the position that the moral end 'demands' or 'proves' the existence of a supreme spiritual principle and the position that a supreme spiritual principle has made man moral or 'wills' the moral end.

5. Forms of Ethical Idealism.—The development of this conception of the moral life varies in different systems. Perhaps one might say that the point of divergence between different systems turns on the interpretation of moral evil, and its place in such a theory. Where the existence of evil is regarded as incompatible with the content of the supreme principle, the idealistic theory of Ethics tends to assign only the fact of the moral law and moral end to the operation of the supreme principle, and to attribute the existence of moral evil to man's imperfect working out of the moral end; in other words, all the good in the moral life is placed to the account of the supreme self-consciousness, all the evil to finite self-consciousness. On this view the idealistic treatment of morality tends to be more or less abstract in character. The law is regarded as an abstract, formal, universal law of 'reason'; the end is one that transcends experience in the sense of never being completely

[1] J. Ward, *The Realm of Ends*, Cambridge, 1911.

realizable in man's life; the moral individual is an independent, or even isolated, being who is an 'end in himself,' isolated from Nature and only contingently related to other moral beings.

On the other hand, where evil is treated as springing from the same source as good itself, both having their common root in self-consciousness, the moral end grasps the human individual concretely; law and sensibility, moral ideal and Nature, are looked upon as forming an indissoluble whole; the moral consciousness is inseparable from Nature, and is essentially a social consciousness. The spiritual principle in man subsumes Nature into itself and is realized most fully in society with its laws and institutions; the supreme spiritual principle takes upon itself the whole burden of man's moral destiny; and, through moral failure, the human spirit can pass, in unbroken unity with itself, to moral completeness and reconciliation.

The first form of the idealistic treatment of Ethics is essentially dualistic in conception and in systematic development: the second is essentially monistic in form and substance. With certain qualifications in matters of detail, we might take, as historical examples of the former, Stoicism in ancient Ethics, and Kantianism in modern Ethics; and as examples of the latter, Plato or Aristotle in ancient Ethics, and Hegel or Neo-Hegelianism in modern Ethics.

It is important to note that in the treatment of Ethics from the idealistic point of view the essential identity of finite and supreme self-consciousness is in general all that is affirmed. The detail of the moral life is not deduced from the supreme principle. Any attempt at such a deduction could only result in the repetition of an abstract formula, which would either leave the specific diversity of content in the moral life unexplained or would blot out its diversity altogether. This is inevitable. For the principle of self-consciousness, as realized in man, is the only form of the principle that is directly relevant for the interpretation of man's moral life, and indeed is sufficient for the purpose. Any deduction of his moral nature and constitution from the absolute principle is, therefore, as unnecessary as it is impossible. This point is sometimes urged in the form that we cannot deduce the details of duty from the conception of a Divine 'perfection.' If by 'perfection' is meant the complete unity of the Divine or Absolute self-consciousness, such a statement may be admitted. With an 'absolute perfection' in the sense of the perfection of the Absolute we have in morality nothing to do. We are concerned in morality with human moral perfection only. From this, however, it may be possible to derive our specific duty, provided we know in what such perfection consists. Perfection is, no doubt, an attribute of the moral ideal; and from the moral ideal we must be able to explain the meaning and content of the moral life.

6. Value of Ethical Idealism.—It may be said that, if we must analyze the operations of human self-consciousness in order to interpret the nature of morality idealistically, there seems little or no value in connecting morality with an idealistic theory of reality. But this is not the case. The significance of the doctrine lies in the fact that, since the principle in finite and in Absolute self-consciousness is essentially the same, the detailed realization of what that principle contains in the case of man's moral life will, equally with the general principle itself, have its warrant and justification in the ultimate meaning of reality. Thus every moral act has a significance for the whole of reality as truly as the moral ideal itself. And this is both practically and theoretically of profound importance. For, on this view, not merely does the individual's moral life as a whole have a place in the supreme purpose of the universe, but every moral act becomes a contribution to the attainment of the plan of the Absolute. Morality and moral individuals have thus a supreme worth in themselves and for the Absolute; and the moral life becomes a factor in the constitution of religion—a fact which all 'ethical religions' have emphasized, whether they have regarded moral laws as 'Divine commands' or regarded the process of the moral life as the working out of a 'Divine will.'

7. Fundamental difficulty of Ethical Idealism.—This close identification of the moral life with the realization of the supreme spiritual principle has always created a difficulty for ethical idealism. For it is obvious that, the more the identification is emphasized, the more we tend to treat the contribution of the moral individual towards the fulfilment of the supreme purpose as the expression, through him, of the operation of that principle itself. The more we assimilate the moral life and the Divine Life, the greater the difficulty in distinguishing between what in a given act is the individual's doing and what is God's. If the distinction is denied, individual self-determination disappears, and with that the spiritual freedom, which is the very basis of the value of the individual to himself. If, on the other hand, the distinction is affirmed, it becomes difficult to consider the supreme purpose as carrying its own necessity within itself; for clearly a supreme purpose which depends for its attainment on the success or failure of individual finite wills is at the mercy of contingency.

8. Solutions of the difficulty.—This difficulty is a very real one, and is of far-reaching significance. It generally divides ethical idealists into two camps. There are those, *e.g.* Green, who seem to treat the finite consciousness as a kind of channel or medium through which in the moral life the spiritual principle realizes or objectifies itself. Assuming that in some sense such a principle is self-contained and self-determining, the individual is little more, if any more, than a self-conscious instrument, a mere manifestation or emanation of the Absolute self-consciousness. It seems impossible to deny that in everything but name such a view is indistinguishable from Spinozism. There is no difference between Spirit and Substance if they take the same method of realizing themselves in finite self-consciousness. A self-consciousness which 'supervenes' upon the material of sensibility and thereby makes the latter its own, may indeed be 'free' relatively to sensibility, in the sense that its operation implies detachment from sensibility, and self-direction in controlling and ordering sensibility. But this freedom is not an 'ultimate fact,' nor is it self-explanatory as long as it is assumed that the finite self-consciousness is itself a specific realization of a wider Absolute self-consciousness which is expressing itself under human limitations. On the contrary, it is thereby implied that the principle on which finite self-consciousness proceeds in asserting its freedom relatively to sensibility derives the laws and conditions of its procedure from, and is itself determined by, this more comprehensive and all-embracing self-consciousness. Freedom, in short, is, in such a case, but the delegated power to exercise, in reference to sensibility, the functions of a superior self-consciousness. It is freedom only *sub specie temporis*, but is necessity *sub specie æternitatis*. And, since the latter point of view is the more ultimate and therefore the more correct, the freedom of finite self-consciousness is barely distinguishable from illusion—which, indeed, Spinoza asserted it to be.

A second method of dealing with the problem is that which treats self-consciousness as a principle that is not so much an actuality in man's life from the start, but is gradually realized in the course of his activity. On this view, man does not begin his finite existence with a fully active organ or function of self-consciousness, by means of which he assimilates a quasi-alien environment to himself and himself to his environment, in the way described, *e.g.*, by Kant, and also to some extent by Green. The whole course and aim of his finite life consists in becoming self-conscious, not in being completely so to begin with. Thus there are grades of self-consciousness in man's life, and differences of degree of self-consciousness amongst mankind. The function of self-consciousness may be, indeed, abstractly the same in all men; but, actually and as a historical fact, it is realized in very varying degrees by individual men and types of mankind. The mistake of the previous view lay in confounding a formal similarity of function—a purely logical function in Kant's theory—with an actual identity of realization in all human individuals. But, if the attainment of self-consciousness is itself a matter of growth and development in the individual life, then, while all may attain it to a certain degree, imperfection of attainment is not inconsistent with individual success, or with the fulfilment of the final end of the supreme self-consciousness. Perfection of attainment is, indeed, a goal; but, if degrees of attainment be admitted to be consistent with the absolute principle, failure to attain perfectly in any individual case cannot imperil the security or validity of the final end. Moreover, on this view, the defects of individuality in one sphere are balanced or compensated in another. Thus, the imperfections of a given individual in his society do not destroy the stability and order of the general life of the community: his life is so supplemented by the lives of others that unity on the whole is maintained. Similarly, the one-sidedness of any given type of society or form of humanity is counterbalanced by another form of society with which it is connected in the general history of humanity; so that, just as a given society comes to the help of the individual's imperfections, the history of humanity as a whole qualifies or removes the imperfect realization of human life in any one form of society.

This view, again, modifies similarly the conception of individual freedom and the difficulties of reconciling the free action of individuals with an all-pervading and triumphant purpose. For freedom, like self-consciousness, is not a quality with which the individual's will is endowed from the outset; it is a result which he achieves for himself. Freedom is not a pre-condition of the moral life, but a state which he gradually attains; and, like self-consciousness, the attainment of it is a matter of degree. Freedom in that sense is the goal of the moral life, not an antecedent condition of it. The organic life of a community is a realization of moral freedom, and the history of humanity is the progress in attainment of its freedom.

In this way it is sought to harmonize the operation of the principle of self-consciousness under finite conditions with the actuality of the Absolute self-consciousness, without destroying the validity of the pursuit of finite ends or the finality of the Absolute end. This view is found in the ethical idealism of Hegel, and more recently of Bradley. The objection to it is the opposite of the objection to the previous view stated. For, on the second view, the realization of finite self-consciousness and of finite freedom is so completely identified with the course of human history that any degree of attainment of the principle is enough to satisfy the requirements of the supreme principle. The supreme principle cannot, on this view, fail to realize its end, no matter what degree of success attends the operations of finite self-consciousness. That being so, the attitude of the supreme principle is one of indifference to the achievements of finite individuals: its end is fulfilled, no matter what finite individuals do or fail to do. This reduces the position of the supreme self-consciousness to that of a spectator, and the position of the finite individual to that of a player: the moral life becomes a mere drama with the Absolute as witness. Or, again, the effect on the finite individual must necessarily be to make him equally indifferent to the accomplishment of his end; while the process of history taken as a whole is indistinguishable in ethical quality from the course of Nature. Ethical idealism in this shape thus closely resembles the position of pure naturalism.

9. Special features of Ethical Idealism.—The characteristic points on which ethical idealism lays stress in the constructive development of the theory are mainly three: (*a*) the logical priority of the conception of value in the moral life; (*b*) the objective independent reality of social institutions; (*c*) the essential unity of individual and social mind.

(*a*) In virtue of the first, ethical idealism insists that the consciousness of an ideal takes priority over all consideration of circumstances, nature, or history. Relatively to the ideal, circumstances, nature, and history provide merely the material of morality; they can never destroy the authority of the ideal or modify its validity. The ideal remains the same throughout all diversity of realization. It moulds its material in different ways, and thus the material becomes the means or condition of the objective expression of the ideal. Thereby the self 'finds itself' in Nature by making Nature the correlate and counterpart of Spirit. Thus the diversity of content presented is reduced to unity; and all the elements in individuality—heredity, historical situation, natural surroundings, etc.—become significant for the moral life, and contribute to the attainment of man's end. Sometimes this logical priority of the ideal is expressed in an extravagant form, as when Kant asserts that the moral law is absolutely binding for all under all circumstances, and duty remains duty whatever hindrances there are in the way of its realization; or again when Fichte seeks to 'deduce' Nature as simply the sphere of human freedom. But these are merely extreme expressions of the fundamental position on which ethical idealism takes its stand—the position that the operative consciousness of the moral ideal is the basis of all the moral worth of action or personality.

(*b*) Not less important is the second point. Institutions are not regarded by idealism as incidents in the moral life, created by and dependent on the wills of separate finite individuals. Institutions are embodiments of the social spirit, from which individuals themselves derive their moral sustenance and support. It is truer, on this view, to say that individuals are incidents in the life of institutions than that institutions are incidents in the life of individuals. The end for man is one, and by its very nature is common to all individuals; this follows from the constitution of the supreme principle which is realizing itself in man's life. Individuals, therefore, because realizing, each in his own case, the same human end, necessarily live a common life. The community of life is just as real in this process as the variety of ways in which all seek their several interests in the one common end. Institutions are the concrete forms in which this community of end as such finds expression. From this point of view institutions are a more objective and permanent embodiment of the supreme principle in man's life than the actions or the life of a given individual; and conversely we see more fully in institutions what the final end of man is.

Ethical idealism has been singularly successful in developing this aspect of its theory of the moral life. The conception of a social will working itself out in the various forms of corporate social life, the family, the city, or again more abstract human institutions such as the Church; the conception of the 'general will' as the basis of the State and the source of its functions in framing, administering, and executing the decrees of government; the conception of property and of contract as fundamental forms of social mind, deriving their origin and ultimate sanction from the idea of the common good which a common will pursues—all these are direct consequences of the objectivity of social institutions as embodiments of the common human end.

(c) Finally, it is of the essence of ethical idealism to hold that the operations of the individual mind in realizing its own end, and the operations of the social mind in realizing a common end, proceed on the same plan. Whether we speak of the social mind as the individual mind 'writ large' or seek to interpret the social mind in psychological terms—terms applicable to the process of the individual mind — the same idea is involved. The similarity of operation is, indeed, very close. Thus we have in the individual the unity of his moral life summed up in the operations of his conscience, which is the outcome of his social consciousness, and the guiding principle of unity in his moral life; in the social mind we have the common spirit actuating a community, pervading all parts as an operative principle of homogeneous social action and of unity of social feeling and sentiment in individuals. In the individual we have the consciousness of moral laws, some vague, some clearly defined and steadily obeyed; the life of a community, again, is maintained by the vague sense of order, and also by the explicit formulation of, and obedience to, laws and decrees required to ensure the maintenance of an orderly unity of individuals. In the individual's moral life, habit and character are the conditions of moral security and continuity of effort; corresponding to this in the social life we have custom, routine, and social automatism. The inter-relation of ideas and purposes in the individual mind is of a piece with the inter-communication of personalities in the social mind. The sense of guilt and remorse in the individual has its parallel in social disapproval and punishment by the community: the moral disorder of the individual is regarded as identical in nature with social disorder in a community.

It is important to notice, in conclusion, that, on the view of ethical idealism, the moral life, while self-contained and determined by its own conditions, is not regarded as an exhaustive expression of man's spiritual life. On the contrary, by its very nature it points to a wider and completer realization of the supreme principle from which it derives its significance. This is put in various forms. It is said that morality 'points beyond itself to religion,' that 'religion transcends morality,' that 'the moral life is part of the wider life of universal history,' that 'the contemplative life is the crowning activity of the spiritual life.' In all these and similar ways the same point is emphasized—the finitude of the moral attitude as a phase of the realization of the one supreme principle. And this logically follows from regarding the moral end of man as an integral but single expression of the comprehensive end of an Absolute self-consciousness.

LITERATURE.—The literature on Ethical Idealism in the sense above discussed is very large. Most of the chief religions have treated Ethics from this point of view, however much they may have differed both in their religious conceptions and in the content they assign to the moral life. In the systematic discussion of ethical problems, which makes up the History of Ethics strictly so called, Ethical Idealism has been stated and developed in a great variety of ways. The most prominent may be said to be the following: (a) Greek Ethics: **Xenophon**, *Memorabilia of Socrates*; Plato, generally, but chiefly in the *Republic*; Aristotle, *Ethics*.—(b) Mediæval Ethics: **Aquinas**, *Summa contra Gentiles*, bk. iii. chs. 1-63 and 111-146.—(c) Modern Ethics: **Cudworth**, *Eternal and Immutable Morality*, 1731; Cumberland, *De legibus Naturæ*, 1672; **Clarke**, *Discourse on Natural Religion*, 1706; Butler, *Sermons*, 1726; Paley, *Principles of Moral and Political Philosophy*, 1785; **Fichte**, *Bestimmung des Menschen*, 1800, *Grundlage des Naturrechts*, 1796, *System der Sittenlehre*, 1798, *Staatslehre*, 1813; Hegel, *Philosophie des Rechts*, 1821, *Philosophie der Geschichte*, 1837; **Vatke**, *Die menschliche Freiheit*, 1841; Green, *Prolegomena to Ethics*[3], 1890; Bradley, *Appearance and Reality*[2], 1897.

J. B. BAILLIE.

ETHICAL MOVEMENT.—1. Origin and history.—The founder of the Ethical Movement was Felix Adler, afterwards Professor of Applied Ethics in Columbia University, New York. At the urgent request of a number of persons who had become acquainted with his point of view, which assigned the supreme place to right conduct and proclaimed that the good life is not necessarily dependent on theological beliefs, he inaugurated, in 1876, the New York Society for Ethical Culture, which soon counted considerably over a thousand members. 'Deed, not Creed' was his motto. He soon attracted a number of able men—W. M. Salter, Stanton Coit, Burns Weston, and W. L. Sheldon —and, as a consequence, Ethical Societies were established in Chicago, Philadelphia, and St. Louis. In 1886 the London Ethical Society was founded. This Society counted among its members Bernard Bosanquet, Sophie Bryant, Edward Caird, J. S. Mackenzie, J. H. Muirhead, J. Seeley, Leslie Stephen, H. Sidgwick, and G. F. Stout. Two years later Stanton Coit came to England as 'minister' of South Place Ethical Society. From that time onwards the Ethical Movement in England developed, until it counted some thirty Ethical Societies, a considerable number of them being in London. Most of these came to be federated in the English 'Union of Ethical Societies.' In 1892 the German Society for Ethical Culture came into being, and soon had some fifteen branches. Not long afterwards the Austrian Ethical Society, the Italian 'Unione Morale,' and two Societies in Switzerland were founded. Recently, a Society in Tokyo has cast in its lot with the Ethical Movement.

As early as 1893 the German Ethical Society organized a meeting at Eisenach, with a view to starting an International Ethical Union. This, however, proved only the precursor of the meeting at Zürich in 1896, when delegates from the various ethical centres were present and an International Ethical Union was founded. Ten years later the Second International Ethical Conference met at Eisenach, when a constitution was drawn up and a programme of work elaborated. In 1908, on the occasion of the very successful First International Moral Education Congress initiated by the Union and organized by its secretary, a further International Conference took place.

2. Work of the Ethical Societies.—In the United States and in England the Ethical Societies meet every Sunday, either morning or evening, or both. In the United States there is usually some kind of music and reading, besides the lecture, which generally deals with some current topic, or with some question of the inner life or of philosophy from the ethical point of view. In England the 'service' is more pronounced: congregational singing is universal, and other features, such as the reading of an Ethical Declaration, or of Closing

Words, are not uncommon. In Germany and Austria the meetings are held on weekdays, and the proceedings consist simply of an ethical lecture followed by discussion. The Ethical Lecture is one distinguishing feature of Ethical Societies, the other is the Ethical Classes for the Young. These are to be found, highly developed, in the American centres, and, less highly developed, in English centres. In Berlin and other places on the Continent such classes also exist. Moral instruction being a special concern of the Ethical Societies, it is natural that the Movement should have done much to promote it in schools. In America, Adler and Sheldon have written text-books on the subject, and the former has gradually built up his now widely famed New York Ethical Culture School. In England, the Union of Ethical Societies founded a Moral Instruction League, which has induced about a hundred Local Education authorities to make some provision for the teaching of morals. In Germany also a Moral Instruction League exists, which numbers about a thousand members; and the International Ethical Union is endeavouring to create such Leagues everywhere. See MORAL EDUCATION LEAGUE.

The practical activities of the Ethical Societies resemble to a large extent those of the Churches. Innumerable charitable and social activities are connected with the New York Ethical Society, and the other American Ethical Societies all engage seriously in similar work. In England, there is relatively little done in this direction, chiefly because so many of the members are individually absorbed in politics and philanthropy. The German Society has also busied itself much with reforms of various kinds. It was the first to establish public libraries and reading-rooms in Germany, and now such institutions are common there; it developed a scheme of cheap theatres, as a result of which there exist a number of *Schiller-Theater*, as they are called, in Germany. The same society has founded a Charity Organization Society in Berlin, which is doing extremely valuable work on an extensive scale; and it has done much to encourage high-class recreation evenings for the people.

3. Principles of the Ethical Movement.—At the International Conference at Eisenach (1906) a constitution was adopted, expressing the following general aim, which was unanimously agreed to by the delegates and has been accepted by all the national ethical centres:

'To assert the supreme importance of the ethical factor in all the relations of life—personal, social, national, and international, apart from theological and metaphysical considerations.'

The English Union of Ethical Societies in the same year determined upon a series of principles which conveniently sum up the distinguishing features of the Ethical Movement generally. They are here reproduced. Attention is specially drawn to the second principle, in which an attempt is made to state the basis of the ethics taught in Ethical Societies.

'(*a*) In all the relations of life—personal, social, and political—the moral factor should be the supreme consideration.

(*b*) The love of goodness and the love of one's fellows are the true motives for right conduct; and self-reliance and co-operation are the true sources of help.

(*c*) Knowledge of the Right has been evolving through the experience of the human race: therefore the moral obligations generally accepted by the most civilized communities should be taken as the starting-point in the advocacy of a progressive ideal of personal and social righteousness.

(*d*) For each individual, after due consideration of the convictions of others, the final authority as to the right or wrong of any opinion or action should be his own conscientious and reasoned judgment.

(*e*) The well-being of society requires such economic and other conditions as afford the largest scope for the moral development of all its members.

(*f*) The scientific method should be applied in studying the facts of the moral life.

(*g*) The moral life involves neither acceptance nor rejection of belief in any Deity, personal or impersonal, or in a life after death.

(*h*) The acceptance of any one ultimate criterion of right should not be made a condition of ethical fellowship.

(*i*) Ethical fellowships are the most powerful means of encouraging the knowledge and love of right principles of conduct, and of giving the strength of character necessary to realize them in action.'

4. The common programme.—The following manifesto, drawn up at the International Conference of 1896, will give a fair idea of the attitude of the Movement towards the great problems of our age:

'i. (*a*) Ethical Societies should declare their attitude towards the great social problems of the time, in the solution of which the highest significance belongs to moral forces. We recognize, accordingly, that the effort of the masses of the people to attain a human standard of existence contains in it a moral aim of the first rank, and we declare ourselves bound to support this effort to the utmost. But we believe there is here a question not only as to the needs of the poorer classes of the people, but in an equal degree as to the moral poverty of the members of the well-to-do classes, who are directly threatened in their moral being by the outward conditions of our modern economic life.

(*b*) We acknowledge that resistance to injustice and oppression is a sacred duty, and that under the existing circumstances the struggle for rights is an indispensable means of clearing up conceptions of justice and in the attainment of better conditions; but we demand that the struggle be kept within the limits prescribed by humanity, and that it be conducted in the interest of the community as a whole, and with continual reference to ultimate social peace.

(*c*) We maintain that in the solution of the so-called labour problem the question is one not only of the material necessities of the labourers, but of their social and legal status, and of their full participation in the highest results of civilization, science, and art.

(*d*) We recognize it as a task of the Ethical Union to assist in such intellectual equipment of the people as shall serve the cause of social progress; for example, scientific efforts which aim at examining the conflicting theories of Individualism and Socialism, with a view to the possibility of their being harmonized in some profounder view of life; further, to establish inquiries and institute research in moral statistics, which, based on well-authenticated facts, shall bring impressively before the eye the need of reforms in our conditions, and to help in the dissemination of the results so obtained, in order to bring the public conscience to bear as a force making for social justice and higher development.

(*e*) We leave it to the various Societies to apply the above tasks according to the circumstances of their own countries, and we call upon all the individual members of our Societies, by simplicity in their manner of life and by active sympathy, to advance the forward social movement.

ii. We regard the institution of pure monogamic marriage as a priceless good of humanity, which is indispensable for the moral development of the individual and for the permanent duration of moral civilization; but we insist that this institution should stamp itself upon sentiment and conduct with a thoroughness which as yet is absent in wide-reaching circles of society.

iii. (*a*) We demand for woman the possibility of the fullest development of her mental and moral personality, and we would strive to bring about in all departments of life an uncurtailed expression of the equal worth of her personality with that of man.

(*b*) Especially we regard the fate of working women in industry (whether in the factory or at home), and also in personal domestic service, as one of the most grievous evils of our time, and would strive to restore, throughout the whole people, the conditions of a healthy family life.

iv. We hold it to be a fundamental task of our age to give again to education its unity, which in great part has been lost, and, by establishing a universal ethical end in all education, to confer that kind of service which denominational religion once rendered to education in elementary and secondary schools.

v. We heartily approve efforts to establish universal peace among nations, and we would direct our share in these efforts towards overcoming militarism in public sentiment, towards checking the power which it exercises upon the imagination—especially of the young—and towards bringing out in some nobler way those morally significant elements which the life of the soldier contains; further, towards opposing national egoism and national passion, which are at least to-day as dangerous enemies to peace as are the prejudices and personal interests of rulers; and, finally, towards bringing about a reign of conscience and calm reason in times of excitement, and when partisan spirit fosters a blind hatred of enemies.'

5. Attitude towards religion.—Fundamentally the Ethical Movement must be regarded as a religious movement. Even such titles of books as *Ethical Religion* (W. M. Salter), *The Religion of Duty* (Felix Adler), *Die ethische Bewegung in der Religion* (Stanton Coit), and *Faith in Man* (Gustav Spiller) are a general proof of the sympathy with fundamental religion in the United States and in

England. Sheldon, speaking of America, says: 'Many a stranger attending the lectures would at first be a little at a loss to know whether or not he was present at the "services" of a church' (*An Ethical Movement*, p. x). This statement is more than borne out by the following passage taken from the Year-Book of the New York Society for Ethical Culture for 1904–05:

'The Society fills more and more the place of a church in the lives of its members. The leaders act as ministers of religion: consecrating marriages; officiating at funerals; consoling the suffering; advising the troubled and confused; dedicating childhood to the higher ends of life in the "name ceremony" [which takes the place of baptism]; teaching and supervising the training of the young in Sunday School, and clubs and classes for young men and women; and seeking to create and maintain an atmosphere of reverent attention to the high mysteries of life and to the sacredness of the obligation, imposed by man's moral nature, to follow without swerving the dictates of duty according to the best light that is in each individual.'

In England the Ethical Movement is almost invariably regarded by its adherents as a religious movement, and both the rather elaborate form and the spirit of the ethical meetings bear this out.

German ethicists, as a rule, strictly separate ethics from religion, and are averse to the Ethical Movement being looked upon as a religious movement. Yet one of the principles of the German Ethical Union is 'through combination to offer its adherents support and assurance, as well as stimulus and help for the inner life.'

Lastly, the *Union pour l'action morale* of Paris, in an official statement, affirms:

'We are bound together by a common principle: to establish a discipline of life in conformity with reason and outside all theology; to illuminate it by free and frank discussion; to animate it with love; to render it effective and progressive by mutual support; to teach it methodically; to realize it in customs and in laws; and, if justice require it, even by a revolution.'

In principle, then, the Ethical Societies all over the world seek to do for their members what the Christian Church, the Jewish Synagogue, and the Muhammadan Mosque endeavour to effect for theirs. The only difference is that those religions assume the existence of a Deity outside the universe, and that the Ethical Movement, as such, is, in substance, non-theological; or, rather, does not connect the right life with theology or metaphysics (see, however, the above-mentioned volumes by Adler, Salter, Coit, and Spiller). In confirmation of the above we shall quote from a lecture on the 'Aims of Ethical Societies,' by Leslie Stephen (*Ethics and Religion*, 1900, p. 260 f.):

'We believe that morality depends upon something deeper and more permanent than any of the dogmas that have hitherto been current in the Churches. It is a product of human nature, not of any of these transcendental speculations or faint survivals of traditional superstitions. Morality has grown up independently of, and often in spite of, theology. The creeds have been good so far as they have accepted or reflected the moral conviction; but it is an illusion to suppose that they have generated it. They represent the dialect and the imagery by which moral truths have been conveyed to minds at certain stages of thought; but it is a complete inversion of the truth to suppose that the morality sprang out of them. From this point of view we must of necessity treat the great ethical questions independently. We cannot form a real alliance with thinkers radically opposed to us. Divines tell us that we reject the one possible basis of morality. To us it appears that we are strengthening it, by severing it from a connection with doctrines arbitrary, incapable of proof, and incapable of retaining any consistent meaning.'

Eloquent passages might be cited from all the ethical leaders to illustrate the rejection of the belief in supernatural help. We content ourselves with a recent utterance by Adler (*The Religion of Duty*, p. 47 f.):

'In former times, when there was drought and famine in the land, men loaded the altars of the gods with gifts intended to placate their anger and to induce them to send the wished-for rain. To-day in famine-stricken India, what is it that the wisest rulers are intent upon? They are studying how to supply on a stupendous scale artificial irrigation, how to increase the facilities of transportation, how to uplift the ignorant peasantry by education, so that they may be able to employ more effective methods of agriculture. In former times, when the plague passed over Europe, mowing down its millions, the churches were thronged with multitudes of worshippers who besieged the Almighty to withdraw the fearful scourge. To-day, when an invasion of cholera threatens a country, the Kochs and Pasteurs are busy in their laboratories, seeking to discover the germs of disease; and rigorous sanitation is everywhere applied to deprive those germs of the congenial soil in which they flourish. This is a commonplace of modern thinking, and I need not enlarge upon it.

The conception of a Heavenly Father, interfering with the operations of nature, arose when the teachings of natural science were unknown. These teachings have been fruitful of substantial results. The progress of mankind has been kept back for centuries by the disposition to expect, of the love and kindness of Providence, the benefits which, if obtainable at all, must be obtained by human effort. The progress of mankind has been incalculably advanced by the appeal to self-help, by the conviction that "the gods help them who help themselves," which, after all, is synonymous with saying that, if we are to be saved, we must save one another.'

LITERATURE.—Felix Adler, *The Religion of Duty*, New York, 1905; W. M. Salter, *Ethical Religion*, Boston, 1891; Stanton Coit, *Die ethische Bewegung in der Religion*, Leipzig, 1890; Walter L. Sheldon, *An Ethical Movement*, St. Louis, 1903; Georg von Gizycki, *Moralphilosophie*, Leipzig, 1888; Gustav Spiller, *Faith in Man*, London, 1908; *Ethics and Religion* (Essays by John Seeley and others), London, 1900; Alfred Moulet, *Le Mouvement éthique*, Paris, 1899; Stanton Coit, *The Message of Man*, London, 1902; *Ethical Hymn Book*, London, 1905. The following periodicals may be noted: *The Ethical World*, monthly, London; *Ethical Addresses*, monthly, Philadelphia; *Ethische Kultur*, twice monthly, Berlin.

GUSTAV SPILLER.

ETHICS.—I. *THE SCOPE OF ETHICS.*—**1. Fact and ideal.**—Everything may be looked at from two different points of view. We may take it simply as it is, seeking to discover how it came to be the thing it is, and how it is related to other things; or we may compare it with some ideal of what it ought to be. We may call a spade a spade, and seek to discover the material of which it is made, who was the maker of it, how it is related to other garden tools; or we may notice that it is of the wrong size, the wrong make, in its wrong place. Corresponding to these two aspects of things, which we may call respectively fact and ideal, we have two kinds of sciences—those which concern themselves with the description and explanation of things as they are, and those which concern themselves with our judgments upon them. The former class have sometimes been called 'natural,' the latter 'normative' or, as is better, 'critical' sciences.

Ethics is critical in the sense explained. Its subject-matter is human conduct and character, not as natural facts with a history and causal connexions with other facts, but as possessing value in view of a standard or ideal. This is sufficient to mark it out not only from natural sciences, but from other less universal disciplines of the same class as itself. It distinguishes Ethics, for example, from law and grammar, which are concerned with types and principles of a comparatively local and temporary interest, and again from therapeutics and musical harmony, which, though of universal application, are concerned with some particular department of life. As contrasted with these, Ethics, like Logic and Æsthetics, is not only of universal application, but refers to constant elements in human nature. This distinction, indeed, may be said to be a vanishing one; there are principles of law (*e.g.* relating to theft or treason), which may be said to be universal, as there are rules of grammar; but, just in proportion as law and grammar deal with what is thus universal, they tend to merge in Logic and Ethics.

2. Relation of Ethics to Psychology.—From what has been said in the previous paragraph the relation of Ethics to the closely allied sciences of Psychology and Sociology ought to be clear. The distinction between Ethics and Psychology does not consist, as has been maintained, in the fact that the one is a study of 'practical' life, while the other is a study of 'fact and theory,' aiming only at the attainment of truth in itself, and having no interest in its practical applications. The difference does not correspond to that between theory and practice, but to that between origin and value, the natural antecedents of a thing and the value that belongs to it in view of the purpose which it serves or the whole of which it is a part. Psychology deals with ideas, feelings, volitions, from the former point of view. It seeks to analyze mental phenomena, and to find the connexions that subsist between the elements as part of the natural world no less than the elements of physics or chemistry. It has nothing to do with the judgments of value which we pass upon them, except in so far as they in turn may be described as natural facts.[1] The business of the psychologist 'is to understand, not to justify or condemn. He is concerned with appearance only. . . . It is not the world as it ought to appear, but the world as it does appear, which is the outcome of psychological development.'[2] Ethics, on the other hand, expressly concerns itself with our justifications and condemnations, considering them not as natural facts but as involving a criticism or standard of reference, which is not merely a natural fact either in the outer or in the inner world, but which, whatever its relation to natural facts, is primarily an ideal in the mind. While Ethics is thus clearly distinguished from Psychology, it stands in the closest relation to it. The leading error of writers who, like Spencer and Haeckel, approach the subject from the side of biology has been the failure consistently to realize that we are dealing here with psychical entities, and that no solid basis for the study can be laid except in a thoroughgoing analysis of the nature of volition, and of its relation to our ideas and emotions.

3. Ethics and Sociology.—The relation of Ethics to Sociology is more difficult to state. This is not wholly due to the indefiniteness of the newer science. For our present purpose it is sufficient to define Sociology as the science of the phenomena of mind and will in so far as they are modified by the social environment and exhibit themselves in changing social conditions—a definition wide enough to include Economics, the History of Societies and Institutions, Anthropology, and the Psychology of peoples. The individual here appears as subject to 'social control' through the accretions of law, custom, tradition, and religion. The chief difficulty arises from the fact that the name itself suggests just such an ideal as that which Ethics claims as its subject-matter. It is, therefore, not surprising to find the claim put forward that Ethics is merely a subordinate department of Sociology, which for the first time has given precision to its conceptions by its demonstration that 'a man's first and last duty is to see and do those things which the social organism of which he is a member calls upon him to do.'[3] The question whether Ethics is 'subordinate' to Sociology or Sociology to Ethics need not trouble us. Every science may be said to be subordinate to that from which it draws its data. On the other hand, a science may be said to be of higher rank in respect to another, in so far as it recognizes differences of value in the data it receives from it, and sets itself to discover the ground on which these differences rest. It is this that marks off Ethics from Sociology. Sociology treats social customs and institutions in the same spirit of impartiality as Psychology treats sentiments, beliefs, and volitions. Ethics, on the other hand, is concerned throughout with values. It considers social forms and institutions from the point of view of their completeness and coherence as expressions of human nature. It asks whether the social life is the best or the only life for a human soul. 'In what way through society, and in what characteristics of society, does the soul lay hold of its truest self, or become, in short, the most that it has in it to be? How does the social life at its best compare with the life of art, of knowledge, or of religion, and can the same principle be shown to be active in all of them?'[1]

Yet, when we have realized the distinction between what may be called the causal and the teleological points of view as the starting-points for different disciplines, it is no less a mistake to insist too pedantically on their separation. The rise of Sociology in modern times may to a large extent be traced to an ethical dissatisfaction with existing forms of political and social organization, and any attempt to exclude reference to distinctions of value as irrelevant to it in its later developments, or to confine it to naturalistic discussions of origin and growth, must be detrimental to the science, depriving it of its legitimate inspiration and hampering its usefulness. Perhaps the attempt to do so is the reason why the abstract study of Sociology has hitherto been in general so disappointing, and why its most conspicuous successes have been in fields in which, as in the study of Pauperism, Criminology, Eugenics, and Education, the practical interest has been dominant. Similarly, from the side of Ethics, the barrenness of many of its discussions and the abstractness of many of its theories are largely due to the neglect of sociological considerations. It is safe to say that there can be no true understanding of the nature and tendencies of forms of moral judgment and of social institution apart from the study of their origin and history. If all our ethical notions are at present on an expanding scale, if we are reaching forward to wider and clearer ideas as to the meaning of charity, temperance, and simplicity in life, commercial honesty, the objects and methods of punishment, the meaning and social value of religion, it is because of the stimulation we have received from sociological investigations into the effects of almsgiving, of luxury, of unregulated competition and speculation, of our present system of prison discipline, of the secularization of morality. If, on the other hand, our minds are still confused as to the demands of the cardinal principle of justice—some desiring to base it on desert, others on need, others on abstract equality—this is probably because we have hitherto, in our speculations upon it, made too little use of the idea, with which Sociology has familiarized us, of life as consisting in the organized efforts of differently endowed individuals towards the realization of a social ideal, and the ultimate claim of each individual to the opportunity of contributing to it according to his ability.

4. Ethics and Metaphysics.—In a time of reaction against metaphysical ideas it is not surprising to meet with a wide-spread suspicion of anything that would seem to make practical truth depend on speculative. This attitude of mind seems to arise from a mistaken view of the nature both of Ethics and of Metaphysics. Of the former we have already said enough. Metaphysics has been defined as only a particularly obstinate effort to think clearly. But the only way to think a thing out into clearness is to think it in its relations to other things, more particularly to the whole to which it belongs; and, seeing that no finite whole stands by itself, but each leads us out into some wider and more embracive system, till we reach the universe of created things, there is no knowledge completely clear except that which seeks to see things *sub specie Universi*. Philosophy, since the time of Plato, has been familiar with the conception of the universe as thus consisting of a hierarchy of systems related to one another in an order of greater or less comprehensiveness or 'concreteness,' and of the higher form of knowledge as metaphysical in the sense just explained. But, for common sense, which is concerned with objects of everyday experience in their relation to human wants, and even for science, which is concerned with the extension and organization of the knowledge necessary for the effective exploitation of material things, such a form of explanation may be said to be so remote as to be of quite negligible importance. The more particular and exclusive an object (*i.e.* the nearer to ordinary sense-perception and ordinary physical needs), the remoter it is from the all-comprehending Whole, and the less is there occasion to raise ultimate questions of its

[1] See recent developments on the 'assumptions' and feelings of value that underlie mental processes, *e.g.* in W. Urban's *Valuation, its Nature and Laws*, London, 1909.

[2] Stout, *Analytic Psychology*, 1896, i. 12.

[3] Sidgwick, *Miscellaneous Essays and Addresses*, xi., London, 1904.

[1] Bosanquet, *Philosophical Theory of the State*, London, 1899, p. 50 [2nd ed. 1910].

place within it. Mind and will are clearly *not* such objects. They are high up in the scale of universality and comprehensiveness. So embracive a universe as that which they constitute might with some justice be itself regarded as the whole, in reference to which such particular objects and even such universals as art and science find their meaning.

It was an instinctive perception of this relation that led Mill and other philosophers of the middle of last century to use Psychology and Metaphysics interchangeably, and that forced so representative an experientialist as William James to admit, in the Preface to the Italian edition of his *Principles of Psychology*, that in the years which had passed since the publication of his book he had become more and more convinced of the difficulty of treating Psychology without introducing some true philosophy of his own.

If this be true of the psychological treatment of the facts of mind, it would seem to be so *a fortiori* of the ethical. The very definition of Ethics as a science of ends or ideals raises the question of the difference of the teleological from the causal point of view, and of their relation to one another. On the other hand, the claim of these ends or ideals to be universal and absolute for human life necessarily raises the metaphysical question of the place of human life itself in the whole scheme of things. This is the reason why the 'metaphysical basis' or (less ambiguously) the metaphysical implications of Ethics are a matter of concern not only to philosophers, but to the community at large, wherever it has begun to reflect on the nature and authority of moral imperatives, and why controversies, *e.g.* as to the educational value of religion, which to modern Gallios seem to be 'questions of words and names,' and to be disturbances of peaceful progress, are in reality indications of alertness to important practical differences.

Whether we shall express the relation here indicated as one of 'dependence' will again turn upon the meaning we assign to the word. If it be meant that Ethics is a deductive science like geometry, consisting of a series of constructions and demonstrations syllogistically derived from principles resting upon metaphysical proofs, nothing could be more foreign to modern notions. It seems doubtful whether there ever has been any serious attempt to treat Ethics in this way. Even Spinoza's classical *Ethica ordine geometrico demonstrata* fails to conceal the essentially inductive character of his operations, and may be said to have only preachéd Baconianism under the form of the syllogism. On the other hand, if we mean that, owing to the universality of the subject-matter, ethical discussion from the outset marches with metaphysical, and that there are points at which it is so difficult—or even impossible—to discover any scientific frontier between them that they may be said to merge in one another, there is sufficient truth in the statement. But it must be understood that it is meant in no other sense than that in which Mechanics may be said to depend on Physics, Economics on Sociology, or any other of the more 'abstract' sciences upon the more comprehensive and concrete with which it stands in immediate relation. And this sense, it should be further noticed, is the opposite of that which is commonly understood by dependence.

II. *THE SPECIAL PROBLEMS OF MODERN ETHICS.*—The preceding abstract statement will become clearer after a glance at the main stages in the development of ethical theory, with a view to indicating the special problems of modern Ethics and the directions in which it seeks for an answer to them.

The first sketch of a complete moral philosophy we owe to Plato and Aristotle. What distinguished their theories and gave them a permanent value was the perception that human goodness is not merely the expression by the individual will of the essential nature of social life—significant and conclusive though their demonstration of this was. To live the good life was not simply to be a citizen; it also expressed the true nature and purpose of the world in general, and thus united the human to the Divine. To Plato the highest form of human life could only be the outcome of a vision of the eternal Good; to Aristotle (herein out-Platoing Plato) it was itself that vision—a putting aside of our mortality that we may ourselves live in the Eternal.[1]

It is true that the dualism latent in all ancient philosophy led in the end to the separation between a human and a Divine order of virtue. Just as Cicero (*de Nat. Deor.* 53) tells us that the stars have two names—one from the appearances by which they are known to mortal men, another from the names of the immortals—so Plotinus (*Enn.* i. 2) distinguished between an earthly and a heavenly form of Temperance, Courage, Wisdom, and Justice. Yet the intention remained of seeking for the ultimate justification of moral goodness in an order which, while it includes humanity, is more than human.

With the development of the dualism between the individual and society on the one hand, and the temporal and the spiritual on the other, which may be said to have been the work of the succeeding period, there came the need to find some justification other than human nature itself for requirements which forced the claims of others in contrast to self, of the spirit in contrast to the flesh, upon the conscience. The main feature of mediæval and early modern Ethics may be said to have been the removal of the centre of moral energy from the vision of a perfected human nature, expressing the Divine upon earth, to that of perfected happiness in heaven. *Credo ut intelligam* had its ethical equivalent in *Credo ut agam.* Only when the spirit of Plato revived, as in the Florentine Platonists of the 16th cent., or in the Cambridge Idealists of the 17th, did the faith begin to be recovered that goodness means participation in the Divine order of Nature and human society. On the other hand, when, with the rationalizing spirit of the 18th cent., the attempt was made to find a natural basis for the moral life, it is not surprising that, in the spirit of the older dualism, moralists should have been driven to seek for it in the only principle other than revelation that seemed to be available—that of self-love.

It was Kant who first clearly struck the note of modern Ethics, in pointing to the idea of humanity, or of fully developed human nature, as the centre of the moral world. Not only is devotion to this the bond of all social union—the condition of realizing a 'kingdom of ends'—but in it is to be found the revelation to the individual soul of the ultimate meaning of things. This note had its most powerful echo in this country in the course of the 19th cent. in the writings of Thomas Carlyle, who taught that fidelity to duty is not only the one condition of inward peace, but the preserving principle of human society and the way of access into the Divine purpose of creation. This doctrine at once carried Kant and his great English interpreters beyond the naturalism of the positive and utilitarian Ethics on the one hand, and the supernaturalism of the orthodox theology of their time on the other. Unfortunately Kant inherited the psychology of his opponents, which reduced all motives to forms of pleasure-seeking, and he could escape its results only by setting up in its place the barren end of obedience to an abstract command of reason, while Carlyle had too great a contempt for the systematizing spirit of his time ever to seek a psychological foundation for truths which he regarded as sufficiently obvious to intuition.

The task to which modern Ethics has set itself may thus be said to be the justification of this transcendentalism in the light of what recent theory has to say (1) on the nature of volition, (2) on the standard of our judgments on voluntary acts, and (3) on the grounds that we have for conceiving of this standard as rooted in the nature of things. A condensed discussion of these three problems, under the headings of the Psychology, the Logic, and the Metaphysics of Ethics, is all that the present article can attempt.

III. *THE PSYCHOLOGY OF ETHICS.*—**1. General nature of volition.**[2]—The recognition of the element of seeking or 'conation' as fundamental to consciousness may be said to be the starting-point of modern Psychology. What gives unity and continuity to conscious life, binding its elements together as a magnetic field binds the particles of loose metal which come within it, is a purposeful tension, appearing under two forms—according as it is directed to change in the inner or in the outer world. Metaphysicians have spoken of this fundamental factor as 'will,' but Psychology is wise in marking the distinction between mere instinctive, involuntary striving, and self-direction towards a consciously conceived end, and in confining will or volition to the latter. It thus arrives at the definition of volition as the self-direction of a conscious subject through the idea of a change, whether in the contents of the mind itself or in the

[1] *Ethics*, x. vii. 8.

[2] The only adequate treatment of volition in English is the series of articles in *Mind*, new ser., vols. x.–xiii.

external world. In the form both of attention and of overt action, volition is closely related to feeling or interest, seeing that it is only on the basis of some intrinsic or acquired attractiveness in the object, some point of affinity between it and the psychical or psycho-physical structure, that desire can be initiated or sustained. There is no such thing as determination by 'pure reason.' Apparent cases, as in the preference of duty to inclination, are cases of determination by a deeper inclination, not of feelingless choice. At the other extreme, actions prompted by vivid ideas or temporary obsessions just cease to resemble volitions in proportion as the vividness comes from the accidental circumstances of the moment, instead of being, as it normally is, a function of a felt affinity between the object and the soul or psycho-physical organism. Whether we shall call the movement towards the source of this feeling in all cases 'desire,' or reserve that term for cases in which, owing to obstruction in the fulfilment of a conation, the object stands out as something merely possible in more or less painfully felt contrast to the present or actual, is a question of terminology. The essential point to notice is that objects attract, as Aristotle saw, *ὡς ἐρώμενα*, or not at all.

2. The development of volition.—The development of will is thus the development of interest. It follows the line of growing susceptibility to objects which are more remote from the mere physical stimulus, and which correspond to a wider and deeper internal organization. The growth of the power of attention (*q.v.*) is the most obvious illustration of this. In its earlier stages attention is controlled by the merely mechanical pressure of presentations and ideas—their vividness, persistence, novelty—or by their merely external connexions of coexistence or sequence, and their superficial resemblances. We have the beginning of self-direction when the succession of presentations passes under the control of some idea of what is wanted, as in purposeful observation or recall. At a higher stage still the process is freed from all immediate reference to an external world, and becomes in the proper sense self-sustained, as in imaginative constructions or trains of reasoning. Intellectual education means the development of the power of the free exercise of the attention in such self-sustaining activities, under the guidance of comparatively abstract and remote intellectual ends. This is rendered possible by the formation, in the mind, of an intellectual 'interest' or appercipient system which acts as a principle of selection and organization in the objects and ideas that come before the mind, and, as it gains strength, extends and deepens its influence over the flow of mental life. Such interests or dominant selective principles are not to be regarded as possessions of the mind, still less as forces acting from without upon it. They are what give character and individuality to a man's intellectual life, and enable us to speak of him in the proper sense as a mind at all.[1]

Precisely parallel with these stages in the development of the 'internal will' are those which are distinguishable in the development of the will in the ordinary sense. Corresponding to the semi-involuntary control of the attention by the external world or by insistent ideas is control by impulse, pressing appetite, or the fascination of isolated practical ideas. What is characteristic of this stage is the absence of any reference to the idea of the self as a whole. Inhibitions and hesitations occur, but they are caused by the conflict of impulses with one another, rather than by the conflict of an idea, with which the mind identifies itself, with any or all of them. Selection and control come with the power of identifying ourselves with remoter objects, and bringing nearer objects into a form which may harmonize with their attainment. It is a further stage when these objects in turn become subordinated to some idea of the self as a whole, which thenceforth becomes the subduing, organizing principle of a life. Such dominating ideas are not something merely possessed by a man. They possess the man, or rather they make him the man he is. They are his will and personality. It is only when they find expression in his actions that we account him fully himself. Where they fail, we set about seeking for some passing state, some accidental circumstance, outside the man himself, which, if it does not 'excuse' him, may give us the clue to the situation.

We have spoken of attention and overt volition as though they were two species of the same genus. But the connexion is much closer. They are rather to be regarded as the beginning and end of the same process. The condition of all action is attention to that which is to be enacted. It is for this reason that, different though ideo-motor action is from true volition, it has been taken as giving us the clue to its underlying nature. Ideo-motor action depends on the accidental occupation of attention by a passing motor suggestion owing to temporary absence of mind, though it ought not to be forgotten that even here the occupation of the attention depends in turn on the interest, instinctive or acquired, which attaches to the object either as an end desirable in itself, or as a means to some further end with which the agent has identified himself. Volition consists in the selective occupation of the attention by an idea owing to its perceived harmony with a permanent interest, and is essentially 'presence of mind.'

3. Will and character.—The analysis of volition thus carries us beyond the single act to the volitional dispositions on which it depends. The totality of these dispositions in the individual is his character, his 'will' in the substantial sense, in distinction from the volitions which go to form it and are the outcome of it. To the formation of will as thus defined a variety of factors contribute—inherited instincts, temperament or emotional disposition, circumstances both physical and social. But by far the most important are the reactions of the will itself to the suggestions which these supply, and the habits which thus become impressed upon it. Character has hence been defined as the habit of the will. It has seemed to thinkers such as Socrates and Rousseau that this definition is a contradiction in terms, seeing that character in any sense in which it is of value must involve freedom from the tyranny of habit. The difficulty is met, not, as by H. Bergson,[1] by drawing a hard and fast line between motor habits which are correlated with cerebral action, and the free life of mind, but by noting the distinction between narrower or mechanical and the wider or, as we might call them, adaptive habits whose office it is to control them in the interest of life as a whole. In this sense Rousseau spoke of the habit of acquiring no habit, and Aristotle defined virtue itself as the habit of aiming at the mean. The above analysis enables us to add that these habits are, in the last resort, habits of attention, and to understand how, by practice in adapting conduct to embracive ends, the habit of being controlled by these ends—in other words, a moral character—may be acquired.[2]

4. The social will.—In the older psychology, which conceived of pleasure or the avoidance of pain as the single ultimate motive, objects of social value could enter into the content of the will only in so far as they could be made to appear as a means to the furtherance of that end, or, through the principle of association, come to be mistaken for it. It was an advance on this individualistic psychology when it came to be seen

[1] See W. Mitchell, *Structure and Growth of the Mind*, London, 1907.

[1] *Matter and Memory*, Eng. tr. 1911, *passim*.
[2] See Stout, *op. cit.* i. 194.

that the experience of pleasure presupposes instinct and desire, and the social instincts were admitted to a place of at least equal importance with the self-preservative or self-assertive. It was a further advance still when it was recognized that the social instincts are merely vague tendencies, apart from the filling and the moulding which they receive from contact with the developed life of the society into which the individual is born. Just as mental development depends for stimulus and guidance on the social medium, and, more particularly, on the social institution of language, so the development of will depends on the assimilation of the purposes represented by social institutions and customs. There was then no longer any difficulty in understanding how corporate ends, *e.g.* family life, which satisfied deep-rooted instincts and claimed attention from the first, should pass into the structure of the mind and become objects of interest in the sense explained above of at least equal compelling power with that of the more personal. Moreover, it was no longer necessary to conceive of the individual and the social as lying outside of each other and requiring to be linked together by any artificial apparatus of 'association.' Their continuity and interdependence were a mere matter of ascertained fact. 'The individual self and the community are not centres of different circles; they may rather be said to be the two foci in relation to which we may describe the course of human activity.'[1]

So far the facts seemed plain. But, on the further questions of the precise description of the process of assimilation and the resulting content, 'social' psychologists were by no means so clear. With respect to the former question, it was probably the genius of G. Tarde which first effectively directed attention to the part played by imitation. Other psychologists, such as Baldwin, were not slow to follow and apply the principle to explain the appropriation of the purposes and the feelings of others and the development of the individual into a *socius*.[2] With respect to the second question, the current view of what is meant by a universal led to the interpretation of the result as a mere reproduction of the same content in an indefinite number of individuals. A closer analysis of what is meant by imitation seems to show that—except in the case of the children's game, or the savage's exaggerated respect for precedent, of which this is perhaps itself an imitation—imitation in the strict sense of the word plays but a small part in social life. Even where the suggestion comes from the action of another, and not from the requirements of a situation, there is adaptation and invention: the suggestion is what Stout calls 'relative.' Where, on the other hand, it is the situation that works, as in reefing a sail or felling a tree (and this is the typical 'social' case), what we have is co-operation and not imitation. Similarly, what is of value in the result of imitation, even where this is prominent, is not the seeing as another sees, or the feeling as he feels (out of this no *socius* could develop), but the formation, in the individual, of the conception of a whole to whose life he contributes, not by doing as another does, but by doing something which is suggested to his own inventive imagination by the situation in which he finds himself.

In what has just been said we have kept strictly within the limits of Psychology, but beyond the psychological problem of the origin of the social will in the individual is the philosophical one of the reality in society of a will which is not something entirely outside the individual will, and yet, as something more comprehensive, continuous and internally harmonious, is something also more substantial than it. If the doctrine of the reality of the social will was not expressly formulated by Plato and Aristotle, it lies very near the view they took of the State as the individual writ large and as 'prior to the family and the individual.' As has recently been clearly shown by Gierke,[1] it formed the assumption of the whole mediæval theory of the State. It was first clearly stated in modern times, though as a brilliant paradox, by Rousseau, and has found its way into modern political philosophy in divers not wholly compatible forms, through Comte, Hegel, Lotze, and Wundt. The statement of it in the last of these writers (*Ethics*, iii. 20), founded as it is on the best available psychological analysis, is of peculiar value at the present time. In our own country it was held in a somewhat mystical form by J. H. Newman, but has been expounded recently as an integral part of Idealistic philosophy by Bosanquet.

5. The freedom of the will.—It is unlikely that so important a transformation in psychological theory as that sketched above should be without bearing on the question of the freedom of the will. So long as the point of view of Psychology was identified with that of the physical sciences, we can understand how there must have appeared to be an *impasse* between Psychology and the assumption on which all judgments of merit and demerit and of moral and civic responsibility rested. So soon, on the other hand, as it was recognized that the central fact from which any true psychology must start is the idea of a progressively realized end, a breach was made in the older form of determinism, and the question was reopened whether it is possible to harmonize the findings of science and morality. Even from the point of view of Biology it ought not to be difficult, except for one who sets out with an invincible prejudice in favour of the exclusive validity of the categories of the inorganic sciences, to admit that to render the facts intelligible they must be seen with other eyes than those of the physicist or the chemist. Life depends on the storage of physical energy, it maintains itself in and through a system of mechanical strains and impacts; but these are taken up into a scheme that goes beyond them; and, in so far as this is so, the life of the humblest plant is free in a sense denied to the motions of the heavens. *A fortiori* all this is true of beings who not only live but can make their life an object—who to adjustment to environment and determination from within can add determination by the idea of the self. Self-conscious mind is still subject to the laws of inorganic matter and of mere life. In the instincts and appetites which it inherits, in the habits which it acquires, it carries about with it a system of forces which, while they stimulate and give stability to its life, constantly threaten its own peculiar nature. Yet, so long as it bears also about with it a spark of human purpose, it contains a principle that enables it to turn all these into means and to vindicate a new form of being, which is free in the still higher sense of having the power to set everything else, even its own freedom, over against itself, and to convert it into an instrument of self-development. Such freedom will be more or less complete, according as more or less of the insight which experience has brought as to the meaning of the life that calls for development is embodied in the action—in other words, according as a man lives more habitually and consistently in his deepest purposes and is more completely self-possessed.

What modern Psychology claims is that in this conception, which we might call that of 'degrees of freedom,' we have a point of view from which the old controversy between libertarian and determinist may cease. As against the old determinism we must admit that reason is free. In Logic this is not denied. In conception and inference the mind first asserts its freedom from the pressure of what is merely external, whether in the apparent connexions of the data or in the vividness and persistence of their presentation to the mind. Yet (as against any theory of mere indeterminism) we must maintain that it is free from these only to submit itself to its own law, and to be more completely under the constraint of logical connexion. In

---

[1] W. R. Sorley, *The Moral Life*, Camb. Univ. Press, 1911.

[2] See esp. *Mental Development in the Child and the Race*, New York and London, 1895.

[1] *Political Theories of the Middle Age*, Cambridge, 1900. For an account of the various forms in which the reality of the general will has been conceived, see M. M. Davis, *Psychological Interpretations of Society*, Columbia University Publications, 1909.

saying, as he does, that he 'could not conclude otherwise,' the reasoner asserts not his bondage, but his freedom. It is only apparently different with conduct. True, there is commonly a wider gulf between seeing what is reasonable and giving effect to it in action than between seeing a logical consequence and admitting it. But this is only because living is a more complicated business than thinking. The principle is the same. The will asserts its freedom (1) in resisting mere impulse, (2) in collecting itself for rational decision, (3) in refusing to allow itself to be diverted from its resolution. At each of these points it is dependent upon forces of habit and suggestion over which it has no direct control. But at each point also it is more than any of these habits, and has the power of taking this something more as its guiding principle. Just in proportion, moreover, as it does so does it feel at the moment of action that it could not do other than it does. But it does not on that account excuse itself for the result; on the contrary, it is all the more ready to accept the issue as its own. Responsibility, in a word, grows, like freedom, with the extent to which our conduct has been forced upon us as the only true expression of what we desire to be. If the question is still pressed upon us whether in actual fact it could have been different, the answer is at once No and Yes—No, if it be meant that, the agent being what he was, his conduct could have been other; Yes, if it be meant that his character was no inevitable result of a history in which moral purpose, individual and social, has failed to enter as a controlling factor.

An unbiased consideration of the implications of our judgments of moral approval and disapproval and of the principles underlying punishment will be found to support these conclusions. It shows that in the case most favourable for moral judgment, viz. that of one's own actions, what gives remorse its sting is not so much that I have done the action as that I was of such a character as to be capable of doing it. If I could persuade myself that the action expressed no permanent features of my will, this conviction, instead of bringing an access of contrition, as it ought to do on the libertarian theory, would bring a feeling of relief analogous to that which I might experience if I discovered that I had done it in my sleep, or had not done it at all. Similarly with regard to punishment. Punishment is the reaction of society against the offences of the individual, and is justifiable only on the assumption, first, that there is a real connexion between action and character, and, second, that through reform or 'example' it makes for better character in the offender, in the community, or in both.

6. Hedonism.—Like the controversy as to free will, that as to the relation of pleasure to desire, if not actually an anachronism in the light of recent analysis, is on the fair way to become so. It follows, from what has been said of the dependence of all conscious processes on the pre-existence of dispositions with which presented objects are in felt harmony or discord, that without feeling there can be no volition. In this sense we might accept Mill's dictum,[1] that 'desiring a thing and finding it pleasant, aversion to it and thinking of it as painful, are phenomena entirely inseparable, or rather two parts of the same phenomenon' (though for 'as painful' we should have to substitute 'with pain'). But, since Mill wrote these words, the distinction between the idea of a thing and the idea of the pleasure to be derived from it has been frequently pointed out; and, seeing that these are clearly *different* phenomena, it seems obvious that to desire a thing, and to desire the pleasure we expect from it, are not one and the same phenomenon, but are entirely separable phenomena. The recognition of this distinction may be said to have rendered the older form of hedonism no longer a tenable account of the nature of will and desire. It can no longer be maintained that it is the pleasure-giving quality of things that makes them objects of desire.

Of the existence of the type of character known as the pleasure-seeking, there can, of course, be no question; but the pleasure-seeker gets his name not so much from his identifying himself with pleasure in the abstract as from his habitually identifying himself with objects which have so little claim to human significance that the pleasures and pains connected with them are their most striking attribute. He seeks satisfaction in the line of least resistance, and runs his life on the cheap. The normal man has acquired, through education, sufficient strength of mind to be able to combat casual impulses and desires by a reference to the concrete interests with which he habitually identifies himself, and to face the effort of attention involved in banishing contradictory suggestions. The mind of the pleasure-seeker, on the other hand, is like a sluice without a gate. Casual suggestions sweep unresisted through it, because of his inability to face the effort required to sustain an inhibiting idea in the centre of attention. His characteristic is, not that he seeks or finds the greatest pleasure in the things he chooses, but that he fails to find sufficient pleasure in anything else.

[1] *Utilitarianism*, p. 58.

This conclusion is confirmed by recent criticism of the second part of the ordinary doctrine of pleasure-seeking, viz. that pleasure operates as a motive in proportion to its anticipated amount, that 'to desire anything, except in proportion as the idea of it is pleasant, is a physical and metaphysical impossibility.'[1] It is a well-known law that feelings 'blunt themselves by repetition.' While this is a loss for feeling, it is a gain for practice. Objects operate as springs of action, in proportion not to the amount of emotional disturbance they cause, but to the influence they have acquired over us through our habits of thought and action, and the deposits of feeling that we call our sentiments in connexion with them. This is the reason why sense-gratifications are sought by the pleasure-seeker himself, under a law of continually diminishing emotional returns and yet of continually increasing motive pressure.

Recent hedonism has sought to accommodate itself to these criticisms by maintaining that they are irrelevant to the main contention, which is that it is their pleasure-giving quality, and not their felt relation to the will as a system of purposes, that gives value to things. But, while avoiding the difficulty of identifying the object of desire with pleasure, this reading of the doctrine comes into conflict with the recognition by recent Psychology that pleasure is a function of need, and not need of pleasure. The satisfaction of felt need necessarily is pleasant, but the degree or amount of the pleasure, while it may be a gauge of the momentary pressingness of the need, can never be the standard of its value for life as a whole. On the contrary, the worth of the pleasure must follow worth of the need, of whose satisfaction it is the sign.

7. Conscience.—The justification of the pressure which conscience (*q.v.*) exercises upon the will is a question of Ethics in the stricter sense of the word. The question of the precise nature and origin of the feeling of constraint which the word represents belongs to Psychology.

The will, we have seen, is identical with the disposition to be attracted by things which are in harmony with the dominant practical interests, and to be repelled from things which are in contradiction to them. From this it follows that these centres of practical interest, whatever they may be, must have the power, either separately or in conjunction, of exercising a certain pressure upon conduct in so far as there exists a consciousness of its general bearing in furthering or obstructing the purposes they represent. In reference to each of them there is a line of conduct which approves itself, another which disapproves itself. Wherever we have such a centre we have the conditions of such a feeling, the degree of pressure thus exercised varying in proportion to the depth and permanence of the interest concerned. The feeling of harmony or discord of conduct with a ruling interest is, in fact, a rudimentary conscience, and by a suggestive use of language is sometimes spoken of in this way. In this sense we hear of the craftsman's conscience and the student's conscience—even the miser's conscience, which makes the profitless expenditure of a sixpenny-piece a positive pain. What differentiates conscience, in the distinctly moral sense, from these consciences is merely the depth and the permanence of the interest in which it has its roots. If the reader is inclined to resent such an account as a cheapening of an element in human nature which he has been accustomed to regard as its highest manifestation, the reply is the same as that already given in regard to the will in general. In seeking to introduce intelligibility and continuity into the moral life by refusing to acknowledge any element without analogy elsewhere—any psychical Melchizedek without father or mother in human experience—we do not deny specific character to the experience we seek thus to understand. It is, therefore, quite consistent with the

[1] *Ib.*

recognition of a conscience *in sensu eminente* to endeavour to conceive of it as merely an extension, to a pre-eminent interest, of the pressure exercised upon conduct in general by any interest whatsoever.

The general nature and ground of this pre-eminence is, as we have seen, a question for Ethics proper. Psychology is concerned with the means and order of its development. It seeks to make it comprehensible how, appearing first as a vague instinctive pressure from within, and finding its counterpart in established custom without, the tribal self comes to dominate every other, moulding the individual into a homogeneous system of habits—*mores* or ἤθη. In its subsequent development this 'morality' follows in the track of developing self-consciousness in general. A definite stage is reached when the social spirit brings forth heroes and 'founders,' who not only embody in their own lives conspicuous forms of social excellence or 'virtue,'[1] but possess the insight of genius into the significance of virtue in general, and are able through individual prestige to give it firm roots in national life. These 'creative souls,' as Plato[2] calls them—'parents of virtue of every kind'—become thenceforth, through the force of suggestion, a living law or conscience to the nation to which they belong. It is another stage when the demand arises to have usage and inherited authority defined and restrained by written law. But it is not until, owing to the growth of reflexion, the social bearing of different types of moral character comes to be realized, and their goodness becomes transparent in the light of the social well-being they serve, that we reach the highest form of social conscience. Virtue is thenceforth knowledge, or at least implies knowledge. Actions and types of character at first approved because they have the stamp of authority, law, or custom come to be approved for their own sake. Yet the same principle works throughout: there is no real break anywhere. Just as Logic works obscurely in the process by which we accept our beliefs from ordinary sense-experience or common hearsay, so morality works obscurely in the earlier manifestations of social solidarity. Fear is the beginning of wisdom, because there is more in it than fear. And, just as the progress of belief is best represented as a continuous process by which the false is separated from the true, and casual *aperçus* and accidentally received opinions become purified in the light of organized science, so the progress of moral feeling is to be conceived of as a continuous development from unconscious acceptance of tribal custom to the enlightened citizenship or humanitarianism of the patriot or the philanthropist.

IV. *The Logic of Ethics*.—1. The idea of a **logic of moral value**, more than once appealed to in the preceding paragraphs, is contrary to two widely held but opposite ethical theories. On the one hand it is maintained that none is needed, on the other that none is possible.

(*a*) The development of morality, it is held, is the result of natural selection. Once understand how in the inter-tribal struggle for existence a form of character in individuals has been developed which favours survival, and you have an answer—the only answer needed—to the question of the ground of its authority. Character is good because it survives, it does not survive because it is good; *de facto* is *de jure*; its might is its right.

After what has already been said as to the development of will, we shall not be accused of under-estimating the value of the history of moral ideas. Conscience, like everything else, stands in relation to historical fact, but it is, in its essence, as we have seen, a form of self-consciousness, and, as such, claims the right to test the fact by its relation to the self. It is for this reason that the appeal to nature (as the name for what actually exists) must remain unconvincing. Unless it can be shown, apart from the actual course of development, that there exists some essential relation between social solidarity and the rational element in human nature, in other words, that will obeys a logic of its own which forbids it to find rest in anything merely individual, it is difficult to see on what foundations our judgments of value, and the feeling of obligation which depends on them, can rest.

Darwin himself noticed the difficulty of explaining, on the principles of natural evolution, the emotions that lead to philanthropic efforts to preserve the weak. More recently W. James[1] has called attention to the feeling of the inward dignity of certain spiritual attitudes—serenity, simplicity, etc.—as quite inexplicable except by an innate preference of the more ideal attitude for its own pure sake. To this it might be added that, as a matter of history, these attitudes seem first to have arisen in nations which had already been absorbed by conquest, and had long ceased to compete effectively for national existence, and to have commended themselves to the human soul not by any perceived utility as a condition of survival, but by their consonance with the general aspirations of mankind after spiritual unity. Psychology, indeed, seeks to make it comprehensible how, through the influence of habit, association, imitation, our admirations deepen and extend. In this way means are transformed into ends, qualities come to be admired for their own sake, and perfections to be sought after which have no immediate relation to practical utility. But these considerations, however useful in explaining the origin of these and similar sentiments, still fail to touch the main difficulty—the justification of the *right* they claim to be regarded as of superior order, and, as such, to control our conduct. Granted that they exercise that pressure on the coarser and more selfish instincts which we call the authority of conscience, by what right do they do so? What gave them that authority?

(*b*) An opposite line is taken by writers who, while insisting that actual fact can establish no right, maintain that we can have no ultimate standard other than that of immediate feeling. The experience of good, like that of blue or yellow, is an ultimate datum of which no definition is possible,[2] and none is needed. A theory like this is not, of course, to be met by denying the place of immediate experience in moral judgment. Where it errs is in taking immediate feeling as an ultimate instead of merely as a starting-point. It is true that our practical as well as our logical and æsthetic judgments are rooted in quite definite and unique experiences. But no one maintains, as regards our logical judgments, that the matter ends there. Even in the simplest case of sensory data, such as colour, there are the circumstances of light, distance, contrast, etc., to be taken account of before we can tell what it is that we experience. If it is, according to a popular way of thinking, different with regard to 'tastes,' this can be seriously maintained only on condition that we are prepared to deny all value to æsthetic criticism—ultimately all essential difference of value in forms of beauty. And, if it be true that there are standards of truth and beauty, it can only again be at the price of denying all unity to human nature that we deny a like standard in the case of moral goodness.

It is impossible, in an article like the present, to

[1] See Hegel's *Philosophy of Law*, sect. 150.
[2] *Symposium*, 209.

[1] See *Will to Believe*, 1902, p. 187 (1st ed. 1897).
[2] 'Good is a simple notion, just as yellow is a simple notion' (G. E. Moore, *Principia Ethica*, p. 7).

draw out this fundamental analogy with anything like the completeness which it deserves. It must suffice to take the leading points which emerge from a consideration of the underlying structure of our logical judgments.

1. The position to which, in the search for a criterion of truth, philosophy is constantly brought back is that this cannot consist in any mere correspondence of idea with an externally given fact (as common-sense theory holds), or in the mere psychical insistence of the idea itself (as Hume believed). The conditions to be fulfilled are: first, that the test shall lie within the world of our experience; second, that it shall lie somewhere beyond the fluctuating states of the individual mind. And the solution of this problem is found, as Kant was the first to see, in the recognition of the fact that knowledge from the outset is the organization of our ideas, so that they may have a consistent meaning. Where there is a question of the truth or falsity of a belief, no other test is available than the extent to which it is possible to establish continuity and coherence between it and the existing system of what we believe we mean and what we mean to believe. It is useless to appeal against such a statement, as Pragmatism does, to the test of working. For this must either mean working for some partial purpose, usually described as the 'anticipation of experience' in a special field, or working as a universally and necessarily recognized principle. In the former case it simply is not true that in such partial working we have a guarantee of truth: a false idea may work well enough for a particular purpose, as a false premiss may be made to support a true conclusion. In the latter case we have only another way of saying that the belief must be consistent with experience as a whole. Cf. art. Error and Truth.

The ethical problem is set, *mutatis mutandis*, by the same conditions. The standard cannot be anything external to the will itself; good and bad, right and wrong, are distinctions that spring up within moral experience. On the other hand, it cannot be the mere fact of subjective satisfaction: the essence of moral judgment is distinction of value between different forms of momentary and individual satisfaction. And the answer is in principle the same as in the case of knowledge; the will or the self acts from the first in the face of casual appetites as organized experience acts amongst the data of sense-perception. In the semi-conscious morality of everyday life we are constantly submitting impulses and desires to the criticism of our larger purpose, as our thought submits the beliefs that come to it in ordinary apprehension to the criticism of its larger experience. The 'working' of a course of action may, again, be accepted as the test, if by working we mean harmony with moral experience as a whole. If, on the other hand, we mean working to secure some casually chosen purpose, we can say nothing of its goodness until we know the relation of this purpose itself to the organism of human purposes as a whole. As the criticism of beliefs becomes conscious, in the case of opposing theories of which the test is their relative power of bringing the facts into systematic connexion with one another, so criticism of our ends becomes conscious in the case of deliberation in which the search is for the course which shall bring the different interests concerned into the completest harmony with one another, and thus the will into completest harmony with itself.

2. The standard of truth as defined above has two sides. There is the side commonly emphasized in logical text-books—the necessity of submitting our theories or interpretations of meaning to the test of their inclusiveness: their power of taking in all the comparatively established meanings we call facts. On the other hand, meanings claiming to be facts have to submit to the criticism of accepted interpretations, the resistance which theories already in possession offer to reputed facts that refuse to fall into line with them.[1] That neither of these requirements—neither comprehension nor inner harmony—can ever be complete goes without saying. So long as there are elements outside the system already established, unrelated to it through their meanings, equilibrium is unstable. Contrariwise, wherever there is the feeling of instability, it is the sure sign that something lies outside whose meaning menaces the established order. In the progress of knowledge the two ideas of fullness and harmony tend to succeed one another, an age of investigation being followed by an age of systematization. But they are not two different standards, but different sides of the same.

Turning to practice, here, too, we have the same duality. The good, like the true, must be inclusive. In an age of expansion, like the present, this is not likely to be overlooked. 'There is but one unconditional commandment,' writes W. James,[2] 'which is that we should seek incessantly, with fear and trembling, so to vote and to act as to bring about the very largest total universe of good which we can see.' But it is easy here to go wrong. Good is no mere sum of satisfactions any more than truth is a sum of facts. Hence the necessity of emphasizing the consistency and systematic unity of goods without which there is no true self, but merely distraction and chaos. It is for this reason that we may prefer W. James's second definition as containing just this addition, and therefore less ambiguous: 'Vote always for the richer universe, for the good which seems most organizable, most fit to enter into complex combinations, most apt to be a member of a more inclusive whole.'[1]

[1] Witness the hesitation we feel with regard to some of the reputed facts of the Society for Psychical Research. They seem well authenticated, but we have no theory to receive them.

[2] *Will to Believe*, p. 209.

3. These two sides of the ideal of knowledge are the starting-points for opposite forms of intellectual failure. We have the type of open-mindedness that means looseness to all unity of principle and ends in incoherence. On the other hand, we have the man who stands out for consistency of principle, and is usually wrong in detail because his principle is too narrow. There is the same defect in practice. We have the looseness that comes from mere unthinking acceptance of lines of conduct suggested from without: the true 'unprincipledness' which begins anywhere and ends nowhere. On the other hand, we have the man whose life is founded on a principle which ignores fundamental facts. Badness, in the ordinary sense, where it does not consist in the mere absence of all guidance, is only a special form of this defect. It means subjection to some isolated and necessarily exclusive passion, the identification of the self with an interest which is at war with the conditions of individual and social stability.

4. If we follow the argument one step further, we can see how the attempt to find the source of moral judgments in the fact of natural evolution has its analogy in the attempt to derive knowledge from sense-impressions. It is true that the moral ideal develops in the individual only through contact with the society around him, as knowledge can develop only under the stimulus of sense. But its true fountain-head, the source of its authority, is in the nature of the will itself. Of morality we might say, paraphrasing Patricius's aphorism as to knowledge, *a voluntate primam originem, a societate exordium habet primum.* The social structure, so far from furnishing an explanation of the ideal as it exists in individuals, can only be explained by it. Its origin is lost in the mists of the past, but its historical development is the result of the growing insight of individuals into the gaps and inconsistencies which render it an inadequate expression of human good. No account of the ethical ideal can therefore be adequate which ignores the soul's presentiment of what is involved in its own nature, or seeks to explain it in terms other than those of will and individuality itself. The force that gives this ideal driving power is conscience or moral sense, which may now be defined as the feeling of unrest caused by the pressure of the ideal upon the actual will, as logical sense is the pressure of the ideal upon the actual intelligence. It is abstractly possible to disown both of them. But, just as to disown the logical ideal is to turn reason against itself, and leave it a prey to stagnation or delusion, so to disown the practical ideal is to disown what is deepest in ourselves, the source of all that is of value in life.

2. Value of the idealist standard.—While there is a wide agreement among idealist writers as to the general theoretic validity of the above analogy, there is much hesitation as to the extent of its application and the practical value to be attached to it.

(*a*) From the former point of view it has been maintained that, while in the world of theory science more and more approximates to the ideal of deduction and the anticipation of new developments, it is wholly different in the world of practice. Such apparently is the view of W. James,[2] who, while insisting on the analogy of Ethics and Science, conceives of it as ending at the stage of inconclusive experiment. Others, like Höffding, admit that a logic is discernible within the limits of particular ideals, *e.g.* that of self-assertion or self-abnegation, or that of the family or the nation, 'so that a person who recognizes it, and is sufficiently acquainted with the actual conditions under which it holds good, could also be brought logically to grant whatever conclusion might be deduced from that standard.' But they deny that any inner logic is discernible between one such standard and another. Here, no such deduction is possible; we have to wait the judgment of history, 'the great voting-place for standards of value.'[3] (*b*) From the point of view of utility there are others, like McTaggart,[4] who, while they admit that of the Good in the abstract no other account than the above is possible, yet find the appeal to it of little or no value in dealing with the concrete situations of life, and are fain to invoke the discarded end of pleasure as the best criterion or working standard of conduct.

To the first of these criticisms it is sufficient to point out that in reality there does not seem to be any essential difference between the ideals of science

[1] *Will to Believe*, p. 210. [2] *Ib.* 207.

[3] Höffding, *Problems of Philosophy*, New York, 1905, p. 160.

[4] *Studies in Hegelian Cosmology*, Cambridge, 1901, 'On the Supreme Good and the Moral Criterion.'

and our moral ideals in the respect referred to. It is, of course, true in general that we have to wait the judgment of experience to confirm our appeal to the ideal: 'das Weltgeschichte ist das Weltgericht.' On the other hand, it becomes more and more possible, as sensitiveness to moral distinctions develops and the ethical consciousness becomes clearer, to perceive what is implied in acknowledged principles. Such anticipations have commonly been made by the great legislators and reformers of the human race, whose efforts have much more frequently been employed in developing the logic of principles already accepted than in establishing new ones. Nor is there here any difference between the movement within particular ideals and that which carries us from one to the other. Where, for instance, to take Höffding's own example, can any line be drawn between progress within the family ideal and progress from the ideal of a strong domestic to a strong political consciousness? What holds of different levels of the social ideal holds also of the spiritual or suprasocial. There is no real discontinuity between the 'political' life and the life of science, art, and religion. Closely regarded, the latter come more and more to appear in the light of a continuation of the work which the commonwealth begins, 'fuller utterances of the same universal self which the general will reveals in more precarious forms, and in the same way implicit in the consciousness of all.'[1]

The second criticism, in like manner, seems to rest on a misunderstanding, of which the analogy of Logic again suggests the correction. The ideal in Logic, in general, is a world of completely coherent ideas; yet in any particular investigation we are concerned, not with this ideal in the abstract, but with carrying forward the mind's work of organization in response to the summons of a particular theoretic situation. The particular point on which attention is concentrated may be wholly insignificant in itself, bearing no obvious relation to truth as a whole, or even to the body of accepted truth in the particular department. Yet the concentration takes place on a general background of conviction that the problem itself is a rational one, and continuous with the general presuppositions of science, by which, in the last resort, the truth of the results must be tested. So in practice. The call for moral choice comes from particular circumstances, without obvious relation to wider ends, and may be met without consciousness of anything in particular that depends upon the choice. Yet what gives actual value to the choice is that it is rooted in the moral order, which it sustains in equilibrium, or that it carries us perhaps unconsciously to a higher plane. 'Pleasure' could be appealed to in conduct, as in belief, only where the issue is so insignificant that we may 'do as we like.'

3. Other definitions.—A reference to one or two of the classical definitions of the moral standard will serve to illustrate the somewhat abstract statement of it to which we have been led.

(*a*) *The mean.*—Aristotle's doctrine, that virtue or excellence is a mean, stands in express relation to the view that life is a developing system of harmonious activities. There is, indeed, an interpretation of the mean which suggests a compromise between opposing elements rather than the union of them in a harmonious whole. But that this is not the sense in which Aristotle intended the doctrine is evident, not only from the emphasis he lays on the 'relativity' of the mean, but from the analogy of the arts, which, in spite of his disclaimer, really underlies his whole discussion. What Aristotle has in view is the limitation imposed on the passions and desires, not by any artificial average or working compromise, but by the ideal form of individual life. As the artist works at the parts with his eye upon the whole, so it is the form of his own life as a whole that the individual must have in view in fixing the limits within which particular impulses and desires may find a place. The order, however, as the latter part of the definition indicates, can never be a merely individual one. The standard is not to be looked for in the broken outlines of the lives of ordinary people, but in the best type of humanity, the 'wise man,' who represents in the fullest manner the unbroken continuity of individual, social, and spiritual existence.[1]

(*b*) *Personality.*—While the harmonious adjustment of the elements in man's nature—material and spiritual, individual and social—is the keynote of classical Greek Ethics, the manifold obstructions to it, which to the next generation seemed to call for a withdrawal from what is irrelevant and for concentration on the relevant, tended to shift the emphasis from society to the individual, from citizenship to independent personality. True as this conception is when rightly interpreted, the ambiguity which surrounds it has proved a snare to the higher ethical thought almost to our own time. Personality (*q.v.*) may be taken as the merely formal aspect of the will—that in virtue of which it is distinguished, or may distinguish itself, not only from all that is external in the material world, but even from the qualities and capacities through which the will itself finds expression: 'I am what I am: all else is mere accident and limitation.' But only a formalism such as that which was the chief snare of the Stoics could seek for the moral standard in such an abstraction. To be a 'person' in this sense is to be the least that we can be without ceasing to be human: 'something,' as it has been called, 'contemptible in the very expression.' We reach a more concrete, though still a partial, view of personality when we conceive of it as the self which, in virtue of the material separation of the body and other forms of 'property,' has claims against other similar selves. It is the prominence assigned in modern times to the rights of personality in this (which is necessarily an exclusive) sense that has given rise to individualistic conceptions of the standard of ethical value. Hegel's motto, 'Be a person, and respect others as persons,' limited by him to the field of abstract or legal right, is taken by the individualist as equivalent to the highest expression of the moral consciousness. It is only when we come to a third sense of the word — which includes the other two while differing from them — that we can accept this equivalence. Giving meaning to the power we have of separating between ourselves and our conditions (including the various elements in our own nature), there is in every rational being the power of moulding them into a definite form for the furtherance of some concrete purpose or interest. Giving meaning also to the capacities of mind and body, and to the material objects which are their instrument, and justifying the claim the individual puts forward to freedom in the use of them, there is the capacity of permeating them with a life which is not merely individual to himself, but unites him with others who have a joint interest in their utilization. If we call this attitude of purposefulness 'personality,' we can see how it is realized, not in proportion to the extent to which concrete interests are excluded and the individual atomized, but in proportion as particular interests find their place in some

[1] Bosanquet *op. cit.* p. 333.

[1] See Bosanquet, *The Principle of Individuality and Value* London, 1912, App. ii.

universal and inclusive interest whereby the individual enters sympathetically into the spirit of the whole of which he is a part, and is thus raised above himself.

'Personality,' says W. Wallace,[1] 'presupposes *within* us a nature which is one and yet many, which has from the beginning a potency of unification of interests and principles, and which can, occasionally at least, raise that potency to an actual symmetry and solidarity. . . . *Without* us, it depends upon a system of society in which each has his place appointed, and therefore occupies a special restricted position; but still, in filling that place, his inner and moral personality must remain intact. He is no doubt a mere unit, but a unit which can embrace and reproduce in himself the whole society of which he forms a part.'

(*c*) *My station and its duties.*—In view of this statement of the full meaning of the principle of personality, we can understand how the latter element in it should have come in recent Ethics to be made the head of one corner. 'To be moral,' says Bradley,[2] 'I must will my station and its duties.' Though associated with a refined form of idealism in Bradley's writings, this takes us back to Plato's homely definition of virtue as τὰ ἑαυτοῦ πράττειν. There is, however, this difference between the ancient and the modern definition, that it is accepted by Plato only on the assumption that society has undergone a transformation which has eliminated the element of accident that plays so large a part in assigning their places to individuals. It was possible, indeed, for a former time to conceive of a man's station as assigned to him by a deeper Wisdom that knew man's needs. But, interpreted in the modern spirit, there is nothing to veil the element of naked accident to which most of us owe our station and function in life, and which makes all talk of a secret harmony, where it is not treason to a better order, in nine cases out of ten an obstructive form of cant. The difficulty can be met only by a return to the Platonic, which is also the modern democratic, point of view, and which conceives of the fullest life alike for individuals and society as attainable only by assigning to each the place which his own developed capacities best enable him to fill.

Even so the difficulty remains for us as for Plato,[3] that at its best the idea of a 'station' suggests fixity and exclusiveness, and in its very terms spells external pressure and spiritual impoverishment for the great mass, and particularly for the industrial part of society. Although no one is likely to claim that the practical difficulty which a period of mechanical industry like the present causes can be overcome by reference to abstract philosophical theory, it is yet important to realize that in principle there is no real contradiction between the ideal of fullness of life and concentration upon one or other of its particular purposes. The assumption that comprehensiveness is identical with multitude of interests and pursuits is a mistake parallel with that of assuming that fullness of intellectual life means universality of knowledge, and is open to the same correction. As it is the depth with which a man realizes the scientific spirit in a particular field, not the variety of his intellectual interests, that is the measure at once of his work and of his satisfaction in it, so it is the depth and intensity with which a man realizes his particular social obligations, not the multitude of the functions he performs or the area he covers, that gives meaning and fullness to his life.

V. *The Metaphysics of Ethics.*—Tempting though it is to pursue the social applications of ethical principle suggested in the previous sections, it is here more important to follow the philosophy of our subject to the point where it connects with the problems of religion.

It was with a true instinct that Kant perceived that, however separable metaphysical problems might be from science, they were bound up with the very existence of morality. Like the corresponding problems in the theory of knowledge, they may be condensed into two. (1) As the recognition of the relativity of human knowledge raises the question of the grounds on which we claim that the world responds to the claims of our intelligence, in other words, is knowable at all, so the discovery of the relativity of ethical ideals to social wellbeing raises the question whether they are applicable beyond it, whether they find any support in the actual course of the world as a whole. (2) As behind the question of the knowledge of the world of reality there emerges that of the kind of reality we must assign to the world of knowledge, so behind the question of the goodness of the world there lies the question of the kind of reality we must assign to the world of goodness.

1. Is the universe good?—To make clear to ourselves the precise form in which the first of these problems faces us to-day, we may start from Kant himself. In answer to the question, What is the foundation of our faith in duty? Kant, as is well known, appealed to the reality of the supersensible source from which its imperatives issue. But, when it was asked, in turn, on what our belief in this reality rests, the only answer forthcoming was that a categorical imperative is inconceivable without it. To this it seemed sufficient to reply that the alternative to which Kant sought to shut up the believer in morality—*either* the reality of a supersensible goodness *or* the unreality of the categorical imperative—does not represent the situation. There is a third possibility. We may deny Kant's identification of morality with a system of absolute imperatives. It is, indeed, impossible, as Kant saw, to base morality on self-interest. But the imperative that overrides the maxims of self-interest carries us, it may be urged, to no absolute Being containing in himself the conditions of the union of Nature and human life, of happiness and virtue, but only to the relative being of human society. Like the world of science, which, on Kant's own showing, has a claim to no more than hypothetical truth, the moral world is founded on a hypothetical, not on an absolute, imperative: not 'Do this, though the heavens fall,' but 'Do this, as you would have social life upon earth.'

This may be said to be the criticism which, in the next generation, Comte passed upon Kant, the Positivism of France upon the Formalism of Prussia. Its effect was to sweep away the point of contact between the supersensible and the sensible, which Kant thought he had discovered in morality, and to carry into the moral sphere the break between the reality of things and the forms under which we know them, which he had sought to establish in logical theory. Man's life founded on the conception of a good which realizes itself in an organism of social activities appears as something rounded off into itself in a *milieu* which stands in no essential relation to its ideals, and contains no pledge of their fulfilment, but, on the contrary, so far as we can see, after engendering them dooms them to ultimate disappointment. With Positivism the main issue of modern Ethics came into view. An exhaustive criticism of the theory is here out of the question (see Positivism). The question it raises is whether the logic which enables us to see that the individual owes all that he is to the unconscious co-operation of society ought not also to convince us that the being of society is rendered possible only through the co-operation of the universe as a whole. It is quite true that the work of civilization, or, as it is better called, of self-development, has been carried on in the face of apparently antagonistic forces of material Nature and human self-seeking. But it is equally true that it is in the conflict with outward and inward forces that all that is of most value in human life has been achieved. Philosophy is wrong when it seeks to minimize the evils of earthquake and pestilence, war and social injustice, as picturesque shading in the best of all possible worlds. It is within its right when it in-

[1] *Lectures and Essays*, p. 286. [2] *Ethical Studies*, p. 163.
[3] See *Rep.* iv. *ad init.*

sists that the good which we know and value is conceivable only in a world governed by just the laws of matter and mind which these disturbances illustrate. So obvious is this extension of the logic of Positivism, that we are not surprised to find the opposition of cosmic forces recognized by Comte himself as a necessary condition of human development. Without it, he tells us, 'man's feelings would become vague, his intelligence wanton, and his activity sterile. If this yoke were taken away, the problem of human life would remain insoluble, since altruism would never conquer egoism. But, assisted by the supreme fatality, universal love is able habitually to secure that personality shall be subordinated to sociality.'[1] The surprise is that, having established this relation between conditioning and conditioned, external Nature and the best in human life, Comte should still speak of the former as mere 'fatality,' of the latter as something 'subjective.' Whether, from the admission that there is a deeper relation than superficially appears between man's moral ideals and the course of Nature, we can advance to the conception of goodness as not only a revelation of the meaning of the forces actually operating in the world, but as the revelation of a conscious purpose latent in them—is a further question. The contention of the older Idealism was that, the general harmony of the world with our ideals being admitted, there is no logical standing-ground short of the conclusion that the universe is in its essence self-conscious Spirit, differing from our spirits only in that it realizes in its completeness and harmony the good which in our lives appears only fragmentarily and incoherently. But it is just this contention that has recently been subjected to penetrating criticism, and no account of the present state of critical thought on the metaphysics of Ethics would be complete which leaves this problem untouched.

2. Is there a higher in the universe than goodness?—In order to establish the supremacy of the Good, the appeal, we have seen, is to the standard of inner coherence. But, having established before this court its rights against its enemies, the bad and the imperfect, the Good has to face the tribunal on its own merits; and recent criticism has not been slow to point out the flaw in its own case.[2] In its efforts after self-expression the will seeks to include all the elements of life in one harmonious whole. The life which we judge to be truly good must, on the one hand, be all-inclusive, and to this end must ever be going outside of itself; on the other, it must bring its powers and possessions into harmonious relation with one another, and be at home with itself. But, however logically inseparable these two requirements may be, they manifest themselves in reality as two separate ideals: on the one hand, the ideal of self-sacrifice (whether this be to persons, as in altruism, or to impersonal objects, as in devotion to science or art); on the other, the ideal of self-realization. And these are, in the last resort, irreconcilable, and leave life broken and distracted between them. Moreover, the ideal of each side, taken by itself, is again self-contradictory. Good, as we have seen, can have no meaning outside the world of will, and will has its being in the conflict of the actual with the ideal. Grant complete fulfilment of need from either side, and goodness disappears. The conclusion seems inevitable that Good falls in the end into the same condemnation as bad: it is in discord with itself, and, even although it were not so, it would be in discord with the universe. Believe, as we may, that the universe is good, this it cannot be *qua* universe, for this would mean that it failed of inner harmony—in a word, was no universe at all. The same conclusion may be reached even more directly if we consider will and morality from the side not of the content of their ideal, but of the temporal form under which they appear. Of all the elements of our experience, time seems to have the slenderest hold upon reality. The very thought of it involves contradiction. It is to be, but is not yet; it is, and it is no longer; it has never been, and yet there is a past. If, therefore, as can easily be shown, all will depends just on the opposition between the 'now' and the 'not yet,' there seems no means of rescuing it from the unreality that infests this relation.

It is not surprising that consequences thus uncompromisingly deduced from idealist principles should have called forth energetic protest. Not only did they run counter to ordinary opinion as to the supremacy of morality; they seemed to threaten the very springs of action. If all we call good and bad is but a passing shadow on the screen of time of a reality in itself timeless and self-contained, human enterprise and effort seem to be doomed to fatuity. All aspiration after the freedom to plan and to achieve is faced by the sphinx-like calm of a universe already at peace with itself and secure against all innovation. The signal for the revolt against these apparent deductions was given by W. James's *Will to Believe*, which for the brilliance and irresponsibility of its attack has no precise parallel in modern philosophy, except it be Jacobi's celebrated protest in favour of the heart against the deadening weight of Kantian formalism. It was followed by a wave of wide-spread reaction against the whole ideal of philosophy, which, under the names of Humanism, Personal Idealism, Pragmatism (*qq.v.*), is as yet far from exhausted. What is common to all who adopt these names is the attempt to restore flesh and blood to the ghostly make-believes which the older Idealism was supposed to have left to do duty for human purposes, and the insistence to that end upon movement and process as constituting the life of things, the openness of the universe to all kinds of untried interpretations, the hospitality it offers to all forms of creative enterprise.

It is not likely that so vigorous a movement springs wholly from ambiguity of words. Yet it is clear that no agreement is possible until the ambiguities which attach to such central ideas as 'appearance,' 'process,' 'purpose,' are removed. With regard to the first, the distinction between appearance and illusion is, of course, vital. Because a thing is not real in the full sense of the word, it does not follow that it is an illusion. In illusion we take something to be what it is not; an appearance is that which cannot be taken simply as it is. It is an illusion to take the sun's rising for an actual movement of the sun over the earth's brim; the rising itself is, on the other hand, an appearance which, before it can be taken for reality, has to be supplemented by other facts which in explaining transmute it. Without itself representing the whole truth, one concept may be nearer to it, *i.e.* include more of the facts and stand for a more harmonious combination of them, than another. From this it follows that to deny ultimate truth is compatible with recognizing a high coefficient of relative validity. This is the logical equivalent of the metaphysical doctrine sometimes known as that of degrees of reality, which might be better called degrees of relativity. It may be summed up in the propositions: everything which exists at all must have attained some measure of internal unity; short of itself being the whole, this unity, just for that reason, must at some point show itself to reflexion to be incomplete and break down in contradiction; this point is more remote according to the degree of inclusiveness and harmony which it represents; but ultimate failure does not affect relative validity, nor does it prove that the whole could be what it is without the relatively invalid part.

Returning, with this distinction in mind, to the case of willed action, it is true that will rests on the distinction of an actual and an ideal, a now and a not yet, and must partake of the unrest of that relation. So far as it does so, it falls short of the highest reality. On the other hand, will represents a high degree of concreteness and internal stability. In it, as we saw, the elements of the inner life find their unity. It faces and breaks down the opposition between the self and not-self, uniting itself with the external world in the works and institutions we call civilization, and in the long run yielding place to nothing that does not come forward as a deeper form of itself. As will may be said to be the reality of blind instinct and desire, so, we have seen, morality is the reality of the will. In morality will comes to its own, and is at one with itself. But it does so in a world which, being in the form of time, has no other reward for the faithful than the opening up of a further vista which dwarfs present achievement and dooms one to a renewal of the conflict at a higher level. This does not

[1] See E. Caird, *Social Philosophy of Comte*, Glasgow, 1885, p. 160.

[2] See, esp., F. H. Bradley, *Appearance and Reality*, London, 1897, ch. on 'Goodness.'

prove that morality is an illusion, or that it rests upon a make-believe. It merely proves that it is not the highest form of experience. Above it stands religion, itself born of the contradictions in which morality ends, and seeking to heal them with the conviction that the aspect the world presents to the good will is not the final and only reality. Yet we must again add that, though transformed, morality is not suppressed. It does not simply fade out of religious consciousness. It survives in religion as it survives in fine art, giving substance and significance to what otherwise would be a vague and meaningless mysticism, and, so far as it is the immediate basis of the form of consciousness that seems to be the most real of our experiences, itself partaking of that reality.

With this account there seems no reason why idealists of all types should not so far agree. Even pragmatic or 'personal idealism' might be willing to accept it as another way of putting its own contention that the real is that which serves a purpose. It enables us to understand how any particular form of human experience may be unsatisfactory without therefore being valueless, and how one may be of more value than another. On the other hand, we can understand how it may still seem to fail to render intelligible the relation of the whole system of relative reality, or, if it be preferred, relative experience, to the absolute reality or the absolute experience. It is here that the pragmatist sees his opportunity to press the question, 'Why hamper ourselves with an absolute at all, which serves only to stultify our previous results: Is the relative and the finite a necessary element in the absolute and the infinite? Then into the latter itself creeps an irreconcilable contradiction, a seed of unreality into the heart of our all real. Is it, on the other hand, unnecessary? Then is the real altogether real, the whole together complete without it; movement and purpose are, after all, illusion.'

There is, we believe, no other way of meeting this difficulty than by insisting on a clearer statement of what is meant by process and creation. If it is an error to represent reality in terms of fixed entities, like the popular conception of the Platonic ideas, it is surely no less an error to represent it as mere change, though that be the change of a conscious will and intelligence. What gives value to life in general, and to the life of mind and will in particular, is not that it initiates change and novelty, but that in the change it maintains or furthers a system of organic relations, participation in which is the condition of its own self-maintenance. This means that there are differences of reality in purposes themselves, according as they embody more or less of the unity of the whole of which they are parts. But to recognize this is to recognize that all time-process gets its value from relation to a whole or ideal which cannot in any intelligible sense be said to be itself a mere series of events in time. Cf. art. ETERNITY.

In asking pragmatists to admit this, we are, in fact, merely asking them to realize more fully the meaning of their own contention for the abandonment of the Spinozistic notion of reality as substance, in favour of that of subject. This, which is the true Copernican revolution in philosophy, must carry with it a far more thorough attempt than is yet common, to substitute the idea of mind or spirit and its manifestations for the idea of things and their attributes. Thinkers of both camps may reasonably be asked to apply more courageously the notion of self-conscious life as governed by the idea not of process but of progress—of thought and will alike as finding their reality not in mere movement but in more fully organized, and thus more deeply established, forms of self-expression. So regarded, the truest conception of the Infinite may well be that of an ideal which represents in its completeness what the finite seeks to be—what it incompletely already is. As an ideal it is more than any of the finites or any aggregate of them, yet it depends upon the expression of itself by the finites in so far as actual reality is itself an element in that completeness. If it is an error in principle to conceive of the absolute reality as an 'already' actual, it is no less an error to conceive of the actual moment of time as possessing any value apart from the degree in which it expresses the absolute reality, and so partakes of eternity. Whether this involves a further advance—a return, it may be, from the notion of subject to an enriched notion of substance—is a question on which other articles may be expected to throw further light. In any case, ethical philosophy has nothing to lose but everything to gain by allying itself with the most thoroughgoing criticism of its ideals in the light of a sane monism.

See also artt. ETHICS AND MORALITY.

LITERATURE.—(A) *CLASSICAL TREATISES* (historical order): Plato, *Republic* (Eng. trs., Jowett; Davies-Vaughan; A. D. Lindsay); Aristotle, *Nicomachean Ethics* (Eng. tr., Peters); Aquinas, *Summa Theologiæ*, pt. ii.; Hobbes, *Leviathan*, 1651; Spinoza, *Ethica*, 1655; R. Cudworth, *Eternal and Immutable Morality*, 1688 (published 1731); Henry More, *Enchiridion Ethicum*, 1668; R. Cumberland, *de Legibus Naturæ*, 1672; S. Clarke, *The Being and Attributes of God*, 1704; Shaftesbury, *Characteristicks*, 1711; J. Butler, *Sermons*, 1726; D. Hume, *Treatise on Human Nature*, iii. (1739), *Inquiry concerning the Principles of Morals*, 1751; F. Hutcheson, *System of Moral Philosophy*, Glasgow and London, 1755; Adam Smith, *Theory of Moral Sentiments*, London and Edinburgh, 1759; W. Paley, *Principles of Moral and Political Philosophy*, London, 1785; J. Bentham, *Introd. to the Principles of Morals and Legislation*, do. 1789; Kant, *Kritik d. praktischen Vernunft*, Riga, 1788, *Metaphysik d. Sitten*, do. 1797 (Eng. tr., Abbott); Hegel, *Philosophie d. Rechts*, Berlin, 1821 (Eng. tr., Dyde); A. Comte, *Philosophie positive*, Paris, 1829–42 (Eng. tr., Martineau, 1853); J. S. Mill, *Utilitarianism*, London, 1861; Lotze, *Microcosmos*, Leipzig, 1856–64, bks. vi. and viii. (Eng. tr. 1885); H. Sidgwick, *Methods of Ethics*, London, 1874; F. H. Bradley, *Ethical Studies*, do. 1876; H. Spencer, *Data of Ethics*, do. 1879; T. H. Green, *Prolegomena to Ethics*, Oxford, 1883; Leslie Stephen, *Science of Ethics*, London, 1882; J. Martineau, *Types of Ethical Theory*, Oxford, 1882; W. Wundt, *Ethik*, Stuttgart, 1886 (Eng. tr., Titchener and others); S. Alexander, *Moral Order and Progress*, London, 1889.

(B) *IDEALIST ETHICS* in the 19th cent. (last editions): besides Hegel, Green, and Bradley, mentioned above, see B. Bosanquet, *Psychology of the Moral Self*, London, 1897, *Philosophical Theory of the State*, do. 1899, *The Principles of Individuality and Value*, do. 1912; J. S. Mackenzie, *Manual of Ethics*[4], do. 1900; J. H. Muirhead, *Elements of Ethics*[3], do. 1910; R. L. Nettleship, *Philos. Lectures and Remains*, do. 1897; R. B. Perry, *The Moral Economy*, New York, 1909; D. G. Ritchie, *Philos. Studies*, London, 1905; Scotus Novanticus (S. S. Laurie), *Ethica*[2], do. 1891; J. Seth, *Study of Ethical Principles*[10], do. 1908; W. R. Sorley, *Ethics of Naturalism*[2], do. 1904, *The Moral Life*, Cambridge, 1911; W. Wallace, *Lectures and Essays on Natural Theology and Ethics*, Oxford, 1898; J. Watson, *Hedonistic Theories*, Glasgow, 1895.

(C) *RECENT CRITICISMS OF IDEALIST ETHICS*: M. J. Guyau, *Esquisse d'une morale sans obligation ni sanction*, Paris, 1885 (Eng. tr., Kapteyn); G. E. Moore, *Principia Ethica*, Cambridge, 1903; H. Rashdall, *The Theory of Good and Evil*, Oxford, 1907; F. C. S. Schiller, *Humanism*, London, 1903; J. A. Stewart, art. 'Ethics,' in *EBr*[10]; A. E. Taylor, *Problem of Conduct*, London, 1901; C. B. Upton, *The Bases of Religious Belief*, do. 1894.

(D) *HISTORIES OF ETHICS*: E. Albee, *Hist. of Eng. Utilitarianism*, London, 1902; F. Jodl, *Gesch. der Ethik in d. neueren Philos.* ii., Stuttgart, 1889; H. Sidgwick, *History of Ethics*, London, 1896; L. Stephen, *The English Utilitarians*, do. 1900; Wundt (see above), vol. ii.

(E) *SOME IMPORTANT RECENT WORKS* (not mentioned under above headings): G. L. Dickinson, *The Meaning of the Good*[3], London, 1906; L. T. Hobhouse, *Morals in Evolution*, 2 vols., do. 1906; H. Höffding, *Ethik*, Leipzig, 1888; S. E. Mezes, *Ethics: Descriptive and Explanatory*, London, 1901; F. Paulsen, *Ethik*, Berlin, 1889 (Eng. tr., Thilly, London, 1899); C. Read, *Natural and Social Morality*, London, 1909; B. Russell in *Philos. Essays*, 1910; G. Simmel, *Einleit. in d. Moralwissenschaft*, Berlin, 1892–93; H. Steinthal, *Allgemeine Ethik*, Berlin, 1885; A. Sutherland, *The Origin and Growth of the Moral Instinct*, 2 vols., London, 1898; E. Westermarck, *The Origin and Development of the Moral Ideas*, London, 1908.

(F) *JOURNALS*: *International Journal of Ethics*, Philadelphia and London, 1891 ff.; *Ethical World* (1898–1900).

J. H. MUIRHEAD.

ETHICS (Rudimentary). — The procedure adopted in the present article is as follows. (1) A broad characterization is attempted of the lower culture, as a concrete phase of life carrying with it a specific type of ethics. (2) The main determinants of this phase of life are briefly analyzed, with the object of showing how physical causes, on the one hand, and spiritual motives, on the other, combine to sway the course of human life; the sphere of moral evolution being identified with that of the spiritual activities in question. (3) The particular determinations to which these moralizing forces give rise are rapidly surveyed, and some of the salient features of savage conduct at its most intelligent are exhibited as the result of ethical or quasi-ethical sanctions.

1. The general type of conduct prevailing in rudimentary society.—It has been assumed that the lower culture is sufficiently homogeneous to lend itself to what might almost be described as the method of the composite photograph. Though it is by no means so clear that the higher culture admits of similar treatment, it is convenient here to figure it as likewise a single phase, for the simple purpose of bringing out the essential features of rudimentary society by way of a contrast with developed society. It is necessary to conceive of two phases of society (they are in no sense 'ages'), which may be severally distinguished as the *synnomic* and the *syntelic*. As the etymology of these terms implies, in the one phase customs form the bond of society; in the other, ends or ideals. The one is a reign of habit, the other a reign of reflexion. The one results from a subconscious, the other from a conscious, selection of ethical standards.

At once the most striking and the most significant of the characteristics of the synnomic life of savages is that it is public, in the sense that it admits of little or no privacy. Gregariousness, it has been said, is not association. A contiguity with others which is too close and constant hinders that development of personality and independent character upon which syntelic society depends. In synnomic society the normal individual has no chance of withdrawing into himself. Hence he does not reflect; he imitates. Now, when every one imitates every one else, it might seem that a vicious circle must be formed, and society must come to a standstill so far as any real progress goes. As a matter of fact this is not the case. For the most part, however, the successful readjustments are of the subconscious order. Tarde's explanation of them as due to a 'cross-fertilization of imitations' may be cited, if only to illustrate how obscure and hard to describe the process is. The nearest analogy, perhaps, which civilization provides is the progress, such as it is, that takes place in fashions of dress. In thus generalizing with regard to a total phase of society, one must not, of course, be taken to ignore the fact that, however far back human evolution is traced—and in a sense it is not very far—the germs of all our higher mental processes are to be discerned. Deliberate policy is not entirely unknown amongst the ruder savages. Thus Spencer-Gillen[a] (p. 11 f.) are quite ready to admit that 'the Australian native is bound hand and foot by custom.' Nevertheless, they argue that powerful individuals are not untruly credited by the native traditions with having brought about fundamental alterations in the marriage system, the mode of initiation, and so on:

> 'If one or two of the most powerful men settled upon the advisability of introducing some change, even an important one, it would be quite possible for this to be agreed upon and carried out.'

Or, again, at a somewhat higher level of savage society, we come upon the conscious and far-sighted innovator in such a man as Chaka, the famous head-chief of the Zulus. Yet these sporadic manifestations of nascent individuality hardly militate against the broad principle that the savage is a blind conservative content to play a part in life which his ancestors have composed for him beforehand.

What are the ethical implications of this fact? Lack of personal initiative, of the capacity for private judgment, is equivalent to a want of moral freedom. The moral sanction of savagery is external, not internal. This must not be misunderstood. All experiences are in a certain sense internal; but they may be regarded as relatively external so long as they consist in perceptions rather than in conceptions. The conduct of savages is best understood in the light of what is known as 'the psychology of the crowd'; though what is true of the civilized crowd as a temporary gathering merely affords a general analogy to what holds of the savage community, which is a permanent and organic association. In a typical crowd the public opinion exercised by the individual members on each other and, reactively, on themselves is not properly their own, since it does not proceed from a critical or intelligent self. A judgment of sense, not of reflexion, directs the flow of natural approbation or resentment. Each man looks outwards, taking his cue from his neighbours in their mass, or at most from the slightly more self-determined ringleader; for, given any amount of sheep-through-the-gapishness, as Lloyd Morgan calls it, there will always be one sheep at the head of the rest. He does not look inwards to principle. He has no standard, in the form of a conception or free idea, that he can transfer at will from the present situation to another. Thus his conduct is merely the expression of a mobbishly caused and received impression. His morality, such as it is, is a customary morality, custom being defined as the aggregate of the forces of social suggestion at work at any time in a given society.

On this primary law certain corollaries depend. Thus (*a*) it follows, from the sheer want amongst savages of the power of maintaining communications at a distance, that the condition of social and moral solidarity at the synnomic stage of society is the capacity to be physically in touch with each other —to keep together in a crowd. Westermarck is quite right in making local contiguity the all-important bond of primitive life, even such a tie as that of kinship being secondary thereto (*MI* ii. 198 f.). This may be termed the principle of *symbiosis*. (*b*) It follows that, since within a given society there is always a plurality of circles, not necessarily concentric, within which symbiosis takes place in varying degree, the true centre and radiating point of moral influence will always be that particular circle within which the closest and most permanent symbiosis occurs. This circle of most effective symbiosis may be termed the *social focus*. It will be for one type of community the family, for another the kin-group, for another the village, whilst more exceptionally and for particular classes it will be the men's house, the secret society, the military regiment, or what not. Even if it be not always easy to answer the question, it is at least worth asking in every case, Where, for these savage folk, is the nearest equivalent to our 'home'? For not only does charity begin at home, when society is at the synnomic stage, but it may almost be said to end there. (*c*) It follows that, corresponding with this social symbiosis, there is likewise what Lévy-Bruhl is justified in calling a *mental symbiosis* in regard to all that concerns the intellectual and ethical life (*Les Fonctions mentales dans les sociétés inférieures*, 94). Or, as Durkheim-Mauss put it ('De quelques Formes primitives de classification,' *ASoc* vi. [1901–02] 70), the mental attitude is fundamentally *sociocentric.* The actual way in which the folk themselves are grouped together provides the notion of the way in which all the things in the universe are grouped together. Exactly the same scheme of sympathies and antipathies governs things in general as governs the men themselves. Certain animals, certain plants, a quarter of the heavens, certain colours, names, and so on, belong to my group and belong together, whereas your group owns another class of things, and the associations thus arising constitute the essential natures of the things themselves. The 'confusion of categories,' with which Hobhouse (*Morals in Evolution*, ii. 9) charges rudimentary thought, is merely a confusion of such categories as we have since obtained by a slowly-developed attention to the intrinsic relations holding between things in themselves. The savage does not confuse his own categories, but these are almost meaningless to us because strictly relative to the idiosyncrasies of his particular little society. If he is a member of the bear-totem, bear-meat is poison (unless taken homœopathically), whether bear-meat in itself injuriously affects the human stomach in itself or not; and so on. Now, whilst this attitude of mind severely limits his practical efficiency (for we conquer Nature only by obeying her), it positively extends, in a way that only the more religious amongst civilized men may faintly appreciate, the sphere of his ethical interests. His whole universe being socialized and anthropomorphized, it becomes for the savage a battle-ground of quasi-personal powers that are in league, or, more strictly, in literal symbiosis, either with him and his, or with other human beings who are more or less against him and his. Consequently, lacking our mechanical control over Nature, he has little or nothing but his ethics to depend upon—his ways of dealing with friend and foe. So far is the savage from being unmoral, as some have called him, that morality may truly be said to be his all-in-all; though doubtless it is a morality which in general and on the whole he does not think out, but rather lives out, feeling his way by sheer social tact with his human neighbours, and with that environing universe which is for him as but human society writ large.

2. The determinants of conduct in rudimentary society.—The synnomic phase of human society having been generally characterized, it becomes necessary in the next place to designate the general factors or determinants that combine to produce it. From an ethical point of view the main object must be to show how, like every other phase of human life, it is hung somewhere between the opposite poles of physical necessity and moral freedom. One set of determinants may be classed as *physical*, in the wide sense which includes the psycho-physical. They will be dealt with under the two broad headings of 'Heredity' and 'Environment.' The other set of determinants may be termed *moral.* They will be considered under the two heads of 'Social tradition' and 'Personal initiative.'

(1) *Heredity.*—That the laws of heredity (*q.v.*) apply to man admits of no doubt. The working of those laws, on the other hand, is at present only dimly understood. Now, it is only too easy to suppose that what science cannot for the moment grasp is not there at all. For another reason, too, Ethics is apt to ignore heredity, namely, because to admit that some men are born with a greater capacity for morality than others is, from the normative point of view, unedifying, at any rate at first sight. Nevertheless, it is important to allow fully for the congenital dispositions that form the *terminus a quo* of moral evolution. The effects of heredity, as it applies to man, are palpably manifested in those differences of physical type which are due to what is vaguely known as race, or the race-factor. Even here science has hitherto failed to establish criteria of a satisfactory kind—neither shape of head, type of hair, colour, nor any other physical feature proving a sufficient mark of descent. The fact remains, however, that certain outstanding varieties of physical type have been handed on, along more or less traceable lines, from the dawn of history, and seem likely to persist so long as sexual selection remains what it is amongst uncivilized and civilized peoples alike. Less palpably, but no less certainly, there is a steady elimination in process within any given human society in favour of those physical types that are relatively immune as regards certain recurrent forms of disease. For the student of Ethics, however, the interest lies chiefly in the mental rather than in the physical effects attributable to heredity. But a satisfactory criterion of these is even harder to find. The modern view of instinct (the term which best sums up the inheritable part of mind) treats it, not as a determinate mechanism, but rather as a disposition to which a certain measure of plasticity essentially belongs. Thus Hobhouse (i. 16) notes that 'instinct throughout the animal world is found to vary greatly in individuals, to be quite fallible, often imperfect and capable from an early stage of employing elementary reasoning in its service.' Again, McDougall, in his *Social Psychology*, seems to admit that instinct, owing to its intrinsic plasticity, passes over into intelligence without observable transition. Nevertheless, he makes the following reservation. Every instinct on its physical side, he maintains, consists of three parts—an afferent, a central, and an efferent or motor. Correspondingly, on its psychical side, cognitive, affective, and conative activities are manifested in the same order. The plasticity belonging to the instinct, however, shows itself mainly at the two ends of the process. To the central part, on the contrary, and hence corresponding with the affective manifestations, he believes a relatively high degree of constancy to attach. His criterion of instinct, therefore, is the presence of some specific emotion. But if this criterion be adopted—and at present no better one seems to be forthcoming—we reach a position which, from the ethical point of view, is almost paradoxical. On the one hand, our emotions become closely associated with the hereditable and predetermined side of our nature. Yet, on the other hand, emotion is a root-factor in morality, so much so that Westermarck's vast collection of facts (in *MI*) is held by him to show that the moral judgments of mankind have a source that is primarily and essentially emotional. Is, then, the moral man born, rather than made by education? And is morality largely a matter of race? If indeed it be so—and science as science must seek the truth, whether it seem at first sight edifying or not—the fact must be faced. If it be, as McDougall suggests, the function of intelligence simply to refine on a pre-existing fund of sound natural tendencies, by providing these with objects on the one hand and modes of realization on the other, whereby they are to be most fully satisfied, then how to breed sound natures becomes the all-absorbing interest of ethical science. The crux of heredity must be faced and solved, instead of blindly trusting to education to turn moral sows' ears into silk purses.

It remains to add that the popular view which ascribes a greater innate susceptibility to emotion to savages as compared with civilized men is in all probability false. The tests devised by experimental psychology, so far as they carry us, tend to show that savages are emotionally more sluggish and obtuse (cf. the experiments on white and on black women [F. A. Kellor, *Experimental Sociology*, London, 1901, p. 77]). The source of the fallacy lies in the prominence given to emotional manifestations by the conditions of the social life of savages. It is the law of life in the crowd, and, analogously, of synnomic society, that emotions are intensified whilst ideas are neutralized; the reason being that the emotions are transferred by imitation of the movements that accompany and assist their outward expression, whereas ideas are not transferred under conditions prejudicial to reflexion. As Lévy-Bruhl (p. 426) puts it, we should speak not so much of the collective ideas of a savage group as of collective mental states of an extreme emotional intensity, wherein idea is as yet not differentiated from the movements and acts that embody it. Nevertheless, the civilized man is not deficient in emotion because his higher training enables him to keep cool. He cannot do without the physical basis, say, of courage, any more than the savage can, but, on the contrary, needs it all the more because an intelligent application of his impulsive tendency to the needs of the situation calls for a repression of those mere detonations of the nerves which are the by-products rather than the springs of intense activity.

(2) *Environment*.—The term 'environment' (*q.v.*) must be taken to cover all those influences, proceeding from the circumstances wherein human experience takes place, which appear to control the course of that experience rather than, conversely, to be themselves controlled thereby. The line between these opposite controls cannot be drawn exactly. Thus the mother's body constitutes an ante-natal environment which the child itself does not in any way control; yet the mother up to a certain point can do so. Or, again, geographical conditions, the distribution of land and water, climate, and so on, might seem at first sight beyond human sway altogether; yet such a work as that of Marsh, *The World as modified by Human Action* (London, 1874), makes it plain that intelligently, and more often unintelligently, man can affect his physical environment for better, or, still more easily, for worse. Once more, food-supply, as dependent on the local fauna and flora, does not absolutely condition human life, inasmuch as this reacts selectively upon it, so that the whole terrestrial globe is made to respond to the requirements of the civilized breakfast-table. Lastly, what may be termed the distribution-factor — covering both the pressure exerted on one area of population by another, with the resultant wars, emigrations, and so forth, and the pressure exerted within the same area of population by the various parts, whence arises such a phenomenon as the rush to the towns—constitutes an objective condition with an influence of its own. Yet, on the other hand, distribution of population, and its ultimate causes, namely, rate of fertility, mobility due to facility of communications, and the like, are within limits subject in their turn to human policy, not to say politics. In short, what is known as force of circumstances must be treated as a determinant of human conduct, even whilst the aspiration to rise above circumstances, that is, to make them rather than allow them to make us, may legitimately figure amongst the highest of our ethical motives.

Thus, there is considerable scope for the new department of science which its founder, Ratzel, names 'Anthropo-geography,' and for the kindred branch of study termed by Durkheim and his school 'Social Morphology.' There is at present a danger, however, lest this type of physical explanation be overdone. Man may be, as Ratzel says, 'a piece of the earth,' but he is not merely that, by any means. Indeed, it may be expected that it is especially at the stage of savagery, when man is far more dependent on his immediate environment, that the application of these methods is likely to prove fruitful. Thus, Mauss in a study of the environing conditions of Eskimo life ('Essai sur les variations saisonnières des sociétés Eskimos,' *ASoc* ix. [1904–05] 39 f.) shows it to be to no small extent a 'function' of the physical factors of climate, food-supply, and distribution of population taken together. On the other hand, when civilization is similarly treated, as in the case of the 'economic materialism' of Marx, there is a manifest failure to take account of 'imponderables,' or, in other words, of ideas and ideals. Even in regard to savagery, however, it must not be forgotten that man, as known to anthropology and pre-historic archæology, is always more or less the 'lord of creation,' the master of his environment; so much so, that even during the great Ice Age in Europe, when the environment on which they depended proved too much for so many animal species, man, thanks to the use of fire and other mechanical devices, managed to hold his ground and to cultivate a high type of fine art into the bargain. Indeed, man's very mastery over the non-human environment, as contrasted with his weakness in coping with the human environment, namely with rate and distribution of population, is perhaps the main source of his need for an effective Ethics. Even at the stage of savagery, and conspicuously under civilization, a leading problem of human life is how to keep pace ethically with the changes in the social economy that are due to material progress.

(3) *Social tradition*.—At this point it becomes necessary to pass to the consideration of another set of determinants, which are not physical, as are heredity and environment, but moral. Social tradition, of course, may readily be represented as a sort of environment or atmosphere whereby the individual is surrounded and conditioned *ab extra*. But it is safer to attend chiefly to the psychical elements, sentiments, ideas, and so on, with which this environment or atmosphere is, so to speak, charged. Another way of putting the same thing is to say that the influence exerted on a man by social tradition makes itself felt within him in a way quite different from that in which environment or even heredity makes itself felt. Social tradition makes itself felt within a man essentially, that is, most characteristically, as a *sanction*. A sanction may be defined as a judgment of validity or invalidity to which some degree of constraining awe is attached (*sanctio* in Roman law is that clause in a legislative enactment which invokes a curse on the offender). Arising as it does in a more or less spontaneous and unenforced imitation, the influence of social tradition soon ripens into a sense of 'ought,' representing the will of society, or, at any rate, of some power greater and wiser and older and more lasting than oneself. Such is the fact, however one may try to explain it. Social Psychology, which is mere science content with a limited type of explanation, unlike Metaphysics, which seeks the ultimate explanation, would account for the fact by postulating, as the complement to our imitative tendency, a tendency to stimulate and assist imitation in others, and especially in the young. Thus, whilst the chick imitates the hen, as we say, 'instinctively,' so likewise does the hen no less instinctively encourage the chick to imitate. In this tendency to encourage imitation we may discern various subordinate types of activity, notably three, namely the tendencies to impress, to punish, and to persuade. Correspondingly, the influences embodied in social tradition may be reduced, in the interests of a broad and drastic treatment of the subject, to three—religion, law, and education. These are the three main types of sanctions.

(*a*) *Religion*.—The function of religion, regarded

as a sanction, is to inculcate the Good by investing it with impressiveness. The religiously impressive is known as the *sacred*. The evolution of the idea of the sacred consists especially in the gradual differentiation of what is both sacred and good from what is or appears to be sacred, but is, nevertheless, at bottom bad. Amongst savages, the notion of *tabu* (a Polynesian term roughly equivalent to the Latin *sacer*, whence our word 'sacred') extends to all sorts of things—human beings, animals, plants, material objects, ghosts, ceremonies, stones, words, places, and times—which have the common quality of being mystically dangerous, or, as Codrington puts it, 'not to be lightly approached' (*The Melanesians*, p. 188). The positive reason in the background is that they are *mana* (another Polynesian term, embodying, like *tabu*, a wide-spread savage notion), *i.e.* mystically powerful. Now, to be dangerous, because powerful, in a mystic (*i.e.* mysterious or supernatural) way, is a quality that may attach to bad things as well as to good. Hence religion, which is concerned with the mystically good, has at first much in common with magic, which only in the long run is cut off from religion to become a synonym for all 'trafficking with the devil,' *i.e.* for all use of mystically impressive means to effect bad and anti-social ends. From the psychological point of view, sacredness corresponds with the sense of awe, as excited by the display of supernatural power. Awe is a complex emotion, which McDougall (*op. cit.* p. 131, cf. 305) plausibly resolves into a trinity of primary emotions, namely, a fear which drives away, a curiosity which attracts, and a submissiveness which disarms resistance. Awe, therefore, may vary, according as one or other ingredient prevails, from an abject and grovelling terror to an admiring respect tempered with humility. Correspondingly, in certain aspects the religion of savages, and even of more advanced peoples, may be a religion of almost pure fear. At its most typical, however, it is in all stages of its development so closely associated with the social tradition that embodies the vital aims of each and all that its appeal is sympathetic rather than minatory and purely coercive. Social tradition at the synnomic stage of society, namely under conditions of symbiosis, when mutual imitation of the outward expression of emotion helps to intensify men's feelings, is capable of exciting awe in several ways at once; and, so long as the congregational forms of religion are kept up, the same phenomena will recur under civilization. Thus, firstly, it is mysterious, abounding in strange prescriptions, the very oddity and uselessness of which invest the sound remainder with the majesty of twilight. Secondly, it is ancient, its origin being lost in the dreadful yet glorious past, and calling upon the myth-making faculty to consecrate it by stories about supernatural Creators, first parents, culture-heroes, totemic ancestors, and so forth. Thirdly, it is always more or less secret, its repositories and editors being a ruling and relatively educated class, which rarely if ever feels awe towards precisely the same objects as do the less enlightened, the women, the young, and, in a word, the uninitiated, but is nevertheless in normal conditions subject to a similar but more refined awe as it confronts some more ultimate secret. In these ways, then, and in others, religion consecrates the Good so far as it is embodied in the rule of life imparted by each generation to the next, and by rendering it impressive helps the rising generation to imitate and assimilate it.

(*b*) *Law*.—The function of law, as a sanction, is to punish transgressions against the Good as embodied in the social tradition. Its remote origin may be what Bagehot (*Physics and Politics*, London, 1873) calls the persecuting tendency, which visits with the common displeasure all departures from the strict imitation of the prevailing fashion. The same author, however, in referring to the 'wild spasms of wild justice' to which the lower savagery is liable, implies that some sense of a social Good to be maintained runs through these outbreaks of passion at first sight almost purposeless and automatic. Indeed, when public vengeance is exacted by the folk as a whole from the traitor, or, again, from the breaker of *tabu* or the person who practises black magic, the mere fact that all assist at the infliction of the sentence must make it an expression of the social will, to which meaning and purpose are felt to attach. It may not be so obvious at first sight how private vengeance incorporates and enforces the social tradition. Let it be noted, however, in the first place, that the juristic maxim applies here, 'What the sovereign permits he commands'; which is to say that in a society lacking a centralized authority the social will must perforce manifest itself in isolated repressions of crime carried out by self-constituted judges. In the second place, private law in savage society is the affair not of individuals but of kin-groups; and the communal responsibility acknowledged by the member of a clan is a socializing force of the first importance.

So much, then, for the purely legal sanction, which with the evolution of society becomes the right arm, and almost the incarnation, of the State, the legislative, judicial, and executive functions of which are mainly concerned with the framing, applying, or enforcing of its punitive enactments. At an earlier stage, however, State, Church, and Society are almost one. For instance, rudimentary law is largely concerned with the violator of *tabu*, who is typically the criminal at this stage, whilst, conversely, rudimentary religion supplies law with dreadful forms of procedure—ordeals, oaths, and so on; with special punishments, such as costly expiatory offerings; and—most effective sanctionary influence of all—with the notion of supernatural powers at the back of the law, such as a Divine legislator, supreme author of all precedents.

(*c*) *Education*.—Under this last head may be summed up all those homelier and gentler forces of persuasion which, without show of coercion, yet none the less effectively, lead the individual member of society to submit to its traditional injunctions. Education is not merely a matter of training children, but proceeds throughout a man's life so long as he is capable of being modified by fresh experiences. Thus, even amongst savages it is not uncommon to find that initiation, which is at least as much an educational as a religious institution, is not completed at the puberty rites, but carried on far into manhood in a series of fuller initiations opening up ever wider horizons of social duty. Education, amongst savages and civilized men alike, is distinguishable only up to a certain point from religion and law, being never on the one hand wholly confined to secular subjects, or on the other able wholly to dispense with punitive machinery. It must not be forgotten, however, that under this head must be included influences so kindly and intimate that the individual is hardly aware that they are the potters and he the clay. Language itself is the greatest of educators; and yet it is the primary source of self-consciousness and self-realization. Unconscious passes into conscious education, as language generates literature, even savages having their literature of folk-tales, proverbs, songs, and so forth. In early society, however, education comes more by way of outer sense than of inward thought, and synnomic life is a perpetual pageant of dances and shows; whereas civilization is essentially the attribute of a reading public. If a single differentia be sought to mark off civilization from savagery, no better one is to be found than the invention of writing. Hereby human intelligence acquires a new dimension. The physical symbols largely make possible those mental symbols which we know as abstract ideas; and these rule our world. Ethics itself is often identified with the theory built upon certain highly abstract ideas, too abstract indeed to be generally understood, and so to exert much influence on society at large. From the historical and comparative point of view, however, Ethics is as wide as the theory of the moral influences which, in the course of man's concrete living no less than in that of his abstract thinking, point the way to the Good. Of these influences social tradition has now been summarily considered in its leading aspects. It remains to take note of another influence, too often overlooked, namely the initiative of the free and responsible individual.

(4) *Personal initiative.*—When full allowance has been made for the influences of a man's heredity, his environment, and his social tradition, is there anything left that could possibly influence him, or, indeed, that would be there to be influenced? Have we accounted for the man completely? Whatever the metaphysician may say for or against the reality of human freedom, it is necessary at the level of science to distinguish the effects of personal initiative as in their way unique. Without entering on the question whether, apart from the individual centres of activity, human society is, or is not, a soulless thing, we need here concern ourselves only with the individual activity that is manifested in so marked a degree as to appear decisively to exert a purposive control over the course of events. History is not merely the history of great men, but, on the other hand, the human drama conceived as the mere product of a complex of impersonal forces would be like the play of Hamlet with its leading character left out. To confine our attention to the moral genius, if Socrates, or Buddha, or Christ be withdrawn from the reckoning, the source of the truly revolutionary movements usually associated with their names is nowhere to be found. At the same time, the type of explanation which relies on social as contrasted with individual forces for its clues can and must delimit the province of personal initiative by showing what external conditions are able to help or hinder its exercise. Thus, the levelling influences of synnomic society prove normally, though not invariably, fatal to individuality, as has already been said. On the other hand, specialization of social functions encourages responsibility, though it does not necessarily produce it. The mere fact that the social system requires individuals to be sorted out and educated each for his special task, gives potential initiative the chance of maturing. For example, it is within the relatively specialized class of medicine-men that the social reformer is especially apt to arise; while in a lesser degree the specialization of sex functions and consequent limitation of the woman to domestic duties permits to the male as such a greater opportunity of realizing such originality as may be in him. It remains to add that, ethically, the selfhood which issues in a high degree of initiative involves a self-respect which is not inconsistent with self-sacrifice, but, on the contrary, tends to unite the two principles as aspects of one and the same real Good. Even the self-respect of savages, whilst it manifests itself in its lower forms as a love of self-decoration, or as boastfulness, or as the habit of retaliating on an affront, leads likewise to the self-devotion of the warrior and leader, and foreshadows the developed individuality which rises above individualism to the disinterested realization of the idea of Good for its own sake.

3. The determinations of conduct in rudimentary society.—That which the determinants of conduct discussed in the previous section combine together to produce may be correspondingly termed the determinations. Of such determinations, those that are reckoned by those concerned to make for the Good are usually known as types of virtuous conduct, or virtues. A classification of virtues so framed as to further the study of their historical evolution must be founded on a consideration of those relations in which the moral subject, the individual who seeks the Good, is involved by the conditions of human life throughout its whole development as presented in history. What, then, are these permanent relations? If we regard the moral subject for the moment as standing simply at the centre of a scheme of relations which are social in the sense that they are relations with other human beings, we perceive him to be ringed round, as it were, with three concentric circles. Firstly, he is the member of a home circle, that 'social focus' of which mention has already been made. Secondly, he is the member of a body politic. Thirdly, he is a member of the human race, and, as such, willingly or unwillingly brought into touch with men belonging to some body politic other than his own. At this point we might seem to have exhausted the categories expressive of his moral relations; but, at the risk of the appearance of a cross-division, two other categories must be added. Fourthly, a man's moral relations extend inwards as well as outwards. He has a duty to himself, and as a self-conscious being is necessarily committed to certain types of conduct that are primarily self-regarding, though they are never exclusively self-regarding, any more than his conduct towards his neighbours can ever be exclusively other-regarding, or altruistic. Fifthly and lastly, there are certain relations in which man seems to himself, by a sentiment which no reflexion can wholly gainsay, to be lifted right above the opposition between the claims of self and of others. These relations, then, appear to be with the Good itself, or, in the language of religion, with 'God.'

To this general scheme of man's moral relations, which is objective in the sense that Sociology and Psychology alike lend support to it, there corresponds a fivefold division of the virtues as follows: (1) the domestic; (2) the political; (3) the international; (4) the personal; (5) the transcendental. Whereas this classification applies to the moral development of man throughout its whole course as known to history, there is likewise sound reason as well as convenience to be pleaded in favour of its use in a study confined to rudimentary society. At heart, savage and civilized man are well-nigh one, despite appearances to the contrary. The same foundation, the same raw material of emotional tendencies, is there. Civilization, to recur to those principles laid down by McDougall in his *Social Psychology*, sharpens human nature at its ends. It gives a man an infinitely better hold on the facts of life, thus improving the afferent channels of his experience; and, correspondingly it affords him an infinitely better grasp of the means of life, thus improving to a like extent his efferent or motor activities. But the central part of his nature remains relatively unaffected by this gain in vital effectiveness. The general orientation of life, the direction of the quest for the real Good, does not seem to change greatly. The best proof of this is that education, that is to say, the mere substitution of one social tradition for another, can do wonders for the born savage; whilst, again, a whole race may shake off the sleep of centuries, as the Japanese have done, and enrol themselves amongst the more highly civilized nations. We speak with Plato of 'conversion,' but the term is inexact; and it would be truer to say that human nature, being polarized towards virtue, needs merely to be relieved of its ignorance of the ways and means by which virtue is acquired. The problem for Eugenics is how to eliminate the unintelligent and unplastic rather than the bad at heart—to eliminate them, as noxious insects are eliminated, not by killing individuals (for such butchery but depraves those who kill), but, more radically and yet mercifully, by preventing them from being born at all.

(1) *The domestic virtues.*—Tylor has said: 'The basis of society is the family' (*CR* xxi. 711), thus endorsing the time-honoured dictum of Aristotle. One school of anthropologists, who favour what may be termed the 'horde-theory' of the origin of society, might be inclined to retort: 'First find your savage family.' Their hypotheses, however, concerning promiscuity, communal marriage, or what not, frankly refer to some remote past which, if it ever existed, lies at any rate quite beyond the range of scientific observation. At most they find amongst existing savages a few alleged survivals of a social condition when there was no marriage proper. Marriage, in a wide sense that extends to certain of the lower animals no less than to man, is defined by Westermarck (*Hist. of Hum. Marriage*[2], 1894, p. 537) as 'a more or less durable connection between male and female, lasting beyond the mere act of propagation till after the birth of the offspring.' Marriage proper, on the other hand, may be defined with Lord Avebury (*Marriage, Totemism, and Religion*, London, 1911, p. 2), as 'an exclusive relation of one or more men to one or more women, based on custom, recognized and supported by public opinion, and, where law exists, by law.' Now, it is a curious fact that marriage proper occurs amongst those savages who in most respects have the most rudimentary culture of all, such as the Andaman Islanders, Veddas, and Bushmen. Yet with societies of a slightly higher grade, notably such as have totemism in one or another form, it is often the case that the family is somewhat overshadowed by the kin-group ('clan' under mother-right, 'gens' under father-right). In other words, whereas the bond between husband and wife is relatively feeble, inasmuch as they belong to different kin-groups, mother and children or father and children are in intimate communion with each other as members of a kin-group which includes persons whose relationship in the actual matter of blood is distant or perhaps non-existent (though usually blood-relationship is imputed by means of the figment of a common ancestry). It remains true, however, that, whether it be represented by the family, or by some quasi-familial institution, the kin-group, the communal household, or what not, there is always for the savage a 'social focus,' a home-circle, where the virtues pertaining to social intercourse are fostered by mutual relations of special intimacy. These relations may be here briefly considered under three broad heads: (*a*) relations between the sexes, and, in particular, between husband and wife; (*b*) relations between young and old, and, in particular, between parents and children; (*c*) relations between kinsmen in general. See also artt. FAMILY.

(*a*) The adult savage woman is normally a wife and mother, and it is as such that she is primarily related to the community regarded as a moral whole. Thus her economic duties follow directly upon her conjugal and parental obligations. Her function is that of directly propagating and nurturing the race, whilst the function of the male is protective, that is to say, is indirectly race-preserving. If happiness consist in the exercise of unimpeded function, both sexes should be happy in the normal savage community, where there are no unmated females free or anxious to have a hand in the work of the men. Physically woman's is perhaps the harder lot. Child-bearing, indeed, is not so great a strain upon the daughter of nature as is the need of continually suckling her child until it is well into its second year. It is a great gain for her when life becomes relatively sedentary. For amongst hunting peoples not only must she carry her infant, but she is also bound to be carrier in general, that the men may be at liberty to use their weapons. When it is added that the sexual life begins early, namely as soon as puberty is reached, or occasionally before, it will not seem surprising that the savage female tends to age more rapidly than the male. The male, however, is far more liable to be cut off whilst still in his prime.

Passing on to note the influence of social tradition, we come at once to the institution which more than any other determines the relative status of male and female, and in particular of husband and wife, for better or worse. This is the custom of exogamy, or marrying outside the kin-group, though usually inside the wider circle of the tribe. A few of the lowest peoples, mostly miserable remnants whose endogamy or marrying-in may be a result of degeneration, are without this practice, but it is typical of rudimentary society as a whole. What exogamy means for the man and woman who marry is that one or other must exchange the home-circle for another. Now, the morality of savages being narrow rather than lacking in intensity, the consequence is that to break with intimates and dwell among strangers involves a sojourn in a moral wilderness for whichever of the two parties is the outsider. Thus, when mother-right takes the form of the woman remaining amongst her kin and the man playing the part of a visitor liable to *corvées*, there can be no doubt that the woman's is the happier lot. Indeed, all the forms of mother-right, the technical differentia of which is merely that the mother, not the father, hands on the family name, appear normally to involve greater consideration for the mother, if Steinmetz's (*Entwicklung der Strafe*) statistical method is to be trusted. As long as her kin-group formally owns her and her children, the husband has to fear their vengeance if he abuses his rights as consort. It remains only to add in this context that the origin of exogamy is quite obscure. There may be, as Westermarck thinks, a race-preserving instinct against in-breeding behind all. As it meets us in history, however, exogamy is a full-fledged institution at once legal and religious as regards its sanctions. See series of artt. under MARRIAGE.

Another world-wide element in the social tradition of savages that bears strongly, and on the whole very hardly, on the moral status of the woman and the wife, is the magico-religious notion concerning the sacredness of women and especially of woman's blood. Hence the long and weakening confinements at puberty and during pregnancy and child-birth. Hence the avoidance, on the part of the male, of what a woman has touched, lest the contagion of effeminacy be handed on. Hence, too, probably in no small part the very forms of the marriage ceremony, designed to neutralize the mystic evils likely to ensue from contact with one who is a woman and a stranger to boot. In the other scale weigh several clear advantages. Woman's dependence on male protection in combination with her sacro-sanctity tends to render her an object of what eventually ripens into chivalry. Thus, amongst the Australians she is the ambassador between warring tribes, whose very body is able to cement a union of souls between them; or, again, many savages, notably such as are warriors, indulge in a strain of romantic love, the product of a kind of awe supervening on a basis of passion. Again, sexual purity develops into a virtue, of far-reaching influence on the character, out of various tabus on sexual intercourse, observed by the hunter, the warrior, the medicine-man, and so forth. Indeed, excessive sexuality, together with its perversions, is not a vice of the lower savages, despite appearances to the contrary (cf. art. CHASTITY), but rather an attribute of advanced societies, especially those that are polygamous, or, again, those in which marriage is deferred for many years past puberty. The so-called orgies of savages, or, again, the wife-lendings, and so on, have normally a ceremonial character, underlying which there is the notion of sexual intercourse as a means of mystic communion. On the other hand, what he considers to be sexual impurity is loathed and abominated by the savage, as when it takes the form of incest, that is, any violation of the exogamous rule that is not countenanced by some mystic requirement of even more primary importance (as, *e.g.*, occasionally in Australia). Incest regularly excites a 'wild spasm of wild justice,' and spells death for the guilty parties. On the other hand, adultery is, so to speak, a civil affair, an offence against property, being a cause of divorce for the most part under mother-right, though under father-right it often entails severer penalties on the erring wife and her lover (the settlement of the question in any case resting less with the individuals concerned than with their respective kins).

Finally, as regards personal initiative, it is in her mystic character rather than as wife and mother that woman occasionally becomes a leader of society, the old woman especially, with her witch-like qualities intensified by her appearance, exerting a sway over the popular imagination that may be for good or for evil. Meanwhile, the female sex as a sex is not without its share of influence in public affairs: partly because it is consolidated through having initiatory and other sacred and secret rites and attributes of its own, *e.g.* a sex totem in parts of Australia, and may thus come to dominate a whole province of social activity, as the Iroquois women did, thanks to their agricultural lore; partly because they possess and know how to wield what Mill has termed 'the shrewish sanction'; and partly because the desire to shine in the eyes of the women is a male weakness, responsible for much head-hunting and similar manifestations incidental to the pursuit of knightly glory.

(*b*) The relations of men and women have been dwelt on at length, because the woman's half of society will scarcely receive further mention here. As regards the relations between old and young, and those between parents and children, the former must be considered first, because primitive society is normally divided into fairly definite age-grades, and its customs tend to relate to these in their wholesale capacity. Thus, religion prescribes food-tabus and other restrictions upon the young as a class, and incidentally teaches them to control their appetites. Or, most conspicuous case of all, the young are subjected as a class to initiation, and their moral education is administered by the society as a whole in a form that is made impressive by solemn rites associated with the infliction of considerable pain. Parental education, on the other hand, tends amongst savages to be mild. They spare the rod, doubtless chiefly because of natural affection, but in some cases, as notably amongst the Indians of N. America, on the principle that a future warrior should brook a blow from no one. The mother tends to look after her daughter until the latter marries, and to impart to her the duties and lore of women. The son, on the other hand, is often taken away from the mother and sisters some time before puberty, and made to join the company of males who tend to live more or less segregated from the females in club-houses and so forth. Education, as imparted by either parent in the case of both girls and boys, is a mixture of technical and moral instruction, reminding us of the Persian system as reported by Herodotus (i. 136), 'to ride a horse, to shoot with a bow, and to tell the truth'; though it would seem that the deepest moral lessons are acquired in the course of public ceremonies such as the tribal initiation or the rites of the kin-group or of the secret society. The elders as a whole display the fullest concern in the rearing of the rising generation, and the dramatic character of the ceremonies embodies the intention to improve the youth in so palpable a form that these can hardly fail to catch the spirit of the effort made on their behalf, whilst they are likewise induced to embody that moral purpose in their lives by sheer faith in the efficacy of the ritual wherein it is enshrined.

So far the relations between old and young have been considered from one side only. We probably have to go back to instinct for an explanation of the fact that the solicitude of parents and elders for their youthful charges is perhaps reciprocated only in a relatively feeble and limited degree. Too much, however, must not be made of the sporadic occurrence of senicide. This, exactly like its converse, infanticide, is normally the direct result of very straitened circumstances, when a useless mouth or a drag on the mobility of the group is a handicap in the struggle for existence too heavy to be borne. The typical savage regards his elders, alive or dead, as the embodiments of a wisdom and power with something supernormal about it, and ancestor-worship (*q.v.*), a special type of cult which emerges from funeral rites which universally show awe and respect rather than mere fear of the dead, and especially of one's own dead, is but the consummation of a natural sentiment which associates the imitation of their elders by the young with the sort of love that develops into filial piety and gratitude. It has been true of man, since the times of the Ice Age, that the grave itself cannot make an end of family affection.

(*c*) With the subject of the relations between kinsmen in general we almost insensibly pass to that of the relations constituting the body politic as a whole. Kin-ly feeling is kindly feeling in the making. As has already been said, however, the development of kin sentiment is normally restricted, under the conditions of society in which the kin-group is paramount even as against the family, in a way that to the civilized mind seems extraordinary, artificial, and unnatural. The child belongs either to his mother's or to his father's kin, and as such participates in a moral system of rights and duties from which one or other parent is cut off by tabus as by a wall of brass, nay, from which he has as an outsider far more to lose than to gain, as, *e.g.*, in case of a conflict between groups, when parent and child may find themselves actually ranged against each other. On the other hand, so far as it extends, the consciousness of kin is a moral factor of the first importance, involving as it does the principle of corporate responsibility manifested in blood-revenge and the kindred developments of private law; whilst in a religious way it implicates the sense of a mystic brotherhood, as is seen notably in totemic ritual, and in what is probably its lineal successor, the ritual of the secret society. When, however, the individual does not live among his kin, as, *e.g.*, when he inherits his kin from the mother but lives amongst his father's people, there is a conflict between the principles of kinship and of symbiosis, the tendency of which is to end in some modification of the system of kinship that allows locality and brotherly love to go together. Kinship of the one-sided sort is normal in those conditions of the social life in which the separate groups are wandering, or at any rate scattered. When the groups can settle down side by side, as especially in the agricultural village, the family on the one hand as the home circle, and the village on the other as the wider circle of group-mates, come each into their own, whether exogamy and kin-organization be retained or dropped. Such generalizations, however, are purely provisional, as the problems connected with the evolution of the social organization of savages are some of the most perplexing that confront the anthropologist.

(2) *The political virtues.*—Whilst the scope of political virtue, in the sense of the moral bond that unites those who are by reason of local contiguity in constant touch with each other, is narrow, because the area of symbiosis is necessarily a restricted one, its emotional quality on the other hand is normally considerable, nay, such as the civilized community, which keeps in touch over a vast area by means of ideas, can only envy in vain. What corresponds with the savage to the sentiment and idea of the body politic is something in which he 'lives and moves and has his being,' sensibly and not merely symbolically. The savage individual is lost in the crowd, by being absorbed heart and soul in its life and movement. Heredity, of course, produces the coward and loafer as occasional variations; but the conditions of a hard life give the pervert and parasite a short shrift. That the savage will normally answer to a call of duty in its sterner forms, as, for instance, when public danger impends, could be illustrated extensively from amongst the lower savages, though in their case the body politic is less often the tribe as a whole than some one of its constituent groups. Nowhere, however, is this more manifest than at that higher level of savagery at which the 'king' (an elastic term) appears, living personification as he tends to be of State and Church in one. Patriotism at this point becomes almost identical with loyalty; and this is absolute. The Fijian criminal stands unbound to be killed, 'for whatever the king says must be done'; and the native of Dahomey exclaims in a similar strain, 'My head belongs to the king; if he wishes to take it, I am ready to give it up.' The king himself, meanwhile, is inclined to play the autocrat in proportion as he is endowed with personal initiative for better or for worse. In most cases, however, he is himself tied hand and foot by the custom that he is there to enforce—witness Wallace's amusing tale of how the Rājā of Umbok took the census (*Malay Archipelago*, London, 1869, i. ch. 12).

Again, the kindlier side of political duty as manifested in friendliness and good-fellowship is well to the fore amongst unspoilt savages, their dances, games, festivals, and perpetual gatherings being possible solely on that condition. And not only are they in general friendly amongst themselves, but they are likewise polite, doubtless in virtue of their predilection for forms and ceremonies. There is, however, a supreme disturber of these amicable and considerate relations, namely inequality of property; on which, more than on any other condition, is based inequality of social degree, a class system. Amongst the lower savages there is wont to reign what is sometimes not unfairly described as a primitive form of communism or socialism. Thus, the rules about the distribution of the spoils of the chase are based on the principle of a fair share for all, almost regardless of the special claims of the actual slayer of the animals, whose meed is rather honour; and the distribution is even State-regulated in the sense that what custom decrees the elders enjoin and, if necessary, enforce. Such a practice of sharing the produce, as distinguished from the means of production, weapons, and so on, which tend to be owned individually, would seem, however, in most cases to be rigidly confined to the actual symbiotic group of food-mates. Outside this narrow circle there is room for generosity and hospitality, which in their international aspect will again be glanced at presently. It is to be noticed that with this socialistic free-handedness there goes, not indeed a want of industry (for the loafer is soon weeded out), but a want of the capacity to save as against a rainy day; so that an alternation of feasts and fasts is the general rule amongst the lower savages. As there is not much scope for generosity, so neither is there for honesty, within the symbiotic circle, both being virtues incidental to a more or less individualistic régime. Thus, stealing within the home-circle is no crime; though in the wider circle of the tribe it may produce complications between groups; whilst contrariwise, as practised against those who are outside that circle, namely strangers and enemies, it is rather a virtue, at any rate amongst peoples of a predatory type. And what is true of honesty holds in the main of veracity: intimates and comrades do not deceive each other; but in regard to outsiders, to lie is to be diplomatic. With the economic development of primitive society, however, and the growth of classes of unequal wealth, things are somewhat changed. Yet the old communistic spirit, assisted by the profuseness that accompanies improvidence, and by the love of the display of power, tends to survive in the obligation to keep more or less open house, and to be ready with gifts, which is laid upon chief and leading man. Indeed, the savage 'king's' duty of feeding his people is often so interpreted that, if the crops fail, his want of mystic control over the powers of Nature is set down either to inefficiency or to sheer ill-will—with the result that he is put out of the way.

Finally, the institution of slavery, which is unknown at the level of the lower savagery, introduces a class of persons without legal rights, who may indeed be war-captives, or a subject-race dominated by invaders, but may likewise be broken men and pawns of the same flesh and blood as their owners. It would seem that, on the whole, the slave receives a larger share of the milk of human kindness at the hands of a savage overlord than he would if exploited in the interests of a developed industrialism; but life, when it is not that of the nearest and dearest, is cheap amongst savages, and the constant association of a slave-owning system with bloody rites involving human sacrifice tells its own tale. Moreover, wherever a slave-trade is established, the attendant horrors are bound to have a demoralizing effect, Africa being the standing instance of a continent rotted to the core by such an institution (for the development of which civilization, however, is most to blame). Nevertheless, it must not be forgotten that slavery, though morally an abomination, is possibly one of the mainsprings of human evolution. 'Here,' says Tylor, 'is one of the great trains of causation in the history of the human race. War brings on slavery, slavery promotes agriculture, agriculture of all things favours and establishes settled institutions and peace' (*CR* xxii. 70).

(3) *The international virtues.*—The subject of slavery paves the way for a consideration of a topic which for the student of Rudimentary Ethics must necessarily prove somewhat meagre. Savage morality, it has all along been maintained, is primarily an affair of the home-circle. Within this, amity of a high emotional quality; and without it, enmity fierce and uncompromising—such is the general rule. But the actual area of symbiosis is ringed round with an intermediate circle. Mates, neighbours, and strangers are, socially and morally, as heart, rind, and husk in some hard-shelled but palatable fruit. We have already glanced at the inter-gentile relations, as they might be termed, which savagery respects, not without a great deal of internecine struggle tempered by a tendency to settle disputes by compromise and mutual arrangement. But inter-gentile relations pass into inter-tribal (or, as we have, with a view to human evolution as a whole, ventured to name them, inter-national) almost without a perceptible break. Thus, notably in Australia, the kin-groups and local groups are loosely combined in tribes, and these again in wider combinations known to ethnologists as 'nations.' Here it seems quite impossible to draw a line between the customs and formalities governing the intercourse of the smaller groups—the sending of messengers and ambassadors, the regulated combat, the lending or exchange of trade-articles and of sacred objects, ceremonies, and songs, the mutual understanding as to marriage, inter-sexual prohibitions and privileges, and so forth—and those that extend so much further afield that a native can, it appears, travel almost from one end of Australia to another without being treated as a complete stranger. Possibly, too, the stranger as such tends here, as among other savages, to be sacred, hospitality having thus a religious sanction, since the fear of the stranger's curse, as Westermarck has shown (*MI* i. 578 ff.), proves a not ineffective substitute for the stimulus of generosity. In Australia, then, where both race and culture are largely uniform, a certain measure of sympathy establishes itself, despite the difficulties set up by a natural suspicion of unknown men (as exemplified by the 'silent trade') or by the want of a common tongue (necessitating such a device as gesture-language).

It is not till a fuller control over the forces of Nature enables population to grow relatively dense that the struggle for room begins in a given area of characterization, and the predatory spirit is let loose. War has evolved like everything else, and the art of killing one's neighbour efficiently was not acquired all at once. In protected areas a mild type of savage flourishes to whom war is unknown. Thus the Todas of the Nīlgiris have literally no man-killing weapons at all. On the other hand, the fighting qualities would appear to go closely with the breed, and to be the result of a struggle for existence waged primarily within the kind, though a fauna that includes dangerous, man-slaying animals (such as are not to be found on the Australian continent) must be an intensifying condition. The accompaniments of primitive warfare are mainly what have given savagery its evil name, constituting precisely that aspect of the life of rudimentary society which is turned, not without good cause, towards the so-called pioneers of civilization; but, as regards themselves, war is often a transitory condition, though there are some definitely predatory peoples—Zulus, Masai, Apaches, and so forth. The characteristic quality of the savage brave is fierceness, an emotional rather than a calm and reasoned form of valour. As such, it sustains itself, partly by war-dances before the event, but partly also by wanton cruelty both during battle and afterwards in the torturing of prisoners, as amongst the American Indians, who thereby not merely satisfied their own feelings, but sought at the same time to 'blood the young whelps,' to wit, the future warriors of the tribe. Again, one form of cannibalism (*q.v.*) is directly associated with warfare. This revolting practice may consist in sheer 'anankophagy,' as usually amongst the lower savages, or in an 'endo-cannibalism,' or ceremonial eating of blood-relations to keep the spirit in the family, or for some similar reason, which is not without high moral value; but a warrior tribe will eat its enemies simply, as it were, to glut its rage. There can, moreover, be little doubt that the institution amounts to an asset in the struggle for existence, as the cannibalism inspires terror amongst the neighbouring peoples; so that a cannibal tribe, as, *e.g.*, the Niam-Niam of the Bahr al-Ghazal, may rank amongst the most vigorous and effective people of a given region. On the other hand, such a practice as the head-hunting of the Dayaks of Borneo or the Nāgās of Assam is to be regarded rather as a by-product of war, a sort of collector's mania that has supervened on a legitimate love of warlike trophies. For the rest, the moral effects of war on the group and the individual alike make scarcely if at all less markedly for good than they do for evil. Collectively, men are knit together by a common purpose that demands from them at once all that Bagehot's phrase 'the preliminary virtues' covers, namely, courage, loyalty, obedience, and a devotion maintained to the point of death. For the individual, again, war is a school of self-respect; and, though the swagger and boasting of the savage brave has its humorous side, his mastery over that lower self which bids him shun danger and live soft is reflected in a strength of character to which there is added, on the intellectual and ideal side, a sense of honour and of duty. This sentiment has probably counted for more in the history of the race than even the religious sense of tabu, inasmuch as 'Do' is more fruitful than 'Do not,' and defiance of a danger that is known more rational than the avoidance of a danger that is unknown and taken to be a danger for that very reason.

(4) *The personal virtues.*—Something has just been said in regard to the self-respect of the savage warrior, of whom the North American brave will serve as a type. On the whole, however, it must be declared that it is precisely in its reference to self, which is almost to say in its reflective aspect, that savage morality is especially weak. The moral subject looks outwards, not inwards, and reads his duty in the movements of his fellows, not in the movements of his own heart. He has his selfish inclinations, which have to be suppressed by social drill and education; but he is incapable of that misbegotten creation of civilized philosophy, a reasoned selfishness. Yet, conversely, he has but little of that moral individuality which enables a man to stand out for the right even against the opinions of his circle. He sees as one of the crowd, and at most applies his crowd-consciousness to himself as to one who is viewed from without. He can see himself cutting a fine or a humble figure, and is moved accordingly to try that it shall be the one rather than the other. But there his notion of self tends to stop. One might say that his most internal of moral sanctions is pride of appearance. His tendency to self-adornment, one that unfortunately does not always carry with it the virtue of personal cleanliness, illustrates this type of self-feeling on its lower side. Again, a desire to cultivate an honourable idleness, and to abstain from such work as may lower his dignity, is directly due to pride of self; indeed, the main reason why the civilized man fails to establish satisfactory relations with the savage is that he forgets, or is incapable

of appreciating, the fact that the savage is a 'gentleman' in all the mixed connotation of that term. On its higher side, the pride of the savage gives him an intense sense of his rights, and especially of his right to a good name; so that he must not brook an insult either to himself or to those who are intimately his. Further, the curious power that man alone of animals has of putting an end to his own life is the occasion amongst some savages of exalting suicide (*q.v.*) to a place amongst the virtues, to die with dignity being, as it were, the projection of the desire to live therewith.

It must not be supposed, however, that self-respect is entirely responsible for the many-sided virtue of a self-regarding type which goes by the general name of self-control. One of the most important spheres of the influence of tabu is the domain of sensual appetite. Thus, in sexual matters, together with the coyness that is but a means of attracting a mate, there goes a shyness, the natural accompaniment of a vitally critical act, which gradually ripens under the sway of tabu into genuine modesty and delicacy of feeling (cf. art. CHASTITY). Similarly, eating and drinking, no less than sexual intercourse, are normally surrounded, in virtue of their very importance in the vital economy, with a network of ceremonial prescriptions that reinforce the sense of crisis, and turn a mere opportunity of carnal enjoyment into a solemn rite. There is plenty of strong lustiness in the background, however, which the emotional type of savage experience is well calculated to foster; so that, though pent up by religion within strict limits, it discharges itself along lawful channels, in the shape of orgies and carnivals, with the force of a torrent. Nay, religion may directly minister to the stimulation of passions that seem for the time being to set all self-control at naught, as, *e.g.*, when the use of drugs and intoxicants is encouraged as a means of obtaining inspiration, or when the gambler is led to stake his all on his own luck conceived more or less clearly as a supernatural power in him and behind him.

In conclusion, it must be pointed out that by means of this same conception of a grace that is in him, yet somehow above him, religion affords the inner life of the savage a great support for reflective self-development, the 'personal totem,' spirit-helper, and similar beliefs being, as it were, the man's own aspiration towards welfare in its more spiritual aspects seen in an enlarging mirror.

(5) *The transcendental virtues.*—It is a common mistake to suppose that the savage is capable of envisaging a material Good only. His whole religion, it is true, may be summed up in the formula, half spell and half prayer—'Let blessings come and evils depart.' But the blessings and evils alike are primarily spiritual. Nature and matter in the modern sense have at most a very restricted sense for the typical savage. His desire is to be in sympathetic relations of a pre-eminently social type with an environment conceived as an array of quasi-personal or personal beings, all mystically powerful and, as such, able to help or to hurt him and his. His universe is thus a moral order, and the savage is a savage just because he is too ready to cope with physical necessities merely by means of moral control or suasion. So much is he already in spirit, if not in effect, the lord of creation that he can imagine no part of creation that is purely unmoral and mechanical in its mode of operation. For him a strong will, a human will augmented by an indefinite *plus*, can directly influence the courses of the stars or the currents of the ocean. Thus the Good for him is always in some sense God, a power analogous to will-power which realizes itself within man himself no less than in the other beings of his environment, and can be good as friend, evil as enemy, like man or any other living being. Such a belief clothes itself in a variety of forms, some of which, *e.g.* the belief in a Supreme Being who makes the tribal laws, or, again, the cult of the dead, and in particular of ancestral heroes, can be seen to make for righteousness more clearly than can the animism or polydæmonism which is distracted by the desire to serve many and alien masters.

Whereas, however, religious beliefs vary infinitely amongst savages, their ceremonial customs, which are far more closely and directly related to their practice, embody much that is common. Thus tabu, starting as a ceremonial aversion, becomes almost universally moralized as a purity of heart, which is fortified by a custom of ceremonial purgation that develops into the confession of sins. Communion, again, is, at its lower end, little more than the crudest kind of sympathetic magic; nevertheless, at the upper end of the evolutionary scale, it expresses the realization of the Good perhaps better than any idea within the purview of religion or philosophy. Once more, sacrifice, as a ritual act, passes insensibly into self-sacrifice. Finally, the central notion of spiritual power or grace lends an orientation to human life which, though since enlarged and purified by continual reinterpretation, is essentially something that civilized men owe to their savage ancestors. To extend the area of human brotherhood by translating the natural feelings of simple folk, who cannot, so to speak, see far beyond the fire-circle of their own camp, into ideas that can unify men across the length and breadth of the world in a mutual understanding—such is the mission of civilization. Savagery, however, must be allowed to have perceived the Good even in its more transcendental aspects, though it be left to civilization to conceive these fully; and, in the meantime, the real Good exists neither for perception nor for conception as such, but for the whole spiritual and moral nature of developing mankind.

LITERATURE.—The subject of Rudimentary Ethics being in certain respects as wide as that of Social Anthropology, it is impossible to offer the reader a complete bibliography here; he must be referred generally to the classical works of Tylor, Frazer, Lang, Hartland, Jevons, etc., not to mention Continental writers. Of works that profess to treat of Ethics in particular, H. Spencer, *Principles of Ethics*, London, 1893, and C. S. Wake, *Evolution of Morality*[3], London, 1878, are both somewhat out of date as regards their anthropological data. Though the same is to some extent true of Waitz-Gerland, *Anthropologie der Naturvölker*, Leipzig, 1859–1872, the high philosophic quality of the treatment makes it still worth consulting. E. B. Tylor's papers in *CR* xxi. and xxii. (London, 1873) are, on the other hand, of almost as much value now as at the time when they were written. Of more recent writings in English, E. Westermarck, *MI*, London, 1906–08, and L. T. Hobhouse, *Morals in Evolution*, London, 1906, are easily the best, though both treatises attempt to cover the whole field of human morals—with the result that the one is relatively weak on the history of civilization and the other on the anthropological side. A. Sutherland, *The Origin and Growth of the Moral Instinct*, London, 1898, is suggestive, but shows gaps. For the social psychology which must form the background for all such studies, W. McDougall, *An Introd. to Social Psychology*, London, 1908, is indispensable; but, when allowance is made for the too exclusive insistence on the function of social tradition as a moralizing agency, L. Lévy-Bruhl, *Les Fonctions mentales dans les sociétés inférieures*, Paris, 1909, brings the reader into closer touch with the facts of Anthropology. For the influence of religion, and again for the bearing of social organization on the moral life of savages, the 11 volumes of *ASoc*, Paris, 1896–1908, should be consulted, and especially the contributions of E. Durkheim and his eminent collaborators M. Mauss and H. Hubert. F. Ratzel is the best authority for Anthropo-geography; see especially his *History of Mankind*, Eng. tr., London, 1896–98. On the side of law, the various works of A. H. Post on Comparative Jurisprudence (in German), and S. R. Steinmetz, *Ethnol. Studien zur ersten Entwicklung der Strafe*, Leyden, 1894, are invaluable. W. Wundt's *Ethik*, Stuttgart, 1886, and *Völkerpsychologie*, Leipzig, 1904 f., despite the fact that their author is among the greatest of psychologists, do not seem to the present writer to be as sound and well-founded on fact as they are incontestably brilliant. As regards the bearing of the anthropological study of Ethics on general philosophy, the present writer may refer to his own essay,

'Origin and Validity in Ethics,' in *Personal Idealism*, ed. H. Sturt, London, 1902, from which the classification of virtues followed in the text is taken over. A short sketch of his, *Anthropology* (Home University Library, London, 1912), covers much the same ground as the present article, in a rather more popular way. For the rest, there is an all too vast bibliography of the subject to be found at the end of Westermarck's work already cited.

R. R. MARETT.

ETHICS AND MORALITY.

ETHICS AND MORALITY (American).—The autochthones of North and South America present levels of culture as varied as their habitats. Moral elevations and depressions are as recurrent as changes in race and environment. It is obviously impossible to characterize the Botocudo and the Quichua, or the Huron and the Pueblo, in one breath. Nevertheless, for the purposes of a concise survey of the moral attainment of the Indian peoples, we may confine ourselves to three broadly distinguished levels. The lowest of these is presented by the great mass of the S. American tribes dwelling east of the Andes, and by sparser examples in the less favoured localities of the N. continent. The second level is typically that of the great forest and plains nations of N. America. Finally, following the western mountains, from Alaska to Chile, there occur a series of culture-centres marked by proficiencies in the arts—wood-, stone-, and metal-working, weaving, pottery, agriculture—and complexities in social organization which, in the culminating civilizations of Mexico and Peru, warrant our treating them as a distinct moral level.

1. The lowest levels.—Garcilasso de la Vega (*Royal Commentaries*, Fr. ed., Paris, 1830, or Markham's ed., Lond. 1869–71) has several passages portraying the moral state of some of the wild tribes with whom the Incas came in contact. Thus (VIII. iii.) the peoples of Huancapampa are described as

'without peace or amity, without lord or government or city; making war never for dominion, since they know not the meaning of rule, nor yet for plunder, since they have no possessions, and go, for the most part, quite naked; their most precious booty is the wives and daughters of the conquered; the men are captured, if possible, and inhumanly eaten; as for their religion, it is as absurd as their manners are fierce.'

In another passage (VII. xvii.) the Chirihuanas are given a yet worse character: the spies of the Incas report that

'they lead a life worse than the beasts, knowing no divinity, no law, no rulers, without towns or houses; they make war in order to obtain prisoners whose flesh they may eat and whose blood they may drink, and, not content with this, they eat their own dead relatives; they never cover their nudity, and have intercourse indifferently with all sorts of women, even their sisters, their daughters, their mothers.'

We recognize in these reports an exaggeration natural enough when the facts reported upon are seen through hostile eyes; yet the offences are of such a nature as to place their perpetrators among the lowest of mankind—and we have evidence enough of the reality of the offences.

The Paumari of Brazil have a 'Song of the Turtle'—'I wander, always wander, and when I get where I want to go, I shall not stop, but still go on'—which, says J. B. Steere (*U.S. Nat. Mus. Rep.* 1901), reflects their own mode of life, passed in roaming from sand-bar to sand-bar of the Brazilian rivers in search of food. This lack of orientation in the physical realm has its intellectual counterpart, shown, *e.g.*, in the utterly rudimentary number-systems of many S. American tribes (cf. Tylor, *Prim. Cult.*[4], London, 1903, ch. vii.; Conant, *The Number Concept*, 1896, p. 22 f.). It is only to be expected that the moral level will be equally low; and this we find to be the fact in wide-spread cannibalism and low sexual standards.

Nevertheless, when Dobrizhoffer, in the very words of Garcilasso, affirms that 'the wild Abipones live like wild beasts,' we should bear in mind that he is speaking with their ignorance of agriculture foremost in mind. As a matter of fact, he shows them to possess not only very respectable arts, but some very stalwart virtues (see *Account of the Abipones*, London, 1822, esp. II. xiii.). To be sure, the equestrian tribes of the pampas have long been superior to the tribes of the tropical forests; but, even with the latter, ferocity and vice are not the dominant characteristics.

Mode of approach has much to do with the impression derived; it is significant that those who have known the lower peoples the most intimately find most in them worthy of regard. Thus, von den Steinen (*Unter den Naturvölkern Zentral-Brasiliens*, Berlin, 1894, p. 59) describes his solitary stay in a village of the Bakairi near the head-waters of the Xingú, in a chapter entitled 'Bakaïri-Idylle,' and he can say of this episode:

'After accompanying the two brave fellows to the landing-place, and seeing them disappear at the first bend of the river, I turned back to my new friends and soon felt so much at my ease in their midst that I regard those idyllic days as unquestionably the happiest that I have ever experienced.'

He found the Indians of this region docile, gay, companionable, trustworthy—mother-naked, but paradisaically innocent of shame. It is incredible that all the difference between such a picture and those drawn by earlier and less unprejudiced pens can represent merely an amelioration due to a casual white influence.

H. H. Prichard is vigorous in his praise of the Tehuelches (*Through the Heart of Patagonia*, London, 1902, esp. ch. vi.):

'a kind-hearted, docile, and lazy race . . . invariably courteous,' whose 'women make excellent mothers, and the father is inordinately proud of his offspring, especially of his sons.' 'The morality of the Tehuelches is, on the whole, admirable. Unfaithfulness in the wife is rare and is not often bitterly revenged.' 'Polygamy is allowed, but not much practised.'

It will be remembered that continence and chastity are virtues which Dobrizhoffer (II. vii., xix.) found especially praiseworthy among the Abipones (*q.v.*), contrasting them with the licentious and degenerate neighbouring tribes; while their over-indulgent fondness for their children was also noted.

Prichard likens the Tehuelches to the Eskimos, at the other extremity of the Americas: 'Both races are eminently sluggish and peaceable. . . . And of both little evil can be said.' The testimony of a recent sojourner among the latter is in point:

'In many things we are the superiors of the Eskimo, in a few we are his inferiors. . . . He has developed individual equality farther than we; he is less selfish, more helpful to his fellow, kinder to his wife, gentler to his child, more reticent about the faults of his neighbour, than any but the rarest and best of our race. As a guest who could not pay for my keep, as a stranger whose purpose among them no one knew, I learnt these things in a winter that, for all its darkness, was one of the pleasantest of my life' (Vilhjálmr Stefánsson, *Harper's Monthly*, vol. 117, p. 721).

Of course not all peoples on the lower levels betray such characters. McGee (*17 RBEW*, pt. i. [1898]) is only the latest among a long series of observers who have found the Seri Indians of Tiburon and the adjacent mainland 'the most primitive and the most bloodthirsty and treacherous of the Indians of North America' (p. 119). 'Their highest virtue is the shedding of alien blood . . . their blackest crime the transmission of their own blood into alien channels' (p. 154). In these traits McGee finds the sources of a character which places the Seri, in spite of physical excellence, very near the bottom of the moral scale. Even animal gratitude is absent:

'The 1894 party was fortunate in successfully treating a sick wife of sub-chief Mashém, and subsequently spent days in the rancheria, distributing gifts to old and young in a manner unprecedented in their experience . . .; yet, with a single possible exception, they succeeded in bringing no more human expression to any Seri face or eye than curiosity, avidity for food, studied indifference, and shrouded or snarling disgust. Among themselves they were fairly cheerful, and the families were unobtrusively affectionate; yet the cheerfulness was always chilled and often banished by the approach of an alien' (p. 132).

2. Typical levels.—The presence of an obvious moral sense, as expressed either in custom or in conscious reflexion upon moral problems, is the fair criterion of the beginnings of moral elevation. Such a sense is the indubitable possession of the great body of N. American Indians, with many of whom it develops conduct of the highest order. We are justified, too, in regarding the morality of the forest and plains tribes of the northern continent as the typical Indian morality; for we find it already inchoate in many of the inferior peoples, while it is the foundation for our understanding of the conceptions of the more civilized groups.

(1) *Social organization.*—With most observers the first impression of Indian societies is of their lack of organization. 'They love justice and hate violence and robbery, a thing really remarkable in men who have neither laws nor magistrates; for among them each man is his own master and his own protector,' writes Père Biard in 1612 of the Canadians (*Jesuit Relations*, ed. Thwaites, Cleveland, 1896–1901, ii. 73). That the Indians have no law is a characteristic judgment; and, understanding law in a constitutional or statutory sense, it is, of course, the general truth; yet it is safe to affirm that no Indian group is so primitive as not to possess its body of customs, to be violated only on peril of outlawry.

As a rule the ostensible authority is vested in the tribal elders, certain of whom have the prestige which we denominate chieftainship. This office may best be defined by characterization:

'The system of authority which prevails in Indian societies is very simple. Each family . . . is ruled over by the father, whose authority is great. As long as he lives, or at least while he is strong and active, his wives, his daughters and their husbands, and his sons, until they marry and thus pass from their own family under the rule of a new house-father, are almost completely under his sway. . . . But the father of each, while retaining his authority over his own family, is to some extent under the authority—that is, under the fear and influence—of the peaiman; and, where several families live in one place, he is also under the authority of the headman of the settlement. The authority of the peaiman . . . depends on the power which the man is supposed to exercise over spirits of all kinds, and, as all diseases are supposed to be the work of spirits, over diseases, and . . . consequently over the bodies of his fellows. The headman, on the other hand, is generally the most successful hunter, who, without having any formal authority, yet because he organizes the fishing and hunting parties, obtains a certain amount of deference from the other men of his village. He settles all disputes within the settlement, and in the not distant days when Indians were in the habit of waging war . . . he used . . . to determine on the commencement of hostilities (E. F. Im Thurn, *Indians of Guiana*, London, 1883, p. 211 f.).

Tribal headman, war-leader, 'medicine-man,' and the group of fathers or elders which forms the tribal council—these are the authorities of the Indian tribe in either continent. They are not always differentiated, however. In the description just cited the office of headman and war-leader is one; and it is, of course, the rule that a capable war-chief should assume an important rôle in civil affairs. Yet in the more advanced tribal organizations—as among the Iroquois, Sioux, Creeks, etc.—there is not only differentiation of military and civil chieftaincies, but well-marked hierarchies of the latter, chiefs and sub-chiefs, having at once legislative, executive, and judicial powers.

The civil chieftaincies are usually hereditary, in the maternal line, though the selection is seldom apart from merit, which with some peoples is apparently the sole criterion. Unquestionably, the ideal of merit, from the lowest to the highest tribes, is the ideal of social service. Stefánsson (*loc. cit.* p. 725 f.) gives an illuminating account of a conversation with an Eskimo chieftain touching the foundations of his office:

'One day, as Ovayuak and I sat in our snow blocks with backs to the wind, fishing, I asked him why he was not satisfied with the huge pile already stored away—more than our family of twenty-two could eat in two years. He then told me that he was a chief. And why, did I suppose, was he a chief? Or, now that he was chief, did I suppose he would continue being a chief if he were lazy? We had plenty fish for ourselves there at Tuktuyaktok, but who could tell if the people who had gone inland after reindeer might not return any day with empty sleds, or possibly with no sleds—carrying their children on their backs because the dogs were dead of starvation? And how about the people west of the Mackenzie at Shingle Point? True, they had caught plenty fish in summer, but they catch none in winter, and they are not sensible now as they formerly were, but will haul a big load of fish a long distance to sell to the traders at Herschel Island for a little tea, which tastes good but does not keep a man alive. And what of the people up the Mackenzie? They depend largely on rabbits. Some years there are plenty of these, and other years, for some reason, there are few or none. Might we not some day see many sleds coming from the southwest along the coast? And may not these sleds turn out to be empty because there are no rabbits in the willows? Did I suppose that if all these people came we would have too much fish? And why was he a chief, if not for the fact that people twenty days' journey away could always say when they became hungry, "We will go to Ovayuak, he will have plenty food"?'

An instance of a reverse order, yet illustrating the same general demand that the chieftain be a giver, is narrated by von den Steinen (p. 285):

'The power of the chiefs was not great. In all the larger villages there were several chiefs, who lived in different houses; our village was always represented by only one. "Representation" was the most important duty in time of peace. The chief was manager of the seedsmen's stores, and he ordered the *beijús* to be baked and the drinks to be prepared on all festive occasions and during visits of strangers. He was simply a householder on a larger scale; but he dared not be stingy if he wished to have the esteem of his fellow-villagers, much less his tribal neighbours. In this respect the chief of the first Batovy village was *kurápa*, 'bad' = 'greedy.' He allowed only a few *beijús* to be baked for the guests. Greediness was looked upon as the most offensive quality. But this method of ruling must have been difficult. Antonio told me about a certain João Cadete in the village of Paranatinga, whose turn it was to become chief, but who preferred to emigrate *com medo de tratar*, for fear that he would have to entertain people; so Felipe was appointed in his stead.'

But chieftaincy among the Indians is not always founded upon beneficence. The career of Tchatka, chief of the Assiniboins, as narrated by Father de Smet (*Life, Letters, and Travels*, 1905, VII. x.), is that of a medicine-man who by means of poison and pure criminality made himself feared and powerful among his people. And, in many other instances, supernatural powers—frequently exercised for good—have elevated the Indian prophet to a position of civil or military primacy (cf. Mooney, 'The Ghost-Dance Religion,' *14 RBEW*, pt. ii. [1896]). In the cases of the Aztec Emperor and the Peruvian Inca it is obvious that civil, military, and sacerdotal functions are united in the one officer, who thus, as it were, figures the whole sovereignty of the nation.

The power of the chieftain thus rests primarily upon some type of personal prestige. Père Biard says of the Algonquian 'Sagamores': 'The Indians follow them through the persuasion of example, or of custom, or of ties of kindred and alliance; sometimes even through a certain authority of power, no doubt' (*Jes. Rel.*, ed. Thwaites, ii. 73). In better organized tribes the chief's authority is grounded in more definite sanctions, especially caste, property, and the religious sanction of his installation (cf. *ib.* xxvi. 155 f.).

In every case, the real source of power lay with the tribal council, comprising the men of quality and character. The council determined all movements of importance, as matters of war and peace, of the hunt, etc. Ability to speak persuasively was hence of much moment, and the orator a man of importance. Police duty fell to the younger and more vigorous warriors,—men of tried and sterling character,—not only in hunting and war parties, but also in the camp, and tribal festivals (cf. Eastman, *Indian Boyhood*, New York, 1902, pp. 40, 186). Quarrelsomeness and violence within the tribe seem to be rare; except when under the influence of liquor, the Indians of both continents appear to be peaceable in their domestic relations. This fact early impressed the Jesuit missionaries in Canada:

'Leaving out some evil-minded persons, such as one meets almost everywhere, they have a gentleness and affability almost incredible for Savages. They are not easily annoyed, and, if they have received a wrong from any one, they often conceal the resentment they feel—at least, one finds here very few who make a public display of anger and vengeance. They maintain themselves in this perfect harmony by frequent visits, by help they give one another in sickness, by feasts, and by alliances' (Thwaites, x. 213).

'They are very much attached to each other, and agree admirably. You do not see any disputes, quarrels, enmities, or reproaches among them. Men leave the arrangement of the household to the women, without interfering with them; they cut, and decide, and give away as they please, without making the husband angry. I have never seen my host ask a giddy young woman that he had with him what became of the provisions, although they were disappearing very fast. I have never heard the women complain because they were not invited to the feasts, because the men ate the good pieces, or because they had to work continually—going in search of the wood for the fire, making the houses, dressing the skins, and busying themselves in other very laborious work. Each one does her own little tasks, gently and peacefully, without any disputes' (vi. 233 ff.).

Crimes of violence, where they do occur, are punished by the injured person or family. In the more primitive societies murder is the occasion for blood-feud (cf., *e.g.*, Thwaites, iii. 93 f.). In more complexly organized groups it may be atoned for or compounded with the relatives of the slain (see EXPIATION AND ATONEMENT [American]). Outlawry—especially for an offence against a clansman—is a normal form of punishment, and is sometimes the prevailing punishment, as among the Seri (*17 RBEW*, pt. i. p. 273).

In the last resort it is the sanction of the community as a whole—at least among the typical tribes—which determines the punishment of the offender, as it upholds the power of the chieftain. Thus, in his chapter on 'The Polity of the Hurons and their Government' (Thwaites, x. 211 ff.), Père Brébeuf states:

'They punish murderers, thieves, traitors, and sorcerers; and, in regard to murderers, although they do not preserve the severity of their ancestors toward them, nevertheless the little disorder there is among them in this respect makes me conclude that their procedure is scarcely less efficacious than is the punishment of death elsewhere; for the relatives of the deceased pursue not only him who has committed the murder, but address themselves to the whole village, which must give satisfaction for it, and furnish, as soon as possible, for this purpose, as many as sixty presents. . . . For it is not here as it is in France and elsewhere, where the public and a whole city do not generally espouse the quarrel of an individual. Here you cannot insult any one of them without the whole country resenting it, and taking up the quarrel against you, and even against an entire village. Hence arise wars; and it is more than sufficient reason for taking arms against some village if it refuse to make satisfaction by the presents ordained.'

(2) *The family and sexual morality.*—Broadly divided, Indian families are of two general types: that in which descent is counted in the male line, with a relative subordination of the woman's social status, and that in which descent is counted through the mother, and marriage is only between members of clearly marked exogamous clans or gentes. In the former case the family authority rests directly with the father; in the latter it devolves upon the brothers of mothers, or even, in a sort of veritable matriarchy, upon the mothers themselves (cf. *17 RBEW*, pt. ii. pp. 269–274), and is merged into a group responsibility. There are numerous degrees of intermediacy between these extremes, as amongst the Guiana Indians, where paternal rule is accompanied by maternal descent and exogamous marriage (see Im Thurn, chs. vii. and x.). On the whole the marked exogamous clan is characteristic of the more advanced societies, with a tendency, in the better type of tribe, to emphasize the power of the father (as distinguished from that of the uncles). These units—family and clan—are the real possessors of the tribal sovereignty, so that in the majority of instances the tribe may be viewed as a federation—based on common language, customs, and convenience—made up of such units.

But the force of the family as a unit in a larger organism is a matter of social structure; the troth of husband and wife, on the other hand, is primarily an individual affair, and it is on this individuality of the sex relation that family morality primarily depends.

The Indian conception of chastity represents great variations, and is determined by many considerations. Most of the restrictions which appear grow directly out of the demand for purity of descent, and hence, as with other races, apply chiefly to the women. Yet there are numerous demands for continence on the part of the men, even within the marriage relation—as in the purifications preceding war excursions or during religious festivals. In S. America the custom is wide-spread for husband and wife to abstain from intercourse during the entire period, two or three years, in which a child is suckled. Dobrizhoffer recounts the consequences of this practice among the Abipones (II. x.):

'The mothers suckle their children for three years, during which time they have no conjugal intercourse with their husbands, who, tired of their long delay, often marry another wife. The women, therefore, kill their unborn babes through fear of repudiation, sometimes getting rid of them by violent arts, without waiting for their birth. Afraid of being widows in the lifetime of their husbands, they blush not to become more savage than tigresses.'

This is no doubt a not unusual consequence in S. America, where divorce is frequently a matter of the husband's whim.

Certainly the fact that white women captured by the Indians of N. America have, as a rule, been respected in the matter of their honour is fair evidence that the Indians are not as a race licentious. And, north and south, conjugal fidelity appears to be the prevailing condition—tempered, perhaps one should add, by facile divorce. 'Little is necessary to separate them,' says Le Jeune (Thwaites, v. 111), 'unless they have children, for then they do not leave each other so easily.' It is worth noting that he adds: 'A man who loved his (deceased) wife—or a wife who loved her husband—and who respects her relatives, will sometimes remain three years without remarriage, to show his love.' Testimony to the mutual affection of Indian couples is frequent, though, of course, the reverse is to be found. Polygamy is found among many tribes, but seldom on any considerable scale, plural wives falling to men of wealth or position, or, in some cases, resulting from the decimation of the male population in war, the survivors customarily taking to wife their wives' sisters.

Virginity in the bride is very differently esteemed in particular tribes. The Huron maidens were in bad repute with the Fathers, and among the northern tribes—Eskimo and Athapascan—the virginity of the bride appears to be of far less moment than her industrial value—skill in clothes-making, house-tending, and the like (see Morice, 'The Great Déné Race,' *Anthropos*, v. [1910] 979 ff.; Parkman, *Jesuits in North America*, Boston, 1871, pp. xxxiii–xxxv). On the other hand, the standard of maidenly morality is often upheld by important tribal sanctions. Eastman (*Indian Boyhood*, pp. 183–187, *The Soul of the Indian*, pp. 95–99) describes the Siouan 'Feast of the Virgins,' at which each girl in turn touched a rock-altar, prepared for the occasion, in token of her purity.

'Any man among the spectators might approach and challenge any young woman whom he knew to be unworthy; but if the accuser failed to prove his charge, the warriors were accustomed to punish him severely.' Furthermore, 'our maidens were ambitious to attend a number of these feasts before marriage, and it sometimes happened that a girl was compelled to give one on account of gossip about her conduct.' See art. CHASTITY (Introd.).

Prostitution among Indian women, where it exists, appears to be largely due to contact with degraded whites, although perhaps in some cases the frequency of temporary and adulterous relations constitutes an aboriginal equivalent of the institution. Unnatural vice occurs, particularly in S. America, where it roused the abhorrence of the Incas to such a degree that conquests were undertaken to eradicate it, and the offenders punished by burning (Garcilasso, VI. x., XIII. xiii.; see also, Westermarck, *MI*, ch. xliii.).

The real clue to the Indian conception of sexual morality and family purity is to be found in their devotion to their children, as vehicles of the tribe's perpetuity. When Père Lalemant rebuked a Montagnais for looseness, telling him he might not be sure of his own children, the Indian replied: 'You French people love only your own children; but we all love all the children of our tribe' (Thwaites, vi. 255). And in the Indian accounts of the battle of Wounded Knee, there is nothing more affecting, as there is no more stinging accusation of the whites, than the evidence of their dear regard for the children:

'. . . There was a woman with an infant in her arms who was killed as she almost touched the flag of truce, and the women and children, of course, were strewn all along the circular village until they were dispatched. Right near the flag of truce a mother was shot down with her infant; the child not knowing that its mother was dead was still nursing; and that especially was a very sad sight. The women as they were fleeing with their babies were killed together, shot right through, and the women who were heavy with child were killed also. . . . Of course it would have been all right if only the men were killed; we would feel almost grateful for it. But the fact of the killing of the women, and more especially the killing of the young boys and girls who are to go to make up the future strength of the Indian people, is the saddest part of the whole affair, and we feel it very sorely' ('Narrative of American Horse,' *14 RBEW*, pt. ii. p. 885 f.).

See artt. CHILDREN (American), EDUCATION (American).

(3) *Property, industry, war.*—The Indian conception of property rights, if not exactly loose, is at least elastic. There is little development of the sense for possessions in so far as this stands for exclusive enjoyment. An 'Indian gift,' as the white man understands it, is a loan; and the Indian's communistic understanding of property, as distinguished from the white's individualism in such matters, is doubtless at the root of many racial conflicts.

Indian communism perhaps explains the great prevalence of the vice of gambling, as, in a better intention, it explains their fine hospitality—even the unwelcome stranger has a right to food, if he be hungry, while the coming of a friend is the occasion for a feast.

'They are very generous among themselves, and even make a show of not loving anything, of not being attached to the riches of the earth, so that they may not grieve if they lose them. Not long ago a dog tore a beautiful beaver robe belonging to one of the savages, and he was the first one to laugh about it. One of the greatest insults that can be offered to them is to say, "That man likes everything, he is stingy." If you refuse them anything, here is their reproach, "Thou lovest that, love it as much as thou wilt." They do not open the hand half-way when they give,—I mean among themselves, for they are as ungrateful as possible toward strangers. You will see them take care of their kindred, the children of their friends, widows, orphans, and old men, never reproaching them in the least, giving them abundantly, sometimes whole moose. This is truly the sign of a good heart and of a generous soul' (Le Jeune's *Relation*, 1634 [Thwaites, vi. 237 ff.]).

'The native American has been generally despised by his white conquerors for his poverty and simplicity. They forget, perhaps, that his religion forbade the accumulation of wealth and the enjoyment of luxury. To him, as to other single-minded men in every age and race, from Diogenes to the brothers of Saint Francis, from the Montanists to the Shakers, the love of possessions has appeared a snare, and the burdens of a complex society a source of needless peril and temptation. Furthermore, it was the rule of his life to share the fruits of his skill and success with his less fortunate brothers. Thus he kept his spirit free from the clog of pride, cupidity, or envy, and carried out, as he believed, the divine decree—a matter profoundly important to him' (Eastman, *Soul of the Indian*, p. 9 f.).

These are perhaps both idealistic representations, yet they do represent the ideal, if not always the attainment, of the great body of the Indian tribes. Where, as is often the case, we find the Indians denominated thieves, the thievery is usually a matter of inter-tribal or inter-racial conflict—in the Indian conception, justified plunder.

'Indians will occasionally steal small articles from one another; but, when questioned, they will say they were in want of them and could not get them any other way,' writes de Smet (p. 1073). 'When they rob whites, they think they are doing right. With them all whites are interlopers, getting rich from the labours of the Indians, and to take a portion of their goods is nothing more than their due long since in arrears.'

In the more primitive societies property is communal, under the control of the chief—even the game captured by the unmarried hunters is his (see, *e.g.*, Thwaites, iii. 87; von den Steinen, p. 285 f.). In more advanced groups, especially in the North-west, where slavery is important, the sense of personal possession becomes intensified. Yet it is significant that the peculiar Indian institution of the 'potlatch'—a feast at which the feast-maker gives away all his wealth—finds its characteristic development among these very tribes, remaining, as it were, an institutional protest against the conception of private property (*e.g.*, among the Tlingit; see *26 RBEW* [1908], pp. 428, 434 ff.). The custom even persists in so advanced a society as the Aztec, in connexion with the worship of Napatecutli. The giver of the feast, says Sahagun (*Hist. gén.*, Paris, 1880, I. xx.), dispenses all his possessions, saying: 'It matters not that I remain without resource, provided my god be satisfied with this feast; whether he return to me goods, whether he leave me in poverty, let his will be done.'

Industrial conditions among the Indians have been as difficult for the white mind to comprehend as is their conception of property. The usual first impression is that the women are the sole burden-bearers, the men altogether lazy.

'These poor women are real pack-mules, enduring all hardships,' writes Père Lalemant (Thwaites, iv. 205). 'When delivered of a child, they go to the woods two hours later to replenish the fire of the cabin. In the winter, when they break camp, the women drag the heaviest loads over the snow; in short, the men seem to have as their share only hunting, war, and trading.'

Yet the truth implies a very considerable modification of the notion that this distribution is one-sided. It is normally the Indian woman's duty to prepare the food and to manufacture such articles as are needed by the household in its home routine—basketry, pottery, clothing, etc. Agriculture is viewed as a feature of the food preparation, and so becomes woman's work; although, in tribes where it is important, the men usually do a fair share of this work. The dangerous occupations, war and hunting, fall to the men, who usually manufacture the implements of chase and weapons of war, and often, also, their own clothing; and upon the men also falls that other occupation which leads abroad, barter—in primitive times itself a semi-military industry, as among the Mexicans (cf. Sahagun, bk. ix.), and one which was thoroughly developed long before the advent of white traders (see *Anthropos*, v. 643 f.).

Thus, in general, domestic and routine work devolves upon the women, foreign and adventurous duties upon the men. The judgment of Im Thurn (p. 215) with respect to the Indians of Guiana, that the work of the men 'is at least equal to, though accomplished more fitfully than, that of the women,' is, on the whole, true of the typical Indian society. What gives the impression of laziness in the Indian man is doubtless the fitfulness of his employments: 'the life of the Indian man is made up of alternate fits of energy and of comparative inactivity,' says Im Thurn (p. 269); and this follows from the nature of his work. Possibly also it is in part due to physical and nervous structure, following upon primitive modes of life, as McGee would explain in the case of the Seri, 'characterized by extreme alternations from the most intense functioning to complete quiescence—the periods of intensity being relatively short, and the intervals of quiescence notably long' (*17 RBEW*, pt. i. p. 156).

War with the Indian is only a more difficult form of the chase. For both employments the same qualities are demanded,—courage, endurance, craft,—and these may be regarded as essentially the masculine virtues in the eyes of the aborigine. Craft and endurance, involving the most painful and unrelenting pursuit of an enemy; fortitude, hardened to the point of stoical endurance of the most fiendish torments—for the cultivation of these traits the braves undergo rigorous fasts, and submit themselves to strenuous and terrible tortures, as in the famous Sun Dance of the Plains tribes (see 'Sun Dance,' *Handbook of American Indians*, ii. 649–652; cf. de Smet, 247 f., 255 f., etc.).

The Indian conception of war has resulted in the most varying notions of his courage. Thus even the same observer—Père Biard (*Relations*, 1616)—can pass such diverse judgments on the one people as:

'Their wars are nearly always . . . by deceit and treachery. . . . They never place themselves in line of battle. . . . And, in truth, they are by nature fearful and cowardly' (Thwaites' ed., p. 91); and: 'These savages are passionate, and give themselves up to death with desperation, if they are in hopes of killing, or doing any one an injury' (p. 69).

As a matter of fact, Indian warfare demanded a very high order of courage, sanctioning, as it did, the most terrible treatment of captives. It was waged, in fact, largely for the sake of making prisoners—thus preserving the character of a hunt—with a view to submitting them to torture.

'When they seize some of their enemies, they treat them with all the cruelty they can devise. Five or six days will sometimes pass in assuaging their wrath, and in burning them at a slow fire; and they are not satisfied with seeing their skins entirely roasted,—they open the legs, the thighs, the arms, and the most fleshy parts, and thrust therein glowing brands, or red-hot hatchets. Sometimes in the midst of these torments they compel them to sing; and those who have the courage do it, and hurl forth a thousand imprecations against those who torment them; on the day of their death they must even outdo this, if they have strength; and sometimes the kettle in which they are to be boiled will be on the fire, while these poor wretches are still singing as loudly as they can' (Thwaites, x. 227).

This is but one of a multitude of such descriptions to be found in the *Jesuit Relations* and elsewhere, illustrating an ingenious cruelty which marks the American Indians among the savages of the world, and is probably equalled only by the inquisitorial and judicial tortures devised by white men. For Indian cruelty is of an intellectual, one might say of a moral, type; it is not a callous incomprehension of suffering, or a brutal indifference to it, as is so often the case with savages; rather it is devilishly devised and inflicted for understanding enjoyment.

The primary motive seems to be to test the fortitude—the supreme virtue—of the sufferer, with whom it becomes a point of honour to make no sign of weakness, but rather to breathe defiance to the last breath: 'Those who dread your torments are cowards, they are lower than women' (de Smet, 249). If the prisoner dies bravely, his flesh, and especially the heart, is eaten, as a kind of sacrament, with the belief that the courage of the deceased will pass into the spirits of the partakers—a rite which becomes apotheosized with the Mexicans into a huge and terrible theanthropic worship (cf. art. INCARNATION [American]). Throughout the Americas we find this custom:

'They tear the heart from the breast, roast it upon the coals, and, if the prisoner has borne bravely the bitterness of the torture, give it, seasoned with blood, to the boys, to be greedily eaten, that the warlike youth may imbibe the heroic strength of the valiant man,' writes Jouvency (Thwaites, i. 268); and in South America, in similar case, Garcilasso states that the women lave their breasts in the blood of the sufferer, that their babes may drink it in with the mother's milk (*op. cit.* I. xi.).

Such a practice could not fail to lead to degradation, in many cases to cannibalism with no such moral purport. Reaction against it is not uncommon among the Indians themselves. Yet it was prevalent enough to be regarded as a racial trait, as it is also the chief ground for the bitter excoriations of Indian character by observers who so frequently have only admiration for the Red Man's domestic virtues.

3. Higher cultures.—The semi-civilizations of Mexico and Peru manifest that natural complication of moral problems and accentuation of moral consciousness which comes with advancing culture. At the same time, the quality of originality with which each is stamped is due to the dominance or emphasis of purely Indian traits.

In Mexico, and particularly among the Aztecs, warlike ferocity is elevated into a veritable religious consciousness, holding whole societies in pitiless grasp and colouring every conception of life. Indeed, Mexican religion so strongly countered the normal instincts of humanity that, in some cases at least, its devotees gave themselves to its practices only with 'tears and dolour of soul' (Sahagun, II. xx.); and it resulted in an attitude toward the world consistently and patiently pessimistic. When a child was born into the world, it was addressed:

'Thou art come into this world where thy parents endure troubles and fatigues, where there are burning heats, where there are winds and cold, where there is found neither pleasure nor content, since it is a place of labours, of torments, and of need.' And if a boy: 'Thy true fatherland is elsewhere; thou art promised to other places. Thou belongest to the shelterless fields where fall the combats; it is for them that thou hast been sent; thy profession and thy science is war; thy duty is to give unto the Sun the blood of thy enemies, that it may drink, and unto the Earth the bodies of thy foes, that it may devour them' (*ib.* VI. xxx., xxxi.).

Certainly the Mexicans had glimpses of a better order, as is shown in some of the myths of Quetzalcoatl, and as is evidenced perhaps by their deep conviction of sin and their readiness to do penance:

'There can be no doubt that the prayers, penances, and confessions described at length by Sahagun indicate a firm Mexican belief that even these strange deities "made for righteousness," loved good, and, in this world and the next, punished evil' (Lang, *Myth, Rit., and Rel.*[2], 1899, ii. 104).

Yet the inevitable impression of their civilization is of a fundamental conflict between brutalizing superstition and the instinct for moral growth, with the latter on the losing side.

Quite the reverse impression is made by the great S. American culture. The two characters that stand out in the Inca empire are communism, or paternalism, in the administration of material affairs, achieved on an immense scale, along with a proselytizer's instinct for reform. The latter may often have been a somewhat hypocritical excuse for conquest, yet the conquest was not regarded as complete without the reform. The whole moral ideal of the Inca civilization may perhaps best be expressed in the words which Garcilasso gives as the address of the Sun to the parents of the Inca race:

'My children, when you have brought the peoples of these lands to our obedience, you should have care to maintain them therein by the laws of reason, of piety, of clemency, and equity; doing for them all which a good father is accustomed to do for the children whom he has brought into the world and tenderly loves. In this you will follow my example, for, as you know, I cease not from doing good to mortals, lighting them with my light and giving them the means of following their affairs; warming them when they are cold, making fertile their fields and their pastures, fructifying the trees, making the herds to multiply, and bringing rain or fair weather as their needs are. It is I who make the tour of the world once each day, in order to see of what the earth has need, to set it in order, to the easing of its inhabitants. I wish that you follow my example, as my well-beloved children sent into the world for the good and the instruction of those wretched men who yet live as the beasts. It is for this that I give you the title of kings, and I wish that your dominion extend to all peoples, that you may instruct them by good reason and good deed, but above all by your example and by your beneficent rule' (*Royal Commentaries*, I. xv.).

The degree in which this ideal was realized is indicated by the most recent writer on the Peruvian civilization, Sir Clements R. Markham (*The Incas of Peru*, 1910, p. 168 f.); and it exemplifies the greatest and most complex moral achievement of the American Indian race:

'The people were nourished and well cared for, and they multiplied exceedingly. In the wildest and most inaccessible valleys, in the lofty *punas* surrounded by snowy heights, in the dense forests, and in the sand-girt valleys of the coast, the eye of the central power was ever upon them, and the never-failing brain, beneficent though inexorable, provided for all their wants, gathered in their tribute, and selected their children for the various occupations required by the State, according to their several aptitudes. This was indeed socialism such as dreamers in past ages have conceived, and unpractical theorists now talk about. It existed once because the essential conditions were combined in a way which is never likely to occur again. These are an inexorable despotism, absolute exemption from outside interference of any kind, a very peculiar and remarkable people in an early stage of civilisation, and an extraordinary combination of skilful statesmanship.'

LITERATURE.—In addition to works cited in the text, see bibliographical materials under artt. AMERICA, ANDEANS, the artt. on Amer. Indian tribal names, COMMUNION WITH DEITY (American), etc. The moral customs and ideals of the Americans are cited in comparative treatments in L. T. Hobhouse, *Morals in Evolution*[2], London, 1908; A. Sutherland, *Origin and Growth of the Moral Instinct*, do. 1898; E. Westermarck, *MI*, 2 vols., do. 1906–8; C. S. Wake, *The Evolution of Morality*[3], do. 1878. Perhaps special mention should be made of C. Eastman's *The Soul of the Indian*, Boston, 1910 (an idealizing, but not unfair, characterization). Valuable guides to literature are the 'Handbook of American Indians,' *Bull. 30 BE*, 1907–10; W. I. Thomas, *Source Book for Social Origins*, London, 1909; and J. D. McGuire, 'Ethnology in the Jesuit Relations,' *Amer. Anthropol.*, new ser., vol. iii.—a guide to the materials in Thwaites' 73-vol. ed. of the *Relations and Allied Documents*.

H. B. ALEXANDER.

ETHICS AND MORALITY (Australian).—According to the earlier explorers and missionaries and the careless travellers of even recent years, the morality of the Australian aborigines was of a very low grade. Almost all such observers agreed in placing them in the very lowest stages of culture. They were described as bestial in habits, naked, lacking all sense of virtue; the men cruel to their children and wives. They were said to be addicted to infanticide and cannibalism, cruel in their disposition, shiftless, lazy, stupid, deceitful—in fact, possessed of all conceivable evil qualities, deaf to the lessons of religion and civilization, ready at theft, and with almost no regard for the value of human life. They were naturally, moreover, given up almost constantly to destructive inter-tribal wars. The investigations of more recent students of the natural races have thrown a somewhat different light upon the matter. It is now recognized that morality is not to be judged by relationship to some fixed and absolute standard, but rather that it is fundamentally related to the system of social control which prevails within the group. It must, moreover, be borne in mind that the 'higher race,' in its first contact with the lower, seldom sees it at its best. Without doubt the ignorance and brutality of many of the first white settlers and explorers of Australia were constantly provocative of retaliation on the part of the natives. The laziness of the latter may be attributed merely to their inability to fall in with the enterprises of the settlers, or to appreciate the objects of their endeavour or their interests. In activities of their own the natives showed the most surprising industry, *e.g.* in the collection of food (Henderson,[1] p. 125), and in the preparation for, and performance of, their elaborate ceremonials. The observations which follow should not, however, be taken as applying to the Australian race as a whole, but only to the sections directly observed; for there is no question that there is much diversity in the customs and characteristics of different tribes and groups.

As to personal virtues, the natives of Queensland were said to be generally honest in their dealings with one another. Apart from murder of a member of the same tribe, they knew only one crime, that of theft. If a native made a 'find' of any kind, such as a honey tree, and marked it, it was thereafter safe for him, as far as his own tribesmen were concerned, no matter how long he left it. The Australian native in general was and is possessed in a marked degree of fortitude in the endurance of suffering. There is abundant opportunity for the development of this quality of mind in the painful ordeals of initiation—a ceremony always accompanied by fasting and the infliction of bodily mutilations of various kinds, differing with the tribe and the locality. These mutilations include the knocking out of teeth, circumcision, sub-incision, and various scoriations of the trunk, face, and limbs. Among some of the tribes there are permanent food-restrictions imposed by custom upon different classes. There are also food-restrictions imposed upon the youth and younger men, and all of these are faithfully complied with, although they involve considerable personal hardship (see Howitt, p. 561; Fraser, p. 90).

The food-restrictions form such an important phase of aboriginal morality that they warrant further discussion. The following regulations of the Kurnai tribe are typical. A man of this tribe must give a certain part of his 'catch' of game, and that the best part, to his wife's father. Each able-bodied man is under definite obligation to supply certain others with food. There are also rules according to which game is divided among those hunting together. In the Mining tribe all those in a hunt share equally, both men and women. In all tribes certain varieties of food are forbidden to women, children, and uninitiated youths; there are also restrictions based upon the totem to which one belongs. The rules regarding the cutting up and cooking of food are as rigid as those regulating that food of which the individual may lawfully partake. Howitt says of these food-rules and other similar customs that they give us an entirely different impression of the aboriginal character from that usually held. Adherence to the rules of custom was a matter on which they were most conscientious. If forbidden food were eaten, even by chance, the offender has been known to pine away and shortly die. Contact with the whites has broken down much of this primitive tribal morality.

'The oft-repeated description of the blackfellow eating the white man's beef or mutton and throwing a bone to his wife

[1] Names of authors throughout this art. stand for works mentioned in the literature.

who sits behind him, in fear of a blow from his club, is partly the new order of things resulting from our civilisation breaking down the old rules' (Howitt, p. 777).

Under the influence of the food-rules, a certain generosity of character was fostered, and unquestionably it was present in the blacks to a marked degree. They were[1] accustomed to share their food and possessions, as far as they had any, with their fellows.

'It may be, of course, objected to this that in so doing he is only following an old-established custom, the breaking of which would expose him to harsh treatment and to being looked upon as a churlish fellow. It will, however, hardly be denied that, as this custom expresses the idea that in this particular matter every one is supposed to act in a kindly way towards certain individuals, the very existence of such a custom . . . shows that the native is alive to the fact that an action which benefits some one else is worthy of being performed' (Spencer-Gillen[a], p. 48).

The apparent absence of any excessive manifestations of appreciation or gratitude in the blackfellow has been interpreted by some adversely; but *giving*, as far as the natives were concerned, was such a fixed habit that gratitude did not seem to be expected. It does not necessarily follow that they could not feel gratitude because they did not show any sign of it to the white man when he bestowed upon them some paltry presents; for, as Spencer-Gillen point out, they might not feel that they had reason to be grateful to one who had encroached upon their water and game and yet did not concede to them a like hunting of his own cattle.

Although, as a rule, perfectly nude, the natives are said to have been modest before contact with the whites (Lumholtz, p. 345). Of the North Australians we are told that the women were never indecent in gesture, their attitude being rather one of unconsciousness (Creed, p. 94). The low regard for chastity, reported by some observers (*e.g.* Mackenzie, p. 131), may, in part, be explained by the failure of the outsider to understand the peculiar marriage customs, on account of which the relation of the sexes is to be judged by different criteria from our own.

Spencer-Gillen, the most recent and the most scientific of all who have studied this race, say of the Central tribes that chastity is a term to be applied to the relation of one group to another rather than to the relation of individuals. Thus, men of one group have more or less free access to all the women of a certain other group. Within the rules prescribed by custom, breach of marital relations was severely punished. No one would think of having sexual relations with one in a class forbidden to himself or to those of his own class. It would thus appear that, within the bounds of their own customs, they were extremely upright. When, under certain conditions, chiefly ceremonial, wives were loaned, it was always to those belonging to the group within which the woman might lawfully marry (see also Cameron, *JAI* xiv. 353). Among the natives of North Central Queensland a competent observer (Roth, p. 184) holds that there was no evidence of the practice of masturbation or of prostitution. The camp as a body punished incest and promiscuity. Howitt, writing of the natives of S.E. Australia, says that the complicated marriage restrictions expressed in a very definite way their sense of proper tribal morality. Here also looseness of sexual relations was punished, although at certain times it was proper to exchange wives, and at other times there was unrestricted licence among those who were permitted to marry.

Of the treatment of wives and children there are conflicting reports, the more recent investigators holding that there was less cruelty than was at first represented. There was, however, doubtless much difference in this respect in different tribes. One early observer (Earp, p. 127) affirms that wives were always secured by force, the girl being seized from ambush, beaten until senseless, and thus carried off by her 'lover.' Others, in like manner, emphasize the brutality of obtaining wives (Angas, p. 225), and Lumholtz says that stealing was and is the most common method. The researches of Spencer-Gillen do not confirm these statements as far as the natives of Central Australia are concerned; Roth refers to the commonness of the practice of stealing wives and eloping, among the North Central Queensland natives. According to Spencer-Gillen, wives may have been so secured, but such was assuredly not the customary method in Central Australia at least. They know of no instances of girls being beaten and dragged away by suitors. It is probable that cases of exceptional cruelty more easily came to the notice of the first travellers, and they inferred that these were characteristic. The last named authors affirm that the method of securing wives among these tribes was definitely fixed by tribal usage, and involved no cruel practices whatsoever. Howitt, the authority on the South-Eastern tribes, says that cruelty was often practised upon elopers; but this is manifestly because they had themselves been guilty of a breach of tribal morality. Looseness of sexual relations among these tribes originally met always with severe punishment.

As to treatment of wives among the Central tribes (Spencer-Gillen[a], p. 50), there were undoubtedly cases of cruelty, but they were the exception rather than the rule. The savage husband had a hasty temper, and in a passion might act harshly, while at other times he might be quite considerate of his wife. Among the aborigines of the Darling River, New South Wales, quarrels between husband and wife were said to be quite rare (Bonney, *JAI* xiii. 129); Brough Smyth says that love is not rare in Australian families; while another observer (Palmer, *JAI* xiii. 281) asserts that the life of the women is hard, and that they are much abused by their husbands. Dawson, who wrote expressly to show that the Australian blacks had been misrepresented, maintained that in Victoria, at least, there was no want of affection between members of a family (p. 37); Lumholtz (p. 161 ff.) holds that the Queensland husband felt little responsibility for his family, and that he was really selfish and hunted only for sport, often consuming the game as caught, and bringing nothing home. The same author refers to one case of a wife being terribly beaten because she refused, one cold night, to go out and get fuel for her husband. Over against this testimony, we have that of Spencer-Gillen, referred to above, that the husband was ordinarily by no means cruel. In hard seasons men and women suffer alike. A woman suspected of breach of marital relations was, indeed, treated with revolting severity. It is pointed out, however, that many things which to us seem harsh were by no means so in Australian eyes, and that the savage woman recovers easily from wounds that to a civilized woman would entail the greatest suffering. Treatment which we should naturally think cruel was to them merely rough and in conformity with the rest of their life. Howitt (p. 738) says that among the Kurnai tribe family duties were shared by husband and wife, each performing an allotted part towards the support of the family. The man's duty was to fight and hunt, the woman's to build the home, catch the fish and cook them, gather vegetable foods, and make baskets, bags, and nets.

With reference to children, much affection was usually shown, and this in spite of the fact that abortion and infanticide were practised in many localities (*e.g.* in N.W. Central Queensland [Roth, p. 183], and among the South-Eastern tribes [Howitt, p. 748 ff.]). In this connexion Howitt says:

'. . . they [the Mining tribe] are very fond of their offspring, and very indulgent to those they keep, rarely striking them, and a mother would give all the food she had to her children, going hungry herself.'

Infanticide was by no means so unrestricted, or so indicative of cruelty of nature and lack of parental affection, as is implied by Mackenzie, writing in the year 1852 (see *Ten Years in Aus-*

[1] As many of the accounts refer to tribes, or at least to customs, which are practically extinct, it seems best to use the past tense consistently throughout.

tralia, p. 130). Among the North Central tribes (Spencer-Gillen[b], p. 608) infanticide was practised, but only rarely except immediately after birth, and then only when the mother thought she was unable to care for the babe. The killing of the new-born child was thus an effort at kindness; it was certainly devoid of cruelty in the eyes of the perpetrators, since they believed that the spirit part went back to the spot whence it came, and was subsequently born again to the same woman. Twins were killed as unnatural—a practice to be explained in part by the natives' dread of everything uncommon or rare. On infrequent occasions a young child was killed, that an older but weaker child might eat it, and thus get its strength. Howitt mentions the same practice among the South-Eastern natives (p. 749). He also says that in some places infants were eaten in especially hard summers. Sometimes, also, after the family amounted to three or four, all additional children were killed, because they would make more work than the women could manage. Among the Kurnai, infanticide unquestionably arose through the difficulty of carrying a baby when there were other young children, some of whom might be unable to walk. Under these circumstances, new-born infants were simply left behind when the family were on the march, it not being regarded as killing to dispose of them in this way (Howitt, p. 750).

Palmer, writing of the natives of Queensland, says that the killing of a new-born child was lightly regarded, but not common. On the Lower Flinders River the fondness of the natives for their children was noted (Palmer, *loc. cit.* p. 280). According to Spencer-Gillen[a], p. 50 f., children were, with rare exceptions, kindly and considerately treated, the men and women alike sharing the care of them on the march, and seeing that they got their proper share of food. Howitt mentions the case of a mother watching a sick child, refusing all food, and being inconsolable when it died (p. 766). One woman carried about a deformed child on her back for nineteen years (Fraser; see Henderson, p. 121). Natural affection was certainly keen, and much grief was manifested over the loss of children.

In the aborigines' treatment of the old and infirm most observers depict them in quite a favourable light. Dawson, it is true, reports that the natives of Victoria killed them, but this is certainly not a widely prevalent custom. Lumholtz (p. 183) says that the Queenslanders were very considerate of all who were sick, old, or infirm, not killing them, as did some savage peoples (cf. Bonney, p. 135). In northern parts of Australia there were many blind, and they were always well cared for by the tribe, being often the best fed and nourished (Creed, p. 94). In the Central tribes the old and infirm were never allowed to starve. Each able-bodied adult was assigned certain of the older people to be provided with food, and the duty was in every case fulfilled cheerfully and ungrudgingly (Spencer-Gillen[b], p. 32). In some tribes the old and the sick were carried about on stretchers.

In the Dalebura tribe, a woman, a cripple from birth, was carried about by the tribes-people in turn, until her death at the age of sixty-six. On one occasion they rushed into a stream to save from drowning an old woman, whose death would have been a relief even to herself (Howitt, p. 766). Fraser emphasizes the respect in which old age is held by the aborigines of New South Wales, and the fact that they never desert the sick (see also Brough Smyth).

Cannibalism among the Australian blacks was by no means a promiscuous and regular practice, as was at first supposed. Lumholtz (p. 101), it is true, says that among those observed by him human flesh was regarded as a great delicacy (see also Bicknell, p. 104, who holds that it is quite common). Palmer, also, writing of Queensland, asserts that cannibalism was practised to a certain extent, the victims being those killed in fights, and often children who had died. An early writer reports that in South Australia bodies of deceased friends were eaten as a token of regard (Angas, p. 225), or as either a sign of regard or in ceremonial (Fraser, p. 56).

Spencer-Gillen found difficulty in gathering evidence of cannibalism being practised among the Central tribes. They were often told by one tribe that it was customary among others who lived farther on, and the latter in turn said the same thing of those beyond themselves. Spencer-Gillen think, in general, that human flesh was eaten as a matter of ceremony or at least for other than mere food reasons. They found much more evidence of it among the Northern tribes. Howitt says that the Dieri tribe practised cannibalism as a part of their burial ceremonies, and that it was a sign of sorrow for the dead. Other tribes ate only enemies slain on their raids; the Kurnai, for instance, would not eat one of their own tribe. Among still other tribes, if a man were killed at initiation ceremonies, he was eaten, as was also any one killed in one of the ceremonial fights; while others did not eat their enemies.

Howitt is positive that there is no such thing among any of the tribes hitherto observed as propitiatory human sacrifice; and he denies emphatically the statement, made current by some, that sometimes a fat *gin* (woman) was killed to appease their craving for flesh when they chanced to have been long upon a vegetable diet. He also says that at the tribal meetings of the Bunya, men, women, and children, killed in fights or by accident, were eaten, but that there is no evidence that women and children were killed for cannibalistic purposes.

The morality of the Australian native was, in a word, the morality of tribal custom, and, if fidelity to duties so imposed may be taken as a criterion, it was of no low order. Recent investigators unite in testifying that the blackfellow, especially before contact with Europeans, was most scrupulous in his obedience to the sacred duties imposed upon him by tribal usage.

Of the Queensland natives Roth declares (p. 139 ff.) that the life of the tribe as a whole seemed to be well regulated. Custom, with the old men as its exponents, was the only law. Where there were few old men, each individual, within limits, could do as he pleased. Howitt (p. 776) writes of the tribes studied by him that custom regulated the placing of huts in the camp, and even the proper position of individuals within the huts. In the Kaiabara tribe, single men and women lived on opposite sides of the camp. The old women kept an ever-watchful eye upon the young people to prevent improprieties. In another tribe the women were not allowed to come to the camp by the same path as the men, a violation of the rule being punishable by death.

The law of custom thus controlled almost every phase of the life of the individual, including many personal matters as well as conduct towards others; the intercourse of the sexes is or was most definitely limited and regulated; the women who were eligible to each man in marriage were also rigidly determined by custom, as well as the proprieties of conduct towards the wife's family. Reference has already been made to the severe restrictions entailed by the initiation and other ceremonies, and also to the minute regulations regarding the choice of food. In all cases these customs were enforced by severe penalties. In some tribes the local group or camp united to punish any member who was guilty of overstepping the bounds, or of complicity in more serious crimes, such as incest and murder, or the promiscuous use of fighting implements within the camp. Most customs were, however, probably obeyed from habit, the native being educated from infancy in the belief that infraction of custom would produce many evils, such as premature greyness, pestilences, and even cosmic catastrophes. In fact, among the tribes observed by Howitt, authority was generally impersonal, though not always, for the headmen were often men of great personal ability, and were greatly feared and respected by the rest of the tribe or group (Howitt, pp. 295–300).

Questions of right and wrong for the Australians seem to have centred chiefly in food restrictions, secrets relating to the tribal ceremonies, the sacred objects, and wives. Moral precepts probably originated in association with the purely selfish idea of the older men, whereby they sought to keep all the best things for themselves (Spencer-Gillen[a], p. 48). In this way at least may be explained many of the regulations regarding what the younger men might eat. So also as to marriage, for, apart from restrictions as to totem and the class into which a man might marry, all the younger women were reserved by the old men, the less desirable ones alone being available to the young men. But, granting the selfish character of many of the rules, there was still a certain amount of morality which transcended anything of this sort.

'The old men, in their leisure time, instructed the younger ones in the laws of the tribe, impressing on them modesty of behaviour and propriety of conduct . . . and pointing out to them the heinousness of incest' (Howitt, p. 300).

The rigid duties of manhood centred especially in the ceremonies of the tribe. The obligations which these involved were regarded as extremely sacred and inviolable.

'As he [the youth] grows older he takes an increasing share in these [ceremonies], until finally this side of his life occupies by far the greater part of his thoughts' (Spencer-Gillen[b], p. 33).

He must continually show strength of character, ability to endure hardship, to keep secrets, and, in general, to break away from the frivolity of youth and all that savoured of femininity. There were, among the Central tribes, certain sacred things which were only gradually revealed by the older men, and, if a young man showed little self-restraint and was given to foolish chattering, it might be many years before he learned all that was in store for him.

It is interesting to see that under the traditional régime the Australian natives lived a harmonious and certainly far from unhappy life. Fraser says they were a merry race (p. 43). Howitt, who was instrumental in gathering together the Kurnai tribe for the revival of their initiation ceremonies some years ago, reports that the people lived for a week in the manner of their old lives, and that the time passed without a single quarrel or dispute (p. 777). In their wild state the Dalebura tribe were noted to have lived most peaceably: *e.g.*, a camp of three hundred is known to have continued for three months without a quarrel. Their method of settling disputes was usually by means of a fight between the parties who were at odds. When blood was drawn, the fighting ceased, and all were henceforth good friends (Dawson, p. 76). They were generous in fighting, taking no unfair advantage. They loved ease and were not quarrelsome, but were, nevertheless, ready to fight (Brough Smyth, i. 30). Mortal wounds in such conflicts were rare (Lumholtz, p. 127). According to Spencer-Gillen[b] also, among the Central tribes, whenever compensation in any form had been made by an offending party, the matter was supposed to be ended and no ill feelings were cherished (p. 31).

In some tribes, theft was regarded as the greatest crime next to the murder of a fellow-tribesman; but, as there was so little private property, crimes arising from this source were rare. The stealing of women is said to have been the most common cause of inter-tribal trouble (Lumholtz, p. 126; Spencer-Gillen[b], p. 32). There were no fights for superiority, no suppression of one tribe by another. Within the tribe there was, in large measure, absolute equality. There were no rich or poor, age being the only quality that gave pre-eminence (Semon, p. 225). The inter-tribal fights were certainly not so serious as some have represented. That they were constantly attacking and trying to exterminate one another is not confirmed by those who have known them best. Their fights were probably half ceremonial, or of a sportive character, and were usually stopped when blood flowed freely. They undoubtedly did fear strangers, and a man from a strange tribe, unless accredited as a sacred messenger, would be speared at once (Spencer-Gillen[b], p. 31). On the other hand, delegations from distant tribes were received and treated with the utmost kindness, if they came in the recognized way. They were even permitted to take a prominent part in the ceremonies of their hosts. The relations subsisting between members of the same tribe or group were, according to Spencer-Gillen, marked by consideration and kindness. There were occasional acts of cruelty, but most of them can be attributed to something else than a harshness of character. Thus, much cruelty resulted from their belief in magic (Spencer-Gillen[a], p. 50, [b]pp. 31–33). The revolting ceremonies practised at initiation were all matters of ancient tribal custom, and hence cast little light upon the real disposition of the native.

All things considered, we are obliged to say that the life of the Australian blacks was moral in a high degree, when judged by their own social standards; and not even according to our standards are they to be regarded as altogether wanting in the higher attributes of character. Dawson holds that, apart from their low regard for human life, they compared favourably with Europeans on all points of morality. Howitt (p. 639) says of the South-Eastern tribes:

'All those who have had to do with the native race in its primitive state will agree with me that there are men in the tribes who have tried to live up to the standard of tribal morality, and who were faithful friends and true to their word; in fact, men for whom, although savages, one must feel a kindly respect. Such men are not to be found in the later generation.'

LITERATURE.—G. F. Angas, *Savage Life and Scenes in Australia and New Zealand*, London, 1847; A. C. Bicknell, *Travel and Adventure in North Queensland*, do. 1895; F. Bonney, 'The Aborigines of the River Darling,' *JAI* xiii. [1883–4] 122; A. L. P. Cameron, 'Tribes of New South Wales,' *ib.* xiv. [1884–5] 344; D. W. Carnegie, *Spinifex and Sand* (West Australia), London, 1898; J. M. Creed, 'The Position of the Australian Aborigines in the Scale of human Intelligence,' *The Nineteenth Century and After*, lvii. [1905] 89; E. M. Curr, *The Australian Race*, London, 1886–7; James Dawson, *Australian Aborigines* (West Victoria), Melbourne, 1881; G. B. Earp, *Gold Colonies of Australia*, London, 1852; John Fraser, *The Aborigines of New South Wales*, do. 1892; Sir George Grey, *Expeditions in North-West and Western Australia*, do. 1841; John Henderson, *Excursions and Adventures in New South Wales*, do. 1851; A. W. Howitt, *Native Tribes of South-East Australia*, do. 1904; Carl Lumholtz, *Among Cannibals* (Queensland), do. 1889; D. Mackenzie, *Ten Years in Australia*, do. 1845; Walter Roth, *Ethnological Studies among the North-West Central Queensland Aborigines*, Brisbane, 1897; R. Semon, *In the Australian Bush*, Eng. ed., London, 1899; R. Brough Smyth, *Aborigines of Victoria*, 2 vols., Melbourne, 1878; Spencer-Gillen, *Native Tribes of Central Australia*, do. 1899 (cited as Spencer-Gillen[a]), and *Northern Tribes of Central Australia*, do. 1904 (Spencer-Gillen[b]).

IRVING KING.

ETHICS AND MORALITY (Babylonian).—

1. The predominating influence of religion.—The civilization of Babylonia was dominated throughout by religion. Every aspect of national and civic life and every phase of human intercourse were governed by a religious conception of the universe. The question as to the connexion between morality and religion was in Babylonia no question at all; for morality, like every other manifestation of mental life, was a part of religion. The commotions produced by political revolutions were always of brief duration. In the annals of Babylonia we meet again and again with the same historical phenomenon: the conquering peoples receive the intellectual, and thus also the religious and ethical, impress of Sumero-Babylonian culture.

In contemplating the ethico-religious conception of the universe which prevailed among the Babylonians, we are amazed at its sublimity. It comes before us as a complete system even in the oldest documents, which, while their literary form is the work of Semitic Babylonians, yet throw light upon Sumerian times. It is true that to a large extent they are purely theoretical. We are unable to say whether the elevated morality presupposed by the injunctions of the priests was ever actually practised by any class of the people. The writers of the tablets idealize their heroes. As the august prologue and epilogue of the Code of Ḫammurabi give expression to religious and ethical ideas which find not the slightest echo in the actual legal provisions of the code, we may venture to assume that even in an earlier age there existed a similar discrepancy between theory and practice. Still, the theory is there; and it dominates the ritual texts even in periods of religious decadence. Lofty moral precepts in catechetic form are uttered by the very priest who will submit to the sorriest witch and the most paltry enchantments.

2. Morality and the cult of Ea, 'the Good.'—One of the oldest religious cities known to us is Eridu. At no period known to history was Eridu a political centre; not only the Code of Ḫammurabi but even the Sumerian inscriptions speak of it as an ancient and venerable city. It was situated 'at the mouth of the rivers,' *i.e.* at the place where formerly the Euphrates and the Tigris flowed separately into the sea. Eridu enjoyed the name of 'the city of the Good' (Uru-dug). The 'Good' is Ea, and his temple is 'the house of the ocean's depth,' or 'the house of wisdom.' Ea inscribes oracles with a 'sacred calamus'—probably beneath the sacred tree of Eridu which is sometimes referred to in the records. His wise counsels he imparts, *e.g.*, to Adapa, 'the seed of the human race,' upon whom he desires also to confer wisdom and immortality (the bread and the water of life). By his wise counsels, according to the Deluge narrative, he saves the Babylonian Noah from the flood. As the Deluge is taken to be a punishment of human wickedness, it would seem that the good Deity saved the man on account of the latter's acceptable behaviour.

The overwhelming majority of the texts that refer to Ea represent him as the god whose worship consists in the rites of ablution and incantation. He heals all manner of disease. Behind disease, however, stands the fact of sin. Although sin appears in the ritual texts as ceremonial transgression, as a conscious or unconscious revolt against ceremonial laws, yet behind this there must certainly be the idea of sin in a deeper sense—as rebellion against the Deity. The motive which prompts men to resort to the ritual worship of Ea is the desire to be cleansed from their sins.

3. Morality and the worship of Šamaš.—Besides Ea, the Good, the other Deity with whom moral ideas are specially connected is Babbar Šamaš, the god who manifests himself in the orb of day, and whose principal sanctuaries were Larsa in S. Babylonia, and Sippar in the northern portion (cf. A. Jeremias, art. 'Schamasch,' in Roscher). Šamaš is the god of retributive justice. All unrighteousness is brought to light by him, just as all darkness melts away when his beams illumine the world. His temple is called *Ê-D-kud-kalamma*, 'the house of the world's judge.' In a description of the New Year festival (cylinder B. 18) Gudea says: 'The sun caused righteousness to shine forth; Babbar caused righteousness to shine forth. Babbar trampled unrighteousness under foot; the city shines like the sun-god.' Ur-engur, king of Ur, who presided over the worship of the sun in that ancient city of the moon, says that in conformity with the just laws of Babbar he had caused righteousness to prevail. In the ritual texts the attendants of Babbar are Kettu and Mesharu, 'justice and righteousness' (cf. Ps 97[2] 89[14]). Thus moral ideas are here personified as Divine, just as in Egypt we find Maat as the protectress of righteousness.

The moral activities of Šamaš, who rewards the righteous judge and punishes the corrupt one, are set forth with great fullness in a hymn of some two hundred lines, which certainly emanated originally from Babylonia, but comes down to us in a transcript found in the library of Aššurbanipal. This hymn represents the effects of the sun's activity as a continuous mystery, by means of which all evil powers above and below are brought to naught.

'At thy rising the gods of the land assemble;
Thy terrible radiance overwhelms the land.
From all lands together resound as many tongues:
Thou knowest their designs; thou beholdest their footsteps,
Upon thee [look (?)] all men together.
Thou causest the evil-doer, who . . . not . . . to tremble;
Out of the depths (?) thou bringest those who perverted justice (?).
O Šamaš! by the just judgment which thou speakest [. . .],
Thy name is glorious, [. . .] is not changed.
Thou standest beside the traveller whose way is toilsome;
To the voyager who fears the flood thou givest [courage (?)].
On paths that were never explored thou [guidest (?)] the hunter;
He mounts [to heights (?)] rivalling the sun-god . . .
O Šamaš! from [thy] net [. . .];
From thy snare [escapes (?)] not . . .
He who, contrary to his oath [. . .];
To him who does not fear [. . .],
Outspread is thy wide [net . . .].
Whoso [lifts his eyes (?)] upon the wife of his companion,
On a day not pre-ordained for him, [. . . takes him away (?)];
For him is appointed (?) burning, the seed (?) . . . [. . .];
If thy weapon reaches him, [there is] no deliverer.
At his trial [his] father does not appear;
At the judgment of the judge, his brothers—they answer not for him;
In a brazen trap he is struck down without knowing it.
Whoso devises wickedness, his horn thou destroyest.
Whoso meditates oppression (?), his dwelling is overturned.
The wicked judge thou causest to see bonds;
Whoso takes a bribe, and does not judge righteously, on him thou inflictest punishment.
Whoso takes no bribe, but makes intercession for the weak,
Well-pleasing is this to Šamaš—he increaseth his life.
An upright judge, who renders righteous judgment,
Prepares for himself (?) a palace; a prince's house is his abode.
Whoso gives money for excessive interest (?), what does he increase?
He overreaches (?) himself for gain, empties his own purse.
Whoso gives money for just interest (?), who takes a shekel for [. . .],
Well-pleasing is this to Šamaš—he increaseth his own life.
Whoso keeps the balance (?) [. . .],
Whoso then changes the weights . . . [he] lowers . . .,
He overreaches (?) himself for gain, empties [his purse].
Of the honest man who keeps the balance, many are [. . .];
All possible things, much . . . [. . .].
He who keeps the measure, who practises . . . [. . .],
[. . .] in the meadow, who lets too much be paid,
[. . .], the curse of the people shall seize him.
[Whoso . . .] his [. . .], demands a tax,
[. . .] shall not possess his inheritance.
In the [. . .] his brothers, they shall not be surety.
The [. . .] who gives corn for [. . .], who furthers the good—
Well-pleasing is this to Šamaš—increaseth his life;
He enlarges his family, obtains possession of riches;
As waters of the deep, inexhaustible, so shall his seed be inex[haustible].
He who charges (?) an unwise man to give good succour,
He who oppresses (?) his inferiors (?), he is noted down (?) with the pen.
Those who work evil, their seed has not continuance;
Whose mouth, full of lying, avails not before thee.
Thou burnest their utterance, rendest it asunder, yea, thou . . .
Thou hearest the down-trodden, as thou movest over them; thou discoverest their right;
Each one, every one, is entrusted into thy hand.
Thou rulest over their judgments; what is bound, thou dost loose.
Thou hearest, O Šamaš, prayer, supplication, and homage,
Submission, kneeling, whispered prayer, and prostration.
From his deepest breast the needy crieth unto thee,
The feeble, the weak, the afflicted, the poor—
With a lament (?), a petition, he ever appeals to thee,
He whose family is far away, whose city is a great way off.
The shepherd, with the fruits of the field, appeals to thee.
The [. . .] . . . (?) in rebellion, the shepherd among the enemy,
O Šamaš, appeals to thee, as he walks on a way of terror.
The travelling merchant, the trader who carries the bag,
[. . .] appeals to thee; the fisher of the deep,

The hunter, the slaughterer, the keeper (?) of cattle,
The fowler in the . . . of the reed fence, appeals to thee.
The house-breaker, the thief—though an enemy of Šamaš—
The vagrant upon the way of the desert, appeals to thee.
The wandering dead one, the fleeting shadow,
O Šamaš, appealed to thee [. . .].
Thou hast not rejected those who appealed [to thee . . .];
Those who thus kneel, for them thou, loosing (them from evil), restorest their purity.
Those who thus render homage, their homage dost thou receive.
But they fear thee; they reverence thy name;
Before thy greatness men continually bow down.'

4. The positive character of Bab. morality.—The Bab. conception of the universe was permeated by the assumption that morality rests upon the commandments of Deity, and hence, should the excavations some day bring to light a Bab. narrative of the Fall, it would be no matter for surprise. According to Bab. ideas, not only wisdom, but also purity and happiness, existed at the beginning of things. The mythological Creation-story of the Babylonians closes with a significant passage telling how Marduk, the victor over Tiāmat, brings the laws of Ea to men, and how they are to be disseminated amongst men like a revelation of doctrine:

'Let them be held fast, and let the "First" teach them;
Let the wise man and the learned meditate upon them together.
The father shall hand them down; let him instruct his son therein.
Let him open the ears of the herdsman and the keeper (?),
That he may rejoice in Marduk, the lord of the gods;
That his land may prosper, and that it may go well with him.
Steadfast is his (Marduk's) word; his decree is not changed;
The word of his mouth is not altered by any (other) god.
If he frowns, he turns not again his neck (to grace);
If he is angry, if he is enraged, no god sets himself against him—
The magnanimous, the sagacious . . .
Against evil and sin . . .'
(Other five lines mutilated.)

The existence of tablets inscribed with Divine commandments is presupposed by the text K 7897, which survives in three distinct transcripts (*Cuneiform Texts*, xiii. 29 f.; cf. Macmillan, *Beiträge zur Assyriologie*, v. 5, no. 2 (Leipz. 1903); for tablet 5, cf. A. Jeremias, *The OT in the Light of the Ancient East*, Eng. tr. 1910, i. 222 f.)—

'Slander not, but speak kindness;
Speak not evil, but show good will;
Whoso slanders and speaks evil—
Unto him will Šamaš requite it by . . . his head.
Open not wide thy mouth, guard thy lips;
If thou art provoked, speak not at once;
If thou speakest hastily, thou shalt afterwards have to atone therefor;
Soothe (rather) thy spirit with silence.
Offer daily unto thy god
Sacrifice, prayer, the incense most meet (for the Deity):
Before thy god shalt thou have a heart of purity (?).
It is that which is due to the deity' (for continuation, see *ERE* iii. 747[a] f.).

5. The identity of moral and ceremonial law.—The relation between men and the Deity is determined by their qualities. It is only the wise man who is acceptable to the gods. Religion is essentially knowledge, and accordingly the intellectual interest enters largely into piety. The ideal first man is the 'keenly sagacious' Atraḫasis. The will of the Deity has to be searched out. Piety consists in a submissive and unflagging performance of the ritual. The afflicted king inquires whether his sufferings are the consequence of ceremonial dereliction or of actual evil-doing. Just as, in the conception of Deity, righteousness and capricious wrath are not discriminated, so we find no distinction between real sin and ritual error. Not only murder and theft, but spitting at the holy place, is regarded as a possible cause of disease, and atonement for transgression is effected by repentance and—closely associated therewith—the use of incantations. In either aspect the source of the disease is sin. For it is necessary that the man who offends against the Deity by transgression should receive evil, and that the devout man should receive good. The perplexities of such a theodicy make themselves felt, but they are not, as in Israel, brought to a solution. The Divine moral law is vitiated by the utilitarian principle. The idea of love to God remains without any ethical development.

The ritual texts composed with a view to the cure of disease enumerate with painful solicitude all possible forms of sin, but we can, nevertheless, trace the ethical ideal that underlies the formulæ. The incantation tablets of the Šurpu series exhibit the particular offences that come under the head of sin:

'Has he estranged father and son?
Has he estranged mother and daughter?
Has he estranged mother-in-law and daughter-in-law?
Has he estranged brother and brother?
Has he estranged friend and friend?
Has he failed to set a prisoner free,
Or not loosed one who was bound?
Is it outrage against his superior (?), hatred of his elder brother?
Has he despised father and mother, insulted his elder sister
By giving to the younger, and withholding from the elder?
To Nay has he said Yea?
To Yea has he said Nay?
Has he spoken impurity,
Spoken wickedness,
Used an unjust balance,
Taken base money?
Has he disinherited a legitimate son, installed an illegitimate?
Has he drawn false boundaries,
Deranged boundary, march, and precinct?
Has he intruded upon his neighbour's house,
Approached his neighbour's wife,
Shed his neighbour's blood,
Stolen his neighbour's garment?
Has he refused to let a man escape his power (?),
Driven an honest man from his family,
Broken up a well-cemented clan,
Revolted against a chief?
Was he honest with his mouth, while false in heart?
With his mouth was he full of Yea, in his heart full of Nay?
Is it because of the injustice that he meditated
In order to disperse the righteous, to destroy (them),
To wrong, to rob, to cause to be robbed,
To have dealings with evil?
Is his mouth unclean?
Are his lips froward?
Has he taught impurity, instilled unseemly things?
Has he concerned himself with sorcery and witchcraft?

Has he promised with heart and mouth, but not kept faith;
Dishonoured the name of his god by (withholding) a gift,
Dedicated something, but kept it back,
Given something (flesh for sacrifice) . . . but eaten it?
By whatsoever thing he is bewitched—let it be revealed!

(Be it revealed) whether he has eaten anything that made an abomination for his city;
Whether he has spread a calumny through his city;
Whether he has brought his city into evil repute;
Whether he has gone to meet an outlaw;
Whether he has had intercourse with an outlaw
(Slept in his bed, sat in his chair, drunk out of his cup).'

On the third tablet of Šurpu it is assumed that a person may have been bewitched

'Because he has helped some one to justice by bribery,
Uprooted plants in the field,
Cut cane in the thicket.
. . . .
(Because) for a day he was entreated for a conduit, and refused it;
For a day he was entreated for a cistern, and refused it;
(Because) he obstructed his neighbour's channel;
Instead of agreeing with his adversaries, he remained their enemy;
Polluted a river, or spat in a river.'

These questions involve the fundamental laws of morality, such as are essential to the very conception of an organized State. They imply that life and property are protected. In the 25th ordinance of the Code of Ḫammurabi it is enacted that, if one who has come to extinguish (a fire) allows himself to covet a possession of the master of the house, and appropriates the property of the master of the house, he shall be cast into the fire (*HDB*, vol. v. p. 600). Theft is a capital offence. Veracity is held in high honour. False witness and evil-speaking are severely punished. Legal cases are decided by oath. Falsehood in word or thought is accounted a base thing.

6. The morality of the 'Penitential Psalms.'—Further materials for the investigation of ethical conceptions are supplied by the so-called *Penitential Psalms* of the Babylonians. In the Assyr. bilingual recensions in which these psalms are found, they are arranged as ritual texts for healing incantations, but in the ancient Bab. period they were doubtless used for specifically religious ends, viz. as 'threnodies for appeasing the heart' (of the Deity). That they are, like the ritual texts themselves, of very remote age may be inferred from the fact that in the one group as in the other explanatory notes have been added to the difficult passages. In these psalms the sufferer is the king himself, who, as the incarnation of Deity, is the ideal man. His sufferings, which are depicted as both physical and mental, bear a vicarious character: he suffers for his people.

A fine example of the *Penitential Psalms*, and one which illustrates the points just noted, will be found in the art. COMMUNION WITH DEITY (Bab.), vol. iii. p. 746 f.

7. The moral practice of the people.—The ritual texts likewise throw light upon the ethics of the middle ranks of Bab. society. Here censure is passed upon the characteristic sins of landowners and the commercial classes: theft and encroachment upon boundaries, damaging one's neighbour or one's competitors in connexion with the irrigation system, perjury and bribery, dishonesty in trade. But we likewise find descriptions of a higher moral practice.

From the age of Ḫammurabi, but in a copy belonging to the library of Aššurbanipal, comes a text containing the so-called 'family laws.' That these laws are older than the Code of Ḫammurabi is shown not only by their being written in the Sumerian language, but by their extreme severity and the primitive character of the legal processes involved:

'If a son says to his father, "Thou art not my father," he (the father) shall set the mark upon him, make him a slave, and sell him for money. If a son says to his mother, "Thou art not my mother," one shall set his mark upon him, lead him through the city, and expel him from the house. If a father says to his son, "Thou art not my son," he (the son) must abandon house and home. If a mother says to her son, "Thou art not my son," he shall abandon house and household goods. If a married woman renounces her husband and says, "Thou art not my husband," she shall be cast into the river. If a married man says to his wife, "Thou art not my wife," he shall pay her half a *mina* of silver. If any one hires a slave, and he (the slave) dies, goes amissing, runs away, is imprisoned, or becomes sick, he (the hirer) shall pay for his hire one *bar* of corn daily.'

From other texts likewise we learn that the relations between parents and children were of a patriarchal character. The mother-in-law, according to the ritual tablets, was held in high esteem. The wife, too, occupied an honoured position. She was capable of going to law, and was safeguarded against marital caprice. The practice of adoption was highly developed. Widows (*Cod. Ḫamm.* §§ 171, 172*b*) and orphans (*ib.* § 177) were protected; the kings pride themselves in being called the guardians of the weak. Drunkenness and debauchery, lust and sensuality, seem to have been very prevalent among the men. And as the people, so the gods. The pictures of carousing deities in the Creation epic—of deities who drink till they fall under the table—reflect the customs of the day. The licentious cult of Ištar, the representations of sexual life given in the Gilgameš epic and in Ištar's descent into the under world, as also the fact that the place of sexual intercourse was the public street, all point to conditions of gross sensuality. So far as the present writer knows, there are no indications of the passion for gambling. In Babylonia, dice-playing and similar games had not yet lost their original cosmic significance, and were resorted to as devices for consulting Fate.

To the attitude of the Babylonians towards the Deity corresponds their attitude towards their kings. The two precepts, 'Fear God, honour the king,' as found in a tablet of the library of Aššurbanipal (*Ilu tapalaḫ šarru tana'ad*), are really identical; and this reverential attitude extends also to the palace, for the palace, the 'high gate,' is the counterpart of the celestial abode of the gods.

The kingly ideal accords with the conception of Deity. A king must be pure, like Ani; kind, like Ea; wise, like Sin; and just, like Šamaš. And, as the Bab. pantheon grew stiff and mechanical under the influence of astrology, which saw the sway of the gods in an inexorable Fate, and surrendered the moral government of the world to a rigid destiny, so the idea of kingship degenerated into that of the Oriental despot, who represents, not the Deity, but iron Fate, and who exercises the power of life and death with pitiless severity.

8. The secular character of Bab. morality.—The morality of the Babylonians, like their religion, is in its essential aspects directed upon the present world. The religion of Nature which originated in their idea of the cosmos is but loosely connected with the cult of the dead. The realm of the dead forms no part of the world at all, but is a locality in the lowest of the three divisions of the celestial universe. The deified spirits of the dead thus live a life apart from earthly things. Our available sources show so far but few traces of a doctrine of future retribution. But the restriction of religion to the present life involves a danger that the foundations of morality may be sapped by excessive self-indulgence. Thus, in a fragment inserted in the Gilgameš epic some Bab. eudæmonist, who, like the speaker in the Heb. book of Qoheleth, had carried the pessimistic and materialistic theory of the universe to its logical issues, gives expression to his thoughts in the following words:

'Gilgameš, why dost thou wander about?
The life that thou seekest, thou shalt not find.
When the gods created men,
Upon men did they also impose death,
And retained life in their own hands.
Thou, O Gilgameš, gratify thy flesh;
Enjoy thyself by day and night;
Make a feast of joy every day;
Day and night be wanton and happy.
Let thy garments be unsoiled;
Let thy head be clean, and wash thyself with water.
Look upon the little ones whom thy hand holds;
Let thy wife rejoice upon thy bosom.'

LITERATURE.—There is no literature on the subject beyond what has been cited in the article.
A. JEREMIAS.

ETHICS AND MORALITY (Buddhist).—

1. General characteristics.—Starting with an eager yearning for emancipation from worldly sorrows and pains, the Buddha attained the solution of his mental struggles in the enlightenment of the Four Noble Truths. The infusion of practical needs with theoretical knowledge, on the one hand, and the stress laid upon the ascetic life as against the worldly, on the other, make up the key-note of Buddhist morality. As its religion is inseparably connected with its philosophy, its morality is based upon its ethical theories, which, again, are the outcome of practical demands and training. In the close connexion between, or identification of, the practical and the theoretical sides, Buddhist ethics betrays clearly its inheritance from the ordinary Hindu mental disposition, and in its ascetic aspects it differs little from the other religious Orders of India. But it exhibits a fundamental contrast with Brāhmanic morality in not adhering to the social institutions and traditions, but seeking the basis of morality immediately in the universal truths, which are to be realized in every one's wisdom and attainment. In both religions practical morality is founded on the *dharmas*, which, however, mean with Brāhmans the Divine ordinances incorporated in the legal codes of the nation, while the same word means to Buddhists the truths taught by the Buddha and to be realized in every one's wisdom. In short, the fundamental feature of Buddhist morality consists in its autonomic and personal principle, in contrast with the legal and social principle of Brāhmanism. This characteristic is, again, a necessary consequence of the starting-point of the religion, viz. the significance of the Buddha's personality. He is revered not only as the founder of the religion, but also as the revealer of final truths and the guide of all beings to the same attainment as his own. He is the saviour, the ferryman who conducts men to the other shore of perfection, which may be attained by all who follow his instructions in accordance with truth. His person is the pivot on which all Buddhist thought turns, and the ideal at which every believer should aim. In him personal perfection is united with universal truths.[1] He is the light of the world (or the eye, *loka-chakkhu*); but every one should discover the same light in himself (*atta-dīpa*), the Master being the revealer of the light and not an intruder from the outside. One takes refuge in the Buddha, in order to take refuge in himself (*atta-saraṇa*), as the Master has done. This autonomic principle and personal basis of Buddhist morality was, indeed, a new departure in the history of Indian religion, and laid the foundation for the universal religion of Buddhism.

The prominence of personality is associated with esteem for individual liberty, or at least for the spirit of toleration and liberalism. The Master gave many precepts, both in the theoretical and in the practical domain, though they are not expected to be followed in the letter but only in the spirit. This comes out very clearly, for example, in the last sermon of the Buddha on the eve of his entrance to the Great Decease, when he urged that his disciples should leave off minor precepts and be themselves their own light. The value of this admonition can never be over-estimated, when we note how the tradition is preserved even among the Theravādins, the advocates of traditions and precedents, as well as among the liberal Mahāyānists. This liberal spirit stands, again, in close connexion with the esteem shown for the Middle Path, which formed, indeed, the introduction of the Buddha's first sermon at Benares, and remained the leading spirit of Buddhism through the various forms and tendencies manifested in the history of the religion. This liberal spirit is what distinguishes Buddhism from other ascetic Orders, especially from the Jains; and this is the reason why, while Jainism remained to the last a formal asceticism, Buddhism was able to achieve its development in almost inexhaustible forms adapted to the needs of the times and peoples.

The Buddhists, as has been hinted above, never distinguished sharply between ethical theories and moral practice, but the practice is regarded as incomplete without the theoretical foundation and the basis of mental training, and *vice versa.* Thus the whole discipline (*sikkhā*) is divided into the three branches, which are to be assisted and accelerated mutually: morality (*śīla*), mental training (*samādhi* or *chitta*), and wisdom (*paññā*).[2] The kernel of the discipline, and especially of morality, is expressed in a very concise résumé of the whole teaching of Buddhism, which runs:

'Not to commit any sin, to do good,
And to purify one's own mind, that is the teaching of (all) the Buddhas.'[1]

The first half of the verse is the kernel of every system of morality, which is here, in the latter half, assisted by mental purification and consummated by the belief in the teaching of all the Buddhas, the belief which shall finally realize the communion of the enlightened. A similar relation between morality and the other attainment of Buddhist perfection (*a-sekkhā*) is shown in the group of the five branches (*khandha*), viz. morality (*śīla*), contemplation (*samādhi*), wisdom (*paññā*), deliverance (*vimutti*), and insight into the knowledge of deliverance (*vimuttiññāna - dassana*).[2] Herein is shown again the inseparable connexion of morality with wisdom and supernatural or mystic attainments. Thus we see that Buddhist morality, both in its discipline and in its perfection, forms a part of the religious ideal of complete enlightenment, and it loses its value and significance apart from these perfections. But morality is not merely a means to perfection, as is the case with most mystical systems; it is an integral part of the perfection, and hence one of the epithets of Buddha—'abounding in wisdom and goodness.' Mere knowledge or a solitary immersion in mystic contemplation, without practical moral actions, is not perfection, and in the same way morality without insight into the depth of truth is baseless. Morality is an integral part of religion, and so ethics should never be a mere system of theoretical discussions or speculations on ethical problems; it must be associated with enlightenment in metaphysical truths and their realization in one's own life. Thus the moral and intellectual perfection of a personality, in spite of the doctrine of the non-ego, is the highest aim of Buddhist morality.

Viewing in this way the system and aim of Buddhist morality, we may divide its exposition naturally into four parts: (1) basis and aim, or metaphysics of the good; (2) virtue and rules of conduct, or practical ethics; (3) efficacy of morality, the ecclesiastical side of ethics; and (4) mental training and spiritual attainments. The first of these answers to *paññā* of the above given division of the discipline, the second and third to *śīla*, and the fourth to *samādhi.*

The sources from which we have to discover the fundamental (or, one might say, primitive) forms of Buddhism are known to us through the Pāli Canons. These, as is well known, are the traditions of the orthodox Theravādins, who in many points deaden the spirit by the letter and are pre-eminently scholastic in their trend of mind. Hence it is quite natural that, together with the kindred schools, they are called the Hinayānists, the followers of the Little Vehicle or the Abandoned Way. On the other hand, the developments or amplifications, whether natural and consequent or not, are represented by the so-called Mahāyānists, whose traditions are handed down to us partly in Buddhist Sanskrit texts and still more in Chinese translations. Here we are not to enter into discussions of the perplexing questions as to the origin of this difference and the mutual relations between these two aspects; but, regarding them as a whole, we might say that the latter deduced many important consequences from the fundamental ideas, though sometimes they run to extremes. Thus we find it desirable, in seeking to discover the kernel and vital spirit of the Buddha's teachings, to interpret the letter of the Pāli books by the light thrown upon them by the spirit of the Mahāyāna.[3] Though these two are never to be confused or their differences minimized, the close relations existing between them should be kept in view more than has been usual. Abandoning the rather misleading nomenclature of the Lesser and the Greater Vehicles, and keeping these points in view, we shall now enter into the details under each head, and endeavour to state the fundamental features and to see their consequences.

[1] *Itiv.* 92: 'One who sees me sees the truth,' etc.; *Dīg.* 27, Aggañña: 'This is the appellation of the Tathāgata, his body is of truth (*dhamma-kāya*)—he is made up of truth (*dhamma-bhūta*),' etc. The present writer cannot at all agree with Oldenberg's view as to the position of the Buddha in his religion (*Buddha*[4], Stuttgart, 1903, p. 372 f.).

[2] *Dīgha*, 4 (*PTS* ed. i. 124), *Aṅg.* 3. 81–90 (*ib.* i. 229–239), etc.

[1] *Dhammapada*, verse 183.

[2] *Saṁy.* 33. 3, 4 (*PTS* ed. i. 99 f.), 47. 13 (*ib.* v. 162), etc. Here *dassana* means more than insight, and may be rendered 'realization.'

[3] This remark may, for instance, be illustrated by the idea of a Tathāgata or of a Bodhisattva (*q.v.*). Further to be noticed are, for instance, the close connexions between the introductory part of the *Saddharmapuṇḍarīka* and the *Itivuttaka* (also the fourth part of the *Aṅguttara*), or between the 15th chapter of the same and the *Nidāna-kāthā* of the Jātaka.

2. Basis and aim; metaphysics of the good.—The fundamental principle of Buddhist ethics and morality is expressly stated, in the very opening of the Buddha's first sermon, to consist in the Middle Path, which is, again, the way to the realization of the ultimate end—the extinction of the pains arising from egoism. Here the Middle Path is recommended, not merely because it lies in the middle between worldly pleasures and ascetic self-tortures, but because therein lies the right or perfect (*sammā*, Skr. *samyak*) way for realizing the ideal in accordance with truth. It is the solid (*khema*) way, in contrast with the crooked (*kumma*); the holy or noble (*ariya*), in contrast with the false (*micchā*) or base (*anariya*); and it leads to the perfect enlightenment (*sambodhigāmin, sambodhiparāyana*).[1] Here arises the question as to what is the content of that enlightenment. The answer is given mostly in a negative way, in the denial of the phenomenal, of human weakness, illusions, and passions—in short, in the teaching of non-ego (*anattā*), extinction (*nirodha*) of pains, and the well-known *nibbāna* (Skr. *nirvāṇa*). There are perplexing questions as to the real meaning of the term, and its negative aspect has led not only many European scholars, but a section of Buddhist thinkers, to a thoroughly negative view.[2] Not entering into these discussions, we shall content ourselves with noting that Buddhism here faced the same problem as Schopenhauer did as to the ultimate nature of his nothingness (*Nichts*), especially in its relation with the mystic experiences of the saints, both Buddhist and Christian.[3] But the difference between Buddha and Schopenhauer consists in this, that the former was not content with the merely theoretical attitude of the latter, but, having himself realized the experience of transcending the phenomenal and of entering into the height of mystic illumination, tried to lead his followers to the same attainment. This ideal of the same attainment is expressed in the term 'One Way' or 'Sole Road' (*eka-yāna*),[4] treading in which is the very essence of Buddhist morality, and the basis of which is found in the stability of truths (*dhamma-ṭṭhiti*).[5] In summarizing positively the highest aim of Buddhist morality, we might say that it consists in entering into the communion of all the Buddhas and Saints, through realizing the oneness and eternity of truths in one's own person. Not only insight and wisdom (*dassana, vijjā*), but morality and mental training are possible on the ground of this assumption, and all virtuous acts flow from this metaphysical source.

Thus, in the *Brahma-jāla*, one of the books which show most vividly the connexions between practical morality and philosophical speculations, the Buddha contrasts mere works, however good and excellent, with his attainments and purposes. Having heard his disciples talking of the others' praise and blame of Buddhist morality, he teaches them not to be anxious about these 'trifling matters, the minor details, of mere morality (*śīla-mattaka*).' The reason is not because morality is a trifling matter in itself, but because it is vain unless founded upon profound knowledge and high attainments. He says:

'There are other things, profound, difficult to realize, hard to understand, tranquillizing, sweet, not to be grasped by mere logic, subtle, comprehensible only by the wise. These things the Tathāgata, having himself realized them and seen them face to face, hath set forth; and it is of them that they who would rightly praise the Tathāgata in accordance with the truth should speak.'[1]

Here we can see very clearly the close connexion between morality and enlightenment in Buddhism, and at the same time the basis of its liberal and broad spirit.

This characteristic of Buddhist morality is, again, closely related to its ideal of universal salvation, as shown in the missionary charge given to the first disciples and manifested in missionary works, even in the Buddha's time and afterwards under King Aśoka's patronage. This universal ideal is further expressed by the Mahāyānists in the oft-repeated saying that every being is a Buddha in his essential quality, and on this account the standard of a perfect Buddhist was transferred from an *arhat* to a *bodhisattva* (see below). After all, the foundation of Buddhist morality rests on the essential capacity of every person for Buddhahood; and the criterion of true morality lies in the tendency to *bodhi*, as attested by the one road (*eka-yāna*) trodden by all the *Tathāgatas* of the past as well as of the present and future. Abandon the false and base conduct of common men (*puthujjana*) and adopt the methods of a Buddha—that is the cardinal maxim of Buddhist morality. Though this expression may sound somewhat vague and self-evident, the latter, the good and holy life, is not to be merely talked about, but to be tested by personal touch, and realized in the exercise of the three methods of discipline as well as by the group of the four perfections. Suppose a traveller perishing of thirst found a well by the wayside; if he saw the water, but had no rope or bucket to fetch it, could he quench his thirst?[2] The answer is evident. The essential aim of any discipline or exercise is to touch the immortal region by the body (*kāyena amatam dhātum phassayitvā*),[3] *i.e.* by personal experience and actual realization. The guide to this end is found in the person of the Buddha; hence the important rôle which faith fills in Buddhist morality, as has been indicated above, and as we shall see later under the head of 'Virtues' (§ 3, below).

Here arise naturally the questions as to the nature and origin of sin and ills, and the opposition of man's moral nature to the good. Buddhist ethics is so anxious to prevent the arising of bad thoughts and actions that it surpasses almost all other ethical systems in enumerating human weaknesses and vices (see below). So manifold are these vices that they can fetter one's mind at any moment and on every possible occasion, just as demons were thought by mediæval Christians to do. Various classifications insist on the dreadfulness of human passions; the method of the four exertions (*padhāna*) supplies guidance for the checking of every germ of evil and the fostering of any good inclination; the doctrine of the source (*samudaya*) of pain tries to explain the origin and genesis of ills. But Buddhism has no story of Adam's fall, except a myth of man's gradual degeneration,[4] nor does it teach that sin is a transgression of Divine law in consequence of free will. The causation or genesis of ills is traced to the one root of thirst (*taṇhā*); and the source of all vices, however classified, is sought in passion and greed (*kāma* and *rāga*).[5] Though these may, again, be traced to, or associated with, ignorance (*avijjā*) or delusion (*moha*), the latter are, for their part, the outcome of the former; and the terms express nearly the same thing in different aspects, and, taken together,

[1] *Majjh.* 19 (*PTS* ed. i. 118), 26 (*ib.* i. 161–163), *Sn.* 38, etc.
[2] The Sarvāstivādins emphasize the reality of the objective world (*dharmas*) and the ultimate nothingness of ego (*ātman*).
[3] See Schopenhauer, *Die Welt*[3], Leipzig, 1859, i. 450–464, ii. 700–703.
[4] See art. TATHĀGATA.
[5] *Aṅg.* 3. 134 (*PTS* ed. i. 286), *Saṁy.* 12. 20 (*ib.* ii. 25), for which see DOCETISM (Buddhist). This was the *punctus saliens* which gave rise to the exaltation and explanation of the Buddha's educative tactfulness (*upāya-kauśalya*) in the *Saddharmapuṇḍarīka* (chs. 2–4), and finally to the revelation of his true personality (chs. 15 and 21).

[1] Rhys Davids, *Dialogues of the Buddha*, London, 1899, i. 26.
[2] *Saṁy.* 12. 68 (*PTS* ed. ii. 118).
[3] *Itiv.* 51 (p. 46), 73 (p. 62).
[4] *Dīgha* 27, Aggañña.
[5] *Majjh.* 13, Dukkha-kkhandha (*PTS* ed. i. 85); 46, Dhamma-samādāna (*ib.* i. 309), etc.

amount to egoism. This is the original sin, so to speak, and the root of all evils (see, further, EGOISM [Buddhist]). In Buddhist ethics no distinction is made between sin and ills, and their sole origin is sought not in the objective world, but in our own mind and acts (*kamma*, Skr. *karma*).

Here again Buddhists faced the same problem as Schopenhauer as to the cause of the individuation of will. The conclusion is to the same effect as that of the German philosopher—that no reason could be sought in this domain. Or, we might say, the question is left theoretically unanswered, and the more emphasis is laid on the necessity and urgency of uprooting the present ills and actual vices.[1] Here we see reflected the very practical character of Buddhist ethics, but we note at the same time that this point gave rise to various speculations among later Buddhist thinkers. Aśvaghoṣa (*q.v.*) tried to answer the question by the idea of an abrupt upheaval of *avidyā* out of the *Tathatā*, nearly on the same line as Schelling's theory of a jump (*Absprung*) of the individual will out of the universal. Another solution tends, as in Leibniz's *Theodicée*, or still more in the Gnostic emanation theory, to explain ills as the imperfect reflexion of the one universal mind. The latter is the case with Vasubandhu and his followers. Whatever might have been tried, the fundamental trait of Buddhist ethics consisted in its practical nature, and it had a very vivid sense of the vices of *human nature* in its actual conditions, and of the ills arising from them, both of which are the irrevocable consequences (*vipāka*) of the *karma* without beginning. This feature appealed to the mind of the Hindus, yearning for emancipation; and also impressed deeply the peoples of the Far East, so that the change of sentiment worked out by Buddhistic influence in Japan, perhaps more than in any other country, is a very remarkable feature in the history of the religion.[2]

It may be said that the identification of sins and ills, the basis of which lies in the theory of *karma*,[3] has the effect of weakening the moral sense of responsibility which we find so strong in the Jewish and Christian religions; but we should not forget that here we have to deal with another sort of morality, whose sole aim is the abandoning of egoism and entering into the vast communion of the enlightened mind. Buddhist morality is, in its principles, completely free from nomistic elements; and the wide-reaching love for all beings, as expressed in the four aspects of the infinite mind (*appamāṇa-chetovimutti*), was possible only on this basis, apart from the love of and for the only Father in Heaven.

The full realization of the holy way (*ariya-magga*) and the attainment of enlightenment (*bodhi*) are necessarily associated with the final uprooting of fundamental vice. This condition is described in the oft-repeated expression '*arhat*-ship': birth is extinguished, purity is perfected, and all is done that is to be done, etc. And this, again, is what is called the footstep of the Tathāgata, the settlement of the Tathāgata, the impress of the Tathāgata.[4] Here an *arhat* is evidently identified with a Tathāgata, so far as the above-mentioned attainments are concerned.[5] At the same time, a distinction is made between the Tathāgata and a *bhikkhu* who has been released by wisdom; there the point lies in the difference between a *pachcheka-buddha* and a fully enlightened Buddha, the former being a self-content saint, and the latter the teacher and benefactor of all beings. Every Buddhist should aim at the attainment of *arahatta* (saintship); and the most significant type, or the only standard, of this attainment is found in the personality of the Buddha who is one of the *arhats*. In this respect we may say that the ideal of Buddhist morality consists in the imitation of the Buddha, and this is the reason why faith in the Master is so strongly insisted upon, for both moral and intellectual perfection. The Buddhists of earlier times never pretended to be themselves Buddhas; they were content to have as their Master the only Buddha who appeared in this world-period, yet their moral ideal was always directed towards the perfection of an *arhat*, who was nothing but a Buddha in his moral perfection. But this point gave rise to a division in moral ideals and, conjointly with that, to the schism of the Mahāyāna and the Hīnayāna.

A section of conservative Buddhists adhered more to the letter than to the spirit of the fundamental teachings, and found their satisfaction in self-culture. Their ideal consisted in the imitation of the Buddha, but they deemed themselves thoroughly unqualified for that perfection, and cherished the hope of being born in the good resort of the heavenly worlds, and of finishing their journey on the way of *bodhi* in the time of the future Buddha *Metteya* (Skr. *Maitreya*). This type of Buddhist ideal is prevalent among the Buddhists of Ceylon, Burma, and Siam.. It is of very ancient origin, and exhibits a great tenacity through the whole history of Buddhism in the other countries as well. Against this stream of moral scrupulosity there arose a school, more broad-minded and daring, which emphasized the importance of following the Buddha's footsteps in spirit. The division may be traced to the schism of the Vajjian monks, ascribed to the second century after the Buddha's death. Whatever the date may have been, the difference resulted in the division of the Hīnayāna and Mahāyāna.

This division involved, *inter alia*, a rupture between the ideal of *arhat* and that of *Bodhisattva* (Pāli *Bodhisatta*). The latter was an appellation of the Buddha in his former births, preparing for his Buddhahood, and meant 'a being seeking for *bodhi*.' Now this was transferred to every Buddhist whose moral aim consisted in the same attainment and practice as that of the Bodhisattva, and this ideal was distinguished from that of the *arhat*, including the self-content *pachcheka-buddhas* and the conservative preservers of the Buddha's sermons (*sāvaka*, Skr. *śrāvaka*, *i.e.* 'hearers').[1] Though this changed notion of ideal saint contained nothing radically different from that of an *arhat*, it showed a departure in favour of a freer development of Buddhist moral ideals, and involved many important consequences for morals.

Reserving these practical bearings for a later section of the present article, we have here to deal with the Mahāyānist theory of the *bodhi-chitta*.[2] It means the primordial essence of our mind, which in itself consists in the supreme *bodhi*, i.e. the very essence of Buddha's enlightenment. This essence is present in every mind, but lies dormant or covered by the dust of ignorance and infatuation. When it is awakened and developed by due training, we may see in ourselves the eternal Buddhahood in its full illumination, and, in this way, the communion with all the Buddhas may be realized. Morality, associated with wisdom and mental training, is the way to this realization, and makes us tread the one and same way (*eka-yāna*) of the Buddhas. Indeed, morality is

1 *Majjh.* 63, Māluṅkya (*PTS* ed. i. 426). See Oldenberg, 318; Warren, *Buddhism in Translations*, Cambridge, Mass., 1900, p. 117.

2 This is the feature in the moral character of the Japanese people that is least known to the West, and, curiously enough, the modern Japanese themselves are unconscious of it. Some hints may be derived from the present writer's article, 'Le Sentiment religieux chez les Japonais,' in *La Revue du mois*, July, 1908.

3 See Rhys Davids, *Hibbert Lecture*, 1881, and art. KARMA.

4 *Majjh.* 27, Hatthipadopama (*PTS* ed. i. 181). Cf. below, the parallel in the *Saddharmapuṇḍarīka*.

5 This identification is confirmed by the description of a perfectly holy *bhikkhu* as a Tathāgata (*Majjh.* 22, Alagaddūpama [*PTS* ed. i. 139 f.]), and also by passages where the *arhats* are exalted as equal to Buddhas (*Saṁy.* 22. 76 [*PTS* ed. iii. 83–84]). Besides these, the training of the four *jhānas*, the four *appamāṇas*, etc., are described in innumerable passages in the same words, both in regard to Buddhas and to *arhats*.

1 See *SBE* xxi. 35, 43, 80, and many other Mahāyāna texts.

2 There are many Mahāyāna treatises on the subject; see, *e.g.*, Nanjio's *Catalogue*, nos. 1181, 1301, 1304, all of which are ascribed to Nāgārjuna.

possible only on this foundation of our essential fellowship with Buddhas and of the substantial identity of our mind with theirs. Morality is the actualized *bodhichitta*, which is, again, the *universalia ante res* of morality. In other words, the *bodhichitta* is the 'stability of truths' translated to the inner heart of man; it is the *bodhi* seen not as an attainment or acquisition, but as the original possession of man's mind. Viewed in this light, the contrast of good and bad, noble and base, amounts to the contrast between the primordial *bodhi* and the fundamental *avidyā*. Thus we see in Buddhist ethics the Jewish contrast of God and Satan transferred to the inner heart of our own mind, which at the same time is substantially identical with that of all beings, including Buddhas, Bodhisattvas, and common men, as well as animals and spirits in the purgatories.[1]

3. Virtues and rules of conduct; practical ethics.—Just as the contrast between the *bodhichitta* and *avidyā* is the ultimate point of theoretical ethics, the contradistinction of virtues and vices forms the fundamental subject of practical ethics. Buddhist teachers are so fond of enumerations and classifications that nearly every topic of thought or of doctrine is arranged in numerical groups. This answered not only the theoretical purpose of classification, but, at the same time—perhaps much more than the former—the practical purpose of extracting the materials according to need. This use is naively expressed, in the explanation of the seven divisions of *bodhi*, by a simile that robes and jewels stored in one case can be easily taken out.[2] The tables of virtues and vices are arranged in this way, partly for the sake of classification, and partly for the practical purpose of easily drawing their items out at any moment, when one of them is present while the associated ones are to be enticed or guarded against.[3]

The fundamental classification of Buddhist discipline is, as we have seen above, the three branches of the *sikkhā*; closely connected with this is the division of actions (*kamma*) or organs of works, *i.e.* body (*kāya*), speech (*vācha*), and mind (*manas*).[4] Among these the mental is the root of actions, but all the three have great influence upon one another, so that, both for repression of the bad and for acceleration of the good, the three are associated and help mutually.

Now we shall first consider the vices to be guarded against. As we have seen above, the radical vice of human nature consists in egoism, and it manifests itself in lust (*kāma*), desire (*chhanda*), and intention (*adhippāya*). These passions manifest themselves in greed (*rāga*), seeking for pleasure, hatred (*dosa*) of pain, stupidity (*moha*), and hopeless indifference. These are cardinal vices, and are called the three roots of the bad (*akusala-mūlāni*), depravities (*upakkilesa*), etc.[5] They may further be divided into five or seven items. The five hindrances (*nīvaraṇa*), or, to express the same thing, covers (*āvaraṇa*), are: (1) sensual desire (*kāma-chchhanda*), (2) ill-will (*vyāpāda*), (3) stolidity and torpor (*ṭhīnamiddha*), (4) excitement or vanity (*uddhachchha*), and (5) perplexity (*vichikichchhā*). The seven fetters (*saññojana*), or incentives (*anusaya*), are: (1) fawning (*anumaya*) or sensual pleasure, (2) repugnance (*paṭigha*), (3) opinion (*diṭṭhi*), (4) perplexity (*vichikichchhā*), (5) pride (*māna*), (6) attachment to existence (*bhava-rāga*), and (7) ignorance (*avijjā*). The fetters are again developed to 10 or 16, 108, etc., and these groups are called depravities, attachments (*upādāna*), streams (*ogha*) of passions, fire, etc., with various nomenclatures, according to the points of view from which these vices fetter, afflict, or stir the human mind, and incite to bad actions. These classifications, as we can easily see, are in some cases cross-divisions, and they are not designed for a scientific purpose. Yet, when we compare them with the vices enumerated in the New Testament, we discover that the Buddhist classifications had psychological analysis more in view than the Christian, which are thoroughly practical. Herein, too, is seen the close relation between Buddhist morality and mental training. The same remark may be applied to the classifications of virtues which we now proceed to consider.

All the virtues and virtuous practices are arranged in seven groups,[1] which are sometimes called the divisions of the way (Skr. *mārgāṅga*), but four of them may better be described under the head of mental training, and the remaining three are groups of virtues combined with the methods of mental exercise. The virtues (*bala*) are also called organs (*indriya*) of moral practice, and their practice consists in the Eightfold Holy Way (*Ariyamagga*). The virtues or organs are: (1) faith (*saddhā*), (2) exertion (*viriya*), (3) mindfulness (*sati*), (4) contemplation (*samādhi*), (5) wisdom (*paññā*).[2] Among these, faith, contemplation, and wisdom are the three cardinal virtues of Buddhism, and are included in every other group of virtues; and, on the other hand, several others are added to the above five, such as shame (*hirī*) and fear of sinning (*ottappa*), or again, blamelessness or clear conscience (*anavajja*), sympathy or altruism (*saṅgaha*), deliberation (*saṅkhā*), etc., which, taken in various groups, make up the seven or nine virtues. The practice of sympathy, for instance, is divided into four: almsgiving or charity (*dāna*), kind word (*peyyavajja*), beneficial act (*atthachariyā*), and all-identification (*samānattatā*). These virtues, applied to practical life, make up the Eightfold Way, which consists in the perfection of (1) opinion (*diṭṭhi*), (2) decision (*saṅkappa*), (3) speech (*vācha*), (4) actions (*kammanta*), (5) livelihood (*ājīva*), (6) effort (*vāyāma*), (7) mindfulness (*sati*), and (8) contemplation (*samādhi*).[2] We see how in these classifications mental training plays a great part.

We shall not enter into the details of these items; suffice it to say that Buddhism lays more emphasis on the intellectual side than is done in Christianity, and in this respect these virtues may be compared with Greek or Confucian virtues.[3] Nevertheless, faith plays the central part, as in Christianity, and this point brings us to the religious or ecclesiastical side of Buddhist morality, as we shall presently see.

Lastly, as regards Buddhist virtues, we have to speak of the *pāramitās*, the virtues which bring us

[1] This point was systematized by the Chinese philosopher Chi'i (A.D. 531–597) of T'ien-T'ai, on the authority of the *Saddharmapuṇḍarīka*, and applied to ethics, among others, by Chi-Hsu (1599–1655) in his commentary on the Mahāyāna *Brahma-jāla*. The influence of this idea was far-reaching and deep in China, and even more so in Japan. A popular song of the 13th cent. says: 'The Buddha was once a common man, we shall be once finally Buddhas; sad and lamentable are the walls separating us from them (who are all one in essence, in the primordial Buddhahood).' Another popular saying, of the 18th cent., runs: 'See the puppet-player, he brings out of the box that hangs from his neck anything he pleases, a Buddha or a devil.'

[2] *Saṁy.* 46. 4 (*PTS* ed. v. 71).

[3] This practice of enumerating in incantation fashion may be witnessed among the Buddhist monks throughout the East. The tables serve not only to keep their contents in memory, but also for mental culture. Side by side with this advantage, its disadvantage is shown in its mechanical routine.

[4] *Majjh.* 56, Upāli (*PTS* ed. i. 372 f.); *Aṅg.* 3. 1–9 (*ib.* i. 101–105), etc.

[5] *Saṁy.* 36, Vedanā-saṁy., esp. 3, 5, etc.; *Aṅg.* 3. 33, 69 (*PTS* ed. i. 134 f., 201); *Itiv.* 50, etc.

[1] *SBE* xi. 61; Rhys Davids, *Dialogues of the Buddha*, ii. 129.

[2] See, further, *Saṁy.* 64. 4 (*PTS* ed. v. 6), where virtues are beautifully described by similes, which may be compared with St. Paul's utterance in Eph $6^{13\text{-}17}$.

[3] The cardinal virtues of Confucianism are wisdom, love, and courage.

to perfection or to the other shore of *nirvāṇa*. As we have seen above, the aim of Buddhist morality is to bring us to the attainment of *arahatta* (saintship) or to Buddhahood, to the final goal of perfect enlightenment. So in this respect every virtue is a *pāramitā*, but in the Pāli books the term is applied exclusively to the moral acts of the Buddha in his innumerable lives in preparation for his Buddhahood. It is told in the introduction to the *Jātaka*[1] that the Brahman Sumedha, the future Buddha, made the promise to himself, as well as to his teacher, to exercise the virtues leading him to the attainment of Buddhahood (*buddhakāre dhamme*). They are enumerated as follows: (1) charity (*dāna*), (2) morality (*śīla*), (3) resignation (*nekkhamma*), (4) wisdom (*paññā*), (5) exertion (*viriya*), (6) forbearance (*khanti*), (7) truthfulness (*sacca*), (8) persistency (*adhiṭṭhāna*), (9) love (*mettā*), and (10) equanimity (*upekkhā*).[2] Now the transition to Mahāyāna morality brought these within the scope of all Buddhists, who must strive for perfect enlightenment; and in this ethical system the *pāramitās* fill a great rôle. Six of them are usually enumerated, viz. charity (*dāna*), morality (*śīla*), forbearance (*kṣānti*), exertion (*vīrya*), meditation (*dhyāna*), and wisdom (*prajñā*). Very often four are added to these, making ten in all, viz. tactfulness (*upāya*), earnest wish or vow (*praṇidhāna*), strength (*bala*), and knowledge (*jñāna*).[3] A résumé of these virtues is given in the Lotus of the True Law, and is regarded by the Mahāyānists as containing the three fundamental maxims of their morality. It runs:

'Any Bodhisattva, Mahāsattva, who, after the *parinirvāṇa* of the Tathāgata, shall set forth this *Dharma-paryāya* to the four classes of hearers, should do so after having entered the abode of the Tathāgata (*Tathāgata-layana*), after having put on the robe of the Tathāgata (*T.-chivara*), and occupied the seat of the Tathāgata (*T.-āsana*).' The abode is explained to mean abiding in love to all beings (*sarva-sattva-maitrī-vihāra*); the robe, the delight in an immense forbearance (*mahākṣānti-sauratya*); and the seat, the entrance to the vacuity of all laws (*sarva-dharma-śūnyatā-praveśa*).[4] This is exactly the same idea as is expressed in the above-quoted expressions, 'the footstep of the Tathāgata,' etc., by transferring the *pāramitās* to the imitation of the Tathāgata.

We omit further comments on these classifications and their mutual relations, but we have to note that in the virtues of the Bodhisattvas more consideration is paid to those virtues that have regard to others, and that the essence of sympathy or love is more prominent than in the virtues above given. This was, indeed, a very important point in the departure of the Mahāyāna. The Mahāyānists are wont to call the Hīnayānists egoists, in contrast with their own altruism. Though this is not literally true, the characteristic difference between the two schools, or between the ideal *arhat* and *bodhisattva*, consists in this, that, while the former sees in self-culture the first requisite of morality, the latter insists on the necessity of altruistic actions and thoughts, even for the sake of self-culture, as in the case of the Buddha's former lives. In other words, the Mahāyānist moral ideal lays special stress on the realization of the *bodhichitta*, by entering into the communion of the saints through the exercise of altruistic virtues. This is, of course, an extension of the fundamental virtue of love or sympathy, but the emphasizing of this point gave rise to another important idea, that of the dedication (*pariṇāmanā*)[1] of all merits and works for the sake of others, in order to lead them to the same enlightenment. It makes it possible for all beings to help each other on the way to salvation and the realizing of the communion of spiritual fellowship. The practical results of this ideal were momentous, and we may say that Buddhist influence in China and Japan turned on this pivot, although unfortunately with its abuses as well.[2]

The consideration of the virtues and their values leads us to the methods by which, and the conditions under which, they could be worked out. The organization for the promotion of morality is established in the Order (*Saṅgha*), including monks and laymen, and the guidance of morality therein was laid down by the Buddha in the rules of obedience (*Vinaya*), including prohibitions and commandments, and also necessary rules of discipline for carrying them out. Leaving the details of these rules to the special art. VINAYA, we shall here examine their general characteristics. Though the vow of taking refuge (*saraṇa*) in the Three Treasures and the Five Commandments (*verāmaṇī*) are common to all members of the Order, a clear demarcation is drawn between the laic and the monastic disciples in regard to the other standards of life. In this respect Buddhism may be said to teach a twofold system of morality—one that of monks and nuns, which is beyond this world (*lokuttara*); and the other that of the laity, which is worldly.[3] A detailed description of worldly morality is given in the sermon to Siṅgālaka,[4] and the practice of filial piety, respect toward teachers, harmony between husbands and wives, etc., are recommended as the deeds which shall bear good fruit in one's being born in heavenly worlds. This, however, is not specially Buddhistic, but generally human. To be perfectly moral, according to the Buddhist ideal, all the conditions of the *śīla* should be fulfilled, for which monastic life or homeless life (*anāgāra*) is a necessary condition. It is evident that the Buddha recommended the life of an ascetic (*samaṇa*) as the fittest for perfect morality, but at the same time it should be noted that the household life (*sāgāra*) was not totally excluded from salvation. The Buddhist communion (*Saṅgha*) is made up of the four classes of members—monks and nuns, laymen and laywomen. These four are always described as making up one body and as equally praiseworthy, when they are well-disciplined.[5] Moreover, we hear a Brahman Vachchhagotta praise the Buddha's laws for their universal application to all his followers, without distinction of the conditions of life.[6] The Buddha is credited with having gone even so far as to say that no difference existed between a layman and a monk, when they had realized perfect purity.[7]

1 *Jātaka*, ed. Fausböll, vol. i. pp. 19–28; Warren, *Buddhism in Translations*, pp. 23–29; Rhys Davids, *Buddhist Birth Stories*, 1880, i. 18–26.

2 This may be compared with the ten dharmas for attaining the *paramām gatim* (highest resort), as stated in Manu, vi. 92–93.

3 See art. BODHISATTVA; also Suzuki, *Outlines of Mahāyāna Buddhism*, London, 1907, pp. 277–330, 391–404. In the latter book the author is, in many points, too anxious to draw sharp distinctions between the Hīnayāna and Mahāyāna, and misses connecting links between these two forms of Buddhism.

4 *SBE* xxi. 222; *Saddharmapuṇḍarīka*, ed. Kern and Nanjio, p. 234. (Kern's rendering of *āsanā* by 'pulpit' is right, but it parts company with Oriental associations.)

1 This is stated in the *Aṣṭasāhasrikā* (Calcutta, 1888), and many other texts. Suzuki expresses this by the word *parivarta*, of which the source is not given.

2 Anesaki, 'Buddhist Influences in Japan,' in the *Transactions of the Congress for the History of Religion*, Oxford, 1908, ii. 155 f.

3 *Majjh.* 117, Chattārīsaka.

4 *Dīgha*, 31, Siṅgālaka.

5 *Saṁy.* 55, Sotāpatti-saṁy. (*PTS* ed. v. 342 f.).

6 *Majjh.* 73, Mahāvachchhagotta (*PTS* ed. i. 491 ff.).

7 *Saṁy.* 55. 54 (*PTS* ed. v. 410). Oldenberg would see in this a later doctrine (*Buddha*[4], 370, note 1). But his suggestion may be controverted by adducing other texts called the Mirror of Truth (*Dhamma-ādāsa*, or *Ginjakā-vasatha*, *PTS* ed. v. 356–360), where several laymen and laywomen are described as having attained *arhat*-ship, and where the difference of the degrees in their attainment is evidently not due to their respective conditions of life, but to the differences of their emancipation from the fetters. Not a few lay disciples (*upāsakas*) are there said to have cut off the five fetters and to have entered perfect *parinibbāṇa*, equally with many *bhikkhus*. Moreover, when we consider that such *upāsakas* as Chitta of Machchhikasaṇḍa, Sura of Ambaṭṭha, and Mahānāma the Sākyan were in no way inferior to monks in their attainment and moral perfection, it cannot be denied that the Buddha allowed them the same

We may thus safely conclude that the Buddha did not make a fundamental distinction between these two classes of his disciples as to the qualification of their moral and spiritual perfection. Nevertheless, it is very evident that the moral ideal of Buddhism can be attained with less difficulty by many by means of the homeless life than by householders (on the same ground as St. Paul [1 Co 7] recommended celibacy to the followers of Christ); hence the pre-eminently monastic character of Buddhist morality, and hence the duty of the lay followers to pay a special respect to monks.

Similar remarks may be applied to the relations between the sexes. In general, women are regarded as less capable of perfect morality, because of their natural weakness and defects, and so female ascetics (*bhikkhunīs*) have to pay special respect to those of the male sex.[1] Buddha was never tired of describing the defects and vices of women and of warning the monks to guard against them. But this should not be ascribed merely to a despising of the weaker sex, for similar warnings are given to women as regards the wickedness of men.[2] Moreover, when we consider what an active part in sexual immorality is taken by men, we are justified in saying that the Buddha was so emphatic on this point for the sake of his male disciples.[3] On the other hand, we see how many excellent women filled their rôles among the Buddha's disciples;[4] and here, again, Vachchhagotta's utterance is justified.

This brings us to consider the exaltation of lay life and of the female sex among the Mahāyānists —a consequence of their conception of the Bodhisattva ethics. They take the former lives of Śākyamuni as the models of morality, which should be at the same time every one's preparation for Buddhahood; and so they find the life of nobles or householders in no way incompatible with the practice of the *pāramitās* and the attainments of *bodhi*. Thus, the Buddhist communion, in the conception of the Mahāyānists, consists of all kinds of beings, both human and angelic,[5] and among them there are various Bodhisattvas, side by side with monks and ascetics. We are not in a position to determine the first origin of this change of ideal, or to assign each Bodhisattva his nativity; but we see in the Gandhāra sculpture the Bodhisattva Maitreya represented exactly like a prince, with garlands and other decorations, as is found in Barhat and Sanchi.[6] Parallel with these plastic representations, literary testimonies to these changes are so abundant in the Mahāyānistic literature that we might say that nearly every Mahāyāna book contains exaltations of various Bodhisattvas and lay saints.

Most conspicuous among many books of the kind are two texts bearing the names of Vimālakīrti and Śrīmālā respectively. The former is said to have lived in Vaiśālī, contemporary with the Buddha, and the superiority of his moral perfection and dialectic power forms the subject of the whole book.[7] He was perfect in the practice of all the *pāramitās*, but he lived the life of a rich man, dressed in fine robes, and drove a fine carriage, etc. His philanthropy was well known throughout the country. He went about the town instructing in Buddhist morality the people whom he met and sought, whether in the palaces, or on the streets, or in gambling-houses, or in infamous places. He also exercised his influence over the politics of the town. Perfect practice of the *pāramitās* in the worldly life was his aim, for which he is said to have been highly praised by the Buddha, and on which account he is regarded as the model *upāsaka* among the Buddhists of the Far East, even to the present day.

Śrīmālā was the daughter of King Prasenajit (Pāli, Pasenadi) and his queen, Mallikā, so well known in the Pāli books, and was married to the king of Ayodhyā. An obedient daughter and faithful queen, she was imbued with the deep insight of Buddhist wisdom, and perfect in her moral practice of the Sole Road of the Bodhisattvas. Her great vows, stated in the presence of the Buddha, and the dialogues between her and the Buddha, serve to show the capacity of lay morality, when associated with true wisdom, to take up the essence of all the rules enjoined upon monks and nuns, and to elevate and broaden them to the all-embracing morality of the Mahāyāna.[1]

In short, for a Mahāyānist, the moral ideal consists in practising all the precepts of morality, in their essence and spirit, regardless of the circumstances and conditions of life.

'His mother,' it is said, 'is wisdom (*prajñā*), his father tactfulness (*upāya*), his kinsmen all beings, his dwelling the vacuity (*śūnyatā*), his wife joy (*prīti*), his daughter love (*maitrī*), his son truthfulness (*satya*), and yet his household life makes him not attached to existence.'[2]

These precepts should be observed both figuratively and literally; therein consists the compatibility of lay morality with the highest ideal of a Bodhisattva. A Mahāyāna text entitled *Brahma-jāla*[3] enumerates all Buddhist virtues and moral precepts, and explains them in higher senses and according to the spirit of the Mahāyāna, re-interpreting the prohibitions in their respective positive counterparts, and referring every rule and precept to the deepest basis and highest aim of the *bodhi*. This has become the standard of Buddhist Vinaya in China and Japan, and has exercised great influence upon the morality of both the nations.[4]

4. Efficacy of moral practice; ecclesiastical side of ethics.—The basis has been established, the aim shown, and the rules and precepts given. The next question is how these could be carried out. Here the *Saṅgha* plays the essential part. The Buddhist *Saṅgha* is neither a mere congregation nor a society of friends or pietists; it is a religious communion and churchly organization, furnished with the disciplines necessary for the realization of the ideals aimed at. It is a church in the full sense of the word, in spite of the dictum of certain scholars to the contrary. The word 'sacramental' cannot be applied to the Buddhist Church, if it were understood exclusively as founded on God's grace; yet the *kammas* (Skr. *karmas*), the religious and ecclesiastical acts, such as ordination (*upasampadā*), the acceptance of the precepts (*śīla-samādāna*), and confession (*pavāraṇā*),[5] were considered as not merely formal acts, but as furnished with religious, if not mysterious, significance. They were thought to have perpetual

honour as the monks. These are in agreement with Vachchhagotta's utterance above cited. See Rhys Davids, *Dialogues of the Buddha*, i. 63.

1 These marks of respect are called the *gāravas*, for which see *Vinaya*, Chullav. 10. 1, and *Aṅg.* 8. 51.

2 *Aṅg.* 8. 17–18 (*PTS* ed. iv. 196–197).

3 This is illustrated by the simile of warriors (*yodhājīva*) (*Aṅg.* 5. 75–76 [*PTS* ed. iii. 89–100]).

4 See Bode, 'Women Leaders of the Buddhist Reformation,' *JRAS*, 1893, p. 517 f.

5 This conception, taken by itself, is not specially Mahāyānistic, but generally Buddhistic. See *Dīgha*, 20, Mahāsamaya, *Sn.* Ratana, etc.

6 See Grünwedel-Burgess, *Buddhist Art in India* (London, 1901). The Mahāyānists explain this difference of dress on the part of *arhats* and *bodhisattvas* by saying that, while the former are concerned about themselves alone, and so are dressed in simple dull-coloured robes, the latter embellish their bodies in every way in order to please and attract others, and so to lead them to conversion and companionship.

7 The *Vimālakīrti-nirdeśa*, one tr. by Ch' Chien in the 3rd cent. (Nanjio, no. 147), and another tr. by Kumārajīva in A.D. 406 (Nanjio, no. 146).

1 The *Śrīmālā-sīhanāda*, tr. by Guṇabhadra in the 5th cent. (Nanjio, no. 59). There are a great many texts of a similar tendency. We hear of Sumati, daughter of the rich Ugra; Ajitā, daughter of King Ajātaśatru; Vimāladattā, daughter of King Prasenajit, etc.

2 Quoted in the commentary of great authority on the *Brahma-jāla*, below cited, by Tā-hsien, a Korean monk of the 8th (?) century. The words are taken from various Mahāyāna texts and works of Nāgārjuna, Vasubandhu, etc.

3 Tr. by Kumārajīva (Nanjio, no. 1087). The title is evidently taken from the same name in the *Dīgha*, and is intended to expand its contents, by amplifying the Buddha's profound knowledge, as regards the foundation of morality, which has been cited above.

4 In China the Mahāyānist morality inclined to quietism and mysticism, having been conjoined with Taoism, especially in the valley of the Yantsu, where Buddhism was most prevalent. In Japan, on the contrary, it entered into union with the warrior spirit of the nation, and exercised its influence in every department of life, down to the arts of fencing, swimming, and even to the spirit and method of the *harakiri*.

5 For these acts, see art. VINAYA.

efficacy for morality through the whole of the present life, and for the future as well. This is the reason why the moral precepts enjoyed by the holy men (*ariyakantāni śīlāni*) are declared to be one of the four objects of the indefatigable faith or repose (*avechcha-ppasāda*), together with the Buddha, the *Dhamma*, and the *Saṅgha*. These precepts are described, in the formula stating the objects of faith, to be 'unbroken, intact, unspotted, unblemished,'[1] and those who have become imbued with this faith are assured that they have entered the stream of emancipation (*sotāpatta*). Naturally, the ceremonies alone have no such efficacy, yet any works and merits without the performance of the ceremony are worldly, and, therefore, not the morality practised and enjoyed by the Buddhist holy men. The authority to give assurance of its efficacy is in the hands of the *Saṅgha*, instituted by the Buddha. Thus, just as the faith in the *Saṅgha* and in morality does not come to stand, so the faith in the Master is incomplete without the faith in the efficacy of morality and the ceremony instituted for the purpose of effectuating and assuring its practice. The *śīla*, together with its inauguration act, is an indivisible whole, as the one instituted by the perfectly Enlightened, and observed faithfully by the whole communion of the *Saṅgha*. It is also untainted and unblemished, not being defeasible by contrary powers. Therefore it is said:

> 'The holy disciples, furnished with these four things, enter into the stream, become unruinable (*avinīta-dhamma*), and turn to the destiny of the perfect enlightenment.'

The four things mean the faith in the Three Treasures and the *śīla*. The life of such men is, indeed, inexhaustible (*amogham jīvitam*).[2] To the Mahāyānistic explanation of this source of morality we shall return below.

Here we have arrived at the point where we must speak of the authority of the *Saṅgha*. Quite naturally, the Buddha was, during his lifetime, the sole authority and leader of morality. After his death, a kind of apostolic succession, though not unified as claimed by the Christian Church, was kept up by a series of ordaining teachers (*upajjhāya*, Skr. *upadhyāya*); and every Buddhist could trace the lineage of his ordination through the series up to the Buddha.[3] This practice of receiving the precepts from an *upajjhāya* was observed, both by monks and by laymen, even in the Buddha's lifetime; and parallel with this a kind of diocese was inaugurated, and is continued to this day. It is called the *Sīmā* (Skr. *Śīmā*), *i.e.* the circle within which the wandering monks and nuns, as well as resident laymen, had to attend regular meetings and ceremonies, conducted by the elders, during the rainy seasons. This practice was extended, in the countries outside of India, beyond the rainy seasons, and its conception developed into that of a diocese, and at last became that of a catholic church.[4]

The emphasis laid on the efficacy (if not sacramental) of the acts for the acceptance of the *śīla* and the respect for the authority performing them gave rise later to disputes as to whether mind alone or body also is influenced by these acts and thereby continues their efficacy.[1] Without entering into the details of these disputes, we here note the close connexion of this point with the teaching of the Bodhisattva morality. The precepts and the religious acts of receiving them are observed, of course with modifications, by the Mahāyānists, but they consider these acts rather vain, unless accompanied by an eager decision for the attainment of the full *bodhi*, and consequently consummated in the deep impression of the will upon the inner kernel of the mind. What is, therefore, more essential for them than any act is the awakening of the radical good, the fundamental nature, we might say the matrix, from which these acts and moral practice derive their source. This is called the *bodhichitta*. Though the value of morality consists in its practice, the latter should be well founded on sound principle, which again should be in accordance with the ultimate matrix. The religious acts for the entrance to moral life awaken the manifestation of the radical good; and the continual efficacy of faith and sacraments causes the *bodhichitta* to manifest itself more and more, and leads finally to its full realization—the enlightenment. Thus, when the *bodhichitta* is once awakened, its essence (*prakṛti*) is manifested in life, and, because the essence in itself is unmade, is of non-action (*akṛti*), the moral life of the initiated needs less and less exertion, and so much the more partakes in the communion of the saints. Morality, in this condition, consists in actions—bodily, oral, and mental—but they are no *opera operata* but *inoperata*, so to speak. In the descriptions of the four *jhānas*, *appamāna-chetovimutti*, so often repeated in the Pāli Canon and not less in the Mahāyāna books, we can see this sense of unexerted morality, and the formula of the *śīla* in the four *pasādas* shows this bearing, at least implicitly. The theory of the matrix of morality played a great part in the Mahāyāna ethics and became the source of various speculations as well as of practical influences. Chi-Hsu, in his commentary on the *Brahma-jāla*, expresses this point as follows:

> 'The entity (of *śīla*, i.e. the *chitta*) manifests itself as the essence (*bodhi*), and the principles (good and bad) manifest themselves in practice; the realization of the essence is induced by practice, and the perfection of practice is derived from the essence, these two being in reality one.'

This is a piece of scholastic analysis of Mahāyāna morality, and may sound very abstract, but it is intended to explain the efficiency of morality on the basis of the *bodhichitta*, which is identical in all beings, and thereby to lay a foundation for the practice of sympathetic acts in the essential quality of the *bodhichitta*. This philosophy, in conjunction with the teaching of the *pāramitās* and dedication, had actual influence over the Far East converted to Buddhism, and made its morality capable of being applied to various conditions of life. It broadened the people's moral ideal so as to admit all beings to their spiritual communion, and to extend their sympathy toward even animals and plants.[2]

5. Mental training and spiritual attainments.—We now come to our last subject—a peculiarity of Buddhist morality, viz. its close connexion with the methods of spiritual exercises. Though, as we have seen above, morality is enumerated side by side with wisdom and contemplation, in the three

[1] *Saṁy.* 55, Sotāpatti-saṁy. (*PTS* ed. v. 342 f.); also *SBE* xi. 27.

[2] *Saṁy.* 55. 51 (*PTS* ed. v. 404 f.). The same thing is told in *Saṁy.* 11. 2, 4 (*ib.* i. 232), and *Aṅg.* 4. 52 (*ib.* ii. 57), 5. 47 (*ib.* iii. 54), etc. Here the faith is described as the virtues of faith (*saddhā*), morality (*śīla*), repose (*pasāda*), and insight into knowledge (*dassana*).

[3] It is to this observance that we owe the tables of the Elders (*Thera*, Skr. *Sthāvira*), who were heads of their respective branches of Buddhism. Whether these tables are credible or not is another question. Cf. art. ELDER (Buddhist).

[4] We hear of a central seat of the *śīmā* at Nālandā, mentioned in a Chinese record of the 8th century. In China it was for the first time instituted by an Indian, Guṇabhadra, in 430, under the auspices of the Emperor, and after that many *śīmās* were started, each of them having a certain right of jurisdiction. In Japan the *śīmā* was established in 754, and some others after that. Nichiren (1222–1282) prophesied the establishment of the sole seat of the *śīmā* over the whole world.

[1] These are found in the *Mahāvibhāṣyā*, ascribed to the reign of King Kaniṣka. A parallel may be found in the differences between transubstantiation and consubstantiation.

[2] It is in this way that Buddhist morality in China, and still more in Japan, has become connected with poetry and plastic arts. Æsthetic sense among them is derived from the source of mental training, and is manifested in their daily life. An art for art's sake used to be an inconceivable thing among them. See the present writer's article in the *Revue du mois*, cited above, and Okakura, *The Book of Tea*, New York, 1906.

branches of discipline they form one whole, and morality dissociated from the other two ends in merely outward works, while these mental exercises are without wisdom, an empty thing; and wisdom is imperfect apart from moral practice. We have stated above that four—a majority—of the seven groups of virtues (or training) are the methods of contemplation, and that even the rest contain in them what we now should call not virtues but rather spiritual exercises. These will be seen from the items that make up these groups. We do not here enter into them in detail (see art. DHYĀNA), but their general bearings upon moral training are not to be overlooked. The cardinal vice of human nature lies in egoism, which manifests itself most conspicuously in the attachment to sensual pleasures, and in the fetters which bind our mind to various impressions and thoughts. The fourfold fixation of mind (*sati-paṭṭhāna*) aims at the extirpation of egoism. Therefore the mind is fixed on the body (*kāya*); and its foulness, instability, etc., are thought of. The next step is to think of the senses (*vedanā*) and of the pains and pleasures arising from them. Further, the mind (*chitta*) itself is closely examined; and, finally, the ultimate nature of things (*dhamma*). In like manner, in the exercise of the right exertion or control (*sammāppadhāna*) the aim is to prevent sinful conditions arising (*saṁvara*), to put them away when they have arisen (*pahāna*), to protect and cherish good conditions as they arise (*anurakkha*), and, lastly, to retain and develop good conditions in existence (*bhāvana*). These qualities are the same in substance as the seven divisions of *bodhi* (*bojjhaṅga*), which are arranged as follows: (1) mindfulness (*sati*)[1] of all that is morally desirable, (2) discrimination of things (*dhamma-vichaya*) good and bad, (3) exertion (*vīriya*), (4) joy (*pīti*) in what one has attained, (5) satisfaction (*pasaddhi*), (6) contemplation (*samādhi*), and (7) equanimity (*upekkhā*). Nearly the same thing is expressed in the eight kinds of the great man's thoughts (*mahāpurisa-vitakka*). A similar kind of meditation, or release of the mind, is extended to all beings, in order, firstly, to prepare in mind, and then to practise, the virtues of love (*mettā*), compassion (*karuṇā*), joy (*muditā*), and equanimity (*upekkhā*).[2]

The close association of these spiritual exercises and moral actions is shown in the personal example of the Buddha himself. He was a mystic visionary, but he lived nearly fifty years of his ministry in constant activities. He passed sometimes whole nights under forest trees, conversing with spirits or angels, as it is told; he lived often in complete seclusion among the woods of Ichchhānaṅgala or elsewhere for weeks and months. But more significant were his activities as the teacher and benefactor of mankind. Visiting of sick people, itinerating in the regions attacked by pestilence, mediation between two combatants, consolation of mothers afflicted by loss of children—these and other things are frequently told in the Pāli books. His care for health caused him to instruct his disciples in the number of meals to be taken, or in the method of bathing, and even in the minutiæ of using the toothpick. Though he himself did not go outside India, some of his disciples emulated his missionary spirit and went to the west and north-west, beyond the Indus. Thus, the two sides of training—self-culture and actions—found a perfect union in the person of the Buddha, but it was inevitable that there should exist differences in the character and tendency among his disciples, as described in the *Aṅguttara* and shown in the

1 Ten kinds of mindfulness are again enumerated, of religious and moral virtues; see *Aṅg.* (*PTS* ed. i. 42).

2 These are the *appamāṇa-cheto-vimutti*; see Rhys Davids, *Dialogues of the Buddha*, i. 318; K. E. Neumann, *Gotamo Buddho's Reden*, Leipzig, 1896–1902, *passim*.

poems ascribed to them.[1] The consequence is easy to see. It resulted in the division of the *Saṅgha* into the conservative and liberal sections, and finally in the contrast between the ideals of *arhat*-ship and *bodhisattva*-ship. Though these divisions were not precisely the direct results of the different characters, we may roughly say that the former represents the tendency to self-seclusion, while the latter is daring enough to emphasize the sanctity of lay morality. Further, a similar difference arose among the Mahāyānists themselves, the more quietistic morality being represented by the adorers of the *Prajñā-pāramitā*, and the activities for the salvation of all fellow-beings being represented by the followers of the *Saddharmapuṇḍarīka*.[2]

LITERATURE.—This is fully given in the footnotes.

M. ANESAKI.

ETHICS AND MORALITY (Celtic).

—I. *GAULS.*—Among the classical authors there is a great divergence of opinion regarding the moral status of the Celts; and, inasmuch as their qualities and defects have been recorded by their enemies, the Romans, whose sympathies were naturally alienated from them, one must be careful not to attach too much importance to naive generalizations founded frequently on superficial observation. Thus, while Cæsar (*de Bell. Gall.* VI. xvi. 1) and Livy (V. xlvi. 3) regard the religious note as the dominant feature of the character of the Celts, Cicero (*pro Fonteio*, xii.) asserts that they lacked all sentiment of piety and justice; and, though most authors attribute to them a simple and frank nature, Polybius (ii. 7) calls them perfidious. Nevertheless, from the points in which the classical writers concur, we can arrive at some idea of the moral character of the primitive Celts. In general the portrait is far from attractive (Dottin, *Manuel pour servir à l'étude de l'antiquité celtique*, Paris, 1906, p. 117), and some modern authors contend that this is due to their religion, which, according to them, had very little influence in regulating moral conduct (Joyce, *Soc. Hist. of Anc. Ireland*, London, 1903, i. 220). While this may be true to a certain degree, it is nevertheless a fact that their firm belief in a hereafter had a marked influence on their moral nature, inspiring them to acts of rare bravery in which their scorn for death is manifest (Cæsar, VI. xiv. 5; Mela, III. ii. 19). Coupled with this, an aptitude for work and a cleanliness exceptional among barbarous peoples tended to elevate them above the level at which one would naturally be inclined to place them.

A few traits of the character of the Celts may be indicated by way of preface, before going into detail.

Though they were easy to be convinced, and often suffered thereby at the hands of ambitious individuals (Strabo, II. iv. 2; Cæsar, VII. xxx. 3, IV. v. 3: 'incertis rumoribus serviant'), they did not lack the power of reasoning, or refuse to listen to the language of prudence (Cæsar, VII. xiv.; Tac. *Hist.* iv. 69; Strabo, *loc. cit.* and IV. i. 5). They were eager to learn, and sought information concerning other nations (Strabo, *loc. cit.*). Turbulent in spirit, and having a marked aversion for order and regularity, they loved war for its own sake, the state of war being so permanent among them that scarcely a year passed without some injury being washed away in blood (Cæsar, VI. xv. 1). Inconstant, they readily abandoned their ideas, morals, customs, all except their character, and became so thoroughly Romanized that the emperor Claudius, in supporting their claim to be represented in the senate, was able to state that they were 'iam moribus, artibus, affinitatibus nostris mixti' (Tac. *Ann.* xi. 24). In appearance they were usually tall (Diod. v. xxviii. 1; Strabo, IV. iv. 3; Ammian. xv. xii. 1), with soft white skin

1 *Aṅg.* i. 14 (*PTS* ed. i. 23–26); *Thera and Therī-gāthā*, tr. K. E. Neumann, *Die Lieder der Mönchen und Nonnen*, Berlin, 1899, tr. C. A. F. Rhys Davids, *Psalms of Early Buddhists*, London, 1909.

2 Very noteworthy are the descriptions in this book of a Sage (or a group of teachers), to appear in the latter days to bring salvation, and of the persecutions he would endure; it contains also the assurance given by the Buddha as to his mission and its effect (*SBE* xxi. chs. xii., xiv., xix., xx.). On the last point there are deviations from the present Skr. text in Kumārajīva's tr., which led to important consequences in China and Japan.

(Diod. *loc. cit.*; Ammian. *loc. cit.*: 'candidi paene omnes') and blond hair (Diod. *loc. cit.*; Ammian. *loc. cit.*: 'rutili'), and possessed a fierce look (Diod. v. xxxi. 1; Ammian. *loc. cit.* 'luminum torvitate terribiles'). They loved beautiful men, which explains in part the sway that Vercingetorix exerted over them. Even their enemies are obliged to testify to the simplicity and frankness of their character, free from all malice (Strabo, IV. iv. 2; *de Bell. Afric.* lxxiii.). Upright and incapable of evil, deception and trickery were repugnant to them (Strabo, *loc. cit.*). Their superabundance of life, love of novelty, and adventurous humour explain that continual state of agitation and excitement in which they lived (Cæsar, III. x. 3). They disputed and fought on the slightest provocation at repasts. In a word, theirs was a country of duels and civil wars (Diod. v. xxviii. 5; Ammian. xv. xii. 1: 'avidi iurgiorum et sublatius insolescentes'). As a natural consequence of this, they were easily discouraged and dejected, and it was usually more advantageous to arouse them by illusions than by appealing to the sentiment of duty (Cæsar, VII. xx., esp. 12; Strabo, IV. iv. 5), although they were quick to recover from any state of demoralization into which they might have fallen (Livy, XXII. ii.). Among the Romans they were celebrated for their love of revolutions, rapid decisions, and continual changes (Cæsar, III. viii. 3, IV. v. 3, VII. xx. 1, etc.; Strabo, IV. iv. 2). In addition to the art of war, according to Cato (*Orig.* ii.), they cultivated with great talent the art of speaking readily, and they had a natural gift for eloquence (Polyb. II. xvii.; Diod. v. xxxi.). Though Cæsar states (VII. xxii. 1) that the Gauls possessed to a high degree the power of imitation, they stubbornly refused to profit by the experience of their defeats. They were proud even in defeat, and showed no inclination to change their manner of fighting (Strabo, IV. iv. 5; Cæsar, I. xiii. 3, etc., xiv. 7). Finally, they gave special attention to the care of the body (Ammian. xv. xii.). According to Pliny (*HN* XII. xxvi. 45, XXVIII. li.), soap made of tallow or ashes was an invention of the Gauls; while certain tribes, such as the Valeriana Celtica, were in the habit of using a kind of perfume. Various classical authors call attention to the fact that the Celto-Iberians preserved urine in reservoirs for washing their bodies and cleansing their teeth (Diod. v. xxxiii.; Strabo III. iv. 16; Catullus, xxxix. 17–19), and Pliny (XXII. lxxxii.) notes also that the Celtic women used beer-foam as a cosmetic. The men usually wore long moustaches (Diod. v. xxviii. 3), and were fastidious in the care of the hair (Ammian. xv. xii. 2). They were often reproached for their love of ornaments, exhibiting a particular preference for purple or golden garments, necklaces and bracelets of bright colours (Diod. v. xxx. 1; Strabo, IV. v. 5; Appian, *Celtica*, 12; Propert. v. x. 40; Florus, I. xx. 2); and Vergil (*Aen.* viii. 659–661) traces a portrait—very poetical, it is unnecessary to state—of 'the golden-haired Celt, wearing a golden tunic, covered with a mantle with stripes of a thousand colours, a necklace of gold surrounding a neck of milky whiteness.'

With this insight into their character, we can, with the aid of the Irish texts, arrive at some definite idea of the condition of their morals.

1. Marriage and immorality.—In regard to marriage, it suffices to say that the bride was purchased by her future husband. As women were usually married only once, the purchase-price (Old Ir. *coibche*) was received in entirety by the father (*Anc. Laws of Ireland*, Rolls Series, London, 1869–73, iii. 314), and in subsequent marriages (until the twenty-first) the *coibche* was divided between the father and the daughter (*ib.* ii. 346). Apparently the *jus primæ noctis* existed among the early Celts, if we may infer that the right exercised by Conchobar, king of Ulster, is an indication of the prevalence of that custom in early times.

In the *Book of Leinster* (p. 106, col. 2) we read that 'in Ulster, every man who had a daughter to marry took her to pass the first night with Conchobar, in order that she might have that king as a husband (*cech fer di Ultaib doberad ingin macdacht a-feiss la Conchobar in-chét aidchi, com-bad he a-cétmunter*)'; and the despotic king does not hesitate to exercise this right over Emer, the bride of Cúchulainn (Windisch, *Ir. Texte*, Leipzig, 1880, i. 590; d'Arbois de Jubainville, *Famille celtique*, Paris, 1905, p. 125, etc.). That this custom was in vogue in Scotland, we shall see later.

As for the marriage itself, the contract was not binding, and later on Irish canonical law protested in vain against the ease with which marriages were dissolved (Wasserschleben, *Die ir. Kanonensammlung*², Leipzig, 1885, p. 185 f.). That divorce was far from being unusual among the Celts is obvious from the fact that the Ancient Laws of Ireland permitted divorce by mutual consent even when the woman was a legitimate wife (*cétmuinter* [ii. 362, line 21 f.]), for which the technical expression is *im toga scartha*, or 'by choice of separation.' Though the *cétmuinter* was considered the *selb*, or property, of her husband, this did not prevent her from having certain very important rights, such, for example, as that of seizing the property intended to be used by her husband towards the purchase of another woman. The *Senchus Mór* is very explicit in that respect:

'If he gives the purchase-price for another woman,' state the Laws, 'even though it should be from his own property, that purchase-price is the property of his legitimate wife, if she acquits herself of her conjugal duties' (ii. 382).

But, with these exceptions, adultery was otherwise unrestrained; for, besides his legitimate wife, the husband was permitted by law to keep in the domicile one or several concubines, so that Diarmaid mac Fergusa, supreme king of Ireland, had four wives, two of whom had the rank of queens (d'Arbois de Jubainville, *Cours de litt. celt.*, Paris, 1883–1902, vii. 210 ff.). That this institution existed from early times among the Celts is obvious from the statement of Cæsar (VI. xix. 3) that after the death of an important personage, if his wives (*uxores*) were suspected of having brought it about, they were put to torture and finally burned. These were without doubt his concubines, for the relatives of his legitimate wife, who was invariably of high birth, would have avenged her death (d'Arbois de Jubainville, *Famille celt.* 104).

In Ireland the concubine was the rival of the legitimate wife, and was called *adaltrach*; she must not be confused with the *cétmuinter ar muin araile* ('wife on the neck of the other'), or second legitimate wife, whom the husband was permitted to take if it chanced that the first legitimate wife was afflicted with an incurable disease (*cró-lige*, *i.e.* on her death-bed). In that case the husband could send his sick wife back to her relatives; but, if she had none, he was obliged to keep her in his home (*Anc. Laws*, v. 144). However, the condition of a legitimate wife having another legitimate wife as a rival was naturally rare, while that of having a concubine as a rival was most frequent. With the latter the husband usually contracted an annual marriage, lasting from the 1st of May to the 1st of May (*ib.* ii. 390). The concubine was of a stage of society much lower in rank than that of her husband, usually a slave.

An example of such a marriage is that of Derdriu and Conchobar, after the murder of the sons of Usnech (Windisch, *Ir. Texte*, i. 81 f.). St. Bridget was the daughter of Dubthach and his *cumal*, or slave, Broicsech (Stokes, *Three Middle Irish Homilies*, Calcutta, 1877, p. 52).

That the legitimate wife had superior rights over the concubine is evident from the honour-price (*enechlann* or *lóg eneich*) assessed in case of moral injury, that of the *cétmuinter* being twice as great as that of the *adaltrach* (*Anc. Laws*, ii. 404). Furthermore, the law permitted her to strike the concubine until blood flowed, without the latter being entitled to demand any reparation for the injury (*ib.* v. 142). This explains why Mugain, the legitimate wife of Conchobar, makes no protest against the presence of Derdriu; while Emer, the wife of the hero Cúchulainn, while tolerating his relations with his concubine, Ethne Ingube, refuses to submit to the presence of his *cétmuinter ar muin araile*, the goddess Fand (Windisch, i. 206 f., 222 ff.). The attitude of the legitimate wife in these cases may have been influenced somewhat by the fact that the husband had the right of life and death over his wives, as well as his concubines (Dottin, 136; see also *ERE* iii. 813ᵇ).

2. Adultery, incest, polyandry, etc.—Strabo says (IV. v. 4) that it was considered quite natural in Ireland for men to have relations with wives of others, with their mothers or sisters, while St. Jerome goes so far as to state that in Ireland the institution of marriage was entirely unknown:

'Scotorum natio uxores proprias non habet; nulla apud eos coniux propria est, sed, ut cuique libitum fuerit, pecudum more lasciviunt' (*adv. Iovin.* ii. 7 [*PL* xxiii. 309]).

In this, of course, we see a reference to the

system of polygamy or concubinage discussed above. While adultery on the part of the man was very common, there are very few examples of legitimate wives failing to observe fidelity to their husbands. We have, to be sure, the legend of Medb, queen of Connaught, and the celebrated hero Fergus—an account that was known without doubt by Strabo (*Leabhar na hUidhre*, 65). Notwithstanding this, the Celtic women were famed among the ancients for their fidelity (d'Arbois de Jubainville, 'La Légende et les femmes,' etc., in *RCel* vii. [1886] 129–144).

Polybius (XXII. xxi.) relates the story of Chiomara, the wife of the Celtic king Ortiagon, who brought to her husband the head of the Roman centurion who had violated her. When the king said to her, 'Woman, fidelity is a beautiful thing,' she answered, 'Yes, but there is something still more beautiful; it is that there is only one man alive to whom I have belonged.' Derdriu kills herself when the king of Ulster, after having passed a year with her, wishes to give her up to the murderer of her husband. For the beautiful story of Camma, wife of the Tetrarch Sinatos, see Plutarch, *Amor.* xxii.

As for incest, we have in Ireland the example of Clothru, the daughter of a king, who, after having been the wife of her three brothers, marries her own son, Lugaid, supreme king of Ireland (*Book of Leinster*, 23, col. 2). It is permissible to conclude from a statement of Cæsar that, at an early date in Ireland, it was not uncommon for brothers to have wives in common—'uxores habent deni duodenique inter se communes et maxime fratres cum fratribus' (V. xiv. 4); and this custom existed also in Caledonia (Dio Cass. lxxvi. 12; cf. lxii. 6). The accusation of pæderasty, borne against the Gauls by several classical authors whose testimony is worthy of very serious consideration, is apparently without foundation (Aristotle, *Pol.* II. vi.; Diod. V. xxxii.; Strabo, IV. iv. 6; Athenæus, xiii. 80; cf. also d'Arbois de Jubainville, *op. cit.* 187–199).

3. Prostitution. In spite of the ease with which the marriage vows could be violated or broken, prostitution did not fail to flourish. The name given by the *Senchus Mór* to the prostitute is *baitsech* (*Anc. Laws*, i. 190, 236), or *merdrech* (*meretrix*), or 'female of grove and bush' (*Anc. Laws of Wales*, London, 1841, p. 42). A curious fact in ancient Irish law is that the head of the family, to whom the purchase-price of the wife was paid, had also a right to a share in the earnings of the prostitute (*cuit in apthaib baitsaide* [*Anc. Laws of Ireland*, iii. 314]; *cuit a n-abad baidside* [iv. 62]). If she had any children, she and her family were obliged to support them (*do fastad cirt ocus dligid* [v. 452]). If she attempted to force any man to assume charge of the child through obligation of paternity, the *Senchus Mór* gave him the power to refuse (i. 192).

If the minute distinctions made in the Ancient Laws in regard to rape are any criterion, we must conclude that this form of seizure was not infrequently practised in ancient Ireland. The *Senchus Mór* distinguishes three kinds of irregular union between man and woman. The first is called *lánamnas foxail*, or 'union by elopement,' an open and violent seizure done with the consent of the woman against the wishes of the family. The woman in this case is called *ben fuataig*, or 'woman of elopement' (*Anc. Laws*, ii. 356, 400, 402). The second, entitled *lánamnas tothla i tdide*, is a secret union formed with the assent of the woman but unknown to her family. She is then called *ben tdide*, or 'woman of theft' (ii. 356, 404, iii. 38). And, finally, a union by violence without the consent of the woman or family is called *lánamnas éicne no sleithe*, i.e. 'union by force,' in which case she bears the name of *ben forcuir*, or 'woman of violence' (ii. 356, 404).

4. Status of women.—From what we can glean from the different authorities, the condition of women among the ancient Celts was quite miserable (Dottin, 138). Seized with the passion of war, the Gauls often abandoned the cultivation of the soil to the women ('feminæ res domesticas agrorumque culturas administrant, ipsi armis et rapinis serviunt' [Justin, xliv. 3]; cf. also Sil. Ital. iii. 344). Later on, however, under the domination of the Romans, the men developed a great interest in agriculture (Strabo, IV. i. 2). Although there are instances of women governing tribes in the British Isles (such as Cartismandua, who was queen of the Brigantes *c.* A.D. 50 [Tac. *Ann.* xii. 36]), the statement of Aristotle (*Pol.* II. vi. 6), that the Celts were free from the domination of women, holds true for the Continent. That they were not without influence, however, is confirmed by Plutarch (*de Mul. Virtut.* vi.), who says that they were admitted into the councils of war as arbiters of the differences between tribes; and Hannibal agreed with his Celtic allies to let all difficulties between them be judged by the women of the Celts. The women of the Gauls were beautiful and courageous (Diod. V. xxxii. 7; Athenæus, xiii. 80); they encouraged their husbands to fight, and accompanied them on the field of battle (Polyb. V. lxxviii. 1; Tac. *Agricola*, xv., *Ann.* xiv. 34, 36); at times they even displayed greater physical strength than their husbands (Ammian. XV. xii.); and, according to Strabo, they were good mothers and could do more work than the men (IV. i. 2, iv. 3).

5. Cruelty.—The cruelty of the Gauls in war terrified the Greeks and Romans (Dottin, 114). According to their national custom, they cut off the heads of the dead and wounded on the battlefield, to offer them up afterwards to the souls of their ancestors or to the gods (Jullian, *Recherches sur la relig. gaul.*, Bordeaux, 1903, p. 82). Oftentimes they sacrificed captives, and they are also accused of having massacred old men and little children (Diod. V. xxxii.; Pausan. X. xxii. 3f.; Athenæus, iv. 51). The heads of dead enemies were sometimes attached to the necks of their horses or fastened on the end of their lances (Livy, V. xxvi. 11; Diod. V. xxix., XIV. cxv.), while at Entremont, near Aix, trophies were raised with heads exposed on them (Reinach, *Catalogue sommaire du Musée des antiquités nationales*, Paris, 1889, p. 40). They displayed with pride the heads of their chiefs or other illustrious personages, which they preserved in a preparation of oil (Strabo, IV. iv. 5; Diod. V. xxix.). In battle their attacks were characterized by a savage fury (Pausan. X. xxi. 3; Florus, II. iv.; Dion. Hal. xiv. 10, 17).

Probably the most striking example of their savagery is in one of the early Irish sagas, the *Scél mucci Mic Dáthó*, or 'History of the Pig of Mac Dáthó.' Conall Cernach, the foster-brother of the great hero Cúchulainn, replies to the opposing hero Cét in the following manner: 'I swear by the oath that my people swear: since the day when I first took a javelin in my hand, it did not often happen to me that I was without the head of a Connaught-man under my head as a pillow when I slept. Not a day or night passed without that I killed some enemy (. . . *nach menic ro bá cen chend Connachtaig fó-m-chind oc cotlud, ocus cen guine duine cech óen lá ocus cech óen aidchi*).' When Cét regrets that Ánlúan is not present to fight with Conall, the latter replies: 'He is here, however,' and 'drawing from his girdle the head of Ánlúan, he threw it upon the bosom of Cét with such force that a stream of blood burst upon his lips (*atá imorro, ar Conall ic tabairt chind Ánlúain as-sa chriss, ocus no-s-leice do Chét ar a bruinni, corroimid a loim fola for a béolu*' [Windisch, *Ir. Texte*, i. 104, lines 15–23]).

However convincing these accounts may appear, it is, nevertheless, true that the Gauls were no more cruel or savage than other barbarous nations, although they inspired the Greeks and Romans with such great fear that the classical authorities do not hesitate to attribute to them all possible crimes and vices (Jullian, *Hist. de la Gaule*, Paris, 1907, i. 332, etc.). Diodorus accuses them of violating tombs (XXII. xii.); Pausanias says that they did not bury their dead, and outraged and massacred women and children (X. xxi. 1, 7); Livy asserts that they continually used false weights (X. xlviii. 9); while Plutarch states that the only right known to them was that of strength and of the sword (*Camill.* xvii.). Such accusations are only what we should expect from a people in constant dread of a powerful enemy.

6. Human sacrifice.—Probably the most serious accusation of cruelty borne against the Gauls by classical authorities is that they practised human sacrifice (Lucan, *Pharsal.* i. 443–445; Diod. v. xxxii. 6; Livy, XXXVIII. xlvii.). Cæsar (VI. xvi. 2 f.) states that those of the Gauls who were afflicted with grave diseases either sacrificed human victims or made a vow to do so, for they believed that, if a human life were not given for a human life, the wrath of the gods would not be appeased. He adds that they were accustomed to construct immense wooden statues, which they filled with living beings and burned in honour of their gods ('quorum contexta viminibus membra vivis hominibus complent; quibus succensis, circumventi flamma exanimantur homines' [VI. xvi. 4]). Cicero, who was always very bitter against the Gauls, exclaims in his defence of Fonteius: 'They have preserved to this day the barbarous custom of sacrificing human beings. What can be the good faith of a people who think they can appease Divine wrath by crime and human blood' (*pro Fonteio*, xii.)? This rite was practised mainly in war; and before the battle, if the omens were unfavourable, they would even kill their wives and children in order to assure themselves of the victory (Justin, xxvi. 2). If they were victorious, they sacrificed their captives as a thank-offering to the gods (Diod. XXII. ix.; Pausan. X. xxiii. 6). Dionysius of Halicarnassus, who finished his *Roman Antiquities* (i. 38) about 8 B.C., maintained that human sacrifice was still practised among the Gauls, although it was prohibited by the Romans as early as 97 B.C. Under Tiberius (A.D. 14–37) this rite was suppressed (d'Arbois de Jubainville, *Cours*, ii. 376–381), although it survived in certain parts of Britain as late as A.D. 77 (Pliny, *HN* XXX. iv. 13). According to Diodorus (V. xxxii.), the Gauls kept criminals for five years before burning them on enormous pyres. That the belief in the immortality of the soul was one of the prime causes of these sacrifices is supported by the statement of Pomponius Mela (III. ii. 19) that relatives of the dead person often threw themselves into the funeral pyre, in the hope of living with him in the hereafter. The article of the *Dinnsenchus*, written about the 6th cent. A.D., contains an account of the 'plain of prostrations,' showing that the bloody practice of human sacrifice was continued in Ireland probably at a very late date; and the author of this treatise states that at some period previous to his time the people were accustomed to sacrifice their firstborn to an idol called *Cromm crúach* ('bloody crescent') which stood on this field (*Book of Leinster*, p. 213, col. 2).

With human sacrifice is closely allied the love of suicide, which, according to the belief of the Gauls, was a kind of personal and spontaneous sacrifice to the gods. Some of the finest examples of self-sacrifice in antiquity occurred among the Celts. Brennus, believing that he was the cause of the misfortunes of his soldiers, committed suicide in order to appease the wrath of the enemy's god Apollo (Diod. XXII. ix.; Pausan. X. xxiii. 12; Jullian, *Hist.* ii. 359). Livy (XXXVIII. xxi.) states that the Gauls scorned their wounds, enlarging them in order to make them more apparent.

7. Courage.—Among the more important doctrines taught by the Druids (*q.v.*) were the scorn of death and the obligation of courage (Cæsar, VI. xiv. 5; Mela, III. ii. 19). In other words, the Gauls made their theology accord with their temperament. Their very great courage, so highly lauded in antiquity (Polyb. II. xxx. 4, xxxiii. 2; Dio Cass. xii. 1. 2 f.; Livy, XXXVIII. xvii. 7; Plut. *Camill.* xli.), was rather a sort of fury (*rabies Gallica*) than a form of will. They considered it shameful to be attacked first (Plut. *loc. cit.*). On the battlefield, they were filled with anger, confidence, and pride, as they cast defiance against the enemy (Diod. V. xxix. 3); but the resistance of an adversary quickly dispelled their confidence (Pausan. X. xxiii. 12), and not infrequently they were victims of panic (*ib.*; Sil. Ital. xv. 719: 'patrius genti pavor'). It was their great desire to enjoy the esteem of posterity—'posteris prodi pulcherrimum' (Cæsar, VII. lxxvii. 13). Furthermore, the brave were recipients of many tokens of esteem from the tribe. For them were reserved the finest pieces of meat at the feasts, and the honour of carving was always left for the great hero (cf. the *Hist. of the Pig of Mac-Dáthó*, mentioned above, and the *Feast of Bricriu*; d'Arbois de Jubainville, *Cours*, v. 71–78, 86–146, 35–47).

8. Intemperance.—The Gauls were celebrated for their intemperance (Diod. V. xxvi. 3; Ammian. XV. xii. 4; Posidon. iv. 36; Cic. *pro Fonteio*); and, according to Pliny (XII. ii. 5), it was the love of wine that caused them to make their incursions into Italy. The southern heat, combined with their excessive activity, aroused in them an irresistible desire to drink alcoholic liquors (Polyb. II. xix. 4; Livy, XXXIV. xlvii. 5: 'minime patientia sitis'). Cicero, with his usual acerbity, says that wine mixed with water was regarded as a poison by the Gauls (*pro Fonteio*, xv.). They delighted in the invention of liquors of all kinds ('ad vini similitudinem multiplices potus' [Ammian. XV. xii. 4]). Although they prepared a beer called *corma*, they preferred the wines of the south, which they drank until they were insane (Ammian. *loc. cit.*; Diod. V. xxvi.); and it was this excessive indulgence in alcohol that finally undermined their vitality and rendered them weaker than women ('postrema minus quam feminarum' [Livy, X. xxviii.]; Florus, II. iv. 1).

9. Avarice and cupidity.—The thirst of the Gauls for booty was insatiable (Plut. *Pyrrhus*, xxvi.; Livy, XXI. xx. 8). They violated tombs in order to secure gold (Diod. XXII. xii.; Plut. *loc. cit.*); they did not even hesitate to rob the most sacred temples (Pausan. X. xxii. 6); they were so venal that they would become mercenaries of any purchaser, and were willing to engage in long expeditions merely for the sake of pillage (Livy, *loc. cit.*; Justin, xxv. 2; Diod. V. xxvii.; Polyb. II. xxii.). Yet, in spite of their love of gold, they amassed great quantities of it in their own temples as an offering to the gods, and no one dared to touch it (Diod. *loc. cit.*).

10. Justice.—While Cicero assures us that the Gauls were entirely lacking in the sentiment of justice (*pro Fonteio*, xii.), Cæsar (VI. xxiv. 3), on the contrary, states that certain tribes were renowned for justice and moderation; and Strabo extols their equity (IV. iv. 2). Tradition relates that the Senones marched against Rome to avenge the right of the people, which had been violated by certain patricians (Livy, V. xxxvi.; Diod. XIV. cxiii.; Plut. *Camill.* xvii.).

11. Hospitality.—Though indiscreet at times, the Gauls practised all the laws of hospitality (Diod. V. xxviii.; Caesar, IV. v. 2); and, even in dealing with the most warlike tribes, Rome had no complaint to make of the reception accorded her ambassadors (Livy, XXXIX. lv., XLIII. v., etc.). Anxious to learn about other people, their homes were always open to bards and strangers (Diod. *loc. cit.*).

12. Piety.—At first the conquered Greeks accused the Gauls of lacking piety, making of Brennus the type *par excellence* of sacrilege (Pausan. X. xxi.; Diod. XXII. ix. 4); but later, when they began to study their enemies, they not only admitted that they were religious, but even declared them to be the most pious of men (Justin, XXIV. iv. 3; Livy, V. xlvi. 3; Dion. Hal. vii. 70). Cæsar (VI. xvi. 1) calls them a people much addicted to religious practices, for which they are praised by classical authors (Livy, V. xxxvi. 3; Arrian, xxxiv.; Dion. Hal. vii. 70). Religious scruples, for example, prevented Dumnorix from accompanying Cæsar to Britain (Cæsar, V. vi. 3).

13. Obedience and devotion.—Especially before a common enemy, the Gauls showed absolute obedience to their chiefs, whom they loved as one would a father (Fustel de Coulanges, *La Gaule romaine*[3], Paris, 1891, pp. 35–44); and the bonds that unite the chief to his followers are described by Polybius (II. xvii.) as ἑταιρεία, *i.e.* fellowship. Cæsar did not fail to admire the devotion of the *Soldurii* to their chief (III. xxii.). These men share the good or bad fortune of the one to whom they have given themselves; and, if he dies, 'there is not an example of one in this case who would wish to remain alive.' It is to their generous and sympathetic nature that this sublime devotion is due. Thus, two sons of the Galatian king Adiatorix vie with one another as to which shall die with their father (Strabo, XII. iii. 35). Prompt in responding to all appeals for help, they rush to the defence of their neighbours (Strabo, IV. iv. 2); even an army making an invasion into Italy stops at the Alps to free a tribe besieged by another (Justin, xliii. 4), while their haste to respond to a request which excites their sympathy often leads them into war. The chief, on his part, never suffered his followers to be tormented or oppressed; if he did so, he lost his authority among his people (Cæsar, VI. xi. 4).

14. Pride.—Though the Gauls were characterized by their devotion and obedience, they had little regard for discipline, owing principally to their excessive vanity (Diod. XXIII. xxi.; Polyb. II. xxi. 2–5, V. lxxviii. 1–3; Arrian, *Anab.* I. iv. 6). It was this pride that rendered them incapable of profiting by experience; for, even though defeated, they were too haughty to admit their mistake and change their manner of fighting (Strabo, IV. iv. 5; Cæsar, I. xiii. 3–7, xiv. 7). They defied the elements, and believed themselves dishonoured if they sought to avoid the fall of a wall (Ælian, *Var. Hist.* xii. 23; Stobæus, *Anthol.* xliv. 41). Their vanity led them to boast (Strabo, IV. iv. 5; Diod. V. xxix.), and before battle the chiefs lauded the exploits of their ancestors and their people, and cast insults at the enemy (Sil. Ital. iv. 279; Cæsar, VII. xxix. 6, xxx. 1).

15. Perfidy.—Though the Gauls were inconstant, changeable, and not inclined to reflexion (Cæsar, IV. v. 1; Strabo, IV. iv. 2; Polyb. II. xxxii. 8, xxi. 2–5; Sil. Ital. iv. 49 f.), few of the classical authors have reproached them with perfidy. This accusation has been brought against them only in an informal way (Polyb. II. vii.; Cic. *pro Fonteio*). Nevertheless, as we might expect, ruse and treachery flourished to some extent, especially in times of war. It is true that we have such traitors as Divitiacus and Dumnorix, while some of the acts of Vercingetorix are certainly not above suspicion; yet, with few exceptions, they were so open and frank that they did not even use strategy, a method of warfare so honoured among the Greeks (Jullian, *Hist.* i. 346). Their constant happiness and the levity of their humour seem to have been a proof against those worse defects of character (Livy XXI. xx. 3; Cæsar, IV. v. 2; Diod. V. xxviii.); and this gaiety, which so frequently manifested itself in face of death, seems to have been aroused in part by their firm belief in the immortality of the soul as well as by the pique of personal honour.

16. Anthropophagy.—From the evidence we have from different authors, there is little doubt that anthropophagy prevailed to a certain extent among the primitive Celts. While we may have reason to refuse to accept the statement of St. Jerome (*adv. Iovin.* ii. 7) that the Atticoti of Britain relished certain parts of the bodies of shepherds and women, Cæsar (VII. lxxvii. 12) makes the formal accusation that the Gauls, at the time of the invasion of the Cimbri and the Teutons, ate the bodies of those amongst them whom age had rendered useless for war. Pausanias (X. xxii. 3) states that the Celtic invaders of Greece often ate the flesh and drank the blood of little children; and Strabo (IV. v. 4) maintains that certain tribes of Ireland had a special predilection for the bodies of their fathers.

17. Frugality.—It is obvious, from lack of evidence to the contrary, that Polybius (XII. iv.) is correct when he states that at least the Cisalpine Gauls were very frugal. Their principal food seems to have been hog-meat.

18. Murder.—It is worth noting that among the Gauls the penalty for the murder of a stranger was greater than for that of a fellow-citizen (Stob. *Anthol.* xliv. 41); in the first case, it was death; in the second, exile. From the scanty information found in the classical authors, it is impossible to state how frequently murder was resorted to among the primitive Gauls (see, further, below, II. § 13, III. § 15, IV. § 4).

19. Theft.—Although the Greeks accused the Celtic invaders of all kinds of theft and brigandage (Jullian, *Hist.* i. 337 f.), it is highly improbable that this was a common practice in times of peace, if we believe what the same authors say of the frankness and simplicity of their character. Furthermore, the punishment for theft and brigandage was extremely severe—the criminals were burned alive (Cæsar, VI. xvi. 5). If a Gaul concealed a part of the booty of war, or stole some object from those deposited in sacred places, he was put to death after undergoing severe torture (Cæsar, VI. xvii. 5). The severity of these punishments must have tended to curb any desire of individual Gauls to appropriate to themselves the property of others (cf. also above, § 9).

20. Punishments.—It is important to note here that, whereas in later times the *éric*, or compensation for murder, and the punishment of thieves and other criminals, were definitely established by the legal statutes, according to the rank of the person killed, or according to the value of the thing stolen, in earlier history it was left to the Druids to decide in such cases and to determine the punishment (d'Arbois de Jubainville, *Cours*, i. 165–189). As they were reputed to be the most just of men, the individual was obliged to accept their sentence; if he did not, he was forbidden to take part in the sacrifices (Dottin, 281). In order not to receive any injury from their contact, the society of those suffering such excommunication was carefully avoided—in other words, the criminal became an outcast from his tribe, so that, if he had any complaint to make, no justice was rendered him.

II. *IRISH.*—Giraldus Cambrensis, who completed his *Topography of Ireland* about 1187, presents a moral portrait of the Irish of that time which is far from attractive (*Opera*, ed. Dimock, London, 1867, v. 19, etc.). He asserts, for example, that the Irish are 'indeed a most filthy race, a race sunk in vice, a race more ignorant than all other nations of the first principles of the Faith' (xix.), and yet, when not influenced by religious prejudices, he is a very valuable source, inasmuch as he was a contemporary of an obscure period of Irish history.

According to this authority, the Irish are not only inconstant, but perfidious. 'This race is inconstant, changeable, wily, and cunning. It is an unstable race, stable only in its instability, faithful only in its unfaithfulness' (v. 21, p. 166). The following sentence is characteristic: 'Their arts are, therefore, more to be feared than their arms, their friendship than their fire-brands, . . . their malignity than their martial spirit, their treachery than their open attacks, their specious friendship than their spiteful enmity' (*ib.*). Through this oratory, however condemning it may be, we can readily see that, in the main, Irish character of the 12th cent. was practically the same as that of the early Celt.

1. Marriage, immorality, etc.—On this subject, Giraldus is as severe as St. Jerome, for he asserts that the Irish 'do not contract marriages or shun incestuous connexions' (*ib.* v. 19, p. 164). 'Nay, what is more detestable,' he continues, 'in many parts of Ireland, brothers (I will not say marry) seduce and debauch the wives of their deceased brothers, and have incestuous intercourse with them' (p. 164 f.). Here, without doubt, the author is attacking the community of women which apparently continued to exist (see above, I. § 2). Elsewhere (v. 35, p. 181), he speaks of the Irish as 'gente adultera, gente incesta, gente illegitime nata et copulata, gente exlege.' Notwithstanding these statements, it is manifest that marriage continued to exist in Ireland in much the same form as in primitive times, from the following remark in the *Book of Leinster* (190, col. 27; O'Curry, *MS Mat.*, Dublin, 1861, p. 15): 'It is from this circumstance that in Erin it is the men that purchase the wives always: while it is the husbands that are purchased in all the rest of the world.' We have already seen the attitude of the *Senchus Mór* towards divorce. As for concubinage, suffice it to say that it continued unrestricted, especially among the higher classes (Joyce, ii. 12 f.). Until the reforms effected by Adamnán at the end of the 7th cent., female slaves were treated with the coarsest brutality (Stokes, *Tripartite Life*, London, 1887, Introd. p. xxii). Polygamy persisted even in Christian times. Dermot, who was king of Ireland from 544 to 565, had two queens (Joyce, ii. 7); and, a century later, Nuada the Sage, king of Leinster, also had two wives (*da banchéle* [Stokes, *Lives of Saints*, Oxford, 1890, p. 237]). Adultery, which was probably not very uncommon among the Irish at a later period (cf. Giraldus' account of the wife of Tiernan O'Rourke, king of Breifny, A.D. 1152, in his *Expugnatio Hibernica*, i. 225), was very severely punished. Cormac's *Glossary* (p. 59) derives *drúth*, 'prostitute,' from *dír*, 'right,' and *aod*, 'fire,' *i.e.* 'as much as to say to burn her were right.' In the story of Corc Mac Lugdach in the *Book of Leinster*, it is stated that 'it was the custom at first to burn any woman who committed lust (*dognid bais*) in violation of her compact' (*RCel* ii. [1873–75] 91). In the *Fotha Catha Cnucha*, 'Cause of the Battle of Cnucha,' Tadg, the Druid of Cond Cétchathach (king of Ireland from A.D. 122 to 157), wishes to have his daughter, Murni, burned for having eloped with Cumall (*ib.* p. 86). According to the Ancient Laws, children begotten illegitimately of a woman who had been abducted belonged to the woman's family, who might sell them if they chose (d'Arbois de Jubainville, *Cours*, vi. 312; *Anc. Laws*, iv. 231, 12, v. 357, 11, v. 439, 5). Under Christian influence, chastity and modesty come to be admired (Stokes, *Lives of Saints*, 239).

2. Cruelty.—A most ferocious act of cruelty is found in the story of the sons of Eochaid Muigmedoin, king of Ireland from A.D. 358 to 366 (*Book of Leinster*, 190, col. 3, line 1). When one of the sons, Fiachra, dies of the wounds received in the victory over the Munster-men, the fifty captives taken in the battle are buried alive round his grave. As this seems to be only an isolated account, it is quite probable that the custom was not much in vogue in ancient Ireland. Decapitation, however, is so frequently mentioned in the Irish saga that it is needless to cite examples. Carnage in battle is often designated *ár-cenn*, 'slaughter of heads' (not 'slaughter of chiefs,' as Stokes translates, *ZCP* iii. [1896] 207). Heads of dead enemies were carefully preserved by individuals, inasmuch as they attested the fact that the family obligation of killing the murderer who refused to pay compensation had been fulfilled (d'Arbois de Jubainville, *Cours*, v. p. xxx). Giraldus (*Expug. Hib.* iv. 233) states that, after the victory of Ossory (A.D. 1169),

'about two hundred of the enemies' heads were collected and laid at the feet of Dermitius, prince of Leinster, who, turning them over one by one, in order to recognize them, thrice lifted his hands to heaven in the excess of his joy, and with a loud voice returned thanks to God most High. Among them was the head of one he mortally hated above all the rest, and taking it up by the ears and hair, he tore the nostrils and lips with his teeth in a most savage and inhuman manner.'

3. Human sacrifice.—Although Joyce (i. 239) maintains that human sacrifice was not practised at all in Ireland, we have already called attention (above, I. § 6) to the account of the *Mag Slechta*, or 'Plain of Prostrations,' to which there is another reference in the account of Taillten (now Teltown, Co. Meath) in the *Dinnsenchus*, where it is stated that Patrick preached at the great fair there 'against the burning of the firstborn progeny' (Joyce, i. 281–284). This would be in accord with the Celtic law giving the father the right of life and death over his children (d'Arbois de Jubainville, *Cours*, vii. 244 f.; Cæsar, VI. xix. 3).

4. Courage.—Giraldus (*Top. Hib.* x. 150) states that the Irish 'go to battle without armour, considering it a burden, and esteeming it brave and honourable to fight without it'; and this accords with the accounts of the bravery of the early Celts as mentioned above. It may be noted here that among the Irish those soldiers who lacked courage were usually fettered in pairs, leg to leg, leaving them free in other respects. In A.D. 250, Lugaidh Mac Con, fearing defection among his Irish allies in his invasion of Ireland against Art Oenfer, supreme king of Ireland, had them fettered to the Britons; and at the Battle of Moyrath in A.D. 637, Congal, the leader of the rebels, resorted to the same measure (Joyce, i. 143 f.).

5. Intemperance.—In spite of the fact that Cormac's *Glossary* (p. 116) indicates that *mesci*, 'drunkenness,' implied 'more of reproach than sense,' intemperance was such a common vice that it is unnecessary to give examples here. We shall merely mention the *Mesca Ulad* in the *Book of Leinster* (ed. by Hennessy, *Proc. Roy. Ir. Acad.* [1889]), which is an account of a drunken raid against Munster. Giraldus (xxvii. 172) accuses even the Irish clergy of excessive indulgence in drink.

6. Hospitality.—As among the Gauls, hospitality was one of the principal virtues of the Irish. According to the *Senchus Mór*, chieftains were bound to entertain guests without asking questions (iv. 237); and elsewhere (iv. 337) cases are specified wherein a king may be excused for deficiency of food if an unexpected number of persons should arrive. The *Glossary* of Cormac (p. 66) gives the word *enech-ruice*, 'face-blush,' for shame at not being able to discharge the due rites of hospitality; and the *Senchus Mór* mentions a 'blush-fine' to be paid when one felt ashamed of the scantiness of his food (i. 123, 11). In accordance with this admiration for hospitality, free lodging-houses were established all over the country at a later date (Joyce, ii. 167).

7. Cupidity.—According to Giraldus, the Irish had a great love for gold, which they still coveted in a way that showed their Spanish origin ('aurum enim . . . quod adhuc Hispanico more sitiunt' [*Top. Hib.* x. 152]).

8. Discipline.—The Irish seem to have had a certain scorn for discipline in the field, and were in this respect much inferior to the Anglo-Normans (Joyce, i. 132); but the monks, on the contrary, were characterized by their unquestioning obedience (Adamnán, 343).

9. **Perfidy.**—In this respect, Giraldus is exceedingly severe on the Irish of his time.

'They are given to treachery,' he says, 'more than any other nation, and never keep the faith they pledged. Neither shame nor fear withholds them from constantly violating the most solemn oaths, which, when entered into with themselves, they are above all things anxious to have observed' (xx. 165); and he concludes: 'From an ancient and wicked custom they always carry an axe in their hands instead of a staff, that they may be ready promptly to execute whatever iniquity their minds suggest' (xxi. 165).

It is probably true that, because of the frequency of its requirement, the oath fell into disrepute, with the exception of that sworn on religious relics in Christian times (Giraldus, ii. 52–54, iii. 33 f.) and the one known as the *cró-cotaig*, or 'blood-covenant.' The latter consisted in drinking each other's blood, which they shed for this purpose (*ib.* iii. 22), and was absolutely binding. The kings of Ulidia and Ireland entered into a 'blood-covenant' in A.D. 598, when they united against Branduff, king of Leinster, at the battle of Dunbolg (*RCel* xiii. [1892] 73); and as late as 1703 this oath was so firmly respected in the western islands of Scotland that one who violated it utterly lost character (Martin, *Western Isles*, London, 1716, p. 109). In primitive times the oaths by the elements and by arms were the most revered (*Atlantis*, i. [1858] 371; Joyce, i. 383 f.).

10. **Chivalry.**—In spite of the accusation of perfidy borne against the Irish of later times, it is apparent from the early literature that they were little inclined to this vice. It is true that there are examples of those who did not hesitate to resort to ambush (*etarnaid*) or other stratagems in war, but these are rare. Thus in the battle between Aed Mac Ainmirech, king of Ireland, and Branduff, king of Leinster, the latter smuggled into Aed's camp 3600 oxen carrying large hampers, in each of which was concealed an armed man (Joyce, i. 140–142). But, on the other hand, according to O'Curry (*Manners and Customs*, Dublin, 1873, ii. 261), the Irish warriors never sought to conceal intended attacks, either letting their adversaries know beforehand or coming to an agreement with them. At the first battle of Moytura, the Firbolg king had to consent to the demands of the invaders for battle each day with equal numbers on both sides, although he had a much larger army (O'Curry, i. 238). Before the battle of Moylena, about the end of the 2nd cent., Owen-More, being hard pressed by Conn, the supreme king, sent to ask him for a truce of three days, which was granted (O'Curry, *Moylena*, p. 23); and in the year 1002, Brian Boru granted King Malachi a delay of a month in which to muster his forces (Joyce, *Short Hist. of Ireland*, Dublin, 1893, p. 208). So much for history. In literature we have the beautiful story of the two intimate friends Cúchulainn and Ferdiad, forced by circumstances to fight one another to death. During their duels they show each other great affection, and, when Ferdiad is slain, Cúchulainn falls on his body in great grief (O'Curry, *Manners and Customs*, ii. 415). A noble example of self-sacrifice is shown in the account of the death of Ailill, king of Connaught, in A.D. 549, for Columkille relates, in the *Annals of Ulster*, that, in order to protect his fleeing army from pursuit and slaughter, Ailill turned his chariot and plunged amidst his foemen, by whom he was slain.

11. **Vengeance.**—The Irish, like the Gauls, were always quick to avenge any insult. 'Woe to brothers among a barbarous race!' exclaims Giraldus (*Top. Hib.* xxiii. 167), 'Woe also to kinsmen! While alive, they pursue them to destruction; and even when dead they leave it to others to avenge their murder.' Every tribe had its *aire-échta*, or 'avenger of insults,' who was not slow in acting, as when Aengus of the Terrible Spear, the *aire-échta* of the Déise or Desii, killed in open court at Tara the son of king Cormac Mac Art who had insulted a woman of that tribe (Joyce, *Soc. Hist.* i. 92; see, further, BLOOD-FEUD [Celtic]).

12. **Slavery.**—It is evident that slavery existed in Ireland from very early times to a comparatively late date. There were three classes of serfs or non-free men, called the *bothach*, the *sencleithe*, and the *fuidir*. Of the *fuidir*, the lowest of the three classes, there were two kinds—the *sáer-fuidir*, or 'free *fuidir*,' and the *dáer-fuidir*, or 'bond *fuidir*,' the latter being escaped criminals, captives taken in war, convicts respited from death, and purchased slaves. That traffic in slavery was still very great in the 12th cent. is evidenced by Giraldus' account of the Synod of Armagh in 1170, which dealt with this question.

According to Giraldus (*Expug. Hib.* i. 18, p. 258), the Irish 'had long been wont to purchase natives of England as well from traders as from robbers and pirates, and reduce them to slavery. For it was the common practice of the Anglo-Saxon people, while their kingdom was entire, to sell their children, and they used to send their own sons and kinsmen for sale in Ireland, at a time when they were not suffering from poverty or famine.'

13. **Murder, etc.**—Murder is the principal topic in the Irish law, which means that it was probably the most common of crimes. Capital punishment, however, was known and practised only outside the courts. 'At this time,' says the writer of the commentary on the *Senchus Mór*, 'no one is put to death (by judicial sentence) for his intentional crimes as long as *éric* is obtained' (*Anc. Laws*, i. 15). But, if the family of the murderer wished to avoid the *éric*, they were required to give up the criminal to the family of the victim, who might then, if they pleased, kill him, or use him, or sell him as a slave (*ib.* iii. 69). Sometimes the murderer was drowned by being flung into the water, either tied up in a sack or with a heavy stone attached to his neck. It was thus that the Danish tyrant Turgesius was executed by King Malachi in A.D. 845 (Joyce, i. 211 f.). It should be noted that bodily harm as well as personal injury of any kind, such as a slight on character or an insult, was punishable by a fine called *díre*—a term that is very frequently used in the Ancient Laws. Furthermore, according to the Ancient Laws (v. 313), if a person wounded another or injured him bodily without justification, he, his family, or his clan was held responsible for 'sick-maintenance,' i.e. *othrus* or *folach-othrusa*, meaning the cost of maintenance until cure or death. There are seven different kinds of injury enumerated by law, which, if inflicted on a wife by her husband, gave her the right to separate from him (*Anc. Laws*, ii. 357, 359, 361, 381, 383).

14. **Old age.**—The respect for old age shown by the ancient Irish is praiseworthy. According to the Ancient Laws (iv. 373), 'the old man is entitled to good maintenance, and the senior is entitled to noble election' (O'Curry, *Manners and Customs*, ii. 30 f., 479, etc.). Furthermore, if the old person was destitute and had no children, it devolved upon his tribe to see to his wants; 'it is one of the duties of the *fine* (tribe) to support every tribesman' (*Anc. Laws*, iii. 55, 2; 57, 9).

15. **Idleness.**—Giraldus (*Top. Hib.* x.) states that the Irish of his time were a pastoral people, living like beasts. 'Abandoning themselves to idleness, and immersed in sloth, their greatest delight is to be exempt from toil, their richest possession the enjoyment of liberty' (*ib.* 152); and elsewhere (p. 173) he states that 'this people are intemperate in all their actions, and most vehement in all their feelings.' 'Thus the bad are bad indeed—there are nowhere worse; and than the good you cannot find better.' Finally, as for jealousy, in the opinion of Giraldus (*ib.* xxvi. 172), 'they are also prone to the failing of jealousy beyond any other nation.'

16. **Cleanliness.**—Giraldus speaks of a tribe of

Connaught 'who did not wear any clothes, except sometimes the skins of beasts, in cases of great necessity' (xxvi. 171). This was not true in the main, for the Irish, like the Gauls, took great pride in their personal cleanliness. The people bathed daily, usually in the evening (Joyce, ii. 185). Kings and chiefs were in the habit, even before battle, of bathing and anointing themselves with scented herbs (for references to baths, see *Ir. Texte*, i. 295, 6; *RCel* xiv. [1893] 417; Hull, *Cuchullin Saga*, London, 1898, p. 130, 12, etc.). According to the Ancient Laws (iv. 373), the head of a family who had retired because of age was to have a bath at least once every twentieth night, and his head was to be washed every Saturday. Long hair was much admired, and baldness was considered a serious blemish (O'Curry, *Manners and Customs*, ii. 144). Women dyed their nails crimson (*Ir. Texte*, i. 79, 11); men and women reddened their faces (Meyer, *RCel* xiii. 220); and oftentimes the women dyed their eyelids black (O'Curry, *MS Mat.*, 309, 595, 6). At table, they ate with their hands (*Vision of Mac Conglinne*, p. 64), though napkins were introduced as early as the 8th or 9th cent. (Zeuss, *Gramm. Celt.*², Berlin, 1871, pp. 653, 45), being called *lambrat*, or 'hand-cloth.'

III. *WELSH*.—The general conclusion that can be drawn from Giraldus (*Descrip. Kambriæ*, i. ch. 8, etc.) and other authorities is that in the 12th cent. the Welsh, like the Irish, were a warlike pastoral people, who were further advanced in matters of intellect than in regard to material prosperity and higher morality. Giraldus states further that, in his time, they were a wild and turbulent race, dangerous neighbours, and impatient of settled control from any quarter. Wynne, in his *History of the Gwydir Family* (Oswestry, 1878), shows how late these disorderly habits continued. According to Giraldus, the Welsh were a light and active people, entirely bred up to the use of arms (i. 8, p. 179). The serious defect of their character was evidently the continual litigation about land among themselves, and their tendency to resort to the common violence of trespassing on the lands of others, that of relatives not excepted.

'Hence arise suits and contentions,' says Giraldus (*ib.* ii. 4, p. 211), 'murders and conflagrations, and frequent fratricides, increased, perhaps, by the ancient national custom of brothers dividing their property amongst each other,' adding that the habit of princes of entrusting their children to the care of the principal men of the country was also the cause of 'frequent disturbances amongst brothers, terminating in the most cruel and unjust murders.'

1. Marriage, divorce, etc.—In regard to marriage, it may be stated at first that even in later times there were customs of a barbaric character which it is surprising to find surviving in a country where the Church had been established for many centuries (Rhys and Brynmor-Jones, *The Welsh People*, London, 1900, p. 212 f.). According to Giraldus (ii. 6, p. 213), the Welsh did not engage in marriage until they had tried, 'by previous co-habitation, the disposition, and particularly the fecundity, of the person' to whom they were engaged. As in Ireland, the marriage tie was loose, the wife having far greater freedom than was afforded to her by the law of the Church or by the English Common Law. Whenever the husband and wife separated, which they were allowed to do if one or both so desired, there was apparently no legal method by which they could be brought together again. The woman usually married very early—'from her fourteenth year unto her fortieth year she ought to bear children,' say the Ancient Laws (100, sec. 5); and after her marriage she enjoyed the greatest liberty—she might go 'the way she willeth freely, for she is not to be home-returning' (*ib.*). The Laws of Gwyned, or North Wales, recognize the influence of the Church as establishing the sanction of marriage, requiring legitimacy in the sons, and introducing a law of primogeniture in the succession to land which did not exist in the Irish system (Skene, *Celtic Scotland*², Edinburgh, 1890, iii. 198).

There were three good reasons for which the wife might separate from her husband without any loss of property: 'If he be leprous, or have fetid breath, or be incapable of marital duties' (*Anc. Laws*, 38, sec. 10). But, on the other hand, 'if a married woman committed any heinous crime, either by giving a kiss to another man, *vel praebendo se palpandum vel stuprandum*,' the husband could separate from her, and she forfeited all of her property rights (*ib.* 40, sec. 19). That this did not operate as a complete divorce, however, is obvious from the following passage in the Venedotian Code (*ib.* 40, sec. 17 f.): 'If the husband take another wife, after he shall have parted from the first wife, the first is free; but, if he part from his wife, and she be minded to take another husband, and the first husband should repent having parted from his wife, and overtake her with one foot in the bed and the other outside the bed, the prior husband is to have the woman.' But, if the wife left her husband and slept away from home for three nights during the first seven years of their marriage, and they separated at the end of the seventh year, she lost all right to her dower (*ib.* ii. sec. 9, p. 39). There is an article in the Venedotian Code (ii. sec. 70, p. 48) which shows the exceptional ease with which divorce was obtainable as well as the very great emphasis laid upon the dower: 'If a woman be given to a man, and her property specified, and the whole of the property had, except one penny, and that be not had, we say that the man may separate from her on that account, and she cannot reclaim any of her property; and that is the single penny,' the Law adds, 'that takes away a hundred.' Without entering into further details concerning divorce, it is obvious from the articles cited above that each party had a right of separation, exercisable without any liability, except a loss of *da* (possessions), varying with the time and circumstances of the parting (for further details, see *Anc. Laws*, pp. 38–50, etc.).

Polygamy was not permissible according to law, and the Venedotian Code states succinctly that 'no man is to have two wives' (*Anc. Laws*, ii. sec. 46, p. 54). As for the *jus primæ noctis*, suffice it to say that, if it was not exercised in Wales, we have at least an indication of it in the transmission of the purchase-price (*gobyr* or *amobyr*) by the bride's father into the hands of the king (*brenhin*) or lord (*arglwyd*) (*Anc. Laws*, p. 258 f.), this signifying that the right was bought back by the bride through her parent or guardian. The payment of this sum could not be avoided, for the Laws (iv. sec. 26, p. 405) state that, if a man asserted that a woman was pregnant by him and the woman denied it, nevertheless he should pay the *amobyr* of the woman to the lord.

2. Adultery.—Provisions against adultery were made at the time of the marriage, when the kindred or parent of the bride gave sureties that she would do nothing culpable against her wedded husband (Rhys and Brynmor-Jones, 211). After that, the restrictions were not severe, for the penalty imposed in the case of adultery was insignificant in comparison with that imposed for other crimes. According to the Dimetian Code (ii. sec. 18, p. 257), 'if a man commit adultery with the wife of another, he is to pay the husband his *saraad* ("disgrace-price") once augmented, because it engenders family animosity.' Apparently this was in the case of violence, for later on it is stated (p. 258, sec. 37) that a man who has committed adultery with the wife of another with her consent 'is to pay him (the husband) nothing while she is consenting; and, if the deed be notorious, the wife is to pay *saraad* to her husband, or the husband may freely repudiate her.'

It is sufficient to say that the Law did not consider this question a very serious one, for it states that, if a woman 'of full age' committed adultery with a man and was afterward deserted, 'upon complaint made by her to her kindred and to the courts, she is to receive, for her chastity, a bull of three winters having its tail shaven and greased, and then thrust through the door-clate; and then let the woman go into the house, the bull being outside, and let her plant her foot on the threshold, and let her take his tail in her hand, and let a man come on each side of the bull with goads to propel the bull; and if she can hold the bull, let her take it for her *wynebwerth* ('face-worth,' or fine for insult) and her chastity; and if not, let her take what grease may adhere to her hands' (*Anc. Laws*, p. 367, sec. 42). The penalty for adultery, like that for murder, was most frequently some kind of compensation paid by the man committing the act to the offended husband; for, according to the Law, there were three women whose husbands were not to have right from them for their adultery: 'one is a woman taken clandestinely; if she do what she may please with another man, she is not to do right to the man who took her clandestinely; the second is, a woman slept with as a concubine, and that publicly known; though she do what she may please, the man she slept with is to receive no right; the third is, a woman of bush and brake; her paramour is to receive no right from her, though she may commit fornication by taking another paramour' (*ib.* sec. 54, p. 260). Finally, if a man committed fornication with a virgin, the Law required that she be paid the compensation that he might have promised to give her (*ib.* sec. 9, 52).

3. **Incest.**—Although Giraldus speaks of this crime as most common among the Welsh, the only formal accusation that he brings against them is that they were not 'ashamed of intermarrying with their relations, even in the third degree of consanguinity,' which, he adds, was due principally to their 'love of high descent' (*Descrip. Kamb.* ii. 6, p. 213).

4. **Concubinage.**—Concubinage does not seem to have flourished to the same extent as in Ireland—possibly because of the greater freedom of the woman in the married state. In all probability the relations with the concubine were of short duration; for, if a woman lived with a man until the end of seven years, 'thenceforward,' says the Law, 'he is to share with her as with a betrothed wife' (sec. 31, p. 42).

5. **Prostitution.**—An important difference from the Irish system with regard to the regulations concerning prostitution is that if a 'female of grove and bush'—the common term for a prostitute—gave birth to a child, its father was obliged to rear it, for the Law (sec. 33, p. 42) enacted that she should not 'suffer loss on account of the man.' The same was true with regard to the household servant, with the addition that the man had to supply her master with another to take her place during her pregnancy (*ib.* ii. sec. 51, p. 45). Otherwise, the prostitute had no privilege; and, even if violence were committed upon her, she could not obtain compensation (*ib.* ii. sec. 80, p. 49).

6. **Abduction.**—Abduction was not dealt with seriously by the Law; for, if a man abducted a virgin, 'her lord and her kindred are to take her away from him, though it may annoy him'; but, if she were not a virgin, they could do nothing without her consent (*ib.* sec. 38, p. 44).

7. **Violence.**—That the punishment for violence or rape was castration is evident from the article in the Dimetian Code (ii. sec. 20, p. 255) which states that this regulation was not enacted in the law of Howel.

8. **Cruelty.**—According to Giraldus (*Descrip. Kamb.* ii. 8, p. 220), the Cymry gave no quarter in warfare, usually beheading their captives.

9. **Courage.**—The Welsh were a very patriotic and courageous people in the opinion of Giraldus (i. 8, p. 180):

'They anxiously study the defence of their country and their liberty; for these they fight, for these they undergo hardships, and for these willingly sacrifice their lives; they esteem it a disgrace to die in bed, an honour to die on the field of battle.'

They were so bold and ferocious that, when unarmed, they did not fear to encounter an armed force (*ib.*). Daring in their first onset, they were unable to bear a repulse, being easily thrown into confusion and flight; but, though defeated on one day, they were ever ready to resume the combat on the next, dejected neither by their loss nor by their dishonour. Unlike the Irish and the early Celts, they continually harassed the enemy by ambuscades and nightly sallies (Giraldus, ii. 3, p. 210). They were able and willing to sustain hunger and cold, showing great resistance against fatigue, and were not despondent in adversity—in fine, they were 'as easy to overcome in a single battle as difficult to subdue in a protracted war' (*ib.*).

10. **Intemperance.**—Though the Welsh were little inclined to drunkenness and gluttony at home, where they were accustomed to fast from morning till evening (Giraldus, i. 9, p. 182), they were immoderate in their love of food and intoxicating drinks whenever they found themselves surrounded with plenty (ii. 5, p. 212)—'as in times of scarcity their abstinence and parsimony are too severe, so, when seated at another man's table, after a long fasting (like wolves and eagles, who, like them, live by plunder, and are rarely satisfied), their appetite is immoderate.' The Ancient Laws prohibit the chaplain of the royal household, the judge of the palace, and the royal mediciner from ever becoming intoxicated, for 'they know not at what time the king may want their assistance' (ii. sec. 19, p. 215). The only other mention of inebriates in the Ancient Laws is where it is stated that they are not amenable to law, and that all their acts are invalid (pp. 389, 587, 604, 656).

11. **Hospitality.**—Giraldus (i. 10, pp. 182, 183) says:

'No one of this nation ever begs, for the houses of all are common to all; and they consider liberality and hospitality amongst the first virtues. When water is offered to travellers, if they suffer their feet to be washed, they are received as guests; for the offer of water to wash the feet is with this people an hospitable invitation. Those who arrive in the morning are entertained till evening, with the conversation of young women and the music of the harp. In the evening, when no more guests are expected, the meal is prepared according to the number and dignity of the persons assembled, and according to the wealth of the family which entertains. While the family is engaged in waiting on the guests, the host and hostess stand up, paying unremitting attention to everything, and take no food till all the company are satisfied; that, in case of any deficiency, it may fall upon them.'

12. **Piety.**—The Cymry were, at any rate outwardly, very religious. 'With extended arms and bowing heads' they asked blessing of every passing priest or monk, and they also showed 'greater respect than other nations to churches and ecclesiastical persons, and to the relics of saints which they devoutly revere' (Giraldus, i. 18, p. 203). According to the Ancient Laws (p. 301), religion was one of the seven legal qualities which a judge ought to possess.

13. **Pride.**—Proud and obstinate, the Cymry refused to subject themselves to the dominion of one lord and king (Giraldus, ii. 9, p. 225). They greatly esteemed noble birth and generous descent, so that even the common people retained their genealogy and could readily repeat the names of their ancestors back to the sixth and seventh generation (i. 17, p. 200).

14. **Perjury.**—According to Giraldus (ii. 1, p. 206), the Cymry were constant only in acts of inconstancy, cunning and crafty.

'They pay no respect to oaths, faith, or truth; and so lightly do they esteem the covenant of faith that it is usual to sacrifice it for nothing. They never scruple at taking a false oath for the sake of any temporary emolument or advantage; so that in civil and ecclesiastical causes, each party is ready to swear whatever seems expedient to its purpose.'

This was a necessary result of a legal system which made an oath an incident of ordinary transactions, and which multiplied the number of compurgators to an unusual degree, sometimes six hundred being required. So the trial depended on a complicated method of swearing and counter-swearing, each party concerned not by what he had actually seen or heard, but in standing by a kinsman in trouble (Rhys and Brynmor-Jones, 258).

15. **Murder.**—The principal indictment borne against the Welsh by Giraldus (ii. 7, p. 216) is that of murder and fratricide, and it is obvious from the lengthy treatment accorded to these crimes in the Ancient Laws that they were among the most frequent to be dealt with.

'They revenge with vehemence the injuries which may tend to the disgrace of their blood,' says Giraldus (i. 290), 'and, being naturally of a vindictive and passionate disposition, they are ever ready to avenge not only the recent but ancient affronts.' 'It is also remarkable that brothers show more affection to one another when dead than when living,' adds the same author elsewhere (ii. 4, p. 212), 'for they persecute the living even unto death, but revenge the deceased with all their power.' According to the Dimetian Code (*Anc. Laws*, p. 197), *galanas*, or murder, with its nine accessaries, is one of three columns of the law.

The important fact in regard to murder among the Cymry was whether the murderer killed a kinsman or not, for the slaying of a man outside one's community might or might not be counted for righteousness, but was not thought of as wrong. While no particular penalty was attached to the killing of a member of the same tribe, the murderer forfeited his rights of kinship, and became a *carl-lawedrog*, or a kin-wrecked man, which meant that he became an object of hatred and was obliged to flee. The cause for this was that in the tribal system the status of individuals depended upon the theory of blood-relationship. 'Since the living kin,' state the Ancient Laws (i. 791), 'is not killed for the sake of the dead kin, everybody will hate to see him.' It is worthy of note that, if an innocent man were accused of murder and neglected to seek justice, 'should he be killed on account of it, nothing is to be paid for him, though innocent' (*Anc. Laws*, p. 200, sec. 33). Furthermore, if a woman killed a man, she received the spear-penny; 'and this is the person who receives, but does not pay' (*ib.* p. 49, sec. 77).

16. Theft.—'This nation conceives it right,' remarks Giraldus (ii. 2, p. 207), 'to commit acts of plunder, theft, and robbery, not only against foreigners and hostile nations, but even against their own countrymen.' Theft (*lladrad*), with its nine accessaries, is one of the three columns of the law, according to the Dimetian Code (p. 197). Afterwards there is supplied a collection of rules relating to moveable property, as well as rules for the punishment of theft and interference with a man's right of possession. In the Ancient Laws, theft is distinguished from surreption, violence, and error (p. 124). Theft, or *lladrad*, is to take a thing in the owner's absence, with a denial of the act. Surreption, or *anghyfarch*, is to take a thing secretly, but without denial of the act. Violence, or *trais*, is to take a thing in a man's presence and against his will. Error, or *annodeu*, is everything that is taken instead of another, *i.e.*, taking a thing one had no right to possess, under the belief that one was acting legally. For error there was no particular fine, only a 'compensation payable to the person for his property' (*Anc. Laws*, p. 124). 'By the law of Howel,' continues the Venedotian Code (sec. 42, p. 123), 'for theft to the value of four pence, the thief is saleable; and, for a greater amount, forfeits his life,' but not his property, 'because both reparation and punishment are not to be exacted, only payment of the property to the loser' (sec. 44, p. 123). If seven pounds were paid by him or on his behalf, he was let off; if not, he was exiled; and, if he remained in the country beyond the time allowed—a day to pass through every *cantref* in the lord's dominions—he might lose his life unless some one bought him. There was no *galanas* (the sum assessed for homicide) for a thief, nor did the Law permit a feud between two kindreds on account of his execution (*ib.* sec. 47, p. 123). To accuse one of theft legally, it was necessary to have seen him with the thing stolen 'from daylight to twilight,' and to swear upon a *rhaith* ('verdict,' usually composed of from 5 to 300 compurgators [see COMPURGATION]) that the accusation was made not 'through hatred or animosity, or for worth, or for reward, but only to show the truth' (*ib.* sec. 21, p. 204). We can readily see, from the severity of the punishments administered, that theft was placed, because of its frequency, no doubt, on an equal basis with homicide.

17. Miscellaneous crimes.—The third 'column of the law,' according to the Venedotian Code, which, it may be said, was written about 1050, was arson (*tan*, 'fire'). The punishment for this was death (*Anc. Laws*, 302). Treason was also recognized by the Law, which states that 'no *galanas* is due for traitors to a lord' (*ib.* sec. 49, p. 124). The punishment was the forfeiture of the patrimonial rights (Rhys and Brynmor-Jones, 239). The third book of the Venedotian Code states with great minuteness the worth of different limbs and members of the human body, etc. As has been pointed out in CRIMES AND PUNISHMENTS (Celtic), the distinction between civil injuries (offences against an individual) and crimes (offences against the State or community) is not developed, though for many wrongful acts the lord had the right to exact fines called *dirwy* or *camlwrw*, and for some the criminal was sold, exiled, or put to death.

18. Sodomy.—Giraldus accuses the Cymry of 'that detestable and wicked vice of Sodom,' to which Mailgon, king of the Britons, and many others were addicted. And he adds that, if they abstained from that vice 'which in their prosperity they could not resist, it may be attributed more justly to their poverty and state of exile than to their sense of virtue' (ii. 6, p. 215). We find additional evidence of the existence of this crime in the Dimetian Code (p. 292), which states that the testimony of 'a person guilty of unnatural crime with man or beast' is of no effect in any case. It is possible that there is further reference to it in the Gwentian Code (sec. 10, p. 380), wherein it is stated that the third shame of a kindred is 'the despoiling of one's wife, being more pleased to spoil her than to be connected with her.'

19. Paternal authority.—The husband was the lord (*arglwyd*) of his household. If his wife uttered 'a harsh or disgraceful word' to him, she was obliged to pay him 'three kine as a *camlwrw*, for he is her lord.' But, if he preferred, he could 'strike her three blows with a rod of his cubit length, on any part he may will, excepting her head' (*Anc. Laws*, sec. 5, p. 252). Furthermore, he had the right of life and death over his children, except the son after the age of fourteen, when he was emancipated (d'Arbois de Jubainville, *Cours*, vii. 244 f., 3). In the 6th cent. St. Teliavus saved the lives of seven children whom the father, being too poor to feed them, had thrown one by one into a river (*Liber Landavensis*, Llandovery, 1840, p. 120). In the 11th cent. (Venedotian Code [*Anc. Laws*, sec. 22, p. 103]), it was common for a parent or kindred to deny a son in order to prevent him from receiving his patrimony. Finally, there were three things for which a wife could be beaten, according to the Venedotian Code, (sec. 39, p. 44), to wit, 'for giving anything which she ought not to give; for being detected with another man in a covert; and for wishing drivel upon her husband's beard.' If he chastised her for being found with another man, the Law did not permit him to have any other satisfaction, 'for there ought not to be both satisfaction and vengeance for the same crime' (*ib.*).

20. Immoderation, cleanliness, etc.—At the close of bk. i. of his *Descrip. Kamb.*, Giraldus, after stating that the Cymry were a quick, impulsive race, wanting in moderation, and indulging in extremes of conduct, resumes their moral portrait in the following manner: 'This nation is earnest in all its pursuits, and neither worse men than the bad, nor better than the good can be met with.' He notes also their wit and pleasantry. 'The heads of different families,' he says (i. 14, p. 190), 'make use of great facetiousness in their conversation; at one time uttering their jokes in a light, easy manner; at another time, under the disguise of equivocation, passing the severest censures.' They were famed for their 'boldness and confidence in speaking and answering, even in the presence of their princes and chieftains' (i. 15, p. 192). In rhymed songs and set speeches they were so subtle and ingenious that they produced 'ornaments of wonderful and exquisite invention, both in words and sentences' (*ib.*). They loved to boast of their strength, and exulted in their ancient name and privileges (ii. 7, p. 216). In regard to their jealousy, Giraldus states (i. 10, p. 183) that, 'as no nation labours more under the vice of jealousy than the Irish, so none is more free from it than the Welsh.' Finally, the same authority contrasts the Welsh with the Irish in regard to cleanliness (*Top. Hib.* iii. 10). There are frequent allusions to the bath in the Ancient Laws. Both sexes cut their hair short—close round to the ears and eyes (Giraldus, *Descrip. Kam.* i. 11, p. 185). They took special care of their teeth, which they rendered like ivory by constantly rubbing them with green hazel and then wiping them with a woollen cloth. The men shaved all their beard except the moustache (*ib.*). Their only garments were a thin cloak and tunic for all seasons of the year.

IV. *SCOTTISH.*—Fordun, who was favourably disposed toward the Gaelic Highlanders, offers the following moral portrait of them during the 13th cent., in contrast with that of the Teutonic Lowlanders. According to him (*Chron.* ii. 38; Skene, *Celtic Scotland*², Edinburgh, 1886–90, iii. 40),

'the Highlanders and people of the islands . . . are a savage and untamed nation, rude and independent, given to rapine, ease-loving, of a docile and warm disposition, comely in person but unsightly in dress, hostile to the English people and language, and, owing to diversity of speech, even to their own nation, and exceedingly cruel. They are, however, faithful and obedient to their king and country.'

The correspondence of a visitor in 1726 shows that after five centuries their character had little changed (Skene, iii. 324 f.). According to this authority, they esteem it the most sublime degree of virtue to love their chief and to pay him a blind obedience. Next to this is the love of the particular branch from which they sprang, and, in a third degree, of the members of the whole clan, whom they will assist, right or wrong, against those of any other tribe with which they are at variance. And, lastly, they have an adherence to one another as Highlanders, in opposition to the people of the Low country, whom they despise as inferior to them in courage, and whom they believe they have a right to plunder whenever it is in their power. During the first half of the 18th cent., half of the Highlanders passed an idle life, using blackmail as their main resource. Half of the men stole, in order that the other half might be employed in recovery (Lang, *Hist. of Scotland*, Edinburgh, 1902, iv. 375). If we compare this portrait with that traced by Dio Cassius of the Caledonii, or Northern Picts, we can readily see that time effected little change in their character. According to this authority, these tribes were a pastoral people, living principally by hunting. 'Naked and unshod, they had wives in common. They were great thieves, "looted most liberally" . . . and they were steady in combat' (Lang, i. 10).

1. Marriage.—In the early period, 'the sanctions of marriage were unknown, and a loose relation between the sexes existed' (Skene, iii. 138). Among the tribes of Northern Scotland, community of women was most frequent, and ten or twelve men—generally brothers or a father with his sons—had wives in common (Lang, i. 4). Annual marriage, or 'hand-fasting,' existed in the Highlands until the 16th century. According to this custom, two chiefs agreed that the son of one should marry the daughter of the other. If, at the end of a year and a day, the young wife had not yet given birth to a child, then they could separate, and each of the parties was permitted to marry again (Skene, *The Highlanders of Scotland*, ed. Macbain, London, 1904, p. 108 f.). The *jus primæ noctis* was exercised in Scotland from very early times; according to Buchanan (*Rerum Scoticarum Historia*, Utrecht, 1697, pp. 99, 200), it was abolished in the 11th cent. A.D. by King Malcolm III.:

'Uxoris etiam precibus dedisse fertur, ut primam novae nuptae noctem, quae proceribus per gradus quosdam lege regis Eugenii debebatur, dimidia argenti marca redimere possent, quam pensionem adhuc marchetas mulierum vocant' (C. J. L. Schmidt, *Jus Primæ Noctis*, Freiburg, 1881, p. 196).

The *merchet*, or 'maiden-fee,' which was paid to the superior on the marriage of the daughter of a dependant, is the equivalent of the *amobyr* or *gobyr* of the Welsh laws mentioned above (III. § 1; cf. Skene, *Celtic Scotland*, iii. 219).

2. Immorality.—Bede, who wrote about A.D. 687 or later, noted the immoral condition of the Scots (Lang, i. 72). In later times illegitimacy was prevalent amongst the royal family, the nobles, the clergy, and the people. Robert I., Robert II., Robert III., and James IV. had many natural children, and the Crown was much weakened by the large number of children whom Robert II. had by his two wives, besides many sons and daughters of illegitimate birth (J. Mackintosh, *Hist. of Civilization in Scotland*, Paisley, 1892–96, i. 428). Although, in 1528, Parliament attached a severe penalty to the crime of rape, it was often passed over with a very light punishment. Bigamy and adultery were common offences; and in 1551 Parliament enacted a measure which proposed severe penalties against them. Divorce was also extremely common among the upper classes (*ib.* ii. 229).

3. Intoxication, idleness, etc.—Drinking of liquor was always very common in Scotland, and Parliament passed numerous acts against this habit, but to no avail (Mackintosh, i. 415). During the 15th cent. the country was overrun with beggars and vagabonds, in spite of the efforts of Parliament to suppress them (*ib.* 422 f.).

4. Murder.—As in Ireland and Wales, there was a system of fines for homicide (Lang, i. 81; Skene, iii. 152 f.; Cosmo Innes, *Scotland in the Middle Ages*, Edinburgh, 1860, p. 192). Until the Reformation, murder and manslaughter were extremely prevalent throughout the Scottish kingdom; and, although many Acts of Parliament were passed for putting an end to these crimes, they seem to have produced little effect. When criminals were convicted, they were often pardoned, and so many pardons were granted that in 1487 Parliament was obliged to interfere (Mackintosh, i. 425, ii. 228).

5. Theft.—Gildas, who wrote about 560, calls the Picts 'a set of bloody freebooters with more hair on their thieves' faces than clothes to cover their nakedness' (Lang, i. 15). In the 12th and 13th centuries, if we believe Fordun (*Chron.* iv. [ed. 1872, ii. 251]), the native population would not, for either prayers or bribes, either treaties or oaths, leave off their disloyal ways, or their ravages among their fellow-countrymen. In the 15th cent. theft and cattle-raiding were the most frequent crimes, against which Parliament acted in vain (Mackintosh, i. 427 f., ii. 228).

See, further, the 'Celtic' sections of CHILDREN, CRIMES AND PUNISHMENTS, etc.

LITERATURE.—This has been sufficiently indicated in the article.

JOHN LAWRENCE GERIG.

ETHICS AND MORALITY (Chinese).—If we are to write of Chinese ethics, we must have in view only the ethics of the Confucian school; for China has no other system. These moral laws, rules, and principles are found embedded in the classical literature which for ages past has formed the one subject studied by every scholar throughout the length and breadth of China. Not only are they accepted without question by all Chinese, educated and uneducated, but they have helped to mould the social life of the people, and have coloured and influenced the national legislation and administration. As religions, Taoism and Buddhism have established themselves by the side of Confucianism, doubtless because they better satisfy that desire for something beyond the present life which is so common and so natural to the human mind; but the morality which they inculcate is entirely borrowed from the Confucian system.

Though **Confucius** has given his name to a school, he did not claim to have founded one. He said of himself, probably with much truth, that he was 'a transmitter and not a maker, believing in and loving the ancients' (*Confucian Analects*, vii. 1). Of an eminently prosaic and practical turn of mind, he was never weary of describing the characteristics of virtue or of drawing distinctions between right and wrong in actual life; but he cared little to speculate on the nature of the moral faculty or any such questions. We know, however, that he considered virtue to be a mean between two extremes, to which some fail to attain, while others go beyond it; and he held the fault of excess to be as bad as that of deficiency (*Conf. An.* vi. 27, xi. 15; *Doctrine of the Mean*, iii., iv.).

These ideas are elaborated in the treatise called *The Doctrine of the Mean*, which contains many quotations of Confucius' words, and is believed to have been written by his grandson. The treatise further declares that man receives his nature from heaven, and, when he acts in accordance with his nature, he is following the proper path, from which he must not wander for an instant (*op. cit.* i. 1–3). Here we find a principle disclosed, concerning which Confucius never expressed himself with definiteness, but which for many generations occupied the minds of his followers more than any other question in ethics, namely, that the nature of all men at their birth is perfectly good.

The doctrine of the goodness of human nature had its most powerful advocate in **Mencius**, the greatest of all the learned men who owned Confucius for their master. In his day a certain philosopher, Kao by name, urged that man's nature is neither good nor bad; but any one may be led to practise either good or evil, just as water, when one makes a hole for it to escape by, has no preference for east or west, but will flow in either direction indifferently. Not so, replied Mencius, when asked his opinion as to this: though water is indifferent to the points of the compass, its tendency is to flow downwards, and only by force can it be made to rise; so the tendency of man's nature is towards what is good, and doing evil is unnatural to him (Mencius, vi. pt. i. 2). Then another theory was brought to his notice—that the nature of some men is good and that of others bad. To this he makes answer with a more serious argument. In saying that man's nature is good, his meaning, he explains, is that 'from the feelings proper to it, it is constituted for what is good'; and, if men do evil, it is not the fault of their natural powers. Every one has the feelings of pity, of shame, of reverence, of approval and disapproval, *i.e.* of appreciating right and wrong. Thus, as he said on another occasion, every one, no matter who, will feel alarmed and distressed if he suddenly sees a child on the point of falling into a well. And this will be a genuine sensation; it will not be merely that he desires to gain either the friendship of the child's parents or the approbation of his own friends, nor yet that he dislikes seeming to be callous. Hence it will be evident that there is no man without the feeling of pity; and it is the same with regard to the other feelings (*ib.* vi. pt. i. 6, ii. pt. i. 6). Mencius further held that a few sages had existed who lived perfect lives; and other men might be like them if they chose, for a perfect life consisted in simple acts which every one was physically able to perform. It was not that men could not do these acts, but simply that they did not do them. People were led into evil because they allowed themselves to be influenced by surrounding circumstances; thus, for instance, in years of plenty the common folk were mostly well-behaved, but in time of dearth they became lawless (*ib.* vi. pt. ii. 2, vi. pt. i. 7).

Though the doctrine of Mencius has found final acceptance among the Chinese, it was not left unchallenged at first. Soon after Mencius' time a distinguished scholar, named **Hsün Ching**, maintained with much force that human nature is evil. He appealed to experience to show that men are not good spontaneously, and that they are made so only by teaching and by the laws. Eyes can see, ears can hear, naturally; they do not need instruction to enable them to do it; but men acquire righteousness only by learning and hard effort. Again, when a man is tired or hungry, his natural feelings prompt him to rest or to eat: if, instead of yielding to them, he gives place to his father or an elder, he acts rightly, but it is against his natural inclination. Indeed, the mere fact that a man *wishes* to do right shows that righteousness is not natural to him.[1]

There remained one more theory to be brought foward—that our nature is partly good and partly evil. This was upheld by the philosopher **Yang Hsiung**, who lived about the time of the Christian era. He taught that man's progress in either direction depends on the development of the good or the bad part of his nature, according as he is influenced by his environment.

Besides *The Doctrine of the Mean*, among the recognized Chinese classics there is another ethical work, known as *The Great Learning*, of which the subjects are the practice of virtue and the art of governing. This treatise, which is extremely short, is most highly praised by the Chinese for its profound wisdom, and is perhaps admired by them beyond all their other canonical books. Modern authorities ascribe its opening and fundamental chapter to Confucius himself; but for more than fifteen hundred years, probably with greater correctness, it was held to be by another hand. In any case it is substantially in accord with Confucius' views, and must have been written not long after his time. At its commencement is a description of what was said to be the process adopted by the ancient princes for promoting virtue throughout the Empire:

> 'With this object they were careful to govern well their own States. In order to govern well their States, they first regulated their own families. In order to regulate their families, they first practised virtue in their own persons. In order to arrive at the practice of virtue, they first rectified their hearts. In order to rectify their hearts, they first sought for sincerity of thought. In order to obtain sincerity of thought, they first extended to the utmost their knowledge. The extension of knowledge lay in the investigation of things.'[2]

The process thus consists of a succession of steps, by the first part of which the individual may arrive at personal virtue, and by the second

[1] Legge, *Chinese Classics*, vol. ii. [1895] p. 79.
[2] Legge, *op. cit.* vol. i. [1893] p. 357; W. A. P. Martin, *Lore of Cathay*, p. 211.

part, the individual being a ruler, virtue may be promoted throughout the land. What is to be understood by the first step of all, the 'investigation of things'? According to the greatest of Chinese commentators, it means 'investigating the principles of all things with which we come in contact' (*Great Learning*, Com. v. 2). This, verily, is no small task to impose upon the seeker after virtue. The third step, sincerity of thought, is explained as being a sincere desire for, and instinctive following of, the good, not a mere doing of what is right from inferior motives (*ib.* vi.). But there seems to be little distinction between this and the next step, rectification of the heart. In the later portion of the chain, one notices how good government is made to spring from the personal excellence of the ruler. This was a favourite point with Confucius, who repeatedly insisted on the necessity of a good example being set by those who govern. Once, when asked by a certain ruler how to deal with the prevalence of robbery, he went so far as to reply: 'If Your Excellency were not covetous, your people would not rob, though you paid them to do it' (*Conf. An.* xii. 19).

It was as a teacher of practical morality that Confucius won his fame. But he left no treatise on the subject; nor did he ever handle it systematically. We have from him merely a quantity of disconnected utterances, which were collected and recorded by his followers or appear as quotations in later writers. The Confucianists hold that there are five virtues (*tê*), or that virtue consists of five parts: *jên* (charity), *i* (righteousness), *li* (propriety), *chih* (wisdom), *hsin* (sincerity). Perhaps the best idea of the sage's teaching will be given by grouping under these heads a few specimens of his more important sayings.

(1) *Jên*—the virtue of man's relation to man, charity (in St. Paul's sense), benevolence, humanity. The descriptions given by Confucius of this quality vary according to the occasion and the questioner. The most concise is that it is 'to love all men' (*Conf. An.* xii. 22); the most elaborate, that it consists in the practice, without intermission, of respectfulness, indulgence, sincerity, earnestness, and kindness (*ib.* xvii. 6). To another inquirer it was said to be found in reverence and the observance of the Golden Rule—'not to do unto others what you would not wish done to yourself.' This great rule is repeated several times by him, and once he gave it as sufficient alone to serve as a guide for one's whole life (*ib.* xii. 2, xv. 23). A man may be pure, be loyal, be capable, and yet not worthy of being called *jên*: Confucius disclaimed for himself any right to be so considered (*ib.* v. 7, 18, vii. 33). Charity is founded on filial piety and fraternal submission; and, if rulers behave properly to their relatives, the people will be roused to charity (*ib.* i. 2, viii. 2).

(2) *I*—righteousness, justice, duty. This is specially the virtue of public life. Thus, to refuse to serve one's country is a failing in duty (*ib.* xviii. 7). The prince must be just in laying burdens upon his people; if he be so, they will willingly submit to his rule (*ib.* v. 15, xiii. 4). If righteousness be absent, courage only leads men of high position into rebellion, and those of low position into brigandage (*ib.* xvii. 23). Without righteousness, riches and honour are but a floating cloud (*ib.* vii. 15).

(3) *Li*—propriety, combining with it an idea of ceremoniousness. It is worth nothing without charity; it must be accompanied by reverence; and it does not consist in gorgeous array (*ib.* iii. 3, 26, xvii. 11). If it be absent, respectfulness will become clumsiness, carefulness become timidity, boldness become insubordination, and straightforwardness rudeness (*ib.* viii. 2). Without a knowledge of propriety a man's character cannot be established; and combined with study it will keep one from erring (*ib.* viii. 8, xii. 15).

(4) *Chih*—knowledge, wisdom. The most important kind of knowledge is the knowledge of men (*ib.* xii. 22). A man ought to know what heaven commands (*i.e.* what is right and what is wrong); he should also know the rules of propriety; and, thirdly, he should know language, in order to estimate the character of those who speak with him (*ib.* xx. 3). When one knows a thing and recognizes that one knows it, when one does not know a thing and recognizes that one does not, that is real knowledge (*ib.* ii. 17). Attempts to acquire virtue will fail if not accompanied by study (*ib.* xvii. 8). One should learn for the sake of one's own improvement, not to win approbation (*ib.* xiv. 25). To study without thinking is labour lost; thought without study is dangerous (*ib.* ii. 15). Confucius once said: 'I have passed the whole day without eating and the whole night without sleeping—occupied with thinking; it was of no use: the better plan is to study' (*ib.* xv. 30). But, after all, knowledge of the truth is not equal to the love of it; and the possessor of literary acquirements is a useless man if he be devoid of practical ability (*ib.* vi. 18, xiii. 5).

(5) *Hsin*—sincerity, truthfulness, belief. The necessity of this virtue is inculcated in many passages. Faithfulness and sincerity should be one's first principles; without truthfulness no man can get on (*ib.* i. 8, ii. 22). In intercourse with friends, one must above everything be sincere; and it is disgraceful to pretend friendship with a man whom one dislikes (*ib.* i. 4, v. 24). Sincerity is one of the requirements of a ruler (*ib.* i. 5).

As we have seen above, Confucius, living in the 6th cent. B.C., inculcated the Golden Rule of our Saviour, which has been described as 'the most unshaken rule of morality, and foundation of all social virtue.' On the other hand, there is one well-known instance where he distinctly falls short of the standard of Christian benevolence. When asked what was his opinion as to the repayment of injury with kindness, he replied, 'With what then will you repay kindness? Repay injury with justice, kindness with kindness' (*ib.* xiv. 36). On another occasion, also, in reply to an inquirer, he declared that, in the case of the murder of a parent, the son must be ready to slay the murderer whenever and wherever he may meet him. This conversation is no doubt authentic, though it does not rest on such a high authority as the *Analects*.

Filial piety cannot be left unmentioned by any one dealing with Chinese ethics. It is often coupled by Confucius with the somewhat similar, but less important, fraternal affection or submission which a younger brother owes to an elder. These two duties formed the corner-stone of both the ethical and the social system of Confucius. For in his view, not only are they the foundation of charity, the greatest of all the virtues, but it is by practising them that the people learn to be obedient to the government and the laws. Filial piety is said to consist in serving parents, when alive, according to propriety, and, when they are dead, in burying them according to propriety and in sacrificing to them according to propriety. Reverence and willingness in service are requisite; mere performance of duties is not enough (*ib.* ii. 5, 7–8).

The *worship of ancestors*, that great offshoot from filial piety, was, as practised by Confucius, merely a commemorative rite. There is no sanction from his authority for its more objectionable features at the present day, namely, the transformation of the deceased into tutelary deities, and the absurd doctrine that the fortunes of a family are determined by the location of its tombs.[1] One charge which foreign critics have not been slow to make against ancestor-worship is that it sanctions and encourages concubinage. There is truth in this. In China the practice of taking concubines is extremely common among the wealthy; but persons of strict morality view it with disapprobation, except where a wife is not likely to bear a son. In such a case the necessity of having male descendants to continue the ancestral sacrifices, in the opinion of all Chinese, completely justifies concubinage, even though it is possible to avoid the practice by the introduction into the family of an adopted child.

LITERATURE.—The Chinese 'Four Books': (i.) The *Lun Yü*, or *Analects of Confucius*; (ii.) Mencius; (iii.) The *Ta Hsüo*, or *Great Learning*; (iv.) The *Chung Yung*, or *Doctrine of the Mean*. The best translations of these are by Legge (*Chinese Classics*, vols. i., ii., Oxford, 1893, 1895). With the translations there are prolegomena and exegetical notes of great value. See, further, E. Faber, *The Doctrines of Confucius*, Hongkong, 1875; J. J. M. de Groot, *The Relig. System of China*, Leyden, 1892 ff.; W. A. P. Martin, *The Lore of Cathay*, Edinburgh, 1901.

T. L. BULLOCK.

ETHICS AND MORALITY (Christian).—I. *HISTORY*.—There is no formal science of Ethics in the NT. The presence of a life-giving Personality, the Source and Norm of Christian Teaching, is dominant. His teaching is not limited to His spoken words; it is an ever-present continuous work. This is taken for granted by the NT writers. Hence we can speak of a real progress in Christian thought concerning conduct. Because Christ is the Fulfiller of Hebrew revelation, the OT is of special, though subordinate, value. As Christianity spread to Græco-Roman soil, Christians, because of their cosmic view of Jesus' Person, appropriated from their new surroundings whatever helped their spiritual life. The history of Christian morality is thus a record of how the Spirit of Christ has been endeavouring to redeem all life to its own service, and the record is still unfinished.

The *Didache*, the *Epistle of Barnabas*, and the Apostolic Fathers show the predominance of the religious-ethical interest, but the beginnings of legalism and externalism are also manifest (*Pastor* of Hermas). The dogmatic interest gradually submerged the ethical; and ascetic withdrawal from the world and superiority of knowledge to faith introduced a division of labour into morality. Hence the distinction between *honestum* and *utile*, between *consilia* and *mandata*.

In Clemens Alexandrinus, and in Ambrose in the West, the ideas and terminology of Hellenism are influential. The organized Church became a law-giving source (Cyprian), and legalism suppressed spiritual spontaneity. The recognition of Christianity by the State deepened this influence. In Justin, Clement, and the Alexandrians generally we see the rationalistic and inclusive tendency of Christian thinking; in Tertullian and the West, its legalistic and exclusive tendency. Notwithstanding the recognition of asceticism, virginity, baptism, and the Eucharist as means of salvation, there existed a vigorous new life of brotherly love and martyr courage.

Augustine is the greatest of the early moralists. His conversion had supreme influence on his teaching. In him are found the germs of the various mediæval tendencies. His teaching on sin and grace, on the Church and on conversion, on God as Highest Good, and on virtue as *ordo amoris*, influenced not only Gregory the Great, Isidore of Seville, and more especially Aquinas, but also the preachers of repentance, the Mystics and Quietists.

The Middle Ages elaborated classifications of sins and virtues, discussed the freedom of the will (Thomists and Scotists), and were rich in casuistic and penitential books. Petrus Lombardus' 3rd book of *Sentences* was an influential moral treatise. Aquinas summed up mediæval teaching. In him the terminology and thought of Aristotle supply the foundation for evangelical Ethics, and the distinctiveness of Christian morality is regarded as a revealed overplus to the Ethics of the world.

A new era began with the Reformation. Faith became personal trust in God, the value of the individual was recognized, and ordinary vocations were regarded as the true sphere of moral life. But its greatest work was the placing of the Scriptures in the hands of the common people. Problems as to the relation of the individual to the State, and of the State to the Church, now arose. There was also a tendency to separate philosophical and Christian Ethics (Melanchthon and Keckermann), though Amesius insisted on Ethics as purely theological. The Counter-Reformation produced Jesuistic casuistry (*q.v.*)—against vigorous individual protests (Pascal). The verbal inspiration theory of Scripture developed in the post-Reformation period a new dogmatism, and Christian Ethics was a part of Dogmatic. The merit of having separated the two is usually ascribed to Danæus and Calixtus.

While Rom. Cath. Ethics largely followed tradition and casuistic refinement in dealing with 'cases,' Protestant Ethics tended to be moulded, from this time onwards, by the current philosophies, and, within the various Churches, by the authorized Confessions of Faith.

Rationalism and Deism (Wolf, Lessing, English Deists) made reason supreme, and the source of indubitable truths; Christianity was an awkward republication of innate moral principles.

Theories as to the origin of the moral sense, natural rights, and sanctions exclusively interested moralists. Biblical Ethics was neglected or confused through the equal valuation of the OT and the NT. Butler deserves mention, because of his insistence on conscience; but it was Kant who routed rationalism and individualistic utilitarianism. Hegel objectified morality in the customs and institutions of the community, and may be regarded as the father of modern socialism. His influence tended to make the Church a part of the State and to intellectualize and externalize morals. Schleiermacher laid stress on the distinctiveness of the Christian consciousness, and on the value of feeling; he occupies in modern Christian Ethics the place that Kant occupies in the philosophical. Rothe is largely influenced by him; Martensen occupies a mediating position; while I. A. Dorner is speculative and Biblical. The Ritschlian school aims at safeguarding the Christian ethical values—against the scepticism of history, the conservatism of dogma, and the lack of finality introduced by science.

The influence of the inductive sciences and of evolution raised questions as to the origin of conscience, and attempts were made to explain morality genetically and associationally. The question of origin is, however, distinct from that of value. The historical study of Scripture has cleared up difficulties in the Ethics of the OT, and has enabled moralists to distinguish between principles and their historical setting in the NT, while it has helped to reveal the distinctiveness of the Christian life. Dogmatic disputes called forth protests in favour of an ethical basis for united action in dealing with grave social problems (Ethical Societies). The Unitarian school emphasized the supremacy of conduct over dogma, and can claim many distinguished names in the ethical field. The various revivals of religion made prominent the power of Christianity in renewing life, and at

[1] W. A. P. Martin, *op. cit.* pp. 269, 277.

present the stress is laid on the psychology of the Christian moral life and the supremacy of the will, while it is also felt that education and State control can do not a little to develop and safeguard morality.

Till recently there was a general tendency even among non-Christians to regard the moral teaching of Jesus as perfect, as far as individual life was concerned, though defective on its social and political side. Lately this has been denied from without and within (Nietzsche and the *Interimsethik* school), on different grounds. Christian moralists are coming to see that the Christian life is bound up with the Christian revelation, and that the ideas of philosophic Ethics or historical theories must not be used so as to crush out the distinctive vitality of the Christian life of faith. Recognition of spiritual facts is more valuable than systematic completeness, and defective views of Christ's Person are found to revenge themselves on Christian morals.

II. *DEFINITION AND SCOPE.*—(*a*) Christian Ethics, analytically defined, is the science which deals with (1) what the Christian man (individual and social) should desire and what he should avoid (*summum bonum*), (2) what he ought and ought not to do (Duty), and (3) what moral power is necessary to attain end and accomplish duty (Virtue). The Christian life, however, is an organic continuum, and any analysis of its contents must be to some extent artificial; but, if we guard against overlapping and repetition due to this trichotomy, we may, for clearness of exposition, adopt it. [Schleiermacher, Paulsen, and A. J. Dorner adopt this analysis for philosophic Ethics; Rothe, Lange, Krarup, and others, for Christian Ethics.]

(*β*) Classificatorily viewed, Christian Ethics is defined by its place in the theological encyclopædia, its boundaries delimited, and its organic relations with the totality of Christian thinking determined (Flint, art. 'Theology,' in *EBr*[9]; cf. artt. in theological encyclopædias). We cannot do more here than mention this way of looking at the science. The present age is anti-dogmatic and anti-metaphysical, and the central position of Christian Ethics, as of Ethics in general, is more and more recognized. This tendency is against confessional and dogmatical Ethics. Men ask rather, 'How much must we believe to live the Christian life?' (Krarup). Christian Ethics, however, presupposes the Christian revelation—the matrix alike of both Ethics and Dogmatics—and is organically bound up with it (see Findlay, *Fernley Lectures*, London, 1894, for a fine treatment of Christian Ethics from this point of view).

(*γ*) The science may be defined also by comparison and contrast with other views of life. Some views of life are inimical to Christian morality, others are preparatory and propædeutic. The task of the Christian moralist is in this region wider to-day than was that of Clement or Tertullian, Augustine or Aquinas, Melanchthon or Calvin, because, thanks to the vast missionary labours of modern times, new systems of life have come before the mind of Christendom. As a practical science, Christian Ethics must take note of earnest ethical speculation, both past and present, outside the Christian Church. In this way it becomes conscious of itself and of the magnitude of its evangelistic task. The analytic method adopted here is not exclusive of the others, though different from them.

1. Christian virtue.—Under this heading we deal (1) with the objective, (2) with the subjective, dynamic of the Christian life.

(1) *The objective dynamic of the Christian life.*—What is needed to initiate Christian morality is not ethical synthesis (Plato), or discipline (Aristotle), or inhibitive control (Stoics), or culture (Goethe), or development (Spencer), or 'the fulfilment of a capability given in human nature itself' (Green), but creation. All the others are needed once we get a beginning; but a beginning is imperative, otherwise man is left within the circle of his own impotence. It is because ethical systems often neglect this that the Christian thinker feels dissatisfied with them. 'It is their main defect not that they conflict with Christianity, but that they fail to touch the problem with which it most directly deals' (Wace, *Boyle Lectures*, v. [ser. 1], 1874–75, cited in *Lux Mundi*, p. 504). The same objection applies to the Ethics of Rabbinic Judaism, where the highest good depends on works, without any real reference to the grace of God (Oesterley, 'Grace and Free will,' *Expos.*, Nov. 1910). The objective dynamic of Christian Ethics is the Holy Spirit, or God exerting moral creative power. The Holy Spirit is not simply the immanent Spirit of God, as that is generally viewed. Its character is revealed and its power acts through Jesus. A great novel activity of God has been manifested in the earthly life of Jesus, consummated in His death, and exhibited as completed in His resurrection, which makes the beginning of specific ethical Christian experience possible. Hence Christianity is a gospel of God (even as an ethical system), not the product of man's working or thinking, but an offer of life impinging on man for acceptance. Christian moral experience, then, takes for granted the Holy Spirit of God uniting His help to our weakness (Ro 8[26]). Christian Ethics is thus primarily neither individual nor social, but theological, and that in a specific sense. Any other ethical basis is synthetically incomplete. 'Ethics must either perfect themselves in religion, or disintegrate themselves into Hedonism' (Martineau, *Study of Religion*[2], 1889, i. 24). The Holy Spirit is viewed here not dogmatically, but as a condition of ethical power.

(*a*) *Relation of the Holy Spirit to human freedom.*—Christian Ethics, like Ethics in general, postulates freedom in the sense that man is not moved simply by instinct or impulse, but can choose between presented alternatives, that his choice depends on himself—at least, as far as to make him responsible for it. Christian Ethics admits freedom in this sense, but it recognizes as a fact of historic experience the moral impotence of man and the necessity of the gift of the Holy Spirit.

(*α*) This gift is a moral one, because its acceptance is based on a receptive response by the human spirit. However deadened the human πνεῦμα may be, in this region the Holy Spirit has its point of appeal. Thus the offer is to all men irrespective of class, disposition, temperament, or past history. It is just the love of God attempting to gain the human heart, and so the Spirit is not an alien power, but the very substratum of the human personality. Before this offer the Stoic distinction of the wise man and the fool, the Aristotelian cleavage between free men and slaves, vanish; the dubiety as to whether virtue can be taught and the bad man made good disappears. This is not simply because the moral ideal has been realized in Jesus, but because the Holy Spirit is offered to man as man.

(*β*) The gift is moral also, because the offer implies a task. We are to work out our own salvation with fear and trembling. Things are not 'offered to our acceptance but to our acquisition' (Butler, *Analogy*, ch. iv. [p. 75 in Bernard's ed., London, 1900]). The task set before men is now a greater one than ordinary Ethics conceives. The demands made on human responsibility are higher than ever before. The moral life is not first a gift and then a task, but from beginning to end these two moments are combined in one real human experience. Christian Ethics, then, does not desire to disparage man's freedom, to overlook his natural virtues and regard them as *splendida vitia*. The question before us is the practical one of how man can begin the attaining of Christian perfection, and of how the race of man can start embodying in itself the Kingdom of God. It is the old question of ἀκρασία, which Plato practically denied, and which Aristotle found a surd in his thinking. In this initiation men historically have failed, and a new activity of God was necessary to meet the bankruptcy of human effort. This is the gospel, which is not the destruction of freedom, but its re-creation.

(*b*) *The Holy Spirit and conscience.*—Christian Ethics also postulates conscience in the sense that man distinguishes between one action as good and another as bad, one conduct as right and another as wrong, and that the good and right ought to be done and the bad and wrong avoided. What conscience needs is the certainty that its laws are those of the absolutely good, and that its judgments are not simply critical but constitutive of conduct. It needs to be freed from its own bewildering perplexity, as freedom needs rescuing from moral impotence. To Christian Ethics, history is a resultant of two moments—one the Divine purpose, the other human free actions; and, as far as the former is concerned, history is a training and a test of conscience. Conscience is thus historically made aware of its own worth (Stoicism and elsewhere), and brought to an impasse when its vision is focused on itself alone. It may act as human before it is discovered to be Divine (cf. Martineau, *op. cit.* i. 22), but it needs to make this discovery. To St. Paul it was one function of the Law and of pagan experience to bring about the ἐπίγνωσις ἁμαρτίας (Ro 3^{20} 7^{7-13}, Gal 3^{19-22}). Through the love of God seen in the death of Jesus this happened. Conscience discovered its own divinity, its 'range of sensibility' was infinitely extended, its perplexity abolished, its aberrations condemned. Its authority was placed in the bosom of God Himself, its fear purified in the tragic tenderness of a Redeemer crucified for sin, and its hope rekindled in the free offer of God's saving love. Thus the enthusiasm necessary for the generating as well as for the safe-guarding of virtue arose, and conscience and freedom were emotionally reconciled, the one enlightened as to its true function, the other set free to carry out its real purpose. The two great questions, 'What must I do to be saved?' and 'What ought I to do after I am saved?' are now answered. The Holy Spirit does not disregard conscience, but, on the contrary, enthrones it.

(*c*) *The Holy Spirit and varieties of temperament and conditions.*—Christian Ethics recognizes the infinite variety of human conditions and temperaments.

(α) There is a class which cannot accept *ab initio*, through a personal moral act, the saving power of God. To the demoniacs our Lord had to apply βασανισμός before moral relations between God and the sufferer could be established. Here we cannot theorize so as to attribute personal responsibility in all cases, yet we are not altogether helpless. Intercessory prayer is open, and it is not without power. Perhaps the name of Jesus is of greater power than we realize (cf. Nevius, referred to by Ramsay, *Expos.*, Feb. 1912). Christian Ethics is not without hope even here.

(β) There are many, in all civilized countries even, who have bartered much of their power of response to the Divine through their own sin, or through the pressure of social evil upon them, or through both. In all such cases the Christian moralist must search for some point of receptive response and seek to remove all hindrances. The appeal of Christianity should be made unreservedly. Responsibility depends on and is proportionate to opportunity, and it is the duty of Christians to present opportunity to all—to heathen, to depraved, to children—through education and training, for the Spirit of God works through means. Hence our Lord healed bodies for the sake of the spirit, fed the hungry in order to reach their souls, and cast the seed of His word everywhere.

(γ) The varieties of temperament are not accidental, but, proleptically viewed, fields of opportunity for the exercise of the manifold Spirit of God, natural bases for its varied *charismata*. Thus the gift of the Holy Spirit is ethically conditioned, not generally, but specifically and individually. Different individuals and different nations have thus been prepared for Christianity, and their varied gifts find here their explanation (πάντων μὲν γὰρ αἴτιος τῶν καλῶν ὁ θεός [Clem. Alex. *Strom.* i. 5]; cf. Calvin, *Inst.* bk. ii. ch. iv. 8). What Christianity aims at is thus not the destruction of natural endowments, but their moral potentiation. Negatively viewed, the Holy Spirit may be resisted not simply by positive moral repugnance, but by neglect, by contentment with life without it, and by searching for the highest along false lines; hence the necessity that the character of the Redeeming Spirit be made known through proclamation, through holy moral living, through the removal of stumbling-blocks in the fabric of society, and through the consecration of all natural endowments and graces. The Holy Spirit is thus the objective dynamic of the individual moral life and of social life as well. It is the condition of social progress.

(2) *The subjective dynamic of the Christian life.*—The subjective dynamic of the Christian life is *faith in God.* This admits of many stages, according to the individual concerned, ranging from the barely reflective movement (often mingled with gross superstition) of the needy heart towards the offered love of God, up to the highly conscious, intensely emotional, and pressing, volitional soul-grasp of the Redeemer. Through faith, ethically viewed, the soul is converted (see art. CONVERSION); it condemns its own past, abandons it in motive (repentance), resists its re-assertion, and finds itself changed in its view of life and duty, and equipped with power to realize the Kingdom of God. It is said that such a theory is wrong because it breaks the law of ethical continuity. But continuity in the moral life is permanently secured only by the presence of the power of God in the character. The false character, fashioned without the aid of the Holy Spirit, is brittle all along the line. Continuity must not be applied to chain the soul to its evil past, but to safeguard the gains of holy living. Hence Christianity takes a view of the past which is distinctive. By the aid of God the individual can break through his evil past and, by resistance to it, 'rise on stepping-stones' of his dead self 'to higher things.' Christian faith does not energize *in vacuo*; it is orientated in Christ as the revelation of God's love to men. Christ is the 'handle by which we lay hold on God' (cf. Rothe, *Theol. Ethik*, iii. 359).

Faith, then, brings the soul into a world of new values, and by it the individual values himself and others after a new fashion. There arises here the sense of the value of the individual. The individual is one for whom Christ died. This, personalized—'He loved me and gave Himself for me'—is now the constraining motive of action.

The will acquiesces in this love, and finds itself reconciled to God. Peace follows which the world cannot give or take away. The individual is garrisoned with the peace of God and rejoices in the Lord. It is impossible to exaggerate the amount of pure joy and calm serenity that Christianity brings to a man. The enthusiasm for virtue it generates is unique. The great danger to the Christian is contentment with the old world which Christ abolished, and which, by believing, he himself has repudiated. This is the world of sin. It is alienation from the life of God through wicked works, the consequent darkening of the conscience and understanding, the deterioration of the will, the deadening of the spiritual affections, and the quasi-cosmos of evil in which men's subjective and social energies act, and which acts through them. It is the destruction of freedom, the darkening of the conscience, and the devaluation of the individual. The Cross shows sin to faith in its true light. It is no longer an error of judgment merely, or a lack of harmony in ourselves, or a crime against society, but a revolt against holy love; and it is all the rest because it is this. Sin is thus not in the actions but in the will, and sins are graded according to this inwardness of view. The Pharisees—the proud, haughty, humility-lacking — are more hopeless than the miserable, restless in their sins.

Faith thus calls upon itself to a battle *à outrance* with sin, and here begins the problem of the formation of character. Christian character-building is just the soul of man habituating itself to the active presence of God, and transforming the natural endowments into spiritual instruments to carry out the will of God (sanctification).

Faith is accompanied by humility, which arises from the sense of God's great love in Christ to us. It is due not simply to a sense of our finiteness and of God's infinity, but much more to a sense of God's activity of saving love so utterly undeserved by us. Intellectually viewed, it is adoration, as we see God's infinite patience with men in history and His provision for their salvation (cf. Ro 11[33-36]). It is the outlook of the soul on its own sinful past, and the recognition of God's forgiveness of it. It is the remembrance also of our present frailty and future difficulties, and the knowledge that we need God every hour. Towards men, humility arises as we realize our indebtedness to others—to Greek and Jew alike. God's varied gifts are meant for common blessing and common service; hence humility condescends to men of low estate. It is the death of pride and vainglory. It expels indifference to the common needs of men. It is the disposition which makes advance in knowledge possible, makes self-sacrifice in action easy, and keeps open the windows of the soul in adoration towards heaven. It also consecrates the meanest service because it is done for God (cf. the widow's mite), and fills the humblest life with sweetness and dignity. One can hardly call it a virtue; it is rather the aroma of a life lived in the sense of God's amazing love (so free and undeserved) to men in Christ. Closely associated with it are the gentle graces of character—regard for the needs of others, sympathy with suffering, respect for the lowly, an eye for the glory of the commonplace, compassion, tenderness, pity, gentleness, obedience, lack of ostentation, thankfulness, a forgiving spirit. When it becomes conscious of itself and tries to ape itself, it loses its peculiar flavour, and thus the monastic conception of humility (doing menial tasks, etc.) tended towards the destruction of this spontaneous Christian grace.

The synthetic character of faith is seen in the fact that in it is also the germ of the manly virtues — independence, courage, endurance. Because faith is sure of God's forgiveness, the character is strengthened into fidelity to God against all odds. Thus is generated an independence based on God, far surpassing anything found on the heights of Stoic αὐτάρκεια, and a courage which is not an ebullition of natural temperament, but a 'habitual mood' of the soul. Faith lifts man above the tyranny of the customary and the accidents of fortune, for it is loyalty to Christ. This loyalty finds sufficient exercise in our ordinary callings: Luther was true to the Christian spirit when he rescued common vocations from the stigma of inferiority implied in the meritorious life of the cloister. The patient endurance (ὑπομονή) of pain and suffering and of the flux of earthly blessings, whether that be directly due to providence or to the hostile opposition of society, is a result of faith. Hence follows contentment. It is neither the ἀταραξία of Epicurus nor the ἀπάθεια of Stoicism. It does not shun difficulties, but it does not create them unnecessarily (Ro 12[18]); it feels pain and injustice keenly, and, where possible, removes them. Patience is the knowledge of what is to be endured and what is not (Clem. Alex. *Strom.* ii. 18). It is thus gentle and stern, passive and active (Rev 2[2]). Patience must never fail, and hence suicide is never allowable. Patience may lead to death, but such a death is the gateway to life.

As the Christian has to live his life in his vocation, he is impelled to exercise discretion in trying to find out God's will. He is a member of society with definite calls on him, involving the welfare of others and the progress of Christ's Kingdom. Hence knowledge is a virtue. Such a knowledge is determined by the interests of the new life. It is practical, and must avoid foolish questionings. It is for the sake of service to men, and must not puff up, or separate the possessor of it from his brethren and the pathway of ordinary duties. It is never perfect in this world, but is a growing intensity of penetration into the active purpose of God.

Faith is thus the personal bond which unites the human person to the Divine redemptive Spirit and submits itself to the dictation of that Spirit. The Christian virtues are implicit in it.

'We may only speak of Christian "virtue" if we keep constantly before us what has been said of the reception of faith as the fountain of all Christian morality; were that fountain dried up, the moral life could not longer be maintained. Christ is and remains the principle, rather the personal originator, of holiness, as He is of that conversion which lays the foundation of the Christian life' (Häring, *Ethics of the Christian Life*, p. 247).

Hence the end of Christian virtue is to be a perfect man in Christ, to live with a sure hold of the world of values which Christ revealed, and to convert these values into reality. Its great means of subsistence and progress is prayer. Prayer is faith seeking and finding power from God, thankfully acknowledging its privilege, becoming conscious of its task, renewing itself to follow the path the Spirit of God indicates. The Church as means of grace is valuable as it helps this, for it is a house of prayer, and all other so-called means of grace should ever be used in holding Christ up before the soul as the Power and the Pattern of Holiness. Prayer is not simply negative and protective, but positive and constructive. It is the Spirit of God re-creating man in God's image, and the work of man's spirit working out his own salvation.

'The Spirit is not merely, in St. Paul's view, an aggressive force leading the human spirit against the flesh, or a defensive power shielding it from attack. Stoicism, as interpreted by Seneca and Epictetus, was able to go some way in that direction. St. Paul opens another door of hope; his indwelling Spirit is also a constructive power which builds up a new life within, co-operating with the spirit of man in the work of restoring human life to the image of God' (Swete, *Holy Spirit in New Test.*, 1909, p. 344 f.).

Faith issues in *hope*, according as it experiences the power of Christ in the pressure of temptation and affliction. Hope rests itself on Christ's victory and on the promise of the victory of His kingdom. It is cognizant of the might of sin and its energy, it knows the tribulation that accompanies righteousness, but it has counted the cost and tasted the worth of the new life. Hope never fails; hence the continual optimism of the Christian character, touched with a seriousness and gravity unknown elsewhere. Hope can 'reach a hand through time to grasp the far-off interest of tears' (Tennyson, *In Memoriam*, canto i.). It is, like prayer, focused in Christ. Christ is the atmosphere of its life and the limit of its longings. It thus faces life with a spontaneity of assurance which sin in all its potent resistance can neither demoralize nor overcome.

Because faith and hope are orientated in Christ, they energize in *love*, and all the virtues and graces are thus determined as to their inner quality. For emotion, intellect, and will are apt to become self-centred. Hence the need of love, lest the emotions should rest in themselves. Thus the 'gift of tongues' has to be used for the benefit of all, the intellect must become conscious of its social task, and the great deeds of self-denial must not become monuments of selfish display (1 Co 13). Christ is the perfect embodiment of love, and the aim of the Christian man is to know the love of Christ which passes knowledge (Eph 3[19]), and to give himself no rest till all men are made participants of the same love (2 Co 5[14f.]). Prayer then becomes intercessory and social, for it knows that common blessings issue from common prayer; and the Christian man, in all his inner and outer activities, feels the worthlessness of all if love be lacking. Christian perfection consists in the possession of such a love as is seen in Christ. This is eternal life.

2. The Christian ideal.—The Christian ideal is, individually viewed, eternal life, and for all men, organically viewed, the Kingdom of God. These two are inseparable and interchangeable, yet are distinguishable as the individual and the common good. What is the content of this good? Christianity makes no attempt to give an exact definition, but seeks to communicate it and let it reveal its nature by its presence and possession.

(*a*) Eternal life is not existence infinitely prolonged. Dives may live after death, but his existence may be a curse. Yet, clearly, eternal life implies immortality. To say that the good is good, however short its existence, 'admits of no answer but produces no conviction' (Hume's *Works*, ed. London, 1854, iv. 176). The tremendous reality of death must be faced by all earnest, ethical thinking. Heartless banter, Stoical indifference, perplexed uncertainty towards it, cannot satisfy serious men, and any ethical ideal limited by death stands self-condemned. Thus Plato thought extinction too good for the unrighteous. Kant postulated immortality in order to harmonize virtue and happiness (see also Green's *Proleg.*³, 1890, p. 195). The worth of eternal life is not, however, in its duration; its duration is implied in its worth. Immortality, as bare existence after death, may be as Sheol or the realm of Hades—both so hazy that one day of labour on earth is preferable to them (cf. *Od.* xi. 489 ff.).

(*b*) Eternal life does not depend on a healthy body or pleasant surroundings, otherwise many would *in limine* be cut off from its possibility. Aristotle could hardly conceive it possible for deformed persons, or slaves, or even artisans to possess the *summum bonum*. The Christian ideal is open to all. We must not forget this truth in our ardour for economic improvement and our advocacy of a living wage. The man clothed in purple and fine linen and faring sumptuously every day may be unaware of what eternal life is, while he who has not where to lay his head may have it. Even though 'friends, leisure, and means' were for ever possessed, the Christian life might still be lacking. Thus the Christian ideal conflicts with all ideals summed up in earthly pleasures, pursuits, and interests with no outlook beyond (cf. Browning's *Old Pictures in Florence* for the difference between Greek and Christian art in this respect).

(*c*) Eternal life is communion with God. Man was created in God's image, re-created in the image of the Son. Hence man's aim is moral likeness to God. The great task of Christian teaching is to awaken in man the practically lost sense of sonship; for, when the prodigal returns to his Father, then he who was dead is alive again. This communion is not the absorption of mystic contemplation or Nirvāṇa. Such an absorption negates moral values and personality. It is not simply the communion of τὸ λογικόν in man with the eternal reason, as Plato tends to make it in the case of Socrates (*Phædo*). That would leave behind the varieties of personal temperament and character in its sublimation. By communion, Christianity does not mean breaking the limits between the Infinite and the finite. These are not moral distinctions at all. They are not barriers to communion. What is aimed at is freedom from sin, and the acquisition of holiness. This communion is a moral life, and it aims at perfection through moral activity. It is, ideally viewed, a real ethical personal communion, in which all endowments and characteristics are morally potentiated to their highest degree. It is a personal life of righteousness saturated in the atmosphere of a Personal Holy Presence. The Christian ideal is at the same time the Highest Good. Viewed as Ideal, it waits its full realization; as the Highest Good, it is a present possession. Thus, while it awaits its full realization, it must be morally operative now. It is otherworldly, but it demands all reality as its content.

(*d*) Eternal life is a fellowship dependent on the possession of a righteous character, and it is maintained in the living of a righteous life. 'Be ye holy, for I am holy.' The way to attain it is not, as Orphism taught, to escape from matter *per se*, through acts having little moral reference in themselves and valuable only as means. The moral life is not a *vita purgativa* or *scala perfectionis* simply, but a permanent moment of the Christian ideal. This aspect of communion and the way to attain it break down the false asceticism and subjectivism that dog Mysticism. For eternal life is a righteousness that demands all for the service of God.

(i.) Eternal life demands Nature. Jonathan Edwards declares that he saw a new beauty in Nature at his conversion; so Lacordaire and many besides. In the light of the ideal, this world is God's world and a theophany, as it was to ancient Psalmists. To make this universal through the æsthetic side of our nature should be the aim of art—to make the lily and the bird bring us to our Heavenly Father. True art should thus be a means of righteousness, and so should true science. Neither material needs, nor pains, nor privations should obstruct this communion by focusing attention solely on themselves. Their pressure should lead us beyond themselves. Nor should the soul attempt to satisfy itself in worldly possessions, to the exclusion of God. That is why Jesus warns against anxiety and riches, because the affairs of business and pleasure, exclusively pursued, turn the will into channels divergent from the will of God; because ideals through these influences are truncated, and the singleness of aim which ought to characterize conscience becomes blinded by the false lights of the world. Experience in this, as in every age, proves that there are no more certain ways of falling out of fellowship with God than these. To act thus towards Nature is to be ruled by it—not to rule it, as is the Christian ideal. Christ's Lordship over Nature is a pledge of ours. There is thus truth in Rothe's view that morality is the gradual spiritualization of Nature. Every advance in science, every subjugation of natural forces, every great work of art, should make righteous communion more easy. When these advances are suborned into the service of injustice, then communion is more difficult. One of the great tasks of Christianity is to convert the material gifts of civilization into means of righteousness, and not suffer them to be held in the bondage of non-moral or immoral purposes.

(ii.) Eternal life demands the whole of mankind and of every man. Just as Nature becomes a theophany in the light of this ideal, the bodily members become ὅπλα δικαιοσύνης τῷ θεῷ. Even in the future perfect communion, Christianity does not offer the abolition of the body.

'Not the destruction of the body but its liberation was the hope which it held forth to the world. Human nature is to be perfected, not by the abandonment of one of its factors, but by the emancipation of the whole man; humanity is to be preserved in its entirety for the coming Christ' (Swete, 355).

Thus righteousness includes care for the bodies of men and for their proper surroundings. Sickness is due to sin, and our Lord's ministry of healing is an integral part of the Kingdom. Hence Seeley (*Ecce Homo*, ch. x.) rightly points out that, on the one hand, Christians cared for the body passionately, while showing, at the same time, a more than Stoic apathy in regard to personal suffering. The passion for social reform, the crusades against disease and degeneration, the desire to regulate labour hours and conditions that would breed weaklings and fill our hospitals, ought to find in Christianity their warmest recruits. Every slum is a dead weight on the Christian heart, making communion with God more difficult. The same applies to nations sunk in superstition and paganism. Righteousness, rightly understood, is the nerve of missionary effort. Till the whole of humanity, intensively and extensively viewed, is in the Kingdom of God, there is something lacking in the fullness of the ideal.

(iii.) Eternal life demands an interpretation of history, for righteousness is the substratum of history. It is the highest good in history; but, because it has not been fully entrenched in any society or any institution, it is an ideal to be realized, though present from the first, and all along moving towards realization. The truth of history is the Kingdom of God. This culminates in Christ, and unfolds itself under His control. We are thus given a standard to evaluate individuals, societies, and movements, and it helps us to fill in concretely the Ideal itself and gain guidance for the future.

(*e*) The inner nature of eternal life, of the Kingdom of God, is thus seen to be love, because it culminates in Christ. Love is not a baseless psychological experience that can be made or forgotten by individuals. It is the Reality. God is Love. Love is the inward spirit of righteousness in man, of order and beauty in Nature. Men may appreciate order in Nature, purpose in history, and righteousness in conduct before realizing the inner nature of all as Holy Love. This is Dorner's justification for contrasting righteousness and love, but the contrast is one of human appreciation, not of inward nature (see R. Law, *The Tests of Life*, 1909, p. 80). To have the love of God shed abroad in our hearts, to see it preparing a world for itself and realizing itself in human relationships, is to have eternal life and to be in the Kingdom. Love tries to reproduce in men a character in which it is itself the inner principle of life and conduct. It takes on itself men's burdens and sins so as to abolish them. This ideal is a historical reality in Christ. Love is the very nature of God, and the aim of the Divine Spirit is to reproduce it in men, just as it is the highest task of faith to make it a reality in the world.

3. Christian duty.—When the Christian acknowledges, through faith, the infinite worth of the Ideal, and is in motive reconciled to it, he imposes on himself the duty of actualizing it. The ideal is a criticism of the actual, and has its own motives and sanctions. These are intrinsically bound up with the ideal itself; hence the charge of hedonism is a misapprehension, though so-called Christian conduct has often justified the charge (cf. Westermarck, *MI* ii. 660). To say that virtue is its own reward, and that duty should not be determined by consequences, is a noble truth; to make that mean that there is no reward and no consequences is to make the moral life unreal. The 'purity' demanded by Kant is consistent with Christian sanctions, because no false sanction can ever be appealed to. The 'medicinal lie' is not a Christian sanction, although Clement and others recognized it. But Christianity can use the fear of punishment if the punishment is the consequence of outraged holiness. Even Christians themselves are not exempt from holy law, *i.e.* from judgment. Those who build with wood, hay, stubble shall have their work destroyed in fire (1 Co 3^{12-15}). That our Lord denounced hypocrisy and brought God's holiness to bear on the issues of human conduct is not immoral. For evil is so self-confident and often so successful in this world that it is a duty to tear the mask off its face and let the light of eternal holiness expose and confound it.

The brevity of life may be appealed to as emphasizing the duty of buying the opportunity. Positively, the appeal can be made to the blessedness of the pure in heart and to the sure reward of persecuted righteousness. In all this, however, we have but coloured spectral rays of the real inward motive and sanction of Christian duty, which is the redeeming love of Christ to all men, constraining us to personal holiness and public righteousness. To lose this love or be faithless to it supplies deterrents more awful than any conceivable punishments, and to have it is a motive compared with which the uncertain promises of the natural life are trifling. There is, thus, no division of duties into commands and counsels; for duty is obligatory love, and merit is excluded. Yet duty is coloured by the position and condition of the individual and society. That we abstain from things offered to idols is no duty for us, but it is a duty to exercise our freedom with a regard to the welfare of others. We cannot thus have an exhaustive classification of duties. It is more important to note that duty is single—the determining of life from the side of God. Hence fidelity to Christ is the primary duty. 'Follow me' is the first as it is the last word of Christ to His people (Mt 4^{19}, Jn 21^{22}).

(1) *Duties to ourselves.*—Self-regarding duties are not prudential, as in Greek Ethics, but Christ-determined. A conflict, thus, cannot arise between them and service for others, as A. E. Taylor (*Problem of Conduct*, 1901, chs. vii., viii.) supposes. For self-regarding duties are not consciously directed towards self, but are the reflex influence on the person of his fidelity to Christ. The duty of self-love has to be qualified in this way, or it may become a misnomer. The question of the 'neces-

sary lie' is also solved by this principle. In actual life either the falsehood or the necessity is lacking. A list of self-regarding duties is impossible. One Christian finds his vocation in science, another in politics; and all may labour in these spheres from a sense of Christian duty. What is important is fidelity to Christ in each sphere. Because of division of labour it is not a Christian duty to cultivate all potentialities, but rather to limit oneself to one's vocation; for fidelity in our vocation does not impoverish but enriches the character and makes it more effective for all providential calls (cf. Dewey, *Outlines of Ethics*, 1891, p. 40). Because self-regarding duties are determined by reference to Christ, not by prudence, the body and bodily actions have spiritual value. The members of the body become instruments of righteousness to God. Hence the duties of chastity and moderation in all things. There is also the duty of work, for the upkeep of the body, for the support of dependants, for the sake of a good example, and in order to have wherewith to exercise charity. St. Paul lays it down as an inexorable duty to support the weak and helpless bound to us by family ties (1 Ti 5[8]). To be conscientious in our work, to keep our souls pure and our minds alert, are duties incumbent on us because we are servants of Christ and are here to advance His Kingdom. A lively interest in all real human questions and an understanding of God's will in our tasks rise before us as obligations.

(2) Thus self-regarding duties merge imperceptibly into *duties to others*. In the family we learn, by working for others, to realize Christ's claim. The family is a nursery of discipline in self-sacrifice and in working for a common good. Here we see the Kingdom of God spiritualizing natural conditions, for marriage is in the Lord. Parents appreciate the love of the Heavenly Father, the need for the correction of natural partiality, and the value of authority and law in dealing with their children, while children are trained to reverence moral values, to understand the need of obedience and the value of common service. The family is of extreme value in the eliciting of sympathy and mutual co-operation. Wider than the family are the community and the State. Through these we learn our dependence on others—the value of division of labour and the possibility and duty of contributing to the common good. For society places so many gifts before us that we are bound to be thankful and to strive for the common welfare with all our might. The gifts of society are not to be exploited for selfish ends, but for the enrichment of Christian character, and for the advancement of the Kingdom of God. The individual is thus constrained to contribute to its welfare. Contribution not acquisition, emulation in service not competition, should be the watchwords of all.

(3) *Duties of institutions to the individual.*—The individual in Christianity is of infinite value; hence the Church, which is the specific Christian institution, should keep this in view.

(*a*) The Church should be the guardian of freedom. Institutions were made for man, not man for institutions. The rights of conscience are inherent in Christian faith, and cannot be ignored in the interests either of despotism or of democracy. Thus the Church must supplement the workings of the general laws of the State and of communities, as well as the customs of societies through the ἐπιείκεια which Aristotle saw was necessary. Christian freedom subserves itself, as St. Paul and Luther saw, to service for all; hence the Church must enlighten all natural institutions as to duty, and supplement their shortcomings. She must not wait for the State or municipality, nor must the real living Church wait for the Church itself as an organized institution. For this reason the Early Church recognized duties of benevolence, of hospitality, of finding work for her members. It may be said she was by necessity a labour bureau. These, of course, are duties for some individual Christians, but they are corporate duties as well. Above all, she should aim at removing stumbling-blocks from the way of righteousness, but her weapons are love, not physical force.

(*b*) The paramount duty of the Church is evangelization. The unrest and suspicion between classes and between nations, the unification, through discovery and commerce, of the whole world, make this most imperative in our time. Lord Acton, referring to Ac 16[6f.], says: 'It is not harder to believe that certain political conditions are required to make a nation fit for conversion than that a certain degree of intellectual development is indispensable' (*History of Freedom*, 1877, p. 202). The passage in Acts may also mean that single individuals may not be fitted to go to certain places evangelizing. If both qualifications hold, yet the Christian Church has not acted up to these limitations. She is in arrears of duty as regards evangelization.

(4) *The State and the individual.*—The State is a limited natural institution, but a Divine ordinance and a real entrenchment of the Kingdom of God as the common good. Christian Ethics should insist on the duty of the Christian State in administration and legislation to look after the welfare of all classes, and to make all contribute to the common good. The means of education and an honest livelihood should be within the reach of all; hence poverty and its causes should be abolished as far as possible. The weak should be protected against aggression and exploitation—possibly against themselves. The Christian conscience is certainly coming to make greater claims on the Christian State in the way of providing work for all, in demanding a living wage, in looking after the aged and the helpless young; and the science of Economics is rapidly providing a basis for scientific legislation. These demands carry with them the corollary that the State has greater control over private interests than was once recognized, whether the interests be those of capital or labour, money or work, land or commerce. What we need, however, both in the State and in the various minor institutions that compose it, even more than legislation, is the spirit of devotion to the common good by all, and the spirit of self-sacrifice among those who have special spiritual and material endowments. We need the Christianizing of the public conscience which determines the State. It is to be deplored that there is no recognized mouthpiece to give voice to the duties of State to State. 'Si vis pacem, para bellum' has converted Europe into arsenals. But war is incompatible with Christianity, and its incompatibility with State duty should be more and more recognized.

We have not, owing to the limits of this article, entered into details. Suffice it to say that the Christian ideal of the Kingdom of God, which is also the Supreme Good, lays on all who accept it duties of brotherhood, service, and self-sacrifice; that, as far as natural institutions are Christianized, the same services are demanded of them; and that the hope of Christianity should make us fall back more and more on the Eternal Spirit who originates, sustains, and shall perfect, through human endeavour, the Kingdom of God.

LITERATURE.—(1) For NT Ethics, see Lit. in H. C. King, *The Ethics of Jesus*, New York, 1910; J. Stalker, *The Ethic of Jesus*, London, 1909; J. Drummond, *Via, Veritas, Vita*, London, 1894; G. B. Stevens, *Theol. of NT*[2], Edinburgh, 1906; Ethical artt. in *DCG*.

(2) For history of Christian Ethics: A. Harnack, *Hist. of Dogma*, Eng. tr., London, 1894–99; E. v. Dobschütz, *Christian Life in the Primitive Church*, Eng. tr., London and New York,

1904; E. Hatch, *Hibbert Lectures*, 1888, London, 1890, ch. vi.; W. Gass, *Gesch. der christl. Ethik*[2], Berlin, 1888–93; C. E. Luthardt, *Gesch. der christl. Ethik*, Leipzig, 1888–93, vol. i. tr. Hastie, *Christian Ethics before the Reformation*, Edinburgh, 1889; K. Werner, *System der christl. Ethik*[2], Regensburg, 1888 (Rom. Cath.); W. E. H. Lecky, *Hist. of European Morals*[9], London, 1890; A. Wuttke, *Christian Ethics*, Eng. tr., Edinburgh, 1873, vol. i., 'History of Ethics'; H. Sidgwick, *Hist. of Ethics*[2], London, 1888, ch. iii.; T. C. Hall, *Hist. of Christian Ethics within Organised Christianity*, London, 1910; see also artt. ABELARD, AUGUSTINE, CALVINISM, LUTHER, etc.

(3) For systems of Christian Ethics: R. Rothe, *Theol. Ethik*[2], Wittenberg, 1870; H. Martensen, *Christian Ethics*, Eng. tr., Edinburgh, 1873, 1881; H. Schultz, *Grundriss der evang. Ethik*[2], Göttingen, 1897; F. C. Krarup, (Danish) *Grundriss der christl. Ethik* (Germ. tr. by Küchler, Freiburg, 1897); C. E. Luthardt, *Kompend. d. theolog. Ethik*[2], Leipzig, 1898; J. Köstlin, *Christl. Ethik*, Berlin, 1899; W. Herrmann, *Ethik*, Tübingen, 1901; L. Lemme, *Christl. Ethik*, Berlin, 1905; O. Kirn, *Grundriss der theol. Ethik*, Leipzig, 1906; T. v. Häring, *Ethics of the Christian Life*, Eng. tr., London, 1907; Newman Smyth, *Christian Ethics*[3], Edinburgh, 1894; W. F. Lofthouse, *Ethics and Atonement*, London, 1906; J. R. Illingworth, *Christian Character*[6], London, 1907; T. B. Strong, *Christian Ethics*, London, 1896; R. L. Ottley, 'Christian Ethics,' in *Lux Mundi*[5], London, 1890, also *Christian Ideas and Ideals*, London and New York, 1909; J. C. Murray, *Handbook of Christian Ethics*, Edinburgh, 1908; T. B. Kilpatrick, *Christian Character*, Edinburgh, 1899; A. Harnack, *What is Christianity?*[3], London and New York, 1904; J. R. Seeley, *Ecce Homo*, London, 1866; W. L. Davidson, *Christian Ethics*[3], London, 1907; W. A. Knight, *The Christian Ethic*, London, 1893; G. F. Barbour, *A Phil. Study of Christian Ethics*, Edinburgh and London, 1911; see also various Encyclopædias, and 'Systematische christl. Religion,' 1909, in *Die Kultur der Gegenwart*—artt. by Mausbach and Seeberg.

DONALD MACKENZIE.

ETHICS AND MORALITY (Egyptian).—**1. Introductory.**—The opinion of the Greeks, that the Egyptians were a profoundly philosophical and reflective people, has been shown by the contemporary inscriptions and monuments to be false. The bent of the Egyptians was essentially practical; and, if they attained some proficiency in mathematics, astronomy, and medicine, it was for the sake of the uses to which these sciences could be put. For the things of the mind, as such, they had little taste; hence their ethical views were without depth, and they had no opposing schools of ethical thought. Nevertheless, it cannot be denied that the Egyptians took a very keen interest in the moral aspect of the world. They were never tired of boasting of their virtues, and the popularity of the Osirian worship bears witness to their strong moral feelings. To put the matter shortly, the Egyptians, though not ethically speculative, were in a high degree ethically minded.

2. Terminology.—Language usually provides a rough criterion of the mental state of a people with regard to any given topic, since thought tends to create its own adequate expression. The Egyptian expressions for moral concepts are neither numerous nor precise. For 'right' the word is *ma'et* (Copt. ⲘⲈ : ⲘⲎⲒ; the older Egyptologists write *maāt*, *ma*, etc.), which seems to be derived from a verb meaning 'to be straight,' 'to move in a direction.' Thus *ma'et* signifies conformity to an ethical norm,[1] though it has also, and perhaps even more frequently, a purely intellectual connotation; it then means 'truth.' The contradictories of *ma'et* are *'iesfet*, 'wrong,' and *'oze*, 'guilt'; *gōrg* more often means 'untruth,' 'falsehood.' For 'good' and 'bad,' *nūfer* and *bo'in* are the commonest terms; they also stand for 'beautiful' and 'ugly' respectively. *Bōte* means 'crime'; for 'sin' is used the phrase *bowt nūter*, 'what God detests.' There is no verb corresponding to 'ought'; 'duty' is represented by *'ere-t*, 'that which is reckoned as against' a man, his debt to the community.[2] The will as a psychological entity is unknown, and is not distinguished from the agent ('I', 'me').[3] The word *'ieb* (=Heb. לֵב), 'heart,' is often found in Egyptian texts for the intellect or reason; but it appears sometimes to mean more than the mere instrument of cognition; it means the faculty which recognizes and suggests the right course of action, 'the conscience.' So in the following passage, which is a good example of Egyptian modes of expression in ethical matters:

> 'Thus saith he. This is my character to which I have borne witness, and there is no exaggeration therein. . . . It is my *heart* (*'ieb*) that caused me to do it through its guidance unto me. It was an excellent prompter unto me; I did not infringe its commands; I feared to transgress its guidance. Therefore I prospered exceedingly, and was fortunate on account of that which it caused me to do; I succeeded by reason of its guidance. Of a sooth, true is that which is said by men: "It (namely the heart) is *the voice of God* that is in every body; happy is he whom it has led to a good course of action!"' (K. Sethe, *Urkunden des äg. Altertums*, Leipzig, 1908 [hereafter cited as *Urk.*], iv. 973 f.; cf. iv. 119, and W. Wreszinski, *Wiener Inschriften*, Leipzig, 1906, p. 160).

The 'thoughts' of men are 'that which is in the body (*'imiu-khat*) or 'the concerns of the heart' (*khert-'ieb*). The very concrete way in which psychological facts were expressed is here conspicuous; for more complex ethical concepts, such as 'motive,' 'responsibility,' 'scruple,' abstract names were wanting.

The moral predicates were represented in language in an equally concrete way, an adjective or participle, metaphorically used, being combined with such substantives as *'ieb*, 'heart' (for qualities of mind or temperament), *ḥor*, 'face' (for qualities that can be detected or conjectured from a man's look or expression), *rō*, 'mouth' (for qualities that manifest themselves in speech), or *'a*, 'arm' (for qualities that manifest themselves in action). Thus *waḥ 'ieb*, 'enduring of heart,' was the phrase used to convey the notion 'kindly,' 'indulgent', *spud ḥor*, 'sharp of face,' for 'intelligent,' 'clever'; *ḥap rō*, 'hidden of mouth,' for 'reserved,' 'discreet'; *'aw 'a*, 'extended of hand,' for 'generous,' 'liberal.' The difficulties which imagery of this kind makes in translation into a modern language may easily be conceived; in particular cases hieroglyphic scholars are often at a loss to decide precisely what qualities are meant.

3. Destiny and free will.—The Egyptians were strong believers in 'Fate' (*shay*),[1] which was occasionally personified; as a rule, however, it is 'God' (*nūter*) in general, or some god in particular (*e.g.*, Rē [*Urk.* iv. 943]), who is supposed to determine the events of a man's career. The uncertainty of human projects is often alluded to:

> 'What men have devised never comes to pass, it is what God commands that comes to pass.' For instance, 'One man plans to plunder another; he ends by giving to him he knoweth not' (*Papyrus Prisse*, 6. 9–10). On this account the precept is given: 'Take no counsel for to-morrow ere it be come' (*Petrie Ostracon*, 11; *Prisse*, 6. 8).

Luckily the Egyptians did not, as a general rule, go on to conclude that their own actions were unchangeably predestined; the influence of Fate seems to have been restricted to the things that might happen to men, and did not extend to their actions (cf. FATE [Egyptian]). We have seen that 'conscience' was compared to the 'voice of God' speaking in men; but there was no compulsion to listen to the voice.

It is quite an exceptional case when Sinuhe in the tale excuses himself for his flight to foreign parts by attributing it to the 'will of the god' (*Sin. B*, 43), 'who decreed this flight' (*ib.* 156). And, when the magician disclaims responsibility for the formulæ he pronounces by saying, 'It is not I who say them, it is not I who repeat them; it is Horus who says them, it is Horus who repeats them' (*Pap. Turin*, 136. 8), this is a statement governed by quite special conditions.

That men are free agents is a necessary assumption in everyday life; that the opposite is true has often appeared to men as a necessary deduction

[1] Very often the best rendering is not 'right' but 'justice.'

[2] The word *'ere-t* is derived from the preposition *er*, 'towards,' 'against'; cf. ⲚⲈⲦⲈⲢⲞⲚ, 'our debts,' in the Coptic versions of the Lord's Prayer, lit. 'those things that are against us.'

[3] The elusive word *ka*, which is usually translated 'double,' may sometimes conveniently be rendered 'will'; so, too, *ba'u*, lit. 'souls.'

[1] Cf., too, the masculine *p-ši*, ψαις, which is rendered in Greek by Ἀγαθὸς Δαίμων.

from the notion of causality or fate. The practical-minded Egyptians accepted the first view without hesitation, and ignored the second.

4. The range of responsibility.—The extent and limits of responsibility are questions on which there is but little Egyptian evidence. It is very probable that madness was attributed to possession by demons—a belief now universal in the Orient; we know for a fact that illness was thought to be due to the presence of haunting spirits of the dead (cf. art. DEMONS AND SPIRITS [Egyp.]). Again, it may have been held that families were jointly responsible for the acts of their individual members, though this cannot perhaps be quite legitimately deduced from the assurance given that a man's children benefit by his good deeds (*Urk.* i. 129), and will have to bear the consequences of his bad ones (Petrie, *Koptos*, London, 1896, pl. 8, 6; Lepsius, *Denkmäler*, Berlin, 1849–59, iii. 140*c*).

5. The question of disinterestedness.—Egyptian moralists may now and again have caught a glimpse of the loftiest heights of ethical thought—the conception of right as its own sufficient reason, regardless of consequences; but in general their teaching was on a lower plane.

'Excellent is right,' exclaims the wise Ptahhotep, 'and endureth and prevaileth'; upon this irreproachable sentiment there quickly follows a prudential consideration which completely spoils its elevated tone:—'Never has wickedness brought its venture safe to port; wrongdoing stealeth away riches' (*Pap. Brit. Mus.* 10509, 2, 7–9 = *Prisse*, 6. 5–6).

The Egyptians were very sensitive about their reputation, and often boasted of having won the approval of their fellows.

'I did what all men approved,' says one noble (*Urk.* i. 75); a hackneyed phrase of the funeral stelæ is, 'I did what men loved and what the gods approved' (e.g. *Urk.* iv. 131, 484). It was an ancient proverb that 'the good deeds of a man are his monument, an evil nature is oblivion' (*PSBA* xviii. [1895–96] 196).

In the desire for a good reputation the extreme limit of Egyptian disinterestedness is reached; it was deemed the highest possible virtue for a man to 'raise up a good name' in his city (*Shipwrecked Sailor*, 159), though, of course, the desire for approval is a self-seeking motive only a little less crass than other selfish motives. Naturally it was more profitable to a man that he should stand well with the king than that he should be respected by the people at large; the Egyptian noble, in the *naïveté* of his soul, esteemed himself even more for the good opinion in which Pharaoh held him than for his fair fame among his equals. Blended with protestations of his generosity, his love of justice, and so forth, we frequently find him describing himself as 'beloved of his master,' or as one 'with whose excellence the lord of the two lands was content.' In such a high degree was the Pharaoh considered to be the patron and recompenser of virtue that he was known as 'the good God,' and 'the lord of Right.'

Thus an official relates, 'I did right for the lord of Right, for I knew he is pleased at it' (*Urk.* iv. 941). To Rameses II. it is said: 'Thy tongue is the shrine of Right' (*Kuban Stele* 18).

Yet, in spite of the absolute form of the government under the Pharaohs, the popular verdict was held of high account. The speech of king Thutmosis III. in appointing his Minister of Justice illustrates this point in rather a remarkable way; among other things it is said:

'If a man inspire fear overmuch, there is some injustice in him in the opinion of men'; and again, 'As for the chief scribe of the Vizier, Scribe of Righteousness is what he is called' (Newberry, *Life of Rekhmara*, London, 1900, p. 10).

6. Virtue rewarded upon earth: Egyptian pessimism.—It was very generally believed that virtue reaps its own reward upon earth. A man who has favoured us with a long catalogue of his virtues ends with an address to mankind:

'I speak to you, O mortals; listen and do the good deeds that I have done, and to you shall be done the like' (*Urk.* iv. 61, cf. 65). To a king it is said: 'Do the right that thou mayest live long in the land' (*ZÄ* xiv. [1876] 108).

The theological expression of this idea was as follows:

'God returns evil to him who does it and right to him who brings it' (*Urk.* iv. 492).

'The fear of God' (*ib.* 64) might also be a powerful inducement to good conduct, inasmuch as

'God knoweth that which is in the body . . . his eyes perceive men's characters in their livers' (Newberry, 8. 39).

Of course the Egyptians were well aware that often it is the bad and not the good who prosper, and a passage in a literary satire illustrates the fact that rank and comfort were sometimes obtained without any superabundant merit (*Anast.* i. 9. 4–6). That all men are sinners is assumed as axiomatic in a passage of the Book of the Dead (ed. Naville, Berlin, 1886, pp. 17, 44). The wickedness of the world and the predominance of vice over virtue form the theme of a whole class of pessimistic writings, of which several specimens have survived. Here social conditions are depicted as topsy-turvy—the slaves have usurped the place of the rich, murder and rapine prevail, the righteous dwell alone and in misery. From this state of affairs one author draws the conclusion that life is not worth living (A. Erman, *Das Gespräch eines Lebensmüden mit seiner Seele*, Berlin, 1896); another gives as the cause the impiety of mankind and the callousness of their ruler (A. H. Gardiner, *The Admonitions of an Egyptian Sage*, London, 1909); for a third writer, anarchy and moral dissolution are but a stock literary theme (*Brit. Mus.* 5645, in *op. cit.*). In all these books the present calamities are either explicitly or implicitly contrasted with a happier condition of Egypt which is clearly regarded as normal, and it seems evident that Egyptian pessimism was less the outcome of philosophic meditation than the literary reflexion of disturbed historical periods like those that followed upon the VIth and XIIIth dynasties. In any case, the ethical thought underlying these writings is that wickedness and misery are things inseparable alike in thought and in reality.

7. Virtue rewarded after death.—That happiness after death depended upon a life of virtue and uprightness was a belief of gradual growth, which ultimately crystallized in the doctrine of the *psychostasia*, or weighing of the heart before Osiris. This doctrine had at all periods to contend with a contrary theory of a more primitive and no less tenacious kind, namely, that funerary rites and the knowledge of potent formulæ were the sole passports to eternal bliss. The stage of opinion that is found in the Pyramid-texts[1] (the oldest religious books of the Egyptians) is almost exclusively of the latter type. Certain passages have been quoted to show that ethical considerations were already beginning to influence the conceptions of the future life (Erman, *Äg. Rel.*², Berlin, 1909, p. 110), but they still play a very unimportant part. It must, however, be remembered that the Pyramid-texts originally applied only to the king, who in a certain sense stood above morals, and it is not quite legitimate to argue thence to the case of private individuals. The stelæ and the tomb-inscriptions of the Old Kingdom display to us the elements from which the later doctrine sprang. On such monuments the virtues of the deceased are very often commemorated—evidently in the hope of inducing passers-by to recite the funerary formulæ, if not actually to bring offerings to the tomb; it was but a short step to the conclusion that virtue upon earth is the necessary condition of happiness in the after life. Again, there was always the danger that a tomb would be damaged or destroyed by enemies or thieves in search of plunder; against

[1] Our most ancient copies date from the Vth and VIth dynasties, but the archetype of many of the chapters may be hundreds of years older.

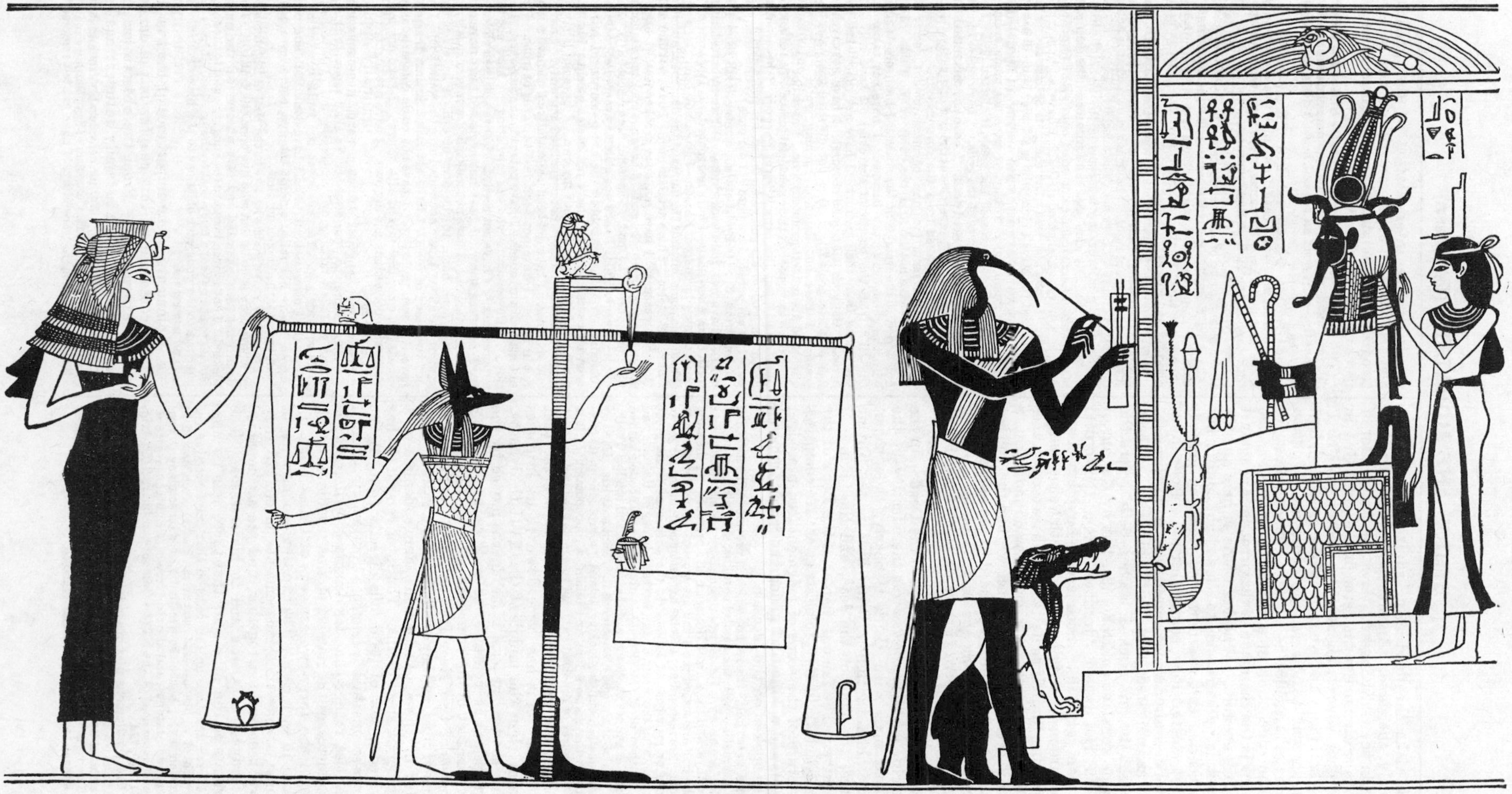

The Psychostasia, or Weighing of the Heart.
From a papyrus in the Cairo Museum.

such risks the dead man had but one weapon, namely, the curse. An oft-repeated formula, current in the Old Kingdom, threatens the violator of tombs with 'judgment through the great God in the place where judgment is given' (e.g. *Urk.* i. 117, 122, 150); and we read of 'the great God, lord of judgment' (A. Mariette, *Les Mastaba de l'ancien empire*, Paris, 1881–84, D 19). These phrases give us the conception of a Divine being who to some extent is the champion of the virtuous dead against wicked enemies. Whether Osiris is here already meant is perhaps open to some slight doubt; but the Osirian cult was now rapidly gaining ground, and it was not long before a certain episode in his history acquired a wide-spread funerary application. It was narrated that Osiris himself had been accused by his wicked brother Seth before the Divine conclave in Heliopolis, but by the aid of Thōth had issued 'justified' from the ordeal (Erman, 41, 116).[1] Soon every Egyptian found pleasure in identifying himself with Osiris, and in regarding himself as destined to share the fortunes of the god, and at last after death and judgment to attain everlasting life; hence we find the epithet *ma'khrow*, 'justified,' appended to the names of all deceased men from the early Middle Kingdom onwards[2] (Maspero [*Études de mythologie*, Paris, 1893 ff., i. 93 ff.] takes a wrong view of the word).

8. Chapter 125 of the Book of the Dead.—In the doctrine of the *psychostasia* the identity of the judged man with Osiris is nearly, though not quite, lost to sight; Osiris here is the Divine judge, the king of the dead, and the 'prince of eternity.' The famous chapter of the Book of the Dead known to Egyptologists as ch. 125 comprises a picture of the scene of judgment (see preceding page), and a long text giving the words supposed to be spoken on the occasion.

In a great hall,[3] the roof of which is crowned with flames of fire alternating with the symbol of Right, sits Osiris enthroned under a canopy. He is accompanied by his sisters Isis and Nephthys, and the sons of Horus are also present. At the back of the hall are seated the dread assessors of Osiris, forty-two in number, corresponding, as some have supposed, to the forty-two nomes or provinces of Egypt. In the foreground is the great balance, with the heart of the deceased in one of its pans and the feather of Ma'et (Right) in the other. The dog-headed Anubis examines the tongue of the balance, and the ibis Thōth, the 'scribe of the gods,' announces the result to Osiris. Hard by there squats a sinister-looking animal, 'a crocodile in its fore-parts, in the midst a lion, and behind a hippopotamus'; it is the 'devourer of the dead' who fail to support the test.

Neither the picture just described nor the text belonging to it has come down to us in copies earlier than the middle of the XVIIIth dynasty. That the text at least is far older is proved by the corruptions it contains, as well as by the very obvious fact of its composite origin. The kernel consists of two Negative Confessions, or Repudiations of Sins, as they would be better called. The older of these (A) contains simple denials of a number of specific sins. The later version (B) has derived a few of its details directly from A, but shows a marked preference for denials of evil qualities rather than for denials of evil deeds; it also increases the number of sins repudiated to 42, one of the forty-two assessors of Osiris being invoked in each case. The two Confessions were, of course, at one time independent; in ch. 125 they have been welded together, and are accompanied by prayers to Osiris and to his assessors. The variants of the MSS show that there was no unanimity in the interpretation of the particular denials, many of which are still obscure to Egyptologists. The following rendering contains all the more interesting parts of the chapter.[1]

(*Title*): *What is said on arriving at the Hall of Righteousness* [lit. *the double Right*, a common but unexplained expression], *the purging of N. from all the evil he hath done, in the sight of the gods.*

'Hail to thee, O great God, lord of Righteousness. I am come to thee, my Lord, I have drawn nigh to see thy beauty. I know thee, and I know the names of the forty-two gods who are with thee in the Hall of Righteousness, who live on the Harbourers (?) of Evil, and who gulp down their blood on that day of the reckoning up of characters before Onnophris [*i.e.* Osiris, 'the good Being']. Behold, thy name is "the twin daughters Merti" [*i.e.*, perhaps, the two all-seeing eyes of God]. Behold, I am come to thee; I have brought Right unto thee, and I have removed wickedness from thee.'

(*Confession A*): 'I have done no wickedness to men. I have not brought misery upon my fellows. I have not wrought injuries in the place of right. I have not known what is not [*sic*; probably corrupt]. I have not done mischief. I have not made the beginning of every day laborious in the sight of him who worked for me. My name has not approached the ship of him who is First [? *i.e.* men have not cried out to Rē execrating my name]. I have not slighted (?) God. I have not impoverished the poor. I have not done what the gods abominate. I have not traduced the slave to him who is set over him. I have not caused hunger. I have not caused weeping. I have not slain. I have not commanded to slay. I have not made every one suffer. I have not decreased the meals in the temples. I have not diminished the loaves of the gods. I have not taken away the oblations to the blessed dead. I have not committed fornication or impurity in the service of the god of my city. I have not added to or taken from the corn-measure. I have not diminished the palm [an unit of measurement; some MSS 'acre']. I have not falsified the cubit of the fields. I have not added to the weights of the scales. I have not tampered with the plummet of the balance. I have not taken away the milk from the mouth of the child. I have not driven the flocks from their pasture. I have not snared the birds, bones of the gods [*sic*; quite obscure]. I have not caught the fish of their pools (?). I have not diverted the water in its season. I have not dammed running water. I have not quenched fire in its (appointed) time. I have not neglected the feast-days in respect of their sacrificial joints. I have not held back cattle from the perquisites of the god. I have not hindered the god in his goings forth (*i.e.* his processions). I am pure! I am pure! I am pure! I am pure!'

(*Confession B*): 'O Broad-of-Gait, coming forth from Heliopolis—I have not done wickedness. O Fire-embracer, coming forth from Kher-Ahau—I have not robbed. O Possessor-of-the-nose, coming forth from Khmūn—I have not been grasping (?). [From this point onwards the names of the demons are omitted.] I have not stolen. I have not slain men. I have not diminished the corn-measure. I have not done crookedness. I have not stolen the property of the god. I have not spoken falsehood. I have not taken away food. I have not been resentful (?). I have not been neglectful. I have not slain any sacred animals. . . . [obscure]. I have not robbed the *ḥnb-t*—loaves. I have not been an eavesdropper. I have not been a gossip. I have not made mischief in matters not my own. I have not lain with a married woman. I have not committed impurity. I have not laid schemes. I have not been neglectful [*sic*]. I have not been hot in reply. I have not been deaf to words of truth. I have not made disturbances. I have not made another weep. I have not . . . the copulator who was copulating. I have not made suppressions.[2] I have not reviled. I have not been violent. I have not been hasty. I have not neglected the nature of the god's satisfaction. I have not multiplied words in speaking. I have not done harm to the doer of evil. I have not railed against the king. I have not waded over the water [*sic*]. I have not been loud of voice. I have not railed against the god. I have not been puffed up. I have not made comparisons with myself [*i.e.* compared myself with others]. I have not made a show with possessions not my own. I have not slighted (?) the god in my city.

Praised be ye, ye gods! I know you and I know your names. I fall not a prey to your swords. Ye shall report to this god whom ye follow nothing evil concerning me. I have had no fault towards you. Ye shall speak the truth concerning me before the Universal Lord. For I have done Righteousness in Egypt, I have not railed against the god, and I have had no fault towards the king of my time.

Praised be ye, ye gods who live in the Hall of Righteousness, in whose body is no lie and who live upon the truth. . . . I have done what men command and that wherewithal the gods are pleased. I have given bread to the hungry, water to the thirsty, clothes to the naked, a ferry-boat to the boatless. I have made offerings to the gods, and oblations to the blessed dead. Save me and protect me. . . .'

9. Comments.—The importance of the two lists of sins contained in this chapter has often been grossly exaggerated. From the observation that no reference is made to family duties, it has been

[1] It was doubtless on this occasion that Osiris received the 'wreath of righteousness' (*woḥ n ma'khrow*) often named in Egyptian texts; hence the wreath depicted on so many Græco-Roman tombstones, and also the 'crown of righteousness (στέφανος δικαιοσύνης) of the NT (see Cumont-Gardiner, *RHR* lxiii. [1911] 210, 214).

[2] The posthumous pilgrimage to Abydos (see below, § 10) is said in at least one place (Thebes, tomb of Amenemhet, no. 83) to have had as its object the 'fetching of justification' (*ma'khrow*).

[3] The vignettes vary considerably; the above description does not adhere to any one particular example.

[1] Another translation, differing considerably from that here given, will be found in art. CONFESSION (Egyptian).

[2] Erman is wrong in translating, 'I have not felt remorse.'

argued that these were not specially emphasized at the time when the lists were drawn up; and the prominence accorded to certain petty offences against religion is urged as a proof that they were considered as heinous as calumny or murder. Far worse than such deductions is the comparison of the two versions in order to distinguish an earlier from a later condition of ethical thought.[1] All such arguments are based on the unproved and wholly unwarranted assumption that the 'Negative Confession' is, as it were, a canonical repudiation of *all* the sins that were considered heinous. The very existence of two lists differing in their details is in itself an indication that neither possessed any high degree of authority; moreover, both exhibit all the signs of careless and hasty compilation. We may be sure, too, that, if great weight had been attached to the precise text, more trouble would have been taken to preserve it from corruption. The truth is that the nature of the sins denied was not the central point of interest to the author or authors of the chapter. Their aim, so far from being an ethical one, was essentially, though perhaps not quite consciously, anti-ethical. Accepting the prevalent belief that happiness in the hereafter is conditioned by a previous life of innocence upon earth, they proceeded to elaborate an incantation such as might hoodwink the Divine Judge and enable the dead man to evade the natural consequences of his sins. Chapter 125 of the Book of the Dead claims to impart knowledge of the words to be spoken on entering the Hall of Righteousness; the tacit assumption is that a knowledge of the names of the judge and his assessors and of what sins to deny was as serviceable a means of attaining eternal felicity as the cleanest of consciences. Whether the sins repudiated had actually been committed or not was a matter of comparative indifference; the main point was that the deceased should be ready with his denials. Nor was it necessary for him actually to commit the chapter to memory; he in whose tomb it was inscribed, or with whom a papyrus containing it was buried, might feel himself perfectly safe as regards the judgment to come. Chapter 125 is, in fact, just such another magical document as that Leyden papyrus (no. 347) which contains spells for aiding a man who had been taken before a court of justice 'to issue thence justified' (*ma'khrow*).

To sum up: it has been seen how a non-ethical theory of the future life, whereby it was contingent on the performance of certain rites and the recitation of certain formulæ, gave rise to a theory in which ethics was of paramount importance; and it has been seen how ch. 125 of the Book of the Dead, while acknowledging the truth of the latter view in principle, finds a means of subordinating it to the earlier view in practice.

10. The story of Osiris.—In the doctrine of the *psychostasia*, Osiris appeared as the perfect judge, the arbiter of human character and ruler of the virtuous dead. The origin and the early nature of Osiris are shrouded in obscurity, but at a very ancient date he became the prototype of the beneficent Pharaoh. Mythology told how Osiris had succumbed, after a long and prosperous reign, to the machinations of his wicked brother Seth, who mutilated his body and scattered his limbs. At length Isis, the faithful wife of Osiris, succeeded in collecting his remains, and infusing new life into them by dint of her magical power; but henceforth Osiris was a shadowy being ruling among the dead, while his son Horus, having taken vengeance upon Seth, sat upon the throne of the living. It is, doubtless, owing to its human interest and pathos that the story of Osiris took so firm a hold on the imagination of the Egyptians; and, as we have seen, every Egyptian who died claimed to be another Osiris, destined at last to conquer the powers of evil, and to awake to a happier and never-ending life. Pilgrims flocked to Abydos, which had become (though not much before the Middle Kingdom) the traditional burial-place of the god; and, as every one sought to establish for himself a cenotaph in that city, it was sometimes called 'the island of the Just' (Gardiner, *Literary Texts*, Leipzig, 1911, i. 7, note 1).[1] In the temple-cults all the other gods were gradually assimilated to Osiris; and the Pharaoh, whom a fiction always represented as the chief officiant, played the part of the 'loving son' Horus (A. Moret, *Le Rituel du culte divin journalier*, Paris, 1901). In Ptolemaic times, Osiris was blended with a newly introduced god, Serapis, and henceforth his importance waned; but at the same time the popularity of Isis increased, and it was in her shrines that the Osirian faith was kept alive throughout the length and breadth of the Roman Empire.

11. The gods as guardians of morality.—As the personification of all that is good, Osiris acquired the title of *Onnofre* (Onnophris), 'the good being,' besides which he was known as 'the great God, the lord of Right.' Seth came to be regarded as the essence of evil; and, though his cult persisted in certain places where the secondary antithesis to Osiris had not been able to dislodge the primitive cult, his image was generally held in abhorrence, and at certain periods was obliterated from the monuments. The gods of the Egyptians were collectively regarded as good, though individually they might be bad or neutral: thus, in narrating his virtues, a noble says, 'I did what all the gods loved' (*ZÄ* xlv. [1908] 125). We have seen above that 'God'—the vague entity which not seldom takes the place of more explicitly named divinities in Egyptian texts—was looked upon as the dispenser of rewards and punishments. This conception was, doubtless, a generalization due to the importance of the local gods. Every Egyptian felt himself specially dependent upon and bounden towards the 'god of his city'; and that deity, whatever his individual name or characteristics, was at bottom nothing but the personified feeling of the community, and hence, as a matter of course, also the guardian of the ethical code. Besides Osiris there were other specific deities, who were thought of as judges or patrons of virtue. Amen-Rē is called the 'Vizier of the poor, who taketh not the bribes of the guilty' (*Pap. Bologna*, 1094, 2, 4). Thōth, the scribe of the gods, is also 'the Vizier in heaven,' and Ptah is the 'lord of Right *or* Truth.' On-hor (Onuris) also was frequently appealed to as arbitrator (Gardiner, *Literary Texts*, i. 16, note 4). That the gods were regarded as righteous judges is indicated by the frequent recourse that litigants had to them; numerous ostraca of the New Kingdom, from the Theban necropolis, tell how cases of petty theft, debt, and commercial disputes were decided in the shrines of the local deity, the deified king Amenhotep, who nodded in answer to the questions put to him by his priest (Erman, *Sitzungsb. d. kön. Preuss. Akad.*, 1909; cf. DIVINATION [Egyp.]). This mode of obtaining justice seems to have superseded all others in the XXIst and following dynasties; and, since

[1] It will be noted that the passages quoted throughout this article are of very various dates. The reason is that it is seldom possible to trace any development of Egyptian ethical ideas, and a historical treatment is therefore precluded. It is likewise impossible, with the evidence at our disposal, to distinguish between the different moralities of different grades of Egyptian society.

[1] Not seldom the pilgrimage was not performed during a man's lifetime, but his mummy was taken to Abydos before the final burial rites.

this is the period at which the power of the priests was paramount, we shall probably not err in interpreting the frequency of trials by oracle as due to a deliberate policy of the priesthood, who would naturally wish to bring secular matters, as far as possible, under their own control. Ma'et, 'Right' or 'Truth,' was from the earliest times conceived of as a goddess (see Lanzone, *Diz. di mitologia egizia*, Turin, 1881–86, pp. 276–280); for the Egyptians, like the Romans, were by no means averse to creating deities out of abstract concepts. Many nobles, and especially the judges, received the title of 'priest of Ma'et'; and in the New Kingdom we even hear of a 'temple of Right.' Whether this was an actual shrine or another name for the law-courts is not certain; it is not unlikely that Ma'et enjoyed a regular cult. The sole significant epithet given to her is 'daughter of Rē'; this relationship is explained by the pleasure that the sun-god was supposed to take in virtue, it being even said that 'Rē lives upon (*i.e.* eats) right' (*ma'et*). In this connexion may be mentioned a ceremony daily practised in the temples: the king (or his substitute, the high priest) offered to the god a small image of Ma'et, seated upon a basket or basket-like vessel, a feather on her head, and the sign of life in her hands. The meaning of this offering is not established; it is not even clear whether Ma'et, in this case, is the goddess of Righteousness or that of Truth, the personification of ethical or of intellectual rightness.

12. Law and punishment.—A few words must be said about Egyptian conceptions of law and punishment. For 'law' the word was *hap*, a term also employed for 'custom'; the etymology is unknown. The Egyptians codified their laws, as indeed everything in Egypt was committed to writing. Of the laws themselves we know little beyond what the Greek writers have to tell us. In the two central courts of justice the vizier sat with the forty parchment rolls of the Law open before him (Newberry, 2); still it was apparently enjoined upon him to pay no less attention to equity than to law (*ib.* 10. 4). The Egyptian word for 'punishment' (*sbōyet*) literally means 'teaching,' punishment probably being regarded in the light of a lesson and example to others. Egyptian punishments seem, on the whole, to have been less severe than those inflicted in Babylonia; but magistrates prided themselves on making penalties proportionate to the offences. Thus, one official states that he 'inflicted hurt on him who inflicted hurt' (*Urk.* iv. 969), and that he 'punished the evil-doer in accordance with his evil-doing' (*ib.* 971).

13. Specific moral concepts.—We now turn to the special side of our subject—the moral judgments concerning particular vices and virtues. The field to be covered is so large that it has been found impossible to emphasize any but the most salient facts; what is here given must be supplemented by the information to be found in special articles.

(1) *Homicide* was, of course, forbidden: 'I have not slain, I have not commanded to slay' (Conf. A). That in certain cases magistrates possessed powers over life and death is implied by the statement of an official: 'There was none who died by my counsel' (*Hannover*, 11 = *RTAP* xvii. 4). Later, in the XVIIIth dynasty, the king reserved to himself these powers; the vizier might inflict only such punishments as did not involve the cutting off of a limb (Newberry, 2. 13). How absolute was the might of Pharaoh is shown by the advice that is given to the king in a St. Petersburg papyrus: 'Do not kill a man whose excellence thou knowest' (*ZÄ* xiv. [1876] 108). In a case of high treason, the condemned were allowed to make away with themselves (T. Deveria, *Le Pap. judiciaire de Turin*, Paris, 1868). To kill an adulterous wife seemed to the Egyptians quite legitimate (*Pap. d'Orbiney*), and a similar punishment might justifiably be exacted from her paramour (*Pap. Westcar*, p. 3 f.). That capital punishment was not unfamiliar to the Egyptians is shown by the phrase which describes any heinous crime as 'a great crime of death.' No compunction was felt in putting captured foes to death (*Amada Stele*); such an act had, indeed, a religious sanction as a sacrifice to the god who had sent Pharaoh forth to war. Magicians made waxen images of those whom they wished to destroy (*Pap. Lee*); but this practice was, of course, condemned by law.

(2) *Human sacrifice* was undoubtedly practised in ancient Egypt, notwithstanding Herodotus' explicit statement to the contrary (ii. 45). The monumental evidence still needs collection and sifting, but there is little doubt that it will confirm the affirmations of the classical writers. Diodorus (i. 88) speaks of offerings of human beings made upon the tomb of Osiris; and Plutarch preserves a tradition (which is not likely to have been invented) to the effect that red-haired men were burnt alive in Eileithyiaspolis (*de Is. et Osir.* 73, with Parthey's valuable note, p. 272 f.). We hear, too, of similar sacrifices in Heliopolis, for which, however, King Amasis caused waxen images to be substituted (Porphyry, *de Abst.* ii. 55). The models of servants who were buried together with their lords very probably exemplify the same kind of substitution. It has been thought that the ceremony of the *tiknu*, which was practised at funerals, involved human sacrifice; but this is by no means certain.

(3) *Cruelty.*—Some of the facts that have already been mentioned might be thought to indicate that the Egyptians were cruel of disposition; but the treatment of enemies, the punishment of criminals, and religious immolations were, in all lands of antiquity, equally ruthless and barbarous. It may be added in this connexion that in warfare the Egyptians were accustomed to cut off the hands or the phalli of the slain. Criminals were frequently deprived of their ears and noses (*Decree of Haremheb; Inscr. of Mes*). The ordinary punishment, however, was the bastinado, which was as freely used under the Pharaohs as in the Egypt of one hundred years ago. Not even men of rank were exempt from chastisement of the kind; an official of the Old Kingdom asserts: 'I have never been beaten before any magistrate since I was born' (*Urk.* i. 75). The general impression gained from the inscriptions is that the Egyptians were too easy-going and good-tempered a people to be cruel. The infliction of unnecessary pain was deprecated: when a Pharaoh suggested to a magician who claimed to be able to replace a severed head that he should try his skill on a condemned prisoner, he was asked to rest content with an experiment on a goose (*Pap. Westcar*, 8. 16).

(4) *Kindness and benevolence.*—Egyptians often claim to have been 'kindly, lovers of men' (*Louvre*, C 41; *Anast.* i. 2, 6). The proverbs of Ptahhotep praise the man who is conciliatory and friendly; he will find his reward in days of misfortune (*Prisse*, 11. 1 f.). 'I have not oppressed (my) fellows,' 'I have not caused weeping,' are assertions made in the Negative Confession (A). The poor and afflicted were held to be particularly in need of kindness:

> 'I was father to the orphan, a husband to the widow, a shelter to the cold' (*Hannover*, 11 = *RTAP* xvii. 4); 'I saved the miserable man from him who was more powerful than he' (Petrie, *Dendereh*, London, 1900, p. 8).

Suppliants were to be treated with exceptional patience:

> 'If thou art a ruler, be willing to listen when a suppliant speaks. Do not repel him until his body is rid of that which he

intended to tell thee. He who is in trouble loves to pour out his heart concerning that on account of which he is come. When a man repels petitions, people say, "Why does he disregard them?"' (*Prisse*, 9. 3-6).

(5) *Charity.*—No virtue was more incumbent upon the rich than generosity to the needy:

'I gave bread to the hungry, clothes to the naked' (*Urk.* i. 122), and like phrases, encounter us at every turn. 'I caused the peasant to carry home corn together with his wife, and the widow together with her son' is the boast of a noble of Syut (F. L. Griffith, *Siût*, London, 1889, pp. 15, 9-10). An ostracon of the New Kingdom bitterly reproaches a rich and childless old man with not having adopted a son (*Berlin Pap.* 10627).

(6) *Hospitality* is partly covered by the quotations already given. In one passage we read:

'Do not make a funeral feast without thy neighbours, in order that they may stand round thee mourning on the day of burial' (*Petrie Ostracon*, 11). In another passage it is said: 'Do not sit at meat while another stands, but stretch forth for him thy hand towards the food'; for 'one is rich and another poor,' and 'he who was rich last year is a wayfarer this' (*Any*, 7. 3-6).

(7) *Regard for old age.*—To succour the aged was regarded as highly meritorious; but it would appear that this was looked upon less as a duty towards a highly respected class than as an act of charity towards the feeble. The disadvantages of old age were vividly present to the Egyptian mind (*Prisse*, 4. 2-5. 3); but, on the other hand, length of years brought with it high honour and esteem (*imakh*). The Egyptians frequently expressed the hope that they would attain the age of 110 years. The vizier Rekhmere says of himself: 'I tended the old man, I gave to him my staff; I caused aged women to say, "This is a happy time"' (Newberry, 7. 23). 'To bury the aged' was a virtuous deed (*PSBA* xviii. [1895-96] 196); to scoff at decrepit old people, a very wicked one (*Petrie Ostracon*, 11).

(8) *Regard for parents and close relatives.*—A Theban high priest thus describes his behaviour towards his father:

'I was a staff-of-old-age by my father's side while he was yet upon earth. I went in and out at his command, and transgressed not the utterance of his mouth. I did not make little of that wherewith he charged me. . . . I did not pierce him with many glances, but my face was downwards when he spoke to me. I made not bold to do that whereof he was unaware. I knew not the handmaid of his house; I lay not with his servingmaid. I did not curse his butler; nor did I enter in before him violently' (*ZÄ* xlvii. [1910] 92). Another great man of the XVIIIth dynasty quaintly remarks that he 'did not strike his father or curse his mother' (*Urk.* iv. 490).

Filial obedience was rigorously inculcated:

'An obedient son is as a follower of Horus; it fares well with him in consequence of his obedience; he groweth old and attaineth reverence, and telleth the same to his children, renewing the teaching of his father' (*Prisse*, 17. 10-12).

It was the duty of a son to take his father's place in his office when the latter had grown old; a son who did this received the honorific title of 'staff-of-old-age' (see the first quotation above, and the references there given). A father had the obligation to treat his son well, as being of his own flesh and blood, but only if he showed obedience; if he neglected this duty, his father was bidden to 'turn him out; he is not thy son, he was not born to thee' (*Pap. Brit. Mus.* 10509, 3, 17). The god Horus, son of Isis and Osiris, was the pious son *par excellence*, and hence earned the epithet 'protector of his father' (*noz hir iotef*). Every son had the obligation to officiate in the burial ceremonies of his father, though it appears that, in the absence of an heir, a priest, called 'his loving son,' could act as a substitute. Even long after the death of the parents, it was considered right for the children to 'pour water to' their 'father and mother who rest within the Valley' (*Maxims of Any*, 3. 4). In return, the deceased parent would come back 'to visit his home of the living, and to be a protection to his children' (*Urk.* iv. 491).

Though, as has been shown, the duties towards the father were considerable, the mother was accounted nearer of kin; the maternal brothers ranked before brothers by the same father only (e.g. *Prisse*, 10. 3); and heirship, at least in the royal and princely families, was reckoned in the line of the mother. But it was, above all, the mother's tender care to her children that gave her so great a claim upon their affection; the Egyptian moralist pleads the cause of the mother in eloquent words:

'Give back twofold the sustenance that thy mother gave thee. Support her as she supported thee. Long did she bear the burden of thee, and forsook thee not. When thou wast born after thy term of months, she carried thee on her shoulder; three years long her nipple was in thy mouth. . . . She put thee to school when thou shouldst be taught thy letters, and waited upon thee daily, bringing food to the hungry ones in her home. Thou becamest a stripling and didst take to thee a wife, and art established in thy house. Cast around thine eye for one who hath borne thee, seek the man who hath nurtured thee as did thy mother! Let her not find cause of complaint in thee, or lift up her hands to God, lest he hear her cry!' (*Any*, 6. 17-7. 3).

So sacred was the maternal tie deemed, that we find the command, 'Do not regard a woman as thy mother who is not' (*Petrie Ostracon*, 11).

A kindly, affectionate spirit in the family was esteemed above other virtues; often in the Old Kingdom a man claims to have been 'loved of his father, praised of his mother, and beloved of all his brethren' (e.g. *Urk.* i. 122). Under certain circumstances the elder brother might take the place of the parents, and in that case exacted complete obedience from his juniors (*d'Orbiney*, pp. 1 and 2).

(9) *Wedlock, love, and the position of women.*—'Get thee a wife while thou art yet a youth' is the advice given by a moralist of the New Kingdom (*Any*, 2. 1); the reason there given is 'in order that she may bear thee a son,' who is to receive a careful education; for 'happy is the man whose household are many; he is respected in proportion to his children.' From the point of view of the man this was the customary condition of opinion; a peasant whose wife has been drowned tells us that he does not regret her for her own sake, but only for the sake of the children she might have borne (Erman, *Lebensmüde*, 79). The wife was, nevertheless, to be well treated and loved:

'If thou art well-to-do, found a house, and love thy wife studiously. Fill her stomach and clothe her back; oil is the medicine of her body. Gladden her heart thy lifetime long. She is a field that is profitable unto its lord' (*Prisse*, 10. 6-8).

The Egyptian monuments everywhere depict husband and wife in attitudes of affection, and the phrases 'his wife whom he loves' and 'his sister whom he loves' are amongst the commonest expressions found in the hieroglyphs. Forbearance is to be shown to the woman who is wayward and given up to amusements: 'Be kind to her for a season, send her not away, give her food to eat' (*Prisse*, 15. 6-7). How tender and passionate the love of an Egyptian could be is shown by the love poems that have survived (see Max Müller, *Die Liebespoesie der alten Ägypter*, Leipzig, 1899). Polygamy seems to have been permitted, but to have been unusual; brother-and-sister marriage was not rare. Divorce seems to have depended on the caprice of the husband; but the latter bound himself by contract, at least in late times, to pay an indemnification if he exercised the right to repudiate his wife without valid reason (see Griffith, *Rylands Papyri*, London, 1909, iii. 116). The divorced woman, like the widow, often stood in sore need of protection (*Eloquent Peasant B 1*, 63); but, since women were allowed to possess property, either position was doubtless often very tolerable. The lady of means, from the most ancient times onwards, bore the title 'mistress of a house' (*nebt pēr*). The position of a woman was higher than in any other land of antiquity; not only could she administer her own possessions, but she had testamentary rights and the power to go to law (see Gardiner, *The Inscription of Mes*, Leipzig, 1905). Egypt had many great queens, of whom several reigned independently and with great prestige, *e.g.* Hatshepsut of the XVIIIth dynasty.

(10) *Sexual morality* (for adultery, see above under the heading '*Homicide*' and art. ADULTERY [Egyptian]).—Pre-nuptial immorality was very lightly regarded; we find no prohibition concerning it in the Negative Confession, and a lord of Elephantinē in the VIth dynasty even boasts of 'having had a good time with women' (*ZÄ* xlv. [1908] 130. Loose women abounded; and the dancing girls who attended the feasts given by grandees doubtless belonged to the prostitute class. The moralist gives a warning against women of this type:

'Beware of the strange woman, who is not known in her town. Approach her not . . . and know her not in bodily wise. A deep and unfathomable water is the woman who is apart from her husband' (*Any*, 2. 13–15).

Religious prostitution is attested by Strabo (xvii. 1. 46) for the priestesses of Amon of Thebes until the age of puberty, when they were given in marriage. The monuments afford no direct confirmation of this statement, but certain indications make it probable that it is no mere invention. Amon was a sensual god, represented, like Min, as ithyphallic; numerous 'chantresses' (*shemayt*) constituted his *harîm* (*khenr*), and the wife of the high priest bore the title 'chief of the ladies of the *harîm* of Amon' (*ZÄ* xlv. [1908] 127). In the New Kingdom most ladies of rank, married to men in high stations, called themselves 'chantresses' of one god or another; even goddesses had their *harîms* (*ZÄ* xlviii. [1910] 50). The Pharaohs had large *harîms*, and it is improbable that concubinage on a considerable scale was confined to the royal house; but we are ill-instructed on this point. The papyri of the New Kingdom give the impression that the lower orders, as, for example, the workmen of the Theban Necropolis, usually formed loose temporary connexions in lieu of legal marriages (see Erman, *Life in Ancient Egypt*, tr. Tirard, London, 1894, p. 154). An erotic papyrus (at Turin), full of pictures of the coarsest kind, shows that few of the sexual vices of the Orient were unknown to Ancient Egypt. In a magical papyrus of the XIIth dynasty, Seth appears as a pæderast seeking to tempt his brother Horus (Griffith, *Hieratic Papyri from Kahun*, 1899, p. 3; cf. *Sphinx*, xiv. [1910] 39–41); and it would appear that this crime, like adultery, was a stock charge in the indictments brought before the law-courts (see *Pap. Turin*, 55. 4). In both versions of the Negative Confession, impurity (masturbation ?) while serving as a lay priest of the god is denied.

(11) *Purity*.—Cleanliness, both of the person and of the clothing, was scrupulously observed; and the houses of the wealthy seldom lacked a bath-room (*Sinuhe B*, 285). The washing of face and hands was considered the necessary preliminary to a meal (Griffith, *Stories of the High Priests*, Oxford, 1900, p. 44), and sexual acts of all sorts were regarded as defiling. Purity in the service of the gods was strenuously insisted upon (Herod. ii. 37); and all grades of priests, professional and lay, shared the name of *wēb*, 'the pure priest' (see, further, PURIFICATION [Egyp.]). The concept of ethical purity was also known, though it did not play a very important part; we find it at the end of the earlier Repudiation of Sins (A); and *wa'b* in the metaphorical sense means 'to be innocent' (*Pap. Mayer B, passim*).

(12) *Slavery*.—On this subject we have strangely little precise information. Prisoners of war were often presented as slaves, both to individuals (*e.g. Urk.* iv. 2. 11) and to the gods (*e.g.* Newberry, 21). There can be little doubt that slaves were very numerous, but we have no early evidence as to the sources whence they were recruited, or as to the question whether they were ever emancipated. From the XXVIth dynasty legal deeds exist recording the sale and transfer of slaves; also voluntary contracts of servitude, involving not only a man's person but also his children (Griffith, *Rylands Papyri*, iii. 50 f.).

(13) *The right of property*.—The official theory in Ancient Egypt was to the effect that the Pharaoh is the sole owner of property; if his subjects hold lands, houses, cattle, and valuables, it is because the king has granted them leave to do so; even the tombs of the dead were 'the gift of the king.' The temples of the gods, too, were the castles which the Pharaoh, their son, had built for them; and each successive monarch confirmed to the gods the possessions accorded by his ancestors (see Moret, *La Royauté pharaonique*, Paris, 1903). Similarly, the booty captured from foreign tribes was theoretically regarded as tribute which rebellious subjects had failed to render. In practice, this theory of property corresponded with the reality just in the degree in which the royal power was on the rise or on the decline. Conquerors who (like Amenemmes I. and Amosis I.) reduced the land to order after a period of anarchy rewarded their subjects with grants of land pretty much as they chose. In periods of prosperity the king had to content himself with a show of confirming (*smīne*) already existing rights; or the latter might, as in the first half of the XIIth dynasty, be actually under the control of feudal families, or, as in the XXIst dynasty, be usurped by a ruling priesthood. The official formula remained the same throughout Egyptian history, and might doubtless have been used to justify taxation, if, indeed, this question was ever raised. In actual fact the land was parcelled out among a variety of proprietors, all tenacious of their proprietorship, which was attested by title-deeds and carried with it rights of testamentary disposition and alienation by sale. The elaborate care with which the land was surveyed and registered is only partly explained by the Egyptians' inveterate love of committing things to writing; documentary records were an absolute necessity in a land where the annual inundation was apt to sweep away all boundary marks. It was a primary duty for those in authority to protect proprietary rights, and the nobles frequently recorded the fact that they had 'succoured him who was debarred from his property by one more powerful than he' (*Urk.* iv. 972), and that they had 'never deprived a man of the estate of his father' (*ib.* i. 123). A great portion of the land was in the hands of the priests, being theoretically considered the property of the gods. To such limits did the encroachments of the priesthood go that, in the XXth dynasty, Amon of Thebes possessed no less than 864,168 *stat* of land, 421,362 head of cattle, 433 gardens and groves, and 86,486 serfs and slaves (see Breasted, *Anc. Records*, Chicago, 1906–7, iv. 97).

The crime of robbery is frequently mentioned:

'Never have I taken away the property of any man by robbery' (*Urk.* i. 75); and the subject of a well-known tale of the Middle Kingdom is a peasant who has been robbed of his ass and its load on a trumpery pretext, and who demands justice from the administrator of the province (Vogelsang-Gardiner, *Die Klagen des Bauern*, Leipzig, 1908).

Robbery is distinguished from theft in Confession B; it is curious that A makes no reference to either sin. Many ostraca and papyri deal with cases of petty theft, but throw no light on the penalties imposed on account of it.

The decree of King Haremheb mentions some stringent reforms carried through by that Pharaoh; the official tax-gatherers had been abusing their opportunities in order to rob and oppress the peasants; these offences were thenceforth to be punished by banishment to the frontier fort of Zaru, after the offender's nose had been cut off, or, in less serious instances, by a hundred blows of the bastinado inflicted so as to leave five open wounds.

The rich equipment of furniture and jewels buried with the wealthy dead was an easy booty to unscrupulous men, and tomb-robbery was committed on a large scale.

In the XXth dynasty it was found that many royal tombs had been tampered with, and the legal investigations then instituted form the subject of some of the most interesting documents from Ancient Egypt (see Newberry-Spiegelberg, *Excavations in the Theban Necropolis*, London, 1908).

(14) *Regard for truth and good faith.*—Truthfulness was highly esteemed and was barely distinguished from 'right,' both concepts being denoted by the same word *ma'et*. In Confession B the deceased says: 'I have not spoken falsehood.' But Egypt would not be the Orient if lying had not been both practised and regarded in many cases as venial. To lie for one's own advantage without harming others was doubtless regarded as clever; it is the root-idea of the Negative Confession and of no small part of magic. Sinuhe tells us that he wilfully misinformed the Syrian prince who was showing him hospitality (*Sin. B*, 61). On the funeral stelæ it is frequently stated that what is there inscribed contains no falsehood and no exaggeration; in Confession B we find the 'suppression' of the truth denied. In ordinary conversation, asseverations were reinforced by such oaths as 'By Ptah, lord of Truth' (Right), 'As Month praises me'; in the law-courts the ordinary oath was 'As Amon liveth, and as the Prince liveth,' but often there were added long and circumstantial self-curses specifying the penalty to be incurred if what is said proves to be untrue (see W. Spiegelberg, *Rechtswesen*, Hanover, 1892, and Gardiner, *Inscription of Mes*). Lying became a serious offence when it involved the interests of others:

'I have not said lies concerning another,' an official maintains (*Urk.* iv. 120); and 'I have not traduced the servant to his master' (A) is a frequent claim.

To render messages faithfully was thought a desirable habit (*Prisse*, 7. 3; *Urk.* iv. 120), and reliability and obedience towards one's masters are virtues everywhere praised. Honesty in commercial transactions is emphasized in those statements of Confession A which refer to the units of measurement and to the balance. The stemming or diverting of running water (A), in a land where irrigation played so important a part as in Egypt, was, of course, a common way of obtaining an unfair advantage over other persons.

(15) *Justice.*—The endeavour of the magistrate was not only to 'cause the two parties to go away satisfied' (Newberry, 4), but to administer the laws fairly and in accordance with the command of Pharaoh (*ib.* 10). Great stress was laid on impartiality:

'Regard him whom thou knowest like him whom thou knowest not.' Again it is said, 'To put upon the one side'—the metaphor seems to be from overweighting one scale of the balance—'is the abhorrence of God' (*ib.*). The judge must, of course, be wholly incorruptible; 'I have not been deaf to the empty-handed, I have not received the bribe of any,' says the vizier Rekhmere (*ib.* 8. 24). In the only civil case of which we have full details (XIXth dynasty), a commissioner was sent out to make some investigations, and came back with a false report to the chief court of which he was a member; it is clear that he had been bribed by one of the parties (Gardiner, *Inscription of Mes*).

The insistence with which the inscriptions refer to incorruptibility and impartiality suggests that these virtues were less common than was claimed; nor does the analogy of modern Egypt discourage this supposition. The ideal picture of the judge drawn in Thutmosis III.'s charge to Rekhmere is up to a high standard of moral enlightenment. Besides the indispensable qualities of justice and incorruptibility, he is required to possess patience, tact, and discretion; not to be over-lenient or over-stern, allowing the litigants to have their say, and making it quite clear on what grounds the verdict is given (Newberry, 10).

(16) *Demeanour in everyday life.*—*Good-temper* was enjoined and admired.

The chief butler, Thuti (Tomb in Gurna, no. 110), takes credit to himself for having been 'of pleasant character, self-restrained, and free from passion.' 'I have not been hot of mouth,' *i.e.* hot in reply, is one of the statements in Confession B.

Pharaoh, indeed, might allow himself to 'be enraged like a leopard of the South' (e.g. *Urk.* iv. 139), but his subjects had no such licence. *Contentiousness* was considered a fault.

One moralist gives the precept, 'Do not persist in fighting with thy neighbours' (*Petrie Ostracon*, 11), and another advises, 'Enter not into the law-court, lest thy name stink' (*Any*, 2. 17).

Rancour was blamed, and men are bidden not to store up memories of small wrongs (*Petrie Ostracon*, 11); and the words 'I have not done harm to the doer of evil' (B) may refer to the virtue of *forgiveness*. Among the fatalistic Egyptians of to-day, *gratitude* is said to be almost unknown. There is no exact phrase for gratitude in the old Egyptian language, for 'to praise God' (*dowe' nūter*) for some one is rather to congratulate him than to thank him; in Coptic 'I am grateful' is rendered by ⲟⲩϩⲙⲟⲧ ϣⲏⲡ, 'a favour has been received.' The forgetfulness of benefits received, however, calls forth bitter comment in several old texts:

'Yesterday is not remembered, and to the doer is not done again in these times' (*Lebensmüde*, 115). 'A man has no household on the day of troubles, . . . he who ate of my food conspired against me' (*Millingen*, 2. 5).

On the subject of *friendship* the ethical writers have much to say.

The reflexion contained in the words last quoted should teach the king to place no confidence in any one (*Millingen*, 1. 2). If a man wishes to keep his friends, he must avoid too close familiarity with their women-folk (*Prisse*, 9. 8–11). If he wishes to ascertain a friend's real feelings, he should commune with him privately, and not seek information from others (*ib.* 14. 6–9). Egyptian dignitaries often assert that they have not had evil associates (e.g. *ZÄ* xlvii. [1910] 93).

Eavesdropping, *gossiping*, *mischief-making*, and *excessive talkativeness* are faults named in the Repudiation of Sins (B). *Self-ingratiation* by improper means is condemned: 'Do not make straight what is crooked in order to win love' (*Petrie Ostracon*, 11). *Deference to superiors* was a duty imposed on all: 'Bow thy back to thy superior, thy overseer from the Palace' (*Prisse*, 13. 9–10). Distinctions of rank were jealously guarded, and etiquette prescribed a strict order of precedence.

The pictures in the tombs, as well as the inscriptions, prove that nobles were approached in deferential attitudes. Before Pharaoh all his subjects grovelled in the dust, touching the earth with their foreheads; and it was deemed the highest favour to be allowed to kiss the king's foot instead of the ground (*Urk.* i. 52).

Courtesy and *tact* were prescribed, especially in the company of men of position:

'If thou art seated at the board of one greater than thee, take what he offers thee. . . . Look straight in front of thee, pierce him not with many glances. . . . Speak when he addresses thee, and laugh when he laughs; it will please him greatly' (*Pap. Brit. Mus.* 10509, 2. 13–16).

That *obedience* was exacted from inferiors goes without saying; but even so high an official as Ineni affirms (*Urk.* iv. 62): 'I was one who hearkened to what my superior said.' *Pride* is very often spoken of as a failing: 'Do not be proud, lest thou be humbled' (*Prisse*, 12. 1). Of intellectual pride it is said:

'Do not exalt thy heart on account of thy knowledge; take counsel with the ignorant as with the wise. For the limit of a craft is not to be reached; there is no perfect craftsman. A good saying lies hidden more than an emerald; it is to be found with slave-girls grinding at the mill' (*Prisse*, 5. 8–10).

The poor man is not to be treated haughtily (*Pap. Brit. Mus.* 10509, 3. 6), for 'he who possesses virtue possesses riches' (*Prisse*, 7. 5). Nor should contempt be shown to him who has no children, for 'there is many a father in misery, and many a mother, and other women are happier than she' (*Prisse*, 7. 6). The Negative Confession has several references to pride and vanity: 'I have not been puffed up,' 'I have not compared myself with others.' No quotations are required to illustrate the great love of ostentation characteristic of the Egyptians. Like their modern descendants, the ancient people were incurable braggarts, never so contented as when airing their virtues and displaying their own cleverness.

One of the favourite books of the XIXth and XXth dynasties has as its subject the rivalry of two scribes, each of whom tries to demonstrate his superiority over the other by boasting about himself, and depreciating the merits of his fellow (Gardiner, *Hieratic Texts*, Leipzig, 1911, i. 1).

Discretion was very highly valued; of many men we are told that they were 'closed of mouth concerning what their eyes saw' (Benson-Gourlay, *Temple of Mut*, London, 1899, p. 326), or 'secretive in the business of the Palace' (*Urk.* iv. 47). The utility of silence was very well understood, and it was prescribed as the best method of coping with many difficulties (*Prisse*, 1. 1; 7. 5; 11. 9). So, too, in B, 'I have not multiplied words in talking.'

(17) *Qualities and defects of character.*—Under this heading we deal with the self-regarding virtues and with various traits of character of which the ethical nature is more or less clearly defined. *Drunkenness* was the invariable ending of feasts, and seems to have been looked upon as a good joke rather than as something culpable. In the tomb-paintings, men are shown being carried home drunk on the shoulders of their companions; and not seldom we are allowed to see a fashionable lady who has been overcome with nausea, while an attendant rushes to her assistance. Drunkenness is, however, sometimes deprecated as a bad habit, as in the following passage:

'Do not corrupt thyself by drinking beer. . . . A speech issues from thy mouth, and thou knowest not who says it. Thou fallest and thy limbs are broken, and no one lendeth thee a hand. Thy companions in drinking stand and say, "Away with this drunkard!" Some one comes to seek thee to speak with thee, and thou art found lying on the ground like a child' (*Any*, 3. 6–11; see, too, *Anast.* iv. 11. 8–12. 5).

Gluttony is blamed only in so far as it constitutes a breach of good manners:

'If thou sittest together with many others, reject the food thou likest. It is but a little moment of self-restraint, and gluttony is bad. . . . A cup of water quencheth the thirst . . . and a little trifle does as a substitute for much' (*Prisse*, 1. 1).

Sexual morality has already been discussed. The Egyptians occasionally preached *moderation* and the curbing of the appetites, as we have seen; and certain restrictions in diet were demanded by religious usage and the rules of purity. Among the subjects of the Pharaohs, however, there is to be discovered hardly a trace of that asceticism which was later to become so marked a feature of Egyptian Christianity. On the whole the *quest of pleasure* was encouraged. Ptahhotep says:

'Follow thy desire as long as thou livest; do not do more than has been enjoined so as to shorten the time of thy enjoyment' (*Prisse*, 7. 9); and the well-known Song of the Harper gives similar counsel, for life is short and death is but decay and annihilation (Max Müller, *l.c.*). But preparation for the hereafter should be made by the building of a tomb (*Any*, 3. 14), for no man can tell when he will die (*Any*, 4. 2–3).

The value of *industry* was not ignored.

One official claims to have been 'a foreman vigilant on behalf of the king's mother, not distinguishing night from day' (*Urk.* iv. 47); another speaks of himself as 'not slothful concerning the things entrusted to him' (*ib.* 959). An ostracon that has often been quoted contains the maxim: 'Do not spare thy body whilst thou art young, for food cometh by the arms and provisions by the legs' (*Petrie Ostracon*, 11).

Courage in battle was always highly rewarded by the Pharaoh, the 'gold of bravery' and lands and other possessions being given to the officers who so distinguished themselves (see *ZÄ* xlviii. [1910] 143). The Pharaoh himself is described as a miracle of valour, and is compared with the lion for prowess and with the bull for strength. The *pursuit of wisdom* is the last personal attribute that will be mentioned under this heading; it falls within the province of ethics as being dependent on voluntary effort, and as being an object of general approval. The man 'who knows things' (*rakh ikhet*) was held in high esteem by the Egyptians, and they often speak with pride of their intellectual attainments.

Thus Rekhmere informs us that he was 'clever in all undertakings, ardent in inquiry, and a ready listener'; 'I was skilled,' he says, 'in the ways of the past, and the things of yesterday caused me to know to-morrow' (Newberry, 8. 35–36).

(18) *Duties towards the dead.*—In view of the care and forethought which the Egyptians expended on the construction of their tombs and on the continuance of their funerary cult, it is strange that public opinion imposed on the living no adequate obligation to fulfil the intentions of the departed. It is an undoubted fact, and one not untinged with tragedy, that magnificent tombs, ornamented with exquisite skill and equipped with the costliest furniture during the life-time of their owners, were within a few years suffered to fall into decay, and even to become the undisputed prey of tomb-plunderers. Filial piety, as we have seen, demanded that the son and heir should accomplish his parent's burial rites; and it may be assumed that none but a few shirked this duty. But this first perfunctory service by no means assured the permanent welfare of the dead; offerings had to be made at the periodical feast-days, not for a few years only, but in perpetuity. It seems certain that the attentions paid to the dead seldom extended beyond a single generation; and in this respect Ancient Egypt stands in signal contrast to China, with its universally-recognized cult of ancestors. The Pharaohs, it is true, were more assiduous in their veneration of their forefathers than the bulk of the people; but, with a little qualification, it may fairly be said that in Egypt the cult of the dead existed only in demand, not in supply. See, further, ANCESTOR-WORSHIP AND CULT OF THE DEAD (Egyptian).

(19) *Duties towards the gods.*—In lands where, as in Ancient Egypt, an official cult of the gods has been established—wherever, in fact, religious observances are not dictated by mere individual desires—this cult and these observances become a duty. The only question is whether the obligation falls on the shoulders of the people at large or is vicariously discharged by a specially-appointed priesthood. The Egyptian priesthood was only in part professional; whence it follows that private persons, so far as their wealth and position prescribed, took part in the public worship of the gods. How far the populace at large attended to, or were supposed to attend to, the gods of the State will be discussed in such articles as WORSHIP (Egyptian); here it will suffice to quote a precept which enjoins on all men generally the observation of the Divine feast days: 'Make the feast of thy god, and repeat it in its season. God is wroth when He is neglected' (*Any*, 2. 3–4). Various religious offences are mentioned in the Negative Confession, including fraudulent diminution of the temple-offerings, the slaying of sacred animals, and blasphemy. There were also prohibitions as to food, rules of purity, and much else that cannot here be discussed. The fact that the gods rewarded virtue (see above) proves that righteousness was regarded in one aspect as a duty towards them; and, owing to this religious side of ethics, the relations of a man with his deity might become very intimate. Certain votive stelæ of the New Kingdom exhibit the nearest approach to *penitence* that is found in Egyptian texts; a certain Nefer-abu, for instance, humbly confesses that he is a 'foolish man,' and prays to his god not to punish him for his 'manifold transgressions' (Erman, *Äg. Rel.*[2] 99, and in detail, *Sitz. d. kön. Preuss. Akad.*, 1911, no. xlix.).

14. Conclusion.—In conclusion, a rough moral estimate of the Egyptians may be attempted.

They were gay, light-hearted, luxurious, and inclined to ostentation; prone to self-indulgence, and not proof against sensual temptations. They were kind, charitable, and courteous; perhaps rather less callous to pain than other nations of antiquity. Honesty and incorruptibility were not among their strong points, but in this respect they were at least able to perceive the ideal standard, if they did not attain to it. Intellectually, the Egyptians were gifted but not deep; their aversion to dull brooding, and their love of all that is artistic and pleasurable in life, are characteristics which have played by no means a small part in helping to endear them to their modern votaries.

LITERATURE.—Besides the authorities quoted throughout the article the following books may be mentioned: E. Amélineau, *Essai sur l'évolution histor. et philos. des idées morales dans l'Égypte ancienne*, Paris, 1895; W. M. Flinders Petrie, *Religion and Conscience in Ancient Egypt*, London, 1898.

ALAN H. GARDINER.

ETHICS AND MORALITY (Greek). — **1. Homeric age.**—The mental attitude of the society which Homer depicts was neither introspective nor agitated by moral doubts. It belonged to an age of action, when bodily strength, courage, and resolution were more highly esteemed than unswerving rectitude or pre-eminent wisdom. The sagacity of Nestor was treated with formal respect, but he had lost in the feebleness of age the position which he had successfully claimed in his prime. On the other hand, the counsel of Odysseus was the more readily welcomed in consequence of his practical resource and military skill. The authority wielded by the chieftains over their feudal retainers depended on their power to enforce it: in the absence of Odysseus and Achilles, Laertes and Peleus were too old to watch effectively over their sons' interests, and Telemachus as a mere stripling was ignored. Similarly, the nominal over-lordship of Agamemnon failed to coerce Achilles, who was strong enough to assert his independence. Thus the exercise of the humaner virtues was restricted to the bounds of family or clan; but within these limits we find evidence of a highly developed morality. The sanctity attached to the marriage bond may be illustrated from the wonderful pictures of Hector and Andromache, and of Odysseus and Penelope; and the supreme happiness of a well-assorted union is recognized in the words of Odysseus to Nausicaa: 'There is nothing greater or better than a husband and wife dwelling together with united minds' (*Od.* vi. 182 ff.). The position of women recognized in the Homeric poems — but always within the limits indicated above — was characterized by greater freedom and influence than was customary at Athens in later times, as may be seen in the several cases of Penelope, Nausicaa, and Arete the wife of Alcinous (*Od.* vii. 66).

Various causes have been assigned for the change, such as (1) the fact that the women described in Homer belonged to a privileged class, (2) the necessary seclusion imposed by the conditions of town life, and (3) the contact with the Ionian civilization of Asia Minor (see Mahaffy, *Social Life in Greece*[2], London, p. 147, and T. D. Seymour, *Life in the Homeric Age*, New York, 1907, p. 117 ff.). Seymour, in suggesting (p. 128) that the society of Homer was Æolic rather than Ionian, refers to the abuse directed against the Æolic poetesses by non-sympathetic Ionians.

There is similar evidence of sympathy with children (see esp. *Il.* xv. 362, xxii. 499). The cases of Euryclea and Eumæus show that slavery was compatible with relations of intimate affection and devoted fidelity between the master and his household. Beggars and suppliants were under the special protection of Zeus, and had an indefeasible claim to hospitality (*Od.* vi. 208, xiii. 213). The same mild spirit was shown in the gentle treatment of the lower animals, such as horses and dogs; and the example of the old dog Argus (*Od.* xvii. 292 ff.), who recognized his master after twenty years' absence, is familiar to every one. The claims of morality as thus acknowledged imposed obligations which could not be broken without offending public opinion. The sense of honour (αἰδώς) corresponded to the feeling of resentment (νέμεσις, as in *Il.* xiii. 122) with which a disregard of propriety was visited. Nevertheless, behind all these manifestations of refinement and generosity there was a dark background of hardness and cruelty.

In his wrath the Homeric hero was a savage. Patroclus slew the son of Amphidamas in anger over a game of knuckle-bones (*Il.* xxiii. 88), and Achilles was afraid lest his passion should drive him to kill the defenceless Priam, who as suppliant and guest could claim his special protection (*Il.* xxiv. 568, 585). Mutilation of an enemy is mentioned over and over again without reprobation (see *Il.* xi. 145, xiii. 202, xiv. 488, etc.). The punishment of the treacherous slave Melanthius is carried out with brutal and repulsive ferocity (*Od.* xxii. 474 ff.). In fact, in dealing with those who were beyond the pale, the heroic warrior showed no pity for unprotected weakness; when a town was captured, the old men and children were slain, and the women were carried off as the property of the victors (see *Il.* xxii. 62; *Od.* viii. 528 ff.).

2. Hesiod.—The poems of Hesiod, whether belonging to a time somewhat later than Homer or expressing the sentiments of a lower grade of society not articulate in the *Iliad* and the *Odyssey*, may be regarded as a bridge which enables us to cross the gap dividing the heroic from the historical age. For in the *Works and Days* we find the earliest signs of a conviction that all is not well with the world, that the gods no longer dwell with men, and that even honour and resentment (αἰδώς and νέμεσις) have departed, abandoning mankind to the workings of harsh and malignant jealousy (200 f.).

'Potter is wroth against potter, carpenter against carpenter; even beggar is envious of beggar, and one minstrel of another' (25). 'Money is a man's soul' (686).

Morality is depressed from the heroic level to suit the work-a-day requirements of the struggling farmer. Life is a continual battle against poverty, and the simple virtues which it needs leave no room for the exercise of elevated sentiment. Industry and fair dealing, temperance and simplicity, are enjoined:

'Hard work is no shame; but idleness is a disgrace' (311). 'Take a good measure and give as much or even better in return, so that in need you may afterwards find sufficiency' (350).

Among the most famous of Hesiod's sayings is his rebuke of the unjust judges who robbed the poor:

'Fools! they know not how much greater is the half than the whole, how mighty a blessing there is in mallow and asphodel' (40).

There is plenty of shrewd and homely wisdom, breathing the spirit merely of commercial prudence; and we are hardly surprised to find a wife enumerated as a part of the necessary agricultural stock-in-trade (375), or to read the advice that she should be chosen after much circumspection, lest the neighbours should have cause to mock (701). But we reach a higher level in the crowning exhortation to Perses.

'Vice is easy of attainment even by the crowd; for the road is smooth and she dwells hard by. But the Immortals have placed Toil in front of Virtue; long and steep and rough at first is the path that leads to her' (287 ff.).

3. The age of the gnomic poets and the Seven Wise Men.—In this period thought began to be consciously directed to moral questions. A change had taken place in the political conditions of Greece: the old feudal monarchies had passed away, and were succeeded by a long period of unrest. At first the domination of an aristocratic class and subsequently the rise of the tyrants, nominally as the champions of the masses, but actually in the interest of absolutism, kept the communities agitated with successive upheavals of internecine strife. Insecure of their lives, men were brought face to face with the hard necessities of a struggle for existence. Hence in all the literature of the time a vein of melancholy may be traced, to be seen in its fullest outcrop when Theognis writes:

'It is best of all things for the sons of earth not to be born, or to see the bright rays of the sun; or else after birth to pass as soon as possible the gates of death, and to lie deep down beneath a weight of earth' (425 ff.).

Debarred by stress of present anxiety from celebrating the glories of the past, the creative instinct found an outlet in recording the lessons of personal experience. The more individual and passionate outbursts of the lyric poets are of less direct importance to a survey of morality. But the elegiac writers, and especially Mimnermus, Solon, Phocylides, and Theognis, contain a mass of proverbial wisdom to which after ages never ceased to appeal. Trite and commonplace as much of their writing seems to a modern reader, their immediate audience judged very differently.

'To obtain concise and abstract maxims upon the ethics of society, politics, and education was to them a new and inestimable privilege. In the gnomic poets the morality which had been merely implicit in Homer and Hesiod received separate treatment and distinct expression. The wisdom which had been gradually collecting for centuries in the Greek mind was tersely and lucidly condensed into a few pregnant sentences. These sentences formed the data for new syntheses and higher generalizations, the topics for enlarged investigation, the "middle axioms" between the scattered facts of life and the unity of philosophical system' (J. A. Symonds, *Greek Poets*[2], London, 1877, i. 102).

The poets were, in fact, the educators of Greece (cf. Isocr. ii. 43, and see K. J. Freeman, *Schools of Hellas*, London, 1907, p. 247); and to this age belongs the formulation of all that was most characteristic in Greek popular morality. The dramatists were steeped in this literature, and their sententious passages often prove to be adaptations from some gnomic poet: thus Sophocles in *Oed. Col.* 1225 reproduced the above-quoted lines of Theognis, just as in fr. 329 he paraphrased Theogn. 255, and in fr. 286 Theogn. 215.

Similar considerations apply to the traditional utterances of the Seven Wise Men. They belonged to the latter part of this era, the age of the tyrants: indeed, one of them, Periander, was himself tyrant of Corinth, and another, Pittacus, tyrant of Mytilene. They were happily described by Dicæarchus (fr. 28 [*FHG* ii. 243]) as 'neither adepts nor students of philosophy, but men of intelligence endowed with some legislative capacity.' Although Thales and Solon distinguished themselves independently, the others were merely convenient eponyms to whom could be attached such scraps of unappropriated wisdom as were handed down from one generation to another (for the details, see Diels, *Fragmente der Vorsokratiker*[2], Berlin, 1907, p. 518). The famous 'Nothing too much,' attributed to Solon and repeated by Cleobulus as 'Measure is best,' comes from the innermost kernel of Greek sentiment.

Phocylides (fr. 18) praised the middle rank as the happiest; Solon (fr. 2) rebuked the insolence (ὕβρις) of the popular faction, arising from the excess which they could not check; and Aristotle followed popular opinion when he defined Virtue as a Mean. Closely akin is the saying of Pittacus, καιρὸν γνῶθι, which is inadequately rendered 'Know the right season,' since καιρός (as may be seen from the Lexicons) is not limited to time. Theognis (401), enlarging upon this text, gave a wider application to the words of Hesiod, who recommended the farmer not to overload his waggons (*Op.* 694).

It should be observed that in recommending moderation the Greeks were impelled as much by æsthetic and intellectual motives as by the strictly moral consideration that the free indulgence of the appetites is harmful. But, in fact, no such distinction was known to them. Sappho had testified to the identity of the beautiful with the good (fr. 101); and the fact that we have no word corresponding to καλός is no less significant than the absence from Greek of terms capable of expressing adequately the ideas of 'duty' and 'sin.'[1] The intellectual aspect of Greek morality appears still more strongly in Chilon's γνῶθι σεαυτόν, 'Know thyself,' which, together with μηδὲν ἄγαν, was inscribed on the front of the temple of Apollo at Delphi. In its most obvious application it recalls the advice given by Pythagoras to his pupils, that they should always, on their return home, put to themselves these questions: 'Whither have I strayed? What have I done? Which of my duties was unfulfilled?' (Diog. Laert. viii. 22). But it was capable of a wider significance, and was interpreted by Plato in the *Charmides* (164 D) as a recommendation of σωφροσύνη, understanding thereby a proper examination by the observer of his own capacity. In this sense it was adopted by the tragic poet Ion (fr. 55): '*Know thyself* is but a brief saying, and yet is a task so great that Zeus himself alone can master it.'

An increased recognition of the importance of justice is characteristic of an age which continued and developed the strain of wisdom introduced by Hesiod (*Op.* 320, etc.).

Solon declared (fr. 13) that unjust gains bring their own retribution; and Theognis (197) writes to the same effect, that riches righteously acquired are a sure possession, but dishonesty, though it seems to prevail for the time, issues finally in ruin. And Chilon said (fr. 10 [Diels]): 'Choose loss rather than shameful gain, for the one will hurt for the moment, but the other will never cease to be a curse.' Phocylides (fr. 15 =Theogn. 147) went so far as to declare that all virtue is comprehended in justice; and this view afterwards exercised considerable influence on the ethical systems of Plato and Aristotle (see Arist. *Eth. Nic.* v. i. 1129^b, 29).

The greater the value attached by men to the observance of justice in their mutual dealings, the keener was the disappointment with which they viewed the apparent tardiness of the gods in visiting with retribution the transgressions of the unjust. The poets were forced to conclude that, while the actual sinner escaped, his crime was expiated by the sufferings of his descendants (Solon, fr. 4, 27–32). Yet no protest follows against the injustice of the gods: their ways are inscrutable and past finding out (fr. 9). Similarly Theognis, while praying that the purpose of the gods may yet be changed, mournfully acquiesced in the punishment of the innocent for the sins of the guilty (731–742). It must at the same time be remembered that the sense of justice was so limited as to exclude any consideration for enemies.

'Beguile your enemy with fair words' says Theognis (363); 'but, when you have him within your grip, wreak your wrath on him, and let no scruple stand in your way.' 'Would that I could drink their blood!' is another of his utterances (349), when he is speaking of those who had robbed him. These are not isolated sentiments. To Pittacus is ascribed: 'Do not speak ill of your friend, or well of your enemy.' Above all, you must not give your enemies cause to exult; therefore hide your misfortunes, as Periander advised.

We can now appreciate the significance of the apologue in Theogn. 215:

'Assume the character of the polypus, which, as it coils round a rock, makes itself of like aspect thereto. So be thou adroit in changing from one appearance to another; for wisdom, let me tell you, is better than an unbending front' (cf. Pind. *Pyth.* ii. 84).

It was reserved for Plato to anticipate Christian ethics by controverting the popular view (*Rep.* 335 B; *Crit.* 49 C), and maintaining that the good man will not harm another. The justification of deceit in the case of enemies leads us to consider the general estimate of truth. Although it would not be difficult to collect passages in which the value of absolute truthfulness is highly esteemed (*e.g.* Hom. *Il.* ix. 312 f.), it can hardly be doubted that public opinion did not seriously disapprove of deception in suitable circumstances. It is sufficient to point to the character of Odysseus (cf. *Od.* ix. 19), and to the conception of the god Hermes as patron of trickery, who had trained Autolycus as his human representative (*Od.* xix. 395). Two fragments of Æschylus (frs. 301, 302) are preserved which, in the absence of their context, ought not to be held to warrant a sinister inference: 'God does not

[1] It is unnecessary to show that καθῆκον (or δέον) and ἁμαρτία do not fill the gap.

withhold his countenance from righteous deception,' and 'There are times when God honours a lie in season.' But Plato (*Legg.* 916 D) explicitly affirms that the many are too fond of saying that at proper times the practice of falsehood may be justified. Sophocles often follows closely the precepts of popular morality; and it may be concluded from the evidence which he affords that falsehood was justified either in cases where it brought final success in a momentous issue (*Phil.* 109; fr. 326), or even where some definite advantage was to be expected. 'Gain is sweet, even when it is the fruit of falsehood' (fr. 749). 'No speech is evil, if fraught with gain' (*El.* 61; cf. Athen. 122 C).

It has been suggested, on the strength of the Attic evidence, that in the period between Homer and the Persian wars, under the influence of the Delphic religion, a higher estimate of truthfulness was prevalent than in the subsequent period (L. Schmidt, ii. 413). This is a mistaken view, due partly to neglect of the fact which has already been emphasized, that the tragedians constantly echoed the sentiments of the gnomic poets, adapting them to the conditions of their art, or ascribing them to their most conventional characters.

4. The era of the Persian wars.—It may be broadly affirmed as a general proposition that the conventional morality which can be gathered from the fragments of the early poets continued to be the standard of the masses throughout the classical period. Although the fifth century—of course, our evidence applies almost exclusively to Athens—was characterized by a revolution of thought which may be fairly described as epoch-making, the time which elapsed before the establishment of the Macedonian empire was far too short for the new radicalism of the advanced thinkers to penetrate the prejudices of the average citizen, even in a community so sensitive to novelty as Athens. The conviction of Socrates is enough to show that the majority shared the sentiments of Strepsiades in the *Clouds*, and would willingly have lent him a hand in setting fire to the 'Reflectory,' so soon as they perceived the danger of an inroad on their cherished prepossessions. Hence it would be a mistake to deduce the bias of contemporary opinion from the sympathies which may be aroused by this or that play of Æschylus or Euripides. Nor must this be understood as applying solely to subjects which excited the keenest controversy. For example, the *Heraclidæ* of Euripides is mainly devoted to a panegyric of Athens as the protector of the weak, and the advocate of generosity to a beaten foe (see Introduction to the edition by the present writer, p. xxvi ff.). Yet, at almost the same time when this play was produced, the assembly was debating the Mytilenæan decree; and the atrocities of Scione and Melos occurred not long after. It is dangerous to infer an advance in general morality because a few enlightened thinkers might condemn the execution of Peloponnesian envoys in retaliation for the similar treatment of traders in contraband (Thuc. ii. 67), or because the ruthless proceedings of a Spartan admiral evoked a general protest from Ionia (iii. 32). But to assign to literary evidence its necessary limitations is not to disparage the value of its guidance. The true spirit of an age is to be gathered from the aspirations of its leading minds; but, when we finally leave the era of the tyrannies and encounter the first fresh breezes of democratic Athens, it behoves us to remember that the individual witnesses will be less likely to conform to a general pattern.

The effect of the Persian wars, following closely upon the democratic reforms of Cleisthenes and the expulsion of Hippias, was to deliver the Athenians from the danger of political slavery, and to open out an almost unlimited field for their practical and intellectual energies (see Gomperz, i. 382 ff.). Athens, at the head of her maritime league, was the leading member of a powerful confederacy, and was soon to aspire to an imperial rule. On the other hand, the combined resistance offered to a common danger had given birth to a new sense of pan-Hellenic unity. The best representative of pan-Hellenic sentiment is Pindar (*q.v.*) the Theban. He belonged to a State which had taken the side of the Persians, and was said to have been heavily fined by his countrymen for his praise of Athens in the poem partly preserved in frs. 76, 78, and 83. As a writer of odes in honour of victorious athletes who competed at the great festivals from every quarter of the Greek world, he displayed an extraordinary sympathy with the local associations of his patrons' families, and testified to the unity of sentiment and tradition in the Greek race which Salamis and Platæa had made a living reality. He was so little a particularist that all Greece could feel proud of his genius. So in part he continued to expound the familiar axioms of the national ethics with a wider outlook, a more elaborate imagery, and a more varied application. No one perhaps so well illustrates the central Hellenic principle of σωφροσύνη, the need of self-control, the reduction of all excess to the normal measure required by the interests of society (Gomperz, i. 301).

Even the highest ambition, the desire for the fame which song alone can give (*Nem.* vii. 17), must be controlled by the fear of going too far. A mortal must shape his aims with a sense of his own weakness; let him not seek to become Zeus (*Isth.* iv. 14). The pillars of Herakles are set as a limit to human emprise (*Ol.* iii. 44). Strain not the eyes too far; the brazen heaven cannot be climbed (*Pyth.* x. 27). But there are those who, like Tantalus and Ixion, cannot bear the stress of great prosperity (*Ol.* i. 56; *Pyth.* ii. 28). Then Surfeit breeds Insolence, whose child is Ruin. The germs of this thought are to be found in Solon and Theognis, but Pindar and Æschylus (*Ag.* 749) invested it with a fuller meaning.

Perhaps the most striking note in Pindar's poetry proceeds from his aristocratic pride. He will have no commerce with the vulgar, and cares nothing for the jealousy of lesser rivals. Birth is the supreme advantage, and natural powers are the gift of heaven, the want of which no training can replace (*Ol.* ix. 100, τὸ δὲ φυᾷ κράτιστον ἅπαν). So he concludes from heroic examples:

'A man who hath the birth-right of nobility prevaileth greatly; but he whose knowledge is a lesson learned is a man in darkness, whose thought is as a veering gale, and who never cometh to port with unerring course, but with ineffectual mind tasteth a thousand excellencies' (*Nem.* iii. 40 ff., tr. Bury).

Great powers should be worthily exercised:

'Happy and meet to be sung in verse is he who, prevailing by might of arm or excellence of speed, so directs his courage and his strength as to win the highest prizes; and who lives to see his son in the bloom of youth crowned with Pythian wreaths as his due' (*Pyth.* x. 22 ff.).

While Pindar sang the glories of the great games, Æschylus (*q.v.*) was making a more direct appeal to the national honour of Athens. Few poets have left with their readers so keen an impression as Æschylus of their deep interest in the highest problems of morality. In his fervour for righteousness he has often been compared to a Hebrew prophet. With the issue of the dramatic conflict is involved the solution of an ethical or religious question which permeates the atmosphere of the play. Thus in the *Prometheus* the sufferings of the chief character and those of Io are inseparably bound up with the justification of the ways of Zeus. It was a leading motive of Æschylus' poetic activity to find a moral lesson which could be traced amidst the horrors and cruelties of the old legends, and especially to discover how the interference of the gods in human affairs could be reconciled with the requirements of justice. It is a mistake to regard Æschylus as a conservative thinker, though he came to be so classed at a later date. Probably to his contemporaries he appeared as a revolutionary. But, however this may be, he was undoubtedly a loftier moralist than any of the earlier poets. We cannot conceive of him as justifying a falsehood for the sake of obtaining a practical advantage: 'The mouth of Zeus knows not how to lie, and all his words he will fulfil' (*Prom.* 1064). It is especially instructive to observe how Æschylus contrives to read a new and higher meaning into the precepts of the old morality. That suffering is learning was an old saw which in Hesiod (*Op.* 218) took the form of 'A child knows when he is hurt.' But Æschylus deduced from it the profound truth that suffering is an education which schools men to wisdom by awakening the conscience.

> 'Stern is the grace and forcèd mercy kind
> By spirits upon their awful bench assigned'

(*Ag.* 192 f., tr. Headlam). 'Whom he loveth he chasteneth.' Again, in the *Eumenides* (520 ff.): 'There are times when terror is in place, and the inquisitor of hearts must bide in his seat. It is good to learn wisdom by duress' (Verrall's tr.).

He was especially concerned to find an answer to the old problem respecting Divine justice, why the sins of the fathers are visited upon the children. In effect Æschylus denied the doctrine that 'the fathers have eaten sour grapes, and the children's teeth are set on edge' as completely as the prophet Ezekiel (18[2]). Agamemnon was not punished for the sin of Atreus. He yielded to the fatal Temptation which lured him to the sacrifice of Iphigenia, as in the days of his triumph over Troy he forsook σωφροσύνη and gave way to ὕβρις (W. G. Headlam in *Cambridge Prælections,* 1906, p. 126). There is always an act of sin breaking out afresh in the new generation—in consequence of the inborn taint in the blood. But how did the first sin come to be committed? Here Æschylus definitely rejected the traditional view which attributed it to the jealousy of the gods aroused by great prosperity:

> 'But single in the world I hold
> A doctrine different from the old:
> Not weal it is but sinful Deed
> More sinners after him doth breed
> Formed in his image' (*Ag.* 754 ff.).

The name of Æschylus was permanently connected with the 'good old days' of the Μαραθωνομάχαι; and old-fashioned citizens at the end of the century still held him to be the greatest of poets (Aristoph. *Nub.* 1366), and attributed to his teaching the virtues of the generation which grew up under the discipline described in the famous speech of the Just Reason (*ib.* 961 ff., 986). When Æschylus and Euripides appear in the *Ranæ* of Aristophanes as candidates for the favour of Dionysus, they agree to base their claims upon their respective merits as teachers of morality (1009, 1055); and Dionysus in proceeding to his final decision proposes to examine them, in order to see which gives the best advice in his country's need (1430). It is important to emphasize this old view of the poets as teachers, since we are now on the threshold of an age in which a class of professional educators arose styling themselves 'teachers of virtue.' In the eyes of the ordinary man, the chief of these Sophists, who claimed to supplant the poets, was Socrates (*Ran.* 1491); and, as the result of his and their labours, the teaching of morality was henceforth to be considered as the proper function of philosophy. (On the subject of this section, see the treatise of Buchholz, *Die sittliche Weltanschauung des Pindaros u. Aeschylos,* Leipzig, 1869.)

5. Influence of religion upon Greek morality.—In the summary description which has been given of the growth of Greek morality, hardly any account has been taken of religious influences; and, before we proceed further, these must be briefly examined. At the present day morality is popularly regarded as an established code of precepts and obligations which has been framed to regulate human action and rests ultimately upon the authority of a religious sanction. But, inasmuch as their religion, so far at least as it related to the cult of the Olympian deities, did not comprise any such code, the Greeks, in the earlier period of their national development, scarcely recognized any connexion between morality and religion. It is true that there existed a vague and misty belief that wrong-doers were visited with retribution after death; but it was not a doctrine which swayed the conscience of the ordinary man. Such exceptional punishment was reserved for exceptional transgressors like Tantalus and Ixion, whose offences culminated in the arrogance of their attempts to share the blessings of the immortals. Each god had his appointed sphere (μοῖρα [Eur. *Bacch.* 302; Headlam on Æsch. *Ag.* 1007]) within which he exercised control; and, though Zeus was supreme over all, even he was subject to the adamantine decrees of destiny (Æsch. *Prom.* 553 f.). The gods were jealous to avenge any infringement of their privileges. But the sinner was punished not as a moral offender, but as a trespasser—and often as an ignorant trespasser—against a vindictive power. Apart from special circumstances, the general attitude towards the conception of a future life, as may be gathered from the well-known utterance of Achilles, was one of contemptuous indifference: 'Sooner would I be a serf on some poor man's farm . . . than lord over all the spirits of the dead' (*Od.* xi. 489 ff.). So little concerned was the Greek to extend his vision to the farther side of the grave.

No less unsubstantial was the belief that wickedness is punished in this life. Such a conception is so notoriously contradicted by the facts of daily experience, that the believer in Divine justice is obliged, as we have already seen, to suppose that punishment is sometimes reserved for another generation, and the scoffer is convinced that the gods do not regard the affairs of man. The fact is that the investment of the gods with moral attributes was an attempt to reconcile tradition with the needs of an awakening conscience. The primitive gods were not moral agents; they were vindictive and inscrutable potencies, to be conciliated and appeased, if need arose, but hardly to be securely venerated as the unswerving champions of righteousness. The natural result was not to stimulate a desire of improvement or a passion for righteousness, but to quell the promptings of Hope as a treacherous seductress into forbidden regions. This consideration will serve to explain the presence of Hope as one of the evils in Pandora's box (Hes. *Op.* 96), and the disparaging language applied to Hope in very many passages of Greek literature.

Thus Theognis (637) puts Hope on a level with Danger, and calls them both 'cruel demons.' Euripides condemned the untrustworthiness of Hope (*Suppl.* 479), which exalts the passions of rivalry and brings one State into conflict with another. And Pindar (*Nem.* xi. 45) spoke of the limbs of men as fettered by importunate Hope, while the streams of foresight are far distant. (Many other illustrations are given by L. Schmidt, ii. 70 ff.; see also Headlam, *Cambridge Prælections,* p. 115 f.)

The power of hope depends upon the uncertainty of the future. It expresses the efforts of man to escape from his destiny, and points at once to his rashness and to his weakness. It is an invitation to man to step beyond his proper limits, to disregard the rule of temperance, even to seek to be a god. But true wisdom will recognize human impotence, and will counsel resignation to a lot which is inevitable. Hence, to acquiesce in destiny (στέργειν μοῖραν), as a mortal to aim no higher (θνητὰ φρονεῖν), and to bear misfortune with a stout heart (κακὰ εὖ φέρειν), are inculcated again and again. The joyful aspect of Greek religion was embodied in its cults. But the recurring cycle of the city festivals and the greater splendour of the pan-Hellenic gatherings hardly touch the sphere of morality.

In relation to the individual, religious contemplation was pervaded by a spirit of melancholy which may be traced without difficulty from Homer to the latest writers of the Anthology (see S. H. Butcher, *Some Aspects of the Greek Genius*[2], London, 1893, pp. 142–176).

If this was the general effect of religion upon the best minds, it is not surprising to find a plentiful crop of evils issuing from the superstitions of the vulgar. Here the old savage beliefs in magic and demons still flourished vigorously, and the superstitious were the victims not only of their own fears, but of all kinds of mercenary impostors. The portrait of the superstitious man, as delineated by Theophrastus (*Characters*, p. 162, ed. Jebb, 1870), will furnish copious illustration. But in Greece, as elsewhere, superstition only ministered to fear; and, when Greek civilization awakened to a consciousness of its inner development, when the animistic conceptions of their forefathers ceased to satisfy the men of the historic era, and when the creative play of the imagination had hardened the outlines and determined the personalities of the anthropomorphic gods, the religious instinct—craving for something which would rescue man from the terrors of supernatural malignity, and assist him in his unceasing struggle towards the light—eagerly welcomed the professions of a purer creed which seemed to promise relief. Such, at least in certain of their aspects, were the tenets of Orpheus. Orphism aimed at a purity of thought and act higher than the common standard, and, in order to stimulate the enthusiasm of its adherents, required of them a general asceticism of life, and in particular the wearing of white garments, the observance of certain tabus, and abstention from a flesh diet. Curiously enough, this vegetarianism was combined with an initiatory ceremony in honour of Dionysus Zagreus—intended to effect an identification with the Divine nature—at which raw flesh was consumed by the novice (Eur. fr. 472, 9 ff.). The leading notion of the Orphic creed, which cannot now be separated from that of the Pythagoreans, was to cleanse the soul from the original sin contracted by its earthly imprisonment in the body. With their consciousness of sin and their systematic attempt to restore the soul to its former purity by the mortification of the body, the Orphics united a belief in metempsychosis and in the purgatorial office of the under world. (The best account of Orphism is in Gomperz, i. 123 ff.)

In a similar way the claims of morality were recognized in the Mysteries (*q.v.*) of Eleusis. Although we are imperfectly informed as to the details of these ceremonies, there is ample evidence to attest their influence on the religious emotions, and especially the promise offered to their votaries of happiness in the world to come (Soph. fr. 753; Pind. fr. 137). Yet, when every allowance has been made for the influence exerted by mysticism upon Greek society, its diffusion was too partial to leaven the character of the community. In the *Hippolytus* of Euripides, Theseus appears to adopt the standpoint of the ordinary citizen when he inveighs against the Orphics as self-satisfied and pretentious hypocrites who veiled a vicious disposition beneath a sour exterior (952 ff.). The Eleusinia, doubtless, were much less the rallying point of a sect; initiation seems to have been the normal proceeding of an Athenian gentleman; and the privilege was so highly prized that Æschylus and Alcibiades had to meet a storm of popular indignation when accused of divulging its secrets. Nevertheless, an occasional festival, however venerable and soul-stirring, was necessarily lacking in sustained influence: the celebrants might, indeed, be moved by a transient enthusiasm, but were scarcely conscious of a new direction given to the current of their lives.

6. Beginnings of ethical inquiry.—The appearance of ethics as a subject of scientific inquiry was directly due to the Sophistic movement, and especially to the commanding personality of Socrates (*q.v.*). Before Socrates, to adopt Hegel's distinction, the morality of the Greeks rested rather upon custom than upon principle. Even the moral teaching of Heraclitus (*q.v.*) and Democritus (*q.v.*), so far as our records go, consisted of *ex cathedra* pronouncements, excelling perhaps in subtlety and penetration, but hardly differing in the form of their presentment from the dogmatic utterances of the Seven Sages.

There are several noteworthy sayings among the fragments of Heraclitus, such as 'Character is a god to every man' (fr. 119), or 'Insolence must be quenched sooner than a conflagration' (fr. 43). When he affirms that opinion is 'the falling sickness,' and that the power of sight is deceitful (fr. 46), we may trace the working of his central doctrine concerning the supremacy of Logos.

Much greater in bulk is the amount of sententious moralizing connected with the name of Democritus. We may select the following as favourable specimens:

'Peace of soul (εὐθυμίη) comes from moderation (μετριότητι) in pleasure and harmony of life' (fr. 191), and 'The crown of righteousness is a mind confident and unamazed; but the end of unrighteousness is the fear of impending calamity' (fr. 215).

The key to these and similar utterances may be found in the results of physical speculation, but they do not profess to rest upon an assured basis of ethical science, and derive such additional weight as may accrue to their intrinsic importance from the personal authority of the teacher who was responsible for them.

'The fact is that a moral system could not satisfactorily be constructed until attention had been strongly directed to the vagueness and inconsistency of the common moral opinions of mankind; until this was done, the moral counsels of the philosopher, however supreme his contempt for the common herd, inevitably shared these defects' (H. Sidgwick in *EBr*[9], viii. 576[a]).

Towards the middle of the 5th cent. B.C. the ontological inquiries of the early thinkers had issued in such conflict of opinion that further progress on the lines hitherto followed became impossible. The failure of repeated attempts to read the secret of the universe led to a fever of scepticism which left no shred of tradition untouched. Nor was it surprising that the intellectual upheaval should spread to the region of morality, and undermine the established rules prescribed by authority. The struggle between the opposing forces was concentrated in a discussion on the mutual limitations of Nature and Convention, where the ambiguity of the term 'Nature' helped to confuse the issue. The advocates of free thought rebelled against settled customs as artificial restraints imposed upon natural freedom.

'Convention,' says Hippias in Plat. *Prot.* 337 D, 'is the tyrant of mankind, and often compels us to do many things which are against nature.' Archelaus, the pupil of Anaxagoras, declared that all moral distinctions were due to convention and not to nature (Diog. Laert. ii. 16). Euripides, who was pre-eminently the poet of the new movement, is perhaps the best witness of the extent to which the revolt against customary bonds had spread itself in cultivated circles. 'The rebuke of bastardy is but a name, for nature levels all' (fr. 168). We have travelled far from Pindar in fr. 336: 'I have but small praise for noble birth: the good man is nature's nobleman, but the unrighteous, though his father be higher than Zeus, is naught but a churl.' 'There is one thing that disgraces a slave—to be so called: in all else no honest slave is inferior to the free' (*Ion*, 854).

Sentiments like these appeal to the universal sympathy which is always ready to take the part of the weak. But Nature could be invoked to serve another turn. Callicles in the *Gorgias* argued that Nature is on the side of the strong, that Might is Right, that the strong man will break through the fetters of Convention, and make himself supreme over the weak (482 E ff.). Laws which proclaim the equality of rights are framed in the interest of the weak, to protect them against the encroachments of the strong. In a similar spirit Thrasymachus in the *Republic* (338 C ff.) says that Justice is the advantage of the stronger, and that only the fool willingly obeys the law, since the wise man knows that he may disregard it if he can. The prominence of this type of argument in Plato's dialogues, and the prejudice attaching to Protagoras' profession of his ability to make the weaker cause appear the stronger (Arist. *Rhet.* ii. 24. 1402[a], 23), have earned for the Sophists as a class an evil reputation which they did not deserve (see Grote's *Hist. of Greece*, 1869, ch. lxvii.; and H. Sidgwick in *JPh* iv. [1872] 288). But, apart from this, they naturally attracted the unpopularity which is the usual portion of innovators. The effect of Sophistic teaching upon the average mind may be gauged by a quotation from the anonymous work known as Διαλέξεις (ii. 18 [Diels, *Vorsokr.*[2] p. 639, 24]):

'I think that if one were to bid all men collect in a heap the several customs which they consider base, and then to withdraw from it those which they hold to be good, nothing would be left, but all would be completely distributed.'

7. Socrates.—It was in such a crisis that Socrates came forward as the founder of Greek ethics. Starting from the proposition that the errors of men were due to a failure to comprehend the extent of their ignorance, and that his own claim to instruct others was founded not on any greater knowledge, but only on the absence in himself of any pretensions to know anything at all (Plat. *Apol.* 23 A), he represented himself as eager to examine, in company with his fellow-learners, the possibility of arriving at knowledge which should have a practical result in conduct. Holding that, for the time at any rate, the opportunity of making further progress in physical science was excluded by the failure of previous investigators to agree upon a common basis of research, he urged that men should clear their minds by discovering the content of such common terms as Piety, Justice, Temperance, and Courage. By a searching examination (ἔλεγχος) of those who were willing to submit themselves to his questions, he convinced them of holding loose and imperfect notions; and afterwards, by the comparison of homely and familiar examples, he sought to obtain their assent to more rational definitions (cf. Arist. *Metaph.* xiii. 4. 1078[b], 28). The leading proposition upon which he sought to base the whole of his moral teaching was the identity of Virtue with Knowledge. He interpreted 'knowledge' as 'practical wisdom' (φρόνησις), holding no other knowledge to be attainable, and considered that right action necessarily results from a properly furnished understanding. No one desires evil, he was wont to argue; and vicious conduct, though it may seem to be founded on deliberate choice, may invariably be traced to ignorance. Virtue is thus a unity, and its separate branches are distinguished as the varying spheres of action in which knowledge is applied. At the same time it follows that virtue can be imparted by teaching. If we inquire, further, to what object our knowledge is to be related, the answer is—to the Good; and this in its turn is expounded as the Useful or Expedient. Thus the virtuous man is required to possess a complete knowledge of the conditions of his own well-being or advantage. However unsatisfying the positive result of Socrates' teaching may appear, his influence upon his successors was so great as to direct the course taken by Greek thought throughout the whole of its subsequent development.

8. Knowledge and virtue.—Critics, both ancient and modern, have not failed to remark upon the extraordinary omission to include any account of the will in the Socratic analysis of moral action; and it has been suggested that Socrates himself exercised so complete a control over his own impulses that he was led to ignore the important results which flowed from the failure of will-power in others. There may be some measure of truth in this, but it is far more important to observe that the Greeks never at any time succeeded in drawing a clear line between the intellectual and the moral qualities, and that with them morality was always rather a concern of the head than of the heart.

Æschylus described insensate *folly* as causing the sin of Laius (*Theb.* 742); Hermes warned the Oceanides not to be led by *folly* into disobedience to the will of Zeus (*Prom.* 1113); and Helen was the *insane* cause of the bloodshed at Troy (*Ag.* 1456). So in Soph. *Ant.* 603, Antigone, the last hope of the royal stock, has been destroyed by *folly* of speech and *frenzy* of the mind.

These examples, taken almost at random, might be multiplied indefinitely; but the tendency is summarized in a fragment of Sophocles (839), 'Folly is most nearly akin to depravity.' It has left its mark on the vocabulary not merely in the moral connotation of such words as ἀμαθής, σκαιός, and ἀπαίδευτος, but in the more general use of σώφρων, κακῶς φρονεῖν, and the rest. It must also be remembered that ἀρετή itself was not entirely a moral quality like our 'virtue,' but included the other gifts and capacities which sustain and enrich life (see also Gomperz, ii. 66 ff.).

The subsequent history of moral philosophy in Greece was so far determined by the influence of Socrates that the various schools founded by his immediate pupils all professed to continue the teaching of the same doctrine, and those who came afterwards followed in the current. Until Christianity set up a new ideal, Socrates continued to be the pattern of moral perfection to the pagan world (M. Anton. i. 16).

9. The Cynics.—The founder of this school was Antisthenes, who is said to have attached himself to Socrates, after a life of hardship, at a later age than was usual (Plat. *Soph.* 251 B). In the school which he established after the death of his master, he emphasized the Socratic principle of the supreme importance of knowledge, by a searching criticism of the ideals of the average citizen. Thus he denounced the false notions which are implicit in the popular estimation of riches, honour, and power. Antisthenes even went so far as to depreciate the patriotic ideals of his fellow-citizens, by declaring that the national victories in the Persian wars were of no great account, as shown by the instability of the results obtained. But his severest condemnation was reserved for pleasure. 'May I be mad sooner than glad' (Aul. Gell. ix. 5. 3). 'If I could lay hands on Aphrodite, I would shoot her' (Clem. Alex. *Strom.* ii. 20, p. 485 P). The popular judgment is an illusion (τῦφος), and the wise man must cultivate complete freedom from such illusions (ἀτυφία). In order to reach this security he must fix his regard entirely upon the requirements of Nature, and distrust everything which is sanctioned only by convention. For this purpose he must be self-sufficient (αὐταρκής), and must train himself to acquire the 'Socratic strength,' the complete self-control which springs from the wisdom of a master mind. The Cynic chose Heracles as his patron saint (Zeller, p. 306, n. 4), glorifying his labours as victories won against cruelty and lust; and loved to contrast him with Prometheus, who had beguiled mankind with the delusive promise of an injurious civilization (Gomperz, ii. 145, 151). It soon became evident that the requirements of a life 'according to Nature' were inconsistent with the habits of ordinary society. The Cynic deliberately adopted the life of a beggar. He wore his beard long and unkempt, dressed himself in a rough coarse cloak, and carried a wallet and a staff.

The leader in this movement of practical asceticism was Diogenes of Sinope, who ultimately settled at Corinth, and to whose name a number of witty sayings were attached by later writers. Cynicism has been termed the philosophy of the Greek proletariat, and, by mixing with the masses and striving to instil their minds with saving knowledge, the Cynics remind us of the wandering friars of the Middle Ages. The power of the movement is shown by the fact that it lasted until at least A.D. 400. Diogenes scornfully adopted as a title of honour the nickname 'Dog' (κύων, whence 'Cynic'), which had been applied to him in contempt. His life was directed especially to prove that the ordinary standards of value are based upon illusion. What the many esteem as goods are impediments to the attainment of happiness. Only when a man has learnt that sickness, death, and dishonour cannot impair his peace of mind is he able to grasp the absolute indifference (ἀδιαφορία) of external goods. But the Cynics were not content to be philosophical anarchists. Their writings advocated a new Utopia founded upon the abolition of all privileges, political and social, and of all distinctions between one nation and another, even of that which to the Greek was fundamental—the distinction between Greeks and barbarians. Diogenes proclaimed himself a 'citizen of the world.' The extremes to which they were prepared to go in combating the prejudices of society—as when they defended incest or cannibalism as natural—are responsible for the degradation of the word 'cynic' in modern usage. But the social communism which led Diogenes to advocate a community of wives and children was no more reprehensible in him than in Plato; and the spirit of the paradoxes by which he startled his hearers was no doubt often misunderstood and misrepresented. (An excellent estimate of the strength and weakness of Cynicism is given by Gomperz, ii. 166 ff.; see also art. CYNICS.)

10. The Megarians (*q.v.*), a school founded by Euclides, are chiefly important to the student of philosophy as the earliest of the Sceptics, who from this time forward, under various leaders, attacked the conclusions of the dogmatic schools; but as to their views in the department of Ethics we have hardly any information. All that can be said is that Euclides, starting from the Socratic position that the good is the highest object of knowledge, proceeded to identify it with the Eleatic Being, and to declare that Good is a Unity, whereof God, Mind, and Prudence are but different names. Further, since Good comprehends all existence, Evil, the opposite of good, is non-existent (Diog. Laert. ii. 106). In his attempt to unite Eleaticism with Socraticism, Euclides reminds us of Plato, who sought to blend with his master's teaching elements derived from Heraclitus and Pythagoras.

11. The Cyrenaics.—Aristippus of Cyrene was the earliest apostle of hedonism. From the Socratic identification of the good with the useful, and his limitation of knowledge to the discovery of the proper end of action, Aristippus deduced that every virtuous action aims at pleasure. The analogy of the irrational impulses of children and animals, who continually strive after pleasure or seek to avoid pain, pointed to this process as a fundamental condition in the operation of Nature. Further, he held that all knowledge is relative to the subject, since we have no knowledge of things in themselves, but only so far as they affect our feelings. Consequently, we can only aim at producing what is gratifying to ourselves. He defined pleasure as a gentle movement, distinguishing it from pain on the one hand, and absence of pain on the other. The pleasure to be pursued is not to be found in the sum of a series of pleasurable activities, although happiness might be so called, but rather in the particular pleasure of the present moment (μονόχρονος ἡδονή [Athen. 544 A]). The past and the future are alike indifferent; only the present is ours to enjoy. Since every pleasure, *qua* pleasure, is good, there is no difference between them; and there is no such thing as a disgraceful pleasure. Nevertheless, a pleasure may be accompanied by such painful consequences that it must be rejected (Diog. Laert. ii. 87, 88). Therefore, on the balance of convenience, a wise man will abstain from pleasures which are forbidden by law or reprobated by custom. Wisdom, in fact, is required as a means to an end—the selection of the greatest good; for, though external circumstances press too hardly to permit the enjoyment of unbroken happiness, the wise man's life will in the main be passed in pleasure, that of the fool in pain (Diog. Laert. ii. 91).

The anecdotes which are related concerning the life of Aristippus, his alternate subservience and indifference to Dionysius the tyrant, his enjoyment of and contempt for wealth, and the importance which he ascribed to intellectual freedom and self-control (Zeller, 362 ff.), illustrate the ideal of cautious cheerfulness and moderation to which he aspired. 'I endeavour,' says Horace, speaking in the person of Aristippus, 'to make things submit to my control, not to submit myself to them' (*Epist.* i. 1. 18). And again: 'No form of life, no condition or situation, came amiss to Aristippus, who, for all his lofty aims, was yet equal to every present need' (*Epist.* i. 17. 23; cf. Diog. Laert. ii. 66). The well-known saying, 'I possess but am not possessed' (Diog. Laert. ii. 75), referred primarily to his connexion with Lais; but it has a wider significance in relation to the general attitude of Aristippus towards the emotions.

It is worth while to mention that one of the developments of Cyrenaic ethics took the direction of Pessimism. The impossibility for the great majority of mankind of attaining pleasure, and the consequent worthlessness of life, were most strongly asserted by Hegesias, who earned his title 'advocate of death' by his treatise on suicide (Diog. Laert. ii. 86). He argued that the best thing to which we can attain is freedom from pain, and that this is most fully realized by death (*ib.* 94; cf. also art. CYRENAICS).

12. Plato.—Of all the pupils of Socrates, Plato (*q.v.*) was the most fully endowed with his master's spirit, and must be accounted the true heir of the succession to his doctrine. By way of contrast with Plato, the philosophers previously discussed have been called the imperfect Socratics. The influence of Plato upon subsequent generations has been extraordinary (Cic. *Tusc.* i. 79; *ad Att.* iv. 16. 3), but has been due at least as much to the charm of his surpassing literary genius as to the character of his philosophical speculations. Plato's philosophical views were presented in a series of dialogues, in which the professed object of investigation often appears not to have been attained, and other questions of equal importance are introduced incidentally, only to be dismissed unsolved. The coherence and development of his system have in consequence given rise to protracted discussion. Fortunately, however, these difficulties are less urgent in the sphere of ethics than in that of ontology. Plato started from the Socratic position that virtue must be acquired through knowledge; but, in his investigation of the conditions upon which the acquisition of knowledge depends, he passed far beyond the Socratic limits. He derived from previous philosophers the conviction that sense-perception of the phenomenal world is thoroughly untrustworthy as a basis for the apprehension of actual existence. Socrates, leaving all such difficulties on one side, had contented himself with affirming that whatever knowledge we have must be of the general conception underlying individual instances, which we endeavour to express by definition; but Plato made the general conception a Reality, something existing in and for itself, at once comprehending and transcending the particulars as they appear to our senses. Further, he was able to identify existence with good, on the ground that each thing exists only so far as it performs its particular good. True knowledge can proceed only from contact with the supreme entities (ἰδέαι or εἴδη), through participation in which the world of appearances comes into being or seems to be. To bridge the gap between apparent and real existence is the lifelong task of the philosopher; and only in so far as he is successful can he attain to knowledge, and consequently to virtue. Hence Plato arrived at the important distinction—corresponding to that which exists between right opinion and knowledge—between ordinary 'civil and political' virtue and the true virtue of the philosopher (*Phædo*, 82 B; *Meno*, 100 A). The former may be acquired by the successful statesman through habituation or by some Divine dispensation (θείᾳ μοίρᾳ); but the latter can be reached only by the arduous path of inquiry into the true nature of absolute virtue. The effect of this rejection of the sensible world as the field for knowledge was to drive the philosopher to the contemplation of the immaterial ideas. He must turn aside from the phenomenal and seek refuge in the Divine; his whole life must be a preparation for death, a purification of his soul from the debasing influences of its association with the body (*Phædo*, 64 ff.). This element of mysticism seems to have been derived from Pythagorean sources, just as the sceptical attitude towards phenomena was suggested by the conclusions of Heraclitus, Parmenides, and Protagoras.

An important part of Plato's ethics can be understood only in connexion with his psychology. As the soul existed before, and will continue to exist after, its period of incarceration in the body, it must contain within it an element akin to the eternal essence of the ideas, at the head of which is placed the idea of the Good (*Rep.* 511 B, with Adam's discussion, ii. 170). On the other hand, it is clearly accessible to earthly influences, and its deterioration must be attributed to the growth of those tendencies which depress its higher aspirations and strengthen its material bonds (*Rep.* 611). From these conditions Plato deduced his doctrine of the tripartite soul. The part which is akin to real existence is known as the ruling part, and as informed with reason (ἡγεμονικόν, λογιστικόν); opposite to it are the two parts which are the seats of the emotions, the one of the nobler promptings of anger (θυμοειδές), and the other of the lower cravings of sensual desire (ἐπιθυμητικόν). How Plato was able to reconcile this triple division with the essential unity of the soul is a question which need not be discussed here. The exposition of the character of virtue rests upon his psychology. Each part of the soul has its own appropriate excellence, or virtue, and, according to their various dispositions, men tend to excel in this or that direction. In this way Plato arrived at his doctrine of the four cardinal virtues. As Wisdom corresponds to the rational (λογιστικόν) part, so does Courage to the spirited (θυμοειδές), and Temperance to the appetitive (ἐπιθυμητικόν). But the exercise of the moderating power of reason over the other two parts, compelling them to subordinate themselves to its guidance, is assigned to the fourth virtue, Justice (δικαιοσύνη). It should be observed that Plato is here using Justice in the wider sense, which common opinion warranted (Adam on *Rep.* 331 E), of general righteousness in relation to others. It comprised the whole duty of man to his neighbour, and was not immediately limited by the requirements of particular values. But Plato would hardly have given to it such a prominent place in the analysis of the individual soul, if he had not been thinking at the same time of the welfare of the body politic. For the correspondence between the parts of the soul was conceived as analogous to the mutual relations of the three classes in the ideal community; and civic justice was the fulfilment by each separate class of its duty to observe the limits prescribed to its activities.

The Highest Good must be found in the complete development of the soul in its proper function of communion with the ideal world. Thus alone can a soul be esteemed happy either in this phase of existence or after death. It is obvious that Plato had moved far from the simple utilitarianism of Socrates. But it is extremely difficult to define Plato's attitude towards Pleasure, which is variously expressed in different dialogues. Whereas in the *Protagoras* (351 A) he seems to identify Pleasure and Good, in the *Gorgias* (497 A) and the *Republic* (509 A) he declares that the two are entirely distinct. Finally, in the *Philebus*, although he denies that Pleasure is the Chief Good, and asserts that in the scale of goods Intelligence and Reason stand far above Pleasure, nevertheless it is admitted that a life without pleasure (or pain) is not to be chosen (21 D, 63 E), and the pure and harmless pleasures of the senses are allowed to possess a certain degree of value (66 C).

13. Aristotle.—The moral philosophy of Aristotle (*q.v.*) should be regarded as the complement of Platonic speculation. Their differences are less important than the particulars in which they agree, although the former are made the more prominent by the fundamental contrast of their method and style. Aristotle formulates and defines conclusions which are implicit in Plato's writings, and, by correcting the relative values to be assigned to certain views which occupy a part of the common field of investigation, he appears to be more in opposition than he really is. Thus, in his treatment of the Socratic ground-work, Aristotle definitely draws the distinction between speculative and practical wisdom (σοφία and φρόνησις) towards which Plato was working in contrasting civil with philosophic virtue. But, whereas Plato employed all the energy at his command in urging the paramount claims of philosophy, Aristotle admitted the supremacy of the theoretic life (*Eth. Nic.* x. 7) as an end in itself, and as an approximation to the Divine through the activity of reason, but concluded that the proper exercise of man is to be found in the moral virtues which belong to a practical life.

The Highest Good, or ultimate aim, of all action is to be found, as every one agrees, in Happiness (εὐδαιμονία), or—to adopt a more accurate equivalent—in well-being. Neither pleasure nor external goods can be identified with Happiness, which can be attained only by rational activity. This activity properly performed is Virtue (*Eth. Nic.* i. 6). Happiness, however, is not to be predicated of single acts, but is commensurate with life taken as a whole, and requires a certain supply of external advantages. No one could call Priam happy. Friendship, health, noble birth, and beauty are all elements which cannot be disregarded in making an estimate of complete happiness. In the same way Aristotle deals with the claims of Pleasure. While fully conscious that it cannot be weighed in the scale against virtue, and that, if it becomes necessary to make a choice between suffering and the abandonment of virtue, every hardship must be borne on behalf of the latter, he refuses to regard pleasure as something indifferent or negligible. On the contrary, he maintains that it is the necessary concomitant of every activity (*ib.* x. 4), and that the purest and best pleasures are those which spring from the exercise of moral and intellectual virtues. The pursuit of pleasure is natural and not to be condemned (*ib.* x. 2, vii. 13). Nevertheless, pleasure and external goods are valuable only in relation to virtuous activities (*ib.* i. 8), whether intellectual (διανοητικαί) or moral (ἠθικαί).

Moral virtue is a permanent condition (ἕξις) of the soul (*ib.* ii. 4), as distinguished from an emotion (πάθος) or a faculty (δύναμις). Virtue is not innate but acquired by practice, not involuntary but dependent on a definite exercise of the will. Again, a virtuous action implies a virtuous agent; unless it proceeds from a right motive, and is such as a virtuous man would perform, no action can properly be described as virtuous (*ib.* ii. 3, v. 13). Virtue requires the presence of certain natural qualities, *i.e.* we are born with a capacity for moral activity (*ib.* vi. 13). But these are not enough in themselves: otherwise children or animals might possess virtue. Virtue is impossible without insight (φρόνησις); but knowledge and virtue are not identical, as Socrates thought. Socrates ignored the irrational part of the soul, and the effect of emotion upon conduct. Virtue implies the free exercise of the will in controlling or yielding to impulse, and is rooted in habit. The repeated performance of moral actions produces as its result a moral character. But how is the will to be exercised? Here Aristotle can only give the rule that the proper mean between the extremes of excess and defect must be preserved, and that it should be determined by reason according to the judgment of the man of practical intelligence (see the definition of Virtue in *Eth. Nic.* ii. 6).

After propounding the definition of Virtue in general, Aristotle proceeds to describe the particular virtues in their character as means lying between two extremes, but without unfolding any principle of classification. Most of the virtues are discussed briefly, but Justice—in the narrower sense as the virtue which aims at equality—is examined at length in book v. Book vi. is devoted to the treatment of Insight (φρόνησις), the virtue of practical reason, which is carefully distinguished from ἐπιστήμη, νοῦς, σοφία, and the rest. This is not the place to enter into the details of the analysis, but it should be observed that Aristotle regards ethics less as an abstract science than as an opportunity for recording the results of his own observation in the sphere of contemporary morality. The general principles reached by this method of induction cannot be so exactly systematized as to fit the varying circumstances of every-day life. Just as a lawyer will refuse to refine upon a broad generalization, by saying that each case must be judged on its own facts, so the philosopher leaves the reciprocal relations of insight and moral virtue to be decided by the experienced judgment of the practical moralist.

14. The Hellenistic age.—There can be no question that the period which closed with the death of Aristotle was one of marked decay in public virtue. After the disastrous issue of the Peloponnesian war, Athens was never again more than a shadow of her former self. She was still to produce eminent citizens, but her political spirit was broken. The venality of her politicians, and the failure of her citizens to make an adequate response to the calls of military and other public services, were continually on the increase. If we make allowance for the universal tendency to idealize the past, there was still sufficient reason for Isocrates to complain (vii. 48) of the increasing idleness and profligacy of the young men, of the want of respect towards their elders, and of the tendency to esteem wit and cleverness more highly than the more solid civic virtues. Sparta, again, had failed conspicuously to realize the opportunities afforded by her success. Her rule was marked by so much cruelty, stupidity, and avarice that she quickly aroused a general opposition to her ascendancy, which never recovered from the shock given to her military power at Leuctra. If Thebes seemed for a season to have revived the ancient Hellenic fire, it proved to be only a temporary flash, quickly extinguished by the death of the heroic leader whose efforts had kindled it. In fact, the conditions under which the city communities had flourished were rapidly passing away. The time had come for the establishment of a wider dominion, and in the person of Philip of Macedon the destined conqueror appeared. The task of his successor Alexander was not so much the establishment of a universal empire as the opening out of every part of the known world to the spread of Greek thought and Greek civilization. Thus, in the words of Plutarch (*Mor.* 329 A), was realized the dream of Zeno the Stoic, that all men should live as members of a single community, since Alexander, by mixing, as in a loving-cup, the lives and characters of all men, had required of them that they should consider the world as their native country. Henceforward the distinctive characteristics of the Greek communities were merged in a general cosmopolitanism; and the mode of life customary at Athens was not widely different from that of Pergamum or Alexandria. The decay of civil interests led to the withdrawal of serious and intelligent people to the seclusion of philosophy, and so fostered the growth of the individual conscience, which is reflected in the teaching of the Stoics and Epicureans.

So far as the morality of the individual is concerned, it is difficult to make a comparison with the earlier era. But the pictures of ordinary life which are presented to us in the plays of the New Comedy—as known to us until quite recently only through the Latin adaptations of Plautus and Terence—are not of an attractive character. The society depicted is narrow and mean, and there is hardly a trace of elevated feeling or generous ambition. The tricks of a cunning slave, and the outwitting of a straitlaced father or a rascally pander were the common stock-in-trade of every dramatist. 'Idleness, frivolity, luxury, self-indulgence, are the attributes of the society which went to see its own reflection upon the stage' (Mahaffy, *Greek Life and Thought*², London, 1896, p. 137). The extent of the decay in public spirit which had set in since the great period of Athenian expansion may be gauged by contrasting—to take a trivial illustration—the caricature of Lamachus in the *Acharnians* with the military braggadocios of the New Comedy, or the speeches of Pericles in Thucydides with the servile compositions which bestowed Divine honours on Demetrius Poliorcetes (*Poetæ Lyrici Græci*, ed. Bergk⁴, Leipzig, 1882, iii. 674). Even the chief ornament of Alexandrian literature, the development of the Theocritean idyll, has been referred, like the case of Rousseau in the 18th cent., to a reactionary movement seeking to find relief, in the freshness of Nature, from the depravity of contemporary society (see Ziegler, 142). But the importance of this evidence must not be exaggerated by omitting certain items on the other side of the account which deserve consideration. Thus, if the characteristic traits of the period showed less vigour, they had lost much of the earlier harshness. The increase of enlightenment brought with it a more widely diffused humanity. The most important sign of progress was the growing influence of philosophy upon daily life. The ancient system of education, which was sufficient for old-fashioned people at the end of the 5th cent., had ceased, after the lapse of a hundred years, to satisfy the needs of their descendants. To attend philosophical lectures, which was a fashionable craze for 'up-to-date' people in the time of the Sophists, had become the established practice. Philosophers, instead of being prosecuted for impiety,[1] were considered worthy of the highest honours which the State could confer. Aristotle had been summoned to Macedonia to superintend the education of the young Alexander, and in the next generation we have the honorific decree in favour of Zeno the Stoic, the intimate friendship of Persæus with Antigonus Gonatas, and the political missions of Xenocrates to Antipater and of Crates to Demetrius.

Philosophy was no longer regarded merely as an educational instrument, or even as an avenue leading to knowledge. The schools of Plato and Aristotle became permanent institutions localized at the Academy and the Lyceum, and organized so as to encourage a spirit of corporate enthusiasm among their members. For the degradation of politics, as has already been mentioned, had driven those who were sufficiently serious to be dissatisfied with the frivolity of ordinary life, and were not preoccupied with commerce or military service abroad, to take refuge in the disputations of the schools. But, in spite of the fame of their founders and the influence which they were destined to exercise over mediæval and modern thought, neither the Academy nor the Lyceum provided exactly what the generation required. The lofty idealism of Plato and the minute and accurate science of Aristotle were alike unsuited to the need which craved a sustaining principle of hope and comfort amidst the sinister influences of a corrupt society. In other words, philosophy was expected to supply what religion was then incapable of affording. Herein lay the opportunity which the new schools of Zeno and Epicurus were not slow to seize. Both Stoics and Epicureans made practical ethics the ultimate end to which their physical and logical speculations were directed; they aspired to discover truth in order to throw open the way to happiness.

15. The Stoics.—Zeno, a native of Citium in Cyprus, who had studied under Xenocrates and Polemo the Academics and Crates the Cynic, established a separate school at Athens in the closing years of the 4th century. Under his successors, Cleanthes (*q.v.*) and Chrysippus (*q.v.*), the distinctive doctrines of the Stoics, so called from the *Stoa Pœcile*, where Zeno had lectured, were developed and defined; and during the following centuries, through which it continued to flourish, the leaders of the school, without abandoning their main positions, succeeded better than any of their rivals in accommodating their teaching to the needs and aspirations of the time. Although Zeno and his immediate successors devoted an immense amount of labour to the study of logic and physics, the supreme importance of ethics was recognized at an early date (*Stoic. Vet. Fragm.*, ed. von Arnim, iii. [Leipzig, 1905] 68), and, as time went on, it tended more and more to be the sole subject of general interest. The ultimate end of moral action was, according to the Stoics, a life in agreement with Nature, whereby they understood a conformity with the workings of Reason as immanent both in the individual and in the universe (*ib.* 4). Reason, which is the Universal Law, is identified with Zeus, and happiness is attained when the individual reason is made to submit itself to the will of the Supreme Governor of the universe. Life in accordance with Nature is identical with a perfect life, and the perfection of anything is the same as its virtue (*ib.* 16). Thus virtue is the only thing which should be chosen for its own sake (*ib.* 39), and is by itself sufficient for happiness (*ib.* 54). The Good was interpreted, as by Socrates, as equivalent to advantage (*ib.* 75), and it was obvious that virtue alone could furnish true profit, and that vice alone could harm (*ib.* 75, 76). It follows that everything except virtue and vice—health, riches, fame, beauty, even life itself—is absolutely indifferent. So far Zeno was in accord with the Cynics; but he refused to draw the same inference from the premisses. Things indifferent are capable of being used either well or ill, and are not all indifferent to the same extent. In other words, things indifferent may have a certain value, positive or negative (ἀξία, ἀπαξία), as contributing towards a life in accordance with Nature or as hindering its development (*ib.* 126). But there are certain things which have so much value that, in the absence of over-riding circumstances, they will always be chosen in preference to their contraries. Such things are natural ability, life, riches, fame, and so forth, and they are consequently described as being preferred (προηγμένα), whereas their opposites are to be rejected (ἀποπροηγμένα [*ib.* 31]). Such advantages, however, will weigh as nothing in the scale against virtue; and, if it becomes necessary to make a choice, we must face death sooner than be guilty of vice (*ib.* 168). All moral action arises from impulse (ὁρμή), that is to say, the movement of the soul directed towards the acquisition of some external object. In man, impulse is controlled by reason; but, where reason does not exist or is not fully developed, as in the case of children and animals, the natural impulses are primarily directed towards self-preservation, and not, as the Epicureans believed, towards pleasure (*ib.* 178). The objects thus sought after (τὰ πρῶτα κατὰ φύσιν) serve as an introduction to the subsequent action of wisdom, which is exercised in the separation of the natural from the unnatural and the rational selection of the former (*ib.* 186, 190).

The impulses given by Nature are directed to the right objects, but the reason may be distracted by the seductions of pleasure or the urgency of associates (*ib.* 228). Nevertheless, virtue can be taught, as experience proves (*ib.* 223). The Socratic view that Virtue is Knowledge is still maintained; but the Stoics, who held that nothing but body exists, were obliged to argue that the virtues also were corporeal, being, in fact, a particular disposition of the soul itself (*ib.* 305). Virtue is thus both one and many—one in so far as it is inseparable from the soul, and many in relation to the sphere of its activities. Thus Insight is the knowledge of what to do and what not to do, Temperance the knowledge of what to choose and what to avoid, Justice is that knowledge which gives every man his due, and Courage that which can distinguish the proper objects of fear (*ib.* 262). The virtues are reciprocally connected with each other, and he who has one necessarily possesses all; nor can he act in the exercise of a single virtue without at the same time employing the others (*ib.* 299). Virtue, being based upon secure convictions, was so completely identified with a man's moral nature that some of the Stoics considered it absolutely indefectible (*ib.* 237). The ordinary man (φαῦλος), however, fails to exercise his reason properly. He is the slave of emotion (πάθος), which may be described either as an excess of impulse, or as an outburst breaking away from the control of reason (*ib.* 379), or again as perverted judgment (*ib.* 456). The Stoics spent much labour in distinguishing the varieties of emotion, grouping them round the four chief classes, two of which, Pleasure and Grief, are concerned with the present, and the others, Desire and Fear, with the future (*ib.* 391). It will be seen that emotion is a disordered condition of the reason itself; we have no longer, as in Plato

[1] The last echoes of the older thunder were the decree for the expulsion of philosophers from Athens in 316, which was repealed within a year; and the unsuccessful prosecution of Theophrastus by Agnonides.

and Aristotle, to think of two rival powers striving for the mastery, but rather of a revolt against the rightful authority. It follows that emotion must be absolutely suppressed, since everything that is contrary to right reason is sinful (*ib.* 445, 448).

The Stoics drew up a classification of actions so as to correspond with the distinction between Virtue as the Absolute Good and things indifferent but yet valuable. Actions proceeding from virtue are Right Actions (κατορθώματα), vicious actions are Sins (ἁμαρτήματα). These classes comprise every act of the wise man on the one hand, and of the fool on the other. Hence the paradox that all sins are equal; for no difference in degree is conceivable (*ib.* 527, 528). But, if we look not at the agent, but at the act in relation to its object, we must distinguish between what is fitting (καθῆκον) and its opposite. A perfectly fitting action (τέλειον καθῆκον), such as to act justly, may be identified with Right Action. Otherwise, fitting actions are such as may be justified on grounds of probability (ὃ πραχθὲν εὔλογον ἴσχει ἀπολογισμόν), as to honour one's parents or to take care of one's health (*ib.* 134 f.). The actual embodiment of the Stoic conception of Virtue is to be seen in their picture of the Wise Man. In the exercise of his knowledge the wise man never makes a mistake, never opines, never changes his mind. He is an expert on every subject, being endowed with every excellence. His body may be in pain, but he never suffers; though he were as unfortunate as Priam, he would still be happy. None but the wise can lay claim to riches, beauty, or freedom; for no one has possessions so valuable, no one is so deserving of love, no one is so unfettered by prejudice. The wise man is the only true prophet, priest, and king. True friendship can exist only between the wise, for they alone can benefit each other: 'If a single wise man anywhere extends his finger with a wise purpose, all the wise men in the world are benefited' (*ib.* 627). The wise man bears no trace of softness; he is unmoved by passion; he never pardons, never pities, and is never surprised. It is not to be wondered at that this doctrine involved the Stoics in controversial difficulties, or that Chrysippus was forced to admit that the wise man was a rarer portent than the phœnix (see E. V. Arnold, *Roman Stoicism*, Cambridge, 1911, p. 298, and cf. art. STOICISM).

16. Epicurus.—The school of Epicurus (see art. EPICUREANS), first established at Mytilene and subsequently removed to Lampsacus, was transferred to Athens in 306. The system was in all essentials the work of the founder, and was faithfully guarded by his successors, remaining practically unchanged so long as the school continued to exist. Epicurus asserted emphatically that the object of all philosophical inquiry is the attainment of happiness by the individual, and that neither knowledge nor virtue has any worth in itself. Thus, his exposition of the true nature of the gods, as absolutely indifferent to human affairs, was intended to remove superstitious fears, which are among the most serious obstacles to human happiness. Similarly, by his inquiry into the essence of the soul, and his demonstration that it could not be immortal, he hoped to destroy entirely the fear of death. He laid the ground-work of his ethics by a psychological examination of the varieties of Pleasure and Pain. The highest grade of pleasure is attained when every painful need is removed, and every natural craving stilled. The condition thus attained is one of complete rest (καταστηματικὴ ἡδονή), and must be contrasted with the pleasure which consists in the satisfaction of a want (ἡδονὴ ἐν κινήσει). The latter is necessarily mingled with discomfort, unless it is merely connected with a variation (ποικιλμός) of the highest good. Wants were accordingly classified as (1) natural and necessary, (2) natural and not necessary, (3) neither natural nor necessary. The second class is not subject to the influence of passion, except when men are misled by a false opinion that the highest good is capable of increase. The third class are products of the imagination, and must be totally rejected (frs. 450–453 [Usener]).

Epicurus differed from the Cyrenaics in three respects: (1) he declared freedom from pain, which the Cyrenaics did not count as a pleasure at all, to be the greatest of all pleasures; (2) he declared that all pleasures of the mind are ultimately referable to and derived from bodily pleasures, whereas the Cyrenaics held that the pleasure of intercourse with friends or the gratification arising from honour is independent of sensation; (3) pleasures of the mind refer to the past and future as well as to the present, and, as being more durable, are greater than immediate bodily pleasures. In other respects his ethical principles are those of undiluted hedonism. Experience shows that pleasure and pain are the only motives which control our actions. The attainment of pleasure and the avoidance of pain are the natural criteria by which the value of our impulses and activities is measured. Reason is a later accretion, which does not alter the ultimate aim, but points out the means of attaining it. Reason teaches us to look not to immediate enjoyment, but to the remoter consequences of our actions. Every pleasure is a good in itself, as being suitable to our nature (οἰκεῖον), but it is not every pleasure which is an object of pursuit (αἱρετόν). Conversely, certain pains are comparatively so unimportant that we must accept them, if on the balance of the account they appear to bring with them a larger amount of pleasure.

The value of the virtues is to be found in the fact that without them we cannot reach the highest good—absence of all pain and of every fear of future disturbance. Insight (φρόνησις) is the root of all the other virtues: it sets us free from false opinion, and puts before us the true goal of our endeavour. Self-control (ἐγκράτεια) imparts the necessary resolution to adhere to the decisions of the judgment, so that we may receive as much pleasure and as little pain as are possible for us; and courage prevents our peace of mind from being destroyed by fear of death, superstition, or pain. Lastly, the violation of justice is incompatible with an agreeable life. For the unjust man, even though his misdeeds are concealed, is continually anxious lest they should be discovered. On the other hand, upright conduct contributes to our enjoyment, by earning the good-will and affection of our fellow-men. On the value of friendship the Epicureans laid great stress: it was grounded ultimately upon mutual advantage, but the happiness of the individual was conceived to reach its highest pitch in the unselfish fellowship of the wise and virtuous (fr. 544). In other respects, Epicurus assigned very little value to the conditions of civil society. Laws would not be needed in a community of the wise; as things are, they exist to protect the wise from injustice (fr. 530). He recommended abstention from politics on the ground that public life interferes with happiness (λάθε βιώσας [fr. 551]). Similarly, he discountenanced marriage as likely to lead to much trouble (fr. 525). The result of Epicurean hedonism is not far removed from the Stoic ideal: the happiness of the Epicurean wise man is no less founded on the secure possession of insight, and is so entirely independent of external circumstances that it endures while its possessor is suffering physical torture (fr. 601).

17. The Græco-Roman age.—In the sketch that has already been given of Stoic ethics, little or nothing has been said of the adaptation of Stoic principles to the needs of daily life. But the influence and vitality of the school were shown by nothing more clearly than by their success in procuring the adhesion to their system of so large an element of Roman society (for the details, see E. V. Arnold, *op. cit.* 99 ff., who shows the importance of the modifications made by Panætius). Stoicism, as it was opened out to the practical Romans, became less a subject of study for the curious than a religious creed to which every serious man might look for support. Its success in this direction was undoubtedly promoted by the attitude which had been adopted towards the popular religion. By an elaborate series of allegorical explanations the Stoics sought to accommodate their pantheistic belief in the universal immanence of the Divine Reason to the existence of the separate personalities represented in popular theology. Hephæstus was fire, Rhea earth, Zeus æther, and so forth. Thus, a breach with tradition was avoided, and an advantage gained which neither the agnosticism of the New Academy nor the outspoken hostility of Epicurus to the orthodox religion was able to secure. The history of the Stoa after Panætius shows a continually diminishing interest in philosophy and an increasing strength in moral exhortation. Seneca (*q.v.*), for instance, laid much stress on the healing powers of philosophy for all who were mentally sick. He prescribed rules for those who were in various stages of progress (προκοπή) towards wisdom; for the removal of vicious habits; for the training of the impulses; for the mastery of the passions; and for the strengthening of the will. The restraint of civil liberty under the Empire imparted a gloomy tone to the discourse of the philosophic preacher. The doctrine of 'a reasonable departure' (εὔλογος ἐξαγωγή)—by which the earlier Stoics had countenanced suicide as an escape from intolerable evils, thereby emphasizing the moral indifference of life and death—was repeated by Seneca with morbid insistence. Musonius and Epictetus admit into their writings even less philosophical discussion than Seneca. Epictetus (*q.v.*) in particular was the preacher of a pure and gentle morality which often approximates to Christian doctrine. His famous maxim, 'Suffer and abstain' (fr. 179), testifies to his belief in a benevolent Providence; and he never fails to recommend the duty of submission to outward events which are not within our power. The same spirit of pious resignation appears in Marcus Aurelius (*q.v.*), the last of the Stoics: the proud independence of the sage had given way before the human sense of helplessness; the soul was hampered by the prison-house of the body, and found life to be 'a sojourn in a strange land.' Thus in its last moments Stoicism came near to Platonism.

Of the four post-Aristotelian schools, neither the Epicurean nor the Peripatetic made any progress, of sufficient importance to be recorded here, beyond the views of their founders. But the Academy had a more chequered history, to which we must briefly refer. The New Academy under Arcesilas and Carneades was precluded by its determined scepticism from admitting the possibility of scientific ethics; but on the basis of probability they gave a general adherence to Platonic teaching. Later, Antiochus of Ascalon, Cicero's teacher, endeavoured to effect a fusion of the doctrines of Plato with those of Stoicism, but his influence soon exhausted itself. In the 1st cent. B.C. there was a notable emergence of mystical asceticism, associated with a revival of Pythagoreanism. Its general tendency was to recommend purity of soul, to be attained by a special restriction of the bodily appetites, as the only proper channel whereby the devotee could acquire a knowledge of the Divine mysteries (see Mahaffy, *Greek World under Roman Sway*, London, 1890, p. 179 ff.). This movement reacted upon Platonism, and the traces of its working may be found in the moral treatises of Plutarch (*q.v.*). According to him, the structure of morality is built upon a religious foundation. Virtue is identified with an assimilation to the Divine, and the Highest Good is the knowledge of God (*Aristid.* 6). Thus his attitude towards religion was conservative; he defended divination, maintained the doctrine of metempsychosis, and believed in the power of demons and spirits to control human action by their interference. To avoid the defilements of sense, and to cultivate the reason as the indwelling source of Divine inspiration, were the supreme duties of man (see *de gen. Socr.* 20, p. 588 E ff.). But the culmination of this mystical tendency was realized in Neo-Platonism (*q.v.*); and Plotinus, who was its chief representative, has been justly regarded as the last of the great thinkers of antiquity. In conformity with Plato, who had denounced the untrustworthiness of sense-impression, Plotinus identified matter with evil, and made purification from the contaminations of sense, withdrawal from the world, and liberation of the soul from its enslavement to the body, the fundamental requirements of his ethical teaching. The ordinary civil virtues are of no value, since they tend to bind the soul to the world of matter. The soul must approach God by re-absorption into the Intelligence (νοῦς) from which it sprang. This process must be encouraged by contemplation; and the love of the Beautiful (the Platonic ἔρως) helps to direct us from the impressions of sense to the ideal world. Constant association with the ideas may lead ultimately to the condition of supreme bliss, when the soul in a moment of ecstasy finds itself by contact with the Divine Unity identified with God Himself.

LITERATURE.—Several of the authorities have been mentioned incidentally, but the chief sources of information are the Histories of Greek Philosophy, and more particularly E. Zeller, *Phil. d. Griechen in ihrer geschichtl. Entwicklung*[5], Leipzig, 1892 (the greater part has been translated into English by various writers from the 3rd Germ. ed.); Th. Gomperz, *Griech. Denker*[2], Leipzig, 1903–8 (three vols. of an Eng. tr. have appeared, London, 1905 ff.); W. Windelband, *Gesch. der alten Philosophie*[2], Munich, 1894. Special treatises on the History of Greek Ethics are the following: L. Schmidt, *Die Ethik der alten Griechen*, Berlin, 1882; J. Denis, *Hist. des théories et des idées morales dans l'antiquité*[2], Paris, 1879; Ch. E. Luthardt, *Die antike Ethik in ihrer geschichtl. Entwicklung*, Leipzig, 1887; Karl Köstlin, *Gesch. der Ethik*, i. 1, 'Die Ethik des classischen Alterthums,' Tübingen, 1887; Th. Ziegler, *Ethik der Griechen und Römer*[2], Bonn, 1886; cf. also L. R. Farnell, *Greece and Babylon*, Edinburgh, 1912.

A. C. PEARSON.

ETHICS AND MORALITY (Hindu).—Hindu ethics is deeply tinged with the belief in transmigration or rebirth according to the doctrine of *karma* ('action') under which every act, whether good or bad, finds its reward, not only in heaven or hell, but in innumerable other bodies, from a god to an insect or plant, or even a stone. The same gradation of rebirths which pervades the entire creation prevails in the more limited circle of human life, from the high-born Brāhman to the low grovelling Chaṇḍāla, all of which stations depend on the various shades of merit and demerit acquired in a previous existence. The hymns of the Vedas, it is true, contain no distinct allusion to metempsychosis; they abound in glowing descriptions of the deified powers of Nature rather than in moral sentiments, though reference is made to the delights of paradise and to the tortures of hell. The Upaniṣads, on the other hand, mention, for instance, the rebirth of virtuous men as Brāhmans or other persons of high caste, of wicked men as dogs, hogs, or Chaṇḍālas, and of those who eat rice as rice (see *Chhāndogya Upaniṣad*, v. 10). The idea of *karma*, or action, and *karmavipākaḥ*, or ripening of acts in future births, pervades the six systems of philosophy, and the earliest lawbooks of the Dharmasūtra class. It is the highest goal of Indian philosophy to get rid of the fetters of action and consequent rebirth by overcoming the inclination to be active. The question of will, whether bound or free, does not concern these philosophers; they rather aim at the entire extinction of individual volition by absorption into the supreme Being. The Dharmasūtras state the special duties of men, as determined by their rebirth in a particular caste, notably the Brāhman caste; and they discuss the obligations of Brāhman ascetics who, by keeping the five vows of abstention from injury to living beings, of truthfulness, of abstention from theft, of continence, and of liberality, by the practice of various austerities, and by concentration of mind, wish to obtain full deliverance from the bonds of *karma* and to reach final emancipation.

The narrowmindedness of Brāhman moralists was objected to by Buddha and his followers. Thus Buddha is said to have been consulted by two Brāhmans as to whether a man becomes a Brāhman by birth or by his acts. His reply was that the station of a Brāhman is not due to birth, but to abhorrence of the world and its pleasures. The Buddhistic *Dhammapada*, a beautiful collection of proverbs and moral sentiments, contains an eloquent exposition of the virtues, such as self-restraint, patience, contentment, mildness, sympathy, which entitle a man to be rightly called a Brāhman. In other respects, there is no essential difference between Brāhmanical and Buddhistic ethics. *Karma* in Buddhism is the cause of the aggregation of the five *skandhas*, which include all mental and physical phenomena, and therefore of birth and rebirth, of the universal passage through a succession of existences (*saṁsāra*). The middle course, which destroys the working of *karma* and leads to the cessation of suffering and to Wisdom and *Nirvāṇa*, is the Eightfold Path, consisting of right views, right thoughts, right speech, right actions, right living, right exertion, right recollection, and right meditation. The five commandments (*pañchaśīla*) of Buddhism—Kill not, Steal not, Commit not Adultery, Lie not, Drink not Strong Drink—closely resemble the above mentioned five special duties enjoined on Brāhmanical ascetics. Buddha made these rules obligatory on all his followers, and added five more severe commandments for his monks—not to eat at forbidden hours; not to attend worldly amusements, such as dancing or singing; not to use wreaths, unguents, or ornaments; not to use high mats or thrones; not to acquire or receive gold or silver. The five first rules of this Decalogue (*daśaśīla*), though binding on all men alike, were made more stringent in the case of Buddhist monks and nuns. Thus chastity means in the case of monks and nuns absolute abstinence from sexual intercourse; in the case of laymen it means refraining from adultery. There are also secondary precepts extending beyond the rules of the *daśaśīla* for those who have renounced the world. This superior morality corresponds in many particulars to the rule of life prescribed for a Brāhmanical *yati* ('ascetic'). That which especially characterizes Buddhism is the sympathy displayed towards all living beings, carried to the extreme of avoiding injury to the smallest insects, and showing kindness to the most noxious animals. It is recorded of the Buddha himself, in those charming tales of his anterior births, the Jātakas, that in former births he often gave himself up as a victim to satisfy the appetites of hawks and beasts of prey; and on one occasion, meeting with a famished tigress, sacrificed his own body to supply the tigress and her cubs with food. This regard for animal life comes out very clearly in the rock and pillar edicts of the Buddhist king Aśoka (*c.* 250 B.C.), which contain ample discourses on Buddhist morality, furnishing an early and authentic record of Buddhist teaching. Reverence to parents, elders, and preceptors, true charity and true ceremonial, toleration for the beliefs and practices of others, kind treatment of slaves and servants, liberality to ascetics and Brāhmans, truthfulness, purity, gentleness, and saintliness are other virtues extolled in the edicts of king Aśoka.

Jainism, which, unlike Buddhism, continues to flourish in India at the present day, goes even beyond Buddhism in the regard paid to animal life. The oath not to hurt animals is exacted from the Jaina ascetic on his entrance into the Order; it demands watchfulness over all functions of the body by which anything living might be hurt, and for this purpose the Jaina ascetic must carry with him a straining cloth for his drinking water, a broom, and a veil before his mouth, in order to avoid killing insects. In his four other oaths the Jaina monk promises, like the Brāhman and the Buddhist, and almost in the same words, not to speak untruth, to appropriate nothing to himself without permission, to preserve chastity, and to practise self-sacrifice. Asceticism, both inward and outward, is made specially prominent in this religion; it embraces repentance of sin, confession of the same to the teacher (as in Buddhism), penance done for it, the study and teaching of the holy faith, pious meditations, the renunciation of all worldly possessions, temperance, begging, different kinds of self-mortification, especially by fasts which may be continued to starvation, voluntary death by withdrawal of food being regarded as a sure entrance to Nirvāṇa. The rules of 'the right way' for the Jaina laity are less severe, the oath of chastity, *e.g.*, being replaced by that of conjugal fidelity, just as the rules for Brāhman and Buddhist laymen are less strict than those destined for the clergy. In practical life Jainism may be said to make of its laity earnest men who excel in an exceptional willingness to sacrifice anything for their religion. The clergy in the education of worldly communities are united again to humanity and its interests, and conversions of people of low caste to the Jaina creed are not uncommon even at the present day.

Later Brāhmanism, as represented in the Code of Manu, the 'Great Epic' (*Mahābhārata*), and many other productions of what is called classical Sanskrit literature, reiterates the old iniquitous law of caste, and tries to enforce the claims of the priestly class to spiritual and social superiority. 'The Hindu code as a whole is savage and antique' (Hopkins). Thus in criminal law the *jus talionis* is carried to an extreme degree (see CRIMES AND PUNISHMENTS [Hindu]). Witnesses in a court of justice are exhorted to speak truth, with many fine sentiments extolling veracity and denouncing falsehood; yet perjury is permitted where an accused of respectable caste may be saved from death by it (see LAW AND LAWBOOKS [Hindu]). Long lists of offences of various degrees are given, which do not differ essentially from the moral code and the notions of right and wrong current among other nations of antiquity, except perhaps in the peculiar sanctity attributed to Brāhmans and all their belongings, and to the cow, the sacred animal of the Hindus. But every sin may be atoned for by performing a penance (see EXPIATION AND ATONEMENT [Hindu]); and these penances were an important source of profit to the Brāhmans. Though each class has its special duties assigned to it, there are also general obligations common to all castes, such as forbearance, veracity, self-restraint, purity, liberality, self-control, regard for animal life, obedience towards elders, visiting places of pilgrimage, sympathy, straightforwardness, contentment, etc. (*Viṣṇusūtra*, ii. 16 f.). The doctrine of *ahiṁsā* (non-injury to living beings) is, however, not so much insisted on as in the Buddhist and Jaina creeds; for a sacrifice, cattle may be slain, and the meat of such cattle may be eaten, although the doctrine of *karma* and of the soul's passage through all kinds of animal bodies, according to its deeds in a previous life, is fully recognized in the Code of Manu. The merit of asceticism, combined with religious meditation, is highly extolled; and the entrance into the order of religious mendicants is supposed to form a regular stage in the life of a Brāhman, preceded by the stage of a hermit in the woods (*vānaprastha*). The sacerdotal element is very strong in the Mahābhārata also, which is, like the codes, a vast thesaurus of Hindu ethics. Thus there is an eightfold path of religious duty, as in Buddhism, but here it consists in sacrifice, study, liberality, penance, truth, mercy, self-control, and lack of greed. The epics contain many touching pictures of domestic and social happiness: children are dutiful to their parents and submissive to their superiors; parents are fondly attached to their children, and ready to sacrifice themselves for their welfare; wives are loyal and devoted to their husbands; husbands are affectionately disposed towards their wives; love and harmony reign through the family circle (M. Williams). The didactic and sententious note prevails in the whole range of Sanskrit literature (Macdonell). It is particularly strong in the old collections of fairy tales and fables, which agree in putting instructive speeches and moral sentiments into the mouths of jackals, cats, elephants, parrots, monkeys, and other animals; and it also pervades Sanskrit lyrics and dramatic works, among which the *Prabodhachandrodaya* furnishes an instance of an allegorical and philosophical play which may be fitly compared to some of our old Moralities. The keynote in Sanskrit moral poetry is the conception of fate, but fate is declared to be nothing else than the result of action done in a former birth, so that every man can by right conduct shape his future fate himself.

Passing to modern developments, we find a general tendency on the part of religious founders such as Basava, the founder of the Liṅgāyats, in the 12th cent., Kabīr, the founder of the Kabīrpanthīs, in the 15th, Nānak, Dādū, and Chaitanya, in the 16th, and many others, to proclaim the social equality of all those who enrolled themselves in their Order. In practice, however, this levelling down of caste distinctions met with only partial and temporary success. As a way of salvation, the 'way of love and faith' (*bhaktimārga*) has been gaining ground, though the 'way of works' (*karmamārga*), *i.e.* the practice of religious rites, austerities, penances, and sacrifices, is held to be equal, and the 'way of true knowledge' (*jñānamārga*) is held to be superior to it. The *puṣṭimārga*, or 'way of enjoyment,' is sometimes recognized as a fourth way. The Reports on the Census of 1901 contain some interesting attempts at establishing the actual standard of morality in India.

'The code of morality of the ordinary Hindu is much the same as that of most civilized nations, though it is nowhere reduced to a code. He knows that it is wrong to commit murder, adultery, theft and perjury, or to covet, and he honours his parents, in the case of the father, at any rate, to a degree exceeding the customs of most nations, which have no ceremony resembling that of *Śrāddh* [funeral oblation]. The influence of caste is, however, of the greatest importance here, and some inquirers have expressed their opinion that the principal sanction attaching to a breach of morality is the fear of caste penalties rather than the dread of divine punishment, and there are many facts which go to support this view. . . . An extreme example of the effect of caste principles may be seen in some of the lowest castes, where adultery is only condemned . . . when committed with a person of different caste. In the case of perjury, the offence may be committed, without public reprobation, on behalf of a caste-fellow, or even an inhabitant of the same village. . . . I believe that the doctrine of *Karma* is one of the firmest beliefs of all classes of Hindus, and that the fear that a man shall reap as he has sown is an appreciable element in the average morality. . . . A man and his wife bathe in the Ganges with their clothes tied together, to ensure their being married to one another in a future existence.' As for Heaven and Hell, they are not merely 'transitory stages of existence in the chain of transmigration,' but 'the soul' when sufficiently purified 'goes to dwell in Heaven for ever. . . . There is no idea of absorption in the deity whose place is far above' (*Census of India*, 1901, Report, p. 363 f.).

The belief in metempsychosis does not prevail all over India; thus the ordinary Hindu peasant in the Central Provinces 'has practically no belief in the transmigration of souls, but has a vague idea that there is a future life, in which those who are good in this world will be happy in a heaven (*sarg*), while those who are bad will be wretched in a hell (*narak*)' (*Central Provinces Report*, p. 78). The general effect of these two different beliefs on the state of morality remains the same, the idea of retribution in a future state being common to both of them. The influence of Christian morality on the religious life of India becomes visible in the teaching and practical working of the various theistical sects called Samājes (see ĀRYA SAMĀJ and BRĀHMA SAMĀJ). Thus the *Ārya Samāj* insists on education both of males and females, and aims at doing good to the world by improving the physical, intellectual, spiritual, moral, and social condition of mankind.

LITERATURE.—A. Barth, *The Religions of India*[3], London, 1890; E. W. Hopkins, *Religions of India*, London, 1896; V. A. Smith, *Early History of India*[2], Oxford, 1908; M. Williams, *Indian Wisdom*[3], London, 1876; L. A. Waddell, *The Buddhism of Tibet*, London, 1895; H. Kern, *Manual of Indian Buddhism*, Strassburg, 1896; G. Bühler, *The Indian Sect of the Jainas*, tr. by Burgess, London, 1903; A. A. Macdonell, *History of Sanskrit Literature*, London, 1900; O. Böhtlingk, *Indische Sprüche*, 3 vols., Petersburg, 1870–73; *Reports on the Census of India*, 1901.

J. JOLLY.

ETHICS AND MORALITY (Japanese).—I. Ancient Japanese.

—The Japanese nation through its long history has cherished several peculiar forms of morality, which, of course, must be admitted to have undergone modifications to some extent, although their essential character has remained unaltered. The characteristic ethical features of the ancient Japanese are to be found in the morality of Japan at the present day. One of them is certainly nationalism. It is recognizable in the old mythology, which, unlike that of any other land, centres in the Imperial family and the State. In the course of the creation, the Divine pair, Izanagi and Izanami (see COSMOGONY AND COSMOLOGY [Japanese]), first produced the country (*i.e.* the earth) and, after a long interval, the Sun-goddess, the Moon-god, and one other son. The first of the three was made ruler of the heaven-world; she afterwards sent her grandson to Japan, gave him a mirror, a sword, and a bead, to be handed down to their posterity as the royal insignia, and said:

'This country has to be ruled by my descendants; thou oughtest to go and reign over it. The sacred dynasty will be so prosperous that it will last eternally, even as heaven and earth do.'[1]

The Sun-goddess is sister to the country, and is regarded as the first ancestor of the Imperial family and of the people in general, which are to be, as her prediction indicates, eternally the ruler and the ruled. A throne occupied by a single dynasty

[1] *Nihongi*, fasc. 2.

is the possession of no nation in the world except the Japanese. A great respect has always been paid by the people to such a sacred throne. At one time they regarded the Mikados as living gods, and, even when they were deprived of ruling power, the people never ceased to pay the respect due to them. This does not mean that they stood in a slavish relation to the Imperial family, which, on the contrary, is related to the people as the main house to branch houses. The Mikados are not their conquerors, as with the majority of other nations. The people are often addressed by the Mikados as 'Our children,' which accounts for the special relation between the two. Submission to the Mikados, therefore, is not merely loyalty but filial piety.[1] In contrast with China, filial piety in Japan comes next to loyalty, though in most cases the two are mentioned side by side. In the Japanese family, parents are absolutely obeyed by their children, and superiors by inferiors, as the Mikados are obeyed by their subjects. Filial piety is not so highly valued as loyalty, which is absolute, and very often bids people sacrifice other virtues for its sake. Dutifulness to parents and obedience to superiors were the chief morals in the Japanese home in ancient days, as they are still. Honesty and righteousness were among the principal virtues in old Japan. Classical scholars are of opinion that the ancient Japanese were honest and upright of themselves without any teaching, and could be governed quite easily, and that neither were detailed laws needed to rule them, nor minute moral doctrines to regulate their daily life, because they were simple, honest, and good, and committed neither illegal nor immoral acts.[2] They were practical and optimistic to an extreme, thinking neither of the future nor of the past, but only of the present.[3] Death was hateful, but not fearful, to them. They seem never to have thought of whither they would go after death—a state of things which was much modified after Buddhism was introduced. In ancient chronicles, we meet with the words *nigitama* (a gentle spirit) and *aratama* (a rough spirit); the former denotes the virtues of gentleness and generosity, the latter those of bravery and chivalry. The old Japanese were gentle and magnanimous on the one hand, and so were kind and indulgent to others, and lived in harmony with the world; but, on the other hand, they had strong wills and brave hearts, which, when duty called them, very often made them face dangers, and, if necessary, sacrifice their lives for the sake of the fatherland.[4]

2. Shintoism.—The word *shinto* is not Japanese, but Chinese; it means 'the Way of the Gods' (*Kami-no-michi*). Some say it is a religion, some a moral system, and others a political way. It may be any or all of these three, for in ancient days no distinction was made between them. It presents no peculiar doctrines, and nothing like a code of ethics; but, as it is the great way of the Empire, all the Japanese, ancient and modern, in spite of different creeds, must be Shintoists. The Shinto scholars (*e.g.* Hirata) say that they are acting and moving in accordance with the Shintoistic teachings when they worship national deities, when they venerate Mikados and parents, when they try to promote the national welfare and happiness, or when they lead an honest and godlike life. Shinto is a mixture of Ancestor-worship and Nature-worship, as may be seen from the nomenclature of the deities worshipped. The Japanese have combined their ancestors with natural phenomena, have deified them, and worship them. In dealing with them in such a manner, they mean that the ancestors are their progenitors, superiors, and benefactors; not only the creators of their bodies, but the furnishers of their life, professions, estates, and all other things. They hold their merits in great esteem, and thank them for their perpetual favours. Esteem for their ancestors being common to all, the sentiments of loyalty, patriotism, and filial piety, the love of family and the feeling of honour are combined, and thus a phase of morality peculiar to the Japanese has been developed.[1] In ancient times no distinction was made between worship and administration, between reverence for the gods and loyalty. Loyal people only could be faithful to the deities or their ancestral spirits, and the Emperors in taking the reins of government were appeasing and worshipping national deities. The very words *matsuri* ('worship') and *matsurigoto* ('worship-matter' or 'administration') signify the identity of these two. Patriarchal monarchy was thus theocratical monarchy as well. Various ceremonies were performed to serve the national deities, of which the most important is the ceremony of purification, or *harai*—important alike from the religious, the moral, and the legal point of view. *Oharai*, or grand purification, was performed at the Court twice a year, and is so still, though nowadays it is a mere ceremony, to drive away the evils resulting from the sinful, immoral, or unlawful deeds of the whole nation during every half-year; and, when any serious offence was committed, a ceremony for the same purpose was performed. *Misogi* (body-washing) was another rite of purification which at first consisted in washing the body when one touched anything unclean, but afterwards became confused with *harai*, so that no distinction was made between them. Defilement, mental or physical, was hateful to the Japanese; and, according to their simple ideas, any guilt, moral or legal, could be as easily removed by the performance of purification as literal dirt can be removed by bathing. See, further, art. SHINTOISM.

3. Bushido.—*Bushido*, or simply *Budo* or *Shido*, is the Chinese term for the Jap. *Mononofu-no-Michi*, lit. 'the Way of Fighting Knights or *Samurai*' (attendants). It is a moral system intended for the military class. Though its full development belongs to later ages of the national history, say the feudal periods—the 12th and following centuries—it may be said to be as old as the race themselves; and *Yamatodamashii* ('the soul of Japan,' *Yamato* being a classical name for this country) is not only the soul of the military men, but that of the whole nation. As Shinto is the indigenous religion of the nation, so Bushido is their national morality, or at least its essence.[2] But here we have only to deal with the Bushido for the Bushi class, and not as national morality. The Bushi should be, in the first place, loyal to lords and filial to parents; these, along with reverence for gods and worship of Buddhas, were considered their chief duties. Indeed, loyalty and filial piety were the fundamental morality of the Bushi class, as is the case with the nation in general. Then they should be brave and fearless in fighting, and calm and never flinching in the face of any danger or death. Bravery, fearlessness, self-possession, and the like, were what they always specially cultivated; but they were not by any means foolhardy or brutal in fighting or in their daily life. Their courage was restrained and softened by the feeling of benevolence and the sense of rectitude and honour; they were not to do anything brutal or underhand, but what was right and manly. Benevolence was one of the chief virtues of the Bushi; and many pathetic stories are told of 'benevolence of warriors.' Kindness, magnanimity, sympathy, and the like, were praised as supreme

[1] Sawayanagi, *op. cit. infra.* [2] Motoori, *Nawonohire*, 1771.
[3] Haga, *op. cit. infra.* [4] Arima, *op. cit. infra.*

[1] Sawayanagi, *loc. cit.* [2] *Ib.*

virtues for the military men, who might otherwise be disposed to coldheartedness or even to cruelty. They should be polite to superiors as well as to inferiors, faithful in the fulfilment of their duties, and simple in their life. These, with a few others of a kindred nature, were the qualifications thought necessary to *Samurai*-ship. The Emperor Meiji gave his soldiers five commandments, in which he recommended loyalty, politeness, bravery, faithfulness, and simplicity; and he concluded with words to the effect that in the fulfilment of these five precepts a sincere spirit is essential, for without this neither good language nor good conduct will be anything more than a mere ornament, of no practical use. These five items are 'the public path of heaven and earth, and the perpetual code of human relations.'[1]

4. Confucianism.—In A.D. 284[2] the Pakchian king sent his minister Achiki to the Japanese Court to offer tributary homage. The minister being a man of letters, the Crown Prince became his pupil and learned from him Chinese literature. In the following year another scholar was invited, who brought with him ten copies of the *Analects* and a copy of the *Book of One Thousand Characters*; he taught the prince Chinese literature and Confucian doctrines. The literature thus introduced influenced the nation in at least three points. (1) They learned Chinese characters, by means of which they could reduce their thoughts to writing. (2) Prior to this time, things had had no distinguishing names: loyalty, filial piety, friendship, for instance, though they were virtues inborn with the nation, had been devoid of particular designations. Now that Chinese wording was introduced, any notions could be expressed in words. (3) The manners, customs, and other things in the neighbouring countries came to be understood among the Japanese, who by and by followed them in these matters.[3] During the following centuries, Chinese moral teaching acquired considerable popularity among the people, especially of the higher classes; but from the 10th cent. it gradually declined, being first crushed out by classical studies, and then neglected on account of successive disturbances. At the commencement of the Tokugawa Shogunate, *i.e.* early in the 17th cent., it revived under the protection of the founder of the dynasty; well-informed Chinese scholars, though divided into several schools, appeared one after another and brought it back to its original glorious state. This dynasty witnessed the best days of the history of Confucian ethics in Japan; and the system has continued to flourish down to the present day, though not free from degeneration. The morality taught in this system, not differing materially from the ancient morals of the nation, has never encountered such vehement opposition as Buddhism; it deepened and elaborated the pre-existing sentiments of loyalty, filial piety, rectitude, truthfulness, and other virtues. A few of the principal points of difference between the Chinese and the Japanese systems are as follows: Chinese ethics is founded on the worship of Heaven, whereas the Japanese worship ancestral spirits; the Chinese pay supreme respect to men of wisdom, and hence admit that unwise or tyrannical monarchs may be dethroned at the people's will, whereas the Japanese regard the Mikados as sacred and inviolable; and, lastly, the chief virtues of the former are benevolence and filial piety, whereas the latter attribute supreme value to loyalty and rectitude, loyalty and filial piety being, according to their national morality, identical.[4]

[1] Shigeno and Kusaka, *Bushido in Japan*; Arima, *loc. cit.*
[2] The official date of its introduction; but the verified one is about A.D. 402.
[3] Endo, 'Confucianism' (*Encyc. of Philosophy, ut infra*).
[4] Arima, *loc. cit.*

Confucius taught that benevolence is the supreme virtue, the highest ideal of man, the *summum bonum*; Mencius connected it with rectitude, declaring that 'the greatest way in the world is only benevolence and rectitude,' and that 'benevolence is the peaceful residence of mankind, and rectitude is the right road of mankind.' Scholars who appeared later on added politeness, knowledge, and truth to these two; and the whole pass under the name of the five cardinal virtues, the sum-total of human virtue. In human society men are related to each other in five different ways, which impose on them as many obligations. They are as follows: rectitude between lord and subject, familiarity between father and son, distinction between husband and wife, grade between elder and younger brother, and confidence between friend and friend. The most important of these are the first two, especially the second; hence filial piety is the root of all virtues, of all moral practices. Generosity, respect, gratefulness, humility, faithfulness, self-control, courage, and manliness are some of the virtues commended in the Confucian teaching. For thirteen centuries the Japanese have lived under this moral teaching, and probably there is no one of them who is wholly uninfluenced by it; but they have wisely adopted only the points suitable to their special culture and national development, neglecting the elements that might be injurious to public morals or fatal to the welfare of the State.[1] See, further, CONFUCIAN RELIGION, CONFUCIUS.

5. Buddhism.—Buddhism was officially introduced into Japan in A.D. 552. Its introduction at once gave rise to a controversy between two parties at the Court—a controversy which was not merely religious but also political and tribal, and which after a violent conflict resulted in victory for the pro-Buddhist party. Prince Shotoku (573–621), one of the wisest and greatest personages Japan had ever produced, did all in his power for the advancement of the newly introduced creed, and well deserves the high respect paid by the Buddhists to his memory. The doctrine of Divine incarnation, according to which some Shinto deities are the incarnations of Buddhas, Bodhisattvas, or certain Indian Devas, was first taught by Prince Shotoku and then by Gyoki (670–749), a learned and virtuous high priest, and was further broadened and deepened by two great men who arose shortly after his death—Saicho and Kukai, who respectively founded the Tendai and the Shingon sects in Japan. Thus Shintoism was seemingly absorbed into Buddhism. Strangely enough, the two somewhat antagonistic creeds co-existed in unity for nearly a thousand years, until their final separation in 1871. Prince Shotoku and other great personages who appeared early in the history of Buddhism in Japan seem to have striven to nationalize its teachings and to bring it into as close contact with the nation as possible. During those days all the work of the Buddhists was designed in the interests of the national welfare and peace. The Emperor Shomu (reigned 724–748), for instance, had a monastery and a nunnery built in each province throughout the Empire, as well as the general monastery, in which the famous *daibutsu* (*q.v.*) is set up, at Nara, then the capital. During the Kamakura age (1190–1333) many new sects were imported from China or sprang up in Japan, and all of them laboured in the interests of the Imperial family and the welfare of the State. In return, Buddhism received great favours from Court and Government, and certainly it is owing to these favours that it has flourished so long in Japan. The national morality, especially Bushido, was reinforced and expanded by it. Its doctrines

[1] Endo, *loc. cit.*

of unselfishness and freedom from desire being in harmony with the essential elements of Yamato-damashii, it has found a ready entrance into the Japanese heart. Its teaching of benevolence softened the otherwise harsh character of the national spirit. It introduced the idea of another world, which was entirely lacking in the ancient Japanese system. The Mahāyānist teachings enlarged the insular spirit. As it was long popular among the people, high and low, no grade of society remained uninfluenced by it, and the highest culture is solely the work of the Buddhist teachers. Japanese Buddhism at the present day is divided into a dozen sects and into some fifty sub-branches, which differ more or less in doctrines, ritual, habits of monastic life, and as a matter of course in their ethical systems. The teachings of some of the sects appear to be quite antagonistic to each other—a fact which shows how inclusive and assimilative the whole system is.

Buddhistic ethics is founded on the assumption that all the creation is sprung from one common Cause, and things in the universe are connected with one another in complicated ways.[1] The naming and location of that Cause may differ with different sects, but all the Mahāyānist sects agree in regarding it as the primary source of all that exists in the universe. Things with and without life are all closely related to one another; and persons of the same household, trade, or social rank, and those who are the same in other respects, have been born thus from one and the same Cause; in other words, they did the same *karma* in a previous existence. Besides, we have transmigrated through the six states of existence, in the course of which we may somewhere have been closely connected with some who are strangers to us to-day. Ought we not then to be kind to others, whether familiar or unfamiliar to us? Of many moral precepts given by the Buddha, as practical morality, the four favours, with their corresponding obligations, must first be mentioned. They are (i.) of parents, (ii.) of fellow-beings, (iii.) of the king, and (iv.) of the triple treasure, *i.e.* the Buddha, the Law, and the Congregation. Next to them come the five or ten precepts and the six *pāramitās*, or perfections. The precepts are as follows: (1) not to destroy life, (2) not to steal, (3) not to have unlawful sexual intercourse, (4) not to tell a lie, and (5) not to drink fermented liquors. Otherwise they are: (1) not to take life, (2) not to steal, (3) not to commit adultery, (4) not to tell a lie, (5) not to talk frivolously, (6) not to slander, (7) not to be double-tongued, (8) not to be covetous, (9) not to be malicious, and (10) not to be heretical. The *pāramitās* are: perfect exercise of (i.) charity; (ii.) morality; (iii.) patience; (iv.) fortitude; (v.) meditation; and (vi.) knowledge. Cf., further, ETHICS AND MORALITY (Buddhist).

LITERATURE.—The *Kojiki, Nihongi, Kujiki*; the works on Shinto, Nationality, and Bushido, of Hayashi Razan (1583–1657), Kamo (1697–1769), Motoori (1730–1801), Hirata (1776–1843), Kaibara (1630–1714), Yamaga (1622–1685), and other authors; T. Inoue's three works on Japanese philosophy (*Yang Ming School*, 1899, *Revival School*, 1902, *Chu Hi School*, 1906); M. Sawayanagi, *Education in Our Country*, Tokyo, 1910; Y. Arima, *Japanese Nationality*, do. 1907; Y. Haga, *Ten Lectures on Japanese Nationality*, do. 1908; R. Endo, *Oriental Ethics*, do. 1909; *Encyc. of Philosophy*, published by the Dobunkwan.

S. TACHIBANA.

[1] Saito, *Outlines of Buddhist Ethics*, 1903.

ETHICS AND MORALITY (Muslim).—**I. Muḥammad and the Qur'ān.**—As Islām in its genesis and development was to some extent influenced by the moral ideas of the ancient Arabs, it will be well to make a brief preliminary reference to these. The social conditions amid which Muḥammad appeared, and which survive to this day with but little change among the denizens of the desert, had reached the stage of tribal organization, and the life of the people was regulated by established custom, *i.e.* by tribal morality. Their moral ideas, so far as we are in a position to judge, reveal an unmistakably secular spirit, alike among the merchants of the cities and among the Bedawīn. The Prophet opened his propaganda among them by denouncing their sins and threatening them with the impending Day of Judgment and the fire of Hell, but at first he encountered nothing but mockery; and it was only when he had in some measure accommodated his message to the present world that they gave heed to his words about the world beyond.

But, while the ancient Arabs were intent upon material advantage and enjoyment, they were not wholly unmindful of higher things. As we may see from the powerful impression produced among them by satirical poems—an impression due only in part to the dread of magic—they had a high sense of both personal and tribal honour. The moral ideal of the Bedawīn found expression in the patient endurance of privations; in a loyalty accorded not so much to the chief of the tribe as to co-equal fellow-members; in a courage which, in open warfare and still more in marauding expeditions, was controlled by a wise policy of sparing the lives of enemies; and, finally, in hospitality—a virtue which, it is true, is ever a native of regions where there is little occasion for its exercise. As compared with the Bedawīn, the people of the cities had, to say the least, a larger share of worldly wisdom. The Meccans, in particular, both before and after Muḥammad's day, were astute enough to put their market under the protection of a sanctuary, and to exploit the very piety of those who came to trade within the sacred precincts. The present inhabitants of the holy city quite frankly avow their adherence to the ethics of the happy mean, asserting that, while the people of Yiddah are very worldly, and those of Medīna very devout, they themselves hold an even balance between heavenly and earthly interests.[1]

In pre-Muhammadan poetry terms expressive of moral sentiments occur only sporadically. We find, indeed, warnings against arrogance and threatenings of Divine vengeance; but such exceptions, in which moral and religious concepts are distinguished from law or custom, are probably traceable to Jewish-Christian influence. It was under that influence, at all events, that Muḥammad stood forth as a reformer—to work, in the words of tradition, 'for the improvement of morals.'

Muḥammad made the demand of personal belief and personal morality.

'No burdened soul shall bear the burden of another.'[2] In the Day of Judgment every one shall be answerable for himself: 'O ye people, fear your Lord, and dread the day when the father shall not atone for the son, nor the child atone at all for his parent.'[3]

Hence, too, the Qur'ān urges—though less insistently than the NT—the necessity of repentance, conversion, the good heart, the changed spirit. Good intentions are commended; unpremeditated lapses from virtue are leniently judged. In short, Allāh makes it no onerous task for His faithful to serve Him: He is forgiving, merciful.

Nevertheless, as Muḥammad's earliest adherents were but a small company, it was no child's play for them to respond to his demand of personal morality. Such a demand shattered the old family ties and came into conflict—at first somewhat too harshly, though afterwards in a milder fashion—with immemorial usage and custom. In this way the moral fellowship of the true believers came to mean more than the tribal relationship. In the light of the ideal thus introduced every believer

[1] Snouck Hurgronje, *Mekka*, ii. 72 f., 149.
[2] Qur'ān, liii. 39. [3] *Ib.* xxxi. 32.

was henceforth the neighbour or brother of every other. Islām was to be a universal brotherhood, in which kindness and equity should count for more than custom and law. Muḥammad was, nevertheless, unable to bring this ideal to its full realization with respect to the right of hospitality and protection and to the practice of blood-revenge. In principle, no doubt, private revenge was superseded by legal punishment, but in practice the former was still permitted, though in a somewhat mitigated form. It had now to be kept within the bounds of moderation, and must involve none but the actual culprit. Moreover, Muḥammad helped to foster a higher regard for human life by prohibiting the heathen custom of killing female infants; but, on the other hand, the practice of fœticide has all along prevailed, without censure, in Muslim countries.

The ethics of the Qur'ān might be summed up in the trite formula: 'Believe and do right.' Belief, of course, is the primary obligation, since without belief all works are vain—a mere mirage in the waste.[1] But, as it does not come within the scope of the present article to deal with belief (see FAITH [Muslim]), or with the duties of religion in the narrower sense, our sole concern here is with the question, What is implied in 'doing right'?

Of human virtues the Qur'ān insists most frequently and most urgently on beneficence—the bestowing of benefits upon the poor, the needy, the orphan, the stranger, the slave, and the prisoner, especially in the form of alms (*zakāt*). By almsgiving a person not only helps others, but also manifests the true spirit of self-denial—in the expectation, it is true, of winning, not indeed the treasures of earth, but the rewards of Heaven. This spirit was displayed by Muḥammad himself, chiefly in the earlier years of his prophetic activity in Mecca, when he declaimed against the rich. Afterwards, when his followers had become a political organization in Medīna, the antagonisms were somewhat less pronounced. A similar development appears in the practice of *zakāt*. Originally a voluntary expression of love, and, in the view of Oriental Jews and Christians, almost identical with piety or the fear of God, *i.e.* with virtue in general, it gradually became a tax upon property, and as such became one of the five pillars of Muslim law.[2] In Muslim countries the *zakāt* came usually to be assessed for the public treasury. The collectors of the tax did not neglect their own interests, while the lawyers or priests (so far as we may speak of a priesthood in Islām) claimed to rank pre-eminently among the poor and needy who had a right to share therein.

Besides almsgiving, many other virtues are spoken of in the Qur'ān as acceptable to God. A series of corresponding commandments which, while lacking systematic form, seems to be dependent upon the Mosaic Decalogue, is given in sūra xvii. 23-40:

'Set not up another god with Allāh, lest thou sit down despised, forsaken. Thy Lord hath ordained that ye shall worship none but Him; and kindness to your parents, whether one or both of them attain to old age beside thee; and say not to them "Fie!" neither murmur against them, but speak to them in gracious words. And defer humbly to them out of compassion; and say, "Lord, have compassion on them, even as they brought me up when I was little." Your Lord well knoweth what is in your souls, whether ye be righteous: And verily, He is forgiving towards those who return to Him with repentance. And to thy kinsman render his due, and also to the poor and the wayfarer; yet waste not wastefully; for the wasteful are ever brethren of the Satans, and Satan is ever unthankful to his Lord. But if thou dost turn away from them, and seekest from thy Lord boons for which thou hopest, in any wise speak to them with kindly words. And let not thy hand be fettered to thy neck; nor yet open it with all openness, lest thou be made to sit down in rebuke and beggary. Verily, thy Lord provideth plenty for whomsoever He will; and He too giveth with measure. Verily, He ever beholdeth and observeth His servants. Kill not your children for fear of poverty; we will provide for them and for you. Beware, for killing them is a great wickedness. Withhold yourselves from adultery, for it is an abomination, and evil is the way thereof. Neither slay any one whom God hath forbidden you to slay, except for a just cause; for, if one be slain unjustly, to his nearest of kin have we given authority; yet let not *him* exceed in slaying; verily, he is ever helped. And touch not the substance of the orphan, except in an upright way, till he attain the years of strength; and perform your covenants; verily, a covenant shall be inquired of. And give full measure when ye measure, and weigh with an equal balance—this is the better, and more just for settlement. And follow not that of which thou hast no knowledge; verily, the hearing and the sight and the heart—these shall all be inquired of. And walk not proudly upon the earth, for thou canst not cleave the earth, and thou shalt not reach the mountains in height. All this is evil, hateful in the sight of your Lord.'

These precepts are intended primarily for Muslims, and apply only in a limited degree to the adherents of other faiths. Towards the heathen, towards the Jews, Christians, and other possessors of sacred scriptures who would not submit to the secular power of Islām, and also towards apostates from the faith, the Muslim policy was the holy war and death. Here we have an instance of the religious restriction of moral obligation. The same thing is observable in the fact that the development of a free personal moral life is seriously cramped by religious considerations. The fundamental principle of Islām is that Allāh is sovereign and that men are his slaves, whose virtue consists in obedience. The will of Allāh—in reality, of course, the mind of His Prophet—alone decides as to good and evil. 'Islām,' indeed, simply means the surrender of believers to the will of Allāh.

The sanctions of morality are also of a religious character. Reward and punishment belong mainly to the other world. The majority of mankind must presumably expiate their sin in the fire of Hell. But those who believe and do right shall enjoy the delights of Paradise, which Muḥammad depicts after a fashion suggested by the wine-shop of the ancient Arabs. For all their self-denial on earth—their abstinence from wine, from games of chance, and from luxury in general—they shall find compensation in the heavenly virgins and κιναιδοι who serve the deathless ones with the goblet that inebriates not.

2. Muḥammad and tradition.—Muḥammad made no claim to be a saint, nor was he one, but shortly after his death devout Muslims endeavoured to order their lives by his example. Hence, as the Qur'ān did not furnish the requisite information on every detail, there arose a demand for definite traditions regarding the Prophet's manner of life, as also that of his companions and most intimate adherents; and, as the pious fraud is not usually accounted the most heinous of sins, the supply corresponded to the demand. In Islām, accordingly, we find several collections of traditions—compounds of the authentic and the spurious—some of which are regarded as canonical, and thus ancient tribal custom came to be superseded, in theory at least, by the *sunnah* of the prophet (cf. art. LAW [Muhammadan]). The true believer felt himself obliged to follow this idealized *sunnah* as loyally as possible, and, while the first sentence of the most celebrated collection, viz. that of Bukhārī, but echoes the teaching of the Qur'ān in asserting that actions are judged by their motive, yet the conformity of the faithful consisted largely in externals, being ritualistic rather than ethical. To 'Umar, the second successor of the prophet, is attributed the saying:

'Nowadays [*i.e.* when the process of revelation mediated by Muḥammad, and therefore also the possibility of discerning the

[1] Qur'ān, xviii. 105, xxiv. 39.

[2] Viz. the third, the others being (1) the creed, (2) the ritual of prayer, (4) fasting, and (5) the pilgrimage. According to an ancient tradition, Muḥammad enjoined as a sixth primary obligation the active love of one's neighbour, *i.e.* the duty of doing to others what one would wish done to oneself.

thoughts of the heart, has ceased for ever] we judge people entirely by their outward actions; we protect him who appears to us to do right, for we know nothing of what is within—Allāh is the judge thereof!—and we do not protect him who appears to do wrong, nor do we find faith in him even if he asserts that his motives are pure.'[1]

It is likely enough, indeed, that many who availed themselves of this pronouncement forgot the parenthetic clause regarding the judgment of Allāh. It was easier, moreover, in conformity with the *sunnah*, to use a toothpick, to rub oneself with water or sand, and to submit to circumcision, than to cleanse the soul from sin, and with pure heart to serve Allāh in spirit and in truth. Thus the great bulk of the moral precepts of Islām, as found even in the Qur'ān, and more particularly in the tradition, bear a somewhat external and—one may venture to say—commercial character.[2] The believer has an account with Allāh. One tradition has it that a convert to Islām has all his previous good deeds put to his credit.[3]

The *sunnah* agrees with the Qur'ān in assigning the leading place among good works to almsgiving. If a man is unable to give alms, let him labour with his hands[4]—in order, of course, to make himself able; for this is the conception of work presented by the tradition. Only by way of exception do the *ḥadīths*—the Qur'ān is silent on the subject—ascribe an independent ethical value to work. Thus the following saying was put into the mouth of the Prophet: 'No man can have a better meal than that which he has earned by the labour of his hands. David, the prophet of God, ate what he had earned by the work of his hands.' But perhaps this saying, and others like it, may simply imply that work is superior to begging, though not to almsgiving.[5] The practice of almsgiving, as indeed the element of self-denial in general that was present in Islām from the outset, was strongly reinforced by the influence of Christianity, and, subsequently, of Indian religions, as appears from the fact that the *sunnah* is much less distinctively Arabian in character than the Qur'ān. When Islām had overspread the Christian provinces of the Roman empire, it assimilated many elements of Christian asceticism.

The assertion that early Islām was absolutely destitute of the ethical spirit has been refuted, above all, by Goldziher.[6] The *sunnah* undoubtedly contains ethical elements. It is true that Arabic has no single specific term for 'conscience,' but the thing itself is quite adequately connoted by such periphrases as 'unrest of heart.' According to one highly esteemed *ḥadīth*, 'virtue is [the sum of] good qualities, iniquity is what disturbs the soul, and what thou desirest others not to know concerning thee.' The last clause certainly savours of conventionalism, but there are other traditions in which the requirement of inward sincerity is more clearly expressed.

Thus, *e.g.*, we read: 'Shall I tell you what work stands higher than all prayer, fasting, and almsgiving? It is to make peace between two enemies'; or, again: 'Of more avail [than ritual prayer] is the prayer which a man utters in his own house, where no one sees him but Allāh, and which has no other motive than the desire to draw near unto Allāh.' Another tradition tells how a pious female devotee who was using insulting language towards her neighbour was consigned to hell by the Prophet; whereas his judgment regarding another woman, who was negligent of prayer and fasting, but gave to the needy and never insulted her neighbour, was 'She is destined for Paradise.' The compassion of Allāh is frequently set forth as a pattern for the faithful, and they are urged to the performance of pious works.[7]

According to a favourite and frequently quoted *ḥadīth*, the best works are: (1) honour towards parents; (2) not to take a niece in marriage against her will; and (3) to pay one's day-labourers well. A tradition of quite another cast, which had its source among the devout, gives the following list of precepts: (1) Love thou the poor, and be accessible to them; (2) look always at those who are beneath you, and gaze not at those who are above you; (3) never solicit anything from any one; (4) be loyal to thy kinsfolk, even if they should vex you; (5) always speak the truth, even when it is unpalatable; (6) be not overawed in the paths of Allāh by the reviling of the reviler; (7) frequently cry aloud, 'There is no might or power save by Allāh,' for this comes forth from the treasure which is hidden under God's throne.

Probably none of these pious counsels was more fervently obeyed than the last; we find it used as a magic formula, as, *e.g.*, in the *Thousand and One Nights*. But in all likelihood the everyday life of Islām was otherwise but little in harmony with such ideal demands. The mass of the people paid less attention to the Qur'ān and the *ḥadīths* than to the actual life lived by Muḥammad in his Medīna period, when his love was given mainly to women, and the objects of his hate and greed were the unbeliever and their possessions. The early annals of Islām, in fact, exhibit the chosen servants of Allāh as world-conquerors, who, whatever might be their hopes of heavenly reward, were meanwhile wonderfully content with earthly spoils.

3. Development of the law.—To the true Muslim, as to the devout Jew, religion means a law which should control and regulate the whole life of man. From the Oriental point of view, not only social, but also political life, is bound up in the closest way with religion, and hence the Jewish and Christian communities that secured toleration and protection within the pale of Islām by paying tribute always formed in a greater or less degree an *imperium in imperio*. Thus, too, for the Muslim community sacred and secular law are one, and this holds good—in theory—universally, even under foreign domination, while the ideal is in some measure realized under sovereigns who are of the faith. A knowledge of this law (*fiqh*)—a law with religious sanctions—has, therefore, been all along imperative upon every educated Muslim. Legally, children under the age of seven, and, in practice, women also—for the most part—are exempt from this requirement: the former, because they cannot as yet discriminate between right and wrong, good and evil; the latter, because, by ancient tradition, they are but fuel for the fire.

This law, then, as based upon the Qur'ān and the *sunnah*, and to some extent influenced by Roman jurisprudence, entered upon a process of independent development. And just as some—to wit, six—of the collections of traditions gradually acquired a special prestige, so in Sunnite Islām four schools or systems of the *fiqh* came to enjoy canonical authority, even before the development of the *ḥadīth* had reached its term. Ever since that development took place—in the first three centuries of Islām—the Qur'ān and the *sunnah* have become almost a dead letter except in matters of ritual, and their place in practical life has been taken by the law. From the handbooks of its schools and the decisions of its more distinguished contemporary exponents, the educated Muslim learns what he must do and forbear to do. But he learns likewise that the world, even the Muslim world, lies in wickedness, so that obedience to the sacred law is possible only in a very limited degree, and, at most, in the spheres of purely religious obligation and of family life. The tolerant Umayyad dynasty (A.D. 661–750) is regarded by Muslim historians as having been excessively worldly. But the Abbāsids (from A.D. 750), though they adopted

[1] Bukhārī, ed. Houdas and Marçais, ii. 209.
[2] Cf. Charles C. Torrey, *The Commercial-Theological Terms in the Koran*, Leyden, 1892.
[3] Bukhārī, ii. 51. [4] *Ib.* i. 469. [5] *Ib.* ii. 11.
[6] *Vorlesungen*, p. 14 ff. [7] *Ib.* 44 ff.

the Persian maxim that religion and government are sisters, were not much better. In the most numerous Muslim sect, the Shī'ites—and elsewhere as well—the divergence between ruling governments and their subjects with regard to the law has had the effect of making hypocrisy a virtue. We refer to the doctrine of *taqīyya* ('prudence'), according to which it is the primary duty of the Shī'ite who sojourns in the land of the adversary—a very elastic term—to disavow his convictions by word and deed, for the sake of his personal security and the welfare of his associates. Everywhere within the bounds of Islām, and at all periods of its history, the discrepancy between ideal law and actual practice has, on the one hand, led to a policy of compromise on the part of the majority, and, on the other, given rise to scruples and conflicts of conscience, and also to numerous attempts, under the leadership of a Mahdī, to supersede a sinful and worldly régime by a better. In Islām, accordingly, endeavours after moral and religious reform are always involved with or accompanied by political action. The work of a man like General Booth, who, as leader of the Salvation Army, seeks to achieve moral and spiritual results among Christian peoples, would be quite impossible in Islām, unless he or his officers tried at the same time to grasp the reins of political power.

The historical development of Muslim jurisprudence cannot be dealt with in detail here, and it must suffice to refer the reader to the works of Goldziher, Snouck Hurgronje, and others (see the Literature at end, and cf. art. LAW [Muhammadan]). We are meanwhile concerned with the *fiqh* only in so far as it bears upon ethical conceptions and leaves room for the free expression of moral life. In this reference the most important point is the classification of actions according to their gradations of legal obligation, and here we find a number of such arrangements more or less in agreement with one another. The most widely accepted division has five legal categories, as follows: (1) absolute duty (*farḍ* or *wājib*), embracing actions the performance of which is rewarded and their omission punished; (2) commendable or meritorious works (*sunnah, mandūb*, or *mustaḥabb*), which are rewarded, but their omission not punished; (3) permitted actions (*mubāḥ* or *jā'iz*), which are legally indifferent; (4) reprehensible actions (*makrūh*), which are disapproved of, but not punishable, by the law; (5) absolutely forbidden actions (*ḥarām*), the doing of which calls for punishment.

As regards the reference of each particular action to its proper category in this arrangement, there is, as might be expected, no unanimity among the learned in Islām. The more easy-going moralists among the sages of the law endeavour to make out that certain forbidden actions are doubtful, *i.e.* permissible, and certain obligatory actions merely commendable. In general, the great regulative principle is public opinion, *i.e.* the consensus of the authoritative scholars of the day. This consensus (*ijmā'*) is binding upon the conscience not merely in matters of faith, but also in the most trifling details of daily life. Yet, in spite of all, many Muslims, whether from want of knowledge or from want of will, order their lives by unauthorized *'ādāt*, or, what is accounted still worse, exercise their own discretion.

Further, the law is not uniformly binding upon every one. It distinguishes between duties incumbent upon all (*farḍ 'ala' l-'ain*) and obligations which affect certain individuals only (*farḍ 'al-kifāyah*). The duty of taking part in the holy war is an instance of the latter class.

Another distinction of importance is that between great and small sins—a distinction elaborated largely in connexion with the doctrine of evidence, which demanded that witnesses must be above reproach. Sins universally regarded as great are murder, unchastity, misappropriation of money belonging to a ward, the taking of interest, the refusal of *zakāt*, and the like. To the class of small sins are assigned such offences as taking part in unlawful games or listening to forbidden music.

As might be expected, the science of the law, in dealing with such distinctions, frequently degenerates into an arid casuistry, or becomes a sophistry which will enable one to cozen and defraud either God or man. The letter of the law kills the spirit of morality. An illustration of this will be found in the *Thousand and One Nights*, Night 296 ff. The manner in which legal luminaries tone down the prohibition of wine-drinking is set forth by Goldziher, *Vorlesungen über den Islām*, p. 63 ff.

4. The development of doctrine.—Islām found in the countries which it conquered not only legal and political institutions, but also systems of doctrine with more or less of an ethical element, as well as a popular didactic literature. With the latter we shall deal below (§ 6); of more immediate importance for the development of the Muslim doctrine of faith are the speculations of Christian theologians.

A factor of the utmost significance for later times was the ethico-religious system of the Mu'tazilites—descendants of the Qādarites. This sect was designated originally 'the people of the righteousness' (of Allāh), because they held that Allāh is the Righteous One who rewards men according to their deserts. This was not a genuine Muslim conception in the early days. The original conception of Allāh—and, somewhat spiritualized, it still holds sway—was that, as the Almighty, He is a vengeance-breathing tyrant towards His enemies, and an indulgent God of mercy towards His friends. In His vengeance He is arbitrary; in His love and mercy, capricious. With many persons, no doubt, this idea was a cause or a consequence of unprincipled conduct. It was possible for a man to transgress the whole law and still remain a believer; confession to Allāh in words, or even in thought—faith without works—was all that was required. Such was the teaching of the Murji'ites, who, though they discriminated between small offences and great sins, yet held that even the latter were forgiven to the Muslim who but uttered the creed.

This Murji'ite teaching was challenged by the originally powerful sect of the Khārijites, who have been called the puritans of Islām. They looked upon the great sinner as an unbeliever, and maintained that there is no true faith without works. This view approximates to the Mu'tazilite ethics, which might indeed be regarded as that of the Khārijites mellowed by the influence of Christianity, and, subsequently, of philosophy. It is certainly true that many of the early Mu'tazilites insisted emphatically on the importance of good works, and in this aspect they might be compared with the Pelagians of the Christian Church.[1] They were neither liberals in theology, nor libertines in ethics.

Their speculations upon the Divine righteousness, moreover, were closely connected with the question of human freedom. No quite unequivocal teaching on this problem could be drawn from either the Qur'ān or the *ḥadīth*; nevertheless the devout multitude was always inclined to believe in predestination. The idea that everything, not even excepting evil and sin, is ordained and brought to pass by Allāh largely dominates the popular mind to this day. The Qādarites and Mu'tazilites, on the other hand, affected probably by the dogmatic controversies of the Eastern Church, preached the

[1] Cf. R. Strothmann, in *Der Islām*, ed. C. H. Becker, ii., Strassburg, 1911, p. 60.

doctrine of free will. In support of their position they could appeal to certain passages of the Qur'ān, according to which Allāh does not cause, but simply allows, the sinner to go astray. They held, accordingly, that man is the author of his own deeds, the artificer of his own good or evil fortune, and that Paradise or Hell lies within his own choice. Evil and sin have their source in the human will; whatsoever comes from Allāh is necessarily good. Subsequently, indeed, they went as far as to say that God can devise nothing but good, and must in all things work for the welfare of His creatures. Here, in effect, we have a theodicy, such as has frequently been propounded from Plato's day, and as frequently shattered by the monistic trend of faith or of reason. The theodicy of the Mu'tazilites was influenced even in its early stages by Neo-Platonic ideas. Their doctrinal system resolved itself in time into a rationalistic theology, with reason as its first principle—the source, not only of knowledge, but also of the laws of conduct. It is reason, they held, that distinguishes between good and evil.

The doctrine of free will became in this way a rational determinism. An action is good when reason finds it good or beautiful; an action is evil when reason finds it evil or repulsive; in short, moral distinctions do not depend upon the will of Allāh. Caprice thus gives place to knowledge, authority to discernment, and obedience to reflexion. Knowledge, discernment, reflexion—it is these, accordingly, that reveal to us what is in itself good or evil. That which is in itself good is binding upon the will of God Himself, and thus involves a limitation of both His omnipotence and His freedom. In order to leave room in human life for a rational freedom and an individual sphere of action, for self determination and moral responsibility, Allāh was represented as being conditioned by the law of His being.

While the Mu'tazilite doctrines maintained their position in Shī'ite literature, the orthodox party in Sunnite Islām adopted a mediating position. They would not cast the shadow of a doubt upon the doctrine of God's omnipotence and unlimited freedom. Human beings are absolutely dependent upon Him: their good purposes, their good works, the ability to carry these into effect—all flow from Him, from His mercy and grace towards mankind. Man, however, as was maintained by the orthodox Ash'arite school, has power to appropriate God's works, and it is this appropriation (*kasb* or *iktisāb*) that constitutes the believer's sole merit. And even his great and heinous sins do not make him an unbeliever, so long as he does not believe, when he commits them, that they are permitted.[1]

5. Ascetic-mystical ethics.—So long as the primitive community of Islām remained comparatively feeble, the Prophet's call to renunciation of the world was generally complied with. But this state of matters did not last; the Arabs, with their predatory instincts, soon learned to appropriate the world, and, in the succeeding generations, to enjoy it. Caring little for supernal rewards, they were in reality a military aristocracy, an oligarchy, in the empire. In no long time, however, the peoples whom they exploited and laid under tribute began themselves to embrace Islām, thus creating a situation that demanded a new policy, even in moral and religious matters. Here and there, moreover, a feeling of satiety began to settle upon the luxurious classes in both the older and the newer centres of culture, and this in turn prepared the way for a system of an ascetic morality—which, it is true, had never been entirely absent from Islām. This ascetic morality had special links of connexion with the ideas of Christian monasticism.

One characteristic feature of monasticism, viz. celibacy, was, however, alien to primitive Islām; nor has it ever at any time gained general recognition. 'There is no monasticism in Islām'—so the Prophet is recorded to have said; and in his later years he showed by his example that woman may be regarded merely as man's plaything. The asceticism preached in the earliest period, whatever its object was, actually served, however, as a species of training for the soldiers of the faith. It consisted in fasting and watching, and accorded admirably with the performance of the ritual of prayer. But, when at a later day the ascetic spirit became more widely diffused, the positive value of the practice as a means of discipline was more and more lost sight of in favour of a purely negative renunciation. To mortify the flesh became the cry. Absolute trust in God led to quietism: in God's hands man should be *perinde ac cadaver*. The mystic eventually becomes a mere will-less pauper, who accepts as a gift the alms he will not ask or hold out his hand to take, and who fills his feeble life with pious ceremonies. Morality is hardly to be looked for in such conditions. The mendicant (*faqīr*) lives only for the moment and for his God; in relation to his contemporaries or to posterity, he is as good as dead. Yet it was but the absolutely consistent application of his convictions that carried him to such extremes.

The ascetics, clothed in their coarse woollen frocks (*ṣūf*), sought to vindicate their manner of life chiefly by appeal to passages in the NT. A sense of sin and a craving for penance were the forces which largely helped to fill their ranks. But amongst them were also a number of brooding idlers, who began to speculate in Oriental fashion; and it was accordingly in Ṣūfī'ism that the practice of asceticism—from about the 8th cent. A.D. onwards—found a theoretical basis. Platonic-Pythagorean doctrines, gleaned from Hermetic and Gnostic writings, here joined hands with Indian speculation. Ascetic morality is always founded upon the conviction that the human body is of little value, if not indeed absolutely evil, or else a mere phantasm; while the soul, on the other hand, is regarded as the essential element in human nature, or at least as forming a stage of transition to the higher life of the Spirit and of God. Thus the supreme object of human endeavour is to free oneself from the bondage of sense, to purge the soul of foul desire, and to become pure Spirit, or God—not merely God-like, but positively Divine. Stage by stage does man advance on the paths of the soul. By the use of intoxicants, by means of macerations and of pious exercises sustained to the point of ecstasy, the finite being dissolves in God, who is viewed in the abstract manner of Pantheism as pure light or absolute truth. The earthly life is of value only in so far as it is animated by love to God and aspiration after things above.

While every age in Islām has had its devout ascetics, men whose moral excellence cannot be disputed, this Ṣūfī'ite fanaticism cannot claim any high degree of moral approval. The Ṣūfī'ites' fervent love of God left no place for the practical love of their neighbour. The aim of all their striving was, not a moral life upon earth, but a fancied salvation in Heaven. Hence Ṣūfī'ism, alike on its practical and on its speculative side, inculcates poverty, self-humiliation, and the surrender of personality; these were its supreme virtues, and could be best acquired by living in a community under strict monastic discipline. The individual members of such communities must yield unconditional submission to their superior. Moreover, the mystics were for the most part at one with the dogmatists in repudiating

[1] For the Mataridite theory, which is akin to that of the Ash'arites, cf. Macdonald, *Development of Muslim Theology*, p. 310 f.

the freedom of the will,[1] and were sometimes even more thoroughgoing in their denial. Likewise in actual practice they went far beyond the jurists, so that their mysticism consorted uncommonly well with despotism of every kind.

From the beginning of the 9th cent. A.D. these mystical and ascetic tendencies occasionally took practical shape in cœnobitism, but not until the 11th cent. was there any extensive development of a regular monastic system. This, while certainly less highly elaborated than the system of Orders in the Christian Church, had nevertheless much in common with it. Those belonging to the Dervish Orders have always been more highly esteemed in Islām than the representatives of the law or the governing classes, and many among them, both male and female, are revered as saints. The common people venerate them as miracle-workers and medicine-men, as their mediators and advocates with Allāh.

The adherents of the ascetic-mystical morality sought in various ways to adapt their views to the official teaching of the law, or at least to reconcile them with it. Of the two classes into which human actions were frequently divided, viz. 'deeds of the bodily members' and 'works of the heart,' the Ṣūfis not unnaturally gave preference to the latter. The extreme mystics regarded the outward act as nothing more than a symbol of the inward sentiment, or else considered the obligations of the law to be utterly beneath their notice, so that the extremes of abstemiousness and of sensual indulgence might both be found in their ranks. Sects of pronounced mystical tendencies, such as the Ismā'īlites, showed a special liking for the classification of mankind into grades. Obedience and sacrifice were imperative only upon the common people and brethren of low degree, while the initiated members of the higher grades, or of the highest, were independent of every law.

Mystical sects and mystical tendencies have always abounded in Islām. But, just as Sunnite Islām had, besides its canonical collections of *ḥadīth* and its schools of the *fiqh*, an orthodox system of theology, so it had also an orthodox mysticism, the fullest exposition of which is found in the writings of Ghazālī (see § 7, below). See also art. ASCETICISM (Muslim), vol. ii. p. 99 ff.

6. Philosophical ethics.—Among the Arabs and other Muslims a popular philosophy of morals, at once international and interconfessional, is found in their fables and proverbs: suffice it to refer to Luqmān, the Arabian Æsop. Luqmān's counsels to his son, which in reality owe their inspiration to Jewish-Christian and Hermetic 'wisdom,' are often quoted in ethical and parenetic writings.

The literary *genre*, which is made up of moralistic aphorisms, and more especially of the maxims of court politics found in the various 'Mirrors for Magistrates,' bulked largely in Persian literature, consisting partly of translations from Indian originals. Even to-day this type of literature maintains a certain popularity, and is highly esteemed among the cultured classes of Persia. The earliest known representative of this Persian school is 'Abdallah ibn al-Muqaffa' (executed *c.* A.D. 757), who translated the *Pañchatantra* from Pahlavi into Arabic. His *al-Durra al-yatīmā*, printed in Cairo and Beirūt, is a short 'Mirror for Magistrates,' with rules for prudent behaviour at court and polite intercourse among friends. In his introduction, after circumspectly assigning the supreme place to faith and the avoidance of great sins, he eulogizes the following virtues: temperance, courage, liberality, and proficiency in discourse and business. It is the morality of worldly-wise politicians and merchants, and is thoroughly typical of this class of literature.[1]

A much larger and more elaborately systematized contribution comes, through Syrian channels, from the philosophical literature of Greece. Collections of biographies, with supplements of moral aphorisms, testaments, letters, etc., were very popular. Pseudepigraphic writings, especially of the Hermetic type, were extensively circulated. Works of Plato and Aristotle, as also compositions falsely ascribed to them, found great favour among philosophers in the stricter sense. Thus Plato's *Republic* was translated by Ḥunain ibn Isḥāq as the *Kitāb al-siyāsa*, and forms the main source of the doctrine of the soul (trichotomy) and of the four cardinal virtues which appears in many Muslim writers on ethics. To Plato also were ascribed a treatise on the education of children (*Adab al-ṣibyān*), and a testament (*waṣīya*) addressed to Aristotle. Of Aristotle's own writings, Arabic authors refer to and quote from the *Nicomachean Ethics* (*Kitāb al-akhlāq*), which is said to have been translated by the afore-named Ḥunain or by his son Isḥāq ibn Ḥunain. Extant quotations from this work show traces of Neo-Platonic redactions.

These and other translated works of the kind helped to mould the development of Mu'tazilite and Ṣūfī'ite ethics. But it was only in the limited circles of sectaries or of scholars and persons of culture that ethical doctrine attained the more independent status of a philosophical science (*'ilm al-akhlāq*). Conformably to the scholastic Aristotelian tradition current in the East, philosophy was defined as 'a knowledge of the essence of things and a doing of the good.'[2] The theoretical side was invariably discussed more exhaustively than the practical, but the latter also received attention from those who dealt with morals and politics as more or less independent of each other.

But it was the pseudepigraphic writings of a spiritualistic and an ascetic and edifying character that produced the most powerful effects in this sphere. These writings were often supplemented by astrological speculations, according to which the natural temperament and even the moral constitution of human beings are conditioned by the influence of the stars. The felicity of man was believed to consist in his being delivered from matter and exalted to the pure spirit-world of the higher spheres. This type of ethics, pervaded by metaphysico-psychological speculation, has left a characteristic deposit in the eclectic writings of the 'Pure Ones' or 'Brethren of Purity' (*Iḥwān aṣ-Ṣafā*).

In the system of the Brethren of Purity, the moral nature of man is determined by the following four causal agencies. (1) The bodily structure: the body is composed of the four elements, and a person whose body contains, say, much earth will be harsh and greedy, while another, with a large proportion of water in his body, will be gentle and gracious, and so on. (2) Climate: those who live in a northern climate have more courage than those of southern lands. (3) Education. (4) The influence of the stars; and this, indeed, is the most powerful of all, since the other three are dependent upon it. Even education, which superposes something upon the natural constitution, is affected by the heavenly bodies and relative positions. All this holds good of the first stage of human nature, the stage of natural morality, in which conduct is instinctively good or bad. But the soul can raise itself above nature, and in the second or psychical stage, where man has freedom

[1] But see *ERE* i. 13.

[1] Cf. also the will of a merchant in *The Thousand and One Nights*, Night 308 ff.

[2] See *Mafātiḥ*, ed. van Vloten, Leyden, 1895, p. 132 f.

of choice, his deeds are praised or blamed according to their quality. Should a man reach the third stage—that of rational deliberation—he acts either wisely or foolishly, nobly or basely. Finally, the fourth or highest stage is that of the Divine cosmic order (*nāmūs*) conformed to by godly prophets and holy angels, and a man is rewarded or punished according as he does or does not associate himself with them in the endeavour to become, as far as in him lies, like God.

The path by which this mystic goal of life is to be reached, according to the Brethren of Purity, is the practice of asceticism. The supreme virtue, the yearning after things above, or the love that presses towards God, must manifest itself upon earth in a pious endurance of, and indulgence to, all creatures, even the animals. Man thereby wins freedom from sensual passion here, and hereafter the ascent to the eternal light. But, if a man does not in this life purge himself of bodily desire, and persists in 'foolish slumber and careless sleep,' he remains after death hovering in the air, trammelled and drawn downward by his fleshly passions. Hell is simply this life in time, whether on the earth or in the air; Paradise, on the other hand, is the eternal world of the celestial spheres to which pure souls ascend.

All men, according to the teaching of the Brethren, are imperfect, though in different degrees. But the sum-total of good qualities is found in the absolutely perfect man, who has the characteristics of the Platonic Idea and the 'wise man' of the Stoics. The Sunnite mystics find the perfect man (*insān kāmil*) in Muḥammad; the Shī'ites in Ali or Ḥusain. The Pure Ones are less definite in their choice, and—apart perhaps from the 'Imām of the age,' whom they greatly honour—it is rather Socrates and Christ that win their enthusiastic homage. In their estimation the ideal of reason was realized in Socrates, and the law of love in Christ; and it is these great ones, accordingly, whom they seek to emulate. In the interests of this *imitatio* they concede a relative value to the earthly life in the flesh; the body should be guarded and cared for, so that the soul may have time for its full development.

The moral theory of the Pure Ones is a mystical intellectualism. It is found—in a somewhat less fantastic form, no doubt—also in the so-called Aristotelians of Islām, from al-Kindī to Ibn Rushd. In keeping with the character of their sources, these thinkers set—to use Aristotle's own words—the dianoetic virtues above the ethical. Thus, *e.g.*, in the *Apophthegmata Philosophorum* of Ḥunain ibn Isḥāq the highest good is identified with the sound understanding. Wit and shrewdness, talent and sagacity, are put on a higher level than goodness and rectitude. Such, too, is the spirit which pervades nearly all the *adab* writings ('the doctrine of good or elegant manners') of the Arabs—often, indeed, mere compilations of extracts, and having hardly the slightest concern with ethics and morality.

A counterpoise to the extravagances of mysticism was provided by the supreme Aristotelian principle of the *mean*—the doctrine of the μεσότης, which was introduced into Islām at an early period. The Mu'tazilite al-Jāḥiẓ († A.D. 869) writes as follows: 'Divine religion approves the conduct of him who neither does too little, nor performs too much, of the Good.'[1] Some professed to find the doctrine in the Qur'ān (cf. ii. 137, 'Thus have we made you an intermediate people'). The principle of the mean came at length to permeate both the popular conception of morality and the ethical science of jurists and philosophers; and it was also combined—especially among the latter—with the

[1] Goldziher, *Muh. Stud.*, Halle, 1889-90, ii. 397 ff.

Platonic doctrine of the four cardinal virtues (σοφία, ἀνδρεία, σωφροσύνη, δικαιοσύνη). As early as the 9th cent. A.D., in the writings of the Mu'tazilite author Dāwūd ibn Marwān al-Maqammis, we find mention of the Platonic series of virtues, which thereafter, with occasional modifications in the order and grouping, gained general currency.[1]

The most notable representative of Neo-Platonic eclecticism in Muslim ethics is Ibn Maskawaih († A.D. 1030), physician, philologist, and historian, who was the treasurer and friend of Sultan 'Adud-addaula, and ranks as an orthodox Muslim. It is true that his ethical doctrine (*Tahdhīb al-akhlāq*, 'the improvement of morals'), like that of the Pure Ones, shades off into mysticism, but it is free from astrological accretions. Its underlying psychology, and, indeed, the structure of the system as a whole, is Platonic, though in matters of detail the author quotes frequently from Aristotle, as well as from Socrates, Hippocrates, Galen, and al-Kindī. The work is divided into six (or seven) parts and may be outlined as follows:

i. By way of introduction we have a Platonizing doctrine of the soul. The soul is of a spiritual nature, and, as an independent and immortal entity, stands on a higher plane than the mutable substance of the body. It finds its peculiar sphere of action in the sciences (dianoetic virtue). After enumerating the parts of the soul—desire, impulse, and reason—the work specifies the four principal virtues: prudence or temperance, courage, wisdom, and the combination of the three in justice. The virtues, with their various sub-species, are then defined, liberality being treated more elaborately in a special paragraph. Liberality is thereafter frequently mentioned along with the cardinal virtues, and in one passage it actually takes the place of wisdom. Each of these virtues is then defined on the Aristotelian principle, *i.e.* as the mean between two vices, justice itself being placed midway between doing wrong and suffering wrong. As regards prudence, however, a defect is said to be better than an excess, while as regards liberality the reverse holds good.

ii. The second section treats of man's natural disposition, of habituation, and education. Ibn Maskawaih adopts Galen's idea that a few men are good by nature, some become good by practice, and very many remain evil to the last. Parts of the chapter on the education of children recall Plato's *Republic*, as, *e.g.*, the assertion that moral education should precede instruction in mathematics and other sciences; while the ancient Arabic poetry is to be treated as having a harmful influence on children. This section discusses also the rules of good breeding.

iii. The third division of the work treats of the supreme good and the supreme happiness (εὐδαιμονία). The supreme good is interpreted absolutely or objectively; it is eternal and the same for all, and hence it is probably identical with the Deity. Happiness, on the other hand, is defined subjectively: it has various gradations, corresponding to differences among individuals. The supreme happiness is attained in the closest possible approximation to the supreme good, *i.e.* in becoming as like God as is possible for man. But there are innumerable gradations of human happiness, and hence also innumerable degrees of human virtue or efficiency. The measure of realization appropriate to each individual constitutes his virtue and determines his happiness. It is, therefore, best for all to live a moral and happy life in the community—in the State. Monasticism is not virtue. So long as man remains man, *i.e.* is composed of body and soul, so long does his happiness remain incomplete without the satisfaction of his bodily wants. Nevertheless, the psychical or purely spiritual enjoyments are the most perfect, since they are the most enduring. The doctrine of the bodily resurrection and the sensual delights of Paradise is treated by this theory with polite silence.

iv. This section deals specially with justice. Aristotle likewise had devoted a whole book of his *Ethics* to this virtue.

v. Here the themes are love and friendship. Two circumstances, viz. that Aristotle had allotted two books (viii. and ix.) to the discussion of friendship, and that love occupies a leading place in the Neo-Platonic system, have conspired to give this part of the treatise a somewhat prolix character. A notable feature of the section is the endeavour to invest religious duties with moral significance. Thus the daily liturgical prayers of the Muslims, which the *sunnah* ranks far above solitary prayer in the silent closet or the monk's cell; the meeting of dwellers in cities with the inhabitants of the surrounding districts at the two official festivals of the year; the flocking of pilgrims—each once in his lifetime—from all countries to Mecca: these things, as enjoined by the law, foster the sense of brotherhood and the universal love of mankind.

vi. The concluding section (sometimes divided, as vi. and vii.) discusses the health and sickness of the soul. The diseases of the soul are the eight vices—the *aṭrāf* of the four cardinal virtues—and their sub-species. Of the four pairs of vices only one—the excess and defect of courage—is handled in detail, its

[1] Goldziher, *Kitāb ma'ānī al-nafs*, Berlin, 1907, p. 18* ff.

extremes being presumption or foolhardiness, and cowardice or want of spirit, with their sub-species. But the actual vices are dealt with less thoroughly than the affections from which they spring—anger and grief, and their varieties.

Thus far Ibn Maskawaih and philosophical ethics. The Platonic-Pythagorean features of the theory, *i.e.* its dualistic psychology and its hyperphysical morality, found special favour among the mystics, while, on the other hand, the scholars of the *ḥadīth* and the *fiqh*, as well as the dialectical theologians (the Mutakallim) and the rationalistic writers, gave the preference to the Aristotelian elements.

7. The ethics of Ghazālī.—The ethical system of the great theologian Abū Ḥāmid al-Ghazālī (A.D. 1059–1111) merits separate treatment, more especially as he is the final authority for orthodox Islām. In his case life and doctrine are one—rooted in his own personality. He was delivered from the snare of vain learning and worldly ambition by becoming convinced of the truth and moral power of Islām. In Islām he holds single-handed a position corresponding to that shared by Augustine and Aquinas in the Christian Church.

Ghazālī's moral philosophy is the synthesis of the various doctrines which we have passed in review. He is also acquainted with philosophical ethics, *i.e.* the doctrines of the four cardinal virtues and of the mean. These he expounds in his *Mīzān al-'amal*, probably one of his early works, and we find traces of them also in his later mystical writings. Thus the narrow bridge which leads to Paradise (*Ṣirāṭ*), and the scales in which the deeds of men are weighed (*mīzān*), he interprets esoterically as the true mean of virtue, just as many Mu'tazilites and speculative Ṣūfīs had done. Ignoring the actual sequence of history, he maintains that the philosophers borrowed their ethical theories from devout Ṣūfīs. Such might certainly be said of his own system, as it is saturated with and held together by the spirit of Ṣūfī'ism, and is intelligible only in the light of the mystics' doctrine of stages (the corporeal earthly life; the sensuous psychical intermediate stage; the spiritual celestial life; the being of God). Ghazālī's theory is, in point of fact, a mysticism that vitalizes the law and doctrine of Islām, as is indeed clearly indicated by the title of his greatest work, *Iḥyā'ulūm al-dīn*, *i.e.* 'the revivification of the religious sciences,' dealing with living religion or the religious life. Faith without works was in his view a dead faith. Religion must be an experience of the soul, and must manifest itself in works. 'He who knows and acts accordingly shall be called great in the kingdom of Heaven.'

The relation between faith and works, knowledge and action (*'ilm* and *'amal*), had formed the theme of much speculation before Ghazālī's time.[1] The philosophic school, and even the mystics, were all more or less influenced by the intellectualism of Greek ethics. Correct thinking was preferred before good conduct. Action, moreover, was restricted to the present life, *i.e.* it was deemed of value only as a preparation for a higher life; while perfection or salvation in the hereafter was thought of as a state of pure knowledge, not indeed without joy, but certainly without action. With Ghazālī, however, as with the mystics, the relation in question is complicated by the introduction of a third factor. Between knowledge (*'ilm*) and action (*'amal*) he places the state of the soul (*ḥāl*), a condition akin to emotion, and having a propensity to good or evil conduct. We have thus a sequence of three causally connected elements: knowledge gives rise to an affective volition, and this in turn produces action.

In connexion with these explanations, the extreme intellectualism (gnosticism) of the philosophers who assert that knowledge without consequent action is better than action without knowledge of the grounds of action is assailed by Ghazālī as sheer folly. Nevertheless, we trace the influence of the philosophical-dogmatic tradition in his own predilection for knowledge, even though he thereby means knowledge of the religious sciences. For him, too, the perfection of the pure spirit consists in intuitive knowledge, *i.e.* the beatific vision of God. In the first book of the *Iḥyā* he fully discusses knowledge—the religious knowledge that is profitable for the life beyond, and is 'a work of the heart'; and in the second book he deals with the knowledge of religious doctrine as man's primary obligation. Religious knowledge, or true doctrine, is in fact the tree whose branches are the various states of the soul (*aḥwāl*), and whose fruits are good deeds.

Ghazālī agrees with the Ash'arite school in teaching that the merit of man's action lies in his appropriation or assimilation (*iktisāb*) of Divine action. The life of the soul, with its activities, stands midway between the absolute freedom of the Divine will and the absolute necessity of bodily and earthly existence. The moral disposition can be improved by education and asceticism. Such is Ghazālī's theory. But his truly religious spirit kept him from saying much about human freedom, or even about human ability. Allāh is omnipotent, and acts as it pleases Him. He will assuredly lay on any soul no burden beyond its power; for so it is written in the Qur'ān (vii. 40); but He might without injustice demand from His servants what they could not give. He is in no sense bound to have regard to the welfare of His bondslaves. These and similar statements, however, should be interpreted as in the first instance polemical, being directed against the Mu'tazilites, and may be regarded as so much theorizing. We shall perhaps best succeed in doing justice to the spirit of Ghazālī's system by setting forth his view as follows: the material world of the body is the sphere of absolute necessity, where God's omnipotent will is all in all; in the realm of the sensuous and psychical, a relative freedom must be recognized; in the kingdom of pure spirit, there is a return to absolute necessity—the law of love, which is at the same time absolute freedom.

Passing, however, from these vague and—in relation to the system as a whole—certainly esoteric speculations, we shall find it of more utility to make a brief examination of his principal ethical work, the *Iḥyā 'ulūm al-dīn.*

The work is in four parts, each comprising ten books.[1] The first part discusses religious duties in the narrower sense (*'ibādāt*); the second, the duties of social and political life (*'ādāt*); and in both parts the substance and its arrangement are taken mainly from books of the *ḥadīth* and the *fiqh*. The third part sets forth that which perverts the soul, and its renunciation of the world; the fourth, that which saves the soul, and its return to God. This second half (the third and fourth parts) is based upon the manuals of ascetic Ṣūfī'ism; but to the author alone belongs the credit of the excellent selection of material, as also of its arrangement and synthesis. In the first half of his work, for instance, he does not deal with the religious duties and the social and political institutions of Islām in the purely external and casuistical manner of most teachers of the *fiqh*, but expounds their 'mysteries' (*asrār*), *i.e.* their import for the inner spiritual life, and with special regard to the hereafter. If he begins, as books of the *ḥadīth* and the *fiqh* usually do, with ceremonial purity, he immediately makes reference to the purity of the heart, the innermost recesses of which, when it has renounced every vice, are free from all that is not God. The same thing holds good of the ritual of prayer, to the outward forms of which inward experience alone lends plenary significance. He deals with religious prayer—prayer in the proper sense—and with such pious practices as the recitation of the Qur'ān, much more fully than with the ceremonies prescribed by the law. At the same time he never forgets to urge that outward compliance with the law is imperative upon all—primarily, no doubt, upon the people in general, but no less upon those who occupy a higher spiritual level. The lower stage must

[1] Cf. Goldziher, *Kitāb ma'ānī al-nafs*, p. 54* ff.

[1] The reader should note this enumeration, as in mystical writings such numbers are never without significance.

always be merged in the higher, and in the light of this fact Ghazālī combines the distinction made by the *fiqh* between *farḍ al-'ain* and *farḍ al-kifāyah* with the doctrine of stages propounded by Neo-Platonic Ṣūfī'ism. So, *e.g.*, in regard to fasting, the fourth of the religious duties; in the first stage, as obligatory upon all believers it means abstinence from food, drink, and the enjoyments of love; in the second, it signifies refraining from the sins of the bodily members—the eye, the ear, etc.; finally, in the third stage, attained only by the few, fasting implies the heart's abnegation of the world and of all that is not God.

Ghazālī's ethical theory is thus, as regards its ideal, out and out ascetic. Divine service, as he says in a later work (*Minhāj al-'ābidīn*), has two sides: a positive—meritorious action; and a negative—the abandonment of sin, or the warfare against the evil world, the creatures, Satan, and the sinful self. The negative side is the more excellent—the higher stage. On certain points Ghazālī has some difficulty in harmonizing his theory with tradition. In the *Iḥyā*, e.g., he raises the question whether marriage or celibacy is the more excellent way. His first answer is that each has its advantages and disadvantages, and neither is expedient for every one. But he inclines, in conformity with his doctrine of stages and the practice of his later life, to hold that, while marriage is good, celibacy is better. The question then arises whether in that case Jesus was not superior to Muḥammad. Ghazālī's answer, which may at a pinch be reconciled with the theory of stages, is that, while the celibate life is intrinsically the better—not for everybody, of course—the best of all, as in Muḥammad's case, is to be married and at the same time to be as the unmarried, *i.e.* to live always in the presence of God and to be susceptive of His manifestations. Had our moralist dealt in earnest with this idea, his system would have assumed a very different character. But his ascetic temperament, while he does not put it forward as the norm for all, dominates the entire work, alike as regards its structure and as regards his selection of the Jewish, Christian, and Muslim traditions which he so plentifully introduces for the edification of his readers.

At the end of the second part of the *Iḥyā*, i.e. after the religious and the social duties have been discussed, Ghazālī utters a panegyric upon Muḥammad as the standard of human virtue, and commends him as a pattern for human conduct. The beauty of his outward appearance and the grace of his speech are highly extolled, as are also his marvellous deeds. Of all men, moreover, he was the most affable, the bravest, the most just, the most temperate, and the most generous; he was chaste and modest above all others; at once reserved and frank, straightforward and without dissimulation—one saw the anger in his face; simple and kindly in his whole manner of life.

The second half of the *Iḥyā* (parts three and four) carries us far beyond this imitation of Muḥammad—as a historical person, at least. 'Man's perfection and happiness,' as Ghazālī expresses himself elsewhere,[1] 'consists in endeavouring to reproduce the characteristics of God and in adorning himself with the true essence of His attributes.' It is only the soul of man that lies in the snare of sense; in his heart—his distinctive spiritual nature—he is the image of God. So the first book of the third part deals with the wonders of the heart, and the second book with the virtues of the soul. It is in this second book that philosophical ethics—the doctrines of the cardinal virtues and of the mean—are discussed. Here, however, Ghazālī, following Plato, remarks that justice has but one antithesis, viz. injustice. The chief virtue is said to be wisdom, which was not mentioned at all in the sketch of the Prophet's character referred to above. The superficial way in which the Platonic and Aristotelian doctrines are attached to the work appears also from the fact that they have no further influence on the contents of parts iii. and iv. The third part discusses, on the basis of the Platonic psychology, the purification of the spirit from carnal and psychical lusts; and the fourth, its turning towards God by means of repentance and fear, patience and thanksgiving, and absolute trust culminating in union with Him in love. The last book of all is a *meditatio mortis*, in which the dying experiences of Muḥammad and the four orthodox Khalīfs are set forth as examples. Parts iii. and iv. have little to do with ethics in the modern sense, but they contain valuable observations in the sphere of religious psychology.

The *Iḥyā* as a whole might be described as the ethics of a pastor. Ghazālī considers that men require such a counsellor. Only a few, he remarks, are perfect by nature: such are Jesus, John the Baptist, and other prophets. All others are weak, and require prophetic guidance, which, after the death of the prophets, is adjusted to human nature in various ways. Consequently Ghazālī thinks it advisable that men should place themselves under the spiritual care of a shaikh, as was done in the religious Orders. The numerous religious brotherhoods in Islām, which have a vast influence among the masses—especially in North Africa—even to the present day, may find a warrant for their existence in his words. But it may justly be doubted whether their moral influence upon the people has realized the hopes of the great theologian.

[1] Cf. Goldziher, *Vorlesungen*, p. 31.

The principles of Ghazālī are very characteristic of the peculiar nature of Oriental civilization. Neither philosopher nor devout mystic has in this sphere ever been able to attain fully to the thought of moral self-development. The Orient lacks the vital idea of autonomy, and of a super-personal law which, written on men's hearts, is binding upon all. Although in the East an all but immutable law has been in operation for centuries, yet the frequent changes of dynasties and rulers have ever and anon been attended with intervals of anarchy. An imperative law is thus always associated in the popular mind with a particular ruler and those who represent him in secular or sacred things. There has as yet been little scope for individual freedom or personal initiative in any sphere of life. The populace submit to the secular power, or to the shaikh of an Order, or to the 'Hidden Imām,' or to some one who claims to be the Mahdī; for neither in social and political affairs nor in the sphere of religion and ethics can they do without a leader.

8. The period after Ghazālī.—For centuries the instability of Oriental life has been hedged round by a remarkable stability of doctrine. Since the 13th cent. A.D. Islām has been content to study and expound the teachings of the ancients. The writings of the earlier ages are constantly being re-issued in lithographed or printed editions—not as mere scientific curiosities, but as real stepping-stones to learning; and this is true also in the sphere of ethics.

In Ghazālī orthodox speculation reaches its culminating point, and in the sphere of religious learning his influence is immense. But other factors continued to operate. The masses still clung devoutly to their *'adat*, teachers of the *fiqh* did not discard their casuistry, while many philosophers and speculative Ṣūfīs ignored the law in its outward form (antinomianism).

Ethics (*'ilm al-akhlāq*) could make no further advance in Islām as an independent science. People found their moral doctrine in the compendiums of the legal schools, or in some guide-book to the Ṣūfī'ite life, or in the manuals of good breeding (*adab* literature). Books of the last-named class found special favour in secular circles. In Persia there exists a marked predilection for the teachings of the ancient poets, and, in particular, for the didactic verses of Sa'adī. An illustration of the way in which ethics has been incorporated with the *adab* literature is found in the *Adab al-dunyā wal-dīn* of Abū 'l-Ḥasan al-Māwardī († A.D. 1058).

This work, which was written before Ghazālī's day, is still used in the higher schools of Stambul, where it serves as a treasury of quotation for the young. After passing the time-honoured encomiums upon reason and knowledge, it gives a profusion of aphorisms, uttered by devout scholars, poets, and sages regarding religion, the world, and the soul. The section that treats of the secular life bears the impress of Aristotelian ideas, while the closing section, dealing with the morals of the soul, shows an ascetic strain, and singles out for special commendation such virtues as humility, meekness, veracity, and contentment. Its counsels are regarded in the same light as in the 11th cent., when Māwardī compiled them, *i.e.* as so many fine sayings.

This continuity of doctrine is certainly a remarkable fact. Even those who have in modern times tried to introduce reforms into Islām appeal for support to the ancient teachings. This is specially true of the Wahhābi movement, which sprang up about the middle of the 18th century; it aimed at restoring Islām to its pristine state, and denounced in puritanical fashion all innovation, the use of tobacco and similar indulgences, the luxury of cities, and the worship of saints. Of greater significance than this Arabian attempt to restore the past is the Persian Bābī movement (see BĀB, BĀBĪS), which took its rise about the middle of the 19th century. It was in its origin associated with ancient mystical ideas, and trafficked in all manner of magical trumpery, speculations about numbers and letters, etc. It has latterly assumed a more progressive aspect, and now advocates the emancipation of women and the brotherhood of all classes and religions. To the present writer, however, it seems highly questionable whether the flaccid mystical utterances of the Bābī prophets are capable of effecting anything—in the face of Oriental despotism—on behalf of a free and active morality. Some look more hopefully to the revival of Muʿtazilite teaching, more especially in British India, where its best-known exponent is Syed Ameer ʿAli. This movement, however, presents but few of the typical features of Islām, and is scarcely to be distinguished from a liberal form of Christianity.

Here, indeed, we have lit upon the characteristic feature of present-day Islām. The culture of Europe and America, with Christian customs and moral ideas in its train, is forcing its way on every hand into Muslim countries, and by means of education and the press is asserting itself everywhere, with the possible exception of Afghanistan and Morocco. The movement is meanwhile largely confined to scientific and technical learning, which is assimilated in a somewhat superficial fashion; but whether it will prove fruitful, not only in the economic, but also in the ethical and the social and political spheres, the future alone can decide.

9. Moral life. — We have now dealt with the foundations and the growth of moral conceptions in Islām; and, although much obscurity still rests upon the subject, we have found it possible, with the help of the extant literature, to trace the main lines of ethical development. A much more difficult question, and one, indeed, that must probably remain in great part unanswered, is that concerning the actual moral life of the people. What was its character, and how did it compare with moral doctrine? Law and doctrine may often act as incentives to good conduct, but they are oftener simply the conscious reflex of actual morality, and sometimes but the drapery which hides the hypocrisy beneath. Our main concern is the people's actual mode of life, and our knowledge of this is very defective.

It has already been remarked that the sacred law, alike in its original form and in its later expansion, has to a great extent the weight only of an ideal canon law; as a rule, the people restricted their observance of it to purely religious duties and the provisions regarding family life. The sentiments and practices of daily life were largely conditioned by racial character, by circumstances, by occupation—in a word, by the stage of civilization that had been attained by society or the individual. A detailed history of the morality of Oriental society—could such a work be written at all, and as yet there is an almost complete lack of competent preliminary studies in this field—would have to depict a vast variety of phenomena, such as, for instance, the various gradations by which nomadism passed into permanent habitation, and, in city life, the practice of confining the inhabitants to certain quarters or streets, according to their creed, nationality, or trade.

The fact that differences in nationality and occupation involve differences in moral characteristics and conduct has attracted attention from ancient times. Thus, according to an early Muslim tradition, 'pride and haughtiness are among the people of horses and camels, the shouters, and the tent-dwellers, but modesty (*sakīna*) among keepers of cattle.'[1] A still greater contrast, and one that pervades the whole course of Muslim history, is that between the predatory semi-nomads and the owners and leaders of city caravans, whose great concern is security of travelling and the undisturbed enjoyment of their gains. The largely inartificial customs of the former are very different from the more comfortable life of townspeople. This more luxurious mode of life was condemned by official Islām, which, however, was long unable to restrain the merchants of the Syrian cities—a gay and humorous class of people—from their wine-bibbing and other self-indulgent habits. In Persia this restriction never proved effective in any real sense. The Arabs did not succeed in assimilating the national character of the Persians to their own, just as they failed afterwards with the Turks and the Mongols. In the polemical literature evoked by the struggle between Arabs and Persians in the 2nd and 3rd centuries A.H., neither side failed to pass judgment upon the qualities of the other, and, as we might expect, each judged with all the bias of mutual animosity. Such estimates must, of course, be utilized with the utmost caution. It will be well also to be somewhat sceptical regarding the jeremiads emanating from teachers of the law, as the class to which they belong has been prone in every age and among all peoples to proclaim the utter wickedness of a world that did not tally with their sacred ideals, or submit to their personal rapacity. Our best course will be to avail ourselves of incidental observations found in poetry, in narrative literature, in historical writings, and books of travel; while for recent times we may have recourse to ethnographical works. As regards the polite literature, in particular, we must certainly bear in mind that the poets, in their vainglory, are wont to magnify out of all measure both their own sybaritism and the munificence of their exalted patrons. Muḥammad himself had it revealed to him that poets do not really do what they say—and the East has never lacked an abundant supply of poets.

When we examine the representations of manners given by the ancient poets in the *Kitāb al-Aghānī* and *The Thousand and One Nights*, we see little indication of a rigorous conformity to the law, or of a profound and vital morality. We generally find ourselves in the sprightly and voluptuous society of princes and merchants—a society whose basis is largely sordid gain, and whose life revolves round 'wine, woman, and song.' These people know the moral code by heart. They also indulge in pious meditations of an ascetic and mystical tendency, but only by way of rhetorical embellishment. At a very early date, even in the holy city of Mecca, then at the Umayyad court in Damascus, and subsequently in the Abbāsid city of Baghdad—in Cordova, Cairo, and other less important centres of Muslim culture—we find, under the mask of religion, a most worldly mode of life among the higher classes of society. Their morality had always much in common with the popular ideas expressed in fables and proverbs—*i.e.* it was altogether mundane. We shall search the fables of Luqmān in vain for any mention of God or the hereafter. Death, which in religious and mystical ethics is always hailed as a deliverer, appears, conformably to the common sentiment, in *The Thousand and One Nights*, as the 'destroyer of all delights.' The enjoyment of life is at once the ideal of popular literature and the grand concern of educated society. To acquire wealth in the easiest possible way—often by means of magic—and to squander it in pleasure, to go in quest of adventures as a cunning thief, a robber, or a warrior, in most cases, however, as a travelling merchant who is a favourite of fortune: such were the visions which, designed originally to captivate the imagination, many endeavoured to realize in practice. Here,

[1] Quoted in Jacob, *Altarab. Beduinenleben*, p. 226.

in fact, we find a society that fostered the virtues of worldly wisdom, polite intercourse, tolerance, and business initiative, and at the same time practised the old and prevalent vices in more refined forms. The higher ranks in Muslim countries, even in cities of more recent foundation, became infected—under the influence, it must be conceded, of Byzantine and Persian ideas—with the vices of the κίναιδοι, who were in great demand as musicians and singers, as also with all the mischiefs attendant upon the practice of keeping *harîms* and eunuchs.

The civilization of Muslim lands, in the first three or four centuries of its development, reached a height that it never again attained after the irruption of the Turks and the Mongols. In the cultivation of science and art, in the refinement of manners, in the systematic provision for the treatment of illness and for other public services, it was, as far down as the 12th cent. A.D., and in part even later, in advance of Christendom and the West. In intelligence and outward culture the Muslim showed himself superior to the Crusader, but whether he stood higher also in an ethical respect it is not easy to decide. What was morally good in him was nurtured and cultivated in secret, and, when it was exercised with the supercilious and ironical air of a Saladin, it was perhaps no longer good at all. But, be this as it may, it is certain that in a moral aspect the Muslim world, even as it exists to-day, is rather to be compared —to leave absolute standards out of account altogether—with mediæval Europe than with the conditions of our modern civilization. In order to put the matter in a clearer light, and in view of the fact that Muslims of the present day are seeking in considerable numbers to assimilate Western culture, it will be well to add a few observations on the point.

Various as are the ways in which the many systems of religion and philosophy set forth the essence and the religious sanction of morality, there is one feature common to all, viz. the requirement that the individual shall, on the one hand, permanently hold in control the moods and pleasures of the moment, and that, on the other, by a process of constant self-expansion towards the ideal of humanity, he shall adjust himself to, and play a useful part in, a smaller or larger whole. Every stage of civilization has its rightful measure of stability and its appropriate sphere of operation—these being conditioned by the sway of the forces of nature without, and of the impulses of nature within; and under this sway, while the West has been making progress, the East has stood still, yielding to its changing destinies with a species of fatalism.

When we go a little more deeply into the popular literature of Islām, we recognize the elementary stage of its underlying morality. In the following paragraph a number of particulars are combined in a sketch which, though its dependence upon romantic sources, such as *The Thousand and One Nights*, will be obvious to all, may nevertheless help us to form at least a relative estimate of Muslim morality.

There is no theme that fills so large a place in this literature as the vicissitudes of fortune. Just as the peasant lies at the mercy of rain and sunshine, so does the citizen depend upon the favour and good-will of his superiors. Human life has no stability: the beggar of to-day may be a king to-morrow, and conversely; while one who to-day drinks deep at the wells of pleasure may to-morrow renounce the world. There is a corresponding lack of perseverance: people live for the day and do not lay by. Then the law against taking interest stands in the way of a profitable investment of capital. The idea that the giving of charity, especially to crazy devotees, is in itself a meritorious work, is an encouragement to idleness. A man's living and prosperity are supposed to be dependent, not upon work, but upon Allāh or some magical power. Many are, of course, often reduced to want, but there are occasional festivals at which everything is surrendered to merry-making, and the savings of a year are squandered in a day. The absence of steady self-control makes itself felt everywhere. Promises are lightly forgotten, and secrets lightly betrayed. Men cannot curb their curiosity, and so bring disaster upon themselves; and it is curiosity also that prompts them to make adventurous journeys. They make gifts freely, but give in order to receive again. They fall in love at first sight, and transfer their affections easily and frequently. Passionate weeping and lamentation alternate with extravagant rejoicing or helpless dismay. It is true that many have acquired the power of controlling their looks and bearing—or, rather, of hiding their feelings; but, when they seem to overlook an injury, and really defer their vengeance till a more favourable opportunity, the ethical character of their emotion or of the eventual deed of revenge is not thereby altered. But the man who has the power to strike never fails to indulge the impulse of the moment; he mutilates and beheads without any serious inquiry as to the guilt or innocence of his victims; and repentance often comes too late, and when it can no longer avail. Great as is the venality of judges and officials, their credulity and caprice are greater still. Mere arbitrariness, finding expression now in extravagant kindness and now in atrocious cruelty, appears to be the sole rule of a society so constituted, while patient submission is its supreme virtue. A typical representative of a class far from uncommon in the smaller Muslim State of mediæval times has been limned by Ibn Baṭūṭa in a single sentence: 'From his gate was never absent the beggar who received an alms, nor the corpse of one who had been executed.'[1] The potentate referred to was Muḥammad Tughluq, Sultān of Delhi (A.D. 1325–51).

The wider psychological explanation of these various phenomena (which are not without significance even for modern Islām) has been given—not perhaps without some indebtedness to Plato's *Republic*—by Ibn Khaldūn (b. Tunis, A.D. 1332; d. Cairo, 1406). He points to the limitations of psychical force within which alone the social and political energy of Islām has hitherto had an opportunity of asserting itself. The most telling instance of this is seen in the soon-exhausted vitality of the various dynasties. A dynasty usually begins with two or three vigorous rulers, who settle and maintain their kingdom; then its energies begin to flag, and the heritage of the fathers is consumed in enervating luxury. A dynasty such as that of modern Morocco—one which, though now apparently approaching dissolution, has lasted since 1659—is a rare exception in Muslim history. In Islām no ruling house has ever been able to maintain its position without the slaughter of relatives and war amongst brothers. And, while it is true that the same sinister features, with all their significance for the state of public morality, are found also in mediæval Christendom, yet it is in Turkey alone that fratricide has been legally sanctioned, as falling within the domestic rights of the Sultan.

10. The present condition.—Islām, in its diffusion from Morocco to the Malay Archipelago, is professed by races of widely different character. In N. Africa negroes of an easy-going and untrustworthy temperament, though often fanatically devout, and Berbers, in part semi-savage and difficult to subdue, live in close proximity to mixed city populations, with whom they have as little in common as with the hard-working, all-enduring Egyptian *fellaḥīn*. In Western Asia the Arab brigand comes in contact with Turkish peasants and soldiers, as also with Persian merchants. The Muslims of India, who are among the most loyal subjects of the British Crown, are very different from the Afghans, a people proud of their independence. In the Dutch East Indies are found the quiet and tractable Javanese as well as the predatory and warlike Achehnese; and many more instances of diversity might be given. Notwithstanding the common faith of these peoples, they do not form a homogeneous ethical whole. The violent political disruptions which have taken place since the shortlived glories of the Umayyad and Abbāsid khalifates have been anything but favourable to the growth of fraternal unity throughout Islām.

Nor is there any lack of social and economic dis-

[1] *Voyages*, tr. Defrémery[2], Paris, 1874–79, iii. 216.

parities in Muslim countries. Slavery still exists, more particularly in the forms of eunuchism and concubinage. As the slaves, both male and female, are kept from motives of luxury and pleasure, they are relatively well treated. Such cruelties of capitalistic exploitation as we hear of in the annals of Greece and Rome, or in the more recent history of the plantation system in the Indies and America, are seldom or never found in Islām. The Muslim owner frequently treats his slaves, and even his dumb animals, more humanely than his fellow-men of equal standing with himself. Here, moreover, it is accounted a good and praiseworthy work to educate slaves and then grant them their freedom.

The further division of Muslim society into classes is not everywhere the same. It strikes the Western mind as primitive, mediæval, or, at least, as pre-revolutional. In India, for instance, Islām has not entirely abolished the system of caste. The inhabitants of cities in Western Asia were still in many cases segregated according to their various trade-gilds. An illustration is furnished by the membership of the first Persian Parliament, which by the constitution of the 5th of August 1906, was composed of the following representatives: (1) those of the princes and the ruling house (the only nobility in the proper sense); (2) those of learned men and students; (3) those of the merchant class; (4) those of landlords and peasants; and (5) those of the various industries—one member for each gild (embracing from three to nine trades).[1]

It is impossible in the space at our disposal, and especially in view of our defective knowledge of the more private life of Islām, to deal exhaustively with the morals of all these peoples and their various social ranks. We shall, therefore, confine ourselves to a few general observations regarding Muslim life as actually affected by the moral code.

Islām lays upon its followers the duty of propaganda—of active effort in spreading the faith, either by the peaceful methods open to merchants and traders, or, where possible, by the holy war. This demand has pronounced moral effects. For the Muslims themselves the result is twofold: on the one hand, sinister—in so far as an impulse is given to fanaticism; and, on the other, favourable—in so far as active virtue is sustained by a manly pride and by the consciousness of belonging to a vast and effectively expanding organization. With regard to this propaganda, nevertheless, the present political situation of Islām is anything but propitious. There are in all some 225 millions of Muslims; but of these about 65 millions live under British rule, 35 under Dutch, 30 under Chinese, 20 under Russian, 20 under French, and so on; while the Turkish empire, the last great power of Islām, and in the 16th cent. the strongest State in Europe, is now being harassed on every side. It is possible, however, that the diffusion of Islām among lower races, like the less civilized tribes of Africa, may prove effective in raising their moral conditions to a higher level.

Throughout Islām the religious law has a powerful influence in family life. Christian writers have usually a good deal to say about the Muslim form of married life—polygamy. The law permits any man who has the requisite means to have four wives, and as many concubines as he wishes. But it should be borne in mind that this permission is circumscribed in practice by the fact that the number of women is not unlimited, as also by the economic conditions, which allow only the prosperous few to maintain more than one wife. Monogamy is all but universal among the peasantry, and is practised by the majority of townspeople. As a matter of fact, polygamy has nothing like such baneful effects as the facility of divorce, also sanctioned by the law. It is not so much the practice of having more than one wife at a time as that of frequently changing the wife that works great moral harm in Muslim society. The husband can put away his wife at any time and for any reason, provided only he repays her dowry or gives her a compensation. This extreme liberty of divorce, which is certainly incompatible with all higher culture, is very widely taken advantage of, and the result is the derangement of domestic relations and the neglected training of the young.

In most Muslim lands the position of women is an inferior one. The Qur'ān explicitly declares the superior status of men. Tradition and popular proverb have it that heaven is full of poor people, and hell of women, and that women are deficient in understanding and religion. But they have, of course, their own peculiar type of intelligence, as also of religion, which the men call superstition. Women attend the mosque much less frequently than men, but are, on the other hand, much more

[1] *Rev. du monde musulman*, i. [1908] 94.

addicted to the magical arts and to the practice of visiting the graves of holy miracle-workers. The latter custom, however, has in many cases no deeper motive than visits to the bazaar or the baths.

The Muslim reckons the preservation of his own life as one of his primary duties. Suicide is rare in Islām. It is prohibited by the Qur'ān, as is also the killing of one's neighbour, though the latter prohibition is not so scrupulously observed.

The moral practice of everyday life is regulated in Islām, as elsewhere, more by circumstances than by religious law. The ordinary offences are due to momentary weakness, sensuality, or defective memory, rather than to evil will. In some respects the religious law, when it is not hypocritically evaded, tends to clog the wheels of progress. The interdict against interest, and the fast of Ramaḍān—the latter being in the main rigidly observed—militate against a settled commercial life; and alms-giving, as was said above, encourages idleness. The theme of perennial interest is either enjoyment or else abstinence therefrom, while a man's daily work is not regarded as having any ethical value. Praying, or begging, or even being insane is thought of by many as providing a more excellent career than working or trading. Study of the law is frequently prized more highly than obedience to it. In the greatest Muslim university, the Azhar, in Cairo, and elsewhere, many continue their study of the sacred sciences till old age—not, however, with a view to becoming useful members of society, but simply in order to win a higher place in Paradise.[1] By way of instructing the faithful as to the right disposal of their wealth, a Cairo newspaper recently published the will of a pious Sayid—a genealogist and a shaikh of the Azhar—who died in 1906. He left one-third of his property for a distribution of bread among the poor; a granddaughter received 3000 piastres; his books were bequeathed to his two sons, and his clothes to the poor students and learned men of the Azhar.[2]

An example of the false analogies to which the Muslim is led by his fatalistic trust in God may be seen in his condemnation of the principle of insurance. A shaikh of the Azhar says in a *fatwa* that life and fire insurance is to be regarded as gambling, and as contrary to the spirit of the Qur'ān.[3]

One great obstacle to the development of social morality in the East has been from time immemorial the corruption of official life. Both in Persia and in Turkey, however, voices are now being raised in favour of a purer public service. Thus a celebrated preacher in Teheran recently uttered the following words from his pulpit: 'We have, thank God, the best law in the world, for we have the Qur'ān, and we do not desire the laws of Europeans. But what we might well take from them is their method of appointing and supervising officials, and of collecting taxes in such a way that none need suffer extortion.'[4] The rapacity of governments and officials has often pernicious results upon pious bequests—the so-called *waqf*-endowments. In various ways, and sometimes doubtless in the interests of justice and morality in a higher sense, the dead hand is compelled to move again. In the hands of devout teachers of the law these funds have been used as a weapon against the State, and the State accordingly encourages their secularization, though, as we might expect, the process is seldom carried out without fraud. Another consequence of the systematic extortion that prevails in Oriental life is that many strive to conceal the fact of their wealth, as they would conceal heretical opinions. The majority, however, lay out their easily won gains on houses, finery, and large retinues of servants.

The middle classes, who devote themselves by preference to trading—industry is everywhere in a backward condition—have generally a bad reputation for self-interest and avarice. This is possibly an exaggeration, and in any case these vices are not confined to Islām. It cannot be denied, indeed, that in the East the policy of fixed prices prevails still less than in Southern Europe, and that many Orientals have little natural repugnance to falsehood. But to say that commercial honour is here unknown, or that lying is not reckoned a sin among Muslims generally, is mere slander, though it may be admitted that the Muslim, like the majority of mankind, judges of truth and falsehood from the standpoint of immediate advantage rather than from that of morality.

The official moral code has less to say about the means by which a man earns his living than about the way in which he enjoys, or refrains from enjoying, his gains. But how does the matter stand in actual practice? One feature that forces itself upon the eye at once is that many morally indifferent commandments and usages are the most widely and most zealously observed of all. The laws against luxury and intemperance are much less strictly adhered to. As regards luxury, indeed, some measure of dressing and finery is permitted to children, who as yet cannot commit sin; and to women, who are lost in any case; while the men as a rule study to be simple in dress and dignified in bearing. Many Muslims produce a favourable impression by their unaffected manner and their temperate habits. The prohibition of wine is observed by the majority; but it must be granted that with many Muslims *ḥashīsh*, opium, and other intoxicants take the place that alcohol has in the West. There are many opium-smokers in Persia and Turkey, and there is also a considerable amount of wine-drinking. In India the use of opium keeps pace with the spread of Islām itself. But the Muslims of the Celestial kingdom are said to be much less addicted to this vice than their Chinese masters.

[1] Cf. Arminjon, in *Rev. de Paris*, v. [1904] 592.
[2] *Rev. du monde musulman*, i. 263.
[3] *Ib.* 276.
[4] *Ib.* ii. [1908] 313 f.

With these insufficient references to the morals of contemporary life in Islām this article must draw to a close. The question as to the ethical significance of Islām for the future is one easier asked than answered. If the sacred law continues to be interpreted literally, then, though it may still prove helpful to peoples at a lower stage of civilization, it will in other circumstances act as an obstacle to moral development. Among more highly civilized peoples, Islām must either degenerate into a mere sect, or else adapt itself anew to new conditions. It must come to realize—as in many quarters, indeed, it has already realized—that the laws of Muḥammad and the tradition were given in view of the primitive conditions of an earlier age. Will the modern Muslim community, in assenting to this idea, be able to raise itself above the Qur'ān and the *sunnah* without surrendering Islām itself?

LITERATURE.—In this article the author is chiefly indebted to the works of I. Goldziher, especially to his admirable *Vorlesungen über d. Islam* (*Religionswissenschaftliche Bibliothek*, i.), Heidelberg, 1910; further, Carra de Vaux, 'La Morale de l'Islam' (in *Morales et Religions; Leçons professées à l'école des hautes études sociales*, Paris, 1909, pp. 189–216); D. B. Macdonald, *Development of Muslim Theology, Jurisprudence, and Constitutional Theory* (*The Semitic Series*, ix.), New York, 1903, also 'The Moral Education of the Young among Muslims,' *IJE* xv. [1905] 286–304.

The following may be consulted in connexion with the various divisions:

1. J. Wellhausen, *Reste arab. Heidentums* (*Skizzen u. Vorarbeiten*, iii.), Berlin, 1887, [2]1897; G. Jacob, *Altarabisches Beduinenleben* (*Studien in arab. Dichtern*, iii.), Berlin, 1897; O. Procksch, *Über die Blutrache bei den vorislam. Arabern u. Mohammeds Stellung zu ihr* (*Leipziger Studien aus dem Gebiete d. Geschichte*, v. 4), Leipzig, 1899; *The Qur'ān*, tr. E. H. Palmer (*SBE* vi. and ix.), Oxford, 1900; H. Grimme, *Mohammed* (*Darstellungen aus d. Gebiete d. nicht-christl. Religionsgesch.* vii. and xi.), Münster, 1892–95, esp. xi. 110–153.

2. Al-Būkhārī, *Les Traditions islamiques*, trad. . . . avec notes et index, par O. Houdas et W. Marçais (*Publ. de l'école des langues orientales vivantes*), 3 vols., Paris, 1903–08.

3. Th. W. Juynboll, *Handb. d. islam. Gesetzes*, Leyden and Leipzig, 1910.

4. *Schahrastâni's Religionspartheien u. Philosophen-Schulen*, tr. Th. Haarbrücker, 2 pts., Halle, 1850–51 (Arab. ed. by Cureton, London, 1842–46).

5. *Hermetis Trismegisti qui apud Arabes fertur de castigatione animæ libellum*, ed. O. Bardenhewer, Bonn, 1873; cf. also 'Muslim' sections of artt. ASCETICISM, BLESSEDNESS, COMMUNION WITH DEITY.

6. Carra de Vaux, 'Akhlāḳ,' in *Ency. des Islam*, ed. Houtsma, Leyden, 1909; A. Merx, *Die Einführung d. aristotel. Ethik in d. arab. Philosophie* (*Verhandl. d. 13ten Orient.-Kongr.* p. 290 ff.), Leyden, 1904; T. J. de Boer, *Gesch. d. Philosophie im Islam*, Stuttgart, 1901, Eng. tr., London, 1903.

7. Al-Ghazālī, *Iḥyā 'ulūm al-dīn*, Cairo, A.H. 1282; the same writer's *O Kind!* Arab. and Germ. by Hammer-Purgstall, Vienna, 1838; M. Asin Palacios, *Algazel dogmática moral, ascética* (*Colleccion de estudios arabes*, vi.), Saragossa, 1901; Carra de Vaux, *Gazali* (*Les grands Philosophes*), Paris, 1902 (esp. pp. 129–174: 'La Morale').

8. Nāṣir al-Dīn Ṭūsī, *Aḫlāq-i Nāṣirī* (various edd.).

9. A von Kremer, *Culturgesch. d. Orients unter d. Chalifen*, 2 vols., Vienna, 1875–77.

10. J. L. Burckhardt, *Notes on the Beduins and Wahábys*, London, 1830; E. W. Lane, *An Account of the Manners and Customs of the Modern Egyptians*, 2 vols., London, 1871; J. E. Polak, *Persien; d. Land u. seine Bewohner*, 2 pts., Leipzig, 1865; C. M. Doughty, *Travels in Arabia Deserta*, 2 vols., Cambridge, 1888; C. Snouck Hurgronje, *Mekka*, 2 vols., The Hague, 1888–89, *The Achehnese*, Eng. tr., A. W. S. O'Sullivan, 2 vols., London, 1906; E. Montet, *De l'État présent et de l'avenir de l'Islam*, Paris, 1911; *Revue du monde musulman*, 12 vols., Paris, 1908–10.

T. J. DE BOER.

ETHICS AND MORALITY (Parsi).—1. The place of ethics in the religious system of the Avesta.

—The religion of Zarathushtra, qualified by the Avesta and the Pahlavi books, is in the fullest sense of the word a religion of morality. When comparing Persian religion with Indian, we see in the former a moral interest take the place of the sacrificial and philosophical interests of the Brāhmans. This moral interest corresponds with the practical and political character of the Persians themselves; but the Zarathushtrian ethic has its real foundation in the religious system of the Avesta. This system we know as a dualistic one (see DUALISM [Iranian]). Already in the theology of the *Gāthās*—the oldest part of the Avesta, originating perhaps in the time of the Prophet himself or in that of his nearest successors—we hear of the two opposing Spirits, the pure and good Spirit Ahura Mazda (Ormazd [*q.v.*]), and the evil and impure Angra Mainyu (Ahriman [*q.v.*]).

'Of these two the wicked Spirit chose to do the most evil things, the holy Spirit chose Righteousness and those men who in performing acts of purity please Ahura Mazda' (*Yasna* xxx. 5). 'And, when the two Spirits first met, they created as the first things *Life and Death*, and as the final end *Hell* for the wicked and *Heaven* for the Righteous' (*ib.* xxx. 4).

The conception of these principles of Life and Death is elaborated in the idea of two real empires, the one being the dominion of Ormazd, the other that of Ahriman. As these two empires are not divided according to the natural division of material and spiritual, they rule together in Nature, and in bodily phenomena as well as in spiritual, as do life and death, good and evil. The motto of Ormazd's empire is 'the furthering of life' (*frādaṭ-gaētha*), and the words are almost a war-cry in the combat; the angels of Ormazd, the *Amesha Spentas* (*q.v.*), 'Immortal Holy Ones,' are always described as the 'furtherers of the living,' that they may not wither or decay; while, on the other hand, the chief of the Evil Spirits is called *Pourumahrka*, 'Full of Death.' From a formal or moral point of view the two principles might be defined as Purity and Impurity—Purity containing all the vital forces of the world, Impurity all the forces of death. It is the sacred duty of man, and constitutes his moral righteousness, to uphold the forces of good; and so we see *purity, holiness, righteousness* appearing as identical conceptions, and all included under the one word *aša*. This *aša* is the fundamental idea of the Zarathushtrian religion. Personified, it is the angel *Aša Vahišta*, 'The Best Righteousness'; and, as the *summum bonum*, *Aša Vahišta* gives its name to Paradise (=New Pers. *Bahišt*). The final aim of religion, the regeneration of the world, corresponds with this idea of righteousness. It endeavours to make the world absolutely pure and righteous, free from every defilement of evil and death.

This dualistic idea, found already in the *Gāthās*, is developed further in a mythological direction in the Pahlavi book *Būndahiš*, where the Evil Spirit attempts to destroy what the Good created. He is conquered, but is allowed to continue his evil work in the world for a time, in order that it may be perfectly manifest how bad the evil is, and that good deeds and a good life constitute the only right in the world. This tolerance of evil is to last for 6000 years, after which period the final processes leading to the victory of Ormazd begin. These 6000 years make up the period of the actual world, and so this world-period is naturally a time of *struggle* between the powers of Good and Evil (cf. AGES OF THE WORLD [Zoroastrian]). The later Avesta (*Vendīdād*, i.) describes the beginning of that struggle as a twofold creation—Ahriman always creating something evil, in imitation of each good thing created by Ormazd. So Nature itself becomes twofold—good things and pure creatures always mingling with the wicked inventions of the Evil One.

The world of spirits is divided into good and evil, and so is it in the world of men: Ahriman is the chief not only of Evil Spirits, but of unbelieving men. The great problem of life is now (1) Who shall prevail—Ormazd or Ahriman? and (2) What can be done to further the cause of Ormazd? *Religion* solves this problem. To believe in Ormazd is to believe in his cause—to believe that he is right, and that he has the power and will obtain the victory at last. This belief must be not only theoretical but practical. To belong to the empire of

Ormazd is to struggle for his cause, to work out his ideas in the world, to realize the good and pure in Nature, as in the life of man. Thus the Good One and his followers struggle *together* against the powers of evil, and the final victory will depend on this collaboration of God and man. No other religion has made the work of man a condition of the ultimate success of the Divinity; and, because the system of Zarathushtra does so, we may truly say that in a unique sense it is the religion of morality: duty being an inherent religious necessity, and moral actions the inevitable consequence of the religious principle.

2. Morality a struggle against the evil spirits.—This morality is, however, no pure morality in our modern sense of the word: the immediate struggle against the evil spirits forms a large part of the duties of man—especially of his sacrificial and ritual duties. For the priesthood the actions involved in the performance of the cult are the most important, but this cult has its meaning only as a combat against the evil spirits, and as a system of purifications to expel the evil spirits found in Nature and in human life. Against the evil spirits the priests are armed with a mighty weapon, consisting of the pure elements, and especially of the holy fire which is always kept burning as an ever active power of purification. In ordinary human life a great multitude of observances are needed for keeping the evil spirits at a distance; among these, *cleansings* are the most important, for evil is always considered as a form of impurity. At the same time the cleansings have the power of expelling the evil spirits; and many performances that would commend themselves to us as being practical and useful are, according to the Persian ideas, in reality effective because they expel the indwelling evil spirits. Water, for example, has a real anti-demoniac efficacy, and not merely a hygienic or æsthetic value, as in our modern view. Again, after an illness all the bed-clothes must be cleansed with the utmost care, not so much to obtain clean bed-clothes as to free them from the indwelling evil spirits. Every sickness and the natural states of organic life, such as menstruation, are understood to pertain to the great realm of death and devils. Every dead thing belongs to Ahriman, is impure, and makes impure; therefore ritual observances of cleansing are needful when one has touched a dead dog, a dead man, or any other dead body—only, however, if the creature, when living, belonged to the realm of purity.

Thus the customs of mourning imply at every step the expulsion of evil spirits, the purification of the house, the family, and the district where the evil spirit of Death has dwelt. The Parsis to-day bring the dead bodies of men and of dogs to the 'Towers of Silence,' where they are exposed to the birds of heaven, in order that earth, fire, or water be not defiled by the burning or other destruction of the bodies. But, on the other hand, the corpses of evil men or of noxious animals convey no impurity, since by their death the demon has left them (*Vend.* v. 35–38; cf. DEATH AND DISPOSAL OF THE DEAD [Parsi], § 3).

3. Morality as an art of civilization.—Besides the actual decease of living creatures, every state implying a poverty of life or a tendency opposed to life, in Nature and practice, is considered as a manifestation of death, and so, naturally, of the action of evil spirits. Therefore unfruitfulness, cold, destructive heat, withering, noxious substances, blight, weeds, harmful insects, etc., all belong to the empire of Ahriman, and are to be striven against in the works of man. Thus religious duties go hand in hand with the work of *civilization*. In the time of Zarathushtra this civilization referred mainly to a nomadic and an agricultural community. The pious man ought to treat his cattle well, to nourish them, and not slay them for useless sacrifices; and this care for the cattle led in later Parsiism to the classic symbol of pious morality. Besides these virtues of the nomad we hear much in the later Avesta of agricultural duties: the cultivation of the fields, cutting of canals, construction of roads and bridges, building of houses, and manufacture of agricultural implements are all important and necessary duties of the faithful. The weeding of the fields and the destruction of noxious insects and beasts are meritorious deeds, tending to obliterate the boundaries of Ahriman's empire. The duties of an agricultural life provide the religious ideals of the Persians, and in the religious texts we continually meet with pictures drawn from agriculture which are used to illustrate the holy life.

To the question where the earth enjoys the best fortune, Ahura Mazda naturally answers: first, 'Where most sacrifices are made, the laws obeyed, and praise given to the Gods.' Then follows the second answer: 'There it is, where a believer builds a house, with priest and cattle, with wife and children; where cattle and holiness flourish, and food and dog, and wife and children, and all abundance.' And thirdly he says: 'There it is, where the believer grows most corn and grass and fruit; where he waters the dry soil and drains the damp' (*Vendīdād*, iii. 1–4). 'For that soil is not blessed which lies long uncultivated, waiting for an husbandman, like a ripe maiden who goes childless, longing for an husband; but to him who works the soil with both arms will she bring riches, as a beloved spouse brings her child to her husband' (*ib.* 24 f.).

With this desire for cultivation goes the representation of its religious meritoriousness and of its holy power.

'Who sows corn sows holiness,' is a saying of the *Vendīdād*, which also declares: 'When the barley is arranged (for threshing), the demons begin to sweat (for fear); when the mill is arranged (for grinding the barley), the demons lose their senses; when the meal is arranged (for leavening), the demons howl; when the dough is arranged (for baking), the demons break wind (for fear). Here let some of this leaven be ever in the house to cast upon the demons; let their mouths be burned by it; they are seen to turn to flight' (*ib.* 31 f.).

4. Higher ideas of morality.—The norm of ethics is based upon the principle of utility contained in the Avesta. But that utility has in many cases an ideal character, and leads, at its height, to a real ethic even in our sense of the word. The productive activity of man is always highly esteemed. Nothing may be done that might curtail life in any sense. Therefore we never find any ascetic elements in the ethics of the Avesta (see ASCETICISM [Persian]); on the contrary, it is the duty of man to be in health and vigour, that he may work well for the cause of Righteousness. He ought to marry and become the father of strong children; every act that could diminish the fertility of man is strongly prohibited. Chastity is a necessary duty; and every form of unnatural sexual relation is forbidden and severely punished, as being under the power of evil spirits and leading not only to impurity but to the destruction of life. In the later contest with the Manichæans in Persia, the positive character of Zarathushtrian ethics is always evident, and a chief point in the policy of the Zarathushtrian priests was to conduct a polemic against the various forms of asceticism, such as celibacy, fasting, self-flagellation, and other forms of mortification of the flesh.

Besides the immediate obligation to care for oneself and for the race, we meet a series of duties always highly esteemed in practical life: for example, industry, temperance, economy, the keeping of early hours, assiduousness in all practical things. But the principle of purity and usefulness in life leads to a still higher ethical plane, where righteousness is understood not only as being outward purity and practical deeds, but as the true realization of right conduct in life, including truthfulness, uprightness, justice, faithfulness, and generosity. These elements are demanded not only as pointing to social instincts necessary to the life of the community, but as being also personal qualities inherent in the highest type of Persian manhood, and giving to it its highest value. The truthfulness praised by Herodotus (i. 136) as one of the elements in Persian education includes, without doubt, the duty of speaking religious truth; so at least the *arš-ukhdha vāxš* ('truth-speaking') of the Avesta is to be understood. Truthfulness in the moral sense is found, if not directly in the Avesta, at least in the ethics of the Pahlavi books; and here we note also how a city civilization in Persia leads to a higher moral state than that of an agricultural utilitarianism. The inward qualities of man—the tender emotions, benevolence, thankfulness—are mentioned in the Table of Duties in the *Dīnā-ī Maīnōg-ī Khraṭ*, ch. 37. Of the thirty-three duties mentioned in that chapter we choose some characteristic ones: benevolence, truthfulness, thankfulness, contentedness, to further the welfare of the good and to be a friend of all men, to marry one's sister, to adopt children, to labour industriously, to respect the capacities and goodwill of every one, to keep maliciousness and untruthfulness far from one's mind, not to show rancour, not to be libidinous, not to be quarrelsome, not to touch the goods of travellers and the unprotected, not to give way to anger, to exercise self-control, to resist laziness, to be happy oneself and to further the happiness of others, to help the good and to protect against the evil, to be careful not to speak untruth, to be scrupulously careful in keeping one's word, to open one's house to the sick, the poor, and the traveller. This is, as we see, a composite scheme of ethics, where a very refined moral outlook is combined with remnants of relatively primitive social customs—*e.g.*, the marrying of a sister, which in the times of the Achæmenians was regarded as a mark of the highest aristocracy.

5. Morality.—Parsiism being in this extreme sense of the word a religion of morality, the community naturally found a special task in upholding morality and educating the people in good works. The daily life of the priests was, of course, much taken up with ritual matters of cleansing and exorcism; but these rites included many moral and pedagogical elements—*e.g.*, to insist that it is the duty of men to cleanse themselves from every defilement, as it is their duty to expel the devils by the doing of useful works. It was the office of the priests directly to oversee and govern these multifarious exercises, and they had also to instruct husbands and wives in their duties and to punish them when these duties were not fulfilled. The name of the priest who had the latter function, *sraoša varez*, 'he who works out obedience,' is very significant of the duty, and to 'work out obedience' he used a scourge called by the same name.

The system of penalties belonging to this sacred pedagogic is codified in the moral law of the Avesta, the *Vendīdād*, whose name, 'given against the demons,' hints once more at the characteristic identification of demonology and morality in the Avesta. The idea of *sin* which usually meets us in this book is, therefore, essentially a juristic one. The *pešō-tanu*, as the sinner is called, is he who deserves corporal punishment. The conception of sin as an inward state of mind is hardly found in the Avesta.

The deepest guilt is not conceived of as sin, but, from a religious point of view, as unbelief; or, in the extreme case, as worship of the evil spirits. The fulfilment of all duties is contained in the Threefold Rule of Good Thoughts, Good Words, and Good Works (*humata, hūkhta, huvaršta*). Every pious man or woman may produce a great store of these three for gaining the bliss of heaven, and very holy persons, such as priests, may sometimes produce more than is needed for their own salvation. This overplus of good thoughts, words, and works is stored up in heaven as a *thesaurus operum supererogatorum*, to be distributed among the souls that are not sufficiently well provided for.

6. The Final Judgment.—It naturally follows from this system that the Final Judgment will turn upon the question of good works. The Zarathushtrian eschatology knows already in the *Gāthās* two stages of Judgment. The one corresponds to the *judicium speciale* of Christian theology, and is a scrutiny of individual souls; the other, the *judicium generale*, is a trial of mankind as a whole. The former is the trial before the tribunal of Mithra, on the mountain *Chakāṭ-ī Dāitih*. There the *souls* will be weighed in the

'balance of the spirits, which renders no favour on any side, neither for the righteous nor yet the wicked, neither for the lords nor yet the monarchs. As much as a hair's breadth it will not turn, and has no partiality; and him who is a lord and a monarch it considers equally, in its decision, with him who is the least of mankind' (*Dinā-ī Maīnōg-ī Khraṭ*, ii. 120 ff. [tr. West, *SBE* xxiv. 18]).

Even the soul that is acquitted is punished for its evil works by the angel Asha; then it may pass the Bridge of Judgment, *Chinvaṭ*, which leads to heaven. The guilty fall from this bridge into the gulf of hell beneath (see, further, BRIDGE, ii. 2 (*e*)).

The Final Judgment is carried out on the Last Day, when the bodily resurrection takes place, and the souls, blessed and wicked together, rise again to join their bodies. This Judgment is an immense ordeal, in which resurrected mankind will be required to pass through the molten metal that will overflow the whole earth. Here the true character of each will be tried; for the wicked the fire will burn very fiercely, to the good it will appear like lukewarm milk; but in all cases the fire will destroy every remnant of impurity, leaving man, as well as the whole earth, in that complete state of purity and holiness which was the original state before Ahriman introduced his defilements.

This Last Judgment, as we see, has much of the character of a natural process of cleansing; but in relation to the individual the formal element in the procedure appears; indeed, the idea is founded upon a principle of merciless retribution. The good Mithra has merely the duty of superintending the procedure; the supreme God Ahura Mazda has no part to play at all, the idea of mercy being absolutely excluded from the accomplishment of human destiny.

Nevertheless, the religious community has the power of releasing men from the consequences of their guilt (1) by means of the *Patēt*, the confession of sin made at the moment of death (see EXPIATION AND ATONEMENT [Parsi]); and (2) by sacramental means, viz. putting the holy juice of *haoma* into the ear of the dying. These dispensations are possible only in virtue of the overplus of good works at the command of the community.

Reviewing the whole field, we note the extremely formal and rather juristic character of the Zarathushtrian ethic, while the Persian genius for utilitarianism and things practical always enters into the scheme of righteousness and justice. In the individual life, this ethic appreciates industry, self-control, and veracity; in social life—righteousness, regularity, and social accord. The reverse of this ethic is an abstract stiffness that will not accommodate itself to life, and whose irrational consequences are often inimical to life. The monotonous opposition of good to evil and evil to good leaves no room for the intermediate stages of real life, for the individual and spontaneous states in the soul of man. The Persians cared little for the emotions of disinterestedness; even in the religious feelings we feel too often the want of lyric elements; on the contrary, we always feel the heavy burden of the juristic spirit. In accordance with this, 'religion' in the Avesta is called 'law' (*daēna*), and the Persians could not distinguish between the two ideas.

LITERATURE.—The only important special treatments of the ethic of the Avesta are in the Introduction to **J. Darmesteter's** tr. of the *Vendīdād* in *SBE* iv. (Oxford, 1895), and in **A. V. W. Jackson's** 'Iranische Religion' viii. (*GIrP* ii. 678–683), based on his 'Moral and Ethical Teachings of the Ancient Zoroastrian Religion,' in *IJE* vii. [1896] 55–62. Many passages bearing on the subject may be found in general works like **J. Darmesteter**, *Le Zend-Avesta*, Paris, 1892–3, i.–iii.; **C. P. Tiele**, *Geschiedenis van den Godsdienst in de Oudheit*, Amsterdam, 1901, vol. ii. (Germ. ed., Gotha, 1896); **Edv. Lehmann**, *Zarathustra*, Copenhagen, 1899–1902, vol. ii.

EDV. LEHMANN.

ETHICS AND MORALITY (Polynesian, Melanesian, and Malayan).—The character of the Polynesians has been painted both in the brightest and in the darkest colours. The truth seems to lie between the two extremes, and the explanation is to be found in the fact that the Polynesian is a child of nature, and, like all children, under the sway of each passing emotion. It was the better side of the Polynesian character which first impressed the early voyagers. Their lightheartedness, their ceremonious courtesy, and their abstinence from petty quarrels led their European discoverers to fancy that there was no darker side to the picture. Yet the same childish superficiality which filled them with unrestrained joy could fill them in an instant with melancholy which might not stop even at suicide. Nor was their lightheartedness always ingenuous; it often formed a cloak for falsehood and treachery. In many of these cases the Europeans were not free from blame, provoking, by their violence and licentiousness, such revenge as the weaker natives could inflict. On the other hand, perfidy was common between the Polynesians themselves, so that wars were conducted by ambuscade rather than by open attack. One of their leading characteristics was revenge, which was often concealed for years with deep secrecy until a fitting opportunity occurred for its gratification. This principle of revenge, which, it must be borne in mind, is reckoned a virtue rather than a vice among many peoples, frequently led to the vendetta. Thievery and robbery were considered commendable and skilful when practised against foreigners; yet among themselves or towards those who had been adopted into their number, as well as in regular barter, the Polynesians evidenced a high code of honour. In like manner, they possessed the primitive virtues of hospitality and generosity, though these qualities, like their honesty, suffered from the coming of the whites. Indolent and fitful at work, the Polynesians were, nevertheless, devoted to war; yet flight was not regarded as a disgrace. The Tahitians regarded wounds in battle as marks of awkwardness and foolishness. Their wars were conducted with the utmost cruelty and with pitiless barbarity towards captives, though, on the other hand, there was in New Zealand and Tonga a noble recognition of a prisoner's valour. Closely allied with their bravery in war was their pride, even though this sometimes degenerated into vanity. In the use of spirituous liquors the Polynesians were originally extremely temperate, but their licentiousness, especially in Tahiti, was almost incredible. The abstract was by no means lacking among the Polynesians. Noble deeds were admired, and the Tongans struck the keynote of hedonistic ethics when they said: 'After a good deed one feels well, therefore we do good deeds.' Shame for theft or other unseemly conduct was by no means rare, and the ethical sense grew steadily higher with ascent in the social scale.

The position of women throughout Polynesia was comparatively high, although they were not considered equal to men. Ill-treatment was rare, and women were often admitted to the councils, possessing an influence which was very real. Heavy toil was spared them; and where, as in Hawaii, they did not eat with the men and were forbidden the enjoyment of certain foods, this was due in most cases to the laws of tabu. Pre-nuptial chastity was unknown, excepting in the higher classes, and the utmost indelicacy in conversation and jests prevailed throughout the islands, especially in Tahiti. After marriage, chastity was more strictly preserved, and the adulterer was severely punished. On the other hand, those who were united to a husband by the blood-covenant might regard his wife or wives as their own. From this must be distinguished a husband's prostitution of his wife, especially to Europeans. Unnatural and secret vices, as well as incest, were disgracefully common, all combining with the general licence to aid in the decay of the Polynesian race. Parents met with scant esteem from their children, yet, despite the prevalence of infanticide and abortion, they were devoted to those who were allowed to survive. The status of slaves was toilsome, yet relatively merciful. Punishment for crime was stern, among the penalties being death and mutilation, while the *lex talionis* was common throughout the Polynesian Islands, and extended not only to the criminal but to his family, although pecuniary compensation was not unknown.

The character of the Melanesians was ethically inferior to that of the Polynesians. Thus theft was extremely common, especially in Fiji, where it was punished only when committed against compatriots. In like manner, the Melanesians were notorious for their falsehoods, except that one's own deeds were never denied. Proud and revengeful to the last degree, they forgot no injury, seeking requital both by murder and by black magic. They were cruel, but were cowardly rather than brave. On the other hand, the Melanesians were very susceptible to civilizing influences, and in their courtesy and hospitality were little inferior to the Polynesians. The position of women was less elevated among them, however, since wives were obliged to do the heavier sorts of work and to surrender the greater part of the adornments to the men. Their condition was particularly debased in the Fiji Islands, where they were in the absolute power of their husbands, and were frequently maltreated. Melanesian women were far more chaste than their Polynesian sisters, even the unmarried girls observing strict chastity. In the Fiji Islands sexual relations were unknown before the young men had reached the age of eighteen or twenty—a restraint which in its time checked the shameless precocity which prevailed in Polynesia. In Melanesia strong affection prevailed, for the most part, between parents and children, and they were carefully educated, although they had no ethical training. The practice of infanticide was shockingly prevalent, two-thirds of the children in Fiji being killed as soon as they were born—often by people who made this their profession; girls were the chief victims, because they could not be warriors. Abortion was also extremely common; yet, if an infant survived the first day, it was safe, and was treated with all tenderness. The immorality of infanticide and the murder of the aged was lessened by the Melanesian belief that human beings lived in the future life in the age and the estate in which they were at death. The aged, or those afflicted with long and tedious illnesses, were put to death either by burial alive or by abandonment. The sick and aged themselves desired to die thus, and it was accounted a tribute of love for sons to put them to death. Whether the practice of cannibalism may properly be considered as appertaining to ethics is somewhat doubtful, but it may be noted that this custom was prevalent throughout both Polynesia and Melanesia. (See CANNIBALISM.)

The characteristics of the Polynesians and Melanesians are most clearly defined in Tahiti and Fiji respectively. The one people was facile, mercurial, social, relatively cultured, kind, and chivalrous, but marred by an all-pervading and enervating sensuality; the other was cruel, treacherous, and inferior to its kindred race in almost every respect save that of sexual purity.

LITERATURE.—Waitz-Gerland, *Anthropologie der Naturvölker* (Leipzig, 1872), vi. 105-118, 120-131, 135-145, 207, 223-227, 622-630, 636-640, 687-690. LOUIS H. GRAY.

ETHICS AND MORALITY (Roman).—*Sources.*—In scarcely any field of Roman life are we so conscious of the paucity of our sources as in that of ethics and morality. For the earliest period we seem at first sight fairly well supplied, for we have, or seem to have, a multitude of anecdotes and figures from which to draw that picture of the virtuous early Roman in which the later and decadent period of antiquity took such retrospective satisfaction. But, once we have caught up with modern scientific progress in the matter of Roman history, these figures, and even the legends of them, lose all value as contemporary documents. Modern theories of anthropology and primitive psychology take their place. With the beginning of Roman literature our situation improves; but this literature is to a high degree dependent upon Greek models; and, even where it reflects Roman feeling, the latter is merely that of the intellectual classes. Nor does the advent of Greek philosophy, with its formal teaching of ethics, succeed in any considerable sense in enlarging our vision. But, during the Empire at least, the multitude of inscriptions and our knowledge of Oriental cults diminish our darkness.

In spite of these obstacles, the following outline seems tolerably sure; in it an attempt has been made to sketch the evolution of the moral attitude of the Romans from the earliest times until the conquest of Christian ideas. It does not attempt to trace the development on Roman soil of ethics as a philosophical discipline. This is not possible, simply because no such development ever took place. Roman philosophy, to be sure, dealt preferably and almost exclusively with ethics; but it took its origin from Greece, not merely at the beginning, but in every individual attempt, during all its history. It does not, therefore, represent so much a Roman development as the reflexion, among Roman writers, of a development which took place in Greece and the Greek-speaking lands.

The ethical development of any people is a continuous process; but, though the process is continuous, it is, nevertheless, subject to change of speed, and may be accelerated or retarded by circumstances. The acceleration is usually due to the pressure of outside influence, while a lack of foreign impact often tends to quiescence and lethargy in the moral sphere. In Rome's history, between the foundation of the city and the accession of Constantine, there are three such accelerations: the first (in the 6th cent. B.C.), caused by the coming of the Etruscans; the second (in the 3rd cent. B.C.), caused by the victories of the Punic wars; and the third (in the Julian-Augustan age), caused by the influence of Greek philosophy and Oriental culture.

1. The period before the coming of the Etruscans.—In the phraseology of the orthodox history of Rome, this is the period of 'the Early Kingdom.' In it we are confronted with a series of pictures of heroic virtue. The majority of those who have discussed the morality of the early Romans have used these stories as evidence, thus unwittingly spreading utterly false views. Before the middle of the 6th cent. B.C. the Romans had obtained, at best, merely the rudiments of civilization. Their moral life was dependent upon the categorical imperative of obedience to those principles and actions which tended to preserve and perpetuate the race in its struggle for existence. The basal concept of ethics was, therefore, the fulfilment of the obligations which society laid upon the individual members. The moral life of the individual was entirely dissolved into that of the race. Actions were good or bad according as they assisted or hindered the race in its struggle for existence. The intensity of the struggle is reflected in the cogency which these ethical demands possessed, and in the extension of moral feeling into regions of activity which a higher and more civilized state regards as ethically indifferent. This attitude of mind can best be illustrated by those two words which together sum up the ethical ideal of early Rome: *virtus* and *pietas*. *Virtus*, which for this earlier period is wrongly translated by 'virtue' or even by 'valour,' has a strongly sexual implication. It is the possession of the power of reproduction, and its opposite is neither 'vice' nor 'cowardice,' but physiological 'impotence.' It is the rating of the individual in regard to his capacity to act for the continuance of the race. Similarly, *pietas* is simply the respect and homage shown to parents in their lifetime, and to the larger company of 'ancestors.' It is, in a sense, the apotheosis of the continuity of the race. This is its pristine significance, and it is only by extension that it comes to refer generally to the attitude of worship towards the gods.

Thus the obligations implicit in *virtus* are those of the individual to labour for the propagation of the race; and the obligations of *pietas* are the homage of the race for its own continuity. These seem to be the most important positive elements, and they are accompanied by one negative condition: the moral obligation of conservatism and the immorality of innovation. This is, of course, the respect for the *mores majorum*, the customs of the ancestors, which bears its philological testimony in the word 'morality.'

We are thus enabled to understand how, owing to misinterpretation, the half-civilized Italic folk, just issuing from the portals of the age of magic, can figure in the traditional history of morals as possessed of 'virtue, piety, and morality.' It was this kind of misinterpretation which assisted the idea of the 'fall of man,' and of the 'Paradise' and the 'Golden Age' in the past.

2. From the coming of the Etruscans to the Punic wars.—Into this primitive community, busied with the processes of self-preservation and propagation, there came, about the middle of the 6th cent. B.C., the race of Etruscans. The origin of this people, and their means of reaching Italy, do not concern us here; it is sufficient for our purpose to realize that they were a people of advanced culture, possessed of a developed form of government, and of a certain appreciation for art. However decadent they may have grown later, they were a strong and virile people in this 6th century. About a century later, *i.e.* about the middle of the 5th cent., their influence began to be eliminated. But their residence had sufficed to introduce to the Roman people developed ideas of government, and to call forth Rome's natural instinct for law. Rome commenced to realize her own destiny, and patriotism began to be a vital force in the community.

In the sphere of religion it is relatively easy to trace the effects of this patriotic instinct. But its effects were also perceived in the moral sphere. The chief end of man, the *summum bonum*, no longer consisted exclusively in physical increase.

The mass of accumulated power must be put to a purpose. The fulfilment of this purpose became a duty. Thus *virtus* adds to virility the idea of valour, and the *patria* takes its place alongside the *patres* as the object of *pietas*. Thus we step forward into the period of the Republic, with its series of wonderful conquests; and the farmer of the old régime becomes the soldier of the new, while still retaining his farming instincts. This state of affairs continued until the end of the Second Punic War, or, in other words, until the beginning of the 2nd cent. B.C. It is scarcely an accident that at the opening of this 2nd cent. we have the remarkable words of the old Cato in the introduction to the treatise, *de Agri Cultura*—words which seem to sum up the whole ethical situation. Speaking of what their ancestors (*majores nostri*) thought, he says:

'And when they praised a man and called him good, they praised him in this fashion, that they called him a good farmer or a good tiller of the soil. And he who was thus praised, they considered to be praised indeed. For from farmers are begotten the strongest men and the bravest soldiers.'

Thus production has had added to it conquest; and the whole ethical system gradually adjusts itself to this new valuation. Henceforward, actions are good or bad, not simply as they assist or hinder increase, but also as they further or retard the progress of the State.

3. The last two centuries of the Republic.—The Second Punic War and the wars of the 2nd cent. B.C. brought to Rome great material prosperity. Riches increased with amazing rapidity, and large private fortunes became less and less uncommon. At first these riches were solemnly and frugally invested in lands, but such investments served only to increase the problem by increasing the riches themselves. Thus began the spending of money for luxury, and, later, for mere extravagance. But, as the rich grew richer, the poor grew, if not correspondingly, at least considerably, poorer; and, in any case, the gulf between the two extremes of society gaped open more widely. The effect of riches and of poverty was in so far similar that each alike begat indifference to ideals. The simple life of the fathers was impossible for either class: for the one, because they were choked with riches; for the other, because they were throttled by poverty. Thus the old life was forgotten; and it was not many decades after Cato's death before a man was 'good' according to the extent of his riches—the essential *bona*—rather than because he was a good farmer or a good citizen. That was already true which Cicero says (*de Republica*, i. 51): 'In their ignorance of virtue, they call those the "best men" who live in riches and plenty.' Similar phrases are found a century and a half earlier in Plautus (*Curculio*, 475; *Captivi*, 583); and, though here they doubtless go back to Greek originals, they could count upon an answering echo in the Roman audience. The commercializing of ethics was the inevitable accompaniment of the general commercializing of human life. The older maxims of severe frugality and patriotic zeal were not entirely forgotten, and they lived on with considerable power among the now despised farming classes; but gradually, in the city at least, goodness and poverty were incommensurable; and the favourite phrase of Cicero, 'all good men' (*omnes boni*), referred in actual practice to respectable well-to-do citizens. Certainly, in Cicero's informal moments, when he would be more likely to express his real feelings, for example, in his correspondence, it is so used (*ad Att.* viii. 1, 3).

But, in spite of their apparent profitlessness, the last two centuries of the Republic, by this very luxury and self-indulgence, were working out an ethical salvation. By a strange psychological antinomy, through self-indulgence ethical individuality was born; and in the reaction from the depths of sensuous luxury we have the new and severe ethic of individual moral responsibility, which is characteristic of our fourth and last period—the Empire to Constantine.

4. The Empire until Constantine.—The result of the general dissolution of ideals which characterized the last centuries of the Republic was such a condition of scepticism in the realm of theory, and of sensuous materialism in the world of practice, that a moral revolution could not fail to follow. This new idea of morality was based upon the concept of the individual, and his responsibility. It was, doubtless, assisted in its development by the ethical theories of Greek philosophy, which now began to be popular in Rome; but it does not owe its rise entirely to these theories. The influence of Oriental cults was, at least among the masses, stronger than that of Greek philosophy. But both these influences worked side by side; and, although they were based on entirely contrary principles, they seem to have lived together without jealousy or interference. Thus we have the two great crusades for moral regeneration: that of the philosophers, especially the Cynics, and their wandering preachers, proclaiming the doctrine that moral regeneration comes from knowledge, that to know the truth is to do it, and, conversely, that sin is merely ignorance; and that of the priests of the various Oriental cults (of Magna Mater, Isis, Mithra), proclaiming that men are saved from sin and its consequences, not by knowledge, but by faith. It was the latter idea especially which affected almost all classes. The attempt to bring philosophy to the masses was destined to failure; but, where Stoicism failed, Mithra conquered. The world has seldom witnessed a more strenuous moral atmosphere than that which existed during the first two centuries of the Empire. Perhaps the most powerful proof of this statement is to be found in the fact that even the Oriental cults themselves were purified and spiritualized by their residence in Rome. See MITHRAISM.

Thus it came to pass that the Christian ethic, radically different as it was in many respects from that of the other Oriental religions which surrounded it, found many of its tenets in accord with the accepted morality of the day; and its teachings, which would have been almost entirely unintelligible to society in the time of Sulla, were in many respects commensurable with the world of Trajan. There were, however, even then, grave points of disagreement; and, by an unfortunate accentuation of certain Oriental interpretations of the Christian ethic, the old Pagan ethic of patriotism engaged in conflict with the whole Christian system. The conflict raged for centuries, through Julian on to Gratian and to the altar of Victoria, and on to Alaric's capture of Rome, until in Augustine's *City of God* it received at least a partial solution.

LITERATURE.—W. Warde Fowler, *The Religious Experience of the Roman People*, London, 1911; J. Benedict Carter, *The Religious Life of Ancient Rome*, Boston and New York, 1911; F. Cumont, *Les Religions orientales dans le paganisme romain*, Paris, 1906.

JESSE BENEDICT CARTER.

ETHICS AND MORALITY (Teutonic).—The term 'ethics' can be used in this connexion only in its general sense of 'ethical ideas' or 'recognition of moral obligations,' for we may be very certain that no idea of a system of ethics had ever suggested itself to the early Teutonic mind.

1. Sources of information.—No race has left so much literature behind it with so little of a merely didactic or theoretical nature. All the heathen Teutonic peoples, so far as we can judge, seem to have been intensely interested in conduct, but mainly as revealing character, not as illustrating abstract principles of right and wrong. In ancient Teutonic society there was no class set sufficiently apart from the ordinary business of life to survey it as a whole, like the poets of early Greece or the Druids of Celtic heathendom. The poets, law-givers, and saga-tellers were fighters and farmers as much as everybody else, and even the priests were not a caste apart—except possibly in England—but only chiefs with priestly functions superadded. Perhaps it is significant that it is in early Anglo-Saxon poetry that we find those traces of reflexion on moral issues, as well as a facility in the expression of ethical ideals, which are so noticeably absent in all other early Teutonic literature; but it is most probable that these characteristics are the result of the early conversion of England to Christianity.

Most of the foreigners who had any opportunity of observing the manners and customs of the Teutonic races were missionaries, to whom the ethical ideas of the heathen made no appeal, so that we can depend very little on outside judgments. From an earlier date, however, the *Germania* of Tacitus gives an admirable outline of the social life of the Germani of the 1st cent. A.D., and everything we know of these races in later times goes to show that Tacitus' observations on their code of morality were in the main correct. Still, in the absence of all open utterance on ethical ideals by the people themselves, we are driven back on the more or less unconscious self-revelation of the old hero cycles and sagas, in which the mere choice of subject betrays where the moral interest of the hearers lay. It is necessary to bear in mind that the period covered is a long one—ten centuries—and that our sources usually reflect the ideas of the ruling classes only.

2. Teutonic virtues.—Such virtues as were vital to the continued existence of the society naturally ranked first in public opinion, and of these (1) the first and foremost was *courage*. Lack of courage is the one unpardonable sin.

Tacitus (*Germ.* vi.) tells us that a German who abandons his shield in battle has committed the basest of crimes, and is shut out thereafter from the sacred rites and from the council; and he adds that many, after escaping from battle, have ended their infamy with the halter. No less emphatic is the curse pronounced on the coward thanes in the Anglo-Saxon *Beowulf*, and it, too, ends significantly: 'Death is better for every well-born man than a shamed life' (*Beowulf*, ed. Harrison and Sharp, 4th ed., Boston, 1901, line 2891 f.).

Many a good man doomed himself to death at the hands of a vastly superior force of enemies because he could not conquer his repugnance to the idea of seeking safety in flight. Even treachery to friends and kinsmen can be condoned or understood, but no one will listen to a justification of an act of physical cowardice.

Many tales reveal how far courage takes precedence of all the other virtues. The faithlessness with which Gunnar and Högni slay their foster-brother Sigurd, in the Völsung story, is wiped out in the eyes of posterity by their heroic defence at the court of Atli, and their still more heroic acceptance of defeat.

The mind unshaken by adversity is the object of the Teuton's highest admiration. An almost American Indian stoicism underlies that grim humour in the acceptance of death or wounds which strikes us so keenly in the Northern stories.

Thormod, St. Olaf's scald, dragging a death-arrow from his breast after the battle of Stiklastad, looks at it as he dies and observes: 'Well hath the King fed us, fat am I yet at the heart-roots' (*Heimskringla*, Morris-Magnússon's tr., 1893-95, ii. 442). When Thorgrim is sent to climb up Gunnar's hall in Iceland to see if he is within, he returns mortally wounded to his comrades, who ask if Gunnar is there. 'You can learn that,' he says, 'what I found out is that his halberd was at home,' and falls dead (*Brennu-Njálssaga*, ed. F. Jónsson, 1908, ch. 77).

Fortitude in bearing the death of friends or kinsmen is also admired, but the betrayal of feeling under such circumstances is readily condoned, especially in the aged, though we can feel the saga-writer's admiration in the tale of the old Viking Thorarin, who hears of the slaying of his son with apparent phlegm, with only a casual inquiry as to his defence, and all the while fumbles with the uncertain hand of age at a dagger with which he attempts to avenge himself ('Thorsteinn the Staff-smitten,' in Morris-Magnússon's *Three Northern Love-Stories*, 1875, p. 261 f.).

(2) *Endurance* and *tenacity of purpose* were allied virtues that ranked with courage. 'Enduring of toil, hunger, and cold, whenever fortune lays it on them,' says Geoffrey of Malaterra of the Normans; and every expedition in the undecked Viking ships must have been a training ground of such qualities. Anglo-Saxon literature, in the poem on the battle of Maldon, supplies us with those two lines which are a very epitome of Teutonic ideals of courage and endurance:

'Our soul shall be the more steadfast, our heart the higher,
Our mettle the more, the more our might is minished.'

(3) But in modern eyes perhaps the noblest of the early Teutonic virtues is the supreme *loyalty* which inspired the followers of any chief or king. A man could choose whom he would follow, or whether he would attach himself to any one, but, once his choice was made and he had become the 'man' of some chief, nothing could wean him from his allegiance. Loyalty transcends all other duties, and will lead men to arraign the gods, and defy Fate itself, as they fall in the last rally by their leader's side, like Bjarki in the story of Hrolf Kraki, as told by Saxo. Tacitus and the *Beowulf* concur in saying that it is a reproach for life to have survived the chief in battle. Even in the 12th cent., when the old heathen virtues were dying out, the young Icelander Ari Thorgeirsson makes a shield of his body for his Norwegian lord, standing weaponless between him and his enemies. This is self-sacrifice born of courage, but the idea of loyalty fostered other virtues besides that of courage—virtues which otherwise would hardly have flourished on Teutonic soil. Tacitus tells us that the chief fights for victory, his vassals fight for their chief; that to ascribe one's own brave deeds to one's chief, to increase his renown, is the height of loyalty. The self-forgetfulness, the abnegation involved can be gauged only by those who realize that personal fame was the highest earthly good of the Teuton warrior. Loyalty was not confined, however, to the warriors by profession, but permeated the whole fabric of Teutonic society. Every little Icelandic farmer expects that his 'home-men,' his farm-labourers, will cheerfully sacrifice their lives on his behalf, and the obligation even extends to the chance guest, so that many a Norwegian merchant in Iceland lost his life in a quarrel that was not his. The call of loyalty is yet sterner in one case on record.

Ingimund the Old has been slain by a base and unworthy hand; and, on receiving the news, one of his old shipmates declares: 'It is not fit for the friends of Ingimund to live,' and falls on his sword. His example is followed by another of Ingimund's old companions (*Vatsdœla Saga*, ch. 23).

We may suppose that this spirit of devotion to a chosen chief had its root in the ancient tribal solidarity which made the whole kindred adopt the cause of any member of it. Only in Northern Germany and the Netherlands, however, do we find this devotion to the kindred unimpaired in historical times, and there it persisted for centuries.

A chronicler of the little land of Dithmarschen, writing after the end of the 16th cent., describes the old kindreds of that country, and how the members of it protected the weakest and poorest against outside aggression, and would risk life and limb for any member of their kin (*Neocorus*, ed. Dahlmann, Kiel, 1827, i. 206). But in Scandinavia loyalty to the chief seems to have been far more binding than loyalty to the kin. Treachery to a master brings infamy, and, in fact, is hardly mentioned in the old tales, but the slaying of kinsmen is frequently dealt with, and, though theoretically disapproved, it does not alienate all sympathy.

Eirik Blodöx is said to have burnt his half-brother Rögnvald in his house, at the bidding of their father, Harald Fairhair, because Rögnvald had become addicted to sorcery; and 'much was that work praised,' says *Heimskringla* (Morris-Magnússon's tr. i. 133).

How far the new idea of loyalty transcends the duty to the kindred is disclosed in the *Egilssaga* (ch. 22 ff., F. Jónsson's ed., Copenhagen, 1886–88), where King Harald Fairhair treacherously attacks and slays Thorolf, one of his own men, wrongly suspected of treachery. Thorolf has kinsmen, as well as comrades, in the king's bodyguard; but, so far from attempting vengeance on the king or the slanderers, they do not even ask for compensation (wergild) for themselves. Hagen, in the *Waltharilied*, overlooks the slaying of his nephew by Walther, his sworn friend, but cannot refuse to attack him when his king's honour is involved (*Ekkehard's Waltharilied*, Germ. tr., H. Althof, Leipzig, 1902, lines 1109, 1112). Rüdiger, in the *Nibelungenlied*, makes a similar choice between lord and friend (line 2152 ff).

In England this loyalty to the king early developed into *patriotism*, finding favourable soil in the sufferings of the country from the Danes, and in the appeal which such a king as Alfred made to the hearts of his subjects. In other Teutonic States, however, an effective patriotism was a plant of slow growth; and of Norway and Iceland it may be truly said that their foes were of their own household.

(4) In return for the loyalty of his subordinates the chief was expected to be *generous*—'mild,' as all the old Teutonic tongues phrase it,—and the Northern praise of princes, as 'gold-scatterer,' 'bracelet-spender,' and so forth, indicates the form which their generosity took. According to modern ideas, this quality was unduly glorified, and we may guess that it could cover a considerable degree of unscrupulousness in the method of acquiring wealth, as well as a disregard for the general welfare of the kingdom. But its glorification was natural in a State where the fighting man had no fixed wages, and where the poets were the servants of the prince. Even Walther von der Vogelweide considers it reasonable to estimate kings by their generosity towards himself. The chronicler of the Normans already quoted tells us that 'their chief men were especially lavish, through their desire of good report.' His previous cryptic utterance, that they hold a certain mean between lavishness and greed, is perhaps to be explained by the system of gifts and counter-gifts prevalent all through Teutonic society. Tacitus, indeed, says that the Germans 'expect no return for what they give' (*Germ.* xxi.), but the testimony of the most worldly-wise of the old Edda poems is perhaps more deserving of acceptance: 'I never found a man so "mild," or so free with food, that he was loath to receive reward' (*Hávamál*, 40). But the generosity manifested itself also in less questionable forms. The quality which makes it a 'nithing's deed' to take advantage of weakness, and the generous appreciation of an enemy's virtues, merge into the love of 'fair play,' so characteristic of the Teutonic races.

Even King Eirik Blodöx, guilty of the death of several of his half-brothers, cannot kill his deadly enemy Egill, who, wrecked on his shores, has thrown himself on Eirik's mercy; because to do so under such circumstances would be a 'nithing's act' (*Egilssaga*, ch. 61). In a similar position, Kári, who has killed over a dozen of Flosi's companions, is not mistaken in going to Flosi's house and relying on his generosity (*Njála*, ch. 159).

The opposite of a 'nithing' is a *góðr drengr*, a characteristic Northern phrase, only to be translated 'a good fellow,' 'an honourable man'—in fact, exactly what is meant by 'gentleman' when that word is used to denote certain moral qualities.

(5) A kindred duty to that of generosity is *hospitality*, which is even more binding. 'To exclude any human being from the roof is thought impious,' says Tacitus (*Germ.* xxi.); and the same idea is found all over Teutonic Europe in early times, and in Iceland to this day.

(6) *Truth* was a highly esteemed virtue among the Germanic race. Tacitus (*Germ.* xxii.) calls them 'a race without natural or acquired cunning'—an estimate which may be partly inspired by the natural attitude of a sophisticated race towards a barbaric one; for the mediæval chronicler already quoted calls the Normans 'gens astutissima,' and the somewhat cynical Edda poem *Hávamál* has no hesitation in advising its hearers to flatter a false friend and to reward deceit with lies (*Háv.* 42, 45). But Saxo, the early historian of the Danes, says that 'the illustrious men of old thought lying most dishonourable'; and it may be said that the sagas reveal a high ideal of straightforwardness in general. It is characteristic of the Northern trend of thought that there was no sin in a slaying openly confessed, but an indescribable baseness in a secret or a midnight slaying, which was qualified as murder. To lie to a friend would certainly have been thought a baseness, and we meet with individuals who would rather risk their lives than impair their self-respect by lying. The accounts of the early Norwegian kings and their courts reveal that flattery, at least, was not one of the besetting sins of the Northmen. Great sanctity attached to oaths and promises of every sort, and nothing was held to excuse breaches of faith, though instances, especially of truce-breaking, are found scattered up and down the sagas—oftener after than before the introduction of Christianity. To the recognition of an obligation to strict veracity in the recital of stories we owe much of our knowledge of ancient Teutonic customs.

(7) *Modesty*, strangely enough, entered into the ideal of the perfect warrior in Iceland, and boastfulness was regarded with more contempt than censure. In the epics of the heroic age, however, boasting is freely indulged in.

So far we have been dealing with qualities or obligations which are still recognized as virtues and duties in modern ethical systems.

(8) *Vengeance*, however, has not only been degraded from its paramount position among duties, but is placed in a different category altogether. We catch glimpses of a time when it was an absolutely binding obligation, but in all Teutonic States the system of money compensation had been adopted before historical times, to mitigate the recognized evils of blood-feuds. But among a race which, from the time of Tacitus onwards (*Germ.* xiv.), rather scorned peaceful methods of money-getting, it was hardly to be expected that every one should be willing to 'put his (slain) kinsman in his pocket,' as the saying went. The Icelandic sagas give such a vivid picture of the havoc wrought by blood-feuds that the custom of vengeance in the early history of that country is a matter of common knowledge, but its persistence in country districts in Germany is not so generally realized. In many parts vengeance was held to be obligatory, not only on nobles, down to the 16th century.

Thus our sources tell us that in 1577 a Holstein peasant named Graumann, who had more or less accidentally slain another, was killed by the deceased's brothers with 48 wounds. These brothers were proceeded against in a court of law, but were never condemned. In Frisia, as late as the 13th cent., it seems to have been customary for the relatives to hang up the corpse of their slain kinsman under their roof until they had acquitted themselves of the duty of vengeance. In England, so early Christianized, the current ideas concerning this duty are quaintly revealed in a verse made on King Edward's death in 979:

> 'Him would not avenge
> his earthly kinsmen,
> him has his heavenly father
> greatly avenged' (*Saxon Chronicle, sub anno* 976 [Gomme's tr. 1909]).

The idea that vengeance alone can wipe out an insult was prevalent, and has persisted to this day in the Continental attitude towards duelling (*q.v.*).

(9) In the matter of *sexual morality* the heathen Germanic races have always had a high reputation since the time of Tacitus, and on this point Christian priests have added their testimony to his (see Salvian, *de Gubern. Dei*, bk. viii.).

'Their marriage code,' says Tacitus, 'is strict, and no part of their manners is more praiseworthy. Almost alone among barbarians they are content with one wife, except a very few among them, and these not from sensuality, but because their noble birth procures for them many offers of alliance' (*Germ.* xviii.). 'Clandestine correspondence is equally unknown to men and to women' (*ib.* xix.).

This description needs little modification to fit the customs of a much later age. It was no reproach to King Harald Fairhair to have several wives, but it must be especially noted that this polygamy involved no *harīm*, for it seems that for the most part each wife continued to live with her own family or in the part of the country where she was born. The Icelandic sagas indicate that divorce was easily obtainable—apparently on trifling grounds; but the fates of Brynhild and Sigurd, of Gudrun and Kjartan in the *Laxdale Saga*, of Björn the Hitdale Champion, and Oddny, show that the persons wrongly mated make no attempt to throw off the marriage bond in order to be free to marry another—presumably because such action was held to be base. It is surely not entirely out of jealousy that the Icelandic Gudrun brings about the death of the man she loves, but because only so can she rid herself of the degradation of preferring another man to her husband, and of the continual temptation of that other's presence. She prefers his death to dishonour.

Tacitus tells us of the punishment of a faithless wife; but later sources, Icelandic and Norwegian, mention no penalty for the woman, though they speak of a heavy fine to be exacted from her lover. The old Norwegian laws make the ecclesiastical fine for conjugal infidelity the same for either sex.

(10) Perhaps the most remarkable feature of the ethical ideas of the Teutons is that *the ethical ideal was the same for both sexes.* Women do not fight, but the wife, according to Tacitus, does not 'stand apart from aspirations after noble deeds or from the perils of war, but is her husband's partner in toil and danger, destined to suffer and to dare with him alike in peace and war' (*Germ.* xviii.); and earlier he tells us how the dauntless courage of the women has been known to rally wavering forces in battle (*ib.* viii.). For Helen of Troy, for the Irish Deirdre, beauty and an unhappy love have been sufficient titles to immortality; but to fire the Germanic imagination women have needed these and more: the character that shapes destiny, the courage which does not blench before responsibility, the truth which scorns to evade consequences. Such are Brynhild, Gudrun, Hervör, Svanhild, and the Anglo-Saxon Hildegyth of the Waldere-fragment (C. W. M. Grein, *Angelsächs. Bibliothek*, i. [1883] 7 f.). It is perhaps significant that Germanic hero-legend exalts no woman who has yielded to a dishonourable love. The Icelandic sagas not only attribute these greater virtues to women, but expect them to urge the love of fair play and a high sense of honour on their men-folk, if these fail to realize their public responsibilities. Griselda is no Teutonic conception. In one minor detail a sharp line is drawn between the sexes: drinking to excess at feasts is no reproach to men, but is unheard of in women.

3. Ethical motives and sanctions.—(1) If we regard the ethical ideas of the Teutonic races as a whole, the main point which emerges is that they are the outcome of a sound *utilitarianism*, not of chance tradition or custom. We cannot even call this in question with regard to the ideals of generosity and vengeance, if we bear in mind the social and economic conditions of the time. Their ideal of generosity has struck moderns as blameable lavishness, but it originated in an epoch when wealth was of little use save to attach warriors to one's cause. Otherwise capital had no beneficent functions to perform, no industrial enterprises to maintain; and, where gold and chattels were hoarded in few hands, they became dangerous to the freedom of the rest of the community, and liable to excite the cupidity of suspicious neighbours. The same defence can obviously be made for the duty of vengeance, which, in the absence of a powerful State executive, must be considered, with Lecky (*Hist. of European Morals*[2], 1897, i. 41), to have been 'the one bulwark against social anarchy.' The moral outlook was limited to the community, and actions were judged—consciously or unconsciously—from its standpoint. This is clearly exemplified in the attitude towards human sacrifice. Persons outside the pale may be immolated for the good of the community, but public opinion condemned and ostracized any individual suspected of practising such rites for his own personal advantage (*Vatsdœla Saga*, ch. 16. 30). The same distinction can be traced in the similar attitude towards magic, and also in the treatment of the aged and infirm at moments when the life of the community was threatened (see OLD AGE [Teutonic]). It is more pleasant to recognize the sense of social obligation, of duty towards the community, in the 'courtesy' so carefully practised between man and man, in the acceptance of arbitration in disputes, and still more in the conscious sacrifice of self-interest to the claims of law and order. 'We must allow Snorri to carry out the law,' says his enemy Arnkell in *Eyrbiggja Saga* (Morris-Magnússon, *The Ere-dwellers*, 1892, ch. 22); and the idea constantly recurs in all Scandinavian literatures. The political genius of the Teutonic races was born out of the conflict between this sense of responsibility—the recognition that man does not live to himself alone—and the intense independence and powerful will of the individual. Perhaps the idea of duty to the community finds its noblest expression in the lofty conception that men are not freed from its claims even in the other world, but must band together in fellowship with the gods for one last vain fight against the forces of evil and of destruction, before the end of the world (see DOOM).

(2) The Teutonic races had too strong a tendency to look to motives, too keen an interest in the clash of character with circumstances, for *custom* to become as binding a social sanction among them as in many primitive societies. *Religion*, also, had little force as a moral sanction, though we note that, in the ancient formula, the 'wrath of the gods' is declared to follow 'truce-breaking.' And there was probably some notion of divine sanction in the carefully ordered duels which in Europe seem to have been the heathen forerunners of the ecclesiastical ordeal. Cf. art. DUELLING.

(3) Of external sanctions, by far the most powerful was *public opinion.* All the condemnation the Icelandic sagas usually allow themselves is to say that such and such an act was 'ill spoken of.' And, if the condemnation of the community was strongly felt as a deterrent to crime, far more did its praise act as an incentive to virtue. From the time of their supremacy in Europe until their racial consciousness was merged in their citizenship of the Roman Church, the quest of glory called forth much that was best in the Teutonic race; and in judging it as a motive we must remember that there has hardly been an epoch in the world's history when a man might gain so wide and lasting a renown—a fame that extended as far as the Teutonic race, so that the selfsame hero might be sung from the north of Africa to Greenland. We cannot

wonder that even the cynical *Hávamál* is inspired to the noble verse:

> 'Chattels die, kinsmen die,
> One dies oneself also;
> But fame dies never
> For him who has won it worthily' (*Hdv.* 76).

(4) But the deepest, most potent sanction of morality was an internal one: the sense of personal integrity, the sturdy *self-respect*, the fear of that sense of degradation which was probably as near as the heathen Teuton ever approached to the sense of sin.

LITERATURE.—**Tacitus**, *Germania*; *the Older Edda* (B. Sijmon's text, Halle, 1888–1901; an English tr. by O. Bray, London, 1907, and in Vigfússon-Powell's *Corpus Poeticum Boreale*, Oxford, 1883); *the Icelandic Sagas* (some of which have been translated by Morris-Magnússon, in the Saga Library, etc.); *Njálssaga* and *Gísla Saga* have been translated by G. W. Dasent (Edinburgh, *Nj.*, new ed. 1900, *Gisla*, 1866); and *Laxdale Saga*, by A. C. Press (London [2nd ed. 1906]). **O. Jiriczek**, *Deutsche Heldensage*, Strassburg, 1898 (Eng. tr. by M. Bentinck-Smith, London, 1902), treats the older epics. Little attention has been paid to the subject by modern scholars. **A. Olrik's** *Nordisches Geistesleben*, Heidelberg, 1908, is an able and sympathetic work; and the last chapter of **Chantepie de la Saussaye's** *Religion of the Teutons*, Boston, 1902, is valuable. See also **H. M. Chadwick**, *The Heroic Age*, Cambridge, 1912, ch. xv. ff. **A. P. Fors**, *The Ethical World-Conception of the Norse People*, Chicago, 1904, should be used with great caution.

B. S. PHILLPOTTS.

ETHNOLOGY.—1. Definition.—Ethnology is that section of Anthropology (the science of man in general) which deals systematically with the various branches of mankind in detail. It is not merely descriptive (Ethnography), but aims at co-ordinating all known data bearing on the inter-relations of the several members of the human family, regarded not as independent groups, but as mutually related divisions of mankind. As so defined, Ethnology assumes a genetic connexion between these divisions; and the most important problem which it has to solve is whether all races really constitute not distinct species, still less genera, but only varieties of a single species of a single genus.

Polygenism, which postulates a given number of distinct groups independently originating in so many distinct geographical areas—the actual number of these distinct groups and areas ranging from about four to sixteen or even more—is certainly not yet extinct. But the tendency of modern thought is undoubtedly towards *Monogenism*, which postulates only one such distinct group and one such distinct area, with four main or relatively fundamental divisions separately evolved in four corresponding geographical areas reached by migration from a single cradle-land. A return is thus made after much 'storm and stress' to the sober teachings of Linné, in whose Order of ANTHROPOMORPHA man appears as one genus with one species, 'cujus varietates *Europæus albus, Americanus rufescens, Asiaticus fuscus, Africanus niger*' (*Systema Naturæ*, ed. 1756, p. 3). This scheme, forming the solid basis of all rightly directed ethnological studies, is frankly accepted by Sir William Flower, in whose Sub-Order of ANTHROPOIDEA the *Hominidæ* (Linné's *varietates*) constitute the fifth and highest family, coming nearest to, but still independent of, the *Simiidæ*, that is, the four groups of the so-called man-apes: Gibbon, Chimpanzee, Gorilla, Orang-utan.

These *Hominidæ*, with their numerous diverging and converging sub-forms, are the proper study of Ethnology, which thus seeks to determine their origin, primeval home, antiquity, and early migrations, their distinctive physical and mental characters, social and cultural developments, and, especially for our purpose, their religious notions, not as separate units, but as interconnected members of the human family.

2. Specific unity of mankind.—(*a*) Perhaps the most convincing proof of common descent from one stock is afforded by what Broca calls their *eugenesis*, the complete and permanent fertility of unions between all races *inter se*. Such crossings between the highest and the lowest and all intervening groups have taken place in all ages, and this physiological test has been so universally applied that there are no longer any pure races, except perhaps a few isolated groups, such as the Andamanese, the Fuegians, and some African and Oceanic negritos. Miscegenation is everywhere the rule, and all peoples are now essentially hybrids, representing both diverging and converging types of the original prototypes, which must now be regarded as mainly ideal. Already in the Stone Ages we have intermingling of long-heads from North Africa with short-heads from Asia, resulting in the present mixed Europeans. In recent times these Europeans migrating to the New World have formed fresh amalgams with the aborigines; and the Hispano-American and Lusitano-American Mestizos now number little short of 50,000,000, and in many places (Mexico, Salvador, Colombia, Peru, Brazil) are steadily increasing, with little accession of fresh blood from Europe. Even in Anglo-Saxon America the present Indians are largely mixed with whites and negroes, and 'we find the rather unexpected result that the fertility among half-breed women is considerably larger than among full-blood women' (F. Boas). The Bovianders of British Guiana form a vigorous half-caste community, 'descendants of the old Dutch settlers by Indian squaws' (Henry Kirke), and most of the present South African Hottentots are also Dutch and native half-breeds. To realize the full force of this argument, we have only to consider how impossible such *eugenesis* would be on the Polygenist assumption. Distinct human species originating in Pliocene or at least early Pleistocene times could not now be racially fertile, and their unions would serve only to illustrate the opposite law of *kakogenesis*.

(*b*) Specific unity is further shown in the prevailing physical and mental uniformity of all peoples. As these points will again engage our attention, it will suffice here to remark with E. B. Tylor that 'all tribes of men, from the blackest to the whitest, the most savage to the most cultured, have such general likeness, in the structure of their bodies and the working of their minds, as is easiest and best accounted for by their being descended from a common ancestry, however distant' (*Anthropology*, p. 5).

But, it is urged on linguistic grounds, languages differ specifically and even generically, and hence cannot be reduced to a single stock, to a common centre of evolution. This, says Abel Hovelacque, 'is for us sufficient proof of the original plurality of the races that have been developed with them'; that is, with these irreducible forms of speech. This reasoning still passes current, and, although involving a patent fallacy, is perhaps the chief present mainstay of the Polygenist school. How fallacious it is will at once become evident when we reflect that the stocks in question are reckoned not by tens or scores, but literally by the hundred, so that *quod nimis probat nihil probat*. In the United States and the Dominion of Canada alone Powell enumerates about sixty stock languages; and as, on this hypothesis, each of these represents a stock race, we should have in North America alone some sixty specifically distinct human groups, though *de facto* all are admittedly very much alike, scarcely distinguishable physically or mentally one from the other. The facts relied upon merely show that race and speech are not convertible terms, that there is no arguing from one to the other; and this may now be taken as axiomatic in Ethnology.

3. Origin: centre of dispersion: migratory routes.—Specific unity may thus be removed from the sphere of speculation, and accepted as an established fact with all its far-reaching consequences. A first consequence is that man, being one, had but one cradle, whence he peopled the earth by migration. This cradle has been sought in all quarters of the globe—in the Arctic regions now covered with ice, in the Austral lands now flooded by the Indian Ocean, in the Eastern and Western hemispheres, in Asia the reputed *officina gentium*, in Africa, and now (by Wilser and others) in Europe, and more particularly in Scandinavia (South Sweden). But none of these lands has made good its claim, and the tendency now is to look for the centre of origin and dispersion in South-East Asia, where it breaks away into the insular Malaysian world.

The latter view, which for the present at least may be said to hold the field, has acquired a certain consistency from the discovery made in 1892 by Eugène Dubois of some distinctly human remains embedded in the late Pliocene deposits of the Solo river in the Trinil district of East Java. These highly fossilized remains of *Pithecanthropus erectus*, as he has been named by the finder, include a femur, two molars, and portion of a skull, and are regarded by Manouvrier, Deniker, Hepburn, and most other competent judges, as undoubtedly those of a human precursor. The great capacity of the skull (900 to 1000 cubic centimetres) shows that it could not have belonged to any of the allied anthropoids, none of which even now exceeds 500 c.c., while the perfectly human femur makes it clear that this Javanese prototype could already walk erect. In the accompanying diagram he is seen to diverge, not from any of the living Simians, but from a common anthropoid stem having its roots far back in the Miocene; and that is the now commonly accepted view regarding the line of

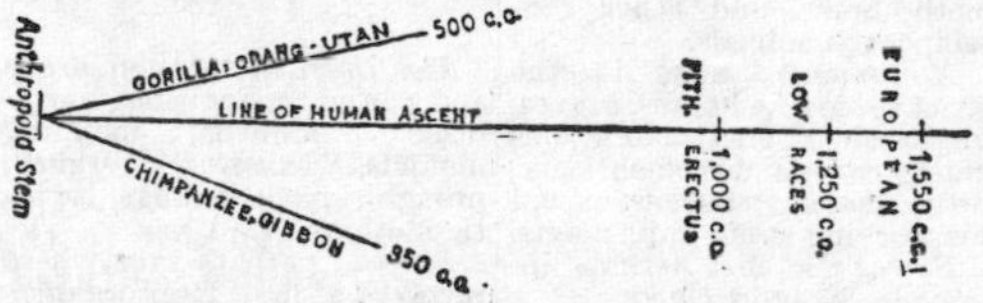

human ascent. The same diagram shows that, as regards its mental powers, as indicated by its cranial capacity, the Javanese 'missing link' held a position about midway between Orang-utan and the present average European, while the present low races (Bushman, Vaalpen, Botocudo, Aeta, and Semang) stand about midway between these two.

Ethnology thus seems to have at last found a sure starting-point for the evolution and dispersion of mankind over the globe. For the Javanese remains, long antedating the *Neanderthal*, that is, the lowest human cranium previously described, present the physical characters which were anticipated in Pliocene as compared with Pleistocene man, should his remains ever be discovered. His erect position implies a perfectly prehensile hand, the chief instrument of human progress, while the cranial capacity suggests vocal organs sufficiently developed for articulate speech. *P. erectus* was thus well equipped for his long migrations round the globe, and it is safe to conjecture that without such equipment he never could have completed the journey. Physically he was far too helpless to contend with the great Pliocene fauna that barred the path. But, armed with stone, wooden, bone, and other weapons that lay at hand, and endowed with mental powers far beyond those of all opponents, he was assured of success from the first, and eventually became the one living species whose *habitat* coincided with the habitable world. He certainly had not yet acquired any knowledge of navigation. But such knowledge was not needed to cross inland seas, open waters, and broad estuaries.

At the time of the first migratory movements, the Indo-African Continent, the existence of which was established by the geologists of the Indian Geological Survey, still presented almost continuous land across the present Indian Ocean, between the Deccan, Madagascar, and South Africa. The shallow inland waters, even now nowhere exceeding fifty fathoms in depth, had not yet transformed into great archipelagoes the Sunda region (Borneo, Sumatra, Java), which is now separated by narrow channels from the Asiatic mainland. The Australian Continent was connected across Torres Strait with New Guinea, and extended much farther west than at present. New Zealand also occupied a far wider area, while the recent borings in the island of Funafuti in the Ellice group (1897) leave little doubt that Polynesia itself is to a large extent a region of comparatively recent subsidence. In the northern hemisphere Africa, as proved by the range of the southern fauna (hyæna, elephant, hippopotamus, cave lion, etc.), was still connected with Europe at least at three points — across the Strait of Gibraltar; between Tunis, Pantellaria, Malta, Sicily, and Italy; and, farther east, between Cyrenaica and Greece, across the present Ægean waters. Lastly, Britain still formed part of the European mainland, while almost continuous land appears to have extended in both directions, across Bering Strait to Alaska, and from North-West Europe through the Faroes and Iceland to Greenland and North America. Here, therefore, are sufficient land connexions for early man to have gradually spread from his Indo-Malaysian home to the uttermost confines of the habitable globe. That he did so is an established fact, as will be seen; and, if the routes here suggested as followed by him may seem somewhat speculative, they must still be accepted, because there were no others available during the required late Tertiary (Pliocene and Pleistocene) period.

4. Areas and lines of specialization from the Pleistocene precursors.—A considerable mass of trustworthy evidence has in recent years been brought together from all quarters to show that the whole world had really been occupied by primitive man during this late Tertiary period, which is synchronous with the last recorded recurrent invasions of ice in the northern and southern hemispheres. The 'Ice Age' — an expression covering a pre-glacial, two or more inter-glacial, and a post-glacial epoch—thus coincides with the first migratory movements, which may be conceived as advancing and receding with the spread and retreat of the ice-cap, but were all completed, if not during the inter-glacial, certainly in the post-glacial (early Pleistocene), epoch. That is to say, the earth was first occupied by a generalized Pleistocene prototype, which became independently specialized into the four fundamental varieties in the four above-mentioned geographical areas. The main divisions of mankind may thus be regarded as respectively descended in their several zones from four undifferentiated Pleistocene ancestral groups.

This view of human origins at once removes some of the greatest difficulties that systematists have hitherto had to contend with, while at the same time accounting in a reasonable way for many phenomena which must otherwise remain inexplicable. Thus the four varieties, springing independently from four generalized Pleistocene ancestors, become each specialized in its own domain, and need no longer be derived one from the other—black from white, yellow from black, and so on,—a theory which both on physiological and on physiographical grounds has always presented all but insurmountable difficulties to the anthropologist. Indeed, no anthropologist has yet seriously grappled with the insoluble problem presented by conditions which, as we now see, have no existence. To suppose that some highly specialized group, say, originally black, migrating from continent to continent, became white in one region or yellow in another is a violent assumption which can never be verified, and should on reflexion be rejected. Had such a group passed from its proper zone to another essentially different environment, it would probably have died out long before it had time to become acclimatized. The fundamental racial characters are the result of slow adaptation to their special surroundings. They are what climate, soil, diet, heredity, natural selection, and time have made them, and are of too long standing to be effaced or blurred except by miscegenation, a process rendered possible by primordial unity.

5. Early works of man: Old and New Stone Ages.—By descent from common Pleistocene ancestors is further readily explained the surprising resemblance, amounting to identity, which is everywhere presented both by the earliest skeletal remains of primitive man and by the first rude objects of primitive culture. Such are the skulls found in West and Central Europe, in Egypt, California, Brazil, and other parts of South America; the stone implements occurring in prodigious quantities in Britain, France, North and South Africa, Somaliland, India, the United States, Argentina, Fuegia; the social and religious institutions of primitive man in Australia, Melanesia, Africa, North and South America. Certain Australian skulls seem cast in the same mould as the Neanderthal, the oldest yet found in Europe. Sir John Evans, the first judge on this subject, tells us that rude stone objects brought from the most distant lands are 'so identical in form and character that they might have been manufactured by the same hands. On the banks of the Nile, many hundred feet above its present level, implements of the European types have been discovered, while in Somaliland Mr. Seton-Karr has collected a large number of implements which . . . might have been dug out of the drift deposits of the Somme and the Seine, the Thames or the ancient Solent' (*Inaugural Address, Brit. Assoc.*, Toronto, 1897). Similarly, the animistic concept is found to be equally well illustrated in the religious notions of the Melanesians, the West African Negroes, and the natives of British Guiana (see below).

To the Pleistocene or Post-Pliocene, answering roughly to the Quaternary of French writers and the Diluvium of the Germans, has been assigned a duration of from 200,000 to 300,000 years, and this may be taken as the measure of early man and all his works. It covers two distinct periods of cultural growth, the PALÆOLITHIC or OLD STONE, and the NEOLITHIC or NEW STONE AGE, these being so named from the material, chiefly flint, everywhere used by primitive peoples in the manufacture of their weapons and implements of all kinds. As many are still in the primitive state, it is obvious that here Old and New do not imply time sequence absolutely, but only relatively to those regions, mainly Europe, North Africa, and America, where the subject has been most thoroughly investigated. Even in these regions Old and New do not always follow in chronological order, since the two stages still flourish side by side in some places, as, for instance, amongst the North American aborigines. The distinction between the two periods is based especially on the different treatment of the material, which during the immeasurably longer Old Stone Age was merely chipped, flaked, or otherwise rudely fashioned, but in the New more carefully worked and polished. Hence experts assure us that they can always tell a *palæolith* from a *neolith*, although a warning note has recently been raised, amongst others, by A. Thieullen, who, speaking from personal observation, declares that 'toutes les formes, même les plus archaïques, ont été fabriquées simultanément avec les formes plus nouvelles, à tous les âges de la pierre, et cela jusqu' aux derniers jours de la pierre polie' (*Hommage à Boucher de Perthes*, Paris, 1904, p. 13). Nevertheless, Sir John Evans' great test of a palæolith—the bulb of percussion—still holds good, while it is safe to say that no well finished and polished neoliths were produced in the early period.

Other distinguishing features of Palæolithic and Neolithic culture are here tabulated in parallel columns for more convenient comparative study:

OLD STONE AGE.	NEW STONE AGE.
Fire: at first known only, later partly under control; could be preserved when kindled by natural means.	*Fire*: under complete control; could be artificially kindled and preserved.
Food: at first mainly vegetable, then animal also; mostly perhaps eaten raw; obtained by hunting and fishing only.	*Food*: vegetable and animal, obtained by hunting, fishing, stock-breeding, and tillage; mostly cooked.
Cultivated plants: none.	*Cultivated plants*: numerous: cereals, vegetables, fruits.
Industries: limited to the making of stone and bone implements, the former never ground or polished, but of progressively improved types, and later embellished with artistic carvings, chiefly of the mammoth, horse, and other contemporary animals.	*Industries*: polished stone implements of diverse types; spinning, weaving, basketry, mining, pottery hand-made without the wheel and poorly ornamented; artistic sense low at first, later well developed.
Monuments: none in the strict sense; no houses, graves, or barrows at first; habitations chiefly caves and rock-shelters; no permanent stations except for working stone implements.	*Monuments*: very numerous and varied: monolithic, megalithic; dolmens, menhirs, mounds, barrows, kurgans, nuraghi, pile-dwellings, aquatic stations.
Speech: at first perhaps inorganic, later involved.	*Speech*: perhaps everywhere involved at first, later organic.
Social groups: the family, later the clan reckoning kinship through the female line.	*Social groups*: the family, the clan, the gens reckoning kinship through the male line, the tribe, the phratry, the *civitas* (city-State).
Letters: none, unless certain pebble-markings found in the Mas d'Azil caves, Dordogne, be regarded, with M. Piette, as a kind of crude script, with ideographic if not phonetic values.	*Letters*: very general, and well developed beyond the pictographic to the ideographic, the syllabic, and even alphabetic (purely phonetic) stage.
Religion: generally supposed to be non-existent. But cave burials in late Palæolithic times suggest funeral rites. The painted figures also lately discovered by MM. Rivière and Capitan in caves of the Madelenian epoch (see below) seem to afford evidence of religious notions at that time. M. Salomon Reinach is inclined to think that some, especially of the animal figures, may have served as totemic or tribal symbols, so that such pictures may have exercised a magic influence. If so, this would imply the existence of religious ideas in still earlier times.	*Religion*: prevalent and well developed everywhere, as attested beyond doubt by solemn burials in dolmens and barrows, and by crematory ceremonies, mortuary urns, the so-called lachrymary vessels, and other indications of a belief in an after-life. In Neolithic times Animism and Psycholatry, lying at the root of all religion, were well established, in fact, universal, so that Haberlandt seems justified in holding that, as all peoples have always been gifted with the faculty of speech, so all, at least since the late Stone Ages, have been endowed with the religious sentiment.

Here it is to be noticed that the 'hiatus'—the gap or break supposed by some ethnologists to intervene between the two early cultural eras—is now generally discredited. Partial breaks of continuity may have been of local occurrence. But the absolute hiatus here in question is an absurdity. It would imply that the first period of human culture was somehow arrested and extinguished everywhere;

and that then, after a blank of unknown duration, a fresh start was made with the sudden appearance of a new and higher culture, as if dropped ready-made from the clouds. Evidence is now accumulating to show that progress was not arrested but continuous throughout the whole of the first cultural era, which thus tended in favourable localities (South France, the Riviera, North Africa) to merge imperceptibly in the second, so that it is not always possible to draw any hard and fast line between the Old and New Stone Ages.

The Old Stone Age is itself divided into a number of successively progressive eras, the most generally accepted of which, at least for Europe, are: (1) The *Chellian*, so called from Chelles on the Marne, where were first found some of the very oldest and rudest chipped flints, now often called *eoliths*. (2) The *Moustierian*, named from the Cave of Moustier on the Vézère River, Dordogne, which has yielded some improved but still rude spear-heads, scrapers, and other flints of a simple type. (3) The *Solutrian*, from the cave at Solutré near Mâcon, whence come the famous 'laurel-leaf' and some other patterns, showing an immense advance in finish and variety, still unpolished, but so delicate and dainty that they have never since been rivalled or even imitated. Hence an object of true Solutrian type is always genuine, as it cannot be forged like most other 'antiques.' Yet vast numbers have been found not only in Europe but in the United States, where occur whole *caches* ('nests') of these beautiful palæoliths. (4) The *Madelenian*, from the rock-shelter of La Madeleine, also on the Vézère, representing a very long inter- or post-glacial period of steady progress, during which was developed quite a Palæolithic 'school of art.' Here were first brought to light some of those remarkable stone, horn, and even ivory scrapers, gravers, 'harpoons,' ornaments, and statuettes with carvings on the round, and skilful etchings of seals, fishes, reindeer, horses, mammoths, snakes, and man himself, considerable numbers of which occur also in many other stations in Dordogne and elsewhere. The remains found in the Placard Cave, the Charente basin, as well as in the Balsi Rossi caves at Mentone on the Riviera, together with the numerous rock carvings of the neighbouring Ventimiglia district, show distinct interminglings of Old and New Stone Age types, and thus the 'hiatus' vanishes for ever.

The Palæolithic Age gives the measure of the antiquity of man. The Palæolithic remains supply the proof of that antiquity. Many of the Chellian eoliths (Gr ἠώς, 'dawn,' *sc.* of culture) are found *in situ* under conditions and in associations which bespeak very great age. They occur, for instance, in the undisturbed glacial drift (sands, gravels, boulder-clays) of the Ouse, Thames, Somme, Seine, Nile, and other rivers which have since scoured their beds down to depths of 50, 100, and even 400 feet. In Tunisia many have been found under a thick bed of Pleistocene limestone deposited by a river which has since disappeared. The now absolutely arid and lifeless Libyan plateau is strewn with innumerable worked flints, showing that early man inhabited this formerly fertile and well-watered region before it was reduced by the slowly changing climate to a waste of sands. Many objects of human industry have been recovered from Kent's Hole and other caves beneath great masses of stalagmite, while others again are found associated with the now extinct Post-Pliocene fauna. And what changes have taken place even in the comparatively recent New Stone Age, which acquired its greatest development in North Africa (pre-dynastic Egypt), in the Ægean lands (pre-Mycenæan culture), in Italy, Central and West Europe, the British Isles, Scandinavia, and South America (Tiahuanaco)! In Scotland the Neolithic era lasted long enough to witness the formation of the Carse clays, which now stand 40 or 50 feet above sea-level, but then formed the bed of a sound or estuary flowing between North and South Britain. Hence Sir W. Turner's suggestion that after the separation of Britain from the mainland, during the Ice Age, another land connexion, a 'Neolithic land-bridge,' may have enabled Neolithic man to reach Scotland while the upheaved terrace was still clothed with the great forest growths that have since disappeared.

6. Pre-Historic and Historic Ages.—The Neolithic era, to which a duration of from 50,000 to 100,000 years has been ascribed, merges in an ill-defined Pre-Historic period, when stone was gradually superseded by the metals—first copper, then bronze, lastly iron, as correctly stated by Lucretius (*de Rer. Nat.* v. 1286–7):

> 'Posterius ferri vis est aerisque reperta,
> Et prior aeris erat quam ferri cognitus usus.'

To these Pre-Historic times may perhaps be referred most of those popular myths, demi-gods, eponymous heroes, and traditions of real events which even still survive and have supplied the copious materials which were eagerly seized upon and worked up by the early rhapsodists, the founders of new religions, and later legislators (Homer, Hesiod, Zoroaster, Manu, Solon, Lycurgus).

7. Antiquity of the primary types.—With these names, shadowy though most of them be, are ushered in strictly historical times throughout the Aryan world, while in Hamitic and Akkado-Semitic lands more certain and far more ancient records are supplied by the dated monuments, the rock and mural inscriptions and clay tablets of the Nile Valley, South Arabia, and Mesopotamia. With the revelations made by archæologists in these earlier seats of the higher cultures the Historic period itself is constantly receding farther into the background, and we are now assured that the Mesopotamian city of Nippur already possessed a history some 8000 years ago. Thus is approached the period of 10,000 years which may have to be assigned to the Historic Age before the archæological exploration of Egypt and Babylonia is exhausted. From the pictorial and plastic remains here brought to light, as well as from other early sources, it is now placed beyond doubt that the great divisions of the human family had at that time already been fully specialized. Even in the Neolithic era the European type had already been established, as shown by the osseous remains of the 'Cromagnon race,' so called from the cave of that name in Périgord where the first specimens were discovered. Professor Virchow has described a skull of the early Iron period from Wildenroth in Bavaria, which had a cranial capacity of no less than 1585 cubic centimetres, and was in every respect a superb specimen of the regular-featured, long-headed North European. In Egypt, where Oppert finds traces of a well-developed social and political organization dating back to over 13,000 years, Professor Petrie discovered in 1897 the portrait statue of Prince Nenkhetftka of the Vth dynasty (3700 B.C.), a man also described as of 'European features.' Still older is the portrait of Enshagsagna, who reigned over the Babylonian Akkad about 4500 B.C., and had quite regular features which might be 'either Semitic or even Aryan.'

Thus we have documentary evidence that the *Caucasic*, that is, the highest human type, had already been not only evolved, but spread over a wide area (Europe, North Africa, Mesopotamia), some millenniums before the new era. The other chief types (*Mongol*, *Negro*, and even *Negrito*) are also clearly depicted on early Egyptian monuments, so that all the primary groups must have already been differentiated at least in Neolithic times.

8. Nomenclature.—As these main divisions will be dealt with separately, it will here suffice to give a summary statement of the more salient physical and mental characters (such as may be regarded as true racial criteria) by which they have been distinguished throughout the strictly Historic period. With regard to the nomenclature, much of which is purely conventional, it should be noted that the *Ethiopic*, *Negro*, and *Black* are taken as practically synonymous, answering roughly to Linné's *Africanus*, but including also the allied Oceanic blacks commonly called *Papuasians* (Papuans and Melanesians), and *Australasians*, with the now extinct *Tasmanians*. The Ethiopic division thus forms two distinct sections—the *African* or *Western*, and the *Australasian* or *Eastern*, now separated by the intervening waters of the Indian Ocean (see above). This remark applies also to the *Negrito* subdivision, of which there are likewise two sections (*African* and *Oceanic* Negritos). *Mongolic* and *Yellow* are similarly equivalent terms, as are also *American* and *Red*, where 'Yellow' and 'Red' are to be taken in a somewhat elastic sense, as in Linné's corresponding expressions *Asiaticus fuscus* and *Americanus rufescens*. Lastly, *Caucasic* and *White* are the same, answering in a general way to Linné's *Europæus albus*. 'European,' however, can no longer be taken in this wide sense, since the division is now known to have also extended from Pre-Historic times to a large part of Asia, as well as to North Africa, where it most probably originated (Sergi, Keane). The forms *Eurafrican* and *Afro-European* have been proposed; but they leave out Asia, so that nothing better has yet been suggested for Blumenbach's somewhat equivocal *Caucasic*. As here used it does not mean a Caucasian, an inhabitant of the Caucasus, but is the collective name of the white division, of which some natives of the Caucasus (Georgians, Circassians) are or were assumed to be typical members. The three now nearly obsolete terms, *Turanian*, *Allophyllian*, and *Alfuro*, are here discarded as useless, and leading to endless confusion.

As the four divisions have not remained stationary in their respective original homes, but have been subject to great fluctuations during Historic times, in the subjoined general Conspectus are given their *cradle-land*, *later expansion or retreat*, and *present domain*, with approximate population.

9. Religions of primitive and later peoples: evolution of the religious sentiment.—In the treatment of religions, with which we are here more nearly concerned, it is assumed, with most unbiased observers (E. B. Tylor, E. im Thurn, A. B. Ellis, E. S. Hartland, E. Clodd, R. H. Codrington, T. Waitz, F. Ratzel, A. de Quatrefages, J. B. Ambrosetti, F. Boas, P. Ehrenreich, J. W. Powell), that all later developments spring from the first vague notions formed by primitive man of himself and his environment. The absolute starting-point, behind which it seems impossible to get, is everywhere the *dream*, which, as soon as the reasoning faculty is sufficiently awakened, enforces the subtle and apparently metaphysical distinction between soul and body, spirit and matter. 'The dreams which come in sleep to the Indian are to him . . . as real as any of the events of his waking life. To him dream-acts and working-acts differ only in one respect—namely, that the former are done only by the spirit, the latter are done by the spirit in its body. Seeing other men asleep, and afterwards hearing from them the things which they suppose themselves to have done when asleep, the Indian has no difficulty in reconciling that which he hears with the fact that the bodies of the sleepers were in his sight and motionless throughout the time of supposed action, because he never questions that the spirits, *leaving the sleepers*, played their part in dream-adventures.' And thus is explained the at first sight strange fact that 'a savage should be able to form for himself a conception of so immaterial a thing as a spirit.' The quotations are from E. im Thurn (*Among the Indians of Guiana*, Lond. 1883, p. 343 f.), one of the closest students of the savage mind, and they have reference to the British Guiana natives (Caribs, Arawaks), whose religious system is perhaps the most primitive of which we have any clear record.

From this starting-point the development proceeds in two directions, which lead on the one hand to Psycholatry (Spirit-worship, Animism) in its simplest form, on the other to Ancestor- and Nature-worship, the two great factors in all primitive religions. For early man, after the concept of an independent soul is thoroughly realized in his own person, the next step is to extend the idea to his fellow-men, and then to other animals and to plants, that is, to all living organisms, and, lastly, to the inorganic world, to such conspicuous and lifelike objects as the raging torrent, the rolling seas, snowy peaks, frowning crests, steep rocky walls, gloomy gorges, dark woods, trees, crags, clouds, storms, lightning, tornadoes, heavenly bodies, until all Nature becomes animated and everything personified and endowed with a living soul. But this soul emanates, so to say, from his own, and consequently resembles it in all respects, has the same passions, feelings, affections, and differs only in being, perhaps, a little more or a little less powerful; and thus is established the universal principle of *anthropomorphism* (*q.v.*), which pervades all religions from the lowest to the highest. The mental qualities of the individual soul become the norm to which everything is referred, and, when in more advanced stages man likens himself to his deities, he is really fashioning his deities to his own likeness. Hence the intensely anthropomorphic character of the gods of the Babylonians (Anu, Ea, Marduk), the Semites (El, Baal, Jahweh), the Greeks (Zeus, Aphrodite, Apollo). So C. Hill Tout, speaking of the British Columbian Sīciatl tribe, tells us that 'their anthropomorphic conceptions of the animal and vegetable worlds coloured all their lives and thoughts. Even to-day . . . there is still a strong belief in *the human or man-like side of animals, plants, and other objects and forces*' (*JAI* xxxiv. [1904] 28). And so it is everywhere.

Why any spirits, all being of a human nature, should be reverenced or worshipped at all is easily explained by the above remark that some may be more, some less, potent than man himself. The latter are, of course, treated with indifference, while the former are respected and even feared, and have often to be appeased, being for the most part ill-disposed towards mortals, whence the saying that *timor fecit deos*. And, if even a human being was more powerful in life—a tribal chief, for instance, or any great warrior—he would also be more powerful in death, since death is only an extended sleep from which he may and does often return, as in dreams. Hence his survivors naturally suppose that 'the spirit of the dead man, yet living, continues to act just as does the living man in dreams' (im Thurn, p. 344). Thus are sown the germs of the wide-spread Ancestor-worship (*q.v.*), which amongst some peoples almost seems to be the only form of religion, and in some places gives rise to such strange and even sanguinary rites as the horrible 'customs,' now everywhere happily suppressed, of the Gold and Slave Coast Negroes; and the curious notions of the East African Wagiryama people, who suppose that the departed spirits appear in dreams and ask for *pombe* to allay their thirst. So, when it is a-brewing, some is poured out on the graves of the dead, who are asked to drink, and when drunk to fall asleep and cease to disturb the living with their brawls and bickerings. Thus also Dengdit (on whom see *ERE* iv. 707 f.), the rain-giver, god of the Nilotic Dinka Negroes, is endowed with 'Dinka propensities'; while Umvile, god of the neighbouring Golos, is actually 'the father of mankind by his wife, Barachi' (S. L. Cummins, *JAI* xxxiv. 164).

These Golos distinguish things and people from their shadows (*vuvu*), which enter the dreamer's mind in sleep, and after death are spoken of as the souls gone to cloudland. Thus is afforded a first clue to those otherwise inexplicable refinements and distinctions made by primitive psychology between the personal soul and other associated spiritual entities, such as the classical *manes* which 'Orcus habet,' the *umbra* which 'tumulum circum volat,' and the *spiritus* which 'astra petit.' Such are the Egyptian *ba*, 'soul,' *akh*, 'mind,' *ka*, 'existence,' 'being,' *khaba*, 'shade'; such the Greek νοῦς, ψυχή, πνεῦμα; and the Malagasy *saina*, 'soul,' 'mind,' which vanishes at death, *aina*, 'life,' which becomes 'air, thin air,' *matoatoa*, 'ghost,' which hovers round the grave. Such is especially the *kra* of the Gold Coast Negroes, an indwelling soul, which is absolutely distinct and independent of the personal human soul. Both lead a separate existence, and both survive death, the disembodied *kra* becoming again a *sisa*, or wandering spirit, still seeking to return to a human body as a *kra*, while the real soul becomes a *srahman*, or ghost-man, which goes to dead-land. This dead-land is itself a ghost-land, its mountains, forests, and rivers being 'the ghosts of similar natural features which formerly existed in the world. The trees, as they die in the earthly forest, go and join the ranks of the shadowy forest in dead-land' (Ellis), since all things have souls which must die, and, like the human soul, become *edsietos*, departed spirits dwelling in *edsie*, Hades.

It might be supposed that these teachings, implying a belief in the sublime doctrine of immortality quite beyond the mental grasp of savage man, cannot be genuine, but are rather the ideas read into the mind of savage man by his civilized interpreters. But it is not so. Life after death does not imply everlasting life, since the *edsieto* and the *edsie* itself must also die. 'The notion of an absolute immortality of the dead does not appear to be held. If left to themselves the natives do not inquire into such matters as how long the dead live in dead-land; but if a European asks them if they live for ever, they nearly always reply that nothing can live for ever, and that the dead must also die; so that the Negroes, when thinking of dead-land, practically only think of it as inhabited by the ghosts of men who lived in times approaching their own' (Ellis, *The Ewe-speaking Peoples*, London, 1890, p. 108).

Stress has here been laid on the difference between the *kra* and the personal soul, because the distinction is lost sight of in most anthropological writings. To this neglect is due, in great part, the prevalent confusion and the contradictory statements regarding the religious notions of primitive man. A clear understanding of the distinction is also important in other respects. Thus, the same train of thought that evolved the *kra* has likewise evolved the many strange superstitions associated with the widely-diffused belief in 'wer-animals,' that is, 'man-animals' (Old English *wer*, Goth. *wair*, 'man'). As the *kra* can become disembodied and re-enter the human body at pleasure, so during its ramblings in quest of adventures it can enter any other body; and later, when the *kra* and the personal soul are merged in one, the real human soul can do the same. Then, if evilly disposed, it will select the fiercest and most dreaded wild beast to effect its purpose—the wolf in Europe (whence 'wer-wolfism' and 'lycanthropy'); the tiger, bear, or crocodile in Asia; the lion, leopard, hyæna, shark in Africa; the jaguar in America; and so round the globe. The principle extends even to the after-life; and Cummins (*loc. cit.*) tells us that the Nilotic Dinkas believe that the spirits of the dead sometimes take the forms of lions, leopards, hyænas, and such beasts. A transition is thus effected to the *vampire*, a nocturnal demon, or the soul of a dead man who, the Slavs think, leaves its buried corpse to suck the blood of the living (Tylor, *PC*[3], 1891, ii. 192 f.).

From these animalistic notions, themselves the outcome of pure Animism (*q.v.*), directly flow snake-, bear-, and all other kinds of animal- and spirit-worship. During the early phases of social life the safety of the tribe is supposed to be largely dependent on the due observance of the prescribed rites. Hence public worship becomes a matter of general concern, and is entrusted to experts, such as the medicine-man, the wizard, the shaman, the priest. These gradually assume an official as well as a sacred character; they are the pleaders between the people and their tutelary deities, and 'Church and State' are inseparably one. In the tribal council chamber—the Hellenic *prytaneum*, the Roman *capitol*, the N. American *kiva*, the Mangbattu *assembly-hall*—all matters spiritual and temporal are transacted in common. Later, with the growth of general intercourse and increasing trade and wealth, a slow divergence takes place, and the agora and forum stand apart from, but still somewhat overshadowed by, the temple. Sacrifice and ceremonial rites of all kinds now acquire their full development, and are entirely controlled by the sacerdotal caste, which long continues to be an *imperium in imperio*, even exercising a direct influence on public opinion, as witness the death of Socrates. But, divorced from State affairs, religion becomes more introspective, concerned more with liturgies, outward forms, and dogmatic teachings than with personal conduct. In Aralu, the Babylonian Hades, the dead are judged by the goddess Beltis-Allat, and punished or rewarded, not according to the good or bad lives they may have led, but according as they may have neglected the service of the temples, or taken part in sacrifices and offerings made at the shrines of the gods. Many religious systems certainly contain immoral elements, and place low ideals before their votaries. The faithful Muslim, for instance, is rewarded in the after-life with gross sensual pleasures, while in this life such a trivial thing as the use of knife and fork is regarded as sinful. But the general attitude of religion towards ethics is a wide question which cannot here be discussed. See the series of artt. under ETHICS AND MORALITY.

Nor need we be detained with the higher forms of religion and their concomitants—polytheism and other forms of theism, Judaism, Brāhmanism, Buddhism, Shintoism, Christianity, metempsychosis (*avatars*, incarnations), immortality, *nirvāṇa*, *karma*, ordeals, and the like—all of which will be separately dealt with in detail.

10. Conspectus.—

ETHIOPIC, NEGRO, OR BLACK DIVISION.

1. *Western* (*African*) *Section.*

Cradle-land: Africa south of the Sahara.

Later expansion: Madagascar, North Africa,

Southern United States, West Indies, Nicaragua, North-East Brazil, the Guianas.

Population (pure and mixed): Africa, 160,000,000; Madagascar, 3,000,000; America, 20,000,000: total, 183,000,000.

Physical characters: *head* dolichocephalic, *i.e.* long from glabella to occiput; *cephalic index* 72, taking length at 100; *jaws* prognathous; *nose* broad at base, short, flat; *lips* thick, everted, showing the red inner skin; *cheek-bones* rather prominent; *brow* arched; *eye* large, round, black, with yellowish sclerotic; *foot* flat, with low instep and larkspur heel; *leg* slender; *calves* undeveloped; *arms* disproportionately long; *colour* very dark brown and blackish, rarely quite black: *hair* short, black, woolly, flat in cross section, sparse or no beard; *height* above the average, 5 ft. 8 in. to 6 ft. and 6 ft. 4 in. (Turkana).

Mental characters: *temperament and culture*: sensual, unintellectual, fitful, passing readily from tragedy to comedy; mind arrested at puberty, hence unprogressive, this trait being attributed to the early closing of the cranial sutures; no science or letters; few industrial arts beyond agriculture, stock-breeding, weaving, dyeing, pottery, woodwork, and metallurgy (iron, copper); in Benin artistic casting and carving in relief and on the round.

Speech: agglutinating, with both prefixes and postfixes; stock languages numerous in Sudan, one only in Bantuland, besides Negrito, Hottentot, and Bushman tongues; in Madagascar, Malayo-Polynesian exclusively; in America, European *patois* exclusively.

Religion: generally at the stage of simple Animism, Ancestor-worship being on the whole much more prevalent than Nature-worship; no *ens supremum* anywhere; chief deities *Munkulunkulu*, with many variants, along the east coast, *Nzambi*, also with many variants, along the west coast, both intermingled in the interior; witchcraft and ordeals very prevalent; *obeah* and *voudoo* rites, with ceremonial cannibalism surviving in the West Indies, especially Hayti, and in the Guianas; human sacrifices and fetishism in its purest form in Upper Guinea.

Chief Sub-Groups: I. SUDANESE (NEGROES PROPER): *Wolof, Serer, Felup, Timni, Kru, Nalu, Vei*, West Sudan; *Gurma, Mossi, Gurunga*, within the Niger Bend; *Tshi, Ewe, Yoruba*, Gold and Slave Coasts; *Sonrhay, Hausa, Kanuri, Baghirmi, Mosgu, Yedina, Bassa, Michi*, Central Sudan; *Igarra, Ibo, Nempé, Benin, Qua, Igbara, Borgu*, Lower Niger and Oil Rivers (Southern Nigeria); *Maba, Nuba, Dinka, Golo, Shilluk, Bari, Fur, Nuer, Shuli, Bongo*, East Sudan and White Nile; *Zandeh* (*Niam-Niam*), *Mangbattu, Momfu, A-Barmbo, A-Babua*, Welle Basin.

II. BANTUS (NEGROID PEOPLES SOUTH OF SUDAN): *Waganda, Wanyoro*, Lakes Victoria and Albert; *Akikuyu, Akamba, Wapokomo, Wanyika, Wagiryama, Waswahili, Wanyamwezi, Wasagara*, British and German East Africa; *Makua, Batonga, Banyai, Basenga, Achawa, Magwangara*, Portuguese East Africa; *Marotse, Makalanga* (Mashona), *Wayao, Zulu-Kafir, Basuto, Bechuana*, British South Africa; *Ovaherero, Ovampo, Bunda, Eshi, Kongo, Bateke, Mpongwe, Ibea, Duala, Batanga*, West Coast between Orange and Oil Rivers; *Aduma, Bangala, Balolo, Tushilange, Babanda, Vuaregga, Manyuema, Kalunda, Vuarunga, Vuafiba, Baluba, Bayansi*, Congo Free State.

III. ABERRANT AND DOUBTFUL GROUPS: *Fula*, West and Central Sudan; *Fan*, Ogowe and Gabun Basins; *Negrito* (*Akka, Wochua, Batwa, Obongo, Dume* [?], *Doko* [?], *Wandorobbo* [?]), Congo-Welle and Ogowe Basins, Masailand; *Bushmen*, British South Africa; *Hottentots* (*Namaqua, Griqua, Gonaqua, Koraqua, Hill Damaras*), Cape Colony, German South-West Africa; *Vaalpens*, Limpopo River.

2. *Eastern* (*Oceanic*) *Section.*

Cradle-land: Malaysia, Andamans, Philippines, New Guinea, Western Polynesia (Melanesia), Australia, Tasmania. No later expansion.

Present domain: Malay Peninsula, Malaysia east of Flores, Andamans, New Guinea, Melanesia, parts of Philippines, and Australia.

Population: 2,000,000 (?), chiefly in New Guinea and Melanesia.

Physical characters: very variable, differing from the African section chiefly in the *height*, which is about or even below the average of 5 ft. 6 in.; the *hair*, though always black, is rather frizzly ('mop-headed' [Papuasians] or shaggy [Australians]); *nose* often large, straight, and even aquiline, with downward tip; *lips* less thick, and never everted. The eastern Negritos often closely resemble the African, the chief difference being the *colour*, which is always darker (blackish), the *stature*, which is greater, and the *gnathism*, which is sometimes more pronounced (Semangs).

Mental characters: *temperament and culture*: Papuasians boisterous, very cruel and treacherous; head-hunting and cannibalism common, generally more savage than the African; Australians better in all these respects, though at a much lower stage of culture (no tillage or navigation, and cruel puberty-rites); no science or letters anywhere; few industrial arts; elaborate wood-carving and good boat-building in Papuasia.

Speech: archaic forms of the Oceanic (Malayo-Polynesian) stock language everywhere in Melanesia: agglutinating tongues with postfixes in Australia and most of New Guinea; have no terms for the numerals beyond 2 or 3. In the Andamans the one stock language has developed agglutination to a surprising degree, numerous prefixes and postfixes being combined with the alliterative harmony of the Bantu tongues.

Religion: Spirit-worship very prevalent, with *tabu* in Melanesia, and *totemism* in Australia; *mana*, a subtle essence or virtue like the Augustinian *grace*, is a distinctive feature of the Melanesian system, which is otherwise essentially animistic, distinguishing between pure spirits (supernatural beings that never were in a human body) and ghosts, *i.e.* men's disembodied spirits. There are prayer, sacrifice, divination, omens, death and burial rites, also a Hades (*Lolomboetogigi*), with trees and houses, and a ghostly ruler, but no Supreme Being. There is none of all this in Australia and New Guinea, where the religious sentiment is so little developed that many close observers have failed to detect it. The Australian *Bunjil* is too grossly anthropomorphic to be regarded as a spiritual being at all, much less a deity; and we are assured that those who credit these natives with a belief in gods 'have been imposed upon' (Giles). But there are mythical heroes, such as *Nurunderi*, who are already a kind of demi-gods, and may eventually tend to develop Ancestor-worship. Meantime, however, there is 'nothing of the nature of worship, prayer, or sacrifice'—a remark which may also be safely applied to the natives of New

Guinea, and to all the Oceanic Negritos. The Australian totemistic and puberty ceremonies must all be regarded as features of the social life, and in no sense religious institutions.

Sub-Sections: *Papuasians*, including the *Papuans* proper and the *Melanesians*. The Papuans, most typical of all the Oceanic Negroes, occupy most of East Malaysia as far west as Flores inclusive, with nearly the whole of New Guinea. The Melanesians give their name ('Black Islanders') to the Melanesian world, most of which they occupy almost exclusively. The chief groups are New Britain, New Ireland, and the Duke of York, now by the Germans renamed the Bismarck, Archipelago; the Louisiades, Solomons, New Hebrides, Banks, New Caledonia, and Loyalty, with the outlying western part of Fiji. The *Australians*, a highly specialized branch, with marked uniformity of type, speech, and usages, originally scattered thinly over the whole continent, now disappearing; *Tasmanians* of Tasmania, somewhat intermediate between the Australians and the Melanesians, all extinct since about 1876. *Negritos*, formerly wide-spread throughout Malaysia, now reduced to three detached groups: *Andamanese* of the Andaman Islands; *Semangs* and others of the Malay Peninsula; and *Aetas* ('Blacks') of the Philippines, where they are extinct in several islands, but have left a distinct Negrito strain amongst all the other inhabitants (Malayans, Japanese, Chinese, Spaniards).

MONGOLIC OR YELLOW DIVISION.

Cradle-land: probably the Tibetan plateau.

Early expansion: Indo-China, China, North and Central Asia, Malaysia, Mesopotamia (?).

Present domain: Japan, Formosa, China, Korea, Manchuria, Mongolia, Siberia, Turkestan, Tibet, parts of Irania, Armenia, and Caucasia; most of Asia Minor; parts of European Russia, Scandinavia, the Balkan Peninsula, and Hungary; most of Malaysia and Madagascar, here intermingled with the African aborigines.

Population: China, 380,000,000; Japan and Korea, 57,000,000; Mongolia and Manchuria, 15,000,000; Tibet, 6,000,000; Turkestan and Siberia, 8,000,000; Indo-China, 35,000,000; Malaysia, 30,000,000; West Asia and East Europe, 15,000,000: total, 546,000,000.

Physical characters: *head* brachycephalic, *i.e.* short between glabella and occiput; *cephalic index* somewhat variable, but mean about 85, ranging from 80 to 90, and even 95; *jaws* fairly orthognathous; *nose* very short and flat, or snub; *lips* thin, never everted; *cheek-bones* very high and prominent laterally; *brow* low and moderately arched; *eye* small, black, oblique, outer angle slightly elevated, vertical fold of skin over inner canthus (a highly characteristic trait); *foot* normal, artificially deformed in Chinese women; *colour* dirty-yellowish and light-brown (Malays); *hair* uniformly black, lank, coarse, lustreless, rather long, round in transverse section, no beard, but moustache common; *height* about or slightly under the average of 5 ft. 6 in., but tall in North China and Manchuria (5 ft. 8 in. to 5 ft. 10 in.).

Note.—Many grouped as Mongols originally, and some of them still speaking Mongolic tongues, are now largely and even completely assimilated to the Caucasic physical type (Finns, Turks, Bulgarians, Magyars). They are the *Allophyllians* and *Turanians* of the early writers.

Mental characters and culture: *temperament* generally somewhat reserved, sullen, apathetic, outwardly very courteous, but supercilious; very thrifty, frugal, and industrious in China and Japan, elsewhere mostly indolent (Malays, Siamese); nearly all reckless gamblers; science slightly, arts and letters moderately, developed; porcelain, bronze work, ivory carving, and decorative painting scarcely surpassed (China, Japan, Korea formerly), but all plastic and pictorial art defective, lacking perspective, and the human figure mostly caricatured.

Speech: three great linguistic families:

1. *Ural-Altaic* (*Mongolo-Turki*), ranging with great lexical and structural diversity from Lapland to Japan, from the Lena Basin through Turkestan and Asia Minor to Turkey in Europe and Hungary. Japanese and Korean stand quite apart; but all the rest are typical members of the agglutinating order of speech, with unchangeable roots and variable postfixes, cemented together by the principle of vowel harmony.

2. *Tibeto-Indo-Chinese*, from the Himalayas to the Pacific, and from the Great Wall to the Indian Ocean; originally agglutinating, now in every transition of phonetic decay towards monosyllabism, which is not a primitive but a very late condition of articulate speech. In the process of decay innumerable homophones are developed, which have to be distinguished by their tones; hence the members of this family may be called monosyllabic toned languages. Structurally they are isolating, the sentence being made up of unchangeable isolated words, the inter-relations of which are determined not by inflexion or affixes, but by their position, as often in English (*James hit John; John hit James*).

3. *Malayo-Polynesian*, the 'Oceanic' family in a pre-eminent sense, ranging from Madagascar across the Indian and Pacific Oceans to Easter Island, and from Hawaii to New Zealand (Maori); all are more or less agglutinating at various stages of dissolution, but untoned; vocalism predominates, and the vowels are more stable than the consonants—a trait peculiar to this group.

Religion: *Psycholatry* in its widest sense is the dominant note, the worship extending both to the disembodied human soul (Ancestor-worship, which is now perhaps the most prevalent form) and to the innumerable spirits, bad and good (*feng-shui* and *fung-shui*), which people earth, air, water, and all natural objects of the Mongol world (pure Animism). The practical Chinese and Annamese combine both cults, and, while passing their lives in terror of the malevolent circumambient genii, keep the anniversary of 'roast pig day,' as they call their 'All Souls' day,' by littering the graves of the departed with pork, chicken, cakes, and other food. This Spirit-worship still persists elsewhere, and lies at the base of the later pre-historic and historic superimposed cults. Amongst uncultured peoples (Siberians, Yukaghirs, Kamchadales) it takes the form of undisguised *Shamanism*, where the shaman (wizard, medicine-man, not yet priest) is the 'paid medium' of communication between his dupes and the surrounding good and evil spirits. Even in Tibet the primitive shamanistic *Bonbo* (*Boa-ho*) still survives beneath the official *Lamaism*. Nor have the Tibetans yet forgotten their red and black demons, the snake-devil, and especially the fiery tiger-god, father of all the secondary members of this truly 'diabolical pantheon.' In North-East Siberia the tiger is ousted by the bear, and here the Gilyaks, Oronches, and Ainus are all *bear-worshippers*. The historical religions are largely a question of race, all true Mongols of Mongolia, Manchus, Chinese, Indo-Chinese, and Tibetans being at least nominal *Buddhists*; the Turks, Tatars, and most Malays *Muhammadans*; the Finns, Lapps, and Magyars now *Christians*. Other so-called State religions—the *Confucianism* and *Taoism* of China and Annam, the *Shintoism* and *Bushidoism* of Japan—are rather ethical codes, fostered and upheld for political purposes. The 'filial piety,' everywhere inculcated, for the most part means devotion to the reigning dynasty, while the great weight attached to the purely civic as distinguished from the theological virtues—self-mastery, courage (the Roman *virtus*, 'valour'), benevolence, and loyalty—shows that the sole aim of these systems is to nurture good citizens in this world without a thought for the hereafter. Here is no antagonism between religion and ethics, but a complete divorce of one from the other.

Chief Subdivisions: Mongolo-Turks, commonly called Mongolo-Tatars. MONGOL BRANCH: *Khalkas* or *Sharas*, *i.e.* Eastern Mongols; *Kalmuks*, *i.e.* Western Mongols; *Buriats*, *i.e.* Siberian Mongols; *Tunguses, Manchus, Lamuts, Oronches, Golds, Gilyaks*, East Siberia and Amur Basin. TURKI BRANCH: *Yakuts* of Lena Basin; *Kirghizes, Uzbegs, Kara-Kalpaks, Turkomans*, West Siberia and Turkestan; *Nogais, Tats, Anatolians, Turks, Osmanli*, Caucasia, East Russia, Asia Minor, Rumelia. UGRO-FINNIC BRANCH: *Soyots, Ostiaks, Voguls, Permians, Siryanians, Samoyeds, Lapps, Finns, Livonians, Vepses, Mordvins, Cheremisses, Bulgars* (now Slavonized in speech), *Magyars*, Altai Mts., West Siberia, North and East Russia, Lapland, Bulgaria, Hungary. TIBETO-CHINESE BRANCH: *Tibetans, Burmese, Shans* or *Laos* (*Siamese Ahoms, Khamti*), *Chins, Nāgās, Mishmis, Annamese, Chinese*, Tibet, Himālayas, most of Indo-China and China. MALAYAN BRANCH: *Malays proper, Sundanese, Javanese, Madurese, Balinese, Sassaks, Bugis, Mankassaras, Dayaks, Tagals, Bisayans, Formosans, Hovas*, and other *Malagasy*, Malaysia, Philippines, Formosa, Madagascar. KOREO-JAPANESE BRANCH: *Koreans, Japanese, Liu-Kiu Islanders*. SUB-ARCTIC BRANCH: *Chukchi, Koryaks, Yukaghirs, Kamchadales*.

AMERICAN OR RED DIVISION.

Cradle-land: the whole of the New World.

Present restricted domain: the unsettled parts and some reservations in the Dominion of Canada; Alaska; numerous reservations and a few tracts in the Western parts of the United States; most of Mexico, Central and South America, partly intermingled with the white and black intruders, partly still independent or in the tribal state.

Population: full blood, 10,000,000; Mestizos, 20,000,000: total, 30,000,000; chiefly in Mexico, Guatemala, Colombia, Venezuela, Peru, Bolivia, and Brazil; 250,000 only in the United States, and 100,000 in Canada.

Physical characters: *head* very variable, long and short in many places, intermingled inextricably; highest known brachycephaly in South America (the extinct Calchaquis with cephalic index 92·6)'; *jaws* slightly prognathous, very large and square; *cheek-bones* moderately prominent; *nose* large, bridged or aquiline; *eyes* small, round, straight, black, rarely with Mongolic fold; *colour* normally reddish or coppery, but variable and rather yellowish in the South American woodlands; *hair* uniformly very long, coarse, lank, black (horse-hair type), round in transverse section, no beard or moustache; *height* generally above the average, 5 ft. 8 in. to 6 ft. (Patagonians), and 6 ft. 4 in. (Brazilian Bororos, almost the tallest known race), others very short, 5 ft. or a little over (Quechuas, Fuegians, some Eskimos), highlanders generally undersized, prairie Indians tall.

Mental characters and culture: *temperament* reserved, moody, taciturn, wary, deep feelings masked by an impassive exterior, strong nervous system with great power of enduring physical pain; great range of culture from almost the lowest savage state (Mexican Seres, Brazilian Botocudos, Fuegians) to the fairly civilized Aztecs, Mayas, Chibchas, Quechuas (Peruvians), and Aymaras. Amongst these architecture, engineering, calendric systems, pictorial writing, pottery, weaving, well developed.

Speech: almost universally of polysynthetic structure, with a great number of irreducible stock languages, some (Algonquian, Athapascan, Siouan, Shoshonean, Nahuatlan, Maya-Quichéan, Tupi-Guaranean, Quechuan) spread over wide areas, but the great majority crowded together in narrow spaces, especially along the West Coast of North America. This order of speech is confined exclusively to the New World, implying separation from the Eastern hemisphere from very remote times, probably the late Palæolithic or early Neolithic Age.

Religion: *Shamanism* (see above) is widely diffused amongst the North American aborigines: *totemistic* systems, presenting analogies with those of the Australians, but apparently of a more religious cast, are highly developed amongst Iroquoians, Algonquians, Dakotans, and the North-West Coast tribes. *Animism* in its simplest form (worship of animated Nature rather than of ancestral spirits) prevails amongst all the uncultured peoples that have any religion at all. With it are associated in Mexico, Argentina, and elsewhere strange superstitions about the terrible *wer-jaguar*, while in the Guianas similar notions are held in connexion with the *kenaimas* and *peaimen*. The former enter the body not of wild beasts, but of man himself, as caterpillars or in other forms, causing sickness which can be cured only by the aid of the *peaiman*, who exorcizes the patient with the usual make-believe incantations. Solar worship prevailed in Peru, while the cultured peoples of Mexico (Mayas, Zapotecs, Aztecs) had developed a complete system of polytheism with ferocious deities (Tezcatlipoca, Quetzalcoatl, Tlaloc, etc.), whose thirst for human blood was insatiable; hence the hecatombs of victims offered to the gods on solemn occasions, and often accompanied by unutterable horrors. Aztec women still cast their infants into the Mexican lagoons, to propitiate the rain-god Tlaloc. Thus the principle of sacrifice, which pervades all advanced religious systems, acquired its highest development in the New World, where some tribes (Seres, Fuegians, Botocudos) have scarcely yet evolved any true religious notions at all.

Subdivisions: I. NORTHERN: *Eskimo* (*Innuit*), with *Aleut* and *Yuit*; *Déné* or *Athapascan* (Chippewayan, Kutchin, Taculli, Hupa, Umpqua, Apache, Navaho); *Algonquin* (Delaware, Fox, Sac, Mohican, Cree, Ojibwa, Shawnee, Massachusett, Illinois, Cheyenne, Blackfoot); *Iroquois* (Erie, Huron, Mohawk, Onondaga, Seneca, Tuscarora, Cherokee); *Tlingit*; *Haida*; *Tsimshian*;

Chinook; Siouan (Dakota, Assinaboin, Omaha, Ponca, Kansa, Osage, Quapaw, Iowa, Oto, Missouri, Winnebago, Mandan, Hidatsa, Crow, Tutelo, Catawba); *Shoshone* (Bannock, Comanche, Ute, Hopi); *Muskhogean* (Choctaw, Chickasaw, Creek, Alibamu, Seminole, Apalachi); *Natchez; Pawnee; Kiowa; Salish* or *Flathead; Pueblo* (Zuñi, Tewa, Taos, Picuri, Tusaya).

II. CENTRAL: *Opata-Pima* (Tarahumare, Yuma, Cora, Papago, Tepehuane); *Sere; Guaycuran; Tarascan; Otomi; Mexican* or *Nahuan* (Aztec, Chichimec, Pipil, Niquiran); *Maya-Quiché* (Toltec [?], Huaxtec, Maya, Lacandon, Quiché, Mamé, Cachiquel, Sutughil, Pocoman, Zendal, Chol, Zotzil, Poconchi); *Zoque; Mixe; Mixtec; Zapotec; Charotegan; Lencan* (Chontal, Wulwa, Rama, Paya, Guatusa); *Bribri; Talamanca; Cuna.*

III. SOUTHERN: *Chibcha; Choco; Chinchasuyu; Quichua* (Inca, Chanca); *Aymara* (Colla, Calchaqui); *Antisuyu; Jivaro; Zaparo; Pano; Ticuna; Puru; Mojo; Barré; Curetu; Caripuna; Charrua; Chuncho; Cocoma; Conibo; Carib* (Macusi, Akawoi, Rucuyenne, Bakairi, Arecuna); *Arawak* (Atorai, Waplana, Maypure, Parexi); *Warrau; Chiquito; Bororo; Botocudo; Hipurina; Tupi-Guarani* (Chiriguana, Caribuna, Paraguay, Tupinamba, Goajire, Tocantins, Omagua, Mundrucu, Tupinambaze); *Payagua; Mataco; Toba; Guaycuru; Gaucho; Araucan; Puelche; Pampas; Tehuelche (Patagonian); Fuegian.*

CAUCASIC OR WHITE DIVISION.

Cradle-land: probably North Africa between the Mediterranean and the Sudan.

Early expansion: all the Mediterranean lands; Central, West and North Europe; Britain, Asia Minor, Syria and Palestine, Arabia, Mesopotamia, Irania, Eurasiatic steppe between Carpathians and Pamir, India, South-East Asia, Malaysia, Polynesia, North-East Asia.

Present domain: nearly the whole of North Africa and Europe; Abyssinia and Arabia; parts of Turkestan, Caucasia, and Armenia; Irania, India, and parts of Indo-China; Malaysia and Polynesia; New Zealand; Australia; South Africa; North and South America.

Population: Europe, 355,000,000; Asia, 300,000,000 (chiefly India and including unclassified low-caste Hindus); America, 115,000,000; Africa, 15,000,000; Australasia, 5,000,000: total, 790,000,000.

Physical characters: Three Types: I. *Homo Europæus: head* rather long; *cephalic index* 74 to 79; *jaws* orthognathous; *cheek-bones* generally small, not prominent; *nose* large and straight; *eyes* blue or grey, white sclerotic, straight; *colour* florid; *hair* rather long, straight or wavy, fair, flaxen, very light brown or reddish ('carroty'), full beard; *height* above the average, 5 ft. 8 in. to 6 ft. 2 in. II. *Homo Alpinus: head* short; *cephalic index* 80 to 90 and even 95; *eyes* brown, hazel, or black; *colour* pale-white, in aberrant groups (East Africa and India) very dark, and even blackish; *hair* brown or chestnut and black, rather short and straight, or wavy, small beard; *height* medium, 5 ft. 5 or 6 in. III. *Homo Mediterraneus: head* long; *cephalic index* 72 to 78; *nose* large, straight, or aquiline; *eyes* black and straight; *colour* pale-olive or swarthy; *hair* black, wavy or curly; *height* undersized, generally under 5 ft. 6 in., except in aberrant groups, which are often tall (Gallas, Somals, Sikhs).

Mental characters and culture: *temperament* of I. slow and somewhat stolid, cool, collected, resolute, tenacious, enterprising; of II. and III. fiery, fickle, bright, impulsive, quick, but unsteady, with more love of show than sense of duty; all three highly imaginative and intellectual; hence science, arts, and letters fully developed, to some extent even from early historic times; most civilizations (Egyptian, Babylonian, Sabæan, Assyrian, Persian, Indian, Mycenæan, Hellenic, Italic) have had their roots in Caucasic soil.

Speech: mainly inflexion (highest order, with complete fusion of root and formative elements), but also agglutinating (Caucasia, Deccan, Polynesia); several stock languages in Caucasia; one (Basque) in Western Pyrenees; apart from these the whole Caucasic domain is covered by four great linguistic families: 1. *Hamito-Semitic*, North Africa, South-West Asia; 2. *Aryan* (*Indo-Germanic, Indo-European*), most of Europe, Armenia and Irania, Northern India, most of America, Australia, Tasmania, New Zealand, parts of North and South Africa; chief branches: Indic, Iranic, Hellenic, Italic, Slavic, Lettic, Teutonic, Celtic; 3. *Dravidian*, Southern India (the Deccan); chief branches: Telinga (Telugu), Tamil, Malayalim, Kanarese; 4. *Kolarian*, formerly perhaps wide-spread throughout India, now reduced to the Vindhyan uplands between Aryan and Dravidian North and South.

Religion: from the first Nature-worship seems to have greatly predominated over Ancestor-worship. The Egyptians did not worship but embalmed the dead, who were supposed to remain human in the after-life. The chief gods of the Semites were the sun and moon, and those of the Aryans—Dyaus, Indra, Zeus, Apollo, Jupiter, Saturn, etc.—were the personified elements of the upper regions. The eponymous heroes, such as Heracles, who may be supposed to have had a human origin, always remained mere demi-gods, and were scarcely worshipped at all. Amongst the Aryans the gods were symbolized in stone, wood, or bronze; and this led to the worship of the image itself—true idolatry, which, despite iconoclastic zeal, still persists amongst the uneducated classes in many parts of Christendom. The picture of St. Anthony is not clearly distinguished from the saint himself, and, when it fails to protect the Italian *bifolco* from accidents, is cursed and stabbed. Out of the general polytheism various shades of monotheism were slowly evolved by a natural process of elimination. The process is now going on amongst some of the lower races, and it is a popular error to credit the Semites with the monotheistic concept from the first, as if it were a sort of racial character, a special privilege of those worshippers of Elu, Baal, Molech, and innumerable other repulsive deities. Out of the monotheism thus evolved arose the historic religions of the West (*Judaism, Christianity, Muhammadanism*), while crass polytheism still dominates the East (*Brāhmanism* in India, a degraded *Buddhism* in Ceylon). Between monotheism and polytheism is the dualistic doctrine which had its home in Persia, where *Ormazd* and *Ahriman*, the good and evil principles, contend for supremacy in the universe. This Zoroastrian system, which refers light and all good things to Ormazd and his host of angels, darkness and all evil to Ahriman and his host of demons, was already denounced by Isaiah, whose Jahweh is the single source of everything, 'formans lucem, et creans tenebras, faciens pacem, et creans malum' (45[7]). Nevertheless, it found its way into the early Christian communities, and explains the *demonology*, with all its attendant horrors, which flourished in mediæval times, and is not yet quite extinct.

Subdivisions : HAMITES : *Egyptians, Bejas, Afars* (Danakil), *Somals, Gallas, Masai, Turkana, Wahuma*, East African seaboard from the Mediterranean to the equator; *Mauritanians, Berbers, Tuaregs*, North Africa between the Mediterranean and Sudan; *Iberians, Picts, Ligurians, Pelasgians, Etruscans, Hittites* (?), the Mediterranean lands, Britain, Syria. SEMITES : *Himyarites, Abyssinians, Arabs, Assyrians, Canaanites* (*Israelites, Idumæans, Philistines, Phœnicians, Syrians*), Arabia, East Africa, Mesopotamia, Syria, Palestine. ARYANS : *Kashmiri, Panjabi, Gujarati, Marathi, Bengali, Assami, Beluchi, Afghans, Persians, Kurds, Armenians, Ossetes*, India, Irania, Armenia, Caucasus; *Thracians, Illyrians, Greeks, Italians*, Balkan Peninsula, Greece, Italy; *Slavs* (*Russians, Poles, Bohemians, Wends, Croatians, Servians, Dalmatians, Montenegrins*), East Europe, Balkan Peninsula; *Teutons* (*Goths, Scandinavians, Low* and *High Germans, Dutch, Flemings, Anglo-Saxons, English, Lowland Scots*); *Letts* and *Lithuanians ; Celts* (*Irish, Highland Scots, Manx, Welsh, Bretons*). CAUCASIANS (Georgians, Circassians, Lesghians). DRAVIDIANS and KOLARIANS : *Telugus, Tamils, Santals, Bhils, Konds.* POLYNESIANS : *Samoans, Tahitians, Tongans, Maori, Hawaiians.* AINUS.

LITERATURE.—J. F. Blumenbach, *de Generis Humani Varietate Nativa*, Göttingen, 1775; J. C. Prichard, *Researches into the Physical History of Mankind*, London, 1836; R. G. Latham, *Natural History of the Varieties of Man*, do. 1850; T. Waitz, *Anthropologie*, Leipzig, 1859–72; C. R. Darwin, *The Descent of Man*, London, 1871; T. H. Huxley, *Collected Essays*, London, 1894: 'Man's Place in Nature'; A. de Quatrefages, *Classification des races humaines*, Paris, 1889; O. F. Peschel, *The Races of Man*, Eng. tr., London, 1876; E. B. Tylor, *Anthropology*, do. 1881; Sir J. Lubbock, *Prehistoric Times*[6], do. 1900; F. Ratzel, *History of Mankind*, Eng. tr., do. 1896–99; A. H. Keane, *Ethnology*[2], Cambridge, 1897, *Man, Past and Present*[2], do. 1899; J. Deniker, *The Races of Man*, London, 1900; H. N. Hutchinson, *The Living Rulers of Mankind*, London, 1902; G. de Mortillet, *Le Préhistorique: Origine et antiquité de l'homme*[3], Paris, 1900.

A. H. KEANE.

ETRUSCAN RELIGION.—I. *ANCIENT SOURCES.*—**1. Etruscan documents.**—Unfortunately we have no original document giving such valuable information regarding the Etruscan religion as the calendar of festivals (Mommsen, *CIL* i.[2] 205 ff.) supplies for the study of the ancient Roman religion. It is true that the Agram linen-roll (§ 3) is regarded by some scholars as a ritual calendar of festivals, but the numerals which stand at the beginning of the several paragraphs, and which accordingly formed the starting-point of the theory, do not seem to serve as monthly dates. It must not be forgotten, however, that the Roman calendar of festivals itself, with its arrangement of kalends, nones, and ides (Etr. *itis*), and perhaps also the actual institution of the liturgical calendar of festivals in Italy, are traceable to the hieratic colleges of the Etruscans. Archives of families, temples, and cities, the sifting of which has proved so important for the history of the primitive Roman religion, must be presumed to have had their counterparts also in Etruria, but none of these survives in the original; and, in particular, among all the 8000 extant Etruscan inscriptions we do not find, or at least have so far failed to identify with certainty, any specimen of such official documents as statutes, minutes, formularies of prayer, or rubrics of the priests' colleges or the religious fellowships of individual *gentes*: the one or two gratifying exceptions from which better results may be expected will be discussed below. Meanwhile we possess definite and reliable evidence of the fact that such documentary records, together with oral traditions, were at an early period brought into an orderly form—probably in rhythmical language—in works ascribed to mythical authors (*e.g.*, the books of Tages and of Begoe, § 29), and bearing mysterious titles ('libri fatales,' 'libri Acherontici,' § 35), and that afterwards, for antiquarian and practical purposes, they were reduced to a learned and complicated system in the 'libri fulgurales,' 'libri haruspicini,' and 'libri rituales' (§§ 30–34), as the *Etrusca disciplina*.

2. Latin adaptations.—These books were often recast in Latin forms, or adapted to Roman conditions, and the history and contents of this derivative literature must now be laboriously gathered from sporadic and casual references in the works of Cicero, Livy, Seneca, and Pliny the Elder, as also of grammarians, antiquaries, commentators on Vergil, *gromatici*, and Church Fathers. More or less prominent among those who dealt with the subject are the following: Tarquitius Priscus (before Vergil's time) made poetical experiments in the field of the *Etrusca disciplina*, and occupied himself with the study of *ostenta* ('unnatural phenomena') as the objects of *haruspicina* (§ 32). A. Cæcina, whose family came originally from the Etruscan city of Volterra, and who was an opponent of Cæsar, wrote on the Etruscan doctrine of lightning (§ 30). P. Nigidius Figulus, the friend of Cicero, wrote, among other works, books *de Extis, de Divinatione, de Animalibus*, in which he can hardly have ignored the *Etrusca disciplina*. The writings of Labeo, *de Diis Animalibus* (§ 20), are mentioned in Servius's commentary on the *Æneid*, while Julius Aquila, Umbricius Melior, Vicellius, and Cæsius are cited by Pliny, Lydus, and Arnobius as authorities in the literature of the Etruscan discipline.

3. The Agram linen-roll.—The Agram linen-roll—by far the longest Etruscan text (some 1500 words in twelve columns) that we possess—has been regarded as an original fragment of the *Etrusca disciplina*. The remains of this *liber linteus* were found in Egypt, carelessly torn into strips and wrapped about a female mummy. They are now preserved in the National Museum at Agram (Croatia). The writing and spelling of the fragment, and the dressing of the mummy, point to the Græco-Roman period. Arguing from the few words and constructions which we understand, scholars are variously inclined to see in this formulary text a sacrificial ritual (Krall, Lattes), a ritual calendar of festivals (Torp), portions of the Etruscan doctrine of the lightning-flash (Skutsch), or a relic of Etruscan religious poetry bearing some analogy to the Eugubine Tables (Thulin). To the present writer the various items of external and internal evidence (the circumstances of its discovery, the manuscript rolls of Etruscan sepulchral monuments, the divine names, litanies, and certain definite appellatives in the text itself) seem to indicate a funerary text, and also to imply a more than merely accidental connexion between the roll and the mummy—in so far, namely, as the funeral liturgies and the ideas of the hereafter found in the *libri Acherontici* (§§ 20, 35) may have in this particular instance been used in the same manner as the Egyptian Book of the Dead.

4. Other sepulchral rolls and longer sepulchral inscriptions.—With the Agram roll we may fitly associate the manuscript rolls and diptychs held in the hands of figures on the lids of Etruscan sarcophagi and ash-chests, or in the hands of the persons or the gods of the under world sculptured on the sides of these memorials, or painted on Etruscan vases; and, above all, the so-called *pulena*-roll, a sepulchral inscription of nine lines upon an open roll which the figure on the lid (*i.e.* the dead person himself) holds up before the onlooker. Nor is the longest Etruscan inscription, the sepulchral tablet of Capua—so far as we are able to interpret it—inconsistent with the conjectural contents of these funerary book-rolls; while the third longest Etruscan text, the *cippus Perusinus*, seems actually to furnish certain analogies to them. In comparison with these as yet very imperfectly interpreted literary remains, however, the furnishings and contents of excavated tombs, such as mural paintings, reliefs on cinerary chests and sarcophagi, figured lids, and also the abundant accessaries of vessels, utensils, clothes, and ornaments warrant much more definite conclusions regarding the cult of the dead and the hopes and fears of the hereafter (§§ 25, 26) that prevailed among the Etruscans.

5. The leaden tablet of Magliano and similar relics.—The text of this inscription introduces us to a different sphere of religious ideas. Certain assonances in language have led some to compare it with the text of the Agram roll. But the external form of the memorial seems rather to connect it with the leaden tablets of Volterra and Campiglia Marittima, which Skutsch has identified as *devotiones*; and, as a matter of fact, the chthonic deities named in the Magliano text are quite in keeping with the personal and non-official magic and imprecatory spells which we are able, with the help of Græco-Roman analogies, to recognize on these tablets. The Etruscan ABC monuments should likewise be assigned to this group. Finally, the simple, semi-anatomical votive gifts—not, it is true, confined to Etruria—which the excavations have brought to light, and which often strikingly suggest the sacred objects of modern shrines and places of miraculous healing (cf. § 28), seem rather to fall outside the sphere of the official religion.

6. The bronze liver of Piacenza.—A singularly important survival of Etruscan haruspicy is found in the bronze liver of Piacenza, a fairly accurate model of a sheep's liver, which is marked off into regions corresponding to the Etruscan divisions of the sky, and is inscribed all over with divine names or abbreviations thereof. We shall hardly err in regarding this hastily written and relatively late document as a kind of index-catechism of Etruscan haruspicy, or as an instrument which the officiating haruspex employed for purposes of orientation. Remarkable analogues have been recently unearthed in Babylonia and at Boghaz-keui.

7. Bronze mirrors, gems, mural paintings, reliefs, coins, and statuettes of deities.—Apart from the bronze liver, our main source for the names of Etruscan deities is the large number of bronze mirrors exhumed from Etruscan tombs. The mythological scenes which they present in such profusion serve better than anything else to enlighten us as to what the Etruscans borrowed from Greek mythology and adapted to their own apparently very sober views. Next in importance come the gems, with their carved figures and names; then the mural paintings of tombs and the reliefs of sarcophagi and cinerary chests, with their representations from the Græco-Italian mythology of deities and heroes, and their occasional inscriptions. Of much less value in this respect are the paintings on the so-called Etruscan vases, which have proved to be, in the main, importations from Greece, and tell us more of Greek than of Etruscan ideas. Finally, coins and statuettes, though they seldom bear inscriptions, are valuable sources of information regarding the characteristics and the various types of the gods.

8. The difficulty of isolating the purely Etruscan element.—One very serious difficulty in regard to both the monumental and the literary sources is that of clearly disengaging the specifically Etruscan from the Greek, Roman, and Oriental factors. If, even in investigating the earlier Greek religion, we find it no easy task to separate the purely Greek elements from those of Oriental origin, or those inherited from the primitive Aryan age, and if it is hard to disentangle the Greek and Italic strands in the history of Roman religion, the difficulty will naturally be greatly intensified in the case of a religion like the Etruscan, where the literary sources in particular are much more scanty and the linguistic memorials remain in great measure unexplained, while the ethnological, linguistic, and religious relationships of the people have not yet been conclusively made out. The old and the new, the exotic and the indigenous, intermingle in the nebulous tradition; and, even where foreign influence can be clearly traced, it is often impossible to distinguish between ideas fused together by later syncretism and those mutually related from the first.

9. The impossibility of a systematic or genetic delineation.—From the sources (the bibliography of which will be found at the end of this article) we gain some impression of the various deities and systems of deities, the worship, and certain phases of the religious and ethical ideas of the Etruscans, and this impression it will be the aim of the succeeding paragraphs to set forth. In view of the defective and fortuitous transmission of the records, and owing to the impossibility of interpreting them clearly and finally, it is out of the question to think of reducing the aggregate mass of data to a system, or of tracing the course of their historical development. Moreover, we lack as yet —apart from a few excellent but still unfinished compilations of particular groups of objects (see lit. under 7)—a critical or relatively exhaustive collection of the materials furnished by the various monumental sources. Such a collection, again, would be of little service without an atlas of illustrations —not only because religious ideas are reflected in the artistic portrayal of the various types of deities, and in the conscientious workmanship, seen in the Etruscan sepulchral monuments and their abundant furnishings, but even more because, by reason of the peculiar character of the Etruscan record, the pictorial and glyptic sources usually speak to us more distinctly than the linguistic sources, which still remain largely inarticulate, and, in their Græco-Latin form, show a considerable admixture of non-Etruscan elements. We should add, further, that the (in part) very imperfectly preserved readings of the all-important Etruscan mirrors—especially of those published some decades ago—require to be collated once more with the originals; while a persevering philological investigation, not, indeed, of the roots—for such were at present a hopeless task —but of the suffixes of the Etruscan divine names, would even to-day be a most serviceable piece of preparatory work (see § 14).

II. *NAMES OF THE DEITIES.* — **10. Ancient Etruscan deities.**—The etymology of the genuinely Etruscan divine names remains for the most part an unsolved problem; nor do the vast majority of these names occur in the literary tradition. Still, the pictorial representations enable us to identify —with certainty, or, at least, with some degree of confidence—a number of them with the names of Roman and Greek deities. That the spheres of connotation in such secondary identifications only partially coincide, and that assimilations of this kind actually obscure the original character of the two deities so compared, is made perfectly clear, for example, from the study of Roman religion. The following pairs are broadly homologous: *tin(i)a* and Juppiter, *śeθlans* and Vulcan, *turms* (*trm·s*) and Mercury, *fufluns* and Bacchus, *turan* and Venus, *θesan* and Aurora. More or less obscurity still hangs over the names *ca(u)θa* (a sun-god? cf. § 11), *cilens, cvlalp, leθam, mantrnś* (cf. *Mantus*, § 25), *θuflθa, tecum, tluscv, laran* (a war-god?), *aminθ* (Amor?), and *svutaf* (a winged youth). For another series of names which cannot be interpreted individually, but are intelligible as a group, see § 23.

11. Italic and Greek deities.—Other deities bear Italic or Greek names, the forms of which have been more or less adjusted to Etruscan phonology. Thus *hercle* (Ἡρακλῆς), *ap(u)lu(n)* (Ἀπόλλων), *χaru(n)* (Χάρων), *aita* (Ἀΐδας), *ar(e)aθa* (Ἀριάδνα), and many names of heroes, seem to have been borrowed directly from the Greek. The Italic pantheon contributes, or may contribute, the following: *uni* (Juno), *mariś* (Mars), *neθuns* (Neptune), *sel(v)ans* (Silvanus), *vetis* (Vedius), *ani* (Janus), *satre* (Saturn), *mae* (Maius), *vesuna* (Umbr. and Mars. Vesune, Uesune [dat. sing.]). It is true that, phonetically, these parallels do not correspond in all respects, and in some instances (*neθuns, sel(v)ans, satre*) it is still an open question whether the Romans did not rather borrow the name and conception from the Etruscans. In some other cases a Greek or Italic name came to be used in place of the original Etruscan one; thus *atrpa* (Ἄτροπος) instead of *vanθ* (§ 25), *usil* (Sab. *ausel*) instead of *cauθa* (ἀμάρακον . . . Ῥωμαῖοι Σῶλις ὄκουλουμ, οἱ δὲ μιλλεφόλιουμ, Θοῦσκοι καυτάμ[-ν] [Dioscor. ii. 147, l. 17]), *herm-* (Ἑρμῆς) for *turms*, and *ani* (Janus) for *culśanś*. As regards the last, the bronze statuette which, according to *CIE* 437, was dedicated to *culśanś*, shows—as the present writer can attest, from a personal examination of the object at Cortona—the two faces of Janus, and we may therefore venture, on the analogy of other votive statues showing the image of the deity to whom they are dedicated, to couple the ancient Etruscan *culśanś* with the Etruscanized *ani*, who was perhaps related to the Faliscan Janus quadrifrons (Serv. *Æn.* vii. 608).

12. Deities mentioned in the literary tradition.—Other Etruscan deities, bearing Latin or Latinized names, are known to us only from the literary tradition. *Vertumnus* is designated 'deus Etruriae princeps' by Varro (*de Ling. Lat.* v. 46). *Voltumna* comes before us as the goddess of the federal temple of the twelve Etruscan city-States (Livy, iv. 25. 7: 'consilia ad movenda bella . . . in Etruria ad fanum Voltumnae agitata. Ibi prolatae in annum res, decretoque cautum, ne quod ante concilium fieret'). The temple of *Nortia*, the goddess of destiny, at Volsinii was noted for the device of registering the years by nails driven into the door (Livy, vii. 3. 7). The Etruscan city of Mantua took its name from *Mantus* (cf. §§ 10, 25), the Etruscan god of the under world (ancient authorities in Müller-Deecke, *Die Etrusker*, i.², note 6). A mythical *monstrum* called *Volta* is mentioned by Pliny (*HN* ii. 53, 140). The nymph *Begoe* and the divine youth *Tages* will be referred to below (§ 29).

13. Oriental deities.—While we are on comparatively safe ground in recognizing certain Greek and Roman deities under their Etruscan disguise, we are quite at a loss with regard to other foreign deities. It is true that the only Etruscan inscription that comes from Carthage contains the name of the Semitic *melkarθ*. But of the identifications of Etruscan and Egyptian deities which the present writer, by inference from the records on mummy dressings brought from Egypt (§ 3), has ventured to suggest, not a single instance is absolutely certain. The question whether pre-Hellenic ('Pelasgian,' 'Ægæo-Anatolian,' 'Carian,' 'Cretan,' 'Hittite,' or the like) types underlie the ancient Etruscan deities—a question which as regards some of these deities, e.g. *fufluns, śeθlans*, and *selvans*, a number of scholars answer affirmatively—is not, in the present writer's opinion, yet ripe for decision. Babylonian and Etruscan affinities will be dealt with below (§§ 30–32).

14. Suffixes of divine names.—Perhaps the suffixes of the Etruscan divine names may yet prove to be the key to further progress in this field, though some of these terminations are so slightly characteristic that they might even be Indo-Germanic, while others may possibly indicate only the Etruscan modifications of Italic, Greek, or Oriental names. The forms noted below may serve at least as a starting-point for further discussion; meanwhile it is important to notice that in some cases the same suffix may occur in the names of both male and female deities.

Suffix.	Names of Deities.
-nθ	ami-nθ, lei-nθ, va-nθ.
-ns	fuflu-ns, neθu-ns, śeθla-ns, selva-ns, culśa-nś, (lasa) isminθia-ns, cile-ns, mantr-nś (§ 25).
-θa	θufl-θa, area-θa, tali-θa, (lasa) racune-ta, mlaχ(u)-ta.
-mn-	Vertu-mn-us, Voltu-mn-a, Volu-mn-us, Volu-mn-a, Vitu-mn-us; probably also Pilu-mn-us, Picu-mn-us, Clitu-mn-us.
-rn-	Mant-urn-a, Iut-urn-a(?), Sat-urn-us, Volt-urn-us, Lavern-a, Numit-ern-us, El-ern-us.
-an	tur-an, θes-an, alp-an, ev-an, me-an, lar-an.
-l	hinθia-l, recia-l, rescia-l.
-χ	puri-χ, malavis-χ, mlacu-χ, munθu-χ.

III. *SYSTEMS OF DEITIES.*—**15. Triad, ennead, dodecad; 'Dei involuti.'**—The various deities of the Etruscans (*æsar*, Hesych. *s.v.* *αἰσοί*; Sueton. *Aug.* 97; Dio Cass. lvi. 29) were grouped in distinct orders or systems. In every city that was founded *Etrusco ritu* special honours were accorded to the divine triad of Tinia, Uni, and Menrva, and a city which had not dedicated three gates and three temples to the triad did not find favour with the *prudentes Etruscæ disciplinæ*. To an ennead of gods, again, there belonged the power of launching certain kinds of lightning (*manubiæ*, 'hand-weapons,' separate flashes); and, as Tinia grasped three such *manubiæ* in his hand, there were in all eleven distinct species of lightning (Plin. *HN* ii. 138); in this connexion the number eleven is probably derived from Bab. ideas (Serv. on *Georg.* i. 33). The *prima manubia* was hurled by Tinia *suo consilio*; the *secunda* was sent with the advice of the dodecad of gods ('hos *Consentes* et *Complices* Etrusci aiunt, quod *una oriantur et occidant una*, sex mares et totidem feminas, nominibus ignotis et miserationis parcissimae: sed eos summi Jovis *consiliarios* ac participes existimari' [Varro, in Arnob. ii. 40]; the connexion of these six pairs of deities, who daily rise and set together in the sky, with the Gr. δώδεκα θεοί, the Græco-Oriental θεοὶ βουλαῖοι, the twelve months, and the Bab.-Oriental signs of the zodiac, is quite unmistakable). The *tertia manubia*, however—the most destructive of all—was sent by Tinia only with the concurrence of the *dei superiores, involuti*, or *opertanei*, whose names and number were unknown, and who, mysterious and inscrutable, sat enthroned above all (Cæcina, in Seneca, *Nat. Quæst.* ii. 41; Varro, in Arnob. ii. 40).

16. Deities of lower rank.—From these exalted gods we must distinguish the groups of spirits associated with persons and places. Here, however, it is more than usually difficult to detach the Etruscan from the Roman element. The *lares* (O. Lat. *lases*), the spirits who attach themselves to particular plots of land, and roam about at the cross-roads (*q.v.*); the *di penates*, who dwell and hold sway in the *penus*, i.e. the storeroom, beside the kitchen and the hearth; the *genii* of men and the *junones* of women, who, as guardian spirits (δαίμονες), are accorded special honours on birthdays—just as in the Rom. Cath. Church the tutelary saint is honoured on the name-day, which by its association with baptism became the true birthday of the Christian; the *aisna hinθu*, or *divina anima*, the deified soul of the dead; the *dei gentiles*, who share the name of their particular *gens*: all these Roman divinities reappear—some quite evanescently, others more palpably, in the Etruscan tradition as well, though we cannot form a clear impression of the several groups, of their derivation from one another or from other types (gods of the under world, ancestral spirits), or of the way in which they were fused together at a later stage.

17. Lares.—But we are able at all events to distinguish the prænomens

Etr. *lar*	Lat. Lar	Gr. Λᾶρος
,, *larθ*	,, Lars	,, Λάρτας

with the long *ā* attested by the spelling and accentuation of names like Lártius, Laaro, Lāronius, Λᾶρος, from the Lat. appellative *lār* (from **lărs*), gen. *lăris*, O. Lat. pl. *lăses*, with *ă* short by nature. But, on the other hand, it is not impossible that the Lăra, the goddess of the nether world (Ov. *Fasti*, ii. 599 ff.), whom scholars are unwilling to detach from the Lăres or Lases, may be akin, alike in name and in function, to the Lasa (quantity of first *a* unknown), seen as a winged and attired goddess of fate or death, unfolding a roll and standing between the seer *hamφiare* (Ἀμφιάραος) and the *aivas* (Αἴας), whose look is submissively bent to the ground (Gerhard, *Etr. Spiegel*, iv. fig. 359). But there is a still unexplained incongruity between this particular *lasa* and the usual *lasa*-types of Etruscan mirrors (§ 23); and the 'Lăra' used by Ovid instead of the ordinary 'Lārunda' may perhaps be peculiar to that writer. The identification of the Etruscan deities *leθn* and *lasa* found on the Piacenza liver with the *Lar militaris* and the *Lar cœlestis* mentioned by Martianus Capella is quite uncertain.

18. Penates.—Our authorities with regard to the Etruscan *penates* are Nigidius and Cæsius, as quoted by Arnobius (*adv. Gent.* iii. 40). Both writers speak of a tetrad of deities. Nigidius distinguishes four *genera*, viz. the *di penates Jovis, Neptuni, inferorum*, and *mortalium hominum*; while Cæsius specifies the four individual deities, Fortuna, Ceres, Genius Jovialis, and Pales. In the four categories of Nigidius may be discerned the four elements—sky, sea, under world, and earth; but whether, or in what manner, the four deities of Cæsius are to be brought into relation with these, the present writer does not venture to decide.

19. Genii and junones.—Whether the term *genius* ('procreator') is the Lat. rendering of an Etr. word, as has been conjectured, and whether the Roman *genii* and *junones* had their counterparts in Etruria, it is likewise impossible to say. A *genius Jovialis* as one of the Etruscan *penates* was cited above (§ 18); in Festus, 359, Tages (§ 29) is designated *genii filius, nepos Jovis*. The serpent, the Roman symbol of the *genius*, is not infrequently depicted on Etruscan monuments.

20. 'Dei animales.'—The practice of deifying the dead has left its impression in the sepulchral art of the Etruscans, and is directly attested by the literary tradition. According to Servius (on *Æn.* iii. 168), Labeo, in 'libris qui appellantur de diis animalibus,' had written: 'esse quaedam sacra quibus animae humanae vertantur in deos, qui appellantur animales, quod de anima fiant'; and Arnobius (*adv. Gent.* ii. 62) explicitly says: 'Etruria libris in Acheronticis pollicetur, certorum animalium sanguine numinibus certis dato, divinas animas fieri et ab legibus mortalitatis educi.' Such a *divina anima* or *deus animalis*—as indicated by the phrase *aisna hinθu* (the deified soul of the dead)—is repeatedly referred to also in the text of the Agram roll.

21. 'Dei gentiles.'—We may safely assume, therefore, that ancestor-worship and the cult of the dead prevailed among the Etruscans. But to determine whether and how far the cult of mythological heroes, which was not very fully developed, and which borrowed most of its materials in a rather superficial way from Gr. mythology (§ 11), was connected with the cult of the dead is certainly very difficult. We are able, however, to distinguish more and more clearly a series of clan deities, though the relation between the deity and the *gens*—even in a chronological respect—is not always evident. In these cases the name of the *gens* is added in adjectival form to that of a well-known deity, or else the clan name and the divine name are simply identical. Thus in funerary text-rolls we can clearly trace the *culšu leprnei*, i.e. a death-goddess of the gens **Leprinia*, and the *uni ursmnei*, the *juno* of the gens *Orsminnia*. The Etr. divine name *satre* is related to the Etr. clan name *saterna* as the Lat.-Etr. clan name *satrius* to the Rom.-Etr. divine name *Saturnus*. The family deity of the *Numitorii* was sometimes called *Numiternus* and sometimes *Mars*; the *gens Numisia* worshipped *Numisius Martius* or *Numesius Mars*; and, similarly, we find in Etruscan inscriptions a *mariś husr-na-na*, and perhaps also a Hermes *huz-r-na-tre*—deities, that is to say, of a *gens Fusia* (**Husia*)—these names being fitted with characteristic Etruscan suffixes and accumulations of suffixes. Nor can it be disputed that the Etruscan or semi-Etruscan goddesses *Ancharia* of Fæsulæ and Asculum, and *Feronia* of the Faliscan Soracte, are connected with the *Ancharii* and the *Heruli* (=**Feruli*; in the Faliscan dialect *fere* is still=**Herus*). The name of the dictator *Egerius Lævius* explains that of the 'nymph' *Egeria*; and, similarly, the name of the Etruscan 'nymph' *Begoe, Vegoia, *Vegonia* (inferred from the adj. *Vegonicus*) is quite identical with the regular feminine form of the clan name *vecu*, i.e. with *vecui, *vecuia, *vecunia*; and, if we are unable to say with certainty whether the *lasa vecu* belongs to the same group, it is only because the spelling with *-u* instead of *-ui* (which would in this case make *lasa vecu=lasa vecui=Lasa Begoe*) has been but rarely found, and because the explanation breaks down when applied to other names with *lasa* (§ 23). The Roman and Etruscan deities *Vitumnus, Vortumnus*, and *Volumnus, Voltumna* (§ 12), as appears from the stems and the common suffix of their names, are connected with Etruscan *gentilicia*; while the names of the death-goddesses *Tarp-eia, Mant-ur-na* (on *Mantus*, cf. § 25), and *Lav-er-na*, to judge from their structure and their stems, may really be pure Etruscan forms of clan names.

22. 'Ani' and 'uni'—clan deities?—Even the names of the well-known Etruscan deities *ani* (m.) and *uni* (f.) cannot be satisfactorily explained on any other hypothesis. The word *Janus*—the original Etruscan name was noted above (§ 11)—is in Latin an *o* or *u* stem; but the Etr. form, instead of being, as we should have expected, **ane* or **anu*, is *ani*, which would yield in Latin an otherwise unknown **Janius*, or would exactly correspond to an *Annius* (cf. Ἄννιος, the Etruscan king [Alex. Polyh. in Plut. *Parall. min.* 40]), and this would imply that an Etruscan clan (=*gens*) god had at a later stage come to be identified with the Lat.-Faliscan Janus, owing to the similarity of their names. The Etr. equivalent of Juno, viz. *uni*, the Faliscan prænomen *iuna*, the Faliscan patronymic *iuneo*, the Roman gens *Junia*, and the month *Junius* (not **Junonius*) are all undoubtedly connected with the Lat. name of the goddess, but the direct link of connexion cannot be made out philologically; the name *Juno, -ōnis*, not yet satisfactorily explained as to the final constituent of its stem, would yield, in Etruscan, the form **unui* or **ununia*; while the Etr. *uni* is the representative of an extinct Latin, or perhaps (in view of the Faliscan cult of Juno in the semi-Etruscan town of Falerii) Faliscan, name-form **Junia*, unless, indeed, it really represents the Indo-Germanic feminine form in -ī of which only fugitive traces survive in Latin itself (Skr. *yūnī-*; cf. Lat. *jūnī-x*).

23. Etruscan 'lasa.'—We find numerous representations of the goddesses whose function it is to serve and adorn others. The majority of these belong to the group of *turan*, and may be most appropriately compared with the *Horai* and the *Charites.* They are depicted as winged, and generally as naked, but they wear trinkets and ornamental shoes, and handle vessels for anointing, hair-pins, and mirrors, or crown others with wreaths, fillets, or sprays. Two of them—*θanr* and *eθauśva*—are seen assisting at the birth of Athene from the head of Jove, just as the Greek *Horai* likewise sometimes act as midwives. They are designated either by the name *lasa* (perhaps an appellative name?), or by this name joined to a personal name, or, again, by a personal name alone. Of such names, most of which remain unexplained, we meet with the following examples: *lasa vecu* (=**vecui*?) (§ 21), *lasa sitmica, lasa θimrae* (=**θimrai*?), *lasa racuneta, alpan, aχvizr, evan, zipanu* (*zipna, zipnu*), *zirna, θalna, θanr, mean* (*meanpe*), *mlacuχ, munθuχ, puriχ, rescial, snenaθ, taliθa*; while *malavisχ* and *hinθial* (Psyche) also seem to belong to the group.

24. Fate-recording goddesses.—Whether the term *lasa* was broad enough to be applied in some cases (§ 17) to the goddesses who record or predict fate—such as *vanθ* or *mlaχ(u)ta*—must remain an open question. It is quite possible that at a later stage the recording Μοῖραι, and, above all, Atropos, took the place not only of the Roman *Parcæ*, but also of the Etruscan death-spirits, and, in particular, of *vanθ*. Whether in any given case the goddesses who appear on Etruscan monuments holding a stylus and a roll or diptych represent the ancient Etruscan *vanθ* or the Etruscanized Atropos (*atrpa*), *mlaχ(u)ta*, or a *lasa*, cannot always be decided.

25. Hell.—The goddess *vanθ* just referred to, together with her companions *culśu* (§ 21) and *leinθ*, introduces us to the Etruscan views of Hell, the horrors of which might seem to be reflected in the demons of Michelangelo and in Dante's *Inferno*. Gruesome figures (*χarun, tuχulχa*), with distorted faces and animals' ears, and with hammers held as if to strike, bear away the dead from the circle of their loved ones. The sad necessity of parting is most touchingly portrayed on ash-chests and sarcophagi; on foot, on horseback, by waggon, or by ship, the dead set out on their long journey to the under world. In paintings on the walls of chambered tombs we see *aita* ('Ἀΐδας) and *φersipnei* (Περσεφόνη) sitting enthroned, and in a bronze-mirror, *turms aitas* ('Hades-Hermes'). It is only in the Latin tradition that Mantus is spoken of as the Etruscan god of the under world, but he seems to be identical with the *mantrnś* of the monuments; while our sole evidence for the Etruscan origin of the death-goddesses *Mant-ur-na* (alongside of *mant-r-nś*), *Lav-er-na*, and *Tarp-eia* is the linguistic structure of their names (§ 21).

26. Paradise.—The ideas of the Etruscans regarding the hereafter, however, had also their brighter side. We referred above (§ 20) to the practice of deifying the souls of the dead—perhaps an Orphic-Pythagorean accretion—which finds expression in the literary sources. It is true that, on the whole, the Etruscans seem not to have been very susceptible to mystical views of the life beyond. The gorgeous displays seen in the cemeteries of Southern Etruria present, not the glorified scenery of a celestial paradise, but the reminiscences rather—and often, indeed, very realistic reminiscences—of earthly splendours. It may well be that the trappings of the sepulchre were used originally for apotropæic purposes, and were designed to pacify the dead or protect the living from being disturbed by them; but, in point of fact, amid the wealth and magnificence of the tombs of aristocrats and merchants in Southern Etruria, death and the dead must surely have lost their terrors. The variety of objects found in these cemeteries baffles description. The shields and weapons of departed warriors hang upon the pillars; while beside the bodies of women are laid gold ornaments of the finest hammered, granular, and filigree work, together with sumptuous toilet articles, including the artistically chased bronze mirrors with their mythological scenes and their unveiled beauties, in which some have vainly tried to discern a mystical and symbolical meaning. The carved figures of the sarcophagi—like the statues of the gods at the *lectisternia*—recline at table as if at some festive meal; whole sets of table services and wine-jars stand ready for them; while the great candelabra would once, no doubt, illuminate the solemn games in honour of the dead, as well as the splendid banquets, the huntings, the dances, and the delights of love, portrayed in the many-coloured frescoes upon the walls.

IV. *WORSHIP OF THE GODS AND THE ETRUSCA DISCIPLINA*.—**27. Priests.**—A striking contrast to the full enjoyment of life which still, after more than two thousand years, sparkles from the mausoleums of Etruscan magnates, is presented by the punctilious and pedantic worship of the gods, as made known to us, in particular, from the remains of the *Etrusca disciplina*. Livy (v. 1. 6) incidentally alludes to the Etruscans as a 'gens . . . ante omnes alias eo magis dedita religionibus, quod excelleret arte colendi eas'; and Clement of Alexandria (*Strom.* i. 306*d*) writes: θυτικὴν ἠκρίβωσαν Τοῦσκοι. The statement, 'Tusci autem a frequentia sacrificii dicti sunt, hoc est ἀπὸ τοῦ θύειν' (Serv. on *Æn.* ii. 781; Varro, in Isidore, xiv. 4, 22), is an example of the superficial etymology of the ancients, but nevertheless gives point to a truth. When the twelve cities assembled *ad fanum Voltumnæ* for their common festival, they chose from among the nobility a *sacerdos* for the *sollemnia ludorum*, who doubtless also enjoyed great political influence (Livy, v. 1. 5). The *Etrusca disciplina* was handed down in the families of the *principes* from generation to generation, and Roman youths were sent to Etruria to study the mysterious science (Cic. *de Leg.* ii. 9. 21, *ad Fam.* vi. 6, *de Divin.* i. 41. 92; Livy, ix. 36. 3; Tac. *Ann.* xi. 15). From the *bilinguis* of Pesaro (*CIL* xi. 6363) and other inscriptions we learn a few of the titles borne by the priests; the Latin terms *haruspe(x)* and *fulguriator*, which correspond in some way to the Etr. *netśvis trutnvt frontac*, indicate at least two such priestly functionaries, viz. the examiner of the liver or entrails and the priest of the lightning, the former of whom is depicted also in the figured cover of an ash-chest from Volterra (*Röm. Mitteil.* xx. [1905] fig. xiv.). The *haruspices* had intimate relations with the Roman aristocracy; they were frequently consulted by the Senate; they were upon the staff of commanders-in-chief and provincial governors; and the Emperors Augustus, Tiberius, Claudius, Alexander Severus, and Julian all had communication with them. Even the drastic measures of the Emperors Constantine and Theodosius did not avail to suppress them entirely. The fact that we find the *ordines haruspicum* in Rome and in the *municipia* seems to warrant us in assuming that special colleges and schools of priests existed also in Etruria.

28. Religious ceremonies.—The cultus consisted in prayers and imprecations, sacrifices and sacrificial meals. The worship of statues and the *lectisternia* feasts (§ 26) seem to have prevailed also in Etruria; while games, dances, music, stately processions, horse-races, and prize-fights (often attended with bloodshed) all had a place in the service of the gods.

We cannot fail to recognize the presence of formal litanies in the Agram roll—especially at the top of column 7; and Varro (*de Re Rust.* i. 2. 27) transmits in Latin form an Etruscan rhythmical charm for diseased feet which he had taken from the book of the Etruscan Sasernæ. Mention was made above of imprecatory tablets and the Magliano lead (§ 5). The epigraphic ABC monuments seem to have been used for the same mystical and apotropæic purposes as their Greek and Roman counterparts.

Besides the ordinary votive gifts, which often take the form of bronze statuettes of the deities to be worshipped, we find in Etruria, as elsewhere on ancient Italian soil, other offerings of a peculiar character, such as clay models of heads, faces and parts of faces, arms and hands, legs and feet, entrails, and external and internal organs of generation, which may have served as expressions of the worshipper's gratitude for restoration to health or the blessing of children, or of his desire for such boons.

Animal sacrifices were of two kinds, *hostiæ animales*, and *hostiæ consultatoriæ* (Serv. on *Æn.* iv. 56). In the former the soul or life of the animal was sacrificed to the gods as a propitiation and a substitute for the soul and life of man; in the latter the offerer solicited a revelation of the deity's will or counsel in the entrails of the victim. But alike in the monumental and in the literary records we find evidence also of such barbarities as the massacre of prisoners and stoning to death.

29. Origin of the disciplina (Tages, Begoe), and its divisions.—The *Etrusca disciplina* was traced to a mythical origin. The wondrous child *Tăges* was cast out of a clod by the plough, and those who crowded round to hear wrote down what he revealed and sang (Cic. *de Divin.* ii. 50, and other writers). The 'nymph' *Begoe* (§ 21) taught Arruns Veltymnus (Etr. *arnθ ultimne*) the sacred law of limitation (§ 33). The doctrine thus revealed falls into three parts—the *libri fulgurales, libri haruspicini,* and *libri rituales.* The *libri fatales* and *libri Acherontici*, to judge from their contents, seem to have belonged to the last-named category.

30. The 'libri fulgurales.'—The *libri fulgurales* contained the Etruscan doctrine regarding the regions of the heavens and the gods of the lightning (§ 15). The *fulguriatores* (§ 27) defined the various species of lightning according to their origin, force, and result; they interpreted the flashes according to the objects struck—places, trees, buildings, sanctuaries, statues, or human beings. They propitiated the lightning by removing the traces of its work ('burying the lightning'); they knew how to mitigate or suspend its effects, but they had it also in their power to call it down by adjurations, and to summon the deity to appear in the flash as guest or counsellor, or to destroy an enemy. With such adjurations the rain-charm would doubtless often be combined.

That the object struck by lightning becomes tabu, sacred, or *religiosum*—a thing in face of which man vacillates between dread and worship—seems to be a universal human belief; but whether the development of the Etruscan doctrine of the lightning by priestly speculations shows in its details the influence of Roman, Greek, or Babylonian ideas, or whether—as was the case with haruspicy—it was the means of conveying Babylonian ideas to the Romans, and perhaps to the Greeks as well, is a problem that awaits further investigation.

31. The 'libri haruspicini.'—The *libri haruspicini* comprised the doctrines relating to the inspection of entrails, and especially of the liver. The reeking entrails of the slaughtered animal were believed to be the media through which the gods spoke to men. The bronze liver of Piacenza (§ 6), with its regions and divine names, shows that the Etruscans, like the Babylonians, assigned to their deities definite localities both upon the liver and in the sky, and that their doctrine of the lightning was inherently related to their haruspicy. The account given by Martianus Capella (*de Nuptiis Merc. et Philol.* i. 41–61) and the Piacenza model both represent the celestial temple of the Etruscans, but each in its own way, so that the regions and deities of the one cannot be summarily identified with those of the other. In Etruscan, as in Babylonian haruspicy, the *caput iocinoris*, the *pars familiaris*, and *pars hostilis* (right and left?), the *fissa* (indentations and crevices seen especially in the sheep's liver), the *fibræ* (tips or edges of the liver), and the gall-bladder all had their special functions. We cannot say as yet whether the clay models of livers with Hittite cuneiform inscriptions which have been found in Boghaz-keui will prove, when deciphered, to be connecting links between the Babylonian and the Etruscan models. But we can even now make out a certain textual connexion between the Babylonian examples and the liver of Piacenza. Thus the two leading types of Babylonian haruspication were as follows: (1) 'If the left side of the gall-bladder is thus or thus, the enemy will capture the sovereign's country'; and (2) 'If [the left side of the gall-bladder is] complete, the flattened middle of the gall-duct is the hand of Ishtar of Babylon'; and, when we compare with these the divine names in the several regions of the Etruscan model, we find that they are abbreviations of the second type. Both the Etruscan and the Greek practice of haruspicy seem to be directly related to the Babylonian; the Roman *extispicium* was no doubt strongly influenced by the Etruscan system, but its sole object was to decide whether the victim was acceptable to the deity or not, whereas the Etruscans read in the liver revelations of the future, even in minute details.

32. The 'libri rituales' ('ostenta').—The Etruscan doctrines of the lightning-flash and of haruspicy were in certain portions closely akin to the doctrine of *ostenta*, which formed a division of the *libri rituales.* Our best source of information regarding the doctrine of *ostenta* is found in the *responsa* given by the Etruscan *haruspices* to the Romans who consulted them. With reference to any particular *prodigium*, the following four points had to be determined: (1) From which deities did the sign proceed? (2) Why had they sent it? (3) What did it portend? and (4) How was it to be propitiated? Examples of such *ostenta* were earthquakes, tempests, showers of stones or blood (fire-balls) in the sky, and comets. Ill-omened trees with black fruits, and unlucky animals (beasts of prey and night-birds) struck terrror into the beholder; white horses and rams with purple or golden spots denoted good luck; serpents might portend either good or evil. Monstrous births, especially hybrids, and grotesque animals stirred the imagination, and such creatures—chimæras, winged beasts, and crosses between lions and birds—appear also on the monuments, but have not as yet received special attention. These terrifying signs were usually propitiated by removing all traces of them. Statues which had been thrown down by tempest or lightning were set up more securely; injured temples were consecrated anew. Monsters and hybrid children were thrown into the sea or buried alive; adults who changed their sex were banished to a desert island. A marriage disturbed by an earthquake or a celestial portent was postponed. Animals that spoke were supposed to be the mouthpieces of deities, and were maintained at the public expense. Whether certain other propitiatory rites, such as sacrifices, gifts, lustrations, and choirs of virgins, are of Greek, Roman, or Etruscan origin can hardly be decided in particular cases; and it is also doubtful whether divination by observing the flight of birds was indigenous to Etruria. Babylonian ideas make their influence strangely felt likewise throughout the Etruscan doctrine of *ostenta*, even in points of detail.

33. The 'libri rituales' (limitation, and ceremonies of consecration and foundation). — The *libri rituales* contained also directions regarding ceremonies on particular occasions. Plots of land, houses, temples, and cities had to be orientated and limited *Etrusco ritu*; *pomerium* and *mundus* seem originally to have been Etruscan terms. The arts of land-surveying and architecture enjoyed the sanction of religion. The books of the *gromatici* contained an oracle of Vegoia (§§ 21, 29) regarding the surveying and allotment of land (*agrimensores*, 350); the word *gruma* itself is most satisfactorily explained—in accordance with Etruscan analogies —as a derivative of the Gr. γνώμων (acc. -ονα). The Etruscan temple-design and the Etruscan *ritus* for the foundation of cities were adopted by the Romans. The excavations made, *e.g.*, at Marzabotto confirm the literary tradition. The investigation of Italian place-names has yielded a surprisingly large number of Etruscan forms; and, as such names are nearly always attached to high places capable of being defended, they are in all likelihood to be explained on the theory that urban colonies of Etruscans, located above and amidst the Italic peasant farm-houses, were founded and named *Etrusco ritu* by the ruling families of Etruscan nationality; though it is not, of course, to be supposed that these settlers, who, being relatively few in numbers, would soon be granted the rights of *connubium* and *commercium* with the neighbouring peoples, were able to maintain the distinctively Etruscan character of their new locations.

34. The 'libri rituales'; law.—In Etruria, legal institutions likewise formed a branch of religion. Thus we hear nothing of a separate legal code; the *jus civile* was merged in the *jus sacrum* of the religious books. The law of property seems to have been connected in the closest way with the sacrosanct art of land-surveying. The saying of Vegoia, found, as noted above, in the writings of the *agrimensores*, finishes with words that suggest the phraseology of Oriental religions: 'propterea neque fallax neque bilinguis sis; disciplinam pone in corde tua.' The perjurer and his offspring were doomed to become fugitives and outcasts. The frightful penalties wreaked upon hermaphrodites in Etruria (§ 32) are found attached to certain crimes also in Roman Law. By a fortunate accident of transmission a representation of the solemn Etruscan rite of adoption has come down to us: a sketch on a mirror shows us the adult Herakles sucking the breast of Juno in the presence of the other Olympians. Here the act of sucking signifies the rite of adoption, the child being admitted into Olympus in virtue of the milk-tie—a relationship which is quite common in the Caucasus, and which, through the influence of Islām, has become a universal law in the East. Cf. art. FOSTERAGE.

35. The 'libri fatales' and 'libri Acherontici.'—The *libri fatales* and *libri Acherontici*—the books of fate and of death—were also included among the *libri rituales*. We have already spoken of the deification of souls (§ 20); and in accordance therewith the Acherontic books would appear to have contained certain elements of the Orphic-Pythagorean doctrine of metempsychosis, and, in the manner of the Orphics, they based the fact upon certain mysterious sacrifices. These books treated also of a certain respite of fate: '. . . sciendum secundum aruspicinae libros et sacra Acheruntia, quae Tages composuisse dicitur, fata decem annis quadam ratione differri . . . primo loco a Jove dicunt posse impetrari, post a fatis' (Serv. on *Æn.* viii. 398). Birthdays and other periods of life were accounted of great, and even critical, importance. The *libri fatales* assigned to human life a duration of twelve hebdomads; but, when life had extended to ten hebdomads, or seventy years, man could no longer delay the incidence of fate by propitiatory rites. From that stage onwards he must ask nothing more from the gods; and, even if he should survive for other two hebdomads, yet his soul is really sundered from his body, and the gods vouchsafe him no further *prodigia* (Varro, in Censorinus, xiv. 6).

36. 'Sæcula'; cosmogony.—The doctrine of the periods of human life was adapted also to the life of the Etruscan city-State, appearing here as the doctrine of *sæcula*, which we meet with again in the sphere of Roman history. It was believed that a respite from the menaces of fate foreboded in the *ostenta sæcularia* could be secured by means of propitiatory ceremonies until the tenth *sæculum*, and that thereafter fate took its inexorable course. The 'secular' festivals were simply propitiations of the *ostenta sæcularia*. Conformably to the tradition regarding the *sæcula* found in the sacred books, the *terminus a quo* of Etruscan chronology was laid down as 967 B.C.—a date which is perhaps not without importance in regard to the appearance of the Etruscans in Italy.

The Etruscan cosmogony was of a very remarkable character. According to the account of it given by Suidas (*s.v.* Τυρρηνία), the demiurge appointed twelve millenniums for his acts of creation, and assigned them severally to the twelve signs of the zodiac. In the first chiliad he created heaven and earth; in the second, the firmament; in the third, the sea, and the waters upon the land; in the fourth, the great lights of heaven—sun, moon, and stars; in the fifth, everything in air, earth, and water that creeps and flies and runs upon four feet; and in the sixth, man. Six thousand years had thus elapsed before the creation of man, and the human race should endure for six thousand years more. The similarity of this creation story to the Biblical account is unmistakable. Whether the source used by Suidas, and very vaguely indicated by him, had been composed under the influence of the Biblical narrative, or whether his account really embodies an ancient Etruscan tradition—in the sense, let us say, that Western Asiatic conceptions underlie both the Biblical and the Etruscan doctrine of the origin and the *sæcula* of the world—is a problem which we are at present unable to solve.

LITERATURE.—I. *GENERAL*: K. O. Müller, *Die Etrusker*, new ed. by W. Deecke, Stuttgart, 1877, ii. 1–195: 'Von der Religion u. Divination d. Etrusker' [still of value, especially for its comprehensive account of the literary sources]; the same writer in Ersch-Gruber's *Allgem. Encyc.*, Leipzig, 1830, *s.v.* 'Hetrurien,' 'Hetrusker' (= *Kleine deutsche Schriften*, Breslau, 1847, i. 173–185); E. Gerhard, *Über d. Gottheiten d. Etrusker: Eine in d. kgl. Akad. d. Wiss. zu Berlin vorgelesene Abhandlung*, Berlin, 1847 [deals with monumental sources, but with untenable mystical interpretations]; G. Dennis, *The Cities and Cemeteries of Etruria*, new ed., London, 1883, i. pp. liii–lx; A. Noël Des Vergers, *L'Etrurie et les Étrusques*, Paris, 1862–64, i. 278–314; J. Martha, *L'Art étrusque*, Paris, 1889, pp. 255–283: 'L'Architecture religieuse,' 313–321: 'La Sculpture religieuse (Les Figures mythologiques)'; the same writer in Daremberg-Saglio, *Dict. des Ant.*, *s.v.* 'Etrusci'; G. Körte, in Pauly-Wissowa, *s.v.* 'Etrusker,' vi. 765–768. L. A. Milani (*Ausonia*, i. [1906] 133) has promised a study on the Art and Religion of the Etruscans. Further bibliographical particulars in G. Herbig, 'Bericht über d. Fortschritte d. Etruskologie für d. Jahre 1894–1907,' in

Jahresber. über d. Fortschritte d. klass. Altertumswissensch. cxl. (Leipzig, 1908) 79 ff. ('Religion,' nos. 488–518; previous reports by **W. Deecke**, cf. *ib.* under no. 5). Short summaries of the literature will be found also in many treatises on Roman and ancient history.

II. *FOR THE SPECIAL SUBJECTS OF THE PARAGRAPHS.*—**1.** For the calendar and astronomy: **Müller-Deecke**, *Etrusker*, ii. 300–316; **C. Thulin**, *Die Götter des Martianus Capella u. der Bronzeleber v. Piacenza*, Giessen, 1906, pp. 75–81; cf. **F. Boll**, in *Berl. philol. Wochenschr.* xxviii. (1908), cols. 1372–79. For calendar dates and the Agram linen-roll: **A. Torp**, 'Etrusk. Monatsnamen,' in *Videnskabs-Selskabets Skrifter*, ii., Histor.-Filos. Kl., Christiania, 1902, no. 4; **G. Herbig**, 'Die etr. Leinwandrolle d. Agramer Nat.-Museums,' in *Abhandl. d. kgl. bayer. Akad. d. Wissensch.*, Philos.-Philol. u. Histor. Kl. xxv. (Munich, 1911), no. 4, p. 43 (with additional literature). Collections of Inscriptions: *Corpus inscr. ital.*, ed. A. Fabretti, Turin, 1867, with three suppl. 1872–78, and G. F. Gamurrini, *Appendice*, Florence, 1880; *Corpus inscr. etr.*, Leipzig, 1893 ff., edd. C. Pauli, O. A. Danielsson, G. Herbig, B. Nogara; more recent discoveries in the current issues of the 'Notizie degli scavi' (*Atti d. R. Acc. d. Lincei*, Rome).

2. For the ancient references to the Etruscan religion and the *Etrusca disciplina*: **Müller-Deecke**, *Etrusker* (as above); **G. Schmeisser**, *Quæstionum de Etrusca disciplina particula*, Inaug. Diss., Breslau, 1872, also *Die etr. Disciplin*, Programm, Liegnitz, 1881; **A. Bouché-Leclercq**, *Histoire de la divination dans l'antiquité*, iv. (Paris, 1882) 3–115; **G. Wissowa**, *Rel. u. Kultus d. Römer*^{2}, Munich, 1912, pp. 543–549; **C. O. Thulin**, *Die etr. Disciplin*, i.–iii., Gothenburg, 1900–09. For Latin writers on the *Etr. disciplina*: **M. Schanz**, *Gesch. d. röm. Lit.* i. 2^3, Munich, 1909, pp. 494–497; *Scriptorum disciplinæ etr. fragmenta*, coll. C. Thulin, i., Berlin, 1906; **E. Bormann**, 'Denkmäler etr. Schriftsteller,' in the *Jahreshefte d. österr. arch. Inst.* ii. (Vienna, 1899) 129–136.

3. For the Agram roll: **I. Krall**, 'Die etr. Mumienbinden des Agramer National-Museums,' *DWAW*, Philos.-Hist. Kl. xli. (Vienna, 1892) 1–70; **E. Lattes**, 'Saggi e appunti intorno alla iscrizione etrusca della mummia,' in *Memorie d. R. Ist.-Lomb.*, Cl. di lett. e scienze stor. e mor. xix. (Milan, 1893) 133–389, and elsewhere; **A. Torp**, *Etr. Beiträge*, i., ii., Leipzig, 1902–03; **G. Herbig**, *Etr. Leinwandrolle* (as above): a new ed. is in preparation for the *CIE*.

4. For sepulchral rolls and the *pulena*-roll: **G. Herbig**, *op. cit.* 11–18, 20–26. For the clay tablet of Capua: **A. Torp**, 'Bemerkungen zu d. etr. Inschrift von S. Maria di Capua,' in *Videns.-Selsk. Skrifter*, ii., Hist.-Filos. Kl., Christiania, 1905, no. 5. For the *cippus Perusinus*: *CIE* 4538.

5. For the leaden tablet of Magliano: **L. A. Milani**, 'Il Piombo scritto di Magliano,' in *Mon. ant. dei Lincei*, ii. (Rome, 1893). For imprecatory tablets: **F. Skutsch**, in Pauly-Wissowa, *s.v.* 'Etrusker,' vi. 785 f., and elsewhere. For ABC monuments: **A. Dieterich**, in *Rhein. Mus. f. Phil.* lvi. (1901) 77–105 (cf. *Kleine Schriften*, Leipzig, 1911, p. 202 ff.). For anatomical votive gifts: **L. Stieda**, 'Über altital. Weihgeschenke,' in *Mitteil. d. kaiserl. deutsch. arch. Inst.*, Röm. Abtheilung, xiv. [1899] 230–243; Anatomische Hefte, Abt. i., xvi. (1901) 1–83.

6. For the bronze liver of Piacenza: **W. Deecke**, 'Das Templum von Piacenza,' *Etrusk. Forschungen*, iv., Stuttgart, 1880, with Supplement, *Etr. Forsch. u. Studien*, ii. [1882] 65 ff.; **C. Thulin**, *Die Götter d. Mart. Cap.* (above under **1**), and cf. **W. F. Otto**, in *Deutsche Lit.-Zeitung*, 1909, cols. 1035-43; **G. Körte**, 'Die Bronzeleber von P.,' in *Röm. Mitteil.* xx. [1905] 348–379. For Oriental analogues, see lit. in **G. Herbig**, *Bericht* (cf. above, under I.), esp. **M. Jastrow**, *Die Religion Babyloniens u. Assyriens*, Giessen, 1905 ff., ii. 213–415. Cf. art. DIVINATION (Roman), vol. iv. p. 825^a, notes 1 and 2.

7. **E. Gerhard**, **A. Klügmann**, **G. Körte**, *Etr. Spiegel*, i.–v., Berlin, 1840–97; **A. Furtwängler**, *Die antiken Gemmen*, i.–iii., Leipzig, 1900; **H. Brunn** and **G. Körte**, *I Rilievi delle urne etrusche*, i., ii., Rome, 1870–96; lit. on mural paintings in **F. v. Stryk**, *Studien üb. d. etr. Kammergräber*, Inaug. Diss. (Munich), Dorpat, 1910; **W. Deecke**, 'Das etr. Münzwesen' (*Etr. Forsch.* ii.), Stuttgart, 1876. There exist as yet no really comprehensive works giving reproductions of the Etr. mural paintings, coins, statues of deities, or vases (with the actual and genuine Etruscan paintings).

8. **Wissowa**'s genetic analysis of the various orders of deities in Rom. religion (*Religion u. Kultus*, pt. ii. sect. 1–5) is a masterpiece of method.

9. A great deal of philological material relating to the names of the gods will be found here and there in the writings of W. Corssen, S. Bugge, W. Deecke, C. Pauli, and E. Lattes. But, grateful as we are for much that has been written on points of detail, we cannot shut our eyes to the fact that nearly every attempt to explain these names etymologically has proved a failure.

10 and **12.** Artt. on individual deities by **W. Deecke** and **C. Pauli**, in Roscher, and by **C. Thulin** and **G. Herbig**, in Pauly-Wissowa, *s.vv.*

11. For Italic and Greek deities in Etruria: **G. Wissowa**, *Religion*, etc.; **W. F. Otto**, in Pauly-Wissowa; **J. B. Carter**, 'Die Etrusker u. d. röm. Religion,' in *Röm. Mitteil.* xxv. (1910) 74–88. For Gr. names of gods and heroes in Etr. form: **W. Deecke**, in *Beiträge z. Kunde d. indogerm. Sprachen*, ed. Bezzenberger, ii. (Göttingen, 1878) 161–186. For (*usil* and) *cauθa*: **Skutsch-Pontrandolfi**, *La Lingua etrusca*, Florence, 1909, p. 16; **G. Herbig**, *Etr. Leinwandrolle*, p. 24 f.; for *herm-* and *turms*: **G. Herbig**, *op. cit.* p. 25; for (*ani* and) *culśanś*: **G. Herbig**, *Glotta*, iv. (1912) 173.

13. On *melkarθ*: **M. Bréal**, *Journal des Savants*, 1899, p. 63 ff. For Egyptian deities in the Agram document: **G. Herbig**, *Etr. Leinwandrolle*, 34–38. For the relations between Etruscans and pre-Hellenic civilization (with very dubious results): **L. A. Milani**, in *Studi e mat. di arch. e numism.* i., ii. (1899–1905), and in the *Rivista critica e storica, promotrice della cultura religiosa in Italia*, vi. (1906); **S. Bugge**, *Das Verhältnis d. Etrusker zu d. Indogermanen u. d. vorgriech. Bevölkerung Kleinasiens u. Griechenlands*, Strassburg, 1909. On *fufluns*: most recently **W. Schulze**, 'Zur Gesch. lat. Eigennamen,' in *AGG*, Philol.-Hist. Kl., new ser., v. 5, no. 5 (Berlin, 1904), p. 589; on *śeθlans* and *selvans*: **C. Pauli**, in Roscher, *s.vv.* For links between Etruria and Babylonia, see lit. to § **6** and §§ **30–32**.

14. For the suffixes of Etr. words: **Müller-Deecke**, *Die Etrusker*, ii. §§ 23, 24, and especially **W. Schulze**, *op. cit. passim.* Precarious conclusions regarding the formation of Etr. divine names in **C. Pauli**, in *Beiträge z. Kunde d. indogerm. Sprachen*, ed. Bezzenberger, xxv. (Göttingen, 1900) 194–227, xxvi. (1901) 48–63.

15. On the divine triad: **C. Thulin**, in *Rhein. Mus. f. Philol.*, new ser. lx. [Frankfort, 1905] 256–261. On the ennead: the same author, *Etr. Disciplin* (see under § **2**), i. 22-27, 32–49. On the dodecad of gods: **G. Schmeisser**, 'De Etruscorum Deis Consentibus qui dicuntur,' in *Commentationes philol. in honorem Aug. Reifferscheidii*, Breslau, 1884, pp. 29–34; **F. Boll**, *Sphæra*, Leipzig, 1903, p. 477 f.; **C. Thulin**, *op. cit.* i. 27–32.

17. On the Roman Lăres: **G. Wissowa**, *Rel. u. Kult. d. Römer*^{2}, 166–175; on the Etr. proper names resembling *lar*: **W. Schulze**, 'Zur Gesch. lat. Eigennamen,' 83 f.; for Lat. *Lāra* and Etr. *lasa*, cf. **Wissowa**, *op. cit.* 174, 235, note 5, and **G. Körte**, *Etr. Spiegel*, v. 9, note 2. Further information in **C. Thulin**, *Götter d. Mart. Capella*, 42–46.

18. On the *Di penates*: **Wissowa**, *op. cit.* 161–166; **C. Thulin**, *op. cit.* 56–58.

19. On the *Genius*: **W. F. Otto**, in Pauly-Wissowa, *s.v.*; dubious conclusions in **C. Pauli**, *Altital. Studien*, i. (Hanover, 1883) 69.

20. On *deus animalis* (*divina anima*), Etr. *aisna hinθu*: **G. Herbig**, *Etr. Leinwandrolle*, 41 f.

21. For the worship of mythological heroes: **Müller-Deecke**, *Etrusker*, ii. 279–292; for clan deities: **W. Schulze**, *op. cit.* (in **13**) 122 f., 165 f., 200, 252; **W. F. Otto**, *Rhein. Mus. f. Philol.*, new ser., lxiv. (1909) 449–468; **G. Herbig**, *Etr. Leinwandrolle*, 25 f.

22. On the Faliscan cult of Janus and Juno, cf. **W. Deecke**, *Die Falisker*, Strassburg, 1888, §§ 33, 31. Latest discussions of the nature and the Lat. names of Juno: **W. F. Otto**, in *Philologus*, lxiv. (1905) 161–223, and **H. Ehrlich**, in *Zeitsch. f. vergl. Sprachforsch.*, ed. Kuhn, xli. (1907) 283–287.

23. On the Etr. *lasa*: **Aem. Schippke**, *De speculis Etruscis quæstionum particula*, i., Inaug. Dissert., Breslau, 1881; see also Lit. under § **17**.

24. For the fate-recording deities: **G. Herbig**, *Etr. Leinwandrolle*, 13–18, 27 f. (with references to E. Lattes' earlier articles on the subject).

25. On *vanθ* and *culśu*, cf. **G. Herbig**, *op. cit.* 12–19; on the Etruscan Charon: **T. A. Ambrosch**, *De Charonte Etrusco*, Breslau, 1837; **S. Rossi**, *Il Tipo e l'ufficio del Charun etrusco*, Messina, 1900; **O. Waser**, *ARW* i. (1898) 177–179.

26. For *mantrnś* (not *muantrnś*), cf. **G. Herbig**, *Glotta*, iv. (1912) 173 f. For the deification of souls, cf. Lit. to § **20**. For the figured covers of Etruscan sarcophagi, and the *lectisternia* deities: **G. Herbig**, *op. cit.* 40. For the Etruscan tombs and their furnishings, cf. (besides numerous Italian monographs), *e.g.*, **B. Modestov**, *Introd. à l'hist. rom.*, Paris, 1907, p. 352 ff.; **Frova**, *La morte e l'oltretomba nell' arte etrusca*, 1908, and the works of **G. Dennis** and **J. Martha** cited above (under I.); **F. v. Stryk** (under § **7**).

27. For lit. on the *Etrusca disciplina*, see under § **2**; on the *haruspices*: **A. Bouché-Leclercq**, in Daremberg-Saglio, *s.v.*; **C. Thulin**, in Pauly-Wissowa, *s.v.* For other priestly titles, see **W. Deecke**, 'Die etr. Beamten- u. Priestertitel' (*Etr. Forsch. u. Stud.* vi.), Stuttgart, 1884.

28. **Müller-Deecke**, *Die Etrusker*, ii. 196–224: 'Von den gottesdienstlichen Spielen, der Musik u. Orchestik der Etrusker'; **C. Thulin**, *Ital. sakrale Poesie u. Prosa*, Berlin, 1906, pp. 1–14, 67–77; also the lit. to § **5**. For human sacrifice: **Müller-Deecke**, *op. cit.* ii. 20, 101, 110.

29. On *Tages* and *Begoe*: **C. Thulin**, *Scriptorum disc. Etr. fragm.* 3–11 (cf. **W. Schulze**, *op. cit.* 240) and 12–21.

30. For the Etr. doctrine of the lightning-flash: **C. Thulin**, *Etr. Disciplin*, i.; cf. **W. F. Otto**, in *Deutsche Lit.-Zeitung*, 1909, col. 1041 f. For Etr.-Bab. astronomy and astrology: **F. Boll**, in *Berliner philol. Wochenschr.*, 1908, cols. 1372–79; **M. Jastrow**, *Religion Bab. u. Assyr.* ii. 742–744.

31. For *haruspicina*: **C. Thulin**, *op. cit.* ii., also lit. to §§ **2**, **6**, and **27**. For the Rom.-Etr. *extispicina*: **G. Wissowa**, *Rel. u. Kult. d. Römer*^{2}, esp. 419; for Etr.-Bab. *haruspicina*: **M. Jastrow**, *op. cit.* ii. 216, 219, 320, note 3, 742.

32. For *ostenta*: **C. Thulin**, *op. cit.* iii. 76–130; for the *responsa haruspicum*: **G. Wissowa**, *op. cit.*, esp. 545 f.; for Etr.-Bab. *ostenta*: **M. Jastrow**, *op. cit.* ii. 744, esp. notes 2 and 3; cf. **Joh. Hunger**, 'Babylonische Tieromina nebst griechisch-römischen Parallelen,' in *MVG* xiv. [1909] 3, 1–178.

33. For 'limitation,' and ceremonies of consecration and foundation, **C. Thulin**, *op. cit.* iii. 3–46. On the Lat.-Etr. *gruma* and Gr. *γνώμονα*, cf. **W. Schulze**, *SBAW*, Berlin, 1905, p. 709. For Etruscan place-names in Italy: **W. Schulze**, 'Zur Gesch. latein. Eigenn.,' 522–582.

34. For Etruscan law: **C. Thulin**, *op. cit.* iii. 52–56; **C. Casati**, *Jus Antiquum*, Paris, 1894, and *Éléments du droit* *étrusque*, Paris, 1895; J. Kohler (and A. Ehrenzweig), 'Milchverwandschaft bei d. Etruskern,' in *ZVRW* xviii. [1905] 73–75.

35. For the *libri fatales* and *libri Acherontici*: C. Thulin, *op. cit.* iii. 57–75; G. Herbig, *Etr. Leinwandrolle*, 34 f., 41 f.

36. On *sæcula*: C. Thulin, iii. 63–75; A. Jeremias, *Das AT im Lichte des alt. Orients*^{2}, Leipzig, 1906, pp. 63, note 2, 154 f.

G. HERBIG.

EUCHARIST (to end of Middle Ages).—The title 'Eucharist,' as applied to the central rite of the Christian Church, has its origin in the thanksgivings pronounced over the bread and cup by Christ at the Last Supper (Mk $14^{22f.}$, Mt 26^{27}, Lk 22^{17-19}, 1 Co 11^{24}). From early times the word was applied to the Christian 'thank-offering,' with special reference to the bread and wine over which the thanksgiving was pronounced (*Didache*, 9; Ignatius, *Philad.* 4, *Smyrn.* 6; Justin, *Apol.* i. 66). On the uses of the words εὐχαριστία, εὐχαριστεῖν, see note by Hort in *JThSt* iii. 594 f.; and on the later history of the parallel word εὐλογία, based on the 'blessing' (εὐλογήσας, Mk 14^{22} [Mt 26^{26}]) pronounced at the institution, see Brightman, *Liturgies Eastern and Western*, Oxford, 1896, Index. There is no instance of these uses of the word εὐχαριστία in the NT, where the terms employed to denote the common meal of the Christians with which the Eucharist was associated are 'the breaking of bread' (ἡ κλάσις τοῦ ἄρτου, κλᾶν ἄρτον, Ac $2^{42.46}$ $20^{7.11}$, 1 Co 10^{16}; in the last 'the cup of blessing' is also referred to) and 'supper of the Lord' (κυριακὸν δεῖπνον, 1 Co 11^{20}; see below). From the presentation in the rite of bread and wine regarded as an offering of the fruits of the earth, along with the prayers and thanksgivings of the worshippers, the term 'sacrifice' (θυσία, *Did.* 14) or 'offering' (Iren. *adv. Hær.* IV. xviii. 1, *ecclesiæ oblatio*; cf. Clement of Rome, *ad Cor.* 40, 44) came to be applied to the rite. Later expansions of this earlier language will be illustrated in the course of the present article. See, further, Drews, *PRE*^{3}, art. 'Eucharistie.'

I. *THE EUCHARIST IN THE NEW TESTAMENT.*—**1. Accounts of the Last Supper.**—The four passages dealing with the Last Supper are Mt 26^{26-29}, Mk 14^{22-25}, Lk 22^{15-20}, 1 Co 11^{23-26}. Of these four accounts Mt. is dependent on Mk.; St. Paul supplies fresh features, while Lk. exhibits important differences from the other three. According to the Synoptists and St. Paul, Jesus on the evening before His arrest, during a meal with His disciples, took bread, and pronounced over it a blessing or thanksgiving (εὐλογήσας, Mt., Mk.; εὐχαριστήσας, Lk., Paul; the words are nearly synonymous—see 1 Co 14^{16}; the 'blessing' or 'thanksgiving' is an act of praise addressed to God). The bread was distributed to the disciples with the words 'This is my body.' Then Jesus took the cup, and, having given thanks (εὐχαριστήσας, Mt., Mk.), He gave it to them and said: 'This is my blood of the covenant which is shed for many' (ὑπὲρ πολλῶν, Mk.; περὶ πολλῶν, Mt.; Paul has 'the new covenant in my blood'; so Lk. acc. to the *textus receptus*). After the words 'This is my body' Paul has 'which is for you (τὸ ὑπὲρ ὑμῶν), and this is expanded by the *textus receptus* of Lk. into 'which is given for you.' Similarly, Mt. expands the words of Mk. about 'the blood shed for many' by the addition 'unto remission of sins.' Mt. alone has the injunctions, after the delivery of the bread and the cup, 'Eat,' 'Drink ye all of it,' while Mk. has simply 'and they all drank of it.' Mk. also records that it was after they had drunk of it that the words 'This is my blood,' etc., were spoken, whereas Mt. connects both the commands to eat and to drink closely with the statements 'This is my body,' 'This is my blood.' Paul and the *textus receptus* of Lk. add the command, 'Do this for my memorial' (τοῦτο ποιεῖτε εἰς τὴν ἐμὴν ἀνάμνησιν) after the words 'This is my body'; and Paul has the same words, with the addition 'as often as ye drink it,' after the words about the cup (the injunction in connexion with the cup is not found in the *textus receptus* of Lk.). Paul and the *textus receptus* of Lk. assert that it was 'after they had supped' that the thanksgiving over the cup was pronounced. In Mt. and Mk. the account concludes with the words, 'Verily I say unto you, I will no longer drink of the fruit of the vine, until that day when I drink it new (Mt. adds 'with you') in the Kingdom of God' ('my Father,' Mt.). The words are absent from Lk. in this connexion, but similar words appear earlier in his account, in connexion with the thanksgiving over a cup and the delivery of it, before the blessing of the bread. St. Paul's account concludes with the words, 'for as often as ye eat this bread, and drink the cup, ye proclaim the Lord's death until he come' (in which Schweitzer sees a reminiscence of the concluding words in the accounts of Mt. and Mk.).

The main problem in the NT account of the institution centres in Lk. Westcott and Hort, on the ground of the omission of vv.$^{19b. 20}$ in some early Western authorities, regard these words as a later insertion (see Sanday, in *HDB* ii. 636). But the resultant text is full of difficulty. According to their reading, in vv.$^{15-18}$ Jesus alludes to His desire to eat this Passover with them before He suffers, and declares that He will not eat of it, until it be fulfilled in the Kingdom of God. Then follows a thanksgiving over a cup, and its delivery to them to be divided amongst them, with no reference to the words about His blood, but merely with the statement that He 'will not drink henceforth of the fruit of the vine, until the Kingdom of God come' (some MSS omit the words ἀπὸ τοῦ νῦν). Then in v.^{19a} follows the account of the thanksgiving over the bread, which is broken and given to them with the words, 'This is my body.'

Those who adopt the reading of Westcott and Hort regard v.^{17} as taking the place of the narrative in Mt. and Mk. about the cup, which thus precedes the blessing pronounced over the bread (for this order, which follows the common Jewish order of the benedictions at meals, cf. *Didache*, 9). According to this interpretation, the sacramental significance of the acts of Jesus is indicated only in the case of the bread. But the omission of the words recorded by the other Synoptists with reference to the cup is in any case difficult to explain. Moreover, the parallelism exhibited in vv.$^{15-18}$ suggests that these verses are closely connected, and form a narrative distinct from that in v.^{19a}, which thus becomes a mere isolated fragment. Hence it may be argued that the text of Westcott and Hort represents a transition between two types of text, the one containing only vv.$^{15-18}$, the other being that represented in the received text of Lk. On the former supposition the whole of v.^{19} would be an interpolation from St. Paul; and Lk., like the Fourth Gospel, would then contain no account of the institution of the rite (Blass, *Philology of the Gospels*, London, 1898, p. 179 f.). There is, however, no manuscript authority for the omission of the first part of v.^{19}. On the other supposition the *textus receptus* of Lk. represents the original reading, and the variations and omissions are explained as due to the difficulty created in the minds of scribes by the existence of two cups in Lk.'s account. Of those who accept the *textus receptus* of Lk., some regard vv.$^{15-18}$ as referring, at least in the intention of the author of Lk., to the Paschal meal (see, however, § 2), and as having no reference to the Eucharist, the account of which follows in vv.$^{19-20}$ (Resch, Holtzmann, Schweitzer). Schweitzer regards the account in Lk. as due to editorial revision, and as possessing no independent value. It has been suggested in this connexion that the rearrangement of his material by Lk. has been carried out with the object of bringing the account into accord with the ritual of the Passover, and that the first cup is intended to represent that which began the Paschal ritual, while the second cup is placed, as in the Paschal ritual, at the end of the meal (cf. Goguel, *L'Eucharistie*, p. 64). Others, however, regard vv.$^{15-18}$ as a doublet, containing a distinct account of the Supper from that found in vv.$^{19. 20}$ (Batiffol, *Études*, 2nd ser., p. 32; Blakiston, *JThSt* iv. 548 f.). A further stage is represented in the opinion which attaches exclusive importance to vv.$^{15-18}$, and finds in them the clue to the real interpretation of the Supper (Loisy, *Les Évangiles synoptiques*, ii. 536 f.; Andersen, *Abendmahl*, 35 f.). But it is a purely arbitrary reconstruction of the history which leaves out of account the tradition preserved in the other Synoptists and in St. Paul.

2. Significance of the Supper.—As to the significance of the words and acts of Jesus at the Supper there has been a wide divergence of opinion in modern discussions of the subject (for useful summaries, see A. Schweitzer, *Das Abendmahl*; Loisy, *Les Évangiles synoptiques*, ii. 535, note 1; Goguel, *L'Eucharistie*, p. 1 ff.). Individual scholars have emphasized severally some particular aspect of the rite, and have denied that it contained any other reference. The brevity of our accounts leaves much unexplained. Possibly Jesus intended His acts and words to be interpreted by the experience of the disciples (cf. Robinson, *EBi*, art. 'Eucharist'), in the light of the events which followed and the new relationship with Him upon which the disciples entered after the Resurrection.

The chief lines along which the interpretation of the Supper has been sought are as follows.

(1) The setting of the meal points to its association with other similar Jewish religious meals, in which there was a solemn benediction of the bread and cup, followed at the close by a prayer of thanksgiving spoken by the president (von der Goltz, *Tischgebete und Abendmahlsgebete*, Leipzig, 1905, p. 7 f.). The prayers of the *Didache* (cc. 9, 10) exhibit the influence of such Jewish formulæ, and the reference to the 'breaking of bread' not only in the early chapters of Acts ($2^{42.46}$), but also in Lk 24^{30-35}, points to the possibility that the Last Supper had links with previous meals which our Lord had shared with His disciples. From this point of view it would sum up and perpetuate that relationship with Him which had been theirs in the days of His ministry.

(2) A second feature of the meal is its connexion with the coming death of Christ. The breaking of the bread and the outpouring of the wine were 'an acted parable' (Jülicher), by which Christ consoled His disciples, declaring to them that His coming death was destined to be a source of blessing to them. This idea, which is clearly expressed in St. Paul's interpretation of the body as 'that which is for you' (τὸ ὑπὲρ ὑμῶν, 1 Co 11^{24}), is implied in Mt. and Mk. by the reference to the blood as 'shed for many' (Mt 26^{28}, Mk 14^{24}), and by the interpretation given to it in Mt. as 'unto remission of sins.' The separate mention of the body and the blood in this connexion shows that it is the body as slain which is spoken of, and rules out all interpretations such as that, *e.g.*, of Andersen, which regards 'the body' as a Pauline phrase, equivalent to 'the Church,' adopted and misunderstood by Mk. from St. Paul. In this way we can explain the idea of the rite as a commemoration of the death of Christ, which is emphasized in the account of St. Paul (1 Co $11^{24f.}$).

(3) A further point is emphasized in our Lord's reference to the cup as 'my blood of the covenant' (Mt., Mk.), or, according to St. Paul (and the *textus receptus* of Lk.), 'the new covenant in my blood.' This aspect has been dwelt upon by Holtzmann (*NT Theol.*, Freiburg, 1896–97, i. 296 f.), who finds in it the clue to the meaning of Christ's action in the Supper. The words refer to Ex 24^8, where, at the ratification of the Sinaitic covenant, Moses sprinkles the people with the blood of the victim, saying, 'Behold the blood of the covenant.' According to this view, our Lord intended by His act to declare the abrogation of the Old Covenant and of the Law, and the inauguration of a new relationship between the disciples and God. In this connexion St. Paul's phrase 'new (καινή) covenant in my blood' is a natural interpretation of the simpler words found in Mk. and Mt., with a probable allusion to Jer 31^{31}. For a fuller expansion of the thought in the light of Christian experience, see He 8–9, where reference is made both to Jer 31^{31-34} and to Ex 24^8. Holtzmann's further contention, that the words of Christ contain no reference to an expiatory death, is not consistent with the language recorded by the Synoptists and St. Paul. The latter, as we have seen, speaks of 'the body which is for you' (τὸ ὑπὲρ ὑμῶν, expanded in the *textus receptus* of Lk. into 'which is given for you'). Similarly, Mt. and Mk. speak of the blood as 'poured out for many,' which Mt. further interprets as 'unto remission of sins.' Moreover, the reference to Ex 24^8 points to a covenant based upon a sacrifice, and in the parallel passage Jer 31^{31-34} there is a reference to the forgiveness of sins in connexion with the new covenant. Such language is fully in accordance with the early Christian interpretation of the death of Christ (cf. 1 Co 15^3, Mk 10^{45}, Mt 20^{28}).

(4) The delivery by Jesus to the disciples of the bread and the cup, accompanied by the command, 'Take' (Mk., Mt.), 'Drink ye all of it' (Mt.), has been interpreted as conveying the idea of a bestowal of spiritual food and drink, of which the bread and wine were representative symbols. The meal as such was to be a memorial feast of the death of Christ, and the bread and wine, received with thanksgiving in remembrance of Christ's death, are designated His body and blood, which are given for the nourishment of the soul (cf. Harnack, 'Brod u. Wasser,' *TU* VII. ii. 117 ff.). This idea is illustrated by St. Paul's implied comparison of the manna and water in the wilderness with the Christian sacraments, and his reference to them as 'spiritual food' and 'spiritual drink' (1 Co 10^{3-4}). It also finds expression in the prayers of the *Didache* (ch. 10). It is this aspect of the Sacrament from which the author of the Fourth Gospel starts in the discourse of ch. 6, which contains an implied reference to the Christian Sacrament, though the author nowhere records its institution. In that chapter we find developed the thought of Christ as the Bread of Life, who gives to men His flesh to eat and His blood to drink. The language used has points of contact with the OT, Rabbinical teaching ('to eat the years of the Messiah,' or 'to eat the Messiah'), and the language of Philo (the Logos the food of the soul); while the terms used ('flesh' and 'spirit') form the starting-point of the theology of Ignatius and Justin, and prepare the way for the conception of the Sacrament as the extension of the Incarnation. The general idea is a spiritual assimilation of Christ in the higher elements of His humanity.

The conception of the Christian Sacrament as a meal following upon a sacrifice lay near at hand in the allusion to Ex 24, where the covenant sacrifice is followed by a sacrificial meal (Ex 24^{11} 'they saw God, and did eat and drink'). A similar reference has been seen in He $13^{10f.}$ where, whatever be the interpretation of the word 'altar,' it is urged that the idea of the writer seems to be that the superiority of the new covenant consists in the fact that, while, in the chief sacrifice of the Day of Atonement, the priests were not allowed to partake of the flesh of the sacrifice, the Christian sacrifice provides at once an atonement and a means of communion. But this interpretation reads more into the passage than can legitimately be inferred from it.

(5) The words with which Mk. and Mt. conclude their account, and in which Jesus declares, 'I will no longer drink of the fruit of the vine, until that day when I drink it new in the Kingdom of God,' contain an allusion to the Jewish belief which represented the coming Messianic age under the form of a banquet, and described its blessings under the form of eating and drinking. Starting from these words in Mk 14^{25}, some modern scholars have explained the words and actions of Jesus at the Supper in an eschatological sense. The pioneer in this interpretation was Spitta (*Urchristenthum*, i.), who illustrates at great length from the Prophets and Wisdom literature of the OT, as well as from Jewish apocalyptic and later Rabbinical writings, the idea of the Messianic feast, in which the Messiah Himself is the food of the subjects of the Kingdom (among the OT passages referred to are Is 25^{6-8} 55^{1-3}, Ps 132^{15}, Pr 9^{2-5}, Sir 15^3 24^{17-21}; cf. Mt $22^{2f.}$, Lk $14^{15f.}$ 22^{28-30}). He further sees in the words of Jesus an allusion to the Davidic-Messianic covenant (see § 4). According to this interpretation, the ideas of Jesus were wholly centred in the future, and had no reference to His death. He turned away from the present, with its prospect of suffering and death, to the future Kingdom, in which, as Messiah, He would bestow on His

disciples the blessings of the coming age. The meal was thus a foretaste of the Messianic feast. Spitta's illustrations of the thought of the spiritual assimilation of the Messiah are instructive and valuable, but his denial that the words and actions of Jesus in regard to the meal have any connexion with His death does great violence to the narratives of the Gospel.

The eschatological view has also been maintained by A. Schweitzer, who in his two works, *Das Abendmahl in Zusammenhang mit dem Leben Jesu und der Gesch. des Urchristenthums* (1901), and *Von Reimarus zu Wrede* (1906), has pleaded for a fuller recognition of the eschatological character of the teaching and acts of Jesus. Starting from St. Mark's account, which he regards as the most authentic, he finds the key to the meaning of the Supper in the words, 'I will no longer drink of the fruit of the vine, until that day when I drink it new in the Kingdom of God.' But, unlike Spitta, he recognizes the connexion of the words of Jesus with the thought of His coming sufferings. The thought of suffering, however, is brought into connexion with the eschatological expectation: Jesus spoke to the disciples, not of His death, but of His death and speedy re-union with them in the feast in the 'Kingdom' (*Abendmahl*, p. 61). Similarly he interprets the feeding of the five thousand as a foretaste of the Messianic meal (*Von Reimarus zu Wrede*, p. 372 f.). By distributing bread to the multitude, He consecrates them to be partakers of the coming Messianic feast, and gives them a pledge that, 'as they had been His table-companions in the time of His obscurity, so should they be also in the time of His glory' (p. 373). The feeding was more than a love-feast or communion-feast. It was a sacrament of deliverance. The Last Supper at Jerusalem had the same sacramental significance. The action of Jesus in distributing the bread and wine is an end in itself, and the meaning of the feast depends upon the fact that He personally distributes the food. The words spoken during the distribution with reference to the propitiatory meaning of His death do not touch the essence of the feast, but are accessary (p. 377). The doubtful feature of this interpretation is the attempt to find the central idea of the Supper in the words of Mk 14^{25} rather than in the words spoken with reference to the bread and wine, and connecting them with the body and blood of Jesus and His coming death. But that there was some such eschatological reference in the Supper, by which the disciples were pointed forward to the coming Kingdom, and their fellowship with Jesus as the Messiah, seems clear not only from the language of the Synoptists, but also from the echo of that language found in the words with which St. Paul concludes his account in 1 Co 11^{26}, 'As often as ye eat this bread, and drink the cup, ye proclaim the Lord's death until He come.'

The eschatological interpretation enables us to reconstruct more exactly the *milieu* amid which the words of Jesus were spoken at the Supper, even if it does not exhaust their reference. It also throws light upon the language of St. Paul, and the spirit in which the early Christian community, with its eager hope of the Second Coming, continued to observe the rite.

(6) The attempt to find a sacrificial meaning in the terms of the command, 'Do this as my memorial,' recorded by St. Paul, and found in the *textus receptus* of Lk., has not gained the general assent of scholars. With the possible exception of St. Paul's words ('ye proclaim the Lord's death until he come') in 1 Co 11^{26}, the NT throws no light upon the way in which the words ποιεῖν ('do') and ἀνάμνησις ('memorial') were interpreted in Apostolic times; and Justin Martyr (*Dial. c. Tryph.* 41) stands alone among 2nd cent. writers in interpreting ποιεῖν in a sacrificial sense ('offer'). The conception of the Eucharist as a sacrifice, which appears already in the *Didache*, arose from more general considerations than the interpretation of the particular words ποιεῖν and ἀνάμνησις used by St. Paul.

In the above discussion the question of the relation of the Eucharist to the Passover meal has been left for separate treatment. The setting of the Supper in the Synoptic accounts implies that it was a Passover meal (see Mt 26^{17}, Mk 14^{12}, Lk 22^{7}). According to that account, Christ sent the disciples to prepare the Passover on 'the first day of unleavened bread,' which Mk. and Lk. identify with the day on which the Passover lamb was killed. The Supper took place on the evening of the same day. Again, the words of Lk 22^{15} ('with desire I have desired to eat this Passover with you'), in the setting in which they occur in the Lucan narrative (see, however, below), imply that the meal was the Passover. Paschal references have been seen in St. Paul's account of the institution (1 Co 11$^{23f.}$), *e.g.* the word 'memorial' (cf. Ex 12^{14}); the 'proclamation' (καταγγέλλετε) of the death, corresponding to the Haggada; the 'cup of blessing,' corresponding to the third cup of the Passover meal (against this reference, see Spitta, *op. cit.* p. 248; Bickell, *Messe und Pascha*, Eng. tr., *The Lord's Supper and the Passover Ritual*, by Skene, Edinburgh, 1891, p. 163). Again, the reference to Christ's death and its sacrificial character undoubtedly arises more naturally out of Paschal associations than it would do if the meal were an ordinary one. On the other hand, the accounts of Mk. and Mt. exhibit no distinctively Paschal features, but refer simply to the covenant-sacrifice of Ex 24^{8} (against this argument, see Lambert, *The Sacraments in the NT*, pp. 253, 297 f.).

But the most serious difficulty connected with the identification of the Last Supper with the Passover meal arises out of the conflicting chronological notices in the Synoptists and in St. John. The day on which Christ sent the disciples to prepare the Passover is identified in Mk 14^{12} (on which Lk. and Mt. depend) with 'the first day of unleavened bread, when they sacrificed the Passover.' Jewish scholars are agreed that this date contains a contradiction, as the first day of unleavened bread was the 15th of Nisan, while the day of the Passover was the 14th of Nisan. It has been suggested that there is some corruption in the source which underlies our Synoptists, and that the original Aramaic text may have had something like 'before the day of unleavened bread' (Resch), or 'the day of unleavened bread drew nigh, and the disciples drew nigh to Jesus' (Chwolson, *Das letzte Passamahl Christi*, ed. Leipzig, 1908, p. 11; on p. 178 f. a different solution is suggested). Other facts in the Synoptic account seem to contradict the idea that the Last Supper was the Passover. Such are the notice of time in Mk 14$^{1.2}$, 'after *two* days was the feast of the Passover,' and the words of the priests, 'not on the feast day, lest there be a tumult of the people.' Again, the reference to the carrying of arms (Mk 14^{47}), the incident of the trial, and the buying of spices are all inconsistent with the idea that the Passover feast had begun, since work of all kinds was prohibited on the feast. Lastly, the account in St. John plainly contradicts the Synoptists in their representation of the Passover feast as the day of the crucifixion (Jn 13^{1}, the Supper was 'before the Passover'; Jn 18^{28}, the Jews would not enter the hall of Pilate, that they might not be defiled, but might eat the Passover; Jn 19^{14}, the day of the crucifixion was 'the preparation of the Passover'; Jn 19^{36}, the identification of Jesus with the Passover lamb, implied in the reference to Ex 12^{46}, Nu 9^{12}). Hence two theories have been propounded: (1) The theory of an anticipated Passover. This view is maintained by Chwolson, *op. cit.* p. 31 f., who explains such anticipation by the suggestion that in the year of the crucifixion the 14th of Nisan fell upon a Sabbath, and that this led to the transference of the day on which the lambs were offered, and to a divergence of custom as to the time of the Passover meal. But this argument is strained and artificial. Another explanation of such a possible anticipation is suggested by M. Power, *The Anglo-Jewish Calendar for every Day in the Gospels* (London, 1902); see Lambert, *JThSt* iv. 192 f. (2) A different interpretation of the problem is supplied by the theory that the Last Supper was the *Ḳiddûsh*, or weekly 'sanctification,' of the Sabbath—a domestic ceremony, in which a cup of wine, and bread, are solemnly blessed and distributed to the household before the evening meal. The *Ḳiddûsh* also preceded great festivals, including the Passover. This theory explains the order in the account of Lk., where the thanksgiving over a cup precedes that pronounced over the bread (cf. 1 Co 10$^{16.21}$; *Didache*, 9). This view was propounded by Box (*JThSt* iii. 357–369), and still earlier by Spitta (*Urchristenthum*, i. 247); cf. also Drews, *PRE*^{3} v. 563, art. 'Eucharistie,' and Batiffol (*Études*, ii. 43–46). According to this view, Christ did not keep the actual Passover with His disciples, but only its preparatory *Ḳiddûsh* (it is in this sense accordingly that Mk 14$^{12.14}$ must be understood). In this connexion it may be noticed that the words of Lk 22^{15} ('with desire I have desired to eat this Passover with you before I suffer'), apart from their context in the Lucan narrative, might indicate an unfulfilled desire (cf. *JThSt* ix. 569 f.). But against this view that we have a description of the *Ḳiddûsh* in the accounts of the Synoptists must be set the order of Mk., Mt., and St. Paul, in which the thanksgiving over the bread precedes the thanksgiving over the cup.

Moreover, according to Mk., it was '*while they were eating*' that Jesus broke bread, and St. Paul describes the blessing of the cup as taking place '*after the supper*' (so Lk. in *textus receptus*). Our accounts are too short, and the writers probably too little interested in the external procedure at the Supper, to enable us to attain any certainty as to the exact details. The general structure of Jewish ceremonial prayers appears to have been much the same as those of ordinary Jewish household prayers, and the parallels adduced prove little more than that our Lord availed Himself of the ordinary Jewish forms of blessing employed at meals.

In any case the Last Supper took place amid the associations of the Paschal season; and, whether in the words and acts of Jesus there is an implied reference to the Passover or not, the association of the Eucharist with the Passover was a natural one, though we may have to admit that the Paschal features in the language of St. Paul represent the later reflexion of a period when the idea of Christ as the true Passover (1 Co 5^{7}, Jn 19^{36}) had influenced the conception of the institution.

3. The Eucharist in Apostolic times.—(1) In the early chapters of Acts mention is made of a meal, 'the breaking of bread' (Ac $2^{42.\,46}$), as one of the characteristics of the life of the early church at Jerusalem. In the former of the two passages (Ac 2^{42}) it occurs in close connexion with the mention of 'the fellowship' which marked the early disciples, and is followed by the mention of 'the prayers' (on the connexion of the clauses, see Robinson, *HDB*, art. 'Communion'). In the second passage (Ac 2^{46}) there is an implied contrast between the daily public attendance of the disciples at the Temple-worship, by which they showed their loyalty to the religion of their countrymen, and the distinctive Christian act of 'breaking bread at home.' The main clause of the sentence in v.^{46}, 'they took their food with gladness and singleness of heart,' (*a*) may indicate that this 'breaking of bread' formed part of an ordinary meal, or (*b*) it may be a general expression summing up the participial clauses προσκαρτεροῦντες . . . κλῶντες, and expressing in Biblical language (cf. Lv 26^{5}) the joy which pervaded the life of the early community (Batiffol). In any case the meal was an expression of fellowship, and doubtless had a religious character (see above, § 2 (1)). Spitta, who sees in Ac $2^{42f.}$ a reference to the Agape, maintains that it was inevitable that the thoughts of those who partook of these meals should go back to the words of Christ at the Supper (*op. cit.* p. 289). Thus the meal would naturally assume a Eucharistic character, and, we may add, include Eucharistic acts. The next mention of the 'breaking of bread' is in Ac 20^{7-11}, where, during St. Paul's stay at Troas, there was a gathering 'on the first day of the week to break bread.' The whole account indicates greater formality than is implied in Ac $2^{42.\,46}$. The mention of the 'first day of the week' (cf. 1 Co 16^{2}), the 'many lights' in the upper room, and the discourse of St. Paul, followed by the breaking of bread, all point to a solemn religious gathering for worship.

(2) St. Paul's account of the Eucharist at Corinth (1 Co 11^{17-34}) throws fuller light upon the fragmentary notices contained in Acts. From his account it appears that the Corinthians assembled for a meal, including, probably at its close [Drews, *PRE*^{3} v. 562, suggests that it was at the beginning; so Box, *JThSt* iii. 365 f.], the Eucharistic commemoration, which, as St. Paul reminds them, had been commanded by the Lord at the Last Supper, and which constituted a solemn memorial of His death 'until he come.' The whole account implies that the Eucharist formed part of a meal (*e.g.* 'when ye come together *to eat*'; 'each one *in eating* [ἐν τῷ φαγεῖν] taketh beforehand his own supper'; lastly, the form in which St. Paul records the institution of the cup, '*as often as ye shall drink*'), though, from its association with the solemn Eucharistic acts, the whole meal should be regarded as 'a supper of the Lord' (κυριακόν is emphatic). To this meal each brought his own provisions; but, instead of waiting for the general distribution, the richer members ate beforehand what they had brought, and by greed and selfishness and excess turned the meal into a private supper (ἴδιον δεῖπνον). Thus the sense of fellowship was lost, and it became impossible to eat a 'supper of the Lord.' Such unworthy participation made a man 'guilty of the body and the blood of the Lord,' and showed a failure to 'discern the body.'

With 'guilty of the body and the blood of the Lord' cf. He 6^{6}, which refers to the sin of those who 'crucify the Son of God afresh,' and He 10^{29} ('who hath trodden under foot the Son of God, and hath counted the blood of the covenant, wherewith he was sanctified, an unholy thing'). Spitta suggests that St. Paul may have had Judas in mind. This guilt arises from the relationship established between the bread of the Eucharist and the Lord's sacrificed body (τὸ σῶμα τὸ ὑπὲρ ὑμῶν) on the one hand, and the Lord's cup and the 'new covenant in his blood' on the other. In the words 'not discerning the body' (omit τοῦ κυρίου with the best MSS), St. Paul is referring primarily to the body of v.^{24}, but it is possible that he has in view the more inclusive sense of 'body' (note τὸ σῶμα, not τὸ σῶμα καὶ τὸ αἷμα, though ἐσθίων καὶ πίνων precedes) referred to in 1 Co $10^{16.\,17}$. By his selfish action the richer brother failed to realize that the sacred meal was a fellowship of believers with Christ and one another. It was the sacrament of their incorporation in Christ. The abuses at Corinth turned it into a private meal.

(3) In another passage of the same epistle (1 Co $10^{16f.}$), St. Paul dwells upon the inconsistency of Christians taking part in idolatrous feasts. In this connexion he refers to the Christian sacrament of the 'fellowship of the body and blood of Christ.' His language is suggested by the associations of the sacrificial feast—an institution which finds a place not only in Semitic life, but also in Greek religion, as well as in early tribal religions. According to this conception, the sacrifice is not merely an offering to the Deity. The worshippers partake of the food of the sacrifice, and in this way a communion is established between the Deity and His worshippers, as well as between the worshippers themselves. Thus to partake of a sacrifice implies fellowship with the Deity who is worshipped (1 Co $10^{18.\,20}$). Similarly, St. Paul says 'the cup of blessing which we bless' and 'the bread which we break' are 'a fellowship' (κοινωνία) of the blood and of the body of Christ, and Christians cannot consistently partake of the table of the Lord and of the table of devils. This aspect of the Christian rite St. Paul develops on striking and original lines. The Christian sacrament is at once a means of spiritual communion with Christ and of corporate fellowship. By participation in the one bread the partakers become one body. The 'fellowship of the body of Christ' would appear to have suggested to him the larger conception of the body of Christ (cf. 1 Co $12^{12.\,13}$), in which Christ and the members of Christ form one whole and are inseparably united (cf. Robinson, *loc. cit.*). In the same way, as we have seen, he interprets the cup to mean 'the new covenant in my blood' (ct. Mk., Mt.), where again the idea is of the fellowship of believers with God and one another, effected through the death of Christ. (For a later development of the whole conception by St. Augustine, see below, II. 3 (2).)

(4) Thus it appears that in the period A.D. 55–57 the Eucharist formed the chief feature of a religious meal, being celebrated probably at its close. St. Paul traces it back to the institution of Christ, and regards its observance as due to His command. This fact throws light upon the earlier references in Acts, and makes it probable that the 'breaking of bread' in Ac $2^{42.46}$ 20^{7-11} included the Eucharist.

The meal with which the Eucharist was associated in Apostolic times has generally been identified with the Agape, which is first expressly mentioned by name in Jude ^{12} (cf. also, on the reading in 2 P 2^{13}, Mayor's note). But St. Paul's account in 1 Co 11 suggests that the gathering there described provided indirectly an opportunity for feeding poorer brethren (vv.$^{21.\,22}$), and that the meal was a pledge of brotherly love and fellowship. But the use of the term Agape and its distinction from the Eucharist, as applied to the conditions described in Ac. and 1 Cor., are possibly anachronisms. As yet there was no sharp distinction between the two parts of the meal. The whole meal in St. Paul's thought had the character of a sacred meal. It was 'a supper of the Lord.' It was only when the social side of the meal came to be distinguished from the solemn liturgical acts connected with it that the Agape came to be thought of as distinct from the Eucharist, and was finally dissociated from it; see, further, Batiffol, *Études*, 1st ser., and art. AGAPE.

4. Critical theories.—The two main questions which have been raised with regard to the early Eucharist in modern discussions are: (1) the significance of the acts and words of Christ at the Last Supper, and (2) the relation of the Last Supper to the later rite, as found, *e.g.*, in St. Paul's account in 1 Corinthians.

(1) It has been maintained that there was no intention on the part of Christ to institute a rite. The meal was simply a parting meal (Andersen). Christ's act was 'a parable' (Jülicher), 'a momentary inspiration,' rather than a premeditated act (Spitta, Holtzmann), in which there was no idea of giving a command for the repetition of the rite. The object of Jesus was to console the disciples by assuring them that His death would not be in vain. The blood 'shed for many' would be the blood of a covenant (Jülicher, and, more fully, Holtzmann). Others, like Spitta and Loisy, think that the thoughts of Jesus at the Supper were wholly directed to the coming Messianic Kingdom. The theory of Schweitzer (see above, § **2** (5)) emphasizes this eschatological reference of the Supper, but does more justice than either of the preceding writers to the connexion of the Supper with the death of Jesus and the mystery of His suffering (*Abendmahl*, p. 61 f.). Both Spitta and Holtzmann deny that there was in the acts and words of Jesus any reference to the sacrificial character of His death. On this see above, § **2** (3).

(2) Many attempts have been made to explain the origin of the meal described in Ac. and 1 Cor. as due to some other cause than a command of Christ at the Last Supper. But, if the Last Supper meant nothing more than some of the theories referred to above represent it to mean, it is difficult to explain how the early disciples came to repeat it or connect their own religious meal with it. By some the early Christian meal has been derived from the Jewish religious meal, adopted by the Christian community as an expression of their sense of fellowship and religious devotion, and enriched by the memory of the Last Supper and the hope of the Second Coming (so Spitta, J. Hoffmann).

Others have emphasized its affinity with the ritual feasts of the heathen world, and have seen in it not an original creation of Christianity, but a particular Christian growth upon the older stock of pre-Christian and non-Christian religious customs. In this case the Eucharist in the form exhibited in 1 Cor. cannot have been a creation of Jesus or have come from strict Jewish circles, but must be explained as due to the reaction upon primitive Christianity of the syncretism of religious beliefs amid which it lived (cf. Heitmüller, *Taufe u. Abendmahl bei Paulus*). In this connexion much is made of the parallel which St. Paul draws in 1 Co 10 between heathen sacrificial feasts on the one hand and the Christian Eucharist on the other, where the 'table of the Lord' is contrasted with 'the table of devils,' while a parallel is sought for St. Paul's implied reference to the Christian sacrament (1 Co $10^{3f.}$) as 'spiritual food' and 'spiritual drink' in the Eleusinian mysteries, where the initiated became ἔνθεοι by means of a meal in which they partook in some mysterious way of the body of Dionysus (cf. Lake, *Earlier Epistles of St. Paul*, pp. 199 f., 213 f.). The attempt has recently been made to trace more explicitly the influence of the mystery religions of the ancient world upon primitive Christianity, especially as seen in St. Paul's Epistles (cf. A. Dieterich, *Eine Mithrasliturgie*², Leipzig, 1910; R. Reitzenstein, *Die hellen. Mysterienreligionen*, do. 1910). This method has been subjected to a searching criticism by A. Schweitzer in his *Geschichte der paulinischen Forschung* (Tübingen, 1911). He discusses the whole question of Hellenizing influence in St. Paul, and repudiates it with characteristic thoroughness. St. Paul, he urges, cannot have been familiar with the mystery religions as known to us, for their general spread in the Græco-Roman world (with the possible exception of the Serapis mystery cult) dates only from the beginning of the 2nd century. Again he emphasizes the danger of constructing from distinct and separate sources a kind of universal mystery religion, possessing a definiteness of contents and ideas such as never really existed, least of all in the time of St. Paul. Nor will he admit that St. Paul's attitude to heathenism was such as to allow of his borrowing from the Nature-worships of heathenism. It is possible that Schweitzer has carried his thesis too far, but he has provided a much-needed caution for those who would press the analogies between Christian and pagan ideas; and, before any satisfactory results can be attained, a more careful sifting of the evidence and dating of the documents are needed. The existence of sacrificial feasts in the pagan world was plainly known to St. Paul, as the passage in 1 Co 10 shows, and provided a *milieu* in which the Christian sacred meal was able to take its place in the life of converts to Christianity. But St. Paul in the same chapter appeals also to similar feasts among the Jews (1 Co 10^{18}), and it is precarious to infer that his own teaching with regard to the Eucharist was moulded by the influence of pagan rather than Jewish customs, especially as the latter formed the original setting of the Christian meal. At the same time it is possible to admit that at Corinth such an influence of pagan customs may have been at work in the case of St. Paul's converts.

Schweitzer's own positive construction connects the sacramental teaching of St. Paul with his eschatology. He finds an earlier parallel to sacraments in Jewish life in the baptism of John, which he maintains was regarded not merely as a symbol of the cleansing of repentance, but as in some way a sacrament of deliverance. Thus the idea of 'eschatological sacraments' would lie near at hand, and St. Paul may have taken it over from the practice of John the Baptist and the early Church. The further question whether the Supper in the view of Jesus was already regarded as bestowing something on those who partook of it, or only first became a sacrament in the primitive Church, would still remain undecided (*op. cit.* p. 189). This attempt to re-state the problem is of importance in two ways: (1) if Schweitzer's criticism proves valid, it sets a limit to the attempt to trace the origin of the Eucharist to the syncretism of Jewish and pagan ideas; (2) it endeavours to find a place for sacraments in connexion with the ideas of the contemporaries of Jesus.

The absence of the command, 'Do this in remembrance of me,' from the narratives of Mt. and Mk. (and according to some texts from Lk.) leaves St. Paul as our ultimate authority for the statement that Jesus commanded the observance of the rite. But it is difficult to believe that in this matter St. Paul was innovating upon the tradition of the Church, or that his account represents a different belief as to the origin of the rite from that current in the primitive Christian community. Nor does his claim to be recording a tradition received 'from the

Lord' (1 Co 11^{23} ἐγὼ γὰρ παρέλαβον ἀπὸ τοῦ Κυρίου) necessarily imply that he is speaking of knowledge given to himself alone, rather than knowledge derived through the medium of the tradition of the Church, though ultimately based on the words of Christ (cf. 1 Co 15^{3} ὃ καὶ παρέλαβον: and for this use of ἀπό to denote the ultimate source, cf. Gal 1^{1} οὐκ ἀπ' ἀνθρώπων οὐδὲ δι' ἀνθρώπου). So Harnack says (*Hist. of Dogma*, Eng. tr. i. 66, n. 1): 'the words of 1 Co 11^{23} are too strong for me.' On the whole, it would seem that the tradition according to which our Lord commanded the observance of the rite was current in the Church in the time of St. Paul, and was not originated by him. Though Mk. and Mt. do not record the command, they would appear to have interpreted the narrative which they give as implying an institution (cf. Goguel, *L'Eucharistie*, p. 190; the writer, however, regards the Synoptic accounts as already influenced by the custom of the Pauline Churches).

Even if we admit that the tradition of the early Church attributed to Jesus the express statement of the command, the question still remains whether this interpretation is the right one. In this connexion we may consider the relation of the Last Supper to the other meals which our Lord had shared with His disciples. Though Schweitzer's suggestion that the feeding of the multitude partook of a sacramental character, and was intended as a foretaste of the Messianic meal, is precarious and improbable, the same objection does not apply equally to the view that this character was first given to the meal by Jesus in the inner circle of the disciples and in close connexion with His coming Passion. In view of the coming separation the 'table-fellowship' which they had shared with Him in His ministry was at this last meal summed up and perpetuated and invested with a new significance. Jesus points them forward to their future reunion with Him in the Messianic feast, and at the same time by the striking symbolism of the Supper points to His death, by which He gives Himself to them and for them, as a source of blessing and a new bond of fellowship between Him and them. The meal was thus at once a sacrament of their deliverance, a pledge of unbroken union through death, and a consecration of them to be partakers of the Messianic feast. That the act was intended to be in some sense sacramental seems implied by the Synoptists when they connect the delivery of the bread and the cup with the words, 'This is my body,' 'This is my blood.' Schweitzer (*Gesch. der paulinisch. Forschung*, 155 ff.) points out that by St. Paul the sacramental meal is represented as a 'fellowship (κοινωνία) of the Body and Blood of Christ,' rather than as an 'eating of the Flesh and drinking of the Blood'—language which he nowhere uses, and which first appears in the Fourth Gospel. But St. Paul elsewhere has the more general phrases 'spiritual food' and 'spiritual drink' (1 Co 10$^{3.4}$); and, though the Fourth Gospel develops—along lines different from St. Paul—the thought of the communion feast as a participation in the Divine life, the accounts in the Synoptists, St. Paul, and the Fourth Gospel alike point to the idea of a sacramental union with Christ effected through His death.

If the words and acts of Jesus can be interpreted, in the sense indicated above, as summing up and perpetuating the fellowship of the disciples with Himself, it is possible to see how the words 'Do this in remembrance of me' would be regarded as a natural interpretation of His meaning. It was thus that the waiting Church of St. Paul's day renewed again and again in the 'breaking of bread' its fellowship with the exalted Lord, and proclaimed His death 'until he should come.' But, while the primitive Church kept vividly before it this hope of the coming in connexion with the Eucharist, it was inevitable that, as time went on, the emphasis should be laid more exclusively upon the death of Christ commemorated in it. Thus, while in the Eucharistic prayers of the *Didache*, which comes from Jewish Christian circles, we find an echo of the eschatological hope, with no reference to the death of Christ, in the Gentile Christian circles represented by Justin the eschatological features have disappeared, and the Eucharist is primarily a memorial sacrifice. The former view seems to be an attenuation of the conception current in the Apostolic age; the latter represents the transition from Jewish to Gentile forms of Christianity.

It has been further contended that the account of Mk. (on which Mt. depends) shows traces of the influence of St. Paul, especially in the language which describes the cup as 'my blood of the covenant which is shed for many.' Thus Goguel (*op. cit.* p. 82) maintains that the relationship between v.^{24} and v.^{25} in Mk 14 is artificial, and that the two distinct ideas associated with the cup—the one referring to the blood of the covenant, the other pointing to the Messianic feast—cannot have thus been brought together by Jesus, as they produce an impression inconsistent with the luminous simplicity of the thoughts and acts of Jesus which we find in His other sayings and acts. But this apparent want of simplicity may be due to the compression of the narratives of the Synoptists and the setting and connexion in which they have recorded the sayings at the Supper. It is insufficient to discredit the sayings themselves. Again, it may be urged that the connexion between the thought of the covenant and the Messianic Kingdom was not so remote as appears on the surface. In the OT the idea of the covenant is associated with (1) the covenant of Sinai (Ex 24^{8}); (2) the 'new covenant' of Jer 31^{31}, cf. Is 42^{6} 49^{8}; (3) the Davidic-Messianic covenant, connected with the promise to David of a kingdom which should last for ever (2 S 7$^{12ff.}$, Ps 89^{28} 132$^{11f.}$, Is 55^{3}, Ezk 34^{23}). The 'covenant' in the two types of prophecy represented in (2) and (3) was in either case associated with the new age, which was identical with the Kingdom. Thus the words 'This is my blood of the covenant' point to Christ's death as inaugurating His Messianic work of bringing in the 'new covenant' or 'the Kingdom,' with an obvious reference to the covenant-sacrifice of Sinai (in the words of Lk 22^{29} 'I appoint [διατίθεμαι] unto you, as my Father hath appointed unto me, a kingdom, that ye may eat and drink at my table in my kingdom,' we find an idea parallel with that of the διαθήκη referred to in the words spoken about the cup). Goguel's theory leads him to the further conclusion that the identification of the cup with 'the blood' was made only by the primitive Church, and he infers from the title of the meal, 'the breaking of *bread*,' that the cup formed no part of the meal in the earliest period described in Acts. But neither of these conclusions can be said to rest on any adequate grounds.

LITERATURE.—The extensive character of the literature makes it impossible to do more than select a few of the more representative works. For useful summaries of the different treatments of the subject, see the works of Schweitzer, Loisy, and Goguel, referred to below. *HDB*, artt. 'Communion' (Robinson), 'Jesus Christ' (Sanday), 'Lord's Supper' (Plummer); *EBi*, art. 'Eucharist' (Robinson); *PRE*^{3}, artt. 'Abendmahl' (Cremer), 'Eucharistie' (Drews), 'Jesus Christus' (Zöckler); C. Weizsäcker, *Apost. Zeitalter*, Freiburg, 1886 (Eng. tr., *The Apostolic Age*, London, 1894–95); P. Lobstein, *La Doctrine de la sainte Cène*, Lausanne, 1889; A. Harnack, 'Brod und Wasser,' in *TU* VII. ii. (1891), also *Dogmengesch.*^{3} i. (Freiburg, 1894); A. Jülicher, 'Zur Gesch. der Abendmahlsfeier in der ältesten Kirche,' in *Theol. Abhandl.*, Freiburg, 1892; F. Spitta, *Zur Gesch. und Litt. d. Urchristenthums*, i. (Göttingen, 1893); W. Brandt, *Die evangel. Gesch. und der Ursprung des Christentums*, Leipzig, 1893; P. Gardner, *Origin of the Lord's Supper*, London, 1893, *Exploratio Evangelica*, do. 1899, *Religious Experience of St. Paul*, do. 1910; E. Haupt, *Ueber die ursprüngliche Form u. Bedeutung der Abendmahlsworte*,

Halle, 1894; R. A. Hoffmann, *Die Abendmahlsgedanken Jesu Christi*, Königsberg, 1896; H. J. Holtzmann, *NT Theologie*, Freiburg, 1896–97; J. Réville, *Les Origines de l'eucharistie*, Paris, 1898; A. Schweitzer, *Das Abendmahl in Zusammenhang mit dem Leben Jesu und der Gesch. des Urchristentums*, Tübingen, 1901, *Von Reimarus zu Wrede*, do. 1906, *Geschichte der paulinischen Forschung*, do. 1911; W. B. Frankland, *The Early Eucharist*, Cambridge, 1902; J. Hoffmann, *Das Abendmahl im Urchristenthum*, Berlin, 1903; W. Heitmüller, *Taufe und Abendmahl bei Paulus*, Göttingen, 1903; J. C. Lambert, *The Sacraments in the NT*, Edinburgh, 1903; A. Andersen, *Das Abendmahl in den zwei ersten Jahrhunderten*, Giessen, 1904; P. Batiffol, *Études d'histoire et de théologie positive*, 2nd ser., 'L'Eucharistie,' Paris, 1905; A. Loisy, *Les Évangiles synoptiques*, 2 vols., Paris, 1907–08; M. Goguel, *L'Eucharistie, des origines à Justin Martyr*, Paris, 1909; R. Reitzenstein, *Die hellenistischen Mysterienreligionen*, Leipzig, 1910; K. Lake, *Earlier Epistles of St. Paul*, London, 1911.

II. *THE EUCHARIST IN THE PATRISTIC PERIOD* (A.D. 100–800). — **I. The 2nd century.** — The materials for the history of the Eucharist in the period immediately following the Apostolic age are scanty, and much of their evidence is obscure. Incidental references in the Epistle of Clement of Rome to the Corinthians, the account in the *Didache* or *Teaching of the Twelve Apostles* (A.D. 100–140), the letter of Pliny to Trajan (*Ep.* x. 97 [96], A.D. 112), and the Epistles of Ignatius (A.D. 110–117) constitute the sole materials before the time of Justin Martyr. Of these the most important are the *Didache* and Ignatius. Their evidence may be summarized as follows.

(1) The name by which the rite is known is the 'Eucharist' (ἡ εὐχαριστία) or 'thank-offering' (Hort, in *JThSt* iii. 594 f.), derived from the 'giving of thanks' at the Institution (εὐχαριστήσας, Mk 14[23] [Mt 26[27]], Lk 22[19], 1 Co 11[24]). Side by side with this 'giving of thanks' the *Didache* still speaks of 'breaking bread' (κλάσατε ἄρτον καὶ εὐχαριστήσατε [c. 14]). The Eucharist is the centre of common worship (Ignat. and *Did.*), and is celebrated on the Lord's Day (*Did.* 14). It appears to be associated, as in Apostolic times, with a common meal. The testimony of Ignatius, indeed, on this point is not conclusive. Lightfoot (*Apost. Fathers*, 'Ignatius,' i. 51 f.) and Loofs (*PRE*[3] i. 39, art. 'Abendmahl') maintain the connexion on the ground of the passage *Smyrn.* 8 ('it is not lawful apart from the bishop either to baptize or to hold a love-feast'), where it is contended that the 'love-feast' (or Agape) includes the Eucharist. But this inference is weakened by the preceding statement that 'that Eucharist is to be considered valid which is under the bishop or him to whom he commits it,' which renders unnecessary any reference to the Eucharist in what follows. The evidence of the *Didache*, however, points more clearly to the association of the two rites. In cc. 9–10 the writer gives some forms of thanksgiving to be used in connexion with the 'thank-offering' (περὶ τῆς εὐχαριστίας οὕτω εὐχαριστήσατε). The first of these prayers is entitled 'for the cup,' the second 'for the broken bread' (περὶ τοῦ κλάσματος). Both prayers are thoroughly Jewish in character, and resemble common Jewish forms for grace at meals (Drews, *PRE*[3] v. 563; Box, *JThSt* iii. 361). There is no reference in them to the words of institution, or to the body and blood of Christ, but only to 'the Holy Vine of David thy servant' (on the title 'Vine of David' as applied to Jesus the Messiah, see Taylor, *Teaching of the Twelve Apostles*, Cambridge, 1886, p. 70). There is, further, a prayer for the gathering of the Church from the ends of the earth into the Kingdom, and the writer sees a symbol of this in the grains of wheat formerly scattered upon the mountains, and now forming the loaf which is broken (this again is probably Jewish rather than Pauline; see Taylor, *op. cit.* 71). The third prayer (c. 11), which is to be said 'after ye are filled,' re-echoes much of the language of the earlier prayers (of which it may be a doublet; see von der Goltz, *Das Gebet in der ält. Christenheit*, Leipzig, 1901, p. 211; Batiffol, *Études*, ii. 114 f.), and speaks, like them, of 'the knowledge and faith and immortality' made known 'through Jesus thy servant,' and of the gathering of the Church into the Kingdom.

Hence it has been maintained that the whole of the thanksgivings in cc. 9–10 refer only to the Agape. There are not wanting, however, references which point to the Eucharist. Such are the direction at the end of c. 9 that none are to eat or drink of the 'thank-offering' (ἀπὸ τῆς εὐχαριστίας) except the baptized, because the Lord has said, 'Give not that which is holy to the dogs'; the words in c. 10 (following the mention of the gift of meat and drink), 'and to us thou didst vouchsafe spiritual meat and drink and life eternal through thy servant' (cf. 1 Co 10[3, 4]); possibly also (though the words may refer to entry into the coming Kingdom) the words at the end of c. 10, 'if any is holy, let him come; if any is unholy, let him repent.' But the most probable explanation is, as Drews suggests (*PRE*[3] v. 563 f.), that for the author of the *Didache* the whole meal constituted a unity, the elements of which are not carefully distinguished.

On the relation of the prayers in the *Didache* to the prayers used at Jewish meals, see von der Goltz, *Tischgebete u. Abendmahlsgebete in der altchr. u. in der griech. Kirche*, Leipzig, 1905, p. 16 f.; Box, *JThSt* iii. 366 ff. The latter suggests that they are forms of thanksgiving for the use of the recipient, not a formula of consecration for the celebrant. Both Drews and Box suggest that the communion precedes the Agape. For other views, see Batiffol, *op. cit.* p. 109 f.; R. A. Hoffmann, *Die Abendmahlsgedanken Jesu Christi*, p. 143 f.; Andersen, *Das Abendmahl*, p. 57 f.; Keating, *The Agape and the Eucharist*, p. 53 f.; Leclercq, art. 'Agape,' in *DACL*; and art. AGAPE in the present Encyclopædia.

That the Eucharist is included in the account which the *Didache* (c. 14) gives of the service on the Lord's Day is shown by the terms employed (συναχθέντες κλάσατε ἄρτον καὶ εὐχαριστήσατε), the mention of the confession of sins, 'that your sacrifice may be pure,' and the injunction which follows in c. 15, 'Elect therefore (οὖν) for yourselves overseers and deacons'—language which could scarcely be used of the Agape alone. These indications, in fact, accord with the evidence of Acts and of Ignatius (*Smyrn.* 8).

Pliny's letter to Trajan (*Ep.* x. 97 [96]), written A.D. 112, has often been adduced in proof of the separation of the Eucharist and Agape in his time. He mentions two gatherings 'on a fixed day' (*stato die*; probably Sunday): (*a*) a gathering before dawn, at which the Christians sang a hymn to Christ as God, and bound themselves by an oath (or 'by a sacrament,' *sacramento*) to abstain from certain crimes; (*b*) a later gathering on the same day, when they partook of an ordinary and harmless meal (*cibum promiscuum tamen et innoxium*). Pliny's informants added that even this had been given up after the Emperor's edict. Lightfoot ('Ignatius,' i. 51) is inclined to the view that the earlier gathering was for the Eucharist, and the later for the Agape. But the inference is doubtful, and the meaning of *sacramento* uncertain (see Robinson, *EBi*, art. 'Eucharist'). The 'ordinary and harmless meal' might quite well, in information given to the heathen, refer to the Eucharist. Possibly in consequence of the Emperor's edict, the common meal may have been given up, and the Eucharist, with this modification, transferred to the earlier hour. The Eucharist was undoubtedly separated from the Agape in the time of Justin and Tertullian. See, further, art. AGAPE.

(2) The nature of the 'thank-offering' (εὐχαριστία) is further illustrated in the *Didache* by the title of 'sacrifice' (θυσία) applied to it. It is to be preceded by a confession of sins, 'that your

sacrifice may be pure'; and in this connexion the writer refers to the words in Mal 1[11] about the 'pure offering.' Light is thrown upon this language by the incidental references of Clement of Rome to the 'offerings' and 'gifts' which it was the duty of the presbyter-bishop to offer (*ad Cor.* 40, 44; cf. 36), the allusion doubtless being to the thanksgivings, prayers, and gifts of bread and wine which were offered in grateful acknowledgment of the bounty of God (cf. the later language of Irenæus). This element of praise, which was a development of the 'giving of thanks' at the Last Supper, forms the starting-point of the later liturgical development of the Eucharistic prayer (the prayer in Clement of Rome, *Ep. ad Cor.* 59–61, is possibly a reminiscence of such a liturgical thanksgiving). Similarly, Ignatius urges the Ephesians 'to come together frequently for thanksgiving to God and for his glory' (*Eph.* 13), and he applies the term 'sanctuary' or 'place of sacrifice' (*θυσιαστήριον*) to the Christian assembly (*Eph.* 5, *Philad.* 4, *Trall.* 7), gathered round the Eucharist.

(3) The conception of the Eucharist as a means of grace is not clearly marked in the *Didache*, and the doubts as to the reference of the prayers in cc. 9–10 to the Eucharist render uncertain any conclusions which may be drawn. The language of the prayers is mystical in character, and the blessings referred to, as has been shown above, do not go beyond the ideas of 'life,' 'knowledge,' 'immortality,' or, more explicitly, 'spiritual food' and 'spiritual drink.' Ignatius is more definite, though in his case, too, there is a mystical strain which makes the interpretation of his language uncertain. Still it is clear that to him the Eucharist is more than a 'thank-offering.' It is a means of union with Jesus Christ, a true participation in the blessings of redemption, and an expression of the unity of the Church.

The chief passages on the subject are: (*a*) *Eph.* 5, 'If any one be not within the sanctuary, he lacketh the bread [of God]'; (*b*) *Eph.* 20, 'Breaking one bread, which (ὅ for ὅς) is the medicine of immortality, the antidote preserving us that we should not die, but live for ever in Jesus Christ'; (*c*) *Philad.* 4, 'Therefore give heed to keep one Eucharist. For there is one flesh of our Lord Jesus Christ, and one cup unto union with his blood. There is one sanctuary, as there is one bishop, together with the presbyter and deacons'; (*d*) *Smyrn.* 6, 'They [*i.e.* the Docetæ] withhold themselves from Eucharist and prayer, because they confess not that the Eucharist is the flesh of our Saviour Jesus Christ, which flesh suffered for our sins, and which in his loving-kindness the Father raised up.' To these may be added, as illustrating the more mystical language of Ignatius, (*e*) *Rom.* 7, 'I desire the bread of God, which is the flesh of Christ, who is of the seed of David; and for drink I desire his blood, which is love incorruptible.'

The language of Ignatius on the Eucharist can be fully understood only when it is viewed in connexion with his whole conception of the Incarnation and the Church. The Incarnation is the reconciliation of the material and the spiritual, the outward and the inward, 'flesh' and 'spirit.' All that represents or embodies the truth of the Incarnation exhibits the same character. Thus the Gospel is spoken of as 'the flesh of Jesus' (*Philad.* 5). The same union of 'flesh' and 'spirit' is exhibited practically in the life of faith and love (*Eph.* 8, 14, *Smyrn.* 13). Hence Ignatius speaks of faith as 'the flesh of Christ,' and of love as 'his blood' (*Trall.* 8, *Rom.* 7). The fullest expression of this 'union of flesh and spirit' is the unity of the Church (*Magn.* 1, 13). In this connexion, Ignatius insists upon the 'one Eucharist,' the 'one sanctuary,' the 'one bishop' (*Philad.* 4). Hence it has been maintained (Andersen, *Das Abendmahl*, p. 67 f.) that the 'flesh of Christ,' when used by Ignatius in connexion with the Eucharist, means 'the Church' (*Smyrn.* 6), and that even *Eph.* 20 has the same reference. But, apart from the unnatural exegesis of these passages, and even allowing for the fact that Ignatius occasionally uses the words 'flesh' and 'blood' in a mystical sense, his references to the Eucharist do not justify a purely symbolical interpretation of his language (cf. Loofs, *PRE*[3] i. 39 f.). When Ignatius speaks of the Eucharist as 'the flesh of Christ . . . *which suffered for our sins, and which the Father . . . raised up*' (*Smyrn.* 6); of the 'one cup unto union with his blood' (*Philad.* 4); and, lastly, when he says that 'if any one be not within the sanctuary, he lacketh the bread [of God],' it seems clear that the rite was to him in some real sense a means of union with Christ, and of participation in the fruits of His Passion and Resurrection. Lastly, we may notice that Ignatius' language re-echoes the Johannine teaching, which associates the flesh of Christ with the gift of life and immortality (*Eph.* 20, 'the medicine of immortality'; cf. Jn 6[54f.]), and in this respect it anticipates much later teaching (see, further, von der Goltz, 'Ignatius v. Antiochien als Christ u. Theolog,' *TU* XII. iii. 69 f.).

About the middle of the 2nd cent. Justin Martyr, in his first *Apology*, refers to the Eucharist (cc. 65–67). His narrative contains two accounts. In the first the Eucharist follows on baptism; in the second he describes the Sunday worship. From the two accounts we can gather the main features of the service. It begins with the reading of the 'memoirs of the Apostles' and the writings of the Prophets (cf. Tertullian, *de Orat.* 14). The elements (bread and a cup of wine and water) are next presented to the president, who offers up prayers and thanksgiving, 'as far as he is able' (*ὅση δύναμις αὐτῷ*, cf. *Did.* 10, 'Suffer the prophets to give thanks as much as they will'), to the Father through the Son and Holy Spirit (c. 65), for the creation of the world and all that is therein for man's sake, also for deliverance from evil and for redemption through the Passion (*Dial. c. Tryph.* 41). To this prayer, which corresponds to the Eucharistic Preface in the liturgy of the *Apostolic Constitutions*, the congregation respond with the Amen. Then follow the reception of the elements, and their conveyance by the deacons to absent members. Mention is also made of the alms, which are collected and laid up with the president for the relief of those in need. To this description, Justin adds his own comment on the meaning of the rite (c. 66): 'This food is called by us Eucharist.' Only the baptized may partake of it. For the elements are not received as common bread or common drink. He draws an analogy between the assumption of flesh and blood by Jesus Christ in the Incarnation and the consecration of bread and wine, which possess the ordinary properties of nutrition (*κατὰ μεταβολήν* refers to the assimilation of the food by digestion), so that they become the flesh and blood of Christ. The Incarnation was 'through the Word of God' (Justin does not clearly distinguish the operations of the Word and the Spirit). The Eucharist becomes Christ's body and blood 'through the prayer of the word which came from Him' (*δι' εὐχῆς λόγου τοῦ παρ' αὐτοῦ*: either (1) a reference to the liturgical thanksgiving derived from the *εὐχαριστήσας* of the institution [see Brightman, *JThSt* i. 112]; or (2) a reference to the operation of the Logos [taking *λόγου* in a personal sense]; see E. Bishop, in Connolly's *Homilies of Narsai*, Cambridge, 1909, p. 158 ff.). Justin then refers to the account of the institution contained in the 'memoirs of the Apostles.' The day on which the Christians assemble for worship is the day of the sun, for it is the first day, on which God made the world, and on which Christ rose from the dead. In this account we may notice: (*a*) the Eucharist, as in the *Didache* and Ignatius, forms a central act of Christian worship on the Sunday. It is a 'thank-offering,' and consists of a service of prayer and praise, in which the blessings of creation and redemption are commemorated. Justin's account shows how the original 'thanksgiving' of the Last Supper has already expanded into the Eucharistic prayer which finds a place in the later liturgies, though this thanksgiving was still mainly extempore in character (ὅση δύναμις αὐτῷ, c. 67). (*b*) Justin marks an advance upon the language of the *Didache* and Ignatius in the greater precision of his description of the Eucharistic gift. The word 'Eucharist' (εὐχαριστία) is applied to the consecrated food, which is expressly identified with 'the flesh and blood' of Christ. It is no longer 'common food' after the thanksgiving has been pronounced over it, but has acquired a sacred character. (*c*) The reference to the sending of the Eucharist to absent members is the earliest indication of a development which received considerable extension in the subsequent period, when, as we learn from Tertullian (*ad Uxorem*, ii. 5), Christians were allowed to keep the Sacrament in private for their own use.

Justin says nothing in the *Apology* of the sacrificial aspect of the rite, though he quotes the words 'Do this as my memorial' (τοῦτο ποιεῖτε εἰς τὴν ἐμὴν ἀνάμνησιν), in referring to the account of the institution. But in the *Dialogue with Trypho* (c. 41) he dwells at greater length on these words, and interprets them in a way which shows that he regards both the words 'do' and 'memorial' as having a sacrificial meaning. 'The offering of fine flour,' he says, referring to Lv 14^{10}, 'was a type of the bread of the Eucharist, which our Lord Jesus Christ commanded us to offer (ποιεῖν) for a memorial of the Passion undergone by Him on behalf of men who are being cleansed in soul from all evil'; and he connects with this offering the giving of thanks to God for the blessings of creation and redemption. Lastly, he refers, like the *Didache*, to the prophecy of Mal 1^{11} (cf. *Dial.* 70, 116, 117). This conception of the Eucharist as a memorial of the Passion, based on the words of institution as found in St. Paul, is, however, peculiar to Justin among 2nd cent. writers.

(*a*) The 'simple realism' (Batiffol) of Justin's language about the Eucharist is re-echoed by Irenæus, the bishop of Lyons, in the last quarter of the 2nd century. In arguing with the Gnostics, who disparaged the material creation as being the work of an inferior power, he appeals to the Eucharist as a witness to the truer view. The Gnostics cannot consistently take part in the Eucharist, for (α) in their view the bread and wine are not creatures of the Father of Jesus Christ, and they cannot offer them to Him or call them the body and blood of His Son (*adv. Hær.* IV. xviii. 4); (β) they deny the future resurrection, and cannot appreciate the efficacy of the Eucharist as a principle of life for the body as well as the soul (*ib.*). Christ, he maintains, confessed the cup to be His blood, and the bread to be His body (V. ii. 2). The bread and the mixed cup, on receiving the word of God (*i.e.* either (1) the invocation [ἐπίκλησιν] of IV. xviii. 4; cf. 1 Ti 4^5; Origen, hom. *in Matt.* [*PG* xiii. 948]; or (2) the personal Word; cf. the passage in Justin, above), become the Eucharist, which is the body and blood of Christ. When consecrated, the bread is no longer common bread, but consists of two elements, an earthly and a heavenly. In like manner our bodies, by partaking of the Eucharist, are no longer corruptible, but have the hope of the resurrection (IV. xviii. 4).

This treatment exhibits the same features as that of Justin, but advances beyond it in emphasizing, more clearly than Justin had done, 'the composite character of the Eucharist' (Swete, *JThSt* iii. 171). By virtue of the invocation the elements become something which they were not before. A 'heavenly element' (πρᾶγμα οὐράνιον) is added to them and operates through them (on the interpretations of the passage, see Loofs, *PRE*³ i. 47 f.). Irenæus also dwells more fully than Justin upon the effects of the Eucharist as a means of imparting life to the body and soul of man (cf. Ignatius, 'the medicine of immortality'). Lastly, Irenæus' theory of the consecration of the elements, and his emphasis upon the invocation (ἐπίκλησις), mark an advance upon the treatment of Justin (Loofs [*PRE*³ i. 42 f.] sees in this last an approximation to Greek conceptions derived from the mysteries).

(*b*) Irenæus' conception of the Eucharist as a sacrifice differs from that of Justin. While Justin dwells upon its connexion with the Passion, Irenæus emphasizes the aspect of it which has already been found in the *Didache*. It is the offering of the first-fruits of the earth. He applies to it, like the author of the *Didache* and Justin, the language of Mal 1^{11}. It is the 'new oblation of the new covenant, which the Church, receiving from the Apostles, offers throughout the world to God,' not because He needs any offering, but as an expression of gratitude, and as sanctifying the creature (IV. xvii. 3 f.). But this offering is connected with the fact that Christ, when instituting the rite, confessed the bread to be His body, and the cup to be His blood (*ib.*): 'Since we are members of Him, and are nourished by the creature, and He Himself provides us with the creature . . . He declared the cup which is supplied by the creature to be His own blood, and affirmed that the bread supplied by the creature was His own body' (V. ii. 2; on this fusion of the oblation with the sacramental meal, see Inge, *Contentio Veritatis*, London, 1902, p. 287). Irenæus further maintains that the Eucharist differs from the offerings of the Jews, as being offered by 'children,' in virtue of their freedom, and not by 'servants' (IV. xviii. 1). Lastly, he refers to the 'altar in heaven' to which the prayers and oblations of Christians are directed (IV. xviii. 5; cf. the prayer in the Roman Canon, and see below).

Subsidiary sources of evidence for the history of the Eucharist during the 2nd cent. are the Gnostic writings, and the epitaph of Abercius, bishop of Hierapolis in Phrygia. The references in Gnostic literature are collected in Struckmann, *Die Gegenwart Christi in der hl. Eucharistie* (Vienna, 1905, p. 90 f.), and are summarized by Batiffol, *Études d'hist. et de théol. positive*, 2nd ser., p. 168 f. Amid much that is grotesque, they re-echo the language of which we have already found traces, and speak of 'the giving of thanks' (εὐχαριστεῖν) and of the 'invocation' (ἐπίκλησις). But they advance beyond this language in their magical conception of the effects of the consecration of the elements, and so exhibit points of contact with pagan thought. Thus, amongst the followers of Marcus we read (Irenæus, I. xiii. 2) of thanks being given over cups in which the wine is turned into blood, and in one fragment of Theodotus (quoted by Clem. Alex. *Exc. Theodoti*, 82) the bread (of the Eucharist), the oil (of Confirmation), and the water (of Baptism), after they have been consecrated 'by the power of the Name,' are spoken of as 'changed into spiritual potency,' though they retain their outward appearances (τὰ αὐτὰ ὄντα κατὰ τὸ φαινόμενον οἷα ἐλήφθη [omitting οὐ before τὰ αὐτά, with Bunsen, Loofs, Batiffol]). On the other hand, we find the opposite tendency towards a mystical rendering of the language of St. John, and the 'flesh of Christ' is interpreted as meaning the Church (*Exc. Theodoti*, 13; see on Ignatius, above).

The epitaph of Abercius exhibits, in language which recalls the pictures of the catacombs, a primitive and simple conception of the Eucharist. In his journeys from the East to 'royal Rome,' faith everywhere led the way, and set before him for food 'the fish from the fountain, mighty and stainless (whom a pure virgin grasped), and gave this to friends to eat always, having good wine, and giving the mixed cup with bread.' The reference in the 'fish' is plainly to the emblem of Christ (ἰχθύς), while 'the fountain' refers to Baptism, which gave admission to the Eucharist (see Lightfoot, *op. cit.* 'Ignatius,' i. 496 f.). See, too, the almost contemporary inscription of Pectorius of Autun in Batiffol, *op. cit.* 166 f., and in *DACL*, art. 'Autun.'

The evidence which has been reviewed shows the main lines on which the rite instituted at the Last Supper was conceived of and developed during the 2nd century. It formed the central feature of the Church's worship, and constituted a great act of thanksgiving—a sacrifice of prayer and praise for the gifts of creation, and a memorial of redemption. Though there was no fixed liturgy, and considerable freedom was allowed to the leaders of the Church in the way of extempore prayer (*Didache*, Justin), the main lines of later liturgical development may already be traced in Justin. The Eucharist was at the same time a means of spiritual refreshment, in which the faithful partook of 'the flesh and blood of Christ' for the nourishment of soul and body unto eternal life. Lastly, it was a pledge of the unity of the One Body. There was as yet no attempt to analyze the exact nature of the gift, or to discuss the relation of the sign to the thing signified. The mystical language of the *Didache* speaks of 'spiritual food and drink,' and there is a strongly mystical strain in the language of Ignatius. But the majority of Christians probably accepted simply, without elaborating any conception of the matter, the words 'This is my body,' 'This is my blood.' See, further, Swete, *JThSt* iii. 176 f.

2. Developments in Eucharistic teaching and practice during the 3rd and 4th centuries.—It was not till many centuries had passed that the Eucharist became a subject of controversy. But during the earlier period considerable developments took place, which gradually affected the conceptions associated with the rite. During the 3rd and 4th centuries the simple faith of the early days was succeeded by a period of greater reflexion and analysis, the results of which appear in the expressions used with reference to the Eucharist, and in the practices associated with it.

(1) As to the nature of the Eucharistic gift, we find that, while in popular belief and practice the elements were more and more identified with the sacred realities of which they were believed to be the vehicle, language was used by both Eastern and Western writers which distinguished between the elements and that which they signified. The former tendency may be illustrated by the use of such language as 'to handle the Lord's body' or 'to offer violence' to it (Tertullian). It is shown, again, in the growing reverence for the consecrated species, and the care bestowed to prevent even a drop or crumb from falling to the ground (Tert. *de Cor.* 3; Origen, hom. *in Exod.* xiii. 3; cf. *Canons of Hippolytus*, 209). Lastly, it is shown in the stories told by Cyprian of the portents which attended the abuse of the Sacrament, as in the case of the defaulter who found the consecrated bread turned to a cinder in his hand (*de Lapsis*, 25 [26]). But, in spite of this growing reverence, and even superstition, with which the consecrated elements were regarded, both Tertullian and Cyprian, when they set down their more deliberate conceptions of the nature of the Eucharistic gift, use language which seems far removed from such ideas. Thus Tertullian speaks of the bread as 'the figure of His body' (*figura corporis*; see *adv. Marc.* iii. 19) and as 'representing His body' (*panem quo ipsum corpus suum repræsentat*; see *ib.* i. 14). Similarly, Cyprian speaks of 'the blood of Christ' as 'shown forth in the wine' (*Ep.* lxiii. 2, 'Christi sanguis ostenditur'; cf. *ib.* 11, 'aqua . . . quae sola Christi sanguinem non possit exprimere'; cf. *ib.* 13).

Nor is this language peculiar to the Latin Church of North Africa, or to the age of Tertullian and Cyprian. It forms the starting-point of the teaching of Augustine (see below), and it appears in the references to the Eucharist made by a series of Eastern writers during the latter part of the 3rd and throughout the 4th century. Thus the *Didascalia* (second half of 3rd cent.), if the text be correct (on this see Struckmann, *op. cit.* p. 225), speaks of 'offering the acceptable Eucharist, which is a symbol (ἀντίτυπον) of the royal body of Christ' (vi. 30). In the *Apostolic Constitutions*, written a century later, and based on the above, the mysteries are described as 'symbols (ἀντίτυπα) of His precious body and of His blood.' The 'unbloody sacrifice' is celebrated to commemorate the Lord's death 'by virtue of the symbols (συμβόλων χάριν) of his body and blood.' In the liturgy thanksgivings are offered for the precious blood and for the body 'of which we celebrate these symbols' (ἀντίτυπα; see v. 14, vi. 23, vii. 25). At the same time the formula employed at Communion is 'the body of Christ,' 'the blood of Christ.' Eusebius of Cæsarea, while speaking of Christians as 'fed with the body of the Saviour' (*de Solemn. Pasch.* 7), says that Christ delivered to His disciples the symbols (σύμβολα) of His Divine Incarnation, charging them to make the 'image (εἰκόνα) of his own body,' and to use the bread, the 'symbol (συμβόλῳ) of his own body' (*Dem. Evang.* viii. [*PG* xxii. 596]). Similarly, Eustathius of Antioch (*PG* xviii. 684 f.) speaks of the bread and wine as 'symbols (ἀντίτυπα) of the bodily members of Christ.' The liturgy of Serapion, bishop of Thmuis (before 361), while speaking of the elements as 'the body and blood,' also speaks of 'offering the bread' as 'a likeness (ὁμοίωμα) of the body,' and 'offering the cup' as 'a likeness (ὁμοίωμα) of the blood' (Brightman, *JThSt* i. 105 f.). Similarly, Gregory of Nazianzus († 390) speaks of offering the external sacrifice, 'the symbol (ἀντίτυπον) of the great mysteries' (*Or.* ii. 95); of the hand 'treasuring aught of the symbols (ἀντιτύπων) of the precious body or blood' (*ib.* viii. 18, cf. xvii. 12). Lastly, Macarius the Egyptian († 390) speaks of bread and wine as offered in the Church as 'a symbol of His flesh and blood' (*Hom.* xxvii. 17). Such language, however, may be easily misunderstood. The Latin words *figura* and *repræsentare* do not necessarily imply that the objects of which they are used are bare symbols and nothing more (on *repræsentare*, see Swete, *JThSt* iii. 173, note 5; Batiffol, *op. cit.* p. 222; Loofs, *PRE*³ i. 59; on *figura*, see Turner, *JThSt* vii. 596); in many cases actual presence is intended (*e.g.* Tert. *adv. Marc.* iv. 22), though in others a representation to the mind seems to be implied. Again, as Harnack (*Hist. of Dogma*, Eng. tr. ii. 144) has said,

'what we now-a-days understand by "symbol" is a thing which is not that which it represents; at that time "symbol" denoted a thing which, in some kind of way, really is what it signifies; but, on the other hand, according to the ideas of that period, the really heavenly element lay either in or behind the visible form without being identical with it.'

In the case of Tertullian and Cyprian, moreover, such language must be qualified by other expressions in which they speak of the elements as 'the body and blood of the Lord' (see, *e.g.*, Tert. *de Idololatr.* 7, *ad Uxor.* ii. 5, *de Orat.* 19; Cyprian, *Ep.* xv. 1). Lastly, we may notice (Steitz, *JDTh* x. 402 f.; Loofs, *PRE*³ i. 58) that in many of the Eastern writers referred to above the sacramental conception of the rite is subordinated to the sacrificial, and it is to the elements as offered, not as received in communion, that the language in question is applied. The same statement is true of Cyprian. It was possibly owing to the emphasis laid upon the commemorative character of the Eucharistic offering that the use of this symbolical language came to be applied to the elements even when conceived of as the food of the faithful. But, as Loofs (*loc. cit.*) and Harnack (*op. cit.* iv. 289, note 2) have said, a purely symbolical representation, in our modern sense of the word, of the Eucharist is to be found practically nowhere in ancient times.

(2) In certain quarters this tendency to distinguish the sign from the thing signified was carried to great lengths. This applies especially to the language of the two great Alexandrian

teachers, Clement and Origen. While witnessing to the current teaching of their day, which adopted the more usual and literal interpretation (νοείσθω δὲ ὁ ἄρτος καὶ τὸ ποτήριον τοῖς μὲν ἁπλουστέροις κατὰ τὴν κοινοτέραν περὶ τῆς εὐχαριστίας ἐκδοχήν, says Origen, *in Joann.* xxxii. 24 [16], ed. Brooke, Cambridge, 1891, ii. 196), they tend to refine upon the language of Scripture about the body and blood, and interpret it, according to their own spiritualizing and allegorical tendency, as denoting 'the participation in the Lord's incorruptibility' (Clem. *Pæd.* ii. 2. 19), 'the apprehension of the Divine power and essence' (Clem. *Strom.* v. 10. 67), or the teaching and words of Christ, which are life-giving, and nourish and sustain the soul (Origen, *in Matt.* 85, hom. *in Num.* xvi. 9; cf. *in Joann., loc. cit.*). This teaching is repeated later on by Eusebius of Cæsarea, who in one passage interprets 'the flesh and blood' of Jn 6[51f.] to mean the words and discourses of Christ (*Eccl. Theol.* iii. 12), and it finds an echo still later in the ardent Origenist, Basil of Cæsarea (*Ep.* viii. 4). In using such language these writers are conscious that they are not speaking the current language of their day, but refining upon it. Elsewhere they use the common phraseology, and speak of the bread 'becoming the body' and as 'being holy, and sanctifying those who use it with right purpose,' in virtue of the prayer (or word) uttered over it (Origen, *c. Cels.* viii. 33, *in Matt.* xi. 14); of 'being fed with the body of the Saviour and partaking of the blood of the Lamb' (Euseb. *de Solemn. Pasch.* 7); of 'partaking of the holy body and blood of Christ' (Basil, *Ep.* xciii.). Outside the immediate circle of Origen's esoteric teaching, we find the Alexandrian writers speaking, like Dionysius in the 3rd cent., of the communicant as 'partaking of the body and blood' of Christ (Euseb. *HE* vii. 9), or, if they venture to dwell upon the nature of the gift, emphasizing, as Athanasius does, the fact that the flesh of Christ is received in a spiritual manner (*Ep. ad. Serap.* iv. 19).

(3) In the *Catecheses Mystagogicæ* of Cyril of Jerusalem (A.D. 347 or 348) we find the first traces of a new development. His language embodies many of the characteristic features of previous teaching. The literal interpretation of the words of institution, the use of the word 'figure' or 'type' (τύπος, ἀντίτυπος), and the terms 'spiritual bread' and 'spiritual drink' (cf. Athanasius) are all employed. After the invocation the bread becomes the body of Christ, and the wine His blood. But Cyril goes further, and attempts to explain the nature of the effect produced upon the elements by the consecration. He uses the word 'change' or 'convert' (μεταβάλλειν) to denote this effect, and he illustrates it from the change of water into wine in the miracle of Cana. This change or sanctification (ἡγίασται καὶ μεταβέβληται, v. 7) is effected by the Holy Spirit. Cyril's treatment marks an epoch in the history of Eucharistic teaching by introducing the conception of a mysterious change of the elements. Taken literally, his language might seem to anticipate the later mediæval doctrine. But his illustration from the miracle of Cana must not be taken too seriously. It is the language of popular teaching, not that of scientific theological statement. Lastly, it must be qualified by the expressions quoted above from the same *Catecheses*. Still it is an indication of the direction in which thought was moving; and, in the period which follows, the conception of a conversion of the elements received considerable extension.

Its great apologist was Gregory of Nyssa († 395), who expounds the idea of the conversion in a striking and original theory. Put briefly, his view is as follows (see *Oratio Catech.* c. 37). As the Word of God Himself, when on earth, received nourishment from bread and wine, so that they became, by the process of digestion, His body and blood, while His body also, by its union with the Word, was raised to the dignity of the Godhead, in like manner in the Eucharist the bread which is consecrated by the word of God is transformed (μεταποιεῖσθαι; cf. μεταστοιχειοῦν in the same chapter), no longer, as in His earthly life, by eating, but immediately, into His body by the Word. Here again, however, the language must not be taken too literally. It is of the nature of an illustration, and presupposes a particular theory of the relation of the 'form' of the body to its constituent elements. The change is a change of relation. The 'constituent elements' (στοιχεῖα) of the bread and wine acquire a new form (εἶδος), 'the body and blood,' and receive fresh properties. Gregory teaches, in fact, 'a qualitative unity' (Harnack) between the bread and the body, not a complete identity (see notes on the passage in the present writer's edition of the *Or. Cat.* in *Cambridge Patristic Texts*, Camb. 1903). But, while the theory in itself is halting and hesitating, its connexion with another statement of Gregory, that, while Baptism is intended for the soul, the Eucharist is a means by which the body of man is brought into union with the Saviour (*Or. Cat., loc. cit.*), and so is raised to incorruption, tended to emphasize the physical character of the Eucharistic food, and so prepared the way for a materialistic interpretation (Gregory, however, insists on the need of faith). There is a similar treatment to that of Gregory in Macarius Magnes, who also repudiates the teaching of those who maintain that the Eucharist is a figure (τύπος) of the body and blood (see Stone, *History of Doctr. of Holy Euch.* i. 65, 73 f.).

None of the later Patristic writers followed Gregory of Nyssa in his attempt to expound the rationale of the Eucharistic mystery, but from this time the language of conversion became common. It is found in Theodore of Mopsuestia († 429), who uses the word employed by Cyril of Jerusalem (μεταβάλλεσθαι, *in Mt.* 26[26]), though side by side with this presentation he speaks of the change as spiritual (*in 1 Cor.* 10[5]), and, like other Eastern Fathers, calls the elements 'symbols' (σύμβολα) of the death of Christ (*in 1 Cor.* 11[34]). It appears again in Chrysostom († 407), who revels in the use of realistic phrases, and speaks of 'eating the body,' of 'burying the teeth in His flesh' (*in Joann.* hom. 47. 1, 46. 3), and of Him who is seated above with the Father being 'held in the hands of all' (*de Sacerd.* iii. 4). But the rhetorical and devotional character of such language prevents us from taking it too seriously, and elsewhere Chrysostom blunts its force by speaking of the gift of the Sacrament as being perceived only with the eyes of the mind, and not by the senses (*in Matt.* hom. 82. 4). Like Gregory, he speaks of the elements as re-fashioned and transformed (μεταρρυθμίζειν, μετασκευάζειν, *in prodit. Jud.* hom. i. 6; *in Matt.* hom. 82. 5), but he does not analyze, like Gregory, the nature of this transformation. He adheres to the literal realism of the popular conception of the rite, and the imaginative fervour and eloquence with which he sets it forth explain the influence of his teaching on later Greek piety.

From the East this way of conceiving the effects of the consecration of the Eucharistic elements passed into the West, finding its earliest exponent in Ambrose, bishop of Milan († 397), who in other respects acted as the interpreter of Greek theology to the West. In his treatise *On Faith* (iv. 10. 125), while using language suggestive of the symbolic sacrificial conception, which we have noted in other writers of the East and the West ('the sacraments of the Lord's death,' 'we proclaim the Lord's death'), he speaks of the elements as 'transformed' or 'transfigured (*transfigurantur*: on this word see Batiffol, *op. cit.* p. 299) by the mystery of the sacred prayer, into the flesh and blood' (cf. *de Incarn.* iv. 23, 'offerre transfigurandum corpus'). In another treatise, *de Mysteriis*, the authenticity of which, however, has been doubted (see Loofs, *PRE*³ i. 61), the doctrine of conversion is expounded at length. The writer emphasizes the importance of the consecration of the elements, which he regards as a miraculous act of God, to which analogies may be found in the miracles of the Old and New Testaments (*e.g.* the miracles of Moses and Elijah, the Virgin Birth). 'How much greater than the blessing of man is the power of the consecration pronounced by God Himself.' For in the Eucharist it is Christ's own word, 'This is my body,' which changes the nature of the material elements on which it is pronounced (*de Myst.* ix. 52–54). Such language, with its repeated insistence on a change of nature in the elements (*præter naturam, naturam mutare, species mutare elementorum*), was new to the West; and even in the treatise in which it is found it is qualified by other expressions which weaken to some extent its force. Thus the writer still uses occasionally the older forms of expression, and speaks of the body as being 'signified' (*corpus significatur*), and of the wine as being 'called' the blood (*sanguis nuncupatur*). Again, he maintains that the food is spiritual, and that the body of Christ is the body of the Divine Spirit, because Christ is Spirit (*ib.* 58). In another treatise, the *de Sacramentis*—also bearing the name of Ambrose, though plainly not his work, but probably written about A.D. 400, somewhere in North Italy (Duchesne)—the influence of the teaching of the *de Mysteriis* is plainly shown, and the doctrine of conversion is expounded on similar lines. Though the writer does not state the spiritual character of the Eucharistic food, he is careful to guard against a physical conception of the Eucharistic gift, and in doing so speaks, like earlier writers in the East, of the sacrament as being received 'in a likeness' (*in similitudinem accipis sacramentum*), though this 'likeness' bestows the virtue of the reality (*naturæ gratiam virtutemque consequeris*, vi. 3; see Batiffol, *op. cit.* p. 305). His language, in fact, shows that he has not completely overcome the influence of the older tradition. Even if neither of these works, the *de Mysteriis* and the *de Sacramentis*, may be ascribed to Ambrose, they still remain authorities of great importance for the history of the Eucharist, as they were later on appealed to as containing the teaching of the great Western Father, and they exercised an undoubted influence on Western conceptions.

But this new train of thought did not succeed as yet in imposing itself on the West. The language of Jerome (*Ep.* 98. 13), of Ambrosiaster (*in 1 Cor.* 11²³⁻²⁶), and of the fragment of the Roman Canon of the Mass, quoted by the author of the *de Sacramentis* (iv. 6), still witnesses to the earlier Western view. The bread 'shows forth' the body of the Saviour (Jerome). The Eucharist is 'a memorial of redemption.' The eating of the flesh and drinking of the blood signify the new covenant. The 'mystical cup of the blood' is received 'in a figure' (*in typum* [Ambrosiaster]). The Eucharistic oblation is 'a figure of the body and blood of Christ' (Roman Canon in *de Sacramentis*; see Batiffol, p. 302 f.).

(4) During this same period the conceptions of the benefits of communion underwent a corresponding development. The idea which had been thrown out in Ignatius' phrase, 'the medicine of immortality,' and which was taken up by Irenæus, finds more definite and precise expression as time goes on. Tertullian speaks of 'our flesh being fed by the body and blood, that the soul may be sated with God' (*de Resurr. Carn.* 8). Cyril of Jerusalem says that the Eucharist makes us 'of one body and one blood with Christ' (σύσσωμοι καὶ σύναιμοι τοῦ Χριστοῦ). In this connexion he quotes 2 P 1⁴, 'partakers of the divine nature' (*Catech. Myst.* iv. 1, 3). By passing into our frame, the Eucharistic food 'helps' body and soul (*ib.* v. 9). But in Hilary of Poitiers and Gregory of Nyssa we meet with a more systematic attempt to exhibit the place of the Eucharist in the economy of the spiritual life. Both writers expound the idea that the Sacrament is the 'extension' of the Incarnation. Thus Hilary maintains (*de Trin.* viii. 13 f.) that the union of the faithful with Christ is more than a union of will, because Christ abides in us *naturaliter*, in that He gives us His body and blood; and He draws a parallel between the union of the Word with flesh, and our union with the Word made flesh in the Sacrament. Gregory of Nyssa (*Or. Cat.* 37) says that Christ 'infused himself into our perishable nature, that by communion with the Deity mankind might at the same time be deified.' As already indicated, Gregory lays special stress upon the value of the Eucharist for the body, and in his whole conception of the sacraments he emphasizes the gift of immortality which they convey (*ib.*). The starting-point of this conception, which appears in a succession of Church writers, is thoroughly Christian, and is based upon the language of Jn 6⁵¹ᶠ·; but, in the more precise form in which it is presented, it exhibits points of contact with the ideas perpetuated in the Greek mysteries.

(5) The conception of the Eucharist as a sacrifice received considerable development during the period under discussion. Hitherto the Eucharist had been spoken of as a 'sacrifice' only in connexion with the Christian interpretation of OT types, and by way of contrasting the spiritual service of Christians with Jewish and pagan ideas of sacrifice. Thus Athenagoras (*Suppl. pro Chr.* 13) speaks of 'the bloodless sacrifice and rational service of Christians' (ἀναίμακτον θυσίαν καὶ τὴν λογικὴν λατρείαν; cf. Ro 12¹; and *Test. of xii. Patr.* [Levi 3], cited by Gore, *Body of Christ*, p. 159, note 2). As we have seen, Justin stands alone among 2nd cent. writers in associating sacrificial ideas with the words 'Do this as my memorial.' Origen appears to follow him in one passage (hom. *in Lev.* xiii. 3 f.), though a little further on he adopts the meaning 'remembrance' (*ib.* c. 5).

But in the Church of North Africa, and in the writings of Cyprian, we find the language of sacrifice freely applied in this connexion. Cyprian speaks of 'celebrating the Lord's sacrifice' (*sacrificium dominicum*; cf. also *hostia dominica* [*de Unit. Eccl.* 17]), of 'offering,' not only the cup, but 'the Lord's blood,' and once of 'sacrificing.' The words 'priest' (*sacerdos*) and 'altar' (*altare*) are employed by him in connexion with the rite (though Tertullian had already used *sacrificium, sacerdos*, and *ara* in a Christian sense; see Swete, *op. cit.* p. 166). Cyprian finds the justification of such language in the account of the institution and in the words 'Do this as my memorial.' Christ offered to God the Father bread and wine, 'that is, his body and blood.' The priest, officiating in Christ's stead (*vice Christi fungitur*), 'offers to God the Father in the Church a true and full sacrifice,' when he imitates what Christ did, and fully carries out His words and acts (he is reproving the custom of using water only). In this sacrifice 'mention is made of his Passion; for the Passion is the Lord's sacrifice which we offer' (*Ep.* lxiii. 4, 14, 17). This close association of the Eucharistic sacrifice with the sacrifice of the Cross opened up a new era. There is no idea of a repetition of the sacrifice of the Cross. For, side by side with phrases which speak of 'offering the blood of Christ,' Cyprian speaks of 'offering the cup *in commemoration of* His Passion' (*loc. cit.* 17). But the transference of the sacrificial idea from the service as a whole to the consecrated elements (Harnack) marks the development of a more specific and clearly defined conception of the sacrifice. It is possible that this had already taken shape in popular thought before Cyprian's time. Another feature, which first appears in the North African Church, is the practice of offering the Eucharist for the departed (*oblationes pro defunctis*, Tert. *de Coron.* 3; *sacrificia pro dormitione*, Cyprian, *Ep.* i. 2).

Traces of a corresponding development appear in the East. Origen already employs the terms 'priest' and 'altar' in a Christian sense (Swete, *loc. cit.*), and in his *Homilies on Leviticus* (xiii. 3) he uses language which prepared the way for the association of propitiatory ideas with the Eucharist. He draws a parallel between the shewbread, which is a type of Christ, the true Propitiation (Ro 3[25]), and the permanent memorial ordained by Christ in the words 'Do this as my memorial.' The shewbread was set before God as a propitiatory memorial. The 'memorial' (*commemoratio*) instituted by Christ has also great propitiatory power. As Steitz has observed (*JDTh* x. 93), it was the development of this conception which gave to the later doctrine of the sacrifice of the Eucharist its essential meaning. This teaching is carried on by Eusebius of Cæsarea (*Dem. Evang.* i. 10), who contrasts the OT sacrifices with the sacrifice of Christ and the 'memorial' (*μνήμη, ὑπόμνησις*) which Christ commanded to be offered to God in place of sacrifice. At the same time he brings this 'memorial' into close connexion with the forgiveness of sins which the sacrifice of Christ won for heathen and Jew alike. Another important feature in his representation is the way in which the conception of 'celebrating' or 'offering' a 'memorial' of the sacrifice of Christ passes over into the idea of an 'offering of his body' (*τοῦ θύματος τὴν μνήμην, τὴν ἔνσαρκον τοῦ Χριστοῦ παρουσίαν, καὶ τὸ καταρτισθὲν αὐτοῦ σῶμα προσενηνέχθαι τῷ θεῷ διδάξας, ib.*). Similarly, in the *Apostolic Church Order* (*c.* A.D. 300) we find the phrase 'the offering (*προσφορά*) of the body and blood' (Harnack, Eng. tr. ii. 137).

But the fullest statement of the sacrificial idea is found in Cyril of Jerusalem. While repeating the language of the earlier period, and speaking of 'the spiritual sacrifice,' 'the bloodless service,' he definitely calls it 'the holy and most awful sacrifice' (*ἡ ἁγία καὶ φρικωδεστάτη θυσία*), 'the sacrifice of propitiation' (*ἡ θυσία τοῦ ἱλασμοῦ*), over which God is entreated for the common peace of the churches. It is Christ sacrificed for sins who is offered (Χ*ριστὸν ἐσφαγιασμένον ὑπὲρ τῶν ἡμετέρων ἁμαρτημάτων προσφέρομεν*), while the loving God is propitiated (*ἐξιλευόμενοι τὸν φιλάνθρωπον θεόν*) on behalf of the living and the dead. Cyril defends such prayers for the departed on the ground of the belief that 'the greatest benefit will accrue to the souls on whose behalf intercession is offered, while the holy and awful sacrifice lies before us.' Allowing for its popular and devotional character, such language shows the increasing awe with which the sacrificial aspect of the rite was invested, and the significance of the intercessions offered immediately after the consecration (the intercessions are found also at this point in the liturgy of Serapion and in that of bk. viii. of the *Apostolic Constitutions*).

Later on in the 4th cent. Chrysostom carries on the teaching of Cyril, and, like him, abounds in the use of sacrificial terms. He speaks of 'the most awful sacrifice,' of 'the Lord sacrificed and lying, and the priest (*ἱερέα*) standing over the sacrifice and praying, and all reddened with that blood' (*de Sacerd.* vi. 4), and of the silence and quiet attending the moment of consecration (*de Cœm. et de Cruce*, 3). But in his exposition of the Epistle to the Hebrews the realism and exuberant rhetoric of this language receive their corrective. There is no repetition of the sacrifice of the Cross. There is one body of Christ, and, therefore, one sacrifice: 'We do not offer a different sacrifice . . . but always the same; or rather we celebrate a memorial of a sacrifice' (*Ep. ad Heb.* hom. xvii. 3). Christ 'offered sacrifice once for all, and thenceforward sat down' (*ib.* xiii. 3). The whole action of the Eucharist lies in the heavenly and spiritual region (*ib.* xiv. 1, 2). And the same thought of the mystical nature of the Eucharistic sacrifice appears in the language of the Western Father, Ambrose, who contrasts the 'shadow' (*umbra*) of the Law with the 'image' (*imago*) of the Gospel on the one hand, and the heavenly 'reality' (*veritas*) on the other. The rites of the Church are an 'image' of heavenly realities. The priests on earth follow, as they can, the offering of their High Priest. Christ Himself is offered, when the body of Christ is offered. Indeed, He Himself is plainly shown (*manifestatur*) to offer in us, seeing that it is His word which sanctifies the sacrifice which is offered, and He Himself stands by us as our Advocate with the Father. But in the Eucharist we have only the 'image.' The 'reality' is to be found 'where Christ intercedes for us as our Advocate with the Father' (*in Psalm.* xxxviii. 25; *de Officiis*, bk. i. xlviii. 238). Ambrose, in fact, views the whole action of the Eucharist from the standpoint of the abiding humanity and intercession of Christ in heaven, and the same thought is implicit, though not so clearly expressed, in the language of Chrysostom (see, further, below, § 3 (2)).

(6) The 4th cent. marks a period of considerable liturgical development in connexion with the Eucharist. The writings of Cyril of Jerusalem and Chrysostom enable us to reproduce with a considerable degree of certainty the liturgy current in their time. To this period also belongs a series of Church manuals, which contain liturgical forms for the celebration of the Eucharist.

Of these the oldest are the *Ethiopic Church Order*, and the Verona *Latin Fragments* (published by Hauler), both of which are based on the same Greek original and may belong to the second half of the third century. For Egypt we have the liturgical prayers of Serapion, bishop of Thmuis (written before 361), and for Syria the liturgy of bk viii. of the *Apostolic Constitutions* (*c.* 375). The *Testament of our Lord* (published by Rahmani, Mainz, 1899, from Syriac MSS) may belong to the same century (Zahn, Morin), or may be a century later. Lastly, in the *de Sacramentis* (*c.* 400) we have some Western prayers, which exhibit the earliest known form of the Roman Canon of the Mass.

Their evidence for the conceptions of the Eucharist may be briefly summarized. (*a*) The primitive character of the rite as a service of praise and thanksgiving for the gifts of creation and the blessings of redemption is emphasized in the long prayer which leads up to the central part of the liturgy. In this respect there is, amid many variations, a general uniformity in these liturgical forms. The following fixed points stand out: (*α*) the *Sursum corda* ('Lift up your hearts'), with the response 'We lift them up unto the Lord' (found in Cyprian, *de Orat. Dom.* 31, and in the *Canons of Hippolytus*; cf. *Eth. Ch. Ord.*, and *Apost. Const.*), followed by the invitation 'Let us give thanks,' and the response 'It is meet and right'; (*β*) the commemoration of God's work in creation, leading up to (*γ*) the angelic hymn, the *Sanctus* (Serapion; *Apost. Const.*). This leads on to (*δ*) the commemoration of the Incarnation, Passion, Resurrection, and Ascension, and the narrative of the institution (*Apost. Const.*; *de Sacramentis*). Then follows (*ε*) the oblation of the elements, and in the Eastern rites the invocation of the Holy Spirit to consecrate them. Thus the structure of this part of the rite sets forth the successive stages of God's revelation, culminating in the work of the Holy Spirit, whose intervention in the mystery is invoked.

(*b*) This invocation of the Holy Spirit upon the elements is found in most of our early sources (*Eth. Ch. Ord.*; *Apost. Const.*; Cyril; Chrysostom). In Serapion it is the Logos who is invoked; in the *Testament of our Lord* it is the Trinity (cf. Cyril of Jerusalem, *Cat.* xix. 7). In the fragments of the Roman Canon in the *de Sacramentis* we find in place of the invocation of the Holy Spirit (1) a prayer to God to make the oblation approved, ratified, reasonable, acceptable, because it is a figure of the body and blood of Christ; (2) a later prayer that the oblation may be received up 'on the altar on high by the hands of Thy angels.' Duchesne suggests (*Chr. Worship*, Eng. tr., London, 1904, p. 181 f.) that the latter prayer may be a symbolical way of expressing the same request for God's intervention in the mystery (others, however, see the equivalent of the invocation in the former of the two prayers [no. 1, above]).

On the question of the precise moment of consecration, see W. C. Bishop, *CQR* lxvi. 398 f.; Procter and Frere, *History of Book of Common Prayer* 3, London, 1910, p. 446; Scudamore, *Notitia Eucharistica* 2, London, 1872, p. 572 ff.; and *DACL*, art. 'Anamnèse.' The Western idea, that the consecration is effected by the recital of the words of institution, appears to be adumbrated in Ambrose and the *de Sacramentis* (Ambrose, *de Myst.* ix. 52, 54; *de Sacram.* iv. 14–23).

(*c*) As to the effects of consecration, the earliest Eastern forms are explicit in identifying the elements with the body and blood of Christ. The words *ποιεῖν* ('make' [Cyril]), *γίγνεσθαι* ('become' [Serapion]), *ἀποφαίνειν* ('show' [*Apost. Const.*], probably a synonym of *ποιεῖν*) are used in the invocation to express the relation of the elements to the body and blood (cf. Roman Canon [Gelasian], where we find *ut nobis corpus et sanguis fiat*). In spite of the use of symbolic language by Eastern writers to denote the oblation, these liturgical forms adhere to the 'simple realism' of early times (cf. Justin, Irenæus). The prayers of the Western Canon in the *de Sacramentis* are less explicit. While using symbolic language of the oblation ('figure of the body of Christ'), the elements are spoken of as 'the holy bread and the cup of eternal life.' This accords with the Western tradition and the language of Jerome and Augustine. But in these prayers the sacramental idea is subordinated to the sacrificial, and, in place of a reference to the body and blood, we find a reference to the gifts of Abel and the sacrifices of Abraham and Melchizedek.

(*d*) The conception of the sacrifice in these sources combines the idea of the oblation of the gifts (cf. *Didache* and Irenæus) with that of the memorial of the Passion (cf. Justin and Cyprian). Thus we find mention made of 'this living sacrifice,' 'this bloodless oblation,' and a reference, before the invocation, to the 'bread scattered upon the mountains' (Serapion; cf. *Didache*); also a prayer for those who have offered the offerings and thanksgivings, after the invocation (Serapion). Similarly the *Apostolic Constitutions* contains the prayer, 'We implore Thee to look graciously upon these gifts lying before Thee,' while the Western prayers in the *de Sacramentis* speak of *oblatio rationabilis*, *immaculata hostia*, and compare the sacrifice with the gifts of Abel and the sacrifices of Abraham and Melchizedek.

Most of these sources contain a prayer of oblation in connexion with the *Anamnesis*, or commemoration of the Passion and Resurrection. In Serapion and the *de Sacramentis* this oblation is conceived of as a 'type' of Christ's offering, and the elements are offered as 'types' and 'figures' of His body and blood. So in the Western Canon the gifts of Abel and the sacrifices of Abraham and Melchizedek may be quoted as 'types' of the offering of Christ.

Serapion accords with the fuller development of the sacrificial idea, as found in Cyril of Jerusalem, in the prayer after the consecration: 'We beseech Thee, through this sacrifice, be reconciled to all of us and be merciful' (ἱλάσθητι). Lastly, in Serapion and the *Apostolic Constitutions* intercessions for the departed and others are offered after the consecration (cf. Cyril Jer. *Cat.* xxiii. 9, quoted above). This development is significant, and helps to explain how the primitive communion feast passed into the 'High Mass' of later times.

3. The Eucharist in the later Patristic period (5th–8th centuries).—The two main developments in Eucharistic teaching which have been traced above may be summarized as follows: (1) the transition from a distinction between the elements and that which they signify (the 'dyophysite' view, Harnack, Batiffol) to the conception of a complete identification of the elements with the body and blood of Christ (the 'conversion' doctrine, Batiffol); (2) the transformation of the idea of sacrifice, according to which the conception of the offering of the gifts and the memorial of the Passion passes into an offering of the body and blood as a propitiatory memorial sacrifice. In the period which followed, these two tendencies were accentuated, though they had to encounter the influence of an earlier tradition, and in the West the authority of Augustine's teaching long resisted the former.

(1) The parallel which Gregory of Nyssa had drawn between the Eucharist and the Incarnation, and the idea that the latter is continued, as to its effects, in the former, concentrated attention on the rite as a living witness and attestation of the practical power of the Church's faith with regard to the Person of Christ. Thus Gregory of Nyssa complains that Eunomius (the Arian) had 'slighted the fellowship of the sacramental customs and tokens from which the Christian profession draws its vigour,' and that he had maintained that 'the sacramental tokens do not, as we have believed, secure spiritual blessings and avert from believers the assaults directed against them by the wiles of the evil one' (*c. Eunom.* bk. xi. [*PG* xlv. 880]). Similarly, Cyril of Alexandria, in his *Third Letter to Nestorius*, appeals to the Eucharist as teaching that the flesh of Christ is 'life-giving' (ζωοποιόν). Thus it witnesses against Nestorius' teaching, which maintains that the flesh of Christ is not the flesh of God the Word. In the Christological controversies of the subsequent period we find the same appeal to the Eucharist made by the orthodox and the Monophysites alike in support of their doctrine. On the one hand, the Monophysites contend that in the Eucharist there is a conversion of the elements into the body and blood of Christ, while their opponents adhere to the 'dyophysite' view, and maintain that the elements retain their own nature, and that the 'change' effected by consecration is in the region of grace (κατὰ χάριν). Such is the argument of Theodoret († 457) (*Eranistes*, i. 56 [*PG* lxxxiii. 87], ii. 165 f. [*ib.* 207]). The same argument re-appears in the *Epistle to Cæsarius* (by an unknown author), and at the end of the 5th cent. it is employed by Pope Gelasius († 496) in his *de Duabus Naturis*. But after the 6th cent. this analogy between the Incarnation and the Eucharist passes out of view (Batiffol, *op. cit.* p. 332), and in the East the doctrine of the conversion of the elements became more and more the accepted teaching, until in the 8th cent. John of Damascus († after 759), whose work *de Fide Orthodoxa* sums up the Church tradition of his time, sets it forth as the established doctrine of the Church. Like Gregory of Nyssa, he illustrates the change in the elements by the transformation of food in our bodies, but he goes beyond Gregory in asserting the complete identity of the consecrated elements with the body and blood of Christ, and he

further maintains the identity of the Eucharistic and the historical body of Christ (though even he shows lingering traces of the earlier view when he speaks of the bread as 'not mere bread, but bread united to the Divinity'). For his whole treatment, see *de Fide Orth.* iv. 13.

In the West the influence of the teaching associated with the name of Ambrose (see above, § 2 (3)) must be reckoned as one of the main factors in introducing the doctrine of conversion. But into the opposite scale was cast the weighty authority of Augustine's teaching, which delayed for some centuries the complete acceptance in the West of the Ambrosian view. Augustine starts from the earlier Western teaching, and is in the same line of tradition as Tertullian and Cyprian. But his importance also consists in the fact that he attempted an analysis of the idea of sacraments, which was epoch-making, and became authoritative for Western Christendom in later times. Thus his definition of sacraments as 'visible signs of divine things,' in which 'the invisible things themselves are honoured' (*de Cat. Rud.* xxvi. 50), his statements that in them 'one thing is seen, another is understood' (*Serm.* cclxxii.), and that 'what is seen has a bodily appearance, what is understood has spiritual profit' (*ib.*), as also his distinction between the *sacramentum* (or outward part) and the *res* (or inward part; cf. *Tract. in Joann.* xxvi. 15) on the one hand, and between the 'sacrament' and the 'virtue' (*virtus*) of the sacrament (*in Joann. ib.* 11; *En. in Ps.* lxxvii. 2) on the other, became classical for the later period, and form the starting-point of mediæval discussions upon the subject. Of importance, too, is his statement that 'the word is added to the element, and a sacrament is constituted, being itself, as it were, a visible word' (*in Joann.* lxxx. 3). But, in accordance with the emphasis which his teaching laid on the spiritual side of things, and the importance which he attached to 'faith' and 'the word,' his language at times seems to pass almost into a figurative or symbolical view of the sacraments, and he has been claimed as teaching such by theological controversialists, as well as by many modern scholars (*e.g.* Harnack and Loofs). Thus he speaks, like Tertullian, of Christ delivering to the disciples 'the figure' (*figuram*) or 'sign' (*signum*) of His body and blood (*En. in Ps.* iii. 1; *c. Adimant.* xii. 3). The bread becomes the body of Christ, because it has been sanctified by the word of God (*Serm.* ccxxvii., ccxxxiv.). Augustine uses the words *consecratio*, *benedictio*, and *sanctificare* to denote this consecration, and this sanctification has the effect of making the elements 'a sacrament of commemoration' of Christ's sacrifice (*c. Faust.* xx. 21). The sign, however, must be carefully distinguished from that which it signifies: 'it is not that which is seen that feeds, but that which is believed' (*Serm.* cxii. 5). 'Believe, and thou hast eaten' (*crede et manducasti* [*in Joann.* xxv. 12]). The 'eating of the body' and 'drinking of the blood' in Jn 6[56] are expounded by him as meaning 'to dwell in Christ and to have Christ dwelling in us.' But elsewhere he shows that the Sacrament is not for him an empty sign. The Eucharist conveys a gift of life. This gift is a spiritual gift, and the eating and drinking are a spiritual process (*Serm.* cxxxi. 1). The Eucharistic body is not the sensible flesh, for of that we could not partake, but of this flesh we receive that which was its essence, the Spirit which quickens it (*in Joann.* xxvii. 5). The presence of Christ is, in fact, a spiritual presence (Augustine, however, nowhere uses this phrase of the Eucharist). Augustine does not identify the Eucharistic body with the historical body of Christ, but seems to conceive of the spiritual essence of Christ's humanity as receiving a new symbolical body (*non hoc corpus quod videtis manducaturi estis . . . sacramentum aliquod vobis commendavi*), and this spiritual essence also becomes the spiritual essence of the Church, which is sometimes spoken of as the body of Christ, and as the *res sacramenti* (see *Serm.* ccxxvii. *in Joann.* xxvi. 15, *Ep.* clxxxv. [*ad Bonifacium*] 50; cf. Gore, *Dissertations*, p. 233, note 1). The latter presentation is in accord with the earlier language of Tertullian and Cyprian (cf. Tert. *de Orat.* 6; Cyprian, *Ep.* lxiii. 13). Again, Augustine has been thought to teach a 'receptionist' view of the Sacrament, and some of his language certainly accords with such an idea. But his treatment is unsystematic, and his teaching on the subject of the reception by the wicked is not consistent. In some passages he seems to identify the eating of the flesh of Christ with believing on Him (see above), and maintains that those who 'abide in Christ' alone eat of the body and blood (*in Joann.* xxvi. 18; *de Civ. Dei*, xxi. 25), though elsewhere he teaches that the 'inward part' (or *res*) is given to all (see *Serm.* clxxiv. 7 ['infants partake of His table, that they may have life in themselves'], and for the reception by the wicked, see *Ep.* cxl. 66; *de Bapt. contra Donat.* v. 8. 9; *Serm.* lxxi. 17; *in Joann.* xxvii. 11). On the whole, Augustine must be ranked with those Eastern and Western writers upon the Eucharist who, during the 3rd and 4th centuries, taught what has been called the 'dyophysite' view. The characteristic of this teaching is, as we have seen (above, § 2), the sharp distinction which it draws between the sign and the thing signified. But, though Augustine emphasizes this point so strongly, and at the same time urges the importance of faith and the spirituality of the gift, there is no real justification for regarding him as teaching a purely symbolical view. His merit consists in his attempt to set forth the nature of the sacramental idea, and in his endeavour to conceive of the body of Christ, as given in the Eucharist, in a way that accords with the highest spiritual conceptions. In this respect his influence was wholly for good, and the authority of his teaching resisted for some centuries to come the inroads of a materializing tendency with regard to the sacraments.

For a further discussion of Augustine's teaching, see Harnack, *Hist. of Dogma*, Eng. tr. v. 155 f.; Loofs, *PRE*[3] i. 61–63; Batiffol, *Études*, 2nd ser., p. 232 f. The last-named criticizes Loofs' symbolical interpretation, and also the view of those who appeal to Augustine as teaching explicitly a belief in an objective presence in the elements (e.g. *En. in Ps.* xcviii. 9; *ib* xxxiii. 1. 10; 2. 2).

These two currents of thought, the Ambrosian and the Augustinian, are exhibited in the writers of the 6th century. The Africans, Fulgentius and Facundus, and the Spaniard, Isidore of Seville, re-echo the language of Augustine, while Cæsarius of Arles and Pope Gregory the Great repeat the teaching of Ambrose (Loofs, *loc. cit.*). The same is true of the language of the prayers in the Western liturgies between the 6th and the 8th century. On the one hand, there are found such phrases as 'the bread changed into the flesh . . . the cup changed into the blood,' 'unto the transformation of the body and blood of our Lord God Jesus Christ,' 'to eat the body,' 'to drink the blood'; on the other hand, there occur 'spiritual food,' 'spiritual cup,' 'the virtue of the heavenly food,' 'the image of the sacrament.' In the early Middle Ages the language of these prayers, as well as the authority of Augustine and Ambrose, was appealed to in the controversies on the Eucharist (Batiffol, *op. cit.* p. 348 f.).

(2) The transformation of the conception of the sacrifice in the Eucharist during the 3rd and 4th centuries, which has been indicated above, affected the course of the developments during the following period. In the East there was little development beyond the standpoint of Cyril of Jerusalem

and Chrysostom. John of Damascus has only a passing reference to the subject, in which he recalls the type of Melchizedek and the prophecy of Mal 1[11], and speaks of the 'pure and unbloody sacrifice' (*de Fide Orth.* iv. 13).

In the West we find, as in the treatment of the nature of the gift, two traditions, represented by Augustine on the one hand, and Ambrose on the other.

Augustine's conception of the sacrifice exhibits two characteristics, both of which may be paralleled from the earlier language current in the West. (*a*) The Eucharist is a 'commemoration of the sacrifice of the Cross' (*sacrificii memoria, sacramentum memoriæ* [*c. Faust.* xx. 18. 21]). The sacrifice of the Cross was prefigured by the OT sacrifices. It was offered in reality on the Cross. It is celebrated by a 'sacrament of commemoration' in the Eucharist (*ib.* 21). This language may be paralleled from Cyprian (*calicem in commemorationem Domini et passionis ejus* [*Ep.* lxiii. 17]), and from the prayers of the Roman Canon in the *de Sacramentis* (the oblation is *figura corporis et sanguinis*). Again, he speaks of the Eucharist as 'the sacrifice of the body and blood of Christ' (*de An. et de Orig.* i. 11 [13]), of 'offering the body of Christ' (*ib.* i. 9 [10]), and of 'the sacrifice of our ransom' (*Confess.* ix. 12 [32]). This also recalls Cyprian (see above, II. 2 (5)). (*b*) But the most distinctive feature of Augustine's teaching is his emphasis on the union of the faithful in the Eucharist with the sacrifice of Christ. The faithful themselves, by partaking of Christ's body and blood, are the sacrifice, and become 'the body of Christ' (*Serm.* ccxxvii.; *de Civ. Dei*, x. 6. 20, xxii. 10). This conception, which is a development of Pauline teaching (1 Co 10[16f.]), had been anticipated by Tertullian (*de Orat.* 6), who connects with the gift of 'daily bread' the idea of continuance in Christ and inseparability from His body (*i.e.* the mystical body), and by Cyprian (*Ep.* lxiii. 13), who finds in the mixture of water with wine in the chalice a representation of the incorporation of the people in Christ.

On the other hand, the teaching of Ambrose (see above, II. § 2 (5)) is reproduced by Gregory the Great in the 6th century (*Dial.* iv. 58). (*a*) The Eucharist is related to the sacrifice of the Cross, which it is said to 'renew' (*reparat*), though this language is qualified by the words 'in a mystery,' and by the comment that it 'imitates the Passion of the Only-begotten Son' (cf. Ambrose, *in imagine*). (*b*) Like Ambrose and Chrysostom, Gregory connects the Eucharist with the heavenly life of Christ. He who is 'immolated for us again in the mystery of the holy oblation' is the Son who dieth no more, but liveth in Himself immortally and incorruptibly. In the mystery of the Eucharist things earthly are united with things heavenly (*ib.*). The whole action is, in fact, as in Ambrose, mystical and transcendental. Moreover, Gregory combines with this presentation two conceptions which further qualify his language, and relate it to that of Augustine. (*a*) The sacrifice of the Eucharist is closely associated with the communion of the faithful. (*β*) The sacrifice is consummated only in the self-oblation of the worshippers (*ib.* 59, 'For then will He be truly the victim [*hostia*] for us to God, when we have made ourselves a victim' [*hostiam*]).

Ambrose, Chrysostom, and Gregory the Great in their teaching upon the sacrifice in the Eucharist exhibit certain common features, which re-appear in later Greek teaching, and in some of the early mediæval writers in the West. Behind their language there lies the Pauline conception of the mystical body of Christ. The Church 'offers' through Christ, the Head of the body, and in union with Him (hence the emphasis of Gregory and Chrysostom on the communion and self-oblation of the worshippers; cf. Augustine). At the same time these Fathers appear to recognize that the Scriptural application (*e.g.* in Hebrews) of the language of sacrifice and priesthood to the heavenly life of Christ is but the language of illustration, used to express the abiding truth of the assumption of humanity in the Person of Christ to the throne of God: 'His Incarnation is itself the offering of our purification' (Greg. Mag. *Moral.* i. 24. 32; cf. Euthymius, quoted below, III. § 6). The Eucharist sets forth that truth 'in an image' or 'in a mystery' (Ambrose, Greg.). The whole action of the rite is 'spiritual' and 'heavenly' (Chrysos.). The same idea is suggested by the earlier language of Irenæus on the 'heavenly altar,' and in the *de Sacramentis* and Eastern liturgies. See Gore, *Body of Christ*, p. 185 f.

(3) The conception of the propitiatory value of the sacrifice in the Eucharist, which has been traced in the earlier Patristic period (Origen, Cyril of Jerus.), received a considerable development later on. The metaphorical language used by some of the Fathers suggested a renewal of the sacrifice of Christ in the Eucharist (*e.g.* Ambrose, *de Off.* i. 48 [*quasi recipiens passionem*]; Greg. Mag. *Dial.* iv. 58 [*mortem unigeniti reparat, iterum immolatur*], hom. *in Ev.* ii. 37. 7 [*iterum patitur*]), and, though qualified by other expressions, it came to be taken in a literal sense. The liturgical custom of offering intercessions for the living and the dead immediately after the consecration led to the same result. Lastly, the practice of offering the Eucharist specially for the departed, which appears first in Tertullian and Cyprian, led gradually to the idea that each offering constituted a distinct sacrifice for sin. The transition was made slowly and almost imperceptibly. In popular religion the propitiatory conception doubtless received a considerable impetus from the influx of pagan ideas into the Church. The language of Gregory the Great shows in this respect the advance made upon the earlier period. He dwells much upon the benefits resulting from the offering of the sacrifice of the Mass for souls in purgatory; in his *Dialogues* (iv. 55) he tells how a priest is visited by the apparition of a departed soul, who offers to him bread, and says, 'Offer this bread to Almighty God on my behalf, that thou mayst intercede for my sins.'

The transition from the Eucharistic to the propitiatory view of the Eucharist is reflected in the Western Sacramentaries, when compared with the earlier prayers (*e.g.* the *de Sacramentis*). Thus in the Leonine Sacramentary (6th cent.), side by side with the older language, which speaks of 'the sacrifice of praise,' we find 'sacrifice of propitiation and praise' (*sacrificium placationis et laudis*).

We may compare also the following prayers from the same source: (*a*) 'O Lord, we beseech Thee, mercifully sanctify these gifts, and, receiving the offering of a spiritual sacrifice, make us to be an eternal gift unto Thee'; (*b*) 'O Lord, mercifully look upon these gifts, which we bring for the commemoration of Thy saints, and offer for our offences' (ed. Feltoe, Cambridge, 1896, pp. 24, 19).

The Western Sacramentaries, in fact, exhibit, in the multitude of their variable prayers, the gradations between the earlier Eucharistic and the later propitiatory view.

LITERATURE.—In addition to the literature quoted under I., reference may be made to the general Histories of Doctrine by Harnack and Schwane, and to Loofs, *Leitfaden z. Stud. der Dogmengesch.*³, Halle, 1893; also to the artt. in *PRE*³, 'Eucharistie' (Drews) and 'Abendmahl II.' (Loofs). The following special treatises or discussions deal with the Patristic period or particular portions of it: G. E. Steitz, 'Abhandl. über die Abendmahlslehre der griech. Kirche,' in *JDTh* ix.–xiii. (1864–68); F. S. Renz, *Opfercharakter der Eucharistie*, Paderborn, 1892; C. Gore, *Body of Christ*, London, 1901; W. B. Frankland, *The Early Eucharist*, Cambridge, 1902; H. B. Swete, 'The Eucharistic Belief of the Second and Third Centuries,' in *JThSt* iii. 161 f. (1902); A. Scheiwiler, 'Die Elemente der Eucharistie in den ersten drei Jahrh.,' in *Forsch. zur chr. Lit. u. Dogmengesch.* iii. 4 (Mainz, 1903); A. Andersen, *Das Abendmahl in den zwei ersten Jahrh.*, Giessen, 1904; V. Ermoni, *L'Eucharistie dans l'Église primitive*, Paris, 1903; P. Batiffol, *Études d'histoire et de théologie positive*, 2nd ser., Paris, 1905; K. G. Goetz, *Die heutige Abendmahlsfrage in ihrer gesch. Entwicklung*, Leipzig, 1907; A. Struckmann, *Die Gegenwart Christi in der hl. Eucharistie*, Vienna, 1905; D. Stone, *A History of the Doctrine of the Holy Eucharist*, 2 vols., London, 1909.

III. *THE EUCHARIST IN THE MIDDLE AGES* (A.D. 800–1500). — **1. Introductory.** — With the Middle Ages we enter upon a period of reflexion and controversy upon the Eucharist, which before the time of Paschasius had never received really systematic treatment at the hands of theologians. From the 9th cent. onwards, however, it continued to occupy a prominent place in theological discussion, which gradually formulated a theory of sacraments, their character, mode of operation, effects, and place in religion. The period from the 9th to the 15th cent. marks the growth of a system of belief and practice, against which the Reformation of the 16th cent. was a reaction and protest. The history, however, is limited mainly to the West, where there was much greater movement of thought and much less unanimity upon the subject than in the East. The Greek Church, as a whole, held by the teaching of John of Damascus, in spite of occasional movements in the direction of a closer accord with later Western teaching (as at the Council of Lyons in 1274, when Greeks and Latins met to discuss re-union, and a statement was drawn up in which μετουσιοῦν occurs as an equivalent for *transubstantiare*). In the Western Church, on the other hand, the history of the doctrine exhibits the stages by which the conversion theory, taught by Ambrose, and established under Greek influence, gradually asserted itself, and was carried to its final development in the doctrine of transubstantiation. The two chief authorities appealed to by early Western mediæval writers upon the Eucharist were Ambrose and Augustine. The teaching of the former was appealed to by those who tended to the view of a miraculous conversion of the elements into the body and blood of Christ. The teaching of Augustine formed the starting-point of those who distinguished sharply the sign from the thing signified, and who inclined to the view of a spiritual presence of power and efficacy—a view which passes in its more extreme forms into a receptionist or commemorative view of the rite. Generally, however, an attempt was made by both parties to harmonize the teaching of these two Fathers and to interpret them in accordance with their own standpoint. There are three reasons why the conversion doctrine finally prevailed during the Middle Ages. (1) It gave to simple minds an easy and literal interpretation of the words 'This is my body,' 'This is my blood.' (2) It fell in with the realism of popular thought, which viewed everything in the concrete, whereas the more vague but spiritual language of Augustine resisted all attempts to materialize it, and it was only by a *tour de force* that mediæval writers made Augustine speak the language of transubstantiation. (3) The language of conversion lent itself to the growing love of the miraculous.

2. The Eucharistic controversies of the early Middle Ages.—The mediæval history of the Eucharist begins with the controversy excited by the appearance of the treatise of Paschasius Radbertus, *On the Body and Blood of the Lord*, in 844. The author was a monk, and afterwards abbot, of Corbey. His book, which was the most complete treatise on the Eucharist that had yet appeared, dealt with the whole subject of the Sacrament, and was inspired by a profoundly religious spirit. Paschasius exhibits clear traces of Greek influence (Cyril of Alexandria, John of Damascus), and no less clearly is he indebted to Augustine, especially in his emphasis on the spiritual character of the gift which is received (*e.g.* ch. 10), and his repudiation of the Capernaite view (cf. Jn 6[52]), which was apparently held in uninstructed circles. He is no metaphysician, but starts from the omnipotence of God, the need of faith, and the words of Christ, 'This is my body.' His treatment follows that of Ambrose in the main. He adduces the miracles of the OT and NT in support of the belief that the substance of the bread and wine is changed into the flesh and blood of Christ. Yet the change is an inward one, and is not apparent to sight or taste. If the elements retain their outward appearance, the object is to call forth faith and to remind believers that the gift is spiritual. He adduces, however, instances in which a miraculous change of the outward appearance has occurred to convince doubters or reward faith. Yet no portents can enhance the value of that which the faithful receive in the Sacrament. He maintains the identity of the Eucharistic and historical body of Christ, and explains its presence in countless places at once by a creative act of God on each occasion.

Paschasius' treatise fell in with popular tendencies and became in the subsequent period the authoritative exposition of the rite. But the influence of Augustine was still too strong to allow such teaching to pass unchallenged. Outside the circle of Paschasius' admirers the language of Augustine was still repeated (Amalarius, Florus, Rabanus Maurus), while John Scotus Erigena appears to have taught a purely symbolical view of the Sacrament. But the great opponent whom Paschasius' book called forth was Ratramnus (also a monk of Corbey), who, in response to a request of Charles the Bald, wrote his treatise, *On the Body and Blood of the Lord*. The two questions submitted to him were: (1) Is the Eucharist the body of Christ in a mystery or in reality? (2) What is the relation of the Eucharistic to the historical body?

(1) He begins by defining the words *figura* and *veritas*. The former denotes the setting forth of something under a veil, as when Christ speaks of Himself as the Bread or the Vine. The word *veritas* denotes the showing of a thing unveiled in its natural character, as when we say that Christ was born of a virgin. The bread and wine show one thing outwardly to the senses, and proclaim aloud another inwardly to the minds of the faithful. There is no material miracle in the Eucharist. Outwardly the elements are the same as before. Inwardly, to the minds of the faithful, they are in a figure (*figurate*) Christ's body and blood. The change is a spiritual one. There are not two different substances, body and spirit, but one thing under two aspects—in one aspect bread and wine, in another the body and blood of Christ. In their bodily nature they are bread and wine; in power and spiritual efficacy they are the mysteries of the body and blood of Christ. Ratramnus throughout represents the older conservative tradition of the West (Tertullian, Jerome, the *de Sacramentis*). He quotes from Augustine the phrase *figura corporis Christi*, to prove that the sacraments are one thing, the thing of which they are the sacrament is another. As visible creatures the elements feed the body; according to their invisible substance (*i.e.* the power of the Divine word) they feed and sanctify the soul.

(2) In dealing with the second question, Ratramnus appeals to a distinction drawn by Ambrose (*de Myst.* 53) between the sacrament of the flesh and the verity of the same, and to a further statement of Ambrose (*de Myst.* 58) that the body of Christ is the body of a Divine Spirit. It is called the body of Christ because in it the Spirit of Christ (*i.e.* the power of the Divine word) feeds and cleanses the soul. Finally, he quotes two prayers from the Mass to show that the elements are the 'pledge' and the 'image' of the verity of Christ's body and blood, but not the verity itself, which will be manifested in open vision only hereafter.

Ratramnus' treatment of the subject exhibits in an acute form the ambiguity attaching generally to the older Western tradition as represented most conspicuously in Augustine, and it is difficult to decide whether Ratramnus believed that the gift bestowed in the Eucharist was merely a mysterious operation of the Divine power through the elements, effecting union with Christ, or a presence in the elements of the body and blood of Christ. His teaching, however, had a certain currency in the subsequent period. Much of it reappears in the *Homilies* of the English Aelfric (10th cent.). Ratramnus' book, which came to be attributed to John Scotus Erigena (see below), also attracted considerable attention at the time of the Berengarian controversy (it was highly esteemed, and quoted by Ridley at the time of the Reformation).

Other writers besides Ratramnus protested against particular views expressed in the work of Paschasius (*e.g.* Rabanus Maurus rejects the view of the identity of the historical and Eucharistic body of Christ), but circumstances favoured the spread of Paschasius' doctrine, which received cruder expression as time went on. The transformation of the elements was regarded as so complete that they could no longer be spoken of as 'signs.' During the 10th cent. the idea of a physical miracle was carried so far in some quarters that, if we may trust the statement of Berengar, expressions were current which countenanced the revolting idea of a *portiuncula carnis* received by the faithful in the Sacrament.

3. The Berengarian controversy (cf. art. BERENGAR).—The wide-spread acceptance of the teaching of Paschasius and the crudities of popular language about the Eucharist aroused a fresh protest against the doctrine of conversion during the 11th century. Berengar, who was head of the school of Tours, had refused to accept the teaching of Paschasius, and re-opened controversy on the subject by addressing a letter to Lanfranc defending the teaching of John Scotus upon the Sacrament of the altar, which Lanfranc had spoken of as heretical.

Berengar was condemned unheard at Rome and Vercelli in 1050. But, though public opinion was against him, he had some powerful friends, and succeeded in 1054 in persuading Hildebrand (then Papal legate at Tours) of his orthodoxy. He appeared before a Synod at Rome in 1059, where he was compelled to submit, and to subscribe a confession of faith put forward by Cardinal Humbert, in which a crude and materialistic conception of the Sacrament was taught ('panem et vinum . . . post consecrationem non solum sacramentum, sed etiam verum corpus et sanguinem domini nostri Jesu Christi esse, et sensualiter non solum sacramento, sed in veritate manibus sacerdotum tractari, frangi, et fidelium dentibus atteri'; see Lanfranc, *de Euch.* 2). (For a more lenient view of this confession, see the language of Innocent III. and Alexander of Hales, quoted by Stone, *Hist. of the Doct. of the Holy Eucharist*, i. 310, 316.) Berengar retired to France, but shortly afterwards renewed the controversy. The accession of Hildebrand to the Papacy did not save him, however, from condemnation (though the Pope showed him much indulgence, and endeavoured to secure for him the opportunity of making a confession of faith couched in general terms), and in 1079 he was required to subscribe a formula couched in milder terms than the earlier one, but still acknowledging the conversion doctrine ('panem et vinum . . . substantialiter converti . . . et post consecrationem esse verum Christi corpus, quod natum est de Virgine . . . non tantum per signum et virtutem sacramenti, sed in proprietate naturae et veritate substantiae'). He again submitted, and spent the rest of his years in retirement.

In Berengar's letter to Lanfranc he expresses his agreement with the opinions of John Scotus. It has been argued, however, with some show of reason, that the work referred to is Ratramnus' book, which was commonly ascribed to John Scotus (Gore, *Dissertations*, p. 240 ff.), and Berengar's position is certainly in the main that of Ratramnus. His more mature view of the subject is set forth in his work, *de Sacra Coena* (written in 1073), which is a reply to Lanfranc (ed. Vischer, Berlin, 1834). He goes back to the tradition of the West before the time of Paschasius, and appeals to the language of Augustine, the *de Sacramentis* (which was ascribed to Ambrose), and the prayers of the Roman Mass in support of his protest against the doctrine of conversion. In his exegesis of the Fathers he is far superior to his opponent. But the novel element in Berengar's treatise is his use of the dialectical method. In this his opponents were no match for him. While they rest their appeal on faith in the omnipotence of God and on the authority of the Fathers, Berengar puts forward the appeal to reason. He attacks the idea that the elements cease to exist, on the ground that 'accidents' cannot exist without a subject—the first appearance of the later Scholastic terminology. By attributing the accidents of the elements to the body and blood, Lanfranc is really teaching that the body and blood are visible (ed. Vischer, pp. 127, 171). He further illustrates the use of the negative in Scripture and the Fathers, in order to prove that it is often employed not to deny the continued existence of that to which it refers, but to emphasize something which it has become, or some aspect of it to which attention is directed. Thus, when it is said that after consecration the elements are not bread and wine, but the body and blood of Christ, it is not necessarily implied that the bread and wine cease to exist (*ib.* p. 177 f.). He attacks Paschasius' idea that the body and blood of Christ are produced by a new act of creation (*per generationem subjecti*), he denies that the wicked receive the body and blood, and, lastly, he protests against the idea of a *portiuncula carnis* as that which is received in the Sacrament. In so doing he states, apparently for the first time among mediæval writers (though he appeals to Augustine for the phrase), that *totum corpus* or *totus Christus* is received. In his positive teaching Berengar appears to have followed Augustine and Ratramnus. As a result of consecration there is a real, though spiritual, presence of the body and blood, which are received with the heart, not with the mouth, of the faithful. He denies that he maintained a merely figurative view. Every sacrament implies a *res sacramenti*, seeing that it is, in Augustine's phrase, 'a visible sign or form of an invisible grace.' Lastly, he has a valuable statement of the nature of the Divine working in its use of natural means. 'Everything which is consecrated is of necessity enhanced, but by no means destroyed.'

To Berengar's opponents such teaching seemed to deny any real presence of Christ in the Sacrament. A purely 'spiritual' presence, such as Berengar taught, seemed scarcely distinguishable from a presence only in the intelligence or memory (so Hugh of Langres; cf. Gore, *op. cit.* p. 256). Hence Berengar's language seemed to lead to a merely figurative view of the Sacrament. Others charged him with teaching a theory of impanation, *i.e.*, that, as Christ took human nature into personal union with Himself and became incarnate, so in the Sacrament He takes bread and wine into the same kind of union, and may be said to be impanate and invinate (see below, § 4). Both these views are attributed to the followers of Berengar by writers of the 11th and 12th centuries (Witmund, Alger of Liège, Gregory of Bergamo).

The controversy produced a series of replies to Berengar (Lanfranc, Hugh of Langres, Witmund of Aversa, Durandus of Troarn), which exhibit traces of the current conceptions (physical manducation, reception by the wicked, incorruptibility of the consecrated species). But Berengar's protest had not been in vain. From this period the cruder views tend to disappear. The rising Scholasticism of the 12th cent. took up the task of formulating the doctrine of conversion. The term 'transubstantiation' had not yet appeared, though Witmund's phrase *substantialiter transmutare* is a close approximation to it. In the task of formulating the Church's belief, however, the Schoolmen learned from the controversy with Berengar to lay aside many of the crude and untenable conceptions which had been current before.

4. The Schoolmen and the doctrine of transub-

stantiation.—During the 12th cent. the development of the doctrine of the Eucharist was affected by two factors in the general history of the period. The first of these was the religious revival which had resulted from the reform of the Papacy and the preaching of the Crusades. It was the age of the Catholic mystics, St. Bernard and the Victorines (Hugh and Richard). And this revival brought with it a revival of the influence of St. Augustine's teaching. The effect of this appears in the greater spirituality of conception shown by writers upon the Eucharist during the period, and in the recoil from the materialism of the preceding century (cf. *e.g.* Hildebert of Tours, *de Sacramento Altaris*: the presence of Christ is real, yet spiritual; Christ is in heaven, yet He is in the Sacrament; His presence is a presence of power and efficacy, yet it is in the elements). The language of St. Bernard (*de Coena Domini*) echoes the Augustinian distinction between the invisible grace and the visible sign, while Hugh of St. Victor speaks of the Eucharist as 'an image of the invisible and spiritual participation of Jesus which is accomplished inwardly in the heart by faith and love' (*de Sacr. Christ. Fid.* ii. 8. 7).

A second influence was the intellectual revival, of which Berengar and Roscellin had been pioneers. The age of the Schoolmen had begun, and the questions raised by the Eucharistic controversy were transferred to the region of metaphysics. Attempts were made to state the nature of the Eucharistic mystery in metaphysical terms. At the same time the whole idea of sacraments was revised, and in this task the influence of Augustine played an important part.

(1) The great problem of the period, which divided Nominalists and Realists, was the nature of 'universals' or 'general ideas.' This question had come to the front through Roscellin's Nominalist teaching on the Trinity. In refuting him Anselm and Abelard, starting from the standpoint of Realism, and with the help of Aristotle, discussed the relation of 'universals' to corporeal existence. In this way the terms *substantia* and *accidentia* came to be used by them. They are first definitely applied to the Eucharist in the 12th cent., though Berengar had anticipated their use when he employed the distinction between *subjectum* and *accidentia*. By *substantia* was denoted 'the impalpable universal which was held to inhere in every particular included under it,' while *accidentia* denoted the 'sensible properties which came into existence when the pure Form clothed itself in Matter' (Rashdall, *Universities of Europe in Mid. Ages*, London, 1895, i. 46 f.). From the 12th cent. onwards the application of this metaphysical language to the Eucharistic mystery dominated Western teaching. (2) A second result of Scholasticism was the revision of the whole conception of sacraments. This was mainly the work of Hugh of St. Victor († 1141) and Peter Lombard († 1164; his *Sentences* became the manual of the Schools in the Middle Ages). They start from Augustine's definition of a sacrament as 'a visible form or sign of an invisible grace,' and distinguish between the *sacramentum* and the *res sacramenti* (Peter Lombard further distinguished in the Eucharist the *res contenta et significata*, i.e. the body and blood, and the *res significata et non contenta*, i.e. the unity of the Church). They maintain that the sacraments 'contain' grace (Hugh of St. Victor) and are 'causes' of grace (Peter Lombard). Their purpose is not only to signify, but to sanctify. These statements became the accepted definitions, and were completed in the 13th cent. by Thomas Aquinas, who taught that the sacraments effect that which they signify, though they are instrumental causes, the principal cause being God.

Both the developments which we have indicated as due to Scholasticism marked in some ways a considerable gain. The metaphysical distinction of *substantia* and *accidentia*, as apprehended by the Schoolmen, made it possible to hold a more refined view of the mode of the Sacramental Presenee. For the *substantia* of the Schoolmen was in the final resort real only to thought, and could be apprehended only by the faith of the believer (popular thought undoubtedly held a far different conception and clung to the cruder notions of the earlier period). Again, the distinction between the outward sign and the inward grace, when clearly defined and held, tended to minimize the dangers of materialism. From this time onwards the language of the Schoolmen shows a growing emphasis upon the spiritual character of the hidden *substantiæ* of the Sacrament, and an increasing tendency to give more reality to the accidents. Thus, in their discussions upon the Eucharist, Hugh of St. Victor and Peter Lombard reject the materialistic views which in the previous century had been associated with the fraction and reception of the consecrated species (see Hugh of St. Victor, *de Sacr. Christ. Fid.* ii. 8. 13; Peter Lombard, *Sent.* lib. iv. dist. 13). In dealing with such questions the mysticism of Hugh comes to his rescue. Thus he says (*op. cit.* ii. 8. 13):

> 'Christ exhibits His bodily presence for a season in order to stir us to seek His spiritual presence. Just as in the Incarnation He withdrew His bodily presence at the Ascension, though His spiritual presence remained, so is it in the Sacrament. The Sacrament is completed. The virtue remains. Christ passes from the mouth to the heart. That food belongs to the soul, not to the body. If, then, after this you seek the bodily presence of Christ, seek it in heaven.'

Both Hugh of St. Victor and Peter Lombard start from the language of conversion, and teach that the elements pass into the body and blood (they teach a change *per transitionem*, not by creation or addition or annihilation: the 'miraculous creation' theory of Paschasius is given up). Peter Lombard discusses the question (*Sent.* lib. iv. dist. 11) whether the change is one of form or substance or some other kind, and inclines, with some hesitation, to the idea of a change of substance. The only substance in the Sacrament is that of the body and blood. The accidents of the bread and wine continue to exist without a subject. They do not inhere in the substance of the body, which is unaffected by them. Hence there is no fraction of the body. He teaches (with other writers of the period) that the whole Christ (*totus Christus*) is received. At the same time he distinguishes between the sacramental and the spiritual eating, quoting Augustine's words, *Crede et manducasti*, and emphasizing the need of faith. The wicked receive sacramentally, but not spiritually.

Neither Hugh of St. Victor nor Peter Lombard employs the term *transubstantiatio*, which is used, however, by Hildebert of Tours early in the 12th cent., while the verb *transubstantiare* is found in Stephen of Autun in the first half of the same century. But they clearly hold the teaching expressed by it, which is that, as a result of consecration, the *substantiæ* of the bread and wine pass into the *substantiæ* of the body and blood of Christ, the sensible properties (or 'accidents') of the bread and wine being all that remains of the original elements.

The doctrine thus expressed became the formally recognized teaching of the West. It fell in with the accepted philosophy of the day, and it gave shape and consistency to the conceptions of popular thought. It secured the belief in a miraculous conversion which was demanded by popular religion, and it minimized the crude materialism of the earlier period. On the whole it seems to have met with little opposition after the middle of the century.

Rupert of Deutz († 1135) represents the standpoint of earlier Patristic teaching (Theodoret, Gelasius) in drawing a parallel between the two natures in Christ and the earthly and Divine elements in the Sacrament. Like Berengar, he denies that the working of the Divine Spirit destroys the substances which are assumed for its own uses. The human nature assumed by Christ was not changed or destroyed by the union. So, too, the bread and wine become the body and blood of Christ, not by being changed into the sensuous realities of flesh and blood, but by assuming invisibly the realities of the immortal substance, Divine and human, which is in Christ (*de Trinitate et operibus ejus: in Ex.* ii. 10). Card. Bellarmine charges Rupert with teaching the theory of impanation (see above, § 3), which was also attributed to Berengar. But in both cases the use of the familiar Patristic analogy lends no support to the view that they carried the parallel as far as their opponents suggested. In both cases, however, the motive which inspired the use of such language was opposition to the popular conception of the conversion of the elements. But such language as that of Rupert is an isolated phenomenon among the Schoolmen of the 12th cent.; it is the language of survival.

The next event of importance in the history is the Fourth Council of the Lateran convened by Pope Innocent III. in 1215. At this Council the Pope put forward a Confession of Faith directed against the errors of the Albigenses. It deals with the doctrine of God, the authority of the Old Testament, the Incarnation, and the sacraments. The statement upon the Eucharist runs as follows: 'There is one universal Church of the faithful, outside which no one at all is in a state of salvation. In this Church, Jesus Christ Himself is both Priest and Sacrifice: and His body and blood are really contained in the Sacrament of the altar under the species of bread and wine, the bread being transubstantiated into the Body, and the wine into the Blood by the power of God, so that, to effect the mystery of unity, we ourselves receive from His what He Himself received from ours.'

The reserve exhibited in the language of this decree has given rise to the question whether the Council intended to impose upon the Church the Scholastic definition of transubstantiation. For, though the term *transubstantiare* is employed, the accompanying term *accidentia* is not found in the decree, and there is no explicit statement to the effect that the *substantiæ* of the elements cease to exist, and that the *accidentia* alone remain. Hence it has been maintained that *transubstantiare* is used in a more general sense to denote a mysterious change (cf. Palmer, *Treatise on the Church of Christ*[3], ii. 166 f.; Pusey, *Real Presence*, p. 14 ff.; Batiffol, *Études*, ii. 383). The language of Pope Innocent III. in his treatise, *On the Mystery of the Mass* (iv. 7-9), has been adduced to show that he speaks without condemnation of the view that the elements of bread and wine continue in their natural substances after consecration. But such a conclusion may be doubted, and the treatise appealed to contains a most careful and explicit statement of the doctrine of transubstantiation. More to the point is Pusey's appeal (*op. cit.* p. 22 f.) to the language used in the 15th cent. by Peter d'Ailly, who, after setting forth the various views upon the subject, decides in favour of that which maintains that the substances of the elements cease to exist, 'although,' he says, 'it does not follow evidently from Scripture that it is so, nor, so far as I can see, from the determination of the Church.' Card. Franzelin (*de S. S. Euch. Sacramento et Sacrificio*, p. 202 f.) adduces against this isolated expression of opinion other language which shows that the Mediæval Church from Thomas Aquinas onwards regarded as heretical any other view than transubstantiation. So, too, the Council of Trent explains it, maintaining the change of the whole substance of the bread and wine into the body and blood of Christ, and denying the continuance of the substance of the bread and wine after consecration, though at the same time it speaks of the sacramental Presence as a 'mode of existence which can scarcely be expressed in words.' See, further, Stone, *History of Doctrine of Holy Eucharist*, i. 313.

Whatever ambiguity there is in the language of this decree, the scholastic doctrine of transubstantiation became the accepted teaching of the Western Church. It found its fullest expression in the *Summa Theologiae* of Thomas Aquinas (III. lxxiii.-lxxxii. 6). In two respects he advanced upon previous teaching. (*a*) He defined more exactly the nature of the Presence. (*b*) He dealt more fully with the question of the accidents.

(*a*) Aquinas affirmed that the whole Christ (*totus Christus*) is present, being entire in each species and every fragment of each species, the body being present by concomitance in the species of the wine, and the blood being present by concomitance in the species of the bread. (This had already been affirmed by some opponents of the Berengarians. In its origin the phrase *totus Christus* maintained the important truth that the gift of the whole Christ is received in the Sacrament, and guarded against the idea of a *portiuncula carnis*. In this sense it had been used by Berengar.) Aquinas denies that the presence of Christ is a local presence (*localiter, in loco*). He is present only *per modum substantiæ* (so also, still earlier, Odo of Cambrai). Hence Christ is not moved in the Sacrament *per se*, but only *per accidens*, in relation to the movement of that in which He is. He denies any fraction of the body, and maintains, like Peter Lombard, that the wicked receive sacramentally, but not spiritually. Lastly, the body remains till the species are corrupted. On all these points he gathers up preceding discussions, and attempts to evade the materialistic conclusions of earlier times by refining and spiritualizing the conception of the Presence.

(*b*) In treating of the accidents, Aquinas, like the later Schoolmen generally, allows them greater reality than had been conceded in the earlier period. The problem was how to reconcile the fact that the elements preserve many of the ordinary effects of a substance with a literal acceptance of the belief that they become Christ's body and blood. Aquinas maintains that the accidents exist without a subject, yet they retain the power of affecting objects and can breed life, nourish, be broken and corrupted. Yet, according to the Schoolmen, the accidents have no independent being, but simply characterize the substance in which they inhere. The solution which Aquinas offers is that they inhere in quantity (*quantitas dimensiva*), as in a subject. This was the great problem of discussion among later Schoolmen, and under the stress of it the metaphysical theory of transubstantiation tended to break down. In the following period the Schoolmen are inclined to allow still greater reality to the accidents. Duns Scotus denies that they require a subject in which to inhere, while Wyclif ridiculed the prevailing uncertainty on the question (*de Eucharistia*, c. 6).

The controversies upon the Eucharist tended to intensify the devotion of the faithful to the Sacrament, which came to be regarded as the mystery of religion *par excellence*. Around the miracle of transubstantiation there gathered a wealth of legend intended to illustrate the mystery and do honour to the Sacrament. Corresponding to this sense of the miraculous character of the Sacrament, we find a growing decrease of communion. Attention came to be concentrated upon the act of consecration. Peter Lombard had affirmed that the form of the Sacrament is to be found in the words of institution, while Aquinas maintained that the Eucharist is completed in the consecration, whereas all other sacraments are completed in the application of the matter to the sanctification of the individual (*Summa*, III. lxxx. 12, where, however, he maintains the necessity of the communion of the priest in both kinds). Worship and adoration formed the central feature of the rite. This in turn led to some important additions to the ceremonial of the Mass, the chief of them being the introduction of the ceremony of the elevation of the consecrated Sacrament.

This ceremony must be distinguished from the earlier ceremony found in the Eastern liturgies and connected with the invitation to communion addressed to the faithful, 'the holy things for them that are holy.' There is no rubric in the Eastern rites prescribing the adoration of the consecrated Sacrament, though later on in the 17th cent., under Roman influence, the Council of Jerusalem (1672) assigned to the Sacramental Presence the same worship (λατρεία) as is paid to the Trinity. In the West, some time during the 12th cent., the practice of elevating the Host and chalice immediately after consecration, and before the close of the canon, came into use. It was intended, doubtless, partly as a protest against the views of the Berengarians, and partly in order to stimulate worship of the mystery of Christ's presence. In earlier days the altar had been veiled with curtains, but the object of this new ceremony was to make a spectacle of the central portion of the rite. Henceforth, the 'gazing upon' the Sacrament plays a prominent part in popular instructions upon the Mass (*e.g.* the *Lay Folks' Mass Book*). The canons of various English Councils in the 13th cent. allude to the custom of elevation for the purpose of adoration, and in the same century Durandus, bishop of Mende, and author of the *Rationale Divinorum Officiorum*, shows acquaintance with the ceremony in a form resembling the present Roman rubric. For the rubric in the use of Sarum, see Frere, *Use of Sarum*, Cambridge, 1898–1902, i. 81, where, however, there is no explicit mention of worshipping the consecrated Sacrament. On the history of the subject, see Drury, *Elevation in the Eucharist*, Cambridge, 1907.

This devotion connected with the Eucharistic mystery culminated in the institution of the festival of Corpus Christi in 1264 by Pope Urban IV. (confirmed and established in 1311). The occasion called forth the noble hymns of Thomas Aquinas, in which the Eucharistic devotion of the Mediæval Church found its loftiest expression.

5. The doctrine of transubstantiation in the later Middle Ages.—The doctrine of transubstantiation remained throughout the later Middle Ages the standard of faith for Western Christendom, and the attempts to challenge it met with little success, and in some cases were visited with severe censures. At the beginning of the 14th cent. John of Paris and Durandus of Pourçain declared that it was possible to believe in the Real Presence without accepting transubstantiation. William of Occam, the Nominalist Schoolman of the same century, suggested that on the grounds of reason alone, apart from the decision of the Church, the permanence of the substances of bread and wine was not improbable. But the greatest of all mediæval opponents of the doctrine was Wyclif. Inspired by the practical abuses of the day, he exposed the inconsistencies of the Scholastic teaching, repudiating the idea of accidents existing without a subject, and charging the popular devotion with idolatry. He is also reported to have taught that the unworthiness of the priest invalidates the Sacrament. Such a theory was undoubtedly held by some of his followers; but Wyclif himself, while holding that the disposition of the priest affected to some extent the value of the Mass celebrated by him, regarded the sanctity which the Sacrament has from Christ's presence as the same in all Eucharists (*de Eucharistia*, c. 4 [Wyclif Society, London, 1892]). Some of Wyclif's language looks like an assertion of a merely symbolical presence. He rejects transubstantiation, identification, impanation, and maintains that the words of institution are used in a tropical sense (*op. cit.* c. 9, p. 291). He attacks the popular idea of a sensible, visible presence of Christ (*op. cit.* c. 1, p. 20 f.), and maintains that the body of Christ is 'virtually in the Host as in a sign' (*op. cit.* c. 8, p. 271). The Sacrament is the form of bread and wine, and not Christ or part of Him (*ib.* c. 1, p. 29). But this language was directed against the materialistic conceptions of his time. Wyclif's positive teaching seems to indicate a belief in a real, though sacramental, virtual, spiritual presence. The Host is not itself the body of Christ, but the very body of Christ is sacramentally hidden in it (*op. cit.* c. 1, p. 15; cf. *Fasc. Ziz.*, London, 1858, pp. 115, 117). The bread is an 'effectual figure' of the body of Christ, and the Sacrament has a special efficacy beyond that of other signs of the OT and NT (*de Eucharistia*, c. 4, p. 84 ff.). But the influence of Wyclif's positive teaching on this subject was less than that of other parts of his teaching. In Bohemia his teaching on transubstantiation did not gain many followers, and John Hus, while protesting against practical abuses connected with the Sacrament (*e.g.* the denial of the cup to the laity), appears to have accepted the doctrine of the Church in its main features.

The great movement in the direction of spiritual religion, originated by the German mystics during the 14th and 15th centuries, did not at first affect the Eucharistic doctrine of the Church. Though some of the mystics, like Eckhardt, were accused of speculative errors in the direction of pantheism, they adopt for the most part the semi-mystical position, which is not indifferent to sacraments, but seeks to interpret them in a way which brings out their spiritual value, as emphasizing the union of the soul with Christ and its devotion to Him (so Ruysbroek and the author of the *Imitatio Christi*). In John Wessel († 1489), however, there is a tendency to break loose from current teaching. Luther regarded Wessel as a precursor of his own teaching in several respects. While emphasizing, with earlier mystics, the spiritual character of the participation of the body of Christ, Wessel held that this spiritual presence was not restricted to particular moments, but extended over the whole life of the believer, and that there is no essential difference between spiritual and sacramental participation. The latter had value only in so far as it rested upon the former. As a sacrament, the Lord's Supper could be celebrated only by a priest. As a spiritual act of participation in Christ by faith, it is possible for all without a priest (*de Sacr. Euch., passim*).

Still earlier than the Mystics, the wide-spread sects of the 12th and 13th centuries promoted a spirit of revolt from the established doctrines. Some, like the Waldenses, appealed to Scripture alone. Others, like the Albigenses, were affected by Manichæan views. From the Franciscans in the 13th cent. there proceeded a famous book, *The Eternal Gospel* (the work of a disciple of the Abbot Joachim of Floris), which preached the near advent of a purely mystical religion, in which the Church system, with its priesthood and sacraments, should find no place.

6. The Eucharistic sacrifice in the earlier Middle Ages.—In the Eastern Church there was little development in the doctrine of the Eucharistic sacrifice beyond the conceptions of the earlier Patristic period, as exhibited in Cyril of Jerusalem and Chrysostom, and in the West by Ambrose and Gregory the Great. The commemorative character of the rite, as a memorial of Christ's sacrifice, and its relation to the sacrifice of the Cross on the one hand, and to the heavenly life of Christ on the other, were clearly affirmed. Later on in the Middle Ages the Greek theologians, Theophylactus (11th cent.), Euthymius Zigabenus and Nicholas of Methone (12th cent.), and Cabasilas (14th cent.) still emphasize these points. The Eucharist is really a sacrifice. That which is offered is the body of Christ, and the moment of the sacrifice is when the bread and wine are changed into the body and blood of Christ (Cabasilas). In this sacrifice Christ offers Himself through His ministers, and unites the Church with Him in His intercession with the Father. The very presence of Christ's humanity before God in heaven constitutes an intercession. 'His very manhood entreats the Father on our behalf' (Euthymius on He 7^{25}). The whole Eucharistic action on earth is, in fact, conceived of as a mystical representation in time of the 'eternal redemption' won for man by Christ. It proclaims aloud the death, resurrection, and ascension of the Lord, and it avails by intercession for the living and the dead, and by communion benefits the faithful (Cabasilas). Lastly, like the mystical commentators of the West, Cabasilas sees in the Eucharistic rite itself a drama of the life, death, and resurrection of Christ. See, further, D. Stone, *op. cit.* i. 156 ff.

The teaching of the West in the 9th and following centuries exhibits some of the main characteristics of Patristic teaching.

(1) The Eucharist is regarded as a commemoration and representation of the Passion. But this representation is found in the ceremonies of the Mass rather than in its wider purposes. The prayers of the Mass are a tableau of the life and death of Christ (Amalarius). The mixture of the chalice represents the water and the blood which flowed from the side of Christ (Paschasius). Others find this representation in those acts of the priest which are based upon what Christ did at the Supper, *e.g.* the fraction of the Host (William of Thierry, 12th cent.), or the double consecration of bread and wine (Peter Lombard, Alexander Hales). On the influence of these ideas on later conceptions of the sacrifice of the Mass, see below, § 7.

(2) Emphasis is laid upon the effects of the sacrifice. The sacrifice is, in fact, explained by, and identified with, the effects which it produces upon the worshippers (cf. Augustine). Thus Paschasius (*op. cit.* c. 9) teaches that the consecration of the gifts renews the Passion, because Christ reiterates daily that which He did upon the Cross, offering himself to the Father to deliver us from our sins. The daily offering is due to our need of daily cleansing. By communion we partake of the fruits of Christ's death. Lastly, he repeats Augustine's saying that by participation we become Christ's body and blood (*op. cit.* c. 7). The same identification of the sacrifice with its effects appears in Alger of Liège (12th cent.; see *de Sacram. Corp. et Sang. Dom.* ii. 2 f.).

(3) Paschasius and Alger of Liège connect the Eucharistic offering with the heavenly intercession of Christ. According to Paschasius, the true priest in every Eucharist is Christ Himself, now made a priest for ever. It is He who offers the gifts presented on the earthly altar, and it is from His offering of Himself that we receive them back as His body and blood. Thus he explains the prayer in the Roman Canon, *Jube hæc perferri.* The lifting up of the gifts is their consecration. The whole act of offering is sacramental, mystical, supra-local. The altar on high, at which the gifts are offered, is the body of Christ, through which and in which He offers to the Father the prayers of the faithful and the faith of believers (*op. cit.* 8, 12; cf. Alger of Liège, *op. cit.* i. 14). This view combines the earlier Western view of the Eucharistic offering, contained in the Roman Canon, with the Greek view exhibited in Chrysostom, and found also in Ambrose and Gregory the Great among the Western Fathers. The Eucharist is no repetition of the sacrifice of the Cross. It is offered, as Paschasius says, in commemoration of the Passion (*op. cit.* c. 9; this expression qualifies the words 'passionem illius reparamus' in the same chapter). But that which connects it with the sacrifice of the Cross is the heavenly priesthood of Christ, who has passed through death and is ever present with the Father, and presents to Him our prayers and intercessions. (Note the identification of the 'altar on high' with the body of Christ. This shows the practical identity of Paschasius' teaching with that of Ambrose and Gregory the Great. See above, II. 3 (2).)

7. The Eucharistic sacrifice in the Scholastic period.—The early Schoolmen paid little attention to the doctrine of the Eucharistic sacrifice, their thoughts being occupied with discussions as to the mode of the presence of Christ in the Sacrament. They content themselves mainly with denying that there is any repetition of the sacrifice of the Cross, and with the simple statement (following Augustine) that there is a representation, or commemoration, or likeness of the sacrifice of the Cross in the Mass. Thus Rupert of Deutz declares that the whole Christ is present upon the altar, 'not that He may again suffer, but that to faith, to which all past things are present, His Passion may be represented by way of a memory' (*de Trin. et op.; in Gen.* vi.). Similar language is used by Peter Lombard (*Sent.* iv. 12. 7).

The Schoolmen of the 13th cent. attempt a more analytical treatment, and endeavour to define the rationale of sacrifice. William of Auvergne, Bishop of Paris († 1249), discusses the chief elements of sacrifice. (*a*) Sacrifice is an act of homage to God with a view to the sanctification of the individual. (*b*) It is, in the form of the sacrificial meal, a means of communion with God, and a source of spiritual refreshment. (*c*) It is an act by which the worshipper is associated with the family of God (*de Legibus*, c. 24). In what follows he maintains that the first and chief sacrifice is that of ourselves, without the offering of which nothing that we present to God is pleasing or acceptable to Him. The essence of the sacrifice of Christ lay in His sinless life of virtue (*ib.* c. 28). By his one oblation on the Cross, Christ has reconciled and sanctified the world. The sacrifice of the Mass is the application by the will of Christ of the benefits which accrue from the sacrifice of the Cross. As a sacrifice the Eucharist propitiates God and averts His wrath. As a sacrament it sanctifies and supplies spiritual refreshment to those who receive it. Without the manifestation of Christ in the Mass faith and devotion would die, and the faithful would be deprived of spiritual food. In it Christ is present as priest and victim, as advocate and healer (see the treatise *de Sacramento Eucharistiæ*, cc. 2, 3, 5). Similarly Albert the Great († 1280), the master of Thomas Aquinas, while combining in an original way the conceptions of earlier writers, and emphasizing the sanctifying effects of the sacrifice of the Cross which are imparted in the Eucharist, regards the Mass as an act of homage to God, and as representing the union of the Church with the self-oblation of Christ (*de Sacram. Euch.* dist. v. 4; *Sent.* iv. 13. 23). At the same time he prepared the way for future developments by discussing the question in what sense the Mass is distinct from the offering of the Cross (*Sent.* iv. 13. 23). See Vacant, *Hist. de la conception du sacrifice de la messe dans l'église latine*, Paris, 1894, p. 39 f.

Nothing shows more clearly the undeveloped character of the doctrine of the Eucharistic sacrifice in the middle of the 13th cent. than the slight treatment which it receives in the *Summa Theologiae* of Thomas Aquinas. Like earlier Schoolmen, he emphasizes the effects of the sacrifice, and maintains that it is a 'representative image' of the Passion (III. lxxxiii. 1). Elsewhere he discusses the nature of sacrifice. It has its roots in the Laws of Nature. 'A sacrifice is something done for the honour properly due to God, to appease Him' (III. xlviii. 3). But he goes beyond previous Schoolmen in his further definition that sacrifice involves the production of a change in the object offered, 'as that animals were killed and burnt, that bread is broken and eaten and blessed' (IIª. IIªᵉ. lxxxv. 3 ad 3). The result of this definition was that the sacrifice was treated independently of the effects which it produced. This opened up a new era. In the later period the main question was, 'What is the physical act accomplished in the Victim which constitutes the essence of the sacrifice of the Mass?' Peter Lombard and Alexander Hales had found a representation of the Passion in the double consecration of bread and wine, and the latter had suggested that it represented the separation of the body and blood in the crucifixion (*Univ. Theol. Summa*, iv. 10. 3). Incidentally Aquinas takes up this idea (III. lxxiv. 1), and later on it was developed (*e.g.*, by Vasquez in the 17th cent.) in discussions upon the sacrificial character of the Mass.

In other respects the teaching of Aquinas associated the sacrifice of the Mass more closely with the consecration, and threw into greater prominence the importance of the priest in the rite. (*a*) In justifying communion in one kind, he argues that it is sufficient for the priest to receive in both kinds, because he receives in the person of all, and because 'the perfection of the sacrifice consists not in the use of the faithful, but in the consecration of the matter' (III. lxxx. 12). This dictum, by isolating the act of the priest, encouraged the separation of the ideas of sacrifice and communion, which had already taken place in practice, and increased the tendency to view the Mass as an *opus operatum* completed in the act of consecration. (*b*) In connexion with the question, 'What is the relation of the priest's action in the Mass to that of Christ?' Aquinas maintained that the priest is the representative of Christ and acts in His person. The sacrifice of the Eucharist has the same value as that of the Cross, being offered directly by Christ Himself (III. lxxxviii. 1 ad 3). (*c*) In one passage (*Sent.* IV. xii. 2 [2 ad 4]), Aquinas asserts that the sacrifice of the Mass has an efficacy, by way of impetration, for all who have a right disposition. Thus it blots out mortal sins, in so far as it obtains for those on whose behalf it is offered, by way of impetration, the grace of contrition. Later on this teaching was used, without the qualification 'a right disposition,' to support the mechanical application of the sacrifice of the Mass, apart from Communion, as a satisfaction for all for whom the intention of the priest applied it.

8. The Eucharistic sacrifice in the later Middle Ages.—The teaching indicated above fell in with certain tendencies of popular religion, the beginnings of which may be traced in the Patristic period.

(1) The practice of offering the Eucharist with special intention, which grew rapidly after the 4th cent., and of associating with each Mass the idea of a distinct offering for sin (cf. above, II. 3 (3)) led to an exaggerated belief in the *ex opere operato* idea of the Mass. An almost magical conception of the operation of sacraments came to be current, which took no account of the spiritual condition of the recipients. Thus the benefits of the Mass were regarded as operating mechanically for the good of those on whose behalf it was offered.

(2) A second feature of the popular religion was the multiplication of Masses. This was a wide departure from primitive usage (*e.g.* the 'one altar,' 'one Eucharist' of Ignatius, and the practice of 'concelebration'). As late as the 6th cent. the Synod of Auxerre (578) forbade the saying of two Masses at the same altar on the same day (Vacant, p. 26). Convenience led to the relaxation of this rule, and the habit of offering Masses with special intention, and of going from one Mass to another, grew from the 9th cent. onwards. From the 11th cent. onwards various decrees were issued forbidding priests to say at first more than three Masses a day; later on, more than one (Vacant, p. 27). This popular practice encouraged a mechanical idea of the rite, and gave ground for the belief that each Mass was a distinct act of propitiation made for sin or to procure some specific benefit.

(3) The system which did more than anything else to externalize the idea of the Mass was the chantry system. Endowments were given to procure the saying of Masses for the souls of the founder and his family. Some of these dated from the 12th cent. in England, but the system became wide-spread in the 14th and 15th centuries. On its better side it represented a touching devotion which followed departed friends beyond the grave, and showed its interest in them by intercession and commemoration (for a defence of it, see Sir Thomas More's *Supplication of Souls*). In practice it led to a traffic in Masses, which degraded the conception of the Mass and excited the cupidity of the clergy (cf. Chaucer, *Canterbury Tales, Prologue*, 507–510).

There are two developments in the later Middle Ages which affected the doctrine of the sacrifice of the Mass.

(*a*) In connexion with the question of the relation of the priest's action in the Mass to that of Christ, the disciples of Aquinas followed their master in maintaining the direct action of Christ Himself in the Mass through the instrumentality of the priest. Duns Scotus (14th cent.), however, departs from this position in two respects. (*α*) He shows a greater anxiety to defend the unique character of the sacrifice of the Cross, and maintains that the sacrifice of the Mass has not the same value as the Passion of Christ, and that in it Christ does not offer immediately by an act of His own will, though He is offered as being contained in the sacrifice (he quotes in support He $9^{25. 28}$). Still the Mass has a special worth, as being a special commemoration of the oblation of Christ upon the Cross, and as beseeching God by it (*Quæst. Quodlibet.* 20. vol. xii. p. 529). (*β*) He emphasizes the fact that the Eucharist is the act of the Church, rather than of the individual priest, and that it is accepted not by reason of the will of Christ acting immediately, but by the will of the Church (*ib.*). This teaching was developed by the later Scotists (*e.g.* Hiquæus and Biel).

In this later teaching upon the Eucharist the thought of the connexion between the worship of the Church and the heavenly intercession of Christ its Head, which had formed the background of the early Christian conceptions of life and worship (cf. *e.g.* Clement of Rome, *ad Cor.* 36, 'the High priest of our offerings'; see also Origen, *de Orat.* 10), and which characterizes the teaching of the later Greek Fathers, and in the West appears in Ambrose, Gregory the Great, and the early mediæval writers, became obscured or even lost. Logically the later Scholastic teaching involved consequences which affected the value not only of the sacrifice of the Mass, but of the priesthood as well. Hence Vacant (*op. cit.* p. 49) says of it that it 'prepared the way for Protestantism' (cf. Kidd, *op. cit.* p. 103 f.).

(*b*) A second development of later mediæval teaching was the idea that, while the sacrifice of the Cross availed for original sin, that of the Mass was an offering for daily sins both deadly and venial. This opinion was mentioned and condemned in the Confession of Augsburg in 1530 (cf. the English Pr. Bk. art. xxxi.). The Roman theologians at first denied that such an opinion had been held. In reply the Reformers appealed to Aquinas. But the sermons appealed to, though ascribed to Thomas Aquinas, and also included in another form among the works of Albert the Great, undoubtedly belong to a later period. The same opinion was attributed to the Dominican Catherinus, who was present at the Council of Trent, and it apparently gained a certain currency, largely because of its association with the two famous Schoolmen mentioned above. It was denounced by Latimer; and, when brought to light in the 16th cent., it was repudiated by the Roman theologians (for the history, see Vacant, *op. cit.* p. 41, note; Kidd, p. 73 f.).

9. The place of the Eucharist in mediæval religion.—The historical development which has been traced above represents the growth of a doctrinal and practical system in which the influence of popular religion played a large part.

(1) In their attempt to formulate a scientific statement of the mode of Christ's presence in the Eucharist the Schoolmen were hampered by the existence of an established belief which had taken shape in the later Patristic and early mediæval period, and which exhibited all the features of a

crude and unreflective piety. They undoubtedly made a sincere attempt to free the doctrine from the materialistic expression which had been given to it before their time, but their influence in this respect, whatever their own conceptions may have been, only very partially succeeded in affecting the general belief. The crude materialism of popular belief continually re-asserted itself (see, *e.g.*, the statement of Archbishop Arundel in 1413, quoted by Stone, *op. cit.* i. 376 f.). Again, the absorption of the Schoolmen in the question of the mode of the Eucharistic presence only served the purpose of keeping the discussion on a lower plane, in which it was continually encumbered by the intrusion of purely physical questions, which withdrew attention from the purpose and significance of the Sacrament as a whole. We must except, however, from this criticism the treatment of the subject by such writers as William of Auvergne (see above, § 7).

(2) One effect of this excessive attention given to the question of the relation of the elements to the spiritual gift bestowed in the Sacrament was to concentrate the thought of worshippers upon the moment of consecration, when by the miracle of transubstantiation the body and blood of Christ were present upon the altar. The elevation of the Sacrament for the purposes of worship (see above, § 4) gave point and precision to this aspect of the rite. Thus the *Lay Folks' Mass Book*, which provides no devotions for communion, directs the worshipper after the consecration to do reverence to Jesus Christ's own presence and to kneel, holding up both hands, and so to behold the elevation and meditate on Christ's Passion. The manifestation of Christ in the Mass was regarded as supplying the greatest incentive to faith and devotion (see the language of William of Auvergne quoted above, § 7), and there is little doubt that in its higher forms this belief fostered a noble and beautiful piety (see, *e.g.*, the prayers in the *Lay Folks' Mass Book* and the *Ancren Riwle*). But on its lower side this 'gazing on' the Sacrament tended to divert attention from the purpose of the Sacrament as a whole, and ministered to the craving for the miraculous and to a magical conception of religion.

(3) Corresponding to this emphasis on the moment of consecration we find a decline in frequency of communion. Amalarius in the 9th cent. still counselled daily communion, but later on a monthly (Langland, *Piers Plowman, Pass.* xix. B. 387 f.) or even yearly communion (Chaucer, *Parson's Tale*) was regarded as sufficient. The Fourth Lateran Council (1215), by prescribing a minimum of one communion a year, had contributed unintentionally to this growing infrequency, though local Councils from time to time sought to secure a higher standard. Among lay-people frequent communion was exceptional (*e.g.*, Fisher mentions as a mark of exceptional piety that the Lady Margaret was 'houselled' well-nigh twelve times a year). Moreover, the custom had sprung up of giving communion outside the time of Mass (see Langland, *Piers Plowman, Pass.* xxii. 4: 'and dyhte me derly . . . and dude me to churche. To huyre holliche ye masse and be housled after'). This dislocation of the rite, by severing the idea of communion from it, marks a wide departure from earlier usage.

(4) Another mediæval departure was the withdrawal of the cup from the laity. This practice began in the 12th cent., and was justified in the 13th by Aquinas (see above, § 4), though he declares the other use permissible. Finally, though communion in both kinds continued even at Rome on Easter Day late in the 14th cent., the Council of Constance in 1415 made communion in one kind compulsory.

(5) The Schoolmen, as we have seen, devoted comparatively little attention to the sacrificial aspect of the Eucharist, though some writers of the 13th cent. have valuable discussions on the rationale of sacrifice in general (*e.g.*, William of Auvergne and Albert the Great). Here again they were hampered by the existence of a popular system of practice which had been growing up since the time of Pope Gregory the Great. This popular system had encouraged, by the frequency of Masses, an external and mechanical conception which led to the belief that each Mass had a distinct propitiatory value apart from the moral condition of the worshipper. The result was that an exaggerated importance came to be attached to the mere hearing of Mass.

(6) Lastly, the loss of the corporate aspect of the Eucharist as an expression of the unity of the faithful, which finds a place in the teaching of St. Paul and St. Augustine, was another consequence of the severance of the idea of communion from that of worship. The Schoolmen, indeed, in their treatises frequently refer to this aspect of the matter, and quote Augustine's language upon the subject, but in popular religion and practice it seems to have found little place.

On the other hand, the mediæval doctrine and practice with regard to the Eucharist rendered important services to religion by the impressive witness which they bore to particular aspects of the rite. (*a*) Worship and adoration found a striking and noble expression in the mediæval Mass, and in the prayers contained in some of the popular books of instruction. To the men of the Middle Ages the Mass was the mystery *par excellence* of the Church. Around it there gathered all the splendour which art and music could provide. The appeal that was made to eye and ear in the public worship of the Church was calculated to enthral the imagination and subdue the will. And there is little doubt that to multitudes the Mass provided a real incentive to devotion and to spiritual worship. (*b*) The mediæval Mass kept the memory of the Passion of Christ vividly before the minds of the worshippers. The popular books of devotion and the mystical commentators on the Mass alike emphasize the conception of the Mass as a sacred drama exhibiting and rehearsing again and again the story of the Lord's Passion 'until He come.' (*c*) The mystical aspect of the Eucharist as a means by which the union of the soul with Christ is effected finds clear expression in the best forms of mediæval religion, alike in the teaching of St. Bernard, Hugh of St. Victor, William of Auvergne, in the hymns of Thomas Aquinas, and the devotions of the *Imitatio Christi*.

LITERATURE.—(*a*) *GENERAL*: A. Harnack, *Hist. of Dogma*, Eng. tr., London, 1894–99, vols. v., vi.; J. Schwane, *Dogmengesch. der mittleren Zeit*, Freiburg, 1882; P. Schanz, *Die Lehre von den heiligen Sacramenten*, do. 1893; C. Gore, *Dissertations on Subjects connected with the Incarnation*, London, 1895, and *Body of Christ*, do. 1901; P. Batiffol, *Études d'hist. et de théol. positive*, 2nd ser., Paris, 1905; K. G. Goetz, *Die heutige Abendmahlsfrage in ihrer gesch. Entwicklung*, Leipzig, 1907; Darwell Stone, *A History of the Doctrine of the Holy Eucharist*, 2 vols., London, 1909.

(*b*) *ON PASCHASIUS, RATRAMNUS, AND BERENGAR*; C. Gore, *Dissertations* (cited above); J. Ernst, *Die Lehre des hl. Paschasius Radbertus von der Eucharistie*, Freiburg, 1896; A. Naegle, *Ratramnus und die hl. Eucharistie*, Vienna, 1903; J. Schnitzer, *Berengar v. Tours, sein Leben u.s. Lehre*, Munich, 1890.

(*c*) *ON TRANSUBSTANTIATION*: art. 'Transsubstantiation,' in *PRE*[3]; C. Gore, *Dissertations*; T. B. Strong, in *JThSt* iv. 28 f.; J. B. Franzelin, *Tractatus de S.S. Euch. Sacram. et Sacrif.*, Rome, 1868; W. Palmer, *A Treatise on the Church of Christ*, London, 1838, ii. 166 f.; E. B. Pusey, *The Doctrine of the Real Presence as contained in the Fathers*, Oxford, 1870, p. 17 f.; P. Batiffol, *op. cit.*; F. Pijper, *Middeleeuwsch Christendom: de vereering der h. hostie; de gods-oordeelen*, Leyden, 1907.

(*d*) *THE EUCHARISTIC SACRIFICE*: J. M. A. Vacant, *Hist. de la conception du sacrifice de la messe dans l'église latine*, Paris, 1894; B. J. Kidd, *The Later Mediæval Doctrine of the Eucharistic Sacrifice*, London, 1898; W. Götzmann, *Das eucharist. Opfer nach der Lehre der älteren Scholastik*, Freiburg, 1901; F. S. Renz, *Geschichte des Messopferbegriffes*, Freising, 1901.

J. H. SRAWLEY.

EUCHARIST (Reformation and post-Reformation period).—I. *GENERAL.*—The first Reformation utterance concerning the nature of the Eucharist is found in Luther's sermon of 1518, 'De digna praeparatione cordis pro suscipiendo Sacramento Eucharistiae.' In order to its worthy reception, the believer must free his mind of all hatred and dissension. No other sins are so incompatible with both the name and the *res* of this sacrament, for its name is communion, and its *res* the unity of hearts. The elements of the Eucharist are a picture of this, for the one bread is made up of many grains and the wine of many grapes.

'Nomen est communio ; Res unitas cordium. . . . Quod et figuratur in speciebus sacramenti, in quibus multa grana, amissa singulorum differentia, in unum panem. Item uvae multae, amissa sua quoque differentia, in unum vinum redactae sunt.'

It has often been remarked that, instead of union, this sacrament brought disunion into the ranks of the Reformers; in place of the 'unitas cordium' there is a bitter sacramental controversy. But, while this is true, it ought not to blind us to the underlying unity of the Protestant doctrine. The Reformed Church in all its branches was and is united in rejecting certain points of mediæval theory and practice. Chief among these are: (1) the doctrine of Transubstantiation; (2) the idea of *any* priestly miracle; (3) the Adoration of the Host; (4) the 'sacrificium propitiatorium' of the Mass; (5) the denial of the cup to the laity. If not so united on the positive side, it has been, and is, practically unanimous in making the following assertions: (1) that the Eucharist—whatever name for it may be in common use—is a sacrament instituted by Christ.

Here the Quakers dissent. They reject the idea of sacraments altogether. The Spirit of God is the only signature and pledge of our Gospel inheritance. 'The communion of the body and blood of Christ is inward and spiritual. . . . Of which things the breaking of bread by Christ and His disciples was a figure, which even they who had received the substance used in the church for a time, for the sake of the weak . . . yet, seeing they are but shadows of better things, they cease in such as have obtained the inheritance' (Barclay, *Apology*, Prop. 13).

(2) That it is the central act of Christian worship.
(3) That it is a means of grace.

At this point a not inconsiderable number part company with the general Protestant doctrine. Historically, they are represented by the Socinians. To them the Lord's Supper is not directly a means of grace. In their Confessional doctrine, they were even loath to speak of sacraments. They called the Eucharist a ceremony (*præceptum Christi cæremoniale*) which it was becoming to retain as a venerable and beautiful custom. It was instituted that believers might call to mind with thankfulness the Lord's death, and for no other purpose (*Cat. Rac.* qu. 337). With them in this matter Winer (*Confessions of Christendom*, Edinburgh, 1873, p. 264) has classed the Arminians who 'regard the Lord's Supper as a mere ceremony of thanksgiving and profession.' But the Brotherhood of the Remonstrants (the representatives of Arminius), while rejecting the full Calvinistic doctrine, have held to a position similar to that of Zwingli at one period of his career, and using largely his language, *e.g.* 'signa repraesentantia rem,' give to the Supper a real though comparatively insignificant place among the means of grace.

(4) That there is a real presence of Christ in the Sacrament.

The phrase 'real presence' would fail to commend itself to many, as being connected with certain dogmas, but the real presence in some sense would not be denied.

Amid all the differences, therefore, of teaching and practice which obtain in the Reformed Churches, there is a profound and wide-spread agreement which must not be overlooked.

II. *THE MAIN CONSTRUCTIONS OF EUCHARISTIC DOCTRINE IN THE CHURCHES OF THE REFORMATION.*—The Reformation, with all its substantial unity, produced three distinct types of doctrine in regard to the Lord's Supper. These are associated with the names of Zwingli, Calvin, and Luther. The main point of divergence lies in the way in which the presence of Christ in the Supper is conceived. H. Schultz (*Zur Lehre vom heiligen Abendmahl*, Gotha, 1886) has called them 'historisch,' 'mystisch,' and 'wunderhaft' respectively. And, subject to certain modifications, this characterization may stand.

1. The doctrine of Luther.—As the differences in doctrine arose largely from different points of departure, something must be said about the mediæval doctrine. In the pre-Reformation Church the Eucharist was regarded not merely as a sacrament, but at the same time as a true sacrifice:

'In quantum in hoc sacramento repraesentatur passio Christi, qua Christus obtulit se hostiam Deo . . . habet rationem sacrificii ; in quantum vero in hoc sacramento traditur invisibilis gratia sub visibili specie, habet rationem sacramenti' (Thomas Aquinas, *Sum. Theol.*, pt. iii. quæst. 79, art. 7).

There had come to be, in fact, two distinct rites—the Mass and the Eucharist. The first time, however, that the distinction was drawn Confessionally was at the Council of Trent, where the doctrines of the 'sanctissimum sacramentum Eucharistiæ' and the 'sacrificium Missæ' are dealt with in two separate sections, the former being defined in 1551, the latter not until 1562.

Now, Luther's great concern was to conserve for the believer all the invisible grace of the Eucharist; Zwingli, on the other hand, attacked the doctrine of the Mass, and, in particular, any thought of the repetition, renewal, or continuance of the sacrifice of the Cross. Luther approached the subject from the point of view of the troubled conscience desiring grace and the assurance of grace, and was content merely to remove the 'superfluous miracles' from the Eucharist; Zwingli from the point of view of the educated layman, sick of priestly claims, and intolerant of any such thought as the manufacture of Deity.

The teaching of Luther, however, is not all of a piece. It has been asserted that there is an obvious Romeward retrogression from the evangelical simplicity of his early doctrine, from the moment he began to enter into controversy with Carlstadt. But over against this may be set the facts that in his earliest teaching he seems simply to have accepted the doctrine of Transubstantiation as he found it, and that, while he was himself conscious of development, he was conscious of it in quite a different direction. In 1545 he asserted that at first, with great humility, he left too many articles to the Pope, which he afterwards condemned as abominations (cf. I. A. Dorner, *History of Prot. Theol.*, Eng. tr., Edinburgh, 1871, i. 124). But he certainly did pass through several stages before reaching the precision of his final doctrine.

It has to be remembered that Luther came to the doctrine of the Eucharist after he had already attained a general theory of the Sacraments. His controversy over the Indulgences and the Sacrament of Penance had given him such a theory—'non sacramentum, sed fides sacramenti, justificat.' To the Scholastic 'sacramenta sunt efficacia signa gratiae,' he added 'si credis, et non amplius' (Serm. *de Pœnitentia*). With such an evangelical theory already to hand, he proceeded to deal in various sermons with the Eucharist. Characteristic is his outburst against the obscuring of the Word in the Sacrament. 'What Devil,' he asks, 'suggested that the words should be hidden from the people?' 'In the Sacrament everything lies in the words that Christ says, which we should verily set with gold and precious stones' (Serm. *Von dem neuen Testament*, Erlangen ed. xxvii. 139 f.). This whole sermon, as A. W. Dieckhoff remarks, reads like a song of victory over the rediscovered word (*Die evangel. Abendmahlslehre im Reformationszeitalter*, Göttingen, 1854, p. 210).

There is, however, no consistent theory in these early sermons—not even consistent progress towards the later doctrine. Throughout, Luther regards the Eucharist as a 'beneficium,' not as an 'officium,' but the details of the exposition vary. In 1518, bread and wine are pictures of the 'unitas cordium' (see above). In 1519, the transformation (*Wandlung*) of bread and wine into body and blood is a picture of our transformation into the spiritual body of Christ. In 1520, the body and blood are present to support the trustworthiness of the word of forgiveness, being outward signs of the death which was necessary before the testament of Christ could have effect. In 1521, the body and blood are present for the same purpose, but now they are identical with the means through which the forgiveness was won (cf. F. Graebke, *Die Konstruktion der Abendmahlslehre Luthers*, Leipzig, 1908, pp. 1–42).

There is here no consistent theory. Luther throughout is operating within Scholastic limits, and has sought to invest the old formulæ with an evangelical meaning. His great aim is to restore the Word to its rightful place in the Sacrament and alongside the Sacrament, and to keep the Sacrament from being regarded as the vehicle of a higher grace than the Word. Indeed, in the *de Captivitate Babylonica*, he asserts that he prefers to speak of one Sacrament—the Word—and several signs ('si usu Scripturae loqui velim, non nisi unum sacramentum habeo, et tria signa sacramentalia').

From the beginning, however, of the controversy with Carlstadt, Luther's doctrine began to be more distinctive, for it had now not only, on the negative side, to be free from the positive errors and 'superfluous miracles' of Rome, but to be developed on the positive side against a theory which denied that the Sacrament was a means of grace at all, and, in particular, refused to allow any real presence of Christ in the Sacrament.

Andrew Bodenstein of Carlstadt was a professor in Wittenberg. When Luther was still in the Wartburg, and Carlstadt was a power in the town, Wittenberg became the scene of tumult and disorder. Hasty reforms were introduced, most of them good; but their hasty execution bred excitement, and the excitement was fanned into uproar and riot by the appearance of the Zwickau prophets. To Luther thereafter Carlstadt was the man responsible for this tumult, a fanatic himself and the associate of fanatics. Carlstadt's Eucharistic teaching was, like Luther's early teaching, not all of a piece. In 1521 he had put forth a small pamphlet on the Eucharist, in which he held, not that the bread was a sign of the body of Christ, but that the body of Christ was a sign of the grace of God. But by 1524, in his treatise 'Von dem wider-christlichen Missbrauch des Herrn Brods und Kelchs,' he had come to another opinion. Much was true and necessary, but there ran through it all the theory that the Lord's Supper was not a pledge and seal of the certainty of reconciliation, but only a mere remembrance with moral influence on the mind, thus setting the Supper on the same plane with any picture or sermon that recalled the death of Christ. In the next year appeared his exposition of the words 'Hoc est corpus meum.' He denied that the presence of Christ in the Supper could be proved from Scripture. When our Lord used the words 'Hoc est corpus meum,' Carlstadt, following an interpretation attributed to the Waldenses, suggested that He pointed to His own body.

Now, of much of Carlstadt's teaching Luther might have been expected to approve. But he never could see Carlstadt as a thinker differing from him in certain points of theology; he always saw him as the representative of a fundamentally different type of piety (cf. K. Jäger, *Luthers religiöses Interesse an seiner Lehre von der Realpräsenz*, Giessen, 1900), or, rather, as devoid of true evangelical religion altogether. And so, in his various answers to Carlstadt and those associated with him, though he always came back to the Sacrament, he attacked their whole conception of salvation and its appropriation. Carlstadt had no conception, he urged, of the needs of a troubled conscience, either in the Sacrament or in Christ Himself. What was needed was comfort through assurance of the forgiving grace of God. This comfort was not to be found in any mere subjective remembrance; some objective guarantee was wanted. Through the necessity of finding this in the Sacrament he never ceased to emphasize his interpretation of the words of institution, and developed rapidly his own distinctive theory (Consubstantiation). The term 'Consubstantiation,' it should here be noted, is mostly used by non-Lutherans. Lutherans in general object to it, because it seems to express the idea of the mixing of two substances so as to form a third, but they have no objection to it when explained as the real co-existence of the two substances (*das reale Zusammensein beider Substanzen*), the earthly and the heavenly.

Luther's interpretation of 'Hoc est corpus meum' always seemed to him the only full Christian one. He claimed that it was literal; but an absolutely literal interpretation would imply rather the Roman Catholic doctrine. By the *hoc* Luther understood the bread—not, however, as bread alone, but as already forming a sacramental unity with the body of Christ, which sacramental unity exists before the words are spoken. This sacramental unity (and this is important) is not the result, therefore, of any word or act of consecration. Having laid down this sacramental unity of bread and body, he then explains the words as a synecdoche, in which the whole (bread and body) stands for a part (body). To this his fertile mind found many analogies, *e.g.* sword and sheath, soul and body, the two natures in Christ, glowing iron, etc. The most homely, 'the child in the cradle' (Erlangen ed. xxix. 267), as when a mother says, 'This (cradle and child) is my child,' led his opponents to say that Luther by *est* understood *continet*. But he never gave up the idea that his interpretation was the natural one, the most literal, and therefore the only legitimate one. In his Larger Catechism he wrote: 'Though infinite myriads of Devils and all fanatics should impudently demand how bread and wine can be the body and blood of Christ, I know that all spirits and learned men put together have not as much intelligence as Almighty God has in His little finger.'

The explanation of the sacramental unity, the co-existence of body and bread, he found in the metaphysics of Scholasticism.

His theory of the mode of presence of Christ's body goes back to certain distinctions made by William of Occam and adopted by Biel and d'Ailly (cf., further, art. UBIQUITY). It appears first in his sermon *Vom Sakrament des Leibes* (1526), and is developed in his other controversial writings against the Swiss reformers. Occam had taught: (1) the *esse repletive* (=omnipresence) of God, (2) the *unipræsentia* of the body of Christ in Heaven, (3) the *esse diffinitive* (=*multivolipræsentia*) of the body of Christ in the Eucharist. The difficulty here lies in the *esse diffinitive*. It is explained by Luther as that which is in space but does not fill any portion of it, and is not circumscribed by it. To Christ's resurrection-body belonged this kind of presence. 'Just as the sealed stone and the shut door remained unaltered, and yet His body was at the place where were mere stone and wood, in the same way is He in the Sacrament where the bread and wine are, and yet the bread and wine remain untransformed and unaltered' (Erl. ed. xxx. 208 f.). The sacramental presence of Christ is not, therefore, conceived in any local or circumscribed fashion. His body is present not after the mode of the *esse circumscriptive*, but after that of the *esse diffinitive*. When the bread is broken, therefore, Luther holds that Christ's body is not broken, but remains complete in every part, even in the smallest particle.

Luther's teaching might have rested finally on the *esse diffinitive* of Occam, had it not been that he was continually faced with the question, 'Christ is seated at the right hand of God, how then can His body be in the Sacrament?' This he met by denying that the right hand of God is local. It is not a particular place 'like a golden chair, or the like.' God's right hand is everywhere. So he turns round on his opponents with this syllogism: 'Christ's body is at the right hand of God—that is acknowledged. But the right hand of God is everywhere—so assuredly it is in the bread' (Weimar ed. xxiii. 143; cf. Hunzinger, *PRE*[3] xx. 187). The *esse diffinitive* has thus been exalted to the *esse repletive*, the *multivolipræsentia* to omnipresence.

To the same conclusion Luther came also from the side of Christology, in which he taught that the conjunction of the two natures in Christ implies a *communicatio idiomatum*—a transference of the attributes of the one to the other—and that, therefore, the body of Christ possessed the Divine attribute of omnipresence.

But all this proved too much, as his opponents were not slow in pointing out. If the body of Christ was everywhere, then it was received in every common meal, and not only in the Eucharist. This difficulty was met by a specific sacramental presence in accordance with the promise. It is one thing for Christ to be present, and another thing for Him to be present for us. 'He is there for thee, when He binds Himself by His word, and says, "Here art thou to find me"' (*ib.* xxiii. 151). The solution is imperfect, as, indeed, must any attempt be to connect a theory of the ubiquity of Christ's body with a real presence in the Sacrament. For either (1) there is the same presence everywhere as in the Sacrament, or (2) a specific sacramental presence must be added to the other, and is so far distinct from the other.

Luther himself did not consider his theorizing to be binding or final. He had outlined an intelligible way in which the almighty power of God could secure the presence of the body and blood. What he did consider as binding and final was the fact of the real presence in, with, and under the bread and wine.

The characteristic Lutheran *in, cum, et sub pane* is not Luther's own. It first appears in the strife between Hesshus and Klebitz in Heidelberg after his death. Luther himself spoke of *in et sub pane*.

In whatever way it might be explained, Luther's strong religious interest made him insist on the real presence being conserved. Sometimes his vehemence led him into language which went beyond his theory; *e.g.*, in his instructions to Melanchthon in 1534 he uses language which might seem to imply that the body of Christ in the Eucharist is eaten after the manner of ordinary food:

'In brief this is our doctrine, that the body of Christ is truly eaten in and with the bread, so that what the bread does and suffers, the body of Christ does and suffers: it is distributed, eaten, and masticated with the teeth (*mit den Zähnen zerbissen*), propter unionem sacramentalem.'

But the qualifying phrase and the heat of controversy ought to keep us from pressing these words too far. And the Formula of Concord (Epitome, Art. 7, neg. 21) expressly rules out any such inference:

'We also utterly reject and condemn the Capernaitic manducation of the body of Christ, . . . as if, forsooth, we taught that the body of Christ is torn by the teeth' (*mit Zähnen zerrissen*).

Luther regarded the *manducatio impiorum* as a decisive test of any supposed doctrine of the real presence. It was self-evident to him that, if the body of Christ were really present, in the sense that he understood the word, even the unbelieving who partook of the bread participated also in the body of Christ. This *manducatio impiorum* was so much a part of his doctrine that he used it from the beginning as an argument to overwhelm Carlstadt. The evangelical nature of the Sacrament he preserved by asserting that, though the unbelieving participated in the body and blood, they had no part in the grace of which body and blood were vehicles.

The main thoughts in Luther's reconstruction are these: (1) that the Eucharist was instituted for the strengthening and comfort of believers through assurance of the forgiving grace of God and communion with the Risen Lord; (2) that the objective guarantee of this assurance and the means of this communion is the real presence of the body and blood of Christ, in (with) and under the elements of bread and wine; (3) that the real presence itself is assured by the ubiquity of Christ's body, and made available by the words of institution; (4) that this real presence entails that the unbelieving participate in the body and blood of Christ, though they have no part in the grace of the Sacrament.

2. The doctrine of Zwingli.—As already mentioned, the difference between Zwingli and Luther largely arose from the different points of departure—the Mass and the Eucharist respectively. To this must be added differences in training and religious experience. Luther's education was monastic, his theological studies originally and essentially Scholastic. Zwingli's education was Humanist, his theological studies originally Patristic. Luther's first Eucharistic controversy was with over-zealous Reformers, Zwingli's with upholders of the Mass. Luther's general idea of a sacrament received its evangelical shape in conflict with Rome over Indulgences and the sacrament of Penance, Zwingli's in controversy with the Anabaptists over Baptism. Against magical ideas of sacramental grace, Luther was led, therefore, to emphasize personal understanding and belief; against individualistic notions, Zwingli brought into prominence the social side of Christianity, the relation of the sacraments to the community.

In Zwingli's *Von Touf und Widertouf* (1525), Baptism is a sign of allegiance, a 'tessera' of the Christian soldier. This expression he probably obtained from Melanchthon, who in his *Loci* (1521) had already spoken of the sacraments as 'tesserae militares.' The Eucharist was the symbol of the communion of all believers in Christ. 'Ergo hunc panem edimus, ut unus panis tandem fiamus' (Letter to Alber). It proclaimed the membership of the believer in the covenant of grace, and pledged him to a life in accordance with his profession. So, while Luther almost always thought of the individual in this connexion, Zwingli gave prominence to the significance of the Supper for the Church community, and this especially when in conflict with Luther.

Zwingli's teaching is divided into three distinct periods. In the earliest and latest periods the same teaching is to be found; in the middle period, during the controversy with Luther, one essential point of his teaching at other times is obscured and even denied. In this article the former is taken to be the true Zwinglian doctrine.

Zwingli set out against the sacrificial aspect of mediæval doctrine. Over against the Mass, with its thought of the repetition of the Sacrifice of the Cross, he set the Supper as a memorial or remembrance of the Sacrifice offered once for all. The thought of remembrance, therefore, is not opposed to any thought of present participation, but opposed simply to any thought of repetition. The bread and wine were signs of the broken body and the shed blood. The primary reference of the Eucharist, therefore, was to the death of Christ, and not to any union with the glorified Christ.

From the beginning of his teaching, Zwingli felt that the words 'Hoc est corpus meum' must be understood in some figurative manner. But in 1522 he came to know of Gerhard Hoen's (Honius) 'de Eucharistia,' where for *est* is understood *significat*. This interpretation he adopted, and supported by many passages of Scripture that seemed to him similar, *e.g.* Gn 41[26] 'The seven good kine are seven years'; 1 Co 10[4] 'That rock was Christ.' But in 1525, after his last disputation with his opponents in Zürich, when he had sought in vain for an absolutely conclusive parallel, he dreamt of one—Ex 12[11] 'Hoc est transitus Domini'—where *est* manifestly stood for *symbolum est* or *figura est*. This discovery further defined his interpretation, and more firmly convinced him of its truth.

Even more essential to the Zwinglian teaching is the emphasis laid on Jn 6. This chapter to him is decisive against all ideas of receiving the body of Christ by the mouth. Faith is the organ of appropriation. And it was by his Johannine conception of faith that Zwingli conceived the presence of Christ in the Eucharist. Faith, to Zwingli, included also the mystical union with Christ—the life of Christ in us, and ours in Him. This life of faith has its fluctuations (*fides labascit*), and so God must continually anew increase our faith. To that end Christ gives Himself for food, and so the prayer of the believer in each succeeding Eucharist is that God may renew this union with Christ. The Eucharist is, therefore, a definite renewal of the one continuous central union with Christ (cf. Ebrard, *passim*). From one side, the Eucharist is a memorial of the death of Jesus, and bread and wine are signs of the broken body and shed blood; from another it is an act of renewed union with Christ, and bread and wine are seals of this union.

So had Zwingli's doctrine developed itself before the controversy with Luther; and, though in that controversy he emphasized only the former side—the relation to the death of Christ—yet in his utterances outside the sphere of the controversy, during this time, his full teaching found expression (cf. his first sermon before the Disputation at Berne, 1528). But in the controversy itself, just as Luther inclined to extremes, not only of language but of doctrine, and used words that seemed to imply a Capernaitic eating, so Zwingli at times would have nothing to do with any presence of Christ save as the object of our subjective contemplation. In so far Schultz is justified in speaking of Zwingli's mode of presence as 'historisch.' 'Nunquam enim aliud obtinebis, quam quod Christi corpus quum in coena quum in mentibus piorum non aliter sit, quam sola contemplatione' (Covering letter sent by Zwingli to Luther with the *Amica Exegesis*).

The main elements of Zwingli's completed doctrine are these, and the obvious Scriptural derivation of all the points should be noted—*e.g.* (2) and (3) are founded on the words of institution, (4) on Jn 6, (5) on 1 Co 10—(1) the Eucharist is not a repetition of the Sacrifice of Christ, but a commemoration of that Sacrifice; (2) the bread and wine are signs or symbols of the broken body and shed blood of Christ; (3) the reference of the Eucharist is, therefore, rather to Christ crucified than to Christ glorified; (4) in the Eucharist, Christ is truly our food, and through Him our spiritual life is nourished, but He is appropriated by faith alone; (5) the Eucharist, as a true communion of the body of Christ, is specially significant for the life of the Church community, being the sign and pledge of united allegiance to Christ and membership in Him.

3. The doctrine of Calvin.—Calvin's teaching on the Eucharist is much easier to define—partly because he appeared on the scene later, when the problems had already been stated and discussed, and partly because his teaching underwent scarcely any change from the beginning to the end. The later Lutheran controversialists regarded Calvin as a cunning Zwinglian intent on making converts to the Zwinglian teaching by the artful use of Lutheran phrases, while many of the Swiss at first regarded him as a pure Lutheran, whose open and declared purpose it was to undermine the teaching of Zwingli. He stands in the middle, not because, like Bucer, he was for ever seeking a *via media*,—a form of words to which both parties could give adherence,—but by reason of his deeper insight into the essentials of sacramental teaching. He stands in the middle, not in virtue of any mere deft manipulation of theological terms, but because his mind and heart demanded an interpretation of the Supper purified from mediæval accretions, while conserving every real religious interest. He had, like Zwingli, a distrust of all the refinements and subtleties of Scholasticism; therefore he could not accept Luther's doctrine of ubiquity. He had, like Luther, a full and rich religious interest in the real presence of Christ; therefore he could not accept the elements as mere signs. By his contemporary admirers his teaching was rightly regarded both as a spiritualizing of Luther's and as a deepening of Zwingli's. His teaching was tolerated by Luther as no other divergent teaching had ever been; it was accepted by Zwingli's successors (cf. *Consensus Tigurinus*). At one time it seemed as if it might have united the divided ranks of the Reformers.

Even in the first edition of the *Institutes*, bread and wine are to Calvin not mere signs, but symbols; and not merely symbols of the death of Christ, as in Zwingli, but also, and indeed pre-eminently, symbols of our living union with Christ; the action of the Holy Supper is an act of real and true reception of Christ (cf. Ebrard, ii. 417). So Calvin speaks habitually not of *signa repræsentantia*, but of *signa exhibitiva*, and of *instrumenta*.

In this first edition there is found already fully developed Calvin's characteristic teaching as to the mode of presence of Christ. Zwingli and Luther had fought over the sitting at the right hand of God. Zwingli had held that the body of Christ, being thus ascended and localized, is not present in the elements; Luther had taught that the right hand of God is everywhere, and that therefore Christ's body is in the elements. Both were sure that any circumscription of the body precluded the real presence otherwise than to faith. But Calvin conceived the *sessio ad dexteram* as participation in the omnipotence and majesty of God. What followed? 'Christus virtutem suam, ubicunque placuerit, in coelo et in terra exserat' (*Inst.*, 1st ed. p. 246, ed. Tholuck, Edinburgh, 1874, IV. xvii. 18). From the glorified Christ there streams a power over and above the ordinary influence of the Holy Spirit, of which, in the Supper, believers are recipients. The body of Christ is not now present on earth anywhere as substance, *i.e.* as material substance, but it is present as power, as *virtus*; if not *naturaliter*, then *vere et efficaciter*. In the Eucharist, Christ is present with *omnia beneficia*. And this, Calvin adds, is the kind of presence that the nature of a sacrament demands. On this account the words of institution do not speak of the body of Christ apart from His benefits, or of the benefits apart from the body and blood whereby they are procured. 'In affirming of his body that it was broken, and of his blood that it was shed for us, he shows that both were not so much his own as ours, because he took and laid down both, not for his own advantage, but for our salvation' (*Inst.* IV. xvii. 3). Calvin, therefore, does not hesitate to give to the elements the name of Christ's body and blood because they are, as it were, instruments whereby Christ distributes them to us. 'Corporis veri et sanguinis nomen eis attributum, quod sit velut instrumenta quibus Dominus Jesus Christus nobis ea distribuit' ('de Coena Domini,' *Opuscula*, Geneva, 1552, p. 133).

The bread does not bring Christ to us; we are not to look to the bread and build ourselves upon it, as if this 'dead creature' had an immanent power to bring Christ to us; but Christ Himself through His spirit gives Himself to us, and the bread is a pledge and seal by which the assurance of this free gift is made victorious over all the fluctuations of our subjective faith. The mode of presence may, therefore, be named mystical, but it is more accurately spoken of as dynamical.

The main distinctive thoughts of Calvin are these: (1) that the bread and wine are signs of the body and blood of Christ, but exhibiting signs and instrumental means of His presence; (2) that, though the body of Christ is in Heaven, there is a real presence of Christ in the Eucharist; (3) that, because Christ is at the right hand of God, He can be present dynamically and efficaciously; (4) that the Eucharist is a real means of grace, because He is present in power to strengthen our real living union with Him.

In regard to doctrine, Calvin stands between Zwingli and Luther; but not so in regard to mode of administration. There is nothing to justify the wide-spread conception that, while Luther accepted all the old forms except such as were inseparably bound up with obnoxious dogmas, Zwingli removed all the ancient customs and, having made a clean slate, constructed thereupon a new form which was meagre and sterile. The truth is that, in respect of the alteration in the celebration of the Eucharist, Zwingli throughout stands on one side with Luther, as against Calvin. Calvin, and more completely à Lasco, went behind mediæval practices to primitive forms. Like Luther, Zwingli removed only the objectionable. He took over the old liturgy, doing away with some parts and altering others (cf. Ebrard, ii. 60 ff., for a description of the Zürich liturgy).

III. *HISTORY OF THE CONTROVERSY OVER THE EUCHARIST AMONG THE REFORMERS.*—The first controversies in Reformed circles concerning the Eucharist were Luther's controversy with Carlstadt, and Zwingli's with the upholders of the Mass. But we begin at the point where the main bodies of Reformed teaching came into conflict with each other. Zwingli's teaching, as above mentioned, arose independently of Luther's and from another point of view. That teaching might have been tolerable to Luther but for three things. (1) He always associated Zwingli with Carlstadt. As early as 1524 he wrote to Amsdorf: 'Carlstadt's poison is spreading in Switzerland.' (2) At first he knew Zwingli's teaching only by inaccurate report. (3) Zwingli represented a different political ideal. He breathed the free democratic air of Switzerland, which to Luther, with his experience of the Peasants' War, was anathema.

Passing over Zwingli's letter to Alber—which, however, is noteworthy as containing his most radical views—the real controversy began with Bugenhagen's attack on Zwingli, 'Contra novum errorem de Sacramento,' etc., which is mostly an echo of Luther against Carlstadt, and seems to know no more of Zwingli's teaching than that by *est* he understood *significat*. Zwingli in his answer meets his opponent on his own ground, and defends his interpretation.

'Which explanation of the words is the more violent—yours, by which you say, "Bread is bread, but in the bread is eaten the body of Christ"; or ours, when we say that the words are figurative, and then explain the figure "Hoc est, nempe symbolum, figura, vel ἀντίτυπον est corporis mei, quod pro vobis traditur"?' (*Respons. ad Bugenhagenii Epistolam*).

Almost simultaneously with the *Responsio* appeared a contribution from Œcolampadius, 'De genuina verborum Domini, etc., expositione.' This work, unlike Zwingli, started from the words of institution, and, also unlike him, set forth no complete theory, and no firm connexion with the death of Christ. To outsiders it therefore conveyed the impression that the whole Swiss teaching was the meagre product of a particular exegesis. This exposition, being dispatched to the Swabian preachers, produced an answer, the Swabian *Syngramma*—the work of Brenz. Here the terminology was Lutheran, the thought a partial anticipation of Calvin. It taught a dynamical presence: the body is in the bread, just as the power of healing was in the Brazen Serpent, through the word ('Jam, ut serpentis verbum sanationem ad serpentem attulit, cur non ita cœnae verbum corpus ad panem ferret?'). Œcolampadius answered in his *Antisyngramma*, taking the *Syngramma* sentence by sentence, replying at length to criticisms of his exegesis, and asserting that the analogy of the Brazen Serpent proved no more than a presence in the Sacrament similar to that in the Word. In the meantime, Pirkheimer of Nuremberg had also replied to the *expositio*. This controversy is for two reasons worthy of mention. It was here that the Lutheran ubiquity theory first made its appearance; and it was from Pirkheimer that Luther got his knowledge concerning the doctrines and personalities of the Swiss Reformers; and Pirkheimer's opinion had been coloured by Erasmus' later view of the Swiss Reformers as fanatics and revolutionaries.

And now, Bucer and the other Strassburg Reformers, who had sought in vain to mediate between Luther and Carlstadt, tried to bring about an understanding between Luther and Zwingli. Their envoy, Chaselius, brought back the answer from Luther that no understanding was possible, 'for either we or they must be in the wrong, one or other of us must be the servant of Satan.' And in his preface to the *Syngramma*, Luther now openly joined in the conflict. The fanatics were wrong, he said, because they were so divided among themselves. To this Œcolampadius answered directly; Zwingli contented himself with his 'Clear Instruction concerning the Lord's Supper'—the first of his sacramental writings in German—in which he developed his views in opposition to Luther, but without naming him. It was written to justify his position to the people. A little later he published his *Amica Exegesis*, to justify his position to the learned. Sent to Luther, it crossed his sermon 'On the Body and Blood of Christ against the Fanatics,' which was answered by Zwingli, immediately on its reception, in his *Fründlich Verglimpfung*. In this he says that 'Martin Luther stands in his poor judgment as high as any individual can, but yet God is higher.' Every year the controversy grew more acute, with an excess of bitterness on the side of Luther. In 1527, Luther issued his 'That the Words of Christ, "This is my body," still stand firm.' Zwingli replied in his 'That the Words of Christ, "This is my body," would eternally keep their ancient and sole meaning; and Martin Luther with his last Book has not made good his own and the Pope's Interpretation,' upon which Luther rejoined with his larger *Bekenntniss vom Abendmahl* (1528).

What were the main points at issue in this controversy? The interpretation of the words of institution stands always in the foreground, but only a minor part of the real difference appeared there. In part it became a Christological controversy—Zwingli accusing Luther, with his *communicatio idiomatum*, of Docetism; Luther charging Zwingli with a Nestorian *alloiosis*. In regard to the Eucharist itself, the whole matter hinged on the real presence. By Zwingli it was expressly denied: (1) that the body of Christ corporeally eaten does or can confirm faith; (2) that the body of Christ corporeally or naturally eaten can or does forgive sin; (3) that the body of Christ is corporeally present in the Eucharist so soon as the words 'This is my body' are spoken over the elements (which, as we saw, Luther never taught); (4) that the body of Christ can be corporeally present in the elements, for He is seated at the right hand of God. By Luther it was asserted: (1) that in the Eucharist Christ is not present only to faith; (2) that whoever accepts the miracle of the Incarnation has no ground for doubting the presence of Christ in and with the elements; (3) that Christ is not shut up in Heaven, *quasi carcere* (which is hardly what Zwingli taught); (4) that it is necessary for Christ's body and blood to be in the Eucharist to assure the believer of the forgiveness of sins.

As the controversy grew more acute, the combatants came more and more to misunderstand each other. And as, all the time, the forces of reaction were gathering strength, Philip of Hesse resolved to bring the two sides together; and, after great difficulty, with the useful help of the usual middleman, Bucer of Strassburg, a conference was arranged for Marburg, and took place in the castle there in October 1529. After private conferences between Luther and Œcolampadius, and Zwingli and Melanchthon, came the public conference. Luther's first action, as eye-witnesses on both sides assert, was to write with chalk upon the table 'Hoc est corpus meum' as a sign that he would not waver. The arguments employed in the controversy were used over again, but with none of the old bitterness. To Luther's interpretation, Zwingli opposed Jn 6 as discrediting it, and the familiar ground of the *sessio ad dexteram* and the 'ubiquity' was gone over again. Only on two occasions did there seem likely to be an open quarrel. But no agreement as to the mode of presence was reached.

The Marburg Conference, says Kolde (*PRE*[3] xii. 255), served more to the true understanding of the differences than to bridging them over. But it certainly was not fruitless. There was a mutual undertaking to cease from controversial writings. The two parties came to an understanding on every point save one—an agreement recorded in the fourteen Articles. In regard to the Eucharist, they came to see that one side had been misinterpreting the other—the Zwinglians in attributing to their opponents a Capernaitic eating, and the Lutherans in regarding their opponents as holding to a mere memorial. After acknowledging in the Supper a spiritual enjoyment of the body and blood of Christ, the document closes with the noteworthy statement: 'But, although we have not at this time come to an agreement as to whether the true body and blood of Christ are corporeally in the bread and wine, still each party ought to manifest Christian love towards the others, as far as the conscience of each will allow; and both parties ought diligently to beseech Almighty God to affirm to us the right understanding by His Holy Spirit.'

Within a few months of the Marburg Articles came the Augsburg Confession. Under what influences the tenth Article was drawn up is a matter of debate. The 'under the form of wine and bread' of the German version seems designed to conciliate the Roman Catholics, though it may be a mere protest against communion in one kind; and certainly the rest of the Article in German and the whole in Latin seems a drawing nearer to Zwingli: 'De Cœna Domini docent, quod corpus et sanguis Christi vere adsint, et distribuantur vescentibus in Cœna Domini; et improbant secus docentes' (Schaff, *Creeds*, New York, 1877, iii. 13). This article, drawn up by Melanchthon, had an important history. Under the influence of Calvin, as some maintain, or by reason of an independent approximation to Calvin's teaching, Melanchthon put forth in 1540 the *Variata*, the altered edition of the Augsburg Confession. At the time no man questioned his right to do this, as he had drawn up the original. Now, in the *Variata* this article reads: 'De cœna Domini docent, quod cum pane et vino vere exhibeantur corpus et sanguis Christi vescentibus in Cœna Domini.' The *Variata*, therefore, leaves out the disapproval of opponents and the 'vere et substantialiter adesse.' It uses Calvin's term 'exhibition.' But it is not fully Calvinistic, for Calvin for *vescentibus* would have read *credentibus*. Witnesses even from the Lutheran side, *e.g.* Chemnitz, trace these alterations to the influence of Luther himself. And, at any rate, though Luther held to his own construction and contended strongly in private letters in its interest, he tolerated the Calvinistic construction as he had not tolerated the Zwinglian, and never entered into the lists of public controversy against it. In 1544, in his last Eucharistic writing, where he attacks erroneous teaching, Zwingli, Œcolampadius, Schwenckfeld, and Carlstadt are all named, but not Calvin; and no passage has been cited which can reasonably be construed into an attack on Calvin's doctrine. The original text and the *Variata*, supposed erroneously to have been disapproved by Luther, came to be a bone of contention between the Philippists and the Gnesio-Lutherans.

After the Marburg Conference, there followed a time of quiet. The place of controversial pamphlets was taken by letters of inquiry, and a possible unifying formula as to the real presence was sought. In Württemberg, *e.g.*, the Zwinglian Blaurer and the Lutheran Schnepff united in this: 'that in the bread and wine Christ's body and blood are present *substantialiter et essentialiter, non autem quantitative aut qualitative vel localiter.*' Bucer, active as ever in mediation, thought he had discovered one in 'Christ's body is bodily present to the soul.' But Luther would have none of it. It used his phraseology to destroy his meaning. After a conference at Cassel between Bucer and Melanchthon, and one at Wittenberg between a larger representation on both sides, came the Wittenberg Concord. Bucer here admitted Luther's phrases, even the statement which was the crucial one, that the body and blood are truly offered to the unworthy, who receive it to their condemnation. Of course, Bucer was able to accept it only by attaching a different meaning to 'unworthy,' by whom he understood, not unbelievers, as Luther, but careless believers. So it was only a seeming unity. And, strive as he would, Bucer could not get the Swiss to accept this. They suspected his explanation of 'indigni,' and on writing to Luther found they had good grounds for doing so.

With the coming of the more positive doctrine of Calvin, hopes of unity waxed brighter. Melanchthon drew nearer to Calvin, until the differences between their teaching became infinitesimal. In 1531 he departed from the ubiquity theory; a little later he gave up the local presence of Christ in the bread; by 1535 he sympathized with the figurative interpretation of the words of institution; and before the end he had given up the 'manducatio impiorum' (cf. Loofs, *PRE*³ i. 66). In his controversy with Westphal, Calvin could write: 'Centies confirmo, non magis a me Philippum quam a propriis visceribus in hac causa posse divelli.' But the union did not come. Zürich, under Bullinger, came over to Calvin; and the *Consensus Tigurinus*, in which they agreed, is the most elaborate Confessional document on the Eucharist. The distinctively Lutheran doctrine was confined to Germany, and even there its limits became narrower.

Within the Lutheran Church there ensued a long and bitter strife, between the Philippists (after Melanchthon's death, Crypto-Calvinists) and the Gnesio-Lutherans. The latter held to the full Lutheran doctrine, but, by asserting it over against Calvin in place of against Zwingli, they were led further than Luther. Some modifications appeared, *e.g.* Chemnitz deserted Luther's later *esse repletive* for the earlier *esse diffinitive*; and in place of *ubiquitas* asserted a species of *multivolipræsentia*: 'Christi carnem reali et essentiali praesentiae modo praesentem esse, non quidem ubique, sed ubicunque et quandocunque vult Christus' (*Explicatio de duabus naturis*). Brenz, now far removed from the *Syngramma*, went beyond Luther. He spoke of a *majestas* of the humanity, under which all Divine properties are embraced, so that from the very moment of its origin the humanity possessed the whole majesty and glory of the Father. In 1577 the strict Lutherans united in the Formula of Concord, which gave prominence to the theory of ubiquity as the basis of the doctrine of the Supper, leaving it undefined whether the ubiquity was absolute or relative (cf. Artt. 7 and 8). The renewed appearance of Crypto-Calvinism was finally suppressed by the Saxon Visitation Articles of 1592. With them the controversy within the Lutheran Church came practically to an end. (For the details of these later Lutheran controversies, see art. UBIQUITY.)

IV. *THE EUCHARIST IN THE REFORMED CHURCHES OF GREAT BRITAIN.*—1. **Scotland.**—The Presbyterian Church of Scotland, like every other Church of the Reformation except the Lutheran, has possessed from the outset a Calvinistic doctrine of the Supper. The Scots Confession of 1560 is a Calvinistic Confession. But in regard to the Supper it uses strong and picturesque language such as would have delighted the heart of Luther. We can imagine Luther better pleased with it than with any other Confession of the Reformation not purely Lutheran.

'In the Supper richtlie used, Christ Jesus is so joined with us, that hee becummis very nurishment and fude of our saules. . . . So that we confesse and undoubtedlie beleeve, that the faithful, in the richt use of the Lords Table, do so eat the bodie and drinke the blude of the Lord Jesus, that he remaines in them, and they in him: Zea, they are so maid flesh of his flesh, and bone of his bones; that as the eternall God-head hes given to the flesh of Christ Jesus . . . life and immortalitie; so dois Christ Jesus his flesh and blude eattin and drunkin be us, give unto us the same prerogatives' (Art. 21).

The change to the Westminster Confession meant in this regard a change simply to a more precise and definite, if less picturesque, statement of the same Calvinistic doctrine.

The Westminster standards involved also the disuse of Knox's Liturgy. This contained not an imposed but a discretionary ritual, *i.e.* it was not supplied to the people for their responses, but supplied to the minister alone, for his guidance as to the matter and manner of worship, leaving freedom of variation. It was widely used, however. In 1620, Scrymgeour, summoned before the Court of High Commission for disregarding the Articles of Perth, pleaded that he conformed to the one valid form (Knox's Liturgy), 'according to the which, likas I have always done, so now I minister that sacrament' (Calderwood, *History*, Wodrow Soc. ed., Edinburgh, 1843-49, vii. 422). In the Westminster Directory this discretionary ritual was replaced by a rubrical provision, consisting of directions without detailed forms.

There has never been a sacramental controversy within the Church of Scotland or any of its branches.

The attempt of Charles I. to impose an alien liturgy, the 'Lifters' among the Seceders who held to the necessity of the manual act of 'taking bread,' and the conflict over the recent overflow of Ritualism from England are the nearest approaches to such a controversy. It may be mentioned that Knox in his Liturgy suggested monthly observance; that this was early departed from, for in 1711 the General Assembly recommended to the Presbyteries a more frequent observance of the Lord's Supper: 'that it be duly observed in their bounds through the several months of the year'; that a little later the practice came to be an annual celebration, frequented, however, also by strangers, so that, though there was only an annual celebration in the individual Church, the communicants observed it more frequently, at different places; that now it is, in general, celebrated twice, thrice, or four times in the year.

2. **England.**—The *Ten Articles* of 1536 were obviously an attempt to construct a doctrine which would be tolerable alike to the mediæval mind and to those who had imbibed the new freedom of Humanism and of Lutheran teaching. The *Six Articles* of 1539 restored Transubstantiation, the Mass, communion in one kind only, under severe penalties. With the reign of Edward VI. the anomalies begin. The Church was endowed with a Zwinglian Creed—the *Forty-two Articles* (1553)—and a *Book of Common Prayer* which in both its versions (1549 and 1552) was alternately Zwinglian and mediæval. With the reign of Elizabeth these anomalies were increased—mainly owing to her precarious position politically—in the *Thirty-nine Articles* (1561) and the revised *Book of Common Prayer* (1559). The 29th Article, expunged by the Queen and restored in 1571, effectually barred Lutheranism.

The doctrine of the *Thirty-nine Articles* has been called Zwinglian, and the close connexion of the English Reformers with Zürich and Bullinger (*Zürich Letters* [Parker Society, Camb. 1842]) has been thought to prove it. But, in regard to the Eucharist, it is to be noted that they arose after the *Consensus Tigurinus*, in which Bullinger had accepted Calvin's doctrine; and in reality they are purely Calvinistic. Expressions in the *Short Catechism* of 1553 point to a Zwinglian origin. 'The Supper is a certain thankful remembrance of the death of Christ, forasmuch as the bread representeth his body.' 'Faith is the mouth of the soul, whereby we receive this heavenly meat' (*Liturgies of King Edward VI.* [Parker Society, Camb. 1844], p. 517). In the 28th Art. it is laid down that 'the Body of Christ is given, taken, and eaten in the Supper, only after an heavenly and spiritual manner. And the mean, whereby the Body of Christ is received and eaten in the Supper, is faith'—which might be either Zwinglian or Calvinistic. In the *Book of Common Prayer* the order of administration has more mediæval elements, but is, after all, not so far removed from the Zürich liturgy (cf. Ebrard, ii. 60 ff.). In distributing the bread the Prayer Book of 1549 had directed to be said: 'The Body of our Lord Jesus Christ, which was given for thee, preserve thy body and soul unto everlasting life'; that of 1552: 'Take and eat this, in remembrance that Christ died for thee, and feed on Him in thy heart by faith, with thanksgiving.' 'The difference represented by the change in these words is between what *might* be the doctrine of transubstantiation and a sacramental theory distinctly lower than that of Luther or Calvin, and which *might* be pure Zwinglianism' (Lindsay, *History of the Reformation*, Edinburgh, 1906-07, ii. 363). That of 1559 simply added the one to the other.

Of some importance is the rubric added in 1552 in response to the demand that the Supper be received seated as at a table, which declares that by kneeling no adoration is intended to the 'Sacramental Bread and Wine there bodily received, or unto any corporal (in 1552, 'real and essential') presence of Christ's natural flesh and blood,' and adds that 'the natural Body and Blood of our Saviour Christ are in Heaven, and not here; it being against the truth of Christ's natural body to be at one time in more places than one.' This rubric was omitted in 1559, as being offensive to Lutherans, and restored in the form quoted above, in the last revision in 1662. This last revision, says Drury (*Elevation in the Eucharist*, Cambridge, 1907, p. 181), 'restored to our Church a complete representation of what our Lord is recorded to have said and done "in the same night that He was betrayed." We "take the Bread" and "take the Cup" as He Himself did, we say the words of Institution which we believe that He said, we break the Bread and bless the Cup as He did, and we perform these significant actions openly in the sight of the people and thus "proclaim the Lord's death till He come."'

As the result of the composite nature of the Prayer Book there has always been a High Church party and a Low Church or Evangelical party in the Church of England. The former came into renewed prominence with the Oxford movement.

In Tract 90, Newman attempted to show that the Articles, 'though the product of an un-Catholic age,' were 'patient of a Catholic interpretation.' By the aid of a return to mediæval ritual, attempts have been made to get behind Article 31, 'Of the one Oblation of Christ finished upon the Cross.' The question of ritual reached its most acute point in the Denison case (1856–58) and the MacConochie case (1867–69). High Churchmen speak of the Eucharist as a Sacrifice. Ridley had spoken of the 'unbloody sacrifice,' but 'as a *representation* of that bloody sacrifice' (*Works* [Parker Society, Cambridge, 1841, p. 250]). The theory advanced by Father Puller at the Oxford Conference of 1899, propounded earlier by Brightman (*The Eucharistic Sacrifice*, 1890), that the Eucharist is a sacrifice because 'our Lord's sacrifice continues for ever and is a perpetual sacrifice,' that it is 'the earthly counterpart of the sacrificial oblation which is being carried on in the heavenly tabernacle,' for which a great weight of authority has been claimed, has been shown by Mortimer (*The Eucharistic Sacrifice*, London, 1901, p. 379 ff.) to have been derived through Mede from Cassander. The controversies concerning the Eucharistic Sacrifice and its ritual continue.

The teaching of the majority of the Nonconformist Churches in England and their sister-Churches in the United States and the Colonies, despite the ultra-Zwinglian Declaration of the Congregational Union of England and Wales of 1833 (Schaff, *Creeds*, iii. 731 ff.), that the Lord's Supper is 'to be celebrated by Christian Churches as a token of faith in the Saviour, and of brotherly love,' is Calvinistic; and in mode of administration they belong to the 'Reformed' type.

V. *THE ROMAN CATHOLIC DOCTRINE.*—The Roman Catholic Church rests entirely on the development described in the preceding article. The Council of Trent first gave Confessional embodiment to the distinction between the Eucharist and the Mass; and, though the decrees gave more space to the 'sanctissimum sacramentum Eucharistiae,' in theory and practice the sacrificial aspect (the Mass) completely overshadows the sacramental character (the Eucharist). The Tridentine decrees were a blend of conflicting mediæval theories, one party wishing to exalt the Sacrifice of the Mass, the other unwilling to obscure the Sacrifice on the Cross.

It is a real propitiatory sacrifice: 'Si quis dixerit, Missae sacrificium . . . neque pro vivis et defunctis pro peccatis, poenis, satisfactionibus et aliis necessitatibus offerri debere: anathema sit' (Sess. xxii. can. iii.). The Mass, unless performed by the priest, is no sacrifice. And yet the priest is not the offerer; Christ offered Himself once on the Cross, and He offers Himself daily in the Mass. The sacrifice is no new suffering for Christ; the once-offered Christ is daily brought before the eyes of God, such presentation (*offere*) being really sacrifice (*immolare*).

But the *Catechismus Romanus* (1566) was a complete victory for the party of the exalters of the Mass. Here the Mass is no representation of a sacrifice, but a repetition (quæst. 53 ff.). Post-Tridentine teaching went far beyond mediæval limits (Scheeben, *La Dogmatique*, Paris, 1882, iii. 399 ff.). Aquinas had taught that the Sacrifice of Christ is impossible of repetition, and the thought of repetition, though current in pre-Reformation times, had little authoritative support, the theologians having been occupied with the dogma of Transubstantiation. Now it became customary to teach that Christ in the Sacrament Himself renews His passion, that in the Mass He is present, not only as *passus*, but much more as *patiens*.

The 'immolation-theory' of Cuesta ran: 'Missa est sacrificium hac ratione, quod Christus aliquo modo moritur et a sacerdote mactatur.' Alongside it stood the 'destruction-theory' of Bellarmine, which attained its fullest expression in De Lugo: 'Consumptio autem quae fit a sacerdote sacrificante non tam est comestio victimae quam consummatio sacrificii.'

These theories appear again and again in various modifications, mainly in Jesuit circles, and were dominant especially during the 17th cent.; but alongside them were theories which did not go beyond the Tridentine decrees, and even sought to spiritualize them, *e.g.* Bossuet: 'Let us not think that the victim which we present in the Eucharist is to be there in truth anew destroyed. . . . We ought to seek therein only a mystical death and destruction' (*Œuvres*, Tours, 1862, vi. 118). Transubstantiation remains as fixed at Trent, and its logical consequences therein mentioned continue, *e.g.* the reservation, adoration (λατρεία), and carrying in procession of the host or consecrated wafer, and the *communio sub una*.

The Old Catholics have not moved far in regard to the Eucharist from Roman dogma and practice. The Synod of 1877 allowed the use of the vernacular in certain parts of the Mass. The Synod of 1883 allowed the partaking of the cup to Anglicans, but resolved to follow among themselves meanwhile their usual practice of communion in one kind.

LITERATURE.—In addition to the works cited and named in the article, and the standard editions of the leading Reformers which are enumerated under the relevant articles, the following are worthy of mention: R. Hospinian, *Historia Sacramentaria*, 2 vols., Zürich, 1598 and 1603; K. B. Hundeshagen, *Die Konflikte des Zwinglianismus, Lutherthums, und Calvinismus in den bernischen Landskirchen, 1552–1558*, Berne, 1842; J. H. A. Ebrard, *Das Dogma vom heiligen Abendmahl und seine Geschichte*, 2 vols., Frankfort, 1845–46; K. F. A. Kahnis, *Die Lehre vom Abendmahle*, Leipzig, 1851; R. I. Wilberforce, *Doctrine of the Eucharist*, London, 1854; C. Sigwart, *Ulrich Zwingli, der Charakter seiner Theologie*, Gotha, 1855; W. Cunningham, *Reformers and Theol. of Reformation*, Edinburgh, 1866; H. Schmid, *Der Kampf der lutherischen Kirche um Luthers Lehre vom Abendmahl*, Leipzig, 1868; C. Hodge, *Systematic Theology*, vol. iii., London and Edinburgh, 1874; F. Schirrmacher, *Briefe und Akten zur Geschichte des Religionsgesprächs zu Marburg, 1529, und des Reichstags zu Augsburg, 1530*, Gotha, 1876; Herrlinger, *Die Theologie Melanchthons*, Gotha, 1879; A. Erichson, *Das marburger Religionsgespräch*, London, 1883; E. B. Pusey, *Doctrine of the Real Presence*, Strassburg, 1880; A. Baur, *Zwinglis Theologie, ihr Werden und ihr System*, Halle, 1885; T. Harnack, *Luthers Theologie*, 2 vols., Leipzig, 1862–86; Pierson, *Studiën over J. Kalvijn*, 3 vols., Amsterdam, 1881–91; J. Schwane, *Die eucharistische Opferhandlung*, Freiburg, 1889; P. Schanz, *Die Lehre von den heiligen Sacramenten*, Freiburg, 1893; W. Sanday, *Priesthood and Sacrifice*, London, 1900; J. Köstlin, *Luthers Theologie*², Stuttgart, 1901; K. Thimme, 'Entwicklung und Bedeutung der Sakramentslehre Luthers,' in *Neue kirchliche Zeitschrift*, 1901; E. F. K. Müller, *Die Bekenntnisschriften der reformierten Kirche*, Leipzig, 1903; K. G. Götz, *Die Abendmahlsfrage*, Leipzig, 1904; R. M. Adamson, *The Christian Doctrine of the Lord's Supper*, Edinburgh, 1905; J. W. Richard, *Confessional History of the Lutheran Church*, Philadelphia, 1909; H. von Schubert, 'Das marburger Gespräch als Anfang der Abendmahlskonkordie,' in *ZKG*, vol. xxx., Gotha, 1909; D. Stone, *History of the Doctrine of the Holy Eucharist*, London, 1909.

HUGH WATT.

EUCHITES (Εὐχῖται or Εὐχῆται, from εὐχή, 'prayer').—A sect whose leading tenet was that sin could be subdued and perfection attained by the practice of perpetual prayer. Originating as an outgrowth of Syrian monachism, they propagated their ideas from the second half of the 4th cent. till the 6th, and traces of their influence are to be found at a much later date. They were otherwise named, after those who at various times were their leaders, Lampetians, Adelphians, Eustathians, and Marcianists; or, from some of their most striking peculiarities, Messalians (their commonest designation [Aram. מְצַלִּין, from צלא, 'to pray,' as in Dn 6^{11}, Ezr 6^{10}]), Choreutes (χορευταί, from their mystic dances), and Enthusiasts (ἐνθουσιασταί, from their claim to possession of the Holy Spirit). It is somewhat difficult to determine their true character and teaching, as nearly all the information that has reached us regarding them comes from their opponents, the heretical literature having almost completely perished. The chief writers who discuss their doctrines and practices are Epiphanius (*Hær.* 80), Theodoret (*HE* iv. 10; *Hær. Fab.* iv. 11), and Timotheus Presb. (in J. B. Cotelerius, *Ecc. Gr. Mon.*, Paris, 1677–86, iii. 400 f.). Their principal writing, which bore the title *Asceticus*, is often referred to, and it furnished John of Damascus with the 'heads of the impious doctrine of the Messalians taken from their own book' (Cotelerius, i. 302).

It is impossible to say whether their practice grew out of their theory, or their theory was squared with their practice. They taught that every one is possessed from his birth by a demon who incites him to sin. For the expulsion of the evil spirit baptism is ineffectual (τὸ ἁγίον βάπτισμα οὐδὲν συμβάλλεται [Timoth. *loc. cit.* 2]). It only 'shears away' the former sins, leaving the root of the evil untouched. The true remedy is intense prayer, unremitted till the departure of the evil spirit is sensibly perceived. Sometimes the Holy Spirit is seen to enter in the appearance of an innocuous fire, and the demon to pass out of the mouth in the form of a sow with her litter (Augustine, *Hær.* 57). Then ensues the happy time when 'the soul is as sensible of union with its heavenly bridegroom as an earthly bride in the embraces of her husband' (Timoth. 4). The Euchite henceforth regards himself as a partaker of the Divine nature. Frequently he ends in 'a pantheistic self-deification' (Neander, iii. 345). If an angel, a patriarch, a prophet, or Christ Himself is named to him, he will reply in each case, 'That am I myself' (Epiphanius, *loc. cit.*). As spiritual men, the Euchites alleged that they had visions such as were not granted to ordinary people. They danced in order to trample on the demons which appeared to them. They had also prophetic gifts, they knew the state of departed souls, and they had power to read the hearts of men. They regarded all the Church's ordinary means of grace, *e.g.* the Eucharist, as well as the discipline of the monastery, with indifference. Professing to give themselves entirely to prayer, they did no work, but lived as mendicants. Bands of Euchites of both sexes roamed about, as persons who had renounced the world and all its possessions. In summer they slept promiscuously in the streets of towns. They were suspected of believing that they could indulge in unbridled licentiousness without falling from their perfection. That may have been a calumny, but undoubtedly a nemesis often overtakes the presumptuous self-confidence which ignores the radical weakness of human nature.

Edessa was one of the first centres of the Euchite heresy. Flavian, bishop of Antioch (*c.* 390), sent a body of monks thither to summon the false teachers before him. As he knew that they would, according to their custom, deny their doctrines and charge their accusers with slandering them, he resorted to a stratagem. Affecting to side with the accused, he induced their aged leader, Adelphius, to disclose all the secrets of the order, and then rounded upon him with the stern words of Daniel, 'O thou that art waxen old in wickedness, now are thy sins come home to thee' (Susanna [52]). Adelphius and his comrades were beaten, excommunicated, and condemned to exile, without the option of recanting. They went to Pamphylia, where they were again condemned in a Synod held at Side, and presided over by Amphilochius of Iconium. Proceedings were also taken against the sect in Armenia, and they gave trouble in Constantinople. Theodosius legislated against them (xvi. Cod. Theod. *de Hær.* vi. 187), and Valerian and Amphilochius of Side had the book *Asceticus* condemned at the Council of Ephesus (431). Lampetius, the first of the sect to obtain the dignity of the priesthood, was summoned before his bishop, Alypius of Cæsarea (Cappadocia), on a double charge of undue familiarity with women and of deriding the musical services of the Church as a legal bondage. He was found guilty, condemned, and degraded. He wrote a book called the 'Testament,' which is lost, but a fragment of Severus the Monophysite's answer to it is preserved (J. C. Wolf, *Anecdota Græca*, Hamburg, 1722–24, iii. 182). The Euchite leader in the 6th cent. was Marcian, whom one of the Popes pronounced orthodox. Little more is heard of the sect till the outbreak of the Bogomil heresy in the 12th century. The Bogomils (*q.v.*) had their origin in Bulgaria, and 'were without doubt the connecting link between the so-called heretical sects of the East and those of the West' (*EBr*[11] iv. 119). They were also known as the 'Paulicians' (from Paul of Samosata), whose doctrines survive in the great Russian sects. See, further, art. PAULICIANS.

LITERATURE.—In addition to authorities cited in the text, see L. S. Tillemont, *Mémoires pour servir à l'hist. eccl.*, Paris, 1690, viii. 527 f.; C. W. F. Walch, *Hist. der Ketzereien*, Leipzig, 1762–85, iii. 481 ff.; J. A. W. Neander, *Church Hist.*, ed. London, 1884, iii. 323; G. Salmon, art. 'Euchites,' in Smith-Wace, *DCB*; Bonwetsch, 'Messalianer,' in *PRE*[3].

JAMES STRAHAN.

EUDÆMONISM.—Eudæmonism may be defined as the theory that the ethical end, the ultimate object to be achieved by action and conduct, the standard and final criterion of what ought to be, is *Welfare* (εὐδαιμονία). Welfare is not to be regarded as identical with happiness, although the latter term has been widely and even generally employed as a rendering of the Greek word, which 'welfare' (*Wohlfahrt*) more truly represents. Happiness may, of course, be so defined and understood by a moral philosopher as to become the technical equivalent of 'welfare' (Aristotle's εὐδαιμονία); but this involves an unnatural divorce from the meaning which it bears in ordinary speech and literature, where 'happiness' undoubtedly connotes pleasure as an essential and predominant, if not as its sole, constituent, and signifies, in fact, 'a life full of pleasures, well selected and arranged' (Mezes, *Ethics*, London, 1901, p. 397). Now, although welfare may be held to consist of pleasure, that theory (Hedonism) imports so great a difference that, in whichever of its several forms it be maintained, it stands apart and calls for separate treatment (see artt. EPICUREANS, HEDONISM, UTILITARIANISM).

Eudæmonism finds its typical exponent in Aristotle, whose famous definition of welfare (εὐδαιμονία), or man's ultimate good (τὸ ἀνθρωπινὸν ἀγαθόν)—'activity, or exercise of the powers, of soul according to virtue or goodness, and that the best and most fully developed'—has the high merit of elasticity, leaving room alike for individuality and for discovery in the conception both of psychical activity and of moral excellence. Only he is clear that well-being is founded and rooted in well-doing.

In modern philosophy Eudæmonism proper, as distinct from Hedonistic Utilitarianism, has few representatives. Perhaps Cumberland,[1] who makes 'furtherance of the common welfare' the ethical end, and, after him, Hutcheson and Butler, have the best claim to be so regarded; and, in our own day, Paulsen, with whom 'acts are called good, when they tend to preserve and promote *welfare*; bad, when they tend to disturb and destroy it' (*System of Ethics*, Eng. tr., London, 1899, p. 222), *welfare* 'consisting in the perfect exercise of all human psychical powers' (*ib.* p. 224).

It is of the essence of Eudæmonism that it is teleological: it looks forward and makes for an end, and that end is not precisely, or mainly, 'righteousness,' which implies a pre-existing rule or lawgiver. Herein it is contradistinguished from all that class of ethical theory which is retrospective and introspective, bidding us look back to a law once delivered, or inward to a perpetual and infallible monitor dictating duty without regard to consequences. Unlike every such 'intuitional' theory of morals, Eudæmonism does take account of con-

[1] *De Legibus Naturæ*, London, 1672, ch. 72.

sequences, not only of those immediate consequences which even for the intuitionist commonly form part of the act or thing to be done or eschewed, but (which is the crucial matter) of manifold consequences that lie, foreseen or pictured, in the far or middle distance.

Of Perfectionism, which is likewise teleological, we may fairly say, with Wundt (*Ethical Systems*, Eng. tr., London, 1897, p. 187), that practically it 'coincides with Eudæmonism,' though with the formal 'superiority' that 'it lays more stress on the duty of moral self-development,' as a means, however, not barely to self-perfection, but thereby to the welfare of our fellow-men. This identification will bring the school of Leibniz into the ranks of the eudæmonists. At the same time it marks the difference between ancient (or Aristotelian) and modern Eudæmonism. The former was primarily individualistic, notwithstanding that for Aristotle membership of a State is indispensable to human welfare, and even to manhood. The latter is predominantly altruistic and universal. Now, individual perfection, excepting for Plato, is not manifestly the same as individual welfare, whereas universal perfection may reasonably be identified with universal welfare—the welfare of all human or, as some authorities would have it, of all sentient beings.

See, further, ETHICS, and the Literature there cited.

J. M. SCHULHOF.

EUDOXIANISM.—Eudoxianism denotes the opinions, more especially on the Arian controversy, held by Eudoxius, who was born about A.D. 300, and became successively Bishop of Germanicia in Commagene, of Antioch (A.D. 358), and of Constantinople (A.D. 360–370). The materials available for ascertaining his views are very scanty, consisting chiefly of his 'Confession,' a fragment of a work on the 'Incarnation,' which has been preserved in a collection made by the presbyter Anastasius. Inferences as to his opinions have also been drawn from his conduct at certain crises, and from one or two sayings he is reported to have uttered. One of these is a scurrilous sentence from a sermon delivered by the 'Bishop of Antioch' and referred to at the Council of Seleucia (Hilary, *c. Constantium*, 13). But it is at least doubtful whether Eudoxius was at the time Bishop of Antioch (see G. Krüger, *Lucifer*, Leipzig, 1886, p. 105): he was the only bishop who signed the Acacian formula at Seleucia (Hahn, *Bib. der Symb.*[3], p. 306) without giving the name of his see (Mansi, iii. 321 B; Loofs, *PRE*[3] v. 579), and the probability is that he was at the time suspended from his diocese. A similar story related by Socrates serves rather to convict him of execrable taste than to identify the school to which he belonged.

Eudoxius was an opportunist and a politician rather than a thinker or a man of principle. During the period of his influence as Bishop of Constantinople, he may be said to have belonged to the left-centre, refraining from committing himself to the Anomœan position of Eunomius, while definitely antagonistic to the Nicene, and critical of the semi-Arian. 'The definite breach which Eudoxius made with Eunomius and Aetius (in the time of Jovian) on the one hand, and on the other the permanent hostility between him and the Homoousians, gave the direction to his theology and Church politics' (Loofs, *loc. cit.*). His Confession is notable for its refraining from the use of the watchwords of the moment, either the Homœan or the Anomœan; for its assertion that Christ was 'made flesh, not made man'; and for its denial of the two natures in Christ. (The text of the Confession is printed by Harnack, *Hist. of Dogma*, iv. 147.)

The ten years of Eudoxius' ecclesiastical domination at Constantinople coincided with the close contact between the Ostrogoths and the capital, and his influence was probably most lasting in the type of Arian teaching which established itself in that race.

See also art. EUNOMIANISM.

LITERATURE.—Athanasius, *de Synodis*, esp. 37, 38 (*PG* xxvi. 760), *Hist. Arianorum*, 4 (*ib.* xxv. 700); C. P. Caspari, *Quellen zur Gesch. des Taufsymbols*, Christiania, 1879, pp. 176–185; A. Hahn, *Bibliothek der Symbole*[3], Breslau, 1897, p. 261; H. M. Gwatkin, *Studies of Arianism*, Cambridge, 1882; A. Harnack, *Hist. of Dogma*, Eng. tr. iv. [1898] 75 ff., 147; F. Loofs, art. 'Eudoxius,' in *PRE*[3] v. [1898] 577; W. M. Sinclair, art. 'Eudoxius,' in *DCB* ii. [1880] 265.

C. A. SCOTT.

EUGENICS.—See MARRIAGE, SOCIOLOGY.

EUHEMERISM.—The term 'Euhemerism' is often applied in a general though quite unwarranted sense to the rationalistic interpretation and disintegration of Greek mythology. As a matter of fact, the romantic tale composed by Euhemerus of Messene marks but a single phase of religious-historical thought in the 3rd cent. B.C. and the period following, and it is only the influence exercised by this work upon the Romans, and, through them, upon modern rationalism, that has given the term a significance by no means commensurate with the actual achievement of the man from whom the movement derives its usual name. For, when all is said, the teaching of Euhemerus has but little claim to be called original. Prior to his time reflexion on religious things had undergone a fairly long process of development. The roots of Greek rationalism lie far in the past. The Ionic historian Hecatæus had already dealt with ancient legends on rationalizing principles, and his example was followed by Herodotus and Herodorus, while the Cynics Antisthenes and Diogenes had sought to re-interpret the myths in a sense peculiar to themselves.

Strictly systematic reflexion on the gods of Greek mythology, however, first made its appearance in the epoch of Alexander the Great, and it was also in this period that romance, stimulated by the marvellous adventures of the campaigns in the East, gained a footing in Greek life. The first name that meets us in this connexion is that of Hecatæus of Teos, who lived in Egypt in the reign of Ptolemy I. (323–285 B.C.), and whose work, entitled Αἰγυπτιακά, was made use of by Diodorus Siculus in the first book of his history (E. Schwartz, in *Rhein. Mus.* xl. [1885] 233–262; Pauly-Wissowa, v. 669 ff.). Hecatæus attempted to explain the general belief in the existence of divine beings by the theory that the gods of Egypt were but the deified benefactors of mankind; and his conclusions were all the more incisive in view of the fact that he regards the gods of Greece, and, indeed, Greek civilization in general, as being of Egyptian origin. Thus, in an age when kings were being accorded the honours of deity, the deities themselves—Helios, Kronos and Rhea, Zeus and Hera, and, above all, Isis and Osiris—were being reduced to the level of ancient monarchs whose efforts on behalf of progress had given men cause to look upon them as higher beings.

Some knowledge of the work of Hecatæus seems to be presupposed in the Ἱερὰ ἀναγραφή of Euhemerus. In this book—written perhaps *c.* 280 B.C. —which purports to be the narrative of a journey, and is composed in the spirit of the numerous political Utopias of the 4th cent. B.C., Euhemerus gives a description of certain Happy Isles that he pretends to have discovered on a voyage from the Red Sea to the Indian Ocean. This romance of travel, the surviving portions of which are found in Diodorus (v. 41–46, vi. 1), as also in the fragments of Ennius preserved by Lactantius (*Div. Inst.* I. xi.

45–48, 63, 65, xiii. 2, 14, xiv. 1–12, xvii. 10, xxii. 21)—Varro perhaps being the intermediary—professes, in particular, to give a sketch of the fabled island of Panchaia, which is here depicted, however, not in the style of a wonder-land, but with a relatively sober and persuasive colouring—an artifice by which Euhemerus hoped to facilitate his readers' acceptance of his theology, for this was in reality his sole concern. Accordingly, he proceeds to tell that he had discovered upon the island a temple of Zeus, and therein a pillar of gold on which Zeus had recorded in sacred script his own deeds and those of Uranos and Kronos. Thus all that had ranked as divine was brought down to the human level, precisely as in the work of Hecatæus, whose views seemed in this way to gain some sort of documentary corroboration. In particular, Zeus himself was now no more than a ruler who had given a powerful impetus to civilization, who had completed the dissemination of his cult by erecting the sanctuary in Panchaia, and who ultimately died and was buried in Crete.

This narrative, of which we have given only the most essential particulars, was generally repudiated and pronounced a fabrication by the more earnest minds among the Greeks (cf. Callimachus, *Hymn.* i. 8 f., frag. 86; Eratosthenes *ap.* Strabo, xlvii. 104 [Polybius]; Plutarch, *de Is. et Osir.* 23); but, as was noted above, it had a great influence upon the Romans, amongst whom it became naturalized in the Lat. rendering of Ennius. It thereby became known to the Roman Christian writers (Minuc. Fel., *Oct.* 21; Lactantius, *loc. cit.*), who were as ignorant of Euhemerus in the original as of the Gr. apologists (Theophilus, *ad Autolycum*, iii. 7, furnishes no evidence on the point), and it was through their influence that Euhemerus and his work became immortal, and his theology passed into a proverb.

It is, accordingly, all the more necessary to insist upon the fact that in Euhemerus we have but a single—though, it may be, the most notable and competent—representative of the spirit of the age. Just as—unless all the evidence is fallacious—he had a forerunner in Hecatæus, so he was followed by others who shared his views. Thus, while we cannot fix precisely the date of Leon of Pella, who fabricated a letter purporting to have been written by Alexander to Olympias—a letter often quoted by the apologists, and setting forth ideas akin to those of Hecatæus—he unquestionably belongs to this period, and must be regarded as an exponent of 'Euhemerism' (cf. Geffcken, *Zwei griech. Apologeten*, Leipzig, 1907, p. 223). Then, in the 2nd cent. B.C., Dionysios Skytobrachion, who is referred to by Diodorus (iii. 56; 57. 2; 60. 3 and 5; 70. 3, 7, 8; 71. 5; 72. 1, 4; 73. 1, 3, 5), followed on the lines of Euhemerus and his predecessor, maintaining that the gods were ancient kings who—as was specially exemplified in the case of Dionysus—had been promoted to divine honours for their services to civilization. Finally, about the end of the 1st cent. A.D., Herennius Philo of Byblus, in his *Sanchuniathon*, applied the same process of transmutation to the Phœnician deities (Euseb. *Præp. evang.* i. 9, p. 29 ff.). The work of Palaiphatos (περὶ ἀπίστων, ed. Festa, in the *Mythogr. græci*, iii. 2, Leipzig, 1902) cannot now be regarded as directly relevant to the point before us. (Cf. with reference to the views developed in the foregoing, E. Schwartz, *Fünf Vorträge über d. griech. Roman*, Berlin, 1896, p. 102 ff.; Jacoby, in Pauly-Wissowa, vi. 952; Wendland, *Die hellenist.-röm. Kultur*², Tübingen, 1912, p. 116 ff.)

The work of Euhemerus, as already remarked, was generally rejected by Greek writers of the more earnest type, and especially, of course, by such as had engaged in research. It is, nevertheless, true that in Greek works of a religious cast we occasionally come upon ideas which, to say the least, emanate from the Euhemeristic sphere of thought. Thus, when certain pagan writers, in seeking to vindicate the practice of idolatry against the vehement onslaughts which Greek scepticism was already making upon it, appeal to man's instinctive craving for the visible presence of deity, and his consequent need of an image (Dio Chrysost. *Orat.* xii. 61; Maximus Tyrus, *Diss.* ii. 10 [p. 28, 12 Hob.]), their argument forms in a manner the basis of the theory by which the Book of Wisdom (14^15ff.) explains the origin of idolatry, viz. that some bereaved father had made an image of the son whom he had lost, and offered sacrifices to it, and that this then became a general practice, till at length the worship of images was legally instituted by kings. In this Judæo-Hellenistic work, therefore, we have a theory of the origin of idolatry that finds no place in extant pagan literature, and shows unmistakably the impress of 'Euhemerism.' Similar ideas found their way also into Hellenistic popular literature, as, e.g., the *Oracula Sibyllina*, which form a medley of heathen, Jewish, and Christian prophecies. In the third book of the Sibyllines, which is known to be the oldest, occurs a myth—relating to Kronos, Titan, Japetos, Rhea, Zeus, and Hera (v. 110 ff.)—whose resemblance to the teaching of Euhemerus found in Ennius was rightly noted by Lactantius, and which is doubtless to be traced back—though hardly in a direct line—to Euhemerus himself. Thus the work of Euhemerus still serves—in the hands of these unintelligent witnesses to religion, who had certainly never read it (even Firmicus Maternus, 3, 6 f., does not imply a direct reading)—as an apologetic weapon against the heathen; and in this fact we may discern the remarkable influence of the writer whose name has come by custom to be associated with the whole intellectual movement to which his original contribution was by no means great.

LITERATURE.—This has been given in the course of the article.

J. GEFFCKEN.

EUMENIDES, ERINYES.—It is not altogether easy to grasp the precise character of the Eumenides, or—to give them their more general and more appropriate designation—the Erinyes; for the traditional representation of these creations of Greek popular belief and poetic fancy is often very indefinite. They sometimes appear as personifications, sometimes as ghosts, and sometimes as really well-defined figures; now the tradition speaks of a single Ἐρινύς, and now of a whole host of these frightful beings. Still, the scientific investigation of this province of religious history has within recent decades to some extent succeeded in discovering the original form and subsequent development of the myth, though we must not expect that every traditional detail will find a place in the resultant delineation. For, while many Greek deities have but little homogeneity of character, and tend rather to coalesce in various aspects with other divine personages, this is especially true of the figures generated by the obscure and primitive popular belief to which we owe also the Erinyes; and the reader who desires to have some idea of the wavering forms shown by the Erinyes in the dawning consciousness of the ancient Greeks will do well to read von Wilamowitz's introduction to his translation of the *Eumenides* of Æschylus (Berlin, 1900, pp. 1–31).

The Erinys—or group of Erinyes—was an earth-deity, who in Thelpusa was identified with Demeter (Pausan. viii. 25. 4). Such chthonic spirits appear nearly always in a dual aspect—one friendly and beneficent, the other dark and sinister, just as the divine pair Demeter and Persephone symbolize, on the one hand, the kindly earth yielding food for man, and, on the other, the gloomy depths of Hades. We find, accordingly, that in the Peloponnesus well-disposed deities of the earth were worshipped as *Eumenides* (Pausan. ii. 11. 4; cf. viii. 34. 1 ff., and Preller-Robert, *Griech. Mythologie*[4], Berlin, 1894, i. 837); elsewhere they are also designated Πότνιαι or Ἀβλαβίαι, and in Athens, on the Areopagus and at the Demos Colonus, the Σεμναί (Paus. i. 28. 6), while this name, as also the title Πότνιαι, was likewise applied in a descriptive sense to Demeter and Kore (cf. Preller-Robert, i. 747). Such deities, in virtue of their chthonic character, were represented in the cultus as bearing not only flowers and fruits, but also the figure of the snake, which is found among many peoples as the symbolic animal of the dark and gloomy under world. For in the earth underneath live the souls of the dead, the haggard spirits whom those who still live on the earth must charm and propitiate; while, under a different name, these earth-deities are the avengers of murder, especially the murder of a blood-relation. It is true that even here the data remain somewhat obscure, for it seems as if the Ἐρινύς was in general the angry soul of the murdered person himself rather than a deity who avenges the crime wreaked upon that soul. To all appearance Hesiod (*Theog.* 217; cf. Æsch. *Sept. contra Theb.* 1054) identifies the Erinyes with the *Kēres*, who must also be regarded as souls. And, since it is thus impossible, as has just been indicated, to attain to absolute certainty at this point, we must be content to verify some of the more outstanding features of the myth in its primitive form.

Now, it is so far an advantage to have ascertained that the avenging deities who punish the crime of slaying a blood-relation are identical with the beneficent spirits of the under world. The cause of a murdered man was in general taken up by his family group; but, when one individual in such a group killed another, the deed was accounted more atrocious than an ordinary homicide; and, as in this case the avenger could not fittingly be supplied by the family itself, the task of executing justice on behalf of the wailing soul of the slain was undertaken by the deities of the sombre depths. Thus the death-blow which Meleager had dealt the brother of his mother is, at her request, avenged upon him by the ἠεροφοῖτις Ἐρινύς (*Il.* ix. 571); and we are told in *Od.* xi. 280 that, though Œdipus was not directly guilty of his mother's death, yet for him Epicaste left pains behind, 'all that the Erinyes ('Avengers' [Butcher and Lang]) of a mother bring to pass' (ὅσσα τε μητρὸς Ἐρινύες ἐκτελέουσιν). Here, however, we can already trace the genesis of the finer and more spiritual idea that the Erinyes are the curse, or curses (ἀραί), of one who has suffered any kind of injury at the hands of a relative. Thus Telemachus is apprehensive of his mother's curses (*Od.* ii. 135; cf. *Il.* xxi. 412), while in Hesiod (*Theog.* 472), Rheia desires that Kronos shall propitiate the ἐρινῦς, *i.e.*—in this case—the curses of his father; and, similarly, in Æschylus (*Eum.* 417) the Erinyes present themselves to Athene as the Ἀραί (cf. Soph. *Œd. Col.* 1375, 1391; Blass, *Einleit. zu d. Eumeniden des Aischylos*, Berlin, 1907, p. 2 f.). In this way the Erinyes came at length to be the protectresses of family law in general; when a household was bereft of parents, their place was taken by the eldest brother, whose prerogative was now maintained by the Erinyes (*Il.* xv. 204). Finally, when they stop the prophetic utterance of the steed of Achilles (xix. 418), they seem to assume the function, if we may so express it, of maintaining the normal order of Nature. As they are thus the handmaids of justice upon earth, they are also the guardians of oaths and the avengers of perjury (xix. 259; Hesiod, *Op.* 803 f.), and, accordingly, in the court of the Areopagus at Athens the judicial oath was taken in the name of the Σεμναὶ θεαί (Dinarchus, i. 47). On all these details, see Rohde, *Psyche*[2], Freiburg, 1898, i. 268 ff., ii. 231 f.

The Erinyes then came to be depicted with all the power of artistic expression of which Hellenism was capable. The ἐρινύς travels amid a dark cloud, is 'one that walks in darkness' (ἠεροφοῖτις, see above); the sombre goddesses, the στυγεραί, the κρατεραί, and the δασπλῆτες, are also figured as huntresses; nothing escapes their eye; and, like a pack of savage hounds, they pursue the criminal —whose trail of blood they have speedily discovered—till they finally bring him to the ground. Hence Æschylus, too, refers to them as the 'mother's hounds' (*Choeph.* 924; cf. *Eum.* 131 f., 146 ff.).

It was, in fact, Greek poetry, and, above all, Greek tragedy, that gave these creations of popular belief their final form. We cannot fix precisely the period in which the repulsive stories of unnatural crime—parricide, matricide, and incest—first took their rise, and to which, therefore, the legends of Œdipus, Alcmæon, and the Atridæ are to be assigned. But in any case the Erinyes filled a great rôle in this particular phase of Greek mythology. This has already been shown in the case of Œdipus (cf. also Æsch. *Sept.* 69, 857), while, as regards the myth of the Atridæ, we read in Stesichorus, who is our chief authority here, and is of importance also for the development of tragedy, that Orestes, who had killed his mother Clytæmnestra, was pursued by the Erinyes, and received from Apollo a bow as a means of defence (frag. 40). The latter detail is one of great interest, as it indicates the early recognition of that conflict between the deities of light and those of the under world which forms so significant a factor in the *Eumenides* of Æschylus. For there the Erinyes are the primeval goddesses whose sole function it is to avenge the violation of kinship; the murder of a husband, which Apollo sets forth before the Erinyes in all its atrocity, is of no concern to them (*Eum.* 212). In Apollo and Athene, as a matter of fact, the Erinyes are confronted with a new ethical point of view—with the Delphic law of expiation—as also with the claim of the Athenian State to deal in its own right with such deeds as the crime of Orestes. As we know, they lose their case, but they are reconciled by Athene, and then, as beneficent spirits, pass into the under world beneath the Areopagus. The Erinyes have become the Eumenides. Thus did Æschylus contrive to introduce ethical harmony into the primitive saga, which, as we saw above, recognized a dual aspect in the earth-deities. Another perpetrator of the crime of matricide was Alcmæon, who was likewise pursued by the Erinyes, but was at length released from the consequences of his impiety (cf. Eurip. in Nauck, *Fragm. trag.*[2], Leipzig, 1889, p. 379; Bethe, *Theban. Heldenlieder*, Leipzig, 1891, p. 138 f.).

We have already noted the fact that the chthonic character of the Erinyes is symbolized by the snake, and on an Argive votive relief (Roscher, i. 1330) each of the three Eumenides carries a serpent in her hand. Æschylus, however, represents them as also having snakes twining about their heads (*Choeph.* 1049 f.), and plastic art sometimes exhibits corresponding figures (Roscher, i. 1334). They are also provided with wings (cf. Eurip. *Iph. Taur.* 289), while their short hunting χιτών is a further indication of their function as the swift pursuers of their prey. In their hands they hold scourges, and also torches (cf. the vase of Canosa, in Roscher, i. 1326), with which they torment the guilty in the under world.

Æschylus does not mention the number of the Erinyes, but speaks of them as many (*Eum.* 585). At the court of the Areopagus the accusing goddesses were three in number—or, by other accounts, two (Preller-Robert, 837, 1; 841, 3). The Argive relief just referred to shows three, and we find the same number in a passage of Euripides (*Orest.* 408). Euripides, however, speaks of them in another passage (*Iph. Taur.* 968) as a large number, and, strange to say, as being split up into two parties, one of which continues to pursue Orestes, while the other acquiesces in the judgment of Athene.

After the age of tragedy the Erinyes or Eumenides show no further phase of development either in character or in outward form. Subsequently, in order to meet the desire for a simpler form of the myth, they were represented only in their more terrible aspects, their more beneficent functions being left out of account, till at length, among the Romans, and even in the description given by Vergil (*Æn.* vii. 323 ff.) they manifest—as the *Furiæ*—a relatively conventional character.

LITERATURE.—In addition to the authorities cited in the article, see A. Rosenberg, *Die Erinyen*, Berlin, 1873; J. E. Harrison, *Proleg. to Study of Gr. Rel.*², Camb. 1908; L. R. Farnell, *The Higher Aspects of Gr. Rel.* (Hib. Lect.), London, 1911, pp. 39, 85, 90, 101. Cf. also the artt. ÆSCHYLUS, CRIMES AND PUNISHMENTS (Greek), EURIPIDES, HOMER, SOPHOCLES.

J. GEFFCKEN.

EUNOMIANISM.—The moral force of Arianism (*q.v.*) was stronger than ever as its end drew near in the East, because the Homœans (those Arians who held the *likeness* of the Son to the Father) were broken up, and there was no more entanglement with the court and politics. Arianism was then represented by Eunomius, who had made no compromises, and had suffered as a martyr to the Anomœan cause (*i.e.* the cause of those who held the *unlikeness* of the Son to the Father). He had to leave his See of Cyzicus, was banished by the Emperor Valens (A.D. 367), and again, when he had returned to Constantinople, by Theodosius—the sole exception to Theodosius' toleration. The Anomœan teaching came to a head, in Eunomius' hands, in the easily understood formula 'that the ἀγεννησία was the essence of the First Person of the Trinity,' whereby a gulf was dug between the Ungenerate and the Generate; in other words, between the Father and the Son.

A passing notice of the word 'Ungenerate' as the equivalent of ἀγέννητος, the catchword of this logician, is necessary at the commencement. It was a term used by the orthodox also as applicable to the Father only, though in a way very different from that in which Eunomius handled it; and, if it were to be translated 'not begotten' or 'unbegotten,' as applicable to the Father only, such a term would confuse the doctrine of the Third Person, who is Himself also 'not made, nor created, *nor begotten*.' Again, 'ingenerate,' which might be suggested as a substitute, is not supported by the Latin usage. 'Unoriginate,' again, bears only one sense of unbeginning, which even with the Arians could be said of the Son. Lastly, 'not generated' does not furnish a corresponding idiomatic expression for ἀγεννησία, 'ungeneracy.' 'Unmade,' 'uncreate' are out of the question for this purpose, both in themselves and because no proper equivalent would be left for ἀγέννητος, and no means of distinguishing it from ἀγένητος. The distinction between these terms was always felt by the Church writers, whether before the 3rd cent. (which Bishop Bull has doubted) or after it (as has been conclusively shown by Lightfoot, *Ignatius*, vol. ii. p. 90 ff.). Thus 'unmade' (ἀγένητος) could be applied to the Son, but not ἀγέννητος. 'Ungenerate' remains, then, as alone capable of representing the word which was put in the forefront of the Eunomian heresy, and from which all its conclusions flowed. As it was a word accepted also by the orthodox, Eunomius' use of it was all the more convincing and plausible.

As to the source of the term 'ungenerate' there can be little doubt. Though Gregory of Nyssa, in the long and bitter controversy with Eunomius, when everything had to be said that would make for the Nicene faith, more than once accuses him of having invented the term (it certainly became a new thing in his hands), we should expect to find it, and we shall not fail to find it, in the Alexandrian philosophy. Gregory accuses Eunomius of Judaizing by means of it, and of introducing also the Greek idolatry, *i.e.* of the creature. This takes us at once to Philo on the one hand, and to the Neo-Platonists on the other. Of course the contemporary philosophy could not enter into the fine distinction between 'ungenerate' and 'uncreate,' so necessary to be drawn in the Christian controversy. Still 'ungenerate' is the term which Plotinus uses of the Supreme Being (*Ennead*, v. iii. p. 517); and Celsus (the Neo-Platonist whom Origen answered) uses it, according to the text of the *Philocalia*, of his eternal world; while Philo, a century and a half before, had treated it as the exact correlative of the Jahweh of the Jews. As for its early use by the teachers of the Church, it is enough to mention that Ignatius writes that 'the *heretics*' (the followers of Simon, who were precursors of the Sabellians) thought that Christ was ungenerate.

It was this word 'ungenerate,' so familiar to Greek philosophy, so consecrated in its application to the First Person of the Trinity, that Eunomius seized upon to destroy the consubstantiality of Nicæa. He saw in it the expression of a positive idea which enabled the mind to comprehend the Deity, and which at the same time, by virtue of the logical opposition between ungenerate and generate, destroyed not only the equality, but also the likeness, of the Father and the Son. As in all other dichotomies arising from privative terms (*e.g.* 'imperishable,' 'unending,' 'uncreate,' etc.), the Trinity stands apart from creation, so in this last dichotomy the First Person stands apart from the Second and the Third. It was the only distinction of this sort that Arianism could seize on for its purpose, and so this distinctive term 'ungenerate' is hypostatized and deified.

1. 'The Ungenerate' as the name of God.—Eunomius asserts 'God is ungenerate, absolutely and independently of aught beside Himself,' and shows at once what he is going to make of this by adding of the term 'ungenerate' itself: 'This name is His glory. It is grafted in our minds from above.' He then constructs the following syllogism: 'No term expressive merely of the absence of a quality can be God's name: *the Ungenerate is God's name*: therefore it does not express a privation.' But how does he prove his second premiss, viz. that 'the Ungenerate' is God's name? The only definite proof he seems to offer is the somewhat curious one that long before the creation of man God had the naming of things, seeing that in the earliest of the sacred records, before the creation of man, the naming of fruit and seed is mentioned; and, if of things, how much more would He have the naming of Himself; and 'Ungenerate,' which includes everything else we predicate of Him (indestructible, unending, etc.)—in fact expresses His essence—commends itself as the name He must have given to Himself. Once he can establish ungeneracy as the Divine essence above all other qualities (which he labours to do by a *constant misapplication of that which constitutes the Person or hypostasis of the Father to the whole essence* [οὐσία] *of Deity*), the heavenly origin of the name follows as a matter of course in accordance with his theory of the sacredness of names.

But Eunomius' most elaborate proof, that 'Ungenerate is God's name,' is a negative and indirect one. He attacks the mental history which Basil and Gregory of Nyssa give of the term. He denies that it is due to a human *conception*, and boldly asserts instead that it is due to a perception as instinctive, spontaneous, and direct as any perception of the senses: the Deity presented this object, and the mind at once grasped it. He pours contempt not only on the orthodox party for treating this and all other privative names of the Deity as merely privative and the result of conception, but also upon the faculty of conception itself. It would be dangerous, he considers, to trust the naming of the Deity to a common operation of the mind. The faculty of conception may, and does, play us false; it can create monstrosities. Besides, if the names of the Father are conceptions, so also are the names of the Son, *e.g.* the Door, the Shepherd, the Axe, the

Vine. But, as our Lord Himself applied these to Himself, He would, according to the orthodox party, be employing the faculty of conception; and it is blasphemous to think that He employed names which we might have arrived at simply by conceiving of Him in these particular ways. Therefore, conception is not the source of the Divine names; but rather they come from a perception implanted in us directly from on high. 'Ungenerate,' above all others, is such a name, and it reveals to us the very substance or essence of the Deity.

It was urged by Basil and Gregory against Eunomius that 'Ungenerate,' as well as every other name of God, is due to a conception. They show the entire relativity of our knowledge of the Deity. In each case of naming Him we perceive an operation of the Deity, or an absence in Him of what attaches to the created, or of evil; and then we *conceive* of Him as operating in the one, as free from the other, and so name Him. But there is no conception, because there is no perception, of the substance of the Deity. Scripture, which has revealed His operations, has not revealed that.

Basil and Gregory both declare the predicate 'Ungenerate' to be a concept; Eunomius declares it to be a thing, to be not privative, but positive.

We recognize in all this a far-off prelude of the battle that had to be fought a thousand years afterwards as to the nature and source of generic names; then, too, the Conceptualists may be considered to have left the field victorious. See artt. CONCEPTUALISM, NOMINALISM, REALISM.

Behind this first assumption,—for it is an assumption for which Eunomius offers no better proofs than those given above,—that the true name of God is 'Ungenerate,' there lies another assumption, namely, that *God is knowable.* On the one hand, Eunomius attacks the orthodox for saying that we know God only through the universe, and through the Son, the author of the universe; on the other, he attacks the older Arians for saying that we know God only in part. He maintains, on the contrary, that it is unworthy of a Christian to profess the impossibility of knowing the Divine nature and the manner in which the Son is generated. Rather the mind of the believer rises above every sensible and intelligible essence, and does not stop even at the generation of the Son, but mounts above, aspiring to the First Cause. Is this bold assertion—so contrary to the teaching of the Fathers, and of Scripture itself—a direct borrowing from Plato and the Neo-Platonists? The language in which it is expressed certainly belongs to these schools; cf. the terms 'transcending,' 'beyond,' 'longing,' 'First Cause,' 'uplifted.' This direct intuition on our part of the Ungenerate manifestly creates an enormous inconsistency in Eunomius' own system. We have to suppose that the creatures whom the Word, the Son, by Eunomius' own showing, created, unconnected as they are with the Ungenerate (since He has *not* made them), nevertheless conceive of and see, beyond their own Creator, a Being who cannot be anything to them!

2. Eunomius' treatment of the doctrine of the Trinity.—It remains to consider the use, in detail, which Eunomius made of this primal dichotomy of 'Ungenerate' and 'Generate' as applied to the whole doctrine of the Trinity. His *résumé* of his re-arrangement of this, as quoted by Gregory from his *Defence of my Defence*, begins as follows:

'There is the Supreme and Absolute Being; and another Being, existing by reason of the First, but after It, though before all others; and a third Being, not ranking with either of these, but inferior to the One as to cause, to the Other as to the energy which produced it.'

This last statement must mean that the Third Person is inferior to the First, as having a cause at all; and to the Second, as proceeding only from the Second and not from the First. In this Eunomius reveals at once the emanationism which marks his teaching throughout. He goes on:

'There must, of course, be included in this account the energies which follow each Being, and the names germane to these energies. Again, as each Being is absolutely single, and is in fact and thought one, and Its energies are bounded by Its works and Its works commensurate with Its energies, necessarily, of course, the energies which follow these Beings are relatively greater and less, some being of a higher, some of a lower order; in a word, their difference amounts to that existing between their works.'

We see that Eunomius in this (and equally so in all that follows) has translated the terms of Scripture straight into those of Aristotle, and changed the ethical-physical of Christianity into the purely physical. Spirit throughout becomes Being (*οὐσία*, a word which, seeing that Eunomius still regards the substance as living, is best translated as above, 'Being'). Nothing else was to be expected after he had so effectually banished the spiritual and moral from his Ungenerate that it becomes as physical as the 'Motionless First Mover' of Aristotle. The contents of the above formula amount to nothing more or less than Gnosticism. In fact, the earlier and this, the later, Arianism are simply the last attempts of Gnosticism to impose the doctrine of emanations upon Christian theology. For, while Arianism held the Logos to be the highest Being after the Godhead, it regarded this Logos as only the mediator between God and man; just as, before the rise of Arianism, it had been the peculiar aim of Gnosticism to bridge over the gulf between Creator and created by means of intermediate beings (the emanations). It is also most significant, in the same direction, that Eunomius, like his master before him, adopted that system of Greek philosophy (the Aristotelian) which had always been the natural ally of Gnosticism. Aristotle is strong in divisions and differences, weak in 'identifications'; he had marked, with a clearness never attained before, the various stages upwards in the physical world; and this is just what Gnosticism, in its wish to exhibit all things according to their various distances from the ungenerate, required, and accordingly made use of. Gregory had reason when he spoke of the followers of Eunomius as 'these Gnostics.'

It is true that Eunomius uses also orthodox terms in dealing with the Trinity. We encounter such in the following creed of his, but the last words preclude any orthodox meaning:

'We believe in the Son of God, the Only-begotten God, the first-born of all creation, very Son, not ungenerate, verily begotten before the worlds, named Son not without being begotten before He existed, coming into being before creation, *not uncreate*' (quoted by Gregory of Nyssa, *c. Eunom.* ii. 7).

The gulf had been dug when once ungeneracy had been proclaimed to be the substance of the Father; and nothing more could pass it. Even the Godhead of the Son seems destroyed, notwithstanding the above articles from Eunomius' creed, in such a sentence as the following: 'No man who has any regard for the truth either calls any generated thing ungenerate, or calls God, who is over all, Son or generate.' The Son is 'subject,' and this subjectivity is proved by the fact of being generated.

'The Father' and 'the Son' are terms which Eunomius avoids as much as possible; he was sure to use them most sparingly—in fact, only to get, and until he could get, a hearing. But, once he can come back to his Ungenerate, his object is secured, and all the details of his system follow by an easy process of drawing inevitable conclusions. The Son is necessarily 'subject.' The opposition of 'ungenerate' and 'generate' admits, he says, of no mean, just like that of 'rational' and 'irrational.' He contemplates, as existing in the 'generate' with reference to the 'ungenerate,' the same difference as there is between 'irrational' and 'rational.' As the special attributes of the rational and irrational are essentially incompatible, so the nature of the generate is one, and that of the ungenerate is another; and as the irrational has been created in subjection to the rational, so the generate is, by a necessity of its being, in a state of subjection to the ungenerate.

As to the mode and manner of the generation of the Son, Eunomius says the Father begat Him at that time which He chose, and quotes Philo: 'God, before all other things that are generated, has dominion over His own power.' This power was under dominion, and was restrained as to its activity, while the due time of the generation of Christ was still about to come, and to set this power to its natural work. What the cause of delay was, and what it was that intervened, Eunomius does not specify. Not time, not space, he says. 'Let there be no questioning among sensible men on this point, why He did not do so before.' That is all. With the same tool of 'ungenerate' and 'generate' God (if he really could still give to Christ the name God), Eunomius shatters, as with a resistless wedge, the article of the Nicene symbol 'Light of Light,' which compares the consubstantiality of Father and Son with the oneness of flame lit from flame. 'As great as is the difference between generate and ungenerate, so great is the divergence between Light and Light.' This is a striking instance of how the avoidance of the Scripture terms 'Father' and 'Son,' implying real oneness of nature, made it possible to say almost anything in this controversy. He goes on:

'We know the true Light; we know Him who created the light after the heavens and the earth: we have heard the Life and the Truth Himself, even Christ, saying to His disciples: "Ye are the light of the world"; we have learned from the blessed Paul, when he gives the title of "Light unapproachable" to the God over all, and by the addition defines and teaches us the transcendent superiority of His Light; and now that we have learnt that there is so great a difference between the one Light and the other, we shall not patiently endure so much as the mere mention of the notion that the idea of light in either case is one and the same.'

With Eunomius, that is to say, the 'true' is one thing, the 'unapproachable' another. The Incarnation was a still further divergence of the Light of the Son.

'This Light carried into effect the plan of mercy, while the other remained inoperative with respect to that gracious action.'

It was even a further degradation:

'If he (*i.e.* Basil) can show that the God over all, who is the Light unapproachable, was incarnate,—or could be incarnate,—then let him say that the Light is equal to the Light.'

As to the Incarnation itself, the true emptying (*kenosis*), which according to Scripture is involved in it, quite disappears in Eunomius' hands. If the Son is created and man is created, He was 'emptied' (Eunomius clings to this phrase) to become Himself, and changed His place, not from the transcendent to the lowly, but from similar (save with regard to the accidental difference of 'bodied' and 'unembodied') to similar both in kind and dignity. The difference between the uncreated and the created no longer constitutes the difference between the two natures in Christ; that difference is marked by dominion and slavery, for 'all things serve God,' while 'the whole creation is in bondage.' But, that difference having disappeared, or rather having never existed between the Son and the world He came to save, it could no longer be shown that the Master was mingled with the Servant, but only that a servant came to be amongst servants. In fact, in Eunomius' scheme, the Incarnation was a fall rather than a condescension.

'The Ungenerate Light is unapproachable, and has not the power of stooping to experience affections; but such a condition is germane to the generate.'

The 'coming in the flesh' was quite akin, with Eunomius, to the declension of a transmigrating soul into a lower order and manner of existence, such as Pythagoras had taught. Eunomius represents the generate as intermediate between heaven and earth, the Divine and the human, so as not to preserve the Divine unsullied, but to have an essence mixed and compounded of contraries, which at once stretched out to partake of the good, and at the same time melted away into a condition subject to affections or emotions. So man need feel no gratitude to the Only-begotten God for what He suffers, since it was by the spontaneous action of His nature that He slipped down to the experience of such affections. His essence, being from the first *capable* of being affected and moved as men are, was thereby naturally dragged down; and such a transaction or change does not demand human gratitude! Nothing could show more clearly than this parody of the Christian doctrine of the Incarnation how wide the gulf is, and always must be, between Christianity and Emanationism or any modern revival of it. It was in the very cradle of this last that the Christian 'theologian' *par excellence* had proclaimed, as the axiom of the new religion, that 'God is Love.'

We do not find the same fullness of statement by Eunomius as to the Spirit as we find in his treatment of the Son. This is little to be wondered at. The doctrine of the Spirit had not yet come to the front in controversy; with the exception of the heresy of Macedonius, who was forming his sect at the very time when Eunomius was teaching, no heresy was connected directly with this, and no Council dealt with it. That was reserved for the next century. The final clauses of the Nicene Creed, which affirm distinctly, amongst other truths, the Deity and personality of the Third Person, were, if we are to accept the entire silence of the leading historians as evidence, not added at the Council of Constantinople; they were entirely ignored even at the Council of Ephesus. The apprehension of the *Homoousion* of the Holy Spirit was little permeated as yet by the Christian consciousness of the unity of God. Still the faith in it was *in* the Church. The expanded form of the Nicene Creed is found in a work written by Epiphanius *seven years before* the Council of Constantinople (A.D. 381), and it is probable that the old Creed of Jerusalem contained such clauses, and that Cyril produced them before the Council of Constantinople. But the times were not ripe for this controversy. Still, his system obliged Eunomius to say something about the Spirit; he had to draw his conclusions; and what he says savours of the purely Greek heresies of the next century: 'After him (*i.e.* the Son), we believe on the Comforter, the Spirit of truth,' says Eunomius. The omission of 'Holy' is to be noticed; doubtless it is because, being aware of the Scripture expressions, 'God is Spirit' (Jn 4^{24} RVm), 'the Lord our God is Holy' (Lv 19^{2}), he may prepare the way, by the omission of one at least of these glorious titles, for the still further subjection of the Spirit. So he continues: 'Once for all made subject,' but does not specify what this subjection is. 'Who came into being by the only God through the Only-begotten.' The term 'the only God' for the Father prepares for what is coming, and shows what value to attach to the whole. The Father employs the Son as an instrument for the production of the Spirit. 'Neither on the same level with the Father, nor connumerated with the Father; nor on an equality with the Son, for the Son is Only-begotten, having no brother begotten with Him.' This is, of course, inconsistent with Eunomius' previous interpretation of the Scripture words πρωτοτόκος τῆς κτίσεως as actually meaning 'first-born amongst many brethren,' *i.e.* the whole creation, including not only the Spirit, but Himself. 'Not yet ranked with any other, for he has gone above all the creatures that came into being by the instrumentality of the Son, in mode of being, and nature, and glory, and knowledge, as the first and noblest work of the Only-begotten, the greatest and most glorious.' Eunomius concedes much to the glory of the Spirit, but he is pledged by his emanationism to His subjectivity. We must discount the value of what follows. Eunomius does not read any text in Scripture about the Spirit in the light of other texts.

'He, too, being one, and first and alone and surpassing all the creations of the Son in essence and dignity of nature, accomplishing every operation and all teaching according to the good pleasure of the Son, being sent by Him, and receiving from Him, and declaring to those who are instructed, and guiding into truth.' Again: 'accomplishing every operation and all teaching,' 'sanctifying the saints,' 'co-operating with the faithful for the understanding and contemplation of things appointed,' 'leading us to that which is expedient for us,' 'strengthening us in godliness,' 'lightening souls with the light of knowledge,' 'emboldening the faint-hearted,' 'acting as a guide to those who approach the mystery,' 'distributing every gift,' 'banishing devils,' 'healing the sick,' 'comforting the afflicted,' 'recovering the distressed.'

Orthodoxy could not have a word to say against all this, for it is true scripturally, only Scripture attributes all these very operations to the Father and to the Son as well, or implies that they must be ascribed to both. But Eunomius, while basing his own doctrine upon Scripture, perforce ignored this. His principle once laid down at the first, 'that the energies and works are commensurate with the Beings which they follow, and are accordingly superior or inferior as the Beings are,' prevents any of these operations of the Holy Spirit from being purely Divine in his eyes. The fatal separation and subordination of the Beings lead to a still more fatal separation and subordination of the works. As redemption itself by the incarnation, being the Son's work and not the Father's, was rather a symptom of weakness in Him than an evidence of the power of Divine mercy, so the work of the Holy Spirit, being not the Son's nor the Father's, is no more to Eunomius than what might be attributed to some human teacher, *e.g.*, to be sent, to receive, to announce, to suggest the truth; it is not God Himself whispering in the heart of man.

To this emanationism ingrained in his system we must, of course, attribute the curious insistence of Eunomius on the Spirit's being the production of the Son alone: the 'energy' of the Son produced the Spirit as the 'energy' of the Father produced the Son. Was it only reverence for the words in Jn 15[26], or was it also the spectacle of Eunomius and many others on this downward road of emanationism, that restrained every Greek Council and every ancient Greek Father from mentioning the Son in connexion with the Procession of the Holy Spirit? Gregory of Nazianzus speaks for them all: 'Standing on our definitions, we introduce the Ungenerate, the Generated, and that which proceeds from the Father (1 *Orat de Filio*, ii.).'

As to Baptism, the views of Eunomius can be speedily stated. He is evidently alluding to it in the following words (as quoted by Gregory of Nyssa, *c. Eunom.* xi. 5): 'But we affirm that the mystery of godliness does not consist in venerable names, nor in the distinctive character of customs and sacramental tokens, but in exactness of doctrine.' He goes on to say that baptism is not into the Father, the Son, and the Holy Spirit, but 'into an artificer and creator'—apparently excluding the Third Person altogether. Accuracy of doctrine and clearness of statement were to the Eunomians salvation, and mysteries worse than nothing, for the claims of the Sacrament of Baptism must disappear altogether with the Divinity of the Spirit, as the claims of the other Sacrament disappear with the Divinity of Christ. Neither could place us, in this system, in communion with this ungenerate God, either in heart and spirit, as the Church could affirm with her living faith in a consubstantial Trinity, or in mind, which was all that the Eunomians would have valued. But for this communion of mind their teacher had provided a better way of his own.

If Eunomius has a title to originality, it must rest on the use he made of this term 'ungenerate,' and it is this peculiar use of it that makes his heresy strange and startling. For 'ungenerate' and 'generate' had been the very terms which the defenders of the *Homoousion* had borrowed from philosophy, to bring home to a cultured but unbelieving world that intimacy between the Father and the Son the mention of which was ever on the Saviour's lips, according to the Gospel records. They had been employed to translate the inmost mystery of the new religion. 'Generate,' which had previously connoted nothing but the opposite of 'ungenerate,' had now been brought into closest correlation and union with the Ungenerate; and expressed that which could not otherwise be expressed, in the current philosophical language. But Eunomius employs the terms in order to destroy that very thing which faith had adopted them to teach—the oneness of the Only-begotten with the God who begat but who is Himself unbegotten. He found these terms within the Church, doing duty, as it were, to make clear that oneness; he employed them, by bringing them back to their former use, to destroy it! Then this dichotomy of his had to be met, *e.g.* by Gregory of Nyssa, with the counter dichotomy of 'created' and 'uncreated,' which, unlike the other, was founded on an *essential* difference, and left that which was within the inviolable circle of the Godhead free for ever from any more dichotomies, whatever other assaults might at any time be made upon it.

'Uncreate, intelligible nature is far removed from such distinctions' (*i.e.* as those of Eunomius), says Gregory (*c. Eunom.* i. 22). 'It does not possess the good by acquisition, or participate only in the goodness of some good which lies above it. . . . It is simple, uniform, incomposite. . . . But it has distinction within itself in keeping with the majesty of its own nature, but not conceived of with regard to quantity, as Eunomius supposes.'

This was the impregnable position that Athanasius also had taken up. To admit that the Son is less than the Father, and the Spirit less than the Son, is to admit, as we have seen, the law of emanation, that is, the gradual and successive degradation of God's substance. By this path Oriental heretics, as well as the Neo-Platonists, had been led to a sort of pantheistic polytheism. Arius had, indeed, tried to resist this tendency, but so far only as to bring back Divinity to the Supreme Being. This was done at the expense of the Divinity of the Son, who was with Arius as much a created intermediate between God and man as one of the Æons. Eunomius treated the Holy Spirit as his master had treated the Son; only by a more complete and decisive method, since his new weapon of ungeneracy created an actual *unlikeness* between the Persons. Arianism, whether the earlier or the later, tended alike to Judaism, and, by making creatures adorable, to Greek polytheism. There was only one way of cutting short the phantasmagoria of Divine emanations, without having recourse to the contradictory hypothesis of Arius; and that was to reject altogether the law of emanations as hitherto accepted. Far from admitting that the Supreme Being is always weakening and degrading Himself in that which emanates from Him, Athanasius lays down the principle that He produces within Himself nothing but what is perfect, and just, and Divine; all that is not perfect is a work, but only a work, of the Divine will, which draws it out of nothing (*i.e.* creates it), and *not out of the Divine substance.*

With regard to the diffusion of Eunomianism, Sozomen says (*HE* vi. 27):

'The heresy of Eunomius was spread from Cilicia and the mountains of Taurus as far as the Hellespont and Constantinople.' In A.D. 380 at Bithynia, near Constantinople, 'multitudes resorted to him; some also gathered from different quarters, a few with the design of testing his principles, and others merely from the desire of listening to his discourses. His reputation reached the ears of the emperor, who would gladly have held a conference with him. But the Empress Flacilla studiously prevented an interview from taking place between them; for she was the most faithful guard of the Nicene doctrines' (*ib.* vii. 6).

At the convention, however, of all the sects, at Theodosius' palace in A.D. 382, Eunomius was present (Socrates, *HE* v. 10). His Ἔκθεσις τῆς πίστεως (to which he added learned notes) was laid before Theodosius in 383. In his answer to Eunomius' Second Book, Gregory of Nyssa finds that Eunomius has still a flock, with whom the former thus expostulated: 'With what eyes will you now gaze upon your guide? I speak to you, O flock of perishing souls!' This could not have been written earlier than A.D. 384.

It was stated at the beginning of this article that Eunomius had been a martyr to his cause, and so he was destined still to be. But it was not till 391 that the Emperor condemned him to banishment to Mœsia. The barbarians, however, drove him from them; and he was brought to Cæsarea, much to the annoyance of the Christians there, who resented the presence amongst them of the enemy of their lost Basil. He died at his birth-place, Dacora in Cappadocia; and his tomb was visited there.

LITERATURE.—The *Apologeticus* of Eunomius in 28 sections is edited by H. Canisius in *Lectiones Antiquæ*, Ingolstadt, 1601–04, i. 172 ff. The beginning and epilogue are in Cave's *Hist. Lit.*, London, 1688, i. 171, Lat. tr. by W. Whiston, in his *Eunomianismus redivivus*, London, 1711. His Ἔκθεσις τῆς πίστεως in the Codex Theodosius is edited by Valesius, in his notes on Socrates, Paris, 1668; by Baluze, in the *Nova Collectio Conciliorum*, Paris, 1683, i. 89; and by Ch. H. Rettberg in his *Marcelliana*, Göttingen, 1794. This is the best edition. See also F. Oehler's ed. of Gregory's 13 Books against Eunomius, in vol. i. of the *Works of Gregory of Nyssa* (Halle, 1865); C. R. W. Klose, *Gesch. und Lehre des Eunomius*, Kiel, 1833; W. Kölling, *Gesch. der arian. Häresie*, Gütersloh, 1875–83; J. Rupp, *Gregors des Bischofs von Nyssa Leben und Meinungen*, Leipzig, 1834; J. A. Fabricius, *Bibl. Græc.*, Hamburg, 1804, ix. 207 ff.

W. MOORE.

EUNUCH.—The operations of castrating males and of spaying females were probably practised on animals earlier than on human beings; and desexualization has always been far more commonly performed on males than on females. Castration of horses was known in Vedic India, as is shown by the frequent occurrence of the proper name *Vadhryaśva* ('He who has castrated horses'), and the repeated mention of the ox beside the bull (*e.g.* *Rigveda*, I. xxxii. 7, X. cii. 12; cf., further, Zimmer, *Altind. Leben*, Berlin, 1879, pp. 231, 226). Homeric Greece was plainly acquainted with the castration of animals (cf. ἔνορχα μῆλα, *Il.* xxiii. 147), and the custom of gelding horses is recorded for the Scythians and Sarmatians by Strabo (p. 312).

1. Methods and purpose of castration.—The most primitive method of castration seems to have been by crushing the testicles, mentioned in *Atharvaveda*, VI. cxxxviii. 2, and implied in a long series of words meaning 'castrated' and connected with bases denoting 'crush' and the like.

Here belong Lat. *capo*, 'capon' (Gr. κόπτω, 'strike'); Old Ir. *molt*, 'wether' (Old Church Slav. *mlatŭ*, 'hammer'); Swab. *raun*, 'gelding' (Skr. *ru-*, 'shatter'); Alban. *treθ*, 'castrate' (Lat. *trudo*, 'thrust'); Gr. θλαθίας, θλιβίας, 'eunuch' (θλάω, θλίβω, 'crush'); Skr. *vadhri*, Gr. ἔθρις, 'eunuch' (Skr. *vadh-*, 'strike,' 'shatter'); O.H.G. *barug*, 'castrated hog,' Old Church Slav. *bravŭ*, 'wether' (Lat. *ferio*, 'strike'). It is also evident, from *Atharvaveda*, VI. cxxxviii. 2, 4–5, that, besides crushing or splitting the testicles with stones, or with a peg, the penis might also be split.

Besides crushing, cutting was also employed, as is shown by such words as Gr. τομίας, 'eunuch' (τέμνω, 'cut'); Lat. *castro*, 'castrate' (Skr. *śās-*, 'cut'); Old Ir. *lún*, 'wether' (Skr. *lu-*, 'cut'); Skr. *nirasṭa*, 'castrated (Skr. *aśri*, 'edge,' 'knife'). The operation of dragging the testicles from the scrotum seems to be implied in Gr. σπάδων, 'eunuch' (σπάω, 'drag'; cf. Skr. *muṣkābarha*, 'castrater' [lit. 'he who puts the testicles outside'], *Atharvaveda*, III. ix. 2); and, if O.H.G. *urfūr*, 'castrated,' Anglo-Sax. *áfýran*, 'castrate,' are connected with Gr. πῦρ, 'fire,' the application of hot iron to the testicles may likewise have been employed (on all these terms, see Schrader, *Reallex. der indogerm. Altertumskunde*, Strassburg, 1901, p. 919; Hirt, *Indogermanen*, do. 1905–07, pp. 291, 658).

A survey of the terms just given shows that castration of human beings was performed in Europe only where Oriental influences were present; and in this case linguistic evidence is not contradicted by any facts thus far known. The reasons for the castration of animals were doubtless the same in early times as they are to-day: greater docility (notably in horses and oxen) and increased savourinesss of meat (as in capons).

Turning to the subject proper of the present art.—the castrated human male, or eunuch—it may be noted that the terms for 'eunuch' give, with perhaps a single exception, no clue as to the reason for the institution of castration. The sources of Skr. *vadhri* and of Gr. θλιβίας, ἔθρις, τομίας, and σπάδων have already been given. The best known term of all, εὐνοῦχος, is of uncertain signification.

The old etymology, found as early as the *Etymologicum Magnum*—ἀπὸ τοῦ τὴν εὐνὴν ἔχειν καὶ ἐπιμελεῖσθαι καὶ φυλάσσειν—and still advanced by Tylor (*EBr* 11, art. 'Eunuch'), by which the word means 'bed-warder,' merits no consideration. Perhaps the best suggestion is that advanced by Jensen, *ZA* i. [1886] 20, who regards εὐνοῦχος as a loan-word from the Sem., comparing Heb. חָנוּךְ, חָנִיךְ, 'trained,' 'tried,' 'experienced' (cf. Syr. *mᵉhaimnā*, 'eunuch' [lit. 'trustworthy,' 'trusted'], and see Lewy, *Sem. Fremdwörter im Gr.*, Berlin, 1895, p. 75).

The Heb. term for 'eunuch' is סָרִיס, which is probably to be regarded, with Jensen, *ZA* vii. [1892] 174, note 1, as borrowed from Assyr. *ša rêši* (*rîši*), 'he who is the head *or* chief,' particularly as this would explain all the offices and duties performed by the סָרִיס in the OT (cf. Zimmern, *ZDMG* liii. [1899] 116, note 2).

EV is, therefore, correct in rendering סָרִיס by 'officer' or 'chamberlain' in the majority of its occurrences, reserving 'eunuch' for passages in which this is obviously the meaning (*e.g.* 2 K 9^{32} 20^{18}=Is 39^{7} $56^{3f.}$; some passages, as Jer 29^{2} 34^{19}, are equally susceptible of either rendering; in any case it seems unnecessary to accept Cheyne's suggestion [*EBi* 1427] that two words originally distinct have been fused in סָרִיס). The precise nature of the operation performed on the ancient Sem. eunuchs is uncertain, but from the antithesis, in Dt 23^{1}, of פְּצוּעַ־דַּכָּה וּכְרוּת שָׁפְכָה (LXX θλαδίας, ἀποκεκομμένος) it is evident that both crushing of the testicles and ablation of the penis must have been among the methods employed (cf. also the Vulg. rendering of the passage, 'eunuchus, attritis vel amputatis testiculis et abscisso veretro').

2. Physical and mental effects of castration.—If castration is performed on a child, and if proper precautions are taken, the operation is not, surgically speaking, a very serious one, although the mortality is enormous among the unfortunate children castrated by African slave-dealers for the Oriental market. After puberty the operation becomes much more grave. In the case of boys, castration prevents the development of the secondary sex-characteristics—the growth of the beard and of hair on the body, and the change of the larynx, the eunuch voice thus approaching the female *timbre*. Males castrated in adult life naturally have the same secondary sex-characteristics as other men. Data are lacking with regard to the castration of girls, though analogically there should be no pubic or axillary hair, and no characteristic development of the pelvis and breasts. Oophorectomy after puberty is commonly alleged to result—though the secondary sex-characteristics remain—in a certain approximation to the male type, as in the quality of the voice and in the growth of hair on the face. Castration of the male does not immediately result in loss of *libido*. On the contrary, the castrate can for some time—at least a year—have sexual intercourse and emit a quasi-semen (probably the secretion of the prostate gland). Accordingly, in the degenerate days of the Roman Empire, eunuchs were regularly made, soon after reaching puberty, for the sensual gratification of Roman dames, particularly 'quod abortivo non est opus' (Juvenal, *Sat.* vi. 365 ff.; cf. Seneca, *de Matrimonio*, ed. Hase, p. 429; Martial, *Epigr.* vi. 2; *Thousand Nights and One Night*, tr. Payne, London, 1882–84, i. 368). Later, however, erections occur much more seldom—almost never after 18 months from the operation—and there is no sensation of seminal ejaculation. In the female oophorectomy usually annihilates the sexual impulse, but there are many exceptions, for in some females *libido* is increased after removal of both uterus and ovaries.

Surgically, castration is generally performed to relieve disease of the testicle, bladder, and prostate gland in the male, and of the ovaries and uterus in the female. In males it is also often done to relieve urinary weakness (retention of urine, etc.). Oophorectomy for ovarian disease of the female hastens the physical changes usually ascribed to the menopause, unless, as is often done, a small portion of ovarian tissue is left *in situ*, or is engrafted upon the uterine body.

The operation of castration affects the body chemistry (metabolism) very strongly. The phosphates in the urine and the carbonic acid in the expired breath diminish, while the weight of the body increases. Many spayed women grow fat and dyspeptic. Congestion to the head and thorax and excessive perspiration appear and may continue for years. Melancholia is developed in a large percentage of cases, together with loss of memory, irritability of temper, impairment of vision, nightmare, insomnia, and skin affections.

On mentality castration appears to produce no essential change. It is true that eunuchs are usually inclined to be malevolent and unscrupulous, that they are apt to be either extremely abased or inordinately haughty. Yet this is due not so much to the physical results of the operation as to the fact that by the hand of their fellow-men they have been put outside the pale of normal humanity, and they feel a not unnatural resentment, accentuated by the aloofness usually felt by all who are marked off, by mental or physical peculiarities, from the ordinary mass of mankind. Nowhere, perhaps, has the mixture of native ability and acquired malignancy been more strikingly exemplified than in the case of Āghā Muḥammad, who, castrated in early life by 'Ādil Shāh, was able to overthrow the Zend dynasty in Persia and, in 1796, to found in blood the Qājār house (cf. Horn, *GIrP* ii. 594–596). But that cruelty is an accident, and that mental and spiritual powers are unabated, is proved by the famous instances of Origen and Abelard (*qq.v.*).

Certain peoples are reported to have practised the excision of one testicle only, as is recorded of the Hottentots by Kolben (*Beschreib. des Vorgebirgs der guten Hoffnung*, Frankfurt, 1745, p. 147). Their motive was to prevent the birth of twins, an event of such ill omen to many peoples (see TWINS); and, Kolben adds, no woman would marry a man unless his left testicle had been excised in childhood, the operation being performed at intervals of eight or nine years on all who might be of the proper age. In Ponape, one of the Caroline Islands, the left testicle is extirpated with a sharp bamboo at the age of seven or eight (on Niuatabutahu, in the Friendly Islands, the age is 12–14), the purpose being to avoid orchitis; and the man on whom this has been performed is deemed particularly handsome by the girls (Finsch, *ZE* xxii. [1880] 316).

The general function of eunuchs was to serve as a superior sort of slave, particularly—in view of their sterility—as guardians of the harîm. It would appear that the castration of human beings was first suggested by analogy with that of animals (cf. Xenoph. *Cyrop.* VII. v. 60–65)—it was supposed to make men more tractable as slaves, and, by depriving them of the distractions of family life, to render them more faithful to their masters. But, effective as this proves in the case of animals, it is far otherwise in the case of man; and the history of the eunuch system is one stained by vilest intrigue and darkened by utter corruption.

3. Birthplace and diffusion of the practice.—Where castration started is an unsolved question, but the tradition recorded by Ammianus Marcellinus (XIV. vi. 17), that it was instituted by the legendary Semiramis, would seem to point to the Mesopotamian region as its first home. Eunuchs were early known in Assyria, where they apparently acted as generals and governors (Jensen, *ap.* Manitius, *ZA* xxiv. [1910] 109, note 1; cf. esp. Klauber, 'Assyr. Beamtentum,' *LSSt* v. 3 [1910], p. 117). They were in Israel at least as early as the reign of Jehu (2 K 9[32]), and in Persia (Brisson, *de Regio Persarum Principatu*, ed. Lederlin, Strassburg, 1710, *passim*), in Greece by the time of the Persian wars (Herod. viii. 105), in Egypt during the XXth dynasty (1202–1102 B.C.; Rawlinson, *Hist. of Anc. Egypt*, London, 1881, ch. xxii.), in Ethiopia (Ac 8[27]), in India at an early date (*Mahābhārata* III. cl. 46); they exercised an evil power at the courts of Gordianus III., Constantius, Honorius, and Arcadius (Gibbon, *Decline and Fall*, chs. vii., xix., xxxii., xxxiii.); and they were introduced into China in the 8th cent. B.C. (cf. Stent, *Chines. Eunuchen*, Leipzig, 1879).

4. The eunuch priest.—Far more important in the present connexion—and far more difficult—is the problem of the origin of the eunuch priest. The Ephesian Artemis was served not only by virgins, but by eunuchs, the name of the latter—Μεγάβυζοι (i.e. **Bagabuxša*, 'having salvation through the Deity' [Justi, *Iran. Namenbuch*, Marburg, 1895, p. 57])—betraying their Oriental origin (Strabo, p. 641); and the priests of Atargatis were also eunuchs (*ERE* ii. 166 f.). A goddess called Hecate—probably an amalgamation of the great mother-goddess of Asia Minor—worshipped at Lagina (the modern Ileina, 2 hours north of Stratonica, Caria), had among her servants eunuchs and *hierodouloi* (Gruppe, *Gr. Mythol. und Religionsgesch.*, Munich, 1906, p. 263); and the eunuch priests of Cybele are universally known (*ERE* iv. 377).

The names applied to the eunuch priests of Cybele and Attis—βάκηλοι and γάλλοι—are of unknown signification. The latter word was derived by the Greeks and Romans (e.g. *Etymolog. Mag.*, *s.v.*; Ovid, *Fasti*, iv. 361 ff.) from the river Gallus in Phrygia, but the stream was more probably so called in honour of some deity; and the attempt to connect γάλλος with Heb. גָּלַל, 'roll,' is merely fantastic (cf. Gruppe, 1542, note 2).

It is in the cult of Cybele (*q.v.*) that the question of the origin of the eunuch priest must centre. That Attis (*q.v.*), her male partner, castrated himself was the subject of very divergent conjectures in ancient times (*ERE* ii. 217; Gruppe, 1542 f.); yet it must be remembered that to ancient religions the problem of origins is in great measure indifferent, the chief duty being minute conformity to traditional rites (cf. Hepding, *Attis, seine Mythen und sein Kult*, Giessen, 1903, p. 98).

The castration of a god is familiar from the Gr. legends regarding Uranos and Kronos (Gruppe, 356, 1114, note 1), although these seem to have little in common with the story of Attis. The foundation of the myth of the mutilation of Uranos and Kronos is probably one 'of the violent separation of the earth and sky, which some races, for example the Polynesians, suppose to have originally clasped each other in a close embrace' (Frazer, *Attis, Adonis, and Osiris*, London, 1907, p. 237; Lang, *Custom and Myth*, do. 1884, p. 45 ff., and *Myth, Ritual, and Religion*, do. 1887, i. 299 ff.; for a convenient summary of the Polynesian myth, see *ERE* iv. 175[a]). Gruppe (1112) is inclined to explain the stories as borrowed from a Sem. source given by Philo Byblius, as quoted by Eusebius, *Præp. evang.* I. x. 12, but Gruppe's explanation, that the series—'Επίγειος (Αὐτόχθων); El, Demarus; Uranos, Kronos, Zeus—represents three periods, viz. unrestricted production, absolute cessation of production, and the orderly and regulated production of like from like (as is the case in the organic world), seems far less likely than the interpretation advanced by Lang and Frazer. But, if the myths of the mutilation of Uranos and Kronos are cosmogonic, it seems equally evident that the origin of the legend of the self-castration of Attis was ætiological, so that, as Frazer declares (p. 221), 'the story of the self-mutilation of Attis is clearly an attempt to account for the self-mutilation of his priests, who regularly castrated themselves on entering the service of the goddess.'

But why, granting Frazer's explanation of the myth of the self-mutilation of Attis, did the *galli* emasculate themselves? First of all, the *galli* were priests of Cybele, a mother-goddess. The cult of this divinity, especially at Rome, is fairly well known (*ERE* ii. 217 f.; and esp. Hepding, *op. cit.*). Here we may note particularly that the self-castration of the *galli* took place probably on 24th March—the third day of the annual festival in honour of the Great Mother the *dies sanguinis*, which typified the grief of Cybele for the death of Attis, and on which her devotees, headed by the *archigallus*, gashed their bodies with potsherds or slashed them with knives to bespatter the altar and the sacred tree with their blood (cf. Frazer, 223, with references, to which may be added the quotations from Ambrosiaster by Cumont, *RHLR* viii. [1903] 423, note 1). We also learn much concerning the *galli* from the Latin accounts of their processions (*e.g.* Lucret. ii. 600 ff.; Ovid, *Fasti*, iv. 181 ff.).

Here one feature must be deemed peculiarly significant, even though little attention seems thus far to have been given it by those who have studied the Attis-Cybele cycle—the *galli* wear female garb.

After his castration Attis wore female clothing (Lucian, *de Dea Syr.* xv.). Varro (*Men.* cxx. [ed. Bücheler]) describes the *galli* as 'partim venusta muliebri ornati stola'; Arnobius (*adv. Gentes*, v. 17), as wearing 'volucra mollium velamenta lanarum'; and the pseudo-Cyprian (*ad Senatorem ex Christiana religione ad idolum servitutem conversum*, 9), as clad 'tunicis muliebribus.' Most important of all in this connexion is St. Augustine (*de Civ. Dei*, vii. 26), who expresses his scorn of the *galli*, who, in their processions, were to be seen 'madidis capillis, facie dealbata, fluentibus membris, incessu femineo.' Small wonder that satirists and Christian apologists even charged the *galli* with being sodomites (Martial, *Epigr.* III. lxxxi. 3–6; Justin Martyr, *Apol.* i. 27)—a charge that was renewed by Rosenbaum (*Gesch. der Lustseuche im Alterthume*, Halle, 1845, p. 120), though there seems to be no certain evidence for the accusation.

In like manner those who castrated themselves in honour of the Syrian Astarte of Hierapolis also wore women's clothing. After performing the mutilation upon themselves, they ran through the city, carrying in their hands the severed parts, which they cast into some house; and the inmates were required to furnish the newly castrated with female attire and female adornments, which were worn by the eunuchs for the remainder of their lives (Lucian, li.).

Outside of Asia Minor the eunuch priest is rare, although Frazer (p. 225, note 4) has succeeded in collecting a few instances.

Among the Ba-sundi and Ba-bwende of the Congo many youths are castrated 'in order to more fittingly offer themselves to the phallic worship, which increasingly prevails as we advance from the coast to the interior' (Johnston, *JAI* xiii. [1884] 473, and *The River Congo*, London, 1884, p. 409). In the western part of the Bellary District of Madras, and in the adjoining portions of Dharwar and Mysore, men who are born eunuchs or in some way deformed are sometimes dedicated to a goddess named Huligamma. They wear female attire and might be mistaken for women. Also men who are, or believe themselves to be, impotent will vow to dress as women in the hope of recovering their virility (Fawcett, *JASB* ii. [1890–92] 331, 343 f.). In Pegu, at a feast called the 'collock,' 'some Women are chosen out of the People assembled, to dance a Dance to the Gods of the Earth. Hermaphrodites, who are numerous in this Country, are generally chosen, if there are enow present to make a Set for the Dance' (Hamilton, *New Account of the East Indies*, Edinburgh, 1727, ii. 57 f.).

What, then, is the origin of the eunuch priest, dedicated to a goddess of fertility and clothed in female garb? Leaving out of account the African usage, which is probably connected with religious sodomy—a custom also widely spread among the ancient Semites and the American aborigines—and likewise dismissing as fantastic the theory reported by Hippolytus (*Refut. omnium hær.* v. 17), on Naassenian authority, that by his castration Attis was raised to 'the celestial essence, where, they say, there is neither female nor male, but a new creation, a new man, who is androgynous,' we may note the principal explanations that have been advanced.

Gruppe (1542–1546) supposes that the self-castration of the *galli* was to secure chastity (cf. Hepding, 162), in conformity with an ascetic desire to renounce the joys of the world, although the idea of the marriage of Cybele and Attis still survived in the practice of burying the severed parts in the earth or in subterranean chambers sacred to Cybele. Westermarck (*MI* ii. 411) suggests that the eunuchization may have been due to 'the idea that the deity is jealous of the chastity of his or her servants,' his basis being a theory of Lactantius (*Div. Instit.* i. 17): 'Deum mater et amavit formosum adolescentem, et eundem cum pellice deprehensum exsectis virilibus semivirum reddidit; et ideo nunc sacra eius a gallis sacerdotibus celebrantur' (further references in Gruppe, 1542, note 3). To say, with Jeremias (in Chantepie de la Saussaye, *Lehrbuch der Religionsgesch.*[3], Tübingen, 1905, i. 361), that 'self-castration is the dedication to the goddess [Astarte]. The castrates are dedicated to the divinity like the Vestals,' is an ambiguous platitude. Frazer (p. 223 f.) conjectures that the self-castration of the *galli*, like the self-gashing of the other devotees, was intended to strengthen the dead Attis for his resurrection.

'Wrought up to the highest pitch of religious excitement, they [the *galli*] dashed the severed portions of themselves against the image of the cruel goddess. These broken instruments of fertility were afterwards reverently wrapt up and buried in the earth or in subterranean chambers sacred to Cybele, where, like the offering of blood, they may have been deemed instrumental in recalling Attis to life and hastening the general resurrection of nature, which was then bursting into leaf and blossom in the vernal sunshine. Some confirmation of this conjecture is furnished by the savage story that the mother of Attis conceived by putting in her bosom a pomegranate sprung from the severed genitals of a man-monster named Agdestis, a sort of double of Attis.

If there is any truth in this conjectural explanation of the custom, we can readily understand why other Asiatic goddesses of fertility were served in like manner by eunuch priests. These feminine deities required to receive from their male ministers, who personated the divine lovers, the means of discharging their beneficent functions: they had themselves to be impregnated by the life-giving energy before they could transmit it to the world.'

Hepding, who, like a number of other scholars, derives the self-mutilation of Attis from the Semites (pp. 128, 161 f., 178, 217), attributes it in part to the anæsthesia-producing frenzy of the general character of the orgiastic rites (pp. 129 f., 160 f.); but this is only a partial explanation, applicable, indeed, to the gashing with sherds and knives, but hardly sufficient to account for the great act of self-castration. He is, however, probably correct in maintaining (p. 127 f.) that this characteristic was introduced subsequent to the time of Herodotus, whose account of the Attis myth (iv. 76) contains no intimation of any orgiastic gallic rites.

Yet all these theories seem inadequate, especially as they do not account for the subsequent donning of female dress and for the general adoption of feminism. The only explanation which seems to fit the facts is that of Farnell (*CGS* iii. 300 f.):

'Even the self-mutilation necessary for the attainment of the status of the eunuch-priest may have arisen from the ecstatic craving to assimilate oneself to the goddess and to charge oneself with her power, the female dress being thereupon assumed to complete the transformation.'

The assumption of women's garb by certain classes of effeminate priests is wide-spread (see above, p. 70, and cf. Frazer, 428 ff.), and in the case before us it may have been furthered by the principle of impersonation often associated with dress (see above, pp. 51ᵇ, 65ᵇ). It seems probable that the *galli*, as devotees of the Great Mother, first donned the garments of her own sex; and that later, to make the resemblance between themselves and their divinity as close as possible, they removed the organs which had rendered them conspicuously not of her sex, and whose ablation made them approximately similar to her. Another contributing factor may perhaps have been that they were thus also assimilated to her virgin attendants of true female sex.

If the explanation here favoured is correct, there would be an interesting analogue in the present writer's suggestion regarding the origin of the Australian operation of *ariltha* (*ERE* iii. 666ᵇ). Moreover, just as in the case of female circumcision (*ib.* 669), there seems to have been a later, reverse tendency to make the female and male types of the devotees of Cybele more alike by amputation of the *mammæ* (Arnobius, *adv. Nationes*, v. 13 f.; cf. also Gruppe, 1545, note 5, whose explanation, however, seems scarcely plausible).

Even within the history of Christianity sporadic instances of self-mutilation have occurred. Of these the best known is that of Origen, who later bitterly repented his un-Christian act, to which he had been led by his incorrect exegesis of Mt 19¹², combined with his anxiety to avoid all scandal in his association with his pupils (Euseb. *HE* vi. 8). In similar fashion

'Leontius made himself an eunuch to avoid suspicion in his converse with the virgin Eustolium: but he was deposed from the office of presbyter for the fact, and it gave occasion to the Council of Nice to renew the ancient canon against such practices; so that, when the Arians afterward ordained him bishop of Antioch, the historians [Socrates, *HE* ii. 26; Theodoret, *HE* ii. 24] tell us, the Catholics generally declaimed against his ordination as uncanonical' (Bingham, *Antiquities of the Chr. Church*, ed. R. Bingham, Jr., Oxford, 1855, ii. 47 f.).

This form of mutilation is, as is well known, the characteristic which gives its name to the fanatical Russian sect of Skoptzy ('castraters'—the writer's rendering, 'circumcisers,' in *ERE* iii. 667ᵇ, is wrong), who also, in addition to mutilation of the female genitals, amputate one or both of the breasts (cf. E. Pelikan, *Gerichtlich-medizin. Untersuchungen über das Skopzenthum in Russland*, tr. Iwanoff, Giessen, 1876). St. Augustine (*de Haer.* xxxvii.), it is true, states that 'the Valesians castrate both themselves and their guests, thinking that they should in this way serve God'; but the existence of these Arabo-Christian heretics is too doubtful for their practices to be considered here, and the Council alleged to have been held in Achæa about the middle of the 3rd cent. to condemn them appears to be equally dubious (cf. Hefele, *Hist. des conciles*, Fr. tr., Paris, 1907 ff., i. 164).

The Skoptzy have not been the only ones who have castrated women. According to Athenæus (xii. 11 [p. 515]), Adramytis thus mutilated women in Lydia, 'using them instead of male eunuchs'; but the most interesting instance is that declared to exist among some Central Australian tribes.

On the authority of Purcell (*Verh. der Berliner Gesellsch. für Anthropol., Ethnol. und Urgesch.*, 1893, p. 288), which is not, however, substantiated by Spencer-Gillen, the operation of *euriltha*, or spaying, is performed on certain selected girls from 10 to 12 years old. The older men prepare a long roll of emu feathers with a loop of hair at the end. This is thrust into the vagina and is left there for some days, after which the old men pull it out, thus tearing away part of the womb. Three days later a small stone knife is inserted, and the neck of the womb is cut horizontally and vertically, the down of geese or eagle-hawks being then introduced, and lumps of fat being used as salve. When the wound is healed, the operation of female circumcision (described in *ERE* iii. 667 f.) is performed. The alleged purpose of this female castration is to prevent the women from bearing children to foreign tribes, and to save them from being encumbered by infants when going through dry and barren country; but, in view of the fact that the Australians do not know that procreation is connected with the sexual act (*ERE* iii. 666ᵇ), this explanation must be accepted with reserve. Milucho-Maclay (*ZE* xiv. [1882] 26 f.) describes a girl who had undergone this operation as having only slightly developed hips, breasts, and *mons Veneris*, and with some hairs growing on her chin. The purpose is said to be the furtherance of prostitution. The same authority was told by E. P. Ramsay, curator of the Sydney museum, that the well-known explorer MacGillivray had seen at Cape York a woman oophorectomized to prevent the birth of dumb children, she herself having been born dumb. Similarly, Roberts (cited by Bischoff in Müller's *Archiv für Anat., Physiol., und wissenschaftliche Medizin*, 1843, p. clix f.) records having seen female eunuchs in India; here again these women, whose age was about 25, approximated in lack of pelvic development, etc., very closely to the male type.

5. Castration as a punishment.—Attention has already been drawn in the artt. CRIMES AND PUNISHMENTS (vol. iv. pp. 251ᵇ, 255ᵇ, 256ᵇ, 266ᵇ, 304ᵇ; cf. also ETHICS AND MORALITY [Celtic], III. § 7), to castration as a punishment. Except in Frisian law, where this was inflicted on a robber of a temple, being preliminary to the penalty of death, emasculation was normally a punishment for rape and similar crimes; and occasionally, as in Welsh law, it was inflicted only when the criminal could not pay the heavy fines required.

In Egypt, castration was the penalty for adultery (Post, *Bausteine für eine allgem. Rechtswissensch.*, Oldenburg, 1880–81, i. 208), while in India a Śūdra who committed adultery with the wife of an Ārya, or who insolently made water on a high-caste man, suffered amputation of the penis (Manu, viii. 282, 374); and a Brāhman who dishonoured the bed of his teacher had, as one of the three modes of death offered him, the option of himself amputating his penis and scrotum, and of then advancing, holding them in his hand, to the south-west (the direction of Nirṛti, 'Destruction') until he should fall dead (Manu, xi. 105). Similarly, those who have sexual relations with women of other castes than their own (excepting, of course, lawful marriages with women of lower castes), who cause animals to be killed, or who violate their teacher's wife, are punished, according to *Mahābhārata*, XIII. cxlv. 52 f., in their next incarnation by being born *klība* (which may mean either 'eunuch,' 'impotent,' or even 'hermaphrodite'). The laws of Alfred the Great (ii. 25) punished by emasculation a servant who raped a female servant (*MI* i. 251), and all male relatives of a Chinaman condemned for treason were doomed to death, excepting the young boys, who were castrated for service in the Imperial palace (*ib.* i. 45, with references).

6. Social and religious status of eunuchs.—The social status of the eunuch has always been of the lowest. (In the following references to Skr. texts it should be noted that the words *klība*, *vadhri*, *ṣaṇḍha*, etc., are somewhat ambiguous in meaning, denoting both 'eunuch' and 'impotent.') The *Mahābhārata* (VIII. xlv. 25) is very explicit here:

'Mlechchhas [barbarians, non-Aryans] are the dirt of humanity; oil-men are the dirt of Mlechchhas; eunuchs are the dirt of oil-men; and they who appoint Kṣatriyas as priests in their sacrifices are the dirt of eunuchs.'

A eunuch, or 'long-haired man,' is neither man nor woman (*Śatapatha Brāhmaṇa*, V. i. 2. 14, iv. 1. 1 f., XII. vii. 2. 12; cf. *Atharvaveda*, VI. cxxxviii. 2; *Mahābhārata*, V. clx. 115; and the references given by Bloomfield, *SBE* xlii. 538 f.), and there is reason to believe that they ministered to unnatural sensuality (R. Schmidt, *Beiträge zur ind. Erotik*, Leipzig, 1902, p. 211). They could not inherit property (*Āpastamba D.Ś.* II. vi. 14. 1; *Gautama D.Ś.* xxviii. 43; *Vāsiṣṭha D.Ś.* xvii. 53 f.), and were to be maintained by the king, who was to take what would have been their inheritance if they had been normal men (*Vāsiṣṭha D.Ś.* xix. 35 f.). They were excluded from the *śrāddha*, or sacrifice to the *manes* (Manu, iii. 165), of which they were unworthy (*ib.* iii. 150), even as they were unfit for the ordeal by sacred libation (*Nārada D.Ś.* i. 332). No Brāhman might eat of a sacrifice performed by eunuchs (Manu, iv. 205 f.), nor might he consume any food prepared by them (*ib.* iv. 211; *Vāsiṣṭha D.Ś.* xiv. 2; *Āpastamba D.Ś.* I. vi. 18. 27; 19. 15) or accept alms offered by them (*Vāsiṣṭha D.Ś.* xiv. 19). They were forbidden to serve as witnesses (*Nārada D.Ś.* i. 179), and were deemed incapable of keeping a secret (*Milindapañha*, IV. i. 6). In contempt for their effeminacy, they might not be struck in battle (Manu, vii. 19), a special penalty being imposed for killing them (*ib.* xi. 134; *Gautama D.Ś.* xxii. 23). Being sterile, and so essentially ill-omened, the very sight of them was defiling (Manu, iii. 239 f.), and they were forbidden to be near the king during his consultations (*Mahābhārata*, XII. lxxxiii. 55), while the neat-herd Gañjā laments (Temple, *Legends of the Panjâb*, Bombay, 1884–1900, ii. 396):

'When I was in my mother's womb, eunuchs danced at the door; and so I am lame, and have no hair on my head.'

A eunuch might not be converted (*Milindapañha*, IV. viii. 53), nor might he be ordained (*Mahāvagga*, i. 61), and a *bhikkhu* was forbidden to castrate himself (*Chullavagga*, v. 7). Eunuchs were permitted to marry (Manu, ix. 79, 204; cf. 'Muslim' section below). Dancers, who are of low caste in India, were castrated (*Mahābhārata*, III. xlvi. 50), and the dancing of eunuchs is already referred to in *Atharvaveda*, VIII. vi. 11. In the *puruṣamedha*, or human sacrifice of the Vedic period, a eunuch was the victim offered to Misfortune [*Pāpman*] and —in this case the victim being neither of Brāhman nor of Śūdra caste—to Prajāpati (*Vājasaneya Saṃh.* xxx. 5, 22).

Among the Hebrews the eunuch was excluded from the assembly of the Lord (Dt 23^{2} [Heb.]), though in the prophetic period the eunuchs that kept the Sabbath and, holding to the covenant of the Lord, pleased Him were to receive, in His house and within His walls, 'a memorial and a name better than of sons and of daughters; I will give them an everlasting name, that shall not be cut off' (Is 56^{3-5}), while from the earliest days of the Church the eunuch has been freely admitted as a layman (Ac $8^{27ff.}$). The question of the ordination of eunuchs has been more perplexing, for, as in the Jewish ritual, only the physically perfect should minister at the altar—a rule which is firmly observed by all Catholic communions. One born a eunuch might be ordained, as was Dorotheus of Antioch (Euseb. *HE* vii. 32), and so might one who had been castrated by a barbarian master, as was Tigris of Constantinople (Socrates, *HE* vi. 15; Sozomen, *HE* viii. 24); but not those who emasculated themselves from pretence of piety or from fear of committing fornication (Gennad. *de Eccl. dogmat.* lxxii.; First Nicene Council, can. 1; Second Arles Council, can. 7; cf. Bingham, ii. 45–48; the rulings have become part of Canon Law).

The whole matter is summed up in the *Apostolic Canons*, xxi.–xxiv.:

εὐνοῦχος εἰ μὲν ἐξ ἐπηρείας ἀνθρώπων ἐγένετό τις, ἢ ἐν διωγμῷ ἀφῃρέθη τὰ ἀνδρῶν, ἢ οὕτως ἔφυ, καί ἐστιν ἄξιος, γινέσθω [*sc.* ἐπίσκοπος].

ὁ ἀκρωτηριάσας ἑαυτὸν μὴ γινέσθω κληρικός· αὐτοφονευτὴς γάρ ἐστιν ἑαυτοῦ καὶ τῆς τοῦ Θεοῦ δημιουργίας ἐχθρός.

εἴ τις κληρικὸς ὢν ἑαυτὸν ἀκρωτηριασει, καθαιρείσθω, φονευτὴς γάρ ἐστιν ἑαυτοῦ.

λαικὸς ἑαυτὸν ἀκρωτηριάσας ἀφοριζέσθω ἔτη τρία· ἐπίβουλος γάρ ἐστι τῆς ἑαυτοῦ ζωῆς.

Already in the Roman Empire both Domitian and Nerva had forbidden castration (Sueton. *Domit.* vii.; Dio Cass. lxvii. 2, lxviii. 2), and this prohibition was repeated in the Digest (xlviii. 8. 4. 2—'nemo liberum servumve invitum sinentemve castrare debet).' Such has also been the position of the Church, the only exception being the practice of castrating boys to preserve their voices, notably for the papal choir. The authorities cited by St. Alfonso Liguori (*Theol. mor.* IV. iv. no. 374) make the custom dependent on the question whether the public welfare promoted by the sweet singing of the *castrati* was of sufficient magnitude to render licit a grave mutilation. St. Alfonso himself inclines to the negative, and the whole practice was definitely condemned by Benedict XIV. (*de Syn. dioces.* XI. vii. no. 4 f.). Since that time there have been no *castrati* in the service of the Church, although the utterly indefensible custom of having male sopranos on the Italian operatic stage lingered on until late in the 19th century. Marriage of a eunuch was declared invalid by the Constitution *Cum frequenter* of Sixtus V. (28th June 1587).

7. Ethical bearing of castration.—The ethical problem of castration has recently come to the front in the question of the sterilization of certain classes of criminals and defectives. The operation, called vasectomy, consists in making an incision into the scrotum and severing the *vas deferens*, the wound being closed by the contraction of the cremaster muscle, and no further medical attention being required. (A similar, but more difficult, operation on the female is oophorectomy by dividing the Fallopian tubes.) The result of vasectomy is sterility, although *libido* is not impaired, and the sexual act may be performed just as before the operation, except that there is no emission of semen. Besides preventing the procreation of offspring likely to inherit the defective or criminal traits of their parents, vasectomy is said to put a stop to such vices as onanism, and it is declared to be absolutely without prejudice to the physical or mental health of the patient (cf. *Journ. Amer. Med. Assoc.*, 4th Dec. 1909; *Maryland Med. Journ.*, Sept. 1910; *Med. Record*, 11th Feb. 1911; *Pearson's Mag.*, Nov. 1909). The operation is widely advocated in the United States, and laws providing for it have been adopted by many individual States. Of these an excellent type is one passed in New Jersey, 21 April 1911 (although up to the date of writing [April 1912], no provision whatever has been made for its enforcement), 'to authorize and provide for the sterilization of feeble-minded (including idiots, imbeciles, and morons), epileptics, rapists, certain criminals, and other defectives.'

After stating that the Board of Examiners shall consist of a surgeon and neurologist, appointed by the Governor by and with the advice of the Senate, and acting with the Commissioner of Charities and Corrections—their duties being 'to examine into the mental and physical condition of the feeble-minded, epileptic, certain criminal and other defective inmates confined in the several reformatories, charitable and penal institutions in the counties and State'—the law proceeds as follows:

'The criminals who shall come within the operation of this law shall be those who have been convicted of the crime of rape, or of such succession of offences against the criminal law as in the opinion of this board of examiners shall be deemed to be sufficient evidence of confirmed criminal tendencies.

Upon application of the superintendent or other administrative officer of any institution in which such inmates are or may be confined, or upon its own motion, the said board of examiners may call a meeting to take evidence and examine into the mental and physical condition of such inmates confined as aforesaid; and if said board of examiners, in conjunction with the chief physician of the institution, unanimously find that procreation is inadvisable, and that there is no probability that the condition of such inmate so examined will improve to such an extent as to render procreation by such inmate advisable, it shall be lawful to perform such operation for the prevention of procreation as shall be decided by said board of examiners to be most effective; and thereupon it shall and may be lawful for any surgeon qualified under the laws of this State, under the direction of the chief physician of said institution, to perform such operation; previous to said hearing the said board shall apply to any judge of the Court of Common Pleas, of the county in which said person is confined, for the assignment of counsel to represent the person to be examined, said counsel to act at said hearing and in any subsequent proceedings, and no order made by said board of examiners shall become effective until five days after it shall have been filed with the clerk of the Court of Common Pleas, of the county in which said examination is held, and a copy shall have been served upon the counsel appointed to represent the person examined, proof of service of the said copy of the order to be filed with the clerk of the Court of Common Pleas. All orders made under the provisions of this act shall be subject to review by the Supreme Court or any justice thereof, and said court may upon appeal from any order grant a stay which shall be effective until such appeal shall have been decided. . . .

No surgeon performing an operation under the provisions of this law shall be held to account therefor, but the order of the board of examiners shall be a full warrant and authority therefor.

The record taken upon the examination of every such inmate, signed by the said board of examiners, shall be preserved in the institution where such inmate is confined, and a copy thereof filed with the Commissioner of Charities and Corrections, and one year after the performing of the operation the superintendent or other administrative officer of the institution wherein such inmate is confined shall report to the board of examiners the condition of the inmate and the effect of such operation upon such inmate. A copy of the report shall be filed with the record of the examination.'

Such measures, while approving themselves very generally to purely secular views of the State and to such medical men and sociologists as consider only the physical side of humanity, are not, however, such a panacea as they appear at first sight. Indeed, from the merely secular side it is only too obvious how readily vasectomy lends itself, in the unscrupulous hands that will, unfortunately, be ready in multitudes, to 'race suicide' and to the most unbridled licentiousness, which then need fear no 'trouble' in the shape of children.

The problem does not appear thus far to have been considered by the Protestant clergy, at least officially; but the Roman Church has devoted considerable study to it, and a lively controversy has been waged, pending decision from the Vatican, in the *Eccles. Rev.* (xlii. [1910] 271-275, 346-348, 474 f., 599-602; xliii. [1910] 70-84, 310-329, 356-358, 553-558; xliv. [1911] 679-705; xlv. [1911] 71-77, 85-98; cf. also *ZKT*, 1911). The results of this discussion may be summarized as follows:

No one can licitly submit to the operation of vasectomy (1) to avoid the procreation of children, (2) to avoid the procreation of degenerates (the way to avoid this is to abstain absolutely from coition, since every sexual act for mere voluptuous pleasure is mortal sin), or (3) to avoid onanism (see St. Thomas Aquinas, *Summa*, IIa. IIae. quæs. lxv. a. 1, *ad* 3; cf. also the citations from Gennadius, the Councils, and *Apostolic Canons*, above, p. 583). The only cases in which vasectomy is licit are for the cure of grave pathological conditions, such as severe erethism arising from disease. Vasectomy is a grave mutilation, and grave mutilations are licit only to save the life of the patient on whom they are performed. But, as proposed by the laws under consideration, vasectomy destroys organs created by God for the propagation of the race, a duty incumbent on man—unless vowed to a life of chastity, even in the married state—toward (1) God, that creatures may come into being to praise Him in this world and to enjoy Him in eternity; toward (2) nature, for the continuance of the race; and toward (3) society, for its strengthening and continuation. The gravest diseases, *e.g.* leprosy, do not constitute an impediment to marriage. Vasectomy cannot, therefore, be performed on the willing. From this it follows that no surgeon can licitly perform vasectomy; nor can the State licitly enact it, for it has no licit right to create impediments to marriage, nor can it mutilate the innocent (under which category the feeble-minded and epileptics certainly come), while in the case of criminals it would compel them, should they perform the sexual act after vasectomy, to commit mortal sin, whereas before the operation the act would not necessarily be sinful.

It may be suggested that what the State can and should do is to confine degenerates and defectives until cured, if they are curable; or, if incurable, for life; that the perils which, waiving entirely theological considerations, may arise from the legalizing of vasectomy have not been duly recognized; and that it is at least open to question whether, in the case of rapists and other criminals, vasectomy does not come within the ban of the Eighth Amendment to the Constitution of the United States, which explicitly declares that 'cruel and unusual punishment' shall not be inflicted.

LITERATURE.—The principal references are given in the course of the article. To these may be added H. H. Ploss, *Das Kind*², Leipzig, 1884, i. 340, ii. 418; C. Rieger, *Kastration in rechtlicher, socialer und vitaler Hinsicht*, Jena, 1911; P. J. Möbius, *Über die Wirkungen der Kastration*, Halle, 1903. (G. Pinot's *Étude médico-légale sur la castration*, Lyons, 1894, is valueless.) The writer's thanks are due to Dr. Ernest M. Lyon, of Newark, N.J., for assistance in the surgical portion of the art., and to Dr. Arno Pöbel, of Johns Hopkins University, for the references to the Assyr.-Bab. eunuchs.

LOUIS H. GRAY.

EUNUCH (Muslim).—In general every mutilation of men and beasts was forbidden by the Prophet (*e.g.* al-Bukhārī, *al-Dhabā'iḥ wal-ṣaid*, 25). Moreover, if we may trust Muslim tradition, Muhammad expressly enjoined his followers not to make themselves or others eunuchs. One day Uthmān ibn Maẓ'ūn asked permission from the Prophet to castrate himself that he might not be tempted to commit fornication. But this was strongly disapproved by Muhammad. 'He who castrates himself or another does not belong to my followers,' he said, 'for castration in Islām may consist only in fasting' (see *Mishkāt al-masābīh*, a collection of the most authentic traditions, tr. A. N. Matthews, Calcutta, 1809, i. 151). It is also related that Muhammad said: 'Let him who cannot marry betake himself to fasting; this will be for him like castration' (al-Bukhārī, *Ṣaum*, 10). These and other sayings of the Prophet are repeated in various forms in the accredited collections of Muslim tradition.

But, although castration is thus strictly forbidden by Muhammadan law, slaves who had undergone this operation were highly appreciated in Muslim countries, and the value of a eunuch was always much greater than that of another slave. This appreciation has caused the continuation of this evil in a great part of the Muslim world; for the slave-traders in the Sudan and elsewhere, who castrated their young slaves for exportation, could expect enormous profits in consequence of this cruel mutilation. During the stay of J. L. Burckhardt in Upper Egypt in the autumn of 1813, the eunuchs who were carried from the Sudan to Egypt had been castrated either in Borgo (west of Darfūr), or in a certain village near Siūt chiefly inhabited by Christians. The operators in this latter place were two Coptic monks, who received the victims (little boys between the age of eight and twelve years) into their house immediately after the arrival of the caravans. Their profession was held in contempt even by the vilest Egyptians (J. L. Burckhardt, *Travels in Nubia*², London, 1822, pp. 294-296). In the *Arabian Nights' Entertainments* it is told that slaves were also, notwithstanding the legal prohibition, sometimes punished with castration by their Muslim owners (e.g. *The Thousand and One Nights*, ed. by W. H. Macnaghten, Calcutta, 1839, i. 324-330; cf. Burckhardt's remark on the castration of captives by Ghālib, the Sharīf of Mecca [*Travels in Nubia*, p. 296]).

Eunuchs were employed by the Muslims either as guardians of the women in the harīms of princes and in the houses of men of high rank and great wealth, or as guardians in sanctuaries. For the latter purpose they were sent as presents, especially to the great mosques at Mecca and Medina. In Cairo a holy relic, the so-called shirt of Muhammad, was guarded by a eunuch, who was sent for that purpose from Constantinople (see A. von Kremer, *Aegypten*, ii. 88).

Burckhardt, Lane, von Kremer, and other travellers in Muslim countries have observed that eunuchs, on account of the important and confidential offices which they filled, were generally treated with great consideration. They were never employed for lower services, and were called usually *Agha* (*i.e.* 'master,' 'lord'). 'I used to remark in Cairo,' says Lane (*The Thousand and One Nights*, London, 1859, i. 57), 'that few persons saluted me with a more dignified and consequential air than these pitiable but self-conceited beings.' It is related by Burckhardt that many of the lower classes at Mecca kissed the hands of the eunuchs of the great mosque on approaching them; their chief was a great personage, entitled to sit in the presence of the Pasha and the Sharīf (Burckhardt, *Travels in Arabia*, London, 1829, i. 288–291). Often eunuchs at the court of Muhammadan princes became men of great influence and power. A well-known example of such statesmen was Kāfūr al-Ikhshīdī, a castrated negro, whose biography is contained in Ibn Khallikān's biographical dictionary (tr. de Slane, Paris, 1843–71, ii. 524–528). He reigned in the 10th cent. A.D. over Egypt and Syria, and public prayers were offered up for him from the pulpits, not only in all the cities of his dominion, but even at Mecca.

Extraordinary as it may appear, the grown-up eunuchs often married, and the legal consequences of such marriages (*e.g.* in the case of divorce) are earnestly discussed in the Muslim law books.

By the time of Burckhardt (1813–1814) the custom of keeping eunuchs had greatly diminished in Egypt as well as in Syria. Undoubtedly by the abolition of slavery the last eunuchs will soon disappear from Muslim territory.

LITERATURE.—Muradja d'Ohsson, *Tableau gén. de l'empire othoman*, Paris, 1820, iii. 302–304; E. Quatremère, *Hist. des sultans mamlouks de l'Égypte*, Paris, 1837, i. 2, p. 132; A. von Kremer, *Aegypten*, Leipzig, 1863, ii. 87–89; C. Snouck Hurgronje, *Mekka*, Hague, 1889, ii. 24.

TH. W. JUYNBOLL.

EUPHEMISM. — *Introductory.* — As far as concerns the religious aspect of the word, 'euphemism'[1] may be defined as the use of names or words of good omen (εὖ, 'well,' φημί, 'I speak') instead of those of evil omen (though in practice it also includes the use of enigmatic words), the object being to avoid the dangers which are inherent in the use of the latter. The being thus named is flattered and conciliated and does not do harm, or he does not know that he is being referred to. Euphemism is thus in speech what propitiatory rites towards evil or demoniac beings are in act. In primitive thought, and surviving into much higher culture, a name is regarded as part of the personality of the being—god, spirit, or man—who bears it; or it is even identical with its owner's soul.[2] Hence, according to the magical view of the universe so commonly entertained, knowledge and use of a name are bound to affect the owner of that name. It may bring him within the power, or force him to do the bidding, of him who utters it. But, on the other hand, when carelessly uttered, it may bring its owner unpleasantly near, or draw his attention to, or bring him into contact with or possession of, the utterer. Obedience by a spirit or demon to the pronouncing of his name was only on compulsion; and he was always watchful for any opportunity of falling upon him who spoke his name 'in vain.' Thus there was danger for the latter in using carelessly the names of dangerous beings. It brought them near, and they had an objection to their names being mentioned. In all cases the use of names is hedged about with many restrictions. Any tabued spirit, person, animal, or thing is apt to receive a circumlocutory or euphemistic name. Great precautions are taken by savages against disclosing their personal or secret names; hence many of them are known by nicknames or circumlocutions, and nothing is more common at certain times than a change of name, often by way of deceiving spirits, *e.g.* those which cause sickness. In many cases a wife may not call her husband by his name, and *vice versa*. Thus the Zulu wife addresses her husband as 'father of so and so,' and the Hindu wife as 'the man of the house,' 'the master.' Or, again, relations who are generally tabu to each other, *e.g.* a man and his mother-in-law, must not utter each other's name. Names of chiefs, kings, or priests are similarly avoided. In all such instances the freakish names, epithets, or circumlocutions which are actually used are euphemistic. But the prohibition extends much further; for if, as often happens, any of these names should be the word used for any object or should occur as part of such a word, another word or a circumlocution must be used for such an object—a practice which gives rise to a constant change of language in some tribes. Further, many words used by men are tabu to women, and *vice versa*; or they may not be spoken in women's hearing, another word, akin to a euphemism, being used.

The beings whose names are generally avoided and a euphemism strictly so-called used in their place, by way of flattering, conciliating, or propitiating them, or of concealing the fact that they are being mentioned, are certain gods, supernatural beings of various kinds, the dead, and animals. Euphemisms are also used for death, or for various things, places, or actions. But it cannot be said that the practice is of universal application, since the actual names of such, or of equally evil beings, etc., are frequently used.[1]

1. Divinities.—As to divinities, the adulatory epithets by which they are characterized, and by which attention is called to their virtues or honorific characteristics, may be looked upon as euphemistic or as serving the same purpose as actual euphemisms. Among the Greeks it was thought unlucky to use the names of the divinities of the under world, because of their connexion with death; and it has been conjectured that the designation of the god and goddess of Hades as ὁ Θεός and ἡ Θεά may be due to such a motive (Farnell, in *Anthrop. Essays*, 1907, p. 91 f.). But much better known examples from Greek soil are the titles given to the dreaded Erinyes by those who feared to use their real name. They were called the *Eumenides* (*q.v.*), 'the well-meaning,' 'the kindly,' or 'the soothed ones'—a name said to have been first given them after the acquittal of Orestes when their anger had been soothed. Another title of the same group of goddesses was 'the venerable goddesses,' σεμναὶ θεαί (Paus. i. 28. 6, ii. 11. 4). Among the Romans the name of the daughter of Faunus was tabued, and she was called *Bona Dea*, 'the good goddess' (Servius, on *Æn.* viii. 315). Similarly, among the Sioux the male water- or earth- divinities are called 'grandfathers,' and the female 'grandmothers' (*11 RBEW*, 1894, p. 438); and in India, Śiva, the god of destruction, is 'the gracious one.'

The Heb. custom of substituting the vowels of *Adonai*, 'Lord, or *Elohim*, 'God,' for those of יהוה, the Tetragrammaton or Sacred Name (*JHWH*), as a sign to the reader to pronounce Adonai or Elohim instead of the mysterious Name, arose from fear of uttering carelessly this sacred name. These substitutions are, therefore, of the nature of euphemisms, and resemble the Bab. usages with regard to the secret names of gods (Lenormant, *La Magie chez les Chaldéens*, Paris, 1874, p. 41). The Jewish custom is connected with the Third Commandment (Ex 20[7]). A similar usage is found in the words which take the

[1] Some writers, including even George Eliot and Mrs. Gaskell, have made the curious mistake of using the word 'euphuism' where 'euphemism' was intended.

[2] In many languages the same word stands for 'name' and 'soul.'

[1] The opposite practice to giving euphemistic names is found in the wide-spread custom of calling a child by an opprobrious name in order to turn away the attention of dangerous spirits from it. Cf. art. EVIL EYE.

place of the Divine name in expletives, exclamations, etc., in popular speech—Eng. *'od's* (*'od's bones*); Germ. *potz* or *kotz* (*potz tausend*); Fr. *bieu, quieu* (*sangbieu*), and the like.

2. Supernatural beings.—Much more common is the use of euphemisms for the names of spirits, demons, fairies, etc. Thus in India the spirits of young men dying without becoming fathers are called *pitris*, 'fathers'—a euphemistic name to which they are least entitled—by way of propitiating them (Monier-Williams, *Rel. Life and Thought in India*, 1883, p. 243 f.). Hindus, who believe that the ghost of some Musalmāns becomes a malignant *rākṣasa*, conciliate it by addressing it as *Mamdūḥ*, 'the praised one' (Crooke, *PR*[2] i. 252). The Arabs and Syrians address the *jinn*, who are in all respects like our fairies (see FAIRY), as *mubarakīn*, 'ye blessed,' or 'blessed ones' (Lane-Poole, *Arabian Society in the Middle Ages*, 1883, p. 37; Hanauer, *Folk-Lore of the Holy Land*, 1907, p. 202). In modern Greece the Nereids, who also correspond to our fairies, are called generally in a euphemistic manner τὰ ἐξωτικά, a name also applied to *Lamiæ* and other supernal powers. Other names, corresponding to 'the Eumenides' and equally conciliatory, are ἡ κυρᾶδες, 'the Ladies'; ἡ καλοκάρδαις, 'the kind-hearted ones'; τὰ κουρίτσιά μας, 'our maidens'; ἡ καλαὶς ἀρχοντίσσαις, 'our good Queens'; ἡ καλλικυρᾶδες, 'our good Ladies'—a name corresponding to αἱ κυρίαι νύμφαι of classical times. Other names are 'outsider women,' 'lucky ones,' 'friends,' or 'brothers.' 'Seizure' by the Nereids is described as ὥρα τὸν ηὗρε, 'an [evil] hour overtook him' (*FL* viii. [1897] 275; Lawson, *Modern Gr. Folklore and Anc. Gr. Religion*, Cambridge, 1910, pp. 132, 143; Dozon, *Contes albanais*, Paris, 1881, p. xxi; Garnett, *Greek Folk Poesy*, 1896, ii. 446). For similar propitiatory reasons, and in order to secure their good offices, the fairies, whose temper is uncertain, are called in Lowland Scotland 'the good folk,' 'the good neighbours,' 'the good ladies'; in Shetland, 'guid folk *or* neighbours'; in the Highlands, *daoine coire*, 'honest people'; and *daoine sith*, 'the people of peace'; in the Isle of Man, 'good people'; in Ireland, 'good people,' 'the gentry,' 'the gentlemen,' or simply 'them';[1] in Wales, *Tylwyth Teg*, 'the fair folk' (Keightley, *Fairy Mythology*, 1900, pp. 164, 351, 363, 397; Scott, *Minstrelsy*, 1839, p. 216; Sikes, *British Goblins*, 1880, p. 123; Rhys, *Celtic Folklore*, Oxford, 1901, *passim*). These names correspond with the title *bonnes dames* given to the mediæval fées—a title probably borrowed from the adopted Roman name *dominæ* given to a group of Celtic goddesses. Certain Teutonic titles for elves are of a euphemistic nature—'das stille Volk,' 'die guten Holden' (*holdo*, a kind or favourably disposed being); cf. Norse *Lieblinge*; Lithuanian *balti z'mones*, 'honest folk' (Grimm, *Teut. Myth.*, 1880–88, pp. 452, 456, 1416; Simrock, *Handbuch der deutsch. Myth.*[6], Bonn, 1887, p. 426). Keightley also refers (p. 495) to a similar title among the Yoloffs of Africa for a race of beings corresponding to fairies, whom they call *Bakhna Rakhna*, 'good people.'

These titles are generic. On the other hand, as many *Märchen* show (*e.g.* 'Tom-Tit-Tot,' 'Whuppity Stoorie,' 'Rumpelstiltskin,' etc.), to know and pronounce the individual name of a fairy brings him within one's power (see *CF*, 26 ff.). The common name for a Brownie, 'Robin Goodfellow,' which seems to be euphemistic, is both individual and generic. 'Hobgoblin' is probably another instance of this conciliatory attitude expressing itself in a friendly diminutive of a proper name, if *Hob*=Robert. Other examples are found in Teutonic names for different sprites, in which occur diminutives of Heinrich, Joachim, Walter, *e.g.* Heinzelman, Hinzemännchen, Chimke, Wolterken, Wouters (Grimm, 503 f.). The *ignis fatuus* regarded as a sprite is also called familiarly 'Will o' the wisp,' 'Jack o' lanthorn,' etc.

In most European languages the devil is commonly spoken of by a variety of euphemisms and softened titles, which have a tendency to degenerate into slang, but which show the fear of using such a name of dread import. In Scotland 'the good *or* guid man' (cf. 'the guid man's croft' = the part of a farmland left uncultivated because dedicated to the devil) probably expresses the devil's tenancy of hell ('guid man' = tenant). Other names are 'Clootie,' 'Auld Hornie,' 'Sandy,' or 'the de'il.' In the Hebrides such names as 'the brindled one,' 'the black one,' 'the great fellow,' 'the nameless,' are found (*FL* x. [1899] 265). English names are 'Old Nick,' 'the Old Gentleman.' In Germany we find *Meister Peter, Peterchen, Meister Sieh-dich-für, Deichel, Gott sei bei uns*, etc.; in France, *diacre*; in Italy, *ceteratojo* (cf. Grimm, 987, 1004, 1606; Farmer-Henley, *Slang and its Analogues*, 1890 ff. *s.v.*).

3. Death and the dead.—For similar reasons such ill-omened names as death, the region of the dead, and also the personal names of the dead are generally avoided, and replaced by euphemisms. Death, being personified, or regarded as the work of spirits or evil-disposed beings, would, if mentioned directly, be apt to draw dangerous attention to him who spoke it. There was probably also the idea of the dread contagion of death (which forced all who handled the dead to be under tabu for a time), working even through the name (name and thing named being one). And, similarly, to refer to a dead man by name would tend to bring his spirit near the living. Among the Ainus figurative words are used for death, *e.g.* 'sleeping,' 'resting,' 'leaving the world behind' (Batchelor, *Ainu of Japan*, 1892, p. 212). Both in Melanesia and in Polynesia there is an unwillingness to speak directly of death, and the usual word for death, *mate*, is used only of the death of an animal or as a term of abuse.

Brown (*Melanesians and Polynesians*, 1910, p. 404) gives the following euphemisms for death: *ua maliu*, 'he has gone'; *ua usu fono* (of an orator), 'he has gone to the council'; *ua gasoloao* (of a chief), 'the titles have passed away,' or *ua taapeape'pāpā*, 'the titles are scattered about.'

In S. Africa, to die is 'to go home,' or 'not to look on the sun again,' or 'not to be here,' or 'to go away,' 'to return to one's fathers' (Macdonald, *JAI* xx. [1891] 121; Casalis, *Les Bassoutos*, Paris, 1859, p. 258). Among the Baganda, when a twin dies (an unlucky event), it is said that the child has 'flown away' or 'gone to gather firewood,' and the death of a king is described as 'the fire is extinguished' (Roscoe, *The Baganda*, 1911, pp. 103, 125). When a sheep dies, lest its spirit should cause a woman to fall ill, she simply says, 'I am unable to untie such a sheep' (*ib.* p. 289; cf. the saying in the Hebrides when a cow dies, 'it is lost'). In Burma, to die is 'to return' (*i.e.* to a state of bliss [Forbes, *British Burma*, 1878, p. 71]). Among the Chinese, dying is expressed by such phrases as 'to enter the measure' (*i.e.* the coffin), 'to leave the body,' 'to pass away,' while the coffin is euphemistically called 'boards of old age' (Friend, 'Euph. and Tabu in China,' *FLR* iv. [1881] 80 f.). In Japan, 'recovery' is used instead of 'death,' and 'clod' for 'tomb' (Aston, *Shinto*, 1905, p. 255). Among the ancient Jews and Greeks, as with many modern races, 'sleep' is a euphemism for death (Heb. שָׁכַב, LXX κοιμᾶσθαι, 'to lie down'), and is constantly used: 2 S 7^{12}, 1 K 2^{10}, 2 Es 7^{32}; *Iliad*, xi. 241; Soph. *Electra*, 509 (cf. Herkenrath, *Stud. zu die griech. Grabschriften*, Feldkirch, 1896). St. Paul speaks of τῶν κοιμωμένων and τοὺς κοιμηθέντας διὰ τοῦ Ἰησοῦ (1 Th $4^{13f.}$); and these phrases passed readily into Christian thought, so that

[1] Cf. the Slavic custom of referring to a demon not by his name, but as 'he' or 'himself.' It is met with elsewhere. 'He,' 'himself,' are often used in Celtic regions as titles of respectful address instead of a superior's name.

'sleep' became almost an equivalent for death rather than a euphemism. 'To sleep in peace,' to 'fall asleep in Jesus,' are common phrases in Christian epigraphy from early times, and *receptus ad Deum, de seculo recessit* (both also classical: cf. *inter deos receptus est* [*recedo* = 'to die']), *natus est in æternum, in pace decessit*, and the like, are found on early Christian tombs. While they are euphemistic, they express the joyful hope of the Christian. In the everyday speech of ourselves 'to pass away,' 'he is gone,' and the like, are used for death (cf. 'to pass out' or 'over,' used by Spiritualists); and in the north-east of Scotland 'he was taken away' means 'he died.' In Germany, death is known as *Freund Hein*, and dying is expressed by a variety of euphemisms—'departing' (in various forms; cf. Gr. οἰχόμενος = θανών), 'faring out,' etc. Our 'to join the majority' occurs in German, and is derived from the Gr. phrase ἐς πλεόνων ἱκέσθαι (cf. the Heb. euphemisms, 'gathered to his fathers,' 'go to his fathers,' 'sleep with his fathers,' etc.).

The reluctance to mention the dead individually or collectively by name is universal among savages and survives in folk-custom (see DEATH AND DISPOSAL OF THE DEAD [Introd.], vol. iv. p. 441[b]). Consequent euphemisms are numerous. Thus, among the aborigines of Victoria a dead man was 'the lost one,' 'the poor fellow that is no more' (Stranbridge, *TES* i. [1861] 299); and among the Abipones he is 'the man who does not now exist' (Dobrizhoffer, *Abipones*, 1822, ii. 273). S. African tribes say 'ye who are above' (Macdonald, *JAI* xx. 121). The Roman *Di Manes*, 'the good *or* kindly gods' (from *manus*, 'good'), applied to the gods of the under world or to the departed, is probably euphemistic; and perhaps the Gr. οἱ ὑποχθόνιοι, οἱ κάτω ἐρχόμενοι, οἱ ἐναγισμοί, 'those below,' or 'those who have gone below,' are of the same nature. οἱ πλέονες, Lat. *majores*, Eng. 'the majority,' are all circumlocutions for the dead. In Scots folk-speech 'them that's awa' expresses a similar reluctance to refer directly to the dead as such. In Japan the old word *mono* applied to the dead means 'the beings,' and is euphemistic (see *ERE* iv. 611[a]). Offended spirits in China are addressed by a euphemism, e.g. *shêng jên*, 'sagely person.' Similarly the region of the dead or of the devil is the subject of euphemistic expressions instead of the word 'hell'—'the ill place,' 'the bad place,' or even, as in the Hebrides, 'the good place.'

4. Diseases.—Among savages, diseases are frequently personified or controlled by spirits, and in either case they are sometimes referred to euphemistically, by way of avoiding such a direct reference as might cause them to afflict the speaker, and also in order to flatter them. In Fiji the word 'leprosy' must not be applied to any one in good society who is suffering from it; and 'many ingenious shifts are resorted to in order to express the meaning without using the word' (Thomson, *The Fijians*, 1908, p. 259). Among the Dayaks, smallpox is not referred to directly, but as 'jungle-leaves,' 'the chief,' 'fruit'; or they ask, 'Has he left you yet?' (St. John, *Forests of the Far East*, 1862, i. 62). In India, the name of the smallpox-goddess, Sītalā, is itself a euphemism, 'she that loves coolness'; but she is also called 'queen of the world,' 'the great mother,' etc. Similarly, the cholera-goddess is 'lady of the flux,' *Olā Bībī* (Crooke, *PR*[2] i. 126; cf. *ERE* ii. 485[a]). In the Cyclades, plague is 'the pardoned disease,' epilepsy is γλυκύ or τὸ καλό, smallpox εὐλίγια; and in Greece, smallpox is συγχωρεμένη, 'the indulgent' (Bent, *The Cyclades*, 1883, p. 74; Crooke, i. 126). Among the Slavs, the demon of fever is called 'aunt,' 'godmother,' by way of making her friendly. The Teutons call disease 'the good,' 'the blessed'; pestilence is 'gossip,' apoplexy 'the blessed,' whitlow 'the unnamed' (Grimm, 1154, 1157, 1656).

5. Animals.—The same custom applies to using the names of animals whose ravages are feared, as well as to other more harmless animals—in the latter case perhaps a survival of some religious tabu in the cult of animals. In Angola, the lion is spoken of as *ngana*, 'sir,' and would punish any one who did not so call him (Monteiro, *Angola and the River Congo*, 1875, ii. 116). In Algeria, the same animal is called *Johanben-el-Johan* (Certeux and Carnoy, *L'Algérie trad.*, Paris and Algiers, 1884, p. 172); and the Bechuanas of S. Africa name it 'the boy with the beard' (Conder, *JAI* xvi. [1887] 84). Among various peoples of Malaysia, the tiger is called 'grandfather,' 'the wild animal,' 'lord,' or 'ancestor,' or, as in Sunda, 'the whiskered one,' 'the honourable one,' etc. In Sunda, the boar is 'the beautiful one.' The Malays also call the elephant 'grandfather,' and beg him not to destroy them, his grandchildren. When catching an alligator, they condole with him and call him 'Raja,' 'Datu,' and 'grandfather'; and in Sarawak the Kenyahs call the crocodile 'the old grandfather' rather than refer to it by name. In all such cases calamity or illness would follow non-observance of these euphemisms (Marsden, *Sumatra*, 1811, p. 292; Mouhot, *Trav. in Indo-China*, 1864, i. 263; Skeat, *Malay Magic*, 1900, pp. 150, 153, 157; St. John, i. 19; Hose-Macdougall, *JAI* xxxi. 186; Frazer, *GB*[2] i. 462). For similar reasons, and lest the dreaded animals should appear, snakes in India are called by various euphemisms—the cobra is 'the good snake' or 'good lord'; and 'worm,' 'insect,' 'rope,' 'creeping thing' are other reptile euphemisms. Similarly among the Cherokees, when a man is bitten by a snake, he is said to be 'scratched by a briar,' lest the feelings of the animal should be hurt (Mooney, *19 RBEW* [1900] pt. i. p. 295). Tigers are called 'the dog,' 'the beast,' 'the jackal,' etc., especially when they are being hunted. Other animals are also denoted euphemistically (Crooke, *PR*[2] i. 275, *TC*, 1896, iii. 249; *FL* viii. 285; *NINQ* i. 70, 104, v. 133). In Syria, the serpent is addressed as 'Thou blessed one' (Hanauer, 202). Similar respectful titles are addressed to the bear by the Finns—'forest apple,' 'golden light foot,' 'old man,' etc., while the Lapps call it 'the old man with the fur coat' (see the *Kalevala, passim*; Tylor, *Early Hist. of Mankind*, 1865, p. 145).[1] Similar forms are used by the Esthonians and Swedes for the bear; and by all these peoples and also generally in Germany the wolf, especially at certain seasons, is called 'grey-legs,' 'golden-tooth,' 'the vermin,' etc., while the fox is 'long-tail,' 'blue-foot,' etc. (Thorpe, *Northern Myth.*, 1852, ii. 83 f.; Tettau and Temme, *Die Volkssagen Ostpreussens*, Berlin, 1837, p. 281; Frazer, i. 454 f.). Similarly, the Sioux call the beaver (or possibly water-monsters) 'water-person' or 'water person female' (*11 RBEW*, p. 439).

6. Euphemisms of occupation, etc.—Some of the above examples have shown that animals while being hunted are spoken of euphemistically, the object being apparently to deceive them by a kind of make-believe, so as to render their capture easy, while at the same time it is sought to avoid falling into their power. In many parts of the world a similar custom is observed while hunting, fishing, or pursuing certain occupations in particular places or at particular times. But here the custom is not confined to the name of the animal or object sought after, but extends to various beings, people, places,

[1] For similar respectful terms addressed to the bear among Ainus and North Asiatic peoples, see *ERE* i. 249, 503.

or things which might be mentioned in conversation. They are either not spoken of for the time being, or they are referred to under some other name, circumlocution, or euphemism. By this elaborate make-believe, men have thought to deceive the spirits or animals or any other being who might be listening, and who, recognizing them or their intentions, would attack them, or avoid and escape them. Thus, if, while hunting, men call themselves, or the animal hunted, or their weapons, by other names, they reckon on deceiving the animal and so obtaining an easy prey. Or, again, if the animal is spoken of in a flattering euphemism, it may be so pleased that it will allow itself to be slain. In other cases, where names of objects or people, allowable at other times, are tabu at certain times or in certain places, there is obviously a fear of disturbing harmful agencies to whom they might be obnoxious. Here, again, the words used are euphemisms of pretence. The beings and creatures swarming around man, whether spirits or animals, are credited with intelligence and understanding, but only up to a certain point. They are weak enough to be open to flattering terms, or ignorant enough not to see through man's elaborate pretences.

Two examples may suffice. Martin (*Descr. of the W. Islands*[2], London, 1716) refers to the custom of the Lewismen, when visiting the sacred Flannan Islands for fowling, of avoiding certain words and employing others in their places—*vah*, 'cave,' for *claddach*, 'shore'; *cruey*, 'hard,' for *creg*, 'rock'; *gaire*, 'sharp,' for *gort*, 'sour,' etc., while the islands themselves must be spoken of only as 'the country.' Similarly, the camphor-gatherers of the Malay Peninsula, while engaged in their task, must speak the *oassa kapor*, or 'camphor language,' because otherwise the spirit in the trees would not be propitiated, and they would not find the object of their quest. Rice is called 'grass-fruit'; gun is 'far-sounding,' etc. In Borneo, and for similar reasons, the same phenomenon is met with, and camphor is here spoken of as 'the thing that smells' (Skeat, 212 ff.; Furness, *Folk-lore in Borneo*, Wallingford, Penn., 1899, p. 27). Among the Bangala no man is addressed by his own name while fishing, but as *mwele*, to hide his identity from the spirits (*JAI* xxxix. [1909] 459). For many other examples, see also Frazer, i. 451 ff. note A, 'Taboos on Common Words.'

7. Certain religious, customary, or unusual actions or things are also spoken of euphemistically, and for reasons similar to those already referred to. Thus, in Samoa, circumcision of a peculiar kind had a recognized name, *tefe*, but in ordinary speech *tafao* was used as a euphemism (Brown, 382 f.). In Fiji, cannibalism, which had a religious aspect, was hedged about by many tabus and had euphemistic names. The trunk was *na vale ka rusa*, 'the house that perishes'; the feet, *ndua-rua*, 'one-two'; or such a desired portion of human flesh as the breast of a virgin was *sese matairua*, 'spear with two points' (Thomson, 104). Among the Yorubas, human sacrifice is euphemistically called 'basket-sacrifice,' because the victim is enclosed in a basket (Ellis, *Yoruba-speaking Peoples*, 1894, p. 105). In the Hebrides, the fire of a kiln is called *aingeal*, not *teine*, because the latter is dangerous and 'ill will come if it is mentioned' (*FL* x. 265); just as, in Scandinavia, fire was sometimes called *hetta*, not *eld* or *ell* (Thorpe, ii. 85). Among the Baganda, when twins were born—an unusual but important event, because they were the gift of the god Mukasa—the midwife, in announcing the birth to the father, did not use the tabued word 'twins,' but 'he has given you,' or some such phrase (Roscoe, *Baganda*, 1911, p. 65).

8. Euphemisms of etiquette.—Etiquette also demands that, in speaking to a superior, particular names or phrases should be used instead of those ordinarily employed. Thus, in China, when a ruler wishes to take a place at an archery meeting and is unable to do so, he should decline on the ground of being ill, and say, 'I am suffering from carrying firewood.' Mencius thus excused himself, and it has been adopted from the manner in which a peasant would speak, as a term of mock humility. This is only one example out of many customary in China (*SBE* xxvii. [1885] 101). Similarly, in Samoa, words of an opposite meaning instead of those supposed to be objectionable were used in speaking to chiefs (for a long list of these, see Brown, 380 ff.). For the same reason ill-omened words are generally avoided in conversation; 'good omen words,' in the Cantonese phrase, being used, as many of the above examples have shown. Thus Helladius says that the Athenians were careful not to use words of ill-omen; so they called the prison 'the chamber,' and the executioner 'the public man' (Phot. *Bibl.*, ed. Bekker, 1825, p. 535). The underlying idea is that by mentioning ill-omened words the action may be itself produced. Survivals of this—but now no more than a shrinking from the use of words calling up disagreeable associations or unpleasant things—are common in civilized life among ourselves. But the old and primitive conception of the connexion between name and thing named, and of the power of the name to produce the effect or to cause the presence of spirit, animal, etc., when the name is spoken, is seen in certain proverbs, the full meaning of which is not realized by those who use them: *e.g.* Talk of the devil and you will see his horns,' 'Speak of the wolf and you will see his tail.'

9. Slang and euphemisms.—Euphemistic language may become merely poetical, and, while it has a different origin from slang, it is also closely connected with it and easily degenerates into it both in English and in foreign languages. The euphemistic names of the devil have in many instances become merely slang expressions, though sometimes used by those who think them softer than such a 'swear-word' as 'devil'; or they have given rise to other slang names. 'The dickens,' 'the deuce,' 'deuce take it,' 'the old boy,' etc., and some of the euphemisms already cited for 'devil,' are examples of such changes. Many people also use slang euphemisms for oaths—'dash,' 'blow,' 'confound,' etc.; while there are many slang expressions for death—'to kick the bucket,' 'to take an earth bath,' 'to go to Davy Jones' locker,' etc.—which in an earlier age would have been euphemisms pure and simple. See Farmer-Henley, *Slang and its Analogues*, 8 vols., 1890 ff.; J. C. Hotten, *Slang Dictionary*, 1859; A. Barrère and C. G. Leland, *Dict. of Slang, Jargon, and Cant*, 2 vols., 1885.

LITERATURE.—There is no work dealing exclusively with the subject, but see R. Andree, *Ethnogr. Parallelen und Vergleiche*, Leipzig, 1889; E. Clodd, *Tom Tit Tot*, London, 1898, p. 125 ff.; J. G. Frazer, *GB*[2], 1900, i. 403 ff., 451 ff.; H. Friend, *FLR* iv. [1881], 'Euphemism and Tabu in China'; B. Thorpe, *Northern Mythology*, London, 1852, ii. 83 f.; E. B. Tylor, *Early Hist. of Mankind*, London, 1865, p. 123 ff.; S. Ehrenfeld, 'Euphemism,' in *JE* v. [1903] 267 f.

J. A. MACCULLOCH.

EURIPIDES, the last of the three great Greek tragedians, is a figure of high importance in the history of Western thought, as well as in that of literature. The present article will say nothing of his life (*b.* before 475, *d.* 406 B.C.), his artistic technique, or his numerous plays (88, of which 18 genuine and one suspect are extant), except in so far as they directly illustrate his ethical and religious position.

The real outlook of a dramatist, for instance, is shown far more by his choice of subjects, and the kind of character that he makes (to use the technical term) 'sympathetic' or 'unsympathetic,' than by the definite sentiments he puts in the mouth of his characters. We may, therefore, notice that Euripides has whole plays upon such subjects as the immorality of the traditional gods (*Ion*, *Auge*, *Melanippe*, *Danae*, *Alope*); the problem of the unjust government of the world (*Bellerophon*, *Troades*); the wickedness or insanity of the 'sacred duty of revenge' (*Electra*, *Orestes*, *Alcmaeon*; cf. *Medea*,

Hecuba, etc.). He once treats the statesman sympathetically (*Philoctetes*); mostly he dwells on the crimes of statecraft (*Iphigenia in Aulis, Hecuba, Troades, Palamedes*), which he associates with such horrors as the persecution of suppliants at an altar (*Heraclidæ, Supplices, Andromache*), or, when backed by superstition, with human sacrifice (*Heraclidæ, Hecuba, Iphigenia in Aulis*, etc.). His virgin-martyrs and his champions of the oppressed stand out against this background of statecraft. He treats often of cruelty and injustice done to women, especially barbarian women (*Medea, Hecuba, Andromache*), and to children (*Heracles, Andromache*), and sometimes of the women's frantic revenge (*Medea, Hecuba*; cf. *Ion*). He has plays on the wise woman (*Melanippe*), the strong and bold woman (*Meleagros*), the wife faithful to death (*Protesilaus, Alcestis*; cf. *Supplices*); on women in love, innocently (*Andromeda*, perhaps *Iphigenia in Aulis*), or with some guilt or trouble (*Hippolytus, Sthenebœa, Cressæ*; also *Æolus* and *Pasiphae*); and on their jealousy and revenge (*Ion, Medea, Andromache*). He has a great play entirely on the evil of war (*Troades*); two on the beauty and the horror of ecstatic religion (*Bacchæ, Cretes*); one in which the hero is a slave, though he proves to be of princely birth (*Alexandros*); and one dealing largely with the contrast of practical and contemplative life (*Antiope*). This is clearly an unusual and characteristic list of subjects.

Euripides as an artist deserves a much fuller treatment than he can receive here. In general, his characteristic is the combination of a highly conventionalized style with an extraordinarily free and original intellect. His technique is as severe as his thought is unconventional. His adherence to the archaic traditional forms of the religious ritual from which drama probably arose—prologue, contest-scene, messenger, epiphany of god or hero —is as marked as that of Æschylus, and forms a strong contrast with the more 'natural' style of Sophocles. His extreme pursuit of σαφηνεία, 'clarity,' makes his speeches often too precise and self-conscious, his scenes too sharply separate and articulate, for modern taste. On the other hand, the persistent thoughtfulness and keenness of his criticism of life alienate those who like poetry to be conventionally poetical.

In his religious and philosophical ideas, though Euripides is not an adherent of any definite school, he can safely be called the poet of the Sophistic movement. A σοφιστής is one who 'makes wise,' an educator; and the Sophistic movement is that great effort towards knowledge and enlightenment which transformed the half-savage Greece of the 6th cent. B.C. into the Greece of Hippocrates, Thucydides, and Plato. Different sophists, of course, emphasized different sides of σοφία; but in its negative aspect the movement was largely one and indivisible. In an age saturated with superstition the first condition of real enlightenment is a drastic rejection of spiritual and intellectual fetters. Criticism attacks first what is immoral or revolting in the accepted beliefs, next what is merely stupid or improbable.

Now, Greek religious belief was never, except in some special communities (Orphic, Pythagorean, etc.), organized into a definite orthodoxy. It rested on innumerable local rituals conforming to a few main types, and explained by traditional stories. Naturally, therefore, while most of the sophists probably agreed with Hecatæus that 'the traditions of the Greeks are many and absurd,' there was no great body of positive doctrine which attempted to replace all the rubbish that was being destroyed. The Sophistic movement was, on the whole, agnostic. It urged men to look for evidence, to use their understanding and their moral sense. But it must always be remembered that the rejection of traditional theology in Greece proceeded almost as much from the craving for a more satisfying faith as from purely critical or scientific causes. This can be seen best by the history of Orphism and the great growth of mystic religions in the emancipated 4th century. And Euripides, being by profession not a dogmatic philosopher, but a philosophic dramatist and student of character, sensitive to all the highest thought of his age, reflects its aspirations quite as much as its denials.

Attempts have been made to show a special connexion between Euripides and the doctrines of particular philosophers (Anaxagoras: the sun as a χρυσέα βῶλος [*Phaethon*, 771, 783; *Or.* 983]; Protagoras: the ἄνθρωπος μέτρον [*Aiolus*, 19, *Phœn.* 499]; Diogenes of Apollonia: the worship of Αἰθήρ [fr. 941, 877; Ar. *Ranæ*, 892], the soul as air [*Hel.* 1013 ff.; *Tro.* 884–86, γῆς ὄχημα = νοῦς βροτῶν]; Heraclitus, Hippocrates, Prodicus, and, in his political theories, Antiphon; cf. Dümmler, *Proleg. zu Platon's Stadt*, 1891, pp. 10 f., 20 ff.; the Orphics: fr. 912, 472, and 638, 833); but the affiliation of each doctrine is often doubtful, their use is almost always dramatic, and the doctrines of no one school can be said to preponderate. On such problems as the existence of the gods, the moral government of the world, the survival of the soul after death, Euripides is full of questions and contradictions, but pronounces no personal judgment.

A question that vexed the age was whether the world is governed by Intelligence (Ξύνεσις), or, more crudely, whether the gods were ξύνετοι, *i.e.* were they like reasonable parents knowing what is in man's heart, or, as the traditions would have it, incalculable creatures ready to punish savagely all who broke their irrational tabus? (The question between monotheism and polytheism gives as little trouble to Euripides as to most Greeks; he uses the singular and the plural indifferently: τὸ θεῖον, in any case, was one.) Euripides at times (*Hip.* 1105) 'has in his secret hope the belief in some great Understanding' (Ξύνεσίν τινα). He is represented as actually praying to Ξύνεσις in Ar. *Ran.* 893. But he sometimes finds the facts against him (*Hip. l.c.*; cf. *Iph. in Aulis*, 394*a*; *Her.* 655). Hecuba's often quoted lines (*Tro.* 884 ff.),

'Base of the world and o'er the world enthroned,
Whoe'er thou art, unknown and hard of surmise,
Cause-chain of things (ἀνάγκη φύσεος) or man's own reason, God,
I give thee worship, who by noiseless paths
Of justice leadest all that breathes and dies,'

express a belief, frequently repeated and denied elsewhere, in the rule of the world by Justice, but in the play the belief is quickly falsified by the event. Cf. the *Bellerophon*, where the righteous hero questions Zeus on this point, and for answer is blasted by a thunderbolt.

If one is to try to conjecture Euripides' own view, it would perhaps be that unknown forces and influences do exist, which shape or destroy man's life, and which may perhaps be conceived as in some sense personal (δουλεύομεν θεοῖς, ὅ τι ποτ' εἰσὶν οἱ θεοί [*Or.* 418]), but that morally they are less good than man, who at least pities and tries to understand. At times, indeed, he deliberately denies the 'miserable tales' of the poets: 'if the gods do shame, they are no gods' (*Beller.* 292); 'God, if He be indeed God, hath need of naught' (*Her.* 1345). Yet, not only are his mere mythological gods (*Ion, Heracles, Electra*) represented as very poor characters, but even the gods of the *Hippolytus* and *Bacchæ*, who clearly represent real forces, if not quite real persons, are by human standards evil. In the magnificent closing scene of the *Troades* he seems to pierce behind all the gods of the poets, first to the primeval worship of the dead who may still love us, then beyond that to a great refusal of all false comfort, an acceptance of the darkness that is God and more than god.

About immortality, Euripides frequently falls into surmise (fr. 638, 833, 'Who knoweth if this life be verily death, and our death life to those that are gone?'; cf. *Phœnix*, fr. 816, *Hip.* 191), and thoughts of an impersonal immortality (*Helene*, 1013: 'The mind [νοῦς] of the dead, though not alive, hath consciousness [γνώμη] immortal, being plunged into the immortal æther'; cf. the 'other shapes of life' in *Ion*, 1068, *Med.* 1039).

Next to the supernatural, sexual morality is the great field for tabus and unreasoning judgments. Euripides' treatment of all such questions is by modern standards high and austere, but shows both sophistic and romantic bias. He treats with sympathy, though with condemnation, the love of married women for men not their husbands (*Phædra*, *Sthenebœa*; cf. *Med.* 635 ff.), but shows no tenderness for men in the same situation. He treats of love within the forbidden degrees (Canace and her brother in the *Æolus*), and even, as a case of heaven-sent madness, of that between Pasiphae and the Bull-god. He often treats legends of the children born of a god and a mortal woman (Creusa, Melanippe, Alcmene, Auge), always making the woman sympathetic and the god hateful, or, at least, suspect and imperfectly justified. Unlike Sophocles and Æschylus, he appears to have no tolerance of pæderastia, which he attributes only to the bestial Cyclops and, as a primeval sin, to Laius. (Ganymedes is mentioned in lyrics.)

Two social institutions of the 5th cent. especially provoked the criticism of sophists—slavery, and the subjection of women. Both had increased with the rapid expansion of city life and commerce. Slavery is never expressly condemned as 'contrary to nature' in our remains of Euripides, though he probably shared this view; but his interest in the question is shown by the innumerable references to it. The influence of slavery is very bad, and most slaves are cowardly and untrustworthy (*El.* 633; fr. 86, etc.). Yet 'many slaves are better men than their masters' (fr. 511). 'Many so-called free men are slaves at heart.' 'A man without fear cannot be a slave.' More important than these abstract statements, which are naturally put as a rule into the mouths of slaves, is the frequent presence of 'sympathetic' slaves (esp. *Alexandros*, see above). The blind devotion of a slave is shown in the *Iph. Aul.* and the *Ion* (cf. *Helene*, 726 ff.). The women of Euripides are famous; they are more prominent in his plays than the men, more closely studied, and treated with more sympathy. Yet, magnificent as his heroines are, they suggest strange conclusions about the real Athenian women of the 5th century. They are apt to be loving, courageous, clever, and often intellectual; but very ignorant and untrained, discontented, and instinctively ready to unite against the man who injures one of them. They are the slaves of their emotions, and turn quickly to treachery and crime (Creusa, Phædra, Electra, as well as the barbarians Medea and Hecuba). Even Iphigenia (Taurica) and Alcestis have their weaknesses. On the other hand, Hecuba in the *Troades* is extraordinarily noble, and so are the various virgin-martyrs. It is one of Euripides' chief glories as a dramatist that he scarcely ever indulges in an ideally 'sympathetic' stage character any more than in stage villains. His strong sympathy with women made him understand them too well to draw them in the conventional man-attracting poses. This enables Aristophanes to represent him as a great enemy of the sex, who has discovered its secrets and betrayed them to the world (*Thesmophoriazusæ*).

Two other questions which vitally interested Euripides were: (1) Is virtue teachable or purely innate? and (2) Is the current conception of a happy life, with its insistence on the possession of a wife and children, correct? On the first he speculates several times, on the whole laying much stress on 'noble birth' (εὐγένεια), if only it is of the true inward sort (fr. 52, 617; *El.* 551, etc.). He generally exalts σοφία, which with him not only means wisdom or 'culture,' but covers such qualities as 'gentleness' or 'mercy' (*El.* 294; *Or.* 491, etc.; *Alc.*, 606, etc.); while ἀμαθία denotes brutality and cruelty (*passim*; cf. the uses of γνώμη, σωφρονεῖν, etc.). Yet he believes greatly in the virtues of 'those in the mean,' especially the free peasants who keep no slaves (αὐτουργοί: cf. *El.*, first half; *Suppl.* 244; *Or.* 920). At times (*Bac.* 393, 428 ff., 1005 ff. (?); *Suppl.* 218; *Hec.* 1192) his characters even denounce the inadequacy or falseness of conventional σοφία. About children, and the intense happiness and more intense sorrow which they are apt to bring, he writes with peculiar interest (*Med.* 1090 ff.; fr. 571, 908, etc.); and he makes a wonderful use of children in his most poignant scenes (*Alc.* 394 ff.; *Andr.*, first half; *Med.*, *passim*, esp. 1270 ff.; above all, *Tro.* 700–800).

We must always remember that Euripides was in the first place a dramatist and poet, only in the second a philosopher. His habitual subject-matter was the heroic saga, which uses supernatural machinery as a matter of course; and, though he cannot keep his mind from criticism, both moral and intellectual, of this subject-matter, his main business was not criticism: it was the writing of tragedy. Further, we must not suppose that a 5th cent. Greek, who rejected superstition and tried to follow σοφία, thereby possessed at once a scientific view of the world. He was only one of the pioneers who eventually made such a view possible. Euripides' habits of often opening with a prologue spoken by a supernatural being, and closing with the appearance of some god or hero in the air, who founds the ritual on which the play is based and explains its αἴτιον (or legendary origin), belong rather to his technique than to his religion. In the development of Greek stage-craft they have their natural place (see note in J. E. Harrison, *Themis*, 1912, pp. 341–362), and theories which explain them away should be read with caution. There are real difficulties, and each case requires separate treatment, but in general we ought probably to realize (1) that an epiphany was an integral part of the old *sacer ludus* from which tragedy is derived, and was usual in Æschylus. (This can be proved from the fragments.) Euripides only stiffened the convention and introduced improved machinery. (2) The epiphany is often beautiful and effective even by our standards; in other cases we must try to imagine what the effect may have been when the mechanical device was new and impressive, and the figure in the Divine mask corresponded with the ordinary man's instinctive expectations, and was not in the faintest degree inherently ridiculous. The thought of Euripides is in many ways so extraordinarily advanced, not only for his own age but for any succeeding age, including even that of the 'Encyclopædists' (*q.v.*) and the present day, that it requires an effort to realize that in other respects he was probably, to our ideas, quite primitive and simple-minded. He was mystic as well as rationalist; and, while rejecting the Olympian mythology and the pretensions of the Delphian priests, it is surprising how often he falls back on some approach to the more primitive strata of religious thought.

Apart from his sheer force of intellect and skill as a playwright, Euripides' distinction as a poet lies partly in a sincerity which often makes him spoil the harmony of his work rather than be content with mere make-believe, and partly in a lyrical gift which can transmute into beauty his most grisly representations of human suffering; but most of all in his unequalled emotional power. It is doubtful if any later dramatist has been born to dispute his right to the tremendous title awarded him by Aristotle, who calls him, in spite of various faults, 'clearly the most tragic of the poets' (*Poet.* 1453*a*, 30).

LITERATURE.—See esp. U. von Wilamowitz-Möllendorff, *Euripides' Herakles*, Berlin, 1889, Einleitung; K. Dieterich, art. 'Euripides,' in Pauly-Wissowa; W. Nestle, *Euripides, der Dichter der griech. Aufklärung*, Stuttgart, 1901, also *Die philosoph. Quellen des Euripides*, Leipzig, 1902; P. Masqueray, *Euripide et ses idées*, Paris, 1908; P. Decharme, *Euripide et l'esprit de son théâtre*, Paris, 1893; A. W. Verrall, *Euripides the Rationalist*, Cambridge, 1895, also *Essays on Four Plays of Euripides*, do. 1905, and *The Bacchantes of Euripides*, do. 1910; G. Norwood, *The Riddle of the Bacchæ*, London, 1908; G. Murray, Introd. essays to his *Euripides*, London, 1902 (=vol. iii. of *Athenian Drama*, ed. G. C. W. Warr), and his trr. of the *Trojan Women, Electra*, etc., London, 1902–10; and the articles in the Histories of Greek Literature (Bergk, Croiset, Mahaffy, Jevons, Murray; also in Gomperz, *Greek Thinkers*, Eng. tr. 1901).

GILBERT MURRAY.

EUROPE.—We have seen (artt. AFRICA, ASIA, and ETHNOLOGY, §§ 8 and 10) that the Caucasic division of mankind was evolved most probably in North Africa, whence it ranged in remote times eastwards into Asia and northwards into Europe. The latter continent was first reached by now vanished land connexions, in company with the late large Pliocene or early Pleistocene fauna whose remains—elephant, hyæna, rhinoceros, hippopotamus, cave-bear, sabre-tooth lion or tiger—are found in association with those of early man in many parts of South and West Europe. We thus get a vast antiquity (estimated by some authorities at three or four hundred millenniums) for the first arrivals, the men of the *Palæolithic*, or *Old Stone, Age*, which nearly coincided with the *Ice Age*, that is, with pre-, inter-, and post-glacial times. All were apparently of somewhat uniform long-headed type, but showed steady progressive developments, both in physical and in mental respects, from the rude *Chellian* and *Moustierian* to the more advanced *Solutrian* and *Madelenian* epochs.

The *Old Stone Age* was followed without any clear intermission, certainly without any marked break or hiatus (now rejected by all leading palethnologists), by the *Neolithic*, or *New Stone, Age*, which had also a very long duration, estimated by Sir W. Turner for Scotland alone at perhaps a hundred millenniums. For a long time Neolithic man was also of the same long-headed type, which in the Cro-Magnon race of Dordogne reveals physical characters that may be called 'European' in the modern sense of the term. Moreover, Quatrefages, who connects all the human remains, both of the Old and of the New Stone Age, with 'the white type,' identifies the Cro-Magnon with the tall, long-headed, fair-skinned, and blue-eyed Berbers (Hamites) who still survive in various parts of Mauretania. To these Neolithic Afro-Europeans are also credited the megalithic monuments—dolmens, menhirs, cycloliths, triliths, barrows, galgals, nuraghi, talayots—which are strewn over Iberia, Gaul, Britain, Denmark, and Sweden, and which in North Africa range from the Atlantic seaboard to Tripolitana. It follows that the men of the Stone Ages form the substratum of the present inhabitants of South and West Europe, and that they are, for the most part, of North African origin.

But before the close of the New Stone Age the uniformity of the long-headed type was disturbed by the advent of numerous short-headed peoples, both in the North-west (Furfuz, Belgium) and in the South (Lozère, Lower Rhone Valley). These everywhere intermingled with the earlier long-headed type, and later became continually more numerous, until, 'towards the close of the Neolithic Age in France, the round and medium types became eight or ten times more numerous than the long in certain parts' (P. Salmon, *Races humaines préhistoriques*, p. 39). In Britain the earlier long barrows are occupied exclusively by long-heads, the later round barrows chiefly by round-heads, whence Thurnam's dictum: 'long barrow, long skull; round barrow, round skull.' In France Paul Raymond, who separates the northern short-heads from the southern long-heads by a diagonal drawn from Cohentin to the Maritime Alps, has recently discovered several short-heads commingled with long-heads in the sepulchral cave of Lirac (Départ. Gard), and infers that

'vers la fin de la période néolithique vivaient dans le sudest de la France des populations dolichocéphales qui présentaient les caractères de la race des Baumes-Chaudes [Cro-Magnon type], avec les variations que leur avait imprimées le croisement de brachycéphales immigrés' (*Revue préhistorique*, Jan 1906, p. 38).

As these Southern short-heads appear to have penetrated inland by the Rhone Valley from the south coast, they too may have come from North Africa, where a very ancient short-headed race, representing the Libyans proper and ranging into the Canary Islands, still forms the substratum in Tunisia and Kabylia, and is declared by Collignon to be remarkably like the short-headed brown French type:

'Si l'on habillait ces hommes de vêtements européens, vous ne les distingueriez pas de paysans ou de soldats français' (*L'Anthrop.*, 1897, p. 424).

It is generally admitted that the more numerous Northern short-heads came from Asia, probably by the Danube route, in the Bronze Age some four or five thousand years ago. These ranged over a vast area in East and Central Europe, and many passed westwards through Brittany into Britain, where they had been preceded by the Afro-Europeans of both Stone Ages. Other Asiatics of a long-headed type arrived, also in the Bronze Age, or perhaps even earlier, by a northern route, and occupied the Baltic lands and Scandinavia, where they are now represented by the North Germans and Norsemen, of tall stature, fair or florid complexion, and blue eyes—Linné's typical *Homo Europæus*. Lastly, another branch of these Asiatics, following a southern route through Asia Minor, passed into the Balkan region, and thence into the peninsulas of Greece and Italy, where they had been preceded by the men of the Stone Ages from North Africa.

We thus see that Europe was first settled in the south and west by North African Hamites, who came later to be known as *Pelasgians* in Greece, *Ligurians* in Italy, and *Iberians* in Spain; in the east and north by Asiatics, who may now be called *Eurasians*, since their original domain comprised the whole of the Steppe-lands between the Carpathians in Europe and the Pamirs in Central Asia (Schrader). They are also commonly called *Aryans*, because all the Eurasians spoke various diverging dialects of the long extinct Aryan stock language. But it is obvious that, strictly speaking, 'Aryan' can be only a linguistic and not an ethnical expression, since it was seen above that the Eurasians were not of one but of two distinct physical types—short-heads and long-heads. Hence, when we speak of 'Aryans,' we really mean very mixed populations of a roughly uniform Caucasic type, and of uniform Aryan speech.

It is more important to note that these Eurasians, coming in the Bronze Age, and consequently more highly cultured, and equipped with better weapons for warfare, everywhere conquered the ruder Afro-European Hamites, imposed their Aryan languages on them, and in the process merged with them into various mixed ethnical groups, which differed from each other in accordance with their different constituent elements. Thus was brought about in remote pre-historic times the Aryanization of Europe, which was so complete that, excluding the much later intrusion of the Finno-Tatar languages, the only non-Aryan form of speech still surviving in Europe is *Basque* (*q.v.*), which is spoken by scarcely 600,000 natives of the Western Pyrenees, and which represents all that remains of the old Iberian language, and is distantly related to the Berber (Hamitic) still current nearly everywhere in North Africa (G. von der Gabelenz, M. Gèze, Morris Jones, and others). Other survivals may have been the Pictish of Britain, since Prof. J. Rhŷs thinks that 'Picts and Iberians belonged to one and the same family which I have ventured to call Ibero-Pictish' (*Academy*, 26th Sept. 1891); and the Pelasgians of Greece, whom W. Wachsmuth calls 'ante-Hellenic,' and of whom Herodotus writes that, according to some evidence, *ἦσαν οἱ Πελασγοὶ βάρβαρον γλῶσσαν ἱέντες* (i. 57). For Homer these Pelasgians were *δῖοι* (*Il.* x. 429; *Od.* xix. 177); for Herodotus 'barbarians' (*loc. cit.*), and for Dionysius Hal. (i. 18 f.) 'Greeks' (*τὸ τῶν Πελασγῶν γένος Ἑλληνικόν*). Such apparently contradictory statements simply mean that, during the course of ages, the pre-Aryan inhabitants of Europe were gradually absorbed and assimilated by the Asiatic intruders of Aryan speech.

This rapid outline explains and agrees with the three great ethnical divisions proposed by Ripley, Sergi, and other leading ethnologists for the historical European populations. These are (1) the tall, fair, long-headed northern type, for which de Lapouge reserves Linné's *Homo Europæus*, and to which Ripley applies the term 'Teutonic,' because the whole combination of physical characters 'accords exactly with the descriptions handed down to us by the ancients.' Thus Tacitus: 'omnibus truces et caerulei oculi, rutilae comae, magna corpora, et tantum ad impetum valida' (*Germania*, iv.).—(2) The central zone of medium-sized roundheads with light brown or chestnut hair, brownish skin, and grey or hazel eyes, the Celts or Celto-Slavs of Broca, the Ligurians or Arvernians of Beddoe, and whom, for want of a better name, Ripley calls *Homo Alpinus*, though also comprising the Slavs of the eastern plains. These are the short-heads both from Africa and from Asia, who may be supposed to have joined hands in the central European uplands, where are met the most pronounced round skulls (*hyperbrachycephalic* in Tirol and Switzerland).—(3) The southern zone of undersized, pale, black-eyed, and black-haired long-heads, who are the primitive Afro-European element in Greece, Italy, Sicily, Sardinia, Corsica, Iberia, West France, and Britain, and are now generally identified with the above-mentioned Pelasgians, Ligurians, and Iberians, who were afterwards modified by Aryan interminglings, but are grouped together by Sergi, Keane, and Ripley as 'Mediterraneans.'

All the present Aryanized inhabitants of Europe, that is, the vast majority, may now be conveniently tabulated in accordance with these three anthropological divisions as follows:

1. HOMO EUROPÆUS (TEUTONS): Swedes, Norwegians, Danes, Icelanders, Frisians, North Germans, Dutch, Flemings, most English, Scotch, and Irish, most Normans and Walloons.
2. HOMO ALPINUS (CELTO-SLAVS): most French, Bretons, and Welsh, South Germans, Swiss, Tirolese, Austrians, Russians, Lithuanians, Poles, Czechs (Bohemians), Croatians, Servians, Dalmatians, Montenegrins, some Albanians, Bulgarians, and Rumanians.
3. HOMO MEDITERRANENSIS (IBERO-LIGURO-PELASGIANS): most Iberians (Spaniards and Portuguese), Provençals, Italians, Sards, Corsicans, Sicilians, Epirots (South Albanians), and Greeks.

On the linguistic basis the groupings naturally vary with the different views taken by philologists regarding the order in which the various members of the Aryan family branched off from the extinct mother-tongue. On this point there is still little accord, although, keeping to Europe, it is now generally allowed that, of the six recognized branches, Hellenic, Slavic, and Lithu-Lettic are more closely related one to the other than they are to the Italic, Teutonic, and Celtic. We thus get two main divisions—an eastern and a western—which, with their numerous sub-groups, may here be tabulated:

ARYAN LINGUISTIC FAMILY: EUROPEAN SECTION.[1]

Eastern Division	*Hellenic branch*:	Æolian, Dorian, Ionian, Attic, Romaic, Old Illyrian, Albanian.
	Lithuanic branch:	Lithuanian, Lettic, Pruczi (Old Prussian).
	Slavic branch:	Old Slavic, Great Russian, Little Russian, Bulgarian, Slovenian, Servo-Croatian, Czech (Bohemian), Polish, Polabish, Lusatian, Slovak.
Western Division	*Italic branch*:	Latin, Oscan, Umbrian, Italian, French, Spanish, Portuguese, Romansch, Walloon, Rumanian.
	Teutonic branch:	*Low German Group*: Gothic, Old Norse, Icelandic, Danish, Swedish, Frisic, Platt-Deutsch, Dutch, Anglo-Saxon, English.
		High German Group: Old, Middle, and New High German, Thuringian, Swabian, Swiss, Tirolese, Austrian.
	Celtic branch:	*Q Group*: Old Irish, Irish, Gaelic (Erse), Manx.
		P Group: Welsh, Cornish (extinct), Low Breton.

Besides the already mentioned Basques, the only non-Aryans now in Europe are the Baltic and other Finns, the Lapps, Samoyeds, and Magyars of Hungary, now assimilated to the normal European type but still speaking a Ugro-Finnic language, the Osmanli Turks, also largely Europeanized but not Aryanized, and lastly a few Kirghiz (Turki) and Kalmuk (Mongol) nomads in Astrakhan. All these arrived from Asia in relatively late historic times, and can in no sense be regarded as European aborigines. Respecting the Finns—about the others there is no question—it is important to note that the views formerly held regarding a western extension of the Finnic race over the whole of Europe and the British Isles are now exploded.

'Despite the fact that all the Finns are distinctly roundheaded, they were identified first with the long-headed cavemen, who retreated north with the reindeer, as was the favourite hypothesis, and then with the early neolithic races who were also long-headed. Elaborate but now forgotten essays were written by learned philologists to establish a common origin of the Basque and the Finnish tongues, which have nothing in common, and half the myths, folklore, and legendary heroes of the western nations were traced to Finno-Ugrian sources' (Keane, *Man Past and Present*, p. 334).

In fact, recent research has shown that the advent of the Finns in Finland itself dates only from about the new era, and the men of the Bronze Age in this region were not Finns but Teutons (A. Hackmann, *Die Bronzezeit Finnlands*, 1897, *passim*). Tacitus (*Germ.* xlvi.) does not know whether his *Fenni* (Ptolemy's Φίννοι) were Germans or Sarmatians (Slavs); but the reference to the children's cradles suspended from the branches of trees shows that they were the Σκριθίφινοι of Procopius (*de Bell. Goth.* ii. 15), and the Scride-Finnas of King Alfred (*Orosius*, i. 12), that is, the *Lapps*, who are still always called Finns by the Norwegians.

During the slow process of fusion between the Afro-European indigenes and the Eurasian intruders, their religious notions also became necessarily intermingled, so that the pre-Christian forms of belief were all of a mixed character like those described in art. ABORIGINES. Even after the fusion, further interminglings took place through

[1] For details, see art. ETHNOLOGY, § 10.

infiltrations from Egypt and Persia, and, more especially, from the Semitic world. Nor were these later influences confined to the contiguous Hellenic and Ægean lands, but were carried by the Phœnician seafarers westwards to Iberia and the British Isles, where they are reflected in the national legends and even in the very language of the Celtic-speaking natives of Ireland, e.g. *Bal Dhia dhuit*, 'God Baal to you'; and there is a district near Cork which is still called *Beal-athamagh-adhoir*, 'Field of the worship of Baal.' Elsewhere this Baal-cult was associated with phallic rites, as in Phœnicia.

To discriminate between all these heterogeneous elements is no longer possible, though it seems safe to say that the higher forms—the Olympian deities and personifications of the natural forces—came in with the more cultured Eurasians, and were by them superimposed on the rude animism and the chthonic gods of the Afro-Europeans, while the mysteries and degrading rites of the Cabiri, of Dionysus, Astarte, and the worshippers of Mithra and Isis (these twice expelled from Rome), were admittedly of Oriental origin. Thus the compound forms *Dyaus-pitar*, Ζεῦ-πάτερ, *Dies-piter* (Jupiter), show at once that Jove was already dominant *before* the Aryan dispersion, and consequently came in with the Eurasians, by whom his supremacy was spread north, through Lithuania (*Diewas*) to Scandinavia (*Týr*), Germany (*Zio*), and west to Britain (A.S. *Tíwesdæg*, Eng. *Tuesday* = 'day of Tíu') and Ireland, where *día* retains all the associated meanings—'sky,' or 'heaven,' 'day,' and 'god.' On the other hand, Jove's counterpart, the goddess *Ertha* (*Herthus, Earth*), was clearly an Afro-European divinity, since she was worshipped with human sacrifices (not customary with the Vedic and other proto-Aryans), and has been identified with Rhea, Ops, Demeter, Cybele, and other distinctly chthonic divinities. But she was early added by the Eurasians to their pantheon, for Tacitus tells us (*Germ.* xl.) that the Angli (Continental English) 'Herthum (variant *Erthum*), id est, Terram matrem, colunt.' He adds that the rites observed in her honour on an island in the ocean (Rügen?) concluded with the sacrifice of the attendant slaves, whom the lake in her hallowed grove (*castum nemus*) 'swallowed up.' With this should be compared the orgies practised by the Corybantes in honour of Cybele, daughter of Terra, or Terra herself, in Phrygia and Thrace, whence her worship passed into Greece (Eleusinian mysteries), and thence into Italy, where her shrine was annually cleansed by the waters of the river Almo, just as Ertha's chariot and raiment were cleansed in the above-mentioned lake at the foot of a high cliff which to this day is called 'Hertha's rock.' The Italic 'Ertha' was called *Bona Dea*, and her non-Aryan origin is admitted, as is also that of the Irish chthonic goddess *Mórrigan*, the 'Great Queen,' who has been identified with Cybele.

That human sacrifices, apparently unknown in the Aryan cradle-land, were everywhere practised by the Eurasians in their new western homes, that is, were adopted from their Afro-European predecessors, is evident from Cæsar's account (*de Bell. Gall.* vi. 16) of the frightful holocausts in Gaul, and from many other less familiar indications. From Tacitus we learn (*Germ.* ix.) that 'deorum maxime Mercurium colunt, cui certis diebus humanis quoque hostiis litare fas habent,' this Mercurius being the Wodan or Odin of the Germans and Scandinavians (as seen in the English *Wednes-day*), and the Greek Ἑρμῆς, who, Herodotus tells us, was specially worshipped by the Thracian kings (v. 7). In Rome, sexagenarians were called *senes depontani*, 'old bridge-castaways'; because old people, when a bridge was finished, were thrown into the water as a sort of bridge-toll to appease the offended river-god for this intrusion on his domain. The tribute had to be paid not once only, but every year, and it was a function of the Vestal Virgins to throw the *depontani* into the river. Later, for the living victims the so-called *argei*—rush or straw figures—were substituted as the *priscorum virorum simulacra.* The statement that the 'sexagenarii de ponte dejiciebantur' occurs in Festus, quoted by Ihering in *The Evolution of the Aryan*, p. 356. An echo of the practice, which appears to have been wide-spread, survives in the Wendland district of Hanover on the Elbe, formerly inhabited by Slavs (Wends), but now by Low Germans, who declare that their exhortation, *kruup unner, kruup unner, de Welt is di gram* ('creep under, creep under, to thee the world is [now] grim'), 'was once used as a prayer [encouragement] when the old people were thrown from the bridge into the water' (*ib.*). Bridge-building was a matter of such importance to the community that a priest called a *pontifex*,[1] or 'bridge-maker,' was appointed to superintend the works, and he gradually became the head of the priestly order, the Pontifex Maximus—a title which still survives as that of the Roman Pontiff, whence Longfellow's

> 'Well has the name of *Pontifex* been given
> Unto the Church's head, as the chief builder
> And architect of the invisible bridge
> That leads from earth to heaven' (*Golden Legend*, v.).

We are told by Tacitus (*Germ.* xxxix.) that the Semnones, who occupied a vast domain between the Elbe and the Oder, opened their national assemblies with horrible barbaric rites at which a human victim was immolated *publice*, that is, on behalf of the people. Even *satī*, or widow-burning, which was post-Vedic in India and unknown to the Greeks, Romans, and Celts, was practised both by the Slavs and by the Germans. After her husband's death the wife mounted the pyre—not, however, as an act of heroic devotion and a voluntary immolation, as amongst the later Hindus, but because she had, *nolens volens*,

> 'to share the fate of all the other possessions which were sent into the grave of a deceased man, perhaps under the impression that he could make use of them in the other world; perhaps because the idea that they should fall into other hands was repugnant to him. Besides his weapons, his horse, his slaves, and his bondmen, his wife also was sent after him' (Ihering, *op. cit.* p. 31).

In Greece we hear little of human offerings, which seem almost excluded by Herodotus, who asks (ii. 45): 'If even animals, except bulls, swine, calves, and geese were unlawful, κῶς ἂν οὗτοι (the Hellenes) ἀνθρώπους θύοιεν?' It was far different in Norseland, where the custom was universal till the introduction of Christianity, and was even observed, or at least threatened, by way of retaliation, by the first converts in Iceland. In the year 1000, the champions of the old faith having offered up two men to the gods, calling upon them not to let Christianity overrun the land, the Christians retorted that they too would make an offering of two men.

> '"The heathens," they said, "sacrifice the worst men, and cast them over rocks or cliffs; but we shall choose the best men, and call it a gift for victory to our Lord Jesus Christ"' (Craigie, *The Religion of Ancient Scandinavia*, p. 58 f.).

In the same spirit, but on the opposite side, the Norwegian king Olaf Tryggvason (998) threatened a great immolation, saying:

> 'I will not choose thralls or criminals, but will select the most distinguished men to give to the gods' (*ib.* p. 58).

So in Denmark, at the great national gathering held every nine years, a holocaust was made of ninety men, with as many horses and dogs. In the Swedish chronicles it is recorded that one of

[1] Walde (*Etymol. Wörterb. der lat. Sprache*[2], Heidelberg, 1910, p. 598 f.) holds that the *pontifex* was the 'performer of holy things.' The question is fully discussed in art. BRIDGE, vol. ii. p. 855.

the early kings was made a 'burnt-offering' to Odin in order to end a famine caused by his slackness in keeping up the sacrifices, while another king immolated nine of his sons in succession to Odin, to obtain long life for himself. Lastly, it is related in the *Guta Saga* that the people of the island of Gotland

'sacrificed their sons and daughters and their cattle. All the land had its highest sacrifices with folk (=human beings), as also had each third (of the country) by itself' (*ib.* p. 57 f.).

For the western Celtic world reference has already been made to Cæsar's account of the inhuman Gaulish holocausts made in huge wickerwork images on special occasions. But at all times such offerings were customary. People stricken with illness, engaged in warfare, or exposed to other risks,

'offered, or promised to offer, human sacrifices, and made use of the Druids as their agents for such sacrifices. Their theory was that the immortal Gods could not be appeased unless a human life were given for a human life. In addition to these private sacrifices, they had also similar human sacrifices of a public character' (Anwyl, *Celtic Religion*, p. 50 f.).

Such rites must have also prevailed in Britain, as may be inferred from the incident mentioned by Nennius, who tells how Vortigern, when building a fort, was much annoyed by the spirits running off with the stones, and was advised by the Druids to kill a fatherless boy and sprinkle his blood upon the foundations of the building. So in Ireland such offerings were not merely threatened, as in Iceland, but actually practised by the early Christians. Some of the legendary underground fiends that went about at night pulling down the walls of churches erected during the day were so troublesome that it was found necessary to revive the old heathen methods of protection, by burying alive a man, woman, or child under the foundations.

'Tradition says that St. Columba, thus tormented, buried St. Oran, at his own request, under the monastery of Iona' (Bonwick, *Irish Druids*, p. 90).

It matters little whether this actually occurred or not, since the mere mention of it as a possibility shows that the early Christian writers were aware of the pagan custom, for which there is in any case abundance of collateral evidence.

Thus in the *Dinnsenchus* it is stated that to Crom Cruach, the chief Irish deity, his votaries offered 'the first-born of all offspring and the first-born of their children'—probably a Phœnician practice (cf. Dt 12[31]). In an old poem on the *Fair of Tailtenn*, St. Patrick is described as preaching against the burning of firstlings; on the summit of Sliabh Crooabh, 'Hill of the Deadly Spear,' there is a ruined altar where the victims of the gods were immolated; and the early Christian Culdees (*q.v.*), the successors of the pagan Druids, are strongly suspected of having offered human sacrifices.

If the proto-Aryans adopted these revolting practices from the Afro-European aborigines, which seems scarcely open to doubt, they made ample amends by the introduction of two social institutions—monogamy and patriarchy—which in pre-Christian times helped more perhaps than all else to raise the ethical standard to a higher level in Europe than in any other part of the world. No doubt the Eurasians were not all monogamists at first, since polygamy was lawful and practised by their rulers. But the great bulk of the immigrants were monogamists, whether on principle or because they could not afford the luxury of many wives. Moreover, the marriage relation received religious sanction, which was even compulsory in certain cases, and already in pre-historic times the whole of Aryanized Europe appears to have been monogamous. The business part of the transaction varied considerably; in Rome the bride brought the *dos* to her husband, while the Germans and Slavs brought the dowry, the *Brautgabe*, to the bride, that is, bought her, as we see in the case of Vladimir the Great (988), who forcibly abducted an undowered Byzantine princess, and then paid her relations for her; cf. Tacitus: 'dotem non uxor marito, sed uxori maritus offert' (*Germ.* xviii.). But such details made little difference; and, when we find monogamy the rule amongst the early Eurasians and later universal, we recognize in the fact the same moral conception of the marriage laws

'which places them so far higher than all contemporary nations of antiquity. In this respect the Aryans are proved to have been a civilized nation of the first rank' (Ihering, *op. cit.* p. 30).

No less beneficial was the patriarchy, with descent through the male line, which everywhere superseded the earlier and ruder matriarchy, with descent through the female line, and for the first time established the family, as now understood, on a solid foundation, by the marriage contract. Recently Lamprecht has proved (*Deutsche Gesch.* i. [1890]) that long before the dispersal the proto-Aryans had reached the patriarchal state through the matriarchal, which implied the absence of marriage, and under which the children belonged to the mother, the father not being considered because unknown. With the introduction of marriage the maternal yielded to the paternal right, and to the father, who now asserts himself, belong the children and the mother herself. It was under this *patria potestas* that the Eurasians entered Europe, where, consequently, no trace now survives of the primitive *matria potestas*. The *paterfamilias*, whose antiquity is shown by the archaic form *familias* for the later *familiæ*, ruled supreme, and in Rome enjoyed the power of life and death over all the household—over the *famuli*, that is, the slaves or servants (cf. the Oscan *famel*=*famulus*, and *famelo*='family'). It was his interest to maintain order amongst these *famuli*, with whom were included his own wife and children, and thus was gradually organized the family circle, as we now see it, throughout the Aryan world. This could never have been under the matriarchal system, which prevailed amongst the early Eurafricans, as it still does amongst many primitive peoples. We see the results in the high esteem in which the domestic virtues were held by the Romans under the kings and during the Republic (Lucretia, Virginia), and by Germans in the time of Tacitus, although here the picture may be somewhat heightened as an object lesson for the decadent Romans under the Empire. Still it is a beautiful picture applicable even to present times ('Numerum liberorum finire . . . flagitium habetur'), and concluding with the memorable words '*plusque ibi boni mores valent* quam alibi bonae leges' (*Germ.* xix.).

In *GB*[2] (vol. i. p. viii) Frazer writes that 'the superstitious beliefs and practices which have been handed down by word of mouth are generally of a far more archaic type than the religion depicted in the most ancient literature of the Aryan race.' So true is this, that all folklorists now admit that the whole of Europe was choked with such rank undergrowths before the arrival of the Eurasians, who, so far from eradicating them, added greatly to their number by fresh importations from Central Asia. Here and there it is possible to distinguish between the old and the new, as in the case of certain spells and spooks characteristically European, but in most instances it would be futile to attempt to draw any dividing line between western and eastern popular notions, which might have sprung up on any soil. Thus witchcraft, lycanthropy, the evil eye, and wind-raising range from Ireland with little interruption to Malaysia, and hence might have been either brought with them by the proto-Aryans or else picked up in their new homes. Even the strange observance of the fire-dance, which from its very nature might be supposed to be restricted in time and place, was already known to the ancients and practised by the Hirpini (Sabines), as it also was by the now extinct

Catawbas of North America, and still is by the Bulgarians, the Japanese, the Hindus, the Tahitians, and the Fijians of the Central Pacific Ocean. Similarly, all sorts of fire-myths are met with, from the Promethean in Hellas to that of the extinct Tasmanians, who had no fire at all until two natives, standing on a hill, threw it about like stars.

'After this no more was fire lost in our land. The two blackfellows are in the clouds; in the clear night you see them like stars. These are they who brought fire to our fathers' (Brough Smyth, *Abor. of Vict.*, Melbourne, 1878, ii. 461).

A closer parallel is the wax effigy of a person, by means of which he was done to death at a distance—a practice found almost everywhere in Europe. The process as described by Ovid (*Ep.* vi. 91)—

'Devovet absentes, simulacraque cerea figit,
Et miserum tenues in jecur urget acus'—

is exactly the same as that adopted by the hapless Princess Caroline to encompass the death of the Prince Regent.

'She made a wax figure as usual, and gave it an amiable addition of large horns; then took three pins out of her garment and stuck them through and through, and put the figure to roast and melt at the fire. . . . Lady —— says the Princess indulges in this amusement whenever there are no strangers at table; and she thinks her Royal Highness really has a superstitious belief that destroying this effigy of her husband will bring to pass the destruction of his Royal person' (S. Clerici, *A Queen of Indiscretion*, F. Chapman's English ed. 1907).

So in Ross-shire the rudely shaped image of the person aimed at

'is stuck all over with pins and thorns and placed in a running stream. As the image is worn away by the action of the water the victim also wastes away with some mortal disease. The more pins that are stuck in from time to time the more excruciating agony the victim suffers. Should, however, any wayfarer discover the *corp* (effigy) in the stream, the spell is broken and the victim duly recovers' (Haddon, *Magic and Fetishism*, p. 20).

In the Isle of Wight the plan is to put a slug under a flower-pot, fix it there with a pin or a needle, and leave it to die, when the victim also is sure to die.

'Our early Teuton forefathers,' remarks F. York Powell (in *Religious Systems of the World*, London, 1901, p. 279), 'were influenced by *anthropomorphism* and *animism*, and thought that inanimate objects, as stones, stars, and the elements, and organisms such as trees, fishes, birds and beasts, were possessed of spirits akin to their own.'

From this root-idea, which belongs to all primitive systems (see art. ETHNOLOGY, § 9), sprang those countless hosts of invisible beings, some good, some bad, some harmless, who have throughout the ages filled the upper, the terrestrial, and the lower regions, and whose numbers were greatly increased by the ancestor-worship which was highly characteristic of the proto-Aryans. As these immigrants failed to sweep away the lower forms of animism (see above), so the Christian system not only left the spirit world untouched, but enlarged it with Lucifer and his fallen angels, and with those δαιμόνια πολλά and πνεύματα ἀκάθαρτα whose name was 'Legion' (Mk 5[9]). Satan and Beelzebub were also recognized, and, demonology having thus received a new lease of existence, it is not surprising that it should continue to flourish throughout Christendom down to the present day. Its name is still 'Legion,' as we read in the *Life and Works of Robert Burns* (ed. R. Chambers, 1851, p. 10), where Betty Davidson, who lived in the family,

'had the largest collection in the country of tales and songs concerning devils, ghosts, fairies, brownies, witches, warlocks, spunkies, kelpies, elf-candles, dead-lights, wraiths, apparitions, cantraips, giants, enchanted towers, dragons, and other trumpery.'

Nor does this exhaust the list, which further includes banshees, leprechauns, cluricauns, good people (*Duine Matha*), tylwyth-teg or Fair Family, tyloethod, Cyweraeth, morrigans, phookas, pixies, spooks, spectres, sprites, nickers or water-kelpies, bogles or bugils, bug-bears, bug-a-bos, goblins, hobgoblins, fays, ogres, duzes, dwarfs, lubber-fiends, pucks, trolls, nissens, damhests, damavoi, rotri, korils, korigans, naiads, nymphs, dryads, sylphs, wer-wolves, vampires, and no doubt many more local and personal *Gespenster* and 'familiar spirits' (cf. Socrates), so that some parts of Europe are said to be more thickly peopled with these invisible spirits than with human beings. And Sir Conan Doyle writes (*Sir Nigel*, 1908) that

'in those simple times [14th cent.] the Devil raged openly upon the earth; he stalked behind the hedge-rows in the gloaming; he laughed loudly in the night time; he clawed the dying sinner, pounced upon the unbaptized babe, and twisted the limbs of the epileptic. A foul fiend slunk ever by a man's side and whispered villainies in his ear. . . . How could one doubt these things, when Pope and priest, scholar and king were all united in believing them, with no single voice of question in the whole wide world?'

Then, as the majority of the spirits were dangerous or ill-disposed, all kinds of devices were naturally invented or developed to thwart their designs and the machinations of those supposed to be in league with them (see artt. DEMONS AND SPIRITS). Thus arose those otherwise unaccountable charms (*carmina*), spells, incantations, divinations, reading of horoscopes, fortune-telling, ordeals, duels, and especially that sinister belief in witchcraft (*q.v.*) which broke out again and again throughout mediæval times, and led to the perpetration of unspeakable horrors by religious and other fanatics. It is scarcely three centuries since James I., the author of a special work on *Demonology*, put two hundred wretched victims of the craze, along with a noble and learned physician, to a horrible death on the charge of having 'raised the wind' against the coming of his Norwegian bride. Whoever wants to understand the full essence of this frightful blend of foulness and ferocity should read Cantù's official revelations of the witchcraft mania, which did not receive its death-blow till the judges of the ecclesiastical courts were themselves struck at by their victims under torture (see Manzoni, *I Promessi Sposi*, Turin, 1827).

Fear in high places thus removed one great evil, but left others which still persist, and all of which have a religious basis. Such is the *duel*, which is the last surviving form of the *ordeal* in Europe. Its great antiquity is shown by its archaic Latin form *duellum*, of which *bellum* is a much later modification (cf. Hor. *Od.* III. v. 38, 'pacem duello miscuit'). The ordeal itself, that is, the A.S. *ordál*, the Germ. *Urteil*, and Lat. *judicium Dei*, persisted under various forms from the earliest times far into mediæval Europe, as seen in Shakespeare's *Richard III.* i. 2, where allusion is made to the test of touch to which suspected murderers were subjected. At their contact the wounds of their victims were supposed to bleed afresh. The close association of these ordeals with early religious beliefs, as pointed out in art. AUSTRALASIA, is clearly illustrated in the pagan Anglo-Saxon *corsned*, under which an accused person was required to swallow a piece of bread or cheese execrated by the priest. If he did so easily, he was innocent; if with an effort, guilty: and it may easily be supposed that, in persons of weak nerves, the awe of the surroundings might produce the effort, even in the case of guiltless persons. In Christian times the *corsned*, like the fire, water, and so many other unpleasant ordeals, was still continued, the consecrated wafer being now substituted for the execrated bread (see, further, artt. DUELLING, ORDEAL).

A still more striking instance of the fusion of the old and new systems is afforded by the mixed or muddled religious notions prevalent amongst the European gypsies, more especially those of Hungary and Austria, who have for some generations been nominal Christians, mostly Roman Catholics, but also Orthodox Greeks in some districts. But none of them is quite clear about the presiding deity, though the prevalent idea is that the dethroned ruler, the *baro puro dewel*, 'great old god,' has long been dead, and that the world is now governed by his son and successor, the *dikno tarno dewel*, the 'small young god,' *i.e.* Jesus Christ. Another theory is that the first still lives, and has only abdicated in favour of the second. Others, again, hold that the old god is really dead, but that the younger is not his son, but the son of a carpenter, having, like Jupiter, usurped the throne on which he is now seated. He controls the elements, and is not a beneficent deity, since, like Saturn, he 'devours his children,' *i.e.* allows them to die. He also has fits of spite and anger, when he sends down thunder and lightning, snow, rain, and hail, which destroy their crops, burn their villages, and cause many other disasters. These gypsies can scarcely be said to have any religion properly so called. They do not worship the old or the new god, they have no kind of rites or ceremonies, and their *beng*, or devil, is borrowed from the Christians. But

'they believe in omens and prognostications; they give credit to the existence of ghosts and spectres, are afraid of the pernicious influence of the evil eye, and object to having their portrait taken lest they might be bewitched' (Featherman, *Dravido-Turanians*, p. 604).

In these respects the eastern gypsies differ in no way from their western kindred, or from the great bulk of the uneducated classes in every part of Europe. The Irish peasantry have endless magic cures for rheumatism, jaundice, whooping-cough, toothache, and other ailments.

Edith Wheeler tells (*Occult Review*, iv. [Nov. 1906]) that the jaundiced are 'mended' by being taken three times over water running south. The whooping-cough is stopped by taking the patient to a child that has never seen its father, and letting it breathe three times over the sufferer and 'the cure will work.' On a headland in Co. Clare there is an old altar, and near it a pool of fresh water and a 'bed of stones'—the saints' bed—to which the pilgrims come and walk round three times; and, if a child of stunted growth be carried round in the same way and then dipped in the pool, it will grow up properly, if the little fishes come to the top of the water.

So in Co. Mayo there is a well from which no woman, though perishing with thirst, would dare to draw water until certain rites are performed with a new-born babe, else it would turn to worms and blood. In the same district another well is visited by women who come to pray for the sick. 'They go round the well seven times on their knees, while telling their beads. If at the conclusion of their devotion any living thing is seen in the well their prayer is answered. I have seen a poor woman kneeling for hours over the well with hands clasped, and gazing with agonized anxiety into the clear water' (Sir H. Blake, in *Man*, 1901, no. 11).

Here is an Irish charm for the toothache: 'May the thumb of chosen Thomas in the side of guileless Christ heal my teeth without lamentation from worms and from pangs,' again showing the blend of old pagan and Christian traditions. The strange keenings of professional mourners at funerals are also very ancient, and certainly pre-Christian, if not pre-Aryan.

Certain observances, which later acquired a religious character or became associated with magical agencies, were originally of a purely practical nature. Such were the totem and tabu (see art. AUSTRALASIA); so also the inspection of the entrails of birds and cattle for divination purposes in Greece, Rome, and Etruria had a similar utilitarian object, as already recognized by Democritus, who thought that not the pleasure of the gods, but the healthiness of the climate and the richness or poverty of the soil, were indicated by the condition of the intestines of the animals living in the district:

'pabuli genus, et earum rerum, quas terra procreet, vel ubertatem, vel tenuitatem; salubritatem etiam, aut pestilentiam extis significari putat' (Cicero, *de Div.* ii. 30).

This view is rejected by Cicero but adopted and revived by Ihering (*loc. cit.*), who concludes generally that all such auspices—the study of the *exta*, the flight and song of birds, *i.e.* the 'avium voces volatusque,' as in Tacitus, *Germ.* x., the feeding of poultry (*tripudia*), and so on—

'owe their origin to practical, essentially secular purposes. The religious idea was in the beginning utterly foreign to them, and has been added, as was the case with so many other primitive institutions, after they had lost their original and practical meaning.'

Those who reject this explanation can take refuge only in the notion that in remote antiquity the people believed that the deity revealed himself in the belly of an ox ('interesse deum singulis pecorum fissis') (Ihering, p. 370). This is, in fact, the natural evolution of such practices, since primitive man must at first have been much more concerned with the quest of food and other material considerations than with costly and elaborate religious ceremonies (see, further, artt. DIVINATION).

Some of the methods of divination are of great age, and may well have been brought by the proto-Aryans from their Asiatic homes. Such is that of the early Germans which is described by Tacitus, *Germ.* x., and is exactly like one practised by the Scythians, as in Herodotus, iv. 67. The ancient oracles have long been silent, but their voices, the messages from above, seem still to linger in the thunder-cloud, in the lightning-flash, in the soughing of the winds, and especially in the church bells, which, like the holy water, are potent, when blessed, to dissipate foul weather and to scare the evil spirits riding in the gale.

It is the blessing, the consecration, which endows the bell, the Agnus Dei, the scapular, and other such talismans with their *mana*, their supernatural virtue (see artt. MELANESIA and AUSTRALASIA), and has caused Hartland to declare that 'all religion is saturated with magic.' Certainly the belief in magic influences is still universal in Europe, and Haddon does not hesitate to declare that 'four-fifths of mankind, probably, believe in sympathetic magic' (*op. cit.* p. 2). By *sympathetic* is meant what Frazer calls *contagious* magic, which requires, if not actual contact, at least some material connexion between the person and the object operated upon. A few hairs, nail-parings, a drop of blood, clothes, personal ornaments, anything will suffice, not only to cause death, but also to produce any other desired effect. Thus in England

'a girl forsaken by her lover is advised to get a lock of his hair and boil it; whilst it is simmering in the pot he will have no rest. In certain parts of Germany and Transylvania the clippings of the hair or nails, as well as broken pieces of the teeth, are buried beneath the elder tree which grows in the courtyard, or are burnt, or carefully hidden, for fear of witches' (*ib.* p. 3).

To this, perhaps, may be due the strange objection some people have to being overshadowed by an elder-tree, one of which the present writer had to remove from his garden to oblige a superstitious neighbour.

All kinds of magic processes are adopted as counter-charms against the baneful effects of the evil eye (*q.v.*), the dread of which is universal in Italy. Any reputed *jettatore*—and Pope Pius the Ninth himself was one—causes a general stampede should he appear in a crowded street, and, 'ever since the establishment of the religious orders, monks have had the special reputation of possessing the fatal influence' (*ib.* p. 34). It is perhaps the very oldest superstition of which there is distinct record. It was known not only to the Greeks and Romans (Plutarch), but even to the early Egyptians, one of whose most common amulets was the so-called 'Eye of Osiris.'

'These mystic eyes were worn equally by the living and the dead as amulets; it being natural, from the associations of homœopathic magic, that representations of the eye itself should have been considered potent amulets against its malign influence' (*ib.* p. 35; cf. also *ERE* iii. 432 f.).

And of Cond of the 'Hundred Battles,' a legendary Irish hero, it is related that he always kept his right eye closed, because its glance was found to be fatal to any one falling under its baneful influence.

As a rule, any one might practise magic if only he or she knew how. But there were specialists—medicine-men, shamans, Druids, magicians, sorcerers, wizards, witches, wise women, and others—who transmitted their lore to their disciples. All had to undergo a severe probation, in which long fastings provocative of visions seem to have played the chief part. Amongst the Finns and Lapps they were constituted in societies or colleges which, like those of the Roman and Etruscan augurs and haruspices, exercised considerable influence even in political matters. But after the suppression of the order of Druids (*q.v.*) by the Emperor Claudius, such societies were never reconstituted in Aryan Europe, and their place was later taken by the Christian hierarchy. Nevertheless, C. G. Leland refers to some such association that still persists in Tuscany, which, however, is shrouded in much mystery. Its professors, mostly women, are said to meet in secret and, like the Anatolian Yezidis, to observe some old-time rites, and to dispense charms and spells to their followers (*Etruscan Roman Remains in Popular Tradition*).

It may be mentioned in this connexion that the term *sacerdotes* occurs more than once in Tacitus (*Germ.* x., xi.), although we learn from other sources that the Germans had no distinct order of priests like the Celtic Druids. Thus Cæsar states positively (*de Bell. Gall.* vi. 21) that the Germans 'neque Druides habent . . . neque sacrificiis student.' Yet Tacitus calls his *sacerdotes* 'ministros deorum,' and adds that they kept order and controlled the proceedings in the public assemblies. On the other hand, we know from the sagas that amongst the pagan Scandinavians there was no distinct priestly caste, but that the priestly and civil functions were vested in the same person—the king, earl, or district chief, spoken of as 'ruler of the sanctuaries,' or *goði*, from *goð*, 'god,' like the English 'divines' from root *divus*, *deus*. It appears, also, that women, to some extent, acted as priestesses, although their precise relation to the priestly chiefs is not clear. The office was hereditary, and, as the *goði* was both a chief and a priest,

'the name did not disappear with the adoption of Christianity . . . though it naturally lost its religious associations and thenceforward dencted only the recognized leader in the various districts' (Craigie, *op. cit.* p. 66).

About the Celtic Druids, their status and functions, much diversity of opinion still prevails, the reason being that the term itself covers three different classes, at least in Gaul and Britain. By Cæsar these are all merged in one, the Druidic as opposed to the military order; but they are carefully distinguished by Diodorus, Pliny, and especially Strabo (after Posidonius), who speak, as we still do, of the Druids proper, the *vates* (seers), and the poets (bards). The Druids were rather philosophers and theologians than priests, though they had to be present at the sacrifices. They taught Pythagorean doctrines, and the immortality of the soul through transmigration, to their disciples gathered in caves and secluded groves where tree-cult may have still survived, and where, in any case, high honour was paid to the oak and to its parasite the mistletoe, the emblem of love, which still plays a part in our Yule-tide festivities. Cæsar (*de Bell. Gall.* vi.) says that these *arcana* came to Gaul from Britain, whither the Continental Druids resorted to complete their education. So in later times the first dawnings of the new learning came also from Britain and Ireland (Pelagius, John Scotus Erigena, founder of the Scholastic philosophy). The true priests were the *vates*, who performed the sacrifices which, till suppressed by the Roman Emperors, were marked by features of a peculiarly atrocious character. They practised divination

'by the slaughter of a human victim, and the observation of the attitude in which he fell, the contortions of the limbs, the spurting of the blood, and the like,' this being 'an ancient and established practice' (Anwyl, *op. cit.* p. 46).

Lastly, the *bards* (*q.v.*) were minstrels and poets, often retainers of powerful chiefs, whose heroic deeds they sang, thus stirring up fierce rivalries between neighbouring clans and septs. But they were also peacemakers, and would at times step in between hostile tribes, and, like the Sabine women, induce them to stop the fight. A volume would scarcely suffice to state the contradictory views held regarding the Irish Druids, bards, brehons (legislators), ollamhs (teachers), and others, all of whom, according to the bias or ignorance of the writers, receive indiscriminate praise or vituperation as priests, philosophers, astronomers, minstrels, poets, learned doctors, law-givers, or physicians, or else as charlatans, impostors, astrologers, sorcerers, necromancers, magicians, and so on. Eugene O'Curry, who knew them best, declares that

'there is no ground whatever for believing the Druids to have been the priests of any special positive worship';

while E. Ledwich tells us confidently that

'the Druids possessed no internal or external doctrine, either veiled by symbols, or clouded in enigmas, or any religious tenets but the charlatanerie of barbarian priests and the grossest gentile superstition' (*Antiquities of Ireland*, quoted by Bonwick, *Irish Druids*, p. 35). Cf. also MacCulloch, *Rel. of Anc. Celts*, 1911, *passim*.

Hence Bonwick (p. 23) shrewdly remarks that

'it is as easy to call a Druid a deceiver as a politician a traitor, or a scientist a charlatan, and a saint a hypocrite.'

One thing is clear, that Druidism was not removed by Patrick, who rather

'engrafted Christianity on the pagan superstition with so much skill that he won the people over to the Christian religion before they understood the exact difference between the two systems of beliefs; and much of this half pagan half Christian religion will be found, not only in the Irish stories of the Middle Ages, but in the superstitions of the peasantry of the present day' (*ib.* p. 29).

The Finns and Magyars call for no special reference, since the former have long been Lutherans, the latter Roman Catholics. But the Lapps, although now also Christians, still cherish many old heathen notions. At one time they were noted shamanists and magicians, and the expression 'Lapland witches' became proverbial, although there were no witches but only wizards in the country. Their idea of an after-life is extremely crude, and many still bury, instead of banking, their money, in the belief that it will be found useful in the next world.

LITERATURE.—O. Schrader, *Sprachvergleichung und Urgeschichte*[3], 1907 (Eng. ed. *Prehistoric Antiquities of the Aryan Peoples*, 1890), and *Reallexikon der indogerm. Altertumskunde*, 1901; H. Hirt, *Die Indogermanen*, 1905–7; R. von Ihering, *Vorgesch. der Indo-Europäer*, 1894 (Eng. ed. *The Evolution of the Aryan*, 1897); A. H. Keane, *Ethnology*, 1896, and *Man Past and Present*, 1900; P. Salmon, *Races humaines préhistoriques*, 1891; J. Bonwick, *Irish Druids and Old Irish Religions*, 1894; G. von der Gabelenz, *Die Verwandtschaft des Baskischen mit den Berbersprachen nachgewiesen*, 1894; J. E. Harrison, *Religion of Ancient Greece*, 1905; C. G. Leland, *Etruscan Roman Remains in Popular Tradition*, 1892; J. G. Frazer, *The Golden Bough*[2], 1900; E. S. Hartland, *The Legend of Perseus*, 3 vols., 1894–6; W. A. Craigie, *The Religion of Ancient Scandinavia*, 1906; A. Featherman, *Dravido-Turanians*, 1891; E. Anwyl, *Celtic Religion*, 1906; A. C. Haddon, *Magic and Fetishism*, 1906; J. Lippert, *Die Religionen der europäischen Culturvölker*, 1881; G. Sergi, *Umbri, Italici, Arii*, 1897; W. Z. Ripley, *The Races of Europe*, 1897; M. de Mortillet, *Formation de la nation française*, 1900; C. Cunningham, *Western Civilization*, 1898; W. Wachsmuth, *The Historical Antiquities of the Greeks* (Eng. ed. 1837); Boyd Dawkins, *Early Man in Britain*, 1880; W. C. Borlase, *The Dolmens of Ireland*, 3 vols., 1897.

A. H. KEANE.

EUSTATHIUS.—Eustathius, bishop of Sebaste in Armenia, was regarded as the apostle of monasticism in the northern part of Asia Minor. Probably he was the author of a work on the ascetic life attributed to St. Basil (*Constitutiones Asceticæ*, see Garnier's Introd. to the Benedict. ed. of St. Basil's works). For these reasons he deserves more generous treatment than he has generally received at the hands of ecclesiastical historians.

Eustathius appears to have been the son of a bishop, Eulalius (Soz. iv. 24. 9; Socr. ii. 43. 1), and was born about A.D. 300. He was the pupil of the heresiarch Arius in Alexandria (Basil, *Epp.* 223, 224). He does not appear to have been profoundly influenced by his master's dogmatic teaching. He acquired, while in Egypt, a great admiration for the lives of the early hermit ascetics. On his return to Asia Minor he commenced to practise asceticism in a manner which brought him into conflict with his father, Bishop Eulalius (Socr. ii. 43. 1), and earned him a reputation as a dangerous man (Basil, *Ep.* 223). He gathered round him a considerable band of disciples, known as Eustathians, who perhaps exaggerated his ascetic practices and teaching. They, though apparently not Eustathius himself, came under the censure of the Council of Gangra (341?). There is no suggestion that they were regarded as dogmatically unsound; what was objected to was the severity and uncatholic nature of some of their forms of asceticism, and the extreme, puritanical narrowness of their efforts to make the clergy in general conform to their standard. Eustathius himself must either have been opposed to this exaggeration of his teaching or must have dissassociated himself from his followers, for, in or about A.D. 356, he became bishop of Sebaste. A few years later his intimate friendship with St. Basil began (Basil, *Ep.* 223).

He was at this time noted as an able preacher, a man of exemplary life (Soz. iii. 14. 36), and a leader of 'very excellent monks' (viii. 27. 4). He founded his ξενοδοχεῖον, a great house for strangers and hospital for the sick, in Sebaste (Epiph. *Hær.* lxxv. 1), and placed it under the charge of monks. This was the model of St. Basil's more famous institution in Cæsarea. Although he lived through the stormy period of the Arian and semi-Arian controversies, his interest in dogmatic questions appears to have been small. He probably believed that some satisfactory middle way could be discovered, and wished to be left in peace to perform his practical work. He signed, without apparently realizing his inconsistency, the creeds of Ancyra (A.D. 358), Seleucia (359), Constantinople (360), and Lampsacus (364) (see ARIANISM). It was this indifference to the importance of the dogmatic issues at stake that was the cause of his quarrel with St. Basil. The great metropolitan was not the man to spare an opponent, and Eustathius has suffered in the estimation of ecclesiastical historians by the account which is given of him by his former friend, after the rupture. We last hear of Eustathius, then an old man, in Basil's *Ep.* 263, written A.D. 377, and we may suppose that his death took place shortly after this date.

LITERATURE.—L. Tillemont, *Mémoires*², Paris, 1701–12, ix.; J. Garnier, *Vita Basilii* (*Op. Bas.*, Bened. ed., Paris, 1721–30); J. A. Fabricius, *Bib. Græc.*, Hamburg, 1790–1809, v., viii.; F. Loofs, *Eustathius von Sebaste u. die Chron. der Basilius-Briefe*, Halle, 1898; H. M. Gwatkin, *Studies of Arianism*, Cambridge, 1882, ii.; O. Zöckler, *Askese u. Mönchtum*², Frankfort, 1897, i.; J. O. Hannay, *Spirit and Origin of Christian Monasticism*, London, 1903; B. Jackson, Introd. to tr. of Basil, in *Nicene and post-Nicene Fathers*; also works cited in text of article.

JAMES O. HANNAY.

EUTHANASIA.—*Introductory.*—Euthanasia may be defined as the doctrine or theory that in certain circumstances, when, owing to disease, senility, or the like, a person's life has permanently ceased to be either agreeable or useful, the sufferer should be painlessly killed, either by himself or by another.

The discussion of the subject, especially from the standpoint of Applied Ethics, is exceedingly difficult for several reasons. In the first place, it may easily be misconstrued as a mere recommendation of suicide or of the wholesale murder of aged or infirm people. Secondly, the effect of such a doctrine on weak or unbalanced minds, incapable of weighing aright the conditions which may be held to render death more desirable than life, is very apt to be pernicious. Thirdly—and this is the greatest difficulty of all—there are obvious and important obstacles in the way of any practical application in a modern civilized community. In order to make euthanasia in any sense a legal proceeding, one would be obliged to encounter, not merely prejudices or even time-honoured religious beliefs, but the healthy and moral feeling that human life is too sacred and valuable to be taken except under a few very definite conditions. In other words, euthanasia would constitute a new form of justifiable homicide, and, unless most strictly regulated, would lead to an appalling increase in sundry forms of crime already far too common. Thus, if it were legally recognized that an infant afflicted with an incurable hereditary disease, or with idiocy, might be put to death, a new excuse for infanticide—terribly prevalent, as is well known, in the case of illegitimate children—would at once be provided. Suicide also—for the most part a mere act of insanity, rashness, or cowardice—would be likely to become more common than it now is if, for instance, persons suffering from a disease known or supposed to be incurable were rather encouraged to take their life than discouraged from such a procedure.

On the other hand, we can hardly refuse to recognize that an application of the doctrine of euthanasia would provide a solution for many grave problems which the modern State is obliged to face. Take a single example, already incidentally mentioned. In all communities a great number of children are born seriously defective in body, or mind, or both. Although a certain proportion of these can be cured by proper medical attention, many cannot, by all the resources of modern surgery and medicine, be made normal; and this applies especially to those who are more or less completely idiotic. Many of these unfortunates are not so obviously abnormal as to make their condition plain to a casual observer, and, especially among the poorer classes, they are frequently treated almost as fully rational beings and allowed to mingle with the community at large and even to propagate their kind. The only substitute for euthanasia here is segregation and training, an able argument for which was put forward some years ago by an eminent worker in that field, M. W. Barr, of the Pennsylvania School for Feeble-minded Children.[1] This writer draws attention to the excellent results produced, within his own experience, in a large number of cases, by industrial training in properly-conducted institutions. His claim is that the feeble-minded can be made actually useful, as many of them have considerable physical skill, and that their lives are far from unhappy under such conditions. But he freely admits that it is only by careful segregation and training that such results can be accomplished; and this obviously involves heavy expense of all sorts, including the diverting of the abilities and energies of a number of physicians, etc., from other fields of activity. Whether, even in the most favourable cases, the result is adequate may be questioned; and this leaves out of account many individuals whose mental disabilities afford little or no hope of any considerable improvement. A carefully controlled system of euthanasia, on the contrary, would eliminate the more hopeless cases at once.

But in the very necessity of control lies the

[1] *IJE* viii. 481.

great, if not the fatal, difficulty. Supposing all objection removed to the taking of life otherwise than in battle, self-defence, or capital punishment, there would still remain the fact that life is, so to speak, a valuable asset, and the question as to where, in any conceivable community, an authority could be found competent to decide whether a given individual deserved to live or not, and to carry out the decision in practice. Apart from all purely moral considerations, if we treat the matter as one of mere calculation, it is obviously most difficult, if not impossible, to judge whether a helpless cripple, known to possess considerable intellectual powers, is or is not more of a burden to the community by reason of the constant attendance he will require than of benefit to it because of his possibilities of brain-work. And, even were this difficulty overcome, we should still have to deal with the vexed question of the limits of the State's functions; for by no means all thinkers, even of those farthest from extreme Individualism, are disposed to allow to any State such wide authority in matters of life and death. Thus Sidney Ball, a writer of rather decided Socialistic tendencies, holds that 'the real danger of Collectivism is . . . that it would be as ruthless as Plato in the direction of "social surgery."'[1] When to these theoretical difficulties are added the certainty of most emphatic opposition from all religious bodies, the protests—less worthy of respect, but still to be reckoned with—of the more squeamish kind of humanitarianism, and the great likelihood, already referred to, of abuse in practice, it is obvious that any extended application of this doctrine is, at present at least, out of the question. This goes a long way to account for the extreme paucity of literature on the subject in recent times. So far as the present writer is aware, no important work by any modern author deals at any length with the topic.[2] And, as a matter of historical fact, euthanasia has never been put into practice. We intend in the remainder of this article to give a brief account of certain approximations to it which have existed or still exist, and of the views of those writers—mainly ancient—who have upheld some form of it.

1. Non-civilized communities.—One of the most noteworthy features of savage and barbarian, as opposed to civilized, society is the relative unimportance of the individual as compared with the community. This is seen, for example, in the frequency of various forms of human sacrifice, which apparently shock no one, and are often accepted quite calmly by the victim himself; in the absolute obedience of most, if not all, savages to the elaborate and often irksome tabus affecting marriage, the obtaining, preparation, and consumption of food, and other essential acts of life; and, most clearly of all, in the practice of a sort of crude euthanasia. This is generally the result of economic forces. When the available food-supply is limited, the numbers of the community must also be kept within bounds; and, if the population becomes too large, the least necessary members are simply got rid of. These are generally young children or very old people (cf. artt. ABANDONMENT AND EXPOSURE, vol. i. p. 3). Perhaps the most striking example of this primitive application of economic laws, regardless of individual feelings, comes from the South Seas, where infanticide—usually a matter for the individual or the family[3]—was actually enforced by law under the native chiefs.

'The Polynesians,' says R. L. Stevenson, a competent and sympathetic observer, though not a professed anthropologist, 'met this emergent danger (of famine) with various expedients of activity and prevention. . . . Over all the island world, abortion and infanticide prevailed. *On coral atolls, where the danger was most plainly obvious, these were enforced by law and sanctioned by punishment.* On Vaitipu, in the Ellices, only two children were allowed to a couple; on Nukufetau, but one.'[1]

That this arose from no callousness on the part of the natives is very clearly shown by the instances he gives of their almost absurd fondness for children. It would be quite wrong, again, to accuse of wanton cruelty those tribes who kill or abandon aged people who are no longer able to get food, or to march, if the tribe is nomadic. To give an ancient example of an island race following this custom—

Ælian tells us[2] that among the Sardinians men of advanced age used to be killed with clubs by their own sons 'because they considered it disgraceful that a man should continue to live when exceedingly old (λίαν ὑπέργηρων).'

Neither these Sardinians nor their modern parallels are to be condemned for cruelty to infants or old people. The proceeding, revolting enough to our feelings, arises from a simple perception of the fact that the necessities of life are too scarce for those members of the tribe to be fed who cannot supply themselves and will never, or not for a long time, be able to do so. The methods of getting rid of them—clubbing, leaving to starve, and the like—are often brutal; this, however, is not deliberate cruelty, but is due partly to the inability of the undeveloped mind to realize another's sufferings, partly to quasi-religious beliefs. Thus, the horror of shedding the blood of a member of the tribe goes far to explain the seeming inhumanity of leaving a helpless person to starve, rather than killing him quickly.[3]

Such 'social surgery' we may call the public application of euthanasia. With regard to its private application, it should be noted that suicide is rare among uncivilized peoples as a rule, and naturally we do not get examples of savages killing themselves as a result of an abstract belief that death is better than life, generally or in particular cases. To call it unknown among savages is, however, as erroneous as the opposite view that it is more common among them than among civilized peoples.[4] Some races, as the Andamanese and Central Australians, seem never to have heard of it; others believe it will be punished in the next world (Dakotas, Kayans), or treat it as an offence against the chief or king (Dahomey); while others regard it as an indifferent, or at most a foolish, action (Accra, Pelew Islanders, Chippewayas), or even as conducive to future happiness (Eskimos of Davis Strait). Some cases may be classed as genuine euthanasia. Thus, among the Karens of Burma,

'if a man has some incurable or painful disease, he says in a matter-of-fact way that he will hang himself, and he does as he says.'[5]

But, on the whole, the natural love of life is strong in savages, although, as we have seen, the vague sense of the importance of the community may at times overpower it.

2. Greece.—Passing now to ancient civilization, we have to note in the case of the Greeks a twofold exemplification of principles which may be roughly identified with euthanasia: first, in the practice of certain States; second, in the precepts, often actually followed, of not a few philosophers.

(1) For many reasons—not least among them being the reverence of the Greeks, on the whole, for old age—we hear little of old people being put

[1] 'Moral Aspects of Socialism,' *IJE* vi. 313. For Plato's views, see below, p. 600.

[2] One or two writers have used the word 'euthanasia' to mean simply 'dying well,' *i.e.* in such a manner as to conduce to happiness hereafter. This has, of course, nothing to do with the present subject.

[3] *E.g.*, among the Wa-Giriama of Brit. E. Africa 'women will sometimes, after deserting their husbands, kill their children to avoid having to hand them back to their father' (*JRAI* xli. [1911] 24). This apparently is done with impunity.

[1] *In the South Seas*, 1901, pt. i. ch. v.

[2] *Var. Hist.* iv. 1.

[3] See, further, Post, *Grundriss der ethnolog. Jurisprudenz*, Oldenburg, 1894–95, i. 174, ii. 11, 43.

[4] Steinmetz *ap.* Westermarck, *MI* ii. 229; Post, *op. cit.* ii. 344 ff.

[5] Westermarck, *MI* ii. 231. Many other examples are given in the same chapter.

to death. There is, however, a curious story [1] that, in Kos,

'very old men come together garlanded as if to a banquet, and drink hemlock (κώνειον [the famous narcotic poison ?=*Conium maculatum*]), when they realize that they are incapable of doing anything useful to their fatherland.'

Passing over this case of voluntary euthanasia, which may or may not be genuine—for Ælian clearly thinks more of edification than of historical verity, and Strabo is doubtful about it—we must next consider that State which, more than any other, claimed and exercised absolute power over the lives of its citizens—Sparta. Plutarch [2] gives us the following information:

'The father had no authority to rear his child, when born, but brought it to a place called the Leschê; here the elders of his tribe sat and examined the infant. If it were well-made and strong, they bade him rear it, and apportioned to it one of the 9000 allotments of land; but, if it were feeble and ill-shaped, they sent it to the so-called Place of Casting-out (Ἀποθέτας)—a chasm near Mt. Taygetos,—considering that for a child ill-suited from birth for health and vigour to live was disadvantageous alike for itself and for the State.'

By this rigid elimination of weaklings, combined with a rough kind of eugenics,[3] Sparta endeavoured, and for several generations successfully, to maintain a high standard of physical efficiency. Other States were less scientific; generally speaking, the parents of a child could choose whether or not they would rear it; if for any reason it was not thought desirable to let it live, it was simply exposed, with certain precautions, one gathers, to keep its ghost from being troublesome. Examples of this are wearisomely frequent in New Comedy, and are often found in earlier drama.[4] But this is not euthanasia; it is a mere shirking of parental responsibility. Also, it did not necessarily result in the death of the infant, which might be found still alive, and in such a case became, it would seem, the absolute property of the finder.[5]

As to suicide, Plato [6] appears to be in accordance with popular feeling when he mentions as justifiable causes intolerable pain or disgrace. We hear very little of it among the Greeks, from Homer down to the end of the Persian Wars. In a somewhat doubtful passage of the *Odyssey* (xi. 271 ff.), Epikaste (=Jocasta) hangs herself on learning of her unconscious incest; but the suicide of Ajax seems to belong to the non-Homeric tradition. One curious instance, which reminds us of Hindu *satī*, is the self-immolation of Euadne on the pyre of her husband Kapaneus;[7] while, among historical examples, we may cite the suicide of Pantitas, one of the two Spartans who survived Thermopylæ, as a result of his disgrace;[8] and of Themistocles, to avoid fighting against his fellow-countrymen.[9] But in Athens at least, although the regular form of capital punishment was enforced suicide, self-destruction in general was looked upon with disfavour, perhaps from fear of the dead man's ghost; at any rate, the right hand of the corpse was severed before burial,[10] with which custom we may compare the mutilation (μασχαλισμός) of a murdered man by his slayers.[11]

(2) The philosophers, and especially the later schools (Stoic, Epicurean, etc.), were interested chiefly in the question of suicide; of euthanasia in other forms we hear little. Plato, however, whose model State is to a great extent an idealized form of the constitution of Sparta, is in favour of a somewhat ruthless application of the principles under discussion to weakly children and also to invalids.

'The children of inferior parents, and any maimed offspring of the others, they (the Guardians) will secretly put out of the way (κατακρύψουσιν) as is fitting,'[1]

are his words on the subject; and a later passage seems also to sanction abortion (μάλιστα μὲν μηδ' εἰς φῶς ἐκφέρειν κύημα μηδέ γ' ἕν [*ib.* 461 C]) in the case of a woman not of the approved age-class for child-bearing. Not dissimilar views were held by Aristotle,[2] in whose ideal State maimed children are not to be reared, and abortion may occasionally be practised. Later, however, the prevalence of exposure drew forth strong protests against the custom from Musonios [3] (1st cent. A.D.). With regard to other applications of euthanasia, Plato considers that invalids ought not to be kept alive by an elaborate regimen, but allowed to die, as they are quite unable to attain to the higher developments of either mind or body.[4] Cf. art. SUICIDE.

3. Rome.—With regard to the Romans, there is almost nothing to add. Their philosophy was borrowed entirely from Greece, and was for the most part either Stoic or Epicurean. The former school inspired most of the famous suicides, such as Cato of Utica; hence Shakespeare's references [5] are really to the results of a foreign teaching. Infanticide and abortion are also offences of comparatively late date. Neglecting myths, mostly of palpable Greek origin, one hears of the former as early as the comedies of Plautus [6]—but the characters in these are Greek; and it is under the Empire [7] chiefly that we hear of wholesale avoidance of maternal responsibility. The *potestas* of the father, however, was supreme, and without his formal recognition of a child it was not reared.

5. Judaism.—It is to the credit of the Jews that we hear nothing of such practices among them, owing partly to their strong desire for offspring,—causing them to rear even a child blind or otherwise helpless from birth,—partly to their regard for human life, and partly to the fact that the *patria potestas* did not, at least in the times of the later kings, extend to life and death.[8] Suicide, though not formally prohibited,[9] seems to have been rare; the denunciations of it which we find in Josephus (*BJ* III. viii. 5) and in various Rabbis are not based on anything in the OT.

6. Christianity.—Christianity, however, soon after its inception, set its face sternly against all forms of self-destruction. The NT, indeed, does not expressly forbid it, and several of the early Fathers justify it in a few cases; but from St. Augustine [10] onwards the Sixth Commandment has been regarded as covering suicide as well as murder, while St. Thomas Aquinas (*Summa*, II. ii. 64, 5) denounces it as (1) unnatural, being contrary to the charity which every man bears towards himself; (2) an offence against the community; (3) a usurpation of God's power to kill and make alive—arguments of which the second is Aristotelian,[11] and the first derived, it would appear, ultimately from Plato (*Laws*, *loc. cit.*).[12] Other forms of euthanasia are equally opposed to orthodox Christianity, at least as heretofore stated, owing to its enormous emphasis on the value of the individual. It is

1 Æl. iii. 37 ff.; Strabo, x. 6, p. 486.
2 *Vita Lycurgi*, ch. xvi.; cf. Grote, *Hist. of Greece*, pt. ii. ch. vi.
3 Plut. *op. cit.* ch. xv.
4 Cf. Eur. *Ion*, 19, 897; Menander, Ἐπιτρέπ. 25 (van Leeuwen); Ter. *Heaut.* 629, 649, etc.
5 Soph. *Oed. Tyr.* 1022 ff.; Men. *l.c.*
6 *Laws*, ix. 873 C; cf. Stallbaum, *ad loc.*
7 Eur. *Suppl.* 990 ff.
8 Herod. vii. 232.
9 Plut. *Vita Themist.* 31; Aristoph. *Equit.* 83.
10 Æschines, *in Ctesiph.* p. 636.
11 Soph. *El.* 445; Æsch. *Choeph.* 437; and Comm. *ad locc.*

1 *Rep.* v. 460 C; cf. 459 D, 461 B, C, and App. iv. in vol. i. of Adam's edition.
2 *Polit.* 1335*b*, 19 ff.
3 Stob. *Floril.* lxxv. 15 and lxxxiv. 21.
4 *Rep.* iii. 405 C ff.
5 Cf. *Ant. and Cleop.* IV. xv. 87; *Macbeth*, v. viii. 1.
6 *E.g.* the *Cistellaria.*
7 Juv. vi. 594 ff., and many other passages.
8 See, *e.g.*, Dt 21[18ff.].
9 Apparently it was not regarded as an offence; *e.g.* Ahithophel is 'buried in the sepulchre of his father' exactly as if he had died a natural death (2 S 17[23]).
10 *De Civ. Dei*, i. 17 f.
11 Arist. *Eth. Nic.* v. 1138*a*, 9.
12 See, further, on the Jewish and Christian attitude towards suicide, Kirn, *PRE*[3] xviii. [1906] 169 f.

perhaps from this source that Islām borrows its prohibition of suicide.

The practice of modern civilized States is for the most part in accordance with this doctrine, even where not actually dictated by it. Thus, the medical profession traditionally keeps a patient alive as long as possible, although an exception has sometimes been made in cases of hydrophobia, where, as readers of George Macdonald will remember, smothering used formerly to be resorted to.[1] The law of murder, again, does not take any account of the physical or mental condition of the victim; and suicide is a legal felony. Theoretical writers are less uncompromising. Thus Sir Thomas More represents suicide as occasionally practised in Utopia — indeed he may be regarded as a euthanasiast.

'But yf the disease be not onelye uncurable, but also full of continuall payne and anguishe; then the priestes and the magistrates exhort the man, seinge he is not hable to doo anye dewte of lyffe, and by overlyvinge his owne deathe is noysome and irkesome to other, and grevous to himselfe, that he wyl determine with himselfe no longer to cheryshe that pestilent and peineful disease,' etc.[2]

Among the morbidities of the inferior type of pessimist we may note a tendency to glorify voluntary death, as in the well-known lines of Thomson (*City of Dreadful Night*, xiv.):

'This little life is all we must endure;
The grave's most holy peace is ever sure,'

and the following lines. But the greatest member of that school, Schopenhauer, regards it as defeating its own ends,[3] since it is not a denial but an assertion of the will to live, the great obstacle to moral freedom. Hume's famous Essay was directed against the older objections to it, and declared it to be no dereliction of duty, human or Divine. Despite the classical argument of Kant,[4] most writers on Ethics would probably agree in substance with Paulsen[5] that to refrain from it in great bodily or mental anguish may be heroic, but is no definite duty: 'Heldentum ist nicht Pflicht.' But, as has been already remarked, euthanasia in general has received little if any discussion. See, further, art. SUICIDE.

LITERATURE.—E. Westermarck, *MI*, London, 1908; F. Paulsen, *System der Ethik*[3], Berlin, 1894; A. Schopenhauer, *Studies in Pessimism*, Eng. tr.[3] by T. Bailey Saunders, London, 1892; I. Kant, *Metaphysik der Sitten*, last vol. of *Werke*, Berlin, 1907; D. Hume, *Essay on Suicide*, vol. iv. p. 535 of the Boston ed. of his works, 1854. For ancient views, see also L. Schmidt, *Ethik der alt. Griechen*, Berlin, 1882, esp. vol. ii. pp. 104, 137; E. Zeller, *Hist. of Gr. Philosophy*, Eng. tr. (several edd.), for views of the various schools; extracts from original texts in Ritter-Preller, *Hist. Philos. Græcæ*[8], Gotha, 1898.

H. J. ROSE.

EUTYCHIANISM.—See MONOPHYSITISM.

EVANGELICAL ALLIANCE. — This is an association of Evangelical Christians of different countries and speaking different tongues, united for the avowal and promotion of Christian union and the advancement of religious liberty. It owed its origin to a wide-spread and growing desire in Protestant Christendom for closer fellowship among true believers holding to the same essentials of faith, and desirous of bearing visible witness to their obedience to the Lord's prayer, 'that they all may be one; as thou, Father, art in me, and I in thee' (Jn 17[21]). The union of Christians of different denominations in the formation of some of the great Foreign Mission Societies, as the London Society and the American Board of Commissioners for Foreign Missions, and in the work of the Bible and Tract Societies as well as in the great Conventions, had demonstrated the possibility of the Alliance.

1. Organization.—The Alliance was organized at an enthusiastic meeting in Freemasons' Hall, London, August 19–23, 1846. Other meetings had prepared the way, especially those held in Glasgow, August 1845; in Liverpool, October 1845; and in London, February 1846. The Convention in London, August 19, 1846, adopted the name and defined the Alliance as a 'confederation.' It was attended by 800 delegates, representing 50 denominations. Among those who took an active part were the following divines from Great Britain: Revs. Edward Bickersteth and Lord Wriothesley Russell (Anglicans); Dr. P. Steane and Hon. Baptist W. Noel (Baptists); Drs. Thomas Binney, J. Angell James, Leifchild, and John Stoughton (Independents); Drs. Jabez and W. M. Bunting and William Arthur (Methodists); Drs. Chalmers, Candlish, Guthrie, and Norman MacLeod (Presbyterians). America was represented by Drs. Samuel H. Cox and William Patton; Germany, by Dr. F. W. Krummacher and Professor Tholuck; France, by Revs. Adolphe Monod and Georges Fisch; Switzerland, by Professor La Harpe and M. Lombard.

The British branch, having its office at 7 Adam Street, Strand, London, has been the most active, and deferred to as the parent branch. Other branches were established in Germany, France, Switzerland, Holland, Denmark, Sweden, Italy, Hungary, Greece, the United States, Canada, and among the Protestant missionaries of India, Japan, and other mission lands.

2. Aims.—The primary aim was to give expression to the substantial unity existing between Evangelical believers and to cultivate brotherly love. The Alliance is a voluntary association, not intended to create a new ecclesiastical organization. It is a union of Christian individuals, not a union of Churches. It claims no legislative or disciplinary authority, and disavows all thought of interfering with the loyalty of members to their respective denominations. The secondary aim, the spread of the principles of religious toleration, was incorporated in the proceedings of the first Conference, and given more full expression in resolutions passed at the General Conference at Paris, 1855. The Alliance is the only association which has made this a distinct aim of its organization.

The doctrinal basis of the Alliance is set forth in nine articles adopted at the London meeting of 1846, which are as follows:

(1) The divine inspiration, authority, and sufficiency of the Holy Scriptures.

(2) The right and duty of private judgment in the interpretation of the Holy Scriptures.

(3) The Unity of the Godhead and the Trinity of the Persons therein.

(4) The utter depravity of human nature in consequence of the Fall.

(5) The incarnation of the Son of God, His work of atonement for the sins of mankind, and His mediatorial intercession and reign.

(6) The justification of the sinner by faith alone.

(7) The work of the Holy Spirit in the conversion and sanctification of the sinner.

(8) The immortality of the soul, the resurrection of the body, the judgment of the world by our Lord Jesus Christ, with the eternal blessedness of the righteous and the eternal punishment of the wicked.

(9) The divine institution of the Christian ministry, and the obligation and perpetuity of the ordinances of Baptism and the Lord's Supper.

These principles, while they were not framed to do so, actually exclude the Unitarians (art. 3), the Friends (art. 9), and the Roman Catholics (artt. 2, 6). The motto of the Alliance expresses well its spirit: *Unum corpus sumus in Christo*—We are one body in Christ.

[1] *Robert Falconer*, ch. 15, p. 249, 'Standard Library' ed.

[2] *Utopia*, pt. ii. ch. vii. 'Of Bondemen, sicke persons,' etc. (p. 122, Cambridge ed.).

[3] *Essay on Suicide*; cf. *Die Welt als Wille und Vorstellung*[2], Leipzig, 1844, 1, § 69.

[4] Kant regards self-preservation as 'the first, if not the highest, duty of man,' and says of suicide: 'The destruction of the moral subject in oneself is tantamount to a driving out of the world, so far as in one lies, of Morality itself.' He adds that it involves the despising of man in general (*homo noumenon*) as represented in one's own person.

[5] *Ethik*, ii. 101 ff.

3. Modes of operation.—The Alliance has sought to accomplish its work mainly in three ways: through the Week of Prayer, General Conferences, and efforts to put a stop to religious persecution.

(*a*) *Annual Week of Prayer.*—This institution was first proposed at a meeting of the Alliance at Manchester, 1846, in a resolution urging 'the friends of the Alliance throughout the world to observe the first week of January as a season for concert in prayer on behalf of the objects contemplated by the Alliance.' Some years later the Alliance broadened its programmes in answer to an appeal from English and American missionaries in India. The British branch issues this year (1912) its 65th programme of topics. These topics have included Union with Christ, Thanksgiving for various benefits, and Prayer for Home, City, and Foreign Missions, for nations and their Rulers, for the Y.M.C.A. and Schools, for the Family, the Observance of the Lord's Day, and other subjects. The Week of Prayer, observed in cities and hamlets in all parts of the Christian world and in missionary territory, has, without a question, exercised a profound influence in promoting the spirit of brotherly love and cordial co-operation among ministers and laymen of the different Protestant communions.

(*b*) *Conferences.*—National or Local Conferences have been held every year by the British branch, and biennially by the American branch, 1875–1893 (with several intermissions). The international or General Conferences, ten in number, have been held in London, 1851; Paris, 1855; Berlin, 1857; Geneva, 1861; Amsterdam, 1867; New York, 1873; Basel, 1879; Copenhagen, 1884; Florence, 1891; London, 1896. The meetings have been called by agreement of the branches, and the entertainment of the delegates and the carrying out of the programme have been left to the branch within whose bounds the Conference met. The topics discussed have included: reports of the religious condition of the nations; the conflict of Christianity with infidelity, Romanism, and superstition; the practical and humanitarian enterprises of the Church; Christian education and revivals. The London Conference in 1851 probably included representatives of more Protestant denominations than had ever sat together since the Reformation. The Conference in New York was the most largely attended and widely influential religious gathering held up to that time in the United States. The large number of foreign scholars and ministers who attended it was incomparably above the attendance of foreign delegates at any convention of any kind held up to that time in the Western World. This result was largely due to the efforts of Dr. Philip Schaff, who made four journeys to Europe to present invitations to attend the meeting and to arouse interest in it.

The Alliance has received the recognition of crowned heads and of the President of the United States. Frederick William IV. of Prussia authorized the invitation to meet in Berlin, was present at one of the sessions, and accorded a reception to the members at Potsdam. The King and Queen of Denmark, the Crown Prince and Princess, and the King and Queen of Greece attended some of the meetings of the Copenhagen Conference. The President of the United States, Mr. Grant, and the Vice-President, Mr. Colfax, by their signatures endorsed the objects of the Alliance and the invitation to the meeting in New York; and President Grant, surrounded by the members of his Cabinet, gave the delegates to the New York Conference a reception at the White House. The then king of Italy sent a cordial letter of greeting to the Conference in Florence.

(*c*) *Opposition to persecution.*—In its earliest period an eloquent appeal was made by Merle d'Aubigné in behalf of the German Lutherans of Russia, and at the same time an appeal was made for the oppressed Armenians. Early cases of successful intervention were the release, through an appeal to the Grand Duke, of the Madiai family of Tuscany (1852), imprisoned for reading the Bible and holding religious meetings; and the release (in 1863) of Matamoras, Carrasco, and their friends in Spain, who were thrown into prison and condemned to the galleys for the same reason during the reign of Isabella. The Alliance interceded for the Methodists and Baptists in Sweden (1858), and through a delegation (in 1871) to the Czar, then sojourning at Friedrichshafen on the Lake of Constance, it sought relief for the Lutherans of the Baltic Provinces. Again in 1874 it sought the Czar's good offices for the Baptists of Southern Russia, and in 1879 it sent a deputation to the Emperor of Austria in behalf of certain Christians in Bohemia, and the request was granted. It helped to secure from the Sultan (1856) rights for the missionaries in Turkey, and has made efforts to secure relief for the Nestorians in Persia, the Stundists in Russia, and other persecuted Christians.

The influence of the Alliance can be traced in the formation of the Pan-Presbyterian Alliance, the Pan-Anglican Synod, and the Pan-Wesleyan Conference, and in the Federation of the Churches of Christ in the United States, which held its first meeting in New York in November 1905, representing 18,000,000 communicants belonging to 35 denominations officially represented.

LITERATURE.—*Conference on Christian Union, Narrative of Proceedings of the Meetings held at Liverpool, Oct. 1845*, London, 1845; *Annual Reports* of the British Branch, London, 1846 ff., and of the American Branch, New York, 1867 ff. The *Proceedings of the General Conferences* have been issued in the tongues spoken at the places of meeting, and for the most part in English reproduction, viz. those of London, Paris, Berlin (Germ. ed. by K. E. Reineck, 1867), Geneva (French ed. by H. Georg, 1861), Amsterdam, New York (ed. P. Schaff and S. Irenæus Prime), Basel (Germ. ed. by C. J. Riggenbach; Eng. ed. by J. Murray Mitchell), Copenhagen (only in Danish, ed. Vahl, 1886), Florence (Eng. ed. by R. A. Bedford), London (the Jubilee vol., ed. A. J. Arnold). Brief but not altogether satisfactory histories of the Alliance may be found in the Alliance vol., New York, 1874, by James Davis, secretary of the British branch, and in the Jubilee vol., London, 1896, by A. J. Arnold. See also *Life of Philip Schaff*, New York, 1897, pp. 252–274, 332 f., 350 ff. Special documents have been issued from time to time by the British and American branches. The more notable of the latter are *The Narrative of the State of Rel. in the U.S.*, by Henry B. Smith, presented to the Amsterdam Conference, 1867; *Report on the Alliance Deputation to the Czar of Russia*, 1871, and *The Reunion of Christendom*, by P. Schaff, 1893, his last literary work, which was presented to the council of the Alliance held in connexion with the Columbian World's Exposition in Chicago, 1893. The art. 'Allianz, Evangelische' in *PRE*³ i. 376, by E. C. Achelis, pronounces an unfavourable judgment on the Alliance as having departed from its original aims, and carrying on 'a hostile separatistic propaganda.' It declares that the Alliance reached the height of its history at the Berlin Conference in 1857, and that, as a religious organization, it has no longer any significance in Germany. This is not the place to enter upon a consideration of the conditions which call forth a judgment so partial and unjust. The British branch issued a monthly, under the title *Evangelical Christendom*, 1847–1899, *The Evangelical Alliance Quarterly*, 1899–1906, and again a monthly, *Evangelical Christendom*, 1906 ff.

DAVID S. SCHAFF.

EVANGELICALISM.—The name given, in English-speaking lands, to a movement of revival which has borne other names in other parts of Christendom. This movement is usually traced to Holland, where it began as Cocceianism or Federalism, being so named from its foremost representative, Cocceius († 1669), professor at Leyden, whose theology was called 'Federal' on account of the prominence given in it to the conception of religion as a covenant (see COVENANT THEOLOGY). The next phase was Pietism (*q.v.*), the principal representatives of which were Spener († 1705), who operated chiefly by prayer-meetings, known as *collegia pietatis*; A. H. Francke (1663–1727), professor at Halle, where he founded the orphanages which still flourish in that academic centre; and J. A. Bengel (1687–1752), the Pietist of South Germany, and author of the well-known *Gnomon*, which may be taken as an index of the devotion to Biblical studies characteristic of the movement. Out of Pietism rose Moravianism, associated with the name of Count Zinzendorf (1700–1760), the passionate lover of Christ and inaugurator of those foreign-mission efforts for the extent and success of which the Moravian Church has so distinguished a name (see MORAVIANS). Methodism, the next phase, was evolved from Moravianism as obviously as the latter was from Pietism. In many respects it is the most remarkable phase of all; and it would be a pleasure to follow the course of its development, first in Great Britain and then in America, where it has achieved phenomenal success; with its great leaders, the two Wesleys and Whitefield, and their many notable successors; with its divisions and reunions; its open-air preachings and camp-meetings; its class-meetings and local preachers; its hymnody and its zeal for education; but all these topics will be dealt with in art. METHODISM.

1. In the Church of England.—The Anglican Church might have retained Methodism within itself, for the original leaders were most unwilling to go out; but different counsels prevailed. After a time, however, there arose within the State Church a number of clergymen who imitated the zeal and efficiency of the Methodists, and earned the name of 'Evangelicals.'

Among these, in the latter part of the 18th cent., the most conspicuous figure was the Rev. John Newton (1725–1807). After a wild youth, spent at sea, he underwent as thorough a conversion as any Methodist, and no Methodist could have had less scruple in making his religious experiences public. Though over forty before being settled in a parish of his own, at Olney in Buckinghamshire, he immediately unfolded an earnestness and force of character which could not fail to make him a centre of influence; and from the time when he was translated to the Church of St. Mary Woolnoth, in Lombard Street, London, in 1779, he exercised, without the name of bishop, a more than episcopal sway over those within the State Church who were coming under the influence of the revival. Before leaving the country, he had won as a convert the incumbent of a neighbouring parish, the Rev. Thomas Scott (1747–1821), who was shaken out of Socinian views and out of the habits of a careless life by hearing Newton preach. At first this adherent fought against his convictions; but, Newton wisely refraining from being drawn into controversy with him, he at last shut himself up with his Bible for three years, determined to discover what was the religion taught in this oracle and to hold to it alone. From these studies he emerged with the conviction that the Evangelical system was the only true gospel; and so convinced was he that a creed obtained as his had been must be the correct one, that he wrote an account of his experiences under the title of *The Force of Truth* (1779)—a book which gained an enormous circulation, and of which John Henry Newman said that he almost owed to it his soul. If Scott was able to prove the new tenets to be Scriptural, another adherent of the school, Joseph Milner (1744–97), undertook to prove, in his *History of the Church of Christ*, that they were the doctrines of the Apostolic Age, of the Reformation, and of the great founders and theologians of the Church of England. The Evangelicals claimed to stand in the footsteps of the Fathers; it was the official Church which had lapsed into error through worldliness and indolence.

But the Evangelical doctrines had the good fortune to secure a means of propagation far more rare and effective than that of either a Biblical expositor or an ecclesiastical historian. While living at Olney, Newton had for a neighbour the poet Cowper (1731–1800); and to the gentle bard this strong man of God became a hero and Great-heart. The literary tribe have persistently represented Newton, indeed, as a tyrant, who drove the poet distracted; but Cowper's insanity was in the blood; he had been in confinement before Newton ever saw him; and, although even this strong friend could not finally rescue him from his fate, he redeemed him from himself and furnished him with employment, by which he was made, in the intervals of his disease, a useful and a happy man. Besides enjoying his collaboration in the writing of the Olney Hymns, Newton suggested other themes for his muse, which drew from him not a few of his happiest efforts; and thus, for the peculiar beliefs and sentiments of Evangelicalism, there was secured the benefit of musical and imperishable expression; for there is no more complete or accurate representation of them than is to be found in Cowper's verse.

In prose, also, the new way of looking at Christianity was to receive brilliant expression from a layman. This was at the hands of William Wilberforce (1759–1833), who, having been turned from a life of frivolity during a tour in Switzerland with Isaac Milner, brother of the ecclesiastical historian, carried his newborn enthusiasm into the business of Parliament, of which he was a member, and into the upper ranks of English society, of which he was an acknowledged leader. To this society his statement of the Evangelical position was addressed, as was shown by its full title, *A Practical View of the prevailing System of professed Christians in the higher and middle Classes of this Country contrasted with real Christianity*; and the grace, the frankness, and the humour of its style made it acceptable in circles into which religious literature seldom penetrated.

But Wilberforce rendered to Evangelicalism a still more important service by leading its accumulating numbers in a crusade against the Slave Trade. In this he enjoyed the support of a section of the community in which the new views had made remarkable progress—the members of the upper middle class, engaged in banking and similar occupations. Of these there happened to be such a concentration in the suburb of Clapham that the whole Evangelical party was sometimes styled 'the Clapham Sect.' Taking this nickname and converting it into a title of honour, the genial historian of Evangelicalism, Sir James Stephen, has, under this caption, in his *Essays in Ecclesiastical Biography* (London, 1907, vol. ii.), penned captivating sketches of such men as Henry Thornton, Granville Sharp, Lord Teignmouth, and Zachary Macaulay, who not only stood by Wilberforce in his prolonged and laborious campaign against slavery, but were distinguished in many other walks of philanthropy. For Evangelicalism had reached and tapped the springs of active beneficence. To whatever it may have been due—whether to the Calvinistic doctrines, believed by Evangelicals, or, as they might rather themselves have said, to the work on their spirits of the Spirit of God—the adherents of the new views not only believed, but turned their beliefs into practice. It was a maxim with them that every one to whom the good news had come was bound, according to his powers and opportunities, to impart it to others. Their first efforts, accordingly, were to propagate the gospel both by personal testimony and by corporate action. They visited the poor, they tended the sick and dying, they instructed the ignorant, they founded schools and colleges, they not only sought out candidates for the ministry, but bought advowsons, in order that parishes might be manned with clergymen of the right sentiments, the force operating behind these efforts being the solemn sense of their own responsibility as well as of the danger and the destiny of those in whose behalf they were exerting themselves. The Church Missionary Society and the Religious Tract Society came into existence in 1779, the British and Foreign Bible Society in 1804. Far, however, from the endeavours of the Evangelicals being confined to the souls of men, they were directed from the first to the body also; and soon philanthropies were devised for prisoners, for children and women working in mines, for the blind, the deaf and dumb, the paralytic, and, in short, for every form of human misery. Wilberforce was succeeded in the next generation by Lord Shaftesbury (1801–85), who, in Parliament, was the unfailing advocate of the poor and needy, and, after a life of unwearying philanthropy, exclaimed, on his deathbed, that he was sorry to quit a world in which so much misery still existed. Through his influence with Lord Palmerston, this nobleman secured for the Evangelicals a fair share of the influential offices in the Church. In one of the universities, Evangelicalism fought its way to power through the weight of the personality of Charles Simeon (1759–1836); and the first heads of the Evangelical divinity halls, founded at Cambridge and Oxford, both rose to be bishops. In the latter half of the 19th cent. the party profited by throwing itself into the revivals which passed over the entire kingdom, coming from American sources; and a centre for the quickening of the spiritual life was provided in conferences, held annually from 1875 at Keswick.

Though, for more than a hundred years, a large and influential party in the Anglican Church, Evangelicalism has never succeeded in permeating that communion completely. W. E. Gladstone, while crediting it with the high merit of pervading the Church as a whole with the preaching of Christ crucified, showed, in an article published in 1879 and republished in *Gleanings of Past Years* (1879–97), that it had manifested a singular incapacity for retaining its own more gifted children, these going off to the left or the right, when they reached maturity. The rise of the Broad Church party in the early half of the 19th cent. furnished evidence of aspirations and needs which Evangelicalism was not satisfying; and the same was still more manifested by the phenomenal development of the High Church and Ritualistic party, which has not yet suffered any check, and has in recent decades eclipsed all rivals. Those who have themselves passed from Evangelicalism to Ritualism are wont to regard the one movement as a preparation for the other, which is, they say, its natural completion. But this is a sanguine view, in which Evangelicals will by no means concur; and a historian will be more likely to recognize in Ritualism a recrudescence of the Anglicanism of King Henry VIII. and Queen Elizabeth, while in Evangelicalism he sees a revival of the Puritanism which long struggled inside the Anglican communion, before it was driven forth into dissent. At the present time the strength of the Evangelical party is estimated by G. R. Balleine at fully a fourth of the entire Church; and the proportion might be reckoned higher if the Anglican Church in the United States and the Colonies were included.

2. In English Nonconformity.—By the Dissenting communities of England it might be contended that, in its essence, Evangelicalism was among them not only before it appeared in the State Church, but even before it was seen in the form of Methodism. Long before the conversion of John Wesley, hymns had been composed by Isaac Watts (1674–1748), which became as truly the language of the revival as those of Charles Wesley, and have even yet lost none of their virtue. Philip Doddridge (1702–51) was preaching and teaching at Northampton the views of Divine truth embodied in his work entitled *The Rise and Progress of Religion in the Soul*, which became a handbook of experience for all, in whatever denomination, touched by the spirit of the revival; and Matthew Henry (1662–1714), in a Presbyterian manse at Chester, had penned a commentary on Holy Scripture, in which mother-wit and common sense are combined with thorough apprehension of the gospel. In fact, such instances point back to a connexion of Evangelicalism with the Puritanism of the 16th and 17th cents., which could, in all probability, be demonstrated also to have lain behind the Cocceianism of Holland, from which, in accordance with the custom of Church historians, the rise of our movement has been traced.

In the Dissenting communities, however, as a whole, as well as in the State Church, in the beginning of the 18th cent. there prevailed a spirit of coldness and deadness. Among the Presbyterians the temperature had sunk so low that not a few of their churches had become the meeting-places of Unitarians. Respectability and solemnity were the attributes to which alone even the better congregations aspired, whereas enthusiasm was among them a name of reproach. It was no wonder, therefore, that the first manifestations of Methodism were beheld with repulsion and alarm, or that the utterances of uncalled and uninstructed earnestness were received with suspicion. As, however, it became manifest that, by such rude and unusual means, the lost children of England were being redeemed from savagery, and publicans and harlots transmuted into saints, the opposition of good men gave way, and the dignified friends of decency and order began to learn the methods of their more ardent neighbours. Great was their reward. Their places of worship, which had been, in most cases, barely holding their own, were filled to overflowing, and larger buildings had to be erected; those who were being saved were daily added to their numbers; and a new joy pervaded the exercises of the sanctuary. From this time onwards, both Baptists and Congregationalists may be regarded as having been captured by Evangelicalism; and to this fact they owe their rapid internal development, as well as their missionary zeal. The London Missionary Society was founded in 1795, and enjoyed, in the century that followed, the services of some of the most eminent missionaries of all time; while the two denominations fully participated in all the home missions and philanthropies which were the new births of the age.

From generation to generation both of these denominations were amply supplied with preachers by whose lips the doctrines of Evangelicalism were interpreted with learning and eloquence; but it may be enough to dwell for a little on the names of two of them, one belonging to each of the denominations, by whose ministries the Evangelical situation was beneficially influenced in the latter half of the 19th century. Charles Haddon Spurgeon (1834–92) was of Congregational extraction, but he joined the Baptists in early life. He was soundly converted in emerging from boyhood, and had scarcely surmounted that period of life when he began to preach, the originality and force of his recent experience giving direction to his efforts, as they never ceased to do all his days; for he said himself that he always preached with the expectation of conversions; and, it is believed, he was not disappointed. Though he had not enjoyed the advantages of academic training, he was throughout life a keen and unwearied student of the subjects likely to help him in preaching, Greek included; and he founded a theological college, of which he was president, delivering lectures on preaching to his students which are esteemed among the best ever produced on the subject. His capacity for business and the warmth of his heart enabled him to carry on a large orphanage; and he maintained, besides, an extensive system of colportage for the circulation of Evangelical literature, and especially his own sermons, which were published every week and sold in thousands. The tabernacle built for him, in South London, held 5000, and was always full, serving, indeed, for a whole generation as a rallying-point for Evangelicals from all corners of the globe. In it was upheld the banner of Evangelicalism, the doctrines of which were preached with clearness, fullness, and spiritual power. In later life, Spurgeon came to believe that the younger ministers of his denomination were forsaking these truths; and, in consequence, he separated himself from the Baptist Union. But the officials of that body denied his accusations, or at least refused to endorse them.

The other leader of Evangelical Nonconformity, R. W. Dale of Birmingham (1829–95), was more open to new light and more inclined to learn from others. He used to speak with earnest conviction of the need for a reconstruction of Protestant theology. At some points he was in sympathy with the Broad Church, especially with Maurice. With him he believed in the creation of humanity in Christ; like him he held strongly by the sacredness of secular life; and, with him, he disbelieved that the wicked would live for ever in torment. Yet he gloried in the peculiar doctrines of Evangelicalism, such as the death of Christ as the ground of divine forgiveness, justification by faith, and the supernatural work of the Holy Spirit in redemption; and equally did he value the Evangelical *ethos*, as he called it—its passion for Christ and for the souls of men.

3. In Scotland.—It was fortunate for Evangelicalism that it was mediated for Scotland through the big brain and big heart of Thomas Chalmers (1780–1847). In England it has sometimes exhibited a somewhat petty aspect. It is impossible, for example, to read of the developments at Cheltenham by which Frederick William Robertson was driven away from his early associations into the Broad Church without recognizing that Evangelicalism could be narrow and unlovely, deservedly bringing down on itself the nickname of 'the hard Church' given to it by R. H. Hutton. But Chalmers (*q.v.*) could not have been the founder of a hard Church. His humanity was broad; he had passed through an intellectual before experiencing a spiritual awakening; he had a distinctly philosophical mind, which delighted in tracing facts to their causes; and his position as an academic teacher could not but intensify this natural bent. Still he was profoundly practical. Among the documents of Evangelicalism there is not one more important than the address he sent to his parishioners at Kilmany when quitting that rural parish, in 1815, for the city of Glasgow. Reviewing the years he had spent among them, first as an opponent and then as an apostle of Evangelicalism, he fixed on this as the essential point—that Evangelicalism works; it actually realizes the righteousness and holiness which his early preaching had utterly failed to produce. Afterwards he was always speculating on the reason for this, and he found it in 'the expulsive power of a new affection.' He did for theology, in his academical prelections, exactly what Schleiermacher was doing for it at the same time in Germany, though these two knew nothing of each other; that is to say, instead of beginning with the mysteries of revelation and coming down from these to human experience, he took his stand on experience and then rose to the supernatural facts without which such experience could not have been enjoyed. His dogmatic consisted of two parts—first, the disease; then, the remedy.

There had, indeed, been an Evangelical party in the Church of Scotland before Chalmers appeared upon the scene; and, outside of the State Church, the doctrines of the gospel had been preached to growing numbers by the ministers of the Secession and the Relief denominations; but it was by the mighty voice of Chalmers that the new views secured the attention of his countrymen as a whole. In the courts of the Church his influence grew apace, till the 'Moderates,' on the opposite side, saw their predominance vanishing. In their straits they sought and obtained the assistance of the civil courts, by which the reforming party was so limited and thwarted that, in 1843, it quitted the State Church and organized itself outside as the Free Church of Scotland.

The virtue of the Evangelical principles by which the Free Church was inspired was made visible by the rapidity with which it not only erected churches, manses, and schools all over the land for its own necessities, but threw itself into mission work of every kind, both at home and abroad. All the foreign missionaries had joined the outgoing movement; and not only were they provided for, but the Church was ready to rise to opportunities, as these presented themselves, to extend its operations. Similarly, the home mission problem was attacked with such vigour that even in Glasgow, where the growth of the city has been phenomenal, the increase of the means of grace has kept pace with that of the population; and at the present moment measures are being organized for meeting the wider needs disclosed by the recent developments of labour. For these missionary and philanthropic exertions the Church was strengthened by wide-spread revivals of religion in 1859–60, 1874, 1881, and 1890, with which the ministers and members associated themselves sympathetically. This also enabled the Church, under the leadership of Principal Rainy (1826–1906), to meet and survive not a few keen theological controversies, of which the most serious was that on Biblical Criticism introduced by Professor Robertson Smith (1846–94). As this scholar recognized the Bible to be the word of God, the only rule of faith and duty, and appealed with full personal conviction to the *testimonium Spiritus Sancti internum*, his views met with a tolerant and patient hearing from his fellow-countrymen, and were, to a large extent, accepted without injury to Evangelical faith.

Meantime the two denominations mentioned above outside the State Church, after uniting in 1847 to form the United Presbyterian Church, had been pursuing a similar course, growing in the same convictions and being educated by similar providences. They outran the Free Church in the development of worship, by adopting earlier the use of hymns and the assistance of organs; and they were earlier in the adoption of a Declaratory Act (1879; the Free Church Act was passed in 1894), by which the Confession of Faith was modified in the direction of a more cordial acknowledgment of the divine love to all men and a less gloomy view of human nature and its destiny. But this branch of the Church excelled particularly in enthusiasm for foreign missions; and, when it and the Free Church united in 1900, there was an expansion within the united Church of this species of Evangelical sentiment.

At the Disruption of 1843 those who remained in connexion with the State were the so-called 'Moderates,' who had stood in opposition to the Evangelicals in the same way as, on the Continent of Europe, the Rationalists had faced the Pietists. But from the first there had been left in the State Church a considerable amount of Evangelical sentiment; and this has grown with time, being favoured by such spirits as Norman Macleod (1812–72) and Robert Flint (1838–1911); and a sign that it is strongly represented among the younger men of light and leading may be seen in the cordiality with which these are now seeking union with those from whom they were separated in 1843. There are few men of mark at the present day in any of the ecclesiastical bodies in Scotland who would be averse to being designated 'Evangelicals.'

4. In America.—An additional proof of the suggestion made above, that the true source of Evangelicalism is to be sought in English Puritanism rather than in the Continental movements to which it is usually traced, is supplied by the fact that in America it arose earlier than it did in England. The date of John Wesley's conversion is 24th May 1738, but as early as 1734 occurred the first of those awakenings which took place at Northampton, in New England, through the preaching of Jonathan Edwards (1703–58), which spread astonishment and awe far and near, and was heard of even in England. In fact, it is known that John Wesley had himself read an account, penned by Edwards, of the experiences in America before anything of the kind had occurred under his own preaching. In later times, influences from German Pietism, from Moravianism, and from English Methodism entered into the religious life of the United States; yet in the revivals which have, from the time of Jonathan Edwards, formed an outstanding and frequently recurring feature of American Christianity, the impulse has always been a native one; and America has, in this particular, been in a position to give to Europe rather than to receive from it. Very remarkable awakenings were experienced in Kentucky and the neighbouring States from 1796 onwards; and in 1857 the whole country was pervaded by a similar movement, which spread thence to Ireland and Great Britain. Not infrequently have such movements had their origin in schools and colleges, and so marked has been their influence upon the young that some psychological observers in America are declaring conversion itself to be a manifestation of puberty. In the early revivals there were physical accompaniments, sometimes of a singular and alarming character; but these have tended to disappear with the progress of time. In the same way, at first, the experiences were looked upon as altogether divine; but, as they became commoner, it was recognized that human agency also had a part to play. Thus, by the setting apart of time for prolonged religious exercises, the mind could be interested in spiritual things, and, by the bringing together of large numbers for a common purpose, social influences could be generated. Certain persons, it was discovered, had the power of awakening appeal or of bringing the hesitating to decision. It was found, in short, that revivals could, to a certain extent, be manufactured; and thus a new danger had to be guarded against, that of merely mechanical excitement passing itself off as religion, or even of revivalism becoming a trade and falling into unworthy hands.

The Puritan religion of New England had originally a national or municipal character. The township and the congregation were identical, all the inhabitants being communicants. But, as population multiplied, it became apparent that there was a growing discrepancy between these two magnitudes; and Edwards became the protagonist of the earnest view that only those should be admitted to the Lord's table who had undergone a religious change, of which evidence was supplied by a consistent life. Indeed, he became the victim of this contention; for so much antagonism was provoked by his severity that he was driven from his pastorate at Northampton and had to betake himself to a mission to Indians; though he did not continue under a cloud, being appointed in 1758 president of Princeton College (see art. EDWARDS). But the demand for a distinct personal experience, of which an account could be given, became more and more general, and the frequent occurrence of revivals, by which this was promoted, fostered a general dependence on this mode of acquiring religious experience, to the disparagement of the regular work of the ministry and the influence of the family. Against this a protest was raised by Horace Bushnell (1802–76), one of the most original of American thinkers, who, in 1846, in a little work entitled *Christian Nurture*, recalled attention, with marked success, to the slower and less exciting processes by which many are brought into the Kingdom.

Still, in spite of drawbacks, the revivals were gifts of infinite value to the Church in America. One of them is said to have added to the Church more than a million members; and devout observers have noted that they seemed to be granted when the country stood on the verge of any particularly trying period, in which new tasks had to be faced or new hardships borne. It was by means of the enthusiasm generated in these seasons of special grace that the Church in America rose to the efforts rendered necessary by the developments of the country's history and the course of Providence; and the Evangelicalism of the United States was not behind that of England or Scotland in the variety or extent of the forms of sin and misery with which it was able to cope. America has all the philanthropies of Europe; and in some spheres, such as the Sunday School and the Young Men's Christian Association, it has specially excelled. But the great task of the Christianity of the country has been the provision of ordinances for the ever-extending population. Failure at this point would have been fatal. But the Church has nobly risen to the occasion, the Methodist and Baptist denominations distinguishing themselves by the zeal and heroism with which they have accompanied the pioneer and settler into the wilds of the West and the South, and helped to lay the foundations of Christian civilization. In spite of the phenomenal growth of the population, the provision of ordinances compares favourably with that of Europe.

Jonathan Edwards was a profound metaphysician and theologian as well as a revivalist; and in his works the seed was sown of a vast theological and philosophical activity which has accompanied the more practical efforts of American Christianity, not a few of those who succeeded him in developing the New England Theology, as it is called, combining, like himself, the characters of metaphysical theologian and powerful evangelist. Edwards' speculations were all directed towards the practical end of reconciling Calvinism with the gracious invitation to all sinners of which he was the mouthpiece; and the ablest of his successors moved in the same sphere. It must, however, be confessed that, in some of the speculations indulged in, any practical aim was difficult to discern; but at the present time there is a return to the best element in Edwards' theology—that dealt with in his great work, *A Treatise concerning Religious Affections* (1746).

5. On the Continent.—While these phases of the Revival movement were disclosing themselves in the English-speaking countries—and for a complete view the Colonies of Australia, South Africa, and Canada would also require to be taken into account—other phases of what was substantially the same movement were manifesting themselves on the Continent of Europe. These were in part derived from Great Britain or America. Thus, a visit paid by one of the brothers Haldane—laymen, who had founded the Congregational body in Scotland, in protest against the reigning Moderatism—led to an outbreak of spiritual life at Geneva in 1817, which spread to neighbouring cantons and produced interesting and influential personalities, such as César Malan (1787–1864), Merle d'Aubigné (1794–1872), and A. R. Vinet (1797–1847). This influence penetrated to France, and a visit of Robert Haldane to Montauban had similar results among the students there. A Free Church came into existence in France, as it had done at more than one point in Switzerland; and here also striking personalities rose to take the direction, such as Adolphe Monod (1802–56) and E. D. de Pressensé (1824–91).

In Germany a decided quickening of spiritual life dates from about the commencement of the 19th cent.; but, the name 'Evangelicalism' not being available on account of its being forestalled for another purpose, this is termed the 'Awakening' (*Erweckung*; so the term *Réveil* in France). As to the origin of this movement, Germans are not themselves very clear. Tracing so many new beginnings to Schleiermacher, they naturally incline to derive this also from him; but its real sources were humbler. It was a re-filling of the channels of Pietism; it sprang out of the prayer-meetings held by Moravians and other 'quiet ones in the land' who were in sympathy with them. Its leader in the beginning of the 19th cent. was Baron von Kottwitz (1757–1843), who flitted about Berlin, holding conferences and succouring the poor and needy; and, in the next generation, his place was filled by Tholuck of Halle (1799–1877), who brought the movement back to science and to public life. In touch with Tholuck were not a few of the most prominent scholars of his own generation, and his disciples were legion in both the pastorates and the professorial chairs of Germany. He himself reckoned that the movement culminated in the forties of his century; but its influence was prolonged in what used to be called the 'Mediating School' of theologians; and it survives still in numerous forms, of which perhaps the most distinctive is the Deaconess movement, which has grown to extraordinary dimensions, and is inspired mainly, though not exclusively, by this type of piety.

See also art. EVANGELICAL ALLIANCE.

LITERATURE.—G. R. Balleine, *Hist. of the Evangelical Party in the Church of England*, London, 1908; H. C. G. Moule, *The Evangelical School in the Church of England*, London, 1901; Sir J. Stephen, *Essays in Ecclesiastical Biography*, new ed., London, 1907; J. Stoughton, *Religion in England, 1800–1850*, London, 1884, vols. viii. and ix.; C. S. Horne, *Popular Hist. of the Free Churches*², London, 1903; W. B. Selbie (editor), *Evangelical Christianity*, London and N.Y. 1911; W. Hanna, *Life of Chalmers*, Edinburgh, 1850–52; G. A. Smith, *Life of Henry Drummond*, London, 1899; P. C. Simpson, *Life of Principal Rainy*, London, 1909; G. P. Fisher, *Hist. of Chr. Doctrine*, Edinburgh, 1896, period v. ch. 2; L. W. Bacon, *Hist. of American Christianity*, N.Y. 1897; F. H. Foster, *A Genetic History of the New England Theology*, Chicago, 1907; E. P. G. Guizot, *Méditations sur l'état actuel de la religion chrétienne*, Paris, 1865; H. Bois, *La Psychologie des réveils*, Paris, 1906; H. Stephan, *Der Pietismus als Träger des Fortschritts in Kirche, Theologie und allgem. Geistesbildung*, Tübingen, 1908, and 'Die Neuzeit,' in Krüger's *Handbuch der Kirchengesch.*, do. 1909; *Princeton Theological Essays*, N.Y. 1846–47, Essay xxi.

JAMES STALKER.

EVE (חַוָּה, *Ḥawwah*; LXX Ζωή, Εὔας; NT Εὔα; Aq. Αὔα; Symm. Ζωογόνος; Vulg. *Heva*).—The name in J for the first woman (for the narrative, see ADAM). Gn 3^{20} explains it by saying that she was called *Ḥawwah*, because she was the mother of all living (חַי, *ḥay*). *Ḥawwah* is connected with the same root, but probably means 'Life' rather than 'Living' (RVm 'Living *or* Life'), or 'Life-giving' (Symm. as above). W. R. Smith (*Kinship and Marriage*², London, 1903, p. 208) connects *Ḥawwah* with *ḥayy*, 'clan,' *Ḥawwah* being a personification of the idea of kinship thought of as consisting in descent from a common mother. An ancient interpretation adopted by Wellhausen and some other modern scholars gives *Ḥawwah* the meaning 'serpent,' and finds in Genesis a trace of the primitive belief that earthly life originated in a serpent, as, in some forms of the Babylonian cosmology, all things spring from Tiāmat, the primeval dragon. Zimmern (*KAT*³, p. 438) suggests that the Eve narrative has been influenced by the Bab. myths of the goddess Ishtar. Skinner (p. 85 f.) writes, with regard to the connexion between the name *Ḥawwah* and Semitic words for 'serpent':

'Quite recently the philological equation has acquired fresh significance from the discovery of the name חות on a leaden Punic *tabella devotionis* . . . of which the first line reads: "O Lady *ḤVT*, goddess, queen . . . !" Lidzbarski sees in this mythological personage a goddess of the under-world, and as such a serpent-deity; and identifies her with the biblical Ḥavvah. Ḥavvah would thus be a "depotentiated" deity, whose prototype was a Phœnician goddess of the under-world, worshipped in the form of a serpent, and bearing the title of "Mother of all living."' Cf. also the OT Ḥivvites.

Probably the references to Eve in Gn 3^{20} and $4^{1.25}$ do not belong to the most ancient form of the Creation story, but to a later stratum of J (so C. J. Ball, 'Genesis,' in *SBOT*). In the older story (Gn 2^{23}) the man names the first woman *'Ishshāh* (the ordinary Heb. word for 'woman,' because she was taken from a man, *'īsh*; or, better, as the LXX and Sam., from her husband, *'īshāh*). But this derivation is not accepted by modern scholars, who derive *'ishshāh* from *'nsh*, 'to be soft *or* delicate,' and *'īsh* from *'ysh*, 'to be strong,' unless, indeed, *'īsh* is a primitive noun, independent of any verbal root (cf. *Oxf. Heb. Lex.*, pp. 35, 61).

P (Gn 1^{27} 5^2) states that mankind was created in two sexes, and tells us that each of the antediluvian patriarchs begat daughters (ch. 5), but says nothing about their wives. In 7^{13}, however, P refers to the wives of Noah and of his three sons. The first woman mentioned by name in P (11^{31}) is Sarai (Sarah); J had already named Lamech's wives, Adah and Zillah, and his daughter Naamah ($4^{19.22}$).

A characteristic feature of the Eve narrative is the sentence (4^1) referring to the birth of Cain, קָנִיתִי אִישׁ אֶת־יהוה. Unfortunately these words are very obscure, and the text may be corrupt. The RV tr. is 'I have gotten a man with the help of the Lord' (similarly LXX, Vulg., Symm.). Another tr. is 'I have gotten a man, even Jahweh' (Gr. tr. in *Hexapla*; Luther), understood as expressing Eve's belief that the Messiah supposed to be promised in Gn 3^{15} had now been born—a mere curiosity of exegesis.[1]

Cheyne (art. 'Adam and Eve,' in *EBi*) maintains that the authors of the Biblical narratives did not put them forth as either purely historical or purely allegorical, but as stating a kernel of fact in a symbolic setting.

The NT interpretation of the narratives is given in the following passages. In Mt 19^6, Mk 10^9, our Lord uses Gn 1^{27} 2^{24} to enforce the sanctity of marriage. In 2 Co 11^3 the beguiling of Eve by the

[1] For a full discussion of the meaning of את־יהוה, see König (who defends the RV tr.), 'Der Evaspruch in Gn 4¹,' in *ZATW*, 1912, pp. 22 ff., 232 ff.

serpent is used as an illustration of the possible seducing of the Church, the bride of Christ, from her Divine Spouse, probably by the devil. On 1 Co 11[2-16], 1 Ti 2[13. 14], and for the expansion of the narratives by Jewish, Christian, and Muhammadan legends, see ADAM.

'The Book of Adam and Eve,' also called 'The Conflict of Adam and Eve with Satan,' extant in an Ethiopic version (Eng. tr., S. C. Malan, London, 1882), was written in Arabic or Syriac by an orthodox Christian of the 5th or 6th cent. A.D. Starting after the Fall, it expands the narrative of Adam and Eve, and in a less degree the account of the patriarchs down to Abraham, and summarizes the history down to the Advent.

LITERATURE.—J. Skinner, 'Genesis' (*ICC*, Edinburgh, 1910), p. 85 f.; A. Jeremias, *The OT in the Light of the Ancient East* (Eng. tr. 1910), i. 221, 321–333; E. G. Hirsch, in *JE* v. 275 f., where the Rabbinical and Muhammadan legends concerning Eve are summarized.

W. H. BENNETT.

EVIL.—See GOOD AND EVIL.

EVIL EYE.—**I. The supposed influence.**—'Evil eye' is the common English term for an influence the belief in which may justly be described as both primeval and universal, and which is in many countries as current to-day as it was in prehistoric times. Its equivalent may be said to exist in every written language, living or dead: Gr. *βασκανία*, whence Lat. *fascinum*, hence modern English, French, Spanish, Portuguese—*fascination*; German—*böser Blick*; Neapolitan and Sicilian—*jettatura*, *mursiana*, and *fascino*. *Fascino* applies to the act as well as to the effect, and consequently, by development, to one of the best known protectives against it. An idea so widespread cannot but have its more common descriptive and colloquial alternatives, such as *malocchio* in Italian, Spanish, and Portuguese, *mauvais œil* in French. By Shakespeare and in English dialects the act implied is forcibly expressed by the verb 'over-look'—'over-looking' used in a well-understood sense, wholly distinct from the literal form meaning 'surveillance' (see *OED*). The word 'evil' is still a household word among English peasantry, though, except in theology, becoming obsolete in literature (*HDB*, *s.v.* 'Evil'). Many diseases of man and beast are so called; *e.g.* 'king's evil,' 'breast evil,' 'udder evil,' 'quarter evil,' and others. In some dialects the word is habitually contracted into 'ill,' and this household word for sickness keeps alive one of its original meanings, viz. sickness or misfortune caused by an evil eye. Bacon (Essay ix., 'Of Envy') says there is a belief in a power of working evil which is ejaculated upon any object it beholds, that has existed in all times and in all countries. Notwithstanding modern science and education, this belief is as strong as ever it was; and, if this were the place, endless authentic stories might be adduced to prove it.

The root conception of the very earliest ages, and still everywhere held by superstitious people, is that certain individuals have the power, by some considered demoniac, whether voluntary or not, of casting a spell or producing some malignant effect upon every object, animate or inanimate, upon which their eye may rest, especially when exercised upon the victims of their displeasure. There does not appear, however, at present, or, so far as recorded, in the past, to be any sort of belief in the power of the eye to produce any good or desirable influence upon the person or thing upon which it may rest, except that doubtful one known as 'love.' From the earliest times the eye *per se* has been supposed to work only evil, and to have a wholly maleficent effect. In Ps 33[18. 19] 34[15] and elsewhere, the effect described is not the direct influence of the eye for good, but must be understood to be the product of a distinctly voluntary and beneficent power, the word 'eye' in these cases being used to denote a personal surveillance. On the 'lifting up upon' of Nu 6[26], Delitzsch (*Babel u. Bibel*, 1905, p. 33 f.) says this is the opposite of the evil eye, the same in meaning as 'make His face to shine upon.' Its supposed manifestations have given rise to many divergent ramifications, finding their expression in more or less descriptive definitions; and these in their turn have further branched out and acquired conventional meanings, which at first sight seem to have no connexion with the original idea of the 'evil eye.' Such, for example, is our Eng. word 'envy,' meaning *malignant* or *hostile feeling* that may be said to arise from natural jealousy—as in 1 S 18[9], where Saul 'eyed David.' It is obvious how close is the connexion here between the definition and the fact denoted. The classic *invideo* describes most accurately what we mean to-day by 'over-look'—'to gaze with evil intent' (see Trench, *Syn. of NT*[8], 1876, pp. 83–106). The Lat. *invidia* not only denotes the feelings connected in our minds with 'envy,' but is to-day an alternative word for the modern Italian *malocchio*.

The Heb. word (קִנְאָה) expressing 'envy' signifies also the evil eye, that is, the natural selfishness, the inbred tendency of humanity, the covetous irritation of unattainable desire. In Scripture, envy and the evil eye are synonymous (Bacon, *loc. cit.*). One of the characteristics of envy is 'to desire the attainment of . . . equality or superiority by the particular means of others being brought down to our own level, or below it' (Butler's Sermon on 'Human Nature,' i. 12, note). So rooted was the belief in this fell influence of the malignant look that in the earliest times every human mischance, all sickness, and whatever was undesirable in life, was looked upon as the certain result of the fatal glance of some person or animal, not necessarily inimical by intention, as will appear later. This conviction remains to the present day among many people, even in England, as strong as ever, while in more backward countries and among so-called savages it is universal and undoubted. In Italy and Southern Europe generally the belief is more prevalent than in more northern countries, and consequently more in evidence. At the present moment, in many parts of England, there are always one or more persons who believe themselves, and are commonly believed to be, slowly dying from being 'over-looked.' This is particularly the case when the disease is at all obscure, and most of all in 'decline,' as *phthisis* is so often called.

Quite recently the present writer knew a respectable, well-to-do farmer who could not be persuaded that his progressive illness was natural senile decay, but maintained to the very last that he was the victim of malignant evil-working on the part of an enemy. Instances of this kind are constantly being reported in local newspapers, and might be multiplied to any extent. A cottager's pig is ill or dies, and at once the conclusion is that it has been spitefully over-looked. A crop is blighted, the cows lose their milk, a horse becomes lame, an accident happens, or any unexpected adversity—it is at once set down as the result of set purpose achieved by some enemy. The evil eye is the cause, and all the inventions of incantation and the magic called 'black art' are but so many reinforcements or helps to quicken the effect of that mysterious influence. Hawker (of Morwenstow), a devout believer, wrote (Aug. 1864): 'The Evil Eye is again at work here. One of my Ewes died yesterday and the ram is taken ill' (C. E. Byles, *Life and Letters of R. S. Hawker*, London, 1905, p. 489).

The evidence to be alluded to later, found upon the earliest known monuments of Babylonia, the cradle of civilization, as well as upon those of Egypt, proves conclusively the importance of the belief, and not only that the dread influence was all-powerful over the living, but that devices many and curious were adopted to protect the dead, and to guard their bodies against it. Ptah, the father of the gods, brought forth all the other gods from his eye, and men from his mouth—a practical rendering of the ancient belief that, of all bodily emanations, those from the eye were most potent. The passages in Scripture referring to the evil eye, such as Dt $28^{54.56}$, Is 13^{18}, Lk 11^{34}, Pr 23^{6} 28^{22}, Mt $6^{22.23}$ 20^{15}, Ps 92^{11}, etc., prove how prevalent the belief was in the ancient East. Among Jews, Muhammadans, Hindus, and all Orientals at the present day it is as firm as ever (see Westermarck, 'The Magic Origin of Moorish Designs,' in *JAI* xxxiv. [1904] 211). Pr 23^{6} ('Eat thou not the bread of him that hath an evil eye,' etc.) is a maxim which holds to-day as firmly as when it was written; and even the suspicion of being the possessor of the evil eye causes people in many countries to avoid a person, or, if that is impracticable, to adopt some of the recognized precautions against it. Hawker, whenever he met one whom he suspected, placed his fingers in the position so well known to Neapolitans (Byles, p. 65). Nowhere—not even among savages—are more precautions used than in Naples, where on the appearance of a reputed *jettatore*, a word or signal is passed; and even in a crowded street there is at once a stampede into shops, entries, or anywhere out of sight and so out of danger, notwithstanding the fact that every one has about him some charm or antidote. Even the mention of the word *fascino* or *jettatura* is enough to cause some to decamp (for a curious instance of this, see Elworthy, *The Evil Eye*, 17).

The antiquity of the belief in the power of the evil eye, as well as its constant persistence, is proved by abundant evidence. In the times of ancient Greece, and in all the subsequent ages, the earliest, the latest, the most familiar, the most constantly portrayed in art of all the possessors of the evil eye, has been the gorgon Medusa, whose fatal glance turned to stone all who beheld her awful face. She was at first depicted in a more or less conventional manner, with staring eyes, wide, grinning mouth, showing wolf-like fangs, and a protruded tongue split down the centre. This was the typical archaic form, and to her fearful ugliness was attributed her baneful influence. The story once started evidently developed rapidly, for at a very early period a parallel version seems to have taken root, and henceforward until comparatively recent times the two ran on concurrently. First the face lost its extreme hideousness, and by degrees, easily traced in ancient art, it became at last in Roman days just as lovely as it had been frightful, while the story grew to match. She was said to have been beautiful at first, and then to have been punished by being changed into a hideousness so terrible that whoever looked upon her was turned to stone (see 'Solution of the Gorgon Myth' in *Folklore*, xiv. [1903] 212 ff.). The belief that her baneful influence arose from her fearful hideousness continued to hold its full force, while, at the same time, the story had developed in the opposite direction to such an extent that her power of *fascinating*, *bewitching*, or *entrancing* was held to be the result of her matchless beauty; yet with all this development the belief has ever remained that the baneful effect sprang from the eyes alone. Thus we see the process by which these terms applied to women in our day derive their meaning. Many Græco-Roman and Etruscan Medusæ are beautiful, but have a sort of horror-struck, agonized expression (see Elworthy, *Horns of Honour*, 61 ff.).

Many theories have been put forward respecting the Medusa and the legend of Perseus—all more or less mythical and speculative. The other famous exploit of Perseus, the rescue of Andromeda, is doubtless still more mythical; by some it is said to be the classic form of the fight between the sun-god of Babylon (Merodach) and Tiâmat, the dragon or power of darkness (cf. Job 9^{12}). Horus slaying the dragon in several forms on Egyptian paintings is but another version; the myth also appears in the fight between Michael and the dragon, and again is perpetuated by St. George on our modern coinage. The representations of Perseus and St. George in art are almost identical, except that the former rides the winged Pegasus, while in some 16th cent. reliefs St. George is represented in plate armour. The panic-stricken lady on the rock, instead of being in the classic nudity of the figure where Perseus is the hero, is dressed in the hoop and farthingale of the Renaissance, in sculptured marbles at the Louvre and Palermo Museums.

Domestic animals of all kinds have ever been specially susceptible of dreaded fascination. The 'ornaments' of Jg 8^{21} (AVm 'like the moon') were none other than the protective charms, some crescent-shaped brasses, some blue glass beads or disks, such as may be seen to-day upon the camels' necks. Young animals of all kinds are now, as ever, thought to be specially liable to injury. Virgil's shepherd (*Ec.* iii. 103) says, 'Nescio quis teneros oculus mihi fascinat agnos.' Plutarch (*Symp.* v. 7) says that certain men's eyes are destructive to infants and young animals. Cows and horses everywhere are to-day subject to the malignant eye, as, indeed, are all kinds of domesticated animals. In the time of Elizabeth, eye-biting witches were executed in Ireland for causing diseases among cattle. One effect of the evil eye on cows to-day is to cause them to lose their milk; this is believed by practically all peasantry in all countries. In the Hebrides it is so well understood as to have a special word (*toradh*) to denote it. If a stranger looks admiringly on a cow, the people believe she will waste away from the evil eye, and they offer him some of her milk so that the spell may be broken (Maclagan, *Evil Eye in the W. Highlands*, 122 f.).

Turks and Arabs have the same belief as to their horses and camels; seldom are any seen harnessed without some protective amulet upon them. In Morocco 'the havoc which the evil eye makes is tremendous. The people say that it "owns two-thirds of the burial ground"' (Westermarck, *loc. cit.*). In Naples the horses, especially those of the street *carrosselli*, are provided with a perfect battery of protective charms; and even in England the apparently useless brass ornaments on horse harness are but the unconscious survival of the self-same idea; each is an amulet, and many of them preserve their undoubted pagan origin. The sun and moon together or separate are among the commonest. In London (May 25, 1905) the present writer saw a horse in a contractor's cart with his head ornamented with blue and red braid, and any number of crescents, suns, and other highly polished brasses on the harness.

The Finns, Lapps, and all Scandinavians are firm believers in the evil eye. In the West of England the baneful influence of envy or ill-wishing is evidenced in the common remark upon any tragic occurrence, bereavement, or serious misfortune, such as a widow being left unprovided for: ''Tis a *wisht* thing for her, sure enough!' Of course, *ill-wisht* is what is understood, but so common is this phrase that 'wisht' is now the accepted and usual word for 'sad.'

The possessors of this power, considered as among the chief agents of mischief-making persons, were mostly females; hence the prevalence (over *wizard*) of the female name of *witch* in English, and its synonyms in other languages. Their spells, incantations, and wicked performances are *witchcraft* (It. *strega*, *stregoneria*). Sorcerers were both male and female, but mostly the latter. This was so in Babylonian times as much as at present. In Jewish, Greek, Roman, and Arabian literature it is clear that sorcery was specially the work of women (on this see *HDB*, *s.v.* 'Magic').

Plutarch, a devout believer, tells us many apt stories (*Symp.* v. 7), and says that the voice, the odour, the breath, are emanations which may easily injure those susceptible to them, producing a wonderful effect, such as the influence of love by the eyes. He says that envy exerts an evil influence through the eyes, and affirms that most direful results are the product of envious looks, which pierce like poisoned arrows. Moors of Morocco still hold the same beliefs (Westermarck, *loc. cit.*). Hindus believe that an invisible spirit is born with the child, and that it is necessary for the mother to keep one breast tied up for 40 days, feeding the child with the other only, by which means the spirit is starved to death. If the child is fed from both breasts it will grow up with the evil eye. Muhammadans are, perhaps, even more fearful of its effects than the Hindus; and texts from the Qur'ān, as in all other countries of Islām, are used as amulets. The legend of the elephant-headed god is the outcome of this belief. Sani, the Hindu Saturn, had been left out of the invitation to the gods to rejoice at the birth of Gaṇeśa, son of Śiva and Pārvatī; he appeared on the scene in a rage, and with the first glance of his eye he caused the child's head to drop off. The other gods instantly cut off the head of a young elephant and stuck it upon the infant's body; hence Gaṇeśa is frequently thus represented.

In Calcutta it is held that a portion of all food bought in the market should be thrown into the fire to avert *nazar* (the native term). It is usual in some parts for a mother to blacken her child's face with a burnt stick to preserve it during the day from the evil influence. Natives of India put *kajal* (lamp-black) on their eyelids, believing that they are thereby protected against, as well as incapable of casting, the evil eye. This blackening of the eyelids, usual all the world over, is not merely a piece of female vanity, but a veritable protective.

The Targum gives a wider reading to Gn 42, explaining that all the sons of Israel went out by one door, lest the evil eye should have sway over them as they went out to buy. Again, Ex 30[8] is rendered 'and looked with the evil eye after Moses.'

Much is said on the subject by A. Goodrich-Freer (*Outer Isles*, 73), Marion Crawford (*Pietro Ghisleri*, 1893, ii. 30), H. Norman (*The Far East*, 1895), and H. G. M. Murray-Aynsley (*Symb.*); while the whole subject is dealt with very exhaustively by Frohmann, *de Fascinatione*.

2. The possessors.—A power so baneful and so steadfastly credited would inevitably lead to much speculation and contention as to the personality of those possessing it; hence arose a multiplicity of canons by which they might be known.

Any abnormal physical peculiarities, whether of beauty or of ugliness, have always been sure evidence of the dread power in all ages associated with the supernatural, with the demons and the powers of darkness. Even the gods were believed to possess it, and to use it when wishing to injure. Juno was particularly so credited; and for this reason Mercury the messenger was provided with a safeguard in his *caduceus*, lest he might be hindered in his flights by the envious eye when on errands for rival deities. Fear of anything uncommon seems to be part and parcel of the nature of all living creatures. All those among the ancients who in any way surpassed conspicuously the common standard, as, for instance, in athletic or physical strength or size, were dreaded as possessors; and so, on the other hand, any one specially defective, particularly a dwarf; the latter, if hunchbacked, was dreaded still more. Squinting or differently coloured eyes were always certain marks of what is now a *jettatore*. In India and in Italy a squinter (*guercio*) is *ipso facto* considered a *jettatore*. We English unconsciously preserve the same idea, for we say 'So-and-so has a "cast" in his eye'—a word purely technical in this sense, and implying the same meaning as the It. *jetare*, 'to cast or throw.' In Armenia very blue or green eyes are evil.

Many animals, particularly those with remarkable eyes, *e.g.* the serpent and the fox, were undoubted possessors of the evil eye. The peacock, Juno's own bird, full of eyes, the symbol of the most envious and ill-natured of the deities, has always been, and still is held to be, a potent mischief-maker. Many well-educated people in England and elsewhere are shocked if peacocks' feathers are put up as ornaments, or even if they are brought into a house; death or at least some evil is believed to be the consequence. The grasshopper's prominent eyes gave it in classic days so evil a reputation as to lead to a certain proverb: 'mantis te vidit' was the exact counterpart of our English, 'Thou art over-looked.' Tycho Brahe would not proceed on his way if a hare crossed his path. The hare is on the Græco-Italian Vase, 2079, Naples Museum, as an emblem of ill-luck. Very much superstition still attaches to the hare; doubtless its prominent eyes are the cause. The Irish thought it cast the evil eye on their cattle; therefore they believed hares to be witches, and consequently there used to be a general slaughter of them on May Day. The hare is still believed in some parts of England, *e.g.* in Somerset, and especially in the Isle of Man, to be the favourite animal into which the witches change themselves (see LYCANTHROPY). Kalmuks regard the rabbit with fear and reverence. Even to-day in Devonshire, fishermen will not pronounce the word 'rabbit,' but describe the animal by some roundabout method (*Devon Assoc. Trans.* 1896). Pregnant Chinese women must not look on a hare lest its eye falling on them should cause the child to be born with a hare-lip. Fishermen almost everywhere avoid mentioning by name not only the hare and rabbit, but also the pig, salmon, trout, or dog, and go out of their way to find some other word. Old gamekeepers do not speak of a fox to each other; it is always a 'thing.'

Pliny (*HN* viii. 34) says that near the source of the Nile is found a wild beast called the *catoblepas*, 'an animal of moderate size . . . sluggish in the movement of its limbs, and its head is remarkably heavy. Were it not for this circumstance, it would prove the destruction of the human race; for all who behold its eyes fall dead upon the spot.'

In Brazil there is a tradition that there is a bird of evil eye which kills with a look. A hunter once killed one of these birds and cut off its head without the eye being turned on him. He killed game thereafter by turning the evil eye upon it. His wife, not dreaming of its destructive power, turned it towards her husband and killed him, and then accidentally turned it towards herself and died at once. The toad's bright eye has always been held to be maleficent. At Bishopsteignton a few years ago lived a reputed witch. Whenever she wished to injure a neighbour she placed a toad at his door, so that when he opened it he might find the toad looking at him, and so receive its first glance.

Snakes have always had a reputation for having the power to fascinate, and there are many marvellous stories of the way in which they hypnotize frogs, birds, and other animals until they seem unconsciously to submit to being swallowed. One kind in particular, *Bucephalus capensis*, is so noted.

At the time of the Black Death in England it was currently believed that even a glance from the sick man's distorted eyes was sufficient to infect those on whom it fell. To this Shakespeare refers in:

> 'Write, "Lord have mercy on us," on those three;
> They are infected; in their hearts it lies;
> They have the plague, and caught it of your eyes'
> (*Love's Labour's Lost*, v. ii. 419 ff.).

Slatin Pasha describes the Khalif's dread of the evil eye. A Syrian blind of one eye was not allowed near him a second time. He declared 'nothing can resist it; illness and misfortune are all caused by the evil eye.' Saul was probably believed to possess it (1 S 18[9]). Heliodorus implies that most, if not all, individuals have it; he says: 'When any one looks at what is excellent with an envious eye, he fills the surrounding atmosphere with a pernicious quality and transmits his own envenomed exhalations into whatever is nearest to him' (*Theag. and Char.* iii. 7). Plutarch says that the Thebans had this faculty so powerfully that they could destroy not only infants, but strong men. Cretans and Cypriotes have had this reputation from ancient times, and retain it even at the present day. So also in Morocco 'whole families have a bad reputation on account of their eyes. People with deep-set eyes, and those whose eyebrows are united over the bridge of the nose, are particularly dangerous' (Westermarck, *loc. cit.*). Pliny says that the Thibii and others possessing the fatal power have a double pupil in one eye, and in the other the figure of a horse, while some have two pupils in each eye; and that in Africa there are families who can cause cattle to perish, trees to wither, and infants to die. Especially the Triballi and Illyrii have such a power of fascination with the eye that they can kill those on whom they fix their gaze. Cicero (Plin. *HN* vii. 2) also declares that 'feminas omnes ubique visu nocere quæ duplices pupillas habeant.' Horace (*Ep.* I. xiv. 37) speaks of the evil power of the 'oculus obliquus.' Bacon (*loc. cit.*) and Frohmann (*de Fascinatione*, p. 11) repeat the same thing. Ovid mentions the double pupils, and says that the Rhodians and Telchines injured whatever they looked at (*Met.* vii. 365 f.). The Greek islanders still in heart worship Fascinus.

Some persons are reputed to have the dread power over special persons or objects. In Italy there are many stories of those known as *jettatori di bambini*, who are of all the most dreaded by mothers, and so are carefully shunned. Another class are supposed to have the faculty of obstruction—such are said to have a *jettatura sospensiva.* If any such person is met on the way to an enterprise, or on setting out on a journey, nothing will succeed, the business will fail, there will be an accident, one must return and give it up for the day.

Pope Pius IX. was confidently affirmed to have the evil eye, and his successor Leo XIII. was said to have it still more; it will probably become part of the reputation of the present Pontiff. It is, moreover, a well-known fact that all ecclesiastics are more or less suspected, especially monks. The murder of King Humbert was confidently ascribed to the *jettatura* of Leo XIII. The Russian peasant is convinced that his or her priest has the evil eye (Norman, *All the Russias*, 1902, p. 44).

In Abyssinia the reputed possessors are called *budas*; they are also magicians, who can work evil at will on any one whose name is known, by taking a certain reed, which the practitioner bends into a circle and places under a stone. At that moment the victim is taken ill; if the reed snaps in bending he will certainly die. All blacksmiths are looked upon as *budas* (Bent, *Sacred City of the Ethiopians*, 1893, pp. 63, 212); cf. our legend of Wayland Smith. These moderns are most likely the descendants in name and reputation of the *Budini* of Herodotus, who refers to them (iv. 105) as evil-minded enchanters; he says that one day in every year they changed themselves into wolves—but he himself did not believe it (see LYCANTHROPY). St. Augustine believed in wer-wolves (see his *de Civ. Dei*, xviii. 18; see also Pliny, *HN* viii. 39).

Not only have the evil-disposed the fatal power, but it is possessed by some involuntarily and much to their own sorrow. Woyciki (*Polish Folklore*, translated by Lewenstein, p. 25) mentions an unhappy Slav who, with the most loving heart, was afflicted with the evil eye, and in sheer desperation blinded himself that he might not be the cause of injury to his dear ones. Cases of involuntary fatal power are related as existing still in England and elsewhere (Mabel Peacock, *Daily News*, Aug. 13, 1895), so that mothers will not venture to expose their infants to the look of their own father. No longer ago than 1901 a farmer of Somerset was said 'to have the evil eye so bad' that if he looked on his own cattle they died. Dt 28[54] is held by Frohmann, the most voluminous writer on the subject, to be a distinct confirmation of the possession of this terrible influence acting against the will of the possessor. Among the Bhuiya and Bhuiyār of India, children born on Saturday have the evil eye, and there are special spells to obviate it (Crooke, *TC* ii. 84, 97).

Perhaps no phase of this superstition is more generally wide-spread than that relating to the danger arising from praise or admiration to the object of it. 'Laudet qui invidet' was believed devoutly by the Romans; it is held and acted on, if unconsciously, among the English to-day, and still more commonly among those belonging to other nations. The conventional or national words uttered instinctively on receiving compliments seem to reflect the notion that danger exists, and that protection must be sought by appeal to a higher power, *e.g.* 'Mashallah!' 'Grazia a Dio!' 'Glory be to God!' 'Lord be wi' us!' Little gratitude is expressed, and certainly no Christianity, but simply a desire to avert the evil expected. This was so strongly felt by the Romans that it became customary even for the speaker of praise or compliment to accompany his speech with the words, 'præfiscini dixerim,' freely translated, 'Fend evil I should say.' In Italy the custom in a like case is to say, *Si mal occhio non ci fosse*, 'No evil eye take effect.' In England it has always been recognized as a rule of good manners not to over-praise; but few reflect that it springs from the old danger (rather than from politeness) lest the speaker should himself fascinate the object of his admiration; for those who were highly praised by others, or even by themselves, were liable to be blasted (Elworthy, *Evil Eye*, 13). In the Hebrides this belief is very strong. Miss Goodrich-Freer writes of horses falling down as if dead (soon after being admired)—the work of the eye (*Outer Isles*, 233). A Highland minister's wife, whose child had been much admired, said, 'Oh, dear, something is sure to happen to that child; I hope she has not given it the Evil Eye!' (Murray-Aynsley, *Symb.* 140). Narcissus was thought to have fascinated himself, hence his untimely fate; so also Eutelidas, who wasted away in consequence of his own admiration of himself. From these old legends we learn why to-day it is not so much ill mannered as directly impious and dangerous to boast of one's belongings, or to praise oneself. Lane (*Mod. Egyp.*, ed. 1895, p. 258) says a modern Egyptian is thereby alarmed, and will reprove one who is over-praising him; he will say to him, 'Bless the Prophet.' If, then, the envier obeys, saying, 'O God, favour him,' no ill effects will be feared. In England, 'bad luck,' it is thought, is certain to follow undue praise or boasting: this is well within the experience of all of us.

'Only yesterday I was saying I had not broken anything for years, and now I have let fall this old glass that belonged to my grandmother! As I was letting loose a favourite dog I said to a friend, "Of all the dogs I ever had, this is the most intelligent, and he will grow up to be a treasure." Half an hour later he picked up a poisoned rat in the road, carried it about ten yards, ran half a mile farther, and died!' (1895).

Just as the hunchback is believed to have the evil eye, so, when his influence has been counteracted, he is thought to be a defender against the malign influence of others; hence, it is said, a notable one gets his living at Monte Carlo by waiting outside the Casino that players may touch him for a consideration, in the belief that so doing will bring luck, *i.e.* prevent evil influence. Luck or good luck is but a negative result depending on the absence of evil or malevolent opposing influence. A very common amulet, made of mother-of-pearl, silver, lava, or other materials, is a *gobbo*, or hunchback, to be found everywhere, even in Moscow, dressed in Russian clothes. An Italian who was wearing one under his waistcoat, having actually received the price agreed, could scarcely bear to part with it; and at last declared that all his good fortune was gone. He died shortly afterwards.

3. Protectives.—A fear so wide-spread and so deeply rooted could not but lead to the invention of innumerable means by which the dread influence could be counteracted. The direct emanations from the eye are the most to be avoided, and the first glance falling upon the susceptible object is the most injurious: if that can be averted or met by some antidote, no harm will be done. It has been shown (Elworthy, *Evil Eye*, 170 ff.) that the devices upon the heads and shields of warriors were originally intended to attract, and so to counteract, the first glance of the adversary in battle. Thus has arisen all that is now understood as heraldic blazonry.

The secondary effects of the evil eye—or of envy, which the term includes—have been produced by many different methods of enchantment, incantation, and mystic rites, under the name of the 'Black Art.' These have been met by analogous acts, so that both bane and antidote fall more properly under the subject of MAGIC; but, inasmuch as many of these acts are confined exclusively to the counteracting of the fatal glance, it is needful to refer to them here at some length. All authorities and all experience agree that to neutralize the look it is essential to attract it towards something striking, by way of diverting it from the object liable to injury. Hence arose the use of bright, shining ornaments of all kinds—of glittering helmets and fantastic head-dresses. Some have even held that this was the origin of the wearing of sparkling gems. The masks of actors, it is maintained (Boettiger, *Kleine Schriften*, 1837–8, iii. 402; Lobeck, *Aglaoph.*, 1829, ii. 973), were first adopted to prevent injury to the persons of those who were necessarily much exposed to the gaze of possible enemies. 'Everything that was ridiculous and obscene was supposed to be inimical to the malignant influence of fascination by the oddness of the sight' (Dodwell, *Class. Tour*, 1819, ii. 34); hence we find that the amulets that were most potent were of this character. Nothing attracts curiosity like obscenity, so amulets of a phallic character have been in all ages the most common, all the world over. Indeed, some writers contend that this is the basis of all protective amulets (J. G. R. Forlong, *Rivers of Life*, 1883). Foremost in this class must be placed that known by classic writers as *turpicula res* (Varro, *de Ling. Lat.* VII. v. 99). For a full description, see Payne Knight's *Worship of Priapus*, 1866, pt. ii. p. 152; Jahn, 'Ueber den Abergl.'; Frohmann, p. 5. Specimens of this amulet, both to be worn on the person and for household suspension, are to be seen in the British and many other Museums.

Amulets against the evil eye are of three classes (for distinction between amulets and talismans see Elworthy, *Evil Eye*, 121): (1) those intended to attract upon themselves the malignant glance, such as were worn on the outside of the dress, or such as were sculptured, painted, or otherwise exposed in or upon houses or public buildings, etc.; (2) all those endless objects worn on or concealed beneath the dress for the purpose of averting evil; (3) written texts from the Scriptures, Qur'ān, or other sacred writings; cabalistic figures and magic formulæ, either in appropriate covering, or carved, painted, or otherwise displayed on houses.

The *turpicula res* was so much in use amongst the Romans that it came to be known by the name of *fascinum*, as in Hor. *Epod.* viii. 18. On this Frohmann (*de Fasc.* p. 5) remarks at length in unquotable language. In fact, *fascinum* became the popular Latin name for *membrum virile*, and survives as *fascino* in modern Italian. Where our present day conventions perceive nothing but obscenity, the ancients saw only the *summum* of everything indispensable to combat successfully the most terrible danger. With them 'fascination was destruction, death—the phallus was life' (Tuchmann, *Mélusine*, ii. [1896] 103). The survivor and obviously less obscene part of the *fascinum* is still to be seen in the ordinary silver charm worn by Roman infants, and known as *mano in fica* (see Elworthy, *Evil Eye*, 152, 256). Its analogue among ourselves survives in the coral and bells of our childhood. Most of the objects worn by the ancients as amulets were generally emblems or symbols (defined in *Evil Eye*, p. 117) of a god, to whom the wearer tacitly appealed by the display of his or her attribute. The amulets denoting one of the four lascivious gods were by far the most common. Of these Priapus, called also Fascinus, according to Lucian, was the special patron of *lascivia*, and the phallus was his special emblem. Infinite in number and in variety of obscenity are the emblems of Priapus, for in all ages and countries his cult seems to have held a prominent position. In Babylonia, Egypt, India, Greece, Rome—among the ancients everywhere—he was in striking evidence, outwardly displayed on the person and in the house. The phallus was consecrated to Osiris, the protector of Egypt. To-day his cult is prominently visible among all savages and so-called Nature-worshippers, while in symbols and cryptic forms it is represented by more civilized people, even by the English. In most museums of antiquity are to be seen specimens of the grosser kind of phallic amulets. That of Naples, containing the remains of Pompeii, shows the greatest number; and few are without specimens of the *turpicula res* before alluded to (on this see Knight, *op. cit.*; Jahn, *op. cit.*; Montfaucon, *Ercolano e Pompeii*; King, *Gems*, 1860, and *Gnostics*, 1864; and Elworthy, *Evil Eye*, 134 ff.). A singular example of obscene Greek fancy is to be seen in a small terracotta (W. 78, Read) at the Brit. Mus., obviously intended as a protective. It consists of two phalli personified, in the act of sawing an eye. Pompeii presents numerous specimens still *in situ*. From mediæval times many are to be found in monastic carvings, *e.g.* the *Shela na gigs* in Ireland, in Glasgow Cathedral, and elsewhere. Publicly exhibited obscene carvings of the Middle Ages were mostly intended as a protection against the evil eye. Cf. art. CHARMS AND AMULETS (Greek), in vol. iii. p. 435 f.

Next to phallic subjects and their developments, perhaps the commonest was a representation of the eye itself, either alone or combined sometimes dramatically with other well-known protective symbols. The best known ancient example is the *uza*, or Eye of Osiris, on most Egyptian coffins or sarcophagi. A good example is on a large wooden sarcophagus in the middle of the Egyptian room at the British Museum. A great eye was carried in Egyptian funeral processions, and, along with the winged scarab, a blue *uza* was placed over the incision made at the embalming of the body as a protector of the dead. Blue and red are everywhere protective colours in Europe, Palestine, India, and throughout the East; in England and all over the world they are the favourite colours for horse ornaments.

The eye as a defence against the evil eye is a good instance of *sympathetic magic* (on this see *HDB*, *s.v.* 'Magic'). As a protective amulet it was certainly used by the Phœnicians, Etruscans, Greeks, Romans, and is used to-day by Turks, Arabs, Nubians, Italians, Russians, and many others. Inghirami (*Pitt. di Vasi Etruschi*, 1852, ii. 164) gives a shield having an eye proper in the centre, as the only device; also (*ib.* iv. 400) Hercules nude has a large eye on each breast and on each thigh, to protect him from the malignant glance of the enemy. A striking shield on a Greek vase in the British Museum has the club of Hercules in the centre, with a large eye upon the appendage beneath (see pl. xix. in Millingen, *Painted Gr. Vases*).

In modern Italy any glass bead or stone having a marking at all like an eye is carefully preserved as an amulet. Bellucci of Perugia has a great number of such, many set in silver and much worn. Ancient Egyptians ornamented their pottery with an eye as a special feature, often in combination with surrounding accessaries. Maspero (*Egyp. Arch.*[5], 1902, p. 245) gives a notable example: three fish having one eye common to all, alternating with three lotus flowers. A remarkable sculptured scene with the eye as the central object is the famous Woburn-relief, first published by Millingen in *Archæologia*, xix. 70, and here reproduced. In

this the evident meaning is the same as that referred to above (Brit. Mus. Read.). Here the eye is being attacked by several hostile animals and by a gladiator, while above it is a man in

Phrygian cap in a well-known indecorous attitude of mocking contempt. This attitude is still practised literally and habitually by Italian sailors against adverse winds, and within the writer's knowledge in England both in act and in words to match. Other curious instances of the eye being attacked by a ring of enemies are found on many ancient gems (see Elworthy, *Evil Eye*, 130), but perhaps the most curious is that (*ib.* 131) where the eye is surrounded by seven symbolic figures, representing the seven powerful and beneficent deities who in turn preside over the days of the week.

This amulet, therefore, provides a protection for every day. Several compound gem amulets having the eye as the centre surrounded by inimical protectors are shown and fully described in *ib.* 130.

The accumulation or piling up of protective agencies is an old-world custom (see Lanciani, *Athenæum*, April 25, 1891). Examples of its prevalence exist in the numerous *disci sacri* of Græco-Roman times, 350 B.C., discovered chiefly at Taranto. One notable specimen is to be seen at the British Museum, and one other at Naples, while two are in the Ashmolean. These have been fully dealt with in the *Soc. Antiq. Trs.* 1898, and more particularly in the present writer's *Horns of Honour*.

The same accumulation of, and unwillingness to ignore, protectives are still in evidence in the dedications of abbeys and churches, *e.g.* to St. Michael and All Angels, to certain Apostles conjointly, to two or more Saints, and, lastly, to All Saints, that none be omitted.

The Gorgoneion already described not only preserves the earliest evidence of the dread of the Evil Eye, but has also been in all ages one of the most favoured amulets against it. Especially has it survived as one of the commonest devices upon the door-knockers, not only of Pompeii, but of modern Naples and all the cities of Europe; thus becoming, even to-day, a potent protector of the house against every new-comer. Birmingham little dreams how persistently she aids in maintaining an ancient myth. One of the most potent of protectives is the *horn* in its various shapes and developments. In modern Italy, especially in Naples, it is so much in use that the word 'horn' has become generic; every kind and description of prophylactic charm against *jettatura* is 'un corno.' The phrase 'non vale un corno' is equivalent to our 'not worth a fig.' On close analysis both phrases are found to bear an identically phallic signification (see HORNS). Plutarch (*Symp.* v. 7) declares that objects fixed up to ward off fascination derive their efficacy from the strangeness or ridiculousness of their forms, which attract the mischief-working eye upon themselves. The same effect is aimed at in the numerous grotesque devices found upon ancient gems. *Grylli*, a quasi-technical term, though included in 'corno,' is the name of all amulets of this comic description. In modern Italian, *grillo* is not only a cricket or grasshopper (a potent protector, because *per contra* a possessor of the evil eye), but also a caprice of fancy, said to be a classic survival. 'Idem [Antiphilus] jocosos nomine Gryllum deridiculi habitus pinxit, unde id genus picturæ grylli vocantur' (Pliny, *HN* xxxv. x. 37).

The likenesses and statues as well as the symbols and emblems of the beneficent gods all continue, both singly and in combination, to be protective amulets against the same danger. The wheel, ladder, club, knife, hook, serpent, fish, snail, cock, lion, pig, dog, elephant, frog, lizard, and many other animals, may all be seen as regular articles for sale in Rome, Berlin, Moscow, Paris, and elsewhere, simply as charms. In Naples and Italy generally they are openly declared to be sold as specifics against the evil eye.

The Scripture *tĕphillîm*, called 'phylacteries' in the NT, are combinations of an object to be worn conspicuously and a hidden writing enclosed within it. Their Greek name proclaims their purpose as protectives, while the Hebrew *tĕphillîm* ('prayers') indicates more clearly their contents (*HDB*, *s.v.* 'Phylacteries'). The Jews are still devout believers in the evil eye, and hence preserve many objects in their ceremonies of a prophylactic nature; among these is the *mezûzāh*, avowedly a literal fulfilment of Dt 6[9]. Strict Jews' doorposts still exhibit this valued safeguard. Persians as well as Jews wear tassels, or *ṭallith*, which have a mystic prophylactic meaning (see *HDB*, *s.v.* 'Fringes').

Luck if analyzed is really the absence of misfortune, *i.e.* of evil wishing, whereby desires and natural expectations are frustrated. Damœtas who, according to Theocritus (*Idyll.* vi. 39), admired his own beauty reflected in the water, knew of the probable consequence, and used the well-known remedy against fascination, spitting three times on his breast. Spitting is a protection against many misfortunes. In Bulgaria it is believed that spitting protects against fascination and also against perjury at a trial.

Many objects besides those already noted, believed to be potent against the evil eye generally, are in some parts held to be specific against certain effects of it. The crescent—symbol of the moon, Ištar, Isis, Hathor, Artemis, Diana, and the Virgin Mary—is everywhere a potent amulet. Along with the sun, it is to be seen on great seals and coats of arms, even episcopal. As a separate amulet, it specially appeals to all those powerful deities for protection, but in Sicily the horned shell called *cacazzi di luna* is worn by children and others against toothache, always considered as the result of maleficence. There also the *operculum*, everywhere a protective amulet from the natural eye upon it, is a certain specific against sore throat (*male di gola*); so also a little wooden cross tied to a piece of crystal is good against sore throat. Small gold earrings are worn by *carbonari* and others, avowedly to ward off the *malocchio*; and our own navvies and showmen wear them for the like purpose, not merely for ornament. A double triangle of silver, a viper's skin in a bag, a silver ring called 'di S. Biaggio,' and many other objects are specifics against various maladies. Many special Sicilian amulets *contro la jettatura* were exhibited by Pitré at the Palermo Exhibition, 1903:

1. A piece of red cloth. Red everywhere is inimical to witchcraft of all kinds, and is constantly used, from Donegal to Japan, both alone and as a strengthener of other amulets against the evil eye. Our plough horses and our recruits alike wear red and white ribbons, and the Kirghiz ornament their horses with bright colours to keep it off. The material on horses is always woollen or worsted. Charms in Italian and Sicilian shops are always tied with red woollen braid or painted red; horns on butchers' shops are always painted red and white.

2. *Virticciu* (Sicilian), *fusajola* (Ital.), the perforated whorl used in spinning. This is but one example of perforated amulets,

of which also the holed stones used everywhere as protectives are another (see Elworthy 'Perforated Stone Amulets,' Paper at Brit. Assoc. 1902, pub. by Anthrop. Inst. in *Man*, 1903, no. 8).

3. *Testa d'agghia* (Sicilian), *aglio* (Italian), stalk of garlic. Alike in Italy, in Greece, and in India may be seen garlic bulbs tied with red worsted. In parts of Greece the mere utterance of the word for 'garlic' is considered a protective, just as 'corno' is in Naples (Murray-Aynsley, 144).

4. *Chiave masculina.* The key everywhere, but always the solid, never the tube key known as *feminina*.

5. *Zabara* (Sic.), *agone* (Ital.), agate—from its likeness to the eye.

6. *Sachetto di sale.* Salt is used as a protective against the evil eye by Jews for their children (Zangwill, *Children of the Ghetto*[4], 1893, p. 190); cf. putting salt on the tongue as part of the Rom. Cath. rite of baptism. Modern Jews put 'a bit of coal' into a child's pocket to ward off the evil eye (*ib.*). So in Ireland, a prisoner carries a piece of coal in his pocket to protect him from the evil eye at his trial. On a child in Corfu was a small silk bag, containing salt, charcoal, a nail, and a clove of garlic.

7. *Ferro di cavallo*, tied with red worsted. The horseshoe to us is perhaps the most familiar of all amulets against the evil eye. It is explained as being merely the conventionalized form of the moon emblem. The Turkish horseshoe, unlike that of Britain, is always shaped like the Byzantine crescent. Power is cumulative; so iron, the bane of witchcraft, is further reinforced by association with the horseshoe (cf. Elworthy, *Evil Eye*, 217).

8. *Anello di chiodo di ferro.* All rings are amulets, but silver ones, Diana's own metal, above all. In Italy the rings sold specially *contro jettatura* are all silver, and frequently augmented by a suspended horn, hand, or flower.

9. *Graccaluora* (Sic.), *gratugia* (Ital.), a common tin grater. At Taormina in 1903 a small tin grater, a spider crab, and a horseshoe, tied together with red braid, were fixed over the door of a house of the better class in a main street.

10. *Fili di seta colorati*, silken threads binding up nine slips of paper on which are cabalistic writings. Threads have always been held to be powerful, both in working enchantments and in countervailing them. The *fattura della morte* (Elworthy, *Evil Eye*, 58) has threads wound in and about the nails and pins to increase the power of the whole. The witch knots her cords to work strangling on her victims; so the Jew and the Persian knot their fringes to guard against witchcraft (see 'Magic' in *HDB*). Threads of many colours, as a charm against fascination, are mentioned by Persius (*Sat.* ii. 31).

11. *Cavaduzza marina*, Hippocampus tied with red braid, specially protective against the *fattura della morte*—invoice of death, a much dreaded spell (Elworthy, *Evil Eye*, 57). The sea-horse is also known in Sicily as a protection against malarial fever.

12. *Nastro giallo intrecciato*, plaited yellow ribbon (braid) shaped to represent the sea-horse. Yellow is also a protective colour. Gubernatis (*Rev. di Trad.*, p. 202) writes: 'per non essere colto da jettatura, si tenga un pezzo di lana gialla, visibile sul vestito che si indossa.' (On the efficacy of coloured threads and ribbons, see Petronius, *Sat.* 131; Story, *Castle St. Angelo*, 211; Jahn, 'Abergl.,' p. 42; Rhys, 'Sacred Wells in Wales,' *Cymr. Soc.*, Jan. 11, 1893; *Hygiene*, Nov. 17, 1893, p. 398; Murray-Aynsley, *Symbols*, p. 142.)

A conspicuous amulet in the Pitré collection was a cow's hoof attached by a red woollen tape to a rapier marked 'contro la jettatura' (on the efficacy of iron as a protective see Elworthy, *Evil Eye*, 221). A curious object for the same avowed purpose is *pettini de telaio*, which is known to us as the sleigh or reeds of a loom.

13. *Carta repiegata sulla quale sono scritti 2 scongiuri Siciliani contro nemici ignoti ed favore di persone cari.* This folded paper is to be worn as both an amulet and a talisman.

14. A boar's tusk mounted in silver with a lobster's claw attached, described as *contro le stregherie*. The tusk is everywhere a protective amulet; even in England it is worn by wild beast showmen to protect them from their savage charges. Tigers' and lobsters' claws mounted with silver rings, etc., are worn as charms by Sicilians, Indians, Japanese, and Greeks in Smyrna. Their efficacy comes from their horn-like shape. Amongst the Jews in Jerusalem the number and variety of charms against the evil eye are equally surprising, and the same remark applies to Russia, Moscow in particular. Miss Goodrich-Freer gives a list of the objects on a necklace from Jerusalem, and the words of a special adjuration even more potent than any, to be worn in a bag hung round the neck: male frog, shoe, comb, stove, lock, dog, pigeon, pestle, hammer, axe, sabre, key, scissors, mallet, pick-axe, camel, pistol, hen, coffee-pot, etc. Every one of these and many more may be bought in Naples, Palermo, and Moscow separately as well as combined (see *Folk-lore*, June 1904, p. 186).

15. Egg (shell filled with wax) stuck with pins and a nail; this is the *fattura della morte*, or 'death charm.' On this subject the mass of evidence is enormous, and the belief in it as a work of Sympathetic Magic is universal. To-day in Somerset and Devon, in the Isle of Man and the Highlands, it is practised as in Italy, as may be seen in the *corp creidh* at the museum at Oxford. The same means are practised to-day as in ancient Thebes and in the Middle Ages. Lytton (*Last of the Barons*) says that Friar Bungay was employed by Jacquetta, mother of Elizabeth Woodville, to make a wax figure to imitate Neville, earl of Warwick, into which she might stick pins so as to cause the Earl's death. An object, evidently of charred flesh, was recently found suspended in a chimney in Somerset, analogous to that described in Elworthy, *Evil Eye*, p. 55 n. (on Sympathetic Magic, see Tylor, *Prim. Cult.*[3] i. 112 ff.; also 'Cucina della strega,' *Corriere di Napoli*, Aug. 9, 1895). To counteract this evil-working artifice, so widely practised, red braid is considered a speciality. To prevent evil-wishers from injuring them, Sicilians wear a *sachetto continente uno spago con molti nodi*, by means of which the evil-worker's schemes are counteracted.

In Italy, Scandinavia, Judæa, China, Japan, and all over the world, every ill that flesh is heir to being the direct result of malignant influences or machination, there are specifics for each to ward them off or to cure. Each trade usually has its own favourite amulet, used singly or in combination (for details see *Evil Eye*). Some, however, deserve to be noticed here. Rome still holds to its own proper children's amulet—the silver *mano in fica* (see *Evil Eye*, p. 256) keeps alive the classic *fascinum* as truly and effectually as do the coral and silver bells of our childhood. Naples, however, utilizes a veritable pantheon for her children's protection, in a combination of many symbols, each of which appeals to one or other of the old pagan deities, and all against dread fascination. A silver ornament, plain on the side worn next the skin, is known as the *cimaruta*, or sprig of rue, represented by three branches, each of which is composed of one or more prophylactic charms (see Günther, *FL*, 1905, p. 132 ff.). The Herb of Grace has ever been held in high esteem, from the time of Pliny down to the present. Pawnbrokers of Florence regard it with especial favour as a protector against the *malocchio*. In most of their shops a pot of growing rue is to be found. In India, rue (*sudāb*) is used in various ways as a charm against the evil eye, as it is in Persia (Jackson, *From Constantinople to the Home of Omar Khayyam*, New York, 1911, p. 119), while the Beriya of India employ *Acacia arabica* (Crooke, *TC* i. 247). True specimens of the *cimaruta* are now scarce, and none is genuine unless of hall-marked sterling silver—which applies equally to the Roman *mano in fica*; all amulets appealing to the moon-goddess must be in her own true metal. Where the story of Ulysses remains enshrined in local topography, of course Parthenope figuratively and literally plays a conspicuous part; consequently, as *all* amulets are 'corno' or 'corna' in Neapolitan, so all of a special class are known as *sirene*. The latter are mostly house amulets for suspension, and are of two classes—a single figure, sometimes as a siren, *i.e.* simply a bird with human head; or more commonly a crowned female whose body ends in a double fish-tail instead of legs, and with silver bells hanging beneath. Others have the same figure in combination with double sea-horses. A siren of this fish-tailed kind—probably an importation from Naples—is embossed on a panel on an old house at Newcastle-on-Tyne. Another favourite house amulet is the sea-horse itself, *cavallo marino*. All Neapolitan house-amulets of this kind are of silver, and ornamented with bells precisely like our old corals, etc. A pendant silver amulet, against the evil eye—a crowned female, ending in a fish with bells, precisely analogous to the *sirene*, said to be German of the 17th cent.—is pictured in the *Connoisseur*, Jan. 1905, p. 56.

It is doubtful at what epoch *bells* (see GONGS AND BELLS) were first used in Europe. The shaking of metal as a means of calling is of extreme antiquity. The clashing of bronze was characteristic of the worship of Demeter. She was called Ἀχαία (the noisy one) from the clanging of cymbals and drums at the searching for Persephone. It is said that the famous Gong of Dodona (see A. B. Cook, *Journal of Hellenic Studies*, 1902, p. 5) consisted of a string of bells, and gave rise to a Greek proverb, which lasted a thousand years—comparing a talkative person to the Gong of Dodona. At the Temple of Jupiter Tonans bells hung down almost to the doors. The use of bells probably came in pre-historic ages from the Far East, and they always have borne a prophylactic character—especially if they were used against the evil eye. This is implied in Ex 28[33]. The colours, too, alternating with the bells, had also their protective value, and have it still, particularly red. Their form, the slit ball, was probably that still to be found in Neapolitan amulets, on Russian horses, on Madeira oxen, and on the coral and bells of our infancy, one of the oldest and most enduring of patterns. Bells on horses and on cattle have been used in all ages—always as protectives. On farm teams in the West of England quite recently a so-called 'housing,' or row of five or six loud-jangling bells, ornamented *de rigueur* with red worsted fringe, was carried above the collar of the leader. The noise was often deafening; the purpose was to drive away evil spirits, while the red colour attracted and so absorbed the first glance of the evil eye. Bells in church towers are not originally intended as calls to prayer, but rather as a preparation for it, by driving away evil spirits, to whom the noise is a terror. The bells of two neighbouring churches, both within sight of the present writer, are rung specially on their respective Saints' Days 'to drive the devil over to the other parish.'

'The sea-horse occurs on many early crosses in the east of Scotland, notably at Aberlemno and Meigle' (*Reliquary*, Oct. 1895, p. 251). Miss Goodrich-Freer says: 'In the Hebrides *caoil-brechan*, water ragwort, called "armpit" flower of St. Columba, is placed in byres, etc., to protect cattle from the same. The cock is sacred to keep off evil spirits' (on this see Elworthy, *Horns of Honour*, 93). In India the excrescences of the Bombax, or cotton tree, are considered protectives; and the tree has the like reputation in Mexico, where it is common. The usual shop amulet of butchers in Naples is a pair of cow's horns, painted red and white, over the door; but, in addition, very many of the better class have a stag's head with branching horns affixed to the inner wall. Many have other objects suspended, such as a horseshoe with a single pendent horn tied with red (see HORNS). Macaroni and provision dealers frequently have several curiously combined amulets hung up inside their shops. Laundresses usually have a glove filled with sand, the thumb and two middle fingers sewn in, so as to make the *mano cornuta*. The sun and moon combined are a common finial for the silver *spada* worn by women in their hair; some have a flower, bird, or piece of coral. Written texts, cabalistic signs (such as the well-known Solomon's seal) of many descriptions are also potent protectors against the dreaded influence. Many are of a double character, *i.e.* possessing power as visible amulets, but with special virtue from the nature of their contents. Magic squares, still worn in modern Italy in bronze, were certainly well-known to the ancient Romans, many in terra-cotta having been found, with numbers arranged precisely as they are to-day. In Scotland, written charms against various ills are still common (*Folklore*, xv. [1904] 350). In Teneriffe it is the custom to scatter mustard-seed through the house after a birth to keep off witches and the evil eye. The Dāngi of India, in similar fashion, burn mustard and pepper, the Dom garlic and pepper on a Tuesday or a Saturday, and the Khairwa salt and pepper (Crooke, *TC* ii. 251, 329, iii. 224). Iron, as being a well-known scarer of demons, is employed to avert the evil eye among the Thāru (*ib.* iv. 393); and the Armenians spit on a stone and turn it under, or make cakes of dough, wet them with water, and throw them into a fire, the evil eye being broken as the cakes crack asunder (Abeghian, *Armenischer Volksglaube*, p. 126 f.). Elsewhere an effort is made to ward off the evil eye by giving a depreciative name to a child, as among the Indian Rāji (Crooke, *op. cit.* iv. 214), though among the Golapūrab this is resorted to only when the first child of a marriage has died (*ib.* iii. 427).

Besides all this multiplicity of concrete objects, there is an endless multitude of incantations, of verbal and ritualistic charms, used for the like purpose, too numerous to be more than referred to. Sayce (*Rel. of Anc. Bab.*[3], App. iii.) gives a long list of magical texts. Abra-Melin also gives a vast number of magical squares, formed of letters, for warding off or producing all sorts of evil.

LITERATURE.—L. Vairus, *de Fascino*, Paris, 1583; J. B. Thiers, *Traité des superstitions*, Paris, 1679, i. 414 f.; J. C. Frommand (Frohmann), *de Fascinatione*, Nuremberg, 1675; V. Alsarius, *de Invidia et Fascino Veterum* (Grævius, *Thesaurus Ant. Rom.* xii., Lugd. Bat. 1699); Jorio, *Mimicha d. Antiche*, Naples, 1832; Jahn 'Ueber den Aberglauben des bösen Blicks' (*SSGW*, Leipzig, 1855); J. Brand, *Popular Antiquities*[2], London, 1870; W. W. Story, *Castle St. Angelo and Evil Eye* London, 1877; G. Pitré, *La jettatura ed il mal' occhio in Sicilia* Klausenburg, 1884; Grossi, *Il Fascino del Oriente*, Milan, 1886; M. Tuchmann, 'La Fascination,' *Mélusine*, ii. f. [1896 f.]; *JASB*, pt. iii., 1888; E. B. Tylor, *Primitive Culture*[3], London, 1891; A. H. Sayce, *Religion of the Ancient Babylonians*[3], London, 1891 (Hib. Lect. 1897); P. Bienkowski, 'Malocchio,' in *Eranos Vindobonensis*, 1893, p. 285 ff.; H. Oldenberg, *Religion des Veda*, Berlin, 1894, p. 503; F. T. Elworthy, *The Evil Eye*, London, 1895, and *Horns of Honour*, do. 1900; W. Crooke, *PR*[2] i. 160, ii. 1 ff., and *TC* i. 30, ii. 478, iii. 82, iv. 405 f.; J. Wellhausen, *Reste arab. Heidentums*[2], Berlin, 1897, p. 164 f.; M. Abeghian, *Armen. Volksglaube*, Leipzig, 1899, pp. 123–127; H. G. M. Murray-Aynsley, *Symbolism of the East and West*, London, 1900; J. G. Campbell, *Superstitions of the Highlands and Islands of Scotland*, Glasgow, 1900; Yrjö Hirn, *The Origins of Art*, London, 1901, ch. xx.; A. Goodrich-Freer, *Outer Isles*, do. 1902; R. C. Maclagan, *Evil Eye in the W. Highlands*, do. 1902; P. W. Joyce, *Soc. Hist. of Anc. Ireland*, do. 1903, i. 309 f.; M. Jastrow, *Rel. Bab. und Assyr.*, Giessen, 1905 [in progress]; S. Seligmann, *Der böse Blick und Verwandtes*, Berlin, 1910; L. Frachtenberg, in *Hoshang Memorial Volume*, Bombay, 1911, pp. 419–424; L. Blau, in *JE* v. 280 f. See also the Literature appended to the various artt. on CHARMS AND AMULETS.

F. T. ELWORTHY.

EVIL-SPEAKING.—See SLANDER.

EVOLUTION (Biological).—In the history of biological thought the term 'evolution' has had more than one meaning. It has, however, been more especially used to denote those views on the interrelation of living things which imply the conception of the mutability of species, now so closely associated with the name of Charles Darwin (1809–82).

1. The idea of the transformation of species, of the origin of new forms from pre-existing ones, is old; it is to be found in the teachings of many of the Greek philosophers. **Aristotle** devotes some attention to it, and his writings doubtless express in large measure the opinions generally prevalent in learned circles during the time in which he lived. He taught that there had been a continuous succession of animal forms, during which the older and less perfect had gradually given rise to the younger and more perfect, themselves in process of giving rise to yet more perfect forms. Life itself arose through the direct metamorphosis of inorganic matter. Plants came early in the succession; for, though endowed with powers of nourishment and reproduction, they have neither feeling nor sensibility. Later came the plant animals or zoophytes; and still later the animals proper, gifted with sensibility and even, to some extent, with powers of thought. Highest of all is man, the one form capable of abstract thought. The process of Nature is a struggle towards perfection, the expression of a perfecting principle inherent in the universe. The result is a gradual evolution from the lower to the higher, owing to the resistance offered by matter to any change of form from that which the perfecting principle seeks to impose upon it. At the back of the perfecting principle is the Efficient Cause; though, whether this Efficient Cause gave the original impulse and thenceforward remained outside the operations of Nature, or whether it is all the time constantly at work, is a question which Aristotle raises without being able to resolve.

In his conception of the processes of Nature, Aristotle had advanced as far as the existing state of knowledge would allow. Though inexact in detail, the idea of progressive change in the organic world stands out clearly enough. But he was unable to point to any natural agency through which change might be brought about. Curiously enough, he considers in one passage a crude form of the survival of the fittest which was advanced by **Empedocles,** though only to reject it. Perhaps he was too deeply impressed by the feeling of design in Nature to sift out the argument for natural selection dimly foreshadowed in the writings of the earlier philosopher. Moreover, the facts at his disposal were insufficient to force him to pay attention to the great amount of variation normally found among living things or to realize its significance.

In the teaching of Aristotle are summed up the contributions of the Greeks to the problems of evolution, and, as Osborn has said, they

'left the later world face to face with the problem of causation in three forms: first, whether Intelligent Design is constantly operating in Nature; second, whether Nature is under the operation of natural causes originally implanted by Intelligent Design; and, third, whether Nature is under the operation of natural causes due from the beginning to the laws of chance, and containing no evidences of design, even in their origin' (*From the Greeks to Darwin*, ch. iv.).

2. The acute and speculative minds of Greece had in large measure formulated the problem of evolution, and for many centuries it rested much where they had left it. The learning of Europe passed into the hands of the Christian Church, where it became a means of extolling the glory of God rather than a pursuit to be followed for its own sake. It was in the order of things that a firm belief in another and better world should draw men's attention from the earthly seat of a sinful and transitory life, and the check thus exerted upon natural curiosity produced its inevitable result in the stagnation of natural knowledge. It is true that some of the more liberal minds in the Church, notably Augustine and Thomas Aquinas, endeavoured to reconcile the teaching of the Greeks with the Mosaic cosmogony, but eventually the precision of the first chapter of Genesis conspired with the inclination of the faithful to behold in the manifold variety of Nature incontrovertible evidence of the manifold power of the Creator. It was only after the lapse of many years that the weakening of the authority wielded by the Church, helped largely by the renaissance of Greek learning, lent a fresh stimulus to curiosity, and enabled men to put aside the temptations of a future life and to devote themselves to the discovery of the world in which their lot was cast. But it was long before definite progress was made with the idea of evolution. In the early revival of science, men were more attracted to the study of the inorganic, where matter was more stable, and where the phenomena encountered were less likely to suggest the derivation of one form of matter from another in orderly sequence. In the provinces of zoology and botany, where these problems are more likely to arise, the naturalists were for long too busy with absorbing into their classifications the facts continuously streaming in to devote much attention to the philosophy of their subject.

3. Starting with the great miscellaneous compilations of Aldrovandus and Gesner in the 16th cent., the process of arrangement gradually took shape through the labours of Ray and others till it reached a definite stage in the monumental work of **Linnæus** (1707–78). The problem of species had been discussed before Linnæus, but it was the *Systema Naturæ* which by its comprehensive and logical arrangement insisted upon the question of the way in which species were related to one another. Linnæus himself, though a man of science, was a good Christian, and held to the Church's teaching of the separate creation of each species of plant and animal. In his later work he allowed himself a little more latitude, and admitted that in certain cases new forms might have come into being through crosses between the original species. But the change so brought about was held to be a degenerative one, tending to obscure the perfection of the original type as it had issued from the mint of the Creator. It was the classification of species that interested Linnæus—the demonstration of criteria by which the vast variety of animal and plant forms could be definitely separated one from another. How these differences might have come about was a question in which he was not greatly interested. Nevertheless, his notable attempt to fix the limits of natural species inevitably forced the botanist and the zoologist to inquire more closely into the nature of species itself.

4. Contemporary with Linnæus lived another great naturalist, who, perhaps more than any one, should be regarded as the father of modern evolutionary thought. In most respects the mind of **Buffon** (1707–88) contrasted sharply with that of Linnæus. Though no less insistent upon exact description as a first necessity in science, he held that the mere accumulation of facts was not an end in itself, but that the scientific mind was fulfilling a proper function in combining and generalizing upon the facts which it had brought to light. For this reason Buffon's writings abound in speculation, and were full of suggestion for many who came after him. To determine precisely the credit due to Buffon in the development of the conception of evolution is a matter of extreme difficulty, for his own standpoint apparently underwent considerable changes during different periods of his life. Like Linnæus, he started with a belief in the fixity of species, each enjoying the attributes with which it was immutably endowed by the Creator. With the riper knowledge that came from his studies in comparative anatomy, we find him questioning the perfection of the plan upon which an animal is built. In his famous dissertation upon the pig he points out that this animal cannot be regarded as formed upon an originally perfect plan, but that it evidently has parts which, though well formed, are of little or no service to it. In fact, it may be regarded as a compound of other animals. From this position it was not a great step to a belief in the frequent mutability of species, and to the conception that the members of a group of species showing family resemblance may have been derived from a common ancestor, some by becoming more perfect, others by degeneration. So might the horse and the ass, so even man and the ape, be related to one another. Yet, after forcibly advancing the claims of a common descent, Buffon will suddenly remember the susceptibilities of his neighbours, and protest that, after all, it cannot be so, since there has been vouchsafed to us a direct revelation that all animals have issued in pairs, completely formed, from the hands of the Creator. How far this attitude was ironical is difficult to say, nor need it greatly concern us here. There is little doubt that in his inmost mind he believed in the mutability of species, and held that changes in animal and plant form could be directly brought about by changes in their environment, and that these changes could become hereditarily fixed. Buffon's great service to the progress of thought lay in his suggestiveness. He questioned the orthodox notions as to the relation of species to one another, and from the width of his learning, the acuteness of his intellect, and the charm of his style he put his questions in such a way that no man thenceforward could afford to ignore them.

5. The seed sown by Buffon soon began to bear fruit, and within a few years **Erasmus Darwin** (1731–1802) in England and **Lamarck** (1744–1829) in France each put forward a theory of evolution. Each accepted the doctrine of the mutability of species, and each adopted almost the same hypo-

thesis to explain how the transformation of species might be brought about. Buffon had expressed the opinion that a change in the external surroundings in which animals lived might directly influence their form. Both to Erasmus Darwin and to Lamarck a changed environment was at the bottom of specific change. And the reaction was an indirect one. The changed circumstances of its life led to an alteration in the habits of an animal; and the altered habits, by causing increased use of some organs, together with decreased use of others, eventually resulted in a change of form. Such changes of form brought about by increased use or disuse of organs—'acquired characters,' as they are now generally called—were assumed by Erasmus Darwin and Lamarck to be inherited. The net result of a permanent change in the environment was a permanent alteration in form, though this was reached only indirectly through a change in the animal's habits. Unless the animal reacted to the altered environment by an alteration in its habits, a change in form could not take place. Evolution was effected only through the co-operation of the animal's nervous system.

6. Though they excited much attention, the views of Erasmus Darwin and Lamarck failed to secure a firm hold on men's minds. At the English Universities, scientific studies were at a low ebb, and the authority of the theologians, including the acute and gifted Paley, was directly hostile and sufficiently powerful to prevent the new doctrines from percolating far. In France the great weight of the learning of **Cuvier** (1769–1832) was cast into the scale against Lamarck, and the younger generation probably grew up to regard him as little better than a madman. The doctrine of the transformation of species implied a unity of plan running through the animal kingdom. To this idea Cuvier, who stoutly upheld the orthodox view of the separate creation of species, was vigorously opposed. He contended that there were several perfectly distinct plans or types upon which different groups of animals were built, and that these different types could not be related to one another. There were instances in which animals built upon one plan might show apparent resemblances to those which were built upon another, but careful anatomical analysis showed that in reality the resemblance was one of analogy only. His great knowledge of comparative anatomy enabled Cuvier to crush his opponents, for it was not until the rise of modern embryology that the fundamental unity of plan common to the great animal groups came to be clearly perceived.

7. Comparative anatomy, as it then existed, was ranged on the side of special creation as opposed to the gradual evolution of species. But another study was already coming into greater prominence. The year (1830) that witnessed the victory of Cuvier over the Lamarckians in the Academy of Sciences at Paris witnessed also the publication of the first volume of **Lyell's** *Principles of Geology*. In that work was set forth what came to be known as the uniformitarian doctrine in geology—'the principle that the past must be explained by the present unless good cause can be shown to the contrary.' Lyell pointed out clearly and forcibly that the formation of the rocks in past ages could be referred to the operation of causes similar to those now at work, and that there was no valid reason for assuming the interpolation of a series of cataclysmal changes such as Cuvier had advocated. By showing that natural causation is competent to account for the non-living part of the globe, Lyell strengthened the hands of those who were trying to show that it could also account for the living. Moreover, the uniformitarian doctrine in geology provided another strong argument for the evolutionist. Palæontology had arisen as a serious study, and in the hands of Cuvier and his pupils had already undergone considerable development. It had been perceived that, on the whole, the different strata of the earth's crust contained different and distinctive collections of fossil forms, and Cuvier had sought to explain this through a series of world catastrophes which blotted out animal life, followed by a series of separate creations which re-peopled the earth with new and distinctive fauna. By abolishing the catastrophe the geologist brought the naturalist face to face with the problem of explaining the connexion between the fossil forms of life and those still living, and, as the science of palæontology developed and fresh discoveries were made, it came to be more clearly seen that the distribution of these various fossil forms in time accorded well enough with the idea that there existed a genetic continuity between them, but that it was not easily to be reconciled with any other hypothesis.

8. The development of the natural sciences during the earlier half of the 19th cent. was rapid, and by the middle of it the evolutionist was able to set forth a goodly array of arguments on his side. In Germany, theories of the transformation of species had excited considerable interest. Through the writings of Oken, Treviranus, von Baer, and others, scientific opinion in that country may be said to have been not only familiar with the idea, but also in large measure sympathetically disposed towards it. In England, on the other hand, isolated as she had been from the solvent action of the Napoleonic wars, scientific opinion was largely represented by men of sincere and orthodox religion, to whom the idea of the mutability of species, and all that it implied, was unwelcome and even repugnant. Indeed, it was not until 1844 that the existing arguments for evolution were actually brought together by **Robert Chambers**, whose work on the *Vestiges of the Natural History of Creation* ran through many editions and excited very considerable discussion and controversy. A brief presentation of these arguments will show that the case for evolution was forcibly stated before 1850, and it is not easy to understand why scientific men in England were not more early sensible of their weight.

(1) *Argument from the general presumption of science against 'supernatural' explanations of phenomena.*—The whole tendency of scientific discovery is to eliminate the miraculous as an element in the causation of natural phenomena, and to regard this causation as having from the earliest times been operative in the same way as we see it now. With the accumulation of facts in the physical sciences the principle of the continuity of natural causation had become so firmly established, through the discoveries of Newton and other great natural philosophers, that it was accepted as axiomatic by those who worked at these branches of knowledge. In deciding, therefore, between two rival theories to account for the causation of the organic world, it was obvious that the presumption was in favour of the one which postulated a continuous and orderly process of natural change, as against that which explained the phenomena by the sporadic intervention of an alien and incalculable force.

(2) *Argument from uniformitarianism in geology.*—The influence of the rise of modern geology, with its doctrine that the past is to be explained by the present, has already been pointed out, and its bearing upon the question of organic evolution as opposed to a series of special creations is sufficiently obvious without further remark.

(3) *Argument from homologies in vertebrates.*—The studies of the comparative anatomists, begun

in the 18th cent. and so brilliantly developed by Goethe, St. Hilaire, Cuvier, and others, had clearly demonstrated that the parts of the skeleton of vertebrates could all be reduced to a common plan. Widely different in appearance as were the wing of a bird, the fin of a whale, and the hand of a man, the anatomist was nevertheless able to demonstrate that there was an intimate correspondence between them, so that the separate parts of the one could be clearly recognized, though greatly modified, in the other. Nor were these homologies confined to the vertebrates; for even at this time cases had been worked out among such groups as the insects and molluscs. Such homologies were obviously in harmony with a theory which implied community of descent through a process of gradual evolution.

(4) *Argument from the variability of existing species.*—Though the study of variation had not yet made much headway, there was one group of facts which pointed clearly to the possibility of species being capable of permanent modification. The various domesticated races of animals offered evidence that certain species were capable of modification, and that such modification could be transmitted. Whatever the origin of the variability, its existence at any rate was positive proof that species could undergo transformation.

(5) *Argument from the sequence of types in palæontology.*—As the fossiliferous strata of the earth came to be more fully explored, it was seen that a rough order was apparent in the succession of the new forms brought to light. The more recent the strata, the higher the types, and the more nearly approximating to living species; while, conversely, the older strata were characterized by a simpler fauna and by the absence of the higher and more specialized types. Though the general import of the sequence of types was unmistakable, the evidence, as it existed in the middle of last century, was for special cases imperfect and often apparently inconsistent. Whole groups of animals might suddenly disappear at the close of a geologic period, and be suddenly replaced by other distinct groups of closely related species, without the appearance of intermediate forms. Such facts were naturally insisted upon by the opponents of the evolutionary doctrine, and its supporters could make little retort beyond alleging the imperfection of the geological record. It may be said that, though palæontology gave a general support to the idea of evolution, the records existing in the earlier half of last century were too scanty to afford that detailed evidence without which it could hardly be admitted as a cogent witness for the evolutionist. More recently, of course, the position is greatly changed; and the palæontological discoveries of the latter part of the 19th cent. have not only gone some way towards filling up clamant gaps in the record, but in certain cases, notably those of the horse and the elephant, have brought to light very beautiful and complete series in which the evolution of an existing animal can be clearly traced back to a geologically remote and widely different ancestor.

(6) *Argument from persistent types in geology.*—Though the palæontological record exhibits on the whole a progressive series of animal forms through the successive geologic strata, there are cases in which a species has remained constant over vast lapses of time. Crocodiles indistinguishable from those now living occur early in Mesozoic times, while the shells of certain primitive molluscs and brachiopods still existing are found as far back as the Silurian. Though clearly not a positive argument for evolution, such facts as these are evidently not what would be expected on the rival theory of successive cataclysms and special creations; and, as such, they have carried weight in favour of the former alternative.

(7) *Argument from the Recapitulation Theory.*—The study of comparative embryology was founded by **von Baer** in the earlier part of the 19th cent., and it was clearly pointed out by him that the early embryos of different animals belonging to allied groups are far more alike than are the adults. Thus the early embryos of a bird and of a fish are to the human eye very much alike, and during the course of its development the embryo bird exhibits such piscine characters as gill-clefts. With the course of development the fish-like characters eventually disappear, until the unmistakable avian form is established. But the fact that the animal higher in the scale tends during its embryological development to recapitulate, as it were, the ancestral history of the race to which it belongs appears more natural on the theory of evolution than on that of special creation. Through the work of F. M. Balfour and others in the latter part of the 19th cent., the study of comparative embryology was largely developed, and many striking instances of recapitulation were added to those previously known. At the same time it must be stated that fuller knowledge has shown that embryological development is no sure guide to ancestral history. Nothing is more certain than that, on the evolution theory, the ancestors of birds were toothed creatures. Yet in no case hitherto investigated in birds is there an embryonic stage in which tooth-germs are present; and numerous other examples could be given in which, during the development of the individual, no traces occur of structures which its ancestors, according to the theory of evolution, must at some time have possessed.

(8) *Argument from rudimentary organs.*—The researches of the comparative anatomists had revealed in many forms the presence, in an undeveloped state, of organs which in allied forms were obviously of use to their possessors. Small teeth had been found in the fœtus of the whalebone whale, traces of hind limbs in certain snakes, small and imperfect additional toes in the splint bones of the horse—all obvious imperfections in the general plan of the animal in which they were found. Chambers made use of these imperfect structures as an argument against the hypothesis of special creation. Their existence alone condemned the idea of a special creation for each organic form, seeing that they, 'on such a supposition, could be regarded in no other light than as blemishes or blunders' (*Vestiges*[4], p. 202). Yet, though discordant with the idea of special creation, they became intelligible and instructive on the hypothesis of a genetic connexion between the different forms of animal life. For, on that hypothesis, horses must be descended from ancestors with more than one toe, baleen whales from whales with teeth, and snakes from reptilian forms with limbs. Not only was the rudimentary organ explicable on these lines, but it might even give a clue to the past history of the forms in which it occurred.

9. From all this it is clear that the idea of evolution had been fully and critically discussed during the earlier half of the 19th cent., and that the arguments for it had been gathered together and forcibly set forth before 1850. Yet it had failed to take root. Nor was this altogether due to religious prejudice. A great obstacle in the way of accepting the evolutionary idea was the difficulty of conceiving a natural process by which it could come about. The suggestions of Buffon and the theories of Erasmus Darwin and of Lamarck all lacked compulsion, nor did the ascription of the process to an innate perfecting principle, as with Aristotle, succeed in investing it with more than a purely academic interest. It was not until **Darwin** and **Wallace** jointly formulated their views in 1858 that a working factor was felt to have been found. In the following year appeared *The Origin of Species*, a work which has influenced human thought more profoundly than any other book of modern times. In that work, Darwin summed up the existing arguments for evolution, and at the same time clearly and convincingly demonstrated a factor by which progressive changes would be brought about. This factor was 'Natural Selection, or the Preservation of Favoured Races in the Struggle for Life.' The idea was not entirely a new one. It had been formulated by Wells in 1813 and by Matthew in 1831, but in both cases it had been thrown out rather as a suggestion in connexion with a small class of facts than as a principle of the first importance and of general application. The greatness of Darwin lay in his appreciation of the profound importance of the principle he advocates, in his patient accumulation of facts, and in his masterly handling of them when brought together.

To Darwin, as later to Wallace, the first hint of natural selection had come from the reading of Malthus' *Essay on the Principle of Population* (London, 1798). The main theme of Malthus was the tendency of population to outrun the available food supply, and stress was laid upon the inevitable struggle for existence that arose unless this tendency was somewhat checked. Malthus concerned himself solely with his own species. For him the struggle was an unpleasant fact, a source of human misery of which some mitigation was much to be desired. What was to Malthus a fact of mainly economic significance became to the wider vision of Darwin a phenomenon of deep philosophical import. For, with a struggle for existence once granted, the logical outcome was the working factor in evolution for which naturalists had long been searching in vain. But to complete the argument two further co-operative factors are needed, and these were demonstrated by Darwin in the Principle of Variation and the Principle of Heredity. According to the former, no two animals or plants are quite alike; but even the offspring of the same parent or parents tend to vary, in greater or less degree, both from them and from one another. According to the latter, the peculiarities exhibited by parents tend to be transmitted to their offspring, to some in greater, to others in less intensity. In other words, offspring are never exactly like their parents, but nevertheless tend to resemble them more than they resemble other members of the same species or variety. If such is the normal condition of a population of living things, and if upon them is imposed a struggle for existence induced by over-multiplication, it follows necessarily that a progressive change will take place in that population. For, since its members are not all alike, some will possess variations through which they will be better equipped than others for survival in the competitive struggle for existence; and these will, therefore, tend to leave more offspring than their less advantaged brethren. These offspring will tend to resemble their parents in exhibiting the favoured variation in greater intensity than their parents; moreover, they will be still more greatly favoured in the struggle, and will tend to leave offspring of whom some will possess the advantageous variation in even greater intensity. The process is a cumulative one. Automatically, the struggle for existence leads to the more favoured variations surviving to become the parents of the next generation. And, as through the principle of variation some of the offspring will show the advantageous variation more marked than in the parents, it follows that this variation must become gradually piled up by small accretions at each generation, until a definite change of type has been brought about. To this automatic process, by which those showing the more favourable variations were picked out for parentage, Darwin applied the term 'natural selection.'

In *The Origin of Species* Darwin's performance was twofold. First, he brought together once more the various arguments for evolution, supplementing them with examples drawn from his own great stores of knowledge, and making use of a new argument in the geographical distribution of animals. Secondly, he endeavoured to show how, through this newly discovered factor of natural selection, evolution might be brought about. That he succeeded in his endeavour, in spite of the most strenuous opposition, is now well known. A few years had to elapse after the publication of *The Origin of Species* before the new doctrine of evolution through natural selection was generally accepted by scientific men, and much vigorous controversy was at first engendered in the clash between the old order and the new. Nevertheless, the new doctrine rapidly won its way in spite of the prejudices it was bound to arouse; and the fact that it has already been accepted for some years in all spheres of thought is not a little due to the pens of **Ernst Haeckel** in Germany, and of **T. H. Huxley** in Great Britain.

10. Though Darwin himself regarded natural selection as the main factor in evolutionary change, he did not consider it to be the only one. He attributed some influence to the effects of use and disuse which he considered to be inherited, thus following the teaching of Erasmus Darwin and of Lamarck (cf. art. ENVIRONMENT). Moreover, he was struck by a class of facts which offered great difficulties in the way of explanation in terms of natural selection. For, to be affected by natural selection, variation must have a utility value, whereas this can hardly be supposed to be the case for a large proportion of those highly ornamental characters which are confined to the male sex, and are generally intensified during the breeding season. It is difficult to ascribe any value, in the struggle for existence, to the tail of a peacock or the plumes of a bird of paradise. Indeed, it might be fairly argued that the reverse is the case, and that such characters as these are actually an impediment to their possessors in the struggle. The difficulty was appreciated by Darwin, who eventually accounted for them on the hypothesis that the more brilliant and attractive males would be preferred by the females. Thus the æsthetic sense of the latter would gradually bring about changes in the males through a process of sexual selection (cf. Darwin's *Descent of Man*). This theory has not met with such general acceptance as that of natural selection, and has been definitely rejected by some authorities. Among these is **A. R. Wallace**, who regards the brilliant ornamentation found in certain males simply as an indication of superabundant vitality. It is in virtue of this extra vitality that such males would be more likely than others to mate successfully and leave numerous offspring. By associating this apparently useless beauty with the utilitarian property of vigour, Wallace seeks to explain it upon grounds of natural selection alone.

11. The influence of *The Origin of Species* resulted in the production of vast quantities of literature on evolution during the remainder of the 19th century. In certain branches of biology, notably in those concerned with morphology, embryology, mimicry, geographical distribution, and palæontology, great numbers of new facts were added; and, on the whole, they may be said to have resulted in a strengthening of Darwin's position without contributing much of novelty to his argument. Perhaps the most interesting additions in this respect have been the essays of **Romanes** and **Gulick** on the importance of isolation, whether geographical or physiological, in the formation of incipient species; and **Pearson's** suggestion of reproductive selection. Pearson pointed out that, if any particular character were definitely associated with greater fertility, that character would tend to establish itself in a population without the help of, and perhaps even in spite of, natural selection.

12. Among the controversial questions which Darwin's work brought prominently forward, none attracted keener interest than that dealing with the transmission of the effects of use and disuse. Darwin always believed that such effects could be transmitted, and in this matter he was supported by Spencer, Haeckel, Cope, and many others. There were some, however, to whom Lamarckianism made no appeal, but who considered that natural selection in itself was sufficient to explain all transformation of species. Of this school, sometimes termed the Neo-Darwinian, **Weismann** has been the chief exponent, and he rendered considerable service to the progress of genetic science in challenging the evidence upon which the alleged transmission of 'acquired characters' rested, and in showing that it generally broke down under critical examination (cf. art. PANGENESIS).

13. Brief mention may here be made of a theory of evolution which regards inheritance as a form of memory; it was independently developed by the physiologist **Hering** and by **Samuel Butler**.

14. Darwin clearly perceived that a true theory of evolution must be based upon an accurate knowledge of the facts of heredity and variation, nor did he less clearly perceive that such knowledge was in his time practically non-existent. In the 6th edition of *The Origin of Species*, the last published in his lifetime, we find him writing that 'the laws governing inheritance are for the most part unknown'; and, again, that 'our ignorance of the laws of variation is profound.' He himself never ceased to accumulate facts and to make experiments bearing upon these matters, and it was largely due to his intimate acquaintance with the great body of facts so patiently brought together that he owed his remarkable sanity of judgment on doubtful questions where direct proof was for the time impossible. But in this work he had few followers, owing largely to the very brilliancy of his achievement. By suggesting in natural selection an acceptable factor through which the transformation of the species might be brought about, he had placed the idea of evolution on a firm basis. It was no longer an upsetting speculation but a definite theory which none in future could afford to neglect. And it was the doctrine of evolution that primarily seized upon men's minds, rather to the momentary exclusion of natural selection; for here was a promise of a clue to that orderly arrangement of the vegetable and animal kingdom towards which the students of natural history had long been striving. If evolution was a true story, it ought to be possible to build up a classification of animals and plants in such a way as to establish the genetic connexions among them. All living things, however aberrant they might seem, should find a place in the single great family tree which the doctrine of evolution postulated. To the construction of that family tree the labours of almost all naturalists were directed during the first few decades after the publication of Darwin's book, and, whether anatomist, embryologist, or palæontologist, this was the central thought in the mind of each. In the countless speculations that ensued as to the past history of living things, it was tacitly assumed that the necessary variations could have occurred and could have been transmitted; but, as different workers made different assumptions, it was not unnatural that widely discrepant views were forthcoming as to the pedigrees of the various groups. The origin of the vertebrates, for example, was traced by various authors to the polychæte worms, to the nemerteans, to the arthropods, and to the enteropneusts; and, as each author usually supported his views with much ingenuity and some little warmth of feeling, the time and labours of most biologists were fully occupied with these engrossing controversies. As time went on, however, and facts accumulated, the doctrine of evolution became firmly established in spite of differences of opinion as to the exact course which it had taken. As the glamour of pedigree-making wore off, the minds of naturalists gradually turned to other problems.

Though the majority of naturalists at this time were testing the theory of evolution by the facts of embryology and comparative anatomy, there were, nevertheless, some who attempted to test the theory of natural selection. In this case the study was that of Adaptation (*q.v.*). If the various characters of animals have arisen through the operation of natural selection, it is evident that the theory demands that they should be of value to their possessors in the struggle for existence. If, on the other hand, it was found impossible to ascribe to them any utilitarian importance, the case for their formation through the operation of natural selection was obviously weakened. Through the observation of animals in their natural surroundings, supplemented, where necessary, by carefully devised experiments, it was hoped that light would be thrown upon this problem. In many cases these hopes were abundantly fulfilled. Numbers of creatures, more especially insects, which at once arrested attention in the collector's cabinet by their striking and often bizarre appearance, were found in life to harmonize so closely with some feature of their external surroundings as to become practically invisible—an obvious advantage, whether for avoiding over-close attention on the part of enemies or for lulling prospective prey into a fancied sense of security. To the form and colour of the leaf insects, of the twig-like 'looper' caterpillars, of the spiders which resemble bird droppings, and of a host of other creatures, it would be difficult to deny a utilitarian value. Nor need utility be confined to those cases where the colour leads to concealment. Conspicuously coloured insects are often endowed with properties disagreeable to a would-be enemy. The sting of a wasp and the unpleasant taste of the black and yellow cinnabar-moth caterpillar are of the nature of 'warning colours,' and there is experimental evidence to show that enemies who have once had experience of them are careful to avoid them subsequently. Another large group of cases is that included under the head 'mimicry.' Many insects, especially among the Lepidoptera, are conspicuously coloured, and are yet lacking in nauseous or hurtful properties. But it frequently happens that such butterflies resemble more or less closely other more abundant species to which there is reason for assigning some disagreeable property. It was first suggested by **Bates** in 1862 that the conspicuously coloured innocuous insect acquired an advantage by mimicking the conspicuously coloured noxious insect, since its enemies would be likely to confuse it with the latter, and to let it alone. If, therefore, the persecuted form varies sufficiently in the direction of the nauseous form, it would have a better chance of preservation through the agency of natural selection. Bates' idea was subsequently extended by **Fritz Müller** to include the many instances in which several nauseous species tend to resemble one another. Müller suggested that in such cases the toll taken by young birds in educating their palate, by being distributed over several species, would fall more lightly on each separate one, and in this manner all would profit by exhibiting a common warning coloration.

15. With the ideas then current as to the nature of variation, natural selection offered the most plausible explanation of these remarkable cases of resemblance. A new note was struck by **Bateson** in 1894, when he pointed out that, while the results attained by the study of embryology and of adaptation could be brought into harmony with the doctrine of evolution and the theory of natural selection, they nevertheless offered no explanation of the origin of specific differences. Each assumed a vague capacity for indefinite variation on the part of living things—a plasticity through which natural selection was able to mould them in this direction or in that, according as was best suited to the course of the author's argument. Bateson insisted on the importance of the study of variation, if further progress was to be made with the problem of species. Naturalists had hitherto given themselves unlimited credit in dealing with variation, whereas they ought first to have inquired what variations actually did and what did not occur. By the systematic collection of facts Bateson was able to show that in many cases variation is certainly of a discontinuous nature. Definite variations are constantly found as part of a population living and presumably breeding together, in the absence of any intermediate forms. As examples may be mentioned the normal orange and the paler yellow form of clouded yellow butterfly (*Colias edusa*), the red and blue of the red underwing moth (*Catocala nupta*), the blue and the scarlet varieties of the common pimpernel (*Anagallis*), or the ordinary brown and the violet-green *valesina* form of the silver-washed fritillary (*Aglaia paphia*)—examples which might be almost indefinitely multiplied.

The existence of such cases is difficult to explain on the view of evolution usually current. In the first place, it is not easy to account for the existence of both forms, on the theory of the survival of the fittest. For, if one of the forms is better fitted to its surroundings than the other, why does the other continue to exist? And, if both forms are equally fitted, how comes it that the one has been evolved from the other? For, where the incipient variety has no advantage over the normal form, it is clear that its becoming established cannot be through the agency of natural selection. Again, if, in the course of evolutionary change, the new variety which is to replace the old one arises through the gradual accumulation of small differences, how is it that, when the new and the old are bred together, there does not result either in the first or in subsequent generations a long series of intermediate forms? For this certainly does not occur in, at any rate, the great majority of cases. In spite of the commingling of the germ-plasms, the characters remain sharply differentiated from one another. Discontinuity in variation and in heredity was evidently not to be reconciled with the idea of the formation of species and varieties by the gradual accumulation of minute variations, whether through natural selection or through some other process. The key to the understanding of these phenomena was given by **Mendel's** work on the heredity of characters in peas (see art. HEREDITY). The result of these experiments, and of many others carried out on the same lines, has been to provide a new conception of the nature of variation and of the process of heredity, thus necessitating some modification in our views as to the manner in which evolutionary change is brought about.

16. Under the stimulus of Mendel's discovery, fresh developments are so rapid that any account of the position to-day with respect to the problems of evolution must necessarily be incomplete. Ideas have gone once more into the melting pot, and as yet it is too soon to forecast clearly what is to be the currency of the near future. Nevertheless, in connexion with evolutionary problems there are certain points which seem to stand out more clearly, and of these one concerns the nature of variation.

Variations are of two kinds—those which are heritable, and those which are not. The latter are for the most part reactions of the organism to its environment, and can play no direct part in the course of evolutionary change, although indirectly they may, by establishing traditions, exert a not inconsiderable influence upon the trend of evolution in the higher animals, and more especially in man. For the moment, however, they may be left out of account. Heritable variations are those which can be represented in the germ-cells. Corresponding to a transmissible character there is a definite something in the minute germ-cells. This something is called a 'factor,' though what these factors are, whether of the nature of ferments or of a different nature, is not at present clear. Generally speaking, however, if, in either one or both of the germ-cells from which an individual is formed, a given factor occurs, then the individual will exhibit the character corresponding to that factor. Moreover, the factor may be handed on from generation to generation, and may pass through crosses of a complicated nature, without apparently undergoing alteration. If present in any individual, the character corresponding to it will, as a rule, appear. If it is not present, the character will not appear. There is reason to suppose that these factors with their attendant manifestation of a given character can pass from body to germ-cells and from germ-cells to body without alteration, much as a chemical atom or radicle can pass unchanged from one compound to another. In other words, the basis of heritable variation is a material one, which is subject, in transmission, to definite ascertained laws. And, unless a variation can be represented by one of these factors, it cannot be transmitted, and cannot therefore play any direct part in evolution. Such, at any rate, is the view to which recent experimental work has led (cf. art. HEREDITY).

We have, therefore, to distinguish between two kinds of variations, viz. those directly due to the environment, and those which are innate, owing their existence to something specific in the germ-cells from which the individual sprang. The former have been termed 'fluctuations,' and the latter 'mutations'; and, though the terms are not free from objection, they may conveniently be made use of. In deciding to which of the two classes any given variation belongs, the only test available is that of its heredity. If it can be experimentally shown to follow the laws of heredity, it is of the nature of a mutation; if, however, it cannot be shown to follow these laws, it must be regarded as a fluctuation. Heredity is a mode of analysis enabling the investigator to decide between these two kinds of variation, and it is at present the only test that can be made use of.

Since the characters of varieties depend on the presence of the appropriate factors in the germ-cells, it is clearly in the germ-cells that the origin of these variations is to be sought. Speaking generally, a new variety comes suddenly into being. This is perhaps to be seen most clearly in the case of certain plants introduced into culture from distant habitats. Neither of the Chinese primulas (*Primula sinensis* and *P. obconica*) is known to show in its native wild state the profusion of form and colour varieties characteristic of the cultivated forms. The historical evidence points to the different varieties having arisen as 'sports' from the wild forms when placed under cultivation in countries remote from their original habitat. The sweet pea offers another instance of the same story. The original purple form first reached England from Sicily at the end of the 17th century. Not long after its introduction, a red and a white variety are recorded in addition to the purple, and by the middle of the 19th cent. several other shades of purple and red were in existence. But the enormous number of varied forms, both in colour and shape, now to be seen are of recent origin, and in some cases, *e.g.* that of the dwarf 'Cupid,' it is certain that they originated in California, from seed sent out there to be grown on. Such examples as these are typical of the experience of the horticulturist. The new variety springs into being suddenly and for no apparent definite reason. Once it has appeared, it is a matter of a few years only to fix it so that thenceforward it breeds true to type. Nevertheless, the tendency to 'sport' or mutate is evidently increased by a sharp change in the environment, such as is to be obtained by transferring it from one country and climate to another. Precisely why this should be is not at present known, but there is reason to suppose that the environmental change leads to abnormal divisions in the ripening germ-cells, and that these abnormal divisions are the starting-point of the new variety.

In a true breeding thing the processes of cell-division by which the germ-cells ripen are symmetrical, and the germ-cells themselves are all alike, in that the factors contained by each are the same, both in point of number and of quality. Should, however, certain of the cell-divisions be abnormal, they must result in an asymmetrical distribution of the factors to different germ-cells, so that some contain one or more factors in excess of the normal, and others one or more factors less than the normal. If two germ-cells each with a factor less than the normal come together, the resulting individual will be completely lacking in a factor possessed by the original form and will breed perfectly true to that state. And, indeed, the evidence from experimental breeding points to the majority of domestic races of animals and plants having arisen in this way (cf. art. HEREDITY). The new form comes into being through the loss of this or that character from the original wild, and this loss must be supposed to be dependent upon the elimination of the appropriate factor or factors somewhere in the cell-divisions which give rise to the germ-cells. Less commonly the new form must be regarded as possessing one or more factors in addition to those present in the form from which it sprang, and it is possible that this is due to the formation, through a process of asymmetrical division, of certain germ-cells with more factors than the normal, and to their subsequent union to produce an individual of a new type.

When once the new variety has arisen, natural selection decides whether it is to persist with or to replace the form from which it sprang. Since the difference between it and the normal depends upon a definite and clear-cut distinction, and since that distinction is respected throughout the hereditary process, the variety, having once arisen, cannot, as Darwin once thought, be swamped by continual crossing with the normal form. On the contrary, as **G. H. Hardy** has shown, a population mating at random, and containing a definite proportion of the new form, will, in the absence of natural selection, retain its constitution. Provided that it is equally fertile, the new form will hold its own even though present in very small numbers, and the population will remain in a position of stability. Positions of stability are exceedingly numerous, and exist when the equation $q^2=pr$ is satisfied, where p and r are the numbers of the pure breeding individuals of the type and variety respectively, while $2\,q$ is the number of hybrid individuals. If, however, the variety be favoured by natural selection, though only in a slight degree, it will gradually supplant the original form until the latter is eliminated. Moreover, the process must be a rapid one. If a population contains ·001 per cent of a new variety, and if that variety has even a 5 per cent selection advantage over the original form, the latter will almost completely disappear in less than 100 generations. Cases of this sort are not unknown to actual experience. Sixty years ago the dark *doubledayaria* form of the common peppered moth (*Amphidasys betularia*) was known only as a rare variety. To-day it has almost entirely ousted the normal form in many parts of England and of the Continent.

17. Considerations of this nature have a bearing upon a class of facts which at first sight are not easy to understand. Speaking generally, a natural species is distinguished by its homogeneity. Colour varieties are numerous in the domestic rabbit; in the wild rabbit they are rare. On a scheme of evolution based upon the mutational nature of variation, it is this homogeneity that offers difficulties in interpretation. But, if the wild form be supposed to possess even a slight selection advantage over the various other colour forms, the rarity of the latter becomes more comprehensible. They may arise; but, with the conditions adverse, though ever so little, they must tend to disappear.

18. There is another aspect of species which is not so generally taken into account. Most species —using the word in the Linnæan sense—are seen, when examined closely, to consist not of a single form, but of a number of slightly different, though perfectly distinct, forms. This was clearly brought out in the middle of the 19th cent. by the French botanist **Jordan** and others. Jordan showed, for example, that the Linnæan species *Draba verna*, the common whitlow grass, can be analyzed into more than 200 forms, each of which is sharply marked off from any other by habit, shape of leaves, etc., and can be bred true from seed. Such is also the case, though generally to a less extent, with many other species. Moreover, it has been shown by experimental breeding that in some cases these varieties—or 'elementary species,' as they have been termed—differ from one another in the same way that domestic varieties differ. They follow in heredity the Mendelian law of segregation, and the differences between them must be supposed to depend upon the presence or absence in their constitution of specific factors for the characters in which they differ from one another. When, as often happens, many of these elementary species are found together, it must be supposed that no one of them has any selection advantage over the rest. Were the conditions of life to alter so that one form was favoured above the others, even to a slight extent, that form would tend rapidly to supplant all the others; and it is conceivable that this may already have happened in many cases of species which exhibit relatively few varieties.

19. The problem of *what constitutes a species* is one that has vexed the minds of many naturalists and philosophers; but, in spite of all that has been written upon it, the problem is yet unsolved. The classification of species at present in vogue is an extension of the Linnæan system, and is mainly based upon external features either of structure or of colour. In most cases these differences are accompanied by the phenomenon of sterility between even closely allied species, though this is not necessarily so. There are cases, such as those of the horse × ass cross and the horse × zebra cross, in which well-formed offspring are produced, but in which the latter are themselves sterile. In some groups of animals, again, hybrids between acknowledged species have been shown to be fertile when inbred or when crossed back with one of the parent species. This is the case with various forms of oxen and buffalo, and especially with the duck and pheasant tribes, where crosses between birds classified as belonging to different genera have been proved to produce fertile offspring. For the systematist, however, whether botanist or zoologist, it is the external features that matter, for upon them he has to base his classifications. But instances are becoming more numerous in which it has been shown that two species founded in this way are fertile together. Whether they are to be regarded as one species or two depends upon whether the criterion made use of is the external features or whether it is sterility. On the whole, it may be said that there is a general consensus of opinion in favour of the latter. If, then, the phenomenon of sterility lies at the root of the problem of species, it becomes of the first importance to form a clear conception of the causes to which sterility is due. There is no doubt that in some cases it is due to mechanical causes, as, for example, where there is great disparity in size, or for some other reason. But the sterility that is associated with species is of a different nature. The germ-cells may come into intimate contact, fusion may occur, and development may even proceed for some way; yet the process stops short of the production of offspring. There would appear to be some incompatibility, probably of a chemical nature, preventing two healthy germ-cells from giving rise to a new individual. Everything seems to point to the problem of species resolving itself into a problem in chemistry, but the present state of knowledge does not permit of more definite statement.

Darwin clearly recognized that the phenomena of sterility could not be explained in terms of natural selection. For the gradual acquisition of sterility on the part of certain individuals cannot be conceived of as advantageous either to those individuals themselves or to the rest of the species. The most natural view of the origin of sterility is to regard it as having arisen through some abrupt physiological change in the organism—a change which at bottom must probably be conceived of as chemical. Sterility is of the nature of mutation; and, if we look upon it as the essential characteristic of species, we must also regard mutation as the bridge between one species and another. The mutational change upon which the sterility depends may become associated with other characters either before or after it first arises. Such associations of characters are not infrequently met with as the facts of heredity are coming to be more carefully studied. External features would then serve to distinguish the new species from that out of which it had arisen, but its origin must be sought in the origin of the fundamental sterility which it shows towards the parent species. Beyond the fact that it is a process initiated in the germ-cells, almost nothing is known at present of the conditions under which a mutation arises. Until such knowledge is forthcoming, that most important link in any theory of evolution—the problem of the nature of species—must remain unsolved.

LITERATURE.—The number of works in the English language dealing with the subject of Evolution from the biological point of view is enormous, and only a very few can be mentioned here. In addition to the classic works of Darwin, Huxley, and Spencer, the following will be found of interest: **W. Bateson**, *Materials for the Study of Variation*, London, 1894; **S. Butler**, *Evolution, Old and New*, do. 1879; **R. Chambers**, *Vestiges of the Nat. Hist. of Creation*[4], Edinburgh, 1845; **E. D. Cope**, *The Primary Factors of Organic Evolution*, London, 1896; **A. H. Lovejoy**, 'The Argument for Organic Evolution before "The Origin of Species"' (*Popular Science Monthly*, 1909); **J. T. Merz**, *History of Scientific Thought in the Nineteenth Century*, vol. ii., Edinburgh, 1903; **T. H. Morgan**, *Evolution and Adaptation*, London, 1903; **H. F. Osborn**, *From the Greeks to Darwin*, New York, 1895; **A. S. Packard**, *Lamarck: his Life and Work*, London, 1901; **K. Pearson**, *The Grammar of Science*[2], London, 1900; **E. B. Poulton**, *Essays on Evolution, 1889–1907*, Oxford, 1908; **G. J. Romanes**, *Darwin and after Darwin*, London, 1892–97; **R. Semon**, *Die Mneme*, etc.[3], Leipzig, 1911; **K. Semper**, *The Natural Conditions of Existence as they affect Animal Life*, London, 1881; **A. C. Seward** (editor), *Darwin and Modern Science*, Cambridge, 1909; **J. A. Thomson**, *The Science of Life*, London, 1899; **H. de Vries**, *The Mutation Theory*, Eng. tr., London, 1910–11; **A. R. Wallace**, *Darwinism*, London, 1889; **A. Weismann**, *The Evolution Theory*, Eng. tr., London, 1904.

R. C. PUNNETT.

EVOLUTION (Ethical).—As its title implies, this article is concerned with ethics as explicable only by the processes of evolution. Until the rise of the science of biology, psychologists, in seeking to explain the constitution of the human mind, assumed it to be different in kind from the animal mind, and postulated certain innate entities and faculties whose analysis would furnish the key to character and to all mental operations. A history of the various theories of the nature and foundation of morals lies outside our province, but, as briefly indicating points of difference between them and the theory summarized in this article, it may be stated that they are mainly resolvable into what are known as the Utilitarian and the Intuitional. The Utilitarian—which Hume was the first among the 18th cent. philosophers to formulate (the doctrine itself is as old as Socrates), and of which Bentham and the Mills are the chief modern exponents—defines virtue as that which is approved, and vice as that which is condemned, the sole standard of morality being utility, whose aim and end is 'the greatest happiness of the greatest number.' Spencer incorporated Utilitarianism into his *Principles of Ethics*, but held that it tends to become wholly altruistic, and modified it by giving play to the egoistic also. The Intuitional, of which Butler is the most famous expositor, and James Martineau the representative modern upholder (see his *Types of Ethical Theory*[2], Oxford, 1866), assumes that there is in each individual a faculty of innate or immediate cognition and perception of what is good or evil, true or false, this intuitive faculty acting without the intervention of reason or the guidance of experience.

A death-blow was dealt to methods of introspective interpretation by the publication of Herbert Spencer's *Principles of Psychology* (London, 1855) and *Principles of Ethics* (do. 1879–1892), and of Darwin's *Descent of Man* (do. 1871), notably in its chapters on 'Comparison of the Mental Powers of Man and the Lower Animals.' Extending the comparative method, which had justified its application in other directions, to the psychical, biology has demonstrated fundamental identity between the mental apparatus of the lowest and highest organisms, and has shown, to quote Baldwin's cogent words, that 'the development of mind in its early stages, and in certain directions of progress, is revealed most adequately in the animals' (*Story of the Mind*, London, 1899, p. 35). It has abolished the ancient and artificial lines of mental demarcation denoted by the terms 'reflex action,' 'instinct,' and 'reason,' and shown that in stimulus from without and in response from within, involving adaptation to needs, lies the explanation of processes linking man, animal, and plant. Mental progress is the result of the activity of fundamental and permanent instinctive impulses (inherited tendencies of which the nervous apparatus is the vehicle) which supply the driving power whereby all mental activities are sustained. From these impulses the complex faculties of the most highly developed minds have their source. 'They are the mental forces that maintain and shape all the life of individuals and societies, and in them we are confronted with the central mystery of life and mind and will' (W. McDougall, *Introd. to Social Psychology*, London, 1908, p. 44).

In the behaviour of the lower organisms there is manifest the potentially psychical 'faint copy of all we know as consciousness in ourselves' (Francis Darwin, *Presidential Address*, Brit. Assoc. 1908). The glandular leaves of the *Drosera* or sundew, and the bladders of *Utricularia*, or bladderwort, entrap the luckless insect which alights on them, and assimilate it for their nourishment. The amœba withdraws its pseudopods when touched, and engulfs the soft organisms on which it feeds. And thus the instinctive impulses might be tracked along the entire line of psychical evolution, the instinctive yielding to the rational in such degree that, in Ray Lankester's phrase, the animal becomes more 'educable' (*Kingdom of Man*, London, 1907, p. 23),

'for if we neglect the psychical aspect of instinctive processes, it is impossible to understand the part played by instincts in the development of the human mind, and in the determination of the conduct of individuals and societies, and it is the fundamental and all-pervading character of their influence upon the social life of mankind which alone gives the consideration of instincts its great practical importance' (McDougall, *op. cit.* p. 30).

They are the fundamental impulses of nutrition and sex, which, Wundt contends, men and animals alike possess 'to form the inalienable foundation of human society as well as of animal association' (*Ethics*, 'The Facts of the Moral Life,' p. 129).

The classification of instincts lies outside the province of this article, and it suffices to refer only to the gregarious or social instinct as the essential factor in ethical development. Man, as a solitary animal, is unknown to us. 'It is not good that the man should be alone' (Gn 2^{18}), and Aristotle follows the writer of the Book of Genesis when he says that 'he who is unable to live in society must be either a beast or a god: he is no part of a State' (*Pol.* i. 2. 14). 'A man not dependent upon a race is as meaningless a phrase as an apple that does not grow upon a tree' (Leslie Stephen, *Science of Ethics*, London, 1882, p. 91); and individual and racial obligation and morality are as interdependent as the personal and the social are inseparable and correlate. The unending struggle for life—'and there is no discharge in that war' (Ec 8^{8})—is a dominant factor in bringing about, on the one hand, individual dependence at maturity in the case of solitary animals, as, *e.g.*, the eagle, cat, and lion; and, on the other hand, collective dependence among social animals, as, among invertebrates, the ant and bee, and, among vertebrates, *e.g.* non-raptorial birds, sheep, horse, dog, and man. Turning to the ant, as corresponding in position among insects to the position of man among mammals, there is, says McCook, 'no trait in emmet character more interesting than the entire devotion of every individual, even unto death, to the welfare of the community' (*Ant Communities*, London, 1909, p. 191). The maxim *salus populi suprema est lex* governs alike ants and men.

Speculating on the social habits of our earliest-known ancestor, *Pithecanthropus erectus* (see art. ANTHROPOLOGY in vol. i. p. 563 f.), who, in expert opinion, represents the stage 'immediately antecedent to the human and yet at the same time in advance of the simian,' we have only analogy to guide us concerning primitive human unions. Arguing from the strength of 'the feelings of jealousy all through the animal kingdom, as well as from the analogy of the lower animals, more particularly of the anthropoid apes,' Darwin formulated the theory that aboriginal man 'lived in small communities, each with a single wife or, if powerful, with several, whom he jealously guarded against all other men' (*Descent of Man*, ch. xx. p. 901). Without question, in one form or another, the family is the social unit, impetus to personal and permanent association being given by the longer period of infancy in the human as compared with that period among the higher mammals (it may be remarked that the larvæ of the ant pass through a prolonged babyhood involving incessant parental care), because the condition of helplessness and dependence strengthens the self-sacrificing instinct of the parent, supremely that of the mother, who, in nourishing her offspring, gives all and receives nothing. John Fiske, who in this matter was preceded by Anaximander two thousand years ago, treats this fully in his *Century of Science*, London, 1899, pp. 100–122.) Hence, in the satisfaction of the physical needs of the child there are developed solicitude, love, self-denial, courage, and—greatest of all—the sympathy out of which the strands of family life are woven, strands multiplying in number and strength until they bind together gentes or groups of the same blood-brotherhood, clan, or totem, these aggregating into tribes which are the foundation of the nation, the patriotism engendered by which is the family bond 'writ large.' One and all are the outcome of social heredity. 'Society is the school in which men learn to distinguish between right and wrong' (Westermarck, *MI* i. 9), and in this lies the key to the nature and origin of the judgments which make up the ethical codes of every age and race. These judgments are wholly subjective, being the outcome of emotions whose beginning and impulses are social. For Nature supplies no standard by which to govern conduct; from obedience or disobedience to her laws invariable consequences follow, but these have no element of the ethical; they are neither rewards nor punishments. The earth may be 'filled with violence' (Gn 6^{11}), her 'dark places' may be 'full of the habitations of cruelty' (Ps 74^{20}), but 'seedtime and harvest, and cold and heat, summer and winter, and day and night shall not cease' (Gn 8^{22}).

Moral concepts have their basis in feeling, not in reason; moral emotions, as Westermarck argues, fall into the two classes of disapproval or indignation, and approval, each belonging to a wider class of emotions which he calls 'retributive,' disapproval being manifested in anger and revenge, and approval in 'retributive kindly emotion,' including gratitude (*op. cit.* i. 21). This assumes organization within the group, which in turn demands an altruistic, rather than an egoistic, individual.

'It is the extension of the application of natural selection to groups rather than its direct application to individuals that has given birth to morals. Morality has arisen because it is socially useful; that is the Darwinian account' (Baldwin, *Darwin and the Humanities*, London, 1910, p. 64).

As J. A. Thomson says, 'progress depends on much more than a squabble around the platter' (*Darwinism and Human Life*, London, 1909, p. 92); and Darwinism recognizes that mutual aid has modified the rigour of the struggle in both the animal and the human. Stripped of a certain coat of exaggeration, the numerous stories of help rendered by one animal to another are not to be dismissed as 'travellers' tales.' For example, in his account of the habits of the viscacha, a S. American rodent, Hudson says that, when one of the burrows is destroyed and the viscachas are buried alive, other viscachas will come from a distance to dig them out (*Naturalist in La Plata*, London, 1892, p. 311).

The degree in which the social and sympathetic impulses have been developed is the measure of the relative place in intelligence reached by man and animal. 'Union is strength,' and the strength is made effective by restraint and subjugation of self-assertion to the interests of the community. An ethical code has warrant and permanence only in the degree in which it secures the healthy interplay of regard for self and for others, and, wherever this is defied in wilfulness or weakness, natural selection, extending its operation from individuals to groups, secures the survival of the fittest, who possess an ethical value in maintaining the health of the social organisms. The weak and wilful, those who detach themselves from the communal life, go under. The solitary animal fights for its own hand; the social animal must be altruistic if the herd is to survive; its tendencies towards self-regardfulness are restrained by communal action whose one end is the common weal. 'That which is not good for the swarm is not good for the bee' (Marcus Aurelius, vi. 54), and the converse is equally true. 'Morality is the sum of the preservative instincts of a society, and presumably of those which imply a desire for the good of the society itself' (Leslie Stephen, *op. cit.* 208). Society being possible only by the compliance of each member with what the community sanctions as necessary to its welfare, or abstinence from what it forbids as inimical thereto, it follows that, in the prohibition or permission of certain acts, we have a fundamental constant, a moral quality in acts which, however much they vary in character, cumulative experience pronounces to be harmful or helpful to the community—in plain language, right or wrong. The means vary, but the end to be achieved is the same, and the achievement is by co-operation. Social acts have a quantitative, not a qualitative value, because man everywhere is psychically, as well as physically, fundamentally the same. His monogenetic origin, with good evidence, is assumed; so is his enormous antiquity, which supplies a sufficient period for the modifications into varieties, and for the different degrees of civilization to which these, be they white, yellow, red, or black, have attained. Man being, at the core, the same everywhere, observation of what, at first sight, seem his vagaries brings home how superficial are the changes which time has wrought since he came to express his philosophy—for such it was in the making—of things. He remains, in the bulk, as his intermittent outbursts of fury and savagery everywhere evidence, a creature of instinctive impulses inherited from his animal ancestry; as an emotional being, his antiquity is dateless; as a reasoning being, he is a late and somewhat rare product. But whatever he has evolved in thought and put into action has justified its existence, because it has responded to some need. It has had, little as might be discerned, some 'soul of goodness' impelling to what, for the time being, seemed to secure the common weal.

Since both religion and ethics are social in origin and, therefore, institutions subject to the law of development, there is no state in man's history on which we can put our finger and say: Here he became a religious and a moral being. It is, therefore, necessary to recognize, as main factors, the impulses to social order which communal life postulates as the primal sources of moral codes. If 'society is the school,' then, as Westermarck adds, 'custom is the headmaster,' and with the ferule of tabu he has kept every race *in statu pupillari*.

'The idea of sin as the individual or national transgression of moral law is extremely modern. In primitive times there was no such individual act and no such moral law. The only misconduct was a breach of custom, the violation of tabu' (Ames, *Psychology of Religious Experience*, London, 1910, p. 131). 'Custom is one of the earliest shapes in which duty presents itself to the consciousness of the savage' (F. B. Jevons, *Introd. to Hist. of Rel.*, London, 1896, p. 190). 'Little by little and, as it were, by stealth, custom establisheth the fact of her authority in us' (Montaigne, *Essays*, i. 136, Dent's Temple ed.). In their derivations both 'ethics' and 'morals' witness to their origin. The one is from ἠθικός, a modification of ἦθος, custom, usage, manners; the other from *mos, moris*, pertaining to manners, therefore to conduct.

Be man savage or civilized, the reluctance to defy or to depart from the usual, the fear of being called 'eccentric,' *i.e.* 'out of the circle,' is in his bones. Conservatism is a permanent force; and it is impossible to overrate either the authority or the value of custom as a factor in conduct. Identity of belief and practice makes for unity and stability, and the force of tradition acts as social cement. To what particular and local causes the great body of customs, infinite in variety, and, not seldom, irrational or inconsequential, is due remains an insoluble problem, because of the remoteness of the social conditions under which they arose. We have only to observe how, among intelligent persons, some chance occurrence will excite or paralyze action, to see, *a fortiori*, how, among unintelligent people, some casual event, followed by fortune or the reverse, will cause this or that line of conduct to be made a rule of life, and obedience thereto to become a rule of conduct, a part of the customary law, of the community. Imitation—'the prime condition of all collective social life' (McDougall, p. 326)—whether in creeds, codes, or clothes, has been a powerful element in the conservation of the decrees of custom. To both savage and civilized are applicable the lines which Henry Sidgwick composed in his sleep:

> 'We think so because all other people think so:
> Or because—or because—after all, we do think so:
> Or because we were told so and think we must think so:
> Or because we once thought so and think we still think so:
> Or because, having thought so, we think we still think so.'

Closely linked with imitation is the influence of suggestion in swaying judgment and conduct, sometimes for good, but, perhaps, as often for evil. The crowd, unquestioning, will believe what each member of it, detached from his fellow, would reject as a fable. Hence, frequently, the worthlessness of collective evidence and judgment; hence, too, often, the valuelessness of concurrent testimony even from men of scientific training as to the validity, say, of so-called spiritual phenomena when, expecting to witness the same, they meet in séances. Hence the aberrations when some dominant idea takes possession of the undisciplined, with mischievous results akin to the epidemic delusions of the Middle Ages, or the corybantic displays of hysterical revivalists, or the terrorism of the Apaches of Paris and the hooligans of London and other crowded centres.

Travelling along the line of least resistance, the general attitude of civilized communities, in which the primitive is persistent, towards innovations explains the conservatism of the savage. So heavy was the weight of the dead hand of custom that the nameless reformer who ventured to resist it must have been shaped in no common mould. For to challenge was to insert the thin edge of the wedge of disruption; it was to assume that he who defied was wiser than his fathers, or, committing rank blasphemy, wiser than the deified ancestors, the traditional framers of the tribal code. What long pre-rational ages of stereotyped acquiescence prevailed is witnessed by the fact of the small part that reason still plays in conduct; the emotions as, primarily, the outcome of the instinctive impulses which are the bases of mental activities show themselves dominant and persistent. 'The progressive state is only a rare and an occasional exception'; and, where the wisest are not supreme, there stagnation rules (see Bagehot's *Physics and Politics*[8], London, 1887, pp. 41, 211). But an ounce of example is worth a ton of exposition.

Herodotus (iii. 38) narrates how 'Darius asked certain Hellenes for what price they would eat their fathers when they died, and they answered that for no price would they do so. After this he summoned those Indians who are called Callatians, who eat their parents, and asked them, in presence of the Hellenes, for what payment they would burn the bodies of their fathers when they died; when they cried aloud and bade him keep silence from such words. Thus then these things were established by usage, and I think Pindar spoke rightly in his verse when he said, "Custom is the King of all."'

Fifteen centuries later, a traveller in High Albania tells us: 'For all their habits, laws, and customs, the people, as a rule, have but one explanation: "It is the custom of Lek," the law that is said to have been laid down by the chieftain Lek Dukaghin. Lek is fabled to have legislated minutely on all subjects. Of himself little is known. He has left no mark on European history—is a purely local celebrity—but that "Lek said so" obtains more than the Ten Commandments. The teachings of Islām and Christianity, the Sheriat and Church law, all have to yield to the Canon of Lek' (M. E. Durham, *High Albania*, London, 1909, p. 25). There is an Albanian proverb which says, 'It is better that a village should fall than a custom' (*ib.* p. 259); and the priests say that, in spite of all their efforts, their parishioners all regard the shooting of a man as nothing compared with the crime of breaking a fast or eating an egg on a Saturday (*ib.* 104). Compare with this the story which Erasmus told four hundred years ago: 'I have just heard that two poor creatures are to be murdered in France because they have eaten meat in Lent' (Froude's *Erasmus*, 1894, p. 360); and a passage from Smollett's *Travels through France and Italy*, 1766 (Letter xxv.): 'A murderer, adulterer, or sodomite will obtain easy absolution from the Church, and even find favour with society; but a man who eats a pigeon on a Saturday without express licence is avoided and abhorred as a monster of reprobation.' How all the ages meet in their assumption of moral qualities in acts which have no bearing on character—the confusion of *malum in se* with *malum prohibitum*—is further seen in comparing a passage which Aulus Gellius (*Noctes*, x. 23) quotes from Cato, that it is for the husband to condemn and punish his wife if she has been guilty of any shameful act, such as drinking wine or committing adultery, with W. G. Palgrave's account of the Wahhaby moral code, in which the great sins are paying Divine honour to a creature and smoking tobacco, while murder, adultery, and false witness are 'merely little sins' (*Journey through Central and Eastern Arabia*, London and Cambridge, 1865, ii. 370).

The literature of the subject of the tabu is enormous, and here it must suffice briefly to refer to that wide-spread institution as a continuous and effective factor, even among the civilized, often in unsuspected form, in human conduct. In *Psyche's Task* (London, 1909), Frazer has shown, in a series of cogent examples, how 'by virtue of his absurdities' man secured stability for the fundamental bases of society, government, private property, marriage, and regard for human life. The belief that dire results will follow breach of rules as to things forbidden is the most powerful deterrent that superstition has begotten. Curses and charms, and all other apparatus of the sorcerer, are more effective than the prosaic bogey, 'Trespassers will be prosecuted,' and the would-be evildoer is kept in check by the fear that some horrible disease will follow the stealing of his neighbour's yams; or that he may go hag-ridden for the rest of his life, if he stealthily removes his neighbour's boundary-mark. The belief that irregular sexual relations will disastrously affect the fertility of the crops is a check on incontinence, and therefore an encouragement to the formation of orderly connexions. The belief that the ghost of a slaughtered man will wreak vengeance on the tribe to which the murderer belongs creates a feeling that shapes codes embodying ideas of the sanctity of human life. Orestes was driven from one land to another, not so much because he had killed his mother, as because of the peril to others brought by him who was pursued by the Erinyes.

In their ultimate analysis the codes of every age and people are found to deal with human relations. 'Pure religion and undefiled before God and the Father is this, to visit the fatherless and widows in their affliction, and to keep himself unspotted from the world' (Ja 1[27]). Murder, theft, lying, slander, unchastity, these are offences of man against his fellows. Of the 'Ten Words,' familiarly known as the 'Ten Commandments,' seven are concerned with social duties. In a document centuries older than the Hebrew code, the *Instruction of Ptah Hotep*, the author 'devotes his work entirely to the principles of charity and duty to one's neighbour' (tr. B. G. Gunn, 1908, p. 33); and the essence of the teaching of Confucius, 'the purest of any in the world,' is—'Act socially' (*Confucian Analects* (tr. Giles, 1907, p. 27).

Sociality is looked upon by the Kaffirs as the essential virtue. The children play in great bands. To loaf about alone would be regarded as a highly penal offence, and every child regards eating in secret as a base act. 'Occasionally a child seems devoid of social tendencies, and in this case a witch-doctor is sent for to cure the child' (Dudley Kidd, *Savage Children*, London, 1906, pp. 72, 119). Among the Euahlayi tribe of Australia the mother's crooning song is, 'Kind be, do not steal; do not touch what to another belongs; leave all such alone; kind be' (K. Langloh Parker, *The Euahlayi Tribe*, London, 1905, p. 54). Papuan youths are thus admonished: 'You no steal, you no borrow without leave. If you take dugong harpoon and break it, how you pay man? You got no dugong harpoon. Give food to father and mother. Spose old man ask you for food or water, spose you not got much, you give half. Never mind if you and your wife go without [cf. Mt 10[42]]. When your brothers (*i.e.* clan brothers) are fighting, you stand side by side. No stay behind to steal women' (A. C. Haddon, in *Agnostic Annual*, 1907, p. 62).

In early social stages, acts of mutual help are restricted to the community. Among existing savage peoples, as the Comanches, Kalmuks, and others, the man who steals from strangers wins admission to higher rank. Speaking of the ancient Germans, Cæsar says that 'robberies beyond the bounds of each community have no infamy, but are commended as a means of exercising youth and lessening sloth' (*de Bell. Gall.* vi. 23). 'Ought' was originally the preterite of 'to owe,' but moral obligations long remained intra-tribal, and the life-struggle which at the outset compelled this, among even the highest civilized communities, has yielded but partially and tardily to a wider sympathy and benevolence which are the fruits of a closer intercourse between, and therefore enlarged knowledge of, peoples—partially and tardily, because racial differences appear to be too deeply engrained to warrant hope that white, yellow, and black will ever be linked in a world-embracing sympathy. (For numerous examples of the distinction between intra-tribal and extra-tribal misdeeds, see Westermarck, ii. 20–24.)

There never has been, probably there never will be, a uniform, unalterable standard of right and wrong, applicable through all times for all men.

'The moral world is as little exempt as the physical world from the law of ceaseless change, of perpetual flux. . . . We can as little arrest the process of moral evolution as we can stay the sweep of the tides or the courses of the stars' (*GB*[3], London, 1911, 'Taboo and the Perils of the Soul,' Pref. p. vii.).

Since the migration of primitive man from a common cradleland, the different environment has been operative in dividing the race into permanent varieties. Sociological differences have resulted, and, since ethics is a branch of sociology, there inevitably arise the contradictions, varieties, and, often, repellent elements whose presence would otherwise perplex the student of the astoundingly complex codes and customs of the world.

'The study of moral advancement is no tracing out of a single straight line, but rather the following of a very winding curve' (L. T. Hobhouse, *Morals in Evolution*, London, 1906, i. 37).

In ethics, as in biology, there is not continuous progress, but adaptation, which sometimes involves retrogression, and adjustment on a lower level.

The sea-squirts, lancelets, and rotifers have their correspondences in degenerate races, in the decline and fall of civilizations whose types of manliness we cannot hope to excel, whose codes embody precepts which are sufficing rules of life, and whose art we may emulate, but can never hope to surpass. The moral standard is the measure of civilization in the highest, and that not a commercial, sense which a community has reached, and that standard advances *pari passu* with it. Hence, even in the course of a few years, changes so momentous that what is approved or tacitly connived at in one generation is condemned and punished in a later. For the code does not create the ethic; it can only embody what, after ages of sore testing, man has felt to be best for man—a result attainable only when acts have their foundation in sympathy disciplined by judgment. We need not travel outside the history of our own criminal code for examples of the relativity of morals, and of their advance along the lines of social evolution.

At the beginning of the 19th cent. there were more than two hundred offences on the statute-book for which death was the penalty. Among these were the cutting-down of young trees, shooting rabbits, and stealing five shillings worth of goods from a shop. Men and women were hanged for sheep stealing, for forgery, and for uttering spurious coin; but they might buy and sell slaves and flog them to death without breaking the law (for further examples, see Hobhouse, *op. cit.* i. 112; G. W. E. Russell, *Collections and Recollections*, London, 1898, pp. 85–87; and Lecky, *Hist. of England in the 18th Century*, do. 1892, vii. 316).

In the later part of the 16th cent. Sir John Hawkins, captain of a slave ship named the *Jesus* (!), gave some of his profits to the founding of Chatham Hospital. He would have made a larger gift, but he explained that 'so many of these wretched creatures, starved or suffocated, had died on the voyage, and they that were left grew into such weakness that it was only by God's grace we were enabled to barter them.' It was not till 1807 that Parliament abolished trading in slaves, and other twenty-six years passed before slavery was abolished in British colonies, the slave-owners receiving twenty million pounds as compensation. The collective conscience had passively acquiesced in what had gone on unquestioned for centuries; only as the moral tone became loftier were such shameful things redressed. The recency of codes that shock us bids us 'nurse no extravagant hope' of an ethical millennium. A survey which embraces the habitable globe shows that 'there are few that be saved.'

Civilization, as Lecky says (*Hist. of European Morals*[9], London, 1890, i. 150), has, 'on the whole, been more successful in repressing crime than repressing vice,' and the primal passions need small incitement to baneful activity. The race is to the swift, the battle to the strong; vast areas of the world remain the arenas of ceaseless turmoil and rapine by tribes whose sole business is fighting—tribes of the marauding type of the Highlanders of two centuries ago, only less barbaric than those of Persian Baluchistan described by a *Times* correspondent (12th July 1911):

'To-day the total population does not probably exceed 200,000, and not 20 per cent are engaged in agriculture. On the other hand, the majority of adult men carry arms of some sort, and find in rapine and violence more congenial means of livelihood. They are mostly of Arab extraction, with a strong admixture of negro blood, but their language is a dialect compounded of Baluch and Persian as well as Arabic; and the ruling class, if any class can be so described in a country where there is no law but that of the strongest, claims to be of Baluch origin, though the real Baluch of British Baluchistan looks upon his mongrel kinsman of Mekran with some contempt. Every district and almost every village has its chief, of varying importance according to the number of *tufenkehis*, or retainers armed with rifles, whom he can muster. These chiefs alone live in mud forts enclosing more or less spacious dwelling-houses of sun-dried mud. The rest abide in squalid huts built up of the ribs of the date-palm branch, and covered with date-palm matting. There are no recognized laws, and the only protection which life and property enjoy is derived from the blood-feud system, which has prevailed from time immemorial. Blood-feuds involve the whole tribe or family in the individual quarrel of any member, and are thus apt to make those responsible for originating them light-heartedly very unpopular with their own people. To this extent they act as a deterrent upon gratuitous violence. Hence, probably, the relatively small amount of bloodshed that accompanies the raids upon which these people are perpetually engaged. The life of every chief is a continuous game of petty intrigue and treachery and predatory warfare, which he plays against his fellows, and of which the stakes, by whomsoever won, are invariably paid by the lesser fry.'

But, while such social chaos, of which the foregoing is a type, prevails, checking optimistic theories of progress, be it remembered that even in the blood-feud—the *lex talionis*—lie germs of social justice.

The transfer of ethics from a social to a supernatural basis was effected in the dim past, when the administration of law became vested in the chief or medicine-man, round whom sanctity gathered, and who was held to derive his authority from the deified ancestors of the tribe. What he did was believed to be done by their aid and in their name; the laws were their laws; and disobedience, as sin against them, was punished here, and in common belief, hereafter. Thus religion

'fixed the yoke of custom thoroughly on mankind.' It 'put upon a fixed law a sanction so fearful that no one could dream of not conforming to it' (Bagehot, *op. cit.* p. 57). 'There is no common wealth where there is not some mixture either of ceremonious vanity or of false opinion, which as a restraint serveth to keepe the people in awe and dutie. It is therefore, that most of them have such fabulous grounds and trifling beginnings, and enriched with supernaturall mistyries' (Montaigne, *Essays*, 'Of Glorie,' Tudor Translations ed., London, 1892–93, ii. 361).

But every institution has served some useful purpose; it has corresponded with some necessity, else it could never have come into being, or survived; and in rude and turbulent times, when men's passions and emotions needed restraint to prevent excesses, the belief that wrongs committed against their fellows were sins against all-powerful gods who were 'angry with the wicked every day' (Ps 7^{11} AV) arrested the course of many an evil-doer. And to this day, wherever the moral tone is lower, and savage instincts are dominant, that belief is a necessary and, often, effective check. In the slow evolution of man from 'the ape and tiger' stage, it seems probable that many ages will elapse before the consciousness of what is due to others, so that no one life shall be the worse through the acts of another, will be the ruling motive of conduct. 'Evil is wrought' not only 'by want of thought, as well as want of heart,' but by ignorance, the mother of so much wrong, and by an accompanying lack of imagination. It is the absence of this which prevents a man from putting himself in the place of those whose actions he may, without warrant, condemn, and deprives him of that sympathy which is the social cement. On the other hand, it is by this faculty of imagination that man has devised instruments of cruelty and torture, and methods of crime which have made him lower than the brute.

Viewed from the standpoint of evolution, the assumed dependence of morals on theology (which, as a body of dogma, is a different thing from religion) is injurious thereto, because the authority of an ethical code is weakened in the degree in which it is bound up with creeds whose truth is questioned, and which, as knowledge advances, become obsolete. Examples of this mischievous connexion are supplied by witchcraft, to give up belief in which, John Wesley contended, was to surrender belief in an infallible Bible, wherein is commanded, 'Thou shalt not suffer a witch to live' (Ex 22^{18}, cf. Dt 18^{10}); and by the justification of the custom of determining guilt or innocence by ordeal given in Nu $5^{11ff.}$. Moreover, the codes of both savage and civilized peoples show that the quality of actions which are held to be sins against supernatural beings is determined by the conceptions entertained regarding those beings. On the lower plane of these sinful acts are omissions of ritual, withholding of offerings, and other offences which have no relation to conduct.

'The gods of the Gold Coast are jealous gods, . . . jealous of the adulation and offerings paid to them; and there is nothing they resent so much as any slight, whether intentional or accidental, which may be offered them' (Ellis, *Tshi-speaking Peoples of the Gold Coast*, London, 1887, p. 11; cf. Ex 20^5). In Australian legend, the god Atnatu expelled man from heaven to earth for neglect of his ceremonies. He made no moral law, but his ritual law as to circumcision and whirling the bull-roarer must be obeyed. In the *Iliad* (xxiv. 66), Zeus says to Hera that Hector was dearest to him of all mortals, 'because he nowise failed in the gifts I loved. Never did my altar lack seemly feasts, drink-offerings, and streams of sacrifice; even the honour that falleth to our due.' Speaking of the modern Greek, J. C. Lawson says: 'In the mental attitude of the worshipper, there is little change since first were written the words, δῶρα θεοὺς πείθει, "Gifts win the gods"' (*Mod. Gr. Folkl. and Anc. Gr. Rel.*, Cambridge, 1910, p. 57). 'With the gods, clearly, nothing goes for nothing. Each blessing has its price. Health is to be had, say, for a calf; wealth, for a couple of yoke of oxen; a kingdom, for a hecatomb' (Lucian, *de Sacr.* 2). Among offences against a supernatural being is that of mentioning his name, or, *per contra*, as in the list of Divine names called *indigitamenta*, it was of immense importance to know the correct name (Warde Fowler, *Religious Experience of the Roman People*, London, 1911, p. 119). How the nature of the offering acceptable to the gods is ruled by the conception of the offerer is seen in the advance from sacrifices of 'thousands of rams' to the social acts of doing justly and loving mercy (Mic 6[7f.]). For the highest moral law is 'expressed in the form, "Be this," not in the form, "Do this"' (Leslie Stephen, *op. cit.* 148).

The comparative method, to which reference was made at the outset of this article, has justified its application to inquiry into the evolution of the moral sense. It has imported order into a realm of speculation and inquiry, where hitherto confusion and chaos ruled. It has made clear the fundamental uniformity of human nature, showing by what like motives the most unlike acts are prompted. It has thrown light on the darkling mysteries which invested what seemed the inscrutable problem of the origin of evil and of the unending and awful tale of human wrong, bloodshed, and tyranny. It explains what part, for the time being, institutions and customs which to the higher moral consciousness are repellent and arresting forces, such as slavery, infanticide, the exposure of infants, blood-feuds, polygamy, polyandry, duelling, torture, the killing of the aged and sick, and cannibalism, have played in social evolution, as subserving what the community believed essential to the welfare of the whole. It has proved that our moral codes, like our theological creeds, are conditioned by the accident of birth, of heredity, and of surroundings. To the fundamental doctrines of Evolution—unity and continuity—it has brought its 'cloud of witnesses.' A survey of the codes and customs of all ages and peoples shows that they are man-made social products; that they are before all creeds and dogmas; that they derive their authority solely from their proved utility; and that they have their origin as the outcome of social needs, increasing their force and securing their permanence because of their adjustment to altered ideas and requirements. Conscience has followed the laws of mental and moral development, and the theory of a definite, rigid, and absolute ethic is a fiction. Montaigne puts the matter with his usual shrewdness: 'The lawes of conscience, which we say to proceed from nature, rise and proceed of custome' (*Essays*, i. 112). It follows that, except in the sense that sin is rebellion against, and attempt to thwart, the universal order, the term is inapplicable. Sin, in essence, is therefore the anti-social.

LITERATURE.—In his *Origin and Development of the Moral Ideas*, London, 1906-8, ii. 747-824, E. Westermarck gives the full titles and dates of about 3000 books bearing on the subject of this article. Here, space permits reference only to the more important which, in addition to those already cited above, should be consulted: S. Alexander, *Moral Order and Progress*, London, 1896; J. J. Atkinson, *Primal Law* (in A. Lang, *Social Origins*, London, 1903); J. M. Baldwin, *Social and Ethical Interpretations in Mental Development*, New York, 1897; B. Bosanquet, *Psychol. of the Moral Self*, London, 1897; H. J. Bridges and others, *The Ethical Movement*, London, 1911; W. K. Clifford, *Lectures and Essays*, London, 1886; G. L. Dickinson, *The Meaning of Good*, London, 1907; H. Ellis, *The Criminal*, London, 1895; G. Gore, *Scientific Basis of Morality*, London, 1899; T. H. Huxley, *Evolution and Ethics*, London, 1894; D. Hume, *Inquiry concerning the Principles of Morals*, London, 1751 (many later reprints); G. Le Bon, *The Crowd*, London, 1903; D. G. Ritchie, *Philosophical Studies*, London, 1905; R. A. P. Rogers, *Short Hist. of Ethics*, London, 1911; G. J. Romanes, *Mental Evolution in Animals*, London, 1883; W. M. Salter, *Ethical Religion*, London, 1905; H. Sidgwick, *The Methods of Ethics*, London, 1901; Boris Sidis, *The Psychology of Suggestion*, London, 1903; Adam Smith, *Theory of Moral Sentiments*, London, 1759 (reprint, 1887); H. Spencer, *Principles of Ethics*, London, 1879-1892; J. A. Thomson, *The Bible of Nature*, Edinburgh, 1908; W. Trotter, art. 'The Herd Instinct,' in *The Sociological Review*, July 1908; E. B. Tylor, *Primitive Culture*[4], London, 1903; M. F. Washburn, *The Animal Mind*, New York, 1908; C. M. Williams, *Ethics founded on Evolution*, London, 1893; W. Wundt, *Ethics* (Eng. tr., London, 1897-1901).

EDWARD CLODD.

EXCOMMUNICATION.—See CURSING AND BLESSING, DISCIPLINE.

EXECUTION OF ANIMALS.

EXECUTION OF ANIMALS.—Belief in kinship between man and animals is universal amongst the lower savages. Their daily, close association with the untamed creatures of hill and jungle impresses upon them similitudes pointing to community of origin and character. Animals move and breathe; they 'certainly seem even to talk' (Im Thurn, *Among the Indians of Guiana*, 1883, p. 351); they are moved by the same passions, securing food by wit and cunning, and mates by strength and violence; they manifest the phenomena from which man derives his conception of spirit; they cast shadows and reflexions; they appear in man's dreams, which to him are not merely 'true while they last,' but actual happenings affecting his waking life. Did space permit, a large number of examples of this primitive psychology could be cited, but the few that follow have the greater weight in being drawn from races above the lowest plane.

One of the septs or sub-tribes of the Kachāris of Assam show traces of their belief in animal descent by going into mourning, fasting, and performing certain funeral rites when a tiger dies (Endle, *Kachāris*, 1911, p. 28). To the Indians of Guiana 'all objects, animate and inanimate, seem exactly of the same nature except that they differ in the accident of bodily form,' and 'have spirits which differ not at all in kind from those of men' (Im Thurn, 350). To the Blackfeet Indians the question 'whether animals have mind and the reasoning faculty admits of no doubt, . . . for they believe that all animals receive their endowment of power from the Sun, differing in degree, but the same in kind as that received by man and all things animate and inanimate' (McClintock, *Old North Trail*, 1910, p. 167).

Hence logically follows belief in the responsibility of the animal for its actions, and punishment for its misdeeds. The Bogos kill a bull or cow which has caused the death of a man; the Maoris killed the pig that strayed into one of their sacred enclosures, as 'in Mohammedan E. Africa, a dog was publicly scourged for having entered a mosque' (Westermarck, *MI* i. 253). Among the Malaccans the buffalo that kills a man is put to death, as under the Hebrew code: 'If an ox gore a man or a woman, that they die, the ox shall be surely stoned, and his flesh shall not be eaten' (Ex 21[28]; cf. Gn 9[5] 'And surely your blood of your lives will I require; at the hand of every beast will I require it, and at the hand of man'). The animal, being regarded as a moral agent, is thus made subject to penal laws whose basis rests on the same motive as that determining all laws of the kind, namely, the resentment of society to acts inimical to its welfare and protection. In his *Theory of Moral Sentiments* (1887 ed.), Adam Smith remarks that

'the dog that bites, the ox that gores, are both of them punished. If they have been the cause of the death of any person, neither the public nor the relations of the slain can be satisfied unless they are put to death in their turn; nor is this merely for the security of the living, but, in some measure, to revenge the injury of the dead' (p. 137).

This explanation, which Westermarck accepts in *MI* (ch. x.), largely accounts for the persistence of the practice of dealing with animals as criminals throughout mediæval times, and even down to the present century.[1] Sufficient warrant for the punishment of animals as criminals would be found in the Hebrew enactment quoted

[1] The *Echo de Paris* of 4th May 1906 reported the condemnation of a dog to death for complicity in a murder committed at Délémont, in Switzerland.

above, as forming an integral part of writings long held to be plenarily inspired; and further support would be derived from the long prevalent belief that animals as well as men could be possessed by demons. 'The period immediately embracing the Christian era saw a vast development of the idea of dæmons or genii' (*EBi*, art. 'Demons,' i. 1070), chiefly due to the influence of Chaldæan on Jewish mythology, and hence the impregnation of the Gospel narratives with that belief, as, *e.g.*, in the reference to Beelzebul, and in the story of the swine of Gerasa (Mk 3^{22} $5^{1ff.}$). Precedent for cursing animal and plant occurs in the sentence pronounced on the serpent in Gn 3^{14}, and on the barren fig-tree, although itself blameless, since, as Mark (11^{13}) adds, 'the time of figs was not yet.'[1] Nor must the influence of the belief in witchcraft and in the metamorphosis of men into animals, as in the superstitions of vampires and werwolves, be overlooked. In these may be found cumulative causes accounting for the permanence of primitive codes which add to the manifold proofs of the survival of primitive ideas, and of the preservation of traces of the earlier stages in man's mental as in his physical structure.

In a chronological list of prosecutions, with resulting excommunications (or, perhaps, more correctly, anathematizations) and execution of animals, given in E. P. Evans, *Criminal Prosecution and Capital Punishment of Animals* (London, 1906), to which work this article is expressly indebted, 194 instances, ranging from A.D. 824 through eleven centuries onwards, are cited; and these may represent only a small proportion of cases of which no record exists. Of the total number thus reported, some in minute detail, 46 are prosecutions against insects; 37 against pigs; 24 each against horses and mares, and against goats, dogs, and she-asses; 16 against cows and bulls; and the remainder against rats and other vermin, snails, etc.

Birds are absent from the list, but there are amusing examples in the commendation of a pastor, Daniel Greysser, of Dresden, by Augustus, Duke and Elector (1559), for having 'put under ban certain sparrows for their extremely vexatious chatterings and scandalous unchastity during the sermon'; and in the anathematizing of swallows by Egbert, Bishop of Trèves, for their sacrilegious defilement of his head and vestments with their droppings when he was officiating at the altar (Evans, pp. 28, 128). The larger percentage of trials of insects in Evans' list may be explained, not so much by the belief in Beelzebul, as by the special ravages wrought by them on crops and fruits. Wholesale destruction of these ubiquitous pests was impossible, and the only weapon to be wielded against them, as in the case of locusts which devastated Botzen in 1338, was excommunication by 'inch of candle,' and anathematization 'in the name of the Blessed Trinity, Father, Son, and Holy Ghost.'

Belief in the magical power of the word and of the curse links together the lower and the higher cultures. Of this the annals of mediæval criminology teem with proof. Even in the Old Testament the prophet Malachi (3^8) warns the people suffering from the plague of devouring things that even conjuration and commination would be unavailing if the tithes to the priests were in arrear. Sometimes the laity were admonished to see in their troubles the anger of the Almighty for this and more serious sins.

The method of procedure in the prosecutions was as elaborate as in any modern criminal trial. The machinery of magic was made effective by the process of law and its attending quirks and quiddities. Counsel were engaged for the prosecution and the defence.

In a 16th cent. trial of weevils, which, twice within a generation, had ravaged the vineyards of St. Julien, their advocate, in reply to the prosecuting counsel's demands for sentence of excommunication, pleaded that the weevils could not thus be banned, because they are outside the pale of the Church; that the Creator would not have commanded them to 'be fruitful and multiply' without giving them the means of subsistence; and that the complainants by their sins had brought on themselves this wrath of God. Rejoinders follow, till the ecclesiastical judge pronounces the weevils guilty, and admonishes them to depart from the vineyard and fields within six days, under penalty of excommunication. As to how the transfer, as in similar cases of condemnation, was effected, the records are silent. Forensic ingenuity comes out in a 15th cent. trial of insects, known as *inger*, which had devoured crops in the district of Lausanne, when the culprits have partial justification as 'irrational and imperfect creatures,' so called because there were none of that species in Noah's Ark. It has further example in a trial of Spanish flies, which were acquitted with a caution because of their small size 'and the fact that they had not yet reached their majority.' In the trial of some caterpillars, whose capture was difficult, a formal citation to appear in court was posted on trees in the infested district—a method which has modern correspondence in the affixing of a writ upon the mast of a ship against whose owner damages are claimed.

As shown above, pigs are prominent as homicides, and as offenders in other ways, in the archives of animal trials. The freedom which permitted them, as scavengers, to run wild in the streets of mediæval towns, as, in fact, they do to this day in many Italian towns, partly accounts for facilities in devouring infants and children. In 1394, one was hanged at Mortaigne for having eaten a consecrated wafer; and in a case of infanticide the pig was accused of eating the flesh, 'although it was Friday'—perhaps tempted thereto by the demon that possessed it, since, as remarked above, the belief that pigs were especially instruments of the devil was strengthened by the narrative of the Gerasene swine. A few cases may be quoted from the records. In 1386, the tribunal of Falaise condemned a sow to be maimed in the head and forelegs (the *lex talionis* is enforced here) and then hanged for having torn the face and arms of a child and caused its death. It was dressed in man's clothes, and executed in the public square. In 1457, a sow was sentenced to be hanged for the murder of the five-year-old son of one Jehan Martin of Savigny, and her six sucklings were charged as accomplices. As their owner refused to go bail for their future good conduct, they were forfeited to the Seigneurie. The reverse occurred when, on the sentencing of a she-ass to death (1750), the inhabitants of the commune bore written witness to her virtuous career, and her pardon and acquittal followed.

Concerning trials and condemnation of other quadrupeds, we find the execution on the common gallows of an ox which killed a villager of Moisy in 1314; of a red bull which killed 'with furiosity' a Beauvais lad of fourteen (this was on the 16th May 1499); of the burning of a mare for homicide by decree of the parliament of Aix (1697); while a humorous variation of the grim records is supplied in the burning of a cock at Basel in 1474 'for the heinous and unnatural crime of laying an egg.' Belief in the impossible being the creed of the superstitious, the fable of the *œuf coquâtre* had such wide credence that a French savant, M. Lapeyronie, read a paper before the Academy of Science in 1710 to disprove it.

LITERATURE.—Nearly all the works treating of the subject of this article are in French or German, and are catalogued by Evans (*op. cit.* pp. 361–371). The most exhaustive is Gaspard Bailly, *Traité des monitoires, avec un plaidoyer contre les insectes*, 1668; see also E. Westermarck, *Origin and Development of the Moral Ideas*, London, 1906–08, i. 249–282; Countess E. Martinengo-Cesaresco, *The Place of Animals in Human Thought*, London, 1909, pp. 347–351; G. G. Coulton, *A Mediæval Garner*, London, 1910, p. 678 f.; R. Chambers, *Book of Days*, London, 1865, i. 127 ff.; and Pausanias, *Description of Greece*, tr., with a commentary, by J. G. Frazer, London, 1898, ii. 371. For primitive peoples, see A. H. Post, *Grundriss der ethnolog. Jurisprudenz*, Oldenburg, 1894–95, ii. 231, and the references given there.

EDWARD CLODD.

EXISTENCE.—See BEING.

EXORCISM. — See DEMONS AND SPIRITS, MAGIC.

EXPEDIENCY.—That character of an action which, in its positive aspect, combines practicability with effectiveness for the end sought, and, in its negative aspect, implies indifference to other characters, especially moral characters. Generalized, it denotes regard for the expedient as determining conduct or as a principle of action.

Expediency bears a threefold relationship to moral values: it may be indifferent to them; it may oppose them; it may be identical with them. The first relationship obtains only where there is a range of conduct recognized as neither moral nor immoral, as held by the Stoics and by Kant (cf. ADIAPHORISM). In such ranges expediency is the only rational governing principle; it becomes, in fact, identical with reason or sound sense. Where the moral value of a given range of conduct is unknown there is opened a similar opportunity for

[1] But upon any theory the interpretation of this incident is difficult (see the Comm.).

resort to expediency. Indeed, the principle of probabilism is, in effect, nothing more than this. Even tutiorism relies upon a kind of expediency, though in this case, since the moral and not the appetitive or personal end is sought, it is a moral expediency—that is to say, the judgment as to moral safety amounts to a judgment that the conduct chosen is the most practicable and effective for the moral standard in the long run.

The antagonistic relation of expediency to morality can occur only in systems which discriminate sharply the ethical obligation from the ethical good—that is, where the 'right' and the 'good' are not necessarily identical. For expediency in conduct only means adopting the most direct means for the end in view. Presumably that end is always (subjectively at least) the good. But, if no other obligation than the realization of this good be recognized, then the expedient means must necessarily be the right means. Intuitional ethics, however, recognizing a moral imperative independent of invariable benefit, and a moral value in action apart from the end of the action, naturally distinguishes actions governed by the sense of right from those dictated by mere practicability. The latter may (though they need not) conflict with the former; and the fact that there are many ends of human desire the attainment of which is not, *per se*, immoral, yet which lend themselves readily to attainment through actions that violate the canons of righteousness, has given a derogatory connotation to the term 'expediency' as designating these means.

It is doubtless the failure on the part of the intuitionists to recognize the twofold regulation of conduct involved in their double reference to a moral sense and an objective good that has led to their reproach of single-principled systems, such as the utilitarian, as endeavours to moralize mere expediency. It is, of course, a fact that systems based only upon a recognition of the objective good as the governance of conduct do determine the righteousness of an action by its expediency to this end; but it is sufficiently evident that, recognizing no conflict between the sense of duty and the realization of the good, right conduct must always be expedient conduct. If the only moral value is the end in view, any means to its attainment is justified. Even Machiavellianism would be beyond criticism if there were no lurking incongruity in the difference of code assigned to prince and citizen.

It is but fair to note, however, that the utilitarian is forced in practice to resort to a kind of expediency differing from moral certainty as much as does the general rule of tutiorism. Such an end as the happiness of the greatest number can only be an object of approximative judgments. Every specific action must be gauged by a kind of calculus of chances of benefit, and in adopting any given estimate a problematical course is being pursued. Granted that the course chosen be the morally plausible one, still the lack of certainty makes its adoption a matter of expediency—moral, to be sure, in motive, but not necessarily so in result. It is, in other words, expedient for the individual to pursue a course which shall justify his moral sense even if it defeat the true moral good as a result of his ignorance. This is a kind of converse to the rule of intuitional ethics that the expedient course to the attainment of benefit is to be condemned if it run counter to the moral sense. Of course, in effect intuitionalism merely sets up an indirect end of action—the integrity of moral feeling,—which is made paramount over its ostensible end—the attainment of objective good.

LITERATURE.—James Mackintosh, *A General View of the Progress of Ethical Philosophy*[2], Edinb. 1837; James Mill, *Fragment on Mackintosh*, Lond. 1835; John Stuart Mill, *Utilitarianism*[13], Lond. 1897; Leslie Stephen, *The English Utilitarians*, Lond. 1900.

H. B. ALEXANDER.

EXPERIENCE (Religious).[1]—*Definition.*—The word 'experience' has two meanings. It signifies practical acquaintance gained by trial or experiment, and also the fruit of the knowledge so obtained. It has, therefore, a twofold religious sense—indicating both the present consciousness of communion with the spiritual and the wisdom accumulated by verification of spiritual facts derived from the inner and outer worlds.

I. *RELIGIOUS EXPERIENCE IN GENERAL.*—Self-analysis reveals the existence of phenomena which the religious man explains as being due to fellowship between God and man. To him spiritual conflict, aspiration, intuition, and the sense of dependence on the unseen are explicable only on the assumption that there is 'some superhuman Power at work within us, lifting us above the narrow limits of our private and particular existence, renewing us and also transforming our relations to our fellowmen' (Eucken, *Christianity and the New Idealism*, 1909, p. 4).

1. Spiritual experience and subjectivism.—It must not be assumed that this method involves a lapse into subjectivism. Experience is not the mere reflex of psychical states, whether intellectual, emotional, or volitional. It is grounded in what Eucken calls the 'life-process itself.' And, when this 'life-process' is examined, it is found that it is not merely subjective, but clothed with a trans-subjective character, inasmuch as the psychical states of the individual are unified and brought into relation with those of others (so that he realizes himself to be a member of a spiritual commonwealth), by the operation of a transcendent spiritual life which is immanent within him. The question has often been asked, Do we, when we speak of spiritual experience, mean that of the individual or that of society? It is possible so to press the antithesis as to give rise to a false alternative. The individual cannot be separated from society, and treated as though he lived *in vacuo*. On the one hand, no one can interpret the spiritual experience of others except in the light of his own. On the other hand, the spiritual experience of the individual is closely linked up with that of others. That which seems to us to be our own peculiar possession has in great part come to us along many channels, *e.g.* heredity, environment, and education. Individual experience cannot, therefore, be isolated, or so purified of the influence of others as to become no more than the individual's own concern.

2. Reality and independence of the spiritual life.—Is the spiritual life truly the Divine life in man, or is it simply the fruit of ordinary psychological processes, extended, it may be, to loftier heights and deeper depths, but still self-originated, and wholly independent of any Power that is not ourselves? We shall endeavour to show that, while it manifests itself through, and utilizes, all the resources of the personality, yet its source is outside of us. For (1) it is a transmuting and unifying power. It is continually working the materials of our human nature into higher forms, creating a new reality out of the old, and resolving the inner antagonism of flesh and spirit. It 'holds forth new ends for our endeavour,' and 'holds before us a regenerated world in the light of which it passes judgment on things as they are,' so that human nature is continually striving to rise above its own level, and to become a 'new creation' (Eucken, *op. cit.* 7). It is difficult to see what resources there are in man himself for the production of this result, the achievement of which 'demands from

[1] For experience in the general philosophical sense, see EMPIRICISM, HUME, KANT, LOCKE, PHILOSOPHY.

us so much toil and sacrifice, such a complete revolution of our being, such a shifting of our life-centre, that it is impossible to think that any natural impulse towards happiness would have led us to it' (*ib.* 9). To the Stoic subjugation of the lower nature by the higher we can attain, but that is the mutilation, not the redemption, of the personality. But to remould all our impulses and passions—not merely to destroy their antagonism, but to bring them into the service of the life of the spirit—is a vastly different task, and one for which the natural man is unequipped. (2) History, properly interpreted, is a struggle for the supremacy of the spiritual life. Underlying all the external events and movements of history are spiritual forces which have provided men with their deepest motives and most potent energies, and linked them together in the fellowship of a hidden life. That inner antagonism which is found in the life of the individual is manifest also in history, and is being resolved by the gradual fulfilment of spiritual purpose. No merely naturalistic hypothesis is sufficient to explain this phenomenon. The evolution of natural forces will not yield the teleological unity of the spiritual life. If an immanent teleology can be traced in history, it is because of the indwelling in man of a spiritual life which has a reality and independence of its own. Thus, from the standpoint of the individual and of history, we are led to the conclusion that spiritual experience is not the mere outcome of subjective psychical states, but has objective reality in fellowship with the Divine life. It is important to notice that the presence of the Divine life in man, as a controlling power, is not destructive of moral freedom, but rather emphasizes and enlarges it. The pre-condition of moral growth is voluntary self-surrender, which brings us increasingly under the liberating influence of the spiritual life. But self-surrender involves conflict and choice. Man is a personality, not an automaton, and has to win his way through to the freedom which chooses the good alone (Aug. *de Civ. Dei*, xxii. 30). Only by struggle and discipline can he attain to willing conformity with the Divine will, and a conscious and ever-increasing participation in the fullness of Divine life.

3. Personality and the spiritual life.—The conception of a transcendent spiritual life, immanent in man, raises very important questions affecting both Divine and human personality. Two dangers must be guarded against. On the one hand, the Divine must not be so identified with the human as to be robbed of all objective reality. On the other hand, the action of the Divine upon man must not be so conceived as to impair his moral freedom. Each of these antagonistic modes of thought ends in the obliteration of the line of demarcation between the Divine personality and the human. The transition from the idea of the Divine immanence to that of Pantheism is made with fatal facility. There can be no doubt that the Hegelian philosophy has, in the hands of some of its exponents, tended in this direction, despite the safeguards which they have endeavoured to set up. These tendencies have been specially characteristic of Mysticism, which is defined by Inge as 'the attempt to realize in thought and feeling the immanence of the temporal in the eternal, and of the eternal in the temporal.' Properly apprehended, it is neither irrational nor destructive of the will, but history shows that it has often been pushed to extremes, and has made for the destruction of the self by the absorption of the human personality into the Divine. Mysticism has indicated three ways in which union with God may be achieved (Inge, *Christian Mysticism*, 1899, pp. 356–368).—(1) *Essentialization.* According to this theory there is a Divine spark in every soul, which is part of the essence of the Deity. Eckhart holds that it is 'so akin to God that it is one with God, and not merely united to him' (cf. Inge, 359). The identification becomes complete in so far as man climbs the *scala perfectionis.* (2) *Substitution.* Man is utterly corrupt and needs the 'substitution of the Divine Will, or Life, or Spirit, for the human' (*ib.* 364). It is clear that, unless they are carefully qualified, both these theories may tend to lessen the value of human personality. The realization of our essential nature, conceived of as a spark of the essence of the Deity, and the substitution of the Divine will for the human, may easily mean the absorption of our personality in God's. The true method of Mysticism is that of (3) *transformation.* The Divine enters into us in ever-increasing fullness, as we are fitted to receive it, and union between God and man is not so much a consummated act as a transforming process. At the same time it is well to remember that, as Inge points out, all three views represent aspects of the truth:

> 'If we believe that we were made in the image of God, then in becoming like Him we are realizing our true idea, and entering upon the heritage which is ours already by the will of God. On the other hand, if we believe that we have fallen very far from original righteousness, and have no power of ourselves to help ourselves, then we must believe in a deliverance from *outside*, an acquisition of a righteousness not our own, which is either imparted or imputed to us. And, thirdly, if we are to hope for a real change in our relations to God, there must be a real change *in* our personality,—a progressive transmutation, which, without breach of continuity, will bring us to be something different from what we were' (p. 366).

What is the authority of mystical states? For the mystic himself they have absolute authority, and he demands no further confirmation. For those who have not experienced them, they 'overthrow the pretension of non-mystical states to be the sole and ultimate dictators of what we may believe' (W. James, *Varieties of Religious Experience*, 1902, p. 427).

4. Psychology of religious experience.—The attempt to connect religious experience with some particular faculty of the mental life has broken down. Faith, which is regarded as the organ of religious experience, is not a separate faculty, but the surrender of our nature to that in which it discerns the promise of the satisfaction of our deepest needs. To discuss adequately the process whereby the surrender is brought about would carry us far afield. It must suffice to insist that personality has the unity of an organism, not that of a bundle of sticks, and that, if faith is to be justified, it must spring out of the necessities of the whole personality. To ground faith only in the speculative reason is to impoverish the spiritual life, and to degrade religious belief into a mere form of intellectual knowledge. This leads to an attempt to explain away those phenomena of religious experience which cannot be rationalistically interpreted. At the same time there are elements of knowledge in faith. The school of which Schleiermacher is the chief representative, which makes faith the product of feeling, fails to solve the problem, because, as J. Caird says, 'to place the essence of religion in feeling is self-contradictory, for a religion of mere feeling would not even know itself to *be* religion' (*Introd. to Phil. of Rel.*, 1880, p. 170). That feeling is a vital element in spiritual experience is undeniable, for the religious life finds its highest manifestation in the emotion of love. But, however blind love may be in its lowest forms, in its highest it must discover a moral ground for the selection of its object, and this cannot be done without the aid of reason.

There is another class of writers who emphasize the place of the will in religious belief, usually associating the will with feeling. This is the view of W. James, who contends that our beliefs are the product of our 'willing nature,' including not only deliberate acts of will, but 'such factors of belief as fear and hope, prejudice and passion, imitation and partisanship, the circumpressure of our caste and sect' (*The Will to Believe*, 1897, p. 9). He would have us take our life in our hands, and make the great venture of faith by deliberately willing to accept the validity of those religious impulses and feelings which 'work.' From James's standpoint, it is no objection to this theory that it sets up an inconstant standard, for he accepts a pluralistic interpretation of the universe. But an objection of another character is not so easily evaded. We are entitled to ask, What is the standard whereby we determine the 'workability' of our beliefs? To say that a belief 'works' is to presuppose a standard of 'workability'—which cannot be arrived at without the aid of reason.

The problem of faith can be solved only when the unity of personality is kept steadily in mind. The reason must gather its materials and sift them, deriving them from no narrow sphere, but from the whole range of knowledge, thought, and feeling, including spiritual instincts and intuitions. The judgment thus arrived at can be made effective only through the emotions and the will. Knowledge does not pass into belief without a decisive act of will, in which emotion is a powerful determining factor—in the sphere of religion, adoration, fear, or love. Thus the whole personality is called into activity before the transition can be made from knowledge to belief. Even yet we have not fully traced the process whereby religious faith is reached. The belief which is the mere outcome of rational, emotional, and volitional processes falls short of faith. And here we are driven back once more upon the reality of that Spiritual Life which, while it transcends man, is immanent within him. To use the language of religion rather than that of philosophy, the Spirit of God entering into us illumines our reason, purifies and quickens our emotions and intuitions, and strengthens our will, so that we are enabled to make a whole-hearted and whole-minded surrender to our beliefs, and all the consequences which come in their train. Faith is, therefore, of ourselves, yet not of ourselves. It is not of ourselves in so far as it is the product of the quickening activity of the Spirit of God; it is of ourselves in so far as it is the rational, willing, and loving response of our whole personality to the power of God.

5. Religious experience and the subliminal self.—Modern psychologists lay great stress on the subliminal self, and by some it is regarded as the organ of religious experience. James holds that the discovery of the subliminal self marks the greatest advance which psychology has made. Myers uses the term to

'cover *all* that takes place beneath the ordinary threshold . . . of consciousness;—not only those faint stimulations whose very faintness keeps them submerged, but much else which psychology as yet scarcely recognises; sensations, thoughts, emotions, which may be strong, definite, and independent, but which, by the original constitution of our being, seldom emerge into that *supraliminal* current of consciousness which we habitually identify with *ourselves*. . . . I conceive also that no Self of which we can here have cognisance is in reality more than a fragment of a larger Self,—revealed in a fashion at once shifting and limited through an organism not so framed as to afford it full manifestation' (*Human Personality*, 1907 ed., pp. 13–15).

James has proposed as an hypothesis

'that whatever it may be on its *farther* side, the "more" with which in religious experience we feel ourselves connected is on its *hither* side the subconscious continuation of our conscious life' (*Varieties*, p. 512).

Following up the line thus opened, Sanday has laid it down

'that the proper seat or *locus* of all divine indwelling, or divine action upon the human soul, is the subliminal consciousness' (*Christologies*, 1910, p. 159).[1]

[1] For criticism of James's and Sanday's views, see *ERE* iv. 53.

This department of psychology is as yet too undeveloped to enable us to arrive at any conclusion approaching definiteness. It is impossible to avoid the use of spatial terms, but such an expression as '*locus* of all divine indwelling' must be received with caution. If God is active in man, He must, above all, be present in that region in which the life of fellowship with Him is consciously lived. His activity may, indeed, penetrate deeper, and it will explain many of the phenomena of the religious life if we believe that the Divine Spirit is present in the hidden depths of our personality, seeking to order our impulses aright. But it does not follow from this that the subliminal self is to be regarded as the peculiar organ of the religious life. It would seem as though it plays as important a part in the development of the artist and mechanic as in that of the saint:

'Religion draws its sustenance from the deep soil of accumulated social experience, and from the wide-spreading roots of individual inheritance and impressionability. The subtle, powerful influences of imitation, suggestion, and subconscious habits operate in religion, giving it stability and intensity. It is by this means that the racial ideas possess such urgency, objectivity, and formative power. They are the result of the long arduous struggles of mankind. It is no wonder that they have been proclaimed with prophetic zeal, and obeyed with tragic devotion. But every interest of society moves forward by the aid of similar forces. In respect, then, to the operation of subconscious elements, religion is not unique. It stands in the normal relations characteristic of all other genuine social interests' (Ames, *Psychol. of Relig. Experience*, 1910, p. 295).

II. *CHRISTIAN EXPERIENCE.*—In the NT we find ourselves in a very different atmosphere from that of philosophy. Its dominant note is not speculation but certainty, and its emphasis is not on the abstract but on the concrete. Spiritual religion is focused in a historic revelation. God has spoken to the world through His incarnate Son, Jesus Christ, whose teaching, life, death, resurrection, and ascension, with the consequent outpouring of the Holy Spirit, are all shown to stand in a vital relationship to spiritual experience.

This connexion is not elaborated in the Synoptic Gospels as in the other NT writings. This is what might be expected, since the Synoptists set out to give a simple record of the earthly ministry of Jesus, and rarely yield to the temptation of reflexion upon the events. Nevertheless, even they afford sufficient material to establish the distinctive features of Christian experience. Jesus Christ is set forth as the Mediator of a new revelation of God to men. He reveals God as Father, and calls on men so to live that they may be the sons of their Father in heaven, and thus receive the Holy Spirit. Israel had already apprehended the Divine Fatherhood in relation to the nation, and even to the individual Israelite through the mediation of the nation; but in the Gospels it is declared to be universal, and is represented as being actually manifested in Jesus Christ, in whom the filial relationship was perfectly realized and exemplified. The purpose of Christ is to reveal and to restore to men their sonship, and to initiate them into a higher spiritual order—the Kingdom of God, or Heaven. Of this Kingdom He is the supreme Mediator. He bids men come to Him, take His yoke upon them, and learn of Him, if they would find rest for their souls (Mt $11^{28f.}$). His blood is shed unto remission of sins (26^{28}); and, though crucified and buried, He is risen from the dead, and is with His people even unto the consummation of the age (28^{20}), and will be the final Judge of all. It is not possible to trace here the development of this teaching in the other NT writings. It must suffice to indicate its main content and implications.

1. The Incarnation and Christian experience.—The Incarnation is a concrete revelation of that which lies at the basis of spiritual experience—

union between God and man. It is the revelation of an eternal affinity between Spirit and Nature, between God and man. Some Unitarians, no less than Trinitarians, prefer the doctrine of Athanasius to that of Arius, on the ground that the former conserves the truth of a union of God with humanity. The NT, however, does not regard the Incarnation as a mere illustration of union between God and man, but as the ground of its realization. It is not simply the revelation of an eternal affinity between the two, but the initiation of a new spiritual process, whereby that affinity is consciously realized by man—a process based not on imitation, but on fellowship in a hidden life, mediated to us by Jesus Christ. 'The law of the Spirit of life in Christ Jesus' liberates us from 'the law of sin and death,' endues us with a moral dynamic, begets in us 'the mind of the spirit' which is 'life and peace,' and leads us into the realization of an affinity with God, which is so close that we are called His sons (Ro 8^{1-17}).

2. Christian experience and the death, burial, resurrection, and ascension of Jesus Christ.—The death, burial, and resurrection of Jesus Christ are regarded in the NT both as objective acts, standing in a real relation to Christian experience, and as symbolizing processes to be reproduced in us. Objectively Christ's death and resurrection are related to deliverance from sin and guilt, and the birth of the new life in the soul. The sense of sin has always been a characteristic mark of Christian experience. Theories of the Atonement lie outside our purview, but it is beyond dispute that the NT sets forth the Cross as the ground of reconciliation, and as that which brings deliverance from the power of sin and the paralysis of guilt—in short, that which makes fellowship with God possible. The Resurrection is regarded as the pledge of the perpetual presence of Christ in the world as the Mediator of the Divine life. It might, however, be contended that an ascended Christ is transcendent, but the Resurrection and Ascension are interpreted in the NT in the light of Pentecost. The Spirit is 'the Spirit of his Son' (Gal 4^6). 'The Lord is the Spirit' (2 Co 3^{17}). The 'Living Christ' is not a mere synonym for the posthumous influence of Jesus. He is present by His Spirit in the hearts of those who love Him, and the Christian hope of immortality is grounded not in speculation, but in participation in His immortal life. But the death, burial, and resurrection of Jesus are also taken by St. Paul as typifying certain inner experiences of the Christian.

'I have been crucified with Christ; yet I live; and yet no longer I, but Christ liveth in me' (Gal 2^{20}). 'We were buried therefore with him through baptism into death: that, like as Christ was raised from the dead through the glory of the Father, so we also might walk in newness of life. For if we have become united with him by the likeness of his death, we shall be also by the likeness of his resurrection' (Ro $6^{4ff.}$).

This is not a mere description of a mystical doctrine of *necrosis*. The spiritual experience has its basis in historic facts, by the aid of which it is initiated. The crucifixion and burial of the old self and the resurrection to newness of life are achieved only by means of the spiritual energies liberated in the death and resurrection of Jesus.

3. The filial consciousness, fellowship with Christ, and the indwelling of the Spirit.—The content of Christian experience may be variously described in these three ways, each of which emphasizes a different aspect of the truth. The filial consciousness is marked by freedom from the spirit of fear and bondage (Ro 8^{15}); fellowship with Christ by victory over sin (1 Jn $3^{6ff.}$); and the indwelling of the Spirit by the discernment and assimilation of Christian truth (1 Co 2). The underlying experience is one and the same. To abide in Christ is to be begotten of God (1 Jn 3^{6-9}), and to be led of the Spirit is to be a son of God (Ro 8^{14}). We have access to the Father, in the Spirit, through the Son (Eph 2^{18}). The three aspects are unified by St. Paul: 'And because ye are sons, God sent forth the Spirit of his Son into your hearts, crying, Abba, Father' (Gal 4^6).

'The one God, Father, Son, and Spirit reveals and communicates Himself; the living Christ invested with the concrete personality of the historical Jesus is the *content*, but since the withdrawal from sight of the historical Jesus, the Spirit is the *mode* in which God shows and gives Himself. It depends on religious temperament and spiritual discernment whether this revelation and communication of the one God will be conceived more vaguely as the operation of the Spirit or more vividly as the presence of the living Christ' (Garvie, *Studies in the Inner Life of Jesus*, 1907, p. 454).

But the NT does not conceive of the indwelling of the Spirit as begetting the filial consciousness, apart from the apprehension of the historical Jesus.

'The Spirit of God, which illumines, is the Spirit of the Lord, and the enlightenment is according to its content nothing else than the saving knowledge of Jesus Christ, that is, not of a principle, which He brought into the world, but of His historical person. If, accordingly, these two moments coincide, the perfect knowledge of Jesus Christ and the enlightenment by the Spirit of God, then indeed they are logically related to one another in such a way that the enlightenment springs out of the knowledge of Jesus Christ, not in the reverse way, that a man might have in the enlightenment of the Holy Spirit, which might occur independently of Christ, the principle of the knowledge of Christ' (Kaftan, quoted by Tasker, *Spiritual Religion*, 1901, p. 133).

4. The witness of the Spirit and the inner light.—The Methodist doctrine of the witness of the Spirit has been expounded in art. CERTAINTY (Religious), vol. iii. pp. 325–331. It may be well here to distinguish between it and the Quaker doctrine of the inner light. The witness of the Spirit is conceived of as operating *ab extra*, the inner light *ab intra*. The former is a development of Christian experience, the latter is its presupposition. The inner light has been compared with the Stoic σπερματικὸς λόγος and *anima mundi*.

'By this Seed, Grace, and Word of God, and Light wherewith we say everything is enlightened, and hath a measure of it, which strives with him in order to save him . . . we understand not the proper Essence and Nature of God, precisely taken, . . . but we understand a Spiritual, Heavenly, and Invisible Principle, in which God as Father, Son, and Spirit dwells: a measure of which Divine and Glorious Life is in all men, as a seed which of its own nature draws, invites, and inclines to God; and this some call *Vehiculum Dei*' (Barclay, *Apology*[6], 1736, p. 137 f.).

It is from this substance that the inward birth arises (Barclay, *op. cit.* 139). It is not to be inferred from this that Christ dwells in all men by way of union and 'inhabitation'; but He is present as in a seed, and 'He never is nor can be separate from that holy, pure Seed and Light, which is in all men; therefore it may be said in a larger sense that He is in All' (*ib.* 143).

Further, this light is not to be identified with any natural faculty such as reason or conscience. Neither is it subject to man's control.

'He must wait for it: which comes upon all at certain times and seasons, wherein it works powerfully upon the Soul, mightily tenders it and breaks it; at which time, if man resists not, but closes with it, he comes to know salvation by it' (*ib.* 141 f.).

Barclay strongly denies that this doctrine is in any way derogatory to the historical revelation of Jesus Christ. He holds it to be 'damnable unbelief' on the part of any one not to believe the Gospel when it has been declared. The remission of sins is obtained only on the ground of the sacrifice of Christ, but it may extend to those who have no knowledge of Christ's work.

'Many may come to feel the influence of this Holy and Divine Seed and Light, and be turned from evil to good by it, though they know nothing of Christ's coming in the flesh, through whose obedience it is purchased unto them. . . . The History then is profitable and comfortable with the Mystery, and never without it; but the Mystery is and may be profitable without the explicit and outward knowledge of the History' (*ib.* 141 f.).

5. Individual and collective experience.—What is the relation of the spiritual experience of the individual to that of the whole society of Christian disciples? The two extremes to be guarded against are the individualism which forgets the organic character of Christian experience, and the authority which eliminates individuality and variety by demanding conformity to a fixed type. Ritschl holds that the Divine life is not a direct gift to the individual, but is mediated to him through his membership in the kingdom of believers. It seems to be more true to the NT and to the facts of experience to represent the individual as coming into immediate fellowship with God in Jesus Christ, and as verifying or correcting his deductions, not merely by reference to the authoritative dicta of the Church, but by spiritual fellowship with those who are partakers of a like experience.

'The basal principle of individual experience' is 'saved from excess by the correction given through the experience of others. . . . In an effective practical fashion the experience of the whole church is brought to bear upon the isolated feelings of the separate member' (H. B. Workman, in *New History of Methodism*, 1909, vol. i. p. 29).

6. Christian experience and philosophy.—The Ritschlians distinguish between theoretical judgments and judgments of value. The validity of Christian experience is to be judged by pragmatic, not by theoretic tests. Ritschl and Herrmann deny that theology needs the sanction of metaphysics. They hold that religious knowledge has no need to be brought into harmony with theoretic knowledge. Kaftan, however, writes:

'The sphere of thought peculiar to the Christian faith, and the sphere of thought identified with the rational knowledge of things, cannot be wholly apart from one another: it must be possible to combine them so as to make a whole' (*The Truth of the Christian Religion*, p. 11, quoted by Mozley, *Ritschlianism*, 1909, p. 27).

What Ritschl means by value-judgments may be seen from his statement that 'we know the nature of God and Christ only in their worth for us' (*Justification and Reconciliation*, Eng. tr., 1900, p. 212). There can be no ultimate divorce between theoretical and religious knowledge. Truth, though many-sided, must be one, and the spiritual and rational universes must finally coincide. But it is not to be assumed that Ritschl conceived of two kinds of knowledge, mutually exclusive and irreconcilable. His emphasis on value-judgments was due to the fact that his interest was practical rather than metaphysical. It seemed to him that they offer the one method of approach to religious truth. And as such they undoubtedly vindicate themselves by enlarging our vision and deepening our sense of certainty. But it is necessary to go further than Ritschl, and to recognize that their authority is greatly increased if they are viewed in the light of all our knowledge, and verified or corrected thereby. The theory of value-judgments embodies, at any rate, two important truths. (1) Experience is a vital factor in the solution of the truth problem. The higher we ascend in the scale of truth, the more scanty does theoretical evidence become, and the more dependent are we on practical motives. (2) Speculation cannot yield an intimate knowledge of the nature of God. Such can be won only by experience—the realization of God's worth *for us*. The inner meaning of the Christian revelation can be apprehended only by those who have experienced its worth in their own lives (cf. 1 Co 2[13-16]). To sum up, value-judgments stand for

'the recognition that proof cannot mean in theology exactly what it means in natural science, but that in theology knowledge must be a matter of personal conviction arising from individual experience.' They are 'the assertion of the presence of the personal element in all knowledge, the protest against excessive intellectualism, the understanding that truth is perhaps not quite so rigid and fixed as in our conceptions we have been inclined to represent it' (Mozley, *op. cit.* 110).

7. Christian experience and doctrine.—Christian doctrine is the outcome of the interpretation of the historical facts of the gospel in the light of Christian experience. The facts of the historic revelation are established independently of experience, which of itself cannot prove their reality, but, once they are given, confirms and interprets them. Doctrine cannot be evolved out of experience alone. The birth, life, teaching, death, resurrection, and ascension of Jesus Christ are facts dependent upon the attestation of history, but no adequate doctrines of the Incarnation, the Person of Christ, the Atonement, the mediatorial work of Christ, and immortality can be formulated unless the facts are approached and interpreted by Christian experience. The doctrine of the Trinity is an outstanding instance of a dogma springing out of the necessities of the experience which is grounded in the facts of the Christian revelation. The eschatological doctrines of Christianity are in a different category. They are based not on historic facts but on revelation, and can be neither deduced from nor confirmed by experience, except in so far as the final principles of judgment are seen to be operating here and now. It is in the development of the doctrines which relate to the new life in Christ that experience exercises the most potent influence. Conversion, regeneration, justification by faith, sanctification, assurance, are phenomena of the inner life, and, however fundamental their relation to the historic revelation, can be translated into doctrine only by the aid of experience. Both the hope and the justification of theological progress lie in the advance which Christian experience is gradually achieving. Doctrines are tentative, not final, efforts to state the truth, and cannot rise above the level of the experience which formulates them. Progress in doctrinal expression will be made in so far as the Church penetrates more deeply into the treasures of wisdom and knowledge that are hid in Jesus Christ (Col 2[3]).

8. Christian experience and history.—As has been shown, Christian experience is based by the NT writers on the historical revelation of God in Jesus Christ. The Ritschlians distrust the mystical side of the religious life, and hold that the Christian knows God and communes with Him through the apprehension of the inner life of the historical Jesus. This view, while it places a necessary emphasis on the historical side of the revelation, does less than justice to the mystical side of NT teaching. The experience initiated by the apprehension of the inner life of Jesus may be developed in fellowship with the living Christ, without any sacrifice of objective reality, or subservience to merely subjective processes. At the other extreme are those who separate the Christ of faith from the Jesus of history. In some instances the historicity of Jesus is denied, and it is held that the Gospel is but a representation of a wide-spread 'Christ-myth' which reflects humanity's struggle for God. The attack on the historicity of Jesus cannot be said to have met with any success, and many of the parallels, so confidently advanced, between the details of the Gospel narrative and mythology, break down on analysis (see Carpenter, *The Historical Jesus and the Theological Christ*, 1911, ch. i., and St. Clair Tisdall, *Mythic Christs and the True*, 1909). In other quarters the conception of the heavenly Christ is regarded as the outcome of a process of gnosticizing which has taken place round the form of Jesus of Nazareth, who, as some think, was the embodiment of a Divine humanity, or, as others believe, merely a well-intentioned, but more or less misguided, Jewish apocalyptist. But such theories are beset with difficulties that are insuperable. (1) They do not explain how the gnosticizing process came to centre in the crucified Jesus of Nazareth, nor do they help us to understand why from earliest days Christian faith has sought its nourishment not in a mystic gnosis, but in the knowledge of the historical Jesus, whom it identifies with the heavenly Christ. (2) Facts of consciousness which are the product of speculation and reflexion, however valid they may seem to the experient, cannot claim the authority and certainty of a revelation which centres in a great historic fact. (3) 'Whenever the Church has treated the historic record with indifference, it has invariably fallen either into scholasticism or mysticism. . . . Christianity, when scholastic, lacks inspiration; when mystical, it lacks reality and balance' (Forrest, *The Christ of History and of Experience*, 1897, p. 335).

LITERATURE.—In addition to the books referred to above, the following may be mentioned:—R. Eucken, *The Life of the Spirit*, London and N.Y. 1909; A. Caldecott, *Philos. of Religion*, London, 1901; J. Caird, *Introd. to Philos. of Religion*, Glasgow, 1880 (new ed. 1889), also *Fundamental Ideas of Christianity*, do. 1899; W. James, *Pragmatism*, London, 1907; W. R. Boyce Gibson, *God With Us*, London, 1909; H. M. Gwatkin, *The Knowledge of God*, Edinburgh, 1906; W. R. Inge, *Faith and its Psychology*, London, 1909; J. Denney, *Jesus and the Gospel*, do. 1908; W. W. Holdsworth, *The Christ of the Gospels*, do. 1911; R. R. Roberts, *The Supreme Experience of Christianity*, Cardiff, 1910; Rufus M. Jones, *Social Law in the Spiritual World*, London, 1904; T. Hodgkin, *Human Progress and the Inward Light*, do. 1911; W. Herrmann, *The Communion of the Christian with God*, Eng. tr., do. 1895; G. A. Coe, *The Spiritual Life*, New York, 1900; E. D. Starbuck, *Psychol. of Religion*, London, 1899; C. C. Hall, *Chr. Belief interpreted by Chr. Experience*, Chicago, 1906; L. F. Stearns, *Evidence of Chr. Experience*, London, 1890; G. Steven, *Psychology of the Christian Soul*, do. 1911; art. 'Religious Experience,' in Hastings' *DCG*.

H. MALDWYN HUGHES.

EXPIATION AND ATONEMENT.

EXPIATION AND ATONEMENT (Introductory and Primitive).—The entire subject of expiation and atonement is inextricably involved with that of sin (*q.v.*), and with the propitiation (*q.v.*) of the Divine being or beings angered by such sin, whether the propitiation be by sacrifice, fasting, penance (*qq.v.*), or any other means. The concepts of expiation and atonement are, however, neither synonymous nor even necessarily connected; the latter involves a far higher type of religious development than does the former. Even on the human plane, the desire to placate an offended fellow-man by no means implies of necessity a wish to be at one with him; the averting of wrath is not inherently prompted by love either for or in the offended. It is true that—from motives of fear as well as of love—there may be a desire not merely to appease, but also to win the favour of, the being appeased; but such desire is accidental, not essential, to the concept of expiation, whereas it forms the inmost kernel of the concept of atonement.

The broad principles motivating expiation may be summed up in fear of Divine anger (cf. ANGER [WRATH] OF GOD) at sin, which, in the words of the Westminster Shorter Catechism (qu. xiv.), is 'any want of conformity unto, or transgression of, the law of God'—a definition which, *mutatis mutandis*, will apply to the lowest as well as to the highest systems of religion.

In the lower stages of religion, what we may conveniently call 'sin' does not necessarily imply infringement of a moral law; it may be merely a violation of an unmoral custom (*q.v.*) or of a non-moral tabu (*q.v.*); it may be one of omission as well as of commission; it may be voluntary, involuntary, or unwitting; it may be grave, or venial, or of any intermediate grade; it may offend various classes of worshipful beings—ghosts, godlings, deities, and the like; it may be entirely physical or ritual. In all such cases of offence, some sort of expiation becomes necessary—some penance must be undergone to placate superhuman beings, just as some surrender of self is needful to appease offended human kind.

It seems safe to conclude that, at its lowest level, expiation is non-ethical, and that non-ethical ideas remain connected with expiation, to a greater or less degree, in relatively advanced religious systems, while in some—notably in Buddhism (see 'Buddhist' section, below)—the concept is non-existent; while in others—as in Muhammadanism (see 'Muslim' section, below)—expiation degenerates into a crass question of debit and credit. The non-ethical aspect seems to characterize the entire Polynesian and Melanesian area, where expiation appears to be simply an endeavour to placate offended ghosts and deities. Yet it must be remembered that, with the exception of the Australians, few of these peoples have as yet been studied with a view to ascertaining their ethico-religious principles—a failure particularly lamentable, since with so many of them the old system of beliefs has practically vanished for ever. Yet it is at least significant that even so competent an observer as Codrington makes no mention of any ethical feeling underlying such sacrifices as are made in Melanesia for the purpose of propitiation (*Melanesians*, Oxford, 1891, p. 127), though it is perfectly evident that the Melanesians and Polynesians had many ethical principles of a high order (see above, p. 516 f.).

In Africa, also, the non-ethical form of expiation is the more usual. As a type may be taken the Shilluk of the Egyptian Sudan. When a Shilluk is seized with a disease as a result of some offence that he has committed, a propitiatory sacrifice is offered, with an appropriately sad and humble frame of mind, to appease the angered worshipful being; and, should the sick man recover, his restoration to health is attributed to the intercession of Nykang (the apotheosized first king of the Shilluk) with Čuok, the 'Great Spirit' (Hofmayr, *Anthropos*, vi. [1911] 121).

In like manner, among the Bantu Wajagga, a sick man inquires of his sorcerer as to the origin of his illness, and, if it be from an offended ghost, this is appeased, according to the sorcerer's directions, either with the sacrifice of a sheep, ox, etc., or with a libation of honey, meal, milk, and the like (Fassmann, *Anthropos*, iv. [1909] 576).

A distinct form of expiation is the rite of confession. Outside Christianity (see PENANCE), confession has been most commonly known from the Assyro-Babylonian, Egyptian, Hebrew (see these sections of CONFESSION; and for a divergent rendering of the Egyptian confession—more accurately 'repudiation'—of sins, see above, p. 478b), and

Parsi (see 'Parsi' section, below) religions. Yet it occurs elsewhere, as among the Eskimos (*q.v.*), the Aztecs and Peruvians (see 'American' section, below; cf. also Waitz, *Anthropologie der Naturvölker*, Leipzig, 1860–77, iv. 129 f., 462 f.), the Dénés (*q.v.*), and the Iroquois (*q.v.*). Here only the Hebrew and the Parsi, together with the Aztec and Peruvian, confessions are prompted by real ethical considerations, from their earliest known history; but the Parsi *patēṭs* are of very late date, while, in the case of the Aztec and Peruvian confessions, there is a possibility (though merely a possibility) that they have been transmitted in too ethical a setting. The Assyro-Bab. confession is, at least originally, largely devoted to ritual offences; and the Egyptian 'repudiation' has no indication of any real sense of sin and repentance—at the most, only attrition is indicated by it (see also 'Egyptian' section, below).

Africa also knows confession. Among the Kikuyu, east of Lake Victoria Nyanza, sin is the violation of some law, custom, ceremony, rite, or prescription, and consists of three parts: *mogiro*, 'prohibition'; *noki*, 'violation'; and *sahu*, 'punishment.' Of this, Fr. Cayzac says (*Anthropos*, v. [1910] 311):

'Sin is essentially remissible; it is enough to confess it. Ordinarily, this is done to the "sorcerer," who expels the sin by a ceremony whose principal rite is a simulation of vomiting (*kotahikio*, derived from *tahika*, "vomit").

There is also a private, non-ritual confession: a man has just committed adultery; his accomplice forbids him to speak of it. If she had said nothing, the man would not have sinned; but, since she has spoken, he has sinned. . . . The man, in this case, then makes a private confession of his act to some friend, and this confession renders him immune against *sahu*.'

Confession is also practised by the Mkulwe (German East Africa), but only by adults, who must perform the rite publicly, fully, and sincerely. Confession is made by all assembled in case of severe illness, or difficult delivery, or before crossing a dangerous stream; individual confession, when the father of the household is starting on a journey.

The confession for severe illness begins: 'The illness is grave. Let us see; perhaps there are sins among the kin. Let him who has sins confess them; let us confess well; let us not confess with double heart. Forgive me, gracious God! I have no other sins than . . . (adultery, breaking of vows, falsehood, theft, etc., as the case may be). I have no other sins at all. I am poor; protect me, gracious God! All my sins are gone forth with the wind!' With the last words the person confessing casts towards the west splinters of wood and bits of straw, that his sins may be carried away by the wind even as the sun sinks in the west, never to return. If the sick man mends, it is attributed to the perfection of the confession; otherwise, it becomes necessary to get a doctor to consult the spirits, in order to discover who is concealing some of his sins, and thus hindering the recovery of the patient (Hamberger, *Anthropos*, iv. [1909] 309–312).

And yet, non-ethical as these African forms of expiation appear to be, it has been declared that the African possesses a real concept of conscience.

Thus Schneider (*Relig. der afrikan. Naturvölker*, Münster, 1891, p. 19 f.) writes: 'The negro is guided at every step by religious conscientiousness (*religiöse Gewissenhaftigkeit*), though, unfortunately, he is very often not led to true morality. . . . His morality is not based upon self-made, secular, and human principles, but upon religious, erroneous though they may often be. What bonds and binds him is not "the categorical imperative of self-ruled reason," but another, higher will, which proclaims to him his religion. . . . The misinterpretation of evil as a power of Nature only fetters, but does not utterly destroy, the sense of responsibility and guilt. No impulse of conscience (*Gewissen*) is alien to the negro; he experiences heaviness and distress of conscience, and comfort and joy of conscience. His constant thought and endeavour is to know and to fulfil the wishes of those invisible powers on whose interference he believes his weal and woe to depend; he knows no worse misfortune than to offend the spirits or fetishes; fear of their anger can plunge him into irremediable dejection; to make them again propitious is the chief matter of his care and his endeavour, and to this end he burdens himself . . . with the most painful renunciations. As he fears the anger of the spirits for his sins, so, with a quiet conscience, he counts upon their help and heartily submits to the ordeal, trusting in their miraculous intervention for the saving of innocence. His prosperity appears to him to be the reward for his good conduct towards the Invisible Ones, and every evil to be a punishment for offending them' (cf. also the 'Egyptian' sections of CONSCIENCE, and ETHICS AND MORALITY).

LITERATURE.—In addition to the authorities cited in the text, see the lists appended to the following series of articles.

LOUIS H. GRAY.

EXPIATION AND ATONEMENT (American).—The conception of expiation is already fundamentally present in the primitive effort to placate evil and to propitiate powers that are or may become unfriendly. Sacrificial rites of all sorts are designed to such ends, the notion being that the worshipper can purchase favour by his sacrifice. Where the sacrifice, in place of a mere offering of goods, involves physical suffering on the part of the donor, we may fairly regard the rite as expiatory—as an effort to make good the punishment which the propitiated power is wont to inflict.

Rites of this type are common among the American Indians. One of the most interesting examples is that given by E. F. Im Thurn (*Indians of Guiana*, London, 1883, p. 368):

'Before attempting to shoot a cataract for the first time, on first sight of any new place, and every time a sculptured rock or striking mountain or stone is seen, Indians avert the ill-will of the spirits of such places by rubbing red-peppers (*Capsicum*) each in his or her own eyes. . . . The extreme pain of this operation when performed thoroughly by the Indians I can faintly realize from my own feelings when I have occasionally rubbed my eyes with fingers which had recently handled red-peppers; and from the fact that, though the older practitioners inflict this self-torture with the utmost stoicism, I have again and again seen that otherwise rare sight of Indians, children and even young men, sobbing under the infliction.'

The same propitiatory notion underlies the severe tortures which the Plains Indians of North America were accustomed to undergo on the eve of going to war, though doubtless here the ethical motive of putting to test the warrior's fortitude also bears a part. A typical description is given by de Smet (*Life, Letters, and Travels*, New York, 1905, p. 255 f.):

'Among the Sioux, as among the Aricaras, warriors preparing for an expedition undergo a very rigorous fast of several days. They have for this purpose a "medicine" lodge, where they spread a buffalo robe and plant a red-painted post: at the top of the lodge is tied a calf-skin containing all sorts of devices. There, to obtain the aid of the Great Spirit, they pierce their breasts, pass leather cords through, attach themselves to the post, and dance thus several times around the lodge to the sound of the drum, singing their warlike exploits and flourishing their war-clubs over their heads. Others make deep cuts under their shoulder-blades, run cords through the gashes, and drag two great buffalo heads to an eminence about a mile away from the village, where they dance until they drop senseless. A last offering before setting out consists in cutting off little pieces of flesh from different parts of their bodies, which they offer to the sun, the earth, and the four cardinal points, to render the Manitous, or tutelary spirits, of the different elements favourable.'

From rites such as these, designed to compound an offence feared or expected, to rites meant as compensation for an offence already given is but the step of reason. Possibly an intermediate case is the acceptance of punishment not with a sense of having offended, but merely as a means of averting a calamity already falling—such as the case of Black Coyote who, after several of his family had died, in obedience to a dream sacrificed seventy pieces of skin from his body to save the remainder (*14 RBEW*, pt. 2 [1896], p. 898). In this instance we have vicarious sacrifice, with no apparent sense of fault; yet expiation readily develops into penance, with the penitential conviction of sin accompanying it, and sometimes into penance viewed as a punishment and acts of compensation viewed as atonement. An excellent instance of this complex sort is the penalty for murder among the Hurons as described by Father Brébeuf (*Jesuit Relations*, ed. Thwaites, Cleveland, 1896–1901, x. 215–223). Not only must the murderer and his family give *compensation*, in the form of presents (as definitely determined as the Anglo-Saxon *wergild*), but he must also give *satisfaction*—probably conceived as a placation of the angry dead. Brébeuf thus describes it:

'The dead body was stretched upon a scaffold, and the murderer was compelled to remain lying under it and to receive upon himself all the putrid matter which exuded from the corpse; they put beside him a dish of food, which was soon filled with the filth and the corrupt blood which little by little fell into it; and merely to get the dish pushed back ever so little would cost him a present of seven hundred porcelain beads . . . ; as for the murderer, he remained in this position as long as the relatives of the deceased pleased, and, even after that, to escape it he had to make a rich present.'

War among the Indians was but an expansion of the primitive blood-feud, of which the above ceremony represents a sort of commutation, as is proved by the fact, noted by Brébeuf, that, 'if the relatives of the dead man avenge themselves for this injury by the death of him who gave the blow, all the punishment fell on them.' Much of the difficulty in maintaining an Indian peace lay with the relatives of the war-slain whose *manes* had not yet been appeased by the death of a foeman. Thus the Assiniboins explained to Father de Smet (p. 1128) their horrible cruelty in slaughtering a whole encampment of unprotected women and children of their Blackfeet enemies, declaring that 'they satiated themselves with cruelty to satisfy the *manes* of their deceased parents and kindred.' Certainly, if captives were spared or adopted, it was usually because the losses of the captors had been negligible in the conflict.

The conception of pollution or uncleanness, with the corresponding need for ceremonial purification, obtains far and wide in the Indian world; but the fasts, purgations, and ordeals which marked the purifying are hardly to be regarded as in a strict sense expiatory; they are of the nature of a cure rather than of a penance. We find, however, that the Indian was more than receptive when the notion of penance, as expiation of sin, was once laid before him. At all events, there is a general unanimity of the Jesuit teachers to the effect that their aboriginal converts were singularly ready to confess and do penance for their faults, often outdoing what the Fathers required of them. The statement, 'they accused and condemned themselves, and pronounced their own sentence, which they carried out' (Thwaites, xxxiii. 33), represents not a particular case but a common attitude.

Le Jeune in the *Relation* of 1640 (*ib.* xviii. 173-177) describes at length one of the rather numerous instances in which a convert had espoused a pagan, and had later come repentant to the Fathers. 'We assembled the principal Christians to ascertain what action would be taken in this matter,' he writes. 'They summarily decided that he should be driven away and forbidden ever to live again with the Christians.' To this severity the Fathers objected, the young man being merely asked publicly to confess his sin. This he did; but more than this, he came in private to his confessor, saying: 'My Father, I have so deeply regretted my fault that I have not dared to approach any Christian since my return; I would not dare even to look at them. I was told, indeed, that you would chide me if I returned to Saint Joseph; but I have come, nevertheless, to see you. I assure you that, since I left this woman, I have fasted every day,—eating only once a day and not more,—so much have I grieved for offending God. I have not dared to take shelter in the cabins of the Christians; I pass before them in silence, with bowed head; I shall go and see them when I have confessed.' Le Jeune adds: 'I carefully examined his behaviour; I found him so little guilty before God that I shuddered within myself for some time with a holy horror. It is true that he had taken this young girl, having already given his word to another; it is true that he lived with her as if they were married, and that was the offence. But it is true also that his fear of offending God and his respect for his baptism had prevented him from touching her, although he was urgently solicited to do so—desiring that she should become a Christian before showing her the evidences of his affection. This, in my opinion, is what passes wonder—to be in the fire, and not be burned; to do an act almost innocent before God, and patiently to bear the penance for it before men.'

The same readiness to confess and do penance is recorded by the Spanish friars in Mexico. There, moreover, the idea had developed independently before the advent of Christians, as is illustrated by the explicit account given by Sahagun (*Hist. gén.*, Paris, 1880, I. xii.; cf. art. COMMUNION WITH DEITY [American], in vol. iii. p. 741). And, indeed, the whole temper of the Aztec religion is that of a deep and unescapable sense of sin—with which a reader of Mexican annals can hardly fail to sympathize. Something very similar among the Peruvians is indicated by Garcilasso (*Royal Commentaries*, ed. Paris, 1830, II. xiii.) in the spirit in which the Inca laws were obeyed. The Inca ruler being regarded as Divine, the laws of the empire were viewed as Divine ordinances, the violation of which was sacrilege.

'Hence,' he says, 'often enough, those who knew themselves culpable, condemned by conscience, went voluntarily to proclaim to the judge their secret faults; for their belief that the soul condemns itself led them to believe that their sins were the cause of all the ills which befell the state—maladies, deaths; unprosperous seasons; disgraces, general or particular. To prevent, therefore, that their private faults should cause their lord to send other ills into the world, they wished to expiate their sin by death.'

There was, in fact, no distinction between crime and sin; every offence was an offence against the Inca, who was himself immune from fault simply because of his Divine origin and sanction (cf. *ib.* II. xii.-xv.).

Garcilasso (VI. xi.) records that in certain tribes the priests were accustomed to fast for the welfare of the community. This is a wide-spread custom among the Indians, being intimately associated with the mystic notion that dream-revelations of importance to the people were to be obtained by such means (see *14 RBEW*, pt. 2 *passim*). The idea of vicarious atonement is, in fact, never very far beneath the surface in a society whose morals are still on the group basis, distributing responsibility to all the relatives of the offender. A quaint development of this notion is detailed in the *Jesuit Relations* (ed. Thwaites, xxxii. 305) by Père Lalemant:

'After the fathers and mothers have confessed, they make such of their children as are fit to receive the sacrament go to confession. But, as regards those who have not sufficient discernment, their mothers bring them to the confessors and relate in their presence their petty acts of naughtiness, and make them ask for a penance, which they themselves perform for their little ones.'

For the final development of this idea of vicarious sacrifice, in its native form, we must turn to the mythologies of the Indians. There we find—among the Iroquois, the Algonquins, the Sioux, the Pawnees, and many others—various developments of the conception of a demiurgic being modelling this world as a habitat for man after the plan of the world which is above the skies and which was before the earth was. This being is at times (as with the Iroquois) a cosmic titan, slain in the making of the earth, so that its body becomes the source of the life of the vegetable and the animal realms, and thus of man himself, who reverences the nourisher of life. At times (as in the legends of Hiawatha) an historical or legendary chieftain, conceived as a benefactor who has won for his people some such gift as the knowledge of agriculture, is identified with the cosmic sacrificial demiurge—thus giving a vicarious turn to the heroic life. Possibly the dominance of the theanthropic conception throughout Mexican religion is but a continuation of the same fundamental conception—of a god dying for mankind (see esp. J. N. B. Hewitt, 'Iroquoian Cosmology,' *21 RBEW* [1903], p. 133; D. G. Brinton, *Myths of the New World*³, Philadelphia, 1896; cf. art. INCARNATION [American]).

LITERATURE.—In addition to the authorities cited in the article, see list appended to COMMUNION WITH DEITY (American).

H. B. ALEXANDER.

EXPIATION AND ATONEMENT (Babylonian).—**I. Personal gods and demons.** — To understand the intricate system of purification from sin in Babylonian religion, it is necessary to start from the unique conceptions of the Sumerian[1] religion regarding the relation of the individual to the gods. The Sumer.-Bab. religion possesses a

[1] The entire structure of Bab. religion is essentially non-Semitic, and borrowed from the primitive inhabitants of Mesopotamia, viz. the Sumerians.

pantheon extraordinary in its ability to represent every element of Nature in its hierarchy, and many abstract ideas as well. The earliest religious literature of the Sumerians represents the social aspect of religion as distinguished from the individualistic. The public worship, in which the entire community joined to sing liturgies in the temples, in praise of the great gods, is apparently older than those forms of worship which touch more closely the individual, which belong to the realm of magic and were excluded from the temple-worship from first to last. But the individual who, by the socialist nature of early worship, felt himself lost in the sight of the gods in the great public liturgies expressed his need of a more personal religion by adopting a personal god, his protecting genius.[1] Each man lived under the protection of his personal god, a good spirit which dwelt in his body, or whose Divine presence permeated his being. Proper names in both languages often refer to this idea.[2] The deity whose name figures in the proper name of any individual is not always his protecting genius. He felt free to choose some other. Usually each individual adopted a god and his consort as his personal gods, so that the Babylonians[3] spoke more often of 'my god and goddess.'[4] So long as the personal god dwelt in a man, he felt himself in communion with divinity, but the evil demons (originally ghosts) often overpowered the protecting spirits and drove them from the body. 'His god is departed from his body, his thoughtful goddess stands afar,' says the priest of one who has fallen to the powers of evil.[5] Ordinarily sickness or any trouble physical or spiritual is regarded as a sign of possession by the demons (see DEMONS AND SPIRITS [Assyr.-Bab.]). It is likely that in the first stages of this religion the demons were regarded as taking the initiative without any cause whatsoever. Thus in the earliest known text of this kind we have the following:

'Namtar,[6] like a god invincible, from on high entered,
He brought headache upon a man
. . . .
To his hand his hand he extended,
To his foot his foot he extended,
This man is the son of my hand, son of my foot is he.'[7]

2. Conceptions of sin.—But only the primitive stages of the religion attribute the flight of the protecting spirits solely to the hostile attacks of the demons. Man himself becomes a factor, and begins to reflect upon his own conduct as a possible cause for the flight of his gods. The first notion of sin is here ritualistic, grossly materialistic.

'When he walked the streets, has he trodden upon a libation poured out? Has he set his foot upon improper water? The water of unclean hands has he seen? A woman of impure hands has he met? A maiden of impure hands has he seen? A woman of poisonous witchcraft has his hand touched?'[1] 'Ban by drinking from an unclean cup (?) (Marduk) dissolves.'[2] 'Ban by having touched a man accursed (Marduk) dissolves.'[3] 'Food (unclean) I have eaten, waters incanted (?) I have drunk, refuse of my god unwittingly I have eaten, rubbish of my goddesses unwittingly I have trod upon.'[4]

The ethical conception of sin and the moral element in religion begin to develop at an early period, if we may judge from the religious aspect in which injustice and violation of civil laws were regarded. Yet it may be safely asserted that ethics and religion were originally independent of each other in Babylonia.[5] The moral transgressions which bring about estrangement between man and his gods are mentioned at great length in the *Šurpu* series:

'Has he failed to deliver the captive, and the bound not set free? Was *yes* in his mouth and *no* in his heart?' 'The boundary of justice has he gone beyond?' Man is inherently prone to sin: 'Who has not been negligent, who has not committed frivolity?'[6]

3. Condition of the sinner.—Corresponding with the advance made in the conception of sin,[7] there are distinctly different conceptions of the condition of the sinner in the various stages of the cults of expiation. The reader will have inferred from the preceding paragraphs that the earliest state of sin was regarded as one of demoniacal possession.[8] Whether disease, sorrow, and calamity were conceived of as due to the attacks of the demons, the machinations of witchcraft, the evil eye, or what not, the actual state of man was described as one of demoniacal possession. Thus in a ritual against a disease we have the curse:

'Evil ghost,[9] evil *alu*,[9] evil *utukku*,[9] evil man, evil eye, evil mouth, evil tongue from the body of the man, son of his god, may they depart.[10]

The technical term for a man in demoniacal possession is *papḫalla* = *muttalliku*,[11] lit. 'one tossing to and fro.' Also the ordinary word for 'sick,' *marṣu*, may be used in a wider sense quite synonymous with 'demoniacal possession.' The man whose protecting gods had deserted him is *lù tu-ra* = *amelu marṣu*.[12] The Sum. word *tur* is probably connected with the root *tar*, 'to curse,' and represents the man as under the curse of the demons. The Sem. root *marāṣu*,[13] indicates a condition of pain and misery, and, unlike the Sumerian, has no magical significance. Another Sum. word, *gig*, is often employed to denote the misery of a sinner.[14] The fundamental idea of this root is 'unclean,' 'worthless.' Sumerian, therefore, in each case employs a term based upon the religious aspect of the case. A sinner is one cursed by the demons, made unclean by the evil spirits so that his gods can no longer dwell in his body. The sinner is often described as one who has a *curse*, for which the technical word is *mamitu* in Semitic.[15] The root of this word, *emû*, Heb. חמה,[16] means 'to speak with a rumbling voice,' probably referring to the ventrilo-

---

1 Sum. *dingir-ni*, Bab. *ili-šu*. More often a man is called 'son of his god,' *dumu dingir-ra-ni* (earliest mention in *Cun. Texts from Bab. Tablets in Brit. Mus.* [*C.T.*] iv. 4*a*, 28), or Bab. *mar ili-šu*.

2 Sum. *Ur-den-zu*, 'servant of the Moon-god'; *Ur-dutu*, 'servant of the Sun-god'; *Lù-dba-ú*, 'man of the goddess Bau'; *Gĭn-dda-mu*, 'maiden slave of Damu'; *dIšḫanna-ama-mu*, 'Išḫanna is my mother'; Bab. *iluMarduk-naṣir*, 'Marduk protects'; *iluEnzu-imguranni*, 'Sin has blessed me.' See esp. Krausz, *Götternamen in den bab. Siegelcylinderlegenden*, Leipzig, 1911.

3 We employ the word in the sense of *inhabitants of Babylonia* attached to the established religion.

4 References to men who have no protecting god are found (*C.T.* xvii. 14 K. 8386. 7, 23, 194), but these are seized upon by disease at once.

5 *Šurpu*, v. 11. One passage represents the protecting god as a man's shepherd, whom the devils seized upon for food.

6 One of the seven demons.

7 *C.T.* iv. 4; see *Babyloniaca*, iii. [1910] 16. The best example of the idea of a soul being wilfully attacked by the demons is the series of incantations known as *Maḳlu*, tablet 1, where the individual attributes his afflictions to the machinations of wizards and witches, one of the most common sources of evil, and the so-called *Utukku limnûti* series, *C.T.* xvi. (tr. by Thompson, *Devils and Evil Spirits*, London, 1903–04). For an example of a man wilfully attacked by restless souls from hell, see King, *Bab. Magic and Sorcery*, 1896, no. 53 = Langdon, 'Bab. Eschatology,' in *Theol. Essays in Honour of C. A. Briggs*, New York, 1911, p. 159. See esp. Morgenstern, *Doctrine of Sin*, 6–21.

1 IV. R. 26, no. 5; cf. *C.T.* xvii. 38.

2 *Šurpu*, iii. 19.

3 *Ib.* 115.

4 IV. R. 10*a*, 28–34. The 'refuse of my god,' *ikkib ili-ia*, and the 'rubbish of my goddess,' *an zil ištariia*.

5 Morgenstern, 2. Dhorme (*Rel. assyr.-bab.* 211 ff.) takes the opposite view. At any rate, the references to moral sin in the rituals of expiation and atonement are found only in the late period.

6 King, *Bab. Magic*, no. 11, obv. 10.

7 For a detailed statement of the Bab. conceptions and technical terms for 'sin,' see SIN (Bab.).

8 Schrank, *Bab. Sühnriten*, 42.

9 One of the seven devils.

10 *C.T.* xvi. 13*a*, 45–48.

11 V. R. 50*b*, 3; *C.T.* xvi. 2, 38.

12 *C.T.* xvi. 4, 149; see Brünnow, *Classified List*, Leyden, 1887, no. 1074.

13 Prt. *imruṣ*, to be distinguished in Assyrian from *marāṣu*, prt. *imras*, 'to be firm, strong.'

14 Translated into Semitic by *marāṣu*.

15 For 'curse,' Sumerian employs *sag-ba* or simply *sag*. *Sag* means lit. 'the throwing,' from the root *sig*; and *ba* means 'to speak,' lit. 'to cast a spell by words.' Another Sumerian technical term is *nam-erim*, the fundamental idea of which is uncertain.

16 The derivation is fixed by *C.T.* xvi. 33, 177, where a demon is called *mutâmû*, 'one who utters a rumbling voice,' and rendered in Sum. by *nam-erim*.

quist.[1] A demon or a witch casts the *mamit* upon a man, or the *mamit* falls upon him as the result of any kind of sin. The individual sometimes represents his condition in more ethical terms in the later stages of the religion. 'May the sickness of my body be removed, may the weariness of my flesh be driven away.'[2] 'Calling and no answer have encompassed me.'[3] 'From the days of my youth much have I been bound with torment. Food I eat not, weeping is my nourishment.'[4] Often the gods (both personal gods and others) are said to be angry with the sinner and to have turned away from him. 'His god and goddess are enraged with him';[5] 'The goddess has turned away from me.'[6]

4. Methods of expiation.—Since the fundamental concept of sin is essentially one of demoniacal possession or of a ban and curse, which enfold man like a great net, the method of overcoming the demons or the curse must be magic. It would be not incautious to say that no religion ever existed in which the entire scheme of atonement is so thoroughly based upon magic. No analysis of the ritual of atonement could possibly convey to the reader an adequate idea of its complexity, its comprehension of all the vital elements in a natural and cultured religion, or the extreme beauty of some of its forms. To restore the protecting gods to a man's body, or to restore a man to his protecting gods, is the essential object of the atonement. It follows, then, that he will be restored to favour with all the gods. To free man from the devils, to loosen the ban cast upon him by the powers of evil, is the problem in the ritual of atonement.

Power to overcome the demons and the ban is obtained through the curse given to the priests by Ea, god of Eridu, the ancient seat of the cult of fresh water. Inherently there is no difference between the curse hurled upon man by the demons and wizards and the curse of salvation uttered by the priests in the name of the water-god. The superiority of the latter lies in the superior mystic power of the god himself.

5. The curse.—The technical term for the curse of expiation is *šiptu* in Semitic, a word borrowed from the Sum. root *šib*, 'to cast, hurl.'[7] Ordinarily the rituals employ the term *nam-šub*, lit. 'the casting, throwing.' We do not possess material from the primitive period to give us an insight into the precise origin of the mystic spell revealed by the water-god, but the act of *casting* a spell of Divine power probably consisted in uttering words attended by conventional movements of the hands.[8] This supreme magical formula was known as the curse of Eridu, and had power not only to overcome the bans of the demons, but also to consecrate any object whatsoever.[9] As in the Christian Church the consecrating formula employed for conveying mystic power to the elements of the mass is preceded by the sacred history of its institution, so in the Bab. rituals the curse of Eridu is employed only after the account of its legendary institution. Ea, the water-god, is said to commission his son Marduk with his own power over the demons. Marduk is represented in the person of the magician (Āšipu), whose words are, therefore, really those of the water-god.[1]

The following passage is the earliest known source for the ritual of expiation, and is employed against headache:

'Go, my son Marduk, this man the son of his god pacify.
Bread at his head place, rain-water at his foot place.
Smite the headache.
The words of the curse of Eridu utter.
Of his limbs the ache allay.
May the headache ascend to heaven like smoke.
Into the beneficent hand of his god restore the man.'[2]

'The words of the curse of Eridu' have not been recorded on tablets. It may well be that they constituted a sacred formula revealed only by oral instruction in the schools.[3] The word *mamit* (Sum. *sag-ba* and *nam-erim*), which, as we have seen above, often denotes the curse of the demons, may also be used for the curse of the gods. 'With the curse of the earth-spirits[4] I curse thee,' says the priest of incantation to the demon.[5] A quasi-philosophic conception of the curse of Eridu is found among the schoolmen: 'Curse, Curse, concept[6] not to be transgressed.'[7] The consecrating, delivering curse belongs to the water-god only, or to the gods connected with fresh water, as Marduk, son of Ea, Ninaḫakuddu, daughter of Ea.[8] The curse was then personified, and a hymn (King, *Bab. Magic*, 61) refers to the curse as created with the gods.

6. Curse without ritual.—Only in the later period do we find the priests of incantation depending wholly upon the curse to banish the powers of evil and bring about reconciliation with the gods.[9] The process here may be described as purely intellectual magic. The priest proclaims himself as commissioned by Ea; and, after describing the demons at great length (it was necessary to obtain a clear idea of the nature of the ban before it could be cursed), finally utters the curse of Eridu, following it by an oath that the demon is cursed.[10] This secondary curse, 'Verily, thou art named,'[10] may be sworn to in the name of any number of gods or sacred objects,[11] and serves only as an assertion that the priest has really discovered the name of the demon to be cursed.

7. The ritual elements.—In the ordinary ritual of atonement water, bread, grain, plants, and animal sacrifices are introduced. The reader will note the passage cited above in § 5, where bread and water are placed at the head and feet. In the primitive ritual, water was undoubtedly employed as a means of purification, and applied in one way or another before the curse of Eridu was uttered. The priest seeks to drive the demons into the water, the bread, the grain, or whatsoever element may be employed. When he utters the curse the evil passes into the water, which is then taken away into 'a clean place' or thrown in the byways. Such water, bread, etc., were regarded as

1 Still another technical term is *arrātu*, 'curse'; the verb is *araru*, Heb. ארר. The Sum. for *arrātu* is *aš*, 'ill-will'; and the verb *aš-bal*, 'hurl the ill-will.' Note the idea of *hurling*, *casting*, the basis of all the expressions for cursing in Sumerian.

2 King, *Bab. Magic*, no. 1, rev. 45.

3 *Ib.* 11. 3.

4 Haupt, *Akkad.-sum. Keilschrifttexte*, Leipzig, 1882, 116, 17-20.

5 IV. R. 29** 14, *zinû itti-šu.*

6 IV. R. 10*a*, 53, *eliia isbusu*; cf. Craig, *Religious Texts*, Leipzig, 1895, i. 13, 5=ii. 7, 8.

7 So first Paul Haupt.

8 Morgenstern supposes that the idea of *casting* refers to the sprinkling or throwing of water; but this is highly improbable. None of the terms employed has any reference to water; on the other hand, they almost universally refer to the casting of *words*.

9 Thus water is consecrated with mystic power by repeating the holy curse over it (IV. R. 22*b*, 12).

1 Sumerian possesses other words for *šiptu*, viz. *tú*, *mŭ*, *én sag-ba*, and *nam-erim*. Of these the two latter may refer either to the curse of life uttered in the name of the gods, or to the curse of the demons (see above, § 3). Both *tú* and *mŭ* refer to a method of speaking. The original idea inherent in the word *én* is obscure (see Langdon, *Sum. Gram.*, Paris, 1911, pp. 213, 268).

2 *Babyloniaca*, iii. 16.

3 Probably the formula was simply *zi* ^{d}*en-ki-ka-ge ge-pad*, 'By the being of Ea thou art named.'

4 Anunnaki, spirits of the nether sea, who guard the waters of life in Hades.

5 *C.T.* xvi. 12, ii. 3.

6 *Uṣurtu*, 'outline,' the form or concept of a thing.

7 *C.T.* xvii. 34, 1.

8 Called 'lady of the curse' (Haupt, *Akkad.-sum. Keilschrifttexte*, 105, 32, and cf. *Babyloniaca*, iii. 28).

9 As in *C.T.* xvii. 34–6 and the *Utukku limnûti* series.

10 Lit. 'thou art spoken against' (*tamâta*; Sum. *ge-pad*, 'be thou named').

11 *C.T.* xvi. 13*a*.

extremely dangerous and capable of exercising a ban upon any one who touched them or even looked at them. On ancient seals the sinner is often represented bringing a goat as an offering, and not infrequently the rituals mention lambs of sacrifice, which appear to have been divided between the priests and the gods. At any rate, neither the blood of the victim nor the sacrifice itself plays any essential rôle in the mystery of expiation.[1] The technical term for putting the elements to the body is *ṭeḫû* (Sum. *teg*), and for removing them *kuppuru* (Sum. *gur*).[2] The bread, water, plants, etc., into which the curse had driven the powers of evil, are called *takpirtu*. *Kuppuru* then developed the sense of 'purge,' 'purify,' *atone*.[3]

8. Scape-goat.—Expiation by means of the scape-goat[4] is often met with. Ea says to Marduk:

'Go, my son Marduk. A man has been seized upon by a ban. Take a scape-goat. Its head to his head put. The king son of his god atone.[5] The venom (of the ban) into its mouth (of the scape-goat) may be cast. May the man[6] be pure, be clean.'[7]

In another ritual a small pig is dismembered, and its parts are applied to the patient, who is washed in holy water and incensed with the censer.[8] In this ritual the pig is said to be a *substitute*[9] for the man. In another ritual the scape-goat is called the image of the man (*nig sag illû*).[10]

9. Sympathetic magic.—In certain rituals, especially those of the fire-cults (*Maḳlu* and *Šurpu*), small images of the sorcerers who have put a man under a ban are destroyed in fire; or tamarisk, dates, onions, etc., are torn and thrown into the fire, attended by prayers that the ban and those who have worked it may likewise perish. In these cases the prayer is said by the patient, and the priest utters the curse of Eridu.

10. Penitential prayers and confession.—Gradually a more ethical element is worked into the rituals of expiation by requiring the sinner to repeat a psalm of adoration to one or several of the gods while the priest performs various acts of the ritual. These prayers are commonly known as 'Prayers of the lifting of the hand,' a scene often represented on seals of the classical period. It is precisely here that the Babylonian religion reaches its highest spiritual development. 'My heart is distressed and my soul faileth. I cry unto thee, O lord in the pure heavens. Faithfully look upon me, hear my supplication,' says the penitent in a prayer to the moon-god.[1] 'May my sin be undone, my frivolity forgotten. May the good genius, the good spirit walk beside me. May evil mouth and tongue stand aside. Before thee I will walk and sing thy praise.' So run the closing lines of a prayer to the god of the new moon.[2] It is probable that sinners read a tablet of their sins before the gods, and that the tablet was then broken in sign that their sins were forgiven. This form of the ritual finally freed itself from magic, and the sinner depended entirely upon confession and prayer in the so-called penitential psalms. The significant act of atonement in this form of the ritual is the appeal of the sinner to various gods to intercede for him with the god whose anger he wishes to appease. Forgiveness is here expressed by the phrase 'remove my sin,' or 'turn thy face unto me,' or 'may thine anger return to its place.'

It will be seen that Bab. religion identifies sin and disease in all its stages, and that atonement and reconciliation depend largely upon magic. The atoning power of sacrifice is a negligible factor, and in any case is not original. The ritual tended to the production of a beautiful literature, and in many cases to symbolic acts of great spiritual power. Finally, the ritual led up to penance and prayer, in which appeal is made directly to the gods.

LITERATURE.—K. L. Tallqvist, *Die assyr. Beschwörungsserie Maqlu*, Leipzig, 1895 (=*Acta Soc. Scient. Fennicæ*, vol. xx. no. 6); H. Zimmern, *Die Beschwörungstafeln Šurpu*, Leipzig, 1900, also *Ritualtafeln*, Leipzig, 1900; J. Morgenstern, *The Doctrine of Sin in the Bab. Religion*, Berlin, 1905; W. Schrank, *Bab. Sühnriten*, Leipzig, 1908; C. Fossey, *La Magie assyrienne*, Paris, 1902; M. Jastrow, *Die Religion Babyloniens und Assyriens*, Giessen, 1905 ff., chs. xvi.–xvii.; L. W. King, *Bab. Magic and Sorcery*, London, 1896; P. Dhorme, *La Religion assyr.-bab.*, Paris, 1911, p. 282 ff.

S. H. LANGDON.

[1] References to the use of blood as a means of expiation are rare. In *C.T.* xvii. 5, 51 the blood of a pig is applied to the side of a bed on which a sick man lay; and in Zimmern, *Ritualtafeln*, no. 26, iii. 20, the blood of a kid is mentioned.

[2] See *ExpT* xxii. [1911] 320–325.

[3] In addition to the special article in *ExpT*, *l.c.*, regarding *kuppuru*, the Babylonian technical term for 'atone,' the present writer would make the following explanatory statement, which must be categorical here. Students of Hebrew who naturally look to Assyriology for a definite statement regarding the meaning of this word should remember that the Babylonians translate the Sumerian word *gur* by *kuppuru*. Now there is not the least doubt that the technical word for 'atone' in Sumerian means 'turn away, remove.' In regard to *kuppuru* the writer is of the opinion that, although the Babylonians employed this word with emphasis upon the *removing* of the objects which had magically absorbed the curse and the uncleanliness, the root meaning involves both the ideas of *cover* and *remove*. The Babylonian ritual gives us, we think, the clue for fixing upon this Semitic conception of atonement from which both Babylonian and Hebrew started. We take the root *kapāru* to mean fundamentally, 'wash away with a liquid'; *apply* and *wipe away* are two concepts inherent in this root, and, although Babylonian appears to have lost almost completely the idea of applying or covering, yet Hebrew has apparently retained traces of it, certainly in Gn 32[21].

[4] The technical word for 'scape-goat' is *mašḫuldubbû*. On the entire subject of the scape-goat in Babylonian religion, see *ExpT* xxiv. [1912] 9.

[5] *U-me-te-gur-gur=kuppir*, i.e. 'take the scape-goat away.'

[6] Here the king.

[7] Haupt, 105.

[8] In this ritual [*C.T.* xvii. 6], fourteen baked cakes are placed at the outer gate of the house.

[9] *Pûḫu*.

[10] *C.T.* xvii. 37, K. 4859. There is another reference to the scape-goat in Craig, *Religious Texts*, i. 18. 8. A scape-goat is also used to purify a sanctuary; and he who carries it away to the fields is unclean for seven days (*RAssyr* viii. [Paris, 1911] 49). Likewise in another ritual, for freeing a house from a ban, he who carries away the water used in the handwashings is unclean seven days (IV. R. 59, no. 1, rev. 3).

[1] King, *Bab. Magic*, no. 6, 60–62.

[2] *Ib.* 31–34.

EXPIATION AND ATONEMENT (Buddhist).

EXPIATION AND ATONEMENT (Buddhist).—In the sense in which these terms are used in Christian theologies, the ideas of expiation and atonement are scarcely, if at all, existent in Indian religions. This holds true especially of Buddhism, constructed without dependence on a deity, and profoundly influenced by the Indian theory of *karma* (*q.v.*). According to the theory of *karma*, as current, it is generally agreed, just before the rise of Buddhism, the fate of a man's soul, in its next birth, was determined by the man's *karma* (lit. 'doing') in this birth. The soul was supposed, in this stage of the theory, to be a very minute creature residing in the cavity of the heart, and resembling in every respect (except in size and in the absence of a soul within it) the visible man. Like a man's, its outward form was material, consisting of the four elements and heat; like a man, it had anger, desire, quality, and other mental traits.[3] This hypothesis of a soul was rejected by Buddhism; but in other respects it adopted and systematized the *karma* theory, and made it one of the foundation-stones of its ethical theory. *Karma* became for it an inexorable law, working by its own efficacy, subject to no Divine or human interference, and resulting in an effect following without fail upon every deed, word, and thought. As to what effect followed on what deed opinions differed (see KARMA). But on the main fact of *karma* all Buddhist schools are agreed. They held that the *karma* and its *vipāka* (the act and its result) were inextricably interwoven; that no exception by way either of expiation or of atonement was either possible or desirable; and that the contrary doctrine, an explaining away or denial of *karma*, was pernicious, immoral, a bar to religious progress.

[3] See Rhys Davids, 'Theory of the Soul in the Upanishads,' in *JRAS*, 1899.

The passages in the canonical books in support of the above doctrine are so numerous that only a small selection can be given.

In *Sutta Nipāta*, 666, the Buddha is reported as saying: '*Karma* is never destroyed, not any one's.' So also an elder[1] is made to say, at *Thera Gāthā*, 144: 'The *karma* a man does, be it lovely, be it evil, that is his inheritance, whatsoever it may have been that he has done.' At *Aṅguttara*, i. 286, it is said: 'Of all woven garments, brethren, a hair shirt is known as the worst. In hot weather it is clammy, in cold weather chilly; it is ugly, evil-smelling, grievous to the touch. Just so, brethren, of all the doctrines commonly known among those of the recluses, that of Makkhali of the Cow-pen is the worst; for that foolish one is of opinion that there is no *karma*, no action, no energy.'[2]

Yet, notwithstanding this uncompromising attitude as to the result of any act done, there are two cases in early Buddhism in which, at first sight, there seems to be some mitigation possible. The first is where a *bhikkhu* is forgiven for a breach of a by-law of the community; the second is in the matter of a *patti-dāna*, or transfer of merit.

The rules as to the first case are translated in *Vinaya Texts*, ii. 330 ff. and iii. 61-65. Stated quite shortly, they amount to this. If a breach of the rules had been reported to the local chapter, the chapter could, under certain conditions, suspend the offender from certain privileges. On his submission, a motion could be brought forward, at a subsequent meeting of the chapter, for rehabilitation. By leave of the chapter the offender was brought in, and, on his acknowledging his offence, the chapter, through the mouth of the mover of the motion, 'took the offence back' (as the standing expression is). Sometimes the Buddha himself, without the matter being laid before a chapter, 'took back' an offence (see, for instance, *Saṁyutta*, i. 123). But in all such cases the offence, it should be noted, is purged only as regards the Order. The law of *karma* is not broken. The *karma* of the offence will work out its inevitable result independently of the fact that the offence, so far as the Order is concerned, has been expiated.

The other apparent exception, the *patti-dāna*, or transfer of merit, is interesting as showing development in doctrine. The belief is not found in the Nikāyas themselves, only in the commentaries upon them.[3] In the latter, however, it is taken so completely for granted that it must have grown up some considerable time before they were written in the 5th cent. A.D.; and, if the present writer's note in *Questions of King Milinda*, ii. 155, be correct, the idea (though not the technical phrase for it) must be as old as the *Milinda*, that is, probably, as old as the 2nd cent. A.D. *Patti* means 'attainment,' 'accomplishment.' To have done a good deed was to have attained the good result that would inevitably follow. By the law of *karma* that result would accrue to the benefactor (to him who has done the good act) either in this or in some future birth. The doctrine of *patti-dāna* (lit. 'gift of the *patti*') was that the benefactor could so direct the *karma* that it would accrue not to his own benefit, but to that of some one else whom he specified. That this amounts to an interference by human will in the action of *karma* cannot, we think, be disputed. And, if the merit of a good action can be thus transferred, it would seem to follow logically that the result of an evil deed could also be transferred. All this brings us very nearly, if not quite, to the Christian doctrine of atonement, of the imputation of righteousness. The Buddhist might deny this; and would point out, quite rightly, that such transfer of merit was supposed possible only in the case of certain good actions of a minor sort. In fact, the *patti-dāna* is most frequently found in the colophons to the MSS, the copyist giving expression to the pious hope that the merit of his having completed the copy may redound to the advantage of all beings. And in other cases, in the stories told in the commentaries, the act of which the merit is transferred is usually the gift of a meal to a *bhikkhu*, the placing of a white flower at the foot of the monument to a departed *arahant*, kindness to animals, or some such simple act of piety.

It is noteworthy that the transfer of merit is usually from a good Buddhist to a non-Buddhist, and that the latter is usually a friend or relation of the benefactor. There is no instance of a good Buddhist desiring or accepting any transfer of merit to himself.

LITERATURE.—V. Fausböll, *Dhammapadam, excerptis ex commentario Palico illustravit*, Copenhagen, 1855; *The Jātaka, together with its commentary*, 7 vols., ed. V. Fausböll, London, 1877-1897; *Sutta Nipāta*, London, 1885; *Aṅguttara Nikāya*, 6 vols. (*PTS*, 1885-1910); *Saṁyutta Nikāya*, 6 vols. (*PTS*, 1884-1904); T. W. Rhys Davids and H. Oldenberg, *Vinaya Texts*, 3 vols. (*SBE*, 1881-1885); Rhys Davids, *Questions of King Milinda*, 2 vols. (*SBE*, 1890, 1894); F. L. Woodward, *The Buddhist Doctrine of Reversible Merit*, Colombo, 1911.

T. W. RHYS DAVIDS.

EXPIATION AND ATONEMENT (Christian).—**1. Scope of the article.**—It is the purpose of this article to trace the history of the doctrine of the Atonement on Christian soil, to distinguish and classify its most important forms, to show their historical antecedents and relations, and to estimate their significance.

The word 'atonement' may be used in two senses: either as a synonym of reconciliation (at-one-ment), or to denote the 'satisfaction or reparation made for wrong or injury, either by giving some equivalent or by doing or suffering something which is received in lieu of an equivalent' (*Cent. Dict.*). It is in the latter sense that the term has been commonly employed in theology. By the Atonement is meant the satisfaction made by Christ for the sins of humanity, however that satisfaction may be conceived in detail. Since the purpose of Christ's atoning work is to reconcile sinners to God, it is not unnatural that some modern theologians should have returned to the original meaning of the word, and maintained that in theology also the true meaning of atonement is reconciliation rather than satisfaction. Such an identification of the process and the result is, however, a departure from the historical usage; and in what follows we shall understand the word in its more technical sense as signifying the action taken by Christ to bring about reconciliation between God and man, rather than the reconciliation itself.

In the sense in which the Atonement has been commonly understood in later theology, both Roman Catholic and Protestant, namely, as an objective satisfaction made by Christ to the Father to secure the forgiveness of man, the doctrine was first clearly formulated by Anselm in the 12th cent. in his famous tract *Cur Deus Homo*. Long before this time, however, the death of Christ had been made the subject of explicit reflexion by Christian theologians; and the answers which they gave to the question why Christ died on Calvary form the necessary introduction to the history of the doctrine of the Atonement. These answers begin within the NT itself, and the rich material which is there contained has proved the point of departure for later speculation.

2. The Biblical basis.—The conceptions which the NT writers bring to the interpretation of the death of Christ fall into five main groups.

(1) The simplest answer finds a sufficient reason for Christ's death in the fact that it took place in fulfilment of OT prophecy. This is the explanation given by St. Peter in Ac 3[18], where no attempt

[1] On the technical meaning of this epithet, see ELDER (Buddhist).

[2] Cf. the note in Rhys Davids, *Dialogues of the Buddha*, London, 1899, i. 76.

[3] *Jātaka* Com. ii. 112; *Dhammapada* Com. 161, 402.

is made to explain why the suffering was necessary. It is enough to know that it was foretold in the sacred book in which the Divine will for man is revealed (cf. Lk $24^{25f.}$).

(2) A more speculative interpretation is suggested by Jesus' own words in Mt 26^{28}. Here the Master compares His death to a covenant-sacrifice sealing the relation between the disciples and God under the new dispensation, as the Paschal lamb marked the union between the Israelites and God under the old. This conception is most fully developed in the Epistle to the Hebrews, where the death of Christ is regarded as at once the fulfilment and the abrogation of the OT sacrificial system. As the High Priest of the New Covenant, Jesus enters the Holy of Holies (*i.e.* the immediate presence of God), not with the blood of bulls and of goats, but with the perfect sacrifice of His own life-blood (He 9^{11-28}), and hence exhibits a type of the true spiritual sacrifice with which alone God is well pleased ($13^{15f.}$). This sacrificial conception underlies the Anselmic doctrine of the Atonement, though in association with other ideas drawn from a different source.[1]

(3) A third interpretation, also suggested by Jesus' own words (Mk 10^{45}), sees in the death of Christ a ransom or purchase price by which His disciples are delivered from the bondage into which they have been brought by sin. The comparison is suggested by the provision made in the Law for the enfranchisement of slaves upon the payment of certain specified sums of money, or by the familiar custom of the ransom of prisoners taken in war. What these money payments accomplished in delivering those in bondage from temporal captivity, that the death of Christ is conceived to effect in securing the deliverance of transgressors from the deadlier bondage of sin (cf. 1 Co 6^{20} 7^{23}, 1 P $1^{18f.}$, Tit 2^{14}, Eph 1^{14}). This idea re-appears in the later history, in the Patristic interpretation of the death of Christ as a ransom paid by God to Satan.

(4) A different explanation again is that which interprets Christ's death after the analogy of the bloody expiation exacted by justice from those who have been guilty of wilful sin (*e.g.* 1 K 2^{31}). The idea of expiation through suffering is a very ancient one. Where a wrong has been done for which the ceremonial system affords no remedy, atonement must be made by the death of the offender or his substitute. This conception finds striking expression in 2 S 24 (cf. 1 Ch 21), where David's sin in numbering the people is atoned for by a pestilence in which seventy thousand of the people perish. It is the pre-supposition of the well-known passage in Is 53, in which the stripes of the righteous servant are the means by which the wicked are healed. In the NT it has its most signal illustration in the Pauline conception of the Crucifixion as the voluntary acceptance on Christ's part, as a result of His self-identification with humanity, of the consequences in suffering, shame, and death to which their own sin had made them liable. This conception re-appears in the later history, in the various forms of the so-called Penal Theory of the Atonement.[2]

(5) In the theology of St. Paul, however, this interpretation of the death of Christ is only one side of his teaching. It is not the death conceived by itself alone which has redemptive significance to St. Paul, but the death as a part of the entire process of the Divine self-identification with humanity, which makes it possible for believers here and now to become partakers of the Divine life of the Christ, and so sharers in His triumph and resurrection. To St. Paul, Christ is not simply the passive Sufferer; He is the conquering Lord, and the benefits both of His suffering and of His conquest are mediated to His disciples by the mystic union with Him which is brought about by faith.

The connexion between the death and the incarnation of Christ is made even closer in the Fourth Gospel. To St. John the suffering of Christ is but an incident in that self-identification of the Divine Word with humanity which constitutes His true redemptive work. It is not the death so much as the life of Christ that has saving power, and Calvary is important not so much for the specific function which it fulfils of itself, as because it is the supreme proof of the completeness of our Lord's subjection to all the conditions of human life.

The contrast just suggested is of importance for the later history. As we follow the interpretation of Christ's death through the centuries, we find two main types of thought predominating. According to the first, the death of Christ is an incident in His incarnate life; according to the second, it is the end for which incarnation takes place. The former is characteristic, on the whole, of the theology of Greek Catholicism; the latter, of that of Roman Catholicism and of Protestantism.

3. The Atonement in Greek theology.[1] — In order to understand the interpretation of Christ's death in Greek theology, we have to bear in mind the general conception of redemption, of which it forms a part. To the Greek, unlike the Latin, the supreme evil from which man needs to be delivered is not guilt, but corruption. Through sin, humanity becomes subject to the law of death. The mind is darkened through ignorance, and the entire nature, as mortal, is destined to destruction. What is needed for the salvation of man, therefore, is not simply forgiveness, but a new transforming power which shall enlighten the mind by the revelation of truth, and transform that which is corrupt and mortal into incorruption. Such a Divine and transforming power entered humanity through the Incarnation. In Christ very God Himself became man, that by partaking of the limitations and sufferings of His human children He might transform them into the likeness of His glorious and Divine life. In the well-known words of Irenæus, 'He became what we are, that He might make us what He is' (*adv. Hær.* v., Preface ['Ante-Nicene Fathers,' ix. 55]).

This conception of redemption finds its classical expression in Athanasius's tract on the Incarnation of the Word (Eng. tr. in 'Nicene and Post-Nicene Fathers,' 2nd ser., iv. 36 ff.). Discussing the problem of redemption, Athanasius asks why it was necessary for man's salvation that God should become man, and answers that it was because thus only could man receive the new life which was the indispensable condition of his salvation. If it were simply a question of guilt, forgiveness might suffice if there were adequate penitence, but forgiveness alone could not deal with the radical corruption of nature which had been produced by sin (vii. 2–4). For this the Incarnation alone was the remedy (xiii. 7). In the Incarnation, Christ became partaker of a complete human experience. He shared our sufferings and limitations; He died the death which was our just due, and so opened the way for us to a share in His Divine and glorious life (viii.). As, when a great king takes up his abode in a lowly village, all the houses share the honour which is conferred by his presence, so all humanity shares the benefits of the Incarnation, and for all a way of salvation and hope is opened (ix. 3, 4). This way of hope is provided through the Resurrection, in which the power of Christ over death is made manifest, and the promise of a like immortality assured to all who put their trust in Him (xxx.–xxxii.). The convincing proof of this victory is found in the fact that Christians—even the weakest of them—no longer fear death, but 'leap to meet it,' preferring it to life on earth (xxviii. f.).

[1] Cf. Ménégoz, *Théol. de l'Ep. aux Hébreux*, p. 231.

[2] On the connexion between the ideas of expiation and of sacrifice, cf. the illuminating discussion of G. F. Moore (art. 'Sacrifice,' in *EBi* iv. 4232 f.).

[1] The references to the Atonement in the ante-Nicene Fathers are discussed by Oxenham (*Catholic Doctrine of the Atonement*, pp. 114–140), and Scott Lidgett (*Spiritual Principle of the Atonement*, p. 420 ff.).

It is clear from this brief review that the death of Christ holds a very different place in this theology from that which it does in the later teaching of the Western world. To Athanasius, as to St. John, death is an incident in the saving work. It is the Incarnation as such that is redemptive. The death takes place because it is a part of the common lot of humanity, which the Redeemer must share. It is described in Biblical language as the payment of a debt (xx. 2), but no theory of its efficacy is given in detail, nor is any of the analogies suggested in the Scripture pressed to its legitimate conclusion.[1]

So far as we find explicit reflexion upon the death of Christ in the Greek Church, it follows the line of the third figure above referred to. In the writings of Origen[2] and of Gregory of Nyssa, as of Irenæus[3] before them, the death of Christ is interpreted as a ransom paid by God to Satan in order to secure the redemption of humanity, which has been brought under his dominion by sin. The theory is differently developed by different writers. Sometimes the right of Satan to the possession of his captives is admitted, and the death is interpreted as a ransom due to the devil on grounds of justice;[4] in other cases this right is denied, and the method actually followed is explained on grounds of fitness, or of God's graciousness in being unwilling to take by force that which was rightfully His.[5]

Gregory of Nyssa regards the deliverance of man as having been secured by deception on God's part, Satan being deceived by the humble appearance of the Redeemer into supposing that he had to do with a mere man, and finding too late that the Deity whose presence he had not perceived escaped his clutches through the Resurrection. This deception he justifies on the ground that it was only paying the devil his due, since he 'effected his deception for the ruin of our nature'; but God, 'Who is at once the just, and good, and wise one, used His device, in which there was deception, for the salvation of him who had perished, and thus not only conferred benefit on the lost one, but on him, too, who had wrought our ruin' (*Great Catechism*, ch. 26, Eng. tr. 'Nicene and Post-Nicene Fathers,' 2nd ser. v. 495).

Fanciful as this theory appears to us to-day, it exercised a great influence, and continued for many centuries to be the prevailing interpretation of the death of Christ. From the Greeks it passed to the Latins, numbering among its adherents such men as Augustine,[6] Gregory the Great,[7] Bernard of Clairvaux,[8] and Peter Lombard.[9] Often the presentation is extremely fanciful, as when Gregory compares our Lord's humanity to the bait placed upon the hook of His divinity (*Moralia*, xxxiii. 7, Eng. tr., Library of Fathers, Oxford, iii. 569), or when Peter Lombard describes the Cross as a mouse-trap baited by our Lord's blood (*Liber Sententiarum*, III. Dist. xix. 1). Yet, it would be a mistake to regard this theory as a mere idle speculation. To the men who held it, it expressed a genuine conviction, and the fact that it secured the endorsement of such teachers as Origen and Augustine shows that it had its roots deep in experience. It is the most signal illustration of the dualistic conception of the world which played so great a rôle in the early history of Christianity—a conception which led in the realm of speculation to the various mediating theories of a Demiurge or Logos, and in the world of practice to monasticism and the ascetic life. To the early Christian theologians, Satan and his angels were very real existences, and a redemption which delivered mankind from the power of the devil was the supreme need of man.[1]

Yet, important as is the place held in history by the theory of a ransom to Satan, it would not be true to say that it is the only point of view represented in the Greek Church. The Greek theology, like that of the later Church, had its different schools of thought, and no single formula can express the point of view completely. If there had been no other influence at work, the study of Scripture, with its varying interpretations of our Lord's death, would have prevented uniformity of statement. So we find different theologians using different figures, and even the same theologian varying his language at different times. The germs of the Moral Influence Theory are found in Irenæus (*adv. Hær.* V. i.), and of the Satisfaction Theory in Origen (*in Num.* hom. xxiv. 1; cf. hom. *in Joann.* xxxviii. 20). Tymms[2] finds in Gregory of Nazianzus anticipations of the Governmental Theory later developed by Grotius; while Origen, in his profounder teaching, regards even the Incarnation itself as but a sort of picture-teaching, through which the Divine Logos prepared the way for that higher insight into truth which constitutes man's true redemption.[3] Thus all the points of view which reappear in the later history are found in germ in the Greek theology.

4. The Atonement in Latin theology.—Latin theology took over from the Greeks the conception of salvation through incarnation; but, in contrast to the Greeks, the Latins found the evil from which man needed deliverance not so much in corruption as in punishment. Where the Greeks thought of God as the Ultimate Reality, the Latins regarded Him as the Supreme Lawgiver or Judge. Hence the death of Christ acquired in Roman theology an independent significance which it did not possess in that of the Greek Church. It was the Divinely appointed atonement for the guilt of man's sin, and incarnation took place primarily in order that this atonement might be wrought. While this theory first finds clear and consistent expression in Anselm's *Cur Deus Homo*, it has its antecedents in the earlier history. Among these may be mentioned Augustine's development of the concept of original sin in his anti-Pelagian writings, and the application of the concept of satisfaction to the problem of forgiveness by Tertullian and Cyprian.

Augustine agrees with Athanasius in his concept of sin as inherited corruption. He differs from the Greek theologian in the emphasis which he places upon the guilt of this sin. It is not mortality, as such, from which man needs to be

[1] Athanasius speaks of the death on the cross, in Pauline fashion, as necessary, in order that Christ might 'bear the curse laid upon us' (xxv. 2); but the context shows plainly that his interest lies along other lines. He tells us that a public death was necessary in order that the Resurrection might be openly established (xxiii.); that the outstretched hands on the cross typify the bringing together of Jews and Gentiles (xxv. 3, 4); that it was fitting that He die in the air, since the purpose of His death was to defeat the prince of the power of the air (5, 6). It is clear that the death, as such, apart from the Resurrection in which it issues, holds no central place in Athanasius's thought. On Athanasius's teaching, cf. Moberly, *Atonement and Personality*, pp. 348–365.

[2] On Origen's view, cf. Scott Lidgett, 432 ff.; Oxenham, 134 ff.; Moberly, 345 ff.

[3] On Irenæus, cf. Scott Lidgett, 430 ff.; Oxenham, 130; Moberly, 343 ff.

[4] So by Augustine, *de Trinitate*, bk. xiii. ch. xiv.

[5] Cf. Irenæus, *adv. Hær.*, bk. v. ch. i.

[6] *de Trinitate*, bk. xiii. chs. xii.–xv.

[7] *Moralia in Librum Job.*

[8] 'Tractatus ad Innocentium II. Pontificem contra quaedam capitula errorum Abaelardi' (*Ep.* 190).

[9] *Liber Sententiarum*, III. dist. xix.

[1] An interesting parallel to the theory of a ransom to Satan is found in Marcion's view that the death of Jesus was a price paid to the God of the Law by the God of grace, in order to secure the redemption of sinners (cf. Burkitt, *The Gospel History and its Transmission*, London, 1906, p. 298 ff.). Tymms (*The Christian Idea of Atonement*, 1904, p. 22) finds in Marcion 'the truest precursor of Anselm in the Ante-Nicene period.'

[2] *Op. cit.* p. 31. The passage in question (wrongly cited by Tymms as xlii. 48) occurs in *Orat.* xlv. 22, where Gregory, after rejecting both the idea that the death of Christ was due to Satan, and that it was required by the Father, accounts for it as necessary to secure the accomplishment of the Divine plan of salvation (οἰκονομία); cf. Ullmann, *Gregorius von Nazianz, der Theologe*, Darmstadt, 1825, p. 456 f.

[3] Cf. W. Adams Brown, *Essence of Christianity*, 1903, p. 66 f.

delivered so much as the separation from God, which is the judicial consequence of his sin. Through the fall of Adam all mankind has become guilty in God's sight, and is justly exposed to His wrath and curse. So great was the guilt of this sin that it has involved all his descendants in a common doom, and, apart from Christ's redemption, even infants dying in infancy are justly condemned to eternal punishment.[1]

A further preparation for Anselm is found in the development of the theory of satisfaction by the earlier Latin theologians, notably Tertullian and Cyprian. According to their teaching, it is possible for man by good works to make satisfaction to God for the sins which he has committed. Tertullian (*de Baptismo*, xx.; cf. *de Oratione*, xxiii.) holds that such satisfaction should precede baptism, while Cyprian contends that it is a remedy for sins committed after baptism (*de Lapsis*, 36). While they did not apply the concept of satisfaction to the death of Christ, their teaching undoubtedly prepared the way for Anselm's theory by making men familiar with the world of thought in which it moves,[2] and, in connexion with similar ideas which had grown up independently on German soil, provided the forms through which his doctrine found natural expression.[3]

Anselm's theory, as is well known, is set forth in his treatise, *Cur Deus Homo*.[4] The title explains the purpose of the book. The words *Cur Deus Homo* should be translated, 'Why a God-man?' not, as they are often rendered, 'Why did God become man?' It is the problem of Christ's Person that engages Anselm's thought. He wishes to know not simply why incarnation took place, but why Christ must unite in a single person the two natures, Divine and human. Why could not God or man alone have answered the purpose just as well? Why was it necessary that there should be a God-man? The answer, in a word, is that it was necessary in order to make possible the Atonement. Only thus could a person be constituted who could render to God the satisfaction necessary for man's sin, and so make possible the redemption which he desired.

The work, which takes the form of a dialogue between the writer and his disciple Boso, begins with an examination of objections to the doctrine of the Atonement, as well as of earlier theories which Anselm rejects as inadequate. Among these is the theory of a ransom to Satan. Anselm finds no reason in justice why God was under any obligation to Satan, in the case of man, which prevented Him from redeeming him by force, if that were necessary (bk. i. ch. vii.). In contrast to this view, Anselm maintains that Christ's Atonement concerns God and not the devil. Man by his sin has violated the honour of God and defiled His handiwork. It is not consistent with the Divine self-respect that He should permit His purpose to be thwarted. Yet this purpose requires the fulfilment by man of the perfect law of God, which by his sin man has transgressed. For this transgression, repentance is no remedy, since penitence, however sincere, cannot atone for the guilt of past sin (bk. i. ch. xx.); nor can any finite substitute, whether man or angel, make reparation. Sin, being against the infinite God, is infinitely guilty, and can be atoned for only by an infinite satisfaction. But this no finite creature can pay (bk. i. ch. xxi.).

Here, then, is the situation: either man must be punished and so God's purpose fail; or else finite man must make an infinite satisfaction, which is impossible. There is only one way of escape, and that is that some one should be found who can unite in his own person the attributes both of humanity and of infinity. This consummation is brought about by the incarnation of Christ. In Christ we have one who is very man, and can therefore make satisfaction to God on behalf of humanity, but who is at the same time very God, and whose person therefore gives infinite worth to the satisfaction which He makes (bk. ii. ch. vii.).

But why, it may be asked, the necessity for the death of Christ? Why could not the life alone atone? Here we reach the most original part of Anselm's theory. The life of Christ, according to Anselm, however perfect, is not available for the purpose of satisfaction, because, as man, Jesus' duty is to do right, and, when He has done all, there is no merit to spare. Not so with His death. This, which, in the case of other men, is the judicial consequence of sin, is, in the case of Christ, the sinless God-man, a work of supererogation—a voluntary offering or sacrifice not due to God, which He freely gives in exchange for the forgiveness of man. This death voluntarily borne when it was not due is the infinite satisfaction which secures the salvation of man (bk. ii. chs. x. and xiv.).

The analogy between this theory and that of a ransom to Satan is obvious. In each case man's deliverance is secured by the acceptance, on the part of the one whose rights need to be conserved, of a substitute which he considers an equivalent in value. But, in the former case, it is the devil whose rights need to be protected; in the latter, it is God. In the former case, again, the satisfaction which is offered, while great in value, is not necessarily infinite, since Satan, as creature, is himself a limited being, whereas in the latter case it is the essence of the theory that the satisfaction rendered should be of infinite value. So far as the infinity of Christ enters into the former theory, it is as an element in the deception which is practised upon Satan. Had he perceived our Lord's Divinity, he would never have consented to the substitution. Humanity was the bait, Divinity the hook, on which Satan was caught. In Anselm's theory, on the other hand, it is Divinity which gives the atoning sacrifice of Christ the priceless worth in God's eyes, through which alone man's redemption is made possible.

There is so much in Anselm's theory which, from our modern point of view, is fanciful and unreal that it is easy to overlook its true significance in the history of doctrine. This is to be found in its clear perception of the fact that that which gives value to the death of Christ is not its penal quality as suffering, but its moral quality as obedience. Christ is not punished for our sins, as in the later Penal Theory; His death is rather a precious gift brought to God, having its value in the spirit of self-sacrifice by which it is inspired. Thus, in spite of the later connexion between Anselm's theory and that of the Reformers, the two belong to distinct types. Anselm's theory, as Ménégoz[1] has rightly shown, is a development of the sacrificial theory of the Epistle to the Hebrews, and has close points of contact with the later ethical satisfaction theories. The Reformers, on the other hand, reject the alternative, which is the major premiss of Anselm's argument, and deny that satisfaction can ever be admitted as a substitute for penalty. This fundamental difference has been obscured by the familiar usage which classes Anselm's and the Reformation theories together as theories of satisfaction.

Few treatises of equal length have exercised so great an influence on the history of thought as the *Cur Deus Homo*. Apart from its influence in Protestantism, of which we shall speak presently, it provided the theoretical basis for the practice of indulgences, which in Anselm's time had already begun to assume substantial proportions. Through the death of Christ, there is laid up a store of supererogatory merit which is available for the remission of the penalties incurred for sins committed after baptism. The administration of this deposit is entrusted to the Church, and is exercised by her through the penitential system. The whole conception of works of supererogation, which fills so great a rôle in the theology of the later Roman Catholicism, has its most signal illustration in the death of Christ. What Christ did in voluntarily submitting to a death which was not His due, gives an example which the saints are to imitate, who thus by their good works increase the store of merit which the Master has begun.

In the later Roman Catholic theology the theory

[1] In his treatment of the death of Christ, Augustine follows the lines laid down by earlier theologians. While different points of view appear in his writings, the theory of a ransom to Satan may be taken as his prevailing view (*de Trinitate*, bk. XII. x.–xv.; cf. Scott Lidgett, 435–441).

[2] Cf. Harnack, *Dogmengeschichte*, iii. 341 (Eng. tr. vi. 54).

[3] On the influence of the Germanic law on the doctrine of satisfaction, cf. Harnack, iii. 288 ff. (Eng. tr. v. 323 ff.).

[4] Eng. tr. by Deane (*St. Anselm*, Chicago, 1903, p. 173 ff.). On Anselm's theory, cf. Harnack, iii. bk. ii. ch. vii. 4 (Eng. tr. vi. 54 ff.); G. Blot, *Étude comparative de l'idée de satisfaction dans le Cur Deus Homo de St. Anselme et dans la théol. antérieure et postérieure*,

[1] *Op. cit.* p. 231; cf. p. 237.

of Anselm is modified at two points. In the first place, the conception of supererogatory merit is extended beyond Christ's death to take in His life of service. In the second place, the principle of strict equivalence, so fundamental to Anselm, is abandoned in favour of a theory which makes the efficacy of the Atonement depend upon the gracious acceptance of God rather than upon its own inherent merit. The first of these changes meets us in the theology of Thomas Aquinas;[1] the second is characteristic of the Scotist theology, and gives rise to the so-called Acceptilation Theory of the Atonement.[2] Both changes have their parallels in the theology of Protestantism.

Contrasting the theology of the Roman with that of the Greek Church, we are struck by the greater prominence of the legalistic element in the former. The older realistic conception of salvation is not denied; it is, indeed, the assumption of the later development, but its significance is altered. Baptism and the Eucharist lose their central position as the sacraments *par excellence*, and become part of a complicated system in which penance and indulgence are the controlling elements. The Eucharist is no longer, as in the Greek Church, a mystic rite through which we become partakers of the incorruptible nature of the Divine Christ; it is the repetition of the sacrifice of Christ upon the cross, and a means of increasing the store of merit which is available for the remission of sins.

Yet here, again, we must beware of too hasty generalizations. In the Roman Church, as in the Greek, many points of view were represented, and no single type of thought adequately expresses the wealth of teaching which its theologians present. In the theory of Scotus, as in the earlier teaching of Gregory of Nazianzus, we have a recognition of principles which reach their full development in the Governmental Theory of the Atonement. Abelard, in his commentary on Romans,[3] anticipates, with a clearness which is remarkable, the later Moral Influence Theories; while in the writings of the mystics, as in Origen's teaching of old, all external media fall away, and salvation is sought and found in the immediate vision of God.[4]

5. The Atonement in the older Protestant theology.—Great as is the importance of the doctrine of the Atonement in Catholic theology, its importance in Protestantism is even greater. To the Catholic theologian the Atonement forms the basis of the whole system of ecclesiastical machinery upon which man's salvation is supposed to depend. To the Protestant it is his warrant for rejecting this machinery as superfluous. Through the atonement of Jesus Christ the price of man's redemption has been paid once for all, and henceforth nothing remains but to appropriate the benefits of this accomplished salvation through faith.

The central importance thus given to the doctrine appears in the language by which it is described. In Protestantism the Atonement and redemption are frequently used as synonyms. Thus the Westminster Confession (iii. 6) speaks of the elect who have 'fallen in Adam' as being 'redeemed by Christ,' whereas the context makes it plain that the reference is to the Atonement.

[1] *Quæst.* XLVIII. art. i.: 'From the beginning of his conception Christ merited eternal salvation for us.' Cf. the following context, where the merit of the life is contrasted with the merit of the death.

[2] *i.e.* the theory that Christ's death owed its efficacy, not to any inherent value which constituted it an exact equivalent for the punishment due from man, but to the good pleasure of God, who was graciously pleased to accept it. On Scotus's view of the Atonement, cf. Seeberg, *Die Theol. des Johannes Duns Scotus*, Leipzig, 1900, p. 281 ff.

[3] iii. 22-26. To Abelard the Cross is the supreme revelation of the love of God, and the means through which a corresponding love is brought about in man.

[4] On the doctrine of the Atonement in the theology of modern Roman Catholicism, cf. Oxenham, *op. cit.* pp. 271-300.

G. B. Stevens' work, entitled *The Christian Doctrine of Salvation*, is really, as an analysis of its contents shows, a treatise on the doctrine of the Atonement; and James Denney, in *The Atonement and the Modern Mind* (London, 1903), says of the Atonement that

'for those who recognise it at all it is Christianity in brief; it concentrates in itself, as in a germ of infinite potency, all that the wisdom, power, and love of God mean in relation to sinful men' (p. 2). So much is this the case that, 'when we speak of the Atonement and the modern mind, we are really speaking of the modern mind and the Christian religion' (*ib.*).

No doubt it is true that not all Protestants carry their emphasis so far. Where the mystic conception of Christianity is made prominent, the older Greek thought, in which incarnation is the central reality, lives on. Thus, to Luther, as to Athanasius and to St. John, the death of Christ is only the culmination of that self-identification with humanity through which we are freed from our bondage into the glorious liberty of the children of God. In Christ we see the revelation of the gracious Father, and are conscious of our own adoption as sons. In Christ we see our present Deliverer, the One who has fought the battle against sin and death and come off victor, and with whom even now we may live and reign in heavenly places. Important as are the sufferings of Christ on our behalf—and no one knew how to paint more vividly than Luther the pain and tears of the Redeemer—they are only a part of a work of redemption which is as varied and many-sided as humanity's needs.[1]

This recognition of the wider aspect of Christ's redeeming work has never been altogether absent from Protestant theology. If there were no other cause, the Bible itself would have compelled a wider outlook. Yet, almost from the first, the death of Christ became the central point upon which the thought of Protestantism was fixed, and in which the redeeming love of God was seen supremely manifested. This central position was due to the fact that it was interpreted not as satisfaction, but as punishment, and hence given a substitutionary significance even greater than that attributed to it in the Anselmic theory.

We may illustrate this changed point of view in the case of Calvin. Calvin, like Luther, takes over many of the presuppositions of the Anselmic view. While denying any absolute necessity on God's part for the death of Christ, he holds with Anselm that, if man is to be redeemed, it must be through the Incarnation and its resulting Atonement. This is necessary because of the infinite guilt of man's sin, which has so 'utterly alienated' mankind from the Kingdom of Heaven that 'none but a person reaching to God can be the medium of restoring peace' (*Inst.* II. xii. 1). Such an efficient Mediator is found in the Person of Christ alone, the Incarnate Redeemer, through whose atoning death the price of man's forgiveness is paid and a way of salvation made open. So far Calvin agrees with Anselm, but in his conception of the nature of the atoning work he differs from him. This he interprets not as a meritorious satisfaction accepted as a substitute for punishment, but as the vicarious endurance by Christ of that punishment itself. While Calvin denies 'that God was ever hostile to Christ or angry with him,' yet in His Divine providence He suffered His Son to go through the experience of those against whom God is thus hostile. In His own consciousness, Christ 'bore the weight of the Divine anger, was smitten and afflicted, and experienced all the signs of an angry and avenging God' (II. xvi. 11). The descent to hell is to Calvin no mere synonym for the experience of death or the entrance to the under world; it involves a literal bearing in the soul of the 'tortures of condemned and ruined man' (*ib.* 10).

In order to understand this change of emphasis, we have to recall Calvin's conception of God. To Calvin, retributive justice is of the essence of Deity. It is not simply a question of God's honour, which cannot be satisfied without the obedience which He has commanded; it is a question of His holiness, which is in eternal opposition to sin. God is gracious indeed, in the sense that He desires to forgive; but this grace or mercy can be exercised only if justice is satisfied, and justice requires, in every case, a punishment commensurate to the sin; hence the necessity for giving the death of Christ penal significance. In Him, God the Father has graciously provided a substitute to

[1] On Luther's view of the Atonement, cf. Köstlin, *Luthers Theol., in ihrer geschichtl. Entwickl. und ihrem inneren Zusammenhange*[2], Stuttgart, 1883, ii. 402 ff. (Eng. tr. by Hay, *The Theology of Luther*, Philadelphia, ii. 388 ff.).

take the place of guilty men, and so make possible a forgiveness which is at the same time consistent with justice.

It would be unjust to Calvin's views to ignore the ethical aspects of Christ's suffering. Like Anselm, he refers more than once to the part which Christ's obedience had in bringing about man's salvation; nor did this obedience begin with His death. In Ro 5[19] St. Paul teaches that the ground of pardon which exempts from the curse of the Law extends to the whole life of Christ. From the moment when He assumed the form of a servant, He began, in order to redeem us, to pay the price of deliverance (II. xvi. 5). Thus, the modern conception which sees in the death the culmination of the life-work of Christ is already anticipated in the *Institutes*.

In the later Calvinistic theology the close connexion between the death and the life of Christ is no longer maintained. The obedience of Christ is separated from His suffering as having a distinct significance. It is the means through which Christ fulfils our righteousness, and so merits for us the reward which we are ourselves unable to earn; even as His death is the payment of our penalty, and so the means of securing our forgiveness (cf. *Westm. Conf.* viii. 5; A. A. Hodge, *The Atonement*, p. 248).

But it is in its view of the means by which the connexion is made between the atoning work of Christ and those for whose benefit it was accomplished that Protestantism differs most signally from Catholicism. In the Calvinistic theology this connexion is brought about by the Divine decree. God who, from all eternity, foreordained the atonement of Christ, determined also those who should receive its benefits; and in due course, through His Holy Spirit, creates in them the new life which Christ has merited by His obedience. Infinite as is the value of Christ's atoning work, it avails for those, and for those only, for whom, in the Divine plan, it was determined from the first (see, further, art. ELECTION).

With the rise of Arminianism (*q.v.*) this doctrine of limited atonement became a subject of increasing protest. Men who had no difficulty in accepting the Calvinistic doctrine of atonement as substitutionary punishment shrank back appalled from the conception of an arbitrary limitation of its scope. In order to reconcile their view of the limited effects of the Atonement with a belief in the universal love of God, they took refuge in a theory of the will which gave man himself the power to accept or to reject the mercy offered in Christ, and hence made him the arbiter of his own destiny. This conception of a universal atonement, limited in its results by man's freedom, has become characteristic of Arminian theology, and has not been without its influence in Calvinistic circles as well.

But the Penal Theory was subjected to even severer criticism by the Socinians.[1] They attacked the entire conception of substitutionary punishment, which was the premiss of the traditional theory. According to the *Racovian Catechism* (§ v. ch. 8), punishment and forgiveness are inconsistent ideas. If a man is punished, he cannot be forgiven, and *vice versa*. Under the theory of distributive justice, punishment, being a matter of the relation between individual guilt and its consequences, is strictly untransferable. But if, for argument, it be granted that this is not the case, then God is clearly unjust if, having received an infinite atonement, He does not forgive all. What kind of a God must He be, it is asked, who, when one drop of Christ's blood would have sufficient value to atone for a world's sin, yet suffered His own Son to endure such needless torture?[2]

So far as their positive teaching was concerned, the Socinians held a form of the Moral Influence Theory, Christ's death being regarded as a declaration of God's love and an incentive to lead men to seek salvation through Him; but their great importance is historical rather than constructive. It was as a result of their criticisms that Hugo Grotius wrote his well-known work on the *Satisfaction of Christ*, in which for the first time the so-called Governmental Theory of the Atonement found systematic expression. This theory has exercised so extended an influence that it needs careful consideration.

Grotius himself is apparently unconscious of any departure from the traditional view. As the title of his book implies,[1] he proposes to write a defence of the orthodox view of the satisfaction of Christ against Socinian objections; yet it needs only a superficial survey of his work to show how profoundly he has been influenced by the arguments which he opposes. He begins by denying, with Socinus, the applicability of the category of distributive justice to the atoning work of Christ. But he differs from Socinus in substituting therefor the category of public justice. God does not, indeed, deal with men as a judge, who administers strict justice in the individual sense, but He does deal with them as a governor who is obliged to conserve the interests of the common welfare. In the course of His rectoral justice He may relax the law if sufficient cause appear, provided it can be done without danger to the interests of public justice (ch. iii. [Eng. tr. p. 72 f.]). This is what actually happens in the atonement of Christ. Christ's death is a substitute for punishment, a suffering inflicted by God and voluntarily accepted by Christ, which works upon men by moral influence (cf. pp. 107–109) in order to conserve the ends of righteousness. Such suffering on Christ's part is necessary, since forgiveness on the basis of repentance alone might be misinterpreted by men and lead to grave carelessness (ch. v. [p. 102 f.]). It is no more inconsistent with God's justice than any other suffering on the part of the innocent for the guilty. The Socinians themselves admit that such suffering is a part and a consequence of our common relationship as members one of another (ch. iv. [pp. 82, 85]). The Governmental Theory simply draws the conclusion which naturally follows from this premiss.

We have already pointed out the fact that certain features of the Governmental Theory were anticipated in the Greek Church in the teaching of Gregory of Nazianzus. In the Latin Church it has its analogies both in the Scotist theory of the *Acceptilatio* and in the Moral Theory of Abelard. It agrees with the Scotist view in its denial that punishment is necessary to satisfy any inherent need of God's nature. It differs from it, however, in that it conceives God as governor, and as being under a constraint, as real as, if different in kind from, that which moved the Deity of distributive justice. The governor, unlike the judge, may temper justice with mercy, but the motives which lead him so to temper it are never arbitrary, but are found in the state of society itself, of which he is the guardian and the ruler. The Governmental Theory agrees with the Moral Theory in that it conceives the nature of the Atonement as determined by the moral effects which it is designed to promote; but it differs from the latter in the fact that the motive to which the Atonement appeals is conceived as fear rather than as love. In Christ's death, men see what will be their fate if they do not repent, and so are moved to repentance and faith.

In the extent and permanence of its influence upon Protestant thought the Governmental Theory is comparable with the Penal Theory alone. Among thoughtful Arminians it has practically supplanted the older Penal Theory, and is declared by Professor Miley[2] to be the only theory of the Atone-

[1] The Socinian view is most fully set forth in the writings of Faustus and Lælius Socinus, collected in the *Bibliotheca Fratrum Polonarum* (6 vols., Amsterdam, 1626). Its official statement is found in the *Racovian Catechism* (1605, Eng. tr. by Rees, London, 1818).

[2] It is interesting to note that a similar objection was made by William Pynchon, a New England Puritan, in his *Meritorious Price of Our Redemption* (London, 1650)—a book which Foster describes as 'the first outbreak of the independent spirit of Congregationalism. . . . The book was first burned and afterwards refuted by order of the General Court, and Mr. Pynchon found it convenient to return to England, where he died' (*Genetic Hist. of the New England Theology*, Chicago, 1907, p. 16 f.).

[1] *Defensio fidei Catholicæ de satisfactione Christi*. The work was written in 1638, and is printed in vol. iv. of the Amsterdam ed. of 1679 (p. 293 ff.). An Eng. tr. by F. H. Foster appeared in the *Bibliotheca Sacra* for 1879, and was reprinted in Andover in 1889.

[2] *Systematic Theology*, New York, 1894, ii. 169.

ment logically consistent with Arminian principles. But its influence is by no means confined to Arminianism. Through Jonathan Edwards (*q.v.*) and his successors it has passed over into Calvinism and has been widely held, not only by New England Congregationalists, but also by the New School Presbyterians, with whom they have been closely affiliated. Albert Barnes has left on record, in the introduction to his well-known treatise on the Atonement (Philadelphia, 1859, p. 4), the difficulty which he felt with the older form of the doctrine, and the relief which was afforded to his mind by the Governmental Theory. Those Calvinists, trained in the older orthodoxy, who have shared Barnes' sense of difficulty with the legal categories of the older theories have commonly found their relief where he did.[1]

6. The Atonement in modern Protestantism.—With the growing acceptance of modern critical methods we find an increasing disposition to emphasize the moral and spiritual elements in the atonement of Christ and, in particular, to relate His death more closely to the life-work of which it forms a part. While the older theories still live on in Protestantism, and some of the most able expositions both of the Penal and of the Governmental Theories have been written within the last half-century, the pre-suppositions upon which they rest in their older form have been gradually undermined. The conception of God as a being with whom justice is necessary and mercy optional, so characteristic of the older Calvinism, has been largely abandoned. The notion of atonement as satisfying some mysterious necessity in God, apart from the realization of the redemptive purpose which Christ has revealed as His supreme aim, appears increasingly unsatisfactory. Even where the fact of the Atonement is still heartily accepted and the death of Christ made central in Christian teaching, we find the effort to get a conception of it which shall relate it more closely to the principles and ideals that have made themselves controlling in other departments of Christian theology.

A potent influence in bringing about this change has been the new view of the Bible. It was characteristic of the older discussions of the Atonement that, whatever might be the particular view advocated, whether Legal or Governmental or Moral, it was identified without question with the teaching of the Divine word.[2] With the breaking down of the older mechanical theories of inspiration, such an easy identification is no longer possible. It is clear that what we have in the Bible is a series of parallel and, in part, differing interpretations, rather than a single consistent dogmatic theory; and no one of the later interpretations can claim exclusive Biblical authority for itself.

The recognition of this diversity of view-point has sometimes been made an excuse for abandoning altogether the attempt to frame a consistent doctrine. A distinction is drawn between the *fact* of the Atonement, faith in which is essential, and the *theory*, as to which men may differ without loss; and even theologians who along other lines would be the first to repudiate the Roman doctrine of an implicit faith have, in the case of this particular doctrine, declared themselves frankly agnostic.[1] But such an attitude, however convenient as a temporary resting-place, is difficult to maintain for any length of time. If the Atonement is permanently to retain in Protestantism the strong hold which it has hitherto had upon the faith of Christians, it must be related to the world of thought in which modern men are living, and shown to be as capable of explanation and defence in the moral and spiritual terms which have become controlling for our modern thought of God as in the legal and judicial categories so familiar to the older theology. It is characteristic of recent works on the Atonement that they attempt such a re-translation. This attempt is not confined to the members of any particular party or school of thought. It is as noticeable in the case of those who still hold the substance of the older theories as in those who reject them. An example in point is R. W. Dale's well-known treatise on *The Atonement.*[2]

Dale's book is interesting as the most serious effort which has been made in recent times to retain a penal significance in the death of Christ, while avoiding the artificiality and legalism of the older statements. It is not easy to give a brief account of the author's discussion, but the essence of it consists in the fact that he conceives the death of Christ as the suffering justly inflicted upon Christ as the voluntary representative and head of the race, in order to satisfy the eternal law of righteousness which is one in essence with the will of God.

'The only conception of punishment,' he writes (p. 383), 'which satisfies our strongest and most definite moral convictions, and which corresponds to the place it occupies both in the organisation of society and in the moral order of the universe, is that which represents it as pain and loss inflicted for the violation of a law.'

If the older theologians were at fault in their treatment of the Atonement, it was not, says Dale, in their insistence upon the penal element in Christ's sufferings, but in their arbitrary limitation of its effects, and, above all, in their failure to give adequate expression to the moral and spiritual side of the relationship which constitutes Him, not only the substitute, but the head and representative of the race (p. 433).

Even more striking, as an example of the effort to translate an older theory into modern terms, is Scott Lidgett's suggestive book, *The Spiritual Principle of the Atonement, as a Satisfaction made to God for Sins of the World.*[3] Lidgett agrees with Dale in his conception of the nature of punishment, but he differs from him in finding the necessity for penal satisfaction in the very nature of fatherhood itself.

'Of course,' writes Lidgett (p. 268), 'the magnanimity of fatherly love raises it above the treasuring up and the exact vindication of merely personal wrongs. But, in the case of true fatherhood, what is personal stands for something that is more than personal. In dealing with a disobedient and rebellious child, the father has to do justice to his own character and will as an authority over the child—an authority representing the ideal of what the child should become, and guiding him on the way to its realisation. He has to assert the sanctity of the law which has been broken, and to secure its recognition. He has to bring home to the child the consciousness of wrongdoing. All this is the work of punishment. It is most truly in the interests of the child himself. . . . The punishment which has been inflicted by the father is made the very means of uttering the conversion of the child.'

Both Lidgett and Dale, in common with the older Protestant writers on the Atonement, agree that that which gives the death of Christ its saving power is its penal quality, or, in other words, the suffering which Christ endured as our substitute or representative. This principle is, however,

[1] On the later history of the Governmental Theory, cf. Miley, ii. 158 f.; F. H. Foster, Introd. to his tr. of Grotius, pp. xii–lvii; McLeod Campbell, *The Nature of the Atonement*, p. 65 ff.; and esp. Park, *The Atonement*, Boston, 1863; a collection of Discourses and Treatises by Edwards, Smalley, Maxey, Emmons, Griffin, Burge, and Weeks, illustrating various phases of the so-called 'Edwardean' (*i.e.* Governmental) Theory of the Atonement.

[2] This is especially noticeable in the discussion between Socinus and Grotius. On either side the Biblical proof is given a place of central importance.

[1] So Horton, in *Faith and Criticism*, New York, 1893, p. 187 ff.; cf. Dale, *loc. cit.* 3; Scott Lidgett, 490 ff.

[2] The Congregational Union Lecture for 1875, 14th ed., London, 1892.

[3] 27th Fernley Lecture, July 1897, 3rd ed., London, 1902.

challenged by an increasing number of writers, who deny that there is anything redemptive in suffering as such, and find the essence of Christ's atoning work in its moral quality as obedience. We may illustrate this position in the case of two works which have exercised a potent influence upon recent English thought concerning the Atonement. The first is McLeod Campbell's *Nature of the Atonement*;[1] the second, Horace Bushnell's *Vicarious Sacrifice*.[2]

Campbell's interest, as the title of his book implies, centres in the question of the nature of the Atonement, or, in other words, the question, What is the quality in Christ's sufferings and death which gives them value for God and fits them to promote the redemptive ends which they are designed to serve? The older Protestant theology, both in its Penal and in its Governmental form, found this atoning quality in the pain of Christ's sufferings considered as pain. In the Penal Theory this pain was regarded as satisfying a demand in the Divine nature itself; in the Governmental Theory, as necessary to provide an example to influence men. Neither of these answers seems to Campbell satisfactory. The Penal Theory is unsatisfactory, since it interposes between man and God an obstacle which is unreal. The Governmental Theory is unsatisfactory, since the motive on which it relies, being that of fear rather than that of love, is inadequate to produce that spiritual transformation which it is the object of the theory to secure. Both failures are due to the lack of a consistent application of the Biblical principle concerning the condition of forgiveness. This condition, according to Campbell, is repentance, and repentance alone. The difficulty in the way of God's forgiving sin is not that there is any barrier on His part to be cleared away which penitence cannot remove, but that, as a matter of fact, men do not truly repent; and this, in turn, is due to the fact that no motive has yet been brought to bear upon them strong enough to overcome their existing sinful habits and desires. In this condition of things Campbell finds the key to the true nature of the Atonement. What is necessary, if mankind is to be saved, is that some man shall be found who shall estimate at its full heinousness the significance of human sin, shall accept in filial reverence and submission the consequences in suffering and pain which this sin has inevitably brought in its train, and so shall set in motion those moral influences by which other men, following his example, shall be drawn to a like repentance. This is what happens in the atonement of Christ. In the spirit in which He met His suffering and death we have the supreme revelation of the true attitude which man should take toward sin. Christ on the cross identifies Himself by sympathy with suffering humanity. He utters in reverent submission His Amen to God's judgment of sin, and so, for the first time, exhibits in the most impressive way the condition upon whose fulfilment alone forgiveness depends (p. 117).

Campbell's critics have objected that in substituting for the older doctrine of vicarious punishment his newer teaching concerning vicarious repentance, he has simply replaced one difficulty by another. They argue that the conception of vicarious penitence is no easier to hold than that of vicarious punishment; indeed, it is less easy, since repentance as a personal act of the individual is strictly untransferable, whereas punishment, being inflicted by another, may conceivably be visited upon a substitute. Such a criticism, however, does not touch Campbell's main contention. He is not concerned primarily with the problem how the benefit of Christ's repentance can be transferred to others, but rather with the question what condition must be fulfilled if man is to be forgiven at all. This he maintains to be repentance pure and simple, and in this contention he has been followed by not a few leading writers on the doctrine who differ from him at other points.[1]

To the question how the penitence of Christ avails for others, Campbell has a very simple answer. It is by the moral influence of His example. There is in every one of us the conviction that we ought to repent if only we knew how. In Christ we have presented to us the ideal penitent. As He identifies Himself with our sin, so in faith and trust we identify ourselves with His repentance, and through this self-identification there is gradually wrought in us that moral transformation which enables us in our turn to repeat Christ's supreme condemnation of sin, and so to enjoy that full forgiveness which God is ever ready to grant to genuine repentance (p. 153).

This conception of the death of Christ, as primarily efficacious through the moral influence which it exerts upon those who witness it, finds classic expression in the second of the books referred to, Bushnell's *Vicarious Sacrifice*. The problem which Bushnell sets himself to solve is that of the possibility and the nature of substitution in religion; and the conclusion to which he comes is that in the case of a moral and spiritual religion, like Christianity, this is possible only in the sphere of the moral and spiritual relationships, of which the family rather than the law-court or the civil government gives us the most helpful example. In love, Bushnell discovers a vicarious principle, involving, on the one hand, the self-identification of the lover with the object loved, and, on the other, a corresponding transformation of the one loved through the response of his spirit to the new moral influences of which he is thus made the subject. He illustrates this principle in the case of motherhood, of friendship, and of patriotism, and finds in it the revelation of a universal law which goes back, in the last analysis, to God Himself. All good beings, he maintains, are in the principle of vicarious sacrifice (i. 53), and a cross is in God's perfections from eternity (i. 73).

Upon the fact of this law of sacrifice, valid both for God and for man, Bushnell bases his doctrine of the Atonement. In the sufferings and death of Christ the Holy God identifies Himself in sympathy with the sins and sufferings of His human children, feels in His own experience the burden of the painful consequences which have been brought upon them by their misdeeds, and through the revelation of His self-sacrificing love calls forth on their part that corresponding love for Him which makes possible their forgiveness and ultimate restoration. All the old sacrificial symbols which are so deeply inwrought into the NT language and which were so efficacious in the older revival preaching are, according to Bushnell, simply symbolical ways of illustrating this profound truth (i. 449 ff.).

In contrast to the theory of McLeod Campbell, where emphasis is laid on the value for God of Christ's sufferings, that of Bushnell is sometimes described as purely subjective (so, most recently, by Stevens in his *Christian Doctrine of Salvation*). There is a certain plausibility in this description, in that in Bushnell's case, as in that of Abelard before him, interest centres in the manward rather than the Godward aspect of Christ's work; but, if by the term 'subjective' it is meant to describe a theory which conceives it possible to express the full significance of Christ's work in terms of human experience alone, the characterization is plainly misleading. To Bushnell, as well as to Campbell, the Atonement is a matter which concerns God as well as man, and that which gives Christ's sufferings their redemptive power is the fact that in the form of a human experience they reveal to us what from the beginning has been God's own attitude towards human sin.[2]

---

[1] *The Nature of the Atonement in Relation to Remission of Sins and Eternal Life*[6], London, 1886.

[2] *The Vicarious Sacrifice grounded in Principles interpreted by Human Analogies*, 2 vols., New York, 1891.

[1] *e.g.* R. C. Moberly and W. L. Walker.

[2] The Godward aspect of the Atonement is more fully developed in vol. ii. of the *Vicarious Sacrifice*. Here Bushnell propounds a theory of the Divine self-propitiation through suffering in which the analogy of human experience is used to illustrate the nature of God's attitude towards sin. The volume,

Both Bushnell and Campbell are concerned primarily with the Atonement as it affects the relation between God and the individual; but, from the first, it has been recognized that the work of Christ has a larger meaning. It was designed not simply to save individuals, but to redeem humanity, and has as its result the establishment of the Kingdom of God among men. One of the most striking features of modern thought regarding the Atonement is its emphasis on this wider social significance. Apart from the Governmental Theory, to which we have already alluded, this emphasis takes two forms. The first, which is more prominently represented among Anglican theologians, regards the Church as an institution, as the continuation of the Incarnation, and emphasizes the connexion between the Atonement and the Sacraments. The second, more ethical in its conception of salvation, takes its departure from the social nature of personality, and finds the primary object of Christ's death in the creation of a community in which the bond of union is the acceptance of his principle of self-sacrificing love. We may take Moberly's suggestive book on *Atonement and Personality*[1] as an example of the first type, and Ritschl's *Justification and Reconciliation*[2] as an example of the second.

So far as his conception of the Atonement itself is concerned, Moberly agrees with Campbell in finding its essence in penitence (p. 110). Like Campbell, he maintains that a perfect repentance, if it could be found, would constitute an adequate atonement. Like Campbell, again, he denies that such repentance is possible to man alone. But what is not possible for man alone is possible for the God man. In the sinless Christ we have one in whom God's ideal for humanity has been for the first time realized, and in His perfect obedience and penitence an adequate atonement for the sin of humanity has at last been made.

But how are the benefits of the Atonement to be imparted to others? It is at this point that Moberly finds Campbell's view inadequate. The moral influence on which Campbell relies he finds not enough. There must be a real identity, if the atonement which Christ makes is to be really ours (p. 405). This identity Moberly secures through his doctrine of the Holy Spirit. In the Spirit, Christ Himself enters humanity and becomes the basis of its higher life.

'The Spirit of the Incarnate Christ, [is] made, through the Incarnation, the Spirit of Man' (p. 203). 'He is the subjective realization within, and as, ourselves, of the Christ who was first manifested objectively and externally, for our contemplation and love, in Galilee and on the Cross. He is more and more, as the Christian consummation is approached, the Spirit within ourselves of Righteousness and Truth, of Life and of Love. He is more, indeed, than within us. He is the ultimate consummation of ourselves' (p. 204). Only through this indwelling Spirit who is 'Christ in the man' (p. 227) is it possible to realize, what true personality means.

But where and how do we actually find this mysterious union realized among men? Moberly answers—in the Church. In organized Christianity with its sacramental system we find the sphere and instrument of the Spirit's influence, nay, more, the Spirit Himself become incarnate in the lives of living men.

'The Church, then, is, in fact, the Spirit of Christ, communicated to the spirits of those who recognize, and believe in, His Person and work; it is the disciples of Christ, made Christian in very deed by participation in the Spirit of Christ' (p. 259).

Like Moberly, Ritschl emphasizes the social significance of the Atonement; but, in place of the mystic bond of an identity of nature mediated through the Sacraments, he puts the ethical conception of community of purpose. According to Ritschl, the purpose of God is not primarily the salvation of individuals as such, but their union in the redeemed society of the Kingdom of God. But this is possible only as there is revealed to men an end at once simple enough and far-reaching enough to transcend all legal and limited ideals, and reinforced by motive power strong enough to secure its inner appropriation in spite of every obstacle. Such a revelation is given to us in the life-work of Christ. In him we see One whose life was dominated from the beginning to the end by the principle of trust in God and love for others, and who, in this trust and love, found a power able to make Him victor over obstacles otherwise insuperable. As such a moral conqueror, He becomes to others the pledge of the possibility of like victory in their case, if only they in turn accept His life-purpose in similar love and trust.

This is the meaning of Ritschl's much-discussed teaching concerning the Church as the object of the Divine justification (vol. iii. ch. ii. 20 [Eng. tr. p. 108 ff.]). By this he means not simply that the life of faith, upon which the Reformers based their assurance of the forgiveness of sins, carries with it inevitably devotion to that universal purpose of love which Jesus has revealed as the will of the Father; he means that the experience of forgiveness itself is possible only as a man makes Jesus' wider social purpose his own. The life of trust and the life of service are not two independent elements in the Christian life; they are two aspects of one and the same experience. As Jesus fulfilled His own true relation to His Father through His willingness to suffer even death itself for the sake of His brothers, so His disciples in their turn realize their true relation to their Father by following Him in like devotion.

It is in the light of this conception that we are to understand Ritschl's view of the Atonement. In his chapter on the 'Person and Life-work of Christ' (ch. vi.) he criticizes the older Protestant treatment of the work of Christ on the ground that it separates things which belong together. It contrasts the sufferings and death of Christ, as an evidence of His humiliation, with His resurrection and second advent, as the proof of His exaltation. But, according to Ritschl, this contrast is misleading. The priestly work of Christ is not something apart from His kingly work—a condition which must be fulfilled in order that that may be accomplished. It is itself an element in that moral victory over sin and death which evidences His Divine power and constitutes Him the world's Redeemer. The sufferings of Christ have not merely ethical value as a price paid by Christ to God for the redemption of man. They have religious value as a revelation of God's purpose towards man, and, above all, as an assurance of that Divine power which is able to make man the victor over the worst foes. As such a revelation, they are harmonious with His whole life-work—a necessary condition of the accomplishment of His purpose, namely, the establishment of God's Kingdom among men.[1]

So we see the latest German thought about the Atonement turning back to the point of view of the earliest Greek theology, and trying to gain a conception of Christ's redemption which shall represent it less as a single act performed once for all in the death upon the cross than as the natural outworking and consummation of the meaning and purpose of His entire life.

which was composed eight years after the first, was originally designed to take the place of its third and fourth sections, but the advice of friends led to the abandonment of the plan, and the two versions stand side by side as vols. i. and ii.

[1] London, 1901.

[2] *Die christliche Lehre von der Rechtfertigung und Versöhnung*, 3 vols., Bonn, 1870–74; 3rd ed. 1888–89 [Eng. tr. of vol. iii. by Mackintosh and Macaulay, Edinburgh, 1900].

[1] In his suggestive book, *The Cross and the Kingdom, as viewed by Christ Himself and in the Light of Evolution* (Edinburgh, 1902), W. L. Walker follows Ritschl in bringing out the close connexion between the Atonement and the Kingdom of God (cf. esp. p. 271 ff.).

7. Summary and conclusion.—As we look back over the history which we have thus briefly passed in review, we are struck by the great variety of opinion represented in our survey.[1] Whether we consider the Atonement from the point of view of its nature, its object, its necessity, or the means by which it is made practically effective in men's lives, we find differences of view so striking as to make any attempt at harmony seem hopeless. The atoning character of Christ's death is now found in its penal quality as suffering, now in its ethical character as obedience. It is represented now as a ransom to redeem men from Satan, now as a satisfaction due to the honour of God, now as a penalty demanded by His justice. Its necessity is grounded now in the nature of things, and, again, is explained as the result of an arrangement due to God's mere good pleasure or answering His sense of fitness. The means by which its benefits are mediated to men are sometimes mystically conceived, as in the Greek theology of the Sacrament; sometimes legally, as in the Protestant formula of imputation; and, still again, morally and spiritually, as in the more personal theories of recent Protestantism. Surveying differences so extreme, one might well be tempted to ask, with some recent critics, whether, indeed, we have here to do with an essential element in Christian doctrine, or simply with a survival of primitive ideas whose presence in the Christian system constitutes a perplexity rather than an aid to faith.

Yet, such an opinion, however natural, would be misleading. The differences which we have discussed are not greater than may be paralleled in the case of every other Christian doctrine. When we isolate any doctrine from its environment, it is easy to represent it as a record of inconsistencies and contradictions; but, when we look below the surface and consider the underlying causes of the changes in question, we find it necessary to revise so superficial a judgment. These causes have to do with the conception of God and of His relations in the world. Where God is conceived, as in the old Greek theology, in physical or metaphysical terms, as the absolute Spirit, immutable and incorruptible, who saves man by making him partaker of his own immortal life, the Atonement necessarily becomes a mere incident in the life of the Incarnate One, and the type of thought represented by Athanasius is the result. Where, as in the theology of Roman Catholicism and the earlier Protestantism, God is conceived primarily as Governor or Judge, dealing with men in terms of justice, either private or public, legal phraseology becomes the natural expression of religious faith, and the various substitutionary theories, whether in the form of satisfaction or of penalty, are the result. Where, on the other hand, as in modern times, the ethical and spiritual categories are controlling, the Atonement will in like manner be given an ethical and spiritual interpretation; and the various questions as to its nature, its necessity, and its effects will be answered along the lines followed by the later Protestant writers whom we have passed in review. The attitude which one will take towards any of the specific questions under discussion will be determined in the last analysis by his answer to the underlying question, Which of these general ways of conceiving God is, on the whole, most adequate to express the Christian view?

LITERATURE.—1. On the history of the doctrine in general, cf. the relevant sections in J. C. Baur, *Die christl. Lehre von der Versöhnung*, Tübingen, 1838; W. F. Gess, *Christi Person und Werk*, Basel, 1870 ff.; A. Harnack, *Dogmengeschichte* [Eng. tr., *Hist. of Dogma*, 1894–9]; F. Loofs, *Dogmengeschichte*[4], Halle, 1906; F. Nitzsch, *Dogmengeschichte*, Berlin, 1870; H. N. Oxenham, *Catholic Doctrine of the Atonement*, London, 1865; A. Ritschl, *Rechtfertigung und Versöhnung*[4], Bonn, 1895–1902, vol. i. [Eng. tr. 1872], vol. iii. [Eng. tr. 1900]; J. Rivière, *Dogme de la rédemption*, Paris, 1905; G. Thomasius, *Christi Person und Werk*, Erlangen, 1886 f. Cf. also J. Scott Lidgett, *Spiritual Principle of the Atonement*, London, 1901, pp. 419–88; R. C. Moberly, *Atonement and Personality*, do. 1901, pp. 324–412; G. B. Stevens, *Christian Doctrine of Salvation*, Edinburgh, 1905, pp. 136–261.

2. On the Biblical basis of the doctrine, besides the relevant sections in the Biblical Theologies and Dictionaries of the Bible, cf. A. Cave, *The Scriptural Doctrine of Sacrifice*[2], Edinburgh, 1890; T. J. Crawford, *The Doctrine of Holy Scripture respecting Atonement*[2], do. 1875; R. W. Dale, *The Atonement* London, 1875 ([14]1892), pp. 65–264; J. Denney, *The Death of Christ; its Place and Interpretation in the NT*[2], London, 1902; C. C. Everett, *The Gospel of Paul*, Boston, 1893; E. Ménégoz, *La Théologie de l'épître aux Hébreux*, Paris, 1894; G. F. Moore, art. 'Sacrifice,' in *EBi*; Ritschl, *op. cit.* vol. ii.; W. Sanday, *Priesthood and Sacrifice*, London, 1900.

3. Systematic treatises: besides the works mentioned in the body of the article, cf. A. Barry, *The Atonement of Christ*, London, 1871; R. S. Candlish, *The Atonement, its Efficacy and Extent*, Edinburgh, 1867; W. N. Clarke, *Outline of Christian Theology*, do. 1898, pp. 321–362; D. C. Davies, *The Atonement and Intercession*, do. 1901; C. A. Dinsmore, *Atonement in Literature and Life*, Boston, 1906; C. C. Hall, *The Gospel of the Divine Sacrifice*, New York, 1896; T. Häring, *Zur Versöhnungslehre: eine dogmatische Untersuchung*, Göttingen, 1893; A. A. Hodge, *The Atonement*, Philadelphia, 1867; J. T. Hutchinson, *A View of the Atonement*, New York, 1897; C. Hodge, *Systematic Theology*, London, 1872–73, vol. ii. pp. 464–591; T. W. Jenkyn, *The Extent of the Atonement in its Relation to God and the Universe*, Boston, 1835; B. Jowett, *Com. on Romans*, London, 1894; J. Kaftan, *Dogmatik*, Tübingen, 1897, p. 531 ff.; G. Kreibig, *Die Verhsöhnungslehre auf Grund des christlichen Bewusstseins dargestellt*, Berlin, 1878; J. F. D. Maurice, *The Doctrine of Sacrifice*, new ed., London, 1893; L. Pullan, *The Atonement*, do. 1906; A. Sabatier, *La Doctrine de l'expiation et son évolution historique*, Paris, 1901 [Eng. tr., London, 1904]; W. G. T. Shedd, *Dogmatic Theology*, New York, 1889–94, vol. ii. p. 378 ff.; D. W. Simon, *Reconciliation by Incarnation*, Edinburgh, 1898; G. Smeaton, *The Doctrine of the Atonement*, do. 1868; A. H. Strong, *Systematic Theology*, New York, 1907, vol. ii. p. 713 ff.; Turretin, *On the Atonement of Christ*, Eng. tr., New York, 1859; T. V. Tymms, *The Christian Idea of Atonement*, London, 1904; R. Wardlaw, *The Extent of the Atonement*, Glasgow, 1830; J. M. Wilson, *The Gospel of the Atonement*, London, 1899; *The Atonement in Modern Religious Thought; a theological Symposium*, do. 1900; S. Plantz, art. 'Vicarious Sacrifice,' in Hastings' *DCG*.

W. ADAMS BROWN.

EXPIATION AND ATONEMENT (Egyptian).—No certain trace of any rite or ceremony analogous to the Sem. atonement-sacrifice (*kippûrîm*) or the Gr. piacular expiation can be found in Egyp. religion so long as it was uninfluenced by Sem. observances. The close connexion with Palestine, which began in the time of the XVIIIth and reached its height under the XIXth and XXth dynasties, resulted in the temporary introduction of many Sem. deities into the Egyp. pantheon; and with them, no doubt, came many Sem. religious observances, among them that of the atonement-sacrifice. But the anti-Semitic feeling, which was brought about by the national resistance to the Assyrians in the 8th and 7th cent. B.C., resulted in the expulsion of the Sem. deities, at any rate from the official pantheon; and with them went their cult-observances. Any trace which may be found of the *kippûrîm*-rite in Egypt is probably to be regarded as of this Sem. origin (as was certainly the rite of burnt-offering), and dating from this period of Sem. religious influence. The Egyp. conception of sacrifice does not seem to have included any idea of expiation for sin. The Egyptian placed fruit, cakes, and cooked meat on a mat before the painted and robed figure of his deity, and burnt incense before it, in order to feed him, please him, and ward off his wrath in case the offerer had offended him by doing something wrong. But this idea of wrong-doing was probably rather that of *crime* than of *sin*. The Egyptian does not seem to have had the same idea of *sin* as the Semite, and the *sin-offering* was, therefore, probably unknown to him originally. When he sacrificed from fear of the Divine wrath, it was

[1] An interesting attempt to classify the different theories of the Atonement according to scientific principles has been made by D. W. Simon, in his *Redemption of Man* (Edinburgh, 1889, p. 6 f.). Cf. also Stevens, *Christian Doctrine of Salvation*, p. 174.

because he had committed a crime 'against the king's peace' or that of the god, not because he had 'sinned' in the Bab. and Jewish sense, or even in the less emphasized Greek sense. Wickedness for him was a sin against society rather than against God. But the gods would punish such wickedness, and so were propitiated, if necessary, by pacifying sacrifices. H. R. HALL.

EXPIATION AND ATONEMENT (Greek).—The word 'atonement' belongs to Christian theology, and inevitably suggests that conception of sin and its remedy which is peculiar to Christianity. Writers on the religion of Greece have either omitted any distinct treatment of this topic, or have discussed it (like Nägelsbach, *Homer. Theol.* and *Die nachhomer. Theologie des griech. Volksglaubens*) from the Christian standpoint. Yet, if 'sin' be used as a general term for conduct which tends to destroy the natural bond between man and his god, and which consequently is followed by manifestations of Divine anger, it is possible to discuss the conception of sin in Greek religion; and by a similarly broad definition we may speak of expiation for sin as that process by which the sin is removed, the anger of the god appeased, and the natural relation of god and man restored. In the present article sin is treated only in so far as is necessary to make clear the remedy for it. Further, the special rites for appeasing Divine anger will be treated in the art. PROPITIATION (Greek).

Some ethical content is almost inevitably connected with our conception of sin and its expiation. In Greece, however, defilement (*μίασμα*), which may have nothing to do with a man's moral conduct, was frequently regarded as the cause of Divine anger. Although we must assume that rites of purification had originally no moral content, yet no sharp line was ever drawn between physical, ritual, and moral purity, and it is necessary to consider the expiation of sin by rites of this character. Again, any disregard of what is due to the gods is an exhibition of man's neglect or self-assertion, which may be considered as sin against the gods. Such acts are a *lèse-majesté* demanding punishment, though sometimes the latter may at least be lessened by expiatory rites. It will be noted that this conception of sin goes with the belief in the gods as Divine rulers, which is emphasized in the Homeric poems. Thirdly, the time came when morality so far rested on a religious basis that transgression of moral principles was punished by the gods. To break a moral law became a sin against the gods when the sanctions of religion were added to morality—in other words, when it became the function of the gods to punish wrong-doing. At this point, and perhaps only at this point, the Greeks clearly recognized the connexion between morality and religion. The certainty of Divine punishment for sin was emphasized in their literature from Homer to Plutarch; and, if the moral ideas were often different from ours, or if religion did not enforce all the precepts of Greek morality, the fact remains that the sinfulness of immorality was generally recognized. As to the Divine punishment of sin there was no doubt; whether expiation had any utility for the sinner was a question not so easily answered.

It appears that the expiation of sin must be considered from these three standpoints: (*a*) the purification from the taint of evil, (*b*) the allaying of Divine anger caused by intentional or unintentional disregard of what is due to the gods, and (*c*) the restoration of a man who has transgressed some moral law to harmony with the gods. The emphasis on these points of view varies, but from Homer onward they are all three present.

1. Pre-Homeric period.—For the period which precedes that in which the Homeric poems were composed our knowledge of religion has made some progress in recent years, but not sufficient to shed much light on the present question. All that we can affirm with any confidence is that the early Greeks, like other primitive peoples, undoubtedly practised rites to drive away evil spirits, and that from these rites arose many later practices, the object of which was to remove some taint of evil. In so far as the evil was the cause of Divine anger and separated men from communion with the gods, it may perhaps be called 'sin,' and its removal the expiation of sin. The idea that evil itself is a substance which can be absorbed in a specially prepared fleece (Διὸς κῴδιον), or removed by some potent cleansing material like blood or clay, or instilled into a person who can bear it out of the city, is perhaps nearer to the facts than is our thought of evil spirits. In a period much later than the one under consideration, the *Thargelia*, a festival of Apollo at Athens, included a peculiar rite in which one or two men (φάρμακοι) were first fed at the public expense, then beaten with branches and leeks, and finally put to death. The connexion with Apollo was not very marked; it seems rather to be an ancient rite which had to do with the safety of the ripening crop. Nor does it presuppose the Divine anger, though doubtless more stress was laid on such a ceremony in time of famine or pestilence, when men felt that their gods were angry with them. It was primarily a means of removing any taint of evil which might bring danger to men or destruction to their ripening crops. Because rites of this character were out of line with the development of Greek religion from Homer onward, it is perhaps safe to regard them as survivals from a very early period. In themselves they shed little light on the present question, except as they indicate that men feared the possible anger of their gods, and possessed means to remove the cause of such anger, if not to allay the anger itself. Still these rites of riddance (ἀποτρόπαια) must be taken into account as the source of later purificatory rites, and perhaps as the starting-point of propitiatory sacrifice.

2. In the Homeric poems.—In contrast with the earlier ages, for which the evidence is largely based on inference, the picture of religion in the Homeric poems is clear cut and reasonably complete. But, strange as it may appear at first sight, while the account of sin and its punishment is definite enough, there is no mention of rites of expiation, no word for 'expiation' or 'atonement,' nor even any distinct form of worship designed to propitiate the anger of the gods. Any direct reference to sin as a sort of defilement demanding purification a taint dangerous because it invites either evil spirits or the wrath of the greater gods—is avoided. It is true that Agamemnon's army purified themselves after the plague which Apollo sent (*Il.* i. 313 f.), and that, after the death of the suitors, Odysseus purified his palace with fire and sulphur (*Od.* xxii. 481–494); in the same spirit, Hector feared to approach the gods with the stain of battle on his hands (*Il.* vi. 266). In none of these cases, however, is it clear that the defilement was itself a possible cause of Divine anger.

But, while the view of sin as a defilement is avoided, the place of sin in the economy of the world is definitely given. The gods are supreme rulers, governing the world in accordance with moral principles; any slight to their dignity is sin, and any infraction of the moral law they uphold is sin. And sin, *i.e.* such action as provokes the anger of the gods, is all but inevitably followed by punishment. It remains only to add that the Divine anger may also be aroused by some injury to a favourite of the gods, as when Odysseus blinded Polyphemus the Cyclops and incurred Poseidon's anger; the apparent inconsistency between such private anger and anger at some moral (or religious) wrong is explained at once by the fact that the gods are rulers, with children and favourites among men.

The conception of sin as an affront to Divine rulers which provokes their anger is illustrated by Ajax's boast that he had saved himself from the sea against the will of the gods (*Od.* iv. 504), whereupon Poseidon shattered the rock on which he had found safety; or by the recklessness of Odysseus' followers in eating the cattle of Helios (*Od.* i. 7–9, xii. 379); or by the affront to Athene when the city of Troy was sacked. In this last instance Agamemnon thought to allay the anger of the goddess by sacrifices, for he did not recognize that the purposes of the gods are not lightly changed (*Od.* iii. 143 ff.). The omission of sacrifices that were due to the gods brought down their wrath on Calydon (*Il.* ix. 533 ff.), and prevented the departure of Menelaus from Egypt (*Od.* iv. 469 ff.). In such cases it was necessary to make good the omission as promptly as possible. Menelaus must go back and offer the sacrifices; Agamemnon must restore Chryseis to her father, the priest of Apollo (*Il.* i. 98 f.). Often, however, it was impossible to undo the evil, in which case men might seek to propitiate the anger of the gods, but with little or no hope of success. So the companions of Odysseus foolishly thought to set right the slaughter of Helios' cattle by vowing to build him a splendid temple, and to dedicate many valuable votive offerings (*Od.* xii. 345 ff.). The sacrifices offered to the gods under these circumstances did not differ from the ordinary ones; but, inasmuch as sacrifice always expressed man's desire to gratify the gods by paying them their due, it might propitiate their anger. Probably the same thought lay behind the vow to bring votive offerings, though such costly gifts might be regarded as the effort to expiate a sin. But from the Homeric point of view neither gifts nor sacrifices had much efficacy; the affront to the gods was certain to bring punishment.

The result of transgressing moral law was much the same; for the gods hate wickedness, and honour just and right deeds (*Od.* xiv. 83 ff., xvii. 485 ff.). Naturally the wrong deeds which gods punished were other than the crimes against human law. In particular, the suppliant, *i.e.* the traveller outside his own country who threw himself on the mercy of the gods, was thought to be under their special protection (*Od.* ix. 479, xiii. 213). No human law punished oath-breaking, but this was a crime against the gods (*Il.* iv. 235, 270 f., xix. 264). The suitors for the hand of Penelope broke no law of man; so much the more the gods permitted their high-handed insolence to develop until it demanded punishment at their hands (*Od.* xv. 329, xx. 215, xxii. 39 f.). And the sin of Aegisthus in marrying Clytæmnestra was primarily a sin against the gods that protect the family; nor could any sacrifices and votive offerings—perhaps sacrifices of thanksgiving—win him the Divine favour (*Od.* iii. 273 ff.).

From the standpoint of the Homeric poems, sin, whether moral transgression or direct affront to the gods, received its due punishment. It was natural for men to seek to allay the anger of the gods, but there were no rites specifically for this purpose, and men had no assurance that their efforts in this direction would meet with any success. The only expiation for sin, strictly speaking, lay in the effort to set right the wrong that had been done.

3. In later Greek history.—While all three conceptions of sin and expiation are found in the later and better known periods of Greek history, the first to develop seems to have been the thought of sin as *a pollution which demanded purification.* In connexion with the spread of the worship of Dionysus early in the 6th cent B.C., a new emphasis was laid on purification. Undoubtedly rites of this character originated in the effort to free men from the taint of evil—in other words, from the dangerous influence of infecting evil spirits. It seems that the Dionysus religion, like the more organized Orphic religion, developed these rites to secure relief from those evil influences which separated man from the divinity. In the 5th cent. some of the rites had been adopted by the State religion, while others were branded as superstition.

The question with which we are now concerned is whether the evil banished by purificatory rites ever gained a moral content, which certainly it did not have at first, or whether impurity in itself provoked the anger of the greater gods, so that its removal could in any sense be called expiation. The second point is more easily answered than the first. Although rites of purification originated quite independently of the greater gods, a connexion was established before the 5th cent. B.C., so that these rites became a part of the State religion. The murderer was banished because he was hated by the gods (Sophocles, *Œd. Tyr.* 95 ff., 236 ff., 1519; cf. Antiphon, *Tetral.* i. 1. 3 and 10; Thucyd. i. 126). On shipboard he was a source of danger to his fellow-passengers; and, when sacrifices were offered to the gods, his presence made the worship unacceptable (Antiphon, *Herodes*, 81–83). Purifications were performed before every religious festival, for any impurity would provoke Divine anger. The more dreadful the cause of the impurity, the greater the Divine curse, so that, for example, the murder of Cylon and his companions demanded peculiar and effective rites of purification. Moreover, the rites themselves came under the worship of Zeus Meilichios, whose statue, erected after great bloodshed at Argos, was distinctly an expiation for that sin (Pausan. II. xx. 1). The ordinary practice of purification, however, was the removal of a possible cause of Divine anger, rather than the expiation of any sin.

It is clear that most of the rites of purification have nothing to do with any real sin. Contact with death, sickness, and birth demands a purification which has no moral significance. Probably the same is true of purification for manslaughter, though at Athens it was permitted only in case of justifiable homicide. At the same time, all shedding of human blood must have been regarded as a kind of wrong, for which some expiation was welcome. The restoration of the murderer to his place in society involved two elements, viz. an adjustment with the family of the murdered man (often a money recompense), and a religious purification; both these demands would be regarded as expiation just in so far as the murder was felt to be a sin. Herodotus (vi. 139) tells how the Lemnian Pelasgians cruelly murdered their Athenian wives and children; and, when a plague came upon them, they were informed by the Delphic oracle that they must pay whatever penalty the Athenians might demand. A similar answer was made to the inhabitants of Apollonia when they sought relief from a plague which followed the blinding of Euenius (Herod. ix. 93 f.; elsewhere, i. 167, Herodotus uses for this process the phrase ἀκέσασθαι τὴν ἁμαρτάδα). Although purification for manslaughter did not originate in the religion of the Olympian gods, we must conclude that it was brought into connexion with that religion; and the Delphic oracle encouraged the belief that murder was a polluting sin against the gods, which demanded expiation.

Further, it would seem that the ritual purity demanded, for example, by the Eleusinian mysteries was at times carried over into the ethical field. Most of the evidence for this view may be questioned, since it comes through Christian writers (*e.g.* Tert. *de Præscript.* 40: '[diabolus] ipse . . . expiationem delictorum de lavacro repromittit'; cf. *de Bapt.* 5); yet it is probable that men did come to the mysteries with a feeling of guilt from which they sought relief (Diod. Sic. v. xlix. 6; Schol. ad Aristoph. *Pax*, 277; cf. also Plato, *Polit.* 364 C: ἀδίκημα . . . ἀκεῖσθαι). Although rites of purification commonly had no element of expiation, sometimes the pollution involved a feeling of guilt for which these rites provided relief by expiation.

That it was a sin *to neglect the gods or to offer them any direct affront* was recognized in later times as clearly as in the Homeric poems. And in later practice, as in the epic picture of society, the expiation of such sin consisted, first, in setting right one's attitude toward the gods; secondly, in appeasing the Divine anger. A mythical example is found in the legend of the Trojan war: Agamemnon pursued a hind into the sacred precinct of Artemis; no expression of humble repentance was sufficient to set the matter right, but Iphigeneia must be sacrificed to the goddess to satisfy her anger before the Greeks could sail. It was an affront to Apollo for Crœsus to test the truthfulness of the Delphic oracle; in this case rich gifts were sufficient to atone for the sin and appease Apollo's anger (Xenophon, *Cyrop.* vii. ii. 19). A plague fell on the inhabitants of Phigaleia; the Delphic oracle explained it as the result of the neglected worship of Demeter, and it ceased when that ancient cult was restored (Pausan. viii. xlii. 5). To kill Cylon and his companions at the altar of Athene was an affront to the goddess for which it was necessary to seek an unusually potent means of atonement (cf. also Herod. vi. 91 f.).

Ordinarily, anything like an affront to the gods was the act of some individual, while the anger of the gods was visited on the State; it was, therefore, the business of the State to deal with the matter, first by punishing the individual, and, secondly, by appeasing the Divine anger. Such acts were the mutilation of the *hermæ* at Athens, and the profanation of the mysteries. Regular courts existed to punish individuals who were responsible for the profanation of religious objects. And to appease the anger of the gods the State had recourse to special rites of propitiation [which will be discussed in the article under that heading]. Here it should be noted that the punishment of the individual was the only expiation (in distinction from propitiation) which could be offered.

The third point of view from which the Greek conception of sin may be regarded is found in *the Divine government of the world.* The Homeric conception that moral law received the sanction of the gods is found in later literature from Hesiod (*Erga*, 333 f.) onwards. 'That old saying, "The doer suffers"' (Æsch. *Choeph.* 306), expresses the Greek view of the inevitableness of punishment (cf. Sophocles, *Œd. Tyr.* 863 ff., *Electra*, 209 ff.; Euripides, *Electra*, 1155). For any expiation which should do away with inevitable punishment, Greek thought found no place. On the other hand, the punishment itself was sometimes regarded as an expiation of the guilt. So the death of Laius' murderer was to 'loose,' *i.e.* undo, the effect of the original deed (Sophocles, *Œd. Tyr.* 100 f.); so the chorus pray that Orestes' deed, a just manslaughter, may 'loose' the blood of long past murders (Æsch. *Choeph.* 803 f.; cf. Eurip. *Her. Fur.* 40). It is not difficult to see how this principle works out in the case of Œdipus. In Sophocles' *Œdipus Tyrannus* the king is self-willed, quick to anger, relying on his own great powers; after years of suffering the same man appears in the *Œdipus Coloneus*, his temper chastened and brought into harmony with the will of the gods, for in the results of his unwitting sin he has made his expiation for it. More commonly, however, the penalty for a grave sin was death; the law was satisfied, *i.e.* expiation was made, but at the expense of the man's life.

The idea of *penance* finds no place in Greek religion, nor are there any practices by which some self-inflicted penalty may take the place of the full consequences of sin. The word 'expiation' naturally refers to some process by which the sinner may free himself either from some of the results of sin, or from the sin itself, or from both. We have seen that the idea of sin was never clearly developed and unified in Greece. Along with other forms of pollution to be removed by purification there was included the pollution due to some evil deed; at times purification came to be a sort of expiation. An affront to the gods was sin; costly gifts might expiate such sin, though here it is simpler to speak of Divine anger and its propitiation. Finally, for sin as moral wrong-doing there was no expiation other than full punishment, since the punishment of sin was regarded as something unchanging and absolute.

Literature.—C. Petersen, 'Griechische Religion,' in Ersch and Gruber's *Encyclopädie*, Leipzig, 1885–89, vi. v. 2 f.; C. F. von Nägelsbach, *Homer. Theologie*, 1840, 3rd ed. by Autenrieth, Nuremberg, 1884, *Die nachhomer. Theol. des griech. Volksglaubens*, do. 1857; E. von Lasaulx, *Studien des classischen Alterthums*, Regensburg, 1854, esp. 5, 'Die Sühnopfer der Griechen und Römer'; K. Lehrs, *Populäre Aufsätze aus dem Alterthum*, Leipzig, 1875, esp. 'Vorstellung der Griechen über den Neid der Götter und die Ueberhebung'; L. F. A. Maury, *Hist. des religions de la Grèce antique*, Paris, 1851, ch. ix., 'Le Culte: sacrifices et offrandes'; G. Anrich, *Das antike Mysterienwesen in seinem Einfluss auf das Christentum*, Göttingen, 1893; E. E. G., *The Makers of Hellas*, London, 1903; L. Campbell, *Religion in Greek Literature*, do. 1898, Index, *s.v.* 'Atonement,' 'Sin'; L. Schmidt, *Die Ethik der alten Griechen*, Berlin, 1882, ch. iii. 'Die Ursachen der Abweichung vom Guten'; G. F. Schömann, *Griech. Altertümer*⁴, ed. J. H. Lipsius, do. 1902, v. 'Das Religionswesen.'

Arthur Fairbanks.

EXPIATION AND ATONEMENT (Hebrew).

—i. In AV 'expiation' occurs only once, Nu 35[33] marg. ('and there can be no expiation for the land' after a murder 'except by the blood of him that shed it'; see further below), and 'expiate' in Is 47[11] marg.: in RV this tr. of Nu 35[33] is brought into the text; 'to make expiation for' occurs also in RV in Dt 32[43], and 'expiated' in the marg. of 1 S 3[14], Is 6[7] 22[14] 27[9]. In all three passages the Heb. word used is *kipper*. 'Atonement' occurs in the priestly laws of the OT for *kippûrîm*, a subst. cognate with *kipper* (as in the 'Day of *Atonement*'); and 'to make atonement' regularly in the same laws for *kipper*. In AV of the NT 'atonement' occurs once only (Ro 5[11]), for καταλλαγή; in RV it does not occur at all, 'reconciliation' being substituted for it in Ro 5[11] on account of other compounds of ἀλλάσσω being, even in AV, rendered by 'reconcile' and 'reconciliation.'

In both AV and RV, it should further be premised, 'atonement' means always, not *amends* or *reparation*, which is the sense the word has acquired in modern English, but 'at-one-ment,' or *reconciliation*, which is the sense in which both 'atone' and 'atonement' are regularly used by Shakespeare, and other writers of the same age: e.g. *Othello*, iv. i. 234, 'I would do much to *atone* them,' *i.e.* to reconcile them; and *2 Hen. IV.*, iv. i. 221, 'If we do now make our *atonement* (reconciliation) well, Our peace will, like a broken limb united, Grow stronger for the breaking'; *Rich. III.*, i. iii. 36 (see further examples in Aldis Wright's *Bible Word-Book*, London, 1866, *s.v.*).

It will be apparent from this preliminary synopsis that *kipper* is the Heb. word corresponding to both 'make expiation' and 'make atonement'; our first step, therefore, must be to examine this word, with its cognates, and try to ascertain what ideas are associated with it.

2. The primary meaning of *kipper* is uncertain, and, with our present knowledge, cannot be made the starting-point of an investigation. In Arabic the corresponding word, *kafara*, means to *cover*, being used, for instance (Lane, *Arab. Lex.* 2620), of clouds *covering* the sky, or of the wind *covering* a trace or mark with dust; and formerly it was customary to derive the senses of *kipper* from this, as though the meaning were properly to *cover* sin (so, though with reserve, and allowing it to be uncertain, the present writer in 1902, in *HDB*, art. 'Propitiation'). In Syriac *kĕphar*, and esp. the Pael conjug. *kappar*, means to *wipe*, or *wipe away* (as to *wipe* the mouth, to *wipe away* tears, the stain of sin, etc.); and W. R. Smith (*OTJC* [1881], 438 f., more briefly *OTJC*[2] [1892], 380 f.) explained the senses of *kipper* from this, supposing it to denote properly the *wiping away* of sin. Recent progress in Assyriology has, however, thrown new light upon the word. In its Assyr. form, *kuppuru* (with a derivative, *takpirtu*), it is now known to occur repeatedly in a ritual connexion in Assyr. texts; and, though the primary idea expressed by the term is still disputed among experts,[1] it seems clear that in actual usage it expresses the idea of *ritual purgation*: by certain specified ceremonial acts a priest is directed, for instance, to 'purge' or 'purify' a king (*šarra tukappar*), a sick person, or a house.[2] The ceremonies prescribed are largely, it should be noted, of a magical nature; and their supposed effect is to remove diseases, and especially to expel the demons who were regarded as the cause of both these and other troubles in those whom they possessed (see above, p. 638[a]). The word is used in a much deeper sense in Heb. than in Assyr.; but the applications in the two languages are sufficiently kindred to leave no doubt that there must be some ultimate connexion between them. Whether, in the remote age in which the Hebrews and the Assyrians separated from each other, the word had already acquired a ritual signification, which was afterwards developed along different lines in the two languages, or whether (Zimmern) the word was *borrowed* by the Hebrews from the Assyrians at a later date, and the ritual sense then attaching to it was afterwards modified independently by the Hebrews, it is hardly possible at present [1912] to determine; but, in one way or the other, the Heb. and Assyr. applications of the word must have sprung from a common origin.

It will be convenient in the sequel to indicate the action denoted by the verb either by the inf. *kappēr*, or by the post-Biblical subst. *kappārāh*.

3. The following are the general ideas expressed by *kappēr*. Either the guilt of sin or the stain of some ritual (non-moral) 'uncleanness' rests upon a man: the appropriate *kappārāh* expiates the guilt, or ritual stain, clears the offender, and at the same time appeases the Divine anger, which the sin has aroused, and effects the 'at-one-ment,' or reconciliation, between God and man. The means by which the *kappārāh* operates is usually some ritual ceremony, especially a sacrifice in which *blood* is shed. The effect might be thought of as produced mechanically; but, as religious ideas became more spiritualized, it was seen that the rite must depend for its efficacy upon the moral state of the sinner, upon his penitence and desire for pardon. A particular case was the guilt of bloodshed, which (according to ancient ideas) had to be avenged by the kinsmen of the murdered man, and which, moreover, was regarded as both implicating the murderer's clan and polluting the land in which the blood was shed. For wilful manslaughter there was no sacrificial *kappārāh* in Israel; but the payment of a *kōpher*, or expiation-price for a life, though recognized by the law only in certain exceptional cases, seems to have been a well-known practice (see § 7).

Kipper, whatever its primary physical meaning may have been, seems to have been in early use in Israel with the idea of *ritual purgation* attaching to it; it then gradually acquired the more definite ideas of *expiation*, *purification from sin*, *propitiation*, and *reconciliation*, just referred to.

4. Let us now examine in greater detail the use of *kipper* in the OT. We may begin with the non-priestly parts. It is doubtful whether it occurs in any passage with its presumed primary meaning; but, if the text is correct, it will do so in Is 28[18] ('And your covenant with death shall be *disannulled*,' where the idea of annulment, or obliteration, might be derived either [see § 2] from that of *to cover* or from that of *to wipe out*); but *kuppar* here is very probably an error for *huphar* (from *pārar*), the word ordinarily used of annulling a covenant.

In the other non-priestly passages of the OT in which the word occurs the subject is sometimes a *lay* Israelite, sometimes God; the object is usually the guilt, but occasionally it is the offender.

In Gn 32[20] Jacob, fearing (v.[7]) to meet Esau, lest (v.[11]) he should slay both himself and his family for the wrongs he had formerly done him, says 'I will *kappēr* his face with a present.' Here the meaning *might* be either '*cover* his face' with a present, the figure being that of a person whose eyes are blinded by a gift so as not to notice something (cf. Gn 20[16] and Job 9[24] [though the Heb. word is not the same], Ex 23[8]), or (W. R. Smith, *l.c.*) '*wipe clean* the face,' blackened by displeasure, as the Arabs say similarly 'whiten the face'; but, in view of what has been said above, it is more probable that the word is borrowed from the ritual terminology, and that the meaning is 'I will *appease* his face with a present' (LXX, ἐξιλάσομαι τὸ πρόσωπον αὐτοῦ—ἐξιλάσομαι being the word by which LXX almost always render *kipper*).

In Ex 32[30] Moses, after the sin of the golden calf, when about to go up to the mount to God, says, 'Peradventure I shall *make expiation* for your sin'—viz. by appeasing God's wrath, either by intercession (v.[31]) or, as some think, by offering to die for the people himself (v.[32]). As in Gn 32[20], the term is borrowed from the priestly terminology; but evidently no priestly ceremonial is implied by its use.

1 S 3[14], 'The iniquity of Eli's house (the sins of his sons) shall not be *expiated* by sacrifice or offering (*minḥāh*) for ever,' is a clear allusion to expiation by sacrifice.

5. The four following passages, all dealing with expiation for the guilt or pollution occasioned by *bloodshed*, should be considered together:

2 S 21[3]. David, inquiring about the cause of a long and continued famine, is told by the oracle, 'Upon Saul and upon his house there resteth blood [so read with LXX], because he slew the Gibeonites,' to whom the Israelites had sworn protection (Jos 9[15. 20f.]). Thereupon David asks the Gibeonites, 'What shall I do for you? and wherewith shall I *make expiation*, that ye may bless the inheritance of Jahweh?' They reply that it is no matter of silver or gold between themselves and Saul or his house, nor have they power to put any one to death in Israel. David thereupon offers to do for them whatever they wish; and they ask for two of Saul's sons, and five of his grandsons, that they may 'hang them up to Jahweh in Gibeon [so LXX].' Their request is granted, and they do this. The Gibeonites are now satisfied: the injury done to them by Saul is expiated; Jahweh's anger also is appeased, and He is reconciled to His land. The narrative sets before us vividly the feeling in Israel in David's time on the subject. The guilt of the blood shed by Saul rests upon his family; and its penal consequences affect the entire nation. The answer of the Gibeonites shows that, whatever the law in Israel at the time might be, expiation could be made for a murder either by a money-compensation (the 'blood-wit,' or ποινή [see § 7]), or by the principle of life for life (Ex 21[12]), and

[1] Zimmern (*Beiträge zur Kenntnis der bab. Relig.*, 1896, p. 92; *KAT*[3], 601 f.) supposes its primary meaning to be to *wipe away* ('*abwischen' von Schmutz*); and the word certainly occurs in the sense of 'wiping away' a tear in *KB* vi. 78, line 20. S. H. Langdon (*ExpT* xxii. [1911] 320 ff.) contends that its primary meaning is to *remove*. C. F. Burney (*ib.* p. 325 ff.) and C. J. Ball (*ib.* p. 478 f.) argue, largely from the evidence afforded by a syllabary, that it means properly to *be bright*, or, in the causative conjug. *kuppuru*, to *make bright*. The theological import of the word, as used in the OT, is, however, unaffected by the question of its primary, *physical* meaning; for it is doubtful if this was at all present to the Hebrews when they used it in a ritual or theological sense.

[2] See the collection of passages given by Langdon, *ExpT* xxii. 320 f. and 380 f.; and the texts translated by Zimmern, *op. cit.* (see Index, *s.v.* 'Kuppuru').

the surviving kinsmen of the murdered man might decide which they would accept. The Gibeonites choose the latter.

Dt 21^{8}. A man is found murdered; the murderer cannot be traced; and the guilt of his blood rests upon land and people. The elders of the city nearest the spot on which the murdered man was found, it is enjoined, are in such a case to perform a symbolical ceremony, slaying a cow (representing the murderer) over running water, and washing their hands over it, to symbolize their own innocence. The ceremony having been duly performed, they are to pray to God in these words: 'Our hands have not shed this blood, neither have our eyes seen it. *Expiate*[1] (or *Declare expiated*), O Jahweh, thy people Israel, whom thou hast redeemed, and lay (=leave) not innocent blood in the midst of thy people,' after which it is added, 'And the blood(-guilt) shall be *expiated* for them.' Jahweh does not 'expiate' the guilt by a priestly ceremony; but, satisfied with the ceremony which the elders have performed, He regards it as 'expiated,' and no longer treats His people with disfavour.

Dt 32^{43} (at the end of the Song attributed to Moses). Jahweh, it is said, will 'avenge the blood of his servants, and will render vengeance to his adversaries, and *expiate* his land, his people' [read, with LXX, *the land of his people*]. The land of Canaan has been polluted by the blood of Israelites slain by their foes: the pollution will be removed by the blood-revenge wrought upon the enemy by Israel.

Nu 35^{33} (in P's law of homicide; a passage which, though belonging to P, does not prescribe any priestly ceremony). 'And ye shall not pollute the land wherein ye are [viz. by allowing the murderer to live]; for blood, it polluteth the land; and no *expiation can be made* for the land for the blood that is shed therein, save by the blood of him that shed it.'

6. We now come to passages from the prophets.

Is 6^{7}. In his vision, Isaiah's 'iniquity is taken away,' and his 'sin *expiated*,' by the seraph touching his lips with the hot stone from the altar.

Is 22^{14}. For their untimely merriment in presence of the foe, the prophet pronounces sentence against the people of Jerusalem in these words: 'Surely this iniquity shall not be *expiated* for you until ye die, saith the Lord, Jahweh of hosts.' Cf. 1 S 3^{14} above.

Is 27^{9} (post-exilic). The 'iniquity of Jacob will be *expiated*' only by Israel's altogether abandoning idolatry, making the stones of (idolatrous) altars into pounded chalk-stones, and discarding entirely *'ăshērîm* and sun-images.

Is 47^{11} (addressing Babylon), 'Therefore shall evil come upon thee, which thou shalt not know how to charm away [but read probably שחדה, *to bribe off*, for שחרה]; and mischief shall fall upon thee, which thou shalt not be able to *propitiate*' (fig. for *arrest*, *avert*; cf. '*expiare* signa' [Cic. *Div.* ii. 130]).

Jer 18^{23} (in a prayer against his foes), '*Expiate* not their iniquity, neither blot out their sin from before thee: but let them be made to stumble before thee; deal thou with them in the time of thine anger.'

Ezk 16^{63} (in a promise of restoration of favour), 'When I *expiate* thee (clear thee from guilt), in regard to all that thou hast done.' The figure is suggested by the priestly terminology: Jahweh produces directly, and by His own free grace, an effect which the priest produces by means of a sacrifice.

Ps 65^{3}, 'Iniquities are too strong for me, As for our transgressions do *thou* (emph.) *expiate* them.'

Ps 78^{38}, 'But he is compassionate, he *expiateth* iniquity, and destroyeth not.'

Ps 79^{9}, 'And deliver us, and *expiate for* our iniquities, for thy name's sake.'

In the next two passages the term is used figuratively.

Pr 16^{6}, 'By kindness and faithfulness iniquity is *expiated*; and by the fear of Jahweh men depart from evil.'

Cf. the teaching of Ben Sira, Sir 3^{3}, ὁ τιμῶν πατέρα ἐξιλάσεται ἁμαρτίας; ^{30}, καὶ ἐλεημοσύνη ἐξιλάσεται ἁμαρτίας; 35^{3} [Swete, 32 (35) ^{5}], εὐδοκία κυρίου ἀποστῆναι ἀπὸ πονηρίας, καὶ ἐξιλασμὸς ἀποστῆναι ἀπὸ ἀδικίας; also 34^{19} [Swete, 31 (34) ^{23}], οὐκ εὐδοκεῖ ὁ ὕψιστος ἐν προσφοραῖς ἀσεβῶν, οὐδὲ ἐν πλήθει θυσιῶν ἐξιλάσκεται ἁμαρτίας.

Pr 16^{14}, 'The wrath of a king is (as) messengers of death (*i.e.* it threatens death); but a wise man will *propitiate* it,' viz. by prudent and conciliatory behaviour.

2 Ch 30^{18-19}, 'The good Jahweh *expiate* (clear from guilt) every one that setteth his heart to seek God, though he be not cleansed according to the purification of the sanctuary.'

Dn 9^{24}, 'Seventy weeks are determined upon thy people and upon thy holy city, to finish transgression, and to make an end of sins, and to *expiate* iniquity, and to bring in everlasting righteousness,' etc., *i.e.* to bring in an age free from all sin.

7. It is now necessary to consider the subst. *kōpher*. *Kōpher* (RV, except Am 5^{12}, always 'ransom') is the *expiation-price for a life*, the money offered for the life of a murdered man to appease his kinsmen's wrath, the ποινή, or 'wergild,' so common among uncivilized and semi-civilized nations (see BLOOD-FEUD, vol. ii. p. 720 ff.). As the allusions to it show, the *kōpher* must have been an institution familiar to the Hebrews: but in Hebrew *law*, from the earliest period in which we know it, the principle, in the case of murder, was life for life (Ex 21^{12}, 'He that smiteth a man, so that he die, shall be put to death'); and in P the acceptance of a money-compensation is strictly prohibited (Nu $35^{31.\,32}$, no *kōpher* to be accepted for the life of a murderer; v.^{33}, murder can be 'expiated' only by the death of the murderer); it was admitted only in the case of a man being killed by a vicious ox, in which case, if the victim's kinsmen were content, the owner might pay such a ποινή as they might fix (Ex 21^{30}, 'If there be laid on him a *kōpher*, he shall give for the redemption of his life whatsoever is laid upon him'). The *kōpher* is also mentioned in the following passages:

1 S 12^{3}. Samuel, in protesting his integrity as a judge, asks, 'Of whose hand have I taken a *kōpher*?'—*i.e.* a bribe to spare a murderer's life. Cf. Am 5^{12}, 'Ye that afflict the just, that take a *kōpher* (a bribe to spare a murderer's life), that turn aside the needy in the gate (from their right).'

Is 43^{3}, 'I have given Egypt as thy *kōpher*, Ethiopia and Seba instead of thee' (Egypt represented poetically as the 'ransom' which Jahweh gives Cyrus in lieu of Israel).

Ps 49^{7}, 'No man can redeem [notice 'redemption' in Ex 21^{30}, above] a brother from death, or give God a *kōpher* for him,' *i.e.* a price sufficient to save his life.

Pr 6^{35} (said of an injured husband, who will accept no price to spare the life of an adulterer), 'He will not regard any *kōpher*; neither will he be content though thou give many bribes.'

Pr 13^{8}, 'The *kōpher* of a man's soul (life) is his riches.'

Pr 21^{18}, 'The wicked is a *kōpher* for the righteous; and the treacherous (cometh) instead of the upright.' Cf. Is 43^{3}; and Pr 11^{8}, 'The righteous is delivered out of trouble, and the wicked *cometh in his stead*.'

In Job 36^{18} the discipline of sickness, and in 33^{24} the penitence brought about by it, are regarded poetically as the *kōpher*, or price, for which God will spare a man's life.

Ex 30^{12} (P). A half-shekel is to be paid by every one, at the time of a census, as the *kōpher* of his life, 'that there be no plague among them, when thou numberest them,' as might be apprehended (cf. 2 S 24) on such an occasion. In v.^{15} the half shekel is said to be given to *make expiation* for their lives, and in v.^{16} it is called *expiation*-money.

Cf. the two following passages, in which, though the word *kōpher* is not used, the idea is present, and the verb *kipper* is used exactly as in Ex 30^{15}, just referred to:—

Nu 8^{19}. The Levites are 'given as a gift to Aaron and to his sons (*i.e.* to the *priests*) from among the children of Israel,' to perform for them menial duties about the sanctuary, and 'to *make expiation* for the children of Israel: that there be no plague among the children of Israel, through the children of Israel coming nigh unto the sanctuary.' The lay Israelites, in approaching the holy vessels, etc., would do so, according to the representation of P, at the risk of their lives (Nu 18^{22} $1^{51.\,53}$): the 'Levites,' doing it in their stead, prevent Jahweh's wrath from manifesting itself in a plague (cf. Ex 30^{12}, just cited), and are therefore said to 'make expiation' on their behalf.

Nu 31^{50}. The army which had returned from the war against Midian without losing a man bring as an offering to Jahweh the jewels which they had obtained from the spoil, 'to *make expiation* for their lives before Jahweh.' This may have been either because (v.^{49}) they had been numbered (cf. Ex 30^{12}), or because they had all returned alive from the war; in either case, the spoil is an expiatory offering for lives which, though they *might* have been forfeited, had been preserved. The narrative, as it stands, is not historical; but the passage exemplifies the feeling on the subject which prevailed.

The *kōpher* was thus the *expiation-price of a life*. The word is particularly associated with *kipper* in Ex $30^{12.\,15}$ and Nu 35^{31-33} (§ 5). For blood shed in murder there is, according to the law, no 'expiation,' save by the death of the murderer. No *kōpher*, therefore, will save his life; but it will, in certain cases, save other lives. At the same time, the allusions appear to show that, in actual practice, a money-*kōpher* might be both offered and accepted. In this connexion, 2 S 21^{3-6} (§ 5) should also be noticed. Though the term *kōpher* is not used, the silver and gold with which the Gibeonites will have nothing to do would be properly described as a *kōpher*; but the only *kappārāh* which, in reply to David's offer, the Gibeonites will accept is the lives of Saul's sons and grandsons.

8. We come, lastly, to consider the use of *kipper* in the *priestly* passages of the OT, *i.e.* in Ezk 40–48, in P, and in 1 Ch 6^{49}, 2 Ch 29^{24}, Neh 10^{33}. In these the subject is always either the *priest*, or (Lv 1^{4} 17^{11}; and, in passages already considered, Ex $30^{15.\,16}$, Nu 31^{50} 35^{33}) an offering of some kind;

[1] We now speak only of 'expiating' an *action*; but, for the sake of preserving the connexion, it is used here (and sometimes in the sequel) in its old sense, which it shares with the Lat. *expiare*, of purifying a *person* from guilt or pollution—properly by religious ceremonies.

the object is never the *guilt* (as in many of the passages cited above), and indeed, as a rule, is unexpressed, the usual expression being to *make expiation for* (or *on behalf of*) a person or (see § 9 (*a*)) thing; the means is a *sacrifice*, except in the few cases in which some other act, or offering, is regarded as having an expiatory force.

(*a*) Of the *blood* of sacrificed animals (as containing the 'soul,' or life, Dt 12^{23}): Lv 17^{11} (in the 'Law of Holiness'), 'I have given it to you upon the altar to *make expiation* for your souls (lives); for the blood, it *maketh expiation* by means of the soul (life), which is in it.'

(*b*) Rarely of the *burnt*-offering: Lv 1^{4} (generally: 'and it shall be accepted for him to *make expiation* for him'); 14^{20} 16^{24} (on the Day of Atonement, after the principal ceremonies are over, when Aaron comes out of the tent of meeting, and offers a burnt-offering to 'make expiation' for himself and his people); also sometimes when prescribed in conjunction with a sin-offering (see § 8 (*c*)). Cf. Ezk $45^{15\text{-}17}$.

(*c*) Most frequently of the *sin*-offering: Ex $29^{36.\,37}$ (to *make expiation* for the altar of burnt-offering at its consecration: so Lv 8^{15}, Ezk $43^{20.\,26}$); 30^{10} (for the altar of incense, on the annual Day of Atonement); Lv $4^{20.\,26.\,31.\,35}$ $5^{10.\,*\,13}$ † (for sins consisting in any act prohibited by Jahweh, committed in ignorance or inadvertence by either the community or an individual); 5^{6} (for withholding evidence in a court of law, for touching the carcass of any unclean animal, or any uncleanness of man, and for taking a rash oath such as would imply a lack of reverence for Jahweh); 6^{30} (on a point of ritual; so 10^{17}); 8^{34} (for Aaron and his sons at their consecration; the sin-offering not expressly mentioned); 9^{7} * (when the high priest enters solemnly upon his duties, for himself and the people); $12^{7.\,*\,8}$ * (for the 'uncleanness' arising out of childbirth); $14^{19.\,31}$ * (after purification for leprosy); $15^{15.\,*\,30}$ * (after the cessation of unclean issues in man or woman); $16^{6.\,10.\,11.\,16\text{-}18.\,30\text{ff.}}$ (on the Day of Atonement, for Aaron and his house, for the goat sent to Azazel, for the Holy of holies [v.^{16}] 'because of the uncleanness of the children of Israel, and because of their transgressions, even of all their sins,' for the tent of meeting, v.^{16} [here = the Holy place], 'that dwelleth with them in the midst of their uncleannesses,'[1] for the altar of burnt-offering [v.$^{18\text{f.}}$] 'to hallow it from the uncleannesses of the children of Israel,' for the other priests, and for the whole people); 23^{28} (on the Day of Atonement); Nu 6^{11} * (at the close of the purification of the Nazirite, when rendered unclean by a person dying suddenly beside him); 8^{12} * (at the dedication of the Levites); $15^{24\text{f.}\,*\,28}$ (for unintentional sins; cf. Lv 4); 28^{22} (on each day [see v.^{24}] of the feast of unleavened bread); ^{30} (on the feast of weeks); 29^{5} (on New Year's Day); ^{11} (on the Day of Atonement); Ezk 45^{20} (for the sanctuary, on the first day of the 1st, and [LXX] of the 7th month—the *two* days of annual purification and atonement, prescribed by Ezekiel); 2 Ch 29^{24} (for all Israel, at the purification of the temple by Hezekiah, as described by the Chronicler); Neh 10^{33} (the people agree to make provision, among other things, 'for the sin-offerings to *make expiation* for Israel'): cf. 1 Ch 6^{49}.

(*d*) Of the *'āshām*, or *guilt*-offering (which was prescribed for cases in which an injury had been done to the rights of another person: if the injury could be estimated in money, the value *plus* one-fifth was returned to the injured person, and the *'āshām* was offered as an acknowledgment of the sin against God): Lv $5^{16.\,18}$ 6^{6} (for different cases of fraud and sacrilege—withholding Jahweh's sacred dues, and breaking generally His commands; perjury in the denial of betrayal of trust, robbery, exaction, misappropriation of lost property, and similar offences); 7^{7} (on a point of ritual); $14^{18.\,21.\,29}$ (in the ritual of purification for leprosy); 19^{22} (for illicit intercourse with the female slave of another man); Nu 5^{8} (for wrongful possession of lost property, etc.; cf. Lv $5^{16.\,18}$ 6^{7}).

(*e*) Of the 'ram of installation' (מִלֻּאִים)—a species of *peace*-offering, offered at the consecration of the priests (Ex $29^{19\text{-}26.\,31\text{-}34}$), the blood of which was sprinkled upon the priests and their garments—and seemingly, also, of the cakes of bread eaten by the priests with it (Ex 29^{33}). Cf. Driver, *Exodus*, Camb. 1911, *ad locc.*

(*f*) Of the blood of a bird (*not* offered in sacrifice), to be sprinkled upon a house infected with leprosy, after it has been pronounced clean by the priest, to 'un-sin' it (Lv $14^{49.\,52}$; see § 9 (*d*)), and 'make expiation' for it (v.^{53}).

(*g*) *Kipper* is also predicated generally of the *meal*- and *peace*-offering (together with the burnt- and sin-offering) in Ezk $45^{15.\,17}$.

(*h*) Of Aaron, when, by kindling incense from the fire on the altar, and carrying it rapidly among the people, he appeased Jahweh's anger, and arrested the plague (Nu $16^{46\text{f.}}$).

(*i*) Of Phinehas, when he slew with the sword two conspicuous offenders, and thereby 'turned away' Jahweh's wrath from Israel, and stayed the plague (Nu 25^{13}).

See also Ex $30^{15.\,16}$, Nu 8^{19} 31^{50} (cited in § 7), and Nu 35^{33} (see § 5).

9. The following facts respecting the use of *kipper* in Ezk and P ought to be noticed:—

(*a*) Though the object of *kipper* is usually an individual or the community, it is sometimes a *material* object, or an animal—in particular, the altar of burnt-offering (Ezk $43^{20.\,26}$, Ex $29^{36.\,37}$, Lv 8^{15} $16^{18.\,20.\,33}$); the altar of incense (Ex $30^{10\text{b}}$); the sanctuary (Ezk 45^{20}, Lv $16^{16.\,20.\,33}$); a house infected with leprosy, on the occasion of its purification (Lv 14^{53})[1]; the goat sent to Azazel (Lv 16^{10}).—(*b*) The verb is a denominative,[2] meaning to *perform an expiatory ceremony* for (or on behalf of) a person or thing: the object follows in the *accus.* only in Lv $16^{20\text{-}33}$, Ezk $43^{20.\,26}$ 45^{20} (each time of a material object).—(*c*) It is followed by 'and it shall be forgiven him (them),' in the case of the *sin*-offering, Lv $4^{20.\,26.\,31.\,35}$ $5^{10.\,13}$, Nu $15^{25.\,28}$ (cf. v.^{26}); and in the case of the *guilt*-offering, Lv $5^{16.\,18}$ 6^{7} 19^{22}.—(*d*) It is closely associated (but only when predicated of the *sin*-offering) with 'to be clean' (טָהֵר) or 'to cleanse' (טִהַר): Ezk 43^{26}, Lv $12^{7.\,8}$ $14^{20.\,52.\,53}$ $16^{19.\,30}$, Nu $8^{21\text{b}}$, cf. 2 Ch $30^{18\text{b}}$; 'to sanctify': Ex $29^{33.\,36.\,37}$, Lv 8^{15} 16^{19}, Nu 6^{11}; 'to free from sin,' or 'un-sin' (חִטֵּא): Ezk $43^{20.\,22.\,23\text{a}}$, Ex 29^{36}, Lv 8^{15}, all of the altar of burnt-offering (EVV, very inadequately, and obliterating altogether the distinctive idea of the Hebrew, 'cleanse' or 'purify'); Ezk 45^{18}, of the sanctuary (EVV 'cleanse'); Lv $14^{49.\,52}$ [see v.^{53}], of the leprous house (EVV 'cleanse'); Nu $8^{21\text{a}}$, of the Levites (RV 'purified themselves from sin').[3]

10. *Kappōreth*, 'mercy-seat' (LXX mostly ἱλαστήριον; Wyclif, 'propitiatory'), though it has been supposed to mean properly a *cover* or *lid* (cf. § 2), can hardly, when the use made of it is considered, be dissociated from *kipper*. As a derivative of *kipper*, *kappōreth* would mean properly *expiation*, and then (cf. *pārōkheth*, a thing that *shuts off*, of the *veil* in front of the Holy of holies) an *expiating thing*, or *means of expiation*. The blood was the actual means of expiation in the Levitical system; but the term may have been applied to the 'mercy-seat,' as being the means of bringing the blood as near as possible to Jahweh on the Day of Atonement. Even if *kappōreth* did originally signify *lid*, it is difficult not to think that the associations of *kipper* must have been felt to attach to it (König: *Sühndeckel*). The word occurs in Ex $25^{17\text{-}22}$, Lv $16^{14.\,15}$, and elsewhere (but, except 1 Ch 28^{11}, only in P).

11. From all that is stated, or may be inferred, it is probable that the primitive ideas of expiation and propitiation among the Hebrews were very similar to those of other primitive nations (p. 635 ff.); but that, as was the case with other primitive ideas and customs, they were developed by the Hebrews along their own lines, made the vehicle of important religious truths, and more and more spiritualized. Early passages implying the idea of appeasement are 1 S 26^{19} (where David says, 'If it be Jahweh who hath incited thee against me, let him accept [Heb. *smell*] an offering' [*minḥāh*]), 2 S $24^{21.\,22.\,25}$ (burnt- and peace-offerings offered to appease Jahweh's anger [v.^{1}] for David's census, and to stay the plague), Gn 8^{21} (where Jahweh 'smells' with satisfaction the 'soothing odour' of Noah's burnt-offerings, and promises no more to curse the ground for man's sake); but neither in these passages nor in 1 S 3^{14}

* Together with a *burnt*-offering.

† Lv $5^{7\text{-}13}$ is the continuation of $4^{1\text{-}35}$.

1 With this annual expiation of the sanctuary, cf. the noticeable parallel in the ritual for the purification of the shrine of Nebo on the 4th and 5th days of the Bab. New Year's festival, published by Dhorme (*RAssyr* viii. [1911] 48 f.), and (in part) translated into English by R. W. Rogers, *Cuneiform Parallels to the OT*, 1911, p. 197 (cf. Langdon, *ExpT* xxii. [1911] 380 f.). In this ritual (to describe it briefly), the priest of incantation first sprinkles the shrine with water 'from a well of the Tigris and a well of the Euphrates,' and burns incense in it; then the head of a male sheep is cut off, and with its body he purges (*ukappar*) the house, and recites incantations to exorcize it; after this he carries away the body, and casts it into the river Nala (cf. Lv $16^{16.\,20\text{-}22}$).

1 Cf. '*expiare* forum' (Cic. *Phil.* i. 30; *pro Rab.* 11).

2 But whether it is derived directly from *kōpher* is uncertain. *Kōpher* is the expiation-price for bloodshed *only*; the use of *kipper* is much wider. Perhaps, however, *kōpher* was once used more widely.

3 The Hebrews understood 'sin' in a wider sense than we do, and applied it to objects and actions to which we should not attribute it (cf. § 13).

(where the word *kipper* is used; see § 4) is any special form of sacrifice adopted; the ordinary burnt- and peace-offering suffices. But, though the special applications of *kipper* found in Ezk. and P will be of later growth, the word itself, as a technical ritual term, must have been in early use in Israel: it appears already in Isaiah and Deut., if not in Gn 32^{20}, in senses derived to all appearance from its ritual use. As the preceding synopsis will have shown, in Ezk. and P *kipper* is especially associated with the *sin*-offering, of which it designates the most distinctive and characteristic operation; it is also frequently, though not so characteristically, predicated of the *'āshām*, or '*guilt*-offering,' the sacrifice prescribed for cases in which some right or due, whether of God or man, had been withheld. The sin- or guilt-offerings are not mentioned in any legislation before those of Ezk. (40^{39} 42^{13} 44^{29}) and P; but they appear to be presupposed in 2 K 12^{16} [Heb. ^{17}]; and the *idea* implied in the *'āshām* is already clearly recognized in 1 S $6^{3ff.}$, where the Philistines, anxious to make some reparation to Jahweh for their desecration of the ark, and to appease His anger, are represented by the Hebrew narrator as sending to Him an *'āshām*—though it is one which consists not in a sacrifice, but in golden images symbolical of the plague-boils which Jahweh had sent upon them. Of the *burnt*-offering, offered alone, *kipper* is predicated in P only in Lv 1^4 14^{20} 16^{24}, on the ground, probably, that, though not a proper expiatory sacrifice, it was a mark of the worshipper's devotion, and, being offered 'for his favour (acceptance) before Jahweh' (Lv 1^3 לִרְצֹנוֹ), and accepted (וְנִרְצָה לוֹ) accordingly, moved Him to regard him graciously and to overlook his moral insufficiency (cf. Gn 8^{21} etc., cited above; and also Job 1^7 42^8). Elsewhere in P, *kappēr* is attributed to the burnt-offering only when it is prescribed in conjunction with the sin-offering (see the passages in § **8** (*c*)), for the purpose, as it seems, of enhancing the significance of the latter. In Ezk $45^{15.\ 17}$, in an enumeration of the principal sacrifices to be provided in the restored Temple to 'make expiation' for the people, the peace-offering, and even the unbloody meal-offering, are included; but probably the expression is intended to refer only to the sin- and burnt-offering.

12. The *kappārāh* is specially the function of the *blood*¹—though not, except in Lv 14^{53} (§ **8** (*f*)), of blood as such, but of the blood of an animal slaughtered 'before Jahweh' (Lv 1^5, etc.), and offered upon the altar. (In the normal ritual, the only exception is Lv $5^{11\text{-}13}$, where a person who cannot afford even a couple of small birds [vv.$^{7\text{-}10}$] is allowed to offer *meal* as a sin-offering.) Thus in the sin-offering the blood was not, as in the other sacrifices, thrown from a bowl against [not, as EVV, *sprinkled upon*; see Comms. on Ex 29^{16}, Lv 1^5] the sides of the altar of burnt-offering; it was applied to specially sacred places—to the horns (Lv $4^{25.\ 30.\ 34}$ 8^{15} 16^{18}), or side (5^9), of the altar of burnt-offering, or to the horns of the altar of incense, and sprinkled before the veil ($4^{6f.\ 17f.}$), or, on the Day of Atonement, before and upon the mercy-seat itself ($16^{14.\ 15}$). Notice also the application of the blood to various parts of the altar of burnt-offering at its consecration in Ezk 43^{20}, and of the Temple at its two annual purifications in Ezk 45^{20}; in the ritual for purification from leprosy, the blood, both of a bird (not killed sacrificially) and of the guilt-offering, was applied to the person to be cleansed (Lv $14^{5\text{-}7.\ 14.\ 25}$), and the blood of the slain bird was sprinkled on the leprous house (14^{51}); the blood of the 'ram of installation' also is sprinkled upon the priests and their garments (Ex $29^{20.\ 21}$). Among primitive and semi-primitive peoples the idea that blood, as charged with latent life, possesses a mysterious potency, was, and still is, widely diffused; it may form a sacramental bond uniting men between themselves or with their God (cf. W. R. Smith, *Rel. Sem.*² 312–20, 336–50, 400); it is powerful, especially when shed in sacrifice, to protect against disease, misfortune, and death (Curtiss, *Primitive Semitic Religion To-day*, Lond. 1902, p. 181 ff.; cf. Driver, *Exodus*, Camb. 1911, pp. 90, 253, 411), to remove uncleanness and the stain of sin, and to restore to 'holiness' (see Blood, vol. ii. pp. 715–719, especially 719; Moore, in *EBi*, art. 'Sacrifice,' col. 4217–9). Blood, as the seat of life, was too sacred to be used as food (Dt $12^{16.\ 23f.}$), but it was so much the more potent as a sacramental agency; in Lv 17^{11} (quoted above, § **8** (*a*)) its expiatory efficacy is expressly ascribed to the 'life' that is in it. And its purifying and sanctifying efficacy was the greater, when it was the blood of an animal consecrated—as in the cases contemplated in Lv 17^{11}—by being sacrificed upon the altar, and especially when it was that of the sin-offering, which was brought (symbolically) nearer to Jahweh than that of other offerings. No doubt, also, later the idea would arise that the 'soul,' or life, of an innocent animal involved in the blood was likely to be the more suitable and the more acceptable as an offering to God, as being the purest and most immaterial gift that could be offered to Him.

13. The *effect* of the *kappārāh* is a purification, usually from sin, but sometimes (Lv 12. 14. 15, Nu 6) from merely ceremonial defilement—ritual and moral defilement being not clearly distinguished by the Hebrews (cf. the use of חִטֵּא, to 'un-sin,' of the altar, a leprous house, or other material object [§ **9**], and of a person after the purely physical 'uncleanness,' occasioned by contact with a corpse [Nu $19^{12.\ 13.\ 19.\ 20}$]). The aim of the priestly legislation is to maintain, by a detailed and comprehensive ceremonial, the *ideal holiness* of the theocratic community; and the *kappārāh* is the primary means by which this is effected. Sometimes cleansing (moral or ceremonial) is expressly mentioned as the effect of the rite (see § **9**; and note esp. Lv 16^{30} 'On this day shall expiation be made for you to *cleanse you*; from all your sins *ye shall become clean* before Jahweh'). As prescribed on behalf of the priests (Ex 29^{33}, Lv 9^7) and Levites (Nu $8^{12.\ 21}$), before entering upon their sacred duties, it is a readily intelligible rite of preliminary expiation. Enjoined for a *material* object, the altar or the sanctuary (§§ **8**, **9**), its aim is to secure, or to preserve, its holiness: the altar prior to its consecration, as the work of human hands, is regarded as affected by a natural uncleanness, which has to be removed; the sanctuary, frequented by a sinful and unclean people, is contaminated by them, and requires periodical purification; the leprous house is conceived as tainted by sin; and the 'scape-goat,' offered by the sinful people, must be purified before it can discharge the solemn functions assigned to it.

On the part of God, the effect of the *kappārāh* is more particularly specified—at least in the sin- and guilt-offering—as *forgiveness* (Lv $4^{20.\ 26.\ 31.\ 35}$ $5^{10.\ 13}$, Nu $15^{25.\ 26.\ 28}$, Lv $5^{16.\ 18}$, and, after graver offences, 6^7 19^{22}). In view of the constant teaching of the prophets that there was no merit or value in sacrifice as such, and that repentance and amendment of life are the indispensable conditions of God's pardon and favour, the forgiveness, we may reasonably suppose, would be understood, at least by the more spiritual Israelites, to be conditional on the penitence of the offender, though this is not stated in the laws as explicitly as might have been

¹ In the Assyr. ritual, it may be noticed, blood is rarely mentioned in connexion with *kuppuru*, and no stress is laid upon it (above, p. 640ᵃ).

expected (*confession* is enjoined only in Lv 5^{5} 16^{21}, Nu 5^{7}: on the formulæ prescribed for use in later days, see below, p. 660 f., and *HDB* i. 201^{b}).

What, however, are the sins expiated by the *kappārāh*? According to Lv $4^{2.\,13.\,22.\,27}$ $5^{15.\,18}$, Nu 15^{24-29} (cf. v.^{22}; Ezk 45^{20} 'for him that *erreth*'), only such as are committed in 'error,' *i.e.* through ignorance or inadvertence, unintentionally: sins committed with a 'high hand' (Nu $15^{30f.}$), *i.e.* presumptuously, in defiance of God's will, cannot be expiated; whoso doeth them is to 'bear his iniquity,' and to be 'cut off from among his people.' On the other hand, some offences, including even grave ones, which can hardly be anything but intentional (Lv $5^{1.\,4}$ 6^{2-4} 19^{20-22}), may be expiated by a sin- or guilt-offering; and, so far as the *words* of Lv 16^{16} go, *all* transgressions of any kind are expiated on the Day of Atonement. This, however, cannot be the intention of the passage: the Day of Atonement is designed partly to clear the *nation*, as a whole, from the sins of individuals which were clinging to it, partly to clear *individuals*, in so far as they were penitent; but it is inconceivable that it could be intended to clear individuals from unrepented sins. The Mishna (*Yōmā*, viii. 8–9) is careful to teach explicitly that its ceremonies are ineffectual unless accompanied by repentance (see below, p. 660). In spite of Lv $5^{1.\,4}$ 6^{2-4} 19^{20-22}, the general scope of the *kappārāh* must have been to make expiation only for venial and unintentional sin, or, in the case of graver sins, after sincere and heartfelt repentance.

14. What, lastly, it may be asked, is the most prominent idea expressed by *kipper*? The ideas of expiation, purification from sin, propitiation, and 'at-one-ment,' or reconciliation, are intimately connected; one and the same rite effects them all; and all, if not included in, are at least immediately suggested by, *kipper*. The oldest rendering of *kipper* that we have is that of the LXX, who express it all but uniformly by ἐξιλάσκομαι, with ἱλασμός and ἱλαστήριον for its derivatives. Ἱλάσκομαι is a well-known Greek word, construed from Homer onwards with an accus. of the deity (or person) propitiated. In the LXX, however, to 'propitiate God' is never said, any more than it is said in the Hebrew: the construction of *kipper* is to *make expiation* (or *propitiation*) *for* a person—usually absolutely, with at most the addition sometimes of *before God* (Lv 6^{7} $14^{18.\,29.\,31}$ 15^{30} 19^{22}, Nu 31^{50}). The difference marks a distinction between the heathen and the Biblical points of view; though the idea of propitiating God may be involved in the phrases used in the OT, it is much less prominent than in heathen writers. The expiatory rite has, no doubt, as its ultimate object the restoration of God's favour, and the worshipper's forgiveness; but there is not the same thought of directly appeasing an angry deity as would be implied if the deity were the direct object of the verb. In the normal sacrificial system, *kipper* is never spoken of as allaying Jahweh's anger; it is so described only in certain exceptional cases (§ **8** (*h*, *i*); cf., as *averting* it, Ex 30^{15}, Nu 8^{19} 31^{50}, § 7). Hence, though the idea of propitiation is, no doubt, involved in *kipper*, it must not be unduly pressed; and the idea most distinctively conveyed by the word was probably that of 'expiation.' Still, as LXX rendered *kipper* by (ἐξ)ιλάσκομαι, and, as ἱλάσκομαι, ἱλασμός, and ἱλαστήριον are used in the NT, in very important passages, of the redemptive work of Christ (He 2^{17}, 1 Jn 2^{2} 4^{10}, Ro 3^{25}), it is to be regretted that in EVV the corresponding words should be rendered 'atonement' in the OT and 'propitiation' in the NT, and that thus a significant link, connecting the NT with the OT, should be lost to English readers.[1]

15. A few words must, in conclusion, be said with regard to the famous prophecy, Is 52^{13}–53^{12}, in which, though the term *kipper* is not used, the idea of expiation is nevertheless clearly present. The prophet here draws a picture of Jahweh's Servant, ideal Israel, describing his exaltation after an antecedent period of humiliation and persecution ending in death; the heathen, who were astonished at the spectacle of his suffering, will be not less amazed by his new and unexpected greatness ($52^{14.\,15}$ [read *startle* for *sprinkle*]). As the Book of Job shows, suffering was to the Hebrews evidence of sin; and for a while those who witnessed the Servant's sufferings thought that he was suffering for his own sins (53^{4b}); but at last the truth was borne in upon them that he was, in fact, suffering for *their* sins, and relieving them of the penal consequences which were their due ($53^{4a.\,5.\,6.\,8b.\,10.\,11.\,12b}$). Ideal Israel's voluntary sufferings thus bring home to others the sense of their own guilt, and restore them to spiritual health (53^{5}); then, after his soul (life) has been made a 'guilt-offering' (*'āshām*, 53^{10}), he will rise again, see God's 'pleasure' (*i.e.* his religious mission to the world, $41^{1.\,4.\,6}$) prospering in his hand, and, as a final reward for his voluntary submission to death, be honoured with a place among the conquerors and great ones of the earth (53^{12}). The use of the word *'āshām* shows (see § **8** (*d*)) that sin is here regarded as a *sacrilege*, an invasion of God's honour; the *'āshām* is the expiation made for it, viz. the innocent life of the ideal Righteous Servant. The voluntary sufferings of the Righteous Servant are accepted on behalf of the wicked; and so the prophecy preaches at the same time the doctrine of vicarious suffering.

16. The theological importance of the ideas which thus had their centre in the *kappārāh* will now be apparent. The dim and at first confused ideas of the nature of sin, of its antagonism to the holiness of God, of its effect in arousing His punitive wrath, and of the need of allaying this, first gave rise to expiatory rites. Gradually, the ideas connected with them became cleared: 'sin' and 'holiness,' which were both at first intermingled and confused with non-moral elements,[1] were seen to be exclusively ethical; and so in Israel, where, in the ancient world, spiritual illumination was greatest, expiatory rites became a permanent witness both to the holiness of God, and to the need of means for annulling the penal consequences of sin, and effecting 'at-one-ment,' or reconciliation, with God. As the *kappārāh*-rites threw the stress on the ceremonial side of religion, there was danger that its moral and spiritual side might be overlooked or forgotten; but the prophets guarded against this, by insisting strongly and repeatedly on repentance and amendment of life as the *sine qua non* of the forgiveness and favour of God. The ritual thus 'served as a great educational agency inculcating in the hearts and minds of participants and spectators right conceptions of the sinfulness of man, and the holiness and mercy of the just God' (J. M. P. Smith, *BW*, 1908, p. 217). And so the way was prepared for the use made in the NT of the ideas, and terminology, and symbolism of the *kappārāh*-ritual, in the interpretation of the highest and most perfect of atoning sacrifices, the death of Christ. See EXPIATION AND ATONEMENT (Christian).

LITERATURE.—E. C. A. Riehm, *Der Begriff der Sühne im AT*, Gotha, 1877; R. Schmoller, in *SK*, do. 1891, pp. 208–288; W. R. Smith, *Rel. Sem.*^{2}, London, 1894, pp. 312–20, 336–52, 396–406, 419–35; A. B. Davidson, *Expos.*, Aug. 1899, p. 92 ff. (on 'atone' in the extra-ritual Literature); J. Herrmann, *Die Idee der Sühne im AT*, Leipzig, 1905 (with an account of the views of Hofmann, Ritschl, Riehm, and Schmoller, and discussion of

[1] The 'atoning' work of Christ, in the proper sense of the word ('reconciling'), is described in the NT by καταλλαγή and καταλλάσσω (Ro $5^{10.\,11}$, 2 Co $5^{18.\,19.\,20}$).

[1] Cf. above, p. 652^{b}.

passages; on Ritschl, see also *HDB* iv. 132); L. R. Farnell, *Evolution of Religion*, London, 1905 (parts of Lect. iii., on the Ritual of Purification); L. Pullan, *The Atonement*, do. 1906, pp. 61-91; H. P. Smith, *AJTh*, 1906, p. 412 ff.; J. M. P. Smith, *BW* xxxi. (1908) 22 ff., 113 ff., 207 ff.

S. R. DRIVER.

EXPIATION AND ATONEMENT (Hindu).—Atonement or expiation (*prāyaśchitta*) forms one of the three principal parts of the sacred law (*dharma*) of India, judicial procedure (*vyavahāra*) and religious custom (*āchāra*) being the other two. It appears that the Indian system of religious atonement for an offence was not originally devised by the Brāhmans, as it goes back to the Indo-Iranian epoch, the penances ordained in the book *Vendīdād* of the Avesta being closely analogous to the penances of the Sanskrit lawbooks. On Indian soil, the *Sāmavidhāna-brāhmaṇa* of the Sāmaveda seems to be the earliest work in which a somewhat detailed exposition of the system of penances is given, but it is to the lawbooks that we have to turn for a full description of the various modes of atonement prevalent in ancient India. The penances for deadly sins are very heavy, and extend even to death. Thus one who has committed the mortal sin of drinking intoxicating liquor is to drink the same liquor when boiling hot; when his body has been completely scalded by that process, he is freed from guilt (Manu, xi. 91). The killer of a Brāhman shall become in battle the target of archers who know his purpose; or he may thrice throw himself headlong into a blazing fire. A Brāhman who has stolen gold belonging to another Brāhman shall go to the king and, confessing his deed, say 'Lord, punish me!' The king himself shall strike him once; by his death the thief becomes pure (Manu, xi. 74, 100 f.). In other penances, fasting is carried to an astonishing extent. Thus the 'lunar penance' (*chāndrāyaṇa*) consists in eating no more than fifteen mouthfuls on the day of the full moon, and diminishing this quantity of food by one mouthful every day for the waning half of the lunar month, until the quantity is reduced to nothing at the new moon, and then increasing it in the same way during the fortnight of the moon's increase. This penance is required to be performed, *e.g.*, for stealing men and women, and for wrongfully appropriating a field, a house, or the water of wells and cisterns (Manu, xi. 164). The cow being the sacred animal of the Hindus, everything coming from, or anyhow connected with, a cow is supposed to be a means of purification. The five products of a cow (*pañchagavya*), viz. milk, sour milk, butter, urine, and cow-dung, have to be swallowed, as a part of various penances, *e.g.* of the penance called *govrata*, which consists in following and serving a herd of cows for a whole month, washing oneself with cow-urine, and subsisting on the five products of the cow during that time. Drops of water falling from the horns of a cow are declared to expiate all the sins of those who bathe in them, and even scratching the back of a cow is said to destroy all guilt (*Viṣṇu-sūtra*, xxiii. 59 f.). The Arabian traveller al-Bīrūnī (*c.* A.D. 1030) mentions, as an expiation performed by Hindu slaves on their return from captivity in a foreign country, that they were buried in the dung, stale, and milk of cows for a certain number of days, till they got into a state of fermentation, and were given similar dirt to eat afterwards. The muttering of prayers, and the chanting of songs from the Sāmaveda, constitute a lighter sort of penance. Some of these prayers and songs have special names indicating their purificatory effect. Religious gifts to the Brāhmans are also greatly recommended. A rich man would give his own weight in gold or silver to the Brāhmans; this is called *tulāpuruṣa*, 'a man's weight,' and of this practice several instances are recorded in Indian history. Visiting one of the sacred places of pilgrimage (*tīrtha*) in which India abounds is another favourite mode of atonement. Such pilgrimages, as an atonement for heinous sins committed, are very common even at the present day; nor have the other old forms of expiation disappeared, though fines or dinners given to the caste are now by far the most common sort of penance. Thus, *e.g.*, when a man has been outcasted for travelling into Europe, crossing the sea in a vessel being a heinous sin under the Hindu law, he may be admitted into his caste again if he gives a dinner to the entire caste. An offender, having been tried and found guilty by his caste, is still occasionally addressed with the old Sanskrit formula: *Āchāryam labhasva prāyaśchittaṃ samāchara*, 'Take a spiritual adviser and perform a penance.' In cases of difficulty, some learned Brāhmans are invited to send in a written declaration (*vyavasthā*) in which their opinion of the case and of the particular penance to be inflicted is stated. The offender is re-admitted on performing the penance enjoined by the Brāhmans. This Brāhman interference naturally was far more common in the times before British rule than it is now, and the spiritual power thus exercised by Brāhmans acquainted with the sacred law must have been considerable, especially as they were consulted by Courts of Justice as well, in cases of civil and criminal law. There never was in India a strict line of demarcation between religious and secular law. Offenders, after having been duly punished, might be compelled to do penance in order to obtain readmission into their caste. The kings did not inflict worldly punishments only; they dictated also the penances by which religious offences were to be expiated. In the Hindu kingdom of Kashmir the Mahārāja, as late as 1875, was in the habit of looking after the due performance of the *prāyaśchittas* ordained by the five learned jurists (*dharmādhikārin*) of the country. The readiness of the people to submit to the prescribed course of atonement for their sins was enhanced by a superstitious dread of the tortures of hell and of the pangs to be suffered in future births. Many diseases and natural infirmities were viewed as the consequence of sins committed in a previous existence, lepers, for instance, being required to do penance in order to expiate the crime in a former birth to which their illness was considered to be due, and to avoid being afflicted with the same illness in a future birth. Secret penances (*rahasya-prāyaśchitta*) are also mentioned; they were, and are still occasionally, performed for offences not publicly known.

LITERATURE.—J. Jolly, *Recht und Sitte*, Strassburg, 1896; *The Laws of Manu*, tr. in *SBE*, xxv., Oxford, 1886; *The Institutes of Vishnu*, tr. in *SBE* vii. do., 1880; A. Steele, *The Law and Custom of Hindoo Castes*, new ed., London, 1868.

J. JOLLY.

EXPIATION AND ATONEMENT (Jewish).—I. It is necessary, though somewhat difficult, to draw a distinction between penitence, or repentance, and expiation, or atonement. This differentiation cannot be entirely rigid, for, in dealing with atonement, it is impossible to exclude all references to penitence, and *vice versa*. It may be laid down as a convenient axiom that penitence is the consciousness of sin; atonement, the desire or effort to be free from sin. Penitence must precede atonement, for penitence is an attitude of the mind, while atonement is a subsequent activity of the body, directed towards the realization of that attitude, although sometimes, as will be seen, penitence was in itself an atonement. The question then resolves itself into an examination of the process which a Jew, guided by Rabbinic ideas and direction, would adopt in order to free his soul from the stain of sin, it being more or less taken for granted that the recognition of his sinfulness has already been awakened in him.

The regular word for repentance is תְּשׁוּבָה, 'returning' (as opposed to מְשׁוּבָה, 'backsliding' [Hos 14^{5}]). The term for 'atone' is כִּפֵּר, the original idea of which was probably 'to wipe out' rather than 'to cover up' (but see König, in *ExpT* xxii. [1911] 232, 378), the כֹּפֶר, 'ransom,' 'bribe,' being the instrument. The ransom to wipe out sin, and purging by means of the blood of sacrifices, gradually gave way to a more spiritual idea. It would not be correct to regard this absolutely as progressive development. Sacrifice was but the outward form of the atonement, a concomitant of the ideal. In course of time it was found possible to maintain the inward process independently of the outward form, but this must not be taken to mean that the idea of physical sacrifice was condemned. In many cases sacrifices were brought without the proper feeling of penitence on the part of the sinner; this abuse was sternly reprobated by the prophets (Am 5$^{21-24}$, Mal 1^{10} Mic 6$^{6-8}$; cf. *JE* x. 616) and Rabbis (*Numb. Rabba* xix. § 4=line 15, outer col., fol. 68*a*, ed. Warsaw, 1868; see also *Tosefta Baba Qamma*, x. 18, cited by Abrahams in *Camb. Bib. Essays*, London, 1909, p. 189; Qimḥi on Jer. 7^{21}; Montefiore, *JQR* xvi. 209; see Maimonides, *Guide*, pt. iii. ch. xlvi.; Friedländer's tr., p. 359; cf. p. 325). But it is an open question whether sacrifice as a means of atonement for sin is categorically repudiated, or whether these denunciations merely refer to the misuse of the practice. On the other hand, the same doubt may be traced in Rabbinic writings and in the Liturgy. It is true that the Prayer-book of all the Orthodox and of some Reform Synagogues contains abundant references to sacrifices and prayers for their restoration as a means of atonement for sin (Singer, pp. 225, 234, but contrast p. 267; see also *JE* x. 628), and that the daily and festival services correspond to the Temple Offices; nevertheless it must be remembered that most of these prayers were composed at a time when the overwhelming calamity was still fresh in the mind of every Jew, and that very often the return to Zion and the rebuilding of the Temple are but other expressions denoting the Messianic age. The thirteen articles of the Creed, composed by Maimonides († 1205), contain no reference to sacrifice (Singer, p. 89), although the tenth and eleventh articles, which deal with God's cognizance of sin and with reward and punishment, naturally imply the doctrine of atonement, and the twelfth makes obligatory the belief in the Messiah. The substitution of prayer and penitence for sacrifice as a means of atonement, as taught by Hosea, Micah, Amos, and Isaiah, was the keystone of the Rabbinic penitential theory; but this did not involve a condemnation of the sacrificial system of the Temple.

The Day of Atonement itself is, of course, the outstanding feature in the Rabbinic scheme of repentance. The cessation of sacrifices naturally magnified its importance, and caused many associations to gather round it. The Synagogue liturgy contains many an echo from the Temple ritual. The humblest Jew in a Russian Ghetto confesses his sins in the identical formula used by kings and high priests. Penitence and atonement occupy so prominent a position in the life of a Jew, as conceived by the Rabbis, that their writings are full everywhere of the necessity and means of obtaining freedom from sin. In particular, the end of Mishna *Yoma* should be studied, but on the whole it will be convenient to examine the treatise on Atonement and Penitence of Maimonides (*Yad*, הִלְכוֹת תְּשׁוּבָה), and to incorporate, where necessary, references from Talmud and Midrash, and finally to consider the Liturgy and Synagogue practices.

2. The Mishnaic atonement consists in a complete repentance, coupled with affliction of the flesh according to the prescribed requirements of the Day of Atonement. If the sin has been against man, restitution must precede everything else. Avowal is also necessary. Death can atone in certain cases. Death-bed repentance is effective, but it is not the highest form of atonement. Fasting, almsgiving, the study of the Torah, submission to stripes—all these can atone; but all forms of atonement depend for their success on the grant of Divine grace.

The Mishna and Gemara *Yoma* deal, in the main, with the ceremonies of the Day, but the concluding sections may here be cited, as referring more particularly to the abstract idea (*Yoma* viii. 8–9). The sin-offering (חַטָּאת) and the offering brought for certain trespasses (אָשָׁם וַדַּי) are adequate to atone; death and the Day of Atonement are adequate, if there is due repentance; repentance alone is adequate for light transgressions, whether of affirmative or of negative commandments. In the case of grievous sins, pardon is suspended until the advent of the Day of Atonement, which brings the pardon. To one who says, 'I will sin and thereafter repent,' the power of repentance is not vouchsafed. If a man says, 'I will sin and rely on the Day of Atonement to bring forgiveness,' the Day will not bring pardon to him. The Day brings pardon for sins between man and God, but for sins between man and man only if the sinner has previously appeased and made restitution to his victim. This R. Eleazar b. 'Azarya (fl. A.D. 100) deduced from Lv 16^{30}, 'From all your sins before the Lord shall ye be clean,' thus taking חַטֹּאתֵיכֶם with לִפְנֵי ׳׳.

R. Aqiba († A.D. 135) said: 'Happy are ye, Israel; before whom are ye purified and who is it that purifies you? It is your Father in Heaven, as it is said in Ezk 36^{25} "And I will sprinkle upon you clean water and ye shall be clean, from all your impurities and from all your abominations will I purify you"; and the verse (Jer 17^{13}) saith, "O thou *Miqwēh* of Israel, O Lord" [*miqwēh* having the double meaning of 'hope' and of 'ritual bath,' the root occurring in the latter sense in Gn 1^{9} 'Let the waters be gathered together']. Just as the *miqwēh* purifies the unclean, so the Holy One, blessed be He, purifieth Israel.' See also *Yoma* 86, quoted in full in art. 'Atonement' in *JE* ii. 280 (this art. is very important).

In the treatise on Penitence, mentioned above, Maimonides summarizes all that is essential in connexion with atonement. (Citations are translated from the Venice ed. of Pietro Bragadino, 1615, and will be marked by the letters *H.T.* = *Hilkhoth Teshubah.*) Reference has already been made to the obligation of avowal. The necessity of public confession is strongly maintained by Maimonides in the opening laws of the first *pereq*. The technical term is וִדּוּי (מִתְוַדֶּה, הִתְוַדּוֹת), from the root יָדָה, and *Widdui* comes between *Teshubah* and *Kapparah*. The duty of confession is itself a positive commandment, because it is written (Lv 26^{40}), 'And they shall confess (וְהִתְוַדּוּ) their sin and the sin of their fathers,' and this implies verbal confession. If a man, having transgressed any single command of the Torah, be it affirmative or prohibitive, be it in presumptuous sin or in unwilling error, desire to repent, he is bound (חַיָּב) to confess his sin before God (*H.T.* i. 1). The duty of confession was, of course, Biblical in origin, and the triple confession of the high priest (Lv 16$^{6.11.21}$, Mishna *Yoma* iii. 8 and iv. 2, vi. 2) was the model which was adopted by private persons, and which still remains in the Atonement liturgy. The formula may be found in any Maḥzor for the Day of Atonement (*e.g.* Davis, vol. ii. 'Atonement,' p. 161, etc.). For the use of individuals it ran thus: 'O God, I have sinned, acted perversely, transgressed before Thee, and I have done . . .

Verily I have repented and am ashamed of my deeds, and I will never return to such an act' (*H.T.* i. 2). The last sentence is, according to Maimonides, the integral factor of the whole confession; and every one who is profuse in confession (special emphasis is laid on this point) is accounted worthy of praise. The Divine name is, of course, omitted; הַשֵּׁם, just as in the Temple formula, representing the Tetragrammaton, which was uttered only by the high priest. No sin-offering could procure pardon without penitence and confession, nor could the infliction of capital punishment suffice to wipe away guilt without these two adjuncts. Moreover, theft, even if restitution had already been made, could be forgiven only if the thief had made public confession and resolved to abandon theft for all time (*H.T.* i. 3). Confession is just as vital in the case of the community; hence the high priest, in sending away the scapegoat, made a public avowal, laying his hand on the head of the goat, because it was to be an atonement for all Israel. But, although the scapegoat was a general national atonement for all sins—light and grievous, presumptuous and unwitting, with or without avowal—yet this was the case only if the sinner repented; without due repentance on the part of the individual the public atonement of the scapegoat was of no avail except for 'light' (קַלּוֹת) transgressions. According to the legal definition, the difference between light and grievous (חֲמוּרוֹת) transgressions lay in the penalty; in the latter category were all sins for which the penalty was capital punishment at the hands of the *Beth Din*, and excision (see CRIMES AND PUNISHMENTS [Jewish]); but vain swearing and perjury, although not subject to this condition, are yet included under the head of 'grievous' (*H.T.* i. 5). The destruction of the Temple has made repentance itself the means of atonement. So powerful is repentance that even on the death-bed of a lifelong sinner it is effective. Further, to those who repent, the Day of Atonement is itself the means of pardon. There are some sins which are forgiven as soon as repentance is exercised, while in the case of others pardon is deferred.

Four main distinctions may be traced (*H.T.* i. 7; *Yoma* 86*a* [Gold. 1021, Rodk. 134]). Thus, if a man repents of a 'light' sin of omission, his pardon is immediate. In the case of a man who repents of a 'light' sin of commission, his repentance suspends his condemnation and punishment, and the Day of Atonement brings his pardon. If a man has committed 'grievous' sins of commission, penitence and the Day of Atonement will suspend his condemnation and punishment, and the chastisement which will be inflicted on him will complete his pardon. In no case can complete pardon be obtained without penance or chastisement (יִסּוּרִין; see conclusion of art. DISEASE AND MEDICINE [Jewish]). The only exception is in the case of blasphemy. By blasphemy (lit. the profanation of the Name) more is understood than the English equivalent implies. It almost includes deliberate atheism (cf. the opposite קַדֵּשׁ אֶת־הַשֵּׁם, 'suffer martyrdom'), and is the only sin to which the distinction of presumption (זָדוֹן) and ignorance (שְׁגָגָה) does not apply (אֶחָד בְּשׁוֹגֵג וְאֶחָד בְּמֵזִיד בְּחִלּוּל הַשֵּׁם [*Aboth* iv. 4; Singer, p. 196]). In the case of a man who has 'profaned the Name,' repented and remained constant in his repentance, passed a Day of Atonement, and suffered the chastisements, his absolute pardon is deferred until his death; but by the effects of repentance, Day of Atonement, and chastisement, his punishment is suspended (*H.T.* i. 6–9).

The principles underlying these differentiations are clear. It is far easier to repair a sin of omission than a sin of commission (see also the footnote in Singer, p. 262); the reality of repentance in the case of a sinner who is guilty of evil practices is tested by time, for he must prove that he has had the power and opportunity to relapse and has not yielded. The greater the sin, the longer is the period necessary to attest repentance. Repentance itself is also more severe and lengthy if the traces of the crime have to be effaced. If the element of chastisement did not enter into the question of pardon, it might lead to a false repentance to avoid punishment.

The question of the reality of penitence is discussed by R. Yehuda in Gemara *Yoma* 86*b* (Gold. 1024, Rodk. 136), and repeated by Maimonides in *H.T.* ii. 1 ff. The decisive test is time and complete opportunity to repeat the offence. With this is also connected the question of validity of death-bed repentance. Maimonides is very decisive. Even if a man has been a sinner all his days and repents in his old age, when all opportunity for sin is gone, in spite of the fact that this is not the highest form of penitence, nevertheless his penitence is a valid atonement. Even if he has sinned all his life and repented only on his death-bed, his sins are all pardoned, in accordance with Ec 12^2 (*H.T.* ii. 2). On the other hand, see *Aboth* ii. 15 (Singer, p. 189): 'Repent one day before thy death' (*i.e.* at once, since thy death may be to-morrow). The difficulty, of course, which the Rabbis felt was how to keep the gates of repentance open to the dying sinner, without, at the same time, making it easy for a man to sin all his life, relying on his last hour to make his peace.

It has already been pointed out that penitence is itself held by the Rabbis to have been a means of atonement; consequently a warning is uttered against the futility of hypocritical atonement. Since the act of repentance had taken the place of sacrifices as the agency by which pardon could be gained, there must be no danger of the means once more being mistaken for the end. Any man who confesses his sins, without the firm intention of abandoning them, is like one who bathes while holding in his hand an unclean insect (שֶׁרֶץ). His bathing will be useless until he abandons the contaminating object (*H.T.* ii. 4). The act of repentance must be a real μετάνοια, 'change of mind,' and must involve a deep recognition of the heinousness of sin. A penitent should be continually praying and giving charity, according to his means. He should flee from temptation, he should even change his name, as much as to say: 'I am now another person, I am not he who did so and so.' He must change all his actions for good; he should exile himself, because exile is in itself an atonement and will involve him in humiliation and affliction which will cause him to become humble and meek in spirit (*H.T.* ii. 5).

It is also praiseworthy to make public confession; for, if a man is too proud to reveal his transgressions, his penitence is imperfect. Here, however, a distinction is drawn. A man should confess publicly sins against his neighbour, but not those against God (*H.T.* ii. 7; *Yoma* 86*b* [Gold. 1024, Rodk. 137]). Penitence and confession, although acceptable at all times, are especially desirable at the period of atonement, that is to say, from the beginning of the New Year (1st Tishri) until the Day of Atonement. (For an investigation of the time and manner of confession, the formula of confession, the manner in which a man must reconcile himself with his neighbour, and the lengths to which he must go, see the last sections of *H.T.* ii. and iii. 5 ff.)

The question of punishment can scarcely be considered here, but eternal damnation requires treatment in so far as it is affected by atonement. The idea of everlasting doom was utterly repugnant to the Rabbis; and, when it was limited to a very small number, great pains were taken to prove that almost every individual or class for whom there seemed no hope was, in fact, sure of ultimate salvation. There was always some mitigating circumstance which had been overlooked, some Scriptural authority to be found. In the end, there were but few, indeed, for whom there was no hope. Maimonides, in his Commentary on Mishna *Sanhedrin*, gives much attention to the question, and also in *H.T.* iii. 11 ff.; it is in the latter passage that the famous words occur: חֲסִידֵי אוּמּוֹת הָעוֹלָם יֵשׁ לָהֶם חֵלֶק לָעוֹלָם הַבָּא, 'the righteous of all nations have a share in the world to come.' It is noteworthy that, when Maimonides proceeds to particularize those who are eternally damned, he is careful to begin each section with 'The following *Israelites*,' because the beliefs which he stigmatizes are frequently held by other religions. Having stated that those of other creeds, holding these beliefs, who live a righteous life have a share in the world to come, he does not want to depart from his pragmatic position. At the same time, there must be no excuse for any Israelite holding these beliefs. In such a case, a Jew may not rely on justification by good works.

There is no atonement for the following classes, if they die impenitent: the Epicureans; those who deny the Torah, the resurrection, the coming of the Messiah; those who cause the multitude to sin; those who separate themselves from the ways of the congregation; those who sin publicly and with a high hand, like Jehoiakim; the betrayers; those who put the Congregation in terror, not for the sake of heaven; those who shed blood; the slanderers; and those who draw back the *'orlah.* Six kinds of Israelites are said to be יוֹצְאִין: he who denies the existence of a God; he who says that the world has no guiding power; he who says that the world has two or more guiding powers; he who admits that there is a Lord, but affirms that it is a star or some being endowed with a likeness; he who denies that the Eternal was the first, or the universal Creator; he who worships a star, in order to have an intermediary between himself and the Lord.

The Epicurean among the Jews is he who repudiates prophecy and inspiration in its widest terms ('he who says that there is no knowledge from the Creator that reaches man's heart'): he who denies the prophecy of Moses and the Divine knowledge of human actions. The Jew who denies the Torah is he who says that it is not from God (even one veres or one word), or who says that Moses wrote it on his own authority; so also he who denies the oral Law; who denies its expounders, as, for example, Zadoq and Baithos; who says that the Creator changes one demand for another, or that the present Law, though originally Divine, is now superseded.

All these sinners, as well as the others enumerated by Maimonides (*H.T.* iii. 16–23), but who cannot, through lack of space, be included here, are definitely cut off from the life to come. But this clear statement is at once mitigated by Maimonides:

'Under what conditions are the above-mentioned sinners precluded from the hereafter? If they have died in sin. But, if a man turn from his wickedness and die (at once), then he is a penitent. He is one of those who shall have a part in the coming world, for there is nothing that can withstand penitence. Even a man who has denied the cardinal principle (כּוֹפֵר בָּעִיקָּר) all his days, and repented at the end, has a share, as it is said (Is 57[19]), "Peace, peace to the far off and near, saith the Lord, and I will heal him." So too, all the wicked, the sinners and transgressors, when they return, be it openly or secretly, they are accepted, as it is said, "Return ye backsliding children" (Jer 3[14]); although such a man be still a backslider, since he has returned in secret without making avowal, yet he is received by reason of his repentance' (*H.T.* iii. 24–25).

The obstacles to repentance are dealt with in *H.T.* iv., but in this connexion penitence is not the means of atonement itself, but a necessary preliminary to it; consequently the fourth and subsequent *p^erāqîm*, which deal with different subjects also, may be neglected here. It is important, however, to study carefully the Gemara at the end of *Yoma* 85*b* (Gold. 1019–1033, Rodk. 132–142) and ch. xi. of *Sanhedrin, Ḥēleq*, with the commentary of Maimonides (see Lit. at end), and also the other Rabbinic references given in *JE*, art. 'Atonement.' A fair number of Midrashic extracts are given by Rapaport in *Tales and Maxims from the Midrash*, London, 1907, p. 261.

3. It remains to consider the question of atonement from the liturgical and ceremonial point of view, apart, of course, from the Day of Atonement itself, to which special treatment is accorded (see FESTIVALS AND FASTS [Heb.]). The keynote of the Liturgy is the oft-quoted trilogy: וּתְשׁוּבָה וּתְפִלָּה וּצְדָקָה מַעֲבִירִין אֶת־רֹעַ הַגְּזֵרָה, 'Repentance, prayer, and charity avert the evil decree' (Jer. *Taanith* ii. 65, fol. *a*, outer col., line 5 [ed. princ.] = vol. vi. p. 153 of Schwab's tr.; see M. Schuhl, *Sentences . . . du Talmud*, Paris, 1878, p. 91, no. 252). These words are the climax of the additional services for the New Year and the Day of Atonement (see Davis, p. 150; also Heidenheim, *Maḥzor*, ed. Roedelheim, 1859, and others, fol. 24*a*). They are printed in exceptionally large type, and beneath them are added explanatory glosses, viz. צוֹם, קוֹל, מָמוֹן. Fasting is thus associated with תְּשׁוּבָה; קוֹל, corresponding to תְּפִלָּה, may either be an allusion to confession or, more probably, to prayer, while מָמוֹן explains צְדָקָה as = charity, on the basis of Pr 10[2] 11[4], which the Rabbis translate 'Charity delivereth from death.' In Rabbinic צְדָקָה, like Syr. *zedq^etha*, always has that meaning, being reserved for 'righteousness.' Mention must also be made of a curious example of Gematria in this connexion. It will be observed that the letters of each of the words צוֹם, קוֹל, מָמוֹן are numerically equivalent to 136, and the three words thus total 408. This corresponds to זאת and explains Lv 16[3], בְּזֹאת יָבֹא אַהֲרֹן אֶל־הַקֹּדֶשׁ, 'With זאת shall Aaron enter the Holy of holies,' *i.e.* he shall make atonement for all Israel by prayer, fasting, and charity.

This theme might be abundantly illustrated: *e.g.*, the conclusion of the Pethiḥāh Seliḥāh for Yoṣer of the Day of Atonement: 'What though our errors be many, yea theft and violence, cause us to turn, O God of our salvation, and annul our wickedness. Repentance and good works are ever as shield and buckler, but it is upon Thy mighty mercies that we rely' (Davis, p. 82). (The main thought is derived from *Shabbath* 32*a*, *Yoma* 87*a*, and *Aboth* iv. 13 [Singer, p. 196, foot].) See also the reference in the Ne'īlāh Service (Davis, p. 263): 'Gates of tears that are never closed,' the same being also said of the Gates of Prayer and of Repentance in *Pesiḳta* xxv. § 4, 157 *a*, ed. Buber, Lyck, 1868.

Reference has been made to the Divine grace as a means of atonement, in the Liturgy; every Seliḥāh Service begins with this idea. Thus the *Pethiḥāh* always ends with כִּי עַל־רַחֲמֶיךָ הָרַבִּים אָנוּ בְטוּחִים, 'For it is on Thy mighty mercies that we rely,' or some similar phrase, in order to lead up to the next Seliḥāh, which is never varied and which begins, 'For it is on Thy mighty mercies that we rely, on Thy charities that we trust' (Davis, pp. 222, 82, 169). A similar idea, a mystic or poetic development, is the mention of the thirteen *middôth*, or Divine attributes (Ex 34[6, 7]), as means of atonement. As instances may be cited the two prayers אֵל מֶלֶךְ יוֹשֵׁב (Davis, p. 258), and the Seliḥāh in the Shaḥarith of the Day of Atonement, beginning שְׁלֹשׁ עֶשְׂרֵה מִדּוֹת (*Seliḥōth*, ed. Proops, fol. 56*b*, no. 105). In the Ne'īlāh Service (Davis, p. 263) this idea has even been pushed so far as to personify, poetically, the *middath hāraḥămîm*, or quality of mercy, and to beseech it to intercede with the Almighty for atonement. This has been eliminated by some modern Maḥzorim, including Davis, by changing the reading (but see Roedelheim text, or Durlacher, *Erech Hatephiloth, Kippour* 2, ed. ii., Paris, 1866, p. 324, where the Seliḥāh occurs in Minḥah). It is, of course, impossible to offer anything more than typical references, since the whole of the vast Seliḥāh and penitential liturgies is replete with passages that might well serve as illustrations. This remark applies to all of the liturgical section of this article.[1]

Jewish theology never contained the idea of original sin, and thus this idea is absent in the scheme of atonement. It has been well shown by S. Levy (*Original Virtue*, London, 1906) that Judaism held the converse idea under the form of זְכוּת אָבוֹת, or the merits of the Patriarchs. The germ of

[1] Under this heading belongs the idea of God atoning 'for his Name's sake' (cf. Singer, pp. 57 and 160, near foot).

this idea is old; 'God of Abraham, Isaac, and Jacob' occurs in the 'Amidāh (Singer, p. 44, and Mt 22³²), and in the Pentateuch (Gn 24¹² 31⁵³ 32⁹). In the end great stress is laid on the merits of the Patriarchs as a claim on the Divine grace and a means of salvation and atonement. If children are not to suffer for the sins of the fathers, it would seem that they may not benefit by their virtues. But in the Seliḥôth the refrain, 'but we and our Fathers have sinned,' occurs, although this is merely stating a fact, not recording a feeling of helplessness at an accumulation of sin. In any case it is held very strongly that, by the Divine grace, the merits of the ancestors may be accounted to their descendants as atonement for sin (*e.g.* the Seliḥāh אַנְשֵׁי אֱמוּנָה אָבָדוּ [Proops, fol. 68*b*, no. 129]; cf. the Seliḥāh beginning with almost the same words, in the Sephardic rite [Gaster, i. 39 or iii. 30]; the prayer מִי שֶׁעָנָה לְאַבְרָהָם אָבִינוּ בְּהַר הַמּוֹרִיָּה הוּא יַעֲנֵנוּ [Davis, *Atonement*, pt. i. pp. 53–55]; for similar prayers, see Gaster, iii. 28–34). This motive has, of course, no connexion with any idea of a personal mediator or intercessor—an idea not found anywhere in the Liturgy.

As a corollary to the merits of the Patriarchs is the idea of the *'ăqēdāh*, or binding of Isaac. God is prayed to recall the *'ăqēdāh*, and pardon the sin of Isaac's descendants. Every Seliḥāh Service contains an *'ăqēdāh* (*e.g.* Davis, 87–89, 228, 176; see also the beautiful Piyyuṭ of Judah Samuel Abbas in the Sephardic rite עֵת שַׁעֲרֵי רָצוֹן לְהִפָּתֵחַ [Gaster, ii. 106, and Singer, p. 8, § 2, also Gaster, i. 4 ff.]). One of the reasons for the blowing of the ram's horn is that God may recall the *'ăqēdāh* and grant atonement to the seed of Isaac. Among the Sephardim, the seventh day of Tabernacles (*Hosha'ana Rabba*) is more penitential in character than among the Ashkenazim; the ram's horn is sounded and Seliḥôth are said, for this is an additional means of atonement; those who did not completely repent, or whose fate was not adjudged on the previous Day of Atonement, may have a last chance. Seven penitential circuits are made, referring to the three patriarchs, Moses, Aaron, Pineḥas, and David, and their merits are urged as means of atonement (Gaster, iv. 148 ff.).

The Confession was greatly elaborated in the Liturgy (for Talmud see *Yoma* 87*b* [Gold. ii. 1030, Rodk. vi. 140]); three chief formulæ require notice. They are all arranged in alphabetical order, to facilitate recitation by memory. The first two are congregational, and the first person plural is employed throughout. They are, on this account, recited aloud. The first formula is the *'Ashamnu* (Singer, p. 258), and is elaborated at the conclusion of every Seliḥāh Service: אָשַׁמְנוּ מִכָּל־עָם, בּוֹשְׁנוּ מִכָּל־דּוֹר (Proops, fol. 6*b*, or Gaster, iii. 37). The second is the *'al-Ḥēṭ* (Singer, p. 259). This is not recited aloud in its entirety. The third formula cannot be quoted so readily; it is the one intended for private use and silent meditation. Several examples of this kind of *Widdui* exist. There is the beautiful composition of R. Isaac b. Israel in the Sephardic Minḥah for Kippur (Gaster, iii. 225). See also the *Widdui* for Musaph by R. Shem Tob b. Ardutiel (Gaster, iii. 181), and the great *Widdui* by R. Nissim of Babylon (*ib.* 123). For a confession for the reader alone, cf. *ib.* 125. In the long prayer (יְהִי רָצוֹן) which concludes the Seliḥôth for 'Erev Rosh hash-Shanah, a *Widdui* has been interwoven (fol. 24 of Proop's ed., Amsterdam, 1711). The former of the public confessions is repeated at all the five services of the Day of Atonement, the *'al-Ḥeṭ*, however, only at the first four; at Ne'īlāh there is substituted for it a very beautiful prayer, אַתָּה נוֹתֵן יָד לַפּוֹשְׁעִים (Singer, p. 267), which should be read very carefully.

Other fasts for atonement may be briefly noticed; the 'Second and Fifth' after the three festivals: the private fast of the bride and bridegroom on the wedding day, because they begin a new life purged of sin (Jer. *Bik.* iii. 65, fol. *b*, cols. *c*, *d* [ed. princ. = vol. ii. p. 386 of Schwab's tr., Paris, 1873–79]); a private fast undertaken in fulfilment of a vow in order to atone for a sin; finally, on the historical fasts Seliḥôth are said, because the calamities which are commemorated were due to sin, and penitence may bring pardon and restoration. On the ninth of Ab, although no actual Seliḥôth are recited, yet the recognition of sin and the prayer for atonement is implied in many of the *Qinôth*. The doctrine of vicarious atonement in the Christian sense finds no place in Rabbinic Judaism, because the Rabbis denied original sin. Man had his two *yeṣers*, but there was no necessity or room for a Messiah suffering for the sins of his people. 'Happy are you, Israel, God it is who purifies you,' said Aqiba (*loc. cit.*). Although passages could be produced which might seem to point to the vicarious idea, such a sense proves, on examination, to be untenable. Other means of atonement—study of the Torah, etc.,—may be found in *JE* ii. 280, outer column.

Reference may also be made to punishment and death as means of atonement. Thus poverty (*'Erubin* 41*b* [Gold. ii. 135, Rodk. 93]), exile (*Sanh.* 37*b*), suffering (*Ber.* 5*a*), can procure it (see DISEASE AND MEDICINE [Jewish]). The death-bed confession (Singer, p. 317, based on *Ber.* 60*a*) is that 'my death may be accepted as an atonement for my sins.' In the Seliḥāh מַשְׂאַת כַּפַּי (Proops, *ed. cit.* no. 131, fol. 69*b*; Davis, p. 224) by Mordecai b. Sabbattai, the poet prays:

'May the words of my mouth be a sweet savour before Thee, Rock of Ages, accept my fat and my blood, diminished by fasting, instead of the fat and blood of the sacrifices; may the meditation of my heart that I have laid before Thee, these ten days, be as the sin-offering, the trespass-offering, and the Minhah' (see Ber. 17*a*, Gold. i. 61).

Baptism can scarcely be said to have been a means of atonement in Judaism. On the eve of Kippūr, after receiving flagellation (see J. Caro, *Shulḥan 'Arukh*, ch. 607, § 6) it became the custom to bathe; but ritual bathing was associated with rather than a means of atonement, though another water-ceremony has been introduced. On the New Year, after service in the place of worship, the congregation repairs to running water, and prays 'that God may cast our sins into the depths of the sea.' The last two verses of Micah, where these words occur, are, with other passages from Scripture, there recited; and it is from Micah that the ceremony takes its name of *Tashlih*, 'Mayest Thou cast' (Abrahams, *Festival Studies*, London, 1906, p. 91; and *JE* xii. 66).

On the eve of the Day of Atonement the ceremony of *Kappōreth* took place (see Oesterley and Box, *Religion and Worship of the Synagogue*², p. 445). It consisted in swinging a fowl, afterwards given to the poor as a symbolic atonement. (The origin of this custom, and also the objections raised against it, may be studied in *JE* ii. 282, and vii. 435; see also *Shulḥan 'Arukh*, ch. 605.) Probably the original aim was charity—to provide poor Jews with a meal before the fast began.

LITERATURE.—C. G. Montefiore, in *JQR* xvi. (1904) 209 (very important); *JE*, art. 'Atonement'; cf. *ERE*, art. CRIMES AND PUNISHMENTS (Jewish); Oesterley and Box, *Religion and Worship of the Synagogue*², London, 1911. For Hebrew books on the subject of Atonement, see the chapter on ethical literature in Israel Abrahams, *Short Hist. of Jewish Literature*, London, 1906. See also *Authorized Daily Prayer-book*, ed. Singer, London, 1911, and *Maḥzor*, ed. A. Davis and H. Adler (cited as Davis), do. 1904, also ed. David Levi, do. 1824, 1860, etc.; *Seliḥôth*, ed. Proops, Amsterdam, 1711; Sephardic *Maḥzor*, ed. Gaster, Oxford Press, 1901 ff.; do. ed. de Sola, London, 1836–38 and 1852. Talmudic references are best studied in L. Goldschmidt's ed. (cited as Gold.), with German tr. and notes, Berlin, 1901, or in Rodkinson's (cited as Rodk.) Eng. tr., New York (vol. vi. = 1899). Mishn. *Yoma* is edited by H. L. Strack (*Schriften des Inst. Jud.*, Berlin, no. 3), Berlin, 1888. See also *Shulḥan*

'Arukh of Joseph Caro in any modern edition. For Maimonides on *Ḥeleq*, see J. Holzer, *Zur Gesch. der Dogmenlehre in der jüd. Religionsphilosophie des Mittelalters*, Berlin, 1901; also E. Pocock, *Porta Mosis*, Oxford, 1655 (with Latin tr.); see also Strack's ed. of *Sanhedrin* in *Schriften des Inst. Jud.*, Berlin, 1910; and Maimonides, *Hilkhoth Teshubah*.

HERBERT LOEWE.

EXPIATION AND ATONEMENT (Muslim).—The formulæ whereby duties and rights are designated in Islām are identical with those used for debts and credits. Hence the acts prescribed by the code are regarded as debts due from man to God, incurred by acceptance of Islām; other debts may be incurred by undertaking obligations voluntarily or by violating prohibitions. In the third case expiation is necessary; in the second it may be permissible; in the first it has no place.

Man's debts to God are the five daily prayers, fasting in Ramaḍān, payment of alms, and pilgrimage. If he omit to pray at the right time, all he need do is to say an extra prayer at a later time; no 'expiation' (*kaffārah*) is required. There is some question whether one who has temporarily apostatized and been re-converted to Islām ought to make up for all the prayers which he has omitted in the interval, and whether the same obligation is incumbent on one who has been ignorantly brought up, so as to be unaware of the obligations. The majority hold that this obligation does exist (*Fatāwā* of Ibn Taimiyyah, A.H. 1326, ii. 238). 'Payment' of prayer, *i.e.* saying it at the proper time (*adā'*), is distinguished from 'repayment' of this sort (*qaḍā*). Similarly, one who has for any reason omitted to fast should make up for the omission by fasting the requisite number of days out of season. Unpaid alms can also be given when the year in which they should have been paid has elapsed; or they may be taken out of the inheritance. An omitted pilgrimage can be made good by deputy, *i.e.* by paying some one to perform it in a dead man's stead. What distinguishes all these cases from those which follow is that there is no substitution of one performance for another; the identical act is performed, though out of the time, or by another person.

'Expiation' in the case of obligations voluntarily undertaken means the substitution of a different act for the act originally promised. This is not permissible in the case of a vow, but is so in the case of an oath (Ibn Qayyim al-Jauziyyah, *Works*, A.H. 1325, ii. 240). The Qur'ān emphasizes the principle that an oath uttered with full intent may be broken on condition of some act pleasing to God being performed, such act being the manumission of a slave, the feeding of the poor, or, if these be beyond the means of the perjurer, fasting (*Qur.* v. 91); the substituted act is called *kaffārah* (a word borrowed from the Hebrew), and the proceeding itself is called 'profaning of the oath' (*taḥillat al-yamīn* [*Qur.* lxvi. 2], otherwise interpreted as 'loosening of the bond'). The theory that it removes the guilt incurred is rejected by some jurists, on the ground that in many cases such perjury is approved. It does not appear that any oath is exempted from this principle; and the discussions of the jurists are ordinarily confined to the question of the formulæ which constitute 'oaths' and the amount of compensation to be paid by the perjurer. The Prophet is supposed to have said: 'If a man swear to do something, and afterwards find a better course, let him do what is better and make *kaffārah* for the oath' (Yāqūt, *Dictionary of Learned Men*, vi. 116).

Where a debt has been incurred by violation of a prohibition, the latter may take the form of a capital offence or a mild offence. For the former the code provides specific punishments, which may, indeed, be regarded as expiations (*kaffārāt* [Ibn Qayyim, ii. 218]), and are probably so in the sense that they redeem the Muslim criminal from hell-fire; though in the case of the wilful murder of a Muslim some further expiation is required for this purpose. For certain mild offences, *e.g.* the slaughter of wild beasts in the sacred area, the Qur'ān prescribes expiations; they take the form of the sacrifice in each case of a tame animal equal in value to the wild animal killed—a camel for an ostrich, a cow for a wild ass, etc. Where the means of the offender are insufficient, fasting must serve instead. For minor offences, which are not treated in the code, according to one theory expiation is to be found in abstention from capital offences; while another doctrine is that the prescribed ordinances count as expiation for them.

Where in a Muslim's account with God there is a deficit, it appears that this will be expiated by temporary punishment after death; and, indeed, the Ṣūfī Abū Ṭālib al-Makkī argues that the fire will have the effect of cleansing on the soul of believers, owing to their affinity with air and earth, whereas it will merely attract those of unbelievers to itself, owing to their affinity with fire (*Qūt al-qulūb*, A.H. 1310, ii. 150). This view, which is based on one solution of a difficult theological problem (whether the believer will in any case remain for ever in hell), gives the punishment subjective value, but does not make it an objective off-set for the offences; and the writer, in agreement with this, makes the act of fasting itself agreeable to God, and thereby fit to rank with those charitable deeds which otherwise serve as expiations.

As between human beings, expiation of offences is a matter for private arrangement. One who has received an injury may agree to accept expiation, or may prefer to avenge it (if he have the power), or to leave it to be settled at the Last Judgment. Ghazālī gives special treatment to the case where the offence committed is *slander*; unless the slanderer expiates and obtains forgiveness from his victim, some of his good deeds will be transferred to the credit of the latter, or some of the latter's misdeeds transferred to his account on the Day of Judgment (*Revival of the Religious Sciences*, A.H. 1306, iii. 116).

Although the cases of expiation contemplated by the Muslim code are thus strictly limited, certain practices, involving the idea of expiation, survived from pagan times, and certain others are to be ascribed to the natural belief that bad actions of various sorts can be cancelled by acts of supererogation. To the former class belong the sacrifices which the law permits rather than enjoins—such as the offering of two ewes for the birth of a male and one for the birth of a female child, where the number corresponds with the rule in the Law of Inheritance that the male counts as two females. The practice doubtless originally signifies that the life of the animal is to serve as a substitute for that of the child which the god may claim; but the jurists seem unwilling to formulate this theory. The sacrifice which forms part of the pilgrimage ceremony is regarded as winning favour rather than as expiating sin; but, according to a tradition, the weight of the animal is to be put into the scale of the sacrificer's good deeds on the Day of Judgment, and so will serve as an off-set against evil deeds which will be found in the other scale.

LITERATURE.—This has been given in the article.

D. S. MARGOLIOUTH.

EXPIATION AND ATONEMENT (Parsi).—**1. Expiatory prayers.**—The Avestan words *paitita* and *āpereti*, 'expiation,' occur in the *Vendīdād* (iii. 21, vii. 52 [gloss in the Pahlavi tr.], iii. 38 f., viii. 107, xviii. 68) in connexion with the penalties prescribed for various crimes. Neither the Gāthās nor the extant Avestan texts have preserved for us any expiatory prayer composed in the Avestan language. The *frastuye* prayer incorporated in the Khordah Avesta from *Yasna* xi. 17–xii. 7 is sometimes spoken of as a specimen of the Avestan expiatory prayer; but it is rather a confessional prayer than an expiatory one, containing, as it does, simply a declaration on the part of the faithful that he accepts all good thoughts, good words, and good deeds, and renounces all evil thoughts, evil words, and evil deeds. For the expiatory prayer proper we have to turn to the Pāzand texts of the later period. There is a penitential prayer called *Patēṭ-ī Pashimānī*, composed in Pāzand, the authorship of which is attributed to Dastur Adarbad Mahraspand, the high priest and premier of King Shāpūr II. (A.D. 310–379). In addition to this, there is an abbreviated *Patēṭ* known as the *Patēṭ-ī Khūd*.[1] These expiatory prayers enumerate all sins of commission and omission; those done knowingly or unknowingly, actually committed or merely contemplated; sins pertaining to thought, word, or deed, body or soul, this world or the next; those committed against Ahura Mazda, the Amesha Spentas, or their respective creations; against parents or children, kinsmen or countrymen, friends or neighbours —in short, all sins that it is possible for human beings to commit.

2. Expiation absolves sins.—Fasting from food is prohibited; the only fast inculcated in the Mazdayasnian religion is from sin (*Sad Dar*, lxxxiii. 3–5). The faithful should not commit sins voluntarily (*Mainōg-ī Khraṭ*, lii. 16). Not to sin is better than to expiate sin (*Dāṭistān-ī Dīnīk*, xli. 11). But, if one has sinned through thoughtlessness or otherwise, he should take the first opportunity to atone for it. A sin unatoned for increases every year in dimension, whereas by atonement its growth is stunted, and it withers like a tree (*Sad Dar*, xlv. 5). Owing to a man's sins, he incurs the condemnation of Ahura Mazda; but sincere penance restores him again to the right relation to his heavenly father, and he is forgiven. The efficacy of expiation is such that, whereas the recital of every sacred Gāthā routs one demon, the expiation of one's sins routs every fiend (*Shāyast lā-Shāyast*, xx. 11). The best time for making atonement for one's sins is during one's life (*Dāṭistān-ī Dīnīk*, xli. 10). It is said that men should make it a habit to recite a short penitential formula every night before going to bed (*Sad Dar*, lxxxiv. 1). For who knows but the Demon of Death may capture him while asleep, and he may not rise to atone for his sins in the light of the day? If an individual dies without expiating his sins, his way to heaven is blocked, for it is ordained in the religion of Ahura Mazda that the only means of entering heaven or to escape hell is the making of expiation while living (*Dāṭistān-ī Dīnīk*, xli. 10). The religion of Mazda extirpates all kinds of sins by means of atonement (*Vendīdād*, iii. 41, 42, viii. 29, 30). As the sins already atoned for in this life stand cancelled in the book of life, no account is taken of them when the soul approaches the seat of judgment on the dawn of the fourth day after death (*Dāṭistān-ī Dīnīk*, xiii. 2, 3). We are told in another place that such a soul does receive punishment at the Chinvat bridge, but is spared the tortures of hell (*ib.* xli. 8; *Sad Dar*, xlv. 10), and is given a place in *Hameshtagān*, a place specially reserved for the souls whose good and evil deeds are equal (*Rivāyat-i Dārāb Hormazdyār*, pp. 497, 498, Navsari, 1896).

In one of his communings with Ahura Mazda, Zarathushtra sees the soul of king Jamshed in the torments of hell. Jamshed becomes penitent before the prophet, and craves forgiveness. Zarathushtra thereupon asks Ahura Mazda to show mercy to the fallen king. The soul is then removed from hell and sent to *Hameshtagān*. There it remains for a period of one thousand years, and, after further penance and expiation, is forgiven all sins and sent to *Garonmāna* (*ib.* 498–500).

If a follower of Mazda who has sinned apostatizes to another religion and dies without atonement, his soul goes to hell, and remains there till the final Renovation (*Dāṭistān-ī Dīnīk*, xli. 5, 6).

3. The nature of expiation.—True repentance must bring about a change of will. The penitent must resolve to abstain from ever repeating the sinful act (*Dīnkarṭ*, tr. Sanjana, Bombay, 1874 ff., bk. vi. ch. 50). Loud confession with the lips and bathing the face with a torrent of tears are of no avail, if the heart is not affected. If the individual really amends his ways and does not commit the sin any more, his former sin is absolved for ever (*Vend.* iii. 21, v. 26, ix. 50), and is swept away from him even as the mighty wind swiftly sweeps over the plain and carries away with it every blade of grass (*Mainōg-ī Khraṭ*, lii. 18, 19); if not, the first sin comes back (*Sad Dar*, xlv. 11). The soul becomes pure only when the atonement is heartfelt (*Dīnk.* vol. i. p. 9), and is accompanied by a firm resolve on the part of the individual to redeem his past by good deeds in the present and future. Such an expiation washes away all sins and removes future punishment (*ib.* vol. ix. p. 598).

4. Expiation before a qualified Dastur.—Sin is the disease of the spirit, and requires to be cured. The Dastur, or high priest, cures sickness of the soul, even as the physician heals bodily diseases (*Dīnk.* vol. i. p. 9). If one commits a sin, whether through weakness of the flesh or through ignorance, he should penitently approach the Dastur for remedy (*Mainōg-ī Khraṭ*, lii. 17), and confess the sin in his presence (*Patēṭ-ī Pashimānī*, 10). But, if one lives in a place where a Dastur is not found, he should travel to distant lands to find a high priest at least once a year, more particularly on the day Rām of the month Mihr (*Rivāyat*, p. 500). Thus, as far as possible, one should make expiation in the presence of a Dastur (*Sad Dar*, xlv. 2). The Dastur who presides at the confession should himself be righteous. If a layman who is eager to atone for his sins has no faith in the holiness of the priest, or knows him to be wicked, he shall approach others for the purpose (*Rivāyat*, p. 501). A Dastur is guilty of the *margarzān* sin, if he prescribes greater penalties than the guilt of the sinner requires, or if he reveals the secrets of the man who has confessed before him (*ib.* p. 500).

5. Other sources to which one can have recourse for expiation.—The texts mention that, in the absence of a Dastur to officiate at the expiatory rites, any righteous man may take his place, and the penitent may atone for his sins before him (*Sad Dar*, xlv. 8). One may offer one's penitential prayers even before sun, moon, and fire (*Mainōg-ī Khraṭ*, liii. 8); before *haoma* or *baresman* (see BARSOM); before the Amesha Spentas; before Mithra, Sraosha, and Rashnu; or before one's own soul (*Patēṭ-ī Pashimānī*, 3). But the best of all expiations is that accomplished before Ahura Mazda (*Dīnk.* vol. ix. p. 630 f.).

6. Retributive expiation.—The penitent sinner has to perform other duties besides the recital of the *Patēṭs*, the confession of his sins before the high priest, and the sincere atonement wrought within his own spirit. When he sincerely desires

[1] The *Patēṭ-ī Pashimānī* is edited in Pāzand by Edalji Kersāspi Antiā (*Pāzend Texts*, Bombay, 1909, pp. 118–125), and translated by Spiegel (*Avesta übersetzt*, Leipzig, 1852–63, iii. 207–215); the *Patēṭ-ī Khūd* is edited in Pahlavi by de Harlez (*Manuel du pehlevi*, Paris, 1880, pp. 140–151), and in Pāzand by Antiā (pp. 146–152), and translated by Spiegel (pp. 215–219). Mention should also be made of the two other Parsi expiatory prayers: the *Patēṭ-ī Irānīg*, edited by Antiā (pp. 134–146), and translated by Spiegel (pp. 219–229) and by Darmesteter (*Le Zend-Avesta*, Paris, 1892–93, iii. 167–180); and the *Patēṭ-ī Viṭarṭakān*, or 'Renunciation for the Dead,' edited by Antiā (pp. 125–134), and as yet untranslated.

pardon, he must be prepared to undergo any corporal punishment, or to pay any amount as penalty, or to perform any other deeds of righteousness that the Dastur may prescribe (*Sad Dar*, xlv. 6; *Dāṭistān-ī Dīnīk*, lxxv. 5). Bodily punishment in this world saves the sinner from future punishment. But, if he does not submit to the penalty in this world, his soul goes to the abode of the *Druj* (*Vend.* viii. 107). The penitent is generally ordered either to arrange a certain number of marriages between the faithful poor, or to offer *zaothra* libations, or to carry certain loads of sweet-scented wood to the fire, or to consecrate *baresman* twigs, or to throw bridges over canals, or to kill noxious creatures such as snakes, frogs, and ants, or to practise other good works as compensation for the wrong he has done (*Vend.* xiv. 1–18, xviii. 67–74; *Dāṭistān-ī Dīnīk*, lxxviii. 17, 19, lxxix. 10, 12; *Mainōg-ī Khraṭ*, liii. 9). The pulling down of the *dakhmas*, wherein lie interred the dead bodies of men, or the killing of the noxious creature Zairimyangura, which kills the creatures of the good spirit by thousands, is also a means of the expiation of one's sins in thought, word, and deed, and is equivalent to the recital of a *Patēṭ* (*Vend.* vii. 51, xiii. 5–7).

7. Inexpiable sins.—The sins of burying or burning corpses, eating dead matter, and sodomy are termed *anāperetha*, 'unatonable' (*Vend.* i. 11, 12, viii. 27). The man who knowingly lets a corpse remain interred in the earth for a period of two years becomes guilty of *anāperetha* (*ib.* iii. 36–39). Ahriman has seduced men into the cooking of corpses—an inexpiable sin, the penalty for which is death (*ib.* i. 16, viii. 73 f.; Strabo, p. 732).

8. Reciting 'Patēṭs' for the expiation of the sins of others.—It is customary among the modern Parsis to hire a priest to recite *Patēṭs* before a dead body as long as it remains in the house. The recital of this expiatory prayer forms an important part of the ceremonials performed in honour of the dead, even after the removal of the corpse to its final resting-place. The relatives and friends of the deceased join in reciting the same prayers for the expiation of the soul which is now embarking on its journey to the next world. They generally keep up this observance daily for at least a month, or in many cases throughout the first year.

If one man has been requested by another to offer penitential prayers for him after he dies, and if he has consented to do so, he should hasten to perform his obligation as soon as he hears of the death of the said person, or, at the latest, on the dawn of the fourth day after death, at the momentous period when the soul approaches the threshold of the celestial world. If the man sincerely recites the *Patēṭ* as he has consented to do, the benefit of it reaches the soul of the deceased at the Bridge (*Rivāyat*, p. 501). If he fails to do so, he is guilty of neglecting his sacred duty towards the dead, and should make atonement (*Patēṭ-ī Pashimānī*, 11).

If a man during his lifetime is unable, for any reason, to recite *Patēṭs* for the expiation of his sins, he may ask the priests to do so for him on payment. But in this case he should himself recite at least the shortest expiatory formula three times a day (*Rivāyat*, p. 501).

LITERATURE.—The sources are indicated in the article. Of modern writers on the subject, the following may be cited: A. V. W. Jackson, *Persia Past and Present*, New York, 1906, p. 387; Rastamji Sanjana, *Zarathushtra and Zarathushtrianism*, Leipzig, 1906, p. 194; D. F. Karaka, *History of the Parsis*, London, 1884, i. 166, 213, ii. 171 f.; V. Henry, *Le Parsisme*, Paris, 1905.

MANECKJI NUSSERVANJI DHALLA.

EXPIATION AND ATONEMENT (Roman).—The attribute of *pietas*, according to Roman ideas, pertained to all who faithfully and conscientiously discharged the duties they owed to the gods (Cic. *de Nat. Deor.* i. 116: 'pietas est justitia adversum deos'; *de Inv. Rhet.* ii. 66: 'religionem eam quae in metu et caerimonia deorum sit, appellant pietatem'), and who thus lived in perfect harmony with the higher powers (cf. Plaut. *Rud.* 26: 'facilius si quis pius est a dis supplicans, quam qui scelestust, inveniat veniam sibi'; Catull. lxx. 2 ff.: 'homini cum se cogitat esse pium; nec sanctam violasse fidem, nec foedere in ullo divom ad fallendos numine abusum homines' . . . *ib.* 26: 'o di, reddite mi hoc pro pietate mea'). Any one who, on the other hand, had forfeited the *pax deorum* by transgressing the sacred ordinances of the *ius divinum* was said to be *impius*, i.e. outside the laws and covenants regulating legitimate intercourse between mortals and the gods, and was therefore subject to Divine punishment—so far, at least, as he failed to purge himself of his guilt by the proper expiatory acts, and so to regain his former legal relations to the gods. The idea of thus making atonement for transgression (Festus, p. 228: 'piamentum et exsolutio omnis contractae religionis'), and by this means recovering the condition of *pietas*, is denoted by the verb *piare* or *expiare* (the prefix *ex-* is here simply an intensive, as in *exsecrare*), and the corresponding substantive *piaculum* is applied both to the trespass itself, the ritual dereliction (so Gell. x. 15, 10: 'eo die verberari piaculum est'), and the act by which it is expiated (so Macrob. *Sat.* i. 16. 10, 'porco piaculum dare debere'), and in the latter sense, therefore, corresponds exactly to the *multa* of the secular penal code. A more lax (and indeed altogether incorrect) usage of the term *piaculum* is met with in writers (*e.g.* Gell. xvi. 6. 10: 'ostentum enim est et piaculis factis procurandum'; cf. Tac. *Hist.* v. 13: 'prodigia, quae neque hostiis neque votis piare fas habet gens,' etc.) who apply it likewise to expiatory acts designed to assuage the Divine anger manifested in prodigies, *i.e.* unnatural and terrifying occurrences in the external world (see PRODIGIES AND PORTENTS), and speak, *e.g.*, of 'piacula irae deorum' (Liv. xl. 37. 2); for *piare* in its original acceptation is in no sense equivalent to *placare*, while those *qui piantur* are not the gods and their wrath, but sinful men and their conduct.

The ritual transgressions which demanded an expiation are of very diverse kinds. A large number of them consist of offences against the minutely detailed provisions of the ceremonial law (Serv. on *Aen.* iv. 646: 'et sciendum, si quid caerimoniis non fuerit observatum, piaculum admitti'), for the slightest deviation from the ritual directions (the formula for such a deviation is 'non rite factum est'; cf. Liv. v. 17. 2, xxii. 9. 9; Cic. *de Har. Resp.* 23), or even a trifling and insignificant disturbance of a religious act—a sacrifice, or the games—not only rendered the whole ceremony invalid and necessitated its being repeated, but also required to be atoned for by a *piaculum*.

At the *feriae Latinae*, for instance, if, in the distribution of the sacrificial flesh, one of the participators was overlooked (Liv. xxxii. 1. 9, xxxvii. 3. 4), or if in the prayer the name of one of the interested communities was omitted (Liv. xli. 16. 1), it was enough to invalidate the whole celebration; while, as regards the games, Cicero (*de Har. Resp.* 23; cf. Arnob. iv. 31) gives quite a list of the irregularities—manifestly of frequent occurrence—which necessarily entailed an *instauratio* of the proceedings. Thus, if a dancer suddenly stopped dancing, if the flutist ceased playing, if the boy who accompanied the chariot of the gods let go the reins, if the presiding aedile made a slip of the tongue while praying, or spilled some drops of the libation—in all such eventualities, Cicero expressly tells us, not only had the games to be repeated from the beginning, but, in addition, a *piaculum* was required: 'ludi sunt non rite facti, eaque errata expiantur et mentes deorum immortalium ludorum instauratione placantur.'

Similarly, every breach of the rigorous injunctions against doing work during the *feriae publicae* (such offence was spoken of as *ferias polluere* [Gell. ii. 28. 3; Macrob. i. 16. 9; Serv. on *Georg.* i. 268]) was subject to the penalties of religious law. Thus, if a prætor gave judgment on a *dies nefastus* (Varro, *de Ling. Lat.* vi. 30), if a general issued an order calling out the efficient troops on one of the days of the *feriae publicae* (Varro, *ap.* Macrob. i. 16. 19: 'viros vocare feriis non licet; si vocavit, piaculum esto'), if the farmer chose a feast-day for any of those agricultural operations which the regulations regarding the period of rest did not explicitly exclude as urgent and not to be deferred (Colum. ii. 22. 4; lists of the sanctioned operations in Cato, *de Agri Cult.* 2. 4, Verg. *Georg.* i. 268 ff., Colum. ii. 22, xi. 1. 20)—such actions had to be atoned for by a *piaculum.* There were also numerous possibilities of incurring guilt in the sphere of the *ius manium*—the law relating to the dead and their tombs.

The provisions of this law were violated by such acts as the following: burying the dead within the city (*Lex Col. Jul. Genet.* [*CIL* ii. Suppl. 5439, cap. 73]), removing a corpse from its tomb (Paul. *Sent.* i. 21. 4; cf. *CIL* vi. 1884, x. 8259), omitting to make the requisite purification of the *funesta familia* after a death in their house, or not performing the rite in the prescribed manner (Gell. iv. 6. 8), failing to perform the *humatio* by casting earth (*iniecta gleba*) upon a corpse found unburied (Paul. p. 223; cf. Varro, *ap.* Non. p. 163), or becoming responsible for disposing of the dead in a manner forbidden by the ritual code (Cic. *de Leg.* ii. 57: 'in eo, qui in nave necatus, deinde in mare proiectus esset . . . porcam heredi esse contractam et habendas triduum ferias et porco femina piaculum pati; si in mari mortuus esset, eadem praeter piaculum et ferias').

The laws were specially stringent in regard to acts of encroachment upon things consecrated to the gods. A *res sacra* was inviolable, and to damage it in any way, or to remove from the sacred precincts any object that belonged to the holy place, was a penal offence; thus, the ancient law of the grove at Spoleto begins with the sentence: 'honce loucom ne qu(i)s violatod neque exvehito neque exferto quod louci siet' (*CIL* xi. 4766). If a Roman magistrate or a company of Roman soldiers desecrated the property of a temple, even the temple of a foreign deity, then not only did the actual perpetrators become liable to Divine punishment, but the State likewise had to purge itself, by numerous acts of expiation, of all complicity in the misdeeds of its officials or its soldiery. Thus, *piacula* were offered on the State's behalf after the sacking of Proserpina's temple at Locri by the legate Q. Pleminius in 204 B.C. (Liv. xxix. 19. 9, 21. 4), after a theft committed by Roman troops at the same sanctuary in 200 B.C. (xxxi. 12. 4, xxxii. 1. 8), and after the act of sacrilege perpetrated by the Censor, Q. Fulvius Flaccus, in carrying away the marble roofing of the temple of Juno Lacinia in 173 B.C. (Liv. xlii. 3. 10). But an expiation was no less necessary even when the proprietary rights of the gods were infringed without any evil intent. Thus, the pardon of a criminal who was under sentence of 'consecratio capitis et bonorum' demanded a *piaculum*, because such an act of pardon deprived the deity of something that was legally his (as when absolution was granted to the Horatius who murdered his sister; cf. Liv. i. 26. 13, also Mommsen, *Röm. Strafrecht*, Leipzig, 1899, p. 903), and the *piaculum* required for the soldier who had been devoted to the gods but had survived the battle, as also for the loss of the lance on which the general had stood while pronouncing the formula of devotion (Liv. viii. 10. 12, 14), is to be explained in the same way.

Of the numerous other contingencies in which satisfaction had to be made by acts of expiation, the following examples may be cited: if a widow married again before the expiry of the regular ten-months' period of mourning (Plut. *Numa*, 12); if a slave who, while being conveyed to the place of punishment, met the Flamen Dialis and threw himself at his feet, was nevertheless punished the same day (Gell. x. 15. 10); if a concubine (*pælex*) touched the altar of Juno (Paul. p. 222; Gell. iv. 3. 3); if a person uttered the names of the goddesses Salus, Semonia, Seia, Segetia, and Tutilina (Macrob. *Sat.* i. 16. 8), etc.

In order to form a proper estimate of the Roman practice of expiation, it is necessary to bear in mind the fact that, for the most part, it was concerned not with actual sins against the gods—sins emanating from an irreligious spirit—but with purely formal offences against the letter of the religious law, which was regarded as holy and inviolate, and was not to be altered even when its provisions had become altogether effete and quite irreconcilable with the exigencies of the day. In such cases the only available course was to transgress with open eyes the ceremonial regulations whose observance had come to be impossible, and then to make reparation for the unavoidable impiety by an act of expiation. Such an expiation was not only definitely fixed, alike as to its kind and as to its magnitude, but was in many cases actually performed beforehand, *i.e.* in anticipation of the forbidden action. Thus the farmer who saw himself compelled to undertake any such urgent and pressing work as sowing, hay-cutting, grape-gathering, or sheep-shearing, on a feast-day, simply sacrificed a dog as a prevenient *piaculum*, and thus, as he believed, freed himself from every imputation of guilt (Colum. ii. 22. 4: 'sed ne sementem quidem administrare, *nisi prius catulo feceris*, nec fenum secare aut vincire aut vehere ac ne vindemiam quidem cogi per religiones pontificum feriis licet nec oves tondere, *nisi prius catulo feceris*'). Similarly, the conveyance of a dead body from one place of sepulture to another—even when the *pontifices* had given their consent—could be effected only 'piaculo prius dato operis faciendi' (*CIL* x. 8259; cf. vi. 1884: 'piaculo facto'). Above all, it was quite impossible, in a higher state of civilization, to observe the law against the use of iron for sacred purposes—a law which had come down from the Bronze Age (Henzen, *Acta Fratrum Arvalium*, Berlin, 1874, p. 128), and which, *e.g.*, made it necessary for the Arval Brothers of the Imperial period to offer an expiatory sacrifice on the annual occasion when they made use of iron in having the record of their proceedings carved on the marble slabs of the temple-wall ('ob ferrum inlatum in aedem scripturae [et scalpturae] causa'), as also afterwards ('ob ferrum elatum' [Henzen, 128 ff.]). When, in a sacred grove, the necessary operations of thinning and pruning the branches, or of cutting up and clearing away dead and fallen trees, had to be performed, and when repairs were required in the edifice of a temple, it was impossible to avoid transgressing the ordinances of the *ius divinum* in two ways, *i.e.* both by the act of introducing iron instruments into the sacred precincts, and by that of removing things that belonged to the holy place, viz. branches, trees, and dilapidated portions of the building. It is true that later temple-regulations made express provision for such cases. The statutes of the temple of Juppiter Liber at Furfo, in the country of the Vestini (*CIL* ix. 3513), direct: 'utei tangere sarcire tegere devehere defigere mandare ferro oeti promovere referre fasque est'; while the ordinances of the grove of Spoleto (*CIL* xi. 4766) permit the felling of trees—at least for use at the annual sacrificial feast: 'neque cedito, nesei quo die res deina anua fiet. eod die quod rei dinai cau(s)a [f]iat, sine dolo malo cedre [l]icetod.' But, wherever the rigorous ancient law remained in force, all infringement of it necessarily entailed guilt, and this guilt could be annulled only by a *piaculum*.

Thus Cato the Elder (*op. cit.* 139) records the prayer which the farmer coupled with the expiatory offering called for by the operation of clearing a grove ('lucum conlucare'), and we find here an interesting regulation to the effect that, if the work was interrupted, or if feast-days intervened while it was in process, the sasrifice must be repeated at its resumption. Similarly, the Arval Brothers invariably performed *piacula* when they removed trees that had fallen from age or had been overthrown by a tempest (Henzen, 136 ff.), though the great sacrificial rite of the *lustrum missum*, which they performed twice in special circumstances, and which Henzen (p. 140 ff.) discusses under the term *piacula*, comes under the head, not of expiation at all, but of lustration. The *piaculum* performed by the Arval Brothers as an atonement for pruning the trees of their grove ('luci coinquiendi et operis faciundi'), and corresponding to the sacrifice described by Cato, was offered annually on the second day of their annual festival, immediately before the principal oblation to Dea Dia (Henzen, 19 ff.). But, as the season of the year in which the festival occurred—the month of May—scarcely seems suitable for the pruning of trees, there is much to be said for Henzen's conjecture that, on the occasion of the annual festival, all operations of the kind requiring to be done during the year were atoned for by a single *piaculum* (p. 22). Such procedure would find a parallel in the sacrifice of the *porca praecidanea* which originally was required *piaculi gratia* (Gell. iv. 6. 8) only from one 'qui mortuo iusta non fecerit' (Paul. p. 223; cf. Mar. Vict. p. 25 [Keil]: 'qui iusta defuncto non fecerunt aut in faciendo peccarunt'), *i.e.* had in some way violated the injunctions of the *ius manium* (cf. also Varro, *ap.* Non. p. 163; Gell. *loc. cit.*). This sacrifice was not only performed at the time when the offence was committed, but was also offered annually before the beginning of harvest; hence the erroneous explanation of the name as if 'antea quam novam frugem *praeciderent*' (Paul. p. 219), while in reality *praecidanea*, as the counterpart to *succidanea*, was the 'porca quae ante sacrificium caeditur'—the idea being that every one had, consciously or unconsciously, committed an offence of the kind during the year, and thus made satisfaction for it in a single act. An account of this ceremony is given by Cato (*op. cit.* 134), who also furnishes valuable particulars regarding the ritual of the sacrifice.

Expiatory sacrifices seem to have been combined also with other important religious ceremonies—*i.e.* a *piaculum* was offered in consideration of all offences that might have been committed, whether consciously or unconsciously, but was performed apart from any particular instance, and by way of gaining a general absolution. There seems at least to be hardly any other explanation of the fact that, at the dedication of the *spolia opima*, not only were sacrifices rendered to Juppiter, Mars, and Quirinus, but a *piaculum* was also offered (Fest. p. 189); while, again, the oblation of the *propudianus porcus*, which was offered in 'sacrificio gentis Claudiae velut piamentum et exsolutio omnis contractae religionis' (p. 238), can be explained most naturally as an inclusive expiation of similar character.

The expiatory rite of the *piaculum*, in the great majority of cases, was an act of sacrifice. Now and again, indeed, the observance of feast-days (*ferias observare*) was prescribed, either as a concomitant of (Cic. *de Leg.* ii. 57), or as a substitute for (Macrob. *Sat.* i. 16. 8), a sacrifice. By way of indemnity for the soldier who had been devoted but had not fallen, it was necessary, in addition to the sacrifice, to present an image not less than seven feet in height, and bury it in the earth (Liv. viii. 10. 12); and the fine 'in tem(plum) Iovis d . . . (denarium) I. d(ato),' exacted, according to *CIL* xii. 2426, for polluting a stream, should also perhaps be regarded as a *piaculum*. The general practice, however, was to offer a *piacularis hostia*. The recipient of the indemnity was, of course, the particular deity whose rights had been infringed: thus the *piaculum* for damaging a sanctuary, or violating its statutes, was rendered to the god to whom the sanctuary belonged; that for breaking the rest enjoined on feast-days, to the deity to whom the feast-day was dedicated; that for violating the *ius manium*, to Tellus (who, along with Ceres, is rightly named by Varro [*ap.* Non. p. 163] in connexion with the sacrifice of the *porca praecidanea*, though Ceres alone is mentioned by our other authorities) and to the Manes. If there was any uncertainty in the matter, and, in particular, if the expiation was required on behalf of the State, the *pontifices* were consulted, and had authority to decide 'quae piacula quibus diis quibus hostiis fieri placeret' (Liv. xxix. 19. 8); if it was found impossible to determine exactly to which deity a *piaculum* was justly due, a sacrifice was offered in accordance with the formula, 'si deus si dea est, quorum illud sacrum est, uti tibi ius est . . . piaculum facere' (Cato, 139). The choice of a victim depended upon the particular deity to whom it was offered. Frequently a deity received as a *piaculum* the kind of animal specially associated with his ordinary worship. Thus Juppiter received an ox (*CIL* xi. 4766), Mars *suovetaurilia* (Liv. viii. 10. 14), Juno a she-lamb (Paul. p. 222; Gell. iv. 3. 3), the Manes a black sheep (*CIL* x. 8259); the cow in calf offered as a *piaculum* by a widow who married again during the recognized period of mourning (Plut. *Numa*, 12) would seem to have been assigned to Tellus, to whom *fordae boves* were sacrificed at the *Fordicidia* (Varro, *de Ling. Lat.* vi. 15; Ovid, *Fasti*, iv. 629 ff.); while the rustic practice of offering a dog as an atonement for breaking the law enjoining rest on feast-days (Colum. ii. 22. 4) finds a parallel in the immolation of a dog at the agrarian festivals of the *Robigalia* (Ovid, iv. 908, 936 ff.; Colum. x. 34. 3) and the *Augurium Canarium* (Fest. p. 285; Philarg. on Verg. *Georg.* iv. 425). But the animal most frequently made use of in expiatory sacrifices—at once the most ancient and the least ostentatious victim—was the pig (*porcus* and *porca*; among the Arval Brothers also *porciliae*), as, *e.g.*, in cases of *pollutio feriarum* (Macrob. i. 16. 10), of violating the laws relating to the disposal of the dead (Cic. *de Leg.* ii. 57), of clearing a grove and removing fallen trees (Cato, 139; cf. Henzen, 22, 135 ff.). The abovementioned expiatory offerings, the *porca praecidanea* and the *propudianus porcus*, derive their names from this animal.

Not every ritual transgression, however, admitted of expiation. Some offences were beyond atonement, and placed the offender, as *impius*, outside the *pax deum*, so that he became liable to Divine punishment without any legal means of escape; as Cicero (*de Leg.* ii. 22) puts it: 'sacrum commissum, quod neque expiari poterit, impie commissum esto.' But the words with which Cicero continues, 'quod expiari poterit, publici sacerdotes expianto,' do not on a strict interpretation harmonize with the religious practice of the Romans; for here expiation was not effected by the priests at all, but simply came about on the ground of the expiatory sacrifice presented by the offender in the name of the State and the magistrates. The sole function of the priests in this regard was, when consulted by the individual or by the community, to deliver an authoritative judgment as to the possibility of expiating a given offence (*ib.* 37: 'publicus autem sacerdos imprudentiam consilio expiatam metu liberet, audaciam . . . damnet et impiam iudicet'), and as to the kind of atonement required—and it is possibly in this sense that the 'expianto' of Cicero (*ib.* 22) is to be understood. But they had no part whatever in the performance of the expiatory sacrifice offered in name of the community—the earliest exception to this took place in the reign of the Emperor Claudius, who (according to Tac. *Ann.* xii. 8) in 49 B.C. directed 'sacra ex legibus Tulli regis piaculaque apud lucum Dianae per pontifices danda'—nor did it lie with them to pronounce judgment or inflict punishment in connexion with religious offences (cf. Mommsen, 36 f.). Nor could either priest or magistrate exercise any penal procedure against an *impius* who had committed an inexpiable offence, or had failed to make atonement for an offence that was expiable; such offender simply remained subject to Divine punishment, which he could not avert by any subsequent efforts towards reparation (Cic. *de Leg.* ii. 22: 'impius ne audeto placare donis iram deorum'); from the human side, one guilty of perjury, and, as we may assume, every other *impius*, incurred nothing beyond the censor's reprobation (cf. A. Pernice, *SBAW*, 1885, p. 1164 ff.).

In course of time, however, the sphere of ritual transgression came to be encroached upon by the secular element, the ceremonial penalty (*piaculum*) being conjoined with, or in part superseded by, the legal penalty of the fine (*multa*). Every offence committed wittingly and wilfully ('sciens dolo malo') against the *ius sacrum* was, in a strict sense, accounted inexpiable; thus, *e.g.*, the praetor who had knowingly administered justice on a *dies nefastus* was proclaimed inexpiably guilty by the Pontifex Maximus, Q. Mucius Scævola (Varro, vi. 30; cf. Macrob. i. 16. 10); but in the law of the grove of Spoleto (*CIL* xi. 4766: 'honce loucom ne qu(i)s violatod . . . si quis violasit, Iove bovid piaclum datod. sei quis scies violasit dolo malo, Iovei bovid piaclum datod et a(sses) CCC moltai suntod. eius piacli moltaique dicator[ei] exactio est[od]') unconscious and conscious, or intentional, injuries are differentiated by the circumstance that, in addition to the *piaculum* incurred in all cases, the voluntary offence demanded also a *multa*, and to this extent the latter found its way even into the sphere of religious law, while the legally actionable character of the *multa* came to be assigned likewise to the *piaculum*. The juxtaposition of *multa* and *piaculum*, as found in Macrob. i. 16. 9f. in connexion with the violation of the feast-day repose, is to be explained on similar grounds; and by the municipal law of the Colonia Julia Genetiva (*CIL* ii. Suppl. 5439), *cap.* 73, not only were those who interred a body within the city obliged to pay a fine of 5000 sesterces—for which any citizen might take legal action—and threatened with the removal of the grave, but it was also ordained that, 'si adversus ea mortuus inlatus positusve erit, expianto uti oportebit,' *i.e.* a *piaculum* was required. On the other hand, the law of the grove of Luceria (*CIL* x. 782) enjoined that one who had polluted the grove ('in hoce loucarid stircus ne[qu]is fundatid neve cadaver proiecitad neve parentatid') should be punished either by a fine (which was recoverable at law by any citizen) or by a *multa* of the magistrates ('sei quis arvorsu hac faxit, [civ]ium quis volet pro ioudicatod n[ummum] L manum iniect[i]o estod. seive mac[i]steratus volet multare, [l]icetod'); while by the ordinances of the temple of Furfo (*CIL* ix. 3513) one who rifled the sanctuary was liable only to the *multa* of the aedile ('sei qui heic sacrum surrupuerit, aedilis multatio esto, quanti volet'), nothing whatever being said of an expiation.

Since the Romans, as has been shown in the foregoing, regarded guilt in relation to the gods, and its remission by expiation, from the standpoint of mere legality, it is obvious that penitence, in the sense of a repentant and contrite spirit, and of a course of conduct directed by such a spirit, did not come into consideration at all. This is seen unmistakably in the prayer accompanying the expiatory sacrifice for the *lucum conlucare* (Cato, 139), inasmuch as it contains no expression of regret or apology for the offence against the sacred ordinances, but simply decrees: 'uti *tibi ius est* porco piaculo facere.'

LITERATURE.—J. Marquardt, *Röm. Staatsverwaltung*, iii.², Leipzig, 1885, pp. 179 f., 257 ff., 459 f.; G. Wissowa, *Religion und Kultus der Römer*², Munich, 1912, p. 392 ff.

G. WISSOWA.

EXPIATION AND ATONEMENT (Teutonic). — Among the ancient Teutons expiation was the act by which peace was restored between the wrong-doer on the one hand, and the wronged or his kindred on the other. An act of expiation prevented the outbreak of a feud, or put an end to one already going on. It was either a purely private transaction, or else was effected with the co-operation of the legislative community, or in virtue of a legal judgment. In the latter case it falls within the sphere of criminal jurisprudence. That which was rendered by the wrong-doer for the purpose of expiating his violation of the peace was the 'boot' (O.N. and A.S. *bót*, O.H.G. *buoza*, Germ. *Busse*), 'redress,' 'indemnity,' 'atonement.'

1. Intervention of the community.—In pre-historic times expiation and atonement must have been the concern exclusively of the families to which the doer and the sufferer of the wrong belonged, and even in the historical period we still find cases in which the families were reconciled without any intervention on the part of the larger community. Thus the Icelandic sagas tell repeatedly how the murderer made unconditional surrender to the slain man's next of kin, put his freedom and his life unreservedly into the latter's hands, and so made atonement for his crime. If, however, the man-slayer did not take this course, there ensued the family feud, which formed so important a feature of ancient Teutonic life. But, in general, even in the early historical period, the entire legislative community had a share in the business of reconciliation. For the rupture of amicable relations which demanded expiation affected not the injured family only, but also the community at large. It was the community, accordingly, which proscribed the wrong-doer, and thus made him an outlaw. This implied, however, that, when the outlawry was revoked and reconciliation effected, the community could claim a share in the indemnity, and even had the right to fix what the latter should be. In this way arose the practice of exacting fines, systematic regulations regarding which are found in the codes of all the Teutonic peoples. In the earlier period fines were paid in cattle (Tac. *Germ.* 12: 'equorum pecorumque numero convicti multantur'), or in food, or other materials of general utility (corn, linen, etc.). This form was longest retained in Scandinavia, but was subsequently superseded—first of all in Southern Germany—by metals or monetary equivalents. Of such payments the injured party received the largest share, usually two-thirds, while the smaller portion was assigned to the public authority—in particular, to the ruler—or to the common good. The latter portion was the price of peace, the *compositio*, the recompense paid to the community for its share in the re-establishment of peaceful relations.

2. Feud and outlawry.—Expiation presupposes a wrongful act. The party injured by such might be either an individual or a community (sacrilege, treason, desertion). In the former case the culprit ruptured the peace with one of his fellows or with the kindred of the injured person; in the latter, with the community at large. The wronged individual and his kindred had the right of revenge. If the offender was caught in the act 'red-handed,' summary vengeance could be executed upon him; if not, the family of the person injured had the right of feud against the wrong-doer. The feud (O.H.G. *fêhida*; A.S. *fæhð*) was a state of hostility between two families or clans (see BLOOD-FEUD [Teutonic], vol. ii. p. 735). The earliest documents recognize the feud only in connexion with homicide; in later sources it extends also to such offences as the abduction of women, adultery, and gross violation of honour. The exercise of this right lay entirely in the hands of the injured person and his relatives, and to them belonged also the right of fixing the expiation and indemnity by which the two groups might be formally reconciled. If, however, the crime was perpetrated against the community, the criminal was publicly proscribed; he was put out of the protection of the law, and, according to our northern authorities, was accounted *úheilagr*, as *vargr í véum*, 'a wolf in the league,' who was at everybody's mercy, and whose property any one might seize. This was also done when the cause of the wronged individual was espoused by the legislative community—a practice found among most of the Teutonic peoples as far back as the early historical period. Even then, however, the prosecution of the culprit—*i.e.* the proclamation of outlawry against him—was solely the affair of the injured party, and was sanctioned only in the case of wilful injury. In cases of unintentional injury, the doer, according to the Scandinavian codes, had voluntarily and without delay to make satisfaction to the injured party, or, by the laws of the German tribes, had to maintain by an oath, and with the aid of a compurgator, that his act was really unintentional. But even outlawry was not usually permanent; it was circumscribed both as to time and as to locality, and could always be reversed by indemnity and expiation; while offences not involving feud and outlawry could also be absolved by the payment of compensation.

3. Conditions of reconciliation.—The act of expiation involved certain formal conditions. To begin with, it had to take place within a given period, the length of which varied among the different tribes. Then the offender had to present himself almost as a suppliant before the person whom he had wronged, or his legal representative; and, finally, he had to assert upon oath that, had he been the injured party, he would have been satisfied with the indemnity which he now offered. The two parties then took the oath of peace, *i.e.* declared the feud at an end, and sealed their reconciliation by a mutual embrace and the kiss of peace.

4. Compensation and fine.—While the right of private vengeance and feud, together with the right to fix the indemnity, remained in force among the northern Teutons till far on in the Middle Ages, among the other Teutonic peoples proscription gave place at an early date to a system of fines. Outlawry was, in fact, resorted to only when such fines were not paid, and even then in a greatly mitigated form. In the earlier period it lay with the wronged individual to decide whether he would adopt the policy of vengeance and outlawry, or accept compensation; subsequently he was compelled to take the latter course. Thus the system of compensation at length carried the day, as we find it in the *Leges barbarorum*, and the Frisian, Anglo-Saxon, and Scandinavian codes. In the various nationalities the measure of the compensation fluctuated in successive periods, but in all cases the extent and character of the injury, and the standing or family of the injured, were important considerations in its assessment. The indemnity for injury to any part of the person was estimated according to the utility of that part in earning a living. The legal tender of such compensation originally consisted of cattle. In this connexion, as was noted above, Tacitus mentions horses and small cattle; according to the Scandinavian codes, the standard of value in fixing compensation was the cow (*kúgildi, kýrlag*). But we often find reference likewise to cloth (O.N. *váðmál*; Fris. *wede*), and also to corn, butter, and wax. It was only in a later age that animals and produce were superseded by the precious metals, and, among the southern Teutons, by coin. In North Scandinavia the pieces of metal were unstamped, and were paid simply by weight, or in the form of rings (*baugr, bauggildi*). The nature and amount of the indemnity were not, of course, matters of public concern in every case, but were sometimes arranged between the injurer and the injured. The Icelandic sagas in particular make frequent mention of such private negotiations. Thus Gunnlaugr, having stunned the slave of a peasant with a blow, offered a mark as compensation to the master, who, though at first he thought the sum inadequate, finally accepted it (*Isl. Sögur*, ii. 210 f.). But, where the compensation was settled by the intervention of the community—which, as the custodian of law and peace, was, according to Teutonic ideas, conjointly affected by an injury to any of its members—then the community, or its representative, the ruler, received a share of the indemnity (O.H.G. *fridu*, and Fris. *fretho*, latinized as *fredus*; A.S. *wíte*). Among some of the Teutonic peoples (N. Teutons and Franks) this *fredus*, or 'price of peace,' was a part of the compensation, and, together with what was given to the injured person, formed the *compositio*, while in other tribes (Saxons, Frisians) it was rendered in addition to the indemnity.

5. 'Wergild.'—A peculiar form of expiation is found in the *wergild* (O.H.G. *werageld*; Germ. *Wergeld*; O.N. *manngiöld, mannbœtr*), the sum of money which was paid for killing a human being, and which came to be substituted for outlawry. The *wergild*, which was recognized by nearly all the Teutonic codes, might be doubled, or even trebled, in cases where the victim was a man held in special esteem. The family of the slayer and that of the slain had each a part in the transaction. The former was required to produce the legal amount—a practice which was confined to this form of indemnity—while the compensation was likewise received by the relatives of the slain man in a body. Nor was this rule departed from when the man-slayer had fled or was dead. This fact suffices to show that the *wergild* was regarded not as a penalty but as an indemnification. The share which the individual relatives of the person slain had in the compensation was also regulated by law, but the mode of allotment was not everywhere the same. The custom of excluding women from participation was almost universal. The share of the male relatives was computed according to the principle that it must be directly in proportion to their nearness of kin to the slain man. According to the Icelandic sagas, which in this as in many other respects reflect older conditions, the amount of the *wergild* was arranged privately between the families of the individuals involved. When the money had been paid, or, at least, when payment had been legally guaranteed, the reconciliation of the two groups of relatives was consummated in a ceremonial similar to that observed at the termination of a feud. In later times the murderer or his kindred were often required to erect a piacular cross at the scene of the crime.

6. Indemnity and punishment.—In cases other than the *wergild*, the compensation was graduated according to the damage entailed by the offence. Loss of property had to be made up by a reparation of equal amount, or by an equivalent in money; an imputation on a person's honour had to be made amends for by a solemn withdrawal, etc. A peculiar form of requital is found among the Franks from the 6th cent. A.D., viz. the 'ban-forfeit,' or the 'king's ban.' This originated with the Merovingian kings, and forms a contrast to the other provisions of the Frankish tribal codes. Here the 'ban' was the sum of money paid to the king by those who did not comply with his decrees. Thus the 'king's ban' partakes of the nature of penalty rather than of indemnity. The latter, we must remember, was not originally a penalty, but simply a payment made in order to recover the protection of the law, and to indemnify the injured party or the community. It was only after the wrong-doer was no longer liable to proscription, and the wronged was forbidden to avenge himself, that compensation was superseded by punishment and the right to demand punishment, including not only legal penalties but also the private vengeance of which the community acted as the medium. Thereafter the injured party had merely the right to prefer an accusation, and the intervention of his family was disallowed. The penalty was thus no longer a matter for the injured person to decide, but was regulated by law. Then corporal and capital penalties were added to those which consisted of monetary fines.

7. Human sacrifice.—In the sphere of religion, expiation took a peculiar form. When a man committed an offence against the gods, he was held guilty of a crime against the community as well, since the vengeance of the offended deity fell upon the community as a whole, so that some—and, in certain circumstances, as *e.g.* famine and storm, even many—of its members were put in peril of their lives. In such cases the deity could be propitiated only by the gift of a human life, and the practice was to immolate the criminal himself. Again, however, such a sacrifice was not a penalty, but an expiatory act. The criminal was first of all declared an outlaw, and thus excluded from the legal union. Thus in Iceland, shortly before the introduction of Christianity, we have the case of a man who was proscribed for sacrilege (*Isl. Sögur*, i. 11); he was thereby numbered among those who were unprotected by law, and could be dealt with as a sacrificial victim whenever such was required. But the sentence of outlawry by the community does not seem to have been pronounced in every case. One who had committed sacrilege was excluded from the legal confederacy without any act of proscription or process of law, and was then treated as a slave or outlaw, by the offering of whose life alone the deity could be propitiated. It is recorded, for instance, that King Olaf Trételgja of Sweden was offered up by his own people during a time of famine, because he had acted perfunctorily as a sacrificer, and was thus a scorner of the gods (*Heimskringla*, p. 37). A crime against the gods, especially when their retribution manifested itself in storm or failure of crops, could be expiated by nothing less than a human sacrifice. If the anger of the gods broke forth at a time when the community had no sacrilegious person within its pale, or did not know of any, attempts were made to assuage the Divine wrath by an oblation of slaves or prisoners of war. When even such victims were not to hand, the person to be sacrificed was discovered by casting lots. It thus appears that among the ancient Teutons human sacrifice (*q.v.*) was not a punishment, but an expiation. Cf. art. CRIMES AND PUNISHMENTS (Teut. and Slav.), vol. iv. p. 304, *et passim*.

LITERATURE.—W. E. Wilda, *Strafrecht d. Germanen*, i., Halle, 1842; C. G. von Wächter, *Das german. Fehderecht u. d. Kompositionen*, Leipzig, 1881; R. Schröder, *Lehrbuch d. deutschen Rechtsgesch.*[5], Leipzig, 1907; H. Brunner, *Deutsche Rechtsgesch.*, Leipzig, i.[2] (1906), ii. (1892); K. von Amira, in Paul's *Grundriss d. germ. Philol.* vol. iii.[2], Strassburg, 1900; F. Dahn, 'Fehdegang u. Rechtsgang d. Germanen,' in *Bausteine*, 2nd ser., Berlin, 1880; P. Frauenstädt, *Blutrache u. Totschlagsühne im deutschen Mittelalter*, Leipzig, 1881; K. Binding, *Die Entstehung d. öffentlichen Strafe*, Leipzig, 1909; H. Siegel, *Deutsche Rechtsgesch.*[3], Berlin, 1895; B. W. Leist, *Altarisches jus civile*, 2 vols., Jena, 1893–96; J. Kohler, *Zur Lehre von d. Blutrache*, Würzburg, 1885; R. Hildebrand, *Recht u. Sitte auf d. verschiedenen wirtschaftlichen Stufen*[2], Jena, 1908; J. Grimm, *Deutsche Rechtsaltertümer*[4], Leipzig, 1899; R. His, *Das Strafrecht d. Friesen im Mittelalter*, Leipzig, 1901; E. Osenbrüggen, *Das Strafrecht d. Langobarden*, Schaffhausen, 1863; H. M. Chadwick, *Studies on Anglo-Saxon Institutions*, London, 1905: His, 'Totschlagsühne u. Mannschaft' (in *Festgabe für K. Güterbock*), Berlin, 1910; L. Huberti, 'Friede u. Recht,' in *Deutsche Ztschr. für Geschichtswissensch.*, Freiburg, v. (1891); H. Geffcken, *Fehde u. Duell*, Leipzig, 1899; v. Müller, *Das Wergeld des Täters u. des Verletzten*, Bonn, 1898; Vinogradoff, 'Wergeld u. Stand,' in *Ztschr. f. Rechtsgesch.* xxiii. (Weimar, 1902); Brandt, *Forelaesninger over d. norske Retshistorie*, 2 vols., Christiania, 1880–83; Björling, *Om Bötesstraffet i den svenska Medeltidsrätten*, Lund, 1893; K. von Amira, *Das altnorweg. Vollstreckungsverfahren*, Munich, 1874; K. Maurer, *Vorlesungen über altnord. Rechtsgesch.*, v., Leipzig, 1910; Merker, *Das Strafrecht d. altisländ. Grágás*, Altenburg, 1907; K. Lehmann, *Die Königsfriede d. Nordgermanen*, Berlin, 1886; E. Mogk, *Die Menschenopfer bei d. Germanen*, Leipzig, 1909.

E. MOGK.

EXTREME UNCTION.—1. Purpose and efficacy.—By the official teaching both of the Roman and of the Orthodox Greek Church the anointing of the sick and dying is recognized as one of the seven Sacraments. The Council of Trent in its 14th Session deals with the subject at some length. It declares that the Redeemer of mankind, having provided all spiritual aids for the different emergencies of human life, wished also to 'guard the close of life by the Sacrament of Extreme Unction, as with a most firm defence.' It urges the need of such help, on the ground that at the hour of death the assaults of the tempter are redoubled. Hence Christ, it is stated, instituted this unction as 'truly and properly a Sacrament of the New Law.' The rite, we are told, was foreshadowed in the anointing of the sick by the Apostles, spoken of in Mk 6[13], but it was 'promulgated' in Ja 5[14f.]: 'Is any among you sick? let him call for the priests (Gr. πρεσβυτέρους; Vulg. *presbyteros*, AV and RV 'elders') of the church; and let them pray over him, anointing him with oil in the name of the Lord: and the prayer of faith shall save him that is sick, and the Lord shall raise him up; and if he have committed sins, it shall be forgiven him.' In these words are indicated not only 'the matter, the form, and the proper minister of this sacrament,' but also the effect.

'For "the thing signified" here is the grace of the Holy Ghost, whose anointing cleanses away sins if there be any still to be expiated, as also the remains of sins, and raises up and strengthens the soul of the sick person by exciting in him a great confidence in the Divine mercy, whereby the sick man being supported bears more easily the inconveniences and pains of his sickness, and more easily resists the temptation of the devil who lies in wait for his heel, and at times obtains bodily health when expedient for the welfare of his soul.'

In the Eastern Church the principal stress is laid upon bodily healing. Thus the Shorter Russian Catechism simply states that the Sacrament 'consists in this, that the sick man is anointed with oil, while grace is prayed for to heal him.' But the Longer Russian Catechism and the *Confessio Orthodoxa* of Mogilas emphasize also its spiritual effects, the last-named declaring (cap. 119) that, 'though health is not always obtained, nevertheless the forgiveness of sins is always most assuredly thereby received.'

To the Tridentine decree four anathemas are appended. The first condemns those who deny the Divine institution of the Sacrament and declare it to be only of Patristic origin or a human figment. The third and fourth anathematize those who maintain that the ritual of the Roman Church does not fully accord with the text of St. James, as well as those who would allow others than priests to administer the Sacrament. The second runs as follows:

'If any one saith that the sacred unction of the sick does not confer grace, nor remit sin, nor comfort (*alleviare*) the sick, but that it has now lost its virtue (*sed jam cessasse*), as though it were a grace of working cures in bygone days, let him be anathema.'

The view that St. James was not speaking of any truly sacramental unction (cf. Loisy, *Autour d'un petit livre*, Paris, 1903, p. 251) was condemned in 1907 with other 'Modernist errors' in the decree *Lamentabili sane*, no. 48 (Denzinger-Bannwart, *Enchiridion*[10], Freiburg, 1908, no. 2048).

Speaking generally, it may be said that this account of the purport and effects of the Sacrament is in close accord with the teaching of Aquinas and the mediæval scholastics. Some difference of opinion there was between the Thomists and the

Scotists regarding the primary object (*effectus principalis*) for which it was instituted, the former maintaining that it was the comforting of the soul, the latter that it was rather the final remission of venial sins (see Kern, *de Sac. Extr. Unctionis*, pp. 215–240), but the dispute was a metaphysical one and was without much practical bearing upon the popular conception of the Sacrament and its effects.

2. Ritual.—In the Church of Rome at the present day the rite of administration is brief and simple. Apart from one or two short and unessential prayers which precede and conclude the ceremony, the rite consists in the anointing of the eyes, ears, nostrils, lips, hands, and feet of the sick person, the following formula being repeated at each unction: 'Through this holy unction and His own most tender mercy, may the Lord pardon thee whatever offences thou hast committed (*quidquid deliquisti*) by sight (by hearing, smell, etc.).' Formerly, in the case of men, the loins were also anointed, and the *Rituale* still retains the formula provided, but in practice this is now always omitted. Only a properly ordained priest can confer the Sacrament validly, and the oil used must be the *oleum infirmorum* consecrated for this special purpose by the bishop on Maundy Thursday. If by some mistake a mineral oil should be used, or if one of the two other holy oils, viz. the chrism or the *oleum catechumenorum*, should be substituted for the *oleum infirmorum*, the validity of the Sacrament would be doubtful. Further, the proposition that in case of necessity, when episcopally blest oil cannot be procured, a priest may validly use oil blessed by himself has been censured so far as concerns the Western Church. On the other hand, permission has long been accorded by the Holy See to the Uniat Greeks to adhere to the ancient tradition of Eastern Christendom, according to which any simple priest who administers the Sacrament blesses the oil himself. That this was also, at least in some localities, the earlier practice in the West seems highly probable.[1]

According to both the present and the former practice of the Western Church, the Sacrament is administered only to those who are suffering from serious illness, and thus at least remotely in danger of death. It may be reiterated, but not in the same illness, or at any rate not unless some new crisis has supervened. Among the Greeks and some other Orientals (it is not now recognized by the Nestorians) the Sacrament of the Prayer-Oil (εὐχέλαιον), as they call it, though a much more elaborate ceremony, requiring when possible the assistance of seven priests, is often administered in maladies of no gravity, and it is received on certain days of the year by persons in normal health as a preparation for Holy Communion. It is consequently very commonly administered in the church, and the forehead, nostrils, cheeks, chin, breast, and both sides of the hands are anointed with a brush or twig, the ceremony being repeated by each priest in turn. The form used begins as follows: 'Holy Father, physician of souls and of bodies, who didst send Thy only-begotten Son our Lord Jesus Christ as the healer of every disease and our deliverer from death, heal also Thy servant N. from the spiritual and bodily infirmity that holds him, and restore him to life, through the grace of Christ,' etc. After this, a number of saints are named, and amongst the rest 'the holy and moneyless physicians Cosmas and Damian' (see Maltzew, *Sakramente*, 493 ff.). The oil used is commonly mixed with wine, and it is blessed by the principal priest present. In practice the Sacrament among the Greeks, as in the West, is often deferred until the sick man is *in extremis*, but the hope of a cure is always entertained. See, for example, Tolstoi's great novel *Anna Karenina*, bk. v. chs. 19–20. In both the Eastern and the Western Church an abbreviated form is sanctioned for cases when the danger of death is imminent.

3. History.—As the anointing of the sick with oil was a primitive form of medical treatment (see Is 1[6]; Jos. *BJ* I. xxxiii. 5; Lk 10[34]), and, like all other remedial measures, was peculiarly apt to be associated with religious observances (see ANOINTING, vol. i. p. 549 ff.), it is not altogether surprising that the early history of sacramental unction should be somewhat obscure. It was an observance which would not have provoked controversy by arousing the hostile criticism of pagans, and the faithful had no special reason to draw attention to it, since it was only the Christianized counterpart of customs, medicinal or magical, which every one recognized. Further, the existence of a non-sacramental use of consecrated oil is clearly deducible from the epistle of Innocent I. (*ad Decentium*, 8 [*PL* xx. 559]), from Cæsarius of Arles (*PL* xxxix. 2238), and from the *Vita S. Genovefæ* (ed. Künstle, cc. 38 and 40), the oil being applied to the sick by themselves or by a woman. Moreover, in other cases oil seems to have been employed in charismatic healing (Mk 6[13]), under which we may include the instance mentioned by Tertullian (*ad Scap.* iv.), when Septimius Severus was cured by the Christian Proculus. Nor can we leave out of account the use of oil from the lamps in the basilicas, or oil sanctified by relics, etc. (see *e.g.* Chrysos. hom. 32 *in Matt.* [*PG* lvii. 384]; Cassian, *Coll.* vii. 26 [*PL* xlix. 706]; Greg. Tur. *Hist. Franc.* iv. 36 [*PL* lxxi. 299]). But, just as the healing of Gorgonia after anointing herself with the sacred species of the Eucharist (Greg. Naz. *Orat.* viii. 18, and cf. *JThSt* xi. [1910] 275–279; a Western example of the same outward application of the Eucharistic species seems to be found in Cæsarius of Arles [*PL* xxxix. 2238]) could not be cited as an argument against the sacramental character of the Eucharist at the same period, so this domestic use of consecrated oil does not seem to militate against the existence of an authorized and official sacramental rite of which the priests were the recognized ministers. In this light the letter of Innocent I. to Decentius, A.D. 416 (Denzinger-Bannwart[10], no. 99) seems quite intelligible. Decentius had doubted whether he, a bishop, was free to anoint the sick, seeing that only priests were mentioned by St. James.

Most certainly you are, the Pope replies in substance; 'even the simple faithful are allowed to *use* the blessed oil, and with much greater reason the bishop, who has power to consecrate it, has power to anoint with it and to bless the sick. But such unction ought not to be administered to penitents (*i.e.* those undergoing penitential discipline), for it is a sacred rite (*quia genus est sacramenti*), and, if the other sacred rites are denied to penitents, why should this particular rite be conceded? (*Nam quibus reliqua sacramenta negantur, quomodo unum genus putatur posse concedi?*)'

No doubt, this answer implies that the unction was not then regarded as specially belonging to those *in extremis*, for penitents at the point of death would not have been refused the sacrament of reconciliation and the Eucharist. On the other hand, the formula for blessing the oil which we find in 'Serapion's Prayer-Book' (A.D. 356) is associated by its position in the series with the rites of interment, though its terms clearly specify the restoration of health to both soul and body.

'Send the healing power of the only begotten upon this oil.' God is asked '. . . for a driving out of every infirmity, for good grace and remission of sins, for a medicine of life and salvation, for health and soundness of soul, body, spirit, for perfect strengthening.'

[1] See Magistretti, *Pontificale Ambrosianum* (p. 95), who quotes the decisive words of Bonizo of Piacenza (*c.* A.D. 1089): 'This *oleum infirmorum* used formerly at all seasons to be consecrated by priests during Mass after the *per quem haec omnia bona creas*. Nowadays, however, it is consecrated only by Bishops, and that on Maundy Thursday, at the same point in the Mass' (*PL* cl. 864).

The *Vita S. Genovefæ* clearly shows that even then (*c.* A.D. 550) it was believed in Gaul that only a bishop had power to consecrate the oil (*forte accidit ut Genovefa oleum non haberet nec adesset in tempore pontifex qui ad praesens oleo gratiam sanctificationis infunderet* [c. 40]). Similarly the *Vita S. Hypatii* (*AS*, 17 June, p. 251) tells us how Hypatius, who was long infirmarian of his monastery, used, when any illness grew serious, to send for the abbot, 'since he was a priest' and Hypatius himself was not, in order that the sick man might be duly anointed. This *Life* is assigned by Bardenhewer to about the year 450. With the 8th cent. the evidence regarding the nature and rite of Extreme Unction grows more abundant. Bede speaks of it in some detail in his commentary on St. James (*PL* xciii. 39), and St. Boniface (about 745) in his Canons orders priests to have the oil for the sick constantly at hand, and to instruct the faithful, when they feel ill, to apply for the Unction. Similarly in the 9th cent. many Councils, beginning with those of Chalons (813), Aachen (836), and Mainz (847), issue various injunctions on the subject, generally making allusion to the Epistle of St. James. The term 'Extreme Unction' seems to occur for the first time in the 15th of the Canons ascribed to Bishop Sonnatius: 'Extrema unctio deferatur laboranti et petenti' (Mansi, x. 599). These Canons may be as early as the 7th cent., but we have no certainty on this point. The name 'Extreme Unction' became common only at a considerably later epoch. It was in all probability suggested by its being the last in order of the unctions a man was likely to receive, but no doubt the association of the Unction with the *Viaticum* and approaching death made the term seem specially appropriate.

LITERATURE.—The fullest and most recent discussion of the subject from the Roman standpoint is that of **J. Kern**, *de Sacramento Extremæ Unctionis Tractatus Dogmaticus*, Regensburg, 1907, a treatise that has been largely utilized by **P. J. Toner**, in the *Cath. Encycl.* v. 716–730. An excellently condensed summary of the historical aspects of the case is given by **J. de Guibert**, *s.v.* 'Extrême Onction,' in the *Dict. apol. de la foi catholique*, i. 1868–1872. See also **A. Tanquerey**, *Synopsis Theol. Dogmat. Specialis*[10], Tournai, 1906, ii. 567–589; **C. Pesch**, *Prælectiones Dogmaticæ*[3], Freiburg, 1909, vii. 249–281; **Wilhelm-Scannell**, *Manual of Catholic Theology*, London, 1898, ii. 485–493; **Lejay**, in *RHLR* x. [1905] 606–610; **F. Probst**, *Sakramente und Sakramentalien*, Tübingen, 1872, p. 373 ff.; **M. Heimbucher**, *Die heilige Oelung*, Regensburg, 1888; **I. Schmitz**, *de Effectibus Sacr. Extremæ Unctionis*, Freiburg, 1893; **M. Chardon**, *Hist. des sacrements*, Paris, 1745; **J. Pohle**, *Lehrbuch der Dogmatik*[3], Paderborn, 1907, iii. 523–548; **E. Martène**, *de Antiquis Ecclesiæ Ritibus*, Venice, 1788, i. 296–350; **W. McDonald**, in *Irish Theol. Quarterly*, 1907, pp. 330–345.

As regards the Orthodox Greek Church, see **A. v. Maltzew**, *Sakramente*, Berlin, 1898, cccxxiii. and 450–553; **Petrovskij**, *Hist. of the Akoluthia of the Prayer-Oil*, Christianskoje Ctenje, 1903 (Russ.); **Rhalles**, *On Penance and the Prayer-Oil*, Athens, 1905 (Greek); **Jacquemier**, 'L'Extrême Onction chez les Grecs,' in *Echos d'Orient*, ii. Apr.–May, 1899.

Of writers unsympathetic to the Roman view may be mentioned the important work of **F. W. Puller**, *The Anointing of the Sick in Scripture and Tradition*, London, 1904; **J. B. Mayor**, *The Epistle of St. James*[3], London, 1910, p. 370 ff.; **W. E. Scudamore**, in *DCA* ii. 2000; and **Kattenbusch**, in *PRE*[3] xiv. 304–311.

HERBERT THURSTON.

F

FABIAN SOCIETY.—1. Origin and aims.— The Fabian Society, a small but influential body of English Socialists, was founded in 1884. At that time began the revival of Socialism in England which was attributable mainly to two influences. The teaching of Karl Marx was becoming popularized, chiefly through the exertions of French and German refugees; while the crusade of Henry George, whose *Progress and Poverty* (1880) had a remarkable circulation in England, led to the formation of a number of small societies, some of which carried his doctrines much further than he had himself intended, and developed into Socialist organizations. Within three years of one another there were established the Social Democratic Federation, the Socialist League, and the Fabian Society. The first of these was, and remains, saturated with the spirit of Marx, and has had little influence in practical affairs. The League carried on a vigorous agitation for a few years, under the inspiration of William Morris; but it belonged properly to Anarchism, and soon disappeared. The Fabian Society, from the outset, rejected much of the economic teaching of Marx, and very soon discarded also certain Anarchist tendencies which were manifest in its earliest publications. It seems to have owed more to George than to Marx, but its leaders were young men of exceptional capacity, like Sidney Webb and George Bernard Shaw, who combined with propagandist zeal an originality and a lack of reverence for authority which soon gave to the Society a distinctive position in the Socialist movement.

Professor Thomas Davidson had gathered around him in London a little group of earnest men who met in one another's houses, and, under the name of the 'Fellowship of the New Life,' sought to cultivate perfection of individual character. A schism in this Fellowship was the origin of the Fabian Society, when the Socialist section became an independent group and adopted its name as descriptive of its method of action. Accepting the desirability of progress towards Socialism, it concentrated attention upon the manner of achieving that end, and quickly purged itself of the revolutionary attitude which characterized the other Socialist organizations. Socialism could not be attained by a catastrophic class-war, but by gradual adaptation and development of existing institutions through legislative, constitutional, and peaceful action. Moreover, it was unnecessary to wait until the majority of the people placed themselves under the Socialist banner; a small body of zealous and enlightened men, who had made clear to themselves the next steps needed towards the Socialist goal, might influence all parties in that direction. Hence the Society did not organize a political party, but sought to permeate the existing parties and to work out, in a form adapted to English conditions, the administrative changes which would lead in the direction of Socialism. An open Socialist campaign in politics appeared to offer little chance of success, and individualism could not be defeated by any single encounter; therefore it was thought that more could be achieved by indirect action, by working as a leaven in existing parties, by concentrating upon a few changes which would command wide support outside the Socialist ranks, but which led in the desired direction. While thus remaining thoroughly Socialistic in its aims, its method was of a strictly practical, and even opportunist, kind. To its members it gave absolute freedom to choose any means they thought fit for the permeation of all parties and schools of thought; and, though it has latterly shared in establishing the Labour Party, it still has members who belong to the Liberal Party both within and without the House of Commons, and its emphasis is still upon permeation.

For this avoidance of a sharp encounter and the policy of indirect and detailed activity an analogy was found in the tactics of Fabius Maximus (surnamed *Cunctator*, on account of his seeming dilatoriness), and in the earliest publications of the Society the plan of campaign was indicated by the following motto, the latter part of which will not bear exact historical scrutiny:

'For the right moment you must wait, as Fabius did most patiently when warring against Hannibal, though many censured his delays; but, when the time comes, you must strike hard, as Fabius did, or your waiting will be in vain and fruitless.'

The policy of delay did not, however, mean inactivity, but preparation of plans, training of forces, and seizing of small opportunities. Having no belief in the efficacy of separatist communities apart from the ordinary economic and political life (cf. COMMUNISTIC SOCIETIES OF AMERICA), the Fabians turned their back on Utopianism, and declared that Socialism must be not a withdrawal from existing conditions, but a transformation of them. Rejecting also the naive faith of the revolutionist—that, after a sudden outburst in which the proletariat were to be victorious, society would somehow settle down into an ordered Collectivism—they undertook the more arduous task of educating themselves and others regarding the means by which that social transformation might be achieved.

The standpoint of the Society was explicitly stated in the following 'Basis':

'The Fabian Society consists of Socialists.

It therefore aims at the re-organization of Society by the emancipation of Land and Industrial Capital from individual and class ownership, and the vesting of them in the community for the general benefit. In this way only can the natural and acquired advantages of the country be equitably shared by the whole people.

The Society accordingly works for the extinction of private property in Land and of the consequent individual appropriation, in the form of Rent, of the price paid for permission to use the earth, as well as for the advantages of superior soils and sites.

The Society, further, works for the transfer to the community of the administration of such industrial Capital as can conveniently be managed socially. For, owing to the monopoly of the means of production in the past, industrial inventions and the transformation of surplus income into Capital have mainly enriched the proprietary class, the worker being now dependent on that class for leave to earn a living.

If these measures be carried out, without compensation (though not without such relief to expropriated individuals as may seem fit to the community), Rent and Interest will be added to the reward of labour, the idle class now living on the labour of others will necessarily disappear, and practical equality of opportunity will be maintained by the spontaneous action of economic forces, with much less interference with personal liberty than the present system entails.

For the attainment of these ends the Fabian Society looks to the spread of Socialist opinions, and the social and political changes consequent thereon, including the establishment of equal citizenship for men and women. It seeks to achieve these ends by the general dissemination of knowledge as to the relation between the individual and Society in its economic, ethical, and political aspects.'

This basis, to which every member is required to subscribe, sufficiently indicates the main objects of Fabian Socialism; but it is upon the detailed application of these generalizations to concrete problems of the day that the actual work of the Society has been concentrated. Unlike some other groups of Socialists, it has refused to take sides on subjects which it views as outside its special province, such as religion and marriage. It wastes no time on futile discussions as to the precise form of currency to be used in the future State. But, whenever a political or social problem is being discussed or seems ripe for treatment, it devotes to it careful study, propounds the Socialist solution, and opposes any measure which cannot be brought into harmony with the Socialist principles. Thus, it has rejected peasant proprietorship as a solution of agrarian problems, and co-operative production by self-governing groups of workmen as an alternative to capitalism, the former being simply an extension of landlordism and the private appropriation of rent, while the latter is merely a form of joint-stock individualism. Both perpetuate the conditions which the Fabian desires to extirpate, and, while granting that there are very many questions of Socialist organization that are as yet unsettled, he strives to set the current of reform in a definite direction. Opportunist in the sense of seizing the favourable moment for propaganda, and making the most of existing materials, he is not opportunist in the sense of accepting any kind of solution which comes first to hand. He acts on principle, by advocating measures that appear to be consistent with the Socialist consummation.

2. Forms of activity. — In carrying out this method of social transformation the Society has done an unusual amount of educational work of a very practical nature, and may perhaps claim to have brought Socialism into closer relation with present-day problems and institutions than has any other group. Fortnightly meetings for discussion of these subjects are held in London, where the majority of its members reside. An individual or a group of members devotes prolonged study to some single social question, and presents the results to the Society, by which they are again discussed; and, when conclusions have been reached that meet with the general approval of the members, they are printed and widely circulated in the form of penny pamphlets. About 160 of these 'Tracts' have now been published, and, being generally well-informed and severely practical in tone, they, along with *Fabian Essays*, may be taken as the text-books of Fabian Socialism. The educational work has also taken the forms of circulating libraries supplied to trade unions, workmen's clubs, co-operative societies, and similar bodies; of the publication of select bibliographies on social subjects; and of supplying lecturers to various societies and classes; while a small monthly *News* is sent to the members. In this department of its work the Society had no small influence in the foundation of the London School of Economics, now a constituent college of the University of London.

3. Influence.—As might naturally be expected, the Society has appealed mainly to the more educated Socialists, and its members are usually of the middle class. It has made little effort to increase its own numbers, except by the encouragement of branches in the Universities; but since 1906, when there were about 1000 members, there has been a relatively rapid increase, until now (1912) there are over 2600, besides many associates who are not committed to the basis, but are interested in the work and subscribe to its funds. Yet its power has been quite out of proportion to its numbers, chiefly because of the exceptional ability of its leaders; and, besides spreading Socialist opinions among the educated middle classes who stood aloof from other Socialist bodies, it has had no small share in influencing the tone of the English Labour movement, and has also occasionally had a marked effect upon political programmes and measures.

4. Demands.—The more immediate demands of Fabianism, as indicated in the Tracts, are the following: (1) nationalization or municipalization of the larger public services, such as tramways, railways, lighting, electric-power, liquor traffic, and land, with the gradual extension of the principle to other industries, as it becomes administratively possible. It is not, however, proposed that the State should monopolize industry as against private enterprise or individual initiative further than may be necessary to make the livelihood of the people and their access to the sources of production completely independent of both. Subject to this condition,

'the freedom of individuals to test the social value of new inventions; to initiate improved methods of production; to anticipate and lead public enterprise in catering for new social wants; to practise all arts, crafts, and professions independently; in short, to complete the social organization by adding the resources of private activity and judgment to those of public routine, is as highly valued by the Fabian Society as any other article in the charter of popular liberties' (*Tract* no. 70, p. 6).

(2) The organization and development of a trained Civil Service, capable of managing the industries and functions taken over by the State, including the co-ordination of the medical and sanitary services, poor-law and other hospitals, under an enlarged public health authority which shall replace much of the private practice by a State service. (3) The imposition of public burdens on the wealthy by such means as death duties and super-taxes. (4) The expansion of public education, raising the age for leaving school, increasing the facilities for poor children to obtain higher education and to enter the universities. (5) Enlarged opportunities for recreation, by means of public parks, playgrounds, and baths. (6) Extension of factory and mines regulation in such directions as will provide not only a national minimum of sanitation and safety, but also a national minimum wage below which the standard of life shall not be permitted to fall.

On the negative side, as against some schools of Socialists, Fabianism repudiates the doctrine of the individual's 'right to the whole produce of his labour,' insisting that wealth is social in its origin and must be social in its distribution, since it is impossible to distinguish the particular contribution that each person makes to the common product. It also rejects doctrines of equal wages, equal hours of labour, equal official status, and equal authority for every one. Such conditions it declares to be not only impracticable, but incompatible with the equality of subordination to the common interest which is fundamental in modern Socialism. While most of the Tracts deal almost exclusively with economic questions, this ethical note frequently recurs; and the Society has issued a few publications on moral aspects of Socialism, besides insisting elsewhere upon the obligation of all to personal service, and the subordination of individual aims to the common welfare. But it does not advocate Socialism as 'a panacea for the ills of human society, but only for those produced by defective organization of industry and by a radically bad distribution of wealth' (*Report on Fabian Policy*, 1896, p. 8).

5. Criticisms.—The Fabian Society has been subjected to much criticism both by Socialists and others. Objection has been taken to its indirect, insidious, and underground methods of permeation, which, indeed, were at one time more questionable than they now are. Mr. Shaw boasted in 1892 of the solid advantages they had gained by joining Liberal and Conservative associations and adroitly pulling all the wires they could lay their hands on. This is denounced both by friends and by opponents of Socialism as sailing under a false flag; but latterly the artfulness has taken the more legitimate form of obtaining support for Socialist measures by attempting to convince people that the new reform is only an extension of long-recognized principles. So long as every one knows that the Fabian aim is Socialism, there can be little objection to enlisting even conservative instincts in the cause of a particular change. Indeed, there is no little conservatism in the Fabian conception of utilizing existing institutions; and some of its leaders have such a dread of any form of destruction that they are censured by the more revolutionary Socialists. These not only condemn Fabian opportunism, but sneer at the Society as the cult of the Civil Service, composed of middle-class men, who may naturally be expected to decry the class-war and to work for a bureaucracy staffed from its own ranks.

Other criticism comes from moderate Socialists, who are much more sympathetic towards its aims, but are not satisfied with its methods. While granting that the waiting policy was defensible in the early years of the movement, these critics consider that the Society has retained it even when the time has come to 'strike hard,' and that now it should employ all its resources in furthering an open Socialist campaign in politics. Socialism, it is urged, will be more effectively achieved by making people Socialists than by insidiously attempting to get Socialistic measures adopted without the electorate knowing that they are such. Indeed, it is pertinently asked if there can be much real benefit in securing a few socialized industries, unless there is a wide diffusion of Socialist ideals. Mere nationalization or municipalization is not an end in itself; and, if it is to be of much social service, it must be accompanied by an expansion of the Socialistic spirit, which is best awakened by proselytizing. There seems at present to be no little difference of opinion within the Society itself in this respect. Some urge it to give whole-hearted support to the Labour party, and to exclude from its membership all who will not do so. Others desire the establishment of a Socialist party quite independent of the Labour party. But the dominant opinion remains favourable to complete liberty of the members to act as they please in party politics, and to the traditional policy of permeation, since it is a delusion that all reform must be effected through a single party.

It is also alleged that the habit of limited action has had an enervating effect, while hostility to revolution and the policy of utilizing existing machinery for new functions have tended to an excessive reverence for the present institutions. In particular, it has been complained by H. G. Wells, who was once a member of the Fabian Society, that its insistence upon continuity 'developed into something like a mania for achieving Socialism without the overt change of any existing ruling body' (*New Worlds for Old*, p. 268). This led to the advocacy of public operation of industries, even in small and unsuitable areas, under incompetent boards and councils, with effects that have sometimes tended to discredit Socialism. Hence it is urged that the socialization of industries cannot proceed much further without a reconstruction of administrative areas, and the typical Fabian policy of building Socialism on the foundation of the existing machinery of Government has almost reached its limit. The areas of local government were not created for the operation of industrial enterprises, and are at present ill-adapted to many of them. Recently, however, the Society has devoted some attention to this phase of the Socialist reconstruction, and has issued a number of Tracts under the *New Heptarchy Series*, advocating changes in administrative areas to render them more suitable to the requirements of public trading.

LITERATURE.—The best known literary product of the Society is the volume of *Fabian Essays in Socialism*, London, 1890. Most of the *Fabian Tracts* may still be obtained from the Secretary, 3 Clement's Inn, London, and some of them have been grouped together and reprinted in the volumes of the *Fabian Socialist Series*. G. Bernard Shaw, *The Common Sense of Municipal Trading*, London, 1908; Sidney and Beatrice Webb, *Industrial Democracy*, do. 1901, and *Problems of Modern Industry*, do. 1898, are also distinctively Fabian works. The following contain expositions or criticisms of Fabianism: Sidney Webb, *Socialism in England*, London, 1890; T. Kirkup, *History of Socialism*, do. 1906; H. G. Wells, *New Worlds for Old*, do. 1908; Brougham Villiers, *The Socialist Movement in England*, do. 1908; J. E. Barker, *British Socialism*, do. 1908.

STANLEY H. TURNER.

FABLE.—Fable originally meant 'a thing said,' and thus a story or narration (as in Horace's 'Mutato nomine, de te fabula narratur' [*Sat.* I. i. 70]); and Dryden wrote 'Fables' of men and women. But in modern English usage the word is mainly restricted to Beast-Fables, or short narratives about animals, having a moral application which is generally expressed in an explicit 'moral' at the end. The fable in this more restricted sense has to be distinguished from the Beast-Anecdote, and especially from the Beast-Satire, in which beasts, by their antics and wiles, parody and satirize the worst qualities of men, as in 'Reynard the Fox' (see MacCulloch, *CF*, *passim*). There is one further quality inherent in the fable which should be emphasized at the outset for reasons shortly to be given; they appeal largely to the sense of fun; the first thing George Eliot remembered laughing at was one of Æsop's Fables (*Life*, by Cross, 1885, i. 20). A German might, accordingly, on the analogy of *Tendenzroman*, define the fable as a 'Moral-Tendency Beast-Droll.'

Taking 'fable' in this strict sense, its independent and original production is practically restricted to two countries—Greece and India. Sporadic instances occur elsewhere, as in Jotham's (Jg 9^{8-15}) and Jehoash's (2 K 14^{9}) fables in the OT, or in the fable of 'The Belly and Members' given in Livy (ii. 32), and repeated by Shakespeare in *Coriolanus*, though even here the 'moral' is not explicitly given; but for any large body of fables we have to look to Greece and to India. In the former country they are associated with the name of Æsop; in the latter they can, in many instances, be connected with the *Jātakas*, or birth-stories of the Buddha. The main problem suggested by the fable is the connexion between the two. This, again, is mainly a literary problem, though there can be no doubt that originally fables both in Greece and in India were current among the folk.

The fables known as *Æsop's Fables*, which have spread throughout Europe, can be traced back to a collection in Latin and German published soon after the invention of printing by Heinrich Stainhowel, printed about 1480, and, within the next ten years, translated into Italian, French, Dutch, English (by Caxton), and Spanish. This consists of a *Life* of Æsop (connected with the legend of Aḥiqār [*q.v.*]), four books derived from a mediæval collection of fables known as *Romulus*, a selection of the fables of Avian, some from a previous selection made by Ranutio, others called 'extravagant,' and two collections of rather coarse anecdotes from Poggio and Petrus Alphonsi. The *Romulus* has turned out to be entirely mediæval prose renderings of Phædrus, a Greek freedman of Augustus, who flourished in the early years of the 1st cent. A.D. It contains survivals of Phædrine fables which are no longer extant in verse form, such as 'The Town and the Country Mouse,' 'The Ass and the Lap-Dog,' and 'The Lion and the Mouse.' It may accordingly be said that our *Æsop* is Phædrus with trimmings.

Besides these prose renderings of Phædrus, which form the bulk of the modern European *Æsop*, there exist a number of Greek prose renderings which were, for a long time, supposed to be the original *Æsop*, but have been proved by Bentley and others to have been derived from a metrical collection in choriambics by one Valerius Babrius, tutor to the son of the Emperor Severus, who flourished about A.D. 235, and part of whose fables were discovered on Mt. Athos by Minoides Menas in 1840. Babrius, in his preface, refers to two sources—Æsop for Hellenic fable, and Kybises for 'Libyan' fable; and Jacobs has suggested that the latter collection ran to about one hundred in number, and was derived directly or indirectly from a Sinhalese embassy which came to Rome about A.D. 52. Similarly Phædrus refers (iii., *Proleg.* 52) not only to Æsop but to Anacharsis the Scythian, as his sources; and some of the Indian elements which exist in Phædrus may be due to this source. That there were such Indian elements in Phædrus and Babrius as well as in Avian (who flourished *c.* A.D. 375) can scarcely be doubted after a glance at Indian fable.

In India, fables in the strict sense, *i.e.* humorous Beast-Stories with 'morals,' are found not only in the Bidpai literature, but, much earlier, in the *Jātakas.* These were brought over to Ceylon in the 3rd cent. B.C., and are probably a couple of centuries earlier. They consist of a 'Story of the Present,' in which some adventure of Buddha is told, which reminds the Master of a 'Story of the Past,' which he proceeds to relate, summing up its moral in a *Gāthā* in verse, and then concludes with the connexion of the 'Story of the Past' with that 'of the Present' by pointing out that one of the characters was a previous incarnation of either a disciple or an enemy, while the chief character was a previous incarnation of himself. Now, several of these 'Stories of the Past' are fables in the strict sense of the word, and several are actually identical with some of the most familiar of Æsop's Fables. Jacobs in his *History of the Æsopic Fable* has pointed out thirteen of these, including 'The Wolf and the Crane,' 'The Ass in the Lion's Skin,' 'The Wolf and the Lamb,' 'The Fox and the Crow,' 'The Bald Man and the Fly,' and 'The Goose that lays the Golden Eggs.' Other parallels are given by the same writer between Greek fables and Indian ones that occur in the *Mahābhārata* and in the earlier strata of the Bidpai literature. These include 'The Oak and the Reed,' 'The Belly and Members,' 'The Lion and the Mouse,' 'The Farmer and the Serpent,' 'The Two Pots,' and 'The Cat turned into a Maiden.' The critical problem of the fable is to determine whether the Indian form is derived from the Greek or *vice versa.*

The solution to this problem is given by the thirty fables which occur in the Talmud and Midrashic literature. Except in three or four cases, all these can be paralleled either in Indian or in Greek fable or in both. In the last instance the Talmudic form invariably follows the Indian wherever it differs from the Greek. Thus, in 'The Two Pots' the Talmudic proverb (*Esther Rabba* 2), 'If a stone falls upon the pot, woe to the pot; if the pot fall upon the stone, woe to the pot,' resembles the strophe of the Bidpai, 'Like a stone that breaks a pot, the mighty remain unhurt,' rather than the fable familiar to us. So too, in the fable of 'The Wolf and the Crane,' both Talmud and *Jātaka* have the lion as the animal with the sore throat, and the Jewish form of 'The Belly and Members' is closer to the Indian than to the Æsopic form. The Talmud itself mentions (*Sukka* 28*a*) that Rabbi Joḥanan ben Zakkai (*c.* A.D. 80) knew both the 'Fables of Foxes' and the 'Fables of Kobsim,' and it has been suggested by Jacobs that the latter is a misreading for 'Kubsis,' and thus identical with the Kybises mentioned by Babrius as one of his sources. It is practically impossible that the Greek fables should have been translated into Hebrew and changed by the Rabbis and then taken to India. The process must have been in the reverse order, especially as the *Jātakas* are earlier than the first collection of Æsopic fables made by Demetrius of Phaleron, who founded the

Library of Alexandria about 300 B.C. and there collected Greek proverbs and the sayings of the Seven Wise Men, as well as Æsop's Fables—all from the mouths of the people (Diog. Laert. v. 80).

Quite apart, however, from the Talmudic evidence, the probabilities are in favour of India on general grounds. India is the home of incarnation, and it was, therefore, natural for the Indians to imagine animals acting as men, whose predecessors they were, whereas in Greece such a belief was at best a 'survival,' and was no longer living in the thoughts of the people. The existence of the 'moral' in the fable properly so called may be traced back to the *Gāthās*, which formed the nucleus of the *Jātakas*, the two 'Stories of the Present and Past' being given as explanations of these metrical morals. In earlier Greek literature only eight complete fables are known, with a dozen others only referred to, the latter, however, including 'The Ass's Heart,' 'The Countryman and the Snake,' 'The Dog and the Shadow,' 'The Cat turned into a Maiden,' all of which can be traced to India, though the occurrence of these fables is in most instances earlier than Alexander's invasion.

The possibility of the same fable having arisen independently in the two countries may be at once dismissed. Two minds in different countries may hit upon the same story to illustrate a simple wile of woman or a natural act of revenge, but it is in the highest degree improbable that two moral teachers, trying to inculcate the dangers of the lowly vying with the proud, should express it by the imagery of two pots floating down a stream. In one case, indeed, we have practically absolute evidence of the direct derivation of classical fables from India. There is a fable of 'The Farmer and the Serpent,' in which the farmer receives benefits from the serpent, but he or his son strikes it, which brings the friendship to an end. This occurs both in Latin (*Romulus* ii. 10), derived from Phædrus, and in Greek (Halm, 1852, p. 96), derived from Babrius. Both forms, however, are imperfect, whereas the Indian, given in the *Pañchatantra* (iii. 5), assigns the motive for every incident, and practically combines the Greek in the Latin forms, which are thus shown by Benfey (*Pantschatantra*, Leipzig, 1859, i. 359) to have been derived from it.

But, while the presumption is in favour of India, where both collections of fables contain the same stories with the same morals, it would be hazardous to assume that all the Greek fables came from India. Of those extant in Latin — running to about 260—56, or about one quarter, have been traced with more or less plausibility to India; the remainder, till evidence is shown to the contrary, may be regarded as originating in Greece and connected with the name of Æsop. Very little is known of the putative father of Greek fable. Herodotus (ii. 134) reports that he was, together with Rhodopis, a slave in Samos, which would fix his date at about 550 B.C.; he also reports that Æsop was murdered and that his master's grandson received *wergild* for him by direction of the Delphic oracle. As all this occurred within a century of Herodotus' period, there is no reason to doubt its substantial accuracy. But it does not follow that Æsop was necessarily the author of the Greek fables passing under his name and referred to by Aristophanes and by Socrates, the latter of whom occupied some of his days in prison, while waiting for his end, in putting a few Æsopic fables into verse. The casual way in which references are made to fables in classical Greek literature would seem to imply that they passed from mouth to mouth among the folk, and the problem connected with them in Greece is to account for their being associated with the name of a special person. This was probably due to their humorous colouring, since it is usual for folk-drolls to be associated with special names of persons, as in the case of Pasquil, Joe Miller, Punch, and the like; the folk mind seemingly requires a jest to be associated with a name which has previously elicited guffaws. As Æsop's period was that of the Tyrants, his connexion with the fable possibly consisted in applying it to political purposes. The only fable directly connected with his name by Aristotle (*Rhet.* ii. 20) was of this kind. The association of the name of Æsop with what was practically a branch of Greek (or partly Indian) folklore was thus due to its humorous character in the first place, and then to its political application. Wherever we can trace the introduction of the fable, it is almost invariably associated with political applications. Both the Biblical fables and that in Livy are applied politically. Rabbi Joshua ben Hananiah applied the fable of 'The Wolf and the Crane' to prevent a revolution of the Jews against the Romans (*Gen. Rabba*, lxiv.). Kriloff and his followers made use of the fable in Russia to reflect upon the bureaucracy; and, when Æsop was first translated into Chinese, the officials soon suppressed the edition because they considered the fables to be directed against them.

Throughout the history of the Greek fable a distinction was made between the Æsopic and the 'Libyan' fable; Aristotle makes this distinction, as well as Babrius and the Emperor Julian. Hence it would appear that the Greeks themselves recognized that a certain section of fables had an exotic origin which, with our later knowledge, may be assumed to be, in its ultimate form, Indian. As before mentioned, the Æsopic fables current among Greeks were collected and written down by Demetrius Phalereus, and it was from this collection that Phædrus derived his fables, since he included among them an anecdote about Demetrius himself. His collection contains several that can be traced back to India, so that these must have percolated thence in the wake of Alexander's army, or even at an earlier stage, since 'The Cat Maiden' fable, ultimately derived from India, occurs in Greece, being quoted by the dramatist Strattis about 400 B.C. Whether the Indian forms started the practice of attaching a 'moral' to a fable corresponding to the *Gāthās* cannot be determined.

The earlier history of the fable in India, before it was taken up into the birth-stories of the Buddha, cannot be definitely traced, though it is remarkable that almost all the *Jātakas* containing fables begin with the formula 'Once on a time, when Brahmadatta was reigning in Benares,' and the previous incarnation of the Buddha was in the person of Kāśyapa, the son of this Brahmadatta. It is possible, therefore, that a separate collection of Beast-Fables existed connected with this Kāśyapa, which was incorporated in the *Jātakas* by assuming him to be a pre-incorporation of the Buddha. It was thus easy for the Buddhist authorities to assume that these fables represented the experiences of the Master in his previous lives. Thus the lamb in the fable of 'The Wolf and the Lamb,' and the crane in the fable of 'The Wolf and the Crane,' are both incarnations of the Buddha. The stories, however, probably existed as Beast-Tales among the folk, before they were incorporated into the Buddhist canon.

Thus, both in Greece and in India the fable existed first as a piece of folklore in oral tradition, and was applied to moral purposes by the Buddhists, and to political satire by Æsop and his followers. In India they were written down in order to form part of the Buddhist canon, while in Greece they were collected by Demetrius in his search for the wisdom current among the folk, whether in the form of proverbs, sayings of wise men, or fables. Fables are thus an interesting and early example of the transformation of oral into written literature.

Very few additions were made to the original stock of fables current in the classical world—in Latin by Phædrus and Avian, and in Greek by Babrius; the former being turned into poor Latin prose (*Romulus*), the latter into equally ineffective Greek prose (collected by Neveletus, 1617). But towards the end of the 12th cent. a couple of sets of new fables made their appearance. Marie de France translated from the Middle English a set of 103 fables, a third of which are unknown to classical antiquity. Many of these also occur in a set of 107 fables with the Talmudic title *Mishle Shu'alim* ('Fox Fables'), written by one Berachyah ha-Naqdan, who has been identified with an English Jew known in the contemporary records as Benedict le Puncteur, mentioned as living in Oxford in 1194. Both these collections contain Oriental elements found in Arabic literature, but their exact provenance has not yet been traced. Stainhowel inserted a dozen or so of them in the fifth section of his *Æsop*; other additions to the fable were made by La Fontaine, mainly from Oriental sources. These include the story of Perrette, who counted her chickens before they were hatched, which Benfey, and after him Max Müller, traced all the way from India to France. Gellert in Germany, Gay in England, and Kriloff in Russia have imitated the Æsopic fable, but their additions have not been accepted by the people, and the European *Æsop* to this day is practically identical with the collections of classical antiquity.

Fable with its explicit 'moral' is thus a highly differentiated form of the Beast-Tale, and it must not be considered remarkable that it occurs in full force only in one or two countries. Anecdotes and tales about beasts are found everywhere—in South Africa (Bleek) and among the American negroes ('Uncle Remus'). An attempt has been made by Sir Richard Burton to trace the fable, properly so called, to Africa, and to suggest that it recalls reminiscences by man of his animal ancestors. The sole basis of this bizarre theory, however, is an Egyptian paraphrase of the fable of 'The Mouse and the Lion,' found in a late demotic papyrus, which also contains Coptic versions of the 'Ritual of the Dead'; and it must, therefore, be summarily rejected. Wherever we find the fable with its distinctive moral, it can be traced either by derivation or imitation to Greece or India.

Yet the conceptions at the root of the fable are primitive enough; they contain almost the first moral abstractions, or at least personifications of the cruder virtues and vices; in them courage is personified by the lion, greed by the wolf, cunning by the fox, innocence by the lamb, etc. Early man may in this way have learnt his first lessons in moral abstraction; to him cunning was foxiness, magnanimity leoninity, cruelty wolfhood. Even to the present day we have no other way of referring to one of the ruling motives in a capitalistic society than by speaking of 'The Dog in the Manger.' Hence the appeal of fables to the primitive mind of children, which is the more direct owing to the absence of any reference in them to the sex-motive. The touch of fun, which forms an essential element of fables, is another attraction for childish minds; on the other hand, the morals they inculcate are not very lofty, since they are necessarily confined to animal qualities. The higher elements of culture—knowledge, love, beauty, consideration for others—are beyond their purview. But the appeal of a fable to the mind of the child remains to-day as strong as ever, and the Æsopic fable is probably, outside of the Bible, the only literature known to practically all Europeans.

Cf. also artt., FICTION, FOLKLORE and REYNARD THE FOX.

LITERATURE.—The above account summarizes a somewhat elaborate *History of the Æsopic Fable*, which forms the first volume of the edition of Caxton's *Æsop*, edited by Joseph Jacobs, London, 1889. This contains a full account of the previous literature and critical investigations by Crusius on Babrius, Hervieux on the Latin Fable, Benfey and others on Indian Fable, Mall on Marie de France, etc., together with connecting links suggested by the editor. His results have generally been accepted by scholars; see, for example, S. Arthur Strong, *Collected Essays*, London, 1912. A more popular account will be found in Jacobs, *Fables of Æsop*, London, 1894. The following works may also be consulted: J. A. MacCulloch, *Childhood of Fiction*, London, 1905; W. W. Skeat, *Fables and Folk-Tales from an Eastern Forest*, London, 1901; J. Jacobs, in *JE* i. 221 f., v. 324. Cf. the Bibliography in MacCulloch, *op. cit.*

JOSEPH JACOBS.

FA-HIAN.—The first Chinese traveller in India. As to his *Record of the Buddhist Kingdom*, see YUAN CHWANG.

FAIRY.—Fairies or elves may be described at this stage as a non-human race, the belief in whom is mainly known as it exists among the Celts and Teutons. There is little difference in attributes, characteristics, and actions between Celtic fairies and Teutonic or Scandinavian elves, dwarfs, and trolls; and much the same cycle of stories and beliefs is common to both. But among other European folk, Slavic or Latin, there are similar stories told of fairy-like beings, while Arabs, Hindus, Chinese, and savages of all regions believe in more or less supernatural beings of whom many things are told which offer a curious parallel to the Celtic and Teutonic fairy superstition. Thus, though the popular idea of fairies is that of a supernatural race existing in the fancy of the folk of North and West Europe, a scientific explanation of the belief must take a wider sweep. And, while the popular idea mainly regards the fairies whose occupation it is to dance in the moonlight, our investigation must also include house fairies and fairies of wood, stream, or other parts of wild Nature.

From the abstract Lat. noun *fatum*, 'fate,' was derived a late Lat. or Italian personal noun *Fata*, equivalent to *Parcæ*. Ausonius uses the word in this sense, speaking of *tria Fata*; and Procopius (*de Bello Goth.* i. 25) makes τὰ τρία Φάτα the Roman equivalent of the Μοῖραι; hence in Romance languages the words for 'fairy,' Ital. *fata*, Span. *hada*, Provençal *fada*, Fr. *fée* (see, for connexion of *fées* and the Fates, § 4). From *fatum* came in med. Lat. *fatare*, 'to enchant,' which became in Fr. *faer*, with a p.p. *faé* (cf. the common phrase in romances, *les dames faés*, 'enchanted ladies'; and a 14th cent. passage, 'les fées ce estoient deables qui disoient que les gens estoient destinez et faés les uns à bien, les autres à mal'). The same sense is found in Scots 'fey.' From *faé* was formed a noun *faerie*, *féerie*, 'enchantment,' 'illusion,' which was adopted into English, but with different senses—(1) the region of the *fées*, (2) the people of fairyland, (3) an individual fairy, with pl. 'fairies.'

'Elf' comes from O.N. *álfr*, A.S. *ælf*; cf. M.H.G. *alp*, 'genius,' pl. *elben*. It is generally connected with Skr. *ṛbu*, 'artisan sprite.' The German word 'elf' was borrowed in the 18th cent. from the same English word.

I. Varieties of fairies.—In the Edda the *Liosálfar* ('light elves') dwell in Alfheim, and are divided from the *Döckálfar* ('dark elves') dwelling underground, who, again, are separated from the *Dvergar* ('dwarfs'), perhaps = the *Svartálfar*, who originated as maggots from Ymir's flesh, and now, in likeness of men, dwell in earth and stones. But the latter can hardly be distinguished from *Döckálfar*, and are sometimes identified with them, or in their proper names the word *álfar* occurs. In folk-belief the distinction between light and dark elves is not clear, and elves are both light and dark by turns, while the widest class is an earth- or under-earth-dwelling race, though there are elves of air or sky. Other kinds are associated with the house, with woods and fields, with waters, and with the mine (scarcely to be distinguished from dwarfs). Such a division generally holds good for all Teutonic, Scandinavian, or Anglo-Saxon lands, and it corresponds, on the whole, to the Celtic groups of fairies, though the chief class of the latter in Ireland—the *Daoine sidhe*—are not always a small folk. The Celts have also their dwarf-like fairies, as well as house, water, and (to a less extent) woodland fairies. But these divisions hold good in folk-belief all over Europe, both in ancient and modern times. It should be noted also that the dwarfs strictly so called—*dvergar, zwerge, drows, bergmännlein, nains, cluricauns*—are metal-workers, but this is also true of elves in the Edda.

2. Characteristics.—Fairies are generally regarded as of a nature between spirits and men, or as spirit beings with the semblance of a body which, to quote Kirk (*Secret Commonwealth of Elves, Fauns, and Fairies*, ed. Lang, 1893), is 'spungious, thin, and defecate.' In many aspects they are like mankind. They have their occupations, amusements, fightings. They marry and bear children. But they have powers beyond those of ordinary mortals, yet like those attributed to medicine-men, sorcerers, and witches. They are regarded as a separate race of superior beings, as many of their titles suggest—'fair *or* still folk,' 'people of peace,' etc.—while in the Edda the *álfar* are a distinct class of beings. They have a king or queen, usually the latter, and the names of some of these are known—Fionnbhar, Aine, Aoibhinn, Cliodna, Miala, Gwion, Huldra, Oberon (=Alberon). There are also single fairies—the Irish leprechaun, the Brownie, etc.—not living in communities. In their dwellings, as seen occasionally by mortals, there is great splendour and luxury. But often all this proves to be mere glamour when the mortal comes to himself (perhaps one source of the fairy glamour conception is to be found in the rude awakening to the grim realities of life after a happy dream experience).

Separate fairy bands are sometimes at enmity; this is already found in old Celtic tales of the *síd* folk (*RCel* xvi. [1895] 275). Frequently fairies are regarded as a diminutive folk, but there is much contradiction on this subject, and many fairies (the *fées* of S. Europe, the Slavic *vilas*, and the *síd* folk of Ireland) are hardly to be distinguished in size from mortals. In the same region some groups of fairies may be tall, others pygmies, but the varying size is sometimes due to their power of changing their form. Once fairies were regarded as small, their smallness would tend to be exaggerated. Usually great beauty is ascribed to female fairies, but certain groups of fairies—dwarfs, kobolds, etc.—are ugly and misshapen. Their clothing is often of a green or red colour, though the Teutonic dwarfs are dressed in grey (cf. the 'elfin gray' in *Tamlane*). They are all intensely fond of music, singing,[1] and dancing (as also are witches), as well as of feasting, and are often represented as spending the whole night in revelry, which has an inevitable attraction for mortals, who are lured into the dance to their own eventual discomfort or worse. No picture is more charming than that drawn by folk-belief of the nightly fairy revels on the greensward. The marks of these form the fairy-rings in which it is dangerous to tread or sleep, and which are also attributed to the witches' 'Sabbat.' This feature may connect fairies with actual rites of an orgiastic character among the folk, performed for purposes of agricultural magic, or with folk-festivals in which music and dancing figure. In part the Sabbat is also connected with these (see Grimm, *Teut. Myth.* 187, 470; Scott, *Minstrelsy*, 213; Delrio, *Disq. Mag.*, 1599–1600, p. 179). The fairies disappear from their revels at dawn, or their power ceases then—a trait shared by other supernatural beings and by witches (MacCulloch, *CF*, 1905, p. 195). They dislike being seen by mortals, and he who looks upon them or their doings is usually brought within their power. They punish with blindness those who possess or have gained the power of seeing them when they are invisible to others, and again their look is of itself sufficient to bewitch. It is also dangerous to enter their domain without due precautions (see § 11).

[1] Some folk-songs and lullabies are said to have been learned from fairies(see, *e.g* *Journ. of Folk-Song Soc.* iv. 3 [1911], 174, and *passim*)

But it is in their magical powers that the special characteristics of fairies appear. They have the power of invisibility, *e.g.* by wearing a magic cloak or hat, or by means of some herb, *e.g.* fern-seed (see *1 Hen. IV.* Act ii. Sc. 1). This power they could also confer on mortals. Immortality is sometimes ascribed to them, especially in poetry (Ariosto, *Orlando Fur.* x. 47; Beaumont and Fletcher, *Faithful Shepherd*, Act i. Sc. 2), but more usually they are mortal, though gifted with longer life than man (Kirk, 15; Grimm, 458). They have the power of assuming different shapes, or of causing others to do so, or of giving an unreal and valuable appearance to objects of no value (fairy gold), or of putting a spell upon mortals which holds them bound for long periods of time. Their knowledge, especially of the hidden powers of Nature, is often more extensive than man's. The fairy glamour has already been referred to, and it corresponds with their power of making time appear long or short to those mortals who are lured into their company. They have also the power of seeing invisible or hidden things, or of divining where they are. Thus it is easy to see why powers of this kind (divination, second-sight) should be regarded sometimes as fairy gifts to mortals.

Yet, in spite of all their powers, fairies are curiously dependent on men. They seek to reinforce their own race by stealing human children; or they steal young women or women in child-bed, in order to unite with them or that they may nurse their children. In such cases the place of the stolen child or woman is often taken by a fairy (see CHANGELING). They compel women to come and assist at child-birth their females or those whom they have stolen. They fall in love with and marry mortals, or they steal men, usually by luring them into the fairy dance (cf. the luring of men into the Sabbat), or by taking them by fascination or force to fairyland (see an early instance in O'Grady, *Silva Gadelica*, 1892, ii. 204 ff.). The purpose of these kidnappings and unions is to improve the fairy race, to obtain human strength or beauty, or perhaps to share in the spiritual benefits of the religion from which fairies are supposed to be excluded (cf. de la Motte Fouqué's *Undine*, Eng. tr., 1875). On the other hand, men often steal fairy brides. Cattle are also stolen by fairies, an illusory appearance being sometimes left in their place.

There is no doubt that the idea of the fairy theft of mortals is connected with the more primitive and wide-spread idea of the anxiety of the dead to obtain the living by causing their death. In many fairy instances the theft is also connected with death or a death-like state (trance). Or the fairies steal the soul, which then sometimes returns to animate the body. The old belief that death is unreal and accidental survives here, and death and trance are both explained as fairy thefts of the real personality (the soul).

To the fairy midwife motive is attached the wide-spread idea of the fairy ointment with which the midwife has to anoint the child. Accidentally it touches her eye, and gives her the power of seeing invisible things. Ultimately she loses her sight, because she is able to see fairies when they wish to be invisible (see many instances in Hartland, *Science of Fairy Tales*, p. 59 ff.). This is also told of *dracs* and water fairies (Bérenger-Féraud, *Superstitions et survivances*, Paris, 1896, ii. 2 ff.; Rhys, *Celtic Folk-lore*, Oxford, 1901, i. 213 ff.).

Fairies are also tricky with men. They carry

them off by night and make them travel long distances, sometimes using them as steeds; the men when they awake in the morning are more or less conscious of this. The trick is also alleged sometimes as an explanation of 'falling sickness.' It is obviously connected with the phenomena of somnambulism and nightmare, though the belief itself might sometimes be exploited by unscrupulous mortals to explain any mysterious absence on their part.[1] In other ways they torment men (cf. the Poltergeist and the house-fairy when insulted). A favourite trick is to give men gold which turns into worthless articles (but worthless things offered as a reward for human services often turn to gold [Hartland, 48 f., 184; Simrock, *Handbuch der deutschen Mythologie*[6], Bonn, 1887, p. 427]). They are easily irritated, capricious in their character, and given to resentment. More than this, they are dangerous and even cruel, especially when despised or ill-treated, causing injury, illness, madness, or death, usually by a 'fairy stroke' (§ 6). Hence the folk seek to placate them or to flatter them by euphemistic names—'good people,' 'guid neighbours,' 'gute Holden,' 'gentry,' etc. (see EUPHEMISM, § 2).

On the other hand, fairies often assist mortals, especially in return for some small service (articles borrowed, advice given, etc.), and are very generous. This is especially true of the house-fairy, who is sufficiently rewarded with a little milk or food. They give gifts of great value (cf. stories of magic swords, etc.). But these objects are often stolen by mortals from fairyland. Supernatural and magic powers are also given by them to mortals (cf. the gift of prophecy—'the tongue that could not lie'—to Thomas the Rymer; and see Scott, *Demonology*, 1898, Letter 5, *Minstrelsy*, p. 212). They also preside at birth, and confer talents on the child.

Thus the relation between men and fairies is a reciprocal one. Each seeks help from the other. Each harms the other. Men are now contemptuous, now afraid of fairies. Fairies are now friendly, now hostile to men. We may see here the survival of older religious ideas—of gods now kind, now evil, and of benefits rendered by them to men out of all proportion to the attention paid to them. This is an old aspect of sacrifice—*do ut des*.

Fairies in Christian lands are generally regarded as pagans. Sacred names, signs, and things keep them at a distance, and they fear sacred days (see an early instance in Adamnan, *Vita S. Columb.* cap. 9), while a demoniac character is attributed to them. A mass was celebrated in mediæval and later times in the church of Poissy to preserve the land from the anger of evil *fées*, and in the *procès* of Jeanne d'Arc the curé of Domremy is said to have sung the Gospel annually near the Tree of the Fées to drive them off. The fairies mourn over their lost supremacy, as the ancient Nature-spirits are held to have done after the coming of Christianity, while in many folk-traditions the earnest preaching of the gospel is said to have dispersed them. The Church was generally opposed to fairies, associating them with paganism, the devil, and witchcraft. Nevertheless, they have a desire to be saved, and many pathetic stories express this, or their anxiety with regard to their position at the Day of Judgment. In other cases they believe themselves Christians and hope for salvation.

The supernatural lapse of time in the fairy dance or in fairyland, while connected with the excitement and exaltation of the orgiastic dance, is perhaps based upon trance experiences, loss of memory, and the like, in which the person, when he comes to himself, takes up the thread of his life where it was left off, the intervening period being thus short to him. Exaggeration of such experiences—especially since in trance men's pre-conceived notions led them to believe they had been in fairyland, the other world, etc.—would result in the incident of the supernatural lapse of time[1] (see Hartland, 223 ff.). On the other hand, in many fairy stories the opposite experience is found—the consciousness of having spent a lifetime during a moment as a result of a fairy spell. This, combined with the fact of similar trance or dream experiences, points to these as its true source.

3. The origin of fairies.—The folk-explanations of the origin of fairies are various. Sometimes they are regarded as descendants of rebellious angels, cast out of heaven, and doomed to remain in sea, land, air, or underground; or they are supposed to have stopped on the way to hell and remained in these places.[2] This is a Celtic and Slavic belief (Curtin, *Tales of the Fairies*, p. 42; Sikes, *British Goblins*, 1880, p. 134; Ralston, *Songs of the Russian People*, 1872, p. 106), and it may be compared with the Arabic belief that the *jinn* are a pre-Adamite race who rebelled against God and were driven to the distant regions of earth (Lane, *Arab. Society*, 1883, p. 30). Other folk-beliefs regard fairies as souls, *e.g.* of Druids, of infants dying unbaptized, of pre-historic races, or of the dead generally (Keightley, *Fairy Mythology*, 1900, pp. 298, 412; Wentz, *The Fairy Faith in Celtic Countries*, Oxford, 1911, pp. 147, 176). Or they are people who refused to accept Christianity and were cursed (Keightley, 432; Wentz, 169).

The learned have attempted many explanations. Maury (*Fées du moyen âge*) found the *fées* in old Celtic and Teutonic Nature-goddesses, *Matræ*, *Matronæ*, akin to the Fates, Junos, Nymphs, etc., and in a folk-memory of 'druidesses' with magic power, who had been their priestesses. To these the people then gave the names *fata*, *fées*, 'enchantresses,' etc.[3] There is no evidence that such 'druidesses' were priestesses of these goddesses (see MacCulloch, *Rel. of the Anc. Celts*, Edin., 1911, p. 316). Others have seen in them the ghosts of a small and swarthy pre-historic race transformed in popular fancy into an actual supernatural people dwelling underground (G. Allen, 'Who were the Fairies?' *Cornhill Magazine*, xliii. [1891] 338 ff.). Another theory is that which regards them as a folk-memory of a pre-historic small race, dwelling underground, with weapons of stone, and generally hostile to their Celtic conquerors.

This was already hinted at by J. Cririe, *Scottish Scenery*, 1803, by Sir W. Scott, following Dr. Leyden (see *Minstrelsy*, 189, *Demonology*, 102 f.), and by Grimm (p. 459), as a partial explanation of the fairy belief. Its main exponent in later times is D. MacRitchie, with his theory of an earlier pygmy race dwelling in what are now regarded as sepulchral mounds (see his *Testimony of Tradition*, 1890, *Fians, Fairies, and Picts*, 1893; cf. also A. S. Headlam, *NC*, Feb. 1908).

But no one cause can be alleged for the origin of the fairy superstition; and, taking into account the precisely similar characteristics ascribed also to spirits, ghosts, demons, witches, etc., in all parts of the world, we may trace it back to animistic beliefs modified and altered in different ways in different localities, but undoubtedly influenced also in various ways by traditions about older races, by beliefs in ghosts, and by the débris of older myths and religions. We may also regard dreams, trance experiences, and psychic phenomena as formative and moulding influences. W. Y. Evans Wentz has recently sought to prove that 'fairies

[1] The witches' aerial flight to the Sabbat and the aerial transportation of their victims resemble this, as does also the alleged flight of mediums (see MacCulloch, *CF*, 222).

[1] In Ireland a trance is recognized as the presence of the entranced person in fairyland.

[2] This resembles the myth in the Edda of elves of air, and of under-earth.

[3] Cf. also L. Shaw, *Province of Moray*, 1775, p. 287.

exist, because in all essentials they appear to be the same as the intelligent forces now recognized by psychical researchers' (*op. cit.* p. 490), whether these are phantasms of the dead or other orders of beings, acting on men, seen by them, or producing the alleged phenomena which the folk ascribe to fairies. But he attaches too much importance to the evidence of modern Celtic seers, and too little to the phenomena of hallucination. Similar evidence, if rashly accepted, would equally prove the existence of many other mythical beings. Fairies, wherever found, are mythical beings, creations of fancy utilizing existing beliefs, traditions, experiences, and customs. In the following sections the connexion of fairies with earlier divinities, ghosts, or actual races will be discussed.

4. Fairies as earlier divinities.—Fairies, as a race of supernatural beings, have many of the traits of earlier divinities; in some instances they may have been originally Nature-spirits or Nature-divinities. In Ireland this is especially true of the *Daoine sídhe*, still associated in popular belief with the Tuatha Dé Danann, the ancient gods of the Irish Celts. Dispossessed by the Milesians—in other words, defeated by the coming of Christianity to Ireland—they retired to the *síd*, or mounds. This is the constant tradition of Irish story, and one class of fairies in Ireland are tall, handsome beings, much more divine than any other class of fairy folk (see CELTS, v. § 3). Specific earlier divinities—Fionnbhar, Aine, Cliodna, Aibell, etc.—are kings and queens of the fairy hosts of different regions. The pagan Celts or the pre-Celtic folk of Ireland may have believed in a race of *síd*-folk other than the Tuatha Dé Danann, with whom the latter were assimilated or became their kings and leaders (MacCulloch, *Rel. of. Anc. Celts*, 65 f.). What is certain is that earlier gods, connected with agriculture and growth, have for centuries been regarded as fairies, while yet preserving some of their divine traits. Other Irish fairies are unconnected with the gods, and others again are lineal descendants of river-, well-, or tree-spirits (MacCulloch, *op. cit.* 43, 173). The Celts of Gaul worshipped *niskas* and *peisgi* (groups of water-divinities), some of whom have personal names, and these are the nixes and perhaps the piskies of later belief (*ib.* 185). Sirens, mermaids, and other fairy beings haunting the waters, the Welsh fairy-brides who emerge from lakes, often accompanied by a venerable old man, and to whom offerings are made—are all alike earlier divinities or spirits. Similarly, Brythonic divinities appear in later legend as fairy-like beings or fairy kings. So also in Italy, some of the older divinities are still remembered, and fairy-like characteristics are ascribed to them (Leland, *Etruscan Roman Remains*, 1892, *passim*), while the domestic Roman gods resemble the Brownie, as already noted by Reginald Scot; the Romans had also their *minuti dei* (Plaut. *Cist.* ii. 1. 45) and their *dei campestri*.

Offerings of food or milk are made to Celtic fairies to appease them; when this has not been done, vengeance is said to have followed. As with sacrifices to gods, it is the invisible essence of the food which is supposed to be taken by them —the *toradh*—the outward appearance being left (Campbell, *Superstitions of the Highlands and Islands of Scotland*, Glasgow, 1900, p. 32).[1]

The northern *álfar* are coupled in the Edda with the Divine *aesir* (cf. the A.S. connexion of *és* and *ylfe*); the dark elves are allied with gods against their enemies, and work for them (Simrock, 424). They have also great magical powers. The general impression which one receives from the older sources is that of the divine character of the *álfar*. And, as Grimm (pp. 179 f., 187, 456) has shown, there was a connexion between the *álfar* and Donar or Thor, as well as with Holda; and he adds (p. 187): 'An intimate relation must subsist between the gods and the elves, though on the part of the latter a subordinate one.' This is also seen in the elf cult. Besides the homely offerings of later folk-custom, in older custom there was the *álfablót*—animal sacrifices to the elves—and in one instance in *Kormaks-saga* the elf-hill is to be reddened with the blood of a bull, and the flesh used as a feast for the elves (Grimm, 448, 1411; Simrock, 426; see also Meyer, *Germ. Myth.*, Berlin, 1891, § 175 ff.).

The activity of fairies and elves at certain seasons—May-day (Beltane) and November-eve (Samhain)—is significant. In the early history of Celts and Teutons these were times of great sacredness. They were festivals, in part orgiastic, and included ritual dances. In so far as fairies are connected with older gods (as in Ireland), it is natural that their power should be more in evidence at these times sacred to the older gods. But in any case, just as ghosts of the dead were active at Samhain, all beings of popular fancy were found to be attracted to these seasonal occasions. And, as dancing was a feature of these festivals, so the fairies are supposed to dance at them (cf. Maury, 39). The striking formula in many tales—that he who has been captured by the fairies through entering into their dances cannot be set free until a year after—points of itself to a recurring festival celebrated annually, the observance of which has been transferred in part to the fairies by the folk who still observed it as a survival.

The three fairies who attend at the birth of a child and foretell its future or give it gifts, and to whom many folk-traditions are attached, are well-known in popular tales from all parts of Europe. They are also the subject of many old tales, especially in the Romance languages, in which they are met by a wayfarer in the forest or coming out of a fountain, and offer him their love, or render assistance in various ways (see stories of them in T. Wright, *Celt, Roman, and Saxon*[2], 1861, p. 285 ff.). In Burchard of Worms' collection of decrees (11th cent.), women are said to have sacrificed to them, spreading a table with meat and drink (Grimm, 1746). In Brittany a table was spread for them at a birth, just as the Romans then placed a couch for Juno Lucina (Maury, 31). They are often called *fées* or *fata*, and are connected with the Parcæ, goddesses associated with birth. Or they are called *Bonnes Dames, Dames Blanches*, 'white women,' *Bé Find, Bonnes Pucelles*; cf. the names *Bonæ Parcæ* and *Puellæ*, given to the Fates and Nymphs. They are primarily, however, descendants of the Celtic and Teutonic *Matres* and *Matronæ*—goddesses generally represented as three in number, and associated with fertility, with springs and rivers, and also with child-bearing and love (MacCulloch, *op. cit.* 45 ff., 73), though they also continue the functions of the Scandinavian *Nornæ*, the Slavic *Vilas*, and the Roman *Parcæ* with regard to birth, and they are sometimes called goddesses (Grimm, 1400). In modern Greece the Fates play a similar part at the birth of children to that which they played in ancient times (Bent, *JAI* xv. [1886] 393), and in ancient Egypt their closest parallel is the seven Hathors, who presided at birth and played the part of fairy god-mothers (Wiedemann, *Rel. of anc. Egyptians*, 1897, p. 143; Maspero, *Contes pop. ég.*[3], Paris, 1905, p. 76 ff.).[1] All these goddesses and fairies as associated with birth are probably 'refractions of the human "spae-women" (in the Scots term) who attend at birth and derive omens of the child's future from various signs' (Lang, *EBr*[11] x. 134*b*, *s.v.* 'Fairy').

Individual fairies, like Abonde, Viviane, Morgen le Fée, Esterelle, Aril, etc.—so often mentioned in mediæval romances, and some of whom figure as fairy queens—as well as the individual white women or *banshees* haunting hills, woods, or castles, are probably connected with the *Matres* or with individual Celtic or Teutonic or other

1 This is also true of fairy thefts of cows or corn; the substance is taken and the empty semblance is left.

1 For the Slavic fairy-like Fates, see *ERE* iv. 626.

goddesses, *e.g.* the Roman Nymphæ as worshipped in Gaul, just as in Romance tales and in popular Italian belief the Roman Orcus has become a wood-fairy or ogre (Grimm, 486; Leland, 75). All these were generally helpful, but occasionally hostile, to men. Generally, too, it may be said that the love of fairies for music and dancing connects them with divinities in whose cult these were common, while the fairy moonlight dance may be a reminiscence of the cult itself, like the witches' Sabbat in another direction. The powers of fairies—shape-shifting, invisibility, magic, etc.—also link them on to the world of the gods.

5. Fairies and the dead.—While the fairy belief cannot be derived merely from a belief in ghosts, since the two exist side by side, the latter forms one of the strands from which the former has been woven. It should also be observed how much is common to the two beliefs. Both fairies and ghosts can benefit or harm the living. Both steal children (see CHANGELING), while both fairy changelings and ancestral ghosts are always hungry. Both can cause death—usually by a 'stroke,' producing a pining sickness—or warn of sudden death. To see them often means death to the seer (see *ERE* iv. 739[b]). Both can be avoided or repulsed by the same means (broom and iron tabu, running water, etc.). Both are active on May-day and Hallowe'en, and both have offerings made to them. Both love the night for their revels (dancing on meadows, etc.; cf. Grimm, 830), but both must vanish at cockcrow (as must the witch and vampire [MacCulloch, *CF*, 195]). Both possess enchanted objects of which daring mortals try to rob them. Both dislike untidiness and uncleanness (cf. Curtin, 178). In fairyland and the world of the dead time passes like a dream (see Hartland, 167 f.), while the same tabu with regard to eating fairy food or the food of the dead—in both cases dangerous to mortals—exists (see *ERE* iii. 561 f., iv. 653, and add to reff. there Brown, *Melanesians and Polynesians*, 1910, p. 194; Seligmann, *Melan. of Br. N. Guinea*, 1910, pp. 656 f., 734). The warning not to eat the food usually comes from a mortal imprisoned in fairyland or from the dead person whose rescue from Hades is sought. It may also be noted that in Brittany the whole superstition regarding the dead is exactly like that regarding fairies, both there and elsewhere.

In folk-belief and *Märchen*, fairies are associated with tumuli or burial-mounds. These are sometimes called 'Fairy-hills,' 'Elf-howes,' 'Alfenbergen,' etc.; but they are also believed to be haunted by the ghosts of those buried in them, or at least are associated with these.[1] In certain cases fairies have succeeded the ghostly tenants of the tumulus, forgotten by the folk—a natural result, since any mysterious structure tends to be associated with mysterious beings. In other cases they are merged with them, and it is hardly possible to discriminate rigidly between them, while both are regarded with awe. The Teutonic dwarfs are *unterirdische* (cf. cognate names in other Northern languages [Grimm, 454, 1415]), as are the dead, the *ὑποχθόνιοι, οἱ κάτω ἐρχόμενοι* or *ἐναγισμοί* of Greek belief (see EARTH, § 8). The Haugbuie, who haunted the tumuli and was feared by the Scandinavian howe-breakers, is at once a ghost and a goblin, like the similar tenant of Brynyr-Ellyllon, near Mold, the hill of the goblin or fairy (Windle, *Life in Early Britain*, 1897, p. 113; J. Anderson, *Scotland in Pagan Times*, Edinburgh, 1886, p. 278). Such a confusion is also found in Madagascar, where the graves of the *vazimba* (at once the aboriginal folk and a species of spirits) are regarded with awe (Ellis, *Hist. of Madagascar*, 1838, i. 424).

In many cases fairies and ghosts are one and the same in popular belief. This is true of much of the fairy belief in Ireland (see Wentz, 40, 58, etc.). The Welsh *Ellyllon* are sometimes regarded as souls of the Druids (Keightley, 412); the Teutonic *dvergar* are closely associated with the *náir*, or ghosts, and the *álfar* are probably in part souls of the dead (Grimm, 445 f., 1415; Simrock, 425, 435 f.; Vigfusson-Powell, *Corpus Poet. Boreale*, Oxford, 1883, i. 418; see *ERE* iv. 633; Wright, *Purgatory of S. Patrick*, 1844, p. 89). The Celtic 'fairy hosts,' *sluagh*, though regarded in the Hebrides in some cases as the dead (the 'Furious Host' of Teutonic belief [Grimm, 918 ff.]), are also a kind of fairies hurtling through the air, and resembling the fairy hunt or ride of other Celtic districts (Wentz, 56, 94, 104, 106, 108; Carmichael, *Carmina Gadelica*, Edinburgh, 1900, ii. 330; Keightley, 355, 384, 401, 414, 520). In Brittany the fairy 'washer at the ford' (*kannerezed noz*) is now a *revenant*, and, like the Irish and Highland fairy washer (also occasionally a ghost), warns of approaching death (Le Braz, *La Légende de la mort*[2], Paris, 1902, i. p. xli). It is interesting to note that Kirk (p. 10 f.) associates the 'co-walker,' or double, seen by second-sighted persons, with the fairies, and equates it with a fairy.[1] The speech of fairies, like that of ghosts, civilized and savage, is said to be a kind of twittering (Kirk, 14; cf. Tylor, *PC* i. 457).

The dead are sometimes associated with fairies in fairyland, and are seen there by those who visit it, and are warned by them not to eat or drink. According to Scottish superstition in the 16th–17th cent., witches were in league not only with Satan but with the court and queen of fairyland, and they saw there many persons known to be dead (Scott, *Minstrelsy*, 207 ff., *Demonology*, 108, 124 f.; Dalyell, *Darker Superstitions of Scotland*, Glasgow, 1835, p. 536 f.). The same idea is found in the Romance writers and in Chaucer, who make Hades into fairyland and change Pluto and Persephone into the king and queen of Faery. Fairyland is also in close association with the Christian Other-world in the ballad of Thomas the Rymer. So, already in early mediæval Welsh belief, Gwyn is king of Faery, and is associated with Annwfn (Elysium) in its later aspect as hell, and hunts the souls of the wicked (MacCulloch, *Rel.* 115). Similarly the water-fairy keeps souls of the drowned in his under water-world (Simrock, 448 f.; Grimm, 496).

The demoniac spirits, with uncertain temper, in whom the West Africans believe, and whom they localize in the air or in natural objects, are ghosts of the dead (Nassau, *Fetichism in W. Africa*, 1904, p. 58), and the Arabic *'afrit*, evil *jinn*, is a name applied also to ghosts (Lane, *Modern Egyptians*, 1846, ii. 41).

In *Märchen* of the 'Dead Wife' cycle, in which a dead mother is recovered from Hades, there is the same incident as in tales of women carried off to fairyland. In both the mother re-appears to suckle her child, and in both she is recovered by her husband, who avoids certain tabus. In the latter series the wife apparently dies, but the 'corpse' is an adult fairy changeling or an illusory appearance. Or, again, the changeling is in effect a double or 'co-walker' (Curtin, 158; see also CHANGELING, § 6; DESCENT TO HADES [Ethnic], § 3). In Ireland the idea is wide-spread that people who die young are taken by fairies; and there is also the belief that the soul is taken, leaving the body dead.

There is one species of fairy which is closely connected with, if not in all cases actually derived from, ancestral or other household spirits—the house-fairy or Brownie,[2] already mentioned as the *Portune* by Gervase of Tilbury in the 13th cent.,

[1] Dawkins, *Early Man in Britain*, 1880, p. 433; *FLJ* v. [1887] 333; Hartland, 231; Kirk, 23.

[1] For the similar Norwegian belief, see Craigie, *Blackwood's Magazine*, cxci. (1912) 304 ff.

[2] For the various names and characteristics of the house-fairy in Germany and Scandinavia, Britain, etc., see Grimm, 500 f.; Bérenger-Féraud, i. 33 ff.; Simrock, 450 ff.; Keightley, *passim*. He is the 'lubber fiend' of Milton.

who dwells in house or stable, and loves to do the work of either. He dislikes disorder or laziness; and, where either is shown or the usual offering is not made to him, he is disagreeable to the person responsible. Food and milk are laid out for him, and he usually receives an annual gift of a new hat or coat, though in some instances this causes him to leave the house. He is particularly associated with the hearth, and to some extent corresponds with the mediæval and later familiar spirit who worked for his master and advised him (Calmet, *Traité sur les apparitions*, Paris, 1751, i. 245 f., 260). His analogues are the Roman household *Lar* (see Plaut. *Aulularia*, prologue), whose worship culminated at the hearth; the Greek *θεοὶ ἐφέστιοι*; the Italian *lasio* and *attilio* (Leland, 80 ff., 141 f.); the Slavic *dedushka domovoj*, 'Grandfather of the house,' who haunts the stove; and the Teutonic and Celtic ancestral and household spirits. The close connexion of the ancestral spirit with the house is perhaps partly to be accounted for by the wide-spread practice of house-burial, found among many savage tribes, as well as among the ancient Semites (1 S 25[1], 1 K 2[34]; Jastrow, *Rel. of Babylonia and Assyria*, Boston, 1898, p. 599), among the early Mycenæan folk, and possibly among Greeks and Romans (Reinach, *L'Anthrop.* vii. 327; Plato, *Minos*, 315; Servius, on *Æn.* vi. 151), among the Celts, and possibly the Slavs (Ralston, 326), and among the Hindus (see DOOR). The practice may have arisen in the Stone Age, when men lived in rock-shelters and caves, and buried their dead there. In any case, the house-burial resulted in, and also guaranteed, the presence of the ancestral spirit in the dwelling. In Europe it is probably as the result of ecclesiastical influences that the house-spirit has taken a more or less demoniac form. In some cases the Brownie appears as a small animal, snake, etc.—a trait common to ancestral spirits elsewhere. The main ideas of the house-fairy superstition and of the household-ghost belief, whether savage or more civilized, are the same—the house-haunting, the offering of food, the assistance rendered to the inmates. The relation of house-spirit and house-fairy is well marked in the case of the Slavic *domovoj*, the shaggy, stove-haunting being, kindly when respected, dangerous when neglected. He is closely associated with the older ancestral cult, is honoured along with the ancestors, is called 'grandfather,' and is, when seen, believed to resemble the head of the house. In many of these respects he corresponds to the house-spirit of the northern Chuds and to the Lithuanian *kaŭkas*, domestic spirits about 1 foot high, haunting the hearth (cf. Lasicius, *de Diis Samagitarum*, Basel, 1615, pp. 42, 51, 55; and, for the *domovoj*, *ERE* iv. 626 f.). The Swedish *tomte* or *nissar*, regarded often as ghosts, who act and are treated exactly as the Brownie, may also be compared (Thorpe, *Northern Mythology*, 1852, ii. 93). Sometimes, in fact, the Brownie is regarded as the spirit of a former servant.[1]

The house-fairy becomes a malicious, noisy, tormenting sprite, when neglected or insulted, and is thus again connected with phenomena in which the link between ghost and fairy is seen—those of the Poltergeist, in which furniture, etc., is moved or thrown about, fire is raised, balls of fire float about, the touch of a tiny hand is felt, etc. Some of these are extreme forms of *telekinesis*—the movement of objects without apparent cause, in presence of a medium,—or of the noises, from rappings upwards, in connexion with coincidental phantasmal appearances. The Poltergeist phenomena were known in ancient as well as in mediæval and modern times, and they still occur among savages and civilized men.[2] The phenomena, as yet unexplained, rest on sufficient evidence in certain cases to establish their authenticity. But phenomena, similar in many of the details, are often attributed to fairies in Ireland, the Highlands, France (the *follets* already mentioned as stone-throwers by Gervase of Tilbury), etc. (see Clodd, *Tom Tit Tot*, 1898, p. 83; Lang, in Kirk, p. li; Curtin, 179; Wentz, 476), also in Germany (where the Poltergeist is half fairy or goblin, half ghost [Grimm, 505]), Russia (where the *domovoj* sometimes acts as a Poltergeist [Ralston, 132]), Greece (where the Nereids [= fairies] throw stones [J. G. Hahn, *Griech. und alban. Märchen*, Leipzig, 1864, nos. 79, 80]), and in Egypt (where the *jinn* [also = fairies] act as the Poltergeist [Lane, ii. 40]). Thus phenomena, whether caused by unseen agency or trickery, or the result of hallucination, are uniformly ascribed to ghosts or to fairies, these being in many respects one and the same.

That the phenomena ascribed to the house-fairy—doing house- or stable-work secretly—may be real in some cases, in the sense of being done by human beings for some private end or under the influence of somnambulism, need not be doubted (see Bérenger-Féraud, i. 114, 137; Lang, in Kirk, p. xxxviii, refers to the 'Brownie of Bodsbeck'). The unexplained work would then be ascribed to house-spirits, and the tradition would be handed down and augmented by every fresh occurrence.

The close connexion between fairies and ancestral spirits is obvious, and there is little doubt that the belief in the latter and the usages regarding them have done much to affect the fairy superstition. Nor is it impossible that the small size attributed to them in many regions may have been suggested by the common belief in the soul as a mannikin, not only among savages but in ancient Greece (on vases the soul issuing from the body as a pygmy), in Egypt (*ka* as a pygmy in bas-reliefs), and in India (*Mahābhārata*, III. ccxcvi. 17).[1] This is in accordance with the belief in the double or 'co-walker' or *ka*, a duplicate of the living person (though not always a pygmy) who at his death 'goes to his own herd,' according to Kirk (p. 10 f.).

6. Fairies as actual people.—The origin of the fairy superstition in the relationships between a small dispossessed race and a taller conquering race has its most convinced exponent in D. MacRitchie (cf. art. DWARFS AND PYGMIES), who connects fairies with Finns, with the Irish Feinn, and the Picts. But the Feinn (*q.v.*) were not dwarfs, nor are they traditionally regarded as fairies; it is doubtful whether Celts ever had relations with Finns, and the Picts may have been a Celtic group. No argument can be based upon the fact that underground dwellings, duns, circles, etc., are ascribed to fairies, for they are ascribed equally to giants, the devil, Picts, and Feinn, just as in Greece the ruins of Mycenæ were ascribed to the Cyclopes. Nor is there any evidence that tumuli were ever dwellings, though there may be a link of connexion between them and dwellings, if they are successors of dwellings, perhaps not unlike them, in which their owners were buried while the living continued to dwell there (§ 5). The existence of a pygmy race in Europe, other and smaller than the pre-Aryan, neolithic folk, is supported by Sergi (*Mediterranean Race*, 1901, p. 233 f.), Kollmann, Dawkins, etc., on evidence furnished by archæological discoveries. Pygmy races are now known to exist in many parts of the world, and they would give rise to a pygmy tradition, as found, *e.g.*, in classical writers and in the folklore of China, Japan, the Ainus, the Malagasy, New Britain, India, Paraguay, and even among the Eskimos, themselves a small people.[2]

---

1 Besides the house-haunting Brownie, fairies in general are often represented as doing household work for those whom they like.

2 See Burton, *Anat. of Melancholy*[16], 1836, p. 124 f.; Calmet, i. 254; Girald. Camb. *Itin. Camb.* i. 12; Seligmann, 277; St. John, *Forests of Far East*, 1862, i. 91; H. J. Bell, *Obeah Witchcraft in the W. Indies*, 1889 [W. Indies]; *ERE* iii. 9[a] [Buriats]; Dennys, *Folk-Lore of China*, 1876, p. 86; also, for mysterious stone-throwing, Liebrecht, *Zur Volkskunde*, Heilbronn, 1879, p. 356 [Java]; Kingsley, *Trav. in W. Africa*, 1897, p. 517; Leslie, *Among Zulus*[2], Edinburgh, 1875, p. 120; and, for the Poltergeist generally, *Proc. Soc. for Psych. Res.* xii. 45, xxv; Myers, *Human Personality*, 1901, ii. 65, 71 ff., 461 ff.; Gurney, *Phantasms of the Living*, 1886, ii. 54, 129, 150, 636, and *passim*; Podmore, *Studies in Psych. Research*, 1897, p. 142 ff., *Modern Spiritualism*, 1902, i. 25 ff.; Lang, *Cock Lane and Common Sense*, 1894, *Making of Religion*, 1898, p. 352 ff.

1 See Crawley, *Idea of Soul*, 1909, pp. 186, 200; Frazer, *GB*[2], i. 248 ff.; Wiedemann, *Ancient Eg. Doct. of Immort.*, 1895, p. 10 f.; Jahn, *Arch. Beitr.*, Berlin, 1847, p. 128 f.

2 See Tyson, *A Philolog. Essay concerning the Pygmies*, 1699, ed. Windle, 1894, p. xv; *L'Anthrop.* xii. 371 f., xiv. 548; *Ko-ji-ki*, tr. Chamberlain, 1883, pp. 141, 207; Brown, 243;

Such a pygmy race in Europe might well be connected in tradition with fairies. But this is not to say that in all respects they gave rise to the fairy belief. Nevertheless, some characteristics are ascribed to pygmy races which resemble those ascribed to fairies.

Thus pygmies are often feared and propitiated, and they are supposed to have magical powers—a trait shared by all aboriginal peoples. They barter with the taller folk (cf. Grimm, 454, note), giving produce or animals for weapons, utensils, or cultivated food-stuffs (Ling Roth, *JAI* xxv. [1895–96] 266; *L'Anthrop.* iv. 86; Johnston, *Uganda Protectorate*, 1902, p. 516). They are shy of being seen, or of their dwellings being discovered or entered. Invisibility is ascribed to them—probably as a result of their quick powers of concealment (Johnston, 513; *L'Anthrop.* iv. 86; *18 RBEW* i. 480 f.). They dwell in caves or concealed structures, suggesting underground residence. The dwarf people believed in by the Ainus are said to have hidden under large burdocks—a habit recalling that of fairies hiding under mushrooms. Johnston says of the Congo dwarfs: 'Any one who has seen as much of the Central African Pygmies as I have, and has noted their merry, impish ways; . . . unseen, spiteful vengeance; quick gratitude; and prompt return for kindness, cannot but be struck by their singular resemblance in character to the elves and gnomes and sprites of our nursery stories' (p. 516 f.). At the same time he warns against reckless theorizing.

It cannot be denied that many stories about fairies suggest an actual people (cf., *e.g.*, the stories cited in Grimm, 451, 469). The frequent reference to fairies as earth- or mound-dwellers may be reminiscent of fact in some cases,[1] especially when it is found that the Bushmen (dwellers not only in the bush but in subterranean caves) are also called 'Earth-men' (*JRAS* xviii. pt. i.). In many stories, fairies resent mortals building over their subterranean dwellings or mounds—possibly a trait derived from actual experience of incomers being plagued by aborigines lurking in subterranean places over which they had built. On the other hand, it might be derived from fear of aboriginal ghosts haunting the mounds. In some cases, as in 'Childe Rowland,' the fairy-mound is surrounded by terraced circles—the markings of an earlier form of terrace agriculture still seen on hills (Jacobs, *English Fairy Tales*, 1898, pp. 117, 242; Gomme, *Village Community*, 1890, p. 75 ff.). In many tales it is obvious that fairies dislike the civilization of mortals, and flee from it (while themselves possessed of much secret lore), though they sometimes take advantage of it. These facts suggest the dislike of an aboriginal race to the ways of their conquerors, yet their occasional desire to benefit by them. Similarly the incident in many tales of fairies receiving articles left out for them, which they replace by gifts of their own, points to actual methods of barter. Their thefts of produce, animals, etc., and more particularly their kidnapping of women and children, reflect incidents in the contact of conquered and conquering races. The occasional cannibalism attributed to fairies is obviously derived from primitive custom, while their shyness, their retiring before the approach of mortals, easily suggesting invisibility, give the impression of a conquered race avoiding its conquerors. Finally, the dislike of fairies to metal, especially iron, by which they are kept off, or which they cannot pass, is significant, though this dislike is also shared by ghosts and other spirits, witches, *jinn*, etc. The dislike is primarily a human one; and, though the tabu concerns iron, it must first have concerned bronze.

The mystery with which the working of metal was surrounded, and the suspicion which attached to its first use, as well as the supposed result of ill-luck following upon its use, must all have contributed to the curious feeling with which it is regarded in folk-belief. Conservatism in religion prohibits its use in ritual; hence it easily came to be regarded as obnoxious to gods and to all supernatural beings. Thus, by a slight change of thought, it became effective against the inroads of the latter. Bronze was regarded as an apotropæic and a warder-off of pollutions, and this belief attached to it long after iron was introduced (Harrison, *Proleg. to Study of Gr. Rel.*[3], Cambridge, 1908, p. 591). Any race which did not use metal would also be easily scared by those who did (for an instance from New Guinea, see Hoernes, *Primitive Man*, London, n.d., p. 86). Hence stories in which fairies flee before the establishment of forges. Thus, those who now used metal came to see its power against both stone-using people and supernatural beings. These two, in course of time, would be inextricably mingled in popular thought; and thus the fairy or ghost iron-tabu doubtless contains some reminiscence of the human fear of metal. (See, on the whole subject, Goldziher, *ARW* x. [1907] 41 f., 'Eisen als Schutz gegen Dämonen'; Frazer, *GB*[2] i. 344 ff.; Hartland, 306; Bertrand, *La Gaule avant les Gaulois*, Paris, 1891, pp. 226 f., 260 f., 313.)

In so far as the fairy tradition is connected with actual people, it probably goes back to the hostile relations which may have existed between Palæolithic and Neolithic folk, these forming the basis of traditions which may have been handed on to metal-using races (to whom the Neolithic folk were equally hostile) by the captives made by them, and then adopted by them with the necessary changes.[1]

Some support is given to the theory of fairies as an actual race by the fact that in Polynesia, where there is a belief in fairies, the traditions concerning them are probably connected with the relations existing between an aboriginal race driven to the mountains and forests and immigrant conquerors. They are fair-skinned, and have a different culture from the latter, are merry, and fond of dancing and singing, but are shy of being seen, and flee from the approach of daylight. Generally they are harmless, but not always so, *e.g.* they steal the women of the conquerors. Yet, many of the traits ascribed to them are non-human—their tiny size, their spirit nature, the glamour which hides their dwellings from mortals, the parallel alleged between them and ghosts. Other Polynesian fairies, connected with the gods or with the sky and the waters, have no human origin.[2] Thus the Polynesian fairy-belief is also composed of various strands. Similarly, the Arapaho belief in a demon mannikin who shoots invisible arrows which cause illness is possibly connected with traditions of an actual small aboriginal people, though here also an animistic groundwork is clear (Talbot, *My People of the Plains*, New York, 1906, p. 259). African dwarf races also do many such things as are ascribed to European fairies, but this again is probably a result of animistic notions, mingling with actual experience of their characteristics. Many of the traits ascribed to the Roman *Fauni* are perhaps due to traditions of an older race which came to be regarded as half-demoniac, half-human (Fowler, *Roman Festivals*, 1899, p. 261; Virgil, *Æn.* viii. 314 ff.).

Allowing for every possibility, an earlier small race does not account for the whole fairy tradition or for its origin. Similar beliefs are recorded elsewhere of other beings—in Japan, foxes; in Greece, nereids or vampires; or, generally, ghosts, spirits, witches, etc. Primitive animistic or even pre-animistic ideas are the true basis of the fairy belief, and have attached themselves indifferently now to groups of imaginary spirits, now to all kinds of supernatural beings, now to actual men. Yet traditions about an actual race may have given a certain definiteness to the fairy creed.

In Scotland the 'fairy-stroke,' which causes death or wasting sickness in men or cattle, is ascribed to 'elf-arrows,' 'elf-darts,' 'elf-bolts,' or 'elf-shot,' thrown by fairies or by mortals in their company compelled by them, or by witches. No wound is seen. This is also a Teutonic belief (cf. the A.S. *ylfagescot*, Germ. *albschosse*, and cognates), and it is found in Ireland.[3] This stroke often caused the real person to be carried off, when a semblance or changeling was left in his place (see CHANGELING). Popular belief has seen these elf-arrows in the flint arrow-heads or axes of pre-historic times, found by the folk; and this belief must have attached to them when their true use was forgotten. (It is also a wide-spread belief—ancient, modern, savage, and civilized—that stone axes are thunderbolts; see Cartailhac, *L'Age de pierre*, Paris, 1877, p. 70 ff.) These flint relics, when found, were worn as amulets, as a preservative against this or other evils. This superstition, which might be regarded as supporting the human origin of fairies, in reality does not do so. The belief that spirits or ghosts can harass

FL vi. [1895] 245; *JAI* xxxi. [1901] 289; Rink, *Tales and Trad. of the Eskimo*, 1875, pp. 403, 470; *18 RBEW* [1899], pt. i. p. 480.

1 Earlier races may have had underground or semi-underground dwellings (like the winter houses of the Eskimos), of which sepulchral mounds may have been more durable copies.

1 The opposition was not necessarily between Celtic and pre-Celtic folk, as Celts had also a Stone Age in Europe.

2 See J. M. Brown, *Maori and Polynesian*, 1907, pp. 30 ff., 235; Clarke, *Maori Tales and Legends*, 1896, pp. 20, 98, 112; Tregear, *JAI* xix. [1890] 120; Gill, *Myths and Songs from the S. Pacific*, 1876, pp. 256 f., 265 f.; Dittmer, *Te Tohunga*, Hamburg, 1907, p. 74 f.; Grey, *Pol. Myth.*, ed. 1906, pp. 209, 212.

3 For a similar Slavic belief regarding the *Vilas* (=fairies), see Grimm, 436.

the living, or enter them, causing sickness or death, is very wide-spread, and this action of theirs is often thought to be produced by invisible weapons (Dayaks [St. John, i. 179]; Andamans [*JAI* xii. (1882) 160]; Santa Cruz [O'Ferrall, *JAI* xxxiv. (1904) 226, 229]; Amer. Indian [*ERE* iii. 362]). Among the Malays the weapon is not invisible, but, as in the fairy belief, is an old stone relic (Skeat-Blagden, *Pagan Races of Malay Pen.*, 1906, i. 244), and this is also alleged of Japanese spirits (Cartailhac, 40). As man caused death by weapons, so must spirits; but, as they were generally invisible, so must their weapons be. For similar reasons, sorcerers could cause death by invisible bolts (Gulf tribes [Palmer, *JAI* xiii. (1884) 292]; Melanesia [Seligmann, 640]; Araucanians [*ERE* iii. 548b]; Napo Indians [Simson, *JAI* xii. 23]). But, when mysterious stone objects were found, it was easy to believe that they were the missiles of fairies, spirits, etc.

7. Fairies as Nature-spirits.—There is little doubt that, in some aspects, fairies are derived from older Nature-spirits, or from the animistic beliefs which led to the creation of the latter in popular fancy. Their close association with fields, woods, hills, streams, and the sea is suggestive of this, and is significant when taken in connexion with the Nature-worship of the Celts, Teutons, etc. The forbidden cults rendered at trees, wells, etc., became connected with fairy-beliefs as well as with sorcery. Hence it was in forests or at fountains that *fées* appeared (see also the evidence in the *procès* of Jeanne d'Arc). But a consideration of actual instances of Nature-spirit beliefs among savage or barbaric peoples is also suggestive, since such spirits, peopling every part of Nature, so much resemble fairies. The connexion is still more clearly seen when particular groups of fairies are considered—those of the woods or of the waters.[1]

The Teutonic wood-spirit, *Schrat*, always male, and the wood- or moss-folk or wood-wives whose life is wrapped up with that of a tree, and to whom offerings of food were made; the elves who change into trees (Keightley, 93; Grimm, 450 ff., 478 ff.; Simrock, 439 ff.; de la Saussaye, *Rel. of the Teutons*, Boston, 1902, p. 322); the Celtic fairies haunting wood and forest, or dwelling in or on trees (Sébillot, *Folk-lore de France*, Paris, 1904 ff., i. 262, 270); the Roumanian *mama padura*, or forest-mothers, haunting forest glades (Gerard, *Land beyond the Forest*, 1888, ii. 9); the various Slavic woodland beings (*Lješyj*, *Dziwozony*, *Vilas*, *Rusalkas*, etc. [*ERE* iv. 628 f.]); the mediæval *Dominæ*, *Puellæ*, and *Matronæ*, haunting forests, and to whom a cult was paid (Grimm, 286 f.)—all point to earlier tree-, wood-, or forest-spirits or -divinities. The latter are known to all religions and mythologies, savage or civilized. They are (as the Baganda believe) friendly to man if the tree is not interfered with (Roscoe, *Baganda*, 1911, p. 317)—a belief corresponding to that which holds that it is not safe to interfere with trees associated with fairies. A stage midway between the purely animistic and the fairy belief is seen in the W. Finn conception of the *Tapio*, a forest-divinity with a wife and many daughters (tree-spirits), who closely resemble the Teutonic wood-folk (Abercromby, *Pre- and Proto-Historic Finns*, 1898, i. 285), or in the E. African sprites residing in trees, from which they descend to torment men (Baumann, *Usambara*, Berlin, 1891, p. 57); or in the *jinn* who, according to the Gallas, haunt sacred trees (Paulitschke, *Eth. Nordostafr.*, Berlin, 1896, p. 34 f.); or in the demons in human form who haunt trees in Central Celebes (Frazer, *GB*² i. 183); or in the Australian bush demons, or the Andamanese demons of the woods who do harm to wayfarers (Tylor, *PC*³ ii. 222; Man, *JAI* xii. 159). But tree- or wood-spirits or -gods are often quite detached from these and made anthropomorphic. This was the case with gods like Pan and Silvanus, or the Panisci and the Fauni, or the Satyrs—the three last groups bearing a close resemblance to the woodland beings of the North, and being generally hostile or mischievous to men. To all woodland elves and fairies were ascribed most of the characteristics of fairies in general.

In Teutonic, Celtic, and Slavic lands, as well as in S. Europe, there is a great variety of water-beings of fairy nature—*Merimanni*, *Wassermann*, *Strömkarl*, *Nix* and *Nisse*, *Mümmelchen*, Celtic river- and lake-fairies, *Morgans*, *Rusalkas*, and the mermaids and mermen of all the European coasts. The males among them often appear singly; the females usually in company, youthful and beautiful. All are fond of music and dancing, and are often associated with a gorgeous world below the waters. Offerings are made to them, to render them propitious, or to procure their good offices. They are often regarded as dangerous to mortals. The drowned are their victims, or they clamour for such victims—a reminiscence of human sacrifice. They entice mortals to their watery element, and there destroy them. But a milder aspect is seen in cases where they fall in love with mortals and take or ravish them to their abodes, or, again, where they are thought to guard the souls of the drowned in their domain. In other cases they become wives of mortals on earth, who lose them by not observing a certain tabu. They often come ashore to market, or seek human wives or midwives or nurses, like the fairies of the land (see Simrock, 445 ff.; Grimm, 487 ff.; de la Saussaye, 323; Ralston, 139 f.; Abercromby, i. 157, 270, 309). The beautiful and attractive, as compared with the more fearsome, aspect of water-fairies is connected by Wundt (*Völkerpsychol.*, Leipzig, 1907, ii. 2, 279) with the various emotions set up by moving water. Many of the traits of water-fairies are already possessed by the Sirens, Naiads, and Nymphs (cf. the tale of Hylas), the Celtic *Peisgi*, *Niskas*, and other water-divinities; and in many cases the tales of the water-beings show their divine or semi-divine character. Such beings or water-monsters are universally believed to be hostile to those who trespass on their domain without an offering, or to seize all who fall into the water, or to steal people or lure them to their destruction, or to take those who look into the water, by means of their reflexion (=soul; cf. Narcissus; see *FLJ* v. 319 [Guiana]; Roscoe, 318 f.; Brown, 198; Macdonald, *JAI* xx. [1891] 124; Theal, *Kaffir Folk-lore*, 1882, p. 196). The belief in such beings also gave rise to a belief in a water-world—that of the Greek Nereus and the Nereids, of the Japanese king and queen of the sea (Griffis, *Jap. Fairy World*, 1887, p. 144; *Ko-ji-ki*, p. 120), of the Slavic water-king and his daughters (Ralston, 148). Many savages also believe in similar water-worlds tenanted by supernatural beings (Africa [MacCulloch, *CF*, 112, 256, 260, 267; Ellis, *Yoruba-speaking Peoples*, 1894, p. 70]; Andaman Islands [Man, *JAI* xii. 159]; Guiana [*FLJ* v. 319]). Such water-worlds resemble the land under waves, with fairy denizens, in Celtic folk-belief.

In both Teutonic and Celtic regions there are water-beings who appear as horses or cattle, or in more monstrous forms—the *kelpie*, *afanc*, *each uisge* ('water-horse'; cf. the Australian *Bunyip*, a monster said to have a house full of beautiful things below a pool). These may be regarded as demoniac forms of earlier water-divinities in animal form.[1]

8. The fairy belief as a result of psychic experiences.—Some recent writers attribute the belief in fairies, etc., as well as myths generally, to dream experiences, or to the dreamlike character of waking experiences, common to savages (and therefore to older races of men), in which conceptions not unlike those of dreams, and endowed, like them, with actual objectivity, are produced.[2] Records of actual dreams show appearances of small figures or of figures which change their size (Ellis, 270). This is also true of trance experiences; while in migraine and epileptic aura visions of small creatures are occasionally experienced, and the diminution of objects is a phenomenon of microptic vision. Hence L. Brunton saw here the origin of fairies. In waking hallucinatory experiences, swarms of phantasmal shapes, often dwarfish, have been seen by modern and ancient percipients.[3] Similar hallucinations have

[1] The old cult of Nature-spirits developed in another direction—that of the Cabalistic and Rosicrucian elementals.

[1] They are to be distinguished from the cattle possessed by water-fairies, which sometimes come on land.

[2] K. Abraham, *Traum und Mythus*, Vienna, 1909; Rank, *Der Mythus von der Geburt des Helden*, do. 1909; Laistner, *Das Rätsel der Sphinx*, Berlin, 1889; Ellis, *World of Dreams*, 1911; Wiedemann, *Rel. of Anc. Egyptians*, 179.

[3] Gurney, *Phantasms of the Living*, ii. 196; *Proc. Soc.*

been experienced in hypnotic states, or in drunkenness.[1] Here probably we have another of the roots of the fairy belief. On the other hand, all such states are fruitful of visions of beings already believed in by the percipient. Preconceived notions colour dreams, just as preconceived notions of hell or heaven have caused visions of these regions. Again, any belief in abnormal creatures which is strongly held is certain to produce mental images of them which are confused with reality.[2]

The changeling belief, as far as it concerns adults, may have been partly shaped by the phenomena of alternating personality. The person stolen by fairies is replaced by a fairy, who resembles, but acts differently from, that person. In one Irish instance, the father said of an afflicted daughter whom he believed to be a changeling that she had the 'tongue of an attorney,' the daughter herself being a 'quiet, honest girl' (Curtin, 157). Actual adult changeling stories often read like a transcript of this.

Those who can see fairyland impart the vision to one who is in contact with them (Rhys, *Celtic Folk-lore, passim*), just as in Russian folk-tales a dead man will place a sod cut from the churchyard on the head of a living person, who then sees the under world (Ralston, *Russian Folk Tales*, 1873, p. 306). The same belief is found with regard to second-sight—physical contact with the percipient enables another to share the vision; this is also true of clairvoyance (Gurney, ii. 189). Modern experiments in telepathy show that contact increases the power of communication, and cases are on record where the percipient of a phantasm could cause another to see it by touching him (Parish, *Hallucinations*, 1897, p. 94). Thus, what is perhaps an actual psychic fact, experienced by the folk, has been applied to fairy, ghost, and other beliefs.

9. Fairy-like beings outside Europe.—That no single cause peculiar to European lands has operated in the formation of the belief in fairies may be seen from the fact that in every part of the world there are to be found beliefs in a variety of beings, all more or less like the fairies of Europe, with similar qualities, characteristics, and powers.

The Battaks of Sumatra believe in mountain-dwarfs hostile to encroaching mortals, who carry off men or women, or have amours with handsome mortals (*L'Anthrop.* iv. 85 f.). In Formosa, tales are told of a mysterious little people to be seen in the forests, with houses which change into boulders; as well as of goblins living in caves, and causing famine, sickness, and death (*FLJ* v. 143, 149). The Siamese *phi* are spirits dwelling in forests, etc., with many fairy traits (Hardouin, *Rev. trad. pop.* v. [1890] 257 ff.; for Annam, see *ERE* i. 538[a], 539[b]).

Turning to Africa, we find the Baganda believing in elves or sprites called *ngagwe*; and the W. African Bantu in *asiki* seen at night wearing a comb, which, if a mortal can snatch it, will bring him riches (Johnston, 677; Nassau, 299). Callaway compared the Zulu belief in ghosts (*amatongo*) with the Irish fairy creed. They call the living to join them or produce disease or pain in men. They live underground, where the living may visit them and see their dead friends, as the dead are seen among fairies. There is also a belief in a 'Little Chieftainess' with a troop of children, to see whom is fatal (*op. cit.* 226 f., 253). The Malagasy believe in dwarfs who come to houses to get milk, and who have a small voice like birds. Another dwarf, *Kotely*, resembles the Brownie. They also enter houses at night and cook rice; but it is dangerous to prevent their leaving before dawn (Ferrand, *Contes pop. malgaches*, Paris, 1893, p. 82 ff.).

Among American Indians, the belief in tiny sprites of rocks, streams, etc., resembling fairies, is wide-spread. They dance in moonlight; and, when seen, vanish at once. They assist or trouble men; *e.g.*, among the Shoshones they steal infants, leaving a changeling (*NR* iii. 157); among the Ojibwas they attack poultry and cattle, which die, or throw stones into the Indian dwellings; among the Algic tribes they cause sleep by striking men with their small clubs; among the Micmacs they tie people when asleep. Generally their form is that of tiny men. The Musquakie Indians believe in sprites produced by Meechee Manito-ah, who cause melancholy, quarrels, ill-health (Owen, *Folk-lore of Musq. Ind.*, 1902, p. 38 f.). On the Mosquito coast, gnomes are thought to carry off wanderers by night, and are mischievous in other ways. There is also a water-spirit which drowns bathers, and another which has the form of a horse.[1] The Eskimos believe in *ingnersiut*, an underground fairy-like folk (Rink, 460).

In Polynesia the 'Peerless Ones,' daughters of Miru, queen of Hades, come to the dances of mortals and leave at dawn. There are also fairies of sky and fountain, the latter sometimes mating with men. Other fairies, *ponatui*, dwell in the sea, appearing only by night, for the sun is fatal to them. Others carry off mortals, and are much dreaded (Gill, 265 f.; Clarke, 98, 112, 172; Tregear, *JAI* xix. 121). The Melanesian *vuis*, a race of spirits, have many fairy characteristics, and many of them are 'a lesser folk of dwarfs and trolls,' with magic powers, yet easily deceived. In some tales they assist mortals, like our fairies (Codrington, *Melanesians*, Oxford, 1891, p. 152). In Torres Straits a mischievous female bogey called *Dorgai* seduces men, steals children, etc., but she can be outwitted and destroyed (Haddon, *JAI* xix. 323). The Fijians have a race of little gods of the sea, a timid race to whom a secret cult is paid, and who sometimes come ashore. They give immunity from wounds, and are fond of singing. Their songs, like those of some of our fairies, have been recorded (Williams, *Fiji*, 1858, i. 237, 240; Thomson, *Fijians*, 1908, p. 189). In New Britain an order of *tebaran* is called *ingal*, mischievous and annoying sprites. Others are friendly and live around men, or enter their bodies to teach them charms, dances, etc., by which they make a profit. There is also a belief in mermaids, and in their unions with mortals (Brown, 81, 200, 242). In New Guinea there is a belief in an underground folk, *not* the dead, who may unite with mortals, and from whom men steal valuable things; as well as in other beings in the forest or swamp, shy of being seen, and with other fairy habits (Seligmann, 386 f., 646 f.).

The Arunta believe in *iruntarinia*, spirits of the Alcheringa (*q.v.*) age, living in winter in underground caves where there is sunshine, and wandering on earth in summer. They have each a double, the *arumburinga*, which, when the spirit is reincarnated, follows it or dwells with the others. These are not visible to all. The *iruntarinia* are very real to the native, and are dreaded for their power of placing pointing sticks in his body. They are visible only to medicine-men and children born with eyes open, and are like men, but thin and shadowy. They steal from men, and carry off women and imprison them in caves, but to those who can communicate with them they impart sacred ceremonies (Spencer-Gillen[a], 515–521).

The beings which most resemble fairies, however, are the Arab *jinn* or *jān*. They live underground, but also haunt doorsteps and other places, and are usually invisible, though they also appear

Psych. Res. iii. 77; Wentz, 126, 133; Scott, *Demonology*, 24; *CQR* lxiv [1907] 124; cf. Callaway, *Rel. of Amazulu*, Natal, 1868, p. 246.

[1] Gurney, ii. 206; Campbell, *Superstitions of the Scottish Highlands*, 1900, p. 102.

[2] See Gurney, i. 118; *County Folk-Lore, Suffolk*, 1892, p. 189; Scott, *Minst.* 210; Campbell, 80.

[1] See *19 RBEW* [1900], pt. i. 330 f., 475 f.; *NR* iii. 497; Dorman, *Origin of Prim. Super.*, Philad. 1881, p. 23 ff.; Boyle, *JAI* xxx. [1900] 265; Wentz, 47; *ERE* i. 806, iii. 362[a], 504[b]; Longfellow, *Hiawatha*, canto 18. Leland thought the Algonquin elves were borrowed from early Norse visitors.

in various forms. They travel about in sand-storms. The *jinn* are arranged in clans, propagate their species, and are subject to laws like mortals. Many are evil and cause sickness, madness, etc., act like the Poltergeist, carry off beautiful women for wives or others as midwives, or their females force men to remain with them for years. Some are friendly to men and even marry them, or by means of talismans men can obtain power over them. Iron, Divine names, etc., are all powerful against them; and, like the fairies, they are euphemistically called *mubarakīn*, 'blessed ones.' Indeed, there is scarcely an article of the fairy creed which does not equally apply to them.[1]

Fairies and *fées* of all kinds[2]—Celtic and Teutonic, Slavic *vilas*, Greek nereids, Arabian *jinn* and *peris*, Hindu *apsarases*, and other supernatural females, like the *dorgai* of Torres Straits, or the *awiri* wife of W. Africa (MacCulloch, *CF*, 330), or the *omangs* of the Battaks (*L'Anthrop.* iv. 85), or the swan-maidens and mermaids of universal folk-belief—carry on amours with men, or marry and bear them children, either on earth or by luring them into their abodes, as the Queen of Faery lured True Thomas. Yet, on the other hand, one of the most characteristic traits of female fairies is their seductive power over men, and the fatal results which follow from amours with them—'the inconvenience of their succubi' (Kirk, 25). This, however, is a feature found even in the case of fairy wives, whether captured by men or not, when the mortal husband breaks a tabu, and was already noted by Gervase of Tilbury (*Otia Imper.* ch. 13; see MacCulloch, *CF*, ch. xii.).

But what is important as illustrating the likeness of various ethnic supernatural beings to our fairies is the fact that precisely similar dangers await him who sees and falls in love with the being who appears in seductive form. The Celtic or Teutonic fairy mistress is dangerous (cf. the Lorelei), but so also is the supernatural mistress of other lands. The unhappy mortal lover is killed, dies, goes mad, or takes to wandering listlessly (νυμφοληψία, 'Peri-stricken' [cf. Keightley, 21]). This was the case with him who had amours with the nymphs and sirens of ancient Greece, like the nereids in modern Greece (Bent, *Cyclades*, 1883, p. 13; Lawson, *Modern Greek Folklore*, Cambridge, 1910, p. 142), as it is the case with him who is lured by the Hindu *rākṣasī* or *churel* (Crooke, *PR*², 1896, i. 253, 269; *ERE* ii. 489b). So in Japan a youth is slain by the monster, who takes the form of a lovely girl (Joly, *Legend in Jap. Art*, 1908, p. 45). The Arabs have transformed the *ka* which haunts the pyramids into a beautiful nude woman, whose lovers become restless lunatics (Maspero, *Études de myth. et arch. ég.*, Paris, 1893, i. 79).

Similar beliefs are found in Melanesia regarding sea-snakes which take female form, or the *tavogivogi* which appears as youth or girl to entice mortals of the opposite sex. In either case death or madness is the result. Another species of sprites, called in New Britain *toltol*, inflict serious wounds on the sexual organs of their male or female lovers (Codrington, 172, 188 f.; Brown, 197; Lang, in Kirk, p. xxxi; cf. Williams, *Fiji*, 1870, i. 239).

The same ideas are found among the American Indians; *e.g.*, the Yuroks believe in a seductive being who lures men into the forest, changes to a panther, and kills them (*FLR* v. [1882] 99 f.); and the Mayas have stories of the *xtabai* and the *xhoh chaltun* of the forests, who turn into a thorn-bush when the pursuing mortal clasps them. He then speedily succumbs to fever and delirium (*FLJ* i. [1883] 255). For the Central American belief in the intercourse of women with *naguals*, see Brinton, *Proc. Amer. Philos. Soc.*, xxxiii. [Phil. 1894] 29.

Risks were also run by women who had intercourse with Pilosi, Panisci, Satyrs, Fauns, Silvani—the *incubi* and *succubæ* of mediæval times, demons who had amours with women or men. They correspond to the Celtic *dusii*, shaggy demons who sought the couches of women to gratify their desires, and perhaps caused madness (MacCulloch, *Rel. of Anc. Celts*, 355); the Hindu *bhūts*, who abduct women, and other demons who tire out women by their nightly amours, so that they die of exhaustion (Dubois, *Hindu Manners*, Oxford, 1897, ii. 389; Crooke, *PR*² i. 264); the *jinn*, who beget children by women (Curtiss, *Prim. Semitic Religion*, 1902, p. 115); the Maya *ekoneil*, an imaginary snake which sucks the breasts of mothers (*FLJ* i. 256); the Samoan *hotua poro*, which makes women pregnant and causes nightmare (Waitz, *Anthrop.*, Leipzig, 1860, vi. 315); the *kruijt*, a spirit who begets children by women; and the Dayak *buan*, ghosts who carry off women and beget monsters by them (Ling Roth, *Natives of Sarawak*, 1896, i. 308; St. John, i. 174).[1] It should be added that ghosts of the dead can cause conception in women (Brittany [Le Braz, *La Légende de la mort*², ii. 146 and *passim*]; Syria [Curtiss, 115]; Borneo [Wood, *Nat. Hist. of Man*, 1870, v. 508 f.]; Egypt [*ERE* iv. 589b]; Ovaherero [*ib.* iv. 860a]; Uganda [Roscoe, 48]; cf. Post, *Ethnol. Jurisprud.*, Oldenburg, 1895, ii. 11, for the Amer. Indian and African belief in monstrous births as products of evil spirits). These beliefs were connected with the erotic hallucinations of hysteria (Ellis, *Psychol. of Sex*, London, 1897–1900, ii. 152 f.), and with erotic dreams in general in which women believed themselves abandoned to sexual embraces, or men thought they had amours with beautiful females. They are also connected with the phenomena of nightmare, as the name as well as its cognates in other languages—*incubus*, *succuba*, ἐφιάλτης, etc.—shows. These are nocturnal spirits which torment men in sleep, while the nightmare personified is in Teutonic belief sometimes the fairy bride or mother.[2] These beliefs are also connected with the idea that the gods could have amours with women.

Thus, when we find that in all parts of the world there exist beliefs either in fairy-like beings or in spirits who act like fairies, while the same precautions are taken against them, the same tabus hold regarding them, the relations between them and men are the same, and the same quasi-cult is rendered to them, we see that the European fairy belief is but a special aspect of a much more widely spread belief in supernatural beings, to whom very much the same characteristics are everywhere attributed, these being probably in no case the result of any one cause. At the same time we are led to discover the real origin of the fairy belief in man's myth-making fancy and his animistic beliefs, and in his applying the conditions of his own life to the creatures of his fancy. These fancies sometimes, however, cluster round the facts of life, actual races being sporadically envisaged as fairies.

10. Witch and fairy.—That no one source can be considered as the origin of the fairy belief is seen in the fact that the parallel between witch and fairy is a very close one. The fairy-revel and the Sabbat had much in common, and both owe

[1] See Westermarck, *JAI* xxix. [1899] 252 ff.; Lane, *Arab. Soc.* 29 ff.: Sykes, *FL* xii. [1901] 263; Hanauer, *Folklore of the Holy Land*, 1907, p. 188 ff.; W. R. Smith², 119 ff.

[2] See Baring Gould, *Curious Myths*, 1888, 'Melusine,' p. 471 ff.

[1] Cf. the Jewish idea of the fall of the angels through their lust for mortal women.

[2] Simrock, 437; see Tylor, *PC*³ ii. 189 f.; Bodin, *La Démonomanie des sorciers*, Paris, 1580, p. 109; Grimm, 464; Strahl, *Der Alp: sein Wesen und seine Heilung*, 1833; J. Franck, *Praxeos Medicæ Universæ Præcepta*, Leipzig, 1832, ch. i. 'de Incubo.'

something to reminiscences of earlier sex-festivals with music and dancing (see MacCulloch, *CF*, 223). The wayfarer is attracted into both, and often pays dear for it. He is forced to pipe or dance, and finds himself in the morning worn out, while all that so attracted him has vanished. Both revels and Sabbat must terminate before dawn or cock-crow (see Reuss, *La Sorcellerie*, Paris, 1871, pp. 39, 43, 54, 56, and reff. there). Similarly the beliefs in bodily or spirit transportation through the air on the part of or by witches or fairies—the objective aspect of a trance or drugged condition (see MacCulloch, *CF*, 223; Wood-Martin, *Elder Faiths of Ireland*, 1902, ii. 8, 21; Nassau, 223 [W. Africa]; Seligmann, 401 [New Guinea])—in child-stealing (see CHANGELING), in cannibalism (*CF*, 223; Français, *L'Eglise et la sorcellerie*, Paris, 1910, pp. 68, 119, 145; Sébillot, i. 229; Wentz, 128), in gifts of money which turns to rubbish, in shape-shifting and invisibility, in taking the substance of milk, corn, or of an animal (cf. a similar belief in W. Africa [*JAI* xxix. 23], in E. Africa [Macdonald, *Africana*, 1882, i. 212]; and see Scott, *Demon.*, 82, 223), in the power of killing cattle by mysterious means, or horses by riding them furiously at night, in the force of similar tabus against both—all apply equally to fairies and witches. Both the mediæval Church and 17th cent. Presbyterians placed fairydom and witchcraft under the same ban; and, in their trials, witches were accused of appealing or repairing to fairies and their queen (Dalyell, 536 f.; Scott, *Demon.*, 129, 135, 266, *Minst.*, 207). Witches used for their nefarious deeds elf-arrows, which were manufactured by fairies and the devil, and supplied to them (Pitcairn, *Criminal Trials*, Edinburgh, 1833, i. 191 ff.; Scott, *Demon.*, 135, 235). In popular Scots tradition the elf-queen and the mother-witch, or *Gyre Carline*, are identical. The three *Fées* who are present at births are sometimes three witches, and both groups are associated with the earlier 'wise woman.' Finally, fairies and witches were supposed to ride through the air headed by a Hecate called *Nic Neven* (Scott, *Demon.*, 111).[1]

Beliefs similar to those associated with fairies are also elsewhere connected with the dead (§ 5), or with other beings—in Japan, foxes; or, among savages, spirits of all kinds; in our own and other lands, the devil or demons, or vampires. But the best example is found in the belief in the 'fairy eddy'—a sudden puff of wind or whirl of dust, leaves, etc., in which fairies or witches are supposed to be (Rhys, ii. 590; Ralston, *Songs*, 382; Frazer, *GB*[2] i. 127). Among the Arabs the *jinn* (in India *shaiṭān*) cause, or travel in, such whirlwinds or sandstorms. In ancient Persia a demon caused the whirlwind (*Bundahiš*, xxviii. 24). In Brittany, the damned, who tried to carry off the wayfarer as fairies carried off men, were seen in such eddies (Le Braz[2], ii. 239); among the Ainus, whirlwinds are embodiments of evil spirits (*ERE* i. 244); among the Baganda, a dust eddy is believed to be caused by ghosts at play (Roscoe, 282); among the Yoruba, an eddy of wind is a manifestation of a forest-god (Ellis, 79); among the Kurnai, it is thought that Brewin travels in a whirlwind (Howitt, *JAI* xiii. 194); or, as in Fiji and among the Pawnees, the whirlwind is caused by ghosts (Frazer, *GB*[2] i. 128). With all these peoples much the same methods of avoiding the eddy or of overcoming the beings in it are found; while, comparing these customs with that of attacking a storm with weapons, we see that both eddy and storm were first personified and then believed to contain hostile beings.

Thus, considering the similarity of what is attributed equally to fairies, witches, ghosts, demons, and spirits of all kinds, it is obvious that certain primitive ideas easily attached themselves to all these indifferently, and that the origin of fairies must be sought in no one recent source, but ultimately in very ancient beliefs of man regarding the beings of his imagination. At the same time, we must not omit that which his poetic fancies have lent to the whole fairy belief, for to do so would be to omit what has always been a most vital element in all folk-lore.

The fairies who figure in the earlier romances and in the Renaissance and later poets are in part the creatures of folk-tradition, in part the creations of the poetic imagination, and concern us but little here.[1]

II. **Situation of fairyland.**—Fairyland as a separate region is variously situated. Most generally it is a subterranean region, sometimes directly below men's dwellings, or within hills and mountains; and to the latter corresponds the mediæval tradition regarding the court of Venus in the 'Venusberg,' of which there were several (Venus here = a fay; see Grimm, 935). We may compare also the Irish tradition regarding the Tuatha Dé Danann and the *sid*, or mounds. The entrance to fairyland was through a cavern (or fairyland was in a cavern), crevice, pit, or wells on tops of hills: the oldest recorded example of this is found in Gervase of Tilbury's story of the Welsh Elidurus, who was taken by two small men through a subterranean passage to fairyland (*Itin. Cambr.* i. 8). In this aspect fairyland corresponds to Hades, as well as to Hell or Purgatory, the entrance to which is also often through a cave or cleft. Both in Teutonic and in Celtic regions, fairies are also associated with tumuli, or with old raths or forts, which are often seen lit up at night (for an early instance, see William of Newburgh, *Historia*, Oxford, 1719, i. 28). Fairyland is also within the waters, and accessible through wells or by diving beneath river or lake or sea (in this corresponding to one aspect of the Celtic Elysium; see BLEST, ABODE OF THE [Celtic]). This dwelling is both that of water-fairies and of other water-beings (§ 7). It is also on islands in lake or sea, which sometimes are seen by the gifted seer (Wentz, 147; Davies, *Mythol. and Rites of Brit. Druids*, 1809, p. 155). Here, again, there is a close correspondence with the island Elysium of the Celts (see *ERE* art. cited). Fairyland may also be all around, a kind of fourth dimensional region interpenetrating ours;[2] or it may suddenly be entered in a mist; or, again, it may be in the air. These various conceptions are connected with the original character of fairies, whether as Nature-spirits or ghosts; and in some instances the abode of older gods has become fairyland.

It is usually dangerous to violate any sacred fairy spot—tree, dwelling, etc.—as it is dangerous to enter the charmed fairy circle, or to cross the night ride of fairies. These are tabus to which many parallels from lower and higher cultures, with respect to sacred places, abodes or haunts of spirits, gods, or ghosts, might be adduced (see Codrington, 177, 218 f.; Seligmann, 184; MacCulloch, *CF*, ch. xi.).

LITERATURE.—There is no work covering the whole ground of the fairy belief, but T. Keightley's *Fairy Mythology*, new

[1] The mediæval writers against witchcraft condemned also fairies and all traffic with them, and the fairy-rings where their revels took place were assimilated to the blasted sward of the witches' Sabbat. This is seen in the trial of Jeanne d'Arc, in whose *procès* witches and fairies are mingled. In several French legends, fairies dance the Sabbat.

[1] See Nutt, *Fairy Myth. of Shakespeare*, 1900; Goyau, *La Vie et la mort des fées*, Paris, 1910; Delattre, *English Fairy Poetry*, Oxford, 1912.

[2] Cf. the New Britain saying regarding *matana nion*, the place of the dead: 'If our eyes were turned so that what is inside the head were now outside, we would see that *matana nion* was very near to us and not far away at all' (Brown, 192).

ed. 1900, is generally useful. Besides the principal collections of *Märchen*, see also W. Bell, *Shakespeare's Puck, and his Folklore*, 3 vols., London, 1852; J. Curtin, *Tales of the Fairies and the Ghost World*, London, 1895; J. Grimm, *Teutonic Mythology*, Eng. tr., London, 1880–1888, ch. 17; Introduction, 'Ueber die Elfen,' to T. C. Croker's *Fairy Legends*, Germ. tr., Leipzig, 1826; E. S. Hartland, *Science of Fairy Tales*, London, 1891; R. Kirk, *Secret Commonwealth of Elves, Fauns, and Fairies*, ed. Sir W. Scott, Edinburgh, 1815, A. Lang, 1893; L. F. A. Maury, *Les Fées du moyen âge*, Paris, 1843, new ed. in *Croyances et légendes du moyen âge*, do. 1896; H. Schreiber, *Die Feen in Europa*, Freiburg, 1842; Sir W. Scott, *Minstrelsy of the Scottish Border*, Introd. to 'Tale of Tamlane,' 1839, *Letters on Demonology and Witchcraft*⁴, 1898; W. Y. Evans Wentz, *The Fairy Faith in Celtic Countries*, Oxford, 1911 (a curious mixture of science and credulity). See also the other authorities cited in the article.

J. A. MacCulloch.

FAITH.

Buddhist.—See Bhakti-Mārga.
Christian (W. Morgan), p. 689.
Greek (I. F. Burns), p. 694.
Hindu.—See Bhakti-Mārga.
Muslim (E. Sell), p. 695.
Roman (I. F. Burns), p. 697.

FAITH (Christian). — Every act of religious faith shows two sides or aspects—a cognitive and a volitional. It is at once an affirmation of truth and a surrender to the truth affirmed. Apart from the first, it would be blind; apart from the second, without practical significance. The fact that the emphasis is sometimes placed on the one and sometimes on the other leads to two relatively distinct notions of faith. When the volitional aspect is emphasized, we have the notion commonly denoted by the word 'trust' (*q.v.*); when the cognitive, that denoted by the word 'belief' (*q.v.*). It is with faith as belief that we are concerned in the present article. The notion of trust is, indeed, vital for religion, but it has played no part in theological controversy.

1. Scripture doctrine of Faith.—(1) *In Jewish canonical and extra-canonical writings.*—Although there are only two OT passages (Dt 32²⁰, Hab 2⁴) in which the RV admits the substantive 'faith,' the idea is far from being infrequent. Every word of God comes with a claim to be received as true; to believe it is an act of obedience to God, as unbelief is rebellion and a mark of hardness of heart (Ex 14¹¹, Dt 1³², Ps 78³², Is 7⁹). At the same time, faith is not among the cardinal conceptions of OT religion. What God requires of men is less that they believe His word than that they fear, love, serve, obey, and trust Him. God's word is thought of rather as a commandment to be obeyed than as a message to be believed.

What first brought the notion of faith into the foreground was the loosening of the bond between religion and nationality, and the rise of a propaganda. When Hebrew religion entered, with a claim to universal acceptance, into competition with other religions and became a matter of personal choice, the question whether a man believed in the God of Israel and received His laws and promises as true inevitably advanced into a position of cardinal importance. The initial religious act became one of belief; and persistence in belief, the presupposition of fidelity to God. We can thus understand why in the later Jewish literature the notion of faith should be considerably more prominent than it is in the OT (En 46⁷ 58⁵, *Apoc. Bar.* 54⁵· ¹⁶· ²¹; Philo, *de Abrah.* 268; 2 Es 5¹ 9⁷ᶠ·).

(2) *In the teaching of Jesus.*—Evidence for the increasing importance that was being attached to faith will hardly, however, be discovered in the teaching of Jesus. Often as He uses the word, it is nearly always with the meaning of trust in the power and goodness of God (Mt 17²⁰, Mk 4⁴⁰). This is the meaning even when He speaks of faith in Himself. What He has in view is not belief in His Messiahship or in any doctrine, but trust in the Divine power that works through Him (Mt 8¹⁰ 9² 15²⁸). Though He is conscious of bringing a new message, He lays the stress not on the acceptance of His word, but on the doing of it. 'This do, and thou shalt live' (Lk 10²⁸). The message is so simple and self-evidencing that the question of believing it hardly comes into view.

(3) *In the writings of Paul.*—It was with the Christian proclamation that the idea of faith really entered on its great career. From the first the gospel was preached, not primarily as a law to be obeyed, but as a message to be believed (Ac 2⁴⁴ 4⁴); and the cardinal article of belief, that which included all others, was that Jesus is Lord and Christ. The doctrine of salvation through believing was, therefore, not introduced by Paul; in his controversy with Peter at Antioch he could assume it as common Christian ground. None the less, he marks a decisive stage in its development. He was the first to establish it on a reasoned basis, and to bring the Church to a clear consciousness of the new significance which faith had acquired. This he accomplished by demonstrating the congruence of faith with the nature of the Christian gospel. Since the gospel comes as a revelation of Divine grace and of a righteousness freely offered to guilty man, the fitting response on man's part can only be that of humble and thankful acceptance of the gift. Putting away the proud thought that he can stand on his own merits, he must believe in Him who justifies the ungodly (Gal 3, Ro 4). It is evident that faith as here conceived is a thing of the heart rather than of the intellect. It implies moral earnestness, the sense of sin and need, submissiveness and openness towards God, and is indistinguishable from the trust of which Jesus speaks. Doubtless the Apostle included in his notion of faith the acceptance of what we should describe as doctrine (Ro 10⁹). The grace of God had no meaning for him apart from the redemption drama in which it presented itself to his imagination and thought. Nevertheless, Wrede's assertion (*Paulus*, Tüb. 1904, p. 67), that what Paul means by faith is nothing more than the obedient affirmation of the preaching of redemption, is wide of the mark. In his doctrinal constructions, Paul has no other object than to set forth the sin-forgiving, salvation-bringing grace of God; and at bottom it is this grace he asks men to believe in and to trust.

In vindicating the title of faith to be regarded as the sole and sufficient condition of salvation, Paul considers it exclusively in its relation to justification. What he establishes is justification by faith. Does he think of faith as also the inner spring of the new life? In two or three passages he approaches this idea. He speaks of faith as working by love, and declares that whatever is not of faith is sin (Gal 5⁶, Ro 14²³). But in general the activities of the new life are traced not to faith, but to the transcendent working of the Holy Spirit. The Christian virtues and graces are fruits of the Spirit (Gal 5²², Ro 8²). Our modern method of psychological derivation is foreign to his thought.

Much more important is the question whether faith, as defined in Ro 4, is an adequate description of the religious relation as Paul habitually conceives it. Is the bond that unites the believer with Christ nothing else than trust in the Divine grace manifested in His Cross? The truth is that it is only in connexion with justification that the Apostle thinks of it in this way. In general, the union with Christ appears as something more intimate and close than can be described in ethical terms. The believer has died with Christ and risen with Him; he is in Christ, and Christ lives in him. While this has for Paul a strongly ethical meaning, to interpret it in purely ethical terms, as signifying nothing more than a death to sin and resurrection to righteousness, a reproduction of Christ's mind or spirit in the believer, is to miss its secret. The union he has in view is a mystical union. Like all mystics, he finds the idea of faith inadequate to express the religious relation. Whether he regards this mystical union as only a deeper interpretation of faith, or as something that follows on it, is not easy to decide (Gal 2[20], Eph 3[17]).

(4) *In the Fourth Gospel.*—As compared with that of Paul, the conception of faith found in the Fourth Gospel is distinctly more intellectualistic in character. The writer shows unmistakable affinities with the Greek thinkers. Faith appears as a result of the impression made on the onlookers, not so much by the grace and truth manifested in Christ's words and deeds, as by His miracles. His whole earthly career is presented in the light of a series of Divine attestations of His claim to be the Son of God (Jn 2[11] 4[53] 14[11] 20[31]). Believing and knowing are brought into the closest connexion with each other, are, indeed, treated as identical. Like the Greeks and Philo, the Evangelist attributes a saving significance to knowledge. At the same time, it is far from his intention to exhibit faith as a mere intellectual assent to the proposition, 'Jesus is the Son of God.' Everywhere the ethical factor, perhaps in conscious opposition to Gnostic tendencies, is strongly emphasized. Knowledge is not understood as a predominantly intellectual function; it includes sympathy and kinship with its object, a personal relation to Christ, and is morally conditioned (Jn 6[44] 5[44] 8[43] 7[17]).

Like Paul, the writer of the Fourth Gospel knows of a deeper relation of the soul to Christ than that of faith or knowledge. Everywhere the mystical union is in the foreground: 'I in them, and thou in me, that they may be perfected into one' (Jn 17[23])—that is the profoundest secret of his piety. It is in virtue of this mystical union that the eternal and Divine life which belongs to Christ as His native possession is imparted to the believer. 'He that abideth in me, and I in him, the same beareth much fruit' (Jn 15[5]). The mystical vein of piety, which passed into Christianity from the Oriental religions, runs side by side with the Hebrew vein, and is suffused with the ethical spirit of the latter.

(5) *In the Epistle to the Hebrews.*—In the Epistle to the Hebrews we find a conception of faith which is modelled on that of Philo. Faith is the vision of the eternal realities of the unseen world—God, His righteousness, His salvation, the better country—the vision of these realities and the conviction that they are more enduring than the things we see and touch (He 11). As such it is the spring of all heroic action. Christ is related to it as its author and perfecter. He is the great example of faith, and through Him the salvation which the saints of the old time could only greet from afar has become a realized fact (vv.[13. 40]). Of all NT conceptions of faith, that of Hebrews is perhaps the broadest.

2. Catholic doctrine of Faith.—We have seen that, from the outset of the Christian community, faith was related to a doctrinal construction of Christ's Person and work. Always it implied belief in His power and dignity as Messiah and Lord, and in the reality of His redemption. If, notwithstanding this, the NT cannot be said to show, except in the latest books, any serious intellectualizing of the notion of faith, the explanation is to be found in the fact that doctrine was still sufficiently simple, ethical, and elastic to serve as a vehicle of the gospel. It still made its appeal less to the intellect than to the heart and conscience. But a time speedily arrived when this in large measure ceased to be true. The passing of the great constructive thinkers, and the Church's experience in Gnosticism of the dangers incident to unfettered speculation, led to the fixing of doctrine as an authoritative norm, the fitting attitude to which was intellectual submission. Nor was this all. More and more, doctrine was elaborated in a direction that removed it from the domain of the heart and conscience into that of the speculative reason. In determining the inner relations of the Trinity and the constitution of Christ's Person, the Church doubtless sought to safeguard what seemed to it vital religious interests. At the same time, such determinations were far removed from the simple truths of the gospel, and the importance attached to them had the result of throwing the latter into the shade. When assent to the creeds was made a condition of salvation, it was inevitable that faith should come to be understood as fundamentally an act of the intellect. By Augustine it is defined as 'cum assensione cogitare' (*de Prædest. Sanctor.* 5), and by Aquinas (*Summa*, II. 2, qu. 2, art. 2) as an act of the intellect which is moved to assent through the will. Three elements were distinguished in it—*notitia*, *assensus*, and *fiducia*; the first two being purely intellectual, and the third having but the slenderest claim to be regarded as ethical. Not only was faith intellectualized; it was conceived in the main as an act, not of insight and independent conviction, but of intellectual submission. The highest mysteries of the faith, being inaccessible to reason, could be received only on the ground of an external authority. Early Scholasticism, it is true, proceeded on the assumption that the doctrines of the Church were capable of being demonstrated to the reason; still the doctrines were first, and reason second. Moreover, the attempt to justify this assumption was in the end abandoned. Faith, in the Catholic conception of it, is authority-faith. And the authority that guarantees the truth of the doctrines is, in the last resort, the Church: 'Evangelio non crederem, nisi me catholicae ecclesiae commoveret auctoritas' (Aug. *contra Ep. Manich.* 6). The Church, therefore, is the real object to which *fiducia*, the practical element in faith, is referred. The notion was still further eviscerated when the Church came to recognize that an intelligent assent to its doctrines was more than could be expected from unlettered people, and to accept a *fides implicita*, or readiness to affirm these doctrines, though not precisely known, as sufficient for salvation.

So emptied of all ethical and religious meaning, faith could no longer sustain the weight of importance that had formerly been attached to it. While it continued to be regarded as indispensable for salvation, the goods of the Christian life were not connected with it in any organic way. The only bond was the external one of merit. God rewarded faith by bestowing forgiveness and infusing love. As the principle of justification, faith was supplanted by good works; as the principle of moral action, by love. One may say that its significance shrank to this, that it represented submission to the Church, and was on that account the condition of participation in the supernatural gifts which the Church dispensed to her children.

It is not to be denied that there were other

currents of thought in the Catholic Church. It would be easy to quote from Augustine and Aquinas passages in which faith is based not on authority, but on inner apprehension of Divine truth. Divine things, Augustine asserts, cannot be understood except by the pure in heart, and Aquinas guards against the idea that faith is an arbitrary choice. It presupposes a certain amount of natural trust and natural grace. Still the main drift was as described.

3. Protestant doctrine.—(1) *Luther.* — Luther restored faith to the place it occupies in the theology of Paul. Against the Roman doctrine of justification by works he set the Pauline doctrine of justification by faith only. In the act of believing, the sinner has full assurance of salvation; his assurance is not contingent on the good works he has done or may do, much less on any ceremonial observance. For salvation is a Divine promise; and, as 'without a promise we have nothing to believe, without faith the promise is useless, since it is through faith that it is established and fulfilled' (*de Captiv. Babyl. Eccl.*). Luther even went beyond Paul in making faith the principle not of justification alone, but of the whole Christian life. Its awakening is itself the new birth. Love does not require to be brought in as something additional; it is included in faith. Only believe, and you will do all good works from your own impulse. It is, indeed, from the faith behind them that good works derive their moral quality: 'Dum bonus aut malus quisquam efficitur, non hoc ab operibus sed a fide vel incredulitate oritur' (*de Libertate*).

The new significance attached to faith implies a deepened conception of it. It is no longer conceived as primarily an affair of the intellect. Luther defines it as a 'certa fiducia cordis et firmus assensus quo Christus apprehenditur' (*Commentary on Gal.* i.). It is nothing else than personal trust in the sin-forgiving grace of God; and it is the product not of reason, but of the impression which the Divine word makes on the heart and conscience.

This conception of faith sets up a new standard for doctrine. If doctrine is to be the object of faith, it must embody the gospel, must exhibit Christ in the characters that render Him our Saviour and awaken our trust. Of this Luther was dimly conscious. He saw that we apprehend Christ only in our experience of His merciful will: 'Misereri arguit eum esse Deum et distinguit ab aliis qui non possunt misereri, cum sint miseri; igitur qui miseretur et bonus est, Deus est.' But, though in these words Luther criticized the metaphysical formulæ of the Greek creeds, he did not seriously raise the question whether they fulfilled the requirement he had proposed. They imposed themselves upon him as something sacrosanct; and he was content to leave them unaltered, and to read into them as much evangelical meaning as they could carry.

(2) *The Reformed Church after Luther.*—Far from working out Luther's epoch-making ideas about faith, the Protestant Churches after the Reformation reverted in large measure to the Roman view. The traditional dogmas, supplemented by that of justification by faith, were elevated to their old position. In the object of faith the sum of the *articuli fidei* was included. As a consequence, the existence of a purely intellectual element in faith was again emphasized. While *fiducia* was regarded as decisive for salvation, *notitia* and *assensus* were made to precede it as necessary preliminary steps. More and more the ground of assent was again sought in authority, with this difference that for the authority of an infallible Church there was substituted that of an infallible Bible.

4. Modern discussions.—In the modern period of theology, which may be dated from the Illumination, discussions regarding faith have turned mainly on two points—its cognitive character; and its relation to the historical facts, above all to the fact of Christ.

(1) Every act of faith involves a judgment, an affirmation of truth or of what is regarded as truth. Faith is thus in one aspect *a cognitive process.* What is the nature of this process? On what grounds do the affirmations of faith ultimately rest? Are the grounds on which we affirm the justice or the goodness of God the same in kind as those on which the affirmations of science are based? The question is one which has far-reaching significance for theology; it is, one may assert, the only epistemological question with which theology has any deep concern.

For its theory of religious knowledge, Protestant orthodoxy was indebted to the theologians of the Catholic Church, above all to Aquinas. It distinguished between the knowledge of God which comes to us through the exercise of our natural reason, and a supplement of supernaturally communicated knowledge resting on authority. Eighteenth-century Rationalism, while it allowed the first, rejected the second. For Rationalism, all religious truths were truths of reason. But neither Protestant orthodoxy nor Rationalism thought of subjecting what it called reason to critical analysis.

(*a*) It was **Kant** who first undertook this task, and his account of reason forms one of the great landmarks in epistemological investigation. As the result of his analysis, Kant distinguished a twofold process in knowledge—that of the theoretical, and that of the practical reason. As theoretical, reason has for its domain the world of sense-experience, and for its instrument the categories—above all, the great category of causality. Within this domain it moves with logical certainty, rising from effect to cause and connecting fact with fact as parts of a single, ordered system. But there its competency ends. When the theoretical reason attempts to transcend the phenomenal world of sense-experience, and to explore, by means of its categories, the ultimate reality which lies behind that world, its incompetence is at once demonstrated by the paralogisms in which it finds itself involved. The transcendent objects with which religion is concerned cannot be established in a theoretical way. To reason as theoretical they are inaccessible. Only through reason as practical, *i.e.* as imposing itself upon us as the law of our conduct, do we attain to any knowledge of the unconditioned. Our religious knowledge comes to us as postulates of our moral consciousness, and the certainty with which we hold it is not a logical but a moral certainty. If our consciousness of being under obligation to obey the categorical imperative of our reason is not to be stultified, we must assume that our will is free, that beyond death there lies an opportunity for approximation to the moral ideal, and that the ultimate power in the universe is on the side of the good.

The Kantian account of knowledge has the great merit of bringing out the fact that our religious affirmations, unlike those of science, are morally conditioned. In other respects, however, it is open to grave objections. It leaves room for no knowledge of God unless as a postulate. Communion with God is possible only in the form that we fulfil our moral duties as God's commands. A theory which so limits the range of religious experience cannot be regarded as adequate.

(*b*) Fruitful as **the Hegelian movement** proved in many ways for theology, on the side of epistemology it represented a reaction in the direction of Rationalism. For Hegel, religion was but the forecourt of philosophy, and religious apprehension but an undeveloped form of philosophical. Firm ground is reached only when the highest truth is logically developed from the idea and recognized as a necessity of thought. The distinction drawn by Kant between the theoretical and the practical reason completely disappears.

(*c*) Meanwhile the problem of knowledge was being attacked from another side. **Herbart** drew attention to the part which feeling plays in cognition. Not only is it involved in all our thinking, but in a particular class of judgments—the æsthetic and moral—it is the determinative factor. **De Wette** showed that in such judgments what we predicate of an object is not existence but worth. We arrange the objects of our experience in a scale of values, rising from hedonistic values to spiritual, the morally good forming the climax of the series. The idea of 'value-judgments' was taken up by **Lotze**, and still further developed. More definitely than De Wette he established their basis in feeling and connected them with religion. Faith, he declared, is the feeling that is appreciative of values (*Microcosmus*, Eng. tr.[4] i. 244 f.). Through our feeling for values we reach a knowledge of things as authentic as that given us in science. Nay, it is precisely such faith-knowledge that takes us to the heart of reality; for it is not in the world of forms with which science deals, but in the world of values, that the inner nature of things comes to expression.

(*d*) It belongs to the epoch-making significance of **Albrecht Ritschl** that he was the first to introduce the 'value-judgment' into theology, and to explain by it the character of faith-knowledge and faith-certainty. According to the Ritschlian view, all religious judgments are judgments of value, or rest on such. They have their ground not, as in the case of theoretical judgments, in the compulsion of perception and thought, but in our feeling for values. Our belief in the personality of God, for example, rests on the fact that we rank ourselves above Nature and claim dominion over it—rank the personal above the impersonal. We proceed on the principle that the highest in rank must be the ultimate in being. The impulse to set the good on the throne of the universe has behind it a feeling for the claim which the good makes on our will. In proportion as we seek the good, we are convinced that our efforts cannot be in vain, but that it is the fundamental law of things, and must assert its right against all resistance. It is the same feeling for values that lies at the basis of the affirmations which faith makes about Christ. The assertion that in Christ God meets us has no other ground than a valuation of the ends for which He lived and of the spirit that breathes through His every word and deed. His holy love authenticates itself to us as the love of the Father for this single reason, that it is the Divinest thing that has come within our experience. Always faith is concerned, not with causal explanation, but with values.

This theory of value-judgments is put forward as an analysis of the actual process of faith-knowing. It rests on the assumption that the certainty of faith is different in kind from the certainty with which we hold a scientific hypothesis. Is this assumption justified? Certainly the objects of faith—God, the Divinity of Christ, the immortality of the soul—do not present themselves to the religious mind as hypotheses, the validity of which has to be tested by the ordinary scientific canons. The assurance with which we affirm them is not measured by our ability to fit them into a causal or logical scheme of things. On all hands it is admitted that a complete theoretical demonstration of their reality is out of the question. From the conservative side we have, indeed, ever renewed attempts to establish Christ's Divinity in a theoretical way, by an appeal to such facts as His miracles, His sinlessness, His superhuman consciousness, and His bodily resurrection. But such a demonstration does not represent the experience in which faith is born, but is purely adventitious. And, even were the facts on which it is built beyond question, it would still remain, when judged by scientific canons, hopelessly inadequate. The truth is that the certainty of faith is not a logical, but a moral certainty. It is rooted not in the intellect, but in the heart and conscience, and is morally conditioned. Its measure is the force of our affirmation of the Good, the Fair, and the True. Faith is the soul's everlasting yea to the Divine realities that appeal to it. If it sets these realities on the throne of the universe, it is because a universe in which they were not central and supreme would be morally intolerable. In the value-judgment theory of religious apprehension the radically moral character of faith-certainty is brought, for the first time, to clear scientific expression.

That judgments of value have to be reckoned with among our cognitive processes is now widely recognized—even by logicians like Sigwart as well as by theologians. Where the Ritschlian epistemology encounters the strongest opposition is in its sceptical attitude towards the speculative reason, and in its demand that the knowledge of faith be kept free from all admixture of speculative elements—in its demand, that is to say, for the extrusion of speculative metaphysics from theology. To many this has seemed equivalent to setting up a double truth, and to a denial of the unity of thought. W. R. Inge, for example, while recognizing the significance of value-judgments for religion, and admitting that we cannot prove that our valuations are anything more than subjective, maintains that there must be a unifying principle in which the different activities of our nature are harmonized as activities of one person, directed towards one satisfying end, and that it is in this unifying experience that faith for the first time comes fully into its own.[1] In other words, faith is securely established only when we have succeeded in building our value-judgments, with all our other knowledge, into a single, coherent system. That the human mind will never cease from the attempt thus to synthesize its knowledge may be regarded as certain. And it would be rash to assert that the syntheses which philosophy offers are without significance for faith. It cannot, however, be admitted that faith is dependent on the constructions of any philosophy. In our Christian religion it is precisely those elements which have been imported from philosophy that have proved themselves the least stable. Christian faith, as distinct from speculative theology, really moves among a few grand, simple, and relatively constant truths; and these truths owe little or nothing to the speculative reason, but are the affirmations of the heart and conscience. While philosophy can render to religion, particularly in the domain of apologetics, a service that is real and indispensable, the idea that it will some day succeed, as Edward Caird hoped, in transforming the moral certainty of faith into logical certainty is purely fantastic.

(2) *To what extent is faith dependent on historical facts, particularly on the fact of Christ?* To state the question in a more general way—What is the medium through which God reveals Himself to the soul? How is the object of faith given?

Traditional theology has always distinguished between a general revelation and a special. The former it regards as given in Nature and in the moral order visible in the life of man. From

[1] *Faith and its Psychology*, pp. 51, 231.

Nature we can rise, by the exercise of our natural powers, to the idea of an almighty and intelligent Creator; from the moral order in human life to that of a righteous Lawgiver and Judge. To general faith, God thus presents Himself as an idea which has been reached through a process of thought. Special revelation, on the other hand, is regarded as consisting in certain 'saving facts' of history, these facts being, above all, the birth into our world of one who was the Son of God, the Second Person in the Trinity, and the atonement for sin He accomplished on the cross. In them specifically Christian faith has its object. While, however, the Incarnation and the Atonement are thought of as facts of history, it is evident that they are not of a kind that can be established by purely historical evidence. They come to us as a speculative construction or interpretation of the Person and work of the historical Jesus, the truth of which is guaranteed in the last resort by inspired Scripture. The immediate object of specifically Christian faith is thus, for traditional theology, not the historical facts of Jesus' life, but a doctrine or series of doctrines; and only when the doctrines have been accepted —whether on authority or as speculatively established—can faith enter. God's special historical revelation is given in the form of doctrine.

(*a*) It was against a historical revelation so conceived that **the Rationalism of the eighteenth century** directed its attack. Rejecting the traditional doctrines of Christianity, it put in their place the simple and self-evident ideas of reason as the one valid content of religious faith. These ideas—the chief of which are God, freedom, and immortality—are independent of Christ and, indeed, of all history; they are in their nature timeless, the same for every age and every race. For the significance of history, whether in religion or in any other department of human life, Rationalism had little feeling. In this respect the Kantian philosophy of religion marked no advance. For Kant, too, the content of religious faith is given in ideas that are timeless and necessary. The conception of a revelation—whether in Nature or in history—was barred for him by his doctrine of phenomenalism. The world of our inner and outer sense-experience, being merely phenomenal, can yield us no knowledge of the hidden power behind it.

(*b*) In **the Hegelian philosophy** the significance of history seems, at first sight, fully recognized. There is no more talk of phenomenalism or of the contingency of historical facts. History is exhibited as controlled by the immanent law of reason, and as the medium of a self-revelation of the Absolute. Of this self-revelation, the historical religions constitute a particular mode, Nature, art, and philosophy forming kindred modes. Christianity—which has as its characteristic that Christ is contemplated as the God-man, the realized unity of the Divine and the human— is established as the culmination of the series and the sole absolute religion. But what Hegel gives to history with one hand he takes away with the other. The religious way of envisaging the oneness of the human spirit with the Divine, the finite with the Infinite—as realized, that is to say, in the Person of Christ—is for him but a step on the road to the philosophical. Firm ground is reached only when the historical is left behind, and the highest truth is developed from the idea itself and recognized as a necessity of thought. Ultimately we are left with a rational idea as the sole adequate content of religious faith. To make this clear was one of the motives that led **Strauss** to write his *Leben Jesu*. He believed that in resolving the Gospel-narrative into a tissue of myth he was doing Christianity a real service, by compelling it to advance from the history-faith of popular religion to the higher faith which receives its object from thought alone. In this epoch-making book, Strauss also brought into the foreground an objection to basing faith on facts of history which had frequently been raised before, though never in so peremptory a fashion. Facts of history are known to us only through human testimony, and human testimony is fallible. How can we build our faith on a foundation that criticism may any day destroy, if it has not already destroyed it? This objection bears with particular force against the traditional conception of a historical revelation, since it is precisely the miraculous facts on which it relies to prove the significance of Christ that are most open to critical attack.

(*c*) Orthodoxy, Rationalism, and Idealistic Philosophy, widely as they differed in many respects, were all agreed in one fundamental assumption, that it is through the appropriation of an idea or doctrine that religion arises. Faith was made dependent for its object on a process of thought. **Schleiermacher's** importance for theology consists in no small degree in this, that he was the first to break with that tradition. Adopting the method of psychological analysis, he sought to demonstrate religion as a function of the Spirit, independent alike of philosophy, ethics, and dogmatics. Religion, he taught, is the immediate response of the Soul in feeling to the Divine reality which besets it behind and before. This reality is not, however, found in Christ or in any historical fact; it is not even anything moral as such. It is the Infinite, the Eternal, the Whole of things. Religion is the inrushing sense of the Infinite in the finite, of the Eternal in the temporal, our feeling that our time-life is a manifestation and organ of the eternal Whole and absolutely dependent on it. Significance is attributed to Christ only as a prototype of a new mode of such 'God-consciousness.' That Schleiermacher gives an adequate account of the content of Christian faith, few would now contend. None the less his demonstration of religion as an immediate experience of Divine reality, and as independent of the constructions of theology and philosophy, stands for all time.

(*d*) **Ritschl** learned from Schleiermacher that faith springs up as the result of contact with Divine reality, and that its object, therefore, is not to be sought in any idea or doctrine. But, holding a definitely ethical and Christian conception of God, he could not regard the Whole of things as the field where the soul finds Him. Not in Nature, but only in the historical life of man, can God reveal Himself in His moral working and as the God of our salvation. And, among the facts of history in which He approaches us, Jesus Christ possesses a significance that is not only supreme but absolutely unique. What gives to Christ such significance is not the miraculous facts on which traditional theology relies to prove His Divinity, but the moral and religious traits of His character as they manifest themselves in word and deed. In contact with His moral might and holy love, we feel the hand of God laid upon us, and know that He has drawn near to us to forgive and overcome our sin and to call us into His fellowship and service.

The historical Jesus, and not any doctrine of His Person and work, is for Ritschl the object of faith. What then is doctrine? It is a product of faith, and intelligible only as an expression of what the soul has found in Christ. This need not be taken as denying to the doctrines of the Church any direct religious value. We know that for countless thousands the doctrine of the Atonement has been the one great medium through which they have apprehended the forgiving and saving love of God. That it does exhibit the holy love of God as manifested in Christ in a powerful and dramatic way, no one with any feeling for reality will deny. This, however, does not affect the question whether it is not something secondary. Behind it lies the historical fact of Jesus dealing with publicans and sinners, His ministry among the weary and the lost. It is from the love which shines out from this ministry that the doctrine of the Atonement derives its living content. The historical reality and not the speculative construction is the primary fact, and the latter cannot be accepted as a substitute for the former.

The Ritschlian view of the historical Jesus as the one ground of Christian faith has been attacked as involving a static conception of revelation. Is not God, it is objected, always revealing Himself to mankind, and in a progressive way? Is He not as active in the present as in the past, and is it not precisely His activity in the present that creates our experience of Him as the living God? Can we regard the Jesus of history as God's last word to us? In order to conserve the constancy and progressiveness of revelation and at the same time to escape the menace of historical criticism, Loisy and Inge, among others, have sought the ground of Christian faith in the living Christ, as He manifests Himself in the Church and the individual soul, rather than in the Jesus of history. The significance of the latter they find in this, that He introduced the movement which in its entirety will constitute a theophany in the life of humanity. It has to be said, however, that the problem which such writers attempt in this way to solve is not that which Ritschl had before him. About the progress of Christian thought Ritschl was not concerned. His one concern was with what he regarded as the fundamental Christian experience, the assurance, namely, that we have a gracious, sin-forgiving God. How can such an experience be reached? In attaching it exclusively to the person of Jesus, Ritschl does certainly give ground for the charge that he denies any other channel of revelation. It would be difficult to deny the fact that many have reached the experience he has in view in other ways than through contact with the historical Jesus. The love of Jesus meets us not only in the written Gospels and in the preaching of the Church, but also in men filled with His Spirit; and, wherever we are brought up before it, it authenticates itself to us as something Divine, and has power to produce within us the assurance that the God of our life is a God of grace. But, while this must be admitted, the history of the Church has made it abundantly clear that Christianity loses its vitality when the Person of its founder is forgotten or obscured. The men and women who have been the driving forces in the Christian community have drawn their inspiration from no secondary source, but from Christ Himself. That in a Christian community there is a power at work which with a certain fitness can be described as 'the living Christ'—an ideal of Christian life and character, as it has shaped itself in the modern mind—is not to be denied. And such a power cannot but possess immense significance for religion, for this among other reasons, that in it God speaks to us in the language of to-day. But can it be accepted as a substitute for the Christ of history? One may assert that the Christ of history, while a child of His time with respect to the forms of His thought, in the essential features of His life and teaching stands above time. A wealth of significance belongs to Him far transcending that of our richest ideals, and a power to awaken and sustain faith in the living God of salvation such as meets us in no other fact of our experience.

LITERATURE.—A. Schlatter, *Der Glaube im NT*[3], Stuttgart, 1905; *Histories of Dogma*, by Harnack (Eng. tr. 1894–99), Loofs[4] (Halle, 1906), and Seeberg (Leipzig, 1910); J. Köstlin, *Der Glaube: sein Wesen, Grund und Gegenstand*, Leipzig, 1895; W. Herrmann, *Communion of the Christian with God* (Eng. tr. 1895); A. Sabatier, *Outlines of a Philosophy of Religion* (Eng. tr. 1897); M. Reischle, *Werturteile*, Freiburg, 1895; W. R. Inge, *Faith and its Psychology*, London, 1909; O. Kirn, *Glaube und Geschichte*, Leipzig, 1900.

W. MORGAN.

FAITH (Greek).—In this article we propose (1) to give some account of religious faith as an actual feature of Greek life, and (2) to indicate the relation between faith and knowledge in Greek philosophy.

1. Faith as a religious force.—(1) *Its nature.*—By religious faith we understand belief coupled with trust in a Divine power. Both these elements enter into the words πίστις and πιστεύειν, although the moral rather than the intellectual notion is prominent in each, especially in the verb (W. R. Inge, *Faith and its Psychology*, London, 1909, p. 3 f.). But, to see the distinctive character of Greek faith, we must turn to its objective aspect. The Greek faith was polytheistic. Its deities were beautiful, and often sublime, conceptions. At the same time—we speak of the national religion rather than of local cults—they were but glorified types of humanity, beings who inspired confidence rather than dread, and with whom the artistic imagination freely played.

(2) *Its history.*—The faith thus described was a living force in Greece till about the middle of the 5th cent. B.C. It is true that in the lyric poetry of the 6th and 7th centuries 'the figure of Zeus dwarfs and obscures all the other divine personalities' (J. Adam, *Relig. Teachers of Greece*, Edinburgh, 1908, p. 83; cf. J. P. Mahaffy, *Social Life in Greece*[2], London, 1875, p. 94). But there is no revolt against the old national faith. The lyric poets 'never advanced even to the most distant hint of atheism, or to a denial that the gods could and did interfere in human affairs' (Mahaffy, 92). Polytheism, gradually purged, indeed, of its grosser elements, was the accepted creed of the Greek poets from Homer to Sophocles. It inspired the masterpieces of the greatest period of Greek sculpture. It was at the heart of every great movement in the formative period of Greek history. Of this, two illustrations may be given. The first is the Apolline cult. The worship of Apollo was, directly or indirectly, a leading factor in the intellectual, moral, social, and political development of the Greeks (for details, cf. L. R. Farnell, in *HDB* v. 145 f.). To take but one instance—the Apolline cult was largely instrumental in introducing and in gradually deepening the vital ethical conception of purification from sin. Our second illustration is from the Persian war. Plato (*Laws*, iii. 699) expressly mentions trust in the gods as one of the great causes of the Greek victory. And the truth of his statement must come home powerfully to every reader of Herodotus. It was faith in the gods that kept Leonidas at Thermopylæ, and the fleet at Salamis (vii. 220, 143). It was this that nerved the Athenians to reject the overtures of Mardonius (viii. 143). And accordingly, when the Athenians appealed to Sparta for aid, they referred to this faith as their own supreme motive: 'We, reverencing Zeus Hellenius, and fearing to betray Hellas, have not accepted the offer of the king' (ix. 7). Finally, Themistocles, addressing his captains after the battle of Salamis, emphatically declares that their deliverance was due, not to themselves, but to the gods (viii. 109), which he would certainly not have done unless he had been sure that he was expressing the uppermost thought of all (E. E. G., *Makers of Hellas*, London, 1903, p. 539). For the above view as to

the power of the traditional faith, cf. also Mahaffy, p. 358.

As Greek faith rested on polytheism, it flourished as long as the latter remained credible. But, about the middle of the 5th cent., rationalism, which had arisen in the Greek colonies of Asia Minor, began to play havoc with traditional belief, and the age of faith was succeeded by the so-called age of illumination (J. Adam, 270 f. ; L. Campbell, *Relig. in Greek Liter.*, London, 1898, pp. 208, 295). This corresponds, roughly speaking, to the latter half of the 5th century. On the other hand, the rapid spread of new ideas provoked a reaction, the most notable incident of which was the condemnation and death of Socrates (399 B.C.). Did the national religion ever regain its old vitality? Mahaffy argues (p. 355 ff.) that Grote and others have greatly exaggerated the scepticism of the last period of Greek history. But even he does not maintain that the old polytheistic creed ever again expressed the prevailing religious attitude of thoughtful minds. There was, indeed, much earnest religious life in the following centuries. This is especially true of the Stoic and the Mystic. But their belief does not concern us here, both because it was not properly national, and also because, being pantheistic, it could hardly be said to embrace the element of trust which belongs to a genuine religious faith.

2. Faith and knowledge.—According to our definition, faith is an act at once intellectual and moral. But such a mode of conceiving man's knowledge of God is foreign to Greek thought. Reason alone, according to Greek philosophy, is adequate to the knowledge of God. This view forms an essential part of Aristotle's teaching, but it is in the *Republic* of Plato (511, etc.) that the superiority of knowledge to faith is most distinctly laid down. According to Plato, πίστις is but a stage in the pathway to knowledge, a stage in which the visible and opinable is regarded as true. 'With Plato, Knowledge and not Faith is "the assurance of things hoped for, the test of things not seen"' (J. Adam, 407).

On the other hand, the opposition between knowledge and faith in Greek philosophy is not so absolute as may at first appear. For knowledge, while ascribed to reason alone, is often brought into closest relation with the moral nature. Thus, Pythagoras viewed the pursuit of knowledge as a means to spiritual emancipation (J. Adam, 193 f.); Socrates, again, viewed knowledge as 'a certain overmastering principle or power that lays hold primarily, indeed, of the intellect, but through the intellect of the entire personality' (*ib.* 329). And, similarly, Plato taught that in the conversion wrought by knowledge the character also is involved. It is a revolution in which the whole nature shares (ξὺν ὅλῃ τῇ ψυχῇ, *ib.* 412; Plato, *Rep.* 518 C). Lastly, the figure by which, in the *Symposium*, Plato sets forth the knowledge of God is that of the soul's marriage with her ideal. It is still knowledge, an *amor intellectualis*, with which he professes to deal. But it is obvious how near the conception brings us to the standpoint of Christian faith.

LITERATURE.—In addition to the authorities cited in the article, cf. the artt. GREEK RELIGION and PHILOSOPHY (Greek), and the Literature appended to them.

I. F. BURNS.

FAITH (Muslim).—The Muham. term for 'faith' is *īmān*, and he who possesses it is called a *mu'min*, or 'believer.' Sūra xxiii. of the Qur'ān, revealed at Mecca, is called the 'Sūra of the Believers'; it begins:

'Happy now the Believers; who humble them in their prayer; and who keep aloof from vain words; and who are doers of almsdeeds; and who restrain their appetites, save with their wives, or the slaves whom their right hands possess, for in that case they shall be free from blame, but they whose desires reach further than this are transgressors; and who themselves tend well their trusts and their covenants; and who keep strictly to their prayers' (vv.1-9).

In two other Meccan sūras (ciii. 3, lxxxv. 11) they are described as 'those who do things which are right'—a form of expression which occurs very frequently in later sūras. The term 'O ye who believe' is found only in the Medīna sūras. All such are called upon to perform various duties and to exhibit certain qualities. Thus, those who believe are to seek help with patience; to retaliate for blood-shedding; to observe the prescribed fast; to hope for God's mercy should they lose their lives in fighting for Him; to take care not to make their alms useless by indulging in reproaches; to fear God and abandon usury (ii. 148, 173, 179, 215, 266, 278). They are not to fear the infidels (viii. 15); they must help God; obey God and the Apostle (xlvii. 8, 35). They are not to take infidels as their friends; they are to avoid intimacy with persons outside the Muhammadan community; they are to be patient and fear God (iii. 27, 114, 200). They are not to devour one another's substance in frivolities, or to come to prayer when drunk (iv. 33, 46). They are to remember God with frequent remembrance, and to praise Him night and morning (xxxiii. 41). They must not make friendship with foes of the Prophet, or with those with whom God is angry (lx. 1, 13). They must carefully observe their engagements, the rites of God, and the sacred month, and must avoid wine and games of chance (v. 1, 2, 92).

It will be seen that Muḥammad associated the profession of faith with the performance of certain duties, without giving any distinct definition of the term 'faith' itself; but in a tradition it is recorded that he said that faith is belief in God, His Angels, His Books, His Messengers, in the Last Day, and in the predestination of good and evil. This is called *īmān-i-mufaṣṣal*, 'the detailed confession.' A briefer form is: 'I believe in God, His name and attributes, and accept all His commands.' This is called *īmān-i-mujmal*, 'the shortened confession.' These definitions refer to the assent to, and the acceptance of, certain dogmas. Muslim theologians have, therefore, defined faith as intellectual acquiescence (*taṣdīq al-qalb*) in the teaching of Muḥammad. This is faith in its simplest form, to which can be added, in order to make it perfect, the open confession of this belief and the practice of good works as flowing from it. Still, in order to be a believer, nothing beyond the intellectual assent is needed. Let a man have that; then, even though he be an evil-doer, he must be regarded as a believer. An illustration used is that a tree may have neither leaves nor fruit and still it is a tree. Believers, therefore, can be classified into men who believe, confess, and do good works; men who believe, confess, and do some good works; and men who believe, confess, and do no good works. A man who openly confesses, 'There is no god but God, and Muḥammad is the Apostle of God,' and does not really believe it, is at heart an infidel; yet he must be called a believer, for no one can know the secret thoughts of another man, and open confession must be assumed to represent inner belief.

These various views, which lay little stress on the moral effect of faith, are not accepted by the Mu'tazilites, the free-thinkers of Islām, who deny that a man who has committed a great sin can any longer be called a believer. They would not call him an infidel, but place him mid-way between believers and infidels. There are some extreme sects, again, who hold that a believer—one who intellectually assents—however wicked he may be, will not enter hell; but the orthodox opinion is that, as all believers, even the most perfect, have committed some sin or other, they must enter hell for such shorter or longer time as each case may require. All will finally be saved; for no Muslim, even the most wicked, can suffer eternal punishment, or be annihilated. Paradise is the final goal of all believers. Thus, speaking generally, the most important element in faith is the intellectual assent, which secures to a man the title and position of a believer, whether the moral results of his belief be good, bad, or indifferent.

There are other definitions of the term *īmān*, framed with reference to the grounds on which it is based, or the means by which it is formed. Traditional faith (*īmān fī taqlīd*) is based on the authority of a teacher (*taqlīd*), without any attempt being made to prove its correctness. This is the faith of the unlearned, who have not the ability to search out things for themselves. Those who have the leisure and the necessary intelligence to investigate religious matters, and who then believe, are said to possess faith founded on knowledge (*īmān fī 'ilm*). Faith which rests on the inner vision (*īmān fī a'yān*), or intuition of the mystic, is progressive in its nature. The last stage is attained only when devotion to God is so absolute that the soul is absorbed in God, the great Reality.

Another point round which many controversies have raged is whether *īmān* and *Islām* are the same. The orthodox view is that they are synonymous, and that a Muslim is a *mu'min*, a believer. By others, *Islām* is looked upon as a larger term than *īmān*. It is said that *Islām* signifies belief with the heart, confession with the tongue, and good works done by the various parts of the body. *Īmān* refers to the first of these, and is, therefore, only a component part of *Islām*. The believer who confesses his belief and practises what he believes unites *Islām* and *īmān*; he who does not so confess and practise possesses *īmān* only. On the other hand, he who confesses and acts, without having any real belief, is not a true believer. Those who hold that confession and action are both essential would not consider assent to the teaching of Muḥammad made on a death-bed to be of much value, as the opportunity for confession of belief and action on it would be gone. The term *Islām*, however, lays great stress on such action. The Muslim is a man who is resigned to the will of God as regards the performance of the five practical duties. It is not so much resignation to the providential dealings of God with a man as submission to, and implicit compliance with, the order to fulfil certain duties. So far, this seems to support the views of those theologians who teach that *Islām* and *īmān* must be kept quite distinct. They say, for instance, that works cannot be a part of faith, for a man who believes and confesses and dies before he does good deeds is a believer and enters Paradise, even if he dies before he makes open confession of his faith.

Another question in dispute is whether faith can decrease and increase. Some say that it does not change, and is not affected by sin, or by the omission of religious duties, though such shortcoming will be punished. Others admit that, in the case of the Companions of the Prophet, faith did increase, for new revelations brought fresh truths to them; but, now that the dogmas of Islām are fixed and there is no further development, faith cannot increase. Ash-Shāfi'ī, however, maintained that, if religious duties were neglected, faith would decrease; to this the reply is made that, at certain times, women do not say the stated prayers, or give alms, yet their faith is not thereby decreased. The view of Ash-Shāfi'ī seems, however, to be supported by a verse of the Qur'ān, revealed to encourage the Muslims when an attack on them was imminent: 'Who, when men said to them, "Now are the Meccans mustering against you; therefore, fear them"—it only increased their faith' (iii. 167). The following further distinctions are made by those who agree with Ash-Shāfi'ī: the faith of men and of the *jinn* increases and decreases; the faith of prophets increases only; the faith of angels neither increases nor decreases.

It is usual to divide mankind into two classes: those who believe in the teaching of Muḥammad, and so have faith and are *mu'mins*, or believers; those who do not so believe, and are, therefore, *kāfirs*, or infidels, to which class all non-Muslims belong. These, if they reject the truth after investigation, are not so blameworthy as if they had declined to accept it through sheer obstinacy. Muslims may have defective faith, but can never be called infidels, though they may be called heretics. In this category the orthodox place all those who have tried to bring reason to bear on religion and have striven to put away the incubus of traditionalism. Again, those who give prominence to the idea expressed by *īmān* would say that infidelity proceeds from ignorance of God and His Apostle; but those who lay stress on the technical meaning of *Islām* assert that it proceeds from disobedience to the law of good works, that is, from neglect of the five duties of Islām. Again, those who reject the Qur'ān as a revelation from God are infidels and have no *īmān*.

One day, Abū Sufyān, Abū Jahl, al-Walīd, and others were in the company of Muḥammad and listened to his revelations, but did not believe them. It is said that a veil was cast over their hearts so that they should not understand, and that, 'though they should see all kinds of signs, they will refuse all faith in them, until, when they come to dispute with thee, the infidels say: "Verily, this is nothing but fables of the ancients"' (vi. 25 and Baiḍāwī's commentary).

Again, all who believe in the Divinity of Jesus Christ are infidels. 'Infidels now are they who say God is the Messiah, Son of Mary' (v. 76).

Muḥammad called Christians the 'people of the book,' and was sometimes friendly towards them, but he entirely misunderstood the Christian doctrine of the Trinity. This, and the fact that he had now lost all hope of winning the Arabian Christians over to his side, led him to burst forth in the latest and most intolerant of the sūras, in strong denunciation of Christians, who are to be shunned, and whom believers may not take as friends (v. 56).

At the time of death both the believer and the infidel see their future lot: heaven in the one case, hell in the other. Should the infidel then repent, his faith is not to be considered trustworthy, because, according to some theologians, faith implies good works. If a person is asked whether he is a believer, he should say, 'I am a believer'; he should not say, 'If God willeth, I am a believer,' as, according to the teaching of Abū Ḥanīfa, such a statement would imply doubt as to the reality of the fact of his being a believer; but Ash-Shāfi'ī considers it right to say, 'If God willeth.'

The conclusion of the whole matter is that a believer, though he may be a very wicked man, and may even hold heretical opinions, does not cease to be a believer, for a great sin does not exclude the person who believes from *īmān*, and does not make him an unbeliever. In order to become an infidel, and so be classed with unbelievers, the man must either deny the existence of God, or associate other gods with Him, or deny the divine mission of Muḥammad, or, with reference to things lawful and unlawful, decline to accept the ruling which by 'general consent' (*ijmā'*) of the Muslim world is current.

LITERATURE.—Almost the only considerable treatment in a Western language on 'Faith' in Islām is L. Krehl's *Beiträge zur Characteristik der Lehre vom Glauben im Islām*, Leipzig, 1877, p. 47 ff. O. Pautz, *Muhammeds Lehre von der Offenbarung*, Leipzig, 1898, p. 153 ff., collects usefully the Qur'ānic phraseology. The reader may consult also T. Haarbrücker's tr. of Shahrastānī's *Religionspartheien*, Halle, 1850; L. Krehl, *D. Leben u. d. Lehre d. Muhammeds*, Leipzig, 1884; H. Grimme, *System d. koran. Theologie*, Münster, 1895; M. Schreiner,

'Beiträge zur Gesch. d. theol. Bewegungen in Islam,' *ZDMG* lii. and liii. (1898–99); I. Goldziher, *Die Zâhiriten*, Leipzig, 1884; E. Sell, *Faith of Islam*[3], London, 1907, p. 185 ff.; D. B. Macdonald, *Development of Muslim Theology*, New York, 1903; *1001 Nights*, in Burton's or Payne's tr. (Nights 436 ff. [Story of Taiwaddud]); Justice 'Abdur Rahim, *Muhammadan Jurisprudence*, Madras, 1911, pp. 51, 249. EDWARD SELL.

FAITH (Roman).—In this short survey we shall notice (1) the general character of Roman religious faith, and (2) its comparative vitality at different epochs.

1. Its character.—The most distinctive feature of Roman religious faith was its vague and largely impersonal character. This is reflected in the Divine beings worshipped. It is generally agreed that the objects of primitive Roman worship were spirits, *numina*, conceived either as inherent in particular objects—which was probably the earlier mode—or as presiding over particular actions. In their close connexion with things or actions, of which they were an ideal reflexion, such *numina* lacked the attribute of independent personality which belongs to gods. Yet even the acquisition of individual names (such as Fons or Robigus) marked a step towards such independence. By and by certain *numina*—Janus, Jupiter, Mars, Quirinus, and Vesta—stood out from the crowd of lesser Divine beings. These, and possibly a few others, through their importance in ritual and consequent prominence in the minds of the worshippers, became in a sense personal deities. But the personality of even the chief Roman divinities, prior to their amalgamation with the Greek gods and goddesses, rested on little more than a name. Now, it is probable that the earliest Greek conception of spirits was similar to the Roman—they were life potencies rather than persons (cf. J. E. Harrison, *Proleg. to the Study of Greek Religion*[2], Cambridge, 1908, esp. ch. iv. p. 162, and ch. v.). But, whereas these first shadowy conceptions of the Divine gave place to the richly personal creations of Greek mythology (see art. FAITH [Greek]), the Roman divinities remained, in comparison, vague and formless.

Closely connected with this lack of personality in the objects of worship was the largely impersonal attitude of the worshipper. Apart from the narrow sphere of strictly family worship (for which cf. W. Warde Fowler, *The Relig. Exper. of the Roman People*, London, 1911, ch. v.), each Roman's religion was undertaken by the State. It was reduced to a science, and gradually incorporated in the *jus divinum*, which laid down the exact and elaborate ritual required for maintaining a right relation between the citizen and his deities. At this ritual the private citizen was an onlooker. It was enough for him to be ceremonially clean, and to keep silence. 'In no other ancient State that we know of did the citizen so entirely resign the regulation of all his dealings with the State's gods to the constituted authorities set over him' (*ib.* p. 226). Yet it is not to be supposed that his religion was a mere form. With the problems, indeed, of the personal religious life the typical Roman had little or no concern. But his faith in his country's gods was real, and it was rooted, moreover, in a profound sense of the supernatural.

2. Its decay and the attempt to revive it.—The faith thus described flourished until the time of the war with Hannibal (218 B.C.). But from that time onwards it suffered a rapid decay. This was due in part to the longing for a more emotional religion, which, though not unknown before, grew to painful intensity amid the stress of the Hannibalic war, especially at moments when the national gods seemed powerless to avert disaster. But it was due also, and far more, to the disintegrating influence of Greek philosophy, which was already, in the 2nd cent. B.C., eagerly studied by many Romans. We can indicate only very briefly the effect produced by these and other causes. In the last age of the Republic, while many sought religious satisfaction in new ways—in Pythagorean mysticism, for example, or in orgiastic foreign worships, and in many forms of allied superstition—there was no Roman religion worthy of the name. The ancient forms no longer expressed a genuine belief either among the people or among their rulers. Even the outward fabric was fast decaying. Old cults and old deities fell into partial or complete neglect. Old priesthoods fell into abeyance, or became mere steps in the ladder of political ambition, while on every side the temples were crumbling into ruins (Hor. *Od.* III. vi.; Propert. ii. 6. 35 f., etc.). And, lastly, the age was as conspicuous for immorality as for unbelief (cf., *e.g.*, Mommsen, *Hist. of Rome*, tr. W. P. Dickson, new ed., 1894, bk. v. ch. xi.).

But the national conscience was not dead. We find in writings of the age a profound sense of national ill-being—here the sense of national guilt, there of misery entailed by neglected duty to the gods (Livy, *Præf.*; Hor. *Od.* III. vi., *Epod.* xvi.; Virg. *Ecl.* iv.; etc.). The superstitious extravagances above described were themselves a symptom of spiritual unrest. Now, it was to such feelings that Virgil appealed in his great poem, wherein he reminded the Roman people of their high destiny, and of the way to its attainment—through a *pietas* like that of his hero, the service of the State with the help of the State's deities. And it was to this task that Augustus, the original of Virgil's hero, devoted himself. His revival of the State religion is described by Fowler as 'the most remarkable event in the history of the Roman religion, and one almost unique in religious history' (*op. cit.* p. 428 f.). He did all in his power to reinstate the old religion in the faith and affections of the people, chiefly by the revival of ancient cults, and by a vast work of temple restoration (*Mon. Ancyr.* iv. 7; Livy, iv. 20. 7; Ovid, *Fast.* ii. 59, etc.), while he sought to strengthen his own dynasty by linking it at many points with the restored religious order (cf. esp. Hor. *Carm. Sæc.*). Finally, the religious policy of Augustus was continued by his successors. If, now, we seek to estimate the general importance of the old Roman religion in the early Empire, we may point, among other evidences, to the curious fact that it was against this rather than the philosophy of the Oriental worships of their time that the Christian Fathers directed their keenest ridicule. If we ask, on the other hand, whether as a spiritual force the Roman faith had any real renascence, the question is not so easy to answer. Here it must suffice to add that both in Rome and in the provinces 'the old religion continued to exist for at least three centuries in outward form, and to some extent in popular belief' (Fowler, 429).

See, further, art. ROMAN RELIGION.

LITERATURE.—An ample bibliography will be found in the work of W. Warde Fowler above referred to, and especially in its introductory chapter.
I. F. BURNS.

FAITH-HEALING.—A term used to express a belief that in the curing of disease the faith of the sufferer (or of others) is a contributory factor. This faith puts its trust in the immediate action of a super-normal being, acting with or without means. In the strictest sense, therefore, faith-healing may be said to exclude the use of visible means of healing; but, in the wider sense—in the sense, that is to say, in which 'faith-healing' occurs as a historical phenomenon—it admits such means as one factor in the process of healing. The principal species are named mental healing, magnetic healing, spiritualistic healing, and spiritual healing. In all, *suggestion* plays a leading part. The most widely spread sub-species of mental healing is that known as Christian Science (*q.v.*), and the strongest form of suggestion is called hypnotism (*q.v.*).

1. **History.** — Faith-healing is the oldest form of healing in the world, or, at any rate, it grew up side by side with medical practice in its earliest and crudest form, and as its predominant partner. The earliest diagnosis gave as the cause of disease the action of some god or spirit (cf. artt. on DISEASE AND MEDICINE), and, therefore, prescribed a homœopathic cathartic. Thus the 'frenzy' of the Dionysiac mysteries was cured by wild music and wilder dancings. 'The Bacchic women are cured of their frenzy by the use of the dance and of music' (Plato, *Laws*, vii. 790). But the dance was a cosmic dance, and the music was the melodies of Olympus taught by Marsyas (Plato, *Symp.* 215); hence the disease which was of Divine causation was cured by faith working with the use of means which were themselves of a Divine nature. If to music, dancing, and incense were added prescriptions of sundry washings, or abstinence from certain animals and plants as food, this was done for religious, not scientific, reasons. The prescription was directed to the faith of the sufferer, bidding him use that faith in an appeal to the deity who had sent the disease.

But it was not the *morbus sacer*, madness, or epilepsy, alone which faith in the god could cure. From the inscriptions of Epidaurus in Argolis we learn that in the 4th cent. B.C. such diseases as spots on the face, blindness, lameness, barrenness, hernia, snake-bite, baldness, headache, suppuration, phthisis, paralysis, and gout were cured by the power of the god joined to the faith of the sufferer (Dittenberger, *Syll. Inscr. Græc.*[2], Leipzig, 1898, 1901; Fiebig, *Kleine Texte*, no. 79; cf. Herodas, *Mimes*, 4). One point which recurs frequently in the inscriptions from Epidaurus is that the sufferer was put to sleep, in this 'temple-sleep' saw a vision, and in the morning awoke cured. In other words, the priests were acquainted with the power of hypnotism and of hypnotic suggestion. Moreover, it is not hazardous to infer from some of the inscriptions that, during the hypnotic sleep, operations were performed and massage and other remedies applied—in one case, the sleeping patient saw the god and his attendants seize him, cut open his abdomen, and stitch it up; and, when he went away on the morrow cured, 'the floor of the sanctuary was full of blood.' The difference between the practice of ancient times and that of to-day is here made clear. The priest of Asklepios based his surgery on the religious faith of the patient. Modern surgery has, as a rule, contented itself with mechanical methods, and abjured or left out of account the therapeutic power of faith.

The close connexion between faith-healing and invisible causal agents of disease is illustrated by the practice of exorcism.

Josephus tells us (*Ant.* VIII. ii. 5) that Eleazar, trusting in the traditional lore and power of Solomon, in the presence of Vespasian and his sons and chiliarchs and a multitude of soldiers, drew out of the nostrils of a certain man a demon who possessed him, by using a certain root that he had placed in his signet ring. As proof of the departure of the demon, the latter had been ordered in departing to overturn a vessel of water placed handy for the purpose, which was done. On another occasion, Vespasian, when in Alexandria, was moved, under the auspices of Serapis, to cure a blind man by anointing with spittle, and a man with a paralyzed hand by letting him be touched by his foot and garment. Both cures were effected in the presence of a great multitude, and were testified to by them all—especially afterwards, Tacitus adds cynically, when there was no temptation to tell lies about the matter (Tac. *Hist.* iv. 81; cf. Sueton. *Vespas.* 7; Dio Cass. *Hist. Rom.* lxvi. 8; Suetonius adds that the sufferers were instigated by a vision seen in dreams).

It is clear, then, that Christianity came into a world which believed in the power of gods (or heroes), as shown in divination (or prophecy), exorcism, and healing, that is, in processes in which a god and the faith of the sufferer were joint-actors. The title *Soter* was bestowed on all healing gods, such as Apollo, Asklepios, and Zeus himself; and, at the beginning of our era, power of healing was regarded as a necessary activity of every being for whom divinity was claimed.

In the earliest documents of the Christian Church faith-healing is frequently referred to, and is a dominant factor in the acts of healing wrought by Jesus Christ. The centurion's servant was healed because of the faith of his master (Mt 8[13]); a paralyzed man was healed on account of the faith of his friends (9[2]); the woman with an issue was made whole by her faith (9[22]); so were the two blind men (9[29]); and so was the daughter of the Canaanitish woman (15[28]). On the other hand, the lunatic boy's cure was delayed through want of faith (17[20]); and it is significant that the sins of the woman who was a sinner were forgiven because of her faith (Lk 7[50]). Moreover, it is expressly recorded that on one occasion Jesus did not (Mt 13[58]), and could not (Mk 6[5]), put forth His power because of the want of faith of the people. The inference is necessary that the method of healing followed by Jesus was of the same general character as that practised by the priests of Asklepios, that is to say, it depended partly on a power put forth by the healer, and partly on an active receptiveness on the side of the sufferer. This, again, corroborates the definition given above of faith-healing, viz. that it consists, as a matter of historical fact, not so much in the power of faith (or of auto-suggestion) as in the power of faith acting in conjunction with some external agency, visible or invisible.

In the Apostolic age the passage 1 Co 12 is classical for its conception of faith-healing. According to it, the power to heal was a gift of the Spirit (v.[9]); it was one among other gifts (v.[11]); it was given not to all (v.[30]); it was one of the greater gifts, and as such was to be sought for (v.[31]); its chief object was the common good (v.[7]), and the royal road to its attainment was love (v.[31]). An instructive comment on this passage is supplied by Ac 3[6], where Peter and John are said to have healed a lame man by calling over him the name of Jesus Christ. The healing of Æneas by Peter (Ac 9[34]) and the raising of Tabitha (v.[40]) both imply the same process, while it is expressly said of the cripple of Lystra that Paul healed him because he saw that he had faith to be healed (14[9]). In Ja 5[14], to the invocation in the name of the Lord are added the agency of the elders and the anointing with oil; and it is expressly added that the prayer of faith will heal (save) the sick man, and that the Lord will raise him—*i.e.*, from his bed of sickness, not eschatologically. In all the cases the implication is that, as cases of faith-healing, they are the joint-product of the work of an invisible agent, Jesus Christ, and of the faith of the sufferer. (On the form and power attributed to the invocation 'in the name of Jesus,' see Heitmüller, 'Im Namen Jesu,' in *Forschungen zur Rel. u. Lit. des A. u. N. Test.* i. [1903] 2.)

As illustrating the nature of faith-healing as practised in the early Church, the ceremony of exorcism is instructive. It is constantly the third with prophecy and healing, as in the case when the activities of the pagan *mantis* are described (Rohde, *Psyche*[4], 357 f.). The exorcism of spirits is but another name for the driving away of disease, wherever the diagnosis in general starts from the postulate that all disease is the work of malignant spirits. For example, Irenæus (*adv. Hær.* II. xxxii. 4) says of his own times and of his own fellows:

'Some do certainly and truly drive out devils, so that those who have thus been cleansed from evil spirits frequently both believe, and join themselves to the Church. Others have foreknowledge of things to come: they see visions, and utter prophetic expressions. Others, again, heal the sick by laying their hands upon them, and they are made whole.'

He goes on to say (§ 5) that Christians work their miracles merely by calling on the name of Jesus Christ in a pure, sincere, and upright spirit, or, in other words, by faith (cf. Just. Mart. *II Apol.* 6, *I Apol.* 30, *Trypho*, 39, 76; Tert. *Apol.* 23, 37, 43, *de Idol.* 11, *de Pud.* 21; Origen, *c. Celsum*, i. 11, iii. 24).

Perhaps the most vivid description of the faith-healing of the Patristic Church is that given by Augustine in his *de Civitate Dei* (xxii. 8. 3). He there tells, among others, the story of a man at Carthage who had been operated on for fistula with partial success only, but who was cured by prayer, and so saved from the necessity of a further threatened operation; and also of a leading Carthaginian lady, named Innocentia, who was healed of an incurable cancer in the breast through the sign of the cross being made over her. The union of divination and healing is here again exemplified by the fact that Innocentia was told in a dream how her cure could be effected. Another man, a doctor, was, at his baptism and after a dream, cured of gout; and an actor, of hernia and paralysis; a paralyzed youth was cured when brought into contact with some earth from Jerusalem. The most graphic story of all is that of a brother and sister being healed of St. Vitus' dance at the tomb of the martyrs in the church where St. Augustine was ministering—the sister, indeed, while he was preaching. He adds many other examples of cures wrought by faith-healing and the agency of the martyrs, and declares that what he gives is but a small sample of similar cures wrought within the two years preceding the writing of this volume—he knows, he says, seventy such cases.

The history of faith-healing knows of no artificial divisions, but runs on unchanged, so that what is true of one age is found true of another. The phenomena of pre-Christian days recur under Christianity, whether in its earlier or in its later forms. Thus the Middle Ages present a rich collection of instances of faith-healing, or miracles of healing, as these were then considered. A few typical examples must suffice, it being understood that they are quoted more as testimony to the belief in faith-healing than as being in every case beyond suspicion.

St. Bridget cured a blind girl named Daria (*Les Petits Boll.* ii. 184) and two lepers with the sign of the cross (Baronius, *Martyr. Rom.*, Antwerp, 1589). The works of healing power of St. Francis of Assisi are numerous, and were recited in the bull of his canonization. Another St. Francis (of Paula), three centuries later, was a still greater wonder-worker: 'He gave eyes to the blind, hearing to the deaf, speech to the dumb; he made the halt to walk, the cripple to have the use of his limbs, and recalled six dead persons to life again' (see *Les Petits Boll.* iv. 143). Similar marvels are told of St. Geneviève (*ib.* i. 100 ff.), of St. Germanus, 'the father, physician, pastor, and love of his people' (Fortunatus, *Lives*), of St. Vincent Ferrier (*Les Petits Boll.* iv. 227), of St. Carlo Borromeo, of St. Cuthbert, St. Patrick, of all great saints indeed, and of numberless lesser saints.

Nor was the religious movement of the 16th cent. able to crush out faith-healing. The saints, it is true, fell out of favour where the Reformers' spirit prevailed; but the witches remained, and Satan remained as an ever-active power of evil. In one striking case, at all events, faith-healing was able to hold its own. English kings since the days of Edward the Confessor, and French kings apparently from Clovis onwards, had touched for scrofula, or 'the king's evil.'

Queen Elizabeth touched, but omitted the sign of the cross; Charles I. invited by proclamation his subjects to come to him to be touched; Charles II. touched 92,107 persons; William III. touched without success; Queen Anne touched 200 persons, including Dr. Johnson when thirteen months old; George I. discontinued the practice.

A case of cure by faith-healing which seems well authenticated is that of Margaret Périer, a boarder at Port Royal, in 1685, who was cured of a persistent lachrymal fistula by the application of a spike from the Saviour's crown of thorns (see R. H. Hutton, *Essays Theol. and Lit.*², 1877, vol. i. pp. xxxiii–xxxv).

But, though faith-healing fell into disrepute in proportion as the spirit of rationalism prevailed, the belief underlying it found defenders continuously. Paracelsus, Glanvill, Valentine Greatrakes, van Helmont (see his *de Magnetica vulnerum curatione*, 1621), the Cambridge Platonists, and John Wesley all set forth that philosophy of life on which faith-healing depends. Moreover, Martin Luther, the Moravians, the Waldenses, the German Pietists, the English Baptists and Quakers, the famous healer of the last century, Prince Hohenlohe-Waldenburg-Schillingsfürst, Father John of Kronstadt, and the Peculiar People have all practised the art. Our own days, moreover, are witnessing its revival, under the influence of the recrudescence of Theosophic and Animistic, Orphic, and Hermetic modes of thought.

2. The means employed.—(1) Foremost among these, though the least important, we must place *some of the ordinary articles of the pharmacopeia.* The majority of these, it is true, such as iron and arsenic for the blood corpuscles, strychnine for the nerves, and pepsine or bismuth for the alimentary canal, call for little or no faith as a co-operant. But, in many cases where the mind reacts on the body through a depressed nervous-system, through fancy, in epilepsy, or in some cases of hysteria, the medical man will use drugs, or other media, not for their own efficacy, but as a means of calling forth that faith through which the *vis medicatrix naturæ* may be stimulated into action. Nor can the therapeutic value of confidence in the medical man be easily overrated as affording that restfulness of the soul which is one necessary condition for faith-healing.

(2) In Roman, Greek, and Christian times alike, great use has been made of *the hand*, and especially *the right hand*, as an instrument of healing. Blindness, child-birth, lameness, abdominal troubles, snake-bites, and strokes of any sort which were attributed to Divine or demonic influence were all treated as curable by the magic power of the Divine or human hand; to these must be added the touch of the *foot*, or of the *dress* as healing agencies, and also *kissing* anything which was thought to possess healing power (Weinreich, *Antike Heilungswunder*, 14 ff.). But, to make such magic power effective, there was obviously needed a co-operant as well as a prevenient faith.

(3) The so-called '*temple-sleep*' of the pagan temple was used as a species of faith-healing. The patient was put to sleep, and in the state of hypnosis he was either operated on or received suggestions that he was healed, which (if the inscriptions may be trusted) were found, when the patient awoke, to have effected their purpose. Modern hypnotism is aware of the part that faith plays in its activities, and is agreed that patients of low intelligence make bad cases, through their inability to make any continuous effort of attention, *i.e.* through their lack of a living faith. The ancient temple-phenomena repeat themselves in many of the miraculous healings performed by Christian saints.

(4) *Miscellaneous objects* used in faith-healing are: blood, oil (St. Cuthbert), spittle (St. Hilarion), hair, the sign of the cross, baptism, holy water (St. Willibrod), or water in which a saint has washed (St. Amandus), the bed on which a saint has died (as in the case of St. Vincent Ferrier), the medal of a saint (St. Francis Xavier), a tooth (St. Maturin), a shroud, relics, indeed anything which has in any way come into contact with a saint. In fact, nothing is a stronger argument for the validity of faith-healing in some sense and to some extent than the predominant place it took in the first 1500 years of our era. When all deduction has been made for credulity, exaggeration, imposture, and the desire to edify, there still remain a large number of healings which must be regarded as genuine, and must be accounted for either by the power of faith or by the power of the saints, or by a union of both. The probability is in favour of the last solution. That such wonder-works began to die out from the 16th cent. is

hardly to be accounted for by a supposed cessation of activity on the part of the saints, but rather by the want of inner and potent subconscious belief in their power. In other words, faith-healing, whether in the narrower or in the wider sense, characterized the West for 1500 years; it became sporadic for the next 400 years, and is now once more raising its head. And the inference is that, where an unquestioned faith—*Massen-illusionen*—in invisible powers holds the field, every individual subject to the influence of this faith is a suitable subject, by virtue of it, either for faith-healing, or, conversely, for falling a victim to any current form of 'possession' or hallucination (*la contagion mentale*) (cf. W. von Bechterew, *Die Bedeutung der Suggestion im sozialen Leben*, Wiesbaden, 1905).

3. The species of faith-healing.—For the sake of clearness, the principal species of faith-healing may be described as magnetic, mental, spiritualistic, and spiritual.

(1) *Magnetic.*—This is described by its supporters as a special case of the use of a primordial and universal force which displays itself in a balance between pairs of allied opposites, *e.g.* attraction and repulsion. Its therapeutic use was familiar to antiquity and is seen in the use of the hand (Weinreich, 1–66). It appears in some of the miracles of Jesus (Mk 5^{30} 8^{22}), was practised by His followers (Ac 5^{15} 9^{17} 19^{12}), and meets us in Roger Bacon, Paracelsus, van Helmont, and Robert Fludd, long before Mesmer in 1775 gave it wide currency. Afterwards the theory of a 'fluid' was discredited by the researches of Puységur and Faria, and, finally, James Braid; and the result has been undeservedly to neglect the unquestionable actuality of a force of some kind known as animal-magnetism, in favour of another known as hypnotism. The mental power has ousted the physical. In both the appeal is made to the nervous system, whether by way of establishing or disturbing its equilibrium; and it is claimed for magnetism that it effects its therapeutic results by the natural use of a force radiating from the operator, which is cognate to a universal force in which the nervous system of all living beings is bathed at its periphery. The chief method of magnetic healing is by passes, by touch, especially at neural centres, and by the application of objects which have been in contact with the operator. But, through the favour shown to hypnotism, magnetic healing has fallen comparatively into the background, though there can be little doubt that it masks a real force of some kind.

(2) *Mental.*—Mental healing is both active and passive. As active, it consists in the impartation of ideas, or suggestion, by the healer to the patient. As passive, it consists in the reception and assimilation of such suggestion. The healing proper, however, is sought in the consequent mental activity of the patient himself. He has been enjoined, for example, to fix his thoughts—by an effort of attention, continuous or repeated—on such virtues as joy, peace, contentment, or love; and, by implication, to exclude their opposites. The soul, it is assumed, will be put by this means in a more favourable condition for the activity of its inherent capacity for health. By some, indeed, faith-healing is identified with this auto-suggestion, on the ground that thought in man is distinctively the Divine in him, and that all that is required for the maintenance or restoration of health is the free play of this inherent Divinity. The phenomena of telepathy, moreover, have been invoked to support the contention that 'absent treatment' by mental healing may be as effectual as that given in the presence of the patient. The difficulties in the way of accepting this whole theory of mental healing lie in the facts that suggestion has less to do with the conscious mind than with the subconscious; that there is no good ground for regarding thought as pre-eminently the Divine in man; that the human mind in its finiteness is too weak a power for the work thus demanded of it; and that such results as mental healing secures are better assigned to spiritual healing, as defined below.

(3) *Spiritualistic.*—It is claimed by spiritualists that the spirits are the only doctors they require, and that these spirits can both diagnose and prescribe the proper remedies because of their superior knowledge. The evidence, however, for such assertions is too slight to call for more than a mere recital of the claim thus made.

(4) *Spiritual.*—Spiritual healing, in its strict and proper denotation, may be said to be synonymous with faith-healing in the stricter sense. The object of this method is to procure for the *soul* of the sufferer an influx of spiritual life, and it reposes on the assumption that physical diseases are the result, directly or indirectly, of psychical disorders, and that, therefore, the wise healer will strike at the causes which lie in the soul rather than at the symptoms which are seen in the body. The power which alone can heal the soul is God, and the link between God and the sufferer is faith. This faith is defined as a quality in the spirit of the healer (and the sufferer also, though in the former actively, in the latter passively) which enables him to render quiescent his 'mortal mind,' and so to place his spirit in a positive state of calm, poised, at peace, and a channel for the Divine spirit to pass through to the sufferer. This state of openness and serenity may be otherwise defined as the normal condition for prayer, and spiritual healing in its turn then comes to be defined as the product of the power of God directed, by faith through prayer, to the soul that needs healing. And its professors maintain that such healing activity, being kinetic, never fails of *some* beneficial result, even though that result may not show itself at once on the physical plane.

4. Suggestion.—It is necessary to say a word on the part suggestion plays in the many theories of faith-healing. The word is used frequently as if it were coterminous with the influence exercised on us by our whole environment, or with any influence exercised by any person on another. Or (Lefèvre) it is applied to all ideas which impinge on the mind without apparent motive and are unconsciously assimilated; or (Forel) to a deliberate alteration, by word or gesture, of another's nervous system by which entrance is afforded to the desired idea; or (Wundt) as a psychical act which blocks up all association-tracks of the nervous system other than the one suitable for the presented idea; or (Binet) as a moral impression which one person exerts on another; or (Sidis) as the invasion of consciousness by an idea without criticism or opposition. It is better, however, with Bechterew (p. 10), to distinguish between perception-activity in which the will takes an active part, and that in which the will is passive. The will is passive in a twofold manner: (*a*) with regard to all objects which lie beyond the centre of the field of consciousness (attention being concentrated exclusively on the one object at the centre); and (*b*) when the nervous system is depressed and, therefore, the power of attention is dissipated. To the latter condition of twofold passivity, suggestion proper belongs, and its proper place in our classification would be under the head of mental healing.

Closely connected with suggestion in general is hypnotism, the name given to a procedure which ensures an enhanced power to suggestion in a state known as *hypnosis*. In hypnosis two factors work jointly—one physical and one psychical. The physical consists in a partial dissociation of the neural dispositions or systems, in such a way that, while some are depressed, others (or one alone) work with increased vigour. In a state of concentration or depression the full flow of nerve currents (ideas) in the patient is arrested, so that the one current which the hypnotizer desires to keep open runs with increased volume. The psychical factor is that of a co-consciousness, or secondary stream of consciousness, which is to the waking consciousness as the stars are to the sun. When one sets, the other rises (see Carl du Prel, *Philos. of Mysticism*). Mental dissociation of tracts of ideas and physical dissociation of groups of nerve-processes seem to be the two poles between which all the phenomena of hypnotism swing.

5. Another question must be touched on. Faith-healing, as we have seen, obeys the same law in its activity as thought does when it depends on subject and object. It is the product of two factors, not of one only. The power which actually heals may be latent and native in the sufferer himself, but it is not called forth except through some stimulus. No account, therefore, of faith-healing can be adequate which omits either the one or the other of its two components.

'In faith-healing the suggestion is that cure will be worked by spiritual or Divine power, especially if this power be appealed to at some particular place, such as a sanctuary, the foot of an idol, a fountain, or pool of water, the resting-place of some sacred relics, such as the bones of a saint, or it may be in presence of the Eucharistic procession, or during High Mass, or the administration of the Holy Sacrament. . . . This Divine power or energy is supposed to act by neutralizing or overcoming sickness, disease, and the ill consequences of accident. The faith-healer does not doubt the reality of matter or of diseases, but believes that he can draw upon a spiritual force to subdue or annihilate an existing evil' (Henry Morris, in *Brit. Med. Jour.*, 18th June, 1910, p. 1458).

The further question whether the theory of faith-healing is that man's organism is self-contained, like a *perfecta societas*, or that it is like an Æolian harp played on by outside forces—in other words, whether as a discrete mass it contains within it all that is necessary for health and wealth, or whether other agents, such as animism and the doctrine of angels postulate, supply its needs—may remain here undetermined as being a question of philosophy or of a *Weltanschauung*. In any case, both may be true, for they are not contradictories but contraries. A place or a thing may be sacred and potent, not merely because we think so, but because unseen powers make it so, and the *vis medicatrix naturæ* latent in us may be reinforced, and not merely stimulated, by external agents, whether visible or invisible. Hence we may conclude, with Clifford Allbutt, that we are not in a position to set any limits to the power of faith-healing. 'No limb, no viscus is so far a vessel of dishonour as to be wholly outside the renewals of the spirit' (*Brit. Med. Jour.*, *ut supra*, p. 1483).

Literature.—Otto Weinreich, *Antike Heilungswunder*, Giessen, 1909; P. Fiebig, 'Antike Wundergeschichten,' in *Kleine Texte*, no. 79, Bonn, 1911; Carl du Prel, *Philos. of Mysticism*, tr. Massey, London, 1889; M. Hamilton, *Incubation*, London, 1906; Worcester-McComb, *Religion and Medicine*, London, 1908, *Grenzfragen des Nerven- und Seelenlebens*, Wiesbaden, esp. Hefte 22, 28, 33, 39, 43, 45; C. Lloyd Tuckey, *Treatment by Hypnotism and Suggestion*[5], London, 1907; J. Milne Bramwell, *Hypnotism, its History, Practice, and Theory*[2], London, 1906; A. Moll, *Hypnotism*[5], London, 1901; A. A. Liébeault, *Étude sur le zoomagnétisme*, Paris, 1883; R. H. Vincent, *The Elements of Hypnotism*[2], London, 1897; L. Deubner, *De Incubatione*, Leipzig, 1900; E. Rohde, *Psyche*[4], Tübingen, 1907; *Brit. Med. Journal* for 18th June, 1910, where the whole subject is discussed by medical men.

W. F. Codd.

FALASHAS.—See Abyssinia, Agaos.

FALL.

FALL (Biblical).—**1. The narrative of Gn 3.**—By 'the Fall' is meant that first act of disobedience to God which is narrated, with its consequences, in Gn 3. If this chapter were in the proper sense history, its interpretation would be easy; it would mean just what it says. But the beginnings of human life lie far beyond the reach of history; there neither is nor can be anything akin to tradition or recollection in a story which deals with the origins either of knowledge or of conscience. Such stories are the fruit of reflexion and imagination, which may be more naive or more philosophical, more childish or more spiritual, more gross or more refined, according to the minds in which they originate, but they are never historical. This is the case with Gn 3. It is a mythical explanation—charged with moral and religious lessons of the highest importance—of some phenomena in human life which especially impressed the writer. In his eyes life was an uncertain term of penal servitude, under the shadow of capital punishment. Both for men and for women it was under a curse. It could not always have been so. God could not have destined man to this misery from the first. There must be some explanation of how man came to be in this condition, and the explanation is given in the story of the Fall.

This view is adopted with practical unanimity by modern scholars, but agreement as to the character and purpose of the narrative does not necessarily result in agreement as to what it means. When we say that the writer gives his explanation in the form of a myth, the question immediately rises how far he was conscious of what he was doing—that is, how far the writer, who certainly did not make the myth out of nothing, was literally bound by its very terms, so that his work is simply one of statement; or how far he was capable of rationalizing or spiritualizing the myth, or feeling that it had significance in the rational and moral world, even if he could not use much liberty with what was probably a more or less sacred form. The various answers which have been given to these questions have issued in different readings of the whole story. Broadly, these may be illustrated as follows:—

(1) Gunkel tries to keep strictly within the limits of the myth. The one false path is that of modernizing. Eden is a garden which is the abode of God. Adam and Eve live in it on the fruit of the trees. They are in a state of childlike innocence, knowing no more than children know. That is the state in which God intends to keep them, and so they are forbidden to eat of the tree of the knowledge of good and evil. This has nothing to do with conscience. To know good from evil, or good from bad, means in Hebrew to know one thing from another; it is to have risen from the age of childhood to that of reason and experience (Dt 1[39], 2 S 19[35], Is 7[15]). The tree is quite accurately described when it is called the tree of knowledge, and the aim of God in forbidding it to man is to keep man in his place. He is not to

become like God—to enter into His secrets and to share His sovereignty. The cunning serpent (who in a more primitive form of the myth must have been an evil god or demon) reveals God's purpose, and prevails on man to eat the fruit of the tree. The result is what he predicted. The eyes of Adam and Eve are opened. The shame which attends on this is not a sense of sin; it is a kind of knowledge to which childhood could not attain. God Himself admits that the disobedience has achieved something. 'The man is become as one of us' in v.[22] is not ironical. Man has actually made something his own which was once exclusively God's, and God punishes with His curse all who have had part in the presumptuous action —the serpent, the woman, and the man. But there is no connexion, rational or moral, between the act and the miseries which God inflicts. They are the revenge of a jealous God on an impious invasion of what He had reserved to Himself; and this invasion and revenge are the mythical explanation of the miseries. Such an interpretation may do justice to the myth used in Gn 3, but it does not do justice to that use of it. The author of the chapter was himself a modernist, compared with the original myth-maker, and it is not modernizing but reading in the spirit in which the chapter was written if we lift the whole to a higher level both of reason and of morality.

(2) It is a higher level which is reached in Wellhausen (*Prolegomena*[4], 306 ff.). He reads the story in connexion with Gn 4 and 11, which tell of the invention of the arts, the progress of civilization, and the building of the Tower of Babel. This whole process is a mistake from the beginning: man was fatally misled when he first tasted of the tree of knowledge. Civilization with all its triumphs is labour and sorrow; we build Babylon only at the cost of losing Eden. Gn 3 is thus an early anticipation of modern moods in which men speak of the bankruptcy of science, the strain of civilization, the happiness of the simple life. But the tragic fact is that the mistake is irreparable. Eden is closed against us with cherubim and a flaming sword, and we can never get back to the idyllic world again.

(3) It will hardly be questioned that thoughts like these were present to the mind of the author, but it is not easy to admit that they exhaust his meaning. While the knowledge of good and evil is undoubtedly in Hebrew the same thing as knowledge or intelligence *simpliciter*, its moral reference is not to be denied. It is not identical with conscience, or the knowledge of right and wrong, but it includes conscience. The Hebrew would not say that a person who could not tell right from wrong had the knowledge of good and evil. And, when we take the story as a whole, and particularly the account of the temptation of the woman by the serpent, and the judicial examination of the man and the woman by God, marked as both are by extraordinary psychological fineness in the domain of conscience, it is very difficult to deny that the centre of the author's interest lay here. Whatever may have been the original motive of the myth, the main concern of the writer who uses it in Gn 3 is not the beginnings of science or the beginnings of civilization, but the beginnings of sin. Of all human origins the origin of the bad conscience is for him the most fateful. It is sin which has robbed man of his primal felicity. All that is distressing in human experience is in some way of a piece with it. The travail of women and the toil of men would not be what they are but for the judgment it involves. It commits man to an exhausting struggle with an ungenial world without, and with creeping poisonous thoughts within, till he returns to the dust from which he was taken. There is no indication in the text that the victory will come at last to man's side. Nothing is said but that, as long as there are men and serpents in existence, they will be at war with one another. This, of course, is literally true, but even for the writer of the chapter (it is suggested) this literal truth did not exhaust the meaning.

With many variations in detail, this is the line of interpretation which is followed by most students—not from a vicious habit of modernizing, but from a conviction that it is what the writer of Gn 3 had in his mind. It has the corroboration of conscience, not, of course, in the sense that conscience turns the myth into history, but in the sense that conscience is directly appealed to in the main matter which interests the writer, and can only assent to his teaching that disobedience to God is that which blights life and works death. The chapter does not contain history or dogma, but ethical experience expressed in a mythical narrative. It is not the story of the first man, but of every man; and, if the key to its form is to be sought in comparative mythology, the key to its contents can be found only in the soul.

It is hardly necessary to inquire into the antecedents of the myth. While we find in other races and religions much that is analogous to Eden (see FALL [Ethnic]), to the tree of life, and to the streams which water the garden, nothing has been discovered analogous to the tree of the knowledge of good and evil. There is no parallel in Babylonian mythology to the story of the Fall as there is to the stories of Creation and the Flood; the Chaldæan Genesis, so far as known, is quite defective here. Nor can it be doubted that, if such a parallel were found, it would be as much inferior as those others, in religious and moral respects, to its counterpart in the Hebrew Scriptures. Neither need we inquire how the writer would have conceived the moral history of man to take shape had Adam resisted the temptation and refused to eat of the forbidden fruit. What he has to do is to explain the actual world, with its suffering, toil, and death; but whether or how he imagined an alternative world without sin and its curse we cannot tell. Probably a mistake is made when we try to deduce from the narrative a conception of man's original state or nature and ascribe it to the writer. In a composition of this sort, we must not make the author responsible for more than he says. The eating of the fruit of the tree of knowledge was forbidden under pain of death; but it is vain to argue from this as to what man's relation to death would have been had he refrained from eating. This is a question the author does not raise. He starts with death and all our woe, as things that in common experience are of one piece with the bad conscience; but, although he avails himself of the mythical form to represent the idea that disobedience to God underlies all the tragedy of human life, the world in which we actually live and have our tragic experiences is the only one which is real to him. We cannot build anything on the idea of another world in which death did not exist—except as a child might, for whom as yet death does not exist. To forget this is to treat the mythical element in the story as if it were science; and it is not doubtful that, when Gn 3 was written, such a view was no longer possible, even if it had once been so.

2. Apocryphal and apocalyptic literature.— Apart from Gn 3 there is no distinct reference to the Fall in the OT. The garden of Eden is mentioned in Jl 2[3], Ezk 36[35]; Eden the garden of God in Ezk 28[13]; and the trees of Eden in Ezk 31[9. 16. 18]; but, though Ezk 28 has various mythological features (including the cherub) which recall Gn 3, there is no allusion to the events of this chapter. The margin of the RV is to be preferred to the text in the two passages (Hos 6^{7}, Job 31^{33}) in which the sin of Adam is directly recalled. But, at a later period, the story of the Fall concentrated upon itself a great deal of attention. In Sirach and Wisdom, and still more in the later apocalypses known as 2 Esdras and Baruch, it is a focus of theological speculation. The poetry of Gn 3, its psychology, its sense of the worthlessness of what civilization brings as compared with what we have to sacrifice to it, are lost; nothing remains but the interest in sin and death, and in their relation to each other. Sir $25^{23f.}$ is the earliest passage. The writer is reflecting in a disparaging tone on various evils which a bad woman may bring into her husband's life, and on this small occasion observes: ἀπὸ γυναικὸς ἀρχὴ ἁμαρτίας καὶ δι' αὐτὴν ἀποθνήσκομεν πάντες. This does not mean that woman was the cause or origin of sin, but that it began with her; and, as death is the doom of sin, we all owe our death to her. There is nothing in this akin to a doctrine of original sin, though it implies that sin only needed a beginning to extend its fatal consequences to all mankind. If Sir 25^{23} might be regarded as merely a passing petulance, such as a cynical person might still indulge in who did not believe in the Fall at all, a much more serious utterance is found in Wis $2^{23ff.}$:

'God created man for immortality (ἐπ' ἀφθαρσίᾳ), and made him the image of His own proper nature [reading ἰδιότητος; others ἀϊδιότητος = of His own eternity]; but by the envy of the devil death entered into the world, and those who are on his side have experience of it.'

Here the myth has been frankly turned into science—rationalized as far as the author could rationalize it, and made to yield a doctrine of human nature. The questions which, as we have seen, Gn 3 does not raise are both raised and answered here. God, as the author has said in the previous chapter (1^{13}), 'did not make death, nor does He delight in the destruction of the living.' He did not make man for death, but for immortality; this is included in 'His own proper nature,' in the likeness of which man was made. This is an idea, if not of Greek origin, peculiarly congenial to the Greek mind, even when Christianized. The serpent has disappeared, and is replaced by the devil: the idea of a close connexion between the two, whether it be that the devil makes use of the reptile, or that the reptile is regarded as an incarnation of the devil, first emerging here, became common (cf. Rev 12^{9} 20^{2}). This, as Gunkel observes, may be one of the points at which in the last stage of the myth a return is made to the beginning, the serpent having been originally a demon or evil god. The author of Wisdom does not explain what he means by the envy of the serpent: the idea was variously expanded in later haggadic treatment of the Fall, sometimes man, with his Paradise and immortal prospect, being the object of envy, sometimes God (Bousset, *Relig. des Judentums*², 469). The main point is that the author finds in Gn 3 an explanation of how a being constituted for immortality lost that high destiny, and became what we see man to be.

A deeper and more despairing kind of reflexion is found in 2 Esdras. The writer of this apocalypse, who lived through the terrible events of A.D. 70, is a pessimist in a profounder sense than the author of Gn 3; but he finds in the Fall of Adam there recorded the explanation of all the sin and misery of the world in his own age. These are universal:

'In truth there is no man among them that be born but he hath dealt wickedly: and among them that have lived there is none which hath not done amiss' (8^{35}).

But the purely mythological element disappears from his speculations on the origin of all this evil. It is connected with Adam certainly, but there is no longer either a serpent or a devil in the case.

'A grain of evil seed was sown in the heart of Adam from the beginning, and how much wickedness hath it brought forth unto this time! and how much shall it yet bring forth till the time of threshing come!' (4^{30}).

Who sowed the grain of evil seed in the heart of Adam *ab initio* he does not tell; but it originated apparently one continuous self-propagating life of sin in the world. It is supposed to be in Adam before he is tempted, and to be, if not the source, the ally of temptation and the cause of the Fall.

'For the first Adam, bearing a wicked heart, transgressed and was overcome; and not he only, but all they also that are born of him. Thus disease was made permanent; and the law was in the heart of the people along with the wickedness of the root; so the good departed away, and that which was wicked abode still' ($3^{21f.}$).

Man, as he is, has two things in him—the wicked heart, which he has inherited from Adam; and the law, which God has given him as a guide to Himself. This does not solve the problems of theodicy; it only raises them. How can man be responsible for his wicked heart if he has inherited it—that is, if it belongs to the natural, not to the moral, world? And how are we to understand the *cor malignum*, the יֵצֶר הָרַע, in Adam, before he had transgressed at all? What dogmatic theology calls 'original sin' is part of 'the sinfulness of that estate whereinto man fell,' but the *cor malignum* or *malignitas radicis* is inherent in Adam before he falls. It is part, apparently, of the constitution of his nature as he came from the hand of God (*ab initio*, 2 Es 4^{30}). It is not, however, the ultimate origin of evil or the idea—which a Jew would not seriously have contemplated—of ascribing it to God that really distresses the author; it is the fact that all men are involved somehow in the sin and doom of the first:

'This is my first and last saying that it had been better that the earth had not given thee Adam; or else, when it had given him, to have restrained him from sinning. For what profit is it for all that are in this present time to live in heaviness, and after death to look for punishment? O thou Adam, what hast thou done? for, though it was thou that sinned, the evil is not fallen on thee alone, but upon all of us that come of thee. For what profit is it unto us, if there be promised us an immortal time, whereas we have done the works that bring death?' ($7^{46\,(116)\,ff.}$).

Further than this the writer does not go. He is depressed by what man is, endures, and has to expect; he is tortured by his sense of the solidarity of the race in sin and death; but, when he tries to connect what he sees and feels with Gn 3, as a story of the origin of sin, he is both intellectually and morally baffled. He is obliged to assume *ab initio* the very thing he has to explain—the existence of the *cor malignum*, or יֵצֶר הָרַע, in Adam; and the moral inequity of allowing Adam's act to decide the destiny of the race is unrelieved.

The writer of the Apocalypse of Baruch represents the same circle of ideas, but probably feels less intensely about them, and seeks moral relief by emphasizing individual liberty as against the solidarity of mankind.

'If Adam did sin first and bring untimely death upon all, yet those too who were born of him each prepared for his own soul its future torment, and again each of them chose for himself his future glory. . . . *Non est ergo Adam causa, nisi animae suae tantum; nos vero unusquisque fuit animae suae Adam*' ($54^{15.\,19}$).

The doctrine, 'Every man his own Adam,' might formally be taken as a direct contradiction of that expressed in 2 Es 7^{118}, but it is probably not meant to be such. It rather suggests that the implication of the race in Adam's sin and its consequences is not so arbitrary as it can be made to appear; it is morally mediated, after all, by the fact that we all somehow make Adam's act our own. We may be hopeless and unhappy, but we are not compelled to rebel and blaspheme.

In comparison with these apocryphal books, in which real problems of the spiritual life are discussed in connexion with Gn 3, it is only necessary to mention that the story of the Fall is elaborated in the Book of Jubilees ($3^{17ff.}$) and the Apoc. Mosis (7 f.), but in ways that have no new interest for thought (Bousset, 411; Couard, *Die religiösen u. sittl. Anschauungen der alttest. Apokryphen u. Pseudepigraphen*, 113); cf. also Enoch 69^{6}.

3. The New Testament.—The ideas which we find in the apocryphal books just examined were, no doubt, familiar to many Jewish minds in NT times; but, apart from St. Paul, there is little trace of them in the NT itself. In the Synoptic Gospels Jesus nowhere alludes to Gn 3; and in Jn 8^{44}, when the devil is described as a murderer from the beginning, it is clear from the parallel in 1 Jn $3^{8ff.}$ that the allusion is not to Adam's forfeiting of life by sin, but to Cain's killing of Abel. In the Apocalypse there are many references to Gn 3, but rather to its scenery than to its incidents; the end of history returns to the beginning, and Paradise is restored (2^{7} $22^{2.14.19}$) with the tree of life. The old serpent, who is the devil or Satan, is cast down from heaven and chained (12^{9} 20^{2}). But there is no speculation or reflexion on the Fall. The same may be said of some of the allusions even in St. Paul. Thus Ro 16^{20} probably borrows its form from a recollection of Gn 3^{15}. In 2 Co 11^{3} there may be a reference not only to Gn 3, but to an idea current in certain Jewish circles, that the serpent seduced Eve to be unfaithful to her husband as well as disobedient to God; so in the same chapter (v.^{14}), where the transformation of Satan into an angel of light is also found in some Jewish elaborations of the OT story (for both, see Schmiedel, *ad loc.*, and Everling, *Die paulin. Angelologie u. Dämonologie*, Göttingen, 1888, p. 58 f.). But there are two passages in St. Paul where more is, or seems to be, based on the OT story, and where we seem to be in close connexion with the circle of ideas in which the authors of Sirach, Wisdom, 2 Esdras, and Baruch move. The interest of both is that St. Paul draws in them a parallel, which is in other respects a contrast, between Adam and Christ.

(1) In the earlier passage (1 Co $15^{21f.}$), as in Wis $2^{23f.}$, death is in view rather than sin: 'As by man came death, by man comes also the resurrection of the dead. For, as in Adam all die, so also in Christ shall all be made alive.' Adam is the head of the old humanity, which (whatever its original constitution or destiny may have been) is, in point of fact, mortal; this is what it is, and it is so in virtue of its connexion with him. Christ is the head of the new humanity, which (in spite of the mortality due to Adam) is destined at last to triumph over death; it is really immortal in virtue of its connexion with Him. The fact that in the two cases the connexion is quite different in nature is disregarded by the Apostle. The connexion with Adam, which involves us in death, is an affair of heredity; we are descended from him in the ordinary course of nature, and stand where we do, liable to death, apart from any choice of our own. But the connexion with Christ is not a matter of heredity, but of faith; it is only those who believe in Christ that are in Him, and will share His triumph over death. There is nothing in the fuller reference in vv.$^{45-49}$ which enables us to say more. In particular, there is no reference in them to sin. What is present to St. Paul's mind is that the creature made of the dust of the ground, the ἄνθρωπος ἐκ γῆς χοικός, cannot as such be immortal. 'Flesh and blood cannot inherit the Kingdom of God,' not because they are sinful, though that is true, but because they are essentially corruptible, and the Kingdom is incorruptible. There can be no such thing as immortality in nature; if there is to be immortality at all, it must be in another mode of being—not that mode of being with which we are familiar from our connexion with Adam, but that which has been revealed to us in the resurrection of Christ. Immortality, in other words, is strictly supernatural. A connexion with Christ of the kind formed by faith is needed to ensure our participation in immortality, just as our mortality is sure in virtue of our connexion with Adam. It is needed to ensure it; and it does. 'As we have worn the image of the man of clay, so shall we wear the image of the heavenly man.' An elevation or transmutation of nature, an evolution in which our being rose to a higher level, rather than the reversal of a doom, might seem to satisfy the terms here employed; but, congenial as this might be to a modern mind, it is improbable that it represents St. Paul's thought. Even if we set aside v.^{56} as a marginal comment which interrupts an inspired text, it is shrewdly to the purpose, and thoroughly in keeping with the other passage in which the Apostle treats of the same subject.

(2) The other passage is Ro $5^{12ff.}$. St. Paul is not dealing here, in the first instance, with immortality, but with the δικαιοσύνη θεοῦ; it is this which is revealed in Christ, and, consequently, when he again draws a parallel between the first and the second Adam, the emphasis falls not on death and life, but on sin and righteousness. Death comes, no doubt, in the train of sin, just as grace reigns through righteousness unto eternal life, but sin and righteousness are here the primary interests. 'As through one man sin entered into the world and through sin death, and so death extended to all men, for that all sinned'; so, we might suppose the Apostle continuing, by one man righteousness entered into the world, and through righteousness life; but we should find it difficult to provide the parallel to the clause 'for that all sinned.' These last words themselves (ἐφ' ᾧ πάντες ἥμαρτον) have been taken very variously. (*a*) Some have ventured to identify Adam and his posterity in such a way that his responsibility became immediately theirs—that is, theirs without any action on their part which mediated it from him to them. As Bengel puts it, '*Omnes peccarunt Adamo peccante.*' This seems to agree with the fact that the individual is involved in the moral responsibilities of the race, awful as these are, without his consent being first asked and obtained; he is born participant in the guilt and doom of mankind. Whether St. Paul would have shrunk from this or not, it raises more moral difficulties than it solves. (*b*) Others would make the ἥμαρτον apply to voluntary individual sins. Every man is his own Adam, and the author of his own fate. Within whatever limits this may be true, to say that it is true absolutely is to ignore the solidarity of the race in sin and its consequences, with which the Apostle is specially concerned at this point. (*c*) The interpretation which appeals for relief to the doctrine of heredity, and assumes that man inherits from Adam that which, when it is morally appropriated, reveals itself in consciousness as sin, is perhaps not unfair to the passage, but cannot directly appeal to anything in it for support. St. Paul is conscious that men are somehow one in sin; but, though he knows that only the faith of the individual unites him to Christ and makes him a partaker in righteousness and life, he never raises the question whether there is anything analogous to faith—an individual and voluntary appropriation of the inherited *cor malignum, granum mali seminis, malignitas radicis*, יֵצֶר הָרָע, or however it is to be called—in virtue of which we are morally involved in the responsibilities of the first man. While the solidarity of the race in sin and death is an immediate datum of experience for him, which he connects (without defining how) with the entrance of sin and death into the world through

Adam's disobedience, he gives us no means of constructing a doctrine of man's original state, or of the origin of evil. Adam, as the head of the old humanity, and as a foil to Christ the Head of the new, is just what we are before we are united to Christ by faith—a creature of clay, or of flesh, sinful, weak, mortal; an Adam before the Fall, in a state of original righteousness, may seem to be logically implied in what St. Paul says of 'the disobedience of the one,' but is a conception of which he makes no use.

It is quite futile to think that a Pauline doctrine of the origin of evil can be deduced from Ro $7^{7\text{ff.}}$. There are undoubtedly allusions here to Gn 3, so far as the expressions are concerned, but no historical doctrine can be based on this piece of generalized and ideal autobiography. If we say that in 1 Co $15^{21\text{ff.}\ 44\text{ff.}}$ the mortality of man is made to depend on his inheritance of Adam's nature, and that in Ro $5^{12\text{-}21}$ the condemnation of man, with all its fatal consequences, is conceived as dependent upon his being involved somehow in the transgression by Adam of God's express command, we go as far as the Apostle does. He really does not transcend theoretically the problems presented by 2 Esdras. He makes no use of the serpent or the devil in explaining the origin of evil. Man is a sinner, all men are sinners, sin is in the stock and has been from the beginning; it is deep, virulent, constitutional, no hurt to be healed slightly. But St. Paul's theodicy is not in a doctrine of its origin, in the act of Adam or otherwise; it is in his doctrine of redemption. Sin in its unity and universality may be taken for granted, and it may also be overcome; but not even on the basis of the Bible—OT or NT—will its origin ever be explained.

LITERATURE.—The Comm. on Genesis, especially Dillmann (Eng. tr. 1897), Gunkel ([2]1902), and Skinner (*ICC*, 1910); J. Wellhausen, *Prolegomena*[4], Berlin, 1895; H. Schultz, *OT Theology*, Eng. tr. Edinburgh, 1892; R. Smend, *Lehrbuch des alttest. Religionsgesch.*[2], Tübingen, 1899; A. Bertholet, *Bibl. Theologie des AT.*, Tübingen, 1911; J. Köberle, *Sünde u. Gnade*, Munich, 1905, p. 65 f.; W. Bousset, *Relig. des Judentums*[2], Berlin, 1906; L. Couard, *Die religiösen u. sittl. Anschauungen der alttest. Apokryphen u. Pseudepigraphen*, Gütersloh, 1907; F. C. Porter, 'The Yeçer Hara,' in *Bibl. and Sem. Studies*, New York, 1901; Sanday-Headlam, *Romans*[5], Edinburgh, 1902, pp. 136 and 146; the Comm. on Corinthians and Romans; the NT Theologies of Holtzmann[2], Tübingen, 1911, Feine, Leipzig, 1910, and Weinel, Tübingen, 1911; C. Clemen, *Christliche Lehre von der Sünde*, Göttingen, 1897.

JAMES DENNEY.

FALL (Ethnic).—i. *ORIGIN OF THE BELIEF.*—1. Man's curiosity regarding the things around him, itself the source of numerous Nature-myths, must early have been aroused by the condition in which he found himself. His speculative faculty had caused him to ask questions regarding the origin of the world and of mankind, and to these questions his cosmogonic and creation myths supplied answers. Hence it is not surprising that he should have sought an explanation of such things as appeared to him evils in his lot—hunger, his battle with the forces of Nature, the difficulty of obtaining food, the existence of disease and death, and, so far as his moral faculty had been awakened, the opposition of good and evil in himself, the struggle he had to follow the law he felt to be right, or even, perhaps, the customary laws of his tribe. These questionings gave rise to innumerable myths, found among many races and at all levels of civilization, which suggest as the answer that in the distant past something had occurred which reduced man to the state in which he now found himself, or that some disaster, perhaps anterior to his appearance on earth, had affected his destinies, or that some being, hostile to man, had injured him physically and morally, or that men had gradually deteriorated from some earlier existing state of happiness. Such occurrences may be comprehensively included under the title Fall, as used in Christian theology, while the stories which embody them are called Fall-myths. As a rule, the form and contents of such myths have been moulded by man's experience of the things which produced, or which he fancied to produce, evil to himself. As breach of tabu, or the breaking of divine commands, frequently produces evil in the actual life of primitive men, so they readily imagined that some such act originally introduced all the evils of life. Man's natural conservatism may have made him look askance at the introduction of the elements of culture: hence the idea that the craving for illicit knowledge on the part of some ancestor produced the Fall. Or it was put down to an early desire to be as the gods. Or man's sensual cravings were believed to have been his ruin, as seen, for example, in myths which told how, at first, he had lived without requiring to satisfy them. Or woman, being at all times regarded as a source of evil, and the subject of a variety of sexual tabus, was sometimes held to be the cause of man's undoing. Occasionally, too, beings exterior to man are blamed for his fall; but, as a rule, he takes the blame upon himself. In a few cases, it is some act, generally regarded as contemptible, which is supposed to have ruined man, as in an Algonquin myth. Goldziher has argued (*Myth. among the Heb.*, Eng. tr. 1877, p. 79) that hunters and nomadic shepherds look down on agricultural races as being slaves to the soil in comparison with themselves, the free wanderers; while, where a people is partly nomadic, partly agricultural, there is a conviction that 'they have taken a step towards what is worse, and have sunk lower by exchanging pasture for crops.' In such cases, myths arise which tell how the downward step was taken, or show how man doomed himself to labour on the soil in the sweat of his brow; and these myths of a Fall are closely connected with others which set forth the dignity of a shepherd life.

This theory, intended to explain the origin of the Fall-story in Genesis, hardly applies to it as a whole, since man is already in charge of a garden and is not a nomad, while his fall is anterior to the curse of tilling the ground. The form of the curse, however, may have been moulded by some lost Fall-myth attributing man's ruin to agriculture—to the conservative nomad a species of illicit knowledge. For some myths which illustrate Goldziher's theory, see ii. 2 (1).

2. A different conception underlies the myths of a Golden Age, especially among the Greeks, whose poets praised agriculture; yet even in them we see a trace of the same idea, since man eats of the fruits of the earth without labour or tillage. When the Golden Age passes away he must eat them in the sweat of his brow. The same idea is present in those myths (Hindu, etc.) which tell how man lived without food, till, having tasted the earth or its fruits, he was forced to live upon them and labour to produce them.

3. Some of these myths have assumed a highly poetical form; on the other hand, even among advanced peoples like the Persians, some are exceedingly crude, and betray their primitive origin. In some cases, notably among peoples of a highly philosophic cast of mind, as well as with individual thinkers, the causes of man's present condition take a profounder form, especially where the doctrine of metempsychosis is made use of. This article will consider (1) myths explaining the presence of death and other evils by man's fault; (2) myths of a Fall; (3) myths of a Golden Age of innocence from which man deteriorated; (4) myths of a lost intercourse between gods and men through the growing wickedness of the latter; (5) myths of a Fall in a former existence; (6) myths of a divine Fall.

It should be observed that the idea of deterioration through a divine curse, usually on account of some act of wrong, is quite a usual one in myths. The existence of apes is commonly believed in Africa to be due to a curse which turned offending men into that shape; while in N. Zealand, among the Indians of Huarochiri, and with the Namaquas, the habits of animals, like those of the serpent in Genesis, are conferred as the result of a curse or blessing (Shortland, *Trad. of N.Z.*[2], 1856, p. 57; *Fables of Yncas*, Hakluyt Soc., p. 127; Hahn, *Tsuni Goam*, 1881, p. 66). Transformation of human beings is, in all mythologies, attributed to Divine anger on account of human wrong-doing.

ii. *VARIOUS MYTHICAL EXPRESSIONS OF THE FALL-BELIEF.*—**1. Myths of the origin of death.**—The existence of death was one of the clearest indications of a serious disorder in human life. Ethnological evidence from all parts of the world proves that man's thoughts about death had everywhere taken much the same form. To man, with his intense love of living, death appeared unnatural; hence his firm belief in a life beyond the grave, or in the possibility of the renewal of life on this earth. The unnaturalness of death from the savage point of view is shown by the universality of the idea that disease and death are due to demonic and magical influences, and that, if men were never bewitched or killed by violence, they would always live on. Death from any natural cause is inconceivable. But, if death is unnatural, the question arises, How was it first introduced into the world? Various mythical answers were given, all tending to show that a time had been when death did not exist, and in some of these we see distinct traces of the idea that its coming was due to man's disobedience or folly. Other causes are alleged, *e.g.* the wrong delivery of a divine message, or a compact between an evil being (*e.g.* Death personified) and the divinities, or the malice of an evil being, or the first man's death establishing a precedent. Traces of such myths may be found in some of the higher mythologies, but they are most common among lower races. We are here concerned only with those in which the origin of death and other evils is due to man's own fault, as in the Hebrew account of the Fall.

(1) In some cases the fault is *man's stupidity or carelessness*, as the following myths will show. The Dog-rib Indians say that after the Thunder-bird had made all things, he gave the Indians a large arrow which they were to keep with great care. But it was lost through the stupidity of the Chippewas, and the creator was so angry that he left the earth for ever, and now men die (Bancroft, *Nat. Races*, 1883, iii. 105). A Shawnee myth relates that there was a time when men could walk on the ocean or restore life to the dead (here death already exists, but is vanquished), but they lost these privileges through carelessness (Schoolcraft, *Ind. Tribes*, 1857, iv. 255). In Jap. mythology, death is introduced because, when the deity Great-Mountain-Possessor sent his ugly elder daughter as wife to the suitor for his younger daughter's hand, he sent her away. Had he not done so, their offspring would have been immortal; as it is, they are as frail as the flowers (*Kojiki*, xxxviii. 115). Where the performance of religious rites according to a prescribed ritual is all-important, myths regarding any breach of ritual are sure to arise. Among the Maoris such a breach is the cause of the entrance of death into the world. When the culture-hero Maui was baptized, his father omitted part of the *karakias*, or prayers to the gods. For this reason men became mortal. As yet there was no death, nor would there ever have been if Maui had been able to pass through the body of Hine-nui-te-po; but because of this omission he failed and died, and now all men must die (Grey, *Polynesian Myth.*, 1857, p. 16). In the Admiralty Island version, death is due to the fact that a certain chieftain's family could not recognize that his spirit, and not his body, which had fallen from a tree, was the real man, so that he makes his spirit return to the dead body, and thus perish (*Anthropos*, iii. [1908] 194 f.).

(2) In other cases, *death results from a quarrel* (cf. the death of Abel), or from *man's wickedness*. An Eskimo myth relates that two of the first human beings quarrelled regarding human immortality. The one who advocated men's dying gained the victory; hence arose death (Nansen, *Eskimo Life*, 1893, p. 272). Among the Hare-skin Indians death is said to have arisen from a quarrel regarding the possession of a screech-owl. An old man fled with it, but was pursued and killed; a relative of his killed the chief murderer; he was in turn slain, and thus death and war arose (Petitot, *Trad. ind.*, 1886, p. 180). The Aleutians say that formerly men, as they grew old, plunged into a lake and renewed their youth. But a woman who had a divine lover made him angry by her peevish complaints. He killed her brother, and so made all men subject to death (Farrer, *Primitive Manners and Customs*, 1878, p. 13). In Blackfoot Indian legend also the folly of woman introduced death (Grinnell, *Blackfoot Lodge Tales*, 1893). The Caribs, Arawaks, and others ascribe death to the fact that the creator, finding men so wicked as to try to deprive him of life, took away their immortality and gave it to skin-casting creatures. A myth current in Polynesia relates that the early part of Rangi's reign was a Golden Age, in which death, war, and famine were unknown; but through a quarrel, death entered into the world, followed by disease and famine, and thus, in spite of Rangi's interposition, the Golden Age passed away (Gill, *Myths and Songs*, 1876, p. 286). In an Admiralty Island legend an old woman strips off her skin, and thus regains her youth; but one of her sons wishes to wed her. In consequence of this evil wish, aggravated by falsehood, the old woman re-dons her skin, and since then death has been in the world (*Anthropos*, iii. [1908] 193).

(3) More usually death is attributed to *man's disobedience*, generally through a breach of tabu, *e.g.* eating some forbidden food; and myths of this nature have very naturally arisen among people who believe that breach of tabu, or eating a totem animal or plant, is inevitably followed by punishment, especially by the death of the tabu-breaker. Wherever such a custom or belief existed, it would be easy to found a myth upon it as the reason for that puzzle—the origin of death and other evils. Some of these myths may have been influenced by the account of the Fall as told by missionaries; on the other hand, they are so consonant with savage customs and methods of thought that they bear marks of originality. A Dog-rib Indian myth relates that the first man, Tschapiwäh, gave his children two kinds of fruit, black and white, forbidding them to eat the former. They were obedient for a time while he was absent to fetch the sun, but disobeyed him when he went away a second time to obtain the moon. He was angry with them, and said that henceforth the earth would produce only bad fruit, and men should be subject to sickness and death. His family bewailed their lot, and he then relented so far as to say that those who dreamt certain dreams should have the power of curing sickness (Klemm, *Culturgesch.*, 1843–52, ii. 155). The tabu is often connected with the idea that eating the fruit of any strange country or people makes one belong to it; hence arise myths that mortal men are immortal beings who were condemned to earth because they ate of its fruits. A Tonga version of such a myth makes certain immortal gods journey from Bolotoo (Hades) and land on Tonga, where they ate of its fruits. Soon some of them died, and all were condemned to live there and people the world with mortals.

Hence arose the race of men, subject to decay and death (Mariner, *Account of the Natives of the Tonga Islands*[2], 1818, ii. 115). The same idea occurs in Sinhalese cosmogony: the immortal beings of the fifth period of creative energy ate certain plants, and so became subject to mortality and lost the power of returning to the heavenly mansions. At the same time arose the division of the sexes (Forbes-Leslie, *Early Races*, 1866, i. 177). In other cases the tabu has nothing to do with eating. The Ningpos of Bengal say that once men were forbidden to bathe in a certain pool. Some one did so; hence men became subject to death (Dalton, *Eth. of Bengal*, 1872). There is an Australian myth to the effect that the first pair were forbidden to go near a tree on which lived a bat, which was not to be disturbed. Gathering firewood, the woman approached the tree; the bat flew away, and death arrived (Brough Smyth, *Abor. of Vict.*, 1878, i. 429). Elsewhere the disobedience is not connected with a tabu. Another Australian myth makes death result from men refusing through fear to carry the fierce dogs of Buhloo (the Moon) across a creek. 'If you had done what I had asked you,' said he, 'you could have died as often as I die, and have come to life again as often as I come to life' (K. L. Parker, *Aust. Legend. Tales*, 1896, p. 8). In Uganda it is thought that death was introduced because when Kintu, the first man, was sent down from heaven, he was told that if he forgot anything he was not to return for it, since Warumbe (death or disease) would assuredly go with him to earth. He forgot millet, and, contrary to his wife's advice, returned for it, with the result predicted (Johnston, *Uganda Protectorate*, 1902, ii. 704). The Basutos say that Matoome, the first man, came out of the earth with his sister Matoomyan, who had a life-preserving medicine. She told him to lead their cattle in one direction; he disobeyed her, and she, in a rage, went back into the earth with her medicine. Thus death and disease came into the world (Campbell, *Travels in S. Afr.*, 1822, i. 306). The following myth was told by a native of Tumele (Cent. Africa). Til made men deathless, and forbade them to kill the beasts; they broke his command, and were all destroyed save one. Til now changed a gazelle into a woman, who bore the survivor four children, two white and two black. These were also deathless; but the frog complained to Til that it was unfair to make harmless animals subject to death, and guilty man immortal. Til saw the justice of this, and made men subject to old age, sickness, and death (*Ausland*, Nov. 4, 1847). In Togo, death is due to the petition of a frog, who reached the Supreme Being before the dog, who sought that man might live again after death (*Anthropos*, ii. [1907] 203; cf. iii. [1908] 277); and in an Admiralty Island version, death comes from the ingratitude of a man who sought to deceive the tree which had saved him from a demon (*ib.* iii. 194). The Melanesians account for death by various myths, one of which turns on an act of disobedience on the part of a woman made by the divine hero Qat. She was stolen by Marawa; Qat urged her to return, but she refused; therefore, while the pair were sleeping, he pulled their teeth, shaved their hair, and covered their eyes with spiders' webs so that their sight became dim. Thus old age and death became the lot of men (Codrington, *Melanesians*, 1891, p. 266). In New Guinea (Mowat), death came upon all men because the mother and grandmother of the first man who died, instead of obeying his injunction to remain until he returned to them as before, went in search of him (Beardmore, *JAI* xix. [1890] 465). An American Indian myth reported by the Jesuit missionaries in 1634, and apparently quite original, has a curious resemblance to the Greek Pandora myth (see below, **2** (3)). After the world had been recovered from the Deluge, the divinity Messon gave a Montagnais Indian the gift of immortality enclosed in a small box, subject to the condition that he should not open it; for, so long as the box remained closed, he would be immortal. His curious and incredulous wife opened the box to see its contents. And thus all Indians became subject to death. This myth was current in other parts of Canada (*Relation de la Nouvelle France*, 1636)—among the Ojibwas in 1857 (Hind, *Labrador*, 1863, i. 61).

These myths of the origin of death and kindred evils through a 'Fall' form the most concrete answer to man's questionings about his evil plight—death being taken as typical of evil generally—while they approach the series of the more complete Fall-myths current among many peoples, which must now be considered.

2. Myths of a Fall.—(1) Some myths of this class bear a striking resemblance to the story of Genesis, and may have arisen as a result of missionary teaching, or through the gradual diffusion of the Hebrew story in the same way as *Märchen* have been diffused over a wide area. In others, the likeness may simply be due to the colouring of an original myth with pigments borrowed from outside sources. Each myth of this kind must be judged on its merits, and with a full appreciation of the possibility of similar stories arising through similar circumstances, surroundings, and psychic conditions, in more places than one. Many others are undoubtedly original—even a few which might seem at first sight to be borrowed. Especially is this the case where, in many of the myths which follow, as in some already referred to, the Fall is due to the eating of a forbidden food. This need not necessarily have been borrowed from Genesis, but shows how emphatically the system of tabus, especially with regard to foods, was connected with punishments meted out automatically to the tabu-breaker, and how naturally all this was reflected in myths of the origin of evil. Man accounted for the latter by that which appealed most easily to his imagination, and of the danger of which he had seen many evidences. His Fall was a punishment visited on him for breaking a divine tabu. Such a view might easily become current among the lowest races, since it is found that the creative beings of, *e.g.*, the Andamanese, Australians, and Bushmen are also moral governors, punishing men for breaches of their commands. The Batutsi say that the Fall was due to Nyinakigwa's breaking of the divine prohibition to tell how, being sterile, she had three children, the gifts of the deity Imana (*Anthropos*, iii. [1908] 2 ff.). Where it had become customary not to eat of certain foods at certain seasons, it would be easy to form a myth suggesting that men had been told by a higher Being not to do so, and that, when they had done so, much evil had resulted. Thus the Andamanese, whose remarkable theology, according to the best authorities, is independent of Christian influence, believe that Puluga, the creator, gave the first man, Tomo, various injunctions, especially concerning certain trees which grew only at one place (Paradise) in the jungle, and which he was not to touch at certain seasons—during the rains, when Puluga himself visits them and partakes. Later, some of Tomo's descendants disobeyed and were severely punished. Others, disregarding Puluga's commands about murder, adultery, theft, etc., and becoming more and more wicked, were drowned in a deluge. Two men and two women survived, and, in revenge, wished to kill Puluga, who, telling them that their friends had been justly punished, disappeared from the earth. But even now these trees are strictly tabu during the rainy season when Puluga visits them invisibly, and it is firmly held that, if any one dares to tamper with them, a new deluge will result (Man, *JAI* xii. [1882] 164, 166f., 154). Here, a native system of tabus has given rise accidentally to a series of myths bearing a certain resemblance to the Genesis story, and this may, quite conceivably, have happened elsewhere. An Australian myth, which might easily have become a Fall-myth, points to this conclusion. When the divine Baiame left the earth, the flowers withered and died. Three trees alone were left which none dared touch, because Baiame had put his mark upon them. When he saw that no one touched them, he sent a kind of manna upon the earth (K. L. Parker, *More Aust. Legend. Tales*, 1898, p. 84). A Fall through breaking a divine tabu regarding food or some other divine orders will be found in several of the myths which follow. Such myths, involving a catastrophe to many, should be compared with *Märchen*, in which an individual comes to grief through disobedience, *i.e.* breaking a tabu. Here, too, the incident reflects actual customs.

A myth, current among the Maidu Indians, may possibly owe some of its details to missionary teaching. The good world-maker, Ko-do-yam-peh, sent man on the earth, where all animals were tame and the soil fruitful. He bade him take all things freely, but always to bring his food home and cook it, never to kindle a fire in the woods. But the evil Hel-lo-kai-eh told man to cook his game in the woods. He did so, with the result that the smoke made the animals wild, as they now are; the ground was changed, and man had only roots and worms to eat; frost, rain, and tempests arose; and death was introduced into the world (*FLR* v. [1882] 118 ff.; cf. the 'Bushman myth,' § 3). In Pentecost Island (New Hebrides) a woman, become the wife of the sun-god, is violated by the moon-god, who enters the tabued precincts of the happy land; she is accordingly driven away, and bears two children, one black (the son of the sun-god) and the other white (the son of the moon-god); they engage in conflict, and the black son, the ancestor of the natives, expels his half-brother, the ancestor of all white men (*Anthropos*, vi. [1911] 902–905). A kind of dualism runs through all American Indian mythology (see DUALISM [American]; here the evil being acts the part of tempter, but the myth, even if some details have been borrowed, is in the main original. Similarly in a Blackfoot Indian myth, when Nāpi the creator makes the first pair out of clay, death is introduced through the folly of the woman, and all later misfortunes arise through disobedience to the creator's laws (Lang, *Making of Religion*, 1898, p. 260). Another myth which, according to Leland, 'gives the fall of man from a purely Indian standpoint' traces all human evils to that idle loquacity which is, above all other things, most contemptible in Indian eyes. A child was born of an Indian girl by the spirit of the mountain. She was bidden never to tell her people of his origin. The child fed them miraculously, and would have made of them a mighty nation, but they never ceased to ask his mother whence he came, and she told them, 'It shall be to you exceeding sorrow that ye ever inquired.' She and the child disappeared, and thus the Indians, who should have been a great, became a little people (Leland, *Algonquin Legends*, 1884, p. 257). The dualistic idea of the origin of evil reappears in a myth current among the Khonds of Orissa. Boora Pennu, the god of light, had a consort, the Earth-goddess, the source of evil. Her jealousy of her husband's love for his creature man caused her to introduce physical and moral evil into the world. Such men as rejected her influence were deified; all others were condemned to suffering, moral degradation, and death (MacPherson, *Mem. of Service in India*, 1865, p. 273). Compare with this the old Mexican belief that the Golden Age of Anahuac came to an end through the envy of the god Tezcatlipoca, who seduced the daughter of king Huemac, whereupon followed a decline in moral purity and the departure of the culture-hero Quetzalcoatl (Hardwick, *Christ and other Masters*, 1855–59, pt. iii. p. 151).

Certain Negro and Malagasy myths may be due to Christian or Muhammadan influence; but here again we cannot assert this with certainty, and indeed a more ancient source may be appealed to. In some of these myths may be seen that contrast between the nomadic and the agricultural life already referred to. Thus in Calabar it is told how the first human pair were called to Abasi (the Calabar high god) by a bell at meal-times. Abasi had strictly forbidden to them both agriculture and the propagation of their kind. Both these commands were broken, more especially through the woman's being tempted, by a female friend who had been given her, to use the implements of tillage. Thus man fell and became mortal, and his agricultural occupation was his curse (Bastian, *Geog. und eth. Bilder*, 1872, p. 191). This is also hinted at in a myth from Madagascar. The first man was subject to none of the present human evils, and was placed in a garden of all delights, but forbidden to taste of its fruits or drink of its limpid streams or partake of any kind of food or drink. His fall was brought about by his great enemy, who painted to him the sweetness of the apple, the lusciousness of the date, and the succulence of the orange. At last he ate, and thus brought about his ruin (Baring-Gould, *Legends of OT Characters*, i. 20). In the sequel a pimple appeared on his leg, and increased till it burst. From it emerged a beautiful girl, who became through him the mother of mankind. The Dahomans and the Agni are credited with a belief in a first pair, a tree and forbidden fruit, and the temptation of the woman by a serpent (Delafosse, *L'Anth.* iv. 434). Such legends may appear to be due to Christian influence, but we must not overlook the capacity of myths to diffuse themselves over wide areas in long-distant ages; hence such stories may have long ago reached Africa from Semitic sources. On the other hand, they may be quite original, like the Andamanese myth. Others would explain their likeness to the story in Genesis by the early presence in Africa of a Semitic element, now represented by such a people as the Masai (Merker, *ZE* xxxv. 373), who possess a mythology which is said to be in many points similar to the narratives in Genesis, but contains no Christian elements. Hence it has not been obtained from Christian sources, and Merker thinks the Masai have preserved these traditions from the time of their separation from the Israelites. They hold that Paradise resulted from the moistening of the sterile earth with the blood of a huge dragon slain by God (cf. the Babylonian combat of Tiāmat and Marduk). The first man was brought down from heaven; his wife came out of the earth. They were forbidden to taste the fruit of one of the trees of Paradise. The woman was tempted to eat by a serpent: she and her husband both enjoyed the fruit; then fear fell on them and, as a punishment, they were expelled from Paradise. We hear nothing of the curse of tilling the soil; the Masai are mainly a nomadic people.

F. Max Müller has found all the elements of the Fall-story in Egypt, and thinks the Israelites derived their story thence. The myth is yet unpublished, but it is possible that all these African myths may also have been derived from it, since we know that many Egyptian customs and beliefs filtered slowly through to the remotest parts of Africa (see the Egyptian Golden Age myth, § 3 (5).

The Madagascar myth of the Fall producing a different sex may be compared with the Sinhalese myth, above, ii. 1 (3).

(2) The idea of a Fall occurs in various forms in the mythologies of several higher races. Among the **Hindus**, who more than any other people have brooded over the problem of evil, various reasons were alleged to account for man's evil plight. A Fall in a previous existence was, as we shall see, a favourite method of accounting for it; in other cases it was regarded as the inevitable consequence of the association of the soul with a material existence; again, the doctrine of emanation, as in the Gnostic view, suggested a gradual deterioration, keeping pace with the increasing distance of souls from the divine; while, as in Greek mythology, a series of successive world-ages, each growing worse than its predecessor, was also postulated.

In the earliest writings (the Vedas) there is no Fall-myth; the story of the incest of Yama and Yami (Rigveda) affords no real parallel to the Genesis story, as is sometimes supposed, but is a crude explanation of origins. In later times the more philosophical views occasionally give place to a concrete myth, *e.g.* that of Brahmā, identified with the first man Manu Svāyambhuva, and Śatarūpa, Manu's wife, the equivalent of the creative principle. Śiva dropped from heaven a blossom of the sacred *vaṭā*, or Indian fig—the *bōdhidruma*, or tree of knowledge of Brahman and Buddhist alike. Ensnared by its beauty, Brahmā gathered it, thinking it would make him immortal and divine. While still exulting in this thought, he was punished by being consigned to an abyss of degradation, whence he could be freed only after a long term of suffering. His wife, adds the myth, had urged him to take the blossom, and on their descendants was the curse entailed.

This myth, which has very frequently been cited as a parallel to Gn $3^{1ff.}$, owes nothing to the latter, is of late origin, and possibly is derived from a Buddhist myth with several variants. One form, cited by Hardy (*Man. of Bud.*, 1864, p. 66), tells how the Brahmas who were born into this world were happy, and peace reigned everywhere. A peculiar scum arose on the surface of the earth; one of them tasted it, found it palatable, and devoured it greedily. The others followed his example, with the result that the glory of their persons faded, and it became necessary to make the sun and moon. Their skins grew coarse; they deteriorated morally and physically; and the world became filled with passion and evil. The Tibetan form of the myth is similar. Men lived to 60,000 years, and were invisibly nourished and able to rise at will to the heavens. But, through covetousness and the consequent eating of a honey-sweet substance (or herb) produced by the earth, they lost these gifts, became vicious, and were forced to practise agriculture for the sake of food (Pallas, *Reise*, 1771–76, i. 334). In the Nepāl version, earth is uninhabited, but visited occasionally by the dwellers of the heavenly mansions (*Ābhasvara*), who were innocent, and androgynous. But desire to eat arose in their minds; they tasted the earth, lost the power of return to Abhasvara, and had to eat the fruit of the earth for sustenance (Hodgson, *Buddhism*, p. 63). The Sinhalese version resembles this, but after eating earth for 60,000 years these visitors became covetous. Earth lost its sweet taste, and brought forth a kind of mushroom of which they ate till it failed them. Thus they proceeded from food to food, till their spirit nature was lost, and they became men, filled with wicked ideas (Upham, *Sacred Books of Ceylon*, 1833, iii. 156).

(3) However lightly the **Greeks** may have estimated moral evil or veiled it under æsthetic forms, they were by no means blind to it, and myth and philosophy alike tried to explain its existence. The early legend of Prometheus accounts for the evils of human life by the fact that the hero, in stealing fire from the gods, was trespassing the limits set to human knowledge and power by them. Hence their resentment. It thus exhibits that aspect of many mythologies, seen even in the Hebrew, of the gods' jealousy of men, of men becoming their equals, while the idea of man's encroaching on something forbidden is parallel with the Semitic Tree of Knowledge and other forbidden things. Hesiod (*Works and Days*, 52 f.) brings the story into connexion with that of Pandora, fashioned by the gods to bring evil to Prometheus and the whole race of men. Within her breast were infused falsehood and guile by Hermes, following the counsel of Zeus. She was received by Epimetheus, in spite of the warning given him by his brother Prometheus. And now evils came into the world, because Pandora removed the lid from a vessel in which they were contained, and so dispersed them among men. In a story mentioned by Proclus, Prometheus himself had deposited this vessel, which he had received from the Satyrs, with Epimetheus. Contrary to warning, Pandora opened it, thus showing her nature. But according to Philodemus, Epimetheus himself opened it, bringing evil and death upon his fellows. Hesiod's intention is to teach that woman is the intermediate cause of human ills (cf. Gn 3^6). Better had it been for man to have remained alone than to have joined himself to this Greek Eve, the later creation of the gods. A similar duplication of the idea of human ills being brought about by rash desire for illicit knowledge as well as by woman occurs in the myth of the Sirens, who say they will send men who listen to them on their way the wiser. For they 'know all things,' 'all that will hereafter be upon the fruitful earth' (*Odyssey*, xii. 191). The close approach of these leading ideas of the Greek myth to those of the Semitic story is remarkable; but, in spite of possible points of contact between early Greeks and Phœnicians on the one hand, and Phœnicians and Hebrews on the other, we need not suppose that the two are interdependent or have any common source except in the similarity of man's psychic conditions and environments leading him to formulate his conception of the world on more or less similar lines. What alone seems certain is that Greeks and Hebrews, in common with some other peoples, believed that the gods were jealous of human advancement in culture, and that human ills were due to the acquisition of such culture and also to female curiosity. The wide-spread belief in woman's power for evil, and the sexual tabus resulting from it, are sufficient to account for her place in many myths as the direct or indirect cause of the Fall. We may here compare a Delaware legend which tells how, in the beginning, men had tails, but for their wickedness these were cut off and changed into women, who would be a perpetual trouble to man (Hunter, *Memoirs of a Captivity among the Indians of N. America*, 1823).

In the story of Pandora later theological animus may be detected. In earlier times she seems to have been a great Earth-goddess, mother of all things. The tabued vessel may have been suggested by the grave-*pithos* from which primitive Greek belief held that the *keres* of death and disease fluttered forth. See J. E. Harrison, *Prolegomena to Greek Rel.*, 1903, p. 284 f. For a comparison of the Semitic and Greek stories, see Symonds, *Greek Poets*, 2nd ser., 1879, p. 115.

(4) In the **Persian** sacred writings a myth occurs which some think to have been borrowed from Jewish sources, while others suggest its influence on the Hebrew story. A careful examination of

the myth (which, possibly through earlier faulty translations, seemed to have closer resemblance to Gn 3 than it really possesses) shows that it may have been quite independent in origin, while it need not have exerted any exterior influence. It occurs in the *Bundahiš*, a work which, in its present form, dates from the 9th cent., but doubtless enshrines material of a vastly older date. There is no reason to suppose that the myth is not archaic, and its contents suggest an exceedingly primitive view of things. The *Bundahiš* describes the covenant made between Ahura Mazda and Ahriman (after the discovery of the former by the latter, towards the end of the first three thousand years) that Ahriman's power should last only nine thousand years. In the first three thousand Ahriman is caused to remain in confusion; in the second, he is triumphant; in the third and last, he is gradually overcome (see AGES OF THE WORLD [Zoroastrian], vol. i. p. 205). At the beginning of his triumphant career Ahriman is said to have made a rush at the creatures, 'springing, like a snake, out of the sky down to the earth.' He first destroyed the primeval ox, from whose body and seed various plants and animals proceeded. Next followed the destruction of Gāyōmarṭ, the archetypal man, but from his seed sprang a human pair, Māshya and Māshyōī, who existed first, apparently, as plants growing out of the earth, and were then changed into human form. To them Ahura Mazda said: 'You are man, you are the ancestry of the world, and you are created perfect in devotion by me; perform devotedly the duty of the law, think good thoughts, speak good words, do good deeds, and worship no demons!' After having washed themselves they acknowledged the power of Ahura Mazda, but now 'antagonism rushed into their minds,' so that they were thoroughly corrupted and declared the evil spirit to be the creator. 'That false speech was spoken through the will of the demons, . . . through it they both became wicked, and their souls are in hell until the future existence.' At first they drank only water and were clad in herbage; but after thirty days they drank the milk of a goat, expressing their delight in it, and by this second false speech enhancing the power of the demons. Thirty days later, they slaughtered and ate a sheep, roasting it with fire 'extracted by them out of the wood of the lote-plum and box-tree, through the guidance of the heavenly angels' (and probably by friction). The skin of the animal served them for clothes; later, they wore woven garments. They dug iron out of the earth, hammering it with a stone, cut down wood, and made a shelter from the sun. Their gracelessness increased; the demons became more oppressive; and they fell to fighting with each other. At the end of fifty years they were moved to desire of each other. A pair of offspring were born to them, but, 'owing to tenderness for offspring,' they devoured them. This 'tenderness' was taken from them by Ahura Mazda, so that their succeeding children remained alive. Here, as in the Hebrew and other Fall-stories, advance in culture is associated with a lapse from righteousness, but temptation is merely hinted at, and we learn only by inference that the drinking of milk and eating of flesh were forbidden. On the whole, the differences are greater than the resemblances, and we may have here an original and ancient myth, which at a later date may have received some colouring from Hebrew sources, but obviously is entirely Parsi in its teaching (*Bundahiš*, chs. i.–xv., in West's *Pahlavi Texts*, pt. i. *SBE* v. [1880]). In other parts of the *Bundahiš* it is clear that Ahriman seduces human creatures to evil, rather than that the evil comes from within themselves. So he announces his intention to the creator: 'I will force all thy creatures into disaffection to thee and affection for myself' (*Bund.* i. 14), and Ahura Mazda says he cannot rest at ease, for he must provide protection for his people against the seductions of Ahriman, who 'casts this into the thoughts of men, that this religion of Ahura Mazda is nought, and it is not necessary to be steadfast in it' (xxviii. 3–5). It is not clear that a taint of evil is inherited. At all events, king Yima, sixth in descent from Māshya, appears to have lived in righteousness 'till his glory (or reason) departed' (*Bund.* xxxiv. 4); when this happened he took a she-demon for wife through fear of the demons, and gave his sister Yimak to a demon as wife. 'From them have originated the tailed ape and bear and other species of degeneracy' (xxiii. 1). Yima is the Yama of the Vedas, who committed incest with his sister Yami, just as, in a later Pahlavi text, Yimak pretended to be Yima's demon-wife, and lay with him (*SBE* xviii. [1882] 419). Yima appears in the earlier Iranian writings (*Vendīdād*, ii.) as a righteous king whose reign was a time of innocence, without cold, heat, age, disease, death, or envy of the *daēvas*, and full of prosperity and productiveness (*Yasna*, ix.; *Yašt* xv.). Here, too, it is said his 'glory' departed through his lie, when he began to delight in falsehood (*Yašt* xix. 34). Firdūsī, in the 10th cent., says that the lie consisted in his pretending to be a god. Yima is not here the first man, though he may in an earlier myth have had that position; this, however, is rendered unlikely by the fact that he is through all the sacred writings placed in a later generation. Disease and death, too, were in the world before his time. He may, therefore, have simply been the ideal righteous king, who at last fell, like all other men, through the seductions of the *daēvas*. In the earliest writings of all, he also bears this righteous character, but is taken as an example of apostasy, apparently because he sinned through flesh-eating after having lived on vegetable food. The interpretation of the passage *Yasna*, xxxii. 8 is much disputed, and Tiele and others do not accept this rendering. There is no doubt, however, that the Iranians believed the earliest state of men to have been one of innocence and prosperity, when they lived on imperishable food and were free from the ills of life, and that all this came to an end through the envy of the *daēvas*, who corrupted men (*Yasna*, ix., xxxii. 5).

(5) The idea of man's hapless plight as a punishment is also suggested in myths which refer it to a wrong choice (like the choice of Plato's pre-existent souls, see § 5) made in the beginning of things. The Ashantis trace all their woes to the folly of their ancestors. In the beginning there were three white and three black men and women, who were told by a divinity to choose either a box or a piece of sealed-up paper. The blacks chose the box and found in it gold, iron, etc.; while the whites chose the paper, which contained wisdom. After their choice the blacks worshipped 'fetishes' instead of their high god (Hutton, *Voy. to Africa*, 1821, p. 320). So the Navahos assert that their ancestors chose a richly decorated jar which contained rubbish, and hence they are now poor and miserable; the Pueblos chose a coarse jar full of flocks and herds, and now enjoy plenty (Schoolcraft, *Indian Tribes*, iv. 90). The Ashanti myth probably existed before the appearance of the whites, and would then have referred to some other race, to judge by the analogy of the Navaho story. With both may be compared a Tongan and Fijian myth, alleged to be archaic, and also to have received its present application after contact with Europeans, to the effect that the first-born of mankind was disobedient to the Creator and grew black, while the second-

born, by virtue of a higher obedience, remained fair, and was the ancestor of the white race (Hale, *Exploring Exped.*, Philadelphia, 1846, p. 177).

The choice of a worse object and the obtaining of many benefits thereby, on the part of a hero or heroine, and the choice of a better object which produces nothing but evil to the malicious chooser, is a favourite theme of *Märchen*, in countless forms and in all parts of the world, civilized and savage (cf. § 5).

3. Myths of a Golden Age.—Combined in some cases with the myth of a Fall, and always predicating man's earlier innocence and happiness, is the legend of a Golden Age, or the more philosophic idea of a series of recurring world ages.

(1) Even among the lowest races, especially after contact with a higher civilization, such a conception is not wanting. The Bushmen tell how once they could 'make stone things that flew over rivers' (Lang, *Myth, Rit., and Rel.*, 1899, i. 169), while their myth of origins relates that once men and animals (who could speak) lived together till men made fire, which they had been forbidden to do, and so startled the animals that they lost the power of speech and fled ever afterwards from man's presence (Stow, *Races of S. Afr.*, 1905, p. 130). Cf. the Amer. Indian myth, ii. 2 (1), and the idea (as in the Prometheus legends) that fire is illicit. In Samoa, as elsewhere, we hear of a primitive Golden Age when all things could talk. The idea of a Golden Age in the past, lost through man's fault, took shape in various ways, but it was more immediately suggested by the almost instinctive conviction (common to old races as to old individuals) that things must once have been better, just as men generally hope that things will be better in the future. In some cases a people dwelling in comparative comfort and plenty in some desirable part of the earth, but driven out to a less pleasant region by a stronger race, would easily shape to themselves a legend of a happier state of things long ago, and with each generation the mythic happiness of that state would be increased. All migrations would tend to do the same, just as in some cases the dim memory of rivers and mountains crossed, joined with the desire to be buried in one's native place, suggested the idea of the journey of the soul over a perilous way to the land of the departed. Occasionally the memory of such migrations appears to be mixed up with myths of human origins; men came from below the earth or descended from the skies (see § 4). In the latter case the myth usually takes the form that men and gods then lived together, or that there was intercourse between heaven and earth; this ceased through some act of human folly (cf. the Tongan myth, ii. 1 (3)). Finally, the idea of the Golden Age may have been suggested to men by observing the happiness of the child, and by thinking that all men were thus happy in the childhood of the race.

(2) The most typical form of the Golden Age myth is the **Greek** one given by Hesiod in his *Works and Days* (following upon, but distinct from, his myth of Pandora), where we learn that a new race was formed in each of the series of successive ages, gradually deteriorating. The first age was that of the golden race of men, who were prosperous and happy, and passed from life as in a sleep. The second was the silver age, in which began sorrow; men could not refrain from injustice, and refused worship to the gods. The third was that of the race of bronze—a race of warriors who took away life with their own hands. Then came the fourth age, that of the men who fought at Thebes and Troy, now in the Isles of the Blest, where Kronos reigns; and, lastly, the iron age, that of the present, full of toil, wretchedness, and corruption. The Attic Cronia, like the Saturnalia, commemorated the fabled Golden Age, while both were a kind of harvest festival. According to Pindar (*Ol.* ii. 70), Kronos now reigns in the fortunate isles in a species of Golden Age. Among the Greek philosophers some trace of this tradition is found. Plato, in his *Critias* (xvi.), teaches that the human race started aright, but by gradual deterioration and loss of the divine admixture in their nature the early promise of mankind was broken. It also coloured **Roman** philosophic thought—Cicero, Seneca, and Lucretius asserting man's degeneration from a purer state, while in Ovid the Golden Age is connected with the native god of agriculture, Saturn, whose festival, the Saturnalia, represented that primitive happy state, though it is possible that the myth may have arisen to explain the festival. Saturn was identified with the Greek Kronos, and made the culture-hero and teacher of the happy people who owned his rule. Ovid's picture, doubtless, represents current mythic conceptions: it was an age without guilt or need of punishment or war: the earth produced its fruits without man's labour; there was eternal spring and abundant prosperity. In the succeeding ages of silver, brass, and iron, degeneracy began until the earth was filled with evil and violence, sorrow and toil and pain (*Metam.* bk. i.). To all this, however, there would be an end, and the Golden Age would return. Hence Virgil's prophecy:

'Jam redit et Virgo, redeunt Saturnia regna' (*Ecl.* iv. 6).

(3) It has been seen (ii. 2 (4)) that the **Iranian** Yima was king of a Golden Age of innocence, without disease or death, though, with the usual inconsistency of myth, death is already present in the world (*Yasna*, ix.), while this age is later than the time of the first man. Yima was directed by Ahura Mazda, after the evils of winter came to his territories, to make an 'enclosure' for his people, within which no evil things could come. Thither he was to bring 'the seeds of men and women of the greatest, best, and finest on this earth,' and seeds of the finest animals and plants; they bring forth two of their kind every forty years, and enjoy uninterrupted happiness (*Vendīdād*, ii.). This earthly Paradise somewhat resembles the kingdom of Yama in the other world, where he rules over the souls of the dead, as represented in the Rigveda (x. 14. 1, 2); and it is not impossible that the Iranian legend may have been coloured by the Indian, which is undoubtedly primitive, since the conception of the first man as ruler of the kingdom of the dead, whither he has first penetrated, is certainly early. But it is more likely that an earlier Iranian myth which made Yima the first to die and his people the souls of the dead who followed him had become corrupted in course of time into a belief in an enclosure filled with more or less supernatural beings (see Darmesteter, *SBE* iv. p. lxxv, *Introduction*; for another interpretation, cf. BLEST, ABODE OF THE [Persian]).

(4) **Confucianism,** which holds that man is made by nature virtuous, and might easily remain so, has its legends of a Golden Age of virtue and the true practice of religion, of innocence and happiness, without disease or death, which issued in the catastrophe of a flood, because, according to the *Li Ki*, men turned away from the Monarch of the universe, bent their eyes earthwards, loving sensuality, desiring knowledge, or, according to Lao-tse, to eat, and so became the prey of all miseries and addicted to all kinds of crime. Or, according to the *Shi King* (iii. 3. 1), men draw their being from heaven, but time and the environment in which they live soon produce error and sin. The primitive lapse is thus reproduced in the life of every man. The *Shi King* also describes the

virtuous and happy reigns of such kings as Wan; while, according to the *Shu King* (pt. v. bk. 27. 2), Khih Yu was the first to produce disorder, which spread among the people. But, as this rebel is held to have lived about 2700 B.C., the Chinese Golden Age is thus brought within historic times. A verse sometimes quoted from the *Shi King* (iii. bk. 3, ode 10, 3, Legge's translation), as proving that the Fall was due to a woman who overthrew her husband's wall of virtue, does not refer to a primitive fall, but only describes in general terms the weakness of even the best of women.

(5) Some trace of a myth of the Golden Age appears in ancient **Egyptian** religion. Maspero says: 'Certain expressions used by Egyptian writers are in themselves sufficient to show that the first generations of men were supposed to have lived in a state of happiness and perfection' (*Dawn of Civ.*[2], 1896, p. 158). They recalled the earthly reign of Rā in the beginning as a Golden Age long ago passed away. Men's wickedness had been the cause of its ending, and of Rā's leaving the earth and causing the death of its people at the hands of a goddess. But with the survivors a compact was made that they would no more be destroyed. Men looked back to that happy time with longing, and expressed it by the phrase 'the times of Rā,' while of anything which was superior of its kind they said that its like had not been seen since the days of Rā (Maspero, *op. cit.*; Lenormant, *Les Origines*, 1880–84, i. 448).

Connected with the legend of a Golden Age is the myth of a Paradise, not always, however, inhabited by the first human pair, as in Genesis, but by gods, or supernatural beings, or deathless men. Among the Greeks there is the conception of Elysium and the Islands of the Blest, as well as that of the Garden of the Hesperides, a home of the gods, in which Hera's golden apples grew on a tree guarded by a dragon which Herakles slew, afterwards stealing the fruit. Some have seen in the last an echo of Genesis (Lenormant, *Origines*, i. 94). But beyond the seductive beauty of both gardens and the mystic tree there is no real parallel: the dragon acts differently from the serpent, and Herakles is unrepresented in Genesis, while there is no temptation or 'Fall.' The Hindu sacred Mount Meru, with its gardens and four rivers, unapproachable by sinful man and guarded by a dragon, has its counterpart in the Iranian Alborz (Hara-berezaiti), the seat of Mithra, where there is no night, darkness, cold, putrefaction, or uncleanness (*Yašt* x. 50). A similar garden mountain, moistened by water flowing from the fountain of immortality and forming four rivers, and guarded by an animal called Kaiming, appears in Chinese mythology, and possibly was suggested by Buddhist influence. The fabled earthly Paradise is the counterpart in space of what the Golden Age is in time. Both are equally remote and usually inaccessible. Possibly the idea that Paradise with its Golden Age had been lost to men in the past led to the idea that it still existed far away, to be reached by adventurous or favoured mortals. The idea that gods dwelt with men in the past suggested the existence of an earthly home of the gods, while it doubtless helped to form myths of a Golden Age. That divine earthly home perhaps became also the inaccessible Paradise.

(6) *World-ages.*—Among various races cosmogonic speculation, in the attempt to conceive a beginning of things, has imagined a series of world-ages, which in some mythologies end each in a catastrophe, and are occasionally connected (as in Hesiod) with the Golden-Age myth. The Hindu world-ages are also connected with the theory of a Golden Age and of the gradual deterioration of mankind. In the Kṛta age all was perfect, men were innocent and happy, they had free intercourse with the gods, who frequently assumed human form and spoke to them of the divine world whither they would go. But in the next, or Tretā, age, men had departed from their primal perfection; in the third, or Dvāpara, age, doubt and atheism flourished; while in the present, or Kali, age, evil of all kinds predominates in human life. These four ages are but divisions of one in a vast series of cycles through which the universe passes, according to Hindu philosophic pantheism. Each cycle endures for 12,000 years, and each year is equivalent to 360 ordinary years (*Laws of Manu*, i. 68–86; *Viṣnu Purāṇa*, bk. i. cap. 3). Similar beliefs are found in Buddhism, while four ages, each terminating with a catastrophe (but unconnected with a Golden Age), were mythically represented in ancient Mexico (Clavigero, *Hist. of Mexico*, 1787, i. 401). With these may be compared the Stoic world-years (Plutarch, *de Orac. Def.*) and Plato's speculations. In other cases (*e.g.* Scandinavian and Persian) four great ages include the whole drama of the universe, and involve gods rather than men; both show, however, how for an age the gods had peace, and assert the coming reign of peace and right (*Corpus Poeticum Boreale*, 1883; *Bundahiš*, xxxiv.). A late Persian legend tells how Ahura Mazda showed to Zarathuštra a tree with four branches, of gold, silver, steel, and iron, representing four periods yet to come—of revelation and its acceptance; of the reigns of two succeeding kings; and, lastly, of the evil sovereignty of the demons. In a variant there are seven branches and seven periods. The whole is couched in the form of a prophecy, while it describes past events; its form may owe something to the Greek myth; and the age of revelation is dimly adumbrated as a true Golden Age (West, *Pahlavi Texts*, i. 192, 198). It is quite distinct from the earlier conception of the great ages of Iranian mythology. See AGES OF THE WORLD.

(7) While these myths of a Golden Age make the deterioration of mankind a gradual affair, those others, of the origin of death or of a Fall, show how it was produced at one fell stroke, though the myths frequently tell how the previous condition of man was a Golden Age of peace, innocence, and plenty. It should be noted, however, especially in connexion with the idea of a series of world-ages, which appears also in primitive mythologies, that, in contradistinction to a primitive Golden Age, it is sometimes held that various races of men were created and then destroyed as being unfit for survival, and inadequate to their surroundings. The existing race is thus a survival of the fittest. We find this in Brāhmanic myths, in the Quiché *Popol Vuh* (with the further idea that some of the earlier peoples degenerated into apes), and among lower races (Lang, *op. cit.* i. 202). This view also resembles a widespread mythical conception of the ancestors of the race being ignorant of the arts and given up to various evil practices, *e.g.* cannibalism, until they were taught better by a god or a divine culture-hero. The race thus improved instead of deteriorating, and an ascent of man is postulated (in line with the teaching of modern science) instead of a descent from better things. The idea of Aristotle (*Pol.* ii. 8) was that men were at first on a level of ignorance and darkness; and that of Æschylus, in his version of the Prometheus story, that men lived in caves and were wretched till enlightened by Prometheus. The latter may point to a Greek myth differing from that of the Golden Age, just as in Egypt a myth, contrary to that already noticed above (5), told how Osiris weaned the first people from a condition of bestial savagery. In Babylon, according to Berosus, Oannes taught men, who till then had lived as beasts, while the Babylonian epic of Gilgameš makes Eabani live with beasts as a beast till the sacred prostitute, Ukhat, shows him a higher life (cf. Jastrow, *Relig. of Bab. and Assyr.*, Boston, 1898, p. 476 ff.). The same people sometimes hold simultaneously the most diverse myths—products, in certain cases, of different tribes or races which have amalgamated—without any thought of their incongruity. Yet even in such cases, so long as the divine culture-hero remains among the people whom he has taught, there is for them a kind of Golden Age. Then he takes his departure, promising to return; but till that time men must live in toil and pain.

This was a frequent myth among all branches of the American Indian race.

The Greek myth of Saturn's reign and the Egyptian of Rā's both postulate the presence of a divine being with men during their state of innocence.

4. Myths of a lost intercourse between gods and men.—Analogous to the idea of the divine culture-hero dwelling with men for a time in a kind of Golden Age is the belief (related to that of a Golden Age), found among many races, that at the earliest period of human existence there was free intercourse between gods and men, heaven and earth, either by some method of reaching the sky or by men having actually dwelt with the gods. This is usually part of a myth explaining the origin of man, who, as was sometimes thought, came from that glad upper world. Various reasons are assigned for that intercourse having ceased; occasionally it is human curiosity, weakness, or error which caused this happy state of things to end; but it may also arise through ancestor-worship, especially where the ancestors worshipped have become gods, from whom the people or their rulers trace their descent. In Andamanese mythology, the high god Puluga lived with men till they tried to kill him. He answered that he was 'as hard as wood,' and that if they persisted in disobeying him he would destroy them and the world with them. This is the last occasion on which he made himself visible (Man, *JAI* xii. 167). Among the Kurnai of S. Australia it is held that a great being, Mungan-ngaua, once lived on earth and taught them all the arts they know. He instituted the Jeraeil (mysteries), but some traitor once revealed the secrets of these mysteries to the women. Mungan sent fire between heaven and earth so that men went mad with fear; then the sea rushed over the earth, drowning all save a few, who became ancestors of the Kurnai. Some of these were changed into animals. Mungan then left the earth and now remains in the sky (Howitt, *Nat. Tribes of S.E. Aust.*, 1904, p. 630). Among the Negroes of Fernando Po it is held that once there was a ladder from heaven to earth by which the divine beings descended to men, until a cripple started to ascend. His mother chased him, and the gods, horrified at the sight, and at the possible intrusion on their domain, threw down the ladder, and have left humanity alone ever since (M. H. Kingsley, *Trav. in W. Afr.*, 1897, p. 507). The Fantis have a myth which tells how the first men lived in a lofty and desirable land, but were driven from it to the lower world in order to learn humility (Smith, *Nouveau Voyage de Guinée*, 1744, ii. 176). The people of Guiana hold that their forefathers once lived happily above the sky. But curiosity tempted them to descend to earth by means of a rope-ladder and to taste its food. One of their number (in one of the variants, a woman) stuck in the hole in the sky, thus preventing all possibility of return. There are several variants of this myth, some of which tell of men's longing to return to heaven, and their condemnation to remain below in spite of their pleading (Brett, *Legends of B. Guiana*, 1880, p. 103 f.). A myth of the same kind, found among the Kirghiz, is also connected with the earlier Golden Age. On the top of Mt. Mustagh-ata is an ancient city built in the days of universal happiness. Since that time ceased there has been no intercourse between its inhabitants, who are still happy, and the fallen race of men (Sven Hedin, *Through Asia*, 1898, i. 221). Instances of divine beings descending to earth and thus losing their immortality have already been referred to (ii. 1 (3), 2 (2), Tongan, Hindu, Tibetan), and exemplify this conception, which is also met with in the myths of various tribes of the Algonquin stock. A divine woman, for some reason which varies in different myths, but which is occasionally said to have been disobedience or immorality, is banished from heaven to earth, and falls on the back of the turtle, who then sends another animal to fish up the earth, where she becomes mother of a dualistic pair of demi-gods and also of the human race (Brinton, *American Hero-Myths*, 1882, p. 54).

5. Myths of a Fall in a former existence.—This latter notion of a fault committed in a higher state leading to banishment to the earth is the basis of those myths and beliefs which trace man's Fall and his present misery to his wrong-doing in a pre-existent state. Metempsychosis, wherever it is held in an ethical form, presupposes the idea of a Fall. In Hindu belief, the souls which departed from the primal essence were condemned to existence in the body within a purgatorial world, and each life is now conditioned by its conduct in the former. The misery of life is thus a direct penalty for the primal Fall as well as for the sins of all succeeding existences (Manu, vi. 77, 78). This idea of human life as a purgatory, whether borrowed from Egypt or not, appears sporadically in Greek religious and philosophic thought. Pythagoras and his school postulated the guilt of the soul in a higher state as the cause of its separation from the divine and its imprisonment in the body, through one or several existences (Zeller, *Pre-Soc. Phil.*, 1881, i. 48), and Empedocles taught that mundane existence was the doom of souls hurled earthwards from the heaven of which they had proved unworthy. This, too, according to Plato, was the Orphic doctrine—the soul expiated in the prison of the body the sins it had committed in a previous existence. Plato himself, while sometimes teaching the belief in a Golden Age, lays stress on pre-existence and a Fall in that earlier state, due either to indolence, weakness, and perverseness, or to a wrong choice of the destinies of life (cf. the Ashanti myth above, 2 (5); *Phædr.* 246; *Repub.* x. 2. 614). A similar doctrine of the Fall appears in Philo and in Origen, and has been upheld by later Christian philosophers, *e.g.* Müller in his *Christian Doctrine of Sin*, Eng. tr., 1885 (see PRE-EXISTENCE).

6. Myths of a divine Fall.—A more profound thought is reached in the occasional myths which tell of the Fall of a god. In most of those myths concerning the Fall of the first of men they are conceived as almost more than human—the first man is sometimes a creator, or, when he dies, he becomes king of the dead. It has been seen, too, how immortal gods lose their immortality and become the first of men through descending to earth and eating its fruits (see ii. 1 (3), 2 (2)). Wherever dualism prevails (and it runs like a coloured thread through the stuff of most mythologies), the divinities are usually subject to the attack of evil beings—titans, giants, wicked divinities, serpents, etc.—and are frequently defeated by them. Though this defeat is not, strictly speaking, a Fall, yet it shows a strain of weakness in the gods, such as is also adumbrated in the thought of an immutable fate to which the gods must be subject, *e.g.* the divinities of Scandinavia could not avert the death of Balder. Again, that strain of weakness is seen in the idea, so prominent in Zoroastrianism, and which occurs even in savage mythologies, that the works of the good creator, and especially man, are subject to, and frequently overcome by, the attacks and wiles of the wicked divinity. Where myths of a divine Fall exist, they occasionally show how it affected for the worse the lot of man. In a Hindu example, Brahmā was seized with a guilty passion for his daughter Sarasvatī, which he could not resist, and, pursued by the reproaches of his creatures, he quitted the body which he had soiled; or, according to a legend in the Purāṇas, being proud of his works and wishing to make himself equal with the supreme Being, he was sunk by him in matter, followed by all his creatures (B. Constant, *De la Religion*, iv. 116, 117). A genuine ancient Mexican myth relates that Quetzalcoatl, Tezcatlipoca, and their brethren were gods in heaven and passed their time in a rose-garden until they began plucking roses from the great rose-tree in the centre of the garden. Thereupon Tonaco-tecutli, in his anger at their action, hurled them to earth, where they lived as mortals (Brinton, *Amer. Hero-Myths*, p. 95). Two curious Scandinavian myths in the *Edda*, both ancient, and the first of them certainly dating from heathen times, suggest a fall of the gods. In the *Völuspá* we read, 'The Æsir met on Ida's plain: They altar-steads and temples high constructed. Their strength they proved, All things tried, Furnaces established, Precious things forged; Formed tongs, and fabricated tools; At tables played at home; Joyous they were; To them was naught the want of gold, Until there came Thurs-maidens three, All powerful from Jötunheim.' There is here a suggested weakening of the gods and an end of their happy state on Ida's plain, through the seductions of these female giants, just as the seductive Pandora brought evil upon men (Thorpe, *Edda of Sæmund*, 1866, 'Völuspá,' stanzas 7 and 8). The other myth, which occurs in 'Bragi's telling,' relates how Loki was seized by an eagle (a giant in that shape) who would not let him go till he took oath to bring to him Iðunn, guardian of the gods' apples of immortality, out of Asgard. Loki agreed, and lured Iðunn into a wood under pretence of comparing her apples with others which he had found. There she was seized by the giant, who fled with her. Loki would have been punished by the sorrowful gods had he not agreed to go and seek her in Jötunheim. Thence he brought her, pursued by the giant, who was slain by the gods (Dasent's translation of *Edda*, p. 86). The seduction of the goddess is involuntary on her part, but the story resembles Loki's final revolt against the gods, of whom he was one, as a result of the giant nature which was in part his.

A war between two classes of supernatural beings, and the utter ruin and banishment of one of them to a lower state, is the subject of various myths—Greek, gods and Titans; Scandinavian, gods and giants; Hindu, gods and demons, etc. (for other examples, see Baring-Gould, *Legends of OT Char.*, i. 5 f.). Some such idea, connected with that of a fall of higher powers, underlies the vague statements in the Bible regarding the fall of the angels, so much developed in Rabbinical and Muhammadan lore (cf. *Book of Enoch*), while it forms a central doctrine in various Gnostic systems and in Manichæism.

The Fall and the Flood.—In some cases peoples who have a myth of the Fall have also a Deluge-myth. Sometimes this is directly brought into connexion with the Fall as its punishment; in other cases it is a separate event, usually resulting as the punishment of further human wickedness. Or, again, it is merely a catastrophe ending one or more of the successive world-ages. In some myths all human beings are swept away and a new race is formed; in others, a few survive who re-people the earth. Andamanese myths are examples of a flood as a direct punishment of a Fall (see ii. 2). The Caribs also say that men at first lived in happiness and to a great age, until they became wicked and a flood came and swept them away (de la Borde, *Reise zu den Caraiben*, 1684, i. 380). See DELUGE; Baring-Gould, *Legends of OT Char.* i. 116–133; Lenormant, *Les Origines*, p. 382 f.

iii. *COMPARATIVE STUDY OF FALL-MYTHS.*—1. With few exceptions, the surveys of Fall-myths have been uncritical. Anxiety to prove the truth of the Biblical story of the Fall has led several writers to find echoes of it in myths and legends from all parts of the world. It was enough for such apologists to discover a myth of a tree, or a serpent, or of both together, or of a woman and a serpent, to see in it a corruption of the Hebrew story, which they suppose to have once been common to all races of mankind. But wherever tree-worship, or serpent-worship, or totemism has prevailed, such myths are inevitable, and it is far from unlikely that all these and other elements were laid under contribution in the gradual formation of the Hebrew myth. But myths involving any or all of these elements need not have any connexion with it. Examples of such forcing of myths into a connexion with Genesis are the Greek story of Eurydice bitten to death by a serpent; the similar Hindu story of Pramadvarā's death and her recovery by her lover Ruru, as told in the Mahābhārata; the Mexican myth, also represented in hieroglyphic pictures, of the mother of mankind attended by a huge serpent; the Babylonian myth of the conflict of Tiāmat and Marduk; the Egyptian myth of the conflict of Typhon and Osiris; the Hindu tales of divinities, such as Kṛṣṇa, striving with, and overcoming, monstrous serpents; or of Indra, victor over the serpent Ahi; the Greek legends of Apollo and the python, or of the dragon slain by Minerva; Mexican stories of a huge serpent slain by Tezcatlipoca; the Scandinavian myth of the Midgard serpent, offspring of Loki, overcome by Thor. All these are held by such apologists as Deane (*Worship of the Serpent*[2], 1833) and Faber (*Horæ Mosaicæ*[2], 1818, i.) to be pagan versions, derived from a distorted reminiscence of primitive history, of the temptation of the woman by the serpent, and of the overcoming of the tempter by a promised Deliverer. On the other hand, Doane (*Bible Myths and their Parallels*[4], 1882) and Higgins (*Anacalypsis*, 1878) throw discredit on the Biblical narrative by the existence of these stories. Both methods are equally uncritical.

2. Again, a Babylonian cylinder showing a horned man and a woman sitting on either side of a tree and plucking its fruits, while a serpent is seen behind the woman; a bas-relief from Rome representing two persons standing near a tree encircled by a serpent; a painted vase from Cyprus, of Phœnician provenance, with a tree from whose branches hang bunches of fruit which a serpent is in the act of taking—are sometimes cited as witnessing to the existence of a myth, akin to the Hebrew, in the lands where they have been found, or, at least, to the diffusion westwards of a Semitic story of the Fall (see Delitzsch, *Babel und Bibel*, 1905, p. 37; Lenormant, *op. cit.* i. 106).

3. **The serpent in mythology.**—It is certainly a striking fact that the serpent or a fabled dragon should so universally be chosen as the symbol of evil, physical or moral. The explanation is probably to be found not in distortions of the story of a primitive temptation and Fall, but in the fact that the serpent or other reptiles, and possibly occasional survivals of extinct monsters, must have struck early man everywhere with terror or aroused his amazement. In many mythologies, Vedic, Amer. Indian, etc., the serpent is the guardian of the waters. We may see in this a memory of the time when such creatures—pre-historic monsters or large serpents—lived in or near the waters and levied a toll on human life, especially from those who came to draw water. Stories of their destruction would easily attach themselves to the mythic cycles of this or the other god, and gradually assume a more ethical form, until a mythic

serpent or dragon became the symbol of darkness or evil (as in the myths referred to above), or elsewhere remained the enemy of man, keeping back the most valuable treasure, water, from him. The mysterious, uncanny, and demoniac nature of the serpent would easily make it the vehicle of man's mythic fancies, sometimes his fabled enemy, but also possessor of a higher wisdom and occasionally man's friend — a character which the serpent of Genesis may have had in the earlier forms of the story (see Barton, *Sem. Origins*, 1902, p. 93). On the other hand, the myths which speak of women overcome by a serpent are not to be confused with the Biblical story in its present form — of a woman tempted by a serpent to evil. The latter, however, may have some connexion with a whole series of myths and *Märchen* in which the serpent has a mysterious relation to woman—her lover, seducer, or husband. These stories arose from the general animistic and totemistic idea that men and beasts had much in common, and that there was a time when their qualities were identical. But the persistent appearance of the serpent rather than other animals in such stories may have some other significance besides, and, taken in connexion with a series of myths showing that menstruation originated from woman's having been bitten by a snake, that significance is possibly phallic.

Ch. Schoebel, in *Le Mythe de la femme et du serpent*, 1876, seeks to show that the story of Genesis and its supposed correlates referred to above have a phallic significance. As soon as man, until then bi-sexual, became two, male and female, the sexual act was committed after having been forbidden. By it, man thought to put himself on a level with the creator and to equal his creative power by the force of the flesh. This failed; hence his shame and also his punishment.

LITERATURE.—Most writers on the subject have written either from the apologetic or from the destructive standpoint—to prove or disprove the truth of Genesis. Their studies are unsatisfactory and forced. In the best commentaries on Genesis some parallels are usually cited, but frequently these are exaggerated, especially that from the *Bundahiš*, where it is doubtful whether the demon had the form of a serpent, as is asserted. The reader may be referred to Kalisch's, Dillmann's, and Driver's Comm. on *Genesis*; C. Geikie, *Hours with the Bible*, Lond. 1881, vol. i. ch. 2; S. Baring-Gould, *Legends of OT Characters*, do. 1871, vol. i. ch. 4; F. Lenormant, *Les Origines de l'histoire*, Paris, 1880, vol. i. ch. 2; B. Constant, *De la Religion*, do. 1824, vol. iv.; C. Hardwick, *Christ and Other Masters*, Camb. 1855–1858; F. R. Tennant, *Sources of the Doctrines of the Fall and Original Sin*, do. 1903, ch. 2; cf. also the other authorities cited in the article.

J. A. MACCULLOCH.

FALL (Muslim).—The Fall (*hubūṭ*) of Adam and his wife from Paradise is repeatedly epitomized in the Qur'ān (ii. 33–36, vii. 18–24, xx. 115–121), with slight variations. The temptation is ascribed to Iblīs ([D]iabolos, the D being mistaken for the Syriac sign of the genitive), determined to injure Adam, before whom he had declined to prostrate himself when commanded to do so. Adam, intended by God to be His deputy on earth, is told that he and his wife are to dwell in the Garden, and eat thereof where they will, only not to approach one tree, 'lest they be wrongdoers'; they are also warned that Satan is their enemy, who will try to drive them out of the Garden. Satan, whose purpose was 'to reveal to them that nakedness of theirs which was concealed from them,' offers to show them a tree of perpetuity and unending sovereignty, assures them that they have been forbidden to eat of it only lest they might become angels or immortal, and swears that he is their true friend. They eat, their nakedness appears, and they begin to stitch leaves from the Garden to cover themselves. Upbraided by God, they implore forgiveness, but are told to descend, enemies of each other.

The hints which the Qur'ān contains were amplified by the Muslims from the Jewish and Christian records and their own fancies. In the chronicle of Ṭabarī († A.H. 310 = A.D. 922) the name of Eve (*Ḥawwā*) is introduced, and the serpent (originally a quadruped,[1] not unlike a camel) is employed to carry Iblīs in its mouth and so elude the guardians of Paradise, who would not have admitted him. It is also Eve who first experiments with the fruit, and, finding it harmless, persuades Adam to eat. There are thus four persons involved in the story—Adam, Eve, Iblīs, and the serpent (who loses his legs in consequence of his service to Iblīs). The four, when thrown down from the Garden, fall in different places: Adam somewhere in India, either on a mountain called Wāsim near a valley called Bahīl between Dahnaj and Mandal, or in Ceylon on a mountain called Budh (for which most authorities [*e.g.* Mas'ūdī, ed. Barbier de Meynard, 1861, i. 60; Muqaddasī, ed. de Goeje, 1877, p. 13] substitute Rahūn); Eve at Jeddah; Iblīs at Maisan or Abolla; and the snake at Iṣfahān or Sijistan (Damīrī, *Zoological Dictionary*, Cairo, 1309, *s.v.* 'Ḥayyah'). Adam's footprint, 70 cubits long, was shown on the mountain in Ceylon; the other foot landed in the sea at two or three days' distance (Ibn Khordadbeh, ed. de Goeje, 1889, p. 64). At first Adam was so tall that, standing on the earth, he could hear the singing of the angels in heaven, but his height was afterwards reduced. He brought down with him various leaves of the Garden, which account for the perfumes of Ceylon; and, according to Mas'ūdī, a sheaf of wheat and branches of some thirty fruit-trees. He and Eve met at 'Arafāt, and this event is commemorated by some other local names connected with the Meccan pilgrimage.

The Fall is of far less consequence in Muslim theology than in Christian, because the former—which employs it to account for weeds, the antipathy to snakes, and the troubles of menstruation and child-bed—does not use it to account for *death*; indeed, it infers from the words of the Qur'ān that man had not been created immortal, whence Satan could tempt Eve by a promise of immortality. Besides this, Adam is invested with the character of Prophet, whence he himself makes good the consequences of the Fall. But a question which gives rise to considerable discussion is the relation of the Garden whence Adam was expelled to the Garden which is promised to Believers. The various opinions held on this subject, with the arguments in support of them, are collected in the Eschatology of Ibn Qayyim al-Jauziyyah († A.H. 751 = A.D. 1350; *Works*, 1325, i. 43–80), who shows that the founders of legal as well as theological schools have expressed themselves on it. Those who (following the example of Ibn Qutaibah [† 276]) are content to supplement the Qur'ānic texts from the OT naturally hold that the scene of the Fall is some place on the earth; and the name 'Eden' is identified by them with '*Adan*, or Aden, in Yemen. But this word is certainly used of heaven in the Qur'ān (xix. 62, etc.); and, if the Qur'ānic texts alone be considered, the result appears to be a drawn battle; it is certain that, according to the *sūras*, Adam was created on and for the earth, and that the Garden whence he fell is the Garden which is promised to Believers. The suggestion that Adam, though created on earth, had been, like the Prophet, taken up into heaven, was, indeed, made, but found few supporters; for such a miracle could scarcely pass unnoticed.

Muslim writers ordinarily assume acquaintance with certain parts of the story which are not found in the Qur'ān, especially the name *Eve* (meaning in Arabic 'black,' just as *Adam* means 'red'), and her causing the Fall and expulsion from Paradise

[1] According to Jewish Midrashic literature, the serpent of the Garden originally had feet (Gray, *XIV Cong. internat. des orientalistes*, i. [1905] 186).

(*Alf Lailah*, ed. Macnaghten, 1839, i. 7, tr. Payne, 1882–84, i. 7). Familiarity with the story of the serpent is often assumed also (*e.g.* Damīrī, *s.v.* 'Ḥayyah').

LITERATURE.—Ṭabarī, Ibn Qayyim al-Jauziyyah, etc., as above.

D. S. MARGOLIOUTH.

FALSEHOOD.—See LYING.

FAMILY.

FAMILY (Primitive).—**1. Rudimentary forms of family life among lower animals.**—Traces of the grouping, more or less permanent, of parents and offspring usually understood by the term 'family' are found among the lower animals: among birds, companionship of male and female after pairing, the sharing of labour in building the nest, of incubation, and of the care of the young while they are unable to look after themselves, present close analogies to the essential functions of the human family. On the other hand, among some mammals, especially the carnivora, the protection which the family organization would demand from the male is lacking, and the offspring sometimes become, or would become but for the protection of the mother, the prey of the male. The quadrumana, especially the anthropoids, in the relation of the parents to one another and to their young, seem to approach more nearly to the human type. It is recorded of the gorillas that they move about in bands consisting of females and one male, while the male builds a nest for the female and sleeps at the foot of the tree to protect her and the young at night. The chimpanzee is said to act in the same manner, and the evidence (Wallace, *Malay Archipelago*, London, 1869, i. 93) points in the same direction in the case of the orang-utan.

The essential features which make it possible to speak of family life among the lower animals are the provision for the needs of the female and the protection of both the female and the young, by which the family becomes an organization directed towards the preservation of the species. The human family is organized upon the same basis, the chief difference being its greater permanence, due in the first instance to the longer period during which the children require the care and protection of their parents.

2. Functions of man and woman as members of family group.—(*a*) *Man.*—Subject to certain qualifications, it may be said that among primitive races the functions of the senior members of the family are clearly recognized. The duties of the male are to protect the female, to supply her with a habitation, and to provide food, sometimes by agricultural labour, more often by the chase. Instances may be quoted of the views of primitive peoples on these points.

The Patwin of California held strongly that it was the duty of the father to support his family (Powers, 'Tribes of California,' *Contributions to N. Amer. Ethnology*, Washington, 1877, iii. 222). Among the Iroquois, during the first year of marriage, the products of a man's hunting belonged entirely to his wife, and subsequently were shared equally with her (Heriot, *Travels through the Canadas*, London, 1807, p. 338). Admiral Fitzroy (*Voyages of the Adventure and Beagle*, London, 1839, ii. 182) records that among the Fuegians a youth who desired to marry must show that he was capable of supporting a wife by hunting and fishing. Among the Botocudos, girls were married at a very early age, but after marriage remained with their father until nubile; the husband, however, was required to support his wife (J. von Tschudi, *Reisen durch Südamerika*, Leipzig, 1866–69, ii. 283). Among the Kurnai, a man was required to support his family with the assistance of his wife (Howitt-Fison, *Kamilaroi and Kurnai*, Melbourne, 1880, p. 206). In Samoa it was considered the duty of a man to support and protect his wife, and the duty of the wife to obey her husband and to wait upon him and upon any visitors (Brown, *Polynesians and Melanesians*, London, 1910, p. 43). Im Thurn records that among the Indians of British Guiana a man must show that he could do a day's work and support a family before he was allowed to marry (*Indians of Guiana*, London, 1883, p. 221). Prowess in fighting as well as in hunting was also required. The head-hunting Dayaks of Borneo, as well as the Nāgās, make marriage depend upon the number of heads taken by the aspirant (Bock, *Headhunters of Borneo*, London, 1881, p. 216; Dalton, *Descrip. Ethnol. of Bengal*, Calcutta, 1872, p. 40). Among the Kafirs and Bechuana of S. Africa, the bridegroom elect must have killed a rhinoceros (Livingstone, *Miss. Travels and Researches in S. Africa*, London, 1857, p. 147). In Burma, failure to support constituted a ground for divorce (Fytche, *Burma Past and Present*, London, 1878, ii. 73). The obligation to contribute to the support of a wife was even continued after the marriage had been dissolved; and, when the husband died, the duty of supporting her devolved on the husband's relatives.

(*b*) *Woman.*—The provision towards the support of his wife and family made by the male parent naturally varied according to the character of the community. Where the staple of life was obtained by hunting and fishing, the provision of food fell largely to the father; and among pastoral peoples the care of the flocks and herds was also his duty. Agriculture originally fell to the lot of the woman, as is still the case among the majority of the Bantu peoples of Africa. In Melanesia, where both men and women work in the plantations, the duties of each sex are strictly defined. The woman was also responsible for such domestic duties as the collecting of fuel, the cooking, the making of pots, weaving, and the care of the children. The position of the woman varied, from the almost complete subjection to her husband of the Australian *gin* to the supreme authority of the woman in the long house of the Senecas. The customs attendant on exogamy and the tracing of descent through the mothers tended to place restrictions upon the power of the husband, while vesting it in the woman's male relatives; but even in the exogamous and matrilineal societies of Melanesia the husband and father was supreme in authority in his own household, and the wife's authority, so far as dependent on status, did not exist. In Africa, among the Bantu races, even where, as is still largely the case, matrilineal descent prevailed, the authority of the husband and father was paramount except in certain matters, in which traces of the authority of the kin remained. Among the Baganda, for instance, the wife's kin hold the husband responsible for negligence in the event of the wife's adultery.

(*c*) *Relation to children.*—The early care of the children naturally devolved upon the mother, but, in the case of the boys, after infancy they passed from her tutelage. Among the Australian tribes, boys were under the care of their father; but in a matrilineal society of primitive type the claims of the kin cause them to pass to the care of their maternal uncle, who is also sometimes responsible for their preparation for initiation. In the Torres Straits this claim is also to some extent recognized in the case of girls; when the time arrives for their initiation, they are handed over to their maternal aunts for instruction and preparation (Haddon, *Head-Hunters*, London, 1901, p. 135). As a rule, however, the children live with their parents until their marriage; or, in the case of boys and where the institution of a men's house is recognized, until their initiation, or attainment to the age of puberty.

3. The dwelling-place and the family.—One of the urgent needs of human existence is some form of shelter against the inclemency of the weather. The dwelling-place, as the centre which, through early habit and by custom, has come to be recognized as the gathering place for those who are closely connected by birth, has played an important part in the development of the family and of the acknowledgment of the common obligations and privileges it entails. In the early stages of human society, a camp-fire, with at most a screen of boughs or some natural hollows in the lee of the rock as a shelter against the wind, served to give warmth and protection to a mother, her children, and their male protector. As the group increased in numbers by the birth of children and the accession of husbands for the daughters, owing to the desire for companionship and the protection of contiguity, the tendency would at first be to enlarge the shelter rather than for the group to split into a number of smaller groups, each with a shelter of its own.

The Rock Veddas of Ceylon, who live in caves and rock-shelters, and in this respect present a parallel to the Palæolithic inhabitants of the Madelenian epoch of Europe, are an example of a people at an early stage in the development of the communal house inhabited by the members of one family or kin. The Veddas reckon descent through the mother, and the husband on marriage joins his wife's family group, of which the head is his maternal uncle, his wife being his cousin. Each group, consisting of husband, wife, daughters, and daughters' husbands, is recognized as the owner of a cave. Within the cave, however, each of the smaller groups within the kin group, *i.e.* the families, has a fire of its own, around which the members sit at night. No family ever usurps the place of another (Seligmann, *The Veddas*, Camb. 1911, p. 625 ff.). This represents the beginnings of the large communal houses which have been found in various parts of the world, the best known examples, perhaps, being the long houses of the N. American Indians, which sheltered not merely one but several kin. Among the Orang Mamaq of Sumatra, each *suku*, or clan, lived under one roof (Wilken, quoted by Hartland, *Primitive Paternity*, London, 1910, i. 264). The communal house has reached its most elaborate form in Borneo in the Lelak village, where as many as 200 families may live under one roof, each in separate apartments, with doors opening out on to a common verandah (Haddon, 331). The raised communal houses of the clan found in Kiwai Island in the Torres Straits resemble the Vedda cave-dwelling in internal arrangement, each family having its own hearth (Haddon, 99). The men's house or club house of Melanesia—found wherever Melanesian influence has penetrated, as, for example, in Fiji—in which all unmarried men live between the time when they leave their own family on attaining puberty and their marriage, is a relic of the communal house. The separate hearth for each member is a record of the distribution of the occupants in families in the earlier stage. A reminiscence of the communal house also exists among the Bontoc Igorot of the Philippines, but in this case the club house belongs to the girls of the village. When it is realized that the secret society to which the club house belongs has in Melanesia taken the place of the social group of the tribe into which young men were introduced by initiation ceremonies which conferred upon them the status of manhood and made them members of the tribe, their relation to the communal house and their position in relation to the development of the family and family life become clear. The custom in Fiji, by which a man leaves his wife and family and returns to the club house for a lengthy period after the birth of a child, is not merely a matter of convenience but a ceremonial reversion to an earlier stage.

The extension of the dwelling, if local circumstances are favourable, is an obvious method of accommodating an increase in numbers, as well as the most likely to impress forcibly upon the outsider the importance of the kin. The Pueblo value daughters more than sons, for the reason that they add to the power and importance of their family by the introduction of their husbands into the group; instead of the newly married pair seeking a home of their own, more apartments are added to the already elaborate cliff-dwellings characteristic of this people (Mindeleff, *13 RBEW* [1896] 197). The communal house, however, is not the only or, indeed, the more usual result of the expansion of the family or the kin. Its construction presents difficulties which can be overcome only in peculiarly favourable conditions, and it is only in localities presenting such conditions that it would be feasible that all the daughters' husbands and families should be permanently accommodated in the parents' dwellings. The normal course of development has rather been in an opposite direction, and it is here that the house has played a more important part in the development of family life.

Sometimes only temporary residence with the wife's family was demanded, the married children subsequently building dwellings for themselves around or near the parents' abode, as among the Arawak. After the death of the parents, the group which had formed around the original home split up, each going its own way to form the nucleus of a new settlement (Im Thurn, 186, 221). The growth of a settlement by the grouping of the dwellings of married children near the parents' house finds a parallel in Florida Island in Melanesia (Codrington, *The Melanesians*, Oxford, 1891, p. 61), where, however, the land appropriated for the dwelling belongs to the husband's kin. Many primitive peoples make the provision of a house a condition of the recognition, partial or complete, of a husband's position and rights over his wife and children. Among the Yaos and Anyanja, when the intending bridegroom has obtained permission to marry from the relatives of his bride and afterwards from his own people, he returns to the bride's village 'to build the house,' the ceremony taking place when it is nearing completion (Werner, *Natives of British Central Africa*, London, 1906, p. 131). The further step, when the husband, usually after the claims of the kin or the bride's parents have been recognized by payment of the bride price, is allowed to take his wife to his own village, involves a more or less complete recognition of the independence of the husband as against the claim of the kin. In the case of the Melanesian custom mentioned above, the distinction between the kin and the family is recognized on both sides; on the female side by residence with the husband's kin, on the male side by the appropriation of communal land, subject to rights of inheritance, to the needs of an individual and his family.

4. Polygamy and the family.—The polygamous marriage presents points of interest in this connexion. The earliest form of this type of marriage is probably the *pirauru* custom found in Australia, whereby a native, when sojourning with a tribe other than his own, is provided with a temporary consort from the class with which marriage would be permissible. Among the Yakuts, a man who travelled a great deal used to marry a woman in each of the villages to which he usually resorted, and in W. Africa the same custom was followed by native traders. In New Guinea, as the different classes lived in separate villages, no wife would live with the husband, and, if all the wives belonged to distinct classes, each would live in a different village (Brown, p. 119). A trace of this form of localized polygamy was preserved, when the bride followed her husband, in the practice of assigning a separate hut to each wife and her children, as, for instance, in the Kafir kraal and the enclosures of the other Bantu races of Africa. The same custom existed in the case of the chiefs in Samoa, where the wife did not enter the family of her husband (Brown, p. 43). Among the Anyanja of Central

Africa, the free wife stayed in her own village; her husband did not necessarily remain with her, as the men, especially the Angoni, spent much time in travelling, usually on trading expeditions. If he had more than one free wife, he divided his time between their different villages. The men also had slave wives, who either followed the husband or lived in his village. If he took up his residence permanently with his chief wife in her village, his slave wives followed him, lived in his wife's hut, and acted as her servants (Werner, 133).

5. Early form of the family.—Widely divergent views have been held as to the origin of the family. One school of anthropologists, of whom Morgan, McClellan, and Bachofen may be taken as the representatives, have maintained that in the earliest stages of the development of human society the family as such did not exist. They hold that within the group individual marriage was non-existent, and that the widely spread custom of tracing descent through the mother, the close connexion existing between the mother's brother and her children, and the nomenclature of primitive relationship point to a state of society in which promiscuity and uncertainty of paternity were the rule, and the children were regarded as belonging to the group and not to a particular family. The family, it is maintained, is a comparatively late development which has slowly evolved within the larger group. On the other hand, it has been held (Atkinson-Lang, *The Primal Law*, London, 1903) that the primitive horde was a single family, from which the young males were driven by the jealousy of the male parent as soon as they had attained maturity. Westermarck (*Hist. of Hum. Marriage*, London, 1891, p. 40 ff.), arguing that man was not originally gregarious, largely on the ground of the difficulty of obtaining an adequate food supply, quotes a number of instances in support of his view that the family and not the group is the original basis of society, and that, even where a group of a few families are found in association, they tend to separate in times of stress.

The Wild Veddas of Ceylon, one of the lowest races in the scale of social organization ever described, were said by Pridham (*Account of Ceylon*, London, 1849, i. 454) to live in single pairs, building their huts in trees, while the Wild, or Nilgala, Veddas were said by Bailey (*Trans. Ethnol. Soc.*, new ser., ii. [1863] 281) to live in pairs or families in caves. Seligmann (p. 62) says that the social group among these Veddas usually consists of the father, mother, daughters, and daughters' husbands. The Fuegians recognized no relationship outside the family (Stirling, *S. Amer. Miss. Magazine*, iv. [1870] 11). The Yahgans of Fuegia live in families, seldom in clans (T. Bridges, quoted by Westermarck, 45). The Bushmen lived in hordes consisting of the members of one family (Fritsch, *Die Eingeborenen Süd-Afrikas*, Breslau, 1873). According to von Tschudi (ii. 283), the Botocudos of Brazil recognized the family as the only tie, while the same thing is stated of other Indian tribes of Brazil. Among the Caishánas, for instance, each family is said to dwell in its own solitary hut (H. W. Bates, *The Naturalist on the River Amazons*, London, 1863, ii. 376). Petroff records of the Eskimos of Alaska that they live in families or groups of families without cohesion, and that a young man will wander away from his family on a hunting expedition, marry, and settle, without regard to his native place of origin, or his original group (*Population, Industries, and Resources of Alaska*, Washington, 1884, p. 135). The Australian tribes of Victoria used, in times of scarcity, to break up into their constituent families, the head of each betaking himself to the land which had been frequented by his father (Brough Smyth, *Aborigines of Victoria*, London, 1878, i. 146). Schoolcraft, in his account of the Indians of North America, speaks of families becoming widely separated in times of scarcity.

It would be possible to extend the number of quotations from the observations of travellers to show that the family is widely recognized among primitive peoples as the social unit, whether the group consists of one or more families. When, however, the composition of that unit and its relation to its social environment are examined, it must be conceded that the evidence, even if it does not go to uphold the group theory of primitive society in its entirety, does demonstrate in many cases a transition from one fundamental basis of social organization to another. The group, which may in a loose sense be termed the family in the earlier form of social organization, has undergone a change of composition. It is only in the later stages that the family, in the strict sense of a group consisting of father, mother, and children, has become the social unit. But the importance of the kin in the early stages does not involve a negation of the existence of a rudimentary family in the strict sense. At this stage, however, certain privileges and duties connected with the disposal of property and the right to control the lives of its members, which later are recognized as essential features in the organization of the family, are vested in the blood relatives or kin. The substitution of patrilineal for matrilineal descent, which would seem at one time or another to have existed among almost every people, has been accompanied or preceded by a re-adjustment of the organization of the social unit; and from this re-adjustment has evolved the family of civilized type, of parents and offspring, with full recognition of relationship on both sides of the house.

6. Relative importance of father and mother, in the early stages of development.—The prevalence of mother-right and the organization of society on a basis which recognizes blood relationship to the kin through the mother, while ignoring the father and his connexion with his children, whether it existed in its logical entirety, as has been inferred from the evidence, or not, necessarily renders the origin of the family obscure. The marriage customs and social organization which accompany matrilineal descent, as well as the use of primitive terms of relationship, have led some writers to deny that the father in the earliest stages of primitive civilization had any place in the family group at all. There is ground for maintaining that the physiological facts of paternity were not fully recognized, even if in the earliest stages of human progress they were recognized at all. The beliefs as to conception and pregnancy current among the Arunta of Australia, as reported by Spencer-Gillen, appear incompatible with any such recognition. Apart from this, the importance of the mother's brother, upon whom devolved the duties which at a later stage fall upon the father, shows that it was he, and not the father, who was regarded as head of the group. But the position of the father begins to be recognized at a very early stage, although he does not attain his full share of family authority, rights, and duties until the patrilineal stage of social development is reached. At the same time, in the stage prior to paternal authority, the existence of a small group of persons, closely related, living more or less in close association, and recognized as forming a unit within the kin to which the term 'family' might be applied loosely, is not only highly probable, but is clearly indicated by the fact that the functions which at first fall to the kin are gradually assigned to the mother's brother, and not to the kin as a whole. Upon the mother's brother fall all the rights and duties which under fully recognized father-right fall upon the father. He is the nearest relative of his sister's children, he is responsible for their well-being, he provides for them, and—most important of all in a primitive society—they inherit his property.

The preponderating importance of the mother in primitive social organization is shown by the fact that in the earliest stages the children belong to the mother's kin and not to that of the father. In a society in which mother-right is the rule, status depends upon the mother; the status of the father is of no consequence. In the Congo, even legitimacy is of no consequence; the fact of birth gives the child status as a member of his mother's family (Dennett, *Journ. Afr. Soc.* i. [1901] 265). Among the Fantis of the Gold Coast, it is stated, the father is hardly known or is disregarded. Although it is not probable that among many peoples at the present day the father is absolutely unknown to his children, numerous instances are recorded where he does not live regularly with the mother. In the Torres Straits Islands men of one island frequently marry women of another; these women stay in their own island, and the husband returns periodically to his village to cultivate his own land (Haddon, 160 f.). In early forms of polygamous union a man may have wives in several villages, the custom being that the wife should not dwell in the husband's village. At this stage the family, as an association of both parents and their offspring, can hardly be said to exist, and, as already suggested, its place is taken by the unit consisting of mother and offspring more or less closely associated with a male head—the mother's brother—within the kin.

7. Position of the husband and father as a resident with the wife's kin or family.—A further stage in the development of the family is reached when the father, instead of being a temporary visitor, lives with his wife's kin.

The Orang Mamaq of Sumatra are organized in *suku*, or clans, which are exogamous. The members of the *suku* live together, and, as no members of the same *suku* can marry, husband and wife do not, as a rule, live under the same roof; but, when they do, the man goes to the woman's clan. His position, however, as regards authority is not affected; the children belong to the mother's clan, and the father has no rights over them. These rights are exercised by the mother's brother (Wilken, quoted by Hartland, *op. cit.*). Arab matrimonial customs furnish instructive instances of the position of the father. Robertson Smith, on the authority of Ibn Baṭūṭa, states that in the 14th cent. the women of Zebid were perfectly willing to marry strangers, but never followed their husbands, on whose departure they themselves took charge of the children. The women of Jâhiliya had the right to dismiss their husbands at will. In reference to Saracen marriages he also quotes Ammianus Marcellinus (xiv. 4), who says that the wife gives her husband a tent and spear as dowry. Robertson Smith interprets this as meaning that she provided her husband with a home, and that he was under an obligation to fight for her kin (*Kinship and Marriage*[2], Lond. 1903, p. 79 ff.). If this interpretation be correct, it is a step in advance of the practice of some primitive races, among whom in case of tribal combat the husband leaves his wife's kin and fights on the side of his own—a custom held to be the origin of the numerous legends of which Sūhrab and Rustam is the type, in which a combat between father and son, who are unknown to one another, results in the death of the former (for an examination of the father and son legend, see Potter, *Sohrab and Rustem*, London, 1902).

Among the Syntengs of Assam, although the husband only visits his wife at her mother's house and himself lives with his own mother, yet, if he dies, his widow keeps his bones after his death, on condition that she does not re-marry. If she marries again, the man's children hand over his bones to his clan, to be placed in a building which the wife may never enter. Among the neighbouring Khasis, however, the husband goes to live with his wife in her mother's house, and may after the birth of one or two children remove her (Gurdon, *The Khasis*, London, 1907, p. 82). A similar juxtaposition is found in Sumatra among the Menangkabau Malays: the husband is only a visitor, and each party lives in his or her birthplace; but among the Tiga Loeroeng the husband goes to live with the wife, or may build her a house in the settlement of her clan (Wilken, quoted by Hartland, ii. 10 ff.). Here the children belong to the mother's clan. A further development is also found. Lower down the river-valley, where one of the two clans is much the stronger, the residence is with the stronger, whether it be the clan of father or of the mother; and descent follows residence.

It is not infrequently the case that the wife does not reside with the husband until a child has been born. This apparently happened in Formosa, where 'Labanism'—the practice by which a son-in-law resided with his bride's family for a term of service—also existed. Sometimes this term of service was extended or became a permanency, and the husband eventually, on the death of the parents, succeeded as head of the family (Davidson, *The Island of Formosa*, London, 1903, *passim*). In Japan also the husband appears originally not to have been a member of the family. In Samoa, the husband resided with the wife's family and acted as a drudge until the birth of the first child (Brown, p. 43). Among the Yakuts, although the bride price was paid at once, the bride was retained at home, often for as long as four or five years, and at each visit the bridegroom brought a present for her parents (Sumner, *JAI* xxxi. [1901] 84). A variant of this custom of regarding the husband as a more or less temporary visitor of his wife is found among the Ossetes. Although the bride is taken to her husband's home, he himself goes to live with friends. The bride visits her parents for the first time at the end of a year, and her first child is born in her parents' home. It is said that no man takes notice of his children in the presence of other people (Darinsky, quoted by Hartland, ii. 17).

It will be noted that a number of the cases cited belong to a stage of transition. The existence of the family is recognized, but claims are made on its behalf which could be enforced in their logical entirety only on a kinship basis.

8. The blood-feud.—The blood-feud (*q.v.*) throws much light upon the early stages of the evolution of the family, particularly at the point at which it passes from an organization based upon kinship to one founded upon the marriage tie.

The supreme influence of the relationship traced through the mother is shown in the custom of the Kumeka, a people of the Caucasus, whereby, if a man murdered a brother by a different mother, the blood-feud arose between himself and the surviving brothers born of the same mother as the murdered man. In Dagestan the murderer of a wife paid blood-money to his own children as well as to his wife's relatives (Darinsky, quoted by Hartland, i. 272). A number of customs among various tribes of Africa are peculiarly significant in this connexion. A husband among the Kunama did not avenge his wife unless she were murdered in his presence; this duty fell primarily on his wife's brothers or her sister's son. Nor were a man's children responsible in case of his own violent death, while the duty of avenging his children's death, should he slay them, fell upon his wife's brothers (Munzinger, *Ostafr. Studien*, Basel, 1883, p. 488 ff.). Among the Herero, though they are patrilineal in other matters, the blood-feud is left to maternal relatives; while, in the case of the death of wife or child through no fault of his, a man pays compensation to his wife's relatives (Dannert, *Zum Rechte der Herero*, Berlin, 1906, p. 10). Analogous customs are found in the Marshall Islands, among the aboriginal tribes of Manipur, in Fiji, among the Maoris, and among the Indians of British Columbia.

In all these cases the blood-feud follows the blood, *i.e.* the duty of vengeance falls first upon those who belong to the mother's kin, and not upon those whose connexion has been brought into existence by marriage.

9. The power to pledge the members of the family.—A similar conception of family ties and rights is shown in the custom, which is common in Africa, of pledging children in payment of debt.

Among the Bavili the mother may pledge her child, but the father must be given the option of pledging his goods in its place, and he may ransom the child (Dennett, *Journ. Afr. Soc.* i. 266). The father cannot pledge the child, but a brother may pledge the sister, or the uncle the niece on the same condition, if the mother is dead. On the Ivory Coast the kin may pledge children, though, if the pledge is a married niece, the husband must have the option of offering goods in her place (*ib.* i. 411). A woman cannot pledge children for her debts without the authority of her brother; and the mother, not the father, is responsible for the children's debts.

10. The bride price.—The institution of a family independent of the bride's parents is not infrequently made to depend upon payment of the bride price, and in these cases the line of descent of the children is changed when the conditions of the marriage bargain have been fulfilled. In the Luang Sermata group of the Moluccas, the payment of the bride price gives the right to reside with the wife, but does not entitle the husband to carry her off. But on the islands of the Ambon and Uliase, on the payment of the bride price, the bride is handed over to the bridegroom, and she is conducted to his dwelling. Side by side with this custom there exists another form of union. Proposals of marriage having been made by the man's relations, if he is accepted, he establishes himself in the bride's dwelling and becomes practically the slave of his wife's parents, acting the part of the secret lover. All children belong to the mother's family. In Wetar, in the same group, although the married pair live at the wife's home until they get a separate dwelling, payment of a bride price secures his children to the husband. On the island of Serang, when the wife enters her husband's family, payment of the bride price is followed by constant gifts to the wife's parents, to keep alive his right in his wife and children (Riedel, quoted by Hartland, ii. 27 ff.). In the Torres Straits Islands, the birth of each successive child involves payment to the wife's parents. On the other hand, in the islands of Mabuiag and Badu, although the husband took up his residence with his wife's people, payment of the bride price annulled the rights over her of her father or her family, except that in the case of the re-marriage of a divorced woman part of the compensation given to her former husband was handed over to her father (Haddon, 159, 161). The two different systems exist side by side on the Wallubela Islands. Here, in the case of the man who lives with his mother's family, payment of the bride price gives the man equal rights over his children as if their mother had formally been handed over to him in the first instance. Marsden (*Hist. of Sumatra*, London, 1811, p. 225 ff.) states that, in Rejang in Sumatra, on payment of the bride price, the woman became the slave of her husband; but, except in case of a quarrel, a small part of the bride price was never paid, in order to keep up the relationship and the family interest. The alternative method of the husband becoming a member of the bride's family was also found. In this case he and his wife might emancipate themselves by payment, but this was made difficult if there were daughters, as their value belonged to the family. The Achehnese have an interesting custom by which, for every twenty-five dollars in the bride price, the parents have to support the bride for one year, the husband giving her only a small monthly present (Hurgronje, *The Achehnese*, Leyden, 1906, i. 295). A right would here seem to have been transformed into a duty. The Belunese of Timor have a double system: the home and the children follow the marriage price, but this is payable by either the man or the woman, the descent being determined accordingly (Wilken, quoted by Hartland, ii. 57).

11. **Residence.**—Throughout Africa, among various tribes, residence with the wife's family is common, whether for a shorter or a longer period. Among the Dinkas the period of residence ended with the birth of the first child (*JAI* xxxiv. [1904] 151). Among the Bambala a man will be required to fight for his father-in-law's village against his own (Torday, *ib.* xxxv. [1905] 399, 410). Both Bushmen and Hottentots required the husband to reside with the wife's parents; among the former it was his duty to provide them with game. In S. America, among the Bakairi (Fritsch, 445), the husband worked in the father's clearing, and on the death of his wife he was bound to marry his wife's sister. This custom was common elsewhere. The Lengua of the Paraguayan Chaco sometimes compromised in the matter of residence, the man and wife spending half their time in the homes of the parents of each (Grubb, *Indians of the Paraguayan Chaco*, London, 1904, p. 61). The husband among the Arawak worked for his bride's father (Im Thurn, 186, 221); when the family became too large to be accommodated in the father's hut, the younger man built a hut for himself near by. When the head dies, the several fathers separate and build houses for themselves, thus each forming the nucleus of a new settlement. Settlements of the same kind are found in Melanesia.

12. **Authority of the father.**—Reference has already been made to the absence of influence of the father in the primitive family, and the vesting of parental rights over children in the mother's kin, and especially in the mother's brother. The gradual recognition of the father as the person responsible for the well-being of his children, and as the holder of the rights to dispose of them and to exact obedience from them, has only very slowly ousted the older conception—by stages which are fairly clear.

The customs of the people of the Lower Congo may be taken as typical of an early, if not of the earliest, stage. There the uncle, who is addressed by the children as 'father,' exercises paternal authority over the children of his sister; the father is without power; and, if the husband and wife separate, the children go with her as belonging to her brother. The children, as they grow up, go to live with their uncle (Bentley, *Pioneering on the Congo*, London, 1900, ii. 333; M. H. Kingsley, *Travels in W. Africa*, London, 1897, p. 224 f.). Among the Bambala the family is beginning to develop its form; there are two types of marriage. In the case of child-marriage, or, more properly, child-betrothal, the boy lives with his chosen bride's parents until he is of marriageable age, and any children of the marriage belong to the maternal uncle. In the case of marriage of adults, a bride price is paid to the father or maternal uncle, and any children then belong to the father. But a father has little authority, and any property he himself has is inherited by his sister's eldest son (Torday, *JAI* xxxv. 410 f.). Kinship is reckoned on the mother's side, but also on the father's, for one or two generations; father-right is beginning to override mother-right. Among the Bangala a man may sell his nephews to pay his debts (Livingstone, 434); so also in Angola. Although the father may have no power over his children, the case is different when the mother is a slave; among the Kunbunda they are reckoned his children, and can inherit from him. The customs of some negro tribes exhibit instructive peculiarities. Among the Ewe of Anglo in Upper Guinea, the nephew accompanies the uncle on trading journeys and acts for him, accounts to his uncle for all that he takes, and receives a share of the profits. But it is the uncle and the father together who negotiate for his marriage; and the father is also consulted as to the marriage of his daughter, and receives a share of the price (Ellis, *Ewe-speaking Peoples*, London, 1890, p. 207 ff.).

Among the Fantis a further step in the organization of the family has been taken. The Fantis are matrilineal; the head of the family is usually the eldest male in the line of descent, and in his compound dwell not only the younger members of his line of descent, but also his own wives and children. His power is limited, however, by the fact that he cannot pawn his children without their mother's consent, and any members who have left to live with their maternal uncle are out of his power (Sarbah, *Fanti Customary Laws*, London, 1897, *passim*). Among the Kunama of Abyssinia the right of the father has been extended to cover the son's earnings, but not his life and liberty, which remain in the power of the maternal uncle (Munzinger, 477 ff.).

The position of the mother's brother and his relation to his nephew are of great importance in Melanesia, and especially in Fiji. But even in this region it has begun to give way to a recognition of the father as head of his family. On the island of Muralug, Torres Straits, patrilineal descent is recognized, but the bride's brother still arranges the details of a girl's marriage, although the father receives the bride price, and his consent to the marriage is required. The bridegroom exchanges a sister for his promised wife; and, if he has no sister, he gives a daughter of his maternal uncle (*Rep. Camb. Exped. Torres Straits*, v. 145, Camb. 1910).

Among the Australian tribes the authority over the children is very slight, but it rests with the father, so far as boys are concerned, until the time of initiation, when it is vested vaguely in the elders of the tribe. In the case of girls, the authority is concerned chiefly with the right of betrothal, while after marriage the power of the husband is practically absolute. Such control as exists is vested mainly in the girl's or her mother's brother. Among the Dieri (Howitt, *Native Tribes of S.E. Australia*, London, 1904, pp. 177, 167, 195, 217) the right of betrothal rests with the mother, who acts with the concurrence of her brothers. The Wallaroi exchange their sisters without the intervention of their mother.

13. The inheritance of power and property.—The gradual growth of the feeling of solidarity in the family as opposed to the kin, *i.e.* in the unit in which the relation of father to offspring is more potent than the connexion which is traced through sister or mother, can be seen in the customs connected with the disposal of power or property. Where the feeling of kinship is predominant, at a man's death his property would be divided among the members of his kin, with whom he was connected through his mother. The 'potlatch' of the Haida of Charlotte Island in N. America, to which the whole kin contributed or in which they shared, is an instance of an analogous character, which shows the solidarity of the kin in relation to personal property. A parallel instance may be quoted from Samoa, where all the relatives contribute to the dower of the *taupou*, or village maid. As the conception of a relationship within the kin increases, it becomes generally recognized that the direct heir is the sister's son rather than the kin as a whole. At this stage of development it is usual for the chieftainship to be elective, and the tendency is for the honour to fall to the wealthiest or to the one who is possessed of the greatest amount of traditional knowledge. A further stage is reached when a man's affection for his own children is strong enough for him to endeavour to break through this restriction. The evidence from Melanesia is of importance in connexion with the evolution of the family, as it offers numerous examples of a transition from one set of customs to another. The peoples in the various islands are divided into exogamous clans, and for the most part trace descent through the mother: husband and wife 'belong to different sides of the house,' and neither at marriage passes over to the side of the other. It is clear that at one time the heir in all cases was the nephew. In Bogotu the chief is the head of the predominant *kema*, or clan. But, it is stated, no *kema* is continuously predominant, because a chief, in order to secure the chieftainship to his children, transfers what he can of his own property to his sons, who are not of his own kin (Codrington, 32 ff.). Property is frequently transferred to the son, or used to secure the son's advancement in the club house during the father's lifetime. In the New Hebrides, the chieftainship tended to become hereditary, as the chief handed on his traditional knowledge to his son. At Motu the headship had become hereditary. In the case of land a distinction was recognized. Land in long occupation, which, it would be assumed, had originally been cleared by the kin, would descend to the sister's son, but land cleared by a man himself—a task in which the sons would assist—would descend to the children. Further, this land would continue to descend from father to son; but, should the fact of its clearing by an individual, and not by the kin, be forgotten or overlooked, it would descend to the nephew. Trees, in which property was recognized as apart from the land, whether planted on land belonging to the planter or on that of another, also descended to the sons. Strictly speaking, personal property was inherited by the nephew, but might be secured to the children in various ways. Frequently it was hidden in the owner's lifetime for the benefit of the children; in Florida a canoe might be given to the son by the father's direction; or the direct heirs might be bought off. In Banks Island, both land and personal property might be inherited by this method.

14. Conclusion.—A general review of the evidence relating to the primitive family—a subject around which in its various aspects much controversy has arisen—would suggest that many of the theories which have been put forward have been based upon superficial observations and imperfect evidence. Early travellers have read into what they have seen much that belonged to the civilized conditions with which they were familiar, while by the use of ill-defined terms of relationship, which did not correspond with the native connotation, they have misled those who relied upon their evidence. If the precise meaning of a group consisting of father, mother, and offspring is to be attached to the term 'family,' it must be recognized that in the early stages of civilization the family as a group, though not necessarily non-existent, as has been maintained, is not so closely-knit an organization as it becomes at a later stage. The economic value of the woman, as an important factor in the production of material comforts and utilities, as a source of the accession of strength from outside, and as the mother of future members of the tribe, was recognized at an early stage; and this accounts largely for the fact that many of the functions of the family of which the father was recognized as the head in a later development were vested in those related to the woman by blood—at first the kin as a whole, later the smaller group within the kin consisting of her immediate male relatives, or, using 'family' in a looser sense, the family connected by blood ties. It is only by gradual stages—through the bride price, the compensation, whether it be the husband's service for his life or a term of years, the exchange of another woman (a sister) for the bride, the loss of all or some of his children, or a payment in goods or money, or through forcible abduction—that the husband has been able gradually to secure independence of the unit of which he becomes the head, in location, in the disposal of property, and in the ordering of the lives of its members.

Cf. also artt. CHILDREN, INHERITANCE, KINSHIP, MARRIAGE.

LITERATURE.—This is given in the article.

E. N. FALLAIZE.

FAMILY (Assyro - Babylonian). — The three meanings usually given to this word were also present in Assyro-Bab.: (1) the head of the household, with his wife, children, and other relatives; (2) a group of people connected by blood or by marriage; (3) the same, including the tribe or clan. The commonest word for 'family' is, perhaps, *qinnu*, from *qanānu*, 'to build a nest,' though this may not have been its original meaning. The word occurs in the Assyr. historical inscriptions; 'his brothers, his family (*qinnu-šu*), the seed of his father's house' (Aššurb. iii. 10); 'his wife, his sons, and all his family' (*qinnaššu gabbi* [letter K. 13, l. 8]); '300 families (*qinnāte*) of the criminals (implicated in the rebellion)' (Tigl. vi. 31). A synonym of this word is *kimtu*, which explains (*WAI* ii. 29, 72–74*fg*) the cognate forms *kîmu*, *kîmatu*, and also *lîmu*, all meaning, probably, something collected—a group, or the like. *Kîmtu* is the Bab. rendering of *ḫammu* in the name *Ḫammurabi*, which the Babylonians translated as *Kîmta-rapaštu*^{m}, 'my family is wide-spread,' or the like; and of *ammi* in *Ammi-ṣaduga* (*-ṣaduqa*), rendered as *Kîmtu*^{m}*-kêttu*^{m}, 'the righteous family'—to all appearance they did not recognize in *ḫammu* or *ammi* the Arab. divinity 'Amm. These examples show that *kîmtu* was regarded as the equivalent of the Arab. *ḥamm*, or *ḥāmmat*, and, though it could be used in the restricted sense of *qinnu*, a wider meaning was sometimes present: *kîmti lurappiš, salati lupaḫḫir, pir'i lušamdil*, 'may I spread abroad my family, may I gather together my relatives, may I extend my offspring' (Meissner and Rost, *Beit. z. Assyr.*, Leipzig, 1893, pp. 254, 255). *Bîtu*, 'house,' also became a synonym of the above words, with the addition of servants and dependents (*Cun. Texts*, xviii. pll. 16, 26).

All these expressions naturally belong to the period following that of the early nomadic times of the Sem. tent-dwellers. The word for town, *âlu*, is probably the same as the Heb. *ôhĕl*, 'tent,' Arab. *ahl*, 'family,' with transferred meaning, implying that the inhabitants of the early centres of population were as one large family. The character expressing *âlu*, however, seems to be rather a large house than a tent.[1]

The members of a Bab. family were the husband (*mutu, ḫa'iru*), the wife (*âššatu, ḫîrtu*) or wives, and their children.[2] More than two wives seem to have been unusual, and, in the case of a double family of this kind, both were expected to interest themselves in their common offspring. A wife might give her maid-servant to her husband (*Code of Ḫammurabi*, § 146; Gn 16[1ff.]), but in that case he could not himself take a concubine. The maid-servant thus honoured was not equal with her mistress, and presumption on her part might result in her being relegated to her old position, even though she had borne children. If the wife were childless, the husband might take a concubine (§ 145); and, if a malady had stricken the wife, the husband might marry again, but the sick wife could not be divorced (§ 148). That there may have been transgressions of these laws is not improbable, but they seem to indicate the composition of the families of the well-to-do. A second wife appears to have been taken sometimes to provide a servant for the first (Pinches, *OT in the Light*[3], p. 175). An ill-treated wife could claim her freedom (*Cod. Ḫam.* § 142).

Descent was always traced through the father, and the Sumer. custom of mentioning the female sex first in certain cases may have had merely a mythological origin, due to the teaching which made Tiāmat, or 'Mother Ḫubur,' the first creator. Her offspring, who overcame her, however, were all gods, not goddesses. Even in the purely Sumer. pantheon, it is nearly always the divine husband who is the more powerful. It was the husband, therefore, who was the more important as a progenitor, and, in the so-called 'family-laws' of the Sumerians, the clause dealing with the denial of a foster-father not only takes precedence of that of the mother, but is also punished more severely (Pinches, *OT in Light*[3], p. 190 f.). The descendants of a man were called his 'seed' (Sumer. *(n)umun*, Assyr.-Bab. *zēru*) or 'progeny' (Assyr.-Bab. *nannabu*). To indicate his parentage, and thus identify him legally, his father's name was given, and generally, in later times, the founder of his tribe, *e.g.* 'Marduk-naṣir-âbli, son of (*âbli-šu ša*) Itti-Nabû-balāṭu, descendant of (*âbil*) Êgibi'; 'Balaṭu, son of (*âbli-šu ša*) Ina-êši-êṭir, descendant of (*âbil*) Bêl'u.' The number of Bab. families thus indicated is considerable, but the Assyrians generally omit these genealogical indications.

The father was supreme in his house. It was he who gave his daughters in marriage, whether adoptive or otherwise (Meissner, *Beiträge z. altbab. Privatrecht*, p. 92; *JRAS*, 1897, pp. 603–606). He gave his adopted children a share of his property, and his sons seem to have had no legal right to complain either of the adoption or of being thus deprived of patrimony (Pinches, 176 f.). The obedience required (by contract) from an adopted son apparently only reflected that expected of a man's own child. A man could disown his son, but the judges had to inquire into the matter *Cod. Ḫam.* § 168), and it needed a repetition of a grave fault to justify cutting off from sonship (§ 169). The denial of a father or mother by adoption, however, might apparently be followed by immediate expulsion (*Cod. Ḫam.* § 186; Pinches, 177). In Sumerian times the penalty of denying a foster-father was slavery (Pinches, 190 f.; cf. also p. 176, where, however, there is the same penalty for denying a foster-mother). The frequency of adoption was very likely due to the desire to carry on the family traditions and name, though the scarcity of slaves (Meissner, 16) may have had something to do with it.

If adoption took place during infancy, a nurse was hired, and maintained for three years (*WAI* ii. pl. 9, 45–50*cd*). At the age of reason mutual liking seems to have been taken into consideration (*ib.* 40–43*b*: 'If he dislike [be hostile to] his father, he shall go forth into [the family of ?] whoever has caused him to enter'). Instruction was not neglected. 'He caused him to know the writing' (concerning himself [?]) (*ib.* 66*cd*). Women might adopt as well as men, and could give their foster-daughters in marriage. The latter were expected to help their adoptive mothers, should they afterwards be in want (*JRAS*, 1899, p. 106). For the legal aspects of adoption, see *ERE* i. 114.

Apparently the father married off his sons in the order of seniority, and any of the younger sons who remained unmarried at his death were provided with a bride-gift by their elder or married brethren (*Cod. Ḫam.* § 166). When the time for the wedding came, the bridegroom conveyed the bride-gift to the father of the woman decided upon, the latter having probably been offered beforehand by one of her parents. As a father could give his sons property without prejudice to their sharing after his death (*Cod. Ḫam.* § 165), in like manner the parents gave them the wherewithal for the bride-gift (Meissner, 14).[1] In return for this, the woman brought a dowry, generally in the form of house-furniture. Ceremonies attended all these transactions, and there was a fixed ritual for the wedding itself (see MARRIAGE [Semitic]). Absolute fidelity—a most important thing in family-life—was expected, and probably generally obtained. In the case of long absence from home on the part of the husband, however, he could expect this only if there were food in the house; otherwise the woman was allowed to become another man's mistress, resuming her former place in the household on her husband's return. Children born in consequence of this custom were credited to the real father (*Cod. Ḫam.* §§ 133, 135). In all probability this was a law of which advantage was seldom taken, being a remnant of a loose state of family-morals. Wilful desertion acted like divorce (§ 136). Unfaithfulness on the part of a wife, except in the above circumstances, was at first punished by drowning (Family Laws), or death by being thrown down from a tower (Ungnad, *Hammurabi's Gesetz*, iv. 86). Later (in the time of Samsu-iluna), she was marked as a slave, and sold (*ib.* 86). Though the wife could not divorce her husband,

[1] This, however, would merely imply that the Sumerians were house-dwellers at the time when they came into contact with the Semitic Babylonians.

[2] Synonyms of *ḫa'iru* are *êrišu*, *išḫu*, and *naḫšu*, those of *âššatu* or *ḫîrtu* being *marḫîtu* and *iššu*. Other forms are *ḫāyaru*, 'husband,' and *ḫîratu*, 'wife' (*WAI* ii. 36, 39–46*cd*). The spouse of the sun-god is called *hîrtum*; Ištar is the *ḫîratu* of Tammuz; the wife of Ut-napištim, the Babylonian Noah, is called *sinništu*, 'woman,' and *marḫîtu*, 'wife.' There was apparently a distinction between a divine and an earthly spouse.

[1] This is naturally a remnant of the old days of wife-purchase. For dowries provided by selling the comeliest maidens by auction, see Herod. i. 196.

the husband could divorce the wife, upon paying her divorce-money. She retained her dowry.

Whether women were looked upon with more respect in earlier (Sumerian) times than in later is uncertain, but it is to be noted that the ideograph for 'mother,' *ama* (also, probably, *aga*), is written with the sign for 'divinity' within that used for 'house' or 'dwelling-place.' This has led to the suggestion that the Sumerians thought of her as 'the divinity within the house.' It seems more likely, however, that a mother was herself regarded as the dwelling-place of some divinity—probably one of the manifestations of Zērpanîtu^{m}, who, as Aruru, created the seed of mankind with Merodach, and was possibly conceived as acting within her (see BIRTH [Assyr.-Bab.], vol. ii. p. 643^{b}).[1] The mother occupied a high place with regard to the children in the family. If she said to her son (or foster-son), 'Thou art not my son,' he had to forsake the house and the furniture; and if, on the other hand, he denied his (adoptive) mother, he was first marked by having his temple shaved, and then, having been led around the town, was expelled from the house. Wives were at liberty (no doubt with the consent of their husbands) to carry on business, and also to appear as witnesses to contracts.

In the absence of the father, the (eldest) son, if old enough, took his place, and administered his property. Otherwise the mother became head of the family, and administered the property for her sons' benefit (*Cod. Ḫam.* §§ 28, 29). On the death of the father, his children divided the property according to the usual custom, and engaged not to bring actions at law against each other with regard to the sharing (Pinches, 178 ff.).

The respect due to parents was apparently willingly given by their children. In a letter from Êlmešu^{m} to his father, of about the time of Ḫammurabi, he prays that Šamaš and Merodach may grant his father enduring days, that he may have health and life, and that his father's protecting god may preserve him. He hopes that his father will have lasting well-being. In the body of the letter, he seems to have regarded the direct pronouns 'thou' and 'thee' as too stiff, so he substitutes the words 'my father' wherever he can, sometimes along with the pronoun required.

The best family-picture of later date is that given in the history of Bunanitu^{m} and her lawsuit with her dead husband's relatives. She had married Abil-Addu-nathānu, bringing with her a dowry of 3½ *mana* of silver, and the pair had one daughter. They traded with the money of her dowry, and bought a house at Borsippa, with grounds, borrowing a sum of money to complete the purchase. In the 4th year of Nabonidus she made an arrangement with her husband, and he willed all the property to her, in consideration of her dowry and the fact that they had always acted together. The next year they adopted a son, Abil-Addu-âmāra, and made known that their daughter's dowry was two *mana* of silver and the furniture of a house. After her husband's death, her brother-in-law laid claim to all her property, including a slave whom they had bought. The judges decided in her favour, and decreed that, according to their tablets, Bunanitu^{m} and Abil-Addu-âmāra, her adopted son, were the rightful heirs.[2] The lender was to receive the money which he had advanced, Bunanitu^{m} was to have her dowry back, and her share of the property besides. The daughter was to receive the slave (Pinches, 459 ff., 462 ff.).

The private letters belonging to the period of the later Bab. empire show the same courteous spirit between members of the same family as of old.

Noteworthy is the letter of a father to his apparently more successful son, in which he tells him that there is no grain in the house, and asks him to send some. He prays to Bêl and Nebo for the preservation of his son's life, and tells him that his mother greets him (*ib.* 453). Affectionate letters between the brothers and the sisters of families are also found, as well as others showing that brothers were not always on good terms. Among the last may be mentioned the letter of Marduk-zēr-ibnî to Šulâ his brother, protesting against the latter's rapacity (*ib.* 453 f.). A noteworthy communication is that of Nabû-zēr-ibnî to his four brothers, protesting against the slandering of their brother Bêl-êpuš (*ib.* 452 f.).

Of the few lists of families extant, those of certain slaves may be quoted to show in what manner the enumerations in such cases were made:

'Ubara, Nabû-banî, his brother, 1 suckling (lit. 'child of milk'), 2 women—total 5; Paliḫ-ka-libluṭ, Nabû-âḫa-êreš, his brother, 1 child of 4 (years), 2 women—total 5; Zazâ, 1 child of 4, 1 woman, 2 daughters—total 5; Ḫarranū (the Haranite), Amat-bêli-uṣur, a child of 5, 3 women—total 5' (S. A. Smith, *Keilschrifttexte Asurbanipals*, Leipzig, 1887–89, pt. iii. p. 63 ff. [and pl. 20]). For the family of the slave Usi'a (Hoshea), see Johns, *Assyr. Deeds and Documents*, Cambridge, 1898–1901, iii. 447.

It is to be noted that the word 'wife' (*âššatu*) is not used in these cases, but simply 'woman' (*sinništu*), implying either that slaves were not regarded, at least sometimes, as regularly married, or that their wives were not held worthy of the more honourable term.

From life-long association and intercourse, slaves or vassals were probably often enough treated as members of a man's family; and, when the women of that class were favoured with the attention of the master of the house, this quasi-membership became a reality. The children of a free man and a slave, however, were not regarded as his legitimate children unless he acknowledged them during his lifetime (*Cod. Ḫam.* §§ 170, 171). The best way to ensure their freedom and inheritance of his property was apparently by emancipating the mother.

LITERATURE.—For further details, see the Code of Ḫammurabi, in C. H. W. Johns, *Oldest Code of Laws*, Edinb. 1903; A. Ungnad, *Hammurabi's Gesetz*, Leipzig, 1904–1910; T. G. Pinches, *The OT in the Light of the Records of Assyria and Babylonia*[3], London, 1908, pp. 187–525, also 169 ff., 430 ff., 553, 554; B. Meissner, *Beiträge zur altbab. Privatrecht*, Leipzig, 1893; H. de Genouillac, *La Société sumérienne*, Paris, 1909, p. xxi ff.

T. G. PINCHES.

FAMILY (Biblical and Christian).—'Here is a social group which, in its present form, is by no means an original and outright gift to the human race, but is the product of a vast world-process of social evolution, through which various types of domestic unity have been in turn selected and, as it were, tested, until at last the fittest has survived' (Peabody, *Jesus Christ and the Social Question*, New York, 1901, p. 134).

I. *IN THE OLD TESTAMENT*.—There are not wanting indications that the Hebrews, like all the other Semites, passed through the stages of exogamy, totemism, and reckoning descent in the female line. But in the earliest historical times the matriarchate is a superseded and forgotten system; the patriarchate is in secure and unquestioned possession. The family is constituted under the headship of the father; the woman passes over to the clan and tribe of her husband; kinship, tribal connexion, and inheritance are all determined by the man. The Hebrew historians assume that through the expansion of the family all the wider groups are evolved, and the genealogists attempt to derive the tribes of Israel, and ultimately all the races of mankind, by male descent from a common ancestor. The Hebrews were always remarkable for the intensity of their family feeling; the strength of their nation lay in the depth, variety, and richness of the characters which were created in their homes; and their moral and spiritual progress is largely the evolution of their domestic life. In their Scriptures the imperfect relations of husband and wife, parent and child, brother and sister, master and servant, host and stranger, were displayed with a fine healthy realism; and under each head there is slowly but surely developed an ethical ideal which is the preparation for the perfect Christian type of the family.

---

[1] The Sumer. saying: *Salla-mu alšaga, kalammaene tilbab-(b)eneše = Uri-mi da[miq?] ina niši-ia gummuranni*, 'My womb being fortunate, among my people they hold me perfect,' if rightly translated, shows in what high honour the mother of a family was held.

[2] Property given to a wife in due form could not be taken from her after her husband's death (*Cod. Ḫam.* § 150).

1. The father.—The reverence paid to the head of the family was due not so much to his superior wisdom and strength as to his position as priest of the household. His unlimited authority rested on a spiritual basis. The family was a society bound together by common religious observances. Every one born into it recognized, as a matter of course, its special cult, in which the worship of ancestors seems to have been originally the distinctive feature. The *tᵉrāphîm* (Gn $31^{19.\,34ff.}$, 1 S $19^{13.\,16}$ *et al.*) are usually understood to have been images or symbols of ancestors. The family burying-place was holy ground, and many of the famous old sanctuaries probably owed their sacredness to their being regarded as the graves of heroes. Ancestor-worship was, of course, family worship. The father was the guardian of the traditional cult, which he passed on to his eldest son, thus securing the continued prosperity of the family. According to the earliest documents, the patriarchs erected altars and offered sacrifice (*e.g.* Gn $12^{7f.}$ 13^{18} 22^{9} [Abraham] 26^{25} [Isaac] 35^{7} [Jacob]). The father presided at the passover, which was a family rite, observed in the home (Ex 12). In the days of Saul, when the tribes had long been united in the worship of Jahweh, each family, or clan (*mishpāḥāh*), still had its *sacra gentilica*, and every member was bound to attend the annual festivals (1 S $20^{6.\,29}$). Any one who cut himself loose from the authority of the father debarred himself from the protection and favour of the ancestral *numina*. As the strength of the family was thus rooted in spiritual causes, it became a matter of sacred duty to secure its continuance. The cult must be handed down from father to son, from generation to generation. Celibacy was at once an impiety and a misfortune, for it threatened the existence of a social unity of worship. When a family became extinct, it was a cult that died.

2. Husband and wife.—The position of woman is the touchstone of civilized society. In ancient Israel the husband had a proprietary right over his wife. He was the owner or master (*ba'al*), she the owned or mastered (*bᵉ'ûlāh*). In the Decalogue she is mentioned as part of his wealth, along with his house, slave, ox, and ass (Ex 20^{17}). To betroth a woman was simply to acquire possession of her by paying the *mōhar*, or purchase-money. A 'betrothed' was a girl for whom the *mōhar* had been paid. Her own consent to the transaction was unnecessary, all the arrangements as to the marriage, and especially as to the purchase-price, being carried through by her father or guardian. So long as this commercial idea of marriage prevailed, certain blemishes marred the beauty of family life.—(*a*) Polygyny was common. If a husband regarded his wife simply as a valuable asset, his power of multiplying wives was limited merely by his purse. It was the ambition of most men of rank and wealth to possess a large *harîm*. In addition, any of the female slaves of the family was at his disposal as a concubine. Sometimes the legal wife took the initiative in suggesting this arrangement, as in the cases of Sarah (Gn 16^{2}), Rachel (Gn 30^{3}), and Leah (Gn 30^{9}). Of course, the approximately equal numbers of the two sexes placed limits to polygyny. In the middle classes, of which Elkanah may be taken as a representative (1 S 1^{1}), it was probably the ordinary practice to have two wives. 'Rival' (צָרָה) was the technical term for one of the two (1 S 1^{6}), and Dt $21^{15ff.}$ deals with the case where one wife is beloved and the other hated. In the nature of things, a large proportion of the poorer classes must have been monogamous.—(*b*) The woman being the man's property, he had the right to divorce her at his pleasure (Dt 24^{1}). He could at any time send her back to her own kin, provided he was willing to return the *mōhar* with her. No moral stigma of any kind attached to her from the mere fact that she had been divorced.—(*c*) While the husband was allowed a wide sexual liberty, law and custom dealt very strictly with the wife. Adultery on her part was a crime punishable by stoning (Dt 22^{22}), and the same sentence might be passed on the wife who at her marriage was found not to have been a virgin (22^{21}).—(*d*) Being herself part of her husband's estate, the wife was incapable of inheriting property. Her right of ownership was confined to presents. She was the mistress of the servants whom she received as personal attendants on leaving her home. But even these were ultimately the property of her husband and his heir, since they could not revert to her own kindred.—(*e*) The husband's authority over the wife easily degenerated into tyranny, and in the lower ranks of society her lot was, doubtless, often hard, since she had not only to fulfil the arduous menial tasks of the household, but might be required to engage in field labour or tend the flocks and herds.

Various causes, however, conspired to improve the position of women, and so to elevate family life. (1) Marriage was not always an affair of the market. Sometimes the heart obtained its rights. In all ranks of society there was a considerable freedom of intercourse between the sexes, and the spirit of romance was not to be quenched. In a simple pastoral society, men and maids naturally met at wells, and love-matches were sometimes the result (Gn $29^{18.\,20}$). The Song of Songs celebrates a rustic love that is strong as death; and in kings' courts, marriages were not always conventional (1 S 18^{20}). (2) The *mōhar* tended to lose its original meaning of purchase-money, and came to be a gift to the bride herself. Laban's daughters complained that he had sold them as slaves and wasted their *mōhar* (Gn 31^{15}). (3) While an injured wife could not divorce her husband, she was not without redress. She always had claims on the protection and aid of her blood-relations, who were ready to defend her if she had any just cause of complaint. The women of the family were its most sacred trust, and any insult offered to them was sure to be avenged. The aim of legislation was also to restrict the man's freedom of divorce. By requiring him to give his wife a bill of divorce, it enabled her to resist any attempt on his part to re-assert his rights over her (Dt 24^{1}). If a man falsely charged his wife with unchastity before marriage (22^{13-19}), or if he had seduced her and been consequently obliged to marry her (vv.$^{28.\,29}$), he was deprived of the right of divorce. (4) The typical 'mother in Israel' was far from being the morally and intellectually stunted creature who is often met with in Eastern lands. If she was a person of rank, she was too powerful and independent to be treated as a mere chattel. If she was a woman of character and ability (Pr 31^{10}), she knew how to increase her husband's affection and to improve her own condition. Once and again the interest of Hebrew history centres in the action of some brave and noble woman. (5) The whole prophetic movement was towards monogamy. Gn 2^{18-24} makes woman the helpmeet of man, and the love of one man for one woman the normal relation of the sexes. When the prophets regard marriage as the symbol of Jahweh's covenant with Israel, and adultery as that of idolatry, they think of monogamy as the ideal. Hosea strikes the keynote of a new doctrine when he tells the story of a love which does not loathe and repudiate a prodigal wife, but cherishes and seeks to redeem her. Malachi (2^{14-16}) proclaims the Divine detestation of divorce. The Hebrew Wisdom reinforced prophecy in the endeavour to purify the family life of the nation, and there is abundant evidence that Israel ultimately began to realize the folly and iniquity of sexual licence on man's part as well as on woman's. Yet the law of monogamy was never placed on the Jewish statute-book; and Justin Martyr (*Dial. c. Tryph.* 134) states that, even in his time, the Talmudists allowed every common man to have four or five wives, while kings might still have as many as eighteen. But by that time humanity had heard the voice of the final Lawgiver. See, further, MARRIAGE (Semitic).

3. Parents and children.—(*a*) To have a numerous progeny was the universal desire in ancient Israel. Children were a heritage of Jahweh, and happy was the man who had his quiver full of them (Ps 127[3-5]). The honour paid to the wife was dependent on her having a son. If she was childless, she endured a reproach; for barrenness was regarded not only as a misfortune, but as a Divine judgment. 'Give me children, or else I die,' was Rachel's heart-cry (Gn 30[1]; cf. 1 S 1[11]). The husband who had no son dreaded the extinction of his house. His fear was probably rooted in ancestor-worship. If he died childless, he would have no one to pay the needful dues to his *manes*. If, therefore, his first wife had no son, it was his sacred duty to take a second or a concubine; and, if he died without an heir, it was an act of piety on his brother's part to marry his widow and raise up children in his stead (Dt 25[5, 6]).—(*b*) The first desire of parents was for sons, the defenders of the hearth and the main support of the home. It was the first-born son who was dedicated to Jahweh (Ex 22[29]). But daughters were also welcome, and that not merely because they were required for the labour of the household, or because a *mōhar* could be demanded for them, but because their beauty was desired and their chastity honoured alike in kings' courts and shepherds' tents (Ps 45, Canticles, *passim*). There was none of that contempt for girls which has always marked many Eastern races. Female infanticide, which was practised among the Arabs, was apparently unknown among the Hebrews.—(*c*) The *patria potestas* was, however, almost absolute. Abraham's readiness to sacrifice Isaac (Gn 22), Jephthah's sacrifice of his daughter (Jg 11[34-40]), and the practice of offering children to Molech (2 K 23[10], Jer 32[35]) rest upon this authority. The father had power to cast out a bond-woman with the child she had borne him (Gn 16[6]). He could sell his daughter into bond-service (with concubinage), though not to foreigners (Ex 21[7-11]). He could not, on any account, sell her into prostitution (Lv 19[29]). He might cause a prodigal son to be stoned to death (Dt 21[18-21]), or a prodigal daughter to be burned alive (Gn 38[24]). Children were required to render the utmost respect and obedience to both their parents (Ex 20[12], Lv 19[3]). Any one cursing his father or his mother was put to death (Lv 20[9]). —(*d*) The early education of the children was mostly in the hands of the mother. The sayings of Lemuel were taught him by his mother (Pr 31[1]). Proverbs contains many references to the instruction (*mūsār*) of the father and the teaching (*tōrāh*) of the mother. Schools are never mentioned in the OT. — (*e*) The solidarity of the Hebrew family was so complete that grave injustice was often done to the children. The sin of Achan was expiated by the destruction of his whole household (Jos 7[24, 25]). It was the task of the prophets to preach the doctrine of individual responsibility, separating 'the soul of the son' from 'the soul of the father' (Ezk 18[4]).—(*f*) The stress which the OT lays upon the family is indicated by its closing words, which contain a promise to 'turn the heart of the fathers to the children, and the heart of the children to their fathers.' A strong and pure domestic life is to save the earth from a curse (Mal 4[6]). See, further, artt. CHILDREN and EDUCATION.

4. Brothers and sisters.—(*a*) Polygyny divided a man's family into sub-families, each presided over by a mother, whose personal jealousies were apt to be shared by her children. The full brother was the natural guardian of his sister. Laban takes precedence of Bethuel in the arrangements for Rebekah's betrothal (Gn 24[50]). The sub-families were so distinct that in early times brothers were permitted to marry half-sisters (20[12]). Tamar, Absalom's daughter, thinks that David will certainly allow her to marry her half-brother Amnon (2 S 13[13]). Ultimately, however, such unions were forbidden by law (Lv 18[9]).—(*b*) There was no difference of legitimacy, in the Græco-Roman sense, between the sons of wives and those of concubines. Even Jephthah, though a prostitute's son, is brought up in his father's house, and rightly complains of his expulsion as an act of violence (Jg 11[1, 7]). The claim not unnaturally made by the wife, that the son of the bond-woman should not share the inheritance with her son (Gn 21[10]), was never sustained by law. Four of the tribes of Israel were descended from the sons of Jacob's concubines. A man's acknowledged children were all legitimate, irrespective of the status of their mother. The bastard (*mamzēr*) was not one born out of wedlock, but the offspring of an incestuous union (Dt 23[2]). —(*c*) The domestic word 'brother' had a wider application to the clan, the tribe, and the nation. Israel and Judah (2 S 19[41]), Israel and Ishmael (Gn 16[12] 25[18]), Israel and Edom (Nu 20[14]), were brethren. But those who were kin were not always kind. The Prophets have to ethicize the ideal of 'a covenant of brethren' (Am 1[9]), the Psalmists sing the praise of brotherly unity (Ps 133[1]), and ultimately Christianity sets itself the task of making humanity a family.

5. Master and servant.—The Hebrew slave was a true member of the family. He was part of his master's wealth, but he was not regarded as an inferior being. He was circumcised, and kept the passover. He was admitted to the family cult. He prayed to the God of his master (Gn 24[12]). In the Deuteronomic law his humane treatment is rooted in his master's remembrance that the Hebrews themselves were once slaves in Egypt (Dt 15[15] 16[12] etc.). It was a still higher consideration that the same Divine creative power made both master and slave (Job 31[15]). The Hebrew religion, perfected in Christianity, enunciated principles which slowly undermined and ultimately abolished slavery. It created a spiritual climate in which bond-service dies a natural death. See SLAVERY.

6. Host and guest.—The Hebrew family was scarcely complete without the 'stranger' or guest (*gēr*, μέτοικος), who, separated for some reason from his own kindred, put himself under Israelite protection, and then was included in the sacred blood-bond. As Jahweh was 'the protector of strangers' (Ps 146[9]; cf. Zeus Xenios), hospitality rested on religious sanctions. There are many exhortations to deal justly and generously with the *gēr* (Ex 22[21] etc.), who worshipped the God of the land in which he sojourned, shared the privilege of the sabbath, and was perhaps admitted to the *sacra* of his patron. This family tie between host and guest was also to be perfected in Christianity.

'The Christians looked upon themselves as a body of men scattered throughout the world, living as aliens amongst strange people, and therefore bound together as the members of a body, as the brethren of one family. The practical realization of this idea would demand that whenever a Christian went from one place to another he should find a home among the Christians in each town he visited' (Sanday-Headlam, *Romans*[5], Edinburgh, 1902, p. 363.

II. *THE CHRISTIAN FAMILY.*—Jesus had personal experience of the privilege and obligation of home life. He spent many quiet years in the Holy Family at Nazareth, which was to Him a shrine of moral culture, a temple of Divine communion. His whole thinking was influenced and inspired by the experience. He came to regard the sacred relation of the family as mirroring the rightful relation between God and man. He had an intuition of the essential oneness of these relations. He saw that of all the immeasurable forms of love none is so beautiful, so lasting, so Divine as the love of husband and wife, parent and child, brother and sister. He grasped this force as the key of all future moral and spiritual progress. By consecrating marriage, by emancipating womanhood, by sanctifying childhood, by expanding brotherhood, and making the domestic group the type of the Divine social order which is to be, He created what may distinctively be called the Christian family.

1. The consecration of marriage.—Both in the lower and in the higher aspect, the union of two personalities is the beginning of family life. Jesus recognizes its physical aspect (Mk 10^{8}), which He never regards as in any way sinful or ignoble. It is scarcely possible to overestimate the importance of the change which He effected by His law of marriage. On many of the burning questions of His age He refused to commit Himself, but in regard to the institution of the family He repeatedly expressed His mind with the utmost emphasis. To the laxity of the time He opposed an austere purity, which startled even His own disciples, and probably seemed to the ordinary intelligence fanatical. It is true that, in spite of the technical lawfulness of polygamy, the Jews had become to a great extent monogamists. But divorce was scandalously common, and the discussions on the subject had fallen to an extremely low level. Between the two great Rabbinical schools of the period there was a standing dispute (based on Dt 24^{1}), not whether divorce was permissible, but for what reasons. The school of Shammai wished to restrict them to acts of unchastity, but the school of Hillel inferred that a divorce was warranted when a wife burned her husband's food in cooking, while Rabbi Akiba thought that a man might lawfully dismiss his wife if he found another more attractive (Mishna, *Giṭṭin*, ix. 10). In opposition to this licentious trifling, Jesus categorically denies the rightness of divorce (Mt 19^{9}, Mk 10^{11}, Lk 16^{18}). In His view marriage is not a creation of law, which can merely recognize and protect it, but an institution based on a Divine creative act. Its true significance is to be sought, not in human customs, but in the human constitution. Moses, indeed, allowed divorce (Mk 10^{5}), but only as an expedient, as the lesser of two evils, regulating what he could not prevent, reducing anarchy to law, while by a legislative compromise he violated human nature. From temporary ethics Jesus passes to absolute morality. He sees that marriage in its true nature is not a legal status, a social contract, a licensed partnership for mutual help and support, but a real union of complementing personalities, a forming of one flesh (10^{6-8}). In His view the question is not, May a man divorce his wife? but, Can he? and the emphatic answer is, He cannot. The sacred bond is essentially indissoluble. It is not to be violated even by a look or a thought (Mt 5^{28}), and, except as a formal recognition of an already broken union, divorce is impossible. Jesus discerned the Divine ideal of the institution, and made that the law of His Church. He directed His legislation to the perfecting of the home in the interest of the Kingdom. It was not so much that He 'changed the family (which till then had only a civil importance) into a religious institution' (Schmidt, *The Social Results of Early Christianity*, Eng. tr., London, 1885, p. 203) as that He discovered its Divine principle, which is inherently and eternally religious.

'To dishonour this first of human relationships is to loosen the bonds of society, to lower present social ideals, to do injury to the essential nature of both the man and the woman. It was, therefore, not in the spirit of a purist or a fanatic that Jesus thus put checks upon divorce, but in that of the ethical and social philosopher' (Shailer Mathews, *The Social Teaching of Jesus*, New York, 1910, p. 90).

2. The elevation of womanhood.—Jesus' lofty conception of the family involves the emancipation of woman. Astonishingly free from Eastern prejudices, He abolishes the idea of a husband's property rights in his wife, and liberates her spirit from the last trace of servility and abjectness. He never commands her to be in subjection to her husband (contrast Eph 5^{22}), and never traces the transgression of mankind to her weakness (1 Ti 2^{14}). 'He simply treats woman as an equal—equal in the matter of marriage and divorce, equal as a companion' (Shailer Mathews, *op. cit.* 97). St. Paul's teaching on this head is not quite self-consistent, but he clearly has the mind of Christ when he enunciates the principle that in Him 'there can be no male and female' (Gal 3^{28}); and Augustine, while he gives celibacy and virginity the exaggerated importance of a more perfect virtue, teaches that the natures of man and woman are equally honourable, and that 'the Saviour gives abundant proof of this in being born of a woman' (*Sermo* 190, § 2). All the Fathers teach that husband and wife must equally honour the sanctity of the home. Errors which are condemned in the one cannot be condoned in the other.

'In consequence of Christian respect for reinstated woman, it is no longer she alone who is thought capable of committing adultery. The doctors of the Church vigorously attack the pagan pride which accused woman alone, whilst man claimed to be free. Henceforth the unfaithful husband was held to be as guilty as the wife who violated her duty' (Schmidt, *op. cit.* 200).

3. The dignity of childhood.—The family exists especially for the child. Jesus was Himself the Holy Child, reared in the shelter of an earthly home, meeting parental authority with filial submission, growing in favour with God and man. His profoundest teaching was coloured by thoughts of family life, and He has left words which have for ever hallowed childhood. He made the spirit of a little child the type of Christian character (Mk 9^{36}), and gave children a share in His kingdom (10^{14}). He did not prescribe minute details for the conduct of parents and children. In general it was His part not to legislate but to inspire. He entrusted to others the task of incarnating His principles in the midst of imperfect human conditions. Under the influence of His spirit paternal authority ceases to be an arbitrary tyranny, and the servile dependence of children is replaced by the truer and gentler dependence of love and gratitude (cf. Eph 6^{1-4}, Col 3^{20-22}). Christianity vitalizes the fine Roman saying, 'Maxima debetur puero reverentia' (Juv. xiv. 47), and gives it the sanction of a far higher faith.

4. The expansion of brotherhood. — In the original condition of mankind, blood was the single tie which bound men together, the family was the sole basis of rights and duties. Every one who was not a brother was counted an enemy. Only the life and property of a kinsman were safe. We have seen how the idea of brotherhood was gradually extended to the tribe and the nation. It was reserved for Jesus to place *all* men in the relation of brethren to each other. In His name St. Paul exhorts Philemon to receive back Onesimus 'no longer as a servant, but as a brother beloved' (Philem ^{16}). The thought of 'the brother . . . for whom Christ died' (1 Co 8^{11}) has been the inspiration of the noblest service of the human race. The Saviour's hope for the world is to be fulfilled through the expansion of those affections which are naturally born and nurtured in the sanctuary of the home. The family is His microcosmic kingdom. He makes the first social unit also the last. 'His entire theology may be described as a transfiguration of the family' (Peabody, *op. cit.* 147). 'Paternal love is His representation of the love of God, and the family. . . . His type of that divine society towards which humanity with a Christ within it must move' (Shailer Mathews, *op. cit.* 104).

5. The subordination of the family. — The dearest relationships may, however, conceal the subtlest temptations, and Jesus was alive to the dangers which lurk in the affections of the home. Love may narrow as well as widen the heart. Domestic selfishness is as disastrous as any other form of selfishness. Just because the devotion of kindred is so intense, it is apt to be exclusive. When Jesus entered on the work of His vocation, and, again, when He began to call men to be disciples, He came into collision with the claims of the family. Then and only then did He seem to depreciate it. 'He that loveth father or mother more than me is not worthy of me' (Mt 10[37]). 'Whosoever shall do the will of God, the same is my brother, and sister, and mother' (Mk 3[35]). The family exists for the sake of ends beyond itself; it is the preparation and equipment of personalities for the service of God and man. It was part of the tragedy of Jesus' life that He was not understood by His own brethren, and that He had to assert, in unequivocal language, His independence of the interests and obligations of His former home. The pain of separation from His kindred, and especially from His mother, was proportionate to the tenderness of His love. By example as well as by precept He taught that, when the call of duty comes into conflict with the claims of affection, the former must prevail. It was not that He loved the family less, but that He loved the Kingdom more. As Bengel notes on Mt 12[48], 'non sprevit matrem, sed anteponit Patrem.'

6. The ultimate social aggregate. — Though the best institutions may easily become the most mischievous when they are perverted and mismanaged, that does not affect their intrinsic value. The character of the teaching of Jesus on the family has never been so adequately appreciated as to-day, when science and politics are concentrating the attention of the educated world on the crucial problem of the ultimate social unit. Many anti-Christian attacks are being directed against the domestic group, but 'it is clear that monogamy has long been growing innate in civilized man,' and this relationship is 'manifestly the ultimate form' (Spencer, *Principles of Sociology*, London, 1876–96, i. 673, 752). The Christian family is the germ of the yet higher civilization of the future. It enfolds in itself the promise and potency of all social progress and pure human happiness.

'It is the mature opinion of every one who has thought upon the history of the world, that the thing of highest importance for all times and to all nations is Family Life. . . . Not for centuries but for millenniums the Family has survived. Time has not tarnished it; no later art has improved upon it; nor genius discovered anything more lovely; nor religion anything more divine' (H. Drummond, *The Ascent of Man*, London, 1894, pp. 378, 407).

Cf. also artt. CHILDREN, MARRIAGE, WOMAN.

LITERATURE.—In addition to the authorities cited in the article, the following may be consulted: J. Fenton, *Early Hebrew Life*, London, 1880; W. R. Smith, *Kinship and Marriage*², London and Edin. 1907; I. Benzinger, *Heb. Arch.*, Freiburg i. B. 1904; W. Nowack, *Lehrb. der heb. Arch.*, do. 1904; H. L. Martensen, *Chr. Eth.* (Social), Eng. tr., Edin. 1884; J. Clark Murray, *A Handb. of Chr. Eth.*, do. 1908, p. 253 f.; Newman Smyth, *Chr. Eth.*, do. 1892, p. 405 f.; W. S. Bruce, *Soc. Aspects of Chr. Morality*, London, 1905, p. 48 f.; T. B. Kilpatrick, *Chr. Character*, Edin. 1899, p. 143 f.; J. Stalker, *The Eth. of Jesus*, London, 1909, p. 331 f.; T. v. Häring, *Eth. of the Chr. Life*, do. 1909, p. 337 f.; Helen Bosanquet, *The Family*, do. 1906; art. 'Familie,' in *PRE*³.

JAMES STRAHAN.

FAMILY (Buddhist).—In the 6th cent. B.C., when Buddhism arose in the valley of the Ganges, the family had already been long constituted, and its every detail settled, in accordance with the tribal customs of the Aryan, Dravidian, Kolarian, and other inhabitants. Neither at the beginning, in the precepts put into the mouth of the Buddha in our earliest documents, was any attempt made to interfere in any way with those customs; nor afterwards, as the influence of the new teaching spread, do we find any decree of a Buddhist Council, or any ordinance of a Buddhist king, prescribing a change there in family relations. When Buddhism was subsequently introduced and more or less widely or completely adopted in other countries, the Buddhists evinced no desire, and probably had no power, to reconstitute the family according to any views of their own on the subject. It is possible, therefore, to speak of the family as Buddhist only in a very modified sense—an observation equally true of all religions so late as, or later than, the Buddhist. But the general tone of the Buddhist teaching, and the adoption by a proportion of the inhabitants of any country of the system of self-culture and self-control we now call Buddhism (the Buddhists called it the *Dharma*), could not fail to exercise a certain influence on the degree in which previously existing customs were modified to suit the new environment. And in our oldest documents, in those portions addressed to beginners in the system, and amounting to little more than milk for babes, we find allusions, not indeed to the re-adjustment of any point of detail, but to the general principles which should guide a good Buddhist in his family relations.

Thus in the edifying story of the partridge,[1] the Buddha is represented as laying especial stress on the importance of reverence being paid to the aged, and as concluding his discourse thus:

'So, since even animals can live together in mutual reverence, confidence, and courtesy, so much more should you so let your light shine forth that you, who have left the world to follow so well taught a doctrine and discipline, may be seen to dwell in like manner together.'

This is here addressed to the *bhikkhus*. Afterwards the same story was included in the popular collection of Jātakas (Fausböll, Lond. 1877–97, i. 217–220); and it was well known to the Chinese pilgrim, Yüan Chwang (Watters, *On Yuan Chwang's Travels in India*, do. 1905, ii. 54). A similar sentiment is found in the popular anthology of favourite stanzas, the *Dhammapada* (verse 109, a celebrated verse found also in other Buddhist anthologies, and repeated, in almost identical words, by later Sanskrit writers).[2]

In the *Sigālovāda Suttanta* the Buddha sees a young man worshipping the six quarters, North, South, East, West, the nadir, and the zenith, and shows him a more excellent way of guarding the six quarters by right conduct towards parents and wife and children, and teachers and friends and dependents.

'In five ways the son should minister to his mother and father, who are the East quarter. He should say: "I will sustain in their old age those who supported me in my youth; I will take upon myself what they would otherwise have to do (in relation to the State and the family); I will keep up the lineage of their house; I will guard their property; and when they are dead and gone I will duly make the customary gifts."

Thus ministered unto, the father and mother in five ways show their affection to their son. They restrain him from evil, and train him to follow that which is seemly, they have him taught a craft, they marry him to a suitable wife, and in due season they give him his portion of the inheritance. . . .

In five ways the husband should minister to his wife, who is the West quarter. He should treat her with reverence; not belittle her; never be false to her; acknowledge her authority; and provide her with things of beauty. Thus ministered unto, the wife should in five ways show her affection for her husband.

1 *Vinaya*, ii. 161, tr. in *Vinaya Texts*, iii. 194 (*SBE* xx.).
2 Manu, ii. 121; *Mahābhārata*, v. 1521.

She should manage her household well; carry out all due courtesies to relatives on both sides; never be false to him; take care of his property; and be able and active in all she has to do.'[1]

Passages of similar tendency are found in other parts of the *Nikāyas* addressed to beginners or householders. The principles set forth in them may certainly be called Buddhist, since they have been adopted into the *Dhamma*. But it is probable that they are a selection from the views as to family and sexual relations already current among the Aryan clans to which the Buddha himself and most of his early disciples—to whom we owe the record—belonged. What is Buddhist about it is the selection. For instance, we know from the later law-books that the pre-Buddhistic Aryans performed, at a marriage, magical and religious ceremonies which bore a striking resemblance in important details to ceremonies enacted at a similar date by other Aryan races in Europe. Other religious ceremonies were performed at the name-giving, the initiation, and other important periods in the history of the family. All these are, of course, ignored and omitted in the exhortation. Buddhists could not countenance practices which they held to be connected with superstition. And they put nothing in their place. There are no Buddhist ceremonies of marriage, initiation, baptism, or the like. Marriage is regarded as a purely civil rite, and the Buddhist clergy, as such, take no part in it. This is probably the reason why Asoka, in his edicts on religion, does not mention it. He considers marriage, and the observance of family customs, a civil affair.[2]

In pre-Buddhistic times, divorce, but without any formal decree, was allowed. So Isidāsī, for instance, explains how she had had to return twice to her father's house, having been sent back by successive husbands owing to incompatibility of temper (the result of her evil deeds in a former birth).[3] No instance is recorded of similar action taken against the husband. In countries under the influence of the Thera-vāda (the older Buddhism) there is divorce on equal terms for husband or wife on the ground of infidelity, desertion, or incompatibility of temper. This is, however, infrequent. Fielding estimates it, for village communities in Burma, at two to five per cent of the marriages;[4] and the present writer, while not able to estimate any percentage, for which there are no statistics available, is able to testify to the very low number of divorces in Ceylon.

The wife, after marriage, retains her own name, and the full control of all her property, whether it be dower or inheritance. Property acquired by the partnership (of husband and wife) is joint property. There is no *harîm* system; marriage is monogamous (that is, among the people; kings often follow the Hindu customs); women go about unveiled, engage in business, can sign deeds, give evidence, join in social intercourse, and have just such liberty as they and their men-folk think expedient. Fielding, who has given the facts for Burma in considerable detail (chs. 13–17), does not discuss the question how far this state of things is due to the influence of Buddhism, and how far to the inherited customs and good sense of the people. But, when we call to mind that the same or closely related races have, under other influences, much less advanced customs, and that in early Buddhism a remarkably high position was allowed to women, we may conjecture that the influence of early Buddhist teaching was not without weight.

LITERATURE.—The authorities are given in the article.

T. W. RHYS DAVIDS.

[1] Tr. from *Dīgha*, iii. 189 ff.; also tr. by S. Gogerly, *Ceylon Buddhism* (ed. Bishop, Colombo, 1908), p. 529 ff., and by R. C. Childers, *CR*, 1876.

[2] There is a reference to docility towards parents in the 3rd Rock Edict. See T. W. Rhys Davids, *Buddhist India*, London, 1903, p. 295.

[3] *Therī-gāthā*, 416, 425, tr. by C. A. F. Rhys Davids, in *Psalms of the Sisters*, *PTS*, 1900, p. 160.

[4] *Soul of a People*, London, 1898, p. 246.

FAMILY (Celtic).—**1.** The evolution of the Celtic family is wrapped in considerable obscurity, and it is by no means easy, from the evidence that has come down to us, from both Christian and pre-Christian times, to conjecture through what phases it had passed before the dawn of history. In the case of Celtic countries, too, it has always to be remembered that the Celtic-speaking inhabitants were comparatively late comers, and that the previous inhabitants had for ages their own social institutions, which may or may not have undergone a similar evolution to those of the invaders of Indo-European speech. Nor can it be supposed that the institutions of the invaders would necessarily supplant those of the earlier inhabitants, especially in the remoter districts, where the indigenous population would be most likely to hold its own. Further, it is not impossible that, in some cases, the institution which survived was neither that of the invaders nor that of the previous inhabitants in its entirety, but a working compromise consisting of elements from both sources, the development of which it is now by no means easy to follow. It may well be, for example, that the curious system of fosterage, which played so large a part in Celtic family life (see artt. CHILDREN [Celtic], and FOSTERAGE), owed its origin to some such fusion of Celtic and pre-Celtic institutions, but it is now, at this distance of time, a fruitless task to speculate upon the matter. Further, it must be borne in mind that, in the documents which describe the social life of the Celts, our information relates almost entirely to the higher circles of the population—that is, to the free members of tribes (doubtless in the main sprung from men of Indo-European speech) who at the earliest did not reach the British Isles before about 1800 B.C. and the West of Europe some centuries before. What the institutions of the 'unfree' tenants of Celtic countries may have been is involved in great uncertainty, and their social organization may well have developed on lines distinctly different from those that were characteristic of the Indo-European conquerors of Gaul and the British Isles, and of the kinsmen of these conquerors in other countries of cognate speech.

2. A study of the various treatises which embody the ancient law of Ireland, together with the documents which describe the social system of ancient Wales, and, similarly, an investigation into the clan organization of the Scottish Highlands, make it abundantly clear that the family basis was patriarchal, and, at any rate in Christian times, essentially monogamic. In Gaul, too, as Cæsar (*de Bell. Gall.* vi. 15) tells us, the family structure was of the same type, and the family groups had attached to them groups of *ambacti* ('clients')—a word of Celtic origin, which is the exact phonetic equivalent of the Welsh *amaeth* ('farmer'). Nor is this development of Celtic institutions to be wondered at, because the type of family in question is the natural correlative of the kind of military and semi-nomadic life which ultimately brought the Celts into a dominant position (until Rome conquered them) in Celtic lands. At the same time, there are indications that there were, at any rate in some parts of these lands, certain unusual features of family life, which impressed some of the observers of the ancient world. For example, Cæsar (vi. 18) acquaints us with the curious fact that, in Gaul, it was thought to be a shameful thing for a boy to be present before the face of his father in public, until he was of age to bear arms. He also tells us (v. 14. 4) that in

Britain ten or a dozen men had wives common to the group, and that in this matter brothers mostly joined with brothers. Strabo (iv. 5. 4), following Posidonius, speaks of a rumour that the Irish had no definite system of matrimony, but he could not vouch for the truth of this view. Dio Cassius (lxxvi. 12. 2) says that the Caledonii had wives in common (ταῖς γυναιξὶν ἐπικοίνοις χρώμενοι); and, in his description of Thule (derived from Pytheas), Solinus (*Polyhistor.* ch. 22) says that the king of that island had no wife of his own. These statements regarding the inhabitants of Britain appear to have gained a wide currency in antiquity, and we find Bardesanes in Eusebius (*Praep. Evang.* vi. 10) repeating the story that several persons jointly had one wife in Britain; while Jerome (*adv. Jovin.* ii. 7, p. 335) says of the Scoti:

'Scotorum natio uxores proprias non habet: et quasi Platonis politiam legerit et Catonis sectetur exemplum, nulla apud eos coniux propria est, sed, ut cuique libitum fuerit, pecudum more lasciviunt' (see, further, above, pp. 456 f., 460[a], 462 f., 465).

It has been thought that the absence in Welsh of any word for 'son' as distinguished from 'boy' (*mab*), or for 'daughter' as distinguished from 'girl' (*merch*), points to an analogous situation in remote times in that country; but this absence of separate terms may easily be one of the accidents of language. Again, the so-called Pictish succession, whereby the Pictish crown descended from the reigning king to his sister's son, has been thought to have had its roots in a remote matriarchal system; but the criticism of this view by d'Arbois de Jubainville, in *La Famille celtique* (p. 88) makes it hazardous to accept it. Nor would it be safe to attach undue importance to certain cases of legendary nomenclature, such as *Conchobar mac Nessa* ('Conchobar, son of Ness') and *Gwydion fab Don* ('Gwydion, son of Don'), where the hero is called after his mother's name. The prominence given also to the grouped goddesses called 'Matres' and 'Matronae' (on whom see *ERE* iii. 280) in certain regions cannot, in view of the scantiness of the general evidence, be regarded as of any significance in this connexion.

3. Still, notwithstanding the rumours of antiquity,—which it would be rash to say were entirely devoid of foundation, at any rate in the more backward districts,—the evidence of Cæsar as to Gaul and the abundant testimony of the Irish and Welsh laws alike reveal, both in Gaul and in Britain, communities where the male head of each social group is in unmistakable prominence. Of the *patria potestas* enjoyed by the husbands in Gaul, Cæsar says (vi. 19): 'Viri in uxores, sicuti in liberos, vitae necisque habent potestatem,' and both the Irish and the Welsh laws show us that women could not be members of the recognized tribes. The organization of the Celts was everywhere based on the tie of blood: in Gaul the tribe, in Ireland the clan under its chief, and in Wales the *cenedl* ('kindred') under its *pencenedl* ('head of the kindred'), were all governed by the idea of a common ancestry. The family proper was the smallest subdivision of the social organism, and was founded on the principle of monogamic marriage. The organization of the family had at one time a very important practical significance, since it was closely connected with the tenure of land and the occupation of the dwelling-houses built upon the land—in other words, with succession, and also with responsibility for the payment of compensation for wrongs committed by a kinsman (see CRIMES AND PUNISHMENTS [Celtic], vol. iv. p. 261, and BLOOD-FEUD [Celtic], vol. ii. p. 725). There were thus reasons for the evolution of the family-group in the direction of greater compactness and definiteness.

4. The Irish legal documents, such as the *Senchus Mór*, with its commentary, the *Book of Aicill*, and other treatises, unfortunately do not present us with a very clear account of the structure of the Irish family, and the descriptions therein contained have given rise to much discussion; see d'Arbois de Jubainville, *op. cit.*; also the 'Introduction to the Book of Aicill,' in *Ancient Laws of Ireland*, vol. iii. p. cxxxix, and especially the Introduction (by Alexander George Richey) to the Brehon Law Tracts, *ib.* vol. iv. p. xlix. The latter Introduction, which deals with this complicated subject most thoroughly, may be supplemented with advantage by a study of R. Atkinson's *Glossary to the Ancient Laws of Ireland* (vol. vi. in the Rolls Series). Both the Introduction in question and the *Glossary* show how little can be gleaned with certainty from the Irish laws as to the precise significance of their fourfold classification of the Irish family into the *gelfine*, the *derbfine*, the *iarfine*, and the *innfine*. Of these family-groups it is evident, from the account given by Atkinson in his *Glossary*, that the *gelfine* was the most living and vigorous form of the family in the times to which the Irish Law Treatises refer, though this form may, even then, owing to the settlement of a large part of the land of Ireland, have lost something of its earlier *raison d'être* in the occupation of new territory. According to Atkinson, it can be stated with certainty that the *gelfine* included two varieties: (1) the *gelfine iar mbelaib* ('frontwards'), and (2) the *gelfine iar culaib* ('backwards'), the former denoting five men of the direct line—father, son, grandson, great-grandson, and great-great-grandson; the latter denoting the similar descendants in the direct line from the father's brother. Of these two varieties it would appear that the former was the more important aspect of the *gelfine*, and Richey in his Introduction has ingeniously suggested that it began with the occupation of new lands, when the father would hold the original dwelling, and, if he had five sons, four of them would during their father's lifetime occupy each a homestead on the land, while the fifth son would in time succeed to his father's homestead. The view held by Whitley Stokes and by d'Arbois de Jubainville, that *gel* in *gelfine* means 'a hand,' and that it is cognate with the Greek χείρ, is improbable; and, consequently, there appears no warrant for the view that the *gelfine* was essentially a 'familia in manu.' Of the other names for family-divisions the term *derbfine* ('true-family') suggests that it may have denoted what was for a time a rival classification with some of the other divisions, and the present writer is inclined to hazard the opinion that these terms, which have given rise to so much ingenious discussion, are in reality surviving traces of different family arrangements, which prevailed at different periods, and that the Irish, instead of discarding the old classifications completely when the *gelfine* came into favour, allowed them to remain as names, and regarded them as being forms of family arrangements which were in reserve in case of need. The process of evolution has doubtless operated here, and has left some of its traces, as in the case of other social institutions.

5. The Scots who carried with them the Gaelic tongue into Scotland brought also their tribal organization, but, as Skene (*Celtic Scotland*, iii. 320) points out, the original clan-organization of the Gaelic-speaking invaders from Ireland appears to have been broken up, and new septs or clans came to appear as a distinct and prominent feature in the organization of the Gaelic population. The basis of the clan-system was, however, essentially the same as in Ireland; and, just as there were in Ireland certain dependent septs, so, too, in Scotland there were, side by side with the clans of kinsmen corresponding to the Irish 'free' tenants, other

'unfree' clans corresponding to the *fuidhir* tenants of Ireland. (For an account of the development of the clan and family system of the Highlands, the reader should consult Skene, iii.)

6. In Wales, the family organization within the tribe (*cenedl*) was only of one type, namely, that corresponding in the main to the *gelfine* of Ireland. It consisted of the ancestor, his sons, his grandsons, and great-grandsons. So far as the occupation of land was concerned, the corresponding territorial division was the *gwely*, upon which a body of members of the same family were settled, occupying the original mansion of the family, and the supplementary *tyddynod* ('homesteads') which were built upon the land to accommodate the sons as they married. This family organization among the Welsh was responsible for the payment of the *galanas* ('blood-fee') in the case of the commission of homicide by a member of the family (see CRIMES AND PUNISHMENTS [Celtic]). It will thus be seen that in Wales, as in Ireland, it was the practical questions of land-tenure and responsibility for the actions of kinsmen that made the family as such so important a factor in social life, with the result that pedigrees were kept with remarkable care. With the introduction, however, of the English manorial system and English law, the pressure of practical necessity upon family organization became less urgent; but, nevertheless, the sense of kinship, even to the recognition of distant relatives, has remained far stronger in Wales than in corresponding circles in England at the present day, and this recognition of kinship shows itself in a marked way in the sense of obligation which most Welshmen feel to attend the funerals even of distant kinsmen—a feature of Welsh life which generally appears strange to Englishmen who come to reside in Wales.

7. The various terms which express family relationship, in spite of their common Indo-European origin, are somewhat different in the two great branches (the Goidelic and the Brythonic) of the Celtic tongue. For example, the term for 'father' in Irish is *athair*, the phonetic equivalent (with the regular loss of Indo-European 'p') of the Latin *pater*, while, in the Brythonic group, the corresponding Indo-European term of endearment, *tăta*, has entirely supplanted the more formal Celtic term for 'father,' giving the Welsh and Breton *tād*, and the Cornish *tas*. Similarly, in Welsh, Breton, and Cornish, the place of *modr* (the equivalent of Lat. *mater*, Irish *mathair*) has been taken by the analogous term of endearment *mam* from *mamma*. Likewise in Brythonic (cf. Welsh *taid*, 'grandfather,' *nain*, 'grandmother') we have survivals of Indo-European terms of endearment. In Ireland, too, the terms for 'foster-father' (*aite*) and 'foster-mother' (*muime*) are, in origin, both survivals of terms of endearment also. The Irish word *mac*, like the Welsh *mab*, can mean both 'boy' and 'son'; and the Irish term *ingen* ('daughter')—a word meaning literally 'one born into the family' (for *eni-gena*)—has the same dual meaning. In both branches of Celtic speech, too, the words which originally meant 'grandson' and 'granddaughter' have come to mean 'nephew' and 'niece.'

8. In modern Welsh the term in regular use for 'family' is *teulu*, but the reader should be on his guard against assuming that in Welsh mediæval documents this word had the same meaning as it now has. Its meaning then, in accordance with its derivation (from *ty*, 'house,' and *llu*, 'host'), was 'the retinue or bodyguard of the head of the household'; and, in the case of the king, this retinue had a special head, the *pen teulu*, and a special bard, *bardd teulu*, of its own. The earlier meaning of the word now survives only in a South Wales term for a 'phantom funeral procession' (pronounced *toili*=*teulu*).

9. The treatment of children among the Celts, as well as the interesting practice of fosterage, is discussed in the artt. CHILDREN (Celtic) and FOSTERAGE, and the place of the wife in the family, together with the conditions of marriage (including the question of marriage gifts) will be considered in connexion with the subject of MARRIAGE (Celtic).

LITERATURE.—Rhys and Brynmor-Jones, *The Welsh People*[4], London, 1906; H. d'Arbois de Jubainville, *La Famille celtique*, Paris, 1905; *Ancient Laws and Institutes of Wales*, ed. Aneurin Owen (Rolls Series, London, 1841); Wade-Evans, *Welsh Medieval Law*, Oxford, 1909; *The Ancient Laws of Ireland* (Rolls Series, London, 1865-1901); R. Atkinson, *Glossary to Ancient Laws of Ireland* (Rolls Series, London, 1901); W. F. Skene, *Celtic Scotland*[2], Edinburgh, 1890.

E. ANWYL.

FAMILY (Chinese).

—*Introductory*.—The analysis of a Chinese character is not always a reliable guide to its primitive meaning. The usual form of the character for 'family,' *i.e.* those under the roof of one paterfamilias, is a pig under a roof, and the *Shuo Wên* (*c.* A.D. 100) says that, originally meaning a pig-sty, it was afterwards metaphorically used for a human home. It is just as likely, however, that originally the part of the character which stands for 'pig' had merely a phonetic value; and in any case the *Liu Shu Ku* (between A.D. 1250 and 1319) sets aside this derivation, and analyzes another form of the character into three persons under a roof.

The institution of the family is ascribed to Fuh-hsi (2852–2736 B.C.). Before his time the people were like beasts, knowing their mothers but not their fathers, and pairing without decency. Fuh-hsi established the laws of marriage, organized clans, and introduced family surnames.

Society in China is predominantly patriarchal. The family is the social unit and the norm of social organization (Williams, *Middle Kingdom*, New York, 1876, i. 296). A mandarin is the parent of his children people. 'The Empire is one family.' 'To the Son of Heaven there is no stranger: he regards the empire as his family.' In accordance with this idea, *hsiao*, filial piety, the duty of a child, and *t'i*, the duty of a younger brother, are the fundamental social virtues. 'Esteem most highly filial piety and brotherly submission, in order to give due prominence to the social relations' (*Sacr. Edict* [A.D. 1670], i.).

A typical Chinese family might consist of father, mother, sons, daughters-in-law, and grandchildren. To have four generations alive in one household is marked felicity; if five are alive at the same time, many are the congratulations, and special announcement of the fact is made in the temple of the City-Guardian.

1. Husband and wife.—Marriages are arranged by the parents of the bridegroom and bride through the agency of a 'go-between.' 'In taking a wife, how do you proceed? Without a go-between, it cannot be done' (*Shi-King*, xv. 6). Betrothal is considered binding, and often takes place at a very early age. In some cases the future daughter-in-law is brought as an infant into her future husband's family, and grows up as a member of it. The custom, however, is not of high repute, and is particularly objectionable where, as in at least one district, the future husband and wife cohabit from their earliest years, and there is no formal marriage. Early marriage is usual. A boy is of age at 15. Prohibition of inter-marriage extends to all persons of the same surname, even though they should belong to widely separated parts of the Empire; and, if a man would marry a near relative on his mother's side, the contracting parties must be of the same generation; *e.g.*, a man may marry his cousin but not his aunt. Otherwise there is no restriction. In practice, of course, regard is paid to equality of social status—'Eight ounces is a match for half a pound'; and the horoscopes of the parties are often taken into consideration. The bride brings her trousseau; but the husband's family have to pay a dowry for her, although among the wealthy this is somewhat of a formality. Marriage arranged in this way is not of affection, and in many cases, at least in the humbler ranks of life, is as much providing a help for the mother-in-law as a wife for the son. But it is evident from popular tales that romance is not unknown in Chinese life, through love stirred by favourable report or accidental glimpse. Doubtless, too, in many cases, however affection may be lacking to begin with, it springs up in the course of years. The virtue of a husband is to be 'a just person,' and of a wife to be obedient. Conjugal harmony is recognized as the foundation of successful family life, and finds its emblem in mandarin ducks—types of conjugal modesty and fidelity (cf. *Shi-King*, i. 1). Owing to the low status of women and the excessive desire for offspring, the wife is too often regarded merely as the possible mother of sons. In the lower ranks of life, where it is her function to 'boil rice' as well as to 'bear children,' it is desired also that she be a capable housewife. Theoretically she is a keeper at home. Her husband refers to her as 'the person within,' with the addition of various depreciatory epithets. Whatever the origin of foot-binding, it is popularly regarded as a salutary check on woman's proclivity to gadding about and to worse evils. Foot-binding, however, is by no means universal; and among the lower classes, especially in certain districts, women are allowed great freedom, and take even too large a share in heavy outdoor work. Owing to the lack of female education, a wife can seldom be a companion to her husband. Nor is this looked for; and a household is apt to fall into two sections, male and female, the women and girls taking their meals apart from and after the men-folk.

Besides the normal form of marriage, in which the bride goes to live in the home of her husband's parents, there are other forms, in which the husband joins his wife's family. This may happen when the wife's parents have no sons, and, instead of marrying their daughter out, bring in a son-in-law to marry her. In this case the husband does not take his wife's surname; but some arrangement is come to, such as that the first son of the marriage shall take the surname of his mother's parents, and carry on the succession for them. A second class of such marriages is where a husband is called in to marry a widowed daughter-in-law. In such cases the wife retains the surname and even the name of her deceased husband, and the children of her second marriage carry on his succession and not that of their own father. In this case the second husband leaves his own clan and is merged in that of his wife, and is regarded with a certain measure of contempt.

Re-marriage of a widower is usual; and re-marriage of a widow is not infrequent, though to remain faithful to the memory of her husband is considered more estimable, and a second marriage is celebrated with 'maimed rites.' The arrangements for the re-marriage of a widow are made by her parents-in-law; but more regard is paid to her will in the matter than would be paid to the wishes of a daughter. There is no fixed rule with regard to the disposal of a widow's children; but it may be taken for granted that not all her sons at least would be allowed to accompany their mother to her new home.

Concubinage.—Chinese law recognizes only one wife, but concubinage is legal. The practice dates from ancient times. Of Yao (2356 B.C.) it is recorded that he gave his two daughters in marriage to his successor Shun, though this is a case rather of polygamy than of concubinage. It may be noted that the marriage of two sisters, as in this case, is now unknown, though marriage of a deceased wife's sister is not forbidden. Concubinage is common among the wealthy classes. Among the poorer it is less common, and usually only for the purpose of securing a male succession. There is no legal limit to the number of concubines that may be taken.

Divorce. — According to law there are seven reasons for which a husband may divorce his wife; but the law recognizes no right of the wife to divorce her husband. The seven legal reasons for divorce are unfilial conduct (towards the husband's parents), adultery, jealousy, loquacity, theft, grievous disease (*e.g.* leprosy), barrenness; but some of these, *e.g.* barrenness, are not recognized by custom. To these legal reasons must be added poverty, which is the commonest cause of all. It is difficult to estimate the percentage of divorces, but divorce is not supposed to be frequent (Dyer Ball, *Things Chinese*, ed. Shanghai, 1903, p. 212; Doolittle, *Social Life*, i. 107). No legal process is necessary, though a writing of divorcement should be given, and is usually demanded by the second husband of the repudiated woman as a precaution. The repudiated wife is married by the aid of a 'go-between.' This is not so difficult as it might seem; for the desire for children is strong, and matrimony is largely a mercantile transaction, in which a woman whose reputation is damaged may be had at a cheaper rate. The husband's somewhat despotic power over his wife is limited in practice, not so much by legal restraints as by public opinion, and in particular by the fear of his wife's relatives, especially if they are of a powerful clan. Short of divorce a man may, if his wife offends, send her back to her parents, as a hint that their family discipline has been defective. This is regarded as a disgrace to them; and it is for them, if the wife has been in the wrong, to placate her husband and persuade him to take her back. In practice, though not in law, a concubine has little protection against her husband, and can be sold at his pleasure.

2. Parents and children.—In the family the father is the supreme authority—a general rule with many qualifications according to the ability and force of character of other members of the family group. A woman is not supposed to rule; as a girl she should obey her father, as a wife her husband, as a widow her grown-up son. But, while it is true that the status of women is low, it would be a great mistake to infer that they can have no influence. Of the twenty-four examples of filial piety, more than half are instances of piety towards mother or stepmother; an aged mother is usually treated with much deference. The duty of a son to his parents takes precedence of his duty to wife or children. The eleventh of the examples of filial piety is a man who, because his means are insufficient to maintain his mother and his child, says to his wife: 'One may get another child, but it is impossible to get another mother,' and proposes to economize by burying his child alive. As he is digging the grave, he is rewarded by finding a pot of gold. According to the same principle, to put away a wife because she is displeasing to her mother-in-law is laudable; and it is considered right to subordinate the wife's interests to the mother's. The object of having children is broadly stated to be that parents may in old age enjoy their ministrations; and *hsiao* has been defined as to serve parents with propriety, to bury them with propriety, and to sacrifice to them with propriety (*Analects*, bk. ii. ch. v.). A parent's birthdays are times of congratulation, particularly from the fiftieth year onwards, men observing their fifty-first, sixty-first birthday, and so on, while women observe their fiftieth, sixtieth, etc. A coffin is considered to be an appropriate gift from a filial son to his parents; and to provide a seemly funeral is an important part of his duty, though extravagance is not favoured by classical precept. The great importance attached to *hsiao* underlies the practice of rewarding a man's merit by granting honours to his deceased parents and ancestors; on the other hand, to say to a child that he lacks family training is, by its reflexion on his parents, felt to be a severe rebuke. Parental authority is not less wide than filial duty. If filial piety suggests the sacrifice of a child to a mother's comfort, paternal authority is warrant for the deed. In practice, if not in law, it lies with the parents to decide whether a new-born child shall be brought up or not. The question, of course, concerns female children only: 'One may kill a girl though she might have become a queen; no one kills a boy though he may become only a beggar.' The extent of infanticide varies in different times and places; in some it is lamentably common. It may seem a paradox to say that a nation in which infanticide is practised, not indeed without protest (cf. Chinese tracts against it), but without grave social reprobation, is also distinguished by love of young children; but the fact is so. Among the poorer classes very young children take their share in the family work, attending to still younger children, herding cattle or geese, and gathering fuel. But, in spite of all that can be fairly urged, it is easy to do less than justice to the happiness of Chinese children. Where foot-binding is practised it is, of course, both crippling and painful.

Corresponding to filial piety the parental virtue is *tz'ŭ*, 'tenderness.' More generally it is the mother who is spoken of as the Family Tenderness, while the father is the Family Gravity (*yen*). 'A grave father makes filial sons,' and paternal severity is recommended by the example of Confucius, who maintained towards his son an attitude of distant reserve (*Anal.*, bk. xvi. ch. xiii.). Manuals of family discipline are not lacking which exhibit an ideal of family life. Of these a well-known example is Chu Fu Tzŭ's *Family Instructor*, with its precepts on cleanliness, moderation, economy, and education, and its hinted darker side in its warnings against the beauty of maids and concubines or the good looks of young serving-lads. Family training is, on the whole, not well carried out. Excessive indulgence and weak retreat before childish obstinacy are apt to alternate with passionate anger and unreasonable harshness. In the case of children who are guilty of extreme disregard for their parents, appeal may be made to a magistrate; or, in spite of legal restrictions, a father may exercise his own disciplinary powers with little fear of question, even in those very rare cases in which he may arrange to have his son removed by death, though, in the case of a son adopted from beyond the family, questions might be raised by his relatives. Crimes against parents are particularly heinous. The guilt of parricide is such as to involve not only the whole family of the parricide, but also his neighbours and his teacher.

Adoption.—Where children are lacking, or an adult son has died unmarried or childless, the family succession is provided for by adoption. The most usual course is to adopt a son. Sometimes—perhaps as a cheaper expedient—a daughter is adopted, and a son-in-law brought in for her. The adopted son is often a nephew, or is one belonging to the family of a near relative, or at least is of the same surname. In one case known to the present writer, adoption from another surname is forbidden under an ancestor's malediction. There is, however, no absolute rule on this point. An adopted son is, as to his rights and his duties towards his adoptive parents, in the position of a son by birth.

Property.—The father's discretion in the division of the family property is strictly limited, and any departure from use and wont would be checked by the collective opinion of the family expressed through the nearer relatives. Daughters do not inherit. The eldest son usually receives a larger share than any of his brothers, in view of his greater responsibility for the carrying out of the rites of filial piety ('Incense lamp fields'); but in this, as in other matters, custom seems to vary (cf. A. H. Smith, *Village Life*, 327). Sons of concubines take a smaller share than sons of the wife. If the family property has not been divided by the father among his sons before his death, they may continue to hold it in common, and to do so is a laudable evidence of fraternal harmony; or they may proceed to a division by mutual agreement. In this case, their mother's brother is considered a proper person to act as 'divider.' A part of the family property may be set aside to provide for the family's ancestral worship. Such property is held in annual rotation by the sons or their representatives, the holder for the year having to provide what is needed for the ancestral worship, while the remainder of the income falls to himself. In some wealthy families an endowment is also provided for the scholars of the family. Before alienating any family property, the seller is supposed to give his near relatives the option of buying.

3. The family and larger groups.—All families descended from a common ancestor recognize in that a bond of union, and a special kinship is recognized between persons who derive from a common ancestor not more than five generations removed. Among such kinsfolk, mourning is regulated according to the degree of propinquity. Theoretically, all persons of the same surname, however widely separated their native places may be, form one great clan. This clan system, though naturally of little influence except where members of the clan are in geographical proximity, is a very prominent feature of Chinese life. There are villages with hundreds or thousands of inhabitants, all of one surname, and tracing their descent from a common ancestor whose sons were the founders of the 'fathers' houses,' to some one of which each villager belongs. These 'fathers' houses' are distinct entities, and may be friendly or hostile to each other. It is, therefore, a matter of no small moment not only to belong to a powerful clan, but in it to belong to a 'father's house' which is powerful, the degree of its power being determined not by seniority, but by its numbers, wealth, or the official persons who belong to it. The bond of common ancestry is recognized, even though the descendants are not congregated in one village. A centre of union is found in the common ancestral temple or grave, although worship of the common ancestor is apt to decay unless there is common property the tenure of which depends on it. A family register is also kept; and to have his name erased from it is one of the greatest disgraces to which a Chinaman can be subjected. In connexion with the register there is an ingenious plan by which the generation to which a man belongs may be known from his family name. In mnemonic verses, chosen characters are arranged in a certain order, and each of these chosen characters is appropriated to a certain generation, and forms part of the name of all the males belonging thereto. Mutual responsibility is a marked feature of Chinese life; senior relatives for their juniors, and the elders of a clan for its members.

4. Servants and slaves.—In the lower ranks, servants or hired workers are treated very much as being of the family, and take their meals with its members. In the higher ranks this is not so. There, on the one hand, servants show to their masters a ceremonious deference; on the other, they often exercise a freedom of intervention in their master's affairs, both of which are strange to Western manners. Slavery is by no means a prominent feature of Chinese life; though, even where it is unknown as such, there may be those who through stress of poverty have been sold, or have sold themselves, into service. A much more usual type of slavery is seen in the slave girls of well-to-do families. They are the property of their owners, and dependent for their happiness on the goodwill of their mistresses. They are distinguished from daughters of the house by not having their feet bound, and by some differences of attire. When they have grown to womanhood, they may remain in the family as female attendants, though this is rare, or be taken as concubines, or (more reputably) be disposed of in marriage, or as concubines to others. Eunuchs employed as slaves are unknown outside court circles.

5. Social changes.—China is in a state of transition, and the family also is sure to undergo change. Among the influences which may modify her social system are education, increased knowledge of other social systems, female education, changes in industrial conditions with the rise of manufactures, greater facilities for travel, the general shock of the recent revolution, and last, though not least, the spread of Christianity.

LITERATURE.—A. H. Smith, *Village Life in China*, Edin. and Lond. 1900; J. Doolittle, *Social Life of the Chinese*, New York, 1866; E. H. Parker, 'Comparative Chinese Family Law,' *China Rev.* viii. [1879–80] 67–107; E. Faber, *The Status of Woman in China*, Shanghai, 1889.

P. J. MACLAGAN.

FAMILY (Egyptian).—The Egyptian family presents many points of contrast both with the Semitic and with the Greek. Its most interesting characteristics are a distinct preservation of matriarchy, the prominent position of women, and a comparative promiscuity of sexual relations. We may, therefore, regard it as in some ways more primitive than the family in other countries of the ancient world. The prominent position of the women in the family led generally to a prominence of women in Egypt much greater than that allowed to them either among the Semites or in later Greece, and analogous to that apparently enjoyed in a greater degree by the women in early (Mycenæan) Greece. There also, among a people probably racially connected with the Egyptians, a matriarchal idea of the family may be assumed to have brought about a feminine prominence even more pronounced than in Egypt. It was no idea of the equal intelligence of women and men that in Egypt placed the two sexes almost on the same level, and in Minoan Crete perhaps made the women quite as important as the men. This equality arose simply from the matriarchal idea that descent is absolutely certain through the mother, but not through the father, so that the family centres in the house-mother rather than in the house-father; and the woman, instead of being the man's slave, as among the Semites, is in many respects his equal or even superior. But this view of family life makes at the same time for what we should regard as sexual immorality. Thus, at any rate in the royal family, the Egyptians, in order to secure the succession of the mothers in the same family, often married their own sisters. In Roman times we find this practice common among ordinary people.

The most important person in the family was, then, not the father, as among the Semites, but the mother. She was the house-ruler, the *nebt-per*, the focus of the family. Nevertheless, she was the inferior of the man, her husband, in that she was always mentioned after him: on the tombstones she is always the wife (*ḥemet*) of the man, he is never the husband (*zai*) of the woman. After all, she could not become *nebt-per* unless she were first *ḥemet*, and that, when all was said and done, depended on the pleasure of the man. So far the man dominated, but never as the Semitic man did, who was the *ba'al*, 'lord' of his wife, his *b*e*rî'ah*, 'chattel,' or as did the Greek man, who, like Hesiod (*Works and Days*, 403), regarded a wife simply as a necessary possession on a level with his ox and his plough; at Athens only the *hetairai* had any freedom or influence. But, on the other hand, the Semite preserved far greater privacy and holiness of the sexual relations. This agrees perhaps with the Egyptian character, which was and is naturally more open and frank than that of the Semite. Actual marriage with sisters was more or less confined to the royal house (with disastrous results to the Pharaohs), but the indefiniteness of the relations of the women of the family to the men is shown in the fact that the word *senet*, 'sister,' was used not only for the real sisters of a man, but also for his concubines, and even for his *ḥemet*, or wife. Similarly 'brother' might mean 'husband.' The woman who sits at the side of a man in some funerary sculptured group may be described as 'his sister, whom his heart loveth,' or as 'his beloved wife.' He might have many of these 'sisters' together with one wife (rarely two), or no wife at all; in that case there was no properly constituted *nebt-per*, for this only a wife could be. If there were two wives, one was the *nebt-per*; if two *nebut-per* are mentioned on a man's tombstone, it means either that the one succeeded the other in the dignity of house-mother, or that the man had maintained two separate establishments, which had no link save the fact that the same man maintained and fathered both. This a noble might do, and besides the regular 'houses' of his 'wives' he might also possess a *harîm* of concubines. But these had nothing to do with his family or families proper, however much he might favour his natural children. The father could, if he wished, make his son his heir, but this was somewhat opposed to usual custom, which, in accordance with the matriarchal theory, preferred that property should descend in the female line. Thus, ordinarily, it was to the eldest son of the man's eldest daughter that his goods went, and a man's maternal grandfather was considered more closely related to him than his own father. Naturally this elaboration of primitive custom was at war with all parental affection, and so the men constantly broke through it; those in high station, and, above all, the kings, consistently did so. It was rarely that a dead monarch was not succeeded by his own son.

The maternal line of descent had the effect of confusing families, so that the Egyptians had little idea of family history, of genealogies and pedigrees, and never developed the surname or 'patronymic.' Even tribal surnames were unknown. The ordinary man was the son born of his mother So-and-so. Only the man of better class is such-and-such a man's son, the son of him who begat him. Until quite late times the Egyptian traced no genealogy further back than three or four generations, even in the case of a noble house. It is only in the decadence, when Egypt was conscious of her great age, that she became interested in her past, and her children reckoned back the generations of men.

Marriage was effected by means of a properly drawn up legal contract, but of these we have none till the Greek period. There may have been, as in later times, a probationary year, after which, by a certain payment, the marriage might be annulled. The concubine, if free, no doubt was taken by force or came of her own accord; if a slave, she had no voice in the matter, and was sold to her master. Whether a slave-woman could legally be made a full wife we do not know. The king was subject to the same laws and customs in this regard as his subjects. In contrast to Assyria, where only one queen appears on the monuments, and only two or three are even mentioned during the whole course of the empire's history, the queen of Egypt is always mentioned, and always appears with her consort, who not infrequently derived his sole right to the crown from her, as in the case of Thutmosis (Thothmes) I. She is called the 'king's wife' simply, or the 'great king's wife,' to distinguish her from other and inferior wives; often she is both 'great king's wife' and 'king's mother' (*ḥemet-nsi ueret*, and *met-nsi*). The 'king's son' (*si-nsi*) might, were he the son of an inferior wife, conceivably have in his veins not a drop of the blood of his father's predecessors on the throne. In this case, his succession could only be assured by force if necessary. Thutmosis III. was related to Amonhatpe (Amenhetep) I. only through the female line, and was actually the son of an inferior wife, if not of a concubine. This last fact rendered his right to the crown so weak that, in order to give him a good claim, it was necessary to marry him to his aunt Hatshepsut, who was wholly of the blood-royal as the eldest daughter of a 'great king's wife' (but whose father, Thutmosis I., was not of royal blood at all). She kept her nephew in the background, herself assuming the royal dignity, not as queen merely but as actual 'king.' In spite of the pre-eminence of the *nebt-per* in the family, there was no precedent for Egypt being directly ruled by a woman; so, as Hatshepsut would have no lord and master in the kingdom, she was obliged to assume, officially, the dress and status of a man. The husband-nephew considered himself wrongfully kept from his rights, for, though the son of a concubine or inferior queen, his marriage with his aunt had at once legitimized his claim to the throne. By herself assuming the crown, Hatshepsut undoubtedly became in law and custom an usurper, and Thutmosis was legally justified in the punishment which he meted out to her adherents after her death.

Difficulties of a similar kind must have repeated themselves indefinitely in the homes of subjects, and yet Egyptian family life was very close and very affectionate. On his tombstone a man's immediate relatives, whether gone before him or surviving him, are all represented bearing the offerings to him and praying that the gods of the dead will give him the kingly funeral meats. The words 'love' and 'beloved' recur more frequently in Egyptian mouths than in those of any other ancient nation, for none, whether father, mother, brother, sister, son, or daughter, seems to have been unbeloved by the rest of his family, judging from the inscriptions of the tombstones. This must at times have been an artificial convention, of course (we may be sure that Thutmosis III. did not love his aunt Hatshepsut), but at the same time the convention would not have grown up had not the reality been there, and we obtain the impression in old Egypt of a very close and very loving family life. It is so still: the modern Egyptian is usually a fond father, though Islām has turned his relation to his wife into a tyranny (albeit often a kind one) which his forefathers did not know. The ancient Egyptian knew no other object in marriage than the possession of children by both man and wife in common; children came normally to all, whether prince or peasant, as one of the best of the good gifts of the gods, and, though not necessary to his soul's health after death, it was at least desirable that a man should have sons to make the funerary offerings and pray for the safety of their father's spirit in the under world. We have not, even in the funerary stelæ of ancient Greece, such constant insistence on family solidarity and affection as we see in the Egyptian gravestones, especially those of the Middle Kingdom; and in later times the same spirit is revealed in the repeated bas-reliefs in the tombs of el-Amarna, which show the heretical king, Akhenaten, with his sister-queen Nefert-iti and their little daughters, always together and represented as exhibiting the closest mutual affection. From Babylonia and Assyria we have nothing of the same kind; king Asshurbanipal is shown once feasting with his queen (with the head of his enemy, the king of Elam, hanging in a bush close by), but no sign of marital affection appears, and the king's children are never represented. The greater harshness of the Semitic nature and the more 'human' character of the Egyptians are very apparent when we compare their 'family life.'

Families were usually large, especially under the Middle Kingdom. No pressure of economic conditions existed, as in modern times, to act as a check upon the increase of offspring; there was subsistence for all, within reason. Only a king could, if he desired, bring an enormous number of children into the world, but we may be sure that not many cared to emulate Rameses II., who is said to have had two hundred children; one hundred and three of his sons and fifty-nine of his daughters are actually known to us. The descendants of these people formed an important body of princely parasites for centuries; reasons of policy would forbid such reckless conduct on the part of later monarchs. As in all societies in a similar stage of development (*e.g.* India and China to-day), pestilence and war served as the natural checks on a too prolific increase of the race. Death took early toll then, as it does now, of the Egyptians; and, though we have many instances of very aged persons, yet the funerary stelæ show how enormous a proportion of the population died young. The age of the deceased is never given, but we see from their representations that they were commonly young: children with the side-lock (see below) constantly appear in rows, one after the other, each with the epithet *ma'at-kheru* ('acquitted,' *sc.* of sin in the Hall of Osiris) or *uḥem-'ankh* ('repeating life'), the usual equivalents of our 'deceased,' after its name. These representations of children, one often a head taller than the next, and so on, remind us of the rows of sons and daughters shown on the brasses of the 15th to 17th centuries in our churches. Of course, as in these modern brasses, all the children or other persons shown on an Egyptian stele are not dead; the whole family is shown, dead and living together, bringing offerings to the tomb of the owner of the stele.

The large number of children often caused confusion in family nomenclature. After the death of a child bearing a certain name, another might be born to whom the same name might be given, and both appear on the same stelæ of their parents. But very often two, sometimes many more, children living at the same time might bear the same appellation—a fact which makes the ancient genealogies often very difficult to unravel.

Children in ancient Egypt were differentiated

from their elders by a special mark—the manner of dressing their hair. Whereas, with the exception of the soldiers and often the peasants, the Egyptian men always shaved the whole head and wore wigs, the boys either shaved or close-cropped only part of it, leaving on one side a long lock, which was always carefully plaited in a pigtail hanging to the shoulder or below it. Sometimes the whole hair seems to have been worn gathered into this single thick pigtail over the ear. Rarely, and only under the Old and Middle Kingdoms, does the tail appear to have been worn at the back of the head. It was usually retained till manhood; sometimes we find portrait-figures of young men who wear both the natural pigtail and a wig, the former coming out of a hole in the latter! In later times the princes seem all their lives to have worn this lock, which marked their position as 'royal children' (in their case it seems sometimes to have been a representation of the lock rather than natural hair). The girls wore the same lock, but often in a number of small braids or not plaited at all, whereas that of the boy was always a single plait. And very often the girls did not shave the rest of the head, but wore the rest of their hair hanging down, the 'lock of youth' being simply tied separately at the side. On reaching womanhood a great wig was often worn on the top of the natural hair, though sometimes the women seem to have shaved their heads or cropped their hair short like the men, always, of course, wearing their long wig over it.

Children of both sexes usually wore no clothing whatever till the age of puberty, and even then the girls often wore nothing but a slight girdle. The mother was assisted in their care by the nurse (*men'at*), who was an important person in the family, and is commonly represented on the tombstones as a member of it. The ideograph of her name shows that she was primarily a wet-nurse or foster-mother. The name was transferred to male nurses (like our 'nurse'), and we find the great nobles who acted as tutors or governors of royal princes bearing it as their official title ('royal nurse').

We thus see that the love of the Egyptians for their children, the important position of their wives, and their interest in their families and dependants enable us to give a very full idea of the ancient Egyptian family and its life.

See also CHILDREN (Egyptian) and MARRIAGE (Egyptian).

LITERATURE.—Good general account in **A. Erman**, *Life in Ancient Egypt*, tr. Tirard, London, 1894, p. 150 ff. For the funerary stelæ, see **Lange** and **Schäfer**, *Grab- und Denksteine des mittleren Reichs*, Cairo Catalogue, Berlin, 1902; and **Hall** and **Scott-Moncrieff**, *Hieroglyphic Texts from Egyptian Stelæ in the British Museum*, pt. 2, London, 1912. The present writer has in this article used his general knowledge of the stelæ in the British Museum. For the reliefs of Akhenaten and his family, see **N. de G. Davies**, *Rock Tombs of El Amarna*, London, 1903 ff., and **A. E. P. Weigall**, *Akhnaton, Pharaoh of Egypt*, London, 1910. On the relationship of Thutmosis III. to Hatshepsut, the present writer's position is midway between that of Naville and that of Sethe and Breasted (see the long controversy in *ZÄ*, *passim*: the matter is not yet settled satisfactorily). On marriage with sisters at Arsinoë in Roman times, see **U. Wilcken**, in *Abhandl. k. preuss. Akad.*, 1883, p. 903.

H. R. HALL.

FAMILY (Greek).—**1. Position of women in society.**—The position of women in Athens in the 5th cent. B.C. and afterwards differs strikingly from their position in Doric States like Sparta, or in the earlier period pictured by the Homeric poems. The *Odyssey* presents Penelope as the honoured wife and queen; Arete is almost on the same plane as her husband Alcinous; and, when Telemachus is entertained by Menelaus in the Spartan court, Helen takes precedence over her husband in caring for the guests, she corrects his mistakes, and her advice is followed in the questions under discussion. In *Il.* xxiv. 200 ff. we find Hecuba present with the men in council, as was Arete in the council of the Phæacians (*Od.* xi. 335). The princes of these poems have each one wife, though they may also have concubines, and the wife shares her husband's position before the world.

While in the Sparta of later days women shared the respect paid to men, since in bearing children they also performed a great duty to the State, the condition of affairs in Athens was decidedly different. Normally a woman could not appear before the courts, but must be represented by her husband or her guardian; in fact, her position legally was almost comparable with that of a slave. Unfair as it would be to accept the estimate of comedy or of such a poet as Euripides, still the whole trend of literature, history, and philosophy, as well as poetry, points to the subordinate place of woman in Athenian life. Her sphere is the home; and, although she is not locked up in an Oriental *harîm*, her life is compared with that of a tortoise in that it is restricted to the home (Plut. *Mor.* 142 B). Silence becomes her, even in her husband's presence; she does not meet his guests; nor is she in any sense his intellectual or social companion. Even in time of war the woman of position is not expected to leave the house without her husband's knowledge or without proper attendants. Under these restrictions she might visit women friends near by, she was expected to attend certain religious festivals, mainly festivals of women, and she performed rites in honour of the dead. In the home the entire administration of the household fell to her: the care of the stores, the arrangement of the meals, and, in particular, the direction of spinning and weaving to provide garments for the family. Her special duty was to care for the children, boys up to the age of eight or ten, and girls till they were married. It was this preoccupation with simple tasks and the seclusion in the house which prevented any real development of intellectual life among women, and consequently any ability to share the husband's intellectual life. Moreover, the education of girls before marriage was extremely limited (see EDUCATION [Greek]). It was primarily of a practical nature—training in morals and manners, in spinning, in weaving, and in the direction of the household. The intercourse even with other girls was limited, and it was only on the occasion of some religious festival that a girl had any opportunity to see men other than her father and the slaves of the household. See, further, WOMAN (Greek).

2. The reasons for marriage.—Such being the position of women at Athens as daughters and wives, it is not strange that some brilliant women, of whom Aspasia is a typical example, should not have conformed to the standards of Athenian family life. It is not so strange at first sight that Athenian society gave great freedom to men, both unmarried and married, in matters of social morality, as it is that the family thus strictly defined should have existed at all. The reason for the existence of the family and for the strictness with which daughters and wives were guarded is the same, namely, the importance of securing sons to continue the activities of the father in service to the State and to the gods. It is true that occasionally the need of a housekeeper is emphasized (Eur. *Alc.* 946 f.; Arist. *Eth. Nic.* viii. 14, p. 1162), but the house might have been managed, as a business was managed, through a competent slave. The Athenian married that he might have sons who would be recognized by law and religion. To them he might safely look for care in his old age, and in their activities he could see with satisfaction the continuation of the work to which he had devoted his life (Plato, *Symp.* 207). In rearing them he performed his best service to the State, for citizenship was limited to men of legitimate birth; and the preservation of the reputation of the family in the State was a very strong incentive to good citizenship. In Sparta the fines for men who did not marry (Stob. *Flor.* lxvii. 16), in Athens the demand that statesmen and generals be married (Dein. *in Dem.* § 71), and the disgrace of daughters who did not find a husband (Soph. *Œd. Tyr.* 1500), illustrate the importance attached to this duty, which naturally is emphasized in Plato's philosophy of the State. Religion also demanded that a man marry and raise up sons to continue his line. The worship of the State-gods was carried on by legitimate citizens, and on this ground also Plato rests the duty of marriage (*Leg.* vi. 773 E). Further, certain forms of religious service were the duty and privilege of particular families, which must be kept up in order that this service may be performed. Finally, the wellbeing of the dead (of a man's ancestors, and his own well-being after death) depended on offerings by his descendants (Isocr. xiv. 60; Plato, *Hipp. Maj.* 291 E), so that actual or adopted sons (Isæus, vii. 30) were necessary to perform this important service.

3. The choice of a wife depends on this conception of marriage as a duty to the State, to the gods, and to one's self. A man's wife is ordinarily chosen by his father, who deals with the father of the proposed bride, and there is little or no opportunity for romance or individual choice, since ordinarily the girl has had no opportunity of seeing her future husband before betrothal, and hardly any opportunity before marriage. Even the consent of the parties themselves need not be asked, for the girl has no occasion to object, and the youth can have his income cut off if he does not agree. The picture of Hæmon and Antigone in Sophocles' *Antigone* is evidently an exception to the rule, even in literature. That marriage was conceived as a duty and arranged by the parents does not, of course, mean that in ancient Athens (any more than in modern countries where marriage is arranged by parents) the husband did not often come to have real regard and love for his wife.

The woman chosen for a wife must, of course, be the daughter of an Athenian citizen, for only the children of such a marriage would be legitimate. She might be, and often was, a near relative of her future husband. Usually the bride would be a girl between fifteen and twenty, unless, indeed, she were a widow; and her husband would be between twenty and thirty years of age. Her beauty would count for something, her skill in the feminine arts, such as spinning and weaving, for more; but the important thing was rather that her social position and her dowry should be comparable with the position and wealth of her future husband. The reason for this is simple, in that a woman with small dowry would often fail to win her husband's respect, while a wife with a very large dowry might make her husband very uncomfortable by interfering with his financial management of the property, if not with other sides of his life (cf. Plato, *Leg.* vi. 774 D; Plut. *de Educ. Puer.* 13 F; Arist. *Eth. Nic.* viii. 10. 5, p. 1161*a*). See, further, MARRIAGE (Greek).

4. The family a religious institution.—While marriage and the family were definitely legal institutions, the religious side must be clearly recognized. Like every other human institution, the family needed the divine blessing, and religious rites to obtain this blessing were not neglected even in times when belief in the gods became vague or insincere. Indeed, they could not well be neglected, for, in so far as the family was recognized by the State, it was a duty to the State to follow the customary rites in invoking the blessing of the gods. So far as the marriage ceremony was concerned, the religious rites attending it resembled in principle the religious rites attending any important undertaking. They consisted in sacrifices to the patron gods of marriage on the day before the wedding, and again in connexion with the wedding banquet. The choice of the gods to whom these sacrifices were offered, rather than the character of the sacrifices, was significant. Zeus and Hera, who, with local deities, were honoured in the preliminary sacrifices, were not only the patrons of marriage as a human institution, but also the gods whose relations represented the type of the human family in the Olympian circle. Similarly, the gods of the household and Aphrodite, who were honoured at the marriage feast itself, were the gods who watched over the relations of the new family. Just as the religious character of any Greek institution finds expression in the gods with whom it is associated, so the religious character of the family is seen in the nature of the gods invoked in the marriage ceremony.

Further, Greek religion was a matter of social groups like the family or the tribe or the State, before it was a matter of the individual. The worship of the family centred in Hestia (Vesta), the personified hearth-flame. At her round altar, hung with fillets, in the main room of the house, libations were offered at each meal, and she was recognized in connexion with every sacrifice that took place in the home. Other gods also were worshipped—Apollo the Guardian, whose symbol or altar stood outside the door; the patron gods of their race, whose shrine might be in a room off the main hall; Zeus Herkeios, whose altar stood in the court; and the gods of property like Zeus Ktesios; even gods from different shrines in the city might be represented by small images in the home. At all the events of family life, such as the birth of a child, the coming of age of a son, or in cases of sickness or death, the gods of the home were worshipped. On home anniversaries such as birthdays, and often on the occasion of public worship in the city, sacrifices were offered in the home. In a word, the Greek family was a religious institution, because every social institution in Greece was essentially religious.

5. The relation of members of the family.—The effort to ascertain from Greek literature the meaning of the family as an ethical institution is complicated by various difficulties. Pictures of private life are not found in the earlier literature, and we are left to deduce the facts from occasional allusions in philosophical writings and speeches, or from the exaggerations of comedy, or from the high ideal plane of tragedy. Xenophon's account of the training he proposed to give his young wife on marriage (in the *Œconomicus*) is a welcome exception, even if Xenophon can hardly be regarded as the type of an Athenian citizen.

If we go back to the Homeric poems, we find charming pictures of the intimate relations of husband and wife, in particular of Hector and Andromache (*Il.* vi.), of Alcinous and Arete (*Od.* vi.–viii.), of Odysseus and Penelope. In the words of Odysseus to Nausicaa (*Od.* vi. 180 f.; cf. Hesiod, *Erga*, 702), 'There is nothing mightier and nobler than when man and wife are of one heart and mind in a house, a grief to their foes, and to their friends great joy, but their own hearts know it best' (tr. Butcher and Lang).

In later literature the references to this subject are few but striking. It is Euripides who describes the chaste wife who makes the home life happy, so that the husband rejoices when he enters, and calls himself fortunate as he goes out (*Iph. Aul.* 1158 ff.). Euripides also speaks of the sweet deceit of a wife who softens the trouble and cheers the illness of her husband (frag. 819). In her husband's absence it is her lot to suffer (Æsch. *Agam.* 861 f.); in his presence there is such complete trust and understanding that burdens are lightened (Soph. *Œd. Tyr.* 769 f., and *passim*). By the time of Aristotle the entire community of life between husband and wife is emphasized (Arist. *Eth. Nic.* viii. 14, p. 1162*a*, 19–29; cf. Isocr. iii. 40); and Plutarch (*Mor.* 59 F) names honour to the wife as one of the essentials of family life.

While these references in literature can hardly be regarded as pure imagination of poets and theories of philosophers, we must not fail to recognize the conditions which limited the development of such relations. In general it is clear that the possibilities of intellectual companionship were limited by the very restricted opportunities of the wife for any intellectual development. Where books hardly existed in the home, and where women never came in contact with any one but slaves, even if the latter were sometimes educated persons, they could not be expected to meet their husbands on common ground intellectually. Certain pleasures belonged to husband and wife in common —pleasure in the comfortable, well-regulated home and in the growing children; perhaps sometimes the pleasures of music. Common purposes and ideals they certainly shared so far as the sons and daughters were concerned. Of affection between husband and wife one can say but little. It seems hardly possible, however, that the pictures of affectionate husbands and wives in Greek tragedy could have been appreciated by the Athenian audience, or even conceived at all, if they had no counterpart in the actual life of the day.

The relation of parents to children is frequently referred to in literature. Three similes in the *Iliad* (iv. 130, xv. 362, xvi. 7) express the tender sympathy of the mother for her child. The joy of Æson in his son Jason and of Telamon in his son Ajax is described by Pindar (*Pyth.* iv. 120 f., *Isthm.* v.); the love of Creon for Hæmon, temporarily blinded by passion, in Sophocles' *Antigone*, the mother's joy in Cleobis and Biton (Herod. i. 31), and the pain Medea inflicted on Jason by killing their children (Eur. *Medea*), are examples that might be multiplied indefinitely. The reverse of the same thought is found in the pain when children turn out badly (Isæus, v. 39; Theog. 271 ff.); and, when this feeling of tenderness to children seems to be lacking, as in the case of Demosthenes, who placed the prosperity of the State above his personal loss in his daughter's death, it is a fit subject for public reproach (Æschin. *in Ctes.* 77).

The visible record of parental affection is preserved to us in the representations of mother and child on Attic vases, and in various representations of the family on Attic grave-reliefs. The duty of parents to bring up their children in right ways, and in particular to develop honour to the State and respect for parents, is ordinarily presupposed rather than stated explicitly (cf. Demosth. *Coron.* 22–23; Eurip. *Antiope*, fr. 219). This training in earlier years was supervised by the mother; and, as girls never passed out from the mother's immediate care till they were married, the relation developed between mother and daughter must have been an intimate one. The son early passed from his mother's hands to the schoolmaster, the training slave (παιδαγωγός), and, in less degree, to the father. As to any intimate relation of father and son, we know little except from the evidence of tragedy. It is clear, however, that both sons and daughters were trained strictly in the feeling for the unity of the family, with the duties and the privileges which this imposed.

The relation between brothers, and between a brother and a sister, is not infrequently mentioned from the Homeric poems onwards. The account of Agamemnon and Menelaus in the *Iliad* (iv. 148 ff., vii. 107) only serves to illustrate the general principle (*Od.* viii. 546). The affection of a brother and sister is best illustrated by the story of Electra and Orestes as it was developed in literature and in art.

The duty of children toward their parents is first a material one, namely, to care for them in their old age (Lysias, xiii. 45; Isæus, vii. 30). More broadly it is described as honour towards parents (Lycurg. *Leocr.* 94; and esp. Pindar, *Pyth.* vi. 23 ff.). Plato goes so far as to say that piety towards parents is the best worship of the gods (*Leg.* xi. 930 E ff.), and the absence of such piety was at Athens a legal bar from public office (Dein. ii. 17). For the Athenians the most repulsive phase of the Sophistic attack on moral ideals concerned this point (Aristoph. *Clouds*, 994 f.; Xen. *Mem.* iii. 5. 15), and the problems which arose for sons, when one parent was turned against another, as in the story of Eriphyle or of Clytæmnestra, proved extremely interesting to the Greeks.

Judged by the only data at our disposal—those of myth and literature and art—the unity of the family was the fundamental conception of Greek society and Greek morals. When the hold of other social and political institutions had begun to weaken, the family still retained its solidarity, and duties to the family were observed with care.

Cf. also the 'Greek' section of artt. CHILDREN, EDUCATION, MARRIAGE.

LITERATURE.—F. H. Müller, *Ueber das Familienleben der homerischen Zeit*, Zeitz, 1866; J. P. Mahaffy, *Social Life in Greece*, London, 1874 (new ed. 1898); G. Glotz, *La Solidarité de la famille dans le droit criminel en Grèce*, Paris, 1904; W. H. S. Jones, *Greek Morality*, London, 1906, p. 83; C. A. Savage, *The Athenian Family*, Baltimore, 1907; T. D. Seymour, *Life in the Homeric Age*, New York, 1907, p. 117.

ARTHUR FAIRBANKS.

FAMILY (Hindu).—**1.** The family in India is of the *joint-family* type, and it is chiefly for this reason that the Indian family law differs so much from that of Europe. Its main principles were early reduced to writing in the well-known legal Sanskrit treatises called *Dharmaśāstras* or *Smṛtis*, all the more important of which have been published in English. This so-called Hindu law is still applied, throughout British India, in all questions relating to the inheritance, succession, and marriage of Hindus, to caste, and to Hindu religious usages or institutions.

2. The state of a family living in union implies a common habitation as well as community of property, of meals, and of cultus. It may be described, with H. Maine, as 'a group of natural or adoptive descendants held together by subjection to the eldest living ascendant, father, grandfather, or great-grandfather. The head of such a group is always in practice despotic' (*Early History of Institutions*, London, 1875, p. 116; cf. *Ancient Law*[10], do. 1907, p. 133). It should be added that, if the family chose to continue united after the father's death, the eldest son would generally become its head, as stated in the lawbook of Nārada: 'Let the eldest brother, by consent, support the rest like a father.' The position of such an eldest son managing the family estate is also a very influential one, though not equal in dignity to that of a father, whose power resembles the *patria potestas* of the paterfamilias in ancient Roman law.

Thus 'a wife, a son, and a slave, these three are declared to have no property; the wealth which they earn is (acquired) for him to whom they belong' (Manu, viii. 416). 'That is declared a valid transaction which is done by the senior or head of a family. That is not valid which has been transacted by one who does not enjoy independence' (Nārada, i. 42).

Even nowadays the manager (*kartā*) does not confine himself to the financial part of the household; there is not a single domestic affair of any importance which may be undertaken without his consent or knowledge; and he is even expected to watch over the spiritual needs of all the members, and to check irregularities of all kinds by his sound discipline. The extent of his sway may be gathered from the facts that married sons in India, with their wives and children, generally choose to remain under the paternal roof, as they marry very early, and avoid the responsibility and expense of a separate establishment; that adopted and illegitimate sons may have to be added to the legitimate sons; that polygamy and concubinage are not forbidden, whereas the re-marriage of widows is objected to; and that a respectable Hindu is often obliged to support indigent relatives together with their families, as well as a hereditary family-priest and other hangers-on. It should be remarked, however, that the general body of an undivided family extends further than the coparcenary, which consists of the three generations next to the owner of certain property in unbroken male descent, and possesses a right of survivorship for all the descendants included in it.

3. The *eldest son* is not infrequently allowed by the father to manage the affairs of the family under his direction, and he may even himself become the *kartā* during the lifetime of the father, if the latter is advanced in years and unable or unwilling to continue to concern himself with matters of a secular nature. After the father's death, the eldest son, as mentioned before, will generally succeed him, though this is no invariable rule. The precept of Nārada is still occasionally followed, that even the youngest brother may govern the family if specially capable, because the prosperity of the whole family depends on ability. It is seldom, if ever, that more than one member of a family takes part in the management, though there is nothing to prevent such democratic methods of family government. The *kartā* is, however, liable to render an account; it has been so held by a full bench of the Calcutta High Court.

4. The *wife* of the manager, called *ghinni*, also occupies a responsible position, as she has to look after the inner department of the household, to see that every one is duly fed, to regulate her expenses according to the means of the family, to exercise a mild and prudent sway over her daughters and daughters-in-law and over the domestic servants, to get her daughters married at an early age, and have their nuptials properly celebrated. As for the task of educating her children, it would be a mistake to expect too much from a mother who herself is in most cases unacquainted with the barest elements of knowledge, entirely governed by religious notions of the crudest kind, and given to superstitious practices.

5. The *daughters* and *daughters-in-law*, whose attitude towards one another is not always that of strict harmony and peace, are not only subject to the control of the female head of the house, shut up as they are in the family *zenana*; they also labour under all the disadvantages and hardships incidental to the difficult position of females in an Eastern country. Thus a young daughter-in-law in a genteel family is regarded as immodest and unmannerly, if she should happen accidentally to enter the outer or male compartment of the house. No married female is permitted to leave the house, without having first obtained the sanction of the male or female head of the family, or otherwise than in a closed conveyance, either a *pālkī* or a carriage. Women take their meals after the men, and the choicest part of the food is first offered to the males, and the residue kept for the females.

6. Most women in India are strictly religious; the *ghinni* in particular hardly ever fails, after breakfast, to go through her morning service in the domestic place of worship, at the close of which she invokes the blessing of her guardian deity. All the inmates of the house, both male and female, are expected to be present at the daily *pūjā* performed by the hereditary priest of the family, and to make their obeisance to the stone or metal image of the tutelary god of the house. In rich families, a sufficient endowment in inalienable landed property is set apart for the permanent support of the idol.

7. From a legal point of view, the subject of *maintenance* is important, especially as this includes defraying the expense incurred for the nuptials and other religious ceremonies, or *saṁskāras*, of the younger male members of the family. Those who, owing to some bodily or mental defect, are disqualified from inheriting under the Hindu law have a claim to maintenance against the head of the house. Illegitimate sons and concubines are also entitled to be maintained.

8. *Partition* is another important subject. According to the 11th cent. *Mitākṣarā* (a well-known authoritative Sanskrit commentary), partition is the adjustment into specific portions of divers rights of the several members of a joint-family, *i.e.* the ascertaining of individual rights which during the joint condition—where the members share in food, worship, and estate—are not thought of. Partition, according to the same authority, may take place at the desire of a single male member, who is therefore at liberty, as far as he is concerned, to terminate the joint-tenancy, the other coparceners having to submit to it whether they like it or not. In Bengal, however, real partition may take place only after the father's death, when any co-sharer is at liberty to demand it. Such is the law as laid down in the 15th cent. *Dāyabhāga*, the author of which is supposed, in order to prevent the growth of disobedience by sons, to have deprived the latter of the right of enforcing partition against the father's wish. It appears probable that throughout India partition against the father's will was, down to very recent times, considered very much *contra bonos mores*, even where it was not forbidden.

9. The early Sanskrit lawbooks contain long lists of *secondary sons* who may be used to supply the place of a legitimate son, if the latter should happen to be wanting. This topic of the secondary sons (*gauṇaputra*) is also treated in the learned Sanskrit commentaries of later times, though all the various ancient modes of filiation had gradually become obsolete except the device of adoption, which has remained a highly important and vigorous institution down to the present day (see ADOPTION [Hindu]). Of the other subsidiary sons, the *kṣetraja*, or son of the wife, was the son begotten of one man's wife by another, after express authorization, the legitimate husband being childless and impotent, disordered in mind, incurably diseased, or dead.

Thus, in the Sanskrit Epics, King Saudāsa is reported to have induced the sage Vasiṣṭha to beget for him a son by his queen; and the two brothers Dhṛtarāṣṭra and Pāṇḍu, the ancestors of the chief heroes of the *Mahābhārata*, are said to have been begotten by the sage Vyāsa for King Vichitravirya. This custom corresponds in part to the *levirate* of the Israelites, and has been found to prevail among many nations of antiquity and recent times in all parts of the globe.

A son secretly born (*gūḍhaja*) from adulterous intercourse is also said to become the son of his mother's husband: if a pregnant young woman marries, her son belongs to the husband, and is called a son received with the bride (*sahoḍha*); and the son of a girl (*kānīna*), if she marries, becomes her husband's son; whereas, should she remain unmarried, he is reckoned as the son of her father. The latter principle is equally applicable in the case of the *putrikāputra*, or son of an appointed daughter, whose son became the son of her father, if the latter had no male issue. Somewhat peculiar is the case of the *paunarbhava*, or son of a woman twice married, who appears among the secondary sons, because women, under the Brahman law of marriage, are not permitted to marry more than once—a prohibition which has only been removed by the English legislation of the last century.

10. The hankering after sons, which is evidenced by the recognition of these various substitutes for a real legitimate son, seems to have originated in the exigencies of a primitive state of society when male issue was greatly prized, because the prosperity of a family used to depend on the number of hands able to cultivate the family property; and the very existence of a tribe surrounded by enemies depended on the number of its male members capable of bearing arms. The happiness of a man even in the next world was connected with the existence of a continuous line of male descendants capable of making the customary offerings to deceased ancestors. Procreation by the father does not appear to have been a necessary element in the conception of sonship, and the chastity of women was not valued very highly.

11. It is not necessary, on the other hand, to explain these anomalies in the early family law of the Brahmans from a supposed universal practice of *polyandry* in ancient India, and to connect them with the polyandrous practices which are no doubt widely prevalent among the non-Aryan races of India. The well-known tale of Draupadī in the *Mahābhārata*, who became the joint-wife of all the five Pāṇḍava brothers, is the only instance of an Aryan woman said to have been the legal wife of several men, and the *Mahābhārata* itself represents the match of Draupadī as unusual and shocking. As for polyandry among non-Aryans, it exists, according to Risley and Gait's *Census Report*, both in the matriarchal form, where a woman forms alliances with a plurality of men not necessarily related to each other, and succession is therefore traced through the female, and in the fraternal, where she becomes the wife of several brothers.

Thus, among the Kannuvans of Madura, a woman may legally marry any number of men in succession, and may bestow favours on paramours without hindrance. Among the carpenter and blacksmith classes in Malabar, the four or five chosen husbands are said to be in the habit of celebrating their polyandrous marriage openly with much pomp. In the Malabar and Canarese *tarwāds* generally, a woman may freely associate with men unrelated to each other, so that the only family group is that of the mother with her children. The family is perpetuated by the female members only, and the person occupying the position of son to a man is the son of his sister. This is the *marumakathayam* law, lit. descent in the line of a nephew or sister's son, which is nowadays confined to the Nāyars or Nairs and other castes on the Malabar coast and in Travancore, but even there is falling into disrepute, and gradually passing into the fraternal form of polyandry or into monandry. The great facilities for divorce which exist in some parts of the Madras Presidency may also be viewed perhaps as a relic of, or akin to, matriarchal polyandry. The fraternal system is still widely spread along the whole of the Himālayan range, including Kashmir, as well as in some parts of S. India, *e.g.* among the Todas in the Nilgīris. In Kashmir the woman is regarded as the wife of all the brothers, as in the case of Draupadī, and the children call them all father.

12. In the Aryan marriage system of India, what strikes a European observer most is the well-nigh universal prevalence of the married state, which is brought about by the custom of *infant marriage* (see CHILD MARRIAGE [in India]). This custom, the gradual growth of which may be traced in the Sanskrit lawbooks, has gone on spreading from the higher castes to the lower till it has become almost universal. There is no greater opprobrium, at least in a genteel family, than to have a daughter unmarried at the age of puberty; hence no father dares run the risk of deferring his daughter's marriage till she is grown up. It may be supposed that the patriarchal power of the *kartā* was adverse, from the outset, to the female members of the family exercising the right of choosing their husbands for themselves. It may be hoped that the movement against infant marriage will gradually gain ground in India, though hitherto it has made but little progress.

13. The prohibition of *widow re-marriage*, which is said to be the social complement of infant marriage, is also a custom of ancient standing which has been spreading from the higher castes to the lower. Among the latter, however, it often meets with strenuous resistance, women being more of a power than in the higher castes, and naturally prone to set their influence against the obstacles placed in the way of their re-marriage. Among the upper classes, also, social reformers have been constantly advocating the propriety and necessity of widow marriage.

14. *Polygamy*, though permitted in the Sanskrit lawbooks, is rarely practised nowadays, the excess of wives over husbands not amounting to more than 8 and 7 in the thousand respectively among Hindus and Buddhists. It is quite unusual to take a second wife, unless the first wife should be barren or afflicted with some incurable disease; and, even then, a man has often to obtain the consent of his first wife, or of his caste *panchāyat*, or of both.

15. The *Śāstras* contain many curious rules regarding *prohibited degrees* in marriage, the principal rule being that bride and bridegroom should never belong to the same *gotra*, or clan (see CASTE, § 11). These exogamous rules are crossed by an endogamous principle, under which intermarriage between persons differing in caste is strictly forbidden (see MARRIAGE [Hindu]). In practice, any marriage may be said to be valid which has been celebrated in the presence, and with the presumed assent, of the relatives and leading members of the caste.

16. It should be observed, perhaps, that the otherwise strict rule against intermarriage between different castes is relaxed in the case of what has been called *hypergamy*, or 'marrying up,' *i.e.* the custom forbidding a woman to marry a man of a group lower than her own, and compelling her to marry into a group equal or superior in rank. This custom is both wide-spread and ancient, the Code of Manu styling marriages between men of a higher class and women of a lower class as according to the order of nature, while marriages of the converse type are unnatural. Social reformers have endeavoured to check the operation of the general rule against intermarriages by a proposed fusion of the existing sub-castes.

17. The universally prevailing custom of celebrating the *nuptials* with great pomp, and often lavish expense, may be cited as a proof of the importance and sanctity of marriage in the eyes of the people. Some of the ceremonies customary at a wedding are extremely ancient, and seem to have come down from Aryan times. It is true that *concubinage* is tolerated, both the concubine or female slave and the illegitimate son being mentioned in the Sanskrit Commentaries as members of a joint-family. Since the abolition of slavery, however, public opinion on this head has greatly changed; and it is only in the case of holders of *rājyās*, or large estates, or among very low-caste people, that concubines living as members of the family of the man keeping them may now sometimes be found. See also ADULTERY (Hindu).

LITERATURE.—H. Zimmer, *Altind. Leben*, Berlin, 1879; G. Bühler, *The Laws of Manu*, Oxford, 1886 (=*SBE* xxv.); W. Stokes, *Hindu Law Books*, Madras, 1865; G. Sarkar, *Hindu Law*[2], Calcutta, 1903; J. D. Mayne, *Hindu Law and Usage*[7], Madras, 1906; B. Mullick, *Essays on the Hindu Family in Bengal*, Calcutta, 1882; J. Jolly, *Recht und Sitte*, Strassburg, 1896 (=*GIAP* ii. 8); E. J. Trevelyan, *Hindu Family Law*, London, 1908; S. C. Bose, *The Hindoos as they are*, Calcutta, 1881; M. F. Billington, *Woman in India*, London, 1895; J. A. Dubois, *Hindu Manners, Customs, and Ceremonies*[3], Oxford, 1906; C. R. Aiyar, *A Manual of Malabar Law*,

Madras, 1883; Risley-Gait, *Report on the Census of India, 1901*, Calcutta, 1903; B. Delbrück, *Indogerm. Verwandtschaftsnamen*, Leipzig, 1889 (=*ASG* xi. 5).

J. JOLLY.

FAMILY (Japanese).—The earliest family system in Japan was that known as *uji*. This word is of the same origin as *uchi*, signifying 'interior' or 'household'; but from the earliest times it has been used exclusively in the sense of 'name,' especially the name of a clan. *Uji* existed from the most ancient times, and constituted the first units of Japanese society.

The organization of the *uji* was quite complex. It was not a matter of blood relationship alone, but of social, economic, and political interests as well. Originally but a few noble families possessed names and received recognition as *uji*. These *uji* included all the members of the given family, and were named after the favour of the Royal *uji*, the occupation of the family members, or the place of residence. As the numbers within the family increased, the branches were made subdivisions, called *ko uji*, or lesser families, under the authority of the central *uji*, *o-uji*, which in turn was governed by its *kami*, or superiors. Each central *uji*, with its various branches, formed a social body, for the most part sufficient unto itself; and its chief interest became that of self-preservation and self-perpetuation along clear and distinct lines.

As early as the reign of Suinin (29 B.C.), there were laws governing the names of *uji*; and the court carefully looked after their preservation, not allowing names once fixed to be changed except by special arrangement; and, later, establishing such historic *uji* as the Fujiwara, the Minamoto, and the Taira. As the offshoots of the various *uji* still further multiplied, they took various family names, often from the locality, such as Hōjō, Ashikaga, Tokugawa, etc. These names were known as *mioji* (the name of a descendant), as distinct from *uji*; but the use of even the *mioji* was not allowed to the common people until after the opening of the Meiji era in 1868.

As economic groups the *uji* were important. Occupations, trades, and professions were considered hereditary; and, while caste system in the strict sense never existed in Japan, very real bonds held a man to the calling of his father, whether that was the making of swords or the teaching of mathematics at the Government University of the time.

As political factors, the *uji* constituted the very material and machinery of government. Theoretically, the people of Japan were all included in the various branch *uji* of the central *uji*, of which the Emperor was the head; and the national administration, such as it was in those early days, was carried on for the most part through the *uji*. In course of time the large *uji* became very powerful, holding many in a kind of serfdom, and defying the central authority of the Court. Such a state of affairs led to the Taikwa reformation in A.D. 645, which sought to strengthen the Imperial authority by the overthrow of certain powerful *uji*, and the organization of provinces and prefectures as political units in their place. This system, copied from China, was not adapted to conditions in Japan at the time, and soon gave way before the influence of other rising families; but during those years the *uji* underwent modification, which led, by the latter part of the 12th cent., to a more complete development of what may be termed the patriarchal system.

In the *uji* the family, as including the members of one household merely, was merged to a great extent in the larger body of the clan, and possessed no real social influence; but in the patriarchal system its organization became more clearly defined and efficient. The patriarchal system reached its most complete development during the period of the *buké*, or warrior; and it remained practically unchanged for centuries, until the Restoration of 1868. The chief characteristic of the family under this system was the absolute authority of its head. A 'house,' consisting of relatives to the third or fourth generation, was governed by one head, who, of necessity a male but not necessarily the father or senior, exercised almost unlimited power over the property, personal conduct, and lives of his subordinates, the only check upon his actions being a council of relatives who held in sacred regard that which was deemed for the honour and best interests of the family. Both legislative and executive power belonged to the head of a family. He controlled the education of the children, the marriage of the young, the occupation of all. Ceremonies of all kinds were under his direction; and punishment even up to the extreme penalty of death was at his bidding. But this great authority was combined with great obligations; upon the head of a family devolved the duty of its support, and the maintenance of its honour under all circumstances.

Thus far we have considered the position mainly of the male members of the family. In the family of early Japan, the wife and daughter held by nature a place of greater influence and importance than was allowed after the coming of Confucian and Buddhist teachings, which won the allegiance of practically the entire country. Woman's duty became that of obedience to her father, her husband, and her son. She was literally given in marriage by her family; and, when married, she had to render absolute obedience to her husband's parents. Whatever property she brought became the possession of her new family; and there were seven reasons recognized by the law for any one of which she could be sent back divorced to her father's household—barrenness, adultery, disrespect towards father-in-law or mother-in-law, loquacity, theft, jealousy, and foul disease. Furthermore, in the family of the strong and wealthy, the wife, whatever her condition and character, was doomed to association with many concubines in proportion to her husband's prosperity and position.

Filial duty was the chief obligation, including that of revenge. When the head of a family, or a grandfather or grandmother, or a relative was injured or slain by one of another family, the duty of private revenge rested upon his subordinates, upon the children or grandchildren. This obligation was publicly recognized; and in its performance all conceivable obstacles were overcome and dangers met, even women feeling the necessity of obedience to this duty. Private revenge may be considered natural in an age and society where laws are not formulated or firmly enforced by organized government, especially in the country where the military ideal has commanded the respect and adoration of the people.

A sacred meaning was attached to the conception of family under this system. The individual was swallowed up in the common family life, not temporarily but permanently. The family, from its first ancestor to the latest generation, was a unit; and its unbroken continuance was all-important. The departed were regarded as still interested in the condition of the family, affected by its doings, and able to aid its undertakings. In a very real sense the past lived in the present, and was to be honoured by it. Ancestor-worship, while not peculiar to Japan but shared by all clan-peoples, attained among the Japanese a remarkable hold through this sense of family unity; and Shinto, the most essentially Japanese of the faiths, developed at a time when the worship of ancestors was strong and vital. The deified spirits of ancestors, *uji-gami*, protected the home and made it a holy place sanctified by their presence.

Loyalty to the family of the past required that the family of the present should take thought for the family of the future. This perpetuity of the family was attained through the perpetuity of the family head. The eldest son and his eldest son preserved the family name, and so preserved the family. Thus the heir to the family headship was obliged to marry; and for him to die without a male descendant to continue the family and pay due respect to the spirits of the departed was a grave offence against the most sacred law of filial piety. Divorce of the barren and the taking of concubines were honourable if intended for this purpose.

Heirship in the family was not so much a matter of property as of birthright to the position of family head. From this fact grew the system of adoption, when no son was born to succeed to the family name. The adoption was preferably of a relative; but, if circumstances required, it might be of a stranger. The obligation which rested upon the head of the family, as representing the hallowed past, and as responsible for the present and the future, was great; and hence it was most important that he should be a man of real character and ability. From this consideration arose the custom of retirement, *inkyo*, by which one resigned his position as the head of a family to his son or another who should succeed him. This was very common, for various family reasons; and, in the case of influential or royal families, it took place, for political reasons, at the age of fifty, or even much earlier.

With the entrance of Western influence at the dawn of the Meiji era (1868) great changes began in the social and family, as well as business and political, life of Japan. Social changes, to be made safely, have to be made slowly; and many elements of the old patriarchal system are strongly operative to-day; but gradually the principle of individualism is gaining ground. The present Civil Code was compiled, after years of careful study in comparative legislation, by scholars and lawyers. It is modelled in many particulars upon German law, taking ancient customs into due consideration. It became operative on 16th July 1898. In the section concerning the family the old calculation of relationship is abolished; and relatives by blood to the sixth degree, husband and wife, and relatives by affinity to the third degree are recognized as forming a family. An adopted son is recognized as related to the other members of the family as a natural son would be. A 'house' is declared to be the sphere of its headship without regard to personality; and, with a view to putting an end to the objectionable custom of early retirement from active life, it is provided that the headship of a family shall not be resigned before the age of sixty. Furthermore, marriage is recognized as an act requiring formality, and is legalized upon report to the proper Government registrar. Mutual consent and judicial decision are recognized as conditions, one of which must obtain, in securing divorce. A legal agreement may be made concerning the property of husband and wife; but the official head of a family may manage the property of a wife—or of a husband if the head be a woman — unless a special arrangement be made. The wife is regarded as the representative of her husband in the ordinary domestic affairs of the home.

In spite of the spirit of the new laws and the changes which are taking place, it must be said that the country people and farmers still follow, in large measure, the old system in all matters of personal family influence, the young being fettered by the family authority of generations living and dead. Among the educated and in the great centres, on the other hand, the individualistic family of the English and American type, consisting of husband, wife, and children, is becoming the rule. There is everywhere a growing recognition of the individual; but beneath the apparent calm a bitter struggle is going on. Two principles are contending for supremacy: the principle of communism within the family—personal absorption in its interests; and the principle of personal freedom—the right of personal initiative and realization. The young men and women who have received a modern education are at present the greatest sufferers from the strife if, as often happens, they are forced by old customs into an uncongenial marriage, or, on the other hand, if they break too thoughtlessly into rebellion. Nevertheless, 'the old order changeth, yielding place to new.'

LITERATURE. — *EBr*[11], art. 'Japan'; **Kazuo Hatoyama**, 'Japanese Personal Relations' in ch. x. of *Fifty Years of New Japan*, ed. Shigenobu Okoma, Tokyo, 1907–08 (Eng. ed. London, 1909); **L. Hearn**, *Japan*, London, 1904.

TASUKU HARADA.

FAMILY (Jewish).[1]—Though considerably affected on the legal side by non-Jewish environments, Jewish family life has retained, throughout the centuries, a distinct character to which Bible and Talmud contributed. The influence of the family relations has been one of the strongest religious and social forces, making for sobriety and purity, and forming an intimate bond between the individual and the community. Family solidarity, in its aspects of piety and altruism, led to the establishment at once of a private code of morality and a communal linking of the generations. On the one hand, the individual was merged in the family; and, on the other, the family was merged in the community. Every Jew found his joy and his sorrow in all Jews' joys and sorrows. He took a personal interest in the domestic life of the community, for the community was in a very real sense one united family. A marriage, a funeral, each was a congregational event. And, more generally, the social outlook of the whole was based on the virtue of the parts. The serenity and purity of the home worked outwards, and made the communal life pure and serene amid even the most sordid of external conditions. Family chastity, affection, piety, forbearance, and joyousness formed the base of the pyramid on which the communal life was securely erected. Hence the life of Jewry, in the Ghetto period, was independent of, and rose superior to, restrictions which must otherwise have proved demoralizing.

The whole of the family life was pervaded by religion; the home ceremonial in general and the special Sabbath and festival rites combined to make the table an altar. The commonest acts of the daily round were sanctified. The Sabbath in particular had this effect. The legalistic observance of its many restrictions was associated with a spirit of joy and beatitude. On the Sabbath eve the children were blessed—a custom which still widely prevails in Jewish homes.

'Before the children can walk, they should be carried on Sabbaths and holidays to the father and mother to be blessed; after they are able to walk, they should go of their own accord, with bowed body, and should incline their heads and receive the blessing' (Moses Henochs, *Brandspiegel*, tr. Heilprin, Basel, 1602, xliii.).

Jewish family life was based on this mutual reverence between parents and children. It was naturally founded also on law. The parent—especially the father—exercised authority over

[1] See also 'Jewish' sections of BIRTH, EDUCATION, MARRIAGE.

children during their minority (which, in important aspects, ended with the boy at the beginning of the fourteenth and with the girl at the beginning of the thirteenth year). Up to this date the father had power to give his daughter in marriage, though she had certain rights of repudiating (*mi'un*) such marriage. The general tendency has, however, been to postpone marriage until the girl has reached her majority, and the parental authority within the family thus becomes moral rather than legal. A first-century saying shows aptly the combination of the legal with the moral side of the father's influence:

'Our masters have taught, He who loves his wife as himself, and honours her more than himself; who leads his sons and daughters in the straight path, and marries them near their time of maturity;—to his house the words of Job apply (5^{24}), "Thou shalt know that thy tent is in peace"' (Bab. *Yebamoth*, 62*b*).

The child, in accordance with Biblical precept, was bound to honour his parents. This duty was far-reaching—the son was not to occupy the father's seat; he was not to contradict him, or call him by his name. The reader of David Qimḥi's commentaries will recall the regularity with which this author cites his father as 'my lord, my father.' The son could be compelled to maintain his parents. The daughter was bound to honour her father and mother, but, as after her marriage she came under her husband's authority, she was not amenable to all the obligations which fell on the son. On his part the father was expected to teach his children, to have his sons apprenticed to a trade, and to avoid putting unnecessary strains on their respect. Thus the text, Lv 19^{14}, 'Thou shalt not put a stumbling-block before the blind,' was taken as a caution against striking a grown-up child (*Mo'ed Qaṭon*, 17*a*); the child might be tempted to retaliate with a passionate blow.

The confined quarters occupied by the Jews in the Middle Ages, as well as the survival of patriarchal sentiments, often led to the dwelling of the whole family, of several generations, under the same roof. After marriage, the bride's parents would frequently provide accommodation for the son-in-law. In the Orient the system sometimes leads to very complicated legal questions of ownership in the large houses occupied in common by many distinct coteries of the family. This system prevailed more extensively while marriages were contracted at an early age. But, though it was the father who mostly remained head of the family, the mother filled a high place in the esteem of her children and more remote descendants. We have a striking instance of this in the Memoirs of Glückel of Hamelin (17th cent.). After her husband's death (1689) she not only brought up her eight children, but carried on her husband's business. She travelled to the great fairs, and spent her days usually in the warehouse. Her influence over her children was extraordinarily complete, her piety no less than her capacity winning their love and veneration. No greater blow was dealt to the Jewish theory of life than was inflicted by such interferences as the *Familianten-Gesetz* which prevailed in Bohemia, Moravia, and Silesia in the 18th century. In those States no Jew could marry without a special permit from the Government. The avowed object was to prevent any increase of the Jewish population. The law was repealed in 1849, but in many parts of the world the problem of harmonizing Jewish with modern legal requirements has much modified the old family relations which, as Heine has made the modern world understand, turned the Jewish home into 'a haven of rest from the storms that raged round the very gates of the ghettos, nay, a fairy palace in which the bespattered objects of the mob's derision threw off their garb of shame and resumed the royal attire of freemen. The home was the place where the Jew was at his best. In the market-place he was perhaps hard and sometimes ignoble; in the world he helped his judges to misunderstand him; in the home he was himself' (I. Abrahams, *Jewish Life in the Middle Ages*, London, 1896, p. 113; see whole of ch. vii.).

LITERATURE.—P. Buchholz, *Die Familie . . . nach mosaisch-talmud. Lehre*, Breslau, 1867; L. Löw, *Die Lebensalter in der jüd. Literatur*, Szegedin, 1875; M. Güdemann, *Gesch. des Erziehungswesens und der Cultur der Juden*, Vienna, 1880–88; D. Kaufmann, *Die Memoiren der Glückel von Hameln*, Frankfort, 1896; S. Schechter, *Studies in Judaism*, London, 1896, Philadelphia, 1908; S. Krauss, *Talmud. Archäologie*, ii., Leipzig, 1911; I. Abrahams, *op. cit. supra*.

I. ABRAHAMS.

FAMILY (Muslim).—The constitution of the Muslim family is very different from that of the Christian family; it is more indefinite, involved, and complicated. Marriage has not the same binding force; the ceremony is far less solemn—in fact, it is scarcely a public ceremony at all. A first marriage does not debar a man from a subsequent union, polygamy being quite legal; and, outside the married state, the husband is allowed to cohabit with an unlimited number of slaves. The status of the children of these concubines is identical with that of the children of the wedded wives, so that even marriage does not precisely decide the question as to the legitimacy of a child. Furthermore, a Muslim marriage is precarious: divorce is more easily obtained than in any Christian sect. Properly speaking, it is not really divorce that is admitted by Islām—it is the husband's right of repudiation, which he may exercise almost as he pleases. Muslim custom does not give the same social importance to marriage as we do: the wife, always secluded in her apartments, or veiled, does not appear in society at all. A guest or a host must never speak to a Muslim about his wives, or ask any news of them. The education of the children, which is the great family duty in Christianity, is reduced almost to vanishing-point in Islām, and is hardly a subject of interest at all to the parents. Finally, the family makes no effort, such as is made among Christian races, to perpetuate or increase its prosperity and glory from generation to generation; it is, especially in despotic countries, at the mercy of the prince's whims, and may pass in a day from wealth to poverty.

The rules controlling the constitution of the Muslim family are supposed to be laid down by the *Qur'ān*; but they are not found explicitly stated there, and accretions have been formed by custom. Muhammad formally sanctioned polygamy—for himself in particular, since he had several wives (nine, according to some traditions; fourteen, according to others), all of whom he regarded as legitimate; and he always had a revelation to justify these various marriages. But he did not approve of this large number of wives for the general mass of his followers. It is generally said that he forbade them to have more than four legitimate wives; the verse containing this rule, however, is not quite precise:

'If ye fear,' says the Prophet (*Qur'ān*, iv. 3), 'that ye cannot do justice between orphans, then marry what seems good to you of women, by twos, or threes, or fours,' that is, do not marry too many wives if you are not sure of being able to bring up the children.

Tradition has set this limit of four wives for ordinary believers, and has authorized the Khalīfs and Sultans, as successors of the Prophet, to have nine. Muslims are also allowed, according to the most generally accepted tradition, to have as many slaves as they choose, to use as concubines at a moderate fee; these slaves are often the women in the service of their legal wives, and hence arises a situation somewhat painful for the latter. This custom of unlimited concubinage does not appear to be formally sanctioned anywhere in the *Qur'ān*; certain Muslims, indeed, do not think it conformable to the pure teaching of their religion. It is, nevertheless, a custom that has always had wide vogue in Islām, and is, no doubt, of ancient Persian origin. A large number of wives is one of the luxuries almost forced upon a personage of high estate by his position.

By legitimate wives are meant women of free or comfortable estate—*e.g.*, among the Turks, the daughter or wife of a Turk. Slaves would include the Circassians, Georgians, and at one time even the Hungarians, Poles, and Muscovites, bought as a rule through the medium of the Jews; and also prisoners of war. The husband has the right to free a slave and take her as his legitimate wife.

Marriage with a woman of free status, which is marriage properly so-called, takes place by means of intermediaries; the husband and wife do not see each other until their union is consummated. Friends of the two families meet together, a matron visits the girl and gives the young man as exact a description of her as possible, and, if the description pleases, the dowry is fixed. The latter is paid by the man; this is not only a custom, but a Qur'ānic law.

'Give women their dowries freely,' says the *Qur'ān* (iv. 3), 'and, if they are good enough to remit any of it to you of themselves, then enjoy it at your ease.'

The dowry really represents a purchase: it is the price paid by the man for his wife, and is handed over to the parents of the girl, who give her up. The wife has full control of the dowry—at least after the necessary furniture has been bought. There is a great contrast in this respect between the Muslim custom and what takes place in Europe, where it is difficult for a girl to get married without a dowry, and the husband ordinarily controls the wife's possessions.

The marriage contract is arranged before the *qaḍī*. The woman is not present at it, but is represented by her father, brother, or nearest relative, who accepts in her name the dowry which the fiancé undertakes to pay. It is this contract that legally constitutes the marriage; as may be seen, it is scarcely more than a simple declaration. After the contract, the parties go to the mosque, with the bride (veiled, of course) and a few relatives and friends, and the *imām* blesses the marriage. The woman is then taken to her husband's house; the wedding is celebrated by two feasts—one for the men and another in the women's apartments; and, at the end of the feast, the husband enters the nuptial chamber and sees his bride for the first time.

Muslim girls are married very early—usually at the age of from twelve to fourteen; sometimes they are betrothed when they are only three or four years old. Their parents are very anxious to have them married, and also re-married as soon as possible after being widowed or divorced. The state of celibacy, either for man or for woman, is scarcely a possibility in the Muslim world.

The *Qur'ān* (iv. 26 f.) indicates what classes of women it is unlawful to marry:

'Unlawful for you are your mothers, and your daughters, and your sisters, and your paternal aunts and maternal aunts, and your brother's daughters, and your sister's daughters, and your foster mothers, and your foster sisters, and your wives' mothers, and your step-daughters who are your wards, born of your wives to whom ye have gone in . . . and that ye form a connexion between two sisters . . . and do not marry women your fathers married.'

It will be noticed here that foster mothers are regarded as real mothers; as to the prohibition against marrying mothers, daughters, and sisters, it may have been necessary in consideration of the teaching of the Mazdæan religion, which allows incest. Mixed marriages, *i.e.* marriages with non-Muslims, are practically forbidden by the *Qur'ān* (ii. 220): it is better to marry a believing slave, according to Muslim opinion, than an unbelieving free woman; the same holds good of a husband. The rite of Abū Ḥanīfa, however, permits marriage with Christians and Jews.

The woman must obey and submit to her husband. Muhammad distinctly regards her as the inferior of man, and gives as one of the reasons of her inferiority that man uses his wealth to dower her (*Qur'ān*, iv. 38); he also holds that the masculine qualities are superior. He grants the husband the right to admonish a disobedient wife, put her into a separate bed-chamber, and even beat her; but he forbids a husband to seek a quarrel with his wife. If a wife commits adultery, the husband is allowed by custom to put her to death. According to a *fatwā* ('judicial decision') of Abdallah Efendi, a husband who takes his wife in adultery and kills both offenders is not liable to any punishment whatever; he even falls heir to the woman's possessions. Among the Turks, the husband may also drown an erring wife. Custom is more severe in this connexion than the *Qur'ān*; for Muhammad does not decree the death penalty for adultery, nor does he allow the injured husband to execute justice for himself. The husband, or any other person accusing a woman, must produce four witnesses; and the accuser who fails to do so is liable to receive eighty stripes (*Qur'ān*, iv. 19, xxiv. 2, 4). If the charge is proved by the agreement of the four witnesses, the offenders are both to be punished with a hundred stripes administered in the presence of a certain number of people; or the husband may imprison his wife for an unlimited period. Of course he may also divorce her. Cf. art. ADULTERY (Muslim).

A man wishing to divorce one of his wives for any reason must wait for four months, keeping the woman at his house but not cohabiting with her (*Qur'ān*, ii. 226); then he dismisses her, giving her a document called a 'certificate of divorce.' The woman retains her dowry. The divorced wife must wait three months before marrying again; if she has just had a child at the time of being divorced, the father may demand that she nurse the child for two years, and in such a case he must provide for the mother's maintenance during this period. A husband may take a divorced wife back again twice; but, if he divorce her a third time, he may not take her back unless she has been married to another man and divorced also by him.

A woman may not leave her husband at will; but she may seek divorce through the judge, and is granted it freely in various circumstances: *e.g.*, if the husband is prodigal or debauched, if he is not a good Muslim, or if he has not the means of supplying all household necessities. It is the husband's first duty to support the household; another and scarcely less important duty is to maintain his wife, children, and domestics in the practice of the Muslim religion. The husband, further, must rest content with the love of the wives and concubines he has in his house, and must never seek for objects of affection outside of it. He is bound also to give satisfaction to his legitimate wives; Muhammad says so expressly, and the commentary upon his words says that he must cohabit with them at least once a week.

Polygamy is a very costly luxury. The four legitimate wives cannot be forced to live together; each one has her house, or at least her apartment, table, and domestics. Economical reasons are a check upon polygamy, and it is only the rich who practise it. Men of moderate means and peasants have usually only one wife; there are even men who prefer not to marry at all, and are content with the commerce of their slaves, the latter being regarded as legitimate wives once they have borne a son. This method of procedure is in agreement with the spirit of *Qur'ān*, iv. 3:

'If ye fear that ye cannot be equitable [*i.e.* that you will not be able to do your duty to the children], then marry only one wife or one slave.'

The Muslim woman's life appears to us a very pitiable condition. She takes no part in the society of men; she seldom goes out, and is always veiled when she does go. The wearing of the veil and a certain amount of seclusion are forced upon her by the *Qur'ān*. The custom of veiling is also found in ancient Greece; it existed likewise among various Arabian tribes before the time of Muhammad; it was meant to protect the dignity of free-born women, and scarcely applied to any others. It was only the women of high social rank that Muhammad had in view when he imposed the rule of covering the face with a veil; his words did not apply to slaves or women of low station. The precept, however, has been put in practice by all Muslims, and peasants and even nomads wear veils; the latter, it is true, do not have them so well fixed on as the town-ladies; they hang loose around the face, and are lowered only when passing a stranger. In Constantinople, after the revolution (A.D. 1909) which dethroned the Sultan Abdul Ḥamīd II., Muslim women began to go out unveiled; and the *shaikh al-islām* had to make a *fatwā* commanding them, on pain of imprisonment, to return to the observance of the law.

Women of high position go out very little; they pay visits to each other, and sometimes visit the shops, but rarely the mosque. Their chief amusement is going to the baths; but in the larger *ḥarīms* there are very elegantly built bathrooms, and so the women are deprived of this motive for going out. The Turkish lady passes her day on a sofa, smoking, singing, spinning, embroidering, or sleeping. Many of them have had keen intellects in their youth, and have received instruction and even learned a little foreign literature; but their intelligence is apt to become dull in their seclusion, and their occupations are of necessity childish. Their chief concern is to please their husband; and they become expert in the arts of dressing and voluptuousness. In the larger *ḥarīms* the musical and dancing slaves have to give festivals from time to time.

Neither the Turks nor the Arabs are a prolific race; and the multiplicity of wives does not increase the number of children. The secluded life must be unfavourable to fecundity, and the desire for luxury gets the better of that of producing children. Many young women, slighted by their lord, pass their youth in enforced sterility in the women's workshop; and the keeping of these, besides, entails the sacrifice of a certain amount of virile force, for it is necessary to make a great number of eunuchs to keep in the paths of chastity a multitude of pretty slaves who are tormented by their sensual appetites and the ennui of the *ḥarīm*.

Children are brought up, to the age of seven, by the women, in the father's house; they are swaddled for eight or ten months, and are usually nursed by the mother, who suckles them for twelve or fourteen months (the *Qur'ān* [xlvi. 14] says thirty months). If a nurse has to be requisitioned, she is treated with the greatest respect; she is called 'the foster mother,' and is generally a young slave who becomes free and is then regarded as a member of the family. The child is laid in a fine cradle and, in rich families, rocked by slaves. A fête is held to celebrate the day when it is put into short clothes or has its hair cut for the first time, and another when it begins to walk. At about seven years of age, boys are circumcised and pass out of the women's care. This ceremony, which they like to perform for a fairly large number of children at a time, is the occasion of great rejoicings. The boys after circumcision may be seen walking in the streets of Muslim towns, dressed in rich clothes, and wearing turbans embroidered in gold and silver and surmounted by plumes, and their families also give gifts to the poor at this time (see, further, CIRCUMCISION [Muhammadan], vol. iii. p. 677). Among the Arabs, this is also the occasion for giving the boys horses. Boys from the age of seven upwards go to school; they are taught reading, writing, arithmetic, and a little of the *Qur'ān*. In towns where there are Christian missionary schools the young Muslims sometimes attend them; even the little Muslim girls go to the schools managed by Christian nuns. Sometimes the richer parents employ governesses to come to their houses, and they may be Europeans. All the girls learn to sew and embroider; they do not take the veil until puberty. See, further, EDUCATION (Muslim).

Muslim children have the greatest respect for their father and mother. This veneration is enjoined in several verses of the *Qur'ān* (xlvi. 14–16, xvii. 24 f.). A Tatar boy never sits down in presence of his father; and a Turkish boy always comes for his father's blessing at the festivals and chief events in his life. In important Arab families the father is a veritable king. The chief of a rich family settles his sons when they reach the age of eighteen or twenty; he gives them houses of their own and finds them wives; this first marriage is arranged by the parents, whom the young man cannot but obey.

The *Qur'ān* lays down some regulations as to wills; but they are not quite clear. The disposable portion is not stated in figures. It is said that

'men should have a portion of what their parents and kindred leave, and women should have a portion of what their parents and kindred leave, whether it be little or much, a determined portion' (iv. 8);

but it is not stated what portion. A son has a right to twice the portion of a daughter. A husband gets one-half of what his wife leaves if there are no children, a quarter if there are children. A widow gets a quarter of her husband's possessions if there are no children, an eighth if there are children. Thus we see that testamentary legislation is ruled by the idea of the woman's inferiority—an idea which dominates the whole system of Muslim family life. See, further, LAW (Muhammadan).

LITERATURE.—It is impossible to select a bibliography on this subject. All books on Muslim religion and all accounts of travels in Muslim countries contain some reference to it. Besides the *Qur'ān* itself, it may be useful to consult d'Ohsson's *Tableau général de l'empire othoman*, Paris, 1787–1820, which gives an account of Turkish customs at the end of the 18th cent.—that is, at a time when the Turks had not yet been influenced by European thought; the general works or manuals recently published on Muhammadanism, *e.g.* by O. Houdas (*L'Islamisme*, Paris, 1904) or M. Hartmann (*Der islam. Orient*, Berlin, 1899 ff.), and the present writer's *La Doctrine de l'islam*, Paris, 1909. There are numerous interesting details regarding life in the Sultans' *ḥarīms* in J. A. Guer, *Mœurs et usages des Turcs*, Paris, 1746 (a very fine work); and a charming description of family life in the castle of an Arab nobleman is found in Emily Ruete's *Mémoires d'une princesse arabe*, Paris, 1905.

BON CARRA DE VAUX.

FAMILY (Persian).

FAMILY (Persian).—Pride in an honoured lineage has always been as characteristic of the Iranians as of other peoples. Thus Darius I. traces his descent to Achæmenes (*Behist.* i. 4–6), and from the O. Pers. inscriptions we learn the Iranian term for 'family,' *taumā* (*ib.* i. 8, 28, 45, etc.), lit. 'seed.'[1] There are, however, only meagre data on the various degrees of relationship, except for those of husband and wife and of parent and

[1] The doubts of Tolman (*Anc. Pers. Lex.*, New York, 1908, p. 91) as to the connexion of O. Pers. *taumā* with Av. *taoxman*, 'seed,' seem exaggerated in view of the Bab. rendering of *taumā* by *zêru*, 'seed, family' (cf. Heb. זֶרַע, 'seed, offspring'; and the plural of Av. *taoxman*, in the sense of 'kindred,' in *Vend.* xii. 21).

child, and for this reason we must especially regret the loss of those portions of the Avesta *Hūspāram Nask* which treated of

'the guardianship of a family; likewise the varieties of it, and the fitness of a man for it. About one's own family, and whatever is on the same subject. About the income of wife and child. . . . About adoption; likewise the varieties of it, and fitness for it; the violation of adoption, the sin of the son who is accepted, and whatever is on the same subject. . . . About property that comes to next of kin through relationship, and that through adoption. . . . About where and in whom, after the father, is the prerogative as to a daughter being given away to a husband' (*Dīnk.* VIII. xxxvi. 7–17). Similar discussions—probably more elaborate—were contained in the lost *Sakāṭūm Nask* of the Avesta (*ib.* xliii. 10–20).

The closeness of bonds between relatives as determined by the godling Mithra, according to *Yašt* x. 116 f., has been quoted above (p. 208b), and in *Vend.* xii. the duration of mourning for various kinsfolk is given in a form which may be summarized as follows:

For a father (*pitar*) or mother (*mātar*) 30 days; for a son (*puthra*) or daughter (*dughdhar*) 30 days; for a brother (*brātar*) or sister (*xvanhar*) 30 days; for a husband (*nmānō-paiti*, 'house-master') or wife (*nmāno-pathnī*, 'house-mistress') 6 months; for a grandfather (*nyāka*) or grandmother (*nyākā*) 25 days; for a grandson (*napāt*) or granddaughter (*naptī*) 25 days; for a brother's son (*brātruya*) or brother's daughter (*brātruyā*) 20 days; for a father's brother (*tūirya*) or father's sister (*tūiryā*) 15 days; for a son of a father's brother (*tūiryō-puthra*) or daughter of a father's sister (*tūirya-dughdhar*) 10 days; for a son of a son of a father's brother or the daughter of a daughter of a father's sister (on these two terms, corrupted in the existing manuscripts, see Bartholomae, *Altiran. Wörterb.*, Strassburg, 1904, col. 748) 5 days. These periods are for those who have died in full religious fellowship; for those who die while under the ban the time of mourning must be doubled.

It should also be noted that each sex mourns for its own dead—'then when a father dies or a mother dies, how long do they mourn for them, the son for the father, the daughter for the mother?' (similarly the father for the son, the granddaughter for the grandmother). But brothers may mourn for sisters, and sisters for brothers; and nothing is directly specified regarding sex distinctions in mourning for nephews, nieces, uncles, aunts, and first or second cousins. Besides these relations, honour is shown to the *fravashis* (*q.v.*) of those next of kin (*nabānazdišta* [*Yasna* i. 18, iii. 22, iv. 24, vii. 22, xxii. 27, xxiii. 4, xxiv. 3, xxvi. 7, lxvi. 19, lxxii. 7 f.; *Yašt* xiii. 156; *Āfrīngān* ii. 2]).

The only terms for relatives in the Avesta besides those just quoted are for husband of one's daughter (*zāmātar*), and for father of one's husband (*xvasura*; both in *Yašt* x. 116), while for great-great-grandfather the O. Pers. (*Art. Sus. a*, 3) has *apanāyaka*. The dual *pitare* ('two fathers') denotes 'parents' (*Yašt* x. 116), and the plural *pterebyō* ('to the fathers') is employed in *Vend.* xv. 13 to denote the father and the oldest members of his family (cf. O. Icelandic *fethgar*, 'father and son(s),' *mœthgur*, 'mother and daughter(s)' [Delbrück, *Festgruss an Roth*, Stuttgart, 1893, pp. 15–17; Brugmann, *Vergl. Gramm. der indogerm. Sprachen*[2], Strassburg, 1897 ff., II. ii. 458, 447]).

Marriage was to the Iranians a sacred duty (see CELIBACY [Iranian]); a good marriage was a boon to be mentioned along with honourable lineage (*Vīsp.* ii. 7); good husbands, to whom the father gave away the bride[1] (*Yasna* li. 17; *Dīnk.* VIII. xx. 89, xxxvi. 17, xliii. 10 f.), were the gift of Haoma (*Yasna* ix. 23), and maidens also prayed for spouses to Ardvī Sūra Anāhita (*Yašt* v. 87), Vayu (*ib.* xv. 39–41), and Aši Vanuhi (*ib.* xvii. 10). Family discords were viewed with horror (*Yasna* lxv. 7), and a good wife was to be easy to guide, obedient to her spiritual head, and pious, while her husband should be fully acquainted with the faith, free from the *kayadha* sin (contempt of religion ?), and diligent (*Vīsp.* iii. 4; *Gāh* iv. 9; cf. *Dīnk.* VIII. xxxi. 5 f.). Terrible punishment awaited the disobedient wife in the world to come (*Arṭā-Vīrāf Nāmak*, ed. and tr. Asa, Haug, and West, Bombay, 1872, xxvi., lxiii., lxx., lxxxii. f.).

The best of all marriages was the 'next-of-kin' (*xvaētvadatha* [*Vīsp.* iii. 3; *Gāh* iv. 8; *Yašt* xxiv. 17]), on which see MARRIAGE (Iranian); and the wife might be of any one of five classes.

A *pādšāh* ('ruling *or* privileged') wife is an unbetrothed maiden, wedded with her parents' consent, her children all belonging to her husband. A *yūkan* or *ayūk* ('only child') wife is similar, except that her first child belongs to her parents, who give her in return one-third of their property. A *satar* ('adopted') wife is one dowered by the relatives of a man dying childless and unmarried; half her children belong to her living husband, and half to the dead one, who also has her in the other world. A *čākar* ('serving') wife is a re-married widow, if she has no children by her first husband, who in any case has her in the future world; she is also a *satar* wife. A *xūd-šarāī* ('self-disposing') wife is one marrying without the consent of her parents, from whom she inherits no property until her eldest son gives her to his father as a *pādšāh* wife (Pers. *rivāyats* summarized by West, *SBE* v. 142, note 10; cf. also *Dīnk.* v. 17, tr. Sanjana, p. 637; Anquetil du Perron, ii. 560 f.).

Polygamy was common, at least among the rich, among the Persians (Herod. i. 135; Strabo, p. 733; Ammian. Marcel. xxiii. 76; Agathias, ii. 30) and Medians (Strabo, p. 526); and it also appears to have flourished among the Zoroastrian Iranians. As Geiger points out (*Ostīrān. Kultur*, pp. 244, 247), there are Avesta passages, such as *Vend.* iii. 3 (in the house of the righteous, women and children are present in rich abundance—*frapithwō nāirika frapithwō aperenāyūkō*), which imply this, while in *Yasna* xxxviii. 1 there is plainly a reference to the 'women' (doubtless the wives) of Ahura Mazda himself (*yāsčā tōi genā ahurā mazdā*), and Zoroaster is represented by tradition as having three wives, two of whom were 'privileged' and the third a 'serving' wife (*Bundahišn*, xxxii. 5–7; cf. also Jackson, *Zoroaster*, New York, 1899, p. 20 f.). In the later period, when the *Māṭigān-ī-Hazār Dāṭistān* was written, polygamy was expressly recognized (West, *GIrP* ii. 117), but in India it was permitted only when the first wife was barren, and then only if she gave consent (Anquetil du Perron, ii. 561).

In regard to concubinage, it would seem that there was a sharp distinction between Zoroastrian and non-Zoroastrian Iranians. The Avesta contains no allusion to the concubine, and the chief references in Pahlavi literature seem to be *Šāyast lā-Šāyast* x. 21, xii. 14, the latter passage reading:

'It is well if any one of those who have their handmaid (*čakar*) in cohabitation (*zanih*), and offspring is born of her, shall accept all those who are male as sons; but those who are female are no advantage, because an adopted son is requisite, . . . and there are many who do not appoint an adopted son with this idea, that: "The child of a handmaid may be accepted by us as a son."'

Among the non-Zoroastrians, on the contrary, concubinage was very common, at least among the wealthier classes (*ERE* iii. 812 f.). There was in the Sasanian period, as there is to-day, a strong disapproval of marriage outside the Zoroastrian community (*Dīnk.* iii. 80, tr. Sanjana, pp. 90–102; the particular case under consideration is the marriage of a Zoroastrian to a Jewess), the reasons being largely those of lack of racial and religious sympathy. On the other hand, the marriage of princesses from foreign lands was very frequent throughout Persian history, even in the Sasanian period (Spiegel, *Erân. Alterthumskunde*, iii. 679 f.). When Zoroastrianism was still a proselytizing religion, a non-Zoroastrian might be wedded after having embraced the Zoroastrian faith; but the modern Parsis have not merely abandoned proselytizing, but object strenuously to receiving converts, so that the problem of intermarriage has become more difficult than it was centuries ago.

The dowry of a widow who marries a second time is less than that of a virgin bride (*Dīnk.* v. 17, tr. Sanjana, p. 637), and, as already noted, half of her children by her second husband really belong to her first husband, as does she herself in the future world.

There was, besides the forms of marriage already mentioned, a quasi-levirate. According to al-Bīrūnī (*India*, tr. Sachau, London, 1888, i. 109 f.), quoting Tansar,

'if a man dies without leaving male offspring, people are to examine the case. If he leaves a wife, they marry her to his nearest relative. If he does not leave a wife, they marry his daughter or the nearest related woman to the nearest related

[1] Apparently an orphan girl without uncles on either side was unmarriageable (*Dīnk.* VIII. xliii. 11).

male of the family. If there is no woman of his family left, they woo, by means of the money of the deceased, a woman for his family, and marry her to some male relative. The child of such a marriage is considered as the offspring of the deceased. Whoever neglects this duty and does not fulfil it, kills innumerable souls, since he cuts off the progeny and the name of the deceased to all eternity.'

The desire of the Iranians for children and their provision for their education have been considered elsewhere (*ERE* iii. 544, v. 207 f.). As supplementary to CHILDREN (Iranian), it may be noted that not only were children a blessing (*Vend.* iv. 47; *Šāyast lā-Šāyast*, x. 22, xii. 15; *Dāṭistān-ī Dīnīk*, xxxvii. 43; *Dīnk.* v. 19 [tr. Sanjana, p. 639], VIII. xx. 139) and childlessness a curse (*Yašt* xvii. 57), but special respect was paid to mothers of heroic sons (*Yasna* i. 6, etc.; *Visp.* i. 5; *Gāh* iv. 2; *Sīrōz* i. 7, ii. 7; *Yašt* ii. 5, 10), and the birth of some of the legendary heroes of Iran was a direct reward for the religious devotion of their fathers (*Yasna* ix. 4 [Yima], 7 [Thraētaona], 10 [Urvāxšaya and Keresāspa], 13 [Zarathuštra]).

The principle of filial obedience was implanted by Ahura Mazda himself (*Yasna* xliv. 7), and the *Dīnkarṭ* declares (IX. lv. 5) that

'whoever teaches to a son reverence unto his father has also appropriated the reward for reverence unto the creator for teaching that person; even for this reason, because express reverence unto parents and service to them are connected with reverence unto the Creator and service to him.'

Even after the death of one's parents and other relatives, one is to celebrate the sacred feast (*myazd*), the consecration of the sacred cakes (*drōn*), and the benedictions (*āfrīngān*) for the souls of the dead, who will then avert misfortunes from the living (*Sad Dar*, xiii.; cf. vi. 2, xlv. 9). Naturally, the father had certain duties toward his child (*Dīnk.* VIII. xxxi. 21, xxxiv. 4 f.); but, if the proper filial obedience was not shown, those who 'in the world distressed their father and mother, and asked no absolution and forgiveness from their father and mother in the world,' had, in hell, 'their chests plunged in mud and stench, and a sharp sickle ever went among their legs and other limbs, and they ever called for a father and mother' (*Arṭā-Vīrāf Nāmak*, lxv.).

In the Pahlavi *Dāṭistān-ī Dīnīk*, elaborate rules are given for inheritance, adoption, and guardianship.

The regulations for inheritance are as follows (lxii. 3 f., 6): 'When there is nothing otherwise in the will and private, property goes to a wife or daughter who is privileged; if one gives her anything by will, then she does not obtain the share pertaining to her. Whenever a share for a son is not provided by it, every one has so much, and the wife who may be a privileged one has twice as much; and the share of that one of the sons, or even the wife of a son, who is blind in both eyes, or crippled in both feet, or maimed in both his hands, is twice as much as that of one who is sound. . . . If there be no son of that man, but there be a daughter or wife of his, and if some of the affairs of the man are such as render a woman not suitable for the guardianship, it is necessary to appoint a family guardian; if there be, moreover, no wife or daughter of his, it is necessary to appoint an adopted son.' The adopted-sonship and guardianship referred to in these sections are thus defined in the same treatise (lvi. 2–4): 'It is requisite, whenever a man of the good religion is passing away, while he is a complete ruler of a numerous household, who has no wife and child that may be privileged and acknowledged, nor associating brother, nor son by adoption, and his property is sixty stirs [about 84 rupees] of income. The controlling of the property is to be publicly provided out of the kindred of the deceased, and is called the adopted-sonship; and he is to be appointed to it who is the nearest of the same lineage, who will manage and keep the property united in its entirety. The guardianship of a family is that when a guardian has to be appointed in that manner over the family of a man whose wife, or daughter, or infant son is not fit for their own guardianship, so it is necessary to appoint some one.' Those who are suitable for such adoption are 'a grown-up man of the good religion who is intelligent, a complete ruler of a numerous household, expecting offspring, and not having sins worthy of death,' such a man being eligible 'even when he has accepted either one adoption, or many adoptions.' 'And a grown-up woman, or even a child, is suitable for one adoption, but when adopted in one family she is not suitable for another adoption. A woman requiring a husband—though a complete worshipper—or a foreigner, or an infidel, or one having sins worthy of death, is unfit for adoption; so also those who are demon-worshippers, she who is a concubine (*šūsar nēšman*) or courtezan, and she who is menstruous are unfit' (*ib.* lvii. 2–4; cf. also lvi. 6 f.). Maladministration of the adopted-sonship is a deadly sin (*ib.* lx.). This adoption is of three kinds—existent, provided, and appointed. 'An adopted son who is existent is such as a wife who may be privileged, or an only daughter is a kind of adopted son owing to confidence in herself, such as happens when there is no wife, and a daughter for whom there is no husband. . . . An adopted son who is provided is such as a son that is acknowledged, who is accepted by oneself, and free from being appointed, or from necessity. And an adopted son who is appointed is he who is to be appointed among the relations who are suitable for adoption—and are nearest to him who is to be appointed as adopted son—and the ministers of religion, and he performs the duty of family guardianship; he who is the appointed one is he who is appointed by the men who are the nearest relations on account of proximity' (*ib.* lviii. 3–5).

From this fictitious adoption we must distinguish the real adoption of a son, to be appointed, in the case of a man dying with neither an own nor an adopted son, by the priests and the relations of the deceased, in order that the soul of the dead man might escape the tortures of hell, especially as 'every duty and good work that he [the adopted son] performs shall be just like that which is performed by one's own hand . . . every time that they appoint an adopted son for any one, it is just as though they have made the deceased alive' (*Sad Dar*, xviii. 12, 19).

LITERATURE.—B. Delbrück, *Die indogerm. Verwandtschaftsnamen* (*ASG* xi. 5), Leipzig, 1889, pp. 41, 76, 86, 96, 100, 107, 129, 140; H. Hirt, *Die Indogermanen*, Strassburg, 1905–07, pp. 704–707; O. Schrader, *Sprachvergleichung und Urgesch.*[3], Jena, 1907, ii. 305–318; F. Spiegel, *Erān. Alterthumskunde*, Leipzig, 1871–78, iii. 676–684; W. Geiger, *Ostīrān. Kultur im Altertum*, Erlangen, 1882, pp. 234–249; A. Christensen, *L'Empire des Sassanides*, Copenhagen, 1907, pp. 49–54; Anquetil du Perron, *Zend-Avesta*, Paris, 1771, ii. 551–564; D. F. Karaka, *Hist. of the Parsis*, London, 1884, i. ch. iv.; E. West, *Pahlavi Texts*, i.–iv. (*SBE* v., xviii., xxiv., xxxvii.); Sanjana, *Dinkarṭ*, Bombay, 1874 ff.; Rapp, *ZDMG* xx. (1866) 107–114.

LOUIS H. GRAY.

FAMILY (Roman).—With characteristic fondness for legal distinction and analysis, the Romans distinguished four relationships in which each individual found himself: (1) the relationship to himself as an individual; (2) that to his family; (3) that to the group of families which formed his clan (*gens*); (4) that to the union of clans (*gentes*) which composed the State. The most elementary of these four relationships, and the one upon which the others were based, was not, as we would suppose, judging by our own day, the individual, but rather the family. The growth of the concept of individuality on Roman soil was retarded by the excessive degree to which the social idea was developed. The individual existed merely for the sake of the family and its derivatives, the clan and the State. At death he passed over into the 'majority,' and lost whatever little of individuality he had gained in life, by being absorbed into the mass of departed spirits; he was mortal and the family was immortal. On the other hand, the family had created the clan, and the clan the State, with the result that the clan soon fell into insignificance and lost its life on behalf of the creature of its own making, the State. Finally, in its turn the State, at least in the earlier phases of its history, was nothing but the magnified reflexion of family life, with its king as the father of the people, etc. From this brief sketch it will be seen that the family occupied a unique place in the make-up of early Roman society. Centuries were destined to pass before individualism attempted to make good any claims of the individual over against the dominating superiority of the family; and, on the other hand, the decline of the clan-idea left the State as the only rival of the family—a rivalry which was chiefly theoretical rather than real.

It was a basic principle of Roman religion that human life was everywhere surrounded by the gods; for what the faith of the Romans lacked in spiritual intensity was, in part at least, compensated by its extensiveness, and the very superficiality of their belief brought it into contact with the whole surface of their life. Thus the gods were interested in the fulfilment of the duties which attached to each of these four above-mentioned relationships. The divine duties of a man as a citizen of the State formed a part of the 'public worship,' or *sacra publica*; the divine duties connected with the other three relationships were included under the term 'private worship,' or *sacra privata*. Of these three relationships, that of a man towards his clan or *gens* sank so soon into insignificance that our knowledge of the *sacra gentilicia* is extremely scanty, and the subject need not trouble us here. The divine duties of the family form the theme of this article, but the individual was so involved with the family that we cannot eliminate him from our discussion. As a matter of fact, those elements which later assumed the characteristics of individualism were in their original state merely phases of family worship, expressing the relations of each individual to the family.

Our sources for a knowledge of the history of the family and of family worship in Rome are relatively scarce when compared with our sources for the history of the State and of the State religion. Official documents, calendars, etc., which are so valuable for the history of the State religion, are of almost no value here. Inscriptions, indeed, are exceedingly numerous, but they are almost all sepulchral, and are therefore valuable only for our study of the cult of the dead. The very homeliness and familiarity of the subject from the standpoint of contemporaries is the cause of our ignorance; very few people take the trouble to speak about what everybody knows; hence our sources are largely incidental, *e.g.* among the poets, especially Plautus, Horace (*Satires*), Tibullus, besides a few late antiquarian writers, and the scholiasts and commentators on the poets. We might well despair of ever obtaining an adequate picture, were it not for one psychological fact, namely, that, though all religion tends to conservatism, there is no part of it which is more conservative and less subject to change than the religion of the family. Hence, though our sources are fragmentary and widely separated chronologically, they can be placed side by side to form a mosaic picture.

The deities worshipped by the family may be divided for convenience of treatment into two classes: those regularly connected with the family, and those who were occasionally interested in family life. We shall deal first with those regularly connected with the family, second with those occasionally interested in family life, and we shall then add as a third section a brief discussion of the relationship of family worship to Christianity.

I. Deities regularly connected with the family.—The deities regularly connected with the family were either not included in the State cult at all, or, if included, were worshipped there as an imitation of the cult of the family, a symbolic representation of the State as merely an enlarged family. Chief among these deities are the Genius (and the Juno), the Lar, the goddess Vesta, and two groups of deities, the Di Manes and the Di Penates.

(1) The most important element in the worship of the family and the supreme duty of the individual was the worship of the deified ancestors, or *Di Manes* (literally, 'good gods'). At death each individual was conceived of as losing his individuality and becoming immortal merely as a part of the great mass of the Di Manes. The prime duty of the head of the family was the regular and scrupulous fulfilment of the ancestral sacrifices; and it was also his paramount duty to provide a successor in the person of a real or an adopted son who could take up the burden of the sacrifices after he had laid it down at death. For further particulars, see art. ANCESTOR-WORSHIP AND CULT OF THE DEAD (Roman).

(2) Quite distinct from this worship of the deified dead *en masse* was the cult of the protecting deity of the living, the guardian of each individual. This guardian was called in the case of a man the *Genius*, in the case of a woman the *Juno*. The connexion of the individual with the family is shown very clearly in the original meaning of the Genius and the Juno, for at first they were thought of in a purely materialistic way, as the physical force employed in the maintenance of the family, the Genius (cf. *gignere*, and Censorinus, iii. 1) as the procreative power, and the Juno as the conceptive power. By degrees these ideas became more and more spiritual, until during the empire the Genius and the Juno stood for a sort of guardian angel. The Genius (we use the word here and onwards to express both Genius and Juno) was thought of as co-existent with the individual, born with him, passing through life with him, and finally dying with him. Hence the birthday of the individual was the chief festival of his Genius. On this day he was worshipped as the 'Genius natalis' or simply as 'Natalis' (cf. Tibullus, ii. 2, iv. 5; Censorinus, ii. 1; similarly 'Juno natalis,' Tibullus, iv. 6. 1); and sacrifice of wine and milk and cake was made to him. The most important of these birthday celebrations was naturally that of the master of the house, the *paterfamilias*. Slaves and freedmen often erected dedicatory inscriptions in honour of this event (cf. *CIL* vi. 257–259, ii. 1980, v. 1868, x. 860, 861, ii. 356; and, for the Juno, ii. 1324). From the time of Augustus the cult of the Genius received an additional emphasis from the fact that the Genius of the living Emperor was an object of worship at first for the State at large, and afterwards for each family. The use of the Genius as a protecting deity of corporations, cities, buildings, etc., lies outside of our present discussion.

(3) But the religion of the family did not content itself with the cult of the deified dead and the worship of the Genius of the living; it paid homage, in addition, to the deities who protected those material things with which the family had to do—the house itself, the store-closet, and the hearth—viz. the Lar Familiaris, the Di Penates, and Vesta.

(*a*) The origin of the *Lar Familiaris*, or protecting deity of the house, is one of the most disputed points in the field of Roman religion; but the most likely view is that the cult of the household Lar (in the singular) is merely a branch of the general cult of the Lares (in the plural) at the cross-roads, the so-called 'Lares Compitales' (for a different view, cf. Samter, *Familienfeste der Gr. und Röm.*, Berlin, 1901; cf. also *ERE* iv. 336[b]). The Lar Familiaris was thus the protector of the house and its inhabitants, especially the slaves (the *familia* in the technical sense). The venerable farm-almanac of Cato directs that the bailiff's wife, the *villica*, should place a wreath on the hearth on the Kalends, Ides, and Nones, and should on those same days pray to the Lar Familiaris for plenty (*de Agric.* 143). The Lar Familiaris formed the sentimental centre for all phases of family life, and offerings of wreaths, incense, and wine were made to him on all family anniversaries. Thus the Lar represented the primitive concept of home, and was the ideal figure about which the associations of the household clung. Before undertaking a journey, the Roman offered up a sacrifice to the Lar (cf. Plautus, *Merc.* 843 ff.), and also on the occasion of a safe return home. When a member of the family, who had been lost, was found (cf. Plautus, *Rud.* 1206 ff.; and *CIL* ix. 925), or when one of the family recovered from an illness, a wreath was put on the Lar; and, when a member of the household died, the ceremony of purification which followed included the sacrifice of sheep to the Lar (Cic. *de Leg.* ii. 55). When a son put on the *toga virilis*, the Lar Familiaris was crowned, and the amulet, the *bulla*, which the boy had worn up to that time, was hung about the neck of the Lar (cf. Pers. v. 31; Petron. 60; Prop. iv. 1, 131 ff.). When the bride entered the house of her husband, she placed one copper coin on the hearth as an offering to the Lar Familiaris, gave a second to her husband, and placed a third on the altar at the nearest cross-roads in honour of the Lares Compitales (Varro, *in Non.* p. 531). Finally, various votive offerings were hung on the wall near the hearth in honour of the Lar, *e.g.* the weapons of the veteran soldier (cf. Ovid, *Trist.* iv. 8. 22; Prop. iii. 30. 21 ff.; Hor. *Sat.* i. 5. 65 ff.).

(*b*) One of the most important rooms in the old Roman house was the *cella penaria*, or store-closet, corresponding to the room which in modern Italian houses is called the *dispensa*, containing the reserve supplies of food products, and to be carefully distinguished from the pantry, where the day's supply of food was kept after it had been taken out of the store-closet. It is characteristic at once of the simplicity and the practical nature of early Roman religion that a group of gods who were supposed to be in charge of this store-room, and who received their names from it, formed one of the most important elements in the cult of the family. These gods were known as the *Di Penates* (*penus* = 'store-closet'), where Penates is not a proper name like *Lar*, *Lares*, but merely an adjective in agreement with *Di*; hence it was frequently a theme of discussion among the antiquarians of Rome as to who the Di Penates were, and whether any particular deity, *e.g.* Vesta, belonged to them or not. The real state of affairs seems to have been as follows. The Di Penates originally were a group of otherwise nameless gods, and Vesta was not included in their number, though she was very closely associated with them, since the hearth, Vesta's altar, was the place where sacrifice was made to them also. When Vesta was worshipped by the State in the forum, this relationship was recognized, and the Penates of the State, the 'Di Penates P.R.Q.,' were worshipped at the same altar. Later the Penates received their own State temple, and were thus in public worship separated from Vesta, so that both they and Vesta preserved their independence. In private worship the reverse process took place, and the original association of Vesta and the Penates was never broken, but, instead, Vesta gradually lost her independent position, and was included under the title of the Penates. This explains the apparent neglect of Vesta in private worship. But, apart from Vesta, there was a constant tendency to abandon the group of nameless deities, and to include certain well-known gods among the Di Penates. The choice in such cases was governed by the particular circumstances and interests of the individual; hence we have many varying combinations, as may be seen in the frescoes on the kitchen walls of many of the houses of Pompeii (cf. Helbig, *Wandgemälde der von Vesuv verschütteten Städte Campaniens*, Leipzig, 1869, p. 19 ff.; de Marchi, *Il Culto privato*, 1896, i. 79 ff.).

2. Deities occasionally interested in the family.—Apart from those deities whom we have already mentioned, and who were constantly protecting the individual himself and his permanent surroundings, his house, his hearth, his store-closet, etc., many others of the gods of Rome were occasionally concerned in family life, so that it is literally true that human life was hedged about by them from the cradle to the grave. Practically every one of the gods of the State came into contact with the family at some time during the life of the individual, and we shall speak here only of the more important of these temporary associations.

(1) The famous sentence of Tertullian (*de Anima*, 39), 'Ita omnes idololatria obstetrice nascuntur,' was from his standpoint a fair enough expression of the part which a host of minor deities was thought to take in the conception and *birth* of each human being. The exact names of these deities, however, and the part which each took, are by no means certain (for further details, cf. the article 'Indigitamenta,' by Peter, in Roscher's *Lexikon*; and de Marchi, *Il Culto privato*, i. 165, note 3); but the chief of these deities was Juno, who, under the cult name of Lucina, was invoked as the goddess of childbirth (cf. *ERE* ii. 649). Another long list of deities cared for the child in his cradle, taught him to walk, protected him from the evil eye, and developed him to young manhood (for these deities, who also are uncertain, cf. Peter, i. 1, and de Marchi, i. 168 f. and notes). Certainty attaches, however, to the celebration of the *dies lustricus* (the ninth day after birth in the case of a boy, and the eighth day in the case of a girl [cf. Marquardt, *Privatleben der Römer*, Leipzig, 1888, p. 83]), when the child was given a name, to the accompaniment of a sacrifice, and probably a banquet. One of the greatest proofs of the essential difference between Roman religion and Christianity, and of the absolute foreignness of Roman religion to our habits of thought, is found in the matter of the training of the child. We miss any act resembling in meaning either baptism or confirmation; religion and the State are so identical that the child as a citizen necessarily partakes of the religious life of the State without any formal act of inclusion. Further, since religion consists so entirely in ritual acts and is so barren of theology, no formal religious instruction is necessary, but the child grows up learning by imitation when and how the ritualistic acts should be performed. The myths he learns partly from his nurse, partly in the schools, but principally by being surrounded by them in wall-decoration, literature, etc. The transition from boyhood to manhood was marked by the putting on of the *toga virilis*, and the offering of a sacrifice. The youth, accompanied by his family, ascended the Capitol, sacrificed to Juppiter, and put a coin into the money-box of the goddess Juventas. The usual day for the performance of this rite was the Liberalia (March 17), the festival of Liber.

(2) From the standpoint of the preservation of the family, the most important act in the life of the individual is *marriage*; hence it is not surprising that it, too, was under the protection of the gods. But, while we see traces of religious observances surrounding all forms of Roman marriage, it is difficult to state exactly in what these ceremonies consisted. Of the three forms of marriage in Rome—*confarreatio*, *usus*, and *coemptio*—only the first was attended by any special religious act, while the last two were affected by religion only as much as were all the acts of life. Common to both *confarreatio* and *coemptio* was the avoidance, on religious grounds, of certain days for marriage. (*Usus*, being merely the legalization of cohabitation at the end of a year, did not permit of the choice of a special day.) The days thus avoided were: the Parentalia, or the feast of the dead, Feb. 13–21; the month of March, because of the festivals of the Salii and of Mars; the month of May, because of the Lemuria—May 9, 11, 13—and because of the procession of the Argei on the 15th; June 7–15, because the temple of Vesta was being cleaned; the three days in the year when the lower world was thought to be open (*mundus patet*)—Aug. 24, Oct. 5, Nov. 8; in general the

dies postridiani, i.e. the days following the Kalends, the Nones, and the Ides; the *dies atri*, or days unlucky because of some great disaster (*e.g.* July 18, the day of the battle of the Allia). In addition to all these days, the day immediately preceding each of them was generally avoided, so that, even if the day of marriage itself was lucky, the first full day of married life might not be unlucky; and, finally, all holidays were avoided, so that there might be no rival attraction to interfere with attendance at the wedding. Further, in connexion with both forms of marriage the auspices were consulted, in early times by the genuine *auspicia*, the observation of the flight of birds, later by the more convenient form of the consultation of the entrails (*haruspicina*). The predominatingly religious form of marriage was, however, the *confarreatio*, which as early as the end of the Republic was more or less of an old-fashioned curiosity. It was undoubtedly originally the only form of marriage for patricians. The marriage took place in the presence of ten witnesses, and the Pontifex Maximus and the Flamen Dialis, or priest of Juppiter. Its chief act, from which it derived its name, was the offering of a cake (*panis farreus*) to Juppiter.

(3) We have seen the gods active at birth and at marriage: and we might expect their presence at the death-bed, but such is not the case. The individual has done his work so far as the family is concerned, he has contributed his share; let him pass now into the mass of nameless Di Manes. He can have no comfort at death, for there is no individual future for him; his only satisfaction is the contemplation of what he has done for the family, and the prospect that the ancestral sacrifices, for which he has provided, will now benefit him along with the rest of the Manes.

3. Family religion and Christianity.—In the minds of a people who loved the customs of their ancestors (*mos majorum*) as much as the Romans did, the simple rites of the family, descending from an indefinite past, had a far greater sanctity than the more gorgeous, but more modern, ceremonies of the official State religion. The preachers of Christianity, therefore, found the pagan far more ready to give up Juppiter and Mars than the Genius and the Lar. On the other hand, the rites of family worship were so often connected with some perfectly innocent family event that the spiritual directors of the Christians thought it improper altogether to forbid the participation of Christians in the family festivals of their pagan friends. Tertullian, who wrote about A.D. 200, has an interesting passage on this (*de Idololatria*, 16), in which he authorizes attendance at the festivals connected with the putting on of the *toga virilis*, betrothals, marriages, and the naming of children, even though sacrifices were connected with them. This reverence on the part of the pagans, and this indulgence on the part of the Christians, caused the *sacra privata* to decline much more slowly than the *sacra publica*. Almost three generations after Constantine had given Christianity an official right of existence, it was necessary for Theodosius (A.D. 392) to issue the famous edict (*Cod. Theodos.* xvi. 10. 2): 'nullus omnino secretiore piaculo Larem igne, mero Genium, Penates odore veneratus accendat lumina, imponat tura, serta suspendat.' But, in spite of this edict, some of the rites of family-worship seem to have existed in the country places for centuries longer.

See also art. ROMAN RELIGION and the 'Roman' sections of CHILDREN, EDUCATION, MARRIAGE.

LITERATURE.—G. Wissowa, *Religion und Kultus der Römer*, Munich, 1902, pp. 141–159, artt. 'Lar' and 'Penates,' in Roscher, and his revision of J. Marquardt, *Röm. Staatsverwaltung*[2], Leipzig, 1885, pp. 121–129, 303–314; de Marchi, *Il Culto privato di Roma antica*, i., 'La Religione nella vita domestica,' Milan, 1896; Preller-Jordan, *Röm. Mythologie*, Berlin, 1881, ii. 61–119, 195–203; Birt, art. 'Genius,' in Roscher; Steuding, art. 'Manes,' *ib.*; W. W. Fowler, *Roman Festivals*, London, 1899, p. 337 f.; J. B. Carter, *Religion of Numa*, London, 1906, pp. 12–19.

JESSE BENEDICT CARTER.

FAMILY (Teutonic and Balto-Slavic).—When the Aryan peoples, including, of course, the progenitors of the Teutons and Balto-Slavs, spread over Europe in pre-historic times, they found, among many of the aboriginal tribes of our continent, certain forms of family life quite different from their own. Of these the most notable was the so-called matriarchy, *i.e.* that family organization—still surviving, as ethnologists tell us, in certain parts of the world—which, while it recognizes a marital relationship of longer or shorter duration, does not recognize the paternal relationship, as the children belong, not to the father, but to the mother, and inherit property, not from the father or paternal uncle, but from the mother, and especially the maternal uncle or grand-uncle. In connexion with the matriarchal family we frequently find, on the one hand, that women are held in high honour and even possess supreme power, and, on the other, that sexual life is marked by an astounding laxity; we hear also of polyandry, of the marriage of blood-relations, and even of complete sexual promiscuity.

A signal contrast to such conditions of family life is presented by what we know of the Aryan or Indo-Germanic stock, in which the existence of the so-called patriarchal or agnatic family is attested by the fact that the words expressive of family relationships are essentially the same in the various cognate languages.

Thus, for example, Goth. *fadar* corresponds to Lat. *pater*, Gr. πατήρ, Skr. *pitár*; O.H.G. *muoter*, O. Slav. *mati*, to Lat. *mater*, Gr. μήτηρ, Skr. *mātár*; Goth. *sunus*, Lith. *sunùs*, O. Slav. *synŭ*, to Skr. *sūnú*; Goth. *daúhtar*, Lith. *dukté*, O. Slav. *dŭšti*, to Gr. θυγάτηρ, Skr. *duhitár*; Goth. *brôþar*, O. Pruss. *brote*, O. Slav. *bratrŭ*, to Lat. *frater*, Skr. *bhrātar*; Goth. *svistar*, Lith. *sesũ*, O. Slav. *sestra*, to Lat. *soror*, Skr. *svásar*; O.H.G. *fatureo*, 'uncle,' to Lat. *patruus*, Gr. πάτρως, Skr. *pítṛvya*; Goth. *avo*, 'grandmother,' to Lat. *avus*; A.S. *nefa*, 'grandchild,' Lith. *nepotis*, to Lat. *nepos*, Skr. *nápāt*; O.H.G. *snura*, 'daughter-in-law,' O. Slav. *snŭcha*, to Lat. *nurus*, Gr. νυός, Skr. *snuṣā*; O.H.G. *suehur*, 'father-in-law,' Lith. *szeszìùras*, O. Slav. *svekrŭ*, to Lat. *socer*, Gr. ἑκυρός, Skr. *śváśura*; Goth. *svaíhrô*, 'mother-in-law,' O. Slav. *svekry*, to Lat. *socrus*, Skr. *śvaśrū*; O.H.G. *zeihhur*, 'husband's brother,' Lith. *dewerìs*, O. Slav. *deverŭ*, to Lat. *levir*, Gr. δαήρ, Skr. *dêvár*; O. Slav. *zlŭva*, 'husband's sister,' to Lat. *glôs*, Gr. γάλως; O. Slav. *jetry*, 'husband's brother's wife,' Lith. *inte*, to Lat. *janitrices*, Gr. εἰνάτερες, Skr. *yātaras*, etc.

These examples of the terms applied to family relationships show incontrovertibly that the foundations of the modern family were already laid in primitive Aryan times, and it is the object of the present article to treat of this institution in fuller detail, more especially as found among the Teutons and Balto-Slavs. We do not propose to deal separately with these two ethnological groups, as it will be seen that in many cases the bearings of the subject in one group become fully intelligible only by reference to the other. The subject-matter will be arranged under the three headings of (1) marriage, (2) husband and wife, and (3) the other inmates of the household.

1. Marriage.—From the earliest times we find in either group two forms of marriage, viz. marriage by purchase and marriage by capture. As regards the ancient Lithuanians, we have the following item of information in *Michalonis Lituani de moribus Tartarorum Lituanorum et Moschorum fragmina*, ed. Grasser (Basel, 1615), p. 28: 'Quemadmodum et in nostra olim gente solvebatur parentibus pro sponsis pretium, quod krieno ('purchase-money': Skr. *krīṇāmi*, 'I buy') a Samagitis vocatur.' Of the ancient Prussians, Peter of Duisburg (in *Script. rer. Pruss.*, Leipzig, 1861, i. 54) writes: 'Secundum antiquam consuetudinem hoc habent Prutheni adhuc in usu, quod uxores suas emunt pro certa summa pecuniae.' With reference to the ancient Slavs, see below. In Old Russian a marriageable girl was called a *kunka*, from *kuna*, 'marten,' because her parents might exchange her for marten-skins, the usual medium of payment in ancient Russia, just as Homer speaks of a maiden as ἀλφεσίβοια, 'cattle-winning,' signifying that she brought her parents a bride-price in the form of cattle. To this day among the Russian peasantry, the first act of the nuptials is the suit or proposal (*svátanie*), which is a purely commercial transaction. The father of the suitor, usually accompanied by a relative, visits the girl's parents and says, 'We have a purchaser; you a commodity: will you sell your ware?' Then follows the bargaining, which, as our informants state, differs in no respect from a negotiation about the sale of a cow.

The well-known reference of Tacitus to the marriage customs of the ancient Germans (*Germ.* 18: 'Dotem non uxor marito, sed uxori maritus offert. Intersunt parentes et propinqui ac munera probant [*i.e.* marriage was an affair of the whole family-group], non ad delicias muliebres quaesita nec quibus nova nupta comatur, sed boves [cf. ἀλφεσίβοια] et frenatum equum et scutum cum framea gladioque. In haec munera uxor accipitur') can hardly refer to anything else than a commercial transaction of similar character. For the fact that marriage by purchase continued to prevail among the Teutons till a much later period is shown by numerous passages in the vernacular records.

Cf. *e.g.* 'êr thea magath habda giboht im te brudiu' (O. Sax.), and 'Cyning sceal mit cêape cwêne gebicgan, bûnum and bêagum' (A.S.). The Teutonic term for the bride-price appears in O.H.G. *widumo* and A.S. *weotuma*, words which in course of time to some extent changed their meaning (cf. N.H.G. *wittum*, 'widow's estate'), but which, alike in form and signification, were originally equivalent to the Homeric ἔεδνον (=Fέδνον), 'gift to the bride's parents.' If we assign to this word a root with a double termination (**ved, vedh*), we can trace the A.S. *weotuma* and Gr. ἔεδνον to the oldest term for marriage in the Aryan tongues: Lith. *wedù*, O. Russ. *voditi*, lit. 'to lead' (*vodimaja*, 'wife'), Skr. *vadhū*, 'young wife,' Avest. *vadhū*, 'woman,' *vadhrya*, 'marriageable'; so that A.S. *weotuma* and Gr. ἔεδνον mean literally 'the price for taking home the bride.'

Side by side with marriage by purchase is found marriage by capture. The co-existence of the two forms is seen most clearly in eastern Europe. Thus, according to the Chronicle of Nestor (ed. Miklosich, Vienna, 1860), cap. x.,

'they [the ancient Slavs] had their customs and the law of their fathers and their traditions; each tribe had its own usages. The Poljans (*i.e.* the Poles in the neighbourhood of Kiev) had the quiet and gentle manners of their fathers, were modest before their daughters-in-law and their sisters, their mothers and parents, and showed great respect for their mothers-in-law and brothers-in-law. They had a marriage (*bračny*) system. . . . But the Drevljans ('forest-folk') lived in brutish fashion; they lived like wild beasts; they killed one another, ate unclean things, and had no marriage (*brakŭ*), but abducted (*umykachu uvody*) the young women. And the Radimičes ('sons of Radim,' on the Soz), the Viatičes ('sons of Viatko,' on the Oka), and the Severes (people of the North), had all identical customs: they lived in the woods like wild beasts, and ate all manner of unclean things; they carried on lewd conversations before their parents and daughters-in-law. They had no marriages (*brakŭ*), but had places for play between the villages, and assembled at these games, dances, and all kinds of devilish sportings, and then each one carried off the woman with whom he had come to terms. Each of them, moreover, had two or three wives.'

Among the Baltic tribes likewise—the Lithuani, Livonienses, and Curetes—as also among the Muscovitæ and Rutheni, as we learn from the *Historia de gentibus septentrionalibus* (Rome, 1555) of Archbishop Olaus Magnus, marriage by capture was quite common. Of the Lithuanians in particular, Lasicius (*de Diis Samagitarum*, cap. 56) writes as follows: 'Nec ducuntur (puellae), sed rapiuntur in matrimonium, veteri Lacedaemoniorum more a Lycurgo instituto. Rapiuntur autem non ab ipso sponso, sed a duobus ejus cognatis.' Cf. also M. Prætorius, *Deliciæ Prussicæ*, ed. W. Pierson (Berlin, 1871), p. 69:

'Erasmus Franciscus, in his *Mirror of Ethics*, lib. 3, c. 3, p. 958, speaks thus of the Prussians: "In many localities their marriageable daughters wore little bells or cymbals, which were fastened to the girdle by a ribbon and hung down to the knees, so as to give a sign to suitors that the fruit was ripe. Nevertheless, they did not offer themselves directly, but allowed themselves to be seized and dragged into the married state. They were carried off, however, not by the bridegroom himself, but by his two nearest friends."'

Among the Russian peasantry the two forms of marriage referred to, viz. marriage in the recognized sense (*brakŭ*)—which, as we saw, was simply marriage by purchase—and 'predatory marriage' (*voróvskaja svádĭba*), marriage by capture (*umykánie*), or whatever else it may be called, still exist side by side, though the latter has receded farther and farther into the wooded country to the east of the Volga. For a fuller discussion of predatory marriage in Russia, see Schrader, *Sprachvergl. u. Urgesch.* ii.[3] 326 ff.

In the Teutonic area, marriage by purchase was much less in vogue than marriage by capture, but that it prevailed there not merely in isolated cases but as a general practice is rendered probable by its existence among related peoples, such as Indians, Greeks, and Romans (Schrader, p. 321). Further, with reference to the Teutons of primitive times, we have the witness of Tacitus (*Ann.* i. 55) to the predatory marriage of Arminius and the daughter of Segestes, who had been betrothed to another—a proceeding that led to a deadly warfare between the two family groups, just as, according to Olaus Magnus (see above), family feuds were rife among the peoples of the North-east 'propter raptas virgines et arripiendas.'

2. Husband and wife.—By purchase or by capture, then, the young woman passed under her husband's authority—a state which the Romano-Teutonic legal documents speak of as *mundium* (O.H.G. *munt*, 'hand'); in other words, the woman became the man's property. The idea that in the married state the man and the woman enjoyed equal rights in relation to each other is, as regards the Teutonic and Slavic peoples in primitive times, absolutely baseless. A specific confirmation of this is found in the fact that originally the man's act of marriage had quite a different terminology from the woman's. This phenomenon has been preserved most faithfully in the Slavic dialects.

Thus we have, *e.g.*, O. Russ. *ženit'sja* ('to provide oneself with a wife'), as predicated of the husband (Lat. *in matrimonium ducere*), and *vyti zámuž* ('to walk behind the man,' *i.e.* when the woman is taken home), as predicated of the wife (Lat. *nubere*). Terms like Fr. *marier* and Ger. *heiraten* (O.H.G. *hîrât*, 'marriage,' lit. 'house-management'), as used of either the man or the woman, are of relatively late origin.

In the original Aryan language the man to whose authority the woman was thus subject was styled **poti-s* (Skr. *páti-s*, *patitvá*, 'domestic sway,' *i.e.* 'married life'), 'lord and master.' This term may still be traced in the Goth. *brûþ-faþs*, 'bridegroom,' lit. 'maiden's-lord,' and appears also in the Slavic compound **gosti-poti*, Russ. *gospodĭ*, 'master,' lit. 'master of the strangers who come into the family' (O. Slav. *gostĭ*, cf. Lat. *hospes*, from **hosti-pets*). At a still earlier stage of Aryan speech the word **poti-s* meant simply 'himself' (cf. Lith. *pàts*, and Avest. *xvaē-pati*, 'himself'), and it is a singular fact that over wide tracts of the Slavic and Teutonic area the master of the house is to this day habitually referred to as 'himself.' Thus, among the Russian commercial class, which maintains the ancient Russian usages with remarkable fidelity, *sam*, 'himself' (in relation to the wife and the household generally), and *samá*, 'herself' (in relation to the children and the home), are the usual designations of husband and wife respectively. Ostrovskij, the brilliant delineator of this old Russian commercial class, has in his comedies given numerous illustrations of the *samodúrstvo* ('autonymity,' 'self-naming'; cf. Russ. *sam*, 'self,' *durak*, 'fool') of the ancient Muscovite merchant, whose wife and children tremble in his presence. But among the White Russians, Czechs, and Poles, as also throughout the Scandinavian Peninsula, corresponding designations are applied to the peasant and his wife (Norweg. *han sjölv*, *ho sjölv*), while in many parts of Britain 'himself' and 'herself' are popularly used in the same way.

We proceed to a more detailed account of the relations between husband and wife in the earliest times. It is beyond question that as regards the Teutons and Balto-Slavs we must start from the stage of polygamy. It was not until A.D. 1249 that the ancient Prussians formally bound themselves to abandon the custom of having three or four wives, as heretofore, and to be content with one (cf. Hartknoch, *Das alte u. neue Preussen*, Frankfort and Leipzig, 1684, p. 117). Polygamy, according to the Chronicle of Nestor, was practised also by the ancient Slavs. We must likewise assume that the same condition of things originally prevailed in the case of the Teutons, among whom, and especially among the Norsemen, a wide-spread practice of polygamy was long maintained (cf. Adam of Bremen, iv. 21); here, indeed, we find that a man might have as many as nine wives. Among the Germans, however, as referred to by Tacitus in *Germ.* 18 ('nam prope soli barbarorum singulis uxoribus contenti sunt, exceptis admodum paucis, qui non libidine, sed ob nobilitatem plurimis nuptiis ambiuntur'), there seems to have been a marked leaning towards monogamy. But the concurrent existence of an extensive system of concubinage is proved by the fact that the term *kebisa* ('concubine') is found in all the Teutonic dialects.

The strongest possible contrast to this sexual freedom on the husband's part is seen in the position of the wife. The fearful penalties wreaked upon the unfaithful wife among Teutons and Slavs are indicated in art. CHASTITY (Teut. and Balto-Slav.), vol. iii. p. 499 ff. That article emphasizes the fact that the erring wife was punished not so much for unchastity in the proper sense as for yielding her person to another without the knowledge and consent of her husband and owner. This may be safely inferred from extant traces of two institutions discussed in the article referred to, viz. vicarious procreation and lending a wife to a guest, both of which are found in the Teutonic, and the former also in the Slavic domain. And in another respect the patriarchal family system was everywhere associated with the depreciation and servitude of women. The idea that woman is in some way a creature of inferior rank prevails to the present day among the rural population of Eastern and South-eastern Europe. The wife of the Russian peasant could not well conceive of a mode of life without the *učit'* ('discipline'), *i.e.* flogging by the husband. If, when she did wrong, her husband did not have recourse to the 'silken whip,' which in Russian folk-song is a standing household article, she would think that he no longer loved her. Nor, except by reference to similar practices, or, at least, to the vestiges of such practices, among the Teutons, is it possible to explain what, according to the writer of the German *Nibelungenlied*, Queen Kriemhild, after her wrathful insults to Brunhild, says of her husband (xv. 894):

> '"Daz hât mich sît gerouwen"—sprach daz edel wîp—
> "ouch hât er sô zerblouwen dar umbe mînen lîp:
> daz ich ie beswârte ir mit rede den muot,
> daz hât vil wol errochen der helt küene unde guot."'

Of no less significance for the position of women was the universal custom which forbade them to eat with the men, and compelled them to take their meals by themselves. Thus, when the Nibelungs came to Bechelâren, they were met by the Margrave Rüedigêr and his wife, and then, as we are told (xxvii. 1671):

> 'Nâch gewonheite dô schieden si sich dâ:
> ritter unde frouwen die giengen anderswâ.'

In many districts, as, *e.g.*, in the island of Sjælland, the men sat, while the women stood, at table, the wife taking her position next to her husband, and then the daughters and maids to her left. In Servia, as recently as the reign of Milosh Obrenovitch, the wife and daughters stood at meals, even when guests were present. The separation of the sexes at meal-times was still a common practice in the Middle Ages, and there is direct historical evidence of the fact that in the Roman Catholic formula of divorce, 'separatio quoad thorum et mensam,' the *mensa* ('board') was a later addition.

On the whole, while we must admit that what Tacitus (*Germ.* 18) says of marriage among the Germans is somewhat idealized, we shall hardly find a more adequate representation of the relations between husband and wife than that given by him in ch. 15:

> 'Quotiens bella non ineunt, non multum venatibus, plus per otium transigunt, dediti somno ciboque. Fortissimus quisque ac bellicosissimus nihil agens, delegata domus et penatium et agrorum cura feminis senibusque et infirmissimo cuique ex familia, ipsi hebent: mira diversitate naturae, cum iidem homines sic ament inertiam et oderint quietem.'

All property belonged to the husband. By the oldest Russian code (cf. L. K. Goetz, *Das russische Recht*, vol. i., Stuttgart, 1910, §§ 118, 120), married daughters inherited nothing, and the unmarried only when there were no sons; though the sons were required to give a dowry to their sisters. The present law of use and wont operates in similar fashion to this day in the larger family of the patriarchal household. The ancient Norse code contained an ordinance to the same effect: 'the man goes to the inheritance; the woman from it.' It is impossible to imagine a more decided contrast to the practice of the non-Aryan peoples of ancient Europe (see above)—the practice, that is to say, by which in many cases the daughters inherited everything, and provided for the sons.

Among the Teutons and Slavs, moreover, the wife—overworked, exposed to all manner of ill-usage, and all but incapable of inheriting—was, so to speak, bound hand and foot to her husband. The *Lex Burgundiana*, xxxiv. 1, ordains: 'Si qua mulier maritum suum, cui legitime iuncta est, dimiserit, necetur in luto'; *i.e.*, she was to suffer the most degrading form of capital punishment—that commonly inflicted upon cowards and perpetrators of unnatural crime (cf. Tac. *Germ.* 12).

Unenviable as was the wife's position during her husband's lifetime, however, it was still preferable to her lot after his death. Here philology reveals the suggestive fact that, while not only the original Aryan language, but also the earliest Teutonic and Slavic dialects, had a special term for 'widow' (Goth. *viduvô*; O. Slav. *vĭdova*; cf. Lat. *vidua*, Skr. *vidhávā*), they had none for 'widower.' The explanation of this is that a material, as apart from a merely formal, import attached only to the position of the bereaved wife. The widower could take another mate whenever he chose, but the widow had no such liberty of action. Not only in ancient India, and among Scythians and Thracians, but among Teutons and Slavs as well, it was the rule that, when a husband died, his wife, or one of his wives, should be put to death at his pyre or grave, and be burned or buried with him, the idea being that she would thus continue to serve him in the life beyond as she had done here. Our earliest information regarding this practice on Teutonic soil comes from Procopius (*de Bell. Goth.* ii. 14). He tells us that the widow who did not wish to become the object of undying scorn and of her kindred's hate hanged herself beside her husband's grave; and Bonifacius (Jaffé, *Monumenta Moguntina*, Berlin, 1866, p. 172) writes of the Slavs to the same effect:

> 'Winedi, quod est foedissimum et deterrimum genus hominum, tam magno zelo matrimonii amorem mutuum observant, ut mulier, viro proprio mortuo, vivere recuset. Et laudibilis mulier inter illos esse iudicatur, quia propria manu sibi mortem intulit, et in una strue pariter ardeat cum viro suo' (cf. art. ARYAN RELIGION, vol. ii. p. 22b).

It must nevertheless be admitted that the somewhat sombre picture of women's position among the Teutons and Slavs of archaic times is here and there relieved by brighter touches. Women were regarded as prophetesses (Tac. *Germ.* 8: 'inesse quin etiam sanctum aliquid et providum putant, nec aut consilia earum aspernantur aut responsa neglegunt'; for their horrible modes of divination, see art. ARYAN RELIGION, vol. ii. p. 54b, and DIVINATION [Teut.], vol. iv. p. 827), as physicians (Tac. *ib.* 7: 'ad matres, ad coniuges vulnera ferunt; nec illae numerare aut exigere plagas pavent'), and as helpers in war (Tac. *loc. cit.*: 'cibosque et hortamina pugnantibus gestant'). These various traits are found also among the Slavs, and especially the southern Slavs, as, *e.g.*, in Montenegro. Over all the Slavic area, moreover, as upon Teutonic soil, women were regarded as specially conversant with the occult powers of Nature, with medicinal roots and plants, and with the most potent charms and incantations.

3. The other members of the household.—As we saw above, the primitive Aryan terms for family relationships included a number of words applied to relations by marriage. Thus we noted terms for 'daughter-in-law,' for 'father-in-law' and 'mother-in-law,' as also for 'husband's brother,' 'husband's sister,' and 'husband's brother's wife.' It will be observed that the names indicated in the latter portion of this list applied only to the husband's kindred in relation to his wife, but a closer examination of the Aryan terms for 'father-in-law' (O.H.G. *suehur*, O. Slav. *svekrŭ*, Lith. *szeszìuras*, Lat. *socer*, Gr. ἑκυρός, Skr. *śváśura*) and 'mother-in-law' (O.H.G. *suigar*, O. Slav. *svekry*, Lat. *socrus*, Gr. ἑκυρά, Skr. *śvaśrū*) shows that those words likewise originally denoted the father and mother of the husband only. Thus, not only in Greek, but in the Lithuanian and Slavic dialects as well, this is the archaic and proper idiom, and we need therefore have no hesitation in affirming that the application of the O.H.G. terms *suehur* (Ger. *Schwäher*) and *suigar* (Ger. *Schwieger*), as also of the Lat. *socer* and *socrus*, to the father and mother of the wife likewise was a later usage. Hence, too, it is impossible to translate the words 'father-in-law' and 'mother-in-law' into a Slavic tongue, such as Russian, unless it be known first of all whether the persons referred to are the parents of the husband or of the wife. Only in the former case does Russian use the words *svěku* and *svekróv'*, corresponding to O.H.G. *suehur* and *suigar*, while for the wife's father and mother idiom demands the palpably more modern terms *testĭ* and *tĕšča*, which are peculiar to the Slavic languages. It follows, therefore, that the Aryan terms for affinities took shape only as applied to the young wife's relation to the kindred of the man into whose home she had come.

Now, the substratum of reality which underlies these linguistic phenomena can be nothing else than what—in contradistinction to the separate family as we now have it—is variously called the 'house-community,' 'hearth-circle,' *Herdgemeinschaft* (Germ.), or 'undivided family,' *i.e.* that family organization in which parents and sons and the wives and children of the latter lived together in a single household. It is no merely accidental circumstance that the Slavs, who have retained not only—like the Teutons—the verbal forms, but also the original usage, of the Aryan terms denoting marriage affinities, should have likewise maintained the institution of the house-community from the earliest times to the present day. Russian writers who essay to depict the life of the common people of their country frequently bring before us such undivided households. Thus, *e.g.*, Turgeniev, in the first sketch in his *Annals of a Sportsman* (1846; Eng. tr., New York, 1885), describes the family life of a peasant who lives in a joint-household with a large group of sons and their wives.

The original Slavic word for 'family' appears in the Russ. *semĭjá*. The young woman who joined such family by marriage was called 'the alien side' (Russ. *čuzája storoná*), while the bridegroom, to whom and to whose kindred she was *nevesta* (probably 'the unknown'), was similarly called *čuzeninŭ*, 'the stranger'—a further evidence of the fact that the family of the husband and that of the wife were originally quite distinct. To the Slavic *semĭjá* corresponds—in meaning and probably also in etymology—the archaic Teutonic root **hîwa* (cf. Goth. *heiva-frauja*, 'master of the house'), the specific term for the Teutonic house-community (cf., most recently, F. Kauffmann, *Wörter und Sachen*, Heidelberg, 1911, ii. 26 ff.). The epoch in which the separate family, *i.e.* the system according to which a son left his father's house at his marriage and founded a home of his own, superseded the house-community on Teutonic soil (where the change occurred earlier than among the Slavs) is a problem that awaits further investigation. But it is beyond question that at one time the same conditions existed among the Teutons as we saw above to have prevailed among the Slavs.

We must now turn to speak of the persons who thus lived together in the undivided household, which is the earliest traceable form of the family among the Aryan and, derivatively, the Teutonic and Slavic peoples.

(*a*) *Parents and children.*—Possibly the term that comes nearest the primitive conception associated with the former word is the Goth. *fadrein*, lit. 'fatherhood,' which Ulfilas uses for 'parents,' and which, in its derivation from the word for 'father,' tacitly includes the designation of 'mother' as well. The absolute authority of the father over his children began from the moment of birth, as it lay within his option either to recognize the newly-born infant by the symbolic rite of 'lifting' it, or to doom it to exposure. With the former act was associated a kind of baptismal initiation, the child being immersed, immediately after its birth, in the waters of the Rhine, 'qui spurios infantes undis abripit, tamquam impuri lecti vindex' (cf. Cluver, *Germania antiqua*, 1663, p. 155). The primitive Teutonic—and therefore pre-Christian—ceremony denoted by the Goth. verb *daupjan*, 'to baptize,' would thus seem to have served as a test of legitimacy, and it is worthy of note that an ablutionary ceremony of similar import is found also among the Babylonians (cf. *ZVRW* xxiii. [1909] 434 ff.). The right of exposing infants, which, notwithstanding the averment of Tacitus (*Germ.* 19: 'numerum liberorum finire flagitium habetur'), was frequently exercised among the Teutons, doubtless bore most heavily upon females, the birth of whom was in ancient times so frequently regarded as a calamity. Even to-day, indeed, if a Lithuanian, whose family numbers five, three sons and two daughters, is asked how many children he has, he will answer 'Three,' as he leaves the females out of account. What Cæsar (*de Bell. Gall.* vi. 19) says of the Gauls ('Viri in uxores, sicuti in liberos, vitae necisque habent potestatem') holds good without qualification also of the Teutons, Letts, and Slavs. Of the Frisians, Tacitus (*Ann.* iv. 72) writes: 'Ac primo boves ipsos, mox agros, postremo corpora coniugum aut liberorum servitio tradebant'; while the Russian peasant, as depicted in folk-song and village tale, could exercise, even down to modern times, the same unlimited authority (*patria potestas*) over his family as was enjoyed by the *paterfamilias* of ancient Rome.

(*b*) *The aged.*—The family circle of the house-community would, of course, include grandfathers and grandmothers, grand-uncles and grand-aunts, and even great-grandparents, living in the 'old people's quarters.' Their lot would scarcely be a happy one, for the temperament of primitive peoples, as of the peasantry of to-day, was hard and unsentimental. In point of fact, we know that among the Teutonic and Baltic tribes, as in Europe and Asia generally, it was a common practice to abandon the aged, with or without their consent; cf. with reference to the Teutonic Heruli, Procop. *de Bell. Goth.* ii. 14: ἐπειδάν τις αὐτῶν ἢ γήρᾳ ἢ νόσῳ ἁλῴη ἐπάναγκές οἱ ἐγίνετο, τοὺς συγγενεῖς αἰτεῖσθαι ὅτι τάχιστα ἐξ ἀνθρώπων αὐτὸν ἀφανίζειν; and, with reference to the ancient Prussians, Hartknoch, *op. cit.* p. 181: 'At the order of the *waidewuti* (*i.e.* priest) they smothered their own parents when they became old or fell into a severe illness, so that they should incur no unnecessary expense in their regard.'

(*c*) *Brother and sister.*—Of the relationships among the younger members of the house-community, that of brother and sister merits special notice. Among Teutons and Slavs, as among other Aryan peoples, the brother might be designated the moral sponsor of his sister, and, after their father's death, her guardian in general. It was the custom in White Russia, when a bride was found on the marriage night not to be a maid, to hang a halter round the neck of her brother, and to compel him to wear it throughout the marriage feast. In Russian folk-song the brother is represented as taking a prominent part also in the transactions regarding the bride-price. We find an indication of the Teutonic practice in a verse of the *Nibelungenlied* (i. 4):

> 'Ir (Kriemhild) pflâgen drî künege edel unde rîch . . .
> diu frouwe was ir swester: die helde hêtens in ir pflegen.

Among the Letto-Lithuanians the strong bond of affection between brother and sister forms at once a special feature of common life and a favourite theme of popular poetry.

(*d*) *Uncle and nephew.*—It was noted above that the Aryan term for 'father's brother' can be traced in the O.H.G. *fatureo*, Lat. *patruus*, Gr. πάτρως, Skr. *pítṛvya*. We find no corresponding Aryan term for 'mother's brother,' who, of course, was not a member of the agnatically constituted house-community; but it is worthy of note that the Teutonic (O.H.G. *ôheim*), Lithuanian (*awynas*), Old Prussian (*awis*), and Slavic (*ujĭ*) forms for 'uncle' are all derived, though in quite different ways, from the Aryan root for 'grandfather' and 'grandmother' (Lat. *avus*, Goth. *avô*). This fact has not as yet been satisfactorily explained. It is beyond question, however, that in several of the Teutonic dialects, as in the Celtic group throughout, the Aryan word for 'grandchild' (Skr. *nápāt*, Lat. *nepos*, etc.) has by a corresponding linguistic process come to mean 'nephew' in the sense of sister's son. Now, these two more recently formed correlatives, uncle and nephew (*i.e.* mother's brother and sister's son), acquired great importance among the Teutonic peoples, as appears not only from the remarks of Tacitus (*Germ.* 20: 'Sororum filiis idem apud avunculum qui apud patrem honor. Quidam sanctiorem artioremque hunc nexum sanguinis arbitrantur'), but also from the fact that in Old English and Old Danish poetry uncle and nephew on the female side are represented as being most intimately associated alike in peace and in war. This is not to be explained by a reference to a matriarchal system among the primitive Teutons, as the ancient law of succession there was of the agnatic form (*Germ.* 20). But it is a possible conjecture that the Teutons were influenced in this respect by non-Aryan peoples who reckoned by female descent, and that among the former the mother's brother thus came to enjoy what was rather a position of honour than a strictly legal status.

(*e*) *Mother-in-law and daughter-in-law.*—As we have seen, the son brought his bride (O.H.G. *brût*, Russ. *nevesta*) into his father's house, and lived with her in the circle of his own kindred. The converse case, *i.e.* where the bridegroom joined the wife's household and became an 'adopted one,' or 'incomer' (Russ.), a 'house-son-in-law' (Serb), or a 're-heater' (Lith. for one who marries a widow), is also, as these terms indicate, to be met with in all parts, but was certainly of sporadic occurrence, and must not be postulated as a characteristic feature of the earliest times. The young wife's residence with her husband's parents was at first no pleasant experience for her. As the Russian folk-songs indicate, with abundance of concrete detail, she was an object of mockery, and the hardest drudgery was laid upon her. She suffered most, however, at the hands of her mother-in-law, who often resorted to the knout; and, indeed, as the house-community was the nursery of *patria potestas*, and of the tutelage of women, so was it the source of the old popular notion of the 'wicked mother-in-law.' That expression applied in ancient times to the husband's mother only, not to the wife's mother (Russ. *tëšča*)—or, at least, not to the latter in relation to the son-in-law (O.H.G. *eidam*, 'one bound by oath,' Russ. *zjatĭ*)—for, as is evident from what has been said above, no proper relationship was supposed to subsist between mother-in-law and son-in-law at all; and, when this type of affinity came at length to be recognized among the various peoples, it was rather the son-in-law that by his effrontery and avarice was accounted the more 'wicked' party, as is the case to-day throughout the East, North-east, and South-east of Europe. The 'mischievous mother-in-law' (as the *wife's* mother) is a product of modern times, and comes into recognition in connexion with the separate household of the young married pair. The 'wicked mother-in-law' in this sense is first heard of *c.* A.D. 1430, in a piece by the German poet Muskatblut.

Further, the frequent existence of licentious relations between *daughter-in-law and father-in-law*—a state of things known as *snochačestvo*, and notoriously characteristic of the Russian peasantry at the present day—should be noted as a typical feature of the house-community (cf. art. CHASTITY [Teut. and Balto-Slav.], vol. iii. p. 501[b]).

(*f*) *The widow.*—The melancholy fate of the widow in the dawn of the Aryan period has already been touched upon. Even when she was not forced to follow her husband in death, she would doubtless be prevented from marrying again (cf. Tac. *Germ.* 19: 'melius quidem adhuc eae civitates in quibus tantum virgines nubunt et cum spe votoque uxoris semel transigitur'). It seems to have been the ancient practice that the son, after his father's death, should take possession of his stepmother or stepmothers; cf. Procop. *de Bell. Goth.* iv. 20: Ῥαδίγερ ὁ παῖς ξυνοικιζέσθω τῇ μητρυιᾷ τὸ λοιπὸν τῇ αὐτοῦ, καθάπερ ὁ πάτριος ἡμῖν ἐφίησι νόμος.

(*g*) *The bachelor.*—The house-community was characterized by the rarity rather than by the frequency of bachelorhood. It cannot be doubted that the primitive Aryan race regarded marriage as an obligation from which there was no discharge (for the grounds of this idea, see art. ARYAN RELIGION, vol. ii. p. 29[a]). This view still prevails throughout Eastern and South-eastern Europe. Thus, P. A. Rovinskij, an eminent authority on the social life of these regions, writes as follows of the Russian and Montenegrin points of view:

> 'With us [*i.e.* in Russia] the people look upon an unmarried youth as imperfect and incomplete; and to live without a wife is regarded as unlawful. In Montenegro this unalterable obligation of marriage is insisted upon still more emphatically: a man

can be designated as a human being (*čoek*) only when he is married. Otherwise he will always be spoken of as but a "youth," lit. "child" (*djete*). In Servia and Bulgaria likewise marriage is held to be a duty absolutely binding upon all.'

Similar views prevail in certain rural districts of Germany.

A man who had died unmarried was still an object of the survivors' solicitude. The Arabic traveller Mas'ūdī, who visited Russia in his commercial journeys, writes thus of the people as he saw them:

'They cremate their dead, laying their weapons, their beasts of burden, and their ornaments upon the same funeral pyre. When a man dies, his wife is burned alive with him; but when the wife dies, the husband does not submit to the like fate. When a man dies unmarried, however, they provide him with a wife after his death.'

Traces of this practice of 'death-marriage' are found both on Slavic and on Teutonic soil (cf., further, *ERE* ii. 22 f.).

It is in full accordance with these data that the terms used for 'bachelor' in the languages of Eastern Europe are of recent formation, and are either loan-words (*e.g.* Turk. *bek'ár*) or derived from epithets applied to the lowest ranks of the people (*e.g.* Russ. *bobylĭ*, lit. 'proletarian,' 'landless peasant,' 'sponge'). Traces of bachelorhood can be followed further back in the West, among the Teutons. One such trace appears in the modern Germ. term for 'old bachelor,' *Hagestolz* (A.S. *hægesteald*). The word means literally 'enclosure-owner,' and was originally the technical term for the peasant who had no allotment in the communal land of the Teutonic settlements, but was restricted to a small fenced-in portion of the soil, quite insufficient for the support of a family. The Danish word for 'bachelor,' *ungkarl*, in contradistinction to *karl*, 'free land-owner,' 'yeoman,' points to similar conditions.

(*h*) *Slaves.*—In the lower stages of civilization there is never any marked outward distinction between bond and free. What Tacitus records of the Germans in this regard (*Germ.* 20: 'Dominum ac servum nullis educationis deliciis dignoscas: inter eadem pecora, in eadem humo degunt, donec aetas separet ingenuos, virtus agnoscat') is proved by the evidence of language to have been true of the Slavs no less than of the Teutons, as the Teutonic and Slavic designations of male and female slaves (*e.g.* A.S. *híwan* [pl.] 'domestics'; O. Slav. *semija*, 'mancipia'; Lith. *szeimyna*, 'retainers') are in many cases derived from the already noted terms for 'house-community,' **híwa* and *semĭjá*, thus showing that the slaves likewise were reckoned among the inmates of the house.

LITERATURE.—In addition to the literature given throughout the art., cf. O. Schrader, *Reallex. d. indogerm. Altertumskunde*, Strassburg, 1901 (2nd ed. in preparation), *Die Schwiegermutter u. der Hagestolz*, Brunswick, 1904, *Totenhochzeit*, Jena, 1904, *Sprachvergl. u. Urgesch.*³, Jena, 1907 (esp. ii.³ 369 ff.), and *Die Indogermanen*, Leipzig, 1911 (esp. p. 74 ff.).

O. SCHRADER.

FAN (Anglo-Sax. 'fann,' from Lat. *vannus* [**uet-no-s*]).—An instrument for purifying grain by throwing it into the air. Cognates of *vannus* are *ventus*, 'wind,' 'winnow' (see Walde, *Lat. etymol. Wörterbuch*², Heidelberg, 1910, *s.v.* 'Vannus'). For variant English forms of the word and historical steps in meaning, see *OED* and the *English Dialect Dictionary* (*s.v.*). The Gr. equivalent of *vannus*, λίκνον, and its by-form, νεῖκλον, go back to a root **neiqō*, 'to clean' (cf. νίζω, 'to wash'); the *l* form specialized in Greek into the sense of cleaning 'grain' (see J. Schmidt, *Kritik der Sonantentheorie*, Weimar, 1895, p. 107 f.). The Gr. word for the fork or shovel form of fan, πτύον, is probably from an onomatopoetic root *pte*, meaning 'to spit out.' The Gr. and Lat. words for 'sieve,' κόσκινον and *cribrum*, mean simply 'separators.' Normally they are used for perforated instruments, but Plato's κόσκινον τετρημένον (*Gorgias*, 493 B) may point to a time when the sieve, like the fan, was not perforated.

1. Shapes of fan and methods of use.—Two principal forms obtain. (1) A long-handled instrument, which may be a fork, a toothed spade, or a shovel. It is used like the modern hayfork. After the grain is threshed, the mixture of broken straw, chaff, and corn is turned and tossed up, so that the wind may blow away the lighter material. The 'fan' and shovel of Is 30[24] are instruments of this kind, such as are still in use in modern Palestine (see *HDB*, art. 'Agriculture' [cf. also *ib.* art. 'Shovel'], where specimens are figured), and, indeed, all over the world. Such instruments lent their symbolism to religion, *e.g.* Lk 3[17] 'whose fan is in his hand, and he will thoroughly purge his floor'; but, so far as we know, they were not employed in Palestine in actual ritual. But on the steatite vase of Hagia Triada in Crete (*JHS* xxiv. [1904] 249, fig. 7; see Literature, *infra*) pronged forks are carried in what seems to be a ritual harvest procession. On an Egyptian sculptured slab of the XVIIIth dynasty, now in Bologna, a winnowing-spade is seen erected on a heap of corn offered to the serpent-goddess of the granary, RNWT. About it are grouped two pairs of hand-scoops, a pair of sweepers, and a three-pronged fork (*JHS*, *loc. cit.*, fig. 1). The custom still prevails in Teneriffe of erecting the winnowing-spade when the work is over. But it seems to have no ritual association. Among the Greeks the winnowing-spade (πτύον) was set up in honour of Demeter. Theocritus at the end of his Harvest Idyll (vii. 155) prays:

'O once again may it be mine to plant
The great fan on her corn heap, while she stands
Smiling, with sheaves and poppies in her hands.'

(2) It is the second form of winnower, the winnowing-basket, that is of cardinal importance in ancient ritual and mysticism, and this for a reason that will appear immediately. Much confusion has been caused by the fact that our word 'fan' has been used indiscriminately to translate alike the Latin *ventilabrum* and *vannus*, and the Greek θρῖναξ, ἀθηρηλοιγός, πτύον, and λίκνον. The confusion is now inevitable, since the beautiful word 'fan' has passed into English literature as the rendering of two quite distinct implements, which have only this in common, that they are both used for cleaning corn. The use of the winnowing-spade or fork (*ventilabrum*, θρῖναξ [poet. ἀθηρηλοιγός], πτύον) has been already explained; the *vannus*, λίκνον, and winnowing-basket, or corb, of modern times remains.

FIG. 1. Fan from France.

Its shape is seen in fig. 1, a modern winnowing-basket (or fan) from France, now in the Ethnographical Museum, Cambridge. The method of its use, now rapidly becoming a lost art, is seen in fig. 2; the essential feature in the winnow-corb, as for clearness and brevity we shall call it, is its shovel shape, one side being left open. The distinguishing point in its use is that, in the winnowing by the corb, as contrasted with the fork, though the mixture of grain and chaff is in a sense ventilated, the wind plays no part in the process. By a particular knack of jerking and working the basket—a knack difficult to acquire and almost impossible to describe—the chaff is gradually propelled forward and out of the basket

FIG. 2. Fan in use.

and the grain left clean. Columella (1st cent. B.C.) knew that the wind played no part in the use of the *vannus*. He says (ii. 21): 'If the wind be low in all quarters, let the grain be cleaned by fans (*vannis expurgentur*).' Broadly speaking, the fork or spade was used for rough preliminary work, the basket for finer cleaning. Some further confusion in terminology was caused by the fact that not only were winnowing-fork and winnowing-basket confused, but winnowing-basket was by later writers identified with winnowing-sieve (*cribrum*, *κόσκινον*). All had, of course, in common this factor only, that they were grain-cleaners; identity in function led to confusion as to form. That the winnowing-*basket* was called a 'fan' or 'van' in England, and was of substantially the same shape and use as that in fig. 2, is happily certain from a 14th cent. brass in the Church of Chartham (C. Boutell, *Monumental Brasses of England*, London, 1849, p. 35). On the surcoat, ailettes, and shield of Sir Robert de Setvans are emblazoned the family arms, the seven 'fans' or baskets.

2. Ritual use and mysticism of the winnow-corb (*vannus*, *liknon*) **among the Greeks and Romans.**—The *locus classicus* as to the sanctity of the winnow-corb is, of course, the passage in the *Georgics* of Vergil (i. 165):

> 'Virgea praeterea Celei vilisque supellex,
> Arbuteae crates, et *mystica vannus Iacchi*.'

It is clear that to Vergil the *vannus* is a *light* agricultural implement made of wicker-work. He assumes its mysticism as known; but Servius in his commentary, though very confused as to forms, (1) makes clear that the *vannus* is our winnow-corb, and (2) gives some cause for the epithet *mystica*. A portion of this long note must be quoted:

> 'The mystic fan of Iacchus, that is, the sieve of the threshing-floor. He calls it the mystic *vannus* of Iacchus because the rites of Father Liber had reference to the purification of the soul, and men are purified in his mysteries as grain is purified by fans. . . . Some add that Father Liber was called by the Greeks *Liknites*. Moreover, the *vannus* is called by them *liknon*, in which he is currently said to have been placed after he was born from his mother's womb. Others explain its being called "mystic" by saying that the *vannus* is a large wicker vessel, in which peasants, because it was of large size, used to heap their firstfruits and consecrate it to Liber and Libera. Hence it is called "mystic".'

The Latin *vannus* being the same as the Greek λίκνον, we can elucidate *vannus* from Greek usage. Harpocration (*s.v.* λίκνον) has left us this remarkable statement:

> 'The *liknon* is serviceable for every rite of initiation, and every sacrifice.'

We begin with sacrifice. The *liknon* was serviceable for sacrifice, simply because it was a convenient basket in which to pile up firstfruits. It was not made to be a carrier—that is clear from the open end, which could only serve the purpose of winnowing—but it could and did serve to hold fruit or grain.

In a fragment of Sophocles (760 [Nauck]) the Athenians are addressed as

> 'Ye who pray
> To Ergane, your bright-eyed child of Zeus,
> With service of your winnow-corbs set up.'

In a Hellenistic relief (fig. 3), now in Munich (Glyptothek, no. 601; T. Schreiber, *Hellen. Reliefbilder*, Leipzig, 1899, Taf. 80*a*), we see such a service: a little circular shrine, past which a peasant is going to market; in the middle of the shrine an ornamental pillar surmounted by the shovel-shaped wicker-basket from which hang bells to scare away evil influences; in the basket are fruits, leaves, and the *phallos*, the sign of fertility. Servius is confirmed by this and many other monuments.

FIG. 3. Hellenistic relief: *liknon* holding firstfruits.

The *liknon*, Servius tells us, was used as a cradle. For this the shoe-shaped basket was obviously convenient; the cradles of to-day are of similar shape. Dionysus as a child was called *Liknites*, 'He of the Cradle.' On the Pashley sarcophagus, now in the Fitzwilliam Museum at Cambridge (fig. 4), we see 'Him of the Cradle' carried by two men bearing torches. The *liknon* as cradle is closed in at the end, lest the child fall out. About this simple and convenient use of the *liknon* as cradle, a primitive mysticism of the 'sympathetic magic' kind speedily grew up.

The scholiast on Callimachus (*Hymn.* i. 48), in telling of the *liknon*-cradle of Zeus, says:

> 'In old times they used to put babies to sleep in winnow-corbs as an omen for wealth and fruits.'

The child was put in the winnow-corb for what we should call 'luck.' Another scholiast (*ap.* Aratus, *Phæn.* 268) says that this was done immediately after birth (τὰ γὰρ βρέφη τὰ πρῶτον γεννώμενα, κτλ.).

The same magical intent, dwindling gradually into mere symbolism, explains the use of the *liknon* in marriage rites. The pseudo-Plutarch (*Prov. Alex.* xvi.) says:

> 'It was the custom in Athens at weddings that a boy, both of whose parents were alive (ἀμφιθαλῆ παῖδα), should carry a *liknon* full of loaves, and thereon pronounce the words, "Bad have I fled, better have I found" (ἔφυγον κακόν, εὗρον ἄμεινον).'

The loaves of bread (ἄρτος, fermented bread) have

taken the place of more primitive offerings; but the symbolism, or rather magic, is the same. At a marriage every precaution is taken to suggest and induce fertility. On a black-figured vase now in the British Museum (Cat. B. 174) we see (fig. 5) a marriage procession. Two of the figures, the

FIG. 4. Pashley Sarcophagus: Dionysus Liknites.

first and third, carry winnow-corbs on their heads. One of the figures stands close to the veiled bride. A handle and the wicker-work of the corb are very clearly seen.

FIG. 5. Black-figured vase: *liknon* in marriage procession.

Marriage is 'an excellent mystery.' The Greek conceived of it as a rite of initiation. The plural word τέλη covered all mysteries and initiation rites, while the singular form τέλος was specially used of marriage. All rites of birth, of puberty, of marriage, and of death were and are to the primitive mind *rites de passage*, *i.e.* rites of transition from one social state to another. The name τέλος, which we translate 'accomplishment,' meant originally 'growing up,' becoming a man; ἀνὴρ τέλειος is a full-grown man. When a boy was full-grown, he was made a tribesman, and initiated into tribal customs, tribal dances, and the like. The various and complex ceremonies that attend this and other initiation have primarily but two ends, which are really one and contain the gist of all magic. They are purification, and the promotion of fertility. This double end was excellently symbolized by the *liknon*. It was a purifier because it was a winnower; it was a fertility-vehicle because it was a basket for firstfruits. Hence, in the rare scenes where initiation-ceremonies are represented, the *liknon* is always figured, usually on the head of the veiled initiate. A good instance is given in fig. 6 from a cinerary urn in the Museo delle Terme at Rome (*Helbig Cat.* 1168). The mysteries are Eleusinian in kind —judging from the fact that on the other side of the urn Demeter and her snake are figured. In fig. 6 we see the pig sacrificed for purification. The veiled candidate is seated with his right foot on a ram's skull. Over his head a priestess holds a *liknon*. Duly purified and fertilized, he will be able to pronounce the words, 'Bad have I fled, better have I found.'

FIG. 6. Cinerary urn: *liknon* at Eleusinian Mysteries.

Briefly to resume: in the mysticism of the 'fan' two elements are distinguishable: (1) purification, and (2) magical promotion of fertility. Any form of winnower, be it fork or basket, might have served as the symbol and vehicle of purification; but, as a matter of actual fact, mysticism gathered only round the basket, *not* the fork. Hence it is probable that the main element of the symbolism focused in the notion of fertility, and that the idea of purification was at first subsidiary. Later, when the idea of sin and release from it became prominent, the fan as purifier was more and more emphasized; and its symbolism was still further developed in relation to its perforated successor, the sieve. It must, however, always be remembered that, alien though it is to modern thinking, to the primitive mind purification and fertility charms are never far asunder. Fertility is largely induced by purification, *i.e.* by the purging away of all evil influences hostile to birth and growth. The other element in its induction is the bringing of things into contact with the source of growth or other living things, —plants, fruits, running water, or whatever is supposed to be charged with life and grace, or, as the Polynesians call it, *mana*. The *liknon* was the vehicle of both procedures, and its use shows very clearly how the highest spiritual mysticism of New Birth and Regeneration may have its source in a rudimentary magic. You lay a child in a winnow-corb, you put a corb of fruits on a boy's head at a puberty rite, you carry a corb of grain and fruits in a marriage procession, and the winnow-corb becomes at once the symbol and the sacrament of the whole physical, moral, and spiritual field covered by the formulary ἔφυγον κακόν, εὗρον ἄμεινον.

[3. The winnowing-basket in India.—The Indian equivalent of the fan, the winnowing-basket (*śūrpa*), also merits attention in this connexion. It is one of the concomitants of the wedding ceremony in the period of the *sūtras*, and on that occasion the *śūrpa*, containing four handfuls of roasted grain mixed with *śamī* leaves, is placed behind the wedding fire (Hillebrandt, *Rituallit.* [=*GIAP* iii. 2], Strassburg, 1897, p. 65 f.). Among the modern Baiswār, after the clothes of the newly-wedded pair have been knotted together,

'they do the usual five revolutions round the cotton tree, while the bridegroom holds a winnowing-fan (*sūp*) into which the bride's brother pours a little parched rice each time as they go round. The bride sprinkles this grain on the ground out of the fan, and both retire into the retiring room' (Crooke, *TC* i. 129).

The winnowing-fan is also used among the Kols and Orāons in selecting a new village priest, since 'by its magical power it drags the person who holds it towards the individual on whom the sacred mantle has fallen' (Crooke, *PR* ii. 189).

But, if the winnowing-basket, through its association with grain, is often associated with rites for prosperity and increase, it is also employed to separate the evil from the good, so that Mātaṅgī Śaktī, a form of Durgā (*q.v.*), 'carries a broom and winnowing-fan with which she sifts mankind' (*PR* i. 133); and the essential difference between the winnowing-basket and the sieve is neatly given by a Sanskrit proverb (Böhtlingk, *Ind. Sprüche*[2], St. Petersburg, 1870–73, no. 6235) which says that 'good men, like a winnowing-basket, cast out faults and retain virtues; but evil folk, like a sieve (*chālanī*), retain faults and let virtues go.'—LOUIS H. GRAY.]

LITERATURE.—J. E. Harrison, 'Mystica Vannus Iacchi,' in *JHS* xxiii. [1903] 292–324 and xxiv. [1904] 241–254; also *BSA* x. [1903–1904]; cf. *Proleg. to the Study of Gr. Religion*[2], Cambridge, 1907, pp. 519–535. To these three articles reference may be made for full details and illustrations of the various forms of fan in use in Egypt, and especially Greece, and for modern forms of fan so far as they illustrate these. For the final clearing up of the peculiar form and use of the winnowcorb the present writer is entirely indebted to Dr. Francis Darwin, who procured for her from France the specimen figured in fig. 1, and whose old gardener, as shown in fig. 2, is one of the few surviving exponents in England of an almost lost art. It is impossible to discuss or even enumerate the slightly variant forms of 'fan' in use all over the world; and for the purposes of religious symbolism nothing would be gained by it, as they are all modifications of either fork, spade, basket, or sieve. It may be noted that in Finland, and, so far as the writer is aware, only there, all three forms appear in use together; see Grotenfelt, *Det primitiva Yordbrukets Metoder i Finland*, Helsingfors, 1899. The three Finnish forms are reproduced from his book in *JHS*, 1903, p. 309, fig. 10, and show very well the phases of transition from one to the other. Reference may, finally, be made to O. Schrader, *Reallex. der indogerm. Altertumskunde*, Strassburg, 1901, pp. 764, 965 f.

J. E. HARRISON.

FANCY.—See ILLUSION, IMAGINATION.

FAQĪR.—See DERVISH.

FĀRĀBI.—**1. Life and writings.**—Al-Fārābi, one of Islām's leading philosophers, was of Turkish origin. His full name was Muhammad, son of Muhammad, son of Tarkhān Abū Naṣr al-Fārābi. He was born at Fārāb, situated on the Jaxartes (*Syr Darya*), the modern Otrar. Coming to Baghdad, he studied under the Christian doctor Johanna, son of Hīlān. Another of his teachers was Abū Bishr Mattā, known as a translator of Greek works. He next proceeded to Aleppo, to the court of Saif ad-Daulah, son of Hamdān, and led a somewhat retired life under his protection, assuming the garb of a Ṣūfī. When this prince captured Damascus, he took the philosopher with him, and there Fārābi died in A.H. 339 (= A.D. 950).

Fārābi's literary production was considerable, but a great number of his works were lost very early; they were neglected in favour of the works of Avicenna (*q.v.*), which were written in a more lucid and methodical style. They were chiefly commentaries or explanations of the Greek philosophers, especially Aristotle. He wrote an *Introduction to Logic*, a *Concise Logic*, a series of commentaries on the *Isagōgē* of Porphyry, the *Categories*, the *Hermeneia*, the *First* and *Second Analytics*, the *Topics*, *Sophistic*, *Rhetoric*, and *Poetics*. The whole formed an *Organon* divided into nine parts. In the sphere of Moral Philosophy he wrote a commentary on the *Nicomachean Ethics*; in that of Political Philosophy, he made a summary of Plato's *Laws*, and composed a short treatise on the *Ideal City*, which has been published. To Psychology and Metaphysics he contributed numerous works, with such titles as *Intelligence and the Intelligible*, *The Soul*, *The Faculties of the Soul*, *The One and Unity*, *Substance*, *Time*, *The Void*, and *Space and Measure*. He also commented on Alexander of Aphrodisias' book *de Anima*. Believing (according to the view of the Musalmān 'philosophers' properly so called, *i.e.* those who gave themselves out as disciples of the Greeks, and for whom the Arabs reserve the title *failāsūf*, 'philosopher') that Greek philosophy was a unity, he laboured to reconcile Plato and Aristotle, and with this idea wrote treatises on *The Aims of Plato and Aristotle*, and *The Agreement between Plato and Aristotle*—works which are known to us. He also discussed certain interpretations of Aristotle proposed by Galen and John Philoponus, and composed an *Intervention between Aristotle and Galen*.

In the sphere of science, Fārābi wrote commentaries on Aristotle's *Physics*, *Meteorology*, *The Heavens*, and *The Universe*, besides commenting on the *Almagest* of Ptolemy. To him also is due an essay explaining some difficult propositions from the *Elements* of Euclid. The occult sciences interested him, and he left writings on *Alchemy*, *Geomancy*, *Genii*, and *Dreams*.

This great philosopher was also a talented musician—a somewhat exceptional combination. In this sphere he was at the same time composer, virtuoso, and theorist. Some songs attributed to him still exist among the Maulavī dervishes (dancing dervishes), and it is to him that we owe the most explicit work on the theory of Oriental music. His musical talent excited the admiration of Saif ad-Daulah.

Fārābi's style is somewhat peculiar. It generally takes the form of aphorisms, short sentences which always appear condensed and profound, but sometimes become obscure by failing to maintain a methodical sequence. Fārābi is indeed a difficult author, and it is not safe to be dogmatic when attempting to interpret the details of his system. In the main body of his teaching he belongs to the so-called 'school of Philosophers,' *i.e.* to the school which represented the Neo-Platonic tradition in his time; his position in this school is between al-Kindi (older than Fārābi, though not so well known) and Avicenna (a younger philosopher, who is very lucid and easy to study). Following Kindi, he prepares the way for the theory that we find explicitly formulated in Avicenna. His system, or at least his style of thought, is, however, more mystical than that of Avicenna. Mystical ideas and terms appear nearly all through his writings, and seem to colour his whole doctrine, whereas Avicenna treats mysticism as a sort of supplementary chapter or a climax, quite distinct and separate from the rest of his system. The Orientals called Fārābi the 'second master,' Aristotle being the 'first.' In giving this title to the Muslim thinker, it was especially his importance as a logician that they had in view.

2. Doctrines.—It is possible, by making a methodical arrangement of his sentences, to disentangle the principal theses of Fārābi's doctrine and present them in a coherent form. This has been done by M. Horten in an important work (see Lit. below) devoted to this philosopher and his commentator Ismā'īl al-Fārānī (pp. 486–491). It is easier to recognize, under his arrangement, the teaching of Oriental scholasticism. The chief subjects of discussion are as follows. (*a*) In Logic: cognition, conceived as a resemblance of objects; perception, a means of cognition; representation, the first stage of cognition; the concept, assimilation and union with the object; abstraction; the predicates; substance and being; the qualities of bodies and the accidents; causality and the relations in the physical world. (*b*) In Psychology: the principle of life, breath; the faculties and their objects; vegetative force; animal force or animal soul, capable of desire, fear, anger; the external senses; the internal senses; common sense (in the scholastic meaning of the term) and memory; imagination, cogitation, instinct; human intelligence, with its logical faculties, the passive intellect and the active intellect which receives illumination from God. (*c*) In Metaphysics: being, the source of being, non-being; the proofs of God's existence; the necessary and the contingent; the possible; potentiality and action; species and individual; substance and accident, causality; God, the origin of causes; the chain of causes; the principle of causality — that every effect produced upon an object otherwise than by its nature comes from a cause exterior to it. (*d*) In Theology: God existing by His very nature, proved by the causal series, and by the consideration of multiplicity and unity; comprising all creatures; being at the same time unity, truth, love, and light (as in Plotinus), pure being and the source of being, endowed with an interior activity and a personal life; knowing Himself and knowing the world, but always maintaining His unity; the cause in a certain way of free actions in man; both visible and invisible; knowable by man as cause, and through ecstasy or revelation. (*e*) In Cosmology: the first being sprung from God, Divine knowledge and power, the world of Ideas, of knowledge, of abstraction; the second being sprung from God, the 'Commandment' or Word (*λόγος*, Arab. *amr*); the celestial spheres and the sublunary world. (*f*) In Ethics: happiness, the end of life, attained by union with God, the return of all things to God.

The following passages are taken from the treatise *Gems of Wisdom*, and will give an idea of the philosopher's style. This work, consisting of 58 articles in very brief form, was much admired and extensively used in the schools; it has been edited by Dieterici and translated by Horten.

There are two worlds: the world of created things—our world—and the world of unseen, invisible things, which is the celestial kingdom and the region of Ideas. The latter is also called the world of the 'Commandment'; the 'Commandment' is the eternal will in relation to created things with their perfections. Fārābi further distinguishes the 'Commandment' (*amr*) from the Spirit (*rūḥ*); we may take *amr* as corresponding to the *Logos*, or Word, of the Neo-Platonists, while the Spirit corresponds to the *Psyche*.

How does the multiplicity that is in evidence in the world arise from a God who is Unity? By a sort of intermediary hypostasis between the absolute One and the world:

'You regard Unity, and it is Power; you regard Power, and it becomes second knowledge, which includes within itself multiplicity,' for the first knowledge of God can know nothing but the One. 'There is the horizon of the world of Sovereignty —the purely Divine world—which is followed by the world of the Commandment where the reed-pen runs along the tablet.' This refers to the tablet on which, according to Qur'ānic eschatology, the deeds of men are inscribed. 'Unity becomes multiplicity at the point where the shadow of the heavenly Lotus falls,' the Lotus which shades the Muslim Paradises, 'and where the Spirit and the Word are projected,' the eternal Word of God inspired by the Spirit and preserved in the Qur'ān. 'There is the horizon of the world of the Commandment, followed by the Tabernacle and the Throne,' the seat of God and envelope of the world, 'then the heavens and all that they contain. Every creature sings the praises of God; the heavens revolve according to the principle,' according to the impulse given by the creator, 'and there is the world of the Creation, whence one comes back to the world of the Commandment, by which all once more become one.'

'When you regard the world of the Creation, you perceive the nature of what is created; when you regard the world of pure Being, you know that there must be something existing by his essence.' 'If you know truth first, you also know its opposite; but if you regard error first,' *i.e.* the contingent world, 'you know error, but you know not truth, inasmuch as it is the reality beyond the contingent. Turn your eyes then to the true Essence; and so you will not love the stars which suffer eclipse'; this is an allusion to a passage of the Qur'ān (vi. 76), 'but will turn your eyes towards the face of Him whose face, and none other, is eternal.'

God, conceived as supreme Unity, is also thought of as necessary Being, existing by itself.

'Necessary Being has neither form nor kind nor difference . . . it is the principle whence all else flows.' God is at the same time interior and exterior, manifest and hidden; this manner of speech is usual in Ṣūfiism: 'God is exterior by His essence, and in virtue of being exterior He is interior'; *i.e.* the brightness when He appears is so great that it blinds, and the Divine unity is thus invisible. 'Everything that is seen is seen by means of Him,' *i.e.* everything is visible in Him, as objects in the light of the sun.

God has a two-fold manifestation: first, the manifestation of unity; He shows Himself as unity either to the human intelligence, which seeks after the absolute, or to the heart by means of mystical illumination. His second manifestation takes place by means of signs, which are the wonderful creations scattered throughout the world. 'This second manifestation is connected with multiplicity, and proceeds from the first manifestation, which is that of unity.'

Does God know the world? According to Aristotle, God can have only an abstract knowledge of things. Fārābi does not agree with this view. According to him, God knows things in their causes, and this kind of knowledge does not lead to any change in His being, because the causes, viz. Ideas, are eternal. Moreover, His knowledge is active, and becomes confused with His power to create; it does not, as with us, result in the impression made upon Him by the objects:

'We cannot say that the First Truth comprehends the things that spring from His decree from the fact of these things themselves, as things of sense are perceived by the fact of their presence and the impression they make on us. . . . It comprehends things by its essence; for, when it regards its essence, it sees the lofty power therein, and in the power it sees what is decreed; it sees all, then, and the knowledge it has of its essence is the cause of the knowledge it has of all other things.'

This theory is dangerous for free will; for, if God knows all the details of the world's life as consequences of His power and His decree, there is not much room left for liberty.

The creation is not conceived as an action analogous to human actions, which would be accompanied by desire and effort; it is merely the immediate expression of the Divine thought. As soon as God imagines a thing to Himself, the existence of that thing follows. According to this conception of the act of creation, it seems absolutely necessary to admit that creation is eternal; for God's thought of the world must have been eternal, and He did not require to wait until a need or a desire brought it to realization; the world must then have flowed from His thought at all times. This conclusion, however, is not so inevitable as one might think: the Oriental scholastics, like all the ancients, did not have quite the same conception of time as we have. For them time began when the world was set in motion, and was measured by the number of revolutions performed by the heavenly spheres. Before the movement of the spheres there was no time, but only a sort of fixed duration not susceptible of measurement. The Creator is therefore placed outside of time; and produces it all at once along with the world. Similarly, according to the Oriental conception of the Middle Ages, mensurable space did not extend beyond the limited sphere of the world.

On the idea of substance, Fārābi expresses interesting but contradictory views. He applies the term to both individuals and species. Species and genera, though real substance, require individuals to actualize them. They become actualized and individualized gradually with the passage from the general to the particular. Material substance is the cause of bodies; bodies are the cause of plants; plants, of animals; animals, of man; and man in general is the cause of the human individual. In a short treatise called *Epistle of the Second Master in Reply to Questions put to him*, Fārābi explains his view as follows:

'How, it is asked, are we to conceive the order of substances which are supported by one another? The first substances are the individuals; nothing else is necessary to their existence. The second substances are species and genera, which in order to be (in action) must have individuals. Individuals, in this sense, are therefore anterior in substantiality, and have more right to the name of substance than have species. But, from another point of view, universals, as being fixed, permanent, subsisting, have more right to the name substance than perishable individuals.' 'Universals,' Fārābi says again, 'do not exist in action; they exist only by individuals, and their existence is then accidental—which does not mean that universals are accidents, but that their existence in action can take place only by accident.'

Munk, in his art. on Fārābi in the *Dict. des sciences philos.*, says that the philosopher Ibn Ṭufail tried to accuse Fārābi of denying the immortality of the soul. But this accusation lacks support. Fārābi's doctrine on this point is the same as that of the philosophic school: the soul, on accomplishing the end of its destiny, must enter into communication with the intellect at work (the philosophical form of the doctrine); or it returns to God (the mystic form). But the fact that the soul is destined to become united with God does not necessitate, according to Fārābi, the annihilation of its personality; nor does it follow, from the fact that the human intellect must receive illumination from the world of Ideas, that the human person must lose all idea of particular things. Fārābi's conception of happiness and the other world is similar to that found in the mystic part of Avicenna's works.

There is a curious passage in which Fārābi speaks of bliss in the other world; it is in *The Ideal City*, the work in which he explains that the end of government on earth ought to be to make souls happy in the other world. The souls of the inhabitants of the city assemble, generation after generation, and their happiness increases as they become more numerous:

'The joy of those long dead increases at the arrival of the newly dead, for each soul then comprehends its essence and the essence of the other souls similar to itself; thus the intensity of its feeling grows—just as the skill of the scribe grows with the number of times he practises writing. The addition of souls to souls corresponds, as regards the progress of each soul's happiness, to the scribe's repetition of his work, by means of which he progresses in facility and skill.'

This passage assumes that each soul is endowed with individual feeling and perception in the other world.

LITERATURE.—M. Horten, 'Das Buch der Ringsteine Farabis († 950) mit dem Kommentare des Emir Isma'il el-Ḥoseini el-Farani (um 1485) übersetzt und erläutert,' vol. v. pt. iii. of *Beiträge zur Gesch. der Philos. des Mittelalters*, Münster, 1906, with bibliography on pp. xviii–xxviii of the Introduction (Fārāni's commentary was published in the East, A.H. 1291); M. Steinschneider, 'Al-Fārābi: des arab. Philosophen Leben und Schriften,' in *Mém. de l'Acad. impér. des sciences de St. Pétersbourg*, vol. xiii. no. 4, St. Petersburg, 1869; F. Dieterici, *Alfārābī's philos. Abhandlungen*, Leyden, 1890 (the Arab. text of nine short treatises), also *Alfārābī's Abhandlung der Musterstaat*, Leyden, 1895 (Arab. text); P. Brönnle, *Die Staatsleitung*, Leyden, 1904; T. J. de Boer, *Hist. of Philos. in Islam*, London, 1903 (see Index); Carra de Vaux, *Avicenne*, Paris, 1900, pp. 91–116.

B^ON CARRA DE VAUX.

FASTING (Introductory and non-Christian).—

1. Purposes and origin.—The purposes of fasting as a religious, magical, or social custom are various. It may be an act of penitence or of propitiation; a preparatory rite before some act of sacramental eating or an initiation; a mourning ceremony; one of a series of purificatory rites; a means of inducing dreams and visions; a method of adding force to magical rites. Its origin has been sought in some of these, and it is not improbable that, as a rite, it may have originated differently in different quarters. But behind all there was first man's frequent periods of enforced fasting through scarcity of or difficulty in obtaining food. His experience of this, as well as of its results, whether on body or on mind, would come in course of time to be used as suggesting the value of voluntary fasting.

Thus, when men wished to obtain vivid dreams, the recollection of the fact that enforced abstinence from food was connected with such dream experiences would suggest recourse to fasting in the hope of obtaining them. Again, when men began to believe that any painful state would be pleasing to, or would propitiate, higher powers, the unpleasant experience of enforced fasting would also point to it as a satisfactory form of suffering. Once more, as a rite of mourning, fasting might originate both from man's incapacity for eating food when seriously distressed—this then tending to become a conventional sign of mourning—and from a real desire to suffer pain on occasions of bereavement. The custom of avoiding certain foods, sometimes because these are regarded as harmful, on certain occasions might readily be extended into a disciplinary practice; or men might resort to extensive and prolonged fasting by way of showing their powers and gaining repute, *e.g.*, among the Algonquin Indians 'to be able to fast long is an enviable distinction' (Tylor, *PC*³ ii. 411). Finally, as suggested in another article, abstinence might be resorted to in order to lessen the inroads upon the food supply, and this might then come to be regarded as a magical way of increasing the latter, the fasting being now more strictly observed (see AUSTERITIES, § 6). In the lower stages of culture all these various origins and methods may be taken for granted, but it is mainly at higher stages that fasting becomes a strictly ascetic practice of self-mortification and discipline or of propitiation.

Fasting may be complete or partial, and in either case for a longer or shorter period. Sometimes, generally upon magical grounds, though often upon grounds of health, only certain foods are abstained from on particular occasions, but these foods occasionally cover many which are liked by or necessary to the savage at other times. Again, in many instances certain foods are forbidden or tabu to women, or to youths and children; but, while this may be invested with some supernatural sanction, it is probably due to selfish causes.

Among the Ba-Yaka, almost every form of flesh as well as fish is tabu to women, and any breach of the tabu would be visited by supernatural punishment (*JAI* xxxvi. [1906] 41, 51). Among the Wagogo of E. Africa, certain parts of meat—liver, kidneys, heart, etc.—are prohibited in childhood (Cole, *JAI* xxxii. [1902] 317). In New Guinea, young people may not eat certain foods, under pain of certain undesirable things happening to them (Seligmann, *Melanesians of Brit. N.G.*, Cambridge, 1910, pp. 139, 352, 580).

Generally speaking, this is true among most savage tribes with respect to women and to youths before initiation; and, though it does not necessarily amount to fasting, it points to abstinence from certain desirable foods, this abstinence being generally enforced by tribal customary law or by the power of fear. Thus, fasting or abstinence, more or less complete, may be regarded as a well-nigh universal practice among lower races at certain times. To this there are exceptions; thus Beardmore asserts of the natives of Mowat, New Guinea, that they never fast (*JAI* xix. [1889–90] 462), but these exceptions are very occasional. The attitude of higher races and religions to fasting will be considered later.

Probably no single cause can be alleged as the origin of the practice of fasting.

W. R. Smith explains it as 'primarily nothing more than a preparation for the sacramental eating of holy flesh' (*Rel. Sem.*², 1894, p. 434); Tylor, as a 'means of producing ecstasy and other morbid exaltation for religious ends' (*PC*³ ii. 410; cf. Wundt, *Völkerpsychol.*, Leipzig, 1904 f., ii. 3, 153 f.). Herbert Spencer suggests that the sacrifice of food to the dead causes a lack of food and so produces hunger, and that fasting arises as a necessary result of such sacrifice (*Principles of Sociology*, 1876, i. 285).

The complex nature of its origin is amply vindicated when the various occasions of fasting, among both savage and higher races, are considered. But in no case should it be thought that fasting as a strictly penitential discipline is of early occurrence. That belongs to a later stage of thought, and it is by no means accepted among all higher religions.

2. Fasting or abstinence at certain stages of life.—As a result of the idea that food has a direct influence upon existence, each kind having its own peculiar effect, it is a wide-spread practice for the mother, and sometimes also the father (who is also in a magico-sympathetic relation with his unborn offspring), to abstain from certain foods before or after the birth of a child. This aspect of fasting is a purely magical one, and was probably not of early or immediate occurrence in the history of mankind. Still, it has been so common that it is of importance in any discussion of the principle of fasting. It helps to show how, for certain definite purposes, man is willing to renounce foods which are pleasant and agreeable to him at all ordinary times, in order that he may prevent certain contingent results following upon his indulgence in them.

Among the Melanesians, this method of abstinence is of general occurrence. Thus, among the Koita of New Guinea, a woman during pregnancy must not eat bandicoot, echidna, certain fish, and iguana; and the husband must observe the same food tabus. Among the southern Massim, the mother is restricted for about a month after a birth to a mixture of boiled taro and the fruit of the *okioki*; while the father has also to abstain from many favourite foods. In other districts, similar tabus hold good, and 'every mother observes certain complicated customs of fasting after the birth of each child, especially after the birth of the first-born' (Seligmann, 84, 86, 487, 580 f.). In New Britain, 'no pregnant woman can eat anything which is *tabanot*, *i.e.* which is complete'—shark, arum, etc.—or again, cuttle-fish, which is said to walk backward, lest the child should become a coward (Brown, *Melanesians and Polynesians*, 1910, p. 33). Similarly, Codrington says of other islanders that both father and mother refrain from certain foods before and after a birth (*Melanesians*, Oxford, 1891, p. 228). Pregnant women among the Andaman Islanders must abstain from pork, turtle, honey, iguana, and parodoxurus; while the husband abstains from the two last (Man, *JAI* xii. [1883] 354). Among the Arunta, as among most Australian tribes, a numerous list of forbidden foods applies to the expectant mother, fewer to the husband, the reasons alleged being those of danger to the unborn child, or occasionally to the parents (Spencer-Gillen[b], 614). The husband and wife among the Coroados of S. America must refrain from all flesh foods before a birth (Spix-Martius, *Travels in Brazil*, 1824, ii. 247). The father, among the Xingu and other Indian tribes, must avoid fish flesh, and fruit; and among the Bororó both parents eat nothing for two days after the birth, while among the Paressí the father may taste only water and *beijú* for five days (von den Steinen, *Unter den Naturvölkern Zentral-Brasiliens*, Berlin, 1894, pp. 334 ff., 434, 503). The Carib father must fast for 40 days after a birth, and at the end of that time has to undergo other austerities (Tylor, *Early Hist. of Mankind*, 1865, p. 294). Among the Baganda, there were many food restrictions for the expectant mother, transgression of which resulted, according to popular belief, in injury to the child (Roscoe, *The Baganda*, 1911, pp. 49, 101). As a final example we may take the tribes of Assam, among whom one of the many food *gennas*, or tabus, is that a woman is denied many articles of food lest she should hurt her unborn child (Hodson, *JAI* xxxvi. [1906] 97).

Similar restrictions are generally observed by savage girls at the time of the first menstrual period. Thus, among the tribes of British Columbia, a girl must fast for four days; and also throughout the whole lengthy period of her seclusion she must abstain from fresh meat, because this would harm her, or because the animals which furnish it might take offence (Hill Tout, *JAI* xxxv. [1905] 136). Among the southern Massim, girls were secluded at this period and had to abstain from all flesh food (Seligmann, 498). For fasting before marriage, see AUSTERITIES, vol. ii. p. 230[b]. The same custom was ordained in ancient China in the *Lī Kī*, along with various purifications (*SBE* xxvii. [1885] 78). Food-tabus are also observed during sickness, as among the Wagogo of E. Africa, with whom the medicine-man forbade certain foods (Cole, *JAI* xxxii. [1902] 317), and among the Ten'a of Alaska, where, after a cure, certain forms of abstinence—from hot food and drink, or from certain kinds of food—were imposed temporarily or for life (Jetté, *JRAI* xxxvii. [1907] 172).

In many cases, tabus are placed upon certain foods for a shorter or longer time, generally for practical purposes, the tabu having really the intention of a 'close season.' This may be done by the chief, or by some society, or by general consent (see Brown, 126; Seligmann, 299). But sometimes a religious sanction is given to this tabu, as among the Andaman Islanders, who abstain from certain fruits, edible roots, etc., at certain seasons, because the god Puluga then requires them, and would send a deluge if the tabu were broken (Man, *JAI* xii. 154, 353). These prohibitions correspond to the magical food-tabus which are observed by various peoples, to prevent the qualities of the animal eaten from entering into the eater.

3. Fasting as an act of mourning.—The origin of this rite has been explained on various grounds—as propitiatory of the ghost, as a practice contrary to ordinary actions and so resembling the actions of the land of ghosts which differ from those of this earth (see *ARW* xii. [1909]), as a prevention of the ghost of the dead man from entering the body with food (Frazer, *JAI* xv. [1886] 92), and as a conventional practice arising out of the actual starvation consequent upon the destruction or sacrifice of food-stuffs at a death (H. Spencer, i. 285). Westermarck suggests that the origin may be found in the fear of swallowing food polluted with the contagion of death—the custom of not preparing or eating food in a house where there is a dead body pointing to this (*FL* xviii. [1907] 403). But, while these or other reasons have doubtless assisted the growth of the custom, it is not unlikely that actual grief, making mourners indifferent to the pangs of hunger, may have given rise to fasting as a conventional sign of mourning, other reasons being later assigned to it. The time during which the fast endures varies considerably, and in some places the fast is absolute, while elsewhere only certain foods are abstained from.

In the Andaman Islands, mourners abstain from pork, turtle, and luxuries (Man, 142). Among the tribes of New Guinea, various foods are abstained from, and in some instances a man voluntarily gives up a favourite food for a time. Among the southern Massim, the widow may not eat the kinds of food eaten by her husband in his last illness until after the funeral feasts—with the result that she is often reduced to a state of inanition (Seligmann, 617, and *passim*). In Fiji, fasting is observed during the day from ten to twenty days (Williams, *Fiji*, 1870, i. 169); and, in Aurora, many foods are abstained from, and what is eaten is usually what grows wild in the bush (Codrington, 281), just as in the Solomon Islands the mourners live on coconuts and a few bananas (*JAI* xvii. [1887–8] 96). In Samoa, mourners fasted entirely during the day (Turner, *Nineteen Years in Polynesia*, 1861, p. 228, *Samoa*, 1884, p. 145; Brown, 54). Many African tribes also fast at a death. Among the Yoruba, widows and daughters are shut up and must refuse all food for at least 24 hours (Ellis, *Yoruba-speaking Peoples*, 1894, p. 156). Tribes on the Gold Coast fast with great severity, and for a long period after a death (Waitz, *Anthrop.*, Leipzig, 1872, ii. 194). Among South African tribes, fasting is observed after the death of a relative or of a chief, in the latter case by the whole tribe for a day or longer (Macdonald, *JAI* xix. [1889–90] 280). The American Indian tribes varied in the extent of their fasting as a mourning custom, but the practice was general among them. Thus, in British Columbia, the Stlatlumh (Lillooet) spent four days after the funeral feast in fasting, lamentations, and ceremonial ablutions (Hill Tout, *JAI* xxxv. [1905] 138). In China, fasting was more rigorous in proportion to the nearness of the relationship, and the foods refrained from were mainly those offered in sacrifice to the dead. The *Lī Kī* orders the custom and shows many examples of extreme devotion of this kind. The present ritual prescribes blows with a bamboo for any participation in festive meals during the period of mourning (de Groot, *Rel. of Chinese*, New York, 1910, p. 70, *Rel. System*, Leyden, ii. [1894] 474 ff., 646 ff.). The worship of ancestors was also preceded by fasting and vigil for seven days according to the prescription of the sacred books (*Lī Kī* [*SBE* xxvii. 87, xxviii. 292]; *Shi King* [*ib.* iii. 300, 304]). In Korea, no food is eaten for one day by the family, and for three days by sons and grandsons (Ross, *Hist. of Corea*, Paisley, 1879, p. 322). While fasting was uncommon in ancient Persia, a fast of three nights after a death is ordered in *Shāyast lā-Shāyast* (xii. 5), and, according to the *Sad Dar Bundahišn*, no fresh meat is to be cooked or eaten (*SBE* v. [1880] 341). In ancient Japan, a vegetable diet of the sparest kind was partaken of by mourners, children observing this for 50 days on the death of a parent (*JAI* xii. 225). In ancient Egypt, fasting was observed by his subjects at the death of a king, no meat, wheaten bread, wine, or any luxury being allowed, nor baths, anointing, or soft beds (Wilkinson, iii. 443). Among the Greeks, the custom was also observed, and Lucian describes the efforts of relatives to induce parents to take food after their two or three days' fast (*de Luctu*, 24). Fasting for the dead was practised by the Hebrews. The men of Jabesh-Gilead fasted for Saul seven days (1 S 31[13], 1 Ch 10[13]); David and his friends fasted until evening on hearing of the death of Saul and Jonathan (2 S 1[12]), and he also fasted until sundown for Abner (2 S 3[35]). In 2 S 12[21] the astonishment of the courtiers that David should fast before, not after, his child's death shows that the custom was a general one.

It should be noticed that as a wide-spread custom a funeral feast follows or, less usually, precedes the fasting at a death (see FEASTING).

In connexion with fasting after a death, it is interesting to notice—as showing that a fear of the contagion of death or of swallowing a revengeful ghost has influenced the practice—that in many instances those who have slain a man must fast, besides undergoing other rites of a purificatory order.

In New Guinea (southern Massim), the killer or captor of a man who was to be eaten would go at once to his house and remain there for a month, living on roast taro and hot coco-nut milk; he did not join in the cannibal feast because he was afraid of the 'blood' of the dead man. Among the Mekeo tribes, the warriors are secluded and must eat but little. Among the Roro-speaking tribes, homicides during their purification must eat little and must not handle their food (Seligmann, 297, 333, 557; cf. also, for the Fijian practice, Thomson, *Fijians*, 1908, p. 98). In the Pelew Islands, young warriors after returning from a fight must eat only coco-nuts and syrup, other food being tabu (Kubary, *Die sozialen Einrichtungen der Pelauer*, Berlin, 1885, p. 131). Similar rules prevailed among many American Indian tribes. Thus, among the Pima, the slayer of an Apache had to fast for sixteen days and to live alone; and among the Natchez young warriors after taking their first scalp had to abstain during six months from all flesh food. If they broke the tabu, the soul of the slain man would kill them (*NR* i. 550; *9 RBEW*, 1892, p. 475 f.; Charlevoix, *Hist. de la Nouvelle France*, Paris, 1744, vi. 186 f.). Similarly, among the Thompson River Indians, those who handled a dead body were secluded, and fasted until it was buried (Teit, *Mem. Amer. Mus. Nat. Hist.* i. [1900] 331).

4. Fasting as a rite of preparation.—As food may convey evil influences into the body, according to savage belief, and as fasting would, in any case, render the body void of impurities, it is often resorted to as a ritual preparation and as a purificatory act.

Thus, before slaying the eagle, a sacred bird, the professional eagle-killer among the Cherokees had to undergo a long vigil of prayer and fasting (Mooney, *19 RBEW*, pt. i., 1900, p. 282). Among the Tlingits, with whom there exists a belief in reincarnation, after a death a girl fasted for eight days, 'unless she were delicate, when half as many sufficed. In the former case she fasted steadily for four days, rested two days, and then fasted for the remaining four,' as a preparation for the spirit incarnating itself through her (Swanton, *26 RBEW*, 1908, p. 429). For similar reasons the Egyptian fasted and performed ablutions before entering a temple (Wiedemann, *Rel. of Ancient Eg.*, 1897, p. 206); and, for the purpose of purity, fasting was resorted to before sacrifice in the cult of Isis (Herod. ii. 40), just as the sorcerer among the Lapps prepares himself by fasting for the offering of a sacrifice (G. von Düben, *Om Lappland och Lapparne*, Stockholm, 1873, p. 256). Hence, before eating new food, the firstfruits of the harvest, etc., fasting is commonly practised, the food possessing a kind of sacramental virtue. Before the yam feast in New Guinea the chief was kept without food for several days (Brown, 413). Among the Cherokees, at the dance at which the new corn was eaten, only those could eat who had prepared for it by fasting, prayer, and purifications (Mooney, 242 ff.); and among the Creeks, at the festival of the firstfruits, those who had not violated the law of marriage or that of the firstfruit offerings during the year were summoned to enter the holy square and observe a strict fast for two nights and a day, purging themselves also with a bitter decoction (Frazer, *GB*² ii. 330). Similarly among the Natchez, at the festival of new fire—a harvest-festival—the people fasted for three days and took an emetic, after which the festival began (Chateaubriand, *Voyage en Amérique*, Paris, 1867, p. 130 f.). Thus, before receiving food which is to all intents and purposes sacred, the body must be purified—this being also seen in the use of emetics in connexion with fasting, found among the Masai (Thomson, *Through Masai Land*², 1887, p. 430). Among the Baganda the person who drank milk fasted for several hours before eating certain foods tabued in connexion with it, and *vice versa* (Roscoe, 418). The Mexicans, before eating the sacrament of Huitzilopochtli, ate no food for a day, just as modern Jews fast from 10 a.m. before eating the Passover. Among the southern Massim, before the Walaga Feast, certain men of the community who are set apart as 'holy' must fast from boiled food, mango fruit, etc., and a number of women are also subject to the same tabus (Seligmann, 590).

In these cases there is clearly seen the aspect of fasting as 'a preparation for the sacramental eating of holy flesh,' whether we regard this as its origin, as does W. R. Smith (p. 434), or not. Another excellent example of this is found in the Greek Eleusinia. According to the myth, Demeter had been persuaded by Baubo to take food after her nine days' fast. This fast was imitated by the *mystæ* at Eleusis, and it was succeeded by the eating and drinking of sacramental food—sacred cakes of sesame and the *cyceon*. Clement of Alexandria has preserved the formula spoken by the initiated—'I have fasted, I have drunk the cyceon' (*Protrep.* ii. 18). So also in the Mithraic ritual the sacramental repast was preceded by many severe trials, which included prolonged abstinence and other austerities. And generally in the Mithraic religion 'abstinence from certain foods and absolute continence were regarded as praiseworthy' (Cumont, *Mysteries of Mithra*, Chicago, 1903, pp. 141, 160). In other instances fasting is a preparation for festival rejoicing. The third day of the Thesmophoria, called νηστεία, was observed by fasting and mourning. 'At Athens the women fast, seated on the ground' (Plut. *de Is. et Osir.* 69). This also was explained as an imitation of Demeter's mourning. In the Roman cult of Ceres, the ritual of which was very largely Greek, there was introduced in 191 B.C. a fast, the *Jejunium Cereris*, which corresponds to the Attic νηστεία. Similarly in the ritual of the *Mater Magna*, the 24th of March, *Dies Sanguinis*, was a day of fasting and mourning, recalling the grief of the Mother for Attis, and was succeeded next day by the *Hilaria*, a great day of festival rejoicing. The *taurobolium* sometimes took place on the *Dies Sanguinis*. Though these fastings are connected with mythic events, they are in origin preparatory, purificatory acts for festal rejoicing. We may compare with them the three days' fast which preceded the great Peruvian festival of Raymi, at the summer solstice (Prescott, *Hist. of Conquest of Peru*, 1890, p. 50).

5. Fasting at initiation.—This, along with the whole complex ritual of initiation to manhood and its privileges, may also be regarded as a preparation for the latter and for the reception either of foods hitherto tabued to the boy or of knowledge until now withheld from him.

Among the tribes of N.S. Wales, boys at the *bora* ceremonies are kept for two days without food, and receive only a little water (Palmer, *JAI* xiii. [1884] 295). The list of foods forbidden to the novices until initiation is complete is a very large one in many of the Australian tribes (Howitt, *ib.* 455, xiv. [1885] 316; Spencer-Gillen[b], p. 612 f.). In these instances the object of the restrictions appears to be that 'of confining the best food to the older men and at the same time inculcating upon the youths the habit of strict obedience.' Such food restrictions are also found in the Andaman Islands, where, as a test of self-denial, until the tabus are removed at initiations (or, in the case of girls, at marriage), young people must not touch certain favourite articles of food for months or years—turtle, pork, fish, honey, etc. (Man, 94, 129). In the Banks Island, at initiation to the secret societies or clubs, a period of fasting has to be undergone. In the New Hebrides the novices at initiation are kept in an enclosed place and given very little food or water, sometimes for 30 days. Great suffering is often involved (Codrington, 80, 87, 93, 107). Among the western tribes of Torres Straits, lads had to abstain from all animal food at the period of initiation (Haddon, *JAI* xix. 309). In New Guinea similar customs are found. Among the Roro-speaking tribes many foods are forbidden to boys at puberty while they are making their ceremonial drums in the forest. Fasting for a day at the end of the seclusion period was usual among some of these tribes. Among the southern Massim, many foods are forbidden to the novices, the abstinence being of a ceremonial character (Seligmann, 258, 261, 496 f.).

Corresponding to these initiatory forms of abstinence are the prolonged fastings and other austerities which the American Indian youth undergoes in seclusion at puberty, in order that by means of a vision he may see the guardian spirit which will be his for the remainder of his life. Here also fasting is a preparatory act, and is generally combined with the purificatory use of strong emetics, and of ablutions, although there is a physiological connexion between the fasting and the visions which are induced in the brain of the youth weakened by hunger and worked up to a pitch of excitement. This connexion has probably been discovered for himself by the savage. This form of fasting is found among all the American Indian tribes, whether of higher or of lower culture, and, in many of the instances recorded, the discipline, whether self-imposed or not, is of a most rigorous kind. A few examples will show this.

Boys among the Musquakie Indians undergo a nine years' training, which becomes steadily more severe. 'The fasts that at first were deprivation from one meal lengthen, till they stretch over days and nights of abstinence from both food and water.' Finally comes the nine days' fast, during which the lad wanders in the woods, and has feverish dreams, in one of which he learns what his 'medicine' is to be (Owen, *Folk-lore of the Musquakie Indians*, 1904, p. 67 f.). Charlevoix (vi. 67 f.) describes the privations of the young tribesmen among the Algonquins and others: 'They begin by blackening the boy's face, then they cause him to fast for eight days without giving him anything to eat.' This induces dreams which are carefully inquired into. 'Nevertheless the fast often ends before the proper time, as few lads can keep it up so long.' Jones, the Ojibwa Indian, describes his own experience of fasting: 'I well remember, in my early days when I used to blacken my face and fast, in order to obtain the favour of some familiar god, that one day, being thirsty, I took a sip of water. The moment I had done so I remembered I was fasting. The thoughtless act filled me with sorrow, and I wept the greater part of the night.' He never was favoured with a vision, and hence never obtained a *manitou* (*Hist. of the Ojibway Indians*, 1861, p. 87 ff.). The fasting, sometimes for a fortnight, would ordinarily kill a man, but the natives believe that he is kept alive by the *tamanous* or *manitou* (Eells, *18 RSI*, pt. i. 1889, p. 674). For many other instances, see the works of Lafitau, Bancroft, Schoolcraft, etc., and those cited by Frazer, *Totemism and Exogamy*, 1910, iii. 370 ff.; also art. COMMUNION WITH DEITY (American), § 3.

In certain mystery cults of the ancient world, fasting was one of the conditions of initiation. Apuleius describes the thrice-repeated ten days' abstinence from luxurious food, the avoidance of the flesh of animals and of wine—'reverential abstinence'—which the candidates had to observe before being fully initiated into the mysteries of Isis (*Metam.* xi. 23, 28, 30). See also § 4 above.

Similar fastings, with the use of strong emetics, narcotics, flagellations, etc., are undergone in many regions by those who wish to become medicine-men. Here too the act is preparatory to the reception of higher knowledge, but it also tends to induce dreams, which are regarded as a necessary part of the medicine-man's means of obtaining revelations.

The Eskimo youth who wishes to become an *angekok* must retire and fast for some time until he obtains visions, in which the spirits are supposed to visit him (Cranz, *Hist. of Greenland*, 1820, i. 210). Among the Lapps, those who wished to be wizards had to fast strictly (Klemm, *Culturgesch.*, Leipzig, 1843–52, iii. 85). In Brazil, the youth who desires to be a *pajé* dwells alone and fasts over a period of two years, after which he is admitted as a *pajé* (Martius, *Von dem Rechtszustande unter d. ur. Bras.*, Munich, 1832, p. 30). Among the Abipones, the postulant for the position of *keebit* had to sit on a tree overhanging a lake for some days, fasting, until he began to see into futurity (Dobrizhoffer, *Abipones*, 1822, ii. 68). Similar methods obtained among the N. American tribes for becoming a medicine-man. These included very severe and prolonged fastings, followed by vivid dreams. So also, among the Zulus, diviners become qualified for their work and for intercourse with spirits by a severe discipline which extends over a protracted period and includes a very rigorous fasting. Thus the youth becomes 'a house of dreams' (Callaway, *Rel. System of the Amazulu*, 1884, p. 387).

This connexion between fasting and other disciplinary methods, and dreams, visions, or revelations, is well established everywhere. Hence also, in order to induce such dreams or to receive communications from supernatural or higher powers, fasting has been very commonly resorted to both among savages and among more advanced peoples, as well as in higher forms of religion. Among the American Indians, with whom fasting as a preparation for the acquiring of a guardian spirit and for becoming a medicine-man occupied so important a place, it is very commonly resorted to as an ordinary means of acquiring hidden knowledge or messages from the spirits in dreams. The hunter fasts until he dreams whether his hunt will be successful or not; the husband fasts until he dreams whether his hopes of becoming a parent will or will not be gratified. The greater the power of fasting, and the more vivid and numerous the consequent dreams, the more was the seer held in reverence and the greater power did he acquire. Even the Great Spirit might appear as a handsome youth to him who had undergone almost superhuman fasts—a vision believed to be of peculiar efficacy. And as a preparation for the state of ecstasy in which the spirits speak through the medicine-man, he fasts much and often and undergoes other austerities (see Schoolcraft, *Indian Tribes*, Philadelphia, 1852, *passim*; *Relation des Jésuites*, 1672, p. 38; Matthews, *Ethnog. and Philol. of Hidatsa Ind.*, Washington, 1877, p. 51; Warren, *Hist. of the Ojibway Nation*, St. Paul, Minn. 1885, p. 64; Dunn, *Hist. of the Oregon Territory*, 1844, p. 253 ff.).

The Zulu diviners also make use of fastings lasting over several days, in order to have visions. For, as their proverb runs, 'The continually stuffed body cannot see secret things,' which agrees with Galen's saying that dreams produced by fasting are clearer than others (Callaway, 387; Grout, *Zulu-land*, 1864, p. 158). The Santal priest also fasts for several days; the result is a wild ecstatic state in which he utters oracles by the power of the god possessing him (H. Spencer, i. 257). The Chinese custom of fasting before a sacrifice to the ancestral spirits may have had the intention of causing communion with them through visions, as the person had at the same time to fill his mind with thoughts of them (*SBE* iii. 304, xxviii. 292). In one of the texts of Taoism a mechanic is described as fasting in order to become of concentrated mind, and after several days he has forgotten all about himself; in other words, he is now fit for Divine revelations (*SBE* xl. [1891] 209). Such fastings were not unknown in the mystic aspects of Greek religion. At the grotto of Acharaca, the vapours of which had a medical virtue, and which was therefore the seat of an oracle, the sick remained several days without food, and the fast was used to aid visions in this place of inspiration (Strabo, xiv. p. 650). Those who consulted the oracle of Amphiaraus abstained from wine for three days and from food on the day of sleeping in the temple (Philostr. *Vita Apol. Tyan.* i. 37). The Pythia, in addition to chewing laurel, drinking the sacred water, and inhaling the vapours of the chasm, fasted as a preparation for her inspiration.

This purpose of fasting was also recognized by the Hebrews, to judge by certain references to it in connexion with revelations, or visions, or communications from God. For these there was preparation by fasting as well as by other methods. Thus, while Moses was with Jahweh on the Mount and received the Law, he fasted forty days and forty nights (Ex 34^{28}, cf. Dt 9^{9}). Daniel, also, before his communion with God and the visions which he experiences, fasts, in one case eating 'no pleasant bread,' flesh, or wine for three months (Dn 9^{3} $10^{2.3}$). It is also noticeable that Elijah's revelation on Mt. Horeb comes after he has gone in the strength of the food provided by the angel forty days and forty nights (1 K $19^{8ff.}$). Later Jewish writers define a necromancer as one who fasts and lodges among tombs in order that the evil spirit may come upon him (H. Spencer, i. 261). This purpose of fasting also passed over to Christian custom (see FASTING [Christian], and cf. Tertullian's opinion that fasting gives rise to dreams [*de Anima*, 38], and Chrysostom's saying that it makes the soul brighter and provides it with wings to mount and soar [*in cap. i. Gen.*, hom. 10]).

6. Fasting in magical ritual.—Here also the power of fasting as a preparation for sacred or ritual actions may be seen. The man who fasts makes his magical act more likely to succeed by his being in a purer state of body for it.

In Banks Island, fasting adds power to the charms used for causing the death of an enemy, and so long would a man fast that, when the day arrived on which he was to use the charm, he was too weak to walk (Codrington, 205 f.). Among the Roro-speaking tribes of New Guinea, a sorcerer who wishes to obtain a magical snake-stone fasts for two weeks, eating merely a few roasted bananas. Then he dreams of the locality of the snake and sets off in pursuit. Before a hunt, the hunt is ritually imitated, and this is itself preceded by abstinence from many customary foods (Seligmann, 282, 292). Among the Motumotu tribe, those who remain at home must abstain from eating certain foods, else the expedition might fail (Chalmers, *JAI* xxvii. [1898] 333). Maori sorcerers, using magic with a victim's hair to cause his death, remained fasting for three days. During war all those at home had to fast strictly while the warriors were in the field, the magical effects acting through the sympathetic connexion of the two. Before setting out on an expedition no food was cooked on the previous day until the priest had gone through his divinatory rites (*Old New Zealand*, by a Pakeha Maori, 1884, p. 114; Tregear, *JAI* xix. 108). In Java, the rain-doctor observes a fast as part of the ritual for the prevention of rain (Batten, *Glimpses of the E. Archip.*, Singapore, 1894, p. 68 f.). Among the Santals, on the other hand, those who visit a sacred hill to beseech the god for rain must go there fasting (Dalton, *TES*, new series, vi. [1868] 35). Among the Natchez, also, wizards fasted and danced, with pipes of water in their mouths, when rain was wanted (*Lettres édifiantes et curieuses*, Paris, 1780–87, vii. 29 f.). Similarly the body of rain-priests among the Zuñis have the special duty of fasting and praying for rain (Stevenson, *23 RBEW*

1904, *passim*). The Haida Indian fasts in order to obtain a fair wind; indeed, of these and other tribes it is true that, 'whether a man were a shaman or not, he could increase his physical power, or obtain property, success in hunting, fishing, war, etc., by rigid abstinence from food and drink, by remaining away from his wife, bathing in the sea, taking sweat-baths, etc. He would drink warmed salt water often, and take fresh water afterwards, when all the contents of his stomach were ejected, leaving him so much the "cleaner"' (Swanton, *Contrib. to the Ethnol. of the Haidas*, 1905, p. 40). In Alaska the wife must remain at home fasting, while her husband is out fishing, in order that he may have a good catch (Holmberg, *Acta Soc. Scientiarum Fennicæ*, iv. [1856] 392). Among the ancient Celts, magical herbs were gathered with a due ritual and after fasting (Pliny, *HN* xxiv. 11). For the Celtic custom of 'fasting against' a person, see *ERE* ii. 231[a].

7. Fasting as an act of penitence.—While some of the methods of fasting discussed above may have had a penitential aspect, especially those connected with initiation to mysteries, they were not penitential in origin. Rather does fasting as an act of penitence form a development from them. The person who fasts suffers inconvenience or pain, and he may well have come to think that by so suffering he would humiliate himself before higher powers whom he believed to be angry with him, and would thus gain their pity. At the same time, his suffering was a self-inflicted punishment for sin, which might have the effect of warding off other or further punishments inflicted *ab extra*. As a penitential act, fasting is invariably combined with prayer. The relation between fasting as a penitential act and fasting as a more or less magical method of forcing the hand of the gods is perhaps to be seen at lower levels of culture.

The Tsimshians think they can force the deity to perform their wishes by strict fasting. Hence they lie in bed for seven days without food, observing also continence (Boas, in Frazer, *Totemism*, iii. 317). When the Indians of Colombia wished to obtain the help of their divinities, they fasted and observed continence for several days (Ternaux-Compans, *Essai sur l'anc. Cundinamarça*, Paris, 1842, p. 44 f.). Here there is no penitence, but it is easy to see how such fastings might become penitential if it were the forgiveness of the deity which was sought. Among the ancient Mexicans, fasting as a penitential act existed, and was intended to assist in purifying the conscience. These fasts varied much in extent,—from one day to several years,—and they were observed either by individuals or by the whole nation on particular occasions, and were usually imposed by the priests after due confession of sins or for specific offences. The high priest fasted and prayed, practising also severe austerities in seclusion, for months at a time, on occasions of public calamity (Clavigero, *Hist. of Mexico*, 1780, i. 397 ff.; Torquemada, *Monarchia Indiana*, Madrid, 1723, ii. 212 f.).

In Egypt, fasting as a method of expiation for sin, either occasional or at fixed times, was recognized. All luxuries had to be abstained from, as well as every form of gratification of the passions. It has been thought that fasting is alluded to in the 'negative confession' (Wilkinson, iii. 396). As many of the Babylonian penitential psalms show, fasting had become a regular ritual act of penance, accompanying these mournful expressions of wrongdoing. The penitent describes how he has neither eaten food nor drunk clear water. But there were also days of fasting appointed in periods of distress and calamity when the people gave themselves up to strenuous fasting and other acts of penitence (Zimmern, *Bab. Busspsalmen*, Leipzig, 1885, p. 34; Maspero, *Dawn of Civ.*, London, 1894, p. 682; Jastrow, *Rel. of Bab.*, Boston, 1898, pp. 320, 688). The latter practice is well exemplified by the Assyrian fasting described in the Book of Jonah, when the whole people (as well as the animals) were covered with sackcloth, wept and fasted, and prayed to God for forgiveness ($3^{5ff.}$).

Among the Hebrews, fasting as a form of penitence was well known from comparatively early times. Originating as a means of exciting the Divine compassion, it came to have a more ethical colouring, and was the outward expression of a real inward penitence. At the same time there was a contrary tendency for the practice to be resorted to in a conventional manner whenever calamity threatened, and as a mere means of keeping it off—a view against which the prophets vainly protested. Individuals fasted on account of their sins or for some special object (1 K 21^{27}, Ezr 10^{6}). On various occasions a general fast was proclaimed as a recognition of sin—the occasion of any public calamity being a proof that the people had sinned (1 S 14^{24}, 2 Ch 20^{3}, 1 K $21^{9f.}$, Jer 36^{9}, Jl $1^{13f.}$). Or it may have been resorted to spontaneously (Jg 20^{26}, Neh 9^{1}). Fasting, if the accompaniment of a due penitential state of heart and the token of humility, was certainly approved by the prophets and regarded as agreeable to God, the reverse being abhorrent to Him and them (Jl 2^{12}, Is 58^{3-5}, Zec 7^{5}; cf. Jer 14^{12}). Days of public fasting might take place on the occasion of any calamity, *e.g.* the lack of autumn rains; but fixed times of fasting are also found. Of these the most significant is that of the Day of Atonement (Lv $16^{29f.}$), whether its origin is to be sought before or after the Exile. On the 10th day of the 7th month the people were to 'afflict their souls.' This may be the fast referred to in Neh 9^{1} as taking place on the 24th day of the month. Four yearly fasts, in the 4th, 5th, 7th, and 10th months, are mentioned in Zec 8^{19} (cf. 7^{5}). These had reference to events in the Chaldæan conquest of Jerusalem. Another fast day of later origin was that of the 13th of Adar, supposed to commemorate the fast of Esther and her maidens and the fast of the people commanded by her (Est 4^{16}). It immediately preceded the Feast of Purim, and may have been of Bab. origin (see Frazer, *GB*² iii. 176; Zimmern, *ZATW* xi. [1891] 157 ff.). Private fasting was also much multiplied during and after the Exile, strict Jews fasting on the 2nd and 5th days of each week in the year (cf. Lk 18^{12}; *Didache*, 8; *Ta'anîth*, 12*a*). These were also the days adopted for special public fastings. Such fasting was done as openly as possible,—a sign of its non-spiritual nature,—and this was rebuked by our Lord (Mt $6^{16ff.}$). At such times it varied in intensity, according as food was taken at the end of 12 or of 24 hours, and according to the omission of various usual actions. Private persons no doubt added to these occasions of fasting, taking no wine or flesh or pleasant food for many days or even over a period of years, as a sign of mourning for sin or as a help to living chastely. This is reflected in the Apocryphal and other writings (Jth $8^{4f.}$; *Test. xii. Patr.* [Reub. 1^{10}, Sim. 3^{4}, Jud. 15^{4}, Issach. 7^{3}, Jos. 3^{4} 9^{2}]). Indeed, so characteristic did fasting as a Jewish custom become that Augustus boasted that he had fasted more earnestly than a Jew (Tac. *Hist.* v. 4).

In Muhammadanism, the principle of penitential fasting is recognized and highly commended by Muhammad himself. The Qur'ān recommends fasting as a penance, for three days on a pilgrimage, and for seven on returning (ii. 193). The believer who kills another believer and cannot find the blood-money must fast for two months as a penance (iv. 94), and the oath-breaker who cannot as a penance feed ten poor men must fast for three days (v. 91). Fasting is often referred to as a good work, and it is one of the recognized duties of the Muslim. Hence there are many stated times of fasting, some of which are obligatory, and others may be regarded as works of supererogation undertaken by the devout. Chief amongst the former class is the fast of the 30 days of Ramaḍān, rigorous and strictly observed, in which no water is allowed between dawn and sunset, and from which only the sick and infirm, travellers, idiots, and young children are exempt (ii. 180 ff.). Devout Muslims seclude themselves in the mosques, and those who observe this fast receive pardon of all past venial sins (*Mishkāt*, vii. 7. pt. 1). It is followed by a great festival of rejoicing, to which it may be regarded as in some sense preparatory. The 13th, 14th, and 15th days of each month are also generally observed as fasting days, also the day *Ashūrā*, the 10th of the month Muḥarram, because Muhammad said he hoped it would cover the sins of the coming year. Strict Muslims fast also on the Monday and Thursday of each week. While Muhammadanism is not an ascetic religion, the value of fasting as a discipline or a good work is clearly recognized, and it is said that 'the very smell of the mouth of a keeper of a fast is more agreeable to God than the smell of musk' (Hughes, *DI*², 125).

While the idea of the Ramaḍān fast may have been derived from the Christian fast of Lent, it is perhaps more closely connected with the Harranian 30 days' fast, in which all food and drink were avoided between dawn and sunset. This fast was in honour of the moon, but the Harranians also observed a 7 days' fast for the sun, and a 9 days' fast in honour of 'the Lord of good luck,' in the former abstaining from fat and wine (Chwolsohn, *Die Ssabier*, St. Petersburg, 1856, ii. 71 f., 226; Jacob, *VI. Jahresber. der geogr. Gesell. zu Greifswald*, i. [1893–6] 5 ff.).

8. Fasting as an ascetic practice.—Most of the examples of fasting already cited are non-ascetic, that is to say, for whatever purpose they are undergone, they occur in religions in which a dualism between body and soul—the former evil, the latter pure—is not recognized, although, in some of the religions referred to, this dualistic view came to prevail amongst individuals or sects. But, wherever asceticism, based on this view, is found, fasting is a more or less recognized ascetic practice, since by observing it the evil body is not pampered by excess in food or drink. Fasting as a penitential practice would easily pass over into an ascetic practice. It is true that, even where the strictly dualistic view does not prevail, fasting may be practised in order to combat the grosser desires of the body, or by way of preparing it for some sacred occasion. This view has already been found in considering fasting as a preparatory act, and in certain instances it very closely approaches strictly ascetic fasting. This is also true of cases where certain foods are avoided as too luxurious—a conception perhaps originally based upon earlier food-tabus.

Thus Plutarch says that the Egyptian priests (of Isis) committed no excess in eating or drinking, and that, while on the 1st day of the 9th month the people feasted on fish, the priests abstained from it, one reason being that it was 'an unnecessary and over-luxurious article of diet.' For a similar reason they abstained from garlic (*de Is. et Osir.* 5 ff.). Abstinence from luxurious food, flesh, and wine was necessary for him who was initiated into the mysteries of Isis (Apuleius, *Metam.* xi.). The Orphic prohibition of animal food was based on the fact that it was used in sacrifice to the dead, though it became an ascetic practice (on this aspect of abstinence generally, see Porphyry, *de Abst. ab Esu Animalium*).

In Greece, where the native religion was opposed to the idea of the acceptableness to the gods of a maceration of the body, this dualistic view leading to a true asceticism is found in Orphism, and here, accordingly, fasting had its place (Diels, 'Ein orphischer Demeterhymnus,' in *Festschr. für Th. Gomperz*, Vienna, 1902, p. 6 f.). Pythagoras also recommended frugality in diet, and commended fasting. Those who went to the temples to pray for some days should not take food all that time—perhaps an example of preparation for Divine revelations rather than of ascetic fasting (Porph. *Vita Pyth.* 34; Iambl. *Vita Pyth.* 27; Diog. Laert. viii. 19). The teaching as to abstinence from all excessive bodily desires, gluttony, drunkenness, etc., is also continued by Plato (*Phædo*, 69–71).

Reference has already been made to the abstemiousness of the Egyptian priests. In the *Maxims of Any* (XIXth dynasty) the same principle is recognized—'Be not greedy to fill thy stomach, for one knows no reason why he should do so' (Petrie, *Rel. and Conscience in Anc. Eg.*, 1898, p. 113). This, however, is not ascetic fasting, but self-control, and generally abundance of good things was an other-world ideal, abnegation in this life not being thought of. Ascetic groups, however, arose in Egypt towards the 4th cent. B.C., perhaps under Indian influences, and at a still later date the Therapeutæ (*q.v.*) are found in large numbers in Egypt. They ate nothing before sunset, and many of them broke their fast once only in three days, or even in six days (Petrie, *Personal Rel. in Egypt*, 1909, pp. 61 f., 70).

Among the later Jews, while fasting was regarded as a meritorious rather than as an ascetic practice, individuals occasionally led strictly ascetic lives, eating as little food as possible. We reach a consistent ascetic view only among the Alexandrian Jews, who held that bodily desires hindered spirituality, and that only through a strict asceticism could the soul be released from their power. Yet Philo did not teach that ascetic practices such as fasting had any value in themselves, though he would have his disciples avoid luxurious excesses.

In Muhammadanism, asceticism was contrary to the Prophet's outlook, but it soon took hold in Islām, and abstinence from various kinds of food, as well as the strict observance of the fasts, was regarded as bringing a man nearer to God. This view was greatly developed in Ṣūfiism (see *ERE* ii. 101 f., 104).

While Buddhism is an ascetic religion and regards the body as evil, Buddha was opposed to excessive ascetic practices of any kind, mainly because excess was evil. Hence, though food was to be taken in moderation as a method of guarding the gateways of the senses, he never advised excessive fasting. One of the ten abstinences is that of eating at forbidden times. Monks must eat but one meal, at mid-day, and nothing after it; they must fast on the days of the new and full moon (a derivative from Brāhmanism), giving themselves also to public confession and hearing of the law. A fast with confession of sins four times a month is now more usual—the *Uposatha* days, which the laity are invited to observe. Köppen says that the Lamaists, on the 14th and 15th, the 29th and 30th days of the month, take nothing but farinaceous food and tea, but the devout refrain from all food until sunset (*Lamaische Hier.*, quoted in Waddell, *Budd. of Tibet*, 1895, p. 501). Another Tibetan ceremony, 'The Continued Fast' (*Nungnas*), lasts for 4 days, of which the first two are preparatory, with confession, prayer, and devout reading, continued till late at night. On the third day there is a strict fast, no one being allowed even to swallow his saliva. Prayer and confession of sins are made in complete silence, and the fast continues till sunrise on the fourth day (Schlagintweit, *Buddhism in Tibet*, 1881, p. 240). The anniversary of Buddha's death on the 15th day of the 4th month is preceded by a five days' abstinence in which even the laity abstain from flesh. This is an example of a preparatory fast, and another example is found in the fast of 24 hours by the priest who conducts the so-called 'Eucharist' of Lamaism (Waddell, 445, 507; cf. p. 501, and see also Monier-Williams, *Buddhism*, 1889, pp. 79, 82, 84, 335; Copleston, *Buddhism*², 1908, p. 127). The Mahāyāna Buddhists fast as a means of being re-born into higher grades (*SBE* xlix. pt. 2 [1894] 192 f.).

9. Fasting discredited as a religious rite.—Examples of this, or rather of a mechanical and formal method of fasting, are familiar from the prophetic books (Is 58⁴, Jer 14¹², Zec 7⁵ etc.). It has also been seen that Buddha taught moderation rather than excessive fasting. In the *Dhammapada* the fasts of the Brāhmans are discredited as against the moderate Buddhist discipline (*SBE* x. [1881] 21, note), and in another passage fasting and other ascetic practices are said to have no effect in purifying a mortal who has not overcome desire. Of themselves they cannot purify the passions (*SBE* x. 38). The ancient Parsi religion, although fasting occurred sporadically (cf. § 3), despised it. In the *Vendīdād* (iv. 48, *SBE* iv. [1880] 47) it is said that 'he who fills himself with meat is filled with the good spirit more than he who does not do so.' And the *Sad Dar* (83, *SBE* xxiv. [1885] 348) says:

'It is requisite to abstain from the keeping of fasts. For, in our religion, it is not proper that they should not eat every day or anything, because it would be a sin not to do so. With us the keeping of fast is this, that we keep fast from committing sin with our eyes and tongue and ears and hands and feet.' 'That which, in other religions, is fasting owing to not eating is, in our religion, fasting owing to not committing sin.'

While this expresses a valuable truth of spiritual religion, it is perhaps aimed at the excessive fasts of the Manichæans. So, too, in one of the writings of the Taoist Kwang-tze, the question is asked:

'Can the fact that we have drunk no spirituous liquor and eaten none of the proscribed foods, be regarded as a fast?' and the reply runs: 'It is the fasting appropriate to sacrificing, but it is not the fasting of the mind,' explained as a purely spiritual process (*SBE* xxxix. [1891] 208 f.).

10. It should be observed that fasting is usually accompanied by other acts of abstinence, *e.g.* continence, by numerous austerities, and generally, in the higher religions, by prayer. Cf. the common Jewish phrase 'prayer and fasting.'

LITERATURE.—This is referred to throughout the article. See also E. B. Tylor, *PC*³, London, 1891, ii. 410 f.; E. Westermarck, 'The Principles of Fasting,' *FL* xviii. [1907] 391 ff.

J. A. MACCULLOCH.

FASTING (Christian).—I. *THE FIRST TWO CENTURIES.*—**1. New Testament.**—Two sayings of our Lord moulded the ideas of early Christianity about fasting: (*a*) that, though His disciples did not fast as the Baptist's disciples did ('often,' Lk 5³³), because the Bridegroom was with them, yet the days would come when the Bridegroom should be taken away, and then they should fast 'in that day' (Mk 2¹⁹ᶠ· RV)—a saying which was interpreted literally and led to a particular rule as to the duration of the Paschal fast; and (*b*) that fasting must be unostentatious (Mt 6¹⁶ᶠᶠ·). Although He Himself fasted for 40 days before beginning His ministry, and probably, as a devout Jew, kept the one fast-day that was obligatory at the time,—the Day of Atonement,—He left no regulations for fasting; He gave the principles, and left His Church to make rules for carrying them out. This explains why the Church was so slow in developing a system of fasts and festivals. No rules on the subject could claim to come directly from the Master Himself. It is hardly probable that the first disciples imitated the stricter Jews in voluntarily adding to the Day of Atonement the two weekly fasts (cf. Lk 18¹²) of Monday and Thursday (days which were chosen because Moses was believed to have gone up to the Mount on the latter and to have come down on the former), for there is no trace of these as Christian fasts in NT. But many Jews increased these fasts voluntarily, as did Anna (Lk 2³⁷), and even the heathen Cornelius, according to some MSS (Ac 10³⁰); and so we read of St. Paul fasting (2 Co 6⁵ 11²⁷: 'fastings often' the mark of the Christian minister), and of the first Christians fasting before ordinations or solemn appointments (Ac 14²³ 13²ᶠ·). The Jewish Christians, doubtless, continued to keep the Day of Atonement, and St. Luke mentions it as an epoch (Ac 27⁹ 'the Fast'), but the Gentiles were almost certainly not pressed to observe it.

2. Second century.—We may now proceed to trace the growth of fasting in the Christian Church, and, in doing so, we must bear in mind the caution that customs varied much, and therefore we must be careful to pay attention to the particular age and country of which our authorities speak, without assuming that, because we find a custom mentioned in one of the older Fathers, it must have been characteristic of the whole Church from the beginning. A broad generalization of Hooker may, however, in the main be accepted. He says that fasts were 'set as ushers of festival days,' and have as their object 'to temper the mind, lest contrary affections coming in place should make it too profuse and dissolute' (*Eccles. Pol.* v. 72, last par.); and the former dictum is true of all but the weekly fasts (below (*c*)). When we review the century and a half that followed the death of St. Paul, we are at once struck by the want of regulations as to fasting; as far as we can gather from the scanty literature before the age of Irenæus, Clement of Alexandria, and Tertullian (end of 2nd cent.), and from the writings of those Fathers, much was left to individual piety. The following facts, however, emerge from the study of this period.

(*a*) There was a general sense of the duty of fasting, and frequent warnings against making it a merely external act. Barnabas (§ 3; *c.* A.D. 100) and Justin Martyr (*Dial.* 15; *c.* A.D. 150) quote Is 58 in this sense; the same warning is given by Clement of Alexandria (*Pæd.* iii. 12, *Strom.* vi. 12). Clement also wrote a separate treatise on fasting (Jerome, *de Vir. Illustr.* 38). Earlier in the century, Polycarp (§ 7; *c.* A.D. 110) urges fasting and prayer as a means of meeting temptation. Hermas (*Sim.* v. 1; written before A.D. 140 [?]) says that he was fasting and keeping a 'station' (a weekly fast) when he saw the Shepherd, who spoke to him of fasting, warning him against the mere external observance: to 'do no evil in your life and to serve the Lord with a pure heart' is the true fast; fasting is very good if the commandments of the Lord be observed.

(*b*) *Paschal fast.*—We hear of this first from Irenæus. He mentions it in his letter to Pope Victor on the Paschal controversy (written *c.* A.D. 195, and quoted by Eusebius, *HE* v. 24), and says that there was great variety in its observance, some fasting for one day, others for two or for several days, others for 'forty hours of night and day,' and that this variety was of long standing; it existed 'long before, in the time of our ancestors.' This shows that the Paschal fast was known early in the 2nd century. The fast of one day and that of forty hours would doubtless be absolute; the latter period would correspond to the time during which our Lord lay in the grave. Tertullian (*de Orat.* 18) says that the 'day of Pascha' (by which he means Good Friday, though the term *Pascha* has other meanings)[1] was a general and, as it were, public fast, on which the kiss of peace was not given. See also below (*e*).

(*c*) *Weekly fasts.*—It was a common custom in the 2nd cent., at least in some countries, to fast on Wednesdays and Fridays; see FESTIVALS AND FASTS [Christian], I (*b*).

(*d*) *Pre-baptismal fast.*—This is mentioned in the *Didache* (§ 7 f.); it was for a day or two days, and was observed by the candidate, the baptizer, and others. It is also mentioned in Justin (*Apol.* i. 61) and in Tertullian (*de Bapt.* 20, and perhaps *de Jejun.* 8). As baptism was ordinarily administered at Pascha (Tertull. *de Bapt.* 19, and later writers *passim*), though it might be deferred to 'Pente-

[1] In Christian literature, *Pascha* means Easter Day, or Good Friday, or Maundy Thursday, or Holy Week, or even the forty days before Easter; and similarly *Pentecost* means either the festival itself or the fifty days before it.

cost,' *i.e.* the 50 days after Easter (*ib.*: 'latissimum spatium'), there was a very close connexion between this fast and that before Pascha; and the suspicion may arise that the former is the real rationale of the latter.

(*e*) The feeling of the non-Montanist Christians in the 2nd cent. with regard to fasting is clearly exhibited by Tertullian's abusive treatise, *de Jejuniis*, written *c.* A.D. 210, after he had become a disciple of Montanus; and it is curious that the great development in fasting which took place later was largely due to the rivalry of this sect. The Montanists kept two weeks of 'xerophagy,' *i.e.* partial fasts, in the year; but of these weeks the Saturdays and Sundays were excepted (*de Jejun.* 15). It is not said at what time of the year they were kept. Both the name and the thing were opposed by the 'Psychics' (the ordinary Christians) as a novelty (§ 2). Xerophagies consisted in not eating flesh or anything juicy, not even succulent fruit, or anything with the flavour of wine, and in abstaining from the bath (§ 1). The 'Psychics' objected to the definite *enjoining* of 'stations,' as these should be voluntary (§ 10); yet (Tertullian says) they were inconsistent, as they sometimes lived on bread and water (§ 13) and had definite fast-days, especially 'when the Bridegroom was taken away' [the Paschal fast, see above, I. 1], and Wednesday and Friday up to the ninth hour, or 3 p.m. (§§ 2, 10); they often fasted even on Saturday, which Tertullian says should never be observed as a fast-day except at Pascha (§ 14); their bishops ordained fasts for their own dioceses, and there were fasts before Councils were held (§ 13). The Montanists kept on the bi-weekly fasts to a later hour (§ 10). With this we may compare Hippolytus' accusation against the Montanists, of 'novelties of fasts, and feasts, and meals of parched food and repasts of radishes' (*Hær.* viii. 12 [*c.* A.D. 220]; cf. x. 21, 'novel and strange [read παραδόξους] fasts'). Thus the difference between the Montanists and the Orthodox seems to have been that the latter were less strict in the custom of fasting, and left more to voluntary observance, while the former made a settled practice of compulsory xerophagies and half-fasts in addition to the complete fast of the *Paraskeue* (Good Friday), or of Paraskeue and the following Sabbath. Tertullian's treatise shows how bitter was the feeling excited by a mere difference of observance.

II. *PERIOD OF DEVELOPMENT* (A.D. 200-500).—**1. Development after Tertullian.**—From the 3rd cent. onwards manuals of instruction and worship, now conveniently called 'Church Orders,' became common, basing their injunctions in most cases on supposed Apostolic authority. What before was a matter of voluntary or customary observance now came under rule. Fasting accordingly was more exactly regulated, and the Orthodox became stricter than the Montanists, who retained the fasting customs mentioned by Tertullian till the 5th cent. (Sozomen, *HE* vii. 19). The growth of strictness in fasting is especially observable in the 4th cent., the age of Councils and organization made possible by the cessation of persecution.

2. The Paschal fast was of slow development, and even well on in the 4th cent. we find only the two days before Easter named as fasts in some authorities (Egyp. Ch. Order, 55; Ethiopic Ch. Ord. 41; Verona Fragments, ed. Hauler, Leipzig, 1900, p. 116; *Test. of our Lord*, ii. 18, 20 [all probably to be dated A.D. 300-350]); the fast ends at midnight (*Test.* ii. 12). No other Paschal fast is mentioned in these works, and sick people who cannot fast on both days are allowed to fast on the *Saturday* only (so also *Apost. Const.* v. 18 [*c.* A.D. 375], for which see below). In the above-named Church Orders, or at least in their sources, the Crucifixion and Resurrection were commemorated on the same day. Epiphanius says that the Quartodecimans fasted only one day (*Hær.* l. 1-3; *Exp. Fid.* 22). But a greater development is found in the *Older Didascalia* (v. 14. 18 [probably 3rd cent.]); a partial fast with bread, salt, and water is enjoined from Monday to Thursday of Holy Week, and an absolute fast on Friday and Saturday. Dionysius of Alexandria (*Ep. ad Basilidem*, can. 1 [early 3rd cent.]) mentions a Holy Week fast, during the six days of which some even ate nothing at all; but he testifies to a diversity of usage, some fasting two, some three, some four days, others not even one day. There was also a diversity (he says) as to the time of ending the fast before Pascha [*v.l.* 'Pentecost'; but this seems to be an error]; in Rome they ended it at cockcrow, elsewhere at nightfall. He mentions the Friday and Sabbath (Saturday) as rigorous fasts.

A forty-days' fast is not found till the 4th cent., and made its way only gradually; a supposed reference in Origen (hom. *in Lev.* x. 2) is due to Rufinus' 'translation.' In some countries the 'forty days' were observed as a solemn season for prayer, without being a fast, as Advent was observed in later times in the West; at Nicæa they are merely mentioned as a well-known space of time, before which Synods were held (can. 5); and in the *Test. of our Lord* (*c.* A.D. 350) the people are told to keep vigil and to pray in the church then, but there is no word of fasting (ii. 8). The name of the season was τεσσαρακοστή, 'Quadragesima'; at first this means the 'fortieth day' before Easter, on which the *competentes*, or selected candidates for baptism, were enrolled (Cyr. Jerus. *Cat. Lect.*, Introd. 4); but soon the name was given to the whole season. An exact parallel is to be seen in the name 'Pentecost' (see above, I. 2 (*b*)). The next stage was that the partial fast before Pascha, of varying duration, was called τεσσαρακοστή, irrespective of its exact length. Some moderns suppose that the name first arose from the forty *hours*' fast; others think that it has nothing to do with the fast, but only with the period of probation of the *competentes*, though it is not quite clear why this was forty days. For less probable reasons, see below.

The 'Festal Letters' of Athanasius show that the forty-days' fast did not develop so soon in Egypt as in Rome (cf. also Egyp. Ch. Order above). In the first (A.D. 329) he speaks of the fast beginning on Monday of Holy Week, and implies that the fasts of Moses, Elijah, and Daniel were longer than those of Christians. So in the letters for A.D. 332, 333, Holy Week only is mentioned. In the intervening years, however, he refers to τεσσαρακοστή, but only tentatively; Holy Week is *the* fast, and so in the letter for A.D. 334 ff. In the year 340 (*Ep.* xii.), writing to Serapion of Thmuis from Rome instead of sending a festal letter, he persuades the people to fast all the forty days, as they did in Rome. In 347 (*Ep.* xix.) he says that any one who neglects to observe the fast of forty days cannot celebrate Easter. Two points appear from these Letters: (*a*) Saturday and Sunday were not fast-days (vi. 13; so A.D. 389 at Milan [Ambrose, *de Elia et Jejunio*, 10] and at Antioch [Chrysostom, hom. xi. *in Gen.* 2]); (*b*) the Holy Week fast ended in Egypt late on the evening of Saturday, as in the days of Dionysius (see above). Like so many earlier and later writers, Athanasius warns his people against making the fast an external matter only (i. 4 f.).

The forty-days' fast is also mentioned by Eusebius (*de Pasch.* 5), and in the *Canons of Hippolytus* as we now have them (*c.* A.D. 320 [?]; can. xx. [154]). The latter prescribe bread and salt and water in Holy Week (can. xxii. [195-8]); sick persons and those who neglect the fast by ignorance of the time should fast after Pentecost. The *Edessene Canons* (*c.* A.D. 350 [?]; can. 7) are the first to give as the reason for the forty-days' fast that our Lord and Moses and Elijah fasted for that period; at Edessa the 'forty days' included all or most of Holy Week [so *Test. of our Lord*, which does not make the forty days a fast], and the Passion and Resurrection were apparently commemorated on the same day (see above). Another development is the *prefixing* of the forty-days' fast to Holy Week, as in the *Apost. Const.* (v. 13, 18, ed. Funk, *Didascalia et Const. Apost.*, Paderborn, 1905); in Holy Week, bread, salt, herbs, and water only are allowed, and the last two days are an absolute fast *if possible*, or, at any rate, the Saturday (see above; the saving clause is an adaptation of the parallel *Didascalia* passage). Holy Week is pre-eminently 'the week of the fast' (v. 20). Pseudo-Ignatius (*Philipp.* 13), who is perhaps the author of *Apost. Const.*, likewise makes Holy Week separate from the τεσσαρακοστή, as does Chrysostom (hom. xxx. *in Gen.* 1). The *Apostolic Canons*, which at any rate are from the same school, do not mention this point, but make the forty days a fast for all, under penalties (can. 69 [*c.* A.D. 400]). The 'Pilgrimage of Silvia' (or 'of Etheria') describes an eight-weeks' Lent at Jerusalem, with forty-one actual days of fasting (*c.* A.D. 385 [?]).

In the 5th cent. Socrates (*HE* v. 22) says that the Paschal fast varied greatly. At Rome three successive weeks before Easter were kept, except Saturdays and Sundays; but the accuracy of his statement that Saturdays were excepted has been doubted. In Illyria and Greece and Alexandria they fasted six weeks, which were called τεσσαρακοστή. Others began the fast in the 7th week before Pascha, and fasted only for three periods of five days, and that at intervals, and yet called it τεσσαρακοστή—a fact which greatly surprised the historian. The mode of fasting also varied; some abstained from things that had life, others ate fish only, others both fish and fowl; some did not eat eggs and fruit; some ate dry bread only, some not even this; others fasted till the 9th hour and then took any kind of food (this applies to the weekly fasts; see below, 3); there was no written command on the subject.

Sozomen (*HE* vii. 19) gives like evidence. In some Churches the fast was 6 weeks, as in Illyria, the West, Libya, Egypt, Palestine; but 7 weeks in Constantinople and the neighbourhood as far as Phœnicia. In some Churches people fasted 3 alternate weeks during the space of 6 or 7 weeks; in others they fasted continuously for 3 weeks just before Pascha; Montanists fasted only for 2 weeks. Earlier in the 5th cent. John Cassian remarks on the variety of custom with regard to the Lent fast (*Collat.* xxi. 24–30, written *c.* A.D. 420); he says that, though some kept it for 6 weeks and others for 7 weeks, both made only 36 days of fasting [this would depend on whether the Saturdays were fast-days or not]; and the number 36 was a tithe of the year. The 36-days' fast was for all, but some devout persons exceeded the number; the observance of Quadragesima was not primitive, and was not originally enjoined by canonical rule, but was a matter of gradual growth The name was adopted because our Lord, Moses, and Elijah fasted for 40 days (cf. *Edessene Canons*, above), and for other reasons. The reference of the name to our Lord's fast is also given by Augustine (*de Doct. Christ.* ii. 16 [25]), Ambrose (*Hom.* 21), Gregory of Nazianzus (*Orat.* xl. 30), and Jerome (*in Is.* xvi. 58; *in Jon.* 3). Socrates (*HE* ii. 43) says that Eustathius, the heretical bishop of Sebaste in Armenia, who was condemned by the Synod of Gangra (*c.* A.D. 380), allowed the prescribed fasts to be neglected, and recommended fasting on Sunday (see also the Synodal letter of Gangra, summarized by Hefele, *Councils*, ii. 327, Eng. tr., Edinb. 1871–96).

During Lent, entertainments, horse-racing, and similar shows were forbidden (see *DCA* ii. 975). The Council of Laodicæa (can. 51 [*c.* A.D. 380]) prohibited the keeping of the festivals of martyrs in Lent except on Saturday and Sunday; so (A.D. 692) the second Trullan Council (can. 52). Among those who wrote on fasting during this period of development were James of Nisibis († *c.* 350) and Maximus of Turin († *c.* 470), both mentioned by Gennadius (*de Vir. Illustr.* i. 41); Maximus wrote on the Quadragesimal Fast, and also on fasting in general, and 'that there should be no jesting on a fast day.' Many sermons on fasting are extant, by Augustine, Leo the Great, Basil, and others.

3. Weekly fasts.—We find the Wednesday and Friday fasts in the 3rd and following centuries, but not as a universal custom till the end of the 4th. In the 3rd cent. they are mentioned by Origen (hom. *in Lev.* x. 2; but in *c. Cels.* viii. 22, 'Paraskeue' must mean Good Friday and not every Friday, for otherwise Wednesday would be mentioned with it) and in the *Older Didascalia* (v. 14, ed. Funk: 'omni tempore' seems to mean 'all the year round'), which hints at the reason for the fasts on these days, which is explicitly given at the beginning of the 4th cent. by Peter I. of Alexandria (*Ep. can.* 15, really a fragment *de Pascha*)—that Wednesday was the day of the conspiracy of the Jews, and Friday of the Crucifixion. Augustine (*Ep.* xxxvi., Benedictine ed. [*aliter* lxxxvi.] 30 *ad Casulanum*) at a later day gives the same reason (for another explanation, see Clem. Alex. *Strom.* vii. 22). Eusebius (*Vit. Constant.* iv. 18) tells us that Constantine enjoined on all his subjects the observance of Sunday *and Friday*; he does not mention Wednesday. But these set weekly fasts were not universal. In the *Test. of our Lord* no fixed fast-days are prescribed in the week,[1] though the possibility of a fast-day falling in the week is allowed for, in which case the Eucharist is to be celebrated then (i. 22); for in some countries a fast-day was chosen for the Eucharist (Tert. *de Orat.* 19—Wednesday and Friday). The *Edessene Canons* prescribe service on Wednesday and Friday, which *may* imply a fast. Etheria at the end of the 4th cent. speaks of the observance of these days as fasts, and seems to say that the Eucharist was celebrated on them at 3 p.m., except in Lent. The *Hippolytean Canons* mention them as fasts, and say that the more devout added other fast-days as well (can. xx. [154]). These fasts are strictly enjoined in Cyprus towards the end of the 4th cent. by Epiphanius (*Hær.* lxv. 6; *Exp. Fid.* 22), who says that they were universal, and that the fasts of the 'stations' ended at the hour of the Lord's death, the 9th hour; also by the *Apost. Const.* (v. 14, 20 incorporating the *Didascalia*, and vii. 23 incorporating the *Didache*), with the same reasons for the choice of the days as we find in Peter of Alexandria; and by pseudo-Ignatius (*Philipp.* 13) and the *Apost. Canons* (can. 69).

In some cases the fast was prolonged to Saturday; the phrase was 'superponere' (ὑπερτίθεσθαι), or, in Tertullian, 'continuare jejunium.' The Council of Elvira in Spain (*c.* A.D. 305) ordered these 'superpositions' once a month, except in July and August, and not every week (can. 23, 26); though Saturday is not mentioned, that day is probably meant, but Hefele (*Councils*, i. 146) takes the phrase to mean an extension of the fast till evening. Saturday was often kept as a fast in the West, especially at Rome (so expressly Augustine, *loc. cit.*, though his words do not involve every Saturday in the year). But, in the East, Saturday was regarded from the 4th cent. as a festival commemorating Creation; and fasting on it, except on Easter Even, was strongly condemned (cf. Tertullian above, I. 2 (*e*); so *Apost. Const.* v. 14, 20, vii. 23, viii. 33; *Apost. Canons*, 64; and, later, the second Trullan Council, A.D. 692, which forbids fasting, as was practised at Rome, on Saturdays in Lent, can. 55). For this reason Saturday as well as Sunday was thenceforward regarded as specially suitable for a *synaxis*, with a Eucharist, as in the *Test. of our Lord* (i. 22, corrected text), the *Arabic Didascalia* (§ 38), the *Apost. Const.* (ii. 59 by implication), and at the Council of Laodicæa (can. 49, 51 [in Lent]); and in Socrates' time this custom was universal, except at Alexandria and Rome (*HE* v. 22; cf. Sozomen, *HE* vii. 19, who says that it obtained at Constantinople; see art. AGAPE in vol. i. p. 172). That the Saturday fast, however, was known in Rome as early as the beginning of the 3rd cent. appears from a remark of Jerome (*Ep.* lxxi. 6 *ad Lucin.*),

[1] But in the derived *Arabic Didascalia* (§ 38 [*c.* A.D. 400]) Wednesday and Friday are fast-days.

who says that Hippolytus discussed the question of the Saturday fast and of a daily reception of the Eucharist.

4. Pre-baptismal fasts.—These are twice prescribed in the *Canons of Hippolytus* for the candidates *and others.* In one place the length of them is not mentioned; in the other the candidates fast on the Friday before Pascha (can. xix. [106, 150–2]). With the last provision the corresponding passages of the Egyp. Ch. Ord. (§ 45) and the Ethiopic (§ 34) agree; the *Test. of our Lord* (ii. 6) says Friday *and* Saturday. In the *Apost. Const.* (vii. 22) the candidate is enjoined to fast beforehand, because our Lord fasted after His baptism. The canons of the '4th Council of Carthage' of A.D. 398 (probably a later compilation [Hefele, *Councils*, ii. 410]) seem to speak of a longer fast, but of a partial nature; the candidates must be proved by abstinence from wine and flesh (can. 85); and so Greg. Naz. (*Orat.* xl. 31) advocates fasting, vigils, and other exercises as part of the preparation. Cyril of Jerusalem (*Cat. Lect.* iii. 7, xviii. 17 [A.D. 348]) refers to pre-baptismal fasting, and says that the *competentes* took part in the Paschal fast, the 'prolonged fast of the Paraskeue.' In the *Clementine Recognitions* (vii. 34, 36, now thought to be of the 4th cent.) a fast of at least one day is mentioned, and this must be observed expressly with a view to baptism. Socrates (*HE* vii. 17) speaks of a Jew who for purposes of his own desired baptism from a Novatian bishop, being made to fast 'for many days.'

5. The Pentecostal fast.—There is some trace of a fast either before or after Pentecost; for ten days before the festival, in Philastrius (*Hær.* 119) and Isidore (*de Off.* i. 38); for a week beginning eight days after it, in *Apost. Const.* v. 20; cf. *Can. Hipp.* for sick persons (above, 2), but this shows that at the time when that manual was compiled the Pentecostal fast was not an ordinary observance. Athanasius alludes to a short fast (of a day or two [?]) after Pentecost in *Apol. de fug.* 6, *c.* A.D. 358. It probably began only in the 4th century.

6. Special and voluntary fasts.—Corresponding to the fast before ordination in NT is a special fast for bishops after their consecration in the *Test. of our Lord* (i. 22) and the *Arabic Didascalia* (23, 38). In several of the Church Orders voluntary fasts are recommended to widows and, indeed, to all Christians (*Test.* i. 42; Egyp. Ch. Ord. 47; Ethiop. Ch. Ord. 36; *Can. Hipp.* xx. [155]). The bishop, however, according to the second of these, ought not to fast except when all the people fast. In some places Jan. 1 was in the 4th cent. observed as a fast with a view to counteracting the influence of heathen New Year's orgies (Ambrose, *Serm.* ii. 'de Kal. Jan.'; Aug. *Serm.* cxcviii. 2, Benedictine ed., 'de Kal. Jan.'); but Augustine says that, if people cannot fast on that day, at least they should dine with sobriety. As monastic communities grew, from the middle of the 4th cent. onwards, special fasts became common in them. For monasticism and its discipline, see artt. ASCETICISM (Christian), MONASTICISM (Christian).

7. Fasting before and after Communion.—The fast before Communion corresponds in some measure to that before Baptism, but is not mentioned at so early a date. It is clear that, if the Agape was connected with and preceded the Eucharist (see the different views given in art. AGAPE), the latter could not have been received fasting: yet the feeling of reverence which dictated fasting before Communion would not be offended by the previous partaking of a sacred meal like the Agape in the same way as it would be offended by the partaking of ordinary food. But there is no evidence of the custom at the time when the Agape and the Eucharist were united.

The first writer who alludes to the custom is Tertullian (*ad Uxor.* ii. 5: 'quod secreto ante cibum gustes'; the reference is to private reservation of the Eucharist by the Christian wife of a heathen husband; cf. also *de Orat.* 19); but there is no hint that it was a novelty in his day. The next certain reference to the custom is in the 4th cent., when we find the rule laid down in the *Canons of Hippolytus* (can. xix. [150–2], xxviii. [205]), in the *Test. of our Lord* (ii. 20, 25), in the Verona Fragments (Hauler, p. 117), in the Egyp. Ch. Ord. (58), and in the Ethiopic Ch. Ord. (44). In some of these passages, but not in all, the rule is inverted: the faithful are to receive the Eucharist before they eat other food. The *Can. of Hippol.* say that no one is to taste anything before receiving the mysteries, especially on the days of the sacred fast; the last words show that the rule was not absolutely rigorous.

Though these passages are (probably) of the 4th cent., their wording shows that they are derived from the common source of these manuals, and therefore the rule goes back to the 3rd century. Of writers of the 4th cent. who insist on the rule may be mentioned Basil (hom. *de Jejun.* i.), Chrysostom (hom. 27 *in 1 Cor.* etc.), and Greg. Naz. (*Orat.* xl. 30). The last treats the custom as universal, though (he remarks) Jesus gave the 'sacrament of the Passover' after supper. Augustine makes it a Divinely established rule ('it seemed good to the Holy Ghost'—a common formula at one time for canonical legislation, from Ac 15[28]), and says that 'for the honour of so great a sacrament the body of the Lord should enter into the mouth of a Christian before other foods, for so is this custom kept throughout the world,' even although the disciples at the Last Supper did not receive fasting (*Ep.* liv. 8, Ben. *ad Januar.* [*aliter* cxviii. 6]). It is clear that in this matter an additional reason for fasting besides that of self-discipline presented itself to the Christian mind, namely, reverence for the heavenly gift.

Later, both in East and West, and among the Separated Orientals as well as among the Orthodox, the rule became very rigid (see, *e.g.*, Councils of Bracara, can. 10 [A.D. 572], Auxerre, can. 19 [*c.* A.D. 580], Toledo [A.D. 646]); but even in Augustine's time the rule was not absolute, for the 3rd Council of Carthage (A.D. 397; can. 29) excuses the fast before Communion on Maundy Thursday (perhaps the officiating clergy are meant), while saying that on other days the 'Sacraments of the Altar' must be celebrated by none but those who are fasting. This exception is attested by Augustine (*loc. cit.*), but was afterwards taken away by the 2nd Trullan Council (A.D. 692; can. 29). Socrates (*HE* v. 22) says that in the 5th cent. the Egyptians near Alexandria and the inhabitants of the Thebaid celebrated the Eucharist on Saturdays in the evening after having eaten; perhaps an Agape is meant. On the other hand, Augustine says that on Maundy Thursday there were two Eucharists—one early for those who did not fast on that day, and one late for those who did (*Ep.* liv. 9, Ben.). On fast-days the Eucharist was often celebrated at a late hour, that the people might remain fasting till then. It is sometimes said that there is a trace of this in Tertullian (*de Orat.* 19). But he seems to say the contrary—that the Eucharist on 'station' days was not deferred till the afternoon, but that scrupulous persons, who thought that by Communion they would break their fast, might carry away the holy gift and consume it after the fast was over. At the end of the 4th cent. Etheria implies that on Wednesday and Friday (the 'station' days) the Eucharist was celebrated at 3 p.m., except in Lent. At a later date an exception was made to the rule of fasting Communion in the case of the sick and of the Viaticum (see Scudamore, *Notitia Eucharistica*[2], London, 1876, p. 1036; and *DCA* i. 418*b*). It will be remembered that fasting Communion was made easier by the common practice of private reservation of the Sacrament (see Scudamore, p. 903, and Maclean, *Ancient Church Orders*, p. 56, for the authorities). The practice is referred to at Cæsaraugusta (Saragossa) in Spain *c.* A.D. 380 (can. 3, which forbids the communicant to keep the Eucharist by him without consuming it, or perhaps forbids the practice altogether).

Of a fast *after* Communion there are some slight traces, but not as early as the period now under consideration, the first *certain* reference being a law of Charlemagne (A.D. 809), which enjoined two or three hours' fasting after reception. This custom was observed by some till the later Middle Ages (Scudamore, p. 808; *DCA* i. 664 f.).

8. Fasting of penitents.—Fasting was enjoined on those under discipline, as appropriate to their penitence (*e.g.* Cyr. Jerus. *Cat. Lect.* ii. 9; Basil, *Ep.* xlv. 1; Socrates, *HE* v. 19). But it was not during this period inflicted as a special penance, the first certain instance being the 29th canon of the Council of Epaon in Burgundy (A.D. 517), included among the canons of Agde or Agatha in South Gaul (A.D. 506; Hefele, *Councils*, iv. 76, 85). Thereafter the practice was common.

9. When fasting was forbidden.—On Sundays and in the season of 'Pentecost' (*i.e.* Eastertide, 50 days after Easter) fasting and kneeling were not allowed, both being considered unsuitable to a time of joy. The prohibition is found first in a fragment of Irenæus quoted by pseudo-Justin, *Quæst. et R. ad Orthod.* 115 (kneeling); then in Tertullian, *de Cor.* 3 (fasting and kneeling) and *de Orat.* 23 (kneeling); in the latter passage Tertullian says that some also abstained from kneeling on Saturdays, and that on fast-days prayer should always be offered kneeling. We find the same prohibition in Peter I. of Alexandria (*Ep. can.* 15, kneeling), in the canons of Nicæa (can. 20, kneeling), in the *Test. of our Lord* (ii. 12, fasting and kneeling in Pentecost), in the *Apost. Const.* v. 20 (fasting; the prohibition is not in the parallel *Didascalia*), and in the canons of Saragossa (can. 2, Sunday fasting). Pseudo-Ignatius (*Philipp.* 13) says that one who fasts on these days is a 'Christ-slayer.' The Council of Gangra anathematizes those who fast on Sunday from pretended asceticism (can. 18). Augustine is equally strong on not fasting on Sundays and in Pentecost (*Ep.* xxxvi. 18, Ben. [*aliter* lxxxvi.] *ad Casulan.*). See also *DCA* i. 725*a*.

III. *MEDIÆVAL AND MODERN PERIODS.*—(A) THE WEST.—**1. Lent.**[1]—Saturdays in Lent were expressly ordered to be kept as fast-days at the beginning of the 6th cent. in South Gaul, by the Council of Agde (can. 12). Yet, even so, 'Quadragesima' consisted of only 36 fasting days, since Sunday was not a fast. At Rome, Gregory the Great († 604) speaks of the fast being six weeks, *i.e.* 36 fasting days (hom. 16 *in Evang.*). So in 653 the 8th Council of Toledo in Spain repeats Cassian's language (above, II. 2) about Lent being a tithe of the year (can. 9). But in the 7th cent., before the Gelasian Sacramentary was drawn up, four days were prefixed to Lent, which thus began on Ash Wednesday, and consisted of 40 fasting days. At Milan the older custom survived; and, according to the Ambrosian rite, the Lenten fast still begins on the 6th Monday before Easter. In Scotland the four extra days were introduced by St. Margaret in the 11th cent. (*Vita S. Marg.* ii. 18); the Mozarabic rite adopted them only *c.* A.D. 1500 (Dowden, *Ch. Year and Kalendar*, p. 83). Gregory the Great recognizes sickness as a reason for not fasting (*Epp.* xxxii. xl.).

2. Advent.—This season, instituted in preparation for Christmas, is not heard of as a fast till just before the 6th century. Hence, from the fact of its once lasting six weeks no argument can be drawn as to the original date of the Western Christmas, as has lately been done by Kirsopp Lake (*Guardian*, 29 Dec. 1911). But the Council of Cæsaraugusta (Saragossa) in Spain (*c.* A.D. 380; can. 4) appointed the days from Dec. 17 to Jan. 6 as a solemn season for prayer and daily church-going, when 'no one may go with bare feet.' It was not, however, a fast. This may indicate that Jan. 6 was then observed in Spain, as in the East at that time, as the Nativity festival. The fast of Advent is first found in the Calendar of Perpetuus, bishop of Tours, A.D. 491 (*PL* lxxi. 566). It lasted from Nov. 11 (Martinmas) to Dec. 25, and was for three days a week. The Council of Mâcon (A.D. 581; can. 9) appointed for all a fast on Mondays, Wednesdays, and Fridays for the same period. For this reason Advent came to be known as 'St. Martin's Quadragesima.' The Council of Tours (A.D. 567) appointed a daily fast from Dec. 1 to 25 for monks (can. 17). At Rome, Advent never lasted for more than five Sundays (so even in the Gelasian Sacramentary [7th cent.]); and usually only for four (so Gregory the Great). Advent fasting soon died out in the West, and the season became merely a solemn time for prayer, as at the present day. But Bede (*HE* iii. 27, iv. 30) mentions a 40-days' fast before Christmas and after Pentecost as being observed by some devout persons in the 7th and 8th centuries.

3. Pentecostal fast.—The Council of Tours, A.D. 567, mentions a week's fast after Pentecost for monks (can. 17). In the 8th, 9th, and 10th centuries we find a 40-days' fast after Pentecost, sometimes called 'the Quadragesima before St. John the Baptist.' This is said by Theodore, Abp. of Canterbury († 690), in his *Pœnitentiale*, to be for all men. We find the same in Ireland *c.* A.D. 700, in Charlemagne's *Capitula*, and in the canons collected by Burchard, bishop of Worms, A.D. 1006 (Dowden, 85). For Bede, see above, III. 2. But this fast soon disappeared in the West.

4. Rogation Days are a Western institution only. They are the three days before Ascension Day (Holy Thursday), a fast preparatory to that festival. They are thought to have been instituted by Mamertus, bishop of Vienne on the Rhone, *c.* A.D. 470, at a time of earthquakes in Auvergne. He introduced penitential 'rogations' or processions for supplication. The Rogation fast was enjoined by the first Council of Orléans, A.D. 511, indirectly by that of Tours, (can. 17), and perhaps by that of Mainz, A.D. 813 (can. 32 f.; the fast not explicitly mentioned); in England by the Council of Clovesho, A.D. 747. It was enjoined by Leo III. at Rome, *c.* A.D. 800, as an intercession for the fruits of the earth. It is found in the *Missale Gothicum* (perhaps of Autun in France), *c.* A.D. 700. The procession still survives, especially in the form of beating parochial bounds; hence the names 'gang days,' 'gang week,' found in the *Anglo-Saxon Chronicle* and in the laws of Athelstan (Dowden, 87).

5. Ember Days also are found only in the West. They are the fasts of the four seasons ('quatuor tempora,' Germ. *Quatember*, whence perhaps the English name, though it is more plausibly derived from A.S. *ymbren*, 'recurring'), being (since the 11th cent.) the Wednesday, Friday, and Saturday after the First Sunday in Lent, Pentecost, Holy Cross Day (Sept. 14), and St. Lucy's Day (Dec. 13). They are particularly interesting as being the relics of the full weekly fasts of the West (above, II. 3), which thus have survived in only four weeks of the year; otherwise, the Friday fast is the sole survival of the weekly observance, though, in and after the Middle Ages, Wednesday and Saturday were sometimes observed as fast-days (see Procter-Frere, *Hist. of Bk. of Com. Pr.*, London, 1901, p. 331; and below, 8). Leo the Great (*c.* A.D. 440) refers to these fasts of the four seasons at Rome, held in Lent (Serm. 39–50), Pentecost (Serm. 78–80), the 7th (Serm. 86–94), and 10th (Serm. 12–20) months, *i.e.* Sept. and Dec.; and from Rome they spread over the West. But at one time they were held in some places only at three seasons, the sowing, reaping, and vintage; afterwards the winter Ember fast was added. The exact weeks, however, have varied. The Gelasian Sacramentary mentions the 1st, 4th, 7th, and 10th month. At the Council of Mainz (A.D. 813, can. 34) they fall in the first week of March, the second week of June, the third week of Sept., and the last full week before Christmas Even. In the *Leofric Missal* they are in the first week of Lent, the week of Pentecost, and in the full weeks before the autumn equinox and Christmas. Pseudo-Callistus (*Ep.* i. 1, part of the False Decretals of pseudo-Isidorus [*Ante-Nic. Chr. Lib.* ix. B, p. 203]) advocates their being held quarterly, with reference

[1] The English name 'Lent' is derived from Ang.-Sax. *lencten*, 'the spring.'

to the four seasons and the fruits of the earth. The Council of Clovesho (A.D. 747) enjoins the fasts of the 4th, 7th, and 10th months, but does not mention that of the spring, probably because it was absorbed in the great Lenten fast.

The original Ember Days had no reference to ordination, but, as seen in the 7th cent. Gelasian Sacramentary and in later authorities (though the custom may be earlier [Duchesne, *Chr. Wor.* p. 353]), it became the rule for bishops to ordain at these seasons, the fasting thus taking the form of a pre-ordination exercise; and this is the present aspect of the Ember Days. Minor orders, however, were conferred at any time. The present rule in the Roman Catholic and Anglican Churches is for ordination to the presbyterate and diaconate to be normally confined to these seasons, though the bishop has a discretion (see, *e.g.*, the preface to the English Ordinal in the Bk. of Com. Pr. and the English Canon 31).

6. Vigils.—These are single fasting days before certain saints' days and other festivals; but as fasts they are purely Western. Originally a 'Vigil' was a night spent in prayer, as often in the earlier periods (*e.g.* Etheria, *Peregrinatio*; Pontius, *Life of Cyprian*, § 15; Chrysos., hom. *de Mart.* ii. 668 D; Socrates, *HE* vi. 8). The substitution of a fast-day for this 'pernoctatio' probably dates only from the end of the 9th century. As Sunday cannot be a fast-day, if the day before a festival which has a Vigil be the Lord's day, the fast is kept on the Saturday.

7. 'Fasting' and 'abstinence.'—The Roman Catholics at the present day make a distinction between these. On a day of abstinence, meat is forbidden, but there is no restriction on the quantity of food taken; on a fast-day the quantity is also restricted. The distinction as regards England is modern; in the Anglican Bk. of Com. Pr. the two terms are used synonymously. The distinction was introduced among the English Roman Catholics in 1761, Fridays and Rogation Days being days of abstinence.

8. Fasts at the present day in the West.—The Church of England and the Church of Rome enumerate as fasts the 40 days of Lent, Ember Days, Rogation Days, all Fridays except Christmas Day if it fall on that day of the week, and Vigils before certain festivals. Roman Catholics in some countries relax the Vigils in favour of a stricter observance of Wednesdays and Fridays in Lent and Advent. Since the Reformation the Church of England, while fixing the fasting days, has made no rule as to how they are to be observed, leaving this to the individual conscience; but Acts of Parliament of Edward VI. and James I. and Proclamations of Elizabeth, vigorously enforced, ordered abstinence from flesh-meat on fast-days, and gave the curious reason for the injunction that the fish and shipping trades might be benefited; also, curiously enough, Saturdays are there mentioned as fast-days (see remarkable instances of the enforcement of these injunctions in *Hierurgia Anglicana*², London, 1902–4, iii. 106 ff., cf. i. 248). The Anglican *Homily of Fasting* (pt. i.) defines fasting as a 'withholding of meat, drink, and all natural food from the body,' and (pt. ii.) 'a restraint from some kinds of meats and drink'; it permits two meals on a fast-day (*Hier. Ang.*² iii. 108). A relic of the pre-baptismal fast is seen in the service for the baptism of such as are of riper years in the Bk. of Com. Pr., where the candidates are to be exhorted to prepare themselves with prayer and fasting (1st rubric). Fasting was markedly retained by the Protestant Reformers in Continental Europe; and the Fast Day (generally Thursday) before the Communion is a well-known feature of Scottish Presbyterian custom, observed with much rigour by the devout up to recent times. See also art. ASCETICISM (Christian) in vol. ii. p. 79. In Roman Catholic countries the days before Ash Wednesday, called 'Carnival' (? from Lat. *carnem levare*, 'to put away meat,' or *carne levamen*, 'solace in the flesh') are given to relaxation and entertainments. A certain relaxation also is permitted in Mid-Lent; the fourth Sunday in Lent, when the Gospel for the day narrates the Feeding of the Five Thousand, has long been called *Dominica Refectionis*, or 'Refreshment Sunday' (but in French *Mi-Carême*).

(B) THE EAST. — **I. The Orthodox Eastern Church.**—(*a*) Lent, the 'Fast of the holy and great τεσσαρακοστή,' in popular language σαρακοστή, begins on the Monday following Quinquagesima, which is called 'the Sunday of cheese fare' (ἡ κυριακὴ τῆς τυρινῆς); but meat is not eaten in the preceding 'week of cheese fare' (ἡ ἑβδομὰς τῆς τυρινῆς or τυροφαγοῦ). During this week cheese and eggs are permitted on Wednesday and Friday as well as on other days. The Sunday corresponding to the Western Sexagesima (that preceding the above mentioned 'cheese fare') is called the 'Sunday of meat fare' (ἡ κυριακὴ τῆς ἀποκρέω, the Carnival being ἀποκρέα or αἱ ἀποκρέω [often αἱ ἀπόκρεω] or, according to Dowden [p. 84], *Apocreos*). The Greeks do not fast on Saturdays and Sundays in Lent, except on Easter Even (Dowden, 84; see also Shann, *Euchology*, Kidderminster, 1891, pp. 261–3).—(*b*) The fast corresponding to that of Pentecost in old times (above II. 5, III. (A) 3) is called the 'Fast of the Apostles' [Peter and Paul], and lasts either a week from the morrow of the Sunday of All Saints (the octave of Pentecost), or till June 29, St. Peter and St. Paul's Day (Shann, 416).—(*c*) From Aug. 1 to 14 incl. is the 'Fast of the Mother of God,' before the festival of the Repose of the Virgin (Aug. 15); it perhaps once lasted for 40 days (*DCA* i. 662).—(*d*) The 'Fast of the Nativity of our Lord' (Advent) begins on Nov. 15, and lasts for 40 days up to Christmas (Shann, 498). This dates from not before the 9th cent. (*DCA* i. 32*b*), and even then was only for monks. Theodore of Balsamon (A.D. 1200) says that there was in his time only one τεσσαρακοστή, that before Pascha; the other fasts were of 7 days only (*ib.*). But now Advent is a fast of 40 days for all. The Greeks sometimes call it the 'Fast of St. Philip,' because St. Philip's Day falls on Nov. 14. The name τεσσαρακοστή is loosely applied to all the above fasts; cf. II. 2 above.—(*e*) Curiously enough, two festivals are observed as strict fasts: the Decollation of John Baptist (Aug. 29), and Holy Cross Day (Sept. 14); see Dowden, p. 91.—(*f*) Wednesdays and Fridays throughout the year are fasting days; but on the day before Ascension Day, oil, wine, and fish are allowed (Dowden, 87).

Of these fasts, Lent, Wednesday, and Friday are most obligatory; Nicolas Bulgaris (*Catechism*, § 119, ed. Bromage, London, 1893, p. 280) says that their observance is one of the five commandments of the Church, while he does not so characterize the keeping of the other fasts. In the *Orthodox Confession* (*ib.* note), another commandment of the Church is the observance of any fast expressly enjoined by the bishop of the diocese. The Orthodox Church combines with its injunctions to fast at certain times many warnings of the importance of fasting not being only external; it should lead to prayer and penitence (see, *e.g.*, *Duty of Parish Priests*, iv. 40–47 [Blackmore, *Doctrine of Russian Ch.*, Aberdeen, 1845, p. 262 ff.]). These warnings are also frequently found in the books of the other Eastern Churches, and need not be referred to again. (All dates given in this and the following sections are according to Old Style.)

2. The Armenians.—See FESTIVALS AND FASTS (Armenian).

3. The Monophysites.—(*a*) The customs of the *West Syrians* or *Jacobites* are less known to us than those of any other Eastern Church. Their Advent, or *Sūbārā* (*Sūbōrō* = εὐαγγελισμός), lasts for six weeks, as compared with 24 days of the Nestorians (below, 4).—(*b*) *Copts and Abyssinians.*—The fasts as enjoined in Filothaus' *Catechism of the Coptic Church* (Eng. tr. ed. Bromage, London, 1892, p. 42 f.) are: 'The holy 40 days followed by the week of the Passion' [they thus exclude Holy Week; see above, II. 2], Wednesday and Friday, the fast of Christmas, the fast *following* the day of Pentecost, the 'days relating specially to our Lady,' and the three-days' Nineveh fast. [For the three-days' fast (*sic*) of the Ninevites in OT, see *Apost. Const.* v. 20; but it is not there mentioned as a Christian fast.] In the fast, meat and butter are forbidden. Fasts are binding on all except 'infants, invalids, women in child-bearing, those worn out by captivity or exile, and the like.' We also learn that ordination among the Copts is *followed* by a 40-days' fast, and that between a death and burial all the near relatives fast (Fowler, *Christian Egypt*, London, 1901, pp. 208, 212). The Abyssinian fasts are still stricter.

4. The Nestorians (known also as *East Syrians, Assyrians*, or *Chaldæans*) are remarkable as fasting more strictly than their own Book of Canon Law, or *Sūnhādhūs*, requires. They abstain on Sundays in the fasting season, though the *Sūnhādhūs* forbids it because of the Manichæans. In some copies a saving clause says that 'a man may fast on Sunday if it is not from an evil and Manichæan intention.' The fasts observed by all are: (*a*) Advent, called *Sūbārā*, also 'The Little Fast,' Dec. 1–24 incl., though the *Sūnhādhūs* makes this a voluntary fast except for monks. (*b*) Lent, called 'The Fast' or 'The Great Fast,' lasting 50 days, including Sundays. The *Sūnhādhūs* mentions 40 days, but the Service-book called *Khūdhrā*, or 'Cycle,' allows for 50 days (with the Sundays included). Mid-Lent is often marked by some entertainment, but the fast is not broken. (*c*) The 'Rogation' (*bā'ūthā*, or 'supplication') of the Ninevites, the three days following the 5th Sunday after Epiphany. (*d*) Every Wednesday and Friday, not excluding Christmas Day.

Other fasts, not now universal, are the 15 days before 'Mart. Mariam' (St. Mary, Aug. 15), observed by many; the two 'Rogations' of Mar Zaia and of the Virgins, respectively the three days following the 2nd Sunday after Christmas and the 1st Sunday after Epiphany; the *shāwū'ā* (or period of seven weeks) of the Apostles (beginning Whit Monday; this is the Pentecostal fast, ending with the festival of the Twelve Apostles, or *Nausardīl*, 50 days after Pentecost—thus the Nestorians, by 'the Apostles' in this connexion, do not mean St. Peter and St. Paul); the *shāwū'ā* of Elijah (beginning 99 days after Pentecost). These two are mentioned by the *Sūnhādhūs* as voluntary fasts, but are now almost, if not quite, obsolete, and the Rogations of Mar Zaia and of the Virgins are nearly so. In the fast, meat, butter, milk, fish, eggs, etc., are prohibited; and the stricter Nestorians, especially those in the Kurdish mountains, will not eat, drink, or smoke in Lent till mid-day, except on Sundays. In other fasting seasons they may eat when they please, as long as they do not partake of the forbidden foods. In practice, the Wednesday and Friday fasts in most parts of the E. Syrian country only begin in the morning, and end at evensong, so that flesh-meat may be eaten thereafter (for the day begins and ends at sunset, and there is some inconsistency in not fasting after sunset on what we should call the day before); and usually from Easter to Pentecost, butter, milk, and eggs may be taken on these days. The usual food in the fast consists of bread, beans, rice cooked with walnut or other vegetable oil; vine leaves stuffed with rice and raisins and cooked in vinegar; treacle, fruit, raisins, and walnuts. A curious rule about the end of the fast reflects the difference of custom in the 4th cent. (see above, II. 2). The Advent and Lenten fasts end at evensong on Christmas Even or Easter Even, if one has communicated at the Eucharist of the Even; otherwise it does not end till the Eucharist of the festival (the rule is not of universal application). On fast-days the Eucharist is celebrated late—often as late as 1 p.m. or 2 p.m.—that all may remain fasting till then (see above, II. 7). Another rule (perhaps now obsolete) is that, if a person does not communicate at or about Easter, he is not to eat meat for a month; if he has communicated on Maundy Thursday, but not on Easter Even or Easter Day, then for a fortnight. (For the information in this section, see Maclean-Browne, *The Catholicos of the East*, London, 1892, p. 340 ff.) In this Church, as now among the Greeks (see above, III. (B) 1), there is no difficulty about a festival and a fast falling on the same day; as a matter of fact, most of the holy days fall on a Friday, but that day is, nevertheless, a fasting day.

All the Eastern Churches are strict about the fast before Communion. In some cases (*e.g.* the East Syrian *Sūnhādhūs* [Maclean-Browne, p. 343]), the clergy who take any part in the Eucharist or baptism or ordination must be fasting.

Cf. art. FESTIVALS AND FASTS (Christian).

LITERATURE.—Besides works cited above, see *DCG*, art. 'Calendar (the Christian)'; *DCA*, artt. 'Advent,' 'Fasting,' 'Lent,' 'Ember Days,' 'Rogation Days,' 'Vigils,' etc.; *PRE*, art. 'Fasten in der Kirche,' etc.; J. Dowden, *The Church Year and Kalendar*, Cambridge, 1910; A. J. Maclean, *Ancient Church Orders*, Cambridge, 1910; V. Staley, *The Liturgical Year*, London, 1907, and *Liturgical Studies*, do.; L. Duchesne, *Christian Worship, its Origin and Evolution*, Eng. tr., London, 1903; J. Wordsworth, *Ministry of Grace*, London, 1901; J. Issavardens, *Rites and Ceremonies of the Armenian Church*, Venice, 1888.

A. J. MACLEAN.

FATALISM.—See FATE, NECESSITARIANISM.

FATE.

FATE.—I. *DEFINITION.*—The idea of Fate is found only in conditions where some attempt has been made to trace all phenomena, and more particularly the phenomena of human life, to an ultimate unity. Fate, indeed, is precisely this unity apprehended as an inevitable necessity controlling all things; it is the absolutely inscrutable power to which all men are subject, and may be either personified or represented as impersonal. It is a conception which prevails wherever the mind of man is unable to frame the idea of rational necessity or of a supreme purposive will, and it survives so long as either of these, though within the field of consciousness, is imperfectly realized. Further, men tend to fall back on the idea of Fate when, at a higher level of intellectual development, they begin to doubt of a rational order, or a rational end, in the universe. If any distinction is to be drawn between Fate and Destiny, it is simply that the latter is but the former regarded as operative in particular cases. The idea of Destiny, however, does not necessarily preclude the rationality of the thing destined; it merely implies that this rationality is not perceived. Destiny, in fact, being a somewhat indefinite conception, may even connote an ethical vocation, and may in that case be applied to the end which a higher will sets before a moral personality as an ideal to be realized in moral endeavour.

II. *HISTORICAL SURVEY*. — **1. Non-Christian religions.**—In the course of history, Fate has assumed various forms. (1) In *polydæmonistic religions* thought is as yet too incoherent to give definite shape to the idea. Crude anticipations thereof emerge when men begin to reflect upon their lot, as, *e.g.*, in the 'Life-Dream' of the American Indians, amongst whom, however, the prevailing idea is that of dependence upon particular spirits, these not being supposed to form a unity. An important place is certainly assigned to the Death-god, the All-Father, or Great Spirit, but he is not figured as Fate, for the simple reason that the conception of necessity, or even of the necessary order of Nature, has not yet dawned upon the mind.

(2) A closer approximation to the idea of Fate is found in *religions which recognize the uniformity of Nature*, more especially as seen in the courses of the heavenly bodies, and which develop an astrology. This stage was reached by the Quichuas and the Aztecs, who, having various astrological beliefs, began to entertain surmises regarding the operation of Fate in human life, and, interpreting this as the will of the gods, sought to get into right relations therewith, and with its actual decrees, by means of magic, oracles, dreams, and haruspication. Among the Aztecs, in fact, there was a special school of astrology, while full credence was given to the manifold evil omens which pointed to the downfall of their kingdom.

(3) We meet with the idea of Fate also in *religions in which the process of Nature forms the dominant factor*, such as the Egyptian, in which the leading motive is the antithesis of life and death; or the Babylonian, which is permeated by the thought of the uniformity of Nature, more particularly as exemplified in the movement of the stars. Yet we must not forget that these religions likewise show a high ethical development, however incongruous with their naturalistic tendencies this may appear.

(*a*) In the religion of *Egypt*, magic papyri are regarded as equally effective with good works in obviating the penalties of the final judgment. The Egyptians speak of Nūter, the Power or Deity; they personify law in the goddess Ma'et, who in reality stands for natural order, but has also moral attributes; they find a place for Destiny in the Hathors, Shai, and Rennenet; and, in fact, as the system in its entirety, notwithstanding its ethical aspects, is dominated by the process of Nature, it exemplifies a stage of development in which Fate takes the form of natural necessity, as may be inferred likewise from the magical arts by which souls are to be delivered at the day of judgment. See, further, FATE (Egyptian) and ETHICS AND MORALITY (Egyptian).

(*b*) The *Babylonians* had a profound sense of the august will of the gods, as that which maintained not only the order of Nature but also the ordinances of the State, and in their penitential psalms the devout make sorrowful confession of their offences against both. Yet we find among them so much in the way of exorcism, magic, and astrology as to make it appear that in their view the order of Nature was simply an all-controlling Destiny: the stars decide the lot of men. The Chaldee astrology, we should note, was still a power in Rome. See, further, FATE (Babylonian).

(*c*) Similar conditions meet us in *China*. The worship of spirits is there associated with reverence for natural law, of which, again, civil law is simply a particular phase. In the religion of ancient China, systematic knowledge of the order of Nature—an order believed to emanate from Heaven, from the Sovereign Deity—was obstructed by the belief in spirits, as appears from the respect accorded to soothsaying and astrology. Here morality really consisted in the due observance of class-precedence, *i.e.* in the recognition of that domestic and civil order which is at the same time the order of Nature. To this impersonal Fate mankind was fettered. The reform inaugurated by Confucius was so far ethical that he laid the supreme emphasis upon practical obedience to the law, and supported his demands by examples culled from the history of the ancient empire. But, while he is convinced that obedience to the moral law is attended with the happiness which is organic to the order of Nature, he does not develop this view to its logical issues. The man who does right should have no anxiety regarding the result.

'If the wise man achieve something, it is well; if he achieve nothing, it is also well: he recognizes Destiny.' 'The perfect man sees danger, and yet bows to Destiny.'

Although Confucius sought to limit the sphere of sorcery and the belief in spirits, he did not identify Destiny with Providence; and, while he yields a certain recognition to Providence, he is, nevertheless, content to ascertain what the order of Nature prescribes; for him Destiny still remains the necessity to which he adjusts himself, though he does not directly assert that it possesses moral attributes. The natural order was recognized still more distinctly by Lao-tse, who actually idealized it as the metaphysical force that he calls *Tao*. Tao is the source of that economy which is manifested both in Nature and in the State. It shows no partiality. To it man must yield himself without desire, and in it, renouncing all passion, he must find peace. Lao-tse takes his stand upon the necessity of this self-adjustment. But Tao, notwithstanding all its ethical accretions, still remains a merely natural power, like Heaven itself. As a matter of fact, the ever-growing practice of soothsaying—the *feng-shui*, or geomancy—shows how firmly-rooted was the belief in Fate, in a country where men had an inkling, but no concrete knowledge, of the order of Nature, and tried to fathom its mysteries by fantastic expedients of all sorts. In reality China is at that stage of development where order is felt to be morally determinative; but, as this order is essentially a natural order, it is neither more nor less than Fate. See, further, FATE (Chinese) and FENG-SHUI.

(*d*) The conception of Fate is found also in the *Teutonic* religion. Though the process of Nature is here combined with the ethical process which terminates in the *Götterdämmerung*, the 'twilight of the gods,' yet guilt and impermanence—to which the gods themselves are subject—operate as a tragic doom hanging over the world. The destructive elements, viz. the Fenris Wolf, the goddess Hela, and the Midgard Serpent, at length gain the upper hand, while Odin himself falls swooning from the world-ash. The cosmic process, in short, comes to its consummation as something destined. From the beginning the worms are gnawing at the tree Yggdrasil. In the waters of Urd dwell the three Norns, daughters of Hela, goddesses of time—past, present, and future—who spin the threads of fortune; goddesses of Destiny, who are older than Odin. Thus the idea of Fate, especially in its tragic form, plays a part in this religion also. The moral element is certainly not absent, but the moral process is mainly one of dissolution. It is a moot point whether the anticipation of a new world under Vali and Vidar belongs to the original Teutonic tradition. In any case this religion looks upon the transitoriness of Nature and human life as the decree of Fate. See DOOM, DOOM MYTHS (Teutonic).

(*e*) The Indo-Germanic peoples of *India* combined Fate and ethics in a somewhat different way. Brāhmanism and Buddhism are both dominated by the doctrine of re-birth—the evil cycle from which no one can extricate himself. The *Ṛta* of the Vedas may be regarded as an analogue of the Greek Μοῖρα, since the ordered process it denotes is by no means thought of as purely ethical. In *Brāhmanism*, it is true, the *Ātman* (*q.v.*) or *Brahma* seems to be something more than Fate. But, on the other hand, later Brāhmanism possesses an emanational doctrine, representing in the *Trimūrti* the cycle of generation and dissolution in Nature; while, again, it shows a wide diffusion of the belief in blind destiny. Even the caste system is simply the malign reflex of the theory of natural necessity, as a force which holds all men in its sway, and from which none can deliver himself, the fate of the individual having been fixed by his birth. The system of caste is fostered also by the doctrine of re-birth. It is true that this doctrine contains the element of retribution, but the exhaustless cycle and the interminable suffering of life which it involves are, after all, a necessity of Nature, a decree of Fate. To wrench oneself free from the chain of re-birth is possible only for those who become absorbed in mystic contemplation and live as ascetics, *i.e.* those who belong to the two higher castes. In other words, the conception of Fate forms the substructure of Brāhmanism in its exoteric form. See, further, FATE (Hindu).

The same holds good of *Buddhism*, the basis of which is the doctrine of universal suffering in an infinite cycle of re-births. In this religion, too, the necessary continuity of Nature is represented as moral retribution; nevertheless, it is predominantly regarded as an inherent Fate, in which man finds himself enmeshed against his will. Deliverance is, indeed, possible for those who renounce all life, all desire, all finitude, in order that they may enter Nirvāṇa; and the way is open to all. But Buddhism in its original form is so closely identified with a fatalistic view of the continuity of Nature that the deliverance which it proffers involves the destruction of personality, the conception of Spirit as something which transcends Nature not having as yet been attained. The latter feature is reflected also in the various magical expedients by which popular Buddhism seeks to dominate Nature, as also by the mechanical formality of the popular worship. Exoteric Buddhism, in short, is destitute of any positive spiritual content. See, further, for a somewhat different view, FATE (Buddhist).

(*f*) Fate plays a considerably less important part in the dualistic religion of *Persia*, but it has not been altogether eliminated. Though in this religion Spirit has won a positive significance, and Ahura Mazda ranks as the Supreme Power, yet the latter is opposed by Angra Mainyu, and the created world is an amalgam of good and evil, benefit and bane. It is believed, indeed, that the conflict between the two powers will eventually eliminate the evil, and that man's part in the campaign is to espouse the cause of Ahura Mazda by obeying the laws of Zarathushtra; meanwhile, however, man is entangled in an evil world, beset upon every side by demons, from whose wiles he must guard himself; and even the Supreme Deity himself, though sure of ultimate victory, is not as yet wholly free, but physically and spiritually circumscribed by the evil spirit. Now, as this evil spirit acts without reflexion, and under the influence of a blind impulse of nature, and as he is supported by a whole host of demons, who shed abroad darkness and sorrow, tempt to robbery and tyranny, stir up hatred and revenge, and disseminate evils of all kinds, including even the unsavouriness of food—men are clearly subject to an alien necessity, from which they may, indeed, with the help of the law gradually free themselves by a struggle, but by which their earthly existence is heavily trammelled. We shall hardly err, therefore, in saying that in Parsiism the conception of Fate has not been fully transcended, though it has certainly fallen into the background. The dependence of the Supreme Deity upon Angra Mainyu, as represented in the later Avesta—even though that dependence be but temporary—bears an ominous resemblance to the idea that the gods themselves are subject to Fate. That Angra Mainyu appears as personal cannot hide from us the fact that he and his demonic hosts alike are under the control of a blind will, thus resembling a natural force which acts in opposition to the highest god and compels him to struggle. The naturalistic limitations of Parsiism are also shown in its fire-worship, and the partial worship accorded to natural deities. Furthermore, *Asha*, the Persian analogue of the Indian *Ṛta*, does not symbolize a purely ethical order. The potent influence of the conception of Fate—an all-controlling factor in human life—in this system of dualism may probably be traced in the later theological idea of *Zrvan Akarana*, or Infinite Time, which forms the apex of the system, and furnishes the starting-point of the dualistic process. Again, in the *fravashi* (*q.v.*), the guardian angel of the good man, we recognize the belief that human beings are surrounded by friendly and beneficent spirits, as well as by assailants of evil intent; while the belief that the latter can be effectively counteracted by oft-repeated prayers opens the door to exorcism and magic—to that mechanical debasement of religion, in fact, which corresponds to a naturalism not yet transcended.

Finally, the various systems of Gnosticism influenced by this religion, as also Manichæism, are largely pervaded by the conception of Fate: thus, they regard mankind as divided by nature into pneumatic, psychic, and hylic groups, the lot of the individual being determined by the extent to which the evil principle intermingles with his being. See, further, FATE (Iranian).

(*g*) Nor had the religions of Greece and Rome quite outgrown the belief in Fate. As regards *Greece*, it is true that Homer places Zeus on the throne of Olympus; but, as the gods are still to some extent liable to envy and caprice, they are shadowed by Μοῖρα, or Necessity; and, although Destiny is spoken of as the 'decree of Zeus' (Διὸς αἶσα), yet it is Μοῖρα who, acting independently of Zeus, assigns the term of human life. In the tragic poets the idea of Fate was superseded by that of a just and beneficent world-order controlled by Zeus: Μοῖρα gives place to Δίκη. They warn men against ὕβρις, the temper which transgresses the limits of human power. The jealousy of the gods was repudiated by Pindar in favour of the idea of retribution. In the hands of the tragedians, Fate acquires an ethical significance: the Μοῖρα combines with the *Erinyes*, who punish ὕβρις. While in Sophocles the distinction between Fate and guilt is frequently obscured, and guilt may sometimes fasten upon the innocent, yet he also expresses the conviction that presumption will be visited with stern retribution, and that hardship and sorrow may lead to glory. In Greek philosophy likewise, the trend of which was towards monotheism, the Deity is extolled as the supreme Idea of the Good, as the supreme Reason, as Providence, though we still hear of Ἀνάγκη (Necessity) and Εἱμαρμένη (Fate). In point of fact, natural necessity and Providence are not as yet sharply distinguished, and, accordingly, the moral personality has not attained to complete emancipation from Nature. Nature, indeed, save where it was interpreted by reason from the æsthetic standpoint, was always a mystery; and, though the Stoics regarded the gods themselves as organs of Providence (not altogether free from natural necessity), we need hardly wonder that even amongst them the occult arts had a place. Nor were the Neo-Platonists, notwithstanding their ὑπερόντως ὄν (super-existent Being), quite free from a natural dualism in their view of matter; and, consequently, they too fell back upon magic and theurgy. In a word, Greek thought did not succeed in fully harmonizing moral reason and natural necessity; it either identified the two, or admitted a residuum of dualism, and, while the conception of cosmic unity became more and more clearly formulated, all the more persistently did some remnant of fatalism maintain its ground, asserting itself alike in ritual and in moral life. See, further, EUMENIDES.

The belief in Fate survived also in *Rome*, where it assumed a largely practical form, being associated with the *Fata*, or destinies of individuals, and with the practice of augury connected therewith and developed mainly from Etruscan sources. The *Fata* were primarily concerned with birth and death. The later period of Roman history was remarkable for its syncretistic tendencies, the city becoming a rendezvous for sorcery of all kinds, Chaldæan astrology, Greek oracles, etc. Fortuna (τύχη) was worshipped as the goddess of Destiny, as were also the Parcæ. The *fatum*, or lot, of the individual or the State was doubtless traced back to the gods; but along with this flourished a belief in Fate as an independent power, manifesting itself in various *prognostica*, the interpretation of which was a craft by itself. Thus there was ever the *Dira Necessitas* hovering above the life of man. See, further, FATE (Greek and Roman).

(4) One might naturally suppose that the idea of Fate would be absent from religions which adhere to a *supranatural theism*, such, *e.g.*, as the leading faiths of the Semitic world. This, however, is by no means the case. We must not forget that in those religions the Divine will, being regarded as absolute sovereignty, really takes the form of inevitable necessity. In the last resort chance and necessity signify the same thing, viz. a necessary force determining human life and not as yet fully illuminated by reason.

(*a*) So far, therefore, as *Judaism* holds by the absolute prerogative of God, it fails to exclude fatalism. Certainly the God of Judaism is supranatural; Nature lies within His power; He assigns reward and punishment according to His righteousness, not according to a necessary law of Nature; He guides His people to a goal fixed by Himself, and disciplines them by dealings adjusted to their conduct towards Him. But, as this righteous régime does not always vindicate itself in the actual lot of the people or the individual, there emerges a kind of scepticism which, as in the book of Ecclesiastes, takes the form of a threnody upon the vanity of earthly things. While the book certainly declares that God will bring every work into judgment (Ec 12[14]), it also says that the sons of men are snared in an evil time when it falleth suddenly upon them (9[12]), and that there is no work, or device, or knowledge, or wisdom in the grave (9[10]). The destiny of man, ending as it does in Sheol, is vanity. Here we discern traces of fatalism, of resignation to an inevitable necessity. Moreover, bearing in mind the Israelite idea of God's peculiar relation to His chosen people, and the relentless spirit of the imprecatory Psalms, we see that the Israelite view of election implies a certain caprice and arbitrariness in the Divine nature. The God of Judaism manifests love and righteousness to His own people, while He leaves the heathen to themselves. Such an arbitrary choice lies upon the Gentiles like an evil doom, which they can do nothing to avert. The idea, promulgated by some of the prophets, that the Gentiles should come to pay homage to Jahweh at Jerusalem, is little more than a religious parallel to that of the political supremacy of Rome and Juppiter Capitolinus. See, further, FATE (Jewish).

(*b*) In *Muhammadanism* the supremacy of omnipotent Will is still more strongly asserted; for, though God is represented as compassionate and just, yet, in face of every attempt to maintain a place for free will, the most rigorously fatalistic doctrine of the Divine omnipotence at length won the day through the advocacy of the Mutaqallim. God being the Creator of all, and indeed, as the Mutaqallim hold, creating the world anew every moment, all freedom is excluded from the world, and man's only course is submission to the will of Allah—*Kismet*. Kismet differs from Fate only in its being referred to an all-powerful Will; all human appeal against either is in vain. Man may follow the law of Allah, but must, none the less, submit to his own destiny; an absolute determinism blights all spontaneity of action, leaving room at best for fanaticism—a phenomenon observed also in the ecstatic dancing of the dervishes, whose frenzies are attributed to Divine possession. Moreover, in view of the fact that the new authoritative doctrine of the non-created character of the Qur'ān, the depository of God's will, proscribes all criticism and clogs all freedom, it is easy to see how in Islām mankind becomes subject to an absolute necessity—even though such necessity is figured as omnipotent Will—and how, in short, the belief in Destiny may still cohere with ethical ideas. The arbitrary will of omnipotence and the blind necessity of Nature thus come eventually to the same thing—the non-moral subjection of mankind to an inevitable necessity. See, further, FATE (Muslim).

2. Fate and Christianity.—Belief in Fate is transcended only when men come to regard themselves as free, as called by the Deity to a responsible moral life, and when the Deity is regarded as ordaining all things in His wisdom and providence, to the end that man may enjoy the liberty of the children of God in a Kingdom of God, so realizing not merely his essential independence of Nature, but his actual lordship over it. Fate, in fact, is transcended whenever dependence upon God becomes the spring of free action, all things being then regarded as necessarily subservient to man's highest interests, and man himself as capable of so utilizing them. Such is, ideally at least, the view held by Christianity, and, accordingly, Christianity repudiates *on principle* all belief in Fate. The Christian religion regards the Supreme Power of the world as a rational Will by which all things are made to promote the ends of the Kingdom. Here omnipotence is not arbitrary, but is one with the all-wise Will; nor is necessity blind, but rational, and likewise identical with the all-wise Will—the Will which always acts as a moral stimulus to the freedom of man. Only when freedom and necessity are recognized as being one in the Deity is it possible for Destiny to give place to Providence; only when man realizes his freedom as that which lays upon him the obligation of self-determination in the sphere of conduct does he cease to resort to the occult arts; and only as he knows that all things can be utilized for the highest ends does he finally break with the idea of Fate. These beliefs, however, constitute in essence the Christian point of view.

Nevertheless, it cannot be said that Christianity is even yet entirely free from the belief in Fate. For one thing, vestiges of the idea have worked their way into Christian doctrine; and, again, traces of it are actually found in Christian practice; while, finally, the Christian world shows a recrudescence of certain theories of the universe which, avowedly opposed to the Christian view, have rehabilitated the belief in Fate in one or other of its forms.

As exemplifying the first of these tendencies we shall speak of Origen and Augustine, the two greatest thinkers of the Patristic period; from the Mediæval period we shall cite Aquinas and Duns Scotus; and from Protestantism, Calvin and Schleiermacher.

i. *Fate in Christian doctrine.*—(1) *Patristic.*—(*a*) In so far as Origen regards the world as originating in a condition where all spiritual beings were of the same sort, and believes that, when the fall of spirits has reached its term, the world will be restored to its primal state, his doctrine is still capable of a Christian interpretation, since, in fact, mankind is being raised, under Divine tuition, from its present sinful condition towards perfection. But, as Origen also conceives of this world-process as eternally recurrent, he does not get beyond the idea of an endless cycle, and thus still retains something of the ancient conception of Fate. Again, while he holds that man may become one with the Divine Logos in virtue of his freedom and his rational nature, thus making Christianity the rational and ethical religion, yet his view of the Father, as supremely exalted above the Logos, and of man's incapacity for perfect oneness with the Father, practically makes God a super-ethical and metaphysical Being. Nor is Origen always consistent in his theory of the relation between the Logos and the Father, the Logos being sometimes spoken of as a natural and necessary efflux from God, and sometimes as a product of the Divine will; and, similarly, God is now the rational Will which reveals itself in the Logos as Love, and now a simple metaphysical Monad, which creates the Logos by natural necessity. This inconsistency repeats itself in Origen's view of the world: now he accepts ἀποκατάστασις, man's final unity with God, while, again, this unity is ceaselessly ruptured by finite free will—the irrational factor in the world. Finally, in Origen's theory it is mere metaphysical caprice which excludes the creature from perfect unity with God and casts him again into the endless cycle of fall and restoration—a process which holds him in its grasp like inevitable Fate itself. The relapse into sacramental magic with which the early Greek Church is sometimes charged is, so far as the charge is valid, attributable to the fact that that Church had not yet fully attained to an ethical conception of God.

(*b*) A similar inconsistency appears in *Augustine.* He interprets God, on the one hand, as a Trinity of conscious loving Will, manifesting itself in the *gratia* of the Holy Spirit, but again, on the other, as a self-identical, metaphysically simple Being; in the last resort, indeed, God is an arbitrary Will, who, precisely as in the Jewish doctrine, elects some out of His mere grace and rejects others. Moreover, God works irresistibly in the elect as an impersonal *gratia*; and, just as these can do nothing to procure their election, so the reprobate likewise are under an absolute decree, shadowed as if by a necessity of Fate, and even children who die unbaptized are consigned to perdition. Such views present us with unmistakable vestiges of the belief in Fate. Further, in Augustine's differentiation of the world from God in virtue of its containing an element of negation which did not originate in Him, we recognize a remnant of the belief in a power antagonistic to God; God is the *summum Esse*, the world the *minus esse.*

(2) *Mediæval.*—(*a*) According to *Aquinas*, God is *purus actus* (pure action) and rational substance, and the world is the stage upon which this rationality is revealed. The world stands in a substantial relation to God, and the Divine reason displays itself in the order, the necessary uniformity, of the world, which forms a whole just because it contains every grade of being, evil itself not excepted. Aquinas, indeed, even maintains that God gives the world a share in His own goodness, His rational existence, though not all in the same degree. Such a view seems to leave no room whatever for Fate, but, in point of fact, Aquinas traverses it by another conception. He holds that the world is differentiated from God by its element of negation, which involves a decrement of substance. Hence, of course, a real union between the human reason and God is possible only by a suspension of this negation. In order, therefore, that man may become one with God, Aquinas introduces a supernatural communication, by which the finite, the natural, the negative, the spontaneous are all annulled in order to make way for the Divine action, as is seen more particularly in the special powers attributed to the sacraments — the channels of Divine grace. Here we recognize an element of dualistic fatalism. As was to be expected, Aquinas makes no mention of Fate, but in this inherent imperfection of things—an imperfection capable of being removed, though only in part, by a supernatural intervention annulling the natural—we may discern traces of a negative anti-Divine power, which, as it is not rational, has something in common with blind necessity, or Fate.

(*b*) On the other hand, *Duns Scotus* premises that God is sovereign and free,—subject to no necessity whatever,—and that the concrete world does not rest upon negation. The perfections of the concrete, in fact, are comprised in God's essence, in the Divine mind and the Divine thoughts, and in these the world can participate. According to Duns, God is a self-knowing, self-affirming, independent, and blessed Will, creating the world voluntarily, and admitting it to a share in His perfections by His voluntary decree. It is the Divine Will alone which determines what kind of perfections the world is to receive, and whether it is to receive them at all; or, in other words, the very existence of the world, the 'that' of the world, depends upon the volition of God. As this Will, however, acts by free choice, the existence of the world is contingent; and this is the real cause of its imperfection. Now, though Duns proceeds to say that God loves the world, and mankind in particular, he traces this love to God's self-love, mankind being, as has been indicated, a sharer in God's own perfection. But in Himself God is all-sufficient, and the very existence of the world remains for Him quite as contingent as the particular character of its structure and order. In His intrinsic essence, therefore, God remains alien to the world, as that which is in its nature contingent.

It also follows from this that man can apprehend the will of God only by revelation through the Church, and must, accordingly, obey the Church's behests. In this contingency of the world we trace once more some residual idea of Fate, for the Divine decree, while emanating from the free sovereignty of God, is, so far as the world is concerned, simply a destiny which it must fulfil. That which for Aquinas is supernatural necessity and negation is for Duns Scotus the arbitrary determination of God, and, consequently, the idea of Fate is not fully surmounted by either.

(3) *Protestant.*—(*a*) The same thing may be said in regard to *Calvin*; nor, indeed, does either Luther or Zwingli differ from him in the matter under discussion. It was Calvin, however, who most consistently developed the fundamental idea, and we may therefore take him as representative, more especially as his view is shared by some theologians at the present day, of whom we may instance Kuyper. It is true that, if we fix our attention upon Calvin's teachings regarding the elect—namely, that God has chosen them in order that they may do His will, that He assures them by His Holy Spirit of their election, that the general grace of God is at work throughout the world, and that, accordingly, secular callings have their rightful place in the Kingdom of God, while the State, as also science and art, may likewise subserve His glory—it may well seem that everything in the nature of Chance or Fate is excluded. But if, on the other hand, we bear in mind that, according to Calvin, everything is subject to the omnipotent Will, and that a certain number of the human race are rejected from the outset, simply because God willed that they should be sinful and should persist in their sin, it is plain that the ethical purpose of God is subordinate to His arbitrary decree. God's *horribile decretum* is thus, so far as the reprobate are concerned, neither more nor less than a Fate from which there is no escape. As, in fact, the Divine decree, once fixed, is carried out with absolute necessity, and as no man can do aught to procure his own salvation unless he is empowered thereto by God, it is clear that Calvin has so far failed to free himself from fatalism.

(*b*) *Schleiermacher* attempts to make good this defect in the doctrine of election by limiting the Divine decree exclusively to the particular time at which an individual shall come to participate in the Christian salvation. He seeks to show that the Divine plan of the world is a unity, and that the communion with God which accords with the nature of man is so realized in Christianity as to become the spring of moral conduct. From this it would appear that his belief in Providence embraces the whole world, and that the entire world-order is illumined by the Divine reason. On the other hand, Schleiermacher's idea of God as the absolute undifferentiated unity of all opposites, and of the world as the sphere in which these opposites fall apart, implies that the world is not only different from God, but permanently imperfect as well. As Schleiermacher has given no definite expression to his view of the world's final purpose, we may fail to observe this lacuna in his thought, but, in point of fact, his philosophy is still burdened with the ancient theory that the world is the realm of negation. The more perfect the world becomes, the more completely must its opposites disappear, and the more nearly must it approximate to the undifferentiated unity of God, *i.e.* cease to be a world at all. Further, the order of Nature, as a product of Divine omnipotence, stands at the centre of Schleiermacher's system, and it is very doubtful whether, on his view, the moral order takes precedence over the natural order and assimilates it, or, on the other hand, the ethical life is not as subject to natural law as Nature itself. In short, neither the metaphysical conception of God as an absolutely simple Being, and of a natural uniformity to which all things are subject, nor the idea that the world's imperfections rest upon its opposites, is calculated to dispel the suspicion of a fatalistic ingredient. Since good and evil, alike in a physical and in a moral sense, have both a necessary place in the world-order, and since the world, on account of its difference from God, is doomed to permanent imperfection by God Himself, its absolute sovereign, the lingering trace of the conception of Fate in Schleiermacher's theory is quite unmistakable.

ii. *Fate in common life.*—It is also obvious that vestiges of fatalism are present in the everyday life of mankind, as, *e.g.*, (1) in the manifold *superstitions* handed down from earlier stages of religion—observance of days, exorcism, astrology, oracles, drawing lots, etc.—as also in the use of amulets, scapulars, images, and miraculous preventives, to all of which magic virtues are ascribed. The same tendency appears in the idea of 'luck' as the condition of success, the underlying thought being that one man is a favourite, and another a victim, of fortune, whether in play or in more serious matters. Such notions are frequently associated with a pleasure-seeking and immoral spirit, as in those who look for success not to their own efforts but to extraneous influences, and are disposed to take what comes with resignation. Similarly, many decline the moral task of deciding questions for themselves, and have recourse to something of the nature of an oracle, which will give a decision by mere chance and without any rational connexion with the matter in hand; or, again, they help themselves out of a practical dilemma by referring to some contingent natural phenomenon which is believed to exert a magical influence, but which has no ethical import at all. The power thus supposed to help or hinder is represented as working, not by rational or moral means, but through the blind mechanism of Nature; while, again, the belief in Providence as applied to ordinary life and practice frequently exhibits traits that really belong to fatalism.

(2) As another instance of the still surviving influence of the belief in Fate we may refer to *poetry*, and in particular to the *drama*, though it is by no means only the dramas of Fate strictly so called which exhibit the feature in question. The dramatist who would portray the tangled skein of life is at no loss for situations in which a blind destiny, a *dira necessitas*, seems to rule. He sees a human being held in bondage by ignorance, and that through no fault of his own; or immured from childhood in a narrow or uncongenial sphere, so that the wing of spiritual aspiration is lamed from the outset. In the drama, again, decisions of the gravest import are often brought about by events that seem purely accidental, so that the individual comes to feel that he is but the plaything of an inexorable power. His very ignorance of the larger concatenation of things prompts the thought that he is in the grasp of a blind destiny. But, even when he is aware of this larger concatenation, he may still feel compelled to bow before an all-ruling necessity, as something actually experienced, and it is this iron sway which the dramatic poet often makes it his task to bring to light. Such an imminent and inexorable necessity, whose causal relations we may so far recognize, though their deeper significance remains inscrutable, must likewise fall under the conception of Fate.

(3) A recrudescence of the conception shows itself also in *certain recent philosophical ideas.* Thus, those who find the sole regulative principle of things in the mechanism of Nature do not seem

very far away from the ancient belief. Herbert Spencer, for instance, if we may judge from the elucidation of his system, sees the necessary causal energy of the Unknowable everywhere in operation, and, while he recognizes a progressive movement in the world as it now is, yet he looks for an eventual disintegration, thus reading, as it were, the inherent destiny of the universe in the merely mechanical cycle of becoming and dissolution. Mention may also be made of the Darwinian theory, in so far as it traces biological phenomena—progress as well as degeneration—to merely mechanical causes, though the actual progress ought to be something more than blind necessity. We may also instance J. S. Mill, who discards the idea of a God at once almighty and morally good, and regards it as most probable that there exists a Superior Being whose purposes of good are constantly thwarted by a hostile necessity—a theory analogous to that of Parsiism, though Mill's representation of the antagonistic power remains quite indefinite. Parallels to these views likewise appear in Germany, *e.g.* in the 'Evangelium der armen Seele.' Again, as a result of the present bias of philosophy towards psychology, with its consequent repudiation of the Ego and the Ego's independent action, and its tendency to explain everything by a psychical mechanism, this mechanism itself has become a kind of Fate, a necessity brooding over all. Finally, if we take as our starting-point the manifold misery of the world, and survey, from the eudæmonistic standpoint, the various forms of evil—the transitoriness of all things and the sufferings associated therewith—we can hardly wonder at the rise of a philosophy which emphasizes the irrationality of existence, traces it to the impulse of a blind Will, and regards the extinction of this Will as the final task of the race. True as it may be that there is, as von Hartmann admits, a relative rationality and purpose in the world, yet, according to the general theory, the world owes its existence to the persistent action of an unconscious volition, *i.e.* Chance, or to blind necessary impulse, the limits of whose action have not been clearly defined by von Hartmann, as there is nothing to show that the extinguished Will may not re-assert itself. In any case it is obvious that this Unconscious Will, as the source of all things, is simply a Fate, a Destiny which cannot be evaded till the Will is brought to extinction. Such is the latest prevalent theory of the universe.

III. *ANALYSIS, INVESTIGATION, AND CONCLUSION.* — From the above outline we see the wide diffusion of the belief in Fate among mankind, and the manifold forms it assumes; we see likewise that vestiges of the belief persist even where a radically different view of the universe prevails, and, further, that the idea is again in various shapes gaining a footing as a kind of reaction to the Christian view. Our survey, however, also indicates that fatalism takes root wherever men regard themselves as subject to an irresistible power thought of as incapable of rational or purposive action. Whether the all-controlling force is figured as immanent or as transcendent, whether it is regarded as a mechanical, physical, unconscious necessity, or is credited with a volition which, though conscious, is absolute and arbitrary in its working—in every case it is to be recognized as inevitable Fate. Fatalism cannot be overcome by the assumption of an omnipotent arbitrary Will represented as supramundane, any more than by a physical pantheism or pan-cosmism; nor is an antidote to it found in the ability to grasp the law of Causality or the order of Nature, so long, at all events, as these are reduced to a mere mechanical necessity enclasping us. Many an absurd superstition may doubtless be dissipated by a knowledge of the uniformity of Nature; but, if in the last resort this uniformity be construed as an aimless necessity enfolding all things, the cramping belief in Fate is not eliminated.

As a matter of fact, the belief can be finally extirpated only by the recognition of a rational Good Will determining the natural order with reference to an end, and harmonizing therewith the law of necessary physical causality. It is, of course, impossible to trace the purposive relations of every phenomenon in the world, and it might therefore appear as if, after all, there were a place for Fate in one or other of its forms. But our inability to trace such a universal purpose in detail does not justify us in denying its existence—so long as we have adequate grounds for admitting the presence of an order in the world as a whole. Moreover, the assumption of such a world-order can be made good only in so far as we abandon the empirical view of things, and recognize that the world is designed to move from one stage of progress to another, and that, in particular, the moral world is intended to consummate the process by means of individual effort upon a basis of Divine action. Considered in this light, every known imperfection in the world will but provide a motive for its own removal, while the knowledge of the contrast between the ideal and the actual, and the consequent perception of defect, furnish an opportunity for ameliorative action. The belief in Fate will, in fact, disappear only as men become convinced that the world has been rationally designed by a rational Will, and that it is their task, as morally endowed beings—as organs of the Divine Will conforming to the plan of Providence—to realize that design.

This brings us, however, face to face with the subjective conditions in which the belief in Fate subsists, and in which, again, its elimination is possible. So long as man feels himself simply impotent in relation to Nature, and thinks of himself as a mere atom in the universal order, he remains subject to Fate, to necessity. So long as he regards his position and his lot as something given, to which he must adapt himself, he cannot rise above the notion of Fate; nor is any deliverance possible, in spite of all attempts to improve his position, so long as he is disposed to eudæmonism, and, consequently, dependent upon circumstances or upon Nature. Eudæmonism, making pleasure the end of life, strikes at the springs of moral energy; it makes man the thrall of the things which promise enjoyment, and which Fate is supposed to bestow or deny. The man who, on the other hand, regards it as his task to realize a Divinely-ordained moral ideal will judge of all things in reference to their possible utility for that purpose. For such an one there exists no blind destiny, no arbitrary will, to paralyze his energy; for him all things are ordered by God with a view to their subserving his Divinely ordained ethical task; and, just because it is God who so orders the world, all thought of an aimless destiny or an arbitrary will is done away. For him no actual state of affairs is unalterably ordained, but every fresh situation is a call to a higher realization of the world's ethical purpose, for which, indeed, the mechanical uniformity of Nature provides the most effective means. For him, too, history acquires a new meaning, its larger canvas showing the progress of man to consist in the fulfilment of his peculiar function, and manifesting the sway, not of a blind destiny, but of Providence. Nor can the existence of evil falsify such a conviction, as the very fact that certain things are reckoned evil evinces the potency of the religious and moral reason which recognizes the ideal, this recognition being, in fact, the first step towards its practical realization. Evil is, therefore, no millstone, no incubus of Fate, weighing down the mind; on the contrary, in the very act of its being overcome it provides a motive for renewed effort and further progress. Of all religions it is Christianity alone which, when rightly interpreted, rings the knell of the belief in Fate.

LITERATURE.—R. Flint, *Anti-theistic Theories*, Edinburgh, 1879; A. M. Fairbairn, *City of God*, London, 1883, Introd. i. 1, ii. 3, iv.; L. D. McCabe, *Foreknowledge of God and Cognate Themes*, Cincinnati, 1878; *Boston Lectures* (1870), i.–v.; F. W. J. v. Schelling, *Syst. d. transcend. Idealismus*, Tübingen, 1800 (*Werke*, Stuttgart, 1856–61, I. iii. 327, 587 f., 603 f.), *Vorlesungen über Methode des academ. Studiums* 3, Stuttgart, 1830, I. v. Lect. 8, p. 286 f.; E. de Pressensé, *Les Origines*, Paris, 1883, Eng. tr. 1883; I. A. Dorner, *System of Chr. Doctrine*, Eng. tr., Edinburgh, 1880–96, §§ 34–37, 65; O. Pfleiderer, *Religionsphilosophie* 3, Berlin, 1896, p. 523 f.; J. Lindsay, *Recent Advances in the Theistic Philosophy of Religion*, London, 1897, chs. 2, 4, 6, 7; P. Le Page Renouf, *Origin and Growth of Religion of Ancient Egypt* (*HL*, 1879), London, 1880, 111 f., 149 f., 180 f., 196 f., 222 f.; F. Lenormant, *La Divination et la science des présages chez les Chaldéens*, Paris, 1875; cf. *SBE* xxv. 'Laws of Manu,' Oxford, 1886, for fatalism among the Brāhmans; A. Weber, *Ind. Studien*, Berlin, 1850–98, i. iv. xiii., 'Zwei vedische Texte über Omina u. Portenta,' *ABAW*, 1858; H. Oldenberg, *Buddha* 5, Stuttgart, 1906, ii.; Rhys Davids, *Buddhism* 18, London, 1899; K. Simrock, *Handbuch der deutschen Mythologie* 6, Bonn, 1887, ii. no. 60, 162 f.; C. Orelli, *Allgemeine Religionsgesch.*, Bonn, 1899, p. 362 f.; C. P. Tiele, *Gesch. d. Religion im Alterthum*, Gotha, 1895, I. II. i. ii.; A. Sprenger, *D. Leben u. d. Lehre d. Mohammad* 2, Berlin, 1861–69, ii. 300 f.; J. H. Plath, 'Religion und Cultus der alten Chinesen' (*Abhandl. d. Akad. zu München*, 1862); E. J. Eitel, *Feng-Shui, or The Rudiments of Natural Science in China*, London, 1873; F. Spiegel, *Erân. Alterthumskunde*, Leipzig, 1871–78, ii.; Orelli (as above), 547, 562; J. G. Müller, *Gesch. der amerikanischen Urreligionen*, Basel, 1855, pp. 148 f., 230, 394 f., 654 f.; W. R. Smith, *Rel. Sem.* 2, London, 1894; Oldenberg, *Religion des Veda*, Berlin, 1894, pp. 195 f., 476 f., 287 f.; for *Ṛta*=Parsi *Asha*, see Tiele, *op. cit.* ii. 142 f., 188 f.

A. DORNER.

FATE (Babylonian).—By the Babylonians and Assyrians the abstract conception of Fate or Destiny was never personified as a separate deity, whose nature and attributes might be cited as evidence in this connexion. But they possessed a special word for 'Fate' (*šîmtu*), and it is desirable to establish as accurately as possible the senses in which the word was used. Apart from such direct evidence it is clear that in Bab. thought a conception of Fate or Destiny may have existed which was not peculiarly associated with the word *šîmtu*, or at any rate may not have left its traces on the context of extant passages in which the word happens to occur. Our inquiry thus falls into two main sections. In the first we shall examine the use and precise meaning of the word *šîmtu*, 'fate'; in the second it will be necessary to inquire whether at any period we may legitimately recognize traces of a fatalistic conception in Bab. popular beliefs or philosophical speculation. The latter inquiry will be the longer of the two, as it touches some points around which a considerable amount of controversy has gathered during recent years.

1. The word *šîmtu*, pl. *šimâti*, derived from the verb *šâmu*, 'to establish,' 'to determine,' is the feminine of the participle *šîmu*.[1] It properly has a passive meaning, 'established,' 'determined,' but in a few passages referring to the *šîmtu* of some of the greater gods it is clearly used with an active meaning, in the sense of 'the act of determining the fate or lot.'[2] From the fact that in its passive sense the word is sometimes used as a synonym for 'death,' it might seem at first sight that death, and, consequently, the length of life were events which were decreed from the beginning. That care should be taken before drawing such a conclusion is suggested by a very interesting passage in the Cylinder-Inscription of Sennacherib, in which the premature death of Kudur-Nankhundi, king of Elam, is said to have taken place by the command of Ashur on a day which was not his *šîmtu*, or pre-ordained fate.[1] From this passage it is clear that *šîmtu* was not an irrevocable destiny, since, at any rate in Kudur-Nankhundi's case, it could be overridden by the special decree of Ashur, the national god of Assyria. By whom then was the *šîmtu*, or 'fate,' determined, which could apparently be altered at will by the head of the pantheon? A study of the Bab. mythology enables us to answer the question with some degree of confidence.

In the legends the power of controlling the fates or destinies of all the gods, in other words, the various departments and sections of the universe, was symbolized by the possession of certain magical tablets, known as the *dupšîmâti*, or 'Tablets of Fate.' In the Bab. Creation-legend, when the monster Tiâmat, after the defeat of her consort Apsû, appointed Kingu the leader of her host, she gave him the Tablets of Fate and laid them on his breast: the Tablets were not merely the symbol of authority, but in themselves conferred the power to rule. So, too, the first act of Marduk, after the conquest of Tiâmat and her host, was to take from Kingu the Fate-Tablets, seal them, and place them on his own breast.[2] It is clear that he did this in order to acquire the power inherent in the Tablets which Kingu had hitherto enjoyed. The magical character of the Tablets and the manner in which their mere possession conferred supreme power upon the holder are well illustrated by the legend of the storm-god Zû, which recounts how he stole them from their rightful owner, Enlil, the god of Nippur.[3] The privileges their possession conferred may be gathered from Zû's soliloquy when contemplating the theft:

'I will take the Fate-Tablets of the gods, and the oracles of all the gods will I direct; I will establish my throne and dispense commands; I will rule every one of the Spirits of Heaven!'

The legend relates how Zû waited for the dawn at the entrance of the hall where Enlil dwelt. And, while Enlil was pouring out the clear water for his morning ablution, Zû swooped down and seized the Fate-Tablets which Enlil had laid aside with his diadem and other insignia on the throne beside him. Zû made off with the Tablets to his inaccessible mountain, where he enjoyed the power they conferred until the Sun-god caught him in his net and recovered them for Enlil.

From these passages in the mythology it is clear that the ultimate arbiter of the fates of gods and men was the chief of the gods, and that he enjoyed his power by virtue of the Fate-Tablets which he possessed. But it is not to be inferred that the Fate-Tablets had any independent existence or any power apart from their possessor. It is also clear that they did not in any sense resemble a Book of Fate, for the whole future was not recorded unchangeably upon them: nor have we any evidence that the Divine holder of the Tablets recorded his decrees upon them from time to time. They appear to have been merely magical insignia, which enabled the god who held them actively to control and mould the course of events. The legends which have been recovered concerning them arose at a period when the Bab. pantheon was already in existence, and the owner of the Tablets, and hence the ultimate arbiter of Fate, was the head of the pantheon. Originally this god was Enlil of Nippur, who retains his early privilege in the legend of Zû; with the rise of Babylon to power Marduk usurps

1 For references to the principal passages in which the word occurs, see F. Delitzsch, *Assyr. HWB*, Leipzig, 1896, p. 653 ff.; and Muss-Arnolt, *Concise Dict. of the Assyr. Language*, Berlin, 1905, pp. 1052 f., 1065 f.

2 Such an expression, for instance, as *šîmatka la šanân seḳarka Anum*, 'Thy *šîmtu* is without rival, thy word is (that of) Anu!' (Creation-series, Tabl. IV. line 4; cf. L. W. King, *Seven Tablets of Creation*, London, 1901, i. 58 f.), where *šîmtu* is paralleled by *seḳru* ('word,' 'command'), proves that the former could be used with an active meaning.

1 The phrase is *ina ûm lâ šîmtišu*; cf. Rawlinson, *WAI* i. (1861) pl. 41, col. v. line 2.

2 Cf. King, *op. cit.* i. 20 f. and 74 f.

3 Cf. E. J. H rper, *Beiträge zur Assyriologie*, ii. (Leipzig, 1894) 409 ff., 467 ff.

the attributes of Enlil, and in the Creation-series in its present form we are told how he became possessed of the Fate-Tablets. In Assyria, on the other hand, Ashur, the national god, inherited in turn the attributes of the supreme Bab. deity—among them the most important being the power to decree fate.

2. From an examination of the uses of the word *šimtu*, and of the legends which refer to the Fate-Tablets, it would seem that, at any rate in popular belief, the fates, both of the universe and of individual gods and men, were not believed to have been fixed from the beginning, but were pictured as in hourly process of development under the personal supervision of the supreme deity. It remains to inquire whether, apart from these legends and beliefs, we may trace evidence that the Babylonians of any period conceived of Fate as an impersonal and inexorable law. To answer this question it will be necessary to refer briefly to one aspect, the so-called 'Astral Theory,' of the Bab. religion, which was elaborated in Germany a few years ago and still retains a considerable following in that country. For upholders of the theory claim that belief in a fixed Fate or Destiny, both of the universe and of the individual, did enter largely into Bab. thought of all periods, including even the pre-historic age.

Perhaps the most characteristic feature of the theory is that, according to the Bab. conception of the universe, everything on earth was a copy of a heavenly prototype. It is well established that the Babylonians, like the Hebrews, conceived the universe as consisting of three parts—the heaven above, the earth beneath, and the waters under the earth. Winckler, the chief exponent of the astral theory, and his followers elaborate this conception of the universe, and would trace in the threefold division of the heavens a parallel to the earth. Thus they would divide the universe, according to their view of Bab. beliefs, into a heavenly and an earthly world, the latter's three divisions (the heaven being confined to the air or atmosphere immediately above the earth) corresponding to the northern heaven, the zodiac, and the southern heaven. The important point to note is that in these threefold subdivisions the zodiac and the earth occupy the second place and correspond to one another. Thus the movements of the sun, the moon, and the five great planets (which are visible to the naked eye) through the ecliptic constellations were held to have a peculiar connexion with events on earth. It is a fact that in the later Bab. period the greater gods were identified with the planets and the lesser gods with the fixed stars, each god having his special house or star in heaven in addition to his temple on earth. By analogy the astral theory assumes that everything on earth had its equivalent in heaven, lands and cities in addition to temples all having their cosmic counterparts. The movements of the stars were, according to the theory, related to events on earth much as a moving object seen in a mirror is related to its reflexion. Their movements were the cause of events on earth; but the movements themselves were not the arbitrary acts of independent deities. They took place in accordance with a cosmic law of harmony, inherent in the universe, and ordained from the beginning of creation. For a further mystical conception is ascribed by the astral mythologists to the Babylonians: that, as the part may be held to correspond in essence to the whole, so any single phenomenon of the universe was believed to reflect the whole in miniature. The course of the world-cycle, for example, was reflected in the struggle of the dual powers of Nature, in light and darkness, in summer and winter, in cold and heat. Moreover, as the succession of day and night may be held to correspond to the changes of the seasons, so the year itself corresponded to greater cycles of time, consisting, on the one hand, in ages of the world during the historic period, and, on the other, in æons of the world-cycle. Thus, according to these mystical doctrines, which are ascribed by the upholders of the astral theory to Babylonians of all periods, every occurrence in both the heavenly and the earthly halves of the universe may be said to have taken place in obedience to the symmetrical but inexorable laws of Fate or Destiny.

It would be out of place in the present article to do more than indicate briefly the false assumptions on which this theory rests. Most theories of interpretation have some historical basis to rest upon, and in making generalizations of this magnitude it is usual to support them by reference to texts of ascertained date. It is characteristic of the representatives of the astral school to do without such aids. Since the inscriptions which have actually been recovered do not in themselves furnish the necessary support for their thesis, they plant the roots of their theory in a purely imaginary age where evidence for or against it is *ex hypothesi* lacking. Thus the oldest monuments that have been recovered upon Bab. sites are not regarded by them as relics of the early stages of Bab. culture. It is assumed that in the periods behind them there existed a most elaborate and highly developed civilization, described as pre-historic and lying back in the darkness beyond the earliest existing records. In the total absence of material evidence it is no difficult task to paint this age in colours which are shared by no other early or primitive race in the world's history. It is assumed that war and violence had no existence in this pre-historic time. Intellect dominated and controlled the passions of this primeval but highly gifted people, and, in particular, one form of intellectual conception, based on a scientific knowledge of astronomy. It is postulated that a purely astronomical theory or conception of the universe lay at the root of their civilization and governed their whole thought and conduct; and this was no secret teaching of a priesthood, but a universally held belief which permeated every branch of the national and individual life. These doctrines in their perfect state perished with the other relics of their supposed pre-historic inventors. But they were inherited by the Semitic immigrants into Babylonia; and, though employed by them in altered and corrupted forms, have, it is said, left their traces in the cuneiform inscriptions. In this way the astral mythologist attempts to explain the unsatisfactory character of his evidence, from which he claims to be able to reconstruct the original beliefs in their entirety. So involved are they in the conception of an inexorable Fate or Destiny of the universe that, according to the upholders of the astral theory, the earliest Babylonians claimed to be in a position to foretell the future in its broader aspects. For it is asserted that they believed themselves able, by a mystical application of a remarkably accurate knowledge of astronomy, not only to disclose the origin of the world from its birth, but also to foretell its renewal in future æons.

To find evidence for their theory the astral mythologists are naturally obliged to rely on texts which have come down to us from the historic period. Assuming the close correspondence between the zodiac and the earth in early Bab. thought (an assumption to which reference has already been made), it is argued that the Babylonians divided the course of the world's history into Ages according to the particular sign of the zodiac in which the sun stood each year at the vernal equinox. This is a most vital point of the theory, and it postulates on the part of the early Babylonians a highly accurate knowledge of astronomy; it assumes a knowledge on their part of the precession of the equinoxes, which could be based only on a very rigid system of astronomical observation and record. The course of Bab. history, from the pre-historic period onwards, was thus divided, according to the theory, into three Ages—those of the Twins, the Bull, and the Ram—according to the sign of the zodiac in which the sun stood at the vernal equinox. Certain myths are supposed to have characterized each of these Ages, not only affecting religious beliefs, but so impregnating Bab. thought that they even influenced historical writings. As the sun at the vernal equinox gradually progressed through the great ecliptic constellations, so, according to the theory, the history of the world was believed to be evolved in harmony with its course, and the pre-ordained Fate of the universe was slowly unrolled.

It will be unnecessary to point out in detail the arbitrary and fanciful system of interpretation which the astral mythologist is forced to apply to his texts in order to make them fit his theory. It will suffice to summarize the damaging criticism which the theory has sustained at the hands of an astronomer,[1] by which its supposed astronomical basis has been completely demolished. In the first place, it may be noted that there is no evidence that even the later Babylonians had a sufficiently accurate system of measuring the heavens to enable them to arrive at a knowledge of the precession of the equinoxes. But in complete independence of this fact, and assuming such a knowledge on the part of the Babylonians of all ages, Kugler has shown that the inferences elaborated from the assumption by Winckler and his school do not follow. It is well known that the different ecliptic constellations which make up the signs of the zodiac do not each occupy thirty degrees of the ecliptic, but that some are longer and some shorter. Also the constellations of the Bab. astronomers during the late periods do not completely coincide with ours. For instance, the most eastern star of our constellation Virgo was counted by the Babylonians of the Arsacid era as belonging to the next ecliptic constellation, Leo, since it was known as 'the hind foot of the lion.' But, fortunately for our purpose, not much doubt can exist as to the eastern limit of the Twins and the western limit of the Ram, which mark the beginning and end of the three World-Ages of the astral mythologists; for the two bright stars, Castor and Pollux, from which the Twins receive their name, were undoubtedly reckoned in that constellation by the Babylonians, and the easternmost star of our constellation of the Fishes (*α Piscium*) was probably well beyond the Bab. constellation of the Ram. Working on this assumption, and assigning thirty degrees to each of the three intervening constellations, Kugler has calculated the years in which the sun entered these signs of the zodiac at the vernal equinox. He is consequently able to state accurately the years in which Winckler's World-Ages would have begun and ended, and his figures entirely dispose of all Winckler's claims to an astronomical basis for his astral system. The Age of the Twins, instead of ending, as Winckler and his followers hold, about 2800 B.C., really ended in the year 4383 B.C. Thus the Age of the Bull began fifteen hundred years before the birth of Sargon I., who is supposed to have inaugurated its beginning, and it ended considerably before the birth of Ḫammurabi, under whom, we are told, the Bull-Age *motifs* were principally developed. Moreover, from the time of the Ist dynasty of Babylon onwards, down to the year 81 B.C., that is to say, during the whole course of her history, Babylon was really living in the Age of the Ram, not in that of the Bull. In short, all the *motifs* and myths which have been so confidently and with such ingenuity connected by the astral mythologists with the Bull sign of the zodiac, ought really to have been connected with the Ram. But even the astral mythologists admit that there is not a trace of a Ram *motif* in the Bab. mythology.[2] Granting all Winckler's assumptions with regard to the astronomical knowledge of the Babylonians, the theory is found not to stand investigation: his astronomy is at fault, and his three astrological World-Ages do not really correspond with his periods of history. It follows that the Babylonians did not divide the history of the world into astral Ages, and all grounds for the further assumption as to their conception at an early period of a world-cycle, evolved through a succession of æons, in accordance with an inexorable Fate or Destiny, are thus removed.

It remains to inquire whether in the later periods of Babylonian history we may not recognize a fatalistic conception in priestly, as opposed to popular, belief. The evidence of Diodorus, Philo of Alexandria, and other writers may certainly be cited in favour of ascribing to the later Chaldæan priesthood the teaching of a religious and cosmic system closely associated with the idea of an impersonal Fate or Destiny. But their evidence is certainly not applicable to any period earlier than the Seleucid era, where it is impossible to separate the nucleus of native tradition from the essentially different form it assumed under Hellenic influence. It is certain that the gradual advance in the Babylonian knowledge of astronomy from the 8th cent. B.C. onwards prepared the way, in the Achæmenian period, for the recognition of law in the heavens as opposed to the earlier conception of a universe under the arbitrary rule of personal deities swayed by human passions. But it is doubtful whether the Babylonian astrologers themselves ever evolved a conception of Destiny, as existing apart from the gods, except under the direct influence of Greek speculation.

To sum up the results of our inquiry: it is probable that at no period much earlier than the Seleucid era had the Babylonians any conception of Fate or Destiny as a blind, impersonal, and inexorable law, whether as applied to the universe or to the individual. In their belief the fate, whether of a man or of a country (which was usually the limit of their speculation), was not irrevocably fixed, but was in continual process of development, under the supervision of the most powerful deity known to them at the time. In the earliest period the city-god was for his worshippers the unchallenged arbiter of fate; but, with the growth of a federation of cities and the accompanying development of a pantheon, his place was naturally taken by the head of the pantheon—at first Enlil of Nippur, but afterwards Marduk of Babylon; and in Assyria, Ashur, the national god. Before the Hellenistic period, Fate was never dissociated in Babylonian belief from the personal direction of the gods, and, when once it had been decreed, it was still capable, in extreme and exceptional cases, of modification.

LITERATURE.—For collections of passages from the inscriptions in which the Bab. word for 'Fate' occurs, see the references cited on p. 778ᵃ, n. 1; and for passages bearing on the subject in the Bab. mythology, see p. 778ᵇ, notes 2 and 3. The best and most detailed criticism of the so-called 'astral theory' of the Babylonian religion is Kugler's *Im Bannkreis Babels*; and for scientific information on Bab. knowledge of astronomy, see the other works cited on p. 780ᵃ, n. 1.

LEONARD W. KING.

FATE (Buddhist).—To Oriental thought in general, and more especially to a mind trained in Buddhist doctrine and possessed by the teaching and preconceptions of Buddhist ethics, the idea of Destiny or Fate presents itself in an entirely different aspect from that to which Greek mythology or philosophy has given currency in the West.

[1] See F. X. Kugler, *Im Bannkreis Babels*, Münster, 1910. Cf. also C. Bezold, 'Astronomie Himmelsschau und Astrallehre bei den Babyloniern' (*Sitzungsberichte der Heidelberger Akademie der Wissenschaften*, 1911, Abh. 2). For a scientific survey of the astronomical knowledge of the Babylonians, see especially Kugler's *Sternkunde und Sterndienst in Babel*, Münster, 1907–1912; and cf. also his *Die babylonische Mondrechnung*, Freiburg im Br. 1900, and Ernst Weidner, *Beiträge zur babylonischen Astronomie* (= *Beiträge zur Assyriologie*, viii. 4, Leipzig, 1911). Jastrow's *Die Religion Babyloniens und Assyriens*, ii. 415–748 (Giessen, 1909–1911), contains a detailed description of much of the astrological material.

[2] According to Winckler's system, the Age of the Ram did not start till about the 8th cent. B.C., being inaugurated by a fresh revision of the calendar under Nabonassar. But no amount of ingenuity can discover material for a Ram *motif* at Babylon. The nearest approach to one is found in the Libyan desert: Jupiter Ammon is represented with the head of a ram, and he is assumed to have been identical in his nature with Marduk. Thus the new reckoning is supposed to have passed over to Egypt, while Babylon remained unaffected and continued to enjoy 'Bull *motifs*.' The only explanation put forward is that the Age of the Ram began at a time when the power of Babylon was on the decline. This example of constructive theorizing is quite typical of the ease with which the astral mythologist is capable of clearing the most stupendous obstacles.

'Fate,' in the sense of an external compelling power, with universal sway and irresistible decrees, is a conception entirely alien to the fundamental principles of either of the great schools of Buddhist thought, and is opposed to the exhortations to personal effort and strife in order to win salvation which in the sacred books the Master is constantly represented as uttering. The disciple of the Hīnayāna works out his own deliverance by his own unaided toil and self-discipline; and, as none can help, so none can hinder in the great task. The kindlier and more liberal creed of the Mahāyāna puts at the disposal of the seeker after truth and rest supernatural and effective aid, whereby his feeble endeavours may be seconded and supported, and brought to certain fruition. In either case the issue of life depends ultimately upon the individual, the determining factor being his own will and moral purpose, and neither is the result foreordained nor is he himself the plaything or helpless victim of an omnipotent force which he can neither influence nor resist.

The place which Fate or Destiny occupies in the systems of Greek and European philosophy and theology is in the East taken by *karma* (*q.v.*). *Karma*, however, implying action with all its results or 'fruits,' so far from being an extraneous and all-compelling force which exercises over the course of human life an irresponsible control that cannot be gainsaid or resisted, is the self-caused and internal constraint of the deeds of the individual in his transient existences upon earth. He is himself his own fate, in that he receives now the due and deserved recompense for what he has himself done, be it good or evil. And his life proceeds, not on lines determined for him from above or from without, but on lines which he has himself marked out and continues to mark out with irrevocable certainty and exactness, as long as a life of fruitful activity is prolonged. Only when his actions cease to bear 'fruit' is the control broken, the power of *karma* rendered ineffective, and he himself set free. Between the conception of 'Fate,' therefore, as defined in the teaching of Greece and the West, and its Buddhist and Eastern counterpart, there is a profound difference as well as a substantial likeness. In both the power is absolute, dominant, and irresistible; its movement can neither be stayed nor turned aside. In the former, however, man has nothing to say to it; he can only bow his head and submit. Fate regulates the course and issue of all, and man can only make the best of his own hard case. According to the scheme of thought of the East, man orders his own destiny. Once determined, it is in each part and at each moment as rigorous and unbending as the most absolute pronouncement of the Fates. What is done cannot be undone; the effect remains, and must be realized in the form of reward or suffering in his own personal experience and life. He may, however, or rather he must, by his own actions and conduct determine what his future shall be. Its course and conditions are entirely laid down by himself. When these have been, as it were, prescribed, they have passed beyond his control and are unalterable and irrevocable. But the future is in his own hands. At each moment by his deeds he is shaping his own destiny. The moulding thereof for good or for evil rests entirely with himself. He ordains and directs his own fate, which is then inexorable and self-operative. All his life long he is under the dominion of *karma*, and cannot escape from its effects.

In a wider cosmical sense it may be said that the conception of Fate prevailed in Buddhism, inasmuch as Buddhist doctrine took over from Hinduism the conception of world-cycles, succeeding one another as the acts of an indefinitely prolonged drama of birth, florescence, decay, and death (cf. AGES OF THE WORLD [Buddhist]). From the Buddhist point of view, each cycle was characterized by the renewed preaching of the true doctrine, which was more or less widely accepted amongst men, ran its course, and then fell into neglect with the increasing prevalence of unbelief and wickedness, and finally disappeared. In each cycle a Buddha is born, who gains for himself illumination and perfect knowledge of the truth, which he then proclaims to the world. But the truth prevails only for a limited period, and is succeeded again by times of ignorance and darkness, dispelled in their turn by a fresh revelation. Thus Gautama, the Buddha of this age, has been preceded by an indefinite number of earlier Buddhas, who in succession taught the Law.[1] He himself prophesied of the end of the present cycle, which would be accompanied by the total disappearance of all knowledge of the truth; thereafter Maitreya, the Buddha of the coming age, would appear upon the earth, would attain to perfect insight and wisdom, and in due time would restore the true doctrine to mankind.[2]

The series of world-cycles, therefore, is independent of human will and endeavour, and so far corresponds to a conception of Fate, relentless and almost mechanical, with supreme and absolute control of the destinies of all, moving forward resistlessly to a predetermined end. The doctrine, however, is purely cosmical, and does not concern itself with the career or fate of the individual, except in so far as the latter may chance to have been born at an age propitious or otherwise for attending to the preaching of a Buddha. This last event, of course, the time and place of his birth within the cycle, like all the other circumstances and conditions of his life, is controlled by *karma*. His existence is comprised, as it were, within the world-scheme, as an item or element in its progress. But it contributes nothing to its determination, and cannot affect its course. The revolution of the ages, the rise and fall of the true teaching, the destruction and resuscitation of the universe, repeat themselves within assigned and unalterable limits, without cessation, and apparently without conceived or conceivable beginning or end.

It would appear, therefore, that from the Buddhist point of view Destiny or Fate, as it affects the individual, is practically equivalent to a theory of strict and determinate causation, the merit or demerit of his own actions resulting in a proportionate increase of freedom and happiness, or involving him in renewed tribulation and punishment. Moreover, both of the great schools, the Mahāyāna and the Hīnayāna, taught the possibility of deliverance or redemption from the power of *karma*, in the attainment of *nirvāṇa*, the state in which actions are performed without desire or 'clinging,' and therefore do not entail any resultant consequences which must be worked out in a renewed existence. In practice, especially in the Mahāyāna, *nirvāṇa* came to be equivalent to paradise or heaven; but it was originally attainable and attained here upon earth during the mundane life. And the broad difference between the doctrines of the two schools consisted in this, that in the endeavour to reach the goal, and to secure final release, the adherent of the Hīnayāna found himself dependent upon his own unaided exertions;

[1] Eighty-one of these, for example, are enumerated in the *Sukhāvatī-vyūha* 3, beginning with Dīpaṅkara, 'long ago in the past, in an innumerable and more than innumerable, enormous, immeasurable, and incomprehensible *kalpa* before now.' Elsewhere predecessors of Dīpaṅkara are named (*Jātaka*, i. 43). Gautama is said to have 'received recognition' from twenty-four of these.

[2] See art. BUDDHA, vol. ii. p. 885

no external aid was either available or possible, and in the most absolute sense of the term he must work out his own salvation. The Mahāyāna, on the contrary, conceived of a hierarchy of supernatural beings, the *Bodhisattvas* (*q.v.*), who were ever willing and able to bring help in the strife; by whose aid man might rise, when his own strength would fail. The entire cycle, however, of human existence, thus regulated in each individual instance by *karma*, was carried out and completed within the larger cosmical cycle, in which *karma* had no meaning or place. The latter proceeded in a fixed and determined order, through æons upon æons of time. It represented, upon the broadest possible scale, the Buddhist or rather Indian conception of a mechanical and all-controlling Destiny, to which the entire universe was subject, alike in its origin, its progress, and its dissolution.

LITERATURE.—For the general literature, see art. KARMA. Cf. *Dhamma-Saṅgaṇi*, iii. 1, tr. C. A. F. Rhys Davids, in *Buddhist Psychology*, London, 1900, pp. 123–155; *Abhidhammattha-Saṅgaha*, v. 8, tr. Shwe Zan Aung, *Compendium of Philosophy*, London, 1910, p. 143 ff.; H. C. Warren, *Buddhism in Translations*, Cambridge, Mass., 1896, pp. 215–221, 226–233, 481–486; D. T. Suzuki, *Outlines of Mahāyāna Buddhism*, London, 1907, p. 196 ff.

A. S. GEDEN.

FATE (Celtic).—As among all imaginative and superstitious peoples, the belief in Destiny was strong among the Gaels. The whole of life was regarded by them as encompassed and ruled by an over-mastering Fate, from which there was no possibility of escape. In the older literature we find constant expression given to this belief.

'If it be here that I am fated to die, I have no power to shun it,' says Diarmaid in the tale of the 'Pursuit of Diarmaid and Gráinne.' 'It is profitless to fly from death; and, though I should avoid the battle, flight never yet saved a wretch,' says Congal before the fatal battle of Magh Rath (ed. O'Donovan, Irish Arch. Soc., Dublin, 1842). 'There are three periods of time that cannot be avoided—the hour of death, the hour of birth, and the hour of conception' (*ib.*). In an old poem attributed to St. Columba we get the same idea of the fixity of Fate:

'When once the fixed period of death arrives,
There is no fortress which can resist it; . . .
But the fortunate in life are protected
Even in the fore-front of a battle . . .
Whatever God has destined for a man
He leaves not the world until he meet it'
(ed. O'Donovan, *Miscel. Celtic Soc.*, Dublin, 1846).

In like manner, the Gaulish tribe of the Cadurci, when reduced to extremity by Cæsar, thought that what was happening was not by the act of man, but by the will of the gods (*de Bell. Gall.* viii. 43. 5).

Though this sense of fatality is as old as pagan times, it is probable that it has rather developed than been checked by Christian teaching. The passivity of mind and the inertia which mark the life of the Gaelic and Breton peasant arise largely out of this feeling that both the good and ill of life lie entirely outside of his control; his stoic acceptance of evil and death rests upon the same idea. The legends and folk-tales both of Brittany and of the Gaelic-speaking peoples are filled with the same overpowering sense of fatality. Connected with this are the omens of death or ill-luck which we find penetrating all Celtic literature, and which are universally believed in at the present day; and, again, the belief in lucky and unlucky days and hours. In the old medical treatises, the cross or unlucky days are set down in order, and in Christian times Biblical events were made to coincide with the days or hours of pagan observance. It was customary to consult a Druid or soothsayer as to the lucky moments for beginning a journey, battle, or other undertaking.

King Dathi requires his Druid to 'let him know his destiny and that of his country,' for a twelvemonth from that day (O'Curry, *MS Mat.*, Dublin, 1861, p. 284). Before the campaign of the Táin bó Cúalnge, the host were kept waiting a fortnight until a good omen was obtained (*Leabhar na hUidhre* [*LU*], 55*a*), and at the muster of the Hill of Slane or Slemain of Meath in this same story the onset is held back until the lucky moment of sunrise (*Leabhar Laignech*, or Book of Leinster [*LL*], 101*a*). Again, Cúchulainn was bound to be famous if he took arms on a particular day (*ib.* 64*b*); and a child, if not born before a certain day foretold by the Druids, would become a great king (S. H. O'Grady, *Silva Gadelica*, London, 1892, ii. 354). Lucky and unlucky days have great prominence given to them in the Coligny Calendar (J. Rhys, 'Celtæ and Galli,' in *Proc. of the British Academy*, London, 1905).

Regular horoscopes were drawn at critical moments in a chief's career (Battle of Magh Lena, ed. O'Curry for the Celtic Soc., 1855). Omens were obtained by means of various Druidical rites. Chief of these was *imbas forosnai*, or the 'knowledge which illumines,' which was gained through a magic sleep, and was associated with offerings to idols. The means of inducing this sleep of incantation is elaborately described in Cormac's *Glossary* (ed. Whitley Stokes, London, 1862, p. 94). Sometimes this knowledge seems to have been obtained by looking into a crystal. The prophetess Fedelm, who declares that she has knowledge of this art, is asked by Queen Medb to 'look for her' what will be the fate of her expedition. Then the maiden 'looked for it,' apparently into a ball or crystal (*LU* 55*b*). Another heathen method of divination was known as *teinm læghda*, which enabled an inquirer to discover such matters as to whom the body of a headless corpse belonged (Cormac's *Glossary*, p. 130). Both these methods of divination are said to have been suppressed by St. Patrick, on account of the idol observances with which they were accompanied (*ib.* p. 94 f.; *Senchus Mór*, vol. i. [Dublin, 1868] pp. 24, 44), but he permitted the use of a means of foresight known as *dicetal dochennaib*, which was gained from some incantations made with the finger-tips, and was not accompanied by offerings to idols. Instruction in these arts formed part of the regular course of the fully-equipped *file*, or Druid of the higher ranks (cf. art. COMMUNION WITH DEITY [Celtic]). At times the decision as to who was to be elected king was reached by Druidical revelation gained in sleep, after a 'bull-feast' (*Bruighen dá Derga*, ed. Stokes, 1902, pp. 14, 15). The stone on which the kings of Ireland were crowned at Tara was called the *Lia Fáil*, or 'Stone of Destiny,' because it was believed to cry aloud when the rightful heir stepped upon it. In the before-mentioned poem, or 'Lorica,' attributed to St. Columba, several means of divination are mentioned as practised by Druids:

'Our destiny is not with the *sreod*,
Nor with the bird on the top of the twig,
Nor with the trunk of the gnarled tree,
Nor with a *sordan*, hand on hand . . .
I adore not the voice of birds,
Nor a *sreod*, nor a destiny, nor this earthly world,
Nor a son, nor chance, nor woman;
My Druid is Christ, the Son of God.'

In an old historical poem relating to the settlements of the Cruithne, or Irish Picts, in Alba (Scotland), among the kinds of divination taught by evil Druids and necromancers were:

'The honouring of *sredhs* and omens,
Choice of weather, lucky times,
The watching the voices of birds,
They practised without disguise . . .'
(Irish Nennius, ed. J. H. Todd, Irish Arch. Soc., 1848, p. 145).

The exact significance of some of these terms of divination is not known, but the word *sreod* is equated with *sén* or *séon*, 'good omen' or 'luck,' in various passages; and in MS Laud, 615, p. 7, we read: *ni h-ág sreoid atá mo chuid*, 'not for me is the luck of the *sreod*.' *Séona-saobha* means 'augury,' or 'sorcery'; and in *LL* 101*a* we read of the 'power of the *séon* and of the *solud*,' *nert don t- séon agus don solud*—evidently omens of good-fortune. A lucky moment is called *séon* in *LU* 55*a*, and *sén* in *LL* 64*a*. It is possible that the *sredh* or *sreod* may be connected with *sraod* or *sraoth*, 'sneezing'—a form of augury known in early times, and frequently condemned by

Synods. See, further, CELTS, vol. iii. p. 300, and DIVINATION (Celtic), vol. iv. p. 787.

The sense of Destiny surrounding each person of importance is expressed in the old tales by means of tabus (called in Irish *gessa* or *geasa*), usually laid on him at birth, and which, when his doom is about to overtake him, are broken through by him, one by one, against his own will, foreshadowing evil. Many of the Irish *gessa* were, no doubt, real tabus actually imposed upon kings and chiefs. We possess a complete tract giving the restrictions which had to be observed by the provincial kings of ancient Ireland (*Leabhar na g-ceart*, ed. O'Donovan for the Celtic Soc., Dublin, 1847, pp. 1–25); but they are used in the old romantic tales, with the definite poetic purpose of representing the unescapable decrees of Destiny. They have all the Greek sense of over-mastering Fate. They are usually, especially the birth-tabus, laid on the hero at birth; but any one seems to have had the power of inflicting them, and they appear to have been equally binding, however they were imposed.

In the story called 'The Tragical Fate of the Sons of Usnach,' the tabu of Fergus to refuse a feast resulted in the death of the three brothers; in the 'Pursuit of Diarmaid and Gráinne,' the death of the hero was due to his neglect of his tabu 'never to hunt a boar'; the breaking of the *gessa* laid upon the boy Conla by Cúchulainn resulted in the slaying of the son by his own father.

Elaborate *gessa* were laid on each of the chief heroes of the older, or Cúchulainn, cycle of tales (see CÚCHULAINN CYCLE), and it is in the gradual and inevitable breaking down of these *gessa* that the tragedy of their doom consists. The approaching end of each, and especially of the central figure of Cúchulainn himself, is surrounded by omens (cf. art. CELTS, in vol. iii. p. 300, § 6). In the Ossianic tales, especially the more recent of them, less stress is laid upon the breaking of tabus, but great prominence is given to the omens of sickness or death, such as the howling of dogs, clouds red like blood, and foreboding dreams (Trans. of the Ossianic Soc.). These signs are still regarded as sure forewarnings of a fatal catastrophe.

Another remnant of a very ancient superstition is the belief that 'banshees,' or female fairies (see DEMONS AND SPIRITS [Celtic]), foretold by their wailings near a house the death of an inmate. The banshee is usually the early pagan goddess of the district which she haunts, but she appears as a weeping woman, mournfully bewailing the expected death. Many families have their own special banshees who always appear before a death in the family. Sometimes, instead of the presiding genius of the country, some woman who has met an accidental death acts the part of the banshee, and is heard crying and moaning. There are examples of the appearances of banshees in the old historical literature.

Queen Aoibhill of Craig Liath, the presiding goddess of Clare and banshee of the Dalcassian race, appears to King Brian Boromhe before the Battle of Clontarf to forewarn him of his death (*War of the Gaedhil with the Gaill*, ed. J. H. Todd, London, 1867, p. 201). The same goddess has been seen in recent times attended by twenty-five other banshees of Clare before an impending disaster.

In many of the ancient tales this forerunner of death takes the form either of a beautiful but weeping maiden or of a gruesome and monstrous hag, who is found in the path of a host going to battle, or of a chief who is doomed to death, stooping over a stream, washing and wringing bloody garments and weapons. She is called the 'washer of the Ford,' and she informs the doomed man or host that it is their own bloody garments that she is wringing out.

As late as 1318, Richard de Clare and his Norman troops met this hideous figure, 'washing armour and rich robes till the red gore churned and splashed through her hands,' when they were on their way to plunder the O'Deas of Dysert. She tells Richard that she is come to invite him to join her among the tribes of Hell. Next day Richard and his son and host lay dead upon the field near the fort of Dysert.

A similar superstition is that of the 'death's coach,' with headless driver and black or headless horses which, if it passes by a house or through a village, must not be stopped on its way. If it meets with any impediment or draws up at a door, some one is sure to die next day within the house. These beliefs are firmly held in all parts of Ireland, and many apparently authenticated cases are recorded of such events actually happening within recent times (*FL* iv. [1893] 352, x. [1899] 119, 122; T. C. Croker, *Fairy Legends*, London, 1870, p. 250). In Brittany the same superstition exists; the 'Coach of the Ankou' is driven by a figure who is the personification of death, imagined as tall and lean with long white hair, or as a skeleton whose head turns about every way inspecting the country. His coach resembles a funeral cart with tandem-horses, and he is escorted by two companions walking beside the cart, who open the gates of fields or the doors of houses and pile the dead upon the vehicle. The 'Ankou' is the last person who has died in each parish during the year, and is replaced at the end of twelve months by a successor (A. le Braz, *La Légende de la mort*, new ed., Paris, 1902, i. 95–99).

LITERATURE.—This has been given in the article. Cf. also the literature appended to art. DEMONS AND SPIRITS (Celtic).

ELEANOR HULL.

FATE (Chinese).—**1. Definition of the term.**—The Chinese equivalent for 'fate,' viz. *ming*, like the original of our English word, means primarily 'something spoken or decreed.' It is composed of the radical for 'mouth' and the symbol for 'law' or 'commandment,' the latter supplying the place of phonetic as well as supplementing the force of the radical. As *fatum* in philosophical language represents the eternal, immutable law of the gods, so *ming* is interpreted as the appointment of Heaven, the unalterable decree which determines man's lot; it is often used as synonymous with 'life'—regarded as the span of existence, whose limits are irrevocably fixed, so that a long *ming* is but another name for long life. To 'calculate the ming' is to forecast one's fortune. Owing to the fact that the term is sometimes applied in connexions which seem to admit of a variety of interpretations, some difference of opinion exists as to whether the Chinese should be described as fatalists, but it may be said without hesitation that the weight of evidence is in favour of such a description. It may be sufficient to note, with regard to the contrary view, that there are circumstances under which it may be possible, according to Chinese theories, to escape one's destiny, which might seem to imply that *ming* was not considered as invariable; but it will be found, on investigation, that in such cases apparent failure of the decree was of the nature of a deprivation of the gifts which Heaven had in store, in consequence of the unwillingness or unworthiness of the intended recipient to receive or retain them, rather than malfeasance on the part of Heaven. From this point of view it might seem that man is regarded as the potential master of his destiny, but, on the other hand, it must be borne in mind that, though he may fail to realize, or deliberately reject, the high position marked out for him by fate, he may by no means attain to a higher station than that which is destined for him.

2. Classical references.—In the Confucian classics the term *ming* frequently occurs, though, as we are informed, it was one of the subjects on which the Master was characteristically reticent. The word is sometimes qualified by the addition of 'Heaven,' *i.e.* 'Heaven's decree'; and sometimes 'Heaven' alone stands for the *decree of Heaven*. The two terms are often found in apposition, as in the statement, 'Death and life have their determined appointment (*ming*), riches and honour depend upon Heaven.'

When a disciple named Po Niu was visited by Confucius, and found to be hopelessly ill, the Master said: 'It is the appointment (*ming*) of Heaven, alas!' The expression is frequently used with regard to the ancient rulers: 'Heaven decreed him the throne.' Again, we read of the 'superior man,' the Confucian ideal, as 'waiting, quietly and calmly, for the appointment of Heaven,' *i.e.* his destiny, in contrast with the 'inferior man' who 'walks in dangerous paths looking for luck.' In another passage Confucius says: 'Without recognizing the decree it is impossible to be a "superior man."' He frequently refers to destiny as influencing his own life, *e.g.*: 'Heaven produced the virtue that is in me'; 'At 50 I knew the decree of Heaven'; 'While Heaven does not let the cause of truth perish, what can the people of Kw'ang do to me?'; 'If my principles are to advance, it is so ordered; if they are to fall to the ground, it is so ordered (*ming*)'; 'Heaven is destroying me.'

From statements such as these it may be argued that, to the mind of the Sage, *ming* meant very much what we mean by destiny or fate: something which he recognized as actively operating in the determination of man's lot, but which he refused to discuss or analyze, regarding it, in common with spiritual beings and other extra-mundane phenomena, as beyond the pale of controversy.

3. Mencius.—The philosopher Mencius agrees with Confucius in regarding *ming* as Heaven's decree, in his references to the ancient 'Emperors' Yao and Shun; and quotes passages from the *Odes* to the effect that 'God, having passed the decree, caused the descendants of Shang to submit to the new dynasty of Chow.' When the prospect of obtaining preferment was suggested to him, he replied, in the words of Confucius: 'That shall be as Heaven directs.' He speaks of Heaven's gift of the kingdom to Shun, though he does not describe it as resulting from *destiny*, but rather as the demonstration of Heaven's will by Shun's personal character and achievements. His pronouncements on the subject are much looser than those of Confucius, since he speaks in one place of calamity and happiness as being in all cases of man's own seeking, and endeavours to illustrate his theory by a quotation from the *Odes*: 'Study always to be in harmony with the ordinances (*ming*), so you will certainly get for yourself much happiness'; and again, in a passage from the *Canon of History*: 'When Heaven sends down calamities, it is still possible to escape from them; when we occasion the calamities ourselves, it is not possible any longer to live.' There is a further explanation in a later phrase of his: 'That which is done without man's doing is from Heaven, that which happens without man's causing it to happen is from the ordinance (*ming*).' There is, therefore, a destiny decreed for every man, 'there is an appointment (*ming*) for everything,' and it is possible for each man to 'establish his destiny,' or fail to realize the favours which Heaven wills to bestow on him. An early and apparently untimely death may be ascribed to destiny, if encountered in the honourable discharge of one's duty; but a disgraceful death cannot be so attributed. Men should calmly await the fate which is decreed for them; but, should they place themselves in needless danger, they may entail upon themselves a 'fate' which is not of Heaven's appointment.

Destiny and Nature are closely associated in some passages of Mencius, and seem to reflect what is said in ch. i. of the *Doctrine of the Mean*: 'What Heaven has conferred (*ming*) is called Nature,' the idea being that Heaven has decreed an ideal destiny for man, and his success or failure in realizing that destiny represents the extent to which his nature is in harmony with the ideal. He may attain to the highest honours, if such are indicated to him by the understood will of Heaven, as in the case of the ancient rulers; or he may, like some of them, be condemned, by his own moral delinquency, to surrender the powers and dignities to which, humanly speaking, his former virtues entitled him. His ideal destiny may assign him a potential longevity, which he may reject by voluntary suicide. It is only when his nature is cultivated so as to correspond with the ideal that he can fulfil his ideal destiny. He discovers his destiny by performance of the eternal law of Right, and thus Mencius, when asked 'Did Heaven confer its appointment on Shun with specific injunctions?' replied 'No, Heaven does not speak, it simply showed its will by his personal actions and conduct of affairs.' By this means Shun was declared to be 'the man after God's own heart,' by the conferring of the Imperial dignity upon him.

The ideal destiny is limited or determined, in the sense that none can reach a higher standard than that appointed for him. In the case of some, that appointed limit may not permit him to rise above the lowest levels of human attainment; in other cases it may allow the happy recipient to secure the position of 'assessor with the Deity.' A recent pronouncement by a Confucian writer states that 'Confucius emphatically denies that all men may be made good' (Lim Boon Keng, in *China*, Jan. 1912, p. 515). Man may represent an early stage in the evolutionary process which, in course of time, may produce a sage; but, in his own person, he can have no hope of reaching that proud position, though he may rejoice in the privilege of advancing the process by strict attention to the limited sphere of his own responsibilities. He may, on the other hand, inherit a noble destiny, and not only fail to attain it, but by his failure retard the evolutionary process, and bring about a condition of atavism.

4. The Chucian school.—The reticence of Confucius with reference to *ming* gave his later expositors the opportunity of elaborating theories of their own; and their materializing tendencies are reflected in the *Doctrine of the Mean*, attributed to Tsze-sze, a grandson of Confucius, who was also, to a great extent, the inspirer of Mencius. A further development is observable in the writings of Chu-hsi (Chucius) (A.D. 1130–1200), who depraves Destiny by explaining it as meaning simply Nature, and Nature as equivalent to Principle, whether existing in the natures of men or beasts. In other words, men and beasts inherit their individual natures, which constitute each of them a law unto himself; but, since Nature, or Principle, may become deflected, an outside standard is necessary for correction of morals, viz. *Tao*, or 'the Way'; and *Kiao*, or 'instruction,' which is furnished by sages and teachers. It should be borne in mind that Chucius was largely influenced by Buddhistic opinions, and that the doctrine of *karma*, no doubt, affected his treatment of the subject; and, since Chucius is admitted to be the most popular exponent of the Confucian school at the present time, it is not surprising that the Chinese should be represented as thorough believers in fatalism. To the latter fact has been credited the universal traffic in astrology, fortune-telling, clairvoyance, mesmerism, necromancy, palmistry, physiognomy, the planchette, and the use of nostrums and charms, all with a view to discovering and influencing one's destiny. For, though the Chinese may sometimes appear to disclaim belief in a predestined and irrevocable fate, and express contempt for the methods by which an equivocal decree is supposed to be adjusted or evaded, it is evident, from many expressions in common use, that they are obsessed with the idea that an unalterable fate attends certain courses of action, and that the only way to obviate that destiny is to refrain from entering upon such courses; and thus the ignorant masses, who cannot attain to that state of enlightenment where individual destiny is understood, flock to the charlatans who profess to lift the veil which hides the future, so that the inquirer may learn the fate which threatens him, and take steps to escape it.

5. Historical illustrations.—Chinese history, especially in its earlier periods, abounds in references to the Decree by which kings reigned, and which was unalterable so long as individuals and dynasties exhibited that congruity with the will of Heaven which justified their appointment and established their fortunes.

An early instance is supplied in connexion with the tripods of Yü (2205–2197 B.C.), of which it is said: 'Their weight depended upon the virtue of the man who endeavoured to lift them. If it was slight, they were heavy and immovable; but if great, they were as light as a feather.' These tripods were given, it was believed, 'by the direct interference of Heaven . . . and none could possess them except by its will.' Fu-kien, king of the State of Ts'in (4th cent. A.D.), said, with reference to the methods suggested for the repression of a suspected rebel, 'To whomsoever Heaven has decreed to give the kingdom, that man shall have it, and not all the wisdom or might of this world can prevent it.' In the following century Siau-tau, a military commander under Ming-ti, was generally regarded 'as a man whom Heaven seemed to have destined for a throne'; and the chronicles of the time show that, in spite of the machinations of the court against him, he ultimately succeeded in founding the dynasty of Ts'i, over which he ruled with the title of Kau ti. During an outbreak of plague in Shensi, at the end of the 6th cent., so great a condition of panic was created that the sick were utterly abandoned by their relatives through fear of infection, and confidence was not restored until Sin-kung, the local governor, having cared for the afflicted in his own residence, gave them back to their relatives when convalescent, with the words, 'Life and death are in the hands of Heaven. Why are you afraid of infection?' When the consort of Ta'i-tsung was about to die (A.D. 637), she heard that steps were being taken to secure the prolongation of her life by an appeal to Heaven, and, calling her son, the prime mover in the matter, to her bedside, said: 'Our life is in the hands of Heaven; and, when it decides that we shall die, there is no mortal power that can prolong it.' The Emperor Ta'i-tsung himself, at a later period (A.D. 645), in view of the disasters which menaced his throne, proposed a general massacre of the ladies of his *harim*, because it was prophesied that from amongst them a queen should arise who would exterminate the royal house of T'ang; but he was dissuaded from adopting such a course by Li-fung, who assured him that the coming events were ordained by Heaven, and that, though he might destroy every individual in the palace, It would raise up another to carry out Its sovereign will. When Chang Shih-kieh, a faithful general of the Sung dynasty (A.D. 1280), was threatened with shipwreck, he refused to save himself by attempting to beach his ship, saying, 'When one Emperor perished, I set up another; he also has disappeared; and now to-day I meet this great storm; surely it must be the will of Heaven that the Sung dynasty should perish.' Noorhachu, the founder of the Manchu dynasty (A.D. 1616), assumed the name of Ti'en Ming='By decree of Heaven,' as his royal title on the establishment of the new dynasty.

6. Proverbial references.—The Chinese view with regard to the interposition of Destiny, as illustrated in the preceding, is confirmed by the everyday language of the people. 'All is Destiny' is a phrase which is constantly heard. 'Tum, tum, tum, life is fixed,' is a proverb which represents the strumming of the fortune-teller's guitar, and expresses the futility of man's efforts to change his lot. 'Nothing proceeds from the machinations of man, one's whole life is planned by Destiny,' conveys a similar lesson. Other common phrases thus express it:

'If it is your fate to gain wealth, you will at last possess it: if it is your fate not to have wealth, do not use violence to get it.' 'If fated to have sons, what matters it early or late?' 'A man's disease can be cured, but not his fate.' 'Ill-gotten gains will not enrich those whose fate it is to be poor.' 'Planning matters pertains to man, completing matters pertains to Heaven.' 'Man contrives, Heaven decrees,' *i.e.* 'Man proposes, Heaven disposes.' 'Heaven decrees happy unions,' *i.e.* 'Marriages are made in Heaven.' 'Everything depends on Heaven and Fate, and not on man.' 'All the plans of man are unequal to the one fixed determination of Heaven.'

7. Popular literature.—The doctrine of Fate in works of fiction is well illustrated in such selections from Chinese literature as *Strange Stories from a Chinese Studio* (see Lit. below); and the 'Book of Fate' is frequently referred to as being consulted in order to discover the terms of one's lease of life.

The inevitableness of Fate is tacitly accepted by the Chinese people, and finds constant illustration in their otherwise inexplicable carelessness in the control of fire, which sometimes devastates enormous areas; the neglect of proper precautions against flood, which has been known to inundate whole counties; and similar remissness in connexion with the outbreak of 'plague, pestilence, and famine,' or even personal afflictions, such as abnormal growths or deformities. The whole tendency of Taoism, which, though sadly depraved by its modern representatives, is, nevertheless, a powerful influence among the thinking classes, may well be described as fatalistic, inculcating, as it does, that absolute compliance with the *Tao*, or 'Course of Nature,' which precludes the stirrings of ambition, and deprecates all restless striving in the direction of self-advancement, whether by virtue of one's individual merits, or by sedulous attention to the desires of the higher or even the highest powers, including the gods themselves.

In conclusion, it may be said that, on this subject, as in the case of many others, the Chinese appear to be able to harmonize what might seem to Westerners to be conflicting and contradictory opinions. They express belief in an unalterable destiny, and yet speak of the possibility of evading that destiny, of a fate which is unaffected by outside agencies, whilst at the same time they seek by every means to anticipate the decree by recourse to horoscopes, fortune-tellers, etc. The explanation is supplied by the theory that the debased may surrender the good fortune in store for them, for Heaven has the right to annul a destiny which proves to be too good for its intended recipient. The ignorant may be unaware of the destiny which Heaven intends for them, and thus neglect to qualify for their predestined lot. Only complete sincerity can attain to the foreknowledge of Heaven's appointment: only he who fashions his life in accordance with 'the Way' can hope to gain the highest places which beneficent Heaven has to bestow. Death is unalterably fixed in the case of all men, and this belief gives rise to that extraordinary resignation with which the Chinese accept the death penalty; but one's lot in life is, to a large extent, in one's own hands; happiness may be secured, and calamity averted, by living in accordance with *Tao*, as set forth in the Confucian classics; for, as the proverb says, 'If Heaven should weary my body, I must set it off by putting my heart at ease.'

LITERATURE.—J. Legge, *Chinese Classics*, London, 1861; J. MacGowan, *Hist. of China*, do. 1897; H. A. Giles, *Strange Stories from a Chinese Studio*, do. 1909; J. Doolittle, *Social Life of the Chinese*, New York, 1867; A. H. Smith, *Proverbs and Common Sayings of the Chinese*, Shanghai, 1888, also *Chinese Characteristics*, New York, 1900.

W. GILBERT WALSHE.

FATE (Egyptian).—The Egyptians had a very definite notion of Fate or Destiny, which was personified as the deity Shai. The word for 'destiny,' *šau*, later *šai* (*shai*), is derived from the verb *ša*, 'decide,' 'define,' the German *bestimmen*; *šai*, therefore, ='was bestimmt ist,' as in the verse, 'Es ist bestimmt in Gottes Rath, Dass man vom Besten was man hat, Muss scheiden, ja scheiden'; *šai*='what *must* be,' unavoidable Fate. We find it in this sense always: even the heresy of Akhenaten did not deny Fate, and the word occurs in the inscriptions of his high priest Merir'a at el-Amarna (1370 B.C.). A prominent example of its use is in the inscription of Amasis describing the overthrow of Apries at Momemphis (560 B.C.):

'The land was traversed as by the blast of a tempest, destroying their ships [*i.e.* those of the Greek allies of Apries], abandoned by the crews. The [Egyptian] people accomplished their fate [that of the Greeks]; killing their prince [Apries] on his couch, when he had come to repose in his cabin.'

Naturally, unavoidable fate was regarded as evil fate, and *šai* can mean this without qualification. In the 'Israel-Stela' of Merenptah (1230 B.C.), which records the ravaging of Palestine by the Egyptians and the destruction of Israel, the word is 'determined' by the ideograph of a devouring dog: an evil animal was destiny!

Death was the destiny of all, whether the rich man who built himself a pyramid of granite, or the poor *fellaḥ meskīn* who died of heat and labour on the canal-dyke or *gisr*, with none but the fish to see him die. It was an evil destiny, death, and, when one thought upon it, one was disturbed, and tears came to the eyes; the very thought of death was pain and grief; never would one come back from the tomb to see the sun. So said his soul to 'Tired-of-Life' in the curious dialogue translated by Erman; but the man himself, seeking rest from the wickedness of the world, saw in death no evil fate, but rather a glorious one, since, when dead, he would become a 'living God,' who would accompany R'a in his sun-ship through the sky, all-seeing and all-knowing, and able to punish evil-doers. So 'Tired-of-Life' rebuked his soul, and so the common fate of man appeared to the religious, then as now, rather a good than an evil destiny, and 'That-which-must-be' (*šai*) was deprived of his terrors. He ceased to be the Devourer, and became, instead, the Benefactor. Shai now appears, in late times, as a popular deity in the form of a serpent, the animal which had become the emblem or image of any and every deity otherwise unprovided with an animal-form. For religious reasons connected with the idea of death, as mentioned above, and for euonymous reasons too, no doubt, Destiny gradually comes to be regarded as a beneficent rather than a maleficent demon, and eventually in Roman times develops into the good angel of mankind and is translated into Greek as Ἀγαθοδαίμων. When the priests wanted to call the Emperor Antoninus Pius 'the good genius of Egypt,' they wrote *p-šai n Kemet*, which to their predecessors of a thousand years earlier could have meant nothing but 'the evil destiny of Egypt'! At Dendūr in Nubia the local god Petisis is similarly called *p-šai Enthūr*, 'the Ἀγαθοδαίμων (not the Μοῖρα) of Dendūr.' It is in his capacity of protecting dæmon that we find the serpent Shai, wearing the crowns of a Pharaoh and bearing the *caduceus* of Hermes and the *thyrsus* of Dionysos (a true type of the *Mischkunst* of the time), represented on either side of the inner doorway of the great family catacomb at Kom esh-Shuḳafa at Alexandria, which dates from the 2nd cent. A.D. In the 3rd cent. magical papyri we find Shai as the *agathodæmon*, the spirit of good rather than of bad luck: in a love-charm he is invoked as 'the great Shai who makes magic for the great (goddess) Triphis, the lady of Koou.' Triphis (*t-ripe(t)*), 'the princess,' was a form of Hathor, the goddess of love, who also from the earliest times had been connected with the idea of Fate: 'the seven Hathors' foretell the destiny of a child at its birth as early as the Vth dynasty. The name of Shai was now very popular in compound personal appellations: thus we find *Senpsaïs* ('Daughter of Shai'), *Tapsaïs* ('She who belongs to Shai'), *Petepsaïs* ('He whom Shai hath given'), and so forth. As the Good Spirit, he was now regarded as watching over the safety of the crops, and appears as a male counterpart of the corn-goddess Ernute (Thermuthis). Such is the history of an Egyptian godling. By this time the word *šai* had probably lost entirely its original signification of 'what is determined,' 'destiny unavoidable.' It does not occur in this sense in Coptic, in which ϣⲁⲩ (*šau*) means 'good,' 'pleasant,' 'proper,' thus preserving rather the altered and later agathodæmonic signification of the word.

LITERATURE.—On the derivation of the word *šai*, see H. Brugsch, *Hierogl. Wörterb.* Leipzig, 1867–82, Suppl. p. 1219; on the divinity, *Book of the Dead*, ch. cxxv.; *Book of Traversing Eternity* (ed. E. v. Bergmann, Vienna, 1877, l. 73, 46, n. 69); G. Steindorff, *ZÄ*, 1890, p. 51; and H. R. Hall, *PSBA* xxvii. (1905) 87–89, where references to inscriptions quoted are given, except that of Amasis (Daressy, *RT* xxii. 1 ff., tr. Hall from Daressy's Egyp. text in *Oldest Civilization of Greece*, 1901, appendix, p. 323 f.; J. H. Breasted, *Anc. Records*, Chicago, 1906–07, iv. 996 ff.) and the 'Dialogue of the Man Tired of Life with his Soul,' for which see A. Erman, 'Gespräch eines Lebensmüden mit seiner Seele,' *ABAW*, Tübingen, 1896. For Shai in the magical papyri, see F. Ll. Griffith, *Stories of the High Priests of Memphis*, Oxford, 1900, p. 54; Griffith and Thompson, *Magical Papyrus of London*, London, 1909, p. 185. On the Hathors, see A. Erman, *Die Märchen des Papyrus Westcar*, Berlin, 1891.

H. R. HALL.

FATE (Greek and Roman).—Fate is the counterpart of Fortune (*q.v.*). They are two ways of looking at life; both are essentially connected with man. From the point of view of Fortune all is indeterminate; from the point of view of Fate all is determined. And Fate, like Fortune, attains to deity before our eyes during the course of Greek literature. From the first the idea of a predetermined order of destiny in the affairs of man was present to the mind of Hellas, and was fostered by the belief in oracles. 'Fatum a fando,' says Augustine (*de Civ. Dei*, v. 9). Fate is by derivation 'that which has been spoken,' with the implication that it shall be fulfilled. The nearest verbal equivalent to this in Greek is τὸ χρεών, since that is connected with the appropriate word for the answer of an oracle; cf. Eur. *Hipp.* 1256:

οὐδ' ἔστι μοίρας τοῦ χρεών τ' ἀπαλλαγή.[1]

But there is a great variety of ways in which the idea of Fate may be expressed in Greek: *e.g.* αἶσα, αἴσιμον, αἴσιμον ἦμαρ, μοῖρα, μόρος, μόρσιμον, τὸ μόρσιμον, μόρσιμον ἦμαρ, αἰὼν μόρσιμος, μοιρίδιον ἆμαρ, εἵμαρται, εἵμαρτο, εἱμαρμένον, ἡ εἱμαρμένη, πέπρωται, πέπρωτο, πεπρωμένον, πεπρωμένη μοῖρα, ἡ πεπρωμένη, κήρ, κῆρες, δαίμων.

1. Homer.—The idea of Fortune (τύχη), as Macrobius (*Sat.* v. 16) has pointed out, is unknown to Homer, but not so the idea of Fate. The latter is everywhere present both in the *Iliad* and in the *Odyssey*, though the three Fates as mythological persons are not yet to be found. Μοῖρα in Homer is always singular, except in *Il.* xxiv. 49:

τλητὸν γὰρ Μοῖραι θυμὸν θέσαν ἀνθρώποισιν.

Μοῖρα is the abstract noun from μείρεσθαι, so that the idea underlying it is that of some Power which apportions to man his destiny. We may conjecture that the same meaning attaches also to Αἶσα, which is used convertibly with Μοῖρα:

Il. vi. 487 f.: οὐ γάρ τίς μ' ὑπὲρ αἶσαν ἀνὴρ Ἄϊδι προϊάψει·
μοῖραν δ' οὔτινά φημι πεφυγμένον ἔμμεναι ἀνδρῶν.
Od. v. 113–115: οὐ γάρ οἱ τῇδ' αἶσα φίλων ἀπονόσφιν ὀλέσθαι,
ἀλλ' ἔτι οἱ μοῖρ' ἐστὶ φίλους τ' ἰδέειν καὶ ἱκέσθαι
οἶκον ἐς ὑψόροφον καὶ ἑὴν ἐς πατρίδα γαῖαν.

Αἴσιμον occurs in *Il.* xxi. 291:

ὡς οὔ τοι ποταμῷ γε δαμήμεναι αἴσιμόν ἐστιν,

and αἴσιμον ἦμαρ in *Il.* viii. 72, xxi. 100.[2]

Μόρος stands to Μοῖρα in the relation of effect to cause, and is therefore less liable to personification:

Il. xix. 421: εὖ νύ τοι οἶδα καὶ αὐτὸς, ὅ μοι μόρος ἐνθάδ' ὀλέσθαι.

An example of μόρσιμον is *Il.* v. 674 f.:

οὐδ' ἄρ' Ὀδυσσῆϊ μεγαλήτορι μόρσιμον ἦεν
ἴφθιμον Διὸς υἱὸν ἀποκτάμεν ὀξέϊ χαλκῷ,

and of μόρσιμον ἦμαρ, *Il.* xv. 613; *Od.* x. 175. νῦν δέ με λευγαλέῳ θανάτῳ εἵμαρτο ἁλῶναι occurs in *Il.* xxi. 281 and in *Od.* v. 312.

Πέπρωται and its cognates come from the root πορ-, which means 'provide,' and so convey the same idea as μόρος of something predetermined.

Il. xviii. 329: ἄμφω γὰρ πέπρωται ὁμοίην γαῖαν ἐρεῦσαι.
Il. iii. 308 f.: Ζεὺς μέν που τόγε οἶδε καὶ ἀθάνατοι θεοὶ ἄλλοι,
ὁπποτέρῳ θανάτοιο τέλος πεπρωμένον ἐστίν.

[1] Cf. *Herc. Fur.* 311; *Elect.* 1301; *Iph. Taur.* 1486; *Bac.* 515.
[2] Cf. oracle of Bacis, in Herod. ix. 43.

In *Il.* xvi. 441 f. (=xxii. 179 f.) *πεπρωμένον* is used of the victim of fate, meaning 'foredoomed'—

> ἄνδρα θνητὸν ἐόντα, πάλαι πεπρωμένον αἴσῃ
> ἂψ ἐθέλεις θανάτοιο δυσηχέος ἐξαναλῦσαι;

Κήρ and Κῆρες represent Fate on its sinister side, and so are generally associated with death.

Il. xxiii. 78 f.: ἀλλ' ἐμὲ μὲν κὴρ
ἀμφέχανε στυγερή, ἥπερ λάχε γεινόμενόν περ.
Il. xvi. 687: κῆρα κακὴν μέλανος θανάτοιο.
Il. ii. 834: κῆρες γὰρ ἄγον μέλανος θανάτοιο.
Od. xi. 171: τίς νύ σε κὴρ ἐδάμασσε τανηλεγέος θανάτοιο;

Hence *κήρ* is sometimes used simply in the sense of death, as in *Il.* i. 228, ii. 352, iii. 32—a sense in which it is personified in *Il.* xviii. 535:

> ἐν δ' Ἔρις, ἐν δὲ Κυδοιμὸς ὁμίλεον, ἐν δ' ὀλοὴ Κήρ.[1]

Δαίμων has affinities with both Fortune and Fate.

Od. x. 64: πῶς ἦλθες, Ὀδυσεῦ; τίς τοι κακὸς ἔχραε δαίμων;
Od. xi. 61: ἆσέ με δαίμονος αἶσα κακὴ καὶ ἀθέσφατος οἶνος.

To derive it from *δαίειν* in the sense of 'divide,' 'distribute,' brings it into line with the conceptions already treated of.

In the *Iliad* there are a number of expressions, such as *ὑπὲρ μοῖραν* (xx. 336), *ὑπὲρ μόρον* (xx. 30, xxi. 517), *ὑπέρμορα* (ii. 155), *ὑπὲρ αἶσαν* (vi. 487, xvi. 780), *καὶ ὑπὲρ Διὸς αἶσαν* (xvii. 321), *καὶ ὑπὲρ θεόν* (xvii. 327), which seem to imply that man could on occasions overpass Fate. But except in xvi. 780—

> καὶ τότε δή ῥ' ὕπερ αἶσαν Ἀχαιοὶ φέρτεροι ἦσαν—

we are never told that he does overpass it. The rest of the passages are conditional, and some god always steps in in time to save the credit of Fate. The one passage, then, which runs counter to the rest may either be set down as hyperbolical or referred to the same range of thought as displays itself in the *Odyssey* (i. 32–36), where a sort of compromise is effected between Fate and free will. Some evils, we are led to suppose, come from the gods, whereas there are others which men bring upon themselves by their own infatuation—for instance, the death of Ægisthus. This is a sound judgment, to which common sense responds. There are sorrows against which no wisdom or virtue can guard, while there are others which are clearly traceable to one's own fault. But even in the *Iliad* the fatalism of the poet is not rigid, but admits of alternatives. Had Patroclus heeded the warning of Achilles, he would have escaped the evil fate (*κῆρα*) of black death (xvi. 685 ff.); and Achilles himself has an alternative destiny—death and immortal glory at Troy or an inglorious old age at home (ix. 410–416).

As men in the *Iliad* are often on the verge of transgressing Fate, so Zeus now and again entertains thoughts of setting it aside, but never actually does so. He sheds tears of blood over his own son Sarpedon (xvi. 431–461), but leaves him to his fate; he pities Hector, but does not save him (xxii. 168–185). The public opinion of the skies is against such an example. Fate is after all *Διὸς αἶσα*, and Zeus is true to himself. Even when he has been entrapped into an oath by Hera, he keeps it, though to his own cost (xix. 95–133). The general attitude of Zeus is shown by the impartial way in which he holds the scales of battle (viii. 69–74, xxii. 209–213), leaving the fates (*αἴσιμον ἦμαρ*) of the combatants to decide the matter by their own weight, the heavier to go down to Hades. Vergil has caught the Homeric spirit when he says (*Æn.* x. 112 f.):

> 'rex Juppiter omnibus idem.
> Fata viam invenient.'

It was the metaphor of spinning the web of destiny to men at their birth which brought into being the mythological persons called the *Μοῖραι*. But the gods in Homer do the work of Fate themselves. Zeus does the spinning in *Od.* iv. 207 f.:

> ᾧ τε Κρονίων
> ὄλβον ἐπικλώσῃ γαμέοντί τε γεινομένῳ τε.

More often it is done by the gods generally, as in *Il.* xxiv. 525 f.:

> ὣς γὰρ ἐπεκλώσαντο θεοὶ δειλοῖσι βροτοῖσιν
> ζώειν ἀχνυμένοις,

and in *Od.* i. 17, iii. 208, viii. 579, xi. 139, xx. 196. In *Od.* xvi. 64, however, the gods are relieved of the task by *δαίμων*:

> ὣς γάρ οἱ ἐπέκλωσεν τά γε δαίμων,

in *Il.* xx. 127 f. by Αἶσα:

> ὕστερον αὖτε τὰ πείσεται ἅσσα οἱ Αἶσα
> γεινομένῳ ἐπένησε λίνῳ, ὅτε μιν τέκε μήτηρ,

and in *Il.* xxiv. 209 f. by Μοῖρα:

> τῷ δ' ὥς ποθι Μοῖρα κραταιή
> γεινομένῳ ἐπένησε λίνῳ, ὅτε μιν τέκον αὐτή.

We have only to pluralize this in order to get the Μοῖραι, and towards this we are helped by *Od.* vii. 196 f.:

> ἔνθα δ' ἔπειτα
> πείσεται ἅσσα οἱ αἶσα κατὰ κλῶθές τε βαρεῖαι
> γεινομένῳ νήσαντο λίνῳ, ὅτε μιν τέκε μήτηρ.

So far then Homer has brought us. There are stern spinning-women who spin to men their destiny at birth.

2. Hesiod, etc.—By the time of Hesiod these stern spinsters have been supplied with the appropriate names of Κλωθώ, Λάχεσις, and Ἄτροπος, having reference severally to the thread of life, to allotment, and to inevitability. It is now definitely their function to dispense good and ill to mortals at their birth; cf. *Theog.* 218 f.:

> αἵτε βροτοῖσι
> γεινομένοισι διδοῦσιν ἔχειν ἀγαθόν τε κακόν τε.

Thus Zeus is relieved of the great responsibility which we find imposed upon him in *Il.* xxiv. 527–532.

As the Fates have now become persons, we expect to hear of their genealogy. But the accounts are conflicting. When they are first introduced to us in the *Theogony* (211–219), we are told that they are the daughters of Night without a father. But on a second mention (901–906) we learn that they are the daughters of Zeus and Themis, and held in the highest honour by their wise-counselled sire. Plato, who is a prose-poet, makes them daughters of Necessity (*Rep.* 617 C). Cicero (*de Nat. Deor.* iii. § 44), following 'the old genealogists,' makes Night the mother of the *Parcæ*, but supplies them with a father in Erebus. According to the Orphic theogony, as represented in Athenagoras (18 B), Clotho, Lachesis, and Atropos were daughters of Heaven and Earth, and sisters of the hundred-handed giants and of the Cyclopes.

Hesiod (*Theog.* 215–222) mentions the Μοῖραι in such close connexion with the Κῆρες that what is said of one may be intended to apply to the other. Now what is said of the Κῆρες would serve for a description of the Furies:

> αἵ τ' ἀνδρῶν τε θεῶν τε παραιβασίας ἐφέπουσαι,
> οὐδέποτε λήγουσι θεαὶ δεινοῖο χόλοιο,
> πρίν γ' ἀπὸ τῷ δώωσι κακὴν ὄπιν, ὅς τις ἁμάρτῃ.

In this way a connexion might seem to be set up at starting between the Fates and the Furies; and it is worth noting that Pausanias (ii. 11. § 4) mentions incidentally how at Sicyon the same rites were paid to the Fates as to the Furies. There was a one day's festival every year with a sacrifice of sheep with young, a libation of mead, and flowers, but not garlands.

The fact that the Fates are essentially concerned with human life, and are naturally most prominent in connexion with its two great terms of birth and death, has led a modern writer (L. Schmidt) to the conjecture that there were at one time two Fates, not three—that Fate, in fact, passed through the numbers of singular, dual, and plural. But the passages from late authors by which this conjecture is supported do not seem to justify it. Thus Pausanias (x. 24. § 4) mentions that in the shrine at Delphi there stood two statues of Μοῖραι, but he immediately adds: 'and instead of the third of them there stood by them Zeus

---

[1] The line occurs also in Hes. *Sc.* 156 with ἐθύνεον for ὁμίλεον.

Moiragetes[1] and Apollo Moiragetes.' Again, in Plutarch (*Mor.* 474 B, *Tranq. An.* 15), where *διτταί τινες . . . μοῖραι καὶ δαίμονες* are spoken of, the context shows that the reference is not to the Fates proper at all, but to the Good and Evil Dæmon. The same author says (*Mor.* 385 C, *de εἰ apud Delph.* 2) that the two Fates at Delphi were intended to awake inquiry, since three were everywhere usual (*πανταχοῦ τριῶν νομιζομένων*). That the Fates should figure among birth-goddesses is only what might be expected. Pindar (*Ol.* vi. 71) couples the Μοῖραι with Eleutho (= Εἰλείθυια) at the birth of Iamus, and addresses Εἰλείθυια as 'assessor of the deep-minded Μοῖραι' (*Nem.* vii. 1), while Euripides bestows upon the Μοῖραι the epithet of λόχιαι (*Iph. Taur.* 206), and Plato in his poetical way speaks of Μοῖρα and Εἰλείθυια in the same breath (*Symp.* 206 D); an early poet of Delos, too, gave to Εἰλείθυια the epithet of εὔλινος, indicating thereby her identity with Fate (*δῆλον ὡς τῇ Πεπρωμένῃ τὴν αὐτήν*), and declared that she was older than Kronos (Paus. viii. 21. § 2).

Pindar has Μοῖρα in the singular (*Nem.* vii. 84) and in the plural (*Ol.* xi. 65, *Pyth.* iv. 259, *Isth.* v. 25); also *θεοῦ* Μοῖρα (*Ol.* ii. 37); he has two mentions of Clotho (*Ol.* i. 40, *Isth.* v. 25), one of Lachesis (*Ol.* vii. 118), but none of Atropos, though he speaks of 'Κλωθώ and her sister Μοῖραι'; he also enriches the vocabulary of Fate with some new expressions, such as *αἰὼν μόρσιμος* (*Ol.* ii. 20), *μοιρίδιον ἆμαρ* (*Pyth.* iv. 454), *μόριμος υἱός* (*Ol.* ii. 70, of Œdipus), and lays down broadly *τό γε μόρσιμον οὐ παρφυκτόν* (*Pyth.* xii. 52).

3. The Greek tragedians, etc.—This gnome might be taken as the key-note of Greek Tragedy. Quite apart from the curse of inherited sin, as in the house of Pelops, man is represented in the Tragedians as the victim of some awful, unseen power, which foredooms him to disaster. It has been said that there is less of this in Euripides than in Æschylus or Sophocles. But it is from the *Orestes* of Euripides (976–981) that we take the following lines:

> 'Ye tear-drown'd, toiling tribes,
> Whose life is but a span,
> Behold how Fate, or soon or late,
> Upsets the hopes of man!
> In sorrow still your changing state
> Must end as it began.'

'Pray not at all,' says the chorus in Sophocles' *Antigone* (1337 f.) to Creon, 'since there is no release for mortals from predestined calamity.' Greek Tragedy is believed by many to culminate in the *Œdipus Tyrannus*, and there, too, the idea of Fate attains its zenith. Œdipus is like a fly in a spider's web; the more he struggles to escape, the faster does Fate entangle him. 'Awful,' says Sophocles (*Ant.* 951), 'is the mysterious power of Fate.' It is perhaps a sense of this awfulness that makes the Tragedians, though they speak sometimes of 'Fates' in the plural, refrain from using the proper names of the goddesses. The thing with them is too serious for mythology. They were studying life as they found it, in the same spirit as that in which we study the laws of Nature.[2]

In the *Prometheus Vinctus* it is darkly hinted that Zeus himself is subject to Destiny, and that Prometheus knows a secret of Fate which will eventually effect his deliverance (511–525). In Æschylus the connexion between the Fates and the Furies comes out strongly. 'Who then,' asks the chorus, 'turns the rudder of Necessity?' to which the answer is (*ib.* 516):

> Μοῖραι τρίμορφοι μνήμονές τ' Ἐρινύες.

And again in the *Eumenides* (962) the Μοῖραι are addressed as *ματροκασιγνῆται* of the Furies—doubtless with reference to the account in Hesiod of both triplets being the unfathered offspring of Night. The metaphor from spinning, which is rare in the Tragedians, occurs in *Eumen.* 335 in connexion with Μοῖρα.

The belief in oracles is assailed by Euripides, though in such a way as to 'save the face' of Loxias.

> *El.* 399 f.: Λοξίου γὰρ ἔμπεδοι
> χρησμοί, βροτῶν δὲ μαντικὴν χαίρειν ἐῶ.

The logical tendency of this would be to upset the belief in Fate, which is so intimately connected with prediction. But, as a matter of fact, Euripides, like the other tragedians, is permeated through and through with a belief in Fate. Take, for instance,

> *Rhesus* 634 f.: οὐκ ἂν δύναιο τοῦ πεπρωμένου πλέον.
> τοῦτον δὲ πρὸς σῆς χειρὸς οὐ θέμις θανεῖν.
> *Herac.* 615: μόρσιμα δ' οὔτι φυγεῖν θέμις.
> *Herc. Fur.* 311: ὃ χρὴ γὰρ οὐδεὶς μὴ χρεὼν θήσει ποτέ.
> *Iph. Taur.* 1486: τὸ γὰρ χρεὼν σοῦ τε καὶ θεῶν κρατεῖ.

In Æschylus (*Prom. Vinc.* 936) and in the *Rhesus*, which the present writer believes to be the work of Euripides, a new power, bearing a close resemblance to Fate, makes its appearance upon the scene. This power is Ἀδράστεια. She is by some identified with Nemesis, in agreement with which it is the custom to propitiate her before dangerous utterances (Plato, *Rep.* 451 A; Eur. *Rh.* 342, 468), while others regard Adrasteia as another name for Atropos (Schol. ad Plato, *Rep.* 451 A), and the philosophers frankly identify her with Fate in general (Plato, *Phædr.* 248 C; Ar. *Mund.* vii. 5; Stob. *Ecl.* i. 188). According to Callisthenes (Strabo, xiii. 588), the name is due to the accident that the first statue of Nemesis was set up by Adrastus; but the more usual derivation is perhaps the true one, which takes the name to indicate the impossibility of escape from the goddess (*ὅτιπερ οὐκ ἄν τις αὐτὴν ἀποδράσειεν*, Schol. on *Rep.* 451 A).

Nemesis, herself a goddess of distribution (*νεμ-*), is akin to Μοῖρα (*μερ-*), and has at the same time affinities with Fortune, who has managed to appropriate her wheel (see FORTUNE [Gr.]). Herodotus, with his notion of 'a jealous god' (iii. 40), is full of the idea of some power which brings disaster upon men, not because they are wicked, but simply because they are fortunate, like Polycrates, or because, like Crœsus, they think themselves so (i. 34). In Herodotus (i. 91) we find a strong assertion of the omnipotence of Fate, where the Pythia declares to Crœsus that it is 'impossible even for a god to escape destiny' (*τὴν πεπρωμένην μοῖραν ἀδύνατά ἐστι ἀποφυγέειν καὶ θεῷ*). Yet, even so, there is a certain amount of elasticity allowed to Fate, for Loxias claims that he had induced the Μοῖραι to postpone the fall of Sardis for three years. How different is this theologian's acquaintance with the hand of God in history from the calm positivism of Thucydides! And how strongly does his ready belief in oracles (viii. 77, 96) stand contrasted with the sceptical remarks of the later historian (Thuc. ii. 54) as to the way in which predictions get accommodated to current events!

The phrase used by Demosthenes in a famous passage of the *de Corona* (p. 296, § 205)—*τὸν τῆς εἱμαρμένης καὶ τὸν αὐτόματον θάνατον*—indicates the same mental attitude as that of the author of the *Odyssey*, in distinguishing between things which are due to Destiny and those which come about through man's free agency: 'He who regards himself as born only for his parents,' says the orator, 'awaits his appointed and natural end,' whereas he who thinks that he is born also for his country will die rather than see her enslaved. Cicero, in an equally famous utterance (*Phil.* i. § 10), has an echo of this, or of the *ὑπὲρ μόρον* of the *Odyssey*

[1] On this title of Zeus, see Paus. v. 15. § 4, viii. 37. § 1. At Megara there was a statue, made partly by Phidias, with the Μοῖραι above the head of Zeus, on which Pausanias (i. 40. § 3) remarks: *δῆλα δὲ πᾶσι τὴν πεπρωμένην μόνῳ οἱ πείθεσθαι.*

[2] For this remark the writer is indebted to Professor E. A. Sonnenschein.

(i. 34 f.), where he says: 'Multa autem impendere videntur praeter naturam etiam praeterque fatum.' Vergil, too, has the same idea when he speaks of Dido's death (*Æn.* iv. 696):

'Nam quia nec fato merita nec morte peribat.'

In the view of all three writers there is a course of destiny, which may yet be infringed by man, either in the way of glorious self-sacrifice or of murder or suicide.

4. Roman writers.—The Romans add but little to the mythology of Fate. Their own birth-goddesses, of whom one was Parca, were identified under the generic name of *Parcæ* with the three Μοῖραι of the Greeks. Varro seems to be right for once in deriving Parca (Parica) from *pario*. The name Morta used by Livius Andronicus in his *Odyssey* must surely be connected with *mors*, which makes it look as though Cæsellius Vindex were right, as against his critic, Aulus Gellius, in taking Morta as the proper name of one Fate, not the generic name of all. Varro, however, gives the Roman names as Parca, Nona, and Decima, in which the allusion to birth is obvious (Aul. Gell. iii. 16, §§ 9–11). The threeness of the Roman goddesses may be due merely to their assimilation to the Μοῖραι.

The symbolism of spinning is used by Tibullus (I. viii. 1):

'Hunc cecinere diem Parcae fatalia nentes
Stamina, non ulli dissoluenda deo,'

by Propertius (IV. vii. 51):

'Iuro ego Fatorum nulli revolubile stamen,'

and by Ovid (*ad Liv.* 239 f.):

'Quondam ego tentavi Clothoque, duasque sorores,
Pollice quae certo pensa severa trahunt.'

It was reserved for the abundant genius of the last-named poet to contribute to poetic thought the following fine picture of the archives of Fate (*Met.* xv. 808–814):

'Intres licet ipsa Sororum
Tecta trium, cernes illic molimine vasto
Ex aere, et solido rerum tabularia ferro;
Quae neque concursum coeli, neque fulminis iram,
Nec metuunt ullas tuta atque aeterna ruinas.
Invenies illic incisa adamante perenni
Fata tui generis.'

5. The philosophers.—We turn now to the treatment of Fate by the philosophers, with whom the great name for it is ἡ εἱμαρμένη. Modern grammarians treat εἵμαρμαι as an irregular perfect of μείρομαι (=σέσμαρμαι); but to the ancient philosophers the word was suggestive rather of εἱρμός (='series'), as appears from their definitions.

Heraclitus, whose floruit is put at about 503 B.C., is reputed to have been the first to employ the term εἱμαρμένη. All things, we are told, took place, according to that philosopher, καθ' εἱμαρμένην.[1] It was further explained by him, if we may trust Stobæus (*Ecl.* i. 178), that the essence of Fate was Reason (λόγος), which pervaded the substance of the universe. Here we have the subsequent doctrine of the Stoics complete already, if it has not been read into the earlier thinker.

It is in his character of poet rather than as a philosopher that Plato speaks of Fate. Into the symbolism of the Vision of Er we need not enter further than to note that Lachesis is treated as the eldest of the Fates, since Lachesis stands for the past, Clotho for the present, and Atropos for the future (*Rep.* 617 C; cf. *Laws*, 960 C; in the Peripatetic *de Mundo*, Atropos stands for the past, and Lachesis for the future). Everywhere Plato takes for granted that there is a predetermined order of destiny, especially in relation to human affairs, without specifying by whom or what it has been determined.[2] In *Phædo* (115 A), Plato makes Socrates in his last moments allude playfully to the prominence of Fate in Tragedy—ἐμὲ δὲ νῦν ἤδη καλεῖ, φαίη ἂν ἀνὴρ τραγικός, ἡ εἱμαρμένη. In *Gorg.* (512 E) his language leads us to think that submission to Fate was a sentiment peculiarly prevalent among women—πιστεύσαντα ταῖς γυναιξὶν, ὅτι τὴν εἱμαρμένην οὐδ' ἂν εἷς ἐκφύγοι. In the bold myth of the *Politicus* he identifies εἱμαρμένη with the 'connatural desire' of the universe, when left by God to its own devices. This is a new light upon the subject altogether.

It is with the Stoics that the interest in Fate really begins. Heraclitus was before his time, and we do not know exactly what he said. Zeno identified Fate (εἱμαρμένη) with Providence (πρόνοια) and Nature (φύσις).[1] Chrysippus said that 'the essence of Fate is a spiritual power (δύναμιν πνευματικήν) arranging the whole in order.' He declared also that Fate is the reason of the universe.[2]

The unwary reader must not be deceived by Chrysippus' speaking of Fate as a 'spiritual' power. We mean by *spirit* something that is not matter; the Stoics meant by it something that is matter. Augustine uses *spiritus vitæ* to express 'spirit' in our sense[3] that something, itself increate, which creates all things.

Posidonius made Fate third from Zeus, Nature being intermediate between them (Stob. *Ecl.* i. 178). Antipater said simply that Fate was God.

With regard to this last view, Augustine, who dislikes the word 'Fate' because of the connexion that had been established by his time between it and astrology, says, if any one means by Fate the will or power of God, 'sententiam teneat, linguam corrigat' (*de Civ. Dei*, v. 1).

Pope's 'Universal Prayer' is instinct with the spirit of Stoicism:

'Yet gave me in this dark estate
To see the good from ill;
And binding Nature fast in Fate,
Left free the human will.'

That is the position on which Epictetus is always insisting. God's will is certain to come about, whether we wish it or not. What is in our power is to make ourselves happy by a cheerful assent to it, or miserable by a futile resistance. There is no doubt that the Stoics held this position. How they made it good by argument it is not very easy to see. But Chrysippus, who was the brain of Stoicism, seems to have reasoned in this way. Everything has its antecedent causes; but we must distinguish between two kinds of causes: (1) those which are complete and primary, or, in one word, efficient; and (2) those which are adjuvant and proximate. If all causes were of the first kind, there would be no room anywhere for freedom; but, as some are of the second, there is. Sense cannot be stirred except by an object striking it; but the causes here are of the latter kind, and do not affect freedom. Assent lies with ourselves. If a man gives a kick to a cylindrical stone, he sets it rolling; but it goes on rolling because of its own nature. Bad minds, according to Chrysippus, rush into errors voluntarily; and it is part of the order of Fate that they should do so, as being a natural consequence of their badness (Cic. *de Fato*, §§ 41–43; Aul. Gell. vii. 2). This does not sound very satisfactory as a vindication of the freedom of the will. Cicero, who had the works of Chrysippus before him, and who was a good judge, did not think that he had made out his case. Neither did he think Epicurus successful, who, in order to leave room in the universe for free will, had recourse to the hypothesis of a slight deviation from the perpendicular on the part of single atoms.

Cicero himself, in his fragmentary *de Fato*, follows Carneades and the New Academy in denying Fate altogether. If there were no such thing as Fate, things would still happen as they do. Nature and Chance are enough to account for them. The

[1] Diog. Laert. ix. § 7: πάντα τε γίνεσθαι καθ' εἱμαρμένην. See frag. lxiii. in Bywater.

[2] The following are some of the passages in which the idea of Fate comes in: *Phædo*, 113 A; *Phædr.* 255 B; *Prot.* 320 D; *Rep.* 566 A; *Menex.* 243 E.

[1] Stob. *Ecl.* i. 178.

[2] εἱμαρμένη ἐστὶν ὁ τοῦ κόσμου λόγος (Stob. *Ecl.* i. 180).

[3] *de Civ. Dei*, v. 9: 'Nam et aër iste seu ventus, dicitur spiritus: sed quoniam corpus est, non est spiritus vitae.'

stone which fell in a cavern on the leg of a brigand Icadius (the reference is to a story told by Posidonius) would have fallen whether Icadius was there or not. But in this case, says Cicero, there is no Fate, because there is no prediction (*de Fato*, § 5)—a remark which brings us to the heart of the matter. For prediction is the stronghold of Fate. Free will is destroyed, says Cicero, if there be such a thing as divination (§ 11). This is an argument which has great power over many minds, but is nevertheless, fallacious. For present knowledge by another of a man's actions is no interference with his freedom. If, then, it be possible for a human being to transcend the conditions of time, and to project himself, or be projected, into the future, he may see what one is freely doing then, just as we see what others are freely doing now. Of course, it may be denied that this is possible; but it cannot be denied that, if it is possible, it renders prediction compatible with free will.

The Stoic belief in Fate as a continuous chain of causation is Determinism, not Fatalism. Fatalism is the belief that a definite event will take place, whatever happens—which is as much a denial of causation as is a theory of pure chance.

See also the 'Greek' and 'Roman' artt. on FORTUNE.

LITERATURE.—Cicero, *de Fato*; Stobæus, *Ecl.* i. 152–192; Aulus Gellius, VIII. i. and ii.; L. Schmidt, art. 'Moira,' in Smith's *Dict. of Gr. and Rom. Biog. and Mythol.*, Lond. 1864–67.

ST. GEORGE STOCK.

FATE (Hindu).—The Skr. language has various equivalents for what we call fate, such as, *e.g.*, *kāla*, lit. 'time,' as leading to events the causes of which are imperceptible to the mind of man; *vidhi*, 'ordinance,' 'rule'; *daiva*, 'divine,' 'celestial,' 'divine power *or* will,' 'destiny,' 'fate,' 'chance'; *adṛṣṭa*, 'what is not seen,' *i.e.* that which is beyond the reach of observation or consciousness, the acts done by each soul in former bodies, which acts exert upon that soul an irresistible power called *adṛṣṭa*, because felt and not seen; *karman* (*karma*), work done in a former existence and leading to inevitable results, fate. *Kāla*, 'time,' is perhaps the earliest of these terms, occurring, as it does, in hymns of the *Atharvaveda* (xix. 53) on the power and Divine nature of Time, which is akin to Destiny or Divine Ordinance. 'It is he who drew forth the worlds and encompassed them. Being their father, he became their son. There is no other power superior to him.' In a subsequent period, Kāla was sometimes identified with Yama, the judge of the dead, or represented, together with Mṛtyu, 'Death,' as a follower of Yama, or invoked as one of the forms of the god Śiva. The *Mahābhārata*, the great epic of India, contains various tales tending to illustrate the relative importance of the various agencies of which Fate may be said to be composed, none perhaps finer than the apologue of the snake (xiii. 1), relating how a boy was killed by a snake, and the snake, after having been caught by a hunter, was released by the boy's mother on the ground of her loss being due to Fate alone.

First, the snake declares its innocence of the boy's death, Mṛtyu, the god of death, having used the snake as an instrument. Thereupon Mṛtyu himself makes his appearance and exonerates himself, asserting that Kāla, 'Time,' has in reality killed the boy. 'Guided by Kāla, I, O serpent, sent thee on this errand. All creatures, mobile or immobile, in heaven or earth, are pervaded by this same inspiration of Kāla. The whole universe is imbued with the same influence of Kāla.' But Kāla in his turn explains that neither Mṛtyu, nor the serpent, nor he himself is guilty of the death of any creature. 'The child has met with death as the result of its *karma* in the past. We all are subject to the influence of our respective *karma*. As men make from a lump of clay whatever they wish to make, even so do men attain to various results determined by *karma*. As light and shadow are related to each other, so are men related to *karma* through their own actions. Therefore, neither art thou, nor am I, nor is Mṛtyu, nor the serpent, nor this old Brahman lady, the cause of the child's death. He himself is the cause here.' On Kāla expounding the matter in this way, the child's mother became consoled, and asked the fowler to release the snake.

The conception of *karma* is closely connected with the celebrated Indian theory of transmigration or metempsychosis, which pervades all post-Vedic religious and philosophical systems of India, and has continued down to the present day to exercise a powerful sway over the popular mind. As observed by Burn (in *General Report of the Census of India*, Calcutta, 1903, p. 364), it is a mistake to suppose that the ordinary Hindu peasant has practically no belief in the doctrine of transmigration. 'The doctrine of Karma is one of the firmest beliefs of all classes of Hindus, and the fear that a man shall reap as he has sown is an appreciable element in the average morality.' It is only in S. India, according to Stuart (*ib.* p. 264), that the influence of Animism is prevalent, the villager's real worship being 'paid to Máriamman, the dread goddess of smallpox and cholera, and to the special goddess of the village'; and misfortunes are regarded as the work of evil spirits or devils who must be propitiated. In the same way, a native observer, G. Sarkar, in his well-known work, *Hindu Law*, points out that the doctrine of *adṛṣṭa*, the mysterious but irresistible power of the acts done in previous lives, is universally held by the Hindus as a fundamental article of faith.

'*Adṛṣṭa*, or the invisible dual force, is the resultant of all good and bad deeds, of all meritorious and demeritorious acts and omissions, done by a person in all past forms of existence and also in the present life, and it is this *adṛṣṭa* which determines the condition of every soul, *i.e.* is the cause of his happiness or misery; the state of a living being depends on his own past conduct' (G. Sarkar, *Hindu Law*[2], Calcutta, 1903, p. 230).

And so it is stated by Deussen in his *History of Philosophy* that the doctrine of metempsychosis has governed the Indian mind from the epoch of the Upaniṣads down to the present time, and is still of eminent practical importance, as affording a popular explanation of the cause of human suffering and operating as a spur to moral conduct. He quotes a blind Indian Pandīt, whom he met in his travels through India, as replying to a question put to him concerning the cause of his deficiency in vision, that it must be due to some fault committed by himself during a previous existence (Deussen, *Allgemeine Geschichte der Philosophie*, vol. i. pt. ii. p. 282).

Historically speaking, the belief in metempsychosis and the lasting effects of *karma*, or action, as determining the fate of man, makes its first appearance in one of the Brāhmaṇas, and, in a more developed form, in the Upaniṣads. These philosophical treatises preach a strict determinism, except in so far as a man, by recognizing his identity with the eternally free *Ātman*, may be released from the bondage of *karma*. The germs of this theory, as supposed by Oldenberg, may be much older; and it has been shown by Schrader, in his suggestive little book, *Die Indogermanen* (Leipzig, 1911, p. 148), that the earliest Indo-European conception of Fate is that of a share inherited from the mother at the time of birth; the Roman *Parcæ* (from *pario*), equally with the Greek Εἰλείθυιαι and the Slav. *Rozdanicy*, being Fate Mothers (*Schicksalsmütter*) assisting at every birth.

From Brāhmanism the theory of *karma* passed into Buddhism, and became one of Buddha's leading tenets.

'When a man dies, the khandhas [elements] of which he is constituted perish, but by the force of his Kamma [Karma] a new set of khandhas instantly starts into existence, and a new being appears in another world, who, though possessing different khandhas and a different form, is in reality identical with the man just passed away, because his Kamma is the same. Kamma, then, is the link that preserves the identity of a being through all the countless changes which it undergoes in its progress through Saṁsāra' (Childers, *Dict. of the Pali Lang.*, London, 1875, p. 198).

Jainism, the rival religion of Buddhism, agrees

in this respect with the latter. There existed in ancient times a large number of philosophical systems, belonging to two principal classes—one asserting the existence of free will, moral responsibility, and transmigration; and the other negativing the same. Both Jina and Buddha belonged to the former class. They believed in transmigration, the annihilation of which was the final aim which they had in view (Pischel). According to the Jaina doctrine, the deeds performed in the bodies by the souls are *karma*, merit, and sin. This drives them, when one body has passed away, into another whose quality depends on the character of the *karma*. Virtue leads to the heavens of the gods, or to birth among men in pure and noble races. Sin consigns the souls to the lower regions, sends them into the bodies of animals or plants, or even into masses of lifeless matter. The addition of new *karma* can be prevented by right faith, strict control of the senses, and austerities on which the Jainas lay special stress (Bühler).

Of modern Hindu sects, the Sikhs may perhaps be said to be the most fatalistic of all. They agree with the adherents of other systems in explaining the glaring difference between riches and poverty, honour and dishonour, by the acts in a former life determining the present condition and circumstances of a person. But they go very far in denying the liberty of human action, everything being subject to the decree of Fate, and the future lot of a person written on his forehead. These ideas have struck root very generally among the Sikhs, who, therefore, are far more rigid fatalists than even the Muhammadans. The *karma* theory occupies the same place in the Sikh religion as elsewhere, and the highest goal of the Sikh is not paradise, but the cessation of re-birth and existence (Trumpp, Macauliffe).

To return to Brāhmanism, it should be observed that the rigid determinism of its view of *karma* is frequently mitigated by admitting the modifying and controlling influence exercised on Fate by human exertion. Thus the Anuśāsana Parvan of the *Mahābhārata* contains the fine discourse on human effort (*puruṣakāra*), in which the relative importance of fate (*daiva*) and human acts is discussed.

'As, unsown with seed, the soil, though tilled, becomes fruitless, so, without individual exertion, Destiny is of no avail. One's own acts are like the soil, and Destiny (or the sum of one's acts in previous births) is compared to the seed. From the union of the soil and the seed doth the harvest grow. It is observed every day in the world that the doer reaps the fruit of his good and evil deeds. Happiness results from good deeds, and pain from evil ones. Acts, when done, always fructify, but, if not done, no fruit arises. By devoted application (or by austerity) one acquires beauty, fortune, and riches of various kinds. Everything can be secured by exertion, but nothing can be gained through Destiny (*daiva*) alone, by a man wanting in personal exertion' (*Mahābhārata*, XIII. vi. 7–12).

And so it is stated in the Vana Parvan that

'those persons in the world who believe in Destiny, and those again who believe in Chance, are both the worst among men. Those only that believe in the efficacy of acts are laudable. He that lies at ease, believing in Destiny alone, is soon destroyed like an unburnt earthen pot in water. So also he that believeth in Chance, *i.e.* sitteth inactive though capable of activity, liveth not long, for his life is one of weakness and helplessness' (*ib.* xxxii. 13–15).

It is also declared in the *Mahābhārata* that only eunuchs worship Fate (*daiva*). In other places, the paramount power of Destiny is upheld, and it is clear that the comparative weight of free will and fate must have furnished a fruitful theme for discussion to these Brāhman theorists.

The part played by Fate in the ordinary relations of human life, according to Hindu notions, may best be gathered perhaps from the view which the Indian jurists take of Fate or Chance (*daiva*). Thus, it is a well-known rule in Indian law that a depositary is not responsible for such damage as may have occurred to a chattel deposited with him by the act of Fate (*daiva*) or of the king, Fate being explained to include ravages caused by fire or water, the falling down of a wall, decay through the lapse of time, an attack by robbers or by inimical forces, and other events of a similar nature corresponding exactly to what is called *vis maior* in Roman law. If, therefore, a deposit should have been destroyed by the act of Fate or of the king, together with the depositary's own goods, he shall not be compelled to restore it. The same rule recurs in the recently discovered *Arthaśāstra*, in the 'Chapter on Deposits,' where it is ordained that a deposit shall not be reclaimed whenever forts or country parts are destroyed by enemies or hill tribes, or villages, caravans, or herds of cattle are attacked, or the whole kingdom destroyed; whenever extensive fires or floods bring about entire destruction of a village or partly destroy immoveable or even moveable properties, owing to the sudden spread of fire or rush of floods; and whenever a ship (laden with commodities) is either sunk or plundered by pirates. A loss caused by Fate is also not chargeable to a carrier transporting certain goods and losing part of them; or to a herdsman neglecting his cattle, after having been struck by lightning, bitten or killed by a snake, alligator, tiger, or other noxious animal, seized with disease, or the victim of an accident; or to one particular partner, when the property of the partnership has been injured through Fate or a gang of robbers, etc.

It is interesting also to examine the references to Fate in medical Sanskrit literature. Thus in Suśruta's system of medicine a certain class of diseases is attributed to the act of Fate (*daivabala*), as having been caused by Divine wrath, or by the mystic potencies of charms or spells, or by contagion. Sudden paroxysms of fever and sudden death or paralysis caused by lightning are quoted as instances of such diseases. There was, besides, a popular belief, originating in the doctrine of *karmapāka*, or ripening of acts, according to which certain aggravating diseases and infirmities were supposed to be due to some offence committed in a previous existence, leprosy, *e.g.*, being regarded as the result of a heinous crime perpetrated in a former life; blindness, dumbness, and lameness as being the consequence, respectively, of killing a cow, cursing a Brāhman, and stealing a horse; stinking breath as being caused by uttering calumnies; an incurable illness as due to injuring a person; epilepsy as the result of usurious practices, etc. This popular superstition was sanctioned by the medical writers of India, who seriously register crimes committed in a former existence among the regular causes of leprosy, and prescribe certain religious ceremonies among the remedies to be used for curing this disease. It is also believed that, when a person dies of leprosy, he will be affected with it in the next life, unless he performs a certain penance, consisting of abstinence for a day, shaving the whole hair of the head, and presenting a certain number of cowries and other articles to Brāhmans, who offer certain prayers, and to whom the person confesses his sins. This ceremony is performed before entering on the treatment of any supposed dangerous disease (T. A. Wise, *Commentary on the Hindu System of Medicine*, London, 1860, p. 258).

The notions of Sanskrit writers regarding the nature and working of Fate may be further illustrated by some miscellaneous sayings collected from their compositions.

'The accomplishment of an object is divided between Fate and exertion. Of these, the Fate is the manifestation of one's acts in former life. Some expect success from Fate, some from accident, some from the lapse of time, and some from effort. Men of genius believe in the efficacy of the combination of all these. As a chariot cannot be put into motion with a single wheel, so does Fate not succeed without exertion' (*Yājñavalkya-*

smṛti, i. 348–350, tr. Mandlik). 'Success in every enterprise depends on Destiny and human acts: the acts of Destiny are out of man's control. Think not on Destiny, but act thyself' (*Manusmṛti*, vii. 205, tr. M. Williams). 'Fate I consider paramount, human effort is futile. Everything is governed by Fate; Fate is the final resort' (*Rāmāyaṇa*, I. viii. 22). 'Fate binds a man with adamantine cords, and drags him upwards to the highest rank, or downward to the depths of misery' (*ib.* VII. xxxvii. 3, tr. M. Williams). 'Banish all thought of Destiny, and act with manly vigour, straining all thy nerve. When thou hast put forth all thy energy, the blame of failure will not rest with thee' (*Hitopadeśa*, Introd. 31, tr. M. Williams).

'What though we climb to Meru's peak, soar bird-like through the sky,
Grow rich by trade, or till the ground, or art and science ply,
Or vanquish all our earthly foes, we yield to Fate's decree,
Whate'er she nills can ne'er take place, whate'er she wills must be' (*Bhartṛhari*, tr. Tawney, Calcutta, 1877, p. 40).

'As a man puts on new clothes in this world, throwing away those which he formerly wore, even so the self of man puts on new bodies, which are in accordance with his acts in a former life' (*Viṣṇusmṛti*, xx. 50, tr. Jolly).

LITERATURE.—Monier-Williams, *Brahmanism and Hinduism*[4], London, 1891; A. Barth, *The Religions of India*[3], do. 1891; P. Deussen, *Allgem. Gesch. der Philosophie*, vol. i.–iii., Leipzig, 1894–1908, also *Vier philos. Texte des Mahābhāratam*, do. 1906; E. W. Hopkins, *The Great Epic of India*, London, 1901; H. Kern, *Manual of Indian Buddhism*, Strassburg, 1896 (=*GIAP* iii. 8); R. Pischel, *Leben und Lehre des Buddha*, Leipzig, 1906; Bühler-Burgess, *The Indian Sect of the Jainas*, London, 1905; O. Böhtlingk, *Ind. Sprüche*[2], St. Petersburg, 1870–73 (cf. A. Blau's *Index* to this collection, Leipzig, 1893, *s.v.* 'Schicksal').

J. JOLLY.

FATE (Iranian).—The Gāthās attribute foreknowledge to Ahura Mazda (*Yasna* xxix. 4, xliv. 2, 6, 9–11, 13–19, xlviii. 2), which is also implied in the whole Iranian scheme of the Ages of the World (*q.v.*). Foreordination, however, scarcely developed in Zoroastrian thought, except in a minor infralapsarian sense, until a comparatively late period. Practically the only Avesta passage which is directly fatalistic in its teaching is *Vend.* v. 8, which states that a man apparently drowned is really carried away by demons, and that 'there, then, Fate is fulfilled, there it is completed' (*athra adhāt frajasaiti baxta adhāṭ nijasaiti*).

In genuine Zoroastrianism fatalism has no place, for the entire spirit generated by the long struggle which each man must help Ahura Mazda to wage against Ahriman and every other power of evil militates against a concept which—whatever its alleged justification—has, as a matter of history, sapped the energy of every people that has held it. And yet fatalism came to be an important doctrine of later Zoroastrianism. What was the source of this new factor — philosophical speculation, the malign influence of Babylonian astrology, the crushing of the national spirit by the foreign dominion under which the Zoroastrians passed, or a combination of all three—it is not easy to tell; yet there is at least a curious and suggestive analogy between the rise of fatalism in Iran and that of *karma* (*q.v.*) in India, which seems to have been evolved from a combination of philosophical speculation with the religious beliefs of the aborigines of India.

The *Dīnkarṭ* (iii. 77, tr. Sanjana, Bombay, 1874 ff., p. 85) teaches a qualified free will when it says:

'It is through the power and the assistance of the Ijaḍs (angels) that man knows the Holy Self-existent (Ahura Mazda), fights with the Darújs (demons) and delivers his body and soul from them, and possesses the power of managing the other creation of this world. Under the design of the Creator, man is born, and has the power to direct himself, under the superintendence of the Ijaḍs. The abode (in man) of the evil qualities of the evil passions is for the purpose of obstructing heavenly wisdom and for contriving to plunge man into sin.'

Within the sphere of orthodox Zoroastrianism, fatalism comes to the front chiefly in two Pahlavi works—the 9th cent. *Dāṭistān-ī Dīnīk* (*DD*), and the *Dīnā-ī Maīnōg-ī Xraṭ* (*MX*) of uncertain date, but probably before the Arab conquest, and possibly in the reign of Chosroës I. (531–579 [*MX*, ed. Sanjana, Bombay, 1895, p. vii f.]). According to *DD* lxxi. 3–5,

'there are some things through destiny, and there are some through action; and it is thus fully decided by them [the high priests] that life, wife, and child, authority and wealth are through destiny, and the righteousness and wickedness of priesthood, warfare, and husbandry are through action. And this, too, is thus said by them, that that which is not destined for a man in the world does not happen; and that which is destined, be it owing to exertion, will come forward, be it through sinfulness or slothfulness, he is injured by it. That which will come forward owing to exertion is such as his who goes to a meeting of happiness, or the sickness of a mortal who, owing to sickness, dies early; and he who through sinfulness and slothfulness is thereby injured is such as he who would wed no wife, and is certain that no child of his is born, or such as he who gives his body unto slaughter, and life is injured by his living.'

Some colour is lent by *MX* viii. 17 to the view which the present writer, like Cumont (*Mysteries of Mithra*, tr. McCormack, Chicago, 1903, p. 124 f.), is inclined to favour, that Zoroastrian fatalism is borrowed, in the main, from Babylonian astrology, when it declares that 'every good and the reverse which happen to mankind, and also the other creatures, happen through the seven planets and the twelve constellations.' It is useless to strive against fate, for, according to *MX* xxiii. 5–9,

'when predestination as to virtue, or as to the reverse, comes forth, the wise becomes wanting in duty, and the astute in evil becomes intelligent; the faint-hearted becomes braver, and the braver becomes faint-hearted; the diligent becomes lazy, and the lazy acts diligently. Just as is predestined as to the matter, the cause enters into it, and thrusts out everything else.' In short, destiny (*baxt*) is 'predominant over every one and everything' (*MX* xlvii. 7; cf. also the polemic of Eznik, *Against the Sects*, tr. Schmid, Vienna, 1900, p. 121 ff.). There is, however, a sharp distinction in *MX* xxiv. 5–7 between destiny (*baxt*) and Divine providence (*bāk-baxt*); 'destiny is that which is ordained from the beginning, and Divine providence is that which they also grant otherwise,' and according to *Vīsp.* vii. 3 there is special Divine intervention (*baghō-baxta*) on behalf of Iranian warriors.

Yet it must be questioned whether the *MX* is, strictly speaking, orthodox, for in xxvii. 10 occur the significant words,

'The affairs of the world of every kind proceed through destiny (*breh*) and time (*damānak*) and the supreme decree of the self-existent eternity (*zōrvān*), the king and long-continuing lord.'

This is strongly suggestive of the Zarvanite heresy (on which see SECTS [Zoroastrian]), according to which both Ahura Mazda and Ahriman are sprung from Zrvan Akarana ('Boundless Time'), who is mentioned as a Divinity in the Avesta itself (*Yasna* lxxii. 10; *Nyāiš*, i. 8; *Vend.* xix. 13). That this belief existed long before the composition of the Pahlavi texts quoted above is shown by a citation from Theodore of Mopsuestia (*apud* Photius, *Bibl.* lxxxi.), on the authority of an Armenian chorepiscopus Mastubius, who regarded Zrvan as the author of all, and who called him Fate (Ζαρουάμ, ὃν ἀρχηγὸν παντῶν εἰσάγει ὃν καὶ τύχην καλεῖ), while both the 5th cent. Armenian polemist Eznik (tr. Schmid, p. 119 ff.) and the Syraic writers (cf. Nöldeke, *Festgruss an Roth*, Stuttgart, 1893, pp. 34–38) make one of their main attacks on the Zoroastrian religion turn upon the fatalism of Zarvanism.[1] In similar fashion the Parsi *'Ulamā-i Islām* (tr. Vullers, *Fragmente über die Relig. des Zoroasters*, Bonn, 1831, pp. 44 f., 46) affirms that Time created Ahura Mazda, who created all good things, this being in direct opposition to the statement of Zāṭsparam (i. 24, tr. West, *SBE* v. 160) that Ahura Mazda was the creator of Time. The latter view is confirmed by a statement of a Persian *rivāyat* (ed. and tr. Spiegel, *Trad. Lit. der Parsen*, Vienna, 1860, p. 161 ff.), according to which Ahura Mazda also created Zrvan dareghō-xᵛadhāta ('long, self-ordained Time'), who differs in many regards from Zrvan Akarana (Spiegel, *Erân. Alterthumskunde*, ii. 4 ff.).

The fatalism of the Zoroastrians also appears in the numerous prophecies of future events (cf., for example, *Yātkār-ī Zarīrān*, tr. Modi, Bombay, 1899, pp. 21 f., 29 f., where Jāmāsp prophesies to King Vištāspa the outcome of battle) and in the

[1] On the adoption of Zarvanism by Mithraism, see Cumont, *op. cit.* pp. 107, 148, and also his *Oriental Religions in Roman Paganism*, Eng. tr., Chicago, 1911, p. 150 f., where the co-operation of Bab. influence is again emphasized.

entire system of Persian divination (*q.v.*). In the Persian epic of the *Šāh-Nāmah* (tr. Mohl, Paris, 1876–1878) the power of Fate is also emphasized. Thus the Emperor of China declares (iii. 112) that 'no one will escape the rotation of heaven (*gardiš-i āsmān*), even though he were able to overthrow an elephant,' and the poet makes a similar reflexion on the violent death of Yazdagird I. (v. 419); but here, as de Harlez observes (*Avesta . . . trad.*, Paris, 1881, p. lxxxvii), we no longer move in a Zoroastrian sphere.

LITERATURE.—**F. Spiegel**, *Erân. Alterthumskunde*, Leipzig, 1871–1878, ii. 7, 11, 14, note 2, *Avesta . . . übersetzt*, do. 1852–1863, ii. 219; **L. C. Casartelli**, *Phil. of the Mazdayasnian Relig. under the Sassanids*, tr. Asa, Bombay, 1889, pp. 9, 31–33, 86, 144, 148 f.; **E. West**, *Pahlavi Texts*, ii., iii. (*SBE* xviii. [1882], xxiv. [1885]).

LOUIS H. GRAY.

FATE (Jewish).—Based on the OT, which on the whole acknowledges freedom of choice, Judaism does not, and consistently cannot, hold the pagan doctrine of Fate. The subject never entered Jewish consciousness, and therefore there is not even a Heb. word in the OT corresponding to *μοῖρα* or *fatum*. חֹק is an engraved statute and hence a law of Nature, but not applied to human affairs. When, therefore, Josephus makes his countrymen state their theological differences in philosophical language and ascribes to the Pharisees a belief in a *εἱμαρμένη* (*Ant.* XVIII. i. 3), he does not mean by it an inflexible power to which gods and men must bow, but has in his mind the late Heb. word גְּזֵרָה (from גזר, 'to divide'; cf. *μείρομαι* from *μέρος*), generally גְּזַר דִּין, a decree of a judge or king, or Divine decision. Not fatalism but foreordination was the belief of Pharisaism.

The new term for God's foreordination was grafted on OT notions evolved from new ideas of God's Providence. The Bab. god Marduk held a solemn assembly of the gods on New Year's Day, when the lot was cast, the year's destiny settled, and Marduk seized anew the reins of government (A. Jeremias, *OT in the Light of the Ancient East*, Eng. tr. 1910, i. 59). It is probable that this largely influenced the Jewish observance of the autumnal New Year, and gave rise to the Pharisaic belief in a *εἱμαρμένη*. For on the first of Tishri, the agricultural New Year and Feast of Trumpets, the sole sovereignty of God is emphasized in the liturgy in a special manner. On that day God holds a court of justice in heaven, before which all mankind are arraigned. Satan is the accuser, and prayers and the sound of the trumpet ascending as a memorial (Lv 23[24]) are the special pleaders. Three books are opened, wherein is inscribed the fate of each individual—one for the perfectly righteous, one for the perfectly wicked, and one for the mediocre; the first two are respectively sealed on that day for life and for death, the third is left open for forensic proceedings, merits and demerits being balanced during the penitential days, and is sealed on the Day of Atonement (*Rosh Hash.* 16*b* ff.). The usual salutation on New Year's Day is: 'May you be inscribed (on the Day of Atonement, 'May you be sealed') for a good year!' The *Musaph* prayers for the New Year say:

> 'On this day sentence is passed upon countries—which of them is to be destined to the sword and which to peace, which to famine and which to plenty; and every creature is visited therein, and recorded for life or for death. Who is not visited on such a day as this?'

Even the extent of man's sustenance is decreed in this session (*Beṣa*, 16*a*). The sentences, however, of this annual assize are not irrevocable. 'Repentance, Prayer, and Almsgiving rescind the evil decree' (Liturgy, and *Rosh Hash.* 16*b*). Hence a converted sinner can be said to annul the Divine *gᵉzar dîn* (*Mo'ed Ḳaṭ.* 16*b*), in so far that it is no longer applicable to him since he became another.

Man, then, remains master of his religious and moral destiny. 'Everything is in God's hands, except the fear of God' (*Ber.* 33; *Meg.* 25*a*). Good and evil are the issues of man's actions (*Deb. R.* iv.). He possesses the power to defile himself and to keep himself clean (*Yoma*, 39*a*). In *Mak.* 10*b* it is proved from the Law, the Prophets, and the Writings that one is guided on the way he desires to walk.

But, when God's Providence is spoken of, we meet in Jewish literature with sentiments expressive of determinism. It is possible that the Stoic philosophy lent a colouring to Jewish speculations on Divine Providence. We know that the ethics of Stoicism agree in many points with those of the Haggada, betraying some acquaintance, on the part of the Rabbis, with the tenets of that school. Strabo identifies Judaism with Stoicism (Reinach, *Textes d'auteurs grecs et romains relatifs au judaïsme*, Paris, 1895, pp. 11, 16, 99, 242). Ben Sira (17[7] 15[11-17]) asserts the freedom of human will in the manner of one attacking a contrary opinion. Josephus (*BJ* VI. i. 8, iv. 8) uses the word *εἱμαρμένη* as if he were a real fatalist. The repeated emphasis laid on Divine foreknowledge is a step in the direction of fatalism. Thus, in the above mentioned *Musaph* prayers for the New Year, God is spoken of as 'looking (צוֹפֶה) and beholding to the end of all generations.' A dictum of R. 'Aḳiba's was (*Ab.* iii. 19): 'Everything is foreseen (צָפוּי, equivalent to Josephus' *ἐφορᾶν*=*providere* [*BJ* II. viii. 14]),' although it is added: 'free will is given.' Man in his nature and environment is a product of a predetermined will. 'He is fashioned, born, lives, dies, and is brought to judgment against his will' (*Ab.* iv. 29). In his ante-natal state his sex, constitution, size, shape, appearance, social position, livelihood, and all that may befall him, are pre-ordained (*Tanḥ.* on Ex 38[21]). Marriages are made in Heaven. Forty days before the birth of a child its future spouse is proclaimed by a herald (בַּת קוֹל), and no prayers can alter it (*Mo'ed Ḳ.* 18*b*; *Sanh.* 22*a*). Throughout his life his feet guide him whither he is destined to go (*Suk.* 55). The very wounding of a finger is previously proclaimed in heaven (*Ab. Zara*, 54). No one dies prematurely, although the plague may rage for seven years (*Sanh.* 29). His mental endowments are likewise prescribed. One has an aptitude for studying Haggada, another for Mishna, another for Gemara, and another for all three. Even the prophetic gift was bestowed in measure. One prophet was the author of two books, another of a chapter, and another of only one verse (*Yalḳuṭ* on Job 9[16]). 'By thine own name, says Ben 'Azai, will they call thee, in thy place will they seat thee, of thine own will they give thee. No one can touch anything that is destined for another. No kingdom can extend a hairbreadth against another' (*Yoma*, 38*a*).

History is shaped in accordance with a pre-ordained plan. Suffering, death, the Deluge, Israel's servitude in Egypt and persecution by Haman, were prescribed before creation (*Tanḥ.* on Ex 3[1]). God revealed to Adam before he was completely formed his righteous descendants (*ib.*). To Moses He showed a list of 'every generation, its kings, guides, and prophets from the creation until the final resurrection of the dead' (*Midr. R.* on Ex 31). The leaders were to appear on the stage of time as they were wanted: *Uno avulso non deficit alter.* Thus, 'before Moses' sun set, Joshua's rose.' Similar was the case with Eli and Samuel. On the day R. 'Aḳiba was slain, Judah the Prince was born, and on the latter's death day Rab Ada bar Ahaba was born,' etc. (*Midr. R.* on Gn 23[1]). Israel's election was decreed from all eternity, and is irrevocable. Their final redemption must be preceded by repentance.

Should they fail to repent at the appointed time, God will force it by raising up for them another tyrant like Haman (*Sanh.* 97*b*, 98*a*). The interference of miracles with the course of Nature, such as the dividing of the Red Sea at the Exodus, the solstice at Gibeon, the Jonah miracle, etc., was in accordance with a Divine 'stipulation' before creation (*Midr. R.* on Gn 1^9).

How far foreordination was compatible with the doctrine of rewards and punishments was a frequent subject of discussion in the Talmudic period. But the Rabbis advanced no solution of the problem beyond the categorical statement that, notwithstanding, man possessed freedom of will. At most it was added that compliance with the law merited greater reward for the righteous and severer punishment for transgressors (*Shab.* 32*a*). The problem wrecked the faith of Elisha ben Abuyah. It was left to the Jewish philosophers of the Middle Ages to reconcile the doctrine of Divine foreknowledge with freedom of will. It being beyond the scope of this article to reproduce their arguments, we conclude that all, with perhaps the exception of Ḥasdai Crescas, rejected fatalism, pointing out that foreknowledge was not identical with causation.

LITERATURE.—*JE*, artt. 'Fate,' 'Predestination'; Hamburger, art. 'Bestimmung'; F. Weber, *Jüdische Theologie*, Leipzig, 1897, Index; L. Stein, *Die Willensfreiheit . . . bei den jüd. Philosophen des Mittelalters*, Berlin, 1882; D. Kaufmann, *Gesch. der Attributenlehre*, Gotha, 1877; S. Bernfeld, *Da'ath Elohim*, Warsaw, 1897; M. Joseph, *Judaism as Creed and Life*, London, 1910, ch. vi.

A. E. SUFFRIN.

FATE (Muslim).—**1. General.**—Islām has often been charged with being a fatalistic religion, but this reproach is not quite merited. For a proper analysis of fatalism in Islām, it is important, in the first place, to distinguish between the popular point of view and the philosophical or theological. Eastern peoples have a psychological tendency to fatalism; but this species of popular fatalism, numerous traces of which are found in their folklore, is a sentiment rather than a doctrine. It is, moreover, limited to the outstanding accidents of human life, and especially to death, which it represents as happening of necessity at such and such a time and in such and such circumstances, no matter what one may do to avoid it; it is, we may say, a physical fatalism. The fatalism of the scholars is rather a moral fatalism; it does not apply specially to death, but refers to all human actions, holding these to be decreed by God. It is true that there have been scholars who taught fatalism in Islām, and that the books of Muslim theologians and the Qur'ān itself contain propositions apparently inculcating fatalism. At the same time, it must be remembered that the doctrine of fatalism has always been expressly repudiated by orthodox Islām, which believes in the free will of man, although it encounters serious difficulty in reconciling this with the all-powerful will of God. We now proceed to indicate briefly how the questions of predestination and free will are treated in the Qur'ān, among various philosophical sects, and among the people.

2. In the Qur'ān.—Muhammad speaks of books, kept in heaven, in which the deeds of men are written down, and which will be used as the basis of the Last Judgment. One of these books is called *'Illiyūn*: 'The book of the righteous is in 'Illiyūn' (Qur'ān, lxxxiii. 18 [*SBE* ix. 324]); another is called *Sijjīn*: 'The book of the wicked is in Sijjīn' (lxxxiii. 7 [*SBE, loc. cit.*]). Tradition has it that these books are eternal, though this is not indicated in the text of the Qur'ān; probably Muhammad thought the lists were written day by day as the deeds took place. There are also books relating to each individual:

'As for him who is given his book in his right hand [at the Last Judgment], he shall be reckoned with by an easy reckoning. . . . But as for him who is given his book behind his back, he shall call out for destruction, but he shall broil in a blaze!' (lxxxiv. 7-12).

Muhammad's idea seems to be that human actions are noted down in the books at the time they are performed. There is still another book, called the 'perspicuous Book,' relating to the whole world:

'Nor shall there escape from it the weight of an atom, in the heavens or in the earth, or even less than that, or greater, save in the perspicuous Book' (xxxiv. 3 [*SBE* ix. 150]).

According to tradition, this book is eternal; but the Qur'ān does not say so. In short, the relevant passages do not justify the popular expression 'It was written' (with 'from all eternity' understood).

While there is no text in the Qur'ān affirming that men's actions are decreed in advance by God, we find passages, on the other hand, which seem to signify that God forces certain men to do evil, that He predestines a certain number to hell; *e.g.* the following verses:

'Had we pleased we would have given to everything its guidance; but the sentence was due from me:—I will surely fill hell with the *jinn* and with men all together' (xxxii. 13). 'We have created for hell many of the *jinn* and of mankind: they have hearts and they discern not therewith; they have eyes and they see not therewith; they have ears and they hear not therewith; they are like cattle, nay, they go more astray! these it is who care not' (vii. 178). 'God leads astray whom He pleases, and guides whom He pleases' (xxxv. 9, etc.).

These passages are probably not to be taken quite literally. Muhammad in the Qur'ān does not speak with the precision of a teacher, but rather expresses himself as an orator, almost as a poet. His very emphatic terms were occasioned by the persistent stubbornness of his audience, and may mean only that God finally hardens the hearts of the wicked who have first scorned His favours. This is more clearly stated in ii. 17 (*SBE* vi. 3):

'Deafness, dumbness, blindness, and they shall not return!'

It will be noticed that the above passages are reminiscent of the Bible; Muhammad applies to the wicked what the Bible says of idols (Ps 115^{5-7} $135^{16f.}$).

3. With the theologians.—It was not until philosophical studies began to flourish that the question of fatalism was thoroughly investigated in Islām. The attributes of God are enumerated; amongst them are specified knowledge, will, power. These Divine attributes must be absolute; what room is left then for the will and power of man? The philosophers knew God as universal agent and creator of all things. If God was the 'agent' of everything, how could man be the 'agent' also (and, so to speak, over and above) of his own actions? In God also they saw the supreme 'cause,' the cause of causes; how then could they admit that man was capable of performing deeds of which God was not the 'first cause'? Such were the philosophical forms in which the question was clothed.

God's will and knowledge, according to Muslim theologians, produce from all eternity a sort of decree which is realized by His power. This decree is called the *qaḍā*; its continual realization is the *qadar* (cf. Jurjānī, in the book of the *Ta'rīfāt*). Now, man, under this Divine decree, must be left enough liberty to give his life a moral significance; at the same time, the morally bad actions of wicked men must not be attributed to God. This was the problem which Muslim theology tried to solve, but we cannot say that it has given a clear solution.

There is a short treatise by an interesting though late author, 'Ab dar-Razzāq (*q.v.*), the Ṣūfī († A.D. 1330 at Kāshān), which well represents the point of view of orthodox Muhammadanism on this question. The work is called *Tract on Predestination and Free Will* (*Risālat fī 'l-Qaḍā wa 'l-qadar*). Amidst many subtleties, we see how the author conceives the rôle and function of the will in human action, and the part he means to leave to it in relation to God's will. Knowledge, says 'Abd ar-Razzāq, is the impression of the form of a known object on the mind of man; perception is the feeling of the object given by the external senses, such as sight, or by the internal senses, such as intelligence or imagination. Power is that faculty of the soul which makes it able to accomplish or leave unaccomplished any action; will is the decision which encourages or forbids its accomplishing. The distinction between the 'power' and the 'will' of man plays an important part in these discussions.

When we perceive a thing, we know it; when we know it, we judge whether it is agreeable or repugnant to us; and it produces in us a certain inclination which makes us pursue it or reject it: this inclination is will; and it is will that acts upon the power which moves the members according to the choice of the will. In cases where we are not compelled to admit the absolute agreeableness or non-agreeableness of the object, our intelligence employs the faculty of reflexion and imagination to find out to which side the balance leans; and the will of the intelligence gives free scope to its opinions in this investigation. It may happen that a thing is agreeable under certain aspects and repugnant under others; *e.g.*, it may please some of our senses and not the others, it may be good for certain members and harmful for others, it may please the senses and repel the mind, or inversely; or, again, it may be of advantage for the present but not for the future, or inversely. Every agreeable motive produces an attraction, every other a repulsion; if the attractions prevail, the result is a free decision in favour of the action. To this decision should be attributed praise or blame, according as the action is good or bad; it is this decision that deserves either reward or punishment. Nevertheless, 'Abd ar-Razzāq continues, there is no doubt that perception, knowledge, power, will, reflexion, imagination, and the other faculties exist by the agency of God and not by ours. He concludes that we must refer all actions to God as the agent who makes them exist, without, however, entirely withdrawing them from their human authors.

Ghazālī has a fairly thorough investigation of the question in his *Epistle to Jerusalem*, a section of his great treatise on the *Ihyā*. The principle is that everything produced in the world is the act and creation of God—'God has created you, and what ye make' (Qur'ān, xxxvii. 94). No single movement escapes the power of God, but the decision lies none the less with man to a certain extent. Every free act is, in a way, decided twice—once by God and once by man; it depends upon God for its production, and upon man for the merit or demerit resulting from it; or even, outside of the moral sphere, for the advantages or disadvantages following upon it, since for God there is no advantage or disadvantage. This quality in actions of being advantageous or disadvantageous, which does not exist except from the human point of view, is called *kasb*, 'gain' (cf. Jurjānī, *Ta'rīfāt*). The choice, therefore, lies with man, the accomplishing of the action with God; the movement is man's, but created by God. God is the creator of the action decided by the human will.

Even before Ghazālī, this doctrine had been very clearly formulated in the work of the theologian Ash'arī. Human power, according to this *imām*, can have no influence upon the production of actions, for everything that exists is produced by a unique decree which is superior to the distinction between substance and accident; and, if man's decision could influence this creative decree, it could also influence the production of natural objects, and almost create the heavens and the earth. We must, therefore, believe that God has arranged man's actions beforehand in such a way that things will happen at their proper time in conformity with the decisions of the human will. Man produces an action in appearance only; it is really created by God; but, from the moral point of view, the action is 'attributed' to man because he decided it. Here we have a veritable system of pre-established harmony.

4. With the School of Philosophers.—The question of providence and evil was thoroughly discussed in the philosophic school. Avicenna (*q.v.*) in particular has some very fine passages on it in his *Najāt* (p. 78, section on Providence, and how evil enters into the Divine judgment), and in a treatise specially devoted to the subject—the *Risālat al-Qadr* (*Treatise on Destiny*, tr. by Mehren). In these we meet with ideas, expressed in very eloquent terms, that might be compared with those of Leibniz.

Providence, for Avicenna, is

'the knowledge of God enveloping everything. . . . The knowledge God has of the kind of beneficence applicable to the universal order of things is the source whence good flows over everything.'

How is evil possible in this world which is enveloped by the thought of the absolutely good Being? Avicenna answers the question by a theory of optimism. He recognizes three kinds of evil—metaphysical, moral, and physical. To moral evil he pays little attention; metaphysical evil does not exist except in potential beings, not yet completely realized, *i.e.* in the corruptible world, which is inferior to the sphere of the Moon; it depends on matter; but in the sphere of the Intelligibles there is no metaphysical evil, since everything there exists in a state of complete perfection. As for physical evil, it is less widely spread than physical good; it is frequent, indeed, but not so frequent as good; not illness, but health, is the normal state. Further, every evil is a good in some sense: the weaker animal torn by the wild beast, and the sparrow carried off by the bird of prey, suffer; but their suffering is for the advantage of the stronger animal. Physical good and evil cannot be the same in the eyes of God as they are to us; His point of view and the motives of His judgment are hidden in a mystery which ought to forbid our condemning His work.

5. With certain theological sects.—The doctrine of 'Abd ar-Razzāq is that of the orthodox theologians of Islām; it strikes a happy mean; on either side there is a sect famous in the history of Islām: the Qadarites, who credit man with full power in the production of his actions, and the Jabarites, who credit him with none.

The Qadarites (from *qudrah*, 'human power,' not from *qadar*, 'the Divine decree') hold that man has the power to create his own actions, and do not allow that his evil actions are produced by God. Ash'arī and 'Abd ar-Razzāq reproach them with positing two principles, one for good deeds—God—and one for bad—Satan. The prophet, writes 'Abd ar-Razzāq, said:

'The Qadarites are the Magi of this generation, since they acknowledge two powerful, independent principles, just as the Magi, who looked upon Yezdan and Ahriman as independent principles, the one of good, the other of evil.'

The Mu'tazilites, who were not exactly, as they have been called, free-thinkers, but theologians with a rationalistic tendency, in the 3rd and 4th centuries of Islām, were interested in the question of human freedom; they treated the subject, with a very few differences, in the Qadarite sense.

The Jabarites are the opposite of the Qadarites. They utterly deny the freedom of man; they do not believe that an action really comes from man, but attribute everything entirely to God. Man, they hold, does not even have the power of choice.

God creates the choice and the action along with the sanctions they involve. The name 'Jabarite' comes from *jabr*, 'constraint,' because in this system man is constrained in his every action by the decree of God; good and evil are necessary in him just as are their consequences.

The best known Jabarite teacher is Jahm, son of Safwān. He began to teach at Tirmiz and was put to death by Sālim, son of Aḥwaz al-Māzini, at Merv at the end of the reign of the Umayyads (8th cent. A.D., according to Shahrastāni, text, p. 59). This teacher held that God creates actions in man as He creates them in things, and that actions are attributed to man only metaphorically, as they are to things, when it is said, *e.g.*, that the tree produces fruits, the water runs, etc. Rewards and punishments are compulsory like the actions themselves.

The name Jabarite with the qualification 'moderate' (or 'mitigated') has, according to Shahrastāni, sometimes been given to those who accord a certain rôle in the production of an action to the power of man, while not allowing him freedom of choice. Jurjānī's definition in the *Ta'rīfāt*, that 'the moderate Jabarites are those who accord man a certain merit or demerit in the action, like the Ash'arites,' is not exact; for this last position is confused with the orthodox view.

It should be observed that those ancient Muslim teachers who deny human freedom always deny it on the ground of the omnipotence of God, and not of a purely natural determinism; they still cling to religion even in the very act of annihilating freedom, the condition of moral life.

'Abd ar-Razzāq criticized both sects—Qadarites and Jabarites—in these terms:

'Both are blind in one eye; the Qadarites in the right eye, the stronger, the eye that perceives essential realities; the Jabarites in the left eye, the weaker, the eye that perceives exterior objects. But the man whose sight is sound enjoys two eyes; he sees the Divine essence with his right eye and refers human actions to it, both good and bad; he sees created things with his left eye, and holds that man influences his own actions, not in an independent fashion, but by God. He thus recognizes the truth of the word [attributed to the] Prophet—not absolute constraint or absolute independence, but something between the two.'

6. In popular belief.—The popular conception of fatalism, as we have said, applies only to the outstanding accidents of life and to death. Man is in the power of certain superior, obscure forces, and, however he may struggle against them, he cannot alter the destiny in store for him. This is exactly the ancient Greek idea of destiny: human freedom is not denied, but it is represented as vain in practice, in face of the all-powerful forces that preside over our lives. For example, if it is decided by the power above that a man shall die under certain circumstances, nothing can ever prevent the fulfilling of this decree.

It was prophesied to Khalīf Ma'mūn, the famous promoter of philosophic studies in Islām, that he would die at Raqqa; he accordingly always avoided the well-known town of that name; but one day, when returning from an expedition, he encamped in a little place, where he was seized with a violent fever; he asked the name of the village, and was told that it was Raqqa; then he understood that this was the place, unknown to him, to which destiny had brought him, and had no doubt that his death would follow soon—as it did, in fact, within a few hours.

This willingness to believe that death cannot come except at a fixed time and place is a source of great courage in battle; for where is the danger in recklessness? If it is not written that one is to die, he will suffer no harm; and, if it is written, then nothing can save him. Orthodox theology, however, does not altogether approve of this sentiment. Khalīf Omar uttered a very wise saying on this subject, which well represents the point of view of sound theology: 'He who is in the fire should resign himself to the will of God; but he who is not yet in the fire need not throw himself into it.' 'Resignation' or, rather, 'abandonment' to God is the form of fatalism admitted by the teaching of Islām. It is the idea of Christian mysticism—the believer should abandon himself to the will of God. The very name of Islām expresses this sentiment: *islām* means 'the action of giving up oneself, of surrendering' (*i.e.* to God).

LITERATURE.—Stanislas Guyard, *Traité du décret et de l'arrêt divins, par le dr. soufi Abd er-Razzaq*, tr. in *JA*, 1873, ed. Paris, 1879, new tr., Nogent-le-Rotrou, 1875; A. F. Mehren, Memoir on *al-Ash'arī* (from *Travaux de la 3ième session du congrès internat. des orientalistes*), n.d. vol. ii. p. 46 f., also *Traités mystiques d'Avicenne*, Leyden, 1889–94, fasc. iv.; Carra de Vaux, *Avicenne*, Paris, 1900, *Gazali*, do. 1902, *La Doctrine de l'Islam*, do. 1909.

B^ON CARRA DE VAUX.

FATEHPUR-SĪKRĪ (Arab. *fatḥ*, 'victory,' Hindi *pur*, 'city,' and *Sīkrī*, the original name of the site).—A famous deserted city, situated in the Agra District of the United Provinces of Agra and Oudh; lat. 27° 5′ N.; long. 77° 40′ E.; 23 miles W.S.W. of the city of Agra. Akbar selected the rocky ridge which passes through the old Hindu village of Sīkrī as the site of his new capital.

The native historian, Niẓāmu-d-dīn Aḥmad, in his *Tabakāt-i-Akbarī* (H. M. Elliot, *Hist. of India*, 1873, v. 332 f.), records that 'the Emperor had several sons born to him, but none of them had lived. Shaikh Salīm Chishtī, who resided in the town of Sīkrī, 12 *kos* from Agra, had gladdened him with the promise of a son. The Emperor went to visit the Shaikh several times, and remained there ten or twenty days on each occasion. He commenced a fine building there on the top of a hill, near the Shaikh's monastery. The Shaikh also commenced a new monastery and a fine mosque, which at the present day has no equal in the world, near the royal mansion.' This noted saint of Sīkrī, a descendant of another great saint, Shaikh Farīd Shakkarganj, was born at Delhi in A.D. 1478, and spent the greater part of his life at Sīkrī, where he died in 1572. The son promised to Akbar was born in the house of the saint, was named Sultān Salīm after him, and became Emperor under the title of Jahāngīr (born 1569, ascended the throne 1605, died 1627).

The new palace was founded by Akbar in 1569, after his return from a victorious campaign at Ranthambhor, and the name 'city of victory' commemorates this success and the conquest of Gujarāt which immediately followed. His design in selecting this site for his capital and palace was to secure for himself, his family, and people the benefits of the intercession of the holy man referred to above. It continued to be the principal residence of Akbar until 1584, and was also occupied by his son and successor, Jahāngīr; but it was abandoned by Shāhjahān in favour of Delhi, partly because the position of the latter was superior, and partly because the site of Fatehpur-Sīkrī was found to be unhealthy and the water supply unsatisfactory. Many of the buildings are now in ruins, but careful restoration has been effected by the Indian Government, and a complete survey of the site was carried out by E. W. Smith. Here it is necessary to describe only two of the most important religious buildings—the tomb of the saint Salīm Chishtī, and the Great Mosque, both situated within the same enclosure, the state entrance to which is by a splendid gateway, the Buland or Baland Darwāza, 'great gate.'

Fergusson describes this gate as 'noble beyond any portal attached to any mosque in India, perhaps in the world,' and points out the skill of its architect. The inscription, cut in bold Arabic characters, records its erection in A.D. 1602 to commemorate the conquest of Khāndesh. Coming from a great builder, it has a pathos of its own: 'Said Jesus, on whom be peace! "The world is a bridge; pass over it, but build no house there. He who hopeth for an hour, may hope for an eternity. The world is but an hour; spend it in devotion; the rest is unseen. He that standeth up to pray, while his heart is not in his duty, exalteth not himself, remaining far from God. Thy best possession is that which thou hast given in alms; thy best traffic is selling this world for the next"' (E. W. Smith, *The Moghul Architecture of Fathpur-Sīkrī*, pt. iv. p. 17).

The Great Mosque is called by Fergusson 'the glory' of the place, and is hardly surpassed by any in India. Bishop Heber (*Journal*, ch. xxi.) characteristically contrasts it with the Oxford and Cambridge quadrangles. A chronogram on the main arch records its erection in A.D. 1571. The tomb of the saint, with its lovely carved arcade enclosing the cenotaph, the body being interred in a vault below, is one of the most beautiful buildings in India. It has been fully illustrated and described by E. W. Smith. The tomb is largely frequented by pilgrims from all parts of N. India, the great fair commencing on the 20th day of the month Ramaḍān, when the chief guardian, known as Imām, or Sajjādanashīn, 'he who sits on the carpet of prayer,' a lineal descendant of the saint, is enthroned. Women, as well as men, come to pray; and, though the former are not allowed within the cenotaph chamber, they wander timidly and silently round the perambulatory. Many, particularly brides and childless women, attach scraps of cloth or pieces of thread to the delicate tracery of the marble screen, not, as Smith supposes, as 'votive offerings,' but as a means of bringing themselves into sacred communion with the spirit of the saint, who is implored to act as their intermediary with the Almighty to secure the boon they crave. The same belief in another form is shown in the silver horse-shoe placed, according to tradition, by Akbar himself upon the outer gate, and carried off by the Jāṭs when they attacked Agra in 1764; and in the 333 horse- and ox-shoes, some beautifully chased, ornamenting the Buland Darwāza, where they have been placed by people who trusted that the saint would intercede for the recovery of their sick animals.

LITERATURE.—The article is based on the personal knowledge of the place by the writer and on the monograph by E. W. Smith, *The Moghul Architecture of Fathpur-Sikri*, 4 parts, Allahabad, 1894–98; see also J. Fergusson, *Hist. of Indian Architecture*, London, 1910, ii. 293 ff.; E. B. Havell, *Handbook to Agra and the Taj*, London, 1904; A. Führer, *Monumental Antiquities of the N.W. Provinces and Oudh*, Allahabad, 1891; W. H. Sleeman, *Rambles and Recollections*, ed. V. A. Smith, London, 1893; L. Rousselet, *India and its Native Princes*, London, 1882; *IGI* xii. [1908] 84 ff. There are numerous references to the place in the *Āin-i-Akbarī*, ed. and tr. Blochmann and Jarrett, Calcutta, 1873–94. For frescoes and other works of art, see V. A. Smith, *A History of Fine Art in India and Ceylon*, 1911, pp. 282, 408 ff., 425, 430, 435, 437, 441, 459 ff., 496.

W. CROOKE.

FATHER.—See CHILDREN, FAMILY.

FATHERHOOD OF GOD.—See GOD.

FEAR.[1]—**1. Definition.**—*Fear* in its most general sense means the anticipation or expectation of evil or pain, as hope is the anticipation of good. In its incidence and kind it may be momentary, transitory, and occasional, or a permanent, persistent, all-pervading influence poisoning the whole mind and character; it may be a natural, healthy resistance to a passing physical danger, or a morbid enslavement, a paralysis of will and effort in the anticipation of some remote and improbable contingency. *Surprise* may be regarded as a mild form of fear—the query as to whether an evil is present or not; *astonishment* is a slightly stronger form of the same emotion; *embarrassment* and *shyness* are social forms; *anxiety* is a more diffuse, indefinite kind; *terror* is usually employed for more extreme and sudden onsets of fear, *fright* for a momentary case, and *horror* for the deepest degree to which the emotion attains (C. Darwin, *Expression of the Emotions*, ed. London, 1892, ch. 12). *Timidity*, again, is the general character or temperament from which fear is likely to spring.

2. Physical concomitants.—In its more pronounced form, fear has correlated with it a distinctive group of physical changes in the organism, which, together with their outward effects, form its 'expression.' These are: (1) *changes in the circulation*: the blood-vessels contract, with resulting pallor and lowered temperature in the skin of the body; the heart beats more rapidly and more violently, as if against a greater resistance. (2) *Changes in the respiration*: the breathing becomes laboured; it is shallower and more rapid, with occasional deep inspirations, while in extreme cases the mouth is opened wide as if for easier breath. (3) *In the glands* also action takes place: the skin perspires freely (a 'cold sweat'); the mouth is dry because of the failure of the salivary glands; the voice is hoarse and whispering. (4) *In the viscera* the digestive processes are checked; extreme fear may produce nausea and sickness. (5) *The muscles* are variously affected: the skin trembles all over the body ('shivering with fear'); the voice is tremulous as well as hoarse, and may fail to act ('the tongue cleaving to the roof of the mouth'); the eyes are opened widely ('staring'), the eyebrows arched, the forehead wrinkled, the lower jaw dropped; the arms are swung upwards, as if warding off an approaching enemy; the body, at first motionless and rigid, may become flaccid, the individual shrinking, crouching, perhaps falling limp to the ground. In children, and in most primitive races, these phenomena are exaggerated; in civilization, they are modified by training and other causes, but some never fail to present themselves wherever fear is. Similar expressions are found in animals; in the rabbit the ears turn pale at any sudden change in the environment, as the barking of a dog, or the flight of a passing bird; so with other animals, where the presence, in any part of the surface of the body, of a rich supply of blood makes changes from redness to pallor visible. Trembling from fear also occurs in most animals, while the motionless crouching and the 'shamming dead' of various species correspond to the paralysis of muscles found in man. The more intense the emotion, the greater is the number of muscles affected, and the greater the amplitude of the movements made, according to Pflüger's law (A. Mosso, *La Peur*, Fr. tr. of 3rd Ital. ed., Paris, 1886, p. 34).

Herbert Spencer suggested that the nervous current follows the line of least resistance; those muscles which are most frequently used, and also those which are nearest the nerve-centres, and which are small and unattached to any resisting weight, will present the most permeable paths. Hence the facility with which the muscles of the face are played upon by fear, as by every other emotion (*Essays*, 2nd ser., 1863, pp. 109, 111). Mosso (p. 113) explains the influence of fear upon the capillary blood-vessels, their contraction and the resulting paleness of the skin, on similar principles. It is known that the centres of all such emotional expressions, including the palpitations of the heart, the trembling of the skin-muscles, etc., lie in the brain below the cerebral mantle (in the optic thalami, etc.), and that they still take place in animals from which the greater part of the fore-brain has been removed. It is only 'associative' fear that is no longer shown: a dog, for example, does not show fear, in such a condition, at the *sight* of the whip, but does so at its *crack*; the former is an acquired, the latter an instinctive fear-reaction (Mosso, 40). Mosso, therefore, rejects Darwin's theory as to the *origin* of such reactions, viz. that they have been voluntarily adopted in some previous generation, and then transmitted as 'acquired habits,' the effect accumulating from generation to generation, until the structure of the animal has been so modified that the action is compulsory and invariable. The wide-open eyes and raised eyebrows, for example, are referred to the effort to *see* better the object of fear; the wide-open mouth of horror is explained partly by the effort to *hear* better, mouth-breathing being less noisy than nose-breathing, partly by the needs of a rapid inspiration; the muscular actions as preparation for flight or for attack; the erection of the hair as a relic of the tendency, found in many species of animals, to make the appearance more terrifying to an opponent, as dogs raise the hair of the back, cats fluff out their hair and rise on tip-toe, reptiles and amphibians swell the body or neck, etc. (Darwin, pp. 100, 110).

Darwin had also considered that the focusing of attention on the object of fear might have the effect of withdrawing nervous energy from the general musculature of the body; hence, perhaps, the hanging jaw, the trembling of the skin, the shrinking of the body in fear. It is to a more general principle such as this that Mosso and Lange prefer to appeal—the tendency of the organism towards equilibrium, when subjected to stimuli of different kinds; circulation and respiration are the processes which are most rapidly modified in different situations—cold and heat (whether local or general), light, sound, taste, etc. The immediate effect of any great mental disturbance, arising from a strong stimulus, is to send blood to the brain, withdrawing it from the skin and muscles and the internal organs. The organism, as it were, draws its forces towards the centre, in order to be able to direct them effectively to the right point of attack. For the same reason the heart beats more rapidly, to

[1] For aspects of fear not discussed in the present art., see RELIGION, REVERENCE.

keep the centres supplied with fresh materials. The withdrawing of the blood from the scalp may be a direct cause of the erection of the hair, and, even when the latter does not occur, and when the terror is prolonged, the trophic disturbance may cause the hair to turn grey or fall out soon afterwards. The circulation of the blood is dependent in its turn on a sufficient supply of air to provide it with oxygen; the panting breath of a great fear is similar in its nature and its origin to the panting after an exertion, or during a cold shower-bath. There is a great drain on the cerebral energy, and all the vital processes are set in action to counteract it or make it good. The trembling of the body, shrinking of the skin, pallor, and the rest, are, as it were, by-products of this general reflex tendency; they are not adaptive, and serve no end for the advantage of either individual or species.

So obviously is the 'expression' of fear in ordinary cases unadapted to assist the organism that Darwin, after suggesting the explanation by 'relics' of useful habits,—no longer useful in present circumstances,—admitted the insufficiency of his explanation. It has even been thought that the fear-reactions were determined by natural selection, not for the good of the terrified species—the victim—but for that of the terrifying species—the beast of prey. This would, indeed, be a bizarre product of evolution. Mosso showed that they have simply no reference to evolution: the trembling of the body, for example, in fear, is similar to the trembling which occurs when lifting a heavy weight, or when exhausted by illness: the nervous excitement prevents us from co-ordinating the movements of the many muscles involved in every—even the simplest—action, as standing, walking, speaking, etc. A man who is afraid does not see better, however widely he opens his eyes; he does not hear better; he is the less prepared for action the greater his terror and therefore, presumably, his danger. Actions which are so injurious to the organism should have been discarded in the course of evolution, but in fear the reaction becomes more ill-adapted, more hurtful to the individual, the greater the actual danger is (Mosso, 122 f.); they are not, therefore, products of evolution, but symptoms of disease, pathological forms taken by normal processes under abnormal conditions.

The principle of adaptation can be applied only when we are dealing with very mild forms of fear—little more than expectation or surprise: the expression in such cases involves several of the attention reflexes—the wide-open eyes, the raised eyebrows, and the frown, which Darwin interpreted as a nascent crying, but Mosso showed to be part of the action of adapting the *sight* to a near object. Any mental effort tends to set in play the muscles used in external attention, just as all higher mental processes tend to have as their 'expression' the same reactions as occur in the corresponding *sensory* processes.

3. The objects of fear.—In its *type* form, fear is a perceptual emotion, felt on awareness of an object or recognition of a situation of some definite kind. In other words, the object in the fear-consciousness is complex and indirect, containing elements which are added to the immediate effect of the stimulus, either from memories of past experience or in some other way. Small and defenceless birds show fear of the hawk and other birds of prey, and of snakes or serpents; horses show fear of the wolf, its appearance, its howl, and even its odour; kittens show fear of dogs; dogs of tigers and lions; cattle of strange dogs, etc. The gnat is said by Hudson to have an 'instinctive' fear of the dragon-fly; the cockroach, according to Belt, of the larger spiders; the child has fear in insecure positions (fear of falling), fear of the dark, of wild animals, etc. It seems, then, as if there were definite classes of objects, corresponding to the most dangerous features in the natural life of every animal, with the perception of which fear is associated. Healthy dogs are said to avoid 'instinctively' a dog which has rabies; they will not attack it, nor do they retaliate when themselves bitten by it. The question arises as to how this is possible. A natural explanation refers the formation of the percept, and its association with the fear impulse, to the experience of the individual, either in memory of actual experience, as a dog 'learns' to reject food seasoned with mustard, or in some sort of inference from past experience, as a child, having fallen from a table to the ground, may feel insecure at any high level afterwards. But, as this explanation is obviously inadequate to account for fear in infants and in young animals, which is exhibited apart from any experience of the injurious influence of the objects feared, the argument has been extended to include the ancestors of the individual. It is *their* experience and not his that conditions his special behaviour towards the object of fear. In the former case, simple and comparatively familiar forms of association account for the result: a cat hears the bark of a dog for the first time, then sees the dog, which springs upon it and shakes it; the painful experience leads to protective reactions of clawing, spitting, etc.; one or more experiences of this kind are sufficient to drive home the association, so that the sound or sight of the dog calls up directly (1) a memory of the sensations of being seized, etc., (2) the feeling of pain, and (3) the impulse to attack or to escape (G. H. Schneider, *Der thierische Wille*, Leipzig, 1880, § 4). It is not a memory of the original feeling, but a new and actual feeling, that is caused by the remembered sensations; but, since the cerebral processes involved in sensation and its 'memory' are probably the same, in part at least, the feelings will also tend to be similar. Thus fear, as a feeling, is a form of *pain*, and its reactions are similar to those of pain. With repetition of this process, the sensations of being seized fail to be remembered consciously, and the feeling and impulse attach directly to the sight or sound of the feared object.

There is ample evidence in human life of this dropping out of links—for example, the frequent cases in which a person or a kind of food is disliked, because of some forgotten experience in the past, perhaps in early childhood. The emotion may in such a case be utterly out of proportion to its immediate object. The cerebral processes, corresponding to the original experience, may really be excited, but not sufficiently to give separate and distinct consciousness of the past. Cases are frequent where one wakes from a light sleep with a vague feeling of depression, dread, or terror, without any object being consciously before the mind; but a search or some chance association through the day may recall a dream in which some situation of terror was actually presented. The emotion caused by the dream persisted after the consciousness of the latter had itself ceased. Such subconscious states have been found to be a common condition in many cases of pathological fear (see below), and the fear has been cured or removed by bringing the cause to full consciousness, so that its irrationality is appreciated.

Similar to the above process, but less direct, is that in which fear is caused in a social animal by the sight of the suffering or death of one of its own kind. It is from these and the former experiences that G. H. Schneider supposes instinctive and congenital fears to have been evolved. The reactions to such percepts become habitual in the individual, modification of the cerebral or other central nerve-elements takes place, and these modifications become congenital in the descendants—either by way of natural or 'organic' selection, or through direct inheritance, if such is possible (*Der thierische Wille*, 108 ff., and *Der menschliche Wille*, Berlin, 1882, pt. i. ch. 4). In either case what is congenital is not the perception or the emotion as such, but the conditions on which their formation depends; there is no inherent difficulty in the conception of 'connate' ideas of this kind; the perception of a particular object, as of a lion, with differential reactions towards it, may be as easily congenital, and may be accounted for in the same way, as the sensation of a colour, *e.g.* red, or green, the power to differentiate which has been undoubtedly 'evolved' from a primitive colourless light-sense. Hence a young animal, as is suggested, might easily have an untaught 'recognition' of a dangerous foe, with the corresponding emotions. A bird, even before leaving the shell, ceases chirping at the warning cry of the mother-bird; within a day after hatching it will crouch motionless under the same conditions, or, if it is a young water-bird, it will dive in the water; later, it will of its own accord shrink and stand quietly still when a hawk appears in the air. Conversely, young cuckoos, it is said, pay no heed to the shrill warnings of their foster-mother. Belt (*Naturalist in Nicaragua*[2], London, 1888, p. 109 f.) describes a tribe of butterflies, 'naturally' fearless because distasteful to most animals, but showing immediate fear of a conspicuous wasp which preyed upon them. But experiments show, whatever be the case with insects, that birds and higher animals have no such instinctive dread of particular objects. Thus there is no congenital fear of man (Hudson, *Naturalist in La Plata*[2], London, 1892, p. 83 ff.); birds crouch with fear not merely at a hawk, but at any large object flying over them; in Aberdeenshire, when grouse are very wild, and are being shot over dogs, a practice of keepers is to fly a paper kite; this has the effect of making the birds lie quiet till the dog is almost upon them. The cry of a hawk frightens, but so does any harsh, shrill, or grating cry; blind kittens show fear, hiss, and bristle at the smell of a dog, but they do the same at any strong odour—such as ammonia (Lloyd Morgan, *Animal Behaviour*, London, 1900, p. 48).

E. L. Thorndike describes experiments on the fears of chicks, corroborating Morgan's decision 'that no well-defined specific fears are present; that the fears of young chicks are of strange moving objects in general, shock in general, strange sounds in general.' No specific reaction occurred, *e.g.*, to the presence of man or to the presence of a cat, unless the cat sprang upon them, when they showed the same sort of terror as when 'a basket or football' was thrown among them. The general fear of a novel object in motion is not present from the beginning, but develops during the first month; this is also true of the fear of man. Among the interesting observations made is that of the great individual differences between chicks, both in the immediate reaction, and in the process of acquiring definiteness of perception. The mew of a cat, for example, caused a great show of terror in one or two chicks, but none at all in others (Thorndike, *Animal Intelligence*, N.Y. 1911, p. 162). Thus, inheritance, as Lloyd Morgan expresses it, only 'provides the *raw material* for effective consciousness to deal with, in accordance with the results which are its data' (*op. cit.* p. 51).

However simple or however complex the fear-consciousness may be, the reactions, and, therefore, probably the feelings themselves, are essentially the same as those of the sensory experience—for example, the feeling and reaction on being clawed, bitten, mauled, or otherwise injured (Schneider, *Der menschliche Wille*, ch. 12). The differences between actual pain and its reaction on the one side, and the mental anticipation of pain in fear and *its* reaction on the other, are differences only in the *extent* of the muscles and organs affected, the *number* of movements made, etc. In no case is *will* concerned with the origin of the fear-reactions; they are neither distinctly intentional, nor the 'traces,' 'relics,' or 'rudiments' of ancestrally willed and supposedly useful actions. Experience may modify them, lead to a selection of their objects, and to the control or even the exaggeration of their movements, but it has had no part in their formation (cf. also Lloyd Morgan, 110).

In the child the first real expression of fear is towards sudden, sharp, and unfamiliar sounds, also to loud, voluminous sounds, and, in some cases, even to musical sounds when first heard (J. Sully, *Studies of Childhood*, London, 1896, p. 194). Occasionally such fears do not show themselves in the early months, until the child is a year old or more; according to Sully, they are not to be explained entirely by the disturbance to the nervous sensibility, but by a sort of 'vague alarm at the unexpected and unknown'; when the sounds have been frequently repeated, the fear disappears. The fear of falling, shown by all children of a few months old, when being awkwardly carried, or later, when first trying to walk, may be referred to the same general cause: the situations are unfamiliar, therefore mentally disturbing. No doubt also the experience of actual falls is a contributory influence. In the case of visual impressions, again, it is mainly the new and strange—a new room, a strange person, a change of dress in a familiar person, any new or distorted form of a familiar object, a grimace, an awkward movement, the play of shadows. Feathers and fur, animals of all kinds when first seen, more especially black animals, and the dark, especially being alone in the dark, are familiar occasions of fear in nearly all children, although these feelings are not developed until the child is several months old. Many children are afraid of being alone even by day. But in this, and in respect of every other 'fear,' children differ so enormously from each other, so much depends on experience, on the suggestions of adults, that the idea of an hereditary or atavistic element in child fear seems unnecessary and even absurd. As in the case of animals, fear of the novel, sudden, startling, or disconcerting, along with fear of what actually causes pain to the child, gives a sufficient basis for experience to work upon. Fears of the imagination, probably because of the very vagueness of the imagery underlying them—such fears as the incautious nurse excites by her tales of 'black man,' 'bogey,' ghost and goblin, ogre and dwarf, robbers and murderers in the dark places, etc.—are of the most intense description, and often seriously weaken a child's character for life (see Mosso, ch. 14).

Is it true, then, that the child in these cases is suffering in a rudimentary form the actual fears, sprung from experience, of its remote ancestors? Mosso holds that it is so:

'Destiny gives as a legacy to each of us a fatal inheritance. Abandoned in the forest, confined in a tower, without guide, without example, without light, the experience of our parents and our most remote ancestors is revealed in us as a sort of mysterious dream. What we call instinct is the voice of extinct generations, resounding as a distant echo in the cells of the nervous system. We have in us the inspiration, the advice, the experience of all men, from those who perished naked in the forests striving against furious wild beasts, and who fed upon acorns, down to our fathers and mothers who transmit to us their virtues, their courage, their anxieties, and their tenderness' (p. 168).

As indicated in art. DEVELOPMENT (Mental), Stanley Hall ('A Study of Fears,' *AJPs* viii. [1897]; see also A. F. Chamberlain, *The Child*[2], London, 1906, p. 265) has greatly extended this view: fear of wind and water, of fire and darkness, of solitude, of strangers, of animals, of fur, of teeth, etc., are all alike referred to various ancestral stages in the life of the human race. But, apart altogether from the extreme unlikelihood of such 'acquired' characters being hereditarily transmitted, the above simple conditions seem sufficient to account for the facts. The varieties observed in children may be explained by an inherited timidity in some, or nervous weakness, with consequent excitability—the same cause which makes women more easily terrified than men, and the victim of alcoholic or other form of nervous disease more easily terrified than his fellows. A peculiarly intense shock of fear in childhood, and especially in early youth, may permanently weaken the system, so that a slighter cause may produce fear or terror than with the normal individual.

4. Theory of fear.—As is well known, these views have led C. Lange[1] and William James[2] to regard the feeling of fear as succeeding, not preceding, the reactions; it is the consciousness of these changes and movements *as* they are occurring and *after* they have occurred—a consciousness conditioned by sensory nerves leading from the various muscles and joints of the body, from the skin, and from the various internal organs, to the brain. In this 'back-stroke' hypothesis, expression precedes feeling or emotion; the reaction (the 'expression') is connected directly with the perception of the object, or with the sensory elements 'integrated' in the perception; further, feeling itself ceases to be a different kind of mental element from sensation; in the last resort *fear* can be analyzed, it is claimed, into the *awareness* of the coldness and shivering of the skin, the perspiration, the trembling muscles, the ineffectual efforts, the dryness of the mouth, the sinking of the stomach, the inability to see clearly, to attend

[1] *Ueber Gemüthsbewegungen* (tr. from Danish), Leipzig, 1887.
[2] *Principles of Psychology*, London, 1891, vol. ii. ch. 25.

or to think steadily, etc.; each of these phenomena has its reflex in consciousness, and these in their sum make up the emotion of fear. Thus, according to Lange (p. 40), *fear* has its characteristic colour from these three processes—the weakening of voluntary innervation (this by itself characterizes *disappointment*), the contraction of the blood-vessels (these two combined represent *sorrow*), and the spasm of the organic visceral muscles. Its diametrical opposite, from this point of view, is *anger* (heightening of the voluntary innervation, dilatation of blood-vessels, but with inco-ordination of action added). In these various manifestations the primary are the vasomotor changes; the muscular weakness, *e.g.*, comes from the fact that the nervous system, like the skin and other organs, receives too little blood (p. 41), owing to the narrowing of the fine arteries. Fear, then, is simply the perception (or other consciousness) of certain changes in the person's body (p. 51):

'Take away the bodily symptoms, let the pulse beat quietly, the eye be steadfast, the colour healthy, the movements rapid and certain, the speech strong, the thoughts clear—what is there left of the fear?' (p. 53).

The chief evidence appealed to by both Lange and James is: (i.) the cases of fear and similar emotions existing without any adequate or conscious cause; these, however, the ordinary theory is quite competent to explain, as above suggested. (ii.) The admitted effect of such drugs as alcohol: fear can be removed by alcohol, and by its abuse fear in the most extreme form (as in *delirium tremens*, or in neurasthenic anxieties, etc.) may be produced without, in either case, the external situation offering any cause. This is because alcohol, at first and in moderate doses, excites the vasomotor apparatus, increases the frequency and strength of the heart-beat, dilates the capillary vessels, heightens the voluntary innervation, etc., while alcohol-poisoning has precisely the opposite effects. In the former case, speech and movement are easy, the subject feels warm and active, the thoughts flow freely; in the latter, speech, action, sensation, thought are all alike paralyzed: the resulting state in the one case is *courage*, in the other *fear*, and the emotions suggest objects, imaginary if no real ones can be fixed upon. The process is therefore (*a*) physical state, (*b*) emotion (its conscious reflex), (*c*) object, in that order of time, whereas, on the ordinary theory, the procession is from object (perception) to emotion, and from emotion to physical state (expression).

It does not belong to this article to discuss the general theory; there can be no question, however, (1) that in our own case, and in that of animals, the fear-reaction is instinctive, and attaches directly to the perception of its object; (2) that the emotion itself, of fear, is in us largely constituted by sensory and perceptual elements arising from our changed organic and muscular state; (3) there are also many associative ideas present, memories and imaginations of evil, from our own direct experience, from tradition, from analogy, etc.; but these factors alone do not account for the emotion; in itself it is (4) a mental attitude, depending in each case partly on the sensations and their feelings (pain), partly on the bodily disposition as a whole, health, fatigue, etc., partly on the cerebral disposition in particular, as modified and determined by past experience. (5) What is now innate, both in the expression and in the discrimination of the objects of fear, had its origin in previous generations in the simple feelings and reactions directly correlated with sensations. The gradual dulling, with growing civilization, of such emotions as fear is explained partly by man's increasing intellectuality—the blood is drained more habitually towards other cerebral centres than the vasomotor—and partly by training in control, the inhibition of these, as of other reflex-actions, through the discipline of family and school life. From both these causes the lower liability to *physical* fear in ourselves as compared with more primitive peoples, or with our own ancestors of a generation or two back, can be explained. But what the modern fear has lost in *intensity* and in materiality it has gained in *extensity*, in persistence, in refinement of torture. Worry is the most common form, and its influence illustrates the two fundamental characters of intellectual and spiritual fear: on the one side, the attention is held only by those sensations or percepts, those passing memories, images, and thoughts which harmonize with or corroborate the emotion; the latter forms a morbid apperceptive system by which the whole outlook upon life, the colour and trend of the thoughts, is modified; on the other side, action is paralyzed, dangers, difficulties, evil consequences, uncertainties are constantly before the mind, so that the individual either does not act at all, or acts on any blind impulse that happens at a given moment to have some strength.

In disease of the brain or of the general nervous system, whether organic or functional, the deficient energy with which the various nervous processes are carried out, the ineffective muscular action, the poorer 'tone' of the whole body, imperfect digestion, shallower breathing, defective circulation, have as their mental correlate a state of nervous anxiety or dread, with confusion of thought, and inability to will or to act. Frequently this vague anxiety becomes fixed upon some special object; the melancholy table given by Féré (*The Pathology of Emotions*, Eng. tr., London, 1899) illustrates the variety of forms in this torturing malady—fear of open spaces, of precipices and of heights, of closed places, of water or of liquids in general, of cold, of draughts, of thunder, of fire, of solitude, of crowds, of animals, of poisoning, of infection, of death, of ruin, etc. In many cases there is some event in the individual's life, the memory of which is revived under the stress of the emotional state, so that it is raised to the intensity and associative force of a dominant idea; in other cases such a real experience has occurred, perhaps in early childhood, but has been forgotten; yet it may be subconsciously revived by the emotion, and so draw to itself the control of thought and of action, without rising into distinct consciousness, except under the analysis of the physician. Superstitious fears are largely of this subconscious type; the intensity of the fear is quite disproportionate to the ideas actually in consciousness. To see the baneful influence of such fears in full force, one must go to the African or Australian native. Thus, R. H. Nassau (*Fetichism in West Africa*, London, 1904) represents fetishism as a monstrous outgrowth from natural beliefs; it is crushing the natives out of existence even more effectively than the white man's competition, destroying independence of mind and freedom of thought among individuals; trust, even in one's nearest relatives, has ceased to exist—there is universal fear and insecurity; as every act has to be carefully deliberated, and all possible measures taken against evil influences, the result is an appalling waste of human effort, waste of human life, and the decay of all hope of progress or even of escape. On the other hand, fear, especially fear of the inexplicable, of the unknown, has formed an almost universal stimulant to religious custom and belief. In the individual, as in the race, the coming of religion—conversion—is, in a very large number of cases, as Starbuck's analysis shows, the sequel of a longer or shorter period of intense anxiety and fear (*Psychology of Religion*[2], London, 1901, ch. 4).

LITERATURE.—The works of Darwin, Spencer, Mosso, Sully, William James, and C. Lange, as referred to in the text; also W. McDougall, *Social Psychology*[3], London, 1911.

J. L. McINTYRE.

FEARLESSNESS.—In the highest forms of *courage* (*q.v.*), fear (*q.v.*) still persists as an element; there is at least the consciousness and, therefore, the anticipation of danger. Many of the bravest soldiers have gone with trembling limbs and palpitating heart through their earlier engagements, and many a moral or religious act of devotion or of self-sacrifice has been carried out 'in fear and trembling,' yet is all the more highly valued on that account. *Fearlessness*, on the other hand, is insensibility to danger, where the natural or normal individual would be keenly conscious of it, as in a situation involving almost certain death, or loss of fortune or social reputation. It may arise from inexperience or ignorance, as in the case of an infant's attitude to fire, or that of the Antarctic penguins to man when first approached by him; or, again, from the absorption of a strong, instinctive impulse, as when a mother-animal turns to defend her wounded young, regardless of her own danger, or as in the case of the sheep-dogs in S. America, described by Darwin, which showed extreme timidity when away from their flock, but turned with the utmost ferocity and fearlessness when back among the sheep with which they had been brought up, and which they probably regarded as their 'pack.'[1] So in man, the consciousness of numbers, as in the 'crowd,' gives a suggestion of strength to the individual, and inhibits in his mind the thought of difficulty, of danger, of possible evil consequences; a naturally timid man may under such conditions become absolutely fearless.

In such cases, fearlessness springs from a *temporary* absorption or concentration of the attention on one group of facts, with correlative anæsthesia for others, especially those inconsistent with the former. The intensity of absorption in its turn is explained by some primary instinct, social or individual, which is stimulated. Such a state may also be natural and *permanent*, as in those fortunate beings who, with a capacity for finding happiness in almost any conditions, never experience evil in their own lives, and fail to appreciate the extent of its presence in those of others: W. James gives Walt Whitman as an instance (*op. cit. infra*, p. 84). So in all great enthusiasms—moral, religious, artistic—even the most ordinary risks, doubts, drawbacks, consequences, do not enter the mind at all; or, rather, they are thought of only as one notes and avoids obstacles in walking across a room, as conditions requiring some adjustment of our action, but not in the slightest degree affecting its successful issue. Such an attitude tends of itself to compel success: confidence is increased; energy, both physical and mental, is economized; the highest possible co-ordination between thought and action is obtained, without any of the irresolution, uncertainty, weakness, which fear connotes. Civilization has not removed the bodily weakness and mental incapacity of animal fear, while it has enormously extended the number of fear-objects, just as it has widened the conception of the self, to include the family, the nation, and the race. In its modern form of 'worry,' as in older animal forms, fear is destructive to the individual, paralyzes activity, and debases the quality of thought.

A religion which gives the sense of an Infinite Power behind the finite individual, and of infinite goodness, tends of itself to remove all fear, to produce fearlessness, so far as the religion is really believed. Christian Science (*q.v.*) and other 'mind-cure' philosophies make this their conscious aim—to produce in the individual, whether by persuasion or by suggestion, a sense of perfect security and trust. All strain, all effort, doubt, hesitation, worry, mental and, to some extent, even physical fatigue, fall away, when the thought of self has been banished. The result that is claimed is a great increase not only in the happiness, but also in the efficiency, courage, and confidence of the individual (see the chapters on 'The Religion of Healthy-Mindedness,' in W. James, *Varieties of Religious Experience*, London, 1902, p. 78 ff.; the characteristics of Saintliness, *ib.* p. 272 ff.; and the striking instance of George Müller, *ib.* p. 468 ff.).

J. L. McINTYRE.

[1] *Naturalist's Voyage*, ch. 8 (ed. 1901, p. 149).

FEASTING.—*Introductory.*—The custom of feasting together is a direct development of the meal partaken in common. The allaying of the pangs of hunger by food taken at more or less regular intervals has had for man very important and unexpected results. Perhaps as a result of food being prepared at the hearth—the seat of ancestral spirits or, ultimately, of gods—the gods came to be recognized at the common meal by being presented with some of the food. Eating thus assumed a religious aspect. But, by the very fact that the meal was partaken of in common, it was in itself a bond of union between the eaters; and, since it was shared with gods, it thus obtained a sacramental character. Hence there was no more usual way of admitting a stranger to kinship than by permitting him to share the common meal. Again, since the partaking of food gave rise to pleasurable sensations, man's social instincts suggested the sharing of these sensations with others when abundance of food or some luxurious form of food was available. In all these ways the common meal easily passes over into the feast, in which there is a religious, a social, and a sensuous aspect, as far as savage and barbaric life is concerned, and frequently at higher levels also.[1] In savage and barbaric life, feasting occupies a considerable place and is indulged in upon every possible occasion. The mere fact that food is abundant frequently leads to a feast in which large quantities are consumed or wasted, with the usual savage lack of forethought. The mere desire for good fellowship and for jollification may lead to a feast at which there are guests from far and near.

Such gatherings are found in the Nicobar Islands, when, invitations having been duly sent out, the guests arrive bringing contributions for the feast of pork, yams, plantains, toddy, etc. (Solomon, *JAI* xxxii. [1902] 203 f.). Among the Eskimos there are festal dances during the winter in the *casine*, or town-house, when the performers and all present indulge freely in fish and berries (Bancroft, *NR* i. 67). Among the Mosquitos there are frequent drinking feasts lasting for many days, whenever liquor is plentiful (*ib.* i. 735).

Such gatherings may have a collective importance if they are of a tribal character.

Among the Andaman Islanders a chief will organize a tribal feast, sending invitations to all within easy reach. Food is prepared in abundance, and feasting and dancing go on all night. Next morning the guests exchange presents with their friends (Man, *JAI* xii. [1883] 388 f.). At a higher stage, as in China, the same is found. The *Li Ki* describes the festive meetings in each territorial district for drinking and feasting. These had also a religious aspect, since sacrifice was offered at them (*SBE* xxvii. [1885] 56, xxviii. [1885] 435 ff.).

In civilized society the same social instinct leads to frequent gatherings, private or public, at which the guests eat and drink and enjoy each other's company. While the motive for these on the part of the giver of the feast may be mere display, none the less the idea of fellowship is there, and the pleasurable sensations aroused also stimulate that fellowship.

In this article we shall consider feasting as it occurs at different periods: birth and name-giving, initiation, marriage, funerals; in connexion with sacrifice; and at various seasonal festivals, including harvest.

[1] Cf. the remarks of Wundt, *Ethics*, London, 1897, i. 171 ff.

1. Feasts in connexion with birth.—Children being generally regarded as a valuable asset among savages and barbaric peoples, rejoicings usually take place either before or soon after birth, often in connexion with the ceremony of name-giving. Thus among the Northern Massim a feast is given when it is certain that the wife is pregnant (Seligmann, *Melanesians of Brit. New Guinea*, Cambridge, 1910, p. 704). Among both Hindus and Muhammadans in the Panjāb, feasting takes place during the 8th and 9th, or the 7th month of pregnancy (Rose, *JAI* xxxv. [1905] 277, 279). In E. Africa, when a young wife is pregnant for the first time, a great feast is held in which only women who have borne children take part (Macdonald, *Africana*, 1882, i. 128 f.). Among the Southern Massim the umbilical cord of a first-born child is placed in the sheath of one of the leaves growing near the base of a banana. 'When it bears fruit, the first of a series of feasts termed *sipupu* is given to the child's maternal uncles, and the produce of the tree forms a part of the feast.' Four or five feasts are given at intervals of a month (Seligmann, 487). At Uvea a feast is held soon after the birth of a child, in connexion with a ceremonial lustration (Ploss, *Das Kind*², Leipzig, 1884, i. 258). Among the Baganda, at the name-giving ceremony, a feast was made for all the relatives present (Roscoe, *The Baganda*, 1911, p. 62). The birth of twins was celebrated with much feasting, as this was regarded as a very lucky event, dancing and promiscuous intercourse being part of the proceedings (*ib.* pp. 68–72). At the baptism of the child among the Muhammadan Swahili the ceremony is ended with a feast (*ZE* xxxi. [1899] 67). Among the Mayas a birth was celebrated with especial rejoicings, and feasts were held when the umbilical cord was cut (Bancroft, *NR* ii. 679). Similarly the Nahuas held a feast a few days after birth, while during the baptism of the child the festivities lasted 20 days, and open house was kept by the parents (*ib.* 270, 276). American Indian tribes usually celebrate name-giving with festivities. Thus the Pottawatomies make a great feast, inviting numerous guests by sending a leaf of tobacco or a small ring (de Smet, *Voyages*, Brussels, 1873, p. 393). On the occasion of the birth of a child among the Pūna Musalmāns, friends are invited to feast on the goat offered as a sacrifice, the parents, however, abstaining from the food (Campbell, *Notes on the Spirit Basis of Belief and Custom*, Bombay, 1885, p. 410). Among the Chinese, when the ceremonial of shaving the child's hair takes place at the end of the 1st month, a feast is held to which neighbours and relatives are invited (see *ERE* ii. 646ᵃ). At the *amphidromia* celebrated by the Greeks on the fifth day after birth, banquets were held for the assembled friends and relatives (Ephippos, in Athen. 370 D), and on the tenth day, at the name-giving ceremony, festival-banquets were also held (Aristoph. *Birds*, 494, 922 f.; Eurip. *Elect.* 1126, fr. 2). In Burma, a fortnight after birth, a fortunate day and hour are fixed by an astrologer for the name rite, and a feast is prepared for all the friends and relatives (Monier-Williams, *Buddhism*, London, 1889, p. 353). Among the Tibetan Buddhists the name-giving ceremony concludes with a feast (Köppen, *Rel. des Buddha*, Berlin, 1857–59, ii. 320). Muhammadans celebrate a birth with great feastings and rejoicings, the father entertaining his friends, usually on the seventh day or on seven successive days after a birth (Lane, *Arabian Society*, 1883, p. 187, *Modern Egyptians*, 1846, iii. 142 f.). In modern times and in Christian countries the festal gathering of relatives after a baptism is analogous to and continues these feasts of ethnic races.

2. Initiation feasts.—Initiation being an important period in the life of the savage youth, it is a time when many ceremonies are performed, and among these a feast has usually a prominent place, since the admission of the youth to full tribal privileges is naturally an occasion of rejoicing. In the Andaman Islands, when a lad breaks his 'turtle fast' (see FASTING [Introd.]) for the first time, a feast is arranged by his friends, consisting mainly of turtle (Man, *JAI* xii. [1883] 130). Among the tribes to the north of the Papuan Gulf, the feast takes place, not at initiation, but when the boy is five years old. The father gives a dedicatory feast in order to declare that the boy will be fully initiated at the proper time (Holmes, *JAI* xxxii. [1902] 419). In Fiji, at the annual initiation to the Mbaki mysteries, a feast was held each night, and on the fifth day a great feast took place at which all kinds of food previously under tabu were prepared. The youths received food sacramentally, after which feasting took place, and was continued for several days (Thomson, *Fijians*, 1908, p. 152 f.). In New Britain, when lads are initiated to the Dukduk mysteries, local feasts, followed by a general feasting, terminate the rites (Brown, *Melanesians and Polynesians*, 1910, p. 66 f.). Similarly, in the Banks Islands, admission to the *suqe*, or club, demands a costly feast, at which much eating takes place and licence is general (Codrington, *The Melanesians*, Oxford, 1891, pp. 53, 103, 106). The initiation of youths among the Basutos was accompanied by a feast and dances (Casalis, *Les Bassoutos*, Paris, 1859, p. 277). Among the American Indians such feasts are wide-spread. Thus, among the Salish, at the initiation of a youth to the secret society, his father feasted the society for five days, masked dances being performed (Boas, *Report of the U.S. Nat. Mus. for 1895*, Washington, 1897, p. 644 f.). Among the Tsimshian, initiation to the secret society is associated with a feast and dancing (*ib.* 659 f.). Circumcision, which is often a species of initiation, is accompanied by festivities. In Fiji it was followed by a great feast and indescribable revelry (Thomson, 157). Among the Bageshu of Mt. Elgon the chief kills an ox to furnish a feast for the boys (Roscoe, *JRAI* xxxix. [1909] 185). The Naivashai Masai have a circumcision feast at which bullocks, sheep, and milk are contributed by the elders. The feast lasts for three months, and is accompanied by dancing, singing, and drinking—the 'warriors' feast.' Before their circumcision the boys themselves have a feast lasting two days (Bagge, *JAI* xxxiv. [1904] 167). Similar feasts often take place when girls attain the age of puberty, and frequently in connexion with their being tatued (see Seligmann, 265). As an example of feasting at initiation in higher religions, the rites of Isis-worship may be cited. After the fasting and baptism of the candidate, he was exposed to the gaze of the multitudes. Then followed a joyous banquet and merrymaking. A religious feast was also held on the third day (Apuleius, *Metam.* xi.).

3. Marriage feasts.—Here the feast has a definitely ritual aspect, since, by eating together, bride and bridegroom, as well as their respective relatives and friends (or in some cases these alone), are bound together, or the feast is an outward expression of this union.[1] In some instances the feast is almost the chief or the only rite of marriage; but in any case it has a ritual aspect, though this tends to disappear in more advanced societies, where the feast is little more than an occasion of merrymaking, expressing, however, mutual friendliness. Among the Roro-speaking tribes of New Guinea,

[1] The Roman rite of *confarreatio* and similar rites elsewhere, though not of the nature of a feast, express even more clearly the same idea of union (see Crawley, *Mystic Rose*, 1902, p. 379 ff.; Hartland, *LP*, 1895, ii. 343 f.).

part of the elaborate ceremonial of marriage consists in the bridegroom's kin bringing many pigs to the bride's folk, who supply a large quantity of fish and bananas, upon which a feast is made. With the Southern Massim the kin of the bride and bridegroom exchange presents of food, upon which they feast, the young couple, however, not partaking. This constitutes a binding marriage (Seligmann, 271, 504). In Fiji the feast, provided by the bridegroom, was an indispensable part of the ceremony, and was followed by the bridegroom taking the bride to his house (Thomson, 202). In New Britain, three days after the bride was taken to the man's house, a feast called *Wawainim*, 'giving to drink,' was held, the friends of the pair exchanging pigs and coco-nuts. Three days later a more elaborate feast was held.

It consisted mainly of a large dish of *taro* and coco-nut milk, and of baskets of puddings, almond nuts, chestnuts, bananas, etc. These were arranged in a line, with bundles of food brought by separate individuals. The guests marched round these, and the chief broke a coco-nut over the heads of the pair. Food was then interchanged, the large dish of *taro* being kept for the second day (Brown, 115 ff.).

In Florida (Melanesia), after the bride has remained two or three months in the house of her father-in-law, her parents bring presents of pigs and other food there, and a feast is made upon this. Neither bride nor bridegroom partakes, but after the feast the young man takes his wife, for now he is married (Codrington, 238). Among the Yoruba, a marriage feast is held at the house of the bridegroom's parents, the bride's parents taking no part in it. There is much merrymaking, and the feast is continued on the next day (Ellis, *Yoruba-speaking Peoples*, 1894, p. 154). Among the Baganda, after the consummation of marriage, the bride visited her own people, who gave her presents of food. Next day she cooked a feast for her husband, who called together his friends to share in it, the first meal prepared for him by his wife (Roscoe, 91). With various S. African tribes, marriage is the occasion of a great feast and dance for the friends, neighbours, and retainers. One head of cattle must be killed, or the marriage would be disputed. Beer and milk also form part of the feast (Macdonald, *JAI* xix. [1889–90] 271). Among the Stlatlumh (Lillooet) of British Columbia, when the bridegroom is conducted by the elders of the bride's family to sit by her, a feast follows at the house of her people. A few days later, the parents of the bride pay a return visit to the parents of the bridegroom, when another feast takes place (Tout, *JAI* xxxv. [1905] 131 f.). With other American tribes, feasts and dances had a prominent place at marriages (Bancroft, *NR* i. 350, 515, and *passim*). The Araucanos held a feast three days after the bride was taken home, to which the relatives of both the young people came (Latcham, *JRAI* xxxix. 359). In higher civilizations the marriage feast still plays an important part. With the Aztecs a banquet shared by all the relatives and friends, but in which the wedded pair took no part, concluded the ceremonies; and among the Mayas a great feast, with lavish quantities of food and wine, was an essential part of the proceedings (Bancroft, ii. 258, 668). In ancient Babylon, the marriage day ended with a feast in which the families of bride and bridegroom and numerous guests participated (Maspero, *Dawn of Civilization*^{4}, 1901, p. 735). Feasting and merriment on a most extensive scale are a necessary part of all Hindu weddings; and among the aboriginal tribes, *e.g.* the Gonds, the wedding feast is equally important, and is characterized by much drunkenness and licence (Monier-Williams, *Rel. Thought and Life in India*, 1883, p. 380 ff.; Hopkins, *Rel. of India*, Boston, 1895, p. 528). Among Buddhists, the principal ceremony of marriage is a feast which is given by the bridegroom or the parents. To this all relatives, priests, and neighbours are invited. There is no religious service (Monier-Williams, *Buddhism*, 359). Among Muhammadans in Egypt, the bridegroom feasts his friends, once or oftener, before the wedding. Feasts also take place on the night before the nuptials and on the wedding night; and, according to Muhammad, 'the first day's feast is an incumbent duty, the second day's a *sunnah* ordinance, and the third day's for ostentation and notoriety.' Feasting also takes place on the seventh and fortieth days after marriage (Lane, *Modern Egyptians*, i. 208 ff., iii. 141 f., *Arab. Soc.* 232 f.). Among Indian Muhammadans also the festivities precede and follow marriage (Hughes, *DI*^{2}, 318). Among the Greeks the wedding feast (γάμος) took place after the procession to the bridegroom's house, and it formed one of the most important parts of the proceedings, as there was no civil or religious ceremony. Women as well as men took part in it, though the women sat at a separate table. The bride was then conducted to the nuptial chamber. Among the Romans, after the bride arrived at the bridegroom's house, he gave a feast to the guests, the *cœna nuptialis*, and sometimes a second feast, the *repotia*, on the following day.

4. **Funeral feasts.**—A meal or feast partaken in common before, at, or after burial is universal among the lower races. Such feasts are often of a most elaborate and prolonged character, affording an opportunity for display and for gluttony. It is also customary to renew them at intervals after a death, or on the anniversary, or there may be a yearly feast of the dead (for many examples, see *ERE* iv. 434 ff.; Seligmann, *passim*; Brown, 201; Roscoe, 120 f.; Seligmann, *The Veddas*, Cambridge, 1911, p. 130).

Wundt (*Ethics*, i. 141) has shown that the reason sometimes alleged as the origin of these feasts—viz. the custom of giving food to all who attended the funeral as a compensation for their trouble in coming, this passing over into a duty and often becoming a means of ostentatious display—does not really explain their origin. There is no doubt that the feasts originated out of a desire at once of propitiating and of holding communion with the dead by means of the food which they were now supposed to share with the living. Hartland has argued that the feasts in which the mourners eat with the dead kinsman are a natural transformation of the cannibal feast *upon* the dead (*LP* ii. 278). Although this is not unlikely, yet, where food was offered to the dead and shared by the living, the practice would originate and exist independently of the cannibal meal.

Among higher races the funeral repast is also found. In Egypt, during the long interval which often elapsed between death and burial, feasts were held in honour of the dead (Wilkinson, *Manners and Customs*, ed. 1878, iii. 432). In Babylon the monthly offerings to the dead formed also the material of a meal by which the living had communion with them (see *ERE* iv. 445). Among the Greeks a funeral repast (περίδειπνον) took place in connexion with the rites of burial, those who took part in it regarding themselves as guests of the dead (Lucian, *de Luctu*, § 24; Artemidor. *Oneirocr.* v. 82; *Il.* xxiii. 52 f.). The anniversary of a death was celebrated by a repast or feast (γενέσια, νεκύσια) as well as in other ways. The Romans ate a funeral repast at the tomb, the *silicernium*, and a banquet in honour of the deceased was held at the house, the *cœna funeris*. Memorial feasts were also celebrated during the *Parentalia*, the family festival of the *cara cognatio* (Ovid, *Fasti*, ii. 117 f.), at the actual anniversary of a death, and at other times. In China the food placed before the dead man is eaten by the family, and after the funeral the food which has been placed on the tomb forms part of the funeral feast. Subsequently, memorial feasts are also held (de Groot, *Rel. System of China*, Leyden, 1892 ff., i. 118, and *passim*). The ancient Teutons celebrated great funeral banquets (*erfiol*, or 'heir beer') in which the soul of the deceased was supposed to participate, and at which the heir entered on his inheritance (de la Saussaye, *Rel. of the Teutons*, Boston, 1902, p. 301). Among the Burmese, great feasting goes on in the house for the benefit of the crowds who come to offer condolence (Monier-Williams, *Buddhism*, 369). In Tibet the relatives and friends are entertained during the funeral rites with much food, beer, and tea—a species of 'wake' at which the dead man is also offered a share. A year after a memorial feast is held (Waddell, *Buddhism of Tibet*, 1895, pp. 491–98). In modern Europe, memorial feasts for the dead occur sporadically among the folk (Tylor, *PC*^{3} ii. 37), and a meal is often partaken of by the relatives after a funeral, this, however, having now little ritual significance. See also ANCESTOR-WORSHIP, COMMUNION WITH THE DEAD, DEATH AND DISPOSAL OF THE DEAD.

5. Sacrificial feasts.—Whatever be the origin of sacrifice, the custom of the worshippers feasting upon part of the offering is wide-spread. The feast has a religious aspect, whether we regard it as an actual eating of slain divine victims, or as eating, together with a spirit or divinity, of food which has acquired a sacrosanct character.[1] The Veddas of Ceylon make offerings of food to the spirits of the recently dead, and then eat the offerings as an act of communion with them (Seligmann, 130). In Florida (Melanesia) at a public sacrifice some of the food was presented to the *tindalo*, and the remainder was eaten by the sacrificer and the assistants (Codrington, 131). In Fiji the gods were supposed to eat the 'soul' of the offering, the worshipper consuming the substance of it (Williams, *Fiji*, 1858, i. 231). In Samoa, men partook of the offerings to Tangaloa, god of the heavens, women and children being excluded. Of another sacrificial feast in the cult of Taisumalie, for which all kinds of food were prepared, only the family of the priest partook (Turner, *Samoa*, 1884, pp. 53, 57). Among the Tshis, after a human sacrifice to the river-gods, a bullock was killed and divided among the inhabitants of the village (Ellis, *Tshi-speaking Peoples*, 1887, p. 66). Among the Baganda the owner of a fetish often sacrificed a fowl to it, dropping the blood upon it. The bird was then cooked and eaten by him and his friends in presence of the fetish (Roscoe, 329). The Zulus feasted on the black cattle sacrificed to the sky-god when rain was required (Callaway, *Rel. System of Amazulu*, 1884, p. 59). The Patāris sacrifice a goat, fowl, and cakes to the Earth-goddess, the males and unmarried girls eating the flesh (Crooke, *PR*^{2}, 1896, i. 32). The ancient Peruvians at the great festival of the solstice feasted on the sacred llamas which were slaughtered sacrificially. Much wine was also consumed, and the feast was closed with music and dancing (Prescott, *Hist. of Conquest of Peru*, 1890, p. 51). Herodotus describes a sacrifice of a pig to the moon in Egypt. Part of it was consumed by fire and the remainder eaten by the worshippers (ii. 48). At the festival of Isis an ox was sacrificed, and the parts which were not burned were eaten by all present (Wilkinson, iii. 378). Among the Greeks the sacrificial feast was well known. Indeed, every meal had a sacrificial aspect, and there, as elsewhere, feast and sacrifice were almost synonymous terms (cf. Athen. v. 19). Part of the victim was burned on the altar, the remainder was cooked and formed part of the sacred feast, the θάλεια δαίς. These feasts were often occasions of great indulgence (Diog. Laert. vi.; *Life of Diog.* § 4), and the gods were believed to take part in them (*Od.* vii. 201 f.). One of the main objects of the religious associations (θίασοι, ἔρανοι) was the celebration in common of sacrifices and feasts in which the flesh of the victim was the staple along with cups of wine (Foucart, *Des Assoc. rel. chez les Grecs*, Paris, 1873, pp. 2, 154, 238). Among the Romans, when the *exta* of the victims had been burned on the altar, the remainder was eaten in a feast with bread and wine by the worshippers, or, in the case of official sacrifices, by the magistrates and senators (Wissowa, *Rel. und Kultus der Römer*, Munich, 1902, p. 353 f.). In the cult of Mithra the sacrificial repast had also a prominent place (see Cumont, *Myst. of Mithra*, Chicago, 1903, p. 160).

The ancient Teutons in sacrificing animals offered only the *exuviæ* to the gods, and a great feast on the flesh followed. On great occasions much cattle was slaughtered, and many people assembled to take part in the ceremony, bringing food with them, and feasting and drinking together, toasting the gods and each other. Here, also, the gods were conceived as sharing the feast with the worshippers (Vigfusson-Powell, *Corpus Poet. Boreale*, Oxford, 1883, i. 404; Grimm, *Teut. Myth.* 1882–88, p. 46 ff.; de la Saussaye, *Rel. of the Teutons*, 369 f.). In India in Vedic times, while the gods were offered a share of food at festive gatherings, the worshippers partook with them of the flesh of victims sacrificed; and god, priests, and men held feast together (Monier-Williams, *Rel. Thought and Life in India*, 12 f.). The drinking of the soma at soma-sacrifices had also a solemn festive aspect, and rendered the recipients immortal (*Rigv.* viii. 48. 3). Animals are seldom offered in sacrifice now, but, when they are, the flesh is partaken of at a solemn feast, *e.g.* in the cult of Sītalā (Risley, *TC*, Calcutta, 1891, i. 179). In general the offerings at most sacrifices are partaken of more or less sacramentally by the worshippers. In Tibet the common service of the 'sacrifice to the whole assembly of Rare Ones,' *i.e.* to all the gods, concludes with the eating of the offerings by the Lamas, the gods having partaken of the essence of the food and so consecrated it (Waddell, 431). Sacrifices of animals are made on mountain passes, and those present dine off the flesh with much singing and dancing (Landor, *In the Forbidden Land*, 1898, ii. 38). In many of these instances the feast upon sacred food is prepared for by propitiatory and other ritual customs, *e.g.* by fasting (*q.v.*).

6. Seasonal feasting.—Among the lower races, with whom, as with higher races, the regulation of the food supply is of the highest importance, the periods connected with sowing, ingathering, the opening of the hunting season, etc., are times of rejoicing, in which after hard work it is natural for them to feast; and, as these seasons are associated with divine influences, feasting has a prominent place. Man feasts with his gods. But, besides these, other seasonal occasions are also celebrated with feasting, *e.g.* the appearance of the new moon, the recurring festivals of divinities, etc. The Abipones celebrated the reappearance of the Pleiades with great rejoicings, ceremonial dancing, and feasting (Dobrizhoffer, *The Abipones*, 1822, ii. 234). The people of the Shortlands group (Solomon Islands) held a festival called *Viloto* when the Pleiades appeared at the nutting season (Brown, 210). Among the ancient Mexicans, at the end of each cycle of 52 years, the passing of the Pleiades across the zenith—the sign of the endurance of the world for another period of 52 years—was the occasion of great rejoicing, eating, and drinking (Bancroft, *NR* iii. 394 f.). Among the Southern Massim a great feast was held during the south-east monsoon. For this enormous quantities of food were prepared and distributed among all present (Seligmann, 584). In Mysore the appearance of the new moon was the signal for a great feast in honour of deceased parents (*TES*, new ser. viii. [1869] 96). The Yoruba also feast when the new moon appears (Ellis, 82). The Baganda

[1] Cf. the excellent remarks of Ames, *Psych. of Rel. Experience*, Boston, 1910, p. 122 f.

celebrate a feast lasting 7 days, at each new moon, in honour of the python god, the people feasting and dancing by day and night (Roscoe, 322). Similarly many American Indian tribes held a feast with sacrifices at the beginning of the hunting season, at which all the victims must be eaten (Tanner, *Narrative of Captivity*, New York, 1830, pp. 195, 287; Schoolcraft, *Indian Tribes*, Philadelphia, 1853–6, iii. 61). But most general is the festival at harvest time, when the firstfruits are either offered to spirits or divinities, or solemnly eaten by priest, chief, or people. Until this is done no one may eat of them, but then follows much feasting and merriment. A few examples of this will suffice. The tribes of the Niger celebrate the yam harvest by a feast to which every one contributes a fowl (Parkinson, *JAI* xxxvi. [1906] 319). The Yoruba at the yam harvest celebrate a festival in honour of the god of agriculture. All partake of the new yams, and quantities of vegetable foods are cooked and set out for general use (Ellis, 78). In Fiji great feasts take place at the time of the presentation of the firstfruits of the yams to the ancestral spirits (Fison, *JAI* xiv. [1884–85] 27). Among the Jakun of the Malay Peninsula there is an annual feast at harvest when, besides dancing and singing, much eating and drinking takes place (Skeat, *JAI* xxxii. [1902] 133). The Dayaks hold a festival when the paddy is ripe. They place the firstfruits on an altar, dance and feast for two days, and then get in their crops (St. John, *Forests of the Far East*², 1865, i. 191, and S. B. Scott, 'Harvest Festivals of the Land Dyaks' *JAOS* xxix. [1908] 236–280). In Celebes at the time of the new rice, fowls and pigs are killed, and some of the flesh with rice and palm-wine is given to the gods. Then the people eat and drink together (Graafland, *Die Minahassa*, Rotterdam, 1869, i. 165). Turning to American Indian tribes, we find that the Seminoles at the 'Green Corn Dance,' having prepared themselves by fasting, ate sacramentally of the new corn, and then enjoyed a great feast (MacCauley, *5 RBEW* [1887] 522 f.). The Natchez at their harvest festival, which was solemnly observed with fasting and offering of the first sheaves of the maize, concluded their rites with a great feast (Chateaubriand, *Voyage en Amérique*, Paris, 1870, p. 136). In India the Hos hold a Saturnalia when the granaries are full. Sacrifice is offered, the dead are commemorated, and feasting and drinking follow (Dalton, *Descr. Ethnol.*, Calcutta, 1872, p. 196 f.). The hill tribes near Rājmahāl hold a thanksgiving festival, when the new grain is ceremonially eaten and sacrifice made. The ceremony concludes with drinking and festivity for several days (Shaw, *Asiatic Res.* iv. [1795] 56 f.). Similarly, the Japanese held a festival of firstfruits of the rice, followed by feasting in holiday dress, songs, and dances (Aston, *Shinto*, 1905, p. 277).

Among the lower races, festivals of the gods are sporadically found, of which one great incident is feasting. The Elema tribes of the Papuan Gulf held tribal feasts for eating, drinking, and merry-making, associating with these one or more tribal gods (Holmes, *JRAI* xxxix. 427). In Samoa, annual feasts were held in honour of the gods (Brown, 229). The Yoruba held many such annual festivals, *e.g.* one in honour of Oro lasting for 3 months, at which the men feasted on dogs and fowls (Ellis, 111). The Gonds held an annual festival in honour of the snake, and another in honour of the sun, both of a licentious and bacchanalian character (Hopkins, 527 f.). Many such annual festivals were held in Mexico, all of them being occasions for great feasts in which much food and drink were consumed, and much licence occurred (Bancroft, iii. 341, 347, 360, and *passim*).

In the higher religions the many recurrent festivals of divinities are usually the occasion of feasting. Men honour the gods; and, feeling themselves on good terms with them, they rejoice before them—the rejoicing being both testified to and stimulated by the consumption of food and drink. See artt. on FESTIVALS AND FASTS.

Thus in most religions, from the lowest upwards, festival occasions are signalized by the consumption of good cheer, which lightens men's hearts and is at once a symbol of their joy in commemorating their gods and a further cause of that joy, passing over frequently into orgiastic excesses. In some instances, however, religions or cults in which even a moderate asceticism is considered right tend to disparage excessive indulgence in food or feasting, *e.g.* Buddhism and also certain aspects of Egyptian religion. Thus in the Maxims of Any it is said: 'That which is detestable in the sanctuary of God are noisy feasts' (Petrie, *Rel. and Conscience in Ancient Egypt*, 1898, p. 160). Christianity, though it does not forbid festal rejoicing, and, though many of its festivals were celebrated with good cheer—even a common meal being associated with the Eucharist (see AGAPE)—teaches that all excessive indulgence, gluttony, and drunkenness are wrong. Moderation in feasting is, however, hardly to be found in the bulk of the ethnic religions and at lower stages. Indeed, these feasts are often the occasion not only of excessive eating, but of drunkenness and sexual abominations (see DEBAUCHERY).

See also the following article; and cf. throughout FESTIVALS AND FASTS.

LITERATURE.—This is cited throughout the article.

J. A. MACCULLOCH.

FEASTING (Hebrew and Jewish).—**1. Religious joy characteristic of Judaism.**—The underlying higher motive for feasting among the ancient Hebrews and pious Jews of the Diaspora down to the present day is religious joy of one degree or another. The occasions of rejoicing may range from celebrations of universal import, such as the ingathering of the harvest, to more or less private family reunions, as at a wedding or the weaning of a child; but the motive of religious joy is to the pious Jew the golden thread that runs through all his seasons of cheer and gladness. It is possible for this high motive to rest on a perverted principle, as was, for instance, the case at the making of the golden calf, when 'the people sat down to eat and drink, and rose up to play,' or perhaps 'to make merry' (Ex 32⁶). But even so a religious element would remain; for all worship, be it ever so perverted, is capable of inspiring its devotees with its own special kind of joy. There is, however, this important difference between idolatrous occasions of rejoicing and those sanctioned and regulated by the pure Jahweh-cult that, whereas pagan festivities were, generally speaking, only too likely to lead to practices which the higher conscience regards as immoral, the close union of all joy with the lofty dictates of Mosaic piety was calculated to restrain the Israelite from indulging in excesses for which there would naturally be much stimulus during seasons of public or private feasting.[1]

The great prominence given in the OT to the idea of religious joy is attested, not only by the stress frequently laid on it in the sacred texts, but also by the series of Hebrew words (שָׂשׂוֹן, מָשׂוֹשׂ, שִׂמְחָה, גִּילָה, חֶדְוָה, דִּיצָה, רִנָּה, besides the verb עָלַז and its cognates and derivatives) employed to express the various gradations of rejoicing. For it is clear that, where there is a full appreciation of the different degrees of any given sensation, there must first of all be

[1] The few exceptions to this wholesome restraint, *e.g.*, the habit of copious drinking at the Feast of Purim (see, *e.g.*, Abrahams, *Jewish Life in the Middle Ages*, Lond., 1896, pp. 103, 382), do not, as a rule, involve more than venial shortcomings.

a strong and fully realized sense of its presence. A mere glance at the rows of passages given in the Hebrew Concordances under the respective roots of the words named will be sufficient to impress the mind with the prevalence of the idea of religious joy in the Hebrew Canon, but it will be useful to refer here especially to such typical passages as the following:

'Ye shall rejoice before the Lord your God seven days' (Lv 23^{40}: Feast of Tabernacles); 'Serve the Lord with rejoicing, come before his presence with singing' (Ps 100^{2}); 'To keep the dedication with gladness, both with thanksgiving, and with singing, with cymbals, psalteries, and with harps' (Neh 12^{27}).

Mosaism, it will be remembered, set itself to discourage all gloomy brooding on a shadowy hereafter in Sheol, and all the uncanny and disquieting practices that were connected with such brooding, and placed before the people instead the ideal of a life of brightness, plenty, and holy rejoicing. Some special illustrations of the continuance of the same cherished ideal among the Jews of later times will be found in § 2, and the reader will do well to consult, *e.g.*, the article 'Freude,' in Hamburger (where a number of Talmudical references bearing on this topic will be found), besides the various articles in the *JE* to be referred to later. The marked development of the idea of the hereafter among the Jews of post-Biblical times had, indeed, its share in fostering a strong ascetic tendency in some members of the race, but the bulk of the nation and the majority of its leaders remained faithful to the old ideal of sacred joy; and, as the later Jewish doctrine of the future life was—to persons of a cheerful disposition, at any rate—not centred in the thought of torment or of a shadowy Hades, but rather in a life of bliss for the good under the wing of Jahweh, they found no contradiction between the newly developed idea of the life to come (העולם הבא) and the ancient Divine command to rejoice in the present (העולם הזה). They, indeed, gave themselves earnestly to fasting and mourning on the days specially set aside for that purpose, but the dominant tendency of their mind remained one of hope, and of the readiness to rejoice which accompanies hope.[1] It is even correct to say that one effect of the many sufferings and persecutions which the Jews had to undergo was to heighten the relish of religious joy on every possible occasion. The Ghetto is generally thought of only as a place of depression and gloom, a kind of mediæval Jewish purgatory, but it had its bright side as well. In their secluded homes, their synagogues, their convivial gatherings, their Sabbaths (when capacity for the pleasures of the table was enhanced by the bestowal of a נשמה יתירה, *i.e.* additional soul), and more particularly their festival rejoicings, they found a welcome refuge from the many ills that beset them in the world around. The inwardness of the hopes and joys that were left to them, as well as their love of ease and good cheer, had a tendency to grow with the dangers, the contumely, and the suspicions that fastened on them so readily from the outside.

2. Occasions of feasting.—A brief survey of the chief occasions of feasting, additional to those of festivals proper, may be fitly grouped under (*a*) special celebrations that were in vogue during the second Temple and partly dated from pre-Exilic times; and (*b*) seasons of rejoicing largely observed down to the present day, partly celebrated in continuation of customs prevalent in OT times, and partly dating from later times. The feasting that was customary at the reunion or parting of friends (*e.g.* Gn 26^{30}), at a time of sheep-shearing (1 S 25^{36}, 2 S $13^{23ff.}$), or on an occasion like that of the home-bringing of the Ark (2 S $6^{12ff.}$, 1 Ch $15^{25ff.}$), when David 'danced before the Lord with all his might,' need not be included in the list chosen for special treatment.[1]

(*a*) First to be noted under this head are the processions from the provinces connected with the *conveyance and presentation of the firstfruits to the Temple priests at Jerusalem*, in accordance with the ordinance contained in Dt 26^{1-11} (v.^{11} 'Thou shalt rejoice in all the good,' etc.). This semi-festive religious observance no doubt goes back to very early times, and has its parallels in the customs of other nations (see *HDB*, art. 'Firstfruits'). The time during which the presentations could be made extended from the Feast of Weeks or Pentecost to the Hasmonæan Feast of Dedication (in the month Kislev [December]) (see *Bikkurim*, and cf. Philo, *de Festo Cophini*, and Jos. *Ant.* IV. viii. 22).

A much greater degree of rejoicing characterized what is commonly known as the *Water-Feast*, which was celebrated during the nights of the Feast of Tabernacles. According to *Sukkah*, v. (where an account of these additional festivities will be found), a person who has not been present at these celebrations 'has never seen joy.' The real character of the festivities is still a matter of dispute. Geiger (*Lehrbuch der Mischnah*, Breslau, 1845, *s.v.* שׁוֹאֵבָה, which he translates by *Fackel*, 'torch') and others consider the torchlight procession to have been its principal feature. Herzfeld and Venetianer (see Lit. at the end of the article) have respectively advocated a connexion with celebrations in honour of Dionysus and with the Eleusinian Mysteries. The extraordinary effort of a chief like Simeon b. Gamaliel I. to amuse the people on these occasions by personally engaging in a grotesque dance with eight lighted torches in his hands (Bab. *Sukkah*, 53*a*) would seem to favour the idea that he had a particular reason for diverting the attention of the populace from the undesirable associations of such festivities. The purpose of giving a higher sanction to an originally pagan celebration may also be discerned in Midrash Rabba on Gn 29^{2} (ch. lxx. § 8), where the water-drawing is made to signify the bestowal of the Holy Spirit (cf. *ExpT* xxiii. [1912] 180, and where also the well-known suggestion of a connexion with the 'rivers of living water' of Jn $7^{38.39}$ is referred to).

Special mention must also be made of the thirty-five days enumerated in *Megillath Ta'anith* (original text begun in the 1st cent. A.D. and completed in the 2nd), on none of which public fasting was allowed, whilst on the most important of them public mourning was also prohibited. The first of these days was the 8th of Nīsān, on which certain Pharisaic statutes were carried in opposition to the Sadducees; and the last date was the 28th of Adar, when news of the close of the persecutions instituted by Hadrian arrived. There is a distinct religious flavour about these half-festive occasions and the entire tone of *Megillath Ta'anith*.

(*b*) The second part of this survey may appropriately begin with the question of *birthday celebrations* among the Jews. There is no clear reference to such celebrations among the ancient Hebrews in the OT. The mention of the 'day of our king' in Hos 7^{5} may quite naturally be taken to refer to the anniversary of the king's accession to the throne, and the other passages quoted in *JE* iii. 221 are still less decisive.[2] The only clear reference to a birthday festivity in the OT is found in Gn 40^{20},

[1] As one of the best illustrations of the prominence given by the Jews to the idea of life's joy, even in seasons of highest seriousness, may be cited the custom of Jewish maidens in Mishnaic times, and possibly earlier, who went out in white apparel to dance in the vineyards on the Day of Atonement (besides the 15th day of Ab) for the purpose of directing the minds of Jewish young men to thoughts of matrimony (so Bab. *Ta'anith*, 26*b*; *Baba bathra*, 121*a*).

[1] The occasion of the feasting referred to in Job $1^{4f.}$ is not clear. As the seven days appear to have been consecutive, they could hardly have been birthdays.

[2] On Job $1^{4.5}$ see the preceding note.

and relates to the Egyptian Pharaoh. The birthday celebrations in the Herodian family (see Jos. *Ant.* XIX. vii. 1; Mt 14⁶) were, no doubt, an imitation of Græco-Roman customs of the time. All one can say of Jewish feeling about it in mediæval times is that the birthday celebration of a private person among pagans lay under a minor kind of ban, its connexion with idolatrous worship not being considered pronounced enough to warrant the cessation of all business connexion with the pagan concerned for three days preceding the festivity, so that the ban lay only on the day itself (see Maimonides, *Mishneh Torah* (הלכות ע"ז וחקות הגויים, ch. ix.).[1] In modern times, however, Jews very largely adopt the custom of birthday celebrations from their neighbours.

The *circumcision feast*, which was celebrated by banqueting in Talmudic times (see *JE* ii. 496), had, of course, a profoundly religious significance; but the attempt of the Rabbis to refer the institution of such feasting to Abraham (see *JE*, *loc. cit.*) rests on a mere quibble. There is no mention of banqueting on the occasion of a circumcision in the OT.

The *weaning* of an infant, on the other hand, which apparently took place at the end of the 2nd or 3rd year of the child's life, was made the occasion of feasting or of sacrifice in very early times (see Gn 21⁸, weaning of Isaac; 1 S 1²²ᶠᶠ·, weaning of Samuel). The reason for the celebration was, no doubt, the entrance of the child on a more independent and more vigorous existence, but under the religion of Jahweh all such thoughts were permeated by a strain of genuine religious joy.

An occasion of festivity, the more title of which suggests its religious character, is that of *bar-miṣwah* ('son of commandment'), a term denoting a youth who has completed his thirteenth year, and thus enters on a life of religious responsibility. On the first Sabbath in his fourteenth year the youth is for the first time in his life called up to read a portion of the *Torah*, and sometimes also the prophetic section entitled the *Hafṭarah*. A family feast, to which the teachers of the youth as well as friends are invited, and at which religious addresses are delivered by the *bar-miṣwah* himself and others, is the natural accompaniment of this institution. The oldest Rabbinical reference to the idea underlying the initiation is found in *Pirḳē Abōth*, v. (near the end), where a youth is declared liable to observe the commandment at the age of thirteen (בן שלש עשרה למצות), although the name *bar-miṣwah* itself appears to be of much later origin (see *JE* ii. 509). The account of our Lord's disputing with the doctors of the Law, when only twelve years of age (Lk 2⁴⁰⁻⁴⁹), has been brought into relation with the same idea. In Morocco a boy becomes, in fact, *bar-miṣwah* when he has passed the age of twelve years (*JE*, *loc. cit.*).

On the subject of festivities connected with *betrothal* (in the old Jewish sense of a ceremony of so binding a character that only divorce could dissolve it) and *marriage* (*i.e.* the home-taking of the bride), only one remark need here be made. Although the Jewish contract of marriage is a purely civil one, in the sense that the presence of a Rabbi and its ratification in a synagogue are unessential, yet the occasion is one of profoundly religious import. Marriage being a Divine ordinance, and the procreation of children a sacred duty, wedding festivities must in the nature of things also bear a decidedly religious character.

A minor occasion of sacred holiday-making in old-fashioned Jewish circles, and more particularly among young students of the Talmud (hence called 'Scholars' Festival'), is *Lag bĕ-'Ōmer*, i.e. *the thirty-third day counted from the second day of the Passover Feast*, when a sheaf of the firstfruits was brought as a 'heave-offering' (Lv 23⁹ᶠᶠ·). The exact reason for the festivity is lost in obscurity (for some Rabbinical guesses, see *JE* ix. 400); but some kind of connexion with the progress of agricultural operations appears to follow from its dating after the heave-offering at Passover time; for, as has already been intimated, religious joy has in the Jewish mode of thought been associated with such occasions from early times.

Worthy of mention are also the various local *Purim festivals*, celebrated in imitation of the Biblical Purim, or Feast of Esther, on anniversaries of deliverance from great calamities. One of the best-known of these is the Purim of Cairo, annually held in that city on the 28th of Adar, in commemoration of their escape from the dangers that threatened the Cairene Jews in 1524 at the hands of Aḥmad Shaiṭān Pasha (see *JQR* viii. [1895-96] 274–288, 511 f.). The reading of a *Megillah*, written in close imitation of the Book of Esther, forms the central part of this religious observance. For a list of similar celebrations (including as late an occasion as that of the Purim of Padua, which is held in commemoration of the extinguishing of a great fire in 1795), see *JE*, art. 'Purims.'

See also artt. FESTIVALS AND FASTS (Hebrew) and (Jewish).

LITERATURE.—In addition to the original texts and the various works already named, the reader should consult J. Hochman, *Jerusalem Temple Festivities*, London, 1908 (i. 'Presentation of the Firstfruits'; ii. 'The Water-Feast'). L. Herzfeld, *Gesch. des Volkes Israel*, Leipzig, 1871, ii. 125, and L. Venetianer, 'Die eleusin. Mysterien im jerus. Tempel,' in Brüll's *Populär-wissenschaftliche Monatsblätter*, 1897, pp. 121–125, 169–181, for theories on the Water-Feast. Among the editions of *Megillath Ta'anith* is that of Neubauer in *Mediæval Jewish Chronicles*, ii. (*Anecdota Oxoniensia*, Semitic Series, vol. i. pt. iv.), and a full account of the work is given in Hamburger, *Realencyc. des Judenthums*², Leipzig, 1896, Supplementband, i. 104–107. On other topics, see *JE*, artt. on 'Banquets,' 'Betrothal,' etc.

G. MARGOLIOUTH.

FEBRONIANISM.—The system of Church government defended by Hontheim, auxiliary Bishop of Trier in the 18th cent. under the pseudonym 'Justinus Febronius.' It is the German form of Gallicanism with an Erastian colouring; it had a great vogue at the time, lasted as a tendency during the early 19th cent., and was not finally expelled from the Roman Catholic Church till the Vatican Council in 1870.

1. **Life of Hontheim.**—Johann Nicholas von Hontheim was born of a distinguished family at Trier on 27th Jan. 1701. His father and most of his relatives were officials in the service of the Bishop Electors. He began his studies at the Jesuit college at Trier, and continued them at the universities of Trier, Louvain, and Leyden. When he was 12 years old, he was tonsured and received a canon's stall at the collegiate church of St. Simeon in his native city. At Louvain he came under the influence of Van Espen. He took his degree in law in 1724, travelled in Belgium, Holland, Germany, and Italy, was three years at the German College at Rome, was ordained priest at Trier in 1728, and taught Canon Law in the university from 1732 to 1738. From 1738 to 1747 he was 'Offizial' (agent) of the Elector at Coblenz, and Director of the Seminary there. In 1747, already overburdened with literary work, he retired to his canonry at Trier. But the Elector (Franz Georg) appointed him auxiliary Bishop in place of the one who had just died. He was ordained at Mainz on 13th May 1748, with the title Bishop of Myriophytus *in part. infidelium*, and he remained auxiliary and Vicar General *in spiritualibus* under the Electors Johann Philipp (von Waldendorf) and Clemens Wenzeslaus (von Sachsen) to the end of his life. The Electors lived at their castle on the Rhine, and were more princes than bishops, so that Hontheim was practically bishop of the diocese. He enjoyed a great reputation for learning and piety. On several occasions he succeeded in composing strife, and in every way he showed himself a zealous and edifying bishop. No one disputes the correctness of his morals, the excellent work he did for the diocese, or the value of his historical writings. From the year 1746 he was Vice-Chancellor of the university of Trier, and in that capacity came into frequent conflict with the Jesuits. Towards the end of his life he was known throughout Europe as the author of the *Febronius*, and was much troubled by the controversy

[1] The birthday celebration of a king, on the other hand, which was a pagan national festivity, lay under the greater ban (see *'Abōda zara*, i. 3, and Excursus 2, p. 19 ff., in W. A. L. Elmslie's edition of the tractate [*TS*, vol. viii. no. 2], who, however, defends an unacceptable construction of the Hebrew text instead of taking יום גנוסיא to signify the day of the Cæsar's apotheosis).

which arose from his book. He had a Schloss at Montquintin on the Rhine. He died here on 2nd Sept. 1790, and was buried in the crypt of the Church of St. Simeon at Trier. In 1803 that church was desecrated, and his body was removed to St. Gervasius in the Neustrasse, where it now lies. He left a number of foundations for various charities in Trier.

2. Writings and system.—Hontheim was the author of a number of works. He is said to have written the lessons of the local Trier breviary (since abolished). F. X. Kraus doubts this, as they do not at all represent his ideas (*Allgemeine deutsche Biographie*, xiii. 83). He deserves well of German historians for his *Historia Trevirensis diplomatica et pragmatica* (3 vols., Augsburg and Würzburg, 1750) and *Prodromus Historiæ Trevirensis* (2 vols., do. 1757). But the work to which he owes his fame is the *Febronius*, published in 1763. It is said that the interference of the Papal Legate Doria at the election of the Emperor Charles VII. (1742–1745) first gave him the idea of writing a work which should distinguish the political from the ecclesiastical power of the Pope. He chose the pseudonym 'Justinus Febronius' from the name of his niece, a nun at Juvigny, in religion Justina Febronia. The MS was taken by his friend von Krufft to a bookseller, Esslinger, at Frankfurt am Main, who promised the strictest secrecy as to the real author, and did not pay any fee for it. In order to keep the secret, an imaginary publisher and place were printed on the title-page. The work appeared as: *Justini Febronii Jcti* (= iurisconsulti) *de Statu Ecclesiæ et legitima potestate Romani Pontificis liber singularis ad reuniendos dissidentes in religione Christianos compositus;* Bullioni apud Guillielmum Evrardi, 1763. The main idea of the work is that the power of the Pope should be reduced and that of the bishops increased; the Christian princes should see to this. There is nothing new in it. The ideas are those of du Pin, Richer, Van Espen, and the Gallican school. It puts these clearly, forcibly, and in a moderate compass. The author declares that, so far from opposing the Papacy, he wishes only to strengthen it by fixing its just limits. Thus he hopes to reconcile Protestants and bring them back to union with the Pope. He dedicates his work to the Pope Clement XIII. (1758–1769), 'summo Pontifici, primo in terris Christi vicario,' to Christian kings and princes, the bishops and doctors of theology and Canon law.

There are nine chapters. Ch. i. ('De exteriore forma regiminis quam in sua ecclesia Christus Dominus instituit') begins by interpreting Mt 16[18], Jn 20[22f.], as not applying to the Papacy. The form of the Church is not monarchic, the 'keys' are given by Christ to the whole Church; all Apostles were equal, though Peter was primate; the Council of Trent did not declare the Church a monarchy; the infallibility of the Pope ('ultramontanorum doctrina') is not recognized by the Church. Ch. ii. ('De Primatu in ecclesia et genuinis eius iuribus') establishes that there is a primacy by Divine right, for the sake of unity. The Pope is the guardian of the Canons for the whole Church. He can make laws 'in the name of the universal Church,' and has a *principatus*, not of jurisdiction but of order and *consociatio*. Ch. iii. is entitled 'De incrementis iurium Primatus Romani, illorumque ausis tum fortuitis et innocuis, tum sontibus.' Many Papal rights have been acquired by devolution; these are no part of the *ius ordinarium*. The False Decretals totally modified the external government of the Church. The Roman Curia must be distinguished from the see. Ch. iv. ('De causis quae vulgo maiores vocantur') describes how these came to be reserved to the Pope. Questions of faith are not reserved; any bishop may condemn heresies. Local synods may re-examine doctrines condemned by Rome. The confirmation and deposition of bishops, erection of new sees, and so on, are rights of the Metropolitan. Cardinal Orsi is quoted against the monarchic claims of the Pope. Ch. v. discusses the right of making laws for the universal Church and the question of appellations to Rome. Lk 22[32] does not apply to the successors of Peter. Papal laws are not binding till they are promulgated in each province by the Metropolitan. Gratian and other collections of canons have only the sanction of custom. 'A wide authority,' but not jurisdiction in the strict sense, over all Churches belongs to the Roman Pontiff. Ch. vi. ('De Conciliis generalibus') declares that no Divine or ecclesiastical law reserves the summoning of General Councils to the Pope; the first eight were convened by the Emperor. A General Council is above the Pope. He may not re-examine its decrees; but many Councils have re-examined decrees of Popes. It is lawful and often expedient to appeal from the Pope's decision to a future General Council. A General Council should be summoned now, as soon as possible, to reform abuses. Ch. vii. establishes that bishops have their jurisdiction not from the Pope, but directly from God. The Pope has no real jurisdiction over other bishops. The immunity of regulars from episcopal jurisdiction is a grave abuse, a 'hard and undeserved wound' to the rights of the ordinaries. Ch. viii. ('De libertate ecclesiae, eiusque restaurandae iure et causis') is about the False Decretals. These destroyed the liberty of provincial Churches, and are the source of the Pope's excessive power and the main impediment to the reunion of Christendom. Ch. ix. declares that Roman Catholics must carefully watch every step of the Roman Curia which may be hurtful to right law. The best remedy would be to summon without delay a free General Council. An agreement of all Roman Catholic princes and a common constitution promulgated by them would be the best way of securing this. Nor need any one fear the censures of the Pope; there is no danger of a schism. The princes should arouse popular feeling against the False Decretals. The end of the book sums up its whole purpose thus: 'It is the interest of the Church certainly to maintain the primacy, but to keep it within proper bounds.'

An obvious criticism of this famous work is that, like many reformers, its author is carried by his principles too far to have any chance of being heard by authority, perhaps further than he himself foresaw. Certainly it was not difficult for his opponents to quote from his book passages which were scandalous to Roman Catholic readers, as coming from a Catholic bishop. F. X. Kraus, who is sympathetic to Hontheim, admits that 'the *Febronius* contains things which must seem highly suspicious even to a very liberal Roman Catholic, if he remains a Catholic at all' (*op. cit.* xiii. 89).

3. The controversy.—The book at once excited enormous interest throughout Europe. A second edition was called for in 1765 and translations appeared immediately in German, French, Italian, Spanish, Portuguese. The effect of Hontheim's principles was soon seen. In 1768, Venice declared that the bishops have jurisdiction over all regulars throughout its territory; the Neapolitan Government abolished the rules of the Roman Cancellaria in that kingdom; Maria Teresa allowed similar laws for the Duchy of Milan. In Portugal the Bishop of Coimbra, who had forbidden the book in his diocese, was forced by Government to withdraw his order. Especially throughout Germany was the effect of the *Febronius* long felt, in spite of its repeated condemnation by the Pope and German bishops. The complaints against the Curia made by the legates of the three episcopal Electors at Coblenz on 13th Dec. 1769, the 'Emser Punktat' in 1786, and much of Joseph II.'s (1780–1790) legislation are influenced by it. In Italy the Synod of Pistoia (1786), and Leopold of Tuscany (1765-1790) follow the same principles: so that most of the later so-called Gallican movement throughout Europe found in *Febronius* a guide, or an expression of its principles.

Meanwhile the book was condemned at Rome and attacked by a great number of opponents. As soon as it appeared, it was denounced by the Nuncio (Cardinal Borromeo) at Vienna; on 27th Feb. 1764 it was put on the Index by Clement XIII., who on 21st May wrote an encyclical to the German bishops telling them to suppress the book in their dioceses (these are reprinted in Roskovány, *Romanus Pontifex*, iii. 234–240). Nine obeyed, including Clemens Wenzeslaus of Trier; sixteen took no step either way (letters of German bishops condemning the book [*ib.*]). In July the Archbishop of Vienna had heard that the book was being read with approval by the princes at court; he ordered it to be destroyed wherever found (*ib.* 238). Clemens Wenzeslaus still did not know, or affected not to know, who was the author. He condemned it as 'a poisonous book which has appeared under the unknown name of Justinus Febronius' (*ib.* 242 f.).

Among the many writers who entered the lists against Febronius, the most noticeable are F. A. Zaccaria, S.J. (*Anti-Febbronio . . . o sia apologia polemico-storica del primato del Papa*, Pesaro, 1767, and *Antifebronius vindicatus*, do. 1772),

P. Ballerini (*de Potestate ecclesiastica Summorum Pontificum*, Verona, 1768), and the archæologist T. M. Mamachi (*Epistolarum ad Justinum Febronium . . . libri tres*, 3 vols., Rome, 1776–1778). Hontheim answered his critics in four more volumes under the same title (Frankfurt and Leipzig, 1770, 1772, 1773, 1774); in 1777 he published a *Febronius abbreviatus*.

At first the secret of the authorship was well kept. But in 1764 it began to leak out, apparently through Hontheim's friend Garampi. Pius VI. (1775–1799) insisted on a retractation, and Clemens Wenzeslaus in 1778 began to urge Hontheim to withdraw. Apparently he threatened, in case of a refusal, to dismiss not only Hontheim himself, but all his relatives as well, from his service. On 14th June 1778, Hontheim sent an incomplete retractation to the Elector, although he still defended 16 propositions which the Elector's theologians had declared heretical. Neither the Elector nor the Pope was satisfied with this, and a formula of entire retractation was presented for Hontheim's signature. After much discussion he signed it, with one modification, the erasing of the sentence: 'Wherefore rightly the government of the Church is called monarchic by Catholic doctors.' The Nuncio accepted this. On 2nd Jan. 1779, Pius VI. published a Brief announcing the retractation. Hontheim was much annoyed by the public announcement (though it always follows, and he had received no guarantee to the contrary), and in letters to his friends began to complain of the way he had been treated. So the idea spread that he had not really meant to retract at all. On 7th April 1780, he published in the *Coblenzer Intelligenzblatt* a statement that he had retracted freely and was about to publish a defence of his retractation. This appeared at Frankfurt in 1781 under the title: *Justini Febronii Jcti Commentarius in suam retractationem Pio VII. Pont. Max. Kal. nov. an. 1778 submissam.* In this work he so explained his action that it was plain that he still held the ideas condemned. So the Roman Curia declared itself not satisfied, and the dispute began again. From now to the end of his life Hontheim showed a curious vacillation. In 1781 he wrote to the *Hamburger Zeitung*:

> 'The world has read, tested, and approved the statements of my book. My retractation will no more persuade thoughtful men to reject these statements than will the many refutations written by pseudo-theologians, monks, and flatterers of the Pope.'

On the other hand, in 1786 he wrote against the 'Emser Punktat,' which only echoed the ideas of the *Febronius*. Towards the end of his life he seems inconsistent and perhaps wilfully ambiguous. He did not actually incur any censure, and died in union with the Church. The effect of the *Febronius* lasted intermittently in Germany into the 19th century. J. V. Eybel took up its ideas to fortify the policy of Joseph II. (*Was ist der Papst?* Vienna, 1782). The final blow to Febronianism was given by the Vatican Council in 1870.

LITERATURE.—Krufft, 'Hist. de la vie de J. N. de Hontheim,' in Otto Mejer, *Febronius*, Freiburg, 1885; F. X. Kraus, 'Hontheim,' in the *Allgemeine deutsche Biographie*, Leipzig, 1881, xiii. 83–94; *Briefwechsel zw. weiland Ihrer Durchlaucht dem Herrn Churfürsten von Trier, Clemens Wenzeslaus, u. dem Herrn Weihbischof, Niklos v. Hontheim, über das Buch Justinus Febronius, u.s.w.*, Frankfurt am Main, 1813; A. de Roskovány, *Romanus Pontifex tamquam Primas ecclesiæ et Princeps civilis e monumentis omnium sæculorum demonstratus*, Nitriæ et Comaromii, 1867, tom. iii. pp. 234–240.

ADRIAN FORTESCUE.

FEELING.—1. Definition and scope.—The equivocal term 'feeling' is now the accepted designation of states of consciousness viewed as agreeable or disagreeable. We have sensations, and they are pleasant or unpleasant; we have ideas, and their presence in the mind creates pleasure or pain; we carry on activities, and along with them goes a glow of delight or a mental disturbance or aversion. The experiences through which we pass create melody or discord, and we are aware of it. Abstracting the hedonic aspect from its sensational, intellectual, or volitional accompaniment, as we readily do whenever it preponderates, we call the state of consciousness one of feeling. The characteristic marks, then, of the feelings are these two: pleasure and pain (in a somewhat broader and more technical sense than popular use attaches to the words), and pure subjectivity, as being simply states of the self, and wanting the objective reference implied in knowing and in willing. Among the feelings, we generally mark off the emotions (affections, passions, sentiments) as at once the most extensive and the most important class.

It was long customary to regard the distinction of intellect and will—the contemplative and the active powers—as exhaustive, feeling being regarded as merged in impulse, desire, and volition, and the emotions as complex products in which cognition and appetency blend; and to this view some still adhere. But, whether we consider the dual or the triple division of mind as psychologically the more exact, it must be admitted that feeling is so unique a fact, and that the feelings are so impressive, bulk so large in consciousness, and are so important for human life, that it has become imperative to give the exposition of feeling a place of co-ordinate rank with that of knowing and of willing. In days past, when the struggle of life was more arduous than it is now, and when men had to gather all their energies for a swift and vigorous reaction on circumstances, feeling was readily lost in impulse and volition, and men had little inclination to view it in abstraction from activity, or to give it an independent value. It is otherwise now, as, among other symptoms, the modern novel proclaims; although even now, in circles where life is hard and stern, feeling is apt to be viewed as an intruder.

The importance of feeling may be realized by a moment's consideration of the consequences of its withdrawal from consciousness. Were we incapable of pleasure and pain, of joy and sorrow, were nothing good in our eyes and nothing evil, we should be as stones, nothing could have any value for us, no event any interest, and life would be bereft of all significance. We familiarly speak of an apathetic man as *dead*. It is only because we are capable of feeling that we are interested in ourselves, or interested in each other, or have any questions to put about life and the universe, or have any reason for desiring any one event to come to pass rather than another. It is feeling that stirs to action the whole animated world. Yet we are not thus laying a basis for hedonistic ethics; for behind this fact of pleasure and pain lies the impulse of self-conservation and self-development, which, setting us in movement, conducts us to the tree of the knowledge of good and evil, the eating of whose fruit starts the tale of man's life. In the case of animals, pleasures and pains receive simply a quantitative valuation, and, as such, absolutely rule their doings; but in the case of a self-conscious being, who can make objective all the contents of his reason, and look before and after, pleasures and pains are valued relatively to his whole complex nature both individual and social, and to that ideal end which gives law to all conduct. Self-conscious desire is a different thing from appetite. Pleasure and pain remain mighty factors in our life, although not sovereign masters prescribing even the moral law of conduct; they are the condition of life having value, but not themselves the standard of value.

2. Classification.—The feelings naturally fall into two classes, according to the nature of their base; that is, the nature of that to which they attach, and from which they rise. (1) There are feelings that have *sensations* for their base—sensuous, or sensation-feelings, *e.g.* the pleasureable feelings arising from the taste of food, from the odour of flowers, from the light of day or the blue sky, or from the healthy functioning of the organism; or the painful feelings arising from gloom or weariness, or jarring sounds. (2) There are feelings that have *ideas* for their base—such as may arise from presentation of an object to sense (such as the sea or the rising sun) when it also conveys a rush of ideas; or such as may arise in the activity of memory, and the constructive imagination. Examples are hope, fear, melancholy, jealousy, moral approbation, the sublime. This class of feelings is commonly distinguished as the emotions.

This distinction between the feelings that have sensations for their base and those that are based upon ideas seems clear, and it is certainly serviceable; but it cannot be pressed too absolutely. In some cases there seems to be a certain representative element present where we might imagine there was only sensation—for example, in the feeling of disgust which is generated by seeing or touching some natural objects, and which is due in all likelihood to association and teaching. Again, a sensation-factor seems to attach even to the highest emotions, as in the sense of warmth suffusing us in the presence of the beautiful, or in the thrill we feel in the presence of the sublime. It must also be noted that the feelings of joy and sorrow, hope and fear, elation and depression, and others, are generated by stimulants and drugs, or even by the secretions of the body, as surely as by ideas—with the qualification that the result in the former case is rather an emotional mood or frame than a definite emotion. Nevertheless, we hold by the useful distinction between feelings that adhere to sensational experiences purely as such, and feelings that, even if they involve sensation, arise in connexion with some further activity of ideation. The presence or absence of an ideational factor furnishes, if not a quite exact, yet a serviceable, principle of arrangement.

(1) Before passing to the emotions, as much the more important, we devote a short space to the *sensation-feelings*. They are our earliest feelings, and belong even to our pre-natal life—and who can tell with what important consequences? They are universal, or common to all men. They are habitual. They sum themselves up into an important aggregate of happiness or misery. The feelings arising from the organic sensibility alone will suffice to bathe the consciousness in sunshine or smother it in gloom; they mainly determine the mood or temperament, and thus tell upon the formation of character. We scarcely realize all we owe of life's joy to the senses—to the song of birds, to the rippling of water, to the common light, to the colours of the earth and sky, to pleasant odours, and the taste of food. Nor do we realize as we ought how ugliness and gloom, a blackened sky, blasted vegetation, a poisoned atmosphere, and all agencies that create sensuous pains, not only make life an oppression, but also degrade and tend to crush the soul into pessimism and atheism (for good statements on the subject of sensuous feelings, see Höffding, *Psychology*, Eng. tr., 1892, pp. 221–233; also Dewey, *Psychology*, New York, 1887, ch. xi. pp. 250–261).

(2) On proceeding now to the *emotions*, it would serve no purpose to enter on the question of classification. There is no agreement among psychologists, nor need any be expected. The emotional life grows and expands like a tree; and can we logically classify its branches? (Any one interested in the question will find a good resumé of methods of classification in Appendix B of Bain's *Emotions and the Will*; also in Sully, *The Human Mind*, 1892, Appendix I. vol. ii.) It will be found more instructive to enter on a consideration of the more prominent characteristics of the emotional life.

(*a*) The first point arresting attention is the *number* of the emotions. It would not be difficult to enumerate scores for which we have names; and we give names only to the more common and more prominent. There is a fleeting vagueness about many emotional states, which makes them as difficult to grasp or name as the sensations of the viscera. It is curious that in certain languages emotions have received names that are untranslatable into other tongues; for example, we have no equivalent for the German *Gemüthlichkeit*; and it is said that no other language has an equivalent for the Scotch word 'eeriness.' Further, each one of the more familiar emotions runs through a gamut of modifications or subdivides into several species. Thus, in the æsthetic emotions, we have the pretty, the graceful, the elegant, the lovely, the picturesque; in the emotions of the ludicrous, we have the witty, the humorous, the funny, the grotesque. Thus, fear becomes alarm, terror, despair; anger becomes resentment, indignation, rage, fury; joy becomes brightness, gladness, cheerfulness, delight, rapture, ecstasy. Probably every modification of consciousness has its own modification of feeling. Language is too scanty to express them all, and is also too rough and coarse; we require to have recourse to music. The human soul is as subtle in its responses of feeling as the thermo-electric pile in relation to degrees of temperature.

(*b*) We may next observe the manner in which the emotions *ramify* in the mental life. As an example, we may take the familiar emotion of fear. We can trace its presence in the religious feelings of reverence, awe, and adoration. It enters into the composition of the emotion of the sublime. According to Kant at least, it belongs to the sense of duty. In timidity, anxiety, diffidence, suspiciousness, caution, prudence, bashfulness, it requires but little insight to detect its colouring. It acts as a check on conceit and arrogance. Superstition, bigotry, and intolerance would more readily slacken their hold, but for fear. The emotion of fear, like all other simple feelings, is in itself neither good nor bad; but it may enter as an element into the very worst and very best qualifications and activities. Similarly we might trace the ramifications of hope, pride, or anger.

(*c*) It is more than doubtful whether there is any fact in mind that can be properly expressed as 'psychical chemistry'; but the nearest approaches to it seem to be found in the emotional life. The emotions *compound* themselves; and there emerge new products, which have all the aspect of ultimate simplicity, until, turning an analytic gaze upon them, we force them to disclose their elements. One of the simplest examples is found in melancholy, in which the pain of regret for loss so fuses with the pleasure of recollection of possession, or the pain of self-commiseration so fuses with the pleasure of self-congratulation, that there emerges a new type of feeling—unpleasant, and yet so pleasant that men will even nurse it with tenderness. A somewhat more complex example is found in jealousy, in which the joy and pride of possession, the fear of loss, anger, indignation, rivalry, all blend to create a remarkable new form of emotion of tragic potency. A more notable example is found in the passion of love. The analysis of its components, as given by Spencer (*Psychology* [2], 1870–72, i. § 215), will be found a marvel of acumen.

(*d*) The emotions, however, do not always fuse. They sometimes even *conflict*. They influence each other in the most various ways. The question as to the result where two or more emotions press on consciousness simultaneously merits examination. (α) Like emotions combine easily and enhance each other. Thus, there is apt to be an easy fusion of disappointment, vexation, anger, envy, and malice; or of success, generosity, kindness, courage, and pride. One hardly expects a generous donation from an angry and disappointed man; but one may readily obtain it when he is elated with the joy of success. Homogeneous emotions not only fuse easily, but in doing so enhance and inflame each other—although this is more observable in the case of the asthenic than of the sthenic emotions. When a man is already down, a slight addition of sorrow may readily prove the last straw; and in the presence of some new trial, in itself not insupportable, he will cry out, 'All his waves and billows have gone over me.' (β) Some emotions are contradictory, and related like salt and sweet, which never blend. Love and hate, arrogance and humility, laughter and devotion, ludicrous contempt and reverence, exclude each other, and do so in proportion to their intensity. Yet they will sometimes press simultaneously on consciousness. King Arthur loves the fallen wife at his feet, while, at the same time, he is inspired with anger and indignation. A friend will sometimes provoke at once our admiration and our contempt. A merchant will be in grief over business losses and in joy over the birth of an heir. An ass has been known to bray at the church door while the congregation was engaged in prayer. What happens? If we could suppose the conflicting emotions to be of equal strength (which is probably never the case), they would simply neutralize each other. It commonly happens that the one supplants the other, as when a ludicrous idea makes devotion impossible; or, if it cannot quite supplant the other, there takes place a trial of strength and a rapid and distracting alternation of moods. We try to end the turmoil by going in search of reinforcements of the emotion we desire to prevail. (γ) There is a third case. Emotions may be simply different, although not contradictory, related like bitter and sweet: for example, joy and the ludicrous, humility and hope. In this case, the result is various and uncertain. If the one feeling is weaker than the other, the predominant emotion absorbs the other, and converts it into itself, while yet receiving from it some modifications. Thus, the self-confident courage with which a speaker advances to an audience is sometimes met by the different feeling of alarm when facing it; and the ordinary result is that his courage is toned down, and the speaking improved. A man does not speak the better for over much confidence and excessive coolness. (On this interesting section of the emotional life, the reader may consult with advantage Hume on the *Passions*, pt. iii. § ix., also his *Dissertation on the Passions*, especially in §§ ii. and vi.; Höffding, *Psychology*, p. 238; various sections in Bain, *Emotions and the Will*).

(*e*) The method of the *spread* of the emotions seems next to demand attention. The main instruments are the laws of contiguity and similarity. Let M stand for an emotion, and C for its cognitive base. But C is connected by contiguity with D, E, F, fuses therewith, and forms the unit CDEF. M now spreads over that larger complex unit. Thus, if a man loves a woman, he is apt also to love everything connected with her, even her very raiment, and the ground on which she stands. A similar expansion takes place by similarity. We are here in presence of a weighty factor in human life, and one of extensive application. Thus, Palestine became the *Holy* Land by virtue of our reverence for Him who lived and died there, extending itself to the very soil with which He was contiguous. Thus, such an emotion as patriotism is created; the colonist, after long years, still turns with longing heart to the hills and rivers associated with parents, friends, and the happy days of youth. Sometimes there result tragic consequences. A man with a bad conscience hates himself; and, as he can never be parted from the self he hates, the odious thing becomes contiguous with all things he sees or handles, with all places he visits, with all associates and all occupations; a dark shadow falls everywhere, he becomes a cynic and misanthrope, and comes to hate existence and curse the universe. Another tragic example may be found in the irrational hostility of renegades and apostates to the creed they have cast away; for the hostility is not proportioned to the logical grounds of the rejection, but to the misery associated with a former belief. Thus do our own emotions, by their tendency to diffuse themselves, colour the universe, making it, perchance, a temple of God or a pit of blackness.

(*f*) Turning our eyes in a somewhat different direction, let us next note the conspicuous fact that the *emotions of the soul are always correlated with commotions of the body*, although in smaller degree in the case of the higher or more intellectual emotions. There is no doubt a correlation between every form of mental life and the physical organism; but it does not obtrude itself as it does in the quickened or impeded pulsation and breathing, the stir in the abdominal viscera, that attend anger and fear, joy and sorrow. This 'somatic resonance' of the emotions is marked in their popular location in the heart, and was more reflected in Oriental speech, which located them in the liver, bowels, and kidneys. A paradoxical doctrine has even found some acceptance in recent years, to the effect that the bodily commotion reported in consciousness constitutes the emotion: that we do not tremble because we are afraid, but are afraid because we tremble, and similarly that we are sad because we weep. Nothing, however, has been adduced at all likely to upset the judgment of common sense that the bodily movement follows as the effect of the mental disturbance. Some bearings of the physical reverberations of the emotional life are important. The undisciplined make no effort to guide or control these movements; like children, they have no stillness and cannot veil their feelings. But we have means, direct and indirect, of determining the direction and measure of the physical excitement. The possession of this skill is part of the self-control so requisite in social intercourse and in the management of affairs. Courtiers and actors show to what perfection it can be brought, and how it gives authority to a man's bearing, and grace and dignity to manners. It is also part of the discipline by which the explosive and impulsive will is converted into the rational and deliberate will of the moralized man. Let us note, further, that the 'somatic resonance' of the emotions explains their bearing on health and life. There are authentic records of sudden death through the abrupt irruption of glad or of evil tidings. There are also those that are pining away into early graves through the starving of the emotions, and to whom love and hope would come as the very breath of life, restoring health and youth. Faith-healings and kindred phenomena show what wonders can be wrought when the emotional thrill discharges itself into all parts of the body through the nervous mechanism.

(*g*) We have next to note the fact that the various emotions are correlated with *definite* bodily movements, and that each has its definite and characteristic expression. From the aspect of the face and attitude we can tell that a man is deep in thought or is fixed in purpose; but we cannot tell what is the thought or resolution. In the case of the emotions, however, we can tell at once the fact of feeling and the definite nature of the feeling. We have familiar examples in the blush of shame, the pallor of fear, the clenched fist and dilated nostrils of rage, the drooped eyes and downward curved muscles of sadness. So close is this correlation that, by assuming artificially the physical attitude or the expression of an emotion, we can in some measure induce the emotion, and by suppression of its expression to some extent destroy the feeling, as when we half conquer a man's anger by persuading him to be seated.

Since Darwin's time and the publication of his *Expression of the Emotions* (1872) there has been much interesting discussion on the genesis of the various emotional expressions. There is force and truth in many explanations adduced, along with not a little that is fanciful or even grotesque (for illustrative examples, see Spencer, *Psychology*, ii. §§ 494–501).

(*h*) The *function* of the emotions is to serve as the connecting link between the intellect and the will, and to furnish us with springs of action. Aristotle (*Ethics*, vi. 2, § 5) uttered a weighty truth when he said, 'Intellect moves nothing.' Ideas, simply as such, have no more power to touch the will than our percepts have. Truths that have no inherent fitness to create feeling never become springs of action; no man ever did anything simply in virtue of his knowledge of algebra. Doctrines, howsoever great and important, never have the smallest real influence on life, unless they become incandescent, and kindle a fire in the heart; the world has seen immoral philosophers, and undevout theologians. It is always emotion that mediates, and translates thoughts into deeds. Victory will always be on the side of the principles that can commend the strongest and most persistent enthusiasm. Nothing great was ever yet accomplished by a man incapable of intense feeling. The practical bearings of this principle are numerous. We single out these two: (α) we do violence to our nature, and demoralize ourselves, if we do not use emotions as the impetus to conduct, or if we permit ourselves to cultivate them simply for the luxury of having them; (β) we need not in any case expect too much from mere teaching and preaching. If a man is already under the power of any emotion or passion, we shall not rescue him unless we succeed in creating a yet stronger emotion or passion; and the creation of this 'potential' is the supreme difficulty in all attempts at moral reformation (cf. Chalmers' Sermon on *The Expulsive Power of a New Affection*).

(*i*) 'The *inertia* of feeling' is a fact of far-reaching consequence. 'The imagination,' says Hume, 'is extremely quick and agile, but the passions (emotions) in comparison, slow and restive' (*Dissertation*, § 3). We can pass with ease and rapidity from one object of thought to another, and from one kind of mental activity to another; and, when we cannot do so, some harassing feeling is the cause; but, as every one knows, we cannot thus rapidly and easily pass from melancholy to gladness, from ill-temper to serenity, from despondency to hopeful courage, from the comic opera to the church. Our emotions detain us; they drag; they move heavily. Hume has happily compared emotions to a stringed instrument that continues to vibrate for a while even after the impulse has ceased, while cognition is like a wind instrument. It follows that emotion is in some respects a hindrance and in other respects advantageous to the movement of thought. The emotion that cleaves to a thought will not move and yield so readily as the thought, and may, therefore, cause a memory to haunt us, from which we desire to be free, and drag a belief back on our mind long after its logical hold has been loosened or destroyed; but we have the compensation that, once a new conviction has been lodged in us, and has been well saturated with emotion, it becomes thereby a possession of which we cannot be easily deprived. Intellect is apt to be a disintegrating force in human affairs; emotion alone welds strongly, and perpetuates securely. Emotion is the slow conservative side of human nature, the custodian of old ideas, old customs, and old institutions. Emotional natures, with strong loves and hates and ardent attachments, are apt to be most conservative; thus, women, as a rule, are more conservative than men. Cold intellectual natures, whose principles are not saturated with feeling, have no difficulty in following out a doctrine to its applications and hearkening to the bidding of logic; they therefore change easily, and are apt to wonder that the world is so slow and irrational. But ours would be a worse world, and not a better, were there no such thing as the inertia of emotional attachment. The inertia of feeling may be used to explain the persistency of character compared with the instability of opinion; also the inevitable relapses and reactions following on too many and too violent changes of habit or thought, whether in the case of individuals or in that of communities: and also, the perpetual bribing and corrupting of the intellect by emotional prejudice.

The doctrine just inculcated may seem to be inconsistent with the undoubted fact that emotional natures are also most impulsive and headlong—the very reverse of conservative. But there is no inconsistency. Emotional natures, having the warmest attachments, are, no doubt, on this very account, with greatest difficulty loosed from their moorings; but *once set in movement they are apt to go farthest.* We may find a good example in the 'perfervidum ingenium Scotorum.' The Scottish people are wedded with intense passion to their own traditions, and move from them with deep reluctance; but what people has gone so far in its reactions and reformations? Nor can Scotland abide compromise in Church and State, after the manner of the English people, on whom that habit sits so lightly, and who find it so useful. The story of the French Revolution might furnish other examples.

(*j*) The ethical importance of the emotions appears when we consider their *relation to character*. It is patent that the springs of conduct lie among the emotions, in emotional dispositions, and in complex emotional formations. Men act from hope and fear, love and hate; from love of money, power, knowledge, distinction; from kindness, sympathy, or perchance from malignity and misanthropy. When we describe the character of men, we, for the most part, do so in terms taken from the emotions; we speak of them as timid, gentle, irascible, sanguine, affectionate, cold-hearted, sentimental. No doubt, we also speak of moral character in terms of intelligence, as when we praise a man for prudence, discretion, and considerateness; but even in such cases we have in view types of intelligence created by a habitual preference for certain forms of emotion. Thus, the prudent and cautious man has had his habit of judgment formed by the emotions that have reference to evil and pain. We also speak of moral character in terms of will, as when we praise a man for being patient, resolute, manly. But here also we have virtues formed by prevalent emotions; for example, the morally resolute man is possessed by a feeling of self-respect, honour, sense of duty, and hatred of meanness and cravenness. A man's moral character is the resultant of his controlling emotional habits and proclivities, and of the ways in which they combine and co-operate. Commonly there are a few emotions of one type; indeed, not infrequently one emotion, potent above all others in a man's soul, gives colour to his whole life and character. Thus the miser is made; thus the recluse; thus the philanthropist. We do nothing to determine a man's life and character unless we can touch his heart. The most potent weapon in a man's hands is power to send an emotional thrill through the soul and kindle the glow of enthusiasm. Eros is King; and the enthusiasms of youth, the most fervent kindlings of emotion, make men what they become.

(*k*) The relation in which emotion stands to *religion* cannot be neglected; and, clearly, it is an intimate one. It is the heart that pants for the possession of religious life, even when the search takes the ostensible form of a longing to penetrate the mystery girding us, and to comprehend the use and meaning of our existence: for how could any such desire awake in us except for a longing to be rid of the feeling of dreariness and worthlessness, and to be able to rejoice in the conviction that life has value? The possession of religion comes to a man as a new emotional experience; as a deepening, expansion, and purification of his feeling; as a power to rejoice in his conscious existence as an inestimable gift of the Creator; as freedom to look abroad over the world with peaceful eyes made glad with love and hope; as a consciousness of inward nobility raising him above the world's vanity; as a new self-consciousness springing from a heart purged from the foulness of a bad conscience; as a revelation of a new capacity for praise and adoration. The religion portrayed in the Psalms and Epistles is a life glowing with emotion; and nowhere else in literature have we any such record of emotional experience. If we compare such Psalms as the 88th and the 103rd, we see how this emotional life has an incomparable depth, and passes from deepest sadness to highest rapture. A religion of this sort requires no evidences. It is like salt, or light, or the aroma of an ointment. It fascinates like a charm, and spreads itself like a contagious enthusiasm. Of this sort was Christianity meant to be: such it was in the beginning; and such will it be again some future day. But emotion cannot feed itself, nor can it support itself. The *summum bonum* revealed in immediate feeling demands reconciliation with the *summum verum*: and here all our difficulties in dealing with religion begin. The experience of the heart enwraps ideas that we have great difficulty in making clear and stable, and in bringing into harmony with the facts of life and the world. The correlated creed has never yet been able to make itself more than just a *reasonable faith*, and in its details has never risen above the fogs of controversy. Nevertheless, no one who has truly experienced the religion of emotion can doubt that it is the greatest and best that can ever enter into the life of man, and that its necessary implications must needs be true.

Our attention is arrested by the fact that there is to be found a fervent emotional religion without moral purity and without stable religious character. This was so often brought under his notice in connexion with revivals that Jonathan Edwards (*q.v.*) wrote his memorable book on *The Religious Affections* in order to set forth the marks by which to discriminate between genuine and spurious religious emotion. But no empirical tests are available; and the outcome of his effort is simply to show that religion must enwrap intelligence and volition as well as emotion—must root itself in enlightened conceptions, and take form in a holy walk and conversation—must grasp consciousness in the unity of reason. It is so; but it deserves, nevertheless, to be made emphatic that religion is centrally an *emotional* experience. Otherwise it is formalism. We thus reduce Dogma, Ritual, and Church to their rightful position of subordination.

(*l*) We are naturally conducted to the question whether emotion can ever be accepted as *a ground of judgment, a basis of belief, and a test of truth.* Emotion is, without doubt, a cause of belief; but a cause of belief is not necessarily a ground or reason. There are cases in which all would admit that emotion must be peremptorily excluded, as, for example, in a judicial trial, and generally in all purely scientific work. It has, however, been held that there are certain cases in which emotion may sit in judgment on truth and error, especially in moral and religious questions. That 'the heart has a logic of its own' is a sentiment preached in many a discourse. Tennyson tells us, in well known lines, that, in virtue of having felt, a man may justly rise in wrath against the freezing reason, that is, the critical understanding, and with superior authority silence it (*In Memoriam*, cxxiv.). In a similar vein Jacobi says, 'There is light in my heart, but, when I seek to bring it into the understanding, it is extinguished'; and pronounces the verdict on himself, 'a heathen with the understanding, but a Christian with the spirit' (quoted in Überweg's *Hist. of Philosophy*, Eng. tr.², 1875, ii. 200). The heart, then, has a co-ordinate title with the judgment to say Yes or No, on a question of truth; nay, a superior title. A writer on Browning says of him that in his poems he assumes that 'love, even in its illusions, may be accepted as a messenger of truth' (Orr, *Handbook*, 1885, p. 337). Right through all the forms of Mysticism there runs a doctrine of this sort. We have before us an example of the fact that, for popular literary purposes, forms of speech may be allowed which are psychologically incorrect. It cannot be correct to speak of emotion as judging of truth and error. We might as well speak of the eye hearing music, or set ourselves to measure feelings with a foot rule. Nothing can judge of truth and error but the logical understanding. Nevertheless, there is truth and meaning in such words as 'The heart has a logic of its own,' and in Tennyson's lines. It is true that there come trying hours when our heart moves us to affirm what our head urges us to deny, or in which arguments point to a conclusion that is repugnant; and occasionally it may well be the case that the instinct of our emotion is found in the end wiser than our logic. The mind is often guided by an implicit logic, vaguely conscious of the pressure of arguments which it is unable to formulate, but which it will readily recognize when expressed by a clearer and more vigorous understanding; and, in such cases, the first appearance is as if emotion alone judged. When emotion seems to judge in moral and religious matters, it is found that the process is one of deductive reasoning assuming as true some such major premiss as 'No doctrine can be true which robs existence of worth and meaning,' or 'The Universe is at bottom wise and good and rational'; and every proposition is straightway rejected that is or involves the contradictory. Further, it is true that all men are not in a position to sit in judgment on certain matters. A man with no vivid religious experience will show his wisdom by declining to pronounce any judgment on religious subjects; for he wants at once the materials for judging and the capacity for appreciation of the factors; and the demand for a decision in morals and religion is addressed to the Ego in the undivided unity of its powers. The majority of men will never be guided in their belief on the highest matter by learned apparatus, by deliberate critical inquiry, and by explicit logic. They will be determined by emotional proclivities and emotional experiences—'feeling doing the work of thought'—and the simple honest soul is not thus necessarily guided amiss. Indeed, are there any matters in which the groping of unclear emotion does not pioneer the way that logic follows? We *feel* the presence of a new thought before it becomes quite luminous to thought; and the inventor or discoverer *feels* the approach of success before his intellect has quite grasped the desired issue. We *feel* the presence of fallacious reasoning before we can state explicitly wherein lies the fallacy.

(*m*) The *proper wealth of reason* consists in its emotional experiences. We disparage neither thought nor volition in saying that we have lived only as we have felt. In Schiller's *Wallenstein* we hear Thekla singing:

'Ich habe genossen das irdische Glück,
Ich habe gelebt und geliebt.'

We may generalize the sentiment: we have lived only as we have glowed with emotion; and the hours of intense feeling stand forth in memory as the shining peaks that catch the eye. It was then we learned into how goodly an inheritance God summoned us when He gave us being. It is to be feared, however, that such hours are few, and that the emotional experiences of most men are meagre and within a narrow compass. The more simple emotions, such as love and hate, hope and fear, are known by all men; but the higher emotions seem to remain an unrealized possibility.

'One may assert,' says Ribot, 'that these higher forms are unattainable by the great majority of men. Perhaps scarcely one person in a hundred thousand or a million reaches them; the others know them not, or only suspect them approximately and by hearsay. They are a promised land only entered by a few of the elect' (*Psychology of the Emotions*, 17).

There is much to justify this strong impeachment and probably not too severe disparagement.

(*n*) The *intellectual* (or logical) emotions, such as arise in connexion with cognitive activity and gather round the idea of *truth*, seem to be unknown to most men, for only a few lead an intellectual life. They are not pained by inconsistencies and contradictions, are easily tolerant of the absence of order and of logic; nor do they know the joy of the entrance of a new thought, of emancipation from error and ignorance, or of grasping unifying principles. All men laugh, and desire to be made to laugh, yet it does not appear that the higher reaches of the emotion of the ludicrous are very common. The sense of humour, with its subtle combination of quick perceptiveness and genial kindness, is not a universal possession; and the want amounts to a fearful impoverishment of reason. Those who want it neither see nor feel. Their souls become like leather. In rudimentary form all men have some *sense of the beautiful*; and the ornamentation of their bodies, their furniture, and their weapons, on the part of the humblest races, shows us from how deep a root in reason the æsthetic emotion springs. It is no superfluous flourish, but deep as the demand for truth and goodness. Yet a true artistic sense is not yet common; nor can heaven and earth reveal their beauty except to one who can suffuse it all with the inner wealth of his own soul. Probably, the emotion of *the sublime* is among the rarest of all experiences—the incipient movement towards it seldom going beyond a vague sense of the imposing, unless to give way to the feeling of awe and terror. Being important for life and conduct, and incessantly demanded, the *ethical sentiment* exists in considerable vigour. No normal human being is lacking in the emotion of moral approbation and disapprobation attendant on the judgment of conscience, or perhaps an integral part of it; and every man is thus constrained to a recognition of a sacred moral order, of a high worth in human existence, and of a sublime End giving law to conduct. And yet the immorality of the world proclaims the feebleness of the moral emotions. Probably, no man is without the germs of the *religious emotion*. In a sense, all men are religious; and they are also irreligious. We cannot extirpate the religious sentiment; nor can all agencies make it strong and fruitful excepting in elect souls, who serve as an offering of the firstfruits of humanity unto God. Religion flares up in a man's spirit in hours when he realizes his nothingness in the immeasurable universe, his weakness in face of its immensity, his vileness in contrast with some radiant form of purity, his bondage under evil in sharp antithesis to the demand of his reason for supremacy, and in numerous other such experiences of his weakness and want; but the fire is apt to die down again, and a man's religion to become only a pitiful remembrance that once he had a few pious days or hours, and that a rift in the clouds gave him a glimpse of untrodden realms. Truly, there are worlds of possible emotional experience yet to be made our own. We have not half lived out the possibilities of our own souls.

3. It is no part of the plan of this article to enter on the **analysis of the emotions** in detail. We content ourselves with indicating the most important principles of explanation: (1) the fundamental impulse of self-conservation and self-realization, moving us to make real the ideal possibilities of our nature; (2) pleasure and pain, joy and sorrow, attaching to the successful or thwarted efforts, with desire for and aversion to all objects according as they aid or hinder us—our conception of good and evil being purely anthropocentric; (3) the Laws of Association; (4) the activity of the constructive imagination; (5) the Law of Relativity: that is, every fresh experience has its nature and effect in consciousness determined by the antecedent and contemporaneous circumstances into the midst of which it enters. These doctrines seem to furnish an adequate explanation of the development of the emotional life throughout, and up to its highest reaches. It seems vain to ask, as is done by Hodgson (*Theory of Practice*, i. 137), 'why there are such feelings as pleasure and pain at all, and why, if there are, they should be attached respectively to successful and unsuccessful effort.' We might as reasonably ask an explanation of the combining power of the ultimate chemical atoms. At some point we have to come to a pause and say, We are so made, and our wisdom was not consulted. When we try to imagine any other arrangement, it seems like setting a suicidal self-contradiction at the heart of things, or as if we were asked to combine the bloom of youth with the decrepitude of age.

See also artt. EMOTIONS, MIND.

LITERATURE.—In the older Psychologies, feeling and emotion are handled in a perfunctory manner; in more recent times, most fully and instructively by **Sully**, **Höffding**, **Baldwin**, and **Dewey**; the sections in **Spencer** being significant on their own lines. In addition, the student may read with advantage: **Spinoza**, *Ethics*, bk. iii.; **Hume**, *Treatise on Human Nature*, ed. Green and Grose, London, 1909, vol. ii., also his *Dissertation on the Passions*, vol. ii. of *Essays*, ed. Green and Grose, 1907; **A. Bain**, *The Emotions and the Will*, London, 1859; **T. Ribot**, *Psychology of the Emotions*, Contemporary Science Series, London, 1897; **S. H. Hodgson**, *Theory of Practice*, London, 1870, vol. i. The best known German works are **J. W. Nahlowsky**, *Das Gefühlsleben*², Leipzig, 1884; **C. Lange**, *Ueber die Gemüthsbewegungen*, Leipzig, 1887. See also the literature appended to art. EMOTIONS.

WILLIAM SALMOND.

FEET-WASHING.—I. Ceremonial cleansing before worship. — (1) *Jewish.*—The defilement attaching to feet imperfectly protected from the dirt of the highway required to be ceremonially washed away before the priests could worthily approach God (Ex 30^{18-21} 40^{30-32}, cf. 2 Ch 4^{6}). Brazen vessels were placed between the Tabernacle and the altar of burnt-offering, and ablutions therein were absolutely necessary before approach to the service of the sanctuary was permitted. According to Tosefta, *Men.* i., to ensure a thorough cleansing, it was the practice of the priests to wash their hands and feet *twice* in the basin. On Sabbaths and on the Day of Atonement (as well as on 9th Ab) the custom was not so rigorously followed, except in the case of one arriving from a journey (see Lampronti, *Paḥad Yiẓḥaḳ*, Venice, 1750–1887, *s.v.* רהיצה). The Jewish ceremonial law of feet-washing as regards laymen is no longer extant. The Temple ritual for the priests is referred to in Philo (*Vita Mosis*, iii. 15: πόδας μάλιστα καὶ χεῖρας ἀπονιπτόμενοι), and in Mishn. *Tamid*. i. 4, ii. 1 (see Surenhusius,

Mischna, Amsterdam, 1698–1703, v. 284–310; Ugolinus, *Thesaurus*, Venice, 1744–69, xix. 1467–1502; Schürer, *HJP* II. i. 278; *JE* v. 357, which gives other instances of ceremonial cleanliness). It must be remembered that the priests always walked about the Temple with bare feet. The ground was sacred, and would have been profaned had the ministrants worn their sandals (cf. Ex 3[5]).

(2) *Roman.*—Ablution of the feet was enjoined as a preliminary to worship of the gods under the Roman and Greek cultus (Jos. Laurentius, *Varia Sacra Gentilium*, in Gronovius, *Thes. Gr. Ant.*, Lyons, 1697–1702, vii. 215).

(3) *Muhammadan.*—The practice of feet-washing before engaging in any religious service is still maintained by Muslims, who have carried over the ceremony from the Mosaic regulations (cf., *e.g.*, W. M. Thomson, *The Land and the Book*, Lond. 1881–86, p. 122).

(4) *Early Christian.*—Churches of the early Christian centuries were provided with an *atrium* or *area* or 'court,' surrounded with porticoes or cloisters, in the middle of which stood a fountain called *cantharus* or *phiala*. In this it was deemed necessary that worshippers should wash their feet and hands before entering the church.

In his panegyric regarding the church erected by Paulinus in Tyre, Eusebius (*HE* x. 4) says: 'On entering within the gates, he has not permitted you to enter immediately, with impure and unwashed feet, within the sanctuary; but, leaving an extensive space between the temple and the vestibule, he has decorated and enclosed it with four inclined porticoes around. . . . Here he has placed the symbols of the sacred purifications, by providing fountains (κρήνας) built opposite the temple, which, by the abundant effusion of their waters, afford the means of cleansing to those that proceed to the inner parts of the sanctuary.'

Further references to this practice are found in Paulinus of Nola, *Ep.* xii. *ad Severum*, where the word *cantharus* is employed. Tertullian (*de Orat.* xi.) inveighs against those who go in to worship, having cleansed the outer person, while they retain a filthy spirit and a polluted soul. Socrates (ii. 38) calls the laver φρέαρ, 'the spring,' when speaking of the bloody conflict between the Catholics and the Macedonian heretics in the church of Acacius at Constantinople, whereby the 'court' with its φρέαρ and its porticoes was overflowed with blood. Chrysostom makes frequent reference to those fountains (hom. lii. *in Matt.*, lxxii. *in Johan.*, iii. *in Ephes.*, *in Psalm.* cxl. etc.); so also Synesius, *Ep.* cxxi. Paulus Silentiarius, in his description of S. Sophia (*Script. hist. Byzant.*, Venice, 1722–33, xiv. 204), calls the fountain φιάλη, the 'basin.' From its being frequently adorned with lions, some modern Greek writers call it the *leontarium* (cf. the fountain in the courtyard of St. Mark's, Venice). Other names are *nymphæum*, ἐμβάτης, and κολυμβεῖον (cf. Bingham, *Orig. Eccles.* II. viii. 6. 3).

(5) *Coptic.*—It would seem from the Canons of Christodulus (11th cent.) that men were required to come barefoot to worship in the ancient Coptic churches in Egypt. A tank was, therefore, placed in the floor, in order to afford facilities for worshippers to cleanse their feet and wipe off the dust of travel before entering on their sacred devotions. The present-day use of shoes in modern Coptic churches has rendered the strict observance of this practice no longer necessary; but the tanks are still employed (as will be pointed out later on) in the services of Maundy Thursday (see A. J. Butler, *Ancient Coptic Churches of Egypt*, i. 23).

The Jewish, Muhammadan, Early Christian, and Coptic ceremonial ablutions of the feet are apparently all of a piece with a ritual of a still earlier era. Flinders Petrie has discovered similar tanks at the entrance to the ancient temple of Serabit el-Khadem in Sinai, parts of which date as far back as Sneferu of the IIIrd Egyptian dynasty (*c.* 4750 B.C.). The tanks, which, however, are probably of a much later date, perhaps of the XVIIIth dynasty, are four in number, and are so situated that it was evidently intended that the worshipper should perform his ablutions over and over again, as he gradually approached the most sacred shrine of all (W. M. Flinders Petrie, *Researches in Sinai*, London, 1906, pp. 105–107).

2. As an act of hospitality.—Providing water for guests, wherewith they might wash their feet, immediately on their arrival at tent or house, was an invariable mark of Oriental courtesy (cf. Gn 18[4] 19[2] 24[32] 43[24], Jg 19[21]). Hospitality was emphasized when the host personally performed the act (cf. 1 S 25[41]). The practice was general throughout most of the ancient world. At Egyptian banquets, guests had their feet washed by slaves, who sometimes used golden basins (Wilkinson [ed. 1837], ii. 210; Herod. ii. 172). For illustrations of the practice among the Greeks and Romans, cf. Hom. *Il.* x. 577, *Od.* iv. 49, xv. 135; Martial, *Epig.* iii. 50. 3; Petron. *Sat.* xxxi.; Plato, *Symp.* 175, 213. In some reliefs, guests are depicted standing, instead of sitting on couches, while their feet are being washed (*Marbles of the Brit. Mus.* ii. 4). Wine and perfumed essences were sometimes used, instead of water, by rich and extravagant hosts (Plutarch, *Phocion*, 20). This has all along been the practice in the East down to modern times, in monasteries and in private houses (cf. Rufinus, in Rosweyde, *Vitæ Patrum*, 1628, p. 348 f.; Niebuhr, *Reisen*, 1837, i. 54; Shaw, *Travels*, 1861, p. 202; Robinson, *Bib. Res.*, 1856, ii. 229 f.; Jowett, *Researches*[3], 1824, p. 78 f.; Doughty, *Arab. Des.*, 1887–88, ii. 136; Butler, i. 291). In India honour is accorded a guest by the women of the village anointing his feet and wiping them with the hairs of their heads (*Women's Miss. Mag. U.F. Ch. of Scot.*, Feb. 1905). Not to wash one's feet was reckoned a sign of deep mourning (2 S 19[24]).

3. The NT instances.—These are three in number. (1) The denial of water to a guest was a distinct mark of discourtesy and unfriendliness. Jesus reproached Simon the Pharisee for this neglect, while He commended the loving action of the woman who was a sinner, who washed His feet with her tears, wiped them with the hairs of her head, kissed His feet, and anointed them with the ointment (Lk 7[36-50]).

(2) The classical example is that recorded in Jn 13[1-17]. Certain misconceptions arising from ambiguous translation need to be guarded against. The renderings 'supper being ended' (AV) and 'during supper' (RV) are both open to criticism. Guests did not require to have their feet washed either at the end or in the middle of a feast, but Eastern etiquette made it necessary before they sat down to a meal. May we not, however, translate δείπνου γινομένου 'at supper-time,' or 'supper being served,' or 'when supper was about to begin'? If so, all is made plain. The upper room had been secured, the disciples had arrived, the feast was spread. But the servants, whose duty it was to wash the feet of the guests on arrival, were absent. All the utensils—the basin, the water, the towels, etc.—had been left in readiness. Yet none of the disciples showed a willingness to take upon himself this task of humility. Luke (22[24]) states: 'there was also a strife among them, which of them should be accounted the greatest.' It may well be that this quarrel really took place at the commencement of the feast, and that its true position should be earlier in the evening's events. It would then furnish a reason why Christ taught them this undying lesson of humility. To quell that 'strife,' Jesus Himself rose from the table, laid aside His upper garments, girded Himself with a towel, poured water into a basin, washed the disciples' feet, and wiped them with the towel.

The well-marked distinction between those who, on the one hand, having already 'been in the bath' (ὁ λελουμένος), now require to have merely the dust wiped off their feet (νίψασθαι), and those who, on the other hand, with feet clean, have nevertheless foul bodies, and especially foul hearts, is admirably drawn out by Cox (Almoni Peloni) (*Expos.*, 2nd ser., iv. 146) and Walter Smith (*ib.*, 4th ser., vii. 300), who illustrate the rich inner spiritual teaching underlying the whole of this symbolic act of Christ.

(3) The tradition of Oriental courtesy, involving, as it did, humility and gracious consideration for others, was carried over into the Christian Church, and made one of the qualifications entitling a widow to be received 'into the number.' Such an applicant must have 'washed the saints' feet' (εἰ ἁγίων πόδας

ἐνιψεν, 1 Ti 5[10])—a phrase which, as Bengel says, may be 'a synecdoche of the part for every kind of humble office,' but which certainly embraces also the literal sense.

4. The feet-washing by Christ illustrated in art.—Pictorial representations of this scene in Christ's life are comparatively rare. One on a sarcophagus in the Catacombs is reproduced in A. Jameson's *The Hist. of our Lord as exemplified in Works of Art*, 1864, ii. 12. For other examples, bringing out different features of the incident, cf. an Anglo-Saxon interlined folio Psalter (c. A.D. 1000; Brit. Mus. Cotton Tiber. c. vi.); Waagen, *Treasures of Art in Gt. Britain*, Lond. 1854, i. 144; Giotto, in the Arena Chapel at Padua (Ruskin, *Giotto and his work in Padua*); the *Byzantine Guide to Painting*, in Didron's *Christian Iconography*, 1851, ii. 314. Fra Angelico has a fine treatment of the subject; there is another erroneously ascribed to Perino del Vaga in the Ambrosian Library at Milan; Gaudenzio Ferrari († 1549) has depicted the scene in a fresco at Varallo; in St. Nicholas Cathedral in Newcastle-on-Tyne there is a painting of it by Tintoretto († 1594), while Ford Madox Brown's picture of the feet-washing is in the Tate Gallery, London (reproduced in *Pre-Raphaelites* [Bell's Series of Art Handbooks] and in *The Gospels in Art*, ed. Shaw Sparrow, 1904).

5. The washing of the feet of catechumens at baptism.—The feet-washing by our Lord came, in the early Christian centuries, to have a definite religious significance attached to it. Hence arose the ceremony of the *Pedilavium*, or the washing of the feet of the newly-baptized. This rite did not obtain very wide observance throughout the Church, yet traces of it are to be met with in several ancient liturgies.

(1) *The Gothic and Gallican Churches.*—The so-called *Missale Gothicum* gives perhaps the earliest rubric as to the baptismal service, and its sway extended over the major part of the Visigothic Church. The seventh item in this service is the 'washing of feet,' and the rubric is 'Dum pedes ejus lavas, dicis "Ego tibi lavo pedes; sicut Dominus noster Jesus Christus fecit discipulis suis, tu facias hospitibus et peregrinis, ut habeas vitam aeternam."' A different order is observed in two other Gallican sacramentaries, but indications are abundant that in the Gotho-Gallican Church it was the practice for the bishop to wash the feet of the neophytes (cf. Martène, *de Ant. Eccles. Rit.* i. 63, 84; Mabillon, *Mus. Ital.* i.; Marriott, in Smith, *DCA* i. 164; Neale-Forbes, *Anc. Liturgies of the Gallican Church*, 1855, pts. ii., iii. pp. 97, 191, 270; Darwell Stone, *Holy Baptism*, 1899, pp. 169, 288; Ceillier, *Hist. gén. des auteurs sacrés*, 1858–69, iii. 670; Herbst, in *Tübinger Quartalschr.*, 1881, p. 40; Duchesne, *Chr. Worship, its Origin and Evolution*, 1904, p. 326).

(2) *Milan.*—It has been asserted, on the supposed authority of St. Ambrose, that the rite was observed in Milan; but the treatises in which the references to the custom are found (*de Sacram.* iii. 1–7 [ed. Bened., Paris, 1868–90, ii. 362] and *de Myster.* 6) are very doubtfully ascribed to that great Latin Father. In the *de Sacram.* the unknown author speaks of the bishop washing the feet of the baptized ('succinctus summus sacerdos pedes tibi lavit'). The rite, however, was never formally established as part of the Roman service, and the utmost the Roman Church would admit was that the *Pedilavium* might be observed as an incitement to the Christian grace of humility, similar to the custom of washing the feet of strangers, but that no stress must be laid on it as if it taught a mystery comparable with that of baptism or regeneration. To this the Church of Milan replied that, besides teaching humility, the rite did proclaim a deep mystery, and revealed a method of sanctification, for Christ had said, 'If I wash thee not, thou hast no part with me.' No traces of the rite can now be found in the Ambrosian ritual.

(3) *Ireland.*—That the feet-washing of the newly-baptized was observed in Ireland is shown in the *Stowe Missal* (ed. Warren, p. 217), and by Warren, *Liturgy and Ritual of the Celtic Church*, Oxford, 1881, pp. 66, 217 f.

(4) *North Africa.*—An unsuccessful attempt has been made to make Augustine responsible for the prevalence of the ceremony in the N. African Church (J. Vicecomes, *de Antiquis baptismi ritibus*, 1618, III. xx. 912). The belief in the Augustinian authorship, however, of the work in which references to the *Pedilavium* in the N. African Church occur has now been given up. The treatise in question (*de Tempore*, 160) is really a sermon by Cæsarius, archb. of Arles († A.D. 540). Cæsarius quotes the words of a Gallican missal still extant (Martène, i. 64): 'Secundum quod ipsis in baptismo dictum est, Hospitum pedes lavent,' etc. But this, of course, has nothing to do with the Church in N. Africa (see Cæsar. Arl. *Serm.* clxviii. 3, cclvii. 2, in App. to Augustine, t. vi. col. 291 f.). It is undoubtedly true that Augustine twice refers to the practice. In his *Ep. ad Januar.* cxviii., he speaks of the catechumens bathing their whole body and not only their feet before Easter, that they might be free from bodily filth. This, he says, however, was not a ceremonial washing, but in order that the bodies of the catechumens might not be offensive to others. In the other epistle (cxix. 18) he specially refers to the practice of washing the feet of catechumens after baptism 'on the day when the Lord first gave this lesson on humility.' But he adds that, lest their *Pedilavium* (which was usually held towards the end of Lent) should be regarded as essential to the proper observance of baptism, it never received general recognition (cf. Casalius, *de Veter. sacr. Christ. rit.*, 1681, p. 49).

(5) *Spain.*—That there were many attempts to introduce the rite into Spain as part of the Gallo-Gothic service is generally admitted. Apparently, however, there was a growing feeling against its celebration, not only in Spain, but in neighbouring territories. Many Churches, indeed, refused to allow it as part of the baptismal service, and relegated its observance to a day further on in the ecclesiastical calendar—either 'the third day of the octave,' or 'the octave after baptism' itself. Others absolutely declined to admit the observance of it at all. Falling thus into general disfavour, the practice was formally abolished by the Spanish Church.

The 48th canon of the Synod of Elvira (Illiberis), A.D. 306, forbids the celebration of the rite in these words: 'Neque pedes eorum [qui baptizantur] lavandi sunt a sacerdotibus vel clericis' (Mansi, ii. 14). The prohibition passed into the *Corpus Juris Canonici* (c. 104, causa i. qu. 1; see Bingham, XII. iv. 10; F. A. Gonzalez, *Collect. Canon. Eccles. Hispan.*, Madrid, 1808 [reproduced by Bruns, *Biblioth. Eccles.* .I ii. 1 ff.]; Hardouin, *Concilia*, 1715, i. 225; Hefele, i. 157; Smith, *DCA* i. 164, art. 'Baptism,' §§ 34, 67, *ib.* ii. 1160, art. 'Maundy Thursday').

No traces of the practice can be discerned in the East; and, as it was never followed at Rome, it is plain that the feet-washing of baptized persons was a purely local peculiarity, introduced at an early date into some parts of the Catholic Church, but never universal. At the present day no trace of the rite can be found anywhere in connexion with the sacrament of baptism.

6. The monastic, imperial, and royal washing of the feet of the poor.—Though the practice of the *Pedilavium* (or *Lavipedium*, as it is sometimes called) was forbidden as regards the reception into the Church of catechumens, the rite was nevertheless encouraged in connexion with the poor. As the practice is wide-spread through both Western and Eastern sections of Christendom, and has secured a place in certain divisions of Protestantism, it will be most convenient to treat of its growth under the headings of the different countries in which it has been practised, in order that local variations may be observed.

i. *THE WESTERN (ROMAN) CHURCH.*—(1) *Rome.*—The earliest reference to the monastic feet-washing of the poor seems to be in *Ordo Romanus X.* of the 11th cent. (Mabillon, ii. 101: 'Pontifex vero ingreditur basilicam S. Laurentii, et sine planeta residens in sede, facit Mandatum duodecim subdiaconorum. Interim cantores cantant vesperas ante eum, ut mos est'). The office is in the *Missale Romanum* from the first ed. (1474) onwards, under 'feria quinta in Coena Domini' (see ed. Balthasarius Moreti, Antwerp, 1696, p. 178). Throughout the Middle Ages the practice was commonly observed in nearly every monastery and court; and the feet of subordinate priests, of the poor, or of inferiors, were washed by priests, bishops, nobles, and sometimes by sovereigns. The frequency of the rite varied. In some places it was performed every Lord's Day. But one day in particular in the ecclesiastical calendar was decreed as being eminently suitable, viz. Holy Thursday, the day before Good Friday. The rubric for that day runs: 'conveniunt clerici ad faciendum mandatum'—'mandatum' being the name given to the ceremony from the words of the first antiphon sung during the performance of the service: 'Mandatum novum do vobis ut diligatis invicem' (Jn 13[34]; hence 'Maundy' [see below under '*England*,' p. 818[b]]).

A description of the rite as it was practised until 1870 by the Popes is given in Picart, *Cerem. and Relig. Customs of the World*, 1733, ii. 21; Tuker Malleson, *Handbook to Christian and Eccles. Rome*, pt. ii. p. 294; M. H. Seymour, *A Pilgrimage to Rome*, 1851, p. 242 f.; Chambers, *Book of Days*, 1863, i. 413; Walsh, *Curiosities of Popular Customs*, 1898, p. 676.

This ceremony of feet-washing, associated with Holy Thursday, is widely practised still in the churches of Italy. In Florence, for example, the archbishop on this day annually washes the feet of twelve poor old men; while in many castles and mansion-houses it is considered to be the correct thing for the nobleman or his private chaplain to see that the *mandatum* is observed. Holy Thursday was also the day on which there took place the restoration of those penitents who had been expelled since Ash Wednesday, their re-admission and reconciliation being gone through with according to the ritual given in the *Pontificale*, and with the chanting of the prescribed 'Penitential Psalms' (*EBr*[9] xviii. 487, art. 'Penance'). A full account of the conditions of restoration is given by H. J. Feasey, *Anc. Eng. Holy Week Ceremonial*, 1897, p. 96 f.

A further ceremony known as the *Lavanda* was maintained until recently in Rome during Holy Week. The Great Hospital of the Holy Trinity was thrown open to the thousands of pilgrims who stream across the Alps from all parts of Europe. A corps of Roman ladies and gentlemen, wearing a distinctive form of dress, superintended the arrangements for the reception of these guests. Only those newly arrived were cared for; and, as the pilgrims were mostly very poor, and had tramped for several hundreds of miles without boots and with their feet enswathed in 20 or 30 yards of linen, they were very grateful to have the blood-stained coils removed, and their sores attended to. They were guided to basement rooms with a low wooden seat round the wall. Here the corps of ministrants, men serving men, and women attending on women, in separate rooms, with warm water and coarse soap washed away the dust and the blood from the pilgrims' feet, and dried them with strong towels. The foul, steamy atmosphere was very trying and disgusting. Relay after relay were thereafter led to a long refectory, where they had set before them abundance of bread and meat, served at deal tables covered with a coarse white tablecloth. They were then guided to St. Peter's, where they participated in the august ceremonies of the Holy Week (Walsh, 809, art. 'Pilgrimage'). Since the Italian Government dismantled the specially fitted rooms the *Lavanda* has ceased (Tuker-Malleson, ii. 251, 294).

(2) *Milan.*—The earliest reference to the practice of feet-washing in the Milanese Church is probably that given by Beroldus in the 12th cent. (see Magistretti, *op. cit. infra*, p. 105). Muratori (*Antiq. Ital. Medii Aevi*, vol. iv. col. 893, 'de Feria quinta') thus explains the rite:

'Interea vero archiepiscopus lavat presbyteris et diaconis et magistro scholarum et primicerio lectorum cum magna reverentia singulis singulos pedes, hisce canentibus hanc antiphonam "Postquam surrexit Dominus a coena." Oratio post mandatum: "Adesto, Domine, officio servitutis nostrae, qui pedes lavare dignatus es tuis discipulis . . . et sicut heic exteriora abluuntur inquinamenta ita omnium nostrorum interiora laventur peccata," etc. His finitis, pro caritate bibit cum eis archiepiscopus, et presbyteris et diaconis et magistro scholarum, et primicerio lectorum duodenos denarios tribuit.'

It may be surmised that this practically was the manner in which the service was carried out in most of the churches of Northern Italy.

(3) *Gaul.*—The earliest reference for Frankish monastic feet-washing is the 24th Canon of the Council of Aachen (Aquisgranense), A.D. 814. It runs thus: 'Statutum ut in Coena Domini pedes fratrum abbas lavet et osculetur, et demum propria manu potum eis porrigat' (can. 24, *Cap. Reg. Fr.* i. 583). The obligation of *kissing* the feet already met with is here most explicitly laid down. The rite was in force in every monastery within the Frankish monarchy, and was observed in substantially the same form, though slight local variations in the ritual are noticeable. The fullest description of these variations is given by Martène (vol. iii. col. 280, and vol. iv. p. 372). The *mandatum* was performed in some convents not by the abbot alone, but by every inmate, and not merely on twelve poor persons, but on as many paupers as there were monks in the cloister. The practice of feet-washing, already so wide-spread in the Roman Church, was still further extended and encouraged by the enthusiasm with which the renowned Bernard of Clairvaux (A.D. 1091–1153) urged its observance. So highly did he regard the rite that he sought to have it placed alongside of Baptism and the Lord's Supper as an eighth sacrament. His words are: 'Nam ut de remissione quotidianorum minime dubitemus, habemus ejus sacramentum pedum ablutionem. . . . Aliquid igitur habet quod necessarium est ad salutem quando sine eo nec ipse Petrus partem haberet in regno Christi et Dei' (*Opera*, i., Serm. 'de Coena Dom,' col. 1950). Though the Papal Court refused to agree to Bernard's plea, such was the greatness of his character and the weight of his example that the ceremony was fixed more securely than ever in the service of the Church. There are references from time to time in history to the royal Maundy of the kings of France. Helgaldus (*Vita Roberti regis*, in Duchesne, *Hist. Francor. Scriptor.* 1636–49, vol. iv.) states that King Robert II. (A.D. 971–1031) daily gathered to his table 300 poor guests, and, after feeding them, was accustomed to lay aside his royal vestments, and, clad in a rough garment of goats' hair, to wash the feet of 160 of them, and to wipe them with the locks of his head. To each he then made a present of two pieces of silver ('duobus solidis remunerans'). Picart (ii. 21) records that in his time the chief physician of the king (Louis XV. [1715–1775]) annually made choice of twelve children whose feet the king washed on Maundy Thursday, and who were afterwards served by his Majesty with dishes of food.

(4) *Spain.*—To Spain belongs the distinction of being the first country in Europe to give a synodal imprimatur to the rite of feet-washing. Canon 3 of the 17th Council of Toledo (A.D. 694), while affirming that the ceremony ought to take place on the anniversary of the day when Christ first performed it, viz. Thursday, the 14th Nisan, goes on to decree: 'Si quisquam sacerdotum hoc nostrum distulerit ad implere decretum, duorum mensium spatiis sese noverit a sanctae communionis perceptione frustratum' (*Conc. Tolet.*, Dec. xvii. c. 3) (see Martène, vol. iii. col. 280). The office is in *Liber Ordinum* (ed. Férotin), col. 192, or Ximenes, *Missale Mixtum* (*Liturgia Mozarabica secundum Regulam beati Isidori*, pars i. in *PL* lxxxv. col. 420, 'ad lavandos pedes'). It is here stated that the rubric as to feet-washing did not exist in the *Missale Toletanum*, but that it had been an ancient custom, kept up on the fifth day of Holy Week, in certain churches of Spain and Gaul, and allowed to

lapse in others. In consequence of this, the Council of Toledo ordered the bishops throughout the whole of Spain and Gaul on this day to follow the example set by Jesus Christ, and to practise the *mandatum*, under the penalty of excommunication for two months for non-performance—whence, it is added, there arose the ceremony of the washing of the feet of poor persons, which everywhere was performed even by Christian princes century after century. At the beginning of the 18th cent. the royal Maundy as observed in Spain was described by Picart (*op. cit.* ii. 23). At the present time, besides being observed in almost every convent and palace in Spain, the rite is still continued by the King, twelve old men and twelve old women having their feet touched with a sponge and a towel by the monarch, who afterwards waits on them at a feast. Hone (*The Every-Day Book*, ii. 405) gives a full account of the ceremony as performed in Seville. In Madrid at the present time all vehicular traffic is forbidden on Holy Thursday. A foolhardy cabman in 1870 nearly lost his life while attempting to defy public opinion on the subject (see Walsh, 677).

(5) *Portugal*.—Feet-washing as a part of the services of Holy Week was not observed by either the ex-king (Manuel) of Portugal or his father. The function as a royal act ceased with the demise of Dom Pedro V. (1861). After the institution of the Republic the ceremony was no longer maintained in the Royal Chapel, but only in a few of the churches of the country. Twelve poor persons had their feet washed amid much pomp and splendour and a great profusion of lights. Those operated upon in the Royal Chapel used each to receive Rs. 6000 (worth to-day 26 shillings). This was done every year.

(6) *Bavaria*.—The ceremony of the feet-washing is still annually observed in Munich on Holy Thursday. It is performed in the 'Hercules-Saal' of the Royal Palace by the King (at present by the Prince Regent) in presence of the members of the Royal Family and the dignitaries of the Church. After the usual religious service, the feet of twelve old men, above 90 years of age, selected from every part of Bavaria, are washed by the sovereign and afterwards kissed by the senior priest of the Royal Chapel. After the ceremony, the King (or Prince Regent) hangs a little blue and white bag containing money over the shoulder of each of these 12 'apostles.' Every 10 years, the rite is also celebrated at Oberammergau, 45 miles S.W. of Munich, in connexion with the famous Passion Play.

(7) *Austria*.—Every Holy Thursday it has for centuries been the custom for the Emperor of Austria to wash the feet of the 12 oldest poor men in Vienna. In one of the halls of the Hofburg, amid a throng of brilliantly uniformed nobles and aristocrats, the scene takes place. First comes a 'feast' given to the old men, who are all dressed in a quaint old German costume, and seated on a row of chairs at a table. The Emperor stands at the end of the table, making the number 13. From a side room emerge 12 nobles, each carrying a tray laden with eatables. The Emperor places the plates in turn before each old man. They remain motionless, not touching a morsel. No sooner are the plates on the table than they are quickly lifted again and carried off by 13 men, who form a bodyguard. Four courses are thus served, and all—dishes and food—are later sent to the houses of the poor guests. Relatives, who have meanwhile been standing behind the chairs, now remove the shoes and hose of the old persons, and spread a roll of linen over their knees. A high church dignitary next reads the Gospel for the day, and at the words 'et coepit lavare pedes discipulorum' the Emperor dips a towel into a basin, and hastily wipes the feet of the old men in turn. The actual washing is very perfunctory, and the whole ceremony is over in a few minutes. Lastly, the Emperor hangs round the neck of each guest a silken bag containing silver pieces, and the old men are sent home in Royal carriages. The late Empress Elizabeth had discontinued the practice of performing a similar rite on old women in Vienna for some years before her assassination. The custom of the *Pedilavium* is still widely practised in the cloisters and churches of Austria (cf. P. H. Ditchfield, *Old English Customs extant at the present Time*, 1896, p. 258).

(8) *England*.—In England, Holy Thursday has received the name of 'Maundy Thursday.' A. Nares (*Glossary*, 1822, *s.v.*), following Spelman and Skinner, derives the word from the Saxon *maund*, 'a basket' (in which the provisions were given away). Cf. Shakespeare, *A Lover's Complaint*, 'A thousand favours from a maund she drew.' *Maund* has also been derived from Fr. *maundier*= 'to beg' ('mendicant'=a beggar); hence 'Maundy Thursday'='the poor people's Thursday' (*Gentleman's Magazine*, July, 1779, p. 354). But Skeat (*Concise Etymol. Dict.*[5], 1901, *s.v.*) emphatically maintains that the true derivation is through the Mid. Eng. *maundee* from Old Fr. *mandé*, and that again from Lat. *mandatum*, 'a command' (Jn 13^{34}), and that the etymology from *maund*='a basket' is 'as false as it is readily believed.' The day is also known as 'Shere Thursday' (also *Sheer*, *Chare*, from Mid. Eng. *shere* or *sheere*='pure,' 'unalloyed,' 'clear'; still seen in the use of 'sheer' to express physical purity).[1] The *Liber Festivalis* (fol. xxxii. b) of 1511 explains the name because 'in old faders dayes the people wolde that day shere theyr hedes, and clypp theyr berdes, . . . and so make them honest agenst Easter-day' (see also Brand, *Popular Antiquities*, 1813, i. 142, and Wordsworth, *Eccles. Biog.* i. 297). Hone (*Every-Day Book*, i. 402) says: 'In the miraculous legend of St. Brendan († A.D. 578) it is related that he sailed with his monks to the island of sheep, "and on *shere-thursdaye*, after souper, he wesshe theyr feet and kyssed them lyke as our lorde dyd to his dyscyples [*Golden Legend*]"' (cf. *Early South-English Legendary* [Early Eng. Text Soc., 1887]).

The Anglo-Saxon Church differed from the national Churches of France, Spain, and other countries in this respect, that it had no distinctive type of liturgy of its own. Roman in origin, owing its existence to Augustine of Canterbury, the A.S. Church was Roman all through. The various missals in use in the A.S. Church were practically the Roman missal with variations, additions, and other modifications which serve to distinguish them from the Continental missals of the same date. Of these A.S. missals, written before the Norman Conquest in 1066, three have survived. Two of them have references to the ceremony of feet-washing: (*a*) *The Missal of Robert of Jumièges* (ed. H. A. Wilson, Henry Bradshaw Soc. xi. [1896] 275), once the property of Robert, prior of the Benedictine monastery of St. Ouen at Rouen, who became abbot of Jumièges in 1037, bishop of London under Edward the Confessor in 1044, and archb. of Canterbury in 1051. The MS is of the end of the 10th cent. and the beginning of the 11th, and was preserved at Rouen. It goes under several titles, *e.g.* 'The Benedictional of Archb. Robert' (*Archæologia*, xxiv. 119); and, wrongly, 'The Book of St. Guthlac' (for which Dibdin is responsible; *Bibliog. Tour*, ed. 1821, i. 165). Here the collect is given without rubrics under the heading 'Benedictio (or Oratio) ad mandatum ipso die.' It runs thus:

[1] On the alleged connexion between 'Chare Thursday' and the German 'Charwoche' or 'Karwoche,' cf. *NQ*, 3rd ser., viii. [1865] 389; and for the derivation of 'Charfreitag,' cf. Graff, *Wörterbuch*, Berlin, 1834-46, iv. 464, and Wackernagel, *Wort zu seinem Lesebuch*, 1838, p. 319.

'Adesto, Domine, officio nostrae servitutis, quia tu pedes lavare dignatus es discipulorum. ne dispiceas opera manuum tuarum quesumus nobis retinenda mandasti. quesumus ut sicut hic exteriora abluuntur inquinamenta. sic a te omnium nostrorum interiora laventur peccata, qui cum Patre,' etc. (cf. the 'Oratio post mandatum,' in the Milanese Church).

(*b*) *The Leofric Missal* (ed. F. E. Warren, 1883), bequeathed to Exeter Cathedral by Leofric, first bishop of that see (1050–1072), is a complex volume with three main divisions: (α) a Gregorian sacramentary, written in Lotharingia early in the 10th cent.; (β) an A.S. calendar, written in English about A.D. 970; and (γ) a number of masses, etc., written in English, from the 10th–11th cent. (see *CQR* xiv. [1882] 278). In it (p. 256) we find the following rubric for 'Feria Quinta in Coena Domini': 'Ante missam vero faciant mandatum cum peregrinis et hospitibus.'

In addition to these surviving pre-Norman service-books, we have scattered historical references to the observance of the rite in the A.S. Church. Wluothus, abbot of St. Albans, ordained a *daily* celebration of the *mandatum*. St. Oswald, archb. of York, washed the feet of 12 poor men and fed them every day. In other religious houses it was the practice to wash the feet of as many poor persons as there were monks in the convent, not only on Maundy Thursday, but on the Saturday before Palm Sunday, which therefore received the name of *Mandatum pauperum* to distinguish it from the regular *Mandati Dies* (T. F. Thiselton-Dyer, *Brit. Pop. Customs*, 1876, p. 139). Aelfric, archb. of Canterbury (A.D. 996–1006), ordered the Saxon priests: 'Imple mandata Domini in coena ipsius,' 'Do on Thursday as our Lord commands you, wash the feet of the poor, feed and clothe them, and with humility wash your feet among yourselves as Christ himself did and commanded us so to do.' Rock (*Church of our Fathers*, iv. 85, 95) describes in full detail the ceremony as observed in the A.S. Church. The rubric for the *mandatum* is given by St. Dunstan as it was carried out in every large church throughout Anglo-Saxondom (*Reg. Conc.* 87). Rupert of Deutz (Tuitensis) († 1135) erroneously ascribed the origin of the rite to the woman who anointed Christ's feet. It was sometimes performed in monasteries for the purpose of comforting the souls of friends and families of deceased persons, and was regularly practised by the A.S. kings (*Biblioth. Patr.* 951, referred to in Fosbrooke, *Encyc. of Ant.*, Lond. 1840, art. 'Maundy,' p. 827). The Clugniac monks merely touched with wetted fingers the feet of these poor men: the Benedictines and Cistercians scrupulously washed the feet of the brethren, the abbot himself not being excused.

Further references to the early English practice will be found in the Cistercian *Consuetudines* (ed. Guignard, p. 110 [1878]); and in H. J. Feasey, *op. cit.* p. 95. References to the observance of the rite in later times are found in several of the missals, service-books, and 'uses.' The *Westminster Missal* (*Missale ad usum Eccles. Westmon.* (ed. J. Wickham Legg, Henry Bradshaw Soc., ii. [1893] 573) has 'ad mandatum pauperum in die cene, Antiphona "Dominus Ihesus"' (see also note in vol. iii. p. 1510 as to the identity of this anthem with that in Lanfranc's rule). The *York Missal* (*Missale ad usum insignis Eccles. Ebor.* [Surtees Soc.] i. 101, ed. Henderson, 1874), a MS of the 12th cent., gives the rubric first for the *mandatum* for the poor, and then that for the brethren (see Maskell, *Anc. Liturg. of the Ch. of England*, 1882). *The Book of Evesham* (*Officium eccles. Abbatum secundum usum Evesham. Monast.* [ed. H. A. Wilson, Henry Bradshaw Soc., Lond. 1893]), a MS of A.D. 1300, gives a full guide to the abbot as to the performance of the *mandatum* (pp. 83–87). The *Concordia Regularis* places the abbot's Maundy (col. 85, line 10) immediately after the *mixtum* (the 'refreshment'), and makes no mention of a *mandatum pauperum* performed by the convent generally. Lanfranc's *Statuta* agree with the Evesham Book in placing here the *mandatum pauperum*, but differ from it in making no mention of the abbot's Maundy (Reyner, *Apost. Bened. in Anglia*, 1626, App. 87, 220). The *Rites of Durham* (1593 [Surtees Soc. 1903], pp. 66–77) gives us a clear statement of the two services—the *mandatum pauperum* and the *mandatum fratrum*—in that cathedral. Recent excavations in Durham have revealed fire-places for heating the water used in these rites. In some form or other the ceremonies of the Maundy existed here from very early times. The constitutions of priors Absolon, German, and Bertram in the 12th cent. provide for the Maundy at Durham (Hutchinson, *Durham*, 1785–94, ii. 69 n., 70 n.). Similarly of the service at Ripon Cathedral we read (*Memorials of Ripon*, iii. 208, 211, 216, 221 [Surtees Soc.]): 'Et in iij buscellis frumenti empt. tam pro mandato in Coena Domini quam Eukaristia pro communione omnium parochianorum contra festum Paschae 4 s. 9d; precium buscell, 19d.' There are also references to the ceremony in the *Use of Sarum* (*The Sarum Customs as set forth in the Consuetudinary and Customary*, ed. W. H. Frere, 2 vols., 1898 [Henry Bradshaw Soc.]), which from the 13th century began to predominate over the other service-books, e.g. *The Use of Bangor* (A.D. 1268), *The Use of Lincoln*, and *The Use of St. Asaph* (both of the middle of the 15th cent.). See also Swete, *Church Services and Service Books before the Reformation*, 1896. Many of the English cathedrals still retain indications of the identical spots where the feet-washing was performed. Thus 'at York Minster, the Maundy seats are probably those in the N. choir aisle: at Worcester in the E. alley of the cloisters is a bench table anciently used at the Maundy; at Westminster on a stone bench in the E. cloister sat the 12 beggars whose feet the abbot washed, and under the nosing of the bench still remain the copper eyes from which hung the carpet on which he knelt during the performance of the ceremony. At Lichfield, and probably other cathedrals destitute of cloisters, the Maundy ceremony took place in choirs' (Feasey, 107, and *Home Counties Magazine*, Nov. 1909).

The monastic and the royal Maundy were observed in England under the Norman, Plantagenet, and Tudor reigns, as many references in history reveal.

Matthew Paris (A.D. 1200-1259), in his *Chronica Majora*, and Johannes de Fordun († 1385), in his *Chronica gentis Scotorum*, lib. v. c. 29, tell how Matilda, Queen of England (1109), 'nec horrebat pedes lavare morbidorum, ulcera sanie distillantia contrectare manibus, longa postremo protelare oscula et mensam apponere, et in servitio Dei audiendo voluptas unica.'

Henry II.'s reign.—The devotion with which Roger, archb. of York (1154–1181), always went about this ceremony of feet-washing, and his habit of paying the expenses, are specially recorded by old writers (Stubbs, *Actus Pontif. Ebor.*, in Twysden, *Hist. Angl. Script.*, 1652, ii. 1723).

Edward I.'s reign.—The accounts of the wardrobe expenses of Edward I. (1272–1307) record the giving of money on Easter Eve to 13 poor persons whose feet the Queen had washed (Thoms, *Book of the Court*, 1844, p. 311).

Edward II.'s reign.—The king fed 200 poor in honour of Pentecost—'according to ancient custom' (*NQ*, 7th ser., xii. 53).

Edward III.'s reign.—William de Wykeham records of Robert Betun, bishop of Hereford, that such was his piety that he *twice* performed this humble office on Maundy Thursday (*Anglia Sacra*, ii. 310). Langland, in his *Vision concerning Piers the Plowman* (ed. Skeat, ii. 488, ch. xvi. line 140), shows the custom at the end of the same reign:

> 'Til it bifel on a Fryday a litel bifore Paske
> The Thorsday byfore there he made his maundee'
> (*ib.* [note] ii. 239).

The close Roll 34 of Edward III. has this entry: 'March 21, at Kenilworth the king washed the feet of 50 poor men'; the previous day there had been an order for slippers, cloth, etc. (*Wardrobe Roll*, 19 Edw. III.). It was in Edward III.'s reign (in 1363) that the practice of granting doles was formally inaugurated (John Brady, *Clavis Calendaria*, i. [1815] 285). The custom of all religious houses and good Catholics of bringing out their broken food in 'maunds' to distribute to the poor gave rise to a veritable fair in many places, *e.g.* Tombland Fair at Norwich, held on the plain before the cathedral close (Brewer, *Dict. of Phrase and Fable*, new ed., 1895, p. 821).

Edward IV.'s reign.—Elizabeth of York, daughter of Edward IV., and future wife of Henry VII., used to bestow 'on xxxvij pore women every woman iijs. jd., for hir maundy upon Shire Thursday' (*Privy Purse Expenses*, i.).

Henry VIII.'s reign.—The king himself on Maundy Thursday washed the feet of as many poor men as he himself was years old, and thereafter distributed to them meat, clothes, and money (A.D. 1509–1547), as Sir Thomas More testified (*Works*, 1319). In the *Household Book* (1770, p. 354 f.) of the Earl of Northumberland, begun in A.D. 1512 (new ed. 1906), there is an inventory of 'Al-maner of things yerly yeven by my lorde of his Maundy, ande my laidis, and his lordshippi's childeren.' At Peterborough Abbey in 1530, Cardinal Wolsey washed and kissed the feet of 59 poor men. After wiping them, he granted to each individual 12 pennies, 3 ells of good canvas to make shirts, a pair of new shoes, a cart of red herrings, and 3 white herrings (Cavendish, *Life of Wolsey* 2, 1827; Holinshed, iii. 914).

In this reign also Catherine of Arragon, while Queen, was wont to observe the day with feet-washing of old women; but, after her divorce, Henry forbade her to do so (1533) except under the title of Princess Dowager.

Mary's reign.—Mary in 1556 gave a dazzling exhibition of her love for pageantry by a celebration of this rite on the grandest scale imaginable. The account of it is given in a letter of Marco Antonio Faitta, Secretary to Cardinal Pole, the Pope's Legate, to a correspondent in Venice of date 3rd April 1556 (*Calendar of State Papers* [Venetian], vi. 428).

Elizabeth's reign.—The royal Maundy was continued when England was no longer Roman. Elizabeth in 1579 very elaborately performed the rite at Greenwich Palace on 39 poor persons (see no. 6183, Add. MSS in Brit. Mus.; Nichols,

Progresses of Queen Elizabeth[2], 1823, i. 325; Hone, *Every-Day Book*, i. 401).

Charles II.*'s reign* (1660–1685).—'On Thursday last His Majesty washed poor men's feet in the Banqueting House, an act of humility used by his predecessors to as many poor men as he had lived years. The Queen did the same to several women about one of the clock at St. James'' (*Rawdon Papers*, 1819, p. 175). Pepys (*Diary*, ed. Wheatley, 1896, vi. 257) states: 'April 4th, 1667.—My wife had been . . . to the Maundy, it being Maundy Thursday; but the King did not wash the poor people's feet himself, but the Bishop of London did it for him.' It was in this reign that 'Maundy pennies' were first coined, coming fresh from the mint to the recipients.

James II.*'s reign.*—The last English sovereign to perform the rite in full was James II. (1685–1701). In Colsoni's *Guide de Londres pour les Etrangers*, 1693, p. 33, it is said: 'Le Jeudy Saint, le Roy, selon un fort ancienne coutume, lave les pieds à tout autant de vieillards qu'il a d'années.' But in the 3rd ed. of the same work (p. 43) there is a reference to the fact that the act was no longer performed by royalty in Britain: 'Mais le Roy G. III. (=William III.) a laissé l'intendence de cette cérémonie à son grand Aumonier ou un Evêque du Royaume.'

George II.*'s reign* (1727–1760).—We possess an elaborate account of how the archb. of York, as Lord High Almoner (on 15th April 1731), performed the annual ceremony of washing the feet of a certain number of poor in the Royal Chapel, Whitehall, in lieu of the monarch (see Hone, *op. cit.* i. 402; *Grub Street Journal*, Friday, 23rd April 1736; and *Old and New London*, iii. 368 f.).

Since 1754 the rite of feet-washing has been wholly obsolete in the Church of England; and in place of the former gifts of provisions and clothing a fixed sum of money is granted. The ceremony in 1814 is described by Hone (*op. cit.* i. 401). In 1818, owing to the advanced age of George III., the number of recipients amounted to 160. During Queen Victoria's reign it was the custom to present Maundy pennies to twice as many aged men and women as the Queen had lived years. King Edward VII. continued the ceremony through the Lord High Almoner, and the practice is kept up similarly by King George V.

The Roman Catholic Church in England still preserves the rite in its entirety, at least in certain places. The Cardinal-Archbishop, clothed in episcopal robes, washes, and wipes with a linen cloth, the feet of 13 choir boys arrayed in cassock and cotta, in the Cathedral at Westminster, each boy afterwards receiving a gift-book (Walsh, *op. cit.* p. 675).

(9) *Scotland.*—The references to the practice are scanty. St. Kentigern is recorded to have washed the feet of *lepers* on the Saturday before Palm Sunday (R. Craig Maclagan, *Scottish Myths*, 1882, p. 139). St. Cuthbert, who may be reckoned as Scottish (A.D. 676), is recorded by St. Bede (*Life of St. Cuthbert*, tr. Stevenson, 1887, p. 33) to have found one day at Ripon a young man sitting in the guest chamber in time of snow. He welcomed him *with the customary forms of kindness*. He bathed his feet for him, wiped them with a towel, placed them in his bosom, himself chafing them with his hands. During his residence in Lindisfarne,

'he would devoutly wash the feet of his brother monks with warm water, and he in his turn was forced at times by them to take off his shoes, and to suffer them to wash his feet; for so entirely had he put off all care as to the body, and so had given himself up to the care of the soul alone, that when once he had put on his long hose, which were made of hide, he used to wear them for several months together. Yea, with the exception of once at Easter, it may be said that he never took them off again for a year until the return of the Pasch, when he was unshod for the ceremony of the washing of the feet which is wont to take place on Maundy Thursday' (*ib.* p. 84; cf. Martène, *De Ant. Eccl. Discip.* c. xxii. pp. 277, 346 [ed. 1706], and *De Ant. Monach. Rit.* iii. 13. 50 f.).

In Turgot's *Life of St. Margaret, Queen of Scotland*, p. 61 (tr. from the Latin by W. Forbes-Leith, 1884), as also in Johannes de Fordun's *Chronica gentis Scotorum*, lib. v. ('The Historians of Scotland') p. 216, it is stated that, 'when the office of matins was finished, she (Margaret), returning to her chamber, along with the king (Malcolm Canmore), washed the feet of six poor persons, and used to give them something wherewith to relieve their poverty.' Her son, Alexander I., the Fierce, copied the example of his mother (*ib.* ch. 28, p. 227). After the Reformation the practice was viewed with great abhorrence (Calderwood, *Hist.* 1678, iii. 703, referring to reign of James VI.).

(10) *Ireland.*—Traces of the monastic celebration of this rite are recorded in the *Missale Vetus Hibernicum* (ed. F. E. Warren, 1879, p. 119, in the service for Maundy Thursday); in the legends of St. Bridgit (Hull, *Early Christian Ireland*, 1905, p. 144; see also *Lives of the Saints from the Book of Lismore* [ed. W. Stokes, 1890]; Carmichael, *Carmina Gadelica*, 1900; cf. also what is said about St. Brendan, above, p. 818[b]).

(11) *Palestine.*—The Latin observance of the *mandatum* takes place in Jerusalem in front of the entrance to the Holy Sepulchre, between the Chapel of the Angel and the Greek church. The rite is described by Mantell, in *PEFSt*, 1882, p. 160.

ii. *THE EASTERN CHURCHES.*—(1) *Greek Orthodox Church.*—The ceremony of the *Lavipedium* was observed with a scrupulosity in the Eastern Church rivalling that of the Western communion. The office—ἡ ἀκολουθία τοῦ θείου καὶ ἱεροῦ νιπτῆρος—is in the ordinary ΕΥΧΟΛΟΓΙΟΝ ΤΟ ΜΕΓΑ. Older forms are noted in Goar, ΕΥΧΟΛΟΓΙΟΝ[2] (p. 591). The variants from *Cod. Basiliensis*, noted by Goar, are the oldest extant, viz. *c.* A.D. 795. (See also Dmitrijewski, *Euchologia*, for further details regarding the ancient office.) The Greek office prescribes a full service of chants and prayers and the acting out in every detail of what our Lord said or did—*e.g.*, at the words 'He poureth water into a basin,' the brother both repeats the sentence and imitates the action. Goar (p. 596) refers to Jerome's practice of washing the feet of the multitudes of pilgrims to Bethlehem, and to that of Laurentius of performing the same office for Christian confessors in prison. At the present time the monastic *Lavipedium*, being regarded as an ordinance by the Greek Church, is performed on Maundy Thursday throughout the area over which the Orthodox Church holds sway (cf. Wheeler, *Voyages*, 1689, ii. 414, and Tournefort, *Voyage into the Levant*, 1718, Letter iii. p. 85: 'The more zealous among the bishops wash the feet of 12 Papas; the exhortation they now excuse themselves from').

(α) *Russia.*—The feet of the 'apostles' are washed in all Russian convents, and especially in St. Petersburg and Moscow. Twelve monks arranged in a semicircle are thus treated by the archbishop in the crowded cathedral. 'The archb., performing all and much more than is related of our Saviour in the 13th ch. of John, takes off his robes, girds up his loins with a towel, and proceeds to wash the feet of them all until he comes to the representative of St. Peter, who rises, and says, "Lord, dost thou wash my feet?" and the same interlocution takes place as between our Saviour and that apostle' (Clarke, *Trav. in Russia* [1810], i. 55; see also Leo Allatius, *de dom. et hebd. Græc.*, 1646, p. 21). The Czar of Russia, as the head of the Greek Orthodox Church, continues to this day at St. Petersburg the practice of the Imperial *mandatum*, which was observed in the Court of the Byzantine Emperors at Constantinople. The fullest account of the ancient Byzantine ritual is given by Codinus, *de Officiis Magnæ Ecclesiæ* (ed. Bekker, Bonn, 1839, p. 70, and notes, p. 318; see also *PG* clvii.; and, for the date of Codinus, to whom the *de Officiis* is erroneously attributed [end of 14th and beg. of 15th cent.], see Gibbon, *Decline and Fall* [ed. Bury, 1896–1900], vi. 517, note). The repetition of the Trisagion; the pouring out of the water into the basin by the Czar; the entrance of the 12 poor men, each carrying a burning taper; the washing and kissing of the *right* foot of each by the Emperor; and the giving to each pauper of three pieces of gold, are all slight variants in practice from the ritual as observed elsewhere.

(β) *Turkey.*—The monastic *mandatum* is carried out yearly on Maundy Thursday by the Greek Metropolitan in Constantinople.

(γ) *Palestine.*—On Maundy Thursday the Greek Patriarch washes the feet of 12 of his bishops in a court in front of the Church of the Holy Sepulchre at Jerusalem. In the centre of the courtyard is an oval rostrum, about 4 ft. above the pavement, protected by an iron railing, and enclosing a space about 8 ft. by 12 ft. Inside and around the railing are seats for the bishops, and at the back a gold and white arm-chair cushioned with red satin for the Patriarch. A priest carries in and places before the Patriarch a large golden pitcher in a basin of gold as large as a foot-bath. Then all rise while prayer is offered. The Patriarch removes his grand gown, and stands in a white silk robe with a gold and white girdle. He twists a long Turkish bath-towel round his loins, and pours water into the basin, while the twelve bishops get their feet out of their gaiters, and pull off their white cotton socks. Each then extends one bare foot to the Patriarch, who sprinkles, dries, and kisses each. The last is 'St. Peter,' who objects, violently gesticulates, and rises. But the Patriarch opens the Bible, reads the words of Christ, shakes his hand at Peter, and the unruly 'apostle' submits. At this moment the bells of the Greek churches all over Jerusalem break into music. The Patriarch descends the steps and, followed by the bishops in double file, marches away. A priest lifts the vase containing the remains of the holy water, dips a large bouquet of roses into it, and therewith sprinkles the upturned faces of the eagerly expectant crowd, who rush forward, wipe up the drops on the floor with their handkerchiefs, and rub their faces with them! (Walsh, 672; a very full account is given by Lieut. Mantell, *PEFSt*, 1882, p. 158).

(2) *Armenian.*—A translation of the office for Maundy Thursday is given by F. C. Conybeare (*Rituale Armenorum*, p. 212):

'For to-day our Lord, the Giver of life, humbled himself for our salvation, to wash the feet of his disciples. And the Maker of heaven and earth in the guise of a servant, in all humility fulfilling the tremendous economy, went down on the knees of dust-created beings, and with the raiment wherewith he was girt, wiped away and cleansed the feet of his apostles, giving them power and authority to trample on asps and vipers and all the hosts of the enemy . . . so then it was the compassionate God Christ, Son of God, who to-day stooped to the feet of the disciples, washing away the scandal from them' (the text is from A, an uncial codex in San Lazaro Monast., Venice, not dated, but probably of 9th cent., not later than 10th).

In the Armenian rite a vessel of water is placed in the choir, and chrism is poured crosswise upon it at the benediction. When the bishop has washed the feet of clergy and people, he also anoints them. Then, resuming his cope, which was laid aside for the feet-washing, he is lifted up on high, and dispenses the people from fasting during Easter-tide (Butler, *op. cit.* ii. 350).

The Armenian services of Holy Week, in the form they have assumed in the later Middle Ages, and retain till to-day, have been published by Amy Apcar of Calcutta (*Melodies of five Offices in Holy Week, according to the Holy Apostolic Church of Armenia*, Leipzig, 1902). In this work the hymns sung by the congregation are printed with modern musical notation (note by Conybeare, *loc. cit.* p. 219).

(3) *Coptic.*—The Text of the Office is in Tuki, Εὐχολόγιον, pp. π–τκς′ (170-226). The present Coptic usage is described by A. J. Butler, ii. 350:

'On Maundy Thursday, called "The Thursday of the Covenant," tierce, sext, and nones are duly recited; after which, if there be no consecration of the holy oils to come first, a procession is formed to a small tank in the nave, where the Patriarch blesses the water with ceremonies similar to those ordained for Epiphany, but the gospels and hymns on this occasion dwell upon the subject of the Lord's washing the feet of the disciples. At the end of the prayers, the Patriarch gives his benison to the assembled priests and people, sprinkling them with water from the tank; then also he washes the feet of sundry persons, both clerical and lay, and dries them with a towel. On this day, immediately after the washing of feet, the door of the "haikal" is opened for the celebration of the Holy Communion, after which it is closed again; but in this Mass the kiss of peace and the commemoration of the dead are omitted.' In the 'Systatical Letter,' or decree of the Synod read by the Deacon from the *ambon* or pulpit, setting forth the duties of the Patriarch, it is expressly mentioned that he is to perform the office of feet-washing on Maundy Thursday (*ib.* ii. 145). Hence Butler thinks the ἐπιχερι mentioned in the ancient rubric must mean a towel, doubtless of fine embroidery, gorgeously woven with silver and gold. It was laid on the patriarch's shoulder at his ordination, with special reference to his performance of this ceremony, to which the Coptic Church attached great importance (see Butler, ii. 122, for the special *fanon* used instead of a mitre on this occasion).

The tank used for feet-washing is a conspicuous feature in Egyptian churches. It is usually a shallow rectangular basin about two feet long and one foot broad, sunk in the floor, and edged generally with costly marbles. The ordinary position for it is in the westward part of the nave, but in many desert churches it lies rather more eastward (*ib.* i. 23).

7. Feet-washing in Protestant Churches.—(1) *Lutheran.*—At the Reformation, Luther denounced the practice of feet-washing with characteristic plainness of speech. To him the ceremony was one

'in which the superior washes the feet of his inferior, who, the ceremony over, will have to act all the more humbly towards him, while Christ had made it an emblem of true humility and abnegation, and raised thereby the position of those whose feet he washed. "We have nothing to do," said he, "with feet-washing *with water*; otherwise it is not only the feet of the twelve, but those of everybody we should wash. People would be much more benefited if a general bath were at once ordered, and the whole body washed. If you wish to wash your neighbour's feet, see that your heart is really humble, and help every one in becoming better"' (*Sämtliche Schriften*, pt. xiii. [Magdeburg, 1743], col. 680).

Similarly the Lutheran J. A. Bengel (1687-1751) followed his master in condemnation of the rite:

'In our day, popes and princes imitate the feet-washing to the letter; but a greater subject for admiration would be, for instance, a pope, in unaffected humility, washing the feet of one king, than the feet of twelve paupers' (*Gnomon* [Eng. tr.[3], 1835-36, ii. 420]; Bengel recommends the study of Ittigius, *de Pedilavio*, 1703).

In 1718 the Lutheran Upper Consistory of Dresden condemned twelve Lutheran citizens of Weida to public penance for having permitted Duke Moritz Wilhelm to wash their feet (*PRE*[3] vi. 325, art. 'Fusswaschung').

(2) *Moravian.*—Amongst the other ancient practices revived by the Moravian Brethren was that of the *Pedilavium*, though they did not strictly enforce it. It used to be performed not only by leaders towards their followers, but also by the Brethren among themselves, while they sang a hymn in which the significance of the rite (called 'the lesser Baptism') was explained. In 1818, at a Synod of the Church held at Herrnhut, the practice was abolished.

(3) *Mennonites.*—Menno Simons (1492-1559) in his work, *The Fundamental Book of the True Christian Faith* (1539), laid stress on feet-washing in addition to Baptism and the Lord's Supper, as a necessary ordinance (Mosheim, *Eccl. Hist.*[2], 1868, iii. 545; Kurtz, *Church History*, ii. 405 [Eng. tr.[2] 1891]). His followers were styled *Podoniptæ.* The *Confession of the United Brethren or Mennonites* (1660) acknowledges the standing obligation of the rite as instituted by Christ. The Mennonite Church in Holland was in 1554 split into 'Flemings' and 'Waterlanders,' the former holding the binding necessity of feet-washing, the latter being not so strict. The Waterlanders now call themselves *Doopsgezinden.* The literal practice of feet-washing led to a split in the American Mennonite Church in 1811 (McClintock-Strong, *Cyclop.* vi. 95, art. 'Mennonites').

(4) *Tunkers* or *Dunkards.*—However divided on other points, the members of this sect are all agreed on the binding obligation to observe the feet-washing. The ceremony takes place twice a year in each congregation before the celebration of the love-feast. But as to the correct mode of feet-washing, *i.e.* whether the person who washes the feet must also wipe them, or whether another person should perform the latter operation, there have been grave disputes. The 'single mode' is insisted on by the oldest churches as being more in line with Christ's example, but the Annual Meeting has prescribed the 'double mode' as the recognized rubric for the general brotherhood (Schaff-Herzog, iv. 24, art. 'Dunkers').

(5) *Winebrennerians*, or *The Church of God.*—The 11th article of their creed says: This Church 'believes that the ordinance of Feet-washing, that is, the literal washing of the saints' feet according to the words and example of Christ, is obligatory upon all Christians, and ought to be observed by all the Church of God.' In every congregation Feet-washing, with Baptism and the Lord's Supper, are 'positive ordinances of perpetual standing in the Church' (see H. K. Carroll, *The Religious Forces of the United States*, i. 102; Schaff-Herzog, iii. 91; *PRE*[3] ii. 389; McClintock-Strong, ii. 338, art. 'Church of God').

(6) The *Amana Society*, or *Community of true Inspiration.*—One of their most sacred religious services is the *Liebesmahl*, or love-feast, celebrated now but once in two years. At this Lord's Supper, the ceremony of feet-washing is

observed by the higher spiritual orders. The participants are arranged into three classes: 'The number of those who were to serve had to be determined in proportion to the great membership. Thus there were appointed for the foot-washing at the first Love-feast 13 brothers and 12 sisters. . . . For the second Love-feast likewise 13 brothers and 14 sisters from the first class' (see AMANA SOCIETY, vol. i. p. 365 f.).

[(7) *Seventh-Day Adventists.*—Among this American denomination the rite of feet-washing 'is observed at the quarterly meetings, the men and women meeting separately for this purpose, previous to the celebration of the Lord's Supper, during which they meet together' (Special Census Report [1906] on *Religious Bodies*, ii. 23, Washington, 1910).

(8) *Baptist sub-sects.*—The Freewill Baptists believe in this rite (*ib.* 124), as do some General (Arminian) Baptists (*ib.* 128), and it is also performed by the Two-Seed-in-the-Spirit Predestinarian Baptists (*ib.* 156) and by more than half of the Primitive Baptists (*ib.* 139). Both the Separate Baptists and the Duck River Baptists (Baptist Church of Christ) hold that there are three ordinances—baptism, the Lord's Supper, and feet-washing (*ib.* pp. 132, 136); while the Coloured Primitive Baptists observe the rite 'not "as a Jewish tradition or custom, but as a matter of faith in Christ, and in obedience to the example given by Him"; the sacramental service is not considered complete until this rite is performed' (*ib.* 151).

(9) *River Brethren.*—Both the Brethren in Christ and the United Zion's Children—two sub-sects of this denomination, which is ultimately derived from the Mennonites—observe this rite, although the United Zion's Children differ from the Brethren in Christ in that among the former the same person both washes and dries the feet, while among the Brethren in Christ one person washes and another dries (*ib.* 173).

(10) *Miscellaneous American sects.*—The *Christian Union* occasionally, though rarely, practise feet-washing (*ib.* 189), but it is a distinctive tenet of the Church of the Living God, or *Christian Workers for Friendship* (to be distinguished from its offshoot, the Apostolic Church, which is also called Church of the Living God) (*ib.* 208), and in the Negro *Church of God and Saints of Christ* the ceremony is performed by an elder (*ib.* 202). One of the reasons for the formation of the *New Congregational Methodist Church* in 1881 was its wish to grant to those who desired it permission to observe the rite of feet-washing in connexion with the administration of the Lord's Supper (*ib.* 477). It is also permitted by the *United Brethren in Christ*, who hold that the practice of feet-washing should be left to the judgment of each individual (*ib.* 646).—LOUIS H. GRAY.]

It remains only to be observed that some of the purest and noblest souls in modern times who have lived for the welfare of their fellow-men have felt so attracted by this rite that they have desired to have it recognized as a sacrament (see A. B. Bruce, *Life of William Denny*, 1888, p. 256).

8. Feet-washing in connexion with marriage.—In many countries, both in ancient times and at the present day, bathing of the whole body, and, more particularly, washing of the feet, have been reckoned essential features to the proper celebration of marriage. Thus Roman brides had their feet washed by the *pronubæ* when they approached their husbands on the wedding day (Festus Pompeius, ii. 6; Macrob. *Sat.* iii.; cf. Matt. Brouerius, *de Pop. Veter. ac Recent. Adorationibus*, 1713, col. 978). In many parts of rural England and Scotland, relics of this custom still survive. On the evening before the marriage takes place, a few of the bridegroom's friends assemble at his house, when a large tub nearly filled with water is brought forward. The bridegroom is stripped of shoes and stockings, and his feet and legs are plunged into the water. While one friend with a besom rubs his feet vigorously, another besmears them with shoe-blacking or soot, while a third practises some other vagary (cf. the practice of the ancient Greeks in daubing their naked bodies with clay and dirt in the Dionysiac Mysteries; see G. L. Gomme, *Folklore Relics of Early Village Life*, 1883, p. 219; Gregor, *Folklore of N.E. Scotland*, 1881, p. 89; and de Gubernatis, *Storia comparata degli usi nuziali in Italia*, Milan, 1869, p. 121). In 1903 a case occurred where the bridegroom was a son of the Provost of Huntly. His feet were thus washed by his friends, and the bride would have been similarly treated had not her health prevented it (W. C. Hazlitt, *National Faiths and Popular Customs*, 1905, ii. 454). It was sometimes customary for the ring to be dropped into the water during the washing of the feet of the bride; whoever recovered it first was deemed to have the best chance of being the next to be married (John Grant, *The Penny Wedding*, Edin. 1836).

In the warm Orient, the practice enters largely into the ceremony of the marriage day. In some parts of Java the bride, as a sign of her subjection, kneels and washes the feet of the bridegroom as he enters the house; and in other places, for the same reason, he treads on a raw egg, and she wipes his foot. Among the peoples inhabiting the Teng'gar Mountains in Java, the bride washes the feet of the bridegroom, while she is still actually bending in lowly reverence before the priest during the marriage service (E. J. Wood, *The Wedding Day in all Ages and Countries*, i. [1869] 156, 157). As it is by means of the hands and feet that *bhūts* (evil spirits) enter the body, it is held necessary in India for feet-washing to form part of the marriage ceremony (Crooke, *Popular Relig. and Folklore of N. India*, 1896, i. 241). Thus, at a Santal wedding, women come forth and wash the feet of the guests who arrive with the bridegroom at the village (E. T. Dalton, *Descr. Ethnol. of Bengal*, Calcutta, 1872, p. 216). So among the Muási, at certain times in the marriage service, the two fathers wash the feet of the bride and the bridegroom respectively (*ib.* 234). If this washing were omitted, some foreign and presumably dangerous spirit might slip into the company, just as (according to the favourite example of the result of neglect of this rule) Āditi's failure to do this allowed Indra to form the Maruts out of her embryo (Crooke, i. 242). Amongst the Marāthās in India, feet-washing is repeatedly observed in connexion with a marriage. When the bridegroom's father sends a relative along with the priest to the girl's father to propose the match, they are welcomed, and water is given them to wash their hands and feet. On the marriage day a married woman of the bride's house pours a dish full of water mixed with lime and turmeric on the bridegroom's feet as he enters the bride's home. As soon as the pair are husband and wife, the bride's father and mother sit on two low stools in front of the bridegroom face to face, and the father washes the feet of the husband, while the mother pours water on them (*Ethnographic Append. to the Census of India*, 1901, p. 96 f.). Similarly among the Deshasth Brāhmans, on the marriage eve the women of the girl's house, especially the girl's mother, wash the boy's mother's feet, and mark her brow with vermilion. On the morning of the marriage the bridegroom dismounts at the door of the bride, and his feet are washed by one of the women servants of the house. On the marriage-feast day all wash their hands and feet at a place prepared for the purpose. The maid who stands at the door with an earthen pot full of water empties it at the feet of the pair, who enter the house, followed by friends and relatives. At a later stage the girl again washes her hands and feet, and takes her seat as before, to the right of her husband. At night the girl washes her husband's feet in warm water, with the aid of her elder sister or some friend, and on his feet paints vermilion and turmeric shoes (*ib.* pp. 115, 117, 119). A feature of the Bengal Brāhman wedding ceremony is the *Jāmātā-baran*, or the bridegroom's welcome by the bride's father. The latter offers his prospective son-in-law water for washing his feet (*pādya-arghya*), which the bridegroom touches in token of acceptance (*ib.* p. 190). On the Malabar coast early in the 19th cent. the bridegroom's feet were washed with milk by a young relative who also put a silver ring upon his toe (Wood, *op. cit.* ii. 141). The Indian theory of the duty of the wife to wash her husband's feet has even been exalted into a means of salvation for the woman. Just as it is taught in the *Tantras* that 'the water of a *guru's* (religious teacher's) feet purifies from all sin' (Morrison, *New Ideas in India*, 1907), so in the *Skānda Purāṇa* (iv. 35) it is laid down: 'Let a wife who wishes to perform sacred oblations wash the feet of her lord, and drink the water; for a husband is to a wife greater than Śiva or Viṣṇu. The husband is her god, her priest, her religion; wherefore, abandoning everything else, she ought chiefly to worship her husband.' Even amongst the ancient Poles, the bride on being led to church was made to walk three times round a fire, then to sit down and wash her husband's feet (Wood, i. 219). In Rabb. literature it is made abundantly plain that feet-washing was a service which a wife was expected to render to her husband (Jerus. *Ket.* v. 30*a*). According to R. Huna, it was one of the personal attentions to which a Jewish husband was entitled, however many maids the wife may have had. A similar duty is laid down in the Bab. Talmud (*Ket.* 61*a*), where washing the husband's feet is part of a wife's necessary service to her lord (cf. Maimonides, '*Yad*,' *Ishut*, xxi. 3; *JE* v. 357).

LITERATURE.—For the Jewish ceremonial washing of the feet: **Surenhusius**, *Mischna*, Amsterdam, 1698–1703, vol. v., and **Schürer**, *GJV*³, Leipzig, 1898–1901 [*HJP*, Eng. tr. of 2nd ed., Edin. 1885–90], Index, *s.v.* 'Waschungen.' The most important references for the baptismal feet-washing are the *Missale Gothicum*; **Martène**, *de Ant. Eccles. Ritibus*, Antwerp, 1738; **Smith's** *DCA*, art. 'Baptism'; **Bingham**, *Orig. Eccles.*, London, 1708–22; **Hefele**, *Hist. of the Christian Councils* (Eng. tr.²), Edinburgh, 1872.

For the monastic and imperial feet-washing the chief authorities are: i. for the Western (Roman) Church—(1) Rome: **Mabillon** and **Germain**, *Mus. Ital.*, Paris, 1687–89; the *Missale Romanum*, Venice, 1491, 1574; **Tuker-Malleson**, *Handbook to Christian and Ecclesiastical Rome*, London, 1897, 1900.—(2) Milan: **Magistretti**, *Beroldus sive Eccl. Ambros. Mediolan. Kalendarium et ordines*, Milan, 1894; and **Muratori**, *Antiq. Ital. Medii Aevi*, Milan, 1738–42.—(3) Gaul: the fullest account of the variations in the rite is given by **Martène**, *op. cit.*; cf. also **Amalarius**, *de Officio Ecclesiastico*, in *PL* cv. 1011.—(4) Spain: the Office is in *Liber ordinum* (ed. Férotin), or Ximenes' *Missale Mixtum*, in *PL* lxxxv. Much information is given in **Isidorus Hispalensis** (ed. Arevalo), *S. Isidori Hispal. Episc. Opera Omnia*, 7 vols., Rome, 1797–1803, reprinted in *PL* lxxxi.–lxxxiv., esp. lxxxiii. 764. The Spanish royal Maundy is described in **Picart**, *Cérémonies et coutumes relig. de tous les peuples du monde*, Amsterdam, 1723–37 (Eng. tr., London, 1733–37), and more recently in **Hone**, *Every-Day Book*, London, 1838–41.—(5) Portugal: the facts relating to the rite have been furnished by the Rev. R. M. Lithgow, of Lisbon, from information obtained by him from the Court Chaplain under the last régime.—(6) Bavaria: information obtained from Dr. von Laubmann, Chief Librarian of the Royal Library at Munich.—(7) Austria: the scene in the Royal Palace is as witnessed by the writer in 1896.—(8) England: for pre-Norman use, see **pseudo-Alcuin**, *de Divinis Officiis*, in *PL* ci. 1203; *Missal of Robert of Jumièges* (ed. H. A. Wilson [Henry Bradshaw Soc.], 1896); the *Leofric Missal* (ed. F. E. Warren, 1883); and, for later use, see the other Missals, Services, and Uses of the Early English Church. **D. Rock**, *Church of our Fathers*, London, 1905, gives a highly coloured picture of the rite as celebrated in the Anglo-Saxon Church.—(9) Scotland: **J. de Fordun**, *Chronica Gentis Scotorum*, Edinburgh, 1871–72, lib. v.—(10) Ireland: *Missale Vetus Hibernicum* (ed. F. E. Warren, Oxford, 1879).—(11) Palestine: **Mantell**, in *PEFSt*, 1882.

ii. For the rite as observed in the Eastern Churches, the principal authorities are: (1) for the Greek Orthodox Church, **Goar**, ΕΥΧΟΛΟΓΙΟΝ², Venice, 1730; and **Dmitrijewski**, *Euchologia*, 1901. The fullest account of the ancient Byzantine service is given in **Codinus**, *de Officiis Magnæ Ecclesiæ* (ed. Bekker), Bonn, 1839, and in *PG* clvii. The Greek Palestinian ceremony is very amply described by **Mantell**, *loc. cit.*—(2) The Armenian service is given most fully in **Conybeare**, *Rituale Armen.*, Oxford, 1905.—(3) For the Coptic rite, see **Tuki**, Εὐχολόγιον; and for the present Coptic use, with an account of the feet-washing tanks, see esp. **A. J. Butler**, *Ancient Coptic Churches of Egypt*, Oxford, 1884, and **F. E. Brightman**, *Liturgies, Eastern and Western*, Oxford, 1896—a perfect mine of information (only vol. i., 'Eastern Liturgies,' is yet published).

For feet-washing in Protestant Churches the articles in *PRE*³, **McClintock-Strong's** *Cyclop.*, 1881, **Schaff-Herzog's** *Encycl. of Religious Knowledge* (art. 'Dunkers'), and **H. K. Carroll**, *The Religious Forces of the United States*, N.Y., 1893, are of importance.

For feet-washing in connexion with Indian marriage customs, the most numerous references are perhaps to be found in the *Ethnographic Appendix to the Census of India*, 1901, and **E. Thurston**, *Castes and Tribes of S. India*, Madras, 1909.

G. A. FRANK KNIGHT.

FEINN CYCLE.—1. This is the third of the three great Celtic mythological cycles. (For the other two, see artt. CELTS, V. 1, and CÚCHULAINN CYCLE.) The story of Fionn and the Feinn is indelibly graven in Gaelic thought. Poems, tales, romances, proverbs, and history all abound in allusions to the wonderful, if somewhat mythical, heroes. Their names, qualities, and exploits have been as familiar to the generations of Gaelic-speaking Celts as the Biblical names and narratives to the Jews. Fionn, son of Cumhail, son of Trenmor, was the ideal chief of the band, full of mighty deeds and highest virtues. With him were associated Oisin, his son (Macpherson's Ossian), renowned in later ages as the so-called Homer of the Celtic people; Oscar, son of Oisin, handsome and kind-hearted, one of the bravest of the Feinn; Diarmad O'Duibhne, with the *ball-seirc*, or beauty-spot, which induced every woman who beheld him to fall in love with him; Caoilte MacRonan, nephew of Fionn, the swiftest of them all; Fergus Finnebheoil, Oisin's brother, on account of his wisdom and eloquence famous as poet, diplomatist, and ambassador; Goll MacMorna, blind of an eye, once the enemy of Fionn, whose father he killed, but afterwards his follower; and Conan Maol, the comic character and Thersites of the party.

These were the outstanding figures among the braves who were banded together for the defence of their country, and who warred and hunted on a scale that has raised them to such pre-eminence that they are sometimes confused with the gods of the Gaelic Olympus.

2. The theatre of their operations was Leinster and Munster in Ireland. That country is therefore regarded by most authorities as the original home of the Feinn or Ossianic romance, which in time extended itself to the west of Scotland, the Hebrides, and the Isle of Man. The greater number of the incidents are represented as having taken place during the reign of Cormac MacArt, MacConn of the hundred battles, and that of his son Cairbre of the Liffey. The former reigned from A.D. 227 to 268 (*Annals of the Four Masters*), but it was during the reign of the latter in the year A.D. 284 that the battle of Gabhra was fought, which for ever put an end to the Feinn power. That power, said to have been due mainly to the knowledge of Fionn, the swiftness of Caoilte, and the combativeness of Conan, had become so unbearable to the Irish, through the strictness with which the Feinn guarded their privileges, that the High-King determined at length to try conclusions with it, and succeeded, though Oscar and he perished in fighting each other. Fionn was not present in this battle, either having met his death shortly before, or, as later and less authentic accounts would have us believe, being absent in Rome.

There are no contemporary records now extant of the Feinn any more than there are of Abraham, of Moses, or of Homer. The earliest references to Fionn (originally Finn) occur in a poem of Gilla Caemhain [d. 1072], and in the *Annals* of Tighernach [d. 1088]. Both of these allude to the manner and date of the hero's death, and may have derived their information from a poem of Cinaeth O'Hartagain, who died in A.D. 985. Translated, this poet's remark runs thus: 'By the Fiann of Luagne was the death of Finn at Ath Brea upon the Boyne' (*Book of Leinster*, fol. 31*b*). As it was the bards and professional storytellers who in those early days handed down by oral tradition the memory of great men and great incidents, it is possible that no tales of the heroes were written, except perhaps in ogham, till the 7th century. The oldest existing MSS in which we have mention of Fionn and the Feinn are the *Leabhar na h'Uidhre*, compiled from earlier documents towards the close of the 11th cent., and the *Book of Leinster*, similarly produced about fifty years later. In the former there is a poem ascribed to Fionn; a remark of his wife's containing Gaelic words so old that they required to be glossed in the 11th cent.; an account of the cause of the battle in which his father was killed; and the story of Mongan, an Ulster king of the 7th cent., who was regarded as Fionn come to life again. In the later MS the references are more numerous. Besides poems ascribed to the Feinn chief, to Oisin, Caoilte, and others, there are passages from the lost *Dinnsenchus*, a topographical tract regarding Fionn; an account of a battle in which he fought; his genealogy as well as that of his famous officer Diarmad O'Duibhne; besides a list of no fewer than 187 historical tales. There are other Finns besides Fionn mentioned in the *Book of Leinster*, but, if the list of tales was really drawn up in the 7th or beginning of the 8th cent., as Hyde thinks d'Arbois de Jubainville has proved (*Literary History of Ireland*, p. 382), then it is evident that Fionn and his heroes were subjects of historical storytelling as early as that period. And in what Whitley Stokes believes to be the oldest portion of the Glossary of Cormac, king-bishop of Cashel (A.D. 837–903), there are two further very definite allusions to the wonderful head of the Feinn, who is therein also mentioned by name.

These earliest written hints and impressions represent Fionn as a real historical personage. The story of his life which they unfold is certainly meagre, but it is perfectly intelligible.

3. Of the various versions of his birth, that in the *Leabhar na h'Uidhre* is probably the most substantial. According to it, Tadg, chief Druid of King Conn, had a beautiful daughter, called Muirne. Cumhail, son of Trenmor, at that time leader of the Feinn, wished to wed this young lady. On coming to know this, her father stoutly opposed their alliance, because he knew by his Druidical foresight that, if Cumhail married her, he himself would lose his ancestral seat at Almhain (present Allen) in Leinster. But the great military champion was not thus to be balked. So he took the beautiful Muirne and married her against her father's wishes. The result was that the old man appealed to the king for redress, and the royal forces were despatched to deal with the arbitrary hero. This army encountered Cumhail and his Feinn at Cnucha, where a deadly struggle took place, during which Cumhail was slain by Aedh MacMorna, who, because he lost an eye in this battle, was ever afterwards known as *Goll*, that is, 'the blind,' MacMorna. Hearing of the fate of her husband, Muirne fled to his sister and gave birth to a son, who was at first called Demni, but subsequently Finn, on account, it is said, of his white head (*Finn* means 'fair'; *Fiann*, gen. *Feinne*, 'band' or 'troop,' pl. *Fianna*, 'troops' or 'soldiers' [*Transactions of the Gaelic Soc. of Inverness*, 1886 and 1898]). When the boy grew up he demanded *éric* from his grandfather Tadg for the death of his father, and thus came into possession of Almhain, as his grandparent had anticipated. He also made peace with Goll, whom he enlisted as one of his band of warriors, and who usually figures in the stories as a kind of Ajax. Like his father Cumhail, Fionn got the command of the Feinn and acquired a great reputation as a poet. In fact, in the oldest setting of the so-called Ossianic tales, the poets of the Feinn were Fergus and he, not Oisin. It was only in later and comparatively recent times, as E. Windisch has shown that the latter ousted his father from the pre-eminence in this respect (*RCel* v. 70 ff.). Fionn learned the art of poetry from Finn Eges or Finnéces, a bard who lived on the banks of the Boyne (for poem attributed to him at this period, see Kuno Meyer's *Four Songs of Summer and Winter*, London, 1903). In a tract written upon a fragment of the 9th cent. Psalter of Cashel, and preserved in a 15th cent. MS in the Bodleian Library, Oxford, it is related how he was sent to this old man to complete his education. There had been a prophecy that, if one of the name of Finn ate a salmon caught in Fiacc's pool, he would no longer be ignorant of anything he might wish to know. The aged poet for seven years fished for the coveted prize, but in vain, till his youthful pupil arrived. When the salmon was landed, the delighted Finnéces sent the lad to cook it, at the same time giving him injunctions that he was on no account to taste it. As destiny would have it, Fionn, while turning the fish, burnt his thumb and thrust it into his mouth to ease the pain. Thereupon he was immediately endowed with the gift of knowledge, and every time he sucked his thumb he saw into the future. On reporting this wonderful experience to his master, the poet asked him his name. 'Demni,' said the youth. 'No,' replied the disappointed Finnéces, 'your name is Finn, and it is you who were destined to eat of the salmon of knowledge. You are the real Finn.' (For translation of tract, see vol. iv. of the *Transactions of the Ossianic Society*.)

The story of *Ordag mhor an eolais* ('the great thumb of knowledge') is differently told in a vellum MS in Trinity College, Dublin. There the injured member is represented as having been not burnt, but squeezed by a door which opened in a hill to admit a strange woman, apparently of the fairy order, whom Fionn's curiosity led him to follow.

4. Though mythic elements have entered largely into these stories, there are three other outstanding events of the hero's career which have an air of historicity. They are mentioned and taken for granted as real from earliest times. These were Fionn's marriage with Gráinne, King Cormac's daughter; her elopement with Diarmad O'Duibhne; and Fionn's subsequent revenge on this offending officer. It is in the 'Pursuit of Diarmad and Gráinne,' one of the most persistent of the Feinn sagas, that the fullest account of these events is given (translated by O'Grady, *Trans. Oss. Soc.* vol. iii.). At a feast in honour of Fionn's betrothal at Tara, Gráinne drugged the wine, sending the guests asleep till she got an opportunity to put Diarmad, of whom she made an exception, under *geasa* (bonds which no hero could refuse to redeem) to flee with her. After the banquet, Diarmad, who was most unwilling to injure his chief, consulted his comrades as to what he should do. He even asked Fionn, concealing the lady's name, and they all answered that no hero could break a *geas* put upon him by a woman. That night the pair eloped, and, when the jilted chief discovered their flight, his wrath knew no bounds. A pursuit was organized, and they were followed all over Ireland. Though at length overtaken, they were permitted to return in peace; for the Feinn would not allow Fionn to punish their popular comrade. But Fionn never really forgave Diarmad, and soon after, with sinister intention, he invited him to the chase of the wild boar on Ben Gulban. This animal Diarmad killed without getting any hurt. Then it was that Fionn ordered him to measure the animal's length against the bristles. While Diarmad was doing this, one of the bristles pierced his heel—his only vulnerable part—and he died of the poisoned wound. Even then his chief might have saved him by administering the antidote of which he held the secret, but he did not. And so to all posterity there is this smirch—the only one recorded—on the character of the truest, wisest, and kindest of the Feinn, one who, if he could help it, would never let any one be in poverty or trouble. He himself met his death, it is said, at the hands of a fisherman, probably a Fian of Luagne who sought the notoriety to be obtained from slaying so famous a warrior. The event was followed by the fateful battle of Gabhra, and from this time the curtain falls on the career of the Feinn as an organized body, who henceforth enter the region of myth and fable.

5. For one reason or another these heroes presented ideals of existence that appealed most profoundly to the Gaelic-speaking race, and continued to appeal, in spite of all change, down to the period when science began definitely to cast men's thoughts into other moulds. After the Feinn *débâcle*, the story of their exploits passed into oral tradition. The common people, the bards, the professional story-tellers, the annalists, and the churchmen were all more or less familiar with the details, and interpreted, rehearsed, and amplified them, each class in its own way—with the result that in course of time a great variety of versions arose and entirely new elements entered into the history.

First of all, the Feinn began to be associated with the supernatural and with personages and incidents belonging to the popular Celtic mythology. As 'distance lends enchantment to the view,' so the old heroes were gradually elevated and idealized in the popular imagination. Qualities that originally belonged to the gods were ascribed to them, and they figured in scenes and incidents similar to those rehearsed in the earlier mythical stories. In fact, the opponents of Fionn and his men were no longer the men of Connaught and Ulster, but underworld deities, and the strife between the two seems like a variant of that between the Tuatha Dé Danann and the Fomorians. Sometimes the former are represented as helping Fionn against his powerful foes. That this deifying process had been carried far before the 11th cent. is evident from the story of the Mongan who, the annalists averred, was a reincarnation of the famous head of the Feinn, and son of the god Manannan MacLir.

By and by the Norsemen began to appear and settle in Ireland, and then another new element entered into the warp and woof of the Feinn saga. Fionn in this later rôle is neither the tribal Leinster chief fighting against the northern clans, nor is he the demigod in conflict with underground deities; he is the leader of all Gaeldom warring against oversea invaders from Lochlann. According to some of the sagas, he was born in Lochlann, and, after his voyage to the giant's land, was put ashore in Ireland, which he then trod for the first time. According to others, he walked from Lochlann to Erinn on a road.

The introduction of the Norse element, like that of the supernatural, has rendered the story of the Feinn exceedingly complicated and contradictory, so that the authorities find it hard to reconcile the various versions with the known facts of history. Commenting on the matter from this point of view, Henderson (*CeR* i. 366) says:

'The only reasonable explanation is that Lochlann meant Norse settlements in Ireland. That fits all versions, and makes this story consistent. Stripped of the mythology, which is partly Scandinavian in character, the framework thus far may be historical. The military leader, Cumal, sets up for himself in Scotland. The Norsemen and the Irishmen tempt him to Ireland, where he is slain on the Irish king's territory. His son is born in Ireland, on one or other of the territories in question. When he grows up he seeks vengeance, like an Icelander in a saga, takes a ship, escapes abroad, comes back to the place where his father set up for himself, tells tales to account for his riches, and then follows his father's example, and fights chiefly in Ireland with Norsemen and Irishmen, turn about, till his power is broken and his men are scattered. Then he becomes mythical, and is like Arthur and other worthies who have disappeared from the world.'

But such a view is surely inconsistent with the earliest impressions of Fionn's origin and history as given in the *Leabhar na h'Uidhre* and elsewhere. J. Rhys's conjecture (*Origin and Growth*, p. 355) seems to offer a more likely solution when he says that *Lochlann*, like the Welsh *Llychlyn*, before it came to mean the home of the Norsemen, denoted a mysterious country in the lochs and seas. The Lochlanners might, in that case, be originally the submarine mythical people or underworld deities corresponding to the Fomorians, with whom the Feinn were represented as fighting when they began to be confused with the personages of the mythological cycle.

A third remarkable element in the saga is the religious or ecclesiastic. It is introduced in the following peculiar way. After the overthrow of the Feinn, Oisin and Caoilte agreed to separate. The former went, as tradition says, to Tir-nan-Og, 'the land of the ever young'; the latter passed over Magh Breagh, southwards, and ultimately joined St. Patrick. When 150 years had passed away, Oisin returned on a white steed to seek his old friend and comrade Caoilte. From this horse he was cautioned not to dismount lest he should lose his immortal youth. On the way he found everything changed. Among other things, instead of the old temples of the gods he observed Christian churches, and the Feinn, alas! were now but a memory. One day, unfortunately, as he attempted to assist some men in raising a stone, he slipped from his magic steed, and as soon as he touched the earth he became a blind and withered old man. His horse rushed off to Tir-nan-Og, after which Oisin was brought to St. Patrick and Caoilte, with whom he lived the rest of his days. Both were the saint's constant companions in his missionary journeys through Ireland, and were useful in giving him the history, legends, and topography of all the places they visited, and many besides. These were written down by Brogan, St. Patrick's scribe, for the benefit of posterity. Oisin loved to recount the exploits of the Feinn and to debate with the apostle of Ireland regarding the new religion, against which he was prejudiced in favour of the ethics of his younger days. Between the saint and the aged pagan there occurred various heated and passionate disagreements, the settlement of which is the subject of 'Oschin's Prayer' (*Scottish Review*, viii. [1886] 350 ff.). The conversations are given in the form of dialogues between the two, the one representing paganism, the other Christianity. Doubtless they were the work of monks or ecclesiastical scribes in the 12th cent. or earlier, and they appear in their pristine form in 'The Colloquy of the Ancients,' which is the longest of all the Feinn saga. It is preserved in MSS dating from the 15th cent., but chiefly in the *Book of Lismore* (tr. in O'Grady's *Silva Gadelica*; Whitley Stokes, *Irische Texte*, vol. iv.).

A fourth element that entered largely into the popular tales and ballads of later times was the wizardry of the Middle Ages. In these, giants, dwarfs, enchanted castles, dragons, palfreys, witches, and magicians figure. When they were introduced it is impossible to say, though James Macpherson fancied they were imposed on the Feinn saga in the 15th century. There is evidence that, even earlier than this, Fionn and his heroes were represented as giants; and Scottish authors such as Hector Boece, Bishop Leslie, and Gavin Douglas refer to them as such.

As the centuries passed, the volume of detail increased, each age contributing its own impressions and its own imaginative setting. In Scotland we have evidence of this extraordinary activity in the Book of the Dean of Lismore in the 16th cent.;

the poems of Stone, Macpherson, Smith, Clark, Maccallum, and others in the 18th and 19th cents.; and much more impressively in the various collections such as J. F. Campbell's *Popular Tales of the West Highlands*, 1862, and his *Leabhar na Feinne*, 1872. The latter alone contains 54,000 lines of Gaelic verse, and Cameron's *Reliquiæ Celticæ* 10,000. (For a detailed account of all the other Scottish collections see Stern's résumé in *Transactions of the Gaelic Society of Inverness*, vol. xxii. pp. 288-292.) In Ireland the same development has been continuously taking place, as witnessed by such representative works as Stokes' *Irische Texte*; O'Grady's *Silva Gadelica*; *Proc. Ossianic Society*; Hyde's *Sgéaluidhe Gaedhealach*; and Larminie's and Curtin's *Tales*. So numerous indeed are the Ossianic poems and stories that O'Curry estimated that, if printed at length in the same form as the text of O'Donovan's edition of *The Four Masters*, they would fill as many as 3000 pages of such volumes. That computation he made before the publication of Campbell's *Leabhar na Feinne*. Apart from the tales, it is believed that the poetry alone in Scotland and Ireland combined amounts to a number somewhere between 80,000 and 100,000 lines, all belonging to the Feinn cycle. And this brings us now to the crux of the whole subject.

6. *Who were the Feinn?* It is a question of the deepest interest, in view of the varied opinions that have been expressed. (*a*) Irish authors have always regarded them as an actual martial caste or militia maintained during several reigns by the kings of Erin for national defence. Tighernach, Keating, the Four Masters, Eugene O'Curry, and Douglas Hyde are representative of the common native opinion which has prevailed from early times. Keating, writing about A.D. 1630, gives the traditional account as he gleaned it from ancient books now lost; and Eugene O'Curry, holding the same view last century, wrote the following as his own conviction in the matter:

> 'I may take occasion to assure you that it is quite a mistake to suppose Finn Mac Cumhail to have been a merely imaginary or mythical character. Much that has been narrated of his exploits is, no doubt, apocryphal enough, but Finn himself is an undoubtedly historical personage; and that he existed about the time at which his appearance is recorded in the Annals is as certain as that Julius Cæsar lived and ruled at the time stated on the authority of the Roman historians' (O'Curry, *MS Materials*, Lect. xiv. p. 303).

The band of Feinn were divided into three, or more usually seven, regiments, and had officers over every nine, fifty, and a hundred men. Before a soldier could be admitted he was subjected to rigid tests, some of them of the most extraordinary kind. His relatives had to renounce their right of *éric* in his case. He himself required to promise—(1) never to receive a portion with a wife, but to choose her for her good manners and virtues; (2) never to offer violence to any woman; (3) never to refuse charity to the weak and poor in the matter of anything he might possess; (4) never to flee before nine champions. Along with these obligations went loyalty to the High-King and sworn fidelity to the commander-in-chief. More difficult accomplishments were the following:—He must have the gift of poetry, and be versed in the twelve books of the Muse according to the rules of the chief bard. With only a hazel stick of a forearm's length and a shield, and standing in a hole up to his belt in the earth, he had to defend himself against a simultaneous attack by nine warriors armed with spears, and separated from him only by a distance of nine field rigs. If he were hurt, he was not received as one of the Feinn. Not a man was taken until, with his hair braided and a start of only a tree's breadth, he was pursued by a war-troop through Ireland's woods, and succeeded in eluding them without letting his hair fall. If even the weapon in his hand trembled, or a withered twig broke under him, he could not be accepted. The candidate had further to leap over a branch the height of his forehead, and bend under another no higher than his knee; to hold a spear horizontally with steady arm; and, without slackening his pace while running, to pull out a thorn from his foot with his nail (15th cent. Vellum in British Museum, marked 'Egerton, 1782').

The duties and privileges of the Feinn were equally well defined. In time of peace they acted as the custodians of the public security, maintaining the right of the ruler and guarding the coasts against strangers. In winter from Samhain to Beltane (1st Nov. to 1st May) they were quartered on the people and under shelter. In summer they lived in the open air, hunting and fishing, and eating but one meal a day, always in the evening. Their bed consisted of branches, moss, and rushes. Even to this day the peasantry of Ireland profess to find the traces of their fires (*fualachtan na bh'Fiann*) in deep layers of the ground (Stokes, *Book of Lismore*, p. xl; O'Grady, *Silva Gadelica*, pp. 92, 258; O'Mahony's tr. of Keating's *History*, pp. 345-350; and O'Curry, *Manners and Customs of the Ancient Irish*, pp. 2, 379).

(*b*) W. F. Skene and D. MacRitchie believed that the Feinn were a race distinct from the Gaels and probably allied to, or even identical with, the Picts. The latter writer went further, suggesting the possibility of their being the fairies of Gaelic tradition. But the theory that the Picts were a non-Celtic race is not now accepted. Duncan Campbell put forward the view that Fionn figures as a Gaelic *gueledig*, the leader, like Arthur, of a militia modelled upon the Roman legions (*Trans. of the Gaelic Society of Inverness*, 1887). Zimmer thinks that he was really the Viking robber, Caittil Find, who commanded the Gall Gaidhil or apostate Irish in the 9th century. The names Oisin and Oscar are, in his opinion, the old Norse Asvin and Asgeirr. Kuno Meyer is equally convinced that all the names of the Feinn are Gaelic, not Norse, and, like Windisch, he holds that in all probability there were real historical characters round whose memory the tales and myths and folk-lore grew.

(*c*) While in the main the Irish and German scholars thus favour the view that primeval heroes corresponding to Fionn and the Feinn actually existed, some recent British authorities, prominent among whom have been Alfred Nutt, John Rhys, and Alexander MacBain, are disposed to uphold the opposite opinion, and look upon the Feinn as simply the gods of Celtic mythology humanized, or regarded as men. This way of construing the history may be gathered from the words of MacBain:

> 'Finn is evidently the incarnation of the chief deity of the Gaels—the Jupiter spoken of by Cæsar and the Dagda of Irish myth. His qualities are king-like and majestic, not sun-like as those of Cuchulain. He is surrounded by a band of heroes that make a terrestrial Olympus, composed of counterparts to the chief deities. There is the fiery Oscar (*ud-scar*, utter-cutter?), a sort of war-god; Ossian, the poet and warrior corresponding to Hercules Ogmius; Diarmat, of the shining face, a reflexion of the sun-god; Caelte, the swift runner; and so on. . . . The stories are racial and general, and can be tied down to neither time nor place' (*Celtic Mythology*, p. 108 f.).

But this theory does not readily square with the facts. In a review of history we find that it is not so much the gods who are degraded as it is the heroes who are exalted. Popular idols, who in their own day were human enough, in course of time were clad with divinity. By a curious working of the human imagination they are credited with attributes and deeds beyond the range of man's experience. It is thus no doubt that, the tales of Fionn and the Feinn becoming mixed up in popular fancy with the earlier mythical accounts of gods and heroes, the incidents of the latter were transferred to the former, until the heroes were at length deified. Indeed, Windisch, impressed with the likelihood of some such transference, looked on the mythic incidents of the Feinn cycle as derived from the previous Cúchulainn cycle, which in turn drew upon Christian legend.

7. If then it be asked, as it is natural to ask, how far the Feinn are historical and how far mythological, the answer may very well be given in the words of D. Hyde, who hits off exactly the impression one gets who is familiar with the varied literature of the Feinn, the actual mythology of to-day, and its history in the past.

'While believing in the real objective existence of the Fenians as a body of Janissaries who actually lived, ruled, and hunted in King Cormac's time, I think it equally certain that hundreds of stories, traits, and legends, far older and more primitive than any to which they themselves could have given rise, have clustered about them. There is probably as large a bulk of primitive mythology to be found in the Finn legend as in that of the Red Branch itself. The story of the Fenians was a kind of nucleus to which a vast amount of the flotsam and jetsam of a far older period attached itself, and has thus been preserved' (Notes to Lady Gregory's *Gods and Fighting Men*, p. 467).

8. It was the publication of the so-called translations of Ossian by James Macpherson in 1760–1763 that principally led to the re-discovery of the great body of Feinn saga in modern times, as well as to the recrudescence of its production. The controversy that raged round the name of the Badenoch bard for upwards of a hundred years has now happily been laid to rest, Celtic scholarship having no difficulty in establishing the fact that, though Macpherson drew upon the names and legends of the past, the poems were his own (Maclean, *Lit. of the Highlands*, Glasgow, 1904, pp. 69–90). His initiative and genius, however, have been most powerful in inaugurating the new era of research into this whole cycle of poetry and romance—a research which has gone on unabated and indeed with growing ardour to this day, and which is proving so fertile in the publication of texts, translations, and all kinds of literature bearing on the subject. The following are among the representative books and papers which may be consulted with advantage:—

LITERATURE.—Windisch-Stokes, *Irische Texte*, Leipzig, 1000 1900; S. H. O'Grady, *Silva Gadelica*, Lond. 1892; G. Keating, *History of Ireland*, tr. O'Mahony, N.Y. 1857; *Annals of the Four Masters*, tr. O'Donovan, Lond. 1848–1851; E. O'Curry, *MS Materials*, Dublin, 1861, and *Manners and Customs of the Ancient Irish*, 1873; James Macpherson, *Ossian*, Lond. 1760–1763, 1773; Whitley Stokes, *Dinnsenchus*, do. 1892, and *Book of Lismore*, Oxf. 1890; *Waifs and Strays of Celtic Tradition*, Argyleshire Series, Lond. 1889-91, esp. vols. ii., iii., and iv., containing Alfred Nutt's Essay and J. G. Campbell's *The Fians*, 1891; A. Nutt, *Ossian and the Ossianic Literature*, Lond. 1899; W. F. Skene, *Celtic Scotland*, vol. i., Edinb. 1876; J. F. Campbell, *Popular Tales of the West Highlands*, do. 1862, and *Leabhar na Feinne*, Lond. 1872; T. Maclauchlan, *The Book of the Dean of Lismore*, do. 1862; A. Cameron, *Reliquiæ Celticæ*, Inverness, 1892–1894; *Proc. of Ossian. Soc.*; *Transac. of Gaelic Soc. of Inverness*; O'Beirne Crowe, *Kilkenny Arch. Journal*; *RCel*, 1870–1906; *ZDA*; H. d'Arbois de Jubainville, *La Littérature ancienne de l'Irlande et l'Ossian de Macpherson*, Paris, 1883; Ludwig C. Stern, *Die Ossian. Heldenlieder*, tr. by J. L. Robertson, 1898; J. Rhys, *Lectures on the Origin and Growth of Religion as illustrated by Celtic Heathendom* (Hibbert Lectures, 1886), Lond. 1888; C. Brooke, *Reliques of Irish Poetry*, 1789 and 1816; Douglas Hyde, *Sgéaluidhe Gaedhealach*, Lond. n.d., and his *Literary History of Ireland*, do. 1899; M. Maclean, *Literature of the Celts*, do. 1902; Lady Gregory, *Gods and Fighting Men*, 1904; C. Squire, *Mythology of the British Islands*, Lond. 1905; P. W. Joyce, *Old Celtic Romances*², do. 1894; J. Curtin, *Hero Tales of Ireland*, do. 1894; Kuno Meyer, *Anecdota Oxoniensia*, do. 1905; J. Rhys, *Celtic Folklore*, Oxf. 1901, vol. ii.; papers in *Archæol. Review*, 1888–1889; *Celtic Magazine*, 1876–1888; *Celtic Review*, 1905–1912.

MAGNUS MACLEAN.

FEMALE PRINCIPLE.—That there is a relationship between femininity and religion is indicated by at least three classes of facts: the existence of female deities, the use of phallic symbols in worship and ritual, and the supposed kinship between love in religion and love of mates. How close the relationship is between these two aspects of life is a matter of much contention. The opinions range from that which regards the connexion as accidental and superficial to the notion that religion is essentially a refinement of and abstraction from a feeling for mates. Between these extremes are many shades of judgment which acknowledge that the two facts have more or less vital connexion. The determination of the nature and extent of this relation is a question of psychological and sociological analysis. This can be made only in connexion with an observation of some of the facts on which the conceptions are based.

1. Female deities.—Amongst many primitive peoples, and at the present time in a large number of less developed cults, goddesses occupy important places in the pantheon. In early Babylonia there were as many goddesses as gods; for each male deity, we may assume, had his female companion. There was at least one goddess as patron of each of the cities, sharing with her lord the devotion of its worshippers. Instances are Nana, patroness of Uruk; 'good lady' Bau, 'mother' of Lagash; Ninlil of Nippur, 'mistress of the lower world' and 'lady of the great mountain'; and the 'glorious and supreme' Ninni of Gishgalla, 'mistress of the world.' These city-goddesses had a precarious and extremely varied history. Some of them sank out of sight as consorts of the gods whose majesty and power they could not equal. They became 'mere shadowy reflections of the gods, with but little independent power, and in some cases none at all' (Jastrow, *Rel. of Bab. and Assyria*, New York, 1898, p. 104). This twilight extinction is especially true in early Babylonia, in Syria, and among other nations that entered upon a heroic programme of world-conquest. As if to complete the logic of this type of subjection, goddesses were changed into male deities. 'In various parts of the Semitic field we find deities originally female changing their sex and becoming gods' (W. R. Smith, *Rel. Sem.*², London, 1894, p. 52). Some of them were eclipsed by other more powerful and more beloved goddesses, as villages were fused into cities and cities into States. A marked instance of this subjection and absorption is found in the rise of Ishtar of later Babylonia and Assyria to the position of 'mother of the gods' (and of goddesses as well), who sometimes absorbs the titles and qualities of all. In the event of an eclipse by a male consort or by a greater representative of her own sex, a goddess did not always forfeit her existence, but was deflected into the performance of some special function of lesser importance.

An instance in point is Gula, 'princely mistress' of Minid. This solar deity, Minid, 'mighty one of the gods,' remains even to the days of Nebuchadnezzar I. as 'king of heaven and earth,' and in Assyria also is honoured with every conceivable epithet as god of war and the chase; whilst Gula is only occasionally invoked by the rulers, and assumes a more modest rôle of healer of diseases. In like manner, Juno came to be 'called by the Romans Juno Lucina, the special goddess of child-birth' (C. M. Galey, *Classic Myths*, Boston, 1904, p. 204). No less a goddess than the beloved Ishtar (Astarte of Phœnicia) often suffers the humiliation, when brought into competition with other deities, of serving as the patroness of sensuality.

Another line of differentiation from the multitude of early municipal goddesses was the borrowing or transportation of favourite deities by other peoples, or the amalgamation of their qualities and names with those of native goddesses of the places into which they came. Nana of Erech was one of the first of the important goddesses of the early Sumerian period of Babylonia. Her name appears in many forms and places during early Semitic times: Nanæa, Nani, Nanya, Anitis, Anæa, Tanath, etc., through a considerable list. In like manner she won a place in the worship of other countries.

'The worship of the Sumerian goddess Nana of Erech is traced with probability in Elam, with certainty in Syria, Bactrian-India, Asia Minor, and Greece. She had affiliations with Ishtar in Assyria-Babylonia, with Anahita in Persia, Armenia, and possibly in Bactria, with Ashtoreth (Astarte) in Phœnicia, and went to the making of Artemis or Diana, of Aphrodite or Venus, and of Athena in the Greek world' (G. W. Gilmore, in *New Schaff-Herzog*, viii. 80).

It is possible, however, that the goddesses of Greece and Rome are instances of the law of fusion rather than cases of borrowing. It would seem that Greece and Rome worshipped goddesses of love in very early times, and that their importance was enhanced through association with foreign female deities.

'The native Greek deity of love would appear to have been Dione, goddess of the moist and productive soil. . . ; Venus was a deity of extreme antiquity among the Romans, but not of great importance until she had acquired certain attributes of the Eastern Aphrodite' (Galey, 424).

2. Personality of female deities.—Goddesses have exercised in some place or time essentially every conceivable office as deity, with mental qualities to fit the part. There is, however, a law of differentiation of function as between male and female deities that sets the gods apart to exercise the sterner qualities as ruler, law-giver, judge, protector, or conqueror, whilst goddesses symbolize the gentler and more heartful qualities of Nature and mind. Illustrations are the Greek Aurora, goddess of the dawn, analogue of Uṣas in India; Venus, the spirit of love and beauty; and the Scandinavian Freya, goddess of the atmosphere and clouds, of marriage, and patroness of the tender affection of married lovers, and of parental devotion. This specialization of function often produces a compassionate goddess whose prevailing presence can breathe solace in times of grief and pain, and inspire hope to the weary and heavy-hearted. Such is the holy Mary in Christian worship, with her almost exact counterpart among the Iroquois, Aztecs, and Mayas of America and elsewhere (D. G. Brinton, *The Religious Sentiment*, New York, 1876, p. 68).

While it is not true, as Max Müller has pointed out (*Contributions to the Science of Mythology*, London, 1897, ii. 818), that female deities are purely abstract principles, it is safe to say that they are generally more spiritual than the gods. The name Minerva, goddess of wisdom and contemplation, is from the Latin, Greek, and Sanskrit words for 'mind.' Among the Tzentals of Mexico was and still is worshipped the highest of goddesses, Alaghom Naom, lit. 'she who brings forth mind.' 'To her was due the mental and immaterial part of Nature; hence another of her names was Iztal Ix, the mother of wisdom' (Brinton, *Myths of the New World*, Philadelphia, 1896, p. 179). This pervasive quality of goddesses causes them to burrow in the deeps of things, whence they fix destinies, like the Fates—Clotho, Lachesis, and Atropos, daughters of Night. Of the members of the Egyptian triad—Osiris, Horus, and Isis—the last was *par excellence* the skilled magician. Whilst many goddesses are resplendent with light, others are, since they dwell in the deeps of things, of a sinister character. Others combine both qualities, as is true of Durgā, Kālī, Chaṇḍika, and Chāmundā of India. These are so tender as to receive the innocent prayers of little children, and at the same time are gloomy and foreboding. Female deities have often, thanks to their spiritual qualities, acted as intermediaries between gods and men. The Hindu Śiva is manifested through his wife 'the Great Goddess,' Mahādevī. She 'with a thousand names and a thousand forms' is able to suffuse the day by her elusive presence (A. Barth, *Religions of India*, London, 1891, p. 199). It should not be supposed that, because goddesses are the more spiritual and pervasive presences, they lack integrity and stability. On the contrary, they often represent permanency in the midst of change. The soil in which such a feeling springs is found in a myth rather wide-spread, that the original creative principle is female, and another belief that woman alone is endowed with immortality.

In making generalizations upon the gentler spiritual traits of goddesses, one should not forget the warlike proclivities of the Assyrian Ishtar, and that Minerva was also 'Pallas' Athene who hurled the thunderbolt (see also ASHTART, BENGAL, §§ 13, 31, DURGĀ, EARTH, etc.).

3. Supreme goddesses. — Female deities have often enjoyed the highest place among the gods. This depends upon the nature of the social organization and the respect in which women are held. Clan-life in which the mother is the head of the group is likely to lift the 'mother-goddess' into a supreme position, provided the nation has risen above the stage of magic. The early Semites, who before their dispersion had a polyandrous social organization, are an illustration. G. A. Barton says of them:

'We only see more clearly [than did even W. Robertson Smith in his *Religion of the Semites*] that the chief deity of the clan was at this primitive time a goddess, and that, in so far as a male deity played any considerable part, he was her son and reflex' (*Semitic Origins*, London, 1902, p. 106).

During Bab. history her later equivalent, Ishtar, rose to a position 'independent of association with any male deity' and 'becomes the vehicle for the expression of the highest religious and ethical thought attained by the Babylonians' (Jastrow, 82 f.). Many other illustrations are found among the natives of America (E. J. Payne, *History of the New World called America*, Oxford, 1892–99, i. 462, ii. 480).

'The goddess Tonantzin, Our Dear Mother, was the most widely loved of Nahuatl divinities, and it is because her mantle fell upon Our Lady Guadalupe that the latter now can boast of the most popular shrine in Mexico' (Brinton, *Myths*, 179).

It seems inevitable that, as the quieter agricultural pursuits in naturally protected valleys favourable to the worship of goddesses have fallen into the background, through the fusion of clans and cities into warring nations in which chivalry and virility are at a premium, male deities have risen supreme, while those of the 'weaker sex' have been degraded to lesser functions, attached as consorts, superseded and forgotten, or, to save themselves, have changed their sex to fit the new demands (cf. Barton, esp. pp. 178–180).

India is unique in having the opposite history—of higher appreciation of goddesses, along with its later development. It illustrates, however, the same principle in a negative way. The Vedas were written before and during the period when the Aryans were conquering the aborigines of India and were engaged in feuds among their own tribes. Under such conditions there are no goddesses, although the literature is richly polytheistic. Since the nation has settled down into a relatively peaceful life of agricultural pursuits, the worship of female deities has risen to a place of supreme importance: Durgā, spirit of Nature and spring; Kālī, soul of infinity and eternity; Sarasvatī, supreme wisdom; and Śakti, mother of all phenomena. This is not so strange in a land in which from the earliest times 'one's daughter is the highest object of tenderness' (Manu, iv. 185) and 'the mother is a thousand times more than the father' (ii. 145), and in which there is the present phenomenon, as in the province of Malabar, of women holding a higher social and political position than men (Sister Nivedita, *The Web of Indian Life*, New York, 1904, p. 76 f.). Hence it is that the Hindu worshipper utters daily the prayer:

'O Mother Divine, Thou art beyond the reach of our praises; Thou pervadest every particle of the universe; all knowledge proceeds from Thee, O Infinite Source of Wisdom! Thou dwellest in every female form, and all women are Thy living representatives upon earth' (Svami Abhedananda, *India and Her People*, New York, 1906, p. 285).

4. Goddesses of 'love.'—The term 'love,' as shown in the sequel, is a fusion of three or four separate meanings. In this connexion it is used in the sense of love of mates and the tender passion. There can be no doubt that certain goddesses of various countries have been patrons of courtship, marriage, and fecundity, and even of sensuality. The function of Venus in Rome, Aphrodite in Greece, Freya in Scandinavia, Ishtar in Babylonia, and Tlazolteotl of the Aztecs witnesses to this fact. The behaviour of many of these consorts of the gods is evidence that their wifely attributes were much in the thought of the worshippers. The gods have often conducted themselves toward their mates in a wanton and sensuous manner. In addition to the worship of the deities of love, both male and female, much use has also been made of other deities supposed to be wholly free from those characteristics in the expression of the tender passion. Ideal marriages to the Mother of God have been not uncommon in Christendom; and the spiritual unions of Christian mystics with Christ have been of a passionate sort.

In the main, according to W. James, the religion of St. Teresa 'seems to have been that of an endless amatory flirtation—if one may say so without irreverence—between the devotee and the deity' (*Varieties of Religious Experience*, New York, 1902, p. 347 f.).

The full extent of feminine attraction in religion cannot well be appreciated, however, without an adequate recognition of the retention of the appropriate symbols of sex even after the goddesses themselves have lapsed into oblivion. The persistence of the symbols betrays how the concept and the accompanying impulse have been fixed, then abstracted, and finally blended into the central stream of religion. Among the commonest of these symbols and the least mistakable in their meaning are representations of the reproductive organs. Phallic symbols have been and still are used in the under currents of Shintoism in Japan (E. Buckley, *Phallicism in Japan*, Chicago, 1898; Griffis, *The Religions of Japan*, New York, 1895, pp. 29, 49, 88, 380–384). The *liṅga* in India is 'the symbol under which Śiva is universally worshipped' (J. Dowson, *Dict. of Hindu Mythology*, London, 1891, p. 177). The 'sign of the Mother Goddess,' the symbol of the female organ of reproduction, ramified through many of the Semitic cults (Whatham, *AJRPE*, July 1911, pp. 252–309). Many writers regard certain pillars and posts of houses and altars, and signs carved upon these, as representations of the threshold of life of the mother-goddess (H. C. Trumbull, *The Threshold Covenant*, 1896, pp. 109–164, 228 ff.; Barton, 101 f., 251, 253, etc.). There are wide-spread serpent-stories and serpent-symbolism in religion (H. Ellis, *Psychology of Sex Auto-erotism*, Philadelphia, 1905, p. 206) which are supposed to typify sex (G. W. Cox, *Myth. of Aryan Nations*, London, 1887, p. 353). Fruit-bearing trees, their boughs, their fruit, bunches of grapes, and even the gum that exudes from the tree, have been regarded as sacred symbols of the reproductive principle of Nature, and perhaps contain a strain of sexual obsession (W. R. Smith, 133). Fire-sticks and fire-drills used in worship in many parts of the world have the same significance (GB^3, London, 1911, pt. i. vol. ii. pp. 207–226, 250). In Egypt and amongst the Saivites in India, the lotus is a symbol of the reproductive act (Creuzer, *Symbolik und Mythologie*, Leipzig, 1836–43, I. i. 412). The Buddhists of the north countries still repeat, without suspecting the origin of the phrase, 'Om! The jewel in the lotus. Amen' (Brinton, *The Religious Sentiment*, 214). In the West, too, these symbols persist, even when, as also among the Buddhists, they contradict the central doctrine of the religion in which they appear. In later Rome, women carried phallic emblems in the processions, and this was prohibited by the Council of Mans in 1247, and again by the Council of Tours in 1396 (*Encyc. Am.*, art. 'Phallus'; on the survivals of old cults, Barton, 233–268). See, further, PHALLICISM.

When one combines the presence of these phallic rites and emblems with the fact that religion has amongst most peoples to a greater or less extent broken out in Bacchanalian, Dionysian, Saturnalian, and other orgiastic revels, and often has with seeming purpose ended in the most unbridled passion, it cannot be doubted that there is something in common between 'love' and the religious sentiment (cf. art. CHASTITY). This is so evident that many students have gone to the extent of affirming their complete identity.

The judgment of Fothergill is typical: 'We find that all religions have engaged and concerned themselves with the sexual passion; from the times of Phallic worship through Romish celibacy down to Mormonism, theology has linked itself with man's reproductive instinct' (*Journ. Med. Science*, 1874, p. 198). Even so careful a student as Barton thinks that the 'beginnings of the Semitic religion go back to the sexual relation' (*Sem. Or.* 107), and 'that the religious and moral development of the race has been closely bound up with fatherhood and motherhood' (p. 307).

Since other writers hold the opposite view of this much debated question, and minimize the sexual content of religion or even deny the connexion altogether, the restrictions and limitations of its unqualified acceptance should be pointed out. An enthusiasm, it is claimed, incited by the pursuit of a new theory, has blinded students to the multitude of facts pointing in the contrary direction. Some of them are as follows. The greater number of female deities have little or no connexion whatever with sex. Such, for example, are Ceres and Minerva of Rome, and Sarasvatī and Lakṣmi of India. Even those of 'love' have often subserved primarily other functions. The Assyrian Ishtar had so departed from the motherly function of her original prototype that, while a chaste love entered into her relationship with her subjects, she was essentially a goddess of war, of battles, of protection, and was oftentimes a violent destroyer (Jastrow, 204 f.). So much does tradition distort her true picture that she has been handed down essentially in her connexion with the tender passion. There is a curious trait in human nature by virtue of which scandal travels farther and faster than sober fact. It must be reckoned with in judging the character of those deities and their worship.

The lively imagination of the supporters of the phallic theory of the nature of religion, it would seem, has led to a confusion and distortion in seeing sexual significance in symbols where none exists. The serpent has clearly been an emblem of lightning, of graceful curves, of sinister presences, and many other things. Its place in religious symbolism cannot justly be called invariably a sign of sex (cf. W. R. Smith, 158, and esp. Brinton, *The Religious Sentiment*, 206–209). The lotus is a token of beauty, of spirituality, and, since it springs forth miraculously from its impure surroundings, of resurrection (Wiedemann, *Rel. of the Anc. Egyptians*, London, 1897, p. 138). Pillars and columns have been loaded down with phallic significance by students from Herodotus to the present day. Others are much more cautious in their generalization (cf. W. R. Smith, 456 f. *et al.*; Moore, 'Ashtoreth' and 'Massebah,' in *EBi*). The way in which doorposts, columns of many kinds, obelisks, towers, and steeples have been seized upon as phallic signs illustrates more clearly perhaps the law of apperception in mental behaviour than the sexual content of religion.

It should be borne in mind, too, that religion has tried to suppress or regulate or even to eliminate every type of eroticism. It has practised and preached celibacy in India, Egypt, Europe, Mexico; and elsewhere it has fostered convents, monasteries, and nunneries with the utmost rigour of discipline (A. Réville, *Native Religions of Mexico and Peru*, London, 1895, pp. 109–111). It has often gone the length of violent sacrifice of virility and femininity in the interest of a life of spirituality (GB^3 ii. 144 f.). As if to purge its highest concepts from too great a strain of amorousness, it has formed doctrines of immaculate conception and virgin birth—notions which are very wide-spread (Brinton, *Myths of the New World*, 172). It has pictured gods as produced full-formed independently of sex, as in the case of Minerva, the virgin goddess, who sprang from the brain of Jove. It has created goddesses who have ignored and transcended any connexion with 'love.' Because Vesta, the guardian of the home and companion of the hearth, rejected all suitors, Jupiter gave her the place of honour in his palace; and in the sacred temples of men on earth she was blessed with a position of highest reverence. Vestal virgins (as also in Mexico and Peru), whose chastity was forfeited at the cost of life, attended her sacred altar. Those who would magnify the erotic element in religion have been wont to think that the presence of priestesses and their attendants in temples is evidence of sensual practices. While there is much evidence for it, there are equally convincing proofs that religion has succeeded in preserving the chastity of its worshippers (cf. Jastrow, 350). The large rôle that priestesses have filled in ritual and worship is sufficiently explained on the ground of the finer nervous organization of women and their capability of more delicate emotional response, and hence their special fitness to act as oracle-givers, witches, sorceresses, mediums, and diviners of the will of the god (Jastrow, 432, 485, 659). It is fair to judge religions, like individuals, at their average best rather than at their worst.

Such considerations as the above would indicate that between eroticism and religion there is at most a *kinship* rather than an *identity*. Their inter-relation comes about for two reasons: first, the similarities of the psychoses involved, and second, the almost uncontrollable intensity of the reproductive instincts which religion is trying to regulate. On the first point the law is stated correctly by Brinton:

'Stimulate the religious sentiment and you arouse the passion of love, which will be directed as the temperament and individual culture prompt. Develop very prominently any form of love, and by a native affinity it will seize upon and consecrate to its own use whatever religious aspirations the individual has. This is the general law of their relation' (*The Religious Sentiment*, 73).

The other aspect of the law is that religion acts as a control or a regulative function of all phases of life. That sensuality breaks out in it is evidence simply that the strength of the sexual life, due to its utility in conserving biological ends, constantly threatens personal well-being and social symmetry, and that religion has had, therefore, an especially difficult task to keep it in control. This regulation it accomplishes in two ways: by repression, as we have seen, and also by refinement. The refining process consists in the suppression on the one hand of the coarser form of the love impulse, and on the other in carrying it up into the higher levels of consciousness, or 'spiritualizing' it, and there blending it completely with all the other instincts and impulses that subserve life's needs. Phallicisms at their best have in this way been softened and dignified and also weakened by being relatively lost in the rich fusion with other strains of mental life. Griffis, for example, in describing the phallic observances in Japan, says: 'I have never had reason to look upon the implements or the system as anything else than the endeavour of man to solve the mystery of Being and Power' (*Religions of Japan*, p. 51). It is the failure to appreciate this law of the suppression of the lower and over-intense forms of the love impulse, and at the same time the effort to spiritualize and harmonize it with the rest of the complex, that has led to much needless debate and false interpretation of its place in religion.

5. The female element in terms of the meaning of religion as a whole.—The older emphasis of the rôle of love in religion is thus due to the supposition that religion exists to subserve some special function of life. It does not seek to gratify any taste or appetite, but is for the sake of getting on. It seems to be a function of life as a whole, and is in terms of adjustment and fulfilment. It has, like life in all its relations, an 'autotelic' or 'telesthetic' quality that feels after ideal situations. It has also its 'axiopathic' or 'cosmothetic' aspect, by which it seeks delicately to adjust life to the immediate situations around it. The worshipper consequently responds to the present and future in terms of what the need is, and symbolizes those needs with whatever is at hand in the accidents of his surroundings. Among the needs are protection and safety. Gods have been especially useful in this relation. Another need is the increase of crops, herds, and children. Goddesses have been the natural and convenient symbols of *fertility and increase*. Many of them have filled the rôle simply and solely of ensuring the increase of crops and herds except in so far as, by an easy and natural process of association, the life of sex has been caught up as an incident in their worship.

Diana was 'a personification of the teeming life of nature' (*GB*[3], pt. i. vol. ii. p. 124). Even the 'marriages' of gods and goddesses performed in her cult were charms to promote the growth of crops (*ib.* p. 121). In Palestine, during drought, the maidens and women clothed a winnowing-fork in the garments of a woman, called it the 'bride of God,' and performed ritual with it to bring rain. There is no evidence of any sentiment connected with the ceremony except that of exercising a magical influence over the weather. In seeking to compel increase and induce prosperity, mankind has used not only human motherhood as a symbol, but the cow, the bull, the grape, and anything that the imagination could conveniently hit upon. Continence has proved even more effective in bringing good crops than a positive observance of erotic customs (*ib.* pp 104–112). In the rich literature of the Rigveda there were endless reiterations of petitions for abundance of crops, herds, and children, and for protection and success; yet all the deities are male, and there is essentially no evidence of amatory religious sentiments among the gods or men.

Another great problem of religion has been the question of the origin of things. Femininity has again proved a natural and convenient symbol of *creation*—but so has the egg, which may, for example, split, one part becoming the heavens and the other the earth.

'Half of the Çivaite religions are, in fact, characterised by the cultus of an androgynous or female divinity. The Çakti . . . has its roots . . . in a sexual dualism, placed at the beginning of things (in a Brāhmaṇa of the Yajur-Veda, for instance, Prajāpati is androgynous), or of a common womb in which beings are formed, which is also their common tomb' (Barth, 200).

Femininity is thus clearly *one* factor only in the larger business of religion as adjustment and fulfilment.

6. Sexless deities.—It is suggestive of the limitation of the place of femininity in religion that, along with growth, religion has progressively not only emphasized virgins, continent priestesses, virgin mothers, and celibate goddesses, but has conceived as well sexless and hermaphroditic deities and angels, and also gods and goddesses who transcend considerations of sex entirely. Centring, as the religious impulse does, in feeling after the larger life or 'the sentiment of continuance,' it has thus sought to express the unity of Nature and life in the purely human. It has, therefore, been fond of combining both sexes in one personality, or of fusing, in a deity who happens to be by name of a certain sex (due, let us say, to the limitations of language), the qualities of the opposite sex.

'In the Vatican Apollo we see masculine strength united with maidenly softness: in the traditional face and figure of Christ a still more striking example of how the devout mind combines the traits of both sexes to express the highest possibility of the species' (Brinton, *The Religious Sentiment*, 67).

Were it not for the fact that gods, irrespective of sex, subserve the higher functions of protector, helper, and unifier, how could one explain the fact that Ishtar sometimes appears as female among the Semites and as male among the others?

In the highest monotheisms the Deity has risen superior to sex. The God of Muhammad, while calling forth a holy prophet from a virgin mother, 'begetteth no children'; to impute such to Him would be so gross an impiety as to threaten the cleaving of the heavens asunder and the destruction of the earth.

'It is not meet for God that He should have a son; God forbid! When He decreeth a thing He only saith unto it "Be" and it is' (Qur'ān, xix.). 'He begetteth not, neither is He begotten' (cxii.).

Such likewise are Brahma and Jahweh.

'In Christianity, and already in the spiritual religion of the Hebrews, the idea of divine fatherhood is entirely dissociated from the physical basis of natural fatherhood. Man was created in the image of God, but he was not begotten; God-sonship is not a thing of nature but a thing of grace' (W. R. Smith, 41).

More barbaric religions, not being able to think in terms of æsthetic or moral values or general concepts, have been compelled to picture things in more concrete terms. Deities have sometimes been, therefore, progenitors, just as at other times they are potters who shape men from clay.

Particularly among uncultured people it has been a convenience to represent 'Reality,' the higher self, and the present and possible relationship of the two in the imagery of human relationships; and it is, therefore, natural that the tender passion should have been seized upon as a convenient analogy. Along with increased enlightenment, however, every aspect of the 'love-life' is either taken up into the higher world of religious values in a softened, refined, or almost imperceptible form, or transcended and left behind. Both these things are likely to happen, each in its own way.

7. Summary of psychological theories.—The interpretations of our problem from the standpoint of psychological discussion have been extremely diverse. Although somewhat antagonistic among themselves, there is doubtless some truth in each and all of them. Characteristic theories are here described, arranged as far as possible in a series from the least to the most satisfactory.

(*a*) *Degeneration.*—A popular conception has been that there is little or no connexion between the female sentiment and religion. Whenever they have mingled, it is because the reproductive passion has broken through its proper bounds. This notion of their antithesis has arisen out of the law of contrast, by which the high and the low, the good and the bad, are sharply set off against each other. This inevitable tendency has gradually produced the two incompatible worlds of 'grace' and 'nature,' the 'sacred' and 'secular'—a contrast unknown to the primitive mind—with 'religion' confined to the one sphere, and the biological function of reproduction to the other; and it has ended in many countries in a radical asceticism. Modern developmental conceptions have undermined such artificial distinctions. The truth of this notion rests upon the vast difference, through development, between the 'lower' and the 'higher' which is the refined, intellectualized, and controlled expression of the tender passion; and upon the fact of the strength and persistence of sex, with its consequent dangers from the crasser forms of its expression. Its falsity centres in the resultant divided and incoherent personality, the sensualizing of the biological function by freeing it from the control of the higher sentiments, and in limiting religion to a relatively narrow field of highly abstracted values.

(*b*) *Identity.*—Many students take exactly the opposite view, and regard the religious impulse as primarily, if not solely, the refinement of reproduction. Love in religion is a spiritualized form of love for mates. In the development of individuals the curve of frequency for conversions and other religious awakenings is essentially coincident with that of the maturing of the reproductive functions (Starbuck, *The Psychology of Religion*, London, 1899, ch. iii.). The phenomena attending the stress of conviction for sin are similar to the disturbances of sex (*ib.* 168, 206). There are marked likenesses between 'love' at its highest and mystical states of religion (Hall, *Adolescence*, New York, 1904, ii. 295–301). A genetic series of 'love-states,' from its physiological setting to its highest spiritualized and mystical qualities, identical with those of religion, is easily describable (*ib.* ii. 126–143). The pathology of the two shows remarkable similarities.

'In the female especially the erotic delusion, unknown to the patient herself, often assumes the color of the religious' (J. T. Dickson, *The Science and Practice of Medicine in Relation to Mind*, New York, 1874, p. 383; cf. Ellis, 231 ff.). Murisier remarks: 'The passion of the religious ecstatic lacks nothing of what goes to make up sexual love, not even jealousy' (*RPh*, Nov. 1898).

The evolutionary background of love is traceable, from reproduction, to sex and the family, and on through the larger tribal self until it includes attachment to humanity and to God (Drummond, *The Ascent of Man*, New York, 1894, pp. 215–318). Added to these psychological and biological evidences are those of a sociological character considered above.

Whilst these massed evidences are on the surface extremely convincing, a more careful analysis will show that, although they are true within limits, the supposition that religion and spiritualized 'love' are identical is a hasty one, with rather more error than accuracy in it when applied to developed religions. The reasons for thinking so are that, looked at empirically, the highest religions of the present, barring exceptions and distortions, look as if they had other than erotic significance, no matter how spiritualized the phallic content; a comparative and genetic study of the facts seems to show that phallic symbols and rites, in so far as they are found at present, are relics, or rudimentary marks, of an earlier attempt to regulate promiscuity; the biographical and autobiographical evidence would indicate that more frequently than otherwise the effect of 'getting religion' is either the control of the passions or their uprooting and the substitution of a set of values which cannot, except by the liveliest play of the imagination, be called irradiations of sex; love in religion has psychologically at least two other sources besides the reproductive impulse; and, finally, religion is the fusion of *all* the instincts and emotions, and not the one alone.

(*c*) *Regulation.*—Religion — man's sentiment of continuance and feeling after perfection, or, as theologians prefer to call it, God's revelation to the mind and guidance in the heart—has been trying to control life as a whole. Among other things it has tried to incorporate the reproductive instinct in order to regulate its intensity and to eliminate promiscuity (Marshall, *Instinct and Reason*, New York, 1898, pp. 309–315). In earlier times, biologically, in the absence of the care of children, the perpetuity of the species depended upon multiplicity of offspring. Under such circumstances there must have been a utility in an uncontrolled passion for reproduction. The laws of heredity and recapitulation have brought up this old strain into human life. The conditions later changed. With the increased advantage to the species of having the family as the basis of social organization, the condition of advancement was the establishment of monogamous marriages, and the consequent weakening of the sexual impulse. Religion is in part the crystallization of this feeling of the need of such regulation. It has, therefore, taken over into itself the function of sex and marriage, and has used every conceivable means of exercising control over them. It has hedged them about with social sanctions, under priests who are frequently celibates or eunuchs, with ritual and ceremony too solemn to be disregarded, and with gods and goddesses whose will could not be withstood. It has made marriage difficult to enter, has tested the fitness of mates by periods of long delay, and has sealed their union by forbidding divorce. It has uttered its admonitions, prohibitions, and punishments; and in every way has attempted to restrain the passions, and direct the mind into a sense of the dignity and sacredness of this phase of life, when limited to the channels of social and spiritual well-being.

(*d*) *Adaptation*.—But religion has at times assumed the positive attitude of stimulating the reproductive impulse under its controlled form. The reason for this is to be found in the social sense of the need of increasing the number of individuals in the tribe or nation, combined with the individual recognition of special fulfilment through progeny. Primitive warring tribes have shown much concern over the birth of the greatest possible number of male children. It is natural that this need should be taken up and made part of the business of religion. No warrior could enter Valhalla in early Germanic times who had not begotten a son. Among the Mormons one's condition and position in heaven depends upon the number of offspring brought forth under the regulation of the 'family.' Modern governments have taken seriously the problem of encouraging marriages and the production of large families. Since, now, the regulation and stimulation of such matters has come over, through specialization, into a body of social customs and also under State control, it has inevitably come about that religion has progressively busied itself, to a greater extent relatively, with ideal adjustments irrespective of the relation of mates. So much is this the case that in the empirical study of the religious confessions of normal persons at the present time there is ample evidence that the instinct in question is a hindrance to the spiritual life and must be curbed (Starbuck, 402).

(*e*) *Composition*.—Religion is a compound of all the instincts and emotions, while the female sentiment is but one of these, and, as we have seen, one that has tended in the higher forms of religion to lapse into relative insignificance. The laws of the refinement of the instincts and of their fusion, already referred to, have carried up into religion a rich blending of fear, self-regard, hunger, self-expression, love, curiosity, and many others. Each of these can be traced from its simple, crude form to its spiritualized expression, where it mingles in some measure with every phase of the mental life. It has been a fascinating theme of students to trace out these relations. Fear, for example, betrays itself by the presence in religion of demons, hell, sacrifice, priestcraft, and the like, and also, with a slight blend from other instincts, as the sense of majesty and reverence, which characterizes religion at its best. Self-regard, likewise, develops from the seeking for mere benefits upwards to the craving for perpetuity through immortality, and at last becomes the æsthetic demand for ideal perfection. The temptation of such procedure, since a certain instinct permeates entirely the higher religious life, is to give way to the fascination of the description, and conclude, therefore, that religion is *nothing else than* the single instinct in question. It is analogous to the procedure of an amateur chemist who should be entirely satisfied with discovering a single element in a compound, because he is sure that it permeates every part of the solution. There is perhaps not an instinct that does not, and with much accuracy of description, seem to be the all-filling source and content of the religious life. The enthusiasm of the sex psychologists in particular, during recent years, has resulted in a strange confusion. Many of the facts that seem to them to prove the identity of the female sentiment with religion only want more careful scrutiny to betray their insufficiency. Much has been made of the coincidence and concomitance during adolescence of reproductive and religious awakenings. (On the similarity of these curves of frequency, see Starbuck, ch. ii.; on the value of this kind of reasoning, consult W. James, 11 f.) There is no evidence, however, of a causal relationship. On the contrary, it is clear that for the most part on the mental side they are contradictory and antithetical. The coincidence seems to be due to the prevalence of initiation ceremonies practised among all primitive peoples. The modern equivalent is a custom of confirmation. These ceremonies celebrate the entrance of young men and women into the social, political, and religious ways of the clan, and mark at the same time the fitness for marriage. A process of long social selection in connexion with these ceremonies, through weeding out the mentally and physically unfit, has called out and accentuated the eventful period of early adolescence, with its marked readjustment in the complex strains of character, and the sudden calling out of latent powers. Since the mental and physical characteristics are the same essentially as are necessary to good citizenship on the one hand, and the responsibility of family life on the other, and, since the social group has sought through these ceremonies to prepare young men and women for both the civic and the marital relationship, it is but a matter of course that the awakenings of sex and religion should be synchronous. Keeping in mind the distinction between the *cause* and the *condition* of a mental happening, one may safely say simply that frequently in adolescence the explosive quality of the 'love' instinct touches off a large stock of activities, insights, and interests which are not of sexual origin, and among these the religious impulse. But religion is 'touched off' also by a score of other adolescent nascencies, such as scientific insight, logical acumen, and the joy of conquest, and much more frequently so than by the sexual impulse. So markedly is this true that it is not safe to conclude that the reproductive instinct furnishes to any considerable degree the raw material out of which religion is constructed.

The reasoning from the pathology of sex and religion is equally at variance with the facts. That the pathologies of eroticism are likely to take on a religious cast none will doubt. This is the correct clue to the psychoses of many religious fanatics. In the case of Swedenborg, for example, the evidences from his journal and from his writings are conclusive that his 'divine love' and 'angelic wisdom' are—not wholly, but in large part—the effluvia from an unstable and over-excitable erotic temperament. Other instances can be found, particularly among the radical mystics. They are the exceptions, however, from which alienists have derived too sweeping generalizations.

Religious and sexual insanities are both extremely complex psychoses. Each draws from many sources. There are on the one hand many religious insanities that have no sexual setting (D. H. Tuke, *Dict. of Psychol. Medicine*, Philadelphia, 1892, p. 1091 f.), and on the other many kinds of sexual insanity that do not take a religious turn. The small part that either sex or religion occupies in the whole range of insanities is indicated by statistical studies. Out of 66,918 male inmates in the asylums of England and Wales during the years 1878–1887 there were but 2·5 % whose disturbances took the form of religious excitement, and only 4·9 % traceable to sexual or reproductive causes (H. Ellis, in Tuke, p. 1154). It is from these two small and relatively incompatible fields that the facts have been found from which wholesale conclusions have been obtained. Not only does the sphere of insanity draw from many other sources than sex, but religion is an indefinitely bigger thing than mysticism, which itself only occasionally shows exaggerated eroticism. That there is more in religion than irradiations of sex is suggested by the fact that alienists often recommend it in the treatment of insanity for its humanizing, restraining, steadying, and stimulating influence (cf. Gasquet, in Tuke, 1088–91). Nor can this be suspected as an instance of *similia similibus curantur.* The occurrence, it should be said, of the interplay of erotic mysticism and sexual insanity is due to the law of association which operates amongst the emotions no less than in the cognitive processes. Religion is the whole-hearted response of the devotee to his sense of absolute values. Its psychoses tend to be completely obsessive and voluminous. This is the character, too, of all the instincts, particularly of the sexual emotion. It is to be expected, therefore, that in the exaggerated form mysticism and eroticism should blend, even if, as is true, they draw for the most part from different sources and have a somewhat independent history.

The gravest oversight of the identity theory of the female sentiment and religion is the supposition that love, which is the central fact of religion, has had its sole origin in sex (cf. Mercier, *Sanity and Insanity*, London, 1890, p. 220 ff.). But love is a compound. It has at least three somewhat independent sources—sex, gregariousness, and Nature appreciation. The evolution of the first has brought into religion the tender affection for kind, while its exaggeration results in phallicism and eroticisms of many sorts. The refinements of gregariousness have created the sentiments of fellowship, sympathy, and loyalty to kind, regardless of sex, and when excessive have produced clannishness on the one hand, and unreflecting missionary zeal on the other. Nature appreciation, the sheer enjoyment of things in and for themselves, has ripened into a sense of presences within objects, and at last into Nature-gods and Nature-religions. Gregariousness, or 'sociality,' as M. J. Guyau calls it (*Non-Religion of the Future*, London, 1897, p. 44), can exist independently of sex. In his fine analysis, Ribot (*Psychology of the Emotions*, London, 1897, pp. 276–303) points out that gregariousness is founded upon nutrition, the will to live, and the attraction of like for like, irrespective of sex, while the tender emotion is founded upon sex and mother-love. These two, although having an element in common, have remained, in the course of evolution, 'distinct and mutually independent' (p. 280). It is, furthermore, in connexion with the gregarious life, irrespective of sex, that the true social and moral feelings are developed, whereas the sentiments that arise in connexion with 'domestic aggregates' based upon the tender emotion are 'restricted to a closed group, without expansive force or elasticity' (p. 281). Societies formed within the same sex, or even among members of different species, or among animals like bees and ants in which reproduction is but a brief incident for perpetuating the species and limited to a few—all such societies, because of their common interests and contacts, show loyalties, fellowships, and loves of the most saving kind. The co-operation is based upon the instinct of conservation, and the attraction is derived from the interplay of personalities which becomes part of the mental and spiritual furnishing of each individual, in the absence of which there is distress, and in its presence enrichment and enlargement. If this dualistic theory of the separate origin of the family group and the social group is correct, as seems highly probable, the evidence of comparative and genetic psychology would be that morality and religion, which are primarily in terms of fellowship, have drawn far more from the gregarious instinct than from sex. The empirical evidences, as we have seen, emphatically support this view. In this connexion it is suggestive that sex is but a specialized form of reproduction, the latter having been performed originally by cell-division, and that both reproduction and sex are functions of the will to live. The reproductive system, for example, is a specialization, embryologically, of the nutritive organs. These considerations would seem to fortify the point of view that religion exists fundamentally in the interest of the adjustment and fulfilment of the developing higher life, and not for the sake of any special sentiment.

The root of the difficulty, then, with the identity theory of sex and religion is, in the first place, the failure to appreciate that love in religion is a compound of the tender emotion, the gregarious instinct, and Nature attachments, the first suffusing the other two with an æsthetic quality, and furnishing them with a basis for external reference; secondly, the failure to see that religion is a compound of all the instincts. The female sentiment is, therefore, but one of the ingredients—more important formerly than now—in a rich compound of sentiments called by the single name 'religion,' whose function is ideal adjustment.

Cf. also artt. PHALLICISM, RELIGION, SEX.

LITERATURE.—This has been indicated in the article.

EDWIN D. STARBUCK.

FENG-SHUI.—Chinese dictionaries give no definition of what is to be understood by Feng-Shui. No native treatises expound it upon scientific lines. *Feng* is 'wind,' *shui* is 'water.' Wind is what cannot be seen, and water what cannot be grasped. 'Wind and water' is the term, therefore, for the occult powers which are always bearing down upon human life. Professors of Feng-Shui prefer that it should remain a mystery, and those who pay them for their services accept the position, declaring that it is not to be expected that common people should understand the unfathomable. Eitel (*Feng-Shui, or the Rudiments of Natural Science in China*) calls it 'a conglomeration of rough guesses at Nature.' It undoubtedly grew out of naturalistic beliefs, though it has become distorted and degraded into a gross superstition.

Practically there is little religion in China but such as springs out of Feng-Shui. The worship of ancestors, the most popular of all religious observances, is indissolubly connected with it. It enters into every important arrangement of daily life. Every proposed change must be brought to the test of its principles. All events which happen, favourable or adverse, are explained by it. It is spoken of with reverence and awe. The common people are its slaves. Confucianist gentry laugh at the Feng-Shui doctor, but are careful to fall in with his theories and commands. Chinese law does not discuss it, but the courts always act on the presumption that its principles are not fictitious. The Government, though not acknowledging it, publishes every year an Imperial almanac giving all the lists, figures, and diagrams which are required by its professors and their victims. When a rebellion breaks out, the first act of the authorities is not to raise troops, but to send messengers to spoil the Feng-Shui of the rebel leaders by despoiling their ancestral tombs. And, when selling land to foreigners, the mandarins are careful to assign them only what is believed to have bad Feng-Shui.

S. Wells Williams (*The Middle Kingdom*, ii. 246) remarks that this geomantic and spiritualistic faith became systematized in the times of Chu Hi, who lived under the Sung dynasty (A.D. 1126–1278). Chu Hi's commentaries on the Chinese Classics are read in every school; and his mode of thinking has been adopted by modern Confucianism. His theory is that the soul has a dual nature, consisting of the *animus* and *anima*—sometimes called the breath of Heaven and the breath of Earth. The *animus* is the male or spiritual element in the soul; the *anima*, the female or material element. So long as a man lives, these two principles co-exist in combination, but at death the union is dissolved. The *animus* returns to heaven, the *anima* to earth. Neither of them wanders at large in space. The *animus* enjoys freedom of movement, but chooses to limit its peregrinations to the vicinity of its former *habitat*, and to the company of the people with whom it was formerly associated. The *anima* lies quiet in the tomb, provided that the tomb has good Feng-Shui. The Chinese believe themselves to be compassed about by a great cloud of witnesses in the persons of their ancestors and forbears generally, and they hold that the spirits of these deceased relatives are omnipresent in the elements of Nature.

Here we arrive at the practical point which is of such extreme interest to believers in Feng-Shui. The selection of a grave is the most vitally important matter in a man's life. The quiet repose of the *anima* in its tomb is essential to the well-being of its mortal relations. The tomb must be in such a position that the *anima* will be undisturbed and quiescent; in which case it will be disposed favourably towards those members of its family who survive. If otherwise, so low is its ethical character in this disembodied state that it will make havoc of their fortunes.

The Feng-Shui Sien-Sang, or doctors of the geomantic art, know how to profit by these delusions. They are ridiculed and satirized, but universally feared. Nothing affecting the welfare of a family can be decided without their help. They are called in for consultation on a great variety of occasions. Guided by a curious compass with cabalistic signs, they solemnly profess to be able to judge whether a grave is in the proper position, whether it is safe to build a house on a particular spot, or whether a business is likely to prosper where the shop or office stands. If the client is rich, it takes a long while, so the Chinese say, for the learned doctor to arrive at a decision. A coffined corpse may have to remain for years on a shelf in a temple, or to lodge under a shed, till all appears secure. Or, disasters may befall the family after the burial of their relative; whereupon the Sien-Sang declares that the bones must be unearthed and stored in a jar until better Feng-Shui has been discovered. In some districts vast sheds are filled with coffins awaiting burial. Elsewhere tens of thousands of great jars with human remains find shelter at the foot of rocks facing the south, all of which are owned by the survivors and respected by the populace. Any one disturbing them would do so at the risk of his life. A temporary pagoda is sometimes erected as a regulative influence in order to test the quality of the Feng-Shui. If the crops are good, and no pestilence breaks out, and some talented youths in the district win honours at the local examinations, the Feng-Shui is proved to be good. A permanent pagoda then takes the place of the temporary one. These pagodas, as regulating the streams of spirit influence in warding off the evil or attracting the good, are supposed to exercise a remarkable power in producing talent in students. For this reason they are shaped with high pointed roofs in imitation of a pencil or writing brush; and they are often spoken of as 'towers of literature,' the topmost storey being furnished with an image and shrine of the god of literature.

As it is necessary sometimes to build a pagoda to attract or to divert streams of lucky influence, so it is sheer madness to build tall chimneys, to place chimneys on houses, to erect telegraph poles and semaphore signals, to cast up a railway embankment, or even to dig for coal. There is no knowing what mischief may be done by such rash adventures.

Some German missionaries near Hong Kong built two little watch-towers on a house. One of these was visible at a tomb a mile away. Its enraged owners threatened to burn down the whole mission premises. The missionaries argued that the spirit of the deceased could see the little watch-tower only if he stood up, but not if he was lying down quietly in his grave. No discussion was of any avail until the disturbance to the dead was compromised by a substantial money payment to the living!

Much of the violence of the people in Canton, Tientsin, and Peking against foreigners and Christianity is due to the erection by Roman Catholics of lofty cathedral buildings, which upset the Feng-Shui of the whole district. The objection to railways, with their cuttings, tunnels, embankments, and signal-posts, is of the same nature. The first railway in China, from Shanghai to the port of Wu-sung, nine miles away, was purchased and destroyed by the Chinese, on the plea that the speed of the train destroyed the Feng-Shui of tens of thousands of people on both sides of the line.

With a view to warding off evil influences which are presumed to exist, the custom prevails of building brick walls as shields or screens. On these are painted lucky symbols, or words of defiance, or the rampant figures of savage beasts.

When the Feng-Shui is bad, it can be improved. A low hill may be raised, or a rugged hill-top may be lowered. A straight road or watercourse may be made serpentine. A pond may be laid out on the south side of a cemetery, or a tree which obstructs the favourable spirit-breezes may be cut down.

The Chinese believe that the British have mastered the whole science and art of Feng-Shui. To quote Eitel's reference to the evidences of this in Hong Kong:

'Hong Kong, with its abundance of rocks and boulders scattered about on the hillside, abounds in malign breath, and the Chinese think our Government very wise in endeavouring to plant trees everywhere on the hill to screen these harbingers of evil. But the most malicious influence under which Hong Kong suffers is caused by that curious rock on the edge of the hill near Wanchai. It is distinctly seen from Queen's Road East, and foreigners generally see in it Cain and Abel, Cain slaying his brother. The Chinese take the rock to represent a female figure, which they call the bad woman; and they firmly believe that all the immorality of Hong Kong, all the recklessness and vice of Tai-ping-shan, are caused by that wicked rock. So firmly is this belief impressed upon the lowest classes in Hong Kong that those who profit by immoral practices actually go and worship that rock, spreading out offerings and burning incense at its foot. None dares to injure it; and I have been told by many otherwise sensible people that several stone-cutters who attempted to quarry at the base of the rock died a sudden death immediately after the attempt.'

From all this it will be perceived that Feng-Shui is not strictly a religious doctrine. It is held by no sect. It has no temple, no priesthood, no ritual. It founds no college, nor has it even an authorized professorship. Yet its occult influences pervade the whole of Chinese society. It might be called a materialistic fatalism, by which not merely happiness and misery, but virtue and vice are generated. Its origin is the current of Nature's breath over the surface of the earth, the configuration of the landscape deciding the limits of its powers. It is a mode of thought characteristic of primitive times. It views heaven and earth as one great fetish, animated (as Eitel points out) by a blind, unintelligent, but omnipotent vitality. Its similarity to astrology is obvious. Instead of stars it speaks of hills. Rivers and lakes take the place of the Milky Way.

Philosophically, it maintains that the primordial cause of all existence was that the 'Absolute Nothing' evolved out of itself the 'Great Absolute.' When it began to move, the great male principle came into being; and when it rested, the female principle was produced. The whole universe is a living organism, in which these two principles are at work. When they are happily combined, favourable influences bear down on human life; and when inharmonious, the malign breath of Nature exhales disasters upon mankind.

How to avert these calamities is the aim and purpose of Feng-Shui. The configuration and character of the soil determine the weal and woe of those who live upon it. Sloping hillsides, groups of trees, pools of water, and especially winding roads, when properly situated and combined, secure the largest measure of peace and happiness, of health and wealth. By means of his almanac and his compass the Feng-Shui doctor can detect and describe what will happen to the relatives of the friend whom they are about to place in his grave.

Buddhism and Taoism have been degraded into the position of the handmaids, or rather the slaves, of this superstition, which holds hundreds of millions of the human race in its grip. The degradation of Taoism, in particular, has been due to its alliance with Feng-Shui. The human heart cries out for fellowship with the powers of Nature. Neither Confucianism (with its materialism) nor Buddhism (with its transcendentalism) ever satisfied the Chinese mind. The craving for communion with Nature found its expression in the curious geomantic system of Feng-Shui, which commands the secret sympathy, if not the distinct approval, of every Chinaman, high and low. This blind groping of the Chinese mind after a system of natural science in which it can rest has been called 'the very audacity of superstition'; but it will not be able, any more than the folklore of Christian nations, to withstand the impact of sound education, of genuine science, of engineering progress, and especially of the enlightenment that comes with Christian faith.

LITERATURE.—Ernest J. Eitel, *Feng-Shui, or the Rudiments of Natural Science in China*, London, 1873; S. Wells Williams, *The Middle Kingdom*, New York, 1883, i. 628, ii. 246; J. Edkins, *Chinese Recorder*, vol. iv. 1871–1872; Storrs Turner, *Cornhill Magazine*, March 1874; *Notes and Queries on China and Japan*, vol. ii. p. 69; E. J. Dukes, *Everyday Life in China*, London, 1886, ch. on 'The Biggest of all Bugbears.'

EDWIN JOSHUA DUKES.

FERTILITY.—See HARVEST, MAGIC.

FESTIVALS AND FASTS.

FESTIVALS AND FASTS (Armenian).[1]—In the ancient Armenian calendar there are two kinds of abstinence—absolute and relative. *Absolute abstinence* (fasting) is practised on the first 5 days of *Aradjavorkh* (three weeks before Carnival Sunday), and for the 6 weeks of Lent, beginning with Ash-Wednesday and continuing till the Saturday before Palm-Sunday (but see below). *Relative abstinence* prevails every Wednesday and Friday in the year, and also during (*a*) the week of Pentecost (the abstinence of the prophet Elijah), 5 days; (*b*) the week preceding the Feast of Gregory the Illuminator (the 3rd week after Pentecost), 5 days; (*c*) the Transfiguration (the 6th week after Pentecost), 5 days; (*d*) the week preceding the Sunday of the Assumption of the Holy Virgin, 5 days; (*e*) the week preceding the Sunday of the Exaltation of the Holy Cross, 5 days; (*f*) the week preceding the Feast of St. George, or the Feast of the Cross of Varag; (*g*) the week preceding the Feasts of Archangels and Angels; (*h*) the week of Jubilee; (*i*) the week preceding the Feast of St. James of Nisibis; (*j*) the 7 days preceding the Christmas Epiphany-Feast.

During Lent there is no fasting on Saturdays and Sundays, and the same holds for all Holy Week, but abstinence is practised. In none of the above-mentioned cases is abstinence practised on Saturdays, except on the eve of the Transfiguration, of the Assumption, of the Exaltation of the Cross, of Christmas, and of Easter; on these days milk-food, eggs, and fish are eaten. During a fast, only vegetables, fruits, and sweetened things are eaten; olives are admitted as fruits, and olive oil is not forbidden. On abstinence days, vegetables, fruits, sweet things, dishes with olive oil, etc., are eaten.

1. Great Feasts (*taghavar* = 'tent,' 'tabernacle').—There are five Great Feasts:

1. Christmas-Epiphany.
2. Easter.
3. Transfiguration.
4. Assumption.
5. Exaltation of the Cross.

All these are preceded by a week of abstinence, and on the eve of them milk-food, eggs, and fish are eaten. These feasts, except Christmas-Epiphany, always fall on a Sunday. The second day of all five is also a holiday devoted to the commemoration of the dead, when the people march to the cemetery in procession, after High Mass.

2. Feasts held in common with the other branches of Christianity.—

1. Purification of the Holy Virgin.
2. The Annunciation.
3. The Ascension.
4. Pentecost.
5. Trinity.
6. Nativity of the Holy Virgin.
7. Presentation of the Holy Virgin.
8. Conception of the Holy Virgin.

The Sunday preceding the weekly abstinences discussed above is called by the Armenians the *Carnival* of the Feast.

3. Feasts peculiar to the Armenians.—

1. The 8th day of Epiphany, the baptism of Christ.
2. The Great Carnival of *Aradjavorkh*; this is a fixed Sunday, the 10th before Easter. On this day the conversion of the Armenians to Christianity is commemorated (see F. Macler, *Mosaïque orientale*, 1907, p. 34, n. 1).

[1] See also art. CALENDAR (Armenian) and the Literature there cited; also Ormanian, *Church of Armenia*, Eng. tr., London, 1912, p. 175 ff.

3. Every Sunday of Great Lent commemorates a parable of the Gospel.
4. For forty days after Easter there is the Feast of the Resurrection; there is no other feast during this period except the first Saturday after Easter, which is the day for commemorating the beheading of John the Baptist.
5. The first Sunday after Easter is called New Sunday, and commemorates the doubt of St. Thomas.
6. The second Sunday after Easter is the Feast of the Church, instituted by Gregory the Illuminator, in commemoration of the pagan feasts; it is called the Sunday of the Chapel of the Native Land, or *Green* Sunday.
7. The third Sunday after Easter is called *Red* Sunday.
8. The fifth Sunday after Easter is the Feast of the Apparition of the Holy Cross.
9. The seventh Sunday after Easter is called the 2nd Sunday of Palms; it is the commemoration of the appearance of the angel to Gregory the Illuminator in his well-prison (*virap*).
10. The second Sunday after Pentecost is the Feast of the Church of Etchmiadzin. It commemorates the appearance of Christ to Gregory the Illuminator in the church of Etchmiadzin.
11. The 2nd of July is the Feast of the Bier of the Holy Virgin.
12. The 31st of August is the Feast of the Ungirding of the Holy Virgin.
13. The second day after the Exaltation of the Cross is the Feast of the Cross of Mount Varag.
14. The Sunday six weeks before Christmas (*hisnagats barekendan*) is Jubilee Sunday.

4. Feasts of the Saints.—As Feasts of the Saints are not allowed on Sunday in the Armenian Church, the important ones are always held on a Saturday, *e.g.* the Feasts of St. Gregory, St. George, St. Sargis, St. Nicolas of Smyrna, the Archangels and Angels, etc.; while the national Armenian saints have their feasts, as a rule, either between *Aradjavorkh* and the Great Carnival, or between Trinity week and the Transfiguration. The list of feasts given by Conybeare (*Rituale Armenorum*, Oxf. 1905, p. 527 ff.) is based on the Armenian months, to be used in the reading in the churches after vespers.

5. Traces of paganism in the Armenian feasts.—(1) *Vardavar.*—The last five days of the year (*awelikh*) were sacred to the goddess Astlik (*vardadzri* = 'she who makes the rose grow'). Gregory the Illuminator, in order to preserve this pagan commemoration and to sanctify this feast, transferred it to the Feast of Transfiguration. Further, the Deluge was commemorated on the first day of the Armenian year; Gregory now fused these two feasts into one. Down to the present day it is customary for the people, on the day of Transfiguration, to asperge one another in the church, in commemoration of the Flood (cf. *ERE* i. 796; for an interesting pagan survival in the celebration of Ascension Day by a water and flower festival, see Abeghian, *Armen. Volksgl.*, Leipz. 1899, pp. 61–66).

(2) *Victory of Haik over Bel.*—This feast was celebrated on the 11th of August. According to tradition, Haik began the year on 11th August, the day of his victory over Bel. This day, then, was called 'Haik's day,' and was a national festival. Gregory the Illuminator wished to retain this feast; and so, on his return from Cæsarea, he brought the relics of St. John the Baptist and St. Athanagenius to Taron, where he built the monastery of Surp Garabed (Karapet), which still stands and is known under the name of Sultan of Mush. Gregory arranged that the Feast of St. John the Baptist should be celebrated on the same date as the pagan feast. After the fall of the Arsacid dynasty, this arrangement was abandoned, and the Feast of St. John the Baptist passed over into the ranks of the simple Feasts of the Saints.

(3) *Feast of Diana* (*Anahit*).—A fortnight after the beginning of the year, on the 15th of Nawasard, came the Feast of the goddess Anahit (on whom see *ERE* i. 797). Gregory the Illuminator transformed this into the Feast of the Image of the Holy Virgin, brought to Armenia by St. Bartholomew. In place of the statue of Anahit he put the picture of the Virgin, and the celebration was fixed for the 15th August, the Feast of the Assumption of the Virgin (cf. Alishan, *Souvenirs of Native Armenia*, Venice, 1869, *passim* [in Armenian]).

F. MACLER.

FESTIVALS AND FASTS (Buddhist).—The Buddhist canon prescribes the following festivals and fasts.—**I. Uposatha.**—The *Uposatha* days owed their existence to the ancient Vedic custom of holding sacred two periods in each month—the times of the new moon (*Darśa*) and the full moon (*Pūrnamāsa*). These feast, or sacred, days were called *Upavasatha*, and offerings of intoxicating soma were made in connexion with the worship of the moon.[1] According to Buddhist tradition,[2] the monks of non-Buddhistic sects were accustomed to meet together at the middle and at the close of every half-month in order to proclaim their new teaching in public. At such times the people gathered together, and the different sects found their opportunity of increasing their numbers and influence. The Buddhists adopted the custom of these periodical gatherings, but confined themselves to meeting twice in each month.[3] In later times the intermediate quarter-moon days were also held sacred, and so the number of *Uposatha* days was increased to four in every month.[4] The words of the canon are: 'I prescribe that you assemble on the fourteenth, fifteenth, and eighth day of each month.'[5] In the *Dhammika Sutta* the wording is: 'Moreover, being of a pious mind, one should observe *Uposatha* on the fourteenth, fifteenth, and eighth day of the lunar fortnight.'[6] The fourteenth and fifteenth days must be taken to mean the fourteenth day from the new moon in short months and the fifteenth in long.[7]

Though the idea of four monthly fast-days was borrowed from Brāhmanism and other non-Buddhistic sources, the manner in which they were kept was entirely original. It was not proper to trade or do any business; hunting and fishing were forbidden; schools and courts of justice were closed. They were also, from ancient times, fasting-days. The laity were to celebrate the days with clean garments and clean minds.[8] Special observance of the moral precepts was inculcated on these days. In the *Dhammika Sutta* the eight precepts are detailed, and it is added: 'Such, they say, is the eight-fold fast (*Uposatha*) declared by Buddha, who came among us to put an end to sorrow.' The eight precepts were: (1) not to destroy life; (2) not to take what is not given; (3) not to tell lies; (4) not to become drinkers of intoxicating liquors; (5) to refrain from unlawful sexual intercourse—an ignoble thing; (6) not to eat unseasonable fruits at night; (7) not to wear garlands or use perfumes; and (8) not to sleep on a mat spread on the ground.[9] Furthermore, the brethren and sisters were to make use of the gatherings to confess to the assembled Order the sins and faults which each had committed, and to take upon themselves the penance which the transgression had incurred.[10]

At this *Uposatha* ceremony the *Pātimokkha*, which forms the second Khandhaka of the *Mahāvagga*, had to be recited. 'This (*Pātimokkha*) will be their *Uposatha* service.'[11] Explicit directions are given in regard to the ceremony: an *Uposatha* was to be held in a clearly defined district;[12] at

1 *SBE* xiii. Introd. p. x; Monier-Williams, *Buddhism*, London, 1889, pp. 84 and 336; Rhys Davids, *Buddhism*, do. 1899, p. 139.
2 *Mahāvagga*, ii. 1. 1.
3 *Ib.* ii. 4. 2.
4 Monier-Williams, 337; *SBE* xi. 254.
5 *SBE* xiii. 240.
6 *Dhammika Sutta*, p. 27.
7 Rhys Davids, 139, etc.
8 H. Kern, *Manual of Indian Buddhism*, Strassburg, 1896 (=*GIAP* iii. 8), pp. 99–101.
9 *Dhammika Sutta*, p. 25 f.
10 *SBE* xiii. Introd. p. x.
11 *Ib.* p. 242.
12 *Ib.* p. 250.

least a given number of *bhikkhus* were to be present;[1] sick ones might be excused attendance;[2] certain offences precluded attendance;[3] directions are given for the preparation of a hall in which the ceremony was to be held;[4] the *Pātimokkha* had to be recited in full at each *Uposatha*, except in certain cases of danger, etc.,[5] and offences were to be confessed.[6]

In addition to the regular fast-days it is laid down that the *Pāṭi-hārika pakkha* should also be duly observed.[7] This name, meaning 'extra fortnight,' applies to three distinct periods: (1) the three months of *Vassa*, or rain; (2) the month succeeding *Vassa*, called *Chīvara Māsa*, or 'robe month,' because it was customary to provide mendicants, who needed them, with new robes; and (3) the first half of the 'robe month,' to which period the term more particularly applies. During these periods the observance of the 'eight precepts' is more common than at other times.[8]

An occasional holiday, only for monks, is the *Sāmaggi-Uposatha*, 'reconciliation holiday,' which was held when a quarrel among the fraternity was made up.[9]

2. Vassa.—Throughout his whole career Gautama was in the habit of travelling about during most of the fine part of the year, teaching and preaching to the people, but during the four rainy months, from June to October, he remained in one place, devoting himself more particularly to the instruction of his followers.[10] *Vassa* was ordained because the people complained to Gautama that the Buddhist priests were going on travels alike during winter, summer, and the rainy season, so crushing the green herbs in the field, hurting vegetable life, and destroying the life of many small living things.[11] The institution of *Vassa* was Gautama's answer to these complaints. It is a retreat prescribed for the rainy season. Buddhaghoṣa says:

> 'The *bhikkhus* are to look after their Vihāra (if it is in a proper state), to provide food and water for themselves, to fulfil all due ceremonies, such as paying reverence to sacred shrines, etc., and to say loudly, once, or twice, or thrice, at the beginning of the retreat, "I enter upon *Vassa* in this Vihāra for these three months."'[12]

The periods fixed by Buddha for entering upon *Vassa* were two: 'the earlier and the later. The earlier time for entering (upon *Vassa*) is the day after the full moon of Āsālha (June–July); the later, a month after the full moon of Āsālha.'[13] The double period was probably due to a similar double period prescribed in the Brāhmanas and Sūtras for most of the Vedic festivals. Thus the sacrifice of *Varuṇapraghāsa*, with which the Brahmans began the rainy season, was to be held either on the full moon day of Āṣādha, or on the full-moon day of the following month, Śrāvana, in complete accordance with Buddhistical rules about the *Vassupanāyikā*. The Brāhmaṇa texts begin the year with the full-moon day of the (Uttarā) Phālguna; the Sūtras mention another New Year's day, the *Chaitrī pūrṇāmāsī*, which falls one month later. It was in connexion with this dislocation of the year that the annual festivals might be postponed accordingly.[14]

The rules for the celebration of *Vassa* are contained in the third Khandhaka of the *Mahāvagga*.[15] No *bhikkhu* was to go on his travels till he had kept the *Vassa* during the earlier or later three months.[16] By the order of a king the retreat might be commenced at the later period.[1] A *bhikkhu* might leave his Vihāra, if sent for, but not for a longer period than seven days.[2] A number of other cases are given, such as a visit to a sick man or father, mother, or relation, where leave of absence was permissible, but was restricted to seven days.[3] The place of retreat could be changed for such reasons as danger from beasts of prey, snakes, robbers, demons, want of food, fire, no proper medicine, etc.[4] For those who entered upon *Vassa* in the later period, the end of the retreat fell on *Komudī* day, *i.e.* the full-moon day in the month Kārttika, frequently called 'Kaumuda day' in epic literature.

3. Pavāraṇā.—This solemn termination of the *Vassa* is inaugurated by an act of the *Saṅgha* in an assembly of the Chapter of at least five monks.[5] The fourteenth and fifteenth days of the half-month were appointed as *Pavāraṇā* days.[6] The ritual for the ceremony forms the fourth Khandhaka of the *Mahāvagga*.[7] Gautama says:

> 'I prescribe that the *bhikkhus*, when they have finished their *Vassa* residence, hold *Pavāraṇā* with each other in these three ways: by what has been seen, or by what has been heard, or by what is suspected. Hence it will result that you live in accord with each other, that you atone for the offences (you have committed), and that you keep the rules of discipline before your eyes.'[8]

The form for the ceremony is: 'I pronounce my *Pavāraṇā*, friends, before you, by what has been seen, or by what has been heard, or by what has been suspected; may you speak to me, sirs, out of compassion towards me: if I see (an offence), I will atone for it.'[9]

4. Kaṭhina.—Immediately after the *Pavāraṇā* there followed a distribution of robes, which believers offered to the fraternity, to the *bhikkhus* composing the *Saṅgha*. The ceremonies are detailed in the seventh Khandhaka of the *Mahāvagga*.[10] The distribution commences with the *Kaṭhinatthāra; atthāra*, 'spreading out,' not being here used literally, for spreading out on the ground or otherwise, but in a secondary, juristic sense. The term is translated according to context, sometimes by 'spreading out,' sometimes by 'ceremony,' and sometimes by 'dedication.'[11]

5. The seasons.—At the time of his ordination each priest received from the master of the ceremonies, *kammachāri*, five ordinances, the second being 'the seasons.' In ancient India the ritual year was divided into three four-monthly periods, the three terms being celebrated with sacrifices, on the full moon day of Phālguna, of Āṣādha, and of Kārttika; or, in each case, one month later, as described above. These three sacrificial festivals inaugurated summer, the rainy season, and winter. The Buddhists retained this division of the year, and celebrated the terms, but, of course, not with sacrificial rites. During the first period the priests were directed to reside at the roots of trees, to have the advantage of silent and profound meditation; during the second to keep *Vassa*; and during the third to occupy *paṇṇasālās* (huts of leaves and branches) for mutual instruction and for reading the *bhāṇa* to the people.[12]

6. Saṅgitas. — Convocations of priests were directed to be held frequently. The Pāli word is from a root which signifies 'to sing,' or 'to sound,' as Indians do when they read sacred books. From this it appears that the object of these assemblies was to read the *bhāṇa* to each other, but particularly to read and expound the *Vinaya* books.

1 *SBE* xiii. 280 ff.
2 *Ib.* p. 268.
3 *Ib.* p. 296.
4 *Ib.* p. 271.
5 *Ib.* p. 260 f.
6 *Ib.* p. 243.
7 *Dhammika Sutta*, p. 27.
8 Rhys Davids, 141.
9 Kern, 99.
10 Rhys Davids, 57 f.; Monier-Williams, 427.
11 *SBE* xiii. 298 f.
12 *Ib.* p. 299.
13 *Ib.* pp. 299, 300.
14 *Ib.* p. 300.
15 *Ib.* pp. 298–324.
16 *Ib.* p. 301.

1 *SBE* xiii. 301.
2 *Ib.* p. 303.
3 *Ib.* pp. 305–310.
4 *Ib.* pp. 312–317.
5 Kern, 99–101.
6 *SBE* xiii. 331.
7 *Ib.* pp. 325–355.
8 *Ib.* p. 328.
9 *Ib.* p. 333.
10 *SBE* xvii. 146–170.
11 *Ib.* p. 148.
12 *Karmawākya, the Ritual of the Buddhist Priesthood*, tr. B. Clough, 1831.

See also the 'Chinese,' 'Nepalese,' 'Siamese,' and 'Tibetan' sections of FESTIVALS AND FASTS.

LITERATURE.—This has been cited in the article.

J. H. BATESON.

FESTIVALS AND FASTS (Celtic).—**1. The division of the Celtic year.**—The division of the Celtic year and the position of its festivals were originally governed by agricultural processes. Probably at first the year was divided into two unequal parts, summer and winter. Later came the astronomical cycles—at first lunar (Plin. xvi. 95), then, as a result of the influence of the Roman calendar, solar. Two important facts must be borne in mind: (1) that, in Celtic belief, night preceded day, and that, in early Celtic literature, 'night' usually means a night and a day, with the result that every festival began on the previous night (Cæsar, *de Bell. Gall.* vi. 18; Loth, *RCel* xxv. 116); (2) that the year began with winter—probably about mid-November, though later the winter festival began on November eve. When we first become acquainted with the Celtic calendar from Irish texts, we find a two-fold division—each half being again subdivided. The winter half (*geimhredh*) began with November on Samhain eve, *i.e.* Oct. 31, and was subdivided into two parts, the second beginning on Feb. 1; the summer half (*samhradh*) began with May and the Beltane feast, and also had its subdivision, its second portion beginning with Lugnasad on Aug. 1 (O'Donovan, *Book of Rights*, Dublin, 1847, p. lii f.). There were thus four quarters, but these do not correspond to those beginning with the solstices and equinoxes. They begin each with a feast, three of which—Samhain, Beltane, and Lugnasad—can easily be traced. The February feast is now replaced by St. Bridget's day (Feb. 1): its pagan predecessor has left scant traces. It is unlikely that this definite subdivision existed in earlier times, as, indeed, the shifting of Samhain from mid- to 1st November suggests—in the Isle of Man it is still held on Nov. 12 (*FL* ii. [1891] 308)—and the arrangement is doubtless due to the analogy of the Roman calendar. But the influence of this calendar had the further effect of displacing some of the festivals. Thus, in Gaul, much of the ritual of Samhain was transferred to the calends of January, while there was a tendency to celebrate Midsummer day instead of Beltane as the summer feast, both being found with similar ritual over the Celtic area, and they are evidently twin halves of one festival. The influence of the Christian calendar, with its lists of feasts and saints' days, must also be taken into account, some of the ritual of the earlier pagan festivals now occurring as survivals on holy days within the range of the pagan festival periods. All these festivals being mainly connected with agriculture, magic as well as religion had its place in the ritual, the object of the magical acts being to promote fertility and to aid the power of the divinities or spirits of fertility.

2. Samhain (perhaps from *sam*, 'summer,' and *fuin*, 'sunset' or 'end' [Windisch-Stokes, *Ir. Texte*, Leipzig, 1880 ff., i. 757], though Stokes [*Urkelt. Sprachschatz*, Göttingen, 1894, p. 293] gives to **samani-* the meaning of 'assembly'), as a festival of the beginning of winter when blight and death were assuming their reign, naturally took account of that fact, and its ritual was intended to assist the powers of growth in their conflict with winter's death. But it had other aspects also, and a complete understanding of the festival can be arrived at only by studying early descriptions of the ritual or actual folk-survivals. With the growth of Celtic religion this feast seems to have gathered up into itself the ritual of certain lesser festivals. It is a festival of beginnings, like the New Year festivals of all primitive folk. Its ritual suggests also the festival of earlier pastoral times, when the flocks and herds were regarded as themselves divine animals. It is also a harvest festival, as is Lugnasad in August; and, though harvest would be over before mid-November, some of the ritual may have been transferred to that date, especially if it had been associated with threshing rather than with the harvest-field. With the coming of Christianity and the adoption of the Roman calendar, the ritual of the festival was once more scattered over the other sacred days in winter.

(1) As a festival of beginnings, some of the ritual had reference to that fact. All fires having been extinguished, new fire was brought from the sacred bonfire (Keating, *Hist.*, Lond. 1866, pp. 125, 300), itself kindled probably by friction. Possibly the blazing Yule-log brought to the hearth at Christmas was originally derived from the Samhain rites, by being dislocated from them as Christmas festivities became more prominent. Merriment and feasting characterize tbe festival in Ireland (Windisch-Stokes, i. 205; d'Arbois, ii. 5), and this may also be traced in the Scots Hallowe'en customs. In other words, it was an orgiastic feast; this is clearly seen from the licentious customs of the calends in Gaul, denounced by the Church over a long period. Such licence always characterizes a festival of beginnings, when the evils of the past year are being ritually got rid of by various means. Rites of divination, forecasting the lives of the inquirers during the coming year, were also in evidence. The most common rite was for each person to throw a stone into the bonfire which was kindled at Samhain. Its position next morning indicated the fate of its owner (Brand, *Pop. Ant.*, London, 1899, i. 390; *Stat. Acc.* xi. 621). Perhaps in earlier times this rite was a casting of lots to obtain a human victim, while the memory of the slaying was long after transformed into a presage of death or misfortune within the year. Other rites of divination, such as those described in Burns' *Hallowe'en*, had an erotic character (Hazlitt, *Dict. of Faiths and Folklore*, London, 1905, pp. 297 f., 340).

(2) The lack of fodder led to the slaughter of cattle at this time, or rather at a date corresponding with Martinmas, which points to the earlier date of the festival in mid-November. This slaughter, like that of the Scandinavian 'Blót-mónath,' was sacrificial in character, and was followed by a feast on some of the animals. Within recent times in Ireland it was customary to offer one of the animals to St. Martin, the successor of some pagan animal-divinity in anthropomorphic form, and ill-luck followed the neglect of this rite (Curtin, *Tales of the Fairies*, Dublin, 1895, p. 72). This semi-religious slaughter dates back to the age when the animals were themselves divine. In this pastoral stage, perhaps associated with totemism, the annual slaying would be limited to one animal in each group; and, the animal being divine, the feast on its flesh was sacramental. If the slaughter had been more general from the first (as it certainly became in later times), it would be accompanied with rites intended to propitiate the divine animals, as in analogous cases elsewhere; but the festival would still be sacramental. The sacramental eating, the divinity of the animal, the gradual anthropomorphic tendency to give the animal-god a human form, and the transference of his personality to a later Christian saint, may be seen in the Irish legend of St. Martin (already associated with the slaying), which tells how he was cut up and eaten in the form of an ox (*RCel* vi. [1884] 254). Possibly the representation of the corn-spirit in animal form may have blended with the divinity of the animals slain at Samhain. Again, in Gaul, at the calends, as formerly at

Samhain, men wore the heads and skins of slaughtered animals in processions, doubtless in order to assimilate themselves further to the animal divinities by contact, as they had already done by eating. This custom was vigorously attacked by Church Councils and by individual preachers (see catena of passages in Chambers, *Mediæval Stage*, Oxford, 1903, App. N ; *PL* xxxix. 2001). In certain recent survivals in the Hebrides a youth dressed in a cow's hide paraded the village and brought a blessing to each house where a person or animal inhaled the fumes of a piece of burning hide carried by him (Chambers, *Pop. Rhymes*, Edin. 1847, p. 297). This custom, which may have taken the place of the carrying of the slain animal in procession, resembles the rite of hunting the wren (see art. ANIMALS, in vol. i. p. 532[b]), which occurred at Christmas. But this, like the animal masquerades, may have been associated with Samhain in earlier times. Masquerading is still common among young people on Samhain in the Highlands, and in some parts of Britain dressing in animal disguise was associated with an autumn date (Hutchinson, *View of Northumberland*, Newcastle, 1778, ii. 45 ; Thomas, *RHR* xxxviii. [1898] 334).

(3) The agricultural aspect of the feast is seen first of all in the bonfire which was (and still is in Celtic and rural districts) lit on Samhain eve. The analogy of the Beltane and Midsummer fires shows that it was intended as a fire-charm to aid the power of the sun by virtue of mimetic magic, while, at the same time, this symbol was virtually the thing symbolized and conveyed its benefits. Hence the new fire was lit from the divine fire, blazing faggots were carried through the village, and the people jumped through the fire in order to be purified and strengthened by contact with the divinity. Numerous references show that various evil powers (perhaps blight and death), represented as demoniac beings or witches, were especially rampant on Samhain eve (*RCel* x. [1889] 214, 225, xxiv. [1903] 172 ; Joyce, *Soc. Hist. of Anc. Ireland*, 1903, ii. 556 ; O'Grady, *Silva Gadelica*, London, 1892, ii. 374 ; *Cymmrodor*. vi. 176), and one of these references shows that they were particularly hostile to the crops and animals. They may have been conceived as combating the powers of light and growth, which were thus assisted by the bonfire. There are also traces of a traditional belief that sacrifice was offered to them. In Welsh folklore the people rushed off as soon as the fire was extinguished, to escape from the 'black sow' who captured the hindmost—perhaps a reminiscence of sacrifice (Rhys, *Celtic Folklore*, Oxford, 1901, i. 225), and early Irish literature refers to the tax of the year's corn and milk, and of two-thirds of the children born within the year, to the evil Fomorians on Samhain eve. Keating (*Hist.* 300) also speaks of a sacrifice to the gods, burned in the fire on Samhain eve. But, though the powers of blight may have been propitiated, it is not unlikely that the primitive slaying of a human representative of the corn-spirit or of some divinity of growth was later conceived as such a propitiatory sacrifice. The process of thought is difficult to follow, but it may have seemed natural that, since the divine fire acted magically upon the life of the sun, it would act also upon the power of the god or spirit who was consumed in it in human form. By dying, the divine life was renewed and strengthened (see Frazer, *Adonis*, 1906, p. 100). At the same time we must not overlook the fact that the powers of growth may themselves have come to be regarded as evil in Christian times, just as the corn-spirit was sometimes given a formidable aspect. The 'black sow' in the Welsh instance may have been an earlier animal embodiment of the corn-spirit, which had come to be looked upon as more or less demoniac. At all events, the slaying of a human representative of the corn-spirit can hardly be kept apart from the victim slain at Samhain, more especially as harvest is late in several Celtic regions ; while, to judge by folk-custom, the slaying was frequently connected with the threshing of the grain, rather than with the harvest-field (Mannhardt, *Myth. Forsch.*, Strassburg, 1884, p. 333 ff.). The slaying of the corn-spirit was probably derived from the similar slaying of the tree-spirit at the summer feast. The corn-spirit, like the latter, had also various embodiments—the last sheaf, an animal, or a human being ; and all of these had powers both of quickening and of strengthening the fruits of the earth, cattle, and women, while there can be little doubt that part of the flesh was also eaten sacramentally (Mannhardt, 317 f. ; Frazer, *GB*[2] ii. 288). Possibly, too, as the representative of the tree-spirit had once been a priest-king, so he who represented the corn-spirit may have been called a king also. This would account for the choosing of a mock-king, *e.g.* the king of the bean, at winter festivals (Hazlitt, 35 ; Chambers, *Book of Days*, Edin. 1863, i. 62). This and the presence of effigies of saints, which were carried in procession, their clothes distributed, and then finally burned (Chambers, ii. 492 ; Hazlitt, 131), form survivals, though somewhat apart from the date of Samhain, which are doubtless derived from the ritual of the corn-spirit, or perhaps that of the divine animal associated in earlier times with it. But, since the last sheaf representing the corn-spirit is usually called by some female name, 'the Maiden,' 'the Mother,' etc., this shows that the corn-spirit had originally been conceived as female—doubtless as a result of the fact that agricultural rites were first in the hands of women ; while in survivals ultimately derived from Samhain rites a 'queen' or 'Yule's wife' is in evidence (Hazlitt, 97 ; Davies, *Mun. Records of York*, London, 1834, p. 270). With this we may also connect the fact that men disguised themselves as women at the calends. The increased power of the fairies—in Ireland the successors of gods of growth and fertility—on Samhain eve is easily explicable by the nature of the festivals, though they may have been sometimes confused with the demoniac powers. The vaguer corn-spirits doubtless became greater and more anthropomorphic divinities, and the slaying of one representative may have been changed to the slaughter of several victims, where death was also considered beneficial to vegetation. A similar evolution occurred in connexion with the vegetation spirit, while a holocaust of victims took the place of his representative. Doubtless among the rural people themselves the vaguer spirits and the older ritual still prevailed with little change. This substitution of several victims for one would account for the so-called sacrifice to the Fomorians, if they were aboriginal gods of fertility, and for the sacrificial cult of Cromm Cruaich, connected in one place with Samhain (see CELTS, V. 2). The gods of growth, evolved from these vaguer spirits, may well have been conceived as in conflict with powers of blight and death at this time, and this may have been ritually represented by a combat. The story of the battle of Magtured might then be regarded as based on a myth which told of this conflict, and which showed that, in spite of the apparent blight in Nature, the powers of growth could not be finally vanquished, but were victorious, like the Tuatha Dé Danann, at this battle.

(4) A yearly festival of the dead took place on Samhain eve at the beginning of winter, when the powers of growth were at their weakest, and when possibly a representative of the corn-spirit was slain. Hence this festival, like that of Lugna-

sad, may have been associated with the spirits of such victims. Or a festival associated with dying powers would easily become a feast of the dead generally, while the dead themselves were connected with the under-world god of fertility. In Scandinavia the dead have female spirit-guardians, *fylgjur*, identified with the *dísir*, also females, living in the hollow hills and apparently earth-goddesses. The Celtic analogy is found in the Matres, also earth-goddesses. Christmas Eve was called *Módraniht*, or 'Mothers' Night' (Bede, *de Temp. Rat.* 15); and, as many aspects of the winter festival were dislocated and transferred to Christmas and at the same time christianized, it is possible that Samhain eve had, in pagan times, been the Mothers' Night. Earth-goddesses probably preceded an earth-god, and hence they received the dead into their keeping before the Celtic Dispater did so. Thus the season of earth's decay was also the time at which her children, the dead, were commemorated (see EARTH). Samhain eve would thus correspond to the Scandinavian *Dísablót* held about this time—a festival of the dead and the *dísir* (Vigfusson-Powell, *Corp. Poet. Bor.*, Oxford, 1883, i. 419). This Celtic festival has left survivals in modern folk-custom. In Ireland all the dead come out of their graves and visit the houses, where a good fire is left for them (Curtin, *Tales*, 157; *FL* iv. [1893] 359). The same belief and custom obtain in Brittany (Le Braz, *La Légende de la mort*[2], Paris, 1902, ii. 115). Thus the festival of the dead brings us back to the hearth, and it is not unlikely that the Yule-log was originally associated with Samhain, when new fire was kindled on the hearth, and that the libations poured on it were intended for the dead. The place of the two Christian feasts of All Saints and All Souls on Nov. 1 and 2 (the time of Samhain) remains to be explained. The first, of earlier origin, was doubtless intended to supplant the pagan festival of the dead. As it failed to do so, a Christian feast of all the dead was then originated to neutralize existing pagan rites (Frazer, *Adonis*, 253 ff.). In this it only partially succeeded, but it is perhaps due to Christian influences that the more friendly aspect of the dead has been largely forgotten, and that they are associated in popular belief with demons, witches, etc., whose power is great on Samhain eve, and who are perhaps the representatives of the old power of blight and death.

3. Beltane and Midsummer.—These two festivals being twin halves of one early summer festival, the object of which was to promote fertility in field, fold, and house, the ritual acts of both may be considered together.

The word *Beltane* was already a puzzle to early Irish philologists, who explain it as meaning (1) *bil tene*, a goodly fire, or (2) *bel dine*, because the newly-born cattle (*dine*) were offered to a god Bel (Cormac, in Stokes, *Three Irish Glossaries*, London, 1862, p. 9, *s.v.* 'Bel, Beltaine'; *Arch. Rev.* i. [1888] 232; cf. Joyce, *Irish Names of Places*[4], Dublin, 1901, i. 278; *RCel* xxv. [1904] 86). The latter derivation is followed by those who connect a Celtic god Bel or Belus with a borrowed Semitic Baal. No such god is known, however, unless Belenos, Belisama, be connected with Beltane, as some suppose. D'Arbois (ii. 243) postulates a god of death, Beltene, deriving the word from **beltu*, 'to die,' and makes the festival his day. But no such god is known, and the feast was one of life and growth, not of death. Stokes (*Three Irish Glossaries*, xxxv.) divides the word into **Belt -aine*, while its root is perhaps the same as that of the Lith. *báltas*, 'white,' and the *-aine* is a termination as in *sechtmaine*, 'week.' In his *Urkelt. Sprachschatz*, 125, 164, he shows, however, that its primitive form was the composite **belo-te<p>niā*, from **belo-s*, 'clear' or 'shining,' the root of the divine name Belenos, and *te<p>nos*, 'fire' (O. Ir. *ten*). Hence *Beltane* would have some such meaning as 'bright fire.'

As at Samhain, the chief ritual act was the kindling of a bonfire by a spark from flint, or by friction from a rotating wheel (need-fire), frequently after the fires of the district had been extinguished. Cattle were driven through the fire or between two fires lit, as Cormac says, by Druids with incantations. By this means, viz. contact with the divine fire, they were preserved from disease. Survivals show that the festival was communal, since all the inhabitants contributed to the fire, while its religious side is seen in the fact that, within recent times, there was a service in church and a procession, and mayor and priest attended the fire. They represented the earlier local chief and pagan priest. The fire was sometimes lit round a tree, representing the vegetation spirit, or round a pole covered with greenery (the Maypole of later survivals); or a tree was cut and thrown into the fire (Hone, *Every-Day Book*, London, 1838, i. 849, ii. 595; Joyce, i. 216; *RCel* iv. [1879] 193). The people, probably clad in leaves in order to assimilate themselves to the vegetation spirit, danced sunwise round the fire to the accompaniment of songs or chants. The dance, imitating the course of the sun, probably was intended to assist it, for the livelier the dance the better would be the harvest. The fire being divine, the people crept through it to avoid disease and ill-luck, to ensure prosperity, or to remove barrenness. They ran through the fields with burning brands, or rolled blazing wheels over them, or sprinkled ashes from the fire upon them, or preserved charred brands till the following year. The tree itself was borne through the fields before being burned. The houses of the folk were decked with green boughs. All these rites had one end, viz. to ensure fertility through contact with the divine fire or the spirit of vegetation. As in the Samhain ceremonies, the fire represented and aided the sun; and, consequently, contact with the fire was equivalent to contact with the divine sun. Animals were sacrificed, probably as representatives of the spirit of vegetation or fertility. Among these was the horse, as is seen by Irish folk-survivals in which a horse's skull and bones were placed in the fire (Hone, ii. 595), or a man wearing a horse's head and representing all cattle rushed through the fire (Granger, *Worship of Romans*, London, 1895, p. 113 f.; for a legend of a speaking horse coming out of a mound at Midsummer eve and giving oracles, see Kennedy, *Legendary Fictions of the Irish Celts*, 1866, p. 135). Some of the flesh may have been eaten sacramentally, and some of it placed on the fields to fertilize them. In French Midsummer survivals, animals were burned, sometimes being enclosed in osier baskets (Bertrand, *Rel. des Gaulois*, Paris, 1897, p. 407; Gaidoz, *Esquisse de mythol. gauloise*, Paris, 1879, p. 21). Human victims seem also to have been burned in the fire, or otherwise slain. Thus, in a Perthshire survival, he who received a blackened portion of a cake, the pieces of which were drawn by lot, was called 'the Beltane carline' or 'devoted,' and a pretence was made of throwing him into the fire, and he was spoken of as dead (*Stat. Acc.* xi. 620); while in France he who stumbled in leaping through the fire was considered unlucky and devoted to the *fadets*, or spirits (Bertrand, 119). In earlier times such persons would be sacrificed. In other places gigantic effigies made of osier were carried in procession or burned (Mannhardt, *Baumkultus*, Berlin, 1875, pp. 514, 523).

Can the sacrifices to which these survivals bear witness be connected with the periodic Celtic sacrifices for fertility referred to by Cæsar, Strabo, and Diodorus, all perhaps borrowing from Posidonius, as Mannhardt (p. 532), followed by Frazer (*GB*[2] iii. 319), has suggested? Human victims or animals were enclosed in large osier images at a quinquennial or yearly festival and consumed by fire. The victims were criminals or prisoners of war, the former usually guilty of murder; and Strabo (iv. 4. 4) says that the greater the number of murders the greater was the fertility of the land, probably meaning that where there were many murders there would be a larger available number of criminal victims for the sacrifice. In the osier images and in the animal victims of late survivals, we may trace a connexion with these rites, while the enclosing of the victims in osier cages may be connected with the custom of decking a person in greenery at the summer festival. In this case the person is a representative of the spirit of vegetation. The Celtic holocausts were in origin more than sacrificial; they had originated in the custom of slaying annually one man who was an incarnation of the vegetation-spirit. Originally this man had been a priest-king who had all the powers of the vegetation spirit, but in later times a surrogate took his place and was slain, though regarded for the time as a god. Gradually this slaying was looked upon as a sacrifice; hence it would naturally be thought that the benefits of the rite would be greater if the number of victims was increased. This would account for those great periodic holocausts, though elsewhere, as modern survivals show, the older rite must have continued as it was. The victim was burned in the fire—a sun-charm—and thus vegetation received beneficial effects from the victim himself and also from the fire in which he was consumed. At first the vegetation-spirit had been a tree-spirit which had power over growth, fertility, and fruitfulness (*GB*² i. 188 ff.). Hence a tree had a conspicuous place in the summer festival, and it had all the virtues of the spirit which it embodied. It was carried in procession, imparting these virtues to fields and houses; branches were placed over houses to obtain them by contact, the tree was burned as a method of slaying the spirit, or it was set up in the village for a year, so that its presence might bestow blessing, and was then burned at the next festival (Mannhardt, 177; *GB*² i. 203; Brand, *Pop. Ant.* i. 222 and *passim*; Hone, ii. 595). Among the Celts, with whom the oak was specially sacred, that tree may have been used in the ritual, since it, above all, represented the spirit of growth and vegetation. Here it is natural to connect the Druids' rite of culling the mistletoe with the burning of the sacred tree. Pliny (*HN* xvi. 249 ff.) says that it was cut on the sixth day of the moon, though he does not specify the time of the year; but magical plants, including mistletoe, are frequently gathered on Midsummer eve in order to be effective, and it is far from certain that he is reporting all that the rite betokened. It may well have been that the mistletoe (called in Gaelic *sugh an daraich*, 'sap of the oak') was culled because it was held to represent the life of the tree, which could not be cut down and burned till its life was secured, in accordance with a wide-spread belief that the soul or life of man or god can be placed outside himself for safety and that he will die if any one secures it (MacCulloch, *CF*, London, 1905, ch. 5). But, as survivals, in which a human effigy and a tree are burned together, show, a human representative of the vegetation-spirit was brought into close connexion with the tree and was also slain (Mannhardt, 515 ff.). The vegetation spirit was given, now a theriomorphic, now an anthropomorphic form—hence it could be represented by beast or man, but in either case the tree itself remained as a constant factor in the ritual. Hence the doubling of the tree-spirit's incarnation. Thus the gathering of the mistletoe secured at once the life of the tree and that of the beast or man who was also slain. Possibly the oxen slain at the mistletoe rite may have been theriomorphic embodiments of the vegetation-spirit, though, as a rule, a human embodiment was found; but at this time human sacrifice had been prohibited in Gaul. Frazer has, therefore, suggested that the myth of Balder slain by the mistletoe was derived from actual ritual in which the mistletoe was plucked before the human incarnation of the vegetation-spirit could be slain (*GB*² iii. 345). Thus in the primitive Celtic summer ritual, the spirit or god of vegetation, the tree, and the animal or human victim were one; their life was in the mistletoe; they could not be slain until it was plucked. This done, they were burned in the fire which represented the sun, the visible power of life and growth. Hence both fire and slain god had a fertilizing power. Flames, smoke, burning brand, ashes, and pieces of the victim aided whatever they touched, purifying, strengthening, fertilizing. Hence people leapt through the fire, or passed their cattle through it, or believed that the fire or smoke fertilized their fields, or carried brands through them, or sprinkled them with ashes, or buried part of the victim in them, or preserved the brands in their houses. Probably part of the victim was eaten sacramentally—a rite to which Pliny may refer when he speaks of the Celtic belief that to eat human flesh was considered most wholesome (*HN* xxx. 1). The virtue of fire and victim was magico-sacramental. Through them, men, animals, and vegetation were brought into touch with the divine spirit. And in like manner fire and slain victim reacted beneficially upon the gods or spirits whom they represented, the fire upon the sun, the dying god upon the god who lived again. From such vegetation-spirits the greater Celtic gods of growth were probably evolved.

The blazing wheel, rolled down a slope or through the fields, imitated the progress of the sun, assisting it and also benefiting the crops. Such an imitation of the sun's motion is found in other rites, *e.g.* circumambulating house, cattle, or crops with fire in the direction of the sun (*deiseil*), with the same intention of benefit to them. Here, too, we see the origin of the common Celtic practice of walking *deiseil* round some object on any important occasion. Originating in the idea that to imitate the action of the sun is beneficial, it was held that to do so brought good luck and repelled evil influences. Thus in the Cúchulainn cycle, when Medb is setting out for the war, her charioteer makes her chariot describe a right-hand turn (*deiseil*) to repel evil omens (*Leabhar na hUidhre*, 55). In late survivals the *deiseil* action occurs in manifold forms. By a further process of thought, it was believed that the blazing wheel in its course carried off evils from the community, just as, in all probability, evils were laid on the slain divine representative (Hone, i. 846; Hazlitt, ii. 346), whether animal or human (see CIRCUMAMBULATION, PRAYER WHEELS).

Thus the two chief rites of the Beltane and Midsummer festivals, as also those of Samhain, were mutually complementary. The vegetation-spirit, slain as tree, animal, or man, died that he might live, and his flesh quickened the energies of earth and man. So, too, the blazing fire assisted the life of the powers of light and growth embodied in the sun, and in doing so aided both man and beast and the earth and vegetation. All these rites survived with little change into Christian times and were vigorously combated by the Church (d'Achéry, *Spicil.*, Paris, 1655–67, v. 216). Again, by associating the pagan Midsummer feast with the festival of St. John Baptist, or the pagan rites with the services and ritual of the Church, an attempt was made to modify their sheer paganism. But in neither case was it effectually stifled.

It was usual to roll 'Beltane cakes' down a slope—again in evident imitation of the sun's action; but in some cases the luck of the owner of the cake was denoted by its remaining whole or breaking—if it broke he would die within the year. Perhaps we may trace here an earlier selection of a victim by lot, as in the case of the lot by the blackened fragment of cake. In another survival, pieces of such a cake were given to unnamed friendly powers and to animals hostile to the flocks (Pennant, *Tour in Scotland*, London, 1774, i. 97). If this was done in the primitive pagan rite, there was a propitiation of beneficent and hostile powers—an example of the double outlook of all primitive religion. But probably in their earliest use the cakes were sacramental in character, and eaten by the folk, as in similar Teutonic instances (Grimm, *Teut. Myth.*, 1880–88, iii. 1239). As moisture was necessary for the growth of the crops, magical methods of obtaining it were in use at both the festivals. Sacred wells were visited, and rain charms performed with their waters. Hence such wells were deemed to be specially efficacious in other ways at these times, and people visited them for healing and other purposes (Hazlitt, i. 38, ii. 340; *New Stat. Acc.*, *Wigtown*, 1834–44, p. 208). The customs of bathing in May dew and bathing in a river at Midsummer were originally connected with the magical methods of producing moisture. There was also a dramatic representation of the conflict between the powers of growth and those of blight, or between summer and winter, with the victory of the former at this period. Traces of this ritual combat are found all over Europe, and notably so in the combat of the forces of the Queen of May with those of the Queen of Winter on Laa-Boaldyn (Beltane) in the Isle of Man (*GB*² ii. 99; Grimm, ii. 765; Moore, *Folk-lore of Isle of Man*, London, 1891, p. 112). These combats had doubtless the intention of aiding the actual powers of growth; and certain myths, *e.g.* that of the Tuatha Dé Danann vanquishing the Firbolgs on May-day, and, in Wales, that of the fight of Gwythur with Gwyn for the possession of Creidylad, probably were based upon the ritual. The presence of the May-king and May-queen in popular survivals, and the fact that their pagan predecessors were incarnations of male and female spirits of fertility or vegetation, suggest that the 'sacred marriage' was also part of the summer ritual. In world-wide agricultural rites the symbols or actual human representatives of these spirits or divinities were united temporarily, the object of the union being to promote the fertility of the soil through mimetic magic (*GB*² ii. 205). Probably a considerable amount of general sexual licence for the same magical end occurred at the same time.

4. Female cults of fertility.—At the winter and summer festivals a divine victim—the king-priest or his surrogate—was slain, in order to aid the processes of growth and fertility. But, as Celtic divinities and spirits were once mainly female, and as the processes of agriculture were once in the hands of women, the rites out of which these elaborate festivals sprang were doubtless also at one time confined to them. The divine victim would then be a female—the priestess or her surrogate—representing a female divine being.

Certain survivals point in this direction. The slaying of a female representative of the spirit is suggested in the name *cailleach bealtine*, 'Beltane carline' or 'old woman,' applied to the devoted person in the Highland survivals (see above, 840[b]). Though this person was a male, the name shows that in earlier times the victim was a woman. In winter festivals derived from Samhain, men masqueraded as women (Chambers, *Med. Stage*, ii. App. N); in local observances of St. Catherine's Day, Nov. 25, a 'queen' was chosen by girls; 'Yule's wife' as well as 'Yule' had her place at the Christmas pageants (Hazlitt, i. 97; Davies, *Mun. Rec. of York*, 270). Again, at the summer festival, the May-queen had frequently in survivals a more prominent place than the May-king. In both cases such 'queens' were the incarnations of a female spirit of fertility, an earth-goddess or vegetation-spirit, and were slain by the women who practised the cult. And if, as is probable, the witch orgies are remains of primitive female cults, the special activity of witches on Beltane eve, especially on hills which were formerly the site of worship (Grimm, iii. 1051), may also point in this direction. Later, gods took the place of goddesses, priests of priestesses, and male victims were accordingly slain. But sporadically the female cults probably still held their ground. This may explain some classical notices of female worship on Celtic ground. Strabo (iv. 4. 6) mentions sacrifices paid to native goddesses, whom he calls 'Demeter and Kore,' on an island near Britain. The cult resembled that of the chthonian goddess at Samothrace, *i.e.* it was a cult of fertility in which female divinities were worshipped. These divinities may still be represented in the sheaves of corn called the Old Woman and the Maiden, the corn-spirits of the past and the future year. The seed of the latter was mixed with next year's seed-corn, that the life of the goddess might pass into the seed sown (Frazer, *GB*[2] ii. 171 ff.). Probably the goddesses were once represented by actual personages, whose blood was used to fertilize the seed-corn. Such a rite may underlie Strabo's account of the Namnite women who worshipped Dionysus on an island at the mouth of the Loire, which no man might visit (iv. 4. 6). Yearly they unroofed the temple and the same day re-roofed it, each woman bearing a supply of materials; but she who dropped her load (and this always happened) was torn in pieces and her remains carried round the temple with wild cries. Dionysius Periegetes (v. 570) says the mysteries took place at night in honour of earth-goddesses, with a great clamour, and that the women were crowned with ivy. The whole reference is obscure, but it might be possible to connect it with rites of fertility, if the flesh of the victim was carried to the mainland and there used to fertilize the soil or the seed-corn. This assumes that she was slain as the incarnation of divinity. Perhaps Strabo was mistaken in saying that a god was worshipped; the cult may have been that of a goddess, as Dionysius reports. Another cult is reported by Pliny (xxii. 1) as occurring among the Britons. In it nude women stained with woad took part. This ritual, which may be connected with that of which the Lady Godiva procession is a survival (Hartland, *Science of Fairy Tales*, London, 1891, p. 84 ff.), is again suggestive of agricultural magic, in which nudity is essential to fertility. The same purpose is effected by dressing in foliage, thus effectively personating the spirit of vegetation, and this may explain why the Namnite women were crowned with ivy, and also why, as Diodorus reports (xxxi. 13 [ed. Dindorf, Paris, 1842, ii. 499]), sacrificial victims were crowned with leaves. The latter custom might be an extension of the more primitive one. Just as sporadically the cults of women held their ground, so earlier goddesses of fertility sometimes remained even after the divinities or spirits of fertility and growth, of corn and vegetation, had been conceived as male. The image of a goddess, called by St. Gregory of Tours Berecyntia (probably a native goddess [? Brigindu] assimilated to Cybele under this name), was borne through the fields and vineyards, on her festival and in time of scarcity, while the worshippers sang and danced before it (*PG* v. 1463; Greg. Tours, *de Glor. Conf.* 77; Sul. Sev. *Vita S. Mart.* 9). Such a lustration of the fields with an image in order to fertilize them is found in many regions (cf. the procession of the Germanic Nerthus [Tac. *Germ.* 40]), and we have already seen that the tree representing the vegetation-spirit was similarly borne through the fields, and probably the image has here replaced such a divine tree. The practice continued even among Celtic religious communities, either with the image of a saint or with his relics (Adamnan, *Vita Columb.* ii. 45). The washing of the image after the lustration—probably as a rain-charm—is not referred to in the local Gaulish instance, but was commonly used elsewhere; hence it may be assumed that it occurred, since on Celtic ground the washing of images of saints for that purpose frequently took place.

5. Lugnasad.—The first day of August, or more probably in earlier times some day in mid-August, occurring midway between Beltane and Samhain, was observed as a festival. It began the autumn or harvest-season, and was probably itself a harvest festival associated with the offering of firstfruits, though it is doubtful whether, in Britain and Ireland at least, the harvest would be ingathered by August 1. This points to mid-August as the earlier date of the festival, while, as we have seen, part of the ritual of the harvest festival passed to the Samhain feast. One name of the day, *Brón Trogain*, is explained as 'the earth is afflicted *or* under fruit,' *Trogan* being a name for the earth ('Wooing of Emer,' *Arch. Rev.* i. 232; O'Donovan, liii.). The day was dedicated among the Celts, as the corresponding Lammas among the Anglo-Saxons, to a sacrifice of the fruits of the soil (Vallancey, quoted by Hone, i. 1063). But the day was associated with the god Lug; hence its Irish name, *Lúgnasad*, in Scots Gaelic *Lùnasdal*, in Manx *Laa-Lhuanys*. Cormac (p. 99) explains Lugnasad as 'a festival or game of Lug mac Eithlenn, which was celebrated by him in the beginning of autumn.' But the Rennes Dindsenchas (*RCel* xvi. [1895] 51) says that Lug's foster-mother Tailtiu was buried on that day, and that Lug directed an assembly and games to be convened then as a yearly memorial of her at her grave-mound. This may be a later explanation of the slaying of the corn-spirit in a human representative. In primitive times, when agriculture was in the hands of women, the victim would be a female, later euhemerized as Tailtiu, perhaps herself at one time regarded as the corn-goddess evolved from an earlier corn-spirit. In other parts of Ireland, as at Carman in Leinster, the festival was associated with the death of a woman Carman who had evil designs upon the corn of the Tuatha Dé Danann, but a variant made it commemorative of the death of a king, Carman (*RCel* xv. [1894] 313 f.). This may suggest different conceptions of the personality of the corn-divinity, now a goddess, now a god, the one having female, the other male representatives; while, in the case of the god, the male victim may have been regarded as a king, on the analogy of the representative of the spirit of vegetation. When the festival, as at Tailtiu, was further associated with Lug, it would be easy to connect the goddess Tailtiu with the god, in the relation of foster-mother, as the euhemerized myth sets forth. The association of Lug, probably a sun-god, with the festival is also suggestive of the victory of the powers of light and growth over those of blight, as evidenced by a plentiful harvest. The people rejoiced in presence of the victorious god. Bonfires may have been lit in honour or in aid of the sun-god, and the magical cult of the waters was also in evidence. Cattle were swum through a pool or river so that they might live through the year, and in recent times in the Isle of Man bottles were filled with the water of sacred wells (Vallancey, quoted by Hazlitt, ii. 340; Rhys, *Celtic Heathendom*, London, 1888, p. 422). Besides this agricultural aspect, the local assemblies at Lugnasad had also their social side. These assemblies were fairs at which horse-races took place—Lug being the introducer of such races (*Leabhar Laignech*, 10, 2)—while marriages were also arranged. Men may have been more inclined to enter upon wedlock when their garners promised to be full. But it is also possible that behind this lies an earlier promiscuous love-making as a result of the frenzied festival gladness, or with the object of magically assisting the fruitfulness of the soil. Possibly, too, the rite of the divine marriage was also a part of the festival proceedings. At all events there are hints that it was connected with Lug's marriage, though the texts explain this as his 'wedding the kingship' on the occasion of his being made king after the battle of Magtured (Rhys, 414)—a phrase which may be an allegorical method of stating what was ritually enacted, viz. the wedding of the divine king, the incarnation of Lug, who received the kingdom by virtue of his marriage with a daughter of the royal house, in accordance with the laws of female succession or the matriarchate. In another text this allegorical interpretation is more plainly seen, for here the kingdom or sovereignty of Erin belongs to an actual though mysterious queen who is found in a magic palace with Lug (O'Curry, *MS Mat.*, Dublin, 1861, p. 618). For this reason Rhys explains *nasad*, not as Cormac = 'festival,' but as 'a wedding,' the word perhaps having the same origin as Lat. *nexus* (*op. cit.* 415). The proper observance of Lugnasad, like that of the festival at Carman held on the same day, though not apparently in connexion with Lug, produced plenty of milk, grain, and fruit, as well as general prosperity and freedom from disease; but evil certainly followed any neglect of it. We cannot doubt that the seed of the last sheaf, representative of the corn-spirit, was preserved to mix with the next year's grain, in order to increase its fertility by contact with the divine cereal, while the cattle were made to eat straw for the same purpose; or that the human incarnation of the corn-spirit was slain, and his blood or flesh mixed with the grain for the same purpose, or eaten by the worshippers. To neglect this rite would cause a less bountiful harvest, and from this thought may have sprung the wider ideas about observance or neglect of the festival itself. Though Tailtiu is mentioned as the place where 'all Ireland' met to celebrate the feast, this is certainly an exaggerated way of describing many such central gatherings, since we know of others held, *e.g.*, at Carman and Cruachan. Probably the gathering of 'all Gaul' at Lugudunum, 'town of Lugus' (Lyons), may be similarly explained. In this case the gathering on August 1, originally in honour of Lugus and of the same nature as the insular Celtic Lugnasad, was held in honour of Augustus, and was called, after his name, the Feast of Augustus. This still survives in Welsh *Gwyl Awst*, the August, or, more probably, the Augustus festival, proving that the romanizing of the native feast had spread to Britain. Similarly the christianizing of the pagan offering of first-fruits has issued in the Lammas customs. But relics of the earlier pagan rites still mark the modern observance of the day.

6. These greater periodic Celtic festivals may be regarded as the final development of village rituals for fertility at certain times throughout the year, which were more or less liable to variation. The festivals concerned the anthropomorphic divinities of growth, and were apparently held as central gatherings. But side by side with them the older village rituals may have continued. How far the folk associated the latter with such anthropomorphic divinities is unknown, but they may simply have concerned themselves with the cult of the older spirits of fertility, of vegetation, of the corn. In any case, no strict line can be drawn between the festivals and the village rituals. Their central purpose was the same, though the festivals may have extended their scope; and what we know of the ritual of the festivals constantly recalls that of popular survivals of the village cults. The ruder aspects of such rituals have been held to be pre-Celtic in origin (Gomme, *Ethnology in Folklore*, London, 1892, p. 30 ff.). That the pre-Celtic peoples had such cults cannot be doubted, but everything goes to show that Celtic institutions had emerged out of a savage past, that much in the ritual of the Celts was rude and cruel, and that, if they accepted aboriginal cults, it was only because such cults were already familiar to themselves.

See also artt. CALENDAR (Celtic), CELTS.

LITERATURE.—J. Brand, *Obs. on the popular Antiquities of Great Britain*, London, 1870; A. Bertrand, *Rel. des Gaulois*, Paris, 1897; H. d'Arbois de Jubainville, *Le Cycle mythol. irlandais*, do. 1894; G. Dottin, *Manuel pour servir à l'étude de l'antiquité celtique*, do. 1906; J. Loth, 'L'année celtique,' *RCel* xxv. [1904] 113 ff.; J. A. MacCulloch, *Rel. of the Anc. Celts*, Edin. 1911; J. O'Donovan, ed. *Book of Rights*, Dublin, 1847; John Rhys, *Celtic Heathendom* (Hib. Lect. 1886), London, 1888 ([3]1898).

J. A. MACCULLOCH.

FESTIVALS AND FASTS (Chinese).—The Chinese work *Ts'ing-Kwei*, 'Regulations of the Priesthood,' contains instructions for the observance of all festivals and fasts throughout the year. They are [Jan. 1912] as follows:

1. National.—(1) The Emperor's birthday. The festival commences three days before and continues for three days after. It is called *Sheng-tsie*, 'sacred festival.' (2) The Empress's birthday. (3) The day of receiving an Imperial message at a monastery. (4) Four monthly feasts—at the new, and full moon, the 8th, and the 23rd days of the month. They are called *Kin-ming sï-chai*, 'the four feasts illustriously decreed.' (5) Anniversaries of Emperors' deaths, of the present dynasty only.

2. Celestial beings.—(1) Day of worshipping Devas. The authority for the observances rests on *Kin-Kwang-ming-king*, 'the bright sūtra of golden light.' (2) Eclipses of sun and moon, the celestial bodies being addressed, in the services, as Bodhisattvas (*q.v.*), and the power of Buddha evoked to deliver them. (3) Sacrifice to the moon on the 15th day of the 8th month, this being the moon's birthday. (4) Prayer for fine weather, to various Buddhas. (5) Prayer to Wei-to, protector of the Buddhist religion. If supplies at the monasteries fail, Wei-to is appealed to to replenish them. (6) Birthday of Wei-to, on the 3rd (or 13th) day of the 6th month. (7) Birthdays of the divine protectors of monasteries: (*a*) *Hwa-kwang*, on the 28th day of the 9th month; (*b*) *Lung-wang*, 'dragon-king'; (*c*) *Kwan-ti*, 'god of war,' on the 13th day of the 5th month, though the 24th day of the 6th month is the date in the national annals. (8) Birthdays of the kitchen-god, on the 24th day of the 6th month, the 3rd of the 8th, and the 24th of the 12th.

3. Buddhas and Bodhisattvas.—(1) Birthday of Mi-li Fo (Maitreya Buddha), 1st day of 1st month. (2) Anniversary of Śākyamuni's entrance into Nirvāṇa, 15th day of 2nd month. (3) Birthday of 'Kwan-shï yin p'u-sa,' or Avalokiteśvara (*q.v.*), 19th day of 2nd month. (4) Birthday of 'P'u-hien p'u-sa,' or Samantabhadra, a fictitious Buddha of northern Buddhism, 21st day of 2nd month. (5) Birthday of the female Buddha, Chun-ti, 6th day of the 3rd month. (6) Birthday of 'Wen-shu p'u sa,' or Mañjuśrī Bodhisattva, 4th day of the 4th month. (7) Birthday of Sākyamuni, 8th day of the 4th month. (8) Birthday of 'Ta-shï-chï p'u-sa,' 1st day of the 7th month. This Bodhisattva, with Kwan-yin and Amitābha, are 'the three sages of the West.' (9) Birthday of Ti-tsang p'u-sa, 30th day of the 7th month. (10) Birthday of Yo-shï Fo (the Buddha who instructs in healing), or Bhaiṣajyaguru Buddha, 30th day of the 9th month. (11) Birthday of O-mi-to Fo, or Amida, Amitābha Buddha, 17th day of the 11th month. (12) Anniversary of elevation of Śākyamuni to the rank of Buddha, 8th day of 12th month.

4. Characters in Chinese Buddhist history.—(1) Death of Pochang, 19th day of 1st month. (2) Death of Hwei-yuen, a founder of the Tsing-tu school, 6th day of 8th month. (3) Death of Tau-siuen, a founder of the discipline school, 3rd day of 10th month. (4) Anniversary of death of Bodhidharma (Ta-mo), the first of the six patriarchs, 5th day of 10th month. (5) Death of Hien-shen, founder of the school bearing his name, 14th day of 11th month. (6) Death of Chi-k'ai, founder of the T'ien-t'ai School, 24th day of 11th month.

5. Supplemental anniversaries.—(1) First day of the year, special worship. (2) End of winter, Kiai-tung, 15th day of 1st month. (3) Birthday of Śakra, 9th day of 1st month. (4) Birthday of Yo-wang p'u-sa, medical king and Bodhisattva, 15th day of the 4th month. (5) Commencement of summer, 16th day of 4th month. (6) Yü-lan-p'en, ceremony for feeding hungry ghosts, 15th day of 7th month. (7) End of summer, 16th day of 7th month. (8) Birthday of the Bodhisattva Lung-shu, or 'Dragon-tree,' 25th day of the 7th month. (9) Birthday of the ancient Buddha Jan-teng, 'Light Lamp' (Dīpaṁkara Buddha), whose disciple, in a former *kalpa*, Sākyamuni was, 22nd day of 8th month. (10) Commencement of winter (Li-tung), 15th day of 10th month. (11) Birthday of the Bodhisattva Hwa-yen, 29th day of the 12th month. (12) Winter solstice; special worship.

In this popular calendar, the *Ts'ing-Kwei*, no mention is made of anything astronomical. The Buddhists have arranged their calendar of festivals and fasts to suit the Chinese months [1] (see CALENDAR [Chinese]).

LITERATURE.—E. J. Eitel, *Handbook for the Student of Chinese Buddhism*, London, 1870; C. F. Neumann, *Catechism of the Shamans*, Eng. tr., do. 1831; S. Beal, *Catena of Buddhist Scriptures from the Chinese*, do. 1871; M. Anesaki, 'Chinese Āgamas and Pali Nikāyas,' *JRAS*, 1901; S. Beal, *Buddhism in China*, London, 1884; J. W. Young, 'Feestdagen der Chineezen door Tshoa-tse-koan,' in *Tijdschr. vor ind. Taal-, Land- en Volkenkunde*, xxxii. [1889]; F. K. Ginzel, *Handbuch der mathematischen und technischen Chronologie*, Leipzig, 1906 ff., i. 483-85.

J. H. BATESON.

FESTIVALS AND FASTS (Christian).—**1. Days of weekly observance.**—The week of seven days was taken over by Christians from the Jewish Church with a change in the sacred day—the first, the day hallowed by Christ's resurrection, occupying the place of the seventh.

(*a*) The observance of *the first day of the week*, as the day when Christians met together specially for 'the breaking of the bread,' is already noted in the NT (Jn 20[19. 26], Ac 20[7], 1 Co 16[2]). In the *Epistle of Barnabas* (end of 1st cent.) the words occur (ch. 15): 'We keep the eighth day for rejoicing, in which also Jesus rose from the dead.' The *Didache* (early in 2nd cent.) contains the passage (ch. 14): 'On the Lord's own day (κατὰ κυριακὴν δὲ Κυρίου) gather yourselves together and break bread and give thanks.' Ignatius in his *Ep. to the Magnesians* (same period) speaks (ch. ix.) of those who had been converted from Judaism as 'no longer observing Sabbaths, but fashioning their lives after the Lord's Day, on which our life (he says) also rose through Him.' The latter passages seem to fix the meaning of 'the Lord's day' (ἡ κυριακὴ ἡμέρα) in Rev 1[10]. Justin Martyr's description of the worship of Christians on the 'day of the sun' is well known (*Apol.* i. 67).

(*b*) From very early times *Wednesdays and Fridays* were observed by Christians as half-fasts—*semijejunia* (Tert. *de Jejun.* 13), so called because they were not prolonged beyond the ninth hour, *i.e.* the middle of the afternoon. They are mentioned in the *Didache* (ch. 8): 'Let not your fasts be with the hypocrites, for they fast on the second and fifth day of the week, but ye shall fast on the fourth day and on the Preparation' (παρασκευή, see Mk 15[42]). The allusion is to the Jewish weekly fasts referred to in Lk 18[12]. In the *Shepherd* of Hermas (1st half of 2nd cent.) (*Simil.* v. 1) the author speaks of himself as fasting and holding a 'station.' This word, which is explained by Tertullian (*de Orat.* 19) as a military term implying that Christians were then specially on guard, is his name for the two weekly fasts (*de Jejun.* 2 and 14). Clem. Alex. (*Strom.* vii. [*PG* ix. 504]) also mentions these fasts, but without using the word 'station.' The fasts of Wednesday and Friday are still continued in the East; in the West, Friday alone, as a rule, is so observed. These days were also marked by assemblies for worship (*synaxes*). In Africa at the end of the 2nd cent. the Eucharist was celebrated as on Sundays (Tert. *de Orat.* 19); and this was also the case in Jerusalem, except during Lent, in the 4th cent. (Etheria, *Peregrin.* iv. 3); but at Alexandria (Socrates, *HE* v. 22) and at Rome (Innocent I., *Ep. ad Decent.* 4 [*PL* xx. 556]) at this latter date the service was non-liturgical.

(*c*) There was a tendency at first, as might be expected, among Christians of Jewish race to continue the observance of *Saturday* (the Sabbath); but this practice came to be regarded as a mark of Judaizing (Col 2[16]; Ignat. *ad Magn.* ix., *Ep. to Diognetus*, 4 [*c.* 150]). We do not hear again of any observance of Saturday until the 4th century. It then in the East had become a day of worship, generally eucharistic, and bore a festal character, fasting being forbidden on it, except on Easter Even (Counc. of Laod. 16 and 49 [Mansi, ii. 567, 571]; *Apost. Const.* v. 14, 20, vii. 23 [ed. Funk]; Basil, *Ep.* 93 [*PG* xxxii. 483]). In the West, on the contrary, except at Milan, Saturday became a day of fasting and was non-liturgical (Aug. *Ep.* xxxvi., liv. [*PL* xxxiii. 137, 201]). Probably the Saturday fast originated in the custom, which arose as early as the time of Tertullian, of occasionally prolonging the Friday fast to the following day. This practice is called by him 'continuare jejunium' (*de Jejun.* 14); subsequently the word *superponere*, regarded as a literal tr. of ὑπερτίθεσθαι, was applied to it (Victorinus, *de Fab. Mundi* [end of 3rd cent.; *PL* v. 304, 306]; Counc. of Elvira [324], canons 23 and 26 [Mansi, ii. 9, 10]).

2. Lent and Easter.—Our Lord's death and resurrection took place about the time of the Passover. It was inevitable, therefore, that the Apostles, who were Hebrews, and their converts, who at the first were of the same race, should attach a new Christian significance to the ancient festival. There seems to be an intimation of this in 1 Co. The letter was written after a winter, yet before

[1] J. Edkins, *Chinese Buddhism*, London, 1880, pp. 205, 212.

Pentecost (16[6, 8]), therefore about the Passover season; and in it (5[7]) St. Paul speaks of Christ as our 'Pascha [here=Paschal victim] which hath been sacrificed.' It is on the occasion of the early dispute about the time of its celebration that we have the first historical notice of the Christian Pascha. Polycrates, Bishop of Ephesus, and Irenæus, Bishop of Lyons, in their letters to Victor of Rome (last decade of 2nd cent.) trace the Quartodeciman custom of proconsular Asia back to Polycarp († 155), who claimed for it the authority of St. John. The custom of Rome is traced by Irenæus up to Bishop Xystus (*c.* 120), further than whom apparently the tradition did not go (Euseb. *HE* v. 24).

3. **Lent.**—(*a*) Easter never stood alone; it came as a day of rejoicing after a fast which commemorated the death and burial of Christ. The word 'Pascha' for the first three centuries signified not Easter, but Good Friday (Tert. *adv. Jud.* 10; *de Bapt.* 19), and this meaning was supported by a singular notion that it was derived from πάσχω (Iren. iv. 10 [*PG* vii. 1000]; Lact. iv. 26 [*PL* vi. 531]). The fast, to which at first more importance was attached than to the festival which followed, was not of long duration. Irenæus, in his letter to Victor (mentioned above, 2), alludes to different usages as prevailing in his time, and long before (πολὺ πρότερον). 'Some think,' he writes, 'they ought to fast one day, others two, others even more: others reckon the period as 40 hours day and night.' The 40 hours may be illustrated by passages from Tertullian (*de Jejun.* 2, 13 [*PL* ii. 1006, 1023]), in which he speaks of the custom of fasting during the days 'when the bridegroom is taken away' (Mt 9[15]), *i.e.* the period from Good Friday evening to Easter morning. In Alexandria, in the middle of the 3rd cent., we are informed that some fasted during the whole week before Easter Day, others for shorter periods, and that the fasting varied in degree of rigour (Dion. Alex. *Letter to Basilides*, in Feltoe, *Dionysius of Alexandria*, Cambridge, 1904, p. 101 f.).

(*b*) The mention of a Lent of forty days (Quadragesima, τεσσαρακοστή) first occurs in the fifth canon of the Council of Nicæa (325) (Mansi, ii. 669); and, the reference being only a note of time (πρὸ τῆς τεσσαρακοστῆς), a well-established custom is implied. The period from henceforth is frequently mentioned as a time of preparation of catechumens for baptism, for the discipline of penitents, and generally of spiritual retreat for Christians. Such exercises naturally involved fasting; but the practice varied in different countries. See, further, FASTING (Christian), II. 2.

4. **Holy Week** (*Major* or *sancta Hebdomas*, ἡ ἑβδομὰς μεγάλη or ἁγία).—(*a*) *Palm Sunday* (*Dominica in Palmis*, ἡ κυριακὴ τῶν βαΐων).—The procession of palm-bearers in memory of Christ's triumphal entry into Jerusalem six days before His passion, from which the title of this Sunday is derived, took its origin in Jerusalem. Etheria (*Peregrinatio*)[1] relates how the whole Christian community there went on the evening of this day to the Mount of Olives, where a religious service was held, and thence returned home in procession carrying branches of palm or olive and singing, 'Blessed is he that cometh in the name of the Lord.' The ceremony was not introduced into the West until much later. Isidore of Seville (early in 7th cent.) is acquainted with the name 'Dies palmarum,' but not with the procession (*de Offic. Eccl.* i. 28 [*PL* lxxxiii. 763]). The *Gelasian* and *Gregorian Sacramentaries* also have the name; but no service for the blessing of palms or for the procession is mentioned until the second half of the 9th cent. (Amalarius, *de Off.* i. 10 [*PL* cv. 1008]).

At an earlier period a rite of general observance on Palm Sunday was the 'traditio symboli,' the imparting to the catechumens who had been under instruction during Lent of the words of the Creed for the first time. This ceremony formed the chief characteristic of the Sunday next before Easter in service-books in which the name Palm Sunday is unknown. Thus in the *Sacramentarium Gallicanum* and the *Missale Gothicum* (ed. Muratori) the service for the day is called 'Missa in Symboli Traditione.'

(*b*) *Maundy Thursday* (*Feria v. in cœna Domini*, ἡ ἁγία καὶ μεγάλη πεμπτή).—Our Lord's institution of the Eucharist on the day before He suffered is commemorated in the liturgical epistle taken from 1 Co 11, in all the Western Service-books and in the Greek rite.[1] In Africa on this day the Eucharist was partaken of after the evening meal, contrary to the usual requirement of fasting communion, in order to reproduce the circumstances of the institution. The 3rd Council of Carthage (397), can. 29, exempts even the celebrant on this one occasion from the rule of fasting: 'Ut sacramenta altaris non nisi a jejunis hominibus celebrentur, excepto uno die anniversario quo coena Domini celebratur' (Mansi, iii. 885). St. Augustine (*Ep.* liv. 7 *ad Januar.* [*PL* xxxiii. 204]) refers to the practice, and gives as an additional reason for it the custom of bathing on this day in preparation for Easter, which he deemed incompatible with fasting: 'quia jejunia simul et lavacra tolerare non possunt.' The Trullan Council (680), can. 29, expressly cancelled the exception allowed by the Council of Carthage, and made the rule of fasting communion absolute (Mansi, xi. 956).

Other features of this day were the reconciliation of penitents (Innocent I., *Ep. ad Decent.* 7 [*PL* xx. 559]), and the consecration of the holy oils for baptism, confirmation, and the unction of the sick (Isidore of Seville, *de Off.* i. 29 [*PL* lxxxiii. 764]). The latter rite is still retained in the Latin Church. The feet-washing of inferiors by superiors which, being known as the 'mandatum,' gave its name to 'Maundy' Thursday, seems to be first mentioned in a canon of the 17th Council of Toledo (694) (Mansi, xii. 98), which complains that it was neglected in some places, and for the future enforces the observance on all bishops and priests. The name is taken from the anthem sung during the ceremony, 'Novum mandatum do vobis' (Jn 13[34]). See FEET-WASHING.

(*c*) *Good Friday* (*Feria vi. in Parasceues*, ἡ ἁγία καὶ μεγάλη παρασκευή or ἡ ἡμέρα τοῦ σταυροῦ or ἡ σωτηρία).—The anniversary of our Lord's death is the only day in the year when by general custom the Eucharist is not celebrated—a custom which was formerly extended to Easter Eve (Innocent I., *Ep. ad. Decent.* 4 [*PL* xx. 556]), as it is still in the Eastern Church. The first part of the service for Good Friday in the Roman Missal—consisting of lessons from Holy Scripture and Collects, followed by a series of intercessory prayers—probably preserves the type of worship originally used in the West on non-liturgical days (Duchesne, *Christian Worship*, 172, 248). At a later date (7th or 8th

[1] The *Peregrinatio Etheriae* is a MS discovered by I. F. Gamurrini at Arezzo, and published by him in 1887. It is an account of a pilgrimage to Jerusalem, addressed by a Spanish nun to her sisters in religion. Her name was at first wrongly supposed to be Silvia (see Duchesne, *Christian Worship*[4], p. 490). An ed. of the *Peregrinatio*, with an Eng. tr. by Bishop Bernard, is published in the Palestine Pilgrims' Text Society London, 1891. The portions relating to the order of church offices at Jerusalem with a tr. are given in Duchesne, Eng. ed.

[1] In the calendar of Polemius Silvius (448) (*PL* xiii. 676) the 24th March is marked as 'Natalis calicis,' the birthday of the chalice. This is in accordance with an early belief that the 25th March was the day of Christ's death, and the 27th of His resurrection. The festival seems to have been generally observed in Gaul, as we have fragments of sermons preached on the occasion by Avitus of Vienne (*c.* 518) (*PL* lix. 302, 306, 308, 321), and it is mentioned by Eligius of Noyon (*c.* 640–659) (hom. 10 [*PL* lxxxvii. 628]).

cent.) this service was elaborated by the introduction of the ceremonies of the Adoration of the Cross and the Mass of the Presanctified. The former appears in the *Gelasian Sacramentary* and in the *Ordines Romani* dating from the 9th cent. (ed. Mabillon in *Museum Italicum*, reprinted *PL* lxxviii.). It is omitted in the *Gregorian Sacram.*, probably because this book gives only the prayers said by the Pope (Duchesne, 248 n.). It came to the West from Jerusalem, where on this day, in the 4th cent., the true cross, discovered, as alleged, by the Empress Helena, was brought out to be kissed by the faithful (Etheria, *Peregrinatio*). The Mass of the Presanctified is the communion of the priest, and formerly of the people also, with the Sacrament consecrated on the previous day. The rite was borrowed from the East, where, on days on which the Eucharist was not permitted to be celebrated, the *Liturgy of the Presanctified*, ἡ τῶν προηγιασμένων λειτουργία, was appointed in its place. The rule in relation to Lent is laid down by the Trullan Council (692), can. 52 (Mansi, xi. 968) (see Neale, *Gen. Introd.* 714 ff.; Allatius, 1531 ff.). The Devotion of the Three Hours, so popular in modern times in the Roman and Anglican Communions, dates only from 1687, when it was introduced in Peru by the Jesuit Alonso Messia (Thurston, *The Devotion of the Three Hours Agony, translated from the Spanish Original*, London, 1899). The name 'Good Friday' is peculiar to the Church of England. Elsewhere in the West the day is popularly known as 'Holy Friday.'

(*d*) *Easter Even* (*Sabbatum sanctum*, τὸ μέγα or τὸ ἅγιον σάββατον).—This is the only Saturday in the year which is kept as a fast in the Eastern Church. For this day no services were appointed in the Latin rite. The office of the Vigil of Easter, held before the dawn of Easter Day, was in the 7th cent. (see *Gelasian Sacram.*) transferred to the afternoon of Saturday, and later on to the morning. Thus the English name is in accord with the ritual aspect of the day. The vigil service proper —consisting of a long series of lessons, chants, and prayers—was followed by the blessing of the font, and the baptism and confirmation of the catechumens. The function was concluded by the Mass, which originally was celebrated at the first signs of dawn. Two other ceremonies were prefixed later on to the vigil service—the blessing of the new fire and of the Paschal candle. The new fire probably took rise from a pagan custom to which, when adopted by Christians, a gospel symbolism was attached. The first notice we have of it is connected with Ireland in the legendary history of St. Patrick (Stokes, *Tripartite Life of St. Patrick*, 1887, p. 278). The custom seems to have been carried to the Continent by Irish missionaries. The mode of lighting it was unknown at Rome in the 8th century (Pope Zacharias [741–752], *Ep.* 13 *ad Bonifacium* [*PL* lxxxix. 951]). The fire, which, according to the rubric, must be produced from flint and steel, is used to kindle the lights throughout the church. In the East, the holy fire is peculiar to the Holy Sepulchre at Jerusalem, and cannot be traced farther back than the 9th century. It has been conjectured that it was introduced by the Latin monks stationed there by Charlemagne, 799–801 (Wordsworth, *Ministry of Grace*[2], London, 1903, p. 384 f., and App. E, p. 462 ff.). The blessing of the Paschal candle was an ancient custom in the countries of the Gallican rite, and perhaps in Africa. It seems to be mentioned by St. Augustine († 430), who quotes verses which he had composed 'in laude quadam Cerei' (*de Civ. Dei*, xv. 22 [*PL* xli. 467]). Two forms of blessing are found in the *Opuscula* (9, 10) of Ennodius of Pavia (521) (*PL* lxiii. 258, 262). Pope Gregory I. († 604) writes of the 'preces quae super Cereum in Ravennati civitate dici solent' (*Ep.* xi. 33 [*PL* lxxvii. 1146]). The 4th Council of Toledo (633) refers (can. 9) to the observance of the ceremony in Spain and in many other parts of the world, and directs that it shall be maintained in the churches of Gaul (Mansi, x. 620). It has a place in the three *Gallican Sacramentaries* (ed. Muratori), and in Alcuin's supplement to the *Gregorian*. It is also in the *Gelasian*, but obviously inserted there (Wilson, xxvii.). Although not adopted at Rome until much later, the *Liber Pontificalis* (ed. Duchesne, i. 225) states that it was permitted in the churches of the suburbicarian diocese as early as the time of Pope Zosimus († 418). The service was read from rolls exquisitely written and illuminated, many of which, dating from the 10th to the 12th centuries, are still preserved. They are called 'exultets,' from the first words, 'Exultet iam angelica turba cælorum!' At the blessing of the font, the Paschal candle is plunged into the water during a prayer for the descent of the Holy Spirit. It is lighted at every service from Easter to Pentecost.

5. Easter.—(*a*) *Easter Day* (*Dominica Resurrectionis*, ἡ ἑορτὴ πασχάλιος, τὸ πάσχα, or ἡ μεγάλη κυριακή).—This, the chief festival of the Christian Church, was not at first distinguished by any special rite from other Sundays. So late as the 6th cent. it was ordained by Pope Vigilius (537–555) that the Mass on Easter Day should differ from that on other days only by the addition of suitable Scripture lessons (*Ep. ad Euther.* 5 [Mansi, ix. 32]). At Rome on this day the custom of communion in both kinds was retained until near the end of the 14th century (*Ordo Rom.* xv. [of Amelius, *c.* 1378–1398] ch. 85, ed. Mabillon, *Mus. Ital.* ii. 505 f.). A Western mediæval rite, which lasted up to the 12th cent., was the blessing of the flesh of a Paschal lamb (*Ordo Rom.* xi. [1143], Mabillon, p. 142; Bona, *Rerum Lit.*, Rome, 1671, iii. 185 ff.). A form of blessing is given in the Missal of Robert of Jumièges, 11th cent., p. 103 (H. Bradshaw Soc.). Another rite, still finding place in the Latin Service-book, formed a conclusion to the ritual of Good Friday. On that day, after the Adoration of the Cross, the cross itself with the reserved Sacrament was placed in the 'sepulchre,' a recess generally situated on the north side of the sanctuary. Before Matins on Easter Day the Host was ceremonially taken from the sepulchre and laid upon the altar, while the antiphon, 'Christ, rising from the dead, dieth no more,' with its response, was sung. This was the source of the special anthems prefixed to the proper Psalms for the day in the Eng. Prayer Book. The English name 'Easter' is probably derived from *Eostre*, an Anglo-Saxon goddess, to whom special sacrifices were offered at the beginning of spring (Bede, *de Temp. Rat.* xv., *Op.*, ed. Giles, London, 1843, vi. 179).

(*b*) *The Sunday after Easter*, with which the Paschal season ends, was formerly called simply *Octava Paschæ*, or *Pascha clausum*; but later it received the name *Dominica in albis* (sc. *deponendis*), because on this day the newly-baptized laid aside their white baptismal robes. In the Greek Church it is styled K. τοῦ ἀντίπασχα or K. Θωμᾶ, the latter title referring to the Gospel for the day. In England it is traditionally called 'Low Sunday,' for which name suggested derivations are 'Laudes,' the first word in the sequence, or 'Close Sunday' (Procter-Frere, *New Hist. of the Book of Common Prayer*[3], London, 1905, p. 543 n.).

6. Ascension Day (*Ascensio Domini*, ἡ ἀνάληψις τοῦ Κυρίου).—The day of our Lord's ascension was commemorated at Jerusalem in the time of Etheria, 380 (*Peregrin.*). It is called by her 'the 40th day after Easter, that is, the fifth feria (Thursday).'

In *Apost. Const.* v. 20 (*c.* 375) it is directed to be kept as a festival. We have sermons preached on this day by Gregory of Nyssa († 395) (*PG* xlvi. 690), Epiphanius († 403; ii. 285, ed. Petavius, Paris, 1622), and Chrysostom (*c.* 405) (*PG* l. 441–452), who speaks of it as an ancient and universal feast. There is Western testimony of about the same date. Five Ascension sermons of St. Augustine († 430) (*PL* xxxviii. 1202 ff.) have come down to us. In the second he says: 'This day is celebrated throughout the whole world.'

7. **The Transfiguration of our Lord** (*Transfiguratio Domini nostri Jesu Christi, ἡ ἁγία Μεταμόρφωσις*), Aug. 6.—This immovable feast may most fitly be mentioned here among other festivals of our Lord. It was first observed in the East, being noted in the Coptic Calendar (ed. Selden, *de Synedriis*, iii. cap. 15, p. 409) and in the *Menology of Constantinople* (8th cent.; i. 102, ed. Morcelli). In the West the Transfiguration formed the subject of the Gospel for the Lent Ember Saturday (St. Leo, *Serm.* 51 [*PL* liv. 308]), but for long was not otherwise commemorated. Probably the Greek festival on Aug. 6 was introduced by the Crusaders; but it did not come into general observance until 1457, when, in thankfulness for a victory on that day over the Turks at Belgrade, it was appointed for the Church by Pope Calixtus III. (Baillet, ii. 84). It is only a Black-letter day in the Eng. Prayer Book; but in 1892 the Church in the United States assigned to it a Collect, Epistle and Gospel, and proper lessons.

8. **Rogation Days.**—See FASTING (Christian), III. 4.

9. **Pentecost.**—By early Christian writers the name 'Pentecost' (sometimes 'Quinquagesima' in Latin authors) was generally given to the whole space of fifty days after Easter. The period was regarded as a continuous festival during which no fast was permitted, and prayer was said standing (Tert. *de Idol.* 14, *de Bapt.* 19, *de Cor.* 3; Basil, *de Spir. Sanc.* 27 [*PG* xxxii. 192]). There is a survival of this use of the word in the Greek Office-books, where the name 'Mesopentecoste' is given to a festival of eight days which begins on the Wednesday before the 5th Sunday after Easter. But even so early as Origen (*c. Cels.* viii. 22 [*PG* xi. 1549]) and Tertullian (*de Cor.* 3) we find the word applied also in the restricted sense to the day which closed the period. The Council of Elvira (305) insists upon the duty of celebrating the day of Pentecost (can. 43 [Mansi, ii. 13]), and subsequently this use of the word prevailed. Etheria (*Peregrin.*) gives this name to the festival, and describes the ceremonial observed at Jerusalem (end of 4th cent.). The Eng. term 'Whitsunday,' according to the most probable derivation, is 'White Sunday,' so termed from the white robes worn by those lately baptized (Procter-Frere, p. 546, n. 4, quoting Skeat), the eve of Pentecost being in the West one of the chief seasons for baptism (Bingham, *Origines*, XI. vi. 7).

10. **Trinity Sunday.**—The Sunday after Whitsunday was at first known simply as the Sunday of the octave of Pentecost (see *Gelasian Sacram.* and appendix to *Gregorian*). Its observance as the festival of the Trinity was of late and gradual introduction. As the day was a *dominica vacans*, without any distinctive office of its own, the custom arose in some places of using on it the Mass of the Trinity drawn up by Stephen, Bishop of Liége (903–920). This practice was discouraged by Pope Alexander II. († 1073), on the ground that any special festival of the Trinity was superfluous, as every day in the year was consecrated to the honour of the Trinity in Unity (*Micrologus*, 59 and 60 [*PL* cli. 1019]). But the observance of the day grew in popularity in England, Germany, and France, and was sanctioned by several diocesan synods, as, *e.g.*, that of Arles (1260) (Mansi, xxiii. 1006). Finally, the festival was appointed to be observed generally by Pope John XXII. in 1334 (Baillet, iv. 154 ff.). According to the Roman use, the succeeding Sundays until Advent still continued to be reckoned as after Pentecost. The usage of numbering them from Trinity was adopted in England and for a time in Germany. It is now peculiar to the English Church. In the Greek calendar the day is called 'All Saints' Sunday,' K. τῶν ἁγίων πάντων.

11. **Corpus Christi.**—This festival, the latest in the year of the movable feasts of pre-Reformation date, is held on the Thursday after Trinity Sunday. The commemoration of the Eucharist on Maundy Thursday, the day of its institution, was necessarily tinged with the sadness of Holy Week. It also became overshadowed by the consecration of the sacred oils and the other ceremonies which had subsequently been appointed for the same day. Thus there arose in the Middle Ages a desire for a festival in honour of the Eucharist at another time. Corpus Christi was first kept in 1247, in the diocese of Liége, by direction of Bishop Robert de Thorote, who was influenced, it is said, by a vision which was seen by a nun named Juliana. It was instituted by a bull of Pope Urban IV. in 1264, which was confirmed by Clement V. in 1311, and by John XXII. in 1316 (Baillet, iv. 167 ff.). The observance of Corpus Christi was discontinued in the Church of England at the Reformation.

12. **Advent.**—See FASTING (Christian), III. 2.

13. **Christmas.**—See sep. art. under that title.

14. **The festivals after Christmas.**—With the festival of the Nativity of Christ were associated, at least from the 4th cent., commemorations of eminent saints of the NT. Gregory of Nyssa, in his oration at the funeral of his brother Basil, states that after Christmas and before 1st Jan., the date of Basil's death (379), the Church kept the festivals of Stephen,[1] Peter, James, John, and Paul (*PG* xlvi. 789); and in an earlier panegyric on St. Stephen he explains the principle on which these names were selected, namely, that it seemed fitting that the praise of the proto-martyr should be followed by a commemoration of Apostles (*ib.* xlvi. 725). This statement of Gregory is confirmed by the Syrian Calendar of the same date and country, which contains the following festivals: Dec. 26, St. Stephen; Dec. 27, SS. John and James; Dec. 28, SS. Paul and Peter. The Armenians do not observe Christmas,[2] yet on Dec. 26, 27, 28 they honour the same saints, with the difference that in their order the feast of SS. Peter and Paul precedes that of SS. James and John (Nilles, i. 373, ii. 629). The Nestorians in their calendar follow the same general principle. Their custom is to commemorate saints on a Friday; and on the Fridays following Christmas they observe the feasts of St. James the Lord's brother, St. Mary, St. John Baptist, SS. Peter and Paul, the four Evangelists, and St. Stephen (Maclean, *East Syrian Daily Offices*, p. 265 f.). A similar series of holy days following Christmas is found in the West, with the substitution of the Holy Innocents (Rome) or Holy Infants (Africa and Gaul) on Dec. 28 for SS. Peter and Paul, who in these countries were already commemorated on June 29. The festivals are thus recorded in the Calendar of Carthage (*c.* 505): 'Dec. 26, S. Stefani primi martyris; Dec. 27, S. Johannis Baptistae[3] et Jacobi Apostoli;

[1] In *Apost. Const.* (*c.* 375) viii. 33, among other festivals and times on which slaves are to rest from work, St. Stephen's day is mentioned, but the date is not given.

[2] On Dec. 25 they commemorate SS. David and James as relatives of our Lord—θεοπάτωρ and ἀδελφόθεος respectively.

[3] 'Baptistae' is doubtless a transcriber's error for 'evangelistae,' as St. John Baptist is commemorated in the same calendar on June 24.

Dec. 28, SS. Infantium.' The Gallican liturgies agree with the African and Syrian calendars in celebrating both the sons of Zebedee on Dec. 27; but in the Roman books St. John's name alone was retained, and St. James was subsequently commemorated on July 25. At Constantinople the Roman date, June 29, for SS. Peter and Paul was observed in the 5th cent. (see below, **22** (*a*)); Holy Innocents' day also, under the title of Holy Infants (τῶν ἁγίων νηπίων), was adopted later on, but on the 29th instead of the 28th December.

15. The Circumcision.—The earliest notices of the Christian observance of Jan. 1 represent it as a fast kept with the object of counteracting a riotous pagan festival held at this time of the year (St. Augustine, *Serm.* 198 [*PL* xxxviii. 1025]). The second Council of Tours (567) (Mansi, ix. 796) enjoins (can. 17) that three days at the beginning of January shall be an exception to the rule that all the days between Christmas and Epiphany shall be treated as festivals. In the *Gelasian* and *Gregorian Sacramentaries* the day is simply called the Octave of Christmas (*Octavas Domini*), and the service bears the character of that festival, with a special reference in the proper Preface to the Virgin Mother. The name 'Circumcision' as given to the day is first found in the canon of the Council of Tours mentioned above. It appears also in the *Hieron. Martyr.* (*c.* 595) and in the Gallican liturgical books of the 7th and 8th centuries, which treat the day as a festival. Byzantine calendars of the 8th and 9th centuries connect Jan. 1 with the Circumcision (*Menology of Constantinople*, i. 83, ed. Morcelli, and Calendar of Naples [Mai, *Nova Collect. Script. Vet.*, Rome, 1821, v. 58]). The Armenian Church, which celebrates the Nativity on Jan. 6 (the Epiphany), naturally observes the Circumcision on Jan. 13 (Nilles, i. 374).

16. Epiphany.—See separate article.

17. Festivals of the Blessed Virgin.—(*a*) It has been noted above (**14**) that the Nestorians hold a festival of St. Mary on the second Friday after Christmas. A similar feast is found in the Coptic Calendar on Jan. 16 (Selden, iii. cap. 15, p. 390).

(*b*) In the West the holding of a festival in honour of the Virgin Mother was at first peculiar to countries of the Gallican rite. Gregory of Tours (6th cent.) states that her festival was held in Gaul in the middle of January (*de Glor. Mart.* 9 [*PL* lxxi. 713]). In the *Hieron. Martyr.* (*c.* 595) the date Jan. 18, the same as that of the Gallican St. Peter's Chair (see **22** (*b*), below), is assigned to it (see Mabillon, *de Lit. Gall.* ii. 118 n.). In the Gallican books the precise date is not given, but it is placed early in the year. In Spain the 10th Council of Toledo (656), ch. i., fixed Dec. 18 as the day of the festival, with the note 'that it could not fittingly be celebrated on the most suitable day,' viz. that of the Incarnation, because it sometimes occurred during Lent or the Paschal season, when, according to ancient rule, festivals of saints might not be held (Mansi, xi. 34). At Rome the only commemoration of the B.V.M. was that which was superadded to the service of Jan. 1 (see above, **15**) until the 7th cent., when four festivals in her honour were introduced from Constantinople. All are mentioned in the *Liber Pontif.* i. 376 (*Life of Sergius*, 687–701), and find place in the *Gelasian Sacramentary*.

(*c*) *The Purification* (*Purificatio B.V.M.*, ἡ ὑπαπαντὴ τοῦ Κυρίου ἡμῶν, Ἰησοῦ Χριστοῦ), Feb. 2.—The earliest of these four festivals was the 'Hypapante'; this name, which always continued in the East and was long retained in the West—sometimes in the translated form 'Occursus Domini nostri J. C.'—refers to the meeting between the infant Saviour and Simeon and Anna. Its later name of 'Purificatio' appears first in the *Gelasian Sacramentary* (7th cent.). The events commemorated took place 40 days after the birth of Christ (Lv 12^{2-8}, Lk 2^{22-24}). The festival, therefore, would be celebrated either on Feb. 2 or on Feb. 14, according as the interval is reckoned from Christmas or Epiphany; and the Armenians still observe it on the latter date. The first notice we have of it is by Etheria (*Peregrin.*), who calls it 'Quadragesimae de Epiphania.' Her account of the sermons preached on the occasion as dwelling upon the episode in the Temple leads us to conclude that originally it was a festival of our Lord rather than of the B.V.M. The first title of the day in the Eng. Pr. Bk., 'The Presentation of Christ in the Temple,' therefore sets forth its ancient significance. In the Roman Missal the preface for the day is that for Christmas, and the Collect speaks only of the Presentation. In 542 the festival began to be observed in Constantinople (Theophanes, *Chronograph*, i. 345, ed. Bonn) (see CANDLEMAS).

(*d*) *The Annunciation* (*Annunciatio*, ὁ Εὐαγγελισμός), March 25.—The date of this festival was fixed as being nine months before Christmas. As marking the time of the Incarnation, it, like the Purification, is more properly a festival of our Lord. It must have been widely known in the East in the early part of the 7th cent., as the *Paschal Chronicle* states that in 624 (*Olymp.* 351), Heraclius and his army started for the East on the feast of the Annunciation (i. 713, ed. Bonn). A difficulty about observing the festival on its natural date arose owing to a canon [51st] of the Council of Laodicea (4th cent.) which forbade the keeping of holy days in Lent except on Saturdays and Sundays (Mansi, ii. 572). The Trullan Council (692), while generally endorsing the rule, made a further exception in favour of the Annunciation, *i.e.* it enacts that on all other days in Lent than these the 'Holy Liturgy of the Presanctified' (see **4** (*c*) above) shall take place (*ib.* xi. 968). As regards the West, when the festival was adopted in Spain, the earlier commemoration of the B.V.M. on 18th Dec. (see (*b*) above) was treated as a subsidiary feast to the Annunciation. In the Mozarabic Missal both festivals appear with the same Mass (*PL* lxxxv. 170, 734; Férotin, 491, 492). At a much later date this example was followed in the Roman Church. In 1725 the feast of the *Expectatio Partus B.V.M.* was placed by Benedict XIII. on Dec. 18, with the collects and lections of the Annunciation.

(*e*) The two other festivals of the B.V.M. which came from the East to Rome refer to her more directly. They are the 'Assumption' (*Assumptio*, ἡ Κοίμησις), Aug. 15, and the 'Nativity' (*Nativitas*, τὸ Γενέθλιον), Sept. 8. The Assumption is said by Nicephorus Callistus (*HE* xvii. 28) to have been instituted by the Emperor Maurice (582–602). It was originally styled the 'Falling asleep' (ἡ Κοίμησις, *Dormitio*)—as it still is in the East—of the B.V.M., and commemorated her death. The later title, 'Assumptio,' appears first in the canons of Bishop Sonnatius of Rheims (*c.* 630) (*PL* lxxx. 446). This is its name in the *Gelasian Sacramentary*, though the service for the day contains no allusion to the legend which assigned a special meaning to the word. This is more definitely expressed in the *Gregorian Sacramentary*. It may be noticed that the Assumption, understood as the translation into heaven after death of the body of the B.V.M., is not an article of faith in the Roman Church.

(*f*) *The Conception*, Dec. 8.—This festival of the B.V.M., which is of later origin than the foregoing, gained importance through doctrinal developments. It arose in the East, where it is dated Dec. 9,[1] and

[1] When the feast was introduced into the West and the Roman Calendar followed, the Nativity being commemorated vi. Idus Sept., the Conception naturally was dated vi. Idus Dec.

is known as ἡ Σύλληψις τῆς ἁγίας καὶ θεοπρομήτορος Ἄννης—the word 'conception' in its Greek equivalent being understood in the East in an active sense. It is first mentioned in a sermon of John of Eubœa (middle of 8th cent.) (*PG* xcvi. 1499), and finds place in the *Menology of Constantinople* (ed. Morcelli, p. 80). Through the Greek settlements in lower Italy—its name in the Calendar of Naples (9th cent., ed. Mai, v. 65) is 'Conceptio S. Anne Marie vir.'—it passed into the Western Church, where it appears first in English Calendars and Service-books of the end of the 10th and beginning of the 11th centuries (Leofric Missal, Calendars of Winchester and Canterbury). The festival was suppressed after the Norman conquest, but was reintroduced, at first into Benedictine monasteries, early in the 12th century (Gasquet-Bishop, *The Bosworth Psalter*, p.43 ff.). About the same time we read of the festival in Normandy, where it became so popular that in the Middle Ages it was known as 'Festum nationis Normannicae' (Kellner, *Heortol.* 253). The feast gradually made its way through Europe, but was not received into the Roman Calendar, Missal, and Breviary until 1477 (by Sixtus IV.). In 1854 it was re-named by Pius IX. the 'Immaculate Conception,' and made a day of general obligation. In the Anglican Calendar all these feasts are found, with the exception of the Assumption, which was omitted at the Reformation; but the Annunciation and Purification are alone ranked as Red-letter days.

18. Festivals in honour of St. John the Baptist.—(*a*) *Nativity* (*Nativitas S. Joannis Baptistae*, τὸ Γενέθλιον τοῦ Προδρόμου), June 24.—The date of this festival, suggested by Lk 1[36], was placed exactly six months before Christmas; or, according to the Roman Calendar, on viii. Kal. Jul. as corresponding with viii. Kal. Jan., *i.e.* on the 24th instead of the 25th June. The Festival is of Roman origin, as the Latin date intimates. It is first mentioned by St. Augustine (*Serm.* 287, *PL* xxxviii. 1301), who remarks that the Church celebrates two birthdays only—that of Christ and that of the Baptist. It appears in the ancient Calendar of Carthage (*c.* 505). The festival was accepted in the East at an early date. Notwithstanding the appropriateness of June 24 for this festival, we have evidence that in earlier times St. John's nativity was celebrated in the East and in Gaul shortly after Christmas-tide. The Armenians placed it on the first day lawful for a festival (*i.e.* not Wednesday or Friday) after the octave of the Theophany (Nilles, ii. 565). The Nestorian festival of the Baptist, probably his nativity, on the 3rd Friday after Christmas, has been noticed above (14), and in the Calendar of Tours (490) the 'Natale' appears between the Epiphany and St. Peter's Chair, *i.e.* at the same time of the year. This Calendar has also the festival of June, but strangely calls it the 'Passio' of the saint.

(*b*) *Beheading* (*Decollatio* or *Passio S. Joan Bapt.*, ἡ Ἀποτομὴ τῆς τιμίας κεφαλῆς τοῦ Προδρόμου), Aug. 29.—This festival was adopted in Constantinople before it reached Rome (*Menology of Constantinople*, ed. Morcelli, ii. 222). It is found also in the Coptic Calendar, but with the date Aug. 30 (Selden, iii. cap. 15, p. 376). In the West it appears first in the Gallican liturgical books, where it is undated, but follows at a longer or shorter distance after the Nativity of the Baptist. It is absent from the *Leonine* and *Gregorian Sacramentaries*, and its presence in the Gelasian is probably due to a Gallican interpolation.

19. Festivals of the Cross.—(*a*) *Holy Cross Day* (*Exaltatio crucis*, ἡ Ὕψωσις τοῦ σταυροῦ), Sept. 14, is a Palestinian festival of the 4th century. It is the anniversary of the dedication in 335 of the two churches built by Constantine at Jerusalem—the Martyrium on Golgotha, and the Anastasis over the Holy Sepulchre. The day chosen for the dedication was, according to Etheria (*Peregrin.*), that on which the true cross had been discovered in 320 by the Empress Helena. Thus the festival was regarded as commemorating both events. Etheria (end of 4th cent.) notes that the festival was continued for eight days and was attended by a large concourse of pilgrims. From Jerusalem the festival passed to Constantinople, and thence to Rome, where it is mentioned first in connexion with Pope Sergius (687–701) (*Lib. Pont.*, ed. Duchesne, i. 374, 378). It appears in the *Gelasian* and *Gregorian Sacramentaries.* With the earlier events celebrated on this day another was subsequently associated, which added much to the renown of the feast, namely, the restoration of the true cross to Jerusalem in 629 by the Emperor Heraclius, after his recovery of it from the Persian king Chosroës II., who had carried it away in 614.

(*b*) *Invention of the Cross* (*Inventio crucis*), May 3.—In the churches of the Gallican rite, where the festival of Sept. 14 was unknown, the discovery of the cross was commemorated on May 3. The festival appears in the lectionary of Silos (650) under the name 'Dies sanctae crucis' (G. Morin, *Liber Comicus*, Bruges, 1893, p. 241), and in the Mozarabic Missal and Breviary (*PL* lxxxv. 739, lxxxvi. 1119). In the *Codex of Laws of the Wisigoths* (Paris, 1579), lib. xii. tit. iii. 6, it is included among the feasts on which Jews are forbidden to work. In the *Missale Gothicum* it is placed between the octave of Easter and the Rogation days, but the precise date is not given. It was subsequently adopted at Rome, but was never known in the East. Both festivals are Black-letter days in the Anglican Calendar.

20. St. Michael (*Dedicatio S. Michaelis Archangeli*), Sept. 29.—This, the most ancient Angel-festival, is noted in the *Leonine Sacramentary* (6th cent.), but on Sept. 30, as the day of the dedication of a church of the archangel in the Via Salaria, six miles from Rome (Natale Basilicæ Angeli in Salaria). A later festival of St. Michael is that of May 8, and is connected with a church on Mount Garganus in Apulia. The feast of St. Michael in the Greek Church is kept on Nov. 8, and is relative to a church in the baths of Arcadius built by Constantine (Sozomen, *HE* ii. 3; Martinov, *Ann. Eccl.* p. 273). Legends of apparitions of the archangel are connected with all three sites. At the last revision of the Pr. Bk. (1662), 'and all angels' was added to 'St. Michael' in the title of the festival of Sept. 29—an addition which had appeared already in the Calendar prefixed to Bp. Cosin's *Private Devotions* (1627). The longer description is also not unknown in the Roman Church. In Baillet, iii. 371, the festival is named 'S. Michel et tous les SS. Anges'; the same title occurs in *AS*, Sept. viii. 4 ff., Antwerp, 1762. The festival of the 'Guardian Angels' (*Angelorum Custodum*), March 1, was first observed in Spain in the 16th cent.; and was admitted to the Roman Calendar by Paul V. in 1608. The date was subsequently changed, except in Germany and a part of Switzerland, to Oct. 2, by Clement X., in 1670. For a general account of the Angel-festivals in West and East, see *AS*, Sept., and Baillet (*loc. cit.*).

21. The Maccabees, Aug. 1.—This, which is the only commemoration of OT worthies in the West, was observed almost universally as early as the 5th century. It is found in the early Calendars of Filocalus, Carthage, Polemius Silvius, and Syria. It is the subject of Sermons by St. Gregory Nazianzen (*PG* xxxv. 912), St. Chrysostom (*PG* l. 617), St. Augustine (*PL* xlvi. 874), and others. In the Roman Calendar, it now yields precedence to the feast of St. Peter ad Vincula (see below, **22** (*c*)), which is observed on the same day.

22. Festivals of apostles.—(*a*) *SS. Peter and Paul*, June 29.—The early Eastern commemoration of these Apostles, which closely followed Christmas, has already been mentioned (see above, **14**). The Roman date of the festival has always been June 29. In the Calendar of Filocalus (336), where it first appears, this date is connected with the translation of their relics to a place called 'Catacumbae,' in the consulship of Tuscus and Bassus (258). The Calendar of Carthage is defective here, but there are clear indications that it originally contained the entry; and sermons by St. Augustine (295, 296) on the Festival show that this must have been the case (*PL* xxxviii. 1348, 1352). The festival occurs, but without date, in the Calendar of Tours (490) (Greg. of Tours. *Hist. Franc.* x. 31), and from thenceforward in all Western Calendars and Martyrologies. The observance of the Western date in Constantinople is first mentioned by Theodorus Lector (*HE* ii. 16 [*PG* lxxxvi. 192]). His statement is that through the influence of Festus, a Roman senator who had been sent on a political mission to the Emperor Anastasius in 491, the festival was celebrated with greater splendour than before. It afterwards came into general observance in the East as in the West. In the *Gregorian Sacramentary*, in addition to the Mass for June 29, a Mass in honour of St. Paul is appointed for June 30; and this commemoration is still marked in the Roman Missal and Calendar. This ancillary festival is accounted for by the difficulty which the bishop found in celebrating Mass at the tombs of both Apostles on the same day, and the consequent postponement of one of them until the morrow (Kellner, *Heortologie*, 285). At the Reformation the Church of England made June 29 a festival of St. Peter only, thus confining the commemoration of St. Paul to his Conversion (Jan. 25).

(*b*) *St. Peter's Chair* (*Cathedra S. Petri*).—Another festival of St. Peter appears in the Calendar of Filocalus on Feb. 22 with the title 'Natale Petri de Cathedra.' From early times this has been regarded as meaning the beginning of St. Peter's episcopate; in the Calendar of Tours (490) it is styled 'Natale S. Petri Episcopatus'; but recently a view has been put forward that it refers to the actual wooden chair used, as was supposed, by St. Peter, which is mentioned in a document of the time of Gregory the Great (de Rossi, *Bull. di archeol. Crist.*, Rome, 1867, p. 37 ff.). Whatever may have been the origin of the festival, the choice of the day on which it was held was apparently prompted by a desire to offer Christians a counter-attraction to a popular pagan festival, the 'Cara Cognatio' or 'Caristia,' observed on Feb. 22 in memory of deceased relatives. The festival of St. Peter's chair soon reached Gaul. It is found in the Calendar of Polemius Silvius (448), but under the incorrect designation 'Depositio SS. Petri et Pauli.' It also appears, as we have seen, in the Calendar of Tours. The second Council of Tours (567) complains that Christians sometimes relapsed into pagan rites on this day (Mansi, ix. 803). In Gaul, however, later on, probably in order to prevent the festival taking place in Lent—an occurrence forbidden by the Council of Toledo (see **18** (*b*) above)—it was transferred to an earlier day, which, after some variation, witnessed to by the liturgical books, was fixed at Jan. 18. The two dates appear in the *Hieron. Martyr.*, where the Gallican editor noted Jan. 18, the date familiar to him, as the Chair of St. Peter at Rome; and, finding another 'Cathedra S. Petri' on Feb. 22, he explained the co-existence of the two commemorations by attributing the latter to the episcopate which tradition assigned to the Apostle at Antioch. This diversity of use as to the date of the feast continued until 1558, when, at the instance of Paul IV., both festivals were appointed to be observed with the Hieronymian distinction (Cherubini, *Bullarium Rom.*, Lyons, 1655, i. 822). The feast of St. Peter's Chair has never been introduced into the East.

(*c*) *St. Peter's Chains* (*S. Petri ad Vincula*), Aug. 1.—This festival, which coincides in date with that of the Maccabees (see above, **21**), commemorates the dedication of the Church of St. Peter on the Esquiline, after its restoration in the time of Sixtus III. (432–440). In this church the chains of the Apostle were believed to be preserved, both those mentioned in Ac 12^{6} and those of his Roman imprisonment. The feast appears first in the 8th cent., having place in the *Gregorian Sacram.* and in the *Martyrology* of Bede. The Eastern Church has a festival of St. Peter's Chains on Jan. 16 (Nilles, i. 71). In the English Calendar the festival is termed 'Lammas Day,' which, according to the most probable derivation, = 'Loaf-mass,' and refers to an Anglo-Saxon custom of offering on this day bread made from the new corn in thanksgiving for the harvest. Lammas is one of the legal quarter-days in Scotland.

(*d*) *Conversion of St. Paul* (*Conversio S. Pauli*), Jan. 25.—This festival in the *Hieron. Martyr.*, where it is first mentioned, is entitled 'Romae, Translatio B. Pauli Apostoli'; the reference doubtless being to some translation of his relics. In the *Missale Gothicum* it appears bearing the name with which it has come down to us. It is not mentioned in the ancient Roman Sacramentaries. The need for it was not felt at Rome, because there a special commemoration of St. Paul was connected with Sexagesima Sunday. The station for that day was held in the basilica of St. Paul on the Ostian Way; the Collect in the Mass invoked the protection of the Apostle, and the Epistle (2 Co $11^{19ff.}$) narrated his sufferings. The festival is peculiar to the Western Church.

(*e*) *St. John Apostle and Evangelist.*—See **14** above.

(*f*) *St. John before the Latin gate* (*S. Joannis ante portam Latinam*), May 6.—This festival probably marks the anniversary of the dedication of the church at this place in the time of Pope Adrian (772–795) (*Lib. Pont.* i. 508). It is first mentioned in the *Sacramentary* (the *Gregorian*) which has come down to us through this Pope. See COLLECT, **2** (1). The legend of the Apostle being thrown into a cauldron of boiling oil and escaping unhurt came subsequently to be connected with it. A Greek festival of St. John on May 8 commemorates a miracle said to have been performed on his tomb at Ephesus; another on Sept. 26 celebrates his legendary assumption (*μετάστασις*) into heaven after death (Nilles, i. 154 f., 285).

(*g*) *SS. Philip and James*, May 1.—These Apostles are commemorated on the anniversary of the dedication of a church at Rome in their honour about 561. The day was selected for the purpose because it was already connected with the memory of St. Philip (*Lib. Pont.* i. 306, see n. 2). As only two St. James's are in the Calendar of the West, and St. James the son of Zebedee is celebrated on July 25, it follows that the saint here associated with St. Philip is St. James the son of Alphæus, who is identified with our Lord's brother of the same name. In the Greek Church, St. James the son of Alphæus is commemorated on Oct. 9, St. James, 'the brother of God,' on Oct. 23, and St. Philip, 'one of the first company of the twelve,' on Nov. 14.

(*h*) *St. Andrew*, Nov. 30.—This festival is of exceptional importance as fixing the date of Advent Sunday. It occurs in the Calendar of Carthage (*c.* 505), in which no other Apostles are mentioned by name except St. James the Great and (probably) SS. Peter and Paul. It appears also in all the Gallican and Roman liturgical books. In the *Leonine Sacramentary* four 'propers' for Masses on this festival are appointed. The date, Nov. 30, is not connected with the dedication of any known church. According to the apocryphal 'Acta Andreae' (*Anal. Boll.* xiii. 349, 372, 378), it was the day of his martyrdom at Patras. It is thus the only festival of an Apostle which makes a claim to being observed on the actual anniversary of his death. The day is held in high honour among the Russians, who reckon St. Andrew as the Apostle and patron of their Church (Martinov, p. 293).

(*i*) The dates of the feasts of other Apostles and Evangelists as celebrated in the West and East are as follows: *St. Matthias*—in West, Feb. 24, in East, Aug. 9; *St. Mark*, Apr. 25; *St. Barnabas*, June 11 (in East, St. Barnabas and St. Bartholomew are commemorated together); *St. James the son of Zebedee*—in West, July 25, in East, Apr. 30; *St. Bartholomew*—in West, Aug. 25, in East, June 11 (see above); *St. Matthew*—in West, Sept. 21, in East, Nov. 16; *St. Luke*, Oct. 18; *SS. Simon and Jude*—in West, Oct. 28, in East, *St. Simon Zelotes*, May 10; *St. Judas* (Thaddæus), June 19; *St. Thomas*—in West, Dec. 21, in East, July 3. We have no evidence for the reason of the assignment of these dates. Probably they mark the anniversaries of the dedication of churches or of the translation of relics.

23. St. Mary Magdalene, July 22.—This festival is first noted in the *Martyrology* of Bede. As regards Service-books, it appears first in a Missal of Verona of the 10th cent. and then in some 11th cent. Missals. It was not received into the official Roman books until the 13th cent. (Kellner, *Heortologie*, p. 313). In the West, St. Mary Magdalene is identified by the Gospel for the day (Lk 7^{36-50}) with the woman who was a sinner. In the Greek Service-books she is described as 'the holy ointment-bearer and equal of the Apostles.' In the English Pr. Bk. of 1549 this festival was retained as a Red-letter day, with Collect, Epistle, and Gospel, the latter being the same as that in the Latin missal. Since 1552 the day has merely been noted in the Calendar.

24. Days of the Martyrs and Confessors.—The earliest martyr festival on record is that of *St. Polycarp*, Jan. 26. The letter of the Church of Smyrna to that of Philomelium giving an account of his martyrdom (*c.* 155) states that it had been thought well to celebrate the 'birthday' of Polycarp at his grave 'as a memorial of those who had finished their course' (*Martyr Polyc.* 18 [*PG* v. 1044])—words which imply that earlier martyrs had not hitherto been commemorated. In this letter we find for the first time the death of a martyr described as his 'birthday,' *i.e.* into a better world—the name by which it came generally to be known (ἡμέρα γενέθλιος, *natale*, or *dies natalis*, or *natalitia*) (cf. also COMMEMORATION OF THE DEAD, vol. iii. p. 718 f.). We find no trace of the commemoration of other individual martyrs until the 3rd cent., to which belong the earliest noted in the Calendar of Filocalus. At first martyr festivals were entirely local, each Church honouring its own saints. There is, therefore, more likelihood of the days of martyrs being real anniversaries of their deaths than those of Apostles. By degrees these local festivals, or some of them, were adopted by the central or mother-church of the country. St. Cyprian († 258) not only directs that the death-days of martyrs shall be noted, in order that they may be locally commemorated, but also promises that, where he is (*i.e.* at Carthage), oblations shall be celebrated in their memory (*Ep.* 33 [*PL* iv. 328]). Before long the practice arose of one Church adopting commemorations from the Calendar of another, so that eminent saints came to be honoured not only in their own country, but elsewhere. Already in the Roman Calendar of Filocalus appear the Carthaginian martyrs *Perpetua* and *Felicitas* (March 7) and *Cyprian* (Sept. 14). Some, like the last named, passed into the common Calendar of the Church. At first martyrs alone were commemorated, but later on saints otherwise eminent were admitted to share their honours. The authority to admit to the roll of saints belonged originally to the Bishop of each diocese. The first canonization (*q.v.*) in its later sense,[1] by a Pope, was that of *Udalric*, Bishop of Augsburg, by John XV. in 995 (Mabillon, *Actt. SS. Ben. Saec.* v., Paris, 1698–1701, *Pref.* lxviii; Gibbings, *The Diptychs*, Dublin, 1864, p. 33).

Among local festivals which in early times came to be observed should be mentioned the anniversaries of the dedication of churches, the burial days (*depositiones*) of bishops, and their consecration days (*natales*), which were kept during their episcopate.

25. All Saints' Day (*Festum omnium Sanctorum*), Nov. 1.—The origin of this festival is obscure. The *Liber Pont.* (i. 317) relates that Boniface IV. (608–615), having received the pagan temple known as the Pantheon as a gift from the emperor Phocas, transformed it into a church of the Blessed Ever Virgin Mary and all Martyrs, no date of the dedication being given. In the *Martyrologies* of Rabanus Maurus and Florus (8th cent.) there appear, on May 13, 'Natale Sanctae Mariae ad martyres' and, on Nov. 1, 'Festivitas omnium Sanctorum.' The origin of the latter festival is assigned in both works to the consecration of the Pantheon by Boniface IV., the passage from the *Liber Pont.* being quoted in the form in which it passed through the chronicle of Bede (*de Temp. Rat.*, cap. 66, ed. Giles, vi. 323). But the festival of May 13 corresponds better in title with the dedication of the Pantheon, and it is apparently older than the festival of Nov. 1, as it is found in the *Gregorian Sacramentary*, a document of somewhat earlier date, in which the Feast of All Saints does not appear. Adon, who worked upon and supplemented Florus, observed this incongruity; and in his *Martyrology* he attributed the origin of both festivals to the dedication mentioned in the *Liber Pontificalis.* He also supplemented the notice of Nov. 1 with the statement that Louis the Pious (778–840), at the instance of Gregory IV., ordained that the festival of All Saints should be perpetually observed on that day in the Gallic territories. As this event would have occurred in Adon's time, we may believe that we are here, at any rate, on solid ground of history (Quentin, *Les Martyrologes historiques*, p. 636 ff.). In the Eastern Church the Festival of All Saints is kept on the 1st Sunday after Pentecost (see **10**, above). It was already observed in Antioch in the 4th cent., as sermons preached on that day by St. Chrysostom have come down to us (*PG* l. 706–712).

26. All Souls' Day (*Commemoratio omnium fidelium Defunctorum*), Nov. 2.—The first distinct notice of the observance of this day is its appointment in 998 by Odilo, Abbot of Clugny, for the monasteries of his order (*Statutum de Defunctis* [*PL* cxlii. 1038]). The first diocese to adopt it seems to have been Liége, where it was introduced by Bishop Notker (*c.* 1008). In the Greek Church the commemoration of the departed is kept on the Saturday before the Sunday called 'Apocreos,' which corresponds to the Western Septuagesima. The Armenians keep it on Easter Monday. The

[1] The word 'canonization' recalls the primitive custom of reciting, during the 'canon' of the Mass, the names of deceased martyrs and saints which had been inserted in the Diptychs.

day ceased to be observed in the Anglican Church at the Reformation.

27. Octaves.—The word 'octave' signifies the eighth day, or the period of eight days after a festival, treated as a repetition or a continuation of the feast. The usage may have been suggested by the rule laid down for the prolongation of the chief OT festivals (Lv 23[6. 34ff.]). The first octave of which we read is that of Easter, during which the newly-baptized continued to wear their white garments. Etheria (*Peregrin.*) notices the custom at Jerusalem in connexion with Epiphany, Easter, and the Dedication days of the churches called the Martyrium and the Anastasis. She speaks of the eight Paschal days as kept everywhere. At first octaves were generally attached only to festivals of our Lord, but in the 8th and 9th centuries a few of the greater saints were similarly honoured (Amalarius, *de Eccl. Off.* iv. 36 [*PL* cv. 1228]). In mediæval times, octaves became more numerous, chiefly owing to the liturgical influence of the Franciscans (Kellner, *Heortol.* 15). In the Eastern Church a similar custom is known by the name 'Apodosis,' but the period observed is not always a week; it may be longer or shorter (Neale, *Eastern Church*, Gen. Introd. 764; Daniel, *Codex Liturg.* iv. 230 n.).

28. Vigils and Ember Days.—See FASTING (Christian), III. 6 and 5.

29. The days of the week.—The Latin and Greek names in liturgical use are 'dies dominica, feria secunda, f. tertia, f. quarta, f. quinta, f. sixta, sabbatum'; (*ἡμέρα*) *κυριακή, δευτέρα, τρίτη, τετάρτη, πέμπτη, παρασκευή, σάββατον.* Why 'feria,' which in classical use means a holy day, should be employed for an ordinary week-day is unknown. The most reasonable explanation is that, as the Jews numbered the days of the week from the Sabbath, saying the 'second of the Sabbath,' the 'third of the Sabbath,' etc., so Christians, adopting the same method, substituted, for 'Sabbath,' 'feria' as an equivalent for 'Lord's day,' the holy day from which they counted (Valesius, *Annotationes in H. E. Eusebii*, Paris, 1678, p. 155 f.). The names for the days of the week which the early Christians found in general use—as, in Latin countries, 'dies solis, lunae,' etc.—were deemed by them inappropriate, as derived from pagan gods. At the Reformation in England, when the vernacular was again used in the Services of the Church, the popular names, which had long lost their pagan associations, were naturally admitted into the Prayer Book.

30. Classification of festivals.—(*a*) Lanfranc († 1089), in his *Statuta pro ordine S. Benedicti* (ed. Giles, i. 126 f.), distributes festivals according to their importance into first, second, and third classes. These came to be known as Doubles, Semi-doubles, and Simples. A double festival probably derived its name from the usage which before the 9th cent. prevailed in Rome and elsewhere on greater feasts, of reciting two offices, one of the *feria* and the other of the festival. In process of time the classification of festivals became more elaborate until it reached the system in force at the present day, according to which there are six grades in the Roman Calendar, viz. Doubles of the 1st class, Doubles of the 2nd class, Greater Doubles, Doubles, Lesser Doubles, Simples.

(*b*) The festivals of the Latin Church are also known as *Festa chori*—i.e. those obligatory on the clergy only, and confined to the celebration of Church offices; and *Festa chori et fori*—i.e. those which lay people are bound to observe by attendance at Mass and rest from labour. In modern times there has been a large transference from the latter class to the former, chiefly owing to the pressure of civil authorities. Thus the festivals of general obligation have been considerably reduced in number, but no uniform rule prevails. In England the settlement made by Pope Pius VI. in 1777 has been but slightly modified since. At present, in addition to Sundays, the following holy days are observed: Christmas, the Circumcision, Epiphany, the Ascension, Corpus Christi, SS. Peter and Paul, the Assumption, and All Saints. To these St. Andrew's Day is added for Scotland, and St. Patrick's Day and the Annunciation for Ireland. In the United States, by Papal decree of 1866, six days only, besides Sundays, are of obligation, viz. Christmas, the Circumcision, the Ascension, the Assumption, All Saints', and the Immaculate Conception. In France, the observance of holy days is reduced to the lowest point. The settlement there dates from the reinstating of the Church after the Revolution. By concordat of the Pope with Napoleon, four days only besides Sundays were made obligatory, viz. Christmas, the Ascension, the Assumption (selected because 15 Aug. was Napoleon's name-day), and All Saints. All other festivals, when they fell on a week-day, were transferred to the following Sunday.

(*c*) In the Church of England, all the feasts for which a special Collect, Epistle, and Gospel are provided (Red-letter days) are appointed to be observed; all others (Black-letter days) are simply noted in the Calendar (see Table of Feasts and Calendar in Pr. Bk.).

(*d*) In the Greek Calendar the festivals are distributed into three classes—Greater, Intermediate, and Lesser—corresponding respectively to the Latin Doubles, Semi-doubles, and Simples. The Greater class is subdivided into three sections: I. † Easter, which stands alone; II. † Christmas, † Epiphany, † Hypapante, † Annunciation, Palm Sunday, † Ascension, † Pentecost, † Transfiguration, † Repose of B.V.M., Nativity of B.V.M., † Exaltation of the Cross, † Presentation of B.V.M.; III. † Circumcision, Nativity of St. John Baptist, SS. Peter and Paul, Beheading of St. John Baptist. The Intermediate class includes the 12 Apostles (except those noted above) and certain Greek saints, such as St. Basil, St. Gregory Nazianzen, St. Chrysostom, with St. Elias the Prophet, St. Michael the Archangel, etc. The Lesser class contains all the other saints whose names appear in the Calendar. In the above lists the festivals marked † are days of general obligation, known as *τελείως ἄπρακτοι*, *i.e.* when work is abstained from; all the rest are described as *ἐν μέρει μὲν ἄπρακτοι, ἐν μέρει δὲ ἔμπρακτοι* (Nilles, i. 34).

31. (*a*) In the Eastern Calendars, OT prophets and Saints are freely commemorated—a feature which is in marked contrast with the omission of all such from the Western Calendar, with the exception of the Maccabees. Thus, to take for example the first and last months of the year, in January the prophets Malachi, Elijah, and Isaiah have days assigned to them; in December, Nahum, Habakkuk, Zephaniah, and Haggai. Among other commemorations which have no parallel in the West are Jan. 22, 'The 6th Oecumenical Council'; May 7, 'The Sign of the Cross which appeared in heaven'; May 11, 'The Birthday of Constantinople'; Aug. 16, 'The Icon of our Lord not made with hands.'

(*b*) Among the Greeks and Armenians, Saturday is still, as in early times (see above, **1** (*c*)), treated as a festal day, almost as a second Sunday. It is marked by a celebration of the Eucharist even at seasons when no other week-days are so honoured. Among the Nestorians, Friday holds a similar position. Throughout the year it has its own name and office like Sunday, and upon it the festivals of the greatest saints are fixed in regular course (see above, **14**).

See also CALENDAR (Christian), FASTING (Christian).

LITERATURE.—H. Lietzmann, *The Three Oldest Martyrologies*, Eng. tr., Cambridge, 1904 [gives in a convenient form the ancient Calendars of Rome (Filocalus), Carthage, and Syria]; de Rossi-Duchesne, *Martyrologium Hieronymianum*, prefixed to *AS*, Nov., t. ii. pt. i., Brussels, 1894; L. Duchesne, *Le Liber Pontificalis*, Paris, 1886; L. A. Muratori, *Liturgia Romana vetus*, Venice, 1748 [contains the three Roman Sacramentaries and Gallican Liturgies]; H. Quentin, *Les Martyrologes historiques du moyen âge*, Paris, 1908; M. Férotin, *Le Liber Ordinum en usage dans l'église wisigothique et mozarabe d'Espagne*, Paris, 1904; N. Nilles, *Kalendarium manuale utriusque eccl. orient. et occident.*, Innsbruck, 1896; L. Allatius, 'Dissert. de dominicis graecorum,' in *De eccl. occid. et orient. consensione*, Cologne, 1648; H. A. Daniel, *Codex Liturgicus*, Leipzig, 1847–53, t. iv. [treats of festivals of Eastern Church]; J. M. Neale, *Hist. of the Holy Eastern Church*, Gen. Introd., London, 1850; S. A. Morcelli, *Kalendarium Eccles. Constantinopolitanae*, Rome, 1788 *; J. Martinov, *Annus eccl. græco-slavicus*, prefixed to *AS*, Oct., t. xi., Brussels, 1864; J. Selden, *De Synedriis . . . vet. Ebraeorum*, London, 1650 [gives ancient Coptic Calendars]; A. J. Maclean, *East Syrian Daily Offices*, London, 1894; M. Ormanian, *Church of Armenia*, Eng. tr., London, 1912, pp. 180–198; A. Baillet, *Les Vies des saints*, Paris, 1724; A. J. Binterim, *Die Denkwürdigkeiten der christlich-kathol. Kirche*, vol. v., Mainz, 1829; J. Bingham, *Origines eccl.*, bks. xx., xxi, ed. Oxford, 1855, vol. vii. p. 221 ff.; J. D. Mansi, *Sacrorum Conciliorum Collectio*, Florence, 1759; L. Duchesne, *Origines du culte chrétien*[4], Paris, 1909 (Eng. tr., *Christian Worship*[4], London, 1912); K. A. H. Kellner, *Heortologie*[2], Bonn, 1906 (Eng. tr., London, 1908); J. Wordsworth, *The Ministry of Grace*, London, 1901; J. Dowden, *The Church Year and Kalendar*, Cambridge, 1910; Gasquet-Bishop, *The Bosworth Psalter*, London, 1908; artt. in *DCA*, *DACL*, *DCG*, *Cath. Encycl.*, *Prayer Book Dictionary*, etc. Other authorities are referred to in the article.

JAMES G. CARLETON.

FESTIVALS AND FASTS (Egyptian).—I. *SOURCES.*—Egypt is extremely rich in this respect.

1. We have first of all *the tables enumerating the festivals* in regular series, or in the form of chronological annals of a religious sanctuary. The ordinary form of the first-named is that of the temple calendars (cf. CALENDAR [Egyp.], VII. 3). The specimens most worthy of mention, in order of date, are those of Karnak (XVIIIth dynasty), Medinet-Habu (XXth dynasty), Edfu (Ptolemaic), Dendereh and Esneh (Roman period). The famous 'Stone of Palermo' (Vth dynasty) is a good example of the second type.

Individual mention of a long series of festivals (sometimes augmented by brief descriptions or explanations as to their value or aim) is made from time to time in the corpus of the Egyptian texts. As principal types we may mention: (*a*) historical mural inscriptions or official stelæ of the temples; (*b*) numerous extracts of temple inscriptions of a non-historical character; (*c*) allusions to or enumerations of private stelæ or inscriptions engraved upon private statues; so-called funerary literature adds a long list in (*d*) the festivals quoted in the collections known as 'Books of the Dead' (cf., *e.g.*, chs. xviii.–xxi.); (*e*) funerary calendars, more or less complete, written on the sides of sarcophagi (the best specimen is the coffin of Babe in the Museum of Cairo, containing a list of a hundred local festivals [VIIIth dynasty]); and, finally, (*f*) the festivals mentioned (and sometimes described) on the walls of *mastabas* or hypogea (cf. for the Theban series, the tombs of Einna, Monna, and Nofirhatep, all belonging to the XVIIIth dynasty).

2. *The representations*, properly so called, of festivals of all kinds are sufficiently numerous to permit of reconstituting in the greatest detail the aspect and material order of these ceremonies. The two sources of information are the bas-reliefs of the temples, and the frescoes or reliefs of private tombs. From the immense list of the former, a good chronological series of types may be derived: (*a*) the representations in the royal chapels of the Pyramids of Abusir (Vth dynasty); (*b*) the temple remains recently found by Petrie in Memphis (XIIth dynasty); (*c*) the famous representations of the procession of the grand colonnade of Luxor (XVIIIth dynasty); those of the 'festival hall' of Thothmes III. at Karnak (XVIIIth dynasty); of the inauguration of the Nubian temple of Soleb (XVIIIth dynasty); of the triumphal procession of Deir el-Bahri (XVIIIth dynasty); (*d*) the ceremonies represented at Gurneh (XIXth dynasty); the great festivals of Mîn represented in the Ramesseum (XIXth dynasty), and at Medinet-Habu (XXth dynasty); (*e*) the jubilee festivals celebrated by Osorkon at Bubastis (XXIInd dynasty); (*f*) the festivals or processions engraved on the walls or ascending passages of the Great Temple of Edfu (Ptolemaic period); (*g*) the representations of processions on the famous staircases of the sanctuary of Dendereh (Roman period). The representations on the tombs, principally under the Theban Empire, add a considerable wealth of episode and detail. We must confine ourselves to mentioning here: (i.) the wonderful series of royal or sacerdotal festivals reproduced in the private tombs of Amarna (of special value for the very individual life of Egyptian society under the heretic Amenhotep IV.); (ii.) the representations dispersed throughout the necropolises of Thebes (XVIIIth–XXIst dynasty). The frescoes of the high priest Iumaduait may be regarded as the most beautiful example descriptive of the great festivals of the Theban cult under the later Ramessids.

* Referred to as *Menology of Constantinople*.

3. The combination of these two sources of information gives the dates, the places, and the material form of the Egyptian festivals. Their nature, their aim, their significance, and a great number of details of every kind, are furnished by the *descriptive texts*. Some of these belong to the inscriptions in the temples (*e.g.* the long descriptions of the festivals of Edfu, or the famous series of the 'Mysteries of Osiris' at Dendereh); others come from a combination of the information furnished by the private stelæ (*e.g.*, in regard to everything connected with the feasts of the battles and death of Osiris at Abydos); the *ex-votos* of cures or oracles (cf. DIVINATION and DISEASE AND MEDICINE [Egyp.]) add a great number; finally, the papyri of administrative or private correspondence (principally for the last centuries) serve to complete our knowledge down to the minutest detail (cf., *e.g.*, the papyri of the Ptolemaic period for the διάβασις of the Theban Ammon).

To these properly Egyptian documents, the classical Græco-Roman world adds the wealth of its knowledge (sometimes, however, to be received with caution, especially as regards the interpretation of origins or the esoteric meaning of festivals). The long series of texts from Herodotus, Strabo, and Plutarch, or Diodorus, down to Latin literature, was collected last century by Wilkinson with a care which leaves very little to be added by modern bibliography.

The total actually known of Egyptian festivals of all kinds—general, local, exceptional, royal, funerary, commemorative, etc.—exceeds, in round numbers, 1500. Of course, this figure must not deceive us as to the real number of festivals taken part in by the national life of Egyptian society (cf. below). It is none the less certain, however, that a classification is necessary for the understanding of this enormous series. The most satisfactory method seems to be a division of the festivals according to their chief character, without taking account of chronological details or geographical divisions. Such a procedure is artificial, but it places the information most quickly at the command of the reader.

II. *CLASSES OF FESTIVALS.*—1. **Local festivals having reference to the life of local gods.**—It has been pointed out in a former article (CALENDAR [Egyp.] VI.) that the repetition or commemoration of the acts of the legendary life of the gods, celebrated at times which were foreseen and *fixed*, marked a decisive advance in the religious civilization of nations. The study of uncivilized peoples makes it possible to follow the series of attempts culminating in the point at which the history of Egypt has already arrived. We may summarize the festivals of the local gods under the following heads:

(*a*) *Anniversary of the birth of the god* (specimens: Stone of Palermo, Sarcophagus of Babe).—Practically speaking, the date of these festivals seems to have been based upon the astronomical determination of the heliacal rising of a star, or upon the reappearance in the firmament of a constellation supposed to be the habitation, or one of the 'souls,' of the divinity (an exception is made, naturally, for the gods of 'Nilotic' character or those of solar character, for whom the system is much more complicated).

(*b*) *Festivals having the character of 'seasons of the year,' associated with a local god* (*not including the feasts 'of the Inundation'*).—These are more especially the festivals of the 'first day of the year,' coinciding with the reappearance of the star Sothis (Sirius), and the beginning of the rising of the Nile (end of June). The festivals of the New Year at Dendereh, where the statue of the goddess is brought on to the terrace of the temple and there receives the first rays of the rising sun, are a good example.

The commemorations of cosmogonic events of the historical period were at first, before theology had made itself felt, simply 'naturist' festivals. Such were, *e.g.*, the festivals of the 'rising of the heaven' (*i.e.* its separation from the primordial earth and water), the anniversary of which was celebrated in a number of Egyptian towns, *e.g.* the great festival celebrated at Heracleopolis on the 1st of the month of Phamenoth.

(*c*) *The legendary episodes of the life of the gods* constitute probably the most ancient festivals. Most of these commemorations consist principally in sham battles, and seem to be reminiscences of fights attributed by local history to the war between the friendly divinities and the monsters who were enemies of man (cf. DUALISM [Egyp.]). The myths of Osiris and of Set disguised them, in the historical period, as the anniversaries of the principal dates of the war between Horus and Set-Typhon. The traces of the pre-historic period may still be found in many typical details (magical dances, disguises, masks, etc.), and suggest instructive connexions between them and the mimetic ceremonies of uncivilized peoples. Some, still more ancient, seem to have been linked, before any attempt at cosmogonic religion had been made, to the magic festivals in connexion with hunting or fishing, such as are still celebrated by races of a lower degree of culture.

(*d*) *The local life of Divine idols.*—Like the local lords and princes, who were their heritors, the Egyptian gods lived in effigy the life of lords of the manor in their sanctuaries. The walks which they took for pleasure or inspection, their excursion into their 'houses of rest' during the fine season, form the *schema* of a series of festivals which the calendar spreads over the whole length of the year. It is of these 'outings' (*khau*) and journeys that the Theban collection, thanks to the exceptional wealth of its contents, gives us an abundant list, illustrated and commented upon by hundreds of texts.

The festivals of Amon, those of Maut his wife, and of their divine son, Khonsu, represent for us the visit paid by Amon to Maut and Khonsu in their sanctuaries; the Mother-goddess or the Son-god paying a visit to the head of the family in the great temple of Karnak represents the joyful excursion of the statues of the three divinities to the Thebes of the south (=Luxor). The διάβασις of Amon on the west side of the capital, and the festival of the valley, the 'great festivals' of Amon-Minu at Medinet-Habu and at the Ramesseum, 'the beautiful festival of Amon in Thebes,' and the small festivals, such as that of the 6th day of the month, are not peculiar to the civilization or the province of Thebes. What we know of Edfu, Dendereh, and Memphis shows us a calendar quite as full of rejoicings. Memphis could enumerate an equally long list for the 'outings' or the 'manifestations' of its god Ptah, in 'great' or in 'small' festivals. The only difference in favour of Thebes arises from its position as capital, for the time being, of Egypt, and from the number of monuments which it has left us by reason of this privileged position. Everywhere, in the same way, the dividing up of the divinity into idols having a special epithet and a particular cult has brought about festivals in keeping with this special 'aspect' of the divinity. Khonsu, 'Lord of Joy' (in Thebes, 'Beautiful Rest'), and Khonsu, 'of the magnificent union,' had distinct anniversaries for their rejoicings or processions, just as Ptah, the 'modeller of the world,' and Ptah, 'of the districts of the South,' had theirs.

(*e*) A series of local festivals of a more essentially 'naturist' character is connected with *the cycles of rejoicings proper to each region of Ancient Egypt.* The gods naturally take part in them, but the connexion with their rôle or their legend is here less evident. The festival of the 'reception of the river' (Beni-Hassan, Kahun, etc.), and the festivals of the 'arrival of the Nile' (Silsileh), of the 'beginning of the rising' or the 'opening of the canals' (*passim*), are the most conspicuous. The popular character of these rejoicings, as revealed in our sources and in the classical authors, shows a strong resemblance to what, during last century, was still the character of festivals such as that of the opening of the *khalig* at Cairo. Similarities are equally evident in festivals such as those of the ὕδρευσις mentioned by the contemporaries of the Alexandrian civilization, and all those popular 'assemblies' where the people went into the country or to the neighbouring necropolises or into the 'valley' (Thebes, Dendereh, etc.), to make bouquets of *honit* or *tekhui* flowers, to eat lentils, or to taste the sweetness of new honey, while repeating the saying: γλυκὺ ἡ ἀλήθεια—as Plutarch tells us (*de Is. et Osir.* 68). The description of rejoicings of this kind gives the impression of something quite analogous to the festival of 'onions' in modern Greece, or to the *shamm an-nasīm* so dear to the hearts of the lower-class people of modern Egypt (see below, p. 884[a]).

2. Inter-provincial festivals.—The statues of the chief divinities of the nomes came out once or twice a year to pay visits of great pomp to their neighbours. Information in the form of accounts of these journeys abounds in the principal temples. Harshafitu of Heracleopolis went to see Hathor of the Fayyum, and the latter came to visit him in her turn. Edfu saw Hathor of Dendereh arriving with an immense suite of priests and followers; and Horus of Edfu afterwards went with as long a train to the festivals of Dendereh. The whole of Egypt was continually being crossed and recrossed by these Divine processions. The rejoicings lasted several days, and sometimes several weeks. Picturesque descriptions of them are not wanting, and show that the whole population took part, augmented by thousands of pilgrims from outside, not to mention, of course, the presence of the princes of the respective provinces of the visiting gods, their officers, and the whole of their clergy. The episodes of sham wars and massacres, of great popular affrays, and certain strange scenes where troops of animals (oxen, goats, etc.) were hunted, whipped, or put to death, connect these ceremonies with the highest antiquity. Over and above the legendary wars of the Osirian myth, we catch glimpses of magical feasts, with propitiatory rites in connexion with hunting or tribal wars, similar to those which are found among modern uncivilized peoples.

3. Festivals of a national character.—The mechanism which set these festivals in motion is easy to re-construct. To begin with, part of them took their rise simply in the successive political preponderance of the large towns of Egypt. The festivals of the local gods of Memphis, Thebes, and the Delta became those of the whole of Egypt as each town in turn was the first city of the valley of the Nile. The nation adopted in each case the local dates of the festivals or anniversaries, and established them as general feast-days. Their splendour tended to pale with the decline of the town to which the god really belonged; it diminished in favour of new-comers. Thus it comes about that at the time of Herodotus the great festivals of the gods of Upper Egypt had given place to those of the divinities of the Delta, because it was in Lower Egypt that the dynasties of the Bubastites, the Tanites, and the Saites had established the political centre of the Empire. The great pilgrimages, which drew the faithful by hundreds of thousands, are held henceforth in connexion with the festival of the divinities of Bubastis, Sais, and Buto. But side by side with this first changing group, a certain number of festivals, throughout almost the entire course of Egyptian history, are celebrated all over Egypt at one time. They are almost all connected, as is only logical, with those gods who, with the chief god Rā, were accepted as the universally adored gods, by the side of the local gods (with whom they are frequently confused). These are, then, festivals in connexion with Ptah-Sokar and with Osiris. As well as having in all the large towns special sanctuaries, where the festivals of their particular calendars were celebrated, their great anniversaries always drew to Memphis, Mendes, or, more especially, to the mysteries of Abydos huge crowds which came from all parts of Egypt.

The famous Osirian festivals of the month of Choiak at Dendereh seem to have acquired a more gradual popularity, and to have become famous only when the festivals of Abydos declined. As to the Heliopolitan festivals, which are as ancient as the very history of Egypt, they seem to have retained a monarchical character of high sacerdotal initiation, which separates them absolutely from the great pilgrimage festivals of the other famous sanctuaries. The national festivals are connected more especially with the funerary life of Ptah-Sokar, Osiris, and their devotees (*e.g.* the festival of the 'Round of the Walls'), and ought, rationally speaking, to be taken rather in connexion with the festivals of the dead (cf. below).

4. Anniversaries of a historical or pseudo-historical character.—Although still having a connexion with the divine life, the festivals in question have reference rather to acts done by human chiefs and to their commemoration. The Thinite monuments and the Stone of Palermo represent for us, as regards the most ancient period, the 'festival of beating Anu' or that of 'constructing the defences of Dewazefa,' which may be connected with memories of the *real* great wars of primitive Egypt (but with reserve as regards the mythological share). More definite anniversaries were instituted by the Pharaohs of the first Theban Empire, and celebrated the conquests of the monarchy. The 'festival of repelling the troglodytes' and that of 'taking captive the Nubians' were still commemorated, after having been instituted by Usirtesen III. (XIIth dynasty), under Thothmes III., in the middle of the New Empire.

At the same time, we ought not to be deceived by these anniversaries. At certain times, some Pharaoh might renew them out of devotion to one of his ancestors, or to show that he was repeating his exploits. But in the interval they had fallen into disuse, and everything tends to prove that festivals of this type rarely survived their founder.

5. Foundation of sanctuaries.—The great decorative compositions and the connected texts in the temples of Deir el-Bahri or Soleb, as well as the frescoes of Amarna, give us, with much wealth of detail, the festivals which took place at the foundation of new temples. The arrival of the royal procession, the ritual of foundation, the laying of the first stone (Edfu), the ceremonies of inauguration, of the first sacrifice, and the rejoicings accompanying all may be followed step by step. As regards Amarna in particular, the biographical pictures left by the principal dignitaries on the walls of their tombs add very valuable information to the official descriptions given by other documents, in that they show in a life-like way the popular gaiety and joyous excitement of the crowd.

6. Coronations and royal jubilees.—The categories of anniversary festivals in relation to the life of sons of gods are not numerous in the history of Egypt. The festival of the birth of the Pharaoh does not seem to have been celebrated in a regular way; the festival of giving the name was necessarily confused, through the mechanism guiding the making of royal names, with the festivals of the great gods. The coronation and the jubilee (*sadu*) are the two great ceremonies. The first divides itself naturally into a series of distinct festivals, ranging from the solemn recognition of the king by the chief of the gods, the presentation to the people in the court of the temple, and the adoption of the 'sacred name,' to the consecration properly so called. This last ceremony was fixed from the very beginning to be held at Heliopolis; the few remaining Memphite monuments represent it as being attached to that town, and it is seen from historical inscriptions that the rule of the Pharaoh was not considered valid till after the traditional solemnities had been accomplished at the Heliopolitan sanctuaries. Piankhi himself, the conqueror of Egypt, was not considered the legitimate king of Egypt until he had undergone, in the ancient capital, all the long ceremonies fixed by the custom of thousands of years. Without discussing here the difficult question of the exact nature of the *sadu*, it is evident that its jubilee nature makes it a repetition of the festivals of the coronation. Through it we obtain part of the material details which are lacking with regard to certain points of the coronation, for the festivals of *sadu* have everywhere been represented on Egyptian monuments either in a shortened form or at full length.

The texts of the Pyramids show that the episodes represented on the monuments commemorative of the *sadu* (*e.g.* at Memphis [XIIth dynasty]) existed as early as the proto-historical period. They are found almost unaltered down to the time of the Ptolemys. In this latter period Heliopolis lost the privilege, which Memphis gained, of seeing the Pharaoh crowned. The most detailed and curious scenes representing the magnificent pomp of these festivals and the concourse of all the dignitaries of Egypt are represented in the bas-reliefs of the 'festival hall' of Osorkon II., found and re-constructed in 1892 by Naville at Bubastis.

7. Royal episodic festivals.—Besides the participation of the Pharaoh in the great festivals of the cult or in the commemorations of his own reign, two distinct series of festivals have been left us by the monuments.

(*a*) *Those having reference to expeditions of war and celebrating the victories of the Pharaoh or his triumphal return.*—The royal procession with its booty and its captives, the solemn arrival of ambassadors or tributes from foreign lands, and sacrifices and offerings presented in thanks to the Divine Lords are the subject of immense decorative compositions on bas-relief and frescoes, either in the temples themselves (Karnak, the tower of Luxor, Ramesseum, etc.) or on the walls of private tombs (necropolises of Thebes and Amarna).

(*b*) *Those accompanying the different acts of royal life* (birth of princes, marriages, journeys, inauguration of palaces, etc.).—The sources, which are still rather incomplete, are furnished especially by the paintings of Amarna, which constitute in this respect a series of historical pages of the highest interest. We must make special mention of the arrival of the famous queen-mother Tyaa at her new palace, and the manifestations of all sorts which marked her arrival from Thebes (banquets, popular rejoicings, midnight banquets, processions of musicians and of torch-bearers, military parades, official processions, etc.).

8. Festivals of a funerary character. — The enumerations or calendars of the Memphite *mas-*

tabas (IVth–VIth dynasties), of Dendereh (VIIth dynasty), of Syut (Xth dynasty), of Bersheh, Gebrawi, and Beni-Hassan (XIth–XIIth dynasties), of the Theban necropolises (XVIIIth-XXVIth dynasties), give us the complete lists. The character of these festivals has been shown in art. CALENDAR (Egyp.). The form of procedure is the same as for the festivals of the gods. The cults of local gods of the dead and the festivals of these funerary gods became, at least in regard to some of the gods, national anniversaries, which were little by little all fused into the great cycle of the cult of Ptah-Sokar-Osiris. The placing of the god in the coffin and then in the tomb, the planting of sacred trees or mystic insignia (ancient fetishes [?]), the mourning of the divine family, the apparent death of the god and his subsequent resurrection, form so many episodes giving rise to distinct festivals, with which are connected the festivals of ordinary dead persons. The participation of the living in the principal anniversaries (see the frescoes of the Theban tomb of Nofirhatep) gradually modifies their character. The *agapes*, the so-called 'funeral banquets,' the general mourning on the days consecrated to the dead, the annual pilgrimages to the necropolises, the days of magic 'navigation' of the souls towards Abydos (festival of boats, the prow of which is turned towards Abydos in the night 'when the officiating priest awakes in tears'), the festival in which the processions go by the light of torches to seek the statues of the dead in the necropolises, and the festival in which 'the round of the walls of the Temple is made praying for the venerated dead,' the festival of new fire, are only *excerpta* which may be quoted in passing. Herodotus (ii. 62) has given a picturesque description of the episode of the 'festival of the Lamps.'

III. *MATERIAL CHARACTERISTICS AND GENERAL CHARACTER.*—The description of the pomp of these great Egyptian festivals cannot be made the object of even the briefest description in a summary so condensed as this. The Theban pictures show their gaiety and magnificence (see Lit.): troops of dancers and singers, companies of soldiers, troops of negroes, orchestras, officers and priests, processions of bearers of offerings or sacred objects, emblems, banners, etc. We have, in a word, along with the local modifications of Egyptian civilization, the signs of rejoicing which are present in festivals all the world over. The three more particularly Egyptian characteristics of these immense processions are: (*a*) the sacred boats, carried on litters, on which are placed the tabernacles of the images of the gods; (*b*) the carrying of insignia and emblems, in which may sometimes be recognized the survival of very curious archaic fetishisms (the 'box' of Min, vases, *didu*, thrones with the emblem *khaibet*, etc.); (*c*) the participation in the festivals of small portable statues of deceased kings or of the reigning king. This participation of the royal 'souls' is made clear by numerous inscriptions and by the bas-reliefs of Medinet-Habu, Deir el-Bahri, Karnak, Ramesseum, Gurneh, and Luxor.

Certain traditional and especially venerated statues (*e.g.* those of Ahmes I. and Nofritarit), which were continually being embellished or re-made in precious material, seem to have played a part similar to that of the most famous images of certain of our Christian sanctuaries. The participation of high dignitaries and the local nobility in these festivals would require a long article for itself alone. It is to be regretted that the magnificent representations on the staircases of Dendereh, and more especially of Edfu, have never been popularized as they should be by modern reproductions.

The frescoes of Amarna and the notes made by Herodotus during his travels illustrate briefly the part played by the populace in all these ceremonies: the noisy and sometimes licentious gaiety of the crowds which flocked to the pilgrimage, the thousands of devotees encamped in the approaches to the sanctuary, give the impression that a festival of modern Egypt, like the famous fair of Tantah, must still present an accurate picture of what a great festival of Egypt at the time of the Pharaohs was like.

The religious ceremonies which were there gone through consisted essentially in the following:

(*a*) A representation of celestial navigation by small sacred boats on the sacred lake of the temples. This is probably the most ancient source of the theme of the procession; it is connected with the organization of mimetic magic in its civilized form. (*b*) Journeys (by land and sea) taken by the statues of gods, visiting their various provincial sanctuaries. As if they were real living guests, they receive gifts on their arrival, and are entertained at solemn feasts; they are washed, anointed, perfumed, and robed. Sometimes they rest for the night 'on a bed of flowers.' During their journey they halt at 'stations of rest,' analogous to the *reposoirs* of Roman Catholic state processions. A solemn sacrifice marks the culminating point of the ceremony. (*c*) Visits of the gods to the tombs of deceased kings or princes in the necropolis, on the great days of commemoration of the dead. (*d*) The presence of divine statues at the solemn acts symbolizing the great events of agricultural life (the rising of the Nile, the cutting of the first sheaf at the harvest). (*e*) Sacred dramas, consisting particularly in representations of wars, battles, and brawls, interspersed with songs and incantations. The 'mysteries' of the type of Mendes, Abydos, and Dendereh are of a more complicated kind; in them was given a representation, lasting for some days and taking place at various points of the sacred territory, of the wars of the god, his death, the battles of his supporters, his entombment, and his resurrection. The making of symbolical images of the god, which had been broken in pieces, associating his death and resurrection with the processes of the death and resurrection of the substances of Nature (corn and vine), is the most salient feature of the famous Osirian festivals of the month of Choiak. Ceremonies like those of the great pilgrimages naturally lasted several days, and in certain cases even several weeks. Festivals of even a local character, like the 'great outing of Amon,' were extended for a whole month throughout the Theban territory.

What has been said in the articles CALENDAR (Egyp.) and DUALISM (Egyp.) explains clearly enough the essential meaning and aim of the elementary acts constituting the framework of the festivals as well as the character of pilgrimages or processions in connexion with the cult of the gods. The very nature of the festivals of foundation or the royal festivals shows us their value and their intention. What must be more strongly emphasized, as belonging specially to Egypt, is the importance which the participation in ceremonies had for an Egyptian. The festival of an Egyptian god was not only a magic reproduction, which became later a symbolical commemoration; the living and the dead really participated in the virtue and the favourable influences which flowed from the accomplishment of these 'outings' of the gods. Men contributed, along with their divinities, towards the maintaining of 'order'; their enthusiastic gratitude for the work accomplished by the gods in the past, combined with their confidence in them for future struggles, led them to consider participation in the sacred dramas as a real religious duty, the performance of which acquired merit and a sure outlook for the future life. In many respects a pilgrimage to the festivals of Abydos must have constituted for the Egyptian a meritorious act analogous to that of a Musalmān s pilgrimage to Mecca.

LITERATURE.[1]—J. H. Breasted, *Ancient Records of Egypt*, Chicago, 1906–7, Index, *s.v.* 'Feast' and 'Festival'; E. A. W. Budge, *Osiris and the Egyptian Resurrection*, London, 1911, *s.v.* 'Feast,' 'Festival,' 'Abydos,' 'Choiak,' 'Dendereh,' 'Mysteries'; * E. Daressy, *Louxor*, Cairo, 1893, pp. 41, 48, *Medinet-Habu*, do. 1897, pp. 116, 126; A. Erman, *Life in Ancient Egypt*, tr. Tirard, London, 1894, pp. 64, 246, 277, 294, * *Die ägyp. Relig.*, Berlin, 1905, Fr. tr., C. Vidal, Paris, 1907, pp. 70, 76, 233, 289, 297–302, Eng. tr., London, 1907, pp. 122, 138, 213 f., 249; * N. de G. Davies, *Rock Tombs of El Amarna*, do. 1903–8; E. Lefébure, *Rites égyptiens*, Paris, 1890; * E. Naville, *Festival-Hall of Osorkon II.*, London, 1892, *Deir-el-Bahari*, do. 1895–1908; W. M. F. Petrie, *Palace of Apriès* (*Memphis*, vol. ii.), do. 1909, pp. 5–11; * H. Schäfer, *Die Mysterien d. Osiris in Abydos*, Leipzig, 1904; A. E. P. Weigall, *A Guide to the Antiquities of Upper Egypt*, London, 1910, pp. 43, 343; J. G. Wilkinson, *Manners and Customs*, ed. London, 1878, i. 84, ii. 318, iii. 37, 83, 89, 93, 354–417; F. K. Ginzel, *Handb. der mathemat. und techn. Chronologie*, Leipzig, 1906 ff., i. 203–212.

GEORGE FOUCART.

FESTIVALS AND FASTS (Greek).[2]—A writer on this subject has abundance—embarrassing abundance almost—of material for the first part of the title, but very little for the second, unless it be made to include all religious rites not of a wholly joyous nature; and, even then, the festivals are still greatly in the majority. Greek religion was, on the whole, a very cheerful affair, and, among a people whose ordinary diet was Lenten enough, actual days of abstinence (νηστεῖαι) were not common. Throughout this article we propose to use 'festival' as a general term, corresponding to ἑορτή, for any kind of a periodical observance, whether joyous or sad. We can hope only to give a bare outline description, with a few illustrations, of the general nature of Greek festivals in the classical period, with some slight account of what we believe to have been their origin. They may be classed thus:

(1) *Agricultural.*—Under this head fall an immense number of festivals in honour of deities who, in origin at least, are gods of ploughing and sowing, harvest and vintage. In this connexion, therefore, it may be well to understand clearly, once for all, at what times in the year various agricultural operations were, and are, carried on in Greece.[3] *Ploughing* comes (*a*) in October, (*b*) in spring. *Sowing* is at the end of October (ἐνωρῆς, 'early,' as it is called nowadays) and in November (ὀψέ, 'late'). *Harvest*, beginning with barley, is from the end of April to the middle of June. Hence the modern peasant calls June Θεριστής, 'harvest-month.' *Threshing* takes place in July ('Αλωνάρης, 'threshing-month'). The *vintage* is in September (Τρυγητής, 'vintage-month').

(2) *National and commemorative.*—Under this head we include such festivals as the Panathenaia, and the anniversaries of victories. Of course, they were often dedicated to 'agricultural' deities; but their intent was to commemorate, not the god's power in Nature, but his dealings with a particular people, or his help on a particular occasion. The Great Games might be brought under this head for convenience' sake, though their origin is not beyond dispute.

(3) *Feasts of heroes and under-world powers generally.*—This is closely connected with (1), but again the view-point is different; the earth-power is worshipped, not so much as making the soil bring forth fruits, but rather as influencing the fate of the dead. The few mournful rites which are recorded are mostly included here.

(4) *Orgiastic ceremonies.*—Most, if not all, of these are foreign. The most important are the Bacchic rites, which come from Thrace. The Orphic worship, which springs from them, cannot be considered here.

1. Agricultural festivals.—The earliest and simplest form of these festivals is nothing more than vegetation-magic, originally without reference to a god at all. Athens celebrated, side by side with festivals of a more civilized type, two curiously archaic ceremonies, the Thesmophoria and the Skirophoria. In classical times they were taken under the protection of State-deities;[4] but we can still see the old magic preserved where it would be risking too much to let any ancient ceremony go, and preserved also by the conservatism of the women, the natural tillers of the soil and workers of earth-magic; for, as they know how to bear children, they can induce the earth to do likewise. γαῖα φίλη, τέκε καὶ σύ· τεαὶ δ' ὠδῖνες ἐλαφραί[1] is in effect what the women of all primitive peoples have always said—since before Rhea bare Zeus.

The *Thesmophoria* was in Pyanopsion (October), and was celebrated by the women alone, and in secret,[2] on the Pnyx. Our accounts, the chief of which is a scholiast on Lucian, *Dial. Meret.*, are vague, and overlaid with mythological interpretations; but this much can be gathered. Into certain chasms (μέγαρα) pigs were thrown,[3] and left to rot and be devoured by the snakes who lived there; and the remains—of last year's pigs, apparently—were taken up by women who had been purified for three days and were called ἀντλήριαι, 'drawers-up.' They were then placed upon an altar, 'and they believe,' says the scholiast, 'that whoever takes some, and mixes it with the seed he sows, will have a good crop.' Here we have a wide-spread form of vegetation-ritual—the preparation of a kind of manure, intended to act, not as ordinary manure does, as the σκίρα, or white earth, was perhaps supposed to do later on in the Skirophoria, but by virtue of its *mana*, due partly to the prolific nature of the pig, partly, it may be, to the influence of the serpents, the regular *avatar* of chthonian powers. The festival lasted three days, which seem to have been called ἄνοδος καὶ κάθοδος, νηστεία, and καλλιγένεια.

In connexion with the corresponding summer festival, the *Skirophoria*, we get the strange rite of the *Arrhephoria*, a word of somewhat doubtful meaning, but probably implying 'the carrying of male things.' In this, little girls—so young that their chastity was absolutely indubitable—prepared by a year's residence on the Acropolis, were given, at night, certain sacred objects, which they carried by a natural underground descent to the temple of Aphrodite in the Gardens; and thence they returned, with certain other covered objects which the priestess gave them. These objects were, no doubt, fertility charms of some sort, probably phallic, and their covering, together with the virginity of their bearers, acted as a sort of non-conductor, and prevented their virtue from being wasted. Here we get all the elements of agricultural ritual, the use of objects having great and mysterious *mana*, and the importance attached to virginity, a state whose magical potency is matched only by pregnancy.

Equally primitive, in part at least of their rites, are two festivals of the god whose name we naturally associate with advanced Hellenic culture—Apollo. These are the Spartan *Karneia* and the Athenian *Thargelia*. In the former we have clear indications of a vintage festival[4] of a sort practised all over Europe, and still surviving in places.

'A certain functionary was decked with garlands, and, after praying for blessings on the city, started off running, pursued by certain young men who must be unmarried and who were called σταφυλοδρόμοι or 'grape-cluster-runners'; if they caught him, it was a good omen for the State, but bad if they failed.'[5]

The Thargelia, in the month Thargelion = May, furnishes us with an example of a still more primitive form of the same rite. The functionary in the Karneia—no doubt an embodiment of the

[1] The works to which an asterisk is prefixed are of primary importance.

[2] Abbreviations: Farn. = L. R. Farnell, *Cults of the Greek States*, 1896 ff.; Mom. = A. Mommsen, *Feste der Stadt Athen*, 1898; Nils. = M. P. Nilsson, *Griechische Feste von religiöser Bedeutung*, 1906; Harr. = J. E. Harrison, *Prolegomena to the Study of Greek Religion*, 1903 ([2] 1908).

[3] The writer is indebted for much of his information here to Dr. Simos Menardos, Lecturer in Byzantine and Modern Greek at Oxford.

[4] See Aristoph. *Thesm.* 295.

[1] Callimachus, *ad Iovem*, 29.

[2] Cf. Aristoph. *Thesm.*, *passim*. For numerous examples of non-Attic Thesmophoria, and an account of their ritual, see Nils. 313 ff. It is one of the few feasts with distinctly mournful acts occurring in them—fasting, sitting on the ground, etc. These are probably vegetation-magic (Nils. 318).

[3] Harr. 120 ff.

[4] The *Karneia* was in the month Karneios = Metageitnion = August, roughly.

[5] Farn. iv. 259 f. For numerous examples of this sort of ritual, see Frazer, *GB*[3], pt. v.; and, for the dressed-up functionary, cf. the English Jack-in-the-Green.

vegetation-spirit—was merely pursued and caught, to get his fructifying power for the Spartan vineyards. The *pharmakoi* in the Thargelia were, some authorities inform us, actually put to death. Our chief authority, Tsetzes (*Hist.* 23, 726–756), assures us that a man selected for his ugliness was led out to sacrifice (τῶν πάντων ἀμορφώτατον ἦγον ὡς πρὸς θυσίαν), and after several rites, intended, obviously, to indicate his connexion with a fertilizing vegetation-power,[1] was burned and his ashes 'scattered to the sea and the winds as a purification of the tainted city.' Harpocration adds that this was done at the Thargelia, and not merely, as Tsetzes says, 'if disaster, by the wrath of heaven, overtook a city.' The intention is obvious: the *pharmakoi* are at one and the same time incarnate vegetation-deities and scapegoats. On both counts, of course, they are liable to be put to death—in the one case, to prevent their powers from waning and give them an opportunity to be re-incarnated, and, in the other, to get utterly rid of them and of the sins with which they are laden.

But they were certainly not actually put to death in civilized Athens. On human sacrifice the Greeks of historical times looked with loathing and abhorrence even keener than ours, because they were nearer to it—just as the N. Amer. Indians, some of whom at least were once ritual cannibals, regard as permanently infamous any of their number whom hunger has driven to such a terrible resource.[2] Yet no enemy of Athens ever accuses her of so awful a practice; Athenians, and notably the author of the *Minos*, are as emphatic as any one in denouncing it; and our authorities for the practice are late and doubtful.[3] Finally, the Thargelia was a festival of Apollo, and there is good reason to believe that not even the righteous execution of a condemned criminal was allowed to sully its purity. The killing of the *pharmakoi* can have been only a form; but no doubt, in earlier times or among more backward sections of the Greek world, it was real. At any rate, it was part of a great ceremony of purification, preparatory to getting in the harvest, of the same culture-stratum as the fertilizing rites of the Thesmophoria and Arrhephoria. Apollo's connexion with it is not very clear; probably in his character of a god of harvest[4] he took over an older ceremonial.

Of especial interest to us, particularly from a literary point of view, are those mimetic vegetation-rites connected with the name of *Dionysos*—the dances and mummings of the 'goat-men,' which ultimately led up to Tragedy[5] and Comedy. In these and many other ceremonies it is not primarily Dionysos the wine-god who is worshipped (a wine-deity pure and simple would hardly *exclude* wine from some of his offerings, as Dionysos did), but rather Dionysos the god of fertility in general, and especially the fertility of the fields. In Thrace there survives to this day[6] a curious ritual in which we get both *phalloi*, reminding us of the phallic choruses out of which, says Aristotle, Comedy sprang, and a masque of men dressed in goat-skins, which provides at last the needed link between τράγος and τραγῳδία and helps to sweep away various absurd etymologies.[7] For this masque is 'tragic,' and turns on the death of one of the characters—no doubt in old times Dionysos himself. It is well known that nothing is more common than the death, followed by the resurrection, of a vegetation-god; Adonis, Osiris, Dionysos, Balder, all come under this head—the good god who is slain by Winter or the Storm, and generally returns again in the spring. No festival of Dionysos comes in the summer; he is worshipped in spring and autumn. His three Attic feasts were in Poseideon = December (Rural Dionysia), Gamelion = January (Lenaia), and Elaphebolion = March (Greater or City Dionysia), and he is also connected with the 'Feast of All Souls' (Ἀνθεστήρια) in Anthesterion = February. Counting the Rural Dionysia and Lenaia as merely two forms of the same festival, we get the three feasts just about where we should expect them in the case of an agricultural deity: one at the time of new wine (Anthesteria), one in full spring (Great Dionysia), and one (Lenaia) to arouse the sleeping vegetation-power in winter. He has no Attic festival, however, in Pyanopsion (October), its place being taken by the older ceremonies already described. Roughly, then, we get ancient agrarian festivals answering in date to Easter, St. Demetrius' day,[1] and Christmas in Modern Greece, while the Anthesteria contains elements of something like Lenten observances.[2] It is a fresh example of the Church's marvellous and far-sighted power of adaptation in making her great feasts come at times of the year already consecrated, in the minds of the common people, by the existence of similar pagan festivals.

But we must pass to a brief discussion of the nature of the two great Athenian feasts, the Lenaia and the Greater Dionysia. In these little is left of the simple and primitive Nature-cult, either on its quasi-magical or on its orgiastic side (to be considered later). The former festival consisted (1) of a procession, managed by the king-archon and certain assistants (ἐπιμεληταί) chosen from the sacred *gentes* of the Eumolpidai and Kerykes; (2) of a contest of lyric and dramatic poetry, managed by the king-archon alone.[3] Only the contest (ἀγών) is important, for it was at this that many of the great dramatic works were produced. In this connexion, it cannot be too carefully kept in mind that the plays were all religious, at least in theory, and that going to see them was an act of worship. A devout Greek did not go to the theatre to see a play of Sophocles or Aristophanes merely because he found it amusing or moving, any more than a devout Florentine goes to Santissima Annunziata on Easter morning merely because the singing is good. Of course, æsthetic enjoyment played its part, as it generally does—the people who built the Parthenon or Cologne Cathedral were moved by a love of beauty as well as religious zeal,—but, in its essence, the State's action in appointing *choregoi*, the *choregos*' fitting out and training his chorus, the dramatist's composition of the tragedy or comedy, and the spectator's presence in the theatre were all parts of the public and private religious duty of Athens and her citizens. It is so long since we have had any such union between Church and State that we are apt to forget that there was a time when the miracle-play was almost as much a part of the service, at some times of the year, as the *Kyrie* or the *Te Deum*. The tragedies, as has already been indicated, are the glorified form of old peasant miracle-plays, very like our own May-day and Christmas mummings in general appearance, representing the contest between the two champions and the death of one of them.[4] Rather harder to

[1] τυρόν τε δόντες τῇ χειρὶ καὶ μάζαν καὶ ἰσχάδας,
ἑπτάκις οὖν ῥαπίζοντες ἐκεῖνον εἰς τὸ πέος,
σκίλλαις συκαῖς ἀγρίαις τε καὶ ἄλλοις τῶν ἀγρίων.

[2] See A. D. Cameron, *The New North*, Appleton, 1910, p. 362 f.

[3] There is better evidence for some other places, as Abdera and Rhodes. See Farn. iv. 267 ff., on the whole question.

[4] It may be necessary to remind some readers that Apollo's connexion with the sun is a mere fancy of late mythologists and syncretizers.

[5] Farn. v. 210 ff.

[6] R. M. Dawkins, in *JHS* xxvi. pt. ii. (1906).

[7] *E.g.* Harr. 421 f.; for another theory, see *ERE* iv. 870.

[1] October 26.

[2] Fasting and purification.

[3] [Arist.] Ἀθ. Πολ. lvii. 1.

[4] Ridgeway, *Origin o Tragedy*, Camb. 1910, takes a different view.

explain is the Old Comedy, with its railing and satire, its wild fun and buffoonery, and its frequent coarseness. Yet this is explicable enough as a survival, and not merely a survival—for the ideas were still alive in Greece—of old notions connected with fertility, magic, and good-luck charms. We have countless examples, many of them Greek, of peasant merry-makings, with their attendant broad fun at the expense of all and sundry, the ancient 'jests from the waggon'; and we shall have occasion to see, later on, that in the highly-developed worship of Demeter and Kore one characteristic of these was still carefully preserved—their deliberate coarseness. The *phallos*, as has already been mentioned, was used in these primitive rites as a symbol of fertility. It had its verbal equivalent—designedly coarse and foul jests. These were no mere wantonness—we hear of respectable women ceremonially using them—but part of the fertility-charm. As to the continual railing against individuals, that may be serious enough sometimes in Aristophanes, but in its ultimate origin it was as often as not a mere method of averting the evil eye; just as a street-boy spits on a new-found coin 'for luck'—really to show, or pretend to show, his contempt for it, and so avoid nemesis. We can now understand why Aristophanes dares to rail against Dionysos himself, painting him as fool, coward, effeminate, and incontinent. It is really (though whether Aristophanes fully realized this is doubtful) a pious mode of address—an averting from the god of any possible φθόνος. Dionysos, though he could be very terrible, was a friendly god who came close to his worshippers in their feastings; and extreme reverence for the beings he worshipped was not a characteristic of the Greek.[1] Cf. artt. DRAMA and DRAMA (Greek).

So much for the spirit of the plays. The details of their production are fully discussed in well-known books, such as Haigh's *Attic Theatre*, Oxford, 1889, and need not be entered into here, any more than the vexed question of stage or no stage. These points have absolutely no bearing on the religious side of the question. It should, however, be noted—what Dörpfeldt has overlooked—that whether his discovery of the precinct ἐν Λίμναις and of the wine-press be all he claims for it or not, the name Ληναῖος has nothing to do with ληνός, 'a wine-vat,' which would give Ληνεῖος, but must come from Λῆναι, an old word for 'Maenads,' and signify 'god of the Bacchantes.'[2] The feast itself, however, has nothing of the orgiastic character which the name might imply.

The chief occasion for the production of plays was the Great or City Dionysia, in Elaphebolion. This began, on the 8th, with a προαγών, including lyric performances—no doubt, as in the Lenaia, dithyrambs, the form from which Tragedy is said to have been evolved—and offerings to Asklepios. The feast proper began, as we gather from Pausanias (I. xxix. 2 and other passages), with a solemn procession, in which the sacred cult-statue of Dionysos of Eleutherai was carried to the precinct of Artemis 'Best and Fairest' near the Academy. In this *kanephoroi*, or girls carrying baskets containing sacred emblems—probably of a similar nature to those borne by the *arrhephoroi*—took part, as also did dancing and singing boys. A phallic procession is also mentioned.[1] Next—perhaps on the 10th and following days—came the dramatic contests in the great theatre of Dionysos on the slope of the Akropolis. Here there assembled, not only the Athenians themselves, as at the Lenaia,[2] but also representatives from all over the Empire, and from foreign States. This was the occasion on which most of the new tragedies were produced; indeed, 'at the new tragedies' (καιναῖς τραγῳδίαις) is sometimes used to mean 'at the City Dionysia.' We hear, nevertheless, of new tragedies being produced even at the minor Peiraic Dionysia; and Aristophanes'[2] frequent references to the Lenaia show that he often produced a new play then, as was natural, since so much of his humour is topical and local.

The most discussed of all these agricultural and quasi-agricultural festivals are the two held yearly in Attica in honour of Demeter and Kore, *the Lesser and Greater Mysteries*. A good deal is known of the external ritual of these great ceremonies (τὰ φανερῶς δρώμενα), but exactly what was taught, or whether anything at all was taught, has been a much-disputed point, ever since Lobeck's learning and common sense cleared away the absurd theories of earlier speculators (*Aglaophamus*, pt. i.).

The Lesser Mysteries took place in Anthesterion, probably about the 20th,[3] at Agra, or Agrai, on the Ilissus. Here, as in the Greater Mysteries, a 'truce of God' was proclaimed throughout Greece, to allow would-be initiates to come to Athens unmolested. We know, unfortunately, next to nothing about the rites, except that they must have been simple, as there was no temple of Demeter, so far as we know, at Agrai, and consequently no place for elaborate δρώμενα to take place.[4] The important thing is that the candidate who had been initiated in these mysteries became a μύστης, and was entitled to admission to the Greater Mysteries the next year but one.

The Greater Mysteries were held in Boedromion,[5] the truce lasting from the full moon of Metageitnion to Pyanopsion 10. They began, it would seem, on the 13th, with a procession of the Athenian *epheboi* to Eleusis to get τὰ ἱερά, certain sacred objects of which we know little, but which probably included ancient and peculiarly holy cult-statues of the two goddesses. They returned the next day. Then on the 15th came the ἀγυρμός, or assemblage of the candidates, who on the next day were solemnly addressed by the king-archon, the hierophant, and *daduchoi*, at the Stoa Poikile. All who were guilty of certain ritual impurities (such as the eating of forbidden foods), all who were unable to understand Greek, all who had been deprived of civic rights, and other disqualified persons, were warned away. What this speech was like one can gather from Aristophanes' parody of it (*Ran.* 354 ff.).

'Let every one stand aside
Who owns an intellect muddled with sins, or in arts like these untried;
If the mystic rites of the Muses true he has never seen or sung,
If he never the magical music knew of Cratinus the Bull-eater's tongue.
. . . .
Behold, I give word; and again give word; and give word for the third, last time;
Make room, all such.'[6]

---

[1] Nor always of mediæval Europe; cf. the following lines from a French mystery-play on the Crucifixion:

'Père éternel, lève-toi! n'as-tu pas vergogne?
Ton Filz est mort, et tu dors comme ung ivrogne!'

This is quite as far removed from the *Dies Iræ* as Xanthias'

ὦ χρυσοῖ θεοὶ
ἐνταῦθ' ἔχεις τὴν καρδίαν;

from the songs of the Initiated in the *Ranæ*. So Bhagavati is elaborately insulted at her great spring-festival at Cranganore (see *GB*[3], pt. i. vol. i. p. 280).

[2] Farn. v. 208; Nils. 276, who aptly compares ληναγέτης. Mommsen and Miss Harrison support the contrary view.

[1] *CIA* i. 31. See Mom. 435 ff., for a detailed account.

[2] Aristoph. *Ach.* 503 ff. This indicates that *The Acharnians* was produced at the Lenaia, but *The Babylonians* at the Greater Dionysia.

[3] Mom., chapter on 'Kleine Mysterien.' The month is furnished by Plutarch, *Demetrius*, 26; the duration of the truce (full-moon of Gamelion-Elaphebolion 10) indicates the 20th as a likely date.

[4] Farn. iii. 169 for the few facts that are known.

[5] Plut. 1. 1; Camill. 19; Phokion, 6; cf. *CIA* i. 4, n. 1 B.

[6] Murray's translation.

Next followed the rite which gave the day its name, ἅλαδε μύσται, 'To the sea, ye *mystai!*' The whole body of the initiate went down to Phaleron, washed themselves in the sea, and also washed their pigs. For in this, as in all rites of a chthonian nature, the pig was a recognized means of purification, generally by means of its blood. Exactly how the animals were used on this occasion we do not know; *Ran.* 338 strongly suggests that they formed the material for some kind of sacrificial feast.

Then followed certain rites of which little is known. On the 17th we hear of a sacrifice of a sucking-pig to Demeter and Kore.[1] On the 18th (?) there was a procession in honour of Asklepios, probably identical with the Epidauria which Philostratos mentions (*Vit. Apoll. Tyan.* iv. 18).[2] On the 19th, late in the day, so as to last well into the night, and therefore, by Greek reckoning, into the 20th, came the great Iakchos-procession to Eleusis, visiting various holy places *en route*, and stopping at a certain bridge[3] over the Cephissos for the rough jesting which, we have already seen, is associated with agricultural rites.[4] Here we have to notice the presence of Iakchos-Dionysos in this festival of Demeter and her daughter. Our earliest document, the Homeric Hymn to Demeter (? 7th cent.), knows nothing of him. Probably, after the Dionysiac cult was imported from Thrace, with the Delphic oracle acting as its vigorous missionary and supporter, Dionysos was simply added to the Eleusinian deities, whom he resembled in many ways.

Arrived at Eleusis, no doubt after a rest—for the journey of some 15 miles, made fasting, with incidental dancing and singing, must have been extraordinarily fatiguing—the *mystai* proceeded to the rites of initiation, perhaps on the nights of the 20th and 21st. Concerning these we know, briefly, the following facts. Firstly, they were connected with the legend of the rape of Persephone, the grief-stricken search of Demeter, her arrival at Eleusis, the gift of corn, and the recovery of her daughter. Secondly, we gather that some part at least of all this was enacted in a sort of mystery-play at the *telesterion*, or Hall of Initiation.[5] That there was also a ἱερὸς γάμος, or mystic marriage ceremony; that at a certain point in the rites the hierophant cried aloud, 'Our Lady Brimo hath borne a holy child Brimos'; that there was some sort of representation of the terrors of the under world—are the vague statements of late authors; and, though quite possibly true for some ritual or other, have not necessarily anything at all to do, really, with Eleusis. One fact, however, we do know, that at the climax of the rites certain 'holy things' were shown. Here again we are in ignorance of what they were.

We know a little about what was *said*—a less important matter than what was *done*. We hear of a sacred formula, ὕε κύε, 'Rain (O Sky), conceive (O Earth),' used by the hierophant—a rain-charm, apparently, belonging to the oldest stratum of the rites; of the mystic formulæ (passwords [?]) employed by the initiate; but exactly what it all meant is unknown. The secret was well kept.

Perhaps the fact is that there was no secret—at least no secret *doctrine*. The glow of ecstasy with which many writers, especially Neo-Platonists, speak of the experiences of the *mystai* does not, even if taken literally, compel us to suppose any notable increase in knowledge. It is rather a heightening of religious emotion, and a feeling of having joined the ranks of the elect. 'Bad have I fled, better have I found,' says one of the formulæ. Something in the rites—perhaps a sort of communion-service[1]—may have induced a feeling of unity with Demeter and Kore, and with the male objects of the worship, Hades-Pluton, Eubuleus, Triptolemos, Iakchos. More than this we cannot say. If there had been any tangible doctrine, it is unthinkable that nothing should have leaked out, when practically any one could be initiated; and the official initiators, hierophant, *daduchos hierokeryx*, etc., were not men of any special training, but simply members of certain old priestly families who possessed traditional knowledge of the rites. We do not hear, in Greece, of a priestly caste claiming vast superiority in religious knowledge over the laity. There were, of course, certain things about the gods which only their priests and priestesses knew; but no mysterious powers or wisdom resulted from them to the priests themselves. They were simply things which must not be noised abroad, for fear some hostile person should make a bad use of them. Euthyphron might try to impress Socrates by claiming to be able to tell him many very extraordinary things about the gods; but neither Socrates nor any one else seems to have been much impressed by these claims.

2. National and commemorative festivals.—These were very numerous. They were held with a definite purpose, usually to honour a national deity, or to return thanks for a particular service. Being frequently rather elaborate and expensive, they were often pentaeteric or quadrennial. We may sub-divide them thus: (*a*) festivals simply in honour of the god or goddess of a State; (*b*) international or pan-Hellenic festivals of a similar kind; (*c*) festivals of purification, associated with a ritual legend and purporting to be a representation of the deity's experiences; (*d*) feasts of thanksgiving for victories, etc.

Of (*a*) a good example is furnished by the great pentaeteric festival at Athens, the *Panathenaia*.[2] This occurred towards the end of Hekatombaion, in the height of summer, the chief day being the 28th of the month—τρίτη φθίνοντος, 3 being Athene's number. The orientation of the Parthenon is so calculated as to allow the rising sun to shine full in through the door on this day, in the year of the temple's completion, 458 B.C. This feast was the celebration of the might of Athens and her power over lesser States—for all the allies were expected to send contributions to it—and of the might of her patron-goddess. It consisted of a series of contests such as a goddess of the arts and of war might be expected to delight in. First came an ἀγὼν μουσικῆς, or contest of singing, instrumental music, and, at least in the days of Peisistratos, recitations from Homer. Next came a gymnastic contest (lasting 2 days), originally held near the Piræus, but later (4th cent.) in the present Stadion. The prizes for this consisted of jars of oil, originally at least the product of the μορίαι, or sacred olives of the goddess. There were two prizes for each contest, the second being $\frac{1}{5}$ of the first; *e.g.* the winner in the boys' *pankration* received 40 jars of oil, the 'runner-up' 8. The contests were of the usual nature—foot-racing, boxing, wrestling, etc. Next came the ἀγὼν ἱππικός—horse-racing of various kinds; then certain minor contests—a pyrrhic dance, an *euandria*, or parade of crack troops, and a torch-light procession — all competitive, each

1 *CIG* 523; *Berliner Klassikertexte*, pt. 5, 1st half, p. 10, provides us with an interesting, though very fragmentary, mythological explanation of the connexion between pigs and Kore.

2 Farn. iii. 171 ff.

3 The modern Kolokythou, approximately; about half an hour from the Dipylon Gate.

4 The procession probably started from the Agora (*Ran.* 320, reading δι' ἀγορᾶς for Διαγόρας). For jesting (γεφυρισμός), cf. *Ran.* 420 ff.

5 The small extent of this hall, whose foundations are now completely laid bare at Eleusis, proves that there can have been no very elaborate spectacular performance, and indeed makes it hard to understand how the numerous μύσται can have got in at all.

1 Farn. iii. 185 ff.

2 See E. Gardner, *Gr. Athletic Fest.*, p. 227 f., and, for more details, *JHS* xxxii. pt. i. p. 179 f.

tribe entering. There was also an all-night festival (*pannychis*), mentioned by Euripides (*Herakl.* 777–783) and other authorities; and, on the principal day of the feast, an elaborate procession, bringing the city's tribute to the goddess—the richly embroidered robe (πέπλος) on which was represented her triumph over the giants. Here, in the midst of this civilized ritual, we get a touch of primitive feeling; the statue of the goddess needs clothing, just as at another period of the year it needed to be taken down to the sea and washed, while the temple was undergoing a house-cleaning process (*Plynteria* and *Kallynteria*). The festival ended with a regatta in the harbour.[1]

(*b*) The great *games at Olympia* and elsewhere were not very different from the gymnastic part of the Panathenaia, which they no doubt suggested. Existing nominally to do honour to Zeus, Poseidon, etc., it is at least possible that they originated from the funeral games of buried heroes. However this may be, and whatever be the origin of the games (Olympian chronology is very uncertain, the list of victors compiled by Hippias of Elis being criticized as early as Plutarch's time), in the 5th and 4th centuries their importance can hardly be exaggerated. They were pan-Hellenic; a truce similar to that proclaimed by Athens before the Mysteries protected all visitors; and all Greece was ready to punish those who dared to violate it. Any one who could satisfy the board of judges that he was of pure Greek blood, and not of a city under a curse, that he was free from crime and impiety, and that he had trained for the past 10 months was entitled to enter. This meant that all Greece proper, Ionia, Sicily, Magna Græcia, and the colonies scattered over the Mediterranean sent representatives to Olympia at least, if not to the other great games. The programme—originally 1 day only—lasted 3 days in later times, and consisted of long and short distance foot-races, races in armour, boxing, wrestling, the *pankration*, and an 'all-round' contest, the *pentathlon*—jumping, running, discus-throwing, javelin-throwing, wrestling—besides the great chariot- and horseback-races. It was to celebrate victories of athletes that the greatest lyric poets wrote, and the victor received almost divine honours from his city. Moreover, no place was so good as one of these great athletic meetings to hear all the latest news, see every one worth seeing, and listen to the latest poets, sophists, or historians. Thus, even where no actual 'musical' contests existed, the games fostered art and literature, as well as the pan-Hellenic spirit, indirectly at least.[2]

(*c*) The best example, perhaps, of this is the great Apolline festival of the *Stepteria*. This was held at Delphi every ninth year (*i.e.* once in each *oktaeteris*), and was supposed to commemorate Apollo's slaying of Python, his flight and exile, and his purification and return.[3] A boy of good family—obviously representing the god—was escorted, along with certain other boys, by torch-bearing women (*oleiai*) to a wooden hut built to represent a palace (the 'abode of Python'). This was set fire to, and the table in it was overturned. Then the boy pretended to go into exile; finally all went—not in mimicry but in actual fact—to Tempe, were purified with laurel, crowned themselves with it, and returned by the sacred Pythian way,[4] entering Delphi in triumph. Here we have a good example of a rite giving rise to an ætiological myth. For, assuming the Apollo-Python story as a basis, why should we have a palace—which serpents do not usually inhabit—and why is it elaborately destroyed, furniture and all? Whereas, starting from the ceremony, it is all plain enough. The boys, headed by the incarnate god, get rid of any miasma they may have, in the 'palace,' which is then disinfected by burning.[1] They then go away, possibly bearing the sins of the people with them, and, instead of negatively purging only, they come back after their purification, radiating purity from themselves and their crowns. This example will suffice to show, in an interesting case, the way in which rites really 'agricultural,' purificatory, or the like, came to be interpreted, *via* ætiology, as purely or chiefly 'commemorative.'

(*d*) The feasts of thanksgiving for victories, etc., form a fairly numerous class, but of no special importance. The best-known instance is the *Marathonia* at Athens, with its annual sacrifice of 500 goats to Artemis Agrotera, in composition for the rash vow to give her a goat for every slain Persian. It occurred in Boedromion, on the 6th according to Plutarch (*de Glor. Ath.* 7). The date is no doubt determined, not by the actual day on which the battle was fought—this was nearer the middle of the month—but by the fact that it is Artemis' day.

3. Feasts of heroes and under-world powers generally.—Chthonian rites, as these are generally called, may be distinguished from Olympian worship by the following characteristics. (*a*) Their object is not so much to please the power addressed, and secure its favour, as to induce it to go away or to remain quiescent; the cult is ἀποτροπή, not θεραπεία.[2] (*b*) Sacrifices (ἐναγίσματα, not ἱερά) are given entirely, not shared—are burned, poured into holes in the ground, thrown into the sea, etc. The altar is not called βωμός but ἐσχάρα, a sort of hearth such as was often placed above or before a tomb for funeral offerings. (*c*) Night rather than day is the time chosen for the ritual. (*d*) The powers invoked, though often called by divine names, are generally seen on examination to be heroic rather than divine. (*e*) When combined with Olympian ritual, these powers are honoured with a subordinate, but quite distinct, ceremonial. Of course, one must except from these general rules a few figures which, though chthonian, are in some sense Olympian. Hermes Χθόνιος, for instance, is invoked by the returning Orestes to help and save;[3] Hades-Pluton is no ordinary under-world power, but the great death-god of an advanced race; and Zeus Χθόνιος is regarded as in some way the same as Zeus Ὀλύμπιος or Ὕψιστος. But of the great mass of chthonians all or most of these rules hold good. It should be added that most of them are nameless, and described by adjectives only. Thus we hear of 'the Kindly Goddesses' (Εὐμενίδες), 'the Reverend Ones' (Σεμναί), 'the Easy-to-be-entreated' (Μειλίχιος); and, over and over again, simply of 'the hero.' Even the name Ἀΐδης or Ἅιδης is adjectival = 'the Invisible One,' while Pluton = 'the Rich One.'

The explanation which the present writer considers the most likely is that most of these beings are, like Mycerinus' deities, 'not gods but ghosts.' This is obvious in the case of heroes; they are simply the buried men living in some vague way underground or in their graves—a notion as widespread as it is primitive. It is less certain in the case of many others. For instance, the Erinyes may be variously explained. Are they embodied curses, or the angry ghosts of murdered and unavenged men? Again, who are the Eumenides, with whom the Erinyes are commonly but wrongly

[1] See Mom. for full particulars as to dates, etc.
[2] For details, see Gardner, p. 31 f.
[3] Farn. iv. 293 ff. [4] *Ib.* 103 ff.

[1] It should be remembered that the primitive mind looks upon moral evil of all sorts much as we regard the bacilli of a disease, as something contagious, and to be got rid of by the action of fire and of certain medicinal substances, and that this idea persists into quite late times, in a more or less unconscious form.
[2] Harr. ch. 1. [3] Æsch. *Choeph.* 1–3.

identified? Though powers to be feared, their functions are kindly enough; they give fertility and general good fortune. (See EUMENIDES.) Did Demeter and Kore develop out of some such figures? Are the winds ghosts or elemental powers? These are questions easy to ask and hard to answer. We think, however, that the close resemblance between the worship of heroes and the worship of other chthonian powers makes the ghost-theory a likely one. But this is not the place to discuss so wide a subject, and we shall merely notice a few typical pieces of ritual in which these powers receive honour.

(1) *Actual offerings to the dead, or to some particular dead persons.*—We find a good example of this at Platæa, where, under the title of οἱ ἥρωες, those who fell in the great battle received offerings—a black steer, wine, milk, oil, unguents[1]—every year on the 6th of Alalkomenios = Maimakterion.

(2) *Worship of heroes in conjunction with Olympians.*—Here a good example is afforded by the ritual of the Hyakinthia at Amyklai. This festival, held in the month corresponding to Hekatombaion, divides sharply into two parts—the one mournful, involving abstinence from cereal food, banqueters ungarlanded, etc.; and the other joyous, with music and other rites such as one associates with Apollo, whose feast it is.[2] The reason is clear. Apollo's ritual has been superimposed upon that of an old chthonian power Hyakinthos, who, being dead (permanently, as a hero, or temporarily, as a vegetation-god), is naturally mourned for; his festival, as he has something to do with harvest, contains the not uncommon tabu on cereals before the harvest begins.

(3) *Heroes and other chthonians with the names of Olympians.* — This does not include genuine Olympians such as Hermes; but it does, on the one hand, include the purely heroic Zeus-Agamemnon, where 'Zeus' is almost an adjective, and, on the other, the Zeus worshipped at the Diasia—Zeus Meilichios.[3] Here the ritual is chthonian; the object of worship is often represented as a snake—a regular chthonian form—yet he is called 'Zeus the Easy-to-be-entreated.' To the present writer this proves, with some approach to conclusiveness, that the powerful Olympian has been superimposed upon a local chthonian god—or ghost, it makes little difference—to such an extent as to blot out his personality, such as it was, and leave merely the gloomy, chthonian nature of certain of the rites; just as a little later in the same month (Anthesterion) Dionysos' vigorous personality all but effaces the ancient All-Souls' festival of Χόες, which still betrays itself, however, in certain points of the ritual.

(4) Finally, we must not omit an important class of chthonian rites, namely, *cursing*. Every Greek city had its Commination Service, and the powers who fulfilled the curse would naturally be chthonian—the Erinyes, for example. One of the best-known of these solemn curses is the so-called 'Dirae of Teos,'[4] with its litany-like refrain of 'May he perish, both himself and his kin' (κεῖνον ἀπόλλυσθαι καὶ γένος τὸ κείνου), while we know, from the parody in Aristoph. *Thesm.* 335 ff., the nature of the curse uttered by every Athenian archon and by the herald at the beginning of each ecclesia.[5]

4. Orgiastic ceremonies.—These, though foreign and never germane to Greece, deserve a word of mention, because they are associated with the great name of Dionysos. This is not the place for a detailed account of them; but it may be said that they rest on a basis quite different from the calm ritual of ordinary Greek worship. Instead of a simple sacrificial meal shared with the god, the key-note of an ordinary Olympian ceremony, or even a quasi-magic rite, such as we have seen surviving in the Thesmophoria, orgiastic religions seek for a mystical union of the worshipper with the object of his worship—either by means of a kind of religious mania or self-hypnotism, induced by wild dancing and the like, or by a sacramental devouring of some animal believed to be the incarnation of the god. This, in the case of Dionysos, was generally a bull or a calf. He himself is hailed as a 'noble bull' in the Elean song preserved in Plut. *Quæst. Græc.* 299 B, and often represented as horned or tauromorphic. But this was really a Thraco-Phrygian worship, and in Greece proper Dionysos was usually the recipient of a more sober and ordinary cult.[1] Of his share in the Mysteries we have already written.

In connexion with orgiastic and enthusiastic worship in general, the frenzy of prophets, and especially of the Pythia at Delphi, may be noticed. Here we have a curious bit of savagery, for it is simply the temporary 'possession' of the shaman by his god, surviving in the most orderly and most thoroughly Hellenic of all cults. The explanation perhaps lies in the fact that Delphi had been a mantic shrine before the coming of Apollo; and that certain traces of an older and cruder worship were not to be eradicated. At any rate, the actual givers of oracles were the official 'interpreters' of the priestess's inspired ravings, and not she herself, as she was in all probability totally unintelligible.[2]

Summary.—The variety of cults mentioned in this art. may perhaps give a wrong impression of the general nature of Greek worship. We close, therefore, by insisting on the fact that the average Greek ceremony, the sort performed by the ordinary worshipper nine times out of ten, was neither orgiastic, chthonian, nor magical, but consisted simply in a sacrifice, partly sublimated by burning, so as to reach the celestial abode of the gods, partly eaten by the sacrificer and his fellow-worshippers. This, from Homeric times onward, was the normal expression of Greek piety. In the following ecclesiastical calendar, so to call it, of Athens, the preponderance of such feasts may be seen at a glance—'O.' indicating a festival of any sort in honour of an Olympian, 'Ch.' a chthonian or a hero-feast, 'O.-Ch.' one combining both elements.

THE ECCLESIASTICAL YEAR AT ATHENS (the dates of the festivals are from Mommsen, to whom the reader is referred).

HEKATOMBAION.
- 12 Kronia (O.).
- 16 Synoikia (in commemoration of the συνοικισμός under Theseus) (? Ch.).
- 20–23 Musical *agôn*.
- 24–25 Gymnastic *agôn*.
- 26 Equestrian *agôn*.
- 27 Pyrrhic and *euandria*.
- 28 Torchlight procession, παννυχίς, procession, sacrifice, and feast.
- 29 Regatta.

(20–29:) Panathenaia (O.); pentaeteric. Lesser Pan. (yearly) at same date.

METAGEITNION.
- Herakleia in Kynosarges (? O.).
- Panhellenia (O.).
- (Dates uncertain.)

BOEDROMION.
- 3 Anniversary of Platæa (? O.).
- ? Genesia (? = Nemeseia) (Ch.).
- 6 Marathonia (O.).
- 12 Charisteria (thanksgiving for the overthrow of the Thirty Tyrants; O.).
- ? Eleusinia (gymnastic *agôn*; O.).

[1] Nils. 455. [2] Farn. iv. 264. [3] Harr. 12 ff.
[4] *CIG* 3044; Hicks and Hill, *Greek Histor. Inscriptions*, Oxford, 1901, p. 23.
[5] We have here omitted the greatest chthonians—Demeter and Persephone—because they are most important in their 'agricultural' functions, especially in the Mysteries (see above). For a plausible account of their origin, see *GB*[3] v. pt. i. p. 35 ff.

[1] For a full discussion of Dionysos worship, see Farn. v. chs. 4 and 5.
[2] Farn. iv. 193 ff.

13 Procession of *epheboi* to Eleusis.
15 Agyrmos.
16 *ἅλαδε μυσται.*
17 Sacrifice (to Asklepios ?).
? 18 Epidauria.
19 Iakchos-procession to Eleusis.
20–22 ? Initiation.
} Greater Mysteries (mostly Ch.).

Pyanopsion or Pyanepsion.

7[1] Pyanepsia.
? 7 Race of *oschephoroi*, Komos, etc., offerings to the dead.
8 Procession, sacrifice, and feast, libations to Theseus.
9–11 *Agôn*, etc.
12[2] Torchlight procession.
12 Race of *epheboi*; ceremonial in Kerameikos: funeral oration for soldiers killed in battle during the year.
} Theseia (Ch.).

12 Anodos.
13 Nesteia.
14 Kalligeneia.
} Thesmophoria (Ch.).

? 19–21 Apaturia, or ceremony of receiving children into their fathers' clans (O.); ? Promethia, Hephaistia, Chalkeia, Athenaia (O.). (Dates uncertain.)

Posideon.

? about 19th Rural Dionysia (O.).
? Haloa (Ch.).
? Prochaireteria (? Ch.).
? Dionysia ἐν Πειραιεῖ (O.).

Gamelion.

? Lenaia; procession; lyric and dramatic contests (O.).
? Theogamia (marriage of Zeus and Hera; O.).

Anthesterion.

13 Pithoigia.
14 Choes.
15 Chytroi.
} Anthesteria (O.-Ch.).

? 20 Lesser Mysteries (Ch.).
? 23 Diasia (? O.).

Elaphebolion.

8 *Proagôn*: offerings to Asklepios.
? 9 Procession.
10 and following days. Theatrical contests.
} City Dionysia (mostly O.).

? Galaxia. To Kybele (? O.).

Munychion.

6 Hiketeria, or suppliant procession to shrine of Apollo Delphinios (O.).
? 16 Munychia and Brauroneia (O.; to Artemis).
? 16 Aianteia. Commemorating Salamis (? Ch.).
? 18 Sacred embassy to Delos (O.).
? 19 Olympeia (O.; to Zeus).

Thargelion.

7 Thargelia (O.; ? Ch.).
17 Beudideia (O.).
19 Kallynteria (O.).
21 Plynteria (O.).

Skirophorion.

12 Skirophoria (O.).
? Dipolia or Bouphonia (O.).

Literature.—(1) On Greek religion: L. R. Farnell, *Cults of the Greek States*, Oxford, 1896–1909; J. E. Harrison, *Prolegomena to the Study of Greek Religion*[2], Cambridge, 1908; C. A. Lobeck, *Aglaophamus*, Königsberg, 1829; A. Mommsen, *Feste der Stadt Athen*, Leipzig, 1906; M. P. Nilsson, *Griechische Feste*, Leipzig, 1906; E. Rohde, *Psyche*[4], Tübingen, 1907; E. Gardner, *Greek Athletic Festivals*, London, 1910.

(2) On the general question of survivals of earth-magic, etc., in higher religions: J. G. Frazer, *GB*[3], London, 1911 ff; Farnell, *Evolution of Religion*, do. 1905; *Anthropology and the Classics* (ed. R. R. Marett, Oxford, 1908) might also be consulted.

H. J. Rose.

FESTIVALS AND FASTS (Hebrew).

—I. *Periodical Festivals.*—i. Weekly.—**The Sabbath.**—From probably an early period every 7th day was observed as the holy day of rest. Since the *šabattu* is described in the cuneiform inscriptions as 'a day of rest for the soul,'[3] Sayce (*Higher Crit. and Mon.*[2], London, 1894, p. 74) argues for a Bab. origin, and compares it with the observance of the 7th, 14th, 21st, 28th days, as days on which it was unlawful to do certain kinds of work. But the Jewish observance of the Sabbath was of a very different kind from that of the ancient Babylonians.

The earliest historical reference to the Sabbath in the Bible is 2 K $4^{22.23}$, but the language used suggests that its observance was a long established custom. The fact that at different times different explanations of it are given points in the same direction. In Ex 23^{12b} (E), Dt 5^{14b} (probably derived from JE), the purpose is that all may rest, including the slaves, the stranger, and the animals, as well as the master and the family. In Dt 5^{15} the reason assigned by D is that it is a memorial of the Exodus, which it seems to assume took place on that day. In Gn 2^{1-3}, Ex 20^{11}, the reason assigned is the Sabbath rest of God on the 7th day, after the 6 days' work of creation. In theory, at any rate, the prohibition of work, even in the earliest laws on the subject (Ex 20^{10} 23^{12}), was absolute. But the only evidence of the extremely literal and rigid observance of this rule belongs to the age of the Priestly Code, in which the reason which had come to be assigned for its observance gave it a more sacred and binding character. Thus the manna might not, and indeed could not, be gathered on the Sabbath (Ex 16^{22-30}); a man is stoned to death for collecting sticks on that day (Nu 15^{32-36}). Nehemiah makes very stringent provision against violating the Sabbath by trading, etc., on it (Neh 13^{15-22}). On the Sabbath two lambs, with the customary meal- and drink-offerings, were sacrificed as a burnt-offering in addition to the daily morning and evening sacrifices (Nu 28^{9-10}).

The extreme minutiæ of detail, the difficulties to which they gave rise, and the ingenious methods of evading them are fully discussed in the Mishnic tract *Shabbath*. They frequently formed the ground of conflict between the Pharisees and Christ, who taught that the Sabbath should be regarded not as a fetish, but as an institution designed for practical benefit to man (Mk 2^{23-28} 3^{1-6}, Lk $6^{1-5.\,6-11}$ 13^{10-17} 14^{1-6}, Jn $5^{9ff.}$). When synagogues were established, the Sabbath services became an important feature of Judaism. Many of the discourses and acts of healing of Christ took place in connexion with them (Mk 1^{21-28} 3^{1-6} 6^{1-6}, Lk 4^{31-37} 13^{10-17} etc.). St. Paul also frequently made use of the synagogue service in his missionary journeys (Ac $13^{14-43.\,44-45}$ 14^{1-6} etc.). Parts of the service—notably the lections and discourse which followed (cf. Lk 4^{31-37})—became the model for early Christian worship, and profoundly influenced the history of the Christian liturgies.

It seems likely that the original purpose of the Sabbath was to consecrate every phase of the moon. It may have been derived in the first instance from some form of moon-worship. If so, the purpose was lost sight of when, if not before, a conventional week of 7 days was substituted for the lunar phase (see Calendar [Hebrew], § 1).

ii. Monthly.—**The New Moon.**—This is frequently mentioned with the Sabbath, as being both festivals of ordinary occurrence (2 K 4^{22-23}, Am 8^{5}, Hos 2^{11}, Is 1^{13}), such as, *e.g.*, a devout woman might be expected to attend at some not very distant sanctuary, even though her husband stayed at home (2 K 4^{23}). In early times the New Moon was marked by a sacrificial feast, at which all the household were expected to be present, unless prevented by some ceremonial uncleanness or other religious cause (1 S $20^{5.\,6.\,26}$). In the Priestly Code a special offering was made of two young bullocks, one ram, seven lambs, and a goat for a sin-offering (Nu 28^{11-15}). Just as the Sabbath was probably the dedication of each phase, so the New Moon was undoubtedly the consecration of the whole moon or month (see Calendar [Hebrew], § 1).

iii. Annual.—These we shall divide into (*a*) those that were certainly pre-exilic, and (*b*) those that were possibly or certainly post-exilic in origin.

(*a*) *Pre-exilic.*—It is not improbable, when every important town had its separate sanctuary, that customs with regard to the festivals, their number and their character, may have varied in different localities. But there is evidence to show that at some sanctuaries, such as Shiloh—probably the most important temple of the early days of Samuel

[1] Evening of the 6th by our reckoning.

[2] Night of the 11th.

[3] The real meaning of the phrase *ûm nûḫ libbi* (II Rawl. 32, l. 16) appears to be a day when the gods rested from their anger (see *HDB* iv. 319[a]).

—there was a great annual festival which, if not the only one, was so important as to be regarded as the great yearly sacrifice (1 S 1^{7-21} 2^{19}), and which all within the district attended, unless hindered for a sufficient reason (1^{22}). These chapters, if not contemporary evidence of the state of things in Samuel's time, may at least be regarded as evidence of what was customary at a typical local sanctuary in the time of the early monarchy. With this we may compare the custom of an annual family feast, of which we have evidence in 1 S $20^{6.\ 29}$, at which the scattered members of the family assembled.

The annual sacrificial feast at Shiloh has been frequently identified with the Feast of Booths at the end of the year. It would probably be more correct to say that the latter was a later development of the annual festival. Jg 21^{19-23} (post-exilic but evidently based on earlier documents) certainly supports the view that this annual feast was originally a vintage celebration.

In the earliest legal codes, we find three annual festivals: (1) Unleavened Bread (*Maṣṣôth*), including perhaps Passover (*Pesaḥ*); (2) Weeks (*Shᵉbû'ôth*); and (3) Ingathering (*'Asîph*) (Ex 23^{16} [E], $34^{18.\ 22-23}$ [J]). That these were agricultural in origin is evident in the case of the last two, and probable in that of the first.

1. Maṣṣôth.—The meaning of this feast is not given in the early documents (its association with the Exodus being probably an afterthought; see below). In later times it included three rites which appear to have been originally distinct: (1) the Paschal meal, or Passover proper, (2) the seven days' Festival of Unleavened Bread, (3) the wave-offering of the first sheaf (*'ōmer*).

(1) The essential feature of the *Passover* proper was the sacrificial feast of the Paschal lamb. There was a very ancient religious tradition that the firstlings and firstfruits belonged by right to Jahweh (Ex 13^{11-13} 22^{29-30} 23^{19} 34^{19-20} [JE]). The tradition that in the last plague the first-born of Egypt had been involuntarily sacrificed to Jahweh (Ex 13^{15}), and that the tribe of Levi was consecrated to Him as a tribe to whom the rights of the first-born had been transferred (Nu 3^{12-13}), as well as the offering of all firstfruits and firstlings, including the redemption of men and unclean animals by the substitution of a lamb (Ex $13^{2.\ 12-13}$ etc.), belongs to the same cycle of ideas. What more natural than that the first lambs of the season should be offered to Jahweh? But, as it came to be a matter of importance, with the consolidation of the tribes, that the festival should be observed by all at the same time, the lambs would in due course have ceased to be necessarily the first-born, and the original intention of the feast have been lost sight of, or overshadowed by its connexion with the Exodus. This view of the origin of the Passover is borne out by the analogy of the Feast of Booths which, originally an agricultural feast, came to have an exclusively historical meaning (see below).

(2) The origin of the Festival of *Maṣṣôth* is more uncertain. It appears to have originated from an old religious custom that all bread offered to Jahweh was to be without leaven (Ex 23^{18}; cf. 34^{25} [J], where the same prohibition appears to be confined to the Paschal meal). In later times this law was not so rigidly observed. At any rate a distinction seems to be made between unleavened cakes actually offered on the altar (Lv 7^{12}) and those which were merely presented, as the wave-offering of loaves at Weeks (see below), and the thank-offering (Lv $7^{13f.}$). Whether the shewbread was made of leavened or unleavened bread is not clear. It is probable that in early times a distinction was made between what constituted the essential part of the feast, as usually the animal sacrifice, and what was merely eaten with it, as the bread. In the case of *Maṣṣôth*, the unleavened bread was the essential part of the sacrificial meal. It is probable that originally the unleavened cakes were the first prepared out of the barley harvest, analogous to the first two loaves of the wheaten harvest at Weeks (Lv 23^{17}). There is no reason to suppose that the festival in early times lasted more than a day, or was even more than a single meal. The use of leaven has sometimes been explained, as by Wellhausen, as arising from the unwillingness to mix the firstfruits of the new season with what belonged to the old, the leaven being a piece of old fermented dough. Even in the earliest account of the festival (Ex 13^{6-10} [J]) it is explained, however, as a memorial of the hurried flight from Egypt when the people had no time to prepare leaven.

In the Priestly Code the Feast of *Maṣṣôth* follows immediately after the Passover, and they practically form one festival, now regarded as commemorating in various ways the sudden flight from Egypt and the events connected therewith. In addition to the use of unleavened bread, the chief provisions were: (α) the selection of a lamb or kid on the 10th day of Abib (Nisan) (Ex 12^{2-4}); (β) the slaying of the lamb on the 14th, 'between the two evenings,' *i.e.* probably just before the evening with which the 15th of Abib began (v.^{6}); (γ) the sprinkling of the blood on the doorposts and the lintel of the house in which it was to be eaten (v.^{7}); (δ) the roasting of the lamb whole (vv.$^{9.\ 46}$). It was to be eaten (ϵ) with unleavened bread (vv.$^{8.\ 15.\ 18-20}$), and (ζ) bitter herbs (v.^{8}), and (η) in haste with loins girded, shoes on feet, and staff in hand (v.^{11}). (θ) Nothing was to be left to be eaten the next day, but all remains were to be burnt with fire (v.^{10}).

Of these (ζ) was to signify the hardship of their bondage in Egypt, (η) their sudden flight; (γ) commemorated, of course, the sprinkling of blood which caused the angel to 'pass over' their houses, when he slew the Egyptian first-born. It is doubtful whether (η) was ever actually practised. There is certainly no reference to it in the Mishnic tract *Pesaḥim*, in which it is expressly declared that 'even the meanest in Israel shall not eat until they have arranged themselves in proper order at ease round the table.' It is not easy to explain (δ) and (θ). Probably the latter was enjoined because, according to the traditional view, the Paschal feast commemorated that one night only of Israel's flight, and therefore everything over was burnt lest it should be desecrated by other use. (δ) has been thought to symbolize the unity of the family, the Passover being originally a purely domestic festival, a bond of union between the participants and Jahweh. But perhaps the idea was that the whole was to be offered to Jahweh, as was the case with the burnt-offering, the eating being regarded as a sacrificial act, continued by the burning of all that was not consumed. It is hardly conceivable that anything analogous to the symbolical explanation given by St. John (19^{34-36}) was originally conceived of.

In the Priestly Code all the 7 days of the festival were marked by special additional sacrifices—two young bullocks, one ram, seven lambs as burnt-offerings, with meal- and drink-offerings; and a goat for a sin-offering; and the 1st and 7th days were holy convocations (Nu 28^{16-25}). In later times several additional customs grew up in connexion with the combined Feast of Passover and *Maṣṣôth*, such as the singing of Psalms (*Hallēl*), and the passing round of cups with words of benediction, etc. The latter custom is of great importance from the Christian point of view, as being one of the symbols chosen by Christ, together with the unleavened bread, in instituting the new rite of the Eucharist (cf. Mishn. *Pesaḥim*). There is also an allusion to the singing of a Psalm in Mt 26^{30}, Mk 14^{26}.

(3) The *sheaf-offering* (*'ōmer*, Lv 23^{10-14} [H]).—Probably at first everybody offered independently his own first-cut barley sheaf, which would have naturally happened on different days. Afterwards a special time was fixed, and one offering was made for all. Dt 16^{9} already speaks of 'the time thou beginnest to put the sickle to the standing corn' as of one which is common to the whole community, and could therefore be made the basis for computing the Feast of Weeks. That it should afterwards have become absolutely fixed was the natural result of the centralization of worship by

Josiah. It does not, however, appear in D to be necessarily connected with the festival of *Maṣṣôth*; and, if the view taken of the latter be correct, it would naturally have preceded it by a few days. According to H, the waving of the sheaf took place on the morrow after the Sabbath in that festival (Lv $23^{11. 15}$). This has generally been explained as the day following the first day of the feast, *i.e.* the 16th of Abib (see Jos. *Ant.* III. x. 5), but the Sabbath is obviously used in its ordinary sense in the immediate context in vv.$^{15. 16}$, and probably should be so understood here (see Driver, *PB*, 'Leviticus,' p. 94). The reason for fixing this day was probably that the cutting of the corn was unlawful on the Sabbath itself. At a later time, when the Sabbath was understood to mean the first day of the Feast, it became a burning question whether the cutting of the sheaf was lawful if the day after happened to fall on an ordinary weekly Sabbath (Edersheim, *Temple: Its Ministry and Services*, p. 222 ff.). The waving of the sheaf was followed by an offering of a lamb with a meal-and-drink-offering, and only thereafter might the new corn, whether parched or in loaves, be eaten (Lv 23^{14}).

2. The Feast of Weeks.—The second festival is described in Ex 23^{16} as 'the feast of harvest, the firstfruits of thy labours,' in 34^{22} as 'the feast of weeks, the firstfruits of wheat harvest.' The name 'feast of weeks' is explained by the fact, stated in Dt 16^{9-10}, that it took place 7 weeks after the beginning of the harvest (*i.e.* the barley harvest); hence the Gr. πεντηκοστή, the 50th day. But the name and the relative date which gave rise to it are both very artificial, and are hardly likely to be original. Though they may not have originated with D, they probably illustrate a custom in vogue at the Temple of Jerusalem, and exemplify the natural tendency, especially in a city, to substitute, for the sake of general convenience, fixed dates for the chances of the natural seasons. It seems likely that the festival was originally known either as 'the day of the harvest' or as 'the day of the firstfruits'—a name which survived even in P (Nu 28^{26}). But the phrase, 'the firstfruits of the harvest,' raises a further question, whether originally the rite may not have consisted in the offering of a sheaf of wheat analogous to the sheaf-offering of barley at the commencement of the barley harvest (see above). If this were so, the festival must originally have been only a few weeks after the Passover. At a later time, at any rate, the firstfruits consisted of the first two loaves made out of the new wheat (Lv 23^{17} [H]), analogous perhaps to the original intention of the Feast of Unleavened Bread. In the Priestly Code the sacrifices were the same as on the 7 days of *Maṣṣôth*.

Just as the Passover became the Easter Feast of the Christian Church, so did Weeks (Pentecost) become the Whitsun Feast, commemorating the outpouring of the Holy Spirit on that day (Ac 2).

3. The Feast of Ingathering (Ex 23^{16} [E] 34^{22} [J]) is described in these ancient codes as taking place at the end of the year, *i.e.* about the autumnal equinox, but otherwise does not appear to have been definitely fixed. It is implied in D (Dt 16^{13-15}) that it is a thanksgiving for the produce of the threshing-floor and the wine-press. It is to be kept with joy for 7 days. No explanation is given of the booths in D, and it is evidently spoken of as a well-known and recognized custom. In H (Lv $23^{34. 36a. 39a. 41-42}$) it is ordered that it should begin on the 15th day, and that it should last 7 days (vv.$^{36b. 39b}$, which speak of an 8th day, are evidently a much later interpolation). On the first day they were to take 'the fruit of goodly trees, branches of palm-trees, and boughs of thick trees, and willows of the brook.' The first phrase suggests the inquiry whether the boughs may not originally have been designed as offerings. If so, the festival must in the earliest times have taken place somewhat earlier in the season, when the fruit was on the trees. Others explain booths as commemorating those used by the gatherers of the vintage, etc. Possibly we should draw a distinction between branches of fruit-trees offered and the boughs of thick trees and willows used in the construction of the booths. The explanation given, however, in v.^{43} is a historical one—to commemorate the dwelling of the Israelites in booths, when they left Egypt. The custom, if it had been restored in the Second Temple, had fallen into abeyance in the time of Nehemiah, and no recollection of it survived (Neh 8^{13-18}). The statement that it had not been observed since the days of Joshua is probably an argument of the Chronicler *e silentio*. It is noticeable, however, that, among the trees mentioned when it was revived, we find not only palms but olives—another fruit-tree (v.^{15}).

In P (Nu 29^{12-38}) the days of Ingathering were marked by special sacrifices, the principal feature being the great burnt-offerings of bullocks, diminishing daily, from thirteen on the 1st day to seven on the 7th. On the 8th there was only one bullock. Besides, there were two rams and fourteen lambs on each of the 7 days, one ram and seven lambs only on the 8th, and a goat for a sin-offering on each of the 8 days. The diminished offerings on the last day point to its being a sort of supplementary day added to the feast. Yet both it and the first were now appointed as days of 'holy convocation,' on which no servile work might be done (cf. Lv 23^{39b}).

(*b*) *Post-exilic.*—1. In the legislation of the Priestly Code an additional festival was added, **the Feast of Trumpets**. This appears to have originated from pre-exilic custom. It was appointed to take place on the 1st day of the 7th month (Tishri). This was the New Year's Day of the pre-exilic calendar (see CALENDAR [Hebrew], 2 A (1)), and it is probable that the blowing of trumpets on that day is comparable with the English custom of ringing in the New Year. It came to be a festival of considerable importance when what appears to have been its original meaning was lost. It was a day of holy convocation, and was marked by a burnt-offering of a young bullock and a ram, seven lambs, and a sin-offering of a goat (Nu 29^{1-6}).

2. The Wood-offering.—The 15th of the 5th month (Ab) was the last of the times appointed for bringing in the wood-offerings for the Temple (Neh 10^{34} 13^{31}). It was observed as 'a popular and joyous festival' (Edersheim, 295 f., Jos. *BJ* II. xvii. 6).

3. The Dedication Festival (*Ḥanukka*) lasted for 8 days, from the 25th of the 9th month (Kislev), and commemorated the re-dedication of the Temple and the new altar of burnt-offering, after their defilement by the idolatrous worship introduced by Antiochus Epiphanes (1 Mac 4^{36-59}). It is called by Josephus (*Ant.* XII. vii. 7) 'Lights,' for which he suggests a symbolical interpretation. It seems more natural to refer the name to the practice of lighting candles ceremoniously in the Temple and in houses during the feast—a custom which was perhaps intended to commemorate the re-lighting of the sacred lamp in the Temple after its reintroduction (1 Mac $4^{49. 50}$; but for traditional beliefs concerning its origin, see Edersheim, 293 f.). According to St. John (10^{22-39}), this festival was the occasion on which an attempt was made to stone Jesus, on the charge of blasphemy, for asserting His Divine Sonship. It has been thought that the date of the feast suggested the date of Christmas Day; and there is certainly a remarkable resemblance in the name and ritual between this and Epiphany, which was also called in ancient times the 'Day of Lights' (see Bingham, *Ant.* XX. iv. 6, 7).

4. **Purim** (called also 'Mordecai's Day' in 2 Mac 15^{36}).—This festival was kept on the 14th and 15th of the 12th month (Adar). It commemorated the vengeance taken by Mordecai and the Jews on their enemies as recorded in the Book of Esther (9^{15-32}). The name is explained as the plural of *pûr*, 'a lot,' and as having reference to the lots cast by their enemies to destroy them (v.^{24}). The Book of Esther is, however, certainly not historical, and appears to be a religious romance written to explain the meaning of the Feast. *Purim* may have been originally a Persian or a Babylonian institution adopted as a secular feast by the Jews, and afterwards invested with a religious character. Even in later times the only religious ritual for many centuries appears to have been the solemn reading of the Roll (*megillah*) of Esther. See, further, art. 'Purim,' in *HDB* and *EBi*; and cf. Frazer, *GB*² iii. 153 ff.; also below, p. 872ᵃ, note.

5. **Feast of Nicanor.**—This was appointed to be kept on the 13th of the 12th month (Adar), in the time of Judas Maccabæus, to commemorate his victory over Nicanor (1 Mac 7^{49}, 2 Mac 15^{36}). But it never appears to have been considered of great importance. Josephus says of it: 'The Jews thereon (*i.e.* the 13th of Adar) celebrate this victory every year, and esteem it as a festival day' (*Ant.* XII. x. 5). From the first it was overshadowed by the Feast of Purim, and came to be kept as a fast in commemoration of the fasting of the Jews connected with the object of that feast (Est 4).

iv. SACRED YEARS.—1. **The Sabbatical year.**—An ancient law provided that the term of service for a Hebrew slave should be 6 years, and that in the 7th year he should at least have the option of going free (Ex 21^{2-6} [E], Dt 15^{12-18}). Another law required that the land should not be sown, or any work done in the vineyard or oliveyard every 7th year, but the self-grown crops were to be for the poor and the beasts of the land (Ex 23^{11} [E]). In D there is no provision for the land lying fallow; but, in addition to the law of slave-release every 7th year, there is another requiring the release from all debts in each 7th year, which in this case was to be proclaimed as 'Jahweh's release' (Dt 15^{1-6}). In this year they were required to read the Deuteronomic Code at the Feast of Booths (Dt 31^{10-13}). There is no reason to suppose that, in the earlier code, at any rate, the fallow law implied one common year for all the land, for every kind of crop, or even necessarily for every field or farm. Such a law would have caused the most dire confusion amongst a people chiefly agricultural. It was different with the condition of the Jews after the Exile, and to some extent in the later history of the Southern Kingdom before it. We find a provision for one common year first in the Law of Holiness, which provides for a definite Sabbatical year (Lv $25^{1-7.\ 19-24}$). It is also implied in Ezk 46^{17} unless that indeed refers to the Jubile.[1] We are told also in Lv $26^{34f.}$ (cf. 2 Ch 36^{21}) that the ancient law had fallen into disuse, and that the Exile was (or would be) a recompense to the land for its neglect. No mention is made, in connexion with the Sabbatical year of Lv 25, of the release either from debts or from slavery, but the first is clearly implied in Neh 10^{31}, where it is evidently referred to as an ancient custom. We find several references to the Sabbatical year in later times. In it all warlike operations ceased (Jos. *Ant.* XIII. viii. 1, *BJ* I. ii. 4). In it they held it as unlawful, or perhaps only as impracticable, to pay tribute; at any rate they requested Alexander that they might be excused (*Ant.* XI. viii. 5). Tacitus complains that the 7th year was given by the Jews to idleness (*Hist.* v. 4).

[1] The spelling 'Jubilee' should be avoided.

2. **The year of Jubile.**—The laws regulating this year are given in Lv $25^{8-17.\ 28-33.\ 50-54}$ 27^{16-24}. As, however, the first and principal passage breaks the context (vv.$^{1-7 \text{ and } 18-22}$ dealing with the Sabbatical year), it is probable that it is a later interpolation into the original law of H, and should be regarded as belonging to the Priestly Code (Driver, on the other hand, in his 'Leviticus,' *PB*, regards vv.$^{8.\ 9a.\ 10a.\ 13-15}$, requiring the restoration of the land, as a genuine part of H). According to the text as it stands at present, every 50th year (or probably every 49th year; see below)—(1) all land is to be restored to its original owners (vv.$^{10b.\ 13-16.\ 28-32}$); (2) all slaves, whether Hebrew or foreign, receive their liberty, and no choice of continual bondage is contemplated (v.^{10} etc.); (3) the land is to lie fallow, as in the Sabbatical year (v.$^{11f.}$); (4) the year itself is to be proclaimed by the sounding of a loud horn on the 10th day of the 7th month (v.^{9}).

(1) The first of these regulations made all possession of real property practically a sort of lease, and calculations were made as to the length of tenure in buying and selling land. Originally it was contrary to the usage of common law to alienate property, which descended from father to son (see 1 K 21^{3}). But the custom had long fallen into abeyance (cf. Is 5^{8}), and the regulation of P was probably an attempt in post-exilic times to enforce a modification of the old custom. (2) The same tendency is shown with reference to slave release. The law in this respect was probably an attempt to enforce, every jubile, what should have been observed every 7 years, but had been neglected. (3) Perhaps the same was intended with reference to the fallow law; but in this case the 7th year's rest was in fact revived and enforced. (4) It has been suggested that the year originally began on what was afterwards not the 1st but the 10th day of the 7th month. This would account for the Atonement being afterwards connected with it. The atonement of the sacred things on probably the 1st day of the 1st and 7th month, proposed by Ezekiel, may be a continuation of a pre-exilic practice (Ezk 45^{20} LXX; see below, III. 2). The absence of any reference to debts is singular if it was intended that the jubile should take the place of the Sabbatical year, but it is partly explained by the law which forbade usury altogether to a Hebrew (Lv 25^{35-38}).

It has been argued that the law of jubile was merely tentative and was never really enforced, on the grounds that (1) it was impracticable to have a second year of fallow immediately following the last, viz. the 49th year; (2) there is no certain reference to it in history, and in fact the only Sabbatical years of which the date is actually known, viz. 164–163, 38–37 B.C., and A.D. 68–69, do not give room for an intercalated year. But these objections depend largely on the assumption that the year of jubile was intercalated after the 49th, and that the next Sabbatical year was reckoned not from the last, but from the year of jubile. But this is nowhere stated. On the contrary, it is quite possible that the jubile was intended to fall every 49th year. 'Then shalt thou send abroad the loud trumpet' (Lv 25^{9}) might as well refer to the 49th as to the 50th year of the cycle. The 10th day of the 7th month is equally difficult to explain in either case, but the difficulty disappears if it was a custom originally belonging to the beginning of the year. So understood, there is no question of two fallow years in succession, and every jubile year was necessarily a Sabbatical one. The analogy of the Feast of Weeks is strongly in favour of this interpretation. It would appear that the chief intention was to mark very specially every 7th Sabbatical year, and require its obligations to be strictly enforced. It was probably part of the system of religious observances introduced by Nehemiah.

II. *OCCASIONAL FESTIVALS.*—Festivals not followed up by a yearly commemoration were appointed to celebrate some important religious or secular event, such as the bringing of the Ark from Kiriath-jearim (2 S 6^{18-19}), the coronation of the king (1 K $1^{9.41}$), the dedication of Solomon's Temple (1 K 8^{63-66}), the victory of Jehoshaphat over the Ammonites and Moabites (2 Ch 20^{26-30}), the laying of the foundation of Zerubbabel's Temple (Ezr 3^{10-13}), the dedication of the city walls by Nehemiah (Neh 12^{27-43}). If the details of the Chronicler cannot always be trusted in his descriptions of such events, there is abundant evidence of the custom itself. Some of the Psalms, esp. the 118th, suggest by their contents that they were written for such occasions.

III. *Periodical Fasts.*—**1.** The earliest appointed fasts were those instituted during the Exile to commemorate **events connected with the siege and capture of Jerusalem** (Zec 7. 8^{18-19}). The fast of the 4th month (17th of Tammūz) commemorated the capture of Jerusalem (Jer 39^{2}, 2 K 25^{3-4} give the 9th as the day that the breach was made by which the king, etc., escaped, but do not make it clear that the city was at once captured). The fast of the 5th month (9th of Ab) commemorated the destruction of the Temple (according to Jer 52^{12-13} it was the 10th day, in 2 K 25^{8-9} the 7th). The fast of the 7th month (the 2nd of Tishri) was said to commemorate the murder of Gedaliah and his companions at Mizpah (Jer 41^{1-10}, 2 K $25^{25f.}$). The fast of the 10th month was on the 10th of Tebeth, on which day the siege of the city began (Jer 52^{4}, 2 K 25^{1}). After the Return, the question arose whether these fasts should be still observed. Zechariah answered it by saying that the observance of them had been, strictly speaking, after all, a purely selfish thing; that what Jahweh really cared for was justice and mercy (8^{18-19}; cf. the similar teaching of Is 58^{3-12}); and that the time was coming when these fasts would be 'joy and gladness, and cheerful feasts.' They still, however, continued, and new traditions arose to account for their origin. Thus the first was said to be the anniversary of Moses' breaking the tables of the Law; the second was held to commemorate also the destruction of the Second Temple by Titus, etc.

2. The Day of Atonement (*yôm hakkippûrim*, 'Day of Coverings,' which came to be known as, *par excellence*, 'the Day') was observed as a complete day of rest and fasting, from the evening of the 9th to the evening of the 10th of the 7th month (Tishri). It was evidently unknown in the time of Zechariah (see above); and even in the time of Nehemiah (ch. 9) it was not made use of for the special purpose of a national humiliation, but a day for the purpose was appointed just a fortnight later, though the Feast of Trumpets was duly celebrated on the 1st, and that of Booths on the 15th–22nd days of the same month. It was probably a very late institution, belonging to the period of a late recension of the Priestly Code, the laws regarding it in Lv 23^{26-32} being a later insertion in the Law of Holiness. Curiously enough, in Ezekiel's Temple (Ezk 45^{18-20}) the atonement for the Temple takes place on the 1st day of the 1st month and on the 1st day of the 7th month (so, probably correctly, LXX); but there is no mention of any atonement for sins. This raises the question whether the atonement was not originally intended as a sort of annual consecration or purification of the Holy Places, the 10th day of the 7th month having been originally, so it has been suggested, the beginning of the year (see above). This purification of the Holy Places continued to be a very prominent feature of the ceremonies of the Day. Of these, as the rite existed in later times (Lv 16), the most important were the offering of a young bullock by the high priest, as a sin-offering for himself and his house, and the selection of two goats by lot—one for Jahweh, which was sacrificed; the other for Azazel, which was sent into the wilderness after the high priest had confessed over it the sins of the people. It is probable that Azazel (*q.v.*) was originally some popular deity, perhaps connected with the goat-gods, *śᵉʿîrîm* (Lv 17^{7}, 2 Ch 11^{15}, Is 13^{21} 34^{14}), which were believed to inhabit desolate places (cf. Mt 12^{43}). It came afterwards to be regarded as an evil spirit, just as the Ekronite god Baalzebub (2 K 1^{2}) came to be taken as the name of the prince of devils (Mk 3^{22} etc.; cf. 1 Co 10^{20}). The meaning would then be that the sins were consigned to destruction. According to the Mishnic tract *Yôma*, the goat was led out and thrown over a rock. The high priest entered at least thrice into the Most Holy Place, purifying it by sprinkling the blood of the bullock and the goat about the mercy-seat, or the stone which afterwards represented it, and censing them with incense. The Holy Place was afterwards purified in the same way. This was the only day on which even the high priest, and then he only, was permitted to enter the Most Holy Place. For a symbolical explanation given by an unknown Christian writer, see He 9^{6-14}.

3. Weekly fasts on Mondays and Thursdays were practised by the stricter Jews between the Feasts of *Maṣṣôth* and Weeks, and between those of Booths and Dedication (cf. Lk 18^{12})—the latter week-day being, according to tradition, the day on which Moses went up Mount Sinai to receive the two tables of the Law, the former that on which he descended (see Lightfoot, *Hor. Heb.* on Mt 9^{14}).

IV. *Occasional Fasts.*—In pre-exilic times there were no regularly recurring fasts, but fasts were proclaimed as acts of humiliation and penitence on the occasion of any great national disaster. Thus we read of the fast at Mizpah in consequence of the oppression of the Philistines, followed by their overthrow (1 S 7^{6}; cf. 2 Ch 20^{3}); that appointed by Jezebel when she got Naboth accused of blasphemy (1 K 21^{9}); that appointed in the reign of Jehoiakim, probably with a view to warding off the threatened attack of the Chaldæans (Jer $36^{6.9}$). We find the practice of special fasts continuing in post-exilic times, and such a fast was appointed by Nehemiah on the 24th day of the 7th month as a national act of penitence (Neh 9; cf. also Jon 3^{5-9}, Jl 1^{14} 2^{12}).

Literature.—J. Lightfoot, *Hor. Heb. et Talmud.*, London, 1658–78, *passim*; A. Edersheim, *The Temple: Its Ministry and Services as they were at the Time of Jesus Christ*, chs. xi.–xvii., London, 1874; *Eighteen Treatises from the Mishna*, tr. D. A. de Sola and M. J. Raphall, London, 1843; Driver-White, 'Leviticus,' in *PB*, London, 1898; S. R. Driver, 'Deuteronomy,' in *ICC*, Edinburgh, 1895, and subsequent edd.; H. Schultz, *OT Theology*, Eng. tr., do. 1892, *passim*; J. Wellhausen, *Prolegomena*⁴, Berlin, 1895, pp. 82–117; *HDB*, artt. 'Sabbath,' 'Feasts and Fasts,' 'Sabbatical Year,' 'Purim'; B. Stade, *GVI* i. (Berlin, 1887) 497 ff.; I. Benzinger, *Heb. Archäol.*, Freiburg i. B. 1894, pp. 464–478; W. Nowack, *Heb. Archäol.*, do. 1894, ii. 138–203; W. R. Smith, *OTJC*², London, 1892, *passim*; F. Buhl, art. 'Gottesdienstliche Zeiten im AT,' in *PRE*³ vii. 19 ff.; R. Smend, *Lehrb. d. alttest. Religionsgesch.*², Freiburg i. B. 1899, *passim*; E. Schürer, *GJV*³, Leipzig, 1898–1901, *passim*.

F. H. Woods.

FESTIVALS AND FASTS (Hindu).

—As described in ancient literature, all Hindu festivals were religious; and this is not due solely to the fact that the literature itself is religious. Either inherently, as in connexion with sacrifice to a god, or artificially, as when a coronation was accompanied by rites which made the whole ceremony a religious festival, all celebrations of a public nature consisted partly in feasting and partly in religious exercises.

i. *Ancient Festivals.*—**1.** Among the seasonal festivals **the moon-feast** always held a high rank, and is important not only on account of its antiquity, but also on account of its prevalence, since even the Buddhists preserved a memory of it in the

Uposatha festival, though reduced in that sober organization to a Sabbath-day observance. In the sacrifice at the new moon, and the full moon, the Hindus themselves recognize the prototype of all sacrifices of similar character, and they are probably right in doing so. The moon-festival lasts two days at the new and one day at the full moon, but neither form has so well preserved the festival character as has the 'four month' celebration (see § 2).

2. The seasonal **'four-month' celebration**, as the name implies, occurs at the end of the seasons of four months each, so that there are three in every year. At the close of winter or the beginning of spring the celebration is ostensibly in honour of the All-gods; at the beginning of the rainy season, in June, it is in honour of the water-god, Varuṇa; and in autumn it becomes the sacrifice of firstfruits. Especially in these seasonal festivals is the old popular participation in the religious rites predominant. The goat and ram which are sacrificed are decorated with phallus-emblems, and the wife of the sacrificer has to confess in public how many lovers she has had and wish them all ill. She and the sacrificer take a bath of purification analogous to the bath taken by savages on like occasions, in which the man and woman wash each other's backs.

3. There is also a special **ceremony of firstfruits**, in which the eating of the firstfruits is regulated religiously.

4. In the **soma-sacrifice** the dramatic element enters in the purchase of the intoxicant. The *Vājapeya*, an autumnal *soma*-festival and sacrifice, has a number of such popular elements. The chief participants were garlanded (with 'golden garlands'), and at a fixed time there was a horse-race over a measured course (seventeen bow-shots), in which three horses were harnessed to one car, and sixteen other four-horse cars took part in the race. This festival was marked by the drinking of *surā* (brandy) as well as *soma*. The crowning of the sacrificial post and the special prominence of agricultural elements point to the fact that it was at first a farmers' festival, though it has become a weak priestly affair, from which the popular character has disappeared. See, further, art. ABHIṢEKA, vol. i. p. 24.

5. Either in autumn or in spring occurred **the consecration-ceremony**, which, as occasion demanded, was celebrated as a sacrifice; but it also contains much of popular usage, such as magical rites, symbolic war, games of chance with dice, and a special ceremony to cure the drunkenness due to debauch. The king is soundly beaten, and the reminiscence of human sacrifice still lingers in the formal ritual of the great occasion. The inhabitants of the realm may not cut their hair for a year after this ceremony—a tabu met with in other parts of the world.

6. Like a public festival is **the horse-sacrifice**, later associated with the assumption of the dignity of emperor, but originally not peculiar to this function. It is one of the oldest of Hindu sacrifices, and must have been originally a carouse of the grossest sort—probably a spring-festival. It is marked by ribald dialogue, obscenity of act as well as of word, and appears to have been from the first associated with reproductive ritual. In the later form it is characterized by the number of priests feasted and presented with valuable gifts; by the attendance of the king and his four wives; by the escort, consisting of hundreds of princesses and daughters of the nobility; by the recitation of old tales; and by the freeing of the horse which is to roam about herded by princes for a year, at the expiration of which period it is brought back and the sacrifice takes place, together with that of a large number of other animals. The rich adornment of the steed, and the music and obscenity of the rite, are given in the ritual; but the impression of the popular character of the festival is more truly conveyed by the description of the horse-sacrifice in popular literature (see, further, art. AŚVAMEDHA, vol. ii. p. 160).

7. Another great event in the Hindu year was the celebration of **the solstice-feast**. Many popular traits connect the old ritual with the modern New Year's festival—music, lute-playing, the dramatic appearance of loose women, and the turn of the sun dramatized by discus-play and by mounting the swing. Each of the two solstice-festivities had its proper divinity and melody, and the melody of the summer solstice was accompanied by drums, to imitate thunder, while that of the shortest day was accompanied by the rattle of war-cars, representing an attack on the evil spirits of winter. The dancing of girls round fire, with full water-jugs, and their singing ('a joyous song') were additional popular elements.

8. **A twelve nights' celebration** occurred after the winter solstice, though little remains in this of festival character, except the recognition of a period which, from remote antiquity, had been considered sacred, when the *Ṛbhus*, the three personified seasonal deities who divided up the year, slept. The weather of this season was taken as a prognostic of the year to come—one of the main reasons to-day for celebrating the similar feast in South India. The eighth day after the full moon of the new year was the exact 'type of the year,' which determined whether the year was to be lucky or not.

9. Apart from these celebrations, the beginning of the great modern festivals which terminate annual pilgrimages may be seen in the early mention of pilgrimages and sacrifices at certain particularly holy spots, such as those to the Sarasvatī and Dṛṣadvatī rivers. The *tīrtha*, or *ghāt*, where a stream is fordable, became, in the case of a holy river, the meeting-place of pilgrims. Such pilgrimages are recognized but not approved by the early writers, who admit only the efficacy of sacrifice at a holy place; but such orthodox objections were set aside after the visits at Buddha's shrines became popular, and already, in the first centuries before our era, hundreds of holy places were known and visited by the devotees of various Brāhmanized gods.

ii. *MODERN FESTIVALS.*—These stand to those of ancient days somewhat in the same relation as private and public festivals stand to each other. They cannot be entirely separated from the old, yet they are so new in their character as to be virtually distinct. The old occasion is preserved, or rather it forces itself upon the notice of the public; but that public is so different, and the ceremony of celebration is so diverse in details, that it is new in effect, though old in general character. The chief local festivities to-day are associated with places and deities unknown to the ancient world of India; but the seasons remain the same, and the celebration of the advent of spring, for example, does not differ in reality from the old spring-festival. To whom the honour is paid is of less importance than that the festivity should be celebrated. The rites in honour of one god have passed over to another without materially altering the celebration, and sometimes even to-day the same celebration is held in honour of different gods. Thus the very pleasing 'lamp-festival,' in which, in autumn, lamps are lighted in every direction, floating lamps are set off down rivers, etc., is celebrated by some as a festival in honour of Viṣṇu's wife, and by others in honour of Durgā (*q.v.*), the wife of Śiva. One thing is to be remarked in regard to the modern festivals, as compared with the old, namely, that whereas the old seasonal festivals, such as those of the New Year, spring, and autumn, were degraded into ritualistic observances, so that in many cases it is hard to recognize the original intent, the modern festivals have thrown off Brāhmanism as far as possible, and are more clearly celebrations of seasons, devoid of priestly ritual and self-sufficient. In other words, in the modern festival we have a reversion to the real meaning of the feast, which, even in the oldest literature, was already so buried in ritual as to be virtually lost. Most of the modern festivals celebrate seasonal changes, or are held in connexion with pilgrimages to some holy place, the shrine, or the river *tīrtha*.

In Northern India the most famous of these types are respectively the spring-festival, the pilgrimage and celebration at the shrine of Jagannath (originally Buddha, now Viṣṇu), and the pilgrimage and fair at the junction of the Ganges and Jumna rivers (Allahābād [*q.v.*]). The seasonal festival is celebrated by all; that at Puri, in Orissa, in honour of Jagannath is supposed to be celebrated by worshippers of Viṣṇu, but is actually celebrated by worshippers of Śiva and Durgā as well; while any religious person may be found making a pilgrimage to Allāhābād, to wash away his sins and enjoy himself at the fair. In South India the spring-festival is celebrated much as in the North, and *tīrtha* pilgrimages and fairs are also held, though with rather more pronounced sectarian feeling. There is, however, a great difference in the character of the different modern festivals. The cleanest is the *tīrtha* celebration. This is really a moral as well as a religious performance, and, though men and women bathe together almost naked, there is no wantonness, and no advantage is taken of the situation by evil-minded men. It is a festivity by accident, due to the immense concourse of people and the resultant fair. It is kept, as it is intended to be, as a purification. On the other hand, the temple and shrine pilgrimages in honour of an erotic deity are naturally more or less erotic in character, and at the spring-festival indecency is part of the recognized programme.

Finally, before passing to a closer consideration of the modern festival, it should be said that between the old and the new there must have been a large number of special festivities now lost sight of, or only faintly reflected in the intermediate literature—not to speak of the many special festivities in honour of gods and goddesses described in the mediæval Purāṇic and Tantric literature. Some of these appear to have been popular as well as sectarian; but we know very little about those not described in religious books, and the latter, as described, consist in childish ritual.

Some of the modern festivals are both sectarian and seasonal. Thus the spring-festival in the South is often a Kṛṣṇa festival and love-feast, and the autumn-festival in the North (Bengal) is indifferently a seasonal or Durgā feast, as it is now called. As in the devil-frightening festival already referred to as the 'lamp-festival,' the original intent of the celebration is merged in the worship of some modern deity. The same sort of a celebration as that in honour of Durgā is held in other parts of India in honour of Sītā, the wife of Rāma. Both were originally a kind of All-Fools' Day; in both the chief observances are buffooneries, pantomimes, processions, music, and the casting of the image into water. Such an All-Fools celebration was known under different auspices in ancient India, and it survives to-day in practically the same form whether as a feast to Durgā or to Sītā. A characteristic feature of all these festivities is mimetic exhibition, which on the stage assumes serious proportions, but on the street is simply licensed vulgarity.

The *Holi* (spring-festival) is, as in other countries, the occasion when this sort of thing is most pronounced. The orgies of obscenity which welcome the return of spring are scarcely veiled. The very cars of the gods are decorated with carvings comparable only with those Pompeian scenes now kept from view, but which in India form the delight of men and women. The law practically permits of any excess, the god encourages it, and the nature of the people, which made the law and the god, revels in its own unbridled enjoyment of indecency. Street dances, bonfires, and the throwing of red and yellow powder upon the passers-by remind the Occidental visitor of a Western carnival; but no Western carnival at its worst is so frankly sensual as is the spring-festival of India. This festival appears under various names and disguises. It is identified with the *Dola-yātrā*, or swing-festival, at Puri (in Orissa), where the idols are swung, and is celebrated for three (sometimes ten) days before the full moon of Phālguna, which corresponds with that of February-March. When celebrated for Kṛṣṇa, games take place in his honour. Sometimes, however, the swing-festival is kept distinct from the *Holi*.

The chief seasonal festivities are the *Makara-saṅkrānti*, when the sun turns north, answering to our New Year's Day, which is the time for the great pilgrimage to Allāhābād and the annual bath of purification in the sacred rivers of the North, while in the South it is the season for the festival called *Pongol*, at which the boiling of the new rice is watched and regarded as an augury for the New Year, and cattle are led about decorated with garlands and treated with veneration. Presents are given to friends at this time, and general rejoicing takes place. The festival lasts for three days, and is officially a celebration of the Vedic gods Indra and Agni, with the addition of the (later) god Gaṇeśa. The cooking of the rice is in the South the main event of the *Pongol*, which has given the name to the festival. Anxious bands await the verdict of the official cooks; and, when the rice boils, a glad cry resounds, 'It boils, it boils,' and all with intense excitement repeat the acclamation. In Bengal the New Year is inaugurated in spring, and here the main features are the worship of the Ganges and the cult of the *dhenki*, or husking-bean; while, at the date of the southern *Pongol*, the bathing-festival, which brings together 100,000 people, absorbs popular interest.

Between the New Year's and the *Holi* festival a special day is devoted to the worship of the goddess of eloquence and arts, Sarasvatī, at which time books are worshipped and fasting is enjoined; but the occasion is also a festival, more especially for children; and boys play games to celebrate the day. Another day is devoted in early spring to Śiva, whose phallic image is worshipped, with fasting and prayer, by pilgrims. The birthdays of the two popular gods, Rāma and Kṛṣṇa, are also observed by adherents of these sects, one of them coming on the ninth of Chaitra (March-April) and the other in July-August, just before which there is a celebration in honour of the fabulous *Nāgas*, although the birthday of Kṛṣṇa is sometimes celebrated as an autumn-festival, in August-September (the eighth and ninth of the month Bhādra). On the fourth of Bhādra, Gaṇeśa, the 'son of Śiva,' is especially worshipped, and his image is thrown into the water. The Durgā festival of Bengal occurs in the month Āśvina, on the tenth day of the light half of the moon, about the time of the autumnal equinox. After this there is the 'lamp-festival' in October (see above), and at the full moon of October-November (in the native month Kārttika) a celebration especially devoted to Śiva. The great goddesses, wives of the great gods, have their special days, but besides these there is a great festival in honour of women and children, or the goddess supposed to be theirs, namely, the 'mother of sons,' who is revered under the form of a banyan tree. This celebration (in Bengal) consists chiefly in processions and music in honour of the mother-goddess. The procession goes to the banyan tree, and the participants worship and pray to her there. On this occasion fathers-in-law are expected to give presents to their sons-in-law, and the time is said to be 'one of the happiest days of the year.' The festival of firstfruits, to which reference has already been made, is not one in honour of a special god. It is held at the season when new grain is ripe; and offerings are made to gods, *manes*, cattle, crows, and jackals. The rites to the *manes* are celebrated with especial unction in February at Gayā (*q.v.*), the old seat of Buddhistic worship—some say because the Buddhists were regarded as most opposed to this cult. It is at present a stronghold of Vaiṣṇavism.

The expense of festive celebrations, which is often considerable, is easily met at places where there is a huge concourse of visitors, as at Puri or at Pandharpur, in the Bombay Presidency, where as many as 50,000 pilgrims gather in a day; but in small communities the cost is met by public contributions, and several villages will often combine to have a festival in common—building a pavilion, honouring the god, and providing the feast. The idol that is made use of on such occasions is a temporary effigy, made of clay and sticks, and is 'animated' by the priest, who, at the end of the celebration, flings the image into the water. At the small village celebrations the prayers and processions are, of course, in honour of the local deity thus represented, but the entertainment is catholic, and often consists in an evening recitation by professional story-tellers (or miracle-plays by professional actors) in honour of any god. Such entertainments sometimes include a nautch dance, theatrical representation of some mythological story, etc., and are not infrequently lewd. In larger towns one of the chief events is the *Ratha-yātrā*, or car-journey, of the god, at which thousands assist, and in the confusion and tumult the worshippers sometimes lose their lives. The cars are lofty structures, unwieldy wooden buildings on wheels, embellished with obscene sculpture, and dragged through the streets by a frantic mob of devotees. Such a *yātrā* at Puri in honour of Viṣṇu, or at Bhuvaneśvara in honour of Śiva, forms the chief public glorification of the god. Like many other traits of modern Hinduism, it was probably borrowed from Buddhism. At Puri there are three *yātrās*, the first being followed by the fair, and being the beginning of the celebration. It is called *Snāna-yātrā*, and celebrates the bathing of Viṣṇu's image.

That there were many festivals not included under the screen of religious rites in ancient times may be taken for granted, and this is supported by external evidence. Only an echo has come down to us of the fairs and theatrical exhibitions of semi-religious character, which used to be held in honour of different gods, and were occasions of public festivity. Wrestlers and boxers gave entertainments to the people and to the court, and the priests among themselves had contests of wit, in which the defeated debater was apt to lose his life. The great epic of India also reveals glimpses of festivals not formally recognized, such as that of the annual branding of cattle, at which the king and court held a sort of royal picnic; while the same work shows that court-festivals, where the royal family bathed and picnicked, were not without sensual elements. The erotic character of the Kṛṣṇa cult was at this time beginning to have effect in the popular shows and festivals, if indeed, as is probable, this element was not already at home. Another grand festival, as depicted in the epic, is the election of a princess, at which she is supposed to elect her future husband in accordance with his prowess and skill as shown in knightly tournament. The scene at such an election resembled more than anything else a similar tournament in the Middle Ages in Europe, and the crowd of spectators, the feasting, and the incidental entertainment made the event one of the greatest of the non-religious festivals of India's storied past. Animal contests, especially reprehended by the Buddhists, also formed part of the festivities of the seasonal fairs, especially fights between tigers and elephants, and cock-fights.

Many of these Hindu festivals have a counterpart in those of other races. One of these is the *Dola-yātrā* (swing-festival), or rather the swinging itself, which represents the sun-course, and was very likely borrowed from the aborigines. Even at the present day the grosser and more cruel form of this ceremony is practised by the wild tribes as well as by civilized Hindus. It consists in inserting hooks in the muscles of the back of the devotee or victim and then making him revolve when suspended by the hooks. This is again a perfect parallel to the swinging practised by the American Indians as described by Catlin (*N. Amer. Indians*, 1903, i. 193). Another rite, now practised and also perhaps borrowed from the same source, is the ploughing-festival, often connected with rain-making—magical or religious in intent, but adventitiously of a festival character. The numerous spring-festivals now in vogue appear to be the *disjecta membra* of a continuous spring-festival, which originally lasted a much longer time. The licence allowed at the *Holi* and other spring-festivals reverts to a time when sensuality was thought to corroborate Nature's vernal productive powers, though no such explanation is needed for the existence of the feeling thus brought by magic into relation with the process of Nature.

iii. *THE CALENDAR.*—The Hindu calendar is so closely connected with the subject of festivals that it may be said to have been an outgrowth of the seasonal character of feast and sacrifice. The priest himself was called the 'seasonal sacrificer' (*ṛtu-ij*), and it was his business to know when the festival to the gods took place, or, in other words, when the seasons began. It was not till later that 'star-man' became the title of a special professional character.

1. Modern and mediæval eras.—Before speaking of the earlier calendar, however, it may be well to distinguish at once the modern eras and explain their origin. Not only are they, but the idea underlying them is, if not exactly modern, at least only mediæval; that is, it reverts at most to an age subsequent to that of the Vedas. There are five such eras in common use—two political, two sectarian, and one popular and universal. The first political era is that of Vikrama, in India regarded as equivalent to the year 57 B.C. This is designated at times simply by the word *Samvat*, 'year,' which leads to confusion, since the second political era is regularly designated in the same way. The latter era is the 'era of the Scythians' (*Śāka*), popularly identified with A.D. 78. The two religious eras are those of the Buddhists, in Burma and Ceylon, and of the Jains, in North India. Buddha was born (probably) 500 years before the Vikrama era, so that his death (at the age of eighty) would have taken place in 477 B.C., though native tradition prefers the year 544. Similarly, the Jains' leader, Mahāvīra, probably died in 662, at which time his era should begin; but it may have been later, as native tradition says that Mahāvīra's death (entrance into *Nirvāṇa*) occurred 470 years or 605 years before Vikrama.[1]

Not essentially different in popular consciousness from the idea leading to these religious eras is that underlying the people's universal era, dating from the death of the man-god Kṛṣṇa at the end of the great war and beginning of the last of the four ages, whence, from the name of this evil age, it is called the Kali-calendar, the first year of which is 3101 B.C. This, it is important to notice, was the era from which years were generally reckoned in India till the Sāka era in the 1st cent. A.D. It implies the calendar of the ages (*yugas*), or the theory that every emanation from the supreme being (*i.e.* human existence) is divided into four stages, each with a length shorter than the preceding.[2]

For dates within a year the popular method has always been to give the day by the asterism (moon-station) in which an event occurred, which designated the month, and by the fortnight; also, to be more exact, by the *muhūrta*, or hour of the day, sometimes by the night-watch (each night having three watches). Thus: 'on such a *muhūrta* of the tenth day of the dark fortnight of the month called after such an asterism.' This mode of reckoning brings us to a discussion of the earlier Vedic calendar.

2. The Vedic calendar.—We notice first that the intercalated month necessary to make uniform the solar and lunar year is already known as the 'later-born month' in the earliest literature of India, the Rigveda; and, since the same work speaks of twelve months and 360 days as year-divisions, it is evident that the five-year cycle of later periods was already recognized. According to this cycle, the solar year and the shorter lunar year were adjusted to each other by the insertion of an extra month on the second and fifth year of the cycle.

The sacrifices and festivals depended upon the moon far more than upon the sun in India, and this also is recognized in the Rigveda, which speaks of the moon as 'determining the seasons'—whether of sacrifice or of the year is not stated; but, from the context, the latter is less probable, and in fact the moon had nothing to do with the annual seasons, of which at this time only three were recognized: Heat, Rains, and Cold (later five and six seasons were known, but these also were named without reference to the moon). Moreover, the names of the months refer only to lunar months. The path of the moon through the heavens was laid out according to the stars or constellations through which it passed in the course of its round. These made 27, later 28, stations of the moon, and formed altogether a sort of lunar zodiac, like that of the Chinese and Arabs.[3]

The fact that the moon-stations called *nakṣatras* were already utilized to make the calendar of the Vedic age has had an important bearing upon the question of the date of Vedic literature.[1] Besides the lunar month the Hindus used the fortnight in their reckonings, but do not seem to have subdivided further, though the week, a 'seven-days,' is a period frequently alluded to in later literature. The lunar fortnight division attracted the attention of the Romans, and Quintus Curtius, in his *Life of Alexander* (viii. 9), speaks of it as a noteworthy fact.

As the five-year cycle was divided into years, each having its special name and divinity—Samvatsara, Parivatsara, Idāvatsara, Anuvatsara, Udavatsara (the divinities being respectively Fire, Sun, Moon, Creator, Rudra)—so the greater cycles afterwards employed by the astronomers were divided in the same way.

3. Apart from these cycles, two popular methods of reckoning are known, one of which is the Kali-cycle, already alluded to. Another, confused with it, is called the cycle of the 'Seven Seers' (*i.e.* the stars of the Great Bear), which are supposed to change their position once in a century, according to the asterism in which the Seers are situated. Thus, as there are twenty-seven asterisms, this cycle consists of 2700 years. Mediæval historians equated this cycle, which was a popular one, with their more learned reckoning. So Kalhaṇa says that the 24th year of the 'people's era' is identical with Sāka year 1070. The popular belief was that the Seven Seers had been for seventy-five years in the asterism Maghā when the Kali-age began. The cycle of the Seven Seers is carried back to a date corresponding with the year 4077 B.C.

The astronomical cycles known as 'eras of Jupiter' (the planet Bṛhaspati) are two, one of one revolution of the planet, that is, of twelve years, in which each year is called after the asterism in which Jupiter heliacally rises, and one of five revolutions, that is, of sixty years, in which the first year corresponds with the initial year of the Kali-cycle. In the South this era is regarded as identical with the solar year. There are locally known other cycles of less importance, such as the 1000-year cycle of Paraśu-Rāma, recognized in the South, but known in the North, even to astronomers, only by name. The only one of these cycles which can claim a respectable antiquity is the sixty-year Jupiter cycle, which perhaps reverts to a time antecedent to the beginning of the Christian era.

Cf. also 'Indo-Chinese' and 'Siamese' sections of art. CALENDAR.

LITERATURE.—H. H. Wilson, *Select Works*, ii., London, 1862, ch. iv. 'Religious Festivals of the Hindus'; Natesa Sastri, *Hindu Feasts, Fasts, and Ceremonies*, Madras, 1903; W. J. Wilkins, *Modern Hinduism*², Calcutta, 1900; Monier-Williams, *Hinduism*, London, 1877; F. K. Ginzel, *Handbuch der mathematischen und technischen Chronologie*, Leipzig, 1906 ff., i. 310–402; E. W. Hopkins, *Religions of India*, Boston, 1895 (previous literature cited on pp. 448 and 592); J. C. Oman, *Brahmans, Theists, and Muslims of India*, London, 1907 (esp. p. 241 ff., 'The Holi Festival'); and for special festivals, A. Hillebrandt, 'Die Sonnwendfeste in Alt-Indien,' in *Roman. Forschungen*, v. [1889] 299–340, and *Vedische Opfer und Zauber*, Strassburg, 1897 (=*GIAP* iii. 2); B. Lindner, 'Das ind. Ernteopfer,' in *Festgruss an Böhtlingk*, Stuttgart, 1888, pp. 79–81; J. Jolly, *Recht und Sitte*, Strassburg, 1896 (=*GIAP* ii. 8).

E. WASHBURN HOPKINS.

1 A sectarian distinction. This is not the place to discuss the probability of any of these dates being correct historically. Another common political era is that of the Guptas, probably identical with the Vallabhī era, A.D. 319.

2 For details, see art. AGES OF THE WORLD (Indian), in vol. i. p. 200. After the Hindus came in contact with foreign teachers, from whom they were ever prone to learn, they acquired the knowledge of the precession and then developed the monstrous system of æons, *kalpas*, and *manvantaras*, known to the Purāṇas, according to which even one age includes 4,320,000 years.

3 The relations between the Hindu 'moon-stations' and the Chinese *Sieu* are not yet determined. The Arabs probably borrowed their *Manāzil* from the Hindus, who, however, could not have borrowed their (lunar) zodiac from the Babylonian solar zodiac. Strictly speaking, only a few of the constellations represent *zoa*. The first, corresponding to stars in Aries, is called 'Horse (head)'; the third is (Pleiades) 'six nymphs'; the fourth (al-Debaran) is called 'Rohiṇī's wain'; the fifth (three stars in the head of Orion) is the 'antelope's head,' etc. For the difficult problem in regard to the origin of the moon-stations in India, see Burgess, *Sūrya-Siddhanta*, 1860; Colebrooke, *Essays* (ed. Cowell, 1873), ii. 281; and Müller, *India, What can it teach us?*, 1883.

1 See Jacobi, *Ueber das Alter des Rig-Vedas*, 1893; Tilak, *Orion*, 1893. The conclusion of these scholars was that the Vedic literature must be at least as early as the third millennium before our era, and the data of the Rigveda itself point to the fifth millennium, so that Vedic literature in general would lie between 4500 and 2500 B.C. This conclusion, however, has not been generally accepted.

FESTIVALS AND FASTS (Iranian).—The extant Avesta contains no specific information regarding festivals, and Pahlavi literature is almost equally silent. Nevertheless, the *Dīnkarṭ* states (VIII. vii. 1, 3, 8, xxix. 8, 10, xlv. 4, tr. West, *SBE* xxxvii. [1892] 15 ff., 95, 167) that the lost Avesta Pājag, Hūspārām, and Hādhōxt Nasks discussed, among other matters,

'whatever is about a season-festival; where the appointed place is, when one celebrates it, and when it has fully elapsed; the assembly of the season-festival, and the donation for the feast; where and when the celebration is possible, in what proportion the provisions are to be given out, and when to be prepared and divided; where its advantage is, and what benefit there is from it to the good creations both spiritually and materially.' The sinfulness of a failure to celebrate the season-festival is also considered in the *Dīnkarṭ*, and there are a number of minor allusions to the festival in Pahlavi, such as *Dinā-ī Maīnōg-ī Xraṭ*, iv. 5, lvii. 13, *Šāyast lā-Šāyast*, xii. 19, xiii. 29, xviii. 3 f., xix. 4.

Besides the season-festivals, we find allusions to the days of the guardian spirits in *Bahman Yašt*, ii. 45, *Šāyast lā-Šāyast*, x. 2, xii. 31, *Sad Dar*, vi. 2.

The 'season-festivals' here mentioned are the *gāhanbārs* (the 'yearly'—*yāirya*—divinities of *Yasna* i. 9, ii. 9, *Vīsp.* i. 2, ii. 2), which have been considered in art. CALENDAR (Persian); and the 'days of the guardian spirits' constitute the festival of Fravardigān (on which see *ERE* i. 455, iii. 717[b]; also art. FRAVASHIS).[1] There is also some reason to believe that there were four lunar festivals in each month. In *Yasna* i. 8 (so also ii. 8, *Yašt* vii. 4) occur the words, *nivaēdhayemi hankārayemi māhyaēibyō ašahe ratubyō antare-manhāi . . . perenō-manhāi vīšaptathāiča*, 'I dedicate, I perform (the sacrifice) for the month (gods), the time-divisions of Aša, for the between-moon [*i.e.* the new moon], . . . for the full moon, and for the intervening seventh(s)'—in other words, for the first, eighth, fifteenth, and twenty-third days, which, as has been seen in CALENDAR (Persian), were all dedicated to Ahura Mazda (cf. also Bartholomae, 1472).

Our chief knowledge of the Zoroastrian feasts is derived, not from Avesta or Pahlavi texts, but from Perso-Arabic authors, the most important of whom, in the present connexion, is al-Bīrūnī (*Chronology of Ancient Nations*, tr. Sachau, London, 1879).

In each month an especially sacred day was the one now called *jašn* (Av. *yasna*, 'praise'), on which the month-name coincides with the day-name, as the day Fravarṭīn of the month Fravarṭīn.

The *jašns* are, accordingly, the 19th day of the 1st month, the 3rd of the 2nd, the 6th of the 3rd, the 13th of the 4th, the 7th of the 5th, the 4th of the 6th (also called *Ādhar-čašn*, 'feast of fire' [al-Bīrūnī, 207; cf. also next paragraph]), the 16th of the 7th, the 10th of the 8th, the 9th of the 9th, the 1st, 8th, 15th, and 23rd of the 10th (cf. the lunar feasts noted above), the 2nd of the 11th, and the 5th of the 12th.

Various legends and popular usages are connected with a number of the *jašns*, among which al-Bīrūnī includes the following: Tīragān, 13th day of the 4th month (205 f.); Mihrajān, 16th day of the 7th month (207–209); Ābānajān, 10th day of the 8th month (210); Ādhar-čašn, 9th day of the 9th month (211; according to Zādawaihi, as quoted by al-Bīrūnī, 207, this name was also applied to Šahrīvaragān, the 4th day of the 6th month [see preceding paragraph], this statement, if correct, probably being due to the retrogression of the calendar); Xurram-rūz, 1st day of the 10th month (211 f.); and Isfandārmadh-rūz, 5th day of the 12th month (216 f.). This list may be supplemented by a Parsi-Persian text made accessible by Unvala (*Spiegel Memorial Volume*, Bombay, 1908, pp. 201–210), which also describes the customs connected with Tīragān and Ābānajān, as well as with Bahmanjanah, the 2nd day of the 11th month. For the modern Indian Parsi celebration of the chief *jašns*, see Karaka, *Hist. of the Parsis*, i. 150–152.

There is reason to believe that at least some of the *jašns* were originally far more important than any of the extant texts imply, for they have given names to several months in Iranian systems outside the Zoroastrian series. Thus Tīragān (the 13th day of the 4th month) serves to designate the 4th month of the Seistanians, Tīrkayān-vā (Marquart, *Untersuchungen zur Gesch. von Eran*, Göttingen and Leipzig, 1896–1905, ii. 199), particularly as this was the month of the summer solstice (cf. Tir, 'Sirius'); the great feast of Mihrajān (on which see below) gives its name to the 7th month of the Sogdians, Baghkānj (Marquart, i. 64, ii. 129, 198; Müller, *SWAW*, 1907, p. 465; Gray, *JAOS* xxviii. [1907] 338),[1] and of the Armenians, Mehekan; and Ādhar-čašn (*i.e.* *Ādharagān, the 9th day of the 9th month) to the 9th month of the Seistanians, Ārgayān-vā (so reading, with Marquart, i. 64, ii. 199, instead of the Ārkabāz-vā or Ārkayāz-vā of al-Bīrūnī, 53, 82), and of the Armenians, Ahekan (Hübschmann, *Armen. Grammatik*, Leipzig, 1897, i. 95).

The two great festivals of the Zoroastrians are the New Year (Naurūz) and the Feast of Mithra (Mihrajān), both of which last six days, the number perhaps being based on the six *gāhanbārs*. The first day of the New Year was called Naurūz-i 'Āmma ('of the people') or Kūčak ('little'), and the sixth was Naurūz-i Ḫāṣa ('noble') or Buzurg ('great'). The general scheme of celebration, according to al-Bīrūnī (203 f.), was as follows:

'In these five days it was the custom of the Kisrās [Persian kings] that the king opened the Naurūz and then proclaimed to all that he would hold a session for them, and bestow benefits upon them. On the second day the session was for men of high rank, and for the members of the great families. On the third day the session was for his warriors, and for the highest Maubadhs [priests]. On the fourth day it was for his family, his relations and domestics, and on the fifth day it was for his children and clients. . . . When the sixth day came and he had done justice to all of them, he celebrated Naurūz for himself and conversed only with his special friends and those who were admitted into his privacy.' For various legends connected with Naurūz, see *ib.* 199–204; Hyde, *Hist. religionis veterum Persarum*, pp. 236–238; Unvala, 203–205: for the modern usages, Karaka, i. 144–146; Jackson, *Persia Past and Present*, New York, 1906, p. 99 f.; for the special importance of the concluding day and for the legends connected with it, see the Pahlavi *Māṭīgān-ī Māh Fravarṭīn rōj Xūrdaṭ*, tr. Asana, *Cama Memorial Volume*, Bombay, 1900, pp. 122–129; for the third day, see Karaka, i. 145 f.

The second great festival was Mihrajān, the celebration of which, according to the ideal Avesta calendar, should begin 7th Sept. The near approach of Mihrajān to Naurūz in honour is well illustrated by a saying of Salmān al-Fārisī, cited by al-Bīrūnī (208):

'In Persian times we used to say that God has created an ornament for His slaves, of rubies on Naurūz, of emeralds on Mihrajān. Therefore these two days excel all other days in the same way as these two jewels excel all other jewels.'

This festival, like that of Naurūz, lasted six days, the first being Mihrajān-i 'Āmma and the last Mihrajān-i Ḫāša, while, again, like Naurūz, the celebration was at one period spread over thirty days, the first five being, according to al-Bīrūnī (203), 'feast days for the princes, the second for the nobility, the third for the servants of the princes, the fourth for their clients, the fifth for the people, and the sixth for the herdsmen.' Thus, instead of each of the six *gāhanbārs* being represented by only one day of the festival, it was at one time honoured both at Naurūz and at Mihrajān by a period of five days.

While we may disregard the numerous legends connected with Mihrajān (al-Bīrūnī, 207–209; Hyde, 245–248; Unvala, 207; Mas'ūdī, *Prairies d'or*, ed. and tr. Barbier de Meynard, Paris, 1861–77, iii. 404; Nuwairī, quoted by Golius, *Notæ in Alferganum*, Amsterdam, 1669, p. 23), the problem of its origin cannot so summarily be dismissed. The festival has given its name to the seventh Armenian

[1] The view of Lagarde (*Purim*, Göttingen, 1887) that Fravardigān was the origin of Purim has long been discarded; and equally suspicious is the theory of Scheftelowitz (*Arisches im AT*, Berlin, 1901–03, i. 49 f., ii. 44–48) that פור is borrowed from O. Pers. *frava = Avesta *fravi*, 'luck' (?), particularly as the Avesta word probably means 'thriving, growth, prosperity' (Bartholomae, *Altiran. Wörterb.*, Strassburg, 1904, col. 991).

[1] On *bagha*, 'god,' as a synonym for Mithra, see Marquart, i. 64, ii. 129, 132–134.

month, Mehekan (Hübschmann, i. 95),[1] and it was evidently known to the Persian kings, as is clear from the statement of Strabo (p. 530) that the satrap of Armenia sent the Persian monarch 20,000 colts annually at the Μιθράκανα. Mihrajān and Naurūz were the two times at which the earlier Sasanian kings gave public audiences (Christensen, *L'Empire des Sassanides*, Copenhagen, 1907, pp. 58, 73 f., 98); and it should also be noted that, according to Ctesias and Duris of Samos (*apud* Athenæus, x. 45), the Mihrajān was the one occasion on which it was permissible for the Persian king to become intoxicated and to dance the national Persian dance.

The remarkable parallelism between Naurūz and Mihrajān finds its very simple explanation in the fact that *both* were New Year festivals. Similar double beginnings of the year existed among the Babylonians (*ERE* iii. 74[a], 76[a]) and the Hebrews (Ex 23[16] 34[22]: 12[18]), and Marquart has argued (ii. 206–212) with good reason that the Avesta year originally began about the time of the autumnal equinox, and that during the closing years of the reign of Darius I. (522–486) it was changed to conform with the regular Bab. year, thus commencing about the vernal equinox.[2]

The remaining festivals of the Avesta year may be discussed more briefly. On 17th Fravartīn was the festival of Zamzamah ('muttering'), on which Sraoša was held to have revealed the murmuring required in reciting the liturgy, as well as in speaking, in case words became absolutely necessary, during eating (al-Bīrūnī, 204; Hyde, 241). The 6th Tīr was the Cašn-i Nīlūfar ('feast of the water lily'), a festival considered by al-Bīrūnī (205) to be of recent date (Hyde, 243, puts it on 17th Amerōdaṭ). The 8th (more probably the 18th; cf. Unvala, 208) Šatvairō was Ḫazān ('autumn'), an autumn feast (Hyde, 244), which also gave its name to the eighth month of the short-lived calendar of Yazdagird III. (*ib.* 197). The 1st Mitrō was Ḫazān-i digar ('second autumn'), a feast for the common people, 'because on that day the work of sowing seeds and cultivation was completed' (Unvala, 208; al-Bīrūnī, 207).

A feast of special interest as being, in all probability, a survival of an ancient Bab. custom was celebrated on the 1st Āṭarō, the Rukūb al-Kausaj or Kūsah barnišīn ('the ride of the thin-bearded'), which was apparently observed also as a popular feast of rejoicing at the departure of winter and the coming of spring, so that al-Bīrūnī (p. 211) calls it Bahār-čašn ('spring-festival').

This festival is described, with trifling variations, as follows (Hyde, 249–251; Unvala, 208; al-Bīrūnī, 211; Mas'ūdi, iii. 413 f.; Anquetil du Perron, *Zend Avesta*, ii. 580 f.). A thin-bearded (or toothless) man rode (naked, in some accounts) on a horse (or ass), holding a fan in his hand and complaining of the heat. Escorted by the servants of the king or governor, he rode through the city, the target for snow and ice, but the recipient of hot foods. In his other hand he held a crow or, according to other accounts, an earthen pot full of reddened water, with which, as also with mud and filth, he bespattered those who refused him the dirham which was his due from each shopkeeper. If he was delayed an instant in receiving his tribute, he had the right to seize everything in the shop. The dirhams which he received between the time of his starting out and the first prayers (7 a.m.) he must give to the king or governor; those which he received between the first and second prayers (11 a.m.) were his own property; after the second prayers he might be beaten with impunity.

Here the facts that (*a*) the chief figure in the 'ride of the thin-bearded' was escorted by the servants of the king or of the governor; that (*b*) between the first and second prayers he could exact tribute from every shopkeeper, and, if refused, could seize all in the shops of the recusants and could inflict punishment upon them; and that (*c*) his authority was shortlived, since he could be roundly flogged after his brief tenure of power, all point to his original identity with the condemned criminal who enjoyed a brief reign during the Bab. Sacæa. Anquetil du Perron (ii. 581) had already suggested that the 'ride of the thin-bearded' had perhaps taken the place of the Sacæa, and the two celebrations have also been connected by Lagarde (51 ff.), and especially by Frazer (*GB*[2] iii. 181–184). It seems, on the whole, most probable to hold, with Meissner (*ZDMG* l. [1896] 296 ff.), Winckler (*Altorient. Forschungen*, II. ii. [1900] 345), Brockelmann (*ZA* xvi. [1902] 391), and Frazer (*Dying God*, London, 1911, pp. 115–117), that the Sacæa was connected with the Bab. New Year, *Zagmuk*; and it is of particular interest to note that at Zela, in Pontus, where the Sacæa was still celebrated in Strabo's time (p. 512), the ruler had formerly been a priest-king (p. 559, καὶ ἦν ὁ ἱερεὺς κύριος τῶν πάντων).

This interpretation of the Sacæa seems to the present writer to be preferable to the theory of Gelzer (*ZÄ* xiii. [1875] 14 ff.), Justi (*GIrP* ii. 412), Prášek (*Gesch. der Meder und Perser*, Gotha, 1906–10, ii. 218), Zimmern (*KAT*[3] 384, note 4, 427, 516), and Jeremias (*PRE*[3] xii. 644), that the feast (on which see Berosus, *apud* Athenæus, xiv. 44; Dio Chrysostom, *Orat.* iv., ed. Dindorf, 76, and the euhemerized account of Strabo, p. 512) was an Ištar-Anaitis festival. This hypothesis leaves the most characteristic features of the Sacæa unexplained, although in its favour may be urged the fact that the great festival of Ištar was celebrated in Āb, which is usually regarded as corresponding to the month of Loos, and the statements of Strabo, which also connect the feast with Anaitis. On the other hand, calendrical retrogression may explain some of the chronological difficulties connected with the date of the celebration of the Sacæa (we know, for example, that in 229 B.C. Loos fell, not in Āb, but in Tammūz [Robertson Smith, *apud* Frazer, *GB*[2] ii. 254, note 1]); and, even if Loos be equated with July–August, we are told that both the Sogdian and the Chorasmian year began in July (al-Bīrūnī, 220, 223), as did the Armenian (*ERE* iii. 70[b]). It seems, on the whole, safe to conclude that the Persian 'ride of the thin-bearded' is the vernal counterpart of the (originally) autumnal Babylonian Sacæa, and that it represents a direct descendant of the Bab. festival of the *Zagmuk*.

The 11th Dīn is regarded as the anniversary of the death of Zarathushtra (Karaka, i. 149). The 14th Dīn (according to Hyde, 254, the 24th) was Sīr-savā ('garlic feast'), when garlic was eaten as an apotropæic (al-Bīrūnī, 212). The 5th Vohūman was Barsadhaq ('above *or* new Sadhaq'), five days before Šab sadhaq (*Canon Masudicus*, quoted by Sachau, *Chronol.* 424).

The latter feast ('night of the bonfire') was falsely understood to be the 'hundredth night' (Pers. *sadah*, from which the Arab. *sadhaq* is borrowed, being taken as equivalent to *sad*, 'hundred'). Šab sadhaq was originally the feast of fire *par excellence* (*Šāh-nāmah.*, tr. Mohl, Paris, 1876–78, i. 26 f.), and its great importance at one period is shown by its frequent mention side by side with the feast of Naurūz (*ib.* v. 73, 284, 448, 551, vi. 109, 506, vii. 27, 327, 374; for other legends, etc., see al-Bīrūnī, 213 f.; Hyde, 254–257 [where it is wrongly identified with the winter solstice]; Unvala, 209 f.; Golius, 37–39). On this night blazing

[1] There is, however, no reason to suppose that the name of this feast appears in the Persian region of Mihrjān-qadhaq (Armen. Mihrakan-k'atak, Syr. Mīhragān-qadaq), which was the see city of an East Syrian diocese in A.D. 577 (cf. Marquart, *Ērānšahr*, Berlin, 1901, p. 20; Justi, *Iran. Namenb.*, Marburg, 1895, p. 214).

[2] As supplementary to art. CALENDAR (Persian), it should be noted that Marquart derives the Zoroastrian and Armenian custom of naming each day instead of numbering it—a practice also found in Polynesia (*ERE* iii. 132 f.)—from Egypt, where the days also had names, though these designations merely meant 'the celebration of so-and-so,' and have no real analogy with the Iranian system (Brugsch, *Thesaurus*, Leipzig, 1883, i. 45–54, *Ägyptol.*, Leipzig, 1891, p. 332 ff.; cf. al-Bīrūnī, 58); and it is now certain that the order of O. Pers. months given by Prášek (*Klio*, i. [1902] 26–50) and King and Thompson (*Inscrip. of Darius the Great*, London, 1907, p. xxxviii), whereby Garmapada comes after Thāigarči (*ERE* iii. 128), is correct; for Tolman (*Amer. Journ. of Philol.* xxxii. [1911] 444 f.) has shown, by a comparison with the fragments of the Aramaic version of the Behistun inscription (Sachau, *Aram. Papyrus und Ostraka*, Berlin, 1911, no. 62), that Garmapada can correspond only to Tammūz. The attempt of Weissbach (*ZDMG* lxii. [1908] 633 f.) to prove Garmapada the first month must be regarded as erroneous, while his equation of Margazana with the eighth month (637) is nullified by the Armenian name of the eleventh month, Margaç, which is borrowed from the O. Pers. name (Marquart, i. 64, ii. 182).

fires were lighted, and cattle and birds were driven into the flames, fettered with dry herbs and the like, so that they might speedily escape. The festival falls five days before the middle of winter, and the fires may have been kindled to hasten, by sympathetic magic, the slowly increasing length of the sun's warm activity, as well as to purify the creatures that passed through them.

The 22nd Vohūman was Bādh-rūz ('wind day'), and was probably connected with the Sogdian Bādh-āghām, which was celebrated on the 24th of the corresponding month (al-Bīrūnī, 222). The feast was also called Bādh-i barrah ('lamb's wind'), because of a tradition that on this day a wind blew, after seven years of windlessness, with sufficient force to move the wool on a lamb (Unvala, 210). The 30th Vohūman was celebrated at Isfahan as the Āfrījagān ('outpouring of water'), a rain-festival which, according to some authorities, coincided with Tīragān (Hyde, 243; Unvala, 206), or, according to others, fell on 20th or 30th Horvadaṭ (Hyde, 242); probably, as Hyde remarks, the day of celebration varied in different localities. The 5th Spendarmaṭ was the Jašn-i Barzgarān ('feast of cultivators'), on which charms are prepared for the extermination of hurtful creatures (for specimens, see Modi, *JASB* v. [1901] 398–405 = *Anthropolog. Papers*, Bombay, 1912, pp. 122–130). This feast Anquetil du Perron (ii. 576–578, where, however, it is wrongly set on the 15th) connects with the festival which Agathias (ii. 59) calls *ἡ τῶν κακῶν ἀναίρεσις*, when as many snakes and other noxious creatures as possible were killed and brought to the priests (*τοῖς μάγοις*) as a proof of hatred of Ahriman. The day following is a celebration called Misk-i tāzah ('fresh musk'; al-Bīrūnī, 217). On the 19th Spendarmaṭ fell Naurūz anhār u miyāh jārī ('new year of rivers and running waters'), when rose-water, perfumes, etc., were cast into the streams (al-Bīrūnī, 217; Hyde, 260); and on the 25th–30th (according to others, only on the 30th) came the Mard-gīrān ('man-seizure'), when the women could lord it over the men and take from them what they would (Hyde, 259).

This festival bears considerable resemblance to the later form of the celebration of the Sacæa, when, according to Berosus, masters were ruled for five days by their servants, one of whom wore a quasi-royal robe (*στολὴν ὁμοίαν τῇ βασιλικῇ*), called *ζωγάνη* (a word held by Meissner, 298, note 2, to represent Assyr. *šaknu*, Heb. סָגָן, 'prefect, ruler'), and was in control of the house (*ἀφηγεῖσθαί τε τῆς οἰκίας*). Since, however, the celebration of Mard-gīrān was separated from that of Rukūb al-Kausaj, which we have seen to be a New Year festival connected with the Sacæa, by three instead of by six months, any association of the 'man-seizure' with the Sacæa seems improbable. If the Rukūb al-Kausaj was a spring-festival, the Mard-gīrān must have been a celebration of the summer solstice. The month of celebration is curiously identical with the Jewish Purim on 14th Adar, but the identity of month is doubtless merely fortuitous, and no connexion can safely be alleged between the two feasts.

The Gemara to Mišna III. of the Talmudic treatise '*Aboda zara*, i. (11^b of Babli, 39^c of Yerušalmi) mentions four feasts of the Persians which are of interest as showing what ones were at that period regarded as of most importance. The list given in Yerušalmi is the more accurate: ניסרדי, טירייסקי, מתירקנה, and מחורי (for the variants, see Jastrow, *Dict. of the Targumim*, etc., London, 1886–1903, pp. 741, 534, 739). The first and the third name clearly stand for Naurūz and Mihrajān; the second doubtless represents Tīragān (on the probable early importance of this feast as that of the summer solstice, see above, p. 872^b); and the fourth may be conjectured to stand for Xurram. These would then represent the four seasonal festivals as celebrated at the time of the composition of the *Aboda zara*.

Our information concerning specifically Persian feasts is scanty. We know that each Persian celebrated his own birthday with a feast (Herod. i. 133), and that the king also gave on his birthday a banquet called *τυκτά* (connected with Av. *taoxman*, 'seed'; O. Pers. *taumā*, 'family'; Skr. *tuc, tuj, toka*, 'posterity'; Jackson, *JAOS* xx. [1899] 57), on which he was bound to grant every request (Herod. ix. 110), while other festivals celebrated the king's marriage (Est 2^{18}; Josephus, *Ant.* XI. vi. 2) and the birth of his first son (Plato, *Alcibiades I.*, 121 C).

A Persian festival of much importance was the Magophonia. According to the usual view (Herod. iii. 79; Ctesias, *apud* Photius, *Bibl.* xxxviii.; Agathias, ii. 25), this was a celebration of the slaying of the Magian Gaumāta, the pseudo-Smerdis, by Darius (cf. *Behist.* i. 35–71), and then 'no Magian may appear in the light, but the Magians keep themselves in their houses that day.' This view, maintained by Spiegel (*Erân. Alterthumskunde*, ii. 310, iii. 586–708), Christensen (15 f.), and Meyer (*EBr*[11] xxv. 253), is attacked by Marquart (i. 64, ii. 132, 135; so also Prášek, ii. 140), who holds that Μαγοφόνια is a corruption of O. Pers. **Bagakāna*,[1] and that it is identical with the feast of Mihrajān, considered above, especially as the uproar (*θόρυβος*) lasted five days (Herod. iii. 80) after the death of Gaumāta, who was killed on 10th Bāgayādi (*Behist.* i. 55–57), the month which corresponds to the Zoroastrian month Mitrō.

Despite the cleverness of this suggestion, it seems open to objection. Marquart is certainly right in identifying the Magophonia with the old New Year feast of Mihrajān, and it is almost certain that the O. Pers. year originally began with Bāgayādi ('[month] of the honouring of the god [Mithra]'), just as the Avesta year at first commenced with the corresponding month Mitrō; though later the O. Pers. New Year was changed to a month of unknown name[2] corresponding to the Avesta Fravarṭīn and the Bab. Nīsan. It seems most plausible to hold, therefore, that it was under the cover of an old festival of uproarious character[3] that they were enabled to kill the usurper, their fury both leading them and inciting the other Persians to slay every Magian they could find (Herod. iii. 79); so that the later celebration to commemorate the slaying of the pseudo-Smerdis came to obscure the real origin of the festival in the popular consciousness.

Why the Magi, so universally honoured in Iran, were obliged to keep within doors during the Magophonia has been a hard problem on the basis of the current explanation; but if, as Marquart holds, it was originally a New Year celebration, to be connected with the Mihrajān, which was also a New Year feast, it may probably be connected further with the Sacæa, which, from the statements of Dio Chrysostom and Berosus, was almost certainly a New Year festival, the prominent feature of which was the killing of a criminal who had for five days been permitted to wear royal robes, to sit on the royal throne, and empowered not only to issue whatsoever mandates he would, but even to consort with the royal concubines, and who, after his brief tenure of office, was scourged and hanged, so that the Sacæa probably represents, in attenuated form, the wide-spread practice (found also in Babylonia) of killing the priest-king (cf. Frazer, *Dying God*, 113–117; against this theory see Lang, *Magic and Religion*, London, 1901, p. 118 ff.). It would then follow that the origin of the Magophonia was the actual killing of a Magus

[1] On Gr. Μεγα as the representative of Pers. *Baga* in proper names, see Justi, 56 f., 59; cf. also the Turfān name, *Baghkānj*, for the month corresponding to the O. Pers. month Bāgayādi.

[2] It may be conjectured, from various names of the first month —Chorasmian Nāusārjī, Sogdian Nūsard, Armenian Navasard, Albanian Navasardus, and the gloss of Johannes Lydus, xxxix. 13, *νέον σάρδιν τὸ νέον ἔτος*—that the opening month of the O. Pers. year was *Navathard(a) ('new year').

[3] The writer is informed by Prof. A. V. W. Jackson that he has long held a similar opinion.

who was at the same time both priest and king. This explains why the Magians were both reverenced and also liable to be killed, although long before the historical period the actual killing had been abandoned, and the festival survived merely in a season of merriment, during which the Magi were perhaps the butt of practical jokes and prudently remained indoors. The success of the attack of Darius and his comrades on the pseudo-Smerdis was very likely due in great part to the fact that Gaumāta was himself a Magian; and later, as already noted, the Magophonia was rationalized to commemorate this event, just as in Strabo's day the Sacæa itself had come to be reinterpreted as commemorating a victory over the Scythians (Σακαί) which may, indeed, have been won at the time of the celebration of the ancient festival of the Sacæa, after it had long since lost its primal signification. The meaning of the word Μαγοφόνια, is, therefore, probably 'Magus-slaying,' representing an O. Pers. **Magujaniya*; and the festival was originally a New Year celebration during which the priest-king was slain.

The four season festivals may, accordingly, be summarized as follows:

Autumnal equinox: (Sacæa), Magophonia, Mihrajān.
Winter solstice: Xurram.
Vernal equinox: (Zagmuk), Rukūb al-Kausaj, Naurūz.
Summer solstice: Tiragān, Mard-gīrān.[1]

The feasts of the Sogdians and Chorasmians are listed by al-Bīrūnī (221–226), the principal festivals —so far as either their names or their celebrations are known—being the following:

New Year's day; 28th day of the 1st month, local Sogdian feast of the Bukhārā Magians at the village of Rāmuš; 1st day of the 3rd month, Chorasmian beginning of summer; 7th day of the 4th month, local Sogdian feast at Baikand; 15th day of the 4th month, Sogdian eating of leavened bread after a fast (read غمش instead of عمس [?]); among the Chorasmians this day was Ajghār ('firewood and flame'), since in former times it had marked the approach of autumn; 18th day of the 5th month, Sogdian Bāba (or Bāmī) X^vāra, marked by drinking good, pure must; 1st day of the 6th month, Chorasmian Faghrubah, when the king went into winter quarters; 3rd and 15th days of the 6th month, Sogdian fairs, the latter lasting seven days; 1st day of the 7th month, Sogdian Nīmsarda ('half of the year') and Chorasmian Azdā Kand X^vār, or 'eating of bread prepared with fat' (as a protection against the cold); 2nd day of the 7th month, Sogdian feast of eating cakes of millet-flour, butter, and sugar; 13th day of the 7th month, Chorasmian Cīrī-rōj ('day of Tīr'), venerated by the Chorasmians just as was Mihrajān by the Persians; 21st day of the 7th month, Chorasmian Rām-rōj ('day of Rām'); 5th–15th days of the 10th month, a Sogdian feast of which neither name nor particulars are given; 11th day of the 10th month, Chorasmian Nīmḫab, which, if it may be read Nīmšab (نيمشب instead of نيمخب), 'half-night,' probably refers to the vernal equinox (according to al-Bīrūnī, 223, 220, 'the beginning of their summer was the 1st of Nāusārjī'); 24th day of the 11th month, Sogdian Bādhagham (see above, p. 874^a); 10th day of the 12th month, Chorasmian Waxš-angām, in honour of 'the angel [Waxš] who has to watch over the water, and especially over the river Oxus'; 30th day of the 12th month, beginning of the Sogdian and Chorasmian feast for the dead.

Some special feasts introduced in the Muhammadan period (al-Bīrūnī, 217), as well as the mythical festivals recorded for the 'Sipāsīān' by the *Dābistān* (tr. Shea and Troyer, Paris, 1843, i. 63), may be disregarded here.

The antithesis of feasting, **fasting**, is absolutely forbidden by Zoroastrianism. According to *Sad Dar*, lxxxiii., 'it is requisite to abstain from the keeping of fasts' (*rūzah-dāštan*), for

'in our religion, it is not proper that they should not eat every day or anything, because it would be a sin not to do so. With us the keeping of fast is this, that we keep fast from committing sin with our eyes and tongue and ears and hands and feet. . . . That which, in other religions, is fasting owing to not eating is, in our religion, fasting owing to not committing sin.'

To this al-Bīrūnī (217) adds that 'he who fasts commits a sin, and must, by way of expiation, give food to a number of poor people.' The reason for the prohibition of fasting lies, not merely in the entire Zoroastrian outlook upon the universe, but in the idea that it is as wrong to torture oneself as any other being of the good creation (cf., further, Modi, *Catechism of the Zoroast. Religion*, Bombay, 1911, p. 35 f.). The Mandæans understand fasting in a very similar sense, and polemize against Christian fasts (Brandt, *Mandäische Religion*, Leipzig, 1889, pp. 93, 143 f.; K. Kessler, *PRE*[3] xii. 173 f.); so also the Yezīdīs (Brockelmann, *ZDMG* lv. [1901] 388 f.); while, on the contrary, fasting formed part of the Sogdian religion (al-Bīrūnī, 221; cf. also above, pp. 760^b, 765^a).

[1] The difference of 8 months between the celebration of Naurūz (1st Fravarṭın) and Rukūb al-Kausaj (1st Aṭarō), and of 8 months 17 days between the celebration of Tīragān (13th Tīr) and Mard-gīrān (30th Spendarmaṭ), although the two pairs seem to mark the vernal equinox and the summer solstice respectively, is probably due to the fact that Naurūz and Tīragān were incorporated in the Zoroastrian calendar at its beginning, when they would coincide with the actual periods of the year which they were to celebrate. At a later period, when the calendar had retrogressed 8 months, the popular festivals of Rukūb al-Kausaj and Mard-gīrān, which had been observed at the vernal equinox and the summer solstice without regard to the theoretical calendar, were inserted on the months and days of the calendar in question on which they happened to fall at the time of their incorporation. Hyde, 254, had already noted the possibility of such insertion of feasts, although his special instance, the festival of Šab sadhaq (on which see p. 873 f.), is incorrect.

LITERATURE.—F. Spiegel, *Erân. Alterthumskunde*, Leipzig, 1871–78, iii. 706–708, *Avesta übersetzt*, Leipzig, 1852–63, ii. pp. xcix–cv; F. K. Ginzel, *Handbuch der mathemat. und techn. Chronologie*, Leipzig, 1906 ff., i. 288–290; al-Bīrūnī, *Chronology of Ancient Nations*, tr. Sachau, London, 1879, pp. 199–226; T. Hyde, *Hist. relig. veterum Persarum*, Oxford, 1700, ch. xix.; Anquetil du Perron, *Zend-Avesta*, Paris, 1771, ii. 574–581; B. Brisson, *de regio Persarum principatu*, ed. Lederlin, Strassburg, 1710, pp. 398–401, 53, 135, 158; Inostrancev, 'Sasanidskii prazdnikŭ vesny,' in *Sasanidskiye Yetyudy*, St. Petersburg, 1909, pp. 82–109; D. F. Karaka, *Hist. of the Parsis*, London, 1884, i. 144–152; Rapp, *ZDMG* xx. [1866] 91–93; J. J. Modi, *Lect. and Sermons on Zoroast. Subjects* [Gujarati], Bombay, 1907, iii. 121–145.

LOUIS H. GRAY.

FESTIVALS AND FASTS (Jain).—There is, perhaps, no shorter road to the understanding of a religion than to study its festivals and fasts, the occasions on which it rejoices, and the things over which it mourns. This is certainly the case with Jainism—a religion which lays special stress on outward observance.

1. Pajjusaṇa.—Amongst all their holy seasons none is regarded by the Jains as more sacred than the closing days of their religious year, when the ascetics and laity of all three sects observe the solemn fast of Pajjusaṇa. At this time they confess the year's misdeeds, and especially those against *ahiṁsā* (non-killing), one of the main tenets of the Jain creed. Mahāvīra, their great religious leader, decreed that Pajjusaṇa should begin 'when a month and twenty nights of the rainy season had elapsed,'[1] his reason apparently being that the lay people would by that time have prepared their houses to brave the elements; and business, too, being less brisk, they would be at liberty to attend to their religious duties. It is a convenient season for the ascetics also, who during the rains give up for a time their peregrinations, lest they should injure any of the abundant life, animal or vegetable, then springing into being.

The fast nowadays includes the last four days of the month of Śrāvaṇa as well as the first four of Bhādrapada, *i.e.* it falls usually in August. The Jains say that formerly, instead of eight days, it lasted for one day only, the fifth of Bhādrapada. The Digambara Jains (the sky-clad or naked sect) usually observe seven additional days for worship at the close of these eight fast-days.

The Jains observe the fast with varying strictness: some fast for the whole eight days from all food and water, others only every other day, eating specially dainty food on the alternate days, whilst others, again, fast for thirty days before Pajjusaṇa begins and for its eight days as well, eating nothing, and drinking only hot water or whey.

[1] *Kalpa Sūtra* (*SBE* xxii. [1884] 296).

During Pajjusaṇa special services are held in the *upāsarā* (monasteries) of the various sects. In those of the Śvetāmbara Jains (the white-clad sect) a well-known monk usually reads from the *Kalpa Sūtra* (one of their famous sacred books); and in those of the Sthānakavāsi (the non-idolatrous sect) readings are given from various books which they consider specially sacred, such as the *Antagaḍa* or some *Life* of Mahāvīra. Only the *sādhus* (ascetics) are given raised seats; but, on agreeing to sit on the floor and to remove leather shoes, the present writer was once courteously admitted to the services. The exposition from the sacred books was of a colloquial character, questions being freely asked and answered, and the preaching *sādhu* generally intoning each paragraph before he expounded it. Noticeable amongst the audience were some laymen wearing only the loin-cloth and scarf which form the scanty dress of the Jain ascetic, their unshaven heads marking them off from the monks present. They were doing *posaha*, *i.e.* they had become monks for the time being, and for twenty-four hours they would not leave the *upāsarā*, but would spend their time in meditation and fasting. *Posaha* may be observed every fortnight; indeed, the *Uttarādhyayana* lays down that the faithful householder 'should never neglect the *posaha* fast in both fortnights, not even for a single night';[1] but there is a special obligation to observe it during the season of Pajjusaṇa. *Posaha* was, according to the *Sūtrakṛtāṅga*, specially instituted for those who said that 'we cannot, submitting to the tonsure, renounce the life of a householder and enter the monastic state, but we shall strictly observe the *posaha* on the fourteenth and the eighth days of each fortnight (on the new moon, and) full-moon days,'[2] and who further undertook to keep the five monastic vows of non-killing, truth-speaking, honesty, chastity, and non-covetousness, so far as the exigencies of lay life permitted. *Posaha* well illustrates the special genius the Jain religion has for making the laity feel themselves intimately connected with the monastic order, which largely accounts for its survival in India to-day.[3]

Some Jains, however, find even during the sacred season of Pajjusaṇa that the twenty-four hours' fast from all food and water entailed by *posaha* is too much for them; for these the less exacting fast of *dayā* or *saṁvara* affords a welcome alternative. Those who observe this fast sit in the *upāsarā* and listen and meditate for any period they like to choose, from ten to twenty-four hours, but they may take food and water at will, provided that the water be hot[4] and the food not specially prepared for them.

Saṁvatsari, the last day of Pajjusaṇa and the last day of the Jain religious year, is the most solemn day of all. Every adult Jain must fast throughout the day, abstaining even from water; the *upāsarā* are more than filled, and gatherings of devout Jains are also arranged in secular buildings, such as the verandahs of schools or the dining-halls of various castes. On the afternoon of this day no ascetics are present at the lay gatherings, but they may be seen in the smaller rooms attached to the *upāsarā*, making their own confessions privately; one notices that the hair has been newly plucked from their heads, for this austerity (peculiar to Jain ascetics) has to be performed before Pajjusaṇa ends.

It is most interesting to visit the various *upāsarās* on this day. Those of the Śvetāmbara sect adjoin their temples, the men and women being in different buildings. The women, bedecked with jewels and arrayed in their brightest clothes, are seated in silence on the floor, with the exception of one woman who may have paid for the privilege of reciting the prescribed *mantras* anything from one rupee upwards. In front of her on a wooden stool is a little tripod from which hangs a rosary of one hundred and eight beads, the number of the qualities of the *Pañcha-parameṣṭi* (the Five Great Ones). On the opposite side of the courtyard adjoining the temple is the men's *upāsarā*, where the laymen are seated, clothed only in their loin-cloths, listening to one of their number reciting *mantras*. In the Sthānakavāsi women's *upāsarā* there was no tripod, but first one woman and then another got up from wherever she might be sitting on the floor and recited *mantras*—a privilege which in this community went by seniority. The Sthānakavāsi men, having been crowded out of their *upāsarā*, were on the verandah of the town school when the present writer saw the ceremony. One of their number was preaching, not merely, as in the other gatherings, reciting *mantras*: he was giving an instruction on the twelve vows of a layman, which corresponded very much to an instruction that might be given on the ethical aspect of the Ten Commandments. In preaching, for instance, on the vow against dishonesty, he showed how this vow would be broken by a shopkeeper over-praising his goods. At the close of the instruction on each vow, the whole audience rose, and in a set form of Māgadhī words confessed their breach of it and asked forgiveness. Although the meetings went on till eight or nine o'clock, no light was permitted. At the close all asked each other's forgiveness for any slights or injuries committed during the year in the following words: 'Twelve months, twenty-four half months, forty-eight and four weeks—if during this time I may have said or done anything annoying to you, pardon me!'

No private quarrel may be carried beyond Saṁvatsari, and letters must be written to friends at a distance asking their forgiveness also. The postal authorities can testify how faithfully this is carried out, for the mail of the Jain community increases extraordinarily at this season of the year.

Kalpa Sūtra procession.—In many towns, on the third day of Pajjusaṇa, the Śvetāmbara community organize a procession in honour of the *Kalpa Sūtra*, a Scripture which they hold in peculiar reverence. Some wealthy Jain, who has outbidden the others when the privilege was up for auction, takes the temple copy of that *Sūtra* (which is preferably written, not printed, and should be illustrated) to his house in the evening. It is placed on a little table and covered with a rich cloth, and all night long the inmates of the house and their friends continue what an English-speaking Jain called 'Harmony-Barmony,' singing songs in its honour and playing on as many instruments as they can get. Next morning the procession is formed to return the book to the temple in state. The details would, of course, vary in different places, but when the writer saw it, it was arranged as follows:

The procession was headed by a drummer on horseback, lent for the occasion by the Rājā, followed by other drummers on foot, who preceded the *indrādhvaja*, a painted wooden trolley surmounted by a gaudy wooden elephant bearing on its back tier upon tier of red and blue flags ornamented with gold brocade. A *pūjārī* (officiant), who is generally of the Brāhman caste, followed, bearing a silver mace, and four boys walked behind him carrying smaller silver sticks, their parents having paid heavily for this privilege and the spiritual advantages accruing from it. A portion of the crowd wedged themselves in at this point before the main figure of the procession, the carrier of the *Kalpa Sūtra*, appeared. The proud distinction of being the carrier is accorded to some child connected with the house in which the *Kalpa Sūtra* has been kept. The child, in this case a little girl of seven or eight, arrayed in her gayest silken garment, was seated on a horse; in her hands she held the *Kalpa Sūtra* wrapped in silk, and on the book lay a cocoanut marked in red with the auspicious *Svāstika* sign  She was followed by more of the crowd playing on musical instruments, and by boys who had paid for the honour of carrying the *ārati* lamps which they held in their hands. The last places in the procession were given to groups of women singing songs in honour of the *Kalpa Sūtra*.

Mahāvīra's birthday.—The birthday of Mahāvīra, the founder of Jainism, has been conventionally fixed for the fourth day of Pajjusaṇa (*i.e.* the first of Bhādrapada), though the Śvetāmbaras believe Mahāvīra to have been born on the bright thirteenth of Chaitra. The Sthānakavāsi Jains would like to keep this festival, but their *gurus* discourage them, fearing that it might lead to idolatry. It is observed with great pomp and rejoicing by the other Jains, and the temples dedicated to Mahāvīra are

[1] *Uttarādhyayana* (*SBE* xlv. [1895] 23).
[2] *Sūtrakṛtāṅga*, 17 (*SBE* xlv. 428).
[3] Cf. Hoernle, *Annual Address As. Soc. Bengal*, 1898, p. 45.
[4] On boiled water, see M. Stevenson, *Notes on Modern Jainism*, p. 27.

decorated with flags. The Śvetāmbaras arrange a cradle procession in honour of the day. This procession very much resembles that of the *Kalpa Sūtra*. The drums, the boys with silver staves and *ārati* lamps, the singing crowds, and the small elephant-trolley are again in evidence; but, instead of the book, the child on horseback carries in the centre of the procession a little wooden cradle covered with gold brocade.

The conventional birthdays of several other *Tīrthaṅkara* are celebrated on various days, when the temples specially dedicated to them are decorated with flags, and the imprints of hands dipped in a red mixture are made on the walls. (The hand, the Jains say, is the special symbol of favour, since it is always used when blessing.) Not only the birthdays but also the days when the various *Tīrthaṅkara* attained *kaivalya* and *mokṣa* are celebrated, the pomp, of course, being all the greater at the actual place where the event is supposed to have happened.

2. Diwālī.—Next to Pajjusaṇa the greatest of all the Jain sacred seasons is Diwālī. If the former owes its importance to the emphasis which Jains lay on the sin of killing, Diwālī derives its position from the importance of wealth to a mercantile community. The Jains assign a special reason for their participation in what is really a Hindu festival in honour of Lakṣmī, the goddess of wealth. They say it originated when Mahāvīra passed to *mokṣa*, and the eighteen confederate kings and others who were present at his passing instituted an illumination, saying: 'Since the light of intelligence is gone, let us make an illumination of material matter.'[1] The festival continues for four days—the last days of Āśvina which close the Hindu year and the first of Kārttika—falling usually within the months of October or November. Amongst the Śvetāmbara Jains, the first day (Dhanaterasa) of the festival is devoted to polishing jewellery and ornaments in honour of Lakṣmī; on the second day (Kālichaudasa) the women try to propitiate evil spirits by giving them some of the sweetmeats they prepare and cook on this day. These they place in a circle at cross-roads (*q.v.*), in order to protect their children from evil influences during the year. The third (Amāsa) is the great day of the feast. It was on this day that Mahāvīra went to *mokṣa*, and Gautama Indrabhūti attained to *kaivalya*. This is the day on which Jains worship their account-books and decorate and illuminate their houses. In the morning, Jains of all three sects go to their monasteries and convents and do reverence to the chief monk or nun present, who preaches to them on the life of Mahāvīra and sings appropriate songs. The more devout lay-people stay and do *posaha*, but the generality go home and make up their accounts for the year. In the evening they summon a Brāhman to direct the *Śāradā pūjā*, or worship of the account-books, for Brāhmans are still the domestic chaplains of the Jains. The Jain having arranged his account-book on a stool, the Brāhman enters and paints a *chāndalo* (auspicious mark) on the Jain's forehead, his pen, and one page of the account-book. He then writes the word *Śrī* (*i.e.* Lakṣmī) on the account-book, either five, seven, or nine times, in such a way as to form a pyramid. A rupee (the oldest possible) is now placed on the book; this rupee for the time being is considered to be Lakṣmī herself, and the placing of it is called *Lakṣmī pūjā*. All the year the owner will carefully guard this particular coin, as it is considered luck-bringing, and will use it again next Diwālī, so that in some Jain families the coin used is of great rarity and antiquity. Besides the coin, the leaf of a creeper is also placed on the account-book, and the Jain waves a little lamp filled with burning camphor before the book, on which he has placed rice, *pān*, betel-nut, turmeric, and various kinds of fruit. The ceremony ends by sprinkling the book with red powder, after which the Brāhman and the Jain feast on sweetmeats. The account-book is left open for several hours, and before closing it they say: *Lakṣa lābha, Lakṣa lābha*, *i.e.* 'a hundred thousand profits!'

[1] *Kalpa Sūtra* (*SBE* xxii. 266).

The various Jain conferences are trying to introduce a new *Śāradā pūjā* of their own in which the Brāhman will play a less important part, and the Jain himself do the eightfold *pūjā* to the rupee; but most Jains are content with the old rite. Some of the stricter Sthānakavāsis refuse to have anything to do with either the old or the new rite, regarding both as idolatrous. The Śvetāmbaras light up their temples at Diwālī with little earthenware saucers containing lighted wicks floating in coco-nut oil; but so many insects perish in these unprotected lights that the conferences now object to the custom.

The fourth and last day of Diwālī, New Year's Day, is the first day of the month Kārttika and of the commercial year; and Jains then go and greet all their friends, much as we might on our New Year's Day, and send cards to those who are absent.

3. Saint-wheel worship.—In every Śvetāmbara temple there is a saint-wheel, or *siddha chakra*—a little eight-sided plate made of either brass or silver with five tiny figures. These figures represent 'The Five Great Ones' (*Pañchaparameṣṭi*), whom the Jains daily salute as they tell their beads. First comes the *sādhu*, or ascetic, to whom alone the path to heaven is open without re-birth; then the *upādhyāya*, or preceptor, representing the next stage in the ascetic's onward course, from which he may rise to be an *āchārya*, or head of a body of ascetics; and, lastly, the *siddha*, or being without caste, birth, death, joy, sorrow, or love, whose personality is completely nullified, and who has thus attained the goal of Jain asceticism. In the centre of the plate is a tiny figure of *Arihanta* (the venerable one) which represents the *Tīrthaṅkara*, the chief objects of Jain reverence. Between the figures are written the names of the three jewels of the Jain faith: *Jñāna*, Right Knowledge; *Darśana*, Right Faith; and *Chāritrya*, Right Conduct; and also the word *tapa*, 'austerity,' on which the Jains lay such overwhelming emphasis in their system. This plate, which thus bears on its surface a complete summary of Jainism, is regarded as of such importance that no Śvetāmbara temple is ever without it. Twice in the year, once in Āśvina (September or October) and once in Chaitra (April or May), it is worshipped for eight days by offering the eightfold *pūjā*[1] to it. Once during each of these eight days the saint-wheel is taken outside the town to some spot, probably near a tank or lake, where, before doing the eightfold *pūjā*, they bathe it with water, and this is called *Jalajātrā*, 'water pilgrimage.' This little pilgrimage is accompanied with much rejoicing, and the pilgrims usually celebrate their return home by a feast.

4. Full-moon fasts.—The phases of the moon are watched with the keenest interest by the Jains (as they are, indeed, by all the inhabitants of an agricultural country like India); and four of the full-moon days, or *punema*, are observed as special fasts. On two of these, Kārttika Punema (October or November) and Chaitri Punema (April or May), they go, if possible, on pilgrimage. The favourite places of Jain pilgrimage are the hills of Śatruñjaya (in the State of Pālitāna), Sametaśikhara (Bengal), Girnār (Junāgadh), and Mount Abu (Rajputānā); but at these full-moon fasts the place they are most eager to visit is Śatruñjaya. It was on Śatruñjaya, they say, that at Kārttika Punema the two sons of Kṛṣṇa—Drāviḍa and Vāllibilla—

[1] For the eightfold *pūjā*, see M. Stevenson, *Notes on Modern Jainism*, p. 103 ff.

obtained *mokṣa* along with about a hundred million monks, and at Chaitri Punema that Puṇḍarīka Gaṇadhara, the chief disciple of Ṛsabhadeva, obtained *mokṣa* with fifty million monks. If it proves impossible to visit not merely Śatruñjaya but any of the other places, Jains still manage to acquire some special pilgrimage merit by taking a map or photograph of Śatruñjaya into the fields outside their town in the direction of that mountain and worshipping it there.

On the two other full-moon fasts, Phālguṇa Punema (in February or March) and Āṣāḍhi Punema (in June or July), Jains of either the Śvetāmbara or the Digambara sect fast, decorate their temples with lamps, and are specially diligent in attendance at the temple-worship, whilst Sthānakavāsi Jains go to their *upāsarā* to hear sermons. Āṣāḍhi is specially important to the ascetics, for in whatever town monks or nuns may be for that fast, there they must remain till the monsoon is over and Kārttika Punema comes round.

5. Jñānapañchami.—Śvetāmbara and Sthānakavāsi Jains observe the 5th day of the bright half of Kārttika, which they call *Jñānapañchami*, since special knowledge is gained by those who worship their sacred books on this day. The institution of this fast has been of incalculable use in preserving Jain literature, for not only are the books worshipped and sandal-wood sprinkled over them, but all the volumes in Jain treasure-houses[1] are supposed to be dusted, freed from insects, and rearranged on this day.

6. Maunagyārasa.—Once a year the very strict ascetics commemorate by a solemn fast the five stages through which a mortal must pass before he can become a *siddha*. Sthānakavāsi laymen do not generally keep this day, though some of the Śvetāmbara laity do. During the whole day absolute silence is observed, together with abstention from both food and water. The Jain, as he tells his beads, meditates on each of the five stages (*sādhu*, or ascetic; *upādhyāya*, or preceptor; *āchārya*, or ruler of monks; *tīrthaṅkara*, or ford-finder; *siddha*, or perfected one) which lie before him. This fast, as its name shows, must be kept on the eleventh day of a month. If possible, it should be observed on the eleventh day of the bright half of Mārgaśīrṣa (November and December); but, if that particular date is inconvenient, the eleventh of any other month may be substituted. On the day following, Śvetāmbaras celebrate the breaking of this eleventh-day fast in a curious way. They choose eleven kinds of things connected with the pursuit of knowledge, and put eleven of each kind, such as eleven pens, eleven books, eleven pieces of paper, eleven inkpots, etc., in front of them, and worship these 121 articles.

7. Oli or Āmbela.—Eight days before Chaitri Punema great fairs are held at the chief places of pilgrimage, which are attended by Jains from all over India. At this time men and women take special vows as to what they will eat, promising, for instance, to eat only one kind of grain throughout the day and to drink only boiled water. Oli or Āmbela is the fast *par excellence* of women, for at this season a royal princess, Mayaṇā Sundarī, by worshipping the saint-wheel, won health and restoration to his kingdom for her husband, Sripāla, who had been a leper. Ever since the days of this princess, women who want a happy married life have been specially diligent in observing this fast, giving up for the time any food they particularly like, such as melted butter or molasses, and eating only one sort of dish.

8. Days of abstinence.—In addition to special days like the above, many careful Jains observe as fasts, with more or less strictness, twelve days in every month. These days are the two second, the two fifth, the two eighth, the two eleventh, the two fourteenth, and the bright and dark fifteenth of each month. (In India a month consists of two sets of fifteen days, the bright fifteen and the dark fifteen of the moon.) Less devout Jains observe only five days of abstinence (the two eighth, the two fourteenth, and the fifteenth of the bright half of the month), whilst others keep only two—Śvetāmbaras observing the eighth (Āṭhama) and the fifteenth (Punema), and Digambaras the eighth and the fourteenth days of the month.

9. The bathing of Gomateśvara.—Three or four times during every century the Digambara Jains hold a great festival at Śrāvaṇa Belgolā (Hassan District, Mysore State) to lave the gigantic statue of Gomateśvara. This statue, which is one of the wonders of India, was cut some 900 years ago from a solid block of stone sixty feet high.

The last festival[1] was held in March 1910, when Jain devotees gave gratis the materials and the labour to erect the immense scaffold which encircled the image on its three sides. On the day of the bathing Indrabhūti was closed to all but Jains, but it was possible to see from a distance the figures on the platform over the head of the image. The actual laving took place in the afternoon, and the gradual darkening of the image, as the mingled stream of curds, milk, melted butter, etc., flowed over it, was noticeable even from afar. The privilege of laving the figure had been previously put up to auction, Jains bidding what price they would pay for every separate cupful of mixture they poured over it. During the festival the question was raised of erecting a glass shelter over the sixty-foot figure, but it was decided that to build this would be to appear wiser than their ancestors, and, furthermore, the laving of the image was considered to have proved a valuable means of protecting it from the elements. It was suggested that the festival should be held more frequently, and the image bathed every three or every seven years.

10. The consecration of an idol.—Perhaps amongst festivals should be included *Añjanaśalākā*, the consecration of a new idol, for it is celebrated with the greatest pomp and magnificence. *Mantras* are recited, and in the case of Śvetāmbara Jains the metal eyes are inserted in the head of the idol,[2] which is then anointed with saffron; until this takes place, the idol is not regarded as sacred. The ceremony is rare nowadays, owing to the enormous expense it entails on the donor of the idol, who has to pay for great processions and feasts in addition to the cost of the image.

11. Hindu festivals and fasts observed by Jains.[3]—In addition to their own fasts and festivals, Jain laymen observe most of the great festivals of the Hindus: for example, *Holi*, the shameless festival of spring (which, however, is not observed by Jain ascetics or by laymen who have taken the twelve vows); *Śitalāsātama*, the festival of the goddess of smallpox, when most of the Jain women and children (despite the efforts of their religious leaders and the conferences) go to her temple and offer drawings of eyes to the goddess and money to the temple Brāhmans to obtain immunity from smallpox for the year. On this day, as the women refuse to cook on the ordinary hearths (believing the goddess of smallpox to be sleeping there for the day), the household has usually to eat stale food, or to cook on some other hearth. Jains also observe *Virapasalī*, which falls on some Sunday in the month of Śrāvaṇa (August), when brothers give presents to their sisters, and sisters bless their brothers; and the corresponding feast of *Bhāi bija*, when sisters invite their brothers to their houses. *Daśerā*, the great Kṣatriya festival, is kept by Jains only to the extent of eating specially dainty food on that day. Another Hindu festival the Jains observe is *Makarasaṅkrānti*, which falls

[1] *i.e.* of books and MSS. The most famous of these treasure-houses are at Pātan, Cambay, and Jesalmir.

[1] See H. Spencer, art. in *Harvest Field*, 1910; for a picture of this famous statue, see Moor, *Hindu Pantheon*, London, 1810, plate 73.

[2] Digambara images are always represented with closed eyes.

[3] Cf. FESTIVALS AND FASTS (Hindu).

in January. On this day they fulfil one of their Four Fundamental Duties[1]—that of charity—by giving away food and clothing to the poor and fodder to cattle.

Many Jain women, even of the non-idolatrous sect, observe the Hindu fast of *Bolachotha*, by abstaining from food till evening, when they worship the goddess Gaurī, wife of Śiva, and then cows and calves, which they mark with red on their foreheads. Jain girls very frequently keep the Hindu fast of *Molākata*, abstaining for a whole day from all food containing salt, in order to obtain a kind husband. Many of the Jains so far observe the *Śrāddha*, or death-ceremonies of the Hindus, as to eat specially good food on that day. (The ceremony of throwing food to the crows at this time has, however, in most cases been discontinued by the Jains.)

In fine, so many festivals do the Jains observe, and such rich food do they eat in celebration of them, that a proverb has sprung up—'To turn Śrāvaka for Śiro'—which accuses folk of turning Jain for the sake of a favourite festal dainty.

LITERATURE.—The information contained in the above article has been derived directly from Jain informants. The reader may consult also *BG* ix. (1901) pt. i. pp. 113–115, and the present writer's *Notes on Modern Jainism*, London, 1910.

MARGARET STEVENSON.

FESTIVALS AND FASTS (Jewish).—**1. Modifications of the ancient feasts.**—Although the post-Biblical period of Judaism witnessed the institution of several semi-festivals and other memorial days, it was marked by the rise of no new festivals invested with the solemnities of the ancient feasts. As an offset to this, however, the feasts prescribed in the OT underwent manifold changes, and the character of not a few was fundamentally modified. More particularly after the destruction of the Second Temple, and the consequent cessation of sacrificial worship, the Jews sought to find a substitute for the latter, partly in the development and institution of an ordered liturgy—the germs of which, it is true, go back to the time when the Temple was still standing—and partly in the establishment of new observances for family devotion, as, *e.g.*, the *Kiddûsh* (lit. 'hallowing'), *i.e.* the ceremony of hailing the dawning Sabbath or feast-day by speaking a benediction over a cup of wine, the *Sēder* (see below) designed for the evening of the Passover, and the like. Other modifications were brought about by the altered conditions of life; thus, *e.g.*, the pilgrim festivals almost entirely lost their agricultural character, and became purely historical celebrations.

One particular modification which affected all the Biblical festivals except the Day of Atonement was the introduction of a second feast-day for the Diaspora, *i.e.* for countries outside Palestine. Among the Jews in the time of the Second Temple, and for centuries afterwards, the beginning of the month was determined, not by calculation, but by observation of the new moon, as it was decreed by the supreme spiritual authorities that the month should begin with the first sight thereof (see art. CALENDAR [Jewish], vol. iii. p. 117 ff.). At first the authorities caused the event to be announced to the various communities by beacon-fires on the hills (cf. Wensinck, in Becker's *Islam*, i. [1910] 101), and afterwards by express messengers (Mishna, *Rōsh Hashshānā*, i. 3–4, ii. 2–4), telling them at the same time whether the foregoing month was 'defective,' *i.e.* one of 29 days, so that the new month began on the thirtieth, or 'full,' *i.e.* one of 30 days, the new month thus commencing on the thirty-first. But, as the Diaspora became more widely spread, it was found impossible for messengers to reach the communities in due time, and accordingly, in order to avoid all possibility of error, these outlying communities observed not only the computed feast-day, but also the day following, which, if the closing month had been a 'full' one of 30 days, would, of course, be the proper date. Thus, *e.g.*, the Diaspora kept the Feast of the Passover from the 15th to the 22nd (instead of to the 21st) of Nisan, and held a solemn celebration on the 15th and 16th and on the 21st and 22nd (instead of the 15th and the 21st only), etc. An exception was made in the case of the Day of Atonement alone, as being a fast, for it was considered dangerous to fast for two days in succession (Jerus. *Ḥalla*, i. fol. 57*c*, l. 14; Bab. *Rōsh Hashshānā*, 21*a*). The New Year festival, again, which fell on the 1st of Tishri—on the first day of a month—was often celebrated on two days, even in Palestine, on the ground that it was never possible to determine whether the previous month, Elul, would be 'defective' or 'full.' Once the fixed calendar was introduced, all uncertainty in the matter was at an end; nevertheless, a second New Year's day was observed in Palestine as elsewhere from the 12th cent. A.D. (cf. 'Responses of the Geonim,' ed. Lyck, 1864, no. 1; Zeraḥia Gerundi's *Ma'ōr* on tr. *Beṣa*, at the beginning). In the Diaspora likewise, the observation of the second day was rendered unnecessary by the introduction of the fixed calendar, but it was allowed to continue for tradition's sake (cf. Bab. *Beṣa*, 4*b*). The first to reject it were the Karaites, who reinstated the observation of the moon, and many modern Jewish communities follow their example.

The several festivals were modified as follows:

(1) *Pesaḥ* (The Passover).—Of the three characteristic symbols of this feast—the sacrificial lamb, the unleavened bread, and the bitter herbs—the first was discarded, while the others survived in family devotion under the name *Sēder*. In Palestine the *Sēder* is observed on the first, and in the Diaspora on the first and the second, evening of the festival, and the ritual for its observance is contained in a book called *Haggādā* ('story,' 'narrative'). A faint vestige of the originally agricultural character of this festival appears in the prayer for dew (*ṭal*), which is recited on the first day (see below).

(2) *Sh'bū'ôth* (The Feast of Weeks).—According to Scripture, this feast was to be celebrated seven full weeks after the Passover. The seven weeks were reckoned from the ממחרת השבת, *mimoḥorath hash-shabbath* (Lv 23[15]), and the interpretation of these words was a subject of controversy between the Pharisees and the Boethusæans. The Pharisees, as also the LXX, Philo, and Josephus, understood them as meaning 'on the next day after the feast,' and counted from the 16th of Nisan; so that the Feast of Weeks fell (when Nisan and Īyyar were both 'full') on the 5th of Sivan, or (when Nisan was 'full' and Īyyar 'defective,' or conversely) on the 6th, or again (if both were 'defective') on the 7th (Jer. *Rōsh Hashshānā*, i. fol. 57*b*, l. 18 from foot). Hence, after the introduction of the fixed calendar, according to which Nisan was always full and Īyyar always defective, the festival fell on the 6th, or (in the Diaspora) on the 6th and 7th, of Sivan. The Boethusæans, on the other hand, interpreting the Biblical phrase as 'on the next day after the Sabbath,' began the commemoration with the first Sunday of the Passover festival, and celebrated the Feast of Weeks always on a Sunday. The Boethusæans were followed in this by all the schismatic communities, down to the Samaritans and Karaites of the present day (cf. Poznański, in *Kaufmann-Gedenkbuch*, Breslau, 1900, p. 173, note 4). But there were others who took the words to mean 'on the next day after the last

[1] These are: charity, virtue, austerity, devotion.

feast-day' (so, *e.g.*, the Syriac Peshiṭta), and therefore counted from the 22nd of Nisan, celebrating the Feast of Weeks on the 12th of Sivan (as, *e.g.*, the Abyssinian Falashas), or—where the reckoning was by months of four weeks or twenty-eight days —on the 15th (so, *e.g.*, the apocryphal *Book of Jubilees*; cf. Epstein, *Eldad ha-Dani*, Vienna, 1891, p. 154 ff.). The Feast of Weeks likewise lost its agricultural character, and became the festival of the Sinaitic legislation, which was delivered in the third month, *i.e.* Sivan (Ex 19; cf. Bab. *Shabbath*, 86*b*). The festival bears this character also among the Samaritans (cf. Cowley, *The Samaritan Liturgy*, Oxford, 1909, i. 335 ff.) and the Karaites.

(3) *Rōsh Hashshānā* (New Year Festival).—In the Pentateuch (Nu 29^1; cf. Lv 23^{24}) this feast, which falls on the 1st of Tishri, is referred to as *Yôm Tᵉrū'a* ('day of blowing the trumpet'), but not as the beginning of the year (the year began with Nisan [Ex 12^2]), though the Feast of Tabernacles, which was likewise celebrated in Tishri, is spoken of as taking place 'at the turn of the year' (Ex 24^{22}). Ezekiel (40^1) speaks of the 10th of the month—probably Tishri is meant (cf. Lv 25^9)—as the beginning of the year. Ezra read the Book of the Law before the assembled people on the 1st of Tishri, and calls the day 'holy to the Lord' (Neh 8^{1-10}), but not New Year's day. The latter designation was first given to the festival in the Talmud (*Rōsh Hashshānā*, i. 1), where it ranks also as a day of Divine judgment. We may perhaps discern here traces of Bab. influence (cf. Zimmern-Winckler, *KAT*³, p. 515). The days from the 1st to the 10th of Tishri came simply to be days of penitence and heart-searching (*'Asereth Yemē Tᵉshūba*; cf. *Rōsh Hashshānā*, 18*a*).

(4) *Yōm Kippūr* (The Day of Atonement).—Here, too, a substitute for the abandoned sacrifice was found in a solemn festival in the synagogues, and this day is regarded as the most important of the Jewish feasts.

(5) *Sukkōth* (The Feast of Tabernacles).—This festival likewise entirely lost its originally agricultural character as a vintage feast. According to a Talmudic ordinance (*Ta'anith*, i. 1), God is to be praised as the sender of rain, in a prayer beginning on the 8th day of the Feast of Tabernacles and ending with the 1st day of the Passover. In keeping therewith, a special prayer for rain (*geshem*) was offered on the former day—as also one for dew (*ṭal*; see above) on the latter—and various hymns were composed for the *geshem* from the 7th or 8th centuries. The 9th and last day of the Feast of Tabernacles—in the Diaspora only, of course—was called *Simḥat Torah*, 'delight in the Law,' because, according to a very ancient custom, the reading of the Pentateuch in public worship was completed, and a fresh beginning made, on that day; this designation, however, is first met with in the 11th or 12th cent. (cf. Zunz, *Ritus*, Berlin, 1859, p. 86). The 21st of Tishri, the last of the semi-festival days, is styled *Hosha'na Rabbā*, 'the great Hosanna,' or *Yōm 'Arāba*, 'the day of willows' (*Sukka*, 45*a*). At this festival it was customary to set up willows about the altar, and march round it once; but on the 21st of Tishri the altar was compassed about seven times, and in commemoration thereof it is still the practice to hold a sheaf of willows during the prayer on that day. In the Middle Ages, mysticism gained a powerful hold upon the day, and converted it into a statutory judging day supplementary to the preceding New Year's day and the Day of Atonement (cf. Berliner, *Randbemerkungen zum hebr. Gebetbuche*, ii. [1912] 25 ff.).

2. Minor festivals of later origin.—Of semi-festivals, besides the Biblical Feast of Purim and the Feast of the Maccabees (*Ḥanukka*)—not found in the Bible—both of which have been referred to in the 'Hebrew' section, the following, together with other memorial days, some of which have been given up and some fallen into decay, may be noted:

(1) If, owing to Levitical uncleanness, or from any other cause, a man was unable to present his Paschal offering on the 14th of Nisan, he could, provided he observed certain regulations, make good his omission on the 14th of Īyyar (cf. Nu 9^{10-12}). Traces of this practice still survive, and the day is known as *Pesaḥ Shēnī* ('Second Passover').

(2) The 15th of Ab was the day on which wood was supplied for the altar of burnt-offering, and was, as such, a day of rejoicing (references in Schürer, *GJV* ii.⁴ 316). The recollection of this fact was subsequently lost, and the Talmud (Jer. *Ta'anith*, 69*c*; Bab. 30*b*) seeks in various ways to explain the significance attached to the day.

(3) Nicanor's Day was the 13th of Adar, and commemorated the victory of Judas Maccabæus over the Syrian general Nicanor at Adasa in 161 B.C. (1 Mac 7^{39-50}, 2 Mac 15^{1-36}; Jos. *Ant.* XII. x. 5). P. Haupt ('Purim,' *Beitr. zur Assyr.* vi. 2, p. 3 ff.) seeks to derive the Feast of Purim from Nicanor's Day, but, as it would seem, without any good reason. Nowadays, as we shall see presently, the 13th of Adar is observed as a fast.

(4) and (5) The Alexandrian Jews celebrated several other festivals of a special character. One of these was designed to commemorate the translation of the Torah into Greek (Philo, *Vita Mosis*, ii. 7); another was a memorial of their marvellous deliverance at the time when Ptolemy IV. (1 Mac 6^{36}) or Ptolemy VII. (Josephus, *c. Apion.* ii. 2) attempted to destroy them by means of elephants. The dates of these festivals, however, are quite unknown.

(6) A little work bearing the title *Megillath Ta'anith* ('Roll of Fasts'), and redacted in Aramaic in the 1st or 2nd cent. A.D., contains a list of days on which, as commemorative of some joyful event, it was not permissible to fast (Lit. in Schürer, i. 157, and *JE*, *s.v.*). Of such days there are no fewer than sixty-two, including, besides the *Ḥanukka*, those mentioned in 1–3 above.

(7) The 15th of Shebaṭ is spoken of in the Mishna (*Rōsh Hashshānā*, i. 1) as the New Year for trees; that is to say, the Biblical ordinances relating to trees and their fruits (as, *e.g.*, in Lv 19^{23-25}) come into operation for the year on that day. This date still retains its associations, and is regarded as a day of rejoicing.

(8) The forty-nine days between the Passover and the Feast of Weeks are called the 'Ōmer days, because the beginning of their enumeration was signalized by presenting a sheaf (*'ōmer*) of barley as an offering. These days were also accounted a time of mourning, as it was said that 12,000 pupils of Aḳiba had perished during the period (*Yebāmoth*, 62*b*); and perhaps we have here a reminiscence of Bar Cochba's revolt under Hadrian, in which Aḳiba took a very active part. Further, it is regarded as improper to marry during this season; but the earliest mention of this restriction is found in post-Talmudic sources (cf. the list of relevant passages in Geiger's *Jüd. Ztschr.* vii. [1869] 83), and many scholars find in it simply an echo of the Roman practice of having no marriages in May, as the spirits of the dead were propitiated by special ceremonies, and the so-called *Lemuria* celebrated, in that month. An exception was made of the thirty-third 'Omer day (*Lag be-'ōmer*; lag = ל״ג = 33), which coincides with the 18th of Īyyar, and is regarded as a semi-festival. The reason for excluding this particular day is far from clear. A felicitous conjecture has been made by Derenbourg

(*REJ* xxix. [1894] 149), viz. that the actual period of mourning lasted only thirty-four days (the twenty-nine of Īyyar and the first five of Sivan), and that these were divided into two equal portions with a festive day inserted between them. The 18th of Īyyar would thus be a kind of *Mi-Carême*.

3. Fasts.—Of fasts falling on stated dates, the Pentateuch prescribes only one, viz. the Day of Atonement on the 10th of Tishri (Lv 16$^{29.31}$ 23$^{27.29}$). Then we read in Zec 8^{19} that the fasts of the 4th month (Tammuz), the 5th (Ab), the 7th (Tishri), and the 10th (Ṭebeth), which, as appears from Zec 7^{5}, were observed during the Exile in Babylon, were henceforth to be days of rejoicing. According to the explanation given in the Talmud (*Rōsh Hashshānā*, 18*b*), and accepted by the majority of modern commentators (as, *e.g.*, among the most recent, Marti and Hoonacker, *ad loc.*), these were four fast-days which had been appointed as memorials of calamitous occurrences connected with the overthrow of the Jewish State and the destruction of the Second Temple by the Babylonians, thus: (1) the fast of the 4th month, to commemorate the taking of Jerusalem on the 9th of Tammuz (Jer 39^{2} 52^{6}); (2) that of the 5th month, in memory of the destruction of the Temple, which took place, according to one account (2 K 25^{8}), on the 7th of Ab, and, according to another (Jer 52^{12}), on the 10th; (3) that of the 7th month, in memory of the slaying of Gedaliah—here, however, the sources (2 K 25^{25}, Jer 41^{1}) mention the month only, not the day; and (4) that of the 10th month, to commemorate the investment of Jerusalem, which began on the 10th of Ṭebeth (2 K 25^{1}, Jer 52^{4}, Ezk 24^{1}).

As might be expected, these fasts were discontinued in the time of the Second Temple, but they were resumed after its destruction, though with several changes of date. The fast of the 4th month was transferred to the 17th of Tammuz, the day on which, in A.D. 70, the daily morning and evening sacrifice had to be abandoned (Jos. *BJ* VI. ii. 1), and to which various other national disasters were assigned (Mishna, *Ta'anith*, iv. 6). The fast of the 5th month was appointed for the 9th of Ab, and began, in fact, on the evening before, *i.e.* the 8th of Ab. This was the day (8th Loos) on which the gates of the Temple were set fire to by command of Titus, though the Temple itself was not burned down till the 10th of the month (see Schürer, i. 631, where the statement of Joḥanan in *Ta'anith*, 29*a*, might have been added to the references); perhaps the 9th was decided upon because Betar, the residence of Bar Cochba, was also taken by storm on that day. The fast of the 7th month was assigned to the 3rd of Tishri, as the first two days of the month were dedicated to the New Year festival, and could not be spent as fasts. Finally, the fast of the 10th month still continued to be observed on the 10th of Ṭebeth.

The Karaites keep strictly to the Biblical dates, fasting on the 9th of Tammuz, the 7th and 10th of Ab, and the 10th of Ṭebeth. On the authority of Neh 9^{1}, they hold the fast of the 7th month on the 24th of Tishri, and they too connect it with the assassination of Gedaliah, though with other events as well. It should be borne in mind, further, that, in the Roll of Fasts above referred to, the 3rd of Tishri is reckoned among festive days, so that this fast must have been instituted at a later date than the others.

To these four fasts was subsequently added a fifth, observed on the 13th of Adar in commemoration of the three days' fast of Queen Esther (Est 4^{16}), and therefore known also as Esther's Fast (*Ta'anith Esther*). The earliest reference to it is found in two post-Talmudic works, viz. the *Sheeltoth*, dating from the 8th cent. A.D., and the *Midrash Tanḥuma* (*Bereshith*, no. 3), probably of still later origin; and in France, even as far down as the 11th cent., the fast was regarded not as an ordinance, but simply as a custom (cf. Isr. Lévi, *REJ* xlvii. [1903] 170). It should also be noted in this connexion that, while the Second Temple was still in existence, the 13th of Adar was a day of rejoicing, and was called Nicanor's Day (see above). The fast itself may possibly go back to an earlier time, when the people actually fasted for three days, precisely as Esther had done. In the extra-canonical Talmudic tractate *Soferim* (xvii. 4, xxi. 1) it is stated that the three fast-days of Purim were not consecutive, but were held on Monday, Thursday, and Monday. In Palestine, however, they were observed *after* Purim, because the 13th of Adar, as Nicanor's Day, and the 12th, as Trajan's Day, were festive days, and could not be spent as fasts; even at that period, accordingly, the observance of Nicanor's Day must have been in force (cf. Neuwirth, *Jüd. Presse*, 1912, no. 11). The Karaites do not recognize this fast, though their founder, 'Anān b. David, enjoined that the crisis connected with Purim should be commemorated by a fast of seventy days, lasting, conformably to Est 3^{13} 8^{1}, from the 13th of Nisan to the 23rd of Sivan (cf. Harkavy, *Stud. u. Mitt.* viii. [1903] 40, 130, 133, 149). But this injunction was, in all likelihood, never put into practice.

Besides the fast-days already specified and associated with stated dates, it was customary to appoint fasts in connexion with various evils of a more general kind, as, *e.g.*, with the preparations for a battle (1 Mac 3^{47}, 2 Mac 13^{12}), drought (Mishna, *Ta'anith*, i. 5), and the like; nor has this practice even yet been wholly abandoned. Moreover, devoutly-minded people fast as a seal of penitence, or from a craving for self-denial. Such fasts usually take place on Mondays or Thursdays, which have from ancient times been accounted specially suitable for fasting, probably because it was on these days that the people of the surrounding districts came into the cities for the purpose of hearing the lesson from the Torah, or of attending the law-courts (cf. Joel Müller, *Masechet Soferim*, Leipzig, 1878, p. 235 ff.). But we find that fasting was practised on other days as well, though never on Sabbaths, or on feast-days, or their preparatory days (cf. Jth 8^{6}).

There are also local fast-days, designed to commemorate particular local calamities, and thus obligatory only upon the Jews resident in the countries concerned (cf. Zunz, *Ritus*, 127 ff.). Of such fasts the best known is the 20th of Sivan, observed as a memorial of the slaughter of Polish Jews by Cossacks in 1648–49.

LITERATURE. This has been sufficiently indicated in the course of the article.

SAMUEL POZNAŃSKI.

FESTIVALS AND FASTS (Muslim).—Properly speaking, Muslims know only two festivals (*'īd*, more rarely *mausīm*), which, however, are not mentioned in the Qur'ān, though they are based on it. Further, they have introduced, in the course of time, a multitude of commemoration days for holy men and sacred events; and, finally, in countries which were arabicized later, they have appropriated the pre-Islāmic holidays to a certain extent. Thus we can distinguish festivals and holidays, properly speaking, from observances purely Islāmic and half Islāmic, universal and local.

1. The greatest festival is **the festival of sacrifices** connected with the Great Pilgrimage (*yaum al-aḍḥā; yaum an-naḥr; al-'īd al-kabīr* or *al-akbar*; Turk. *qurbān bairāmi*), which is celebrated from the 10th to the 13th of Dhū-l-ḥijja by pilgrims in the Valley of Minā (now Munā), east of Mecca, and by non-pilgrims at home. Although the festival rests on a heathen basis (cf. art. CALENDAR (Muslim), vol. iii. p. 126[b]), the Islāmic legends associate it with and explain it by the sacrifice of Ishmael at the hand of Abraham. In the *Sūra al-Ḥajj* (xxii.) of the Qur'ān there is, besides the explicit recognition of the Ka'ba cult, also a mention of the sacrifice of animals (v.[28]):

'And proclaim amongst men the Pilgrimage; let them come to you . . . (29) for the stated days over what God has provided them with of brute beasts, then eat thereof and feed the badly off, the poor . . . (31) Cattle are lawful for you, except what is recited to you; . . . (33) That—and he who makes grand the symbols (*sha'ā'ir*) of God, they come from piety of heart. (34) Therein have ye advantages for an appointed time, then the place for sacrificing them is at the old House [the Ka'ba]; . . . (37) The bulky (camels) we have made for you one of the symbols of God, therein have ye good; so mention the name of God over them as they stand in a row, and when they fall down (dead) eat of them, and feed the easily contented and him who begs. Thus have we subjected them to you; haply, ye may give thanks! (38) Their meat will never reach to God, nor yet their blood, but the piety from you will reach to Him.'

Further, it is customary to interpret the words 'So pray to thy Lord and slaughter (victims)' (Qur. cviii. 2) of the festival of sacrifices. According to the oldest tradition (*ḥadīth*, quoted according to the *Ṣaḥīḥ* of al-Bukhārī, Būlāq, 1296 [vocalized], in 8 parts), the following is the fixed order, partly in common with the other festival (see below), which this festival has. First (Bukhārī, ii. 3. 8, 3. 18, 4. 2, 5. 16, 6. 10, 7. 20, 8. 4; vi. 223. 2, 226. 6, 7) comes the general prayer (*ṣalāt*) accompanied by an edifying address (*ḥuṭba*) by the leader in prayer (*imām*). Only thereafter can the sacrificing of the animals take place. Some wished to make the address precede the prayer, because after it the crowd could not be held in restraint. But this practice is criticized. It is lawful to eat dates before the prayer, but not to slaughter or taste flesh (ii. 3. 15 f., 5. 18, 6. 11, 10. 5, 9). If any one did so, it was not reckoned to him as a sacrifice; he had to repeat the slaughtering after the address. When the *imām* addressed women, they used, in the times of the Prophet, to cast their ornaments as alms (*ṣadaqa*) into the garment of the *mu'adhdhin*, Bilāl, held out to them. During the prayer (ii. 5. 4, 7. 20, 8. 12) an antique weapon (*'anaza*, short spear, or *ḥarba*, dart, javelin) used to be planted in the earth before the *imām* (ii. 7. 10 ff.). (This explains also the name *Ḥarba* for Friday.) It was forbidden to carry arms on festival days (ii. 5 f.). It is told that the Prophet consummated the sacrifice in the following fashion (vi. 224 f.). He took two rams (*kabsh*, cf. Gn 22[13]), placed them in the direction of the Ka'ba, pronounced some pious formulæ (see below), and slaughtered the animals. The following predicates are applied to the victims:—(i.) *amlaḥ*, 'of mixed colours,' black and white (Tweedie, *Arabian Horse*, 1894, p. 263, translates this rare expression 'silver grey'); (ii.) *aqran*, 'with grown horns'; (iii.) in some texts but not all, *maujū'*, *mauji*, *mūja'*, *i.e.* 'with testicles crushed' between two stones or boards, because a sacrificial animal must have no sensuality. The last regulation seems to be pagan; for we may infer from Lv 22[24] (כָּתוּת) and Dt 23[2] (פְּצוּעַ־דַּכָּה) that this practice was also present in the Canaanite cult, and was suppressed only by the Jahweh-religion. The heathen custom, also, of adorning the victim with a necktie (*qilāda*) is mentioned even in Islām (vi. 227. 7 f.). The victim is called *ḍaḥīya*, *uḍḥīya*, *dhabīḥa* (cf. זבח), *nasīka*, and *nusk* (cf. נסך); in the Maghrib *'ayāda*. The flesh was eaten by the owner of the sacrifice, and also often distributed among the poor (vi. 223. 8; Baiḍāwi, i. 632. 6 ff.). The second and the third days, on which the inferior parts were consumed, were called on this account *yaum ar-ru'ūs*, 'day of the heads'; *yaum al-qarr*, 'day of the remnants'; *yaum al-akāri'*, 'day of the legs.' Besides sheep, oxen and camels were allowed as victims. At the slaughtering the following words are pronounced:—(*a*) *Bismillāh!* 'in the name of God!' (cf. Qur. xxii. 37); (*b*) *Allāhu akbar*, 'God is very great' (cf. Qur. xxii. 41); (*c*) *Allāhumma! hādhā minka wa-ilaika* (*laka*)! 'O God! this from Thee and unto Thee,' which probably means, 'From Thee, the angry God, we take refuge in Thee, the gracious God!' (cf. I. Goldziher, 'Ueber eine rituelle Formel der Muhammedaner,' *ZDMG* xlviii. [1894] 95 ff.). The ethical side of sacrifice is emphasized in Qur. xxii. 38 as well as in tradition (ii. 7. 9). It is a means of securing moral purification and blessing, and of coming near to God (acc. to the interpretation of *qurbān*, 'sacrifice'). The puritanic Abū Bakr wished therefore to hold in restraint as far as possible the joyful disposition that such a festival naturally brought with it, and to exclude female singers. But the more tolerant Prophet allowed them (ii. 2 f.). Also in the matter of luxury in clothing, there existed side by side a stricter and a laxer practice. Whoever had neglected the celebration of the sacrifice, or could not be present, had to substitute for it a prayer consisting of two bows (*rak'a*) (ii. 10. 15 ff.). In course of time both festivals have become familiar celebrations, during which the faithful make calls and give presents, put on new clothes, and seek amusements; yet they also visit graves, and hold devotional exercises.

2. The month of fasting and the festival that follows it are closely connected. (*a*) *The fast* (*ṣaum, ṣiyām*) (opp. *ifṭār*).—According to the Arabic tradition, Muhammad commanded first that the faithful should fast on the Day of *'Ashūrā*, the 10th of Muḥarram, after the fashion of the Jews, who fast on the 10th of Tishri, the Day of Atonement (ii. 208. 8, 223. 8, 231. 6, 14; iv. 250 f.). Later this regulation was abrogated, and, instead, the whole month of Ramaḍān was devoted to fasting (cf. CALENDAR [Muslim]). The regulation for this is in Qur. ii. 179 ff.:

'O ye who believe! There is prescribed for you the fast as it was prescribed for those before you; haply ye may fear. (180) A certain number of days, but he amongst you who is ill or on a journey, then (let him fast) another number of days. And those who are fit to fast (but do not) may redeem it by feeding a poor man; but he who follows an impulse to a good work it is better for him; and if ye fast it is better for you, if ye did but know. (181) The month of Ramaḍān wherein was revealed the Qur'ān, for a guidance to men, and for manifestations of guidance, and for a discrimination. And he amongst you who beholds this month then let him fast it; but he who is sick or on a journey, then another number of days; God desires for you what is easy, and desires not for you what is difficult—that ye may complete the number, and say "Great is God," for that He has guided you; haply ye may give thanks . . . (183) Lawful for you on the night of the fast is commerce with your wives; they are a garment unto you, and ye a garment unto them [or, better: for touching, to be touched]. God knows that ye did defraud yourselves, wherefore He has turned towards you and forgiven you; so now go in unto them and crave what God has prescribed for you, and eat and drink until a white thread can be distinguished by you from a black one at the dawn. Then fulfil the fast until the night, and go not in unto them, and ye at your devotions in the mosques the while. These are the bounds that God has set, so draw not near thereto. Thus does God make manifest His signs to men, that haply they may fear.'

The words 'may redeem it by feeding a poor man' were soon abrogated (*mansūḫ*), because they were misused by the wealthy (Qur. ii. 180[b]; Bukhārī, ii. 219). The custom of determining the daybreak by the test of distinguishing a white thread from a black is of Jewish origin. The ethical nature of the fast was strongly emphasized in the earliest tradition (ii. 208. 18, 210. 19, 211. 4 f.), just as it was in the Qur'ān. It is called, on the one hand, 'an atonement' (*kaffāra*), on the other 'a protection against sensuality.' It is of no benefit whatever as a mere *opus operatum*, but it must take place (1) in faith (*īmānan*), (2) intentionally (*nīyatan*), (3) in expectation of a reward and compensation (*iḥtisāban*) from God (ii. 210. 4, 232. 7, 233, 17). Whoever does not give up untruth and deceit will not profit by fasting (ii. 210. 15). Boisterous merrymaking is not allowed (ii. 210. 19). The faithful are exhorted not to insult each other during the fast. Whoever is insulted or attacked while fasting must not resist, but briefly answer, 'I am fasting' (ii. 208. 15, 210. 20, 220. 2). Tradition says of one who keeps the fast in this manner: 'The perfume of the mouth of the faster is more pleasant before God than the odour of musk' (ii. 208. 16, 210. 20). The month may not be shortened, but there must not be any overdoing either (ii. 223 f.). The Qur'ān itself excludes all rigorous practice (ii. 181). Similarly, tradition says that the fasting must be regulated according to the power and ability of each individual (Baiḍāwī, i. 102. 6). Some overzealous people wished to continue (*wiṣāl, muwāṣala, sard*) the fast after sunset through the whole night until the next morning; this met with disapproval, and was even threatened with punishment (ii. 223 f.). To meet different conditions and circumstances of everyday life there are special regulations which partly border on casuistry. The Qur'ān itself makes an exception in favour of the sick and of travellers (ii. 180). Likewise a Bedawī proverb says, *Al-musāfir kāfir*, 'The traveller is (like) an infidel,' *i.e.* he is not bound by ritual precepts. Sexual intercourse or the kissing of a woman is allowed (although restricted by the ethical conception of the fast, ii. 215), just as the swallowing of one's saliva (ii. 215. 20) and the use of a toothpick (*siwāk*). Further, it is allowed to snuff up medicine (*sa'ūṭ*) and to dye the eyes with eye-paint (*kuḥl*) (ii. 216. 7). In view of the question whether vomiting or bleeding breaks the fast, the following principle has been established (ii. 218): the fast concerns that which goes into the body and not that which comes out (contrast the position in Mk 7[18ff.]). Others condemn even the drawing of blood. The pious do not permit smoking, which is a more recent custom. One who is dying in Ramaḍān must appoint a substitute (*walī*) to fast the rest of the month in his place (ii. 221. 11). In time of menstruation, a woman may neither fast nor pray (ii. 221. 4).

Some people fast voluntarily at certain times outside of the month of Ramaḍān, *e.g.* on the Day of 'Ashūrā (ii. 231) (see above); in Sha'bān (ii. 225); on the 13th–15th of each month; during the days of pilgrimage at Mount 'Arafa and in the valley of Minā (Munā) (ii. 229); or three days in each month (i. 101. 18 f.). If a person alternately fasts one day and not the next, that is called 'the fast of the Prophet David' (ii. 226 f.).

More than once fasting is given in the Qur'ān as a penalty, *e.g.* iv. 94, where two months' fast is commanded for a case of murder; lviii. 5, two months' fast for one who wishes to have intercourse with his wife after having once pronounced the formula of divorce; v. 91, three days' fast for breach of faith; all this when the culprit is not able to pay the prescribed material penalty.

The oldest Islāmic legend explains the choice of Ramaḍān, which had no special significance in pre-Islāmic Arabia, as far as we know, by the tradition that it was the month of revelations. The 'leaves of Abraham' (Qur. lxxxvii. 19, cf. liii. 37), the Tōrāh, the Gospel, and the Qur'ān (ii. 181) are said to have been successively 'sent down' in Ramaḍān (Baiḍāwī, i. 102. 19 f.). Owing to the fast and the *Lailat al-qadr* (see below), the month of Ramaḍān is surrounded by a greater halo than any other Islāmic month. The mere sighting of the new moon (*hilāl*, cf. CALENDAR [Muslim]) which inaugurates Ramaḍān causes a joyful excitement in all circles. All that one forgoes in the daytime by fasting is compensated by material and spiritual gratification in the night. Beggars, Qur'ān-readers, *dhikr*-reciters, story-tellers fill the atmosphere with life. And, when Ramaḍān falls in the hot summer of the East, the season becomes one of the highest enjoyment through the pleasant nights. The activity of the State officials is reduced to a minimum by the government. Pious asceticism and mysticism celebrate here real triumphs. In addition to all this, there is the expectation of the 'little festival' which follows the hard month of fasting.

(*b*) When Ramaḍān ends, the first three days of the following Shauwāl are celebrated as *festival days*. It is the 'festival of fast-breaking' (*'īd al-fiṭr*) or 'the little festival' (*al-'īd aṣ ṣaghīr*; in Turkish, *Ramazān Bairāmi*, or *Kiychyk Bairām*). With the exception of the sacrifice, the oldest order of the festival is the same as in the *'īd al-kabīr* (see above), viz. prayer, edifying address, and feasting. The private and public amusements are also of the same nature as those of the great festival. Graves are frequently visited. In Egypt it is customary to lay on the tombs palm-boughs, or basils (*rīḥān*), or myrtle-leaves (*marsīn*), or rosemary (*ḥaṣalbān*).

3. Among the other holidays of the Muslims we must mention (1) 'the Night of Power' (*Lailat al-qadr*; Turk. *Qadr gijesi*), because it is based on the Qur'ān.

In Sūra xcvii. we read: '(1) Verily, we sent it down on the Night of Power! (2) And what shall make thee know what the Night of Power is? (3) The Night of Power is better than a thousand months! (4) The angels and the Spirit descend therein, by the permission of their Lord with every bidding. (5) Peace it is until the rising of the dawn!'

In xliv. 2 mention is made of 'the blessed night' of the revelation. But even the oldest tradition cannot tell which night it is (ii. 233 ff.). The only sure fact is that it falls in Ramaḍān. The following words are put in the mouth of the Prophet (ii. 238. 4): 'Behold, it was granted me to know the Night, then I forgot it again. Seek ye (believers), therefore, in the last ten nights of Ramaḍān and especially among the odd numbers!' In this matter, however, the believers have not got beyond the seeking; some have accepted the 25th night (Baiḍāwī, i. 102. 20); the Egyptians and the Ottomans officially observe the 27th night, *i.e.* the night from the 26th to the 27th of Ramaḍān. Legend and superstition add a good deal to that which the Qur'ān says in regard to the blessing of this night. It is celebrated by illuminating the mosques (at Cairo especially the Mosque of the Citadel), by prayers, devotional exercises, *dhikrs*, and hopes of mystical experiences.

(2) The first ten days of Muḥarram, the old 'Ashūrā days (see above), are held to be sacred, and are observed by the pious with superstitious usages. The last day in this series is especially consecrated by the pre-eminently Shī'ite commemmoration of the death, at Kerbela in A.H. 61, of Ḥusain, the son of the Khalīfa 'Alī. Just as in mediæval Christendom and in antiquity, so also here, the religious imagination, seizing upon this event, worked it into a rich dramatic literature in Persia. For the Sunnites also the 10th of Muḥarram has its significance, for on that day Noah left the ark, and Adam and Eve came together for the first time after their expulsion from Paradise. With the exception of these first ten days of the Islāmic year, the beginning of the new year (*ra's as-sana*) is not observed in the same manner as among us and among the majority of the peoples in antiquity.

(3) The remaining holidays are in part productions of legends, and in part connected with the Great Pilgrimage, while a few stand in close relation with the wide-spread worship of saints. The month of Ṣafar is held to be unlucky (cf. CALENDAR [Muslim]). On the 28th of Ṣafar the anniversary of the death of Ḥasan, brother of Ḥusain, is observed in India. Two memorial days of the Prophet fall in Rabī' I.—his birth on the 12th, and his death on the 13th. In India, however, they re-

verse the order, and commemorate his death on the 12th. The anniversary of the birth (*maulid*, *mūlid*) of the Ḥasanain, *i.e.* of Ḥasan and Ḥusain together, falls in Rabīʿ II. Many other great and small saints also have their *maulids*. In Jumāda I. come the commemoration days of ʿAlī, his birth on the 8th, and his death on the 15th. On the 20th of Jumāda I. the Ottomans celebrate the capture of Constantinople in A.H. 857 (27th May A.D. 1453). Rajab has been regarded as a specially holy month ever since heathen times. On the 12th of this month is the *Lailat ar-raghā'ib*, 'the night of the fulfilled desires,' because the Prophet is said to have been conceived in that night. The night of the 26th of Rajab is the *Lailat al-miʿrāj*, 'the night of the ascension' of the Prophet. This observance is based on the narrative, found in Qur. xvii. 1, of the 'journey by night' (*isrā*, *masrā*) which the Prophet made on a marvellous animal (*Burāq*) from Mecca to Jerusalem and back. This event has been treated both in prose and in poetry in the literatures of all Muslim peoples. The 3rd of Shaʿbān is considered by some as the birthday of Ḥusain. The night of the 15th of Shaʿbān is very important as the 'night of privilege' (*Lailat al-barā'a*); in it the heavenly tree, *Sidrat al-muntahā* (Qur. liii. 14), is shaken to decide who shall die in the following year. Something similar to this is told also of the *Lailat al-qadr* (see above), so that one can apply to both nights what Meissner says about the latter, that it must be regarded as a reminiscence of the Babylonian festival of the New Year (*Zagmuk*) (*ARW* v. [1902] 227; *KAT*³, p. 515). On the 21st of Ramaḍān the Muslims of India commemorate the death of ʿAlī. In the month of Shauwāl, soon after the 'little festival,' the Egyptians begin the preparations for the sending of the *kiswa* to Mecca. But the pilgrims, who used to start on foot or riding about this time, have now come to use extensively European steamers from the Maghrib, Egypt, Syria, and the Ottoman countries. Consequently the celebration of the departure and of the return of the pilgrim caravans is now more and more confined to the sending of the *kiswa* and *maḥmil*. The *ʿīd al-ghadīr*, the festival of the Lake of Ḥumm, where the Prophet is said to have nominated ʿAlī as his successor, is purely Shīʿite, and kept on the 18th Dhū-l-ḥijja.

4. Just as in the worship of Saints, so also in the observance of certain festivals, a syncretism crops out which is otherwise quite unknown in Islām. It is true that the Arabs, though numerically far inferior in the great countries which they had conquered, thanks to some other factors spread their language there more or less successfully. But, on the other hand, they naturally adopted some customs, among which was the observance of certain days, closely bound up with the nature or the history of the subjected peoples. Thus in Egypt the following days are celebrated as general festivals: the second day of the Coptic Easter (*Shamm an-nasīm*, 'smelling the mild west wind'); the *Lailat an-nuqṭa*, 'night of the dropping,' *i.e.* the wonderful drop which causes the rise of the Nile, which night falls in June (*Bā'ūna*); with this is connected the custom according to which the *Munādī an-Nīl*, 'Proclaimer of the Nile,' announces the rise and height of its waters; also the celebration of the *Jabr al-Ḥalīj*, 'cutting of the canal,' when the water used to break into the old —now filled up—canal of Cairo. In Persia the old Persian New Year's Day (*Naurūz*), which falls on the vernal equinox, is one of the greatest festivals, and deeply affects all the social relations of the country. In the Spain of the Arabs, the Muslims observed St. John's Day with the Christians, under the name of *al-ʿAnṣara*, which elsewhere designates the Day of Pentecost. This Day of ʿAnṣara is still observed in Morocco about the beginning of July; others combine it with the Day of ʿAshūrā. The negroes of the Maghrib celebrate in May the *ʿīd al-fūl*, 'festival of beans.' Old style New Year's Day is still observed for three days in the Maghrib (formerly also in Egypt) as *Yennāir* or *Ennāyer*. Similarly in Turkey, Christian festivals, and, in India, Brāhmanic festivals are observed equally by the Muslims.

5. Besides the above yearly festivals, the Muslims have also a weekly holiday, Friday, *Jumʿa*, *Jumuʿa* (cf. CALENDAR [Muslim] and Bukhārī, i. 194 f.). Work is not forbidden on Friday; but every good believer is expected, even if he thinks that he has an excuse for other days, to take part on that day in the common prayer in the mosque (*jāmiʿ*, *masjid*), and to hear the address (*ḥuṭba*) of the *imām* or *ḥaṭīb*, which follows the prayer. The observance of the rest of the day is private, or taken up with the *dhikr* exercises of the dervishes.

LITERATURE.—R. F. Burton, *Pilgrimage to Al-Madinah and Meccah* [on the ceremonies of the *Yaum Naḥr* or the Third Day], ed. Lond. 1906; E. W. Lane, *Manners and Customs of the Modern Egyptians*, Lond. 1846, chs. xxiv.–xxvi.; Mouradja d'Ohsson, *Tableau général de l'empire othoman*, Paris, 1787–1820; J. H. Garcin de Tassy, *Sur les Particularités de la religion musulmane de l'Inde*, Paris, 1831–1832 (also in *L'Islamisme*³, Paris, 1874, pp. 289–403); Budgett Meakin, *The Moors*, Lond. 1902, pp. 239–259; R. L. N. Michell, *Egyptian Calendar*, Lond. 1877–1900; E. Sell, *Faith of Islam*², Lond. 1896, pp. 306–332.

K. VOLLERS.

FESTIVALS AND FASTS (Nepalese).—Buddhism and Hinduism are so closely connected that the festivals of Nepāl are of as mixed a character as are the religions. With the mass of the people the religious character of the festivals is scarcely recognized. They are occasions of festivity and feasting rather than of prayer and worship. All the national, or *Niwar*, festivals have lost a great deal of their importance under Gurkha rule. The share which individual Niwars take in the different festivals is not optional, but depends upon a curious custom. Under the Niwar kings, from the earliest known times, the acting, on festival occasions, was the duty or privilege of certain families or castes; so also were the dancing, the construction of the cars, the making of masks, and the necessary painting. In each instance the privilege was hereditary, and passed from father to son. The custom continues to the present day. The important Niwar festivals are given below. They are arranged in the order in which they are celebrated, commencing with the month of Baisakh, the first month of the Niwar year.

1. 'Bhairabjatra' or 'Biskati,' in the month Baisakh.—Bhairava is an incarnation of Śiva, the most popular deity of Nepāl, and regarded as the guardian-angel of the country. The deity is essentially Hindu, but has been admitted into the Buddhist pantheon. Dancing and the sacrifice of buffaloes characterize the festival, which is always celebrated at night, except every twelfth year, when it takes place in the daytime.

2. 'Gaijatra,' in the month Sawan.—This is a festival in honour of the cow. It commences on the first day after the full moon of Sawan. The Hindu festival, where the cow is worshipped, is confined to one day. The Buddhist part of the festival lasts for half a month. The Buddhist *vihāras* and temples are visited, little wax trees (probably commemorative of the sacred Bo-tree at Gaya) are carried, and offerings are made to various Buddhas. Images and pictures are exposed to view in the *vihāras* for fifteen days—from the fifth day before till the tenth day after full moon (*Dassami*), when the festival closes, and the pictures are taken down and carefully put away in the *vihāras*.

3. **'Banhrajatra,' in the month Sawan.**—The name applies to feasts which are given from time to time to the fraternity of *banhras*. They occur quarterly, in the months Baisakh, Sawan, Kartikh, and Margh. They are celebrated by the giving of alms to the *banhras* on the part of any patron or any one who wishes to acquire merit, and of the people generally. On this occasion the coronet of Amitābha Buddha is taken from his image in his temple and exposed to public view.

4. **Indrajatra,' in the month Bhadu.**—This festival, held in Khatmandu, is peculiar to Nepāl. It is held in the beginning of September. It commences four days before the full moon of the month Bhadu, and lasts until the fourth day after.

5. **'Swayambhumala,' in the month Assin.**—This is the birthday of Swayambhu. It is a great Buddhist holiday, on the day of the full moon, and there is general Buddhist worship throughout the country.

6. **'Sheoratri,' in the month Phagan.**—It is held on the first day of the month, and is a fast, not a feast. It is a purely Hindu festival, but most Buddhists observe it.

7. **Small 'Machendrajatra,' in the month Chait.**

8. **'Neta Devi Rajatra,' in the same month.**

9. **Great 'Machendrajatra.'**—This is the most important Buddhist festival in Nepāl. It consists of three distinct portions: (1) the bathing of the image of Machendra; (2) the dragging of the image in a triumphal car; (3) unrobing the image and exhibiting his shirt to the people.

10. **Festival of 'Narayan.'**—Narayan is a form of Viṣṇu, and Buddhists to some extent enter into the worship of the day.[1]

LITERATURE.—H. A. Oldfield, *Sketches from Nepal*, London, 1880; Monier-Williams, *Buddhism*, do. 1889.

J. H. BATESON.

FESTIVALS AND FASTS (Siamese).—*Introductory*.—Siamese festivals, fasts, and observances are, as a rule, traceable to either Brāhmanism or Buddhism. These two creeds, introduced at a very early date into the country, have ever since existed side by side as rivals for the supremacy, but without any violent struggle, in so far at least as extant records go. The former (in its varied developments, especially Śaivism) was, with few exceptions, patronized by the Court till about 150 years ago, while Buddhism found most support among the masses. This naturally led the rulers of Siam, even when deeply attached to Hinduistic tenets, to assume the rôle of defenders of Buddhism as a matter of policy. Thus in every Siamese capital of the past (as even in the present one, Bangkōk), and in the chief provincial towns, especially in the south (Malay Peninsula), Brāhmanic temples with a body of officiating Brāhmans, who acted at the same time as State and Court priests, were to be found along with numerous Buddhist shrines and monasteries erected, some by pious rulers, but mostly by the people. Of these temples there were at least three in each town, facing the east, and dedicated respectively to Śiva (that on the south), Gaṇeśa (the middle one), and Viṣṇu (that on the north side). The result of all this was, if not an actual blending of the two religions, the gradual introduction into most of the national festivals and ceremonies of both Brāhmanic and Buddhist rites. This process was further intensified during the reigns of staunch Buddhist sovereigns like Song-tham (1618–28) and Mongkuṭ (1851–68), who both ascended the throne after having spent a considerable part of their life in a cloister. It was especially through the endeavours of the latter ruler that the introduction of Buddhist rites into State and Court ceremonies, which had long remained strictly Śaivitic, reached its climax. It thus comes to pass that nowadays in well-nigh all festivals and ceremonies, even those of unquestionable Hindu origin, we find Buddhist rites associated with Brāhmanic practices. Nor is this all, for the prestige of Brāhmanism, especially during the present dynasty (founded in 1782), having even more considerably dwindled, it may be said that in a good many festivals and domestic ceremonies the presence of the so-called Brāhmans (now a somewhat degenerate body) is solicited chiefly out of homage to a time-honoured tradition which renders them indispensable. Their task consists mainly in calculating auspicious dates, making offerings to the gods and goblins, performing lustrations, blowing *śaṅkha* shells, or striking the 'gong of victory,' and waving their Śaivite hour-glass-shaped drum (*ḍamaru*).

[1] H. A. Oldfield, *Sketches from Nepal*, vol. ii.

The private observances and ceremonies of the Siamese will be discussed in art. SIAM (Buddhism in). In this art. only festivals of a public nature are treated.

For the sake of easier comparison and identification of Siamese festivals introduced from Brāhmanic or Buddhist India with those of their land of origin, the Siamese solemnities are here mentioned in the serial order of the months in which they occur, beginning with Chaitra, the Siamese fifth month. It is with this that the Siamese new year now commences, whereas at an uncertain remote period it began with Mārgaśīrṣa (as in North India till about the end of the 10th cent., according to al-Bīrūnī), the present Siamese first month. Along with public festivals, some solemnities now held only at Court, or abolished of late, but which were formerly more or less public, will also be mentioned. It seems fit, moreover, that the principal state ceremonies periodically performed at appointed seasons should not be passed unnoticed, owing to their intimate connexion with most public festivals, of which they often constitute the predominant feature. The national periodically recurring holiday is the Moon-feast, or Buddhist *Uposatha* festival, which till recently was regularly observed on the 8th and 15th days of the waxing and on the 8th and 14th or 15th days of the waning, but is now superseded to a large extent (since the adoption of the solar calendar in 1889) for civil purposes by Sundays.

i. CHAITRA (5th month).—The greater part of this month is occupied with the New Year festivals, which are actually three, intended to solemnize respectively the commencement of the luni-solar, civil (modern solar), and astrological (old solar) years. Leaving out civil New Year's Day—fixed, since the introduction of the modern calendar in 1889, to fall invariably on the first of April, and which is an empty observance—it remains to consider the other two, owing to their being essentially religious, connected with the old calendar adopted from India on the basis of the Śaka era reckoning, and celebrated with as much pomp as ever, despite the introduction of the new calendar.

1. **'Trut,' or popular New Year.**—The festivities last three days: the 15th waning of Phālguna (4th month); the 1st waxing of Chaitra (5th month), or New Year's Day; and the day following. These holidays are an occasion for the people to perform meritorious work and enjoy themselves, after having duly freed the premises from ghosts through exorcistic recitations by Buddhist monks, who are presented with food and requisites. The task is accomplished on a much larger scale in the capital, where recitations of the *Āṭānātiya sutta* (an uncanonical compilation) are held all round the royal palace and the city walls, and guns are fired off from them at regular intervals during the night to frighten the goblins. The people carry protective

rings of unspun cotton cord on the head, and threads of the same material across the shoulders for the same purpose, so as to be freed from evil influence on New Year's Day. On this date (1st of Chaitra), oblations to the gods are made and ancestral worship is performed. At court, after this and a *homa* sacrifice offered on the sacred fire by the Brāhmans, the 'name' of the year is changed. This ceremony, termed *Saṁvachchhara-chinda*, consists in changing the name of the animal denoting the place of the year (*saṁvatsara*) in the duodenary cycle (of the twelve animals; see CALENDAR [Siamese]) after which the year is designated, but not the 'figure' or serial number of the year in the era, the altering of which is to be effected later, on *Meṣa-saṅkrānti*, *i.e.* at the completion of the astrological (solar) year. The people are allowed free gambling—an extraordinary concession of which full advantage is taken. In connexion with this popular New Year festival the following other important ceremonies are performed.

2. 'Snāna,' or 'Gajendrāśva-snānaṁ' ('sprinkling of the lordly elephants and horses,' a later reduced form of it).—This has been but recently abolished. It was originally a lustration of arms, a general purification of the army, like the Hindu *Nīrājanā*, which was restricted later to a formal sprinkling of the elephants and horses from the royal stables, effected from stands with lustral water as they filed past in a stately procession. On the same occasion the *Vṛddhi-pāśa* Brāhmans (*i.e.* those in charge of auspicious rites in connexion with elephants) uncoiled, in the royal elephant warehouses, the ropes and nooses stored therein for elephant-catching, and performed a hook and noose dance in honour of Viṣṇu, simulating the capture of elephants. This took place on the third day of the waning. Next morning the ropes and nooses were coiled up again and stored away. Both these ceremonies were repeated on the 4th new-moon day of the 11th month (Aśvayuja) in connexion with the half-year festival. The purport was a general review of the army, so that all its equipment might be kept in proper order and efficiency.

3. 'Thü-Nam,' or drinking of the water of allegiance.—This is a ceremony performed with the utmost splendour in the royal Buddhist temple of the capital (and in the chief temple of every provincial town) with the concourse of all officials. It takes place on the third day of the waxing, and is repeated in connexion with the half-year festival on the 13th day of the waning of the 10th month (Bhādrapada). Water is loyally drunk, in which royal weapons (symbols of the sovereign power) are dipped, adjurations being pronounced the while, so as to make it fatal to traitors. In essence this is tantamount to a water-ordeal, of the kind that formerly obtained in the Hindu Courts (cf. Bṛhaspati, in *SBE* xxxiii. [1889] 318).

4. 'Songkrān,' or astrological (solar) New Year.—This falls nowadays on either the 12th or the 13th of April, the date of the assumed entrance of the sun into Aries, according to the traditional local (Hindu-imported) reckoning. The day is termed *Mahā Songkrān* day (*Mahā-saṅkrānti* being substantially the same as *Meṣa-saṅkrānti*), and with it commences a three days' festival, the year's serial number in the era being changed with much ceremony on the third day, which is actually regarded as New Year's Day (solar). On this occasion the king performs with much splendour a kind of shower-bath with lustral water, termed *murdhābhiṣeka*, and afterwards he sprinkles the sacred images. The people, amid much rejoicing and free gambling, as on the popular New Year's Day, perform a good deal of meritorious work by washing the Buddha images in the temples, sprinkling the monks and their relatives as an act of respect, and building sand-hillocks in the temple-grounds. They partake of rice gruel, and offer *piṇḍas* of food, and lighted incense-sticks and tapers, to the statues of the Buddha.

ii. VAIŚĀKHA (6th month).—**5. Ploughing festival.**—This important state ceremony, traceable to the remotest antiquity in India, is performed up to the present day in Siam in order to usher in auspiciously the tilling of paddy fields. The people dare not, in fact, commence cultivation till this festival has been held, in which prognostics are also drawn concerning the prospects of the crop. It takes place on a lucky day designated by the astrologers in the waxing part of Vaiśākha (usually in the early days of May). A high official, formerly holding the title of *baladeva*, and representing the king (now the task falls *ex officio* to the Minister of Agriculture), performs the ploughing in a Crown field, attended by the Brāhmans, a large retinue, and crowds of people who naturally take a keen interest in the ceremony. After having cut three concentric furrows with a gilt plough drawn by richly caparisoned bulls (the sacred bulls were formerly employed), he scatters over them seeds which have previously been hallowed by *mantras* (Brāhmanic, and now also Buddhist, recitations). The bulls are next fed with seven different sorts of seeds in order to draw prognostics: those they most relish will be plentiful during the year. In ancient times the king presided in person, but later he delegated authority to the Minister of Agriculture (who held, according to the ancient statutes, the title of *baladeva* in allusion to Baladeva or Balarāma, Kṛṣṇa's brother who accomplished so many wonders with his ploughshare). This dignitary was on such an occasion, till half a century ago, regarded as a mock-king, not only from his appearing in princely attire, surrounded by a retinue carrying princely insignia, but also from his being entitled, during the three days that the festival lasted, to collect all tolls and ship-dues in the capital and its suburbs, while the real king kept retired in his palace without transacting any state business. The present king of Siam, however, did away with this absurd custom by attending on 21st April 1912 the ploughing festival, to which he drove in his motor car, his presence being greatly appreciated by all as a token of the sovereign's interest in promoting the welfare of the national agriculture.

6. 'Viśākha-pūjā.'—This is a strictly Buddhist festival, occurring at the full moon of Vaiśākha, which is held to be the anniversary of the birth, enlightenment, and death of the Buddha. For three days the people bedeck their dwellings festively, suspending flower wreaths, garlands, and lanterns which they light at night. They assemble at the temples to worship the sacred images with flowers, scents, and lamps, and to hear religious addresses. They adorn the holy spires with flags and streamers, present offerings of food, etc., to the monks, distribute alms to the poor, and purchase living animals (especially birds and fish), which they release in homage to the Buddhist precept of showing kindness to all creatures. It goes without saying that the royal temples on the evening of such days are gorgeously illuminated, with the additional attraction of fireworks. None the less the festival is not so intensely popular as the New-Year and Mid-Year ones.

iii. JYEṢṬHA (7th month).—**7. Top-spinning.**—This state ceremony, which was discontinued several centuries ago, used to be attended by crowds of people, to whom it afforded the opportunity of drawing prognostics. Three large tops made of the nine metals (corresponding to the planets that are supposed to rule human destinies), symbolizing the three gods, were carried out in procession by the Brāhmans from the temple of Śiva and set in motion on a board by means of a silken string of five colours. From the duration of their spin and the kind of noise they emitted, omens were drawn.

iv. ĀṢĀḌHA (8th month).—**8. Viṣṇu's sleep.**—It is well known that Viṣṇu is supposed to commence his four months' sleep on the Milk Sea on the 11th waxing of Āṣāḍha, a date which is to this day solemnized in India by a festival. This was certainly the case formerly also in Siam, as is evidenced by the state ceremony recorded to have regularly taken place, in the past, at such a season. It consisted in a lustration (*murdhābhiṣeka*) administered to the king by the household Brāhmans on a dais rising in the centre of a pond (representing the one the sea and the other the serpent Śeṣa, Viṣṇu's mythical couch). Besides the above Vaiṣṇava festival (or in connexion with it), the Āṣāḍha, or Midsummer, festival (7th to 14th day of waxing) was likewise celebrated in Siam in bygone days, and at the end of it the Brāhmans began their retreat and fasts. But the festival became in the course of time entirely absorbed in the following Buddhist one.

9. Beginning of 'Vassa,' or Buddhist retreat.—This is solemnized by a festival lasting three days (14th, 15th of waxing, and 1st of waning), during the first of which elaborate *vassa* tapers are carried in procession to the temples, where they are to be lighted and kept burning for the whole year. Offerings of robes and requisites for the incipient retreat-season are liberally made to the monks; and the days preceding it are widely taken advantage of by the youths who seek to gain admission to the holy Order whether as novices or as monks. There is accordingly much animation at this period in and about the temples. On the 15th the magnificent *vassa* tapers (a sort of Paschal candles) are formally lighted by means of 'celestial fire' (which is obtained from the sunbeams through a burning-glass, or, in default, produced with a flint and steel). Those in the royal temples are lighted from candles sent by the king, which have been kindled from the 'celestial fire.' Rehearsals of the Vessantara Jātaka are held in the *Uposatha* hall of royal and other temples by lay devotees engaged for the purpose; Buddha images in the shrines are sprinkled with scented water, and their attire is changed, a scarf being put on their shoulders as befits the rainy season. Among the presents made to the monks are large quantities of bees' wax formed into tapers, artificial flowers, trees with gilt or silvered branches, and tiny figures of birds perched on them, sometimes even entire landscapes to recreate the recluses; or modelled into pineapple-like cakes gorgeously ornamented with ribbons and flowers—all in order to provide light to the monks during their retreat, as they are not allowed to use oil lamps.

v. ŚRĀVAṆA (9th month).—**10. 'Tulābhara.'**—This state ceremony (well known in India as *Tulāpuruṣa* or *Tulad*), consisting in being weighed against gold, silver, etc., and distributing this in charity, was in the past invariably practised by Siamese kings, and at times also by the queen, at this season; but after the middle of the 18th cent. it fell into disuse.

11. 'Varuṇa-sattram,' or 'Mahā-megha Pūjā.'—This propitiation of Varuṇa and of the clouds was essentially a rain-making ceremony, performed of old in Siam in order to promote the germination of seeds in the fields. It has been since celebrated only in times of great drought, but with the addition of Buddhist rites, whereas it was originally a purely Hinduistic rite, and in it only Brāhmans took part. These, clad in a rudimentary bathing-garb, with streaming hair, read twice a day, for three days in succession, addresses to the rain-gods before a pit, while waving cloud-coloured flags, the images of the gods being exposed to the full heat of the sun all the time.

vi. BHĀDRAPADA (10th month).—A festival termed *Bhādrapada* took place at this season, not explained in the old records, which possibly corresponded either to the *Sakra utsava* (Indra's festival, 12th of the waxing) or to the *Ananta chaturdaśī* (festival of the serpent-god Ananta, 14th). Now the only solemnities observed are the following.

12. Semi-annual renewal of the oath of allegiance.—The adjured water is drunk a second time by all officials on the 13th waning, as at New Year (see no. 3 above).

13. 'Sāt' (Śārada).—This is the Half-Year or Autumnal Festival, termed *Sāt* (*Śārada*) from the autumn season which now begins. The celebration lasts three days (*i.e.* the last one of Bhādrapada and the first two of Āśvina). Originally it was mainly a Śaiva solemnity, connected with the descent of the sun (Śiva) to the realm of the departed (the south), which suggested worship to the *manes*. Of this some traces still survive, although the festival has long assumed a Buddhist character. It is an occasion for merit-making; oblations are made to the gods and goblins, offerings to the monks and novices, especially to such as have joined the Order two months before, and presents of sweetmeats to relatives and friends. Every one partakes of rice cooked with coco-nut milk and sweetened with either honey or sugar.

vii. ĀŚVINA, or AŚVAYUJA (11th month).—**14. Lustration of arms.**—It being now the half-year season, the sprinkling of elephants and horses, as well as the uncoiling, distending, and re-coiling of the elephant nooses was, till recently, performed with similar ceremonies as at New Year (see no. 2 above).

15. Royal regatta.—Until the downfall of the former capital, Ayuddhyā, in 1767, a regatta used to take place at this time of the year between the king and the queen in their respective state barges, in which a number of officials also joined, racing between them. Prognostics were drawn: if the king's barge lost, it betokened prosperity to the realm; but, if it won, it was a sign of impending calamities and famine. This state ceremony was discontinued, but a possible survival of it in a modified form may be the annual regatta that takes place on the 8th waning, in honour of the Pāk-nam Pagoda (a spire rising in the middle of the river Mĕ-nam near its mouth), though this is strictly a Buddhist festival.

16 and 17. Termination of the 'Vassa,' or Buddhist retreat; floating of lamps at night.—These are two festivals occurring contemporaneously on the 14th and 15th of the waxing and on the 1st of the waning. Although now believed to be both connected with Buddhism, there can be little doubt that the second one is merely the traditional continuation of the Hindu *Dyūta* or *Kojāgara* festival, held at full moon in honour of Indra and Lakṣmī, when lamps are also lighted. In Siam little rafts with lamps are floated on the streams these three nights, with the object of thus worshipping the footprint which the Buddha is said to have left on the sandy bank of the Narmadā, at the instance of the Nāgas. Round fish-pies, some of large size, are made and partaken of. The Buddhist festival ending the *Vassa* is celebrated these three days by worshipping the sacred images, offering flowers to the monks wherewith to adorn the *uposatha* hall in which *Pavāraṇā* is to be held, and the halls reserved for recitations of the *Mahā Jāti*.

18. 'Kaṭhin' processions.—From the termination of the Buddhist *Vassa* on till the end of the month, and even for some days later, presents of robes and requisites for the monks to use during the coming dry season of outdoor errands are conveyed to the temples in solemn processions, either by water or by land. Such pageants are termed *Kaṭhin* processions, from the *kaṭhina* robes presented on such occasions to the monks, which, according to old custom, should be made from raw cotton, spun, woven, cut, and stitched together in the course of a single day and night, such a feat being considered highly meritorious. The Royal processions taking place for the same purpose at this season are famed for their magnificence, which makes them well worth seeing. Before A.D. 1630 or so they were held only by water, but since then King Prāsād Thōng instituted also the land *Kaṭhin* or *Kaṭhin Bok*, of which Tachard in 1685, Kaempfer in 1690, and nearly every other traveller in Siam, have spoken in glowing terms.

19. The 'P'hā-pā' serenades.—Robes and requisites are also presented to the monks in a somewhat stealthy manner which enhances the fun of the donation. This is accomplished at night by a surprise party, which proceeds by land or boat in silent procession to the precincts of the monastery singled out for the purpose, and lays the robes and other gifts in and about the bush (whence the name *P'hā-pā*, meaning 'jungle cloths,' *i.e.* robes abandoned in the woods). When everything is ready displayed, the party suddenly bursts into a lively serenade, with musical instruments and singing, thus awaking the monks, who, as soon as daylight sets in, come out to gather the presents.

viii. KĀRTTIKA (12th month).—**20. Feast of Lamps.**—This embraces two distinct festivals: (1) the hoisting of lamps on poles on new-moon day and the lighting of them at night, till the second day of the waning, when they are lowered; (2) the floating of lamps in the streams at night on the 14th, 15th, and 16th days of the moon, with the eventual addition of fireworks. This second form of illumination seems, however, to be connected more especially with the festival hereafter explained (no. **21**). On the other hand, the aerial lanterns hoisted on poles, as aforesaid, are kept burning to scare away goblins as in time of epidemics (cf. the *rakṣā-pradīpas*), and, it is believed, also to retain the water from draining off the paddy fields, for the ears of rice would not attain maturity if the yearly inundation were to abate so early. Hence the festival is a very popular one, like its counterpart, the *Diwāli* or *Dīpāwali*, in India. They closely correspond, although the *ākāśa-pradīpas* (lamps raised on poles in the air) are in India lighted in honour of Lakṣmī. We have here to do essentially with a festival in honour of Viṣṇu and his consort, for it is known that on the 11th day of the new moon of Kārttika the god awakes from his four months' sleep, and that his victory over king Bali (*Vāmana avatāra*) took place at this season.

21. 'Kārttikeya' festival.—The main feature of this in Siam, besides the popular one of lamp-floating, was a state ceremony, recently abolished, held in honour both of Kārttikeya (or Skanda, the Hindu Mars, son of Śiva) and of the Pleiades who fostered him. It took place at the time of the moon's conjunction with this star cluster, *i.e.* shortly before full moon. It was a fire-festival, in agreement with Kārttikeya's legendary birth from fire. Three stands were set up in front of the temples, respectively, of Śiva, Gaṇeśa, and Viṣṇu; and by the four sides of each stand, facing the four points of the compass, hillocks were erected, formed of earth mixed with cow-dung. Three earthen pots containing paddy, beans, and tilseed, and provided with a wick dipped in oil in the centre, were placed on the top of poles, one by each stand; and, the wicks having been lighted, fire was kept burning in the pots for three days. Prognostics were then drawn by means of twelve staves, having rags dipped in oil tied at one end. After the setting of fire to these the staves were hurled, four at a time, in the direction of the four hillocks rising round each stand. From the side on which they fell it was argued that prosperity would grace either the king, the clergy, the officials, or the people. The ceremony ended with oblations of parched rice to the earthen pots, and addresses to the three gods. Similarly in Southern India, on full-moon day, rice-meal buns are made, with a cavity in the centre filled in with *ghī* and provided with a wick which is lit; and bonfires are kindled on the mountain-tops in honour of Kārttikeya. This is practically a Śaivite festival held as a counterpart to the Vaiṣṇavite one mentioned above, which in India is by some celebrated in honour of Durgā, the wife of Śiva. So are eventually the lamps set out afloat on the streams. In Siam this lamp-floating is accomplished more generally and with far more splendour than in the month of Āśvina (see nos. **16** and **17**), because the rains are now at an end and fine weather has set in. Many of the lamps are quite elaborate creations, carved out of squill stalks, some being in the form of rafts and others of barges, with daintily carved figures in them, or neatly arrayed with lanterns, tapers, and fireworks, which are lit when they are set adrift.

ix. MĀRGAŚĪRṢA (1st month).—**22. Feast of speeding the outflow.**—This ceremony, literally 'driving away the water,' of high importance in connexion with agriculture, was not performed regularly every year, but only in years of great floods. The last time it took place was on the occasion of the memorable flood of 1831. It has since fallen into disuse. The purpose was to drive away the flood-demon, or, in plain language, to cause the water in the river to abate rapidly, so that the paddy fields might be drained and the harvest accelerated. To this end the king proceeded down the river in his state barge, escorted by a pompous water-procession, and repeatedly waved the royal flabellum in the direction of down-stream, as a magic intimation to the water to flow off rapidly. Kaempfer and other contemporary writers mistook the royal flabellum for a sword, and thus put on record that the king 'cuts the water with a knife in order to make it fall,' which is, of course, absurd (see Kaempfer, *History of Japan*, Glasgow, 1906, i. 73, where he confounds this ceremony with that of *Kaṭhin-nam*, 'Water Kaṭhin,' for which see no. **18** above).

23. Kite-flying festival.—This was a state ceremony as well as a public festivity. Large paper kites were flown with the object of calling up the seasonal wind by the fluttering noise they made. The festival was obviously connected with husbandry, as the wind prevailing at this season is the north-east monsoon, which, when beginning to blow, sweeps the rain-clouds away, so that fine weather sets in and the yearly flood quickly abates, the fields drying up rapidly. This festival was discontinued after the downfall of the former capital, Ayuddhyā. La Loubère, who was in Siam during the last quarter of 1687, mentions that the kite 'of the king of Siam is in the air every night for the two winter months, and some mandarins are nominated to ease one another in holding the string' (*Historical Relation of the Kingdom of Siam*, London, 1693, p. 49). From this it follows that the kite-flying was continued for many days in succession, till the desired result (the setting in of the north-east monsoon) had been attained.

x. PAUṢA (2nd month).—**24. 'Puṣyābhiṣeka.'**—This state ceremony, discontinued after the downfall of the former capital, Ayuddhyā, consisted in the king ascending a dais bedecked with seven varieties of flowers, upon which he bathed and changed his attire, while the eight household Brāhmans who attended upon him performed a sort of angel dance. The rite corresponds to the Hindu *Puṣyābhiṣeka Snāna*, or ceremonial bathing of a king when the moon stands in the asterism Puṣya (nebula in Cancer).

25. **Worship of the sacred bull.**—This festival, which has dropped out of use for several centuries, consisted in leading the sacred bull (Nandi, the milk-white vehicle of Śiva and the guardian of all quadrupeds) out of the royal stables on to a dais two cubits high, on which it was made to stand facing the North, a sacred fire being kindled in front of it. Its horns and hoofs were decked with golden ornaments studded with the nine gems; golden medallions and tassels hung from its ears; a silken cord was passed through its nostrils; the post to which it was tied was richly ornamented. Gold, silver, and silken cloths were heaped underneath the belly of the sacred animal, which was fed and watered from golden vessels, the king's children themselves helping in handing it grass and dainties. The four chief Brāhmans stood at the four corners of the dais sacrificing to the fire, from evening till next morning, when the king arrived in state preceded by the *baladeva*, or Minister of Agriculture, carrying a tray full of parched rice. The royal pageant circumambulated the bull nine times; then a state banquet followed which ended the ceremony. This festival may have originated from the ancient Hindu one of letting loose the sacred bull (*Vṛṣotsarga*), which was, however, performed on full-moon day of Kārttika, or even in Aśvayuja (see *Pāraskara Gṛhyasūtra*, iii. 9). It was somehow connected with agriculture, or, at any rate, with the welfare or multiplication of cattle.

26. **Swing festival.**—This very popular festivity is held with much pomp for the reception of Śiva, and is followed by a quieter one to welcome Viṣṇu. It has been celebrated from the remotest period in all old Siamese capitals and chief cities, and in some of the latter (*e.g.* Ligor) swing-pillars exist to this day and a semblance of the ceremony is still performed. But it is in Bāngkōk, the present capital, that it survives in all its splendour. As it falls about the vernal solstice, its original purpose was undoubtedly that of a solstitial festival, in which the swinging and the circular dances that follow it symbolize the revolution and, perhaps, the birth of the sun typified in its return to the northern hemisphere. But the celebration is at the same time connected with agriculture, it being presided over by the Minister, the *baladeva*, the mock king who also performs the ceremonial ploughing (see no. 5 above). It is only within the last sixty years or so that other dignitaries have been appointed in succession to relieve him of the task. The descent of Śiva on earth occurs on the 7th waxing, when the rites begin; his departure takes place on the first day of the waning. The swinging in his honour is performed on the 7th day of the waxing in the forenoon, and on the 9th day in the afternoon. The presiding dignitary proceeds on both these dates in great state, escorted by a magnificent procession, to the esplanade opening in front of the three temples of the gods, where the swing-pillars rise. These are a substantial permanent wooden structure, some sixty feet in height; the swinging is performed by four Brāhmans who carry on their heads a sort of snake-like hood, and it is repeated twice over again by two other parties of them, changing the swing-board at every turn. While swinging, each party must snatch away with their teeth a money-bag suspended at some distance from the top of a pole. When the contest is over, the twelve swingers, wielding buffalo horns, perform, in front of a stand, where the mock-king sits, a circular dance in three rounds of three circuits each, during which the dancers dip their horns in a basin full of water and sprinkle it upon one another (cf. the *rāsa*, or sportive dance, performed by Kṛṣṇa's cowherds and cowherdesses). The mock-king must witness all this seated, with his left foot resting on the ground, but with his right foot uplifted and resting upon his left knee. He must retain this posture all the time the performance lasts. When it is over, he leaves, escorted by the procession. Evidently the origin of all this is the Hindu *Dola* or *Dola-yātrā* festival (which is, however, a spring solemnity held on the full-moon day of Phālguna), with which it has some features in common, while others may have become lost in its native land. But the swing pillars are said to represent Mount Meru; the ropes sustaining the swing-board, the serpent Śeṣa; and the three boards or seats employed successively in turns, the three gods Āditya (the Sun), Chandra (the Moon), and Dharaṇi (the Earth); and thus the festival may after all be held in commemoration of the mythical churning of the Ocean of Milk effected by the gods. The legend in connexion with this is, in fact, that the gods made use of Śeṣa (or Ananta, or Vāsuki) as a great rope, which they twisted round the mountain Mandara, made to do duty as a churning-staff resting on Viṣṇu in tortoise form, both ends of the rope being held by the gods in their hands to pull to and fro alternately. The description of so peculiar a sort of churning device closely suggests the image of the swing used in this Siamese festival. The swinging, it should be noticed, is effected from east to west, and, therefore, in the direction of the course of the sun.

27. **The reception of Viṣṇu.**—The Vaiṣṇavite festival immediately following the Śaivite one just described is performed quietly in the temple of Viṣṇu. It begins on the first day of the waning, and ends on the sixth, the date of the god's departure from the world of men. The statues of Viṣṇu, Lakṣmī, and Maheśvarī are carried about the town in procession before moonrise, as befits the god of darkness (the night-sun). In former times the king of Siam, mounted on an elephant, used to escort the gods Śiva and Viṣṇu in procession in and out of the temple.

xi. MĀGHA (3rd month).—28. **'Dhānya-dāha' (or 'Dāhanam'), Festival of burning of the ears of paddy.**—This was another popular agricultural ceremony, associated with the harvest, as a form of thanksgiving for the same; it has since been abolished. It must somehow have originated from the old Brāhmanic rite of partaking of the first-fruits of the harvest (*Āgrayaṇa* sacrifice, for which cf. the Gṛhyasūtras). A canopied dais was set up in the Crown paddy fields, to which the usual mock-king proceeded in state as on the occasion of the Ploughing Festival (see no. 5 above). Before the dais a large *chhattra* (state conical umbrella) was erected, having three storeys, made respectively of a different variety of paddy ears entwined together. To this structure the mock-king set fire; then his followers, divided into four parties differently attired and representing the gods of the four quarters and their retinue, rushed in to contend for the umbrella. Prognostics were drawn according to which of the parties succeeded in obtaining possession of the spoils.

Conveying the paddy home.—The ceremony just described was followed by that of conveying home the harvest. When the threshing of the new paddy had been completed on the Crown fields, the king proceeded thither in state, loaded some of the grain on his paddy sled, and had this drawn by members of the royal family to the palace, by means of a rope made of twisted paddy straws with the ears still on. Upon reaching the palace he caused a large conical umbrella to be made with this rope, while from the fresh ears gathered he had the juice expressed. This was then made into gruel by the addition of coco-nut milk and sugar, and sent as an offering to the head monks of the royal monasteries. It goes without saying that such ceremonies were followed by the people in and about the capital with the keenest interest, while in the country the harvest operations were, and still are, celebrated by the peasantry with oblations to the gods and rites similar to those already described, though on a less pompous scale, but amid lively pastimes and intense rejoicing, of which harvest songs (especially threshing and reaping ditties), joined in alternately by men and women, form the chief and most pleasant feature.

29. 'Śiva-rātri,' Festival of Śiva's night.—This is, as the name implies, strictly Śaivite, and has been celebrated from the remotest period in Siam on full-moon day of Māgha, it being derived from the similar Hindu festival more correctly termed *Mahā Śiva-rātri* (which is, however, held on the 14th day of the waning). An earthen pot full of water, but with a hole in the bottom, is suspended by means of strings to four poles, and beneath the pot a *liṅga* is placed, which rests on a basement of the usual symbolical form, provided with a spout. At night the water is let drop upon the *liṅga*, and collected from under the spout into vessels. Shortly before dawn, rice is cooked in the temple of the god, with the addition of honey, palm-sugar, and other condiments, and when ready it is distributed all round in small portions to the bystanders, to be partaken of. At daybreak all go down to bathe in the river or creeks, and wash their heads with some of the water collected from underneath the *liṅga*. It is believed that all impurities and sinful taints are thereby removed and carried away by the hallowed water.

30. 'Māgha-pūjā.'—This is a purely Buddhist ceremony, revived only some sixty years ago by King Mongkuṭ. It is held on full-moon day, to commemorate the exposition of the *Pātimokkha* made on that date by the Buddha to his 1250 disciples of the four congregations. The celebration takes place in the royal temple, where, after feasting the chief monks in the forenoon, a recitation of the *Pātimokkha* and of the Buddha's discourses relating thereto is held in the evening, after which 1250 tapers are lit round the temple in honour of the saintly company referred to above. The full-moon period of this month is also largely taken advantage of by the people for making religious pilgrimages to various sacred spots and shrines in the country, such as, *e.g.*, the models of Buddha's footprint (*P'hraḥ-bāt*) and shadow (*P'hraḥ C'hāi*), two stone benches on which the Blessed One is reputed to have rested, etc.

xii. PHĀLGUNA (4th month).—There occurs no special observance or celebration, except the preliminary ones connected with the popular New Year festival (see no. 1 above).

LITERATURE.—There is no reliable account of Siamese festivals and fasts, in works that have hitherto appeared on Siam. For the literature of Siamese Buddhism generally see SIAM (Buddhism in).

G. E. GERINI.

FESTIVALS (Slavic).

— Beginning with the winter solstice, the festivals of the pagan Slavs, attested in historic texts, folklore, and popular vocabulary, seem to have been as follows:—

Kračun or *koročun* was the festival of the shortest day. The popular word for the solstice itself is *koleda*, *koliada*, which is simply a transcription of the classical *calendæ*, καλάνδαι. The people, as a rule, personified Koleda and made a mythical character of her (cf. Ital. Befania=*epifania*; Eng. 'Father Christmas,' etc.).

At the coming of spring among the Czechs, the Serbs of Lusatia, and the Poles, a figure called Marena, Marzana, was thrown into the water; this probably symbolized death, that is to say, the numbing of the earth by the cold of winter.

In the month of May there was a festival of roses (*Rusalia*).

At the summer solstice fell the festival of *kupalo* (festival of the bath) among the ancient Russians, coinciding later with the Christian festival of St. John (June 24). This name seems to have been derived from the verb *kupati*, 'to bathe,' perhaps because river-bathing begins in the month of June, perhaps—and this designation would be produced under a Christian influence—because John was baptized by immersion.

The chronicle of Thietmar (bk. vi.) supplies a very detailed description of the annual festival celebrated at Arcona in the island of Rügen in honour of the god Svantovit. The description is too minute to be reproduced here. The festival ended in a great feast, in which it was a religious duty to violate every rule of temperance. According to Helmold (i. 52), the sacrifices of the Baltic Slavs were accompanied by feasts and orgies. The guests kept a cup passing round and round, pronouncing over it meanwhile formulæ not of consecration but of execration (Helmold was evidently thinking of the consecration of Mass).

According to the Czech chronicler Cosmas, prince Bretislav in 1092 suppressed the festivals celebrated by the Czechs about the season of Easter—festivals during which offerings were carried to the springs, and victims were sacrificed to the demon.

One of the biographers of Otto of Bamberg (Ebbo, ii. 12, 13) speaks of annual festivals of a very rustic and warlike character, which were held at Pyritz and Volyn by the Baltic Slavs. For festivals in honour of the dead, see artt. ARYAN RELIGION, in vol. ii. p. 25 ff., and DEATH AND DISPOSAL OF THE DEAD (Slavic), vol. iv. p. 509.

LITERATURE.—Louis Leger, *La Mythologie slave*, Paris, 1901, *passim*.

L. LEGER.

FESTIVALS AND FASTS (Teutonic).

—Among the Germanic races, religious festivals seem to have afforded the earliest occasions for intertribal intercourse. Tacitus relates of the Germans that 'at a certain period all the tribes of the same race assemble by their representatives in a grove consecrated by the auguries of their forefathers and by immemorial associations of terror' (*Germania*, 39). Some seven centuries later a religious festival at Skiringsal, in Southern Norway, seems to have united persons who certainly had no political organization in common; and this was probably the case with the great religious festivals held every nine years at Upsala; for the 11th cent. Adam of Bremen states that it was the custom in all Swedish lands that a common festival should be held at Upsala (*Mon. Germ.* vii. 380). We have Thietmar of Merseburg's authority for a similar nine-yearly festival at Lejre in Denmark (*ib.* iii. 739), but all the other public festivals of which we have any knowledge appear to have been annual. Of these the most important all over Germanic territory were three in number: one in the autumn, one at midwinter (Yule), and one at midsummer. But, though the Germanic peoples were thus more or less agreed as to times and seasons, the religious significance attributed to these festivals varied in different countries. Thus, among the Scandinavians we are repeatedly told that the autumn festival (at the 'winter nights') was 'for plenty,' and it was a favourite time for weddings, whereas among the Saxons this feast seems to have been closely connected with the cult of the dead; and that this was the more usual significance of the autumn festival seems clear from the fact that the Church found it advisable, in the 9th cent., to alter the date of the Feast of All Saints from spring to autumn. In England, we know that the autumn festivities gave the name to the month known as *Blót-mónath* (cf. Swedish dialectic *Blotmånad*), because, as Bede informs us, it was during this month that the people sacrificed to their gods the cattle slaughtered during the autumn. The importance of this festival doubtless originated in the necessity of killing off a large number of cattle on the approach of winter. The old heathen midwinter festival lasted from about Christmas Day till Twelfth Night, and the high esteem in which it was held by the Teutons is recorded by writers of all nationalities, from Constantinus Porphyrogenitus, who describes the Yule-tide observances of the Varangian guard at Constantinople, to Bede. The latter tells of the wearing of animal masks at the Anglo-Saxon festival on *Módranicht*, 'the night of the mothers'—which, he declares, fell on the same date as Christmas Eve. Procopius tells of a festival celebrated by the people of 'Thule' (Norway [?]) to greet the sun on its reappearance—presumably early in January. It was, moreover, at this season—about the date of the Epiphany, says Thietmar—that the great nine-yearly festival at Lejre was held.

The Scandinavians, and possibly also the Anglo-Saxons, seem to have had a festival in spring. According to later writers, this was 'for victory'—no doubt with a view to the Viking expeditions of the summer; but an agricultural festival in spring seems to have been common all over Teutonic Europe.

The midsummer festival may be said to survive to this day in rustic observance, especially in the Scandinavian countries, where bonfires are still lighted on St. John's Eve (June 23). But this festival is rarely mentioned in early times; and the conclusion seems inevitable that it had already sunk into a popular observance, of magical rather than religious significance. The originally agricultural importance of some of these heathen festivals is seldom indicated by the earlier sources, and popular customs of later times afford almost the only evidence for the close connexion of heathen festivals with agricultural operations. Of these rustic observances certain rites, such as ploughing round the fields at Yule tide, and leaping the fire at Midsummer, are so common in all Teutonic countries as to make it almost certain that they formed part of the original heathen festivals. The older sources, however, lay chief stress on the actual feasting and ale-drinking which was no doubt characteristic of all festivals.

Icelandic sources show that the blood of the sacrificial victims was offered to the gods, while the flesh was cooked and eaten. Horses were much valued as sacrifices, so that horseflesh was identified by Christian converts with heathendom, but excavations of Icelandic temples show that other domestic animals were more common victims. The other integral part of the festival was the ale, which seems to have been brewed in vats so large that Saxo Grammaticus declares that a Danish prince, Hunding, was accidentally drowned in one (i. 36). A missionary on the Continent relates how he came across a party of men sitting round an enormous vat of ale, and that they described themselves as worshipping Wodan. Early Norwegian laws enjoin the brewing of ale before all Christian festivals, and its consumption in the company of neighbours, under penalty of a fine. The Swedish laws of the 13th cent. also speak of a 'legally ordained ale-festival' on the Sunday following St. Martin's Day (Nov. 11). In heathen times, toasts were drunk to the gods and to the memory of departed ancestors. Drunkenness seems to have been an inevitable concomitant of a feast. Tacitus tells us (*Ann.* i. 50) that the Romans surprised the Germans at a festival, and were able to massacre an intoxicated foe. It is Saxo, centuries later, who relates that, while Athisl 'was honouring the funeral rites of Rolf with a feast, he drank too greedily, and paid for his filthy intemperance by his sudden end' (iii. 75). Most of the private festivals in the North were actually described as *öl*, 'ale.' For instance, the *erfi-öl*, or funeral feast, which was very important in Scandinavia and in Northern England, survived in the latter country as *arvel* till twenty years ago.

After the Reformation, 'lyke-wake drinking' formed the subject of many restrictive ordinances for Denmark and Norway. Already in 1576 the 'great excess of meat and drink at funerals' was prohibited, and Christian IV., in 1624, finally suppressed all feasting on the occasion of a funeral. Before that date it is usual in the regulations of Danish gilds that on the death of one of their members the heirs of the deceased shall give the gild-brothers a barrel of ale for the *erffue-öll*. On the Continent, memorial (anniversary) feasts were popular, and Christian priests were strictly forbidden to 'drink wine for love of the dead,' or to join in the festivities connected with such observances. Drinking seems also to have been characteristic of wedding-feasts. In the North the 'ale of departure' and the 'greeting-ale' were additional occasions for festivities. A feature of all these feasts was the vows taken by the chiefs, pledging themselves to some deed of valour, such as a Viking expedition, vengeance on a powerful neighbour, and the like. This custom persisted into Christian times, and the attempt of the Jómsvikings to conquer Norway in the latter half of the 10th cent. is attributed to such a vow, made at a funeral feast.

From the hints our sources afford us, it seems as if the actual feasting took place at night, Tacitus and the Icelandic sagas concurring in the mention of games during the day. That the festivals actually took place in the temples is indicated by the use of churches for this purpose in Icelandic and Scandinavian custom. A post-Reformation bishop complains of 'the carousing and drinking and dancing with fife and drum' which took place within the church-doors on the Monday and Tuesday of a 'wedding-week,' and elsewhere he finds it necessary to assure his flock that eating, drinking, and dancing in church are only fit for the children of the devil (*Danske Magazin*, iii. [Copenhagen, 1747] 60).

If we may judge from the silence of our sources on the subject, fasting for religious purposes seems to have been unknown among the Teutonic races until the introduction of Christianity. It was certainly unknown in Scandinavia, for the Icelandic Laxdæla Saga expressly mentions the extreme interest aroused in a neighbourhood by a Christian convert's Lenten fast.

LITERATURE.—Information regarding the religious festivals will be found in all manuals of Germanic religion, but the following deal more especially with the subject: A. Tille, *Yule and Christmas*, London, 1899; G. Bilfinger, *Das germ. Julfest*, Stuttgart, 1901; K. Weinhold, *Über die deutsche Jahrteilung*, Kiel, 1862; O. Schrader, *Reallex. der indogerm. Altertumskunde*, Strassburg, 1901, *s.v.* 'Jahrteilung'; W. Mannhardt, *Wald- und Feldkulte*, Berlin, 1875–77; H. Pfannenschmidt, *Germ. Erntefeste*, Hanover, 1878; J. G. Frazer, *GB*^{3}, 1911, 'Midsummer Observances,' pp. 58–69.

B. S. PHILLPOTTS.

FESTIVALS AND FASTS (Tibetan).—The popular festivals of Tibet are essentially religious in character, and almost all of them are assimilated to a Buddhist type. Even those which manifestly belong to the pre-Buddhist religion, the indigenous *Bon*, are taken part in by the Buddhist lamas as priests.

The word for 'festival' in Tibetan means 'feast-time' (*dus-ston*), which aptly denotes the popular conception of the event, with its cessation from routine work and the preponderance of enjoyment over the religious acts of worship and ceremonial. The term here used for 'feast' (*ston*) is from the same root as 'harvest-season' and 'autumn,' implying plenteous store of food and fruit for feasting upon. It also suggests that originally the great festival was probably in the autumn, after the crops were garnered. The great festivals are called by both lamas and laity 'Great Feast-time' (*dus-ston ch'en-po*), or shortly, 'Great Time' (*dus-ch'en*).

Another term which is less commonly used, and more especially applicable to the Bonist feasts, is *mgron*, or 'banquet,' which in its religious sense denotes a propitiatory feast to the four great classes of beings, namely (1) the Holy Ones, interpreted by Buddhists as the *Triratna* (Buddha, the Law, and the Church), the spiritual teacher of the worshipper and his personal tutelary; (2) the 'Lord'-fiends, she-devils (*ḍākini*), and tutelary fiends; (3) the six classes of beings (the five unhappy existences [cf. *ERE* iv. 133], and the gods [*ib.* 134]); (4) the aboriginal devils called *gdon* and *bgegs*.

1. General characteristics.—The Tibetan festivals may be broadly classed as (1) indigenous, or Bonist, and (2) Buddhist.

(1) The *indigenous* festivals appear to be for the most part Nature-feasts, in the revolutions of the seasons of the year. They are obviously related to the solstices and equinoxes, and display what seems manifestly to be worship of the powers of Nature, conceived mythologically as benign spirits and malignant demons of darkness, drought, and ill-luck, to be appeased or expelled from the land. In addition to this Nature-cult there is an element of ancestral worship to be seen in the festivals given to the dead and malignant ghosts. The survival of the cult of ancestors (in itself opposed to the principles of Buddhism, which teaches that ancestors do not remain in the tomb, but return to life in new forms) is seen in the elaborate ceremonial to secure repose of the spirit of the dead and the lighting up of the funeral monuments (*ch'orten* [*q.v.*]) wherein are deposited the cremated remains of the more wealthy classes and the actual bodies of the higher lamas—amongst whom the Dalai lamas claim to have as their direct lineal ancestors the early kings of the country, whose tombs and those of their nobles studded the country in the pre-Buddhist period (cf. *ERE* iv. 509).

(2) The *Buddhist* festivals commemorate semi-historical and legendary events in the life of Buddha (his birth, attainment of Buddhahood, death, etc.), and in the life of the two great canonized monks of Tibet, namely, the Indian teacher Padmasambhava (*c.* A.D. 748), the founder of Lamaism, and the Tibetan reformer Tsong-khapa (A.D. 1356–1417), the founder of the modern dominant sect of lamas, the yellow-cap sect (*Ge-lug-pa*), to which the Dalai and other Grand Lama hierarchs belong. Some of these Buddhist festivals appear to have been grafted on to pre-Buddhist feast-days, as is evidenced by the aboriginal rites which they embody and the discrepancy between some of the dates and those current in other Buddhist countries.

2. Ritual.—During the festivals, some of which extend over several days, the laity generally cease from their ordinary work or business; and, whilst spending their time mainly in festivities, also devote more time than usual to pious deeds to avoid the five great sins, muttering their mystic spells, plying their prayer-wheels, circumambulating the sacred buildings, and visiting the temple to bow before the chief images. For the clergy these events entail a large amount of additional celebrations, reading of the sacred texts, and austere vigils and fastings. The ritual exhibits generally both indigenous and Buddhistic elements—the latter being most conspicuous in the celebrations of the yellow-cap sect. The indigenous rites of both private and public worship generally include expiatory and sacrificial ceremonies, though the latter do not usually involve the taking of life, and there are saturnal revels and even orgies.

3. Occasions.—The general feasts, annual and monthly, are held mainly at fixed periodical times. One, the Water-Festival, is movable according to the appearance of a particular star, and occasionally there are special festivals, at irregular times, for passing events, such as the installation or death of a Grand Lama, or war, or pestilence.

The dates for the general festivals are at stated times definitely fixed in the lunar calendar of Tibet (cf. *ERE* iii. 63). But, owing to the disparity between the lunar and the solar year (*ib.*), and the rough adjustment of the same by intercalating a month every few years, the relationship between the dates and the natural seasons has become seriously displaced. Further confusion also has been introduced by the date of the ancient Tibetan New Year, which obviously coincided with the winter solstice, having been transferred by the yellow-cap sect to a lunar date corresponding to January-February. This was manifestly done with the object of making it coincide with the Chinese New Year, which, however, it does not do exactly. Hence the seasonal incidence of the festivals seldom coincides precisely with the actual equinoxes and solstices, rainy season, or harvest, as the case may be. As a result we get, among other anachronisms, 'flower-festivals' in icy January–February.

The *monthly* festivals are the usual ones as prescribed for meditation and fasting in all Buddhist countries, following the Brāhmanical rule, namely, the auspicious days of the new and full moon (cf. *ERE* iii. 78). To these were added later the other two lunar quarter days, so that this holy day, recurring four times a month, came to be called 'the Buddhist Sabbath.' In Tibet it is the 8th and 15th day of each month which are mostly observed, and these are holy days rather than 'festivals.' On these days the lamas fast more or less, partaking of nothing except farinaceous food and tea; and many of the laity do likewise, and on no account take animal life. The lamas spend these days in reading the scriptures, make formal confession of sins (*pratimokṣa*), and perform the rite of 'washing away sin' (*tui-sol*).

The *annual* festivals, which include all the festivals properly so-called, are not enumerated or described in any known Tibetan work. In compiling the following list from his own observations and those of others, the present writer has arranged the events in the order of the Tibetan calendar, and has shown within brackets the corresponding approximate month in the European calendar.

1st month, 1st–3rd day (= February), Carnival of New Year (*Logsar*) in new style.—The festival of the New Year is held on this date in Lhasa and the other centres where the yellow-cap sect of lamas is dominant. Elsewhere it is observed on the old date in the 11th month, about the winter solstice. The popular festivities are generally similar to those of Christmas in Europe. It is a season for cessation from work and for general rejoicing, singing, dancing, feasting, and visiting of friends. Even the younger monks have their restrictions relaxed, and are permitted to participate for two or three days in the mirth-making. For the event the roads are swept, the houses whitewashed, and the doorways decorated. There is also a pudding, resembling the Christmas pudding of the West, to the eating of which the head of the family invites to his house all the other members and relatives. The pudding is made with raisins, dried apricots, etc., and is brought into the room often with a red flag stuck into it; at other times, when this is absent, a hole is made in its centre, into which melted butter is poured—which, as the fuel of lamps, is said to symbolize light and life. Thus it may emblemize the advent of the New Year's light dispelling the demons of darkness. The flag is admittedly a demon-driving device in Lamaism. The head of the house first partakes of the pudding, next his wife, and then his guests and the rest of the family. During the festivities the people indulge in more food delicacies than usual; and charitable gifts are freely dispensed. A custom of 'first-footing' also prevails.

E. R. Huc describes how at midnight, when the noise of the festivities commenced, 'we had a good mind to get up to witness the happiness of the inhabitants of Lhasa, but the cold was so cutting that after reflection we decided to remain under our woollen coverlets. Unhappily for our comfort, violent knocks on our door, threatening to smash it into splinters, warned us that we must renounce our project. We therefore donned our clothes, and, the door being opened, some friendly Tibetans rushed into our room, inviting us to the New Year's banquet, saying, "New Year has come with plenty. Rejoice, Take, Eat!"' (ii. 216).

Amongst the festivities at Lhasa is the spectacle of 'Flying Spirits,' by performers who glide down a rope stretched from the summit of Potala palace to its base.

1st month, 4th–15th day (=February), Supplication (*sMon-lam*).—This appears to be prayers and expiatory sacrifice for new growth and prosperity during the new year. It is conducted chiefly at Lhasa and Tashilhunpo, and is the greatest ceremony of the year in the Lamaist church, when yellow-cap monks to the number of 30,000 congregate in Lhasa alone, as described in the present writer's *Buddhism of Tibet* (p. 505 ff.). At this festival largess is distributed to the assembled monks (amounting to about ten shillings per ordinary monk, and several hundreds to the higher lamas) from the treasury of the Dalai Lama's Government, as well as from the emperor of China, who is specially prayed for and officially represented by the Amban on the occasion. The prayers continue till the 15th day of the month, which is the anniversary of Buddha's conception, and on this date the great temple of Buddha (the *Jokang*) is illuminated with lanterns. Thereafter the demons are propitiated, and on the 30th day the celebration of 'Deliverance' (*grol-ston*), a festival of relaxation, concludes the feast. A notable feature of this festival is that the civil government lapses or changes hands during the currency of the New Year's ceremonies, which continue throughout the month. The temporal government of Lhasa is removed from its usual custodians, and for the month is placed in the hands of the chief proctor of Dre-pung monastery (to which the Dalai Lama is affiliated), and that monk becomes for the time a *rex sacrorum*, as with the Romans. It probably represents a period during which the administration of justice was suspended to allow of unrestrained carnival or mirth-making, as in the ἱερομηνίαι of the ancient Greeks and the *dies nefasti* of the Romans. In Tibet, however, it is made the occasion of excessive extortion of taxes, to escape which many of the residents leave Lhasa during this period. The practice appears to have been wide-spread over Tibet. In Ladak, at the present day, during the New Year festivities the Tibetan ex-ruler is permitted by the Kashmir State to assume royal dignities and to occupy the old palace.

1st month, 15th day (=February), Anniversary of Buddha's Conception.

1st month, 27th day, Procession of the Holy Dagger (*Phurba* or *Vajra*).—This is obviously a Bonist celebration for expelling evil influences from the country. About a thousand Buddhist priests, half of whom are dressed in Chinese costume, emerge from the great temple at Lhasa with drums, etc., and, accompanied by about a thousand mounted Tibetan soldiery, and the high priest of the State Oracle of Nechung, whose attendants carry in state a famous miraculous thunderbolt-dagger (*phurba*) from Sera monastery, file past a throne in the open on which is seated the Dalai Lama. After dancing movements to the beat of the drums, there is raised a series of howls 'like the roar of a tiger,' which may possibly be intended to rouse the sleeping god from his winter slumbers, and would be appropriate in connexion with the old-style festival which occurred at the winter solstice. Last of all follows the foremost Lama of Tibet, the successor and representative of Tsong-khapa, the 'Ti-Rinpoche,' who is usually *ex officio* regent of Tibet (and was so during the British mission of 1904), and a Buddhist priest of the most orthodox Mahāyāna type. His duty is to hurl the dagger against the evil spirit, who is called 'The King of the Serpents and Lord-fiends' (*Lu-gon rygal-po*). This concludes the ceremony amidst great rejoicing.

2nd month, 29th day (=March), Chase and Expulsion of the 'Scapegoat' Demon of Ill-luck.—This ceremony as practised in Central Tibet is described in the present writer's *Buddhism of Tibet* (p. 512 f.). In Ladak it is termed *Naghrang*. Two Lamas called *hlooiar* are stripped and their bodies painted black, on which ground a devil's face is painted in red on the chest and back. Other lamas surround the two figures and recite prayers and incantations, whilst others beat drums and blow trumpets. After an interval the *hlooiars* appear to become possessed with devils, and begin to shout and leap about and rush over the roofs of the houses, chased by the people. Whilst in this exalted state they are consulted as oracles, and eventually they fall down exhausted in a swoon.

3rd month, 15th day (=April), Anniversary of 'Revelation' of the Demonist Tantrik-cult (*Kāla-chakra*), with sacred masked plays.

4th month, 8th day (=April–May), Anniversary of Buddha's Renunciation of the World.

4th month, 15th day, Anniversary of Buddha's Attainment of Buddhahood, and of his Death (*parinirvāṇa*), Feast of the Dead, or All Souls' Day.—This corresponds to the first lunar month of the Indian calendar, the month *Vaiśākha*, when the moon is full near the Southern scale, and is deemed by the Brāhmans a most auspicious time, to which Indian tradition ascribes the above great events in Buddha's life.

5th month, 5th day (=May–June), 'Buddha as the Physician,' or 'The Medical Buddhas,' and the beginning of the Buddhist Lent (or Rainy Season).

5th month, 10th day, Anniversary of Birth of Padmasambhava.—This is a festival chiefly of the old sects, and is accompanied by masked plays and devil-dances. That at Hemis, in Ladak, is a celebrated fair.

6th month, 4th day (=July), Anniversary of Buddha's Birth and First Preaching of the Law.—This is the occasion for the display of great pictures of Buddha, or of Maitreya, the Buddhist Messiah.

7th month, 10th day (=August), Birth of Padmasambhava (according to Sikkim style).

8th month, 8th day (= September–October), Water-festival and Harvest-festival.—End of Buddhist Lent or Rainy Season with much bathing in the rivers.

9th month, 22nd day (= Oct.–Nov.), Anniversary of Buddha's miraculous Descent from Heaven.

10th month, 25th day (= December), Anniversary of Tsongkhapa's death, usually termed his Ascension or Transfiguration, Feast of Lamps.

11th month, 1st–5th day (= December), New Year Carnival, old style.—It obviously corresponded to the winter solstice.

12th month, 29th–30th day (= Jan.–Feb.), Expulsion of the Old Year with its ill-luck.—This is now regarded as a sort of New Year's Eve ceremony preparatory to the new-style date for the annual carnival. It is probably, however, the festival of the 'Holy Dagger' now held on the 27th of the 1st month (see above). The Lamas invoke the gods to drive away the evil spirits.

4. Fasting (*smyung*, or *bsñen-gnas*) is generally practised by Tibetan Buddhist monks, and also by the uncelibate priests of all sects, on the periodical monthly fasts (*upavasatha*) prescribed by the common code. It is also generally observed on the festival days, and as a preparatory sacrificial rite or penance. The fasting ordinarily consists in abstention from food or from drink or from both, from sunrise to sunset, and total abstention from animal food or spirituous liquor. So intimately is fasting associated with the conception of holiness in the popular mind that the word for 'virtue' (*dge-ba*) is used as a synonym for 'fasting.' Many of the laity also observe a more or less partial fast during these holy days and feasts, as above noted. Fasting is practised with exceptional strictness by the more ascetic Lamas, who are selected to perform not merely expiatory sacrifices to the gods, but also the exorcizing of evil spirits. In this latter regard it is noteworthy that even the low unorthodox priests of a shamanist type, who practise for purposes of sorcery and exorcism the animistic rites of the Bonist cult, also require, as an indispensable condition, to undergo ceremonial purification and be spiritualized by preparatory periods of fasting.

LITERATURE.—E. R. Huc, *Souvenirs d'un voyage dans la Tartarie, le Thibet, et la Chine*, Paris, 1853, i. 96, 29, ii. 95; E. Kawaguchi, *Three Years in Tibet*, London, 1909; H. L. Ramsay, *Western Tibetan Dictionary*, Lahore, 1890, p. 43, etc.; W. W. Rockhill, *JRAS*, 1891, pp. 209–214; E. Schlagintweit, *Buddhism in Tibet*, Leipzig, 1863, p. 237; L. A. Waddell, *The Buddhism of Tibet*, London, 1895, pp. 501–514.

L. A. WADDELL.

FETICIDE.—See FŒTICIDE.

FETISHISM.

FETISHISM.—1. Definition.—Few words have been used with so bewildering a variety of applications as 'fetish' and 'fetishism.' 'Fetish' is derived, through the French, from the Portuguese *feitiço*, which, in its turn, comes from the Lat. *factitius*. A Portuguese-French Dictionary defines it as 'sortilège, maléfice, enchantement, charme.' As an adjective, it means 'made by art,' 'skilfully contrived.' Miss Kingsley observes (*West African Studies*, p. 44) that

> 'the Portuguese navigators who re-discovered West Africa, noticing the veneration paid by Africans to certain objects—trees, fish, idols, and so on—very fairly compared these objects with the amulets, talismans, charms, and little images of saints they themselves used.'

The above etymology suggests that fetishism was at first regarded as a branch of magic, which, as J. G. Frazer has pointed out, may be either religious or non-religious. The fetish may be a god, or the abode of a god or spirit, helpful to its possessor or devotee; or it may be only a sort of clever device or instrument for attaining ends not otherwise to be accomplished.

The first to draw attention to fetishism as a branch of the study of religion was the French writer, de Brosses, whose interesting and, for the time, remarkable book, *Du Culte des dieux fétiches*, was brought out in 1760. He understands by fetishism 'le culte de certains objets terrestres et matériels,' but includes the religious practices of certain tribes with whom those objects are not so much gods as things endowed with a Divine virtue, such as oracles, amulets, and preservative talismans. He excludes the worship of the Sun.

Auguste Comte, on the other hand, gave prominence to the Sun, Moon, and Earth as 'grands fétiches.' In his Positivist calendar he devoted a whole month to fetishism, instituting festivals to Animals, Fire, the Sun, and the Moon. To him and to his followers fetishism is practically Nature-worship. They apply the term to the first stage in the development of religion, in which the natural object or phenomenon is a direct object of worship, not a more or less anthropomorphic deity who has his abode in it, or controls it. It seems undesirable, however, to use 'fetishism' in a sense so far removed from its ordinary acceptation and conveying an undeserved stigma. Nature-worship, though not the highest form of religion, is pure and noble, compared with the cult of 'something irrationally reverenced'—to use a phrase borrowed from the definition in the *OED*. Other scientific writers have not followed Comte's example.

Herbert Spencer's view of fetishism is radically different from that of Comte. In his *Sociology* (i. 313) he says:

> 'The unusualness which makes an object a fetish, is supposed to imply an indwelling ghost—an agent without which deviation from the ordinary would be inexplicable. . . . Only when there is an unfamiliar appearance, or motion or sound or change, in a thing, does there arise this idea of a possessing spirit. The Chibchas worshipped lakes, rivulets, rocks, hills, and other places of striking or unusual aspect. Indirect evidences from all sides converge to the conclusion that the fetish-worship is the worship of a special soul supposed to have taken up its abode in the fetish, which soul, in common with supernatural agents at large, is originally the double of a dead man.'[1]

It will be seen that the fetishism of Comte and that of Herbert Spencer are mutually exclusive. It is, therefore, not surprising to find that, while the former makes it the primary stage of all religion, the latter regards it as a more recent development. Herbert Spencer's attempt to bring Nature-worship within the scope of his ghost-theory of the origin of religion is a veritable *tour de force* of sophistical ratiocination. Goblet d'Alviella, who calls Nature-worship 'primary fetishism,' is nearer the truth when he says, in his *Hibbert Lectures* (p. 82):

> 'Man, having been led by different routes to personify the souls of the dead on the one hand, and natural objects and phenomena on the other, subsequently attributed to both alike the character of mysterious superhuman beings. Let us add that this must have taken place everywhere, for there is not a people on earth in which we do not come upon these two forms of belief side by side and intermingled.'

[1] Lippert's definition of fetishism as 'a belief in the souls of the departed coming to dwell in any thing that is tangible or visible in heaven or earth' (*Die Religionen der europäischen Culturvölker*, Berlin, 1881), seems little more than an echo of Herbert Spencer's.

No writer has done more to elucidate this subject than Tylor, who, in his *Primitive Culture*[4] (ii. 144), defines fetishism as

'the doctrine of spirits embodied in, or attached to, or conveying influence through, certain material objects'—'vessels or vehicles or instruments of spiritual beings.' 'To class an object as a fetish,' he adds (p. 145), 'demands explicit statement that a spirit is considered as embodied in it or acting through it or communicating by it, or at least that the people it belongs to do habitually think this of such objects; or it must be shown that the object is treated as having personal consciousness and power, is talked with, worshipped, prayed to, sacrificed to, petted or ill-treated with reference to its past or present behaviour to its votaries.'

This is very clear and convenient. It covers a very large proportion of what is usually understood by 'fetish,' and applies with special force to the ideas prevalent in West Africa. It deserves general acceptance, if we are not to consign the word to the terminological scrap-heap as so blurred and disfigured by indiscriminate use that it is unserviceable and misleading. There is much temptation to do so.

Goblet d'Alviella's definition of fetishism is closely akin to that of Tylor. He calls it 'the belief that the appropriation of a thing may secure the services of the spirit lodged within it.' He distinguishes between the talisman or the amulet, in which the spirits act on inanimate things from without, using them as implements, and the fetish, when the spirits are embodied in a concrete object —a distinction which, he says, is already recognized by the greater number of savage races. Max Buchner, on the other hand, thinks that fetishism belongs more to the realm of art than of religion, and that, instead of 'fetish' or 'idol,' we should say 'amulet' or 'medicine.' Others call a fetish a magical appliance, or 'an object conceived of anthropopathically.' Waitz (quoted in Schultze, *Fetishism*, p. 241) says that 'a fetish is an object of religious veneration, wherein the material thing and the spirit within it are regarded as one, the two being inseparable.' Travellers have added their quota to the confusion. Miss Kingsley, for example, means by fetishism the whole system of West African religion, of which, as she points out, the worship of spirits embodied in material objects forms only a part. Other travellers have applied the term to the material symbols of the great Nature-deities. Lexicographers naturally reflect the views of anthropologists and travellers. Perhaps Webster's definition represents as accurately as any the most general use of the word, viz. 'a material thing, living or dead, which is made the object of brutish or superstitious worship, as among certain African tribes.' Littré says: 'Fétiche—objet naturel, animal divinisé, bois, pierre, idole grossière, qu'adorent les nègres des côtes occidentales de l'Afrique et même de l'intérieur des terres jusqu' en Nubie.' No wonder that Max Müller exclaimed—'fetishism, whatever that may mean'!

2. **Classification.**—The variety of definition and opinion indicated above is not due to mere wanton caprice. It is the reflexion of a very great and real complexity in the subject-matter. The evidence on which anthropologists have based their views is enormous in amount, and of a very heterogeneous kind. It comes to us from all parts of the world, though its chief source is West Africa. There are at least five distinct classes of objects to which it relates, all of which fall under the general description of material objects worshipped, honoured, or esteemed for something more than their physical properties or commercial value.

(1) CLASS I.—*Natural objects and phenomena.*—The Sun, the Sky, and the Earth (as a source of food) almost universally hold a leading position among personified things of this class. Æschylus's Prometheus extends the list in his magnificent appeal to the Nature-deities to witness the injustice done him by the later generation of anthropomorphic gods:

'O Sky divine, O Winds of pinions swift,
O fountain-heads of Rivers, and O thou
Illimitable laughter of the Sea,
O Earth, the Mighty Mother, and thou Sun,
Whose orbèd light surveyeth all!'
(*Prometheus Vinctus*, 88 ff., Morshead's tr.).

When once the personification, followed by the worship, of a few of the most striking and most powerful objects (distinguished by the negroes as 'grand fetishes') has been accomplished, others follow easily, as the moon, trees, rivers, wells, mountains, rocks, and thunder. Nor does the process stop here. Having personified the most splendid, benignant, and awful objects of Nature, the active, though by no means powerful, imagination of the savage runs riot and deifies indiscriminately all manner of objects of no intrinsic importance or significance, as curious pebbles, leaves, etc. Japanese myth speaks of a time when trees, rocks, leaves, and foam had the power of speech, and evil deities buzzed like flies in the 5th month. It is on these lower and more frivolous levels of Nature-worship that 'teratism,' or the love of the curious and extraordinary, to which Herbert Spencer (*Sociology*, i. 313) attached an exaggerated importance, finds its chief sphere of action. As a matter of fact, the great Nature-divinities are not of this class. The Sun is not worshipped because he is remarkable, abnormal, or extraordinary, but in gratitude for his daily light and warmth; the Sea and Rivers, because they supply fish for food, or will drown one if he is not careful; the Earth, as the great provider of human wants.

It is not always recognized by anthropologists that Nature-worship in its primary stage is not the worship of a deity or spirit immanent in the material object, or of an anthropomorphic being separate from it but controlling its activities. This would involve a dichotomy of soul and body, mind and matter, which is foreign to the ideas of the primitive man or savage. It is not found in the lowest races, though no doubt, as readers of Tylor's *Primitive Culture* are aware, it plays an important part in the philosophy of tribes of no great enlightenment or cultivation. The earliest cult of all is of the material object itself (Comte's fetishism) considered as alive. The Sun, the Sea, the Mountain, as there is abundant evidence to show, is in this early stage *the* god. There is no suggestion of an indwelling spirit in Æschylus's invocation quoted above. The *θεός par excellence* of the Greek dramatists is simply the Sun. Horace's *Fons Bandusiæ* (*Carm.* III. xiii. 1), to which he promises the offering of a kid, is not a nymph of the well, but the water itself, as the epithet 'splendidior vitro' shows. Of course, nymphs, dryads, and fauns are plentiful enough in pagan myth. But this is a secondary development with which fetishism is not concerned. The two stages of belief, however, merge into one another.

The worship of Nature-deities is sometimes referred to the principle that primitive man, like the savage and the child, conceives of everything as animated by human feelings. This view requires some qualification. Strictly speaking, there is no such thing as a primitive man. Man, at any given period, has ancestors and a long history behind him. But, allowing the term as marking a stage of progress similar to that of the lowest savages of our own time, it will be plain, on reflexion, that the ordinary primitive man, like the lower classes everywhere, troubles himself little about the sentient aspect of the universe. To him, as to the lower animals, the animate is animate, and the inanimate inanimate. It is at all times only a few of the more imaginative individuals of a race to whom their fellows are indebted for religious personification and myth. Religious progress is everywhere the work of the genius, not of the vulgar. Children are sometimes said to treat inanimate objects as alive. But this is exceptional, and usually stops short at make-believe. The child does not attempt to eat his own mud-pies. The boy knows quite well that his father's walking-stick is not a real horse, and, in spite of de Brosses, Schultze, and others, the girl does not really believe that her doll is a living being. A mother of the writer's acquaintance, having remonstrated with her little daughter for her rough treatment of 'poor dolly,' received the reply: 'Poor dolly! it is only a bag of sawdust.' Nor does even the primitive or savage genius discern life in all creation. He does so only in a desultory, fragmentary fashion, singling out such objects or phenomena as stir in him the feelings of gratitude, fear, or wonder. The worship of deified living men and of animals for their beneficent (as the cow) or formidable (as the tiger, crocodile, etc.) character, belongs to this class. But they are not usually called fetishes.

(2) CLASS II.—Some writers apply the term 'fetish' to a material object when worshipped, not for itself, but *as the representative or symbol of a Nature-deity or deified man*. Among the latter we may include the ancestor, though here a distinction is to be made between ancestor-worship proper in which the dead man is credited with imaginary powers, and the more rational honours paid to him by ourselves in common with more uncivilized nations. Fetishes of this class are sometimes a direct representation of the true object of worship, as in the case of the ancient Peruvians, who worshipped a golden disk for the Sun, and a silver one for the Moon. The selection of a snake or serpent in many countries as the representative of a river-god or of water is probably due to the direct resemblance of its sinuous, gliding motion to that of a stream. In other cases, the fetish was originally an offering to the god whom by a long association it had come to represent. Most of the *shintai* ('god-body') of Japan had this origin. The Sun-goddess is represented in the temple of Ise by a mirror offered to her, according to the myth, in order to induce her to leave the 'rock-cave of Heaven,' where she had hidden in disgust at the rude behaviour of her younger brother, the Rainstorm. When the Sun-goddess sent down her grandson to rule the world, she gave him this mirror, saying:

'My child, when thou lookest upon this mirror, let it be as if thou wert looking on me. Let it be with thee on thy couch and in thy hall, and let it be to thee a sacred mirror.' Another myth says: 'This is the Great God of Ise.'

We see here the transition from the offering to the symbol, and from the symbol to the actual deity. Of course, the last development is the work of the most ignorant and dull-minded worshipper. But it is not without parallel. The *inao* of the Ainus of Yezo (see art. AINUS, vol. i. p. 245 ff.), which consist of willow wands whittled into a mass of adherent shavings at one end, are properly mere offerings, but occasionally receive direct worship as 'genuine fetishes,' to use the expression of John Batchelor, a missionary who lived amongst them for many years. In Greece, as Lucian (*Imag.* 14) tells us, the visitors to the temple of Olympia believed that Phidias's statue was Jupiter in person. Plutarch and Seneca rebuked similar superstitious ideas about the gods. In West Africa, the dead ancestor is represented by his skull, or by a mass of chalk saturated with drippings from the putrefying head which is hung up over it.

'The conception,' says Tylor (*Prim. Cult.*[4] ii. 151), 'of such human relics becoming fetishes, inhabited or at least acted through by the souls which formerly belonged to them, will give a rational explanation of much relic-worship otherwise obscure.'

With the Damaras of South Africa, the ancestors are represented by stakes cut from trees or bushes consecrated to them, to which stakes the meat is first offered.

From fetishes of this second class the transition is easy to the idol. In Ancient Greece the primitive memorial erected to a god did not even pretend to be an image, but was often nothing more than a pillar, a board, a shapeless stone, or a post. At the present day in Korea we see these pillar-gods, consisting of upright logs of wood, which have so far approached becoming idols as to have their tops very rudely fashioned into human form. In the Indian Museum at Calcutta is a *liṅga* with a face carved on one side of the top—an incipient idol.

The totem, regarded as the animal, vegetable, or mineral which represents the personified national or tribal unity, belongs to this class of fetish (see TOTEMISM). In other cases, however, the animal may be worshipped as representing a Nature-deity, or as the incarnation of one. It is sometimes difficult to say to which of these categories the animal gods of ancient Egypt belonged.

(3) CLASS III.—In this class the fetish is a material object which is supposed to be *the permanent or temporary abode of a spirit*, and is worshipped or honoured accordingly. This is the most general use of the word, and is especially appropriate to the type of fetishism prevalent in West Africa, the chief home of this institution. It is the fetishism of Tylor and of Goblet d'Alviella, though the latter somewhat narrows its application by introducing the proviso that the spirit's services belong to the person who appropriates the fetish, as in the case of Aladdin and his lamp. Some of the spirits thus attached to material objects may be Nature-spirits, while others are the souls of dead men. In Japan, the spirit of a Nature-deity will descend into the sacred wand with paper scallops attached, which is called *gohei*, and answer questions by the mouth of the hypnotized medium who holds it in his hand. The soul of a dead Carib might be thought to abide in one of his bones, taken from the grave and carefully wrapped in cotton, in which state it could answer questions and even bewitch an enemy. But most fetishes of this class are tenanted by spirits of an indeterminate kind, no doubt originally suggested by the former two, but having lost all specific character. The objects selected by the West African negro to serve as the abode of his guardian spirit are such things as animals, snails, shells, tiger's teeth, antelope hoofs, monkey's paws, horns, snake-skins, bits of metal or ivory, teeth, bones, beads, stones, rags, etc. A much valued fetish, which was the subject of a lawsuit, consisted of a brass pan containing a lump of clay adorned with parrot's feathers. Another was a mixture of clay and various roots in an earthen pot. Many are compounds of a number of strange and disgusting things which remind us of the contents of the witches' cauldron in *Macbeth*. Some of these may have originally belonged to the second class of fetishes, and have been at first symbols rather than receptacles. A spirit may be lodged in the object selected as fetish by simple exposure in the open air, or by invitation. Frequently the intervention of a fetish-priest is necessary, with his ceremonial and hocus-pocus formula of consecration. Again, some chance circumstance may cause an otherwise indifferent object to be made a fetish.

A negro, hastening from his hut in order to escape from an enemy, knocked against a stone and hurt himself. He subsequently took up this stone and constituted it as his fetish. A Kāfir broke off a piece of the anchor of a stranded ship. As he died soon after, the people of the neighbourhood attributed his death to the power of the anchor, and honoured it accordingly.

A fetish is more fully trusted when experience has proved its value by success in trade, war, hunting, or fishing, or as a protection against disease and danger. The owner talks to it, asks its advice, lays his complaints before it, and calls upon it on every urgent occasion. It is rubbed with palm-oil, has palm-wine, beer, rum, or milk poured over it, and is sprinkled with blood of animals or even of man. To swear by the fetish is the most binding of oaths. On the other hand, if it fails, after warnings and reproaches, to perform what is expected of it, it may be punished, thrown away, buried, given away, or sold. Every fetish has its special province of efficiency. One prevents sickness, another heals it, others grant long life, children, wisdom, courage, safety in travelling or in war, protection against thunder, success in trade, fair winds, rain, etc. In short, they are supposed to procure every imaginable blessing and avert every conceivable misfortune. They are to be found everywhere—at the entrance to towns, in the huts and over the doors, by every road, at the foot of rocks and trees, or hung on men's necks. Some fetishes are private, belonging to individuals or families; others are public, and protect villages or tribes from misfortune by war or pestilence. The latter sometimes have priests and temples dedicated to them. The chief's house is the home of numerous fetishes; in fact, he himself may be a fetish endowed with supernatural power, such as that of making rain. The priests of the fetish-deity are naturally assimilated to him, and are credited with the possession of similar powers. In the case of the ordinary fetish, as well as of the idol, there are two currents of opinion. Many fetish-worshippers declare positively that, for example,

'the tree is not the fetish. The fetish is the invisible spirit which has taken up its abode in the tree. It cannot consume the offerings of food which are made to it, but it enjoys the spiritual part of them, and leaves the visible bodily element.'

On the other hand, there is undoubtedly a lower conception by which the material fetish itself is the object of worship, the spirit which inhabits it being forgotten or neglected. Tylor says that the negro usually combines the two as forming a whole, and this whole is (as the Europeans call it) the fetish, the object of his religious worship. Turner, in his *Nineteen Years in Polynesia*, 1861 (p. 527), says:

'On the isle of Nukunono Fakaafo worship used to be paid to the Tui Tokelau, or Lord of Tokelau; and this was a stone wrapped up in matting, and held so sacred that only the king durst view it, and even he only once a year, when it assumed a fresh suit of matting. As this stone was considered so sacred, it was natural for the people to identify it with the deity. Whatever offerings were made to the stone were made to the god; whatever petitions they had to address to the god were addressed to the stone. Which is here the god, the stone or the deity?'

As in the case of Class II., the transition of fetishes of Class III. to the idol is easy. A few dabs of paint or scratches with a knife are sufficient to convert a shapeless stone or post into an anthropomorphic figure. Idols are rare amongst most of the coast tribes of West Africa, but are common among all the interior tribes.

(4) CLASS IV.—The term 'fetish' is frequently used, though more in general literature than by scientific writers, of *non-religious magical appliances, charms, or amulets, which have a virtue quite independent of any gods or spirits.* Such are the piece of the rope with which a man has been hanged carried by the superstitious gambler, and the divining-rod used for the discovery of springs of water. To this class belong such fetishes as the kite's foot hung round the neck of a Basuto child, so that he may escape misfortune with the swiftness of the kite in its flight. Another child wears the claw of a lion, in order that his life may be as firmly secured against all danger as that of a lion. This class of so-called fetishes is dealt with more fully in art. MAGIC.

(5) CLASS V.—Material things are sometimes the objects of *a make-believe worship.* The Devonshire farmer, who at Christmas salutes his apple-trees with much ceremony, offering them a bowl of cider and a toast, does not think of them as tenanted by a tree-god. When a Japanese housewife gives her needle one day's rest in the year, and sets before it a tiny offering of cake, it is not necessary to suppose that the needle is taken for a sentient thing, or is believed to be the abode of a spirit. She does not call it *kami*, or 'god.' Both of these practices are due to the pleasure which men take in dramatic make-believe. The writer is not aware how far this applies to the annual honours paid in India by the artisan to his tools, which Herbert Spencer would include under the term 'fetishism.' Underlying all such cases there is, no doubt, a vague sense of gratitude, whether to the inventor or to Nature, which may eventually result in real worship. The kitchen-furnace in Japan is a recognized *kami*, or 'god,' and tree-worship had probably its origin in some such practices as that described above, which are known all over the world as well as in Devonshire.

The above classes of fetish often merge into one another in the most perplexing way. An object which by one person is worshipped for its intrinsic qualities (Class I.) may be regarded by another as the abode of a spirit (Class III.), or as a mere symbol (Class II.). Tylor (ii. 205) points out that 'the negro can say, "In this river, or tree, or amulet there is a wong [fetish-deity]." But he more usually says, "This river, or tree, or amulet is a wong."' Again, the same writer says (ii. 176): 'So close is the connexion conceived between spirit and image, that the idol is itself called "wong."' The medicine or magical appliance which in one case is purely non-religious may in others be fortified by a prayer or incantation. The practice of prefixing the sign of Jupiter to medical prescriptions is perhaps not wholly obsolete with ourselves. On the other hand, an ostensibly religious fetish may be found to owe its efficacy to some physical property of the material object in question.

3. **Religious value of fetishism.**—Fetishism is, no doubt, an undeveloped or a degraded form of religion; yet it rests on a principle which the higher religions are unable to dispense with altogether. In the nature of things, the spiritual must be represented by the physical. Christianity has its Cross, its Eucharist, its Baptismal water. Unfortunately, the evidence relating to fetish-worship, though plentiful enough, seldom enables us satisfactorily to trace the history of the ideas which underlie it. Missionaries are hampered by their religious prejudices; travellers seldom have the necessary previous training for that thorough knowledge of savage languages without which precision is impossible. Supposing that a Timbuctoo savant, visiting this country, saw an educated English gentleman prostrate himself before a wafer of bread, how wholly false and inadequate an impression he would receive of an institution whose history is traceable back for thousands of years through many varying forms of ritual and belief! Not that the traveller is much to blame. But, under the most favourable circumstances, it would be difficult to learn from the fetish-worshipper, or even from the priest, the reasons for practices which they pursue in imitation of their predecessors. They themselves, in fact, seldom know much about them. Yet all fetishes must have a history of some sort. It is not enough to say with de Brosses (*op. cit.* p. 182):

'On n'est pas obligé de rendre raison d'une chose où il n'y en a point; et ce seroit, je pense, assez inutilement qu'on en cher-

cheroit d'autre que la crainte et la folie dont l'esprit humain est susceptible, et que la facilité qu'il a dans de telles dispositions à enfanter des superstitions de toute espèce. Le Fétichisme est du genre de ces choses si absurdes qu'on peut dire qu'elles ne laissent prise au raisonnement qui voudroit les combattre.'

Fear and folly do, no doubt, play a great part, but Herbert Spencer is nearer the truth when he says (*Study of Sociology*[9], 1880, p. 305): 'The wrong beliefs are superficial, and there is a right belief hidden by them.' There would be no spurious coins if there were not a genuine gold or silver currency. We are sometimes able to catch a glimpse of a striving after, or a lapse from, something higher, associated with what might at first sight appear a gross form of fetishistic superstition.

In 644 a prophet arose in Eastern Japan who persuaded his neighbours to worship a grass-green caterpillar with black spots, promising them that, if they did so, they would enjoy long life and riches. The movement spread so far and so rapidly that the authorities intervened; the prophet was executed, and his religion suppressed. This might seem pure fetishism of a low type. Yet, when we are told that the god was called the God of the Eternal World and the God of Gods, it seems probable that the caterpillar was merely a symbol, and that the movement, recorded by no friendly observer, was, in reality, a protest against the prevailing polytheism of the time. The circumstance that the devotees of the new god threw their property into the highways indicates a degree of religious exaltation hardly to be produced by the mere worship of a caterpillar. Pausanias informs us (ix. 40) that in his time the Greeks worshipped the sword of Agamemnon. Surely it was not simply a bit of metal to which they paid their devotions. Its association with the heroic virtues of the men of the Homeric age must have counted for much in the motives for their reverence. The material object worshipped at the shrine of Ise in Japan is a metal mirror enclosed in a box, and never seen by anybody. Doubtless, some dull-witted devotees take this fetish (Class II.) for the actual deity; others know that, historically, it represents the Sun or, rather, the Sun-goddess; but the majority have reached the higher, though less correct, conception of the god as a great Divine ancestor, who from heaven exercises a providential guardianship over Japan. The animal-worship of the Ancient Egyptians was something more than the mere adoration of bulls and cats.

Fetishism—taking the word in its most comprehensive signification—rests on two principles. The first is what, in modern phrase, we call the immanence of Deity; the second is the necessity which there is for the spiritual to be expressed in terms of the physical. But the savage's conceptions of them are crude and inadequate, and his unintelligent application of them has resulted in a profuse outgrowth of gross superstition.

LITERATURE.—C. de Brosses, *Du Culte des dieux fétiches*, Paris, 1760; Auguste Comte, *Philosophie positive*, do. 1830-42 (tr. H. Martineau, 1896); E. B. Tylor, *Primitive Culture*[4], London, 1903; Goblet d'Alviella, *Hibbert Lectures*, London, 1891; Herbert Spencer, *Sociology*, do. 1874; A. C. Haddon, *Magic and Fetishism*, London, 1906 (contains a useful bibliography); F. Schultze, *Fetichism* (Eng. tr. 1885); R. H. Nassau, *Fetichism in West Africa*, London, 1904; M. H. Kingsley, *West African Studies*, London, 1899; J. G. Frazer, *Golden Bough*[2], London, 1900; W. Schneider, *Rel. der afr. Naturvölker*, Münster, 1891 (a most admirable work, with numerous references to authorities). Mention should also be made of Max Müller, Hartland, Clodd, Réville, Casalis, Brinton, Lang, Ellis, Bastian, Waitz, and Holub, who, as travellers or students, have helped to elucidate this subject. Those who have practical opportunities of investigating fetishism will find *Notes and Queries on Anthropology*, issued by the Royal Anthropological Institute, a useful manual.

W. G. ASTON.

FETISHISM (American).—Among the native tribes of the two Americas, fetishism is rife. They regard the fetish as intrinsically possessing that magic power known to some of the N. Amer. Indians as *orenda*, the essential essence which enables the object to achieve supernatural results. But the ability to perform these, and the sphere of action of the fetish, depend greatly upon the nature of the object containing the magic power. The possession of a fetish presumes possession of its magical properties.

It must be borne in mind that to the untutored Indian intelligence all things—animals, water, the earth, trees, stones, the heavenly bodies, even night and day, and such properties as light and darkness—are regarded as possessing animation and the power of volition. It is, however, the general Indian belief that many of these are under the power of some spell or potent enchantment. The rocks and trees are the living tombs of imprisoned spirits, resembling the Dryads of folklore, so that it is not at all strange to the Indian mind to perceive an imprisoned intelligence, more or less powerful, in any object, no matter how uncommon the vehicle—indeed, the more uncommon, the more probable it would appear as the place of detention of some powerful intelligence imprisoned therein, for revenge or some similar motive, by the spell of some mighty enchanter.

Nearly all the belongings of a shaman or medicine-man are classed as fetishes by the N. Amer. Indians. These usually consist of the skins of beasts, birds, and serpents; roots, bark, powders, and numberless other objects. But the fetish must be altogether divorced from the idea of religion proper, with which it has little or no connexion, being found side by side with religious phases of many types.

The fetish may be a bone, a feather, an arrowhead, a stick carved or painted, a fossil, a tuft of hair, a necklace of fingers, a stuffed skin, the hand of an enemy, or anything which might be suggested to the original maker in a dream or a flight of imagination. It is sometimes fastened to the scalp-lock, the dress, the bridle, concealed between the layers of a shield, or specially deposited in a shrine in the wigwam. The idea in the mind of the original maker is usually symbolic, and is revealed only to one formally chosen as heir to the magical possession and pledged in his turn to a similar secrecy.

Notwithstanding that it has been stated that the cult of fetishism is not, strictly speaking, a department of religious activity, a point exists at which the fetish begins to evolve into the god. This happens when fetishes survive the test of experience, and achieve a more than personal or tribal popularity, as among the Zuñi Indians, examples of which will be adduced in the course of the article. Nevertheless, the fetish partakes more of the nature of those spirits which are subservient to man (as, for example, the Arabian *jinn*) than of gods proper; and, if they are prayed and sacrificed to on occasion, the 'prayers' are more of the nature of a magical invocation, and the 'sacrifices' no more than would be accorded to any other assisting agent. Thus sharply must we differentiate between a fetish, or captive spirit, and a god. But it must further be borne in mind that a fetish is not necessarily a piece of personal property. It may belong collectively to an entire community, and, as will be remarked later, it is not necessarily a small article, but may possess all the appearance of a full-blown idol. An idol, however, is the abode of a god—the image into which a deity may materialize. A fetish, on the other hand, is the place of imprisonment of a subservient spirit which cannot escape, and which, if it would gain the rank of godhead, must do so by a long series of luck-bringing, or, at least, by the performance of a number of marvels of a protective or fortune-making nature.

It is not unlikely that a belief exists in the Indian mind that there are many wandering spirits who, in return for food and other comforts, are willing to materialize in the shape that the savage provides for them, and to assist him in the chase and other spheres of life.

1. The Eskimos.—Among the Eskimos, fetishism presents itself in an almost perfect form, and with them is found one of the few instances of making a fetish of the human body. Nelson (*18 RBEW*, 1899, pt. 1, p. 429) states that along the coast of Norton Sound and the Lower Yukon a new-born child is sometimes put to death for the purpose of having the services of its shade to secure success in hunting. The child must be killed secretly, and its body stolen, so that no one may know of the occurrence. The body is then dried, placed in a bag, and worn on the person or carried in the *kayak* at sea. By carrying the body the hunter believes that he compels its shade, which is clairvoyant, to assist in finding game, and so to direct the flight of his spear that the animals he hunts cannot escape. The Eskimos also employ masks to assist them in the chase. These are carved to represent supernatural beings, the *tunghät*, or wandering genii, and are believed to possess the qualities of the animals they depict, the spiritual essence of which enters into the wearers. They are supposed to watch for game, and, by some clairvoyant power, to see it at a great distance; and the hunter is then guided by the influence of the masks to find it. They are also supposed to guide the spears in flight. Among the people of the Kaviak Peninsula and Kotzebue Sound, the possession of the dried body of a weasel, worn in a pouch or belt, is supposed to endow the owner with agility and prowess as a hunter. In all cases it follows that the owner of any mummified animal carries with it power over its shade, which becomes the servant of the possessor.

The Eskimos naturally attach great importance to those fetishes which they believe bring them success in whale-hunting. To this end they employ images of fabulous and other animals. These are of practically the same class as the mask fetishes alluded to above. A whaling *umiak* always carries a number of fetishes, such as a wolf's skull, a dried raven, the axis vertebra of a seal, feathers, the skin of a golden eagle, or the tip of a red fox's tail. Little stone and crystal images of whales are also worn. The Unalit of Bering Strait believe that their arrows and other weapons, when marked with the sign of the wolf or other totem, become invested with some of the qualities of the animal represented, and are endowed with some special fatality. The women of the wolf *gens* braid strips of wolf-skin in their hair, and boys wear a wolf's tail behind in their belts. In these customs we may trace a curious blending of fetishism and totemism, in the use of the totem animal or its parts as fetishes or amulets.

After an animal is killed, the hunter carefully removes and preserves the bladder. These bladders are used in the 'Bladder Festival,' a feast to the dead, and are supposed to contain the shades of the slain animals. When—in some ceremonies—the bladders are burst in the water, it is believed that they release the imprisoned shade, and that it swims out to sea and enters the body of an unborn animal of its own species. If the shade is well pleased with the treatment given it by the hunter, they say it will not be afraid to meet him in its new form, and will permit him to approach and kill it again without trouble. On the Alaskan mainland, the shamans place a small ivory carving of a whale in a male child's mouth directly after birth, so as to feed him upon something that will make him grow up a fine hunter. It is believed that a pair of gloves having the feet of a sea-parrot sewn to them will bring success in salmon-fishing, as the bird is a clever fisher—an instance of what might be called 'sympathetic' fetishism.

What would seem to be a species of ancestor-worship mingles with the fetishism of the Hudson Bay Eskimos, according to Turner (*11 RBEW*, 1894, p. 201), for he states that certain fetishes are worn 'as remembrances of deceased relatives. These have the form of a headless doll depending from some portion of the garment worn on the upper part of the body,' and, of course, are fetishes into which they hope the spirit of the ancestor may be coaxed to reside, so that by means of its clairvoyant gift it will be of great assistance to the wearer.

Besides those enumerated above, the Eskimos possess many other varieties of fetish. Frequently a shaman is employed to coax a wandering spirit into a fetish body, and it is interesting to note that Nelson (*op. cit.* 434) states that 'an heirloom (*paituk*) may become a fetich by reason of its extreme age and long possession in one family. Such objects are treasured, and are handed down from father to son. They are supposed to be endowed with reason and to be gifted with supernatural powers to aid and protect their owners.'

Eskimo women wear belts made of the incisors of reindeer, taken out with a small fragment of the alveolus adhering to them, and attached scale-like to a rawhide strap. When one of these has been in the family for a long time, it is believed to acquire a certain virtue for curing disease: the affected part must be struck smartly a number of times with the end of the belt. A married woman who desires a son procures a small doll-like image from a shaman, who, after performing certain secret rites over it, advises her to sleep with it under her pillow.

When selling skins they cut off a small fragment, and place it in a pouch; or, if selling an entire seal, they cut off and swallow the tip of its tongue in order to retain the essential essence or spirit of the animal. In several of their folk-tales it is mentioned that certain persons took small pieces from skins, and that afterwards these again became full-sized skins, to the benefit of the owner, thus indicating the meaning of this custom. They place implicit faith in such fetishes, which they believe to have been in contact with supernatural beings and objects which by their general appearance recall the effect expected from the fetish—a well-known phase of sympathetic magic. Other fetishistic objects enumerated by Murdoch ('Point Barrow Expedition,' *9 RBEW*, 1892, pp. 436–441) are bunches of the claws of the bear or wolverine, the metacarpal bones of the wolf, the head or beak of the gull or raven, a small dried flounder, the young unbranched antler of a reindeer, the last three joints of a reindeer fawn's foot, the sub-fossil incisor tooth of some ruminant, the tusk of a young walrus, and the stuffed skin of a black-bellied plover. A charm of great value to the mother who has a young babe is the canine tooth of a polar bear, as she is under the impression that, while she wears it, her milk supply cannot fail.

An instance of tribal fetishism is noticeable in the *Ai-yá-g'ûk*, or 'Asking festival,' when a wand known by the same name is made, having three hollow globe-like attachments hanging to it. It is used by a man, chosen for the purpose, to obtain the wishes of all the various members of the tribe, who in turn ask for something which he obtains for them from the other members. This wand is much respected, and it is considered wrong to refuse any request made with it. In some parts of the Lower Yukon, instead of stating their wishes, they make small images and hang them on to the wand held by the man, who conveys it from one to another.

2. Athapascan family.—The Apaches, both male and female, wear fetishes which they call *tzi-daltai*, manufactured from lightning-riven wood, generally pine or cedar or fir from the mountains (Bourke, *9 RBEW*, p. 587). These are highly valued, and are never sold. They are shaven very thin, rudely carved in the semblance of the human form, and decorated with incised lines, representing the lightning. They are small in size, and few of them are painted.

Bourke describes one which an Apache chief carried about with him, made of a piece of lath, unpainted, having drawn upon it a figure in yellow with a narrow black band, and three snake-heads with white eyes. It was further decorated with pearl buttons and small eagle-down feathers. The reverse and obverse were identical.

Many of the Apaches fixed a small piece of malachite to their guns and bows to make them shoot accurately. Bourke (*op. cit.*) mentions a class of fetish which he terms 'phylacteries.' These are pieces of buckskin, or other material, upon which are inscribed certain characters or symbols of a religious or 'medicine' nature, and they are worn attached to the person seeking to be benefited. They differ from the ordinary fetish in that they are concealed from the public gaze.

Such a phylactery, says Bourke, 'itself "medicine," may be employed to enwrap other "medicine" and thus augment its own potentiality' (*op. cit.* 591). He describes several of those objects. One worn by an Indian named Ta-ul-tzu-je 'was tightly rolled in at least half a mile of . . . saddlers' silk,' and when brought to light was found to consist of a small piece of buckskin two inches square, upon which were drawn red and yellow crooked lines which represented the red and yellow snake. Inside were a piece of malachite, a small cross of lightning-riven pine, and two very small perforated shells. The cross they designated 'the black wind.' Another 'phylactery' consisted of a tiny bag of hoddentin (on which see *ERE* i. 602[b]), holding a small quartz crystal and four feathers of eagle-down. This phylactery, it was explained, contained not merely the 'medicine' of the crystal and the eagle, but also that of the black bear, the white bear, the yellow bear, and the yellow snake.

3. Iroquoian family.—Most things that seem at all unnatural are accepted by the Hurons as *oky*, or supernatural, and therefore it is accounted lucky to find them. In hunting, if they find a stone or other object in the entrails of an animal, they at once make a fetish of it. Any object of a peculiar shape they treasure, for the same reason. They greatly fear that demons or wicked spirits will purloin these fetishes, which they esteem so highly as to propitiate them in feasts and invoke them in song. The highest type of fetish obtainable by a Huron was a piece of the *onniont*, or great armoured serpent, a mythical animal revered by many N. Amer. tribes. The medicinal virtue of some fetishes is regarded as very great, one old woman of the Lower Canada Hurons preserving the mummied embryo of a deer, which, she said, the *manitou* had given her during a severe illness of which it had cured her.

4. Algonquian family. — Hoffman states ('The Menomini Indians,' *14 RBEW*, 1896, pt. 1, p. 74) that at the medicine lodges of the tribe there are preserved fetishes or 'amulets, worn above the elbows, which consist of strands of beaded work, metal bands or skunk skins, while bracelets of shells, buckskin, or metal also are worn.' A great tribal fetish of the Cheyenne was their medicine arrow, which was taken from them by the Pawnees in battle. The head of this arrow projects from the bag which contains it, and is covered with delicate waved or spiral lines which denote its sacred character. It was, indeed, the palladium of the tribe. A peculiar type of fetish consisted of a mantle made from the skin of a deer, and covered with feathers mixed with beadings. It was made and used by them as a mantle of invisibility, or charmed covering, to enable spies to traverse an enemy's country with impunity. In this instance the fetishistic power depended upon the devices drawn.

5. Siouan family.—The principal fetishes among the Hidatsa tribe of the Sioux are the skins of foxes and wolves, the favourite war-fetish being the strip off the back of a wolf-skin, with the tail hanging down the shoulders. They make a slit in the skin, through which the warrior puts his head, so that the skin of the wolf's head hangs down upon his breast. These, of course, are totemic fetishes. The most common tribal fetishes with the Siouan tribes are (or were) buffalo heads, the neck-bones of which they preserve with a view to preventing the buffalo herds from removing to too great a distance from them. At certain periods they perform a ceremony with these bones, which consists in taking a potsherd with live coals, throwing sweet-smelling grease upon it, and fumigating the bones with the smoke. There are certain trees and stones which are regarded as fetishes; beside them the Siouans make offerings of red cloth, red paint, and other articles. But all have their personal fetishes, and in all hunting and warlike excursions the 'medicine,' or fetish, is carried. It usually consists of a head, claws, stuffed skin, or other representative of the fetish animal. Even their horses are provided with fetishes in the shape of a deer's horn, to ensure their swiftness. The rodent teeth of the beaver are regarded as potent charms, and are worn by little girls on their necks to make them industrious.

6. Shoshonean stock.—At Sikyatki in Arizona, a territorial nucleus of the Hopi, Fewkes (*17 RBEW*, pt. 2, p. 729 f.) had opportunities of inspecting many interesting fetish forms. A number of these discovered in native graves were pebbles of botryoidal shape, with a polished surface, or with a fancied resemblance to some animal or other form.

A good example of a fetish which has almost attained godhead is that at the Antelope rock at Walpi, 'around which the Snake dancers biennially carry reptiles in their mouths. There is in one side a niche in which is placed a much larger mass of that material [hematite], to which prayers are addressed on certain ceremonial occasions, and upon which sacred meal and prayer emblems are placed.'

Many of the personal fetishes of this people consist of cephalopod fossils, some of which are wrapped up in sacred bundles which are highly venerated, the latter, of course, being tribal fetishes.

In one grave was found a single large fetish of a mountain lion, made of sandstone, in which legs, ears, tail, and eyes are represented, the mouth still retaining the red pigment with which it was coloured. It is almost identical with those used by the Hopi at the present day.

7. Zuñi family.—Cushing (*2 RBEW*, 1883) seems to think that fetishism among the Zuñis arose from the supposition they entertained that they were kin with animals, or, in other words, that their fetishes were totemistic. It is in this stage that totemism and fetishism meet, and the two are by no means incompatible, though they very often flourish side by side. Fetishism of this description is, indeed, the natural concomitant of a totemistic system. Zuñi fetish objects are usually natural concretions, or objects in which a natural resemblance to animals has been heightened by artificial means. Ancient fetishes are much valued by the Zuñis, and are often found by them in the vicinity of pueblos inhabited by their ancestors, and as tribal possessions are handed down from one generation to another. The shamans believe them to be the actual petrifactions of the animals they represent. The Zuñi philosophy of the fetish is given in the Tale of the Two Sun Children, instanced by Cushing (*op. cit.* 14 f.):

'Now that the surface of the earth was hardened, even the animals of prey, powerful and like the fathers (gods) themselves, would have devoured the children of men; and the Two thought it was not well that they should all be permitted to live, "for," said they, "alike will the children of men and the children of the animals of prey multiply themselves. The animals of prey are provided with talons and teeth; men are but poor, the finished beings of earth, therefore the weaker."

Whenever they came across the pathway of one of these animals, were he great mountain lion or but a mere mole, they struck him with the fire of lightning which they carried in their magic shield. *Thlu!* and instantly he was shrivelled and burnt into stone.

Then said they to the animals that they had thus changed to stone, "That ye may not be evil unto men, but that ye may be a great good unto them, have we changed you into rock everlasting. By the magic breath of prey, by the heart that shall endure forever within you, shall ye be made to serve instead of to devour mankind."

Thus was the surface of the earth hardened and scorched and many of all kinds of beings changed to stone. Thus, too, it happens that we find, here and there throughout the world, their forms, sometimes large like the beings themselves, sometimes shrivelled and distorted. And we often see among the rocks the forms of many beings that live no longer, which shows us that all was different in the "days of the new."

Of these petrifactions, which are, of course, mere concretions or strangely eroded rock-forms, the Zuñis say, "Whomsoever of us may be met with the light of such great good fortune may *see* (discover, find) them and should treasure them for the sake of the sacred (magic) power which was given them in the days of the new."[1]

This tradition furnishes additional evidence relative to the preceding statements, and shows the motive wherein lies the power of fetishes. It is supposed that the hearts of the great animals of prey are infused with a spirit or 'medicine' of magic influence over the hearts of the animals they prey upon, and that they overcome them with their breath, piercing their hearts and quite numbing them. Moreover, their roar is fatal to the senses of the lower beasts. The mountain lion absorbs the blood of the game animals; therefore he possesses their acute senses. Again, those powers, as derived from his heart, are preserved in his fetish, since his heart still lives, even although his body be changed to stone. It happens, therefore, that the use of these fetishes is chiefly connected with the chase. But there are exceptions. The great animals of the chase, although fetishistic, are also regarded as supernatural beings, whose mythological position is absolutely defined.

In the City of the Mists lives Po-shai-an-k'ia, father of the Medicine societies, a culture-hero deity, whose abode is guarded by six beings known as the 'prey-gods,' and it is their counterfeit presentments that are used as fetishes. To the north of the City of the Mists dwells the Mountain Lion prey-god; to the west, the Bear; to the south, the Badger; to the east, the Wolf; above, the Eagle; below, the Mole. These animals possess not only the guardianship of the six regions, but also the mastership, not merely geographic, but of the medicine powers which emanate from them. They are the mediators between Po-shai-an-k'ia and man. The prey-gods, as 'Makers of the Paths of Life,' are given high rank among the gods, but, notwithstanding this, their fetishes are 'held as in captivity' by the priests of the various medicine orders, and greatly venerated by them as mediators between themselves and the animals they represent. In this character they are exhorted with elaborate prayers, rituals, and ceremonials, and sometimes placated with sacrifices. Of the prey-gods of the hunt (*we-ma-á-hâ-i*) the special priests are the members of the Great Coyote People, the chosen members of the Eagle and Coyote *gentes*, and of the Prey Brother priesthood. These prey-gods appear to be almost unique, and may be indicated as an instance where fetishism has become allied with religious belief. They depict, with two exceptions, the same species of prey-animals as those supposed to guard the six regions, the exceptions being the Coyote and the Wild Cat. Each one of the six species of prey-animals is subdivided into six varieties. They are, strictly speaking, the property of the priests, and members and priests of the sacred societies are required to deposit their fetishes, when not in use, with the Keeper of the Medicine of the Deer. These 'medicines,' or memberships, alone can perfect the shape of the fetishes and worship them.

The 'Day of the Council of the Fetishes' takes place a little before or after the winter solstice or national New Year. The fetishes are taken from their place of deposit, and arranged according to species and colour, in front of a symbolic slat altar, quadrupeds being placed upright, and birds suspended from the rafters. The fetishes are prayed to, and prayer-meal is scattered over them. Chants are intoned, and a dance performed in which the cries of the fetish beasts are imitated. A prayer with responses follows. Finally, all assemble round the altar, and repeat the great invocation.

The use of the fetishes in hunting among the Zuñi is extremely curious and involved.

The hunter goes to the House of the Deer Medicine, where the vessel containing the fetishes is brought out and placed before him. He sprinkles sacred meal over the vessel in the direction he intends to hunt, chooses a fetish from it, and presses it to his lips with an inhalation. He then places the fetish in a buckskin bag over his heart. Proceeding to the hunt, he deposits a spider-knot of yucca leaves where an animal has rested, imitates its cry, and is thus supposed to confine it within a narrow circle. He then breathes deeply from the nostrils of the fetish, as though inhaling the magic breath of the God of Prey, and puffs the breath long and loudly in the direction whither the beast's tracks tend, in the belief that the breath he has borrowed from the prey-god will stiffen the limbs of the animal he hunts. When the beast is caught and killed, he inhales its suspiring breath. Then he again breathes into the nostrils of the fetish. He then dips the fetish in the heart's blood of the slain quarry, sips the blood himself, and devours a part of the liver. The fetish is placed in the sun to dry, and replaced in the buckskin pouch with a blessing, afterwards being duly returned to the Keeper of the Deer Medicine.

The Zuñi priesthood of the Bow has three fetishes—the Mountain Lion, the White Bear, and the Knife-feathered Monster. The last is probably a tutelar deity, and was perhaps the Zuñi god of war—an instance of the reversion of a full-fledged deity to the status of a fetish, probably occasioned by the popularity and wide-spread nature of fetishism among this people. They have also an equine fetish borrowed from the Navahos, and known as 'The Pony'; and from the same people they have adopted a sheep fetish, the purpose of which is to ensure fecundity.

8. Mexico and Central America.—Although traces of fetishistic belief undoubtedly make their appearance in the religious systems of both Mexico and the ancient civilizations of Central America, concrete examples of them are rare, owing to the fact that these religions had reached a stage far beyond the fetishistic radius. Nevertheless we cannot point to any particular reaction against fetishism, as we can in the case of Peru in the reign of Manco Ccapac, unless it be the alleged policy of Nezahualcoyotl towards the elimination of the swarming deities of the Mexican provinces, many of which probably were merely overgrown fetishes. But the heresies of the Tlatoani of Tezcuco are possibly fabulous.

The only Mexican idol now in existence was most probably of fetishistic origin. This is the uncouth basalt figure of the so-called Teoyaominqui—in reality Centeotl—the 'Corn-mother.' The image shows signs of having been evolved, in its design, from the bundles of maize carried on the backs of women at her festival, and provided with a face back and front. This figure appears to reproduce the primitive fetish which it superseded, and we seem to have confirmation here of the process noted among the Zuñi Indians. The first missionary of Achiotlan, Fray Benito, cited by Burgoa (*Hist. de la Prov. de Predicatores de Guascaca*, Mexico, 1674, ch. xxviii.), destroyed at Mictlan, or Yoopaa, an 'idol' cut from an emerald of great value, of the size of a thick capsicum pod, on which was skilfully engraved a small bird and a serpent coiled ready to strike. This the present writer suspected to be a fetish, and he was glad to see that Eduard Seler confirmed his suspicions in his 'Deities and Relig. Conceptions of the Zapotecs,'[1] and further identified it, from the hieroglyphs on its surface, with the Mexican god Quetzalcoatl, or 'Feathered Serpent.' But the latter circumstance would seem to make it an amulet bearing the god's name, and not a fetish.[2] There are, however, instances where amulets, especially jewels of great value, have been worshipped owing to their connexion with some great deity, as among the Hindus, and this may be a case in point.

The *tepitoton*, or small household idols of Mexico, were perhaps of fetishistic origin. We know very little about them save that they were broken by the people at the end of every 'sheaf' of fifty-two years, when it was considered that the world might possibly come to an end. The ceremony then held was for the purpose of renewing the sacred fire throughout Mexico, and, if these small figures

1 *28 Bull. BE*, 1904, p. 284 ff.; cf. p. 668.

2 Dorsey ('Siouan Cults,' *11 RBEW*, 1894) calls the amulet 'a personal fetish.' It does not appear to the present writer to be so. An amulet is considered to be *directly symbolic* of a deity, power, faith, or idea; a fetish is rarely symbolic, but is merely an acceptable or suitable (or temptingly grotesque [?]) abode for a spirit, imprisoned therein voluntarily or otherwise. It might, however, be brought against this view that symbols are fetishistic, inasmuch as the wearers believe them to be imbued or surcharged with the spirit or essence of the deity, power, faith, or idea they typify.

represented 'hearth and home,' as in some aspects did the Roman *lares* and *penates*, they would hardly have been destroyed. It is more probable that they were fetishistic, like the household *huacas* of Peru.

Here it may be proper to mention some instances, in a religion so advanced as was that of the Mexicans, of the survival of strictly fetishistic ideas. These are found in close connexion with the corn- and rain-spirit worship. Fetishism has an intimate association with early agriculture. The spirits imprisoned or dwelling voluntarily in the fetishes which protect the fields assist the growth of the crops, and subsequently develop into 'food-gods.' But their natural forces become abated by reason of striving after too much fertility of soil, and they require a rest. Such a rest the Mexicans gave to their rain- and maize-gods every eight years, at the festival of the *Atamalqualiztli*, or 'feast of porridge-balls and water,' when the usual staples of existence were for a space abandoned by the people, so that the productive gods might have repose.

9. California. — Some interesting phases are noticeable among the Seri Indians of the Californian Gulf. McGee (*17 RBEW*, 1898, pt. 1, p. 185*) instances among them the use of pottery fetishes or small figurines used in the manufacture of fictile ware, to ensure that the vessels being fired will not crack. The fetish is moulded at the same time and from the same material as the vessel, and then fired with it 'theoretically as an invocation against cracking or other injury, but practically as a "draw-piece" for testing the progress of the firing.'

In their observances prior to warfare the Seri make use of many fetishistic objects, and in battle strive to obtain those of the enemy, which they treasure as fetishes. Their hereditary enemies, the Papago, reciprocate these customs, a case occurring where an aged warrior long wore an Apache arrow-point as a protective against Apache arrows. A Papago shaman also wore a Seri arrow-head for a similar purpose. The Seri are never without imitations of what they believe to be the fetishes of an enemy.

McGee (*op. cit.* p. 259* f.) says that 'the day before the 1895 expedition entered their stronghold, a band of warriors and women were frightened from a freshly slaughtered cow by a party of *vaqueros* so suddenly that their arms were left behind—and these included a heavy Springfield "remodelled" rifle, lacking not only ammunition but breechblock and firing-pin; while Don Andrés Noriega, of Costa Rica, and L. K. Thompson, of Hermosillo, described a rifle of modern make captured similarly two years before, which was in good working order and charged with a counterfeit cartridge ingeniously fashioned from raw buckskin in imitation of a centre-fire brass shell and loaded with a polished stone bullet.' These weapons are, of course, regarded as symbols of mystical potencies, as were several pseudo-machetes made from rust-pitted cask hoops. Another mock machete was actually carved from paloblanco wood and 'coloured in imitation of iron blade and mahogany handle by means of face-paints, and even furnished with "eyes" replacing the handle-rivets, in the form of embedded iron scales.'

The chief use of the weapons of the whites by the Seri is shamanistic and symbolic. As regards their own weapons, the rude appearance and rarity of their stone arrow-heads would seem to point to their being originally manufactured in fetishistic mimicry of alien devices, and it is notable that they are still made only by the shamans of the tribe. Most of the Seri shields or bucklers are fetishistic, as is proved by the circumstance that they are usually made from pelican or other skins much too thin to turn aside a blow, their magical properties being considered sufficient to deflect an enemy's strokes.

10. Peru.—Garcilasso el Inca de la Vega states[1] that in the earliest times in Peru each district, each nation, each family, each row of houses, even each dwelling, had its own god, each different from those of all others, such as herbs, plants, flowers, stones, pebbles, pieces of jade and jasper. That many of these were fetishes cannot be doubted. He also mentions that many of these lesser deities were animals, which would seem to imply a totemic system. But animals are used as fetishes as well as totems, as in Dahomey[1] and on the Slave Coast.[2] In Peru the population was divided into tribes, or *ayllus*, supposed to be consanguineous, each of which had its own *paccarisca*, or place of origin—usually a fabulous one—which was generally a group of rocks rendered conspicuous by their shape and isolation. These were often treated as fetishistic, and were regarded, in some instances, as the abodes of spirits imprisoned by the gods, or else as folk who had been turned into stone by the same agency. Such stones or monoliths were to be seen at Tiahuanaco, Pucara, Xauxa, Pachacamac, and Caxamarca.

But, most important perhaps of all fetishistic examples to be found on the American hemisphere were the *huacas*. The word now signifies 'treasure-house,' or 'ruins of a treasure-house.' In Incan times it implied that the object was one to which worship should be given, and it denoted objects of worship of all descriptions. We have to do for the most part with portable *huacas*, although some immovable ones were fetishes, such as those mentioned at Tiahuanaca and elsewhere. These portable *huacas* included the *conopas*, which were in reality household gods, and as such are of no more interest here than are the *huacanqui*, or amulets proper. Many of the movable *huacas* were stones or pebbles of unusual shape or colour, unshaped by hand; but often they were carved to resemble fruits, animals, or persons.

One of the most important of the fetishistic *huacas* was the *ccompa* which guarded the irrigation channels from leakage and destruction. Other fetishes, called *chichic* or *huanca*, were set up at the boundaries of the fields. They represented a gigantic stalk of maize, carved in stone, and their supposed office was to induce the maize-spirit to make the plant grow to the greatest possible size. A form of fetishism which marks the transition between primitive agricultural fetishes and deities was that of the 'mother' spirits whose function it was to cause the various plants to take root and grow. Such are the *acsumama*, or potato-mother; the *quinuamama*, or quinua-mother; and the *saramama*, or maize-mother. These were usually embodied in hard stones, laboriously wrought into the shape of the ear of maize and the other plants of which they were the guardians. Abnormal plants themselves were occasionally used as fetishes, as, for example, when the rows of grains were twisted spirally round the core of the ear, instead of being straight. Such a plant, or *pirlina-sara*, was placed as a protective fetish on the top of the *pirlina*, or corn-crib, where the maize was stored. The *saramama* was also placed in one of the *pirlinas*. It was made of the finest new maize-stalks, and was richly clothed. On being asked by a spirit-interpreter whether it could live until next year, if it replied in the affirmative, it remained until the following harvest; but, if it announced its inability to survive until that period, it was burnt, and another figure was substituted for it.

There is evidence that fetishism in Peru lingered until long after the destruction of the national mythology. Bollaert states[3] that in the Pass or Abra of Pichuta he noticed a pile of stones with

[1] *Commentarios Reales*, Lisbon, 1609, lib. i. ch. ix.

[1] J. A. Skertchly, *Dahomey as it is*, London, 1874.
[2] Bosman, *Description of Guinea*, London, 1814, Letter xix.
[3] *Antiquarian, Ethnological and other Researches in New Granada, Ecuador, Peru and Chili*, etc., London, 1860.

quids of coca on it. The stones, called *apachitos*, according to the *Mercurio Peruyano* for 1794, 'were adored as deities.' They are found in all the mountain passes, and doubtless originated in Incan times, when those who were laden with baggage, when they had to face a dangerous track, laid down their load, and as a sign of gratitude offered the first thing they could find or lay hands on to the local spirit, saying '*Apachecha*,' which means 'to him who has given me strength.'

11. Brazil.—'Idols,' says Prince Maximilian in his *Travels in the Brazils* (London, 1820, p. 67), 'are nowhere seen among the Tapuyas, and it is only on the River Amazon that certain images have been found which seem to have a connection with the religious creed of the inhabitants.' This would seem to be borne out by the evidence of Christoval de Acuña,[1] who says that the Amazon River tribes had gods who rendered them active assistance in hunting, fishing, and war. On an expedition of war one of the war-gods was placed in the prow of the boat; on a fishing expedition this place was occupied by a 'god' holding a fish. When not in use these fetishes were kept in baskets; and, should the expedition prove unsuccessful, the images were thrown aside, and replaced by others. Thus we learn how the savage carefully experiments with a chosen spirit before he raises it to the level of a god.

The Uapes River tribes possess 'divine stones' of quartz, jasper, or jade, to the piercing of which they devote several years of labour. On the Upper Jamunda is to be found a lake formerly consecrated to the 'Mother Moon,' into which the fabled Amazons threw their *muirákitim*, or sacred stones, representing animals, fishes, and other symbolic objects. The Ipurinas make fetishes of the bones of their ancestors, as do other S. Amer. tribes, and the ancient Caribs were punctilious in preserving the bones of their forefathers, which, after they had been cleaned, bleached, and painted, they kept in a wicker basket full of spices suspended from the doors of their dwellings.

12. Colombia.—The ancient semi-civilized Muysca-Chibcha race, who inhabited a portion of this Republic, manufactured many fetish-like articles of gold, both in the shape of human beings and in that of frogs and fantastic animals. These they deposited in the tombs of their dead, and in their dwellings. The Goajiras, who inhabit the Colombian peninsula of the same name, keep a number of large golden 'dolls,' called *guaras*, which are veritable fetishes, and are supposed to bring good luck to all who see them. But in order to see them an offering must be made—a heifer at the least—or the loss of sight is risked. These figures have often served as the supreme arbiters of peace and war among the tribes. Any chief who possessed one and sent it to an enemy at once brought about a cessation of hostilities. The *guara* is carefully enclosed in a case wrapped in wadding, from which it is drawn only once a year to be bathed. The day is marked by festivities and the sacrifice of oxen. The origin of the *guaras* is unknown to the Goajiras, who say that they have possessed them from time immemorial, and inherit them from father to son. There are two which are widely celebrated: one at Samenta, and that of the Cacique Iuipara, at Ischamana. Smaller fetishes called *keisesia* are owned by numerous Indians, and partake of the general nature of personal fetishes.[2]

LITERATURE.—J. G. Bourke, 'Medicine-men of the Apache,' in *9 RBEW*, 1892; W. P. Clark, *Indian Sign Language*, Philadelphia, 1884; F. H. Cushing, 'Zuñi Fetishes,' in *2 RBEW*, 1883; *Jesuit Relations*, ed. Thwaites, Cleveland, 1896–1901; J. F. Lafitau, *Mœurs des sauvages amériquains*, Paris, 1724; Max Müller, *Origin and Growth of Religion*, London, 1879; J. Murdoch, 'Point Barrow Expedition,' in *9 RBEW*, 1892; E. W. Nelson, 'The Eskimo about Bering Strait,' in *18 RBEW*, 1899; S. R. Riggs, *Gospel among the Dakotas*, Boston, 1869.

LEWIS SPENCE.

[1] *Descubrimiento del gran Rio de las Amazonas*, 1859, ch. xl.
[2] See H. Candelier, *Rio-Hacha, et les Indiens goajires*, Paris, 1893, p. 189.

FETISHISM (Indian).—1. Universal prevalence and nature.—Fetishism is a phenomenon of the Animism universally inherent in the religious practices of the population of India. It is a very common superstition of the educated, and part of the actual religion of the uneducated masses, and, of course, of the savages in their daily life. It is thus ubiquitous under the surface of all the formal religious beliefs prevalent in the country, and is present everywhere in the domestic and similar customs and in the folklore of the people. The main cause of its universality is to be sought in the eclecticism of that agglomerate of heterogeneous beliefs, aboriginal and imported, which goes by the generic name of 'Hinduism,' and is the prevailing recognized religion of the people, largely colouring every other form, and in the capacity of that religion for absorbing and assimilating parts of all the ancient faiths that happen to survive among its extremely varied adherents. A secondary but important cause lies in the fact that the popular Muhammadanism of India is, in reality, a graft of that faith on the indigenous Hinduism, retaining practically all the superstitions handed down by Hindu ancestors to converts, who, for the most part, do not count many generations.

But, while fetishism is thus in evidence all over India, it exists there fundamentally in the same sense as it is to be found concurrently with the various forms of religion which obtain in the Western world: discredited by the philosopher and man of education, and unrecognized by the exponents of the official creeds, occupying largely the position of magic and witchcraft and their survivals among Christians. The natives of India, in fact, in adopting the ideas giving rise to the practice of fetishism, have much in common with the inhabitants of nearly every other religion of the civilized world.

2. Definition.—In India the root-idea of the fetish is spirit-possession. The fetish is an object containing an in-dwelling spirit, and thus proper for worship as being capable of influencing the lives of those connected with it. And in pursuance of this idea it may safely be said that the Indian villager adopts as a fetish any conceivable kind of object, especially if it presents an unusual appearance.

(*a*) *Spirit-possession.*—Under the influence of the idea of spirit-possession local fetishes are continually being created. Anything which can be imagined to possess a spirit is sufficient for this purpose: a hollow tree, a heap of stones, rags left on a bush, a ruin by the wayside or in the jungle, an isolated grave or hummock that can be conceived to be a possible grave, even a milestone of the British Government. Any kind of cairn, grave, tomb, or monument will serve as a fetish, those of English men and women being not uncommonly brought into requisition. Once a story of sanctity is started by an honest or casual devotee, or by a wary would-be priest in search of a living, its mere currency is sufficient for all the neighbourhood to believe, for the tale to be embroidered with accretions, and for the place to be provided with a holy legend, a special ritual, and a list of miracles. In a Hindu neighbourhood all the virtues of the fetish are attributed to a godling, hero, or demon; in a Muhammadan neighbourhood, to a saint; among savages, to the spirits. But the sense is everywhere the same: it is held to be wisdom to worship the fetish, because of the power of the spirit within for good or evil. These notions are occasionally carried very far indeed, as in the case of the Nukalsaini or Nikarsinghī *faqīrs* (Nicholson's 'devotees'), who worshipped the well-known General John Nicholson, of Panjāb Frontier and Delhi fame, during his lifetime, despite repeated severe punishments at the hands of their fetish for so doing. This worship is nowadays transferred to his monument in the Māargallā Pass.

(*b*) *The sacred fire.*—Attribution of a mystical power to a common object in this way has largely brought about the vogue of the sacred fire fetish in India among all sorts and classes of the population, alike at the shrines of the Hindus and Muhammadans and at the holy places of the Dravidian and other non-Aryan savages. Such fire must be ceremonially produced and tended, and it and the ashes it causes will then become worshipful as containing a guardian spirit and curer of disease. But the volcanic fires, meteoric lights, and *ignes fatui* observed in various parts of the country appear to be venerated as manifestations of the powers of evil, and hardly as fetishes proper, though the border line here is not always easy to define.

3. Family and tribal fetishes.—Families, especially when of considerable social position, are peculiarly exposed to fetish worship, and instances are innumerable throughout India of some object possessed by the guardian spirit of the family being held in veneration thereby. Any handy domestic object serves for the abode of such spirits: a stone in the courtyard, an old pestle and mortar, a doorpost, a flower-jar, a specially planted tree or shrub, and so on. On the same principle the Santāls keep sets of prophylactic symbols beside their houses, which represent the abodes of the powers of Nature: pieces of wood, white stones, arrow-heads, and iron tridents. Among the more civilized tribes, but still low down in the social scale, such symbols become rough wooden images set up together in groups, or rude clay models grouped on platforms, which are regularly worshipped as the tribal protectors.

4. Trade and industrial fetishes.—Closely connected with the notion of the family and tribal fetishes are those revered by trades and occupations. The followers of practically every calling among Hindus worship their tools or means of livelihood, actually or symbolically. The object everywhere is the protection of craft interests and, incidentally, cures in general. Instances are as numerous as the occupations. Thus, in various parts of the country, and usually at fixed periods and feasts, sailors will worship their boats; soldiers their swords and other weapons, and, in some Native States, their colours; merchants and bankers their books; clerks their books, pens, and inkstands; grain-merchants their weights daily; farmers their oxen and ploughs; shepherds their sheep; market-gardeners their scales; artisans their tools daily; working-jewellers their pincers and blowpipes; carpenters their yard-measures and also their adzes, chisels, and saws; shoemakers their lasts; tailors their scissors; potters and many other 'low castes' the potter's wheel and moulding-clay for luck; tanners their scrapers; curriers their axes; navvies their mattocks; oilmakers their presses; barbers their razors, scissors, and mirrors; religious mendicants their begging-bowls and bags; dancing girls their musical instruments.

(*a*) *The Ṭhags.*—The most striking instance of a fetish of this description is the pickaxe of the Ṭhags, a criminal brotherhood now suppressed, who gained their livelihood by professional murder by strangling. The pickaxe was the tool used for burying the victims; it was forged with great ceremony, and was especially venerated as the fetish of the association.

(*b*) *The corn-sieve, house-broom, plough, and rice-pounder.*—In India, as elsewhere in the world, the corn-sieve, the house-broom, and the plough are common fetishes connected with marriages and births, as spirit-scarers and symbols of prosperity. To these in India must be added the rice-pounder.

5. Fetish stones.—The commonest kind of fetish in India to come under general observation consists of a stone or stones regarded as representing the village spirit-guardians. These are to be found practically in every village in the country, and are looked upon, according to the degree of civilization of the inhabitants, either as the natural abodes of the guardians themselves or as their symbols, or as representatives of the godlings, who, in their turn, are symbolical of the various powers of Nature. In any case it is considered right and wise to worship them and to treat them with ceremonial reverence. Curious or eccentric form, such as is exhibited by stalactites in caves, is the usual visible sign of spirit-possessed stones, and for this reason many of them are the remains or fragments of ancient and forgotten Buddhist and Hindu carvings, or even pre-historic implements. So also any stone that lends itself by form to phallic worship is sure to be used as a village fetish. In this way, too, meteoric stones, and, in mountain regions, striking rocks, or boulders that glitter or are in any way remarkable by peculiar cleavage or otherwise, become abodes of the gods which attract special worship.

(*a*) *Footprints: viṣṇupāda.*—Miracle-working and worshipful footprints are very common in India, with both ancient and modern attribution of sanctity—among Muhammadans to saints and to Muhammad himself, and among Hindus to all sorts of heroes and godlings. Elaborately carved *viṣṇupāda*, or footprints of Viṣṇu, which are true fetishes, are to be found in several places, and are probably copies of similar footprints of Buddha, common still in all Buddhist countries.

(*b*) *Phallic stones (liṅga): perforated stones, śālagrāma, grindstones: 'rain' stones.*—The assumption of spirit-possession leads in the ordinary course to that of magical powers available for securing the desire of devotees, and hence of fetishes in general. Hence phallic stones (*liṅga*) in particular are venerated as disease-curers. But the form of stone which is specially associated with the cure of ailments and defects in the human body is that which is naturally or artificially perforated. In addition to the perforated, split, fissured, and tunnelled stones and rocks at shrines and places of pilgrimage, both the *śālagrāma*, a species of ammonite with reputed prophylactic and curative qualities, which is ubiquitous in a religious sense, and the family grindstone must be placed in this category. The same line of reasoning has produced rain-getting stones in parts of the country.

6. Fetish trees and plants.—Fetish trees are almost as common as fetish stones, and the forms that most usually strike the observer are the lotus and the *tulsī* (sweet basil) plant, to be found in or near almost all Hindu dwelling-places. The latter is frequently also grown in conjunction with the *nīm* tree (*Margosa*). The *pīpal* or sacred fig, the *bel* or wood apple, the *ām* (mango), the *sāl*, and the betel-nut (*areca*) palm in S. India are samples of other trees treated as the natural haunts of spirits and therefore worshipped. So, of course, are hollow and unusually large trees, or those that grow in burial and cremation grounds, and the like. Specially dark or 'ghostly' groves are further considered to be the abodes of spirits, and are feared and propitiated accordingly.

7. Fetish myths.—Myths, stories, and legends

about fetishes are, of course, legion, and it is hardly an exaggeration to say that they are as numerous in India as the villages themselves. They are chiefly strictly local folk-tales of a religious cast, usually made up of the traditional incidents peculiar to their class, but occasionally throwing a valuable light on the notions of the people in this connexion. For instance, the great mass of religious legend which attaches to the soil of the Govardhan Hill near Mathura has led to the belief that all its stones are endowed with life. Sometimes such stories acquire a certain general importance, as in the case of the legend of Lorik, a tribal fetish among the widely spread and numerous Ahīr (*q.v.*), brought into vogue to account for the tribe's worship of a particular rock at Benares and of a fissured boulder and an 'elephant' stone near the Mārkundī Pass. Of the same nature and social importance are the very numerous and popular stories to account for the beneficial miracles to be secured at real or reputed shrines and tombs of the more widely known Muhammadan saints, indigenous and imported, such as Sakhī Sarwar, Badru'd-dīn Auliā, Khwājā Khizar, Sālār Ghāzī (Zinda Shāh Madār), Ghausu'l-Azam (Abdu'l-Qādir), Salīm Chishtī, Shaikh Farīd, Shāh Daulā, etc.; or of Hindu godlings, heroes, or holy men, whether of classical antiquity or of comparatively modern or even recent date, such as Bhairon, Bhīmsen, Vetāl, Guru Gorakhnāth, Guru Guggā, Lāl Beg, Jumādī, etc.; or of eclectic mediæval and modern religious reformers, like Kabīr and Rāmānand. Such shrines, tombs, monuments, or 'abodes' contain and constitute real wonder-working fetishes for the whole population, Hindu and Muhammadan alike.

8. Human sacrifices in connexion with fetishism.—There is one point in regard to the ritual connected with fetishism in India that cannot be overlooked in a discussion on the subject. It is the universal practice to smear any and every kind of fetish that can be conveniently so treated with ruddle, or red ochre, or red paint. The bright red stain thus produced represents the blood of sacrifices made to the fetish, which, it is not difficult to show, were originally human. The sacrifice of human beings has been prevalent in India, *sub rosa* at any rate, throughout all historical times to the present day, and there is hardly an important building or architectural structure in the country that has not a story of such a sacrifice connected with its foundation, for the purpose of providing it with a ghostly guardian. Under the influence of civilization and the pressure of governing authorities of various kinds culminating in the fear of British law, actual human sacrifice has taken on modified forms of many sorts until the artificial reddening of the fetish to procure for it the desired power of guardian and curer is all that remains of the original sacrificial ceremony.

Momiāī.—Human sacrifice has given rise to a special fetish known as *momiāī*, still actively believed in and used under the necessary prosaic modifications demanded by British law. But the veritable *momiāī* should consist of the ceremonially distilled fat or essence of a murdered boy, and is believed to be of inestimable value as a cure and prophylactic. At the present day this unfortunate superstition gives rise to an unreasoning political fear in many parts of the country, as its successful concoction is attributed to Europeans. Surgeons with a taste for anatomy, freemasons (always regarded by the ignorant masses as a kind of sorcerers), and anatomical collectors for museums are especially exposed to suspicion in this connexion.

LITERATURE.—There is no book devoted to the subject, but there are very many that may be usefully consulted, among which the following may be specially mentioned: **W. Crooke**, *PR*[2], 2 vols., London, 1896, and *TC*, 4 vols., Calcutta, 1896; **J. M. Campbell**, *Spirit Basis of Belief and Custom*, Priv. Print, Bombay, 1885; **E. T. Dalton**, *Desc. Ethnol. of Bengal*, Calcutta, 1872; **A. C. Lyall**, *Asiatic Studies*[2], 2 vols., London, 1899; **Monier-Williams**, *Brahmanism and Hinduism*[4], do. 1891; **E. Moor**, *Hindu Pantheon*, do. 1810; **W. Ward**, *History, Lit. and Rel. of the Hindoos*[5], Madras, 1863; **H. H. Wilson**, *Works*, 12 vols., London, 1862–77, and *Vishnu Purana*, do. 1840; **A. Barth**, *Religions of India*, do. 1882; **F. S. Growse**, *Ramayana of Tulsi Das*,[5] 3 vols., Cawnpore, 1891; **R. C. Dutt**, *Hist. of Civilization in Ancient India*, 2 vols., London, 1893; **C. Manning**, *Ancient and Mediæval India*, 2. vols., do. 1869; **F. H. Buchanan**, *Eastern India* (ed. R. Montgomery Martin), 3 vols., do. 1838; **Rājendralāla Mitra**, *Indo-Aryans*, 2 vols., London and Calcutta, 1881; **H. H. Risley**, *TC*, 2 vols., Calcutta, 1891; **E. Thurston**, *Castes and Tribes of S. India*, 7 vols., Madras, 1909; **M. A. Sherring**, *Hindu Tribes and Castes in Benares*, 3 vols., Calcutta, 1872–81; **J. Wilson**, *Indian Caste*, 2 vols., Bombay, 1877; **Meer Hassan Ali**, *Obs. on the Mussulmauns of India*, 2 vols., London, 1832; **N. Chevers**, *Med. Jurisprudence for India*, Calcutta, 1870; **H. S. Colebrooke**, *Miscell. Essays*[2], London, 1872; **J. Forbes**, *Oriental Memoirs*, 2 vols., do. 1813; **J. Fergusson**, *Hist. of Indian and Eastern Architect.*, ed. Burgess and Spiers, do. 1910, *Tree and Serpent Worship*[2], do. 1873; **W. E. Hearn**, *The Aryan Household*, do. 1879; **H. B. Rowney**, *Wild Tribes of India*, do. 1882; **W. J. Wilkins**, *Hindu Mythology*, Calcutta, 1882.

An immense quantity of evidence is to be found scattered about in all sorts of books and pamphlets descriptive of the people of India as a whole or in part, esp. the *Gazetteers* (from 1870 onwards) and *Census Reports* (for 1881, 1891, 1901, 1911) of Provinces and Native States; local *Government Reports*, *Settlement Reports*, and official *Handbooks of Districts* and *Native States*, *Archæol. Survey Reports*, *Madras Manual of Administration* (3 vols.), *Bulletin of the Madras Museum*; *JASBe*, *JRAS*, *JRASBo*, *JRAI*, and publications of the Hakluyt Soc. for early European Travels; *As. Quart. Rev.*, *As. Researches* (early), *IA* (Bombay), *Calcutta Review* (Calcutta), *NINQ*, *PNQ* (both Allahabad, 1883–1891); the old travellers not yet edited by the Hakluyt Soc., *e.g.* **F. Bernier**, *Travels in the Moghul Empire*, ed. A. Constable, London, 1891; **J. B. Tavernier**, *Travels in India*, ed. V. Ball, do. 1889; **J. A. Mandelslo**, *Travels from Persia into the East Indies*, do. 1662; **R. Fitch**, *Voyage*, ed. J. H. Ryley, do. 1899; **T. Herbert**, *Travels into Asia and Afrique*, do. 1638; **J. Ovington**, *Voyage to Surratt, 1689*, do. 1696; **E. Terry**, *Voyage to East India*, do. 1777; **W. Schouten**, *Voiage aux Indes Orientales*, Amsterdam, 1707; **J. de Thévenot**, *Travels*, London, 1687; **F. Valentyn**, *Oud en Nieuw Oost Indien*, 5 vols., Amsterdam, 1724.

Of more modern travellers the following are examples: **Bholanauth Chunder**, *Travels of a Hindoo*, 2 vols., London, 1869; **J. P. Ferrier**, *Caravan Journeys*, do. 1856; **G. T. Vigne**, *Travels in Kashmir*, etc., 2 vols., do. 1842; **K. von Hügel**, *aschmir und das Reich der Siek*, 5 vols., Stuttgart, 1840–48 (Eng. tr. 1845); **W. Lloyd and A. Gerard**, *Caunpoor to the Boorendo Pass*, 2 vols., London, 1840; **R. Heber**, *Journey through the Upper Prov.*[3], 2 vols., do. 1828; **W. H. Sleeman**, *Journey through Oude*, 2 vols., do. 1858, *Rambles and Recollections*, ed. V. A. Smith, do. 1893; **V. Ball**, *Jungle Life in India*, do. 1880; **J. Forsyth**, *Highlands of Central India*[2], do. 1872.

There are many local descriptive books, *e.g.* **D. C. J. Ibbetson**, *Panjāb Ethnography*, Calcutta, 1883; **G. A. Grierson**, *Bihar Peasant Life*, do. 1885; **R. C. Temple**, *Legends of the Panjāb*, 3 vols., Bombay, 1883–1900, *Proper Names of Panjabis*, do. 1883; **M. A. Sherring**, *The Sacred City of the Hindus*, London, 1868; **W. R. Lawrence**, *The Valley of Kashmir*, do. 1895; **J. Campbell**, *Thirteen Years among the Wild Tribes of Khondistan*, do. 1864; **P. Carnegy**, *Races, etc., of Oudh*, Lucknow, 1868; **S. C. Macpherson**, *Report upon the Khonds*, Calcutta, 1842; **F. Buchanan**, *Journey through Mysore, Canara, and Malabar*, 3 vols., London, 1807; **J. Tod**, *Annals of Rajast'han*, 2 vols., do. 1829–32; **J. Malcolm**, *Memoir of Central India*, 2 vols., do. 1820; **S. Hislop**, *Aboriginal Tribes of Central Prov.*, Nagpur, 1866; **F. S. Growse**, *Mathura, a District Memoir*[3], Allahabad, 1883; **H. A. Oldfield**, *Sketches from Nipal*, 2 vols., London, 1880; **E. J. Gunthorpe**, *Criminal Tribes of Bombay, etc.*, Bombay, 1882; **G. D. Upreti**, *Proverbs and Folklore of Kumaun and Garhwal*, Lodiana, 1894.

Of definitely historical books the following may be noted: **H. M. Elliot**, *Hist. of India as told by its own Historians*, 8 vols., London, 1867–77; **J. Briggs**, ed. of Ferishta's *Rise of the Mahomedan Power in India till 1612*, 4 vols., do. 1829; **D. Wright**, *Hist. of Nepāl*, Cambridge, 1877.

See also translations of vernacular works on the people: **D. Shea and A. Troyer**, ed. of the *Dābistān*, 3 vols., Paris, 1843; **G. A. Herklots**, *Qanoon-e-Islam*, London, 1832; **Blochmann and Jarrett**, ed. of *Āin-i-Akbarī*, 3 vols., Calcutta, 1873–1894; **E. Sachau**, tr. of al-Bīrūnī, London, 1888. Cf. also the following dictionaries, glossaries, etc.: **S. W. Fallon**, *Dict. of Hindustāni Proverbs*, ed. R. C. Temple, Benares, 1884, etc.; **J. Dowson**, *Class. Dict. of Hindu Mythol.*, London, 1879; **H. H. Wilson**, *Gloss. of Indian Terms*, do. 1855; **H. M. Elliot**, *Suppl. Gloss. of Indian Terms*, ed. J. Beames, 2 vols., do. 1869; **T. P. Hughes**, *DI*, do. 1885; **E. O'Brien**, *Gloss. of Multani Language*, Lahore, 1881; **H. A. Rose**, *Dict. of Ethnog. Panjāb*, 1911.

Of books devoted to folk-tales, see esp. **F. A. Steel and R. C. Temple**, *Wideawake Stories*, Bombay, 1884; **C. H. Tawney**, *Kathā-sarit-sāgara*, Calcutta, 1880; **M. Frere**, *Old Deccan Days*, London, 1868; **L. B. Day**, *Folk-tales of Bengal*, do. 1883, *Govinda Sámanta*, 2 vols, do. 1874; **J. H. Knowles**, *Folk-tales* *of Kashmir*, do. 1888; M. Stokes, *Indian Fairy Tales*, Calcutta, 1879; J. Jacobs, *Indian Fairy Tales*, London, 1892; C. Swynnerton, *Rājā Rasālu*, Calcutta, 1884, and *Romantic Tales from the Panjāb*, London, 1903.

R. C. TEMPLE.

FICHTE.—The philosophical work of Fichte falls into two well-defined divisions, corresponding closely with his periods of residence in Jena and Berlin respectively. The work of the first period is that which has had the greatest influence on subsequent philosophical speculation, for it gave direction to the advance which was made on Kant's position by post-Kantian idealists, while his teaching during the second period was more popular in form and closely bound up with current political events. In the first period we have the *Wissenschaftslehre* (quite inadequately translated as *Theory of Knowledge*), the practical philosophy of the *Theory of Natural Right* (*Naturrecht*) and of the *Ethics* (*Sittenlehre*), and the religious philosophy of the essay *On the Ground of our Belief in the Divine Government of the Universe*. In the second period we find Fichte's final synthesis of *Knowledge* (shown in the *Wissenschaftslehre* to be purely formal), *Will* (established as the ground of reality), and the *Divine Moral Order* (in which the vocation of each individual is grounded).

'From this point onwards the inquiry centres in that divine idea of the world which appears as the guiding principle in the popular works, and which at first sight appears to have no immediate connection with the *Wissenschaftslehre* in its earlier form. In certain minor doctrines, the new expositions differ from the *Wissenschaftslehre* . . . but on the whole we find nothing in them to contradict or supersede the *Wissenschaftslehre*. They contain a wider, more concrete view, to which *Wissenschaftslehre* may be regarded as an introduction' (Adamson, *Fichte*, p. 190).

Before describing the salient features of Fichte's contribution to speculation, we must briefly sketch his life and indicate his chief writings.

1. Life.—Johann Gottlieb Fichte (b. 1762) was the eldest son of a humble handicraftsman at Rammenau in Upper Lusatia, who had married the daughter of a well-to-do manufacturer.

The boy was meditative and earnest, endowed with a remarkable memory, and very fond of reading. These characteristics, along with a certain obstinacy, were to have far-reaching effects upon his life. An accident brought his talents to the notice of a nobleman, who sent him first to a tutor, and then to a monastery-like and antiquated foundation-school at Schulpforta, near Naumberg.

At eighteen years of age he entered the theological faculty at Jena, being transferred, however, to Leipzig in the following year. Theological difficulties, especially those arising out of the relation of Providence to the voluntary action of man, led him to take an eager interest in philosophy, and he frankly adopted the determinist position, in which the reading of Spinoza's *Ethics* only served to confirm him. He was thrown on his own resources even before his University course was completed, and after three years at Leipzig he spent some years as a tutor in various families, first in Saxony, and then in Zürich; it was in Zürich that he met his future wife, a niece of Klopstock. In 1790 he had a hard struggle against poverty in Leipzig, but the autumn of that year brought him more pupils, among them one who desired to study the philosophy of Kant. This was a turning-point in his life.

'A circumstance,' he writes to his betrothed, 'which seemed the result of mere chance, led me to give myself up entirely to the study of the Kantian philosophy—a philosophy which restrains the imagination, always too powerful in me, which gives understanding the sway, and which raises the whole spirit to an indescribable elevation above all earthly considerations. . . . It is difficult beyond all conception, and stands greatly in need of simplification. The principles, it is true, are hard speculations, with no direct bearing upon human life, but their consequences are of the utmost importance for an age whose morality is corrupted at the fountain-head; and to set these consequences before the world in a clear light would, I believe, be doing it a good service. . . . I am now thoroughly convinced that the human will is free, and that to be happy is not the purpose of our being,—but to deserve happiness.'

In 1791, Fichte paid a visit to Kant at Königsberg, and laid before him an essay entitled *Kritik aller Offenbarung*, and by some accident this was published anonymously. The philosophical world, already expecting a work on religion by Kant, assumed that the Königsberg philosopher was the author, with the result that Fichte, once again a private tutor, found his book immediately famous. A tour in Switzerland, after his marriage in 1793, brought him into contact with Pestalozzi and other men of wide reputation. The writing of political pamphlets, and deep reflexion upon the difficulties of the Kantian philosophy, occupied him until, in the spring of 1794, he accepted the post of Extraordinary Professor of Philosophy at Jena, then distinguished as the centre of progressive philosophical and literary movements in Germany. His work at Jena, where his influence among the students was remarkable, was cut short by an unfortunate attack upon him on the ground of his supposed atheism—an attack which he met without much tact. The result was that he resigned the chair, and before long he was compelled to make his way quietly to Berlin. There he at first moved in the circle of Schlegel, Schleiermacher, and others of the Romantic school, but it was not long before he found a more congenial and officially more influential circle of friends. Obtaining permission to lecture in Berlin, he gathered round him an audience containing most distinguished scholars and statesmen. At Erlangen in 1805 he delivered a number of lectures, including the famous course on *The Nature of the Scholar*.

In 1807, at the conclusion of the war with France, which had interrupted his residence in Berlin, Fichte was chosen to frame for the proposed University of Berlin a constitution which should ensure its efficiency and success—a task peculiarly congenial to him. Unfortunately, a change in the management of the scheme led to the rejection of his remarkable and far-sighted proposals.

With patriotic disregard of the risks he was running, he delivered his *Addresses to the German People* during the winter of 1807–8, while Berlin was occupied by the French, and his services towards the regeneration of Prussia were recognized by his election as first Rector of the University of Berlin in 1810. While in the strenuous service of his Fatherland, he was stricken down by a fever contracted from his wife, who had laboured in the overflowing hospitals for five months, and he died on 27th January 1814.

2. Writings.—The *Kritik aller Offenbarung* appeared in 1792; it was an attempt to carry the principles of Kant's critical method into the investigation of the possibility of revealed religion. Its interest lies in the emphasis which Fichte thus early laid upon the practical reason as the clue to speculative problems. In 1794 it was followed by *Über den Begriff der Wissenschaftslehre*, a tract containing a purely formal sketch of his first Jena lectures, which has unfortunately been frequently used as the most adequate source for a knowledge of Fichte's system. While at Jena, Fichte developed his speculative principle (described below) in a series of works dealing with its theoretical and practical grounds and implications, including *Grundlage der gesammten Wissenschaftslehre* (1794), *Grundlage des Naturrechts* (1796), *Erste und zweite Einleitung in die Wissenschaftslehre* (1797), *Versuch einer neuen Darstellung der Wissenschaftslehre* (1797) which expounds the philosophical system as a whole, and *System der Sittenlehre* (1798). After leaving Jena, Fichte came under influences which resulted in a more popular exposition and a less intellectual idealism; the keen dialectic of the *Wissenschaftslehre* made way for the ethical idealism of *Die Bestimmung des Menschen* (1800), the theoretical socialism of *Der geschlossene Handelsstaat* (1801), the elevated spiritual insight of *Über das Wesen des Gelehrten* (1805), the acute analysis of current culture and thought of *Grundzüge des gegenwärtigen Zeitalters* (1806), and for the bold reconciliation of life and thought in religion which is found in the *Anweisung zum seligen Leben* (1806). When Prussia was invaded in 1805 by Napoleon, Fichte's patriotism, which had led him to make the unsuccessful appeal to be allowed to accompany the Prussian troops as a preacher of 'fire and sword,' found expression in the *Reden an die Deutschen*—addresses which survey the characteristics of the German people out of which the new State may be built up, and expound the steps to be taken in order to utilize the freedom and vitality of the nation.

(1) *THE JENA PERIOD.*—(*a*) *Wissenschaftslehre.*—Fichte's problem was set for him by the unresolved difficulties of Kant's system. By an analysis of knowledge and an investigation of the result, for knowledge, of the existence of the unity of self-consciousness, Kant attempted to explain experience. But the result of his method seemed to be that two elements, each of which has meaning only as related to the other, are equally necessary for experience, though the relation is a purely negative one.

'What Kant, however, does not perceive, is that . . . these two worlds are essentially relative to each other, so that either, taken apart from the other, becomes an empty abstraction. He has, indeed, proved that existence unrelated to a conscious life is such an abstraction. But it is clear that the pure self, in its universality—as opposed to all the matter of the desires—is equally abstract. To will the self, and only the self, is to will nothing at all. Self-consciousness always implies consciousness of something else than self, and could not exist without it. Self-determination, therefore, though it may be relatively opposed to determination by the not-self, cannot be absolutely opposed to it, for with the not-self the self also would disappear' (E. Caird, *Hegel*, Edinburgh, 1896, p. 124 f.).

Fichte refused to start with any abstract notion. Certainty to him rested on intuition, though he meant by intuition neither the Kantian mode of knowing things-in-themselves nor the consciousness of the Absolute (of Schelling), but what he called in his later writings the free activity of the Ego.

The best-known expression of this starting-point is found in the *Grundlage der Wissenschaftslehre*, where it is reached by a highly artificial method, which cannot be reproduced in brief. The procedure is to assume that any one who considers what happens when he calls himself 'I' will find that he is at the same time both object and subject. But this primitive activity of consciousness (its self-affirmation) is known to the Ego only through reflexion, that is, through limitation. In other words, 'the Ego determines' and 'the Ego is determined.' The only solution of this contradiction is found in the proposition 'the Ego partly determines itself and is partly determined.' From this position the theoretical *Wissenschaftslehre* analyzes the necessary modes of intelligence which are involved in the opposition between non-Ego and Ego. Fichte was quite aware, and held, that this has only formal worth. The practical *Wissenschaftslehre* (*Sittenlehre*) makes an advance. If the Ego is to unite the pure activity of self-affirmation and the limited, determined activity, 'it must be an activity which is at the same time, though not in the same sense, finite; it must be an infinite *striving*. Striving implies opposition. . . . Thus the practical activity of the Ego is the ground of the *Anstoss* [opposition], which renders intelligence possible' (Adamson, 177).

(*b*) *Practical philosophy.*—The *Theory of Natural Right* and the *Moral Phil.* are deductions from the first principles of the *Wissenschaftslehre*, and lay down a series of stages marking the realization of the practical Ego. The Ego, on the principles of the earlier investigation, must affirm itself, be aware of its own activity. It can be so aware only in so far as it is practical, willing. 'The practical Ego is the Ego of original self-consciousness; a rational being immediately perceives itself only in willing; and, were it not practical, would perceive neither itself nor the world—would not be an intelligence at all. Will is in a special sense the essence of reason' (*Werke*, iii. 20 f.; and see Adamson, 181). This striving is a feature of consciousness only to the extent that consciousness is limited, and the Ego is really a system of impulses, or strivings partially but not absolutely opposed.

Fichte examines the implications of the principle that the Ego, to be self-consciousness, must affirm itself as acting freely; and his results are his theory of right or rights. Freedom of action involves the existence of a sphere of action, a world against which the activity is to be directed. Fichte further deduces the existence of a plurality of individuals, and the external world is the means of communication between such free intelligences. Still further, the co-existence of such free persons is possible only if they stand in a relation of right and law (*Recht*) to each other. The theory of right establishes (1) primitive right, the right to be not a mere means but a cause (involving personal freedom and property). To assure this right, there must also be (2) right of coercion, the agreement in a commonweal by mutual contract that violations of the former shall be annulled by its contrary. Hence (3) the political rights of free contract, of legislative and of executive authority. Socialist principles regarding State-control of trade, labour, and money are deduced (cf. the *Geschlossene Handelsstaat*). The system of rights arises from the conflict of the freedom of one subject with that of others; similarly, the conflict of motives in any one person gives rise to the system of duties of Fichte's *Theory of Morals or Duties* (*Sittenlehre*). The pure spring of action, the tendency to freedom for the sake of freedom, finds beside it the instinct of self-preservation, the aim of which is enjoyment, not freedom. Fichte points out that these are not really contradictory; transcendentally, they are both expressions of the fundamental activity of the Ego. Their union is effected when an act materially (by obedience to the natural principle) regards the world of sense, and formally (obeying the pure principle) affirms freedom from the world of sense. But the Ego, so long as it remains a self-conscious Ego, cannot be completely free from limitation, so that the moral end lies in infinity. Moral action is, therefore, a series of acts, no one of which is indifferent; the moral vocation of man is not one definite thing, but a series of vocations, and the moral law is, 'Continually fulfil your vocation.' Conscience is the feeling of harmony in a given case between the empirical and the pure Ego, an assurance immediately given.

(*c*) *Philosophy of religion.*—In his first Essay in the critical style, the *Critique of all Revelation*, Fichte attempted to apply the critical principles to the question of the possibility, the form, and the content of any revelation, thus filling a gap in the Kantian system. The importance of this Essay lies in the stress which he already lays upon the practical side of that system. Within the earlier system of Fichte there was no place for the conception of God as creative, or as personal. Kant had shown the possibility of the existence of Natural Religion, as involved in the necessity of the practical postulates of God and immortality; Revealed Religion, Fichte tried to show, rests upon the morally imperfect condition of those to whom the revelation is made, and any revelation must be in harmony with the moral law. It is of the Divine moral law, not of God, that we read in the treatise which led to Fichte's removal from Jena. Belief in the moral order of the universe is belief in God, and there is no other; only by reason of the necessities of intelligence do we regard this order as substance or person.

(2) *THE BERLIN PERIOD.*—(*a*) *The Nature of Man.*—The harmony which Fichte had tried to establish between cognition and will, by means of the conception of the moral order, received during the Berlin period more elaborate treatment; the *Wissenschaftslehre*, so often taken as Fichte's last word, is merely introductory to the whole of what is contained in the *Popular Works*. The clearest exposition of the later synthesis is found in *Die Bestimmung des Menschen* of 1800 (*Pop. Works*, i. 321 ff.). The three sections of this work—Doubt, Knowledge, and Faith—state the positions of Naturalism, Theoretical Idealism, and Practical (or Ethical) Idealism. Naturalism leaves us with the conflict of natural necessity and freedom, Knowledge is shown to be purely formal; but in the third book the end of existence is declared to be not knowledge, but action.

In the section entitled 'Faith,' Fichte shows that the attempt to analyze the feeling of free activity by reason only, revives the sceptical doubts described in the section entitled 'Doubt.' We must simply accept the impulse to independence, and realize that 'thought is not supreme, but founded on our striving energies.' 'The true dignity of my understanding fills me with reverence. It is no longer the deceptive mirror which reflects a series of empty pictures, proceeding from nothing and tending to nothing; it is bestowed upon me for a great purpose. Its cultivation for this purpose is entrusted to me; it is placed in my hands, and at my hands it will be required.' 'We do not act because we know, but we know because we are called upon to act. The practical reason is the root of all reason.'

The moral results which follow from this position are clear. 'Not merely to know, but according to thy knowledge to do, is thy vocation.' Fichte would, however, have us remember that others also are busy doing. 'Assume it as already known that they can give a purpose to their own being wholly by themselves, and independently of thee; never interrupt the accomplishment of this purpose, but rather further it to the utmost of thy power.' The vocation of the race is to form itself into one single body, each part of which shall be in intimate contact with every other. All has tended to this end, and much of the way is already passed over. Man has attained to a more comprehensive, more energetic freedom. 'When once every useful discovery made at one end of the earth is at once communicated to all other parts, then, without further interruption, with united strength and equal step, humanity shall move onward to a higher culture, of which we can at present form no conception.' But an even greater Order appears; the Eternal World, in which we are and live even now, the world in which Will is the first link in a chain of consequences that stretches through the whole invisible realms of spirit, rises before us. God, the Divine Will, is the bond of union between finite wills within that world, and our true life is a life of active endeavour to co-operate with other willing persons, fulfilling our respective vocations while respecting their freedom, guided by conscience, which is the felt harmony between the natural tendency and the tendency to freedom.

Creative life reveals itself in a different shape in each corner of the universe as the power by which we ourselves were formed. Here it streams as self-creating and self-forming matter through human veins and muscles, and pours out its abundance into the tree, the plant, and the grass. There it leaps and dances as spontaneous activity in the animal, and appears in ever-new forms. 'Everything that lives and moves follows this universal impulse.' Through that which to others seemed a mere dead mass, Fichte saw this life rising in ever-increasing growth, no longer the ever-recurring circle, or the eternally repeated play. 'It is not Death that kills, but the more living Life which, concealed behind the former, bursts forth into new development. Death and Birth are but the struggle of Life with itself to assume a more glorious and congenial form.'

(*b*) *The Way of the Blessed Life* (tr. under that title in the *Popular Works*).—This deals with the ultimate question of the relation of finite spirits to the universe of which they are parts. In the second part of that work, Fichte offers a history of the different stages (distinguishing five) of that reflexion by which the relation is apprehended. The first three stages are those described in *The Nature of Man*, where it is shown that the life of Faith is the acceptance of, and self-sacrifice for, the ideas on which rest art, science, and political life. But man can rise yet higher, for his failure to realize the Divine Will in his own action forces him in upon himself, so that he may comprehend what that is which he loves and after which he strives. Man so lives that 'in the conduct of each individual there may be manifested purely that form which the Divine nature has assumed in this particular individual; that each individual may recognize God as He is outwardly manifested in the conduct of all other men; that all others may recognize God as He is manifested in the conduct of this particular individual; and that thus God alone may be ever manifested in all outward appearance.' The fifth and last stage is that in which the finite spirit apprehends in thought the intimate relations in which he and all other finite spirits are bound together in one community of free intelligences, moved and upheld by one purpose.

LITERATURE.—*Werke*, the collected works, 11 vols., edited and arranged by Fichte's son, I. H. Fichte (vols. i.–viii., Bonn, 1845–46, and vols. ix.–xi., 1834–35); *The Popular Works of J. G. Fichte*[4], tr. W. Smith, 2 vols., London, 1889, with a memoir of the author prepared from materials derived from *J. G. Fichte's Leben und literarischer Briefwechsel*[2], by I. H. Fichte, 2 vols., Leipzig, 1862; *The Science of Rights* and *The Science of Knowledge*, tr. A. E. Kroeger, with introd. by W. T. Harris, London, 1889; *On the Nature of the Scholar* and *The Characteristics of the Present Age*, tr. W. Smith, both contained in the *Popular Works* already mentioned; C. C. Everett, *Fichte's Science of Knowledge*, Chicago, 1884; R. Adamson, *Fichte*, London, 1881 (see also his *Development of Modern Philosophy*, Edinb. and Lond. 1908); F. C. A. Schwegler, *Hist. of Phil.*, tr. with a note by J. H. Stirling, Edinburgh, 1867 (see also other Histories of Philosophy, notably those of K. Fischer, Erdmann, and Windelband); T. Carlyle, *On Heroes*, Lect. vi.; A. Lasson, *J. G. Fichte im Verhältniss zu Kirche und Staat*, Berlin, 1863; F. Zimmer, *J. G. Fichte's Religionsphilosophie*, Berlin, 1878.

HAROLD E. B. SPEIGHT.

THE END OF VOL. V.